The Wee Rock Discography

The Wee Rock Discography

M. C. Strong

Illustrations by Harry Horse

CANONGATE

Published in 1996 in Great Britain
by Canongate Books Ltd,
14 High St, Edinburgh EH1 1TE

ISBN 0 86241 621 3

British Library Cataloguing in Publication Data

A catalogue for this book is available on request from the British Library

Typeset by Æsthetex Ltd, Edinburgh

Printed and bound in Finland by WSOY

The book is dedicated to …
my mother JEAN FOTHERINGHAM
(born: 6th January 1929,
died: 31st August 1985)

Thank you mum up there for
pulling my strings, and
guiding me through all
the hard times.

* * *

Acknowledgements

I wish to thank the following people who've given me more than a WEE bit of help and encouragement throughout the history of the ROCK DISCOGRAPHY.

My daughters SHIRLEY and SUZANNE, my dad GERRY (GEOFF) STRONG, EILEEN SCOTT-MONCRIEFF, VIC ZDZIEBLO, ALLAN BREWSTER, SANDY McCRAE, MICHAEL FLETCHER, all the regulars at The Commercial Bar, Falkirk (including boss JIMMY LAING), The Pop Quiz Team: TED MOCHAR, DAVIE SEATH and FRANNIE FITZPATRICK (who died 23rd May 1996); HAMISH McLEOD-PRENTICE, STEPHEN McELROY, BRIAN McELROY, PAUL McELROY, DOUGIE NIVEN, DEREK IRVINE, BRIAN and MARGARET HUNTER, TAM MORRISON, The SCOTT-MONCRIEFFs; SIMON, COLIN, ALAN, JAS and SUZANNAH (plus AUDREY, EMILY and MAUREEN); LINDA TONER, LES O'CONNOR (deceased), GEORGE BROWN, COLIN TAYLOR, DAVIE BLAIR, PETER WAUGH, PAUL KLEMM, IAIN McLEAN, IAIN SUTHERLAND, PETER GRAHAM (at the BBC), CHRIS LORIMER, MALCOLM STEWART (Jimpress, Hendrix fanzine), FORREST DUNCAN, CHRIS HILL and LEE HARVEY (National Sound Archive), DEREK KILLAH and staff at Falkirk library, ALAN LAWSON (Aesthetex typesetters), and Canongate Books staff (JAMIE BYNG, NEVILLE MOIR, JAMES CLARK, SHEILA McAINSH, FIONA MURRAY, HUGH ANDREW and STEPHANIE WOLFE-MURRAY).

Thanks to all those around the world who wrote me letters of congratulation and encouragement on the second edition, alongside lists of useful information. Some also sent me their ROCK SURVEYS (see my back pages):

JULIA ARMSTRONG, RUSSELL BAILLIE, STEPHEN BAIRD, DIETER BANSCH, STEFFEN BAUER, JURGEN BELING, MARTIN BERTSCH, ULRICH BEUTEFUHR, MARGARET BLACK, STEVE BOISMAISON, ROB BOLTON (U. S. A.), BERNDT BUCH, CHARLES BUTLER, DAVE CHAMBERS, MICHAEL CHANDLER, PAUL COPE, GUY DEEMING, LESLIE FAIR, SIMON "Fish" FISHER, TIM FOOTMAN, JORG FOTH (also wanted to know the piano lady of the early 70s whose lyrics "And When The War Is Over And The Soldiers Come Home, We'll Be Sitting By The Fireside And Leave The World Alone": fax 030/44 27 263), DALE GARDNER, HARTWIG GIERKE, JURGEN GOLDNER, PETER GOLDSMITH, JAMIE GOODMAN, ALICE GRANDISON, MATTHIAS GUDERJAN, TRISTAN GUY-DEMEN, THOMAS HAMILL, Mr. S. HARKER, JIM HENDERSON, FRANK HERGER, ANDREAS HERGER, SIMON HESS, KARSTEN HOEFT, KELVIN HOLMES, SOREN JAKOBS, IAN JONES, HAROLD KAYSER, LARS KIESEL, RAINER KRAKER, MICHAEL KURENKO (Siberia), HUGH "Shug" MACKIE, JOE MACKLE, ADE MACROW, GRAHAM MILNES, ANDREAS MOLLER, PHIL NEWTON (Australia), MARTIN NISBET, DOUGLAS NOBLE, CHRIS OWEN, NEIL PARRY, BRIAN PATTON, PIPPO PIARULLI (Italy), B.C. PIRES (West Indies), ANA POPVIC and VLADIMIR JOVANDIC (Yugoslavia), SANDY PRENTICE, SIEGFRIED RIEDEL, LIAM RIGBY, IAN ROBERTSON, NEIL ROBINSON, ALEXEI ROUDITCHEV, ARTHUR ROUSSELLE (German *Rolling Stone* reviewer who gave it 5 stars), KEVIN SALT, ULI SCHMIDT, STEFANIE SCHMITT, MATTHIAS SCHOLTEN, STEPHEN SCOTT, RAY SHEPPARD, HARTMUT SIEGEL, JOE SIMPSON, NEIL SPORGO, ALLAN STREETER, GUY SUTTON, DAVID SWIFT, ECKEHARD TEBBE, ANNE-KATRIN TURN, DAVID WARNOCK, PAUL WHITTINGHAM and DON WYNNE.

I apoogize to STEVE BOAST, whose letter I mislaid with many files. Recent letters between deadlines for GREAT ROCK III and WEE ROCK also came from KELVIN HAYES, DOUGLAS NOBLE, ALAN PERRA (U.S.A.) and IAN TRENFIELD.

Preface

Promises, promises. Pre-publication ads for THE WEE ROCK DISCOGRAPHY claimed it would contain a rare vinyl price guide with catalogue numbers. Well, before you start to read this book, (you know what's coming) I'd like to mention that, due to a lack of typesetting space, I couldn't fit this in. Sorry, time wasn't on my side either. Between finishing off THE GREAT ROCK DISCOGRAPHY: THIRD EDITION and the deadline to finish this one, I thought it would be impossible. Hell, it was the summertime too and I needed some breaks to see what the big orange thing in the sky was. Still, I'm sure you'll find that THE WEE ROCK DISCOGRAPHY is well worth the money – and a good deal lighter than the original.

The original – the big one from which this wee one was spawned – contains over 1,000 groups/artists and took over a decade to complete. So it's not surprising that I thought this would be an easier book to compile. Not so. It turned out to be a nightmare. Omitting a large number of artists from the third edition was like deciding which limb to lose in an industrial accident. What would you leave out? ABBA or AC/DC, BLUE OYSTER CULT or THE BLUETONES, RED HOT CHILI PEPPERS or RED HOUSE PAINTERS, DOOP or PETULA CLARK (OK, the last two were binned years ago).

As space was at a premium, I decided to drop all artists pre-BEATLES and BOB DYLAN. ELVIS, in this size of book, would have taken up over 12 pages – which means "The King" ain't in here. Next to go were more pop orientated artists, mainly from the 70s, 80s and 90s, such as ABBA, MICHAEL JACKSON, MADONNA, GEORGE MICHAEL and WET WET WET. To keep as up-to-date as possible, I've managed to squeeze in all the artists' 1996 releases (January – June) and add 30 groups/artists who have made it in the last year and I think deserve inclusion (e.g., OCEAN COLOUR SCENE, SUPER FURRY ANIMALS, PLACEBO, etc.). Obviously all my favourites managed to stay in: T. REX, THE ROLLING STONES, DAVID BOWIE, ALEX HARVEY, PINK FLOYD, MIKE OLDFIELD, GENESIS, YES, SEX PISTOLS, THE FALL (my favourite band of all time), PUBLIC IMAGE LTD and JOY DIVISION – but most, if not all, of these would have made it regardless.

Throughout the compiling process there has been another criteria by which I measure a group or artist's eligibility. Just to remind you of the book's title here:– THE WEE **ROCK** DISCOGRAPHY. Predominantly, this is a book about rock artists not pop artists. To define the difference between rock and pop is not an easy task. I see it like this: ROCK music is written by the artist(s) for his or herself, not with the initial intention of making money, but to make music – and, possibly, to stretch its limits and boundaries a little further. This is music that may last forever, becoming "classic" in the process. Take for example: THE BEATLES; JIMI HENDRIX; and, more recently, R.E.M. These rock artists, I agree, have also become POP icons, although they have not, and never will, lose their ROCK credibility tag. On the other hand, POP music is written with the sole intention (normally) of making a quick buck, either for the artist(s) or (more than likely) their record label. Take for example: CLIFF RICHARD; BAY CITY ROLLERS; BROS and TAKE THAT. You won't find any of them in here and for good reason. This is bound to make some people unhappy but so be it.

I always welcome feedback as no one is infallible, so please feel free to write to me care of my publishers. Thanks for buying the book and I hope it brings you hours of mindless pleasure!

How To Read The Book

GROUP / ARTIST(s)

If lettering is grey, it is one of the non-rock artists which a book of this kind could not do without.

Formed/Born: where . . . when . . . birthplace . . . brief history . . . other info.
Style: music type/sound . . . influences . . . fashion.
Songwriters: the pensmiths . . . covers (originals or hitmakers in brackets).
Trivia/Miscellaneous: virtually anything else (i.e. producers, marriages, colour of underpants, etc.).
Recommended: Top selective recommendation (* 4–10). Amalgamation of music press reviews + myself.

Group:
SINGER (born, when, where) – **vocals** (ex-GROUP)
MUSICIANS (born, when, where) – **instrument(s)** (ex-GROUPS)

Discography listed in chronological order (chart positions shown in **bold**)

		UK-label (a)	US-label (a)	
UK-release date.	(format) **ALBUM or EP name** – (album or EP tracks) *(UK re-issue + if on different label)*	**1**	**99**	US-date
UK-date.	(format) **'A' SINGLE./ 'B'SIDE**	**75**	**10**	

If group leaves label (a), the new record company label (b) appears above the subsequent chart position boxes.

— **NEW SINGER/MUSICIAN** (b. 1 Jan '50) – vocals/ instrument(s) (ex-GROUP?) repl.(aced) out-going member who might have joined another group.

Below single didn't hit UK chart and wasn't issued in US

		UK-label (b)	US-label	
UK-date.	(7")(c-s) **'A' SINGLE ./'B-SIDE** (other format +=) Extra track(s) of above single. (other format ++=) Extra track(s) of above extra. (other format +=) Extra tracks(s) to the above single (other format) ('A' side above)/ any other track(s)/ (no 'B' side).		-	

ARTIST(s)

If they've changed group name more permanently, or if a sub-group is formed.

		UK-label	US-label	
Dec 95.	(cd)(c)(lp) **ALBUM** – Album tracks/ etc. (now in correct sequence, I hope).	**1**	**1**	Oct 95

– compilations, others, etc. –

For the most part the Group/Artist(s) compilation and other releases are shown separately after the main discography. These are ordered chronologically by label.

		Virgin	not issued	
date.	(format) **ALBUM/ EP (or) SINGLE**		-	blank

Formats & Abbreviations

VINYL (black coloured unless stated)

(lp) = The (LONG PLAYER) record . . . circular 12" plays at 33⅓ r.p.m., and has photo or artwork sleeve. Approximate playing time . . . 30–50 minutes with average 10 tracks. Introduced in the mid-50's on mono until stereo took over in the mid-60's. Quadrophonic had a spell in the 70's, but only on mainly best selling lp's, that had been previously released. Because of higher costs to the manufacturer and buyer, the quad sunk around 1978. Also note that around the mid-50's, some albums were released on 10 inch.
Note:- Average cost to the customer as of January 1996 = £8.50 (new). Budget re-issues are around £5 or under. Collectors can pay anything from £1 to £500, depending on the quality of the recording. Very scratched records can be worthless, but unplayed mint deletions are worth a small fortune to the right person. Auctions and record fairs can be the place to find that long lost recording that's eluded you. This applies to all other vinyl below.

(d-lp) = The (DOUBLE–LONG PLAYER) record . . . as before. Playing time 50–90 minutes on 4 sides, with average 17 tracks. Introduced to rock/pop world in the late 60's, to compliement compilations, concept & concert (aka live) albums.[1]
Compilations:- are a selection of greatest hits or rare tracks, demos, etc.
Concepts:- are near uninterrupted pieces of music, based around a theme.
Note that normal lp's could also be compilations, live or concept. Some record companies through the wishes of their artists, released double lp's at the price of one lp. If not, price new would be around £15.

(t-lp) = The (TRIPLE–LONG PLAYER) record . . . as before. Playing time over 100 minutes with normally over 20 tracks. Because of the cost to the consumer, most artists steered clear of this format. Depending on the artwork on the sleeve, these cost over £17.50. (See its replacement, the CD.)

(4-lp-box) = The (BOXED–LONG PLAYER) record (could be between 4 and 10 in each boxed-set). As the triple album would deal with live, concept or compilation side, the boxed-set would be mostly re-issues of all the artist's album material, with probably a bonus lp thrown in, to make it collectable. Could be very pricey, due to lavish outlay in packaging. They cost over £25 new.

(m-lp) = The (MINI–LONG PLAYER) record . . . playing time between 20–30 minutes and containing on average 7 tracks. Introduced for early 80's independent market, and cost around £4.
Note:- This could be confused at times with the extended-play 12" single.

(pic-lp) = The (PICTURE DISC–LONG PLAYER) record . . . as before but with album artwork/ design on the vinyl grooves. Mainly for the collector because of the slightly inferior sound quality. If unplayed, these can fetch between £10 and £250.

(coloured-lp) = The (COLOURED–LONG PLAYER) record; can be in a variety of colours including . . . white/ blue/ red/ clear/ purple/ green/ pink/ gold/ silver.

(red-lp) = The (RED VINYL–LONG PLAYER) record would be an example of this.

(7") = The (7 INCH SINGLE). Arrived in the late 50's, and plays at 45 r.p.m. Before this its equivalent was the 10" on 78 r.p.m. Playing time now averages 4 minutes per side, but during the late 50's up to mid-60's, each side averaged 2 and half minutes. Punk rock/new wave in 1977/78, resurrected this idea. In the 80's, some disco releases increased playing time. Another idea that was resurrected in 1977 was the picture sleeve. This had been introduced in the 60's, but mostly only in the States.
Note:- Cost at the start of 1996, was just under £2. Second-hand rarities can cost between 25p to £200, depending again on its condition. These also might contain limited freebies/gifts (i.e. posters, patches, stickers, badges, etc.). Due to the confusion this would cause, I have omitted this information, and kept to the vinyl aspect in this book. Another omission has been DJ promos, demos, acetates, magazine freebies, various artists' compilations, etc. Only official shop releases get a mention.

(7" m) = The (7 INCH MAXI-SINGLE). Named so because of the extra track, mostly on the B-side. Introduced widely during the early 70's; one being ROCKET MAN by ELTON JOHN.

(7" ep) = The (7 INCH EXTENDED PLAY SINGLE). Plays mostly at 33⅓ r.p.m., with average playing time 10–15 minutes and 4 tracks. Introduced in the late 50's as compilations for people to sample their albums. These had a *title* and were also re-introduced in 1977 onwards, but this time for punk groups' new songs.

1: **Note: –** Interview long players mainly released on 'Babatak' label, have not been included due to the fact this book only gives artists' music discography.

(d7")	=	The (DOUBLE 7 INCH SINGLE). Basically just two singles combined . . . 4 tracks. Introduced in the late 70's for the "new wave/romantics", and would cost slightly more than normal equivalent.
(7" pic-d)	=	The (7 INCH PICTURE-DISC SINGLE). This was vinyl that had a picture on the grooves, which could be viewed through a see-through plastic cover.
(7" sha-pic-d)	=	The (7 INCH SHAPED-PICTURE-DISC SINGLE). Vinyl as above but with shape (i.e. gun, mask, group) around the edge of the groove. Awkward because it would not fit into the collectors' singles box. Initially limited and this can still be obtained at record fairs for over £3. Note:- However, in the book the type of shape has not been mentioned, due to the lack of space.
(7" coloured)	=	The (7 INCH COLOURED SINGLE). Vinyl that is not black (i.e. any other colour; red, yellow, etc.). Note:- (7" multi) would be a combination of two or more colours (i.e. pink/purple).
(7" flexi)	=	The (7 INCH FLEXIBLE SINGLE). One-sided freebies, mostly given away by magazines, at concerts or as mentioned here; free with single or lp. Worth keeping in mint condition and well protected.
(12")	=	The (12 INCH SINGLE). plays at 45 r.p.m., and can have extended or extra tracks to its 7" counterpart (+=) or (++=). B-sides playing speed could be at 33 r.p.m. Playing time could be between 8 and 15 minutes. Introduced in 1977 with the advent of new wave and punk. They were again a must for collectors, for the new wave of British heavy metal scene.
(12" ep)	=	The (12 INCH EXTENDED PLAY SINGLE). Virtually same as above but *titled* like the 7" ep. Playing time over 12 minutes, and could have between 3 and 5 tracks.
(d12")	=	The (DOUBLE 12 INCH SINGLE). See double 7" . Can become very collectable and would cost new as normal 12", £3.50.
(12" pic-d)	=	The (12 INCH PICTURE-DISC SINGLE). As with 7" equivalent . . . see above.
(12" sha-pic-d)	=	The (12 INCH SHAPED-PICTURE-DISC SINGLE). See above 7" equivalent.
(12" colrd)	=	The (12 INCH COLOURED SINGLE). Not black vinyl . . . see above 7" equivalent.
(10")	=	The (10 INCH SINGLE). Plays at 45 r.p.m., and like the 12" can have extra tracks (+=). Very collectable, it surfaced in its newer form around the early 80's, and can be obtained in shops at £4. Note:- also (10" ep)/ (d10")/ (10" coloured)/ (10" pic-d)/ (10" sha-pic-d).

CASSETTES

(c)	=	The (CASSETTE) album . . . size in case 4 and a half inches high. Playing-time same as lp album, although after the mid-80's cd revolution, released some with extra tracks. Introduced in the late 60's, to compete with the much bulkier lp. Until the 80's, most cassettes were lacking in group info, lyric sheets, and freebies. Note:- Cost to the consumer as of January 1996 = £9 new. But for a few exceptions, most do not increase in price, and can be bought second-hand or budget-priced for around £6.
(d-c)	=	The (DOUBLE-CASSETTE) album . . . as above, and would hold same tracks as d-lp or even t-lp. Price between £15–£20.
(c-s)	=	The (CASSETTE-SINGLE). Now released mostly with same two tracks as 7" equivalent. The other side played the same 2 or 3 tracks. Introduced unsuccessfully in the US around the late 60's. Re-introduced there and in Britain in the mid-80's. In the States, it and its cd counterpart has replaced the charting 7" single for the 90's. Cost new is around £1–£2.50, and might well become quite collectable.
(c-ep)	=	The (CASSETTE-EXTENDED PLAY SINGLE). Same as above but *titled* as 12" .

COMPACT DISCS

(cd)	=	The (COMPACT DISC) album. All 5" circular and mostly silver on its groove side. Perspex casing also includes lyrics & info, etc. Introduced late in 1982, and widely the following year (even earlier for classical music). Initially for top recording artists, but now in 1996 nearly every release is in cd format. Playing time normally over 50 minutes and containing extra tracks or mixes. Possible playing time is just under 80 minutes. Marketed as unscratchable, although if they go uncleaned, they will stick just as vinyl. Average price as early 1996 is £15, and will become collectable, possibly early in the next century if, like most predictions, they do not deteriorate with time.
(d-cd)	=	The (DOUBLE-COMPACT DISC) album . . . same as above although very pricey, between £16 and £25..
(cd-s)	=	The (COMPACT DISC-SINGLE). Mainly all 5" (but some 3" cd-s could only be played with a compatible gadget inside the normal cd player). Playing time over 15 minutes to average 25 minutes, containing 4 or 5 tracks. Introduced in 1986 to compete with the 12" ep or cassette. 99% contained extra tracks to normal formats. Cost new around over £5.00, which soon rise to over double that, after a couple years of release.

(pic-cd-s) = The (PICTURE-COMPACT DISC-SINGLE). Has picture on disc, which gives it its collectability. Also on (pic-cd-ep).

(vid-pic-s) = The (VIDEO-COMPACT DISC-SINGLE). A video cd, which can be played through stereo onto normal compatible TV screen. Very costly procedure, but still might be the format of the future. Promo videos can be seen on pub juke-boxes, which has made redundant the returning Wurlitzer style. Note:- This is the only mention of videos in the book, although a selective videography might be introduced for a mid-90's update.

DIGITAL AUDIO TAPE

(dat) = The (DIGITAL AUDIO TAPE) album. Introduced in the mid-80's, and except for Japan and the rich yuppie, are not widely issued. It is a smaller version of the cassette, with the quality of the cd.

Another format (which I have not included) is the CARTRIDGE, which was available at the same time as the cassette. When the cassette finally won the battle in the early 80's, the cartridge became redundant. All car-owners over the world were happy when thieves made them replace the stolen cartridge player with the resurrected cassette. You can still buy these second-hand, but remember you'll have to obtain a second-hand 20-year-old player, with parts possibly not available.

Other abbreviations: repl. = replaced / comp = compilation / re-iss. = re-issued / re-dist. = re-distributed

---

RECORD-LABEL ABBREVIATIONS

Amphetamine Reptile – A. Reptile
Beachheads in Space – Beachheads
Blanco y Negro – Blanco Y N.
Coast to Coast – Coast Coast
Factory Benelux – Factory Ben.
Hypertension – Hypertens

Magnum Force – Magnum F.
Music Of Life – M.O.L.
One Little Indian – O L Indian
Paisley Park – Paisley P.
Regal Starline – Regal Star
Road Goes on Forever – Road Goes
Silva Screen – Silva Screen

Thunderbolt – Thunderb.
Vinyl Solution – Vinyl Sol.
Worker's Playtime – Worker's P.
20th Century – 20th Cent

ABC Paramount – ABC Para
Beat Goes On – B.G.O.
Castle Communications – Castle
Def American – Def Amer.
FanClub – Fan Club
Les Tempes Modern – Les Temps

Marble Arch – Marble A.
Music for Nations – M. F. N.
Pacific Jazz – Pacific J.
RCA Victor – RCA Victor
Regal Zonophone – Regal Zono.
Sacred Heart – Sacred H.
Special Delivery – Special D.

Transatlantic – Transatla.
Vinyl Japan – Vinyl Jap
World Pacific – World Pac.
92 Happy Customers – 92 Happy C.

Alt. Tent. – Alt. Tent.
Beggar's Banquet – Beggar's B.
Cooking Vinyl – Cooking V.
Emergency Broadcast – Emergency
Food For Thought – Food for Tht.
Les Disques Du Crepescule – Crepescule
MintyFresh – Minty Fresh
Music for Midgets – M. F. Midgets
Pye International – Pye Inter
Red Rhino Europe – R.R.E.
Return to Sender – R. T. S.
Seminal Tway – Seminal Tw
Sympathy for the Record Industry – Sympathy F.
United Artists – United Art
Warner Brothers – Warners
4th & Broadway – 4th & Broad.

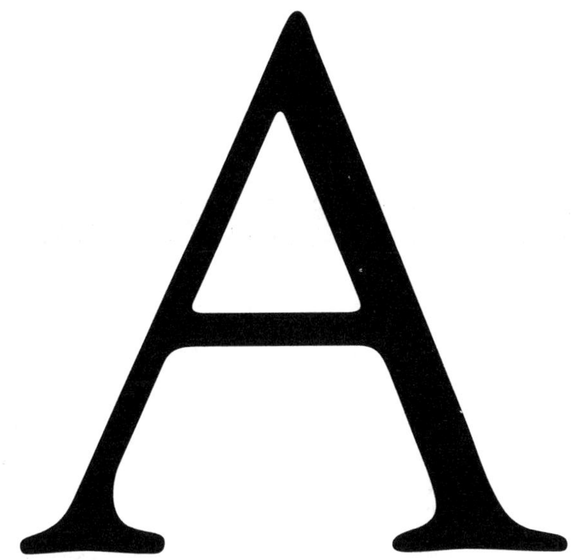

AC/DC

Formed: Sydney, Australia . . . 1973, by brothers MALCOLM and ANGUS YOUNG. By 1974 they had moved to Melbourne, where among other new men, they found petty criminal BON SCOTT. Older brother GEORGE YOUNG and HARRY VANDA (ex-EASYBEATS) set-up contract on their 'Albert' records, and also guided them with production. Early 1976 they signed to 'Atlantic' UK, and moved base to London. With constant touring they were soon to become one of the largest worldwide attractions. In 1980, they even overcame sudden death of BON, by replacing him with soundalike Englishman BRIAN JOHNSON. After the release of No.1 album 'BACK IN BLACK', they grew into top international group in the 80's. • **Style:** Initially branded as punks, probably due to schoolboy uniformed ANGUS. Metal fans started to appreciate his boogie style guitar picking, and also BON's bare-chested high screech vocals. With typical though tongue-in-cheek / double-entendre sexist lyrics, their blend of hard rock heavy metal has and will last for years. • **Songwriters:** Most by YOUNG brothers, some with SCOTT or JOHNSON. Covered; BABY PLEASE DON'T GO (Muddy Waters) / BONNY (trad). • **Miscellaneous:** At two separate US concerts Nov'90 / Jan'91, three youths were killed.

Recommended: HIGH VOLTAGE (UK *8) / DIRTY DEEDS DONE DIRT CHEAP (*7) / LET THERE BE ROCK (*7) / HIGHWAY TO HELL (*7) / BACK IN BLACK (*7) / IF YOU WANT BLOOD . . . (*8) / BALLBREAKER (*7)

ANGUS YOUNG (b.31 Mar'59, Glasgow, Scotland) – guitar / **MALCOLM YOUNG** (b. 6 Jan'53, Glasgow) – guitar / **DAVE EVANS** – vocals / **ROB BAILEY** – bass / **PETER CLACK** – drums

not iss. — Albert AUSTRALIA

Jul 74. (7") **CAN I SIT NEXT TO YOU. / ROCKIN' IN THE PARLOUR** [-] [-]

— When all but the brothers departed, they recruited (i.e.DAVE joined RABBIT) **BON SCOTT** (b.RONALD SCOTT, 9 Jul'46, Kirriemuir, Scotland) – vocals (ex-VALENTINES, ex-FRATERNITY, ex-SPECTORS, ex-MOUNT LOFTY RANGERS) / **MARK EVANS** – (b. 2 Mar'56, Melbourne) – bass (ex-BUSTER BROWN) / **PHIL RUDD** (b.19 May'54, Melbourne) – drums

Albert AUSTRALIA

Jan 75. (lp) **HIGH VOLTAGE** [-] [-]
– Baby please don't go / You ain't got a hold of me / Soul stripper / Show business / Love song / Stick around / Little lover / She's got balls.

1975. (7") **DOG EAT DOG. / CARRY ME HOME** [-] [-]

Dec 75. (lp) **T.N.T.** [-] [-]
– It's a long way to the top (if you wanna rock'n'roll) / Rock'n'roll singer / Can I sit next to you, girl? / T.N.T. / Live wire / High voltage / The jack / School days / Rocker.

Atlantic — Atco

Apr 76. (7") **IT'S A LONG WAY TO THE TOP (IF YOU WANNA ROCK'N'ROLL). / CAN I SIT NEXT TO YOU, GIRL?** [ ] [-]
(re-iss.Jun80 on 'Heavy Metal-Atlantic', hit UK 55)

May 76. (lp)(c) **HIGH VOLTAGE** (comp.from 2 above) [ ] [-]
– It's a long way to the top (if you wanna rock'n'roll) / Rock'n'roll singer / She's got the jack / T.N.T. / Can I sit next to you girl? / Little lover / She's got balls / High voltage / Live wire. *(US-iss.Apr81) (re-iss.+cd.Oct87) (re-iss.cd+c Jul94)*

Aug 76. (7") **JAILBREAK. / FLING THING** [ ] [-]

Oct 76. (7") **HIGH VOLTAGE. / LIVE WIRE** [ ] [-]
(re-iss.Jun80 on 'Heavy Metal-Atlantic', hit UK 48)

1976. (7") **HIGH VOLTAGE. / IT'S A LONG WAY TO THE TOP** [-] [ ]

Dec 76. (lp)(c) **DIRTY DEEDS DONE DIRT CHEAP** [ ] [-]
– Dirty deeds done dirt cheap / Love at first feel / Big balls / Rocker / Problem child / There's gonna be some rockin' / Ain't no fun (waiting round to be a millionaire) / Ride on / Squealer. *(US-iss.Apr81 hit No.3 (UK-re-iss.+cd.Aug87) (re-iss.cd+c Jul94)*

Jan 77. (7"m) **DIRTY DEEDS DONE DIRT CHEAP. / BIG BALLS / THE JACK** [ ] [-]
(re-iss.Jun80 on 'Heavy Metal-Atlantic', hit UK 47)

— **CLIFF WILLIAMS** (b.14 Dec'49, Romford, England) – bass (ex-HOME, ex-BANDIT) repl. MARK

Sep 77. (7") **LET THERE BE ROCK. / PROBLEM CHILD** [ ] [ ]

Oct 77. (lp)(c) **LET THERE BE ROCK** [17] [ ]
– Go down / Dog eat dog / Let there be rock / Bad boy boogie / Overdose / Crapsody in blue / Hell ain't a bad place to be / Whole lotta Rosie. *(cd.Jun89) (re-iss.cd,c,lp Oct94)*

Atlantic — Atlantic

May 78. (lp)(c) **POWERAGE** [26] [ ]
– Gimme a bullet / Down payment blues / Up to my neck in you / Sin city / Gone shooting / What's next to the Moon / Riff raff / Cold hearted man / Kicked in the teeth. *(cd-iss.Jun89) (re-iss.cd,c Oct94)*

May 78. (7")(12") **ROCK'N'ROLL DAMNATION. / SIN CITY** [24] [ ]

Jun 78. (7") **ROCK'N'ROLL DAMNATION. / KICKED IN THE TEETH** [-] [ ]

Oct 78. (lp)(c) **IF YOU WANT BLOOD, YOU'VE GOT IT (live)** [13] [ ]
– Riff raff / Hell ain't a bad place to be / Bad boy boogie / The jack / Problem child / Whole lotta Rosie / Rock'n'roll damnation / High voltage / Let there be rock / Rocker. *(cd-iss.Jun89) (re-iss.cd,c Oct94)*

Oct 78. (7")(12") **WHOLE LOTTA ROSIE (live). / HELL AIN'T A BAD PLACE TO BE (live)** [ ] [ ]
(re-iss.Jun80 on 'Heavy Metal-Atlantic', hit UK 36)

Aug 79. (lp)(c) **HIGHWAY TO HELL** [8] [17]
– Highway to Hell / Girl's got rhythm / Touch too much / Beating around the bush / Shot down in flames / Get it hot / If you want blood (you've got it) / Love hungry / Night prowler. *(re-iss.+cd.Jul87) (re-cd. 1989)*

Aug 79. (7") **HIGHWAY TO HELL. / IF YOU WANT BLOOD (YOU'VE GOT IT)** [56] [-]

Aug 79. (7") **HIGHWAY TO HELL. / NIGHT PROWLER** [-] [47]

Oct 79. (7") **GIRL'S GOT RHYTHM. / GET IT HOT** [ ] [-]
(7"ep) – ('A'side) / If you want blood (you've got it) / Hell ain't a bad place to be (live) / Rock'n'roll damnation.

Jan 80. (7"m) **TOUCH TOO MUCH (live). / LIVE WIRE (live) / SHOT DOWN IN FLAMES (live)** [29] [ ]

— **BRIAN JOHNSON** (b.5 Oct'47, Newcastle, England) – vocals (ex-GEORDIE) repl. BON SCOTT who died 20 Feb'80, after drunken binge.

Jul 80. (lp)(c) **BACK IN BLACK** [1] [4]
– Back in black / Hell's bells / Shoot to thrill / Give the dog a bone / What do you do for money, honey? / Rock'n'roll ain't noise pollution / Let me put my love into you / You shook me all night long / Shake a leg / Have a drink on me. *(re-iss.+cd.Feb87)*

Sep 80. (7") **YOU SHOOK ME ALL NIGHT LONG. / HAVE A DRINK ON ME** [38] [35]

Nov 80. (7")(12") **ROCK'N'ROLL AIN'T NOISE POLLUTION. / HELL'S BELLS** [15] [ ]

Feb 81. (7") **BACK IN BLACK. /WHAT DO YOU DO FOR MONEY HONEY** [-] [37]

Nov 81. (lp)(c) **FOR THOSE ABOUT TO ROCK (WE SALUTE YOU)** [3] [1]
– For those about to rock (we salute you) / Put the finger on you / Let's get it up / Inject the venom / Snowballed / Evil walk / C.O.D. / Breaking the laws / Night of the long knives / Spellbound. *(re-iss.+cd.Jul87) (re-iss.cd+c Jul94)*

Jan 82. (7") **LET'S GET IT UP. / BACK IN BLACK (live)** [13] [-]
(12"+=) – T.N.T.(live).

Jan 82 (7") **LET'S GET IT UP. / SNOWBALLED** [-] [44]

Jun 82 (7") **FOR THOSE ABOUT TO ROCK (WE SALUTE YOU). / T.N.T.** [-] [ ]

Jun 82. (7")(12") **FOR THOSE ABOUT TO ROCK (WE SALUTE YOU). / LET THERE BE ROCK (live)** [15] [ ]

Aug 83. (lp)(c) **FLICK OF THE SWITCH** [4] [15]
– Rising power / This house is on fire / Flick of the switch / Nervous shakedown / Landslide / Guns for fire / Deep in the hole / Bedlam in Belguim / Badlands / Brain shake. *(re-iss.+cd.Jul87) (re-iss.cd,c Oct94)*

Sep 83. (7")(7"sha-pic-d) **GUNS FOR HIRE. / LANDSLIDE** [37] [84]

Jan 84. (7") **JAILBREAK. / SHOW BUSINESS** [-] [ ]

Mar 84. (7") **FLICK OF THE SWITCH. / BADLANDS** [-] [ ]

— **SIMON WRIGHT** (b.19 Jun'63) – drums (ex-A II Z, ex-TYTAN) repl. RUDD

Jul 84. (7")(7"sha-pic-d) **NERVOUS SHAKEDOWN. / ROCK'N'ROLL AIN'T NOISE POLLUTION (live)** [35] [ ]
(12"+=)(c-s+=) – Sin city (live) / This house is on fire (live).
Jun 85. (7")(12")(7"sha-pic-d) **DANGER. / BACK IN BUSINESS** [48] [ ]
Jul 85. (lp)(c)(cd) **FLY ON THE WALL** [7] [32]
– Fly on the wall / Shake your foundations / First blood / Danger / Sink the pink / Playing with the girls / Stand up / Hell or high water / Back in business / Send for the man.
Jan 86. (7")(7"sha-pic-d) **SHAKE YOUR FOUNDATIONS. / STAND UP** [24] [ ]
Nov 85. (7") **SHAKE YOUR FOUNDATIONS. / SEND FOR THE MAN** [-] [ ]
(12"+=) – Jailbreak.
May 86. (7")(7"sha-pic-d) **WHO MADE WHO. / GUNS FOR HIRE (live)** [16] [ ]
(12") – ('A'collectors mix).
May 86. (lp)(c) **WHO MADE WHO (Soundtrack; Maximum Overdrive)**(part compilation) [11] [33]
– Who made who / You shook me all night long / D.T. / Sink the pink / Ride on / Hells bells / Shake your foundations / Chase the ace / For those about to rock (we salute you). *(cd-iss. 1988)*
Jan 88. (7") **HEATSEEKER. / GO ZONE** [12] [ ]
(12"+=)(12"pic-d+=) – Snake high.
Feb 88. (lp)(c)(cd) **BLOW UP YOUR VIDEO** [2] [12]
– Heatseeker / That's the way I wanna rock'n'roll / Meanstreak / Go zone / Kissin' dynamite / Nick of time / Some sin for nuthin' / Ruff stuff / Two's up / Some sin for nuthin' / This means war.
Mar 88. (7") **THAT'S THE WAY I WANNA ROCK'N'ROLL. / KISSIN' DYNAMITE** [22] [ ]
(12"+=)(12"pic-d+=) – Borrowed time.
(cd-s+=) – Shoot to thrill (live) / Whole lotta Rosie (live).

— (Apr88) cousin **STEVE YOUNG** – guitar briefly replaces MALCOLM on tour

— (1989) (ANGUS, MALCOLM, BRIAN & CLIFF) bring in **CHRIS SLADE** (b.30 Oct'46) – drums (ex-GARY MOORE, ex-MANFRED MANN EARTHBAND, ex-FIRM) repl. WRIGHT who had joined DIO.

Atco Atco

Sep 90. (7")(c-s)(10"pic-d) **THUNDERSTRUCK. / FIRE YOUR GUNS** [13] [ ]
(12"+=)(cd-s+=) – D.T. / Chase the ace.
Oct 90. (cd)(c)(lp) **THE RAZOR'S EDGE** [4] [2]
– Thunderstruck / Fire your guns / Moneytalks / The razor's edge / Mistress for Christmas / Rock your heart out / Are you ready / Got you by the balls / Shot of love / Let's make it / Goodbye & good riddance to bad luck / If you dare.
Nov 90. (7")(c-s) **MONEYTALKS. / MISTRESS FOR CHRISTMAS** [36] [23]
(12"+=)(cd-s+=)(12"sha-pic-d+=) – Borrowed time.
Apr 91. (7")(c-s)(7"pic-d) **ARE YOU READY. / GOT YOU BY THE BALLS** [34] [ ]
(12"+=)(cd-s+=) – The razor's edge.
Oct 92. (7") **HIGHWAY TO HELL (live) / HELL'S BELLS (live)** [14] [ ]
(12"pic-d) – ('A'side)/ High voltage (live).
(cd-s+= of above; 2 diff.) – The jack (live)/ or / Hell ain't a bad place to be (live).
Oct 92. (cd)(pic-d-cd)(c)(d-lp) **LIVE (live)** [5] [15]
– Thunderstruck / Shoot to thrill / Back in black / Sin city / Who made who / Fire your guns / Jailbreak / The jack / The razor's edge / Dirty deeds done dirt cheap / Hells bells / Heatseeker / That's the way I wanna rock'n'roll / High voltage / You shook me all night long / Whole lotta Rosie / Let there be rock / Medley:- Bonny – Highway to Hell / T.N.T. / For those about to rock (we salute you). *(In the US, a SPECIAL COLLECTOR'S EDITION hit No.26)*
Feb 93. (12")(cd-s) **DIRTY DEEDS DONE DIRT CHEAP (live). / SHOOT TO THRILL (live)/ DIRTY DEEDS DONE DIRT CHEAP** [68] [ ]
Jun 93. (7")(c-s) **BIG GUN. / BACK IN BLACK (live)** [23] [65]
(12"+=)(cd-s+=) – For those about to rock (live).
(cd-s) – (excludes B-side).
Sep 95. (7"yellow)(cd-s)(cd-s) **HARD AS A ROCK. / CAUGHT WITH YOUR PANTS DOWN** [33] [ ]
Sep 95. (cd)(c)(lp) **BALLBREAKER** [6] [4]
– Whisky on the rocks / The honey roll / The furor / Love bomb / Hard as a rock / Hail Caesar / Cover you in oil / Caught with your pants down / Burnin' alive / Boogie man / Ballbreaker.

. . . Jan – Jun '96 stop press . . .

Apr 96. (single) **HAIL CAESAR** [56] [ ]

– compilations, others, etc. –

Aug 86. Atlantic; (7")(7"sha-pic-d) **YOU SHOOK ME ALL NIGHT LONG. / SHE'S GOT BALLS (live)** [46] [ ]
(12")(12"sha-pic-d) – ('B'extended) / ('A'live).
Aug 84. US= Atco; (m-lp) **JAILBREAK '74** (early demos..) [-] [76]
(re-iss.cd Oct94)
1991. Atco; (3xcd-box) **BOX SET** [ ] [-]
– HIGHWAY TO HELL / BACK IN BLACK / FOR THOSE ABOUT TO ROCK.

– Australian compilations (selective) – (on 'E.M.I.')

Sep 87. (6xbox-lp) **BOX SET** [-] [-]
– (lp's) – TNT / HIGH VOLTAGE / DIRTY DEEDS.. / LET THERE.. / POWERAGE / HIGHWAY. (12"free w/above) **COLD HEARTED MAN. /**
Dec 87. (5xbox-lp) **BOX SET 2** [-] [-]
– (lp's) – BACK IN.. / FOR THOSE.. / FLICK OF.. / FLY ON THE WALL / WHO MADE WHO

ADAM & THE ANTS

Formed: London, England ... April'77 by STUART GODDARD (aka ADAM ANT), LESTER SQUARE – guitar / ANDY WARREN – bass / PAUL FLANAGAN – drums. ADAM acted! in Derek Jarman's controversial punk movie JUBILEE (Released Feb'78). By then DAVE BARBE was on drums / JORDAN extra vocals and MARK GAUMONT – guitar. Recorded 'Plastic Surgery' and 'Deutcher Girls' for film. On latter JOHNNY BIVOUAC had replaced GAUMONT (Oct'77). In mid '78 and with another change of line-up (see below) they signed one-off deal with 'Decca'. The following year indie 'Do-It' label gave them another break. 1980 saw them/him on 'CBS' and taking UK charts by storm. After two 1981 chart-toppers 'STAND AND DELIVER' & 'PRINCE CHARMING', ADAM went solo, immediately striking the top again with 'GOODY TWO SHOES'. Things slowed down and finally ground to a halt by 1985, although a 1990 comeback saw 'ROOM AT THE TOP' hit UK & US Top 20. • **Style:** Punk "indie" pop which in the mid 80's; guided by manager/svengali MALCOLM McLAREN, saw them incorporating old Borundi-style dual drummers. Fashion too had moved ADAM into teeny-bop market as his stage attire moved into and from pirate to highwayman. • **Songwriters:** GODDARD / ASHMAN in the 70's, to GODDARD / PIRRONI in the 80's. • **Trivia:** He acted in stage production of 'Entertaining Mr.Sloane'. After retiring to the States in 1986 he took parts in 'Slam Dance' film, and 'Equalizer' TV serial.
Recommended: DIRK WEAR WHITE SOX (*6) / HITS (1980-1985) (*5)

ADAM ANT (b. STUART GODDARD, 3 Nov'54) – vocals, guitar / **MATTHEW ASHMAN** (b.'62) – guitar, vocals (ex-KAMERAS) / **ANDY WARREN** (b.'61) – bass, vocals / **DAVE BARBE** (b.'61) – drums (ex-DESOLATION ANGELS)

Decca not issued

Oct 78. (7") **YOUNG PARISIANS. / LADY** [ ] [-]
(re-iss.Dec80 hit 9) (re-iss.Oct89 on 'Damaged Goods')

Do-It not issued

Jun 79. (7") **ZEROX. / PHYSICAL (YOU'RE SO) (ltd.3,000)** [ ] [-]
(later Jun79 copies had B-side **WHIP IN MY VALISE**) (This version also re-iss.Jan81 hit 45)
Nov 79. (lp) **DIRK WEARS WHITE SOX** [ ] [-]
– Cartrouble (part 1 & 2) / Digital tenderness / Nine plan failed / Day I met God * / Tabletalk / Cleopatra / Catholic day / Never trust a man (with egg on his face) / Animals and men / Family of noise / The idea. *(re-iss.Jan81 hit 16) (remixed re-iss.Apr83 on 'CBS', track* replaced by; Zerox / Kick! / Whip in my valise). (cd-iss.Jul95 on 'Columbia')*

— **LEIGH GORMAN** – bass (on B-side) repl. WARREN who joined MONOCHROME SET

Feb 80. (7") **CARTROUBLE. / KICK!** [ ] [-]
(re-iss.Jan81 hit 33)

— (Jan80) until (Mar80 when ADAM brought in entire new group) **MARCO PIRRONI** – guitar, vocals (ex-MODELS) repl. ASHMAN / **MERRICK** (b.CHRIS HUGHES) – drums repl. BARBE / **KEVIN MOONEY** – bass, vocals repl. GORMAN (who with above 2 formed BOW WOW WOW) / added **TERRY LEE MIALL** – 2nd drummer (ex-MODELS)

C.B.S. Epic

Jul 80. (7") **KINGS OF THE WILD FRONTIER. / PRESS DARLINGS** [48] [ ]
Sep 80. (7") **DOG EAT DOG. / PHYSICAL (YOU'RE SO)** [4] [ ]
Nov 80. (lp)(c) **KINGS OF THE WILD FRONTIER** [1] [44] Feb81
– Dog eat dog / Ant music / Feed me to the lions / Los Rancheros / Ants invasion / Killer in the home / Kings of the wild frontier / The magnificent five / Don't be square (be there) / Jolly Roger / Making history / The human beings. *(re-iss.cd Oct93 on 'Sony Europe')*
Nov 80. (7") **ANT MUSIC. / FALL IN** [2] [-]
Jan 81. (7")(12") **ANT MUSIC. / DON'T BE SQUARE (BE THERE)** [-] [ ]
Feb 81. (7") **KINGS OF THE WILD FRONTIER. / PRESS DARLING** [2] [ ]
(re-issue)

— **GARY TIBBS** – bass (ex-ROXY MUSIC, ex-VIBRATORS) repl. MOONEY

May 81. (7")(US-12") **STAND AND DELIVER. / BEAT MY GUEST** [1] [ ]
Sep 81. (7") **PRINCE CHARMING. / CHRISTIAN D'OR** [1] [ ]
Nov 81. (lp)(c) **PRINCE CHARMING** [2] [94]

– Prince Charming / The Scorpios / Picasso visita el Planeta de los Simios / 5 guns west / That voodoo / Stand and deliver / Mile high club / Ant rap / Mowhok / S.E.X. *(re-iss.cd Oct93 on 'Sony Europe')*

Dec 81. (7")(7"pic-d) **ANT RAP. / FRIENDS** [3] [ ]

—— (ADAM & THE ANTS broke up Jan82)

Adam ANT

continued solo augmented by **PIRRONI** and sessioners.

May 82. (7")(7"pic-d) **GOODY TWO SHOES. / RED SCAB** [1] [-]

Sep 82. (7")(7"pic-d) **FRIEND OR FOE. / JUANITO THE BANDITO** [9] [ ]

Oct 82. (lp)(c) **FRIEND OR FOE** [5] [16]
– Friend or foe / Something girls / Place in the country / Desperate but not serious / Here comes the grump / Hello I love you / Goody two shoes / Crackpot history and the right to lie / Made of money / Cajun twisters / Try this for sighs / A man called Marco.

Nov 82. (7")(7"pic-d) **DESPERATE BUT NOT SERIOUS. / WHY DO GIRLS LOVE HORSES?** [33] [ ] Mar 83

Jan 83. (7") **GOODY TWO SHOES. / CRACKPOT HISTORY** [-] [12]

Mar 83. (7") **DESPERATE BUT NOT SERIOUS. / PLACE IN THE COUNTRY** [-] [66]

Oct 83. (7")(7"pic-d) **PUSS'N'BOOTS. / KISS THE DRUMMER** [5] [ ] May 84
(12"+=) – ('A'+'B'extended).

Nov 83. (lp)(c) **STRIP** [20] [65]
– Baby let me scream at you / Libertine / Spanish games / Vanity / Puss'n'boots / Playboy / Strip / Montreal / Navel to neck / Amazon. *(cd-iss.Jul84)*

Dec 83. (7")(7"pic-d) **STRIP. / YOURS, YOURS, YOURS** [41] [42]
(12"+=) – ('A'&'B'extended).

Sep 84. (7")(12") **APOLLO 9. / B SIDE BABY** [13] [ ]
(extra 12") – ('A'side) / ('A'instrumental).

Jul 85. (7") **VIVE LE ROCK. / GRETA X** [50] [ ]
(12"+=) – ('A'instrumental).

Sep 85. (lp)(c)(cd) **VIVE LE ROCK** [42] [ ]
– Vive le rock / Miss Thing / Razor keen / Rip down / Scorpio rising / Apollo 9 / Hell's eight acres / Mohair lockeroom pin-up boys / No zap / P.O.E. (c+=) – Human bondage den. (cd+=) – Apollo 9 (acapella). *(re-iss.cd Mar95 on 'Rewind')*

—— ADAM retired for 4 years. MARCO joined SPEAR OF DESTINY

ADAM ANT

brought back MARCO to resurrect career.

M.C.A. M.C.A.

Feb 90. (7")(c-s) **ROOM AT THE TOP. / BRUCE LEE** [13] [17]
(12"+=)(cd-s+=) – ('A'house vocals).

Mar 90. (cd)(c)(lp) **MANNERS & PHYSICIQUE** [19] [57]
– Room at the top / If you keep on / Can't set rules about love / Bright lights black leather / Young dumb and full of it / Rough stuff / Manners & physicique / U.S.S.A. / Piccadilly / Anger Inc.

Apr 90. (7")(c-s) **CAN'T SET RULES ABOUT LOVE. / HOW TO STEAL THE WORLD** [47] [ ]
(12"+=) – Brand new torso.
(cd-s++=) – ('A'-lp version).

Jun 90. (7") **BRIGHT LIGHTS BLACK LEATHER. / ROUGH STUFF** [-] [ ]

—— w/ **PIRRONI** / **BOZ BOORER** -guitars / **BRUCE WITKIN** -bass / **DAVE RUFFY** -drums

E.M.I. Capitol

Jan 95. (7")(c-s) **WONDERFUL. / GOES AROUND** [32] [ ]
(cd-s+=) – Norman / Woman love run through me.
(cd-s) – ('A'side) / If / Phoenix.

Mar 95. (7")(c-s) **BEAUTIFUL DREAM. / LET'S HAVE A FIGHT** [ ] [ ]
(cd-s+=) – Billy boy / Wonderful (acoustic).
(cd-s) – ('A'side) / Shake your hips / Ant music (acoustic) / ('A'-Lucas master mix).

Apr 95. (cd)(c) **WONDERFUL** [24] [39]
– Won't take that talk / Beautiful dream / Wonderful / 1969 again / Yin & Yang / Image of yourself / Alien / Gotta be a sin / Vampires / Angel / Very long ride.

May 95. (c-s) **GOTTA BE A SIN / DOG EAT DOG (live)** [48] [ ]
(cd-s) – ('A'side) / Cleopatra (live) / Beat my guest (live) / Red scab (live).
(cd-s) – ('A'side) / Desperate but not serious (live) / Car trouble (live) / Physical (you're so) (live).

– compilations, others, etc. –

Feb 82. E.G.; (7") **DEUTCHER GIRLS. / PLASTIC SURGERY** [13] [-]

Mar 82. Do-It; (7"ep)(7"pic-d) **THE B-SIDES** [46] [-]
– Friends / Kick! / Physical (you're so).
(12"ep) – ANTMUSIC (+=) – Cartrouble (part 1 & 2).

Jan 88. Old Gold; (7") **ANT MUSIC. / STAND AND DELIVER** [ ] [-]

Nov 90. Old Gold; (7") **PRINCE CHARMING. / GOODY TWO SHOES** [ ] [-]

Sep 86. C.B.S./ US= Epic; (lp)(c)(cd) **HITS** (1980-85) [ ] [ ]
– Kings of the wild frontier / Dog eat dog / Ant music / Stand and deliver / Prince Charming / Ant rap / Goody two shoes / Friend or foe / Desperate but not serious / Puss'n'boots / Strip / Apollo 9 / Vive le rock.

Feb 91. Strange Fruit; (cd)(lp) **THE PEEL SESSIONS** (early 1979 material) [ ] [-]

Jun 91. Columbia; (cd)(c) **ANTICS IN THE FORBIDDEN ZONE** (solo) [ ] [-]
(re-iss.cd Oct94 on 'Rewind')

Oct 94. Columbia; (cd) **THE BEST (ADAM ANT)** [ ] [ ]

Aug 93. Arcade; (cd)(c) **ANTMUSIC – THE VERY BEST OF ADAM ANT ("ADAM ANT / ADAM & THE ANTS")** [6] [-]

Mar 94. Arcade; (cd) **ANTMUSIC -THE VERY BEST OF ADAM ANT** [30] [-]
– (w /free cd) **LIVE (live)**

May 95. Columbia; (cd) **BSIDES BABIES** [ ] [-]

Bryan ADAMS

Born:5 Nov'59, Vancouver, Canada. In 1977 he set up writing partnership with JIM VALLANCE, drummer with techo-rock band PRISM. Numerous groups including LOVERBOY / KISS / BACHMAN-TURNER OVERDRIVE / etc. used their songs before BRYAN ADAMS solo signed contract with 'A&M' early 1979. After 4 years wait, he finally broke into US Top 10 with 'STRAIGHT FROM THE HEART'. He was soon Canada's biggest export, becoming an international star, after the release of 'RUN TO YOU' single in 1984. • **Style:** Hard-edged rock/pop merging at times with 'AOR'. • **Songwriters:** ADAMS continued to write with VALLANCE until 1988, when he added producer MUTT LANGE. Covered: WALKING AFTER MIDNIGHT (D.Hecht /A.Block) / I FOUGHT THE LAW (Sonny Curtis). • **Trivia:** In '91, he stayed a record 16 consecutive weeks at UK No.1 with 'EVERYTHING I DO' from the film 'Robin Hood (Prince Of Thieves)'.

Recommended: SO FAR SO GOOD (*6)

BRYAN ADAMS – vocals, guitar with **JIM VALLANCE** – drums, keyboards, guitar, bass

A & M A & M

Jul 79. (7")(12") **LET ME TAKE YOU DANCIN'. / DON'T TURN ME AWAY** [ ] [ ]

Apr 80. (7") **HIDIN' FROM LOVE. / WAIT AND SEE** [ ] [ ]

Mar 81. (lp)(c) **BRYAN ADAMS** [ ] [ ]
– Hidin' from love / Win some, lose some / Wait and see / Give me your love / Wastin' time / Don't ya say it / Remember / State of mind / Try to see it my way. *(cd-iss.Jan87 + 1988)*

Apr 81. (7") **GIVE ME YOUR LOVE. / WAIT AND SEE** [-] [ ]

now with **TOMMY HANDEL** – keyboards / **BRIAN STANLEY** – bass + **MICKEY CURRY** – drums repl. VALLANCE (he continued to co-write + play piano + percussion for ADAMS until '88).

Mar 82. (7") **LONELY NIGHTS. / DON'T LOOK NOW** [ ] [84]

Apr 82. (lp)(c) **YOU WANT IT, YOU GOT IT** [78] [ ]
– Lonely nights / One good reason / Don't look now / Jealousy / Coming home / Fits ya good / Tonight / You want it, you got it / Last chance / No one makes it right. *(cd-iss.Aug88 + 1988)*

1982. (7") **COMING HOME. / FITS YA GOOD** [-] [ ]

—— **DAVE TAYLOR** – bass repl STANLEY / added **KEITH SCOTT** – guitar, vocals

Feb 83. (7") **CUTS LIKE A KNIFE. / ONE GOOD REASON** [-] [ ]

Apr 83. (7")(12") **STRAIGHT FROM THE HEART. / LONELY NIGHTS** [ ] [-]

Apr 83. (7") **STRAIGHT FROM THE HEART. / ONE GOOD REASON** [-] [10]

May 83. (lp)(c) **CUTS LIKE A KNIFE** [ ] [8]
– The only one / Take me back / This time / Straight from the heart / Cuts like a knife / I'm ready / What's it gonna be / Don't leave me lonely / The best has yet to come. *(re-iss.+cd.Mar86 hit UK 21) (cd re-iss.'88)*

Jun 83. (7") **CUTS LIKE A KNIFE. / LONELY NIGHTS** [-] [15]

Jul 83. (7") **CUTS LIKE A KNIFE. / FITS YA GOOD** [ ] [-]
(12"+=) – Hidin' from love.

Aug 83. (7") **THIS TIME. / FITS YA GOOD** [-] [24]

Nov 83. (7") **THE BEST HAS YET TO COME. / I'M READY** [-] [ ]

Dec 84. (7")(12") **RUN TO YOU. / I'M READY** [11] [6] Oct 84
(12"+=) – Cuts like a knife.
(d7"++=) – Lonely nights.

Feb 85. (lp)(c)(cd) **RECKLESS** [7] [1] Nov 84
– One night love affair / She's only happy when she's dancin' / Run to you / Heaven / Somebody / Summer of '69 / It's only love / Kids wanna rock / Long gone / Ain't gonna cry. *(re-iss.Jul91 hit UK No.29, Apr92 hit No.36)*

Mar 85. (7")(12")(7"pic-d) **SOMEBODY. / LONG GONE** [35] [11] Jan 85

May 85. (7")(12") **HEAVEN. / DIANA** (US B-side='A' live) [38] [1] Apr 85
(12"+=) – Fits ya good / ('A'version)
(d7"+=) – Straight from the heart / You want it, you got it.

Jun 85. (7") **SUMMER OF '69. / THE BEST HAS YET TO COME** [-] [5]

Jul 85. (7") **SUMMER OF '69. / KIDS WANNA ROCK (live)** [42] [-]

(12"+=) – The Bryan Adams mix.

Sep 85. (7") **ONE NIGHT LOVE AFFAIR. / LONELY NIGHTS** [-] [13]

Oct 85. (7")(12") **IT'S ONLY LOVE. (as "Bryan ADAMS & Tina TURNER") / THE BEST WAS YET TO COME** [29] [-]
(d7"+=) – Somebody. / Long gone.

Nov 85. (7") **IT'S ONLY LOVE (w/ TINA TURNER). / THE ONLY ONE** [-] [15]

Dec 85. (7")(12") **CHRISTMAS TIME. / REGGAE CHRISTMAS** [55] [ ]

Mar 87. (7")(12") **HEAT OF THE NIGHT. / ANOTHER DAY** [50] [6]

Mar 87. (lp)(c)(cd) **INTO THE FIRE** [10] [7]
– Heat of the night / Into the fire / Victim of love / Another day / Native son / Only the strong survive / Remembrance day / Rebel rebel / Hearts on fire / Home again. *(re-iss.cd+c Mar93)*

May 87. (7") **HEARTS ON FIRE. / THE BEST HAS YET TO COME** [-] [26]

May 87. (7")(c-s) **HEARTS ON FIRE. / RUN TO YOU** [57] [-]
(12"+=) – Native Sun.

Aug 87. (7") **VICTIM OF LOVE. / INTO THE FIRE** [-] [32]

Oct 87. (7")(c-s) **VICTIM OF LOVE. / HEAT OF THE NIGHT (live)** [68] [-]
(12"+=) – ('A'-live version).

—— BRYAN now used session people?

Jun 91. (7")(c-s) **(EVERYTHING I DO) I DO IT FOR YOU. / SHE'S ONLY HAPPY WHEN SHE'S DANCING (live)** [1] [1]
(12"+=)(cd-s+=) – ('A'extended) / Cuts like a knife.

Aug 91. (7")(c-s) **CAN'T STOP THIS THING WE STARTED. / IT'S ONLY LOVE (live)** [12] [2]
(12"+=)(cd-s+=) – Hearts on fire.

Sep 91. (cd)(c)(lp) **WAKING UP THE NEIGHBOURS** [1] [6]
– Is your mama gonna miss ya? / Hey honey – I'm rockin' you in! / Can't stop this thing we started / Thought I'd died and gone to Heaven / Not guilty / House arrest / Vanishing / Do I have to say the words? / There will never be another tonight / All I want is you / Depend on me / (Everything I do) I do it for you / If you wanna leave me (can I come too?) / Touch the hand / Don't drop that bomb on me.

Nov 91. (7")(c-s) **THERE WILL NEVER BE ANOTHER TONIGHT. / INTO THE FIRE (live)** [32] [31]
(12"+=)(cd-s+=) – One night love affair (live).

Feb 92. (7")(c-s) **I THOUGHT I'D DIED AND GONE TO HEAVEN. / SOMEBODY (live)** [8] [13]
(12"+=) – (Everything I do) I do it for you.
(cd-s+=) – Heart of the night (live).

Jul 92. (7")(c-s) **ALL I WANT IS YOU. / RUN TO YOU** [22] [-]
(12"+=)(cd-s+=) – Long gone.

Sep 92. (7")(c-s) **DO I HAVE TO SAY THE WORDS?. / SUMMER OF '69** [30] [11] Jul 92
(12"+=)(cd-s+=) – Kids wanna rock / Can't stop this thing we started.

Oct 93. (7")(c-s) **PLEASE FORGIVE ME. / C'MON EVERYBODY** [2] [7]
(cd-s+=) – Can't stop this thing we started / There will never be another tonight.

Nov 93. (cd)(c)(lp) **SO FAR SO GOOD** (compilation) [2] [7]
– Summer of '69 / Straight from the heart / It's only love / Can't stop this thing we started / Do I have to say the words? / This time / Run to you / Heaven / Cuts like a knife / (Everything I do) I do it for you / Somebody / Kids wanna rock / Heat of the night / Please forgive me

Jan 94. (7")(c-s) **ALL FOR LOVE. ("BRYAN ADAMS / ROD STEWART / STING") / ('A'instrumental)** [2] [1] Nov 93
(cd-s) – ('A'side) / Straight from the heart (live) (BRYAN ADAMS) / If only (ROD STEWART) / Love is stronger than justice (live) (STING).

—— Above hit from the film 'The Three Musketeers'.

Jul 94. (cd)(c) **LIVE! LIVE! LIVE!** (rec.live Belguim 1988) [17] [ ]
– She's only happy when she's dancin' / It's only love / Cuts like a knife / Kids wanna rock / Hearts on fire / Take me back / The best was yet to come / Heaven / Heat of the night / Run to you / One night love affair / Long gone / Summer of '69 / Somebody / Walking after midnight / I fought the law / Into the fire.

Apr 95. (7")(c-s)(cd-s) **HAVE YOU EVER REALLY LOVED A WOMAN?. / LOW LIFE** [4] [1]

. . . Jan – Jun '96 stop press . . .

May 96. (single) **THE ONLY THING THAT LOOKS GOOD ON ME IS YOU** [6] [52]

Jun 96. (cd)(c)(lp) **18 'TIL I DIE** [1] [31]

– compilations, others, etc. –

Feb 86. A&M; (7") **THIS TIME. / I'M READY** [41] [-]
(12"+=) – Lonely nights.

Jul 86. A&M; (7") **STRAIGHT FROM THE HEART. / FITS YA GOOD** [51] [-]
(12"+=) – ('A'-live version).

Jun 89. A&M; (c) **CUTS LIKE A KNIFE / RECKLESS** [ ] [-]

SWEENY TODD

On the 2nd lp below he had replaced NICK GILDER.

1992. Receiver; (cd)(lp) **IF WISHES WERE HORSES** (re-issue) [ ] [-]

AEROSMITH

Formed: Sunapee, New Hampshire, USA . . . Summer 1970, by PERRY and TYLER, who with others moved to Boston, Massachusetts. By 1972, through a Max's Kansas City gig, they were signed to 'Columbia' by Clive Davis for a six figure sum. Soon became one of America's top live attractions earning platinum record sales in the process. Still going strong in the 90's and unleashed another great slice of rock'n'roll in 1993 'GET A GRIP'. • **Style:** Heavyweight hard glam-rock outfit, fronted by JAGGER lookalike STEVE TYLER. Cited by many new breed heavy bands as major influence. • **Songwriters:** PERRY / TYLER (aka TOXIC TWINS) except; COME TOGETHER (Beatles) / WALKIN' THE DOG (Rufus Thomas) / REMEMBER WALKIN' IN THE SAND (Shangri-la's) / TRAIN KEPT A-ROLLIN' (Johnny Burnette Trio) / MILK COW BLUES (Kokomo Arnold) / CRY ME A RIVER (Julie London) / MY ADIDAS (Run DMC). THE JOE PERRY PROJECT:- GET IT ON (BANG A GONG) (T.Rex) /BIG TEN-INCH RECORD (F.Weismantel; blues artist?) / ALL YOUR LOVE (Otis Rush) / HELTER SKELTER (Beatles) / CHIP AWAY THE STONE (Richie Supa) / . • **Miscellaneous:** In 1978 group appeared in the 'SGT. PEPPER' Beatles film. Early 1981 TYLER was nearly killed in a motorcycle accident, thus delaying 8th lp release.

Recommended: GREATEST HITS (*9) / PUMP (*8) / GET A GRIP (*7).

STEVE TYLER (b.STEVEN TALARICO, 26 Mar'48, New York) – vocals / **JOE PERRY** (b.10 Sep'50) – guitar (ex-JAM BAND) / **BRAD WHITFORD** (b.23 Feb'52, Winchester, Mass.) – guitar repl. RAY TABANO / **TOM HAMILTON** (b.31 Dec'51, Colorado Springs) – bass (ex-JAM BAND) / **JOEY KRAMER** (b.21 Jun'50, New York) – drums

C.B.S. Columbia

Jun 73. (lp)(c) **AEROSMITH** [-] [ ]
– Make it / Somebody / Dream on / One way street / Mama kin / Write me (a letter) / Movin' out / Walkin' the dog. *(UK-iss.Sep74) (US re-iss.Mar76 hit No.21) (US re-iss.Sep87, cd-May88) (UK cd Mar92) (re-iss.cd Dec93 on 'Columbia')*

Nov 73. (7") **DREAM ON. / SOMEBODY** [ ] [59] Oct 73
(UK re-iss.Apr76) (US re-iss.Jan76, reached no.6)

Mar 74. (7") **SPACED. / TRAIN KEPT A-ROLLIN'** [-] [ ]

Jun 74. (7") **S.O.S. (TOO BAD). / LORD OF THE THIGHS** [-] [ ]

Nov 74. (lp)(c) **GET YOUR WINGS** [ ] [74] Mar 74
– Same old song and dance / Lord of the thighs / Spaced / Woman of the world / S.O.S. (too bad) / Train kept a-rollin' / Season of wither / Pandora's box. *(US re-iss.Sep87, cd-May88) (UK-cd Mar92) (re-iss.cd Dec93 on 'Columbia')*

Nov 74. (7") **SAME OLD SONG AND DANCE. / PANDORA'S BOX** [-] [ ]

Jul 75. (lp)(c) **TOYS IN THE ATTIC** [ ] [11] Apr 75
– Toys in the attic / Uncle Salty / Adam's apple / Walk this way / Big ten inch record / Sweet emotion / No more no more / Round and round / You see me crying. *(re-iss.1987 on 'Castle') (US re-iss.Sep87, cd-May88) (UK re-iss.+cd.Apr91 & Nov93 on 'Columbia')*

Jun 75. (7") **SWEET EMOTION. / UNCLE SALTY** [-] [36]

Sep 75. (7") **WALK THIS WAY. / ROUND AND ROUND** [-] [ ]

Nov 75. (7") **TOYS IN THE ATTIC. / YOU SEE ME CRYING** [-] [ ]

Jun 76. (lp)(c) **ROCKS** [ ] [3] May 76
– Back in the saddle / Last child / Rats in the cellar / Combination / Sick as a dog / Nobody's fault / Get the lead out / Lick and a promise / Home tonight. *(re-iss.+cd.Nov89) (US re-iss.+cd.Sep87) (re-iss.cd Dec93 on 'Columbia')*

Aug 76. (7") **LAST CHILD. / COMBINATION** [ ] [21] Jun 76

Sep 76. (7") **HOME TONIGHT. / PANDORA'S BOX** [-] [71]

Feb 77. (7") **WALK THIS WAY. / UNCLE SALTY** [ ] [10] Nov 76

Apr 77. (7") **BACK IN THE SADDLE. / NOBODY'S FAULT** [-] [38]

Oct 77. (7") **DRAW THE LINE. / BRIGHT LIGHT FRIGHT** [-] [42]

Jan 78. (lp)(c) **DRAW THE LINE** [ ] [11] Dec 77
– Draw the line / I wanna know why / Critical mass / Get it up / Bright light fright / Kings and queens / The hand that feeds / Sight for sore eyes / Milk cow blues. *(US re-iss.Sep87, cd-May88) (re-iss.cd Dec93 on 'Columbia')*

Mar 78. (7") **KINGS AND QUEENS. / CRITICAL MASS** [-] [70]

Aug 78. (7") **COME TOGETHER. / KINGS AND QUEENS** [ ] [23]

Nov 78. (7") **GET IT UP. / MILK COW BLUES** [-] [ ]

Jan 79. (d-lp)(d-c) **LIVE! BOOTLEG (live)** [ ] [13] Nov 78
– Back in the saddle / Sweet emotion / Lord of the thighs / Toys in the attic / Last child / Come together / Walk this way / Sick as a dog / Dream on / Mama kin / S.O.S. (too bad) / Train kept a-rollin' / Sight for sore eyes / Chip away the stone / I ain't got you / Mother popcorn. *(US re-iss.Dec87) (re-iss.cd Dec93 on 'Columbia')*

Jan 79. (7") **CHIP AWAY THE STONE (live). / ('A' studio)** [-] [77]

Jan 80. (lp)(c) **NIGHT IN THE RUTS** [ ] [14] Nov 79
– No surprize / Chiquita / Remember (walkin' in the sand) / Cheesecake / Three mile smile / Reefer head woman / Bone to bone (Coney Island white fish boy) / Think about it / Mia. *(US re-iss.Sep87) (UK cd-iss.Mar92) (re-iss.cd Dec93 on 'Columbia')*

Feb 80. (7") **REMEMBER (WALKIN' IN THE SAND). / BONE TO BONE (CONEY ISLAND WHITE FISH BOY)** [ ] [67] Jan 80

'WALK THIS WAY..!!'
-STEVEN TYLER-
'AEROSMITH'

— (Dec79) **JIMMY CREPSO** – guitar (ex-FLAME) repl. JOE PERRY who went solo.

— (Feb80) **RICK DUFAY** – guitar repl. WHITFORD who teamed up with ST. HOLMES

Oct 82. (lp)(c) **ROCK IN A HARD PLACE** [ ] [32] Sep 82
– Jailbait / Lightning strikes / Bitch's brew / Bolivian ragamuffin / Cry me a river / Prelude to Joanie / Joanie's butterfly / Rock in a hard place (Cheshire cat) / Jig it up / Push comes to shove. *(US re-iss.Sep87) (re-iss.cd Dec93 on 'Columbia')*

— (Mar84) original 1970's line-up reform (see above)

Nov 85. (7") **SHEILA. / GYPSY BOOTS** [-] [ ]

Geffen Geffen

Dec 85. (lp)(c) **DONE WITH MIRRORS** [ ] [36] Nov 85
– Let the music do the talking / My fist your face / Shame on you / The reason a dog / Shela / Gypsy boots / She's on fire / The hop. (c+=) – Darkness. *(US cd-Oct87) (UK re-iss.+cd.Jun89 on 'WEA') (re-iss.cd+c Jun94)*

Aug86 AEROSMITH were credited on 45 version of **WALK THIS WAY** by **RUN DMC**

Aug 87. (lp)(c)(cd) **PERMANENT VACATION** [37] [11]
– Heart's done time / Magic touch / Rag doll / Simoriah / Dude (looks like a lady) / St.John / Hangman jury / Girls keep coming apart / Angel / Permanent vacation / I'm down / The movie. *(re-iss.cd+c Jun94)*

Oct 87. (7") **DUDE (LOOKS LIKE A LADY). / SIMORIAH** [45] [14]
(12"+=)(12"pic-d+=) – Once is enough.

Apr 88. (7") **ANGEL. / GIRL KEEPS COMING APART** [69] [3] Jan 88
(12"+=)(12"pic-d+=) – ('A'-AOR remix).

Jun 88. (12") **RAG DOLL. / ST.JOHN** [-] [17]

Aug 89. (7")(c-s) **LOVE IN AN ELEVATOR. / YOUNG LUST** [13] [5]
(3"cd-s+=)(12"+=)(10"pic-d+=) – Ain't enough.

Sep 89. (lp)(c)(cd) **PUMP** [3] [5]
– Young lust / F.I.N.E. / Going down / Love in an elevator / Monkey on my back / Water song / Janie's got a gun / Dulcimer stomp / The other side / My girl / Don't get mad, get even / Vvoodoo medicine man / What it takes. *(re-iss.cd+c Jun94)*

Nov 89. (7")(12")(c-s)(7"sha-pic-d) **JANIE'S GOT A GUN. / VOODOO MEDICINE MAN** [ ] [4]
(12"+=)(cd-s+=) – Rag doll (live).

Feb 90. (7")(7"pic-d)(7"sha-pic-d) **DUDE (LOOKS LIKE A LADY) (remix). / MONKEY ON MY BACK** [20] [-]
(12")(cd-s) – ('A'side) / Love in an elevator (live) / Walk this way (live).

Apr 90. (7") **RAG DOLL. / SIMORIAH** [42] [-]
(12")(cd-s) – ('A'side) / Mama kin (live) / Let it rain (live).

Mar 90. (7")(c-s) **WHAT IT TAKES. / MONKEY ON MY BACK** [-] [9]

Jul 90. (7")(c-s) **THE OTHER SIDE. / MY GIRL** [46] [22] Jun 90
(12"+=) – Theme from 'Wayne's World' / ('A' honky tonk version)
(12") – ('A'side) / Love in an elevator / Dude (looks like a lady) / Walk this way.

Mar 93. (cd-s)(12"pic-d) **LIVIN' ON THE EDGE. / DON'T STOP / FLESH** [19] [18]
(cd-s) – ('A'side) / ('A'acoustic) / Can't stop messin'.

Apr 93. (cd)(c)(lp) **GET A GRIP** [2] [1]
– Intro / Eat the rich / Get a grip / Fever / Livin' on the edge / Flesh / Walk on down / Shut up and dance / Cryin' / Gotta love it / Crazy / Line up / Can't stop messin' / Amazing / Boogie man.

Jun 93. (10"colrd) **EAT THE RICH. / FEVER / HEAD FIRST** [34] [ ] Apr 93
(cd-s+=) – Livin' on the edge (demo).

Oct 93. (12"m) **CRYIN'. / WALK ON DOWN / I'M DOWN** [17] [12] Jul 93
(cd-s+=) – My fist your face
(cd-s) – (first 2 tracks) / Love in an elevator / Janie's got a gun.

Dec 93. (12"m) **AMAZING. / GOTTA LOVE IT / AMAZING (acoustic)** [57] [24] Nov 93
(cd-s+=) – ('A'orchestral).

Jun 94. (7")(c-s) **SHUT UP AND DANCE. / DEUCES ARE WILD** [24] [ ]
(cd-s+=) – Crazy (orchestral) / Line up.

Oct 94. (c-s) **CRAZY. / BLIND MAN** [23] [17] Jun94
(cd-s+=) – Shut up and dance (live) / Blind man (mix).

Nov 94. (cd)(c)(d-lp) **BIG ONES** (compilation) [7] [6]
– Walk on water / Love in an elevator / Rag doll / What it takes / Dude (looks like a lady) / Janie's got a gun / Cryin' / Amazing / Blind man / Deuces are wild / The other side / Crazy / Eat the rich / Angel / Livin' on the edge / Dude (looks like a lady) (live).

Dec 94. (c-s)(cd-s) **BLIND MAN. / ?** [-] [49]

– compilations, others, etc. –

Jan 81. C.B.S./ US= Columbia; (lp)(c) **AEROSMITH'S GREATEST HITS** [ ] [53] Nov80
– Dream on / Same old song and dance / Sweet emotion / Walk this way / Remember (walking in the sand) / Back in the saddle / Draw the line / Kings and queens / Come together / Last child. *(US re-iss.Sep87, cd-Feb88 + UK pic-lp) (UK re-iss.+cd.Nov89) (re-iss.cd Dec93 on 'Columbia')*

Sep 86. C.B.S./ US= Columbia; (lp)(c) **CLASSICS LIVE!** (live 1977-1983) [ ] [84] Apr 86
– Train kept a-rollin' / Kings and queens / Sweet emotion / Dream on / Mama kin / Three mile smile / Reefer head woman / Lord of the thighs / Major Barbra. *(US cd-Nov87) (re-iss.cd Dec93 on 'Columbia')*

Aug 87. C.B.S./ Columbia; (lp)(c) **CLASSICS LIVE II (live)** [-] [ ]
– Back in the saddle / Walk this way / Movin' out / Draw the line / Same old song and dance / Last child / Let the music do the talking / Toys in the attic. *(UK-iss.+cd.Nov89 & Dec92 on 'Columbia')*

Aug 88. Columbia; (3"cd-s) **WALK THIS WAY / DREAM ON** [-] [ ]

Nov 89. C.B.S./ US= Columbia; (lp)(c)(cd) **GEMS** [ ] [ ] Dec 88
– Rats in the cellar / Lick and a promise / Chip away the stone / No surprize / Mama kin / Adam's apple / Nobody's fault / Round and round / Critical mass / Lord of the thighs / Jailbait / Train kept a rollin'. *(UK re-iss.Apr91 & Dec93 on 'Columbia')*

Jun 88. Raw Power; (d-lp)(cd) **ANTHOLOGY** [ ] [-]

Dec 91. Columbia; (t-cd)(t-c) **PANDORA'S BOX** [ ] [45]
– When I needed you / Make it / Movin' out / One way street / On the road again / Mama kin / Same old song and dance / Train kept a-rollin' / Seasons of wither / Write me a letter / Dream on / Pandora's Box / Rattlesnake shake / Walkin' the dog / Lord of the thighs // Toys in the attic / Round and round / Krawhitham / You see me crying / Sweet emotion / No More no more / Walk this way / I wanna know why / Big ten inch record / Rats in the cellar / Last child / All your love / Soul saver / Nobody's fault / Lick and a promise / Adam's apple / Draw the line / Critical mass // Kings and queens / Milk cow blues / I live in Connecticut / Three mile smile / Let it slide / Cheese cake / Bone to bone (Coney Island white fish boy) / No surprize / Come together / Downtown Charlie / Sharpshooter / Shit house shuffle / South station blues / Riff & roll / Jailbait / Major Barbara / Chip away the stone / Helter skelter / Back in the saddle / Circle jerk.

Jun 94. Columbia; (cd) **PANDORA'S TOYS (BEST)** (compilation of '. . .BOX') [ ] [ ]
– Sweet emotion / Draw the line / Walk this way / Dream on / Train kept a rollin' / Mama kin / Nobody's fault / Seasons of wither / Big ten-inch record / All your love / Helter skelter / Chip away the stone.

Aug 94. Columbia; (c-s) **SWEET EMOTION / SUBWAY** [74] [ ] Dec 91
(cd-s+=) – Circle jerk.

JOE PERRY PROJECT

(while not an AEROSMITH member) with **RALPH NORMAN** – vocals / **DAVID HULL** – bass / **RONNIE STEWART** – drums

C.B.S. Columbia

Mar 80. (lp) **LET THE MUSIC DO THE TALKING** [ ] [47]
– Let the music do the talking / Conflict of interest / Discount dogs / Shooting star / Break song / Rockin' train / The mist is rising / Ready on the firing line / Life at a glance.

Aug 80. (7") **LET THE MUSIC DO THE TALKING. / BONE TO BONE** [ ] [ ]

— **CHARLIE FARREN** – vocals repl. NORMAN

Jun 81. (lp) **I'VE GOT THE ROCK'N'ROLLS AGAIN** [-] [ ]
– East Coast, West Coast / No substitute for arrogance / I've got the rock'n'rolls again / Buzz buzz / Soldier of fortune / T.V. police / Listen to the rock / Dirty little things / Play the game / South station blues.

1981. (7") **BUZZ BUZZ. / EAST COAST, WEST COAST** [-] [ ]

— **PERRY** new line-up **MARK BELL** – vocals / **DANNY HARGROVE** – bass / **JOE PET** – drums

M.C.A. M.C.A.

Jan 84. (lp)(c) **ONCE A ROCKER, ALWAYS A ROCKER** [ ] [ ]
– Once a rocker, always a rocker / Black velvet pants / Woman in chains / Guns west / Crossfire / King of the kings / Never wanna stop / Adrianna / Get it on (bang-a-gong) / Walk with me Sally.

WHITFORD / ST.HOLMES

BRAD WHITFORD – guitar, vocals / **ST.HOLMES** – guitar (ex-TED NUGENT) also **DAVID HEWITT** – bass / **STEVE PACE** – drums

not issued Columbia

1981. (7") **SHY AWAY. / MYSTERY GIRL** [-] [ ]

1981. (lp) **WHITFORD / ST.HOLMES** [-] [ ]
– I need love / Whiskey woman / Hold on / Sharp shouter / Every morning / Action / Shy away / Does it really matter / Spanish box / Mystery girl.

AFGHAN WHIGS

Formed: Denver, Colorado, USA . . .Oct'86, by DULLI and McCOLLUM who met in a prison. They moved to Cincinatti, Ohio, after signing for Seattle based indie label 'Sub Pop' in 1989. Now live in California after signing for 'Elektra' in the US and releasing minor 1993 hit album 'GENTLEMEN'. • **Style:** Soulful grunge rock similar to DINOSAUR JR. • **Songwriters:** DULLI, some McCOLLUM except; covers by Diana Ross / Al Green / BAND OF GOLD (Freda Payne) / I KEEP COMING BACK (Austell-Graham).

Recommended: CONGREGATION (*6) / GENTLEMEN (*7)

GREG DULLI – vocals, guitar / **RICK McCOLLUM** – guitar / **JOHN CURREY** – bass / **STEVE EARLE** – drums

not issued Ultrasuede

Oct 88. (lp) **BIG TOP HALLOWEEN** [-] [ ]

– Here comes Jesus / In my town / Priscilla's wedding day / Push / Scream / But listen / Big top Halloween / Life in a day / Sammy / Doughball / Back o' the line / Greek is extra.

Sub Pop | Sub Pop

Aug 89. (7") **I AM THE STICKS. / WHITE TRASH PARTY** [ ] [ ]
Apr 90. (cd)(c)(lp)(orange-lp) **UP IN IT** [ ] [ ]
– Retarded / White trash party / Hated / Southpaw / Amphetamines and coffee / Now can we begin / You my flower / Son of the south / I know your secret. (cd/c+=) I am the sticks. *(re-iss.Aug90 on 'Glitterhouse')*
Oct 90. (7")(7"red) **SISTER BROTHER. / HEY CUZ** [ ] [ ]
Dec 90. (12"ep) **THE RETARD EP** [ ] [ ]
– Retarded / Sister brother / Hey cuz / Turning in two. *(re-iss.+cd-ep May93;)*
Jan 92. (cd)(c)(lp) **CONGREGATION** [ ] [ ]
– Her against me / I'm her slave / Turn on the water / Conjure me / Kiss the floor / Congregation / This is my confession / Dedicate it / The temple / Let me lie to you / Tonight.
Jan 92. (12"ep) **TURN ON THE WATER. / MILES IZ DEAD / DELTA KONG** [ ] [ ]
(cd-ep+=) – Chalk outline.
May 92. (7"white)(7"lavender) **CONJURE ME. / MY WORLD IS EMPTY WITHOUT YOU** [ ] [ ]
(12"+=)(cd-s+=) – My flower.
Oct 92. (7"ep) **UPTOWN AVONDALE EP: BAND OF GOLD. / COME SEE ABOUT ME** [ ] [ ]
(12"+=) – True love travels on a gravel road / Beware.
(cd-s++=) – Rebirth of the cool.
(above release could have been issued earlier in US, early 1990)

Blast First | Elektra

Sep 93. (7") **GENTLEMEN. / MR.SUPERLOVE** [ ] [ ]
(12"+=)(cd-s+=) – The dark end of the street.
Oct 93. (cd)(c)(lp) **GENTLEMEN** [58] [ ]
– If I were going / Gentlemen / Be sweet / Debonair / When we two parted / Fountain and fairfax / What jail is like / My curse / Now you know / I keep coming back / Brother Woodrow – Closing prayer. (lp w /free 7"ep) – ROT. / TONIGHT

—— guests on the album: **HAROLD CHICHESTER** – keyboards / **BARB HUNTER** – cello / **JODY STEPHENS** – b. vocals / **MARCY MAYS** – vocals

Feb 94. (7"ep)(12"ep)(cd-ep) **BROKEN PROMISES EP** [ ] [ ]
– Debonair / My curse / Little girl blue / Ready.
(cd-s) – ('A'side) / Rot / I keep coming back / Tonight.

—— Mar'94, 'MR.SUPERLOVE' was iss. on B-side of ASS PONY's single on 'Monocat'.

. . . Jan – Jun '96 stop press . . .

Mute | Elektra

Feb 96. (single) **HONKY'S LADDER E.P.** [ ] [ ]
Mar 96. (cd)(c)(lp) **BLACK LOVE** [41] [ ]

AIRFORCE (see under ⇒ BAKER, Ginger)

ALARM

Formed: Rhyl, Wales . . . 1977 as punk band The TOILETS. They became "mod" outfit "17" before the same quartet changed again to The ALARM in 1981. After one indie 45 on 'White Cross' label, they signed to Miles Copeland's US based 'I.R.S.' in summer '82. Just over a year later, they entered the UK Top 20, not for the last time, with '68 GUNS'. • **Style:** Inspired by a mixture of The CLASH and U2, although politics differ. Their anthem style basic rock hds its raw and smooth edges plastered into folk and war lyrics. • **Songwriters:** McDONALD / PETERS or SHARP / TWIST, except; THE BELLS OF RHYMNEY (Pete Seeger) / KNOCKIN' ON HEAVEN'S DOOR (Bob Dylan) / WORKING CLASS HERO + HAPPY XMAS (WAR IS OVER) (John Lennon) / ROCKIN' IN THE FREE WORLD (Neil Young). • **Trivia:** Sang in Welsh on single 'A NEW SOUTH WALES (HWYLIO DROS Y MOR)'.

Recommended: STANDARDS (*7).

MIKE PETERS (b.25 Jan'59) – vocals, guitar / **DAVE SHARP** (b.28 Jan'59) – guitar / **EDDIE McDONALD** (b. 1 Nov'59) – bass / **NIGEL TWIST** (b. 18 Jul'58) – drums

17

Vendetta | not issued

Mar 80. (7") **DON'T LET GO. / BANK HOLIDAY WEEKEND** [ ] [-]

The ALARM

White Cross | not issued

Sep 81. (7") **UNSAFE BUILDINGS. / UP FOR MURDER** [ ] [-]

I.R.S. | I.R.S.

Oct 82. (7"m) **MARCHING ON. / ACROSS THE BORDER / LIE OF THE LAND** [ ] [-]
Apr 83. (7") **THE STAND. / THIRD LIGHT** [ ] [-]
(12"+=) – ('A'side) / For freedom / Reason 41.
Jun 83. (7") **THE STAND. / REASON 41** [-] [ ]
Jul 83. (m-lp) **THE ALARM** [-] [ ]
– Across the border / For freedom / Marching on / Lie of the land / The stand
Sep 83. (7")(12") **68 GUNS. / (part 2)** [17] [-]
(12"+=) – Thoughts of a young man.
Nov 83. (7") **68 GUNS. / PAVILLION STEPS** [-] [ ]
Jan 84. (7") **WHERE WERE YOU HIDING WHEN THE STORM BROKE?. / PAVILLION STEPS** [22] [ ]
(12"+=) – What kind of Hell.
Feb 84. (lp)(c) **DECLARATION** [6] [50]
– Declaration / Marching on / Where were you hiding when the storm broke? / Third light / 68 guns / We are the light / Shout to the Devil / Blaze of glory / Tell me / The deceiver / The stand (prophecy) / Howling wind. *(cd-iss.Oct88)*
Mar 84. (7")(7"clear) **THE DECEIVER. / REASON 41** [51] [ ]
(12"+=) – Second generation. (US; b-side)
(ltd.d7"+=) – Lie of the land / Legal matter.
Oct 84. (7") **THE CHANT HAS JUST BEGUN. / THE BELLS OF RHYMNEY** [48] [ ]
(12"+=) – The stand (extended).
Feb 85. (7")(12") **ABSOLUTE REALITY. / BLAZE OF GLORY** [35] [ ]
(ltd.d7"+=) – Room at the top / Reason 36.
Sep 85. (7") **STRENGTH. / MAJORITY** [40] [61]
(12"+=) – ('A'side) / Absolute reality (acoustic).
Oct 85. (lp)(c)(cd) **STRENGTH** [18] [39]
– Knife edge / Strength / awn chorus / Spirit of '76 / The day the ravens left the tower / Deeside / Father to son / Only the thunder / Walk forever by my side. *(also pic-lp) (cd-iss.Apr87) (re-cd.Jan90 on 'M.C.A.')*
Jan 86. (7")(12") **SPIRIT OF '76. / WHERE WERE YOU HIDING WHEN THE STORM BROKE? (live)** [22] [ ]
(12"+=) – Deeside (live).
(d12"++=) – Knockin' on Heaven's door (live) / 68 guns (live).
Apr 86. (7")(7"sha-pic-d) **KNIFE EDGE (edit). / CAROLINE ISENBERG** [43] [ ]
(d7"+=)(12"+=) – Howling wind / Unbreak the promise.
Sep 87. (7") **RAIN IN THE SUMMERTIME. / ROSE BEYOND THE WALL** [18] [71]
(12"+=) – The bells of Rhymney / Time to believe.
(extra 12") – ('A'-Through the haze mix) / ('A'-Lightning mix)
Nov 87. (lp)(c)(cd) **EYE OF THE HURRICANE** [23] [77]
– Rain in the summertime / Newtown Jericho / Hallowed ground / One step closer to home / Shelter / Rescue me / Permanence in change / Presence of love / Only love can set me free / Eye of the hurricane. *(re-cd.May90 on 'M.C.A.')*
Nov 87. (7")(7"blue) **RESCUE ME. / MY LAND YOUR LAND** [48] [ ]
(12"+=) – The Hurricane sessions.
Feb 88. (7")(7"pic-d) **PRESENCE OF LOVE. / KNIFE EDGE (live)** [44] [77]
(12"+=) – This train is bound for glory (live) / Dawn chorus (live).
(cd-s++=) – Rain in the summertime (live).
Oct 88. (m-lp)(c)(cd) **ELECTRIC FOLKLORE LIVE (live)** [62] [ ]
– Rescue me / Rain in the summertime / Permanence in change / Strength / Spirit pf '76 / Blaze of glory.
Sep 89. (7") **SOLD ME DOWN THE RIVER. / GWETHOCH FI I YR AFON** [43] [50]
(10"+=) – Firing line.
(12"+=)(cd-s+=) – Corridors of power.
Sep 89. (lp)(c)(cd) **CHANGE** [13] [75]
– Rivers to cross / A new South Wales / Sold me down the river / The rock / Devolution / Workin' man blues / Love don't come easy / Hard land / Change II / No frontiers / Scarlet / Where a town once stood / Prison without prison bars.
Oct 89. (7")(12") **A NEW SOUTH WALES. / THE ROCK (long version)** [31] [ ]
(cd-s+=) – Working class hero.
(10"white++=) – Rivers to cross (new version).
(7" also in Welsh) – HWYLIO DROS Y MOR. / Y GRAIG
Jan 90. (7") **LOVE DON'T COME EASY. / CROESI'R AFON** [48] [ ]
(12"+=)(cd-s+=) – No frontiers.
(10"pic-d+=) – Change II.
Oct 90. (7")(12") **UNSAFE BUILDINGS (1990). / UP FOR MURDER (1990)** [54] [ ]
(c-s+=)(cd-s+=) – Unsafe Buildings (original mix).
Nov 90. I.R.S.; (cd)(c)(lp) **STANDARDS** [47] [ ]
– The road / Unsafe buildings / The stand / 68 guns / Where were you hiding when the storm broke? / Absolute reality / Strength / Spirit of '76 / Rain in the summertime / Rescue me / Sold me down the river / A new south Wales / Happy Xmas (war is over). (cd/c+=) – Marching on / Blaze of glory.
Apr 91. (7") **RAW. / CHANGE 1** [51] [ ]
(12"+=)(cd-s+=) – Devolution / Workin' man's blues.
Apr 91. (cd)(c)(lp) **RAW** [33] [ ]
– Raw / Rockin' in the free world / God save somebody / Moments in time / Hell or high water / Lead me through the darkness / The wind blows away my words / Let the river run its course / Save your crying / Wonderful world.

— (Jul '91) MIKE PETERS went solo

– compilations, others, etc. –

Apr 88. I.R.S.; (cd-ep) **COMPACT HITS** [ ] [-]
– 68 guns / Blaze of glory / Shout to the Devil / Where were you hiding when the storm broke?.

MIKE PETERS

Crai not issued

Jan 94. (12"ep)(c-ep)(cd-ep) **BACK INTO THE SYSTEM. / 21st CENTURY (demo) / A NEW CHAPTER** [ ] [-]
(cd-s+=) – (Welsh language version).

Apr 94. (12"ep)(cd-ep) **IT JUST DON'T GET ANY BETTER THAN THIS. / DEVIL'S WORLD / WHITE NOISE** [ ] [-]

Oct 94. (cd)(c)(d-lp) **BREATHE** [ ] [-]
– Poetic justice / All I wanted / If I can't have you / Breathe / Love is a revolution / Who's gonna make the piece / Spiritual / What the world can't give me / Levis & bibles / Beautiful thing / Into the 21st century / This is war / The message / Back into the system / It just don't get any better than this / Train a comin' / A new chapter (reprise). *(re-iss.Jan95 as Welsh language 'AER')*

ALICE COOPER (see under ⇒ COOPER, Alice)

ALICE IN CHAINS

Formed: Seattle, Washington, USA . . . 1990 by (see below). Crashed into US chart that year, when debut 'FACELIFT' made Top 50. • **Style:** Heavy grunge merchants, similar to NIRVANA or SOUNDGARDEN. • **Songwriters:** CANTRELL or STALEY or both.

Recommended: DIRT (*5)

LAYNE STALEY – vocals / **JERRY CANTRELL** – guitar, vocals / **MICHAEL STARR** – bass (ex-SADO) / **SEAN KINNEY** – drums, percussion, megaphone

Columbia Columbia

Sep 91. (cd)(c)(lp) **FACELIFT** [ ] [42] Mar 91
– We die young / Man in the box / Love, hate, love / It ain't like that / I can't remember / Confusion / Son of sorrow / Bleed the freak / I know somethin' ('bout you) / Put you down / Sunshine / Real thing.

1991. (c-ep)(cd-ep) **MAN IN THE BOX / SEA OF SORROW / BLEED THE FREAK / SUNSHINE** [-] [ ]

Feb 92. (12"ep)(cd-ep) **SAP** [ ] [ ]
– Brother / Got me wrong / Right turn / Am I inside / Love song.

— Splintered after above, a few became MY SISTER'S MACHINE, and released album in May'92 'DIVA' on 'Caroline'.

Oct 92. (cd)(c)(lp) **DIRT** [42] [6]
– Them bones / Dam that river / Rain when I die / Down in a hole / Sickman / Rooster / Junkhead / Dirt / God smack / Hate to feel / Angry chair / Would?

Jan 93. (7") **WOULD?. / MAN IN THE BOX** [19] [ ]
(12"green+=)(pic-cd-s+=) – Brother / Right Turn

Mar 93. (7") **THEM BONES. / WE DIE YOUNG** [26] [ ]
(cd-s+=) – Got me wrong / Am I inside

May 93. (7") **ANGRY CHAIR. / I KNOW SOMETHIN' ('BOUT YOU)** [33] [ ]
(12"+=) – Bleed the freak / It ain't like that
(cd-s+=) – It ain't like that / Hate to feel

Oct 93. (7")(7"pic-d) **DOWN IN A HOLE. / ROOSTER** [36] [ ]
(12"+=) – A little bitter. / Love hate love.
(cd-s+=) – What the hell I have I. ('A' radio edit)

Jan 94. (cd)(c)(lp) **JAR OF FLIES / SAP** [4] [1]
– Rotten apple / Nutshell / I stay away / No excuses / Whale & wasp / Don't follow / Swing on this. (US-version w /out 'SAP')

Oct 95. (7")(c-s) **GRIND. / NUTSHELL** [23] [ ]
(cd-s+=) – So close / Love, hate, love.

Nov 95. (cd)(c)(d-lp) **ALICE IN CHAINS** [37] [1]
– Grind / Brush away / Sludge factory / Heaven beside you / Head creeps / Again / Shame in you / God a.m. / So close / Nothin' song / Frogs / Good night (by TED LEWIS & HIS ORCHESTRA).

. . . Jan – Jun '96 stop press . . .

Jan 96. (single) **HEAVEN BESIDE YOU** [35] [ ]

MAD SEASON

— were originally called GACY BUNCH with **LAYNE STALEY** -vocals / **MIKE McCREADY** -guitar (of PEARL JAM) / **BARRETT MARTIN** -drums (of SCREAMING TREES)

Columbia Columbia

Mar 95. (cd)(c) **ABOVE** [41] [24]
– Wake up / X-ray mind / River of deceit / I'm above / Artificial red / Lifeless dead / I don't know anything / Long gone day / November hotel / All alone.

ALLMAN BROTHERS BAND

Formed: Jacksonville, Florida, USA . . . 1967 by brothers DUANE and GREGG. Became The HOURGLASS after previously gigging under the ALLMAN JOYS banner with others:- BOB KELLER – bass, BILLY CANELL or MANARD PORTWOOD – drums. HOURGLASS released 2 albums and nearly a third for 'Liberty' before disbanding in 1968. Returned to homeland to augment BUTCH TRUCKS in his outfit 31st OF FEBRUARY, with DUANE also relying on session work for 'Atlantic'. In 1969 all three formed The ALLMAN BROTHERS BAND and moved to Macon, Georgia. They had already signed to the 'Atlantic' distributed label 'Capricorn' run by Phil Walden. The band became one of America's greats of the early 70's, although hindered by the untimely deaths of DUANE and BERRY in 71/72 (see below). Who knows of their real potential?. GREGG carried on regardless, gaining commercial success throughout the 70's and early 80's. • **Style:** Hard Southern-country rock that featured two brilliant guitarists DUANE and BETTS. • **Songwriters:** The ALLMANS and BETTS. In the 90's most were written by BETTS, HAYNES and NEEL. Covered; STATESBORO BLUES (Will McTell) / ONE WAY OUT (Elmore James) / I'M YOUR HOOCHIE COOCHIE MAN (Muddy Waters) / SLIP AWAY (Clarence Carter). • **Trivia:** DUANE ALLMAN played guitar alongside ERIC CLAPTON on his DEREK & THE DOMINOES single 'Layla'. That year (1970) also saw him sessioning for WILSON PICKETT, BOZ SCAGGS, ARETHA FRANKLIN, KING CURTIS, etc, etc . . .

Recommended: A DECADE OF HITS 1969-1979 (*8)

HOURGLASS

GREGG ALLMAN (b. 8 Dec'48, Nashville, USA) – vocals, keyboards, guitar / **DUANE ALLMAN** (b.20 Nov'46) – guitars / **PAUL HORNSBY** – keyboards, guitar, vocals / **MABRON McKINNEY** – bass / **JOHN SANDLIN** – drums

1968. (7") **POWER OF LOVE. / I STILL WANT YOUR LOVE** [-] [ ]

1968. (7") **HEARTBEAT. / NOTHING BUT TEARS** [-] [ ]

Liberty Liberty

Aug 68. (lp) **THE HOUR GLASS** [ ] [ ] Feb 68
– Out of the night / Nothing but tears / Love makes the world 'round / Cast off all my fears / I've been trying / No easy way down / Heartbeat / So much love / Got to get away / Silently / Bells.

— **JESSE WILLARD CARR** – bass, vocals repl. MABRON McKINNEY

1968. (7") **SHE'S MY WOMAN. / GOING NOWHERE** [-] [ ]

1968. (7") **NOW IS THE TIME. / SHE'S MY WOMAN** [-] [ ]

1968. (7") **CHANGING OF THE GUARD. / D-I-V-O-R-C-E** [-] [ ]

Aug 68. (lp) **POWER OF LOVE** [-] [ ]
– Power of love / Changing of the guard / To things before / I'm not afraid / I can stand alone / Down in Texas / I still want your love / Home for the summer / I'm hangin' up my heart for you / Going nowhere / Norwegian wood / Now is the time. *(re-iss. 2 1968 lp's; Mar74 on 'United Art')*

Dec 68. (7") **I'VE BEEN TRYING / SILENTLY** [-] [ ]

3rd album was withdrawn

31st FEBRUARY

DUANE and **GREGG** with **BUTCH TRUCKS** – drums / **SCOTT BOYER** – guitar, vocals / **DAVID BROWN** – bass

Mar 69. (7") **IN THE MORNING WHEN I'M REAL. / PORCELAIN MIRRORS** [-] [ ]

An album DUANE AND GREGG was released 1973 on 'Polydor UK'/'Bold' US cont. these demos.

The ALLMAN BROTHERS BAND

(**GREGG** and **DUANE**) plus **DICKEY BETTS** (b.RICHARD, 12 Dec'43, W.Palm Beach, Florida) – guitar, vocals / **BERRY OAKLEY** (b. 4 Apr'48, Chicago, Illinois) – bass / **BUTCH TRUCKS** (b.Jacksonville, Florida) – drums, timpani / **JAIMO JOHANSON** (b.JOHN LEE JOHNSON, 8 Jul'44, Ocean Springs) – percussion.

Capricorn Atco

Nov 69. (lp) **THE ALLMAN BROTHERS BAND** [ ] [ ]
– Don't want you no more / It's my cross to bear / Black hearted woman / Trouble no more / Every hungry woman / Dreams / Whipping post.

Mar 70. (7") **BLACK HEARTED WOMAN. / EVERY HUNGRY WOMAN** [ ] [ ]

Capricorn Atlantic

Nov 70. (lp) **IDLEWIND SOUTH** [ ] [38]
– Revival (love is everywhere) / Don't keep me wonderin' / Midnight rider / In

memory of Elizabeth Reed / I'm your hoochie coochie man / Please call home / Leave my blues at home. *(cd-iss.Mar89 on 'Polydor')*

Nov 70. (7") **REVIVAL (LOVE IS EVERYWHERE). / LEAVE MY BLUES AT HOME** [ ] [92]

Mar 71. (7") **MIDNIGHT RIDER. / WHIPPING POST** [ ] [ ]

Capricorn Capricorn

Jul 71. (d-lp) **AT FILLMORE EAST (live)** [ ] [13]
– Statesboro blues / Done somebody wrong / Stormy Monday / You don't love me / Hot 'Lanta / In memory of Elizabeth Reed / Whipping post. *(re-iss.Nov74) (d-cd-iss.1986 & Sep95 on 'Polydor')*

— On 29 Oct'71, DUANE was killed in a motorcycle accident in Macon. He had already contributed to 3 tracks on below album.

Feb 72. (d-lp)(d-c) **EAT A PEACH** [ ] [4]
– Ain't wastin' time no more / Les brers in A minor / Melissa / Mountain jam / One way out / Trouble no more / Stand back / Blue sky / Little Martha / Mountain jam (reprise). *(re-iss.Nov74) (cd-iss. 1986 on 'Polydor')*

Apr 72. (7") **AIN'T WASTIN' TIME NO MORE. / MELISSA** [-] [77]

Jul 72. (7") **BLUE SKY. / MELISSA** [-] [86] B-side

Oct 72. (7") **STAND BACK. / ONE WAY OUT** [-] [86] B-side

— (Jan73) **LAMAR WILLIAMS** (b.1947) – bass repl. BERRY OAKLEY who also died in a motorcyle accident, again in Macon, 11 Nov'72.

Sep 73. (lp)(c) **BROTHERS AND SISTERS** [42] [1] Aug 73
– Wasted words / Ramblin' man / Come and go blues / Jelly jelly / Southbound / Jessica / Pony boy. *(re-iss.Jun81) (cd-iss.1986 + Jun87 on 'Polydor')*

Oct 73. (7") **RAMBLIN' MAN. / PONY BOY** [ ] [2] Aug 73

Jan 74. (7") **JESSICA. / WASTED WORDS** [-] [65]

Oct 74. (7") **JESSICA. / COME AND GO BLUES** [ ] [-]

Sep 75. (lp)(c) **WIN, LOSE OR DRAW** [ ] [5]
– Can't lose what you never had / Just another love song / Nevertheless / Win, lose or draw / Louisiana Lou And Three Card Monty John / High falls / Sweet mama.

Sep 75. (7") **NEVERTHELESS. / LOUISIANA LOU AND THREE CARD MONTY JOHN** [-] [67]

[78]

— Jul 76 when GREGG was ostracized by others for giving evidence against convicted drug trafficker and road manager Scooter Herring. GREGG formed his own band. BETTS formed GREAT SOUTHERN and others formed SEA LEVEL who hit US No. 31 Mar 78 with lp 'CATS ON THE COAST'. When rifts were settled **The ALLMAN BROTHERS BAND** re-united early '79. GREGG, DICKEY, BUTCH, JAIMO plus newcomers **DAN TOLFER** – guitar / **DAVID GOLDFLIES** – bass (both ex-GREAT SOUTHERN).

Mar 79. (lp)(c) **ENLIGHTENED ROGUES** [ ] [9]
– Need your love so bad / Pegasus / Just ain't easy / Sail away / Crazy love / Try it one more time / Blind love / Can't take it with you. *(cd-iss.1987 on 'Polydor')*

Apr 79. (7") **CRAZY LOVE. / IT JUST AIN'T EASY** [ ] [29] Mar 79

Jun 79. (7") **CAN'T TAKE IT WITH YOU. / SAIL AWAY** [-] [ ]

Arista Arista

Sep 80. (lp)(c) **REACH FOR THE SKY** [ ] [27] Aug 80
– Hell & high water / Mystery woman / From the madness of the west / I gotta right to be wrong / Angeline / Famous last words / Keep on keepin' on / So long.

Sep 80. (7") **ANGELINE. / SO LONG** [-] [58]

Jan 81. (7") **MYSTERY WOMAN. / HELL OR HIGH WATER** [-] [ ]

Sep 81. (lp)(c) **BROTHERS OF THE ROAD** [ ] [44] Aug 81
– Brothers of the road / Leavin' / Straight from the road / The heat is on / Maybe we can go back to yesterday / The judgement / Two rights / Never knew how much (I needed you) / Things you used to do / I beg of you.

Sep 81. (7") **STRAIGHT FROM THE HEART. / LEAVING** [ ] [39] Aug 81

Nov 81. (7") **TWO RIGHTS. / NEVER KNEW HOW MUCH** [-] [ ]

— **CHUCK LEAVELL** rejoined but they soon disbanded once again. Past member **LAMAR** died of cancer on 25 Jan'83.

GREGG ALLMAN BAND

went solo again in 1987 with **DAN TOLER** – guitar / **DAVID 'FRANKIE' TOLER** – drums / **TIM HEDING** – keyboards / **BRUCE WAIBEL** – bass, vocals / **CHAZ TRIPPY** – percussion

Epic Epic

Jan 87. (7") **CAN'T KEEP RUNNING. / ANYTHING GOES** [-] [ ]

May 87. (lp)(c)(cd) **I'M NO ANGEL** [ ] [30] Feb87
– I'm no angel / Anything goes / Evidence of love / Yours for the asking / Things that might have been / Can't keep running / Faces without names / Lead me on / Don't want you no more / It's not my cross to bear.

May 87. (7") **I'M NO ANGEL. / LEAD ME ON** [ ] [49] Mar 87

Apr 89. (lp)(c)(cd) **JUST BEFORE THE BULLETS FLY** [ ] [ ] Aug 88
– Demons / Before the bullets fly / Slip away / Thorn and a wild rose / Ocean awash the gunwale / Can't get over you / Island / Fear of falling / Night games / Every hungry woman.

Apr 89. (7") **SLIP AWAY. / EVERY HUNGRY WOMAN** [-] [ ]

– other GREGG ALLMAN releases, etc. –

— with **SCOTT BOYER** – guitar, vocals / **TOMMY TALTON** – slide guitar / **CHUCK LEAVELL** – keyboards / **DAVID BROWN** – bass / **BILL STEWART** – drums / etc.

Capricorn Capricorn

Nov 73. (lp)(c) **LAID BACK** [ ] [13]
– Will the circle be unbroken / Don't mess up a good thing / Multi-colored lady / Please call home / Queen of hearts / Midnight rider / Don't mess up a good thing / All my friends / These days. *(cd-iss.Aug87 on 'Polydor')*

Jan 74. (7") **MIDNIGHT RIDER. / MULTI-COLORED LADY** [ ] [19] Dec 73

— (above releases were issued approx.half a year later in UK).

Mar 74. (7") **PLEASE CALL HOME. / DON'T MESS UP A GOOD THING** [-] [ ]

Oct 74. (7") **DON'T MESS WITH A GOOD THING. / MIDNIGHT RIDER** [-] [ ]

Nov 74. (d-lp)(c) **GREGG ALLMAN TOUR (live)** [ ] [50]
– Don't mess up a good thing / Queen of hearts / Feel so bad / Stand back / Time will take us / Where can you go / Double cross / Dreams / Are you lonely for me / Turn on your love light / Oncoming traffic / Will the circle be unbroken?. *(cd-iss.Oct87 on 'Polydor')*

— retained **BILL STEWART** and brought in **STEVE BECKMEIER + JOHN HUG** – guitar / **RICKY HIRSCH** – slide guitar / **NEIL LARSEN** – piano / **WILLIE WEEKS** – bass

Jun 77. (lp)(c) **PLAYIN' UP A STORM** [ ] [42]
– Come and go blues / Let this be a lesson to ya / The brightest smile in town / Bring it on back / Cryin' shame / Sweet feelin' / It ain't no use / Matthew's arrival / One more try.

Aug 77. (7") **CRYIN' SHAME. / ONE MORE TRY** [-] [ ]

ALLMAN AND WOMAN

the (Woman being GREGG's wife and singer CHER) (same line-up)

Warners Warners

Nov 77. (lp)(c) **TWO THE HARD WAY** [ ] [ ]
– Move me / I found you love / Can you fool / You've really got a hold on me / We're gonna make it / Do what you gotta do / In for the night / Shadow dream song / Island / I love makin' love to you / Love me.

Dec 77. (7") **LOVE ME. / MOVE ME** [ ] [ ]

— They soon split and were divorced 16 Jan'79.

The ALLMAN BROTHERS BAND

reformed 1989, **GREGG, DICKEY, JAIMO, BUTCH** and newcomers **ALLEN WOODY** – bass / **WARREN HAYES** – guitar / **JOHNNY NEEL** – keyboards

Epic Epic

Jul 90. (7") **GOOD CLEAN FUN. / SEVEN TURNS** [-] [ ]

Jul 90. (cd)(c)(lp) **SEVEN TURNS** [ ] [53]
– Good clean fun / Let me ride / Low down dirty mean / Shine it on / Loaded dice / Seven turns / Gambler's roll / True gravity / It ain't over yet.

Sep 90. (7") **SEVEN TURNS. / LET ME RIDE** [-] [ ]

Jul 91. (cd)(c)(lp) **SHADES OF TWO WORLDS** [ ] [85]
– End of the line / Bad rain / Nobody knows / Desert blues / Get on with your life / Midnight man / Kind of bird / Come on in the kitchen.

Jun 92. (cd)(c)(lp) **AN EVENING WITH THE ALLMAN BROTHERS BAND** [ ] [ ]
– Southbound / Nobody knows / Revival (love is everywhere) / Midnight blues / Get on with your life / Dreams / End of the line / Blue sky.

May 95. (cd)(c) **2ND SET** [-] [88]

– DUANE & GREGG ALLMAN compilations, etc. –

1972. Polydor/ US= Bold; (7") **MORNING DEW. / (pt. 2)** [-] [ ]

1973. Polydor/ US= Bold; (lp) **DUANE & GREGG ALLMAN** (rec. '68) [ ] [ ]
– Morning dew / God rest his soul / Nobody knows you when you're down and out / Come down and get me / Melissa / I'll change for you / Back down here with you / Well I know you too well / In the morning when I'm real.

– ALLMAN BROTHERS compilations, etc. –

Oct 73. Mercury/ US= Dial; (lp)(c) **EARLY ALLMANS** (as "ALLMAN JOYS") [ ] [ ]

Nov 74. Capricorn/ US= Atco; (d-lp) **BEGINNINGS** [ ] [25] Mar 73
– (first 2 ALLMAN BROTHERS BAND lp's)

1974. Capricorn; (7") **AIN'T WASTIN' TIME NO MORE. / BLUE SKY** [-] [ ]

1974. Capricorn; (7") **MELISSA. / RAMBLING MAN** [-] [ ]

Feb 76. Capricorn; (d-lp) **THE ROAD GOES ON FOREVER** [54] [43] Dec75
– Black hearted woman / Dreams / Whipping post / Midnight rider / Statesboro blues / Stormy Monday / Hoochie coochie man / Stand back / One way out / Blue sky / Hot 'Lanta / Ain't wastin' time no more / Melissa / Wasted words / Jessica / Ramblin' man / Little Martha.

Dec 76. Capricorn; (d-lp) **WIPE THE WINDOWS, CHECK THE OIL, DOLLAR GAS** (demos, rarities recorded live before 1972) [ ] [75]
– Wasted words / Southbound / Ramblin' man / In memory of Elizabeth Reed / Ain't wastin' time no more / Come and go blues / Can't lose what you never had / Don't want you no more / It's not my cross to bear / Jessica.

Aug 80. Capricorn; (lp)(c) **THE BEST OF THE ALLMAN BROTHERS BAND** [ ] [ ]

Jun 81. Capricorn; (d-lp)(d-c) **THE STORY OF THE ALLMAN BROTHERS BAND** ☐ ☐
Sep 83. Polydor; (12"ep) **JESSICA / SOUTHBOUND. / WHIPPIN' POST / RAMBLIN' MAN** ☐ -
Apr 89. Polydor; (6xlp)(4xc)(4xcd) **DREAMS** ☐ ☐
May 92. Polydor; (cd)(c)(lp) **A DECADE OF HITS 1969-1979** ☐ ☐ Nov 91
– Statesboro blues / Ramblin' man / Midnight rider / Southbound / Melissa / Jessica / Ain't wastin' time no more / Little Martha / Crazy love / Revival / Wasted words / Blue sky / One way out / In memory of Elizabeth Reed / Dreams / Whipping post.
Jul 84. Old Gold; (7") **JESSICA. / RAMBLIN' MAN** ☐ -
Feb 88. Old Gold; (7") **JESSICA. / ('b'-Derek & The Dominoes')** ☐ -
Jul 88. Knight; (lp)(c) **NIGHTRIDING** *(cd-iss.Sep89)* ☐ -
May 92. Castle; (cd) **THE COLLECTION** ☐ -
Sep 85. See For Miles; (lp) **THE SOUL OF TIME (as "Hourglass")** ☐ -

DUANE ALLMAN

exploitation compilations featuring all his guitar/sessions
Oct 74. Capricorn; (d-lp) **AN ANTHOLOGY** ☐ 28 Dec 72
– B.B.King medley / Hey Jude / The road of love / Goin' down slow / The weight / Games people play / Shake for me / Loan me a dime / Rollin' stone / Livin' on the open road / Down along the cove / lease be with me / Mean old world / Layla / Statesboro blues / Don't keep me wondering / Stand back / Dreams / Little Martha. *(d-cd.iss.Oct87 on 'Polydor')*
Jan 75. Capricorn; (d-lp) **AN ANTHOLOGY VOL.2** ☐ 49 Jul 74
– Happily married man / It ain't fair / The weight / You reap what you sow / Matchbox / Born to be wild / No money down / Been gone too long / Stuff you gotta watch / Push push / Walk on gilded splinters / Waiting for a train / Don't tell me your troubles / Goin' upstairs / Come on in my kitchen / Dimples / Goin' up the country / Done somebody wrong / Leave my blues at home / Midnight rider. *(d-cd.iss.Oct87 on 'Polydor')*
Sep 79. Capricorn; (lp)(c) **THE BEST OF DUANE ALLMAN** ☐ ☐

RICHARD BETTS

with **CHUCK LEAVELL** – piano / **JOHNNY SANDLIN** – bass, guitar, percussion / **JOHN HUGHEY** – steel guitar / **DAVID WALSHAW** – drums, percussion / etc.

Capricorn Capricorn
Aug 74. (lp)(c) **HIGHWAY CALL** ☐ 19
– Long time gone / Rain / Highway call / Let nature sing / Hand picked / Kissimmee kid.
Sep 74. (7") **KISSIMMEE KID. / LONG TIME GONE** - ☐
Nov 74. (7") **HIGHWAY CALL. / RAIN** - ☐

DICKEY BETTS & GREAT SOUTHERN

with (ex-MELTING POT members) **DAN TOLER** – guitar / **KEN TIBBETS** – bass / **DONNIE SHARBONO** – drums / **TOM BROOME** – keyboards, vocals / **TOPPER PRICE** – harmonica

Arista Arista
May 77. (lp)(c) **DICKEY BETTS & GREAT SOUTHERN** ☐ 31 Apr 77
– Out to get me / Run gypsy run / Sweet Virginia / The way love goes / Nothing you can do / California blues / Bougainvilla.
1977. (7") **NOTHING YOU CAN DO. /** - ☐
1977. (7") **SWEET VIRGINIA. / BOUGAINVILLA** - ☐

— **MICHAEL WORKMAN** – keyboards repl. BROOME / **DAVID GOLDFLIES** – bass repl. TIBBETS / added **DAVID TOLER** – percussion, drums
Apr 78. (lp)(c) **ATLANTA'S BURNING DOWN** ☐ ☐
– Good time feeling / Atlanta's burning down / Leaving me again / Back on the road again / Dealing with the Devil / Shady streets / You can have her / Mr. Blues man.
1978. (7") **ATLANTA'S BURNING DOWN. / MR. BLUES MAN** - ☐

DICKEY BETTS BAND

had sort of comeback album

C.B.S. Epic
Nov 88. (lp)(c)(cd) **PATTERN DISRUPTIVE** ☐ ☐
– Rock bottom / Stone cold heart / Time to roll / The blues ain't nothin' / Heartbreak line / Duane's tune / Under the guns of love / C'est la vie / Far cry / Loverman.

ALMIGHTY

Formed: Glasgow, Scotland . . . 1988 by WARWICK and STUMPY who had evolved from 'FM Revolver' signed band ROUGH CHARM. Broke through in 1990 when a series of heavy 45's slid into the charts 1990. • **Style:** Blistering US-influenced heavy grunge'n'roll, similar to a hard-metal ALICE COOPER. **Songwriters:** Most penned by WARWICK, with some co-written with others. Covered BODIES (Sex Pistols) / YOU AIN'T SEEN NOTHIN' YET (Bachman-Turner Overdrive) / IN A RUT (RUTS) / etc. • **Trivia:** They had meeting with Hell's Angels to discuss!? their similar group emblem/motif. ANDY CAIRNS of THERAPY? provided backing vox on 'CRANK' album.

Recommended: BLOOD, FIRE & LOVE (*7)

RICKY WARWICK – vocals, rhythm & acoustic guitars / **TANTRUM** – lead & rhythm guitars, b.vocals / **FLOYD LONDON** – bass, acoustic guitar, b.vocals / **STUMP MUNROE** – drums, percussion, b.vocals (real surnames of last 3; **JAMES, McAVOY, JULIANS**)

Polydor M.C.A.
Jul 89. (7") **DESTROYED. / LOVE ME TO DEATH** ☐ -
(12"+=)(cd-s+=) – Blood, fire & love (metal version).
Oct 89. (lp)(c)(cd) **BLOOD, FIRE & LOVE** ☐ ☐
– Resurrection mutha / Destroyed / Wild & wonderful / Blood, fire & love / Lay down the law / Gift horse / You've gone wild / Power / Full force lovin' machine / Detroit. (c/cd+=) – New love sensation.
Jan 90. (7"ep)(c-ep) **THE POWER EP** ☐ ☐
– Power / Detroit / Wild and wonderful (live).
(12"ep+=)(12"pic-d-ep+=)(12"clear-ep+=) – ('A'-killerwatt mix).
(cd-ep+=) – Lay down the law (live).
Jun 90. (7")(c-s)(7"pic-d) **WILD & WONDERFUL. / THUNDERBIRD / GOOD GOD ALMIGHTY** 50 ☐
(12"+=)(cd-s+=)(12"pic-d+=) – ('A'extended).
Oct 90. (cd)(c)(10"m-lp) **BLOOD, FIRE & LIVE (live)** 62 ☐
– Full force lovin' machine / You've gone wild / Lay down the love / Blood, fire & love / Destroyed / Wild and wonderful / Resurrection mutha / You ain't seen nothin' yet.
Feb 91. (7")(c-s) **FREE'N'EASY. / HELL TO PAY** 35 ☐
(12"+=)(cd-s+=) – Bodies.
Mar 91. (cd)(c)(lp) **SOUL DESTRUCTION** 22 ☐
– Crucify / Free'n'easy / Joy bang one time / Love religion / Bandaged knees / Praying to the red light / Sin against the light / Little lost sometimes / Devil's toy / What more do you want / Hell to pay / Loaded.
Apr 91. (7")(7"pic-d) **DEVIL'S TOY. / BAD TEMPTATION** 36 ☐
(12"+=)(cd-s+=) – ('A'extended).
Jun 91. (7") **LITTLE LOST SOMETIMES. / WILD ROAD TO SATISFACTION** 42 ☐
(12"+=) – Curiosity (live).
(pic-cd-s+=) – Detroit (live).

— (Apr92) **PETE FRIESEN** – lead guitar (ex-ALICE COOPER) repl. TANTRAM
Mar 93. (12"ep)(cd-ep) **ADDICTION. / ADDICTION (live) / SOUL DESTRUCTION (demo)** 38 ☐
Apr 93. (cd)(c)(lp) **POWERTRIPPIN'** 5 ☐
– Addiction / Possession / Over the edge / Jesus loves you . . . but I don't / Sick and wired / Powertrippin' / Taking hold / Out of season / Life blood / Instinct / Meathook / Eye to eye. *(re-iss.cd Apr95)*
May 93. (7")(c-s) **OUT OF SEASON. / IN A RUT** 41 ☐
(12"+=) – Insomnia / Wild & wonderful (demo).
(cd-s+=) – Free'n'easy / Keep on rockin' in the free world.
(cd-s) – ('A'side) / Fuckin' up / Out of season (demo) / Bodies.
Oct 93. (7")(c-s) **OVER THE EDGE. / TAKING HOLD (live)** 38 ☐
(cd-s) – ('A'side) / Jesus loves you (but I don't) / Powertrippin' (live) / Blind.
(7"colrd) – ('A'side) / Lifeblood.

Chrysalis Chrysalis
Sep 94. (7"clear) **WRENCH. / SHITZOPHRENIC** 26 ☐
(12"pic-d) – ('A'side) / State of emergency / Hellelujah.
(cd-s) – ('A'side) / Do anything you wanna do / Give me fire.
(cd-s) – ('A'side) / Thanks again, again / Knocking on Joe.
Oct 94. (cd)(c)(lp) **CRANK** 15 ☐
– Ultraviolent / Wrench / The unreal thing / Jonestown mind / Move right in / Crank and deceit / United state of apathy / Welcome to defiance / Way beyond belief / Crackdown / Sorry for nothing / Cheat. (cd+=) – Shitzophrenic.
Jan 95. (7"pic-d) **JONESTOWN MIND. / ADDICTION (live) / CRANK (live) / DECEIT (live)** 26 ☐
(12") – ('A'side) / Jonestown dub / The unreal thing (live) / United state of apathy (live).
(cd-s) – ('A'side) / Wrench (live) / Move right in (live).
(cd-s) – ('A'side) / Welcome to defiance (live) / Sorry for nothing (live).

. . . Jan – Jun '96 stop press . . .
Feb 96. (single) **ALL SUSSED OUT** 28 ☐
Mar 96. (cd)(c)(lp) **JUST ADD LIFE** 34 ☐
May 96. (single) **DO YOU UNDERSTAND** 38 ☐

— Have already split in March.

Marc ALMOND (see under ⇒ SOFT CELL)

ALONE AGAIN OR (see under ⇒ SHAMEN)

ALT (see under ⇒ CROWDED HOUSE)

AMBOY DUKES (see under ⇒ NUGENT, Ted)

AMERICAN MUSIC CLUB

Formed: Burnbank, California, USA . . .mid 80's by MARK EITZEL. Progressed steadily for the next half a decade and became Top 50 entrants in 1993 with 'Virgin' label 'MERCURY' album. • **Style:** Gloomy guitar-outfit although similar to R.E.M., GO-BETWEENS or NICK DRAKE. • **Songwriters:** EITZEL. • **Trivia:** The single 'RISE' was a tribute to MARK's friend, who died of AIDS.

Recommended: EVERCLEAR (*8) / SAN FRANCISCO (*7)

MARK EITZEL – vocals, guitar, keyboards / **VUDI** – guitar, accordion, bass / **DAN PEARSON** – bass, guitar, dulcimer, vocals, etc. / **MIKE SIMMS** – drums / **BRUCE KAPHAN** – pedal steel guitar, keyboards, bass, percussion, producer, etc.

Zippo Zippo

Oct 87. (lp)(cd) **THE ENGINE** [ ] [ ]
– Big night / Outside this bar / At my mercy / Gary's song / Night watchman / Lloyd / Electric light / Mom's TV / Art of love / Asleep / This year.

Demon Zippo

Oct 88. (lp)(cd) **CALIFORNIA** [ ] [ ]
– Firefly / Somewhere / Laughing stock / Lonely / Pale skinny girl / Blue and grey shirt / Bad liquor / Now you're defeated / Jenny / Western sky / Highway 5 / Last harbor.

Oct 89. (lp)(cd) **UNITED KINGDOM** [ ] [ ]
– Here they roll down / Dreamers of the dream / Never mind / United kingdom / Dream is gone / Heaven of your hands / Kathleen / The hula maiden / Animal pen. (cd+=) – California (album).

Alias Alias

Oct 91. (cd)(c)(lp) **EVERCLEAR** [ ] [ ]
– Why won't you stay / Rise / Miracle on 8th Street / Ex-girlfriend / Crabwalk / The confidential agent / Sick of food / The dead part of you / Royal cafe / What the pillar of salt held up / Jesus' hands.

Nov 91. (7") **RISE. / ?** [ ] [ ]
(12"+=)(cd-s+=) –

Virgin Int Virgin Int.

Mar 93. (cd)(c)(lp) **MERCURY** [41] [ ]
– Gratitude walks / If I had a hammer / Challenger / I've been a mess / Hollywood 4-5-92 / What Godzilla said to God when his name wasn't found in the book of life / Keep me around / Dallas, airports, bodybags / Apology for an accident / Over and done / Johnny Mathis' feet / The hopes and dreams of Heaven's 10,000 whores / More hopes and dreams / Will you find me?

Apr 93. (c-s) **JOHNNY MATHIS' FEET. / THE AMILNITRATE DREAMS OF PAT ROBERTSON** [58] [ ]
(cd-s+=) – What Godzilla said to God when his name wasn't found in the book of life / Dallas, airports, bodybags (demo).
(c-s)(cd-s) – ('A'side) / Will you find me / The hopes and dreams of Heaven's 10,000.

Jun 93. (c-ep)(cd-ep) **KEEP ME AROUND / CHALLENGER / IN MY ROLE AS THE MOST HATED SINGER IN THE LOCAL UNDERGROUND MUSIC SCENE / MEMO FROM AQUATIC PARK** [ ] [ ]
(cd-s) – (repl. 2nd track w /) / Walking tune / Memo from Bernal Heights.

— **TIM MOONEY** – drums repl. SIMMS (might have been earlier)

Aug 94. (7")(c-s) **WISH THE WORLD AWAY. / I JUST TOOK TWO SLEEPING PILLS AND NOW I'M LIKE A BRIDEGROOM** [46] [ ]
(cd-s+=) – The revolving door (demo).
(cd-s) – ('A'side) / The President's test for physical fitness / Cape Canaveral.

Sep 94. (cd)(c)(lp) **SAN FRANCISCO** [72] [ ]
– Fearless / It's your birthday / Can you help me / Love doesn't belong to anyone / Wish the world away / How many six packs to screw in a light? / Cape Canaverai / Hello Amsterdam / The revolving door / In the shadow of the valley / What holds the world together / I broke my promise / The thorn in my side is gone / I'll be gone / Fearless (reprise).

Oct 94. (7")(c-s) **CAN YOU HELP ME. / THE THORN IN MY SIDE IS GONE** [ ] [ ]
(cd-s+=) – California dreamin'.

Feb 95. (7")(c-s)(cd-s) **CAN YOU HELP ME. / THE THORN IN MY SIDE IS GONE** [ ] [ ]
(cd-s+=) – California dreamin' (alt.version).

MARK EITZEL

Demon Alias

Apr 91. (cd)(lp) **SONGS OF LOVE – LIVE AT THE BORDERLINE (live)** [ ] [ ]
– Firefly / Chanel No.5 / Western sky / Blue and grey shirt / Gary's song / Outside this bar / Room above the club / Last harbour / Kathleen / Crabwalk / Jenny / Take courage / Nothing can bring me down.

. . . Jan – Jun '96 stop press . . .

Virgin Virgin

Mar 96. (cd)(c)(lp) **60 WATT SILVER LINING** [ ] [ ]

— covered THERE IS NO EASY WAY DOWN (Carole King).

AMORPHOUS ANDROGYNOUS (see under ⇒ FUTURE SOUND OF LONDON)

Tori AMOS

Born: MYRA ELLEN AMOS, 22 Aug '63, North Carolina, USA. Daughter of a preacher and Sioux Indian parents. In 1981, she released an independent US single BALTIMORE / WALKING WITH YOU, under her real name Ellen Amos. After signing to Atlantic in 1987 and releasing a miserable pop-metal lp 'Y TORI KANT READ', she finally became a star of 1992. • **Style:** Burnt orange-haired songstress likened to KATE BUSH or JONI MITCHELL. • **Songwriters:** All self-penned, except; SMELLS LIKE TEEN SPIRIT (Nirvana) / RING MY BELL (Anita Ward) / ANGIE (Rolling Stones) / THANK YOU (Led Zeppelin) / LITTLE DRUMMER BOY (UK-hit 1959) / HOME ON THE RANGE (trad.) / IF SIX WAS NINE (Jimi Hendrix Experience) / STRANGE FRUIT (Billie Holliday) / FAMOUS BLUE RAINCOAT (Leonard Cohen). • **Trivia:** Her 1992 album cover, also drew similarities to US version of KATE BUSH's 'THE KICK INSIDE'. TORI sang backing for AL STWEART on 'Last Days of the Century' album, plus STAN RIDGWAY's 'Mosquitos'

Recommended: LITTLE EARTHQUAKES (*8) / UNDER THE PINK (*7) / BOYS FOR PELE (*5)

Y KANT TORI READ

TORI AMOS – vocals, piano with group: **STEVE FARRIS** – guitar (ex MR. MISTER) / **MATT SORUM** – drums /

not issued Atlantic

Jun 88. (7") **THE BIG PICTURE. / YOU GO TO MY HEAD** [-] [ ]

Jul 88. (cd)(c)(lp) **Y KANT TORI READ** [-] [ ]
– The big picture / God on your island / Fayth / Fire on the side / Pirates / Floating city / Heart attack at 23 / On the boundary / You go to my head / Etienne trilogy

Aug 88. (7") **COOL ON YOUR ISLAND. / HEART ATTACK AT 23** [-] [ ]

TORI AMOS

with **STEVE CATON** – guitar / **WILL McGREGOR** – bass / **ERIC ROSSE** – keyboards, co-producer / **JEFF SCOTT** – bass, guitar / **PAULINHO DaCOSTA** – percussion

East West Atlantic

Nov 91. (7") **SILENT ALL THESE YEARS. / ME AND A GUN** [51] [ ]
(12"ep+=)(cd-ep+=) – ME AND A GUN EP: Upside down / Thoughts.

Jan 92. (cd)(c)(lp) **LITTLE EARTHQUAKES** [14] [54] Dec 91
– Crucify / Girl / Silent all these years / Precious things / Winter / Happy phantom / China / Leather / Mother / Tear in your hand / Me and a gun / Little earthquakes.

Jan 92. (7")(c-s) **CHINA. / SUGAR** [51] [ ]
(12"+=)(cd-s+=) – Flying Dutchman / Humpty Dumpty.

Mar 92. (7")(c-s) **WINTER. / THE POOL** [25] [ ]
(cd-s+=) – Take to the sky / Sweet dreams
(cd-s) – ('A'side) / Angie / Smells like teen spirit / Thank you.

Jun 92. (7")(c-s) **CRUCIFY** (remix). / HERE, IN MY HEAD [15] [ ]
(cd-s) – ('A'side) / Little earthquakes / Precious things / Mother (all live).

Aug 92. (7")(c-s) **SILENT ALL THESE YEARS. / SMELLS LIKE TEEN SPIRIT** [26] [ ]
(cd-s) – ('A'side) / Upside down / Me and a gun / Thoughts.
(cd-s) – ('A'side) / Ode to the banana king (pt.1) / Song for Eric / Happy phantom (live).

— Now w / **GEORGE PORTER JR.** – bass / **CARLO NUCCIO** – drums / **ERIC ROSSE** – programming / **STEVE CATON** – drums / **PAULINHO DaCOSTA** – percussion

Jan 94. (7")(c-s) **CORNFLAKE GIRL. / SISTER JANET** [4] [ ]
(cd-s+=) – Piano suite: All the girls hate her – Over it.
(cd-s) – ('A'side) / A case of you / Strange fruit / If Six was nine.

Feb 94. (cd-ep) **GOD / HOME ON THE RANGE (CHEROKEE edition) / HAND SUITE: ALL THE GIRLS HATE HER – OVER IT** [-] [ ]

Feb 94. (cd)(c)(lp) **UNDER THE PINK** [1] [12]
– Pretty good year / God / Bells for her / Past the mission / Baker baker / The wrong band / The waitress / Cornflake girl / Icicle / Cloud on my tongue / Space dog / Yes, Anastasia.

Mar 94. (7")(c-s) **PRETTY GOOD YEAR. / HONEY** [7] [ ]
(cd-s+=) – The black swan.
(cd-s) – ('A'side) / Daisy dead petals / Home on the range (Cherokee version).

TRENT REZNOR of NINE INCH NAILS guested vox on 'Past The Mission'.

May 94. (7")(c-s) **PAST THE MISSION. / WINTER (live)** [31] [ ]
(cd-s+=) – The waitress (live) / Here in my head (live).
(cd-s) – ('A'side) / Upside down (live) / Icicle (live) / Flying Dutchman (live).

Oct 94. (7"pic-d)(c-s) **GOD. / ('A'mix)** [44] [72] Jan94
(12"+=)(cd-s+=) – ('A'remixes from;- The Joy / Carl Craig / CJ Bolland).

. . . Jan – Jun '96 stop press . . .

Jan 96. (single) **CAUGHT A LITE SNEEZE** [20] [60]
Jan 96. (cd)(c) **BOYS FOR PELE** [2] [2]
Mar 96. (single) **TALULA** [22] [ ]

AMPS (see under ⇒ BREEDERS)

Ian ANDERSON (see under ⇒ JETHRO TULL)

Jon ANDERSON (see under ⇒ YES)

ANDERSON BRUFORD WAKEMAN HOWE (see under ⇒ YES)

ANIMALS

Formed: Newcastle, England . . . 1960, as The ALAN PRICE COMBO. When ERIC BURDON joined in 1962, they became The ANIMALS, as so dubbed by their fans due to their wild stage act.. They supported the likes of SONNY BOY WILLIAMSON and JOHN LEE HOOKER, before moving to London in early '64, and signing to EMI's 'Columbia', by then unknown Mickey Most. By summer that year, they were top of the charts on both sides of the Atlantic. The song HOUSE OF THE RISING SUN (a traditional re-working) became standard rock/pop song for many future budding singers. Many top 10 hits followed but splits in ranks froze these by the late 60's, and marred any future. BURDON solo continued to sell records, especially in the States with Top 3 single 'SPILL THE WINE' with soul group WAR. • **Style:** R&B / beat group that heralded introduction of BURDON one of the all-time great and powerful vocalists. When super organ man PRICE departed, they branched out into psychedelic and heavier roots. • **Songwriters:** BURDON lyrics / PRICE arrangements songs, with covers BOOM BOOM + DIMPLES + I'M MAD AGAIN (John Lee Hooker) / I'M IN LOVE AGAIN (Fats Domino) / TALKIN' ABOUT YOU (Ray Charles) / GONNA SEND YOU BACK TO GEORGIA (Timmy Shaw) / DON'T LET ME BE MISUNDERSTOOD (Nina Simone) / PRETTY THING (Bo Diddley) / BABY LET ME TAKE YOU HOME (Russell-Farrell) / BRING IT ON HOME TO ME (Sam Cooke) / WE'VE GOTTA GET OUT OF THIS PLACE (Mann-Weil) / DON'T BRING ME DOWN (Goffin-King) / RIVER DEEP MOUNTAIN HIGH (Phil Spector) / PAINT IT BLACK (Rolling Stones) / etc. • **Trivia:** CHAS CHANDLER gave up bass to produce JIMI HENDRIX, SLADE and other 'Polydor' acts.

Recommended: SINGLES PLUS (*8) / STAR PORTRAIT (*5)

ERIC BURDON (b.11 May'41, Walker, nr.Newcastle, England) – vocals / **ALAN PRICE** (b.19 Apr'41, Fairfield, Durham, England) – keyboards, vocals / **HILTON VALENTINE** (b.21 May'43, North Shields, England) – guitar / **CHAS CHANDLER** (b.18 Dec'38, Heaton, nr.Newcastle, England) – bass / **JOHN STEEL** (b. 4 Feb'41, Gateshead, England) – drums

Columbia M.G.M.

Apr 64. (7") **BABY LET ME TAKE YOU HOME. / GONNA SEND YOU BACK TO WALKER** (US 'A'side) [21] [57] Sep64
Jun 64. (7") **HOUSE OF THE RISING SUN. / TALKING ABOUT YOU** [1] [1] Jul 64
Sep 64. (7") **I'M CRYING. / TAKE IT EASY** [8] [19] Oct 64
Nov 64. (lp) **THE ANIMALS** [6] [7] Sep 64
– Story of Bo Diddley / Bury my body / Dimples / I've been around / I'm in love again / The girl can't help it / I'm mad again / She said yeah / The right time / Memphis / Boom boom / Around and around. *(re-iss.+c.Oct 69 on 'Starline') (US diff. tracks added 'House Of The Rising Sun')*
Nov 64. (7") **BOOM BOOM. / BLUE FEELING** [-] [43]
Jan 65. (7") **DON'T LET ME BE MISUNDERSTOOD. / CLUB A GO-GO** [3] [15] Feb 65
Apr 65. (7") **BRING IT ON HOME TO ME. / FOR MISS CAULKER** [7] [32] May 65
May 65. (lp) **ANIMAL TRACKS** [6] [57] Sep 65
– Mess around / How you've changed / Hallelujah, I love her so / I believe to my soul / Worried life blues / Roberta / I ain't got you / Bright lights, big city / Let the good times roll / For Miss Caulker / Roadrunner. *(re-iss.Sep84 +c on 'Fame')*
Jul 65. (7") **WE'VE GOTTA GET OUT OF THIS PLACE. / I CAN'T BELIEVE IT** [2] [13] Aug 65
Oct 65. (7") **IT'S MY LIFE. / I'M GONNA CHANGE THE WORLD** [7] [23] Nov 65

— **DAVE ROWBERRY** (b.27 Dec'43, Newcastle, England) – keyboards (ex-MIKE COTTON SOUND) repl. PRICE who went solo

Decca M.G.M.

Feb 66. (7") **INSIDE – LOOKING OUT. / OUTCAST** [12] [-]
Mar 66. (7") **INSIDE – LOOKING OUT. / YOU'RE ON MY MIND** [-] [34]

— **BARRY JENKINS** (b.22 Dec'44, Leicester, England) – drums (ex-NASHVILLE TEENS) repl. STEEL

May 66. (lp) **ANIMALISM** [4] [33] Nov 66
– One monkey don't stop no show / Maudie / Outcast / Sweet little sixteen / You're on my mind / Clapping / Gin house blues / Squeeze her -Tease her / What am I living for / I put a spell on you / That's all I am to you / She'll return it.
May 66. (7") **DON'T BRING ME DOWN. / CHEATING** [6] [12]

ERIC BURDON & THE ANIMALS

Sep 66. (7") **SEE SEE RIDER. / SHE'LL RETURN IT** [-] [10]

— ERIC with session musicians incl. BENNY GOULSON

Oct 66. (7") **HELP ME GIRL. / THAT AIN'T WHERE IT'S AT** [14] [29] Dec 66
Apr 67. (lp) **ERIC IS HERE** [-] [ ]
– Help me girl / In the night / Mama told me not to come / I think it's gonna rain today / This side of goodbye / That ain't where it's at / Wait till next year / Losin' control / It's not easy / Biggest bundle of them all / It's been a long time coming / True love.

— ERIC who had earlier moved to California brought back **BARRY JENKINS** in Jan '67

— recruited **VIC BRIGGS** (b.14 Feb'45, London) – guitar (ex-STEAMPACKET) to finally repl ROWBERRY / **JOHN WIEDER** (b.21 Apr'47, London) – guitar, violin repl. VALENTINE who went solo / **DANNY McCULLOCH** (b.18 Jul'45, London) – bass repl. CHANDLER who became producer

M.G.M. M.G.M.

May 67. (7") **WHEN I WAS YOUNG. / A GIRL NAMED SANDOZ** [45] [15] Apr 67
Aug 67. (7") **GOOD TIMES. / AIN'T THAT SO** [20] [ ]
Aug 67. (7") **SAN FRANCISCAN NIGHTS. / GOOD TIMES** [-] [9]
Sep 67. (lp) **WINDS OF CHANGE** [ ] [42]
– San Franciscan nights / Good times / Winds of change / Poem by the sea / Paint it black / Black plague / Yes I am experienced / Man-woman / Hotel hell / Anything / It's all meat. *(re-iss.Apr71) (re-iss.Oct85 on 'Polydor')*
Oct 67. (7") **SAN FRANCISCAN NIGHTS. / GRATEFULLY DEAD** [7] [ ]
Dec 67. (7") **MONTEREY. / AIN'T IT SO** [-] [15]
Feb 68. (7") **SKY PILOT (pt.1). / SKY PILOT (pt.2)** [40] [14] Jun 68
Mar 68. (7") **ANYTHING. / IT'S ALL MEAT** [-] [80]
Apr 68. (lp) **THE TWAIN SHALL MEET** [ ] [79]
– Just the thought / Closer to the truth / No self pity / Orange and red beans / Sky pilot / We love you Lil / All is one.

— **ZOOT MONEY** – keyboards (ex-BIG ROLL BAND, ex-DANTALIAN'S CHARIOT) / **ANDY SOMERS** (aka SUMMERS) – guitar, bass (ex-BIG ROLL BAND, ex-DANTALIAN'S CHARIOT) repl. BRIGGS and McCULLOCH

Aug 68. (lp) **EVERY ONE OF US** [ ] [ ]
– Uppers and downers / Serenade to a sweet lady / The immigrant lad / Year of the guru / St.James infirmary / New York 1963 – America 1968 / White houses.
Nov 68. (7") **WHITE HOUSES. / RIVER DEEP MOUNTAIN HIGH** [-] [67]
Jan 69. (7") **RING OF FIRE. / I'M THE ANIMAL** [25] [ ]
Dec 68. (lp) **LOVE IS** [ ] [ ]
– River deep, mountain high / I'm the animal / I'm dying, or am I / Gemini / The madman / Ring of fire / Coloured rain / To love somebody / As tears go passing by. *(US iss.d-lp) (UK re-iss.d-lp.Apr71 + 1978 on 'ABC')*
May 69. (7") **RIVER DEEP, MOUNTAIN HIGH. / HELP ME GIRL** [ ] [ ]

— Split Feb69. WIEDER joined FAMILY, ZOOT went solo, JENKINS joined HEAVY JELLY, SOMERS became SUMMERS and joined KEVIN AYERS then KEVIN COYNE. He later helped form The POLICE

May 68. (7") **MONTEREY. / ANYTHING** [ ] [ ]

ERIC BURDON & WAR

ERIC BURDON – vocals, and WAR: -**LONNIE (LEROY) JORDAN** – keyboards, vocals / **HOWARD SCOTT** – guitar, vocals / **CHARLES MILLER** – saxophone, clarinet / **HAROLD BROWN** – drums, percussion / **B.B. DICKERSON** – bass / **THOMAS 'PAPA DEE' ALLEN** – keyboards / **LEE OSKAR** – harmonica

Polydor M.G.M.

Sep 70. (lp)(c) **ERIC BURDON DECLARES WAR** [50] [18] May 70
– Dedication / Roll on Kirk / Tobacco road / I have a dream / Spill the wine / Blues for Memphis Slim / Birth / Mother Earth / Mr.Charlie / Danish pastry / You're no stranger. *(re-iss.Oct79 on 'MCA') (cd-iss.Oct95 on 'Avenue')*
Jul 70. (7") **SPILL THE WINE. / MAGIC MOUNTAIN** [ ] [3]

Liberty M.G.M.

Dec 70. (7") **THEY CAN'T TAKE AWAY OUR MUSIC. / HOMECOOKIN'** [ ] [50]
Jan 71. (d-lp)(d-c) **BLACK MAN'S BURDON** [ ] [82] Dec 70

– Black on black in black / Paint it black / Laurel and Hardy / P.C. 3 / Black bird / Paint it black / Spirit / Beautiful new born child / Nights in white satin / Bird and the squirrel / Nuts seed and life / Out of nowhere / Sun – Moon / Pretty colours / Gun / Jimbo / Bare back ride / Home cookin' / They can't take away our music. *(re-iss.Oct79 on 'MCA') (US-cd 1993 on 'Avenue')*

Jun 71. (7") **PAINT IT BLACK. / SPIRIT** ☐ ☐

ERIC BURDON & JIMMY WITHERSPOON

JIMMY WITHERSPOON – blues guitarist + WAR backing.

United Art. United Art.

Aug 71. (7") **SOLEDAD. / HEADIN' FOR HOME** ☐ ☐

Dec 71. (lp)(c) **GUILTY!** ☐ ☐
– I've been drinking / Once upon a time / Steam roller / The laws must change / Have mercy judge / Goin' down slow / Soledad / Home dream / Wicked wicked man / Headin' for home / The time has come. *(re-iss. US 1976 as 'BLACK AND WHITE BLUES')*

ERIC BURDON

performed at Reading festival (Aug73), backed by **AARON BUTLER** – guitar / **RANDY RICE** – bass / **ALVIN TAYLOR** – drums. This line-up also featured on his next long awaited album

Capitol Capitol

Feb 75. (lp)(c) **SUN SECRETS** ☐ 51 Dec 74
– It's my life / Ring of fire / Medley: When I was young – Warchild – The real me / Don't let me be misunderstood – Nina's school / Letter from the County farm / Sun secrets.

Dec 74. (7") **THE REAL ME. / LETTER FROM THE COUNTRY FARM** - ☐ Dec 74

Feb 75. (7") **RING OF FIRE. / THE REAL ME** - ☐ Dec 74

— added **JOHN STERLING** – guitar / **TERRY RYAN** – keyboards / **MOSES WHEELOCK** – percussion / **GEORGE SURANOVICH** – drums / and **KIM KESTERSON** – bass (repl. AARON BUTLER)

Aug 75. (lp)(c) **STOP** ☐ ☐
– City boy / Gotta get it on / The man / I'm lookin' up / Rainbow / All I do / Funky fever / By mine / The way it should be / Stop.

— using different session people

Mar 78. (lp) **SURVIVOR** ☐ ☐ Mar 77
– Rocky / Woman of the rings / The kid / Tomb of the unknown singer / Famous flames / Hollywood woman / Hook of Holland / I was born to live the blues / Highway dealer / P.O. box 500.

— Early '76 the original

ORIGINAL ANIMALS

reformed to record below **BURDON, PRICE, VALENTINE, CHANDLER + STEEL**

Barn United Art.

Aug 77. (lp)(c) **BEFORE WE WERE SO RUDELY INTERRUPTED** ☐ 70
– Brother Bill (the last clean shirt) / Many rivers to cross / Lonely avenue / Please send me someone to love / Riverside county / It's all over now, baby blue / Fire on the Sun / As the crow flies / Just a little bit / The fool.

Aug 77 (7") **PLEASE SEND ME SOMEONE TO LOVE. / RIVERSIDE COUNTY** ☐ -

Oct 77 (7") **MANY RIVERS TO CROSS. / BROTHER BILL (THE LAST CLEAN SHIRT)** - ☐

— PRICE returned to solo work.

ERIC BURDON

solo with many session people.

Polydor not issued

1980. (lp) **DARKNESS DARKNESS** ☐ ☐
– Darkness darkness / On the horizon / Rat race / Gospel singer / Ride on / Baby what's wrong / Cry to me / So much love / Ecstasy / Too late.

Ariola Germany not issued

1981. (lp) **THE LAST DRIVE (as "ERIC BURDON'S FIRE DEPT.")** - -
– The last drive / Power company / Bird on the beach / The rubbing out of long hair / Atom-most-fear / Dry / Female terrorist / The last poet.

ANIMALS

reformed again in 1983.

I.R.S. I.R.S.

Sep 83. (7) **THE NIGHT. / NO JOHN NO** ☐ 48
(12"+=) – Melt down.

Sep 83. (lp)(c) **ARK** ☐ 66
– Loose change / Love is for all time / My favourite enemy / Prisoner of the light / Being there / Hard times / The night / Trying to get to you / Just can't get enough / Melt down / Gotta get back to you / Crystal nights.

Nov 83. (7")(12") **LOVE IS FOR ALL TIME. / JUST CAN'T GET ENOUGH** ☐ ☐

Sep 84. (lp)(c) **RIP IT TO SHREDS – THE ANIMALS GREATEST HITS LIVE (live 1983)** ☐ ☐
– It's too late / House of the rising Sun / It's my life / Don't bring me down / Don't let me be misunderstood / I'm crying / Bring it on home to me / O lucky man / Boom boom / We've gotta get out of this place.

— (split though they did reunion gigs)

ERIC BURDON BAND

with **JOHN STERLING + SNUFFY WALDEN** – guitar / **STEVE GOLDSTEIN + LUIS CABAZA + RONNIE BARRON** – keyboards / **BILL McCUBBIN + TERRY WILSON** – bass / **TONY BRUANAGLE** – drums

Line Blackline

1982. (lp) **COMEBACK** - ☐
– No more Elmore / The road / Crawling King Snake / Take it easy / Dey won't / Wall of silence / Streetwalker / It hurts me too / Lights out / Bird on the beach. *(UK-iss Jun84 as 'THE ROAD' on 'Thunderbolt')*

Bullfrog Carcre

Mar 84. (lp)(c) **POWER COMPANY** ☐ -
– Power company / Devil's daughter / You can't kill my spirit / Do you feel it (today) / Wicked man / Heart attack / Who gives a f*** / Sweet blood call / House of the rising Sun / Comeback. (US-iss. +cd 1988 as 'WICKED MAN on 'Big TIme')

Striped House not issued

Aug 88. (12")(cd-s) **RUN FOR YOUR LIFE. / (2 'A' versions)** ☐ -

Aug 88 (cd)(c) **I USED TO BE AN ANIMAL** - ☐

Rhino Rhino

1990 (c-s) **SIXTEEN TONS / ('A'instrumental)** - -

ANIMALS, – compilations, US imports etc. –

1964. Columbia; (7"ep) **THE ANIMALS IS HERE** ☐ ☐
-House of the rising sun / I'm crying / Gonna send you back to *** /Baby let me take you down.

1965. Columbia; (7"ep) **THE ANIMALS** ☐ ☐
-Boom boom / Around and around / Dimples / I've been around.

Mar 65. US= M.G.M.; (lp) **THE ANIMALS ON TOUR (live)** - 99
– Boom boom / How you've changed / I believe to my soul / Mess around bright lights / Big city / Worried life blues / Let the good times roll / Crying dimples / She said yeah.

1965. Columbia; (7"ep) **THE ANIMALS (No.2)** ☐ ☐
-I'm in love again / Bury my body / I'm mad again / She said yeah.

1965. US= M.G.M.; (lp) **GET YOURSELF A COLLEGE GIRL** - ☐

1965. Columbia; (7"ep) **THE ANIMALS ARE BACK** ☐ ☐

1965. US= M.G.M.; (lp) **BRITISH A-GO-GO** ☐ -

Jan 66. Columbia; (7"ep) **ANIMAL TRACKS** ☐ ☐

Feb 66. US= M.G.M.; (lp) **THE BEST OF THE ANIMALS** - 6
(UK iss.Mar89 on 'Crusader')

Apr 66. Columbia; (lp) **MOST OF THE ANIMALS** 4 ☐
(re-iss.Sep71 +c on 'MFP'; hit no.18)

1965. Decca; (7"ep) **IN THE BEGINNING THERE WAS EARLY ANIMALS** ☐ ☐
– Boom boom / Pretty thing / I just wanna make love to you.

Sep 66. US= M.G.M.; (lp) **ANIMALIZATION** - 20
– Don't bring me down / One monkey don't stop the show / You're on my mind / She'll return it / Cheating / Inside – looking out / See see rider / Gin house blues / Maudie / What am I living for / Sweet little sixteen / I put a spell on you.

Jun 67. Columbia/ M.G.M.; (lp) **THE BEST OF ERIC BURDON & THE ANIMALS VOL.2** ☐ 71

Apr 69. US= M.G.M.; (lp) **THE GREATEST HITS OF ERIC BURDON & THE ANIMALS** - ☐

1971. US= M.G.M.; (d-lp) **POP HISTORY** - ☐

1971. US= M.G.M.; (d-lp) **STAR PORTRAIT** - ☐
– Good times / Sky pilot / We love you Lil / Hey Gyp, dig the slowness / San Franciscan nights / Paint it black / When I was young / See see rider / Ring of fire / River deep, mountain high / True love (comes only once in a lifetime) / Inside – looking out / I'm an animal / Monterey / To love somebody / Anything / I'm dying, or am I?. *(cd-iss. Jul 88)*

Mar 71. M.G.M.; (7") **GOOD TIMES. / SAN FRANCISCAN NIGHTS** ☐ -
(re-iss.Nov82)

Oct 75. M.G.M.; (lp)(c) **ERIC BURDON & THE ANIMALS** ☐ -

Nov 80. M.G.M.; (d-lp)(c) **GREATEST HITS** ☐ -

Nov 76. A.B.C.; (lp)(c) **LOVE IS ALL AROUND (out-takes)** ☐ ☐

Jan 77. A.B.C.; (7") **MAGIC MOUNTAIN / HOME DREAM** - ☐
(above 2 by "ERIC BURDON AT WAR") *(US-cd-iss 1993 on 'Avenue') (cd-iss. Dec 88 on 'Spectrum', US-iss.Nov84 on 'Astan')*

1970. E.M.I.; (lp)(c) **HOUSE OF THE RISING SUN** ☐ ☐

Oct 87. E.M.I.; (lp)(c)(cd) **THE SINGLES (PLUS)** ☐ ☐
(first 10 singles 'A' & 'B')

Jul 90. E.M.I.; (d-cd)(d-c)(d-lp) **THE COMPLETE ANIMALS** ☐ -

Oct 90. E.M.I.; (7")(c-s) **WE GOTTA GET OUT OF THIS PLACE. / THE HOUSE OF THE RISING SUN** ☐ ☐

(12"+=) – Baby let me follow you down.
(cd-s++=) – Blue feeling.

Sep 72. R.A.K.; (7"m) **HOUSE OF THE RISING SUN. / DON'T LET ME BE MISUNDERSTOOD / I'M CRYING** 25
(re-iss. + pic-cd Sep'82 hit No.11)

1973. Pickwick; (lp)(c) **EARLY ANIMALS** -

Apr 76. D.J.M.; (lp)(c) **IN CONCERT FROM NEWCASTLE (live '63)** -
(re-iss Dec 76 as 'LIVE IN NEWCASTLE') (re-iss Jan 77 as 'NEWCASTLE '63 on 'Charly') (re-iss Nov 88 +cd as 'LIVE AT THE CLUB A GO GO, NEWCASTLE' on 'Decal') (cd-iss Feb 93 on 'Charly')

Jan 77. Charly; (lp) **SONNY BOY WILLIAMSON AND THE ANIMALS (live '63)** -
(re-iss.1982) (re-iss.Nov88 on 'Decal')

Feb 77. Charly; (lp) **ERIC BURDON & THE ANIMALS** -
(re-iss.Mar83)

Aug 81. Charly; (lp) **THE ANIMALS** -

Mar 83. Charly; (lp) **HOT ON FILE** -

Dec 88. See For Miles; (lp)(cd) **THE EP COLLECTION** -

Apr 88. Platinum (lp)(c) **GREATEST HITS : ERIC** -

note; next 6 releases as ERIC BURDON solo compilations.

Oct 92. Thunderbolt; (cd) **CRAWLING KING SNAKE** -

Apr 88. Big Time; (lp)(c) **GREATEST HITS 1970-1975** -

1988. Inak; (cd) **THAT'S LIVE (live by "ERIC BURDON & BAND")** -

Sep 92. Prestige; (cd)(c) **RARITIES** -

Feb 91. Raven; (cd) **ROADRUNNERS (live 66-67)** -

Dec 90. Decal; (cd)(c)(lp) **TRACKIN' THE HITS** -

Mar 91. Sequel; (cd)(c)(d-lp) **INSIDE LOOKING OUT (THE 1965-1966 SESSIONS)**(cd+= extra tracks) -

Sep 93. Spectrum; (cd)(c) **INSIDE OUT** -

Jun 90. Nightriding; (cd) **GOLDEN DECADE** -

1992 Blue Wax; (cd) **THE UNRELEASED** -

1992. Old Gold; (7") **HOUSE OF THE RISING SUN. / WE'VE GOTTA GET OUT OF THIS PLACE** -

1993. US= Avenue; (cd) **SUN SECRETS / STOP (ERIC BURDON)** -

May 94. Sixteen; (cd) **16 GREAT HITS (ANIMALS & SONNY BOY WILLIAMSON)** -

Jul 94. Success; (cd)(c) **I USED TO BE AN ANIMAL (ERIC BURDON)** -

Apr 95. Jet; (cd) **LOST WITHIN THE HALLS OF TIME (ERIC BURDON)** -

Oct 95. Avenue; (cd) **SINGS THE ANIMALS GREATEST HITS** -

ANIMALS THAT SWIM

Formed: London, England . . . 1992 by self-proclaimed genius poet HANK STARR, alongside his brothers HUGH and AL BARKER. Released 2 self-financed 45's during the next year; 'KING BEER' and 'ROY'. After another for 'Che' records in 1993, they were snapped up by 'Alt.Tent.' subsidiary 'El-e-mental'. In the autumn of '94, they unleashed the excellent debut album 'WORKSHY', which was plauded by many including NME critics. The rest of the 90s could be theirs for the taking. • **Style:** Melancholy indie-rock outfit whose vox/snare drummer HANK STARRS lets us deja vu on a diet of CATHAL COUGHLAN (Microdisney), MARK GOLDTHORPE (Artery), JULIAN COPE or even 20s caberet star JACQUES BREL. • **Songwriters:** H. STARR'S – H.BARKER and some w/CRABTREE. • **Trivia:** DEL also moonlights for BARK PSYCHOSIS, while ANTHONY does same for MAMBO TAXI.

Recommended: WORKSHY (*10) / I WAS THE KING . . . (*8)

HANK STARRS – vocals, drums / **HUGH BARKER** – guitar / **AL BARKER** – guitar, keyboards, vocals / **DEL CRABTREE** – trumpet / **ANTHONY COOTE** – bass

Beach-heads / not issued

May 92. (7") **KING BEER. /** -

Feb 93. (7") **ROY. /** -

Che / not issued

Aug 93. (10"ep) **50 DRESSES. / CHAPEL MARKET. / HOLLOWAY AVIATOR. / OREGON STATE FAIR** -

El-e-mental / not issued

Sep 94. (7")(cd-s) **MADAME YEVONDE. / ME AND CAPTAIN AMERICA / MAY** -

Sep 94. (cd)(lp) **WORKSHY** -
– How to make a chandelier / Smooth steps / Roy / Pink carnations / St. Francis / Action at Tescos / King Beer / Barney / Susie's friends / Madame Yevonde / Vic / Silent film / Stay with me.

—— They now have a new drummer **KARL** (in Spring '95)

Mar 95. (7"ep)(cd-ep) **PINK CARNATIONS / KANDY KARS. / NEW BOOTS / HARRY DEAN / DEL FRESCO** -

. . . Jan – Jun '96 stop press . . .

Feb 96. (single) **THE GREENHOUSE** -

May 96. (single) **FADED GLAMOUR** -

Jun 96. (cd)(c)(lp) **I WAS THE KING, I REALLY WAS THE KING** -

ANOTHER PRETTY FACE (see under ⇒ WATERBOYS)

Adam ANT (see under ⇒ ADAM AND THE ANTS)

ANTHRAX

Formed: Queen's, New York, USA . . . mid'81, by TURBIN and LILKER. Spotted and signed mid'83 by JOHNNY Z to 'Megaforce' label which was licensed to 'Music For Nations' in Europe. In 1987, their album 'AMONG THE LIVING' was first to chart. • **Style:** Heavy "hard-core" thrash metal with punk ideals. • **Songwriters:** SCOTT IAN except; I'M EIGHTEEN (Alice Cooper) / SABBATH BLOODY SABBATH (Black Sabbath) / GOD SAVE THE QUEEN and FRIGGIN' IN THE RIGGIN' (Sex Pistols) / GOT THE TIME (Joe Jackson) / BRING THE NOISE (Public Enemy) / PROTEST AND SURVIVE (Discharge), LOOKING DOWN THE BARREL OF A GUN (Beastie Boys) / SHE (Kiss) • **Trivia:** DAN SPITZ's older brother DAVID, played bass in mid'80's with BLACK SABBATH. Made an acting/singing appearance on a 1992 showing of US TV sit-com 'Married – With Children'. **Note:** ANTHRAX (US) not to be confused with UK "oi" band same name.

Recommended: SPREADING THE DISEASE (*7) / AMONG THE LIVING (*7) / STATE OF EUPHORIA (*7) / PERSISTENCE OF TIME (*7).

NEIL TURBIN – vocals / **DAN SPITZ** – lead guitar / **SCOTT 'Not' IAN** – rhythm guitar / **DAN LILKER** – bass / **CHARLIE BONANTE** – drums

Music For Nations / Megaforce

Nov 83. (7") **SOLDIERS OF DEATH. / HOWLING FURIES** -

Jan 84. (lp) **FISTFUL OF METAL**
– Deathrider / Metal thrashing mad / I'm eighteen / Panic / Subjagator / Death from above / Across the river / Anthrax. *(re-iss.c+cd+pic-lp.Apr87, cd+=)* – Soldiers of metal / Howling furies. *(re-iss.cd/c/lp Sep95)*

(Mid'84) **MATT FALLON** – vocals repl. TURBIN

—— **FRANK BELLO** (b.19 Jul'65) – bass (ex-roadie) repl. LILKER

—— (Aug'84) **MATT** was replaced by **JOEY BELLADONNA** (b.30 Oct', Oswego, New York) – vocals (ex-BIBLE BLACK)

Feb 85. (m-lp) **ARMED AND DANGEROUS** -
– Armed and dangerous / Raise Hell / God save the Queen / Metal thrashing mad / Panic. *(UK-iss.+cd Aug87 + Nov91 + Sep95)*

Island / Megaforce-Island

Feb 86. (lp)(c) **SPREADING THE DISEASE** Dec85
– A.I.R. / Lone justice / Madhouse / S.S.C – Stand or fall / The enemy / Aftershock / Armed and dangerous / Medusa / Gung ho. *(re-iss.+cd.May86 & Aug91 on 'Island')*

May 86. (7") **MADHOUSE. / A.I.R.**
(12"+=)(12"pic-d+=) – God save the Queen. *(re-iss.Sep86, some with live 'A' side)*

Feb 87. (7")(12")(7"pic-d) **I AM THE LAW. / BUD E.LUVBOMB & SATAN'S BAND** 32
(7"red+=)(12"+=) – Madhouse (live).
(12") – I'm the man.

Apr 87. (lp)(c)(cd)(pic-lp) **AMONG THE LIVING** 18 62
– Among the living / Caught in the mosh / I am the law / Efilnikufesin (N.F.L.) / Among the living / Skeleton in the closet / One world / A.D.I.- horror of it all / Imitation of life.

Jun 87. (7")(12")(7"pic-d)(7"orange)(c-s) **INDIANS. / SABBATH BLOODY SABBATH: TAINT** 44

Nov 87. (7")(7"sha-pic-d) **I'M THE MAN. / CAUGHT IN THE MOSH** 20 -
(12"+=) – I am the law (live).

Nov 87. (m-lp)(c)(cd) **I'M THE MAN** - 53
– I'm the man (censored version) / I'm the man (Def uncensored version) / Sabbath bloody sabbath / I'm the man (live & extremely Def II uncensored version) / Caught in a mosh (live) / I am the law (live).

Sep 88. (7")(7"yellow) **MAKE ME LAUGH. / ANTI SOCIAL (live)** 26
(12"+=) – Friggin' in the riggin'.

Sep 88. (lp)(c)(cd) **STATE OF EUPHORIA** 12 30
– Be all, end all / Out of sight, out of mind / Make me laugh / Antisocial / Who cares wins / Now it's dark / Schism / Misery loves company / 13 / (finale). *(re-iss.cd Apr94)*

Mar 89. (7") **ANTI-SOCIAL. / PARASITE** [44] [ ]
(12"+=)(cd-s+=) – Le-sect.

Island Island

Aug 90. (7") **IN MY WORLD. / KEEP IT IN THE FAMILY** [29] [ ]
(10"+=)(12"+=)(cd-s+=) – ('A'&'B'extended).

Aug 90. (cd)(c)(lp) **PERSISTENCE OF TIME** [13] [24]
– Time / Blood / Keep it in the family / In my world / Gridlock / Intro to reality / Belly of the beast / Got the time / H8 red / One man stands / Discharge. *(pic-lp Jan91) (re-iss.cd+c Apr94*

Nov 90. (7")(10")(c-s) **GOT THE TIME. / WHO PUT THIS TOGETHER** [16] [ ]
(12"+=)(cd-s+=) – I'm the man (live).

Jun 91. (7")(c-s) **BRING THE NOISE. (as "ANTHRAX featuring CHUCK D.") / I AM THE LAW '91** [14] [ ]
(10"+=)(12"+=)(cd-s+=)(10"pic-d+=)(12"pic-d+=) – Keep it in the family (live). CHUCK D. (ex-PUBLIC ENEMY)

Jun 91. (cd)(c)(lp) **ATTACK OF THE KILLER B's** (rare studio) [13] [27]
– Milk (ode to Billy) / Bring the noise / Keep it in the family (live) / Startin' up a posse / Protest and survive / Chromatic death / I'm the man '91 / Parasite / Pipeline / Sects / Belly of the beast (live) / N.F.B. (dallabnikufesin). *(re-iss.cd Apr94)*

— (May92) **JOHN BUSH** – vocals (ex-ARMOURED SAINT) repl. MARK OSEGUEDA who had replaced BELLADONNA.

Elektra Elektra

Apr 93. (7")(c-s) **ONLY. / ONLY (mix)** [36] [ ]
(cd-s+=) – Cowboy song / Sodium pentaghol.
(cd-s) – ('A'side) / Auf wiedersehen / Noisegate.

May 93. (cd)(c)(lp) **SOUND OF WHITE NOISE** [14] [7]
– Potter's field / Only / Room for one more / Packaged rebellion / Hy pro glo / Invisible / 1000 points of hate / Black lodge / C11 H17 N2 O2 SNA / Burst / This is not an exit.

Sep 93. (7") **BLACK LODGE. / ('A'black strings mix)** [53] [ ]
(12"pic-d+=)(10"+=)(cd-s+=) – Pottersfield / Love her all I can.

Nov 93. (7") **HY PRO GLO. / LONDON** [ ] [ ]
(12"+=) – Room for one more (live).

Oct 95. (cd)(c) **STOMP 442** [ ] [47]

. . . Jan – Jun '96 stop press . . .

Jan 96. (single) **NOTHING** [ ] [ ]

– compilations, others, etc. –

Nov 92. Island; (d-cd) **AMONG THE LIVING / PERSISTENCE OF TIME** [ ] [ ]
(re-iss.cd Apr94)

Apr 94. Island; (cd)(c)(lp) **ANTHRAX LIVE -THE ISLAND YEARS (live)** [ ] [ ]

STORMTROOPERS OF DEATH

(SOD)(off-shoot band of **SCOTT IAN & DAN LILKER** with **BILLY MILANO** – vocals

Dec 84. Roadrunner; (lp) **SPEAK ENGLISH OR DIE** [-] [-] Germ'y
– March of the S.O.D. / Sergeant "D" & the S.O.D. / Kill yourself / Milano mosh / Speak English or die / United forces / Chromatic death / Pi Alpha Nu / Anti-procrastination song / What's the noise / Freddy Kruger / Milk / Pre-menstrual princess blues / Pussy whipped / Fist banging mania.

APHEX TWIN

Born: RICHARD JAMES, 1971, Cornwall, England. At a youthful 14, he recorded in his bedroom until breaking out into the dance scene. After an initial release, he put ink on paper with Belgium's 'R&S' label run by Renaat Van De Papeliere, who wanted desperately his 'DIGERIDOO' taping. • **Style:** The wonder lad was best described as an ambient TANGERINE DREAM or a techno Mozart, drawing picturesque rhythms over quite unique techniques. • **Songwriters:** Ideas JAMES; sampled various and covered FILM ME (Luxuria) / ONE DAY (Bjork). • **Trivia:** Was credited on SEEFEEL's 12"single 'Time To Find Me (remixes)'.

Recommended: SELECTED AMBIENT WORKS '85-'92 (*7)

RICHARD JAMES (aka The APHEX TWIN) – keyboards, etc.

Mighty Force not issued

Dec 91. (12"ep) **ANALOGUE BUBBLEBATH EP** [ ] [-]

R&S Outer Rhythm not issued

Apr 92. (12"ep) **DIGERIDOO. / FLAPHEAD / ISOPROPHLEX** [55] [ ]
(cd-ep+=) – Analogue bubblebath 1.

Jul 92. (12"ep)(cd-ep) **XYLEM TUBE EP** [ ] [-]

Nov 92. (cd)(c)(d-lp) **SELECTED AMBIENT WORKS '85-'92** [ ] [-]
– Xtal / Tha / Pulsewidth / Ageispolis / I won't let the Sun go down on me / Greencalx / Heliosphan / We are the music makers / Schotkey / Hedphelym / Delphium / Actium / Ptolemy.

Warp not issued

Dec 93. (12"ep)(cd-ep) **ON. / 73 YIPS. / D-SCAPE / XEPHA** [32] [ ]
– (12"ep)(cd-ep) – ('A'-D-Scape mix) / ('A'reload mix) / ('A'-M-21Q) / ('A'-28 mix).

Mar 94. (d-cd)(d-c)(2xd-lp) **SELECTED AMBIENT WORKS VOLUME II** [11] [ ]
– (12 + 13 of mostly untitled tracks; 1 of them 'Blue Calx')

Feb 95. (cd)(c)(blue-d-lp) **CLASSICS** (collection) [24] [ ]
– Digeridoo / Flaphead / Phloam / Isoproplex / Polynomial-C / Tamphex / Phlange phace / Dodeccaheedron / Analogue bubblebath / En trance to exit / Afx 2 / Metapharstic/ Digeridoo (live).

Mar 95. (12"ep)(cd-ep) **VENTOLIN / ('A'-Salbutanol mix) / ('A'-Marazanovose mix) / ('A'-Plain-an-guarry mix) / ('A'-The Coppice mix) / ('A'-Crowsnegods mix)** [49] [ ]
(12"ep-remixes)(cd-ep remixes) – ('A'-Wheeze mix) / ('A'-Carnarack mix) / ('A'-Cyclob mix) / ('A'-Deep gong mix) / ('A'-Asthma beats mix).

Apr 95. (cd)(c)(d-lp) **. . .I CARE BECAUSE YOU DO** [24] [ ]
– Acrid avid Jan Shred / The waxen path / Wax the nip / Icct Hedral / Ventolin / Come on you slags / Start as you mean to go one / Wet tip hen ax / Mookid / Alberto Balsan / Cow cud is a twin / Next heap with.

Aug 95. (12"ep)(cd-ep) **DONKEY RHUBARB EP** [ ] [ ]
– Icct Hedral (credited with PHILIP GLASS) / Pancake lizard / Mass observation (the crackdown) / Film me and finish off / One day (Sabres of Paradise mix) / Vaz deferenz.

ARCADIA (see under ⇒ DURAN DURAN)

ARMS AND LEGS (see under ⇒ JACKSON, Joe)

ASH

Formed: Downpatrick, County Down, Ireland . . .1992 by TIM WHEELER, MARK HAMILTON and RICK McMURRAY. After a few limited indie 45's, they were signed to 'Infectious', making UK Top 20 in 1995. • **Style:** Youngsters influenced by Ramones and UNDERTONES, on the retro back-lash of 90's punk America. • **Songwriters:** WHEELER or w/ HAMILTON except cover GET READY (Temptations). • **Trivia:** The cover sleeve of their single 'KUNG FU', had a photo of French Man U star footballer ERIC CANTONA, giving his famous throat and neck tackle on an abusive Crystal Palace supporter in 1995.

Recommended: TRAILER (*7) / 1977 (*9)

TIM WHEELER -vocals, guitar / **MARK HAMILTON** -bass / **RICK McMURRAY** -drums

La La Land not issued

Feb 94. (7") **JACK NAMES THE PLANETS. / DON'T KNOW** [ ] [-]

Infectious Generator

Aug 94. (7"ep) **PETROL / THE LITTLE POND. / A MESSAGE FROM OSCAR WILDE AND PATRICK THE BREWER** [ ] [-]
(cd-s+=) – Things.

Oct 94. (cd)(c)(m-lp) **TRAILER** [ ] [-]
– Season / Jack names the planets / Intense thing / Uncle Pat / Get out / Petrol / Obscure thing. (lp w/free 7"yellow) SILVER SURFER. / JAZZ '59

Oct 94. (7") **UNCLE PAT. / DIFFERENT TODAY** [ ] [-]
(cd-s+=) – Hulk Hogan bubble bath.

Mar 95. (7") **KUNG FU./ DAY OF THE TRIFFIDS** [57] [-]
(7"mispressed) – ('A'side) / Luther Ingo's star cruiser.
(cd-s) – (all 3 tracks).

Jul 95. (7")(c-s) **GIRL FROM MARS. / CANTINA BAND** [11] [-]
(cd-s+=) – Astral conversations with Toulouse Lautrec.

Sep 95. (7"clear)(7"gold)("white) **PETROL. / PUNKBOY** [-] [ ]

Oct 95. (7")(c-s)(cd-s) **ANGEL INTERCEPTOR. / 5 A.M. ETERNAL / GIVE ME SOME TRUTH** [14] [-]

Dec 95. (7"red) **GET READY. / ZERO, ZERO, ZERO** [ ] [-]
(above 45 issued on 'Fantastic Plastic')

. . . Jan – Jun '96 stop press . . .

Apr 96. (single) **GOLDFINGER** [5] [ ]
May 96. (cd)(c)(lp) **1977** [1] [ ]
Jun 96. (single) **OH YEAH** [6] [ ]

Daniel ASH (see under ⇒ BAUHAUS)

Tony ASHTON & Jon LORD (see under ⇒ DEEP PURPLE)

ASIA

Formed: London, England based . . . early 1981 by seasoned veteran rockers WETTON, HOWE, PALMER and DOWNES. These supergroup stadium fillers had no trouble finding record contract with 'Geffen'. Their eponymous debut soon climbed to No.1 in the US, and supplanted them as top group over similar challengers YES. • **Style:** AOR catering more for US audiences. • **Songwriters:** All penned by WETTON, HOWE and DOWNES. No covers. • **Trivia:** Their "Asia In Asia" concert at Budokan, Tokyo 6 Dec'83, went live to over 20 million people in US through MTV station

Recommended: THEN & NOW (*5)

JOHN WETTON (b.12 Jul'49, Derby, England) – vocals, bass (ex-URIAH HEEP, ex-ROXY MUSIC, ex-BRYAN FERRY, ex-KING CRIMSON, ex-FAMILY, ex-U.K.) / **STEVE HOWE** (b. 8 Apr'47) – guitar, vocals (ex-YES, ex-BODAST, ex-TOMORROW) / **GEOFFREY DOWNES** – keyboards, vocals (ex-YES, ex-BUGGLES, ex-ISOTOPE) / **CARL PALMER** (b.20 Mar'47, Birmingham, England) – drums, percussion (ex-EMERSON, LAKE & PALMER, ex-P.M.)

Geffen | Geffen

Apr 82. (lp)(c)(pic-lp) **ASIA** [11] [1]
– Heat of the moment / Only time will tell / Sole survivor / One step closer / Time again / Wildest dream / Without you / Cutting it fine / Here comes the feeling. *(re-iss.Sep86.cd.iss.Feb87) (c+cd.re-iss.Apr91)*

Jun 82. (7") **HEAT OF THE MOMENT. / TIME AGAIN** [46] [4] Apr 82

Aug 82. (7")(7"pic-d) **ONLY TIME WILL TELL. / RIDE EASY** [54] [17] Jul 82

Oct 82. (7") **SOLE SURVIVOR. / HERE COMES THE FEELING** [ ] [ ]

Aug 83. (7")(7"sha-pic-d) **DON'T CRY. / TRUE COLOURS** [33] [10] Jul 83

Aug 83. (lp)(c) **ALPHA** [5] [6]
– Don't cry / The smile has left your eyes / Never in a million years / My own time (I'll do what I want) / The heat goes on / Eye to eye / The last to know / True colours / Midnight Sun / Open your eyes.
(c.+=) – Daylight. *(re-iss.Sep86 / cd-iss.Feb87 + Jun89) (c+cd.re-iss.Apr91)*

Oct 83. (7") **THE SMILE HAS LEFT YOUR EYES. / LYING TO YOURSELF** [ ] [34]
(12"+=)(12"red+=) – Midnight Sun.

— (Oct83) **GREG LAKE** (b.10 Nov'48, Bournemouth, England) – vocals, bass (ex-EMERSON, LAKE & PALMER, ex-Solo Artist, ex-KING CRIMSON) repl. WETTON

(Mar84). **ARMAND 'Mandy' MEYER** – guitar (ex-KROKUS) repl. HOWE who returned to YES and formed G.T.R. **JOHN WETTON** returned to replace LAKE (re-joined E.L.P.)

Nov 85. (7") **GO. / AFTER THE WAR** [ ] [46]
(12"+=) – ('A'instrumental)

Dec 85. (lp)(c)(cd) **ASTRA** [68] [67]
– Go / Voice of America / Hard on me / Wishing / Rock and roll dream / Countdown to zero / Love now till eternity / Too late / Suspicion / After the war.

Jan 86. (7") **WISHING. / TOO LATE** [-] [ ]

— (early 1986, disbanded) **WETTON** teamed up with **PHIL MANZANERA**

GEOFFREY DOWNES

released solo album.

Geffen | Geffen

Sep 87. (lp)(c)(cd) **THE LIGHT PROGRAMME** [ ] [ ]
– Ethnic dance / East west / Urbanology / Symphonie electrique / Oceania electronique.

ASIA

reformed late 1989 (WETTON, DOWNES, PALMER plus **PAT THRALL** – guitar (ex-AUTOMATIC MAN). He was replaced by session men **STEVE LUKATHER, RON KOMIE, MANDY MEYER** and **SCOTT GORHAM.**

Geffen | Geffen

Aug 90. (cd)(c)(lp) **THEN & NOW** [ ] [ ]
– (THEN) hits compilation / (NOW) – Days like these / Prayin' 4 a miracle / Am I in love? / Voice of America / Summer (can't last too long). *(re-iss.c+cd.Aug91)*

Sep 90. (c-s)(cd-s) **DAYS LIKE THESE. / VOICE OF AMERICA** [-] [64]

— **JOHN PAYNE** -vocals, bass repl.WETTON

— **AL PITRELLI** – guitar (ex-DANGER DANGER) repl. THRALL

— **STEVE HOWE** also made guest appearance

Re-volver FM | Sony

Jun 92. (cd)(c)(lp) **AQUA** [ ] [ ] Mar 92
– Aqua (part one) / Who will stop the rain / Back in town / Love under fire / Someday / Little rich boy / The voice of reason / Lay down your arms / Crime of the heart / A far cry / Don't call me / Heaven on Earth / Aqua (part two).

Musicdisc | Sony

Aug 92. (12")(10"pic-d) **WHO WILL STOP THE RAIN. / AQUA (part 1). / HEART OF GOLD** [ ] [ ]
(cd-s+=) – Obsessing.

— **MICHAEL STURGIS** – drums repl. PALMER

Bul-let Proof | M.F.N.

May 94. (cd)(c)(lp) **ARIA** [ ] [ ]
– Anytime / Are you big enough? / Desire / Summer / Sad situation / Don't cut the wire (brother) / Feels like love / Remembrance day / Enough's enough / Military man / Aria.

— **VINNIE BURNS + TREVOR THORNTON** repl.PITRELLI and the injured HOWE

– compilations, etc. –

Dec 91. Cromwell; (cd) **ASIA LIVE 09-X1-90 MOCKBA (live)** [ ] [-]

ATTILA (see under ⇒ Billy JOEL)

AUTEURS

Formed: Southgate, London, England . . . early 1992 by LUKE HAINES and girlfriend ALICE READMAN. They quickly signed to up and coming Virgin off-shoot label 'Hut', and charted the following year, with debut album 'NEW WAVE'. • **Style:** Glossy garage indie/punk outfit, fronted by the flamboyant but cynical HAINES. • **Songwriters:** HAINES. • **Trivia:** HAINES had lived in London, then Portsmouth, before joining DAVID WESTLAKE in The SERVANTS. 'LENNY VALENTINO', was named after their 'NEW WAVE' album sleeve, depicting LENNY BRUCE dressed as RUDOLPH VALENTINO.

Recommended: NEW WAVE (*6) / NOW I'M A COWBOY (*8) / AFTER MURDER PARK (*7)

LUKE HAINES (b. 7 Oct'67, Walton-On-Thames, Surrey, England) – vocals, guitar (ex-SERVANTS) / **ALICE READMAN** (b. 1967, Harrow, England) – bass (ex-SERVANTS) / **GLENN COLLINS** (b. 7 Feb'68, Cheltenham, England) – drums (ex-DOG UNIT, ex-VORT PYLON)

Hut | Caroline

Dec 92. (12"ep)(cd-ep) **SHOWGIRL. / GLAD TO BE GONE / STAYING POWER** [ ] [-]

— added **JAMES BANBURY** – cello

Mar 93. (cd)(c)(lp) **NEW WAVE** [35] [ ]
– Show girl / Bailed out / American guitars / Junk shop clothes / Don't trust the stars / Starstruck / How could I be wrong / Housebreaker / Valet parking / Idiot brother / Early years / Home again. (free 7"w/lp on cd+c+=) – Untitled.

May 93. (10"ep)(12"ep)(cd-ep) **HOW COULD I BE WRONG. / HIGH DIVING HORSES / WEDDING DAY** [ ] [ ]

— **BARNEY CROCKFORD** – drums repl. COLLINS

Nov 93. (7") **LENNY VALENTINO. / DISNEY WORLD** [41] [ ]
(12") – ('A'side) / Car crazy / Vacant lot / ('A'original mix).

Apr 94. (7") **CHINESE BAKERY. / ('A'acoustic)** [42] [ ]
(cd-s+=) Government book store / Everything you say will destroy you.
(12"+=) – Modern history.

May 94. (cd)(c)(lp) **NOW I'M A COWBOY** [27] [ ]
– Lenny Valentino / Brainchild / I'm a rich man's toy / New French girlfriend / The upper classes / Chinese bakery / A sister like you / Underground movies / Life classes – Life model / Modern history / Daughter of a child. (lp w /free 1-sided 7") **MODERN HISTORY (acoustic).**

Nov 94. (m-cd)(m-lp) **THE AUTEURS VS U-ZIQ** (remixes) [ ] [ ]
– Lenny Valentino No.3 / Daughter of a child / Chinese bakery / Lenny Valentino No.1 / Lenny Valentino No.2 / Underground movies.

Dec 95. (7"ep)(c-ep)(cd-ep) **BACK WITH THE KILLER E.P.** [45] [-]
– Unsolved child murder / Back with the killer again / Former fan / Kenneth Anger's bad dream.

. . . Jan – Jun '96 stop press . . .

Feb 96. (single) **LIGHT AIRCRAFT ON FIRE** [58] [ ]

Mar 96. (cd)(c)(lp) **AFTER MURDER PARK** [53] [ ]

May 96. (single) **"KID'S ISSUE" EP** [ ] [-]

AZTEC CAMERA

Formed: East Kilbride (nr.Glasgow), Scotland . . . Early 1980 by 15 year-old at the time RODDY FRAME. Released two independent 45's on ALAN HORNE's now semi-famous 'Postcard' label, before moving on to 'Rough Trade' in 1982. The following year, RODDY & group hit the top in indie charts and national Top 30 with album 'HIGH LAND, HARD RAIN'. This led to a signing to 'Warners' and another top selling album 'KNIFE', which was produced by MARK KNOPFLER (Dire Straits). • **Style:** Intelligent, and mostly acoustic, melodic rock/pop. Ballads fused with romance. • **Songwriters:** All by FRAME, except JUMP (Van Halen) / DO I LOVE YOU (Cole Porter) / I THREW IT ALL AWAY (Bob Dylan) / BAD EDUCATION (Blue Orchids) / IF PARADISE WAS HALF AS NICE (Amen Corner). • **Trivia:** In Autumn'83, while in US supporting ELVIS COSTELLO, he lied about age; 19 to get into the country.

Recommended: HIGH LAND, HARD RAIN (*8)

RODDY FRAME (b.29 Jan'64) – vocals, acoustic guitar / **DAVE MULHOLLAND** – bass / **CAMPBELL OWENS** – drums (He replaced ALAN WELSH)

Postcard not issued

Mar 81. (7") **JUST LIKE GOLD. / WE COULD SEND LETTERS** [ ] [-]
Jul 81. (7") **MATTRESS OF WIRE. / LOOK OUTSIDE THE TUNNEL** [ ] [-]

(mid'82) added temp.member **BERNIE CLARK** – keyboards / **DAVE RUFFY** – drums (ex-RUTS) repl. MULHOLLAND

Rough Trade Sire

Aug 82. (7")(7"pic-d) **PILLAR TO POST. / QUEEN'S TATTOO** [ ] [-]
Jan 83. (7") **OBLIVIOUS. / ORCHARD GIRL** [47] [-]
(12"+=) – Haywire.
Apr 83. (lp)(c) **HIGH LAND, HARD RAIN** [22] [ ] Aug 83
– Oblivious / The boy wonders / Walk out to winter / The bugle sounds again / We could send letters / Pillar to post / Release / Lost outside the tunnel / Back on board / Down the dip. *(re-iss.+cd.Feb87)*
(cd+=) – Haywire / Queen's tattoo / Orchard girl. *(re-iss.cd+c Sep93 on 'WEA')*
May 83. (7")(12") **WALK OUT TO WINTER. / SET THE KILLING FREE** [64] [ ]

W.E.A. W.E.A.

Oct 83. (7") **OBLIVIOUS. / ORCHARD GIRL** [18] [ ]
(d7"+=)(12"+=) – We could send letters (live) / Back on board (live).

— **RODDY FRAME** retained **DUFFY** and brought into line-up. **CRAIG GANNON** – bass (ex-BLUEBELLS) repl. OWENS / added **MALCOLM ROSS** – guitar (ex-ORANGE JUICE, ex-JOSEF K) / guest / **GUY FLETCHER** – keyboards

Aug 84. (7")(12") **ALL I NEED IS EVERYTHING. / JUMP** [34] [ ]
Sep 84. (lp)(c)(cd) **KNIFE** [14] [ ]
– Still on fire / Just like the U.S.A. / Head is happy (heart's insane) / The back door to Heaven / All I need is everything / Backwards and forwards / Birth of the true / Knife. *(re-iss.cd+c Sep93)*
Nov 84. (7")(7"sha-pic-d) **STILL ON FIRE. / WALK OUT TO WINTER** [ ] [ ]
(12"+=) – Mattress of wire (live) / The boy wonders (live) / The bugle sounds again (live).
Apr 85 (10"m-lp) **AZTEC CAMERA (live)** [-] [ ]
– Birth of the true / Mattress of wire / Jump / Bugle sounds again / Backwards and forwards.

— **FRAME & DUFFY** plus alongside other session musicians **MARCUS MILLER** – bass / **DAVID FRANK** – keyboards (ex-SYSTEM) / **STEVE JORDAN** – guitar

Sep 87. (7") **DEEP AND WIDE AND TALL. / BAD EDUCATION** [ ] [ ]
(12") – ('A'&'B'extended).
Oct 87. (lp)(c)(cd) **LOVE** [10] [ ]
– Deep and wide and tall / How men are / Everybody is a number one / More than a law / Somewhere in my heart / Working in a goldmine / One and one / Paradise / Killermont Street. *(highest chart position Jun88) (re-iss.cd+c Sep93)*
Jan 88. (7") **HOW MEN ARE. / THE RED FLAG** [25] [ ]
(12"+=) – Killermont Street (live) / Pillar to post (live).
(cd-s+=) – Oblivious / All I need is everything.
Apr 88. (7") **SOMEWHERE IN MY HEART. / EVERYBODY IS A NUMBER ONE '86** [3] [ ]
(10+=)(12"+=) – Down the dip / Jump.
(cd-s+=) – Walk out to winter / Still on fire.
Jul 88. (7") **WORKING IN A GOLDMINE. / I THREW IT ALL AWAY** [31] [ ]
(12"+=) – ('A'version).
(cd-s++=) – How men are.
Sep 88. (7") **DEEP AND WIDE AND TALL. / BAD EDUCATION** [55] [ ]
(12"+=)(cd-s+=) – More than a law.

— (live band '88: augmenting **FRAME + DUFFY**) **EDDIE KULAK** – keyboards / **GARY SANFORD** – guitar / **PAUL POWELL** – bass

— (By 1990, **FRAME** had lost **DUFFY**) retained **POWELL /** and new **GARY SANCTUARY** – keyboards / **FRANK TONTOH** – drums / guests **PAUL CARRACK, EDWYN COLLINS, MICKEY GALLAGHER & STEVE SI DELYNK.**

Jun 90. (cd)(c)(lp) **STRAY** [22] [ ]
– Stray / The crying scene / Get outta London / Over my head / How it is / Good morning Britain (featuring MICK JONES) / The gentle kind / Notting Hill blues / Song for a friend. *(re-iss.cd+c Sep93)*
Jun 90. (7") **THE CRYING SCENE. / TRUE COLOURS** [70] [ ]
(12"+=)(cd-s+=) – Salvation. *(above re-iss.Nov90)*
(extra-10"+=) – I threw it all away (live).

— (next single featured **MICK JONES** – co/vocals (of BIG AUDIO DYNAMITE)

Sep 90. (7")(c-s) **GOOD MORNING BRITAIN. / ('A'live version)** [19] [ ]
(12"+=) – ('A'remix)
(cd-s+=) – Consolation prize.

(with **EDWYN COLLINS** – co/vocals)

Jul 92. (7")(c-s) **SPANISH HORSES. / JUST LIKE THE U.S.A. (live)** [52] [ ]
(cd-s) – ('A'side) / Killermont street / Birth of the true / Song for a friend.
(cd-s) – ('A'live version) / Stray (live) / The bugle sounds again (live) / Dolphins (live).
Apr 93. (7")(c-s) **DREAM SWEET DREAMS. / SISTER ANN** [67] [ ]
(cd-s+=) – Good morning Britain (live) / How men are (live).
(cd-s) – ('A'side) / Mattress of wire (live) / Let your love decide (live) / Orchid girl (live).
May 93. (cd)(c)(lp) **DREAMLAND** [21] [ ]
– Birds / Safe in sorrow / Black Lucia / Let your love decide / Spanish horses / Dream sweet dreams / Piano's and clocks / Sister Ann / Vertigo / Valium Summer / Belle of the ball.
Jun 93. (7")(c-s) **BIRDS. / DEEP AND WIDE AND TALL** [ ] [ ]
(cd-s) – ('A'side) / Working in a goldmine / Knife.
(cd-s) – ('A'side) / Somewhere in my heart / Oblivious / Good morning Britain.
Oct 95. (c-s) **SUN / SUNSET** [ ] [ ]
(cd-s+=) – The crying scene (live).
(cd-s) – ('A'side) / We could send letters / Black Lucia / The rainy season.
Nov 95. (cd)(c) **FRESTONIA** [ ] [ ]
– The rainy season / Sun / Crazy / On the avenue / Imperfectly / Debutante / Beautiful girl / Phenomenal world / Method of love / Sunset.

– compilations, others, etc. –

Sep 90. Old Gold; (7") **SOMEWHERE IN MY HEART. / OBLIVIOUS** [ ] [-]
Nov 90. Chrysalis; (7") ('A'side by "Pogues / Kirsty MacColl") [ ] [ ]
(12"+=)(cd-s+=) – DO I LOVE YOU? (from 'Red, White & Blue' Cole Porter tribute album with proceeds going to AIDS)
Oct 94. Windsong; (cd) **LIVE ON THE TEST (live)** [ ] [-]

BABYBIRD

*** NEW ENTRY ***

Formed: Sheffield, England . . .1995 by Telford born singer STEVEN JONES. He had been prolific in his bedroom, writing over 400 songs, some of which appeared on five well-received albums between mid-'95 and mid-'96. Each album came with a voting section on which the buyer was asked to write in with their "best of" lists. The top 12 appeared on BABYBIRD's "GREATEST HITS" later in '96. • **Style:** Strange romantic performance art-type, as seen on kitsch stage shows. Could be the next BONO or JARVIS COCKER. • **Songwriters:** JONES.

Recommended: I WAS BORN A MAN (*8) / BAD SHAVE (*7) / FATHERHOOD (*6) / HAPPIEST MAN ALIVE (*8)

STEVEN JONES – vocals, guitar – with band; **LUKE SCOTT** – guitar / **HUGH CHADBOURN** – keyboards / **JOHN PEDDER** – bass / **ROB GREGORY** – drums

		Baby Bird	not issued
Jul 95.	(cd) **I WAS BORN A MAN** – Blow it to the Moon / Man's tight vest / Lemonade baby / C.F.C. / Cornershop / Kiss your country / Hong Kong blues / Dead bird sings / Baby bird / Farmer / Invisible tune / Alison / Love love love.		-
Sep 95.	(cd)(d-lp) **BAD SHAVE** – KW Jesus TV roof appeal / Bad jazz / Too handsome to be homeless / Steam train / Bad shave / Oh my God, you're a king / The restaurant is guilty / Valerie / Shop girl / W.B.T. / Hate song / 45 and fat / Sha na na / Bug in a breeze / It's okay / Happy bus / Swinging from tree to tree.		-
Dec 95.	(cd)(d-lp) **FATHERHOOD** – No children / Cooling towers / Cool and crazy things to do / Bad blood / Neil Armstrong / I was never here / Saturday / Goodnight / I don't want to wake up with you / Iceberg / Aluminium beach / Goddamn if you're a kid / Daisies / Failed old singer / Fatherhood / Dustbin liner / Not about a girl / Good weather / But love / May me.		-
Mar 96.	(cd)(d-lp) **HAPPIEST MAN ALIVE** – Razorblade shower / Sundial in a tunnel / Little white man / Halfway up the hill / Horse sugar / Please don't be famous / Louse / Copper feel / Seagullaby / Dead in love / Candy girl / Gunfingers / Married / In the country / Planecrash Xmas / Beautiful disease / You'll get a slap / In the morning.		-

— 5th album and a 'best of' package will be released in the final half of the year. Seymour Stein of 'Sire' records is currently bidding for BB's signature. In the UK 'Echo' (home of JULIAN COPE) won over from 'E.M.I.'. A debut! single 'GOODNIGHT' / 'JULY' released in July.

BABYLON ZOO

*** NEW ENTRY ***

Formed: Wolverhampton, England . . .1993 by ex-SANDKINGS frontman JAS MANN. He was born in Fresno, California, to a Sikh father and Native American (Indian). In 1987, he formed quartet The SANDKINGS who released several singles (4 for own label 'Long Beach' + 3 for 'Sugar Beach' / 'London') over the next five years. After an appearance at Glastonbury in '92 they split. JAS MANN sent solo demo to CLIVE BLACK, who signed them to 'Parlophone'. When he took top job at 'WEA', JAS went too, and little was heard of his protege, until they released some promos of 'SPACEMAN' mid 1995. Later that year, CLIVE and JAS returned to 'EMI', and the track was used on the terrific TV ad for Levi's. Demand for the release of 'SPACEMAN' grew, and when it was finally unleashed on the public early '96, it became fastest selling single of all-time, hitting No.1 in the UK for about six weeks. This also made peak spot all around Europe. However, critics soon became cynical, awaiting them to be classed as one-hit wonders. After a mediocre Top 10 album, they hit Top 20 in Spring '96 with 'ANIMAL ARMY'. • **Style:** Extroverted and flamboyant showman, JAS chose influences of SUEDE and BOWIE, in a futuristic pop/rock fashion. His use of animal noises (i.e. elephants, tigers and monkeys), did nothing but irritate the listener. • **Songwriters:** JAS MANN (SANDKINGS; group).

Recommended: THE BOY WITH THE X-RAY EYES (*4) / WELCOME TO ENGLAND (SANDKINGS; *5)

SANDKINGS

JAS MANN -vocals / **GLENN DODD** – guitar / **DAVE BROWN**– bass / **TERRY KIRKBRIDE**– drums

		Long Beach	not issued
Jul 88.	(7") **RAIN. / ONE OF THESE DAYS** (12"+=) – Spiral steps.		-
Feb 89.	(12"ep) **HOPE SPRINGS ETERNAL. / TRANCE DANCE / SHOW HER UP / UP TIGHT**		-
Aug 89.	(7") **ALL'S WELL WITH THE WORLD. / SWING** (12"+=) – Say goodbye to the railway side / Colour.		-
Mar 90.	(7") **CIRCLES. / NEED TO KNOW** (12"+=) – Kissable.		-

		London	not issued
Nov 90.	(7") **EARTHWHEEL. / SOUND THE WHEEL (2ND DREAM ON THE EARTHWHEEL)** (12"+=) – Respect and criticize. (cd-s+=) – ('A'-cultural mix) / ('A'-pushy mix).		-
Aug 91.	(7") **TEMPLE REDNECK. / PLUG IN BUG OUT!** (12"+=)(cd-s+=) – Monkey face.		-
Nov 91.	(12")(cd-s) **SHAKE YOUR HEAD. / ALL'S WELL WITH THE WORLD / TOMORROW NEVER KNOWS**		-
Apr 92.	(12"purple-ep)(cd-ep) **LET IT GROW / SMOKE CULTURE. / FRAGILE / TOY**		-
Jun 92.	(cd)(c)(lp) **WELCOME TO ENGLAND** – Temple redneck / Let it grow / When the bow breaks / Phoney Maloney / Second skin / Pinstripe ghetto / Hope springs eternal / Circles / Bye bye Erica Grey / I still believe in you.		-
Jul 92.	(12"ep)(cd-ep) **PINSTRIPE GHETTO. / HOPE SPRINGS ETERNAL / COLOUR BLIND**		-

— Disbanded just after above.

BABYLON ZOO

JAS MANN – vocals, guitar

		E.M.I.	E.M.I.
Jan 96.	(c-s) **SPACEMAN / METAL VISION** (cd-s+=) – Blue nude / Spaceman (the 5th dimension). (12") – ('A'side) / Spaceman (the 5th dimension) / Spaceman (Arthur meets the spaceman) / Spaceman (e before i).	1	
Feb 96.	(cd)(c) **THE BOY WITH THE X-RAY EYES** – Animal army / Spaceman / Zodiac sign / Paris green / Confused art / Caffeine / The boy with the x-ray eyes / Don't feed the animals / Fire guided light / Is your soul for sale? / I'm cracking up I need a pill.	6	
Apr 96.	(c-s) **ANIMAL ARMY / ANIMAL ARMY (Arthur plays with animals)** (cd-s+=) – ('A'-Babylon bass mix) / ('A'-Arthur dubs with animals). (12") – Spaceman: the mixes (kiss mix – remixed by Sunrise & Capital mix – touched by the Zupervarians).	17	

— cancelled tour, due to live bass player CARRIE MELBOURNE tearing ligaments in her arm.

BACHMAN-TURNER OVERDRIVE

Formed: Vancouver, Canada . . . 1972 by brothers RANDY, ROBBIE and TIM. They, with FRED TURNER signed to 'Mercury' in 1973 and began steady inroads onto US airwaves. By late '74, they had No.1 US hit with the stuttering 'YOU AIN'T SEEN NOTHIN' YET'. (In the 90's, its intro featured on Harry Enfield's UK TV show DJ creations Chas Smash and NIcey Nice). Subsequent releases provided BTO with more hits, but they couldn't reproduce any of the earlier quality. • **Style:** Heavy hard driving rock, mainly for "blue collar" brigade. • **Songwriters:** RANDY and FRED, no covers. • **Trivia:** Being of Mormon religion, the BACHMANS were not typical rock band, as their faith did not allow alcohol, drugs, tea or coffee, just women.

Recommended: THE BEST OF BTO (SO FAR) (*5)

RANDY BACHMAN

with **DAN TROIANO** – guitar / **GARRY PETERSON** – drums / **WES DAKUS** – steel guitar

		not issued	R.C.A.
1970.	(lp) **AXE**	-	

– Zarahemia / Not to return / Pookie's shuffle / Tally's tune / Take the long way home / La Jolla / Tin Lizzie / Suite theam / Noah.

BRAVE BELT

RANDY BACHMAN (b.27 Feb'43) – vocals, guitar (ex-GUESS WHO) / **CHAD ALLAN** – keyboards, vocals (ex-GUESS WHO) / **C.F. (FRED) TURNER** (b.16 Oct'43) – bass, vocals / **ROBBIE BACHMAN** (b.18 Feb'53) – drums, percussion

		not issued	Reprise
1971.	(lp) **BRAVE BELT**	-	

– Crazy arms, crazy eyes / Lifetime / Waitin' there for me / I am the man / French kin / It's over / Rock and roll band / Wandering fantasy girl / I wouldn't give up my guitar for a woman / Holy train / Anyday means tomorrow / Scarecrow.

Date	Release	not issued	Reprise
1971.	(7") **ROCK AND ROLL BAND. / ANY DAY MEANS TOMORROW**	-	
1971.	(7") **CRAZY ARMS, CRAZY EYES. / HOLY TRAIN**	-	
1972.	(7") **NEVER COMIN' HOME. / CAN YOU FEEL IT**	-	
1972.	(lp) **BRAVE BELT II**	-	

– Too far away / Dunrobin's gone / Can you feel it / Put it in a song / Summer soldier / Never comin' home / Be a good man / Long way round / Another way out / Waterloo country.

Date	Release	not issued	Reprise
1972.	(7") **ANOTHER WAY OUT. / DUNROBIN'S GONE**	-	

BACHMAN-TURNER OVERDRIVE

TIM BACHMAN – guitar repl. CHAD

Date	Release	Mercury	Mercury
Aug 73.	(7") **GIMME YOUR MONEY PLEASE. / LITTLE GAWDY DANCER**	-	
Aug 73.	(lp)(c) **BACHMAN-TURNER OVERDRIVE**		70

– Gimme your money please / Hold back the water / Blue collar / Little gandy dancer / Stayed awake all night / Down and out man / Don't get yourself in trouble / Thank you for the feelin'. *(cd-iss.Jan93)*

Date	Release	Mercury	Mercury
Sep 73.	(7") **STAYED AWAKE ALL NIGHT. / DOWN AND OUT MAN** *(re-iss.Jan77)*		
Nov 73.	(7") **BLUE COLLAR. / HOLD BACK THE WATER**	-	68
Jan 74.	(7") **LET IT RIDE. / TRAMP**	-	23
Mar 74.	(7") **LET IT RIDE. / BLUE COLLAR**		-
Mar 74.	(lp)(c) **BACHMAN-TURNER OVERDRIVE II**		4 Jan 74

– Blown / Welcome home / Stonegates / Let it ride / Give it time / I don't have to / Takin' care of business / Tramp.

Date	Release	Mercury	Mercury
Aug 74.	(7") **TAKIN' CARE OF BUSINESS. / STONEGATES**		12 Jun 74

—— **BLAIR THORNTON** (b.23 Jul'50, Vancouver) – guitar repl. TIM who became producer

Date	Release	Mercury	Mercury
Oct 74.	(7") **YOU AIN'T SEEN NOTHIN' YET. / FREE WHEELIN'**	2	1 Sep 74
Oct 74.	(lp)(c) **NOT FRAGILE**	12	1 Aug 74

– Not fragile / Rock is my life and this is my song / Roll on down the highway / You ain't seen nothin' yet / Free wheelin' / Sledgehammer / Blue moanin' / Second hand / Givin' it all away.

Date	Release	Mercury	Mercury
Jan 75.	(7") **ROLL ON DOWN THE HIGHWAY. / SLEDGE-HAMMER**	22	14
May 75.	(7") **HEY YOU. / FLAT BROKE LOVE**		21
Jun 75.	(lp)(c) **FOUR WHEEL DRIVE**		5 May 75

– Four wheel drive / She's a devil / Hey you / Flat broke love / She's keepin' time / Quick change artist / Lowland fling / Don't let the blues get you down. *(cd-iss.Jan93)*

Date	Release	Mercury	Mercury
Nov 75.	(7") **DOWN TO THE LINE. / SHE'S A DEVIL**	-	43
Jan 76.	(7") **AWAY FROM HOME. / DOWN TO THE LINE**		-
Feb 76.	(lp)(c) **HEAD ON**		23 Jan 76

– Find out about love / It's over / Average man / Woncha take me for a while / Wild spirit / Take it like a man / Lookin' out for #1 / Away from home / Stay alive.

Date	Release	Mercury	Mercury
Feb 76.	(7") **TAKE IT LIKE A MAN. / WONCHA TAKE ME FOR A WHILE**	-	33
Apr 76.	(7") **LOOKING OUT FOR #1. / FIND OUT ABOUT LOVE**	-	65
May 77.	(7") **MY WHEELS WON'T TURN. / FREE WAYS**	-	
May 77.	(7") **MY WHEELS WON'T TURN. / LIFE STILL GOES ON**		-
May 77.	(lp)(c) **FREEWAYS**		70 Mar 77

– Can we all come together / Life still goes on / Shotgun rider / Just for you / My wheels won't turn / Down, down / Easy groove / Freeways. *(cd-iss.Jan93)*

Date	Release	Mercury	Mercury
Sep 77.	(7") **SHOTGUN RIDER. / JUST FOR YOU**		-
Sep 77.	(7") **SHOTGUN RIDER. / DOWN, DOWN**	-	
Dec 77.	(7") **LIFE STILL GOES ON. / JUST FOR YOU**	-	

B.T.O.

—— **JIM CLENCH** – guitar, vocals repl. RANDY who went solo

Mar 78.	(lp)(c) **STREET ACTION**		

– I'm in love / Down the road / Takes a lot of people / A long time for a little while / Street action / For love / Madison Avenue / You're gonna miss me / The whole world is waiting for a love song.

Mar 78.	(7") **DOWN THE ROAD. / A LONG TIME FOR A LITTLE WHILE**	-	
Mar 79.	(7") **HEARTACHES. / HEAVEN TONIGHT**	-	60
Mar 79.	(7") **HEARTACHES. / ROCK'N'ROLL NIGHTS**		-
Apr 79.	(lp)(c) **ROCK'N'ROLL NIGHTS (live)**		

– Jamaica / Heartaches / Heaven tonight / Rock'n'roll nights / Wastin' time / Here she comes again / End of the line / Rock and roll hell / Amelia Earhart.

Jun 79.	(7") **END OF THE LINE (live). / JAMAICA (live)**	-	

—— Broke-up 1979.

BACHMAN-TURNER OVERDRIVE

Re-united mid-84 with below line-up 1984. **RANDY, TIM, FRED TURNER** and newcomer **GARRY PETERSON** – drums

		Compleat	Compleat
Sep 84.	(7") **FOR THE WEEKEND. / JUST LOOK AT ME NOW**		
Nov 84.	(lp)(c) **BACHMAN-TURNER OVERDRIVE**		Sep 84

– For the weekend / Just look at me now / My sugaree / City's still growin' / Another fool / Lost in a fantasy / Toledo / Service with a smile.

		Compleat	Compleat
Jan 85.	(7") **SERVICE WITH A SMILE. / MY SUGAREE**	-	
Mar 85.	(7") **MY SUGAREE. / (Part 2)**	-	

		M.C.A.	Curb
Aug 86.	(lp)(c) **LIVE! -LIVE! -LIVE!**		

– Hey you / Mississippi queen / Sledgehammer / Fragile man / Bad news travels fast / You ain't seen nothin' yet / Roll on down the highway / Takin' care of business.

RANDY later joined with (ex-TROOPER) FRANK LUDWIG, in UNION. He also became songwriter for BEACH BOYS, etc.

- compilations, others, etc. -

Mar 75.	Reprise; (lp) **BACHMAN-TURNER OVERDRIVE AS BRAVE BELT**		
Sep 76.	Mercury; (7") **GIMME YOUR MONEY PLEASE. / FOUR WHEEL DRIVE**	-	70
Sep 76.	Mercury; (7") **TAKIN' CARE OF BUSINESS. / WON'T CHA TAKE ME FOR A WHILE**		-
Nov 76.	Mercury; (lp)(c) **THE BEST OF B.T.O. (SO FAR)**		19 Aug 76
1977.	Mercury; (lp) **JAPAN TOUR (live)**	-	
Aug 81.	Mercury; (lp)(c) **GREATEST HITS**		

– Lookin' out for #1 / Hey you / Takin' care of business / You ain't seen nothin' yet / Flat broke love / Rock'n'roll nights / Roll on down the highway / Freeways / Down, down / Let it ride / Can we all come together / Jamaica.

Oct 83.	Mercury; (lp)(c) **YOU AIN'T SEEN NOTHIN' YET**		
Oct 84.	Mercury; (7") **YOU AIN'T SEEN NOTHIN' YET. / ROLL ON DOWN THE HIGHWAY**		
Aug 93.	Mercury; (d-cd) **ANTHOLOGY** *(re-iss.Sep95)*		
Mar 88.	Old Gold; (7") **YOU AIN'T SEEN NOTHIN' YET. / (other artist)**		-
Jul 88.	Knight; (c) **NIGHTRIDING**		-
Aug 94.	Spectrum; (cd)(c) **ROLL ON DOWN THE HIGHWAY**		-

RANDY BACHMAN

solo with **BURTON CUMMINGS** – keyboards / **IAN GARDINER** – bass / **JEFF PORCARO** – drums / **TOM SCOTT** – saxophone.

		Polydor	Polydor
Jun 78.	(7") **JUST A KID. / SURVIVOR**		
Jul 78.	(lp)(c) **SURVIVOR**		

– Just a kid / One hand clappin' / Lost in the shuffle / Is the night too cold for dancin' / You moved me / I am a star / Maybe again / Survivor.

IRONHORSE

was formed by **RANDY** with **TOM SPARKS** – guitar / **JOHN PIERCE** – bass / **MIKE BAIRD** – drums / **BARRY ALLEN** – vocals

Scotti B. Scotti B.

Mar 79. (7") **SWEET LUI-LOUISE. / WATCH ME FLY** [60] [36]

May 79. (lp)(c) **IRONHORSE** [ ] [ ]
– One and only / Sweet Lui-Louise / Jump back in the light / You gotta let go / Tumbleweed / Stateline blues / Watch me fly / Old fashioned / Dedicated to Slowhand / She's got it / There ain't no clue.

Jul 79. (7") **ONE AND ONLY. / SHE'S GOT IT** [ ] [ ]

—— **FRANK LUDWIG** – vocals, keyboards repl. BARRY / **RON FOOS** – bass / **CHRIS LEIGHTON** – drums repl. JOHN and MIKE

Nov 80. (7") **WHAT'S YOUR HURRY DARLIN'. / TRY A LITTLE HARDER** [ ] [ ]

Nov 80. (lp)(c) **EVERYTHING IS GREY** [ ] [ ]
– Everything is grey / What's your hurry darlin' / Symphony / Only way to fly / Try a little harder / I'm hurting inside / Playin' that same old song / Railroad love / Somewhere sometime / Keep your motor running.

BAD COMPANY

Formed: Based various areas of England (see below). Late summer 1973 the four got together taking name from 1972 western film starring Jeff Bridges. Peter Grant (Led Zeppelin's manager) signed them for his new 'Swan Song' label in 1974, and they soon had US No.1 debut album. For the next several years, they become one of top rock groups, hitting charts on both sides of the Atlantic. • **Style:** Classic power rock outfit, with frontman RODGERS providing heavy but soulful lyrics. By the 80's they had moved into AOR, which all but loyal fans panned. • **Songwriters:** RALPHS penned most. In the 90's RALPHS and HOWE individually co-wrote with THOMAS. • **Trivia:** MEL COLLINS (ex-King Crimson) played sax on debut.

Recommended: STRAIGHT SHOOTER (*8) / BAD CO. (*6)

PAUL RODGERS (b.12 Dec'49) – vocals, piano (ex-FREE) / **MICK RALPHS** (b.31 Mar'48) – guitar, piano (ex-MOTT THE HOOPLE) / **BOZ BURRELL** (b.RAYMOND, 1946) – bass, vocals (ex-KING CRIMSON, ex-SNAFU) / **SIMON KIRKE** (b.28 Jul'49) – drums (ex-FREE)

Island Swan Song

May 74. (7") **CAN'T GET ENOUGH. / LITTLE MISS FORTUNE** [15] [5]

Jun 74. (lp)(c) **BAD CO.** [3] [1]
– Can't get enough / Rock steady / Ready for love / Don't let me down / Bad company / The way I choose / Movin' on / Seagull. *(re-iss.Jan78 + Jun81) (cd-iss.Oct94 on 'Atlantic')*

Jan 75. (7") **MOVIN' ON. / EASY ON MY SOUL** [-] [19]

Mar 75. (7") **GOOD LOVIN' GONE BAD. / WHISKEY BOTTLE** [31] [36]

Apr 75. (lp)(c) **STRAIGHT SHOOTER** [3] [3]
– Good lovin' gone bad / Feel like makin' love / Weep no more / Shooting star / Deal with the preacher / Wild fire women / Anna / Call on me. *(re-iss.Jan78 + Jun81) (cd-iss.Oct88 on 'Swan Song') (re-iss.cd Feb93 on 'Warners') (re-iss.cd Jul94 on 'Atlantic')*

Aug 75. (7") **FEEL LIKE MAKIN' LOVE. / WILD FIRE WOMEN** [20] [10] Jul 75

Feb 76. (lp)(c) **RUN WITH THE PACK** [4] [5]
– Live for the music / Simple man / Honey child / Love me somebody / Run with the pack / Silver, blue and gold / Young blood / Do right by your woman / Sweet lil' sister / Fade away. *(re-iss.Jan78 + Jun81) (cd-iss.Oct88 on 'Swan Song') (re-iss.cd Feb93 on 'Warners') (re-iss.cd Jul94 on 'Atlantic')*

Mar 76. (7") **RUN WITH THE PACK. / DO RIGHT BY YOUR WOMAN** [ ] [-]

Mar 76. (7") **YOUNG BLOOD. / DO RIGHT BY YOUR WOMAN** [-] [20]

Jul 76. (7") **HONEY CHILD. / FADE AWAY** [-] [59]

Feb 77. (7") **EVERYTHING I NEED. / TOO BAD** [ ] [ ]

Mar 77. (lp)(c) **BURNIN' SKY** [17] [15]
– Burnin' sky / Morning Sun / Leaving you / Like water / Everything I need / Heartbeat / Peace of mind / Passing time / Too bad / Man needs woman / Master of ceremony. *(re-iss.cd Feb93 on 'Warners') (cd-iss.Oct94 on 'Atco')*

May 77. (7") **BURNIN' SKY. / EVERYTHING I NEED** [-] [78]

Swan Song Swan Song

Mar 79. (7") **ROCK'N'ROLL FANTASY. / CRAZY CIRCLES** [ ] [13]

Mar 79. (lp)(c) **DESOLATION ANGELS** [10] [3]
– Rock'n'roll fantasy / Crazy circles / Gone, gone, gone / Evil wind / Early in the morning / Lonely for your love / Oh, Atlanta / Take the time / Rhythm machine / She brings me love. *(re-iss.cd Feb93 on 'Warners')*

Jul 79. (7") **GONE, GONE, GONE. / TAKE THE TIME** [-] [56]

Aug 82. (lp)(c) **ROUGH DIAMONDS** [15] [26]
– Electricland / Untie the knot / Nuthin' on the T.V. / Painted face / Kickdown / Ballad of the band / Cross country boy / Old Mexico / Downhill ryder / Racetrack. *(cd-iss.Oct94 on 'Atlantic')*

Sep 82. (7") **ELECTRICLAND. / UNTIE THE KNOT** [-] [74]

—— (mid'83) Disbanded. RODGERS went solo before joining The FIRM. KIRKE played with WILDFIRE. BURRELL sessioned on ROGER CHAPMAN (Family) lp's.

—— **BAD COMPANY** reformed 1986. **RALPHS, KIRKE, BURRELL** and the incoming **BRIAN HOWE** – vocals (ex-TED NUGENT)

Atlantic Atlantic

Oct 86. (lp)(c)(cd) **FAME & FORTUNE** [ ] [ ]
– Burning up / This love / Fame and fortune / That girl / Tell it like it is / Long walk / Hold on my heart / Valerie / When we made love / If I'm sleeping. *(re-iss.cd Nov93)*

Nov 86. (7") **THIS LOVE. / TELL IT LIKE IT IS** [ ] [85] Oct 86
(12"+=) – Burning up / Fame & fortune.

Jan 87. (7")(12") **FAME AND FORTUNE. / WHEN WE MADE LOVE** [ ] [ ]

Aug 88. (lp)(c)(cd) **DANGEROUS AGE** [ ] [58]
– One night / Shake it up / No smoke without fire / Bad man / Dangerous age / Dirty boy / Rock of America / Something about you / The way it goes / Love attack. (cd+=) – Excited.

Apr 89. (7") **SHAKE IT UP. /** [-] [82]

—— **GEOFF WHITEHORN** – guitar (ex-BACK STREET CRAWLER) repl. RALPHS / **PAUL CULLEN** – bass repl. BURRELL / added **DAVE COLWELL** – keyboards (ex-ASAP)

Atco Atco

Jul 90. (cd)(c)(lp) **HOLY WATER** [ ] [35] Jun 90
– Holy water / Walk through fire / Stranger stranger / If you needed somebody / Fearless / Lay your love on me / Boys cry tough / With you in a heartbeat / Never too late / I don't care / Dead of the night / I can't live without you / 100 miles.

Jul 90. (7") **HOLY WATER. / I CAN'T LIVE WITHOUT YOU** [ ] [89]
(12"+=)(cd-s+=) – Love attack.

Apr 91. (7") **IF YOU NEEDED SOMEBODY. / DEAD OF NIGHT** [ ] [16] Nov 90
(12"+=)(cd-s+=) – Love attack.

Jul 91. (c-s) **WALK THROUGH FIRE. / ?** [-] [28]

—— (May91) **STEVE WALSH** – vocals (ex-KANSAS) repl. HOWE / **MICK RALPHS** also returned briefly.

Sep 92. (7")(c-s) **HOW ABOUT THAT. / HERE COMES TROUBLE** [ ] [38]
(12") – No smoke without a fire (remix) / Stranger stranger.
(cd-s+=) – No smoke without a fire (remix) / If you needed somebody.

Sep 92. (cd)(c)(lp) **HERE COMES TROUBLE** [ ] [40]
– How about that / Stranger than fiction / Here comes trouble / This could be the one / Both feet in the water / Take this town / What about you / Little angel / Hold on to my heart / Brokenhearted / My only one.

Nov 92. (c-s)(cd-s) **THIS COULD BE THE ONE. / ?** [-] [87]

—— **RALPHS / KIRKE + HART / COLWELL / LISTER**

Jul 95. (cd)(c) **COMPANY OF STRANGERS** [ ] [ ]
– Company of strangers / Clearwater highway / Judas my brother / Little Martha / Gimme gimme / Where I belong / Down down down / Abandoned and alone / Down and dirty / Pretty woman / You're the only reason / Dance with the Devil / Loving you out loud.

– compilations, others, etc. –

Jan 86. Atlantic; (lp)(c)(cd) **10 FROM 6** [ ] [ ]
– Can't get enough / Feel like makin' love / Run with the pack / Shooting star / Movin' on / Bad company / Rock'n'roll fantasy / Electricland / Ready for love / Live for the music.

Mar 90. Atlantic; (7") **CAN'T GET ENOUGH. / BAD COMPANY** [ ] [ ]
(12"+=)(cd-s+=) – No smoke without fire / Shake it up.

Ginger BAKER

Born: PETER BAKER, 19 Aug'39, Lewisham, London. Gained experience in the late 50's with jazz bands such as ACKER BILK, but chose new style when he joined BLUES INCORPORATED in 1962. Early in '63, he joined GRAHAM BOND ORGANISATION, but left them mid 1966 to form CREAM with ERIC CLAPTON. After their demise late '68, he and ERIC formed BLIND FAITH, but they split after only one album. Late 1969, BAKER formed AIRFORCE ensemble, which released eponymous UK Top 40 album early 1970. After a number of collaborations, he and ADRIAN GURVITZ joined forces in BAKER GURVITZ ARMY mid 70's. BAKER was to many, the greatest drummer of all-time, his CREAM live work certainly cemented that opinion. • **Style:** His range of sounds, moved from jazz, to blues and to Nigerian/African by the early 70's. • **Songwriters:** Collaborated with many other musicians, including FELA KUTI. Covered SWEET WINE (Staple Singers) / TWELVE GATES OF THE CITY (Graham Bond) / STRAIGHT NO CHASER (Thelonius Monk) etc. • **Trivia:** As a schoolboy he also played the trumpet. He married in the mid-90's, and took surname of wife, and became GINGER LOUCKS-BAKER.

Recommended: GINGER BAKER AT HIS BEST (*6)

GINGER BAKER'S AIRFORCE

with **GRAHAM BOND** – keyboards / **DENNY LAINE** – guitar / **RICK GRECH** – bass / **HAROLD McNAIR** – saxophone / **REMI KABAKA** – percussion / plus guests **STEVE WINWOOD, CHRIS WOOD, PHIL SEAMAN & BUD BEADLE**

Polydor / Atco

Feb 70 (lp)(c) **AIRFORCE** [37] [ ]
– Da da man / Early in the morning / Don't care / Toad / Aiko biaye / Man of constant sorrow / Do what you like / Doin' it.

Mar 70. (7") **MAN OF CONSTANT SORROW. / DOIN' IT** [ ] [ ]

— guests now were mainly African percussionists, vocalists and keyboard players.

Sep 70. (lp)(c) **GINGER BAKER'S AIRFORCE II (live)** [ ] [33] May 70
– Let me ride / Sweet wine / Do u no hu yor phrenz r? / We free kings / I don't want to go on without you / Toady / Twelve gates of the city.

Oct 70. (7") **ATUNDE (WE ARE HERE). / (by "GINGER BAKER DRUM CHOIR") / (part 2)** [ ] [ ]

1972. (lp)(c) **STRATAVARIOUS** [ ] [ ]
– Ariwo / Something nice / Ju Ju / Blood brothers / 69 coda.

— In 1971, he had moved to Akeja, Nigeria to buy land to build studio. He was augmented by FELA RANSOME-KUTI and African musicians SALT.

Regal Zono. / Signpost

1972. (lp) **FELA RANSOME-KUTI AND THE AFRICA '70 WITH GINGER BAKER LIVE! (live)** [ ] [ ]
– Let's start / Black man's cry / Ye ye de smell / Egbe mi o.

— He retired for a while early 1973, but returned to form

BAKER GURVITZ ARMY

with **ADRIAN GURVITZ** – guitar / **PAUL GURVITZ** – bass (both ex-GUN)

Vertigo / Janus

Dec 74. (lp)(c) **BAKER GURVITZ ARMY** [22] [ ]
– Help me / Love is / Memory Lane / Inside of me / I wanna live again / Mad Jack / 4 Phil / Since beginning.
(re-iss.May77 on 'Mountain')

Mar 75. (7") **HELP ME. / I WANNA LIVE AGAIN** [ ] [ ]

— added **SNIPS** – vocals (ex-SHARKS) / **PETER LEMER** – keyboards (ex-SEVENTH WAVE)

Mountain / Atco

Aug 75. (7") **SPACE MACHINE. / THE DREAMER** [ ] [ ]

Sep 75. (lp)(c) **ELYSIAN ENCOUNTER** [ ] [ ]
– People / The key / Time / The gambler / The dreamer / Remember / The artist / The hustler. *(cd-iss.Sep93 on 'Repertoire')*

Oct 75. (7") **THE GAMBLER. / TIME** [ ] [ ]

Nov 75. (7") **NIGHT PEOPLE. / ?** [-] [ ]

— Trimmed slightly when PETER LEMER departed.

Apr 76. (7") **TRACKS OF MY LIFE. / THE ARTIST** [ ] [ ]

May 76. (lp)(c) **HEARTS ON FIRE** [ ] [ ]
– Hearts on fire / Neon lights / Smiling / Tracks of my life / Flying in and out of stardom / Dancing the night away / My mind is healing / Thirsty for the blues / Night people / Mystery.

Jun 76. (7") **DANCING THE NIGHT AWAY. / NIGHT PEOPLE** [ ] [ ]

GINGER BAKER & FRIENDS

with loads of session people.

Mountain / Sire

Jan 77. (lp)(c) **ELEVEN SIDES OF BAKER** [ ] [ ]
– Ginger man / Candlestick maker / High life / Don Dorango / Little bird / N'kon kin' n'kon n'kon / Howlin' wolf / Ice cream dragon / Winner / Pampero / Don't stop the carnival.

Jan 77. (7") **DON DORANGO. / CANDLESTICK MAKER** [ ] [-]

— Retired again to breed ponies, but formed **ENERGY** in 1980 with **JOHN MIZAROLLI** – guitar / **MIKE DAVIS** – guitar / **HENRY THOMAS** – bass. In the early 80's, he joined ATOMIC ROOSTER briefly and HAWKWIND. In 1982, he emigrated to Italy with his 2nd wife where she ran a drama school.

GINGER BAKER & BAND

recorded 1982. **DOUG BROCKIE** – vocals, guitar / **KARL HILL** – bass, vocals

C.D.G. / not issued

Jun 83. (lp)(c) **FROM HUMBLE ORANGES** [-] [-] Italy
– The eleventh hour / Too many apples / It / Under the Sun / On the road to granma's house / The land of Morder / This planet / Sore head in the morning blues / Wasting time / Lament.

In 1985, he joined PUBLIC IMAGE LTD, recording ALBUM with them. In 1986 with RAVI SHANKER and BILL LASWELL iss.HORSES AND TREES on 'Celluloid'.

Onsala Int / not issued

Apr 87. (lp) **GINGER BAKER IN CONCERT (live 1982)** [ ] [-]
– Chemical blues / Perfect nation / Everything I say / Wheelchair dance festival / Lost in space / Where are you?

GINGER BAKER & AFRICAN FORCE

with **AMPOFO** – percussion, vocals / **ANSOU MANA BANGOURA** – perc., vocals / **FRANCIS MENSAH** – percussion / **JC COMMODORE** – percussion, vocals / **KAZDA** – co writers

I.T.M. / not issued

1989. (lp)(c)(cd) **AFRICAN FORCE** (rec'86) [ ] [-]
– Brain damage / Sokoto / Ansoumania / Aboa / African force.

Apr 90. (cd)(lp) **PALANQUIN'S POLE** [ ] [-]
– Go do / Brain damage / Ansoumania / Palaquin's pole / Abyssinia-1.2.7. / Ginger's solo / Want come? go!.

Nov 92. (cd) **THE ALBUM** [ ] [-]
– Sunshine of your love / Dream battle / Black audience / Nice -jam / Brain damage.

— now with **BILL LASWELL, JAH WOBBLE + NICK SKOPELTIS**

Axiom-Mango / Axiom

Feb 92. (cd)(c)(lp) **MIDDLE PASSAGE** [ ] [ ]
– Mektoub / Under black skies / Time be time / Altamont / Basil / South to the dust.

— Having backed old friend JACK BRUCE on early 1994 live album 'CITIES', he became part of their trio BBM, alongside GARY MOORE. Their album 'AROUND THE NEXT DREAM' on 'Virgin' hit UK Top 10.

GINGER BAKER TRIO

with **CHARLIE HAYDEN** – bass (of ORNETTE COLEMAN band) / **BILL FRISWELL** – guitars (of NAKED CITY + POWER TOOLS)

Atlantic / Atlantic

Dec 94. (cd)(c) **GOING BACK HOME** [ ] [ ]

– compilations, others, etc. –

1973. Polydor/ US= R.S.O.; (d-lp)(c) **GINGER BAKER AT HIS BEST** [ ] [ ]
(re-iss.Feb76)

Jan 93. Traditional Line; (cd) **LIVE IN LONDON 1975 (BAKER GURVITZ ARMY live)** [ ] [-]

Dave BALL (see under ⇒ SOFT CELL)

BAND

Formed: 1967 after these ex-patriate Canadians had once backed RONNIE HAWKINS. That year in fact, they recorded the legendary once bootlegged THE BASEMENT TAPES, backing BOB DYLAN. Their debut album, recorded around same period at their communal home (Big Pink, Woodstock), became first-off to hit US Top 30. • **Style:** Electric folk played with effortless relaxation, mixing traditional with progressive, shifting through country, jazz and blues. • **Songwriters:** After first albums collaboration with DYLAN, ROBERTSON took over as main writer, with songs about the civil war and 30's depression. One of his songs THE NIGHT THEY DROVE OLD DIXIE DOWN was a big hit for JOAN BAEZ. They covered; TEARS OF RAGE + WHEN I PAINT MY MASTERPIECE (Bob Dylan) / DON'T DO IT (Holland-Dozier-Holland) / LONG BLACK VEIL (Wilkin-Dill) / MYSTERY TRAIN (Elvis Presley) / THE GREAT PRETENDER (Platters) / 4% PANTOMINE (co-Van Morrison / etc. • **Trivia:** In 1980, ROBERTSON went into small acting parts, noteably in THE COAL MINER'S DAUGHTER (starring Sissy Spacek) + THE RIGHT STUFF (1983). ROBBIE had earlier produced 1976 album 'Beautiful Noise' for NEIL DIAMOND. PETER GABRIEL guested on his long-awaited solo album in '87.

Recommended: TO KINGDOM COME – THE DEFINITIVE COLLECTION (*7) / THE LAST WALTZ (*8).

CANADIAN SQUIRES

ROBBIE ROBERTSON (b. 4 Jul'44, Toronto, Canada) – guitar, vocals / **RICHARD MANUEL** (b. 3 Apr'45, Stratford, Canada) – piano, vocals, drums, sax / **RICK DANKO** (b. 9 Dec'43, Simcoe, Canada) – vocals, bass, violin, trombone / **GARTH HUDSON** (b. 2 Aug'37, London, Canada) – organ, saxophone, accordion / **LEVON HELM** (b.26 May'42, Marvel, AR) – drums, vocvals, mandolin, guitar

not issued / Apex

1964. (7") **UH-UH-UH. / LEAVE ME ALONE** [-] [ ]
(re-iss. on 'Ware')

LEVON AND THE HAWKS

		Atlantic	Atlantic
Mar 65.	(7") **THE STONES I THROW. / HE DON'T LOVE YOU**		
		not issued	Atco
1968.	(7") **GO GO LIZA JANE. / HE DON'T LOVE YOU**	-	

The BAND

(same line-up)

		Capitol	Capitol	
1968.	(7") **JABBERWOCKY. / NEVER TOO MUCH LOVE**	-		
Aug 68.	(lp) **MUSIC FROM BIG PINK**		30	

– Tears of rage / To kingdom come / In a station / Caledonian mission / The weight / We can talk / Long black veil / Chest fever / Lonesome Suzie / This wheel's on fire / I shall be released. *(re-iss.+c Jun81, cd-iss.May87)*

Sep 68.	(7") **THE WEIGHT. / I SHALL BE RELEASED**	21	63	Aug 68
Jan 70.	(lp) **THE BAND**	25	9	Sep 69

– Across the great divide / Rag mama rag / The night they drove old Dixie down / When you awake / Up on Cripple Creek / Whispering pines / Jemima surrender / Rockin' chair / Look out Cleveland / Jawbone / The unfaithful servant / King harvest (has surely come). *(re-iss.+c Aug86, cd-iss.Aug88 on 'EMI')*

Oct 69.	(7") **UP ON CRIPPLE CREEK. / THE NIGHT THEY DROVE OLD DIXIE DOWN**		25	
Feb 70.	(7") **RAG MAMA RAG. / UNFAITHFUL SERVANT**	16	57	
Oct 70.	(lp) **STAGE FRIGHT**	15	5	Sep 70

– Strawberry wine / Sleeping / Time to kill / Just another whistle stop / All la glory / The shape I'm in / The W.S. Walcott medicine show / Daniel and the sacred harp / Stage fright / The rumor. *(re-iss.Jun81 on 'Greenlight')(cd-iss.Mar91)*

Oct 70.	(7") **TIME TO KILL. / SLEEPING**			
Oct 70.	(7") **TIME TO KILL. / THE SHAPE I'M IN**	-	77	
Mar 71.	(7") **THE SHAPE I'M IN. / THE RUMOR**			
Oct 71.	(lp) **CAHOOTS**	41	21	

– Life is a carnival / When I paint my masterpiece / Last of the blacksmiths / Where do we go from here? / 4% pantomime / Shoot out in Chinatown / The Moon struck one / Thinkin' out loud / Smoke signal / Volcano / The river hymn. *(re-iss.Jun81 on 'Greenlight') (cd-iss.May89)*

Oct 71.	(7") **LIFE IS A CARNIVAL. / THE MOON STRUCK ONE**		72	
Dec 71.	(7") **WHEN I PAINT MY MASTERPIECE. / WHERE DO WE GO FROM HERE?**	-		
Aug 72.	(d-lp)(c) **ROCK OF AGES (live)**		6	

– Don't do it / King harvest (has surely come) / Caledonia mission / Get up Jake / The W.S. Walcott medicine show / Stage fright / The night they drove all Dixie down / Across the great divide / This wheel's on fire / Rag mama rag / The weight / The shape I'm in / The unfaithful servant / Life is a carnival / The genetic method * / Chest fever / (I don't want to) Hang up my rock and roll shoes. *(re-iss.Jul83 on 'EMI') (re-iss+cd Apr87 omitted*) (US d-cd-iss.1990 cont.track)*

Nov 72.	(7") **DON'T DO IT (live). / RAG MAMA RAG (live)**	-	34	Sep 72
Feb 73.	(7") **CALEDONIA MISSION. / (I DON'T WANT TO) HANG UP MY ROCK AND ROLL SHOES**	-		
Dec 73.	(lp)(c) **MOONDOG MATINEE**		28	

– Ain'y got no home / Holy cow / Share your love / Mystery train / The Third Man theme / The promised land / The great pretender / I'm ready / Saved / A change is gonna come. *(cd-iss.Mar91)*

Nov 73.	(7") **AIN'T GOT NO HOME. / GET UP JAKE**		73	

— Late '73, they renewed association with BOB DYLAN, helping out on album 'PLANET WAVES' and more so 'BEFORE THE FLOOD' a live album credited to BOB DYLAN / THE BAND. In '75 The BAND returned with brand new material.

Feb 74.	(7") **THE THIRD MAN THEME. / THE W.S. WALCOTT MEDICINE SHOW**	-		
Nov 75.	(7") **TWILIGHT. / ACADIAN DRIFTWOOD**	-		
Dec 75.	(lp) **NORTHERN LIGHTS – SOUTHERN CROSS**		26	

– Forbidden fruit / Hobo jungle / Ophelia / Acadian driftwood / Ring your bell / It makes no difference / Jupiter hollow / Rags and bones. *(cd-iss.Mar91)*

Feb 76.	(7") **OPHELIA. / HOBO JUNGLE**	-	62	
Mar 76.	(7") **RING YOUR BELL. / FORBIDDEN FRUIT**			
Apr 77.	(lp)(c) **ISLANDS**		64	Mar 77

– Right as rain / Street walker / Let the night fall / Ain't that a lot of love / Christmas must be tonight / Islands / The saga of Pepote Rouge / Georgia on my mind / Knockin' lost John / Livin' in a dream. *(cd-iss.Mar91)*

1977.	(7") **GEORGIA ON MY MIND. / THE NIGHT THEY DROVE OLD DIXIE DOWN**	-		
Apr 77.	(7") **RIGHT AS RAIN. / KNOCKIN' LOST JOHN**			

— Joined by guests BOB DYLAN, NEIL YOUNG, RONNIE HAWKINS, JONI MITCHELL, ERIC CLAPTON, VAN MORRISON, NEIL DIAMOND, MUDDY WATERS, PAUL BUTTERFIELD, BOBBY CHARLES and DR. JOHN etc. Jams were from STEPHEN STILLS, RINGO STARR and RONNIE WOOD

Apr 78.	(t-lp) **THE LAST WALTZ** (live 25 Nov76 – film soundtrack)	39	16	

– Theme from the last waltz / Up on cripple creek / Who do you love / Helpless / Stage fright / Coyote / Dry your eyes / Such a night / It makes no difference / Mystery train / The shape I'm in / The night they drove old Dixie down / Mannish boy / Further on up the road / The shape I'm in / Down south in New Orleans / Ophelia / Tura lura lural (that's an Irish lullaby) / Caravan / Life is a carnival / Baby let me follow you down / I don't believe you (she acts like we never have met) / Forever young / I shall be released / The well / Evangeline / Out of the blue / The weight / The last waltz refrain / Theme from the last waltz (with orchestra). *(cd-iss.Jul88)*

Jun 78.	(7") **THEME FROM THE LAST WALTZ (live). / OUT OF THE BLUE (live)**			
Nov 78.	(7") **OUT OF THE BLUE (live). / THE WELL (live)**	-		

— After their official split in 1978, HUDSON and MANUEL went into sessions. MANUEL hung himself 6 Mar'86, after a fit of depression. RICK DANKO and LEVON HELM went solo. In 1980, ROBBIE wrote score for film CARNY, before finally getting around to recording solo album in 1987.

— Re-formed (now studio / earlier live) with **DANKO, HELM, HUDSON + JIM WEIDER** – bass / **RICHARD BELL** – piano / **RANDY CIARLANTE** – drums

		Castle	Pyramid	
Feb 94.	(cd)(c) **JERICHO**			Nov93

– Remedy / Blind Willie McTell / The caves of Jericho / Atlantic City / Too soon gone / Country boy / Move to Japan / Amazon (river of dreams) / Stuff you gotta watch / Same thing / Shine a light / Blues stay away from me.

– compilations, etc. –

Sep 76.	Capitol; (d-lp)(c) **THE BEST OF THE BAND** *(cd-iss.May89)*		51
Oct 76.	Capitol; (7") **THE WEIGHT. / TWILIGHT**		
Jan 79.	Capitol; (d-lp)(c) **ANTHOLOGY** *(cd-iss.May89, 2 Vols.)*		
Jul 84.	E.M.I. Gold; (7") **RAG MAMA RAG. / THE WEIGHT**		-
Oct 89.	E.M.I./ US= Capitol; (t-lp)(d-cd) **TO KINGDOM COME – THE DEFINITIVE COLLECTION**		
May 92.	Castle; (cd) **THE COLLECTION**		-

– Back to Memphis / Tears of rage / To kingdom come / Long black veil / Chest fever / The weight / I shall be released / Up on Cripple Creek / Loving you is sweeter than ever / Rag mama rag / The night they drove old Dixie down / Unfaithful servant / King Harvest (has surely come) / The shape I'm in / The W.S.Walcott medicine show / Daniel and the sacred harp / Stage fright / Don't do it (baby don't do it) / Life is a carnival / When I paint my masterpiece / 4% pantomine / The river hymn / Mystery train / Endless highway / Get up Jake / It makes no difference / Ophelia / Arcadian driftwood / Christmas must be tonight / The saga of Peopote rouge / Knockin' lost John.

Nov 94.	Capitol; (3xcd-box) **ACROSS THE GREAT DIVIDE**		
Apr 95.	Capitol; (cd) **LIVE AT WATKINS GLEN (live)**		-

Tony BANKS (see under ⇒ GENESIS)

Lou BARLOW (see under ⇒ DINOSAUR JR.)

Syd BARRETT

Born: ROGER KEITH BARRETT, 6 Jan'46, Cambridge, England. Founder member and songwriter for PINK FLOYD in 1967 until his acid-related L.S.D. dropout from band. His personality made him unreliable and withdrawn, leading to reclusive period in the late 60's. With help from other PINK FLOYD members, except NICK MASON, he recorded two albums released in 1970. These were not regarded highly until later, as anything but whimsical oddities, by critics and public alike. He has since been tributed and stylised by many, including TELEVISION PERSONALITIES and ROBYN HITCHCOCK (Soft Boys). • **Style:** Psychedelic eccentric/genius whose songs although brilliant, were little more than acoustic FLOYD. • **Songwriters:** All written by SYD. • **Trivia:** PINK FLOYD paid homage to SYD on their album SHINE ON YOU CRAZY DIAMOND track from album 'WISH YOU WERE HERE'. SYD attended these sessions but didn't contribute.

Recommended: THE MADCAP LAUGHS (*8) / BARRETT (*6).

SYD BARRETT – vocals, guitar (ex-PINK FLOYD) augmented by **DAVID GILMOUR** and **ROGER WATERS** (Pink Floyd) with **MIKE RATLEDGE** – keyboards / **HUGH HOPPER** – bass / **ROBERT WYATT** – drums (all of SOFT MACHINE) plus **JOHN 'WILLIE' WATSON + JERRY SHIRLEY** – rhythm

		Harvest	Harvest
Oct 69.	(7") **OCTOPUS. / GOLDEN HAIR**		
Jan 70.	(lp)(c) **THE MADCAP LAUGHS**	40	

– Terrapin / No good trying / Love you / No man's land / Dark globe / Here I go / Octopus / Golden Hair / Long gone / She took a long cold look / Feel / If it's in you / Late night. *(cd-iss.May87) (re-iss.cd Jun94)*

— SYD retained GILMOUR, SHIRLEY and WILSON adding **RICK WRIGHT** – keyboards (of PINK FLOYD) and guest on 1 **VIC SAYWELL** – tuba

Nov 70. (lp)(c) **BARRETT**
– Baby lemonade / Love song / Dominoes / It is obvious / Rats / Maisie / Gigolo aunt / Waving my arms in the air / Wined and dined / Wolfpack / Effervescing elephant / I never lied to you. *(cd-iss.May87) (re-iss.cd Jun94)*

— His solo career ended and he formed short-lived STARS early in '72, with **TWINK** – drums + **JACK MONK** – bass (they made no recordings)

In 1982, he was reported to be living with his mother having hung up guitar.

- compilations, others, etc. -

Sep 74. Harvest; (d-lp) **SYD BARRETT**
(re-iss. of his 2 albums from 1970)

Oct 88. Harvest; (lp)(c)(cd) **OPEL** (recorded 68-70)
– Opel / Clowns and daggers (Octopus) / Rats / Golden hair (vocal) / Dollyrocker / Word song / Wined and dined / Swan Lee (Silas Lang) / Birdie hop / Let's split / Lanky (Pt.1) / Wouldn't you miss me / Golden hair (instrumental). *(re-iss.cd Jun94)*

Oct 87. Strange Fruit; (12"ep) **THE PEEL SESSIONS (24.2.70)** [-]
– Terrapin / Gigolo aunt / Baby lemonade / Two of a kind / Effervescing elephant. *(cd-iss.Apr88)*

Apr 93. E.M.I.; (3xcd-box) **CRAZY DIAMOND – THE COMPLETE SYD BARRETT**

Apr 94. Cleopatra; (cd) **OCTOPUS** [-]

Oct 95. Strange Fruit; (cd) **THE PEEL SESSION** [-]

BAUHAUS

Formed: Northampton, England . . . late 1978, first calling themselves BAUHAUS 1919. Obtained one-off deal with indie 'Small Wonder' label releasing an 8 minute epic 'BELA LUGOSI'S DEAD'. By early '81, they signed to 'Beggar's B.', although throughout 1980 they had been on its subsidiary '4.a.d'. In 1982, having scored some minor hits, they smashed into UK Top 20 with a 1972 BOWIE song 'ZIGGY STARDUST'. A year later they were no more as MURPHY went solo and the others formed LOVE AND ROCKETS (who had been under the guise of splinter TONES ON TAIL, while DAVID J moonlighted solo). They had surprise US Top 3 hit in 1989 with 'SO ALIVE'. • **Style:** Combined goth, glam & punk rock, although at first accused of plagiarising BOWIE. • **Songwriters:** Group compositions, except other covers TELEGRAM SAM (T.Rex) / THIRD UNCLE (Eno) / WAITING FOR THE MAN (Velvet Underground). PETER MURPHY solo, wrote with STREATHAM and covered; FINAL SOLUTION (Pere Ubu) / THE LIGHT POURS OUT OF ME (Magazine) / FUNTIME (Iggy Pop). LOVE AND ROCKETS covered BALL OF CONFUSION (Temptations) / BODY AND SOUL (trad). DAVID J covered 4 HOURS (ClockDva) / SHIP OF FOOLS (John Cale). • **Trivia:** Late 1981 onwards, PETER MURPHY appeared in a TV ad for Maxell Tapes. In '82 group performed 'BELA LUGOSI . . . ' for the vampire film 'The Hunger', which starred Bowie and Catherine Deneuve.

Recommended: BAUHAUS 1979-1983 (*9) / NIGHT MUSIC (TONES ON TAIL *6) / LOVE AND ROCKETS (LOVE AND ROCKETS *5)

PETER MURPHY – vocals / **DANIEL ASH** – guitar, vocals / **DAVID JAY** (b.HASKINS) – bass, vocals / **KEVIN HASKINS** – drums, percussion

Small Wonder — not issued

Aug 79. (12"+12"white) **BELA LUGOSI'S DEAD. / BOYS / DARK ENTRIES** [-]
(12" re-dist.Mar81 & Mar82) (re-iss.Sep86 on 12"blue) (re-iss. 1987,12"pic-d) (cd-iss.May88)

Axis — not issued

Jan 80. (7") **DARK ENTRIES. / UNTITLED** [-]
(re-iss.Feb80 on '4.a.d.' some mispressed on 'Beggar's B.')

4.a.d. — not issued

Jun 80. (7") **TERROR COUPLE KILL COLONEL. / SCOPES / TERROR COUPLE KILL COLONEL II** [-]
(7") – ('A'remix).

Oct 80. (lp) **IN A FLAT FIELD** [72] [-]
– Double dare / In a flat field / A god in an alcove / Dive / Spy in the cab / Small talk stinks / St. Vitus dance / Stigmata martyr / Nerves. *(cd-iss.Apr88)* (+=) – Untitled.

Oct 80. (7") **TELEGRAM SAM. / CROWDS** [-]
(12"+=) – Rosegarden funeral of sores.

Beggar's B. — A&M (later)

Mar 81. (7")(12") **KICK IN THE EYE. / SATORI** [59] [-]

Jun 81. (7") **PASSION OF LOVERS. / 1: 2: 3: 4:** [56] [-]

Oct 81. (lp)(c) **MASK** [30]
– Hair of the dog / The passion of lovers / Of lillies and remains / Dancing / Hollow hills / Kick in the eye / Muscle in plastic / In fear of fear / Man with x-ray eyes / Mask. *(re-iss.Feb88 + cd-iss.Oct88)* (cd+=) – Satori / Harry / Earwax / In fear of dub / Kick in the eye.

Feb 82. (7"ep) **SEARCHING FOR SATORI** [45] [-]
– Kick in the eye / Harry / Earwax.
(12"ep+=) – In fear of dub.

Jun 82. (7")(7"pic-d) **SPIRIT. / TERROR COUPLE KILL COLONEL (live)** [42]

Sep 82. (7") **ZIGGY STARDUST. / THIRD UNCLE (live)** [15]
(12"+=) – Party of the first part / Waiting for the man.

Oct 82. (lp)(d-c) **THE SKY'S GONE OUT** [4]
– Third uncle / Silent hedges / In the night / Swing the heartache / Spirit / The three shadows (parts 1, 2, 3) / Silent hedges / All we ever wanted was everything / Exquisite corpse. *(cd-iss.Feb88)* (+=) – Ziggy Stardust / Watch that grandad go / Party of the first part / Spirit (extended).

Oct 82. (free lp,+ on d-c) **PRESS THE EJECT BUTTON AND GIVE ME THE TAPE (live)**
– In a flat field / Rosegarden funeral of sores / Dancing / Man with the x-ray eyes / Bela Lugosi's dead / Spy in the cab / Kick in the eye / In fear of fear / Hollow hills / Stigmata martyr / Dark entries. *(iss.lp/c/cd.Feb88)* (cd+=) – Terror couple kill colonel / Double dare / Waiting for the man / Hair of the dog / Of lillies and remains. (lp, had free 7"ep) – SATORI IN PARIS (live)

Jan 83. (7") **LAGARTIJA NICK. / PARANOIA! PARADISE** [44]
(12"+=) – Watch that grandad go / In a flat field.

Apr 83. (7")(7"pic-d) **SHE'S IN PARTIES. / DEPARTURE** [26]
(12"+=) – Here's the dub.

Jul 83. (lp)(c)(pic-lp) **BURNING FROM THE INSIDE** [13]
– She's in parties / Antonin Artaud / King Volcano / Who killed Mr. Moonlight? / Slice of life / Honeymoon croon / Kingdom's coming / Burning from the inside / Hope. *(re-iss.Feb88.=cd.Sep88)* (cd+=) – Lagartija Nick / Departure / Here's the dub / The sanity assassin.

Disbanded mid 1983. DAVID J. continued splinter solo venture, before forming LOVE AND ROCKETS with DANIEL and KEVIN, who had come from own TONES ON TAIL. MURPHY went solo (see below).

- compilations, others, etc. -

Sep 83. 4 a.d.; (12"ep) **THE 4.A.D. SINGLES** [-]
– Dark entries / Terror couple kill colonel / Telegram Sam / + 1.

Oct 83. Beggar's Banquet; (12"ep) **THE SINGLES 1981-83** [52] [-]
– The passion of lovers / Kick in the eye / Spirit / Ziggy Stardust / Lagartija Nick / She's in parties. *(re-iss.3"pic-cd.Dec88)*

Nov 85. Beggar's Banquet; (d-lp)(d-cd) **BAUHAUS 1979-1983** [36]
(re-iss.d-cd Sep95)

Jul 89. Beggar's Banquet; (d-lp)(cd) **SWING THE HEARTACHE (the BBC sessions)**
(re-iss.cd Sep95)

DALI'S CAR

were formed by **PETE MURPHY** – vocals and **MICK KARN** – bass, multi (ex-JAPAN) / **PAUL VINCENT LAWFORD** – rhythms

Paradox-Beggar's — not issued

Oct 84. (7") **THE JUDGEMENT IS THE MIRROR. / HIGH PLACES** [66] [-]
(12"+=) – Lifelong moment.

Nov 84. (lp)(c)(cd) **THE WAKING HOUR** [84]
– Dali's car / His box / Cornwall stone / Artemis / Create and melt / Moonlife / The judgement the sanity mirror. *(re-iss.+cd.Jan89 on 'Lowdown-Beggar's')*

PETER MURPHY

went solo, augmented by **JOHN McGEOGH** – guitar / **HOWARD HUGHES** – keyboards / **ROBERT SUAVE** – bass / **STEVE YOUNG** – rhythm prog. / **PLUG** – harmonica

Beggar's B. — Beggar's B.

Nov 85. (7") **FINAL SOLUTION. / THE ANSWER'S CLEAR**
(12"+=) – ('A'full version).
(12"pic-d+=) – ('A'club mix).

Jun 86. (7")(12") **BLUE HEART. / CANVAS BEAUTY**

Jul 86. (lp)(c) **SHOULD THE WORLD FAIL TO FALL APART** [82]
– Canvas beauity / The light pours out of me / Confessions / Should the world fail to fall apart / Never man / God . . .sends / Blue heart / The answer is clear / Final solution / Jemal.*(re-iss.+cd.Jul88)*

Oct 86. (7") **TALES OF THE TONGUE. / SHOULD THE WORLD FAIL TO FALL APART**
(12"+=) – ('A'-2nd version).

— **MURPHY** brought in **PAUL STREATHAM** – co-composer, keyboards / **EDDIE BRACH** – bass / **PETER BONAS** – guitar / **TERL BRYANT** – drums

Feb 88. (7") **ALL NIGHT LONG. / I'VE GOT A SECRET CAMERA**
(12"+=) – Funtime (in cabaret).

Mar 88. (lp)(c)(cd) **LOVE HYSTERIA**
– All night long / His circle and hers meet / Dragnet drag / Socrates the python / Indigo eyes / Time has got nothing to do with it / Blind sublime / My last two weeks / Funtime. (cd+=) – I've got a miniature secret camera / Funtime

(cabaret mix).
Apr 88. (7") **INDIGO EYES. / GOD SENDS (live)**
(12"+=) – Confessions (live).
Apr 90. (7") **CUTS YOU UP. / STRANGE KIND OF LOVE** 55
(12"+=)(cd-s+=) – Roll call (reprise).
May 90. (cd)(c)(lp) **DEEP** 44
– Deep ocean vast sea / Crystal waters / Marlene Dietrich's favourite poem / Seven veils / The line between the Devil's teeth (and that which cannot be repeated) / Cuts you up / A strange kind of love / Roll call. (cd+=) – Strange kind of love (alt.version).
Apr 92. (7") **YOU'RE SO CLOSE. / THE SWEETEST DROP**
(12"+=)(cd-s+=) – Cuts you up (live) / All night long (live).
May 92. (cd)(c)(lp) **HOLY SMOKE**
– Keep me from harm / Kill the hate / You're so close / The sweetest drop / Low room / Let me love you / Our secret garden / Dream gone by / Hit song.
Jul 92. (7") **HIT SONG. / SEVEN VEILS**
(12"+=)(cd-s+=) – The line between the Devil's teeth (and that which cannot be repeated).
Apr 95. (cd-ep) **THE SCARLET THING IN YOU / CRYSTAL WRISTS / WISH / DRAGNET DRAG (live)**
Apr 95. (cd)(c) **CASCADE**
– Mirror to my woman's mind / Subway / Gliding like a whale / Disappearing / Mercy rain / I'll fall with your knife / Scarlet thing in you / Sails wave goodbye / Wild birds flock to me / Huuvola / Cascade.

TONES ON TAILS

GLEN CAMPLING – vocals, bass, keyboards (roadie of BAUHAUS) / **DANIEL ASH** – guitar, vocals (of BAUHAUS) / **KEVIN HASKINS** – drums (of BAUHAUS)

4.a.d. not issued
Apr 82. (7"ep)(12"ep) **A BIGGER SPLASH / COPPER. / MEANS OF ESCAPE / INSTRUMENTAL** -
Beggar's B. not issued
Sep 82. (7")(12") **THERE'S ONLY THIS. / NOW WE LUSTRE** -
Situation 2 not issued
May 83 (7")**BURNING SKIES. / OK THIS IS THE POPS** -
(12"+=) – When you're smiling / You the night and the music.
— In 1983, they broke from BAUHAUS. ASH and HASKINS joined The JAZZ BUTCHER. **TONES ON TAILS** soon re-actified line-up.
Beggar's not issued
Mar 84. (7") **PERFORMANCE. / SHAKES**
(12"+=) – ('A'dub version).
Apr 84. (lp)(c) **POP**
– Performance / War / Lions / Happiness / The never never / Real life / Slender fungus / Movement of fear / Rain.
May 84. (7")(12")(12"red) **LIONS. / GO (LET'S GO TO YA YA'S NOW)**
Nov 84. (7")(12"blue) **CHRISTIAN SAYS. / TWIST**
— Split from this set-up.

– compilations, others, etc. –

Feb 85. Situation 2; (lp)(c) **TONES ON TAILS** (the singles)
Oct 88. Beggar's Banquet; (cd) **NIGHT MUSIC** (nearly all work) -

LOVE AND ROCKETS

ASH + HASKINS were joined by **DAVID J.** – vocals, bass, keyboards (also ex-BAUHAUS + a solo artist)

Beggar's Big Time
May 85. (7")(12") **BALL OF CONFUSION. / INSIDE THE OUTSIDE**
Sep 85. (7")(12") **IF THERE'S A HEAVEN ABOVE. / GOD AND MR.SMITH**
Oct 85. (lp)(c) **7th DREAM OF TEENAGE HEAVEN**
– If there's a Heaven above / A private future / 7th dream of teenage Heaven / Saudade / Haunted when the minutes drag / The dog-end of a day gone by / The game. *(re-iss.+cd Jan89)* (cd+=) – Ball of confusion (USA mix) / God and Mr.Smith (Mars mix) / If there's a Heaven above (Canadian mix).
Jun 86. (12"m) **KUNDALINI EXPRESS. / LUCIFER SAM / HOLIDAY ON THE MOON**
Sep 86. (7")(12") **YIN AND YANG (THE FLOWERPOT MEN). / ANGELS AND DEVILS**
Sep 86. (lp)(c) **EXPRESS** 72
– Kundalini express / It could be sunshine / Love me / All in my mind / Life in Laralay / Yin and Yang (the flowerpot men) / An American dream / All in my mind (acoustic version). *(cd-iss Jan89)*
Sep 87. (lp)(c)(cd) **EARTH, SUN, MOON** 64
– The light / Mirror people / Welcome tomorrow / Here on Earth / Lazy / Waiting for the flood / Rainbird / Telephone is empty / Everybody wants to go to Heaven / The Sun / Youth.
Oct 87. (7")(12") **THE LIGHT. / MIRROR PEOPLE (slow version)**
Mar 88. (7") **NO NEW TALE TO TELL. / EARTH, SUN, MOON**
(12"+=) – 7th dream of teenage Heaven.
May 88. (7") **MIRROR PEOPLE. / DAVID LANFAIR**
(12"+=) – ('A'live version).
Aug 88. (7") **LAZY. / THE DOG-END OF A DAY GONE BY**
(12"+=) – The purest blue.
Beggar's B. Beggar's B.
Jan 89. (12"ep) **MOTORCYCLE / I FEEL SPEED. / BIKE / BIKEDANCE**
Jul 89. (7")(12")(c-s) **SO ALIVE. / DREAMTIME** 3 May 89
(cd-s+=) – Motorcycle / Bike. *(re-iss.Jan90)*
Sep 89. (lp)(c)(cd) **LOVE AND ROCKETS** 14
– **** (Jungle law) / No big deal / The purest blue / Motorcycle / I feel speed / Bound for Hell / The teardrop collector / So alive / Rock and roll Babylon / No words no more.
Oct 89. (7") **NO BIG DEAL. / NO WORDS NO MORE** 82 Sep 89
(12"+=) – 100 watts of your love.
Jul 94. (12")(cd-s) **THIS HEAVEN. / (3 other 'A'mixes)**
Sep 94. (12")(cd-s) **BODY AND SOUL. / (2 extended mixes)**
Sep 94. (cd)(c)(d-lp) **HOT TRIP TO HEAVEN**
– Body and soul (parts 1 & 2) / Ugly / Trip and glide / This Heaven / No worries / Hot trip to Heaven / Eclipse / Voodoo baby / Be the revolution / Set me free. *(re-iss.cd Sep95)*
. . . Jan – Jun '96 stop press . . .
Mar 96. (cd)(c) **SWEET F.A.** -

DANIEL ASH

Beggar's B. Columbia
Jun 91. (cd)(c)(lp) **COMING DOWN**
– Blue Moon / Coming down fast / Walk this way / Closer to you / Day tripper / This love / Blue angel / Me and my shadow / Candy darling / Sweet little liar / Not so fast / Coming down.
— Above features covers DAY TRIPPER (Beatles) / BLUE MOON (Rodgers / Hart) / ME AND MY SHADOW (Al Jolson/+).
Jun 91. (7") **WALK THIS WAY. / HEAVEN IS WAITING** -
(12") – ('A'side) / ('A'groovy vox) / ('A'groovy guitar).
(cd-s) – (all 4 tracks).
Apr 93. (12"ep)(cd-ep) **GET OUT OF CONTROL. / THE HEDONIST / GET OUT OF CONTROL (farewell mixes)**
May 93. (cd)(c)(lp) **FOOLISH THING DESIRE**
– Here she comes / Foolish thing desire / Bluebird / Dream machine / Get out of control / The void / Roll on / Here she comes again / The hedonist / Higher than this.

DAVID J.

4 a.d. not issued
Sep 81. (7") **NOTHING. / ARMOUR (by "DAVID JAY / RENE HACKETT")** -
Situation 2 not issued
Aug 83. (7") **JOE ORTON'S WEDDING. / THE GOSPEL ACCORDING TO FEAR**
(12"+=) – Requiem for Joe / Point of venture.
Oct 83. (lp) **ETIQUETTE OF VIOLENCE** -
– The gospel according to fear / I hear only silence now / No one's sending roses / The fugitive / Betrayal / Joe Orton's wedding / The promised land / With the Indians permanent / Say uncle / Disease / Roulette / Saint Jackie.
Glass not issued
Nov 83. (7") **THE PROMISED LAND. / SAINT JACKIE (by "DAVID J. & The J.WALKERS")** -
(12"+=) – A seducer, a doctor, a card you cannot trust.
Jun 84. (12"ep) **V FOR VENDETTA (by "DAVID J. & ALAN MOORE")**
– This vicious cabaret / V theme (intro) / V's theme (outro).
Sep 84. (7")(12") **I CAN'T SHAKE THIS SHADOW OF FEAR. / WAR GAME** -
Mar 85. (lp) **CROCODILE TEARS & THE VELVET COSH** -
Apr 85. (7") **CROCODILE TEARS & THE VELVET COSH. / ELEGY**
(12"+=) – Rene.
Jun 85. (12"ep) **BLUE MOODS TURNING TAILS** -
– 4 hours / The conjurors hand / Ship of fools.
Mar 86. (lp) **DAVID J. ON GLASS** (compilation) -
— w/ **MAX KIDER** – guitar / **ANGUS WALLACE + OWEN JONES** – drums / **DAVE ANDERSON** – steel guitar / **ALEX GREEN** – sax / **BEN HEANEY** – violin / **BEN GREENAWAY** percussion / **JANIS ZAKIS** – accordian.
Beggar's B. Beggar's..
Jun 90. (7") **I'LL BE YOUR CHAUFFEUR. / THE MOON IN THE MAN**
(12"+=) – ('A'original version).
Jul 90. (cd)(c)(lp) **SONGS FROM ANOTHER SEASON**
– Fingers in the grease / A longer look / Sad side to the sand boy / New woman

is an attitude / Sweet ancenthexra / On the outskirts (of a strange dream) / I'll be your chauffeur (original) / The Moon in the man / Little star / Stranded Trans-Atlantic hotel nearly famous blues / The national anthem of nowhere / Nature boy.

BBM (see under ⇒ BRUCE, Jack)

BEACH BOYS

Formed: Hawthorne, Los Angeles, California, USA . . . 1961 by WILSON brothers BRIAN, DENNIS and KARL. They were joined by AL JARDINE and cousin MIKE LOVE. After one minor hit SURFIN' on local 'Candix' label, they signed to 'Capitol' appropriately in summer '62. Surf type hits continued with 'SURFIN' U.S.A.', etc. but surpassed this in '66 when 'GOOD VIBRATIONS' became regarded as a classic, and also UK No.1. They continued to hit both charts for the rest of the 60's, and had a major comeback in the late 70's. BRIAN WILSON became increasingly involved with 60's drug scene, and dropped out of group in 1967, although he returned to the fold full-time in 1976. • **Style:** Fun loving, girl loving, car crazy, pop combo, whose surfy FOUR FRESHMEN style close harmonies became trademark. A little more sophisticated in the 70's, but hits dried up. Nine years later (1988), the soppy 'KOKOMO' gave them return to US top spot. • **Songwriters:** Early hits were co-written by BRIAN and neighbour GARY USHER, but BRIAN soon took control, with others complimenting on some. Covered:- THE TIMES THEY ARE A-CHANGIN' (Bob Dylan) / PAPA OOM MOW MOW (Rivingtons) / I CAN HEAR MUSIC (Ronettes) / BARBARA ANN (Regents) / LOUIE LOUIE (Kingsmen) / WHY DO FOOLS FALL IN LOVE? (Frankie Lymon & the Teenagers) / MONSTER MASH (Bobby Pickett & the Crypt..) / JOHNNY B. GOODE (Chuck Berry) / DO YOU WANNA DANCE (Bobby Freeman) / YOU'VE GOT TO HIDE YOUR LOVE AWAY + I SHOULD HAVE KNOWN BETTER (Beatles) / ALLEY OOP (Hollywood Argyles) / BLUEBIRDS OVER THE MOUNTAIN (Ersel Hickey) / THEN I KISSED HER (Crystals) / COME GO WITH ME (Del-Vikings) CALIFORNIA DREAMIN' (Mamas & the Papas) / THE WANDERER (Dion) / ROCK AND ROLL MUSIC (Chuck Berry) / BLUEBERRY HILL (Fats Domino) / MONA (Bo Diddley) / PEGGY SUE (Buddy Holly) / THE AIR THAT I BREATHE (Hollies) / HOT FUN IN THE SUMMERTIME (Sly & The Family Stone) / WALKING IN THE SAND (Shangri-la's) / UNDER THE BOARDWALK (Drifters). etc. KOKOMO (co-written with John Phillips; ex-Mamas & the Papas). • **Miscellaneous:** The WILSON's father died 4 Jun'73. DENNIS was drowned at sea off Marina Del Ray on 28 Dec'83.

Recommended: THE VERY BEST OF THE BEACH BOYS (*8) / PET SOUNDS (*9)

BRIAN WILSON (b.20 Jun'42, Inglewood, California) – vocals, percussion / **CARL WILSON** (b.21 Dec'46) – guitar, vocals / **DENNIS WILSON** (b.4 Dec'44) – vocals, drums / **MIKE LOVE** (b.15 Mar'44, Baldwin Hills, California) – vocals / **AL JARDINE** (b. 3 Sep'42, Lima, Ohio) – vocals, guitar

not issued / Candix

Dec 61. (7") **SURFIN'. / LUAN** [-] [75]

— **DAVID MARKS** – vocals repl. JARDINE who became dentist

Capitol / Capitol

Oct 62. (7") **SURFIN' SAFARI. / 409** [ ] [14]

Nov 62. (lp) **SURFIN' SAFARI** [ ] [32]
– Surfin' safari / County fair / Ten little indians / Chug-a-lug / Little girl (you're my Miss America) / 409 / Surfin' * / Heads you win – tails I lose / Summertime blues / Cuckoo clock * / Moon dawg / The shift. *(UK-iss.Apr63) (re-iss.Jun79 omitting *)*

Jan 63. (7") **TEN LITTLE INDIANS. / COUNTY FAIR** [ ] [49]
(re-iss.Jun79)

Mar 63. (lp) **SURFIN' U.S.A.** [17] [2]
– Surfin' U.S.A. / Farmer's daughter / Misirlou / Stoked / Lonely sea / Shut down / Noble surfer / Honky tonk / Lana / Surf jam / Let's go trippin' / Finders keepers.

Jun 63. (7") **SURFIN' U.S.A.. / SHUT DOWN** [34] [3] [23]
(re-iss.Jun79)

— **AL JARDINE** – vocals returned to repl. MARKS

Aug 63. (7") **SURFER GIRL. / LITTLE DEUCE COUPE** [-] [7] [15]

Sep 63. (lp) **SURFER GIRL** [13] [7]
– Surfer girl / Catch a wave / Surfer Moon / South bay surfer / Rocking surfer / Little deuece coupe / In my room / Hawaii / Surfer's rule / Our car club / Your summer dream / Boogie woogie. *(re-iss.Aug86)*

Oct 63. (lp) **LITTLE DEUCE COUPE** [ ] [4]
– Little deuce Coupe / Ballad of ole' Betsy / Be true to your school / Car crazy cutie * / Cherry, cherry Coupe / 409 / Shut down / Spirit of America / Our car club * / No-go showboat / A young man is gone / Custom machine. *(re-iss.Jun81 omitting *) (re-iss.Aug86)*

Nov 63. (7") **BE TRUE TO YOUR SCHOOL. / IN MY ROOM** [-] [6] [23]

Dec 63. (7") **LITTLE SAINT NICK. / THE LORD'S PRAYER** [-] [ ]

Jan 64. (7") **PAMELA JEAN (as "The SURVIVORS"). / AFTER THE GAME** [-] [ ]

Mar 64. (7") **FUN, FUN, FUN. / WHY DO FOOLS FALL IN LOVE** [ ] [5]

Jul 64. (lp) **SHUT DOWN VOL.2** [ ] [13] Apr 64
– Fun, fun, fun / Don't worry baby / In the parkin' lot / "Cassius" Love vs "Sonny" Wilson / The warmth of the sun / This car of mine / Why do fools fall in love / Pom-pom play girl / Keep an eye on summer / Shut down (pt.II) / Louie louie / Denny's drum. *(re-iss.Jun89 on 'C5')*

Note:- SHUT DOWN was a various artists surf US-lp issued Jul63 reaching No.7. It contained two BEACH BOYS tracks; 409 / Shut down.

Jun 64. (7") **I GET AROUND. / DON'T WORRY BABY** [7] [1]
(re-iss.Jun79)

Jul 64. (lp) **ALL SUMMER LONG** [ ] [4]
– I get around / All summer long / Hushabye / Little Honda / We'll run away / Carl's big chance / Wendy / Do you remember? / Girls on the beach / Drive-in / Our favourite recording session / Don't back down. *(UK-iss.Jun65) (re-iss.Jul73 on 'MFP', re-iss.+c Aug86)*

Oct 64. (7") **WHEN I GROW UP (TO BE A MAN). / SHE KNOWS ME TOO WELL** [27] [9]
(re-iss.Jun79)

Oct 64. (lp) **BEACH BOYS CONCERT (live)** [ ] [1]
– Fun, fun, fun / The little old lady from Pasadena / Little deuce Coupe / Long tail Texan / In my room / Monster mash / Let's go trippin' / Papa-oom-mow-mow / The wanderer / Hawaii / / Graduation day / I get around / Johnny B. Goode. *(re-iss.Jun81 on 'Greenlight')*

Nov 64. (7"ep) **WENDY DON'T BACK DOWN / LITTLE HONDA / HUSHABYE** [-] [44]

Dec 64. (7") **THE MAN WITH ALL THE TOYS. / BLUE CHRISTMAS** [-] [ ]

Jan 65. (7") **DANCE, DANCE, DANCE. / THE WARMTH OF THE SUN** [24] [8]

— **GLEN CAMPBELL** – vocals (on tour) repl. BRIAN who suffered breakdown. However BRIAN did stay as writer/producer (6th member) (also see other US releases for further imports)

Mar 65. (7") **DO YOU WANNA DANCE?. / PLEASE LET ME WONDER** [-] [ ]

Mar 65. (7") **ALL SUMMER LONG. / DO YOU WANNA DANCE?** [ ] [ ]
(re-iss.Jun79)

Apr 65. (lp) **BEACH BOYS - TODAY!** [6] [4]
– Do you wanna dance? / Good to my baby / Don't hurt my little sister / When I grow up (to be a man) / Help me Rhonda / Dance, dance, dance / Please let me wonder / I'm so young / Kiss me baby / She knows me too well / In the back of my mind / She knew me too well. *(re-iss.UKJan72 as 'DO YOU WANNA DANCE' on 'MFP')*

— **BRUCE JOHNSTON** – vocals (ex-his combo) repl. GLEN CAMPBELL who went solo

May 65. (7") **HELP ME RHONDA. / KISS ME BABY** [27] [1]
(re-iss.Jun79)

Jul 65. (lp) **SUMMER DAYS (AND SUMMER NIGHTS!!)** [4] [2]
– The girl from New York City / Amusements parks U.S.A. / Then I kissed her / Salt Lake City / Girl don't tell me / Help me Rhonda / Let him run wild / You're so good to me / Summer means new love / I'm bugged at my ol' man / And your dream comes true. *(re-iss.+c-Jun78, re-iss.Aug86)*

Aug 65 (7") **CALIFORNIA GIRLS. / LET HIM RUN WILD** [26] [3]
(re-iss.Jun79)

Dec 65. (7") **THE LITTLE GIRL I ONCE KNEW. / THERE'S NO OTHER (LIKE MY BABY)** [ ] [20]
(re-iss.Jun79)

Feb 66. (7") **BARBARA ANN. / GIRL DON'T TELL ME** [3] [2]
(re-iss.Jun79)

Feb 66. (lp) **BEACH BOYS' PARTY!** [3] [6] Nov 65
– Hully gully / I should have known better / Tell me why / Papa-oom- mow-mow / Mountain of love / You've got to hide your love away / Devoted to you / Alley oop / There's no other (like my baby) / I get around – Little deuce Coupe / The times they are a-changin' / Barbara Ann. *(re-iss.Aug86)*

Apr 66. (7") **SLOOP JOHN B. / YOU'RE SO GOOD TO ME** [2] [3]

May 66. (lp) **PET SOUNDS** [2] [10]
– Wouldn't it be nice / You still believe in me / That's not me / Don't talk (put your head on my shoulder) / I'm waiting for the day / Let's go away for awhile / Sloop John B. / God only knows / I know there's no answer / Here today / I just wasn't made for these times / Pet sounds / Caroline, no. *(re-iss.May82 on 'Fame') (re-iss.Aug86, cd-iss.Jun90 w/+= tracks)* – Hang on to your ego / Trombone Dixie. *(re-iss.cd+c Nov93 on 'Fame')*

Jul 66. (7") **GOD ONLY KNOWS. / WOULDN'T IT BE NICE** [2] [39] [8]

(re-iss. Jun79)

Oct 66. (7") **GOOD VIBRATIONS. / LET'S GO AWAY FOR AWHILE** [-] [1]

Oct 66. (7") **GOOD VIBRATIONS. / WENDY** [1] [-]
(re-iss.Jun79)

Apr 67. (7") **THEN I KISSED HER. / MOUNTAIN OF LOVE** [4] [ ]
(re-iss.Jun79)

Capitol Brother

Aug 67. (7") **HEROES AND VILLAINS. / YOU'RE WELCOME** [8] [12]
(re-iss.Jun79)

Nov 67. (lp) **SMILEY SMILE** [9] [41] Sep 67
– Heroes and villains / Vegetables / Fall breaks and back to winter / She's goin' bald / Little pad / Good vibrations / With me tonight / Wind chimes / Gettin' hungry / Wonderful / Whistle in.

Nov 67. (7") **WILD HONEY. / WIND CHIMES** [29] [31]
(re-iss.Jun79)

Dec 67. (7") **DARLIN'. / HERE TODAY** [-] [19]

Jan 68. (7") **DARLIN'. / COUNTRY AIR** [11] [-]
(re-iss.Jun79)

Mar 68. (lp) **WILD HONEY** [7] [24] Dec 67
– Wild honey / Aren't you glad / I was made to love her / Country air / A thing or two / Darlin' / I'd love just once to see you / Here comes the night / Let the wind blow / How she boogalooed it / Mama says.

May 68. (7") **FRIENDS. / LITTLE BIRD** [25] [47]
(re-iss.Jun79)

Jul 68. (7") **DO IT AGAIN. / WAKE THE WORLD** [1] [20]

Sep 68. (lp) **FRIENDS** [13] [ ] Jun 68
– Meant for you / Friends / Wake the world / Be here in the mornin' / When a man needs a woman / Passing by / Anna Lee, the healer / Little bird / Be still / Busy doing nothin' / Diamond head / Transcendental meditation.

Dec 68. (7") **BLUEBIRDS OVER THE MOUNTAIN. / NEVER LEARN NOT TO LOVE** [33] [ ]
(re-iss.Jun79)

Feb 69. (7") **I CAN HEAR MUSIC. / ALL I WANT TO DO** [10] [24]

Feb 69. (lp) **20/20** [3] [68]
– Do it again / I can hear music / Bluebirds over the mountain / Be with me / All I want to do / The nearest faraway place / Cotton fields / I went to sleep / Time to get alone / Never learn not to love / Our prayer / Cabinessence.

Jun 69. (7") **BREAKAWAY. / CELEBRATE THE NEWS** [6] [ ]
(re-iss.Jun79)

Capitol Brother / Reprise

Feb 70. (7") **ADD SOME MUSIC TO YOUR DAY. / SUSIE CINCINATTI** [-] [ ]

May 70. (7") **COTTON FIELDS. / THE NEAREST FARAWAY PLACE** [5] [ ]
(re-iss.Jun79)

Stateside Brother / Reprise

Sep 70. (7") **SLIP ON THROUGH. / THIS WHOLE WORLD** [ ] [ ]

Nov 70. (7") **TEARS IN THE MORNING. / IT'S ABOUT ME** [ ] [ ]

Nov 70. (lp)(c) **SUNFLOWER** [29] [ ] Sep 70
– Slip on through / This whole world / Add some music to your day / Got to know the woman / Deirdre / It's about time / Tears in the morning / All I wanna do / Forever / Our sweet love / At my window / Cool, cool water. *(re-iss.Nov81. on 'Caribou'; adding 'Cotton fields') (re-iss.+cd.Jul91 on 'Epic')*

Feb 71. (7") **COOL, COOL WATER. / FOREVER** [-] [ ]

Jun 71. (7") **LONG PROMISED ROAD. / DEIRDRE** [ ] [ ]

Oct 71. (7") **LONG PROMISED ROAD. / TILL I DIE** [-] [ ]

Nov 71. (7") **DON'T GO NEAR THE WATER. / STUDENT DEMONSTRATION TIME** [ ] [ ]

Nov 71. (lp)(c) **SURF'S UP** [15] [29] Aug 71
– Don't go near the water / Long promised road / Take a load off your feet / Disney girls (1957) / Student demonstration time / Feel flows / Lookin' at tomorrow / A day in the life of a tree / 'Til I die / Surf's up. *(re-iss.Nov81 on 'Caribou') (re-iss.+cd.Jul91 on 'Epic')*

Nov 71. (7") **SURF'S UP. / DON'T GO NEAR THE WATER** [-] [ ]

—— **BLONDIE CHAPLIN** – guitar repl. JOHNSTON who later went solo added **RICKY FATAAR** – drums (DENNIS now just vocals)

Reprise Reprise

May 72. (7") **YOU NEED A MESS OF HELP TO STAND ALONE. / CUDDLE UP** [ ] [ ]

Jun 72. (d-lp)(c) **CARL AND THE PASSIONS – SO TOUGH** [25] [50]
– You need a mess of help to stand alone / Here she comes / He come down / Marcella / Hold on dear brother / Make it good / All this is that / Cuddle up. (w/ 'PET SOUNDS') *(re-iss.+cd.Jul91 on 'Epic')*

Aug 72. (7") **MARCELLA. / HOLD ON DEAD BROTHER** [-] [ ]

Jan 73. (lp)(c) **HOLLAND** [20] [36]
– Sail on sailor / Steamboat / California saga (on my way to sunny Californ-i-a (medley):- Big sur – Beaks of eagles – California / The trader / Leaving this town / Only with you / Funky pretty.
(7"ep free-w/a) – Mount Vernon and Fairway (A fairy tale). / I'm the pied piper / Batter get back in bed / Magic transistor radio / Mount Vernon and Fairway / I'm the pied piper / Radio King Dom. *(re-iss.+cd.Jul91 on 'Epic')*

Feb 73. (7") **CALIFORNIA SAGA. / FUNKY PRETTY** [-] [ ]

Feb 73. (7") **CALIFORNIA SAGA: CALIFORNIA. / SAIL ON SAILOR** [37] [-]

Nov 73. (d-lp)(c) **THE BEACH BOYS IN CONCERT (live)** [ ] [25]
– Sail on sailor / Sloop John B. / The trader / You still believe me / California girls / Darlin' / Marcella / Caroline, no / Leaving this town / Heroes and villains / We got love / Don't worry baby / Surfin' U.S.A. / Good vibrations / Fun, fun, fun / Funky pretty / Let the wind blow / Help me Rhonda / Surfer girl / Wouldn't it be nice.

1974. (7") **I CAN HEAR MUSIC (live). / LET THE WIND BLOW (live)** [-] [ ]

1974. (7") **CHILD OF WINTER. / SUSIE CINCINNATI** [-] [ ]

Aug 74. (7"ep) **CALIFORNIA SAGA: CALIFORNIA. / SAIL ON SAILOR / MARCELLA / I'M THE PIED PIPER** [ ] [ ]

—— **JAMES GUERICO** – bass (on tour) repl. BLONDIE and RICKY / **DENNIS** returned to his drums

Jun 75. (7") **SAIL ON SAILOR. / ONLY WITH YOU** [ ] [49]

—— **BRIAN** returned to live work

Jul 76. (7") **ROCK AND ROLL MUSIC. / THE T.M. SONG** [36] [ ]

Jul 76. (lp)(c) **15 BIG ONES** [31] [8]
– Rock and roll music / It's O.K. / Had to phone ya / Chapel of love / Everyone's in love with you / Talk to me / That same song / The T.M. song / Palisades park / Susie Cincinatti / A casual look / Blueberry Hill / Back home / In the still of the night / Just once in my life. *(cd+c.iss.Jul91 on 'Epic')*

Aug 76. (7") **IT'S O.K. / HAD TO PHONE YA** [ ] [ ]

Nov 76. (7") **SUSIE CINCINNATI. / EVERYONE'S IN LOVE WITH YOU** [-] [ ]

Apr 77. (7") **HONKIN' DOWN THE HIGHWAY. / SOLAR SYSTEM** [-] [ ]

Apr 77. (lp)(c) **THE BEACH BOYS LOVE YOU** [26] [53]
– Roller skating child / I'll bet he's nice / Airplane / Love is a woman / Johnny Carson / Let us go on this way / I wanna pick you up / Let's put our hearts together / Solar system / The night was so young / Ding dang / Mona / Honkin' down the highway / Good time. *(cd+c.iss.Jun91 on 'Epic')*

Aug 77. (7"ep) **MONA. / ROCK AND ROLL MUSIC / SAIL ON SAILOR / MARCELLA** [ ] [ ]

Sep 78. (lp)(c) **M.I.U. ALBUM** [ ] [ ]
– She's got rhythm / Come go with me / Hey little tomboy / Kona coast / Peggy Sue / Wontcha come out tonight / Sweet Sunday kinda love / Belles of Paris / Pitter patter / My Diane / Match point of your love / Winds of change. *(cd+c.iss.Jul91 on 'Epic')*

Oct 78. (7") **PEGGY SUE. / HEY LITTLE TOMBOY** [ ] [ ]

Dec 78. (7") **KONA COAST. / SWEET SUNDAY KINDA LOVE** [ ] [ ]

—— Returned **BRUCE JOHNSTON** – vocals to DENNIS, CARL, AL, MIKE and BRIAN

Caribou Caribou

Mar 79. (7") **HERE COMES THE NIGHT. / BABY BLUE** [37] [44]
(12"+=)(12"blue+=) – ('A'-disco version).

Apr 79. (lp)(c) **L.A. (LIGHT ALBUM)** [32] [100]
– Angel come home / Baby blue / Love surrounds me / Good timin' / Goin' south / Shortenin' bread / Lady Lynda / Sumahama / Full sail / Sumahama / Here comes the night. *(re-iss.Aug86) (cd-iss.Jul89 on 'Pickwick') (also on pic-lp)*

May 79. (7") **GOOD TIMIN'. / LOVE SURROUNDS ME** [-] [ ]

Jun 79. (7") **LADY LYNDA. / FULL SAIL** [6] [ ]

Aug 79. (7") **SUMAHAMA. / ANGEL COME HOME** [6] [ ]

Sep 79. (7") **SUMAHAMA. / IT'S A BEAUTIFUL DAY** [-] [ ]

Nov 79. (7") **GOOD TIMIN'. / GOIN' SOUTH** [ ] [40]

Mar 80. (7") **GOIN' ON. / ENDLESS HARMONY** [-] [ ]

Mar 80. (7") **OH DARLING. / ENDLESS HARMONY** [ ] [ ]

Mar 80. (lp)(c) **KEEPIN' THE SUMMER ALIVE** [54] [75]
– Endless harmony / When girls get together / School day (ring! ring! goes the bell) / Sunshine / Santa Ana winds / Goin' on / Some of your love / Oh darlin' / Livin' with a heartache / Keepin' the summer alive.

Jun 80. (7") **KEEPIN' THE SUMMER ALIVE. / WHEN GIRLS GET TOGETHER** [ ] [ ]

Jul 80. (7") **LIVING WITH A HEARTACHE. / SANTA ANA WINDS** [-] [ ]

Jul 80. (7") **SANTA ANA WINDS. / SUNSHINE** [ ] [ ]

—— **ADRIAN BAKER** – vocals (ex-solo) repl. CARL and BRUCE

—— **CARL WILSON** returned after short solo career

Feb 82. (7") **COME GO WITH ME. / DON'T GO NEAR THE WATER** [ ] [18]

—— Tragically on 28 Dec83, DENNIS was drowned in his swimming pool. The other original 4 (BRIAN, CARL, AL and MIKE) carried on. Next credited with **JULIO IGLESIAS** – co-vocals

1984. (7") **SHE BELIEVES IN LOVE AGAIN. / IT'S JUST A MATTER OF TIME** [-] [ ]

Mar 85. (7") **THE AIR THAT I BREATHE. / BAMBOU MEDLEY** [ ] [ ]

May 85. (7") **GETCHA BACK. / MALE EGO** [ ] [ ]
(12"+=) – Here comes the night / Lady Lynda.

Jun 85. (lp)(c) **THE BEACH BOYS** [60] [52]
– Getcha back / It's gettin' late / Crack at your love / Maybe I don't know / She

believes in love again / California calling / Passing friend / I'm so lonely / Where I belong / I do love you / It's just a matter of time. (cd+=) – Male ego.

Aug 85. (7") **PASSING FRIEND. / IT'S O.K.** [ ] [ ]

Sep 86. (7") **CALIFORNIA DREAMING. / LADY LIBERTY** [ ] [ ]
(12"+=) – (Ballads medley).

— BRIAN now departed to go solo, the rest did on-off with "FAT BOYS" ('A'side) on their hit single WIPE OUT

Nov 88. (7")(12") **KOKOMO. / TUTTI FRUTTI (by 'Little Richard')** [25] [1]
above single was from the film 'Cocktail'

Aug 89. (7") **STILL CRUISIN'. / KOKOMO** [ ] [ ]
(cd-s+=) Rock'n'roll to the rescue (mix) / Lady Liberty.
(12"+=) – Beach Boys Medley.

Jul 90. (c-s)(cd-s) **PROBLEM CHILD /** [-] [ ]

— **MIKE LOVE, CARL WILSON, AL JARDINE, BRUCE JOHNSTON** (now keyboards), **MELCHER** (keyboards + co-writer w/**LOVE**), **ADRIAN BAKER** (backing vocals), **KEITH WECHSLER** (keyboards / some drums), **CRAIG FALL** – guitar, keyboards / **ROD CLARK** – bass / **SAMMY MERENDINO** – drums / **VAN DYKE PARKS** – accordion, keyboards / **DANNY KORTCHMAR** – guitars / **JOEL PESKIN** – saxophone / **JOHN WESTON** – pedal steel

Brother Brother

Jun 93. (cd)(c) **SUMMER IN PARADISE** [ ] [ ]
– Hot fun in the summertime / Surfin' / Slow summer dancin' (one summer night) / Strange things happen / Remember walking in the sand / Lahaina aloha / Under the boardwalk / Summer in Paradise forever. *(re-iss.cd May95 on 'Fame')*

. . . Jan – Jun '96 stop press . . .

— guested on STATUS QUO's hit version of their 'FUN FUN FUN'.

Sub Pop Sub Pop

Jun 96. (single) **I JUST WASN'T MADE FOR THESE TIMES** [ ] [ ]

– compilations, exploitations, etc. –

Nov 64. Capitol; (lp) **BEACH BOYS CHRISTMAS ALBUM** [ ] [ ]
(re-iss.Dec77)

Oct 66. Capitol; (lp) **THE BEST OF THE BEACH BOYS** [2] [8]

Oct 67. Capitol; (lp) **THE BEST OF THE BEACH BOYS VOL.2** [3] [50] Aug 67

Nov 68. Capitol; (lp) **THE BEST OF THE BEACH BOYS VOL.3** [3] [ ] Sep 68
(U.S. title 'STACK O'TRACKS') *(re-iss.Dec76)*

Aug 69. Capitol; (d-lp) **CLOSE UP (SURFIN' USA / ALL SUMMER LONG)** [-] [ ]

Sep 70. Capitol; (lp)(c) **GREATEST HITS** [5] [ ]

Jan 71. Capitol; (d-lp) **THE CAPITOL YEARS** [ ] [ ]

Aug 72. Capitol; (7"ep) **WOULDN'T IT BE NICE. / FUN FUN FUN / CALIFORNIA GIRLS** [ ] [ ]

Aug 72. Capitol; (lp)(c) **LIVE IN LONDON (live 1969)** [ ] [75] Dec76
(re-iss.Sep77 on 'MfP')

Nov 72. Capitol; (7"ep) **BARBARA ANN. / DANCE DANCE DANCE / YOU'RE SO GOOD TO ME** [ ] [ ]

Nov 73. Capitol; (7") **LITTLE SAINT NICK. / THE LORD'S PRAYER** [ ] [ ]

May 74. Capitol; (7") **ALL SUMMER LONG. / SURFIN' SAFARI** [ ] [ ]

Aug 74. Capitol; (d-lp) **WILD HONEY / 20-20** [ ] [50]

Nov 74. Capitol; (d-lp)(c) **ENDLESS SUMMER** [ ] [1] Jul 74
(re-iss.Sep81 on 'MfP') (cd-iss.Feb87 on 'EMI')

Oct 74. Capitol; (d-lp) **FRIENDS / SMILEY SMILE** [ ] [ ]

Apr 75. Capitol; (d-lp) **SPIRIT OF AMERICA** [ ] [8]

Jun 75. Capitol; (7") **BREAKAWAY. / CELEBRATE THE NEWS** [ ] [ ]

Jun 76. Capitol; (7") **GOOD VIBRATIONS. / WOULDN'T IT BE NICE** [18] [ ]

Jul 76. Capitol; (lp)(c) **20 GOLDEN GREATS (on 'EMI')** [1] [ ]
(cd-iss.Nov87) (also issued 1979 on blue vinyl) (re-iss.cd+c Sep94)

Nov 77. Capitol; (7") **LITTLE SAINT NICK. / SANTA CLAUSE IS COMING TO TOWN / ('A'instrumental)** [ ] [ ]

May 78. Capitol; (7") **LITTLE DEUCE COUPE. / ('B' by 'Sunrays & Superstocks')** [ ] [ ]

Jun 78. Capitol; (7") **CALIFORNIA GIRLS. / YOU'RE SO GOOD TO ME / DO IT AGAIN** [ ] [ ]

Jun 79. Capitol; (26x7"box) **THE BEACH BOYS SINGLES COLLECTION** [ ] [ ]
(7"free-w/a) – (as "The SURVIVORS" – Pamela Jean / After the game.

Jun 80. Capitol; (7") **GOD ONLY KNOWS. / GIRLS ON THE BEACH / IN MY ROOM** [ ] [ ]

Jun 80. Capitol; (lp)(c) **GIRLS ON THE BEACH** [ ] [ ]

Aug 81. Capitol; (7") **BEACH BOYS MEDLEY. / GOD ONLY KNOWS** [47] [12]
(re-iss.Jul83)

Jul 83. Capitol; (lp)(c) **THE VERY BEST OF THE BEACH BOYS** [1] [ ]
– Surfin' safari / Surfin' U.S.A. / Shut down / Little deuce Coupe / In my room / Fun, fun, fun / I get around / Don't worry baby / When I grow up (to be a man) / Wendy / Little Honda / Dance dance dance / All summer long / Do you wanna dance / Help me Rhonda / California girls / Little girl I once knew / Barbara Ann / You're so good to me / Then I kissed her / Sloop John B. / God only knows / Wouldn't it be nice / Here today / Good vibrations / Heroes and villains / Wild honey / Darlin' / Country air / Here comes the night / Friends / Do it again / Bluebirds over the mountain / I can hear music / Breakaway / Cottonfields.

Dec 84. Capitol; (d-lp)(d-c) **TEN YEARS OF HARMONY (1970-1980)** [ ] [ ]

Jul 86. Capitol; (7")(12") **ROCK'N'ROLL TO THE RESCUE. / GOOD VIBRATIONS (live)** [ ] [ ]

Aug 86. Capitol; (d-lp)(c)(cd) **MADE IN THE U.S.A.** [ ] [96]

Jun 90. Capitol; (7") **WOULDN'T IT BE NICE. / I GET AROUND** [58] [ ]
(12"+=)(cd-s+=) – Medley of hits.

Jun 90. Capitol; (cd)(c)(d-lp) **SUMMER DREAMS** [2] [ ]

Aug 90. Capitol; (cd) **WILD HONEY / SMILEY SMILE** [ ] [ ]

Jun 91. Capitol; (7")(c-s) **DO IT AGAIN. / GOOD VIBRATIONS** [61] [ ]
(cd-s+=) – Wouldn't it be nice.

Jun 90. Capitol; (cd) **SURFIN' SAFARI / SURFIN' USA** [ ] [ ]
(contains extra tracks) (c-iss.Jul91)

Jun 90. Capitol; (cd) **SURFER GIRL / SHUTDOWN VOL.2** [ ] [ ]
(contains extra tracks) (c-iss.Jul91)

Jul 90. Capitol; (cd) **LITTLE DEUCE COUPE / ALL SUMMER LONG** [ ] [ ]
(contains extra tracks) (c-iss.Aug91)

Jul 90. Capitol; (cd) **FRIENDS / 20-20** [ ] [ ]
(contains extra tracks) (c-iss.Aug91)

Jul 90. Capitol; (cd) **PARTY / STACK O-TRACKS** [ ] [ ]
(contains extra tracks) (c-iss.Aug91)

Aug 90. Capitol; (cd) **TODAY / SUMMER DAYS (AND SUMMER NIGHTS!!)** [ ] [ ]
(contains extra tracks) (c-iss.Aug91)

Aug 90. Capitol; (cd) **BEACH BOYS' CONCERT (live) / LIVE IN LONDON (live)** *(contains extra tracks) (c-iss.Aug91)*

Jul 93. Capitol; (6xcd-box) **GOOD VIBRATIONS – THIRTY YEARS OF THE BEACH BOYS** [ ] [ ]

Also released albums with JAN & DEAN on flip side ORIGINAL HITS, etc.

May 70. Regal Starline; (lp)(c) **BUG-IN** [ ] [-]

Jul 71. Regal Starline; (lp)(c) **THE BEACH BOYS** [ ] [-]
(re-iss.Oct84 on 'Audio Fidelity')

Dec 80. Replay; (7") **SURFIN' SAFARI. / SURFIN' / SURFER GIRL** [ ] [-]

Jan 81. World Records; (7xlp-box) **THE CAPITOL YEARS** [ ] [-]

1983. Cambra; (d-c) **BEACH BOYS** [ ] [-]

Oct 83. E.M.I.; (lp)(c) **THE BEACH BOYS' RARITIES** [ ] [-]

Nov 84. Topline; (lp) **SURFER GIRL** (different) [ ] [-]

Oct 86. Meteor; (lp) **WIPE OUT** [ ] [-]

Jun 70. M.F.P.; (lp)(c) **THE BEACH BOYS** [ ] [-]

Oct 75. M.F.P./ US= Brother; (lp)(c) **GOOD VIBRATIONS – THE BEST OF BEACH BOYS** [ ] [25] Jul 75

Oct 86. M.F.P.; (lp)(c) **DO IT AGAIN** [ ] [-]

May 88. Rhino; (cd-s) **LIL' BIT OF GOLD: THE BEACH BOYS** [ ] [-]
– California girls / Help me Rhonda / Wouldn't it be nice / Good vibrations.

Jun 93. Fame; (cd)(c) **CRUISIN'** [ ] [-]

Jul 94. Success; (cd)(c) **BEACH PARTY (w / JAN & DEAN)** [ ] [-]

Nov 94. Capitol-M.F.P.; (cd)(c) **THE BEACH BOYS' CHRISTMAS ALBUM** [ ] [-]

Feb 95. B.A.M.; (cd) **PEARLS OF THE PAST** [ ] [-]

Jun 95. EMI; (cd)(c) **THE BEST OF THE BEACH BOYS** [26] [ ]

BRIAN WILSON

Capitol Capitol

Mar 66. (7") **CAROLINE NO. / SUMMER MEANS NEW LOVE** [ ] [32]

Warners Warners

May 87. (7") **LET'S GO TO HEAVEN IN MY CAR. / TOO MUCH SUGAR** [-] [ ]

Reprise Reprise

Jul 88. (lp)(c)(cd) **BRIAN WILSON** [ ] [54]
– Love and mercy / Walkin' the line / Melt away / Baby let your hair grow long / Little children / One of the boys / There's so many / Night time / Let it shine / Rio Grande / Meet me in my dreams tonight. *(re-iss.cd Dec95 as 'LOVE AND MERCY')*

Aug 88. (7") **LOVE AND MERCY. / HE COULDN'T GET HIS POOR OLD BODY TO MOVE** [ ] [ ]
(12"+=)(cd-s+=) One for the boys

Nov 88. (7") **NIGHT TIME. / ONE FOR THE BOYS** [ ] [ ]
(12"+=)(cd-s+=) Being with the one you love.

1989. (7") **MELT AWAY. / BEING WITH THE ONE YOU LOVE** [-] [ ]

— with musicians **JIM KELTNER** -drums / **JAMES HUTCHINSON** -bass / **BENMONT TENCH** -keyboards / **MARK GOLDENBERG + WADDY WACHTEL** -guitar / **DAVID McMURRAY** -sax, flute

M.C.A. M.C.A.

Sep 95. (cd)(c) **I JUST WASN'T MADE FOR THOSE TIMES** [59] [ ]
– Meant for you / This whole world / Caroline, no / Let the wind blow / Love and mercy / Do it again / The warmth of the sun / Wonderful / Still I dream of it / Melt away / 'Til I die.

— Late in 1995, BRIAN released 'ORANGE CRATE ART' with VAN DYKE PARKS

BRIAN WILSON and MIKE LOVE

Capitol Capitol

Sep 67. (7") **GETTIN' HUNGRY. / DEVOTED TO YOU** [ ] [ ]

MIKE LOVE

(first 3 releases as with CELEBRATION)

M.C.A. Pacific Arts

1977. (lp) **CELEBRATION** [ ] [ ]
– Gettin' hungry / Sailor / Lovestruck / She's just out to get you / I don't wanna know / Starbay / Go and get that girl / How's about a little bit / Song of creation / Country pie.

Apr 78. (7") **ALMOST SUMMER. / LOOKIN GOOD** [ ] [ ]
Jul 78. (7") **IT'S O.K. / ISLAND GIRL** [ ] [ ]

Epic Epic

Oct 81. (lp)(c) **LOOKING BACK WITH LOVE** [ ] [ ]
– Looking back with love / On and on and on / Running around the world / Over and over / Rockin' the man in the boat / Calendar girl / Be my baby / One good reason / Teach me tonight / Paradise found.

Creole not issued

Nov 83. (7")(12") **JINGLE BELL ROCK. / LET'S PARTY** [ ] [ ]

DENNIS WILSON

Stateside Brother

Dec 70. (7") **SOUND OF FREE. / RUMBO (with "RUMBO")** [ ] [ ]

Caribou Reprise

Sep 77. (lp)(c) **PACIFIC OCEAN BLUE** [ ] [96]
– Pacific Ocean blue / River song / What's wrong / Friday night / Moonshine / Dreamer / Thoughts of you / Farewell my friend / Rainbows / Time you and I / End of the show. *(re-iss.+cd.Jul91 on 'Epic')*

Sep 77. (7") **RIVER SONG. / FAREWELL MY FRIEND** [ ] [ ]

Elektra Elektra

1980. (lp)(c) **ONE OF THESE PEOPLE** [ ] [ ]

CARL WILSON

Caribou Caribou

Apr 81. (lp)(c) **CARL WILSON** [ ] [ ]
– Hold me tight / Bright lights / The right lane / Seems so long ago / What you gonna do about me / Hurry love / The grammy / Heaven.

Apr 81. (7") **HEAVEN. / THE RIGHT LANE** [ ] [ ]
Feb 83. (lp)(c) **YOUNGBLOOD** [ ] [ ]
– What more can I say / She's mine / Youngblood / Given you up / One more night alone / Rockin' all over the world / One of the times / What you do to me / Too early to tell / Time / If I could talk to love.

May 83. (7") **WHAT YOU DO TO ME. / TIME** [ ] [ ]

— BRUCE JOHNSTON also had his own solo career when he wasn't with BEACH BOYS. In '77 he made an album and 3 singles all in UK/US. That year also saw BLONDIE CHAPLIN releasing a UK/US album and single.

BEASTIE BOYS

Formed: Greenwich Village, New York, USA . . . 1981 by YAUCH and DIAMOND. They recruit HOROWITZ to replace 2 others, and after two US indie releases they sign 1984 to 'Def Jam' run by DJ scratcher RICK RUBIN. Early in 1987, they took the States & Britain by storm, after unleashing the ultimate youth anthem '(YOU GOTTA) FIGHT FOR YOUR RIGHT (TO PARTY)'. Sustained commercial impact for a few years, until buying public were finally sickened from over-the-top bad boy press & media attention. • **Style:** Started off playing hardcore, but by mid 80's incorporated white rap and hard rock/punk. A fusion lying somewhere between rappers RUN DMC and the anti-social SEX PISTOLS. • **Songwriters:** Although they released little cover versions, they sampled many LED ZEPPELIN songs. In 1992 they covered JIMMY JAMES (Jimi Hendrix) + TIME FOR LIVIN' (Stewart Frontline), and collaborated with NISHITA. • **Trivia:** ADAM HOROWITZ is the son of playwrite ISRAEL. Volkswagen car owners were up in arms when fans of the group tore by the thousands, the "VW" metal emblems which they wore round necks. HOROWITZ plays cameo role in TV serial 'The Equalizer' circa '88.

Recommended: LICENSED TO 'ILL (*8) / CHECK YOUR HEAD (*7) / ILL: COMMUNICATION (*9)

'MCA' ADAM YAUCH (b.15 Aug'67, Brooklyn, New York) – vocals / **'MIKE D' MIKE DIAMOND** (b.20 Nov'65, New York) – vocals / **'KING AD-ROCK' ADAM HOROWITZ** (b.31 Oct'66, Manhattan, New York) – vocals (ex-The YOUNG & THE USELESS) repl. JOHN BERRY and KATE SCHELLENBACH.

not issued Ratcage

Nov 82. (12"ep) **POLLY WOG STEW** [-] [ ]
– Riot fight / Transit cop / Holy snappers / Egg raid on mojo / Beastie Boys / Jimi / Ode to . . . / Michelle's farm.
(UK-iss.Apr88 +c-s)(re-iss.12"ep/c-ep/cd-ep Feb93)

Aug 83. (7") **COOKIE PUSS. / BEASTIE REVOLUTION** [ ] [ ]
(UK-iss.Jan85, re-iss.Jul87; cd-iss.Dec87)
(re-issues +=) – Bonus bater / Cookie dub / Censored. (re-iss.12"ep/c-ep/cd-ep Feb93)

added **RICK RUBIN** – scratcher DJ

Def Jam Def Jam

Oct 85. (7") **ROCK HARD. / ?** [-] [ ]
Jan 86. (7")(12") **SHE'S ON IT. / SLOW AND LOW** [ ] [ ]
May 86. (7") **HOLD IT, NOW HIT IT. / ('A'-acappella)** [ ] [ ]
(12"+=) – ('A'instrumental).
Sep 86. (7") **SHE'S ON IT. / SLOW AND LOW** [ ] [ ]
(12"+=) – Hold it, now hit it.
Nov 86. (7") **IT'S THE NEW STYLE. / PAUL REVERE** [ ] [ ]
(12"+=) – ('A'&'B'instrumentals).
(d12"++=) – Hold it, now hit it / Hold it, now hit it (Acapulco version) / Hold it, now hit it (instrumental).
Nov 86. (lp)(c)(cd) **LICENSED TO 'ILL** [7] [1]
– Rhymin and stealin' / The new style / She's crafty / Posse in effect / Slow ride / Girls / (You gotta) Fight for your right (to party) / No sleep till Brooklyn / Paul Revere / Hold it now, hit it / Brass monkey / Slow and low / Time to get ill. *(re-iss.Nov89 on 'Capitol') (re-iss.cd+c Jun94) (cd-iss.Jul95)*
Feb 87. (7") **(YOU GOTTA) FIGHT FOR YOUR RIGHT (TO PARTY). / TIME TO GET ILL** [11] [7] Dec 86
(12"+=) – No sleep till Brooklyn.
May 87. (7")(12")(7"sha-pic-d) **NO SLEEP TILL BROOKLYN. / POSSE IN EFFECT** [14] [ ]
Jul 87. (7")(12") **SHE'S ON IT. / SLOW AND LOW** [10] [ ]
Sep 87. (7")(7"sha-pic-d) **GIRLS. / SHE'S CRAFTY** [34] [ ]
(12"+=) – Rock hard.
Mar 88. (7") **BRASS MONKEY. / POSSE IN EFFECT** [-] [48]

no more **RICK RUBIN** as DJ

Capitol Capitol

Jul 89. (12"ep)(cd-ep) **LOVE AMERICAN STYLE** [ ] [36]
(*=+7"only) – Hey ladies *. / Shake your rump * / 33% God / Die yourself in '89 (just do it).
Jul 89. (lp)(c)(cd) **PAUL'S BOUTIQUE** [44] [14]
– To all the girls / Shake your rump / Johnny Ryall / Egg man / High plains drifter / The sound of science / 3-minute rule / Hey ladies / 5-piece chicken dinner / Looking down the barrel of a gun / Car thief / What comes around / Shadrach / Ask for Janice / B-boy bouillabaisse medley:- A year and a day – Hello Brooklyn – Dropping names – Lay it on me – Mike on the mic – A.W.O.L.
1989. (7") **SHADRACH. /** [-] [ ]

— Trio now also on instruments; MCA – bass / **AD ROCK** – keyboards / **MIKE D** – drums

Apr 92. (12"ep)(c-ep) **PASS THE MIC** [47] [ ]
– Pass the mic / Time for living / Drunken praying mantis style / Professor Booty.
(cd-ep+=) – Nethy's girl.
May 92. (cd)(c)(d-lp) **CHECK YOUR HEAD** [ ] [10]
– Jimmy James / Funky boss / Pass the mic / Gratitude / Lighten up / Finger lickin' good / So what'cha want / The biz vs. the Nuge (with TED NUGENT) / Time for livin' / Something's got to give / Blue nun / Stand together / Pow / The maestro / Groove Holmes / Live at PJ's / Mark on the bus / Professor Booty / In 3's / Mamaste. *(re-iss.Sep94)*
Jun 92. (12"white-ep) **FROZEN METAL HEAD EP** [55] [-]
– Jimmy James / The blue nun / Drinkin' wine.
(cd-ep+=) – Jimmy James (original).
Jun 92. (c-s) **SO WHAT'CHA WANT. / ?** [-] [93]

Grand Royale Capitol

May 94. (cd)(c)(d-lp) **ILL: COMMUNICATION** [10] [1]
– Sure shot / Tough guy / Freak freak / Bobo on the corner / Root down / Sabotage / Get it together / Sabrosa / The update / Futterman's rule / Alright hear this / Eugene's lament / Flute loop / Do it / Rick's theme / Heart attack man / The scoop / Shambala / Bodhisattva vow / Transitions.
Jun 94. (7"green)(c-s) **GET IT TOGETHER. / SABOTAGE / DOPE LITTLE SONG** [19] [ ]
(10") – (1st 2 tracks) / ('A'buck wild remix) / ('A'instrumental).
(cd-s) – (1st 2 tracks) / ('A'remix) / Resolution time.
Nov 94. (7"maroon) **SURE SHOT. / MULLET HEAD** [27] [ ]
(10"+=) – ('A'mix) / The vibes.
(cd-s+=) – Son of neck bone / (2-'A'remixes).
Jun 95. (m-cd)(m-c)(m-lp) **ROOT DOWN EP** (some live) [23] [50]
– Root down (free zone mix) / Root down / Root down (PP balloon mix) / Time to get ill / Heart attack man / The maestro / Sabrosa / Flute loop / Time for livin' / Something's got to give / So what'cha want.

. . . Jan – Jun '96 stop press . . .

Mar 96. (cd)(c) **THE IN SOUND FROM WAY OUT!** (instrumental) [45] [45]

– compilations –

Feb 94. Honey World/ US= Capitol; (cd)(c) **SOME OLD BULLSHIT**  46

– (compilation of 1st 2 EP's)

BEATLES

Formed: Liverpool, England . . . by LENNON and McCARTNEY as The QUARRYMEN in 1957 at school. In 1958 HARRISON joined but they split late '59. As The SILVER BEATLES, they reformed in Spring 1960, adding PETE BEST and STU SUTCLIFFE. They soon dropped SILVER, and employed manager Alan Williams, who got them local gigs. Later that year they toured Hamburg, West Germany but had to return because GEORGE was deported for being under 18. On 21st March 1961, they debutted at Liverpool's 'Cavern Club', which was followed by a return to Hamburg for 3 months. While there, they recorded for 'Polydor' records, backing cabaret-type pop singer TONY SHERIDAN. (These recordings were later released when at the peak of their popularity). Around mid-'61, STU stayed in Hamburg to get married and study art. He was to tragically die there of a brain haemorrhage on 10th April 1962. With PAUL now on bass, and BRIAN EPSTEIN as new manager, they laid down a demo for 'Decca', but this was disregarded by DICK ROWE who instead signed BRIAN POOLE & THE TREMELOES. (Dick soon had consolation when he contracted rivals-to-be The ROLLING STONES). Summer '62 brought sunshine when George Martin brought them to EMI's 'Parlophone' label, but during rehearsals BEST was fired and replaced by RINGO. By the end of 1962 their debut single 'LOVE ME DO' was in the UK Top 20. Their follow-up 'PLEASE PLEASE ME' hit No.2 and from then on with a few exceptions, they had a continuous run of UK No.1's, until their split in 1970. In the States, where they later signed to 'Capitol' late '63, they also became greatest pop/rock group of all time. They created history there on the 4th April, 1964 when they filled the Top 5 placings in singles chart. (1. – CAN'T BUY ME LOVE, 2. – TWIST AND SHOUT, 3. – SHE LOVES YOU, 4. – I WANT TO HOLD YOUR HAND, 5. – PLEASE PLEASE ME). Later that year they starred in their own film, A HARD DAYS NIGHT. Later filmography in the 60's included 'HELP!', 'HOW I WON THE WAR' (Lennon only from 1967), 'MAGICAL MYSTERY TOUR', 'YELLOW SUBMARINE' (cartoon), 'GET BACK' and 'LET IT BE'. On the 15th August 1965, they set an audience record (56,000) when they played outdoor at Shea Stadium, New York. The end of that year saw them being awarded the M.B.E. by the Queen. • **Style:** The fab four created new melodic pop sound and image, that progressed into more cultured rock. This was due to their introduction to guru MAHARISHI and the world of pot/dope. The resulting album REVOLVER in 1966, was first to highlight sitar and other Eastern instruments. On 1st June 1967, their masterpiece 'SGT. PEPPER' was born and was soon to become regarded by pop critics as the greatest album of all time. Tragedy struck, when manager BRIAN EPSTEIN died of a drug overdose 27th August 1967. To end 1968, their largely experimental double 'WHITE ALBUM' also became regarded by many as another classic. The following year saw them announce their imminent break-up, although two albums 'ABBEY ROAD' + 'LET IT BE' were released just prior to the split. • **Songwriters:** Mostly LENNON / McCARTNEY, but HARRISON penned a few from each album. RINGO also wrote a few. Covered TWIST AND SHOUT (Isley Brothers) / A TASTE OF HONEY / THERE'S A PLACE / MONEY (Barrett Strong) / ROLL OVER BEETHOVEN + ROCK AND ROLL MUSIC (Chuck Berry) / YOU REALLY GOT A HOLD OF ME (Miracles) / PLEASE MR.POSTMAN (Marvelettes) / KANSAS CITY (Wilbert Harrison) / WORDS OF LOVE (Diamonds) / CHAINS (Cookies) / BABY IT'S YOU (Shirelles) / etc. • **Trivia:** They form own label 'Apple' in 1968. Release own records and sign others including BADFINGER, MARY HOPKINS, JAMES TAYLOR, etc.

Recommended: SGT.PEPPER'S LONELY HEARTS CLUB BAND (*10) / REVOLVER (*9) / THE BEATLES 'White Album' (*10) / THE BEATLES 1967-70 (*10) / THE BEATLES 1962-66 (*10) / LIVE AT THE BBC (*8) / RUBBER SOUL (*9) / PLEASE PLEASE ME (*6) / WITH THE BEATLES (*7) / A HARD DAY'S NIGHT (*7) / BEATLES FOR SALE (*6) / HELP (*6) / ABBEY ROAD (*8) / LET IT BE (*7).

JOHN LENNON (b. JOHN WINSTON LENNON, 9 Oct'40) – vocals, rhythm guitar
PAUL McCARTNEY (b. JAMES PAUL McCARTNEY, 18 Jun'42) – vocals, guitar
GEORGE HARRISON (b.25 Feb'43) – vocals, lead guitar
STU SUTCLIFFE (b. STUART, 23 Jun'40, Edinburgh, Scotland) – bass
PETE BEST (b.1941) – drums

TONY SHERIDAN & The BEATLES

Polydor Decca

Jan 62. (7") **MY BONNIE. / THE SAINTS**  Apr 62

(UK re-iss.May63 hit 48 / UK re-Feb64 + US re-on 'MGM 26.(above 'A' was rel.Aug61 in Germany as TONY SHERIDAN & The BEAT BROTHERS)

—— Were a quartet at the time, STU stayed in Germany, died 10 Apr'62 of brain haemorrhage. McCARTNEY moved to bass and vocals.

BEATLES

(Aug62) **RINGO STARR** (b.RICHARD STARKEY, 7 Jul'40) – drums (ex-RORY STORM & THE HURRICANES)repl. BEST

Parlophone not issued

Oct 62. (7") **LOVE ME DO. / P.S. I LOVE YOU** [17] [-]
(UK re-iss.Oct82 hit 4. (UK re-iss.cd-s.1989, re-iss.Oct92, hit UK 53) (US-iss.Apr64 on 'Tollie' 1+10)

Parlophone Vee Jay

Jan 63. (7") **PLEASE PLEASE ME. / ASK ME WHY** [2] [ ]
(UK re-iss.Jan83 hit 29. (re-iss.cd-s.1989)

Mar 63. (lp) **PLEASE PLEASE ME** [1] [-]
– I saw her standing there / Misery / Anna (go to him) / Chains / Boys / Ask me why / Please please me / Love me do / P.S. I love you / Baby, it's you / Do you want to know a secret / A taste of honey / There's a place / Twist and shout. *(UK re-iss.Nov88 on 'EMI', cd-iss.Feb87 hit 32.)(c.!70's)*

Apr 63. (7") **FROM ME TO YOU. / THANK YOU GIRL** [1] [ ]
(UK re-iss.Apr83 hit 40. (re-iss.cd-s.1989)

Jul 63. (lp) **INTRODUCING . . . THE BEATLES** [-] [2] Feb 64
-(tracks nearly same as UK debut)

Aug 63. (7") **SHE LOVES YOU. / I'LL GET BY** [1] [ ]
(UK re-iss.Aug83 hit 45. (re-iss.cd-s.1989) (US-Jan64 on 'Swan' hit 1).

Nov 63. (lp) **WITH THE BEATLES** [1] [-]
-It won't be long / All I've got to do / All my loving / Don't bother me / Little child / Till there was you / Please Mr.Postman / Roll over Beethoven / Hold me tight / You really got a hold of me / I wanna be your man / Don't bother me / Little child / Roll over Beethoven / Devil in her heart / Not a second time / Money. *(re-iss.Nov88 on 'EMI') (cd-iss.Feb87 hit 40. (c-iss.70's)*

Nov 63. (7") **I WANT TO HOLD YOUR HAND. / THIS BOY** [1] [-]
(UK re-iss.Nov83 hit 62) (re-iss.cd-s.1989)

Jan 64. (7") **PLEASE PLEASE ME. / FROM ME TO YOU** [-] [3]

Parlophone Capitol

Jan 64. (7") **I WANT TO HOLD YOUR HAND. / I SAW HER STANDING THERE** [-] [1] [14]

Jan 64. (lp) **MEET THE BEATLES!** [-] [1]
– I want to hold your hand / I saw her standing there / This boy / It won't be long / All I've got to do / All my loving / Don't bother me / Little child / Till there was you / Hold me tight / I wanna be your man / Not a second time.

Mar 64. (7") **CAN'T BUY ME LOVE. / YOU CAN'T DO THAT** [1] [1]
(UK re-iss.Mar84 hit 53) (re-iss.cd-s.1989)

Apr 64. (lp) **THE BEATLES' SECOND ALBUM** [-] [1]
– Roll over Beethoven / Thank you girl / You really got a hold on me / Devil in her heart / Money / You can't do that / Long tall Ally / I call your name / Please Mr.Postman / I'll get you / She loves you.

Jul 64. (7") **A HARD DAY'S NIGHT. / THINGS WE SAID TODAY** [1] [ ]
(UK re-iss.Jul84 hit 52) (re-iss.cd-s.1989)

Jul 64. (7") **A HARD DAY'S NIGHT. / I SHOULD HAVE KNOWN BETTER** [-] [1] [53]

Jul 64. (lp) **A HARD DAY'S NIGHT (Soundtrack)** [1] [1]
– A hard day's night / I should have known better / If I fell / I'm happy just to dance with you / And I love her / Tell me why / Can't buy me love / Anytime at all / I'll cry instead / Things we said today / When I get home / You can't do that / I'll be back. *(UK re-lp+c.Jan71 hit 39. re-iss.Nov88 on 'EMI') (cd-iss.Feb87 hit 30.*

Aug 64. (7") **I'LL CRY INSTEAD. / I'M HAPPY JUST TO DANCE WITH YOU** [-] [25] [95]

Aug 64. (7") **AND I LOVE HER. / IF I FELL** [-] [12] [53]

Sep 64. (7") **MATCHBOX. / SLOW DOWN** [-] [17] [25]

Nov 64. (7") **I FEEL FINE. / SHE'S A WOMAN** [1] [1] [4]
(UK re-iss.Nov64 hit 65) (re-iss.cd-s.1989)

Dec 64. (lp) **BEATLES FOR SALE** [1] [-]
– No reply / I'm a loser / Baby's in black / Rock and roll music / I'll follow the sun / Mr.Moonlight / Kansas City / Eight days a week / Words of love / Honey don't / Every little thing / I don't want to spoil the party / What you're doing / Everybody's trying to be my baby. *(re-iss.Nov88 on 'EMI') (cd-iss.Feb87 hit 45. (c-iss.70's)*

Jan 65. (lp) **BEATLES '65** [-] [1]
– (track listing near as above)

Feb 65. (7") **EIGHT DAYS A WEEK. / I DON'T WANT TO SPOIL THE PARTY** [-] [1] [39]

Apr 65. (7") **TICKET TO RIDE. / YES IT IS** [1] [1]
(UK re-iss.Apr85 hit 70) (re-iss.cd-s.1989)

Jul 65. (lp) **BEATLES VI** [-] [1]
– Kansas City / Eight days a week / You like me too much / Bad boy / I don't want to spoil the party / Words of love / What you're doing / Yes it is / Dizzy Miss Lizzy / Tell me what you see / Every little thing.

Jul 65. (7") **HELP!. / I'M DOWN** [1] [1]
(UK re-iss.Jul85) (re-iss.cd-s.1989)

Jul 65. (lp) **HELP! (Soundtrack)** [1] [1] Sep 65
– Help! / The night before / You've got to hide your love away / I need you / Another girl / You're gonna lose that girl / Ticket to ride / Act naturally / It's only love / You like me too much / Tell me what you see / I've just seen a face / Yesterday / Dizzy Miss Lizzy. *(UK re-lp+c.Jul71 33. re-iss.Nov88 on 'EMI') (cd-iss.Apr87 hit UK 61)*

Sep 65. (7") **YESTERDAY. / ACT NATURALLY** [-] [1]

Dec 65. (7") **DAY TRIPPER. / WE CAN WORK IT OUT** [1] [5] [1]
(UK re-iss.Dec85) (re-iss.cd-s.1989)

Dec 65. (lp) **RUBBER SOUL** [1] [1]
– Drive my car / Norwegian wood (this bird has flown) / You won't see me / Nowhere man / Think for yourself / The word / Michelle / What goes on? / Girl / I'm looking through you / In my life / Wait / If I needed someone / Run for your life. *(UK re-iss.Nov88 on 'EMI') (cd-iss.Apr87, hit UK 60) (c-iss.70's)*

Feb 66. (7") **NOWHERE MAN. / WHAT GOES ON** [-] [3] [81]

Jun 66. (7") **PAPERBACK WRITER. / RAIN** [1] [1] [23]
(UK re-iss.Jun86) (re-iss.cd-s.1989)

Aug 66. (7") **YELLOW SUBMARINE. / ELEANOR RIGBY** [1] [2] [11]
(UK re-iss.Aug86 hit 63) (re-iss.cd-s.1989)

Aug 66. (lp) **REVOLVER** [1] [1]
– Taxman / I love you to / I want to tell you / Eleanor Rigby / Here, there and everywhere / Good day sunshine / For no one / Got to get you into my life / I'm only sleeping / She said she said / And your bird can sing / Doctor Robert / Tomorrow never knows / Yellow submarine. *(UK re-iss.Nov88 on 'EMI') (cd-iss.Apr87, hit UK 55) (c-iss.70's)*

Feb 67. (7") **PENNY LANE. / STRAWBERRY FIELDS FOREVER** [2] [1] [8]
(UK re-iss.Feb87 hit 65) (re-iss.cd-s.1989)

Jun 67. (lp) **SGT. PEPPER'S LONELY HEARTS CLUB BAND** [1] [1]
– Sgt.Pepper's lonely hearts club band / With a little help from my friends / Lucy in the sky with diamonds / Getting better / Fixing a hole / She's leaving home / Being for the benefit of Mr.Kite / Within you without you / When I'm sixty-four / Lovely Rita / Good morning, good morning / Sgt.Pepper's lonely hearts club band (reprise) / A day in the life. *(re-iss.Nov'88 on 'EMI') (cd-iss.Jun87, hit UK 3) (re-iss.Jun92 hit UK No.6) (pic-lp.1979) (c-iss.70's)*

Jul 67. (7") **ALL YOU NEED IS LOVE. / BABY YOU'RE A RICH MAN** [1] [1] [34]
(UK re-iss.Jul87 hit 47) (re-iss.cd-s.1989)

Nov 67. (7") **HELLO GOODBYE. / I AM THE WALRUS** [1] [1] [56]
(UK re-iss.Nov87 hit 63) (re-iss.cd-s.1989)

Dec 67. (d7"ep) **MAGICAL MYSTERY TOUR** [2] [-]
– Magical mystery tour / Your mother should know / Flying / Fool on the hill / Blue Jay way / I am the walrus.

Dec 67. (lp) **MAGICAL MYSTERY TOUR (Soundtrack)** [31] [1]
– (above UK-ep, plus 1967 singles) *(UK-iss.Oct76, cd-iss.Sep87, hit UK 52)*

Mar 68. (7") **LADY MADONNA. / THE INNER LIGHT** [1] [4] [96]
(UK re-iss.Mar88 hit 67) (re-iss.cd-s.1989)

Apple Apple

Aug 68. (7") **HEY JUDE. / REVOLUTION** [1] [1] [12]
(UK re-iss.Aug88 hit 52) (re-iss.cd-s.1989)

Nov 68. (d-lp) **THE BEATLES (White Album)** [1] [1]
– Back in the U.S.S.R / Dear Prudence / Glass onion / Ob-la-di-ob-la-da / Wild honey pie / The continuing story of Bungalow Bill / While my guitar gently weeps / Happiness is a warm gun / Martha my dear / I'm so tired / Blackbird / Piggies / Rocky raccoon / Don't pass me by / Why don't we do it in the road / I will / Julia / Birthday / Yer blues / Mother nature's son / Everybody's got something to hide except me and my monkey / Sexy Sadie / Long long long / Revolution 1 / Honey pie / Savoy truffle / Cry baby cry / Revolution 9 / Good night. *(re-white-lp.Sep78) (cd-iss.Aug87 hit 18. (re-iss.Nov88 on 'EMI')*

Jan 69. (lp) **YELLOW SUBMARINE (Soundtrack)** [4] [2]
– Yellow submarine / Only a northern song / All together now / Hey bulldog / It's all too much / All you need is love / Pepperland / Sea of time / Sea of holes / Sea of monsters / March of the Meanies / Pepperland laid waste / Yellow submarine in Pepperland. (with GEORGE MARTIN ORCHESTRA) *(UK re-iss.+cd.Aug87, hit UK 60) (re-iss.Nov88 on 'EMI')*

Apr 69. (7") **GET BACK. / DON'T LET ME DOWN** [1] [1] [35]

—— (above credits **BILLY PRESTON** ;on organ) (UK re-iss.Apr89 hit 74) (re-iss.cd-s.1989)

May 69. (7") **THE BALLAD OF JOHN AND YOKO. / OLD BROWN SHOE** [1] [8]
(UK re-iss.May89) (re-iss.cd-s.1989)

Sep 69. (lp) **ABBEY ROAD** 1 1
– Come together / Maxwell's silver hammer / Something / Oh darling / Octopus's garden / I want you (she's so heavy) / Here comes the sun / Because / You never gave me your money / Sun king / Mean Mr.Mustard / Polythene Pam / She came in through the bathroom window / Golden slumbers / Carry that weight / The end / Her majesty. *(UK re-iss.Oct87 hit 30. (re-iss.Nov88 on 'EMI')*
Oct 69. (7") **SOMETHING. / COME TOGETHER** 4 3 / 1
(UK re-iss.Oct89) (re-iss.cd-s.1989)
Mar 70. (7") **LET IT BE. / YOU KNOW MY NAME (LOOK UP MY NUMBER)** 2 1
(UK re-iss.Mar90) (re-iss.cd-s.1989)
May 70. (lp)(c) **LET IT BE** 1 1
– Two of us / Dig a pony / Across the universe / I me mine / Dig it / Let it be / Maggie Mae / I've got a feeling / One after 909 / The long and winding road / For you blue / Get back. *(re-iss.Nov88 on 'EMI') (cd-iss.Oct87 hit 50.)*
May 70. (7") **THE LONG AND WINDING ROAD. / FOR YOU BLUE** - 1
—— Officially disbanded April 1970. All 4 had released, or were due to release, own albums. See **Paul McCARTNEY ⇒ , John LENNON ⇒ , George HARRISON ⇒ , Ringo STARR ⇒ .**

– compilations, others, etc. –

(TONY SHERIDAN & THE BEATLES)
Jan 64. Polydor; (7") **SWEET GEORGIA BROWN. / NOBODY'S CHILD** -
Mar 64. M.G.M.; (7") **WHY. / CRY FOR A SHADOW** - 88
May 64. Polydor; (7") **AIN'T SHE SWEET. / IF YOU LOVE ME BABY** 29 -
Jun 64. Polydor; (lp) **THE BEATLES FIRST** -
(re-iss.Jun71 as THE EARLY YEARS on 'Contour')(re-iss. as 'THE FIRST ALBUM' cd+c May93 on 'Spectrum', credited to TONY SHERIDAN & THE BEATLES)
Jun 64. Atco; (7") **SWEET GEORGIA BROWN. / TAKE OUT SOME INSURANCE ON ME BABY** -
Jul 64. M.G.M.; (7") **AIN'T SHE SWEET. / NOBODY'S CHILD** - 19
(BEATLES)
Mar 64. Tollie; (7") **TWIST AND SHOUT. / THERE'S A PLACE** - 2 / 74
Apr 64. Vee Jay; (7") **DO YOU WANT TO KNOW A SECRET. / THANK YOU GIRL** - 2 / 35
May 64. Swan; (7") **SIE LIEBT DICH. / I'LL GET YOU** - 97
Jul 63. Parlophone; (7"ep) **TWIST AND SHOUT** 2 -
– Twist and shout / A taste of honey / Do you want to know a secret / There's a place.
Sep 63. Parlophone; (7"ep) **THE BEATLES HITS** 14 -
– From me to you / Thank you girl / Please please me / Love me do.
Nov 63. Parlophone; (7"ep) **THE BEATLES (No.1)** 19 -
– I saw her standing there / Misery / Chains / Anna (go to him).
Feb 64. Parlophone; (7"ep) **ALL MY LOVING** 12 -
– All my loving / Ask me why / Money / P.S. I love you.
Jun 64. Parlophone; (7"ep) **LONG TALL SALLY** 14 -
– Long tall Sally / I call your name / Slow down / Matchbox.
Jun 64. Capitol; (7"ep) **FOUR BY THE BEATLES** - 92
– All my loving / This boy / Roll over Beethoven / Please Mr.Postman.
Aug 64. Capitol; (lp) **SOMETHING NEW** - 2
Nov 64. Parlophone; (7"ep) **EXTRACTS FROM THE FILM 'A HARD DAY'S NIGHT'** 34 -
– I should have known better / If I fell / Tell me why / And I love her.
Dec 64. Parlophone; (7"ep) **EXTRACTS FROM THE FILM 'A HARD DAY'S NIGHT' 2** -
– Anytime at all / I'll cry instead / Things we said today / When I get home.
Dec 64. Capitol; (lp) **THE BEATLES' STORY (narrative)** - 7
Feb 65. Capitol; (7"ep) **4-BY THE BEATLES** -
– Honey don't / I'm a loser / Mr.Moonlight / Everybody's trying to be my baby.
Apr 65. Parlophone; (7"ep) **BEATLES FOR SALE** -
– No reply / I'm a loser / Rock and roll music / Eight days a week.
Jun 65. Parlophone; (7"ep) **BEATLES FOR SALE No.2** -
– I'll follow the sun / Baby's in black / Words of love / I don't want to spoil the party.
Dec 65. Parlophone; (7"ep) **THE BEATLES MILLION SELLERS** -
– She loves you / Can't buy me love / I feel fine / I want to hold your hand.
Mar 66. Parlophone; (7"ep) **YESTERDAY** -
– Yesterday / Act naturally / You like me too much / It's only love.
Jul 66. Capitol; (lp) **YESTERDAY . . . AND TODAY** - 1
Dec 66. Parlophone; (lp) **A COLLECTION OF BEATLES OLDIES** 7 -
(re-iss.+c.Oct83 on 'Fame')
Jul 67. Parlophone; (7"ep) **NOWHERE MAN** -
– Nowhere man / Drive my car / Michelle / You won't see me.
Mar 76. Parlophone; (7") **YESTERDAY. / I SHOULD HAVE KNOWN BETTER** 8 -
Below on 'Parlophone' UK/ 'Capitol' US unless otherwise mentioned.
Jun 76. (lp)(c) **ROCK AND ROLL MUSIC** 11 2
(UK re-iss.Nov80 as . . . VOL.1 / . . . VOL.2 both on 'MfP')
Jun 76. (7") **GOT TO GET YOU INTO MY LIFE. / HELTER SKELTER** - 7
Jul 76. (7") **BACK IN THE U.S.S.R. / TWIST AND SHOUT** 19 -
Apr 77. (d-lp)(d-c) **LIVE AT THE STAR CLUB, HAMBURG, GERMANY 1962**
May 77. (lp)(c) **THE BEATLES AT THE HOLLYWOOD BOWL (live)** 1 2
(UK re-iss.Sep84 on 'MfP')
Dec 77. (d-lp)(d-c) **LOVE SONGS** 7 24
1977. (7") **OB-LA-DI, OB-LA-DA. / JULIA** -
Sep 78. (7") **SGT.PEPPER'S LONELY HEARTS CLUB BAND-WITH A LITTLE HELP FROM MY FRIENDS. / A DAY IN THE LIFE** 63 71
Nov 78. (14xlp-box) **THE BEATLES COLLECTION**
– (all original albums boxed)
Oct 79. (lp)(c) **RARITIES** 71 21 Apr 80
Nov 80. (lp)(c) **BEATLES BALLADS** 17
Dec 81. (14x7"ep's) **THE BEATLES EP COLLECTION**
– (all ep's above plus new SHE'S A WOMAN)
– She's a woman / Baby you're a rich man / This boy / The inner light.
Apr 82. (lp)(c) **REEL MUSIC** 19
May 82. (7") **BEATLES MOVIE MEDLEY./ I'M HAPY UST TO DANCE WITH YOU** 10 12
– ('A'medley); Magical Mystery Tour – All You Need Is Love – You've Got To Hide Your Love Away – I Should Have Known Better – A Hard Day's Night – Ticket To Ride – Get Back.
Oct 82. (d-lp)(d-c) **20 GREATEST HITS** 10 50
Oct 88. (lp)(c)(cd-box-set) **THE ULTIMATE BOX SET**
Jun 92. (cd-ep x14-box) **COMPACT DISC EP'S** -
Mar 70. Apple; (lp)(c) **HEY JUDE** - 2
(UK-iss.May79 on 'Parlophone')
Apr 73. Apple; (d-lp)(d-c) **THE BEATLES 1962-1966** 3 3
– Love me do / Please please me / She loves you / From me to you / She loves you / I want to hold your hand / All my loving / Can't buy me love / A hard day's night / And I love her / Eight days a week / I feel fine / Ticket to ride / Yesterday / Help! / You've got to hide your love away / We can work it out / Day tripper / Drive my car / Norwegian wood (this bird has flown) / Nowhere man / Michelle / In my life / Girl / Paperback writer / Eleanor Rigby / Yellow submarine. *(red-lp's iss.Sep78) (d-cd-iss.Jul91) (re-iss.d-cd Sep93 on 'Apple-Parlophone', hit UK No.3)*
(re-iss.red vinyl Feb94)
Apr 73. Apple; (d-lp)(d-c) **THE BEATLES 1967-1970** 2 1
– Strawberry fields forever / Penny lane / Sgt. Pepper's lonely hearts club band / With a little help from my friends / Lucy in the sky with diamonds / A day in the life / All you need is love / I am the Walrus / Hello, goodbye / The fool on the hill / Magical mystery tour / Lady Madonna / Hey Jude / Revolution / Back in the U.S.S.R / While my guitar gently weeps / Ob-la-di, ob-la-da / Get back / Don't let me down / The ballad of John and Yoko / Old brown shoe / Here comes the sun / Come together / Something / Octopus's Garden / Let it be / Across the universe / The long and winding road. *(blue-lp's iss.Sep78) (d-cd-iss.Jul91) (re-iss.d-cd Sep93 on 'Apple-Parlophone', hit UK No.4) (re-iss.blue vinyl Feb94)*
Feb 88. E.M.I./ US= Capitol; (d-lp)(c)(cd) **PAST MASTERS VOL.1** 49
Feb 88. E.M.I./ US= Capitol; (d-lp)(c)(cd) **PAST MASTERS VOL.2** 46
Aug 91. E.M.I.; (c-s x all) **THE SINGLES** -
– (all 7"singles boxed)
Aug 76. Polydor; (d-lp)(c) **THE BEATLES TAPES (interviews)** 45 -
Jul 81. Phoenix; (lp)(c) **EARLY MUSIC VOL.1** -
Jul 81. Phoenix; (lp)(c) **EARLY MUSIC VOL.2** -
Feb 82. Phoenix; (lp)(c) **RARE BEATLES** -
Aug 81. A.F.E.; (d-lp)(c) **HISTORIC BEATLES** -
Sep 82. A.F.E.; (lp) **THE COMPLETE SILVER BEATLES** -
Sep 83. A.F.E.; (lp) **COMETS** -
Jul 82. Charly; (10"lp) **THE SAVAGE YOUNG BEATLES** -
(re-iss.as THE BEATLES FEATURING TONY SHERIDAN, HAMBURG on 'Topline, cd-iss. Feb 93 on 'Charly')
Nov 83. Berkeley; (lp) **AUDITION TAPES** -
Dec 83. Breakaway; (lp) **HAMBURG TAPES VOL.1** -
Dec 83. Breakaway; (lp) **HAMBURG TAPES VOL.2** -
Dec 83. Breakaway; (lp) **HAMBURG TAPES VOL.3** -
Apr 86. Showcase; (lp)(c) **LIVE BEATLES (live)** -
Oct 87. Topline; (lp)(c)(cd) **THE DECCA SESSIONS (1/1/62)** -
Jun 92. Columbia; (cd) **ROCKIN' AT THE STAR-CLUB (live)** -
Dec 94. Apple; (d-cd)(d-c)(d-lp) **LIVE AT THE BBC (live)** 1 3
– Beatle greetings / From us to you / Riding on a bus / I got a woman / Too much monkey business / Keep your hands off my baby / I'll be on my way / Young blood / A shot of rhythm and blues / Sure to fall (in love with you) / Some other guy / Thank you girl / Sha la la la la! / Baby it's you / That's all right (mama) / Carol / Soldier of love / A little rhyme / Clarabella / I'm gonna sit right down and cry (over you) / Crying, waiting, hoping / Dear Wack! / You really got a hold on me / To know her is to love her / A taste of honey / Long tall Sally / I saw her standing there / The honeymoon song / Johnny B Goode / Memphis, Tennessee / Lucille / Can't buy me love / From Fluff to you / Till there was you // Crinsk Dee

night / A hard day's night / Have a banana! / I wanna be your man / Just a rumour / Roll over Beethoven / All my loving / Things we said today / She's a woman / Sweet little sixteen / 1882! / Lonesome tears in my eyes / Nothin' shakin' / The hippy hippy shake / Glad all over / I just don't understand / So how come (no one loves me) / I feel fine / I'm a loser / Everybody's trying to be my baby / Rock and roll music / Ticket to ride / Dizzy Miss Lizzy / Medley: Kansas City – Hey! hey! hey! hey! / Set fire to that lot! / Matchbox / I forgot to remember to forget / Love these Goon shows! / I got to find my baby / Ooh! my soul / Ooh! my arms / Don't ever change / Slow down / Honey don't / Love me do.

Mar 95. Apple; (cd-ep) **BABY IT'S YOU / I'LL FOLLOW THE SUN / DEVIL IN HER HEART / BOYS** [7] [67]

Nov 95. Apple; (d-cd)(d-c)(t-lp) **ANTHOLOGY 1** [2] [1]
– Free as a bird / Speech (by JOHN LENNON) / That'll be the day / In spite of all the danger / Sometimes I'd borrow (speech by PAUL McCARTNEY) / Hallelujah I love her so / You'll be mine / Cayenne / First of all (speech by PAUL) / My Bonnie (w/ TONY SHERIDAN) / Ain't she sweet / Cry for a shadow / Brian was a beautful guy (speech by JOHN) / Secured them an audition (speech by BRIAN EPSTEIN) / Searchin' / Three cool cats / The Sheik of Araby / Like dreamers do / Hello little girl / Well, the recording test (speech by BRIAN) / Besame mucho / Love me do / How do you do it? / Please please me / One after 909 (sequence) / One after 909 (complete) / Lend me your comb / I'll get you / We were performers (speech by JOHN) / I saw her standing there / From me to you / Money (that's what I want) / You really got a hold on me / Roll over Beethoven / She loves you / Till there was you (music man) / Twist and shout / This boy / I want to hold your hand / Boys, what I was thinking (speech by The BEATLES and MORECAMBE & WISE) / Moonlightbay (w/ MORECAMBE & WISE) / Can't buy me love / All my loving / You can't do that / And I love her / A hard day's night / I wanna be your man / Long tall Sally / Boys / Shout / I'll be back (take 2) / I'll be back (take 3) / You know what to do / No reply (demo) / Mr.Moonlight / Leave my kitten alone / No reply / Eight days a week (sequence) / Eight days a week (complete) / Kansas City – hey, hey, hey.

— (below single was recently re-recorded from JOHN LENNON's 1977 cut)

Dec 95. Apple; (7")(c-s) **FREE AS A BIRD. / CHRISTMAS TIME (IS HERE AGAIN)** [2] [6]
(cd-s+=) – I saw her standing there (take 9) / This boy (take 13).

. . . Jan – Jun '96 stop press . . .

Mar 96. (single) **REAL LOVE** [4] [11]
Mar 96. (d-cd)(d-c)(t-lp) **ANTHOLOGY 2** (compilation) [1] [2]

BE-BOP DELUXE (see under ⇒ NELSON, Bill)

BECK

Born: 1971, Los Angeles, USA. He moved to New York in the late 80's and was initially signed to indie 'Bongload', until David 'Geffen' came along in '93. He had released an album (ONE FOOT IN THE GRAVE) in the States with CALVIN JOHNSON of The BEAT HAPPENING. Early the next year 'LOSER' cracked the US Top 20 and paved the way for debut album 'MELLOW GOLD'. • **Style:** Laid back controversial soft-grunge rock experimentalist, with one-man band explorations into other territories (samplers /synths /psychedelia). • **Songwriters:** BECK writes some with KARL STEPHENSON. 'LOSER' used a sample of DR.JOHN's 'I Walk On Guilded Splinters'. • **Trivia:** Also featured a track 'BOGUSFLOW' on 'Geffen Rarities Vol.1'.

Recommended: MELLOW GOLD (*7) / ODELAY (*7)

BECK – vocals, acoustic guitar with guests **RACHEL HADEN** – drums, vocals / **ANNA WARONKER** – bass, vocals / **PETRA HADEN** – violin, vocals / **MIKE BOITO** – organ / **DAVID HARTE** – drums / **ROB ZABRECKY** – bass

not issued / Bongload

1993. (12") **LOSER. /** [-] [ ]
1993. (7") **STEVE THREW UP. /** [-] [ ]
(both above UK-iss.Jan95)

not issued / Fingerpaint

1993. (cd) **A WESTERN HARVEST FIELD BY MOONLIGHT** [-] [ ]

Geffen / Geffen

Feb 94. (7")(c-s) **LOSER. / ALCOHOL / FUME** [15] [10]
(cd-s) – ('A'side) / Totally confused / Corvette bumper / MTV makes me want to smoke crack.

Mar 94. (cd)(c) **MELLOW GOLD** [41] [13]
– Loser / Pay no mind (snoozer) / Fuckin with my head (mountain dew rock) / Whiskeyclone, Hotel City 1997 / Soul suckin jerk / Truckdrivin neighbors downstairs (yellow sweat) / Sweet sunshine / Beercan / Steal my body home / Nitemare hippy girl / Motherfuker / Blackhole. (hidden track cd+=) – Analog odyssey.

May 94. (7")(c-s) **PAY NO MIND (SNOOZER). / SPECIAL PEOPLE** [ ] [ ]
(12"+=)(cd-s+=) – Trouble all my days / Supergold (sunchild).

not issued / Flipside

1994. (cd) **STEREOPATHETIC SOUL MANURE** [-] [ ]
–
(UK-iss.Dec95)

K / K

Nov 95. (cd) **ONE FOOT IN THE GRAVE** [ ] [ ]
-

. . . Jan – Jun '96 stop press . . .

BECK!

Jun 96. (single) **WHERE IT'S AT** [35] [75]
Jun 96. (cd)(c)(lp) **ODELAY** [18] [16]

Jeff BECK

Born: 24 Jun'44, London, England. He began solo career early 1967 after replacing the great ERIC CLAPTON in The YARDBIRDS (Mar65). His first 3 singles all made the UK Top 30, and he soon formed own credited band. It featured ROD STEWART, and gave him and BECK first inroads into US charts with 1968 lp 'TRUTH'. • **Style:** Mickie Most, his producer, was responsible for early use of pop material. All this was disregarded when BECK formed his own heavy rock group in the late 60's. With ROD STEWART taking most vocal chores, they were heavy fused with blues. Veered disappointingly into jazz-rock market on 1975's 'BLOW BY BLOW'. • **Songwriters:** BECK with covers being; HI HO SILVER LINING (Scott English & Larry Weiss) / TALLYMAN (Graham Gouldman) / ALL SHOOK UP + JAILHOUSE ROCK (Leiber – Stoller) / I'VE BEEN DRINKIN' (D.Tauber & J.Mercer) / SHAPES OF THINGS (Yardbirds) / I AIN'T SUPERSTITIOUS (Willie Dixon) / MORNING DEW (Tim Rose) / SUPERSTITIOUS + CAUSE WE'VE ENDED AS LOVERS (Stevie Wonder) / GREENSLEEVES (trad.) / OL' MAN RIVER ('Showboat' musical) / GOODBYE PORK PIE HAT (Charlie Mingus) / SHE'S A WOMAN (Beatles) / STAR CYCLE (Jan Hammer) / WILD THING (Troggs) / etc. • **Trivia:** Played guitar on 1990 JON BON JOVI album BLAZE OF GLORY. His song 'STAR CYCLE' (written by band members Hymas & Philips), became theme tune for 'The Tube'.

Recommended: ROUGH AND READY (*7) / THE BEST OF BECKOLOGY (*6)

JEFF BECK (solo) – vocals, lead guitar (ex-YARDBIRDS) with **JET HARRIS** – bass (ex-SHADOWS) / **VIV PRINCE** – drums (ex-PRETTY THINGS)

Columbia / Epic

Mar 67. (7") **HI HO SILVER LINING. / BECK'S BOLERO** [14] [ ]

— **RAY COOK** – drums repl. PRINCE

Jul 67. (7") **TALLYMAN. / ROCK MY PLIMSOUL** [30] [ ]
Feb 68. (7") **LOVE IS BLUE. / I'VE BEEN DRINKING** [23] [ ]

JEFF BECK GROUP

with **ROD STEWART** – vocals (also a solo artist, who sang on BECK's last 'B'side) / **RON WOOD** – bass (ex BIRDS) / **MICKY WALLER** (b. 6 Sep'44) – drums / **NICKY HOPKINS** – keyboards

Aug 68. (lp) **TRUTH** [ ] [15]
– Shapes of things / Let me love you / Morning dew / You shook me / Ol' man river / Greensleeves / Rock my plimsoul / Beck's bolero / Blues de luxe / I ain't superstitious. *(re-iss.1985) (re-iss.Jun86 on 'Fame')*

— **TONY NEWMAN** – drums repl. WALLER

— (mid'69) The JEFF BECK GROUP teamed up with ⇒ DONOVAN, on their joint hit GOO GOO BARABAJAGAL (LOVE IS HOT). (see ⇒ DONOVAN)

Jul 69. (lp) **BECK-OLA** [39] [15]
-All shook up / Spanish boots / Girl from Mill Valley / Jailhouse rock / Plynth (water down the drain) / The hangman's knee / Rice pudding. *(re-iss.+c Jul85)*

Sep 69. (7") **PLYNTH (WATER DOWN THE DRAIN). / HANGMAN'S KNEE** [ ] [ ]

— Split (Sep69) when ROD STEWART and RON WOOD joined The FACES.

JEFF BECK GROUP reformed (Apr71) with **JEFF BECK** – guitar (only) plus **BOBBY TENCH** – vocals / **MAX MIDDLETON** – keyboards / **CLIVE CHAPMAN** – bass / **COZY POWELL** – drums (ex-BIG BERTHA, ex-ACE KEFFORD STAND, ex-SORCERORS)

Epic / Epic

Oct 71. (lp)(c) **ROUGH AND READY** [ ] [46]
– Got the feeling / Situation / Short business / Max's tune / I've been used / New ways – Train train / Jody. *(re-iss.Mar81 + Aug84) (quad-lp 1974)*

Jan 72. (7") **GOT THE FEELING. / SITUATION** [ ] [ ]

Jul 72. (lp)(c) **THE JEFF BECK GROUP** [ ] [19] May 72
– Ice cream cakes / Glad all over / I'll be staying here with you / Sugar cane / I can't give back the love I feel for you / Going down / I got to have a song / Highways / Definitely maybe. *(quad-lp 1974)*

— Broke-up when COZY POWELL went solo & joined BEDLAM. Later to RAIN-

BOW, etc. TENCH joined STREETWALKERS then VAN MORRISON. **JEFF** formed supergroup

BECK, BOGERT & APPICE

with **TIM BOGERT** – bass, vocals / **CARMINE APPICE** – drums (both ex-VANILLA FUDGE, etc.) plus **DUANE HITCHINS** – keyboards / **JIMMY GREENSPOON** – piano / **DANNY HUTTON** – vox

Mar 73. (7") **BLACK CAT MOAN. / LIVIN' ALONE**

Apr 73. (lp)(c) **BECK, BOGERT & APPICE** 28 12
– Black cat moan / Lady / Oh to love you / Superstition / Sweet sweet surrender / Why should I care / Love myself with you / Livin' alone / I'm so proud. *(re-iss.Sep84) (re-iss.+cd.Nov89 on 'Essential') (quad-lp 1974)*

This trio, also released widely available (JAP-import Nov74 d-lp) LIVE IN JAPAN

JEFF BECK

group reformed as instrumental line-up, **BECK + MIDDLETON / PHILIP CHEN** – bass / **RICHARD BAILEY** – drums.

Mar 75. (lp)(c) **BLOW BY BLOW** 4
– You know what I mean / She's a woman / Constipated duck / Air blower / Scatterbrain / Cause we've ended as lovers / Thelonius / Freeway jam / Diamond dust. *(re-iss.Sep83) (re-iss.May94) (re-iss.cd Nov95)*

May 75. (7") **SHE'S A WOMAN. / IT DOESN'T REALLY MATTER**

Jul 75. (7") **CONSTIPATED DUCK. / YOU KNOW WHAT I MEAN** -

—— **JAN HAMMER** (b.1950, Prague, Czechoslavakia) – drums, synthesizer / **MICHAEL NARADA WALDEN** – keyboards, drums (both ex-MAHAVISHNU ORCHESTRA) / **WILBUR BASCOMBE** – bass (all 3 replaced CHEN)

Jul 76. (lp)(c) **WIRED** 38 16 Jun 76
– Play with me / Goodbye pork pie hat / Sophie / Led boots / Head for backstage pass / Blue wind / Love is green / Come dancing. *(re-iss.Mar82) (cd-iss.1988)*

Aug 76. (7") **COME DANCING. / HEAD FOR BACKSTAGE PASS** -

JEFF BECK with The JAN HAMMER GROUP

(BECK, HAMMER)plus **TONY SMITH** – drums / **FERNANDO SAUNDERS** – bass / **STEVE KINDLER** – violin, synth.

Mar 77. (lp)(c) **LIVE (live)** 23
– Freeway jam / Earth (still our only home) / She's a woman / Full Moon boogie / Darkness / Earth in search of a sun / Scatterbrain / Blue wind. *(re-iss.Jun85)*

JEFF BECK

with **TONY HYMAS** – keys / **MO FOSTER** – bass / **SIMON PHILLIPS** – drums

Jul 80. (lp)(c) **THERE AND BACK** 38 21
– Star cycle / Too much to lose / You never know / The pump / El Becko / The golden road / Space boogie / The final peace. *(re-iss.Aug84)*

Jul 80. (7") **THE FINAL PEACE. / SPACE BOOGIE** -

Aug 80. (7") **THE FINAL PEACE. / TOO MUCH TO LOSE** -

Feb 81. (d7") **THE FINAL PEACE. / SCATTERBRAIN/ / TOO MUCH TO LOSE. / LED BOOTS**

—— Retired from studio for half a decade, before returning 1985 with **HAMMER, APPICE, HYMAS** and **JIMMY HALL** – vocals

1985. (7") **GET US ALL IN THE END. / YOU KNOW WE KNOW** -

Jun 85. (7") **PEOPLE GET READY** (as"**JEFF BECK with ROD STEWART**) **. / BACK ON THE STREET** 48
(12"+=) – You know we know. *(re-iss.Feb92, hit UK No.49)*

Aug 85. (lp)(c) **FLASH** 83 39
– Ambitious / Gets us all in the end / Escape / People get ready / Stop, look and listen / Get workin' / Ecstasy / Night after night / You know, we know. *(re-iss.Jan89) (re-iss.cd Mar94 on 'Sony')*

Sep 85. (7") **GETS US ALL IN THE END. / YOU KNOW WE KNOW** -

Sep 85. (7") **STOP, LOOK AND LISTEN. / YOU KNOW WE KNOW** -
(12"+=) – ('A'remix).

Mar 86. (7")(12") **AMBITIOUS. / ESCAPE**

Jul 86. (7") **WILD THING. / GETS US ALL IN THE END**
(12"+=) – Nighthawk.

In 1987, JEFF BECK went to session with MICK JAGGER on his 2nd album.

JEFF BECK'S GUITAR SHOP

with TERRY BOZZIO and TONY HYMAS + still on 'Epic'.

Oct 89. (lp)(c)(cd) **JEFF BECK'S GUITAR SHOP** 49
– Guitar shop / Savoy / Behind the veil / Big block / Where were you / Stand on it / Day in the house / Two rivers / Sling shot.

Oct 89. (7") **GUITAR SHOP. / PEOPLE GET READY**
(12"+=)(cd-s+=) – Cause we've ended as lovers / Blue wind.

In 1990, sessioned for JON BON JOVI on his BLAZE OF GLORY album.

—— In Sep 91 JEFF collaborated with BUDDY GUY on single 'MUSTANG SALLY' on 'Silvertone'.

JEFF BECK & THE BIG TOWN PLAYBOYS

with **MIKE SANCHEZ** – vocals, piano - / **IAN JENNINGS** – bass, vocals / **ADRIAN UTLEY** – rhythm guitar / **CLIVE DENVER** – drums, vocals / **LEO GREEN** – tenor sax / **NICK HUNT** – baritone sax.

Epic Epic

Jun 93. (cd)(c)(lp) **CRAZY LEGS**
– Race with the devil / Cruisin' / Crazy legs / Double talkin' baby / Woman love / Lotta lovin' / Catman / Pink thunderbird / Baby blue / You better believe / Who slapped John? / Say mama / Red blue jeans and a pony tail / Five feet of lovin' / B-i-bickey-bi-bo-bo-go / Blues stay away from me / Pretty, pretty baby / Hold me, hug me, rock me

—— Above was a tribute to GENE VINCENT & HIS BLUE CAPS.

- compilations, others, etc. -

Oct 72. R.A.K./ US= Epic; (7"m) **HI HO SILVER LINING. / BECK'S BOLERO / ROCK MY PLIMSOUL** 14
(re-iss.Oct82 nearly hit UK 62)

Apr 73. R.A.K./ US= Epic; (7"m) **I'VE BEEN DRINKING. ("JEFF BECK and ROD STEWART") / MORNING DEW / GREENSLEEVES**

Nov 77. Embassy-CBS; (lp) **GOT THE FEELING**

Feb 83. Epic; (d-c) **BLOW BY BLOW / WIRED**

Feb 92. Epic; (3xcd-box) **BECKOLOGY**
(re-iss.3xcd+3xc May94)

Mar 92. Epic; (cd)(c) **THE BEST OF BECKOLOGY**
– Heart full of soul (YARDBIRDS) / Shapes of things (YARDBIRDS) / Over under sideways down (YARDBIRDS) / Hi ho silver lining / Tally man / Jailhouse rock / I've been drinking / I ain't superstitious / Superstition (BECK, BOGART & APPICE) / Cause we've ended as lovers / The pump / Star cycle (theme from 'The Tube') / People get ready (w / ROD STEWART) / Wild thing / Where were you (w /TERRY BOZZIO & TONY HYMAS) / Trouble in mind (TRIDENTS).

Mar 93. Epic; (3xcd-box) **FLASH / BLOW BY BLOW / THERE & BACK**

May 85. Fame-EMI; (lp)(c) **THE BEST OF JEFF BECK featuring ROD STEWART** -

Sep 88. E.M.I.; (cd) **LATE 60's WITH ROD STEWART** -

Feb 91. E.M.I.; (cd)(c) **TRUTH / BECK-OLA** -

May 89. That's Original; (d-lp)(d-cd) **JEFF BECK GROUP / ROUGH & READY** -

Oct 94. Charly; (cd) **SHAPES OF THINGS** -

Dec 95. MFP; (cd)(c) **THE BEST OF JEFF BECK** -

BEEFEATERS (See under ⇒ BYRDS)

BELLY

Formed: Newport, Rhode Island, USA ... Dec'91 by ex-THROWING MUSES and BREEDERS co-leader TANYA DONNELLY. Progressed that year and were tipped for greater things in 1993. • **Style:** Guitar-orientated indie band, not too dissimilar to THROWING MUSES. • **Songwriters:** DONNELLY except; HOT BURRITO 2 (Flying Burrito Brothers) / TRUST IN ME (Sherman Sherman; for 'Jungle Book') / ARE YOU EXPERIENCED (Jimi Hendrix). • **Trivia:** DYLAN ROY guested on late '92 single 'GEPETTO'.

Recommended: STAR (*8).

TANYA DONNELLY – vocals, guitar / **FRED ABONG** – bass / **CHRIS GORMAN** – drums / **THOMAS GORMAN** – guitar

4 a.d. Sire

Jun 92. (12"ep)(cd-ep) **SLOW DUST**
– Dusted / Slow dog / Dancing gold / Low red Moon.

—— **LESLIE LANGSTON** – bass (ex-THROWING MUSES) repl. FRED ABONG

Nov 92. (12"ep)(cd-ep) **GEPPETO / SEXYS. / SWEET RIDER / HOT BURRITO 2**

Jan 93. (7")(c-s) **FEED THE TREE. / DREAM ON ME** 32 95
(12"+=)(cd-s+=) Trust in me / Star

Jan 93. (cd)(c)(lp) **STAR** 2 59
– Someone to die for / Angel / Dusted / Every word / Gepetto / Witch / Slow dog / Low red Moon / Feed the tree / Full Moon, empty heart / White belly / Untogether / Star / Sad dress / Stay.

Mar 93. (12"ep)(cd-ep) **GEPETTO. / HOT BURRITO 1. / SEXY S / SWEET RIDE** 49

(c-ep)(cd-ep) – ('A'side) / It's not unusual / Star (demo) / Dusted (demo).
Jan 95. (7")(c-s) **NOW THEY'LL SLEEP. / THIEF** [28] [ ]
(12"+=)(cd-s+=) – Baby's arm / John Dark.
Feb 95. (cd)(c)(lp) **KING** [6] [57]
– Puberty / Seal my fate / Red / Silverfish / Super-connected / The bees / King / Now they'll sleep / Untitled and unsung / Lil' Ennio / Judas my heart.
Jul 95. (7"clear) **SEAL MY FATE. / BROKEN / JUDAS MY HEART (live)** [35] [ ]
(cd-s) – ('A'-U.S. radio mix) / Spaceman / Diamond rib cage / Think about your troubles.
(cd-s) – ('A'live) / White belly (live) / Untitled and unsung (live) / The bees (live).

Dickey BETTS (see under ⇒ ALLMAN BROTHERS BAND)

Bev BEVAN (see under ⇒ ELECTRIC LIGHT ORCHESTRA)

B-52's

Formed: Athens, Georgia, USA . . . late '76, by PIERSON, SCHNEIDER, STRICKLAND, RICKY WILSON and sister CINDY. Took name from bouffant hairdo the girls had which was named after a bomb. After one self-financed 45 sold out its 2,000 copies, they drew the attention of Island's Chris Blackwell. He signed them after a residency at Max's Kansas City late 1978, and soon re-issued debut 'ROCK LOBSTER' 45, which made UK Top 40 lists in 1979. For the next decade or so, The B-52's brightened up the rock and pop world, hitting the charts on many occasions. However life was not plain sailing, as RICKY died of AIDS on 12 Oct'85, after suffering a few years with the virus. • **Style:** Outwardly weird and visual, mixing new wave REZILLOS-type dual harmonies and danceable futuristic fun rock'n'roll. • **Songwriters:** All mainly STRICKLAND or group compositions. PLANET CLAIRE (w/ Henry Mancini) • **Trivia:** DAVID BYRNE (Talking Heads) produced their 1982 mini-lp 'MESOPOTAMIA'. In 1981, during lay-off, STRICKLAND, PIERSON and CINDY WILSON did one-off Japan venture as "MELON" with group The PLASTICS and ADRIAN BELEW. Late 1990, PIERSON contributed on singles by IGGY POP (Candy) and R.E.M. (Shiny Happy People). DON WAS and NILE RODGERS each produced half of 1992 album.

Recommended: DANCE THIS MESS AROUND THE BEST OF THE B-52's (*9)

KATE PIERSON (b.27 Apr'48, Weehawken, New Jersey) – vocals, organ, bass / **CINDY WILSON** (b.28 Feb'57) – vocals, percussion, guitar / **RICKY WILSON** (b.19 Mar'53) – guitar / **FRED SCHNEIDER** (III) (b. 1 Jul'51, Newark, Georgia) – vocals, keyboards / **KEITH 'Julian' STRICKLAND** (b.26 Oct'53) – drums

not issued / Private . . .
Jul 78. (7") **ROCK LOBSTER. / 52 GIRLS** [-] [ ]
(re-iss.Nov78 on 'Bouffant') (some copies given free with debut lp)

Island / Warners
Jul 79. (7") **ROCK LOBSTER. / 6060-842** [-] [56]
Jul 79. (7") **ROCK LOBSTER. / RUNNING AROUND** [37] [-]
(re-iss.Jul81)
Jul 79. (lp)(c) **THE B-52's** [22] [59]
– Planet Claire / 52 girls / Dance this mess around / Rock lobster / Lava / There's a Moon in the sky (called the Moon) / Hero worship / 6060-842 / Downtown. *(re-iss.Jun86 + Oct86) (cd-iss.Jan87) (re-iss.lp Jan94 + May94)*
Sep 79. (7") **6060-842. / HERO WORSHIP** [ ] [ ]
Nov 79. (7")(7"pic-d) **PLANET CLAIRE. / THERE'S A MOON IN THE SKY (CALLED THE MOON)** [ ] [ ]
(re-iss.Jul81)
Jul 80. (7") **GIVE ME BACK MY MAN. / STROBE LIGHT** [61] [ ]
Sep 80. (lp)(c) **WILD PLANET** [18] [18]
– Party out of bounds / Dirty back road / Runnin' around / Give me back my man / Private Idaho / Devil in my car / Quiche Lorraine / Strobe light / 53 miles west of Venus. *(cd-iss.May90)*
Oct 80. (7") **PRIVATE IDAHO. / PARTY OUT OF BOUNDS** [-] [74]
Nov 80. (7") **DIRTY BACK ROAD. / STROBE LIGHT** [ ] [ ]
Jan 81. (7") **QUICHE LORRAINE. / LAVA** [-] [ ]
Feb 82. (m-lp)(c) **MESOPOTAMIA** [18] [35]
– Loveland / Deep sleep / Mesopotamia / Cake / Throw that beat in the garbage can / Nip it in the bud. *(cd-iss.May90)*
1982. (7") **DEEP SLEEP. / NIP IT IN THE BUD** [-] [ ]
1982. (7") **MESOPOTAMIA. / THROW THAT BEAT IN THE GARBAGE CAN** [-] [ ]
Apr 83. (7") **SONG FOR A FUTURE GENERATION. / ('A'instrumental)** [63] [ ]
(12"+=) – Planet Claire.
(d7"++=) – There's a Moon in the sky (called the Moon).
May 83. (lp)(c) **WHAMMY!** [33] [29]
– Legal tender / Whammy kiss / Song for a future generation / Butterbean / Trism / Queen of Las Vegas / Don't worry / Big bird / Work that skirt. *(cd-iss.May90)*
Jul 83. (7") **LEGAL TENDER. / MOON 83** [-] [81]
Oct 83. (7") **SONG FOR A FUTURE GENERATION. / ?** [-] [ ]

RICKY suffering from full blown AIDS, finally dies 12 Oct'85. Group carry on, augmented by session man **RALPH CARNEY – guitar**

Jun 87. (7")(7"pic-d) **WIG. / SUMMER OF LOVE** [ ] [ ]
(d7"+=) – Song for a future generation / 52 girls.
(12"+=)(c-s+=) – Song for a future generation / Give me back my man.
Jul 87. (lp)(c)(cd) **BOUNCING OFF THE SATELLITES** [74] [85] Sep 86
– Summer of love / Girl from Ipanema goes to Greenland / Housework / Detour thru your mind / Wig / Theme for a nude beach / Ain't it a shame / Juicy jungle / Communicate / She brakes for rainbows. *(cd-iss.May90)*
Sep 87. (7") **SUMMER OF LOVE. / HOUSEWORK** [-] [ ]

—— added on tour **PAT IRWIN – keyboards / ZACH ALFORD** – drums / **PHILIPPE SASSE** – (studio keyboards) / **SARA LEE** – bass (ex-GANG OF FOUR) (also studio)

Reprise / Reprise
Jul 89. (lp)(c)(cd) **COSMIC THING** [ ] [4]
– Cosmic thing / Dry country / Deadbeat club / Love shack / Junebug / Roam / Bushfire / Channel Z / Topaz / Follow your blues. *(re-dist.Apr90, hit UK No.8)*
Aug 89. (7") **LOVE SHACK. / CHANNEL Z** [-] [3]
Sep 89. (7") **CHANNEL Z. / JUNEBUG** [61] [-]
(12")(cd-s) – ('A'side) / ('A'rock mix) / ('A'dub mix). *(re-iss.Aug90)*
Dec 89. (7") **ROAM. / BUSHFIRE** [-] [3]
Feb 90. (7") **LOVE SHACK. / PLANET CLAIRE** [2] [-]
(c-s+=)(cd-s+=)(7"pic-d+=) – Rock lobster (live).
(12") – ('A'side) / ('A'remix) / ('A'Ben Grosse mix).
Apr 90. (7") **DEADBEAT CLUB. / PLANET CLAIRE** [-] [30]
May 90. (7")(c-s)(cd-s) **ROAM. / WHAMMY KISS (live) / DANCE THIS MESS AROUND (live)** [17] [-]
(12") – ('A'side) / (2-'A'mixes).
Sep 90. (7")(c-s) **DEADBEAT CLUB. / LOVE SHACK** [ ] [-]
(12"+=)(cd-s+=) – B-52's megamix.

—— now trimmed to basic trio of **PIERSON, SCHNEIDER** – vox / **& STRICKLAND** – guitar with guest musicians **IRWIN / ALFORD / LEE /** plus **JEFF PORCARO + STERLING CAMPBELL** – drums / **DAVID McMURRAY** – sax / **JAMIE MULHOBERAC + RICHARD HILTON** – keyboards / **LENNY CASTRO** – percussion / **TRACY WORMWORTH** – bass

Jun 92. (7")(c-s) **GOOD STUFF. / BAD INFLUENCE** [21] [28]
(12"+=)(cd-s+=) – Return to Dreamland.
(12") – (4 'A'mixes).
Jul 92. (cd)(c)(lp) **GOOD STUFF** [8] [16]
– Tell it like it t-i-is / Hot pants explosion / Good stuff / Revolution Earth / Dreamland / Is that you Mo-Dean? / The world's green laughter / Vision of a kiss / Breezin' / Bad influence. *(re-iss.cd/c Feb95)*
Sep 92. (7")(c-s) **TELL IT LIKE IT T-I-IS. / THE WORLD'S GREEN LAUGHTER** [61] [ ]
(12")(cd-s) – ('A' 4 other mixes).
Nov 92. (7")(c-s) **IS THAT YOU MO-DEAN?. / ('A'-Moby mix)** [ ] [ ]
(12"+=)(cd-s+=) – ('A'-2 other mixes) / Tell it like it t-i-is.
Feb 93. (7")(c-s) **HOT PANTS EXPLOSION. / LOVE SHACK** [ ] [ ]
(cd-s+=) – Channel Z / Roam.

—— **SCHNEIDER, PIERSON + STRICKLAND**
next from the new film 'The Flintstones' on 'M.C.A.'.
Jun 94. (7")(c-s) **(MEET) THE FLINTSTONES. ("BC-52's") / ('A'mix)** [3] [33] May94
(cd-s+=) – (2 'A'mixes).

– compilations, others, etc. –

Jul 81. Island/ US= Warners; (m-lp)(c) **THE PARTY MIX ALBUM** [36] [55]
Aug 81. Island; (7") **GIVE ME BACK MY MAN (party mix). / PARTY OUT OF BOUNDS** [ ] [ ]
Apr 86. (7")(7"pic-d)(7"sha-pic-d) **ROCK LOBSTER. / PLANET CLAIRE** [12] [ ]
(d7"+=) – Song for a future generation / 52 girls.
(12"+=) – Song for a future generation / Give me back my man.
Jun 90. (cd)(c)(lp) **DANCE THIS MESS AROUND THE BEST OF THE B-52's** [36] [ ]
– Party out of bounds / Devil in my car / Dirty back road / 6060-842 / Wig / Dance this mess around / Private Idaho / Rock lobster / Strobe light / Give me back my man / Song for a future generation / Planet Claire / 52 girls. (cd+=) – (2 extra mixes).
Feb 91. Reprise; (cd)(c) **PARTY MIX / MESOPOTAMIA** [-] [ ]
Nov 92. Reprise; (cd) **WILD PLANET / B-52's** [ ] [ ]
Sep 95. Spectrum; (cd) **PLANET CLAIRE** [ ] [-]

FRED SCHNEIDER

solo, recorded 1984 and written with COTE.

Reprise Reprise

May 91. (cd)(c)(lp) **FRED SCHNEIDER** [ ] [ ]
– Monster / Out the concrete / Summer in Hell / Orbit / I'm gonna haunt you / It's time to kiss / This planet's a mess / Wave / Boonga (the New Jersey caveman).

Jun 91. (c-s)(cd-s) **MONSTER /** [-] [85]

. . . Jan – Jun '96 stop press . . .

Jun 96. (cd)(c) **JUST . . .FRED** [ ] [ ]

Jello BIAFRA (see under ⇒ DEAD KENNEDYS)

BIG AUDIO DYNAMITE

Formed: London, England . . . 1984 by MICK JONES who still was under contract with 'CBS' records. Amongst others he recruits film-maker/friend and non-musician DON LETTS. Although their late 1985 debut 'THE BOTTOM LINE' soon became a favourite, it missed out on chart placing. However the follow-up 'E=Mc2', gave them near UK Top 10 hit in 1986, and resurrected sales of critically acclaimed but flop album. • **Style:** Punk/dub rock, mixed with samples and tapes. Because of Mick's unique punk vocals and his last band's break-up; circa 1985, their sound was not unlike a danceable CLASH. • **Songwriters:** Mainly JONES and LETTS, with other members contributing. Covers: DUELLING BANJOS (Arthur Smith's theme from 'Deliverance' Soundtrack) / BATTLE OF NEW ORLEANS (trad.). • **Trivia:** While recording 2nd album, JOE STRUMMER (Clash) came in to co-write and produce a couple of songs. For half a year in 1990, MICK was hospitalized while he recovered slowly from viral pneumonia and chicken pox. In 1991 he was credited guesting on AZTEC CAMERA top 20 UK hit 'GOOD MORNING BRITAIN'.

Recommended: THIS IS BIG AUDIO DYNAMITE (*8)

MICK JONES – vocals, guitar (ex-CLASH) / **DON LETTS** – effects, vocals / **DAN DONOVAN** – keyboards / **LEO WILLIAMS** – bass / **GREG ROBERTS** – drums.

C.B.S. Columbia

Sep 85. (7")(12")(ext-12") **THE BOTTOM LINE. / BAD** [ ] [ ]

Nov 85. (lp)(c) **THIS IS BIG AUDIO DYNAMITE** [ ] [ ]
– Medicine show / Sony / E=Mc2 / The bottom line / Sudden impact / Stone Thames / B.A.D. / A party. *(cd-iss.Jun86)*

Mar 86. (7")(12") **E=Mc2. / THIS IS BIG AUDIO DYNAMITE** [11] [ ]

May 86. (7") **MEDICINE SHOW. / A PARTY** [29] [ ]
(12") – ('A'extended). / ('B'dub)
(d12"+=) – E=Mc2 (remix) / Albert Einstein the human beatbox.

Oct 86. (7") **C'MON EVERY BEATBOX. / BADROCK CITY** [51] [ ]
(12"+=) – Beatbox's at dawn.
(12"++=) – The bottom line.

Oct 86. (lp)(c)(cd) **No.10 UPPING STREET** [11] [ ]
– C'mon every beatbox / Beyond the pale / Limbo the law / Sambadrome / V thirteen / Ticket / Hollywood boulevard / Dial a hitman / Sightsee M.C! (c+=)(cd+=) – Ice cool killer (dial a hitman-instrumental) / The big V (V thirteen – instrumental). *(re-iss.Oct89)*

Feb 87. (7") **V THIRTEEN. / HOLLYWOOD BOULEVARD** [49] [ ]
(12"+=) ('B'club)

Jul 87. (12"m) **SIGHTSEE MC! (radio cut) / ANOTHER ONE RIDES THE BUS / SIGHTSEE MC! / SIGHTSEE - WEST LONDON** [ ] [ ]

May 88. (7")(ext.12") **JUST PLAY MUSIC. / MUCH WORSE** [51] [ ]

Jun 88. (lp)(c)(cd) **TIGHTEN UP VOL.88** [33] [ ]
– Rock non stop (all night long) / Other 99 / Funny names / Applecart / Esquerita / Champagne / Mr.Walker said / The battle of All Saints Road, incorporating:- Battle of New Orleans – Duelling banjos / Hip neck and thigh / 2000 shoes / Tighten up vol.88 / Just play music. *(re-iss.cd+c Oct94 on 'Columbia')*

Jul 88. (7") **OTHER 99. / WHAT HAPPENED TO EDDIE?** [ ] [ ]
(12")(cd-s) – ('A'extended) / Just play music (club mix)

Sep 89. (lp)(c)(cd) **MEGATOP PHOENIX** [26] [85]
– Start / Rewind / All mink and no manners / Union, Jack / Contact / Dragon town / Baby don't apologise / Is yours working yet? / Around the girls in 80 ways / James Brown / Everybody needs a holiday / Mick's a hippie burning / House arrest / The green lady / London Bridge / Stalag 123 / End.

Oct 89. (7") **CONTACT. / IN FULL EFFECT** [ ] [ ]
(12"+=)(cd-s+=) – Who beats / If I were John Carpenter.

BIG AUDIO DYNAMITE II

was formed by **JONES** and **DONOVAN** (left mid'90) **NICK HAWKINS** – guitar / **GARY STONEDAGE** – bass / **CHRIS KAVANAGH** – drums (ex-SIGUE SIGUE SPUTNIK)all repl. others who formed SCREAMING TARGET in 1991. (album 'Hometown Hi-Fi')

Oct 90. (cd)(c)(lp) **KOOL-AID** [55] [ ]
– Change of atmosphere / Can't wait / Kickin' in / Innocent child / On one / Kool-aid / In my dreams / When the time comes.

Columbia Columbia

Jul 91. (cd)(c)(lp) **THE GLOBE** [63] [72]
– Rush / Can't wait (live) / I don't know / The globe / Innocent child / Green grass / Kool-aid / In my dreams / When the time comes / The tea party.

Jul 91. (7") **THE GLOBE (remix). / CITY LIGHTS** [ ] [76]
(12"+=)(cd-s+=) – ('A'dub).

Nov 91. (7")(c-s) **RUSH (New York mix). / (A3 version)** [ ] [32] Sep 91
(cd-s+=) – City lights (full version).
(12") – ('A'side) / ('A'-3 other mixes).

(above 'A'side was issued Feb91 on other side of CLASH single 'Should I Stay Or Should I Go')

BIG AUDIO

Nov 94. (c-s)(cd-s) **LOOKING FOR A SONG. / MODERN STONE AGE BLUES** [68] [ ]
(12"+=)(cd-s+=) – ('A'-Zonka remix) / ('A'-Shapps remix).

Nov 94. (cd)(c)(lp) **HIGHER POWER** [ ] [ ]
– Got to wake up / Harrow Road / Looking for a song / Some people / Slender Loris / Modern stoneage blues / Melancholy maybe / Over the rise / Why is it? / Moon / Lucan / Light up my life / Hope.

BIG AUDIO DYNAMITE

Radio-active M.C.A.

Jun 95. (c-s) **I TURNED OUT A PUNK / WHAT ABOUT LOVE** [ ] [ ]
(cd-s+=) – ('A'-Live fast, live fast mix).
(12") -('A'side) / ('A'-Live fast mix) / ('A'-Live fast instrumental) / ('A'-Feelin' lucky mix).

- compilations, others, etc. -

Nov 88. C.B.S.; (d-cd) **THIS IS BIG AUDIO DYNAMITE / No.10 UPPING STREET** [ ] [ ]

Sep 95. Columbia; (cd)(c) **PLANET B.A.D.** [ ] [ ]

BIG BROTHER & THE HOLDING CO.

Formed: San Francisco, California, USA . . . 1966 by SAM ANDREW, etc. They recruited Texan JANIS JOPLIN who had just turned down opportunity to join 13th FLOOR EVEVATORS. They signed to 'Mainstream' records in Aug'66, and after excellent Monterey festival performance, released debut album. In 1968 when they signed to 'Columbia', where they had top selling US album 'CHEAP THRILLS', which hit No.1 for 7 weeks. When JANIS JOPLIN left with SAM ANDREW, this all but killed any further success for BIG BROTHER. • **Style:** Powerful bluesy rock, that gave light to tremendous vocal talent of JANIS JOPLIN. In the 70's, they mellowed with her absence. • **Songwriters:** Group compositions. • **Trivia:** see under JANIS JOPLIN.

Recommended: CHEAP THRILLS (*8)

SAM ANDREW (b.18 Dec'41, Taft, California) – guitar, vocals / **PETE ALBIN** (b. 6 Jun'44) – bass, vocals / **JAMES GURLEY** – guitar repl. DAVE ESKERSON (left Nov65) / **DAVID GETZ** – drums repl. CHUCK JONES (left Feb66) also on occasion / **ED BOGAS** – violin (left before Summer'66, to NEW RIDERS OF THE PURPLE SAGE)

—— (Jun66) added **JANIS JOPLIN** (b.19 Jan'43, Port Arthur, Texas) – vocals

not issued Mainstream

Aug 67. (lp) **BIG BROTHER & THE HOLDING COMPANY** [-] [60] Aug 67
– Bye bye baby / Easy rider / Intruder / Light is faster than sound / Call on me / Coo coo / Women is losers / Blind man / Down on me / Caterpillar / All is loneliness / The last time. *(UK-iss.'68 on 'Fontana') (re-iss.May71 on 'Columbia' 2 extra tracks 'Coo Coo' & 'The Last Mile' which were also 'A' & 'B' US single)(cd-iss.Apr93 as 'FIRST ALBUM' on 'Sony Europe')*

1967. (7") **BLIND MAN. / ALL IS LONELINESS** [-] [ ]

1967. (7") **DOWN ON ME. / CALL ME** [-] [ ]
(re-iss.Aug68 in US on 'Columbia' reached No.43) (UK-iss.'69)

Fontana Mainstream

1967. (7") **BYE BYE BABY. / INTRUDER (US) / ALL IS LONELINESS (UK)** [ ] [ ]

1968. (7") **WOMEN IS LOSERS. / LIGHT IS FASTER THAN SOUND** [-] [ ]

C.B.S. Columbia

Aug 68. (7") **PIECE OF MY HEART. / TURTLE BLUES** [ ] [12]

Sep 68. (lp) **CHEAP THRILLS** [ ] [1] Aug 68
– Combination of the two / I need a man to love / Summertime / Piece of my heart /

Turtle blues / O sweet Mary / Ball and chain. *(re-iss.+c-Mar81) (cd-iss.Jan91 & Jun92)*

— Folded late 1968. JANIS JOPLIN went solo, taking SAM ANDREW. In Aug69 GETZ and ALBIN re-formed BIG BROTHER & THE HOLDING COMPANY with **NICK GRAVENITES** – vocals / **MIKE PRENDERGAST** – guitar / **TED ASHBURTON** – piano

— soon split again, GETZ was also in NU BUGALOO EXPRESS.

— **GETZ, GURLEY, ALBIN, SAM ANDREW** and **NICK GRAVENITES** – vocals re-grouped

— **BIG BROTHER & THE HOLDING COMPANY** with **KATHI McDONALD** – vocals and **MIKE FINNEGAN** – keyboards / **DAVID SCHALLOCK** – guitar (both ex-NU BUGALOO EXPRESS)

C.B.S. | Columbia

Jan 71. (lp)(c) **BE A BROTHER** | | Nov 70
– Keep on / Joseph's coat / Home on the strange / Someday / Heartache people / Sunshine baby / Mr.Natural / Funkie Jim / I'll change your flat tire Merle / Be a brother.

Sep 71. (lp)(c) **HOW HARD IT IS** | - | Aug 71
– How hard it is / You've been talkin' 'bout me, baby / House on fire / Black widow spider / Last band on side one / Nu Boogaloo jam / Maui / Shine on / Buried alive in the blues / Promise her anything but give her Arpeggio.

Sep 71. (7") **BLACK WIDOW SPIDER. / NU BOOGALOO JAM** | - |

— Split Feb72. ALBIN rejoined COUNTRY JOE (McDONALD) & THE FISH. He and GETZ were part of them in 1969. FINNEGAN played live with STEPHEN STILLS etc. GRAVENITES tried to revitalise ELECTRIC FLAG.

– compilations etc. –

Nov 68. Mainstream; (7") **COO COO. / ?** | - | 84
Jun 83. Island; (12") **ADVENTURES IN SUCCESS (FIRST ADVENTURE). /** | |
1985. Edsel/ US= Making Waves; (lp) **CHEAPER THRILLS** (live 26th July '66) | - | Jan 84
Oct 84. Code; (7") **BIG BROTHER. / IF YOU TRY** | |
Apr 86. Edsel; (lp) **JOSEPH'S COAT** (best of 71's two albums) | | -

BIG COUNTRY

Formed: Dunfermline, Scotland ... Autumn 1981 by ADAMSON and WATSON. They recruited brothers PETER (keyboards) and ALAN WISHART (bass) plus CLIVE PARKER (drums, ex-SPIZZ ...). Early 1982 the latter three had been replaced by BRZEZICKI and BUTLER. After they turned down 'Ensign' contract, they signed to 'Mercury-Phonogram' Spring '82. They soon were based in London, England, and stormed the charts with 'FIELDS OF FIRE' & 'IN A BIG COUNTRY'. • **Style:** Anthemic heavy pop/rock, featuring live-like Scots 'bagpipe' sound from twin-guitars. • **Songwriters:** Mostly ADAMSON / WATSON, except TRACKS OF MY TEARS (Smokey Robinson & The Miracles) / HONKY TONK WOMAN (Rolling Stones) / AULD LANG SYNE (trad.) / ROCKIN' IN THE FREE WORLD (Neil Young) / FLY LIKE AN EAGLE (Steve Miller) / BLACK SKINNED BLUE EYED BOYS (Equals / Eddy Grant). OH WELL (Fleetwood Mac) / (DON'T FEAR) THE REAPER (Blue Oyster Cult) / WOODSTOCK (Joni Mitchell) / CRACKED ACTOR (David Bowie) / PARANOID (Black Sabbath). • **Trivia:** Their song 'ONE GREAT THING' was used on Tennent's lager advert. In August 1988, they tour major venues in Soviet Russia.

Recommended: THROUGH A BIG COUNTRY – GREATEST HITS (*8)

STUART ADAMSON (b.see SKIDS) – vocals, lead guitar, synthesizer (ex-SKIDS) / **BRUCE WATSON** (b.11 Mar'61, Ontario, Canada) – guitar (ex-DELINX) / **TONY BUTLER** (b. 3 Feb'59, London, England) – bass (ex-ON THE AIR) / **MARK BRZEZICKI** (b.21 Jun'57, Slough, England) – drums (ex-ON THE AIR)

Mercury | Mercury

Sep 82. (7") **HARVEST HOME. / BALCONY** | |
(12"+=)(12"clear+=) – Flag of nations (swimming).

Feb 83. (7") **FIELDS OF FIRE. / ANGLE PARK** | 10 | 52 Feb84
(7"sha-pic-d+=) – Harvest home.
(12"+=)(12"clear+=) – ('A'alternative mix).

May 83. (7") **IN A BIG COUNTRY. / ALL OF US.** | 17 | 17 Oct 83
(12"+=) ('A'pure mix)
(extra-12"++=) – Heart and soul.

Jun 83. (lp)(c) **THE CROSSING** | 3 | 18 Jul 83
– In a big country / Inwards / Chance / 1,000 stars / The storm / Harvest home / Lost patrol / Close action / Fields of fire / Porrohman. (c+=) 4 remixes. *(re-dist.+cd-Mar84) (re-cd.1986)*

Aug 83. (7") **CHANCE. / TRACKS OF MY TEARS (live)** | 9 |
(12")(12"pic-d) – ('A'extended) / The crossing.

Jan 84. (7") **WONDERLAND. / GIANT** | 8 | 86
(12"+=)(12"clear+=) – ('A'extended).
(d7"+=) – Lost patrol (live – parts 1 & 2).

Apr 84 (m-lp) **WONDERLAND** | - | 65
– Wonderland / Angle park / The crossing / All fall together.

Sep 84. (7") **EAST OF EDEN. / PRAIRIE ROSE.** | 17 |
(12"+=) – ('A'extended).

Oct 84. (lp)(c)(cd) **STEELTOWN** | 1 | 70
– Flame of the west / East of Eden / Steeltown / Where the rose is sown / Come back to me / Tall ships go / Girl with grey eyes / Rain dance / The great divide / Just a shadow. *(re-cd.1986) (re-iss.cd+c.May93 on 'Spectrum')*

Nov 84. (7") **WHERE THE ROSE IS SOWN. / BELIEF IN THE SMALL MAN** | 29 |
(d7"+=) – Wonderland (live) / In a big country (live) / Auld Lang Syne (live).
(12"+=) – ('A'extended) / Bass dance.

Jan 85. (7") **JUST A SHADOW. / WINTER SKY.** | 26 |
(12"+=) – ('A'extended).

Apr 86. (7")(7"sha-pic-d) **LOOK AWAY. / RESTLESS NATIVES** | 7 |
(12") – ('A'-outlaw mix) / ('B'-soundtrack part 1).
(d7"+=) – Margo's theme / Highland scenery.

Jun 86. (7") **THE TEACHER. / HOME COME THE ANGELS** | 28 |
(12") – ('A'mystery mix) / Restless natives (part 2).

Jun 86. (lp)(c)(cd) **THE SEER** | 2 | 59
– Look away / The seer / The teacher / I walk the hill / Eiledon / One great thing / Hold the heart / The seer / Remembrance day / The red fox / The sailor. *(re-iss.cd Aug94 on 'Vertigo')*

Sep 86. (7") **ONE GREAT THING. / SONG OF THE SOUTH** | 19 |
(12"+=) – ('A'mix).
(d7"+=) – Wonderland (live) / Chance (live).
(12"+=) – Look away (outlaw mix).
(c-s+=) – In a big country (pure mix) / Fields of fire (live).

Nov 86. (7")(12") **HOLD THE HEART. / HONKY TONK WOMAN (live)** | 55 |
(d12"+=) – (interview part 1 & 2).

added on tour **JOSS PHILIP-GORSE** – keyboards

Mercury | Reprise

Aug 88. (7") **KING OF EMOTION. / THE TRAVELLERS** | 16 |
(12"+=) – Starred & Crossed.
(c-s+=) – On the shore.
(cd-s++=) – Not waving but drowning.

Sep 88. (lp)(c)(cd) **PEACE IN OUR TIME** | 9 |
– King of emotion / Broken heart (thirteen valleys) / Thousand yard stare / From here to eternity / Everything I need / Peace in our time / Time for leaving / River of hope / In this place / I could be happy here. *(cd+=)* – The travellers.

Oct 88. (7") **KING OF EMOTION. / IN A BIG COUNTRY** | - |
Oct 88. (7") **BROKEN HEART (THIRTEEN VALLEYS). / SOAPY SOUTAR STRIKES BACK** | 47 |
(12"+=) – When a drum beats / On the shore.
(cd-s+=) – When a drum beats / Made in Heaven.
(cd-s+=) – Wonderland (12"mix).

Jan 89. (7") **PEACE IN OUR TIME. / PROMISED LAND** | 39 |
(12"+=) – The longest day / Over the border.
(extra-12"+=) – In a big country (live) / Chance (live).
(cd-s+=) – The longest day / Chance.

(Feb90) **PAT AHERN – drums** repl. BRZEZICKI who joined PRETENDERS

Apr 90. (7")(c-s) **SAVE ME. / PASS ME BY** | 41 |
(12"+=) Wonderland (live) / 1,000 yard stare (live) / Dead on arrival (live) *(not on cd)*
(cd-s++=) – World on fire.

May 90. (cd)(c)(lp) **THROUGH A BIG COUNTRY – GREATEST HITS** (compilation) | 2 |
– Save me / In a big country / Fields of fire / Chance / Wonderland / Where the rose is sown / Just a shadow / Look away / King of emotion / East of Eden / One great thing / The teacher / Broken heart (thirteen valleys) / Peace in our time. (c/cd+=) – Eiledon / The seer / Harvest home.

Jul 90. (7")(c-s) **HEART OF THE WORLD. / BLACK SKINNED BLUE EYED BOYS** | 50 |
(12"+=) – Broken heart (thirteen valleys) (acoustic) / Peace in our time (acoustic).
(cd-s+=) – Restless Natives.

Vertigo | Reprise

Aug 91. (7"ep) **REPUBLICAN PARTY REPTILE. / COMES A TIME / YOU, ME AND THE TRUTH** | 37 |
(7"ep)(12"ep)(10"ep) – Comes a time. *(re-iss.cd+c Feb93)*
(cd-ep+=) – ('A'side) / Freedom song / Kiss the girl goodbye / I'm only waiting.

Sep 91. (cd)(c)(lp) **NO PLACE LIKE HOME** | 28 |
– We're not in Kansas / Republican party reptile / Dynamic lady / Keep on dreaming / Beautiful people / The hostage speaks / Beat the Devil / Heap of faith / Ships / Into the fire. (cd+=) – You, me and the truth / Comes a time. *(re-iss.cd Aug94 on 'Vertigo')*

Oct 91. (7")(c-s) **BEAUTIFUL PEOPLE. / RETURN OF THE TWO HEADED KING** | 72 |
(cd-s+=) – Rockin' in the free world (live).
(12"pic-d+=) – Fly like an eagle.

— **ADAMSON, BUTLER + WATSON** were joined by session men **SIMON PHILLIPS** – drums / **COLIN BERWICK** – keyboards

Com-pulsion | Fox-RCA

Mar 93. (7")(c-s) **ALONE. / NEVER TAKE YOUR PLACE** [24] [ ]
(12"pic-d+=) – Winter sky / Look away.
(cd-s) – ('A'side) / Chance / Rockin' in the free world / Eastworld.

Mar 93. (cd)(c)(lp) **THE BUFFALO SKINNERS** [25] [ ]
– Alone / Seven waves / What are you working for / The one I love / Long way home / The selling of America / We're not in Kansas / Ships / All go together / Winding wind / Pink marshmallow moon / Chester's farm. *(re-iss.Sep94)*

Apr 93. (7")(c-s) **SHIPS (WHERE WERE YOU). / OH WELL** [29] [ ]
(12"+=)(cd-s+=) – (Don't fear) The reaper / Woodstock.
(cd-s+=) – The buffalo skinners / Cracked actor / Paranoid.

Jun 94. (cd)(c)(lp) **WITHOUT THE AID OF A SAFETY NET (live)** [35] [ ]
– Harvest home / Peace in our time / Just a shadow / Broken heart (thirteen valleys) / The storm / Chance / Look away / Steeltown / Ships / Wonderland / What are you working for / Long way home / In a big country / Lost patrol.

Trans-atlantic | not issued

May 95. (c-ep)(cd-ep) **I'M NOT ASHAMED / ONE IN A MILLION (1st visit) / MONDAY TUESDAY GIRL / ('A'edit)** [69] [-]
(cd-s) – ('A'side) / Crazytimes / In a big country / Blue on a green planet.

Jun 95. (cd)(c) **WHY THE LONG FACE?** [48] [ ]
– You dreamer / Message of love / I'm not ashamed / ail into nothing / Thunder & lightning / Send you / One in a million / God's great mistake / Wild land in my heart / Thank you to the Moon / Far from me to you / Charlotte / Post nuclear talking blues / Blue on a green planet.

Nov 95. (cd-ep) **NON!** [ ] [-]
– Post nuclear talking blues / Blue on a green planet / God's great mistake / All go together.

— above was an action awareness record for Greenpeace.

- compilations -

Aug 94. Nighttracks; (cd) **RADIO 1 SESSIONS** [ ] [-]
Aug 94. Legends In Music; (cd) **BIG COUNTRY** [ ] [-]
Aug 95. Spectrum; (cd) **IN A BIG COUNTRY** [ ] [-]
Oct 95. Windsong; (cd) **BBC LIVE IN CONCERT (live)** [ ] [-]

BIRTHDAY PARTY

Formed: Caulfield, Melbourne, Australia . . . late 1977 as BOYS NEXT DOOR, by CAVE, HARVEY, PEW and CALVERT who knew each other since 1973. After over a year on 'Mushroom' records, they move to England as BIRTHDAY PARTY. They were soon snapped up mid 1980 by IVO on then new indie label '4ad'. In 1982, they achieved a Top 75 placing with lp 'JUNKYARD', but by the following year, all had splintered into other ventures. • **Style:** Avant-garde gothic/new wave, similar to PERE UBU or POP GROUP, but fronted by the near mental NICK CAVE. • **Songwriters:** Some CAVE / some HOWARD and others. BOYS NEXT DOOR cover; THESE BOOTS ARE MADE FOR WALKING (Nancy Sinatra). • **Trivia:** The band were miffed when 'MISSING LINK' released 'IT'S STILL LIVING' without their consent 1985. While PEW was in jail, others CAVE, HOWARD and HARVEY teamed up as TUFF MONKS with fellow Australians The GO-BETWEENS to issue one-off single 'AFTER THE FIREWORKS'.

Recommended: PRAYERS ON FIRE (*7) / HITS (*9)

BOYS NEXT DOOR

NICK CAVE – vocals / **MICK HARVEY** – guitar / **TRACY PEW** – bass / **PHIL CALVERT** – drums

Suicide | not issued

May 78. (7") **THESE BOOTS ARE MADE FOR WALKING. / BOY HERO** [-] [-] Aust.

— (Dec78) added **ROWLAND S. HOWARD** – guitar (ex-YOUNG CHARLATANS)

Mushroom | not issued

May 79. (7") **SHIVERS. / DIVE POSITION** [-] [-] Aust.
May 79. (lp) **DOOR DOOR** [-] [-] Aust.
– The nightwatchman / Brave exhibitions / Friends of my world / The voice / Roman Roman / Somebody's watching / After a fashion / Dive position / I mistake myself / Shivers. *(cd-iss.1987 Australia) (cd-iss.Mar93 on 'Grey Area-Mute')*

not issued | Missing L.

Dec 79. (12"ep) **HEE-HAW** [-] [-] Aust.
– Catholic skin / The red clock / Faint heart / The hair shirt / Death by drowning. *(re-iss.Dec83 Australia; credited as BIRTHDAY PARTY)*

Feb 80. (7") **HAPPY BIRTHDAY. / THE RIDDLE HOUSE** [-] [-] Aust.

BIRTHDAY PARTY

(same line-up) (Australian record label in brackets)

Jul 80. (7") **MR.CLARINET. / HAPPY BIRTHDAY** (gig freebie) [-] [-]

4.a.d. | not issued

Oct 80. Missing Link; (7"m) **THE FRIEND CATCHER. / WAVING MY ARMS / CATMAN** [-] [-] Aust.

Nov 80. Missing Link; (lp) **THE BIRTHDAY PARTY** [-] [-] Aust.
– (original copies by BOYS NEXT DOOR) – The friend catcher / Waving my arms / Catman / The red clock / Etc.+?

May 81. (lp) **PRAYERS ON FIRE** [ ] [-]
– Zoo music girl / Cry / Capers / Nick the stripper / Ho-ho / Figure of fun / King Ink / A dead song / Yard / Dull day / Just you and me.
(not iss.AUSTRALIA) *(cd-iss.Apr88)* (+=) – Blunder town / Kathy's kisses. *(also its first release in Australia on 'Virgin' red-lp + cd, also +=)*

Jun 81. Missing Link; (12"m) **NICK THE STRIPPER. / BLUNDER TOWN / KATHY'S KISSES** [-] [-] Aust.

Aug 81. (7") **RELEASE THE BATS. / BLAST OFF** [ ] [-]
(12"-issued Australia Apr83)

Oct 81. (7") **MR.CLARINET. / HAPPY BIRTHDAY** [ ] [-]

Feb 82. (m-lp) **DRUNK ON THE POPE'S BLOOD (live)** [ ] [-]
– Pleasure heads / king Ink / Zoo music girl / Loose.
(above other side by LYDIA LUNCH)

— (Dec81) while **TRACY PEW** was in jail for drunk driving he was replaced on tour only by either BARRY ADAMSON, CHRIS WALSH or **HARRY HOWARD**

May 82. (lp)(c) **JUNKYARD** [73] [-]
– She's hit / Dead Joe / Dim locator / Hamlet (pow-pow-pow) / Several sins / Big-Jesus-trash-can / Kiss me back / 6" gold blade / Kewpie doll / Junkyard. *(Australian release 1985, also iss.1991 on 'Virgin' pink-lp / +cd. +=) (cd-iss.Apr88)* (+=) – Release the bats / Blast off / Dead Joe (version).

1982. Missing LInk; (7") **NICK THE STRIPPER. / BLUNDERTOWN** [-] [-] Aust.

— Now quartet when **CALVERT** joined **PSYCHEDELIC FURS**. (HARVEY now drums)

Feb 83. (12"ep) **BAD SEED** [ ] [-]
– Sonny's burning / Wild world / Fears of gun / Deep in the woods.

— **JEFFREY WEGENER** – drums (ex-LAUGHING CLOWNS) repl. HARVEY Also **BLIXA BARGELD** – guitar (of EINSTURZENDE NEUBAUTEN) repl. absent HOWARD

Mute | not issued

Nov 83. (12"ep) **MUTINY** [ ] [-]
– Jennifer's evil / Mutiny in Heaven / Swampland / Says spell.

— Disbanded Autumn 1983. TRACY joined The SAINTS. (He was later to die late '86 of epileptic fit aged 28). ROWLAND HOWARD formed CRIME & THE CITY SOLUTION. NICK CAVE went solo, forming his BAD SEEDS taking with him MICK HARVEY.

- compilations, others, etc. - (all mostly UK)

Jun 83. 4 a.d.; (12"ep) **THE BIRTHDAY PARTY EP** [ ] [-]
– The friend catcher / Release the bats / Blast off / Mr.Clarinet / Happy birthday.

Aug 89. 4 a.d.; (cd) **HEE-HAW** [ ] [-]
(contains tracks from THE BIRTHDAY PARTY lp)

Aug 89. 4 a.d.; (cd) **MUTINY (ep) / THE BAD SEED (ep)** [ ] [-]

Oct 92. 4 a.d.; (cd)(c)(d-lp) **HITS** [ ] [-]
– The friend catcher / Happy birthday / Mr Clarinet / Nick the stripper / Zoo music girl / King Ink / Release the bats / Blast off / She's hit / 6" Gold blade / Hamlet (pow, pow, pow) / Dead Joe / Junkyard / Big-Jesus-Trash-Can / Wild world / Sonny's burning / Deep in the woods / Swampland / Jennifer's veil / Mutiny in Heaven.

Apr 85. MIssing Link; (d-lp) **IT'S STILL LIVING (live)** [-] [-] Aust.
(Australian re-iss.1991 on 'Virgin' green-lp +cd)

1985. Missing Link; (lp) **A COLLECTION - BEST AND RAREST** [-] [-] Aust.
(cd.iss.1991 Australia. w/diff 2nd side)

Feb 87. Strange Fruit; (12"ep) **THE PEEL SESSIONS** (21.4.81) [ ] [-]
– Release the bats / Rowland around in that stuff (sometimes) / Pleasure heads must burn / Loose. *(cd-s.iss.Aug88)*

Oct 88. (12"ep)(cd-ep) **THE PEEL SESSIONS** (2.12.81) [ ] [-]
– Big-Jesus-trash-can / She's hit / Bully bones / 6" gold blade.

ROWLAND S.HOWARD & LYDIA LUNCH

Sep 82. 4 a.d.; (12") **SOME VELVET MORNING. / I FELL IN LOVE WITH A GHOST** [ ] [-]

BIS

*** NEW ENTRY ***

Formed: Glasgow, Scotland . . .late 1994 by AMANDA and brothers SCI-

FI STEPHEN and JOHN. First UK release 'DISCO NATION', was issued on local independent DIY label 'Chemikal Underground', run by The DELGADOS. Managed by Ritchie Dempsey and John Williamson, they were the first unsigned group to play live on Top Of The Pops in March '96. The song 'KANDY POP' from 'THE SECRET VAMPIRE SOUNDTRACK EP', duly zoomed up into the Top 30 the following week. In June '96, they had another Top 50 hit, and the 'Wiiija' label, finally won the battle of over 50 majors to sign them. • **Style:** D.I.Y. alternative pop brat-punk, fusing early ALTERED IMAGES with The SLITS and adding electronic power pop and a drum machine. • **Songwriters:** SCI-FI or group.

Recommended: album release late summer '96.

AMANDA RIN (MacKINNON) – vocals, keyboards, recorder / **SCI-FI STEPHEN DISKO (CLARK)** – vocals, synthesizers / **JOHN DISKO (CLARK)**– guitar

		Chemikal U	not issued
Aug 95.	(7"m) **DISCO NATION. / PLASTIK PEOPLE / CONSPIRACY A GO-GO**		-

— In Dec95, 'Che' issued 7"lp; ICKY-POO AIR-RAID.

Mar 96.	(7"ep)(cd-ep) **THE SECRET VAMPIRE SOUNDTRACK** – Kandy pop / Secret vampires / Teen-c power! / Diska.	25	-
Jun 96.	(7"m)(cd-s) **BIS VS. THE D.I.Y. CORPS** – This is fake d.i.y. / Burn the suit / Dance to the disco beat.	45	-
		Southern	K
Jun 96.	(7") **KEROLEEN. / ("Heavenly":- Trophy Girlfriend)**		

BJORK

Formed: 21 Oct'66, Reykjavik, Iceland. The SUGARCUBES were formed by BJORK and EINAR who had been part of KUKL. In 1987, they were signed by Derek Schulman (ex-Gentle Giant) to indie label 'One Little Indian'. Their classic debut 45 'BIRTHDAY', soon became a John Peel favourite, also making UK Top 75. • **Style:** SUGARCUBES; Underground avant-garde outfit featuring the tortured English speaking vocal talents of petite BJORK, intertwined with weird background squeaks of EINAR. Drew similarities to a futuristic SLITS minus the off-beat reggae. • **Songwriters:** All written by BJORK and EINAR, except TOP OF THE WORLD (Carpenters) / MOTORCYCLE MAMA (Sailcat). Solo BJORK with producer NELEE HOOPER also covered LIKE SOMEONE IN LOVE (J. Van Heusen & J. Burke) / IT'S OH SO QUIET (hit c.1948; Betty Hutton). • **Trivia:** BJORK issued her eponymous solo album in 1977 at the age of 10. She also made a number of homeland recordings with her group TAPPI TIKARRAS between 81-83. BJORK was married to THOR, but after they had child, he soon married new SUGARCUBE; MAGGA. SIGGI and BRAGI were former brother-in-laws who were married to twins. In 1989, they divorced and moved to Denmark to get married to each other!. The first openly gay marriage in rock/pop history.

Recommended: LIFE'S BEEN GOOD (SUGARCUBES; *9) / STICK AROUND FOR JOY (SUGARCUBES; *8) / HERE TODAY, TOMORROW, NEXT WEEK (SUGARCUBES; *8) / DEBUT (*10) / POST (*8)

KUKL

BJORK GUNDMUNDSDOTTIR – vocals, keyboards (ex-TAPPI TIKARRAS) / **EINAR ORN BENEDIKTSSON** – trumpet, vocals / **SIGTRYGGUR 'Siggi' BALDURESSON** – drums, percussion

		Gramm	not issued
Sep 83.	(7") **SONGULL / POKN FYRIR BYRJENDUR**	-	- ICELAND
		Crass	not iss
Nov 84.	(m-lp) **THE EYE** – Dismembered / Assassin / Anna. *(re-iss.Jun89)*		-
Mar 86.	(m-lp) **HOLIDAYS IN EUROPE**		-

SUGARCUBES

BJORK, EINAR + SIGGI recruited **THOR ELDON** – guitar / **BRAGI OLAFFSON** – bass / **EINAR MELLAX** – keyboards

		O. L. Indian	Elektra
Sep 87.	(7") **BIRTHDAY. / BIRTHDAY (Icelandic)** (12"+=) – Cat. Dec 87.(cd-s++=) – Motorcrash.	65	-
Feb 88.	(7") **COLD SWEAT. / DRAGON (Icelandic)** ('A'remixed-12"+=) – Traitor (Icelandic) / Birthday (demo). (cd-s+=) – Traitor (Icelandic) / Revolution.	56	-
Apr 88.	(7") **DEUS. / LUFTGITAR** (12"+=) – Steel of lift. ('A'remixed-10"+=) – Cowboy / Organic prankster. (cd-s+=) – Organic prankster / Night of steel (Icelandic).	51	-
Apr 88.	(lp)(c)(cd)(dat) **LIFE'S TOO GOOD** – Mama / Delicious demon / Birthday / Traitor / Blue eyed pop / Petrol / F***ing in rhythm and sorrow / Cold sweat / Deus / Sick for toys. (cd+=) – I want.	14	54 Jun 88
May 88.	(12"ep)(cd-ep) **COLD SWEAT / COLD SWEAT (meat mix). / BIRTHDAY (Icelandic) / DELICIOUS DEMON / COLD SWEAT (instrumental)**	-	

— **MARGRET 'Magga' ORNOLFSDOTTIE** – keyboards repl. MELLAK

Sep 88.	(7") **BIRTHDAY. / BIRTHDAY CHRISTMAS** (12")(cd-s) – ('A'side) / Fucking in rhythm and sorrow (live) / Cowboy (live) / Cold sweat (live). (12")(cd-s) **BIRTHDAY CHRISTMAS MIX** – Christmas eve – Christmas day – Christmas present – Petrol (all live). (US-green-ep title 'DELICIOUS DEMONS')	65	-

Above single was produced by The JESUS & MARY CHAIN brothers.

Dec 88.	(c-s) **MOTORCRASH (live) / POLO** (12"+=)(3"cd-s+=) – Blue eyed pop.	-	
Aug 89.	(7") **REGINA. / REGINA (Icelandic)** (12")/ /(12"+=)(cd-s+=) – (2 different-12"mixes)./ / Hot meat.	55	
Oct 89.	(lp)(c)(cd)(silver-lp) **HERE TODAY, TOMORROW, NEXT WEEK** – Tidal wave / Regina / Speed is the key / Dream T.V. / Nail / Pump / Eat the menu / Bee / Dear plastic / Shoot him / Water / Day called Zero / Planet. (cd+=) – Hey / Dark disco! / Hot meat.	15	70
Feb 90.	(7") **PLANET. / PLANET (somersault version)** (12"+=)(cd-s+=) – Planet (Icelandic) / Cindy.		

Early 1991, BJORK contributed her vox to 2 songs on 808 STATE album EX-EL.

Dec 91.	(7") **HIT. / HIT-INSTRUMENTAL** (12"+=) – Theft. (cd-s++=) – Chihuahua – instrumental. (7"ep++=) – Leash called love.	17	
Feb 92.	(cd)(c)(lp) **STICK AROUND FOR JOY** – Gold / Hit / Leash called love / Lucky night / Happy nurse / I'm hungry / Walkabout / Hetero scum / Vitamin / Chihuahua.	16	95
Mar 92.	(7") **WALKABOUT (remix). / STONEDRILL** (12"++=)/ /(cd-s+=) – Top of the world./ / Bravo pop.		
Aug 92.	(12"ep)(cd-ep) **VITAMIN. / ('A'Babylon's Burning mix) / ('A'earth dub) / ('A'laser dub in Hell mix) / ('A'decline of Rome part 2 & 3) / ('A' meditation mix)** (cd-ep+=) – ('A' E-mix).		
Oct 92.	(d-cd)(c)(lp) **IT'S IT** (remixes)	47	

— Officially disbanded late 1992.

– compilations, others, etc. –

Apr 90.	One Little Indian; (ltd-7"box) **BOXED SET**		-
Sep 92.	One Little Indian; (12"ep)(c-ep) **BIRTHDAY REMIX EP** – ('A'-Robertson remix) / ('A'-Tommy D remix) / ('A'-Jesus & Mary Chain remix). (cd-s+=) – ('A'other mix). (cd-s+=) – Mama / Hit (remix).	64	

BJORK

solo, with **MARIUS DE VRIES, PAUL WALLER, MARTIN VIRGO + GARRY HUGHES** – keyboards / **NELLEE HOOPER** (co-writer of some), **LUIS JARDIM** (also bass) + **BRUCE SMITH** – drums, percussion / **JON MALLISON** – guitar / **TALVIN SINGH** – tabla / **CORKI HALE** – harp / **JHELISA ANDERSON** – backing vocals / **OLIVER LAKE, GARY BARNACLE, MIKE MOWER** – brass.

		O. L. Indian	Elektra
Jun 93.	(c-s) **HUMAN BEHAVIOUR. / ATLANTIC** (12")(cd-s) – (3 or 4 'A'mixes)	36	
Jul 93.	(cd)(c)(lp) **DEBUT** – Human behaviour / Crying / Venus as a boy / There's more to life than this recorded live at the Milk Bar toilets / Like someone in love / Big time sensuality / One day / Aeroplane / Come to me / Violently happy / The anchor song. *– (re-iss.cd+c Nov93+= Play dead).*	3	61
Aug 93.	(7")(c-s) **VENUS AS A BOY. / ('A' dream mix)** (cd-s+=) – Violently happy / There's more to life than this (mix). (cd-s) – ('A'side) / Stig du mig / Anchor song (black dog mix) / I remember you.	29	
Oct 93.	(7")(c-s) **PLAY DEAD. ("BJORK with DAVID ARNOLD") / ('A'mixes)** (12"+=)(cd-s+=) ('A' instrumental + film mixes).	12	

— (above single on 'Island' and from film 'The Young Americans'. It featured JAH WOBBLE on bass & was remixed by TIM SIMENON (of BOMB THE BASS)

Nov 93.	**BIG TIME SENSUALITY. / SiDASTA** (cd-s+=) – Gloria / Come to me (black dog productions). (12")(cd-s) – ('A'-Dave Morales def radio mix) / ('A'-Fluke mixes) / ('A'-Justin Robertson Lionrock wigout mix) / ('A'-Dom T. mix) / ('A'others).	17	88

— In Mar'94, BJORK was accused by SIMON FISHER (LOVEJOY) of not crediting him on 4 of her songs on her 'DEBUT' album.

Mar 94. (c-s) **VIOLENTLY HAPPY. / ('A'-Fluke mix)** 13 [ ]
(cd-s) – ('A'side) / Anchor song (acoustic) / Come to me (acoustic) / Human behavior (acoustic).
(d-cd-s) – ('B'side) / ('A'-5 other mixes).
Sep 94. (cd)(c)(lp) **BEST MIXES FROM THE ALBUM** [ ] [ ]
Apr 95. (c-s) **ARMY OF ME / ('A'-ABA All-Stars mix)** 10 [ ]
(cd-s) – ('A'side) / Cover me.
(cd-s+=) – You've been flirting again / Sweet intuition.
(cd-s+=) – ('A'-Massey mix) / ('A'-featuring SKUNK ANANSIE) / ('A'-ABA All-Stars instrumental).
(cd-s) – (all 4 mixes).
Jun 95. (cd)(c)(lp) **POST** 2 32
– Army of me / Hyper-ballad / The modern things / It's oh so quiet / Enjoy / You've been flirting again / Isobel / Possibly maybe / I miss you / Cover me / Headphones.
Aug 95. (c-s)(cd-s) **ISOBEL / CHARLENE (Black Dog mix) / I GO HUMBLE / VENUS AS A BOY (harpsicord version)** 23 [ ]
(cd-s) – ('A'side) / ('A'-Goldie mix) / ('A'-Eumir Deodato mix) / ('A'-Siggi mix).
Nov 95. (c-s) **IT'S OH SO QUIET / YOU'VE BEEN FLIRTING AGAIN (flat is a promise mix)** 4 [ ]
(cd-s+=) – Hyper-ballad (Over the edge mix) / Sweet sweet intuition.
(cd-s) – ('A'side) / Hyper-ballad (Girl's blouse mix) / Hyper-ballad (with The Brodsky Quartet) / My spine (featuring Evelyn Glennie).

. . . Jan – Jun '96 stop press . . .

Feb 96. (single) **HYPER-BALLAD** 8 [ ]

— On the 19th Feb'96, she attacked a persistent female journalist at a Bangkok airport for saying "Welcome to Bangkok". BJORK and metalheadz man GOLDIE are an item, as we say.

Frank BLACK (see under ⇒ PIXIES)

BLACK CROWES

Formed: Atlanta, Georgia, USA . . . 1988 originally as MR.CROWE'S GARDEN by ROBINSON brothers. Now as BLACK CROWES they signed worldwide to Rick Rubin's 'Def American' label May 1989. Their debut 1990 album 'SHAKE YOUR MONEY MAKER' eventually went platinum, climbing to US Top 5 a year later. • **Style:** Hard blues/glam rock band influenced by GUNS'N'ROSES, AEROSMITH or The FACES. • **Songwriters:** All written by ROBINSON brothers, except HARD TO HANDLE (Otis Redding) / RAINY DAY WOMAN NOS.12 & 35 (Bob Dylan) / TIME WILL TELL (Bob Marley) /DREAMS (Allman Brothers). • **Trivia:** Their father STAN ROBINSON had a minor US hit in '59 with 'BOOM-A-DIP-DIP'. Chuck Leavell (ex-ALLMANS) produced and guested on 1992 lp.

Recommended: SHAKE YOUR MONEY MAKER (*9) / THE SOUTHERN HARMONY AND MUSICAL COMPANION (*9) / AMORICA (*7)

CHRIS ROBINSON (b.20 Dec'66) – vocals 'Young' / **RICH ROBINSON** (b.RICHARD, 24 May'69) – guitar / **JEFF CEASE** (b.24 Jun'67, Nashville, USA) – guitar / **JOHNNY COLT** (b. 1 May'66, Cherry Point, NC.) – bass (repl. 2 earlier) / **STEVE GORMAN** (b.17 Aug'65, Hopkinsville, Kentucky) – drums (repl. 5 earlier)

Def American / Def American

May 90. (cd)(c)(lp) **SHAKE YOUR MONEY MAKER** [ ] 4 Oct 89
– Twice as hard / Jealous again / Sister luck / Could I've been so blind / Hard to handle / Seeing things / Thick'n'thin / She talks to angels / Struttin' blues / Stare it cold. *(finally hit UK No.36 Aug91) (re-dist.Sep92)*
Jun 90. (7") **JEALOUS AGAIN. / THICK'N'THIN** [ ] 75 May90
(12"+=)(cd-s+=)(12"pic-d+=) – Waitin' guilty.
Aug 90. (7")(c-s) **HARD TO HANDLE. / JEALOUS AGAIN (acoustic)** 45 45 Jul 90
(12"+=)(12"sha-pic-d+=) – Twice as hard / Stare it cold (both live).
(cd-s+=) – Twice as hard (remix).
Jan 91. (7")(c-s) **TWICE AS HARD. / JEALOUS AGAIN (live)** 47 [ ]
(12"+=)(cd-s+=) – Jealous guy (live).
(12"pic-d+=) – Could have been so blind (live).
Mar 91. (c-s)(7") **SHE TALKS TO ANGELS. / ('A'live video version)** - 30
Jun 91. (7") **JEALOUS AGAIN. / SHE TALKS TO ANGELS** 70 [ ]
(cd-s+=) – ('B'live) / Could I've been so blind.
(d12"+=) – ('A'&'B'acoustic) / Waitin' guilty / Struttin' blues.
Jun 91. (7") **HARD TO HANDLE. / WAITIN' GUILTY** - 26
Aug 91. (7") **HARD TO HANDLE. / SISTER LUCK (live)** 39 -
(cd-s+=) – Sister Luck (live).
(12"+=) – Dreams.
(7"sha-pic-d) – ('A'side) / Stare it cold (live).
Oct 91. (7")(c-s) **SEEING THINGS. / COULD I'VE BEEN SO BLIND (live)** 72 [ ]
(12"+=) – She talks to angels (live) / Sister luck (live).
(cd-s) – ('A'side) / Hard to handle / Jealous again / Twice as hard.

— **MARK FORD** – guitar (ex-BURNING TREE) repl. CEASE added **EDDIE HAWRYSCH** – keyboards

Apr 92. (7")(c-s) **REMEDY. / DARLING OF THE UNDERGROUND PRESS** 24 48
(12"+=)(cd-s+=) – Time will tell.
May 92. (cd)(c)(lp) **THE SOUTHERN HARMONY AND MUSICAL COMPANION** 2 1
– Sting me / Remedy / Thorn in my pride / Bad luck blue eyes goodbye / Sometime salvation / Hotel illness / Black moon creeping / No speak, no slave / My morning song / Time will tell.
Sep 92. (c-s) **THORN IN MY PRIDE. / STING ME** - 80
Sep 92. (7")(c-s) **STING ME. / RAINY DAY WOMEN NOS.12 & 35** 42 -
(live-cd-s) – ('A'side) / Jealous again / Seeing things / Boomer's story.
(live-ep-s) – ('A'side) / She talks to angels / Thorn in my pride / Darling of the underground press.
Nov 92. (7")(c-s) **HOTEL ILLNESS. / RAINY DAY WOMEN NOS.12 & 35** 47 [ ]
(12"clear+=) – Words you throw away.
(cd-s+=) – (interview 2 different with CHRIS or RICH).
Jun 93. (7")(c-s) **REMEDY / HARD TO HANDLE** [ ] -
(12"+=)(cd-s+=) – Hotel illness / Jealous again.
Nov 94. (cd)(c)(lp) **AMORICA** 8 11
– Gone / A conspiracy / High head blues / Cursed diamond / Non-fiction / She gave good sunflower / P.25 London / Ballad in urgency / Wiser time / Downtown money waster / Descending. *(cd+=)(c+=)* – Tied up and swallowed.
Jan 95. (7"blue) **HIGH HEAD BLUES. / A CONSPIRACY / REMEDY (live)** 25 [ ]
('A'extended/'B'live-12"+=) – Thick n' thin (live).
('B'live-cd-s+=) – P25 London (live).
(cd-s) – ('A'side) / A conspiracy / ('A'extended) / Thick n' thin (live).
Jul 95. (7") **WISER TIME. / CHEVROLET** 34 [ ]
(cd-s+=) – ('A'-rock radio mix) / She talks to angels (acoustic).
(cd-s) – ('A'acoustic) / Jealous again (acoustic) / Non fiction (acoustic) / Thorn in my pride (acoustic).

BLACK GRAPE

Formed: Manchester, England . . .late 1994 by ex-HAPPY MONDAYS men SHAUN RYDER and BEZ. They were joined by KERMIT and JED from The RUTHLESS RAP ASSASSINS, plus a host of extras. SHAUN's brilliant return from oblivion was complete by summer 1995, when 'REVEREND BLACK GRAPE' returned him to Top 10 status. However the song and video were banned from TV, due to the Catholic church saying it condoned the Venezuelan terrorist Carlos The Jackal, which also angered the New York based ADL (Anti-Defamation League). Another Top 10 classic 'IN THE NAME OF THE FATHER' preceeded the No.1 album 'IT'S GREAT WHEN YOU'RE STRAIGHT'. During this time, they were one of the successes at Hamilton Park's 'T In The Park' 2-day festival (near Glasgow), even though KERMIT broke his leg and had to sit most of the time on a speaker! • **Style:** Groovy but controversial anthemic dance rap/rock featuring a new revamped, but not totally drug-free SHAUN RYDER. • **Songwriters:** SHAUN & KERMIT, although in October '95, INTASTELLA members MARTIN WRIGHT and MARTIN MITTLER served a writ, claiming they co-wrote with SHAUN on early demos before they departed.

Recommended: IT'S GREAT WHEN YOU'RE STRAIGHT . . .YEAH! (*9)

SHAUN RYDER -vocals (ex-HAPPY MONDAYS)/ **BEZ** -dancer (ex-HAPPY MONDAYS) / **KERMIT (PAUL LEVEREDGE)** -rapper (ex-RUTHLESS RAP ASSASINS)/ **JED BIRTWHISTLE** – (ex-RUTHLESS RAP ASSASSINS) / **WAGS** -guitar (ex-PARIS ANGELS) / **CRAIG GANNON** -guitar (ex-SMITHS) who replaced INTASTELLA guitarists **MARTIN WRIGHT + MARTIN MITTLER**

Radio-active / Radio-active

May 95. (c-s) **REVEREND BLACK GRAPE / STRAIGHT OUT OF TRUMPTON (BASEMENT TAPES)** 9 [ ]
(cd-s+=) – ('A'-dark side mix).
(12") – ('A'side) / ('A'-dub collar mix) / ('A'-dark side mix).
Jul 95. (7")(c-s) **IN THE NAME OF THE FATHER. / LAND OF A THOUSAND KAMA SUTRA BABIES** 8 [ ]
(cd-s+=) – ('A'-chopper's mix) / ('A'-chopper's instrumental).
(12") – ('A'side) / (above 2).
Aug 95. (cd)(c)(lp) **IT'S GREAT WHEN YOU'RE STRAIGHT . . .YEAH** 1 [ ]
– Reverend Black Grape / In the name of the father / Tramazi party / Kelly's heroes / Yeah yeah brother / Big day in the north / Shake well before opening / Shake your money / Little Bob.

Shaun Ryder
BLACK GRAPE

Nov 95. (c-s) **KELLY'S HEROES / ('A'-The Milky Bar Kid mix)** 17
(cd-s+=) – ('A'-The Archibald mix) / Little Bob (live).
(cd-s) – ('A'live) / In the name of the father (live) / Fat neck.

. . . Jan – Jun '96 stop press . . .

— BEZ quit due to argument with SHAUN over his role in the group.

— On Channel 4's TFI Friday, SHAUN caused more controversy by adding loads of live f words on their version on SEX PISTOLS 'Pretty Vacant'.

May 96. (single) **FAT NECK** 10
Jun 96. (single) **ENGLAND'S IRIE** 6

— above featured JOE STRUMMER & KEITH ALLEN

BLACKMORE's RAINBOW (see under ⇒ DEEP PURPLE)

BLACK SABBATH

Formed: Aston, Birmingham, England . . . early 1969 out of jazz fusion combo EARTH. (IOMMI had also filled in for 2 weeks as JETHRO TULL guitarist.) BLACK SABBATH name lifted from Dennis Wheatley novel. They signed to 'Fontana' late '69 and after flop single, they were shifted to progressive 'Vertigo' label 1970. Due to earlier constant gigging and press attention, their debut album immediately made inroads into UK Top 10. Their popularity grew even more, when they had classic UK Top 5 hit single PARANOID. Although they released more singles, they were mainly marketed as an album band, with most hitting Top 10. When OZZY finally departed in 1979, they seemed doomed, but with new wave of heavy-metal music taking off again, they/IOMMI managed to survive. • **Style:** Occult influenced heavy outfit, with IOMMI on doom-laden basic guitar riffs, fused with the banshee screech of OZZY. Lyrically morbid with futuristic / medieval outlook, part of their tongue-in-cheek protest against God. Not a band for the easily-led and weak-minded, as blame for suicide attempts were always laid at their door. Did have a softer track on each album (i.e. FLUFF / CHANGES / EMBRYO / DON'T START). • **Songwriters:** Mainly group compositions. Covered EVIL WOMAN (DON'T PLAY YOUR GAMES WITH ME) (Crow) / WARNING (Aynsley Dunbar). • **Trivia:** Group moved to Los Angeles in 1979 and recruited manager Don Arden who had replaced Patrick Meehan in 1974. The original SABBATH reunited on 13 Jul'85 for LIVE AID concert in Philadelphia. Now famous producer ROGER BAIN brought in RICK WAKEMAN to play keyboards on CHANGES from 'VOLUME 4'.

Recommended: WE SOLD OUR SOULS FOR ROCK'N'ROLL (*9) / BLACK SABBATH (*7) / PARANOID (*7) / MASTER OF REALITY (*8) / VOLUME 4 (*8) / SABBATH BLOODY SABBATH (*7) / SABOTAGE (*6).

OZZY OSBOURNE (b.JOHN, 3 Dec'48) – vocals / **TONY IOMMI** (b.19 Feb'48) – guitars / **TERRY 'GEEZER' BUTLER** (b.17 Jul'49) – bass / **BILL WARD** (b. 5 May'48) – drums

Fontana Warners

Jan 70. (7") **EVIL WOMAN (DON'T PLAY YOUR GAMES WITH ME). / WICKED WORLD**
(re-iss. Mar70 on 'Veritgo')

Vertigo Warners

Feb 70. (lp)(c) **BLACK SABBATH** 8 23 Jul 70
– Black Sabbath / The wizard / Behind the wall of sleep / N.I.B. / Evil woman (don't play your games with me) / Sleeping village / Warning. *(re-iss.Jun80 + Nov85 on 'NEMS', cd-iss.Dec86 += Wicked world)*

Aug 70. (7") **PARANOID. / THE WIZARD** 4 61
Sep 70. (lp)(c) **PARANOID** 1 12 Feb 71
– War pigs / Paranoid / Planet Caravan / Iron man / Electric funeral / Hand of doom / Rat salad / Fairies wear boots. *(re-iss.Jun80, hit 54/ + Nov85 + pic-d on 'NEMS') (cd-iss.Jun89 on 'Castle')* (cd+=) – Tomorrow's world (live).

Aug 71. (lp)(c) **MASTER OF REALITY** 5 8
– Sweet leaf / After forever / Embryo / Children of the grave / Lord of this world / Solitude / Into the void / Orchid. *(re-iss.Jun80 + Nov85 on 'NEMS') (cd-iss.Jun89 on 'Castle')* (cd+=) – Killing yourself to live (live).

Jan 72. (7") **IRON MAN. / ELECTRIC FUNERAL** - 52
(re-iss. US 1974)

Sep 72. (7") **TOMORROW'S DREAM. / LAGUNA SUNRISE**
Sep 72. (lp)(c) **BLACK SABBATH VOL.4** 8 13 Oct 72
– Wheels of confusion / Tomorrow's dream / Changes / FX / Supernaut / Snowblind / Cornucopia / Laguna sunrise / St.Vitus' dance / Under the sun. *(re-iss.Jun80 on 'NEMS') (cd-iss.Jun89 on 'Castle')* (cd+=) – Children of the grave (live).

Oct 73. (7") **SABBATH BLOODY SABBATH. / CHANGES**
Nov 73. (lp)(c) **SABBATH BLOODY SABBATH** 4 11 Jan 74
– Sabbath bloody sabbath / A national acrobat / Fluff / Sabbra cadabra / Killing yourself to live / Who are you? / Looking for today / Spiral architect. *(re-iss.Jun80+Nov85 on 'NEMS') (cd-iss.Jun89 on 'Castle')* (cd+=) – Cornucopia (live).

(all lp's above moved to 'W.W.A.' Dec73)

N.E.M.S. Warners

Sep 75. (lp)(c) **SABOTAGE** 7 28
– Hole in the sky / Don't start (too late) / Symptom of the universe / Megalomania / Thrill of it all / Supertzar / Am I going insane (radio) / The writ. *(re-iss.Jan86) (cd-iss.Jun89 on 'Castle')* (cd+=) – Sweat leaf (live).

Feb 76. (7") **AM I GOING INSANE (RADIO). / HOLE IN THE SKY**

Oct 76. (lp)(c) **TECHNICAL ECSTACY** 13 51
– Back street kids / You won't change me / It's alright / Gypsy / All moving parts (stand still) / Rock'n'roll doctor / She's gone / Dirty women. *(re-iss.Aug83; cd-iss.Jun89)*

Nov 76. (7") **IT'S ALRIGHT. / ROCK'N'ROLL DOCTOR** -

— Late '77 OZZY leaves and is briefly repl. by **DAVE WALKER** (ex-SAVOY BROWN) Early 1978 **OZZY** returned.

May 78. (7") **NEVER SAY DIE. / SHE'S GONE** 21
Sep 78. (7")(7"purple) **HARD ROAD. / SYMPTOM OF THE UNIVERSE** 33

Oct 78. (lp)(c) **NEVER SAY DIE!** 12 69
– Never say die / Johnny Blade / Junior's eyes / Hard road / Shock wave / Air dance / Over to you / Breakout / Swinging the chain.. *(re-iss.May83)(re-iss.cd+c Sep93 on 'Spectrum')*

— **RONNIE JAMES DIO** (b.1949, New Hampshire, USA) – vocals (ex-(RITCHIE BLACKMORE'S) RAINBOW, ex-ELF etc.) repl.OZZY who went solo.

Apr 80. (lp)(c) **HEAVEN & HELL** 9 28 Jun 80
– Neon knights / Children of the sea / Lady evil / Heaven and Hell / Wishing well / Die young / Walk away / Lonely is the word. *(re-iss.May83, cd-iss.'87) (re-iss.cd+c May93 on 'Spectrum')*

Jun 80. (7") **NEON KNIGHTS. / CHILDREN OF THE SEA** 22
Nov 80. (7")(12") **DIE YOUNG. / HEAVEN AND HELL (live)** 41

— **VINNIE APPICE** – drums, percussion repl. WARD

Oct 81. (7")(12") **MOB RULES. / DIE YOUNG** 46
Nov 81. (lp)(c) **MOB RULES** 12 29
– Falling off the edge of the world / Voodoo / Mob rules / The sign of the southern cross / E 5150 / Slipping away / Turn up the night / Country girl / Over and over. *(re-iss.+cdJan85)*

Feb 82. (7")(12")(7"pic-d)(12"pic-d) **TURN UP THE NIGHT. / LONELY IS THE WORD** 37

Jan 83. (d-lp)(c) **LIVE EVIL (live)** 13 37
– E 5150 / Neon knights / N.I.B. / Children of the sea / Voodoo / Black Sabbath / War pigs / Iron man / Mob rules / Heaven and Hell / Sign of the southern cross / Paranoid / Children of the grave / Fluff. *(re-iss.Apr86)*

— **IAN GILLAN** – vocals (ex-DEEP PURPLE, ex-GILLAN) repl. RONNIE who formed DIO. **BILL WARD** – drums returned replacing VINNIE who also joined DIO. **BEV BEVAN** – drums (ex-ELECTRIC LIGHT ORCHESTRA) repl BILL, only originals in band were IOMMI and BUTLER

Sep 83. (lp)(c) **BORN AGAIN** 4 39
– Trashed / Stonehenge / Disturbing the priest / The dark / Zero the hero / Digital bitch / Born again / Hot line / Keep it warm.

Oct 83. (7") **STONEHENGE. / THRASHED** -

— **DAVE DONATO** – vocals repl. GILLAN who rejoined DEEP PURPLE

— **TONY IOMMI** recruited **GLENN HUGHES** – vocals (ex-DEEP PURPLE, etc.) repl. DONATO / **DAVE SPITZ** (b.New York) – bass repl. BUTLER / **ERIC SINGER** (b.Cleveland, Ohio) – drums repl. BEVAN / added **GEOFF NICHOLLS** (b.Birmingham) – keyboards (ex-QUARTZ) had toured '79.

Feb 86. (lp)(c)(cd) **SEVENTH STAR ("BLACK SABBATH with TONY IOMMI")** 78
– In for the kill / No stranger to love / Turn to stone / Sphinx (the guardian) / Seventh star / Danger zone / Heart like a wheel / Angry heart / In memory.
TONY IOMMI again added **BOB DAISLEY** – bass / **BEV BEVAN** – percussion / **TONY MARTIN** – vocals repl. HUGHES

Nov 87. (lp)(c)(cd) **THE ETERNAL IDOL** 66
– The shining / Ancient warrior / Hard life to love / Glory ride / Born to lose / Scarlet Pimpernel / Lost forever / The eternal idol.

— **IOMMI + MARTIN** recruited **COZY POWELL** – drums (ex-RAINBOW, ex-ELP) **LAURENCE COTTLE** -bass (on session)

I.R.S. I.R.S.

Apr 89. (7")(c-s) **HEADLESS CROSS. / CLOAK AND DAGGER** 62
(12"+=) – ('A'extended).

Apr 89. (lp)(c)(cd) **HEADLESS CROSS** 31
– The gates of Hell / Headless cross / Devil and daughter / When death calls / Kill in the spirit world / Call of the wild / Black moon / Nightwing. *(re-iss.cd Apr94)*

Jun 89. (7")(12")(7"pic-d) **DEVIL AND DAUGHTER. / (15 min.interview)**

— **NEIL MURRAY** -bass (ex-VOW WOW) joined mid'89 repl.COTTLE

Aug 90. (cd)(c)(lp) **TYR** 24
– Anno Mundi / The lawmaker / Jerusalem / The sabbath stones / The battle of Tyr / Odin's court / Valhalla / Feels good to me / Heaven in black. *(re-iss.cd Apr94)*

Sep 90. (7") **FEELS GOOD TO ME. / PARANOID (live)**

(12"+=)(cd-s+=) – Heaven and Hell (live).

— The 1981-83 line-up reformed Oct91, **IOMMI, GEEZER, VINNIE** and **R.JAMES DIO.**

I.R.S. Reprise

Jun 92. (cd)(c)(lp) **DEHUMANIZER** [28] [44]
– Computer god / After all (the dead) / TV crimes / Letters from Earth / Masters of insanity / Time machine / Sins of the father / Too late / I / Buried alive. *(re-iss.cd Apr94)*

Jun 92. (7") **TV CRIMES. / LETTERS FROM EARTH** [33] [ ]
(12"+=)(cd-s+=)(12"pic-d+=) – Paranoid (live).
(cd-s+=) – Mob rules (live).
(cd-s+=) Heaven and Hell (live).

— **TONY MARTIN** returned on vocals to repl.DIO

— **BOBBY RONDINELLI** -drums (ex-RAINBOW) repl.APPICE

Feb 94. (cd)(c)(lp) **CROSS PURPOSES** [41] [ ]
– I witness / Cross of thorns / Psychophobia / Virtual death / Immaculate deception / Dying for love / Back to Eden / The hand that rocks the cradle / Cardinal sin / Evil eye.

— The 1990 line-up was once again in force although COZY departed once again to be repl. by the returning RONDINELLI

Jun 95. (cd)(c)(lp) **FORBIDDEN** [71] [ ]
– The illusion of power / Get a grip / Can't get close enough / Shaking off the chains / I won't cry for you / Guilty as hell / Sick and tired / Rusty angels / Forbidden / Kiss of death.

– compilations etc. –

N.E.M.S. Warners

Dec 75. N.E.M.S./ US= Warners; (d-lp)(c) **WE SOLD OUR SOULS FOR ROCK'N'ROLL** [35] [48] Feb 76
– Black sabbath / The wizard / Warning / Paranoid / Wicked world / Tomorrow's dream / Fairies wear boots / Changes / Sweet leaf / Children of the grave / Sabbath bloody sabbath / Am I going insane (radio) / Laguna sunrise / Snowblind / N.I.B. *(re-iss.Nov80) (re-iss.d-lp,c,cd.Apr86 on 'Raw Power')*

Dec 76. N.E.M.S.; (7") **PARANOID. / SABBATH BLOODY SABBATH** [ ] [ ]

Dec 77. N.E.M.S./ US= Warners; (lp)(c) **BLACK SABBATH'S GREATEST HITS** [ ] [ ]

Sep 78. N.E.M.S.; (7") **PARANOID. / SNOWBLIND** [14] [ ]
(re-iss.Jun80)

Jun 80. N.E.M.S./ US= Warners; (lp)(c) **LIVE AT LAST (live)** [5] [ ]
– Tomorrow's dream / Sweet leaf / Cornucopia / Wicked world / Killing yourself to live / Snowblind / Children of the grave / War pigs / Paranoid / Cornucopia.

Aug 82. N.E.M.S.; (7"pic-d) **PARANOID. / IRON MAN** [ ] [ ]
(12"+=) – Fairies wear boots / War pigs.

Dec 85. N.E.M.S.; (7xlp-box) **BOXED SET FIRST 6 LP'S + LIVE AT LAST)** [ ] [ ]

Aug 85. Castle; (d-lp)(cd) **THE COLLECTION** [ ] [ ]

Jun 86. Archive 4; (12"ep) **CLASSIC CUTS FROM THE VAULTS** [ ] [ ]
– Paranoid / War pigs / Iron man / Black sabbath.

Jun 88. Vertigo; (d-lp)(d-c)(d-cd) **SABBATH BLOODY SABBATH / BLACK SABBATH** [ ] [-]

Nov 89. Vertigo; (d-lp)(c)(cd) **BLACKEST SABBATH** [ ] [ ]

Jan 90. Masterpiece; (d-cd)(d-c)(d-lp) **BACKTRACKIN'** [ ] [-]

Mar 89. Old Gold; (cd-s) **PARANOID / ELECTRIC FUNERAL / SABBATH BLOODY SABBATH** [ ] [-]

Mar 90. Old Gold; (7") **PARANOID. / IRON MAN** [ ] [-]

May 91. Essential; (3xcd) **THE OZZY OSBOURNE YEARS** [ ] [-]
– (features first 6 albums)

Sep 94. Spectrum; (cd) **IRON MAN** [ ] [-]

Nov 95. EMI; (3xcd-box) **HEADLESS CROSS / TYR / DEHUMANISER** [ ] [-]

BLIND FAITH

Formed: London, England . . . May69 . . . as supergroup of musicians. Played Hyde Park in June that year, supporting The ROLLING STONES. Their first and only album recorded virtually live in the studio, was massive seller on both sides of the Atlantic. Toured the States in the Autumn, but then aborted this project for pastures new. • **Style:** Roots blues, played with remarkable depth of feeling. • **Songwriters:** CLAPTON and WINWOOD, with cover WELL ALL RIGHT (Buddy Holly). • **Trivia:** GINGER BAKER's 11 year-old daughter was controversially used posing semi-naked on UK album sleeve. This was soon banned in USA.

Recommended: BLIND FAITH (*7)

STEVE WINWOOD – vocals, keyboards (ex-TRAFFIC, ex-SPENCER DAVIS GROUP) / **ERIC CLAPTON** – guitar, vocals (ex-CREAM, ex-JOHN MAYALL . . . , ex-YARDBIRDS, etc) / **RIC GRECH** – bass (ex-FAMILY) / **GINGER BAKER** – drums (ex-CREAM, ex-GRAHAM BOND ORGANISATION, ex-BLUES INC.)

Polydor Atlantic

Aug 69. (lp)(c) **BLIND FAITH** [1] [1] Jul 69
– Had to cry today / Can't find my way home / Well all right / Presence of the Lord / Sea of joy / Do what you like. *(re-iss.Nov77 & Aug83 on 'RSO') (cd-iss.Apr86 & Sep95)* (cd+=) – Exchange and mart.

— Disbanded later 1969. GINGER BAKER formed AIRFORCE with STEVE WINWOOD. The latter returned to TRAFFIC before carving out a solo career. RIC GRECH went solo. As did ERIC CLAPTON who also formed DEREK & THE DOMINOES in 1970.

– compilations, others, etc. –

Obviously none were released but some BLIND FAITH tracks did surface on ERIC CLAPTON compilations CROSSROADS and THE HISTORY OF ERIC CLAPTON (see ⇒)

BLIND MELON

Formed: Newport Beach, Los Angeles, California, USA . . . 1989. Had to wait four years and a contract on 'Capitol', before breaking through, initially at home, where their eponymous debut album, made Top 3. • **Style:** Laid back 70's influenced jangly and at times funky hard rock outfit. • **Songwriters:** Group. • **Trivia:** Supported LENNY KRAVITZ on late '93 tour.

Recommended: BLIND MELON (*6).

SHANNON HOON – vocals / **ROGER STEVENS** – guitar / **CHRIS THORN** – guitar / **BRAD SMITH** – bass / **GLEN GRAHAM** – drums

Capitol Capitol

Jun 93. (12"pic-d-ep)(12"ep)(cd-ep) **TONES OF HOME / NO RAIN (live). / DRIVE (live) / SOAK THE SIN (live)** [62] [ ]

Aug 93. (cd)(c) **BLIND MELON** [53] [3]
– Soak the sin / Tones of home / I wonder / Paper scratcher / Dear ol' dad / Change / No rain / Deserted / Sleepy house / Holyman / Seed to a tree / Drive / Time. *(re-iss.Jul94 free cd w /cd, hit UK 56)*

Dec 93. (7"yellow)(c-s) **NO RAIN. / NO BIDNESS (live)** [17] [20] Aug 93
(cd-s)(12"pic-d) – ('A'live) / Soak the sin / Paper scratcher / Deserted.
(12"+=)(cd-s+=) – I wonder.

Jun 94. (7"green)(c-s) **CHANGE. / PAPER SCRATCHER (acoustic)** [35] [ ]
(12"pic-d)(cd-s) – ('A'side) / No rain (live) / Candy says (live) / Time (live).

Jul 95. (cd-s) **GALAXIE / WILT / CAR SEAT (GOD'S PRESENT)** [37] [ ]
(12"+=) – 2 x 4.
(cd-s) – (first 2 tracks) / Change.

Aug 95. (cd)(c) **SOUP** [48] [28]
– Galaxie / 2 x 4 / Vernie / Skinned / Toes across the floor / Walk / Dumptruck / Car seat (God's presents) / Wilt / The duke / St.Andrew's fall / New life / Mouthful of cavities / Lemonade.

— On October 21, frontman RICHARD SHANNON HOON died of drug overdose.

BLONDIE

Formed: New York, U.S.A . . . August 1974, by former playboy bunny girl DEBBIE HARRY and boyfriend CHRIS STEIN. Other original members excluding female backing singers, were BILLY O'CONNOR – drums / FRED SMITH – bass (later to PATTI SMITH group) and IVAN KRAL – guitar (later TELEVISION). With a change of line-up they soon supported the likes of punk legend IGGY POP, issuing debut album on Richard Gottehrer's 'Private Stock' label early '77. 'Chrysalis' records reputedly bought the contract out for $500,000 in August that year. It payed off, when their first 45 for the label 'DENIS' rose to No.2 in UK. They surpassed this in early 1979, when 'HEART OF GLASS' went top. They had a further 4 No.1's in the next two years; ''SUNDAY GIRL', 'ATOMIC', 'CALL ME' & 'THE TIDE IS HIGH'. DEBORAH HARRY went on to have a relatively successful career as a solo artist, as well as moving into film. • **Style:** New wave pop, that later diversed into disco. Visual focus being the peroxide Marilyn Monroe of the seventies DEBBIE HARRY. • **Songwriters:** Most written by STEIN-HARRY except; DENIS (aka DENISE) (by Randy & The Rainbows) / HANGING ON THE TELEPHONE (Jack Lee; Nerves) / THE TIDE IS HIGH (Paragons; John Holt) / RING OF FIRE (Johnny Cash) / HEROES (David Bowie) / CALL ME (co-w / Giorgio Moroder) / her duet WELL, DID YOU EVAH (Cole Porter). Producers CHINN / CHAPMAN provided hit material 1978. • **Trivia:** DEBBIE HARRY filmography:- UNION CITY (1979) / ROADIE

(1980) / VIDEODROME (1982) / HAIRSPRAY (1982) / Broadway play 'TEANECK TANZI: THE VENUS FLYTRAP' (1983), which bombed after one night. She also appeared on 'The Muppet Show' circa 1980. Temporarily retired in 1983, to nurse STEIN through a long debilitating illness.

Recommended: THE COMPLETE PICTURE – THE VERY BEST OF DEBORAH HARRY & BLONDIE (*9) / PARALLEL LINES (*8).

DEBBIE HARRY (b.DEBORAH, 1 Jul'45, Miami, Florida) – vocals (ex-WIND IN THE WILLOWS) / **CHRIS STEIN** (b. 5 Jan'50, Brooklyn, New York) – guitar / **JIMMY DESTRI** (b.13 Apr'54) – keyboards (ex-KNICKERS) / **GARY VALENTINE** – bass / **CLEM BURKE** (b.CLEMENT, 24 Nov'55) – drums (ex-SWEET REVENGE)

Private Stock | Private Stock

Dec 77. (7") **X-OFFENDER. / IN THE SUN** [-] [ ]
Feb 77. (lp)(c) **IN THE FLESH. / MAN OVERBOARD** [-] [ ]
Apr 77. (lp)(c) **BLONDIE** [ ] [ ] Feb 77
– X offender / Little girl lies / In the flesh / Look good in blue / In the sun / A shark in jet's clothing / Man overboard / Rip her to shreds / Rifle range / Kung Fu girls / The attack of the giant ants. *(re-iss.Sep77 on 'Chrysalis', re-iss.Mar79 hit UK 75) (re-iss.+c.Oct82 on 'Hallmark') (re-iss.+c.Apr85 on 'MfP')*
May 77. (7") **IN THE FLESH. / X OFFENDER** [ ] [-]

Chrysalis | Chrysalis

Nov 77. (7")(12") **RIP HER TO SHREDS. / IN THE FLESH / X OFFENDER***(12"re-iss.Dec81)* [ ] [ ]

— (Oct77) **FRANK INFANTE** – bass (ex-WORLD WAR III) repl. VALENTINE

Feb 78. (7")(12") **DENIS. / CONTACT IN RED SQUARE / KUNG FU GIRLS***(12"white; re-iss.Dec81)* [2] [ ]
Apr 78. (lp)(c) **PLASTIC LETTERS** [10] [72] Feb 78
– Fan mail / Denis / Bermuda Triangle blues (Flight 45) / Youth nabbed as sniper / Contact in Red Square / (I'm always touched by your) Presence, dear / I'm on E / I didn't have the nerve to say no / Love at the pier / No imagination / Kidnapper / Detroit 442 / Cautious lip.
Apr 78. (7")(12") **(I'M ALWAYS TOUCHED BY YOUR) PRESENCE, DEAR. / POET'S PROBLEM / DETROIT 442** [10] [ ]
(12"re-iss.Dec81)

— (Nov77 on recording of 2nd lp) added **NIGEL HARRISON** – bass (b.England) now sextet with **INFANTE** – now on rhythm guitar

Aug 78. (7")(7"yellow) **PICTURE THIS. / FADE AWAY (AND RADIATE)** [12] [ ]
Sep 78. (7") **I'M GONNA LOVE YOU TOO. / JUST GO AWAY** [-] [ ]
Sep 78. (lp)(c)(white-lp) **PARALLEL LINES** [1] [6]
– Fade away (and radiate) / Hanging on the telephone / One way or another / Picture this / Pretty baby / I know but I don't know / 11:59 / Will anything happen / Sunday girl / Heart of glass / I'm gonna love you too / Just go away. *(re-iss.Jun88) (re-iss.+c+cd.Nov83 on 'Fame')*
Nov 78. (7") **HANGING ON THE TELEPHONE. / WILL ANYTHING HAPPEN** [5] [-]
Nov 78. (7") **HANGIN' ON THE TELEPHONE / FADE AWAY AND RADIATE** [-] [ ]
Jan 79. (7") **HEART OF GLASS. / RIFLE RANGE** [1] [-] Feb 79
(12"+=) – ('A'instrumental). *(12"re-iss.Dec81)*
Mar 79. (7") **HEART OF GLASS. / 11:59** [-] [1]
May 79. (7") **SUNDAY GIRL. / I KNOW BUT I DON'T KNOW** [1] [ ]
(12"+=) – ('A' French version). *(12"clear;re-iss.Dec81)*
Jun 79. (7") **ONE WAY OR ANOTHER. / JUST GO AWAY** [-] [24]
Sep 79. (7") **DREAMING. / SOUND ASLEEP** [2] [27] Oct 79
Oct 79. (7") **DREAMIN'. / LIVING IN THE REAL WORLD** [-] [ ]
Oct 79. (lp)(c) **EAT TO THE BEAT** [1] [17]
– Dreaming / The hardest part / Union city blue / Shayla / Eat to the beat / Accidents never happen / Die young stay pretty Slow motion / / Atomic / Sound-a-sleep / Victor / Living in the real world. *(re-iss.+cd.Jun87)*
Nov 79. (7") **UNION CITY BLUE. / LIVING IN THE REAL WORLD** [13] [ ]
Dec 79. (7") **THE HARDEST PART. / SOUND-A-SLEEP** [-] [84]
Feb 80. (7") **ATOMIC. / DIE YOUNG STAY PRETTY.** [1] [39] May 80
(12"+=) – Heroes. *(12"re-iss.Dec81)*
Apr 80. (7")(12") **CALL ME. / ('A'instrumental)** [1] [1] Feb 80
(12"+=) – ('A' Spanish).
Oct 80. (7") **THE TIDE IS HIGH. / SUZIE AND JEFFREY** [1] [1] Nov 80
Nov 80. (lp)(c) **AUTOAMERICAN** [3] [7]
– Europa / Live it up / Here's looking at you / The tide is high / Angels on the balcony / Go through it / Do the dark / Rapture / Faces / Do the dark / T-Birds / Walk like me / Follow me.
Jan 81. (7") **RAPTURE. / WALK LIKE ME** [5] [1]
(12") – ('A'side) / Live it up.
Apr 82. (7")(12")(7"pic-d) **ISLAND OF LOST SOULS. / DRAGONFLY** [1] [37] May 82
May 82. (lp)(c)(pic-lp) **THE HUNTER** [9] [33]
– Orchid club / Island of lost souls / Dragonfly / For your eyes only / The beast / War child / Little Caesar / Danceaway / (Can I) Find the right words (to say) / English boys / The hunter gets captured by the game.
Jul 82. (7")(12")(7"pic-d) **WAR CHILD. / LITTLE CAESAR** [39] [ ]

— (Aug82) STEIN formed own 'Animal' label through 'Chrysalis'. CLEM BURKE joins EURYTHMICS and later RAMONES. He also teams up with HARRISON to form CHEQUERED PAST. A solo album HEART ON THE WALL was released by JIMMY DESTRI in 1982 and featured most of BLONDIE. DEBBIE (DEBORAH). HARRY continued solo career.

– compilations, others, etc. –

Oct 81. Chrysalis; (lp)(c) **THE BEST OF BLONDIE** [4] [30]
(cd-iss.1983)
Dec 82. Chrysalis; (d-c) **EAT TO THE BEAT / AUTOAMERICAN** [ ] [-]
Nov 88. Chrysalis; (7") **DENIS (remix). / RAPTURE (remix)** [50] [ ]
(12"+=)(cd-s+=)(12"pic-d+=) – Heart of glass (remix) / Atomic (remix).
Dec 88. Chrysais; (lp)(c)(cd) **ONCE MORE INTO THE BLEACH (GREATEST HITS)** [50] [ ]
– Denis / Heart of glass / Call me / Rapture / Rapture (bonus beats) / The tide is high / The jam was moving (DEBBIE HARRY) / In love with love (DEBBIE HARRY) / Rush rush (DEBBIE HARRY) / French kissin' in the U.S.A. (DEBBIE HARRY) / Feel the spin (DEBBIE HARRY) / Backfired (DEBBIE HARRY) / Sunday girl (French version).

— (above included DEBBIE HARRY solo material)

Feb 89. Chrysalis; (7") **CALL ME. / CALL ME (version)** [61] [ ]
(12"+=)(cd-s+=) – Backfired (DEBBIE HARRY).
Mar 91. Chrysalis; (cd)(c)(d-lp) **THE COMPLETE PICTURE – THE VERY BEST OF DEBORAH HARRY & BLONDIE** [3] [ ]
– Heart of glass / I want that man / Call me / Sunday girl / French kissin' in the USA / Denis / Rapture / Brite side / (I'm always touched by your) Presence dear / Well, did you evah! / The tide is high / In love with love / Hanging on the telephone / Island of lost souls / Picture this / Dreaming / Sweet and low / Union city blue / Atomic / Rip her to shreds.
Jan 94. Chrysalis; (cd)(c) **BLONDE AND BEYOND – RARITIES AND ODDITIES** [ ] [ ]
Aug 94. Chrysalis; (12")(c-s)(cd-s) **ATOMIC (remix). / ('A'mixes by Diddy & Alan Thompson)** [19] [ ]
(cd-s) – ('A'side) / Sunday girl / Union City blues.
Nov 94. Chrysalis; (d-cd) **THE PLATINUM COLLECTION** [ ] [ ]
Jun 95. Chrysalis; (12") **HEART OF GLASS. / CALL ME** [15] [ ]
(c-s) – ('A'side) / Rapture / Atomic.
(cd-s+=) – ('A'mixes).
Jul 95. Chrysalis; (cd)(c) **BEAUTIFUL – THE REMIX ALBUM** [25] [ ]
Oct 95. Chrysalis; (12"blue)(cd-s) **UNION CITY BLUE (remix) / I FEEL LOVE (live)** [31] [ ]
(cd-s) – (other mixes by Diddy / The Burger Queens / OPM / Vinny Vero & Jammin' Hot).
Re-issued /remastered all albums on cd (D.HARRY's) Sep94. PLASTIC LETTERS / AUTOAMERICAN / THE HUNTER + KOO KOO contained bonus tracks. PARALLEL LINES / EAT TO THE BEAT / DEBRAVATION + THE COMPLETE PICTURE were also on cassette, with the latter also released on vinyl & video.
Feb 87. Old Gold; (7") **DENIS. / PICTURE THIS** [ ] [-]
Feb 87. Old Gold; (7") **SUNDAY GIRL. / HANGING ON THE TELEPHONE** [ ] [-]
Feb 87. Old Gold; (7") **CALL ME. / UNION CITY BLUE** [ ] [-]
Feb 87. Old Gold; (7") **HEART OF GLASS. / THE TIDE IS HIGH** [ ] [-]
Feb 87. Old Gold; (7") **DREAMING. / ATOMIC** [ ] [-]
Mar 91. FM-Revolver; (lp) **BLONDIE HIT COLLECTION** [ ] [-]

DEBBIE HARRY

solo, with **NILE RODGERS** and **BERNARD EDWARDS** on production, etc.

Chrysalis | Chrysalis

Jul 81. (7")(12") **BACKFIRED. / MILITARY RAP** [32] [43]
Aug 81. (lp)(c) **KOO KOO** [6] [23]
– Jump jump / The jam was moving / Chrome / Under arrest / Inner city spillover / Surrender / Backfired / Now I know you / Military rap / Oasis.
Sep 81. (7") **INNER CITY SPILLOVER. / THE JAM WAS MOVING** [ ] [ ]
(12"+=) – Chrome.

now worked with various session musicians.

Chrysalis | Geffen

Jan 84. (7")(12") **RUSH RUSH. / RUSH RUSH (dub)** [ ] [ ]
(US b-side = DANCE, DANCE, DANCE)
Nov 86. (7")(12")(12"pic-d) **FRENCH KISSIN' IN THE U.S.A. / BUCKLE UP** [8] [ ]
Nov 86. (7") **FRENCH KISSIN' IN THE U.S.A. / ROCKBIRD** [-] [ ]
Nov 86. (lp)(c)(cd) **ROCKBIRD** [31] [ ]
– I want you / French kissin' in the U.S.A. / Buckle up / In love with love / You got me in trouble / Free to fall / Rockbird / Secret life / Beyond the limit.
Feb 87. (7")(12") **FREE TO FALL. / SECRET LIFE.** [46] [ ]
(12"+=) – Feel the spin.
Mar 87. (7") **IN LOVE WITH LOVE. / SECRET LIFE** [-] [ ]
Apr 87. (7")(12") **IN LOVE WITH LOVE. / FRENCH KISSIN' (in French)** [45] [ ]

not issued | Reprise

1988. (7") **LIAR, LIAR. / QUEEN OF VOODOO (by "VOODOOIST CORPORATION"** [-] [ ]

DEBORAH HARRY

with **CHRIS STEIN** – guitar / **LEIGH FOXX** – bass / **TERRY BOZZIO** – drums / **TOMMY PRICE** – drums / **PHIL ASHLEY** – synthesizers / **STEVE GOLDSTEIN** – keyboards, etc.

		Chrysalis	Sire
Sep 89.	(7") **I WANT THAT MAN. / BIKE BOY**	13	
	(12")(12"pic-d) – ('A'side) / ('A'remix) / ('A'instrumental) (cd-s+=) – (all 4 tracks above).		
Oct 89.	(lp)(c)(cd) **DEF, DUMB AND BLONDE**	12	
	– I want that man / Lovelight / KIss it better / Bike boy * / Get your way / Maybe for sure / I'll never fall in love / Calmarie / Sweet and low / He is so / Bugeye / Comic books / Brite side / End of the run *. *(cd+=*)*		
Nov 89.	(7")(c-s) **BRITE SIDE. / BUGEYE**	59	
	(12"+=) – In love with love. (cd-s++=) – French kissin' in the U.S.A.		
——	Her touring group at time included **STEIN** and **FOXX** plus **SUZY DAVIS** – keyboards / **CARLA OLLA** – rhythm guitar / **JIMMY CLARK** – drums		
Mar 90.	(7")(c-s) **SWEET AND LOW. / LOVELIGHT**	57	
	(12")(cd-s) – ('A'side) / (2 other 'A'mixes).		
May 90.	(7")(c-s) **MAYBE FOR SURE. / GET YOUR WAY**		
	(12"+=)(cd-s+=) – ('A'extended).		
	one-off duet, which featured on Cole Porter tribute album 'Red Hot & Blue'.		
Dec 90.	(7")(12") **WELL, DID YOU EVAH (by "DEBORAH HARRY & IGGY POP"). /** ('B'by THOMPSON TWINS)	42	
	(cd-s+=) – (track by 'Aztec Camera').		

BLUE NILE

Formed: Glasgow, Scotland . . . 1981 by BUCHANAN, MOORE and BELL. After debut 45 on 'R.S.O.', they were offered unusual record contract by Scottish (East Lothian) label 'Linn', in which their sound/album was tested for hi-fi equipment. Later in 1984, with the album 'A WALK ACROSS THE ROOFTOPS' selling enough, due to rave reviews, 'Virgin' took over distribution. Although it took five years for the miraculous follow-up 'HATS', no momentum was lost and it was worth the wait. Currently in the studio again in 1993, so expect an album from them before the year 2000. • **Style:** Emotion riddled, atmospheric music that resurrects sophistication. Singer/crooner PAUL BUCHANAN has all the potential of being the next SINATRA. • **Songwriters:** All BUCHANAN penned with others contributing. • **Trivia:** As said before, basically a studio outfit, until they toured U.S.A. Spring 1990. The trio guested on ROBBIE ROBERTSON's 1991 solo album 'STORYVILLE'.

Recommended: A WALK ACROSS THE ROOFTOPS (*8) / HATS (*9) / PEACE AT LAST (*6)

PAUL BUCHANAN – vocals, guitar, synthesizer / **PAUL JOSEPH MOORE** – keyboards, synthesizer, etc. / **ROBERT BELL** – bass, synthesizer, etc.

		R.S.O.	not issued
Oct 81.	(7") **I LOVE THIS LIFE. / SECOND ACT**		–
——	added guests **CALUM MALCOLM** – keyboards, vocals (ex-BADGER, ex-HEADBOYS) / **NIGEL THOMAS** – drums		
		Linn-Virgin	A&M
Apr 84.	(7")(12") **STAY. / SADDLE THE HORSES**		1985
	(re-iss.Jan89 also as (d7"+=) – Tinseltown in the rain / Heatwave.		
Apr 84.	(lp)(c) **A WALK ACROSS THE ROOFTOPS**	80	1985
	– A walk across the rooftops / Tinseltown in the rain / From rags to riches / Stay / Easter parade / Heatwave / Automobile noise. *(re-iss.+cd Jan89)*		
Jul 84.	(7") **TINSELTOWN IN THE RAIN. / HEATWAVE (instrumental)**		–
	(12") – ('A'extended) / Regret.		
——	Basic trio, plus session musicians.		
Sep 89.	(7") **THE DOWNTOWN LIGHTS. / THE WIRES ARE DOWN**	67	
	(12"+=)(cd-s+=) – Halfway to Paradise (TV theme).		
Oct 89.	(lp)(c)(cd) **HATS**	12	
	– Over the hillside / The downtown lights / Let's go out tonight / Headlights on the parade / From a late night train / Seven a.m. / Saturday night.		
Sep 90.	(7")(c-s) **HEADLIGHTS ON THE PARADE (Bob Clearmount mix). / ('A'-lp version)**	72	
	(12"+=)(cd-s+=) – Easter parade (w / RICKIE LEE JONES)		
Jan 91.	(7")(c-s) **SATURDAY NIGHT. / ('A'version)**	50	
	(12"+=)(cd-s+=) – Seven a.m. (live in the U.S.) / or / Our lives.		
	. . . Jan – Jun '96 stop press . . .		
		Warners	Warners
Jun 96.	(cd)(c)(lp) **PEACE AT LAST**	13	

BLUE OYSTER CULT

Formed: Long Island, New York, USA . . . 1970 as SOFT WHITE UNDERBELLY by BUCK DHARMA, ALLEN LANIER and AL BOUCHARD. They became STALK-FORREST GROUP and signed to 'Elektra', where they had album rejected. Late 1971 they transformed to BLUE OYSTER CULT and gained contract to 'Columbia' through guru manager Sandy Pearlman. • **Style:** Heavy guitar-laden blues-influenced rock inspired by LED ZEPPELIN. By the mid 70's, on massive hit 'DON'T FEAR THE REAPER', they mellowed to a more mid-60's BYRDS feel. • **Songwriters:** Group compositions, except CAREER OF EVIL (written by LANIER's one-time girlfriend PATTI SMITH) / BLACK BLADE (co-written w / MICHAEL MOORCOCK – Hawkwind) / WE GOTTA GET OUT OF THIS PLACE (Animals) / BORN TO BE WILD (Steppenwolf) / 2nd album contained lyrics by producer RICHARD MELTZER. • **Trivia:** AL BOUCHARD claimed on 1988 album 'IMAGINOS', he was inspiration.

Recommended: CAREER OF EVIL: THE METAL YEARS (*7).

ERIC BLOOM – vocals, "stun" guitar / **BUCK DHARMA** (b.DONALD ROSIER) – lead guitar, vocals / **ALLEN LANIER** – rhythm guitar, keyboards / **JOE BOUCHARD** – bass, vocals / **ALBERT BOUCHARD** – drums, vocals

		C.B.S.	Columbia
1972.	(7"ep) **LIVE BOOTLEG (live)**	–	
May 72.	(lp)(c) **BLUE OYSTER CULT**		
	– Transmaniacon / I'm on the lamb but I ain't no sheep / Then came the last days of May / Stairway to the stars / Before the kiss (a redcap) / Screams / She's as beautiful as a foot / Cities on flame with rock and roll / Workshop of the telescopes / Redeemed. *(re-iss.1981)*		
Jun 72.	(7") **CITIES ON FLAME WITH ROCK AND ROLL. / BEFORE THE KISS, A REDCAP**	–	
Mar 73.	(7") **SCREAMING DIZ-BUSTERS. / HOT RAILS TO HELL**	–	
Mar 73.	(lp)(c) **TYRANNY & MUTATION**		
	– The red and the black / O.D.'d on life itself / Hot rails to Hell / 7 screaming diz-busters / Baby ice dog / Wings wetted down / Teen archer / Mistress of the Salman salt (quickline girl).		
1974.	(7") **CAREER OF EVIL. / DOMINANCE AND SUBMISSION**	–	
Sep 74.	(lp)(c) **SECRET TREATIES**		53 Apr 74
	– Career of evil / Subhuman / Dominance and submission / M.E. 262 / Cagey cretins / Harvester of eyes / Flaming telepaths / Astronomy. *(re-iss.Mar82)*		
Nov 75.	(d-lp) **ON YOUR FEET OR ON YOUR KNEES (live)**		22 Mar 75
	– Subhuman / Harvester of eyes / Hot rails to Hell / The red and the black / 7 screaming diz-busters / Buck's boogie / Then came the last days of May / Cities on flame / M.E.262 / Before the kiss, a redcap / I ain't got you / Born to be wild. *(re-iss.Sep87)*		
Nov 75.	(7") **BORN TO BE WILD (live). / (part 2)**	–	
Jun 76.	(lp)(c) **AGENTS OF FORTUNE**	26	29
	– This ain't the summer of love / True confessions / (Don't fear) The reaper / E.T.I.(Extra Terrestrial Intelligence) / The revenge of Vera Gaming / Sinful love / Tattoo vampire / Morning final / Tenderloin / Debbie Denise. *(re-iss.1988) (cd-iss. Jun94 on 'Sony') (cd-iss.May95 on 'Columbia')*		
Jul 76.	(7") **(DON'T FEAR) THE REAPER. / TATTOO VAMPIRE**		12
1976.	(7") **DEBBIE DENISE. / THIS AIN'T THE SUMMER OF LOVE**	–	
Dec 77.	(lp)(c) **SPECTRES**	60	43 Nov 77
	– Godzilla / Golden age of leather / Death valley nights / Searchin' for Celine / Fireworks / R U ready 2 rock / Celestial the queen / Goin' through the motions / I love the night / Nosferatu. *(re-iss.Feb86)*		
Dec 77.	(7") **GOING THROUGH THE MOTIONS. / SEARCHIN' FOR CELINE**		
May 78.	(7")(12") **(DON'T FEAR) THE REAPER. / R U READY 2 ROCK**	16	–
Jun 78.	(7") **GODZILLA. / GODZILLA (live)**	–	
Aug 78.	(7") **I LOVE THE NIGHT. / NOSFERATU**		–
Sep 78.	(lp)(c) **SOME ENCHANTED EVENING (live)**	18	44
	– R U ready 2 rock / E.T.I.(Extra Terrestrial Intelligence) / Astronomy (kick out the jams) / Godzilla / (Don't fear) The reaper / We gotta get out of this place.		
Oct 78.	(7") **WE GOTTA GET OUT OF THIS PLACE. / E. T. I. (EXTRA TERRESTRIAL INTELLIGENCE)**	–	
Nov 78.	(7") **WE GOTTA GET OUT OF THIS PLACE (live). / STAIRWAY TO THE STARS**		–
Aug 79.	(lp)(c) **MIRRORS**	46	44 Jul 79
	– Dr.Music / The great Sun jester / In thee / Mirrors / Moon crazy / The vigil / I am the storm / You're not the one (I was looking for) / Lonely teardrops.		
Aug 79.	(7") **MIRRORS. / LONELY TEARDROPS**		
Sep 79.	(7") **IN THEE. / LONELY TEARDROPS**	–	74
Oct 79.	(7") **IN THEE. / THE VIGIL**		–
Feb 80.	(7") **YOU'RE NOT THE ONE (I WAS LOOKING FOR). / MOON CRAZY**	–	
Jul 80.	(lp)(c) **CULTOSAURUS ERECTUS**	12	34
	– Black blade / Monsters / Divine wind / Deadlines / Here's Johnny (The Marshall plan) / Hungry boys / Fallen angel / Lips on the hills / Unknown tongue.		

Jul 80. (7") **HERE'S JOHNNY (THE MARSHALL PLAN). / DIVINE WIND** [-] [ ]
Jul 80. (7") **FALLEN ANGEL. / LIPS IN THE HILLS** [ ] [ ]
Oct 80. (7") **DEADLINES. / MONSTERS** [ ] [ ]
Jul 81. (lp)(c) **FIRE OF UNKNOWN ORIGIN** [29] [24]
– Fire of unknown origin / Burnin' for you / Veteran of the psychic wars / Sole survivor / Heaven metal / The black and silver / Vengeance (the pact) / After dark / Joan Crawford / Don't turn your back.
Aug 81. (7") **BURNIN' FOR YOU. / VENGEANCE (THE PACT)** [-] [40]
Sep 81. (7") **BURNIN' FOR YOU. / THE BLACK AND SILVER** [ ] [-]
(12") – ('A'side) / Dr.Music / Flaming telepaths.
May 82. (d-lp)(d-c) **EXTRATERRESTRIAL LIVE (live)** [39] [29]
– Dominance and submission / Cities on flame / Dr. Music / The red and the black / Joan Crawford / Burnin' for you / Roadhouse blues / Black blade / Hot rails to Hell / Godzilla / Veteran of the psychic wars / E.T.I.(Extra Terrestrial Intelligence) / (Don't fear) the reaper.
Jun 82. (7") **BURNIN' FOR YOU (live). / (DON'T FEAR) THE REAPER (live)** [-] [ ]

—— (late 1981) **RICK DOWNEY** – drums repl. ALBERT

Nov 83. (lp)(c) **THE REVOLUTION BY NIGHT** [95] [93]
– Take me away / Eyes on fire / Shooting shark / Veins / Shadows of California / Feel the thunder / Let go / Dragon lady / Light years of love.
Nov 83. (7") **TAKE ME AWAY. / FEEL THE THUNDER** [ ] [-]
(12"+=) – Burnin' for you / Dr.Music.
Feb 84. (7")(12") **SHOOTING SHARK. / DRAGON LADY** [ ] [83]
May 84. (7") **TAKE ME AWAY. / LET GO** [-] [ ]

—— **TONY ZVONCHEK** – keyboards (ex-ALDO NOVA) repl. LANIER

—— **TOMMY PRICE** – drums repl. DOWNEY.

Oct 85. (7") **DANCIN' IN THE RUINS. / SHADOW WARRIOR** [-] [ ]
Dec 85. (lp)(c)(cd) **CLUB NINJA** [ ] [63]
– White flags / Dancin' in the ruins / Rock not war / Perfect water / Spy in the house of the night / Beat 'em up / When the war comes / Shadow warrior / Madness to the method.
Dec 85. (7") **WHITE FLAGS. / ROCK NOT WAR** [ ] [ ]
(12"+=) – Shooting shark.
Feb 86. (7") **PERFECT WATER. / SPY IN THE HOUSE OF NIGHT** [-] [ ]

—— added **ALBERT BOUCHARD** – guitar, percussion, vocals
ALLEN LANIER – keyboards returned to repl. TONY

Sep 88. (lp)(c)(cd) **IMAGINOS** [ ] [ ] Aug 88
– I am the one you warned me of / Les invisibles / In the presence of another world / Del Rio's song / Siege and investitune of Baron Von Frankenstein's castle / Astronomy (new version) / Magna of illusion.
Oct 88. (7") **ASTRONOMY. / MAGNA OF ILLUSION** [ ] [ ]
(12"+=) – ('A'wild mix).
(cd-s++=) – (Don't fear) The reaper.

—— (early '89 tour) **JON ROGERS** – bass repl. JOE BOUCHARD / **RON RIDDLE** – drums repl. RICK DOWNEY

– compilations, others, etc. –

Below on 'CBS'/ 'Columbia' unless otherwise mentioned.
1984. (7") **(DON'T FEAR) THE REAPER. / I LOVE THE NIGHT** [ ] [ ]
Apr 90. (cd)(c)(lp) **CAREER OF EVIL: THE METAL YEARS** [ ] [ ]
– Cities on flame / The red and the black / Hot rails to Hell / Dominance and submission / Seven screaming Diz-busters / M.E. 262 / E.T.I. (Extra Terrestrial Intelligence) / Beat 'em up / Black blade / The harvester of eyes / Flaming telepaths / Godzilla / (Don't fear) The reaper.
Jun 84. Old Gold; (7") **(DON'T FEAR) THE REAPER. / R U READY TO ROCK** [ ] [-]
Jan 92. Castle; (cd) **LIVE 1976 (live)** [ ] [-]
Jun 94. Fragile; (cd)(c) **CULT CLASSICS** [ ] [-]
Jul 94. Fragile; (7")(c-s)(cd-s) **DON'T FEAR THE REAPER. / BURNIN' FOR YOU** [ ] [ ]

—— Note: An recording EP was issued on 'Skydog' FRANCE, but very rare.

BLUESBREAKERS (see under ⇒ MAYALL, John)

BLUESOLOGY (see under ⇒ Elton John)

BLUES TRAVELER

Formed: New York, USA . . .mid 80's by JOHN POPPER. While at school in Connecticut, he became friends with BLUES BROTHERS keyboard player PAUL SHAFFER, who at the time was arranger for the DAVID LETTERMAN show. They soon appeared on his show (many times) as The BLUES BAND, but after moving from Princeton, New Jersey to New York, they opted for appropriate BLUES TRAVELER. By the late 80's, their distribution of demo tapes, helped BILL GRAHAM, set up fruitful support slots to SANTANA and The ALLMAN BROTHERS, which led to contract with 'A&M'. Further appearances on the LETTERMAN show, boosted sales of their 1990 debut. In the Autumn of '92, POPPER was seriously hurt in a motorcycle accident, but he returned just over half a year later, albeit on stage in a wheelchair!. Their biggest highlight came when celebrating the 25th year of WOODSTOCK Festival in August '94. The following year now signed to 'Polydor', saw them go Top 10 with album 'FOUR' and single 'RUN-AROUND'. • **Style:** Basic organic blues inspired by the film BLUES BROTHERS (especially late actor JOHN BELUSHI). • **Songwriters:** POPPER, some w/ SHEEHAN or others. • **Trivia:** GREGG ALLMAN (Allman Brothers) and close friend CHRIS BARRON (Spin Doctors) guested on their 2nd album.

Recommended: FOUR (*7)

JOHN POPPER (b.1967, Cleveland, Ohio) -vocals, harmonica, guitar / **CHAN KINCHLA** -guitar / **BOBBY SHEEHAN** -bass / **BRENDAN HILL** -drums, percussion

A&M A&M
Nov 90. (cd)(c)(lp) **BLUES TRAVELER** [ ] [ ]
– But anyway / Gina / Mulling it over / 100 years / Dropping some NYC / Slow change / Warmer days / Gotta get mean / Alone / Sweet talking hippie. (cd+=) – Crystal flame.
Sep 91. (cd)(c)(lp) **TRAVELERS & THIEVES** [ ] [ ]
– The tiding / Onslaught / Ivory tusk / What's for breakfast / I have my moments / Optimistic thoughts / The best part / Sweet pain / All in the groove / Support your local emperor / Bagheera / Mountain cry. *(w/ free cd)* ON TOUR FOREVER (live)
Apr 93. (cd)(c) **SAVE HIS SOUL** [ ] [72]
– Trina magna / Love and greed / Letter from a friend / Believe me / Go outside and drive / Defense and desire / Whoops / Manhattan Bridge / Love of my life / My prophesie / Save his soul / Bullshitter's lament / Conquer me / Fledgling.

Polydor Polydor
Mar 95. (c-s) **RUN-AROUND / SAVE HIS SOUL** [ ] [8]
(cd-s+=) – Escaping.
Apr 95. (cd)(c) **FOUR** [ ] [9] Sep94
– Run-around / Stand / Lok around / Fallible / The mountains win again / Freedom / Crash burn / Price to pay / Hook / The good the bad and the ugly / Just wait / Brother John.
Nov 95. (c-s)(cd-s) **HOOK /** [-] [23]

BLUETONES

Formed: Hounslow, London, England . . .1994 by brothers MARK and SCOTT MORRISS. Appeared on a 'Fierce Panda' compilation ep 'Return To Splendour', before being signed to A&M's 'Superior Quality' label early in 1995. • **Style:** Young Brit-pop pack influenced by STONE ROSES, CHARLATANS, The LA'S and even The SMITHS for songs. • **Songwriters:** Group.

Recommended: EXPECTING TO FLY (*9)

MARK MORRISS -vocals / **ADAM DEVLIN** -guitars / **SCOTT MORRISS** -bass, vocals / **EDS CHESTERS** -drums, percussion

Superior not issued
Feb 95. (7"blue; mail order) **SLIGHT RETURN. / FOUNTAIN HEAD** [-] [-]
Jun 95. (7") **ARE YOU BLUE OR ARE YOU BLIND?. / STRING ALONG** [31] [ ]
(12"+=)(cd-s+=) – Driftwood.
Oct 95. (7")(c-s) **BLUETONIC. / GLAD TO SEE Y'BACK AGAIN?** [19] [ ]
(12"+=)(cd-s+=) – Colorado beetle.

. . . *Jan – Jun '96 stop press* . . .

Jan 96. (single) **SLIGHT RETURN** [2] [ ]
Feb 96. (cd)(c)(lp) **EXPECTING TO FLY** [1] [ ]
Apr 96. (single) **CUT SOME RUG / CASTLE ROCK** [7] [ ]

BLUE VELVETS (see under ⇒ CREEDENCE CLEARWATER REVIVAL)

BLUR

Formed: Colchester, Essex, England. . . 1989. Initially were SEYMOUR then The GREAT WHITE HOPES, before succuming to name BLUR by 1990. They soon were on the books of David Balfe's Parlophone subsidiary label 'Food', where they secured first UK Top 10 hit 'THERE'S NO

OTHER WAY'/ They went from strength to strength with each release, peaking quite deservedly with 'PARKLIFE' from which their first UK Top 5 classic 'BOYS AND GIRLS' was lifted. The following year, 1995 saw them win the battle to No.1 with 'COUNTRY HOUSE' over rivals OASIS. who were sharpening their tongues for an onslaught of media slagging. • **Style:** Groovy psychedelic pop influenced by rave and SYD BARRETT, which evolved into mod-ish pop/rock influenced by The SMALL FACES, The KINKS, due to DAMON's Cockney barra-boy delivery. • **Songwriters:** Group songs, ALBARN lyrics. Covered MAGGIE MAY (Rod Stewart) / LAZY SUNDAY (Small Faces). • **Trivia:** Producer – STEPHEN STREET. DAMON's father KEITH ALBARN used to be the manager of 60s rock outfit THE SOFT MACHINE.

Recommended: LEISURE (*7) / MODERN LIFE IS RUBBISH (*9) / PARKLIFE (*10) / THE GREAT ESCAPE (*8)

DAMON ALBARN (b.23 Mar'68, Whitechapel, London) – vocals / **GRAHAM COXON** (b.12 Mar'69, W.Germany) – guitars / **ALEX JAMES** (b.21 Nov'68, Dorset, England) – bass, vocals / **DAVE ROWNTREE** (b. 8 Apr'63) – drums

Food-EMI S.B.K.

Oct 90. (7")(c-s) **SHE'S SO HIGH. / I KNOW** [48] [-]
(12"+=) – ('A'definitive mix).
(cd-s+=) – Down.

Apr 91. (7")(c-s) **THERE'S NO OTHER WAY. / INERTIA** [8] [82] Dec 91
(12"+=) ('A'extended)
(12"+=)(cd-s+=) – Mr.Briggs / I'm all over.
(extra-12") – ('A'remix). / Day upon day (live).

Jul 91. (7")(c-s) **BANG. / LUMINOUS** [24] [ ]
(12"+=) – Explain / Uncle Love.
(cd-s++=) – Beserk.

Aug 91. (cd)(c)(lp) **LEISURE** [7] [ ]
– She's so high / Bang / Slow down / Repetition / Bad day / Sing / There's no other way / Fool / Come together / High cool / Birthday / Wear me down.

Mar 92. (7")(c-s) **POPSCENE. / MACE** [32] [ ]
(12"+=) – I'm fine / Garden central.
(cd-s++=) – Badgeman Brown.

Apr 93. (12")(c-s) **FOR TOMORROW. / INTO ANOTHER / HANGING OVER** [28] [ ]
(cd-s) – ('A'side) / Peach / Bone bag.
(cd-s) – ('A'side) / When the cows come home / Beachcoma / For tomorrow (acoustic).

May 93. (cd)(c)(lp) **MODERN LIFE IS RUBBISH** [15] [ ]
– For tomorrow / Advert / Colin Zeal / Pressure on Julian / Star shaped / Blue jeans / Chemical world / Sunday Sunday / Oily water / Miss America / Villa Rosie / Coping / Turn it up / Resigned.

Jun 93. (7"red)(c-s) **CHEMICAL WORLD. / MAGGIE MAY** [28] [ ]
(12")(cd-s) – ('A'mix) / Es schmecht / Young and lovely / My ark.
(cd-s) – ('A'side) / Never clever (live) / Pressure on Julian (live) / Come together (live).

Oct 93. (7") **SUNDAY SUNDAY. / TELL ME, TELL ME** [26] [ ]
(cd-s) – ('A'side) / Daisy bell / Let's all go to the Strand.
(cd-s) – ('A'side) / Dizzy / Fried / Shimmer.
(12") – ('A'side) / Long legged / Mixed up.

Mar 94. (7")(c-s) **GIRLS AND BOYS. / MAGPIE / PEOPLE IN EUROPE** [5] [59] Jun94
(cd-s) – (tracks 1 & 3) / Peter Panic.
(cd-s) – (tracks 1 & 2) / Anniversary waltz.

Apr 94. (cd)(c)(lp) **PARK LIFE** [1] [ ] Jun94
– Girls and boys / Tracy Jacks / End of a century / Park life / Bank holiday / Bad head / The debt collector / Far out / To the end / London loves / Trouble in the message centre / Clover over Dover / Magic America / Jubilee / This is a low / Lot 105.

May 94. (12")(c-s)(cd-s) **TO THE END. / GIRLS AND BOYS (Pet Shop Boys remix)** [16] [ ]
(cd-s) – ('A'side) / Threadneedle Street / Got yer!.

— Above 'A' featured LETITIA of STEREOLAB. Next 'A'; actor PHIL DANIELS.

Aug 94. (c-s)(cd-s) **PARKLIFE. / SUPA SHOPPA / THEME FROM AN IMAGINARY FILM** [10] [ ]
(12") – (1st 2 tracks) / To the end (French version).
(cd-s) – (1st track) / Beard / To the end (French version).

Nov 94. (7")(c-s) **END OF A CENTURY. / RED NECKS** [19] [ ]
(cd-s+=) – Alex's song.

Aug 95. (7")(c-s) **COUNTRY HOUSE. / ONE BORN EVERY MINUTE** [1] [ ]
(cd-s+=) – To the end (with FRANCOISE HARDY).
(live-cd-ep) ('A') / Girls and boys / Parklife / For tomorrow.

Sep 95. (cd)(c)(lp) **THE GREAT ESCAPE** [1] [ ]
– Stereotypes / Country house / Best days / Charmless man / Fade away / Top man / The universal / Mr. Robinson's quango / He thought of cars / It could be you / Ernold Same / Globe alone / Dan Abnormal / Entertain me / Yuko and Hiro.

Nov 95. (c-s) **THE UNIVERSAL / ENTERTAIN ME (the live it! remix)** [5] [ ]
(cd-s+=) – Ultranol / No monsters in me.
(cd-s) – ('A'side) / Mr.Robinson's quango (live) / It could be you (live) / Stereotypes (all live from the Beeb).

. . . Jan – Jun '96 stop press . . .

Feb 96. (single) **STEREOTYPES** [7] [ ]

Apr 96. (single) **CHARMLESS MAN** [5] [ ]

— BLUR were joint winners (with rivals OASIS; NOEL) of the Ivor Novello Award for songwriter of the year.

May 96. (d-cd; ltd on 'EMI Japan') **LIVE AT THE BUDOKAN (live)** [-] [-]

BODY COUNT (see under ⇒ ICE-T)

Marc BOLAN

Born: MARK FELD, 30 Sep'47, London, England. After abandoning his performing name TOBY TYLER and career as a male model, he went solo 1965 signing to 'Decca'. In spring 1967 after 3 flop singles, he replaced GEOFF McLELLAND in JOHN'S CHILDREN. With him, they issued controversial DESDEMONA single on the 'Track' label. Early '68, he teamed up with STEVE PEREGRINE TOOK under TYRANNOSAURUS REX name. With airplay on John Peel's night-time show, they gained enough underground attention to hit pop charts. In 1970, with MICKEY FINN replacing TOOK, and under an abbreviated name T. REX, they had biggest hit 'RIDE A WHITE SWAN'. This was followed-up by 8 consecutive Top 3 hits, including 4 UK chart-toppers 'HOT LOVE', 'GET IT ON', TELEGRAM SAM' & 'METAL GURU'. • **Style:** Effeminate superstar, who glided through period of acoustic and electric psychedelia in the 60's, to blatant but excellent glam-rock pop in the 70's. • **Songwriters:** Most written by BOLAN, except SUMMERTIME BLUES (Eddie Cochran) / DO YOU WANNA DANCE (Bobby Freeman) / DOCK OF THE BAY (Otis Redding) / TO KNOW HIM IS TO LOVE HIM (Teddy Bears) / RIP IT UP (Little Richard) / ENDLESS SLEEP (Joey Reynolds) / A TEENAGER IN LOVE (Dion). • **Trivia:** At the end of 1973, he split with wife and assistant manager June Child, and soon became involved with coloured singer GLORIA JONES. She had been part of T. REX backing singers for some months. In '74 the pair virtually emigrated to Los Angeles and Monte Carlo as tax exiles. Moved back to London for comeback Granada TV show "MARC" in 1977. Gloria was seriously hurt when driving the car which hit a tree and killed MARC on 16 Sep'77. The tree which is said to be near Barnes Common, London has since become a shrine for fans. MARC BOLAN still has a fan club "MARC ON WAX" who are also responsible for numerous exploitation/high demand releases.

Recommended: THE ULTIMATE COLLECTION (*9) / MY PEOPLE WERE FAIR... (*6) / PROPHETS, SEERS... (*6) / UNICORN (*7) / A BEARD OF STARS (*6).

Marc BOLAN

solo, using session men

Decca not issued

Nov 65. (7") **THE WIZARD. / BEYOND THE RISING SUN** [ ] [-]

Jun 66. (7") **THE THIRD DEGREE. / SAN FRANCISCO POET** [ ] [-]

Parlophone not issued

Dec 66. (7") **HIPPY GUMBO. / MISFIT** [ ] [-]

— BOLAN then joined JOHN'S CHILDREN before forming own band

TYRANNOSAURUS REX

MARC – vocals, guitars / **STEVE PEREGRINE TOOK** (b.28 Jul'49, London) – bongos, vocals

Regal Zono. A&M

Apr 68. (7") **DEBORA. / CHILD STAR** [34] [ ]

Jun 68. (lp) **MY PEOPLE WERE FAIR AND HAD SKY IN THEIR HAIR ... BUT NOW THEY'RE CONTENT TO WEAR STARS ON THEIR BROWS** [15] [ ]
– Red hot mama / Scenesof / Child star / Strange orchestras / Chateau in Virginia Waters / Dwarfish trumpet blues / Mustang Ford / Afghan woman / Knight / Graceful fat shake / Weilder of words / Frowning Atahuallpa. *(re-iss.May85+c. on 'Sierra')*

Regal Zono. Blue Thumb

Aug 68. (7") **ONE INCH ROCK. / SALAMANDA PALAGANDA** [28] [ ]

Oct 68. (lp) **PROPHETS, SEERS AND SAGES, THE ANGELS OF THE AGES** [ ] [ ]
– Deboraarobed / Stacey grove / Wind quartets / Conesuala / Trelawny lawn /

with
my Les paul
I Know I'm SMALL
But I enjoy
living Anyway
Harry Horse

Aznagell the mage / The friends / Salamanda Palaganda / Our wonderful brownskin man / Oh Harley (the Saltimbanques) / Eastern spell / The travelling tragition / Juniper suction / Scenes of dynasty. *(re-iss.May85 on 'Sierra') (re-iss.cd Oct94 on 'Disky')*

Jan 69. (7") **PEWTER SUITOR. / WARLORD OF THE ROYAL CROCODILES** [ ] [ ]

May 69. (lp) **UNICORN** [12] [ ]
– Chariots of silk / 'Pon a hill / The seal of seasons / The throat of winter / Cat black (the wizard's hat) / Stones of Avalon / She was born to be my unicorn / Like a white star, tangled and far, Tulip that's what you are / Warlord of the royal crocodiles / Evenings of Damask / The sea beasts / Iscariot / Nijinsky hind / The pilgrim's tale / The misty coast of Albany / Romany soup. *(re-iss.May85+c. on 'Sierra')*

Jul 69. (7") **KING OF THE RUMBLING SPIRES. / DO YOU REMEMBER?** [44] [ ]

— **MICKEY FINN** (b. 3 Jan'47) – bongos, vocals repl. TOOK who joined PINK FAIRIES (He died Nov80)

Jan 70. (7") **BY THE LIGHT OF THE MAGICAL MOON. / FIND A LITTLE WOOD** [ ] [ ]

Mar 70. lp,c) **A BEARD OF STARS** [21] [ ]
– Prelude / A day laye / The woodland bop / First heart mighty dawn dart / Pavillions of sun / Organ blues / By the light of the magical Moon / Wind cheetah / A beard of stars / Great horse / Dragon's ear / Lofty skies / Dove / Elemental child. *(US-import had free 7" BLUE THING)(UK re-iss.+c.May86 on 'Sierra')*

T.REX

Fly/E.M.I. — Reprise

Oct 70. (7"m) **RIDE A WHITE SWAN. / IS IT LOVE / SUMMERTIME BLUES** [2] [76] Jan 71

— added **STEVE CURRY** (b.21 May'47, Grimsby, England) – bass / **BILL LEGEND** (b. 8 May'44, Essex, England) – drums

Dec 70. (lp)(c) **T.REX** [13] [ ]
– The children of Rarn / Jewel / The visit / Childe / The time of love is now / Diamond meadows / Root of star / Beltane walk / Is it love / One ich rock / Summer deep / Seagull woman / Sun eye / The wizard / The children of Rarn (reprise). *(re-iss.Mar78 + Oct81 on 'Cube', re-iss.May85 on 'Sierra') (cd-iss.May92 on 'Castle')*

Feb 71. (7"m) **HOT LOVE. / WOODLAND ROCK / KING OF THE MOUNTAIN COMETH** [1] [-]

Apr 71. (7") **HOT LOVE. / ONE INCH ROCK / SEAGULL WOMAN** [-] [72]

Jul 71. (7"m) **GET IT ON (BANG A GONG). / THERE WAS A TIME / RAW RAMP** [1] [10] Dec 71

Sep 71. (lp)(c) **ELECTRIC WARRIOR** [1] [32] Nov 71
– Mambo sun / Cosmic dancer / Jeepster / Monolith / Lean woman blues / Get it on (bang a gong) / Planet queen / Girl / The motivator / Life's a gas / Rip off. *(also iss.pic-lp) (re-iss.Mar78 + Oct81 on 'Cube',+cd.May85) (cd-iss.Apr90 on 'Castle') (cd+=)* – Hot love / Deborah.

Nov 71. (7") **JEEPSTER. / LIFE'S A GAS** [2] [-]

Nov 71. (7") **JEEPSTER. / RIP OFF** [-] [ ]

T.Rex-E.M.I. — Reprise

Jan 72. (7"m) **TELEGRAM SAM. / CADILLAC / BABY STRANGE** [1] [67] Apr 72
(re-iss.Mar82; hit 69)

E.M.I. — Reprise

May 72. (7"m) **METAL GURU. / LADY / THUNDERWING** [1] [ ]

Jul 72. (lp)(c) **THE SLIDER** [4] [17] Sep 72
– Metal guru / Mystic lady / Rock on / The slider / Baby boomerang / Spaceball ricochet / Buick MacKane / Telegram Sam / Rabbit fighter / Baby strange / Ballrooms of Mars / Chariot choogle / Main man. *(re-iss.Oct83 on 'Marc On Wax') (cd-iss.Nov89) (also on pic-lp) (re-iss.cd Jul94 on 'Demon')*

Jul 72. (7") **THE SLIDER. / ROCK ON** [-] [ ]

Sep 72. (7"m) **CHILDREN OF THE REVOLUTION. / JITTERBUG LOVE / SUNKEN RAGS** [2] [ ]

Dec 72. (7") **SOLID GOLD EASY ACTION. / BORN TO BOOGIE** [2] [ ]

Mar 73. (7") **20th CENTURY BOY. / FREE ANGEL** [3] [ ]

Mar 73. (lp)(c) **TANX** [4] [ ]
– Tenement lady / Rapids / Mister mister / Broken hearted blues / Shock rock / Country honey / Electric Slim and the factory man / Mad Donna / Born to boogie / Life is strange / The street and the babe shadow / Highway knees / Left hand Luke and the beggar boys. *(also iss.on pic-lp)(re-iss.Oct83, cd-iss.Nov89 on 'Marc On Wax') (re-iss.cd Jul94 on 'Demon')*

Jun 73. (7") **THE GROOVER. / MIDNIGHT** [4] [-]

Jun 73. (7") **THE GROOVER. / BORN TO BOOGIE** [-] [ ]

— added **JACK GREEN** – guitar (plus 3 female b.singers inc.**GLORIA JONES**)

Nov 73. (7") **TRUCK ON (TYKE). / SITTING HERE** [12] [-]

MARC BOLAN & T.REX

(T.REX = FINN, CURRIE, GREEN, JONES – keys, vocals) / **DAVY LUTTON** – drums (ex-HEAVY JELLY)repl. LEGEND (2 more female singers)

Feb 74. (7") **TEENAGE DREAM. / SATISFACTION PONY** [13] [ ]

Mar 74. (lp)(c) **ZINC ALLOY AND THE EASY RIDERS OF TOMORROW** [12] [ ]
– Venus loon / Sound pit / Explosive mouth / Galaxy / Orange / Nameless wildness / Teenage dream / Liquid gang / Carsmile Smith & the old one / You've got to jive to stay alive – Spanish midnight / Interstellar soul / Painless persuasion and the meathawk / Immaculate / The avengers (superbad) / The leopards (featuring Gardinia and The Mighty Slug). *(also iss.on pic-lp) (re-iss.Oct83, cd-iss.Nov89 on 'Marc On Wax') (re-iss.cd Jul94 on 'Demon')*

T.REX

(same line-up)

Jul 74. (7") **LIGHT OF LOVE. / EXPLOSIVE MOUTH** [22] [-]

— added **DINO DINES** – keyboards

Nov 74. (7") **ZIP GUN BOOGIE. / SPACE BOSS** [41] [-]

Feb 75. (lp)(c) **BOLAN'S ZIP GUN** [ ] [ ]
– Light of love / Solid baby / Precious star / Zip gun boogie / Token of my love / Think zine / 'Til dawn / Girl in the thunderbolt suit / I really love you baby / Golden belt. *(re-iss.Oct83, cd-iss. on 'Marc On Wax') (also iss.on pic-lp) (re-iss.cd Jul94 on 'Demon')*

— members MICKEY FINN and JACK GREEN departed. The latter to PRETTY THINGS Now 5-piece band comprising **BOLAN, JONES, CURRIE, LUTTON** and **DINES.**

Jul 75. (7") **NEW YORK CITY. / CHROME SITAR** [15] [-]

— next with **BILLY PRESTON** – keyboards

Oct 75. (7") **DREAMY LADY (as "T.REX DISCO PARTY"). / DO YOU WANNA DANCE / DOCK OF THE BAY** [30] [-]

Feb 76. (lp)(c) **FUTURISTIC DRAGON** [50] [ ]
– Futuristic dragon / Jupiter lion / All alone / Chrome sitar / New York City / My little baby / Calling all destroyers / Theme for a dragon / Sensation boulevard / Ride my wheels / Dreamy lady / Dawn storm / Casual agent. *(also on pic-lp) (re-iss.Oct83, cd-iss.Nov89 on 'Marc On Wax') (re-iss.cd Jul94 on 'Demon')*

Feb 76. (7") **LONDON BOYS. / SOLID BABY** [40] [-]

Jun 76. (7") **I LOVE TO BOOGIE. / BABY BOOMERANG** [13] [-]

Sep 76. (7") **LASER LOVER. / LIFE'S AN ELEVATOR** [41] [-]

Jan 77. (7") **TO KNOW YOU IS TO LOVE YOU (as "MARC BOLAN & GLORIA JONES"). / CITY PORT** [ ] [-]

— now comprised BOLAN and DINES who brought in **MILLER ANDERSON** – guitar (ex-SAVOY BROWN) repl. GLORIA JONES who went solo / **HERBIE FLOWERS** – bass repl. CURRIE who went into sessions **TONY BRENNAN** – drums repl. LUTTON who joined WRECKLESS ERIC

Mar 77. (7") **THE SOUL OF MY SUIT. / ALL ALONE** [42] [-]

Mar 77. (lp)(c) **DANDY IN THE UNDERWORLD** [26] [ ]
– Dandy in the underworld / Crimson moon / Universe / I'm a fool for you / I love to boogie / Visions of Domino / Jason B. Sad / Groove a little / Hang-ups / The soul of my suit / Pain and love / Teen riot structure. *(also iss.pic-lp)(re-iss.Oct83, cd-iss.Nov89 on 'Marc On Wax') (pic-lp.Sep87) (re-iss.cd Jul94 on 'Demon')*

May 77. (7") **DANDY IN THE UNDERWORLD. / GROOVE A LITTLE** [ ] [-]

Aug 77. (7") **CELEBRATE SUMMER. / RIDE MY WHEELS** [ ] [-]

— On 16 Sep77 MARC BOLAN died when his car driven by GLORIA hit a tree. ANDERSON joined SOUTHSIDE JOHNNY and FLOWERS formed SKY.

– compilations, others, etc. –

On 'Fly' UK / 'Reprise' US unless mentioned otherwise.

Jul 71. (lp)(c) **THE BEST OF T.REX** [21] [ ]

Mar 72. (d-lp) **PROPHETS, SEERS AND SAGES . . . / MY PEOPLE WERE FAIR . . .** (US-title 'TYRANNOSAURUS REX – A BEGINNING') [1] [ ]

Mar 72. (7"m) **DEBORA / ONE INCH ROCK. / WOODLAND BOP / SEAL OF SEASONS** [7] [ ]

May 72. (lp)(c) **BOLAN BOOGIE** [1] [ ]
– Get it on (bang a gong) / The king of the mountain cometh / She was born to be my unicorn / Dove / Woodland bop / Ride a white swan / Raw ramp / Jeepster / First heart mighty dawn dart / By the light of the magical Moon / Summertime blues / Hot love. *(re-iss.Mar78 on 'Cube-Pye', Oct81 on 'Cube-Dakota') (re-Feb85 on 'Sierra') (re-iss.+cd.Apr89 on 'Castle')*

1973. (7") **BANG A GONG. / TELEGRAM SAM** [-] [ ]

1973. (7") **METAL GURU. / JEEPSTER** [-] [ ]

1973. (7") **HOT LOVE. / RIP OFF** [-] [ ]

Apr 78. (7") **CRIMSON MOON. / JASON B. SAD** [ ] [ ]

Oct 72. M.F.P.; (lp)(c) **RIDE A WHITE SWAN** [ ] [-]

Nov 72. Cube; (d-lp) **A BEARD OF STARS / UNICORN** [44] [ ]
(re-iss.Mar78 + Oct81) (re-iss.d-lp,c,cd.Sep88 on 'That's Original') (re-iss.cd Oct94 on 'Disky')

Apr 76. Cube; (7") **HOT LOVE. / GET IT ON** [ ] [-]

Sep 77. Cube; (7"ep) **BOLAN'S BEST + 1** [ ] [-]
– Ride a white swan / Motivator / Jeepster / Demon queen.

Mar 78. Cube; (7"m) **HOT LOVE. / RAW RAMP / LEAN WOMAN BLUES** [ ] [-]
Apr 78. Cube; (d-lp)(c) **MARC, THE WORDS AND MUSIC OF MARC BOLAN** [ ] [-]
Jul 79. Cube; (12"ep) **LIFE'S A GAS / FIND A LITTLE WOOD. / BLESSED WILD APPLE GIRL / ONCE UPON THE SEAS OF ABYSSINIA** [ ] [-]
Aug 81. Cube; (7") **JEEPSTER. / GET IT ON** [ ] [-]
(re-iss.Aug82 on 'Old Gold')
Jun 84. Cube; (7") **RARE MAGIC: SAILOR OF THE HIGHWAY. / DO YOU REMEMBER** [ ] [-]
(12"+=) – Demon queen / Pewtor suitor / The wizard.
Sep 73. E.M.I.; (7") **BLACKJACK (as "BIG CARROT"). / SQUINT EYED MANGLE** [ ] [-]
Nov 73. E.M.I./ US= Reprise; (lp)(c) **GREAT HITS** [32] [ ]
Jun 79. E.M.I./ US= Reprise; (lp)(c) **SOLID GOLD T.REX** [51] [ ]
(re-iss.May82 on 'Fame')
Sep 80. E.M.I.; (lp)(c) **THE UNOBTAINABLE T.REX** [ ] [-]
Jul 82. E.M.I.; (7"ep) **CHILDREN OF THE REVOLUTION / I LOVE TO BOOGIE. / LONDON BOYS / SOLID GOLD EASY ACTION** [ ] [-]
Sep 82. E.M.I.; (7"ep) **TRUCK ON (TYKE) / ZIP GUN BOOGIE. / TEENAGE DREAM / LIGHT OF LOVE** [ ] [-]
Sep 82. E.M.I.; (7"ep) **TELEGRAM SAM / THE SOUL OF MY SUIT. / METAL GURU / LASER LOVE** [ ] [-]
Feb 74. Track; (lp)(c) **THE BEGINNING OF DOVES** [ ] [ ]
(re-iss.+cd.Sep89 on 'Media Motion') (re-iss.Oct91 on 'Receiver')
Jun 74. Track; (7"m) **JASPER C.DEBUSSY. / HIPPY GUMBO / THE PERFUMED GARDEN OF GULLIVER SMITH** [ ] [ ]
Nov 74. Sounds Superb; (lp) **GET IT ON** [ ] [-]
(re-iss.Jun86 on 'Fame')
Apr 78. Pickwick; (d-lp)(c) **THE T.REX COLLECTION / GREATEST HITS** [ ] [-]
Jun 78. Hallmark; (lp)(c) **GREATEST HITS VOL.1** [ ] [-]
(re-iss.Jan87 as 'THE VERY BEST OF VOLUME 1')
Oct 87. Hallmark; (lp)(c)(cd) **TEENAGE DREAM** [ ] [-]
Mar 81. Rarn; (7"ep)(12"ep)(12"clear-ep) **THE RETURN OF THE ELECTRIC WARRIOR** [50] [-]
– Sing me a song / Endless sleep / The lilac hand of Menthol Dan. *(re-iss.7"pic-d.Jul82)*
Jul 82. Rarn; (12")(12"blue) **DEEP SUMMER. / OH BABY / ONE INCH ROCK** [ ] [-]
below on 'Marc On Wax' until otherwise mentioned.
Aug 81. (lp)(c) **T.REX IN CONCERT (live)** [35] [-]
(re-iss.on pic-lp)
Jan 82. (7")(7"blue) **MELLOW LOVE. / FOXY BOX / LUNACY'S BACK** [ ] [-]
(12"+=) – Rock me.
Dec 82. (7"ep) **CHRISTMAS BOP. / SHY BOY / RIDE A WHITE SWAN** [ ] [-]
(12"ep)(12"pic-d-ep+=) – King of the rumbling spires / Savage Beethoven.
Jun 83. (7")(7"pic-d) **THINK ZINC. / MAGICAL MOON / TILL DAWN** [ ] [-]
(12") – ('A'side) – Rip it up / A teenager in love.
Sep 83. (lp)(c) **DANCE IN THE MOONLIGHT** [83] [-]
Oct 83. (lp)(c) **CHILDREN OF THE REVOLUTION** [ ] [-]
(free one-side 7".w/above) – MISTER MOTION
Aug 84. (red-lp)(c) **BILLY SUPER DUPER** [ ] [-]
(re-iss.lp Apr85)
Aug 84. (lp)(c) **T.REXTASY** [ ] [-]
(free 12"w/above) – JAM (live). / ELEMENTAL CHILD (live)
May 85. (7"ep) **MEGAREX 1 (MEDLEY). / CHARIOT CHOOGLE / LIFE'S AN ELEVATOR** [72] [-]
(12"+=) – Solid baby.
May 85. (12"ep) **MEGAREX 2 (MEDLEY). / TAME MY TIGER / CHROME SITAR / SOLID BABY** [ ] [-]
—— (MEGAREX 3: was a 7"sha-pic-d / + 12"pic-d)
Jul 85. (7"m) **SUNKEN RAGS. / JITTERBUG LOVE / DOWN HOME LADY** [ ] [-]
(12"+=) – Funky London / Childhood.
Nov 85. (lp)(c)(cd) **TILL DAWN** [ ] [-]
Feb 87. (7") **CHILDREN OF THE REVOLUTION (remix). / THE SLIDER(remix) / TEAR FOR THE HIGH STAR** (by 'Dave Ashby') [ ] [-]
(12"+=) – Free angel (TV remix).
May 87. (7") **GET IT ON. / JEEPSTER** [54] [-]
(12"+=)(c-s+=)(cd-s+=) – Cadillac.
Sep 87. (7") **I LOVE TO BOOGIE. / RIDE A WHITE SWAN / HOT LOVE** [ ] [-]
(12"+=)(cd-s+=) – Hot George.
Aug 89. (lp)(cd) **THE MARC SHOWS (Granada TV shows)** [ ] [-]
Aug 91. (7")(c-s) **20th CENTURY BOY. / MIDNIGHT / THE GROOVER** [13] [-]
(12"+=)(cd-s+=) – Telegram Sam.
Oct 91. (7")(c-s) **METAL GURU. / THUNDERWIND / BOLAN'S ZIP GUN** [ ] [-]
(12"+=)(cd-s+=) – Solid baby (remix).
Nov 91. (7") **SLEEPY MAURICE. / (1968 interview)** [ ] [-]
Dec 91. (cd)(c)(d-lp) **BORN TO BOOGIE (live & poetry)** [ ] [-]

- MARC BOLAN compilations, etc. -

Sep 81. Cherry Red; (7")(12")(7"pic-d) **YOU SCARE ME TO DEATH. / THE PERFUMED GARDEN OF GULLIVER SMITH** [51] [-]
Oct 81. Cherry Red; (lp) **YOU SCARE ME TO DEATH** [88] [-]
(re-iss.cd+c Nov94 on 'Emporio')
Oct 81. Cherry Red; (7") **CAT BLACK. / JASPER C.DEBUSSY** [ ] [-]
May 82. Cherry Red; (7"m) **THE WIZARD. / BEYOND THE RISING SUN / RINGS OF FORTUNE** [-] [ ]
Dec 91. Cherry Red; (cd) **LOVE AND DEATH** [ ] [-]
Dec 91. Essential; (3xcd) **ANTHOLOGY** [ ] [-]

- T.REX & MARC BOLAN compilations -

Nov 81. Dakota; (d-lp)(c) **THE PLATINUM COLLECTION OF T.REX** [ ] [-]
Jan 82. Dakota; (lp)(c)(pic-lp) **ACROSS THE AIRWAVES** [ ] [-]
Aug 82. Dakota; (7") **HOT LOVE. / JEEPSTER** [ ] [-]
Aug 82. Dakota; (7") **GET IT ON. / DEBORA** [ ] [-]
Aug 82. Dakota; (7") **RIDE A WHITE SWAN. / ONE INCH ROCK** [ ] [-]
below on 'Old Gold' until otherwise mentioned.
Aug 82. (7") **HOT LOVE. / RIDE A WHITE SWAN** [ ] [-]
Aug 82. (7") **DEBORA. / ONE INCH ROCK** [ ] [-]
(above was also iss.1,000 w/'B'side BELTANE WALK)
Jan 85. (7")(7"sha-pic-d) **METAL GURU. / CHILDREN OF THE REVOLUTION** [ ] [-]
Jan 85. (7") **TELEGRAM SAM. / I LOVE TO BOOGIE** [ ] [-]
Jan 85. (7") **SOLID GOLD EASY ACTION. / THE GROOVER** [ ] [-]
Feb 89. (7") **GET IT ON. / JEEPSTER** [ ] [-]
Mar 89. (cd-s) **TELEGRAM SAM / METAL GURU / CHILDREN OF THE REVOLUTION** [ ] [-]
May 89. (cd-s) **SOLID GOLD EASY ACTION / 20th CENTURY BOY / THE GROOVER** [ ] [-]
Oct 82. Countdown; (lp) **T.REX** [ ] [-]
Apr 84. Cambra; (d-lp)(d-c) **BEYOND THE RISING SUN** [ ] [-]
May 85. Cambra; (d-lp)(c) **THE MAIN MAN** [ ] [-]
(7"pic-d. w/above) – TEENAGE DREAM. / SOLID GOLD SEGUE
Nov 84. Sierra; (d-lp)(c) **OFF THE RECORD WITH T.REX** [ ] [-]
May 85. Sierra; (12"ep) **GET IT ON / THERE WAS A TIME. / RAW RAMP / ELECTRIC BOOGIE** *(re-iss.Apr86)* [ ] [-]
May 87. Sierra; (cd) **GREATEST HITS** [ ] [-]
Apr 85. K-Tel; (d-lp)(d-c) **THE BEST OF THE 20th CENTURY BOY** [5] [-]
Jul 85. Dojo; (lp) **A CROWN OF JEWELS** [ ] [-]
Dec 91. Dojo; (cd) **THE EARLY YEARS** [ ] [-]
(re-iss.+lp+c)
Jun 86. Archive 4; (12"ep) **CLASSIC CUTS** [ ] [-]
– Jeepster / Ride a white swan / Get it on / Hot love.
Mar 87. Castle; (d-lp)(d-c)(d-cd) **THE SINGLES COLLECTION** [ ] [-]
Aug 87. Strange Fruit; (12"ep) **THE PEEL SESSIONS (27.10.70)** [ ] [-]
– Jewel / Ride a white swan / Elemental child / Sun eye.
1987. Connoisseur; (lp)(c)(cd) **STAND BY ME** [ ] [-]
Jan 88. Special Edition; (3"cd-s) **HOT LOVE / GET IT ON / TELEGRAM SAM / METAL GURU** [ ] [-]
1988. Fun; (lp) **18 GREATEST HITS** [ ] [-]
Jul 88. Knight; (c) **NIGHTRIDING** [ ] [-]
1990. Rhino; (4xlp-box) **WHERE THERE'S CHAMPAGNE** [-] [-]
Apr 91. S.P.S.; (lp)(cd) **RARITIES VOLUME ONE** [ ] [-]
Jun 91. Music Club; (cd) **THE VERY BEST OF MARC BOLAN & T.REX** [ ] [-]
Sep 91. Telstar; (cd)(c)(lp) **THE ULTIMATE COLLECTION** [4] [-]
– 20th century boy / Metal guru / I love to boogie / Deborah / New York City / Telegram Sam / Hot love / Dreamy lady / One inch rock / The soul of my suit / London boys / Ride a white swan / Get it on / Light of love / Children of the revolution / Jeepster / Laser love / Zip gun boogie / The groover / King of the rumbling spires / Plateau skull / Truck on (Tyke) / Solid gold easy action / Teenage dream. *(cd has 4 extra above)*
Apr 93. Windsong; (cd) **BBC RADIO 1 LIVE IN CONCERT (TYRANNOSAURUS REX live)** [ ] [-]
Apr 93. Deram; (cd-ep) **THE WIZARD / BEYOND THE RISIN' SUN / THE THIRD DEGREE / SAN FRANCISCO POET** [ ] [-]
Jun 93. Deram; (cd) **THE WIZARD** [ ] [-]
Jun 93. Zinc Alloy; (cd-ep) **BLOWIN' IN THE WIND / THE ROAD I'M ON (GLORIA) / BLOWIN' IN THE WIND (session version)** [ ] [-]
Apr 94. Remember; (cd) **20th CENTURY BOY** [ ] [-]

Jun 95. Edsel; (cd) **T.REX UNCHAINED: UNRELEASED RECORDINGS 1972 VOL.1** [ ] [-]
Jun 95. Edsel; (cd) **T.REX UNCHAINED: UNRELEASED RECORDINGS 1972 VOL.2** [ ] [-]
Aug 95. Old Gold; (cd-s) **TELEGRAM SAM / 20th CENTURY BOY** [ ] [-]
Sep 95. Polygram TV; (cd)(c) **THE ESSENTIAL COLLECTION** [24] [-]
Sep 95. Emporio; (cd)(c) **PREHISTORIC** [ ] [-]
Oct 95. Edsel; (cd) **T.REX UNCHAINED: VOLUME 3: 1973 PART 1** [ ] [-]
Oct 95. Edsel; (cd) **T.REX UNCHAINED: VOLUME 4: 1973 PART 2** [ ] [-]
Oct 95. Edsel; (cd) **CHANGE (THE ALTERNATIVE ZINC ALLOY)** [ ] [-]

BON JOVI

Formed: Sayreville, New Jersey, USA ... Spring '83, by JOHN and BRYAN. Signed worldwide by 'Phonogram' records who released RUNAWAY, a recent BONGIOVI solo effort which had been included on local radio station compilation lp. By 1986, they had become one of America's top selling rock bands, unleashing 'SLIPPERY WHEN WET' that year. • **Style:** Hard hookline rock that slipped into mainstream metal, due to influence of BRUCE SPRINGSTEEN and 70's heavy rock. • **Songwriters:** All penned by BON JOVI, SAMBORA and some collaborations with DESMOND CHILDS. Covered: IT'S ONLY ROCK'N'ROLL (Rolling Stones) / WITH A LITTLE HELP FROM MY FRIENDS (Beatles) / I DON'T LIKE MONDAYS (Boomtown Rats). • **Miscellaneous:** April 1988 saw their manager DOC McGEE convicted for drug offences and sentenced to five years suspended, but doing community work. BONGIOVI married childhood sweetheart Dorothea Hurley on 29 April'89. He was given cameo role in film 'YOUNG GUNS II'.

Recommended: NEW JERSEY (*7) / SLIPPERY WHEN WET (*7) / CROSS ROAD (*9)

JON BON JOVI (b.JOHN BONGIOVI, 2 Mar'62) – vocals, guitar / **RICHIE SAMBORA** (b.11 Jul'59) – lead guitar / **DAVID BRYAN** (b.DAVID RASHBAUM, 7 Feb'62) – keyboards / **ALEC JOHN SUCH** (b.14 Nov'56) – bass (ex-PHANTON'S OPERA) / **TICO 'Tar Monster' TORRES** (b. 7 Oct'53) – drums (ex-FRANKIE & THE KNOCKOUTS)

Vertigo Mercury

Apr 84. (lp)(c) **BON JOVI** [71] [43] Jan 84
– Runaway / Roulette / She don't know me / Shot through the heart / Love lies / Breakout / Burning for love / Come back / Get ready. *(cd-iss. 1986)*
May 84. (7")(12") **SHE DON'T KNOW ME. / BREAKOUT** [ ] [48]
Oct 84. (7")(12") **RUNAWAY. / BREAKOUT (live)** [ ] [39] Feb 84
(12"+=) – Runaway (live).
Apr 85 (7") **ONLY LONELY. /** [-] [54]
May 85. (lp)(c) **7800° FAHRENHEIT** [28] [37]
-In and out of love / The price of love / Only lonely / King of the mountain / Silent night / Tokyo road / The hardest part is the night / Always run to you / To the fire / Secret dreams. *(cd-iss. 1986)*
May 85. (7")(7"pic-d) **IN AND OUT OF LOVE. / ROULETTE (live)** [ ] [69]
(12"+=) – Shot through the heart (live).
Jul 85. (7") **THE HARDEST PART IS THE NIGHT. / ALWAYS RUN TO YOU** [68] [ ]
(12"+=) – Tokyo Road (live).
(d7"++=) – Shot through the heart (live).
(extra-12"red/clear) – ('A'side) / Tokyo Road (live) / In and out of love (live).
Aug 86. (7")(10"sha-pic-d) **YOU GIVE LOVE A BAD NAME. / LET IT ROCK** [14] [1] Sep 86
(12"+=) – Borderline.
(12"blue+=) – The hardest part is the night (live) / Burning for love (live).
Sep 86. (lp)(c)(cd) **SLIPPERY WHEN WET** [6] [1]
– Let it rock / You give love a bad name / Livin' on a prayer / Social disease / Wanted dead or alive / Raise your hands / Without love / I'd die for you / Never say goodbye / Wild in the streets. *(re-charted UK Dec90 hit 46, Jun91 No.42 , Sep92 re-issue) (re.pic-lp Aug88)*
Oct 86. (7")(7"pic-d) **LIVIN' ON A PRAYER. / WILD IN THE STREETS** [4] [1] Dec 86
(12"green+=) – Edge of a broken heart.
(d12"+=) – Only lonely (live) / Runaway (live).
Mar 87. (7") **WANTED DEAD OR ALIVE. / SHOT THROUGH THE HEART** [13] [7] Apr 87
(12"+=) – Social disease.
(12"silver++=) – Get ready (live).
(cd-s) – ('A'extended) / ('A'radio) / ('A'acoustic).
Aug 87. (7") **NEVER SAY GOODBYE. / RAISE YOUR HANDS** [21] [ ]
(12"+=)(c-s+=) – ('A'acoustic).
(12"yellow+=) – Wanted dead or alive (acoustic).
Sep 88. (7") **BAD MEDICINE. / 99 IN THE SHADE** [17] [1]
(12"+=)(cd-s+=) – Lay your hands on me.
(extra-12") – ('A'side) / You give love a bad name / Livin' on a prayer (live).
Sep 88. (lp)(c)(cd) **NEW JERSEY** [1] [1]
– Lay your hands on me / Bad medicine / Born to be my baby / Living in sin / Blood on blood / Stick to your guns / Homebound train / I'll be there for you / 99 in the shade / Love for sale / Wild is the wind / Ride cowboy ride. *(re-iss.cd+c Mar93)*
Nov 88. (7") **BORN TO MY BABY. / LOVE FOR SALE** [22] [3]
(12"+=)(12"pic-d+=) – Wanted dead or alive.
(cd-s++=) – Runaway / Livin' on a prayer.
Apr 89. (7") **I'LL BE THERE FOR YOU. / HOMEBOUND TRAIN** [18] [1] Mar 89
(12"+=) – Wild in the streets (live).
(cd-s+=) – Borderline / Edge of a broken heart.
Aug 89. (7")(c-s)(7"red/white/blue) **LAY YOUR HANDS ON ME. / BAD MEDICINE** [18] [7] May 89
(10"pic-d+=) – Blood on blood.
(12"+=)(cd-s++=) – Born to my baby (acoustic).
Nov 89. (7") **LIVING IN SIN. / LOVE IS WAR** [35] [9] Oct 89
(12"+=)(12"silver+=)(box-cd-s+=) – Ride cowboy ride / Stick to your guns.

JON BON JOVI

solo material inspired by the film 'Young Guns II'.

Aug 90. (7") **BLAZE OF GLORY. / YOU REALLY GOT ME NOW** [13] [1] Jul 90
(12"+=)(cd-s+=) – Blood money.
Aug 90. (cd)(c)(lp) **BLAZE OF GLORY** [2] [3]
– Billy get your guns / Miracle / Blaze of glory / Blood money / Santa Fe / Justice in the barrel / Never say die / You really got me now / Bang a drum / Dyin' ain't much of a livin' / Guano City. *(re-iss.cd/c Apr95)*
Nov 90. (7")(c-s) **MIRACLE. / BANG A DRUM** [29] [12] Oct 90
(12"+=)(cd-s+=) – Dyin' ain't much of a livin' / (interview).

RICHIE SAMBORA

(solo with **BRYAN + TORRES + TONY LEVIN** – bass)

Mercury Mercury

Aug 91. (7") **BALLAD OF YOUTH. / REST IN PEACE** [ ] [63]
(12"+=)(cd-s+=) – The wind cries Mary.
Sep 91. (cd)(c)(lp) **STRANGER IN THIS TOWN** [20] [36]
– Rest in peace / Church of desire / Stranger in this town / Ballad of youth / One light burning / Mr.Bluesman / Rosie / River of love / Father time / The answer. *(re-iss.cd/c Apr95)*

BON JOVI

were back for '92.

Mercury Jambco

Oct 92. (7")(c-s) **KEEP THE FAITH. / I WISH EVERYDAY COULD BE CHRISTMAS** [5] [29]
(cd-s+=) – Living in sin.
(cd-s+=) – Little bit of soul.
Nov 92. (cd)(c)(lp) **KEEP THE FAITH** [1] [5] Oct 92
– I believe / Keep the faith / I'll sleep when I'm dead / In these arms / Bed of roses / If I was your mother / Dry country / Woman in love / Fear / I want you / Blame it on the love of rock'n'roll / Little bit of soul.
Jan 93. (7")(c-s) **BED OF ROSES. / STARTING ALL OVER AGAIN** [13] [10]
(12"+=) – Lay your hands on me (live).
(cd-s) – Lay your hands on me (live) / I'll be there for you (live) / Tokyo road (live).
May 93. (7")(c-s) **IN THESE ARMS. / BED OF ROSES (acoustic)** [9] [27]
(cd-s) – ('A'side) / Keep the faith (live) / In these arms (live).
(c-s) – ('A'side) / Blaze of glory (acoustic).
Jul 93. (7")(c-s) **I'LL SLEEP WHEN I'M DEAD. / NEVER SAY GOODBYE (live acoustic)** [17] [97]
(cd-s) – ('A'side) / Blaze of glory / Wild in the streets (both live).
(cd-ep) 'HITS LIVE EP' ('A'side) / Blaze of glory / You give love a bad name / Bad medicine.
Sep 93. (7")(c-s) **I BELIEVE (Clearmountain mix). / ('A'live)** [11] [ ]
(cd-s) – ('A'side) / Runaway (live) / Livin' on the prayer (live) / Wanted dead or alive ('HITS LIVE PART 2 EP').
(cd-s) – ('A'side) / You give love a bad name (live) / Born to be my baby (live) / I'll sleep when I'm dead (live).
Mar 94. (7")(c-s) **DRY COUNTY. / STRANGER IN THIS TOWN (live)** [9] [ ]
(cd-s+=) – Blood money (live).
(cd-s) – ('A'side) / It's only rock'n'roll / Waltzing Matilda (all live).
Sep 94. (c-s) **ALWAYS. / THE BOYS ARE BACK IN TOWN** [2] [4]
(12"colrd) – ('A'side) / Prayer '94.
(cd-s) – ('A'side) / ('A'mix) / Edge of a broken heart.
Oct 94. (cd)(c)(lp) **CROSS ROAD – THE BEST OF BON JOVI** (compilation) [1] [8]
– Livin' on a prayer / Keep the faith / Someday I'll be Saturday night / Always / Wanted dead or alive / Lay your hands on me / You give love a bad name / Bed of roses / Blaze of glory / In these arms / Bad medicine / I'll be there for you / In and out of love / Runaway / Never say goodbye.

Dec 94. (7"pic-d)(c-s) **PLEASE COME HOME FOR CHRISTMAS / BACK DOOR SANTA** [7] [ ]
(cd-s+=) – I wish every day could be like Christmas.

Feb 95. (7"pic-d)(c-s) **SOMEDAY I'LL BE SATURDAY NIGHT. / GOOD GUYS DON'T ALWAYS WEAR WHITE (live)** [7] [ ]
(cd-s+=) – Always (live) / With a little help from my friends (live).
(cd-s+=) – ('A'mixes).

May 95. (c-s) **THIS AIN'T A LOVE SONG. / LONELY AT THE TOP** [6] [14]
(cd-s+=) – The end.
(cd-s) – ('A'side) / When she comes / Wedding day / Prostitute.

Jun 95. (cd)(c)(d-lp) **(THESE DAYS)** [1] [9]
– Hey God / Something for the pain / This ain't a love song / These days / Lie to me / Damned / My guitar lies bleeding in my arms / (It's hard) Letting you go / Hearts breaking even / Something to believe in / If that's what it takes / Diamond ring / All I want is everything / Bitter wine.

Sep 95. (c-s) **SOMETHING FOR THE PAIN / THIS AIN'T A LOVE SONG** [8] [76]
(cd-s+=) – I don't like Mondays.
(cd-s) – ('A'side) / Living on a prayer / You give love a bad name / Wild in the streets.

Nov 95. (c-s) **LIE TO ME / SOMETHING FOR THE PAIN (live)** [10] [ ]
(cd-s+=) – Always (live) / Keep the faith (live).
(cd-s) – ('A'side) / Something for the pain / Hey God (live) / I'll sleep when I'm dead (live).

. . . Jan – Jun '96 stop press . . .

Feb 96. (single) **THESE DAYS** [7] [ ]
Jun 96. (single) **HEY GOD** [13] [ ]

BOOMTOWN RATS

Formed: Don Laoghaire (near Dublin), Ireland . . . 1975 by ex-New Musical Express journalist BOB GELDOF and others (see below). Moved to England late 1976 and signed to newly formed 'Ensign' records. Numerous chart hits followed, with them peaking in 1979 with UK No.1 'I DON'T LIKE MONDAYS'. They had earlier been the first punks to hit No.1 with 'RAT TRAP'. • **Style:** Initially a new wave/punk outfit fused between EDDIE & THE HOT-RODS and The ROLLING STONES, due to GELDOF's energetic stage aura. They mellowed quickly into pop/rock field, hense their slow demise. • **Songwriters:** Most written by GELDOF except; BAREFOOTIN' (Robert Parker). GELDOF covered SUNNY AFTERNOON (Kinks). • **Trivia:** I DON'T LIKE MONDAYS was written about schoolgirl Brenda Spencer, who snipered/shot dead several of her school collegues. GELDOF starred in the feature films THE WALL (1982) & NUMBER ONE (1984). Late in 1984, BOB and MIDGE URE (of ULTRAVOX) masterminded BAND AID. They assembled together all the major stars of the time to sing DO THEY KNOW IT'S CHRISTMAS. It was top selling 45 making millions of pounds for famine relief in Ethiopia. Not content with this BOB and MIDGE assembled most of them again at Wembley Stadium for the LIVE AID concert on 13th July 85. This was simultaneously broadcast over the Atlantic at JFK Stadium, Philadephia. At the time it amassed well over £10m, and was spread around other needy charities as well as Ethiopia. The charity ended at the end of 1991 making over £100m. Already in June 1986, BOB was now Sir BOB GELDOF as he was knighted by the Queen. Two months later he married long-time fiancee PAULA YATES (a TV presenter and writer) who had had their child FIFI TRIXIBELLE and was in 1989 to give birth to another daughter PEACHES. BOB had continued to work with BAND AID until the late '80s, while continuing less strenuous solo career.

Recommended: THE BOOMTOWN RATS (*6) / TONIC FOR THE TROOPS (*5) / LOUDMOUTH – THE BEST OF THE BOOMTOWN RATS AND BOB GELDOF (*8).

BOB GELDOF (b. 5 Oct'54, Dublin) – vocals / **JOHNNIE FINGERS** (b.JOHNNY MOYLETT) – keyboards, vocals / **GERRY COTT** – guitar / **PETE BRIQUETTE** (b.PATRICK CUSACK) – bass / **GERRY ROBERTS** – guitar, vocals / **SIMON CROWE** – drums, vocals

Ensign / Mercury

Aug 77. (7"m)(12"m) **LOOKIN' AFTER No.1. / BORN TO BURN / BAREFOOTIN' (live)** [11] [-]

Sep 77. (lp)(c) **THE BOOMTOWN RATS** [18] [ ]
– Lookin' after No.1 / Neon heart / Joey's on the street again / Never bite the hand that feeds / Mary of the 4th form / (She gonna) Do you in / Close as you'll ever be / I can make it if you can / Kicks. *(re-iss.Dec83 on 'Mercury')*

Nov 77. (7") **MARY OF THE 4th FORM. / DO THE RAT** [15] [-]

Ensign / Columbia

Mar 78. (7") **SHE'S SO MODERN. / LYING AGAIN** [12] [ ]
Jun 78. (7") **LIKE CLOCKWORK. / HOW DO YOU DO?** [6] [ ]
Jul 78. (lp)(c) **A TONIC FOR THE TROOPS** [8] [ ]
– Like clockwork / Blind date / (I never loved) Eva Braun / Living in an island / Don't believe what you read / She's so modern / Me and Howard Hughes / Can't stop * / (Watch out for) The normal people / Rat trap. *(US version repl.* w/ Joey) (UK re-iss.Dec83 on 'Mercury')*

Oct 78. (7") **RAT TRAP. / SO STRANGE** [1] [-]
(re-iss.Nov84 on 'Mercury')

Nov 78. (7") **RAT TRAP. / DO THE RAT** [-] [ ]
Jul 79. (7") **I DON'T LIKE MONDAYS. / IT'S ALL THE RAGE** [1] [73] Jan 80
(re-iss.Nov84 on 'Mercury')

Oct 79. (lp)(c) **THE FINE ART OF SURFACING** [7] [ ]
– Someone's looking at you / Diamond smiles / Wind chill factor (minus zero) / Having my picture taken / Sleep (Fingers' lullaby) / I don't like Mondays / Nothing happened today / Keep it up / Nice'n'neat / When the night comes. *(re-iss.Nov84 on 'Mercury')*

Nov 79. (7") **DIAMOND SMILES. / LATE LATE NIGHT** [13] [ ]
Jan 80. (7")(12") **SOMEONE'S LOOKING AT YOU. / WHEN THE NIGHT COMES** [4] [ ]
Feb 80. (7") **SOMEONE'S LOOKING AT YOU. / I DON'T LIKE MONDAYS (live)** [-] [ ]

Mercury / Columbia

Nov 80. (7") **BANANA REPUBLIC. / MAN AT THE TOP** [3] [ ]
Dec 80. (lp)(c) **MONDO BONGO** [6] [ ]
– Please don't go / The elephant's graveyard (guilty) / Banana republic / Fall down / Hurt hurts / Whitehall 1212 * / Mood mambo / Straight up / This is my room / Another piece of red / Under their thumb . . .is under my thumb / Go man go. (US version repl.* w/ Don't talk to me)

Jan 81. (7") **THE ELEPHANT'S GRAVEYARD (GUILTY). / REAL DIFFERENT** [26] [ ]

—— (Mar81) Trimmed to a quintet when GERRY COTT left to going solo.

Nov 81. (7") **UP ALL NIGHT. / ANOTHER PIECE OF RED** [-] [ ]
Nov 81. (7") **NEVER IN A MILLION YEARS. / DON'T TALK TO ME** [62] [ ]
Mar 82. (7")(12") **HOUSE ON FIRE. / EUROPE LOOKED UGLY** [24] [ ]
Mar 82. (lp)(c) **V DEEP** [64] [ ]
– Never in a million years / The bitter end / Talking in code / He watches it all / A storm breaks / Charmed lives / House on fire / Up all night / Skin on skin / Little death.

Jun 82. (7") **CHARMED LIVES. / NO HIDING PLACE** [ ] [ ]
(d7"+=) – Nothing happened today (live) / A storm breaks (instrumental).
(12") – ('A'side) / A storm breaks.

Aug 82. (7") **CHARMED LIVES. / NEVER IN A MILLION YEARS** [-] [ ]
Jan 84. (7") **TONIGHT. / PRECIOUS TIME** [73] [ ]
(12"+=) – Walking downtown.

May 84. (7") **DRAG ME DOWN. / AN ICICLE IN THE SUN** [50] [ ]
(12"+=) – Rat trap / She's so modern.

Nov 84. (7")(7"pic-d) **DAVE. / HARD TIMES** [ ] [ ]
(d7"+=) – I don't like Mondays / It's all the rage.
(12"+=) – Banana republic (live) / Close as you'll ever be (live).

Dec 84. (lp)(c) **IN THE LONG GRASS** [ ] [ ]
– A hold of me / Drag me down / Dave / Over again / Another sad story / Tonight / Hard times / Lucky / Icicle in the Sun / Up or down.

Feb 85. (7") **A HOLD OF ME. / NEVER IN A MILLION YEARS** [ ] [ ]
(12"+=) – Say hi to Mick.

May 85. (7") **ICICLE IN THE SUN. / RAIN** [-] [ ]

—— Had already split Nov'84. FINGERS and CROWE formed GUNG HO. BOB GELDOF, as I've said, pieced together BAND/LIVE AID before going solo. (see above/below)

– compilations, others, etc. –

Dec 83. Mercury; (7"box 6) **RAT PACK (6 best of singles pack)** [ ] [-]
Jan 88. Old Gold; (7") **I DON'T LIKE MONDAYS. / RAT TRAP** [ ] [-]

BOB GELDOF

solo, with guests **DAVE STEWART, ERIC CLAPTON**, etc.

Mercury / Atlantic

Oct 86. (7")(12") **THIS IS THE WORLD CALLING. / TALK ME UP** [25] [82]
Nov 86. (lp)(c)(cd) **DEEP IN THE HEART OF NOWHERE** [79] [ ]
– Love you like a rocket / In the pouring rain / This heartless night / Words from Heaven / Deep in the heart of nowhere / Night turns to day / I cry too / The beat of the night / When I was young / This is the world calling / August was a heavy month. (cd+=) – Pulled apart by horses / Good boys in the wrong / Truly true blue.

Jan 87. (7") **LOVE YOU LIKE A ROCKET. / THIS IS THE WORLD CALLING** [61] [ ]
(12"+=) – ('A'extended).
(cd-s+=) – Pulled apart by horses / Truly true blue.

Mar 87. (7") **LOVE YOU LIKE A ROCKET. / PULLED APART BY HORSES** [-] [ ]
Jun 87. (7") **THE HEARTLESS NIGHT. / PULLED APART BY HORSES** [-] [ ]

Jun 87. (7") **I CRY TOO. / LET'S GO**
(12"+=) – Night turns to day / Deep in the heart of nowhere.

— He was now augmented by his **VEGETARIANS OF LOVE** backing band **GEOFF RICHARDSON** – viola, clarinet, etc. / **BOB LOVEDAY** – violin, bass, penny whistle / **PETE BRIQUETTE** – bass, keyboards / **PHIL PALMER** – guitars / **STEVE FLETCHER** – keyboard ALUN DUNN – accordion, organ / **RUPERT HINE** – keyboards, percussion, producer,

Jun 90. (7")(c-s) **THE GREAT SONG OF INDIFFERENCE. / HOTEL 75** [15]
(12"+=)(cd-s+=) – In the pouring rain.

Jul 90. (cd)(c)(lp) **THE VEGETARIANS OF LOVE** [21]
– A gospel song / Love or something / Thinking Voyager 2 type things / The great song of indifference / Crucified me / Big romance stuff / The chains of pain / A rose at night / Let it go / No small wonder / Walking back to happiness / The end of the world.

Aug 90. (7")(c-s) **LOVE OR SOMETHING. / OUT OF ORDER**
(12"+=) – The great song of indifference (mix) / Friends for life / One of these girls.

Nov 90. (7")(c-s) **A GOSPEL SONG. / VEGETARIANS OF LOVE**
(12"+=)(cd-s+=) – The warmest fire.

— now with The HAPPY CLUBSTERS (same as last)

Vertigo Mercury

Jun 92. (7")(c-s) **ROOM 19 (SHA LA LA LA LEE). / HUGE BIRDLESS SILENCE**
(cd-s+=) – The great song of indifference / Sweat for you (BRIQUETTE & SHARKEY CO.).

Sep 92. (7")(c-s) **MY HIPPY ANGEL. / MAYBE HEAVEN**
(cd-s+=) – Love or something / ('A'extended).

Oct 92. (cd)(c)(lp) **THE HAPPY CLUB**
– Room 19 (sha la la la lee) / Attitude chicken / The soft soil / A hole to fill / The song of the emergent nationalist / My hippy angel / The happy club / Like down on me / Too late God / Roads of Germany (after BD) / A sex thing / The house at the top of the world.

Apr 94. (7")(c-s) **CRAZY. / THE HAPPY CLUB** [65]
(cd-s) – ('A'side) / Room 19 (sha la la la lee) (live) / The beat of the night (live) / Rat trap (live).

Note; below single by BOOMTOWN RATS (also compilation tracks *)

Jun 94. (7"colrd)(c-s) **I DON'T LIKE MONDAYS. / BORN TO BURN / DO THE RAT** [38]
(cd-s) – ('A'side) / Looking after No.1 / Mary of the 4th form / She's so modern.
(cd-s) – ('A'side) / Rat trap / Someone's looking at you / Banana republic.

Jul 94. Vertigo; (cd)(c) **LOUDMOUTH – THE BEST OF THE BOOMTOWN RATS & BOB GELDOF** (compilation) [10]
– I don't like Mondays * / This is the world calling / Rat trap * / The great song of indifference / Love or something / Banana republic * / Crazy / The elephant's graveyard (guilty) * / Someone's looking at you * / She's so modern * / House on fire * / The beat of the night / Diamond smiles * / Like clockwork * / Room 19 (sha la la la lee) / Mary of the 4th form * / Looking after No.1 *.

BOO RADLEYS

Formed: Liverpool, England . . . 1988, by SICE, etc (see below). Moved to 'Creation' late '91 and soon were favourites of the NME, etc, who praised the release of the masterful 'GIANT STEPS' album. • **Style:** Psychedelic and heavy BYRDS influenced outfit, full of flowing spicy jangly pop, fused with screeching guitars and brassic accompaniment. • **Songwriters:** CARR lyrics / group music, except TRUE FAITH (New Order) / ALONE AGAIN OR (Love) / ONE OF US MUST KNOW (Bob Dylan). • **Trivia:** MERIEL BARHAM of The PALE SAINTS provided vocals on 2 tracks for GIANT STEPS album.

Recommended: GIANT STEPS (*9) / EVERYTHING'S ALRIGHT FOREVER (*7) / WAKE UP! (*8)

SICE (b.18 Jun'69, Wallasey, Lancashire, England) – vocals, guitar / **MARTIN CARR** (b.29 Nov'68, Thurso, Highlands, Scotland) – guitar / **TIMOTHY BROWN** (b.26 Feb'69, Wallasey) – bass / **STEVE DREWITT** (b.Northwich, England) – drums

Action not issued

Jul 90. (lp) **ICHABOD AND I** [-]
– Eleanor everything / Bodenheim Jr. / Catweazle / Sweet salad birth / Hip clown rag / Walking 5th carnival / Kaleidoscope / Happens to us all.

— **ROBERT CIEKA** (b. 4 Aug'68, Birmingham, England) – drums repl. DREWITT to BREED

Rough Trade not issued

Oct 90. (12"ep)(cd-ep) **KALEIDOSCOPE** [-]
– Kaleidoscope / How I feel / Aldous / Swansong.

Apr 91. (12"ep)(cd-ep) **EVERY HEAVEN** [-]
– Finest kiss / Tortoise shell / Bluebird / Naomi.

Sep 91. (12"ep)(cd-ep) **BOO UP! (Peel sessions)**
– Sometime soon she said / Fosters van / Everybird / Song for up.

Creation Columbia

Feb 92. (12"ep)(cd-ep) **ADRENALIN**
– Lazy day / Vegas / Feels like tomorrow / Whiplashed.

Mar 92. (cd)(c)(lp) **EVERYTHING'S ALRIGHT FOREVER** [55]
– Spaniard / Towards the light / Losing it (song for Abigail) / Memory babe / Skyscraper / I feel nothing / Room at the top / Does this hurt / Sparrow / Smile fades fast / Firesky / Song for the morning to sing / Lazy day / Paradise.

Jun 92. (7") **BOO! FOREVER / DOES THIS HURT** [67]
(12"+=)(cd-s+=) – Buffalo Bill / Sunifly II: Walking with the kings.

Nov 92. (7") **LAZARUS. / LET ME BE YOUR FAITH**
(12"+=)(cd-s+=) – At the sound of speed / Petrolium.

— added **STEVE KITCHEN** – trumpet, flugel horn / **JACKIE ROY** – clarinet / **LINDSAY JOHNSTON** – cello

Jul 93. (7") **HANG SUSPENDED. / RODNEY KING (Saint Etienne mix)**
(12"+=)(cd-s+=) – As bound a stomorrow / I will always ask where you have been though I know the answer.

Jul 93. (cd)(c)(lp) **GIANT STEPS** [17]
– Hang suspended / Upon 9th and Fairchild / Wish I was skinny / Leaves and sand / Butterfly McQueen / Rodney King (song for Lenny Bruce) / Thinking of ways / Barney (. . . and me) / Spun around / If you want it, take it / Best lose the fear / Take the time around / Lazarus / One is for / Run my way runway / I've lost the reason / The white noise revisited.

Oct 93. (7")(c-s) **WISH I WAS SKINNY / PEACH KEEN** [75]
(12"+=)(cd-s+=) – Futhur / Crow eye

Feb 94. (7")(c-s) **BARNEY (. . .AND ME). / ZOOM** [48]
(12"+=)(cd-s+=) – Tortoiseshell / Cracked lips, homesick.

May 94. (7")(c-s) **LAZARUS. / (I WANNA BE) TOUCHDOWN JESUS** [50]
(cd-s+=) – ('A'acoustic) / ('A'-Saint Etienne mix) / ('A'-Secret Knowledge mix.
(12"+=) – ('A'-Ultramarine mix).
(cd-s) – ('A'-Secret Knowledge mix) / ('A'-Ultramarine mix) / ('A'-Augustus Pablo mix) / ('A'-12"mix).

Feb 95. (c-s) **WAKE UP BOO! / JANUS** [9]
(cd-s+=) – Blues for George Michael / Friendship song.
(12") – Wake up Boo!: Music for astronauts / Janus / Blues for George Michael.
(cd-s) – Wake up Boo!: Music for astronauts / . . .And tomorrow the world / The history of Creation parts 17 & 36.

Mar 95. (cd)(c)(lp) **WAKE UP!** [1]
– Wake up Boo! / Fairfax scene / It's Lulu / Joel / Find the answer within / Reaching out from here / Martin, Doom! it's 7 o'clock / Stuck on amber / Charles Bukowski is dead / 4am conversation / Twinside / Wilder.

May 95. (c-s) **FIND THE ANSWER WITHIN / DON'T TAKE YOUR GUN TO TOWN** [37]
(cd-s+=) – Wallpaper.
(cd-s) – ('A'-High Llamas mix) / The only word I can find / Very together.

Jul 95. (c-s) **IT'S LULU / THIS IS NOT ABOUT ME** [25]
(cd-s+=) – Reaching out from here (High Llamas mix / Martin, doom! it's seven o'clock (Stereolab mix).
(cd-s) – ('A'side) / Joel (Justin Warfield mix) / Tambo / Donkey.

Sep 95. (7")(c-s) **FROM THE BENCH AT BELVIDERE. / HI FALUTIN'** [24]
(cd-s+=) – Crushed / Nearly almost time.

. . . Jan – Jun '96 stop press . . .

EGGMAN

— i.e. SICE

Creation Rykodisc

May 96. (single) **NOT BAD ENOUGH**
May 96. (cd)(c)(lp) **FIRST FRUITS**

BOOTH AND THE BAD ANGEL (see under ⇒ JAMES)

BOSTON

Formed: 1975 by SCHOLZ who had set-up his own basement studio in Boston, Massachusetts, USA. He surrounded himself with local musicians and sent successful demo to 'Epic' in 1976. They released two massive selling albums, before going into hibernation for 8 years. They resurfaced on 'MCA', but only US public took notice, with album 'THIRD STAGE'. • **Style:** Mainstream hard rock, featuring twin lead guitars softened with light harmonies. • **Songwriters:** SCHOLZ wrote all. • **Trivia:** In their hiatus, SCHOLZ experimented on his 'Rockman', a device that amplified guitar sound at low volume for home recording.

Recommended: BOSTON (*6)

BRAD DELP (b.12 Jun'51) – vocals. guitar / **TOM SCHOLZ** (b.10 Mar'47, Toledo, Ohio) – guitar, keyboards, vocals / **BARRY GOUDREAU** (b.29 Nov'51) – guitar / **FRAN**

SHEENAN (b.26 Mar'49) – bass / **SIB HASHIAN** (b.17 Aug'49) – drums repl. debut lp session drummer JIM MASDEA

		Epic	Epic	
Dec 76.	(7") **MORE THAN A FEELING. / SMOKIN'**	22	5	Sep 76
Dec 76.	(lp)(c) **BOSTON**	11	3	Sep 76

– More than a feeling / Peace of mind / Foreplay / Long time / Rock and roll band / Smokin' / Hitch a ride / Something about you / Let me take you home tonight. *(re-iss.Apr81 hit UK 58) (cd-iss.Mar87)*

Feb 77.	(7") **LONG TIME. / LET ME TAKE YOU HOME TONIGHT**		22	Jan 77
Jun 77.	(7") **PEACE OF MIND. / FOREPLAY**		38	May 77
Aug 78.	(7") **DON'T LOOK BACK. / THE JOURNEY**	43	4	
Aug 78.	(lp)(c)(US-pic-lp) **DON'T LOOK BACK**	9	1	

– Don't look back / The journey / It's easy / A man I'll never be / Feelin' satisfied / Party / Used to bad news / Don't be afraid. *(re-iss.Jun81; cd-iss.Mar87)*

Dec 78.	(7") **A MAN I'LL NEVER BE. / DON'T BE AFRAID**		31	
Mar 79.	(7") **FEELIN' SATISFIED. / USED TO BAD NEWS**		46	

— -(broke up for a while, after 3rd album was shelved / not completed) BARRY GOUDREAU made solo album late '80 before in '82 forming ORION THE HUNTER He was augmented by SCHOLZ and DELP. HASHIAN joined SAMMY HAGAR band.

BOSTON re-grouped around **SCHOLZ** and **DELP** plus **GARY PHIL** – guitar and the returning of **JIM MASDEA** – drums

		M.C.A.	M.C.A.	
Oct 86.	(7")(12") **AMANDA. / MY DESTINATION**		1	Sep 86
Oct 86.	(lp)(c)(cd) **THIRD STAGE**	37	1	

– Amanda / We're ready / The launch: Countdown – Ignition – Third stage separation / Cool the engines / My Destination / A new world / To be a man / I think I like it / Can'tcha say (you believe in me) / Still in love / Hollyann.

Jan 87.	(7") **WE'RE READY. / ?**	-	9	
Apr 87.	(7") **CAN'TCHA SAY (YOU BELIEVE IN ME). / STILL IN LOVE**		20	Mar 87

(12"+=) – Cool the engines.
(cd-s+=) – The launch: Countdown – Ignition – Third stage separation.

— Early in '90 SCHOLZ (aka BOSTON) won $million lawsuit against CBS.

RTZ

(RETURN TO ZERO)
were formed by **BRAD + BARRY** with **BRIAN MAES** – keyboards

		Giant-Reprise	Giant	
Aug 91.	(c-s)(cd-s) **FACE THE MUSIC /**	-	49	
Apr 92.	(cd)(c)(lp) **RETURN TO ZERO**			Aug 91

– Face the music / Devil to pay / Hard time / Rain down on me / Livin' for the rock / Until your love comes around / This is my life / Return to zero.

Apr 92.	(7")(c-s) **UNTIL YOUR LOVE COMES BACK AROUND. / EVERY DOOR IS OPEN**		26	Jan 92

(12"+=)(cd-s+=) – Return to zero / ('A'other mix).

Jun 92.	(c-s)(cd-s) **ALL YOU'VE GOT / ?**	-		

BOSTON

— Another comeback album.

		M.C.A.	M.C.A.	
Jun 94.	(cd)(c) **WALK ON**	56	7	

– I need your love / Surrender to me / Livin' for you / Walkin' on the night / Walk on / Get organ-ized / Get re-organ-ized / Walk on (some more) / What's your name / Magdalene / We can make it.

Jul 94.	(c-s) **I NEED YOUR LOVE / WE CAN MAKE IT**		51	

(cd-s+=) – The launch: The countdown – Ignition – Third stage separation.

– compilations etc. –

Sep 79.	Epic; (7"m) **DON'T LOOK BACK. / MORE THAN A FEELING / SMOKIN'**		-	
Apr 83.	Old Gold; (7") **MORE THAN A FEELING. / DON'T LOOK BACK**		-	
Aug 83.	C.B.S.; (d-c) **BOSTON / DON'T LOOK BACK**		-	

David BOWIE

Born: DAVID ROBERT JONES, 8 Jan'47, Brixton, London. In 1964 he formed The KING BEES with schoolmate GEORGE UNDERWOOD. After one single they split after BOWIE joined The MANNISH BOYS. They too only lasted half a year and DAVID went solo with backing from The LOWER THIRD. Early 1966, he became DAVID BOWIE and signed to 'Pye', but still flopped. After three years trying he finally charted with 'SPACE ODDITY', a classic that introduced his character Major Tom. That year (1969) his father died, but he was compensated by his introduction to ANGIE, his future wife. Although he was regarded as one of top newcomers to rock/pop scene, it took him until 1972 to finally establish himself as *the* rock star. He formed his now famous backing band The SPIDERS and announced to the music press his bisexuality. The single 'STARMAN' and album 'ZIGGY STARDUST' (an archetype alter-ego) were to hit UK top 10. He was now on 'RCA' records, who re-issued past 3 albums, which broke into UK charts. His follow-up 'ALADDIN SANE' was his first of many albums to hit No.1. • **Style:** Moved from 60's ANTHONY NEWLEY copyist, to innovator of risque glam-rock. He fashioned many styles including 'the feathercut' hairdo, make-up for men, and stage-mime (the latter being learnt from Lindsay Kemp). In 1975, his music dramatically diversed into Philadelphia soul/disco. This was thrown by the wayside for experimental/avant-garde type rock on (1977's) 'LOW', augmented by the obscure ENO. After HEROES album, same year, he returned to more conventional type rock, gaining another No.1 hit with his resurrection of Major Tom on 'ASHES TO ASHES'. After a virtual two and a half year hiatus he returned with CHIC producers for 'LET'S DANCE' album. It featured controversial video single 'CHINA GIRL' (once the co-product of his great friend IGGY POP). In recent years the public have seen him slightly stumble from top 10 positions. When he introduced his TIN MACHINE project, it was regarded by many critics to be far from classic BOWIE. Unshifted by opinions, he carried on with this set-up in 1991, but could not substantiate any major hits. • **Songwriters:** He wrote all his own material even managing some for others (e.g. ALL THE YOUNG DUDES for (Mott The Hoople) / OH YOU PRETTY THINGS (Peter Noone) / THE MAN WHO SOLD THE WORLD / (Lulu) / PINK ROSE (Adrian Belew) / etc. He produced 'RCA' acts LOU REED (Transformer) / MICK RONSON (Slaughter on Tenth Avenue) / IGGY POP (The Idiot) / etc. BOWIE's cover album PIN-UPS featured SORROW (Merseys) / ROSALYN (Pretty Things) / HERE COMES THE NIGHT (Them) / SHAPES OF THINGS (Yardbirds) / FRIDAY ON MY MIND (Easybeats) / ANYWAY ANYHOW ANYWHERE + I CAN'T EXPLAIN (Who) / SEE EMILY PLAY (Pink Floyd) / WHERE HAVE ALL THE GOOD TIMES GONE (Kinks) / DON'T BRING ME DOWN + I WISH YOU WOULD (Pretty Things) / EVERYTHING'S ALRIGHT (Mojos) /. Other covers:- LET'S SPEND THE NIGHT TOGETHER (Rolling Stones) / KNOCK ON WOOD (Eddie Floyd) / ALABAMA SONG (Brecht-Weill) / DANCING IN THE STREET (Martha & The Vandellas). I FEEL FREE (Cream) / NITE FLIGHT (Scott Walker) / I KNOW IT'S GONNA HAPPEN SOMEDAY (Morrissey) / DON'T LET ME DOWN & DOWN (Tacha-Valmont) / THE SEEKER (Who). – TIN MACHINE :- He co-wrote with GABRELS except MAGGIE'S FARM (Bob Dylan) / WORKING CLASS HERO (John Lennon, who also co-wrote FAME for BOWIE in 1975) / IF THERE IS SOMETHING (Roxy Music). • **Trivia:** BOWIE'S acting career started in 1976 with the film 'THE MAN WHO FELL TO EARTH' and 'JUST A GIGOLO' (1978). After starring in stage production of ELEPHANT MAN in 1980, he returned to films THE HUNGER (1982) / MERRY XMAS MR. LAWRENCE (1983) / LABYRINTH (1986) / ABSOLUTE BEGINNERS (1986) / THE LAST TEMPTATION OF CHRIST (1989). In 1985, he was one of the major stars of LIVE AID concert, and co-sang on 'DANCIN' IN THE STREET' with MICK JAGGER.

Recommended: CHANGES ONE BOWIE (*10) / ZIGGY STARDUST *10) / ALADDIN SANE (*9) / THE MAN WHO SOLD THE WORLD (*9) / LOW (*10) / HUNKY DORY (*7) / HEROES (*9) / SPACE ODDITY (*6) / STATION TO STATION (*8) / SCARY MONSTERS (*7) / DIAMOND DOGS (*6) / PIN-UPS (*5) / YOUNG AMERICANS (*5) / LODGER (*4) / LET'S DANCE (*6) / TIN MACHINE (*4) / BLACK TIE, WHITE NOISE (*5).

DAVIE JONES with THE KING BEES

		Vocalion	not issued
Jun 64.	(7") **LIZA JANE. / LOUIE LOUIE GO HOME**		-

(re-iss.Sep78 on 'Decca')

The MANNISH BOYS

		Parlophone	not issued
Mar 65.	(7") **I PITY THE FOOL. / TAKE MY TIP**		

DAVIE JONES

with The LOWER THIRD

Aug 65.	(7") **YOU'VE GOT A HABIT OF LEAVING. / BABY LOVES THAT WAY**		

(above re-iss.Mar79 as 7"ep also cont. "MANNISH BOYS" 7" on 'EMI')

DAVID BOWIE with The LOWER THIRD

Pye Warners

Jan 66. (7") **CAN'T HELP THINKING ABOUT ME. / AND I SAID TO MYSELF**

DAVID BOWIE

the name he was to keep forever

Pye Warners

Apr 66. (7") **DO ANYTHING YOU SAY. / GOOD MORNING GIRL** –

Aug 66. (7") **I DIG EVERYTHING. / I'M NOT LOSING SLEEP** –

Deram not issued

Dec 66. (7") **RUBBER BAND. / THE LONDON BOYS** –

Apr 67. (7") **THE LAUGHING GNOME. / THE GOSPEL ACCORDING TO TONY DAY** –

(above re-iss.Sep73 reaching No.6 in UK, re-iss.Jun82)

Jun 67. (lp) **LOVE YOU TILL TUESDAY** –

– Uncle Arthur / Sell me a coat / Rubber band / Love you till Tuesday There is a happy land / We are hungry men / When I live my dream / Little bombadier / Silly boy blue / Come and buy me toys / Join the gang / She's got medals / Maids of Bond Street / Please Mr. Gravedigger. *(cd-iss.Apr89)*

Jul 67. (7") **LOVE YOU TILL TUESDAY. / DID YOU EVER HAVE A DREAM** –

— (Jul68-Feb69) **BOWIE** formed FEATHERS with girlfriend **HERMOINE FARTHINGALE** and **JOHN HUTCHINSON** – bass. BOWIE went solo, recording solo album with session players **RICK WAKEMAN** – keyboards / etc.

Philips Mercury

Jul 69. (7") **SPACE ODDITY. / THE WILD EYED BOY FROM FREECLOUD** 5 –

Nov 69. (lp) **DAVID BOWIE – MAN OF WORDS MAN OF MUSIC** –

– Space oddity / Unwashed and somewhat slightly dazed / Letter to Hermione / Cygnet committee / Janine / An occasional dream / The wild eyed boy from Freecloud / God knows I'm good / Memory of a free festival. *(re-iss.lp,c Nov72 on 'RCA' re-titled "SPACE ODDITY" reached No.17 UK, No.16 US, re-iss.+cd Apr90 hit 64 on 'EMI' += Conversation piece / Don't sit down)*

— **BOWIE** formed backing band **HYPE** with **TONY VISCONTI** – bass / **MICK RONSON** – guitar / **JOHN CAMBRIDGE** – drums

Mercury Mercury

Mar 70. (7") **THE PRETTIEST STAR. / CONVERSATION PIECE** –

— **MICK 'Woody' WOODMANSEY** – drums repl. CAMBRIDGE

Jun 70. (7") **MEMORY OF A FREE FESTIVAL Pt.1. / Pt.2**

Jan 71. (lp) **THE MAN WHO SOLD THE WORLD**

– The width of a circle / All the madmen / Black country rock / After all / Running gun blues / Saviour machine / She took me cold / The man who sold the world / The supermen. *(re-iss.lp,c Nov72 on 'RCA' reached No.26 UK, re-iss.Apr83 on 'RCA' hit 64, cd-iss.Oct84, re-iss.+cd Apr90 hit 66 on 'EMI' +=)*– Lightning frightening / Moonage daydream / Holy holy / Hang on to yourself.

Jan 71. (7") **HOLY HOLY. / BLACK COUNTRY ROCK**

— Became **SPIDERS FROM MARS (BOWIE, RONSON, WOODMANSEY), TREVOR BOULDER** – bass repl. VISCONTI

R.C.A. R.C.A.

Dec 71. (lp)(c) **HUNKY DORY** 93

– Changes / Oh! you pretty things / Eight line poem / Life on Mars? / Kooks / Quicksand / Fill your heart – Andy Warhol / Song for Bob Dylan / Queen bitch / The Bewlay Brothers. *(re-dist.Sep72 reached No.3 UK) (re-iss.Jan81 reached No.32 UK, cd-iss.Oct84, re-iss.+cd Apr90 on 'EMI' hit UK No.39 +=)*– Bombers / The supermen (alt.) / Quicksand (demo) / The Bewlay Brothers (alt.). *(pic-lp Mar84)*

Jan 72. (7") **CHANGES. / ANDY WARHOL** 66 Apr 72

(re-iss.Dec74 reached No.41 UK)

Apr 72. (7") **STARMAN. / SUFFRAGETTE CITY** 10 65 Jun 72

Jun 72. (lp)(c) **THE RISE AND FALL OF ZIGGY STARDUST AND THE SPIDERS FROM MARS** 5 75

– Five years / Soul love / Moonage daydream / Starman / It ain't easy / Lady Stardust / Star / Hang on to yourself / Ziggy Stardust / Suffragette city / Rock'n'roll suicide. *(pic-lp Mar84) (re-iss.Jan81 reached No.33 UK, cd-iss.Oct84, re-iss.+cd Apr90 on 'EMI' hit No.25)*(cd+=) – John, I'm only dancing (demo) / Velvet goldmine / Sweet head / Ziggy Stardust (demo) / Lady Stardust (demo).

Sep 72. (7") **JOHN, I'M ONLY DANCING. / HANG ON TO YOURSELF** 12

Nov 72. (7") **THE JEAN GENIE. / ZIGGY STARDUST** 2 –

Nov 72. (7") **THE JEAN GENIE. / HANG ON TO YOURSELF** – 71

Apr 73. (7") **DRIVE-IN-SATURDAY. / ROUND AND ROUND** 3

— with guests **MIKE GARSON** – piano / **KEN FORDHAM** and **BUX** – saxophone, flute

Apr 73. (lp)(c) **ALADDIN SANE** 1 17 May 73

– Watch that man / Aladdin Sane (1913-1938-197?) / Drive-in Saturday / Panic in Detroit / Cracked actor / Time / The prettiest star / Let's spend the night together / The Jean genie / Lady grinning soul. *(re-iss.Feb82 reached No.49 UK, re-iss. pic.lp Jun84, cd-iss.Jun85)*(cd-iss.Jul90 hit 43 on 'EMI'+=) – other rare tracks

1973. (7") **TIME. / THE PRETTIEST STAR** –

1973. (7") **LET'S SPEND THE NIGHT TOGETHER. / LADY GRINNING SOUL** –

Jun 73. (7") **LIFE ON MARS. / THE MAN WHO SOLD THE WORLD** 3

— **AYNSLEY DUNBAR** – drums repl. WOODY

Oct 73. (7") **SORROW. / AMSTERDAM** 3

Oct 73. (lp)(c) **PIN-UPS** 1 23

– Rosalyn / Here comes the night / I wish you would / See Emily play / Everything's alright / I can't explain / Friday on my mind / Sorow / Don't bring me down / Shapes of things / Anyway anyhow anywhere / Where have all the good times gone!. *(re-iss.Sep81, re-iss.Apr83 hit UK 57, pic.lp-iss.Sep84, cd-iss.Jun85) (cd-iss.Jul90 hit 52 on 'EMI')*

— **DUNBAR** and **TONY NEWMAN** – drums / **HERBIE FLOWERS** – bass / **MIKE GARSON** – keys

Feb 74. (7") **REBEL REBEL. / QUEEN BITCH** 5 64 May 74

May 74. (lp)(c) **DIAMOND DOGS (as "BOWIE")** 1

– Future legend / Diamond dogs / Sweet thing / Candidate / Sweet thing (reprise) / Rebel rebel / Rock'n'roll with me / We are the dead / 1984 / Big brother (including 'Chant of the ever circling skeletal family'). *(re-iss.Feb81, re-iss.May83 hit 60, pic-lp+cd-iss.May84) (cd-iss.Jun90 hit 67 on 'EMI' +=) Dodo / Candidate.*

Jun 74. (7") **DIAMOND DOGS. / HOLY HOLY** 21

— added **EARL SLICK** – guitar / **DAVID SANBORN** – saxophone

Sep 74. (7") **KNOCK ON WOOD (live). / PANIC IN DETROIT (live)** 10

Nov 74. (d-lp)(c) **DAVID LIVE (live at the Tower theatre Philadelphia '74)** 2 8

– 1984 / Rebel rebel / Moonage daydream / Sweet thing / Changes / Suffragette city / Aladdin Sane (1913-1938-197?) / All the young dudes / Cracked actor / Rock'n'roll with me / Watch that man / Knock on wood / Diamond dogs/ Big brother / The width of a circle / The Jean genie / Rock'n'roll suicide. *(re-iss.May84) (cd-iss.Jun90 on 'EMI' +=)* -(band intro) / Here today, gone tomorrow / Time. *(re-iss.d-cd Jun95 on 'EMI')*

— **ANDY NEWMARK** – drums / **WILLIE WEEKS** – bass / **CARLOS ALOMAR** – guitar / **EARL SLICK** – guitar / guests **LUTHER VANDROSS and JOHN LENNON** – backing vocals

Feb 75. (7") **YOUNG AMERICANS. / SUFFRAGETTE CITY** 18 28

Mar 75. (lp)(c) **YOUNG AMERICANS** 2 9

– Young Americans / Win / Fascination / Right / Somebody up there like me / Across the universe / Can you hear me / Fame. *(re-iss.Sep81, re-iss.+cd Oct84) (c+cd.iss.Apr91 hit 54 on 'E.M.I.'+=) – Who can I be now? / John I'm only dancing again / It's gonna be me.*

Jul 75. (7") **FAME. / RIGHT** 17 1 Jun 75

— retained **SLICK + ALOMAR**

— **GEORGE MURRAY** – bass + DENNIS DAVIS – drums repl. WEEKS + NEWMARK

Nov 75. (7") **GOLDEN YEARS. / CAN YOU HEAR ME** 8 10

Jan 76. (lp)(c) **STATION TO STATION** 5 3

– Station to station / Golden years / Word on a wing / TVC 15 / Stay / Wild is the wind. *(re-iss.Sep81, re-iss.+cd Nov84) (c+cd.iss.Apr91 hit 57 on 'E.M.I.'* – Word on the wing (live) / Stay (live).

May 76. (7") **TVC 15. / WE ARE THE DEAD** 33 64

Jul 76. (7") **SUFFRAGETTE CITY. / STAY**

— now collaborated with **BRIAN ENO** – synthesizers

— **RICKY GARDINER** – guitar repl. SLICK

Jan 77. (lp)(c) **LOW** 2 11

– Speed of life / Breaking glass / What in the world / Sound and vision / Always crashing in the same car / Be my wife / A new career in a new town / Warszawa / Art decade / Weeping wall / Subterraneans. *(re-iss.Jan81, re-iss.Jun83 hit 85, re-iss.+cd Nov84) (c+cd-iss.Aug91 hit 64 on 'E.M.I.')*

Feb 77. (7") **SOUND AND VISION. / A NEW CAREER IN A NEW TOWN** 3 69

Jun 77. (7") **BE MY WIFE. / SPEED OF LIFE**

— next guest **ROBERT FRIPP** – guitar who repl. RICKY GARDINER.

Oct 77. (7") **HEROES. / V2-SCHNEIDER** 24

Oct 77. (lp)(c) **HEROES** 3 35

– Beauty and the beast / Joe the lion / Heroes / Sons of the silent age / Blackout / V-2 Schneider / Sense of doubt / Moss garden / Neukoln / Black out / The secret life of Arabia. *(re-iss.Jan81, re-iss.Jun83 hit 75, re-iss.+cd Nov84) (c+cd-iss.Apr91 on 'E.M.I.' +=)*– Joe the Lion (1991 remix) / Abolumajor.

— added **ADRIAN BELEW** – guitar / **SIMON HOUSE** – violin / **SEAN MAYES** – piano

Jan 78. (7") **THE BEAUTY AND THE BEAST. / SENSE OF DOUBT** 39

Sep 78. (d-lp)(c) **STAGE (live)** 5 44

– Hang on to yourself / Ziggy Stardust / Five years / Soul love / Star / Station to station / Fame / TVC 15 / Warszawa / Speed of life / Art decade / Sense of doubt / Breaking glass / Heroes / What in the world / Blackout / Beauty and the beast. *(re-iss.+cd Jul84) (also on yellow vinyl) (cd-iss.Feb92 on 'EMI', w/ extra tracks)*

Oct 78. (7"ep) **BREAKING GLASS (live). / ZIGGY STARDUST (live) / ART DECADE (live)** [54] [ ]

Apr 79. (7") **BOYS KEEP SWINGING. / FANTASTIC VOYAGE** [7] [ ]

May 79. (lp)(c) **LODGER** [4] [20]
– Fantastic voyage / African night flight / Move on / Yassassin / Red sails / D.J. / Look back in anger / Boys keep swinging / Repitition / Red money. *(re-iss.Sep81, re-iss.+cd Oct84) (c+cd-iss.Aug91 on 'E.M.I.' – += 2 tracks)*

Jul 79. (7") **D.J. / REPITITION** [29] [ ]

Dec 79. (7")(12") **JOHN I'M ONLY DANCING (AGAIN). / JOHN I'M ONLY DANCING (1972)** [12] [ ]

Feb 80. (7") **ALABAMA SONG. / SPACE ODDITY** [23] [ ]

— guest **ROBERT FRIPP** – guitar repl. BRIAN ENO

Aug 80. (7") **ASHES TO ASHES. / MOVE ON** [1] [ ]

Sep 80. (lp)(c) **SCARY MONSTERS** [1] [12]
– It's no game (No.1) / Up the hill backwards / Scary monsters (and super creeps) / Ashes to ashes / Fashion / Teenage wildlife / Scream like a baby / Kingdom come / Because you're young / It's no game (No.2). *(re-iss.+cd Oct84) (re-iss.+cd.Jun92 on 'EMI', +=)*– Space oddity / Panic in Detroit / Crystal Japan / Alabama song.

Oct 80. (7")(12") **FASHION. / SCREAM LIKE A BABY** [5] [70]

Jan 81. (7")(c-s) **SCARY MONSTERS (AND SUPER CREEPS). / BECAUSE YOU'RE YOUNG** [20] [ ]

Mar 81. (7")(c-s) **UP THE HILL BACKWARDS. / CRYSTAL JAPAN** [32] [ ]

— (next single "UNDER PRESSURE" was a No.1 collaboration w/ "QUEEN".

Nov 81. (7")(12") **WILD IS THE WIND. / GOLDEN YEARS** [24] [ ]

Feb 82. (7"ep)**BAAL'S HYMN** [29] [ ]
– Baal's hymn / The drowned girl / Ballad of the adventurers / The dirty song / Remembering Marie.

Apr 82. (7")(12") **CAT PEOPLE (PUTTING OUT FIRE). / PAUL'S THEME** [26] [67]

— (above single taken from the feature film of the same name on 'MCA-UK' / 'Backstreet' US)

Nov 82. (7")(12") **LITTLE DRUMMER BOY ("DAVID BOWIE & BING CROSBY" rec. '77). / FANTASTIC BOY** [3] [ ]

— now with **NILE RODGERS + STEVIE RAY VAUGHAN** – guitar / **BERNARD EDWARDS + CARMINE ROJAS** – bass / **OMAR HAKIM + TONY THOMPSON** – drums / **SAMMY FIGUEROA** – perc.

EMI America / EMI America

Mar 83. (7")(12")(c-s) **LET'S DANCE. / CAT PEOPLE (PUTTING OUT FIRE)** [1] [1]

Apr 83. (lp)(pic-lp)(c) **LET'S DANCE** [1] [4]
– Modern love / China girl / Let's dance / China girl / Without you / Ricochet / Criminal world / Cat people (putting out fire) / Shake it. *(cd-iss.Jan84) (re-iss.cd Nov95 on 'Virgin')*

Jun 83. (7")(12")(7"pic-d) **CHINA GIRL. / SHAKE IT** [2] [10]

Sep 83. (7")(12") **MODERN LOVE. / MODERN LOVE (part 2)** [2] [14]

Feb 84. (7") **WITHOUT YOU. / CRIMINAL WORLD** [-] [73]

— retained **HAKIM, ROJAS, FIGUEROA** / brought back **ALOMAR** and recruited **DEREK BRAMBLE** – bass, snyths, etc.

Sep 84. (7")(12") **BLUE JEAN. / DANCING WITH THE BIG BOYS** [6] [8]

Sep 84. (lp)(c)(cd) **TONIGHT** [1] [11]
– Loving the alien / Don't look down / God only knows / Tonight / Neighbourhood threat / Blue Jean / Tumble and twirl / I keep forgetting / Dancing with the big boys. *(re-iss.cd Nov95 on 'Virgin')*

Nov 84. (7")(12") **TONIGHT. / TUMBLE AND TWIRL** [53] [53]

— next, from the film "Falcon And The Snowman")

Jan 85. (7")(12") **THIS IS NOT AMERICA ("DAVID BOWIE and The PAT METHANY GROUP"). / ('A'instrumental by The PAT METHANY GROUP)** [14] [32]

May 85. (7") **LOVING THE ALIEN. / DON'T LOOK DOWN** [19] [ ]
(12"+=)(12"sha-pic-d+=) – ('A' club mix).

Sep 85. (7") **DANCING IN THE STREET. ("DAVID BOWIE & MICK JAGGER") / ('A' instrumental)** [1] [7]
(12"+=) – ('A'dub) / ('A'extended).

(below single from film & album of the same name, cont. 3 BOWIE tracks, album reached No.19 UK) (the next, was from animated film of the same name)

Virgin / Virgin

Mar 86. (7")(12")(7"sha-pic-d) **ABSOLUTE BEGINNERS. / ('A'dub version)** [2] [53]
(cd-s+=) – ('A'versions).

Nov 86. (7")(12") **WHEN THE WIND BLOWS. / ('A'dub version)** [44] [ ]

— (below single from the feature film "Labyrinth" which cont. 5 BOWIE tracks, album reached No.38 UK)

— now with **ALOMAR, ROJAS + ERDAL KIZILCAY** – keyboards, etc. / **PHILIPPE SAISSE** – keyboards, etc. / **PETER FRAMPTON** – guitar

EMI America / EMI America

Jun 86. (7")(12")(7"sha-pic-d) **UNDERGROUND. / ('A'instrumental)** [21] [ ]

Mar 87. (7") **DAY-IN DAY-OUT. / JULIE** [17] [21]
(12"+=) – ('A'&'B'extended versions).

Apr 87. (lp)(c)(cd) **NEVER LET ME DOWN** [6] [34]
– Day-in day-out / Time will crawl / Beat of your drum / Never let me down / Zeroes / Glass spider / Shining star (makin' my love) / New York's in love / '87 and cry / Bang bang / Too dizzy. *(cd+=)* – Time will crawl (extended dance) / Never let me down (version) / Day-in day-out (Groucho mix).*(re-iss.cd Nov95 on 'Virgin')*

Jun 87. (7")(12") **TIME WILL CRAWL. / GIRLS** [33] [ ]

Aug 87. (7")(7"pic-d) **NEVER LET ME DOWN. / '87 AND CRY** [34] [27]
(12"+=) – Time will crawl (extended) / Day-in day-out (Groucho mix).

TIN MACHINE

was the name of **BOWIE's** next project/band. **DAVID BOWIE** – vocals, saxophone / **REEVES GABRELS** – lead guitar / **TONY SALES** – bass / **HUNT SALES** – drums (both ex-IGGY POP, ex-TODD RUNDGREN RUNT)plus p/t member **KEVIN ARMSTRONG** – guitar

EMI Manhattan / EMI Manhattan

May 89. (lp)(c)(cd) **TIN MACHINE** [3] [28]
– Heaven's in here / Tin machine / Prisoner of love / Crack city / I can't read / Under the god / Amazing / Working class hero / Bus stop / Pretty thing / Video crimes / Run * / Sacrifice yourself * / Baby can dance. *(cd+= *) (re-iss.cd Nov95 on 'Virgin')*

Jun 89. (7") **UNDER THE GOD. / SACRIFICE YOURSELF** [51] [ ]
(12"+=)(10"+=)(c-s+=)(cd-s+=) – (interview).

Aug 89. (7")(c-s)(7"pic-d)(7"sha-pic-d) **TIN MACHINE. / MAGGIE'S FARM (live)** [48] [ ]
(12"+=) – I can't read (live).
(cd-s++=) – Bus stop (live country version).

Oct 89. (7")(c-s)(7"pic-d)(7"sha-pic-d) **PRISONER OF LOVE. / BABY CAN DANCE (live)** [ ] [ ]
(12"+=)(cd-s+=) – Crack city (live)

London / Victory

Aug 91. (7")(12") **YOU BELONG IN ROCK'N'ROLL. / AMLAPURA** [33] [ ]
(pic-cd+=) – Stateside / Hammerhead.

Sep 91. (cd)(c)(lp) **TIN MACHINE II** [23] [ ]
– Baby universal / One shot / You belong in rock'n'roll / If there is something / Amlapura / Betty wrong / You can't talk / Stateside / Shopping for girls / Big hurt / I'm sorry / Goodbye Mr.Ed / Hammerhead.

Oct 91. (7")(c-s) **BABY UNIVERSAL. / YOU BELONG IN ROCK'N'ROLL** [48] [ ]
(12") – ('A'side) / A big hurt / ('A'new mix).
(cd-s) – ('A'side) / Stateside / Is there is something / Heaven's in here.

— In Feb'92, BOWIE's song 'SOUND AND VISION (remix)' was re-done with himself and 808 STATE on label 'Tommy Boy'.

Victory / Victory

Jul 92. (cd)(c)(lp) **OY VEY BABY (live)** [ ] [ ]
– If there is something / Amazing / I can't read / Stateside / Under the god / Goodbye Mr. Ed / Heaven's in here / You belong in rock'n'roll.

DAVID BOWIE

(solo again) and starred in the film 'THE LINGUINI INCIDENT'.

Warners / Warners

Jul 92. (7")(c-s) **REAL COOL WORLD. / ('A'instrumental)** [53] [ ]
(12") – ('A'club) / ('A'dub thing 1 & 2) / ('A'dub overture).
(cd-s+=) – (2 more 'A'mixes).

— with **NILE RODGERS** – guitar, co-producer / **DAVE RICHARDS + RICHARD HILTON + PHILIPPE SAISSE + RICHARD TEE** – keyboards / **BARRY CAMPBELL + JOHN REGAN** – bass / **PUGI BELL + STERLING CAMPBELL** – drums / **GERADO VELEZ** – percussion. Plus guests **MICK RONSON** – guitar / **LESTER BOWIE** – trumpet / **REEVES GABRELS** – guitar / **MIKE GARSON** – piano / **AL B.SURE!** – vocals / **WILD T.SPRINGER** – guitar

Savage-Arista / Savage-Arista

Mar 93. (7")(c-s) **JUMP THEY SAY. / PALLAS ATHENA (Don't Stop Praying Mix)** [9] [ ]
(cd-s) – ('A'side) / ('A'-Brothers In Rhythm mix) / ('A'-Brothers In Rhythm inst.) / ('A' Leftfield vocal).
(12") – ('A'side) / ('A'-Hard Hands mix) / ('A'-Leftfield vocal) / ('A'-dub oditty mix).

Apr 93. (cd)(c)(lp) **BLACK TIE, WHITE NOISE** [1] [39]
– The wedding / You've been around / I feel free / Black tie white noise / Jump they say / Nite flight / Pallas Athena / Miracle tonight / Don't let me down & down / Looking for Lester / I know it's gonna happen someday / The wedding song / Jump they say (alternate mix) / Lucy can't dance.

Jun 93. (7")(c-s) **BLACK TIE, WHITE NOISE. / YOU'VE BEEN AROUND (Meat Beat Manifesto mix)** [36] [ ]
(12"+=)(cd-s+=) – ('A'club mix with AL B.SURE!) / ('A'-John Waddell mix).

Oct 93. (7")(c-s) **MIRACLE TONIGHT. / LOKING FOR LESTER** [40] [ ]
(12")(cd-s) – ('A'mixes).

Nov 93. (7")(c-s) **BUDDHA OF SUBURBIA. / DEAD AGAINST IT** [35] [ ]
(cd-s+=) – South horizon / ('A'-Lenny Kravitz rock mix).

Nov 93. (cd)(c) **BUDDHA OF SUBURBIA (TV soundtrack)** [ ] [ ]
– Buddah of suburbia / Sex and the church / South horizon / The mysteries / Bleed like a craze, dad / Strangers when we meet / Read against it / Untitled No.1 / Ian Fish / UK heir / Buddah of suburbia (featuring LENNY KRAVITZ).

— now with **ENO** -synthesizers, co-writer (on most) / **REEVES GABRELS / ERDAL KIZILCAY / MIKE GARSON / STERLING CAMPBELL / CARLOS ALOMAR / JOEY BARON / YOSSI FINE**

R.C.A. Arista

Sep 95. (c-s)(cd-s) **THE HEARTS FILTHY LESSON / I AM WITH NAME** [35] [92]
(cd-s+=) – ('A'-Bowie mix) / ('A'-Trent Reznor alt.remix) / ('A'-Tony Maserati remix).
(12"pic-d) – (5-'A'mixes; Bowie / alt. / Rubber / Simple text / Filthy).

Sep 95. (cd)(c)(d-lp) **OUTSIDE** [8] [21]
– THE NATHAN ADLER DIARIES: A Hyper Cycle:- Leon takes us outside / Outside / The hearts filthy lesson / A small plot of land / segue – Baby Grace (a horrid cassette) / Hello spaceboy / The motel / I have not been to Oxford Town / No control / segue Algeria touchshriek / The voyeur of utter destruction (as beauty) / segue – Ramona A. Stone – I am with name / Wishful beginnings / We prick you / segue – Nathan Adler / Strangers when we meet.

Nov 95. (7")(c-s) **STRANGERS WHEN WE MEET. / THE MAN WHO SOLD THE WORLD (live)** [39] [ ]
(cd-s+=) – ('A'side again) / Get real.
(12") – ('A'side) / The seeker / Hang ten high.

. . . Jan – Jun '96 stop press . . .

Feb 96. (single) **HALLO SPACEBOY** [12] [ ]

– compilations, exploitation, etc. –

Mar 70. Decca; (lp)(c) **THE WORLD OF DAVID BOWIE** [ ] [ ]
(re-iss.Feb73)

May 75. Decca; (d-lp)(c) **IMAGES 66-67** [ ] [ ]

May 75. Decca; (7") **LONDON BOYS. / LOVE YOU TILL TUESDAY** [ ] [ ]

Apr 81. Decca; (lp)(c) **ANOTHER FACE** [ ] [ ]

Oct 72. Pye; (7"ep) **DO ANYTHING YOU SAY / CAN'T HELP THINKING ABOUT ME. / I DIG EVERYTHING / I'M NOT LOSING SLEEP** [ ] [-]

Note; All below on 'RCA' unless otherwise mentioned.

Jan 73. (7") **SPACE ODDITY. / THE MAN WHO SOLD THE WORLD** [-] [15]

Apr 74. (7") **ROCK'N'ROLL SUICIDE. / QUICKSAND** [22] [ ]

Nov 75. (7"m) **SPACE ODDITY. / CHANGES / VELVET GOLDMINE** [1] [-]

Jun 76. (lp)(c) **CHANGESONEBOWIE** [2] [10]

Apr 81. (lp) **CHRISTIANE F. – WIR KINDER VOM BAHNHOF ZOO (soundtrack)** [-] [ ]

Nov 81. (lp)(c) **CHANGESTWOBOWIE** [24] [68]
(cd-iss.May84)

Dec 82. (10x7"pic-d) **FASHIONS** [ ] [ ]
– SPACE ODDITY / LIFE ON MARS / THE JEAN GENIE / REBEL REBEL / SOUND & VISION / DRIVE-IN SATURDAY / SORROW / GOLDEN YEARS / BOYS KEEP SWINGING / ASHES TO ASHES

Jan 83. (lp)(c) **RARE** [34] [ ]

Aug 83. (lp)(c) **GOLDEN YEARS (live recent)** [33] [99]

Oct 83. (d-lp)(d-c) **ZIGGY STARDUST – THE MOTION PICTURE (live '73 film)** [17] [89]
(re-iss./+cd.Sep92 on 'EMI')

Oct 83. (7") **WHITE LIGHT WHITE HEAT (live). / CRACKED ACTOR (live)** [46] [ ]

Jan 84. (7") **1984. / TVC 15** [-] [ ]

Apr 84. (lp)(c) **FAME AND FASHION (ALL TIME GREATEST HITS)** [40] [ ]

Dec 80. K-Tel; (lp)(c) **THE VERY BEST OF DAVID BOWIE** [3] [-]

Jun 81. P.R.T.; (10"mlp) **DON'T BE FOOLED BY THE NAME** [ ] [-]

Oct 87. P.R.T.; (m-lp)(c)(cd) **1966: DAVID BOWIE** [ ] [-]
(pic-lp Jun88) (re-iss.Dec89 on 'Castle')

1985. Castle; (d-lp)(c) **THE COLLECTION** [ ] [-]
(cd-iss.Aug92)

May 85. Krazy Kat; (12"ep) **HANG ON TO YOURSELF. / LOOKING FOR A FRIEND / MAN IN THE MIDDLE (by "ARNOLD CORNS & THE SPIDERS FROM MARS")** [ ] [-]

Apr 86. Krazy Kat; (lp)(c) **RARE TRACKS** [ ] [-]

Aug 86. Archive 4; (12"ep) **ARCHIVE 4** [ ] [-]
– London boys / Love you till Tuesday / Laughing gnome / Maid of Bond Street.

May 84. Deram; (lp)(c) **LOVE YOU TILL TUESDAY (soundtrack)** [53] [ ]

Jan 89. Deram; (cd) **CHAMELEON** [ ] [ ]

Sep 89. E.M.I./ US= Rykodisc; (cd) **SOUND + VISION** [ ] [97]

Mar 90. E.M.I./ US= Rykodisc; (7")(7"pic-d)(c-s) **FAME '90 (mix). / ('A'rap version)** [28] [ ]
(12"+=) – ('A'house mix) / ('A'hip hop mix).
(cd-s++=) – ('A'interminable variations/ mixes).

Apr 90. E.M.I./ US= Rykodisc; (cd)(c)(d-lp) **CHANGESBOWIE** [1] [39]
– Space oddity / John, I'm only dancing / Changes / Ziggy stardust / Suffragette city / The Jean genie / Diamond dogs / Rebel rebel / Young Americans / Fame ('90 remix) / Golden years / Heroes / Ashes to ashes / Fashion / Let's dance / China girl / Modern love / Blue Jean.

Nov 93. E.M.I./ US= Rykodisc; (cd)(c)(lp) **THE SINGLES COLLECTION** [9] [ ]
(re-iss.cd/c Nov95)

Apr 91. Rhino; (cd)(c) **EARLY ON (1964-66)** [-] [ ]

May 93. Spectrum; (cd)(c) **THE GOSPEL ACCORDING TO DAVID BOWIE** [ ] [-]

May 94. Trident; (cd)(c)(d-lp) **SANTA MONICA '72 (live)** [74] [-]

Jul 95. Trident; (cd) **RARESTONEBOWIE** [ ] [-]

BOX OF FROGS (see under ⇒ YARDBIRDS)

BOY HAIRDRESSERS (see under ⇒ TEENAGE FAN CLUB)

BOYS NEXT DOOR (see under ⇒ BIRTHDAY PARTY)

Billy BRAGG

Born: STEVEN WILLIAM BRAGG, 20 Dec'57, Barking, Essex, England. In 1977, he formed PETERBOROUGH based R&B/punk band RIFF RAFF. When they split in 1981, he joined the army but bought himself out after 90 days. Complete with amplifier and guitar he busked around the cities, until he got studio time in 1983 by Charisma's indie subsidiary 'Utility'. LIFE'S A RIOT WITH SPY VS SPY was soon released and with help and distribution of new label 'Go! Discs' it finally hit UK top 30 early 1984. He continued with the label, issuing 45's for under a £1, due to initially not having to pay any band members. • **Style:** Socially aware rock that dubbed him 'the one-man Clash / Jam', mixing politics, love and basically songs about real people. • **Trivia:** He formed 'Red Wedge' in 1986 to help raise funds for the Labour Party through star gigs (i.e.STYLE COUNCIL, COMMUNARDS, himself, etc.). His stance with CND and anti-apartheid, anti-poll tax, etc, has often saw him on wrong side of the law. For the 90's it looks as though he will become a bit more cosmopolitan, but still ungagged. • **Songwriters:** Mostly all penned by himself except later collaborations with JOHNNY MARR, PETER BUCK and WIGGY. Covered; WALK AWAY RENEE (Four Tops) / SHE'S LEAVING HOME + REVOLUTION (Beatles) / JEANE (Smiths) / SEVEN AND SEVEN IS (Love) / THERE IS POWER IN A UNION (trad.new words) / THINK AGAIN (Dick Gaughan) / CHILE YOUR WATERS RUN RED THROUGH SOWETO (B.Johnson Reagan) / TRAIN TRAIN (Z.Delfeur) / DOLPHINS (Fred Neil) / EVERYWHERE (Sid Griffin-Greg Trooper) / JERUSALEM (William Blake) / WHEN WILL I SEE YOU AGAIN (Three Degrees).

Recommended: BACK TO BASICS (*9) / DON'T TRY THIS AT HOME (*8)

RIFF RAFF

(BILLY BRAGG – vocals, guitar) and other members

Chiswick not issued

May 78. (7"ep) **I WANNA BE A COSMONAUT** [ ] [-]
– Cosmonaut / Romford girls / What's the latest? / Sweet as pie.

Geezer not issued

Oct 80. (7") **EVERY GIRL AN ENGLISH ROSE. / U SHAPED HOUSE** [ ] [-]

Oct 80. (7") **KITTEN. / FANTOCIDE** [ ] [-]

Oct 80. (7") **LITTLE GIRLS KNOW. / SHE DON'T MATTER** [ ] [-]

Oct 80. (7") **NEW HOME TOWN. / RICHARD** [ ] [-]

BILLY BRAGG

went solo

Utility not issued

Jun 83. (m-lp) **LIFE'S A RIOT WITH SPY VS.SPY** [30] [-]
– The milkman of human kindness / To have and have not / A new England / The man in the iron mask / The busy girl buys beauty / Lover's town revisited / Richard. *(re-iss.+c.Jan84 on 'Go! Discs')*

— added for back-up **KENNY CRADDOCK** – organ / **DAVE WOODHEAD** – trumpet.

Go! Discs Go! Discs

Oct 84. (lp)(c) **BREWING UP WITH BILLY BRAGG** [16] [-]
– It says here / Love gets dangerous / The myth of trust / From a Vauxhall Velox / The Saturday boy / Island of no return / St.Swithin's Day / Like soldiers do / This guitar says sorry / Strange things happen / A lover sings.

Feb 85. (7") **ST. SWITHIN'S DAY. / A NEW ENGLAND** [-] [ ] EURO

Mar 85. (7"ep) **BETWEEN THE WARS** [15] [-]

– Between the wars / Which side are you on? / World turned upside down / It says here.

Dec 85. (7"m) **DAYS LIKE THESE. / I DON'T NEED THIS PRESSURE RON / SCHOLARSHIP IS THE ENEMY OF ROMANCE** 43 -

— + guests **JOHNNY MARR** – guitar / **KIRSTY MacCOLL** – b.vocals / **KENNY JONES** – drums, co-producer / **JOHN PORTER** – bass, co-producer / **SIMON MORTEON** – perc. / **BOBBY VALENTINO** – violin.

Jun 86. (7"m) **LEVI STUBBS' TEARS. / THINK AGAIN / WALK AWAY RENEE** 29 -
(12"+=) – Between the wars (live).

Sep 86. (lp)(c) **TALKING WITH THE TAXMAN ABOUT POETRY** 8
– Greetings to the new brunette / Train train / The marriage / Ideology / Levi Stubbs' tears / Honey, I'm a big boy now / There is power in a union / Help save the youth of America / Wishing the days away / The passion / The warmest room / The home front. *(cd-iss.May87)*

Nov 86. (7"m) **GREETINGS TO THE NEW BRUNETTE. / DEPORTEES / THE TATLER** 58 -
(12"+=) – Jeane / There is power in a union (instrumental).

Oct87 he is credited with OYSTER BAND backing **LEON ROSSELSON** on his single **BALLAD OF A SPYCATCHER** (Upside Down records)

— May88, he's credited with **CARA TIVEY** on 45 **SHE'S LEAVING HOME** the B-side of **WET WET WET** – With A little Help From My Friends. This UK No.1 single issued on 'Childline' gave all proceeds to children's charity, with backing including his usual friends.

May 88. (12"ep) **HELP SAVE THE YOUTH OF AMERICA (LIVE AND DUBIOUS)**
– Help save the youth of America / Think again / Chile your waters run red through Soweto / Days like these (DC mix) / To have and have not / There is power in a union (with The PATTERSONS).

Go! Discs Elektra

Aug 88. (7"m) **WAITING FOR THE GREAT LEAP FORWARD. / WISHING THE DAYS AWAY / SIN CITY** 52

Sep 88. (lp)(c)(cd) **WORKER'S PLAYTIME** 17
– She's got a brand new spell / Must I paint you a picture / Tender comrade / The price I pay / Little timb-bomb / Rotting on demand / Valentine's day is over / Life with the lions / The only one / The short answer / Waiting for the great leap forward.

Nov 88. (7") **SHE'S GOT A BRAND NEW SPELL. / MUST I PAINT YOU A PICTURE** -

May 90. (cd)(c)(m-lp) **THE INTERNATIONALE** (on 'Utility' UK) 34
– The internationale / I dreamed I saw Phil Ochs last night / The marching song of the convent battalions / Jerusalem / Nicaraguita / The red flag / My youngest son came home today.

— still holding on to **MARR, MacCOLL, TIVEY** (keyboards) and WOODHEAD. plus **WIGGY** – guitar, bass / **J.F.T.HOOD** – drums / **AMANDA VINCENT** – keyboards / etc.

Jun 91. (7") **SEXUALITY. / BAD PENNY** 27
(12"+=)(cd-s+=) – (2 'A'mixes).

Aug 91. (7") **YOU WOKE UP MY NEIGHBOURHOOD. / ONTARIO, QUEBEC AND ME** 54
(12"+=)(cd-s+=) – Bread and circuses / Heart like a wheel.

(above single 'A'featured **MICHAEL STIPE and PETER BUCK (R.E.M.)** with first 12"extra track with **NATALIE MERCHANT (10,000 MANIACS) – also b.vocals**

Sep 91. (cd)(c)(d-lp)(8x7"box) **DON'T TRY THIS AT HOME** 8
– Accident waiting to happen / Moving the goalposts / Everywhere / Cindy of a thousand lives / You woke up my neighbourhood / Trust / God's footballer / The few / Sexuality / Mother of the bride / Tank park salute / Dolphins / North sea bubble / Rumours of war / Wish you were here / Body of water.

Feb 92. (7"ep) **ACCIDENT WAITING TO HAPPEN (Red Star version) / SULK. / THE WARMEST ROOM (live) / REVOLUTION** 33 -
(12"+=)(cd-s+=) – ('A'live version) / Levi Stubbs' tears / Valentine's day is over / North Sea bubble.

– compilations, others, etc. –

May 87. Strange Fruit; (12"ep) **THE PEEL SESSIONS** -
– A new England / Strange things happen / This guitar says sorry / Love gets dangerous / A13 trunk road to the sea / Fear . . .

Jun 87. Go! Discs; (d-lp)(d-c)(cd) **BACK TO BASICS** (best 83-85 material) 37 -
(re-iss.all albums Nov93 on 'Cooking Vinyl')

Feb 92. Strange Fruit; (cd)(lp) **THE PEEL SESSIONS ALBUM** -

Nov 93. Cooking Vinyl; (cd)(c)(d-lp) **VICTIM OF GEOGRAPHY** -

BREEDERS

Formed: Boston, USA . . . 1989 by TANYA DONNELLY (of THROWING MUSES) and KIM DEAL (of The PIXIES). Released an album 'Pod' in 1990, although TANYA was soon to leave for BELLY. In 1993, the BREEDERS were back with another gem album 'Last Splash' which sold massively in the States. • **Style:** Guitar-oriented but experimental indie rock act. • **Songwriters:** KIM DEAL wrote bulk from 1992 onwards. • **Covered:** HAPPINESS IS A WARM GUN (Beatles / George Harrison) / LORD OF THE THIGHS (Aerosmith). The AMPS covered JUST LIKE A BRIAR (Tasties).

• **Recommended:** POD (*7) / LAST SPLASH (*9)

TANYA DONNELLY – rhythm guitar, vocals (of THROWING MUSES) with others **KIM DEAL** – guitar, vocals (of The PIXIES) / **JOSEPHINE WIGGS** – bass (of PERFECT DISASTER) repl. 2 from HUMAN SEXUAL RESPONSE. / **SHANNON DOUGHTY** – drums repl. NARCIZO.

4 a.d. 4 a.d.

May 90. (cd)(c)(lp) **POD** 22
– Glorious / Happiness is a warm gun / Oh! / Hellbound / When I was a painter / Fortunately gone / Iris / Opened / Only in 3's / Limehouse / Metal man.

— **DONNELLY, KIM DEAL, JO WIGGS + JON MATLOCK** (of SPIRITUALIZED)

Apr 92. (12"ep)(cd-ep) **SAFARI** 69
– Safari / So sad about us / Do you love me now? / Don't call home.

— now **KIM** her sister **KELLEY DEAL** – guitar, vocals / **JO WIGGS** – bass, vox / **JIM MacPHERSON** – drums, vocals (living from 1989 Dayton, Ohio)

Aug 93. (12"ep)(cd-ep) **CANNONBALL. / CRO-ALOHA / LORD OF THE THIGHS / 900** 40 44

Sep 93. (cd)(c)(lp) **LAST SPLASH** 5 33
– New Year / Cannonball / Invisible man / No aloha / Roi / Do you love me now? / Flipside / I just wanna get along / Mad Lucas / Divine hammer / S.O.S./ Hag / Saints / Drivin' on 9 / Roi (reprise).

Oct 93. (7"clear)(c-s) **DIVINE HAMMER. / HOVERIN'** 59
(10"ep+=)(cd-ep+=) – I can't help it (if I'm still in love with you) / Do you love me now Jr (J.Mascis remix).

Jul 94. (10"ep) **HEAD TO TOE. / SHOCKER IN GLOOMTOWN / FREED PIG** 68 -
(cd-ep+=) – Saints.

AMPS

KIM DEAL / JIM MacPHERSON / NATHAN FARLEY + LUIS LERMA

4 a.d. 4 a.d.

Oct 95. (12"ep)(cd-ep) **TIPP CITY / JUST LIKE A BRIAR. / EMPTY GLASSES (Kim's basement 4 track version)** 61

Oct 95. (cd)(c)(lp) **PACER** 60
– Pacer / Tipp city / I am decided / Mom's drunk / Bragging party / Hoverin' / First revival / Full on idle / Breaking the split screen barrier / Empty glasses / She's a girl / Dedicated.

BRITISH LIONS (see under ⇒ MOTT THE HOOPLE)

Dave BROCK (see under ⇒ HAWKWIND)

Gary BROOKER (see under ⇒ PROCOL HARUM)

Jackson BROWNE

Born: 9 Oct'48, Heidelberg, W. Germany. His father was in US Army, but moved back to Orange County, California. In 1966 after brief stint with NITTY GRITTY DIRT BAND, Jackson went solo signing for 'Elektra', at first as house songwriter, then to David Geffen's new 'Asylum' label in 1971. Due to his songs being covered by many, 'DOCTOR MY EYES' (Jackson 5) / 'SHADOW DREAM SONG' (Tom Paxton), his eponymous debut album hit US Top 60. He continued to score with many more albums, and also several 45's. • **Style:** Singer-songwriter/balladeer with easy-listening but intelligent appeal. • **Songwriters:** Self penned, except STAY (Maurice Williams & the Zodiacs) / also co-wrote TAKE IT EASY with GLENN FREY (Eagles). • **Miscellaneous:** Disaster hit him when his wife PHYLLIS committed suicide on the 25th March 1976. He found new love in the 80's with actress girlfriend DARRYL HANNAH.

Recommended: THE PRETENDER (*6)

JACKSON BROWNE – vocals with **CRAIG DOERGE** – keyboards / **LELAND SKLAR** – bass / **RUSS KUNKEL** – drums / **CLARENCE WHITE** – guitar / **DAVID CROSBY** – b.vocals

Asylum Asylum

Mar 72. (7") **DOCTOR MY EYES. / I'M LOOKING INTO YOU** 8

Apr 72. (lp)(c) **JACKSON BROWNE** 53 Mar 72
– Jamaica say you will / A child in these hills / Song for Adam / Doctor my eyes / From Silver Lake / Something fine / Under the falling sky / Looking into you / Rock me on the water / My opening farewell. *(re-iss.Jun76) (cd-iss.Jan87)*

Aug 72. (7") **ROCK ME ON THE WATER. / SOMETHING FINE** 48

—— added **DAVID LINDLEY** – guitar, violin, etc. (ex-KALEIDOSCOPE)

Sep 73. (7") **REDNECK FRIEND. / THE TIMES YOU'VE COME** [-] [85]

Dec 73. (lp)(c) **FOR EVERYMAN** [ ] [43] Nov 73
– Take it easy / Our lady of the well / Colors of the sun / I thought I was a child / These days / Redneck friend / The times you've come / Ready or not / Sing my songs to me / For everyman. *(cd-iss.Jan87)*

Apr 74. (7") **TAKE IT EASY. / READY OR NOT** [ ] [ ]

—— retained **LINDLEY** and brought in **JAI WINDING** – keyboards / **DOUG HAYWOOD** – bass, vocals / **LARRY ZACK** – drums

Nov 74. (7") **WALKING SLOW. / THE LATE SHOW** [ ] [-]

Oct 74. (7") **WALKING SLOW. / BEFORE THE DELUGE** [-] [ ]

Dec 74. (lp)(c) **LATE FOR THE SKY** [ ] [14] Oct 74
– Late for the sky / Fountain of sorrow / Farther on / The late show / The road and the sky / For a dancer / Walking slow / Before the deluge. *(quad-lp 1977) (cd-iss.Jan87)*

Mar 75. (7") **FOUNTAIN OF SORROW. / THE LATE SHOW** [ ] [ ]

—— **KUNKEL, SKLAR, DOERGE and LINDLEY** plus **JEFF PORCARO** – drums / **JIM GORDON** – drums / **BOB GLAUB and CHUCK RAINEY** – bass / **ROY BITTAN and BILL PAYNE** – organ / **LUIS F.DAMIAN** – guitar / etc.

Nov 76. (lp)(c) **THE PRETENDER** [26] [5]
– The fuse / Your bright baby blues / Linda Paloma / Here come those tears again / Daddy's tune / The only child / Daddy's tune / Sleep's dark and silent gate / The pretender. *(cd-iss.Jan87)*

Feb 77. (7") **HERE COME THOSE TEARS AGAIN. / LINDA PALOMA** [ ] [23]

Jul 77. (7") **THE PRETENDER. / DADDY'S TUNE** [ ] [58] May 77

Jan 78 (7") **YOU LOVE THE THUNDER. / COCAINE** [ ] [ ]

Jan 78. (lp)(c) **RUNNING ON EMPTY** [28] [3]
– Running on empty / The road / Rosie / You love the thunder / Cocaine / Shaky town / Love needs a heart / Nothing but time / The load-out / Stay. *(cd-iss.Jan87)*

Mar 78. (7") **RUNNING ON EMPTY. / NOTHING BUT TIME** [ ] [11] Feb 78

Jun 78. (7") **STAY. / ROSIE** [12] [-]

Sep 78. (7") **STAY. / THE LOAD-OUT** [-] [20]

Nov 78. (7") **THE ROAD. / YOU LOVE THE THUNDER** [-] [ ]

Jul 80. (7") **BOULEVARD. / CALL IT A LOAN** [ ] [19]

Jul 80. (lp)(c) **HOLD OUT** [44] [1]
– Disco apocalypse / Hold out / That girl could sing / Boulevard / Of missing persons / Call it a loan / Hold on hold out. *(cd-iss.Jan87)*

Oct 80. (7") **DISCO APOCALYPSE. / BOULEVARD** [ ] [-]

Oct 80. (7") **THAT GIRL COULD SING. / OF MISSING PERSONS** [-] [22]

—— next single was from "Fast Times at Ridgemont High" Soundtrack featuring **GRAHAM NASH + DAVID LINDLEY**

Aug 82. (7") **SOMEBODY'S BABY. / THE CROW ON THE CRADLE** [ ] [7] Jul 82

—— **BROWNE** retained **KUNKEL, DOERGE, HAYWOOD, GLAUB RICK VITO** – guitar repl. LINDLEY

Jul 83. (7") **LAWYERS IN LOVE. / SAY IT ISN'T TRUE** [ ] [13]

Aug 83. (lp)(c)(cd) **LAWYERS IN LOVE** [37] [8]
– Lawyers in love / On the day / Cut it away / Downtown / Tender is the night / Knock on any door / For a rocker. *(cd-iss.Jul87)*

Oct 83. (7") **TENDER IS THE NIGHT. / ON THE DAY** [ ] [25] Sep 83

Jan 84. (7") **FOR A ROCKER. / DOWNTOWN** [-] [45]

—— Early in '86, JACKSON was credited on US Top 20 single 'You're A Friend Of Mine', with CLARENCE CLEMONS (ex-BRUCE SPRINGSTEEN). His girlfriend DARRYL HANNAH guested, backing vocals.

Feb 86. (lp)(c)(cd) **LIVES IN THE BALANCE** [36] [23]
– For America / Soldier of plenty / In the shape of a heart / Candy / Lawless avenues / Lives in the balance / Till I go down / Black and white.

Feb 86. (7")(7"sha-pic-d) **FOR AMERICA. / TILL I GO DOWN** [ ] [30]

Elektra Elektra

Oct 86. (7") **IN THE SHAPE OF A HEART. / VOICE OF AMERICA** [66] [70] Jun 86
(d7"+=) – Running on empty / The pretender.

Jan 87. (7")(12") **EGO MANIAC. / LOVE'S GONNA GET YOU** [ ] [ ]
(above single on 'Warners')

Jun 89. (lp)(c)(cd) **WORLD IN MOTION** [39] [45]
– World in motion / Enough of the night / Chasing you into the light / How long / Anything can happen / When the stone begins to turn / The word justice / My personal revenge / I am a patriot / Lights and virtues. *(re-iss.cd Feb95)*

Jun 89. (7") **WORLD IN MOTION. / PERSONAL REVENGE** [-] [ ]

Oct 89. (7") **ANYTHING CAN HAPPEN. / LIGHTS AND VIRTUES** [-] [ ]

Jan 90. (7") **CHASING YOU INTO THE NIGHT. / HOW LONG** [-] [ ]

—— with **DAVID LINDLEY, MARK GOLDENBERG, SCOTT THURSTON, MIKE CAMPBELL, WALLY WACHTEL** – guitars / **KEVIN McCORMICK** – bass / **BENMONT TENCH** – organ / **MAURICIO LEWAK** – drums / **LUIS CONTE + LENNY CASTRO** – percussion / plus guests **DAVID CROSBY / DON HENLEY / JENNIFER WARNES / SWEET PEA ATKINSON + SIR HARRY BOWENS**

Oct 93. (cd)(c) **I'M ALIVE** [35] [40]
– I'm alive / My problem is you / Everywhere I go / I'll do anything / Miles away / Too many angels / Take this rain / Two of me, two of you / Sky blue and black / All good things.

Nov 93. (7")(c-s) **I'M ALIVE / TOO MANY ANGELS** [ ] [ ]
(cd-s) – ('A' side) Late for the sky / Running on empty / The pretender.

Jun 94. (7")(c-s) **EVERYWHERE I GO. / I'M ALIVE (live)** [67] [ ]
(cd-s+=) – The pretender (live) / Running on empty (live).
(cd-s) – ('A'side) / Take it easy / Doctor my eyes / In the shape of a heart.

Nov 94. (c-s) **HAND IN HAND. / TENDER IS THE NIGHT** [ ] [ ]
(cd-s+=) – Everywhere I go.

. . . Jan – Jun '96 stop press . . .

Feb 96. (cd)(c) **LOOKING EAST** [47] [36]

– compilations etc. –

Sep 76. Asylum; (7") **DOCTOR MY EYES. / TAKE IT EASY** [ ] [ ]

Oct 82. Asylum; (d-c) **THE PRETENDER / LATE FOR THE SKY** [ ] [-]

Nov 83. Asylum; (d-c) **JACKSON BROWNE / RUNNING ON EMPTY** [ ] [-]

Jack BRUCE

Born: 14 May'43, Bishopbriggs, Lanarkshire, Scotland. At 17 he won scholarship to R.S.A. of music. He joined local band JIM McHARG'S SCOTSVILLE JAZZBAND, before moving to London to join BLUES INCORPORATED with ALEXIS KORNER. In 1963 he became member of GRAHAM BOND ORGANISATION. In Oct'65 he joined JOHN MAYALL'S BLUESBREAKERS, also releasing debut solo 45. Late 1965, MANFRED MANN recruited him for six months, until his greatest move co-forming CREAM. After their demise late 1968, he went solo with 'Polydor' retaining contract. His debut 'SONGS FOR A TAILOR' hit the UK Top 10, but thereafter this was his only commercial success. • **Style:** One of greatest bass players of all-time, his new blues, with jazzy improvisations alongside superior underated vocals, gave him unique appeal. • **Songwriters:** Wrote most work with PETE BROWN. • **Trivia:** During 1970, he was also part of US jazz-rock outfit TONY WILLIAMS' LIFETIME, releasing album of same name.

Recommended: GREATEST HITS (*6)

JACK BRUCE – vocals, bass (ex-BLUES INCORPORATED, ex-GRAHAM BOND ORGANISATION) with session people.

Polydor not issued

Dec 65. (7") **I'M GETTIN' TIRED. / ROOTIN' AND TOOTIN'** [ ] [-]

—— (see above for details between 1966 and 1968.) He brought in friends **JON HISEMAN** – drums / **DICK HECKSTALL-SMITH** – sax / **CHRIS SPEDDING** – guitar / etc.

Polydor Atco

Sep 69. (lp)(c) **SONGS FOR A TAILOR** [6] [55]
– Never tell your mother she's out of tune / Theme of an imaginary western / Tickets to water falls / Weird of Hermiston / Rope ladder to the Moon / The ministry of bag / He the Richmond / Boston ball game, 1967 / To Isengard / The clearout. *(re-iss.May84) (cd-iss. May 88)*

—— **JOHN McLAUGHLIN** – guitar (solo artist), repl. SPEDDING.

Apr 71. (lp)(c) **THINGS WE LIKE ("JACK BRUCE, JOHN McLAUGHLIN, DICK HECKSTALL-SMITH, JON HISEMAN")** [ ] [ ]
– Over the cliff / Statues / Sam enchanted Dick (medley:- Sam's back / Rill's thrills) / Born to be blue / Hchhh blues / Ballad of Arthur / Things we like. *(re-iss.1979)*

—— retained some past musicians, bringing in **LARRY COYRELL** – guitar / **MIKE MANDEL** – keyboards / **MITCH MITCHELL** – drums

1971. (lp)(c) **HARMONY ROW** [ ] [ ]
– Can you follow? / Escape to the Royal wood (on ice) / You burned the tables on me / There's a forest / Morning story / Folk song / Smiles and grins / Post war / Letter of thanks / Victoria sage / The consul at sunset. *(cd-iss.1980's)*

1971. (7") **THE CONSUL AT SUNSET. / LETTER OF THANKS** [ ] [ ]

—— In 1972/73, he became part of WEST, BRUCE & LAING (see; MOUNTAIN ⇒) He also collaborated on lp ESCALATOR OVER THE HILL with PAUL HAINES and CARLA.

—— now with **MICK TAYLOR** – guitar / **CARLA BLEY** – piano / **RONNIE LEAHY** – keyboards / **BRUCE GARY** – drums

R.S.O. R.S.O.

Oct 74. (7") **KEEP IT DOWN. / GOLDEN DAYS** [ ] [ ]

Nov 74. (lp)(c) **OUT OF THE STORM** [ ] [ ]
– Pieces of mind / Golden days / Running through our hands / Keep on wondering / Keep it down / Into the storm / One / Timeslip. *(cd-iss.!)*

—— now with **SIMON PHILIPS** – drums / **HUGH BURNS** – guitar / **TONY HYMAS** – keyboards

Mar 77. (lp)(c) **HOW'S TRICKS ("JACK BRUCE BAND")** [ ] [ ]

– Without a word / Johnny B '77 / Times / Baby Jane / Lost inside a song / How's tricks / Madhouse / Waiting for the call / Outsiders / Something to live for.

— Friends: **DAVID SANCIOUS** – guitar, keyboards / **DAVE CLEMSON** – guitar / **BILLY COBHAM** – drums

Epic Epic

Dec 80. (lp)(c) **I'VE ALWAYS WANTED TO DO THIS ("JACK BRUCE & FRIENDS").**
– Hit and run / Running back / Facelift 318 / In this way / Mickey the fiddler / Dancing on air / Livin' without ja / Wind and the sea / Out to lunch / Bird alone.

In 1981 he teamed up with BILL LORDAN and ROBIN TROWER to release lp 'B.L.T. Early the following year he and ROBIN TROWER (see ⇒ released TRUCE album).

— He returned to solo work after below 45 was featured on TV car advert.

Virgin Virgin

Jun 86. (7")(12") **I FEEL FREE. / MAKE LOVE**

President Intercord

Jan 87. (lp)(c) **AUTOMATIC**
– A boogie / Uptown breakdown / Travelling child / New world / Make love (part 2) / Green and blue / The swarm / Encore / Automatic pilot.

— next with **ANTON FIER** – drums (ex-PERE UBU) / **KENJI SUZUKI** – guitar

Epic Epic

Jan 88. (lp)(c)(cd) **INAZUMA SUPER SESSION – ABSOLUTELY LIVE ("JACK BRUCE, ANTON FIER & KENJI SUZUKI" live)**
– Generation breakdown / White room / Out into the field / Working harder / Sittin' on top of the world / Sunshine of your love / Crossroads / Spoonful – Beat of rock.

— now with **VERNON REID, NICKY HOPKINS, ALLAN HOLDSWORTH, GINGER BAKER**

Jan 90. (cd)(c)(lp) **A QUESTION OF TIME**
– Life on Earth / Make love / No surrender! / Flying / Hey now princess / Blues you can't lose / Obsession / Kwela / Let me be / Only playing games / A question of time. *(re-iss.Feb91)*

— with **PETE BROWN** still lyricist / plus **ERIC CLAPTON** – lead guitar / **STUART ELLIOT** – drums / **PETER WIEHE** – rhythm guitar / **MAGGIE REILLY** – b.vocals / **CLEM CLEMPSON** – rhythm guitar, etc / **TRILOK GURTU** – percussion / and guests on 1 each **DICK HECKSTALL-SMITH + DAVID LIEBMAN** – saxophones

C.M.P. C.M.P.

Mar 93. (cd)(c)(lp) **SOMETHIN ELS** [-]
– Waiting on a word / Willpower / Ships in the night / Peace of the East / Close enough for love / G.B. dawn blues / Criminality / Childsong / F.M.

— with **GARY MOORE** – guitar, vocals / **MAGGIE REILLY** – vocals / **GARY 'Mudbone' COOPER** – vocals, percussion / **CLEM CLEMPSON** – guitars / **DICK HECKSTALL-SMITH** -saxophone / **BERNIE WORRELL** – keyboards / **PETE BROWN** – vocals, percussion / **GINGER BAKER + SIMON PHILLIPS + GARY HUSBAND** – drums / **FRANCOIS GARNY** -bass / **MALCOLM BRUCE** – acoustic guitar, keyboards / **JONAS BRUCE** -keyboards / **ART THEMIN** – saxophone / **HENRY LOWTHER** -trumpet / **JOHN MUMFORD** -trombone / + **KIP HANRAHAN**

Mar 94. (d-cd)(d-c) **CITIES OF THE HEART (live)**
– Can you follow? / Running thro' our hands / Over the cliff / Statues / First time I met the blues / Smiles & grins / Bird alone / Neighbor, neighbor / Born under a bad sign // Ships in the night / Never tell your mother she's out of tune / Theme for an imaginary western / Golden days / Life on Earth / NSU / Sitting on top of the world / Politician / Spoonful / Sunshine of your love. *(re-iss.Aug94 + Nov94)*

Sep 95. (cd) **MONKJACK** [-]
– Third degree / The boy / Shouldn't we / David's harp / Know one blues / Time repairs / Laughing on music / Street / Folksong / Weird of Hermiston / Tightrope / The food / Immoral ninth.

BBM

(aka GINGER BAKER, JACK BRUCE & GARY MOORE) A near reformation of CREAM with MOORE taking the place of CLAPTON.

Virgin Virgin

Jun 94. (cd)(c)(lp) **AROUND THE NEXT DREAM** [9]
– Waiting in the wings / City of God / Where in the world / Can't fool the blues / High cost of living / Glory days / Why does love (have to go wrong) / Naked flame / I wonder (why are you so mean to me?) / Wrong side of town.

Jul 94. (7")(c-s) **WHERE IN THE WORLD. / DANGER ZONE** [57]
(cd-s+=) – The world keeps on turnin'.
(cd-s) – ('A'side) / Sittin' on top of the world / I wonder (why are you so mean to me?).

– compilations, others, etc. –

1974. Polydor/ US= R.S.O.; (d-lp)(d-c) **AT HIS BEST**
Nov 80. Polydor; (lp) **GREATEST HITS**
Jul 89. Polydor; (d-lp)(c)(cd) **WILLPOWER**
(re-iss.cd Apr95)
May 92. Castle; (cd) **THE COLLECTION** [-]
May 94. Atonal; (cd) **THIS THAT ("HECKSTALL / BRUCE / STEVENS")** [-]
Sep 95. Windsong; (cd) **BBC LIVE IN CONCERT** [-]

B.T.O. (see under ⇒ BACHMAN-TURNER OVERDRIVE)

Lindsey BUCKINGHAM / BUCKINGHAM-NICKS (see under ⇒ FLEETWOOD MAC)

Harold BUDD, Elizabeth FRAZER, Robin GUTHRIE, Simon RAYMONDE (see under ⇒ COCTEAU TWINS)

BUFFALO SPRINGFIELD

Formed: Los Angeles, California, USA . . . March 1966 by STEVE STILLS, NEIL YOUNG, RICHIE FUREY and BRUCE PALMER. They emigrated from various places and odd groups around North America (Canada) and soon signed to 'Atco' label releasing eponymous debut. Early in 1967, they scored a US Top 10 hit with classic 'FOR WHAT IT'S WORTH', but due to various changes in personnel, they didn't last long, and members went on to greater things (see below). • **Style:** Harmonious electric-rock that veered into protest and underground. • **Songwriters:** Mainly STILLS, YOUNG or FUREY. • **Trivia:** Took their name from type of steamroller.

Recommended: THE BEST OF . . . RETROSPECTIVE (*8)

STEPHEN STILLS (b. 3 Jan'45, Dallas, Texas) – lead guitar, vocals / **NEIL YOUNG** (b.12 Nov'45, Toronto, Canada) – lead guitar, vocals / **RICHIE FURAY** (b. 9 May'44, Dayton, Ohio) – vocals, guitar / **BRUCE PALMER** (b. 1944, Liverpool, Canada) – bass repl. KEN KOBLUN / **DEWEY MARTIN** (b.30 Sep'42, Chesterfield, Canada) – drums (ex-DILLARDS)

Atlantic Atco

1966. (7") **NOWADAYS CLANCY CAN'T EVEN SING. / GO AND SAY GOODBYE** [-]
Jan 67. (lp) **BUFFALO SPRINGFIELD** [80] Oct 66
– Don't scold me (*) / Go and say goodbye / Sit down I think I love you / Nowadays Clancy can't even sing / Everybody's wrong / Hot dusty roads / Flying on the ground / Burned / Do I have to come right out and say it? / Leave / Pay the price / Out of my mind. *(re-iss.'71 with below 'A' side repl. (*)) (cd-iss. Feb93)*
Jan 67. (7") **FOR WHAT IT'S WORTH. / DO I HAVE TO COME RIGHT OUT AND SAY IT?** [7]

— On stage **KEN KOBLUN** and **JIM FIELDER**, latter of The MOTHERS, repl. PALMER, although PALMER did return occasionally. / **DOUG HASTINGS** – guitar repl. YOUNG (also DAVID CROSBY guested at Monteray)

— **BOB WEST** – bass & CHARLIE CHIN – banjo deputise for above reshuffles

Jul 67. (7") **BLUEBIRD. / Mr.SOUL** [-] [58]

— **STILLS, FURAY, MARTIN** and the returning **YOUNG** recruit **JIM MESSINA** – bass repl. FIELDER who joined BLOOD SWEAT & TEARS

Oct 67. (7") **ROCK'N'ROLL WOMAN. / A CHILD'S CLAIM TO FAME** [44] Sep 67
Jan 68. (lp) **BUFFALO SPRINGFIELD AGAIN** [44] Nov 67
– Mr.Soul / A child's claim to fame / Everydays / Expecting to fly / Bluebird / Hung upside down / Sad memory / Good time boy / Rock'n'roll woman / Broken arrow. *(re-iss.'71)*
Feb 68. (7") **EXPECTING TO FLY. / EVERYDAYS** [98] Jan 68
Jun 68. (7") **UNO-MUNDO. / MERRY-GO-ROUND**
Aug 68. (7") **KIND WOMAN. / SPECIAL CARE** [-]

— with original line-up they recorded another album, but they had split May. MESSINA who had always been their sound recordist posthumously assembled

Sep 68. (lp) **LAST TIME AROUND** [42] Aug 68
– On the way home / It's so hard to wait / Pretty girl why / Four days gone / Carefree country day / Special care / The hour of not quite rain / Questions / I am a child / Merry-go-round / Uno mundo / Kind woman. *(re-iss.'71) (cd-iss.Mar94 on 'Atco')*
Oct 68. (7") **ON THE WAY HOME. / FOUR DAYS GONE** [-] [82]

— After their split, NEIL YOUNG went solo and joined STEPHEN STILLS in CROSBY, STILLS NASH & YOUNG. FURAY formed POCO adding later MESSINA. DEWEY MARTIN tried in vain to use BUFFALO SPRINGFIELD name.

– compilations etc. –

Mar 69. Atlantic/ US= Atco; (lp) **RETROSPECTIVE – THE BEST OF BUFFALO SPRINGFIELD** [42] Feb 69
– For what it's worth / Mr. Soul / Sit down I think I love you / Kind woman / Bluebird / On the way home / Nowadays Clancy can't even sing / Broken arrow / Rock and roll woman / I am a child / Go and say goodbye / Expecting to fly. *(cd-iss. Jul 88)*
Oct 69. Atlantic; (7"ep) **PRETTY GIRL WHY / QUESTIONS / BLUEBIRD / MR. SOUL / ROCK'N'ROLL WOMAN / EXPECTING TO FLY.** [-]
Oct 70. Atlantic; (lp) **EXPECTING TO FLY** [-]

Oct 72. Atlantic; (7"ep) **BLUEBIRD / MR.SOUL. / ROCK'N'ROLL WOMAN / EXPECTING TO FLY** [ ] [-]
Dec 73. Atlantic/ US= Atco; (d-lp)(d-c) **BUFFALO SPRINGFIELD** [ ] [ ]
— Some tracks appeared on NEIL YOUNG's comp.lp JOURNEY THROUGH THE PAST

BUFFALO TOM

Formed: Boston, Massachusetts, USA . . . 1986 by trio below. • **Style:** Like a grunge hybrid of HUSKER DU and VAN MORRISON. • **Songwriters:** Group except SHE BELONGS TO ME (Bob Dylan) / HEAVEN (Psychedelic Furs) / THE SPIDER AND THE FLY (Rolling Stones). • **Trivia:** Produced by J.MASCIS of DINOSAUR JR.

Recommended: (BIG RED LETTER DAY) (*7) / LET ME COME OVER (*8)

BILL JANOVITZ – vocals, guitar / **CHRIS COLBOURN** – bass / **TOM MAGINNIS** – drums

S.S.T. S.S.T.

Oct 89. (lp)(c)(cd) **BUFFALO TOM** [ ] [ ] Jul 89
– Sunflower suit / The plank / Impossible / 500,000 warnings / The bus / Racine / In the attic / Flushing stars / Walk away / Reason why. *(re-iss.Oct92 on 'Beggar's B.' with extra tracks) (+=) – Blue / Deep in the ground.*

Caff not issued

Feb 90. (7"ltd) **ENEMY. / DEEP IN THE GROUND** [ ] [-]

Megadisc ???

Jun 90. (12") **CRAWL. / ?** [ ] [-]

Situation 2 ???

Oct 90. (12"ep)(cd-ep) **BIRDBRAIN. / REASON WHY (live acoustic) / HEAVEN (live acoustic)** [ ] [ ]
Oct 90. (cd)(c)(lp) **BIRDBRAIN** [ ] [ ]
– Birdbrain / Skeleton key / Caress / Guy who is me / Enemy / Crawl / Fortune teller / Baby / Directive / Bleeding heart. *(cd+=)* Heaven / Reason why (acoustic). *(re-iss.cd Sep95)*
May 91. (12"ep)(cd-ep) **FORTUNE TELLER. / WAH WAH** [ ] [ ]
Feb 92. (12"ep)(cd-ep) **VELVET ROOF / SHE BELONGS TO ME. / CRUTCH / SALLY BROWN** [ ] [ ]
Mar 92. (cd)(c)(lp) **LET ME COME OVER** [49] [ ]
– Staples / Taillights fade / Mountains of your head / Mineral / Darry / Larry / Velvet roof / I'm not there / Stymied / Porch light / Frozen lake / Saving grace. (cd+=) – Crutch.
May 92. (10"ep)(12"ep)(cd-ep) **TAILLIGHTS FADE / BIRDBRAIN (live). / LARRY (live) / SKELETON KEY (live)** [ ] [ ]

Beggar's B Beggar's B

Oct 92. (7")(7"green) **MINERAL. / SUNFLOWER SUIT** [ ] [ ]
(cd-s+=) – Crawl / The bus.
Sep 93. (cd)(c)(lp) **(BIG RED LETTER DAY)** [17] [ ]
– Sodajerk / I'm Allowed / Tree House / Would Not Be Denied / Latest Monkey / My Responsibility / Dry Land / Torch Singer / Late At Night / Suppose / Anything That Way
Sep 93. (12"ep)(cd-ep) **SODA JERK / WOULD NOT BE DENIED. / WITCHES / THE WAY BACK** [ ] [ ]
Nov 93. (7") **TREEHOUSE. / ANYTHING THAT WAY (Acoustic)** [ ] [ ]
(12"+=)(cd-s+=) – Late At Night (Acoustic)
Apr 94. (12")(cd-s) **I'M ALLOWED. / FOR ALL TO SEE / BUTTERSCOTCH** [ ] [ ]
Jun 95. (10"ep)(cd-ep) **SUMMER. / CLOUDS / DOES THIS MEAN YOU'RE NOT MY FRIEND?** [ ] [ ]
Jul 95. (cd)(c)(lp) **SLEEPY EYED** [31] [ ]
– Tangerine / Summer / Kitchen door / Rules / It's you / When you discover / Sunday night / Your stripes / Sparklers / Clobbered / Sundress / Twenty-points (the ballad of sexual dependency) / Souvenir / Crueler.
Nov 95. (7") **TANGERINE. / BREATH** [ ] [ ]
(cd-s+=) – The spider and the fly.

The BUNCH (see under ⇒ FAIRPORT CONVENTION)

Eric BURDON (see under ⇒ ANIMALS)

J. J. BURNEL (see under ⇒ STRANGLERS)

BUSH

Formed: Kilburn, London, England . . .1994 although they soon re-located to the States, highlight being playing New York's CBGB's. Soon became million sellers there, when their 1995 album 'SIXTEEN STONE' hit the Top 20. • **Style:** Grunge rock; the English answer to NIRVANA or PEARL JAM. • **Songwriters:** Group except REVOLUTION BLUES (Neil Young).

Recommended: SIXTEEN STONE (*4)

GAVIN ROSSDALE -vocals, guitar / **NIGEL PULSFORD** -guitar / **DAVE PARSONS** -bass / **ROBIN GOODRIDGE** -drums

Atlantic Interscope

Apr 95. (c-s) **EVERYTHING ZEN. / BUD** [ ] [ ]
(12"+=)(cd-s+=) – Monkey.
May 95. (cd)(c) **SIXTEEN STONE** [ ] [4]
– Everything zen / Swim / Bomb / Little things / Comedown / Body / Machinehead / Testosterone / Monkey / Glycerine / Alien / X-girlfriend.
Jul 95. (5"ltd.)(c-s) **LITTLE THINGS / X-GIRLFRIEND** [ ] [ ]
(cd-s+=) – Swim.
Aug 95. (c-s) **COMEDOWN / REVOLUTION BLUES** [-] [30]
(cd-s+=) – Testosterone.

. . . Jan – Jun '96 stop press . . .

Jan 96. (single) **GLYCERINE** [-] [28]
May 96. (single) **MACHINEHEAD** [48] [43]
Jun 96. (re-issue)(cd w/bonus cd)(c) **SIXTEEN STONE** [42] [-]

Kate BUSH

Born: CATHERINE BUSH, 30 Jul'58. Bexleyheath, Kent, England. In 1974, she formed own K.T.BUSH band with brother PADDY and future boyfriend DEL PALMER. By summer '76, with help from DAVE GILMOUR (Pink Floyd), she obtained contract with EMI. After a surprise No.1 hit early '78, she finally released 'THE KICK INSIDE', an album worked on for past 2+ years, which set her on the road to stardom. All her albums over the next decade or so made UK Top 10, and included nearly 20 Top 50 hits. • **Style:** A shy beauty, with dreamy childlike vocals to complement her innovative, experimental work. Her brilliant and extremely visual videos captured completely her imagination and choreography. • **Songwriters:** All or most written by KATE, except covers; ROCKET MAN + CANDLE IN THE WIND (Elton John) / I'M STILL WAITING (Diana Ross) / WHEN YOU WISH UPON A STAR (Walt Disney s/track). • **Trivia:** Her first major tour came in April'79, and although it was mildly successful, she only once appeared live again at 'The Secret Policeman's Third Ball' in 1987. She had always concentrated on studio work, but said she might tour soon. Actor Donald Sutherland appeared in her video for 'CLOUDBUSTING' 45.

Recommended: THE WHOLE STORY (*9) / THE SENSUAL WORLD (*7).

KATE BUSH – vocals, keyboards with **PADDY BUSH** – mandolin, etc. / **DEL PALMER** – bass / **IAN BAIRNSON** – guitar / **DUNCAN MACKAY** – keyboards / **ANDREW POWELL** – keyboards / **STUART ELLIOTT** – drums / **DAVID PATON** – bass / **MORRIS PERT** – percussion / **BRIAN BATH** – guitar / + others (her backing musicians changed from time to time, see 2nd edition)

E.M.I. EMI America

Jan 78. (7") **WUTHERING HEIGHTS. / KITE** [1] [ ]
Feb 78. (lp)(c) **THE KICK INSIDE** [3] [ ]
– Moving / The saxophone song / Strange phenomena / Kite / The man with the child in his eyes / Wuthering heights / James and the cold gun / Feel it / Oh to be in love / L'amour looks something like you / Them heavy people / Room for the life / The kick inside. *(pic-lp iss.1979) (cd-iss.Jan84) (re-iss.Oct88 on 'Fame'+cd) (re-iss.cd+c Sep94)*
May 78. (7") **THE MAN WITH THE CHILD IN HIS EYES. / MOVING** [6] [85] Feb 79
Nov 78. (7") **HAMMER HORROR. / COFFEE HOMEGROUND** [44] [ ]
Nov 78. (lp)(c) **LIONHEART** [6] [ ]
– Symphony in blue / In search of Peter Pan (incl. When you wish upon a star) / Wow / Don't push your foot on the heartbrake / Oh England my lionheart / Fullhouse / In the warm room / Hammer horror / Kashka from Baghdad / Coffee homeground / Hammer horror. *(re-iss.Apr84 & Oct88 on 'Fame'+cd) (cd-iss.Jan85) (re-iss.cd+c Sep94)*
Mar 79. (7") **WOW. / FULLHOUSE** [14] [ ]
Sep 79. (d7"ep) **KATE BUSH ON STAGE (live)** [10] [ ]
– Them heavy people / Don't put you foot on the heartbrake / James and the cold gun / L'amour looks something like you.
Apr 80. (7") **DREAMING. / THE EMPTY BULLRING** [16] [ ]
Jun 80. (7") **BABOOSHKA. / RAN TAN WALTZ** [5] [ ]
Sep 80. (lp)(c) **NEVER FOR EVER** [1] [ ]
– Babooshka / Delius / Blow away / All we ever look for / Egypt / The wedding list / Violin / The infant kiss / Night scented stock / Army dreamers / Breathing. *(cd-iss.Mar87)*
Sep 80. (7"m) **ARMY DREAMERS. / DELIUS / PASSING THROUGH THE AIR** [16] [ ]
Nov 80. (7") **DECEMBER WILL BE MAGIC AGAIN. / WARM AND SOOTHING** [29] [ ]
Jul 81. (7") **SAT IN YOUR LAP. / LORD OF THE REEDY RIVER** [11] [ ]
Jul 82. (7") **THE DREAMING. / DREAMTIME (instrumental)** [48] [ ]

Sep 82. (lp)(c) **THE DREAMING** [3] [ ]
– Sat in your lap / There goes a tenner / Pull out the pin / Suspended in Gaffa / Leave it open / The dreaming / Night of the swallow Houdini / Get out of my house / All the love. *(cd-iss.Jan87) (re-iss.cd/c/lp.Mar91)*

Nov 82. (7") **THERE GOES A TENNER. / NE T'ENFUIS PAS** [ ] [ ]

Aug 85. (7") **RUNNING UP THAT HILL. / UNDER THE IVY** [3] [30]
(12"+=) – ('A'instrumental).

Sep 85. (lp)(c)(cd) **HOUNDS OF LOVE** [1] [30]
– Running up that hill / Hounds of love / The big sky / Mother stands for comfort / Cloudbusting / And dream of sheep / Under ice / Waking the witch / Watching you without me / Jig of life / Hello Earth / The morning fog. (cd+=) – Cloudbusting (extended).

Oct 85. (7") **CLOUDBUSTING. / BURNING BRIDGES** [20] [ ]
(12"+=) – My Lagan Love.

Feb 86. (7") **HOUNDS OF LOVE. / HANDSOME CABIN BOY** [18] [ ]
(12"+=) – ('A'instrumental) / Jig of life.

May 86. (7")(7"pic-d) **THE BIG SKY. / NOT THIS TIME** [37] [ ]
(12"+=) – The morning fog.

—— In Oct 86, she did duet **DON'T GIVE UP** with **PETER GABRIEL** which hit for 'Geffen' UK No.9 / US No.72.

Nov 86. (7") **EXPERIMENT IV. / WUTHERING HEIGHTS (vocal)** [23] [ ]
(12"+=) – December will be magic again.

Nov 86. (lp)(c)(cd) **THE WHOLE STORY** [1] [ ]
– Wuthering heights / Cloudbusting / The man with the child in his eyes / Breathing / Wow / Hounds of love / Running up that hill / Army dreamers / Sat in your lap / Experiment IV / The dreaming / Babooshka.

E.M.I. / Columbia

Sep 89. (7")(c-s) **THE SENSUAL WORLD. / WALK STRAIGHT DOWN THE MIDDLE** [12] [ ]
(12")(cd-s) – ('A'extended)/ ('A'instrumental).

Oct 89. (lp)(c)(cd) **THE SENSUAL WORLD** [2] [43]
– The sensual world / Love and anger / The fog / Reaching out / Heads we're dancing / Deeper understanding / Between a man and a woman / Never be mine / Rocket's tail / This woman's work. (cd+=) – Walk straight down the middle.

Nov 89. (7")(7"pic-d) **THIS WOMAN'S WORK. / BE KIND TO MY MISTAKES** [25] [ ]
(12"+=)(cd-s+=) – ('A'version) / I'm still waiting.

Mar 90. (7")(c-s) **LOVE AND ANGER. / KEN** [38] [ ]
(12"+=) – The confrontation / Just one last look.
(cd-s++=) – One last look around the house before we go.

Apr 90. (7") **LOVE AND ANGER. / WALK STRAIGHT DOWN THE MIDDLE** [-] [ ]

Nov 91. (7")(c-s) **ROCKET MAN. / CANDLE IN THE WIND** [12] [ ]
(12"+=)(cd-s+=) – ('B'instrumental).

—— (above single on 'Mercury')

—— with **STUART ELLIOTT** – drums / **JOHN GIBLIN** – bass / **DANNY McINTOSH** – guitar / **GARY BROOKER** – hammond organ / **PADDY BUSH + COLIN LLOYD TUCKER** – vocals / **PAUL SPONG + STEVE SLOWER** – trumpet / **NEIL SIDWELL** – trombone / **NIGEL HITCHCOCK** – sax / **NIGEL KENNEDY** – violin / + guests **PRINCE + ERIC CLAPTON**

Sep 93. (7")(c-s) **RUBBERBAND GIRL. / BIG STRIPEY LIE** [12] [88]
(cd-s+=)(12"pic-d+=) – ('A'extended remix).

Nov 93. (cd)(c)(lp) **THE RED SHOES** [2] [28]
– Rubberband girl / And so is love / Eat the music / Moments of pleasure / The song of Solomon / Lily / The red shoes / Top of the city / Constellation of the heart / Big stripey lie / Why should I love you? / You're the one.

Nov 93. (7")(c-s) **MOMENTS OF PLEASURE. / SHOW A LITTLE DEVOTION** [26] [ ]
(12") – ('A'side) / ('A'instrumental) / Home for Christmas.
(cd-s) – ('A'side) / December will be magic again / Experiment IV.

Apr 94. (7")(c-s) **THE RED SHOES. / YOU WANT ALCHEMY** [21] [ ]
(cd-s+=) – Cloudbursting (video mix) / This woman's work.
(cd-s) – ('A'shoedance mix) / The big sky / Running up that hill.

—— In Jul 94, KATE partnered LARRY ADLER on 'Mercury' single 'THE MAN I LOVE'. It hit UK No.27, and was from his tribute album 'The Glory Of Gershwin'.

Nov 94. (7"pic-d)(c-s) **AND SO IS LOVE. / RUBBERBAND GIRL (U.S.mix)** [26] [ ]
(cd-s+=) – Eat the music (U.S. mix).

– compilations, others, etc. –

Jun 83. EMI America; (m-lp) **KATE BUSH** [-] [ ]

Oct 83. Old Gold; (7") **WUTHERING HEIGHTS. / THE MAN WITH THE CHILD IN HIS EYES** [ ] [-]

Jan 84. E.M.I.; (7"x13) **THE SINGLES FILE** [ ] [-]
– (all previous singles +) NE T'ENFUIS PAS. / UN BAISER D'ENFANT

Oct 90. E.M.I.; (9xcd)(8xc)(8xlp)(box) **THIS WOMAN'S WORK – ANTHOLOGY 1978-1990** [ ] [ ]

Aug 94. E.M.I.; (cd)(cd-vid) **LIVE AT HAMMERSMITH ODEON (live)** [ ] [-]

—— (a complete history of all her songs, re-issuing albums)

Oct 92. U.F.O.; (12"-box+cd) **NEVER FOREVER** [ ] [-]
(above issued w / free booklet & T-shirt)

BUTTHOLE SURFERS

Formed: San Antonio, Texas, USA . . . 1980 originally as ASHTRAY BABY HEELS by ex-accountant GIBBY and PAUL who met at Trinity College, San Antonio. By 1983, they were signed to JELLO BIAFRA's (Dead Kennedys) label 'Alternative Tenticles'. Around the mid-80's, due to lack of US interest, they came to the UK, where with the help of airplay from John Peel, they made it into indie charts. • **Style:** Heavy psychedelia that mixes noise, confusion and futuristic punk with the manic GIBBY (complete with loudspeaker, etc). Always offensive and disturbing, their weird stage aura included nude dancer KATHLEEN who covered herself in green jello. • **Songwriters:** GIBBY and co., except AMERICAN WOMAN (Guess Who) / HURDY GURDY MAN (Donovan). • **Trivia:** PIOUHGD is Red Indian for 'pissed off'.

Recommended: LOCUST ABORTION TECHNICIAN (*8) / HAIRWAY TO STEVEN (*7)

GIBBY (b. GIBSON JEROME HAYNES) – vocals / **PAUL 'PABLO' LEARY WARTHALL** – guitar / **KING KOFFEE** – drums repl. ? / **ALAN ?** – bass

Alt. Tent. / Alt. Tent.

Apr 84. (m-lp) **BUTTHOLE SURFERS (BROWN REASONS TO LIVE)** [ ] [ ] '83
– The Shah sleeps in Lee Harvey's grave / Hey / Something / Bar-b-que / Pope / Wichita cathedral / Suicide / The legend of Anus Presley. *(US title 'A BROWN REASON TO LIVE')(re-iss. Sep93)*

Jan 85. (12"ep) **LIVE PCPPEP (live 45rpm)** [ ] [ ]
– (contains most of last mlp)

—— **TERENCE** – bass repl. ALAN (?)

not issued / Touch & Go

Apr 85. (7") **LADY SNIFF. / ?** [-] [ ]

Fundament. / Fundament.

Jul 85. (lp) **PSYCHIC . . . POWERLESS . . . ANOTHER MAN'S SAC** [ ] [ ] '84
– Concubine / Eye of the chicken / Dum dum / Woly boly / Negro observer / Butthole surfer / Lady sniff / Cherub / Mexican caravan / Cowboy Bob / Gary Floyd (cd-iss.Jan88.+=) – (includes below 12" CREAM CORN FROM THE SOCKET OF DAVIS)

—— **MARK KRAMER** – bass (of SHOCKABILLY) repl. TREVOR who had repl. TERENCE

Oct 85. (12"ep) **CREAM CORN FROM THE SOCKET OF DAVIS** [ ] [ ]
– Moving to Florida / Comb – Lou Reed (two parter) / Tornadoes.

Red Rhino / Touch & Go

Apr 86. (lp) **REMBRANDT PUSSYHORSE** [ ] [ ]
– Creep in the cellar / Sea ferring / American woman / Waiting for Jimmy to kick / Strangers die / Perry / Whirling hall of knives / Mark says alright / In the cellar.. *(cd-iss.May88)*

—— **JEFF 'TOOTER' PINKUS** – bass repl. KRAMER who formed BONGWATER

Blast First / Blast First

Mar 87. (lp)(cd) **LOCUST ABORTION TECHNICIAN** [ ] [ ]
– Sweet loaf / Graveyard 1 / Pittsburgh to Lebanon / Weber / Hay / Human cannonball / U.S.S.A. / Theoman / Kintz / Graveyard 2 / 22 going on 23 / The G-men.

—— added **THERESA NAYLOR** – 2nd drummer / **KATHLEEN** – naked dancer(above with GIBBY, PAUL, COFFEY and PINKUS)

Apr 88. (lp)(c)(cd) **HAIRWAY TO STEVEN** [ ] [ ]
– Hairway Part 1 / Hairway Part 2 / Hairway Part 3 / Hairway Part 4 / Hairway Part 5 / Hairway Part 6 / Hairway Part 7 / Hairway Part 8 / Hairway Part 9 (9 tracks marked as rude symbols as titles)

Aug 89. (12"ep)(10"ep)(cd-ep) **WIDOWMAKER** [ ] [ ]
– Bong song / 1401 / Booze tobacco / Helicopter.

Rough Trade / Capitol

Nov 90. (7") **THE HURDY GURDY MAN. / BARKING DOGS** [ ] [ ]
(12"+=)(cd-s+=) ('A'-Paul Leary remix)

Feb 91. (cd)(c)(lp) **PIOUHGD** [68] [ ]
– Revolution pt.1 & 2 / Lonesome bulldog pt.1 & 2 / The hurdy gurdy man / Golden showers / Lonesome bulldog pt.3 / Blindman / No, I'm iron man / Something / P.S.Y. / Lonesome bulldog pt.IV. (cd+=) – Barking dogs. *(cd-iss.Dec 94 on 'Danceteria')*

In Apr'92, GIBBY guested for MINISTRY on single 'Jesus Built My Hotrod'.

Capitol / Capitol

Mar 93. (cd)(c)(lp) **INDEPENDENT WORM SALOON** [73] [ ]
– Who was in my room last night / The wooden song / Tongue / Chewin' George Lucas' chocolate / Goofy's concern / Alcohol / Dog inside your body / Strawberry / Some dispute over T-shirt sales / Dancing fool / You don't know me / The annoying song / Dust devil / Leave me alone / Edgar / The ballad of a naked man / Clean it up.

Nov 94. (7"pic-d) **GOOD KING WENCENSLAUS. / THE LORD IS A MONKEY** [ ] [ ]

. . . Jan – Jun '96 stop press . . .

May 96. (cd)(c)(lp) **ELECTRICLARRYLAND** 44

– compilations, others, etc. –

Jun 89. Latino Bugger; (d-lp)(c)(cd) **DOUBLE LIVE (live ltd.)** -
Apr 95. Trance; (cd) **THE HOLE TRUTH & NOTHING BUTT**
(early demos)

JACK OFFICERS

off-shoot with **GIBBY, JEFF & KATHLEEN**

Na-ked Brain Shim-my DIsc

Dec 90. (cd)(c)(lp) **DIGITAL DUMP**
– Love-o-maniac / Time machine pt.1 & 2 / L.A.name peanut butter / Do it / Swingers club / Ventricular retribution / 6 / Don't touch that / An Hawaiian Christmas song / Flush.

PAUL LEARY

Rough Trade Capitol

Apr 91. (cd)(c)(lp) **THE HISTORY OF DOGS**
– The birds are dying / Apollo one / Dalhart down the road / How much longer / He's working overtime / Indians storm the government / Is it milky / Too many people / The city / Fine home.

DRAIN

aka KING COFFEY + DAVID McCREETH (ex-SQUID)

Synd. Trance Synd. Trance

Apr 91. (12")(cd-s) **A BLACK FIST**

BUZZCOCKS

Formed: Manchester, England . . . April 1976 by DEVOTO and SHELLEY who met at Bolton Institute Of Higher Education. First gig was on 20th July'76 supporting SEX PISTOLS. Early '77, they released first ever non-Stiff punk "indie" 45 on 'New Hormones' in the form of SPIRAL SCRATCH EP. They suffered major bust up when DEVOTO departed, but carried on, signing to 'United Art' after featuring on the now famous 'LIVE AT THE ROXY' Various compilation ('Breakdown' + 'Love Battery'). Early 1978 they stormed the British charts with moping love gem 'WHAT DO I GET', which was followed by 3 bigger hits that year. More followed, but with the decline of new wave/pop, they disbanded in 1981. SHELLEY had mildly successful solo career, and BUZZCOCKS returned to good style but not the charts (yet!) early 1990. • **Style:** Punk rock/pop that had influences from STOOGES to RAMONES. Mellowed a little when SHELLEY took over with his romance'n'roll effeminate wordings. • **Songwriters:** DEVOTO wrote material until he left. SHELLEY took over with DIGGLE writing and vocalising on some. Covered HERE COMES THE NICE (Small Faces). • **Trivia:** In 1978, SHELLEY produced fun group ALBERTO Y LOST TRIOS PARANOIAS. His solo single 'HOMOSAPIAN' went No.1 in Australia.

Recommended: ANOTHER MUSIC IN A DIFFERENT KITCHEN (*9) / SINGLES – GOING STEADY (*9).

HOWARD DEVOTO (b.HOWARD TRAFFORD) – vocals / **PETE SHELLEY** (b.PETER McNEISH, 17 Apr'55) – guitar, vocals / **STEVE DIGGLE** – bass, vocals / **JOHN MAHER** – drums

New Hormones not issued

Jan 77. (7"ep) **SPIRAL SCRATCH** -
– Breakdown / Times up / Boredom / Friends of mine. *(re-iss.Aug79 credited as "BUZZCOCKS with HOWARD DEVOTO" hit* No.31) *(re-iss.as 12"+cd-ep on 'Document')*

— (Mar77) **GARTH SMITH** – bass repl. DEVOTO who later formed MAGAZINE. **SHELLEY** now lead vocals, guitar / **DIGGLE** switched to guitar, vocals

United Art not issued

Oct 77. (7") **ORGASM ADDICT. / WHATEVER HAPPENED TO . . . ?** -

— **STEVE GARVEY** – bass repl. GARTH (on tour at first)

Jan 78. (7") **WHAT DO I GET?. / OH SHIT** 37 -

United Art I.R.S.

Mar 78. (lp)(c) **ANOTHER MUSIC IN A DIFFERENT KITCHEN** 15
– Fast cars / No reply / You tear me up / Get on our own / Love battery / 16 / I don't mind / Fiction romance / Autonomy / I need / Moving away from the pulsebeat. *(re-iss.Aug85 on 'Liberty') (re-.blue-lp.Jun87 on 'Fan Club') (re-iss.lp/c/cd.May88 on 'Fame') (re-cd.Jul88 on 'E.M.I.')*

Apr 78. (7") **I DON'T MIND. / AUTONOMY** 55 -
Jul 78. (7") **LOVE YOU MORE. / NOISE ANNOYS** 34
Sep 78. (7") **EVER FALLEN IN LOVE WITH SOMEONE YOU SHOULDN'T'VE. / JUST LUST** 12
Sep 78. (lp)(c) **LOVE BITES** 13
– Real world / Ever fallen in love with someone you shouldn't've / Operator's manuel / Nostalgia / Just lust / Sixteen again / Walking distance / Love is lies / Nothing left / E.S.P. / Late for the train. *(re-iss.Mar87 on 'Fame') (re-iss.blue-lp.Jun87 on 'Fan Club') (cd.iss.Jul88 on 'E.M.I.')*
Nov 78. (7") **PROMISES. / LIPSTICK** 20
Mar 79. (7") **EVERYBODY'S HAPPY NOWADAYS. / WHY CAN'T I TOUCH IT?** 29
Jul 79. (7") **HARMONY IN MY HEAD. / SOMETHING'S GONE WRONG AGAIN** 32 -
Sep 79. (7") **YOU SAY YOU DON'T LOVE ME. / RAISON D'ETRE** -
Sep 79. (lp)(c) **A DIFFERENT KIND OF TENSION** 26
– Paradise / Sitting round at home / You say you don't love me / You know you can't help it / Mad mad Judy / Raison d'etre / I don't know what to do with my life / Money / Hollow inside / A different kind of tension / I believe / Radio Nine. *(re-iss.blue-lp.Jun87 on 'Fan Club') (cd-iss.Jul88 on 'E.M.I.')* (initial copies cont. previous 45)
Oct 79. (7") **I BELIEVE. / SOMETHING'S GONE WRONG AGAIN** -
Nov 79. (lp)(c) **GOING STEADY – THE SINGLES** (compilation) -
– Orgasm addict / What do I get / I don't mind / Love you more / Ever fallen in love with someone you shouldn't've / Promises / Everybody's happy nowadays / Harmony in my head / Whatever happened to . . . ? / Oh shit! / Autonomy / Noise annoys / Just luck / Lipstick / Why can't I touch it / Something's gone wrong again. *(UK-iss.Nov81 on 'Liberty', re-iss.Aug85) (cd-iss.Jun87 + Jun88 on 'E.M.I.')*

Liberty I.R.S.

Aug 80. (7") **WHY SHE'S A GIRL FROM THE CHAINSTORE. / ARE EVERYTHING** 61
Oct 80. (7") **STRANGE THING. / AIRWAVES DREAM**
Nov 80. (7") **RUNNING FREE. / WHAT DO YOU KNOW**

— (split Feb81) **DIGGLE** went solo and formed FLAG OF CONVENIENCE, with **MAHER**

PETE SHELLEY

solo, augmented by **STEVE GARVEY** – bass / **JIM RUSSELL** – drums.

Genetic-Island Arista

Aug 81. (7")(12") **HOMOSAPIAN. / KEAT'S SONG**
Sep 81. (lp)(c) **HOMOSAPIAN** Jun 72
– Homosapian / Yesterday's here / I generate a feeling / Keat's song / Qu'est-ce que c'est que ca / I don't know what it is / Guess I must have been in love with myself / Pusher man / Just one of those affairs / It's hard enough knowing. *(re-iss.cd Sep94 on 'Grapevine')*
Nov 81. (d7")(12") **I DON'T KNOW WHAT IT IS. / WITNESS THE CHANGE/ / IN LOVE WITH SOMEBODY ELSE. / MAXINE**
Apr 82. (7")(12") **HOMOSAPIAN. / LOVE IN VAIN**

— **BARRY ADAMSON** – bass (ex-MAGAZINE, ex-BIRTHDAY PARTY) repl. GARVEY

added **MARTIN RUSHENT** – keyboards, producer

Island Arista

Feb 83. (7")(12") **TELEPHONE OPERATOR. / MANY A TIME** 66
Apr 83. (lp)(c) **XL-1** 42 Jul 83
– Telephone operator / If you ask me (I won't say no) / What was Heaven? / You better than I know / Twilight / (Millions of people) No one like you / Many a time / I just wanna touch / You and I / XL-1 *. (c+= dub tracks) (track* = only playable on ZX Spectrum computer) *(re-iss.cd Sep94 on 'Grapevine')*.

Im-maculate not issued

Nov 84. (7") **NEVER AGAIN. / ONE ONE ONE** -
(12"+=) Give it to me.

— **SHELLEY** brought in new **JOHN DOYLE** – drums / **MARK SANDERSON** – bass / **NORMAN FISCHER-JONES** – guitar / **GERARD COOKSON** – keyboards / **JIM GARDNER** – synth.

Mercury Mercury?

Mar 86. (7")(12") **WAITING FOR LOVE. / DESIGNER LAMPS**
May 86. (7")(12") **ON YOUR OWN. / PLEASE FORGIVE ME . . . BUT I CANNOT ENDURE IT ANY LONGER**
Jun 86. (lp)(c)(cd) **HEAVEN AND THE SEA**
– Never again / My dreams / Blue eyes / You can't take that away / No Moon . . . / Waiting for love / On your own / They're coming for you / I surrender / Life without reason / Need a minit. *(re-iss.May88 on 'Line')*
Aug 86. (7")(12") **BLUE EYES. / NELSON'S RIDDLE**
Nov 86. (7")(12") **I SURRENDER. / I NEED A MINUTE**

— In 1988, **SHELLEY** formed **ZIP** with COOKSON and SANDERSON.

– his compilations, others, etc. –

Apr 80. Groovy; (12") **SKY YEN** (recorded 1974) [ ] [-]

Im-maculate / not issued

Apr 89. (7")(12") **HOMOSAPIAN. PETE SHELLEY VS. POWER, WONDER AND LOVE / ('A'mix)** [ ] [-]
(3"cd-s+=) – ('A'icon mix) / ('A'shower mix).

STEVE DIGGLE

Liberty / not issued

Feb 81. (7"m) **SHUT OUT THE LIGHTS. / 50 YEARS OF COMPARATIVE WEALTH / HERE COMES THE FIRE BRIGADE** [ ] [-]

FLAG OF CONVENIENCE

was formed by **DIGGLE, MAHER** and **DAVE FARROW** – bass / **D.P.** – keyboards

Sire / not issued

Sep 82. (7") **LIFE ON THE TELEPHONE. / OTHER MAN'S SIN** [ ] [-]

— **DIGGLE, MAHER** plus **GARY HAMER** – bass / **MARK** – keyboards.

Weird Systems / not issued

Dec 84. (7") **CHANGE. / LONGEST LIFE** [ ] [-]

— **JOHN CAINE** – drums repl. MAHER and MARK

M.C.M. / not issued

Apr 86. (7") **NEW HOUSE. / KEEP ON PUSHING** [ ] [-]

Flag of . . . / not issued

Apr 87. (12") **LAST TRAIN TO SAFETY. / ?** [ ] [-]

F.O.C.

M.C.M. / not issued

Oct 87. (12"ep) **SHOULD I EVER GO DEAF / PICTURES IN MY MIND. / THE GREATEST SIN / DROWNED IN YOUR HEARTACHES** [ ] [-]

Aug 88. (12"ep) **EXILES / I CAN'T STOP THE WORLD. / SHOT DOWN WITH YOUR GUN / TRAGEDY IN MARKET SQUARE** [ ] [-]

BUZZCOCKS F.O.C.

DIGGLE, HAMMER plus **ANDY COUZENS** – guitar / **CHRIS GOODWIN** – drums.

Thin Line / not issued

Jul 89. (12")(cd-s) **TOMORROW'S SUNSET. / LIFE WITH THE LIONS / ('A'version)** [ ] [-]

BUZZCOCKS

reformed in 1990 **SHELLEY, DIGGLE, GARVEY** and **MIKE JOYCE** – drums (ex-SMITHS) repl. ANDY and CHRIS who formed The HIGH.

Plan-et Pacific / not issued

Apr 91. (7"ep)(12"ep)(c-ep)(cd-ep) **ALIVE TONIGHT** [ ] [-]
– Alive tonight / Successful street / Serious crime / Last to know.

— **JOHN MAHER** – drums returned to repl. MIKE who joined PIL.

Essential / Rykodisc

Jun 93. (cd)(c)(lp) **TRADE TEST TRANSMISSION** [ ] [ ]
– Innocent / Smile / Palm of your hand / Last to know / Do it/ Who will help me to forget / Energy / Alive tonight / Inside / Isolation / Never gonna give it up / Crystal night / 369 / Chegga / It's unthinkable / Somewhere. (free 7"/12"/cd-s INNOCENT from Apr93)

Aug 93. (12")(cd-s) **DO IT. / TRASH AWAY / ALL OVER YOU** [ ] [ ]

Apr 94. (12")(cd-s) **LIBERTINE ANGEL. / ROLL IT OVER / EXCERPT FROM PRISON RIOT HOSTAGE** [ ] [-]

Dojo / not issued

Nov 95. (cd) **FRENCH (live in Paris 12th April 1995)** [ ] [-]
– I don't mind / Who'll help me to forget / Get on our own / Unthinkable / Strange thing / Energy / Breakdown / Innocent / Roll it over / Why she's a girl from the chainstore / Last to know? / Running free / Libertine angel / Why can't I touch it / Noise annoys / Isolation / Boredom / Do it / Harmony in my head / I believe.

. . . Jan – Jun '96 stop press . . .

Apr 96. (cd)(lp) **ALL SET** [ ] [-]

– compilations, others, etc. –

Apr 87. Weird Systems; (lp)(c) **TOTAL POP** (c+=extra tracks) [ ] [-]

Jan 88. Strange Fruit; (12"ep) **THE PEEL SESSIONS** (7.9.77) [ ] [-]
– Fast cars / What do I get / Moving away from the pulsebeat.

Feb 90. Strange Fruit; (cd)(lp) **THE PEEL SESSIONS** [ ] [-]

Oct 88. R.O.I.R.; (c) **LEST WE FORGET (live)** [-] [ ]
(cd-iss.1990)

Sep 89. Absolutely Free; (lp)(cd) **LIVE AT THE ROXY CLUB, APRIL 1977 (live)** [ ] [-]
(cd= 1 extra track) *(re-iss.Jul90 on 'Receiver')*

Oct 89. E.M.I.; (7"ep) **THE FAB FOUR** [ ] [-]
– Ever fallen in love with someone you shouldn't've / Promises / Everybody's happy nowadays / Harmony in my head.

Nov 89. E.M.I.; (4xlp)(2xd-c)(2xd-cd) **PRODUCT** [ ] [-]
(above cont. first 3 albums + 1 live and rare) *(re-iss.May95)*

Sep 91. E.M.I.; (cd)(c)(d-lp) **OPERATOR'S MANUEL** [ ] [-]

May 92. E.M.I.; (cd) **ENTERTAINING FRIENDS** [ ] [-]

Oct 92. Old Gold; (cd-s) **EVER FALLEN IN LOVE WITH SOMEONE . . . / WHAT DO I GET / PROMISES** [ ] [-]

Feb 94. Anagram; (cd) **THE BEST OF . . . THE SECRET PUBLIC YEARS 1981-1989 ("STEVE DIGGLE & THE FLAG OF CONVENIENCE")** [ ] [-]

Apr 94. E.M.I.; (cd) **ANOTHER MUSIC IN A DIFFERENT KITCHEN / LOVE BITES** [ ] [-]

Jun 94. Strange Fruit; (cd) **THE PEEL SESSIONS ALBUM** [ ] [-]

Jul 95. Dojo; (cd) **TIME'S UP** [ ] [-]

Nov 95. Old Gold; (cd-s) **EVER FALLEN IN LOVE WITH SOMEONE YOU SHOULDN'T HAVE FALLEN IN LOVE WITH / PROMISES** [ ] [-]

STEVE DIGGLE

solo once more.

3:30 / not issued

Nov 93. (cd-ep) **HEATED AND RISING / OVER AND OUT / TERMINAL / WEDNESDAYS FLOWERS** [ ] [-]

Ax-s / not issued

Oct 95. (cd) **HERE'S ONE I MADE EARLIER** [ ] [-]

BYRDS

Formed: Los Angeles, California, USA ... 1964 by McGUINN, CLARK and CROSBY. After one flop single on 'Elektra', they signed to 'CBS/Columbia' where they gained instant success with 'MR.TAMBOURINE MAN', which hit the top on both sides of the Atlantic. For the next 7 years, through many personnel changes, they became one of America's finest, hitting the charts many times. • **Style:** Initially influenced by The BEATLES and DYLAN, but by 1966 they had established own unique electric folk sound that many since have emulated. In 1968 they broke into country-rock territory, with help of new bluegrass method member GRAM PARSONS. • **Songwriters:** All had turns, mostly by 12-string Rickenbacker player McGUINN or CROSBY or HILLMAN. Covered:- MR.TAMBOURINE MAN + ALL I REALLY WANT TO DO + THE TIMES THEY ARE A-CHANGIN' + YOU AIN'T GOIN' NOWHERE + MY BACK PAGES + LAY LADY LAY + IT'S ALL OVER NOW, BABY BLUE + etc. (Bob Dylan) / TURN! TURN! TURN! + THE BELLS OF RHYMNEY (Pete Seeger) / WASN'T BORN TO FOLLOW + GOIN' BACK (Goffin-King a hit by Dusty Springfield) / COWGIRL IN THE SAND (Neil Young) / etc. • **Trivia:** McGUINN changed name to ROGER in 1967 due to his new-found Subud religion.

Recommended: THE BYRDS' GREATEST HITS (*9) / SWEETHEART OF THE RODEO (*8) / GREATEST HITS VOL.2 (*7)

BEEFEATERS

McGUINN, CLARK and CROSBY

Elektra / Elektra

Oct 64. (7") **PLEASE LET ME LOVE YOU. / DON'T BE LONG** [ ] [ ]

The BYRDS

GENE CLARK (b.HAROLD, 17 Nov'41, Missouri, USA) – vocals, tambourine / **JIM McGUINN** (b.13 Jul'42, Chicago, Illinois, USA) – guitar, vocals / **DAVID CROSBY** (b.14 Aug'41) – guitar, vocals / **CHRIS HILLMAN** (b. 4 Dec'42, L.A.) – bass, vocals (ex-HILLMEN) / **MICHAEL CLARKE** (b. 3 Jun'43, New York City) – drums

C.B.S. / Columbia

Jun 65. (7") **MR. TAMBOURINE MAN. / I KNEW I'D WANT TO** [1] [1] May 65

Aug 65. (7") **ALL I REALLY WANT TO DO. / I'LL FEEL A WHOLE LOT BETTER** [4] [40] Jul 75

Aug 65. (lp) **MR. TAMBOURINE MAN** [7] [6] Jun 65
– Mr.Tambourine man / I'll feel a whole lot better / Spanish Harlem incident / You won't have to cry / Here without you / The bells of Rhymney / All I really want to do / I knew I'd want you / It's no use / Don't doubt yourself, babe / Chimes

of freedom / We'll meet again. *(re-iss.'74 on 'CBS Embassy', re-iss.Jul78)*

Oct 65. (7") **TURN! TURN! TURN!. / SHE DON'T CARE ABOUT TIME** [26] [1]

Feb66. (7") **SET YOU FREE THIS TIME. / IT WON'T BE WRONG** [ ] [79]

[63]

Mar 66. (lp) **TURN! TURN! TURN!** [11] [17] Dec 65
– Turn! Turn! Turn! / It won't be wrong / Set you free this time / Lay down your weary tune / He was a friend of mine / The world turns all around her / Satisfied mind / If you're gone / The times they are a-changin' / Wait and see / Oh! Susannah. *(re-iss.'76 on 'CBS Embassy', re-iss.Jul78)*

— trimmed to a quartet when GENE CLARK went solo

Apr 66. (7") **EIGHT MILES HIGH. / WHY?** [24] [14]

Jul 66. (7") **5D (FIFTH DIMENSION). / CAPTAIN SOUL** [ ] [44]

Sep 66. (lp) **FIFTH DIMENSION** [27] [24] Aug 66
– 5D (Fifth Dimension) / Wild mountain thyme / Mr. Spaceman / I see you / What's happening?!?! / I come and stand at every door / Eight miles high / Hey Joe / John Riley / Captain Soul / 2-4-2 Foxtrot (the Lear jet song). *(re-iss.Jul83)*

Oct 66. (7") **MR. SPACEMAN. / WHAT'S HAPPENING?!?!** [ ] [36] Sep66

Feb 67. (7") **SO YOU WANT TO BE A ROCK'N'ROLL STAR. / EVERYBODY'S BEEN BURNED** [ ] [29] Jan 67

Apr 67. (lp) **YOUNGER THAN YESTERDAY** [37] [24] Mar 67
– So you want to be a rock'n'roll star / Have you seen her face / C.T.A. – 102 / Renaissance fair / Time between / Everybody's been burned / Thoughts and words / Mind gardens / My back pages / The girl with no name / Why. *(re-iss.+cd.Mar 87 on 'Edsel') (cd+c-iss.Oct 94 on 'Columbia')*

May 67. (7") **MY BACK PAGES. / RENAISSANCE MAN** [ ] [30] Mar 67

Jun 67. (7") **HAVE YOU SEEN HER FACE. / DON'T MAKE WAVES** [-] [74]

Sep 67. (7") **LADY FRIEND. / DON'T MAKE WAVES** [ ] [82]

— **GENE CLARK** – guitar, vocals returned to repl. DAVID who formed CROSBY, STILLS and NASH (JIM also changed name to ROGER McGUINN)

Dec 67. (7") **GOIN' BACK. / CHANGE IS NOW** [ ] [89] Nov 67
(re-iss.Jun77)
Now a trio of **McGUINN, HILLMAN and CLARKE** (GENE continued solo career)

Apr 68. (lp) **THE NOTORIOUS BYRD BROTHERS** [12] [47] Jan 68
– Artificial energy / Goin' back / Natural harmony / Draft morning / Wasn't born to follow / Get to you / Change is now / Old John Robertson / Tribal gathering / Dolphin's smile / Space odyssey. *(re-iss.Aug88 on 'Edsel' +cd)*

— **KEVIN KELLEY** (b.1945, California) – drums (ex-RISING SONS) repl. MICHAEL who joined DILLARD & CLARK. Also added **GRAM PARSONS** – guitar, vocals, keyboards (ex-INTERNATIONAL SUBMARINE BAND) guests on album – **SNEAKY PETE** – pedal steel guitar / **DOUG DILLARD** – banjo

May 68. (7") **YOU AIN'T GOING NOWHERE. / ARTIFICIAL ENERGY** [45] [74]

Sep 68. (lp) **SWEETHEART OF THE RODEO** [ ] [77] Aug 68
– You ain't going nowhere / I am a pilgrim / The Christian life / You're still on my mind / Pretty Boy Floyd / You don't miss your water / Hickory wind / One hundred years from now / Blue Canadian Rockies / Life in prison / Nothing was delivered. *(re-iss.+cd.Jun87 on 'Edsel')*

Oct 68. (7") **PRETTY BOY FLOYD. / I AM A PILGRIM** [ ] [ ]

— **CARLOS BERNAL** – guitar played on US tour replacing GRAM who joined FLYING BURRITO BROTHERS alongside HILLMAN and SNEAKY PETE. Soon McGUINN recruited entirely new members **CLARENCE WHITE** (b. 6 Jun'44, Lewiston, Maine, USA) – guitar, vocals (ex-NASHVILLE WEST) repl. BERNAL / **GENE PARSONS** (b.1944) – drums, vocals (ex-NASHVILLE WEST) repl. KELLEY / **JOHN YORK** – bass, vocals repl. HILLMAN

Mar 69. (7") **BAD NIGHT AT WHISKEY. / DRUG STORE TRUCK DRIVIN' MAN** [ ] [ ]

Apr 69. (lp) **DR. BYRDS AND MR. HYDE** [15] [ ] Mar 69
– This wheel's on fire / Old blue / Your gentle way of loving me / Child of the universe / Nashville West / Drug store truck drivin' man / King Apathy III / Candy / Bad night at the Whiskey / My back pages – B.J.blues – Baby what you want me to do.

Jun 69. (7") **LAY LADY LAY. / OLD BLUE** [ ] [ ]

Sep 69. (7") **WASN'T BORN TO FOLLOW. / CHILD OF THE UNIVERSE** [-] [ ]

Oct 69. (7") **THE BALLAD OF EASY RIDER. / WASN'T BORN TO FOLLOW** [-] [5]

Jan 70. (lp) **THE BALLAD OF EASY RIDER** [41] [36] Dec 69
– The ballad of Easy Rider / Fido / Oil in my lamp / Tulsa County / Jack Tarr the sailor / Jesus is just alright / It's all over now, baby blue / There must be someone / Gunga Din / Deportee (plane wreck at Los Gatos) / Armstrong, Aldrin and Collins.

Feb 70. (7") **JESUS IS JUST ALRIGHT. / IT'S ALL OVER NOW, BABY BLUE** [ ] [97]

— **SKIP BATTIN** (b. 2 Feb'34, Gallipolis, Ohio) – bass, repl. YORK

Nov 70. (d-lp) **UNTITLED (1/2 live)** [11] [40] Oct 70
– Lover of the bayou / Positively 4th Street / Nashville West / So you want to be a rock'n'roll star / Mr.Tambourine man / Mr.Spaceman / Eight miles high / Chestnut mare / Truck stop girl / All the things / Yesterday's train / Hungry planet / Just a season / Take a whiff (on me) / You all look alike / Well come back home.

Dec 70. (7") **CHESTNUT MARE. / JUST A SEASON** [19] [ ]

May 71. (7") **I TRUST (EVERYTHING'S GONNA WORK OUT FINE). / THIS IS MY DESTINY** [ ] [ ]

Aug 71. (lp) **BIRDMANIAX** [ ] [46] Jul 71
– Glory, glory / Pale blue / I trust / Tunnel of love / Citizen Kane / I wanna grow up to be a politician / Absolute happiness / Green apple quick step / My destiny / Kathleen's song / Jamaica say you will.

Oct 71. (7") **GLORY, GLORY. / CITIZEN KANE** [ ] [ ]

Jan 72. (lp) **FARTHER ALONG** [ ] [ ] Dec 71
– Tiffany queen / Get down your line / B.B. class road / Bugler / America's great national pastime / Antique Sandy / Precious Kate / So fine / Lazy waters / Bristol steam convention blues / Farther along.

Jan 72. (7") **AMERICA'S GREAT NATIONAL PASTIME. / FARTHER ALONG** [ ] [ ]

— They split mid '72, SKIP joined NEW RIDERS OF THE PURPLE SAGE. CLARENCE WHITE was killed in a road accident 14 Jul73. / **JOHN GUERRIN** – drums (session men) took over briefly when reforming

— **McGUINN** then re-formed the original **"BYRDS"** Himself, **CROSBY, CLARK, HILLMAN** and **CLARKE**

Asylum Asylum

Apr 73. (lp)(c) **THE BYRDS** [31] [20] Mar 73
– Full circle / Sweet Mary / Changing heart / For free / Born to rock'n'roll / Things will be better / Cowgirl in the sand / Long live the King / Borrowing time / Laughing / (See the sky) about to rain. *(re-iss.Feb93) (re-iss.May93 on 'Elektra')*

May 73. (7") **THINGS WILL BE BETTER. / FOR FREE** [ ] [-]

Jun 73. (7") **FULL CIRCLE. / LONG LIVE THE KING** [ ] [ ]

Jul 73. (7") **COWGIRL IN THE SAND. / LONG LIVE THE KING** [-] [ ]

— McGUINN, HILLMAN and CLARK all went solo, later teaming up together on album. CROSBY re-formed CROSBY, STILL and NASH. Sadly, MICHAEL CLARKE was to die of liver failure 19th December '93.

– (BYRDS) compilations, etc. –

On 'CBS' / 'Columbia' unless mentioned otherwise.

Dec 65. (7"ep) **THE TIMES ARE A-CHANGING** [ ] [ ]

Oct 66. (7"ep) **EIGHT MILES HIGH** [ ] [ ]

Oct 67. (lp) **THE BYRDS' GREATEST HITS** [ ] [6] Aug 67
– Mr.Tambourine man / I'll feel a whole lot better / Bells of rhymney / Turn! turn! turn! / All I really want to do / Chimes of freedom / Eight miles high / Mr.Spaceman / 5D (Fifth Dimension) / So you want to be a rock'n'roll star / My back pages. *(re-iss.+c Jan84, re-iss.+cd Jun89) (REMASTERED cd.Feb91)*

Oct 71. (lp)(c) **THE BYRDS' GREATEST HITS VOL.2** [ ] [ ]
– The ballad of Easy rider / Jesus is just alright / Chestnut mare / You ain't goin' nowhere / I am a pilgrim / Goin' back / I trust / Lay lady lay / Wasn't born to follow / The times they are a-changin' / Drug store truck drivin' man / Get to you.

May 73. (d-lp)(c) **THE HISTORY OF THE BYRDS** [47] [-]
– Mr.Tambourine man / Turn! turn! turn! / She don't care about time / Wild mountain thyme / Eight miles high / Mr.Spaceman / 5D (Fifth Dimension) / So you want to be a rock'n'roll star / Time between / My back pages / Lady friend / Goin' back / Old John Robertson / Wasn't born to follow / You ain't goin' nowhere / Hickory wind / Nashville West / Drug store truck drivin' man / Gunga Din / Jesus is just alright / The ballad of Easy Rider / Chestnut mare / Yesterday's train / Just a season / Citizen Kane / Jamaica say you will / Tiffany queen / America's great national pastime. *(re-iss.Sep87)*

Jul 73. (7") **MR. TAMBOURINE MAN. / TURN! TURN! TURN!** [ ] [ ]

Feb 76. (7") **CHESTNUT MARE. / ALL I REALLY WANT TO DO** [ ] [ ]

Jul 76. (7") **TURN! TURN! TURN!. / YOU AIN'T GOIN' NOWHERE** [ ] [ ]

Jul 76. (d-lp)(c) **SWEETHEART OF THE RODEO / THE NOTORIOUS BYRD BROTHERS** [ ] [ ]

Feb 80. (lp)(c) **THE BYRDS PLAY DYLAN** [ ] [ ]
(cd+c-iss.Apr94 on 'Sony')

Aug 80. (lp)(c) **THE ORIGINAL SINGLES 1966-1967** [ ] [ ]
(re-iss.Nov81)

Feb 82. (lp)(c) **THE ORIGINAL SINGLES 1968-1969** [ ] [ ]

Jul 82. (7") **CHESTNUT MARE. / WASN'T BORN TO FOLLOW** [ ] [ ]

Jul 84. (7") **MR. TAMBOURINE MAN. / WASN'T BORN TO FOLLOW** [ ] [ ]

1989. (3"cd-ep) **MR. TAMBOURINE MAN / TURN! TURN! TURN!. / ALL I REALLY WANT TO DO / LAY LADY LAY** [31] [ ]

Nov 90. Columbia; (4xcd-box) **THE BYRDS** [ ] [ ]

1990. Columbia; (7"ep) **FOUR DIMENSIONS** [ ] [ ]
– Eight miles high / Mr.Tambourine man / Turn! turn! turn! (to everything there is a season) / I feel a whole lot better

Oct 94. Columbia; (cd) **THE BEST** [ ] [ ]

Mar 93. Columbia; (cd)(c) **20 ESSENTIAL TRACKS** [ ] [ ]

Sep 73. Bumble/ US= Together; (lp) **PREFLYTE (demo recordings of '64)** [ ] [ ] Sep 69

Aug 75. Asylum; (7") **FULL CIRCLE. / THINGS WILL BE BETTER** [ ] [ ]

Sep 83. Scoop; (12"ep) **SIX TRACK HITS** [ ] [ ]
– Lay lady lay / Turn! turn! turn! / Goin' nowhere / So you want to be a rock'n'roll star / Chestnut mare / All I really want to do.

Sep 86. Castle; (d-lp)(c) **THE BYRDS COLLECTION** [ ] [-]
(cd-iss.1987, omits some tracks)

Jan 88. Old Gold; (7") **MR. TAMBOURINE MAN. / TURN! TURN! TURN!** [ ] [-]

May 88. Re-Flyte; (lp) **NEVER BEFORE (Import)** [-] [ ]
(cd-iss.Aug89 on 'Murray Hill')

Feb 91. Raven; (cd) **FULL FLYTE 1965-1970** [ ] [ ]

Dec 92. Edsel; (cd) **RETURN FLYTE (McGUINN, HILLMAN & CLARK)** [ ] [-]

Jul 93. Edsel; (cd) **RETURN 2 FLIGHT (McGUINN, HILLMAN & CLARK)** [ ] [-]

Oct 94. Edsel; (cd-ep) **TURN TURN TURN. / (other artists)** [ ] [ ]

(above from 'Epic' records soundtrack of 'Forrest Gump')

ROGER McGUINN

C.B.S. Columbia

Jun 73. (7") **DRAGGIN'. / TIME CUBE** [-] [ ]

Jun 73. (lp)(c) **ROGER McGUINN** [ ] [ ]
– I'm so restless / My new woman / Lost my drivin' wheel / Draggin' / Time cube / Bag full of money / Hanoi Hannah / Stone / Heave away / M'Linda / The water is wide. *(cd-iss.Feb91) (re-iss.Jul88 on 'Edsel')*

1974. (7") **SAME OLD SOUND. / GATE OF HORN** [-] [ ]

1974. (lp)(c) **PEACE ON YOU** [ ] [92]
– Peace on you / Without you / Going to the country / One more time / Same old sound / Do what you want to / Together / Better change / Gate of horn / Lady.

Sep 74. (7") **PEACE ON YOU. / WITHOUT YOU** [ ] [ ]

1975. (lp)(c) **ROGER McGUINN AND BAND** [ ] [ ]
– Somebody loves you / Knockin' on Heaven's door / Bull Dog / Painted lady / Lover of the bayou / Lisa / Circle song/ So long / Easy does it / Born to rock and roll.

1975. (7") **SOMEBODY LOVES YOU / EASY DOES IT** [-] [ ]

1975. (7") **LOVER OF THE BAYOU. / EASY DOES IT** [-] [ ]

1976. (7") **TAKE ME AWAY. / FRIEND** [-] [ ]

Jun 76. (lp)(c) **CARDIFF ROSE** [ ] [ ]
– Jolly Roger / Take me away / Rock and roll time / Partners in crime / Friend / Up to me / Round table / Prettly Polly / Dream land.

1977. (lp)(c) **THUNDERBYRD** [ ] [ ]
– All night long / It's gone / Dixie highway / American girl / We can do it all over again / Why, baby why / I'm not lonely anymore / Golden loom / Russian Hill.

May 77. (7") **AMERICAN GIRL. / RUSSIAN HILL** [ ] [-]

May 77. (7") **AMERICAN GIRL. / I'M NOT LONELY ANYMORE** [-] [ ]

—— **McGUINN** used session people **STAN LYNCH** – drums / **GEORGE HAWKINS** – bass / **DAVID COLE** – acoustic guitar / **JOHN JORGENSEN** – guitar / **BELMONT TENCH** – keyboards / **MICHAEL THOMPSON** – acoustic guitar

Arista Arista

Feb 91. (cd)(c)(lp) **BACK FROM RIO** [ ] [44] Jan 91
– Someone to love / Car phone / You bowed down / Suddenly blue / The trees are all gone / king of the hill / Without your love / The time has come / Your love is a gold mine / If we never meet again.

Feb 91. (7") **KING OF THE HILL. / YOUR LOVE IS A GOLD MINE** [ ] [ ]
(cd-s+=) – The time has come.

Columbia Columbia

Mar 92. (cd)(c)(lp) **BORN TO ROCK AND ROLL** (his compilation) [ ] [ ]

GENE CLARK

(solo, after he left The BYRDS first time) with The **GODSIN BROTHERS (REX** and **VERN** – both guitars + vocals)

C.B.S. Columbia

Apr 67. (lp) **GENE CLARK & THE GODSIN BROTHERS** [ ] [ ]
– Echoes / Think I'm gonna feel better / Tried so hard / Is yours mine / Keep on pushing / I found you / So you say you lost your baby / Elevator operator * / The same one / Couldn't believe her / Needing someone. *(US remixed & re-iss.1972 as 'EARLY L.A. SESSIONS' extra track *) (re-iss.May88 on 'Edsel') (re-iss.1991 original) (CBS re-issued it as 'ECHOES' in 1991 w/ 6 extra BYRDS tracks)*

1967. (7") **ECHOES. / I FOUND OUT** [-] [-]

1967. (7") **SO YOU SAY YOU LOST YOUR BABY. / IS YOURS MINE** [-] [ ]

—— briefly in Oct67 he rejoined The BYRDS. In Aug68, GENE CLARK and occasional ex-BYRD; **DOUG DILLARD** – banjo formed

DILLARD & CLARK

MICHAEL CLARKE – drums (ed-BYRDS) / **DON BECK** – pedal steel / **BERNIE LEADON** – guitar, vocals / **DAVID JACKSON** – bass (both ex-HEARTS & FLOWERS)

A&M A&M

Oct 68. (lp) **THE FANTASTIC EXPEDITION OF DILLARD & CLARK** [ ] [ ]
– Out on the side / She darkened the sun / Don't come rollin' / Train leaves here this mornin' / With care from somewhere / The radio song / Git it on brother (git in line brother) / In the plan / Something's wrong / Why not your baby / Lyin' down the middle / Don't be cruel.

Nov 68. (7") **OUT ON THE SIDE. / TRAIN LEAVES HERE THIS MORNIN'** [-] [ ]

Feb 69. (7") **LYIN' DOWN THE MIDDLE. / DON'T BE CRUEL** [-] [ ]

May 69. (7") **WHY NOT YOUR BABY. / THE RADIO SONG** [-] [ ]

—— (Jan69) **JON CORNEAL** – drums (ex-FLYING BURRITO BROTHERS) repl. MICHAEL CLARKE who joined FLYING BURITTO BROTHERS / **DONNA WASHBURN** – guitar, vocals repl. BECK

—— (May69) **BYRON BERLINE** – fiddle repl. LEADON to FLYING BURRITO BROTHERS

Sep 69. (lp) **THROUGH THE MORNING, THROUGH THE NIGHT** [ ] [ ]
– No longer a sweetheart of mine / Through the morning, through the night / Rocky top / So sad / Corner street bar / I bowed my head and cried holy / Kansas city southern / Four walls / Polly / Roll in my sweet baby's arms / Don't let me down.

Nov 69. (7") **ROCKY TOP. / DON'T LET ME DOWN** [-] [ ]

—— DOUG DILLARD continued with other solo albums

GENE CLARK

after a rest period continued solo

A&M A&M

1971. (lp) **GENE CLARK (WHITE LIGHT)** [ ] [ ]
– The virgin / With tomorrow / White light / Because of you / One in a hundred / Spanish guitar / Where my love lies asleep / Tears of rage / 1975.

Ariola not issued

Dec 72. (lp) **ROADMASTER** [-] [-] Dutch
– She's the kind of girl / One in a hundred / Here tonight / Full circle song / In a misty morning / Rough and rocky / Roadmaster / I really don't want to know / I remember the railroad / She don't care about time / Shooting star. *(re-iss. 1988 on 'Edsel', cd-iss. Jun 90).*

Asylum Asylum

Oct 74. (lp) **NO OTHER** [ ] [ ]
– Life's greatest fool / Silver raven / No other / Strength of strings / From a silver phial / Some misunderstanding / The true one / Lady of the north. *(re-iss.1988 on 'Edsel')*

Jan 75. (7") **NO OTHER. / THE TRUE ONE** [ ] [ ]

Mar 75. (7") **LIFE'S GREATEST FOOL. / FROM A SILVER PHIAL** [ ] [ ]

Polydor R.S.O.

Mar 77. (lp) **TWO SIDES TO EVERY STORY** [ ] [ ]
– Home run King / Lonely Saturday / In the pines / Kansas city southern / Silent crusade / Give my love to Maria / Sister moon / Mary Lou / Hear the wind / Past address.

1977. (7") **HOME RUN KING. / LONELY SATURDAY** [-] [ ]

Spindrift Takoma

1984. (lp) **FIREBYRD** [ ] [ ]
– Mr. Tambourine man / Something about you / Rain song / Rodeo rider / Vanessa / If you could read my mind / Feel a whole lot better / Made for love / Blue raven. *(cd-iss.1995 as 'THIS BIRD HAS FLOWN' on 'Edsel' +=)* – C'est la Bonne Rue / Dixie flyer / All I want.

—— other solo (import) releases below **CARLA** – vocals of TEXTONES)

Demon Razor&Tie

Apr 87. (lp) **SO REBELLIOUS A LOVER (as "GENE CLARK & CARLA OLSON")** [ ] [ ]
– The drifter / Gypsy rider / Every angel in heaven / Del gato / Deportee / Fair and tender ladies / Almost Saturday night / I'm your toy / Are we still making love / Why did you leave me today / Don't it make you want to go home. *(cd+=)* – Lover's turnaround.

—— GENE CLARK died of natural causes in Feb 1991.

1992. (cd) **SILHOUETTED IN LIGHT (live with CARLA OLSON)** [ ] [ ]
– Your fire burning / Number one is to survive / Love wins again / Fair and tender ladies / Photograph / Set you free this time / Last thing on my mind / Gypsy rider / Train leaves here this morning / Almost Saturday night / Delgato / Feel a whole lot better / She don't care about time / Speed of the sound of loneliness / Will the circle be unbroken.

CHRIS HILLMAN

Asylum Asylum

1977. (lp)(c) **SLIPPIN' AWAY** [ ] [ ]
– Step on out / Slippin' away / Falling again / Take it on the run / Blue morning / Witching hour / Down in the churchyard / Love is the sweetest amnesty / Midnight again / Lifeboat.

Jul 76. (7") **STEP ON OUT. / TAKE IT ON THE RUN** [ ] [ ]

May 77. (7") **SLIPPIN' AWAY. / YOUR LIFEBOAT** [ ] [ ]

1977. (lp)(c) **CLEAR SAILIN'** [ ] [ ]
– Nothing gets through / Fallen favourite / Quits / Hot dusty roads / Heartbreaker / Playin' the fool / Lucky in love / Rollin' and tumblin' / Ain't that peculiar / Clear sailin'.

McGUINN, CLARK & HILLMAN

(nearly a BYRDS reformation)

		Capitol	Capitol	
1979.	(7") **SURRENDER TO ME. / BYE BYE BABY**		-	
Feb 79.	(lp)(c) **McGUINN, CLARK & HILLMAN**		39	

– Long long time / Little mama / Don't you write her off / Sad boy / Surrender to me / Backstage pass / Stopping traffic / Feeling higher / Release me girl / Bye bye baby.

Apr 79.	(7") **DON'T YOU WRITE HER OFF. / SAD BOY** *(re-iss.Apr86)*		33	Mar 79
Jun 79.	(7") **SURRENDER TO ME. / LITTLE MAMA**	-		
Sep 79.	(7") **BYE BYE BABY. / BACKSTAGE PASS**	-		
Jan 80.	(lp)(c) **CITY ("CHRIS HILLMAN / ROGER McGUINN")**			

– Who taught the night / One more chance / Won't let you down / Street talk / City / Skate date / Givin' herself away / Let me down easy / Deeper in / Painter fire.

Feb 80.	(7") **STREET TALK. / ONE MORE CHANCE**	-	
Apr 80.	(7") **CITY. / DEEPER**	-	
Mar 81.	(lp)(c) **McGUINN / HILLMAN – MEAN STREETS (as "McGUINN & HILLMAN")**		

– Mean streets / Entertainment / Soul shoes / Between you and me / Angel / Ain't no money / Love me tonight / King for a night / A secret side of you / Turn your radio on. *(cd-iss.Feb91)*

Mar 81.	(7") **TURN YOUR RADIO ON. / MAKING MOVIES**	-	
May 81.	(7") **LOVE ME TONIGHT. / KING FOR A NIGHT**	-	

McGUINN-HILLMAN

		not issued	Universal
1983.	(7") **YOU AIN'T GOIN' NOWHERE. / DON'T YOU HEAR JERUSALEM MOAN**	-	

CHRIS HILLMAN

(solo again)

		not issued	Sugarhill
1982.	(lp) **MORNING SKY**	-	

– Tomorrow is a long time / The taker / Here today and gone tomorrow / Morning sky / Ripple / Good time Charlie / Don't let your sweet love die / Mexico / It's happening to you / Hickory wind. *(UK-iss.Nov87 on 'Sundown', re-iss.Mar89)*

		A&M	Spindrift
Nov 84.	(lp) **DESERT ROSE**		

– Why you been gone so long / Somebody's back in town / Walk around your heart / Rough and rowdy ways / Desert rose / Running the roadblocks / I can't keep you in love with me / Treasure of love / Ashes of love / Turn your radio on. *(UK-iss.Nov87 on 'Sundown') (re-iss.Mar89)*

EVER READY CALL

CHRIS HILLMAN / BERNIE LEADON / AL PERKINS / DAVID MANSFIELD + JERRY SCHEFF

		not issued	A&M
1985.	(lp) **EVER READY CALL**	-	

– River of Jordan / I'll be no stranger there / Don't let them take the bible out of our schoolroom / God loves his children / It's beginning to rain / Living in the name of love / Boat of love / Men are so busy / I'm using my bible for a roadmap / Panhandle rag.

DESERT ROSE BAND

HILLMAN with **HERB PEDERSON** – guitar, banjo, vocals (also on early-mid 80's lp's) / **J.D. MANESS** – pedal steel guitar (also on '84 lp) / **JOHN JORGENSON** -lead guitar, vocals / **BILL BRYSON** – bass / **STEVE DUNCAN** – drums

		Curb-MCA	Curb-MCA
Jan 87.	(lp)(c)(US-cd) **DESERT ROSE BAND**		

– One step forward / Love reunited / He's back and I'm blue / Leave this town / Time between / Ashes of love / One that got away / Once more / Glass hearts / Hard times.

Feb 87.	(7") **ASHES OF LOVE. / LEAVE THIS TOWN**	-	
Jun 87.	(7") **LOVE REUNITED. / HARD TIMES**	-	
Oct 87.	(7") **ONE STEP FORWARD. / GLASS HEARTS**	-	
Feb 88.	(7") **HE'S BACK AND I'M BLUE. / ONE THAT GOT AWAY**	-	
Jun 88.	(lp)(c)(cd) **RUNNING**		

– She don't love nobody / Running / Hello trouble / I still believe in you / Summer wind / For the rich man / Step on out / Homeless / Livin' in the house / Our songs.

Jul 88.	(7") **SUMMER WIND. / OUR SONGS**	-	
Oct 88.	(7") **I STILL BELIEVE IN YOU. / LIVIN' IN THE HOUSE**	-	
Mar 89.	(7") **SHE DON'T LOVE NOBODY. / STEP ON OUT**	-	
May 89.	(7") **HELLO TROUBLE. / HOMELESS**	-	
Oct 89.	(7") **START ALL OVER AGAIN. / FOOLED AGAIN**	-	
Jan 90.	(cd)(c) **PAGES OF LIFE**		

– Story of love / Start all over again / Missing you / Just a memory / God's plane / Darkness in the playground / Our baby's gone / Time passes me by / Everybody's hero / In another lifetime / Desert rose.

Feb 90.	(7") **IN ANOTHER LIFETIME. /**	-	
Jun 90.	(7") **STORY OF LOVE. /**	-	
Jan 91.	(7") **WILL THIS BE THE DAY. /**	-	
Mar 91.	(cd)(c)(lp) **ONE DOZEN ROSES: GREATEST HITS** (compilation) *(re-iss.1994 as '16 ROSES' with extra tracks)*		

— also; **TOM BRUMLEY** – steel / **JEFF ROSS** – guitar / **TIM GROGAN** – drums repl.J.D., JORGENSON + DUNCAN

1992.	(cd) **TRUE LOVE**	-	

– You can go home / It takes a believer / Twilight is gone / No-one else / A matter of time / Undying love (Alison Kravis duet) / Behind these walls / True love / Glory and power / Shades of blue.

1993.	(cd) **LIFE GOES ON**	-	

– What about love / Night after night / Walk on by / Love refugees / Life goes on / That's not the way / Till it's over / Hold on / A little rain / Throw me a lifeline.

— Disbanded in 1993.

– other CHRIS HILLMAN recordings –

SCOTTSVILLE SQUIRREL BARKERS:- **HILLMAN / KENNY WERTZ / LARRY MURRAY**

1962.	Crown; (lp) **BEST OF BLUEGRASS FAVOURITES (as "SCOTTSVILLE SQUIRREL BARKERS")** *(re-iss.Dutch 1974 as 'THE KENTUCKY MOUNTAIN BOYS' on 'Ariola')*	-	

HILLMEN:- **HILLMAN / VERN + REX GROSDIN + DON PARSLEY**

1969.	Together; (lp) **THE HILLMEN (as "The HILLMEN")** *(re-iss.1988 on 'Sugarhill', cd-iss.Nov95)*	-	

David BYRNE (see under ⇒ TALKING HEADS)

David BYRON (see under ⇒ URIAH HEEP)

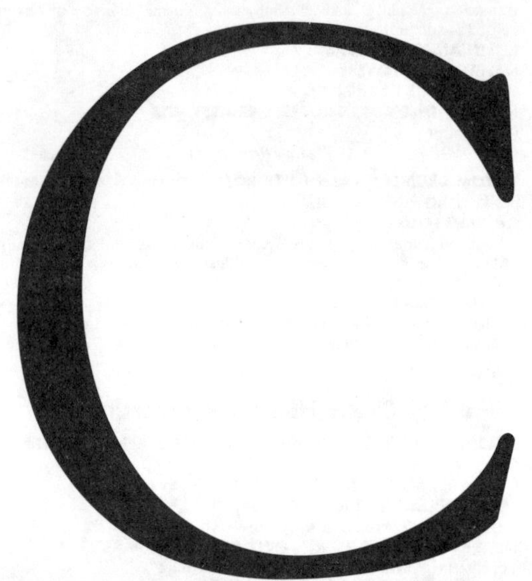

Randy CALIFORNIA (see under ⇒ SPIRIT)

Robert CALVERT (see under ⇒ HAWKWIND)

CAN

Formed: Cologne, Germany ... 1968 by CZUKAY, SCHMIDT and KAROLI. Signed to 'United Art' in 1970 and released debut lp 'MONSTER MOVIE', before unleashing the improvised beauty 'TAGO MAGO' (1971). Continued to be part of continental scene, and signed to Richard Branson's 'Virgin', where they had surprise UK Top 30 hit 45 with 'I WANT MORE' (1976). • **Style:** Avant-garde free-form experimental rock, that was influenced by JOHN CAGE, TERRY RILEY and The VELVET UNDERGROUND. The latter more so, in which hypnotic basic rhythms were interspersed with dour but effective vox. By 1977 they shifted into African /reggae style with introduction of ROSKO. • **Songwriters:** Group compositions, except I WANT MORE (David Gilmour) / CAN-CAN (Offenbach). • **Trivia:** The FALL payed homage to them by crediting a song as 'I AM DAMO SUZUKI'.

Recommended: CANNIBALISM (*8) / TAGO MAGO (*7)

IRMIN SCHMIDT – keyboards / **HOLGER CZUKAY** – bass, electronics / **DAVID JOHNSON** – flute / **MICHAEL KAROLI** (b.28 Apr'48) – guitar, violin / **JAKI LIEBZEIT** – drums / **MALCOLM MOONEY** – vocals

not issued / Music Factory G'MANY

Nov 68. (7") **KAMA SUTRA. /** [-] [-]

— Now a quintet when JOHNSON departed

Aug 69. (lp-500 copies) **DELAY 1968** [-] [-]
– Butterfly / Pnoom / 19th century man / Thief / Man named Joe / Uphill / Little star of Bethlehem. *(re-iss'81 on 'Spoon' GERMANY)(cd-iss.Jun89 on 'Spoon/Mute')*

United Art / United Art G'MANY

May 70. (lp) **MONSTER MOVIE** [ ] [-]
– Father cannot yell / Mary, Mary so contrary / You doo right / Outside my door. *(cd-iss.Jun89 on 'Mute')*

— **KENJI 'DAMO' SUZUKI** – vocals repl.MOONEY who suffered nervous breakdown

not issued / Liberty

Sep 70. (lp) **SOUNDTRACKS** [-] [-] Germ'y
– Deadlock / Tango whiskeyman / Don't turn the light off / Leave me alone / Soul desert / Mother sky / She brings the rain. *(UK-rel.Jun73 on 'United Artists') (cd-iss.Jun89 on 'Mute')*

1970. (7") **SOUL DESERT. / SHE BRINGS THE RAIN** [-] [-]

Feb 71. (d-lp) **TAGO MAGO** [ ] [-] Feb 72
– Paperhouse / Mushroom / Oh yeah / Halleluwah / Aumgh / Peking O / Bring me coffee or tea. *(cd-iss.Jul89 on 'Mute')*

1971. (7") **TURTLES HAVE SHORT LEGS. / HALLELUWAH (edit)** [-] [-]

1971. (7") **SPOON. / SHIKAKO MARU TEN** [-] [-]
(from now just UK releases are mentioned to avoid confusion!?)

United Art / United Art

Nov 72. (7") **SPOON. / I'M SO GREEN** [ ] [ ]

Nov 72. (lp) **EGE BAMYASI** [ ] [ ]
– Pinch / Sing swan song / One more night / Vitamin C / Soup / I'm so green / Spoon. *(cd-iss.Jun89 on 'Mute')*

Jun 73. (lp) **FUTURE DAYS** [ ] [ ]
– Future days / Spray / Moonshake / Bel Air. *(cd-iss.Jun89 on 'Mute')*

Oct 73. (7") **MOONSHAKE. / FUTURE DAYS (edit)** [ ] [ ]

— Trimmed to a quartet when DAMO SUZUKI left to become Jehovah's witness. Now **SCHMIDT / KAROLI** (shared vocals) **CZUKAY** and **LIEBEZEIT**

Nov 74. (lp) **SOON OVER BABALUMA** [ ] [ ]
– Dizzy dizzy / Come sta la luna / Splash / Chain reaction / Quantum physics / Soon over Babaluma. *(cd-iss.Jun89 on 'Mute')*

Dec 74. (7") **DIZZY DIZZY (edit). / SPLASH (edit)** [ ] [-]

Virgin / Polydor

Sep 75. (lp) **LANDED** [ ] [ ]
– Full moon on the highway / Half past one / Hunters and collectors / Vernal equinox / Red hot Indians / Unfinished. *(cd-iss.Jun87)*

— approx Mar76, tried two vocalists one a Malayan, the other **MICHAEL COUSINS** (English). added **DAVID GILMOUR** – guest/composer (3) b.vocals of PINK FLOYD

Jul 76. (7") **I WANT MORE. / ... AND MORE** [26] [ ]
(re-iss.May81)

Oct 76. (lp) **FLOW MOTION** [ ] [ ]
– I want more / Cascade waltz / Laugh till you cry . . . live till you die / . . .And more / Babylonian pearl / Smoke (E.F.S. No.59) / Flow motion. *(cd-iss.Jun87)*

Nov 76. (7") **SILENT NIGHT. / CASCADE WALTZ** [ ] [ ]

— added **ROSKO GEE** – bass (ex-TRAFFIC) (HOLGER now synths., samplers)

Mar 77. (lp) **SAW DELIGHT** [ ] [ ]
– Don't say no / Sunshine day and night / Call me / Animal waves / Fly by night. *(cd-iss.Jun87)*

Apr 77. (7") **DON'T SAY NO. / RETURN** [ ] [ ]

— HOLGER went on a few holidays. The rest of the band below (**SCHMIDT, KAROLI, LIEBEZEIT & GEE**) recorded album. CZUKAY went solo

Lightning / not issued

Jun 78. (7") **CAN-CAN. / CAN BE** [ ] [ ]

Jul 78. (lp) **OUT OF REACH** [ ] [ ]
– Serpentine / Pauper's daughter and I / November / Seven days awake / Give me no roses / Like Inobe God / One more day. *(re-iss.Jun86 on 'Thunderbolt')*

— The split late '78. JAKI formed PHANTOM BAND and collaborated with HOLGER. IRMIN went solo and formed BRUNO SPOERRI. MICHAEL in '84 went solo. All their releases were mainly German only. **CAN** reformed 1969 line-up 20 years on.

Mercury / not issued?

Oct 89. (lp)(c)(cd) **RITE TIME** [ ] [-]
-On the beautiful side of a romance / The without law man / Below this level (patient's song) / Movin' right along / Like a new world / Hoolah hoolah / Give the drummer some. *(cd-iss.Oct94 on 'Spoon')*

White Label / not issued

Sep 90. (cd)(c)(lp) **FISHERMAN'S FRIEND REMIXES** [ ] [-]

– compilations etc. –

Aug 74. United Artists; (lp) **LIMITED EDITION** (ltd 15,000) [ ] [-]

Oct 78. United Artists; (lp) **CANNIBALISM** [ ] [-]
– Uphill / Pnoom / Connection / Mother Upduff / Little star / T.V. spot / Doko E. / Turtles have short legs / Shikaku maru ten / Gomorrha / Blue bag / Red hot Indians / Half past one / Flow motion / Smoke / I want more . . .and more / Laugh till you cry / Aspectacle animal waves / Sunshine day and night / E.P.S. No.7 / Melting away. *(cd-iss.Nov92 on Grey Area-Mute)*

May 76. Caroline; (d-lp) **UNLIMITED EDITION (early rare)** [ ] [ ]
(cd-iss.Nov91 on 'Spoon')

Nov 76. Sunset; (lp) **OPENER (71-74 material)** [ ] [-]

Jul 79. Laser; (lp) **CAN** [ ] [ ]
(re-iss.Feb85 as 'INNER SPACE' on 'Thunderbolt', cd-iss.Jun87)

May 81. Virgin/ US= Polydor; (12") **I WANT MORE. / SILENT NIGHT / ... AND MORE** [ ] [ ]

Oct 81. Virgin/ US= Polydor; (lp) **INCANDESCENCE** [ ] [ ]

Mar 83. Cherry Red; (12"ep) **MOONSHAKE. / TURTLES HAVE SHORT LEGS / ONE MORE NIGHT** [ ] [-]

Feb 95. Spoon; (cd) **CANNIBALISM III** [ ] [-]

Sep 95. Strange Fruit; (cd) **LIVE AT THE BBC** [ ] [-]

Oct 95. Strange Fruit; (cd) **THE PEEL SESSIONS** [ ] [-]

HOLGER CZUKAY

Music Factory | not issued

1968. (lp) **CANAXIS 5 ("HOLGER CZUKAY with ROLF DAMMERS")** - - Germ'y

– Boat woman song / Canaxis. *(cd-iss.Feb95 on 'Spoon')*

CZUKAY with other CAN members augenting

E.M.I. | not issued

Nov 79. (7") **COOL IN THE POOL. / OH LORD GIVE US MORE MONEY** *(re-iss.Jul83)* -

Jan 80. (lp)(c) **MOVIES** -

– Cool in the pool / Oh Lord give us some money / Persian love / Hollywood symphony.

Feb 82. (lp)(c) **ON THE WAY TO THE PEAK OF NORMAL** -

– Ode to perfume / On the way to the peak of normal / Witches multiplication table / Two bass shuffle / Hiss'n'listen.

Mar 82. (7") **ODE TO PERFUME. / PERSIAN LOVE**

— next 2 as **HOLGER CZUKAY, JAKI LIEBEZEIT & JAH WOBBLE**

Virgin | not issued

1982. (lp)(c) **FULL CIRCLE** - - Germ.

Island | not issued

Jun 81. (12"ep) **HOW MUCH ARE THEY? / WHERE'S THE MONEY?. / TRENCH WARFARE / TWILIGHT WORLD** -

(re-iss.1988 on 'Licensed')

Oct 82. (m-lp)(c) **SNAKE CHARMER (as "HOLGER CZUKAY, JAH WOBBLE & THE EDGE")**

– Snake charmer / Hold on to your dreams / It was a camel / Sleazy / Snake charmer (reprise).

Virgin | not issued

May 84. (lp)(c) **DER OSTEN IST ROT** -

– The photo song / Bankel rap '82 / Michy / Rhonrad / Collage / Esperanto socialiste / Der osten ist rot / Das massenmedium / Schave vertraucnsvdl in die zukunft / Traun mal wieder. *(re-iss.Apr86)*

May 84. (7") **THE PHOTO SONG. / DAS MASSENMEDIUM** -

(12"+=) – Biomutanten.

Jan 87. (lp)(c)(cd) **ROME REMAINS ROME** -

– Hey ba ba re bob / Blessed Easter / Sudentenland / Hit hit flop flop / Perfect world / Music in the air. (cd+=) – DER OSTEN IST ROT (lp)

collaborated next Mar88 on album PLIGHT AND PREMONITION with DAVID SYLVIAN (see: JAPAN ⇒).

— Next with **SHELDON ANGEL** – vocals / **M.KAROLI** – guitar / **J.LIEBEZEIT** – drums

Jan 91. (cd)(c)(lp) **RADIO WAVE SURFER** -

– Rhine, water / It ain't no crime / I got weird dreams / Saturday night movie / Dr.Oblivion / We can fight all night / Get it sweet / Ride a radio wave / Atmosphere tuning / Voice of Bulgaria / Late night radio / Through the freezing snow / Encore.

HOLGER CZUKAY also released in Germany 1980 with CONRAD PLANK & AXEL GROS, a 12"m LES VAMPYRETTES on 'Electrola' label.

JAKI LIEBEZEIT

with his group (who released on German labels)

PHANTOM BAND with others **DOMINIK VON SENGER** – guitar / **HELMUT ZERLETT** – keys / **ELEK GELBA** – percussion

Sky | not issued

1980. (lp) **PHANTOM BAND** - -

1981. (lp) **FREEDOM OF SPEECH** - -

Spoon | not issued

1984. (lp) **NOWHERE** - -

— In 1981 he and CZUKAY teamed up with PHEW on lp PHEW. ('Pass' label)

IRMIN SCHMIDT

(solo) on German labels

Spoon | not issued

1980. (lp) **FILM MUSIK** - -

1981. (lp) **TOY PLANET ("with BRUNO SPOERRI")** - -

1981. (lp) **FILM MUSIK VOL.2** - -

Jun 84. (d-lp) **FILM MUSIK VOLS. 3 & 4** - -

— In 1983 he issued other German album 'ROTE ERDE' on 'Teldec'.

W.E.A. | not issued

1987. (lp)(c) **MUSIC AT DUSK** -

– Left into silence / Love / Roll on, Euphrates / The great escape / Villa wunderbar / The child in history / Alcohol.

Venture | not issued

Apr 90 (cd)(c)(lp)**TOY PLANET** -

– The seven game / Toy Planet / Two dolphins go dancing / Yom tov / Spring lite rite / Rapido de noir / When the workers came to life.

Mute | not iss.

Nov 92. (cd) **IMPOSSIBLE HOLIDAYS**

– Dreamtime / Le weekend / Surprise / Shudder of love / Lullaby big / Time the dreamkiller / German ghast drift.

— Virgin issued 'FILM MUSIK VOL.5' in 1989.

MICHAEL KAROLI with **POLLY ESTES** also released DELUGE (lp) in 1984 on 'Spoon'

— **DAMO SUZUKI** with band DUNKEIZIFFER, released in 1984 (lp) **IN THE NIGHT**

CANADIAN SQUIRES (see under ⇒ BAND)

CANDLEBOX

Formed: Beverly Hills, California, USA . . . 1992 by (see below). Their eponymous debut album released on MADONNA's 'Maverick' label in mid-93, made a steady rise to the US Top 10 a year later. • **Style:** Grunge /hard rock. • **Songwriters:** MARTIN lyrics / group compositions except VOODOO CHILE (Jimi Hendrix). • **Trivia:** For Info write to; CANDLEBOX, 11012 Ventura Bl., Suite 299, Studio City, CA 91604.

Recommended: CANDLEBOX (*6)

KEVIN MARTIN – vocals / **PETER KLETT** – guitar / **BARDI MARTIN** – bass / **SCOTT MERCADO** – drums

Maverick-Sire | Maverick-Sire

Jul 93. (cd)(c) **CANDLEBOX** 7

– Don't you / Change / You / No sense / Far behind / Blossom / Arrow / Rain / Mothers dream / Cover me / He calls home.

Mar 94. (c-s)(cd-s) **YOU. /** - 78

Aug 94. (7")(c-s) **FAR BEHIND. / YOU (live)** 18

(cd-s+=) – Live medley: Far behind – Voodoo chile (slight return).

Sep 95. (cd)(c) **LUCY** 11

– Simple lessons / Drowned / Lucy / Best friend / Become (to tell) / Understanding / Crooked halo / Bothered / Butterfly / It's amazing / Vulgar before me / Butterfly (reprise).

CANNED HEAT

Formed: Los Angeles, USA . . . 1966 by HITE and WILSON. Appeared at 1967 Monterey Festival, which led them to sign for 'Liberty'. During the late 60's and early 70's, they clocked-up a few classic hit singles including 'ON THE ROAD AGAIN', 'GOING UP THE COUNTRY' and 'LET'S WORK TOGETHER'. • **Style:** Hard – rock boogie that evolved from jug-band music, and which featured HITE the very large bearded dual singer. His and WILSON's death put paid to any real kind of group reincarnation (see below). Inspired in almost every way by black bluesman JOHN LEE HOOKER. • **Songwriters:** HITE and WILSON, except LET'S WORK TOGETHER (Wilbert Harrison) / ROLLIN' AND TUMBLIN' (Muddy Waters) / WOOLY BULLY (Sam The Sham & The Pharoahs) / SUGAR BEE (Cleveland Crotchet) / BULLDOZE BLUES (Henry Thomas). • **Trivia:** 'Blind Owl' WILSON was so-called due to his bespectacled eyes.

Recommended: CANNED HEAT COOKBOOK (*9).

BOB 'THE BEAR' HITE (b.26 Feb'45, Torrance, California) – vocals, harmonica / **AL 'BLIND OWL' WILSON** (b. 4 Jul'43, Boston, Mass) – vocals, guitar, harmon.. / **HENRY VESTINE** (b.25 Dec'44, Washington DC) – guitar (ex-MOTHERS OF../**ZAPPA) / LARRY TAYLOR**(b.SAMUEL TAYLOR, 26 Jun'42, Brooklyn, New York) – bass repl. MARK ANDES who had repl. STUART BROTMAN (to KALEIDOSCOPE) / **FRANK COOK** – drums

Liberty | Liberty

Aug 67. (lp) **CANNED HEAT** 76

– Rollin' and tumblin' / Bullfrog blues / Evil is going on / Goin' down slow / Catfish blues / Dust my broom / Help me / Big road blues / The story of my life / The road song / Rich woman. *(re-iss.Feb73 as 'ROLLIN' & TUMBLIN'' on 'Sunset') (re-iss.Jun89 on 'See for Miles' cd-iss.Aug90)*

1968. (7") **ROLLIN' AND TUMBLIN'. / BULLFROG BLUES**

— **FITO 'ADOLPHO' DE LA PARRA** (b. 3 Feb'46, Mexico) – drums (ex-BLUESBERRY JAM) repl. COOK

Mar 68. (7") **EVIL WOMAN. / THE WORLD IS A JUDGE** -

May 68. (7") **ON THE ROAD AGAIN. / BOOGIE MUSIC** - 16

May 68. (7") **ON THE ROAD AGAIN. / THE WORLD IN A JUG** 8 -

(re-iss.Sep75 on 'United Art')

Jun 68. (lp) **BOOGIE WITH CANNED HEAT** 5 16 Feb 68

– Evil woman / My crime / On the road again / World in a jug / Turpentine moan / Whiskey headed woman No.2 / Amphetamine Annie / An owl song / Marie Laveau / Fried hockey boogie. *(re-iss.Feb86 on 'See for Miles', cd-iss.Feb90)*

Dec 68. (7") **GOING UP THE COUNTRY. / ONE KIND FAVOUR** 19 11

Dec 68. (d-lp) **LIVING THE BLUES** 18

– Pony blues / My mistake / Sandy's blues / Going up the country / Walking by myself / Boogie music / One kind favour / Parthenogenesis:- Nebulosity – Rollin' and tumblin' – Five owls – Bear wires – Snooky flowers – Sunflower power – Ragi Kafi – Icebag – Childhood's / Refried the boogie (part 1 -live) / Refried the boogie (part 2 -live). *(re-iss.Jul87 on 'See for Miles' cd-iss.Feb90)*

Apr 69. (7") **TIME WAS. / LOW DOWN** [ ] [67] Mar 69

— **HARVEY MANDEL** (b.1946, Detroit, Michegan) – guitar (+ solo artist) repl. VESTINE

Aug 69. (lp) **HALLELUJAH** [ ] [37]
– Same all over / Change my ways / Canned Heat / Sic 'em pigs / I'm her man / Time was / Do not enter / Big fat / Huautla / Get off my back / Down in the gutter, but free. *(re-iss.Feb89 on 'See for Miles', cd-iss.Aug90)*

Sep 69. (7") **POOR MAN. / SIC 'EM PIGS** [ ] [ ]
Dec 69. (7") **CHANGE MY WAYS. / GET OFF MY BACK** [-] [ ]
Jan 70. (lp) **CANNED HEAT COOKBOOK** (compilation) [8] [86]
– Bullfrog blues / Rollin' and tumblin' / Going up the country / Time was / Boogie music / On the road again / Same all over / Sic 'em pigs / Fried hockey boogie / I will wait for you. *(re-iss.Nov75 on 'Sunset')*

Jan 70. (7") **LET'S WORK TOGETHER. / I'M HER MAN** [2] [26] Oct 70
Jun 70. (7") **SUGAR BEE. / SHAKE IT AND BREAK IT** [49] [-]
Jun 70. (lp) **CANNED HEAT '70 CONCERT (live in Europe)** [15] [ ] Jul71
– That's all right mama / Bring it on home / Pulling hair blues / Back out on the road – On the road again / London blues / Let's work together / Goodbye for now. *(re-iss.1988)*

— **ANTONIO DE LA BARREDA** (aka TONY OLAV) – bass repl. LARRY TAYLOR

Sep 70. (7") **FUTURE BLUES. / SKAT** [ ] [-]
Sep 70. (lp)(c) **FUTURE BLUES** [27] [59]
– Sugar bee / Shake it and break it / That's all right mama / My time ain't long / Scat / Let's work together / London blues / So sad (the world's in a tangle) / Future blues. *(re-iss.+cd Jul89 on 'B.G.O.')*

— On 3rd Sep70, **AL WILSON** suffering depression died of drug o/d. He appeared on the releases below until stated.

Dec 70. (7") **CHRISTMAS BLUES. / DO NOT ENTER** [ ] [-]
Jan 71. (7") **WOOLY BULLY. / MY TIME AIN'T LONG** [ ] [ ]

— **HENRY VESTINE** – guitar returned to repl. MANDEL who returned to JOHN MAYALL.

Mar 71. (d-lp)(d-c) **HOOKER'N'HEAT ("CANNED HEAT / JOHN LEE HOOKER")** [ ] [73] Feb 71
– Messin' with the Hook / The feelin' is gone / Send me your pillow / Sittin' here thinkin' / Meet me in the bottom / Altmonia blues / Drifter / You talk too much / Burning Hell / Bottle up and go / The world today / I got my eyes on you / Whiskey and wimmen' / Just you and me / Let's make it / Peavine / Boogie chillen No.2. *(re-iss.Sep88 as lp 'THE BEST OF HOOKER'N'HEAT' on 'See for Miles') (also cd-iss.Aug89 as 'HOOKER'N'HEAT (THE BEST OF PLUS)')*

— **HOOKER** – blues guitarist

— **JOEL SCOTT HILL** – guitar, vocals finally repl. AL WILSON, now alongside **HITE, BARREDA, PARRA and VESTINE**

United Art | United Art

Mar 71. (7") **LET'S MAKE IT (w/JOHN LEE HOOKER). / WHISKEY AND WIMMEN** [-] [ ]
Sep 71. (7") **LONG WAY FROM L.A.. / HILL'S STOMP** [ ] [ ]

— **LITTLE RICHARD** – piano, vocals guested on next album

Mar 72. (lp)(c) **HISTORICAL FIGURES AND ANCIENT HEADS** [ ] [87]
– Sneakin' around / Hill's stomp / Rockin' with the king / I don't care what you tell me / Long way from L.A. / Cherokee dance / That's all right / Utah. *(re-iss.+cd.Aug90 on 'B.G.O.')*

Apr 72. (7") **ROCKIN' WITH THE KING. / I DON'T CARE WHAT YOU TELL ME** [ ] [88] Mar 72
Jul 72. (7") **CHEROKEE DANCE. / SNEAKIN' AROUND** [-] [ ]

— **RICHARD HITE** – bass (BOB's brother) (ex-POPPA HOP) repl. BARREDA. Added **JAMES SHANE** – guitar / **ED BEYER** – keyboards

Jun 73. (7") **KEEP IT CLEAN. / YOU CAN RUN, BUT YOU SURE CAN'T HIDE** [ ] [ ]
Sep 73. (lp)(c) **NEW AGE** [ ] [ ]
– Keep it clean / Harley Davidson blues / Don't deceive me / You can run, but you sure can't hide / Rock and roll music / Lookin' for my rainbow / Framed / Election blues / So long wrong *(cd-iss.May91 on 'B.G.O.')*

Sep 73. (7") **LOOKIN' FOR MY RAINBOW. / ROCK AND ROLL MUSIC** [-] [ ]
Nov 73. (7") **HARLEY DAVIDSON BLUES. /** [-] [ ]

Atlantic | Atlantic

Feb 74. (7") **ONE MORE RIVER TO CROSS. / HIGHWAY 401** [ ] [ ]
Mar 74. (lp) **ONE MORE RIVER TO CROSS** [ ] [ ]
– L.A. town / I need someone / Bagful of boogie / I'm a hog for you baby / You am what I am / Shake rattle & roll / Bright times are comin' / Highway 401 / We remember Fats.

1975. (7") **THE HARDER THEY COME. / ROCK 'N' ROLL SHOW** [-] [ ]

— **RICHARD HITE**and **FITO DE LA PARRA** took over control of band when BOB & HENRY got stoned. ED BAYER also departed. Recruited **CHRIS MORGAN** – guitar / **GENE TAYLOR** – keyboards (both ex-POPPA HOP)

Sonet | Takoma

Dec 78. (lp) **THE HUMAN CONDITION** [ ] [ ]
– Strut my stuff / Hot money / House of blue lights / Just got to be there / You just got the rock / Human condition / She's lookin' good / Open up your backdoor / Wrapped up.

— (later in 70's) **BOB HITE** returned (he was to die of heart attack 4th Apr81)

— re-united + re-formed with **FITO, VESTINE,** and **TAYLOR** and others, **RAUL E. RODRIGUEZ + F.M. HALEY.**

not issued | Destiny

1981. (lp) **KINGS OF THE BOOGIE** [-] [ ]
– Kings of the boogie / Stoned bad street fighting man / So fine / You just can't get close to me / Hell's just on down the road / I was wrong / Little crystal / Dog house blues / Sleepy hollow baby / Chicken shack.

not issued | A.L.A.

1984. (12"ep) **THE HEAT BROS '84** [-] [ ]

— **JAMES THORNBERRY** – guitar repl. VESTINE.

Bedrock | ?

Dec 87. (lp-blue) **THE BOOGIE ASSAULT (LIVE IN AUSTRALIA)** [ ] [ ]
– Kings of the boogie / Stoned bad street fighting man / So fine / You just can't get close to me / Hell's just on down the road / I was wrong / Little crystal / Dog house blues / Sleepy hollow baby / Chicken shack.

Topic | Topic

Sep 93. (cd)(c) **BURNIN' (Recorded live in Australia 1990)** [ ] [ ]
– Let's work together / Gamblin' woman / Hucklebuck / Sunnyland / Rollin' and tumblin' / Nitwit / Gunstreet girl / One way out / J.J. jump / Mercury blues.

Aim | Aim

Jul 95. (cd) **INTERNAL COMBUSTION** [ ] [ ]

- compilations etc. -

Aug 89. Liberty; (7") **LET'S WORK TOGETHER. / GOIN' UP THE COUNTRY** [ ] [ ]
(12"+=) – Rollin' and tumblin'.
(cd-s+=) – Amphetamine Annie.
Sep 89. Liberty; (lp)(c)(cd) **LET'S WORK TOGETHER (THE BEST OF CANNED HEAT)** [ ] [ ]
-On the road again / Bullfrog blues / Rollin' and tumblin' / Amphetamine / Annie / Fried hockey boogie / Sic 'em pigs / Poor Moon / Let's work together / Going up the country / Boogie music / Same all over / Time was / Sugar bee / Rockin' with the king / That's alright mama / My time ain't long.
Jan 70. Pye Int./ US= Janus; (lp) **VINTAGE HEAT** [ ] [ ]
Jun 70. Pye Int./ US= Janus; (7") **SPOONFUL. / BIG ROAD BLUES** [ ] [ ]
Jul 75. Barclay France; (lp) **MEMPHIS HEAT (with MEMPHIS SLIM)** [-] [-]
Nov 76. United Artists; (7"ep) **REMEMBER CANNED HEAT** [ ] [ ]
– On the road again / Let's work together / Going up the country.
Nov 76. D.J.M./ US= Scepter; (lp)(c) **LIVE AT TOPANGA CORRAL (live)** [ ] [ ]
(re-iss.'81 pic-lp as 'DOG HOUSE BLUES')
May 84. EMI-Golden; (7") **ON THE ROAD AGAIN. / LET'S WORK TOGETHER** [ ] [ ]
Nov 92. E.M.I.; (3xcd-box) **THE BIG HEAT** [ ] [ ]
1987. Rhino; (d-lp) **INFINITE BOOGIE** [-] [ ]
Feb 88. Rhino; (lp)(c)(cd) **HOOKER'N'HEAT VOL.2 (with JOHN LEE HOOKER)** [-] [ ]
Oct 88. Beat Goes On; (lp)(c) **70: LIVE IN EUROPE (live)** [ ] [ ]
(cd-iss.Sep89)
Feb 92. Thunderbolt; (cd) **STRAIGHT AHEAD** [ ] [-]
Apr 93. Pulsar; (cd) **BIG ROAD BLUES** [ ] [-]
Jul 94. Success; (cd)(c) **ROLLIN' AND TUMBLIN'** [ ] [-]
Aug 94. E.M.I.; (d-cd) **UNCANNED** [ ] [-]
Feb 95. B.A.M.; (cd) **PEARLS OF THE PAST** [ ] [-]

Jim CAPALDI (see under ⇒ TRAFFIC)

CAPTAIN BEEFHEART & HIS MAGIC BAND

Formed: Los Angeles, California, USA . . . 1964 by VAN VLIET, former school mate of FRANK ZAPPA. Adopted his name from B-movie CAPTAIN BEEFHEART MEETS THE GRUNT PEOPLE. He and his band signed to 'A&M' in 1965 and recorded two singles before moving to 'Buddah' records to record seminal 'SAFE AS MILK' lp 1967. For the next 15 years, he and his band, became one of rock's most diverse acts. • **Style:** From early R&B roots, to weird and wonderful rock that held no barriers, supplanting new styles and imagery concocted by the grunting, HOWLIN' WOLF influenced BEEFHEART. The British public hailed

'TROUT MASK REPLICA' as one of all-time classics, although it verged between mad eccentricity or just alien being. • **Songwriters:** BEEFHEART with DRUMBO arranging/dictating instruments played. Covered: HARD WORKIN' MAN (Jack Nitzche). • **Trivia:** Championed by many bands as major influence (e.g. PERE UBU, STUMP, SHRUBS, MacKENZIES, etc., etc.).

Recommended: SAFE AS MILK (*9) / TROUT MASK REPLICA (*9) / MIRROR MAN (*8) / LICK MY DECALS OFF, BABY (*8) / THE SPOTLIGHT KID (*8) / CLEAR SPOT (*7).

CAPTAIN BEEFHEART (b.DON VAN VLIET, 15 Jan'41, Glendale, California, USA) -vocals, harmonica, occasional guitar, wind instruments / **ALEX ST.CLAIRE** – guitar / **DOUG MOON** – guitar / **JERRY HANDLEY** – bass / **PAUL BLAKELY** – drums

not issued | A&M

1966. (7") **DIDDY WAH DIDDY. / WHO DO YOU THINK YOOU'RE FOOLING (*)** [-] [ ]

1966. (7") **MOONCHILD (*). / FRYING PAN** [-] [ ]
(these tracks became a UK 7"ep in '71. Also resurfacing as UK 12"ep Oct84 'THE LEGENDARY A&M SESSIONS' + 'Here I am, I always am' re-iss.Oct86 on 'Edsel', cd-iss.May92)*

— **The CAPTAIN** recruited an entire new band . . . **RY COODER** – slide guitar repl. MOON and ST.CLAIRE (they later joined DENNY KING) / **HERB BERMANN** – bass, co-composer repl. HANDLEY / **JOHN FRENCH** (DRUMBO) – drums repl. BLAKELY

Pye Int. | Kama Sutra

Jan 68. (7") **YELLOW BRICK ROAD. / ABBA ZABA** [ ] [ ]

Feb 68. (lp) **SAFE AS MILK** [ ] [ ]
– Sure 'nuff 'n yes I do / Zig zag wanderer / Call on me / Dropout boogie / I'm glad / Electricity / Yellow brick road / Abba zaba / Plastic factory / Where there's woman / Plastic factory / Grown so ugly / Autumn's child. *(re-iss.'69, re-iss.Jan82 on 'PRT', re-iss.Jul85 on 'Buddah')*

— **JEFF COTTON** (ANTENNAE JIMMY SEMENS) **-guitar** repl. COODER who went solo

not issued | Buddah

1968. (lp) **MIRROR MAN** (rec.1965) [-] [ ]
– Tarot plane / Kandy korn / 25th century Quaker / Mirror man. *(finally released UK May71, reached No.49)(re-iss.Aug74, re-iss.May82 on 'PRT', re-iss.Apr86 on 'Edsel')*

Liberty | Blue Thumb

Dec 68. (lp) **STRICTLY PERSONAL** [ ] [ ]
– Ah feel like acid / Safe as milk / Trust us / Son of Mirror Man – Mere man / On tomorrow / Beatles bones 'n' smokin' stones / Gimme that harp boy / Kandy korn. *(cd-iss.Aug94 on 'EMI')*

— **The CAPTAIN** retained **DRUMBO** and **ANTANNAE** plus new members **ZOOT HORN ROLLO** (b.BILL HARKLEROAD) – brass, narrator, guitar, flute / **ROCKETTE NORTON** (b.MARK BOSTON) – bass, narrator repl. HERB / **THE MASCARA SNAKE** (b.VICTOR HAYDEN) – clarinet / guest **DOUG MOON** returned

Straight | Straight

Nov 69. (d-lp) **TROUT MASK REPLICA** [21] [ ]
– Frownland / The dust blows forward 'n dust blows back / Dachau blues / Ella guru / Hair pie: bake 1 / Moonlight on Vermont / Hair pie: bake 2 / Pena / Well / When big Joan sets up / Fallin' ditch / Sugar 'n spikes / Ant man bee / Pachuco cadaver / Bills corpse / Sweet sweet bulbs / Neon meate dream of an octafish / China pig / My human gets me blues / Dali's car / Orange claw hammer / Wild life / She's too much for my mirror / Hobo chang ba / The blimp (mousetrap replica) / Steal softly thru snow / Old fart at play / Veteran's day poppy. *(re-iss.May75 on 'Reprise') (re-iss.cd Sep94 on 'WEA')*

— **ED MARIMBA** (ART TRIPP) – marimba (ex-MOTHERS OF INVENTION) repl. THE MASCARA SNAKE

Jan 71. (lp) **LICK MY DECALS OFF BABY** [20] [ ]
– Lick my decals off, baby / Doctor Dark / I love you, you big dummy / Peon / Bellerin' plain / Woe-is-uh-me-bop / Japan in a dishpan / I wanna find a woman that'll hold my big toe till I have a go / Petrified forest / One rose that I mean / The Buggy boogie woogie / The Smithsonian Institute blues (or the big dig) / Space-age couple / The clouds are full of wine (not whiskey or rye) / Flash Gordon's ape. *(re-iss.Jul73 on 'Reprise')*

— **THE WINGED EEL FINGERLING** (r.n. ELLIOT INGBER) – guitar, etc. (ex-MOTHERS etc.) repl. SEMENS who had already formed MU

Reprise | Reprise

Jan 72. (7") **CLICK CLACK. / I'M GONNA BOOGLARIZE YOU BABY** [-] [ ]

Feb 72. (lp) **THE SPOTLIGHT KID ("CAPTAIN BEEFHEART")** [44] [ ]
– I'm gonna booglarize you baby / White jam / Blabber 'n smoke / When it blows its stacks / Alice in Blunderland / The spotlight kid / Click clack / Grow fins / There ain't no Santa Claus on the evenin' stage / Glider.

— **ROY 'OREJON' ESTRADA** – bass (ex-LITTLE FEAT, ex-MOTHERS OF INVENTION) repl. INGBER. ROCKETTE moved to guitar, and augmented by backing vocals The **BLACKBERRIES / RUSS TITELMAN** – guitar (guested, as he did on "Safe as Milk")

Nov 72. (lp) **CLEAR SPOT** [ ] [ ]
– Low yo yo stuff / Nowadays a woman's gotta hit a man / Too much time / Circumstances / My head is my only house unless it rains / Sun zoom sparks / Clear spot / Crazy little thing / Long neck bottles / Her eyes are a blue million miles / Big eyed beans from Venus / Golden birdies. *(US re-iss.Jul87)*

Mar 73. (7") **TOO MUCH TIME. / MY HEAD IS MY ONLY HOUSE UNLESS IT RAINS** [ ] [ ]

— **ALEX ST.CLAIRE** – guitar returned to repl. ROY. Added **MARK MERCELLO** – keyboards

Virgin | Mercury

Apr 74. (lp)(c) **UNCONDITIONALLY GUARENTEED** [ ] [ ]
– Upon the my-oh-my / Sugar bowl / New electric ride / Magic be / Happy love song / Full Moon, hot Sun / I got love on my mind / This is the day / Lazy music / Peaches. *(re-iss.Aug82+Aug85 on 'Fame') (cd-iss.Jun88)*

Apr 74. (7") **UPON THE MY-OH-MY. / MAGIC BE** [ ] [-]

Apr 74. (7") **UPON THE MY-OH-MY. / I GOT LOVE ON MY MIND** [-] [ ]

— **ELLIOT INGBER** – guitar returned to repl. ST.CLAIRE plus session men **MARK GIBBONS, MICHAEL SMOTHERMAN, JIMMY CARAVAN** – all keyboards repl. MARCELLO.

— **DEAN SMITH** – guitar / **BOB WEST** – bass / **GENE PELLO** – drums / **TV GRIMES** – percussion

Nov 74. (lp)(c) **BLUEJEANS AND MOONBEAMS** [ ] [ ]
– Party of special things do / Same old blues / Observatory crest / Pompadour swamp / Captain's holiday / Rock'n'roll's evil doll / Further than we've gone / Twist ah luck / Bluejeans and moonbeams. *(re-iss.Mar84) (cd-iss.Jun88)*

— Late '75 **BEEFHEART** collaborated with **FRANK ZAPPA** on **"BONGO FURY"** album. This was a near live album with 2 studio tracks.

— His new touring band featured past members **ELLIOT, INGBER** and **JOHN FRENCH** plus **DENNY WHALLEY** – slide guitar / **BRUCE FOWLER** – trombone (both on bongos)

— His '76 band were **DRUMBO, WHALLEY, JEFF MORRIS TEPPER** – guitar, and **JOHN THOMAS** – piano. They recorded first sessions for the next album

— **ERIC DREW FELDMAN** – keyboards, bass repl. THOMAS / **ROBERT WILLIAMS** – drums repl. DRUMBO / **RICHARD REDISS** – slide guitar repl. WHALLEY / **ART TRIPP** – marimba returned from MALLARD. **BRUCE FOWLER** also returned.

Virgin | Warners

Feb 80. (lp)(c) **BAT CHAIN PULLER** (US-title 'SHINY BEAST') [ ] [ ]
– The floppy boot stomp / Tropical hot dog night / Ice rose / Harry Irene / You know you're a man / Bat chain puller / When I see mommy I feel like a mummy / Owed t'Alex / Candle mambo / Love lies / Suction prints / Apes-ma. *(re-iss.Aug85, re-iss+cd.Jun87)*

— **GARY LUCAS** – guitar repl. REDISS

Virgin | Virgin

Aug 80. (lp)(c) **DOC AT RADAR STATION** [ ] [ ]
– Hot head / Ashtray heart / A carrot is as close as a rabbit gets to a diamond / Run paint run run / Sue Egypt / Brickbats / Dirty blue Gene / Best batch yet / Telephone / Flavour bud living / Sheriff of Hong Kong / Making love to a vampire with a monkey on my knee. *(re-iss.Aug85) (cd-iss.Jun88)*

— The CAPTAIN brought in **HATSIZE SNYDER, CLIFF MARTINEZ, WILLIAMS, LAMBOURNE FOWLER and DRUMBO**

Aug 82. (12") **LIGHT REFLECTED OFF THE OCEANS OF THE MOON. / ICE CREAM FOR CROW** [ ] [ ]

Virgin | Epic

Sep 82. (lp)(c) **ICE CREAM FOR CROW** [90] [ ]
– Ice cream for crow / The host, the ghost, the most holy-o / Semi-multi-(coloured) caucasian / Hey Garland, I dig your tweed coat / Evening bell / Cardboard cut-out sundown / The past is sure tense / Ink mathematics / The witch doctor life / "81" poop hatch / The thousand and tenth day of the human totem pole / Skeleton makes good. *(re-iss.Aug86) (cd-iss.Apr88)*

He retired from music business to concentrate on painting/sculpting in his recently bought Mojave desert home.

– compilations etc. –

Jul 70. Buddah; (lp) **DROPOUT BOOGIE** [ ] [ ]
(a re-iss. of "SAFE AS MILK" 2 tracks less)

1975. WRMB; (lp) **WHAT'S ALL THIS BOOGA-BOOGA MUSIC (live)** [-] [ ]

1978. Impossible; (d-lp) **EASY TEETH** [-] [ ]

Jan 78. Buddah; (7") **SURE 'NUFF 'N' YES I DO. / ELECTRICITY** [ ] [ ]

Aug 76. Reprise; (d-lp) **TWO ORIGINALS OF . . .** [ ] [ ]
(re-iss. of "DECALS" + "SPOTLIGHT KID")

Feb 91. Reprise; (d-cd) **THE SPOTLIGHT KID / CLEAR SPOT** [ ] [ ]

Nov 77. Pye; (d-lp) **THE CAPTAIN BEEFHEART FILE** (first 2-lp's) [ ] [-]

M.C.A. | M.C.A.

May 78. M.C.A.; (7") **HARD WORKIN' MAN. / ('B'side by Jack Nitzche)** [ ] [ ]

— Above also features RY COODER – on guitar

1978. Virgin/ US= Warners; (7"pic-ep) **SIXPACK** [ ] [ ]

– Sugar bowl / Same old blues / Upon the My-Oh-My / Magic be / Rock'n'roll's evil dol / New electric ride.

Jul 83. P.R.T.; (10"lp) **MUSIC IN SEA MINOR** [ ] [-]
Jul 84. Breakaway; (lp)(pic-lp) **TOP SECRET** [ ] [-]
Jun 88. That's Original; (d-lp)(d-cd) **SAFE AS MILK / MIRROR MAN** [ ] [-]
(re-iss.d-cd.May91 on 'Castle')
Jun 92. Sequel; (cd) **I MAY BE HUNGRY BUT I SURE AIN'T WEIRD – THE ALTERNATIVE CAPTAIN BEEFHEART** [ ] [-]
Jun 93. Flarenasch; (cd) **THE BEST BEEFHEART** [ ] [-]

CARDIGANS

*** NEW ENTRY ***

Formed: Malmo, Sweden . . .1993 by (see below). Released an album in Sweden and signed to 'Polydor'. In 1995, they had minor success with follow-up 'LIFE', which included hits 'CARNIVAL' and 'SICK AND TIRED'. • **Style:** Dreamy SAINT ETIENNE like outfit, influenced by BURT BACHARACH, ABBA and BLACK SABBATH!. • **Songwriters:** SVENSSON – SVENINGSSON, some w/ PERSSON except MR.CROWLEY (Ozzy Osbourne) / BOYS ARE BACK IN TOWN (Thin Lizzy).

Recommended: LIFE (*8)

NINA PERSSON -vocals / **PETER SVENSSON** -guitar / **MAGNUS SVENINGSSON** -bass / **LASSE JOHANSSON** -keyboards / **BENGT LAGERBERG** -drums, flute

Stockholm Polydor

Nov 94. (c-s) **SICK & TIRED. / PLAIN PARADE** [ ] [ ]
(cd-s+=) – Laika / Pooh song.
May 95. (7")(c-s) **CARNIVAL. / MR. CROWLEY** [72] [ ]
(cd-s+=) – Emmerdale. *(re-iss.Nov95, hit No.35)*
Jun 95. (cd)(c) **LIFE** [58] [ ]
– Carnival / Gordon's garden party / Daddy's car / Sick & tired / Tomorrow / Rise & shine / Beautiful one / Travelling with Charley / Fine / Celia inside / Hey! get out of my way / After all.
Sep 95. (c-s) **SICK & TIRED / PLAIN PARADE** [34] [ ]
(cd-s) – ('A'side) / Pooh song / The boys are back in town / Carnival (Puck version).
Feb 96. (7") **RISE & SHINE. / PIKE BUBBLES** [29] [ ]
(cd-s+=) – Cocktail party bloody cocktail party.

CARS

Formed: Boston, Massachusetts, USA . . . 1976 by ORR, HAWKES and EASTON who started out touring as CAP'N'SWING. Manager Fred Davis got demo of 'JUST WHAT I NEEDED' playlisted on US radio and they duly signed to 'Elektra' 1978. This was their first of many US Top 30 hits, and had best time in 1984 with 3 massive sellers 'YOU MIGHT THINK', 'MAGIC' & 'DRIVE'. • **Style:** Mainstream "new-wave" band, that drifted into fashionable pop/rock. • **Songwriters:** All written by OCASEK, ORR and EASTON, except THINK IT OVER and MAYBE BABY (Buddy Holly). • **Trivia:** The song 'DRIVE' was used for LIVE AID concert and re-released with proceeds to famine relief/BAND AID. Most members also produced bands noteably RIC OCASEK for SUICIDE ('81), BAD BRAINS ('83), etc.

Recommended: THE CARS' GREATEST HITS (*7)

RIC OCASEK (b.RICHARD OTCASEK, 23 Mar'49, Baltimore) – vocals, guitar / **BENJAMIN ORR** (b.ORZECHOWSKI, in Cleveland, Ohio) – vocals, bass / **ELLIOT EASTON** (b.ELLIOT SHAPIRO, 18 Dec'53, Brooklyn, New York) – guitar / **GREG HAWKES** – keyboards, saxophone (ex-MILKWOOD, with ORR and OCASEK) / **DAVID ROBINSON** – drums (ex-The POP, ex-DMZ, ex-MODERN LOVERS)

Elektra Elektra

Aug 78. (7") **JUST WHAT I NEEDED. / I'M IN TOUCH WITH YOUR WORLD** [-] [27]
Aug 78. (lp)(c) **THE CARS** [29] [18] Jun 78
– Good times roll / My best friend's girl / Just what I needed / I'm in touch with your world / Don't cha stop / You're all I've got tonight / Bye bye love / Moving in stereo / All mixed up. *(US-cd.-iss.Jan84)*
Oct 78. (7")(7"pic-d) **MY BEST FRIEND'S GIRL. / MOVING IN STEREO** [3] [-]
Oct 78. (7") **MY BEST FRIEND'S GIRL. / DON'T CHA STOP** [-] [35]
Jan 79. (7")(7"pic-d) **JUST WHAT I NEEDED. / I'M IN TOUCH WITH YOUR WORLD** [17] [-]
May 79. (7") **GOOD TIMES ROLL. / ALL MIXED UP** [ ] [41] Mar 79
Jun 79. (lp)(c) **CANDY-O** [30] [3]
– Let's go / Since I held you / It's all can do / Double life / Shoo be doo / Candy-O / Nightspots / You can't hold on too long / Lust for kicks / Got a lot on my head / Dangerous type. *(US-cd.iss.Jan84)*
Jul 79. (7")(7"pic-d) **LET'S GO. / THAT'S IT** [51] [14] Jun 79
Sep 79. (7")(7"pic-d) **DOUBLE LIFE. / COME AROUND** [ ] [-]
Oct 79. (7") **IT'S ALL I CAN DO. / GOT A LOT ON MY HEAD** [-] [41]
Jan 80. (7") **DOUBLE LIFE. / CANDY-O** [-] [ ]
Jan 80. (7") **IT'S ALL I CAN DO. / CANDY-O** [ ] [-]
Sep 80. (lp)(c) **PANORAMA** [ ] [5]
– Panorama / Touch and go / Gimme some slack / Don't tell me now / Getting through / Misfit kid / Down boys / You wear those eyes / Running to you / Up and down. *(re-iss.Nov81) (US-cd.iss.1987)*
Sep 80. (7") **TOUCH AND GO. / DOWN BOYS** [ ] [37]
Jan 81. (7") **DON'T TELL ME NO. / DON'T GO TO PIECES** [-] [ ]
Mar 81. (7") **GIMME SOME SLACK. / DON'T GO TO PIECES** [-] [ ]
Nov 81. (lp)(c) **SHAKE IT UP** [ ] [9]
– Since you're gone / Shake it up / I'm not the one / Victim of love / Cruiser / A dream away / This could be love / Think it over / Maybe baby. *(US-cd.iss.1986)*
Nov 81. (7")(7"grey/pink)(7"black/pink)(7"pic-d) **SHAKE IT UP. / CRUISER** [ ] [4]
Mar 82. (7") **SINCE YOU'RE GONE. / THINK IT OVER** [-] [41]
May 82. (7") **SINCE YOU'RE GONE. / MAYBE BABY** [37] [-]
Jun 82. (7") **THIS COULD BE LOVE. / VICTIM OF LOVE** [-] [ ]
Aug 82. (7") **THINK IT OVER. / I'M NOT THE ONE** [ ] [-]
Mar 84. (7") **YOU MIGHT THINK. / HEARTBEAT CITY** [-] [7]
Mar 84. (lp)(c) **HEARTBEAT CITY** [25] [3]
– Hello again / Magic / Stranger eyes / It's not the night / I refuse / Looking for love / Drive / You might think / Why can't I have you / Heartbeat city. *(US-cd.iss Jul84)*
Apr 84. (7") **WHY CAN'T I HAVE YOU. / JACKIE** [ ] [-]
May 84. (7") **MAGIC. / I REFUSE** [-] [12]
Sep 84. (7") **DRIVE. / STRANGER EYES** [5] [3] Jul 84
(UK.re-iss.Jul85, hit No.4)
Oct 84. (7") **HELLO AGAIN. / ('A'-dub version)** [-] [20]
Nov 84. (7") **YOU MIGHT THINK. / I REFUSE** [ ] [-]
(12"+=) – Let's go.
Feb 85. (7") **WHY CAN'T I HAVE YOU. / HEARTBEAT CITY** [ ] [33] Jan 85
(12"+=) – Hello again (remix) / Moving in stereo.
Sep 85. (7") **HEARTBEAT CITY. / WHY CAN'T I HAVE YOU** [ ] [ ]
(12"+=) – Chemistry / Hello again.
Oct 85. (7") **TONIGHT SHE COMES. / JUST WHAT I NEEDED** [-] [7]
Nov 85. (7") **TONIGHT SHE COMES. / BREAKAWAY** [ ] [-]
(12"+=) – Just what I needed.
Nov 85. (lp)(c)(cd) **THE CARS' GREATEST HITS** (compilation) [27] [12]
– Just what I needed / Since you're gone / You might think / Good times roll / Touch and go / Drive / Tonight she comes / My best friend's girl / Heartbeat city / Let's go / Magic / Shake it up. (c+cd+=) – I'm not the one.
Jan 86. (7") **I'M NOT THE ONE. / HEARTBEAT CITY** [-] [32]
Mar 86. (7") **I'M NOT THE ONE (remix). / SINCE YOU'RE GONE** [ ] [-]
(12"+=) – Shake it up.
Aug 87. (lp)(c)(cd) **DOOR TO DOOR** [72] [26]
– Leave or stay / You are the girl / Double trouble / Fine line / Everything you say / Ta ta wayo wayo / Strap me in / Coming up you / Wound up on you / Go away / Door to door.
Sep 87. (7") **YOU ARE THE GIRL. / TA TA WAYO WAYO** [ ] [17] Aug 87
(12"+=) – Tonight she comes.
Nov 87. (7") **STRAP ME IN. / DOOR TO DOOR** [-] [ ]
Jan 88. (7") **COMING UP YOU. / DOUBLE TROUBLE** [-] [ ]

—— disbanded early 1988. OCASEK married Paulina Porizkova (23 Aug'89.)

RIC OCASEK

Geffen Geffen

Feb 83. (lp)(c) **BEATITUDE** [ ] [28]
– Jimmy Jimmy / Something to grab for / Prove / I can't wait / Connect up to me / A quick one / Out of control / Take a walk / Sneak attack / Time bomb. *(re-iss.Sep86)*
Mar 83. (7") **SOMETHING TO GRAB FOR. / CONNECT UP TO ME** [-] [47]
Jun 83. (7") **A QUICK ONE. / JIMMY JIMMY** [-] [ ]
Oct 86. (7") **EMOTION IN MOTION. / P.F.J.** [ ] [15]
(12"+=) – Step by step.
Nov 86. (lp)(c)(cd) **THIS SIDE OF PARADISE** [ ] [31]
– Keep on laughin' / True to you / Emotion in motion / Look in your eyes / Coming for you / Mystery / True love / P.F.J. / Hello darkness / This side of Paradise.
Jan 87. (7") **TRUE TO YOU. / HELLO DARKNESS** [-] [ ]

Sire Sire

Jul 91. (cd)(c)(lp) **FIREBALL ZONE** [ ] [ ]
– Rockaway / Touch down easy / Come back / The way you look tonight / All we need is love / Over and over / Flowers of evil / They tried / Keep that dream / Balance / Mister Meaner.

ELLIOT EASTON

		Elektra	Elektra
Apr 85.	(lp)(c) **CHANGE NO CHANGE** – Tools of your labour / (Wearing down) Like a wheel / Shayla / Help me / (She made it) New for me / I want you / Change / The hard way / Fight my way to love / Wide awake.		99
Apr 85.	(7") **THE HARD WAY. / (WEARING DOWN) LIKE A WHEEL**	-	
Jun 85.	(7") **WEARING DOWN LIKE A WHEEL. / SHAYLA**	-	

BENJAMIN ORR

		Elektra	Elektra
Dec 86.	(lp)(c) **THE LACE** – Too hot to stop / In circles / Stay the night / Skyline / When you're gone / Spinning / Hold on / The lace / That's the way / This time around.		86
Jan 87.	(7")(12") **STAY THE NIGHT. / THAT'S THE WAY**		24
Apr 87.	(7") **THE LACE. / TOO HOT TO STOP**	-	

CARTER THE UNSTOPPABLE SEX MACHINE

Formed: Streatham, South London, England . . . 1988 by FRUITBAT and JIM BOB. They had been in early 80's outfit The BALLPOINTS, and after a lengthy period with real jobs, they formed the group JAMIE WEDNESDAY in 1984. They signed to 'Rough Trade' subsidiary label 'Pink', and released 2 singles before disbanding Feb87. The following year they became CARTER . . . and after more indie releases, they were contracted to 'Rough Trade' then 'Chrysalis' for whom they started to chart by 1991. • **Style:** D.I.Y. agit punk rock, with a little of the humour that HALF MAN HALF BISCUIT once had. • **Songwriters:** All penned by LES and JIM BOB, except RENT (Pet Shop Boys) / RANDY SCOUSE GIT (Monkees) / EVERYBODY'S HAPPY NOWADAYS (Buzzcocks) / BEDSITTER (Soft Cell) / THIS IS HOW IT FEELS (Inspiral Carpets) / PANIC (Smiths) / MANNEQUIN (Wire) / KING ROCKER (Generation X) / DOWN IN THE TUBE STATION AT MIDNIGHT (Jam) / ANOTHER BRICK IN THE WALL (Pink Floyd) / THE IMPOSSIBLE DREAM (Mitch Leigh/Joe Darion) / HIT (Sugarcubes) / SPEEED KING (These Animal Men) / SILVER DREAM MACHINE (David Essex). • **Trivia:** Surprizingly it was JONATHAN KING who gave them tabloid exposure in his 'Sun' column.

Recommended: 30 SOMETHING (*8) / 1992 THE LOVE ALBUM (*7) / POST-HISTORIC MONSTERS (*8) / 101 DAMNATIONS (*10).

JAMIE WEDNESDAY

JIM 'Jim Bob' MORRISON (b.22 Nov'60)– vocals, acoustic guitar / **LES 'Fruitbat' CARTER** (b.12 Feb'58)– bass / **LINDSEY HENRY** – trumpet / **SIMON LOWE** – brass / **DEAS LEGGETT** – drums

		Pink	not issued
Nov 85.	(12"ep) **VOTE FOR LOVE / THE WALL. / WHITE HORSES / BUTTONS AND BOWS**		-
May 86.	(12"ep) **WE THREE KINGS OF ORIENT AREN'T. / LAST NIGHT I HAD THE STRANGEST DREAM / I THINK I'LL THROW A PARTY FOR MYSELF**		-

— disbanded Feb87.

CARTER THE UNSTOPPABLE SEX MACHINE

was duo formed by **JIM BOB & FRUITBAT** who now both played guitar with back-up of tape machines & **JIM BOB** – vocals

		Big Cat	not issued
Aug 88.	(12"m) **SHELTERED LIFE. / IS THIS THE ONLY WAY THROUGH TO YOU? / GRANNY FARMING IN THE U.K.** *(re-iss. cd-ep Jul 94 on 'Southern')*		-
Nov 89.	(12"ep) **SHERIFF FATMAN / R.S.P.C.E. / TWIN-TUB WITH GUITAR / EVERYBODY'S HAPPY NOWADAYS**		-
Jan 90.	(lp)(c)(cd) **101 DAMNATIONS** – A perfect day to drop the bomb / Midnight on the murder mile / The road to Domestos / An all-American sport / 24 minutes to Tulsa Hill / Good grief / Charlie Brown / Everytime a churchbell rings / Good grief / Sheriff Fatman / G.I. blues. *(re-dist.Sep91, hit No.29)*		-
May 90.	(12")(cd-s) **RUBBISH. / RENT / ALTERNATIVE ALF GARNET**		

		Rough Trade	not issued
Oct 90.	(7") **ANYTIME, ANYPLACE, ANYWHERE. / RE-EDUCATING RITA** (12"+=)(cd-s+=) – Alternative title (randy sarf git).		-
Jan 91.	(7")(c-s) **BLOODSPORTS FOR ALL. / 2001: A CLOCKWORK ORANGE** (12"+=)(cd-s+=) – Bedsitter.	48	-
Feb 91.	(cd)(c)(lp) **30 SOMETHING** – Surfin' USM / My second to last will and testament / Anytime anyplace anywhere / Prince in a pauper's grave / Shopper's paradise / Billy's smart circus / Bloodsport for all / Sealed with a Glasgow kiss / Say it with flowers / Falling on a bruise / The final comedown. *(US-iss.Aug91 on 'Chrysalis' / UK re-iss.Jan92 on 'Rough Trade', hit 21) (re-iss.cd/c Feb95)*	8	-

		Chrysalis	Chrysalis
Jun 91.	(7") **SHERIFF FATMAN. / R.S.P.C.E.** (12"+=)(c-s+=)(cd-s+=) – Twin-tub with guitar / Everybody's happy nowadays	23	
Oct 91.	(7")(c-s) **AFTER THE WATERSHED (EARLY LEARNING THE HARD WAY). / THE 90's REVIVAL / A NATION OF SHOPLIFTERS** (12"+=)(cd-s+=) – This is how it feels.	11	
Dec 91.	(7")(c-s) **RUBBISH. / ALTERNATIVE ALF GARNET** (12"+=)(cd-s+=) – Rent.	14	
Apr 92.	(7"ep)(12"ep)(c-ep)(cd-ep) **THE ONLY LIVING BOY IN NEW CROSS. / PANIC / WATCHING THE BIG APPLE TURN**	7	
May 92.	(cd)(c)(lp) **1992 – THE LOVE ALBUM** – 1993 / Is wrestling fixed? / The only living boy in New Cross / Suppose you gave a funeral and nobody came / England / Do re mi, so far so good / Look mum, no hands / While you were out / Skywest and crooked / The impossible dream. *(re-iss.cd/c Mar94 & Feb95)*	1	
Jun 92.	(7"ep)(12"ep)(c-ep)(cd-ep) **DO RE MI, SO FAR SO GOOD / MANNEQUIN. / KING ROCKER / DOWN IN THE TUBE-STATION AT MIDNIGHT**	22	
Nov 92.	(7"ep)(12"ep)(c-ep)(cd-ep) **THE IMPOSSIBLE DREAM / TURN ON, TUNE IN AND SWITCH OFF / WHEN THESAURUSES RULED THE WORLD / BRING ON THE GIRLS**	21	
Aug 93.	(7")(c-s) **LEAN ON ME I WON'T FALL OVER. / HIT** (12"+=)(cd-s+=) – Always the bridesmaid never the bride.	16	
Sep 93.	(cd)(c)(lp) **POST HISTORIC MONSTERS** – 2 million years B.C. / The music that nobody likes / Mid day crisis / Cheer up, it might never happen / Stuff the jubilee! / A bachelor for Baden Powell / Spoilsports personality of the year / Suicide isn't painless / Being here / Evil / Sing fat lady sing / Travis / Lean on me I won't fall over / Lenny and Terence / Under the thumb and over the Moon. *(re-iss.Feb95)*	5	
Feb 94.	(7")(c-s) **GLAM ROCK COPS. / LEAN ON ME (I WON'T FALL OVER) (by The FAMILY CAT)** (12"+=)(cd-s+=) – ('A'-GRID mixes). (cd-s) – ('A'side) / Bloodsports for all (by SULTANS OF PING F.C.) / Lenny and Terence (by BLADE) / Falling on a bruise (by PUBLIC WORKS).	24	
Mar 94.	(cd)(c)(lp) **STARRY EYED AND BOLLOCK NAKED (A COLLECTION OF B-SIDES)** (compilation) – Is this the only way to get through to you? / Granny farming in the UK / R.S.P.C.E. / Twin tub with guitar / Alternative Alf Garnett / Re educating Rita / 2001: A clockwork orange / The 90's revival / A nation of shoplifters / Watching the big apple turn over / Turn on, tune in and switch off / When Thesauruses ruled the Earth / Bring on the girls! / Always the bridesmaid never the bride / Her song / Commercial f**king suicide / Stuff the jubilee (1977) / Glam rock cops. *(re-iss.Feb95)*	22	

— added **WEZ BOYNTON** – drums (ex-RESQUE)

Date	Release	UK	US
Nov 94.	(7")(c-s) **LET'S GET TATTOOS. / ESPECIALLY 4 U** (cd-s+=) – Speed king / Silver dream machine. (cd-s) – ('A'side) / Turbulence / King for a day.	30	
Jan 95.	(7"colrd)(c-s) **THE YOUNG OFFENDER'S MUM. / TROUBLE** (cd-s+=) – This one's for me. (cd-s) – ('A'side) / Rubbish (live) / Suicide isn't painless (live) / Falling on a bruise (live).	34	
Feb 95.	(d-cd)(c)(d-lp) **WORRY BOMB** – Cheap'n'cheesy / Airplane food -airplane fest food / The young offender's mum / Gas (man) / The life and soul of the party dies / My defeatest attitude / Worry bomb / Senile delinquent / Me and Mr.Jones / Let's get tattoos / Going straight / God, Saint Peter and the guardian angel / The only looney left in town / Ceasefire. **DOMA SPORTOVA . . . LIVE IN ZAGREB, 20/5/94** – Alternative Alf Garnett / Do re me so far so good / A bachelor pad for Baden Powell / Re-educating Rita / The only living boy in New Cross / Lean on me I won't fall over / Granny farming in the U.K. / Travis / Sing fat lady sing / Lenny and Terence / Commercial fucking suicide part 1.	9	
Sep 95.	(7"red)(c-s) **BORN ON THE 5th OF NOVEMBER. / D.I.V.O.R.C.E.F.G.** (cd-s) – ('A'side) / Tomorrow when you die / The aftertaste of Paradise / Airplane food.	35	
Oct 95.	(cd)(c)(lp) **STRAW DONKEY . . .THE SINGLES** (compilation) – A sheltered life / Sheriff Fatman / Rubbish / Antime anyplace anywhere / Bloodsport for all / After the watershed (early learning the hard way) / The only living boy in New Cross / Do re mi, so far so good / The impossible dream / Lean on me (I won't fall over) / Lenny and Terence / Glam rock cops / Let's get	37	

tattoos / The young offender's mum / Born on the 5th of November.

– compilations, others, etc. –

Oct 90. Big Cat Export; (m-lp)(cd) **HANDBUILT FOR PERVERTS** [-] [ ]

CAST

Formed: Liverpool, England . . .1994 by ex-LA'S guitarist JOHN POWER. Spent just under a year perfecting their rhythmic debut album 'ALL CHANGE', which was preceeded by two UK Top 20 hits 'FINETIME' & 'ALRIGHT'. • **Style:** Well-structured psychedelic rock likened to possibly OASIS. • **Songwriters:** JOHN POWER.

Recommended: ALL CHANGE (*7)

JOHN POWER -vocals, guitar (ex-LA'S) / **PETER WILKINSON** -bass / **KEITH O'NEILL** -drums / **LIAM 'SKIN' TYSON** -guitar

Polydor M.C.A.

Jul 95. (7"green)(c-s)(cd-s) **FINETIME. / BETTER MAN / SATELLITES** [17] [ ]

Sep 95. (7"blue)(c-s)(cd-s) **ALRIGHT. / FOLLOW ME DOWN / MEET ME** [13] [ ]

Oct 95. (cd)(c)(lp) **ALL CHANGE** [7] [ ]
– Alright / Promised land / Sandstorm / Mankind / Tell it like it is / Four walls / Finetime / Back of my mind / Walkaway / Reflections / History / Two of a kind.

. . . Jan – Jun '96 stop press . . .

Jan 96. (single) **SANDSTORM** [8] [ ]
Mar 96. (single) **WALK AWAY** [9] [ ]

CATCH (see under ⇒ EURYTHMICS)

Nick CAVE & The BAD SEEDS

Formed: Berlin, Germany . . . 1983 by Australian NICK CAVE, who at the time also lived in London. For a few gigs in '83, he was backed by The CAVEMEN until change of name. Around this time, CAVE had been credited on DIE HAUT album BURNIN' THE ICE, writing and singing 4 songs. CAVE was still contracted to the 'Mute' label from his BIRTHDAY PARTY days, so he stuck with them for release of UK Top 40 entry 'FROM HER TO ETERNITY'. • **Style:** Avant-garde alternative rock with CAVE'S weird but wonderful gruff vocals the forte. • **Songwriters:** All songs by CAVE, except IN THE GHETTO (Elvis Presley) / RUNNING SCARED (Roy Orbison) / BLACK BETTY (Ram Jam) / BY THE TIME I GET TO PHOENIX (Jim Webb) / MUDDY WATER (Johnny Rivers) / HEY JOE (Jimi Hendrix) / ALL TOMORROW'S PARTIES (Velvet Underground) / THE CARNIVAL IS OVER (Seekers) / SOMETHING'S GOTTEN HOLD OF MY HEART (Gene Pitney) / HELPLESS (Neil Young) / WHAT A WONDERFUL WORLD (Ray Charles) / etc. mainly from his covers album KICKING AGAINST THE PRICKS. • **Trivia:** He is the author of two books AND THE ASS SAW THE ANGEL and KING INK. By the late 80's, he had also starred in the film GHOSTS . . . OF THE CIVIL DEAD, also supplying soundtrack.

Recommended: THE FIRSTBORN IS DEAD (*7) / THE GOOD SUN (*8) / HENRY'S DREAM (*8) / LET LOVE IN (*8) / FROM HER TO ETERNITY (*6) / MURDER BALLADS (*7)

NICK CAVE – vocals (ex-BIRTHDAY PARTY, ex-BOYS NEXT DOOR) / **MICK HARVEY** – guitar, keyboards (ex-BIRTHDAY PARTY, ex-BOYS NEXT DOOR) / **BLIXA BARGELD** – guitar (of EINSTURZENDE NEUBAUTEN, ex-BIRTHDAY PARTY) / **BARRY ADAMSON** – bass, guitar (ex-MAGAZINE, ex-PETE SHELLEY) / **HUGO RACE** – drums

Mute Elektra

Jun 84. (7") **IN THE GHETTO. / THE MOON IS IN THE GUTTER** [ ] [ ]

—— added **ANITA LANE** – synthesizers (ex-solo artist)

Jun 84. (lp)(c) **FROM HER TO ETERNITY** [40] [ ]
– Avalanche / Cabin fever / Well of misery / From her to eternity / Wings of flies / Saint Huck / A box for black Paul. *(cd-1987 +=)* – In the ghetto / The Moon is in the gutter / From her to eternity (1987).

—— **THOMAS WYLDER** – drums (ex-DIE HAUT) repl. **HUGO and ANITA**

Jun 85. (lp)(c) **THE FIRSTBORN IS DEAD** [53] [ ]
– Tupelo / Say goodbye to the little girl tree / Train long suffering / Black crow king / Knockin' on Joe / Wanted man / Blind Lemon Jefferson. *(cd-iss.Apr88)*

Jul 85. (7") **TUPELO. / THE SIX STRINGS THAT DREW BLOOD** [ ] [-]

Jun 86. (7") **THE SINGER. / RUNNING SCARED.** [ ] [-]
(12"+=) – Black Betty.

Aug 86. (lp)(c)(cd) **KICKING AGAINST THE PRICKS** [89] [ ]
– Muddy water / I'm gonna kill that woman / Sleeping Annaleah / Long black veil / Hey Joe / The singer / Black Betty * / Running scared * / All tomorrow's parties / By the time I get to Phoenix / The hammer song / Something's gotten hold of my heart / Jesus met the woman at the well / The carnival is over. *(cd+= *)*

Nov 86. (lp)(c)(cd) **YOUR FUNERAL . . . MY TRIAL** [ ] [ ]
– Sad waters / The Carny / Your funeral . . . my trial / Stranger than kindness / Jack's shadow / Hard on for love / She fell away / Long time man. (cd+=) – Scum.

—— **CAVE** retained **HARVEY, BARGELD** and **WYDLER,** bringing in **ROLAND WOLF** – bass / **KID CONGO POWERS** – guitar (ex-CRAMPS, ex-GUN CLUB)

May 88. (7")(12") **THE MERCY SEAT. / NEW DAY** [ ] [-]
(12"+=) – ('A'video mix).
(cd-s+=) – From her to eternity (film version) / Tupelo (version).

Sep 88. (lp)(c)(cd) **TENDER PREY** [67] [ ]
– The mercy seat / Up jumped the Devil / Deanna / Watching Alice / Mercy / City of refuge / Slowly goes the night / Sunday's slave / Sugar, sugar, sugar / New morning. *(cd+=)* – The mercy seat (video mix). (free-12"ep.w/above) **AND THE ASS SAW THE ANGEL** (narration/book) – One Autumn / Animal static / Mah sanctum / Lamentation.

Sep 88. (12") **DEANNA. / THE GIRL AT THE BOTTOM OF MY GLASS** [ ] [-]

Mar 89. (lp)(c)(cd) **GHOSTS . . . OF THE CIVIL DEAD (Soundtrack w/ dialogue) ("NICK CAVE, MICK HARVEY, BLIXA BARGELD")** [ ] [-]
– The news / Introduction – A prison in the desert / David Hale – I've been a prison guard since I was 18 years old / Glover – I was 16 when they put me in prison / David Hale – you're danglin' us like a bunch of meat on a hook / Pop mix / Glover – we were united once / David Hale – the day of the murders / Lilly's theme ("A touch of warmth") / Maynard mix / David Hale – what I'm tellin' is the truth / Outro – The free world / Glover – one man released so they can imprison the rest of the world.

—— (now a 5-piece, without WOLF)

Mar 90. (7")(12")(cd-s) **THE SHIP SONG. / THE TRAIN SONG** [ ] [-]
Apr 90. (cd)(c)(lp) **THE GOOD SON** [47] [ ]
– Foi na cruz / The good son / Sorrow's child / The weeping song / The ship song / The hammer song / Lament / The witness song / Lucy.
(w/-7"/cd-s) **THE MERCY SEAT / CITY OF REFUGE / DEANNA (all acoustic)**

Sep 90. (7") **THE WEEPING SONG. / COCKS'N'ASSES** [ ] [-]
(12"+=)(cd-s+=) – Helpless.

Mar 92. (7") **STRAIGHT TO YOU. / JACK THE RIPPER (acoustic)** [68] [ ]
(12"+=)(cd-s+=) – Blue bird.

Apr 92. (cd)(c)(lp) **HENRY'S DREAM** [29] [ ]
– Papa won't leave you Henry / I had a dream, Joe / Straight to you / Brother, my cup is empty / Christina the astonishing / When I first came to town / John Finn's wife / Loom of the land / Jack the ripper.

Aug 92. (7") **I HAD A DREAM, JOE. / THE GOOD SON (live)** [ ] [ ]
(12"+=)(cd-s+=) – Henry's dream / The Carney (live) / The mercy seat (live) / The ship sons (live).

Nov 92. (7")(c-s) **WHAT A WONDERFUL WORLD. ("NICK CAVE & SHANE McGOWAN") / A RAINY NIGHT IN SOHO / LUCY 2** [72] [-]

Sep 93. (cd) **LIVE SEEDS (live)** [67] [ ]
-Mercy seat / Deanna / The ship song / Papa won't leave you Henry / Plain gold ring / John Finn's wife / Tupelo / Brother my cup is empty / The weeping song / Jack the ripper / The good son / From her to eternity.

Mar 94. (7")(12")(cd-s) **DO YOU LOVE ME? / CASSIEL'S SONG / SAIL AWAY** [68] [ ]

Apr 94. (cd)(c)(lp) **LET LOVE IN** [12] [ ]
– Do you love me? / Nobody's baby now / Loverman / Jangling Jack / Red right hand / I let love in / Thirsty dog / Ain't gonna rain anymore / Lay me low / Do you love me? (part 2).

—— **JAMES JOHNSON** – guitar (of GALLON DRUNK) repl. on tour only BLIXA

Jul 94. (7")(12")(cd-s) **LOVERMAN. / (I'LL LOVE YOU) TILL THE END OF THE WORLD** [ ] [ ]

Oct 94. (7"red) **RED RIGHT HAND. / THAT'S WHAT JAZZ IS TO ME** [ ] [ ]
(cd-s+=) – Where the action is.

Oct 95. (7")(c-s) **NICK CAVE AND THE BAD SEEDS + KYLIE MINOGUE:- WHERE THE WILD ROSES GROW. / BALLAD OF ROBERT MOORE & BETTY COLTRANE** [11] [ ]
(cd-s+=) – The willow garden.

. . . Jan – Jun '96 stop press . . .

Feb 96. (cd)(c)(lp) **MURDER BALLADS** [8] [ ]
Feb 96. (single) **HENRY LEE (with PJ HARVEY)** [36] [ ]

Roger CHAPMAN (see under ⇒ FAMILY)

Tracy CHAPMAN

Born: 1964, Cleveland, Ohio, USA. After graduating from Medford University (Tufts), she signed to 'Elektra' records in 1986. She toured with stablemates 10,000 MANIACS, until her transatlantic US/UK No.1 eponymous debut album was released 1988. • **Style:** Folk balladeer who critics hailed as the new JOAN ARMATRADING. • **Songwriters:** All penned by TRACY, who started writing from age 8. She also interpreted traditional song HOUSE OF THE RISING SUN (Glenn Yarborough). • **Trivia:** She won 'Best New Artist, etc.' at the 1989 US grammy awards. She's also a supporter of human rights, and appeared at Nelson Mandela Concert on 11 June 1988.

Recommended: TRACY CHAPMAN (*7)

TRACY CHAPMAN – vocals, acoustic guitar / with **JACK HOLDER** – guitar, organ / **LARRY KLEIN** – bass / **DENNY FONGHEISER** – drums

Apr 88. (lp)(c)(cd) **TRACY CHAPMAN** [1] [1]
– Talkin' 'bout a revolution / Fast car / Across the lines / Behind the wall / Baby can I hold you / Mountains o' things / She's got her ticket / Why? / For my lover / If not now . . . / For you.

May 88. (7") **FAST CAR. / FOR YOU.** [5] [6]
(12"+=) – Behind the wall.

Aug 88. (7")(12") **TALKIN' 'BOUT A REVOLUTION. / IF NOT NOW . . .** [ ] [ ]
(cd-s+=) – She's got her ticket.

Nov 88. (7") **BABY CAN I HOLD YOU. / ACROOS THE LINES** [ ] [48]
(12"+=)(cd-s+=) – Mountain o' things.

Sep 89. (7") **CROSSROADS. / BORN TO FIGHT** [61] [ ]
(12"+=) – Fast car.
(cd-s+=) – Mountain o' things (live).

Oct 89. (lp)(c)(cd) **CROSSROADS** [1] [9]
– Crossroads / Bridges / Freedom now / Material world / Be careful of my heart / Subcity / Born to fight / A hundred years / This time / All that you have is your soul.

Feb 90. (7") **ALL THAT YOU HAVE IS YOUR SOUL. / SUBCITY** [ ] [-]
(12"+=) – Freedom now.

Feb 90. (7") **ALL THAT YOU HAVE IS YOUR SOUL. / MATERIAL WORLD** [-] [ ]

Apr 92. (7")(c-s) **BANG BANG BANG. / WOMAN'S WORK** [ ] [ ]
(12"+=)(cd-s+=) – House of the rising Sun.

May 92. (cd)(c)(lp) **MATTERS OF THE HEART** [19] [ ]
– Bang bang bang / So / I used to be a sailor / The love that you had / Woman's work / These are the things / Short supply / Dreaming on a world / Open arms / Matters of the heart. *(re-iss.cd+c Nov93)*

Jul 92. (7")(c-s) **DREAMING ON A WORLD. / WOMAN'S WORK** [ ] [ ]
(cd-s+=) – ('A'extended) / House of the rising Sun.

Nov 95. (cd)(c) **NEW BEGINNING** [ ] [4]
– Heaven's here on Earth / New beginning / Smoke and ashes / Cold feet / At this point in my life / the promise / The rape of the world / Tell it like it is / Give me one reason / Remember the tin man / I'm ready.

. . . Jan – Jun '96 stop press . . .

May 96. (single) **GIVE ME ONE REASON** [ ] [3] Mar 96

CHARLATANS

Formed: Northwich, Cheshire, England . . . late 1989 as a quintet. Formed own 'Dead Good' records, which after their debut single, was taken over by 'Situation 2'. Following 2 major UK hits, they went in at No.1 with debut album 'SOME FRIENDLY' in 1990. • **Style:** Influenced by friends The STONE ROSES and also the 60's (i.e. PINK FLOYD). Organ-orientated Manchester inspired "rave" rock. • **Songwriters:** Group compositions except I FEEL MUCH BETTER ROLLING OVER (Small Faces). On their eponnymous 1995 album the track 'HERE COMES A SOUL SAVER' borrowed? a guitar riff from PINK FLOYD's 'Fearless'. • **Trivia:** Steve Harrison is the manager.

Recommended: SOME FRIENDLY (*8) / BETWEEN 10th & 11th (*6) / UP TO OUR HIPS (*7) / THE CHARLATANS (*8)

TIM BURGESS (b.30 May'68) – vocals (ex-ELECTRIC CRAYONS) repl. BAZ KETTLEY / **ROB COLLINS** (b.1967) – organ / **JON BAKER** (b.1969) – guitar / **JON-BOY BROOKS** (b.1969) – drums / **MARTIN BLUNT** (b.1965) – bass (ex-MAKIN' TIME, ex-TOO MUCH TEXAS w / TIM)

Dead Good / not issued

Feb 90. (7") **INDIAN ROPE. / WHO WANTS TO KNOW** [89] [-]
(12"+=) – You can talk to me. *(re-iss.+cd-s.Jul 91, hit No. 57)*

Situation 2 / Beggar's B

May 90. (7") **THE ONLY ONE I KNOW. / IMPERIAL 109** [9] [ ]
(12"+=) – Everything changed.
(cd-s+=) – You can talk to me (version).

Sep 90. (7") **THEN. / TAURUS MOANER** [12] [ ]
(12"+=)(cd-s+=) – ('A'alternative mix) / ('A'instrumental).

Oct 90. (cd)(c)(lp) **SOME FRIENDLY** [1] [73]
– You're not very well / White shirt / The only one I know * / Opportunity / Then / 109 pt.2 / Polar bear / Believe you me / Flower / Sonic / Sproston Green. *(cd+= *)*

Feb 91. (7"ep)(12"ep)(c-ep) **OVER RISING. / WAY UP THERE / HAPPEN TO DIE** [15] [ ]
(cd-s+=) – Opportunity Three (re-work).

— **MARK COLLINS** – guitar (ex-CANDLESTICK PARK) repl. BAKER

Oct 91. (7")(c-s) **ME IN TIME. / OCCUPATION H. MONSTER** [28] [ ]
(12"+=)(cd-s+=) – Subtitle.

Feb 92. (7")(c-s) **WEIRDO. / THEME FROM 'THE WISH'** [19] [ ]
(12"+=)(cd-s+=) – Sproston Green (remix) / ('A'remix).

Mar 92. (cd)(c)(lp) **BETWEEN 10th AND 11th** [21] [ ]
– I don't want to see the lights / Ignition / Page one / Tremelo song / The end of everything etc / Subtitle / Can't even be bothered / Weirdo / Chewing gum weekend / (No one) Not even the rain. *(re-iss.cd Sep95 on 'Beggar's Banquet')*

Jun 92. (7") **TREMELO SONG (alternative take). / HAPPEN TO DIE** [44] [ ]
(cd-s+=) – Normality swing (demo).
(cd-s+=) – Then (live) / Chewing gum weekend (live).
(12"+=) – (4 tracks, including 'A')

— ROB COLLINS was given a jail sentence in Sep'93 for his part in an armed robbery. He was released approximately 3-4 months later.

Beggar's B. / Beggar's B.

Jan 94. (c-s) **CAN'T GET OUT OF BED. / WITHDRAWN** [24] [ ]
(7"+=)(12"+=)(cd-s+=) – Out.

Mar 94. (cd-ep) **I NEVER WANT AN EASY LIFE IF ME AND HE WERE EVER TO GET THERE. / ONLY A BOHO / SUSTERRAINIA / CAN'T GET OUT OF BED (demo)** [38] [ ]

Mar 94. (cd)(c)(lp) **UP TO OUR HIPS** [8] [ ]
– Come in number 21 / I never want an easy life / If me and he were ever to get there / Can't get out of bed / Feel flows / Autograph / Jesus hairdo / Up to our hips / Patrol / Another rider up in flames / Inside – looking out. *(re-iss.cd Sep95)*

Jun 94. (c-ep)(12"ep)(cd-ep) **JESUS HAIRDO / PATROL (Dust Brothers remix) / STIR IT UP -cd(or)12"- FEEL FLOWS (Van Basten remix)** [48] [ ]
(cd-s) – ('A'side) / I never want an easy life / Another rider up in flames / Up to our hips (BBC Radio 1 live sessions).

Dec 94. (7")(c-s) **CRASHIN' IN. / BACK ROOM WINDOW** [31] [ ]
(12"+=)(cd-s+=) Green flashing eyes.

May 95. (7")(c-s) **JUST LOOKIN'. / BULLET COMES** [32] [ ]
(cd-s+=) – Floor nine.

Aug 95. (c-s) **JUST WHEN YOU'RE THINKIN' THINGS OVER / FRINCK / YOUR SKIES ARE MINE** [12] [ ]
(cd-s+=) – Chemical risk (toothache remix).
(12") – (first 2 tracks) / Chemical risk dub / Nine acres (Dust Brothers mix).

Aug 95. (cd)(c)(d-lp) **THE CHARLATANS** [1] [ ]
– Nine acre court / Feeling holy / Just lookin' / Crashin' in / Bullet comes / Here comes a soul saver / Just when you're thinkin' things over / Tell everyone / Toothache / No fiction / See it through / Thank you. (d-lp+=) – Chemical risk (toothache remix).

CHEMICAL BROTHERS

Formed: North London, England . . .1992 by resident DJ's ED SIMONS and TOM ROWLANDS. Both had been students at Manchester University, where they worked under the borrowed name of The DUST BROTHERS (US rap producers) to work on versions of 'Song to The Siren' and 'Chemical Beats'. Due to an objection by said rap artists, they became The CHEMICAL BROTHERS and appeared on numerous production work for the likes of CHARLATANS, PRIMAL SCREAM and The MANICS. They finally unleashed their debut album 'EXIT PLANET DUST', which made UK Top 10 lists. • **Style:** Young techno wizards of distorted hip-hop and a wide variety of sounds. • **Songwriters:** ROWLANDS-SIMONS except samples of Blake Baxters 'Brothers Gonna Work It Out' on 'LEAVE HOME'/ Borrowed Swallow's; 'Peekaboo' & 'Follow Me Down'.

Recommended: EXIT PLANET DUST (*8)

TOM ROWLANDS + ED SIMONS with voices by **TIM BURGESS** (CHARLATANS) + **BETH ORTON** (PORTISHEAD)

Junior Boy's Own / Virgin

Jun 95. (d12")(cd-s) **LEAVE HOME (Sabres Of Paradise mix). / LEAVE HOME (Underworld mix) / LET ME IN MATE** [17] [ ]

Jun 95. (cd)(c)(d-lp) **EXIT PLANET DUST** [9] [ ]

– Leave home / In dust we trust / Song to he siren / Three little birdies down beats / Fuck up beats / Chemical beats / Chico's groove / One too many mornings / Life is sweet / Playground for a wedgeless firm / Alive alone.

Aug 95. (12")(cd-s) **LIFE IS SWEET. / ('A'-daft punk remix) / ('A'remix 1) / (A'remix 2)** 25 –
(cd-s) – (A-remix 1, repl.by) Leave home (terror burns).
(cd-s) – ('A'remix 1) / If you kling to me I'll klong to you / Chico's groove (mix 2).

. . . Jan – Jun '96 stop press . . .

Jan 96. (single) **LOOPS OF FURY EP** 13 –

CHICAGO

Formed: Chicago, Illinois, USA ... 1966 as CHICAGO TRANSIT AUTHORITY on the idea of friend/manager/producer James William Guercio. The band (KATH and PARAZAIDER, etc.) moved to Los Angeles and recorded hit debut eponymous album for 'CBS/Columbia' 1969. That year, due to legal threats, they shortened name to CHICAGO. They became one of America's top bands of the 70's & 80's, and scored 2 US No.1's with 'IF YOU LEAVE ME NOW' (1976) & 'HARD TO SAY I'M SORRY' (1982). • **Style:** Brass-laden jazz-pop rock in the 60's, moving into soft-AOR in the mid 70's. Due to this new guaranteed formula for hits, they stayed with this style throughout the 80's. • **Songwriters:** LAMM wrote lyrics, KATH and group the music. Covered I'M A MAN (Spencer Davis Group). • **Trivia:** 80's newcomer JASON SCHEFF was son of Elvis Presley's bassman JERRY.

Recommended: CHICAGO IX GREATEST HITS (*6).

ROBERT LAMM (b.13 Oct'44, Brooklyn, New York) – vocals, keyboards / **TERRY KATH** (b.31 Jan'46) – vocals, guitar / **PETER CETERA** (b.13 Sep'44) – vocals, bass / **DAN SERAPHINE** (b.28 Aug'48) – drums / **LEE LOUGHNANE** (b.21 Oct'46) – trumpet, vocals / **JAMES PANKOW** (b.20 Aug'47) – trombone / **WALTER PARAZAIDER** (b.14 Mar'48) – reeds

C.B.S. – Columbia

Sep 69. (d-lp) **CHICAGO TRANSIT AUTHORITY** (as "CHICAGO TRANSIT AUTHORITY") 9 – 17 May69
– (introduction) / Does anybody really know what time it is? / Beginnings / Questions 67 and 68 / Listen / Poem 58 / Free form guitar / South California purples / I'm a man / (prologue, August 29, 1968) / Someday / Liberation. *(re-iss.+c+cd.Sep87) (cd-iss.Oct93 on 'Sony Europe') (re-iss.cd+c Jun94 on 'Columbia')*

Jul 69. (7") **QUESTIONS 67 AND 68. / LISTEN** – 71
Dec 69. (7") **I'M A MAN. / DOES ANYBODY REALLY KNOW WHAT THE TIME IS?** 8 –
Mar 70. (d-lp) **CHICAGO II** 6 – 4 Feb 70
– Movin' in / The road / Poem for the people / In the country / Wake up sunshine (ballet for a girl in Buchannon) / Make me smile / So much to say, so much to give / Anxiety's moment / West Virginia fantasies / Colour my world / To be free / Now more than ever / Fancy colours / 25 or 6 to 4 / (prelude) / A.M. mourning / P.M. mourning / Memories of love / It better end soon (movements 1-5) / Where do we go from here. *(cd-iss.Oct93 on 'Sony Europe')*

Apr 70. (7") **MAKE ME SMILE. / COLOUR MY WORLD** – 9
Jul 70. (7") **25 OR 6 TO 4. / WHERE DO WE GO FROM HERE** 7 – 4
Nov 70. (7") **DOES ANYBODY REALLY KNOW WHAT THE TIME IS?. / LISTEN** - – 7
Feb 71. (7") **FREE. / FREE COUNTRY** – 20
Mar 71. (d-lp) **CHICAGO III** 31 – 2 Jan 71
– Sing a mean tune kid / Loneliness is just a word / What else can I say / I don't want your money / Flight 602 / Motorboat to Mars / Free / Free country / At the sunrise / Happy 'cause I'm going home / Mother / Lowdown / A hard risin' morning without breakfast / Off to work / Fallin' out / Morning blues again / When all the laughter dies in sorrow / Canon / Once upon a time / Progress? / The approaching storm / Man vs. man / The end. *(cd-iss.Oct93 on 'Sony Europe')*

May 71. (7") **LOWDOWN. / LONELINESS IS JUST A WORD** – 35
Jul 71. (7") **BEGINNINGS. / COLOUR MY WORLD** – 7 Jun 71
Nov 71. (q-lp) **LIVE AT CARNEGIE HALL (live)** – 3
– In the country / Fancy colours / Does anybody really know what time it is? / Free form guitar / South California purples / Questions 67 and 68 / Sing a mean tune kid / Beginnings / It better end soon (5 movements) / (introduction) / Mother / Lowdown / Flight 602 / Motorboat to Mars / Where do we go from here / I don't want your money / Happy 'cause I'm going home / Wake up sunshine (ballet for a girl in Buchannon) / Make me smile / So much to say, so much to give / Anxiety's moment / West Virginia fantasies / Colour my world / To be free / Free / Now more than ever / A song for Richard and his friends / 25 or 6 to 4 / I'm a man. *(cd-iss.Apr89)*

Jan 72. (7") **QUESTIONS 67 AND 68 (live). / I'M A MAN (live)** - –
Aug 72. (7") **SATURDAY IN THE PARK. / ALMA MATER** – 3
Sep 72. (lp)(c) **CHICAGO V** 24 – 1 Jul 72
– Saturday in the park / A hit by Varese / All is well / Now that you've gone / Dialogue (part 1 & 2) / While the city sleeps / State of the union / Alma mater / Goodbye. *(re-iss.Apr84 on 'Hallmark') (cd-iss.1988) cd-iss.Nov93 on 'Sony Collectors')*

Nov 72. (7") **DIALOGUE (pt.1 & 2). / NOW THAT YOU'VE GONE** – 24 Oct 72
Aug 73. (7") **FEELIN' STRONGER EVERY DAY. / JENNY** – 10 Jun 73
Aug 73. (lp)(c) **CHICAGO VI** – 1 Jul 73
– Critic's choice / Just you 'n' me / Darlin' dear / Jenny / What's this world comin' to / Something in this city changes people / Hollywood / Jenny / In terms of two / Rediscovery / Feelin' stronger every day.

Sep 73. (7") **JUST YOU 'N' ME. / CRITIC'S CHOICE** - – 4
Oct 73. (7") **JUST YOU 'N' ME. / FEELIN' STRONGER EVERY DAY** – -
Apr 74. (7") **(I'VE BEEN) SEARCHIN' SO LONG. / BYBLOS** – 9 Mar 74
May 74. (lp)(c) **CHICAGO VII** – 1 Mar 74
– (prelude to Aire) / Aire / Devil's sweet / Halian from New York / Hanky panky / Life saver / Happy man / (I've been) Searchin' so long / Mongonucleosis / Song of the evergreens / Byblos / Wishing you were here / Call on me / Woman don't want to love me / Skinny boy. *(cd-iss.May88)*

Oct 74. (7") **CALL ON ME. / AIRE** – 6 Jun74
Oct 74. (7") **WISHING YOU WERE HERE. / LIFE SAVER** - – 11
Nov 74. (7") **WISHING YOU WERE HERE. / SONG OF THE EVERGREENS** – -
Mar 75. (7") **HARRY TRUMAN. / TILL WE MEET AGAIN** – 13 Feb 75
Apr 75. (lp)(c) **CHICAGO VIII** – 1
– Anyway you want / Brand new love affair (pt.I & II) / Never been in love before / Hideaway / Till we meet again / Harry Truman / Oh, thank you great spirit / Long time no see / Ain't it blue / Old days.

Jun 75. (7") **OLD DAYS. / HIDEAWAY** – 5 Apr 75
Aug 75. (7") **NEVER BEEN IN LOVE BEFORE. / (part 2)** –
Oct 75. (7") **BRAND NEW LOVE AFFAIR. / HIDEAWAY** – 61
Oct 75. (lp)(c) **CHICAGO IX GREATEST HITS** (compilation) – 1
– 25 or 6 to 4 / Does anybody really know what time it is? / Colour my world / Just you 'n' me / Saturday in the park / Feelin' stronger every day / Make me smile / Wishing you were here / Call on me / (I've been) Searchin' so long / Beginnings. *(re-iss.Nov84) (cd-iss.Jul87)*

Jul 76. (7") **ANOTHER RAINY DAY IN NEW YORK. / HOPE FOR LOVE** – 32 Jun 76
Jul 76. (lp)(c) **CHICAGO X** 21 – 3
– Once or twice / You are on my mind / Skin tight / If you leave me now / Together again / Another rainy day in New York City / Mama mama / Scrapbook / Gently I'll wake you / You get it up / Hope for love. *(cd-iss.1988)*

Sep 76. (7") **IF YOU LEAVE ME NOW. / TOGETHER AGAIN** 1 – 1
Feb 77. (7") **YOU ARE ON MY MIND. / GENTLY I'LL WAKE YOU** - – 49
Sep 77. (lp)(c) **CHICAGO XI** – 6
– Mississippi Delta queen blues / Baby, what a big surprise / Policeman / Till the end of time / Take me back to Chicago / Vote for me / Takin' it on uptown / This time / The inner struggles of a man / (prelude) / Little one. *(cd-iss.1988)*

Sep 77. (7") **BABY, WHAT A BIG SURPRISE. / TAKIN' IT ON UPTOWN** 41 – 4
Jan 78. (7") **TAKE ME BACK TO CHICAGO. / POLICEMAN** – 63 May 78
Mar 78. (7") **LITTLE ONE. / TILL THE END OF TIME** – 44 Feb 78

—— On the 23rd Jan'78, TERRY KATH died, accidentally shooting himself in the head. Later in year, he was repl. by **DONNIE DACUS** – guitar (ex-STEPHEN STILLS)

Sep 78. (lp)(c) **HOT STREETS** – 12
– Alive again / The greatest love on Earth / Little Miss Lovin' / Hot streets / Take a chance / Gone long gone / Ain't it time / Love was new / No tell lover / Show me the way. *(re-iss.cd+c May93 on 'Sony Collectors')*

Oct 78. (7") **ALIVE AGAIN. / LOVE WAS NEW** – 14
Mar 79. (7") **NO TELL LOVER. / TAKE A CHANCE** – 14 Dec 78
Apr 79. (7") **GONE LONG GONE. / THE GREATEST LOVE ON EARTH** - – 73
Aug 79. (7") **MUST HAVE BEEN CRAZY. / CLOSER TO YOU** – 83
Sep 79. (lp)(c) **CHICAGO 13 - STREET PLAYER** – 21 Aug 79
– Street player / Mama take / Must have been crazy / Window dreamin' / Paradise alley / Aloha mama / Reruns / Loser with a broken heart / Life is what it is / Run away.

Oct 79. (7") **MAMA TAKE. / WINDOW DREAMIN'** – -
Apr 80. (7") **STREET PLAYER. / WINDOW DREAMIN'** –

—— **CHRIS PINNICK** – guitar repl. DACUS

Jun 80. (7") **THUNDER AND LIGHTNING. / I'D RATHER BE RICH** - – 56 Aug 80
Aug 80. (7") **SONG FOR YOU. / I'D RATHER BE RICH** - –
Sep 80. (7") **THE AMERICAN DREAM / SONG FOR YOU** – -
Sep 80. (lp)(c) **CHICAGO XIV** – 71 Aug 80
– Manipulation / Upon arrival / Song for you / Where did the lovin' go / Birthday boy / Hold on / Overnight cafe / Thunder and lightning / I'd rather be rich / The American dream.

Dec 81. (lp)(c) **CHICAGO - GREATEST HITS, VOLUME II** (compilation) –
– Baby, what a big surprise / Dialogue (part 1 & 2) / No tell lover / Alive again / Old days / If you leave me now / Questions 67 and 68 / Happy man / Gone long gone / Take me back to Chicago.

— added **BILL CHAMPLIN** – vocals, bass, guitar (ex-SONS OF CHAMPLIN)

Full Moon / Full Moon

Jun 82. (lp)(c) **CHICAGO 16** [44] [9]
– What you're missing / Waiting for you to decide / Bad advice / Chains / Hard to say I'm sorry / Get away / Follow me / Sonny think twice / Rescue you / What can I say / Love me tomorrow. *(cd-iss.1983)*
Aug 82. (7") **HARD TO SAY I'M SORRY. / SONNY THINK TWICE** [4] [1] Jun 82
Nov 82. (7") **LOVE ME TOMORROW. / BAD ADVICE** [ ] [22] Sep 82
Jan 83. (7") **WHAT YOU'RE MISSING. / RESCUE YOU** [-] [81]
Jun 84. (7") **STAY THE NIGHT. / ONLY YOU** [ ] [16] Apr84
Jul 84. (lp)(c)(cd) **CHICAGO 17** [24] [4] May 84
– Stay the night / We can stop the hurtin' / Hard habit to break / Only you / Remember the feeling / Along comes a woman / You're the inspiration / Please hold on / Prima Donna / Once in a lifetime.
Oct 84. (7") **HARD HABIT TO BREAK. / REMEMBER THE FEELING** [8] [3] Aug 84
Jan 85. (7") **YOU'RE THE INSPIRATION. / LOVE ME TOMORROW** [14] [3] Nov 84
(12"+=) – Once in a lifetime. (US B-side)
Mar 85. (7")(12") **ALONG COMES A WOMAN. / WE CAN STOP THE HURTIN'** [ ] [14] Feb 85

— **JERRY SCHEFF** – bass repl. CETERA who goes solo.

Oct 86. (7") **25 OR 6 TO 4 (remix). / ONE MORE DAY** [ ] [48] Sep 86
(12"+=) – Hard habit to break.
Oct 86. (lp)(c)(cd) **CHICAGO 18** [ ] [35]
– Niagara Falls / Forever / If she would have been faithfull / 25 or 6 to 4 / Will you still love me? / Over and over / It's alright / Nothin's gonna stop us now / I believe / One more day. *(re-iss.cd Feb93)*
Nov 86. (7") **WILL YOU STILL LOVE ME? / 25 OR 6 TO 4** [-] [3]
Feb 87. (7") **WILL YOU STILL LOVE ME? / FOREVER** [ ] [-]
(12"+=) – Hard habit to break.
Jul 87. (7") **NIAGARA FALLS. /** [-] [91]
Oct 87. (7") **IF SHE WOULD HAVE BEEN FAITHFUL. / FOREVER** [ ] [17] Mar 87
(12"+=) – 25 or 6 to 4.

Warners / Reprise

Jun 88. (lp)(c)(cd) **CHICAGO 19** [ ] [43]
– Heart in pieces / I don't want to live without your love / I stand up / We can last forever / Come in from the night / Look away / What kind of man would I be? / Runaround / You're not alone / Victorious.
Aug 88. (7")(c-s) **I DON'T WANNA LIVE WITHOUT YOUR LOVE. / I STAND UP** [ ] [3] Jun 88
(12"+=) – 25 or 6 to 4.
(cd-s+=) – Will you still love me?.
Sep 88. (7")(c-s) **LOOK AWAY. / COME IN FROM THE NIGHT** [ ] [1]
(12"+=)(cd-s+=) – 25 or 6 to 4.
Jan 89. (7")(c-s) **YOU'RE NOT ALONE. / IT'S ALRIGHT** [-] [10]
May 89. (7")(c-s) **WE CAN'T LAST FOREVER. / ONE MORE DAY** [-] [55]
Jan 90. (cd)(c)(lp) **GREATEST HITS 1982-1989** (compilation) [ ] [37] Dec 89
Feb 90. (7") **WHAT KIND OF MAN WOULD I BE? / 25 OR 6 TO 4** [ ] [5] Dec 89
(12"+=)(cd-s+=) – You're the inspiration / Hard to say I'm sorry.
Jul 90. (7") **HEART'S IN TROUBLE. / ('B'side by 'Hans Zimmer')** [ ] [75]
(12"+=)(cd-s+=) – (track by other artist) *(above on 'D.G.C.' US)*

— Trimmed when SERAPHINE departed Aug90.

Jan 91. (c-s) **CHASIN' THE WIND. / ONLY TIME CAN HEAL THE WOUNDED** [-] [39]
May 91. (cd)(c)(lp) **TWENTY 1** [ ] [66] Feb 91
– Explain to my heart / If it were you / You come to my senses / Somebody somewhere / What does it take / One from the heart / Chasin' the wind / God save the Queen / Man to woman / Only time can heal the wounded / Who do you love / Holdin' on.

not issued / Giant

Jun 95. (cd)(c) **NIGHT AND DAY** [-] [90]

– other compilations, etc. –

(all 'C.B.S.' releases were on 'Columbia' counterpart in US)

Apr 73. C.B.S.; (7") **25 OR 6 TO 4. / MAKE ME SMILE** [ ] [ ]
(re-iss.Mar75 & 76)
1975. C.B.S.; (7") **BEGINNINGS. / QUESTIONS 67 AND 68** [ ] [ ]
1975. C.B.S.; (7") **COLOUR MY WORLD. / I'M A MAN** [ ] [ ]
1975. C.B.S.; (7") **DOES ANYBODY REALLY KNOW WHAT THE TIME IS? / FREE** [ ] [ ]
1975. C.B.S.; (7") **SATURDAY IN THE PARK. / DIALOGUE** [ ] [ ]
Aug 75. C.B.S.; (7") **WISHING YOU WERE HERE. / LIFESAVER** [ ] [ ]
Jan 77. C.B.S.; (7") **WISHING YOU WERE HERE. / GENTLY I'LL WAKE YOU** [ ] [ ]
Mar 79. C.B.S.; (7") **I'M A MAN. / 25 OR 6 TO 4** [ ] [ ]
Nov 82. C.B.S.; (7") **IF YOU LEAVE ME NOW. / 25 OR 6 TO 4** [ ] [ ]
Nov 82. C.B.S.; (lp)(c) **IF YOU LEAVE ME NOW** [ ] [ ]
(re-iss.Apr86, cd-iss.Dec92)
Jan 83. C.B.S.; (c-ep) **GREATEST ORIGINAL HITS** [ ] [-]
– If you leave me now / 25 or 6 to 4 / Baby, what a big surprise / Wishing you were here.
Aug 88. C.B.S.; (3"cd-s) **25 OR 6 To 4. / MAKE ME SMILE** [-] [ ]
Nov 82. Virgin TV; (lp)(c) **LOVE SONGS** [42] [-]
Dec 83. Meteor; (lp) **BEGINNINGS** [ ] [-]
(re-iss.Jan85 on 'Topline') (cd-iss.Feb93 on 'Charly')
Jul 84. Design; (pic-lp) **TORONTO ROCK'N'ROLL REVIVAL (live)** [ ] [-]
(cd-iss.Jul91 on 'Thunderbolt')
Apr 86. Showcase; (lp)(c) **CHICAGO LIVE (live)** [ ] [-]
(cd-iss.Dec88 on 'Spectrum')
Feb 89. Crusader; (lp) **THE BEST OF CHICAGO** [ ] [-]
May 89. That's Original; (d-lp(c)(cd) **THE COLLECTION** [ ] [-]
– (CHIGAGO XIII / STREET PLAYER)
Nov 89. Warners; (lp)(c)(cd) **THE HEART OF CHICAGO** [9] [ ]
– (c/cd+=3 extra) *(re-iss.cd+c Feb94, re-hit UK No.6)*
Apr 93. Pulsar; (cd) **I'M A MAN & OTHER GREAT HITS LIVE (live)** [ ] [-]
May 94. Columbia-Legacy; (4xcd-box)(4xc-box) **GROUP PORTRAIT** [ ] [ ]
Aug 94. Legends In Music; (cd) **CHICAGO** [ ] [-]
Sep 94. Prestige; (cd) **25 OR 6 TO 4** [ ] [-]

ROBERT LAMM

C.B.S. / Columbia

1974. (lp)(c) **SKINNY BOY** [ ] [ ]
– Temporary Jones / Love song / Crazy ways to spend a year / Until the times run out / Skinny boy / One step forward, two steps back / Fireplace and Ivy / Someday I'm gonna go / A lifetime we / City living / Crazy brother John.

CHUMBAWAMBA

Formed: Burnley /Barnsley, Yorkshire, England . . . 1980 by sextet who shacked up in Leeds commune (see below). In 1982, they appeared as SKIN DISEASE on a single 'BACK ON THE STREETS'. CHUMBAWAMBA toured a year later with CRASS, while releasing 3 cassettes independently. In 1985 /86, they caused controversy by issuing records arguing the merits of the BAND /LIVE AID charity causes. Needless to say, these were banned from radio airplay. More publicity surrounded them around this time, when they poured red paint over The CLASH, when they arrived in Leeds for their 'Busking Britain Tour'. The early 90's saw them finally appreciated by the new hippy crustie scene, culminating in their 1994 album 'ANARCHY' cracking the Top 30. • **Style:** Vegan / non-smoking politicised and animal-rights outfit, like MADDY PRIOR (Steeleye Span) fusing with CRASS. • **Songwriters:** Group, except some traditional Hungarian folk tunes. Also sampled JOHN LENNON (Imagine), ELVIS, ALTERNATIVE TV, GANG OF FOUR, CRASS, FALL, X-RAY SPEX, STIFF LITTLE FINGERS, DAGMAR KRAUSE and GERSHWIN!. The lp 'ENGLISH REBEL SONGS' were all traditional. Covered on 'JESUS H CHRIST'; ALRIGHT NOW (Free) / MONEY, MONEY, MONEY (Abba) / SOLID GOLD EASY ACTION (T.Rex) / HEY YOU GET OFF MY CLOUD (Rolling Stones) / STAIRWAY TO HEAVEN (Led Zeppelin) / BIGMOUTH STRIKES AGAIN (Smiths) / I SHOULD BE SO LUCKY (Kylie Minogue)/ MANNEQUIN (Wire) / HUNCHBACK OF NOTRE DAME (Frantic Elevators; Mick Hucknall). • **Trivia:** In 1982, track 'THREE YEARS LATER' appeared on 'Crass' label album 'BULLSHIT DETECTOR 2'. ALICE NUTTER was named after a 17th century witch. DANBERT NOBACON released a single before he joined them, which featured a picture of his utensil on the cover!. 'NEVER SAY DI' single (proceeds to charity) was surprisingly in support of Princess Diana, as they were anti-royalists. 'BEHAVE!' was a tribute ha!, about 'The Hit Man And Her' (aka PETE WATERMAN & MICHAELA).

Recommended: PICTURES OF STARVING CHILDREN SELL RECORDS (*7) / SHHH (*8) / ANARCHY (*9)

ALICE NUTTER – vocals / **ALAN WHALLEY** – guitar, vocals / **(FRANK) BOFF** – guitar, vocals / **LOUISE MARY WATTS** – keyboards, vocals / **MAVIS DILLON** – brass / **BILLY McCOID** – drums

— (released 3 cassettes before the mid-80's)

Agit Prop / not issued

Sep 85. (7"ep) **REVOLUTION** [ ] [-]
–
Apr 86. (7") **WE ARE THE WORLD. / A STATE OF MIND** [ ] [-]
In 1986, they issued DESTROY FASCISM as The ANTIDOTE; alongside The EX.

Oct 86. (lp) **PICTURES OF STARVING CHILDREN SELL RECORDS** [ ] [-]
– How to get your band on television / British colonialism and the BBC – flicking pictures hypnotise / Commercial break / Unilever / More whitwashing / . . .An interlude: Beginning to take it back / Dutiful servants and political masters / Cocoa colanisation / . . .And in a nutshell 'food aid is our most powerful weapon' / Invasion.

Jul 87. (lp) **NEVER MIND THE BALLOTS: HERE'S THE REST OF YOUR LIFE** [ ] [-]
– Always tell the voter what he voter wants to hear / Come on baby (let's do the revolution) / The wasteland / Today's sermon / Ah-men / Mr. Heseltine meets his public / The candidates find common ground / Here's the rest of your life.

— Under the name SCAB AID, they issued 'Let It Be' on the 'Scum' label.

Jul 88. (7") **FIGHT THE ALTON BILL. / SMASH CLAUSE 28** [ ] [-]

Oct 88. (10"lp) **ENGLISH REBEL SONGS 1381-1914** [ ] [-]
– The Cutty wren / The diggers song / Colliers march / The triumph of General Ludd / Chartist anthem / Song of the times / Smashing of the van / World turned upside down / Poverty knock / Idris strike song / Hanging on the old barbed wire / The Cutty wren (reprise). *(re-iss.lp Nov89) (re-iss.+cd Feb93 & Feb95 on 'One Little Indian')*

— In Dec89; they appeared on 'Agit Prop' Various Artists (SPORTCHESTRA) lp '101 SONGS ABOUT SPORT'. Another Various 'THIS SPORTING LIFE' was iss.Aug90.

Jul 90. (cd)(lp) **SLAP!** [ ] [-]
– Ulrike / Tiananmen Square / Car trouble / Chase PC's flee attack by own dog / Rubens has been shot! / I never gave up (Rappoport's testament) / Gave up / Slap! / That's how grateful we are / Meinhof. *(re-iss.+c Feb95 on 'One Little Indian')*

— In Mar91, CHUMBAWAMBA AND OTHER SUBVERSIVES released 7"; GREATEST HITS for 'Peasant Revolt'. At the same time ALICE and LOUISE (I think?) as The PASSION KILLERS released mail-order EP 'FOUR WAR IS SHIT SONGS' featuring tracks 'Shipbuilding', 'Reuters' + 2 for 'Rugger Bugger' records.

— now a 8-piece group **ALICE, LOUISE, BOFF** (NIGEL HUTTER), **ALAN** (DANBERT BACON) plus **DUNSTON BRUCE** – vocals, percussion / **HARRY** (DARREN HAMMER) – drums, percussion / **MAVE** (MAVIS DILLON) – keyboards / **PAUL GRECO** – bass w / **MATTY** (MC FUSION) – vocals (of CREDIT TO THE NATION) / **COMMON KNOWLEDGE** – keyboards, accordion, vocals / **NEIL FERGUSON** – guitar, keys

Jan 92. (7") **I NEVER GAVE UP (RAPPAPORT'S TESTAMENT). / LAUGHING** [ ] [ ]
(12") – ('A'-Rondo mix) / ('A'cass mix).
(cd-s) – (all 4 tracks). *(re-iss.Jul94 on 'Southern')*

Jun 92. (cd)(c)(lp) **SHHH** [ ] [-]
– Shhh / Big mouth strikes again / Nothing that's new / Behave! / Snip snip snip / Look! no strings! / Happiness is just a chant away / Pop star kidnap / Sometimes plunder / You can't trust anyone nowadays / Stitch that. *(re-iss.Nov94 on 'Southern')*

Jul 92. (7") **NEVER SAY DI. / FOR THE LOVE OF A PRINCESS** [ ] [-]

Nov 92. (12")(cd-s) **SOMEONE'S ALWAYS TELLING YOU HOW TO BEHAVE!. / (2-'A'mixes by PAPA BRITTLE)** [ ] [-]

Dec 92. (cd)(c)(lp) **JESUS H CHRIST** [ ] [ ]
– Alright now / Money, money, money / Solid gold easy action / Silly love songs / Hey you get off my cloud / Stairway to Heaven / Bigmouth strikes again / I should be so lucky.

O. L. Indian Elektra?

Sep 93. (12"ep)(c-ep)(cd-ep) **ENOUGH IS ENOUGH. / HEAR NO BULLSHIT (on fire mix) / THE DAY THE NAZI DIED (1993 mix)** [56] [ ]

— (above was with CREDIT TO THE NATION)

Nov 93. (12"ep)(c-ep)(cd-ep) **TIMEBOMB. / TECHNO THE BOMB / THE WORLD TURNED UPSIDE DOWN** [59] [ ]

Dec 93. (12"ep)(c-ep)(cd-ep) **LOVE IS ON THE WAY. / ?** [59] [ ]

May 94. (cd)(c)(lp) **ANARCHY** [29] [ ]
– Give the anarchist a cigarette / Timebomb / Homophobia / On being pushed / Heaven – Hell / Love me / Georgina / Doh! / Blackpool rock / This year's thing / Mouthful of shit / Never do what you are told / Bad dog / Enough is enough / Rage.

— Next credited with The SISTERS OF PERPETUAL INDULGENCE

May 94. (12"ep)(c-ep)(cd-ep) **HOMOPHOBIA (with The SISTERS OF PERPETUAL INDULGENCE). / MORALITY PLAY IN THREE ACTS / ('A'acappella mix) / SONG FOR DEREK JARMEN** [ ] [ ]
(cd-s) – ('A'side) / Enough is enough (w / CREDIT TO THE NATION) / The day the Nazi died (w / CREDIT TO THE NATION) / Morality play in three acts.

Mar 95. (cd)(c)(lp) **SHOWBUSINESS! CHUMBAWAMBA LIVE (live)** [ ] [-]
– Never do what you are told / I never gave up / Give the anarchist a cigarette / Heaven-Hell / That's how grateful we are / Homophobia / Morality play in three acts / Bad dog / Stitch that / Mouthful of shit / The day the Nazi died / Time bomb (Jimmy Echo vocal) / Slag aid.

Oct 95. (7")(c-s) **UGH! YOUR UGLY HOUSES!. / THIS GIRL** [ ] [-]
(cd-s+=) – Mannequin / Hunchback of Notre Dame.

Oct 95. (d-cd)(c)(d-lp) **SWINGIN' WITH RAYMOND** [70] [ ]
– This girl / Never let go / Just look at me now / Not the girl I used to be / The morning after (the night before) / Love can knock you over / All mixed up / This dress kills / Salome (let's twist again) / Oxymoron / Waiting, shouting / Hey you! outside now! / Ugh! your ugly houses.

. . . Jan – Jun '96 stop press . . .

Apr 96. (cd+book) **PORTRAITS OF ANARCHISTS** [ ] [-]

– compilations, others, etc. –

Feb 92. Agit Prop; (cd)(lp) **FIRST 2** [ ] [-]
– (as said 1st 2 albums, originally Aug89 as '100 SONGS ABOUT SPORT') (re-iss.d-cd/d-c Feb95 on 'One Little Indian')

CICCONE YOUTH (see under ⇒ SONIC YOUTH)

CLANNAD

Formed: Donegal, Ireland . . . 1970, the offspring of Irish bandleader LEE O.BRAONAIN. CLANNAD means "Family" in Gaelic. After noteable Irish album releases in the 70's and early 80's, they signed worldwide to 'RCA', where they hit the charts with TV 'Theme from HARRY'S GAME'. It received an Ivor Novello award in 1983, with 1984's ROBIN OF SHERWOOD also gaining British Academy Award. BONO of U2, a great fan, provided dual vocals on their 1986/89 Top 20 hit IN A LIFETIME. • **Style:** Traditional folk group, that moved into well crafted mystical folk rock for the 80's. • **Songwriters:** POL and CIARAN penned most except covers I SEE RED (Jim Rafferty) / and lots of traditional Irish tunes. • **Trivia:** In 1987, American producers RUSS KUNKEL and GREG LADANYI were used on SIRIUS album, which also featured guests J.D. SOUTHER, BRUCE HORNSBY and STEVE PERRY.

Recommended: PASTPRESENT (*8)

MAIRE NI BHRAONAIN – vocals, harp / **POL O. BRAONAIN** – guitar, keyboards, vocals / **CIARAN O. BRAONAIN** – bass, synthesizer, vocals / **NOEL O. DUGAIN** – guitar, vocals / **PANDRAIG O. DUGAIN** – mandolin, guitar, vocals(twin uncles)

Philips not issued

1973. (lp) **CLANNAD** [-] [-] Ire
– Nil se ina la / Thois chois na tra domh / Brian Boru's march / Siobhan ni dhuibhir / An mhaighdean mhara / Liza / An toilean ur / Mrs. McDermott / The pretty maid / An phairc / Harvest home / Morning dew.. *(re-iss. 1982 as 'THE PRETTY MAID').*

1974. (lp) **CLANNAD II** [-] [-] Ire
– An gabhar ban / Eleanor Plunkett / Coinleach ghlas an fhomain / Rince philib a' cheoil / By chance it was / Rince briotanach / Dheanainn sugradh / Gaoth barra na dtonn / Teidhir abhaile riu / Fairly shot of her / Chuargh me ha. *(re-iss.May79, UK re-iss.+cd Jan89 on 'Shanachie')*

Gael-Linn not issued

1976. (lp) **DULAMAN** [-] [-] Ire
– Dulaman / Cumha coghain vi Neill / Two sisters / Eirirgh suas a stoirin / The Galtee hunt / Eirigh ic cui ort do chuid eadaigh soiriu / Siuil a run / Mo Mhaire / Dtig eas a damhsa / Cucanandy -The Jug of brown ale.*(re-iss.May79, UK re-iss.+cd.Jan89 on 'Shanachie') #010*

Ogham not issued

Sep 79. (7") **DOWN BY THE SALLY GARDENS. / ELEANOR PLUNKET** [-] [-] Ire

Sep 79. (lp) **CLANNAD IN CONCERT (live)** [-] [-] Ire
– Bhean a ti / Fairies hornpipe off to California / Neansai mhile gra / Mhaire Bruineall / Planxty Burke / An giobog / Down by the Sally gardens / Nil se'n la. *(re-iss.'82 on 'Tara', UK-iss.+cd.1987+Jan89 on 'Shanachie')*

Philips not issued

1981. (lp) **CRANN ULL** [-] [-] Ire
– Ar A Ghabhail 'n A 'chuain Damh / The Last Rose Of Summer / Cruscin LÆn / Bacach Shile Andai / La Coimhtioch Fan Dtuath / Crann Ull / Gathering Mushrooms / Bunan Bui / Planxty Browne. *(Ire-iss.'80 on 'Tara', UK re-iss.Nov82 on 'Philips')*

— added **ENYA NI BHRAONAIN** – vocals, keyboards

Tara not issued

1982. (lp) **FUAIM** [-] [-] Ire
– Na buachailli alainh / Mheall si lena ghoithai me / Bruach na carraige baine / La brea fan btuath / An tull / Strayed away / Ni la na gaoithe la na scoilb? / Lish young buy-a-broom / Mhroag's na horo gheallaidh / The green fields of Gaothdobhair / Buai reamh phosta. *(re-iss.cd/c/lp Apr90 on 'Cooking Vinyl')*

1982. (7") **MHORAG'S NA HORO GHEAHAIDH. / STRAYED AWAY** [-] [-] Ire

1982. (7") **THEME FROM HARRY'S GAME. / STRAYED AWAY** [-] [-] Ire

— reverted to original quintet when ENYA went solo

R.C.A. Atlantic

Oct 82. (7") **THEME FROM HARRY'S GAME. / STRAYED AWAY** [5] [ ]

Feb 83. (lp)(c) **MAGICAL RING** [26] [ ]
– Theme from 'Harry's Game' / Tower hill / Seachran charn siall / Passing time / Coinleach glasan fhomhair / I see red / Ta me no shui / Newgrange / The fairy queen / Thios fa'n chosta. *(re-iss.May84, hit 91) (re-iss.+cd Oct87)*

Mar 83. (7") **I SEE RED. / TA ME NO SHUI** [ ] [ ]
May 83. (7") **NEWGRANGE. / SEARCHRAN AND TISAIL** [65] [ ]
Apr 84. (7") **ROBIN (THE HOODED MAN). / LADY MARIAN** [42] [ ]
May 84. (lp)(c) **LEGEND (MUSIC FROM ROBIN OF SHERWOOD)** [15] [ ]
– Robin (the hooded man) / Now is here / Herne / Together we / Dark mere / Strange land / Scarlet inside / Lady Marian / Battles / Ancient forest. *(cd-iss.'87)*

Jun 84. (7") **NOW IS HERE. / TOGETHER WE** [ ] [ ]
Mar 85. (7") **SCARLET INSIDE. / ROBIN (THE HOODED MAN)** [ ] [ ]
(12"+=) – Theme from Harry's Game.

R.C.A. R.C.A.

Sep 85. (7") **CLOSER TO YOUR HEART. / BUACHAILL AN EIREN** [ ] [ ]
(12"+=) – Theme from Harry's Game / Robin (The hooded man). *(re-iss.Feb86)*

Oct 85. (lp)(c) **MACALLA** (means 'Echo') [33] [ ]
– Caislean oir / The wild cry / Closer to your heart / In a lifetime / Almost seems (too late to turn) / Indoor / Buachaill on Eirne / Blackstairs / Journey's end / Northern skyline. *(cd-iss.'87) (re-iss.cd Sep93)*

Nov 85. (7") **ALMOST SEEMS (TOO LATE TO TURN). / JOURNEY'S END** [ ] [ ]
(12"+=) – Theme from Harry's Game / Robin (The hooded man).

Jan 86. (7") **IN A LIFETIME ("CLANNAD featuring BONO"). / INDOOR** [20] [ ]
(12"+=) – Northern skyline / Newgrange.

Sep 87. (7") **SOMETHING TO BELIVE IN. / SECOND NATURE** [ ] [ ]
(12"+=) – In a lifetime.

Oct 87. (lp)(c)(cd) **SIRIUS** [34] [ ]
– White fool / Something to believe in / Live and learn / Many roads / Sirius / In search of a heart / Second nature / Turning tide / Skelig / Stepping stone.

Jan 88. (7") **WHITE FOOL. / MANY ROADS** [ ] [ ]
(12"+=) – Closer to your heart.

Jan 89. (lp)(c)(cd) **ATLANTIC REALM (BBC soundtrack)** [41] [ ]
– Atlantic realm / Predator / Moving thru / The Berbers / Signs of life / In flight / Ocean of light / Drifting / Under Neptune's cape / Voyager / Primeval sun / Child of the sea / The kirk pride. *(issued on 'BBC' records)*

Feb 89. (7") **THE HUNTER. / ATLANTIC REALM** [ ] [ ]
(12"+=) – Skelig / Turning tide.

Apr 89. (lp)(c)(cd) **PAST PRESENT** (compilation) [5] [ ]
– Theme from Harry's Game / Closer to your heart / Almost seems (too late to turn) / The hunter / Lady Marian / Sirius / Coinleach glas an fhomair / World of difference / In a lifetime / Robin (the hooded man) / Something to believe in / Newgrange / Buachaille an Eirne / White fool.
(cd/c+=) – Second stone / Stepping stone. *(re-iss.cd Oct95)*

May 89. (7")(c-s) **IN A LIFETIME. ("CLANNAD featuring BONO") / SOMETHING TO BELIEVE IN** [17] [ ]
(12"+=) – Caislean Oir / The wild cry.
(cd-s++=) – Atlantic realm.

Jul 89. (7")(c-s)**HOURGLASS. / THEME FROM HARRY'S GAME** [ ] [ ]
(12"+=) – World of difference.
(cd-s++=) – Journey's end.

Nov 89. (7")(c-s)(cd-s) **A DREAM IN THE NIGHT. / THE PIRATES AND THE SOLDIER BOY** [ ] [ ]

Dec 89. (lp)(c)(cd) **THE ANGEL AND THE SOLDIER BOY (narrator; Tom Conti)** [ ] [ ]
– A dream in the night / The pirates / The soldier boy / The angel / The flies / The spider / The cat / The Jolly Rodger / Into the picture / Pirates merrymaking / Finding the key / Pirates on the island / Sea and storm / The love theme / The chase / The toys / The rescue / Back to the door / A dream in the night (instrumental). *(re-iss.cd Apr95)*

— now quartet, when POL left

Oct 90. (cd)(c)(lp) **ANAM** [14] [ ]
– Mi na cruinne / Anam / In fortune's hand / The poison glen / Wilderness / Why worry? / Uirchill an chreagain / Love and affection / You're the one / Dobhar. *(re-iss.US Apr93 hit No.46)*

Nov 90. (7") **IN FORTUNE'S HAND. / DOBHAR** [ ] [ ]
(12"+=)(cd-s+=) – An mhaighdean mhara.

— In mid-'91 teamed up with PAUL YOUNG on 'MCA' single 'BOTH SIDES NOW' which hit UK No.74.

— usual quartet plus guests **ANTO DRENNAN** – guitar / **JOHN DONNELLY** – drums / **MEL COLLINS** – sax, flute / **IAN PARKER** – keyboards / **FRANKIE KENNEDY** – flute, whistle / **BRIDIN BRENNAN** – vocals / **DENIS WOODS** – keyboards, synth prog.

May 93. (cd)(c)(lp) **BANBA** [5] [ ]
– Na laethe bhi / Banba oir / There for you / Mystery game / Struggle / I will find you / Soul searcher / Ca de sin do'n te sin / The other side / Sunset dreams / A gentle place.

. . . Jan – Jun '96 stop press . . .

Mar 96. (cd)(c) **LORE** [14] [ ]

– compilations etc. –

May 86. R.C.A.; (7"ep) **ROBIN OF SHERWOOD. / CAISLEAN OIR / NOW IS HERE / HERNE** [ ] [ ]
Sep 92. R.C.A.; (7") **THEME FROM HARRY'S GAME. / ROBIN (THE HOODED MAN)** [ ] [ ]
Jul 86. Starblend; (lp)(c)(cd) **ROBIN OF SHERWOOD** [ ] [-]
Dec 88. K-Tel Ireland; (lp)(c)(cd) **THE COLLECTION** [ ] [-]

Eric CLAPTON

Born: ERIC CLAPP, 30 Mar'45, Ripley, Surrey, England. Raised by grandparents, due to parents' separation. He became a busker until he joined The ROOSTERS in 1963, but he left after six months, joining CASEY JONES & THE ENGINEERS. In October that year, he replaced ANTHONY TOPHAM in The YARDBIRDS. Their manager Giorgio Gomelsky nicknamed him "Slowhand", due to relaxed guitar style. With his roots still in blues, he joined JOHN MAYALL'S BLUESBREAKERS in Mar65, but finally departed Jun'66 to form CREAM with JACK BRUCE and GINGER BAKER. After their demise late '68, ERIC soon formed another supergroup BLIND FAITH. They were around for a year, making Transatlantic No.1 album. After a brief spell with DELANEY & BONNIE, mainly on tour, he went solo in 1970. Later in the year he formed DEREK & THE DOMINOES. In his time with the said groups, he also sessioned for GEORGE HARRISON, playing lead on WHILE MY GUITAR GENTLY WEEPS. He had previously guested on his WONDERWALL album. In 1971 he retired from the music scene as his drug addiction took over. He marked his return 13 Jan'73 at The Rainbow, London by releasing hit album that year. In 1974, he signed to Robert Stigwood's label 'RSO', and soon released 461 OCEAN BOULEVARD, his first in the studio for 4 years. He had already beaten his drug addiction by electro-acupuncture. In the mid-70's, he married PATTI ex-wife of Beatle GEORGE HARRISON, who he had been going out with for some time. They divorced in the late 80's, and tragically his 4 year old son CONOR fell to his death, from the open window of a 53rd storey building. • **Style:** Greatest living guitarist, who is described by fans as GOD. His heavy blues style in the 60's, was nearly abandoned, with his laid back mainstream rock in the mid 70's. His live shows though, were always filled with all his old work, as well as new. • **Songwriters:** CLAPTON wrote most (even attributing LAYLA and WONDERFUL TONIGHT to his wife Patti). Covered AFTER MIDNIGHT + COCAINE + I'LL MAKE LOVE TO YOU ANYTIME (J.J. Cale) / I SHOT THE SHERIFF (Bob Marley) / MAY YOU NEVER (John Martyn) / KNOCKIN' ON HEAVEN'S DOOR (Bob Dylan) / SWING LOW SWEET CHARIOT (spiritual/gospel trad.) / FURTHER ON UP THE ROAD (?) / WILLIE AND THE HAND JIVE + CRAZY COUNTRY HOP (Johnny Otis) / HAVE YOU EVER LOVED A WOMAN (Billy Myles) / NOBODY KNOWS YOU WHEN YOU'RE DOWN AND OUT (Jimmy Cox) / KEY TO THE HIGHWAY (Sager/Broonzy) / KNOCK ON WOOD (Eddie Floyd) BEHIND THE MASK (Yellow Magic Orchestra) / WATCH YOURSELF (Buddy Guy) / WORRIED LIFE BLUES (Mecio Merryweather) / HOODOO MAN (Sonny Boy Williamson) / HOUND DOG (hit; Elvis Presley) / DOUBLE TROUBLE (Otis Rush) / SIGN LANGUAGE (Bob Dylan) / FLOATING BRIDGE and EVERYBODY OUGHTA (Sleepy John Estes) / LEAD ME ON (Womack/Womack) / BEFORE YOU ACCUSE ME (Bo Diddley) / RUNNING ON FAITH + PRETENDING (Williams) / RUN SO FAR (Wilbert Harrison) / DON'T KNOW WHICH WAY TO GO (Willie Dixon) / etc. • **Trivia:** In 1966, with JACK BRUCE, PAUL JONES, STEVE WINWOOD and PETE YORK, he briefly formed The POWERHOUSE which recorded 3 songs for 'Elektra' compilation WHAT'S SHAKIN'. This biography is in no way an attempt to wholly register every detail, but is a summary of his notable work. This job must be left to another biographer, who would do justice to this legend.

Recommended: BACKTRACKIN' (*9)

ERIC CLAPTON (solo) – vocals, guitar (ex-DELANEY & BONNIE, ex-BLIND FAITH ex-CREAM, ex-JOHN MAYALL'S BLUESBREAKERS, ex-YARDBIRDS, etc) featured his **DOMINOES** musicians plus **STEPHEN STILLS** – guitar.

Polydor Atco

Aug 70. (lp)(c) **ERIC CLAPTON** [17] [13] Jul 70
– Slunky / Bad boy / Lonesome and a long way from home / After midnight / Easy now / Blues power / Bottle of red wine / Lovin' you lovin' me / I've told you for the last time / I don't know why / Let it rain. *(re-iss.Nov82 & Feb83)*

— In Oct 70, CLAPTON guested on KING CURTIS single 'TEASIN'. / SOULIN'

Nov 70. (7") **AFTER MIDNIGHT. / EASY NOW** [ ] [18] Oct 70

DEREK AND THE DOMINOES

ERIC CLAPTON – vox, guitar with **BOBBY WHITLOCK** – keyboards, vocals / **CARL RADLE** – bass / **JIM GORDON** – drums / **and guest DUANE ALLMAN** – guitar

Sep 70. (7") **TELL THE TRUTH. / ROLL IT OVER** [ ] [ ]
Dec 70. (7") **LAYLA. / BELL BOTTOM BLUES** [ ] [51] Mar 71
Dec 70. (d-lp)(c) **LAYLA & OTHER ASSORTED LOVE SONGS** [ ] [16] Nov 70
– I looked away / Bell bottom blues / Keep on growing / Nobody knows you when you're down and out / I am yours / Anyday / Key to the highway / Tell the truth / Why does love got to be so sad? / Have you ever loved a woman / Little wing / It's too late / Layla / Thorn tree in the garden. *(re-iss.Aug74 + Feb77) (re-iss.Jan84) (cd-iss.Mar91)*
Feb 71. (7") **BELL BOTTOM BLUES. / KEEP ON GROWING** [-] [91]
Jul 72. (7") **LAYLA. / I AM YOURS** [7] [10] Apr72

— They split Spring '71 but left behind posthumous album below, etc

R.S.O. R.S.O.

Sep 72. (7") **LET IT RAIN. / EASY NOW** [-] [48]
Mar 73. (d-lp)(d-c) **DEREK AND THE DOMINOES – IN CONCERT (live)** [36] [20] Jan 73
– Why does love got to be so sad? / Got to get better in a little while / Let it rain / Presence of the Lord / Tell the truth / Bottle of red wine / Roll it over / Blues power / Have you ever loved a woman.
Apr 73. (7") **WHY DOES LOVE GOT TO BE SO SAD? (live). / PRESENCE OF THE LORD (live)** [ ] [ ]
Jun 73. (7") **BELL BOTTOM BLUES. / LITTLE WING** [ ] [78] Feb 73

— In '71 ERIC had virtually retired into session work. He appeared in GEORGE HARRISON's Bangla Desh concert, 1 Aug71.

ERIC CLAPTON

returned for a one-off concert at the Rainbow, 13Jan73 with **PETE TOWNSHEND** – guitar / **RON WOOD** – guitar / **STEVE WINWOOD** – keyboards / **JIMMY KARSTEIN & JIM CAPALDI** – drums / **REE BOP** – percussion / **RIC GRECH** – bass

Polydor R.S.O.

Sep 73. (lp)(c) **THE RAINBOW CONCERT** [19] [18]
– Badge / Roll it over / Presence of the Lord / Pearly queen / After midnight / Little wing. *(re-iss.Aug83) (cd-iss.1988 & May95)*

ERIC CLAPTON went solo again with **GEORGE TERRY** – guitar (ex-sessions) / **CARL RADDLE** – bass (ex-DEREK AND THE DOMINOES, ex-DELANEY & BONNIE) / **DICK SIMS** – keyboards (ex-BOB SEGER) / **JAMIE OLDAKER** – drums (ex-BOB SEGER) / **MARCY LEVY** – b.vocals (ex-BOB SEGER) / **YVONNE ELLIMAN**

R.S.O. R.S.O.

Jul 74. (7") **I SHOT THE SHERRIF. / GIVE ME STRENGTH** [9] [1]
Aug 74. (lp)(c) **461 OCEAN BOULEVARD** [3] [1] Jul 74
– Motherless children / Give me strength / Willie and the hand jive / Get ready / I shot the sheriff / I can't hold out / Please be with me / Steady rollin' man / Mainline Florida. *(re-iss.Aug83) (cd-iss.Nov89)*
Oct 74. (7") **WILLIE AND THE HAND JIVE. / MAINLINE FLORIDA** [ ] [26]

— added **MARCY LEVY** – vocals, tambourine

Apr 75. (7") **SWING LOW SWEET CHARIOT. / PRETTY BLUE EYES** [19] [ ]
Apr 75. (lp)(c) **THERE'S ONE IN EVERY CROWD** [15] [21]
– We've been told (Jesus' coming soon) / Swing low sweet chariot / Little Rachel / Don't blame me / The sky is crying / Singing the blues / Better make it through today / Pretty blue eyes / High / Opposites. *(re-iss.Mar85) (cd-iss.Nov86)*
Aug 75. (7") **KNOCKIN' ON HEAVEN'S DOOR. / SOMEONE LIKE YOU** [38] [ ]
Sep 75. (lp)(c) **E.C. WAS HERE (live)** [14] [20]
– Have you ever loved a woman / Presence of the Lord / Drifting blues / Can't find my way home / Ramblin' on my mind / Farther on up the road. *(re-iss.Aug83)*

— added **SERGIO PASTORA** – percussion (ex-BOB SEGER)

Aug 76. (lp)(c) **NO REASON TO CRY** [8] [15] Sep 76
– Beautiful thing / Carnival / Sign language / County jail blues / All our past times / Hello old friend / Double trouble / Innocent times / Hungry / Black summer rain. *(re-iss.Aug83) (cd-iss.Dec86)*
Oct 76. (7") **HELLO OLD FRIEND. / ALL OUT PAST TIMES** [ ] [24]
Feb 77. (7") **CARNIVAL. / HUNGRY** [ ] [ ]

— Augmented by five piece when ELLIMAN then PASTORA both went solo.

Nov 77. (7") **LAY DOWN SALLY. / COCAINE** [39] [3]
Nov 77. (lp)(c) **SLOWHAND** [23] [2]
– Cocaine / Wonderful tonight / Lay down Sally / Next time you see her / We're all the way / The core / May you never / Mean old Frisco / Peaches and diesel. *(re-iss.+cd Aug83)*
Mar 78. (7") **WONDERFUL TONIGHT. / PEACHES AND DIESEL** [ ] [16] May 78

— **ERIC CLAPTON & HIS BAND**

ERIC now backed up only by **SIMS, OLDAKER** and **RADLE** when MARCY LEVY went solo and GEORGE TERRY went into sessions.

Sep 78. (7") **PROMISES. / WATCH OUT FOR LUCY** [37] [9] [40]
Nov 78. (lp)(c) **BACKLESS** [18] [8]
– Walk out in the rain / Watch out for Lucy / I'll make love to you anytime / Roll it / Tell me that you love me / If I don't be there by morning / Early in the morning / Promises / Golden ring / Tulsa time. *(re-iss.Aug83) (cd-iss.Jan89)*
Mar 79. (7") **IF I DON'T GET THERE BY MORNING. / TULSA TIME** [ ] [ ]

— added **ALBERT LEE** – guitar (ex-solo artist, etc.) to complete new band, **DAVE MARKEE** – bass repl.CARL / **HENRY SPINETTI drums** repl.JAMIE

May 80. (d-lp)(d-c) **JUST ONE NIGHT (live at Budokhan)** [3] [2]
– Tulsa time / Early in the morning / Lay down Sally / Wonderful tonight / If I don't be there by morning / Worried life blues / All our past times / After midnight / Double trouble / Setting me up / Blues power / Ramblin' on my mind / Cocaine / Farther on up the road. *(cd-iss.Nov88)*
Jul 80. (7") **TULSA TIME (live). / COCAINE (live)** [ ] [30] Jun 80
Oct 80. (7") **BLUES POWER (live). / EARLY IN THE MORNING (live)** [-] [76]

— **GARY BROOKER & CHRIS STAINTON** – keyboards repl. DICK

Feb 81. (7") **I CAN'T STAND IT. / BLACK ROSE** [ ] [10]
Feb 81. (lp)(c) **ANOTHER TICKET** [18] [7] Mar 81
– Something special / Black rose / Blow wind blow / Another ticket / I can't stand it / Hold me Lord / Floating bridge / Catch me if you can / Rita Mae. *(re-iss.Apr84) (cd-iss.Feb87)*
Apr 81. (7") **ANOTHER TICKET. / RITA MAE** [ ] [78]

— **ERIC CLAPTON** retained **LEE** and recruited **RY COODER, ROGER HAWKINS, DONALD 'DUCK' DUNN** plus backing vocalists **JOHN SAMBATAO** and **CHUCK KIRKPATRICK**

Duck-Warners Duck

Feb 83. (7") **I'VE GOT A ROCK'N'ROLL HEART. / MAN OVERBOARD** [ ] [18] Jan 83
(12"+=) – Everybody oughta make a change.
Feb 83. (lp)(c) **MONEY AND CIGARETTES** [13] [16]
– Everybody outta make a change / The shape you're in / Ain't going down / I've got a rock'n'roll heart / Man overboard / Pretty girl / Man in love / Crosscut saw / Slow down Linda / Crazy country hop. *(cd-iss. 1984 & Feb95)*
Apr 83. (7")(7"pic-d) **THE SHAPE YOU'RE IN. / CROSSCUT SAW** [75] [ ]
(12"+=) – Pretty girl.
May 83. (7") **SLOW DOWN LINDA. / CRAZY COUNTRY HOP** [ ] [ ]
(12"+=) – The shape you're in.

— **CLAPTON** put together a new band. **TIM RENWICK** – guitar (ex-SUTHERLAND BROTHERS & QUIVER) / **CHRIS STAINTON** – keyboards (ex-solo, ex-JOE COCKER) / **DONALD 'DUCK' DUNN** – bass (ex-BOOKER T. AND THE M.G.'s) / **JAMIE OLDAKER** – drums (returned) **MARCY LEVY** (returned) **& SHAUN MURPHY** – backing vocals

Mar 85. (7") **FOREVER MAN. / TOO BAD** [51] [26]
(12"+=) – Something's happening.
(12"+=) – Heaven is one step away.
Mar 85. (lp)(c)(cd) **BEHIND THE SUN** [8] [34]
– She's waiting / See what love can do / Same old blues / Knock on wood / Something's happening / Forever man / It all depends / Tangled in love / Never make you cry / Just like a prisoner / Behind the sun. *(re-iss.cd Feb95)*
May 85. (7") **SEE WHAT LOVE CAN DO. / SHE'S WAITING** [-] [89]
Jul 85. (7") **SHE'S WAITING. / JAILBAIT** [ ] [-]
Dec 85. (7") **EDGE OF DARKNESS (by "ERIC CLAPTON & MICHAEL KAMEN"). / SHOOT OUT** [65] [-]
(12"+=) – ('A'side) / Escape from North Moor.
(c-s+=) – (all 3 tracks). *(re-iss.cd-s.Feb89)*
(above from 'BBC' TV Edge Of Darkness on 'BBC' records.
Nov 86. (lp)(c)(cd) **AUGUST** [3] [37] Dec 86
– It's in the way that you use it / Run / Tearing us apart / Bad influence / Hung up on your love / Take a chance / Hold on / Miss you / Holy mother / Behind the mask. (cd+=) – Grand illusion. *(re-iss.cd Feb95)*
Jan 87. (7") **BEHIND THE MASK. / GRAND ILLUSION** [15] [ ]
(12"+=) – Wanna make love to you.
(d7"+=) – White room (live) / Crossroads (live).
Mar 87. (7") **IT'S IN THE WAY THAT YOU USE IT. / BAD INFLUENCE** [ ] [ ]
(d7+=)(12"+=) – Old ways / Pretty girl.

— **GREG PHILLINGANES** also joined

Jun 87. (7") **TEARING US APART. (by "ERIC CLAPTON & TINA TURNER") / HOLD ON** [56] [ ]
(12"+=) – Run.
Nov 87. (7") **HOLY MOTHER. / TANGLED IN LOVE** [ ] [ ]
(12"+=) – Behind the mask / Forever man.

— now backed in concert by BUCKWHEAT ZYDECO

Feb 89. (lp)(c)(cd) **HOMEBOY (Soundtrack w/ others on 'Virgin' records UK)** [ ] [ ]
– Travelling east / Johnny / Call me if you need me (MAGIC SAM) / Bridge / Pretty baby (J.B. HUTTO & THE NEW HAWKS) / Dixie / Ruby's loft / I want to love you baby (PEGGY SCOTT / JO JO BENSON) / Bike ride / Ruby / Living in the real world (The BRAKES) / Final flight / Dixie / Homeboy. (cd+=) – Country bikin' / Party / Training / Chase.

— now with **ALAN CLARKE, ROBERT CRAY, GEORGE HARRISON, PHIL**

COLLINS, etc

Nov 89. (lp)(c)(cd) **JOURNEYMAN** 3 16
– Pretending / Anything for your love / Bad love / Running on faith / Hard times / Hound dog / No alibis / Run so far / Old love / Breaking point / Lead me on / Before you accuse me.

Jan 90. (7") **BAD LOVE. / BEFORE YOU ACCUSE ME** 88 Mar 90
(12")(cd-s)(c-s) – ('A'side) / Badge / Let it rain (both live).

Mar 90. (7")(c-s) **NO ALIBIS. / RUNNING ON FAITH** 53
(12"+=) – Behind the mask (live) / Cocaine (live).
(cd-s+=) – No alibis / Cocaine (live).

Jun 90. (7") **PRETENDING. / HARD TIMES** 55 Nov 89
(12"+=) – Knock on wood.
(cd-s++=) – Behind the Sun.

— with **ALAN CLARKE** – keyboards / **NATHAN EAST** – bass / **STEVE FERRONE** – drums / **PHIL PALMER** – guitar / **RAY COOPER** – guitar / **RICHARD TEE** – piano / **CRAIG PHILLINGAMES** – keyboards, synths. and The NATIONAL PHILHARMONIC ORCHESTRA.

Oct 91. (cd)(c)(lp) **24 NIGHTS (live)** 17 38
– Badge / Running on faith / White room / Sunshine of your love / Watch yourself / Have you ever loved a woman / Worried life blues / Hoodoo man / Pretending / Bad love / Old love / Wonderful tonight / Bell bottom blues / Hard times / Edge of darkness.

Nov 91. (7") **WONDERFUL TONIGHT (live). / EDGE OF DARKNESS (live)** 30
(12")(cd-s)(c-s) – ('A' side) / Layla (band version) / Cocaine.

Jan 92. (cd)(c) **RUSH (Soundtrack)** 24
– Tears in Heaven / Will Gaines / Tracks and lines / Realization / New recruit / Preludia fugue / Kristen and Jim / Help me up / Cold turkey / Don't know which way to go. *(re-iss.cd Feb95)*

— **CHUCK LEAVELL** – keyboards (ex-ALLMANS) repl. CRAIG and RICHARD / **ANDY FAIRWEATHER-LOW** – guitar (ex-AMEN CORNER, ex-solo) repl. PHIL backing singers **KATIE KISSOON + TESSA MILES**

Jan 92. (7")(c-s) **TEARS IN HEAVEN. / WHITE ROOM (live)** 5 2
(12"+=)(cd-s+=) – Tracks & lines / Bad love (live).

In Jul92, ERIC teamed up with ELTON JOHN on single 'RUNAWAY TRAIN'. A month later, STING was his co-collaborator on another hit 'IT'S PROBABLY ME'.

Sep 92. (7")(c-s) **LAYLA (acoustic). / TEARS IN HEAVEN (acoustic)** 45 12
(cd-s+=) – (MTV unplugged interview).

Sep 92. (cd)(c)(lp) **UNPLUGGED (acoustic)** 2 1
– Signe / Before you accuse me / Hey hey / Tears in Heaven / Lonely stranger / Nobody knows when you're down & out / Layla / Running on faith / Walkin' blues / Alberta / San Francisco Bay blues / Malted milk / Old love / Rollin' & tumblin'.

Sep 94. (cd)(c)(lp) **FROM THE CRADLE** 1 1
– Third degree / Hoochie coochie man / Standin' round cryin' / Groanin' the blues / Blues before sunrise / Reconsider baby / Five long years / I'm tore down / How long blues / Goin' away baby / Blues leave me alone / Sinner's prayer / Motherless child / It hurts me too / Someday after a while.

Oct 94. (c-s) **MOTHERLESS CHILD. / DRIFTIN'** 63
(12"+=)(cd-s+=) – County jail blues / 32-20 blues.

— In Mar'95, alongside CHER, CHRISSIE HYNDE and NENEH CHERRY, he hit UK No.1 with charity Comic Relief single 'LOVE CAN BUILD A BRIDGE'.

– more compilations, etc –

Note that 'Polydor' releases were issued on 'Atco' US.

Aug 72. Polydor; (lp)(c) **THE HISTORY OF ERIC CLAPTON** 20 6 Apr 72

Feb 73. Polydor; (lp)(c) **CLAPTON** - 67

Apr 73. Polydor; (lp)(c) **AT HIS BEST** 87 Oct 72

1970. Polydor; (7") **TEASIN'.(by "ERIC CLAPTON & KING CURTIS") / SOULIN'** -

Jan 82. R.S.O.; (7")(12") **LAYLA 'Derek and the Dominoes'. / WONDERFUL TONIGHT** 4

Mar 82. R.S.O.; (7") **I SHOT THE SHERIFF. / COCAINE** 64
(12"+=) – Knockin' on Heaven's door (live).

Apr 82. R.S.O.; (d-lp)(d-c) **TIME PIECES – THE BEST OF ERIC CLAPTON** 20
(cd-iss.1983, re-iss.Dec92 & Apr95)

Aug 82. R.S.O.; (d-c) **SLOWHAND / BACKLESS**

Nov 82. R.S.O.; (t-lp-set) **461 OCEAN BOULEVARD / BACKLESS / SLOWHAND**

May 83. R.S.O.; (lp)(c) **TIME PIECES VOL.II – 'LIVE' IN THE SEVENTIES**
(cd-iss.1985)

Jun 83. R.S.O.; (d-c) **461 OCEAN BOULEVARD / ANOTHER TICKET**

Polydor R.S.O.

Apr 84. Polydor/ US= R.S.O.; (7") **WONDERFUL TONIGHT. / COCAINE**
(re-iss.Aug87)

Aug 87. Polydor; (7") **WONDERFUL TONIGHT. / I SHOT THE SHERIFF**
(12"+=) – Layla (full version).
(cd-s++=) – Swing low sweet chariot.

Sep 87. Polydor; (d-lp)(c)(cd) **THE CREAM OF ERIC CLAPTON** 9
(re-charted Sep92, hit UK No.49) (re-iss.cd/c Mar94, US re-iss.Mar95 hit No.80)

Apr 88. (6xlp)(4xc)(4xcd) **CROSSROADS** 34

— (above features all his work of past 25 years) (YARDBIRDS to solo)

Jul 88. Polydor; (7") **AFTER MIDNIGHT. / I CAN'T STAND IOT**
(12"+=) – What you doing today.
(cd-s++=) – Sunshine of your love (by "CREAM").

Nov 90. Polydor; (cd)(c) **THE LAYLA SESSIONS (Derek & The Dominoes)**

Jul 91. Polydor; (7") **LAYLA. (Edit) / BELL BOTTOM BLUES**

Nov 91. Polydor; (cd)(c)(d-lp) **THE BEST OF ERIC CLAPTON (w /CREAM)**
(re-iss.cd/cJul93)

Mar 94. Polydor; (d-cd)(d-c) **LIVE AT FILLMORE (DEREK & THE DOMINOES)**

May 84. Starblend; (d-lp)(d-c) **BACK TRACKIN'** 29
– I shot the sheriff / Knockin' on Heaven's door / Lay down Sally / Promises / Swing low sweet chariot / Wonderful tonight / Sunshine of your love (CREAM) / Tales of brave Ulysses (CREAM) / Badge (CREAM) / Little wing (DEREK & THE DOMINOES) / Layla (DEREK & THE DOMINOES) / Cocaine / Strange brew (CREAM) / Spoonful (CREAM) / Let it rain / Have you ever loved a woman? (DEREK & THE DOMINOES) / Presence of the Lord (BLIND FAITH) / Crossroads (CREAM) / Roll it over (DEREK & THE DOMINOES live) / Can't find my way home (live) / Blues power (live) / Further on up the road (live).
(re-iss.+d-cd Feb85 on 'Polydor') (re-iss.all formats. Feb91)

Nov 84. Astan; (lp)(c) **TOO MUCH MONKEY BUSINESS**

Mar 86. Thunderbolt; (lp)(c) **SURVIVOR**
(re-iss.Mar88)

Jul 84 Old Gold; (7") **LAYLA (Derek & the Dominoes) / ONLY YOU KNOW AND I KNOW**

Mar 86. Old Gold; (7") **I SHOT THE SHERIFF. / KNOCKIN' ON HEAVEN'S DOOR** -

Apr 86. Arcade; (lp)(c) **GREATEST HITS** -

1987. Castle; (d-lp)(c)(cd) **THE CLAPTON COLLECTION** -
(cd re-iss.Jun92)

1992. Castle; (cd)(c)(lp) **THE EARLY COLLECTION** -

May 88. Big Time; (lp)(c) **FIVE LONG YEARS** -

Jun 81. Decca; (lp)(c) **STEPPIN' OUT (live)** -

Feb 89. Venus; (lp)(c) **THE MAGIC OF ERIC CLAPTON** -
(re-iss.cd+c.Jun93 on 'Royal Collection')

Apr 93. Pulsar; (cd) **MISTER SLOWHAND** -

Dec 93. Immediate; (cd) **THE EARLY YEARS** -

Aug 94. Charly; (cd) **BEGINNINGS** -

Sep 95. Polydor; (d-cd) **LIVE AT THE FILLMORE (DEREK & THE DOMINOES)**

Nov 95. Polydor; (3xcd-box) **SLOWHAND / 461 OCEAN BOULEVARD / THERE'S ONE IN EVERY CROWD**

(also see under CREAM)

Gene CLARK (see under ⇒ BYRDS)

CLASH

Formed: London, England . . . mid'76, by JONES, SIMONEN, STRUMMER and CHIMES. KEITH LEVENE future PIL member also had a brief spell with them in '76. Manager BERNIE RHODES attained deal with 'C.B.S.' early '77, and soon hit charts with 2 minute classic 'WHITE RIOT'. • **Style:** Punk rock, raw with energy, fuelled by politics and mixed with sporadic dub reggae. After two attempts (1978/1979 lp's) to go near commercial and "sell-out" punk roots, they returned with budget triple album SANDINISTA!, that experimented with all musical styles. In 1982 they achieved major success in America, but when most of band dispersed into new ventures in 83/84, their long-awaited return CUT THE CRAP virtually didn't. • **Songwriters:** Either STRUMMER / -JONES until 1980 group penned, except POLICE AND THIEVES (Junior Murvin / LEE PERRY) / PRESSURE DROP (Maytals) / I FOUGHT THE LAW (Sonny Curtis) / POLICE ON MY BACK (Equals) / ARMAGIDEON TIME (Willie Williams) / JUNCO PARTNER + ENGLISH CIVIL WAR (unknown trad) / EVERY LITTLE BIT HURTS (Ed Cobb) / BRAND NEW CADILLAC (Vince Taylor). • **Trivia:** Early 1980, the band featured live in the docu-film 'Rude Boy' about a fictionalized CLASH roadie. JOE STRUMMER went into acting 1986 (Straight To Hell) / 1989 (Lost In Space). A surprise return to the charts in 1991, with re-issue SHOULD I STAY OR SHOULD I GO was due to a TV-ad for Levi jeans.

Recommended: THE CLASH (*10) / THE STORY OF THE CLASH (*9) / GIVE 'EM ENOUGH ROPE (*7) / LONDON CALLING (*8) / SANDINISTA! (*7) /

COMBAT ROCK (*6)

JOE STRUMMER (b.JOHN MELLORS, 21 Aug'52, Ankara, Turkey./ raised London) – vocals, guitar (ex-101'ers) / **PAUL SIMONEN** (b.15 Dec'55, Brixton, England) – bass, vocals / **MICK JONES** (b.MICHAEL JONES, 26 Jun'55, Brixton) – guitar, vocals / **TORY CRIMES** (b.TERRY CHIMES, 25 Jan'55) – drums

C.B.S. | not issued

Mar 77. (7") **WHITE RIOT. / 1977** | 38 | -

Apr 77. (lp)(c) **THE CLASH** | 12 | -

– Janie Jones / Remote control / I'm so bored with the U.S.A. / White riot / Hate and war / What's my name / Deny / London's burning / Career oportunities / Cheat / Protex blue / Police and thieves / 48 hours / Garage land. *(re-iss.Nov82)(cd-iss.May89 + Jun91)(US-release Jul79 on 'Epic' tracks differed, cont free 7"* **GROOVY TIMES. / GATES OF THE WEST.** *This lp version iss.UK – Jan91 on cd)*

— (Jan77) (NICKY) **TOPPER HEADON** (b.30 May'57, Bromley, Kent, England) – drums repl. CHIMES who later joined COWBOYS INTERNATIONAL and GENERATION X.

May 77. (7") **REMOTE CONTROL. / LONDON'S BURNING (live)** | | -

Sep 77. (7") **COMPLETE CONTROL. / THE CITY OF THE DEAD** | 28 | -

Feb 78. (7") **CLASH CITY ROCKERS. / JAIL GUITAR DOORS** | 35 | -

Jun 78. (7") **WHITE MAN IN HAMMERSMITH PALAIS. / THE PRISONER** | 32 | -

C.B.S. | Epic

Nov 78. (lp)(c) **GIVE 'EM ENOUGH ROPE** | 2 | Mar 79

– Safe European home / English civil war / Tommy gun / Julie's been working for the drug squad / Guns on the roof / Drug-stabbing time / Stay free / Cheapstakes / All the young punks (new boots and contracts). *(re-iss.1984) (cd-iss.May89 + Jan91)*

Nov 78. (7") **TOMMY GUN. / 1-2, CRUSH ON YOU** | 19 |

Feb 79. (7") **ENGLISH CIVIL WAR. / PRESSURE DROP** | 25 |

May 79. (7"ep) **THE COST OF LIVING** | 22 |

– I fought the law / Groovy times / Gates of the west / Capital radio.

Jul79. (7") **I FOUGHT THE LAW. / WHITE MAN IN HAMMERSMITH PALAIS** | - |

— added on tour 5th member **MICKEY GALLAGHER** – keyboards (ex-IAN DURY)

Dec 79. (7") **LONDON CALLING. / ARMAGIDEON TIME** | 11 |

(12"+=) – Justice tonight ('B'version) / Kick it over ('B'version).

Dec 79. (d-lp)(c) **LONDON CALLING** | 9 | 27 Jan 80

– London calling / Brand new Cadillac / Jimmy Jazz / Hateful / Rudie can't fail / Wrong 'em Boyd / Death or glory / Koka Kola / The card cheat / Spanish bombs / The right profile / Lost in the supermarket / The guns of Brixton / Lover's rock / Four horsemen / I'm not down / Revolution rock / Train in vain. *(cd-May88)*

Feb 80. (7") **TRAIN IN VAIN (STAND BY ME). / LONDON CALLING** | - | 27

Aug 80. (7") **BANKROBBER. / ROCKERS GALORE . . . UK TOUR** | 12 |

Nov 80. (7") **THE CALL-UP. / STOP THE WORLD** | 40 | -

Dec 80. (t-lp,d-c) **SANDINISTA!** | 19 | 24

– The magnificent seven / Hitsville UK / Junco partner / Ivan meets G.I. Joe / The leader / Something about England / Rebel waltz / Look here / The crooked beat / Somebody got murdered / One more time / One more dub / Lightning strikes (not once but twice) / Up in Heaven (not only here) / Corner soul / Let's go crazy / If music could talk / The sound of the sinners / Police on my back / Midnight log / The equaliser / The call up / Washington bullets / Broadway / Lose this skin / Charlie don't surf / Mensforth Hill / Junkie slip / Kingston advice / The street parade / Version city / Living in fame / Silicone on sapphire / Version pardner / Career opportunites (version) / Shepherds delight. *(iss.as lp in US)(d-cd.iss.1989)*

Jan 81. (7") **HITSVILLE UK. / RADIO ONE** | 56 | -

Feb 81. (7") **HITSVILLE UK. / POLICE ON MY BACK** | - |

Mar 81. (7") **THE CALL-UP. / THE MAGNIFICENT SEVEN** | - |

(12"+=) – The magnificent dance / The cool-out.

Apr 81. (7") **THE MAGNIFICENT SEVEN. / THE MAGNIFICENT DANCE** | 34 | -

(12"+=) – (2-'A'extra mixes).

Nov 81. (7") **THIS IS RADIO CLASH. / RADIO CLASH** | 47 |

(12"+=) – Outside broadcast / Radio 5.

— **TERRY CHIMES** returned to replace HEADON who later went solo.

Apr 82. (7") **KNOW YOUR RIGHTS. / FIRST NIGHT BACK IN LONDON** | 43 |

May 82. (lp)(c) **COMBAT ROCK** | 2 | 7

– Know your rights / Car jamming / Should I stay or should I go / Rock the Casbah / Red angel dragnet / Straight to Hell / Overpowered by funk / Atom tan / Sean Flynn / Ghetto defendant / Inoculated city / Death is a star. *(re-iss.Nov86) (cd-iss.Sep88 + Jan91)*

Jun 82. (7") **ROCK THE CASBAH. / INOCULATED CITY** | - | 8

Jun 82. (7") **ROCK THE CASBAH. / LONG TIME JERK** | 30 |

(12") – ('A'side) / Mustapha dance.

Jul 82. (7") **SHOULD I STAY OR SHOULD I GO. / COOL CONFUSION (or) FIRST NIGHT BACK IN LONDON** | - | 45

Sep 82. (7")(12")(7"pic-d) **SHOULD I STAY OR SHOULD I GO. / STRAIGHT TO HELL** | 17 | -

— (Feb83-Jan84) **STRUMMER & SIMONEN** brought in new musicians **PETE HOWARD** – drums (ex-COLD FISH),repl. CHIMES who later joined HANOI ROCKS. / **NICK SHEPHERD** – guitar (ex-CORTINAS) + **VINCE WHITE** – guitar repl. JONES who formed BIG AUDIO DYNAMITE

Sep 85. (7") **THIS IS ENGLAND. / DO IT NOW** | 24 |

(12"+=) – Sex mad roar.

Nov 85. (lp)(c) **CUT THE CRAP** | 16 | 88

– Dictator / Dirty punk / We are The Clash / Are you red..Y / Cool under heat / Movers and shakers / This is England / Three card trick / Play to win / Fingerpoppin' / North and south / Life is wild. *(cd-iss.Dec92 on 'Columbia')*

— disbanded Dec'85. STRUMMER went solo (see below). SHEPHERD formed HEAD. In the 90's, SIMONEN formed HAVANA 3 a.m.

- compilations, others, etc. -

Oct 80. Epic; (10"m-lp) **BLACK MARKET CLASH** | - | 74

– Time is tight / Capital radio / Bank robber / Presure drop / The prisoner / City of the dead / Justice tonight – kick it over (version). *(UK-iss.c+cd.Sep91+Nov93 on 'Columbia')*

Nov 82. C.B.S.; (7"ep) **COMPLETE CONTROL / LONDON CALLING. / BANKROBBER / CLASH CITY ROCKERS** | | -

Sep 86. C.B.S.; (c-ep) **THE 12" TAPE** | | -

– London calling / The magnificent dance / This is Radio Clash / Rock the Casbah / This is England / Last dance.

Mar 88. C.B.S./ US= Epic; (7") **I FOUGHT THE LAW. / THE CITY OF THE DEAD / 1977** | 29 |

(12"+=)(cd-s+=) – Police on my back / 48 hours.

Mar 88. (d-lp)(c)(cd) **THE STORY OF THE CLASH** | 7 |

– The magnificent seven / Rock the Casbah / This is Radio Clash / Should I stay or should I go / Straight to Hell / Armagideon time / Clampdown / Train in vain / Guns of Brixton / I fought the law / Somebody got murdered / Lost in the supermarket / Bank robber / White man in Hammersmith Palais / London's burning / Janie Jones / Tommy gun / Complete control / Capital radio / White riot / Career opportunities / Clash city rockers / Safe European home / Stay free / London calling / Spanish bombs / English civil war / Police and thieves. *(re-iss.cd/c/lp.Mar91 as THE STORY OF THE CLASH VOL.1, on 'Columbia', and charted 13)*

Apr 88. C.B.S.; (7") **LONDON CALLING. / BRAND NEW CADILLAC** | 46 |

(12"+=) – Rudie can't fail.

(cd-s+=) – The street parade.

Jul 90. C.B.S.; (7")(c-s) **RETURN TO BRIXTON (remix). / ('A'-SW2 mix)** | 57 |

(12"+=)(cd-s+=) – The guns of Brixton.

Feb 91. Columbia; (7")(c-s) **SHOULD I STAY OR SHOULD I GO. / Rush (by "BAD II")** | 1 |

(12"+=)(cd-s+=) – ('B'dance mix) / Protex blue.

(cd-s) – ('A'side) / London calling / Train in vain / I fought the law.

Apr 91. Columbia; (7")(c-s) **ROCK THE CASBAH. / MUSTAPHA DANCE** | 15 |

(12"+=)(cd-s+=) – The magnificent dance / This is Radio Clash.

(cd-s) – ('A'side) / Tommy gun / White man in Hammersmith Palais / Straight to Hell.

Jun 91. Columbia; (7") **LONDON CALLING. / BRAND NEW CADILLAC** | 64 |

(12"+=) – Return to Brixton (remix).

(cd-s++=) – The call-up.

Oct 91. Columbia; (7")(c-s) **TRAIN IN VAIN (STAND BY ME). / THE RIGHT PROFILE** | |

(cd-s+=) – Groovy times / Gates to the west.

(pic-cd-s+=) – ('A'remix) / Death or glory.

Nov 91. Columbia; (cd)(c)(lp) **THE SINGLES COLLECTION** | 68 |

May 94. Columbia; (3xcd)(3xc) **ON BROADWAY** | |

The CLASH also appeared under different guises for singles below

May 83. Celluloid; (12") **ESCAPADES OF FUTURA 2000 ("FUTURA 2000 featuring The CLASH")** | | -

Dec 83. Big Beat; (7") **HOUSE OF THE JU-JU QUEEN. / SEX MACHINE ("JANIE JONES & THE LASH")** | | -

— They can also be heard backing **TYMON DOGG** on 45; Lose This Skin (May80)

JOE STRUMMER

C.B.S. | Epic

Oct 86. (7")(12") **LOVE KILLS. / DUM DUM CLUB** | 69 |

Virgin | Virgin

Feb 88. (lp)(c)(cd) **WALKER (Soundtrack)** | |

– Filibustero / Omotepe / Sandstorm / Machete / Viperland / Nica libre / Latin romance / The brooding side of madness / Tennessee rain / Smash everything / Tropic of no return / The unknown immortal / Musket waltz.

Epic | Epic

Jun 88. (7") **TRASH CITY. / THEME FROM A PERMANENT RECORD** | |

(12"+=)(pic-cd-s+=) – Norfitili rock.

— He's augmented by new band **JACK IRONS** – drums (of RED HOT CHILI PEPPERS) **ZANDON SCHLOSS** – guitar (ex-CIRCLE JERKS) / **RONNIE**

MARSHALL – bass (of TONE LOC)

Aug 89. (7")(c-s) **GANGSTERVILLE. / JEWELLERS AND BUMS** [ ] [ ]
(7"ep+=) – Passport to Detroit / Punk rock blues.
(12"+=)(cd-s+=) – Don't tango with my django.

Sep 89. (lp)(c)(cd) **EARTHQUAKE WEATHER** [58] [ ]
– Gangsterville / King of the bayou / Island hopping / Slant six / Dizzy's goatee / Shouting street / Boogie with your children / Leopardskin limousines / Sikorsky parts / Jewellers and bums / Highway on zero street / Ride your donkey / Passport to Detroit / Sleepwalk.

Oct 89. (7") **ISLAND HOPPING. / CHOLO VEST** [ ] [ ]
(12"+=)(cd-s+=) – Mango street / Baby o' boogie.

STRUMMER joined The POGUES on tour, deputising when SHANE McGOWAN was under the bottle. At the start of 1992, he had begun writing with them, so who knows? At least it will quell the dogged persistent rumours of a CLASH reformation.

Adam CLAYTON & Larry MULLEN (see under ⇒ U2)

Joe COCKER

Born: JOHN ROBERT COCKER, 20 May'44, Sheffield, England. In 1964, he issued one flop single 'I'LL CRY INSTEAD', before forming his GREASE BAND with CHRIS STAINTON, etc. In 1968, he returned to the studio for solo career with band, and had classic UK No.1 'WITH A LITTLE HELP FROM MY FRIENDS'. (see discography.) Continued to be a major star for the next 2 decades. • **Style:** Often compared to RAY CHARLES, he used powerful vox chords to supplant himself as great white blues singer. In the mid-70's, like so many of his contemporaries he shifted music and body to the West Coast. • **Songwriters:** Pens some with band (GREASE BAND) member CHRIS STAINTON. Covers:- I'LL CRY INSTEAD + WITH A LITTLE HELP FROM MY FRIENDS + SHE CAME IN THROUGH THE BATHROOM WINDOW + YOU'VE GOT TO HIDE YOUR LOVE AWAY (Beatles) / DELTA LADY (Leon Russell) / THE LETTER (Box Tops) / YOU ARE SO BEAUTIFUL (Billy Preston-Jim Price) / JUST LIKE A WOMAN + I SHALL BE RELEASED + WATCHING THE RIVER FLOW (Bob Dylan) / DON'T LET ME BE MISUNDERSTOOD (Nina Simone) / DARLING BE HOME SOON (Lovin' Spoonful) / BIRD ON THE WIRE + I'M YOUR MAN (Leonard Cohen) / HONKY TONK WOMEN (Rolling Stones) / I'VE BEEN LOVING YOU TOO LONG (Otis Redding) / GIVE PEACE A CHANCE (John Lennon) / ST.JAMES INFIRMARY (Graham Bond) / LAWDY MISS CLAWDY (Little Richard) / A WHITER SHADE OF PALE (Procol Harum) / MANY RIVERS TO CROSS (Jimmy Cliff) / I HEARD IT THROUGH THE GRAPEVINE (Barrett Strong) / TALKING BACK TO THE NIGHT (Steve Winwood) / INNER CITY BLUES (Marvin Gaye) / UNCHAIN MY HEART (Ray Charles) / UP WHERE WE BELONG (Buffy Sainte Marie-Will Jennings-Jack Nitzchse) / DON'T LET THE SUN GO DOWN ON ME (Elton John) / CAN'T FIND MY WAY HOME (Blind Faith) / THE MOON IS A HARSH MISTRESS (Jimmy Webb) / FIVE WOMEN (Prince)/TWO WRONGS DON'T MAKE A RIGHT (Bendith-Schwartz) / TEMPTED (Squeeze) / I STILL CAN'T BELIEVE IT'S TRUE (. . . Cadd) / LET THE HEALING BEGIN (Tony Joe White) / HAVE A LITTLE FAITH IN ME (John Hiatt) / THE SIMPLE THINGS (Shanks-Neigher-Roy) / SUMMER IN THE CITY (Lovin' Spoonful) / THE GREAT DIVIDE (J.D. Souther) / HIGHWAY HIGHWAY (Steven Allen Davis) / TOO COOL (G.Sutton-K.Fleming) / SOUL TIME (Will Jennings-Frankie Miller) / OUT OF THE BLUE (Robbie Robertson) / HELL AND HIGHWATER (John Miles) / STANDING KNEE DEEP IN A RIVER (Bob McDill-Dickey Lee-Bucky Jones) / TAKE ME HOME (Kipner-Capek-Jordan) / and many more. • **Trivia:** 'UP WHERE WE BELONG' won a Grammy for best song in 1983.

Recommended: THE LEGEND: THE ESSENTIAL COLLECTION (*7)

"JOE COCKER" – vocals, (touring band JOE COCKER'S BIG BLUES) with **DAVE HOPPER** – guitar / **VERNON NASH** – piano / **DAVE GREEN** – bass / **DAVE MEMMOT** – drums Record company used session men instead incl. **BIG JIM SULLIVAN** – guitar

Decca / not issued

Oct 64. (7") **I'LL CRY INSTEAD. / PRECIOUS WORDS** [ ] [-]

— He formed **The GREASE BAND** in '67 retaining **NASH** and **MEMMOTT** and recruited **CHRIS STAINTON** – bass, and **FRANK MYLES** – guitar. But once again opted for session musicians incl. **CLEM CATTINI** – drums / **J. PAGE & A. LEE** – guitar. Although STAINTON did appear. (JIMMY PAGE also appeared on next 45)

Regal Zono. / A & M

Sep 68. (7") **MARJORINE. / THE NEW AGE OF LILY** [48] [ ]

— **JOE COCKER & THE GREASE BAND** with **STAINTON** brought in new guys **TOMMY EYRE** – keyboards / **MICKEY GEE** – guitar / **TOMMY REILLY** – drums

Sep 68. (7") **WITH A LITTLE HELP FROM MY FRIENDS. / SOMETHING'S COMING ON** [1] [68]

— **MENRY McCULLOCH** – guitar repl. MICKEY GEE (he later joined SHAKIN' STEVENS) **KENNY SLADE** – drums repl. REILLY Plus of course a huge selection of session people

May 69. (lp) **WITH A LITTLE HELP FROM MY FRIENDS** [ ] [35]
– Feeling alright / Bye bye blackbird / Change in Louise / Marjorine / Just like a woman / Do I still figure in your life / Sandpaper Cadillac / Don't let me be misunderstood / With a little help from my friends / I shall be released. *(re-iss.Oct81, cd-iss.1988 on 'Cube') (re-iss.Feb90 on 'Castle')*

Jun 69. (7") **FEELING ALRIGHT. / SANDPAPER CADILLAC** [-] [69]
(re-iss.Dec71 on 'A&M')

— **JOE'S GREASE BAND** retained **STAINTON** – now keyboards and **McCULLOCH ALAN SPENNER** – bass repl. TOMMY EYRE who joines AYNSLEY DUNBAR, etc.

BRUCE ROWLANDS – drums repl. KENNY SLADE who went into sessions

Sep 69. (7") **DELTA LADY. / SHE'S GOOD TO ME** [10] [69]

Nov 69. (lp)(c) **JOE COCKER!** [ ] [11]
– Dear landlord / Bird on the wire / Lawdy Miss Clawdy / She came in through the bathroom window / Hitchcock railway / That's your business now / Something / Delta lady / Hello little friend / Darling be home soon. *(cd-iss.May91 on 'Castle')*

Dec 69. (7") **SHE CAME IN THROUGH THE BATHROOM WINDOW. / CHANGE IN LOUISE** [-] [ ]

Jun 70. (7") **THE LETTER. / SPACE CAPTAIN** [39] [7] Apr 70

— Early '70 he retained **STAINTON** and assembled his **MAD DOGS AND ENGLISHMEN** entourage which included **LEON RUSSELL & THE SHELTER PEOPLE** – guitar, piano / **DON PRESTON** – guitar CARL RADLE – bass / **BOBBY KEYS** – sax / **JIM PRICE** – trumpet / **JIM KELTNER** – drums plus even more session people, over 10, which was documented on film in '71.

A&M / A&M

Sep 70. (d-lp)(c) **MAD DOGS & ENGLISHMEN (live)** [16] [2]
– (introduction) / Honky tonk women / Sticks and stones / Cry me a river / Bird on the wire / Feeling alright / Superstar / Let's go get stoned / Blue medley: I'll drown in my own tears – When something is wrong with my baby – I've been loving you too long / Girl from North Country / Give peace a chance / She came in through the bathroom window / Space captain / The letter / Delta lady. *(re-iss.1983, cd-iss.1988)*

Fly / A&M

Oct 70. (7") **CRY ME A RIVER (live). / GIVE PEACE A CHANCE (live)** [ ] [11]

— JOE retained **STAINTON** and some of his past session men

May 71. (7") **HIGH TIME WE WENT. / BLACK EYED BLUES** [ ] [22]

— now with the CHRIS STAINTON BAND" (a 12-piece) retaining **KEYS, PRICE** and **KELTNER.** (also had loads of session men)

Cube / A&M

Aug 72. (7") **MIDNIGHT RIDER. / WOMAN TO WOMAN** [ ] [27] [56]

Dec 72. (lp)(c) **SOMETHING TO SAY** [ ] [30]
– Pardon me sir / High time we went / She don't mind / Black eyed blues / Something to say / Midnight rider / Do right woman / Woman to woman / St.James infirmary. *(US title 'JOE COCKER') (UK re-iss.May85 on 'Sierra') (UK re-iss.+cd.Dec90 on 'Castle')*

Feb 73. (7") **PARDON ME SIR. / SHE DON'T MIND** [ ] [-]

Feb 73. (7") **PARDON ME SIR. / ST. JAMES INFIRMARY** [-] [51]

— now (complete new line-up) **STAINTON** joined TUNDRA / **HENRY McCULLOCH** – guitar / **MICK WEAVER** (aka WYNDER K. FROG) – keyboards / **BUFFALO GELBER** – bass / **JIMMY KARSTEIN** – drums

Jun 74. (7") **PUT OUT THE LIGHT. / IF I LOVE YOU** [ ] [46]

Aug 74. (lp)(c) **I CAN STAND A LITTLE RAIN** [ ] [11]
– Put out the light / I can stand a little rain / I get mad / Sing me a song / The moon is a harsh mistress / Don't forget me / You are so beautiful / It's a sin when you love somebody / Performance / Guilty. *(re-iss.Oct81) (re-iss.+cd.Apr89 on 'Castle')*

Dec 74. (7") **YOU ARE SO BEAUTIFUL. / I GET MAD** [ ] [-]

Jan 75. (7") **YOU ARE SO BEAUTIFUL. / IT'S A SIN WHEN YOU LOVE SOMEBODY** [-] [5]

— He then formed **JOE COCKER & The COCK'N'BULL BAND** with **WEAVER** plus **ALBERT LEE** – guitar / **PETER GAVIN** – drums / **ANDY DENNO** – bass

JOE COCKER retained **LEE, GAVIN** plus touring band **RICHARD TEE** – keyboards / **GORDON EDWARDS** – bass / **CORNELL DUPREE** – guitar / **KENNY SLADE** – percussion and three girl backing singers

Jul 75. (7") **I THINK IT'S GONNA RAIN TODAY. / OH MAMA** [-] [ ]

Aug 75. (lp)(c) **JAMAICA SAY YOU WILL** [ ] [42]
– (That's what I like) In my woman / Where am I now / I think it's going to rain today / Forgive me now / Oh mama / Lucinda / If I love you / Jamaica say you will / It's all over but the shoutin' / Jack-a-diamonds.

Oct 75. (7") **IT'S ALL OVER BUT THE SHOUTIN'. / SANDPAPER CADILLAC** [ ] [ ]

Oct 75. (7") **JAMAICA SAY YOU WILL. / IT'S ALL OVER BUT THE SHOUTIN'** [-] [ ]

— **JOE COCKER & STUFF** retained **TEE, EDWARDS** and **DUPREE** added **ERIC GALE** – guitar repl. LEE who went solo **STEVE GADD drums** repl. GAVIN

A&M A&M

Apr 76. (7") **THE MAN IN ME. / (part 2)** [-] [ ]
Apr 76. (lp)(c) **STINGRAY** [ ] [70]
– The jealous kind / I broke down / You came along / Catfish / Moon dew / The man in me / She is my lady / Worrier / Born thru indifference with you / A song for you.
Jul 76. (7") **THE JEALOUS KIND. / YOU CAME ALONG** [ ] [ ]
Sep 76. (7") **I BROKE DOWN. / YOU CAME ALONG** [ ] [ ]

— JOE then joined **KOKOMO** for a month late '76 (no recordings). Took a long time off from studio & stage. Returned with a host of session people

Asylum Asylum

Sep 78. (7") **FUN TIME. / WATCHING THE RIVER FLOW** [-] [ ]
Sep 78. (lp)(c)(pic-lp) **LUXURY YOU CAN AFFORD** [ ] [76]
– Fun time / Watching the river flow / Boogie baby / A white shade of pale / I can't say no / Southern lady / I know (you don't want me no more) / What you did to me last night / Lady put the light out / Wasted years / I heard it through the grapevine.
Sep 78. (7") **FUN TIME. / I CAN'T SAY NO** [ ] [-]
Jan 79. (7") **A WHITER SHADE OF PALE. / WATCHING THE RIVER FLOW** [ ] [ ]

— In Sep81 JOE was credited on a single 'I'm So Glad I'm Standing Here Today' and guested on 'Standing Still' by the CRUSADERS.

JOE COCKER returned to solo work '82, (first w/SLY DUNBAR + ROBBIE SHAKESPEARE)

Island Island

Jun 82. (7")(12") **SWEET LITTLE WOMAN. / LOOK WHAT YOU'VE DONE** [ ] [ ]
Jul 82. (lp)(c) **SHEFFIELD STEEL** [ ] [ ]
– Look what you've done / Shocked / Sweet little woman / Seven days / Marie / Ruby Lee / Many rivers to cross / So good so right / Talking back to the night / Just like always.
Aug 82. (7") **MANY RIVERS TO CROSS. / TALKING BACK TO THE NIGHT** [ ] [ ]

below from the film 'An Officer and a Gentleman'

Jan 83. (7") **UP WHERE WE BELONG.(by "JOE COCKER & JENNIFER WARNES") / SWEET LITTLE WOMAN** [7] [1] Aug 82
Jun 83. (7") **THREW IT AWAY. / EASY RIDER** [ ] [ ]

Capitol Capitol

Jun 84. (7") **CIVILIZED MAN. / A GIRL LIKE YOU** [ ] [ ]
Jun 84. (lp)(c)(cd) **CIVILIZED MAN** [100] [ ] May 84
– Civilized / There goes my baby / Come on in / Tempted / Long drag off a cigarette / I love the night / Crazy in love / A girl like you / Hold on (I feel our love is changing) / Even a fool would let go. *(re-iss.Jul88)*
Nov 84. (7") **EDGE OF A DREAM (from film 'Teachers'). / TEMPTED** [ ] [69] Oct 84
Jan 85. (7") **CRAZY IN LOVE. / COME ON IN** [-] [ ]
Feb 86. (7") **SHELTER ME. / TELL ME THERE'S A WAY** [-] [91]
Mar 86. (7") **SHELTER ME. / ONE MORE TIME** [ ] [-]
(12"+=) – If you have love, give me some.
Apr 86. (lp)(c)(cd) **COCKER** [ ] [50]
– Shelter / A to Z / Don't you love me anymore / Living without your love / Don't drink the water / You can leave your hat on / Heart of the matter / Inner city blues / Love is on a fade / Heaven. *(re-iss.Oct89 on 'Fame') (re-iss.cd+c Jul94)*
Apr 86. (7")(12") **YOU DON'T LOVE ME ANYMORE. / TELL ME THERE'S A WAY** [ ] [-]
(re-iss.May88) (12"+=) – All our tomorrows.
(cd-s++=) – With a little help from my friends.
May 86. (7") **DON'T YOU LOVE ME ANYMORE. / DON'T DRINK THE WATER** [-] [ ]
Jun 86. (7")(12") **YOU CAN LEAVE YOUR HAT ON. / LONG DRAG OFF THE CIGARETTE** [ ] [ ]
1987. (7") **LOVE LIVES ON. / ON MY WAY TO YOU** [-] [ ]
(above on 'MCA')
Oct 87. (7")(12") **UNCHAIN MY HEART. / YOU CAN LEAVE YOUR HAT ON** [46] [-]
(12") – ('A'side) / ('A'rock mix) / The one.
(cd-s+=) – ('A'dance mix). *(re-iss.Jun92, hit UK No.17)*
Oct 87. (7") **UNCHAIN MY HEART. / SATISFIED** [-] [ ]
Oct 87. (lp)(c)(cd) **UNCHAIN MY HEART** [ ] [89]
– Unchain my heart / Two wrongs (don't make a right) / I stand in wonder / The river's rising / Isolation / All our tomorrows / A woman loves a man / Trust in me / The one / Satisfied. *(re-iss.Jun89)*
Dec 87. (7")(12") **LOVE LIVE ON. / MY WAY TO YOU** [ ] [-]
Dec 87. (7") **TWO WRONGS (DON'T MAKE A RIGHT). / ISOLATION** [-] [ ]

— (above from 'Bigfoot & The Hendersons' US title 'Harry & The Hendersons', on 'M.C.A.')

Jul 89. (lp)(c)(cd) **ONE NIGHT OF SIN** [ ] [52]
– When the night comes / I will live for you / I've got to use my imagination / Letting go / Just to keep from drowning / The unforgiven * / Another mind gone / Fever / You know it's gonna hurt / Bad bad sign / I'm your man / One night of sin. *(cd+= *) (re-iss.cd+c Mar94)*
Oct 89. (c-s) **WHEN THE NIGHT COMES. / ONENIGHT OF SIN** [-] [11]
Nov 89. (7") **WHEN THE NIGHT COMES. / RUBY LEE** [65] [-]
(12"+=)(cd-s+=) – ('A'extended).

— **JOE COCKER BAND** is **DERIC DYER** – sax, keys, perc. / **STEVE HOLLEY** – drums / **PHIL GRANDE** – lead guitar / **JEFF LEVINE** – keys / **KEITH MACK** – rhythm guitar / **CHRIS STAINTON** – keys / **T.M. STEVENS** – bass, vocals / **DOREEN CHANTER** – vocals / **MAXINE GREEN** – vocals / **CRYSTAL TALIEFERO** – vocals, perc. / **The MEMPHIS HORNS:- WAYNE JACKSON, ANDREW LOVE, GARY GAZAWAY**

Jun 90. (cd)(c)(d-lp) **JOE COCKER LIVE (live)** [ ] [95]
– Feeling alright? / Shelter me / Hitchcock railway / Up where we belong / You can leave your hat on / Guilty / When the night comes / Unchain my heart / With a little help from my friends / You are so beautiful / The letter / She came in through the bathroom window / High time we went / What are you doing with a fool like me (studio) / Living in the promise land (studio).
May 90. (c-s) **WHAT ARE YOU DOING WITH A FOOL LIKE ME? / ANOTHER MIND GONE** [-] [96]

(studio:- **KENNY RICHARDS** – drums / **EARL SLICK** – guitar / **BASHARI JOHNSON** – perc. / backing vocals – **TAWATHA AGEE, VANEESE THOMAS & FONZI THORNTON.**)

Oct 91. (cd)(c)(lp) **NIGHT CALLS** [ ] [ ]
– Love is alive / Little bit of love / Please no more / There's a storm coming / You've got to hide your love away / I can hear the river / Don't let the Sun go down on me / Night calls / Five women / Can't find my way home / Not too young to die of a broken heart / Out of the rain. *(re-iss.Apr92, hit UK No.25)*
Oct 91. (7")(c-s) **NIGHT CALLS. / OUT OF THE RAIN** [ ] [ ]
(12"+=)(cd-s+=) – Not too young to die of a broken heart.
Mar 92. (7")(c-s) **(ALL I KNOW) FEELS LIKE FOREVER. / WHEN THE NIGHT COMES** [25] [ ]
(cd-s+=) – Up where we belong / With a little help from my friends.
May 92. (7")(c-s) **NOW THAT THE MAGIC HAS GONE. / FIVE WOMEN** [28] [ ]
(12"+=)(cd-s+=) – Two wrongs don't make a right / The letter.
Nov 92. (7")(c-s) **WHEN THE NIGHT COMES. / YOU'VE GOT TO HIDE YOUR LOVE AWAY** [61] [ ]
(cd-s+=) – Tempted / I still can't believe it's true.
(cd-s) – ('A'side) / The Moon is a harsh mistress / I'm your man / She came in through the bathroom window.

— now w / **JACK BRUNO** – drums / **BOB FEIT + TONY JOE WHITE + TIM PIERCE** – guitar / **CHRIS STAINTON** – keyboards / **LENNY CASTRO** – percussion / **C.J. VANSTON** – organ

Aug 94. (c-s) **THE SIMPLE THINGS. / SUMMER IN THE CITY** [17] [ ]
(cd-s+=) – With a little help from my friends (live).
(cd-s) – ('A'side) / Angeline / My strongest weakness.
Sep 94. (cd)(c)(lp) **HAVE A LITTLE FAITH** [9] [ ]
– Let the healing begin / Have a little faith in me / The simple things / Summer in the city / The great divide / Highway highway / Too cool / Soul time / Out of the blue / Angeline / Hell and highwater / Standing knee deep in a river / Take me home.
Oct 94. (7")(c-s)(cd-s) **TAKE ME HOME. (featuring BEKKA BRAMBLETT) / TEMPTED / UNCHAIN MY HEART (90's version)** [41] [ ]
(cd-s) – ('A'side) / Up where we belong / You can leave your hat on.
Dec 94. (7")(c-s)(cd-s) **LET THE HEALING BEGIN. / SUMMER IN THE CITY (2-mixes)** [32] [ ]
(cd-s) – ('A'side) / You are so beautiful (live) / The letter (live).
Jun 95. (c-s) **HAVE A LITTLE FAITH IN ME / THE SIMPLE THINGS (live) / LET THE HEALING BEGIN (live)** [ ] [ ]
(cd-s) – ('A'side) / Summer in the city (live) / Angeline (live).
(re-iss.Sep95, hit No.67 UK)

– compilations etc. –

Apr 71. Flyover/ US= A&M; (lp)(c) **COCKER HAPPY** [ ] [ ]
(re-iss.May85 on 'Sierra') (cd-iss.Oct94 on 'Disky')

Note; All releases on 'Cube' were issued on 'A&M' US.

Apr 72. Cube; (d-lp) **WITH A LITTLE HELP FROM MY FRIENDS / JOE COCKER!** [29] [ ]
Dec 76. Cube; (lp)(c) **LIVE IN L.A. (live)** [ ] [ ]
(re-iss.May86 on 'Sierra')
1977. Cube; (7") **CRY ME A RIVER. / FEELING ALRIGHT** [-] [ ]
Oct 81. Cube; (d-lp)(d-c) **THE JOE COCKER PLATINUM COLLECTION** [ ] [ ]
Dec 81. Cube; (7") **LET IT BE. / MARJORINE** [ ] [ ]
Apr 82. Cube; (lp)(c) **SPACE CAPTAIN (live)** [ ] [ ]
Oct 82. Cube; (lp)(c) **COUNTDOWN JOE COCKER** [ ] [ ]
May 83. Cube; (7") **YOU ARE SO BEAUTIFUL. / MARJORINE** [ ] [ ]
May 78. Hallmark; (lp)(c) **GREATEST HITS VOL.I** [ ] [ ] Nov 77
Jul 82. Old Gold; (7") **WITH A LITTLE HELP FROM MY FRIENDS. / DELTA LADY** [ ] [-]
Nov 84. Sierra; (d-lp)(c) **OFF THE RECORD** [ ] [ ]
May 86. Sierra; (lp)(c) **REPLAY ON . . .** [ ] [ ]

Apr 86. Castle; (d-lp)(d-c)(cd) **THE COLLECTION** [ ] [ ]
May 86. Telstar; (lp)(c)(cd) **THE VERY BEST OF JOE COCKER** [ ] [ ]
Sep 86. Archive 4; (12"ep) **WITH A LITTLE HELP FROM MY FRIENDS / MARJORINE / THE LETTER / DELTA LADY (live).**
(3" cd-iss.'88)
Mar 88. That's Original; (d-lp)(c) **JAMAICA SAY YOU WILL / COCKER HAPPY** [ ] [ ]
(d-cd.iss-Sep91)
1988. Knight; (cd) **THE BEST OF JOE COCKER** [ ] [ ]
Jul 88. Knight; (c) **NIGHTRIDING** [ ] [ ]
1988. Fun; (lp) **16 GREATEST HITS** [ ] [-]
Jan 92. Raven-Topic; (cd) **CONNOISSEUR'S COCKER** [ ] [-]
Jun 92. Polygram TV; (cd)(c)(d-lp) **THE LEGEND** [4] [-]
– Up where we belong (with JENNIFER WARNES) / With a little help from my friends / Delta lady / The letter / She came in through the bathroom window / A whiter shade of pale / Love the one you're with (live) / You are so beautiful / Let it be / Just like a woman / Many rivers to cross / Talking back to the night / Fun time / I heard it through the grapevine / Please give peace a chance (live) / Don't let me be misunderstood / Honky tonk woman (live) / Cry me a river (live).
Oct 93. Spectrum; (cd)(c) **THE FIRST TIME** [ ] [-]
Jul 94. BR Music; (cd)(c) **THE VERY BEST OF JOE COCKER** [ ] [-]
Oct 94. BR Music; (cd) **FAVOURITE RARITIES** [ ] [-]
Aug 94. E.M.I.; (cd)(cd-vid) **THE BEST OF JOE COCKER – LIVE (live)** [ ] [-]
Oct 94. Woodford; (cd) **MIDNIGHT RIDER** [ ] [-]
Oct 94. Woodford; (cd) **SIMPLY THE BEST** [ ] [-]
Sep 95. Spectrum; (cd)(c) **THE ESSENTIAL JOE COCKER** [ ] [-]
Dec 95. A&M; (4xcd-box) **THE LONG VOYAGE HOME** [ ] [-]

COCTEAU TWINS

Formed: Grangemouth, Scotland . . . late 1981 when the then trio visited London to give DJ John Peel a demo tape. He booked them for sessions on his Radio 1 night time show, and they signed to IVO's indie label '4 a.d.'. Throughout the 80's, they refused many "big deal" offers and issued albums at their own unrushed pace. • **Style:** Pastel and picturesque beauty, fused with LIZ's intentionally incoherent but heart-felt vox. • **Songwriters:** All by COCTEAU TWINS. • **Trivia:** In 1983, LIZ and ROBIN guested for THIS MORTAL COIL (Ivo/4.a.d. assembly of musicians) on SONG TO THE SIREN (45). ROBIN has since produced many '4.a.d.' outfits, and also The GUN CLUB in 1987. An item for some time, LIZ and ROBIN became parents in 1989. Early in 1991, LIZ was surprisingly but not undeservedly nominated for Best Female Vocalist at the 'Brit' awards.

Recommended: TREASURE (*9) / VICTORIALAND (*8) / GARLANDS (*7) / HEAD OVER HEELS (*8) / BLUE BELL KNOLL (*7) / HEAVEN OR LAS VEGAS (*7) / THE PINK OPAQUE (*8) / MILK AND KISSES (*7)

ELIZABETH FRASER – vocals / **ROBIN GUTHRIE** – guitar, drum programming, keyboards / **WILL HEGGIE** – bass

4 a.d. not issued

Jul 82. (lp) **GARLANDS** [ ] [-]
– Blood bitch / Wax and wane / But I'm not / Blind dumb deaf / Grail overfloweth / Shallow than halo / The hollow men / Garlands. *(c-iss.Apr84 +=)* – Dear heart / Blind dumb deaf / Hearsay please / Hazel. *(cd-iss.1986 ++=)* – Speak no evil / Perhaps some other acon.
Sep 82. (12"ep) **LULLABIES** [ ] [-]
– It's all but an ark lark / Alas dies laughing / Feathers-Oar-Blades.
Mar 83. (7")**PEPPERMINT PIG. / HAZEL** [ ] [-]
(12"+=) – Laugh lines.

—— Trimmed to a duo, when HEGGIE left to form LOWLIFE.

Oct 83. (lp) **HEAD OVER HEELS** [51] [-]
– When mama was moth / Sugar hiccup / In our anglehood / Glass candle grenades / Multifoiled / In the gold dust rush / The tinderbox (of a heart) / My love paramour / Musette and drums / Five ten fiftyfold. *(c-iss.Apr84, cd-iss.1986)* (c/cd+=) – Sunburst And Snowblind EP
Oct 83. (12"ep) **SUNBURST AND SNOWBLIND** [ ] [-]
– Sugar hiccup / From the flagstones / Because of whirl-Jack / Hitherto.

—— added **SIMON RAYMONDE** – bass, keyboards, guitar (ex-DROWNING CRAZE)

Apr 84. (7") **PEARLY DEWDROPS DROP. / PEPPER-TREE** [29] [-]
(12"+=) – The spangle maker.

4 a.d. Relativity

Nov 84. (lp)(c) **TREASURE** [29] [-]
– Ivo / Lorelei / Beatrix / Persephone / Pandora – for Cindy / Amelia / Aloysius / Cicely / Otterley / Donimo. *(cd-iss.1986)*
Mar 85. (7") **AIKEA-GUINEA. / KOOKABURRA** [41] [-]
(12"+=) – Rococo / Quiquose.
Nov 85. (12"ep) **TINY DYNAMITE** [52] [-]
– Pink orange red / Ribbed and veined / Sultitan Itan / Plain tiger.
Nov 85. (12"ep) **ECHOES IN A SHALLOW BAY** [65] [-]
– Great spangled fritillary / Melonella / Pale clouded white / Eggs and their shells *(cd.iss.Oct86 contains TINY DYNAMITE ep)*

—— **RICHARD THOMAS** – saxophone, bass (of DIF JUZ) repl. SIMON who fell ill.

Apr 86. (lp)(c)(cd) **VICTORIALAND** [10] [ ]
– Lazy calm / Fluffy tufts / Throughout the dark months of April and May / Whales tales / Oomingmak / Little Spacey / Feet-like fins / How to bring a blush to the snow / The thinner the air.

—— **SIMON RAYMONDE** returned replacing temp. RICHARD (back to DIF JUZ)

Oct 86. (7") **LOVE'S EASY TEARS. / THOSE EYES, THAT MOUTH** [53] [-]
(12"+=) – Sigh's smell of farewell.

—— next a COCTEAU TWINS one-off collaboration with '4.a.d' new signing **HAROLD BUDD** – piano

Nov 86. (lp)(c)(cd) **THE MOON AND THE MELODIES (as HAROLD BUDD, ELIZABETH FRASER, ROBIN GUTHRIE, SIMON RAYMONDE)** [46] [-]
– Sea, swallow me / Memory gongs / Why do you love me? / Eyes are mosaics / She will destroy you / The ghost has no home / Bloody and blunt / Ooze out and away, one how.

4 a.d. Capitol

Sep 88. (lp)(c)(cd) **BLUE BELL KNOLL** [15] [ ]
– Blue bell knoll / Athol-brose / Carolyn's fingers / For Phoebe still a baby / The itchy glowbo blow / Cico buff / Suckling the mender / Spooning good singing gum / A kissed out red floatboat / Ella megablast burls forever.
Oct 88. (7") **CAROLYN'S FINGERS. / BLUE BELL KNOLL** [-] [ ]

—— In Apr 90, **LIZ** was heard on IAN McCulloch's (ex-ECHO & THE BUNNYMEN) 'Candleland' single.

Aug 90. (7")(c-s) **ICEBLINK LUCK. / MIZAKE THE MIZAN** [38] [ ]
(12"+=)(cd-s+=) – Watchiar.
Sep 90. (cd)(c)(lp) **HEAVEN OR LAS VEGAS** [7] [99]
– Cherry coloured funk / Pitch the baby / Iceblink luck / Fifty-fifty clown / Heaven or Las Vegas / I wear your ring / Fotzepolitic / Wolf in the breast / Road, river and rail / Frou-frou foxes in midsummer fires.

—— on U.S. tour, augmented by **MITSUO TATE & BEN BLAKEMAN** – guitars

Fontana Capitol

Sep 93. (7")(c-s) **EVANGELINE. / MUD AND LARK** [34] [ ]
(12"pic-d+=)(cd-s+=) – Summer-blink.
Oct 93. (cd)(c)(lp) **FOUR CALENDAR CAFE** [13] [78]
– Know who you are ate every age / Evangeline / Blue beard / Theft and wandering around lost / Oil of angels / Squeeze-wax / My truth / Essence / Summerhead / Pur.
Dec 93. (cd-s) **WINTER WONDERLAND. / FROSTY THE SNOWMAN** [58] [ ]

—— (above festive tracks, were thankfully deleted after 1 week in UK Top60)

Feb 94. (7")(c-s) **BLUEBEARD. / THREE SWEPT** [33] [ ]
(12"+=) – Ice-pulse.
(cd-s++=) – ('A'acoustic).
Sep 95. (d7"ep)(cd-ep) **TWINLIGHTS** [59] [ ]
– Rilkean heart / Golden-vein / Pink orange red / Half-gifts.
Oct 95. (cd-ep) **OTHERNESS** (An Ambient EP) [59] [ ]
– Feet like fins / Seekers who are lovers / Violaine / Cherry coloured funk.

. . . Jan – Jun '96 stop press . . .

Mar 96. (single) **TISHBITE** [34] [ ]
Apr 96. (cd)(c)(lp) **MILK & KISSES** [17] [99]
Jun 96. (single) **VIOLAINE** [ ] [ ]

– compilations, others, etc. –

1985. 4 a.d./ US= Relativity; (cd) **THE PINK OPAQUE** [ ] [ ] Sep85
– The spangle maker / Millimillenary / Wax and wane / Hitherto / Pearly-dewdrops' drops (12" Version) / From the flagstones / Aikea-Guinea / Lorelei / Pepper-tree / Musette and drums.
Nov 91. Capitol; (cd-s-box-10) **THE SINGLES COLLECTION** [ ] [-]

—— (above featured previous 9 singles + new 1) (all sold separately Mar92)

Leonard COHEN

Born: 21 Sep'34, Montreal, Canada. In the 50's and early 60's he wrote poetry which was later to become lyrics for his songs. In 1963 COHEN published first novel THE FAVOURITE GAME, before attending Columbia Uni. In 1966 he signed to 'Columbia', after songs (most notably SUZANNE for JUDY COLLINS) had been covered. Around the same period, his second novel BEAUTIFUL LOSERS was published, and a film documentary 'LADIES & GENTLEMEN . . . ' was issued. In 1968, his debut album 'THE SONGS OF LEONARD COHEN' gained lots of interest, mostly in the UK where it hit Top 20. Relying on mostly album sales, his work though never massive, made him most respected and enduring artists of all-time. He was back in 1992, when 'THE FUTURE' gave him another album success. • **Style:** Droning narrative-like vocals, not unlike LOU REED in tone, made him loved by college beatnik circuit, although parodied and panned by music press critics. However, in recent years he has become more appreciated. I'M YOUR FAN Various Artists tribute album released late 1991. • **Songwriters:** He penned all material. Also covered; ALWAYS (Irving Berlin) / THE PARTISAN (A.Marly & H.Zaret-Bernard) / BE FOR REAL (Frederick Knight). • **Trivia:** His long-time dual backing singer and solo artist JENNIFER WARNES released album 'FAMOUS BLUE RAINCOAT' which contained all songs written by COHEN.

Recommended: GREATEST HITS (*9)

LEONARD COHEN – vocals, guitar(with various session people)

C.B.S. Columbia

Feb 68. (lp) **THE SONGS OF LEONARD COHEN** [13] [83]
– Suzanne / Master song / Winter lady / The stranger song / Sisters of mercy / So long, Marianne / Hey, that's no way to say goodbye / Stories of the street / Teachers / One of us cannot be wrong. *(re-iss.+cd.Nov91)*

May 68. (7") **SUZANNE. / SO LONG, MARIANNE** [ ] [ ]

Apr 69. (lp)(c) **SONGS FROM A ROOM** [2] [63]
– Bird on the wire / Story of Isaac / Bunch of lonesome heroes / The partisan / Seems so long ago, Nancy / Old revolution / The butcher / You know who I am / Lady midnight / Tonight will be fine. *(re-iss.Nov81) (cd-iss.Feb88)*

May 69. (7") **BIRD ON THE WIRE. / SEEMS SO LONG AGO, NANCY** [ ] [ ]

Mar 71. (lp)(c) **SONGS OF LOVE AND HATE** [4] [ ]
– Avalanche / Last year's man / Dress rehearsal rag / Diamonds in the mine / Love call you by your first name / Famous blue raincoat / Sing another song / Boys / Joan of Arc. *(re-iss.Sep82) (re-iss.cd+c Jun94 on 'Columbia')*

Jul 71. (7") **JOAN OF ARC. / DIAMONDS IN THE MINE** [ ] [ ]

Jul 72. (7"ep) **McCABE & MRS. MILLER** [ ] [ ]
– Sisters of mercy / Winter lady / The stranger song.

— w / **RON CORNELIUS** – guitar / **BOB JOHNSTON** – organ, guitar, harmonica / **CHARLIE DANIELS** – bass, fiddle / **ELKIN FOWLER** – banjo, guitar / **JENNIFER WARNES** – vocals / **PETER MARSHALL** – bass / **DAVID O'CONNOR** – guitar

Apr 73. (lp)(c) **LEONARD COHEN: LIVE SONGS (live)** [ ] [ ]
– (minute prologue) / Passing through / You know who I am / Bird on the wire / Nancy / Improvisation / Story of Isaac / Please don't pass me by (a disgrace) / Tonight will be fine / Queen Victoria. *(re-iss.Mar84, cd-iss. May88)*

Apr 73. (7") **NANCY (live). / PASSING THROUGH (live)** [-] [ ]

Jul 74. (7") **BIRD ON THE WIRE (live). / TONIGHT WILL BE FINE (live)** [ ] [ ]

— now w/ loads of sessioners

Aug 74. (lp)(c) **NEW SKIN FOR THE OLD CEREMONY** [24] [ ]
– Is this what you wanted / Chelsea hotel No.2 / Lover lover lover / Field Commander Cohen / Why don't you try / There is a war / A singer must die / I tried to leave you / Who by fire / Take this longing / Leaving Green sleeves. *(cd-iss.Feb88)*

Nov 74. (7") **LOVER LOVER LOVER. / WHO BY FIRE** [ ] [ ]

Nov 75. (lp)(c) **GREATEST HITS** [ ] [ ]
– Suzanne / Sisters of mercy / So long, Marianne / Bird on the wire / Lady Midnight / The partisan / Hey, that's no way to say goodbye / Famous blue raincoat / Last year's man / Chelsea hotel No.2 / Who by fire / Take this longing. *(re-iss.+cd.Apr85) (re-iss.Jul88, hit UK 99)*

Nov 77. (lp)(c) **DEATH OF A LADIES MAN** [35] [ ]
– True love leaves no traces / Iodine / Paper thin hotel / Memories / I left a woman waiting / Don't go home with your hard-on / Fingerprints / Death of a ladies man. *(cd-iss.Feb88 & May95 +c)*

Dec 77. (7") **MEMORIES. / DON'T GO HOME WITH YOUR HARD-ON** [ ] [ ]

Oct 78. (7") **TRUE LOVE LEAVES NO TRACES. / I LEFT A WOMAN WAITING** [ ] [ ]

Sep 79. (lp)(c) **RECENT SONGS** [ ] [ ]
– The guests / Humbled in love / The window / Came so far for beauty / The lost Canadian (un Canadien errant) / The traitor / Our lady of solitude / The gypsy's wife / The smokey life / The ballad of absent mare. *(cd-iss.May88) (re-iss.cd.Dec93 on 'Sony Europe') (re-iss.cd+c May94 on 'Columbia')*

C.B.S. Passport

Feb 85. (lp)(c) **VARIOUS POSITIONS** [52] [ ]
– Dance me to the end of love / Come back to you / The law / Night comes on / Hallelujah / The captain / Hunter's lullaby / Heart with no companion / If it be your will. *(cd-iss.Feb88)*

Feb 85. (7") **DANCE ME TO THE END OF LOVE. / THE LAW** [ ] [ ]

Jan 88. (7") **FIRST WE TAKE MANHATTAN. / SISTERS OF MERCY** [ ] [ ]
(12"+=)(cd-s+=) – Bird on the wire / Suzanne.

Feb 88. (lp)(c)(cd) **I'M YOUR MAN** [48] [ ]
– First we take Manhattan / Ain't no cure for love / Everybody knows / I'm your man / Take this waltz / Jazz police / I can't forget / Tower of song. *(re-iss.cd Dec95)*

May 88. (7") **AIN'T NO CURE FOR LOVE. / JAZZ POLICE** [ ] [ ]
(12"+=)(cd-s+=) – Hey that's no way to say goodbye / So long, Marianne.

Columbia Columbia

Nov 92. (cd)(c)(lp) **THE FUTURE** [36] [ ]
– The future / Waiting for the miracle / Be for real / Closing time / Anthem / Democracy / Light as the breeze / Always / Tacoma trailer.

Dec 92. (cd-ep) **THE FUTURE EP** [ ] [ ]

May 93. (cd-ep) **CLOSING TIME / FIRST WE TAKE MANHATTAN / FAMOUS BLUE RAINCOAT / WINTER LADY** [ ] [-]

– compilations etc. –

Note; on 'CBS/ Columbia' until otherwise stated.

Mar 73. (7") **SUZANNE. / BIRD ON THE WIRE** [ ] [ ]

May 76. (7") **SUZANNE. / TAKE THIS LONGING** [ ] [ ]

May 88. (cd) **THE BEST OF LEONARD COHEN** (UK-iss.Oct94) [ ] [ ]

Aug 83. Pickwick; (7"ep)(c-ep) **SCOOP 33** [ ] [-]
– Suzanne / Hey, that's no way to say goodbye / Joan of Arc / Bird on the wire / Paper thin hotel / Lady midnight.

Sep 92. Sony-Columbia; (d-cd) **NEW SKIN FOR THE OLD CEREMONY / SONGS FROM A ROOM** [ ] [ ]

Oct 93. Sony-Columbia; (3xcd-box) **SONGS OF LEONARD COHEN / SONGS OF LOVE & HATE / LIVE** [ ] [ ]

Nov 93. Sony Collectors; (cd)(c) **SO LONG, MARIANNE** [ ] [-]
(re-iss.Dec95 on 'Columbia')

Feb 95. Columbia; (d-cd) **SONGS FROM A ROOM / SONGS OF LOVE & HATE** [ ] [-]

Lloyd COLE

Formed: Glasgow, Scotland . . . Summer '83, COLE and BLAIR COWAN formed LLOYD COLE & THE COMMOTIONS. They recruited CLARK, DONEGAN and Scots lightweight boxing champ IRVINE. They almost immediately signed with 'Polydor', becoming college circuit darlings by the mid 80's. They/he had enduring string of albums accompanied by several hit singles, starting with 'PERFECT SKIN'. • **Style:** Intelligent laid-back rock with looks/image courtesy of COLE. • **Songwriters:** COLE penned, except GLORY (Television) / MYSTERY TRAIN (Elvis Presley) / I DON'T BELIEVE YOU (Bob Dylan) / CHILDREN OF THE REVOLUTION (T.Rex). • **Trivia:** 60's chanteuse/singer SANDIE SHAW had minor UK chart hit in 1986 with their 'Rattlesnakes' lp track, 'ARE YOU READY TO BE HEARTBROKEN?'. By 1990, COLE had flitted to New York, also beginning a brief modelling career.

Recommended: 1984-1989 (*8)

LLOYD COLE & THE COMMOTIONS

LLOYD COLE (b.31 Jan'61, Derbyshire, England) – vocals, guitar / **NEIL CLARK** (b. 3 Jul'55) – guitar / **BLAIR COWAN** – keyboards, vocals / **LAWRENCE DONEGAN** (b.13 Jul'61) – bass (ex-BLUEBELLS) / **STEPHEN IRVINE** (b.16 Dec'59) – drums

Polydor Geffen

Apr 84. (7") **PERFECT SKIN. / THE SEA AND THE SAND** [26] [ ]
(12"+=) – You will never be so good.

Aug 84. (7") **FOREST FIRE. / ANDY'S BABIES** [41] [ ]
(12"+=) – Glory

Oct 84. (lp)(c)(cd) **RATTLESNAKES** [13] [ ]
– Perfect skin / Speedboat / Rattlesnakes / Down on Mission Street / Forest fire / Charlotte Street / 2CV / Four flights up / Patience / Are you ready to be heartbroken?. (cd.+=) – The sea and the sand / You will never be no good / Sweetness / Andy's babies. *(re-iss.c+cd. 1991)*

Oct 84. (7") **RATTLESNAKES. / SWEETNESS** [65] [ ]
(12"+=) – Four flights up

Aug 85. (7") **BRAND NEW FRIEND. / HER LAST FLING** [19] [ ]
(12"+=) – Speedboat (live) / 2CV (live).

Oct 85. (7")(10") **LOST WEEKEND. / BIG WORLD** [17] [ ]
(12"+=) – Never ends.

Nov 85. (lp)(c)(cd) **EASY PIECES** [5] [ ]
– Rich / Why I love country music / Pretty gone / Grace / Cut me down / Brand new friend / Lost weekend / James / Minor characters / Perfect blue. *(c+=)* – Her last fling / Big world. *(cd++=)* – Never ends. *(re-iss.c+cd.1991) (re-iss.cd+c May93 on 'Spectrum')*

Jan 86. (7") **CUT ME DOWN (remix). / ARE YOU READY TO BE HEARTBROKEN? (live)** [38] [ ]
(12"+=) – Forest fire (live).
(d7"++=) – Perfect blue (instrumental).

— Trimmed to studio quartet, when COWAN became only part-time (gigs only)

Polydor Capitol

Sep 87. (7") **MY BAG. / JESUS SAID** [46] [ ]
(12"+=)(cd-s+=) – Perfect skin.

Oct 87. (lp)(c)(cd) **MAINSTREAM** | 9 | |
– My bag / From the hip / 29 / Mainstream / Jennifer she said / Mister malcontent / Sean Penn blues / Big snake / Hey Rusty / These days.
Oct 87. (7") **MY BAG. / LOVE YOUR WIFE** | - | |
Jan 88. (7") **JENNIFER SHE SAID. / PERFECT BLUE** | 31 | |
(12"+=) – Mystery train (live) / I don't believe you (live).
(cd-s+=) – My bag (mix).
Apr 88. (7"ep)(12"ep)(cd-ep) **FROM THE HIP** | 59 | |
– From the hip / Please / Lonely mile / Love you wife.
Mar 89. (lp)(c)(cd) **1984-1989** (compilation) | 14 | |
– Perfect skin / Are you ready to be heartbroken? / Forest fire / You will never be so good / Rattlesnakes / Perfect blue / Brand new friend / Cut me down / Lost weekend / Her last fling / Mr.Malcontent / My bag / Jennifer she said / From the hip.
Apr 89. (7") **FOREST FIRE ('89 remix). / PERFECT BLUE** | | |
(12"+=)(cd-s+=) – ('A'&'B'extended).

— DONEGAN decided to leave, and the group folded Apr'89.

LLOYD COLE

went solo with **BLAIR COWAN** – keyboards / **DARYLL SWEET** – bass / **ROBEDRT QUINE** – guitar / **FRED MAHER** – drums, etc / **NICKY HOLLAND and PARKER DU LANY backing vocals. /** (on tour; DAN McCARROLL repl. MAHER / **DAVID BALL repl. SWEET)**

Jan 90. (7")(c-s) **NO BLUE SKIES. / SHELLY I DO** | 42 | |
(10"+=)(12"+=)(cd-s+=) – Wild orphan.
Feb 90. (cd)(c)(lp) **LLOYD COLE** | 11 | |
– Don't look back / What do you know about love? / Loveless / No blue skies / Sweetheart / To the church / Downtown / A long way down / Ice cream girl / I hate to see you baby doing that shift / Undressed / Waterline / Mercy killing. *(re-iss.cd Apr95)*
Mar 90. (7")(c-s) **DON'T LOOK BACK. / BLAME MARY JANE** | 59 | |
(10"+=)(12"+=)(cd-s+=) – Witching hour.
Oct 90. (7")(c-s) **DOWNTOWN. / A LONG WAY DOWN (live)** | | |
(12"+=)(cd-s+=) – Sweetheart (live).

— **COLE** now with **COWAN & CLARK**

Aug 91. (7") **SHE'S A GIRL AND I'M A MAN. / WEIRD ON ME** | 55 | |
(12"+=)(cd-s+=) – Children of the revolution.
Sep 91. (cd)(c)(lp) **DON'T GET WEIRD ON ME BABE** | 21 | |
-Butterfly / Theme for her / Margo's waltz / Half of everything / Man enough / What he doesn't know / Tell your sister / Weeping wine / To the lions / Pay for it / The one you never had / She's a girl and I'm a man.
Oct 91. (7") **WEEPING WINE. / TELL YOUR SISTER** | | |
(12"+=)(cd-s+=) – Somewhere out in the east.
Mar 92. (7")(c-s) **BUTTERFLY. / JENNIFER SHE SAID** | | |
(12"+=)(cd-s+=) – ('A'the Planet Anne Charlotte mix).

| | Fontana | Fontana |
Sep 93. (7")(c-s) **SO YOU'D LIKE TO SAVE THE WORLD. / VICIOUS** | 72 | |
(cd-s+=) – Mystic lady.
(cd-s) – ('A'side) / For your pleasure for your company / 4 M.B.
Oct 93. (cd)(c)(lp) **BAD VIBES** | 38 | |
– Morning is broken / So you'd like to save the world / Holier than thou / Love you so what / Wild mushrooms / My way to you / Too much of a good thing / Fall together / Mister Wrong / Seen the future / Can't get arrested.

— above w/ **ADAM PETERS, ANN CHARLOTTE VENGSGAARD, JOHN MICCO, JOHN CARRUTHERS, NEIL CLARK, MATTHEW SWEET, DAN McCARROLL, ANTON FIER, CURTIS WATTS, FRED MAHER, DANA VLCEK, Lightning BOB HOFFNAR + PETER MARK**

Nov 93. (7")(c-s) **MORNING IS BROKEN. / RADIO CITY MUSIC HALL** | | |
(cd-s+=) – Radio City music hall / Eat your greens.
(cd-s+=) – The slider / Mannish girl.

| | Mercury | Mercury |
Sep 95. (c-s) **LIKE LOVERS DO / I WILL NOT LEAVE YOU ALONE** | 24 | |
(cd-s+=) – Rattlesnakes.
(cd-s) – ('A'side) / Brand new baby blues (demo) / Perfect skin.
(cd-s) – ('A'side) / Traffic / Forest fire.
(cd-s) – ('A'side) / Forest fire / Rattlesnakes / Perfect skin.
Sep 95. (cd)(c) **LOVE STORY** | 27 | |
– Trigger happy / Sentimental fool / I didn't know that you cared / Love ruins everything / Baby / Be there / The June bride / Like lovers do / Happy for you / Traffic / Let's get lost / For crying out loud.
Nov 95. (c-s) **SENTIMENTAL FOOL / BRAND NEW FRIEND** | 73 | |
(cd-s+=) – Lost weekend / Cut me down.
(cd-s) – ('A'side) / Most of the time / Millionaire / Sold.

. . . Jan – Jun '96 stop press . . .

May 96. (single) **BABY** | | |

COLLECTIVE SOUL

Formed: Stockbridge, Georgia, USA . . .late 80's by ED ROLAND, who had studied at Boston's Berklee School Of Music. After numerous rejections from major record companies, he split band in 1992. He continued to try his hand at writing songs for other artists and made songwriting demo for some radio stations. Interest in the song 'SHINE' let 'Atlantic' take note and they duly signed him/them in 1993. He brought in musicians, including his brother DEAN and original drummer SHANE EVANS. SHINE became a near Top 10 hit in the States, as did debut album 'HINTS . . .', helped by playing the Woodstock 25th Anniversary Festival '94. • **Style:** Catchy hard and sometimes alternative rock act. • **Songwriters:** ED ROLAND.

Recommended: HINTS, ALLEGATIONS AND THINGS LEFT UNSAID (*6)

ED ROLAND -vocals, guitar / **ROSS CHILDRESS** -lead guitar / **DEAN ROLAND** -guitar / **WILL TURPIN** -bass / **SHANE EVANS** -drums

| | Atlantic | Atlantic |
May 94. (c-s) **SHINE / LOVE LIFTED ME / BURNING BRIDGES** | | 11 |
(12"+=)(cd-s+=) – ('A'version).
Sep 94. (cd)(c) **HINTS, ALLEGATIONS AND THINGS LEFT UNSAID** | | 18 May 94 |
– Shine / Goodnight, good guy / Wasting time / Sister don't cry / Love lifted me / In a moment / Heaven's already here / Pretty Donna / Reach / Breathe / Scream / Burning bridges / All.
Oct 94. (c-s)(cd-s) **BREATHE /** | - | |
May 95. (c-s)(cd-s) **GEL /** | - | |

— (above was featured in the comedy film 'The Jerky Boys')

May 95. (cd)(c) **COLLECTIVE SOUL** | | 23 Mar95 |
–
May 95. (c-s)(cd-s) **DECEMBER /** | - | 20 |
Dec 95. (cd-s) **THE WORLD I KNOW /** | - | 19 |

Allen COLLINS BAND
(see under ⇒ LYNYRD SKYNYRD)

Edwyn COLLINS

Born: 23 Aug'59, Edinburgh, Scotland. Formed ORANGE JUICE in Glasgow, Scotland . . . 1977 initially as the NU-SONICS. In 1979, ORANGE JUICE signed to local indie label 'Postcard'. After 4 well-received 45's, they transferred to 'Polydor', helped by manager Ian Crann. After 2 minor hits, they progressed early 1982 with debut Top 30 album 'YOU CAN'T HIDE YOUR LOVE FOREVER'. They split in 1984 and after a few singles in the mid 80's, EDWYN finally issued his debut album in 1989 'HOPE AND DESPAIR'. However, it took just over half a decade for him to climb back into the charts with his gorgeous hit single 'A GIRL LIKE YOU'. • **Style:** Jangly alternative pop outfit, fronted by throaty deep vox of COLLINS. He and Nigerian newcomer ZEKE MANYIKA moved into a more funkier territory in 1982. • **Songwriters:** Most written by COLLINS, some with MANYIKA. Note that KIRK was the writer of FELICITY, and Ross provided PUNCH DRUNK. Covered L.O.V.E. (Al Green). COLLINS solo covered MY GIRL HAS GONE (Smokey Robinson) + TIME OF THE PREACHER (Willie Nelson). • **Trivia:** COLLINS was raised in Dundee while of school age, until he moved to Bearsden, near Glasgow.

Recommended: THE ESTEEMED ORANGE JUICE (THE VERY BEST OF ORANGE JUICE) (*9) / GORGEOUS GEORGE (*8)

EDWYN COLLINS – vox, guitar, occ.violin / **JAMES KIRK** – guitar, vocals / **DAVID McCLYMONT** – bass, synths repl. ALAN DUNCAN/ **STEPHEN DALY** – drums

| | Postcard | not issued |
Feb 80. (7") **FALLING AND LAUGHING. / MOSCOW** | | - |
(free 7"flexi) – FELICITY (live).
Aug 80. (7") **BLUE BOY. / LOVE SICK** | | - |
Dec 80. (7") **SIMPLY THRILLED HONEY. / BREAKFAST TIME** | | - |
Mar 81. (7") **POOR OLD SOUL. / (part 2)** | | - |

| | Polydor | Polydor |
Oct 81. (7") **L.O.V.E . . . LOVE. / INTUITION TOLD ME** | 65 | - |
(12"+=) – Moscow.
Jan 82. (7") **FELICITY. / IN A NUTSHELL** | 63 | - |
(12"+=) – You old eccentric.
Feb 82. (lp)(c) **YOUR LOVE CAN'T LAST FOREVER** | 21 | |
– Tender object / L.O.V.E . . . love / Falling and laughing / Wan light / Untitled melody / Dying day / Upwards and onwards / Felicity / Three cheers for our side / Intuition told me / Satellite city / In a nutshell / Consolation prize.

— **MALCOLM ROSS** – guitar (ex-JOSEF K) repl. KIRK who formed MEMPHIS /

ZEKE MANYIKA (b. Nigeria) – percussion, vocals, synths repl. DALY to above

Jul 82. (7")(10") **TWO HEARTS TOGETHER. / HOKOYO** 60 -

Oct 82. (7") **I CAN'T HELP MYSELF. / TONGUES BEGIN TO WAG** 42
(12"+=) – Barbeque.

Nov 82. (lp)(c) **RIP IT UP** 39
– Rip it up / Turn away / I can't help myself / Breakfast time / Tender hook / A million pleading places / Flesh of my flesh / Mud in your eye / Louise Louise. *(re-iss.Jul89)*

Feb 83. (7") **RIP IT UP (remix). / SNAKE CHARMER** 8
(12") – ('A'extended) / A sad lament.
(d7"++=) – (all tracks).

May 83. (7")(7"pic-d) **FLESH OF MY FLESH. / LORD JOHN WHITE AND THE BOTTLENECK TRAIN** 41

— basically now a duo of **COLLINS + MANYIKA** with session people replacing ROSS (who joined AZTEC CAMERA) and McCLYMONT (to The MOODISTS)

Feb 84. (7") **BRIDGE. / OUT FOR THE COUNT** 67
(12"+=) – ('A' Summer '83 mix).
(free 7"flexi w/7") – Poor old soul (live).

Feb 84. (m-lp)(c) **TEXAS FEVER** 34
– A sad lament / Craziest feeling / A place in my heart / The day I went down to Texas / Punch drunk / Bridge.

Apr 84. (7") **WHAT PRESENCE?!. / A PLACE IN MY HEART** 47
(12"+=) – ('A'extended).
(free c-s w/7") – In a nutshell (live) / Simply thrilled honey (live) / Dying day (live).

Oct 84. (7") **LEAN PERIOD. / BURY MY HEAD IN MY HANDS** 74
(12"+=) – ('A'extended).
(free 7"flexi w/7") – Rip it up / What presence?!.

Nov 84. (lp)(c) **THE ORANGE JUICE – THE THIRD ALBUM**
– Get while the goings good / Salmon fishing in New York / I guess I'm just a little sensitive / Burning desire / The artisan / Lean period / What presence?! / Out for the count / All that mattered / Searchager. (c+=) – (extra versions)

— Disbanded after above album. MANYIKA went solo, as did EDWYN COLLINS.

He had already in Aug84 hit UK 72 with PAUL QUINN on 7"/12" 'PALE BLUES EYES' (a Velvet Underground cover) released on 'Swamplands'.

– compilations, others, etc. –

Jul 85. Polydor; (lp)(c) **IN A NUTSHELL** -
(w/free 7"flexi) – FELICITY.

Jan 91. Polydor; (cd)(c) **THE ORANGE JUICE / YOU CAN'T HIDE YOUR LOVE FOREVER** -

Jul 92. Polydor; (cd)(c)(lp) **THE VERY BEST OF ORANGE JUICE (THE ESTEEMED ORANGE JUICE)** -
– Falling and laughing / Consolation prize (live) / Old encentric / L.O.V.E. love / Felicity / In a nutshell / Rip it up / I can't help myself / Flesh of my flesh / Tenterhook / Bridge / The day I went down to Texas / Punch drunk / A place in my heart / A sad lament / Lean period / I guess I'm just a little too sensitive / The artisans / Salmon fishing in New York / What presence?! / Out for the count. *(re-iss.cd Sep95)*

Jul 92. Postcard; (cd)(c)(lp) **OSTRICH CHURCHYARD (live in Glasgow)** -
(re-iss.cd Oct95)

May 93. Postcard; (7") **BLUEBOY. / LOVESICK** -
(cd-s+=) – Poor old soul (French version) / Poor old soul (instrumental).

Jul 93. Postcard; (cd)(lp) **THE HEATHER'S ON FIRE** -
– Falling and laughing / Moscow / Moscow Olympics / Blue boy / Love sick / Simply thrilled honey / Breakfast time / Poor old soul / Poor old soul pt.2 / Felicity / Upwards and onwards / Dying day / Holiday hymn. *(re-iss.cd Oct95)*

EDWYN COLLINS

solo, with **DENNIS BOVELL, MALCOLM ROSS, ALEX GRAY + CHRIS TAYLOR**

Creation Elevation

May 87. (7") **DON'T SHILLY SHALLY. / IF EVER YOU'RE READY** -
(12"+=) – Queer fish.

Elevation not issued

Nov 87. (7")(12") **MY BELOVED GIRL. / CLOUDS (FOGGING UP MY MIND)** -

— now with **BERNARD CLARKE** – keys / **DENNIS BOVELL** – bass / **DAVE RUFFY** – drums

Demon not issued

Jun 89. (lp)(c)(cd) **HOPE AND DESPAIR** -
– Coffee table song / 50 shades of blue / You're better than you know / Pushing it to the back of my mind / The wheels of love / Darling, they want it all / The beginning of the end / The measure of the man / Testing time / Let me put my arms around you / The wide eyed child in me / Ghost of a chance. *(re-iss.cd Sep95)*

Jul 89. (7") **THE COFFEE TABLE SONG. / JUDAS IN BLUE JEANS** -
(12"+=) – Out there.

Oct 89. (7") **50 SHADES OF BLUE (new mix). / IF EVER YOU'RE READY** -
(12"+=) – Kindred spirit / Just call her name / Ain't that always the way.

— (on cd-s last track repl. by) – Judas in blue jeans.

Oct 90. (cd)(c)(lp) **HELLBENT ON COMPROMISE** -
– Means to an end / You poor deluded fool / It might as well be you / Take care of yourself / Graciously / Someone else besides / My girl has gone / Everything and more / What's the big idea? / Hellbent medley:- Time of the preacher – Long time gone. *(re-iss.cd Oct95)*

EDWYN COLLINS

w / **STEVEN SKINNER** – guitar / **PHIL THORNALLEY** – bass / **PAUL COOK** – drums

Setanta not issued

Aug 94. (cd)(c)(lp) **GEORGEOUS GEORGE** -
– The campaign for real rock / A girl like you / Low expectations / Out of this world / If you could love me / North of Heaven / Georgeous George / It's right in front of you / Make me feel again / You got it all / Subsidence / Occupy your mind. *(re-iss.Jul95, hit UK No.8)*

Nov 94. (12"ep)(c-ep)(cd-ep) **EXPRESSLY** 42
– A girl like you / Out of this world / Don't shilly shally (spotter's '86 demo).
(cd-ep) – A girl like you / A girl like you (Macrame remix by Youth) / Out of this world (I hear a new world) remixed by St.Etienne / Occupy your mind.

Mar 95. (12"ep) **IF YOU COULD LOVE ME (radio edit). / IN A BROKEN DREAM / INSIDER DEALING / ('A'-MC Esher mix)**
(cd-s) – (first 3 tracks) / Hope and despair.
(cd-s) – ('A'side) / If ever you're ready / Come to your senses / A girl like you (mix).

Jun 95. (7") **A GIRL LIKE YOU. / YOU'RE ON YOUR OWN** 4 32
(c-s+=) – If you could love me (acoustic version).
(cd-s++=) – Don't shilly shally (Spotter's 86 demo version).

. . . Jan – Jun '96 stop press . . .

Feb 96. (single) **KEEP ON BURNING** 45

Phil COLLINS (see under ⇒ GENESIS)

CONNELLS

*** NEW ENTRY ***

Formed: Raleigh, North Carolina, USA . . .mid 80's by brothers MIKE and DAVID CONNELL. Released debut mini-lp 'DARKER DAYS' in 1985, which found its way to UK via indie label 'Demon'. A follow-up took time, as did their third 'RING' in 1993. MTV in Europe picked up on one particular song '74-75', which gave them massive hit in 1995. • **Style:** Acoustic rock outfit, fusing more than a little of R.E.M. and The LA's. • **Songwriters:** MIKE CONNELL most initially. Some by MacMILLAN or HUNTLEY. Covered LIVING IN THE PAST (Jethro Tull).

Recommended: RING (*5)

MIKE CONNELL – guitar, vocals / **DAVID CONNELL** – bass / **DOUG MacMILLAN** – vocals, guitar / **GEORGE HUNTLEY** – guitar, vocals, mandolin / **PEELE WIMBERLEY** – drums, percussion / **STEVE POTAK** – piano, organ, keyboards

Demon Mammoth

Nov 85. (m-lp) **DARKER DAYS**
– Darker days / Much easier / 1934 / Brighter worlds / In my head / Hats off / Holding pattern / Seven / Unspoken words.

1986. (12"ep) **HATS OFF**

Oct 89. (lp)(cd) **FUN AND GAMES**
– Something to say / Fun and games / Sal / Upside down / Fine tuning / Motel / Hey wow / Ten pins / Inside my head / Uninspired / Sat nite (USA) / Lay me down. *(cd+=)*– Fine tuning.

TVT-London TVT

Jul 95. (7") **'74-'75. / NEW BOY** 14
(cd-s+=) – Logan Street / Fun and games. *(re-iss.Feb96, hit UK 21)*

Sep 95. (cd)(c) **RING** 36 1993
– Slackjawed / Carry my picture / '74-'75 / Doin' you / Find out / Eyes on the ground / Spiral / Hey you / New boy / Disappointed / Burden / Any day now / Running Mary. *(UK-iss.+=)*– Logan Street / Wonder why / Living in the past.

CONTRABAND (see under ⇒ SCHENKER, Michael)

Ry COODER

Born: RYLAND COODER, 15 Mar'47, Los Angeles, California, USA. He sessioned for likes of JACKIE DE SHANNON and TAJ MAHAL, before moving on to CAPTAIN BEEFHEART in '67. He nearly replaced BRIAN JONES in The ROLLING STONES, but chose to only guest on their LET IT BLEED album, before going solo. He signed to 'Reprise' in 1970, and was used on debut album by LITTLE FEAT and STONES' 'Sticky Fingers'. • **Style:** His repertoire shifted through folk / blues, Tex-Mex, and jazz with his bottleneck style a feature. • **Songwriters:** All by COODER except; VIGILANTE MAN (Woody Guthrie) / GET RHYTHM (Johnny Cash) / HE'LL HAVE TO GO (hit; Jim Reeves) / LITTLE SISTER (Pomus-Shuman) / 13 QUESTION METHOD (Chuck Berry) / MONEY HONEY (hit; Drifters) / STAND BY ME (Ben E.King) / IT'S ALL OVER NOW (Bobby Womack) / GOODNIGHT IRENE (Leadbelly) / NEED A WOMAN (Bob Dylan) / BLUE SUEDE SHOES (Carl Perkins) / ALL SHOOK UP (Elvis Presley) / and loads more. The JAZZ album had early 1940's covers, etc. • **Trivia:** He also wrote score for 1980 film SOUTHERN COMFORT which sadly was not issued on soundtrack.

Recommended: WHY DON'T YOU TRY ME TONIGHT (*7)

RY COODER – vocals, guitar (ex-CAPTAIN BEEFHEART & HIS MAGIC BAND) plus session people too numerous to mention

Reprise Reprise

Oct 70. (7") **GOIN' TO BROWNSVILLE. / AVAILABLE SPACE** [-] [ ]

Dec 70. (7") **ALIMONY. / PIGMEAT** [-] [ ]

Jan 71. (lp)(c) **RY COODER** [ ] [ ] Dec70
– Alimony / France dance / One meat ball / Do re mi / Old Kentucky home / How can a poor man stand such times and live? / Available space / Pig meat / Police dog blues / Goin' to Brownsville / Dark is the night. *(cd-iss.May95 on 'Warners')*

May 71. (7") **HOW CAN A POOR MAN STAND SUCH TIMES AND LIVE. / GOIN' TO BROWNSVILLE** [ ] [ ]

Feb 72. (7") **ON A MONDAY. / DARK IS THE NIGHT** [-] [ ]

Feb 72. (lp)(c) **INTO THE PURPLE VALLEY** [ ] [ ]
– How can you keep on moving / Billy the kid / Money honey / F.D.R. in Trinidad / Teardrops will fall / Denomination blues / On a Monday / Hey porter / Great dreams from heaven / Taxes on the farmer feeds us all / Vigilante man.

Feb 72. (7") **MONEY HONEY. / ON A MONDAY** [ ] [ ]

Apr 72. (7") **MONEY MONEY. / BILLY THE KID** [-] [ ]

Oct 72. (7") **BOOMER'S STORY. / BILLY THE KID** [-] [ ]

Nov 72. (lp)(c) **BOOMER'S STORY** [ ] [ ]
– Boomer's story / Cherry ball blues / Crow black children / Axe sweet mama / Maria Elena / Dark end of the street / Rally 'round the flag / Comin' in on a wing and a prayer / President Kennedy / Good morning Mr. Railroad man.

May 74. (lp)(c) **PARADISE AND LUNCH** [ ] [ ]
– Tamp 'em up solid / Tattler / Married man's a fool / Jesus on the mainline / It's all over now / Fool about a cigarette – Feelin' good / If walls could talk / Mexican divorce / Ditty wa ditty.

— next with **FLACO JIMINEZ** – accordion / **GABBY PAHINHI** – steel guitar / **BOBBY KING** – gospel vocals

Oct 76. (lp)(c) **CHICKEN SKIN MUSIC** [ ] [ ]
– The bourgeois blues / I got mine / Always lift him up / He'll have to go / Smack dab in the middle / Stand by me / Yellow roses / Chloe / Goodnight Irene.

Mar 77. (7") **HE'LL HAVE TO GO. / THE BOURGEOIS BLUES** [ ] [ ]

Warners Warners

Aug 77. (lp)(c) **SHOW TIME (live)** [ ] [ ]
– School is out / Alimony / Jesus on the mainline / ark end of the street / Viva sequin – Do re mi / Volver, volver / How can a poor man stand such times and live? / Smack dab in the middle. *(cd-iss.Nov93)*

Aug 77. (7") **SCHOOL IS OUT (live). / JESUS ON THE MAINLINE (live)** [-] [ ]

Jun 78. (lp)(c) **JAZZ** [ ] [ ]
– Face to face I shall meet him / Davenport blues / In a mist / Big bad Bill is sweet William now / Happy meeting in glory / We shall be happy / Nobody / Shine / Flashes / Dream / Pearls / Tia Juana.

Jun 79. (7") **LITTLE SISTER. / DOWN IN HOLLYWOOD** [-] [ ]

Aug 79. (lp)(c) **BOP TILL YOU DROP** [36] [62]
– Little sister / Go home girl / The very thing that makes you rich (makes me poor) / I think it's gonna work out fine / Down in Hollywood / Look at granny run run / Trouble, you can't fool me / Don't mess up a good thing / I can't win.

Aug 79. (7") **LITTLE SISTER. / GO HOME GIRL** [ ] [ ]

Oct 79. (7") **THE VERY THING THAT MAKES YOU RICH (MAKES ME POOR). / LITTLE SISTER** [-] [ ]

Jun 80. (lp) **THE LONG RIDERS (Soundtrack)** [ ] [ ]
– (main title) The long riders / I'm a good old rebel / Seneca square dance / Archie's funeral (hold to God's unchanging hand) / I always knew that you were the one / Rally 'round the flag / Wildwood boys / Better things to talkabout / My grandfather / Cole Younger polka / Escape from Northfield / Leaving Missouri / Jesse James.

Oct 80. (lp)(c) **BORDERLINE** [35] [43] Jan81
– 634-5789 / Speedo / Why don't you try me / Down in the Boondocks / Johnny Porter / The way we make a broken heart / Crazy 'bout an automobile (every woman I know) / The girls from Texas / Borderline / Never make a move too soon.

Oct 80. (7") **BORDERLINE. / THE GIRLS FROM TEXAS** [-] [ ]

Oct 80. (7") **634-5789. / THE GIRLS FROM TEXAS** [ ] [-]

Dec 80. (7") **CRAZY 'BOUT AN AUTOMOBILE. / BORDERLINE** [-] [ ]

Aug 81. (7") **CRAZY 'BOUT AN AUTOMOBILE (EVERY WOMAN I KNOW). / THE VERY THING THAT MAKES YOU RICH (MAKES ME POOR)** [ ] [ ]
(12"+=) – If wall could talk / Look at granny run run.

Mar 82. (lp) **THE BORDER (Soundtrack)**(on 'Backstreet-MCA') [ ] [ ]
– Earthquake / Across the borderline / Maria / Building fires / Texas bop / Highway 23 / Palomita / Rio Grande / Too late / No quiro / Skin game / El Scorcho / Nino.

Apr 82. (lp)(c) **THE SLIDE AREA** [18] [ ]
– UFO has landed in the ghetto / I need a woman / Gypsy woman / Blue suede shoes / Mama, don't treat your daughter mean / I'm drinking again / Which came first / That's the way love turned out for me.

May 82. (d7") **GYSPY WOMAN. / ALIMONY / TEARDROPS WILL FALL / IT'S ALL OVER NOW** [ ] [ ]

Feb 85. (lp)(c) **PARIS, TEXAS (Soundtrack)** [ ] [ ]
– Paris, Texas / Brothers / Nothing out there / Cancion Mixteca / No safety zone / Houston in two seconds / She's leaving the bank / On the couch / I knew these people / Dark was the night.

London Slash

Aug 85. (lp) **MUSIC FROM ALAMO BAY (Soundtrack)** [ ] [ ]
– Theme from Alamo Bay / Gooks on main street / Klan meeting / Too close / Sailfish evening / The last stand / Glory / Search and destroy / Quatro vicios.

Warners Warners

Mar 86. (lp)(c)(cd) **WHY DON'T YOU TRY ME TONIGHT (THE BEST OF RY COODER)** (compilation) [ ] [ ]
– How can a poor man stand such times and live? / Available space / Money honey / Tattler / He'll have to go / Smack dab in the middle / Dark end of the street / Down in Hollywood / Little sister / I think it's gonna work out fine / Crazy 'bout an automobile (every woman I know) / 634-5789 / Why don't you try me tonight.

Jul 86. (lp)(c) **BLUE CITY (Soundtrack)** [ ] [ ]
– Blue city down / Elevation 13 foot / True believers – Marianne / Nice bike / Greenhouse / Billy and Annie / Pops and 'timer – Tell me something slick / Blue city / Don't take your guns to town / A leader of men / Not even Key West.

Jul 86. (7") **BILLY AND ANNIE. / TELL ME SOMETHING SLICK** [-] [ ]

Jul 86. (7") **CROSSROADS. / FEEL IT (BAD BLUES)** [-] [ ]

Jul 86. (lp)(c) **CROSSROADS** [ ] [85] May 86
– Crossroads / Down in Mississippi / Cotton needs pickin' / Viola Lee blues / See you in Hell, blind boy / Walkin' away blues / Nitty gritty Mississippi / He made a woman out of me / Feelin' bad blues / Somebody's callin' my name / Willie Brown blues.

Dec 87. (lp)(c) **GET RHYTHM** [75] [ ] Nov 87
– Get rhythm / Low-commotion / Going back to Okinawa / 13 question method / Women will rule the world / All shook up / I can tell by the way you smell / Across the borderline / Let's have a ball.

Jan 88. (7") **GET RHYTHM. / GOING BACK TO OKINAWA** [-] [ ]

Apr 88. (7") **ALL SHOOK UP. / GET YOUR LIES STRAIGHT** [-] [ ]

Apr 88. (7")(10") **GET RHYTHM. / GET YOUR LIES STRAIGHT** [ ] [ ]
(3"cd-s+=)(12"+=) – Down in Hollywood.

Oct 89. (lp)(c)(cd) **JOHNNY HANDSOME (Soundtrack)** [ ] [ ]
– Main theme / I can't walk this time – The prestige / Angola / Clip joint rhumba / Sad story / Fountain walk / Cajun metal / First week at work / Greasy oysters / Smells like money / Sunny's tune / I like your eyes / Adios Donna / Cruising wife Rafe / How's my face / End theme. *(re-iss.cd Feb95)*

— In 1991 he recorded Soundtrack for Robin Williams film PECOS BILL. He also teamed up with NICK LOWE, JOHN HIATT and JIM KELTNER in band LITTLE VILLAGE.

Sire Sire

Jan 93. (cd) **TRESPASS** (soundtrack w/ other artists) [ ] [82]
– Video drive-by / Trespass / East St.Louis toodle-oo / Orgil Bros. / Goose and lucky / You think it's on now / Solid gold / Heroin / Totally boxed in / Give 'm cops / Lucy in the trunk / We're rich / King of the street / Party lights. *(re-iss.Feb95)*

RY COODER & V.M. BHATT

RY – bottle neck guitar with **VISHWA MOHAN BHATT** – mohan vina / **JOACHIM COODER**(14 year old son) / **SUKHVINDER** – tabla

Water lily Water Lily

Dec 93. (cd) **A MEETING BY THE RIVER** [ ] [ ]
-A meeting by the river / Longing / Ganges Delta blues / Isa Lei.

ALI FARKA TOURE / RY COODER

World Circuit World Circuit

Mar 94. (cd)(c) **TALKING TIMBUKTU** [44] [ ]
– Blonde / Soukora / Gomni / Sega / Amandrai / Lasidan / Keito / Banga / Ai du / Diaraby.

– (RY COODER) compilations, etc. –

May 93. Columbia; (cd) **THE RISING SONS ("The RISING SONS featuring RY COODER & TAJ MAHAL")** [ ] [ ]

Alice COOPER

Formed: Phoenix, Arizona ... 1965 as The EARWIGS, by VINCENT FURNIER son of a preacher. The following year, they became The SPIDERS, and gained good airplay for 45 'DON'T BLOW YOUR MIND', released on local record label 'Santa Cruz'. In '68 they briefly took NAZZ for a name, but dropped it for ALICE COOPER when they signed to FRANK ZAPPA's 'Straight' records. In the 70's, VINCENT adopted group name, when he virtually went solo. By 1971, they sealed a deal with 'Warners', and soon appeared on Top of the Pops, with teen anthem 'SCHOOL'S OUT'. Hits continued throughout the 70's, with ALICE taking time off to recuperate in a mental home. By the late 80's, ALICE was back in the Top 20 with new heavy-metal assault. • **Style:** From 60's garage rock, to gory/glam shocking stage shows in the 70's (his use of pet snake, simulated hangings & guillotine, bloody toy babies, was well documented at the time). In the late 70's, due to alcohol addiction, he mellowed into soft AOR, leaving true fans and burgeoning punks stunned. By the 80's he had backtracked into past themes, culminating in hard-rock image in 1989. • **Songwriters:** ALICE wrote / co-wrote with band most of material, also using producer BOB EZRIN. DICK WAGNER to BERNIE TAUPIN also contributed in the 70's. On 'CONSTRICTOR' album, ALICE co-wrote with ROBERTS, some with KELLY and WEGENER. Collaborated with DESMOND CHILD in '89 and JACK PONTI, VIC PEPE, BOB PFEIFER in 1991. Covered:- SUN ARISE (trad. Rolf Harris) / SEVEN AND SEVEN IS (Love) / FIRE (Jimi Hendrix). **Trivia** Film cameo appearances have been DIARY OF A HOUSEWIFE (1970) / SGT.PEPPER'S LONELY HEARTS CLUB BAND (1978) / ROADIE (1980) / PRINCE OF DARKNESS (1987) / FREDDIE'S DEAD: THE FINAL NIGHTMARE (1991 also acted). In 1975 he sang 'I'M FLASH' on Various Artists concept album 'FLASH FEARLESS VS.THE ZORG WOMEN Pts.5 & 6'. VINCENT PRICE guest narrated on concept 1975 album 'WELCOME TO MY NIGHTMARE'. On 7 Apr'88 during a stage rehearsal he nearly hung himself with noose/prop. Appeared in the film 'Wayne's World'.

Recommended: BEAST OF ALICE COOPER (*8) / WELCOME TO MY NIGHTMARE (*8) / KILLER (*8) / LOVE IT TO DEATH (*8) / BILLION DOLLAR BABIES (*7).

The SPIDERS

ALICE COOPER (b.VINCENT DAMON FURNIER, 4 Feb'48, Detroit) – vocals / **GLEN BUXTON** (b.17 Jun'47, Washington DC) – lead guitar / **MICHAEL BRUCE** (b.21 Nov'48, California) – rhythm guitar, keyboards / **DENNIS DUNAWAY** (b.15 Mar'46, California) – bass / **NEAL SMITH** (b.10 Jan'48, Washington DC) – drums

not issued | Santa Cruz

1967. (7") **DON'T BLOW YOUR MIND. / NO PRICE TAG** [-] [ ]

not issued | Very

1967. (7") **WONDER WHO'S LOVING HER NOW. / LAY DOWN AND DIE, GOODBYE** [-] [ ]

ALICE COOPER

Straight | Straight

Dec 69. (lp) **PRETTIES FOR YOU** [ ] [ ] Jul 69
– Titanic overture / 10 minutes before the worm / Sing low sweet cheerio / Today Mueller / Living / Fields of regret / No longer umpire / Levity ball / B.B. on Mars / Reflected / Apple bush / Earwigs to eternity / Changing, arranging.

Jan 70. (7") **LIVING. / REFLECTED** [-] [ ]

Jun 70. (lp) **EASY ACTION** [ ] [ ]
– Mr. and Misdemeaner / Shoe salesman / Still no air / Below your means / Return of the spiders / Still no air / Laughing at me / Refridgerator Heaven / Beautiful flyaway / Lay down and die, goodbye.

Jun 70. (7") **CAUGHT IN A DREAM. / EIGHTEEN** [-] [ ]

Nov 70. (7") **RETURN OF THE SPIDERS. / SHOE SALESMAN** [-] [ ]

Straight | Warners

Mar 71. (7") **EIGHTEEN. / IS IT MY BODY** [ ] [21] Feb 71

Jun 71. (lp)(c) **LOVE IT TO DEATH** [ ] [35] Mar 71
– Caught in a dream / Eighteen / Long way to go / Black Juju / Is it my body / Hallowed be thy name / Second coming / Ballad of Dwight Fry / Sun arise. *(UK re-iss.Dec71 on 'Warner Bros.', Sep72 hit 28.*

Warners | Warners

Jun 71. (7") **CAUGHT IN A DREAM. / HALLOWED BE THY NAME** [-] [94]

Dec 71. (7") **UNDER MY WHEELS. / DESPERADO** [ ] [59]
(re-iss.Aug74)

Dec 71. (lp)(c) **KILLER** [27] [21] Nov 71
– Under my wheels / Be my lover / Halo of flies / Desperado / You drive me nervous / Yeah yeah yeah / Dead babies / Killer. *(cd-iss.Sep89 on 'WEA')*

Feb 72. (7") **BE MY LOVER. / YOU DRIVE ME NERVOUS** [ ] [49]

Jul 72. (7") **SCHOOL'S OUT. / GUTTER CAT** [1] [7] Jun 72

Jul 72. (lp)(c) **SCHOOL'S OUT** [4] [2]
– School's out / Luney tune / Gutter cat vs. the jets / Street fight / Blue Turk / My stars / Public animal No.9 / Alma mater / Grande finale. *(re-iss.+cd.Sep89 on 'WEA')*

Oct 72. (7") **ELECTED. / LUNEY TUNE** [4] [26]

Feb 73. (7") **HELLO HURRAY. / GENERATION LANDSLIDE** [6] [35]

Mar 73. (lp)(c) **BILLION DOLLAR BABIES** [1] [1]
– Hello hurray / Raped and freezin' / Elected / Billion dollar babies / Unfinished sweet / No more Mr. Nice guy / Generation landslide / Sick things / Mary Ann / I love the dead.

Apr 73. (7") **NO MORE MR. NICE GUY. / RAPED AND FREEZIN'** [10] [25]

Jul 73. (7") **BILLION DOLLAR BABIES. / MARY ANN** [-] [57]

Jan 74. (lp)(c) **MUSCLE OF LOVE** [34] [10] Dec 73
– Muscle of love / Woman machine / Hard hearted Alice / Man with the golden gun / Big apple dreamin' (hippo) / Never been sold before / Working up a sweat / Crazy little child / Teenage lament '74.

Jan 74. (7") **TEENAGE LAMENT '74. / HARD HEARTED ALICE** [12] [48] Dec 73

Mar 74. (7") **MUSCLE OF LOVE. / CRAZY LITTLE CHILD** [-] [ ]

Jun 74. (7") **MUSCLE OF LOVE. / EIGHTEEN** [-] [ ]

— **ALICE** sacked rest of band, who became BILLION DOLLAR BABIES. He brought in **DICK WAGNER** – guitar, vocals / **STEVE** (DEACON) **HUNTER** – guitars / **PRAKASH JOHN** – bass / **PENTII 'Whitey' GLAN** – drums / **JOSEF CHIROWSKI** – drums. (all ex-LOU REED band)

Anchor | Atlantic

Feb 75. (7") **DEPARTMENT OF YOUTH. / COLD ETHYL** [ ] [67] Aug 75

Mar 75. (lp)(c) **WELCOME TO MY NIGHTMARE** [19] [5]
– Welcome to my nightmare / Devil's food / The black widow / Some folks / Only women bleed / Department of youth / Cold Ethyl / Years ago / Steven / The awakening / Escape. *(re-iss.+cd.Sep87 on 'Atlantic')*

Apr 75. (7") **ONLY WOMEN BLEED. / COLD ETHYL** [-] [12]

Jun 75. (7") **ONLY WOMEN BLEED. / DEVIL'S FOOD** [ ] [-]

Aug 75. (7") **DEPARTMENT OF YOUTH. / SOME FOLKS** [-] [ ]

Oct 75. (7") **WELCOME TO MY NIGHTMARE. / COLD ETHYL** [-] [45]

Nov 75. (7") **WELCOME TO MY NIGHTMARE. / BLACK WIDOW** [ ] [-]

Warners | Warners

Jun 76. (lp)(c) **ALICE COOPER GOES TO HELL** [23] [27]
– Go to Hell / You gotta dance / I'm the coolest / Didn't we meet / I never cry / Give the kid a break / Guilty / Wake me gently / Wish you were here / I'm always chasing rainbows / Going home.

Jul 76. (7") **I NEVER CRY. / GO TO HELL** [ ] [12]

Apr 77. (7") **YOU AND ME. / IT'S HOT TONIGHT** [-] [9]

May 77. (7") **(NO MORE) LOVE AT YOUR CONVENIENCE. / IT'S HOT TONIGHT** [44] [ ]

May 77. (lp)(c) **LACE AND WHISKEY** [33] [42]
– It's hot tonight / Lace and whiskey / Road rats / Damned if I do / You and me / King of the silver screen / Ubangi stomp / (No more) Love at your convenience / I never wrote those songs / My God.

Jul 77. (7") **YOU AND ME. / MY GOD** [ ] [-]

— **FRED MANDEL** – keyboards repl. JOSEF

Dec 77. (lp)(c) **THE ALICE COOPER SHOW (live)** [ ] [ ]
– Under my wheels / Eighteen / Only women bleed / Sick things / Is it my body / I never cry / Billion dollar babies / Devil's food – The black widow / You and me / I love the dead / Go to Hell / Wish you were here / School's out.

— **Alice COOPER** now basically a solo artist with session people, which retaining **MANDEL, DAVEY JOHNSTONE** – guitar (ex-ELTON JOHN) / **MARK VOLMAN + HOWARD KAYLAN** – backing vocals (ex-TURTLES)

Dec 78. (7") **HOW YOU GONNA SEE ME NOW. / NO TRICKS** [61] [12] Oct 78

Dec 78. (lp)(c) **FROM THE INSIDE** [68] [60]
– How you gonna see me now / Wish I were born in Beverley Hills / The quiet room / Nurse Rozetta / Millie and Billie / Serious / How you gonna see me now / For Veronica's sake / Jacknife Johnny / Inmates (we're all crazy).

Jan 79. (7") **FROM THE INSIDE. / NURSE ROZETTA** [-] [ ]

— above w / **JOHN LO PRESTI** – bass / **DENNIS CONWAY** – drums

May 80. (lp)(c) **FLUSH THE FASHION** [56] [44]
– Talk talk / Clones (we're all) / Pain / Leather boots / Aspirin damage / Grim facts / Nuclear infected / Model citizen / Dance yourself to death / Headlines.

Jun 80. (7") **CLONES (WE'RE ALL). / MODEL CITIZEN** [ ] [40] May 80

Sep 80. (7") **DANCE YOURSELF TO DEATH. / TALK TALK** [-] [ ]

— now w / **MIKE PINERA + DAVEY JOHNSTONE** – guitar / **DUANE HITCHINGS** – keyboards / **ERIC SCOTT** – bass / **CRAIG KRAMPF** – drums

Sep 81. (7") **WHO DO YOU THINK WE ARE. / YOU WANT IT, YOU GOT IT** [-] [ ]

Sep 81. (lp)(c) **SPECIAL FORCES** [96] [ ]
– Who do you think we are / Seven and seven is / Skeletons in the closet / You're a movie / You want it, you got it / Vicious rumours / Perfect cop on the block / Generation landslide '81 / You look good in rags / Don't talk old to me.

Feb 82. (7") **SEVEN AND SEVEN IS (live). / GENERATION LANDSLIDE '81 (live)** [62] [ ]

May 82. (7")(7"pic-d) **FOR BRITAIN ONLY. / UNDER MY WHEELS (live)** [66] [ ]
(12"+=) – Who do you think we are (live) / Model citizen (live).

— now w / **MIKE PINERA + DAVEY JOHNSTONE** – guitar / **DUANE HITCHINGS** – keyboards / **ERIC SCOTT** – bass / **CRAIG KRAMPF** – drums

Oct 82. (7") **I LIKE GIRLS. / ZORRO'S ASCENT** [-] [ ]

Oct 82. (lp)(c) **ZIPPER CATCHES SKIN** [ ] [ ]
– Zorro's ascent / Make that money / I am the future / No baloney homosapiens / Adaptable (anything for you) / I like girls / Remarkably insincere / Tag, you're it / I better be good / I'm alive (that was the day my dead pet returned to save my life).

— **COOPER + WAGNER** re-united w / **EZRIN + PRAKASH** and recruited **GRAHAN SHAW** – synth / **JOHN ANDERSON + RICHARD KOLINGA** – drums

Mar 83. (7") **I AM THE FUTURE (remix). / ZORRO'S ASCENT** [ ] [ ]

Mar 83. (7") **I AM THE FUTURE. / TAG, YOU'RE IT** [-] [ ]

Nov 83. (lp)(c) **DADA** [93] [ ]
– Dada / Enough's enough / Former Lee Warner / No man's land / Dyslexia / Scarlet and Sheba / I love America / Fresh blood / Pass the gun around.

Nov 83. (12"m) **I LOVE AMERICA. / FRESH BLOOD / PASS THE GUN AROUND** [ ] [ ]

— Band now consisted of **KANE ROBERTS** (b.16 Jan'59) – guitar, vocals / **DAVID ROSENBERG** – drums / **PAUL DELPH** – keyboards, vocals / **DONNIE KISSELBACK** – bass, vocals, **+ KIP WINGER.**

M.C.A. M.C.A.

Oct 86. (7") **HE'S BACK (THE MAN BEHIND THE MASK). / BILLION DOLLAR BABIES** [61] [ ]
(12"+=) – I'm eighteen.

Oct 86. (lp)(c) **CONSTRICTOR** [41] [59]
– Teenage Frankenstein / Give it up / Thrill my gorilla / Life and death of the party / Simple disobedience / The world needs guts / Trick bag / Crawlin' / The great American success story / He's back (the man behind the mask).

Apr 87. (7") **TEENAGE FRANKENSTEIN. / SCHOOL'S OUT (live)** [ ] [ ]
(12"+=) – Only women bleed.

— **KEN K. MARY** – drums repl.ROSENBERG / **PAUL HOROWITZ** – keyboards, repl. DELPH + KISSELBACH.

Oct 87. (lp)(c) **RAISE YOUR FIST AND YELL** [48] [73]
– Freedom / Lock me up / Step on you / Give the radio back / Step on you / Not that kind of love / Prince of darkness / Time to kill / Chop, chop, chop / Gail / Roses on white lace. *(cd-iss.+pic-lp.May88)*

Mar 88. (7") **FREEDOM. / TIME TO KILL** [50] [ ]
(12"+=) – School's out (live).

— retained **KIP WINGER** bringing in guests **JON BON JOVI, RICHIE SAMBORA** plus **JOE PERRY, TOM HAMILTON, JOEY KRAMER** etc.

— **COOPER + WAGNER** re-united w / **EZRIN + PRAKASH** and recruited **GRAHAN SHAW** – synth / **JOHN ANDERSON + RICHARD KOLINGA** – drums

Epic Epic

1988. (7") **I GOT A LINE ON YOU. / LIVIN' ON THE EDGE** [-] [ ]

Jul 89. (7") **POISON. / TRASH** [2] [7]
(12"+=) – The ballad of Dwight Fry / Cold Ethyl (live) =(12"only)
(cd-s+=) – I got a line on you (live).

Aug 89. (lp)(c)(cd) **TRASH** [2] [20]
– Poison / Spark in the dark / House of fire / Why trust you / Only my heart talkin' / Bed of nails / This maniac's in love with you / Trash / Hell is living without you / I'm your gun. *(re-iss.cd+c Sep93)*

Sep 89. (7")(c-s)(7"green)(7"red)(7"blue) **BED OF NAILS. / I'M YOUR GUN** [38] [ ]
(12"+=)(12"pic-d+=) – Go to Hell (live).
(cd-s++=) – Only women bleed (live).

Dec 89. (7")(c-s) **HOUSE OF FIRE. / POISON (live)** [65] [56]
(7"red)(7"yellow)(7"sha-pic-d) – ('A'side) / This maniac's in love with you.
(12"+=)(cd-s+=) – Billion dollar babies (live) / Under my wheels (live).
(12"+=) – Spark in the dark (live) / Under my wheels (live).
(12"pic-d+=) – Poison (live).

Apr 90. (c-s)(cd-s) **ONLY MY HEART TALKIN'. / UNDER MY WHEELS** [-] [89]

— (Mar90) touring band **PETE FRIEZZEN** – guitar / **AL PITRELLI** – guitar / **TOMMY CARADONNA** – bass / **DEREK SHERINIAN** – keyboards / **JONATHAN MOVER** – drums

— (1991 sessions) **STEVE VAI, JOE SATRIANI, STEF BURNS** (on tour), **VINNIE MOORE, MICK MARS, SLASH** – guitars / **HUGH McDONALD, NIKKI SIXX** – bass / **MICKEY CURRY** – drums / **ROBERT SALLEY, JOHN WEBSTER** – keyboards / **STEVE CROES** – synclaiver

Jun 91. (7") **HEY STOOPID. / IT RAINED ALL NIGHT** [-] [78]

Jun 91. (7") **HEY STOOPID. / WIND-UP TOYS** [21] [-]
(12"+=)(cd-s+=)(12"pic-d+=) – It rained all night.

Jun 91. (cd)(c)(lp) **HEY STOOPID** [4] [47]
– Hey stoopid / Love's a loaded gun / Snakebite / Burning our bed / Dangerous tonight / Might as well be on Mars / Feed me Frankenstein / Hurricane years / Die for you / Little by little / Dirty dreams / Wind-up toys.

Sep 91. (7")(c-s)(7"pic-d) **LOVE'S A LOADED GUN. / FIRE** [38] [ ]
(12"+=)(12"pic-d+=) – Eighteen (live '91).
(cd-s++=) – Love gun.

Jun 92. (7") **FEED ME FRANKENSTEIN. / BURNING OUR BED** [27] [ ]
(cd-s+=)(12"pic-d+=) – Poison / Only my heart talkin'.
(cd-s+=) – Hey stoopid / Bed of nails.

— w / **STEF BURNS** – guitar, vocals / **GREG SMITH** – bass, vocals / **DEREK SHERINIAN** – keyboards, vocals / **DAVID VOSIKKINEN** – drums

May 94. (c-s) **LOST IN AMERICA. / HEY STOOPID (live)** [22] [ ]
(12"pic-d+=)(pic-cd-s+=) – Billion dollar babies / No more Mr.Nice Guy (both live).

Jun 94. (cd)(c)(lp) **THE LAST TEMPTATION** (w /free comic) [6] [68]
– Sideshow / Nothing free / Lost in America / Bad place alone / You're my temptation / Stolen prayer / Unholy war / Lullaby / It's me / Cleansed by fire.

Jul 94. (c-s) **IT'S ME. / BAD PLACE ALONE** [34] [ ]
(12"pic-d+=)(pic-cd-s+=) – Poison / Sick things.

Oct 95. (cd)(c) **CLASSICKS** (compilation) [ ] [ ]
– Poison / Hey stoopid / Feed my Frankenstein / Love's a loaded gun / Stolen prayer / House of fire / Lost in America / It's me / Under my wheels (live) / Billion dollar babies (live) / I'm eighteen (live) / No more Mr. Nice guy (live) / Only women bleed (live) / School's out (live) / Fire.

– compilations, others, etc. –

Jun 73. Warners; (d-lp)(d-c) **SCHOOLDAYS** (1st-2 lp's) [ ] [ ]

Mar 73. Warners; (7") **BE MY LOVER. / UNDER MY WHEELS** [-] [ ]

Sep 74. Warners; (lp)(c) **ALICE COOPER'S GREATEST HITS** [ ] [8] Aug 74
(cd-iss.Jun89)

Feb 75. Warners; (7"ep) **SCHOOL'S OUT / NO MORE MR.NICE GUY. / BILLION DOLLAR BABIES / ELECTED** [ ] [ ]

Feb 76. Warners; (7") **SCHOOL'S OUT. / ELECTED** [ ] [ ]
(re-iss.Dec80) (re-iss.Sep85 on 'Old Gold')

1978. Warners; (7") **I'M EIGHTEEN. / SCHOOL'S OUT** [-] [ ]

Dec 77. Anchor; (12"ep) **DEPARTMENT OF YOUTH** [ ] [-]
– Department of youth / Welcome to my nightmare / Black widow / Only women bleed.

Apr 84. Design; (pic-lp) **ROCK'N'ROLL REVIVAL: TORONTO LIVE '69 (live)** [ ] [ ]
(above re-iss.Apr86 as **FREAKOUT SONG** on 'Showcase')

Apr 87. Thunderbolt; (m-lp)(c) **LADIES MAN (live'69)** [ ] [ ]
(cd-iss.Aug88) (re-cd.Jun91)

Dec 89. W.E.A.; (lp)(c)(cd) **THE BEAST OF ALICE COOPER** [ ] [ ]
– School's out / Under my wheels / Billion dollar babies / Be my lover / Desperado / Is it my body? / Only women bleed / Elected / I'm eighteen / Hello hurray / No more Mr.Nice guy / Teenage lament '74 / Muscle of love / Department of youth.

May 92. Edsel; (cd) **LIVE AT THE WHISKEY, 1969 (live)** [ ] [ ]

Apr 93. Pulsar; (cd) **NOBODY LIKES ME** [ ] [-]

Julian COPE

Born: 21 Oct'57, Bargeld, Wales, raised Liverpool, England. In the Autumn of 1978 TEARDROP EXPLODES formed, originally as A SHALLOW MADNESS by ex-CRUCIAL THREE member COPE, FINKLER and SIMPSON. Late '78, they attained deal with local indie label 'Zoo', and became TEARDROP EXPLODES. After three critically acclaimed singles, they transferred to major label 'Mercury' in July 1980. They captured first hit with 'WHEN I DREAM', which was cut from classic album 'KILIMANJARO'. He ventured solo in 1983 sticking with 'Mercury' records, for whom he released 2 albums in 1984. He signed for 'Island' in 1985 leaving behind unissued (until 1990) SKELLINGTON lp. Around the same time he suffered marriage break-up and drug problems, but soon recovered when he re-married in 1986. • **Style:** Keyboard-biased (TEARDROP EXPLODES) and mostly influenced by 60's pop psychedelia, and sounds like a modern post new wave SCOTT WALKER. Public stage antics cutting (IGGY POP-like) his stomach in 1984, and singing perched on high pole in 1986, saw rise to new but weird character. Although it was sometimes his alter-ego (SQWUBBSY a seven foot giant) at work. • **Songwriters:** COPE penned except; READ IT IN BOOKS (co-with; Ian McCulloch, ex-CRUCIAL THREE). He wrote all material, except NON-ALIGNMENT PACT (Pere Ubu) / BOOKS (Teardrop Explodes) / RAVE ON (Buddy Holly). • **Trivia:** The album DROOLIAN, was released for campaign to free from jail ROKY ERICKSON (ex-13th FLOOR ELEVATORS). In '90, COPE marched on Anti-Poll tax march from Brixton to Trafalgar Square.

Recommended: PEGGY SUICIDE (*8) / SAINT JULIAN (*7) / FLOORED GENIUS…(*9) / WORLD SHUT YOUR MOUTH (*7) / FRIED (*7) / MY NATION UNDERGROUND (*6) / JEHOVAHKILL (*7) / TEARDROP EXPLODES:- KILIMANJARO (*9) / WILDER (*7).

TEARDROP EXPLODES

JULIAN COPE (b.21 Oct'57, Bargoed, Wales) – vocals, bass / **PAUL SIMPSON** – keyboards / **MICK FINKLER** – guitar / **GARY DWYER** – drums

Zoo / not issued

Feb 79. (7"m) **SLEEPING GAS. / CAMERA CAMERA / KIRBY WORKERS' DREAM FADES** [ ] [-]

— **GERARD QUINN** – keyboards repl. SIMPSON who formed The WILD SWANS

May 79. (7") **BOUNCING BABIES. / ALL I AM IS LOVING YOU** [ ] [-]

— **DAVID BALFE** – keyboards (ex-LORI & THE CHAMELEONS, ex-BIG IN JAPAN, ex-THOSE NAUGHTY LUMPS) repl. QUINN who also joined The WILD SWANS

Mar 80. (7") **TREASON (IT'S JUST A STORY). / READ IT IN BOOKS** [ ] [-]

— **ALAN GILL** – guitar (ex-DALEK I) repl. FINKLER now (COPE, DWYER, BALFE + GILL)

Mercury / Mercury

Sep 80. (7") **WHEN I DREAM. / KILIMANJARO** [47] [ ]

Oct 80. (lp)(c) **KILIMANJARO** [24] [ ]
– Ha, ha, I'm drowning / Sleeping gas / Treason (it's just a story) / Second head / Poppies in the field / Went crazy / Brave boys keep their promises / Bouncing babies / Books / Thief of Baghdad / When I dream. *(re-iss.Mar81+=)* – Reward. *(re-iss.Jul84, re-iss.+cd.May89)*

(below trumpet by – **RAY MARTINEZ**)

Jan 81. (7") **REWARD. / STRANGE HOUSE IN THE SNOW** [6] [ ]

Apr 81. (7") **TREASON (IT'S JUST A STORY). / USE ME** [18] [ ]
(12"+=) – Traison (French remix).

Jun 81. (7") **POPPIES IN THE FIELD. / HA HA I'M DROWNING** [ ] [ ]
(d7"+=) – Bouncing babies / Read it in books.

— **TROY TATE** – guitar, vocals (ex-INDEX, ex-SHAKE) repl. GILL

Sep 81. (7") **PASSIONATE FRIEND. / CHRIST VS. WARHOL** [25] [ ]

— on session/**gigs ALFIE ALGIUS** (b.Malta) – bass / **JEFF HAMMER** – keyboards

Nov 81. (lp)(c) **WILDER** [29] [ ]
– Bent out of shape / Tiny children / The culture bunker / Falling down around me / Passionate friend / Colours fly away / Pure joy / Seven views of Jerusalem / The great dominions / Like Leila Khaled said / . . .And the fighting takes over. *(re-iss.Jun87, cd-iss.1989)*

Nov 81. (7") **COLOURS FLY AWAY. / WINDOW SHOPPING FOR A NEW CROWN OF THORNS** [54] [ ]

— **DAVID BALFE** returned. **RON FRANCOIS** – bass (ex-SINCEROS) repl. guests

Jun 82. (7") **TINY CHILDREN. / RACHEL BUILT A STEAMBOAT** [44] [ ]
(12"+=) – Sleeping gas.

— now a trio of **COPE, DWYER + BALFE** plus sessionman **FRANCOIS.** TROY TATE went solo and joined FASHION.

Mar 83. (7") **YOU DISAPPEAR FROM VIEW. / SUFFOCATE** [41] [ ]
(12"+=)(d7"+=) – Soft enough for you / Ouch monkeys / The in-psychlopedia.

— Disbanded early '83. BALFE went into producing films. JULIAN COPE went solo augmented by DWYER.

– compilations, others, etc. –

Jun 85. Mercury; (7") **REWARD (remix). / TREASON (IT'S JUST A STORY)** [ ] [-]
(12"+=) – Strange house in the snow / Use me.

Jan 90. Fontana; (7") **SERIOUS DANGER. / SLEEPING GAS** [ ] [-]
(12"+=)(cd-s+=) – Seven views of Jerusalem.

Mar 90. Fontana; (cd)(c)(lp) **EVERYBODY WANTS TO SHAG THE TEARDROP EXPLODES** – (Their long lost 3rd album) [72] [-]
– Ouch monkeys / Serious danger / Metranil Vavin / Count to ten and run forever / In-psychiopaedia / Soft enough for you / You disappear from view / The challenger / Not only my friend / Sex / Terrorist / Strange house in the snow.

Apr 90. Fontana; (7") **COUNT TO TEN AND RUN FOR COVER. / REWARD** [ ] [-]
(12"+=)(cd-s+=) – Poppies / Khaled said.

Jan 91. Document; (cd)(lp) **PIANO** [ ] [-]
– (early 'Zoo' material)

Dec 93. Windsong; (cd)(lp) **BBC RADIO 1 LIVE IN CONCERT (live)** [ ] [-]

JULIAN COPE

JULIAN COPE – vocals, bass, rhythm guitar, organ (ex-TEARDROP EXPLODES) with **GARY DWYER** (ex-TEARDROP EXPLODES), **STEVE CREASE + ANDREW EDGE** – drums / **STEPHEN LOWELL** – lead guitar / **RON FRANCOIS** – bass / **KATE ST.JOHN** – oboe.

Mercury / Mercury

Nov 83. (7") **SUNSHINE PLAYROOM. / HEY HIGH CLASS BUTCHER** [64] [ ]
(12"+=) – Wreck my car / Eat the poor.

Feb 84. (lp)(c) **WORLD SHUT YOUR MOUTH** [40] [ ]
– Bandy's first jump / Metranil Vavin / Strasbourg / An elegant chaos / Quizmaster / Kolly Kibber's birthday / Sunshine playroom / Head hang low / Pussy face / The greatness and perfection of love / Lunatic and fire pistol. *(cd-iss. 1986)*

Mar 84. (7") **THE GREATNESS AND PERFECTION OF LOVE. / 24a VELOCITY CRESCENT** [52] [ ]
(12"+=) – Pussy face.

Nov 84. (lp)(c) **FRIED** [87] [ ]
– Reynard the fox / Bill Drummond said / Laughing boy / Me singing / Sunspots / Me singing / Bloody Assizes / Search party / O king of chaos / Holy love / Torpedo. *(cd-iss. 1986)*

Feb 85. (7") **SUNSPOTS. / I WENT ON A CHOURNEY** [ ] [ ]
(d7"+=) – Mick mack mock / Land of fear.

— **COPE** recruited Americans **DONALD ROSS SKINNER** – guitar / **JAMES ELLER** – bass / **DOUBLE DE HARRISON** – keyboards / **CHRIS WHITTEN** – drums

Island / Island

Sep 86. (7") **WORLD SHUT YOUR MOUTH. / UPTEENTH UNNATURAL BLUES** [19] [84] Feb 87
(d7"+=) – Non-alignment pact / Transportation.
(c-s+=) – I've got levitation.
(12"++=) – (all extra 3 above).
(12"+=) ('A'version).

Jan 87. (7") **TRAMPOLENE. / DISASTER** [ ] [ ]
(7"ep+=)(12"ep+=) – Mock Turtle / Warwick the kingmaker.
(12"+=) – ('A' version).

Feb 87. (m-lp) **JULIAN COPE** [-] [ ]
– World shut your mouth / Transportation / Umpteenth unatural blues / Non-argument pact / I've got levitation.

Mar 87. (lp)(c)(cd) **SAINT JULIAN** [11] [ ]
– Trampolene / Shot down / Eve's volcano (covered in sin) / Spacehopper / Planet ride / Trampolene / World shut your mouth / Saint Julian / Pulsar NX / Space hopper / Screaming secrets / A crack in the clouds. *(re-iss.c+cd.Aug91)*

Apr 87. (7") **EVE'S VOLCANO (COVERED IN SIN). / ALMOST BEAUTIFUL CHILD** [ ] [ ]
(12"+=) – Pulsar NX (live) / Shot down (live).
(12"+=) – Spacehopper-annexe.
(cd-s++=) – (all 3 extra above).

— **DAVE PALMER** – drums (studio) / **MIKE JOYCE** – drums (tour) repl. WHITTEN / added **RON FAIR** – keyboards / **ROOSTER COSBY** – percussion, some drums

Sep 88. (7") **CHARLOTTE ANNE. / CHRISTMAS MOURNING** [35] [ ]
(12"+=) – Question of temperatures / Books.

Oct 88. (lp)(c)(cd) **MY NATION UNDERGROUND** [42] [ ]
– 5 o'clock world / Vegetation / Charlotte Anne / My nation underground / China doll / Someone like me / Easter everywhere / I'm not losing sleep / The great white hoax. *(re-iss.c+cd.Aug91)*

Nov 88. (7") **5 O'CLOCK WORLD. / S.P.Q.R.** [42] [ ]
(12"+=)(cd-s+=) – Reynard in Tokyo (live 12 minute version).

Jun 89. (7") **CHINA DOLL. / CRAZY FARM ANIMAL** [53] [ ]
(cd-s+=) – Desi.
(10"+=)(12"+=) – Rave on.

— **COPE** retained **SKINNER & COSBY** plus **J.D.HASSINGER** – drums / **TIM** – keyboards / **BRAN** – bass (both of Guernsey)

Jan 91. (7")(c-s) **BEAUTIFUL LOVE. / PORT OF SAINTS** [32] [ ]
(12"+=)(cd-s+=) – Love (L.U.V.) / Unisex cathedral.

Mar 91. (cd)(c)(d-lp) **PEGGY SUICIDE** [23] [ ]
– Pristeen / Double vegetation / East easy rider / Promised land / Hanging out & hung up on the line / Safesurfer / If you loved me at all / Drive, she said / Soldier blue / You . . . / Not raving but drowning / Head / Leperskin / Beautiful love / Uptight / Western Front 1992 CE / Hung up & hanging out to dry / The American Lite / Las Vegas basement. *(re-iss.cd Aug94)*

Apr 91. (7")(c-s) **EAST EASY RIDER. / BUTTERFLY E** [51] [ ]
(12"+=)(cd-s+=) – Almost live / Little donkey.
(12"pic-d+=) – Easty Risin' / Ravebury stones.

Jul 91. (7") **HEAD. / BAGGED - OUT KEN** [57] [ ]
(12"+=)(cd-s+=) – Straw dogs / Animals at all.

Oct 92. (7")(c-s) **FEAR LOVES THE SPACE. / SIZEWELL B** [42] [ ]
(12"pic-d+=) – I have always been here before / Gogmagog.

Oct 92. (cd)(c)(d-lp) **JEHOVAHKILL** [20] [ ]
– Soul desert / No harder shoulder to cry on / Akhenaten / The mystery trend / Upwards at 45° / Cut my friends down / Necropolis / Slow rider / Gimme back my flag / Poet is priest / Julian H Cope / The subtle energies commission / Fa-fa-fa-fine / Fear loves this place / Peggy Suicide is missing. *(re-iss.cd Aug94)*

— Next was last in the 90's album trilogy about pollution. Its theme this time was the car, (coincidentally he had just passed his driving test). It featured usual musicians.

Echo / Def American

Jul 94. (cd)(c)(lp) **AUTOGEDDON** [16] [ ]
– Autogeddon blues / Don't call me Mark Chapman / Madmax / I gotta walk / Ain't no gettin' round gettin' round / Paranormal in the West Country / Paranormal / Archdrude's roadtrip / Kar-ma-kanik / Ain't but the one way / Starcar.

Aug 95. (7"ep)(c-ep)(cd-ep) **TRY TRY TRY / WESSEXY. / BABY, LET'S PLAY VET / DON'T JUMP ME, MOTHER** [24] [ ]

Aug 95. (cd)(c)(d-lp) **20 MOTHERS** [20] [ ]
– Wheelbarrow man / I wandered lonely as a child / Try try try / Stone circles

'n' you / Queen – Mother / I'm your daddy / Highway to the sun / 1995 / By the light of he Silbury moon / Adam and Eve hit the road / Just like Pooh Bear / Girl-call / Greedhead detector / Don't take roots / Senile get / The lonely guy / Cryingbabiessleeplessnights / Leli B. / Road of dreams / When I walk through the land of fear.

– compilations, others, etc. –

May 90. Capeco-Zippo; (cd)(lp) **SKELLINGTON** (1985 lost lp) [ ] [-]
– Doomed / Beaver / Me & Jimmy Jones / Robert Mitchum / Out of my mind on dope and speed / Don't crash here / Everything playing at once / Little donkey / Great white wonder / Incredibly ugly girl / No how, no why, no way, no where, no when / Comin' soon.

Jul 90. Mofoco-Zippo; (lp) **DROOLIAN** [ ] [-]

Feb 85. Bam Caruso; (7") **COMPETITION (as "RABBI JOSEPH GORDON"). / BELIEF IN HIM** [ ] [-]

Jul 92. Island; (7")(c-s) **WORLD SHUT YOUR MOUTH (remix). / DOOMED** [44] [ ]
(12"+=)(cd-s+=) – Reynard the fox / The elevators / Levitation.

Aug 92. (cd)(c)(d-lp) **FLOORED GENIUS – THE BEST OF JULIAN COPE AND THE TEARDROP EXPLODES 1981-1991** [22] [ ]
– Reward / Treason / Sleeping gas / Bouncing babies / Passionate friend / The great dominions (all TEARDROP EXPLODES) / The greatness & perfection of love / An elegant chaos / Sunspots / Reynard the fox / World shut your mouth / Trampolene / Spacehopper / Charlotte Anne / China doll / Out of my mind on dope & speed / Jellypop perky Jean / Beautiful love / East easy rider / Safesurfer.

Nov 92. (d-cd) **SAINT JULIAN / MY NATION UNDERGROUND** [ ] [ ]

Stewart COPELAND (see under ⇒ POLICE)

Hugh CORNWALL (see under ⇒ STRANGLERS)

Elvis COSTELLO

Born: DECLAN McMANUS, 25 Aug'55, Paddington, London, England. Grew up in Liverpool the son of bandleader ROSS McMANUS. He took his mother's maiden name and in the 70's played live as D.P. McMANUS. In Dec'76, he signed to Jake Riviera's new indie label 'Stiff', recording debut album under the wing of stablemate producer NICK LOWE. His success from then on was similar to DYLAN, in the way he had mostly UK-Top 10 albums, and at times sporadic UK-Top30 45's. By the late 70's, RIVIERA had taken him to new labels 'Radar' then 'F-Beat'. He continued to impress the buying public during the 80's and early 90's. • **Style:** On the crest of the "new-wave", but branched out into country-rock, melodic pop and even melancholy soul. His musical directions have held no limitations or barriers to most styles of rock music. • **Songwriters:** All penned by COSTELLO, bar NEAT NEAT NEAT (Damned) / I CAN'T STAND UP FOR FALLING DOWN (Sam & Dave) / SWEET DREAMS (Patsy Cline) / A GOOD YEAR FOR THE ROSES (Jerry Chestnut) / DON'T LET ME BE MISUNDERSTOOD (Nina Simone) / I WANNA BE LOVED (Farnell Jenkins) / THE UGLY THINGS (Nick Lowe) / YOU'RE NO GOOD (Swinging Blue Jeans) / FULL FORCE GALE (Van Morrison) / YOU'VE GOT TO HIDE YOUR LOVE AWAY (Beatles) / STEP INSIDE LOVE (Cilla Black) / STICKS & STONES (Ray Charles) / FROM HEAD TO TOE (Smokey Robinson) / CONGRATULATIONS (Paul Simon) / STRANGE (Screaming Jay Hawkins) / HIDDEN CHARMS (Willie Dixon) / REMOVE THIS DOUBT (Supremes) / I THREW IT ALL AWAY (Bob Dylan) / LEAVE MY KITTEN ALONE (Little Willie John) / EVERYBODY'S CRYIN' MERCY (Mose Allison) / I'VE BEEN WRONG BEFORE (Randy Newman) / BAMA LAMA BAMA LOO (Little Richard) / MUST YOU THROW DIRT IN MY FACE (Louvin Bros.) / POURING WATER ON A DROWNING MAN (James Carr) / THE VERY THOUGHT OF YOU (Ray Noble) / PAYDAY (Jesse Winchester) / PLEASE STAY (Bacharach-David) / RUNNING OUT OF FOOLS (Jerry Ragavoy) / DAYS (Kinks) / etc. • **Trivia:** He has also produced The SPECIALS (1979) / SQUEEZE (1981) / POGUES (1985) retaining a latter acquaintance in CAIT O'RIORDON, whom he married on 16 May'86. He acted (played bit-parts) in most of playwright / friend Alan Bleasdale's work including SCULLY (1985 TV series), NO SURRENDER (1988 film). He provided score for the film 'The Courier' in 1987 alongside HOTHOUSE FLOWERS. Around the same time he collaborated with PAUL McCARTNEY writing BACK ON MY FEET for McCartney, and VERONICA for himself in 1989. Costello was produced by T-BONE BURNETT on his 'KING OF AMERICA' + 'SPIKE' albums.

Recommended: THE BEST OF ELVIS COSTELLO THE MAN (*8) / THIS YEAR'S MODEL (*9) / MY AIM IS TRUE (*8) / ARMED FORCES (*7) / GOT HAPPY! (*6) / TRUST (*6) / ALMOST BLUE (*5) / IMPERIAL BEDROOM (*6) / PUNCH THE CLOCK (*8) / GOODBYE CRUEL WORLD (*6) / KING OF AMERICA (*7) / SPIKE (*6) / BLOOD AND CHOCOLATE (*7) / MIGHTY LIKE A ROSE (*5).

"ELVIS COSTELLO" (solo) – vocals, guitar with backing band The **SHAMROCKS,** (alias CLOVER) / **JOHN McFEE** – guitar / **ALEX CALL** – guitar, vocals / **SEAN HOPPER** – keyboards / **JOHN CIAMBOTTI** – bass / **MICHAEL SHINE** – drums

Stiff Columbia

Mar 77. (7") **LESS THAN ZERO. / RADIO SWEETHEART** [ ] [-]
May 77. (7") **ALISON. / WELCOME TO THE WORKING WEEK** [ ] [ ]
(US 'B'side of above= **MIRACLE MAN**)
Jul 77. (7") **(THE ANGELS WANNA WEAR MY) RED SHOES. / MYSTERY DANCE** [ ] [-]
Jul 77. (lp)(c) **MY AIM IS TRUE** [14] [32] Nov 77
– Welcome to the working week / Miracle man / No dancing / Blame it on Cain / Alison / Sneaky feelings / (The angels wanna wear my) Red shoes / Less than zero / Mystery dance / Pay it back / I'm not angry / Waiting for the end of the world. (US version included **Watching the detectives.**) *(UK re-iss.+cd.Jul86 on 'Demon') (re-iss.cd Mar93 w/extra tracks)*

ELVIS COSTELLO & THE ATTRACTIONS

STEVE NIEVE (b.NASON)– keys repl. HOPPER to HUEY LEWIS & THE NEWS
BRUCE THOMAS – bass, vocals (ex-QUIVER)repl. CIAMBOTTI, CALL and McFEE
PETE THOMAS (b.9 Aug'54, Sheffield, England)– drums (ex-CILLI WILLI, ex-WILKO JOHNSON)repl. SHINE

Oct 77. (7"m) **WATCHING THE DETECTIVES. / BLAME IT ON CAIN (live) / MYSTERY DANCE (live)** [15] [ ]

Radar Columbia

Mar 78. (7") **(I DON'T WANT TO GO TO) CHELSEA. / YOU BELONG TO ME** [16] [ ]
Mar 78. (lp)(c) **THIS YEAR'S MODEL** [4] [30]
– No action / This year's girl / The beat / Pump it up / Little Triggers / You belong to me / Hand in hand / (I don't want to go to) Chelsea / Lip service / Living in Paradise / Lipstick vogue / Night rally. *(re-iss.1984/ cd-iss.1986/ Mar93/ Feb95 on 'Demon' w/extra tracks)* (free-7"w/above) **STRANGER IN THE HOUSE. / NEAT NEAT NEAT**
May 78. (7") **PUMP IT UP. / BIG TEARS** [24] [ ]
Oct 78. (7") **RADIO RADIO. / TINY STEPS** [29] [ ]
Jan 79. (lp)(c) **ARMED FORCES** [2] [10]
– Senior service / Oliver's army / Big boys / Green shirt / Party girl / Goon squad / Busy bodies / Sunday's best / Moods for moderns / Chemistry class / Two little Hitlers / Accidents will happen. (free 7"w/ above) WATCHING THE DETECTIVES. / ALISON / ACCIDENTS WILL HAPPEN *(re-iss.1984/ cd-iss.Jan86/ Mar93/ Feb95 on 'Demon' w/extra tracks)*
Feb 79. (7") **OLIVER'S ARMY. / MY FUNNY VALENTINE** [2] [ ]
May 79. (7"m) **ACCIDENTS WILL HAPPEN. / TALKING IN THE DARK / WEDNESDAY WEEK** [28] [ ]

ELVIS COSTELLO

solo, but still used ATTRACTIONS

F-Beat Columbia

Feb 80. (7") **I CAN'T STAND UP FOR FALLING DOWN. / GIRLS TALK** [4] [ ]
Feb 80. (lp)(c) **GET HAPPY!** [2] [11]
– Love for tender / Opportunity / The imposter / Secondary modern / King Horse / Possession / Man called Uncle / Clowntime is over / New Amsterdam / High fidelity / I can't stand up for falling down / Black and white world / Five years in reverse / B movie / Motel matches / Human touch / Beaten to the punch / Temptation / I stand accused / Riot act. *(re-iss.1984, cd-iss.Jan86, re-iss.cd Mar93 on 'Demon') (re-iss.cd May94 on 'Demon' w/extra tracks)*
Apr 80. (7") **HIGH FIDELITY. / GETTING MIGHTY CROWDED** [30] [ ]
(12"+=) – Clowntime is over.
Jun 80. (7")(7"pic-d) **NEW AMSTERDAM. / DR.LUTHER'S ASSISTANT** [36] [ ]
(7"pic-d-ep+=) – Ghost train / Just a memory.

ELVIS COSTELLO & THE ATTRACTIONS

(same line-up)

Dec 80. (7"m) **CLUBLAND. / CLEAN MONEY / HOOVER FACTORY** [60] [ ]
Jan 81. (lp)(c) **TRUST** [9] [28]
– Clubland / Lovers walk / You'll never be a man / Pretty words / Strict time / Luxembourg / Watch your step / New lace sleeves / From a whisper to a scream / Different finger / White knuckles / Shot with his own gun / Fish'n'chip paper / Big sister's clothes. *(re-iss.1984,cd-iss.Jan86,re-iss.cd Mar93 on 'Demon') (re-iss.cd May94 on 'Demon' w/extra tracks)*
Feb 81. (7") **FROM A WHISPER TO A SCREAM. / LUXEMBOURG** [ ] [ ]
Sep 81. (7") **GOOD YEAR FOR THE ROSES. / YOUR ANGEL STEPS OUT OF HEAVEN** [6] [ ]
Oct 81. (lp)(c) **ALMOST BLUE** [7] [50]
– Why don't you love me (like you used to do) / Sweet dreams / Sucess / I'm your toy / Tonight the bottle let me down / Brown to blue / Good year for the roses / Sittin' and thinkin' / Colour of the blues / Too far gone / Honey hush / How much I lied. *(re-iss.1984, cd-iss.Jan86, re-iss.cd Mar93 on 'Demon' w/extra tracks)*
Dec 81. (7") **SWEET DREAMS. / PSYCHO** [42] [ ]
Apr 82. (7"m) **I'M YOUR TOY (live). / CRY CRY CRY / WONDERING** [51] [ ]
(12") – ('A'side) / My shoes keep walkin' back to you / Blues keep calling / Honky tonk girl. (with The ROYAL PHILHARMONIC ORCHESTRA)
Jun 82. (7"m) **YOU LITTLE FOOL. / BIG SISTER / THE STAMPING GROUND** (3rd track credited to **The EMOTIONAL TOOTHPASTE)** [52] [ ]
Jul 82. (lp)(c) **IMPERIAL BEDROOM** [6] [30]
– Beyond belief / Tears before bedtime / Shabby doll / The long honeymoon / Man out of time / Almost blue / . . . And in every home / The loved ones / Human hands / Kid about it / Little savage / Boy with a problem / Pidgin English / You little fool / Town cryer. *(re-iss.1984, cd-iss.Jan86, re-iss.cd Mar93 on 'Demon' w/extra tracks)*
Jul 82. (7") **MAN OUT OF TIME. / TOWN CRYER** [58] [ ]
(12"+=) – Imperial bedroom.
Sep 82. (7") **FROM HEAD TO TOE. / THE WORLD OF BROKEN HEARTS** [43] [ ]

—— (below from the film 'Party Party')

A & M A & M

Nov 82. (7") **PARTY PARTY. / IMPERIAL BEDROOM** [48] [ ]

Imp-Demon Columbia

May 83. (7") **PILLS AND SOAP.(as "The IMPOSTER") / ('A'extended version)** [16] [ ]

F-Beat Columbia

Jul 83. (7") **EVERYDAY I WRITE THE BOOK. / HEATHEN TOWN** [28] [36]
(12"+=) – Night time.
Jul 83. (lp)(c) **PUNCH THE CLOCK** [3] [24]
– Let them all talk / Everyday I write the book / The greatest thing / The element within her / Love went mad / Shipbuilding / T.K.O. (boxing day) / Charm school / The invisible man / Mouth almighty / King of thieves / Pills and soap / The world and his wife. *(re-iss.+cd.Sep84/ Jan88 on 'Demon') (cd-iss. Mar93/ Feb95 on 'Demon' w/extra tracks)*
Sep 83. (7")(12") **LET THEM ALL TALK. / KEEP IT CONFIDENTIAL** [59] [ ]
Apr 84. (7") **PEACE IN OUR TIME.(as "The IMPOSTER") / WITHERED AND DEAD** [48] [ ]
Jun 84. (7") **I WANNA BE LOVED. / TURNING THE TOWN RED** [25] [ ]
(12"+=) – ('A'extended).
Jun 84. (lp)(c) **GOODBYE CRUEL WORLD** [10] [35]
– The only flame in town / Room with no number / Inch by inch / Worthless thing / Love field / I wanna be loved / The comedians / Joe Porterhouse / Sour milk cow blues / The great unknown / The deportees club / Peace in our time. *(re-iss.Jan87,cd-iss.Mar86 + Oct87, re-iss.cd Mar93 & Mar95 on 'Demon' w/extra tracks)*
Aug 84. (7") **THE ONLY FLAME IN TOWN. / THE COMEDIANS** [71] [56] Jul 84
(12"+=) – Pump it up (dance mix).

Imp-Demon Columbia

Jul 85. (7") **THE PEOPLE'S LIMOUSINE.(as "The COWARD BROTHERS" feat. T-BONE BURNETT) / THEY'LL NEVER TAKE THEIR LOVE FROM ME** [ ] [ ]

The COSTELLO SHOW

featuring The ATTRACTIONS and The CONFEDERATES
added **JAMES BURTON** – guitar / **MITCHELL FROOM** – keyboards / **JERRY SCHEFF** – bass / **JIM KELTNER** – drums / **RON TUTT** – drums (i.e.The CONFEDERATES)

F-Beat Columbia

Jan 86. (7") **DON'T LET ME BE MISUNDERSTOOD. / BABY'S GOT A BRAND NEW HAIRDO** [33] [ ]
(12"+=) – Get yourself another girl.

Demon-Imp Columbia

Feb 86. (lp)(c)(cd) **KING OF AMERICA** [11] [39]
– Brilliant mistake / Loveable / Our little angel / Don't let me be misunderstood / Glitter gulch / Indoor fireworks / Little palaces / I'll wear it proudly / American without tears / Eisenhower blues / Poisoned rose / The big light / Jack of all parades / Suit of lights / Sleep of the just. *(re-iss.Jan87) (cd-iss.Mar93/ Feb95 w/extra tracks)*

ELVIS COSTELLO & THE ATTRACTIONS

(ELVIS, BRUCE, STEVE & PETE) plus guest **NICK LOWE** – guitar

Imp Demon Columbia

Aug 86. (7") **TOKYO STORM WARNING. / (part 2)** [73] [ ]
(12"+=) – Black sails in the sunset.
Sep 86. (lp)(c)(cd) **BLOOD AND CHOCOLATE** [16] [84]
– Uncomplicated / I hope you're happy now / Tokyo storm warning / Home is anywhere you hang your head / I want you / Honey are you straight or are you blind? / Blue chair / Battered old bird / Crimes of Paris / Poor Napoleon / Next time around. *(re-iss.cd Mar93/ Feb95 w/extra tracks)*
Nov 86. (7") **I WANT YOU. / I HOPE YOU'RE HAPPY NOW (acoustic)** [ ] [ ]
(12"+=) – I want you (part 2).
Jan 87. (7") **BLUE CHAIR. / AMERICA WITHOUT TEARS No.2** [ ] [ ]

(10"+=) – I want you.
(12"+=) – Shoes without heels.
May 87. (7")(12") **A TOWN CALLED BIG NOTHING.(as "McMANUS GANG" featuring SY RICHARDSON) / RETURN TO BIG NOTHING** [ ] [ ]

ELVIS COSTELLO

solo, with mostly **FROOM, KELTNER, PETE THOMAS** (2), **MICHAEL BLAIR** – percussion / **MARC RIBOT** – guitar / **JERRY MAROTTA** – drums / **PAUL McCARTNEY, ROGER McGUINN, CAIT O'RIORDAN, T-BONE BURNETT, CHRISSIE HYNDE** on 1 or 2, plus The DIRTY DOZEN BRASS BAND (GREGORY DAVIS, EFREM TOWNS, ROGER LEWIS, KEVIN HARRIS, KIRK JOSEPH, C.JOSEPH. (plus loads more)

Warners Warners

Feb 89. (lp)(c)(cd) **SPIKE** [5] [32]
-. . . This town . . . / Let him dangle / Deep dark truthful mirror / Veronica / God's comic / Chewing gum / Tramp the dirt town / Stalin Malone / Satellite / Pads, paws and claws / Baby plays around / Miss Macbeth / Any king's shilling / Coal train robbers * / Last boat leaving. *(cd.+= *) (re-iss.cd Nov93 w/extra tracks)*
Feb 89. (7") **VERONICA. / YOU'RE NO GOOD** [31] [19]
(12"+=)(cd-s+=) – The room nobody lives in / Coal train robbers.
May 89. (7")(c-s) **BABY PLAYS AROUND. / POISONED ROSE** [65] [ ]
(7"ep+=)(10"+=)(cd-s+=) – Almost blue / My funny valentine.
(12")(cd-s) – ('A'side) / (++=) – Point of no return.
Apr 91. (7")(c-s) **THE OTHER SIDE OF SUMMER. / COULDN'T CALL IT UNEXPECTED No.4** [43] [ ]
(12"+=)(cd-s+=) – The ugly things.
May 91. (cd)(c)(lp) **MIGHTY LIKE A ROSE** [5] [55]
– The other side of summer / How to be dumb / All grown up / Invasion hit parade / Harpers bizarre / Hurry down doomsday (the bugs are taking over) / After the fall / Georgie and her rival / So like Candy / Interlude: couldn't call it unexpected No.2 / Playboy to a man / Sweet pear / Broken / Couldn't call it unexpected No.4. *(re-iss.cd Feb95)*
Oct 91. (7")(c-s) **SO LIKE CANDY. / VERONICA (demo)** [ ] [ ]
(12"+=)(cd-s+=) – Couldn't call it unexpected (live) / Hurry down doomsday (the blues are taking over).

In 1992, he wrote material for WENDY JAMES (Transvision Vamp)

ELVIS COSTELLO / THE BRODSKY QUARTET

with **MICHAEL THOMAS + IAN BELTON** – violins / **PAUL CASSIDY** – viola / **JACQUELINE THOMAS** – violincello (all co-wrote music with him)

Jan 93. (cd)(c) **THE JULIET LETTERS** [18] [ ]
– Deliver us / For other eyes / Swine / Expert rites / Dead letter / I almost had a weakness / Why? / Who do you think you are? / Taking my life in your hands / This offer is unrepeatable / Dear sweet filthy world / The letter home / Jacksons, Monk and Rowe / This sad burlesque / Romeo's seance / I thought I'd write to Juliet / Last post / The first to leave / Damnation's cellar / The birds will still be singing.
Feb 93. (c-ep)(cd-ep) **JACKSON MONK AND ROE / THIS SAD BURLESQUE / (interview excerpts)** [ ] [ ]

Elvis COSTELLO

Mar 94. (7")(c-s) **SULKY GIRL. / A DRUNKEN MAN'S PRAISE OF SOBRIETY** [22] [ ]
(cd-s+=) – Idiophone (with the ATTRACTIONS).
Mar 94. (cd)(c) **BRUTAL YOUTH** [2] [34]
– Pony St. / Kinder murder / 13 steps lead down / This is Hell / Clown strike / You tripped at every step / Still too soon to know / 20% amnesia / Sulky girl / London's brilliant parade / My science fiction twin / Rocking horse road / Just about glad / All the rage / Favourite hour.
Apr 94. (7")(c-s) **13 STEPS LEAD DOWN. / DO YOU KNOW WHAT I'M SAYING?** [59] [ ]
(cd-s) – ('A'side) / Puppet girl / Basement kiss / We despise you.
Jul 94. (7")(c-s) **YOU TRIPPED AT EVERY STEP. / YOU'VE GOT TO HIDE YOUR LOVE AWAY** [ ] [ ]
(cd-s+=) – Step inside love / Sticks & stones.
Nov 94. (c-s) **LONDON'S BRILLIANT PARADE. / NEW AMSTERDAM** [48] [ ]
(cd-ep+=) – Beyond belief / Shipbuilding.
(cd-ep+=) – From head to toe / The loved ones.
(12") – ('A'side) / My resistance is low / Congratulations.
May 95. (cd)(c) **KOJAK VARIETY** [21] [ ]
– Strange / Hidden charms / Remove this doubt / I threw it all way / Leave my kitten alone / Everybody's cryin' mercy / I've been wrong before / Bama lama bama loo / Must you throw dirt in my face / Pouring water on a drowning man / The very thought of you / Payday / Please stay / Running out of fools / Days.

. . . Jan – Jun '96 stop press . . .

ELVIS COSTELLO & THE ATTRACTIONS

Apr 96. (single) **IT'S TIME** [58] [ ]
May 96. (cd)(c)(lp) **ALL THIS USELESS BEAUTY** [28] [53]

– compilations, others, etc. –

Mar 82. Old Gold; (7") **OLIVER'S ARMY. / GOOD YEAR FOR THE ROSES** [ ] [-]
Apr 85. Telstar; (lp)(c)(cd) **THE BEST OF ELVIS COSTELLO – THE MAN** [8] [-]
– Watching the detectives / Oliver's army / Alison / Accidents will happen / Pump it up / High fidelity / Pills and soap (THE IMPOSTER) / (I don't want to go to) Chelsea / New lace sleeves / A good year for the roses / I can't stand up for falling down / Clubland / Beyond belief / New Amsterdam / Green shirt / Everyday I write the book / I wanna be loved / Shipbuilding (THE IMPOSTER). *(re-iss.Jan87, re-iss.cd Mar93 on 'Demon')*
Nov 80. Columbia; (lp)(c) **TAKING LIBERTIES** [-] [28]
Apr 85. F-Beat; (7")(7"green) **GREEN SHIRT. / BEYOND BELIEF** [68] [-]
(12"+=)(12"green+=) – ('A'extended).
Nov 85. Stiff; (12"ep) **WATCHING THE DETECTIVES / RADIO SWEETHEART. / LESS THAN ZERO / ALISON** [ ] [-]
Mar 80. Imp-Demon; (lp)(c) **TEN BLOODY MARY'S & TEN HOW'S YOUR FATHERS** [ ] [-]
(re-iss.1984, cd-iss.1986) (re-iss.cd Mar93)
Oct 87. Imp-Demon; (lp)(c)(cd) **OUT OF OUR IDIOT** [ ] [ ]
—— (above credited to "VARIOUS ARTISTS" but all by his pseudonyms) *(re-iss.cd Mar93)*
Oct 89. Imp-Demon; (lp)(c)(cd)(dat) **GIRLS GIRLS GIRLS** [67] [-]
Jul 91. Imp-Demon; (cd)(c)(lp) **GBH SOUNDTRACK** [ ] [-]
—— (above was credited to "ELVIS COSTELLO & RICHARD HARVEY")
Nov 94. Imp-Demon; (cd)(c) **THE VERY BEST OF ELVIS COSTELLO** [57] [ ]
Nov 95. Demon; (4xcd-box) **2 1/2 YEARS** [ ] [-]

The first 4 singles were also re-issued together around 1980 and could be found on 'Stiff' 10-pack Nos.11-20).

The ATTRACTIONS released two singles and an album (Aug80) **MAD ABOUT THE WRONG BOY** on 'F-Beat'.

ELVIS COSTELLO & BILL FRISELL

Nonesuch Nonesuch

Aug 95. (cd) **DEEP DEAD BLUE** [ ] [ ]
– Weird nightmare / Love field / Shamed into love / Gigi / Poor Napoleon / Baby plays around / Deep dead blue.

John COUGAR (see under ⇒ MELLENCAMP, John Cougar)

COUNTING CROWS

Formed: Bay Area, San Francisco, USA . . . 1992 out of early 90's outfit SORDID HUMOR. This band cut an album 'LIGHT MUSIC FOR DYING PEOPLE' for 'Capricorn', which remained unreleased until after COUNTING CROWS became massive in 1994. A year earlier the much-lauded album 'AUGUST AND EVERYTHING AFTER' had breeched the US charts. • **Style:** Melodic rock similar to JAYHAWKS. • **Songwriters:** DURITZ; some w /BRYSON, except THE GHOST IN YOU (Psychedelic Furs). • **Trivia:** Debut was produced by T-BONE BURNETT, and featured MARIA McKEE on backing vocals.

Recommended: AUGUST AND EVERYTHING AFTER (*8)

ADAM DURITZ – vocals, piano, harmonica (ex-SORDID HUMOR) / **DAVID BRYSON** – guitar, vocals (ex-SORDID HUMOR) / **MATT MALLEY** – bass, guitar, vocals / **CHARLIE GILLINGHAM** – piano, organ, accordion, chamberlain, vocals / **STEVE BOWMAN** – drums, vocals

Geffen Geffen

Oct 93. (cd)(c)(lp) **AUGUST AND EVERYTHING AFTER** [16] [4]
– Round here / Omaha / Mr.Jones / Perfect blue buildings / Anna begins / Time and time again / Rain king / Sullivan Street / Ghost train / Raining in Baltimore / A murder of one.
—— added **DAN VICKREY** – guitar
Apr 94. (7")(c-s) **MR.JONES. / RAINING IN BALTIMORE** [28] [ ]
(cd-s+=) – Rain king / ('A'acoustic).
Jun 94. (7")(c-s) **ROUND HERE. / GHOST TRAIN** [70] [ ]
(cd-s+=) – The ghost in you (live).
Oct 94. (c-s) **RAIN KING. / ?** [49] [ ]
(cd-s+=) –

COVERDALE PAGE (see under ⇒ WHITESNAKE)

COWBOY JUNKIES

Formed: Toronto, Canada . . . 1985 by MICHAEL TIMMINS, with young brother PETER and sister MARGO. In the late 70's and early 80's, MICHAEL had been in groups HUNGER PROJECT and GERMINAL, before moving to New York and London in the process. In the mid 80's, The COWBOY JUNKIES recorded debut lp WHITES OFF EARTH NOW! in garage releasing it on their own Canadian indie label 'Latent'. By 1988 they were on the roster of 'R.C.A.', with 'Cooking V.' licensing them in UK. In 1990, they achieved major international success with album 'THE CAUTION HORSES'. • **Style:** Minimalist country/blues rock, influenced by SPRINGSTEEN, described as EMMYLOU HARRIS meeting The VELVET UNDERGROUND. • **Songwriters:** MICHAEL wrote & produced songs, except SHINING MOON (Lightning Hopkins) / STATE TROOPER (Bruce Springsteen) / ME AND THE DEVIL + CROSSROADS (Robert Johnson) / DECORATION DAY + I'LL NEVER GET OUT OF THESE BLUES ALIVE + FORGIVE ME (John Lee Hooker) / BABY PLEASE DON'T GO (Bukka White) / POWDERFINGER (Neil Young) / SWEET JANE (Velvet Underground) / COWBOY JUNKIES LAMENT + TO LIVE IS TO FLY (Townes Van Zandt) / IF YOU'VE GOTTA GO, GO NOW (Bob Dylan) / LOST MY DRIVING WHEEL (Wiffen). • **Trivia:** Their second lp 'THE TRINITY SESSION' was recorded one day in a church, and eventually sold over a million worldwide. They used many session people for the 90's albums.

Recommended: THE TRINITY SESSION (*6)

MICHAEL TIMMINS (b.21 Apr'59, Montreal, Canada) – guitar / **MARGO TIMMINS** (b.27 Jun'61, Montreal) – vocals / **PETER TIMMINS** (b.29 Oct'65, Montreal) – drums / **ALAN ANTON** (b.ALAN ALIZOJVODIC, 22 Jun'59, Montreal) – bass

not issued — Latent

1986. (lp) **WHITES OFF EARTH NOW!** [-] [ ] CAN
– Shining Moon / State trooper / Me and the Devil / Decoration day / Baby please don't go / I'll never get out of these blues alive / Take me / Forgive me / Crossroads. *(UK-iss.cd,c,lp.Feb91 on 'RCA')*

Jan 88. (lp) **THE TRINITY SESSIONS** [-] [ ]
– Mining for gold / Misguided angel / Blue moon revisited (song for Elvis) * / I don't get in / I'm so lonesome I could cry / To love is to bury / 200 more miles / Dreaming my dreams with you / Working on a building * / Sweet Jane / Postcard blues / Walking after midnight. *(UK-iss.lp/c/cd.Mar89 on 'Cooking Vinyl') (re-iss.cd Feb94) (US iss. Jan89 on 'RCA', hit No.26)*

Cooking Vinyl — R.C.A.

Mar 89. (7") **SWEET JANE. / 200 MORE MILES** [ ] [ ] Nov 88
(12"+=) – Postcard blues.

May 89. (7") **MISGUIDED ANGEL. / POSTCARD BLUES** [-] [ ]

Jul 89. (7") **BLUE MOON REVISITED (SONG FOR ELVIS). / TO LOVE IS TO BURY** [ ] [ ]
(12"+=)(cd-s+=) – ('A'live version).
(10"+=) – You won't be loved again / Shining moon / Waking after midnight.

R.C.A. — R.C.A.

Feb 90. (7") **SUN COMES UP, IT'S TUESDAY MORNING. / WITCHES** [ ] [ ]
(12"+=) – Powderfinger.
(c-s+=) – Dead ponies.
(cd-s+=) – Misguided angel.

Mar 90. (cd)(c)(lp) **THE CAUTION HORSES** [33] [47]
– Sun comes up, it's Tuesday morning / 'Cause cheap is how I feel / Thirty summers / Mariner's song / Powderfinger / Where are you tonight / Witches / Rock and bird / Escape is so easy / You will be loved again. *(re-iss.cd Feb94)*

Jun 90. (7") **'CAUSE CHEAP IS HOW I FEEL. / THIRTY SUMMERS** [ ] [ ]
(12"+=)(cd-s+=) – Declaration day / State trooper / Take me.

Sep 90. (c-s) **ROCK AND BIRD. / ?** [-] [ ]

Jan 92. (cd-ep) **SOUTHERN RAIN / MURDER, TONIGHT, IN THE TRAILER PARK / LOST MY DRIVING WHEEL / IF YOU'VE GOTTA GO, GO NOW** [ ] [ ]

Feb 92. (cd)(c)(lp) **BLACK EYED MAN** [21] [76]
– Southern rain / Oregon hill / This street, that man, this life / A horse in the country / If you were the woman and I was the man / Murder, tonight, in the trailer park / Black eyed man / Winter's song / The last spike / Cowboy Junkies lament / Townes' blues / To live is to fly. (w/ free cd-cp) DEAD FLOWERS / CAPTAIN KIDD / TAKE ME / 'CAUSE CHEAP IS HOW I FEEL.

Mar 92. (7") **A HORSE IN THE COUNTRY. / OREGON HILL** [ ] [ ]
(cd-s+=) – Five room love story.

Nov 93. (cd)(c) **PALE SUN, CRESCENT MOON** [ ] [ ]
– Crescent Moon / First recollection / Ring of the sill / Anniversary song / White sail / Seven years / Pale Sun / The past / Cold tea blues / Hard to explain / Hunted / Floorboard blues.

. . . Jan – Jun '96 stop press . . .

Feb 96. (cd)(lp) **200 MORE MILES (live)** [ ] [ ]

Geffen — Geffen

Feb 96. (single) **A COMMON DISASTER** [ ] [ ]

Mar 96. (cd)(lp) **LAY IT DOWN** [ ] [55]

CRACKER

Formed: North Carolina, California, USA . . . 1990 by LOWERY and LOVERING (former members of top cult US acts). While LOVERING had been sidekick of FRANK BLACK in The PIXIES, LOWERY had been in CAMPER VAN BEETHOVEN, who were famous for 5 albums for 'Rough Trade' in the 80's and the classic track 'TAKE THE SKINHEADS BOWLING'. • **Style:** Acoustic laid-back hard rockin' grunge cowpunks, fusing TOM PETTY or IAN HUNTER like songs with twanging country rock. • **Songwriters:** LOWERY or LOWERY-HICKMAN-FARAGHER on second album. Covered LOSER (Grateful Dead). • **Trivia:** Produced by DON SMITH.

Recommended: KEROSENE HAT (*7)

DAVID LOWERY – vocals, guitars (ex-CAMPER VAN BEETHOVEN) / **JOHNNY HICKMAN** – guitar, vocals / **BOB RUPE** – bass (ex-SILOS)/ **DAVE LOVERING** – drums (ex-PIXIES)

Virgin America — Virgin

Mar 92. (7") **TEEN ANGST (WHAT THE WORLD NEEDS NOW). / CAN I TAKE MY GUN TO HEAVEN** [ ] [ ]
(12"+=) – China.
(cd-s++=) – ('A'version).

Apr 92. (cd)(c)(lp) **CRACKER** [ ] [ ]
– Teen angst (what the world needs now) / Happy birthday to me / This is Cracker soul / I see the light / St.Cajetan / Mr.Wrong / Someday / Can I take my gun to Heaven / Satify you / Another song about the rain / Don't f*** me up (with peace and love) / Dr.Bernice.

— **DAVEY FARAGHER** – bass, vocals repl. RUPE

— **MICHAEL URBANO** – drums repl. LOVERING

May 94. (7")(c-s) **LOW. / TEEN ANGST (WHAT THE WORLD NEEDS NOW)** [43] [64]
(cd-s) – ('A'side) / I ride my bike / Sunday train / Whole lotta trouble.
(10") – ('A'side) / River Euphrates / Euro-trash girl / Bad vibes everybody.
(all above single re-iss.Nov94, hit 54 UK)

Jun 94. (cd)(c)(lp) **KEROSENE HAT** [44] [59] Sep93
– Low / Movie star / Get off this / Kerosene hat / Take me down to the infirmary / Nostalgia / Sweet potato / Sick of goodbyes / I want everything / Lonesome Johnny blues / Let's go for a ride / Loser.
(cd+=) – No songs: Eurotrash girl + I ride my bike / Hi-desert biker meth lab.
(c+=) – No songs; Euro-trash girl + I ride my bike / Kerosene hat (acoustic).

Jul 94. (c-s)(cd-s) **GET OFF THIS / HAPPY BIRTHDAY TO ME / CHINA / DR.BERNICE** [41] [ ]
(cd-s) – ('A'side) / Fucking up (live) / Blue Danube / Don't fuck me up (with peace and love).
(10") – ('A'side) / Steve's hornpipe / Mr.Wrong / I want everything (acoustic).

. . . Jan – Jun '96 stop press . . .

Apr 96. (cd)(c) **THE GOLDEN AGE** [ ] [83]

CRAMPS

Formed: Ohio, U.S.A . . . 1975 by LUX INTERIOR and POISON IVY. After two singles on US indie label, they signed to Miles Copeland's 'Illegal' label 1979. Legal wrangles dogged them throughout the 80's, and output was never massive. Their early 1986 lp 'A DATE WITH ELVIS', gave them deserved UK chart entry, hitting Top 40. • **Style:** Bass-less "psychobilly" punk rock'n'roll, fusing 50's rockabilly and 60's garage punk. Frontman LUX and his female sidekicks seemed to wear less and less with each passing phase. • **Songwriters:** Most written by LUX and IVY except SURFIN' BIRD (Trashmen) / FEVER (Little Willie John) / THE WAY I WALK (Robert Gordon) / GREEN DOOR (Jim Lowe) / JAILHOUSE ROCK (Elvis Presley) / MULESKINNER BLUES (Fendermen) / PSYCHOTIC REACTION (Count Five) / LONESOME TOWN (Ricky Nelson) / HARD WORKIN' MAN (Jack Nitzche) / HITSVILLE 29 B.C. (Turnbow) / WHEN I GET THE BLUES (Larry Mize) / HOW COME YOU DO ME? (. . .Joiner) / STRANGE LOVE (. . .West) / BLUES BLUES BLUES (. . .Thompson) / TRAPPED LOVE (Kohler-Fana) / SINNERS (. . .Aldrich) / ROUTE 66 (. . .Troup) / etc. • **Trivia:** Produced by former BOX TOPS singer ALEX CHILTON in 1979/1980. Their fan club surprisingly was based in Grangemouth, Scotland.

Recommended: OFF THE BONE (*9) / A DATE WITH ELVIS (*7) / SMELL OF

FEMALE (*6)

LUX INTERIOR (b.ERICK LEE PURKHISER) – vocals / **POISON IVY RORSCHACH** (b.KIRSTY MALANA WALLACE) – guitar / **BRIAN GREGORY** – guitar / **NICK KNOX** (b.NICK STEPHANOFF) – drums repl. MIRIAM LINNA who had repl. PAM BALAM GREGORY

not issued | Vengeance

Apr 78. (7") **THE WAY I WALK. / SURFIN' BIRD** [-] [ ]
Nov 78. (7") **HUMAN FLY. / DOMINO** [-] [ ]

Illegal | I.R.S.

Jul 79. (12"ep) **GRAVEST HITS** [ ] [-]
– Human fly / The way I walk / Domino / Surfin' bird / Lonesome town. *(re-iss.Sep82- 7"blue-ep) (re-iss.Mar83- 7"red-ep)*
Mar 80. (7") **GARBAGEMAN. / FEVER** [ ] [-]
Mar 80. (lp)(c) **SONGS THE LORD TAUGHT US** [ ] [ ]
– TV set / Rock on the Moon / Garbageman / I was a teenage werewolf / Sunglasses after dark / The mad daddy / Mystery plane / Zombie dance / What's behind the mask / Strychnine / I'm cramped / Tear it up / Fever. *(re-iss.+cd.Feb90)*
Jul 80. (7"m) **DRUG TRAIN. / LOVE ME / I CAN HARDLY STAND IT** [ ] [-]
Jul 80. (7") **DRUG TRAIN. / GARAGEMAN** [-] [ ]

— **KID CONGO POWERS** (b.BRIAN TRISTAN) – guitar repl. JULIEN BOND who had repl. GREGORY for two months mid 1980.

I.R.S. | I.R.S.

May 81. (7")(7"yellow) **GOO GOO MUCK. / SHE SAID** [ ] [ ]
May 81. (lp)(c) **PSYCHEDELIC JUNGLE** [ ] [ ]
– Green fuzz / Goo goo muck / Rockin' bones / Voodoo idol / Primitive / Caveman / The crusher / Don't eat stuff off the sidewalk / Can't find my mind / Jungle hop / The natives are restless / Under the wires / Beautiful gardens / Green door.
Sep 81. (7") **THE CRUSHER. / SAVE IT** [ ] [-]
(12+=) – New kind of kick.

— (LUX, IVY & NICK were joined by . . .) **IKE KNOX** (Nick's cousin) – guitar repl. KID CONGO who returned to GUN CLUB (appeared on live tracks 83-84)

New Rose | New Rose

Mar 83. (7")(7"brown)(7"clear)(7"green)(7"orange) **I AIN'T NUTHIN' BUT A GOREHOUND. / WEEKEND ON MARS** [ ] [-] France

Big Beat | New Rose

Nov 83. (m-lp)(red-lp)(pic-lp) **SMELL OF FEMALE (live)** [74] [ ] France
– Faster pussycat / I ain't nuthin' but a gorehound / Psychotic reaction / The most exhalted potentate of love / You got good taste / Call of the wig hat. *(cd-iss.May87) (re-iss.lp,c,cd.Feb90)* (cd+=) – Beautiful gardens / She said / Surfin' dead.

— **CANDY FUR** (DEL-MAR) – guitar repl. IKE

Nov 85. (7")(7"orange) **CAN YOUR PUSSY DO THE DOG?. / BLUE MOON BABY** [68] [ ]
(10")(12")(10"red)(10"blue) Georgia Lee Brown.
Feb 86. (lp)(c)(cd) **A DATE WITH ELVIS** [34] [ ]
– How far can too far go / The hot pearl snatch / People ain't too good / What's inside a girl? / Can your pussy do the dog? / Kizmiaz / Cornfed dames / Chicken / (Hot pool of) Woman need / Aloha from Hell / It's just that song.
May 86. (7") **WHAT'S INSIDE A GIRL?. / GET OFF THE ROAD** [ ] [ ]
(12"+=) – Give me a woman.
(cd-s++=) – Scene / Heart of darkness.

Enigma | Enigma

Jan 90. (7")(c-s)(7"sha-pic-d) **BIKINI GIRLS WITH MACHINE GUNS. / JACKYARD BACKOFF** [35] [ ]
(12"+=)(cd-s+=) – Her love rubbed off.
Feb 90. (cd)(c)(lp) **STAY SICK** [62] [ ]
– Bop pills / Goddam rock'n'roll / Bikini girls with machine guns / All woman are bad / Creature from the black leather lagoon / Shortenini' bread / Daisy's up your butterfly / Everything goes / Journey to the centre of a girl / Mama oo pow pow / Saddle up a buzz buzz / Muleskinner blues (cd.+=) – Her love rubbed off. *(re-iss.cd Feb94)*
Apr 90. (7")(c-s) **ALL WOMAN ARE BAD. / TEENAGE RAGE (live)** [ ] [ ]
(12"+=)(cd-s+=)(12"pic-d+=) – King of the drapes (live) / High school hell-cats (live).
Aug 90. (7") **CREATURES FROM THE BLACK LEATHER LAGOON. / JAILHOUSE ROCK** [ ] [ ]
(12"+=)(cd-s+=) – Beat out my love.

— **LUX & IVY** are joined by **SLIM CHANCE** – guitar (ex-PANTHER BURNS) / **JIM SCLAVUNOS** – drums

Big Beat | Enigma

Sep 91. (7") **EYEBALL IN MY MARTINI. / WILDER WILDER FASTER FASTER** [ ] [ ]
(12"+=)(cd-s+=) – Wilder wilder faster faster.
Sep 91. (cd)(c)(lp)(pic-lp)(cd) **LOOK MOM, NO HEAD!** [ ] [ ]
– Dames, booze, chains and boots / Two headed sex change / Blow up your mind / Hard workin' man / Miniskirt blues / Alligator stomp / I wanna get in your pants Bend over, I'll drive / Don't get funny with me / Eyeball in my Martini / Hipsville 29 B.C. / When I get the blues (the strangeness in me).

— **NICKY ALEXANDER** – drums (ex-WEIRDOS) repl. JIM

— **HARRY DRUMDINI** – drums repl. NICKY

Creation | Rykodisc

Oct 94. (7") **ULTRA TWIST!. / CONFESSIONS OF A PSYCHO CAT** [ ] [ ]
(12"+=)(cd-s+=) – No club love wolf.
Oct 94. (cd)(c)(lp) **FLAME JOB** [ ] [ ]
– Mean machine / Ultra twist / Let's get f*cked up / Nest of the cuckoo bird / I'm customized / Sado country auto show / Naked girl falling down the stairs / How come you do me? / Inside out and upside down (with you) / Trapped love / Swing the big eyed rabbit / Strange love / Blues blues blues / Sinners / Route 66 (get your kicks on).
Feb 95. (7") **NAKED GIRL FALLING DOWN THE STAIRS. / LET'S GET F*CKED UP** [ ] [ ]
(cd-s+=) – Surfin' bird.

– compilations, others, etc. –

Illegal | I.R.S.

May 83. I.R.S.; (lp)(c)(pic-lp) **OFF THE BONE** [44] [ ]
– Human fly / The way I walk / Domino / Surfin' bird / Lonesome town / Garbageman / Fever / Drug train / Love me / I can't hardly stand it / Goo goo muck / She said / The crusher / Save it / New kind of kick.
(US-title-BAD MUSIC FOR BAD PEOPLE) *(UK cd-iss.Jan87)*
(re-iss. cd 1992 on 'Castle' +=) – Uranium Rock / Good taste (live)
Feb 84. New Rose France; (7")(7"pic-d) **FASTER PUSSYCAT. / YOU GOT GOOD TASTE** [-] [-]
1984. New Rose; (4x7") **I AIN'T NUTHIN' BUT A GOREHOUND. / WEEKEND ON MARS / FASTER PUSSYCAT. / YOU GOT GOOD TASTE / CALL OF THE WIGHAT. / THE MOST EXHALTED POTENTATE OF LOVE / PSYCHOTIC REACTION. /** (one sided) [-] [-]
(all 4 either blue/white/black/green)
May 86. New Rose France; (7") **KIZMIAZ. / GET OFF THE ROAD** [-] [-]
(12"+=) – Give me a woman.
Nov 87. Vengeance; (lp) **ROCKIN' AND REELIN' IN AUCKLAND, NEW ZEALAND (live)** [-] [ ]
(cd-iss.Sep94 on 'Ace')
1989. Big Beat; (4x7"diff.colours) (singles from Mar83/ Feb84/ Nov85/ May86) [ ] [-]

CRANBERRIES

Formed: Limerick, Ireland . . . 1990, initially as covers band The CRANBERRY SAW US, until the inclusion of DOLORES. An independent single 'UNCERTAIN' on 'Xeric' appeared late 1991. They went into the studio late in 1991, and soon re-surfaced on 'Island' in 1992 /3 with 'DREAMS', 'LINGER' and 'PUT ME DOWN'. These were tracks featured on 1993's debut album 'EVERYBODY ELSE IS DOING IT . . .', which went on to sell a million in the US initially, and a year later in the slow-warming UK. • **Style:** An indie style major outfit, initially described as The Irish SUNDAYS, although DOLORES maintains her Heavenly deep-rooted Irish accent in song. • **Songwriters:** DOLORES / N.HOGAN, except (THEY LONG TO BE) CLOSE TO YOU (Carpenters). • **Trivia:** Supported MOOSE in the summer of '91. DOLORES guested on MOOSE's 1992 album 'XYZ'. In the summer of '95, 'ZOMBIE' was discofied into the UK Top 20 by pop/rave artist AMY . . .'nough said.

Recommended: EVERYBODY ELSE IS DOING IT . . . (*8) / NO TIME TO ARGUE (*6) / TO THE FAITHFUL DEPARTED (*5)

DOLORES O'RIORDAN (b.1971) – vocals, acoustic guitar / **NOEL HOGAN** – guitar / **MIKE HOGAN** – bass / **FERGAL LAWLER** – drums

Xeric | not issued

Oct 91. (12"ep)(cd-ep) **UNCERTAIN / NOTHING LEFT AT ALL. / PATHETIC SENSES / THEM** [ ] [-]

Island | Island

Sep 92. (7") **DREAMS. / WHAT YOU WERE** [ ] [ ]
(12"+=)(cd-s+=) – Liar.
Feb 93. (7")(c-s) **LINGER. / REASON** [74] [8]
(12"+=)(cd-s+=) – How (radical mix).
Mar 93. (cd)(c)(lp) **EVERYBODY ELSE IS DOING IT, SO WHY CAN'T WE?** [64] [18]
– I still do / Dreams / Sunday / Pretty / Waltzing black / Not sorry / Linger / Wanted / Still can't . . . / I will always / How / Put me down. *(re-iss.Nov93) (re-iss.Mar94, hit UK No.1)*
Jan 94. (7")(c-s) **LINGER. / PRETTY (live)** [14] [-]
(cd-s+=)(10"+=) – Waltzing black (live) / I still do (live).
Apr 94. (7")(c-s) **DREAMS. / WHAT YOU WERE** [27] [42]
(cd-s+=) – Liar.
(cd-s) – ('A'live) / Liar (live) / Not sorry (live) / Wanted (live).

— Jun 94; DOLORES featured on JAH WOBBLE's Top 50 hit 'The Sun Does Rise'.

Sep 94. (7")(c-s) **ZOMBIE. / AWAY** | 14 | |
(cd-s+=) – I don't need.
(cd-s) – ('A'side) / Waltzing black (live) / Linger (live).

Oct 94. (cd)(c)(lp) **NO NEED TO ARGUE** | 2 | 6 |
– Ode to my family / I can't be with you / 21 / Zombie / Empty / Everything I said / The icicle melts / Disappointment / Ridiculous thoughts / Dreaming my dreams / Yeat's grave / Daffodil lament / No need to argue.

Nov 94. (7")(c-s) **ODE TO MY FAMILY. / SO COLD IN IRELAND** | 29 | |
(cd-s+=) – No need to argue / Dreaming my dreams.
(cd-s) – ('A'side) / Dreams (live) / Ridiculous thoughts (live) / Zombie (live).

Feb 95. (7")(c-s) **I CAN'T BE WITH YOU. / (THEY LONG TO BE) CLOSE TO YOU** | 23 | |
(cd-s+=) – Empty.
(cd-s) – ('A'side) / Zombie (acoustic) / Daffodil lament (live).

Jul 95. (7")(c-s) **RIDICULOUS THOUGHTS. / LINGER** | 20 | |
(cd-s+=) – Twenty one (live) / Ridiculous thoughts (live).

. . . Jan – Jun '96 stop press . . .

Apr 96. (single) **SALVATION** | 13 | |
May 96. (cd)(c)(colrd-lp) **TO THE FAITHFUL DEPARTED** | 2 | 4 |

compilations, etc

Nov 95. (d-cd) **EVERYBODY ELSE IS DOING IT . . . / NO NEED TO ARGUE** | | |

CRASH TEST DUMMIES

Formed: Winnepeg, Canada . . . early 90's by ROBERTS and brother DAN. Released initially in Canada-only the eventually platinum selling 'THE GHOST THAT HAUNT ME', which hosted US Hot 100 breakthrough single 'SUPERMAN'S SONG'. They finally released the acclaimed return in 1994, with the deliciously titled 'MMM MMM MMM MMM', which went worldwide Top 3. • **Style:** Angst lyrically, although BRAD's deep vox fuses in well with semi-acoustic backing. • **Songwriters:** BRAD ROBERTS except ALL YOU PRETTY GIRLS (Xtc). • **Trivia:** Co-produced w/ JERRY HARRISON (ex-TALKING HEADS).

Recommended: GOD SHUFFLED HIS FEET (*6)

BRAD ROBERTS – vocals, guitars / **ELLEN REID** – keyboards, accordion / **BENJAMIN DARVILL** – mandolin, harmonicas / **DAN ROBERTS** – bass / **MITCH DORGE** – drums, percussion

Arista Arista

Sep 91. (c-s)(cd-s) **SUPERMAN'S SONG. / THE VOYAGE** | | 56 |
Nov 91. (cd)(c) **THE GHOSTS THAT HAUNT ME** | | |
– Winter song / Comin' back soon (the bereft man's song) / Superman's song / The country life / Here on Earth (I'll have my cake) / The ghosts that haunt me / Thick-necked man / Androgynous / The voyage / At my funeral. *(re-iss.cd Oct95)*

R.C.A. Arista

Apr 94. (7")(c-s) **MMM MMM MMM MMM. / HERE I STAND BEFORE ME (live)** | 2 | 4 | Jan94
(cd-s+=) – Superman's song (live).

May 94. (cd)(c)(lp) **GOD SHUFFLED HIS FEET** | 2 | 9 | Feb94
– God shuffled his feet / Afternoons & coffee spoons / Mmm mmm mmm mmm / In the days of the caveman / Swimming in your ocean / Here I stand before me / I think I'll disappear now / How does a duck know? / When I go out with artists / The psychic / Two knights and maidens / Untitled.

Jun 94. (7")(c-s) **AFTERNOONS & COFFEE SPOONS. / IN THE DAYS OF THE CAVEMAN (live)** | 23 | 66 |
(cd-s+=) – The ghosts that haunt me / Androgynous (live).
(cd-s) – ('A'side) / Mmm mmm mmm mmm (live) / God shuffled his feet (live).

Oct 94. (7")(c-s)(cd-s) **GOD SHUFFLED HIS FEET. / AFTERNOONS & COFFEE SPOONS (live)** | | |
(12"+=)(cd-s+=) – Winter song / Mmm mmm mmm mmm.

Below feat. vocals by ELLEN REID

Apr 95. (c-s) **THE BALLAD OF PETER PUMPKINHEAD. / GOD SHUFFLED HIS FEET** | 30 | |
(cd-s+=) – Afternoons and coffeespoons (live) / Swimming in your ocean.
(cd-s) – ('A'side) / Afternoons and coffeespoons (live) / When I go out with artists (live) / Swimming in your ocean (live).

Robert CRAY

Born: 1 Aug'53, Columbus, Georgia, USA. He later moved to Tacoma, Washington and toured West Coast 1973, alongside high school idol ALBERT COLLINS. This led to CRAY forming own band in 1975. They cut album in 1978, but WHO'S BEEN TALKIN' finally saw light 1980 on 'Tomato' records. After another long wait, the 'Hightone' label, licensed to 'Demon' for UK, and released follow-up BAD INFLUENCE. From then on, he won many awards, including Best Blues Guitarist / Album for 1984 and '86 respectively, leading to contract with 'Mercury'. His 1986 album 'STRONG PERSUADER' was first to give UK chart status, which continued into the 90's. • **Style:** Black blues guitarist, influenced by Texas style, and heroes ELMORE JAMES, B.B.KING, STEVE CROPPER and ALBERT COLLINS. • **Songwriters:** Mostly CRAY compositions with group collaborations. 1992 producer DENNIS WALKER wrote most with CRAY or PUGH. The same album saw CRAY co-write with BOZ SCAGGS and STEVE CROPPER on 'A PICTURE OF A BROKEN HEART' & 'ON THE ROAD DOWN' respectively. Covered; GOT TO MAKE A COME-BACK (Eddie Floyd) / DON'T TOUCH ME (Johnny 'Guitar' Watson) / TOO MANY COOKS (Willie Dixon) / YOU'RE GONNA NEED ME (Albert King) etc. • **Trivia:** In 1980 he and band appeared in the film 'Animal House' as OTIS DAY's house group.

Recommended: DON'T BE AFRAID OF THE DARK (*7) / MIDNIGHT STROLL (*7) / BAD INFLUENCE (*6) / FALSE ACCUSATIONS (*6) / STRONG PERSUADER (*6)

ROBERT CRAY – vocals, guitar / **RICHARD COUSINS** – bass / **DAVE OLSON** – drums / also **MIKE VANNICE** – sax, keyboards / **WARREN RAND** – sax / **CURTIS SALADO** – guest harmonica

ROBERT CRAY BAND

Tomato not issued

1980. (lp) **WHO'S BEEN TALKIN'** | - | |
– Too many cooks / The score / The welfare (turns its back on you) / That's what I'll do / I'd rather be a wino / Who's been talkin' / Sleeping in the ground / I'm gonna forget about you / Nice as a fool can be / If you're thinkin' what I'm thinkin'. *(UK-iss.+c.Oct86 on 'Charly') (US-re-iss.lp,c,cd.May88) (re-iss.cd/c 1992 as 'THE SCORE' on 'Charly')*

Demon Hightone

Mar 84. (lp) **BAD INFLUENCE** | | | 1983
– Phone booth / The grinder / Got to make a comeback / So many women, so little time / Where do I go from here / Waiting for a train / March on / Don't touch me / No big deal. *(US-re-lp,c,cd.Mar87.) (UK-re-lp/cd.Jul87)* (cd+=) – I got loaded / Share what you've got, Keep what you need.

— **PETER BOE** – keyboards, vocals repl. SALADO, VANNICE and RAND.

Oct 85. (lp)(c) **FALSE ACCUSATIONS** | 68 | |
– Porch light / Change of heart, change of mind (S.O.F.T.) / She's gone / Playin' in the dirt / I've slipped her mind / False accusations / The last time (I get burned like this) / Payin' for it now / Sonny. *(cd-iss.1986)*

Nov 85. (12"ep) **CHANGE OF HEART, CHANGE OF MIND (soft) / I GOT LOADED. / PHONE BOOTH / BAD INFLUENCE** | | |

Mercury Mercury

Oct 86. (7") **I GUESS I SHOWED HER. / DIVIDED HEART** | | |
(12"+=) – Got to be a comeback / Share what you've got, keep what you need.

Nov 86. (lp)(c)(cd) **STRONG PERSUADER** | 34 | 13 |
– Smoking gun / I guess I showed her / Right next door (because of me) / Still around / More than I can stand / Foul play / I wonder / Fantasized / New blood.

Feb 87. (7") **SMOKING GUN. / FANTASIZED** | | 22 |
(12"+=) – Divided heart.

May 87. (7") **RIGHT NEXT DOOR (BECAUSE OF ME). / NEW BLOOD** | 50 | 80 |
(12"+=) – Share what you've got, keep what you need.
(10"+=) – I wonder / Smoking gun.

Aug 87. (7") **NOTHIN' BUT A WOMAN. / I WONDER** | | |
(12"+=) – Still around / New blood.
(10"+=) – Right next door (because of me).

Aug 88. (7") **DON'T BE AFRAID OF THE DARK. / AT LAST** | | 74 |
(12"+=) – Without a trace.

Aug 88. (lp)(c)(cd) **DON'T BE AFRAID OF THE DARK** | 13 | 32 |
– Don't be afraid of the dark / Don't you even care? / Your secret's safe with me / I can't go home / Night patrol / Acting this way / Gotta change the rules / Across the line / At last / Laugh out loud.

Oct 88. (7") **NIGHT PATROL. / MORE THAN I CAN STAND** | | |
(12"+=) – Divided heart.
(cd-s+=) – I wonder.

Jan 89. (7")(12") **ACTING THIS WAY. / LAUGH OUT LOUD** | | |
(cd-s+=) – ('A'guitar version) / Smoking gun.

ROBERT CRAY

solo, retained only **COUSINS** plus **JIMMY PUGH** – keyboards / **KEVIN HAYES** – drums, percussion / **TIM KAIHATSU** – guitar / **& MEMPHIS HORNS: WAYNE JACKSON** – trumpet, trombone / **ANDREW LOVE** – tenor saxophone credited later as **ROBERT CRAY BAND with The MEMPHIS HORNS**

Aug 90. (12"ep)(cd-ep) **THE FORECAST (CALLS FOR PAIN) / HOLDIN' COURT. / LABOUR OF LOVE / MIDNIGHT STROLL** | | |

Sep 90. (cd)(c)(lp) **MIDNIGHT STROLL** [19] [51]
– The forecast (calls for pain) / These things / My problem / Labour of love / Bouncin' back / Consequences / The things you do to me / Wall around time / Move a mountain / Midnight stroll. (cd.+=) – Holdin' court. *(re-iss.cd/c Mar93)*

Jan 91. (7") **CONSEQUENCES. / SMOKING GUN** [ ] [ ]
(12"+=)(cd-s+=) – Right next door (because of me).

— **KARL SEVAREID** – bass repl. COUSINS

Aug 92. (cd)(c)(lp) **I WAS WARNED** [29] [ ]
– Just a loser / I'm a good man / I was warned / The price I pay / Won the battle / On the road down / A whole lotta pride / A picture of a broken heart / He don't live here anymore / Our last time. *(re-iss.cd Apr95)*

— **EDWARD MANION** – saxophone / **MARK PENDER** – trumpet repl. horn section

Oct 93. (cd)(c) **SHAME + A SIN** [48] [ ]
– 1040 blues / Some pain, some shame / I shiver / You're gonna need me / Don't break this ring / Stay go / Leave well enough alone / Passing by / I'm just lucky that way / Well I lied / Up and down.

Nov 93. (7")(c-s) **I HATE TAXES. / SMOKING GUN** [ ] [ ]
(cd-s+=) – 1040 blues / Right next door.

— with **PUGH / SEVAREID / HAYES**

May 95. (cd)(c) **SOME RAINY MORNING** [63] [ ]
– Moan / I'll go on / Steppin' out / Never mattered much / Tell the landlord / Little boy big / Enough for me / Jealous love / Will you think of me / Holdin' on / Love well spent.

. . . Jan – Jun '96 stop press . . .

— Apr'96, he returned to the UK chart (at 65) augmenting JOHN LEE HOOKER on single 'BABY LEE'.

– compilations, others, etc. –

Nov 85. Sonet/ US= Alligator; (lp) **SHOWDOWN!** [ ] [ ]

— above by **"ROBERT CRAY, ALBERT COLLINS & JOHNNY COPELAND"**

Jan 92. Tomato-Rhino; (cd)(lp) **TOO MANY COOKS** (1978 session) [ ] [ ]
(cd re-iss.Jun93)

CREAM

Formed: London, England . . . mid'66 as earliest ever supergroup by ERIC CLAPTON, GINGER BAKER and JACK BRUCE. All had initial experience with top early 60's bands (see below). This stature, made Robert Stigwood of new 'Reaction' records ('Atco' US), give them contract after seeing them debut at The National Jazz & Blues Festival on 3rd Jul'66. Their initial single 'WRAPPING PAPER', gave them first of many Top 40 hits on both sides of the Atlantic. They played their farewell tour in Nov'68, ending at a sell-out Royal Albert Hall. All members went on to more success from 1969 onwards. • **Style:** Improvised ,blues-rock mixed at times with superb and subtle heavy pop. One of the first bands to introduce long solo pieces, featuring GINGER's superb drumming and of course ERIC's legendary axe-playing, best seen live. • **Songwriters:** Bulk of material written by JACK BRUCE with lyrics by poet/non-member PETE BROWN. They also covered; ROLLIN' AND TUMBLIN' (Muddy Waters) / I'M SO GLAD (Skip James) / FROM FOUR TILL LATE + CROSSROADS (Robert Johnson) / BORN UNDER A BAD SIGN (Booker T. Jones ?)/ made famous by Albert King) / SPOONFUL (Howlin' Wolf) / etc. GEORGE HARRISON co-wrote 'BADGE' with ERIC CLAPTON. • **Trivia:** Producer FELIX PAPPALARDI became unofficial 4th member in 1968.

Recommended: DISRAELI GEARS (*8) / STRANGE BREW – THE VERY BEST OF CREAM (*9) / WHEELS OF FIRE (*7) / (also CREAM tracks on CLAPTON comps.)

ERIC CLAPTON (b.ERIC PATRICK CLAPP, 30 May'45, Ripley, Surrey, England) – guitar, vocals (ex-YARDBIRDS, ex-JOHN MAYALL'S BLUESBREAKERS)
JACK BRUCE (b.JOHN BRUCE, 14 May'43, Glasgow, Scotland) – vocals, bass (ex-GRAHAM BOND, ex-JOHN MAYALL'S BLUESBREAKERS, ex-MANFRED MANN) / **GINGER BAKER** (b.PETER BAKER, 19 Aug'39, Lewisham, London, England) – drums (ex-GRAHAM BOND ORGANISATION, ex-ALEXIS KORNER'S BLUES INCORPORATED)

Reaction / Atco

Oct 66. (7") **WRAPPING PAPER. / CAT'S SQUIRREL** [34] [ ]

Dec 66. (lp) **FRESH CREAM** [6] [39]
– N.S.U. / Sleepy time time / Dreaming / Sweet wine / Spoonful / Cat's squirrel / Four until late / Rollin' and tumblin' / I'm so glad / Toad. *(re-iss.Jan69, reached No.7 UK, re-iss Oct70 as 'FULL CREAM' & Mar75 as 'CREAM' + 2 tracks on 'Polydor') (cd-iss.Jan84)* (+=) – Wrapping paper / The coffee song.

Dec 66. (7") **I FEEL FREE. / N.S.U.** [11] [ ]

Jun 67. (7") **STRANGE BREW. / TALES OF BRAVE ULYSSES** [17] [ ]
(re-iss.Jul84 on 'Old Gold')

Nov 67. (7") **SPOONFUL. / (part 2)** [-] [ ]

Nov 67. (lp) **DISRAELI GEARS** [5] [4]
– Strange brew / Sunshine of your love / World of pain / Dance the night away / Blue condition / Tales of brave Ulysses / S.W.L.A.B.R. / We're going wrong / Outside woman blues / Take it back / Mother's lament. *(re-iss.Nov77 on 'RSO', cd-iss.Jan 84 on 'Track')*

Jan 68. (7") **SUNSHINE OF YOUR LOVE. / SWLABR** [-] [5]
(UK-iss.Sep68 hit No.25.)

Polydor / Atco

May 68. (7") **ANYONE FOR TENNIS. / PRESSED RAT AND WARTHOG** [40] [64]

— **FELIX PAPPALARDI** – producer, instr. guested as 4th p/t member

Aug 68. (d-lp) **WHEELS OF FIRE** [3] [1] Jul 68
(re-iss.'72)(re-iss.Jan84 on 'RSO')(above lp was released as d-lp & 2 lp's) (cd-iss.Jan84 & Feb89)

Aug 68. (lp) **WHEELS OF FIRE – IN THE STUDIO** [7] [ ]
– White room / Sitting on top of the world / Passing the time / As you said / Pressed rat and warthog / Politician / Those were the days / Born under a bad sign / Deserted cities of the heart. *(re-iss.Nov77 on 'R.S.O.')*

Aug 68. (lp) **WHEELS OF FIRE – LIVE AT THE FILLMORE (live)** [ ] [ ]
– Crossroads / Spoonful / Traintime / Toad. *(re-iss.Nov77 on 'R.S.O.')*

Jan 69. (7") **WHITE ROOM. / THOSE WERE THE DAYS** [28] [6] Oct 68

— They split around mid-'68. The rest of their releases were posthumous and CLAPTON went solo after forming BLIND FAITH with BAKER. He also went solo. JACK BRUCE went solo, etc.

– compilations, others, etc. –

Note; Below 'Polydor' releases issued on 'Atco' in the US.

Jan 69. Atco; (7") **CROSSROADS. / PASSING THE TIME** [-] [28]

Mar 69. Polydor; (lp)(c) **GOODBYE** [1] [2]
– I'm so glad * / Politician * / Sitting on top of the world * / Badge / Doing that scrapyard thing / What a bringdown. *(* – live, re-iss.Nov77 & Aug84 on 'RSO') (cd-iss.Jan84. +=) – Anyone for tennis)*

Apr 69. Polydor; (7") **BADGE. / WHAT A BRINGDOWN** [18] [60]
(re-iss.Oct72)

Nov 69. Polydor; (lp)(c) **BEST OF CREAM** [6] [3] Jul 69
(re-iss.Nov77 on 'RSO') (re-iss.Apr86 on 'Arcade')

Jun 70. Polydor; (lp)(c) **LIVE CREAM (live)** [4] [15] Apr 70
– N.S.U. / Sleepy time time / Lawdy mama / Sweet wine / Rollin' and tumblin'. *(re-iss.Nov77 & Mar85 on 'RSO') (cd-iss.May88)*

Jul 70. Polydor; (7") **LAWDY MAMA (live). / SWEET WINE (live)** [-] [ ]

Jul 71. Polydor; (7") **I FEEL FREE. / WRAPPING PAPER** [ ] [ ]
(re-iss. Jul84 on 'Old Gold')

Jun 72. Polydor; (lp)(c) **LIVE CREAM VOL.2** [15] [27] Mar 72
– Deserted cities of the heart / White room / Politician / Tales of brave Ulysses / Sunshine of your love. *(re-iss.Nov77 on 'RSO')(cd-iss.May88)*

Apr 73. Polydor; (d-lp)(c) **HEAVY CREAM** [ ] [ ] Oct 72

Oct 80. Polydor; (lp-box) **CREAM BOX SET** [ ] [ ]

Oct 83. Polydor; (lp)(c) **THE STORY OF CREAM VOL.1** [ ] [ ]

Oct 83. Polydor; (lp)(c) **THE STORY OF CREAM VOL.2** [ ] [-]

Apr 78. R.S.O.; (lp)(c) **CREAM VOLUME TWO** [ ] [ ]

Feb 83. R.S.O.; (lp)(c) **STRANGE BREW – THE VERY BEST OF CREAM** [ ] [ ]
– Badge / Sunshine of your love / Crossroads / White room / Born under a bad sign / Swlabr / Strange brew / Anyone for tennis / I feel free / Tales of brave Ulysses / Politician / Spoonful.
(cd-iss.Nov87 on 'Polydor')

Aug 82. R.S.O.; (7") **BADGE. / TALES OF BRAVE ULYSSES** [ ] [ ]
(12"+=) – White room.

Jul 86. R.S.O.; (7") **I FEEL FREE. / BADGE** [ ] [ ]

Jul 84. Old Gold; (7") **WHITE ROOM. / BADGE** [ ] [-]

Jul 84. Old Gold; (7") **SUNSHINE OF YOUR LOVE. / ANYONE FOR TENNIS** [ ] [-]

Feb 89. Koine; (cd) **LIVE 1968 (live)** [ ] [-]

Dec 91. U.F.O.; (cd) **IN GEAR (w/ booklet)** [ ] [-]

Nov 92. I.T.M.; (cd) **THE ALTERNATIVE ALBUM** [ ] [ ]

Dec 92. Pickwick; (cd)(lp) **DESERTED CITIES: THE CREAM COLLECTION** [ ] [-]

Feb 95. Polydor; (cd)(c) **THE VERY BEST OF CREAM** [ ] [ ]

CREATION

Formed: Hertfordshire, England . . . 1961 as 5-piece! MARK FOUR by KENNY PICKETT, JACK JONES and EDDIE PHILLIPS. Under the guidance of manager ROBERT STIGWOOD, they released a couple of flop singles for 'Mercury'. After two more for others, they changed their line-up in mid-66 and became The CREATION. They also employed new manager TONY STRATTON-SMITH, who found American producer

SHEL TALMY and a new label 'Planet'. They unleashed 2 superb 45's in 1966 'MAKING TIME' and 'PAINTER MAN', which both hit UK Top 50, helped by alleged chart hyping from TONY. The latter also gave them a bit pocket money by hitting No.1 in Germany. However, when they moved to 'Polydor' in 1967 they ran out of steam and split the year after. Unfortunately their only lp release had been in Germany, where they had found some other success. • **Style:** Pop-art loud + heavy mods similar to The WHO or The KINKS. PHILLIPS was the first person to play guitar with a violin bow, a feat later achieved by JIMMY PAGE of LED ZEPPELIN. • **Songwriters:** PICKETT or PHILLIPS plus covers:- ROCK AROUND THE CLOCK (Bill Haley) / TRY IT BABY (Marvin Gaye) / LIKE A ROLLING STONE (Bob Dylan) / BONY MORONIE (Larry Williams). • **Trivia:** In 1970, PICKETT co-wrote UK No.1 hit 'Grandad' for CLIVE DUNN (Dad's Army) with HERBIE FLOWERS. PICKETT was later to write 'TEACHER TEACHER' for DAVE EDMUNDS, before he co-wrote some more songs with BILLY BREMNER. **Legacy:** PAINTER MAN was a 1979 UK Top 10 hit for BONEY M, while much later The GODFATHERS (in 1990) and RIDE (in 1994) covered HOW DOES IT FEEL TO FEEL. Many have been inspired by them including TELEVISION PERSONALITIES / TIMES / BIFF BANG POW and the label 'Creation'.

Recommended: HOW DOES IT FEEL TO FEEL (*8) / THE CREATION (*7)

MARK FOUR

KENNY PICKETT (b. 3 Sep'47, Ware, England) – vocals / **EDDIE PHILLIPS** (b.EDWIN, 15 Aug'45, Leytonstone, England) – lead guitar / **MICK THOMPSON** – rhythm guitar / **JOHN DALTON** – bass / **JACK JONES** (b. 8 Nov'44, Northampton, England) – drums

	UK	US
	Mercury	not issued
May 64. (7") **ROCK AROUND THE CLOCK. / SLOW DOWN**		-
Aug 64. (7") **TRY IT BABY. / CRAZY COUNTRY HOP**		-
	Decca	not issued
Aug 65. (7") **HURT ME IF YOU WILL. / I'M LEAVING**		-
	Fontana	not issued
Feb 66. (7") **WORK ALL DAY (SLEEP ALL NIGHT). / GOING DOWN FAST**		-

—— Split after final gig on 6th June 1966. DALTON joined The KINKS.

CREATION

BOB GARNER – bass (ex-TONY SHERIDAN BAND) repl. THOMPSON

	UK	US
	Planet	Planet
Jun 66. (7") **MAKING TIME. / TRY AND STOP ME**	49	-
Oct 66. (7") **PAINTER MAN. / BIFF BANG POW**	36	-

KIM GARDNER – bass (ex-BIRDS) repl. GARNER

	UK	US
	Polydor	not issued
Jun 67. (7") **IF I STAY TOO LONG. / NIGHTMARES**		-
Oct 67. (7") **LIFE IS JUST BEGINNING. / THROUGH MY EYES**		-
Feb 68. (7") **HOW DOES IT FEEL TO FEEL. / TOM TOM**		-

RON WOOD – guitar (ex-BIRDS) repl. DIGGER who had briefly repl. PICKETT

—— **PICKETT** returned to repl. PHILLIPS + GARDNER

	UK	US
May 68. (7") **MIDWAY DOWN. / THE GIRLS ARE NAKED**		-

—— Disbanded soon after above. PICKETT continued to write for SHEL TALMY and he also became road manager for LED ZEPPELIN in America. RON WOOD joined The FACES and later became a member of The ROLLING STONES. GARDNER co-formed ASHTON, GARDNER & DYKE who had a 1970 Top 3 hit with 'RESURRECTION SHUFFLE'. He later formed BADGER. JACK JONES drifted into cabaret session work.

—— CREATION re-formed in the mid-80's with **PHILLIPS, PICKETT, NOBBY DALTON** – bass (ex-KINKS) + **MICK AVORY** – drums (ex-KINKS).

	UK	US
	Jet	not issued
Apr 87. (12"ep) **A SPIRIT CALLED LOVE. / MAKING TIME / MUMBO JUMBO**		-

—— **PHILLIPS**, etc, without PICKETT formed pub band CUCKOOS NEST. In 1994, The CREATION re-formed with **PICKETT, JONES + PHILLIPS.**

	UK	US
	Creation	Rykodisc
Jul 94. (7")(cd-s) **CREATION. / SHOCK HORROR / POWER SURGE**		-

... Jan – Jun '96 stop press ...

	UK	US
Mar 96. (cd)(lp) **THE CREATION**		

– compilations, etc. –

	UK	US
Sep 73. Charisma; (lp) **CREATION '66-67**		-
Oct 73. Charisma; (7") **MAKING TIME. / PAINTER MAN** *(re-iss.Nov77 on 'Raw')*		-
Sep 82. Edsel; (lp) **HOW DOES IT FEEL TO FEEL**		-

– How does it feel to feel / Life is just beginning / Through my eyes / Ostrich man / I am the walker / Tom Tom / The girls are naked / Painter man / Try and stop me / Biff bang pow / Making time / Cool jerk / For all that I am / Nightmares / Midway down / Can I join your band?. *(cd-iss.Aug90)*

	UK	US
May 84. Edsel; (7") **MAKING TIME. / UNCLE BERT**		-
Feb 84. Line; (lp) **WE ARE PAINTERMEN**	-	- GERM

—— (bove originally released in Germany 1967)

	UK	US
Feb 84. Line; (lp) **RECREATION**	-	-
1985. Bam Caruso; (7"ep) **LIVE AT THE BEAT SCENE CLUB**		-

CREATURES (see under ⇒ SIOUXSIE & THE BANSHEES)

CREEDENCE CLEARWATER REVIVAL

Formed: California, USA . . . late 1959 as schoolgroup The BLUE VELVETS by JOHN FOGERTY, STU COOK and DOUG CLIFFORD. JOHN soon invited other multi-instrumentalist and brother TOM. After one 45 on a local label, they became The GOLLIWOGS in 1964. They signed to 'Fantasy' records by boss Hy Weiss. Around mid-1967, they became CREEDENCE CLEARWATER REVIVAL after JOHN and DOUG were earlier drafted. Late in 1968, their first single 'SUSIE Q', helped by live stature, broke them into the US Top 20. The following 2 years, saw them hit No.1 in the US with single 'BAD MOON RISING', and peak on both sides of the Atlantic with album chart topper 'COSMO'S FACTORY' in 1970. • **Style:** Fused swamp rock with traditional country blues and basic rock'n'roll. The GOLLIWOGS had been influenced by British beat combos of '63-64. • **Songwriters:** JOHN wrote most of material. Also covered; SUSIE Q (Dale Hawkins) / I PUT A SPELL ON YOU (Screamin' Jay Hawkins) / I HEARD IT THROUGH THE GRAPEVINE (hit; Marvin Gaye) / OOBY DOOBY (Roy Orbison) / HELLO MARY LOU (Ricky Nelson) / etc. • **Miscellaneous:** TOM FOGERTY was to die of tuberculosis on 6 Sep'90.

Recommended: CREEDENCE GOLD (*8)

The BLUE VELVETS

JOHN FOGERTY (b.28 May'45, Berkeley, California)– vocals, guitar / **TOM FOGERTY** (b. 9 Nov'41, Berkeley)– rhythm guitar, piano / **STU COOK** (b.25 Apr'45, Portland, Califonia)– bass / **DOUG 'COSMO' CLIFFORD** (b.24 Apr'45, Palo Alto, California)- **drums**

	UK	US
	not issued	Orkhestra
1962. (7") **HAVE YOU EVER BEEN LONELY. / BONITA**	-	

The GOLLIWOGS

same line-up (TOM sang lead on first)

	UK	US
	not issued	Fantasy
Nov 64. (7") **DON'T TELL ME NO LIES. / LITTLE GIRL**	-	
1965. (7") **YOU CAME WALKING. / WHERE YOU BEEN**	-	
1965. (7") **YOU CAN'T BE TRUE. / YOU GOT NOTHIN' ON ME**	-	
	Vocalion	Scorpio
Jan 66. (7") **BROWN-EYED GIRL. / YOU BETTER BE CAREFUL**		
Mar 66. (7") **FRAGILE CHILD. / FIGHT FIRE**		
Dec 66. (7") **WALKING ON THE WATER. / YOU BETTER GET IT**	-	
Nov 67. (7") **PORTERVILLE. / CALL IT PRETENDING**		

(above single was soon later credited to below group name)*(also a compilation album of some singles above was released in '74 on 'Fantasy')*

CREDENCE CLEARWATER REVIVAL

same line-up

	UK	US
	Liberty	Fantasy
Sep 68. (7") **SUZIE Q (Pt.1). / SUZIE Q (Pt.2)**	-	11
Nov 68. (7") **I PUT A SPELL ON YOU. / WALK ON THE WATER**	-	
Apr 69. (lp) **CREEDENCE CLEARWATER REVIVAL**		52 Jul 68

– I put a spell on you / Suzie Q / The working man / Ninety-nine and a half (won't do) / Get down woman / Porterville / Gloomy / Walk on the water. *(re-iss.Mar73 & Jul84 & Aug87 +cd.on 'Fantasy')*

	UK	US
May 69. (7") **PROUD MARY. / BORN ON THE BAYOU**	8	2 Jan 69
Jun 69. (lp) **BAYOU COUNTRY**		7 Feb 69

– Born on the bayou / Bootleg / Graveyard train / Good golly Miss Molly / Penthouse pauper / Keep on chooglin' / Proud Mary. *(hit UK 62 May70) (re-*

iss.Mar73 & Aug87 on 'Fantasy' +cd)

Aug 69. (7") **BAD MOON RISING. / LODI** 1 | 2 / 52 May 69

Nov 69. (7") **GREEN RIVER. / COMMOTION** 19 | 2 Jul 69 / 30

Dec 69. (lp)(c) **GREEN RIVER** 20 | 1 Sep 69
– Green river / Commotion / Tombstone shadow / Wrote a song for everyone / Bad moon rising / Lodi / Cross-tie walker / Sinister purpose / Lodi / Wrote a song for everyone / Night time is the right time. *(re-iss.Mar73, Jul84, & cd Aug87 on 'Fantasy')*

Feb 70. (7") **DOWN ON THE CORNER. / FORTUNATE SON** 31 | 3 Oct 69 / 14

Mar 70. (lp)(c) **WILLY AND THE POOR BOYS** 10 | 3 Dec 69
– Down on the corner / It came out of the sky / Cotton fields / Poor boy shuffle / Feelin' blue / Fortunate son / Don't look now (it ain't you or me) / The midnight special / Side of the road / Effigy. *(re-iss.Mar73 & Jul84 & Aug87 +cd on 'Fantasy')*

Mar 70. (7") **TRAVELLIN' MAN. / WHO'LL STOP THE RAIN** 8 | 2 Jan 70

Jun 70. (7") **UP AROUND THE BEND. / RUN THROUGH THE JUNGLE** 3 | 4 Apr 70

Aug 70. (7") **LONG AS I CAN SEE THE LIGHT. / LOOKIN' OUT MY BACK DOOR** 20 | 2 B-side

Sep 70. (lp)(c) **COSMO'S FACTORY** 1 | 1 Jul 70
– Ramble tamble / Before you accuse me / Travelin' band / Ooby dooby / Lookin' out my back door / Run through the jungle / Up around the bend / My baby left me / Who'll stop the rain / I heard it through the grapevine / Long as I can see the light. *(re-iss.Mar73, Jul84, & cd.Aug87 on 'Fantasy')*

Jan 71. (lp)(c) **PENDULUM** 23 | 5 Dec 70
– Pagan baby / Sailor's lament / Chameleon / Have you ever seen the rain / (Wish I could) Hideaway / Born to move / Hey tonight / It's just a thought / Molina / Rude awakening No.2. *(re-iss.Mar73 & Nov89 +cd. on 'Fantasy')*

Mar 71. (7") **HAVE YOU EVER SEEN THE RAIN / HEY TONIGHT** 36 | 8 Jan 71

— now a trio when TOM FOGERTY departed to go solo (Feb 71).

United Art | Fantasy

Jul 71. (7") **SWEET HITCH-HIKER. / DOOR TO DOOR** 36 | 6

Jul 71. (lp)(c) **MARDI GRAS** | 12 Apr 71
– Lookin' for a reason / Take it like a friend / Need someone to hold / Tearin' up the country / Hello Mary Lou / Someday never comes / What are you gonna do / Hello Mary Lou / Door to door / Sweet hitch-hiker. *(re-iss.Mar73) (re-iss.Jul84 & cd-iss.Nov89 on 'Fantasy')*

Apr 72. (7") **SOMEDAY NEVER COMES. / TEARIN' UP THE COUNTRY** - | 25

— Split Oct72.

– compilations etc. –

Mar 72. Fantasy; (d-lp)(d-c) **COSMO'S FACTORY / WILLY AND THE POOR BOYS**

Dec 72. Fantasy; (7") **BORN ON THE BAYOU. / I PUT A SPELL ON YOU**

Jan 73. Fantasy; (lp)(c) **CREEDENCE GOLD** | 15 Nov 72
(cd-iss.Sep91)
– Proud Mary / Down on the corner / Bad Moon rising / I heard it through the grapevine / Midnight special / Have you ever seen the rain / Born on the bayou / Suzie Q.

Mar 73. Fantasy; (7") **IT CAME OUT OF THE SKY. / SIDE O' THE ROAD**

Sep 73. Fantasy; (lp)(c) **MORE CREEDENCE GOLD** | 61 Jul 73
(cd-iss.Sep91)
– Hey tonight / Run through the jungle / Fortunate son / Bootleg / Lookin' out my back door / Molina / Who'll stop the rain / Sweet hitch-hiker / Good golly Miss Molly / I put a spell on you / Don't look now / Lodi / Porterville / Up around the bend.

May 74. Fantasy; (lp)(c) **LIVE IN EUROPE (live)** | Nov 73
– Born on the bayou / Green river / It came out of the sky / Door to door / Travellin' band / Fortunate son / Porterville / Up around the bend / Suzie Q / Commotion / Lodi. *(re-iss.+cd.Feb90)*

Mar 76. Fantasy; (d-lp)(c) **CREEDENCE CHRONICLE**
– Suzie Q / I put a spell on you / Proud Mary / Bad Moon rising / Lodi / Green river / Commotion / Down on the corner / Fortunate son / Travellin' band / Who'll stop the rain / Up around the bend / Run through the jungle / Lookin' out my back door / Long as I can see the light / Have you ever seen the rain? / Hey tonight / Sweet hitch-hiker / Someday never comes.
(cd-iss.Jun87 on 'Big Beat' += I heard it through the grapevine)

Mar 76. Fantasy; (7") **I HEARD IT THROUGH THE GRAPEVINE. / GOOD GOLLY MISS MOLLY** | 43 Dec 75

Jul 77. Fantasy; (7") **BAD MOON RISING. / PROUD MARY / GREEN RIVER**

Nov 78. Fantasy; (7") **WHO'LL STOP THE RAIN. / PROUD MARY / HEY TONIGHT**

Jun 79. Fantasy; (lp)(c) **GREATEST HITS (20 GOLDEN)** 35 |

Jul 79. Fantasy; (7") **I HEARD IT THROUGH THE GRAPE-VINE. / (ROCKIN' ALL OVER THE WORLD ("JOHN FOGERTY")** | 43

(12") ('A'side) / Keep on chooglin' (extended).

Feb 81. M.F.P./ US= Fantasy; (lp)(c) **LIVE AT THE ROYAL ALBERT HALL (live)** | 62 Dec 80
(re-iss.+cd.Aug89 as 'THE CONCERT')

Feb 82. M.F.P./ US= Fantasy; (lp)(c) **THE HITS ALBUM**

Aug 81. Golden Grooves; (7") **PROUD MARY. / UP AROUND THE BEND**

Oct 81. Golden Grooves; (7") **BAD MOON RISING. / GOOD GOLLY MISS MOLLY**

Sep 85. Old Gold; (7") **BAD MOON RISING. / GOOD GOLLY MISS MOLLY** | -

Sep 85. Old Gold; (7") **PROUD MARY. / TRAVELLIN' BAND** | -

Oct 85. Impression; (d-lp)(c) **THE CREEDENCE COLLECTION** 68 |

Jun 88. Ace-Fantasy; (7") **BAD MOON RISING. / HAVE YOU EVER SEEN THE RAIN?**
(12"+=) – Keep on chooglin'.

Jun 88. Ace-Fantasy; (lp)(c) **THE BEST OF – VOLUME 1**

1988. Ace-Fantasy; (cd) **CHOOGLIN'** - |
(re-iss.Nov92)

Aug 88. Ace-Fantasy; (lp)(c) **THE BEST OF – VOLUME 2**

Dec 92. Ace-Fantasy; (cd) **CREEDENCE COUNTRY**

May 88. Arcade; (cd) **THE COMPLETE HITS ALBUM VOL.1** | -

May 88. Arcade; (cd) **THE COMPLETE HITS ALBUM Vol.2** | -

Apr 92. Epic; (7") **BAD MOON RISING. / AS LONG AS I CAN SEE THE LIGHT** 71 |
(cd-s+=) -

Aug 95. Old Gold; (cd-s) **TRAVELIN' BAND. / WHO'LL STOP THE RAIN** | -

Sep 95. Old Gold; (cd-s) **UP AROUND THE BEND / RUN THROUGH THE JUNGLE** | -

BLUE RIDGE RANGERS

was JOHN FOGERTY's first total solo venture

Fantasy | Fantasy

Dec 72. (7") **JAMBALAYA (ON THE BAYOU). / WORKING ON A BUILDING** | 16

Apr 73. (lp)(c) **BLUE RIDGE RANGERS** | 47
– Blue ridge mountain blues / Somewhere listening (for my name) / You're the reason / Jambalaya (on the bayou) / She thinks I still care / California blues (blue yodel #4) / Workin' on a building / Please help me I'm falling / Have thine own way, Lord / I ain't never / Hearts of stone / Today I started loving you. *(re-iss.Sep87, + cd-iss. 1991)*

May 73. (7") **HEARTS OF STONE. / SOMEWHERE LISTENING (FOR MY NAME)** | 37 Mar 73

Oct 73. (7") **YOU DON'T OWE ME. / BACK IN THE HILLS** - |

JOHN FOGERTY

solo, plays, sings everything

not issued | Fantasy

Mar 74. (7") **COMING DOWN THE ROAD. / RICOCHET** - |

Asylum | Asylum

Sep 75. (7") **ROCKIN' ALL OVER THE WORLD. / THE WALL** | 27

Oct 75. (lp)(c) **JOHN FOGERTY** | 78
– Rockin' all over the world / You rascal you / The wall / Travelin' high / Lonely teardrops / Almost Saturday night / Where the river flows / Sea cruise / Dream – Song / Flyin' away. *(re-iss.+cd.Sep87 on 'Ace-Fantasy')*

Dec 75. (7") **ALMOST SATURDAY NIGHT. / SEA CRUISE** - | 78

May 76. (7") **YOU GOT THE MAGIC. / EVIL THING** | 87

JOHN FOGERTY

returned after 9 years complete with new session people.

Warners | Warners

Jan 85. (7") **THE OLD MAN DOWN THE ROAD. / BIG TRAIN (TO MEMPHIS)** | 10 Dec 84

Feb 85. (lp)(c) **CENTERFIELD** 48 | 1 Jan 85
– The old man down the road / Rock and roll girls / Big train (from Memphis) / I saw it on T.V. / Mr. Greed / Searchlight / Centerfield / I can't help myself / Zant Kant danz. *(cd-iss.Nov93)*

Jun 85. (7") **ROCK AND ROLL GIRLS. / CENTERFIELD** | 20 Mar 85 / 44

Aug 86. (7") **CHANGE IN THE WEATHER. / MY TOOT TOOT** - |

Oct 86. (lp)(c)(cd) **EYE OF THE ZOMBIE** 44 | 26
– Goin' back home / Eye of the zombie / Headlines / Knockin' on your door / Change in the weather / Violence is golden / Wasn't that a woman / Soda pop / Sail away.

Oct 86. (7") **EYE OF THE ZOMBIE. / CONFESS** | 81
(12"+=) – I can't help myself.

Peter CRISS (see under ⇒ KISS)

CROSBY, STILLS, NASH (& YOUNG)

Formed: Los Angeles, California, USA . . . Summer 1968 as a superband trio (DAVID) CROSBY, (STEPHEN) STILLS and (GRAHAM) NASH. Their eponymous first offering, came out in Summer '69 and soon broke into US Top 10. After lifting 2 US Top 30 hits, later in the year, they were joined by another semi-star at the time, NEIL YOUNG, who had already played an electric set on their mid-69 gigs. The 4 supported The ROLLING STONES on their ill-fated Altamont concert (when a fan was murdered) on 6 Dec'69. In 1970, after lifting the coveted Best Newcomers award at the Grammys, they released their magnum-opus 'DEJA VU', which hit US No.1 and UK Top 5. Internal disruption and friction between the 4, led to them parting for solo ventures late 1970 (see below discography for all details). • **Style:** Critically acclaimed supergroup, experimental in both vocal harmony, and laid back folk and country rock. A band that inspired many others, including POCO, EAGLES, etc, etc. • **Songwriters:** All 4 took a hand individually and later together in all songs. Also covered; WOODSTOCK (Joni Mitchell) / DEAR MR.FANTASY (Traffic) / and a few more. • **Miscellaneous:** CROSBY's late 60's drug problem was to rear its ugly head again in 1982, when he was arrested twice for possessing cocaine and a gun. The following year, he was convicted and sentenced to 5 years, but after an appeal was sent to a drug rehabilitation center to recover. In Mar'85, he reneged on agreement and was sent to jail. He was released a couple of years later and soon married long-time girlfriend Jan Dance. Early in 1989, he was back again with a solo album 'OH YES WE CAN', which followed a re-union CROSBY, STILLS, NASH & YOUNG comeback album 'AMERICAN DREAM'.

Recommended: DEJA VU (*8) / THE BEST OF CROSBY & STILLS, (*5) / STILL STILLS – THE BEST OF STEPHEN STILLS (*6) / (best solo:-) GRAHAM NASH – SONGS FOR BEGINNERS (*7)

For NEIL YOUNG, albums and reviews, see own discography ⇒.

CROSBY, STILLS & NASH

DAVID CROSBY (b.DAVID VAN CORTLAND, 14 Aug'41, Los Angeles, California) – vocals, guitar (ex-BYRDS) / **STEPHEN STILLS** (b. 3 Jan'45, Dallas, Texas)– vocals, guitar, bass, keyboards (ex-BUFFALO SPRINGFIELD) / **GRAHAM NASH** (b. 2 Feb'42, Blackpool, England)– vocals, guitar (ex-HOLLIES) with **DALLAS TAYLOR** – drums

Atlantic Atlantic

Jun 69. (lp) **CROSBY, STILLS & NASH** [25] [6]
– Suite: Judy blue eyes / Marrakesh express / Guinnevere / You don't have to cry / Pre-road downs / Wooden ships / Lady of the island / Helplessly hoping / Long time gone / 49 bye-byes. *(re-iss.'72) (re-iss.+cd.Jul87)*

Jul 69. (7") **MARRAKESH EXPRESS. / HELPLESSLY HOPING** [17] [28]

Oct 69. (7") **SUITE: JUDY BLUE EYES. / LONG TIME GONE** [ ] [21]

CROSBY, STILLS, NASH & YOUNG

—— added **NEIL YOUNG** – guitar, vocals (ex-solo, ex-BUFFALO SPRINGFIELD) also **GREG REEVES** – bass

Mar 70. (lp)(c) **DEJA VU** [5] [1]
– Carry on / Teach your children / Almost cut my hair / Helpless / Woodstock / Deja vu / Our house / 4 + 20 / Country girl: Whiskey boot hill – Down, down, down – Country girl / Everybody I love you. *(re-iss.'72) (re-iss.+cd.May87)*

Apr 70. (7") **TEACH YOUR CHILDREN. / COUNTRY GIRL** [ ] [16] Jun 70

May 70. (7") **WOODSTOCK. / HELPLESS** [ ] [11] Mar 70

Jun 70. (7") **TEACH YOUR CHILDREN. / CARRY ON** [-] [ ]

Aug 70. (7") **OHIO. / FIND THE COST OF FREEDOM** [ ] [14]

Nov 70. (7") **OUR HOUSE. / DEJA VU** [ ] [30] Sep 70

—— (May70) **CALVIN 'FUZZY' SAMUELS** – bass repl. REEVES **JOHN BARBATA** – drums (ex-TURTLES) repl. TAYLOR

—— (Aug70) split before release of posthumous album below with last line-up

Apr 71. (d-lp)(d-c) **FOUR-WAY STREET (live)** [5] [1]
– On the way home / Teach your children / Triad / The Lee shore / Chicago / Right between the eyes / Cowgirl in the sand / Don't let it bring you down / 49 bye-byes / Love the one you're with / Pre-road downs / Long time gone / Southern man / Ohio / Carry on / Find the cost of freedom. *(re-iss.'72) (re-iss.+cd.Jul87) (d-cd-iss.Aug92)*

—— Their solo recordings, excluding NEIL YOUNG's, are below

STEPHEN STILLS

– solo, – vocals, guitar with **STEPHEN FROMHOLTZ** – guitar / **PAUL HARRIS** – keyboards / **DALLAS TAYLOR** – drums / **CALVIN SAMUELS** – bass / **plus Memphis Horns**

Atlantic Atlantic

Nov 70. (lp)(c) **STEPHEN STILLS** [30] [3]
– Love the one you're with / Do for the others / Church (part of someone) / Old times, good times / Go back home / Sit yourself down / To a flame / Black queen / Cheroke / We are not helpless. *(re-iss.'73) (cd-iss.Oct95)*

Dec 70. (7") **LOVE THE ONE YOU'RE WITH. / TO A FLAME** [37] [14]

May 71. (7") **SIT YOURSELF DOWN. / WE ARE NOT HELPLESS** [ ] [37] Mar 71

Jul 71. (lp)(c) **STEPHEN STILLS II** [22] [8]
– Change partners / Nothin' to do but today / Fishes and scorpions / Sugar babe / Know you got to run / Open secret / Relaxing town / Singin' call / Ecology song / Word game / Marianne / Bluebird revisited. *(re-iss.'78)*

Jul 71. (7") **CHANGE PARTNERS. / RELAXING TOWN** [ ] [43] Jun 71

Sep 71. (7") **MARIANNE. / NOTHIN' TO DO BUT TODAY** [ ] [42] Aug 71

STEPHEN STILLS & MANASSAS

STILLS retained **SAMUELS, HARRIS** and **TAYLOR,** brought in **CHRIS HILLMAN** – guitar, vocals / **AL PERKINS** – steel guitar, guitar / **JOE LALA** – percussion / **KENNY PASSARELLI** – bass (ex-JOE WALSH)repl. SAMUELS.

Atlantic Atlantic

May 72. (d-lp)(d-c) **MANASSAS** [30] [4] Apr 72
– Fallen eagle / Jesus gave love away for free / Colorado / So begins the task / Hide to the deep / Don't look at my shadow / It doesn't matter / Johnny's garden / Bound to fall / How far / Move around / The love gangster / Song of love / Rock'n'roll crazies – Cuban bluegrass / Jet set (sigh) / Anyway / Both of us (bound to lose) / What to do / Right now / The treasure (take one) / Blues man. *(cd-iss.Feb93 & Oct95)*

May 72. (7") **IT DOESN'T MATTER. / ROCK'N'ROLL CRAZIES – CUBAN BLUEGRASS** [-] [61]

Aug 72. (7") **IT DOESN'T MATTER. / FALLEN ANGEL** [ ] [ ]

Nov 72. (7") **ROCK'N'ROLL CRAZIES. / COLORADO** [-] [92]

May 73. (lp)(c) **DOWN THE ROAD** [33] [26]
– Isn't it about time / Lies / Pensamiento / So many times / Business on the street / Do you remember the Americans / Down the road / City junkies / Guaguanco de Vero / Rollin' my stone. *(cd-iss.Nov93)*

May 73. (7") **ISN'T IT ABOUT TIME. / SO MANY TIMES** [ ] [56] Apr 73

Jul 73. (7") **GUAGUANCO DE VERO. / DOWN THE ROAD** [ ] [ ]

—— (Sep73) **HARRIS, PERKINS and HILLMAN joined SOUTHERN HILLMAN FURAY BAND. STEPHEN STILLS** formed his own band, retaining **PASSARELLI** and **LALA** plus **DONNIE DACUS** – guitar / **JERRY AIELLO** – keyboards / **HUSS KUNKEL** – drums

CROSBY, STILLS NASH & YOUNG

(May74) re-formed, mainly for concerts. Augmented by **TIM DRUMMOND** – bass / **RUSS KUNKEL** – drums / **JOE LALA percussion**

STEPHEN STILLS

went solo again (Feb75) with new band **LALA, DACUS, AIELLO** plus **GEORGE PERRY** – bass / **RONNIE ZIEGLER** – drums

C.B.S. Columbia

Jun 75. (lp)(c) **STILLS** [31] [19]
– Turn back the pages / My favorite changes / My angel / In the way / Love story / To mama Christopher and the old man / First things first / New mama / As I come of age / Shuffle just as bad / Cold cold world / Myth of Sisyphus.

Jul 75. (7") **TURN BACK THE PAGES. / SHUFFLE JUST AS BAD** [ ] [84]

—— added **RICK ROBERTS** – guitar, vocals (of FIREFALL)

Apr 76. (7") **BUYIN' TIME. / SOLDIER** [-] [ ]

May 76. (lp)(c) **ILLEGAL STILLS** [54] [30]
– Buyin' time / Midnight in Paris / Different tongues / Closer to you / Soldier / The loner / Stateline blues / No me nieges / Ring of love / Circlin'.

Jul 76. (7") **THE LONER. / STATELINE BLUES** [ ] [ ]

STILLS-YOUNG BAND

STEPHEN STILLS – vocals, guitar / **NEIL YOUNG** – vocals, guitar with **AIELLO, PERRY, VITALE** and **LALA.**

Reprise Reprise

Sep 76. (7") **LONG MAY YOU RUN. / 12:8 BLUES** [ ] [ ]

Oct 76. (lp)(c) **LONG MAY YOU RUN** [12] [26]
– Long may you run / Make love to you / Midnight on the bay / Black coral / Ocean girl / Let it shine / 12/8 blues (all the same) / Fontainebleau / Guardian angel.*(cd-iss.Jul93)*

Dec 76. (7") **MIDNIGHT ON THE BAY. / BLACK CORAL** [-] [ ]

—— CROSBY, STILLS & NASH re-formed in '77 (see further on for more solo

STILLS)

DAVID CROSBY

with loads of session people, too numerous to mention.

Atlantic Atlantic

Feb 71. (lp)(c) **IF I COULD ONLY REMEMBER MY NAME** [12] [12]
– Music is love / Cowboy movie / Tamalpais High (at about 3) / Laughing / What are their names / Traction in the rain / Song with no name (tree with no leaves) / Orleans / I'd swear there was somebody here. *(cd-iss.Nov93)*

Apr 71. (7") **MUSIC IS LOVE. / LAUGHING** [-] [95]

Jul 71. (7") **ORLEANS. / TRACTION IN THE RAIN** [-] [ ]

CROSBY & NASH

duo (DAVID & GRAHAM with more sessioners and left over GRATEFUL DEAD members which were included on DAVID's debut solo album.

May 72. (lp)(c) **GRAHAM NASH & DAVID CROSBY** [13] [4] Apr 72
– Southbound train / Whole cloth / Black notes / Strangers room / Where will I be / Page 43 / Frozen smiles / Games / Girl to be on my mind / The wall song / Immigration man.

May 72. (7") **IMMIGRATION MAN. / WHOLE CLOTH** [-] [36]

Jul 72. (7") **SOUTHBOUND TRAIN. / WHOLE CLOTH** [ ] [ ]

Jul 72. (7") **SOUTHBOUND TRAIN. / THE WALL SONG** [-] [99]

— after CROSBY, STILLS, NASH & YOUNG reunion May74-Feb75

— resurrected partnership, with steady band members **CRAIG DOERGE** – keyboards / **LEE SKLAR & TIM DRUMMOND** – bass / **DANNY KOOTCH & RUSS KUNKEL** – drums / **DAVID LINDLEY** – guitar, violin.

Polydor A.B.C.

Jan 76. (lp)(c) **WIND ON THE WATER** [ ] [6] Oct 75
– Carry me / Mama lion / Bittersweet / Take the money and run / Naked in the rain / Love work out / Low down payment / Cowboy of dreams / Homeward through the haze / Fieldworker / To the last whale. *(cd-iss.Nov91 on 'Thunderbolt')*

Nov 75. (7") **CARRY ME. / MAMA LION** [ ] [52]

Mar 76. (7") **TAKE THE MONEY AND RUN. / BITTERSWEET** [-] [ ]

May 76. (7") **LOVE WORK OUT. / BITTERSWEET** [ ] [ ]

Jul 76. (lp)(c) **WHISTLING DOWN THE WIRE** [ ] [26]
– Spotlight / Broken bird / Time after time / Dancer / Mutiny / J.B.'s blues / Marguerita / Taken at all / Foolish man / Out of the darkness.

Aug 76. (7") **OUT OF THE DARKNESS. / LOVE WORK OUT** [ ] [-]

Aug 76. (7") **OUT OF THE DARKNESS. / BROKEN BIRD** [-] [89]

Oct 76. (7") **SPOTLIGHT. / FOOLISH MAN** [-] [ ]

— CROSBY STILLS & NASH reformed '77 (see further on)

GRAHAM NASH

solo using C,S & N past members plus GRATEFUL DEAD main men

Atlantic Atlantic

Jun 71. (lp)(c) **SONGS FOR BEGINNERS** [13] [15]
– Military madness / Better days / Wounded bird / I used to be a king / Be yourself / Simple man / Man in the mirror / There's only one / Sleep song / Chicago / We can change the world. *(cd-iss.Feb93)*

Jun 71. (7") **CHICAGO. / SIMPLE MAN** [ ] [35] May 71

Sep 71. (7") **MILITARY MADNESS. / I USED TO BE A KING** [ ] [-]

Sep 71. (7") **MILITARY MADNESS. / SLEEP SONG** [-] [73]

Nov 71. (7") **I USED TO BE A KING. / WOUNDED BIRD** [-] [ ]

Nov 73. (7") **PRISON SONG. / HEY YOU (LOOKING AT HTE MOON)** [-] [ ]

Mar 74. (lp)(c) **WILD TALES** [ ] [34] Dec 73
– Wild tales / Hey you (looking at the Moon) / Prison song / You'll never be the same / And so it goes / Oh! Camil (the winter soldier) / I miss you / On the line / Another sleep song.

Mar 74. (7") **ON THE LINE. / I MISS YOU** [ ] [ ]

Aug 74. (7") **GRAVE CONCERN. / ANOTHER SLEEP SONG** [ ] [ ]

— GRAHAM rejoined below and had more solo releases later.

CROSBY, STILLS & NASH

reformed in '77, with various session men.

Atlantic Atlantic

Jun 77. (lp)(c) **CSN** [23] [2]
– Shadow captain / See the changes / Carried away / Fair game / Anything at all / Cathedral / Dark star / Just a song before I go / Cold rain / In my dreams / I give you give blind. *(cd-iss.Oct94)*

Jun 77. (7") **JUST A SONG BEFORE I GO. / DARK STAR** [ ] [7] May 77

Oct 77. (7") **FAIR GAME. / ANYTHING AT ALL** [ ] [43] Sep 77

Dec 77. (7") **CARRIED AWAY. / I GIVE YOU GIVE BLIND** [-] [ ]

STEPHEN STILLS

more solo releses with session people & his tour band **DALLAS TAYLOR** – drums / **GEORGE PERRY** – bass / **MIKE FINNEGAN** – keyboards / **JERRY TOLMAN & BONNIE BRAMLETT** – b.vocals

C.B.S. Columbia

Sep 78. (7") **CAN'T GET NO BOOTY. / LOWDOWN** [ ] [ ]

Oct 78. (lp)(c) **THOROUGHFARE GAP** [ ] [83]
– You can't dance alone / Thoroughfare gap / We will go / Beaucoup yumbo / What's the game / Midnight rider / Woman Lleva / Lowdown / Not fade away / Can't get no booty.

Nov 78. (7") **THOROUGHFARE GAP. / LOWDOWN** [-] [ ]

GRAHAM NASH

solo, with usual and past session people + CROSBY, STILLS & YOUNG

Capitol Capitol

Jan 80. (7") **IN THE 80'S. / T.V. GUIDE** [-] [ ]

Mar 80. (7") **OUT ON THE ISLAND. / HELICOPTER SONG** [-] [ ]

Mar 80. (lp)(c) **EARTH & SKY** [ ] [ ]
– Earth & sky / Love has come / Out on the island / Skychild / Helicopter song / Barrel of pain / T.V. guide / It's alright / Magical child / In the 80's.

May 80. (7") **EARTH & SKY. / MAGICAL CHILD** [-] [ ]

CROSBY, STILLS & NASH

reformed mid '82, with session men.

Atlantic Atlantic

Jun 82. (7") **WASTED ON THE WAY. / DELTA** [ ] [9]

Jul 82. (lp)(c) **DAYLIGHT AGAIN** [ ] [8]
– Turn your back on love / Wasted on the way / Southern cross / Into the darkness / Delta / Since I met you / Too much love to hide / Song for Susan / You are alive / Might as well have a good time / Daylight again. *(cd-iss.Oct94)*

Nov 82. (7") **SOUTHERN CROSS. / INTO THE DARKNESS** [ ] [18] Sep 82

Jan 83. (7") **TOO MUCH LOVE TO HIDE. / SONG FOR SUSAN** [-] [69]

Jun 83. (lp)(c) **ALLIES (live)** [ ] [43]
– War games / Raise a voice / Turn your back on love / Barrel of pain / Shadow captain / Dark star / Blackbird / He played real good for free / Wasted on my way / For what it's worth. *(cd-iss.1984)*

Jul 83. (7") **WAR GAMES (live). / SHADOW CAPTAIN (live)** [ ] [45] Jun 83
(12") – ('A'side) / Dark Star (live) / Keep your . . .

Sep 83. (7") **RAISE A VOICE (live). / FOR WHAT IT'S WORTH (live)** [-] [ ]

— Split Aug82, when CROSBY is sentenced to 5 years for drugs. He gets leniency when he agrees to rehabilitate himself in drug hospital Dec84.

STEPHEN STILLS

solo again (2nd single featured WALTER FINNEGAN)

W.E.A. Atlantic

Sep 84. (lp)(c) **RIGHT BY YOU** [ ] [75]
– 50/50 / Stranger / Flaming heart / Love again / No problem / Can't let go / Grey to green / Only love can break your heart / No hiding place / Right by you. *(cd-iss.Nov93)*

Aug 84. (7") **STRANGER. / NO HIDING PLACE** [-] [61]

Oct 84. (7") **CAN'T LET GO. / GREY TO GREEN** [-] [67]

(above as STEPHEN STILLS featuring MICHAEL FINNIGAN)

Dec 84. (7") **ONLY LOVE CAN BREAK YOUR HEART. / LOVE AGAIN** [-] [ ]

not issued Goldhill

1990. (cd) **STILLS ALONE** [-] [ ]
– Isn't it so / Everybody's talkin' / Just isn't like you / In my life / Ballad of Hollis Brown / Singin call / The right girl / Blind fiddler medley / Amazonia / Treetop flyer.

GRAHAM NASH

solo, he had rejoined The HOLLIES between Sep81-Apr83.

Atlantic Atlantic

Apr 86. (7") **INNOCENT EYES. / I GOT A ROCK** [ ] [84]

Apr 86. (lp)(c) **INNOCENT EYES** [ ] [ ]
– See you in Prague / Keep away from me / Innocent eyes / Chippin' away / Over the wall / Don't listen to the rumours / Sad eyes / Newday / Glass and steel / I got a rock.

Jul 86. (7") **SAY EYES. / NEWDAY** [-] [ ]

Oct 86. (7") **CHIPPIN' AWAY. / NEWDAY** [-] [ ]

CROSBY, STILLS, NASH & YOUNG

reformed yet again

Atlantic Atlantic

Nov 88. (7") **GOT IT MADE. / THIS OLD HOUSE** [-] [69]

Nov 88. (lp)(c)(cd) **AMERICAN DREAM** [ ] [16]

– American dream / Got it made / Name of love / Don't say goodbye / This old house / Nighttime for the generals / Shadowland / Drivin' thunder / Clear blue skies / That girl / Compass / Soldiers of peace / Feel your love / Night song.

Jan 89. (7") **AMERICAN DREAM. / COMPASS** [55] [ ]
(12"+=) – Soldiers of peace.

DAVID CROSBY

solo again

A & M A & M

Feb 89. (lp)(c)(cd) **OH YES I CAN** [ ] [ ]
– Drive my car / Melody / Monkey and the underdog / In the wide ruin / Tracks in the dust / Drop down mama / Lady of the harbour / Distances / Flying man / Oh yes I can / My country 'tis of thee.

Feb 89. (7") **DRIVE MY CAR. / TRACKS IN THE DUST** [ ] [ ]
(12"+=) – Flying men.

Apr 89. (7")(12") **LADY OF THE HARBOR. / DROP DOWN MAMA** [ ] [ ]

— with band **LELAND SKLAR** – bass / **RUSSELL KUNKEL + JEFF PORCARO** – drums / **CRAIG DOERGE** – keyboards / **ANDY FAIRWEATHER-LOWE** – guitar / **DEAN PARKS** – guitar, flute / **BERNIE LEADON** – acoustic guitar / **C.J. VANSTON** – keyboards / with many guests **JACKSON BROWNE + DON WAS** plus outside writers + on session **PHIL COLLINS, JONI MITCHELL, MARC COHN, JIMMY WEBB, PAUL BRADY, STEPHEN BISHOP, JOHN HIATT, BONNIE HAYES + NOEL BRAZIL.**

Atlantic Atlantic

May 93. (7")(c-s) **HERO. ("DAVID CROSBY featuring PHIL COLLINS") / COVERAGE** [ ] [44]
(cd-s+=) – Fare thee well.

Jun 93. (cd)(c) **THOUSAND ROADS** [ ] [ ]
– Hero / Too young to die / Old soldier / Through your hands / Yvette in English / Thousand roads / Columbus / Helpless heart / Coverage / Natalie.

Mar 95. (cd)(c) **IT'S ALL COMING BACK TO ME NOW (live '93)** [ ] [ ]
– In my dreams / Rusty and blue / Hero / Till it shines on you / 1000 roads / Cowboy movie / Almosy cut my hair / Deja vu / Long time gone / Wooden ships.

CROSBY, STILLS & NASH

with **JOE VITALE** – drums, organ, synth bass / **LELAND SKLAR** – bass / **CRAIG DOERGE** – keyboards / **MIKE LANDAU** – guitar / **MIKE FISHER** – percussion.

East West Atlantic

Jun 90. (cd)(c)(lp) **LIVE IT UP** [ ] [57]
– Live it up / If anybody had a heart / Tomboy / Haven't we lost enough / Yours and mine / (Got to keep) Open / Straight line / House of broken dreams / Arrows / After the dolphin.

Aug 94. (cd)(c) **AFTER THE STORM** [ ] [98]
– Only waiting for you / Find a dream / Camera / Unequal love / Till it shines / It won't go away / These empty days / In my life / Street to lean on / Bad boyz / After the storm / Panama.

– their compilations etc. –

Aug 74. Atlantic; (d-lp)(c) **SO FAR – THE BEST OF . . .** [25] [1]
– Woodstock / Marrakesh express / You don't have to cry / Teach your children / Love the one you're with / Almost cut my hair / Wooden ships / Dark star / Helpless / Chicago – We can change the world / Cathedral / 4 + 20 / Our house / Change partners / Just a song before I go / Ohio / Wasted on the way / Southern cross / Suite: Judy blue eyes / Carry on – Questions / Horses through a rainstorm / Johnny's garden / Guinnevere / Helplessly hoping / The Lee Shore / Taken it all / Shadow captain / As I come of age / Drive my car / Dear Mr.Fantasy / In my dreams / Yours and mine / Haven't we lost enough? / After the dolphin / Find the cost of freedom. *(cd-iss.Oct94)*
(re-iss.+cd.Jan87)

Nov 80. Atlantic; (lp)(c) **REPLAY** [ ] [ ]
(cd-iss.Oct94)

Dec 91. East West; (4xcd)(4xc) **CROSBY, STILLS & NASH** [ ] [ ]

Feb 92. East West; (7")(c-s) **OUR HOUSE. / MARRAKESH EXPRESS** [ ] [ ]
(12"+=)(cd-s+=) – Carry on / Dear Mr.Fantasy (STEPHEN STILLS / GRAHAM NASH

(above was re-actified on a famous building society TV ad).

Feb 92. East West; (d-cd)(d-c) **THE BEST OF CROSBY, STILLS & NASH** [ ] [-]

Oct 75. Atlantic; (d-lp) **TWO ORIGINALS OF STEPHEN STILLS (1st 2 lp's)** [ ] [ ]

Dec 75. Atlantic; (lp)(c) **STEPHEN STILLS – LIVE (live)** [ ] [ ]

Jan 77. Atlantic; (lp)(c) **STEPHEN STILLS – THE BEST OF STEPHEN STILLS** [ ] [ ]
– Love the one you're with / It doesn't matter / We are not helpless / Marianne / Bound to fall / Isn't it about time / Change partners / Go back home / Johnny's garden / Rock and roll crazies – Cuban bluegrass / Sit yourself down.

STEPHEN STILLS was credited on Aug68 lp 'SUPER SESSION' alongside AL KOOPER & MIKE BLOOMFIELD.

Nov 77. Polydor/ US= A.B.C.; (lp)(c) **LIVE (live)) ("CROSBY & NASH")** [ ] [52]

Jan 79. Polydor/ US= A.B.C.; (lp)(c) **THE BEST OF CROSBY & NASH** [ ] [ ] Oct 78
(re-iss.Nov80)

CROSS (see under ⇒ QUEEN)

Sheryl CROW

Born: Feb'62, Kennett, Missouri, USA. She left university where she studied classical music and moved to St.Louis. In the mid-80's, she set off to L.A and finally cut her teeth as SHIRLEY CROW on MICHAEL JACKSON's 1988 'Bad' tour. She then earned her crust singing back-up for ROD STEWART, DON HENLEY and JOE COCKER. Always wanting to be a solo singer, she handed a demo to producer HUGH PADGHAM, who with a recommendation from STING, got her signed to 'A&M' in '91. An album of unproductive songs was shelved, but with the help of a second producer BILL BOTTRILL, they emerged late in 1993 with debut 'TUESDAY NIGHT MUSIC CLUB'. Although it didn't sparkle immediately, it became a deserved smash a year later after a support slot to the re-formed EAGLES and a well-received appearance at WOODSTOCK II. Suddenly her album turned gold and a single 'ALL I WANNA DO' was nearly hitting peak spot. • **Style:** Storyteller songstress like EDIE BRICKELL or ROSIE VELA. • **Songwriters:** Writes lyrics mainly / songs by BILL BOTTRELL or BAERWALD-GILBERT-McLEOD, etc. except I'M GONNA BE A WHEEL SOMEDAY (Fats Domino) / D'YER MAKER (Led Zeppelin). • **Trivia:** The track 'HUNDREDS OF TEARS' featured on 'Pointbreak' soundtrack. Another 2 'STRONG ENOUGH' and 'NO ONE SAID IT WOULD BE EASY' appeared in the 1994 film 'Kalifornia'.

Recommended: TUESDAY NIGHT MUSIC CLUB (*6)

SHERYL CROW – vocals + sessioners incl. **BILL BOTTRILL**

A & M A & M

Sep 93. (7")(c-s) **RUN BABY RUN. / ALL BY MYSELF** [ ] [ ]
(cd-s+=) – The na-na song / Reach around jerk.

Oct 93. (cd)(c) **TUESDAY NIGHT MUSIC CLUB** [68] [3]
– Run baby run / Leaving Las Vegas / Strong enough / Can't cry anymore / Solidify / The na-na song / No one said it would be easy / What I can do for you / All I wanna do / We do what we can / I shall believe. *(re-dist.US Feb94) (re-dist.Sep94 hit UK No.22 & 8 early '95) (re-iss.cd May95 w/ free cd '6 TRACK LIVE MINI-ALBUM')*

Feb 94. (7")(c-s) **WHAT I CAN DO FOR YOU. / VOLVO COWGIRL 99** [ ] [ ]
(cd-s+=) – ('A'version) / I shall believe.

Apr 94. (7")(c-s) **RUN BABY RUN. / LEAVING LAS VEGAS (acoustic)** [ ] [ ]
(cd-s+=) – All by myself / Reach around jerk.

Jun 94. (7")(c-s) **LEAVING LAS VEGAS. / ('A'live)** [66] [60] Apr94
(cd-s) – ('A'side) / I shall believe (live) / What I can do for you.
(cd-s) – ('A'side) / No one said it would be easy (live) / The na-na song (live).

Oct 94. (7")(c-s) **ALL I WANNA DO. / SOLIDIFY** [5] [2]
(cd-s+=) – I'm gonna be a wheel someday.
(cd-s) – ('A'side) / Run baby run / Leaving Las Vegas.

Jan 95. (7")(c-s) **STRONG ENOUGH. / NO ONE SAID IT WOULD BE EASY** [33] [5]
(cd-s+=) – All I wanna do.
(cd-s) – ('A'side) / ('A'mix) / All by myself / Reach around jerk.

May 95. (c-ep)(cd-ep) **CAN'T CRY ANYMORE / ALL I WANNA DO / STRONG NOUGH (U.S.version) / WE DO WHAT WE CAN** [33] [36]
(cd-ep) – ('A'side) / What I can do for you (live) / No one said it would be easy (live) / I shall believe (live).

Jul 95. (c-s) **RUN, BABY, RUN / LEAVING LAS VEGAS** [24] [ ]
(cd-s) – ('A'side) / Can't cry anymore / Reach around jerk / I shall believe (the live Nashville sessions).
(cd-s) – ('A'side) / Strong enough / No one said it would be easy / The na na song (the live Nashville sessions).

Oct 95. (c-s) **WHAT I CAN DO FOR YOU / LEAVING LAS VEGAS (live)** [43] [ ]
(cd-s) – ('A'side) / D'yer maker / I'm gonna be a wheel someday / No one said it would be easy.
(cd-s) – ('A'live) / All I wanna do (live) / Strong enough (live) / Can't cry anymore (live).

CROWDED HOUSE

Formed: virtually as SPLIT ENDS in Oct'72 by TIM FINN and PHIL JUDD. Soon slightly altered their name to SPLIT ENZ, stylising their own brand of humour pop fused somewhere between SPARKS and ROXY MUSIC. In fact PHIL MANZANERA of ROXY produced and remixed their 'SECOND THOUGHTS' album in 1976. They were soon joined by brother NEIL FINN, which became nucleus of CROWDED HOUSE, although TIM didn't join until later. CROWDED HOUSE were based in Melbourne, Australia . . . 1985 (NEIL FINN, PAUL HESTER and NICK SEYMOUR). They moved to Los Angeles, California 1986 and signed to 'Capitol', working with MITCHELL FROOM for eponymous US hit debut the following year. • **Style:** From once zany men from SPLIT ENZ, to mainstream romantic pop / rock. In 1991 CROSBY, STILLS & NASH were cited as influence. • **Songwriters:** NEIL FINN penned except MR. TAMBOURINE MAN (Bob Dylan) + EIGHT MILES HIGH + SO YOU WANT TO BE A ROCK'N'ROLL STAR (Byrds). SPLIT ENZ; either NEIL or TIM. • **Trivia:** SIX MONTHS IN A LEAKY BOAT was banned by the BBC in 1982, due to the Argentian / Falklands conflict. Big brother TIM married actress GRETA SCAACHI in 1985. The FINN brothers were awarded OBE's for their services to New Zealand's music industry. NICK is brother of MARK SEYMOUR, vox of other Aussie band HUNTERS + COLLECTORS.

Recommended: WOODFACE (*9) / TOGETHER ALONE (*8) / RECURRING DREAM (*9) / HISTORY NEVER REPEATS (SPLIT ENZ *7)

SPLIT ENZ

TIM FINN – vocals, piano / **PHIL JUDD** – vocals, guitar / **JON CHUNN** – bass / **MILES GOLDING** – violin / **MICHAEL HOWARD** – drums

Vertigo | not issued

Apr 73. (7") **FOR YOU. / ?** [ ] [-]

SPLIT ENZ

EDDIE RAYNOR – keyboards repl. MILES / **WALLY WILKINSON** – guitar + **NOEL CROMBIE** – percussion repl. **HOWARD**

Mushroom AUSTRALIA | not issued

Jun 75. (lp) **MENTAL NOTES** [-] [-]
– Late last night / Walking down a road / Titus / Lovey dovey / Sweet dreams / Stranger than fiction / Time for a change / Matinee idyll / The woman who loves you / Mental notes. *(UK-iss.Aug76 on 'Chrysalis')*

Jun 75. (7") **TITUS. / ?** [-] [-]
Sep 75. (7") **LOVEY DOVEY. / ?** [-] [-]
May 76. (lp) **SECOND THOUGHTS** (re-mixes of debut lp) [-] [-]
– (In 1977, UK 'Chrysalis' issued it)

—— **NEIL FINN** – vocals, guitar repl. JUDD. WALLY, JON and drummer PAUL CROWTHER were repl. by Englishmen **NIGEL GRIGGS** – bass / **MALCOLM GREEN** – drums

(next iss. Australia; May77 on 'Mushroom')

Chrysalis | Mushroom AUST

1977. (7") **LATE LAST NIGHT. / WALKING DOWN THE ROAD** [ ] [ ] 1976
1977. (7") **ANOTHER GREAT DIVIDE. / STRANGER THAN FICTION** [ ] [-]
Oct 77. (lp) **DIZRHYTHMIA** [ ] [ ]
– Bold as brass / My mistake / Parrot fashion love / Sugar and spice / Without a doubt / Crosswords / Charley / Nice to know / Jambouree. *(re-iss.1983)*
Oct 77. (7") **MY MISTAKE. / CROSSWORDS** [ ] [ ]
(12"+=) – The woman who loves you.

—— JUDD re-joined but quit again

Mushroom AUSTRALIA | not issued

1978. (lp) **FRENZY** [-] [ ]
1978. (7") **I SEE RED. / ?** [-] [ ]

Illegal | not issued

Nov 79. (7"m) **I SEE RED. / GIVE IT A WHIRL / HERMIT McDERMOTT** [ ] [-]

—— Initial A&M material iss.Australia 1979 'Mushroom'.

A & M | A & M

Aug 80. (lp)(c) **TRUE COLOURS** [42] [40]
– Shark attack / I got you / What's the matter with you / I hope I never / Nobody takes me seriously / Missing persons / Poor boy / How can I resist her / The choral sea. *(re-iss.Nov85, cd-iss.1988)*
Aug 80. (7") **I GOT YOU. / DOUBLE HAPPY** [12] [53]
Nov 80. (7") **NOBODY TAKES ME SERIOUSLY. / THE CHORAL SEA** [ ] [-]
Jan 81. (7") **POOR BOY. / MISSING PERSON** [ ] [ ]
Jan 81. (7") **I HOPE I NEVER. / THE CHORAL SEA** [-] [ ]
Mar 81. (7") **NOBODY TAKES ME SERIOUSLY. / WHAT'S THE MATTER WITH YOU** [-] [ ]
Mar 81. (lp)(c) **WAIATA** [ ] [45] May 81
– Hard act to follow / One step ahead / I don't wanna dance / Iris / Whale / Clumsby / History never repeats / Walking through the ruins / Ships / Ghost girl / Albert of India.
Apr 81. (7"m) **HISTORY NEVER REPEATS. / SHARK ATTACK / WHAT'S THE MATTER WITH YOU** [63] [ ]
Jun 81. (7") **ONE STEP AHEAD. / IN THE WARS** [ ] [ ]

—— MALCOLM GREEN left and NOEL now on drums.

Apr 82. (7") **SIX MONTHS IN A LEAKY BOAT. / MAKE SOME SENSE OF IT** [ ] [ ]
Apr 82. (lp)(c) **TIME AND TIDE** [71] [58]
– Dirty creature / Giant heartbeat / Hello Sandy Allen / Never ceases to amaze me / Lost for words / Small world / Take a walk / Pioneer / Six months in a leaky boat / Haul away / Log cabin fever / Make some sense of it.
Aug 84. (7") **MESSAGE TO THE GIRL. / BON VOYAGE (KIAKATIA)** [ ] [ ]
Aug 84. (lp)(c) **CONFLICTING EMOTIONS** [ ] [ ] Jul 84
– Strait old line / Bullett brain and cactus head / Message to my girl / Working up an appetite / Our day / No mischief / The devil you know / I wake up every night / Conflicting emotions / Bon voyage. *(cd-iss.1988)*

—— Now a quartet (**EDDIE RAYNOR, NEIL FINN, NIGEL GRIGGS + NOEL CROMBIE**) when TIM FINN married actress Greta Saatchi and went solo.

1985. (m-lp) **SEE YOU ROUND** (live) [ ] [ ]

—— Disbanded 1985, NEIL formed CROWDED HOUSE, which later included TIM.

– compilations, others, etc. –

Dec 80. Chrysalis; (lp)(c) **BEGINNING OF THE ENZ** [ ] [-]
1992. Chrysalis; (cd) **HISTORY NEVER REPEATS (THE BEST OF SPLIT ENZ)** [ ] [ ]
– I got you / Hard act to follow / Six months in a leaky boat / What's the matter with you / One step ahead / I see red / Message to my girl / History never repeats / I hope I never / Dirty creature / Poor boy.
Sep 87. Concept; (d-lp) **COLLECTION: 1973-1984 . . . THE BEST OF SPLIT ENZ** [ ] [-]

—— (above issued in Australia with diff.track listing)

Feb 94. Chrysalis; (cd)(c) **THE BEST OF SPLIT ENZ** [ ] [ ]

CROWDED HOUSE

NEIL FINN (b.27 May'58, Te Awamutu, New Zealand) – vocals, guitar, piano (ex-SPLIT ENZ) / **NICHOLAS SEYMOUR** – bass / **PAUL HESTER** – drums, vocals with many guests **TIM PIERCE** – guitar / **MITCHELL FROOM** – keyboards, producer / **JOE SATRIANI** – b.vox / **JORGE BERMUDEZ** – percussion etc.

Capitol | Capitol

Aug 86. (7") **WORLD WHERE YOU LIVE. / THAT'S WHAT I CALL LOVE** [ ] [ ]
('A'ext.12"+=) – Can't carry on.
('A'ext.c-s+=)(cd-s+=) – Something so strong / Don't dream it's over.
Mar 87. (7") **DON'T DREAM IT'S OVER. / THAT'S WHAT I CALL LOVE** [27] [2] Jan 87
(12"+=)(c-s+=) – ('A'extended).
Mar 87. (7") **LOVE YOU 'TIL I DIE. / MEAN TO ME** [-] [ ]
Mar 87. (lp)(c)(cd) **CROWDED HOUSE** [ ] [12] Aug 86
– World where you live / Now we're getting somewhere / Don't dream it's over / Mean to me / Love you 'til the day I die / Something so strong / Hole in the river / I walk away / Tombstone / That's what I call love. (cd+=) – Can't carry on. *(re-iss.cd+c Mar94)*
Jun 87. (7") **SOMETHING SO STRONG. / I WALK AWAY** [ ] [7] Apr 87
(12"+=) – Don't dream it's over (live).
Aug 87. (7") **WORLD WHERE YOU LIVE. / HOLE IN THE RIVER** [-] [65]
Nov 87. (7") **NOW WE'RE GETTING SOMEWHERE. / TOMBSTONE** [-] [ ]
Jun 88. (7") **BETTER BE HOME SOON. / KILL EYE** [ ] [42]
(12"+=)(cd-s+=) – Don't dream it's over (live).
Jul 88. (lp)(c)(cd) **TEMPLE OF LOW MEN** [ ] [40]
– I feel possessed / Kill eye / Into temptation / Mansion in the slums / When you come / Never be the same / Love this life / Sister madly / In the lowlands / Better be home soon.
Aug 88. (7") **INTO TEMPTATION. / BETTER BE HOME SOON** [-] [ ]
Aug 88. (7")(c-s) **SISTER MADLY. / MANSION IN THE SLUMS** [ ] [ ]
(12"+=)(cd-s+=) – Something so strong (live).
Nov 88. (7") **I FEEL POSSESSED. /** [-] [ ]

—— added **TIM FINN** (b.25 Jun'52, New Z.) – vocals, piano (ex-SPLIT ENZ)

Jun 91. (cd)(c)(lp) **WOODFACE** [34] [83]
– Chocolate cake / It's only natural / Fall at your feet / Tall trees / Four seasons in one day / Weather with you / Whispers and moans / There goes God / Fame is / All I ask / As sure as I am / Italian plastic / She goes on / How will you go. *(above album hit UK No.6 after Feb92 single)*

Jun 91. (7")(c-s) **CHOCOLATE CAKE. / AS SURE AS I AM** [69] [ ]
(12"+=)(cd-s+=) – Anyone can tell.

Oct 91. (7")(c-s) **FALL AT YOUR FEET. / DON'T DREAM IT'S OVER** [17] [75]
(cd-s) – ('A'side) / Six months in a leaky boat (live) / Now we're getting somewhere (live) / Something so strong (lp version). (extra cd-s+=) – Sister madly / Better be home soon.

— reverted to a trio again, when TIM departed Autumn '91. He was replaced on tour by US session man **MARK HART**

Feb 92. (7")(c-s) **WEATHER WITH YOU. / INTO TEMPTATION** [7] [ ]
(cd-s) – ('A'side) / Mr.Tambourine man / Eight miles high / So you want to be a rock'n'roll star (all live).
(cd-s) – ('A'side) / Fall at your feet / When you come / Walking on the spot (all live).

Jun 92. (7")(c-s) **FOUR SEASONS IN ONE DAY. / THERE GOES GOD** [26] [ ]
(cd-s) ('A'side) / Dr.Livingstone / Recurring dream / Anyone can tell (all live).
(cd-s) – ('A'side) / Weather with you / Italian plastic / Message to my girl (all live).

Sep 92. (7")(c-s) **IT'S ONLY NATURAL. / CHOCOLATE CAKE** [24] [ ]
(cd-s+=) (7 minute songs medley) It's only natural – Six months in a leaky boat – Hole in the river / The burglar's song.

Sep 93. (7")(c-s) **DISTANT SUN. / WALKING ON THE SPOT** [19] [ ]
(cd-s+=) – Throw your arms around me (live) / One step ahead (live).
(cd-s) – ('A'side) / This is massive (live) / When you come (live).

Oct 93. (cd)(c)(lp) **TOGETHER ALONE** [4] [73]
– Kare Kare / In my command / Nails in my feet / Black & white boy / Fingers of love / Pineapple head / Locked out / Private universe / Walking on the spot / Distant Sun / Catherine wheels / Skin feeling / Together alone.

Nov 93. (7")(c-s) **NAILS IN MY FEET. / ZEN ROXY** [22] [ ]
(cd-s+=) – Don't dream it's over (live).

Feb 94. (c-s) **LOCKED OUT. / DISTANT SUN (live)** [12] [ ]
(cd-s+=) – Hole in the river (live) / Sister Madly (live).
(10"+=) – Private universe (live) / Fall at your feet (live).
(cd-s) – ('A'side) / (above 2-10" tracks) / Better be home soon (live).

Jun 94. (c-s) **FINGERS OF LOVE (live). / NAILS IN MY FEET (live)** [25] [ ]
(cd-s) – ('A'side) / Skin feeling / Kare Kare (live) / In my command (live).
(10") – ('A'side) / Love u till the day I die (live) / Whispers and moans (live) / It's only natural (live).
(cd-s) – ('A'side) / Catherine wheels / Pineapple head (live) / Something so strong (live).

Sep 94. (c-s) **PINEAPPLE HEAD (live). / WEATHER WITH YOU** [27] [ ]
(10"+=)(cd-s+=) – Don't dream it's over / Together alone.

— NEIL and TIM were awarded O.B.E.'s in Queen's birthday honours.

. . . Jan – Jun '96 stop press . . .

Jun 96. (single) **INSTINCT** [12] [ ]
Jun 96. (cd)(c)(lp) **RECURRING DREAM – THE VERY BEST OF CROWDED HOUSE** (compilation) [1] [ ]

— They are now no longer, having disbanded June '96.

compilations, etc

Nov 95. EMI; (3xcd-box) **CROWDED HOUSE / TEMPLE OF LOW MEN / WOODFACE** [ ] [ ]

TIM FINN

(solo with SPLIT ENZ members)

Epic / A&M

Nov 83. (7") **GRAND ADVENTURE. / THROUGH THE YEARS** [-] [ ]
Nov 83. (7") **FRACTION TOO MUCH FRICTION. / BELOW THE PAST** [ ] [ ] Apr 84
Jan 84. (7") **MADE MY DAY. / GRAND ADVENTURE** [-] [ ]
Jun 84. (lp)(c) **ESCAPADE** [ ] [ ] Sep 83
– Fraction too much friction / Staring at the embers / Through the years / Not for nothing / In a minor key / Made my day / Wait and see / Below the belt / I only want to know / Growing pains. *(re-iss.cd Oct93 on 'Sony Europe') (re-iss.cd+c Jun94 on 'Epic')*

Virgin / Virgin

Mar 86. (7") **NO THUNDER NO FIRE NO CAR. / SEARCHING FOR THE STREETS** [ ] [ ]
Apr 86. (lp)(c) **BIG CANOE** [ ] [ ]
– Are we one or are we two? / Searching the streets / Hole in my heart / Spiritual hung / Don't bury my heart / Timmy / So into wine / Hyacinth / Big canoe. *(re-iss.cd Mar94 on 'Virgin')*
Jun 86. (7")(12") **CARVE YOU IN MARBLE. / HOLE IN MY HEART** [ ] [ ]

Capitol / Capitol

Apr 89. (lp)(c)(cd) **TIM FINN** [ ] [ ]
– Young mountain / Not even close / How'm I gonna sleep / Parihaka / Tears inside / Birds swim fish fly / Suicide on Downing Street / Show a little mercy / Crescendo / Been there, done that. *(re-iss.Oct92)*

Jul 89. (7") **HOW'M I GONNA SLEEP. / CRUEL BLACK CROW** [ ] [ ]
(12"+=)(cd-s+=) – Six months in a leaky boat.

— with **RICHARD THOMPSON / ANDY WHITE / LIAM O'MAONLAI**

Jun 93. (c-s) **PERSUASION. / STRANGENESS AND CHARM (version)** [43] [ ]
(cd-s) – ('A'side) / Parihaka / Secret heart / ('A'acoustic).
(cd-s) – ('A'side) / Six months in a leaky boat (live) / Not even close (live) / Protected (live).

Jun 93. (cd)(c) **BEFORE AND AFTER** [29] [ ]
– Hit the ground running / Protected / In love with it all / Persuasion / Many's the time (in Dublin) / Funny way / Can't do both / In your sway / Strangness in charm / Always never now / Walk you home / I found it *(re-iss.Sep94)*

Sep 93. (7")(c-s) **HIT THE GROUND RUNNING. / NO MORE TEARS** [50] [ ]
(cd-s+=) – Not made of stone / You've changed.
(cd-s) – ('A'side) / Walk you home (live) / Charlie (live w / PHIL MANZANERA) / ('A'live).

ALT

— **TIM FINN** / + **ANDY WHITE** -vocals, guitar (former solo artist) / **LIAM O'MAONLAI** -vocals, guitar (ex-HOTHOUSE FLOWERS). ALT (ANDY, LIAM & TIM) recorded in Australia, although initiated in Dublin.

Parlophone / Capitol

Jun 95. (cd)(c) **ALTITUDE** [67] [ ]
– We're all men / Penelope tree / When the winter comes / Favourite girl / Swim / The refugee tree / What you've done / Second swim / Girlfriend guru / Mandala / I decided to fly / The day you were born / Halfway round the world.

FINN

TIM + NEIL duo

Parlophone / Capitol

Oct 95. (c-s) **SUFFER NEVER / WEATHER WITH YOU (demo)** [29] [ ]
(cd-s+=) – Prodigal son (demo) / Catherine wheel (demo).
(cd-s) – ('A'side) / Strangeness and charm (demo) / In love with it all (demo) / Four seasons in one day.

Oct 95. (cd)(c) **FINN** [15] [ ]
– Only talking sense / Eyes of the world / Mood swinging man / Last day of June / Suffer never / Angels heap / Niwhai / Where is my soul / Bullets in my hairdo / Paradise ((wherever you are) / Kiss the road of Rarotonga.

Nov 95. (c-s)(cd-s) **ANGELS HEAP / IT'S ONLY NATURAL (demo) / CHOCOLATE CAKE (demo)** [41] [ ]
(cd-s) – ('A'side) / There goes God (demo) / How will you go (demo).

CULT

Formed: Bradford, England . . . 1982 as SOUTHERN DEATH CULT by IAN ASTBURY who was then called IAN LINDSAY. He and his family had once stayed in Scotland before emigrating to Canada. By Spring '83, they had become DEATH CULT, leaving only a single FAT MAN, and demo album behind them. They stuck with 'Beggar's B.' subsidiary label 'Situation 2' for a couple more singles, and moved to Manchester. Early in 1984, they shortened name again to become The CULT, also relocating to London, with 'Beggar's B.' now taking full reins. Soon became one of Britain's biggest crowd-pullers worldwide, setting up home in Los Angeles 1988. • **Style:** Initially "gothic"-punks, which shifted into LED ZEPPELIN-ish heavy-metal by '85. ASTBURY always focal point as Red Indian influenced warrior of rock. • **Songwriters:** From '83 onwards, all by ASTBURY / DUFFY. Covered WILD THING (Troggs) / LOUIE LOUIE (Kingsmen) / CONQUISTADOR ? / FAITH HEALER (Alex Harvey). • **Trivia:** RICK RUBIN (Def Jam boss) produced ELECTRIC lp.

Recommended: LOVE (*8) / DREAMTIME (*6) / SOUTHERN DEATH CULT (*6) / ELECTRIC (*6) / PURE CULT (*7)

The SOUTHERN DEATH CULT

IAN LINDSAY (b.ASTBURY, 14 May'62, Heswell, Cheshire, England)– vocals / **BUZZ BURROWS** – guitar / **BARRY JEPSON** – bass / **AKY (NAWAZ QUERESHI)** – drums

Situation 2 / not issued

Dec 82. (7") **FATMAN. / MOYA** [ ] [-]
(12"+=) – The girl.

Beggar's B. / not issued

Jun 83. (lp)(c) **SOUTHERN DEATH CULT** [43] [-]
– All glory / Fatman / Today / False faces / The crypt / Crow / Faith / Vivisection / Apache / Moya.

— (Apr'83) (as BUZZ, AKY and BARRY formed GETTING THE FEAR)

DEATH CULT

with now **IAN ASTBURY** recruited new people– BILLY DUFFY (b.12 May'61)– lead guitar (ex-THEATRE OF HATE, ex-NOSEBLEEDS) / **JAMIE STUART** – bass (ex-RITUAL, ex-CRISIS) / **RAY MONDO** (r.n.SMITH)– drums (ex-RITUAL)

Situation 2 / not issued

Jul 83. (12"ep) **BROTHERS GRIMM / HORSE NATION. / GHOST DANCE / CHRISTIANS** [ ] [-]

— **NIGEL PRESTON** – drums (ex-SEX GANG CHILDREN) repl. MONDO

Nov 83. (7")(12") **GOD'S ZOO. / GOD'S ZOO (THESE TIMES)** [ ] [ ]
(re-iss.Nov88)

The CULT

(same line-up)

Situation 2 / not issued

May 84. (7") **SPIRITWALKER. / FLOWER IN THE DESERT** [ ] [-]
(12"+=) – Bone bag.

Beggar's B. / Sire

Aug 84. (lp)(c)(pic-lp) **DREAMTIME** [21] [ ]
– Horse nation / Spiritwalker / 83rd dream / Butterflies / Go west (crazy spinning circles) / Flower in the desert / Dreamtime / Rider in the snow / Bad medicine waltz. *(re-iss.Oct88.+cd+=) – Bone bag / Sea and sky / Resurrection Joe. (free live-lp.w/above, also cont. on c)* **DREAMTIME AT THE LYCEUM** – 83rd dream / God's zoo / Bad medicine / Dreamtime / Horse nation / Bone bag / Brother Grimm / Moya.

Sep 84. (7") **GO WEST (CRAZY SPINNING CIRCLES). / SEA AND SKY** [ ] [-]
(12"+=) – Brothers Grimm (live).

Dec 84. (7")(12") **RESURRECTION JOE. / ('A' hep cat mix)** [74] [-]

May 85. (7") **SHE SELLS SANCTUARY. / NUMBER 13** [15] [ ]
(12"+=) – The snake.
(c-s+=) – Assault sanctuary.

— **MARK BRZEZICKI** – drums (of BIG COUNTRY) deputised repl. PRESTON

Sep 85. (7") **RAIN. / LITTLE FACE** [17] [ ]
(12"+=) – Here comes the rain.

Oct 85. (lp)(c)(cd) **LOVE** [4] [87]
– Nirvana / Big neon gliter / Love / Brother Wolf, Sister Moon / Rain / The phoenix / The hollow man / Revolution / She sells sanctuary / Black angel. (cd+=) – Judith / Little face.

— **LES WARNER** (b.13 Feb'61) – drums (ex-JOHNNY THUNDERS, etc) repl. MARK

Nov 85. (7") **REVOLUTION. / ALL SOULS AVENUE** [30] [ ]
(d7"+=)(12"+=) – Judith / Sunrise.

Feb 87. (7") **LOVE REMOVAL MACHINE. / WOLF CHILD'S BLUES** [18] [ ]
(c-s+=) – ('A'extended).
(d7"+=)(12"+=) – Conquistador / Groove Co.

Apr 87. (lp)(c)(cd) **ELECTRIC** [4] [38]
– Wild flower / Peace dog / Lil' devil / Aphrodisiac jacket / Electric ocean / Bad fun / King contrary man / Love removal machine / Born to be wild / Outlaw / Memphis hipshake. *(also on gold-lp)*

Apr 87. (7") **LIL' DEVIL. / ZAP CITY** [11] [ ]
(12"+=) – Bonebag (live) / She sells sanctuary (live).
(d12"+=)(c-s+=) – Wild thing (live) / Louie Louie (live) / The phoenix (live) / She sells sanctuary (live). (cd-s+=) – Love removal machine (live) / The phoenix (live) / She sells sanctuary (live).

Aug 87. (7")(7"pic-d) **WILDFLOWER. / LOVE TROOPER** [24] [ ]
(12"+=) – ('A'dub version).
(d7"+=)(cd-s+=) – Horse nation (live) / She sells sanctuary (live) / Outlaw (live).

— **MICKEY CURRY** – (on session) drums repl. WARNER and KID CHAOS

Mar 89. (7") **FIRE WOMAN. / AUTOMATIC WOMAN** [15] [46]
(12"+=)(cd-s+=) – Messin' up the blues.

Apr 89. (lp)(c)(cd) **SONIC TEMPLE** [3] [10]
– Sun king / Fire woman / American horse / Edie (ciao baby) / Sweet soul sister / Soul asylum / New York City / Automatic blues / Soldier blue / Wake up time for freedom. *(cd+=)* – Medicine train.

— **ASTBURY, DUFFY and STUART** were joined by **MATT SORUM** – drums / **MARK TAYLOR** – keyboards (on tour)

Jun 89. (7")(c-s) **EDIE (CIAO BABY). / BLEEDING HEART GRAFFITI** [32] [93]
(12"+=) – Medicine train / Love removal machine (live).
(c-s+=)(cd-s+=) – Revolution (live) / Love removal machine (live).
(pic-cd+=) – Lil' devil (live).

Nov 89. (7") **SUN KING. / EDIE (CIAO BABY)** [39] [ ]
(12"+=) – She sells sanctuary.
(cd-s++=) – ('A'version).

Feb 90. (7")(c-s) **SWEET SOUL SISTER. / THE RIVER** [42] [ ]
(12"+=)(cd-s+=)(12"pic-d+=) American horse (live) / Soul asylum (live).

— (Apr-Oct90) **MARK MORRIS** – bass (ex-BALAAM AND THE ANGEL) repl. STUART

— (1991) **ASTBURY and DUFFY** brought in **CHARLIE DRAYTON** – bass / **MICKEY CURRY** – drums / **RICHIE ZITO** – keyboards, producer / **BELMONT TENCH** – piano, mellotron / **TOMMY FUNDERBUCK** – backing vocals

Sep 91. (7") **WILD HEARTED SON. / INDIAN** [40] [ ]
(12"+=) – Red Jesus.
(cd-s++=) – ('A'extended version).

Sep 91. (cd)(c)(lp) **CEREMONY** [9] [25]
– Ceremony / Wild hearted son / Earth mofo / White / If / Full tilt / Heart of soul / Bangkok rain / Indian / Sweet salvation / Wonderland.

Feb 92. (12"ep)(cd-ep) **HEART OF SOUL / HEART OF SOUL (acoustic) / EARTH MOFO (radio mix) / EDIE (CIAO BABY) (radio mix)** [51] [ ]

Jan 93. (cd-ep) **SHE SELLS SANCTUARY (DOG STAR RADIO) / ('A'live) / ('A'slutnostic mix) / ('A'sundance mix)** [15] [ ]
(12") – ('A'side) / ('A'original mix).
(cd-s+=) – ('A'-Phlegmatic mix) / ('A'-Flustersquish mix).

Feb 93. (d-cd)(c)(d-lp)(4x12") **PURE CULT** compilation) [1] [ ]
– She sells sanctuary / Fire woman / Lil' devil / Spiritwalker / The witch / Revolution / Wild hearted Sun / Love removal machine / Rain / Edie (ciao baby) / Heart of soul / Love / Wildflower / Go west / Ressurection Joe / Sun king / Sweet soul ister / Earth mofo. *(d-lp w/other d-lp)* LIVE AT THE MARQUEE '91

Sep 94. (c-s) **COMING DOWN. / ('A'remix)** [50] [ ]
(12"+=)(cd-s+=) – Gone.

Oct 94. (cd)(c)(lp) **THE CULT** [21] [69]
– Gone / Coming down / Real girl / Black Sun / Naturally high / Joy / Star / Sacred life / Be free / Universal you / Emperor's new horse / Saints are down.

Dec 94. (c-s) **STAR. / BREATHING OUT** [65] [ ]
(12"+=)(cd-s+=) – The witch (extended).

— In Apr'95, they cancelled tour, due to new guitarist JAMES STEVENSON returning to the re-formed GENE LOVES JEZEBEL.

– compilations, others, etc. –

Dec 88. Beggar's Banquet; (cd) **THE MANOR SESSIONS** [ ] [-]
Dec 89. Beggar's Banquet; (pic-cd-ep) **THE LOVE MIXES** [ ] [ ]
Dec 89. Beggar's Banquet; (pic-cd-ep) **THE ELECTRIC MIXES** [ ] [ ]
Aug 91. Beggar's Banquet; (10xcd-ep) **1984-1990** [ ] [-]

— (above 10 ep's later sold seperately)

Jun 92. Beggar's Banquet; (video w/free cd-ep) **FAITH HEALER / FULL TILT (live) / LOVE REMOVAL MACHINE (live)** [ ] [ ]

. . . Jan – Jun '96 stop press . . .

HOLY BARBARIANS

— IAN ASTBURY

Beggar's B / Beggar's B

Apr 96. (single) **SPACE JUNKIE** [ ] [ ]
May 96. (cd)(c)(lp) **CREAM** [ ] [ ]

CUPOL (see under ⇒ WIRE)

CURE

Formed: Crawley, Sussex, England . . . 1976 initially as The EASY CURE until 1977 (see below line-ups). In 1978, after a brief liason with the 'Hansa' label the previous year, they recorded one-off 45 'KILLING AN ARAB' for 'Small Wonder'. Around the same time (Jul78), they signed to Chris Parry's new 'Fiction' label who re-released debut early '79. They soon broke into the UK 50 with first album 'THREE IMAGINARY BOYS'. Six years later on 'Elektra', they began inroads into burgeoning US market, culminating in a near chart topper in 1989 with 'LOVESONG'. • **Style:** Moved quickly from punky new wave to experimental pop-rock, which combined elements of danceable sensual alternative music. • **Songwriters:** Group compositions, except cover of FOXY LADY (Jimi Hendrix), HELLO I LOVE YOU (Doors). • **Trivia:** SMITH married childhood sweetheart Mary Poole on 13 Aug'88.

Recommended: STANDING ON THE BEACH / STARING AT THE SEA (*9) / THREE IMAGINARY BOYS (*8) / THE TOP (*7) / DISINTIGRATION (*8) / THE HEAD ON THE DOOR (*6) / PORNOGRAPHY (*6) / WISH (*6) / KISS ME, KISS ME, KISS ME (*7) / SEVENTEEN SECONDS (*5) / FAITH (*5).

ROBERT SMITH (b.21 Apr'59) – vocals, lead guitar / **LAWRENCE TOLHURST** – drums, keyboards / **MICHAEL DEMPSEY** – bass

Small Wonder / not issued

Aug 78. (7") **KILLING AN ARAB. / 10.15 SATURDAY NIGHT** [ ] [-]

Fiction-Polydor / not issued

Jan 79. (7") **KILLING AN ARAB. / 10.15 SATURDAY NIGHT** [ ] [-]
May 79. (lp)(c) **THREE IMAGINARY BOYS** [44] [-]

– 10.15 Saturday night / Accuracy / Grinding halt / Another day / Object / Subway song / Foxy lady / Meat hook / So what / Fire in Cairo / It's not you / Three imaginary boys. *(cd-iss.Apr90)*

May 79. (7") **BOYS DON'T CRY. / PLASTIC PASSION** [ ] [-]

— **SIMON GALLUP** – bass, keyboards repl. DEMPSEY who joined The ASSOCIATES

Oct 79. (7") **JUMPING SOMEONE ELSE'S TRAIN. / I'M COLD** [ ] [-]

— added **MATHIEU HARTLEY** – keyboards, synthesizers

Nov 79. (7") **I'M A CULT HERO (as "CULT HEROES"). / I DIG YOU** [ ] [-]

Mar 80. (7")(12") **A FOREST. / ANOTHER JOURNEY BY TRAIN** [31] [-]

Apr 80. (lp)(c) **SEVENTEEN SECONDS** [20] [-]
– The final sound / A forest / M / At night / Seventeen seconds / A reflection / Play for today / Secrets / In your house / Three . . . *(cd-iss.Jan86)*

— reverted back to trio of **SMITH, TOLHURST & GALLUP** when HARTLEY left forming CRY.

Mar 81. (7")(12") **PRIMARY. / DESCENT** [43] [-]

Fiction-Polydor | P.V.C.

Apr 81. (lp)(c) **FAITH** [14] [ ]
– The holy hour / Primary / Other voices / All cats are grey / The funeral party / Doubt / The drowning man / Doubt / Faith. *(cd-iss.Jan86)* (c+=) – ('CARNAGE VISORS' film soundtrack)

Oct 81. (7") **CHARLOTTLE SOMETIMES. / SPLINTERED IN HER HEAD** [44] [ ]
(12"+=) – Faith (live).

Fiction-Polydor | Sire

Apr 82. (lp)(c) **PORNOGRAPHY** [8] [ ]
– One hundred years / A short term effect / The hanging garden / Siamese twins / The figurehead / A srange day / Cold / Pornography. *(cd-iss.Jan86)*

Jul 82. (7") **THE HANGING GARDEN. / KILLING AN ARAB (live)** [34] [ ]
(d7"+=)(12"+=) – One hundred years (live) / A forest (live).

— **STEVE GOULDING** – bass repl. GALLUP who also joined CRY. (LOL now keyboards)

Nov 82. (7")(12") **LET'S GO TO BED. / JUST ONE KISS** [44] [ ]

— Trimmed to duo of **SMITH & TOLHURST**

Jul 83. (7")(7"pic-d) **THE WALK. / THE DREAM** [12] [ ]
(12"+=) – Lament.
(free 12"w/12") – Let's go to bed / Just one kiss.

— added **PHIL THORNALLEY** – bass / **ANDY ANDERSON-drums** (ex-BRILLIANT)

Oct 83. (7")(7"pic-d) **THE LOVECATS. / SPEAK MY LANGUAGE** [7] [ ]
(12"+=) – Mr. Pink eyes.

Dec 83. (m-lp)(c) **JAPANESE WHISPERS** [26] [ ]
– Let's go to bed / The walk / The lovecats / The dream / Just one kiss / The upstair's room / Lament / Speak my language.

Mar 84. (7")(7"pic-d) **THE CATERPILLAR. / HAPPY THE MAN** [14] [ ]
(12"+=) – Throw your foot.

Apr 84. (lp)(c)(cd) **THE TOP** [10] [ ]
– The caterpillar / Piggy in the mirror / The empty world / Bananafishbones / The top / Shake dog shake / Birdman girl / Wailing wall / Give me it / Dressing up.

— added **PORL THOMSON** – guitar, saxophone, keyboards (a member in '77)

Oct 84. (lp) **CONCERT-THE CURE LIVE (live)** [26] [ ]
(d-c) **CONCERT AND CURIOSITY-CURE ANOMALIES 1977-1984**
– Shake dog shake / Primary / Charlotte sometimes / The hanging garden / Give me it / The walk / One hundred years / A forest / 10.15 Saturday night / Killing an Arab. CURE ANOMILIES – Heroin face / Boys don't cry / Subway song / At night / In your house / The drowning man / Other voices / The funeral party / All mine / Forever.

— **SIMON GALLUP** returned to repl. PORL. **BORIS WILLIAMS** – drums (ex-THOMPSON TWINS) repl. ANDERSON who joined JEFFREY LEE PIERCE (of The GUN CLUB)

Fiction-Polydor | Elektra

Jul 85. (7") **IN BETWEEN DAYS. / EXPLODING BODY** [15] [-]
(12"+=) – A few hours after this.

Aug 85. (lp)(c)(cd) **THE HEAD ON THE DOOR** [7] [59]
– In between days / Kyoto song / The blood / Six different ways / Push / The baby screams / Close to me / A night like this / Screw / Sinking.

Sep 85. (7") **CLOSE TO ME. / A MAN INSIDE MY MOUTH** [24] [-]
(10"+=)(12"+=) – Stop dead / New day.

Jan 86. (7") **IN BETWEEN DAYS. / STOP DEAD** [-] [99]

Mar 86. (7") **CLOSE TO ME. / SINKING** [-] [ ]

Apr 87. (7")(12") **WHY CAN'T I BE YOU. / A JAPANESE DREAM** [21] [54]
(d7"+=) – Six different ways (live) / Push (live).

May 87. (d-lp)(c)(cd) **KISS ME, KISS ME, KISS ME** [6] [35]
– The kiss / Catch / Torture / If only tonight we could sleep / Why can't I be you / How beautiful you are / Snakepit / Hey you / Just like heaven / Hot hot hot!!! / All I want / One more time / Like cockatoos / Icing sugar The perfect girl / A thousand hours / Shiver and shake / Fight. *(pic-lp iss.Dec87)* (free-ltd.12"orange / or green,w/cd) – A Japanese dream / Breathe / Chain of flowers / Sugar girl / Snow in summer / Icing sugar (remix).

— added **ROBERT O'CONNELL** – keyboards (ex-PSYCHEDELIC FURS (on tour).

Jul 87. (7")(7"clear) **CATCH. / BREATHE** [27] [ ]
(12"+=) – Chain of flowers.
(7"+=)(12"ep+=) – Night like this (live) / Kyoto song (live).

Oct 87. (7")(7"white)(7"pic-d) **JUST LIKE HEAVEN. / SNOW IN SUMMER** [29] [-]
(12"+=) – Sugar girls.

Oct 87. (7") **JUST LIKE HEAVEN. / BREATHE** [-] [40]

Feb 88. (7") **HOT HOT HOT!!!. / HEY YOU** [45] [65]
(12"+=)(cd-s+=) – ('A'remix).

Apr 89. (7")(7"clear) **LULLABY (remix). / BABBLE** [5] [-]
(12"+=)(12"pink+=)(3"cd-s+=) – Out of mind / ('A'extended).

Apr 89. (c-s) **LULLABY (remix). / HOMESICK** [-] [74]

May 89. (lp)(c)(cd) **DISINTIGRATION** [3] [12]
– Plainsong / Pictures of you / Closedown / Lovesong / Lullaby / Fascination street / Prayers for rain / The same deep water as you /Disintigration / Untitled. (cd+=) – Last dance / Homesick. *(pic-lp Apr90)*

May 89. (7") **FASCINATION STREET. / BABBLE** [-] [46]

Aug 89. (7") **LOVESONG. / 2 LATE** [18] [2]
(12"+=)(c-s+=) – Fear of ghosts.
(cd-s+=) – ('A'-12"mix).

— (Mar89) reverted to a quintet when TOLHURST left **SMITH, GALLUP, THOMPSON, WILLIAMS and PERRY BAMONTE** – keyboards

Mar 90. (7")(c-s)(7"green)(7"purple) **PICTURES OF YOU (remix). / PRAYERS FOR RAIN (live)** [24] [71]
(some 'B'sides repl. above with – LAST DANCE (live)
(12"+=)(12"green+=)(12"purple+=) – Disintigration (live).
(cd-s+=) – Fascination street (live). (W.H. Smith's released ENTREAT (May90) a live EP, which featured the 5 tracks +=) – Closedown / Homesick / Untitled.

Sep 90. (7")(12") **NEVER ENOUGH. / HAROLD AND JOE** [13] [ ]
(12"+=)(cd-s+=)(12"pic-d+=) – Let's go to bed (milk mix).

Oct 90. (7") **CLOSE TO ME (closet remix). / JUST LIKE HEAVEN** [13] [97] Jan 91
(12"+=)(cd-s+=) – ('A'dizzy mix) / Primary (red mix).
(cd-s+=) – Why can't I be you (extended).

Nov 90. (cd)(c)(d-lp) **MIXED UP (remix album)** [8] [14]
– Lullaby (extended mix) / Close to me (closer mix) / Fascination Street (extended mix) / The walk (everything mix) / Lovesong (extended mix) / A forest (tree mix) / Pictures of you (extended dub mix) / Hot hot hot!!! (extended mix) / The caterpillar (flicker mix) / Inbetween days (shiver mix) / Never enough (big mix).

Apr 91. (cd)(c)(lp) **ENTREAT (live)** (see above) [10] [ ]
– (finally nationally released)

Mar 92. (7")(c-s) **HIGH. / THIS TWILIGHT GARDEN** [8] [42]
(12"+=) – Play.
(cd-s+=) – High (higher mix).

Apr 92. (12"clear) **HIGH (trip mix). / OPEN (fix mix)** [44] [43]

Apr 92. (cd)(c)(d-lp) **WISH** [1] [2]
– Open / High / Apart / From the edge of the deep green sea / Wendy time / Doing the unstuck / Friday I'm in love / Trust / A letter to Elise / Cut / To wish impossible things / End.

May 92. (7")(c-s) **FRIDAY I'M IN LOVE. / HALO** [6] [18]
(12"+=)(cd-s+=) – Scared as you.
(cd-s++=) – ('A'-Strangelove mix).

Oct 92. (7")(c-s) **A LETTER TO ELISE. / THE BIG HAND** [28] [ ]
(12"+=) – A foolish arrangement.
(cd-s++=) – ('A'version).

Sep 93. (d-cd)(d-c)(d-lp) **SHOW (live)** [29] [42]
– Tape / Open / High / Pictures of you / Lullaby / Just like Heaven / Fascination Street / A night like this / Trust / Doing the unstuck / The walk / Let's go to bed / Friday I'm in love / In between days / From the edge of the deep green sea / Never enough / Cut / End.

— PORL departed after the above.

Oct 93. (cd)(c)(d-lp) **PARIS (live Oct'93)** [56] [ ]
– The figurehead / One hundred years / At night / Play for today / Apart / In your house / Lovesong / Catch / A letter to Elise / Dressing up / Charlotte sometimes / Close to me.

. . . Jan – Jun '96 stop press . . .

Apr 96. (single) **THE 13TH** [15] [44]

May 96. (cd)(c)(lp) **WILD MOOD SWINGS** [9] [12]

Jun 96. (single) **MINT CAR** [31] [ ]

– compilations, etc. –

Aug 80. Fiction/ US= P.V.C.; (c) **BOYS DON'T CRY** [ ] [ ]
(lp – re-iss.Aug83 hit 71) (cd-iss. early 1986)

Apr 86. Fiction; (7") **BOYS DON'T CRY. / PILLBOX BLUES** [22] [-]
(12"+=) – Do the Hansa.

May 86. P.V.C.; (7") **BOYS DON'T CRY. / LET'S GO TO BED** [-] [ ]

May 86. Fiction/ US= Elektra; (lp)(cd)(d-c) **STANDING ON THE BEACH** ('A'45's) / **STARING AT THE SEA** ('B'45's) [4] [48]
– Killing an Arab / Boys don't cry / Jumping someone else's train / A forest /

Primary / Charlotte sometimes / The hanging garden / Let's go to bed / The walk / The lovecats / The caterpillar / In between days / Close to me. (cd+=) – 10.15 Saturday night / Play for today / Other voices / A night like this. *(re-iss.Feb91)*

Oct 88. Fiction; (vid-cd) **WHY CAN'T I BE YOU (video) / JAPANESE DREAM / HEY YOU / WHY CAN'T I BE YOU** [ ] [-]

Oct 88. Fiction; (vid-cd) **IN BETWEEN DAYS (video) / SIX DIFFERENT WAYS (live) / PUSH (live)** [ ] [-]

Oct 88. Fiction; (vid-cd) **CATCH (video) / CATCH / BREATHE / A CHAIN OF FLOWERS / ICING SUGAR (new mix)** [ ] [-]

May 88. Strange Fruit; (12"ep) **THE PEEL SESSIONS** [ ] [-]
– Killing an Arab / Boys don't cry / 10:15 Saturday night / Fire in Cairo.

CYPRESS HILL

Formed: Los Angeles, California, USA . . . 1991 by MUGGS, B.REAL and SEN DOG. In the early 90's, after signing to US 'Ruffhouse' label, they cracked the Top 40 their with eponymous debut. After many tours alongside other rappers HOUSE OF PAIN, they smashed straight into US top slot, with 2nd album 'BLACK SUNDAY'. • **Style:** Hardcore rapping Latinos, who were renowned for liking a joint. • **Songwriters:** Group penned. I AIN'T GOIN' OUT LIKE THAT sampled; THE WIZARD (Black Sabbath) / WHEN THE SH-- GOES DOWN sampled; DEEP GULLY (Outlaw Blues Band) / LIL' PUTOS sampled; ODE TO BILLY JOE (Boobie Gentry) / etc. • **Trivia:** MUGGS also produced HOUSE OF PAIN, BEASTIE BOYS and ICE CUBE.

Recommended: BLACK SUNDAY (*8) / CYPRESS HILL (*7).

B-REAL (b.LOUIS FREESE, 1970) – MC, lead rapper / **SEN DOG** (b.SENEN REYES, 1965) – MC / **DJ MUGGS** (b.LARRY MUGGERUD, 1969) – DJ, producer

Columbia Ruffhouse

Dec 91. (c-s) **HAND ON THE PUMP. / REAL ESTATE** [-] [ ]
(12"+=) – ('A'instrumental).

Jan 92. (cd)(c)(lp) **CYPRESS HILL** [ ] [31] Nov 91
– Pigs / How I could just kill a man / Hand on the pump / Hole in the head / Ultraviolet dreams / Light another / The phuncky feel one / Break it up / Real estate / Stoned is the way of the walk / Psycobetabuckdown / Something for the blunted / Latin lingo / The funky Cypress Hill shit / Tres equis / Born to get busy. *(re-iss.May94)*

Feb 92. (7") **HOW I COULD JUST KILL A MAN. / THE PHUNKY FEEL ONE** [-] [77]

1992. (12"ep)(cd-ep) **HAND ON THE PUMP (Mugg's extended mix) / ('A'-instrumental) / HAND ON THE GLOCK** [-] [ ]

1992. (12"ep)(cd-ep) **LATIN LINGO (Prince Paul mix) / STONED IS THE WAY OF THE WALK (reprise) / HAND ON THE GLOCK** [-] [ ]

Jul 93. (12")(cd-s) **INSANE IN THE BRAIN (radio version). / WHEN THE SH-- GOES DOWN (radio version)** [32] [19]

Jul 93. (cd)(c)(lp) **BLACK SUNDAY** [13] [1]
– I wanna get high / I ain't goin' out like that / Insane in the brain / When the sh--goes down / Lick a shot / Cock the hammer / Interlude / Lil' putos / Legalize it / Hits from the bong / What go around come around, kid / A to the K / Hand on the glock / Break 'em off some.

Sep 93. (12")(cd-s) **WHEN THE SH-- GOES DOWN (extended). / ('A'-instrumental) / THE PHUNCKY FEEL ONE (extended) / HOW COULD I JUST KILL A MAN (the Killer mix)** [19] [ ]

Dec 93. (12"ep)(c-ep)(cd-ep) **I AIN'T GOIN' OUT LIKE THAT. / HITS FROM THE BONG / WHEN THE SH-- GOES DOWN (Diamond D mix)** [15] [65]

Feb 94. (c-s) **INSANE IN THE BRAIN. / STONED IS THE WAY OF THE WALK** [21] [ ]
(12"+=) – Latin lingo (Prince Paul mix).
(cd-s) – ('A'side) / Something for the blunted.

Apr 94. (c-s) **LICK A SHOT (Baka Boys remix). / I WANNA GET HIGH** [20] [ ]
(12"+=)(cd-s+=) – Scooby Doo.

Sep 95. (c-s) **THROW YOUR SET IN THE AIR / KILLA HILL NIGGAS** [15] [45]
(12"+=)(cd-s+=) – ('A'-Slow roll remix) / ('B'instrumental).

Oct 95. (cd)(c)(d-lp) **III (TEMPLES OF BOOM)** [11] [3]
– Spark another owl / Throw your set in the air / Stoned raiders / Illusions / Killa hill niggas / Boom biddy bye bye / No rest for the wicked / Make a move / Killafornia / Funk freakers / Locotes / Red light visions / Strictly hip hop / Let it rain / Everybody must get stoned. (w/ free cd or lp) DJ MUGGS BUDDHA MIX:- Hole in the head – How could I just kill a man – Insane in the brain – Stoned is the way of the walk – Hits from the bong – Hand on the pump – Real estate – I wanna get high.

. . . Jan – Jun '96 stop press . . .

Feb 96. (single) **ILLUSIONS** [23] [ ]

—— SEN DOG went solo (DOGWOOD) and was repl. by DJ SCANDALOUS

Jun 96. (single) **BEAM BIDDY BYE BYE** [-] [87]

Holger CZUKAY (see under ⇒ CAN)

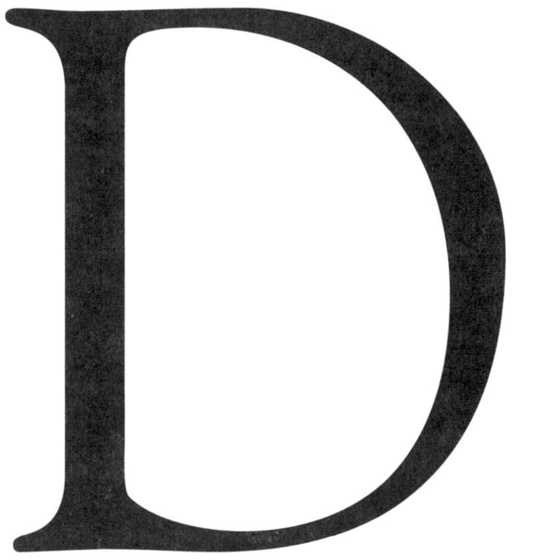

DALI'S CAR (see under ⇒ BAUHAUS)

Roger DALTREY (see under ⇒ The WHO)

DAMNED

Formed: London, England . . . May 1976 by BRIAN JAMES and RAT SCABIES who soon found The CAPTAIN and former undertaker VANIAN. They were signed to new UK indie label 'Stiff' by JAKE RIVERA, and released classic song NEW ROSE produced by stablemate NICK LOWE. Became first "New Wave punks" to release and chart with an album (Mar'77). A number of bust-ups dogged their career until 1985 when major label 'M.C.A.' gave them new pop sensibility. • **Style:** Punk pioneers with extrovert members giving live appeal. Like the STRANGLERS they moved into slight experimental 80's new wave, before drifting into pop-rock and final obscurity. • **Songwriters:** Most written by JAMES, until he left, when group took over. Covered:- HELP! (Beatles) / I FEEL ALRIGHT (Stooges / Iggy Pop) / JET BOY JET GIRL (New York Dolls) / CITADEL (Rolling Stones) / ELOISE (Paul & Barry Ryan) / WHITE RABBIT (Jefferson Airplane) / ALONE AGAIN OR (Love) / WILD THING (Troggs) / LET THERE BE RATS (aka DRUMS) (Sandy Nelson). • **Trivia:** NICK MASON (Pink Floyd drummer) produced disappointing 2nd album MUSIC FOR PLEASURE. CAPTAIN SENSIBLE had UK-No.1 in 1982 with (Rogers-Hammerstein's) HAPPY TALK, and although briefly, became a top disco/pop act abroad.

Recommended: DAMNED DAMNED DAMNED (*8) / BEST OF THE DAMNED (*8)

DAVE VANIAN (b.DAVE LETTS) – vocals / **BRIAN JAMES** (b.BRIAN ROBERTSON) – guitar (ex-LONDON S.S.) / **CAPTAIN SENSIBLE** (b.RAY BURNS, 23 Apr'55) – bass, vocals / **RAT SCABIES** (b.CHRIS MILLER, 30 Jul'57) – drums (ex-LONDON S.S.)

		Stiff	not issued
Nov 76.	(7") **NEW ROSE. / HELP!**		-
Feb 77.	(7") **NEAT NEAT NEAT. / STAB YOR BACK. / SINGALONGASCABIES**		-
Feb 77.	(lp)(c) **DAMNED DAMNED DAMNED**	36	-

– Neat neat neat / Fan club / I fall / Born to kill / Stab yor back / Feel the pain / New rose / Fish / See her tonite / 1 of the 2 / So messed up / I feel alright. *(re-iss.+cd.Apr87 on 'Demon',+pic-lp 1988 + 1991)*

— added (ROBERT) **LU EDMUNDS** – guitar

Sep 77.	(7") **PROBLEM CHILD. / YOU TAKE MY MONEY**		-
Nov 77.	(lp)(c) **MUSIC FOR PLEASURE**		-

– Problem child / Don't cry wolf / One way love / Politics / Stretcher case / Idiot box / You take my money / Alone / Your eyes / Creep (you can't fool me) / You know. *(re-iss.coloured lp +cd.Apr88. on 'Demon')*

Dec 77.	(7")(7"pink) **DON'T CRY WOLF. / ONE WAY LOVE**		-

— **DAVE BERK** – drums (ex-JOHNNY MOPED) repl. SCABIES who formed various bands.

— **JOHN MOSS** – drums replaced BERK. They split Feb 78. VANIAN joined DOCTORS OF MADNESS. SENSIBLE formed SOFTIES then KING. EDMUNDS & MOSS formed THE EDGE. MOSS later joined ADAM & THE ANTS then CULTURE CLUB. EDMUNDS later joined ATHLETICO SPIZZ 80, The MEKONS, SHRIEKBACK, PIL. etc. BRIAN JAMES formed TANZ DER YOUTH, then The HELLIONS. Later he formed LORDS OF THE NEW CHURCH. Reformed Autumn '78 as The **DOOMED** with LEMMY of MOTORHEAD on bass. (1 gig) **HENRY BADOWSKI** – bass (ex-CHELSEA) replaced LEMMY.

— Group reverted to name The **DAMNED** with originals VANIAN, SENSIBLE (now guitar, keyboards) **& SCABIES. ALGY WARD** – bass (ex-SAINTS) replaced BADOWSKI who went solo.

		Chiswick	not isssued.
Apr 79.	(7")(7"red) **LOVE SONG. / NOISE NOISE NOISE / SUICIDE**	20	-

(re-iss.7"blue Feb82 on 'Big Beat')

Oct 79.	(7") **SMASH IT UP. / BURGLAR**	35	-

(re-iss.7"red Mar82 on 'Big Beat')

Nov 79.	(lp)(c) **MACHINE GUN ETIQUETTE**	31	-

– Love song / Machine gun etiquette / I just can't be happy today / Melody Lee / Anti-Pope / These hands / Plan 9 channel 7 / Noise noise noise / Looking at you / Smash it up (parts 1 & 2). *(re-iss.Jun85 on 'Big Beat', 1986 cd)* (cd+=) – Ballroom blitz / Suicide / Rabid (over you) / White rabbit.

Nov 79.	(7") **I JUST CAN'T BE HAPPY TODAY. / BALLROOM BLITZ / TURKEY SONG**	46	-

— **PAUL GRAY** – bass, vocals (ex-EDDIE AND THE HOT RODS) repl. WARD who formed TANK.

Jun 80.	(7") **WHITE RABBIT. / RABID OVER YOU**		-

(12"+=) – Seagulls / Curtain Call (version).

Sep 80.	(7")(12") **THE HISTORY OF THE WORLD (part 1). / I BELIEVE THE IMPOSSIBLE / SUGAR AND SPITE**		-
Nov 80.	(d-lp)(c) **UNTITLED (THE BLACK ALBUM)**	29	-

– Wait for the blackout / Lively arts / Silly kids games / Drinking about my baby / Hit and miss / Doctor Jekyll and Mr. Hyde / 13th floor vendetta / Twisted nerve / Sick of this and that / History of the world (part 1) / Therapy // Curtain call / live side:- Love song / Second time around / Smash it up (parts 1 & 2) / New rose / I just can't be happy today / Plan 9 Channel 7. (1/2 studio, 1/4 live, 1/4 concept) *(re-Aug82 on' Big Beat' as lp) (c-iss.Jun85, cd-iss.Mar90 omits live tracks)*

Nov 80.	(7") **THERE AINT NO SANITY CLAUS. / LOOKING AT YOU**		-

(12"+=) – Anti-Pope.

		N.E.M.S.	not issued.
Nov 81.	(d7"ep) **FRIDAY THE 13th**	50	-

– Disco man / The limit club / Citadel / Billy bad breaks.

		Bronze	not issued.
Jul 82.	(7") **LOVELY MONEY. / I THINK I'M WONDERFUL**	42	-
Sep 82.	(7") **DOZEN GIRLS. / TAKE THAT**		-
Oct 82.	(lp)(c) **STRAWBERRIES**	15	-

– Ignite / Generals / Stranger on the town / Dozen girls / The dog / Gun fury / Pleasure and the pain / Life goes on / Bad time for Bonzo / Under the floor again / Don't bother me. *(re-iss.Mar86 in red vinyl +c. on 'Legacy') (re-iss.+cd.Dec86 on 'Dojo') (cd-iss.Apr94 on 'Cleopatra')*

Nov 82.	(7") **GENERALS. / DISGUISE / CITADEL ZOMBIES**		-

		Damned	not issued.
Nov 83.	(lp)(pic-lp) **LIVE IN NEWCASTLE (live) - ltd 5000**		-

(cd-iss.Jan94 on 'Receiver')

May 84.	(7")(7"pic-d)(7"red)(7"blue)(7"white)(12")(12"marble) (12"multi-colrd)(12"sha-pic-d) **THANKS FOR THE NIGHT. / NASTY**		-

(re-iss.12"-ltd.1985 +=) – Do the blitz)

— **VANIAN** and **SCABIES** recruited new guys **ROMAN JUGG** – guitar, keyboards / who replaced the CAPTAIN who carried on with solo career. **BRYN GUNN** – bass repl. GRAY

		M.C.A.	M.C.A.
Mar 85.	(7")(7"pic-d) **GRIMLY FIENDISH. / EDWARD THE BEAR**	21	

(12"+=) – ('A'version).

Jun 85.	(7")(10") **SHADOW OF LOVE. / NIGHTSHIFT**	25	

(12"+=) – Would you.
(d7"+=) – Let there be Rats / Wiped out.

Jul 85.	(lp)(c)(pic-lp)(colrd-lp) **PHANTASMAGORIA**	11	

– Street of dreams / Shadow of love / There'll come a day / Sanctum sanctorium / Is it a dream / Grimly fiendish / Edward the bear / The eighth day / Trojans. *(free 7" w.a.-)* I JUST CAN'T BE HAPPY TODAY *(re-iss.'86 cont.free 12"blue ELOISE)*

Sep 85.	(7") **IS IT A DREAM?. / STREET OF DREAMS(live)/**	34	

(12"+=) – Wild thing (live).

Jan 86.	(7")(12") **ELOISE. / TEMPTATION /**	3	

(12"+=) – Beat girl.

Nov 86.	(7") **ANYTHING. / THE YEAR OF THE JACKAL**	32	

(12"+=)(10"+=) – Thanks for the night.

Nov 86.	(lp)(c)(cd) **ANYTHING**	40	

– Anything / Alone again or / The portrait / Restless / In dulce decorum / Gigolo / The girl goes down / Tightrope walk / Psychomania.

Feb 87. (7"clear)(12"clear) **GIGOLO. / PORTRAIT** [29] [-]
Apr 87. (7") **ALONE AGAIN OR. / IN DULCE DECORUM** [27] [-]
(12"+=) – Psychomania.
(d7"++=) – Eloise.
Nov 87. (7") **IN DULCE DECORUM. / PSYCHOMANIA** [72] [-]
(12"+=) – ('A' dub version.)

—— Disbanded in the late 80's, although re-union gigs were forthcoming.

Essential / not issued

Aug 89. (lp)(c) **FINAL DAMNATION** (live '88 reunion) [ ] [-]
– See her tonite / Neat neat neat / Born to kill / I fall / Fan club / Fish / Help / New rose / I feel alright / I just can't be happy today / Wait for the blackout / Melody Lee / Noise noise noise / Love song / Smash it up (parts 1 & 2) / Looking at you / The last time. *(cd-iss.Apr94 on 'Castle')*

– compilations, others, etc. –

Nov 85. Stiff; (12"ep) **NEW ROSE / NEAT NEAT NEAT. / STRETCHER CASE / SICK OF BEING SICK** [ ] [-]
Jul 86. Stiff; (blue-lp) **NOT THE CAPTAIN'S BIRTHDAY PARTY – LIVE AT THE ROUNDHOUSE** [ ] [-]
(re-iss.Nov91 on 'Demon')
Jun 86. Strange Fruit; (12"ep) **THE PEEL SESSIONS (10.5.77)** [ ] [-]
– Sick of being sick / Stretcher case / Feel the pain / Fan club. *(c-ep.iss.1987, cd-ep.iss.May88)*
Jul 87. Strange Fruit; (12"ep) **THE PEEL SESSIONS (30.11.76)** [ ] [-]
– Stab yor back / Neat neat neat / New rose / So messed up / I fall.
Nov 93. Strange Fruit; (cd) **SESSIONS OF THE DAMNED** [ ] [-]
Nov 81. Chiswick; (lp)(c) **THE BEST OF THE DAMNED** [43] [-]
– New rose / Neat neat neat / I just can't be happy today / Jet boy jet girl / Hit or miss / There ain't no sanity claus / Smash it up (parts 1 & 2) / Plan 9 channel 7 / Rabid (over you) / Wait for the blackout / History of the world (part 1). *(cd-iss.Oct87 on 'Big Beat')*
May 82. Big Beat; (7")(7"pic-d) **WAIT FOR THE BLACKOUT. / JET BOY JET GIRL** [ ] [-]
Nov 82. Big Beat; (lp) **LIVE AT SHEPPERTON 1980 (live)** [ ] [-]
– Love song / Second time around / I just can't be happy today / Melody Lee / Help / Neat neat neat / Looking at you / Smash it up (parts 1 & 2) / New rose / Plan 9 channel 7. *(c-iss.Jun85) (cd-iss.Jun88)*
Jun 88. Big Beat; (lp)(c)(cd) **THE LONG LOST WEEKEND: BEST OF VOL.1/2** [ ] [-]
Oct 87. I.D.; (lp)(cd) **MINDLESS, DIRECTIONLESS, ENEMY (live)** [ ] [-]
Oct 82. Nems import; (7")(10")(7"green) **LIVELY ARTS. / TEENAGE DREAM** [ ] [-]
Jan 86. Dojo; (lp)(c)(cd) **DAMNED BUT NOT FORGOTTEN** [ ] [-]
Dec 91. Dojo; (cd) **TOTALLY DAMNED (live + rare)** [ ] [-]
Dec 87. M.C.A.; (d-lp)(c)(cd) **THE LIGHT AT THE END OF THE TUNNEL** [87] [-]
Dec 90. Castle; (d-lp)(c)(cd) **THE COLLECTION** [ ] [-]
Jan 91. Deltic; (7") **FUN FACTORY ('82). / A RIOT ON EASTBOURNE PIER** [ ] [-]
May 93. Receiver; (cd) **SCHOOL BULLIES** [ ] [-]
Jun 94. M.C.I.; (cd)(c) **ETERNALLY DAMNED – THE VERY BEST OF . . .** [ ] [-]
Jul 94. Success; (cd)(c) **LIVE (live)** [ ] [-]
Dec 94. Cleopatra; (cd) **TALES FROM THE DAMNED** [ ] [-]
May 95. Spectrum; (cd) **FROM THE BEGINNING** [ ] [-]
Sep 95. Emporio; (cd)(c) **NOISE – THE BEST OF: LIVE** [ ] [-]

DAVE VANIAN & THE PHANTOM CHORDS

Big Beat / not issued

Mar 95. (cd) **BIG BEAT PRESENTS . . .** [ ] [-]
– Voodoo doll / Screamin' kid / Big town / This house is haunted / You and I / Whiskey and me / Fever in my blood / Frenzy / Shooting Jones / Jezebel / Tonight we ride / Johnny Guitar / Chase the wild wind / Swamp thing.

DAMN YANKEES (see under ⇒ NUGENT, Ted)

Dave DAVIES (see under ⇒ KINKS)

Spencer DAVIS GROUP

Formed: Birmingham, England . . . August 1963, when DAVIS met YORK and the WINWOOD brothers at local jazz clubs. After a year on the circuit they signed to 'Fontana' records, helped by owner of 'Island' label CHRIS BLACKWELL who had recommended act. They soon became one of the top hitmakers of 1966, although the following year the young WINWOOD joined TRAFFIC. SPENCER DAVIS soldiered on but original momentum was lost. • **Style:** Basic 'R&B' outfit, with STEVE's vox heavily influenced by 'Motown' sound. After his departure, they unsuccessfully turned to psychedelia 1967. • **Songwriters:** Most surprisingly written by 16-17 year old STEVE. They also covered DIMPLES (John Lee Hooker) / EVERY LITTLE BIT HURTS (Brenda Holloway) / KEEP ON RUNNING (Jackie Edwards) / etc. • **Trivia:** Late 1967, they made small cameo appearance as the group in the film 'HERE WE GO ROUND THE MULBURRY BUSH'.

Recommended: THE BEST OF THE SPENCER DAVIS GROUP (*7)

SPENCER DAVIS (b.17 Jul'42, Swansea, Wales) – guitar (ex-SAINTS) / **STEVE WINWOOD** (b.12 May'48, Birmingham) – vocals, keyboards, guitar / **MUFF WINWOOD** (b.Mervyn, 14 Jun'43, Birmingham) – bass, vocals / **PETER YORK** (b.15 Aug'42, Redcar, Cleveland, England) – drums

Fontana / Fontana

Aug 64. (7") **DIMPLES. / SITTIN' AND THINKIN'** [ ] [-]
Oct 64. (7") **I CAN'T STAND IT. / MIDNIGHT TRAIN** [47] [ ] Mar 65
Jan 65. (7") **EVERY LITTLE BIT HURTS. / IT HURTS ME SO** [41] [-]
May 65. (7") **STRONG LOVE. / THIS HAMMER** [44] [-]
Jul 65. (lp) **FIRST ALBUM** (hit-Jan66) [6] [-]
– My babe / Dimples / Searchin' / Every little bit hurts / I'm blue (gong gong song) / Sittin' and thinkin' / I can't stand it / Here right now / Jump back / It's gonna work out fine / Midnight train / It hurts me so. *(re-iss.1980's on 'Wing')*

Fontana / United A..

Nov 65. (7") **KEEP ON RUNNING. / HIGH TIME BABY** [1] [76]
Jan 66. (lp) **SECOND ALBUM** [2] [-]
– Look away / Keep on running / This hammer / Georgia on my mind / Please do something / Let me down easy / Strong love / I washed my hands in muddy water / Since I met you baby / You must believe me / Hey darling / Watch your step.
Mar 66. (7") **SOMEBODY HELP ME. / STEVIE'S BLUES** [1] [47] Jun 67
Aug 66. (7") **WHEN I GET HOME. / TRAMPOLINE** [12] [ ]
Sep 66. (lp) **AUTUMN '66** [4] [-]
– Together till the end of time / Take this hurt off me / Nobody knows you when you're down and out / Midnight special / When a man loves a woman / When I come home / Mean woman blues / Dust my blues / On the green light / Neighbour, neighbour / High time baby / Somebody help me.
Oct 66. (7") **GIMME SOME LOVIN'. / BLUES IN F** [2] [7] Jan 67

—— (above 'A'side was different remix in the States)

Jan 67. (7") **I'M A MAN. / CAN'T GET ENOUGH OF IT** [9] [10] Mar 67
Mar 67. (lp) **GIMME SOME LOVIN'** [-] [54]
– Keep on running / When a man loves a woman / Take this hurt off me / Georgia on my mind / You must believe me / Here right now / When I get home / I'm a man. *(UK-iss 1988 on 'Capitol')*

—— **EDDIE HARDIN** (b.EDWARD HARDING, 19 Feb'49) – organ, vocals replaced STEVE who joined TRAFFIC and later BLIND FAITH then solo. / **PHIL SAWYER** (b.8 Mar'47) – lead guitar replaced MUFF who became A&R man, / also **CHARLIE McCRACKEN** – bass (guest).

Jul 67. (lp) **I'M A MAN** [-] [83]
– Dimples / Every little bit hurts / Stevie's blues / On the green light / Searchin' / Midnight train / My babe / Georgia on my mind / I can't get enough of it / I'm a man / I can't stand it / Look away.
Jul 67. (7") **TIME SELLER. / DON'T WANT YOU NO MORE** [30] [100]

United Art / United Art

Dec 67. (7") **MR. SECOND CLASS. / SANITY INSPECTOR** [35] [ ]
Mar 68. (7") **AFTER TEA. / MOONSHINE** [ ] [ ]
1968. (lp) **WITH THEIR NEW FACE ON** [-] [ ]
– With his new face on / Mr.Second class / Alec in transitland / Sanity inspector / Feel your way / Morning sun / Moonshine / Don't want you no more / Time seller / Stop me, I'm fallin'.
1968. (7") **SHORT CHANGE. / PICTURE OF HEAVEN** [-] [ ]

—— (Nov68) **DEE MURRAY** – bass / **NIGEL OLSSON** – drums repl. HARDIN & YORK who formed self named duo.

1969. (lp) **HEAVIES** [-] [ ]
– Please do something / Waltz for lum umba / I'm blue (gong gong song) / Hey darling / Mean woman blues / Watch your step / Drown in my own tears / Together til' the end of time / Take this hurt off me / Back into my life again.

—— Split mid '69. MURRAY and OLSSON joined ELTON JOHN's Band.

SPENCER DAVIS & PETER JAMESON

United Art / United Art

1970. (lp) **IT'S BEEN SO LONG** [ ] [ ]
– It's been so long / Crystal river / One hundred years ago / Balkan blues / Brother can you make up your mind / Mountain lick / Jav's tune / King of her / It's too late now.

SPENCER DAVIS

1972. (lp) **MOUSETRAP** [ ] [ ]
– Rainy season / Listen to the rhythm / What can I be / Tried / Easy rider / Tumbledown tenement row / Sunday walk in the rain / I washed my hands in muddy water / Sailor's lament / Hollywood Joe / In the hills of Tennessee / Ella speed.
1972. (7") **LISTEN TO THE RHYTHM. / SUNDAY WALK IN THE RAIN** [-] [ ]

1972. (7") **RAINY SEASON. / TUMBLEDOWN TENEMENT ROW** [-] [ ]

— now re-united w / **HARDIN, YORK, FENWICK + CHARLIE McCRACKEN** – bass

Vertigo Mercury

1972. (7") **CATCH YOU ON THE REBOB. / THE EDGE** [ ] [ ]
1973. (lp) **GLUGGO** [ ] [ ]
– Catch you on the Moon / Don't it let it bring you down / Alone / Today Gluggo, tomorrow the world / Feeling rude / Legal eagle shuffle / Trouble in mind / Mr.Operator / Tumbledown tenement row.
1973. (7") **MR OPERATOR / TOUCHING CLOTH** [ ] [ ]
Oct 73. (7") **LIVING IN A BACKSTREET. / SURE NEED A HELPING HAND** [ ] [ ]
1974. (lp) **LIVING IN A BACKSTREET** [ ] [ ]
– Living in a backstreet / One night / Hanging around / No reason / Fasted thing / On four wheels / Backstreet boys / Another day / Sure need a helping hand / We can give it a try / Let's have a party.

— SPENCER retired from solo work until 1983.

Allegience not issued

May 84. (7") **PRIVATE NUMBER. (by "SPENCER DAVIS & DUSTY SPRINGFIELD") / DON'T WANT YOU NO MORE** [ ] [-]
Apr 84. (lp)(c) **CROSSFIRE** [ ] [-]
– Blood runs hot / Don't want you no more / Love is on a roll / Crossfire / Private number / Just a gigolo / Careless love / A pretty girl is like a melody / When the day is done / Hush-a-bye.

SPENCER became an executive at Island records in the mid 70's. In 1990 **SPENCER DAVIS GROUP** reformed with others **DON KIRKPATRICK, EDDIE TREE** – guitars / **RICK SERATTE** – keys / **CHARLIE HARRISON** – bass / **BRYAN HITT** – drums (ex-WANG CHUNG).

- compilations, others, etc. -

1964. Fontana; (7"ep) **YOU PUT THE HURT ON ME** [ ] [-]
1965. Fontana; (7"ep) **EVERY LITTLE BIT HURTS** [ ] [-]
1966. Fontana; (7"ep) **SITTIN' AND THINKIN'** [ ] [-]
Mar 68. United Artists; (lp) **SPENCER DAVIS' GREATEST HITS** [-] [ ]
1969. Philips; (c-ep) **THE HITS OF THE SPENCER DAVIS GROUP** [ ] [-]
1972. Island; (lp)(c) **THE BEST OF THE SPENCER DAVIS GROUP** [ ] [-]
(re-iss.Oct 86)
Aug 76. Island; (7") **GIMME SOME LOVIN'. / WHEN I GET HOME** [ ] [-]
May 78. Island; (7"ep) **KEEP ON RUNNING** [ ] [-]
– Gimme some lovin' / Somebody help me / Every little bit hurts / I'm a man.
May 91. Island; (7")(c-s) **KEEP ON RUNNING. / HIGH TIME BABY** [ ] [ ]
(12"+=)(cd-s+=) – Somebody help me / This hammer.
1984. Inak; (cd) **LIVE TOGETHER** [ ] [-]
1985. Inak; (cd) **24 HOURS – LIVE IN GERMANY** [ ] [-]
May 93. Royal Collection; (cd)(c) **KEEP ON RUNNING** [ ] [-]
Jun 94. R.P.M.; (cd) **TAKING OUT TIME 1967-69** [ ] [-]
Oct 94. Charly; (cd) **KEEP ON RUNNING** [ ] [-]
Jun 95. RPM; (cd) **CATCH YOU ON THE REBOP – LIVE IN EUROPE 1973** [ ] [-]

John DEACON (see under ⇒ QUEEN)

DEACON BLUE

Formed: Glasgow, Scotland … 1985, by former remedial teacher RICKY ROSS who finds four other guys, who soon took name from a STEELY DAN song. By sheer accident/inspiration ROSS invited girlfriend LORRAINE to sing/accompany his vocals, and she soon became sixth member. By this time they had already been signed to 'CBS' by their manager MUFF WINWOOD (ex-SPENCER DAVIS GROUP). Their first division breakthrough came in 1989, when that year's album hit No.1. • **Style:** Classy rock-pop, slightly similar to early PREFAB SPROUT. • **Songwriters:** All written by ROSS, except covers ANGELIOU (Van Morrison) / TRAMPOLENE (Julian Cope) / I'M DOWN (Beatles) / I'LL NEVER FALL IN LOVE AGAIN and the 3 others on 1990 EP (Bacharach & David). • **Trivia:** Their re-issue of WHEN WILL YOU (MAKE MY TELEPHONE RING) featured future LONDON BEAT group.

Recommended: OUR TOWN (*9)

RICKY ROSS (b.22 Dec'57, Dundee) – vocals / **JAMES PRIME** (b. 3 Nov'60, Kilmarnock) – keyboards (ex-ALTERED IMAGES) / **GRAEME KELLING** (b. 4 Apr'57, Paisley) – guitar / **EWAN VERNAL** (b.27 Feb'64, Glasgow) – bass, keyboard bass / **DOUGLAS VIPOND** (b.15 Oct'66, Johnstone) – drums, percussion / **LORRAINE McINTOSH** (b.13 May'64, Glasgow) – vocals

C.B.S. Columbia

Mar 87. (7") **DIGNITY. / RICHES** [ ] [ ]
(12"+=) – Ribbons and bow.
(c-s+=) – (edit, excerpts 'RAINTOWN' lp)
Jun 87. (7")(c-s) **LOADED. / LONG DISTANCE FROM ACROSS THE ROAD** [ ] [ ]
(12"+=) – Which side of the world are you on / Kings of the western world.
Aug 87. (7") **WHEN WILL YOU (MAKE MY TELEPHONE RING). / CHURCH** [ ] [ ]
(12") – ('A'side) / A town to be blamed (live) (US B-side) / Angeliou (live).
Jan 88. (7") **DIGNITY. / SUFFERING** [31] [ ]
(10"+=) – Shifting sands.
(cd-s++=) – Just like boys.
(7"ep+=) – Ronnie Spector / Raintown (piano).
(12"+=) – Ronnie Spector / Just like boys.
Feb 88. (lp)(c)(cd) **RAINTOWN** [14] [ ]
– Born in a storm / Raintown / Ragman / He looks like Spencer Tracy now / Loaded / When will you (make my telephone ring) / Chocolate girl / Dignity / The very thing / Love's great fears / Town to be blamed. *(re-packaged Aug88 free with above lp+c)* RICHES – Which side are you on / King of the western world * / Riches * / Angeliou / Just like boys / Raintown / Church / Suffering / Shifting sand / Ribbons and bows / Dignity. *(cd+= *)*
Mar 88. (7") **WHEN WILL YOU (MAKE MY TELEPHONE RING). / THAT BRILLIANT FEELING** [34] [ ]
(12"+=)(cd-s+=)(pic-cd-s+=) – Punch and Judy man / Disneyworld.
Jul 88. (7") **CHOCOLATE GIRL. / S.H.A.R.O.N.** [43] [ ]
(7"ep+=)(cd-ep+=) – The very thing / Love's great fears.
(12"+=) – Loves great fears (live) / Dignity (live).
Oct 88. (7") **REAL GONE KID. / LITTLE LINCOLN** [8] [ ]
(7"ep+=)(cd-ep+=) – Born again / It's not funny.
(12"+=) – ('A'extended).
Feb 89. (7") **WAGES DAY. / TAKE ME TO THE PLACE** [18] [ ]
(7"ep+=)(cd-ep+=) – Take the saints away / Trampolene.
(12"+=) – ('A'extended).
Apr 89. (lp)(c)(cd) **WHEN THE WORLD KNOWS YOUR NAME** [1] [ ]
– Queen of the New Year / Wages day / Real gone kid / Love and regret / Circus lights / This changing light / Fergus sings the blues / Sad loved girl / The world is hit by lightning / Silhouette / One hundred things / Your constant heart / Orphans.
May 89. (7") **FERGUS SINGS THE BLUES. / LONG WINDOW TO LOVE** [14] [ ]
(12"+=) – ('A'extended).
(7"ep+=)(c-ep+=) – London A-Z.
(10"++=)(cd-ep++=) – Back here in Beano land.
Sep 89. (7")(c-s) **LOVE AND REGRET. / DOWN IN THE FLOOD** [28] [ ]
(12"+=) – Undeveloped heart.
(10")(cd-s) – ('A'side) / Spanish moon – Down in the flood (live) / Dark end of the street (live) / When will you make my telephone ring (live).
Dec 89. (7") **QUEEN OF THE NEW YEAR. / MY AMERICA** [21] [ ]
(12"+=) – Circus light (acoustic).
(7"ep+=)(c-ep+=)(cd-ep+=) – Sad loved girl (extended) / Las Vegas.
(7"ltd.) – ('A'side) / Chocolate girl.
(12")(c-s) – (above 2) / Undeveloped heart / A town to be blamed.
Aug 90. (7"ep)(12"ep)(cd-ep) **FOUR BACHARACH AND DAVID SONGS** [2] [ ]
– I'll never fall in love again / The look of love / Message to Michael / Are you there (with another girl).

Columbia Columbia

Sep 90. (d-cd)(c)(d-lp) **OOH LAS VEGAS** ('B'sides, sessions) [3] [ ]
– Disneyworld / Ronnie Spector / My America / S.H.A.R.O.N. / Undeveloped heart / Souvenirs / Born again / Down in the flood / Back here in Beanoland / Love you say / Let your hearts be troubled/ / Gentle teardrops / Little Lincoln / That country / Is it cold beneath the hill? / Circus lights / Trampolene / Las Vegas / Killing the blues / Long window to love / Christine / Take me to the place / Don't let the teardrops start.
May 91. (7")(c-s) **YOUR SWAYING ARMS. / FOURTEEN YEARS** [23] [ ]
(cd-s+=) – Faifley.
(12"++=) – ('A'extended).
(10") – ('A'-12"alternative mix) / ('A'-Drumapella mix) / ('A'-7"mix) / ('A'-dub mix).
May 91. (cd)(c)(lp) **FELLOW HOODLUMS** [2] [ ]
– James Joyce soles / Fellow hoodlums / Your swaying arms / Cover from the sky / The day that Jackie jumped the jail / The wildness / A brighter star than you will shine / Twist and shout / Closing time / Goodnight Jamsie / I will see you tomorrow / One day I'll go walking.
Jul 91. (7")(c-s) **TWIST & SHOUT. / GOOD** [10] [ ]
(12"+=) – ('A'extended) / I'm down.
(cd-s+=) – Golden bells.
Sep 91. (7")(c-s) **CLOSING TIME. / I WAS LIKE THAT** [42] [ ]
(cd-s+=) – Into the good night.
(12"++=) – Friends of Billy the bear.

Dec 91. (7")(c-s) **COVER FROM THE SKY. / WHAT DO YOU WANT THE GIRL TO DO / CHRISTMAS (BABY PLEASE COME HOME)** 31
(12"+=) – Real gone kid / Loaded / One hundred things.
(cd-s+=) – Wild mountain thyme / Silhouette / I'll never fall in love again.

Sony-Columbia Sony-Columbia

Nov 92. (7")(c-s) **YOUR TOWN. / ALMOST BEAUTIFUL** 14
(cd-s+=) – I've been making such a fool.
(12") – ('A'perfecto mix) / ('A'extended)

Feb 93. (7")(c-s) **WILL WE BE LOVERS. / SLEEPER** 31
(cd-s+=) – Paint it red.
(12") – ('A'side) / (4 other 'A' mixes)

Mar 93. (cd)(c)(lp) **WHATEVER YOU SAY, SAY NOTHING** 4
– Your town / Only tender love / Peace and jobs and freedom / Hang your head / Bethlehem's gate / Last night I Dreamed of Henry Thomas / Will we be lovers / Fall so freely down / Cut lip / All over the world.

Apr 93. (7")(c-s) **ONLY TENDER LOVE. / RICHES** 22
(cd-s+=) – Which side are you on? / Shifting sand.
(12") – ('A'side) / Pimp talking / Cracks you up.
(cd-s) – (above 3) / Your town (perfecto mix).

Jul 93. (c-ep)(cd-ep) **HANG YOUR HEAD EP** 21
– Hang your head – freedom train (live) / Here on the wind / Indigo sky.
(cd-ep) – (1st track) / Ribbons & bows / Just like boys / Church.

Mar 94. (7")(c-s) **I WAS RIGHT AND YOU WERE WRONG. / MEXICAN RAIN** 32
(cd-s+=) – Goin' back / Wages day.
(cd-s) – ('A'extended) / Kings of the western world / Suffering / Raintown (piano version).

Apr 94. (cd)(c)(d-lp) **OUR TOWN – THE GREATEST HITS** (compilation) 1
– Dignity / Wages day / Real gone kid / Your swaying arms / Fergus sings the blues / I was right and you were wrong / Chocolate girl / I'll never fall in love again / When will you (make my telephone ring) / Twist and shout / Your town / Queen of the New Year / Only tender love / Cover from the sky / Love and regrets / Will we be lovers / Loaded / Bound to love / Still in the mood. (d-lp+=) – Beautiful stranger.

May 94. (7")(c-s) **DIGNITY. / BEAUTIFUL STRANGER** 20
(cd-s+=) – Waves of sorrow / Bethlehem's gate.
(cd-s) – ('A'side) / Fergus sings the blues (live) / Loaded (live) / Chocolate girl (live).

— Disbanded after above release, as it looks certain ROSS will go solo. VIPOND has already secured a regular spot on a Scottish TV programme.

. . . Jan – Jun '96 stop press . . .

RICKY ROSS

Columbia Sony

May 96. (single) **RADIO ON** 35
Jun 96. (cd)(c) **WHAT YOU ARE** 36

DEAD CAN DANCE

*** NEW ENTRY ***

Formed: Sydney or Melbourne, Australia . . .1982 by BRENDAN PERRY and LISA GERRARD. After one homeland lp (very ltd), they came to London and signed to up and coming indie '4ad'. Their eponymous debut in 1984, was critically acclaimed and soon soared to the higher regions of the indie charts in Britain. They selected a few venues for gigs with 15-piece ensemble, but never toured consistantly. After several albums, they secured a Top 50 spot in 1993 with 'INTO THE LABYRINTH'. LISA then released a few solo outings, one as a pseudonym. • **Style:** Deep alternative and at times ambient group with Eastern OFRA HAZA, COCTEAU TWINS singing with JOY DIVISION like backing. • **Songwriters:** GERRARD / PERRY (some w/ others & some trad samples). • **Trivia:** Engineered by JOHN A. RIVERS. They also can be heard on 4ad amalgam THIS MORTAL COIL and featured on various lp 'LONELY AS AN EYESORE'.

Recommended: DEAD CAN DANCE (*8) / SPLEEN AND IDEAL (*7) / WITHIN THE REALM OF A DYING SUN (*8) / THE SERPENT'S EGG (*8) / AION (*7) / A PASSAGE IN TIME (compilation *8) / INTO THE LABYRINTH (*8) / TOWARD THE WITHIN (*7) / SPIRITCHASER (*8)

BRENDAN PERRY – multi-instrumentalist, vocals / **LISA GERRARD** – vocals, percussion / **PETER ULRICH** – percussion, drums, tapes with **JAMES PINKER** – timpani, mixer / **SIMON RODGER** -trombone plus **MARTIN McCARRICK + GUY FERGUSON** – cello / **CAROLYN LOSTIN** – violin / **RICHARD AVISON** – trombone / **TONY ATERS** -timpani / **ANDREW NUTTER** – soprano vox

4 a.d. RoughTrade

Feb 84. (lp) **DEAD CAN DANCE** -
– A passage in time / Threshold / The trial / Frontier / Ocean / Fortune / East of Eden / The fatal impact / Wild in the woods / Musical eternal.
(cd-iss.Feb87, includes below EP)

Sep 84. (12"ep) **THE GARDEN OF ARCANE DELIGHTS** -
– Carnival of light / The arcane / Flowers of the sea / In power we entrust the love advocated.

Nov 85. (lp)(c)(cd) **SPLEEN AND IDEAL** -
– De profounds (out of the depths of sorrow) / Ascension / Circumradiant dawn / The cardinal sin / Mesmerism / Enigma of the absolute / Advent / Avatar / Indoctrination. (cd+=) – This tide / A design for living.

— now a basic duo of **BRENDAN + LISA** when ULRICH departed (SIMON + JAMES formed HEAVENLY BODIES). Retained **FERGUSON + AVISON** and recruited **ALISON HARLING + EMLYN SINGLETON** – violin / **PIERO GASPARINI** – viola / **TONY GAMMAGE + MARK GERRARD** (bother) -trumpet / **RUTH WATSON** -oboe, bass trombone / **JOHN + PETER SINGLETON** -trombone / **ANDREW CAXTON** – tuba, bass trombone

Jul 87. (lp)(c)(cd) **WITHIN THE REALM OF A DYING SUN**
– Dawn of the Iconoclaust / In the wake of adversity / New age / Summoning of the muse / Anywhere out of the world / Cantara / Windfall / Xavier / Persephone (the gathering of flowers).

— **LISA + BRENDAN** brought in **DAVID NAVARRO SUST** (retained **ALISON + TONY**), new **REBECCA JACKSON** -violin / **SARAH BUCKLEY + ANDREW BEESLEY** -viola

Oct 88. (lp)(c)(cd) **THE SERPENT'S EGG**
– The host of Seraphim / Orbis de Ignis / Severance / Chant of the Paladin / The writing on my father's hand / Echolalia / In the kingdom of the blind, the one-eyed are kings / Song of Sophia / Mother tongue / Ullysses.

Jul 90. (cd)(c)(lp) **AION**
– The arrival and the reunion / Saltarello / Mephisto / The song of the Sibyl / Fortune presents gifts not according to the book / As the bell rings the maypole spins / The end of the words / Black Sun / Wilderness / The promised womb / The garden of Zephirus / Radharc.

Oct 91. (cd)(c) **A PASSAGE IN TIME** (part compilation)
– Salterello / Song of Sophia / Ullyses / Cantara / The garden of Zephirus / Enigma of the absolute / Wilderness / The host of Seraphim / Anywhere out of the world / The writing on my father's hand / Severance / The song of the Sibyl (traditional version. Catalan 16th Century) / Fortune presents gifts not according to the book / In the kingdom of the blind the one-eyed are kings / Bird / Spirit.

Sep 93. (cd)(c)(d-lp) **INTO THE LABYRINTH** 47
– Yulunga (spirit dance) / The ubiquitous Mr. Lovegrove / The wind that shakes the barley / The carnival is over / Ariadne / Saldek / Towards the within / Tell me about the forest (you once called home) / The spider's Stratagem / Emmeleia / How fortunate the man with none. (d-lp+=) – Bird / Spirit.

Oct 94. (cd)(c)(d-lp) **TOWARD THE WITHIN**
– Rakim / Persian love song / Desert song / Yulunga (spirit dance) / Piece for solo flute / The wind that shakes the barley / I am stretched on your grave / I can see now / American dreaming / Cantara / Oman / Song of the Sibyl / Tristan / Sanveen / Don't fade away.

Jun 96. (cd)(c)(d-lp) **SPIRITCHASER** 43
– Nierika / Song of the stars / Indus / Song of the dispossessed / Dedicaci outr / The snake and the Moon / Song of the Nile / Devorzhum.

compilations, etc.

1991. Emperion; (cd) **THE HIDDEN TREASURES** (out-takes, live, rare) -

DEAD KENNEDYS

Formed: San Francisco, California, USA . . . 1978 by BIAFRA. Formed own label 'Alternative Tenticles', which was initially licensed to 'Fast' then 'Cherry Red' in the UK 1979-81. • **Trivia:** Always the height of controversy, their FRANCHENCHRIST album with free "penis landscape" poster by Swiss artist HR Giger, led to BIAFRA being tried in court for distributing harmful material to minors. The case was dropped, and since then BIAFRA has protested on spoken word albums against his treatment. He was later to stand for mayor of San Francisco, coming 4th!. • **Style:** Raw hard-core politically aware punks, who scathed their attack on US imperialism and power hunger. They were pro-animal rights campaigners, and also anti-nuclear, anti-abortion, etc. • **Songwriters:** All/most written by BIAFRA, except RAWHIDE (Link Wray – hit) / TAKE THIS JOB AND SHOVE IT (Coe) / CESSPOOLS IN EDEN (?). **More trivia:** A 'DEAD KENNEDYS' tribute album by Various Artists was released May'92 on their own label.

Recommended: GIVE ME CONVENIENCE OR GIVE ME DEATH (*7)

JELLO BIAFRA (b.ERIC BOUCHER, Bolder, Colorado) – vocals / **EAST BAY RAY** (VALIUM) – guitar, (synthesisers-later 80's) / **KLAUS FLUORIDE** – bass, vocals / **TED** – drums

		Fast	Alt.Tent.
Oct 79.	(7") **CALIFORNIA UBER ALLES. / MAN WITH THE DOGS**		

		Cherry Red	Alt.Tent.
Jun 80.	(7")(12") **HOLIDAY IN CAMBODIA. / POLICE TRUCK** (also on I.R.S. in US) *(re-iss.Sep81) (re-iss.7"/cd-s Jun88 & Mar95)*		
Sep 80.	(lp)(c) **FRESH FRUIT FOR ROTTING VEGETABLES** – Kill the poor / Forward to death / When ya get drafted / Let's lynch the landlord / Drug me / Your emotions / Chemical warfare / Calilfornia uber alles / I kill children / Stealing people's mail / Funland at the beach / Ill in my head / Holiday in Cambodia / Viva Las Vegas. *(re-iss.'82) (cd-iss.Mar95)*	33	
Oct 80.	(7")(12") **KILL THE POOR. / IN SIGHT** *(re-iss.7"/cd-s Mar95)*	49	
May 81.	(7")(12") **TOO DRUNK TO F***. / THE PREY** *(re-iss.7"/cd-s.May88 & Mar95)*	36	

— **BRUCE SLEZINGER** – drums repl. TED

		Alt.Tent.	Alt.Tent.
Dec 81.	(10"ep) **IN GOD WE TRUST INC.** – Religious vomit / Moral majority / Kepone factory / Dog bite / Nazi punks f*** off / We've got a bigger problem now / Rawhide.		
1981.	(7") **NAZI PUNKS F*** OFF. / MORAL MAJORITY**		

— **J.H. PELIGRO** – drums, vocals repl. BRUCE

Jul 82.	(7")(12") **BLEED FOR ME. / LIFE SENTENCE**		
Nov 82.	(lp)(c) **PLASTIC SURGERY DISASTERS** – Government flu / Terminal preppie / Trust your mechanic / Well paid scientist / Buzzbomb / Forest fire / Halloween / Winnebago warrior / Riot / Bleed for me / I am the owl / Dead end / Moon over Marin. *(re-iss.Oct85 on 'Static')* (cd-iss.Nov86 +=) – IN GOD WE TRUST (ep)		
Nov 82.	(7")(12") **HALLOWEEN. / SATURDAY NIGHT HOLOCAUST**		

— meanwhile other projects included

KLAUS FLUORIDE

May 82.	(12") **SHORTNING BREAD. / DROWNING COWBOY**		
Aug 84.	(12"ep) **CHA CHA CHA WITH MR. FLUORIDE** – Ghost riders / etc.		

EAST BAY RAY

Jun 84.	(7") **TROUBLE IN TOWN. / POISON HEART**		

DEAD KENNEDYS

(regrouped, see last line-up)

Dec 85.	(lp)(cd) **FRANKENCHRIST** – Soup is good food / Hellnation / This could be anywhere (this could be every-where) / A growing boy needs his lunch / Chicken farm / Macho-rama (invasion of the beef-patrol) / Goons of Hazzard / At my job / M.T.V. – Get off the air / Stars and stripes of corruption.		
Dec 86.	(lp)(c) **BEDTIME FOR DEMOCRACY** – Take this job and shove it / Hop with the jet set / Dear Abby / Rambozo the clown / Fleshdunce / The great wall / Shrink / Triumph of the swill / I spy / Macho insecurity / Cesspools in Eden / One-way ticket to Pluto / Do the slag / Gone with the wind / A commercial / Anarchy for sale / Chickenshit conformist / Where do ya draw the line / Potshot heard round the world / D.M.S.O. / Lie detector.		

Split Dec86 when RAY departed. KLAUS FLUORIDE went solo (lp) BECAUSE I SAY SO.

- compilations, etc. -

Jun 87.	Alt.Tent.; (lp)(cd) **GIVE ME CONVENIENCE OR GIVE ME DEATH** – Police truck / Too drunk to f*** / California uber alles / Man with the dogs / In sight / Life sentence / A child and his lawnmower / Holiday in Cambodia / Night of the living rednecks / I fought the law / Saturday night holocaust / Pull my strings / Short songs / Straight A's / Kinky sex makes the world go round / The prey / Buzzbomb from Pasadena (free flexi with above)	84	
Feb 92.	Alt.Tent.; (cd-ep's re-iss) **IN GOD WE TRUST / HALLOWEEN / BLEED FOR ME**		
Jun 92.	Alt.Tent.; (cd) **PLASTIC SURGERY DISASTERS / IN GOD WE TRUST**		-
Jun 93.	Subterranean; (7"ep) **NAZI PUNKS **** OFF / ARYANISMS. / ('A'live) / CONTEMPTUOUS**		-

JELLO BIAFRA

(solo)(first 2 albums were spoken word)

		Alt.Tent.	Alt.Tent.
Nov 87.	(d-lp) **NO MORE COCOONS** *(re-iss.cd Mar93)*		
1988.	(lp) **HIGH PRIEST OF HARMFUL MATTER (TALES OF THE TRIALS, LIVE)** *(re-iss.cd Mar93)*		

LARD

BIAFRA, AL JOURGENSEN + PAUL BARKER (Ministry) / **JEFF WARD** – drums

		Alt.Tent.	Alt.Tent.
1989.	(12"ep)(c-ep)(cd-ep) **THE POWER OF LARD / HELL FUDGE. / TIME TO MELT (31 mins.)**		
Jul 90.	(cd)(lp) **THE LAST TEMPTATION OF LARD** – Forkboy / Pineapple face / Hate, spawn and dic / Drug raid at 4a.m. / Can God fill teeth? / Bozo skeleton / Sylvestre Matuschka / They're coming to take me away / I am your clock.	69	

JELLO BIAFRA & D.O.A.

— w/ **JOE KEITHLEY + CHRIS PROHOM** – guitar, vocals / **BRIAN GORLE** – bass, vocals / **JON CARD** – drums

		Alt.Tent.	Alt.Tent.
May 90.	(cd)(lp) **THE LAST SCREAM OF THE MISSING NEIGHBOURS** – That's progress / Attack of the peacekeepers / Wish I was in El Salvador / Power is boring / We gotta get out of this place / Full metal jackoff.		

JELLO BIAFRA & NO MEANS NO

with **TIPPER GORE BOB WRIGHT** – guitar / **JOHN WRIGHT** – drums / **JON CARD** – percussion

		Alt.Tent.	Alt.Tent.
Mar 91.	(cd)(c)(lp) **THE SKY IS FALLING AND I WANT MY MOMMY** – The sky is falling and I want my mommy (falling space junk) / Jesus was a terrorist / Bruce's diary / Sad / Ride the flume / Chew / Sparks in the Gene pool / The myth is real – let's eat.		

JELLO BIAFRA

		Alt.Tent.	Alt.Tent.
Jun 91.	(cd)(c)(d-lp) **BLOW MINDS FOR A LIVING** – Pledge of allegience / Talk on censorship – let us prey / Die for oil, sucker – higher octane version / I was a teenage pacifist / If voting changed anything . . . / Running for mayor / Grow more pot / Lost orgasm / Talk on censorship-Better living through new world orders + Fear of a free planet.		

TUMOR CIRCUS

— **DARREN MOR-X / DALE FLAT-UM + MIKE MDRASKOID** (of STEEL POLE BATH TUB) / **KING GRONG CHARLIE (TOLNAY)** (of LUBRICATED GOAT) + **J.BIAFRA**

		Alt.Tent.	Alt.Tent.
Nov 91.	(cd)(c)(lp) **TUMOR CIRCUS – HIGH VOLTAGE CONSPIRACY FOR RADICAL FREEDOM** – Hazing for success / Human cyst / The man with the corkscrew eyes / Fireball / Calcutta a-go-go / Turn off the respirator. (cd+=) Swine flu / Take me back or I'll drown our dog / Meathook up my rectum.		
Feb 92.	(7") **MEATHOOK UP MY RECTUM. / (etched side)** (12"+=)(cd-s+=) – Take me back or I'll drown the dog / Swine flu / Fireball.		

JELLO BIAFRA & MOJO NIXON

		Alt.Tent.	Alt.Tent.
Nov 93.	(7") **WILL THE FETUS BE ABORTED?. / THE LOST WORLD** (cd-s+=) – Drinkin' with Jesus / Achey raky heart.		
Feb 94.	(cd)(lp) **PRAIRIE HOME INVASION** – Buy my snake oil / Where are we gonna work (when the trees are gone) / Convoy in the sky / Atomic power / Are you drinkin' with me Jesus / Love me, I'm a liberal / Burgers of wrath / Nostalgia for an angel that never existed / Hammer chicken plant disaster / Mascot mania / Let's go burn de Nashville down / Will the fetus be aborted / Plastic Jesus.		

DEATH CULT (see under ⇒ CULT)

DEEP PURPLE

Formed: London, England ... 1968 intially as ROUNDABOUT, by then member CHRIS CURTIS. He recruited JON LORD and RITCHIE BLACKMORE, who was living in Germany at the time. By Spring '68, they had become DEEP PURPLE, soon signing to 'Parlophone UK', and 'Tetragrammation' (US label run by comedian Bill Cosby). HUSH gave them near immediate chart success in the States, but had to wait until summer 1970 with BLACK NIGHT for a home Top-3 hit. From then on, but for a few other hits, albums became their tour de force. • **Style:** DEEP PURPLE Mk.I were initially influenced by VANILLA FUDGE, but by the late 60's and Mk.II moved into a more powerful riff heavy rock. Mk.III saw their sound mellow into bluesy funk rock due to new vox of DAVID COVERDALE. Easily the best line-up (Mk.II) reformed in 1984 but they did nothing to resurrect past glories, although albums did net some cash. • **Songwriters:** Mk.I:-Mostly BLACKMORE / EVANS / LORD. Mk.II:-Group. Mk.III:- BLACKMORE / COVERDALE, adding at times LORD and PAICE. Mk.IV:- Permutation 2 of COVERDALE, BOLIN or HUGHES. Covered HUSH (Joe South) / WE CAN WORK IT OUT + HELP (Beatles) / KENTUCKY WOMAN (Neil Diamond) / RIVER DEEP MOUNTAIN HIGH (Ike & Tina Turner) / HEY JOE (Jimi Hendrix) / I'M SO GLAD (Cream). GILLAN covered; LUCILLE (Little Richard) / LIVING FOR THE CITY (Stevie Wonder) / SOUTH AFRICA (Bernie Marsden). RAINBOW; STILL I'M SAD (Yardbirds). • **Trivia:** In the Guinness Book of Records, according to decibel reading meter, they were recorded as "The Loudest Rock Group In the World". To obtain charity monies for the Armenian earthquake disaster late 1989, BLACKMORE, GILLAN and others (i.e. BRUCE DICKINSON, ROBERT PLANT, BRIAN MAY etc.) contributed to Top 40 new version of SMOKE ON THE WATER.

Recommended: MACHINE HEAD (*7) / MADE IN JAPAN (*8) / DEEPEST PURPLE (*9) / COME HELL OR HIGH WATER (*7). RAINBOW:- THE BEST OF RAINBOW (*6) GILLAN:- THE VERY BEST OF GILLAN (*6)

RITCHIE BLACKMORE (b.14 Apr'45, Weston-Super-Mare, Avon, England) – guitar (ex-MANDRAKE ROOT, ex-OUTLAWS, ex-SCREAMING LORD SUTCH, etc.) / **JON LORD** (b.9 Jun'41, Leicester, England) – keyboards (ex-FLOWERPOT MEN) / **NICK SIMPER** (b. 1946, Southall, London) – bass (ex-JOHNNY KIDD & PIRATES) / **ROD EVANS** (b. 1945, Edinburgh, Scotland) – vocals (ex-MAZE, ex-MI5) / **IAN PAICE** (b.29 Jun'48, Nottingham, England) – drums (ex-MAZE, ex-MI5)

Parlophone Tetragramme

Jun 68. (7") **HUSH. / ONE MORE RAINY DAY** [ ] [4]

Sep 68. (lp) **SHADES OF DEEP PURPLE** [ ] [24]
– And the address / Hush / One more rainy day / (prelude) Happiness – I'm so glad / Mandrake root / Help / Love help me / Hey Joe. *(re-iss.Feb77 on 'EMI Harvest') (cd-iss.Mar89) (cd-iss.Feb95 on 'Fame')*

Nov 68. (7") **KENTUCKY WOMAN. / WRING THAT NECK** [ ] [38]

Jan 69. (7") **RIVER DEEP – MOUNTAIN HIGH. /** [-] [53]

Feb 69. (7") **EMMARETTA. / WRING THAT NECK** [ ] [ ]

Harvest Tetragramme

Jun 69. (lp) **BOOK OF TALIESYN** [ ] [54]
– Listen, learn, read on / Wring that neck / Kentucky woman / Shield / Anthem / Exposition / We can work it out / River deep – mountain high. *(re-iss.Jun85 on 'EMI') (re-iss.+cd Aug89)*

Nov 69. (lp)(c) **DEEP PURPLE** [ ] [ ]
– Chasing shadows / Blind / Lalena: (a) Faultline, (b) The painter / Why didn't Rosemary? / The bird has flown / April. *(re-iss.Jun85 on 'EMI') (re-iss.lp/c/cd.Mar89) (re-iss.cd May95 on 'Fame')*

(In Jun69 below two were used on session for 'HALLELUJAH'. They became regular members after the recording of 'DEEP PURPLE' album.) / **IAN GILLAN** (b.19 Aug'45, Hounslow, London) – vocals (ex-EPISODE SIX) replaced EVANS who joined CAPTAIN BEYOND. / **ROGER GLOVER** (b.30 Nov'45, Brecon, Wales) – bass (ex-EPISODE SIX) replaced SIMPER who later formed WARHORSE.

Harvest Warners

Jul 69. (7") **HALLELUJAH (I AM THE PREACHER). / APRIL (part 1)** [ ] [ ]

Jan 70. (lp) **CONCERTO FOR GROUP AND ORCHESTRA WITH THE ROYAL PHILHARMONIC ORCHESTRA (live)** [26] [ ]
– First Movement: Moderato – Allegro / Second Movement: Andante (part 1) – Andante conclusion / Third Movement: Vivace – Presto. *(cd-iss.Aug 90 +=)* – Wring that neck / Child in time.

Jun 70. (7") **BLACK NIGHT. / SPEED KING** [2] [-]

Jun 70. (lp)(c) **IN ROCK** [4] [ ]
– Speed king / Blood sucker / Child in time / Flight of the rat / Into the fire / Speed king / Living wreck / Hard lovin' man. *(re-iss.May82 on 'Fame', cd-iss.Apr88) (pic-lp.Jun85) (re-iss.cd Jun95)*

Jul 70. (7") **BLACK NIGHT. / INTO THE FIRE** [-] [66]

Feb 71. (7") **STRANGE KIND OF WOMAN. / I'M ALONE** [6] [ ]

Sep 71. (lp)(c) **FIREBALL** [1] [32]
– Fireball / No no no / Demon's eye / Anyone's daughter / The mule / Fools / No one came. *(re-iss.Mar84 on 'Fame') (re-iss.+cd.Jan88 on 'EMI') (pic-lp.Jun85 on 'EMI')*

Oct 71. (7") **FIREBALL. / DEMON'S EYE** [15] [-]

Nov 71. (7") **FIREBALL. / I'M ALONE** [-] [ ]

Purple Warners

Mar 72. (7") **NEVER BEFORE. / WHEN A BLIND MAN CRIES** [35] [ ]

Apr 72. (lp)(c) **MACHINE HEAD** [1] [7]
– Highway star / Maybe I'm a Leo / Pictures of home / Never before / Smoke on the water / Lazy / Space truckin'. *(re-iss.Jun85 on 'EMI') (re-iss.Oct86, cd-iss Mar89 on 'Fame', cd-iss.Mar87 on 'EMI')*

Jun 72. (7") **LAZY. / WHEN A BLIND MAN CRIES** [-] [ ]

Oct 72. (7") **HIGHWAY STAR. / (part 2)** [-] [ ]

Dec 72. (d-lp)(d-c) **MADE IN JAPAN (live)** [16] [6] May 73
– Highway star / Child in time / Smoke on the water / The mule / Strange kind of woman / Lazy / Space truckin'. *(cd-iss.Sep88 on 'EMI')*

Feb 73. (lp)(c) **WHO DO YOU THINK WE ARE!** [4] [15]
– Woman from Tokyo / Mary Long / Super trouper / Smooth dancer / Rat bat blue / Place in line / Our lady. *(re-iss.Jun85, cd-iss.Oct87 on 'EMI')*

Apr 73. (7") **WOMAN FROM TOKYO. / SUPER TROUPER** [-] [60]
(re-iss.Sep73)

May 73. (7") **SMOKE ON THE WATER. / (part 2)** [-] [4]

— **BLACKMORE, LORD** and **PAICE** brought in new members / **DAVID COVERDALE** (b.22 Sep'49, Saltburn-by-the-sea, Cleveland, England) – vocals replaced GILLAN who later formed own band. / **GLENN HUGHES** (b.Penkridge, England) – bass (ex-TRAPEZE) repl. GLOVER who became top producer.

Feb 74. (lp)(c) **BURN** [3] [9]
– Burn / Might just take your life / Lay down stay down / Sail away / You fool no one / What's goin' on here / Mistreated / "A" 200. *(re-iss.Jun85) (cd-Jul89)*

Mar 74. (7") **MIGHT JUST TAKE YOUR LIFE. / CORONARIAS REDIG** [ ] [91]

May 74. (7") **BURN. / CORONARIAS REDIG** [-] [ ]

Nov 74. (lp)(c) **STORMBRINGER** [6] [20]
– Stormbringer / Love don't mean a thing / Holy man / Hold on / Lady double dealer / You can't do it right / High ball shooter / The gypsy / Soldier of fortune. *(re-iss.Jun85) (re-iss.+cd.Oct88 on 'EMI')*

Nov 74. (7") **HIGH BALL SHOOTER. / YOU CAN'T DO IT RIGHT** [-] [ ]

Jan 75. (7") **STORMBRINGER. / LOVE DON'T MEAN A THING** [-] [ ]

— **TOMMY BOLIN** (b.1951, Sioux City, Iowa, USA) – guitar (ex-JAMES GANG, ex-ZEPHYR) repl. BLACKMORE who formed RAINBOW. (see further below)

Oct 75. (lp)(c) **COME TASTE THE BAND** [19] [43]
– Coming home / Lady luck / Gettin' together / The dealer / I need love / Drifter / Love child / This time around – Owed to the 'G' / You keep on moving. *(re-iss.Jun85 on 'EMI') (cd-iss.Jul95 on 'Fame')*

Mar 76. (7") **YOU KEEP ON MOVING. / LOVE CHILD** [ ] [-]

Mar 76. (7") **GETTIN' TIGHTER. / LOVE CHILD** [-] [ ]

Nov 76. (lp)(c) **MADE IN EUROPE (live)** [12] [ ]
– Burn / Mistreated (interpolating 'Rock me baby') / Lady double dealer / You fool no one / Stormbringer / Mistreated. (US album title DEEP PURPLE LIVE)

— They split Spring 76. TOMMY BOLIN went solo. He died (of an overdose) 4 Dec 76. HUGHES reformed TRAPEZE. COVERDALE formed WHITESNAKE, he was later joined by LORD and PAICE, after they had been in PAICE, ASHTON and LORD. Remarkably **DEEP PURPLE** reformed 8 years later with early 70's line-up. **GILLAN, BLACKMORE, LORD, PAICE** and **GLOVER.**

Polydor Mercury

Nov 84. (lp)(c)(cd)(pic-lp) **PERFECT STRANGERS** [5] [17]
– Knocking at your back door / Under the gun / Nobody's home / Mean streak / Perfect strangers / A gypsy's kiss / Wasted sunsets / Hungry days. *(cd+=)* – Not responsible.

Jan 85. (7")(7"pic-d) **PERFECT STRANGERS (edit). / A GYPSY'S KISS** [48] [ ] Mar 85
(12"+=) – Wasted sunsets / Hungry daze.

Jun 85. (7")(12") **KNOCKING AT YOUR BACK DOOR. / PERFECT STRANGERS** [68] [61] Jan 85

Jan 87. (lp)(c)(cd) **THE HOUSE OF BLUE LIGHT** [10] [34]
– Bad attitude / The unwritten law / Call of the wild / Mad dog / Black and white / Hard lovin' woman / The Spanish archer / Strangeways / Mitzi Dupree / Dead or alive.

Jan 87. (7")(12") **CALL OF THE WILD. / STRANGEWAYS** [ ] [ ]
(12")(12"pic-d) – ('A'side) / ('B' long version).

Jun 88. (7") **HUSH (live). / DEAD OR ALIVE** [62] [ ]
(12"+=)(cd-s+=) – Bad attitude.

Jun 88. (d-lp)(c)(cd) **NOBODY'S PERFECT (live)** [38] [ ]
– Highway star / Strange kind of woman / Perfect strangers / Hard lovin' woman / Bad attitude / Knocking on your back door / Child in time / Lazy / Space truckin' / Black night / Woman from Tokyo / Smoke on the water / Hush. *(re-iss.Mar91 all formats on 'EMI')*

— **JOE LYNN TURNER** – vocals (ex-RAINBOW, ex-YNGWIE J.MALMSTEEN'S RISING FORCE) repl. GILLAN who continued solo.

R.C.A. Giant-Reprise

Oct 90. (7") **KING OF DREAMS. / FIRE IN THE BASEMENT** [70] [ ]
(12"+=)(cd-s+=) – ('A'version).

Nov 90. (cd)(c)(lp) **SLAVES AND MASTERS** [45] [87]
– King of dreams / The cut runs deep / Fire in the basement / Truth hurts / Breakfast in bed / Love conquers all / Fortune teller / Too much is not enough / Wicked ways. *(re-iss.cd Apr94)*

Feb 91. (7")(c-s) **LOVE CONQUERS ALL. / TRUTH HURTS** [57] [ ]
(12"+=)(cd-s+=) – Slow down sister.

— early 70s line-up again after TURNER was sacked.

Jul 93. (cd)(c)(lp) **THE BATTLE RAGES ON** [21] [ ]
– The battle rages on / Lick it up / Anya / Talk about love / Time to kill / Ramshackle man / A twist in the tale / Nasty piece of work / Solitaire / One man's meat. *(re-iss.cd Oct95)*

Nov 94. (cd)(c)(d-lp) **COME HELL OR HIGH WATER (live mid-93)** [ ] [ ]
– Highway star / Black night / Twist in the tail / Perfect strangers / Anyone's daughter / Child in time / Anya / Speed king / Smoke on the water.

— **STEVE MORSE** – guitar (ex-DIXIE DREGGS) repl. JOE SATRIANI who repl. BLACKMORE on European tour late '93-mid '94

. . . Jan – Jun '96 stop press . . .

Feb 96. (cd)(c) **PURPENDICULAR** [58] [ ]

– compilations, exploitation releases, etc. –

Note; All releases on 'Purple' issued on 'Warners' US.
Sep 72. Warners; (lp) **PURPLE PASSAGES** [-] [57]
Oct 72. Warners; (7") **HUSH. / KENTUCKY WOMAN** [-] [ ]
Jun 75. Purple; (lp)(c) **24 CARAT PURPLE (1970-73)** [14] [ ]
– Woman from Tokyo / Fireball / Strange kind of woman / Never before / Black night / Speed king / Smoke on the water / Child in time. *(re-iss.Sep85, cd-iss.Oct87 on 'Fame')*
Mar 77. Purple; (7"m) **SMOKE ON THE WATER. / CHILD IN TIME / WOMAN FROM TOKYO** [21] [ ]
Sep 77. Purple; (7"ep) **NEW LIVE & RARE** [31] [ ]
– Black night (live) / Painted horse / When a blind man cries.
Jan 78. Purple; (lp)(c) **POWERHOUSE** (early 70's line-up) [ ] [ ]
(re-iss.Jun85)
Sep 78. Purple; (7"ep) **NEW LIVE & RARE VOL.2** [45] [ ]
– Burn (edit) / Coronarias redig / Mistreated (live).
Apr 79. Purple; (lp)(c) **THE MARK II PURPLE SINGLES** [24] [ ]
(singles 'A' & 'B's – 1970-1973)
(re-iss.+cd.Nov88 on 'Fame')
Jan 93. Harvest; (cd) **SINGLES A'S AND B'S** [ ] [-]
Note; All releases on 'Harvest' issued on 'Warners' in US.
Apr 79. Harvest; (7")(12") **BLACK NIGHT. / STRANGE KIND OF WOMAN** [ ] [ ]
Jul 80. Harvest; (lp)(c) **DEEPEST PURPLE** [1] [ ]
– Black night / Speed king / Fireball / Strange kind of woman / Child in time / Woman from Tokyo / Highway star / Space truckin' / Burn / Demon's eye / Stormbringer / Smoke on the water.
(cd-iss.Aug84, re-iss.all formats 1989 on 'EMI')
Jul 80. Harvest; (7") **BLACK NIGHT. / SPEED KING (live)** [43] [ ]
Oct 80. Harvest; (7"ep) **NEW LIVE & RARE VOL.3** [48] [ ]
– Smoke on the water (live) / The bird has flown / Grabsplatter.
Dec 80. Harvest; (lp)(c) **IN CONCERT 1970-1972 (live)** [30] [ ]
– Speed king / Child in time / Wring that neck / Mandrake root / Highway star / Strange kind of woman / Maybe I'm a Leo / Never before / Lazy / Space truckin' / Smoke on the water / Lucille.
Aug 82. Harvest; (lp)(c) **DEEP PURPLE LIVE IN LONDON (live '74)** [23] [ ]
– Burn / Might just take your life / Lay down, stay down / Mistreated / Smoke on the water / You fool no one / The mule.
Jun 85. Harvest; (d-lp)(d-c) **THE ANTHOLOGY** [50] [ ]
(cd-iss.1990+=) – (3 extra tracks).
May 92. Harvest; (d-cd) **IN CONCERT 1970-72 (live)** [ ] [-]
Nov 87. Telstar; (lp)(c)(cd) **THE BEST OF DEEP PURPLE** [ ] [-]
(cd+=) – (1 extra track).
1989. Connoisseur; (d-lp)(c)(d-cd) **SCANDINAVIAN NIGHTS (live)** [ ] [-]
Aug 91. Connoisseur; (d-cd)(d-c)(d-lp) **KNEBWORTH '85 (live)** [ ] [-]
Jul 93. Connoisseur; (cd) **THE DEEP PURPLE FAMILY ALBUM** [ ] [-]
(associated releases)
Mar 91. E.M.I.; (d-cd)(d-c)(t-lp) **ANTHOLOGY** [ ] [ ]
Sep 91. E.M.I.; (cd)(c)(lp) **PURPLE RAINBOWS** [ ] [-]
– (all work including RAINBOW, GILLAN, WHITESNAKE, etc.)
Nov 93. E.M.I.; (3xcd-box) **LIVE IN JAPAN (live)** [ ] [-]
Apr 92. Polygram; (cd) **KNOCKING AT YOUR BACK DOOR** [ ] [-]
May 93. Spectrum; (cd)(c) **PROGRESSION** [ ] [-]
Jun 95. EMI; (12")(cd-s) **BLACK NIGHT (remix). / SPEED KING (remix)** [66] [-]
Sep 95. Spectrum; (cd) **CHILD IN TIME** [ ] [-]
Nov 95. EMI; (3xcd-box) **BOOK OF TALIESYN / SHADES OF DEEP URPLE / DEEP PURPLE IN CONCERT** [ ] [-]

JON LORD

solo (first 3 albums while still a **DEEP PURPLE** member) with the **LONDON SYMPHONY ORCHESTRA** and guests.

Purple / Warners
Apr 72. (lp)(c) **GEMINI SUITE** [ ] [ ]
– Guitar / Piano / Drums / Vocals / Bass guitar / Organ. *(re-iss.Nov84 on 'Safari')*

— now with the MUNICH CHAMBER OPERA ORCHESTRA and guests.

Apr 74. (lp)(c) **WINDOWS** [ ] [ ]
– Continuo on B.A.C.H. / Windows: Renga – Gemini – Alla Marcia – Allegro.

TONY ASHTON & JON LORD

ASHTON – keyboards,vocals (ex-ASHTON GARDNER and DYKE, ex-FAMILY, ex-REMO FOUR, ex-CHRIS FARLOWE)
Apr 74. (lp)(c) **FIRST OF THE BIG BANDS** [ ] [ ]
– We're gonna make it / I've been lonely / Silly boy / The jam / Downside upside down / Shut up / Ballad of Mr.Giver / Celebration / The resurrection shuffle. *(cd-iss.Jun93 on Windsong)*
1974. (7") **WE'RE GONNA MAKE IT. / BAND OF THE SALVATION ARMY BAND** [ ] [-]

JON LORD

solo again, plus guests.
Sep 76. (7") **BOUREE. / ARIA** [ ] [ ]
Nov 76. (lp)(c) **SARABANDE (live)** [ ] [ ]
– Fantasia / Sarabande / Aria / Gigue / Bouree / Pavane / Caprice / Finale. *(cd-iss.1989 on 'Line')*

PAICE, ASHTON and LORD

formed Aug76 and recruited **BERNIE MARSDEN** – guitar (ex-BABE RUTH) / **PAUL MARTINEZ** – bass (ex-STRETCH)

Oyster / Oyster
Feb 77. (lp)(c) **MALICE IN WONDERLAND** [ ] [ ]
– Ghost story / Remember the good times / Arabella / Silas and Jerome / Dance with me baby / On the road again / Sneaky rivate Lee / I'm gonna stop drinking / Malice in Wonderland. *(cd-iss.Jul95 on 'Repertoire')*

— When this bunch split up MARTINEZ joined JOHN OTWAY and more sessions. ASHTON became noted producer. MARSDEN was followed by LORD and then PAICE into WHITESNAKE.

JON LORD

and more solo work. (with **MARSDEN, PAICE, NEIL MUNRO, COZY POWELL** and **BAD COMPANY** most of group.

Harvest / Harvest
May 82. (7") **BACH INTO THIS. / GOING HOME** [ ] [ ]
Jul 82. (lp) **BEFORE I FORGET** [ ] [ ]
– Chance on a feeling / Tender babes / Hollywood rock and roll / Bach onto this / Before I forget / Say it's alright / Burntwood / Where are you. *(cd-iss.Mar93 on 'R.P.M.')*

Safari / not issued
Mar 84. (lp)(c) **COUNTRY DIARY OF AN EDWARDIAN LADY** [ ] [-]
Mar 84. (7") **COUNTRY DIARY OF AN EDWARDIAN LADY. / ?** [ ] [-]

RITCHIE BLACKMORE'S RAINBOW

RITCHIE BLACKMORE – guitar with (ex-ELF) men **RONNIE JAMES DIO** – vocals / **MICKEY LEE SOULE** – keyboards / **CRAIG GRUBER** – bass / **GARY DRISCOLL** – drums

Oyster / Oyster
Aug 75. (lp)(c) **RITCHIE BLACKMORE'S RAINBOW** [11] [30]
– Man on the silver mountain / Self portrait / Black sheep of the family / Catch the rainbow / Snake charmer / The temple of the king / If you don't like rock'n'roll / Sixteenth century Greensleeves / Still I'm sad. *(re-iss.Feb78, Aug81 -hit UK 91- & Aug83 on 'Polydor') (cd-iss.1988 on 'Polydor')*
Oct 75. (7") **MAN ON THE SILVER MOUNTAIN. / SNAKE CHARMER** [ ] [ ]

— RITCHIE only retained **DIO**, recruiting new members **TONY CARBY** – keyboards / **JIMMY BAIN** – bass / **COZY POWELL** – drums.

Polydor / Oyster
May 76. (lp)(c) **RAINBOW RISING (as "BLACKMORE'S RAINBOW")** [11] [48]
– Tarot woman / Run with the wolf / Starstruck / Do you close your eyes / Stargazer / A light in the black. *(re-iss.Aug83) (cd-iss.Nov86)*

RAINBOW

Jul 77. (d-lp)(c) **RAINBOW ON STAGE** (live) [7] [65]
– Kill the king: (a) Man on a silver mountain, (b) Blues, (c) Starstruck / Catch the rainbow / Mistreated / Sixteenth century Greensleeves / Still I'm sad. *(re-iss.Jan84) (cd-iss.Nov86)*
Aug 77. (7") **KILL THE KING: MAN ON THE SILVER MOUNTAIN. / MISTREATED** [44] [ ]
(re-iss.Jul81. reached 41)

— **MARK CLARKE** – bass (ex-COLOSSEUM, ex-URIAH HEEP) repl. BAIN who joined WILD HORSES / **BOB DAISLEY** – bass (ex-WIDOWMAKER, ex-CHICKEN SHACK) repl. CLARKE / **DAVID STONE** – keyboards (ex-SYMPHONIC SLAM) repl. CAREY

Polydor / Polydor
Mar 78. (7") **LONG LIVE ROCK'N'ROLL. / SENSITIVE TO LIGHT** [33] [ ]
(re-iss.Jul81)

Apr 78. (lp)(c) **LONG LIVE ROCK'N'ROLL** [7] [89]
– Long live rock'n'roll / Lady of the lake / L.A. connection / Gates of Babylon / Kill the king / The shed / Sensitive to light / Rainbow eyes. *(re-iss.Aug83)*

Sep 78. (7"red) **L.A. CONNECTION. / LADY OF THE LAKE** [40] [ ]
(re-iss.7"black Jul81)

— **BLACKMORE** retained only **COZY POWELL / GRAHAM BONNET** – vocals (ex-Solo artist, ex-MARBLES) repl. DIO who went solo / **ROGER GLOVER** – bass, vocals (ex-DEEP PURPLE) repl. DAISLEY / **DON AIREY** – keyboards repl. STONE

Aug 79. (lp)(c)(clear-lp) **DOWN TO EARTH** [6] [66]
– All night long / Eyes of the world / No time to lose / Makin' love / Since you've been gone / Love's no friend / Danger zone / Lost in Hollywood. *(re-iss.Apr84) (cd-iss.Dec86)*

Aug 79. (7") **SINCE YOU'VE BEEN GONE. / BAD GIRLS** [6] [57]
(re-iss.Jul81)

Feb 80. (7") **ALL NIGHT LONG. / WEISS HEIM** [5] [ ]
(re-iss.Jul81)

— **JOE LYNN TURNER** – vocals, repl. BONNET who continued solo career. / **BOBBY RONDINELLI** – drums repl. POWELL who later joined E.L.P.

Jan 81. (7") **I SURRENDER. / MAYBE NEXT TIME** [3] [50]
(re-iss.Jul81)

Feb 81. (lp)(c) **DIFFICULT TO CURE** [3] [50]
– I surrender / Spotlight kid / No release / Vielleicht das nachster zeit (Maybe next time) / Can't happen here / Freedom fighter / Midtown tunnel vision / Difficult to cure. *(re-iss.+cd.Aug84)*

Jun 81. (7") **CAN'T HAPPEN HERE. / JEALOUS LOVER** [20] [ ]

Nov 81. (m-lp) **JEALOUS LOVER** [-] [ ]
– Jealous lover / Can't happen here / I surrender / Weiss Helm.

— **DAVE ROSENTHAL** – keyboards repl. AIREY who joined OZZY OSBOURNE.

Polydor Mercury

Mar 82. (7"blue)(12"blue) **STONE COLD. / ROCK FEVER** [34] [40]

Apr 82. (lp)(c) **STRAIGHT BETWEEN THE EYES** [5] [30]
– Death alley driver / Stone cold / Bring on the night / Tite squeeze / Tearin' out my heart / Power / Miss Mistreated / Rock fever / Eyes of fire. *(cd-iss.1983) (cd-iss.Apr94)*

— **BLACKMORE** still had in his ranks **GLOVER, TURNER, ROSENTHAL, /** and **CHUCK BURGI** – drums (ex-BRAND X) repl. RONDINELLI

Aug 83. (7")(7"pic-d) **STREET OF DREAMS. / ANYBODY THERE** [52] [60]
(12"+=) – Power (live)

Sep 83. (lp)(c)(cd) **BENT OUT OF SHAPE** [11] [34]
– Stranded / Can't let you go / Fool for the night / Fire dance / Anybody there / Desperate heart / Street of dreams / Drinking with the devil / Snowman / Make your move.

Oct 83. (7")(7"sha-pic-d) **CAN'T LET YOU GO. / ALL NIGHT LONG** [43] [ ]
(12"+=) – Stranded (live).

— Split late '83 . . .BLACKMORE and GLOVER as said reformed DEEP PURPLE

RITCHIE BLACKMORE'S RAINBOW

— re-formed for comeback concerts & an album. His new band:- **DOOGIE WHITE** - vocals / **PAUL MORRIS** -keyboards / **GREG SMITH** -bass / **JOHN O'REILLY** -drums

Arista Arista

Sep 95. (cd)(c) **STRANGER IN ALL OF US** [ ] [ ]
– Wolf to the Moon / Cold hearted woman / Hunting humans (insatiable) / Stand and fight / Ariel / Too late for tears / Black masquerade / Silence / Hall of the mountain king / Still I'm sad.

RAINBOW – compilations etc. –

Sep 78. Polydor; (d-lp) **RITCHIE BLACKMORE'S RAINBOW. / RAINBOW RISING** [ ] [ ]

Nov 81. Polydor; (d-lp)(d-c) **THE BEST OF RAINBOW** [14] [ ]
– All night long / Man on the silver mountain / Can't happen here / Lost in Hollywood / Since you've been gone / Stargazer / Catch the rainbow / Kill the king / 16th century Greensleeves / I surrender / Long live rock'n'roll / Eyes of the world / Starstruck / A light in the black / Mistreated. *(cd-iss.1983)*

Feb 85. Polydor; (d-c) **DOWN TO EARTH / DIFFICULT TO CURE** [ ] [ ]

Feb 86. Polydor; (d-lp)(d-c)(d-cd) **FINYL VINYL (live 80's material)** [ ] [87]

Feb 88. Old Gold; (7") **SINCE YOU'VE BEEN GONE. / ALL NIGHT LONG** [ ] [-]

Jun 93. Old Gold; (cd-s) **I SURRENDER / SINCE YOU'VE BEEN GONE / ALL NIGHT LONG** [ ] [-]

1989. Connoisseur; (d-lp)(c)(cd) **ROCK PROFILE VOL.1** [ ] [-]
(above credited to RITCHIE BLACKMORE contains early sessions and PURPLE work) (cd.omits interview tracks + 1 song)

Dec 90. Connoisseur; (d-cd)(c)(d-lp) **LIVE IN GERMANY 1976 (live)** [ ] [-]

Jul 91. Connoisseur; (cd)(d-lp) **ROCK PROFILE VOLUME 2** [ ] [-]
(above also credited to RITCHIE BLACKMORE contains RAINBOW material, etc.)

Jan 94. R.P.M.; (cd) **SESSION MAN** [ ] [-]

Jun 94. R.P.M.; (cd) **TAKE IT! – SESSIONS 63-68** [ ] [-]

IAN GILLAN BAND

GILLAN – vocals / **RAY FENWICK** – guitar (ex-SPENCER DAVIS GROUP, ex-AFTER TEA) **MIKE MORAN** – keyboards / **JOHN GUSTAFSON** – bass (ex-BIG THREE, ex-EPISODE SIX, ex-QUATERMASS) / **MARK NAUSEEF** – drums (ex-ELF)

Oyster-Polydor Oyster

Jul 76. (lp)(c) **CHILD IN TIME** [55] [ ]
– Lay me down / You make me feel so good / Shame / My baby loves me / Down the road / Child in time / Let it slide. *(cd-iss.Apr90 on 'Virgin') (cd-iss.Mar94)*

— **COLIN TOWNS** – keyboards repl. MICKEY LEE SOULE who had briefly repl. MIKE TOWNS also contributed some songs.

Island Antilles

Apr 77. (lp)(c) **CLEAN AIR TURBULANCE** [ ] [ ]
– Clean air turbulance / Five moons / Money lender / Over the hill / Goodhand Liza / Angel Manchenio. *(re-iss.Jun82, Aug88 on 'Virgin', cd-iss.Apr90)*

Oct 77. (lp)(c) **SCARABUS** [ ] [ ]
– Scarabus / Twin exhausted / Poor boy hero / Mercury high / Pre release / Slags to bitches / Apathy / Mad Elaine / Country lights / Fool's mate. *(re-iss.Jun82, Aug88 on 'Virgin', cd-iss.Apr90 +=)* – My baby loves me.

Feb 78. (7") **MAD ELAINE. / MERCURY HIGH** [ ] [ ]
This band also recorded LIVE AT BUDOKAN VOL 1 & 2, only released in Japan.– Clear air turbulence / My baby loves me / Scarabus / Money lender / Twin exhausted / Over the hill / Child in time / Smoke on the water / Mercury high / Woman from Tokyo. *(UK-issue 1987 on 'Virgin. cd-iss.Nov89) (re-iss.cd Sep93 as 'GILLAN – THE JAPANESE ALBUM' on 'R.P.M.')*

GILLAN

he only retained TOWNS and brought in **STEVE BYRD** – guitar / **JOHN McCOY** – bass / **PETE BARNACLE** – drums. An album GILLAN was released in Japan (only May78).

— (May79) **BERNIE TORME** – guitar (ex-solo artist) repl. BYRD / **MICK UNDERWOOD** – drums (ex-EPISODE SIX, ex-QUATERMASS, ex-STRAPPS, etc.) repl. BARNACLE

Acrobat Arista

Sep 79. (lp)(c) **MR. UNIVERSE** [11] [ ]
– Second sight / Secret of the dance / She tears me down / Roller / Mr Universe / Vengence / Puget sound / Dead of the night / Message in a bottle / Fighting man. *(re-iss.Jan83 on Fame)*

Oct 79. (7") **VENGENCE. / SMOKE ON THE WATER** [ ] [ ]

Virgin Virgin/RSO

Jun 80. (7") **SLEEPIN' ON THE JOB. / HIGHER AND HIGHER** [55] [ ]

Jul 80. (7"m) **NO EASY WAY. / HANDLES ON HER HIPS / I MIGHT AS WELL GO HOME** [ ] [ ]

Aug 80. (lp)(c) **GLORY ROAD** [3] [ ]
– Unchain your brain / Are you sure? / Time and again / No easy way / Sleepin' on the job / On the rocks / If you believe me / Running, white face, city boy / Nervous / Your mother was right. *(re-iss.Mar84)* (free lp w.a.) **FOR GILLAN FANS ONLY** (limited 15000) *(cd-iss.Nov89) (containing free album)* – Redwatch / Abbey of Thelema / Trying to get to you / Come tomorrow / Dragon's tongue / ost fade brain damage / Egg timr / Harry Lime theme.

Sep 80. (7") **TROUBLE. / YOUR SISTER'S ON MY LIST** [14] [ ]
(free live-7"w.a.) **MR.UNIVERSE. / VENGEANCE / SMOKE ON THE WATER**

Feb 81. (7") **MUTUALLY ASSURED DESTRUCTION. / THE MAELSTROM** [32] [ ]

Mar 81. (7") **NEW ORLEANS. / TAKE A HOLD OF YOURSELF** [2] [ ]

Apr 81. (lp)(c) **FUTURE SHOCK** [2] [ ]
– Future shock / Night ride out of Phoenix / The ballad of Lucitania express / No laughing in Heaven / Sacre bleu / New Orleans / Bite the bullet / If I sing softly / Don't want the truth / For your dreams. *(re-iss.Aug88) (re-iss.cd/c May95 on 'Virgin-VIP')*

Jun 81. (7"ep) **NO LAUGHING IN HEAVEN / ONE FOR THE ROAD. / LUCILLE / BAD NEWS** [31] [ ]

— **JANICK GERS** – guitar (ex-WHITE SPIRIT) repl. TORME (later to DESPERADO)

Oct 81. (7") **NIGHTMARE. / BITE THE BULLET (live)** [36] [ ]

Nov 81. (d-lp)(d-c) **DOUBLE TROUBLE (live)** [12] [ ]
– I'll rip your spine out / Restless / Men of war / Sunbeam / Nightmare / Hadely bop bop / Life goes on / Born to kill / No laughing in Heaven / No easy way / Trouble / Mutally assured destruction / If you believe me / New Orleans. *(cd-iss.Nov89)*

Jan 82. (7")(7"pic-d) **RESTLESS. / ON THE ROCKS (live)** [25] [ ]

Aug 82. (7") **LIVING FOR THE CITY. / BREAKING CHAINS** [50] [ ]
(7"pic-d) – ('A'side). / PURPLE SKY

Sep 82. (lp)(c)(pic-lp) **MAGIC** [17] [ ]
– What's the matter / Bluesy blue sea / Caught in a trap / Long gone / Driving me wild / Demon driver / Living a lie / You're so right / Living for the city / Demon driver (reprise). *(re-iss.Aug88 +cd.Aug89) (cd-iss.Mar94)*

Oct 82. (7") **LONG GONE. / FIJI** [ ] [ ]

— **IAN GILLAN** then joined BLACK SABBATH, before the reformation of DEEP

PURPLE in Nov84. GILLAN left PURPLE again to go solo

Jun 88. (7") **SOUTH AFRICA. / JOHN** [ ] [ ]
(12"+=) – ('A'extended).

After GILLAN's departure from DEEP PURPLE in late 80's, he made 2 other albums (Jul 90) NAKED THUNDER for 'East West' records, and a year later 'TOOLBOX'. He re-joined DEEP PURPLE late '92

– GILLAN compilations etc. –

Aug 84. Thunderbolt; (lp) **ROCKS ON! (by GILLAN / DEAN)** [ ] [ ]

Jun 86. 10-Virgin; (d-lp)(c)(cd) **WHAT I DID ON MY VACATION** [ ] [ ]
– On the rocks / Scarabus / Puget sound / No easy way / If I sing softly / I'll rip your spine out / New Orleans / Mutally assured destruction / You're so right / Long gone / If you believe in me / Bluesy blue sea / Lucille. (d-lp+=) – Mad Elaine / Time and again / Vengeance / Unchain your brain / No laughing in Heaven.

Dec 90. Raw Fruit; (cd)(c)(lp) **LIVE AT READING ROCK FESTIVAL 1980 (live)** [ ] [-]

May 91. V.I.P.; (cd)(c) **TROUBLE – (THE BEST OF GILLAN)** [ ] [-]
– Trouble / New Orleans / Fighting man / Living for the city / Helter skelter / Mr.Universe / Telephone box / Dislocated (GILLAN-GLOVER) / Sleeping on the job / MAD (Mutally Assured Destruction) / No laughing in Heaven / Nightmare / Restless / Purple sky / Born to kill (live) / Smoke on the water (live). *(re-iss.cd+c Dec93 on 'Virgin-VIP')*

Sep 91. Music Club; (cd)(c) **THE VERY BEST OF GILLAN** [ ] [-]

1992 R.P.M.; (cd) **CHERKAZOO AND OTHER STORIES** [ ] [-]

Jul 95. Connoisseur; (cd) **ROCK PROFILE** [ ] [-]

ROGER GLOVER

(solo)

Purple UK

Dec 74. (lp)(c) **BUTTERFLY BALL (Soundtrack)** [ ] [ ] Jan 76
– Dawn / Get ready / Saffron doormouse and Lizzy bee / Harlequin hare / Old blind mole / Magician moth / No solution / Behind the smile / Fly away / Arena / Sitting in a dream / Waiting / Sir Maximus mouse / Dreams of Sir Bedivere / Together again / Watch out for the bat / Little chalk blue / The feast / Love is all / Homeward. *(re-iss.Nov84 on 'Safari') (cd-iss.1989 on 'Line') (re-iss.cd Jul95 on 'Repertoire')*

Aug 76. (7") **LOVE IS ALL. / OLD BLIND MOLE** [ ] [ ]

Polydor Polydor?

Apr 78. (lp)(c) **ELEMENTS** [ ] [ ]
– The first ring made of clay / The next a ring of fire / The third ring's water flow / The fourth ring's with the wind / Finale.

May 84. (lp)(c) **MASK** [ ] [ ]
– Divided world / Getting stranger / The mask / Fake it / Dancin' again / (You're so) Remote / Hip level / Don't look down. *(cd-iss.Apr93 w/ ELEMENTS on 'Connoisseur')*

Polydor 21 records

Jun 84. (7") **THE MASK. / (YOU'RE SO) REMOTE** [ ] [ ]

— **GLOVER** also rejoined DEEP PURPLE (late '84)

GILLAN / GLOVER

10-Virgin Virgin?

Jul 87. (7") **DISLOCATED. / CHET** [ ] [ ]
(12"+=) – Purple people eater.

Jan 88. (7")(12") **SHE TOOK MY BREATH AWAY. / CAYMAN ISLAND** [ ] [ ]

Feb 88. (lp)(c)(cd) **ACCIDENTALLY ON PURPOSE** [ ] [ ]
– Cloud and rain / She took my breath away / Can't believe you wanna leave / Dislocated / Viva! Miami / I can't dance to that / Lonely avenue / Telephone box / I thought no. (cd+=) – Cayman Island / Purple people eater / Chet.

DEEP WOUND (see under ⇒ DINOSAUR JR.)

DEF LEPPARD

Formed: Sheffield, England . . . 1977 by youngsters initially as ATOMIC MASS (see below). In 1978, ELLIOT's dad loaned them money to issue debut EP on own indie label 'Bludgeon Riffola'. The following year, after tours supporting AC/DC, etc., they were signed to 'Vertigo' by Roger Bain. This also prompted a move to London, and in 1980, their debut album 'ON THROUGH THE NIGHT', broke the UK 20, and also nearly hit the US 50, where they soon became massive attraction. • **Style:** Heavy metal, that through the years has mellowed into glam-metal pop. The most easy listening metal band of the time, hated by critics, but loved by their loyal ever growing legion of teenage fans. • **Songwriters:** Group compositions, except ONLY AFTER DARK (Mick Ronson) / ACTION (Sweet) / YOU CAN'T ALWAYS GET WHAT YOU WANT (Rolling Stones) / LITTLE WING (Jimi Hendrix) / ELECTED (Alice Cooper). Roadie STUMPUS MAXIMUS sung; PLEASE RELEASE ME (Engelbert Humperdink). • **Miscellaneous:** The group has been dogged by accidents and deaths (see discography for correct details).

Recommended: VAULT 1980-1995 – DEF LEPPARD'S GREATEST HITS (*8).

JOE ELLIOT (b. 1 Aug'59) – vocals / **PETE WILLIS** – lead guitar / **STEVE CLARK** (b.23 Apr'60) – guitar / **RICK SAVAGE** (b. 2 Dec'60) – bass / **FRANK NOON** – drums.

Bludgeon not issued

Jan 79. (7"m) **OVERTURE. / RIDE INTO THE SUN / GETCHA ROCKS OFF** [ ] [-]

— **RICK ALLEN** (b. 1 Nov'63) – drums, repl. FRANK who later joined LIONHEART, then WAYSTED.

Vertigo Mercury

Feb 79. (7"ep) **OVERTURE. / GETCHA ROCKS OFF / RIDE INTO THE SUN** [ ] [ ]

Nov 79. (7") **WASTED. / HELLO AMERICA** [61] [ ]

Feb 80. (7") **HELLO AMERICA. / GOOD MORNING FREEDOM** [45] [ ]

Mar 80. (lp)(c) **ON THROUGH THE NIGHT** [15] [51]
– Rock brigade / Hello America / Sorrow is a woman / It could be you / Answer to the master / When the walls came tumbling down / Wasted / Rocks off / It don't matter / Satellite / Overture. *(re-iss.+cd Jan89)*

1980. (7") **ROCK BRIGADE. / WHEN THE WALLS COME TUMBLING DOWN** [-] [ ]

Jul 81. (lp)(c) **HIGH'N'DRY** [26] [38]
– High 'n' dry (Saturday night) / You got me runnin' / Let it go / Another hit and run / Lady Strange / Mirror, mirror (look into my eyes) / No no no / Bringin' on the heartbreak / Switch 625. *(US re-iss.May84 +=)*– Bringin' on the heartbreak (remix) / Me and my wine. *(re-iss.+cd Jan89)* (cd+=) – You got me runnin' (remix) / Me and my wine.

Aug 81. (7") **LET IT GO. / SWITCH 625** [ ] [ ]

Jan 82. (7") **BRINGIN' ON THE HEARTACHE (remix). / ME AND MY WINE** [ ] [ ]
(12"+=) – You got me runnin'.

Jan 83. (7") **PHOTOGRAPH. / BRINGIN' ON THE HEART-BREAK** [66] [12] Mar 83
(12"+=) – Mirror, Mirror (look into my eyes).

— **PHIL COLLEN** (b. 8 Dec'57) – lead guitar (ex-GIRL) repl. PETE

Mar 83. (lp)(c)(cd) **PYROMANIA** [18] [2]
– Rock! rock! (till you drop) / Photograph / Stagefright / Too late for love / Die hard the hunter / Foolin' / Rock of ages / Comin' under fire / Action! not words / Billy's got a gun.

Aug 83. (7")(12")(7"pic-d)(7"sha-pic-d) **ROCK OF AGES. / ACTION! NOT WORDS** [41] [16] Jun 83

Nov 83. (7") **FOOLIN'. / TOO LATE FOR LOVE** [ ] [28] Aug 83
(12"+=) – High'n'dry.

Jun 84. (7") **BRINGIN' ON THE HEARTBREAK (remix). / ?** [-] [61]

Aug 85. (7") **PHOTOGRAPH. / BRINGIN' ON THE HEART-BREAK** [ ] [-]
(12"+=) – Mirror, mirror.

— Remained a 5-piece although **RICK ALLEN** lost an arm in a car crash (31 Dec84). He now used specially adapted programmable drum pads and foot pedals.

Jul 87. (7") **ANIMAL. / TEAR IT DOWN** [6] [19] Oct 87
(12"+=)(12"red+=) – ('A'extended).
(cd-s++=) – Women.

Aug 87. (lp)(c)(cd)(pic-lp) **HYSTERIA** [2] [1]
– Women / Rocket / Animal / Love bites / Pour some sugar on me / Armageddon it / Gods of war / Don't shoot shotgun / Run riot / Hysteria / Excitable / Love and affection. *(cd+=)* – I can't let you be a memory.

Aug 87. (7") **WOMEN. / ?** [-] [80]

Sep 87. (7")(c-s)(7"sha-pic-d) **POUR SOME SUGAR ON ME. / I WANNA BE YOUR HERO** [18] [2] Apr 88
(12"+=)(12"pic-d+=) – ('A'extended mix).

Nov 87. (7")(c-s) **HYSTERIA. / RIDE INTO THE SUN ('87 version)** [26] [10] Jan 88
(12"+=) – Love and affection (live).
(cd-s++=) – I wanna be your hero.

Apr 88. (7") **ARMAGEDDON IT!. / RING OF FIRE** [20] [3] Nov 88
(12"+=) – ('A'atomic mix).
(pic-cd-s++=) – Animal / Pour some sugar on me.

Jul 88. (7") **LOVE BITES. / BILLY'S GOT A GUN (live)** [11] [1]
(12"+=)(cd-s+=) – Excitable (orgasmic mix).

Jan 89. (7") **ROCKET. / RELEASE ME** [15] [12]
(12"+=)(cd-s+=)(12"pic-d+=) – ('A'rock mix) / Rock of ages (live).

— **STEVE CLARK** was found dead 8 Jan'91 after drinking/drugs session. Replaced by **VIV CAMPBELL** – guitar (ex-DIO, ex-WHITESNAKE, ex-SHADOWKING)

Mar 92. (7")(c-s) **LET'S GET ROCKED. / ONLY AFTER DARK** [2] [15]
(12"pic-d+=) – Too late for love (live).
(pic-cd-s+=) – Women (live).

Apr 92. (cd)(c)(lp) **ADRENALIZE** [1] [1]
– Let's get rocked / Heaven is / Make love like a man / Tonight / White

lightning / Stand up (kick love into motion) / Personal property / Have you ever needed someone so bad / I wanna touch u / Tear it down. *(pic-lp iss.Dec92, w / 2 extra tracks)*

Jun 92. (7")(c-s) **MAKE LOVE LIKE A MAN. / MISS YOU IN A HEARTBEAT** [12] [36]
(12"+=) – Two steps behind (acoustic).
(cd-s++=) – Action.

Sep 92. (7")(c-s) **HAVE YOU EVER NEEDED SOMEONE SO BAD. / FROM THE INSIDE** [16] [12] Aug 92
(cd-s+=) – You can't always get what you want / Little wing.

Dec 92. (c-s) **STAND UP (KICK LOVE INTO MOTION). / ?** [-] [34]

Jan 93. (7"etched)(c-s) **HEAVEN IS. / SHE'S TOO TOUGH** [13] [ ]
(pic-cd-s+=) – Let's get rocked (live) / Elected (live).
(12"pic-d) – ('A'side) / Let's get rocked (live) / Tokyo road (live).

Apr 93. (7")(c-s) **TONIGHT. / NOW I'M HERE (live)** [34] [62]
(cd-s+=) – ('A'demo).
(cd-s+=) – Photograph (live).

Sep 93. (c-s)(cd-s) **TWO STEPS BEHIND. / TONIGHT (demo)** [32] [12] Aug 93
(12"+=)(cd-s+=) – S.M.C.

(above single from the film 'Last Action Hero' on 'Columbia')

Oct 93. (cd)(c)(lp) **RETRO ACTIVE** [6] [9]
– Desert song / Fractured love / Two steps behind (acoustic) / Only after dark / Action / She's too tough / Miss you in a heartbeat (acoustic) / Only after dark (acoustic) / Ride into the Sun / From the inside / Ring of fire / I wanna be your hero / Miss you in a heartbeat / Two steps behind.

Jan 94. (7")(c-s) **ACTION. / MISS YOU IN A HEARTBEAT** [14] [ ]
(cd-s+=) – She's too tough.

Oct 95. (c-s) **WHEN LOVE & HATE COLLIDE / POUR SOME SUGAR ON ME (remix)** [2] [59]
(cd-s+=) – Armageddon it (remix).
(cd-s++=) – ('A'demo).
(cd-s) – ('A'side) / Rocket (remix) / Excitable (remix).
(cd-s) – ('A'side) / Excitable (remix) / ('A'demo).

Oct 95. (cd)(c)(lp) **VAULT 1980-1995 DEF LEPPARD GREATEST HITS** (compilation) [3] [15]
– Pour some sugar on me / Photograph / Love bites / Let's get rocked / Two steps behind / Animal / Heaven is / Rocket / When love & hate collide / Action / Make love like a man / Armageddon it / Have you ever needed someone / So bad / Rock of ages / Hysteria / Bringin' on the heartbreak. (cd w/free cd) **LIVE AT DON VALLEY, SHEFFIELD (live)**

. . . Jan – Jun '96 stop press . . .

Apr 96. (single) **SLANG** [17] [ ]
May 96. (cd)(c)(lp) **SLANG** [5] [14]
Jun 96. (single) **WORK IT OUT** [ ] [ ]

DEL AMITRI

Formed: Glasgow, Scotland . . . 1983 by JUSTIN CURRIE, etc. (see below). Made one single on indie label 'No Strings' before signing to major 'Chrysalis' records in 1984. Finally broke through early in the 90's on 'A&M', with hit 45 'NOTHING EVER HAPPENS'which was lifted from the Top 10 album 'THE WAKING HOUR'. • **Style:** Intelligent acoustic outfit, led by CURRIE, drawing on similarities to Scottish 'Postcard' era. • **Songwriters:** CURRIE-HARVIE composed except covers; DON'T CRY NO TEARS (Neil Young) / BYE BYE PRIDE (Go-Betweens) / CINDY INCIDENTLY (Faces). • **Trivia:** Means 'from the womb' in Greek.

Recommended: THE WAKING HOUR (*8) / CHANGE EVERYTHING (*6)

JUSTIN CURRIE (b.11 Dec'64) – vocals, bass, acoustic guitar / **IAIN HARVIE** (b.19 May'62) – guitar / **BRYAN TOLLAND** – guitar / **PAUL TYAGIS** – drums, percussion

No Strings / not issued

Aug 83. (7") **SENSE SICKNESS. / THE DIFFERENCE IS** [ ] [-]

Chrysalis / not issued

May 85. (lp)(c) **DEL AMITRI** [ ] [ ]
– Heard through a wall / Hammering heart / Former owner / Sticks and stones girl / Deceive yourself (in ignorant Heaven) / I was here / Crows in a wheatfield / Keepers / Ceasefire / Breaking bread. *(re-iss.cd+c Mar93)*

Jul 85. (7") **STICKS AND STONES GIRL. / THE KING IS POOR** [ ] [-]
(12"+=) – The difference is.

Oct 85. (7")(12") **HAMMERING HEART. / LINES RUNNING NORTH** [ ] [-]

— **MICK SLAVEN** – guitar (ex-BOURGIE BOURGIE) repl. TOLLAND / sessions from **ANDY ALSTON** – keyboards / **ROBERT CAIRNS** – violin / **BLAIR COWAN** – accordion / **STEPHEN IRVINE** – drums / **JULIAN DAWSON** – harmonica / **JAMES O'MALLEY** – bass / **CAROLINE LEVELLE** – cello / **WILL MOWAT** – seq, keyboards

A & M / A & M

Jul 89. (7") **KISS THIS THING GOODBYE. / NO HOLDING ON** [59] [ ]
(12"+=)(cd-s+=) – Slowly / It's coming back.

Jul 89. (lp)(c)(cd) **THE WAKING HOUR** [6] [95] Mar 90
– Kiss this thing goodbye / Opposite view / Move away Jimmy Blue / Stone cold sober / You're gone / When I want you / This side of the morning / Empty / Hatful of rain / Nothing ever happens. *(re-iss.cd/c Mar95)*

Oct 89. (7") **STONE COLD SOBER. / THE RETURN OF MAGGIE BROWN** [ ] [ ]
(12"+=)(cd-s+=) – Talk it to death.

Jan 90. (7")(c-s) **NOTHING EVER HAPPENS. / SO MANY SOULS TO CHANGE** [11] [ ]
(12"+=)(cd-s+=) – Don't I look like the kind of guy you used to hate? / Evidence.

Mar 90. (7")(c-s) **KISS THIS THING GOODBYE. / NO HOLDING ON** [43] [35] Mar 90
(12"+=)(cd-s+=) – *(all a straight re-issue of Jul89 diff.cat.no.)*

Jun 90. (7")(c-s) **MOVE AWAY JIMMY BLUE. / ANOTHER LETTER HOME** [36] [ ]
(12"+=) – April the first / This side of the morning.
(12"+=)(cd-s+=) – April the first / More than you'd ever know.

Oct 90. (7")(c-s) **SPIT IN THE RAIN. / SCARED TO LIVE** [21] [ ]
(10"+=)(12"+=)(cd-s+=) – The return of Maggie Brown / Talk it to death.

— **DAVID CUMMINGS** – guitar repl. SLAVEN / **BRIAN McDERMOTT** – drums (who guested on last) repl. TYGANI

Apr 92. (7")(c-s) **ALWAYS THE LAST TO KNOW. / LEARN TO CRY** [13] [30] Jul 92
(12"+=)(cd-s+=) – Angel on the roof / The whole world is quiet.

Jun 92. (cd)(c)(lp) **CHANGE EVERYTHING** [2] [ ]
– Be my downfall / Just like a man / When you were young / Surface of the Moon / I won't take the blame / The first rule of love / The ones that you love lead you nowhere / Always the last to know / To last a lifetime / As soon as the tide comes in / Behind the fool / Sometimes I just have to say your name. *(re-iss.cd/c Mar95)*

Jun 92. (7")(c-s) **BE MY DOWNFALL. / WHISKEY REMORSE** [30] [ ]
(10"+=)(cd-s+=) – Lighten up the load / The heart is a bad design.

Aug 92. (7")(c-s) **JUST LIKE A MAN. / SPIT IN THE RAIN (remix)** [25] [ ]
(cd-s) – ('A'side) / Don't cry no tears / Bye bye pride / Cindy incidentally.
(cd-s) – ('A'side) / Carry on Colombus / I want to take the blame (acoustic) / Scared to live.

Jan 93. (7")(c-s) **WHEN YOU WERE YOUNG. / THE ONES THAT YOU LOVE LEAD YOU NOWHERE** [20] [ ]
(cd-s+=) – Kiss this thing goodbye (live) / Hatful of rain (live).
(cd-s) – ('A'side) / Long journey home / The verb to do / Kestral road.

Feb 95. (c-s) **HERE AND NOW / SOMEONE ELSE WILL** [21] [ ]
(cd-s)(10") – ('A'side) / Long way down / Queen of false alarms / Crashing down.
(cd-s) – ('A'side) / Always the last to know (live) / When I want you / Stone cold sober (live).

Feb 95. (cd)(c) **TWISTED** [3] [ ]
– Food for songs / Start with me / Here and now / One thing left to do / Tell her this / Being somebody else / Roll to me / Crashing down / It might as well be you / Never enough / It's never too late to be alone / Driving with the brakes on. *(re-iss.d-cd Aug95)*

Apr 95. (7")(c-s) **DRIVING WITH THE BRAKES ON. / LIFE BY MISTAKE** [18] [ ]
(cd-s+=) – A little luck / In the meantime.
(cd-s) – ('A'side) / Nothing ever happens / Kiss this thing goodbye / Always the last to know.

Jun 95. (c-s) **ROLL TO ME / IN THE FRAME** [22] [10]
(cd-s+=) – Food for songs (acoustic) / One thing left to do (acoustic).
(cd-s) – ('A'side) / Spit in the rain / Stone cold sober / Move away Jimmy Blue.

Oct 95. (c-s) **TELL HER THIS / A BETTER MAN** [32] [ ]
(cd-s+=) – The last love song / When you were young (alt.version).
(cd-s) – ('A'side) / Whiskey remorse / Fred Partington's daughter / Learn to cry.

DEPECHE MODE

Formed: Basildon, Essex, England . . . 1980 by CLARKE, GORE and FLETCHER. First appeared on Various Artists lp 'Some Bizzare Album' early '81, having already been signed to Daniel Miller's 'Mute' label. Their second single 'NEW LIFE', nearly reached the UK Top 10, and was the first of 24 consecutive Top 30 hits. Became worldwide Euro + US stars from the mid-80's onwards. • **Style:** Socially aware electronic rock-pop outfit, initially influenced by KRAFTWERK. • **Songwriters:** MARTIN GORE wrote music after the departure of YAZOO then ERASURE bound VINCE CLARKE. Covered: ROUTE 66 (hit; Nat King Cole) • **Trivia:** MARTIN GORE's solo album contained 6 cover versions incl. NEVER TURN YOUR BACK ON MOTHER EARTH (Sparks). He later re-done Leonard Cohen's COMING BACK TO YOU.

Recommended: THE SINGLES 1981-1985 (*9) / VIOLATOR (*8) / CONSTRUCTION TIME AGAIN (*7) / BLACK CELEBRATION (*8) / SOME GREAT REWARD (*7) / MUSIC FOR THE MASSES (*7) / SPEAK AND SPELL (*6) / A BROKEN FRAME (*7).

VINCE CLARKE (b. 3 Jul'60) – keyboards, synthesiser / **DAVID GAHAN** (b. 9 May'62) – vocals / **MARTIN GORE** (b.23 Jul'61) – keyboards, synthesiser, vocals / **ANDY FLETCHER** (b. 8 Jul'61) – guitar, synthesiser, drum machine

Mute Sire

Mar 81. (7") **DREAMING OF ME. / ICE MACHINE** [57] [ ]
Jun 81. (7") **NEW LIFE. / SHOUT** [11] [ ]
(12"+=) – (extended versions).
Sep 81. (7") **JUST CAN'T GET ENOUGH. / ANY SECOND NOW** [8] [-]
(12"+=) – (extended versions).
Oct 81. (lp)(c) **SPEAK & SPELL** [10] [ ]
– New life / Just can't get enough / I sometimes I wish I was dead / Puppets / Boys say go / No disco / What's your name / Photographic / Tora! Tora! Tora! / Big Muff / Any second now. *(re-iss.+cd.Apr88)* (cd+=) – Dreaming of me / New life (extended) / Shout (Rio mix) / Any second now (altered mix).
Nov 81. (7") **JUST CAN'T GET ENOUGH. / TORA! TORA! TORA!** [-] [ ]

— **ALAN WILDER** (b. 1 Jun'59) – electronics (ex-HITMEN) repl. VINCE who formed YAZOO.

Jan 82. (7") **SEE YOU. / NOW, THIS IS FUN** [6] [ ] Aug 82
(12"+=) – (extended versions).
Apr 82. (7") **THE MEANING OF LOVE. / OBERKORN** [12] [ ]
(12"+=) – (extended versions).
Aug 82. (7") **LEAVE IN SILENCE. / EXCERPT FROM MY SECRET GARDEN** [18] [ ]
(12"+=) – ('A' version).
Sep 82. (lp)(c) **A BROKEN FRAME** [8] [ ]
– Leave in silence / My secret garden / Monument / Nothing to fear / See you / Satellite / The meaning of love / A photograph of you / Shouldn't have done that / The sun and the rainfall. *(re-iss.+cd.Jul88)*
Feb 83. (7") **GET THE BALANCE RIGHT. / THE GREAT OUTDOORS** [13] [ ]
(12"+=) – Tora! Tora! Tora! (live).
(12") – ('A'side) (live +=) – My secret garden / See you / Satellite / Tora! Tora!.
Jul 83. (7") **EVERYTHING COUNTS. / WORK HARD** [6] [ ]
(12"+=) – (extended versions).
(12") – ('A'side) / Boys say go (live) / New life (live) / Nothing to fear (live) / The meaning of love (live).
Aug 83. (lp)(c) **CONSTRUCTION TIME AGAIN** [6] [ ]
– Love in itself / More than a party / Pipeline / Everything counts / Two minute warning / Shame / The landscape is changing / Told you so / And then . . . *(re-iss.+cd.Jul88)*
Sep 83. (7") **LOVE IN ITSELF 2. / FOOLS** [21] [ ]
(12"+=) – (extended versions).
(12") – ('A'side) (live+=) – Just can't get enough / Photograph / A photograph of you / Shout.
Mar 84. (7") **PEOPLE ARE PEOPLE. / IN YOUR MEMORY** [4] [13] May 85
(12"+=) – ('A' On-U-Sound remix).
Jul 84. (lp)(c) **PEOPLE ARE PEOPLE** [-] [71]
– People are people / Everything counts / Get the balance right / Love in itself / Now this is fun / Leave in silence / Told you so / Work hard.
Aug 84. (7") **MASTER AND SERVANT. / SET ME FREE (RENOVATE ME)** [9] [ ] Sep 85
(12"+=) – (extended versions).
(12") – ('A' On-U-Sound mix) – Are people people.
Sep 84. (lp)(c) **SOME GREAT REWARD** [5] [51] Jul 85
– Something to do / Lie to me / People are people / It doesn't matter / Stories of old / Somebody / Master and servant / If you want to / Blasphemous rumours. *(re-iss.+cd.Sep87)*
Nov 84. (7") **BLASPHEMOUS RUMOURS. / SOMEBODY** [16] [ ]
(d7"+=) – Told you so (live) / Everything counts (live).
(12"+=) – Ice machine / Two minute warning.
May 85. (7") **SHAKE THE DISEASE. / FLEXIBLE** [18] [ ]
(12"+=) – (extended versions).
(12"+=) – Master and servant (live) / Something to do (metal mix).
Sep 85. (7") **IT'S CALLED A HEART. / FLY ON THE WINDSCREEN** [18] [ ]
(12"+=) – (extended versions).
(extra-d12"+=) – (versions).
Oct 85. (lp)(c) **THE SINGLES 1981-1985** (compilation) [6] [ ]
– People are people / Master and servant / It's called a heart / Just can't get enough / See you / Shake the disease / Everything counts / New life / Blasphemous rumours / Leave in silence / Get the balance right / Love in itself / Dreaming of me. *(cd-iss.Sep87 with 2 extra tracks, as cass.)* (above US-title 'CATCHING UP WITH DEPECHE MODE')
Feb 86. (7") **STRIPPED. / BUT NOT TONIGHT** [15] [ ]
(12"+=) – Breathing in fumes / Fly on the windscreen / Black day.
Mar 86. (lp)(c)(cd) **BLACK CELEBRATION** [4] [90]
– Black celebration / Fly on the windscreen – final / A question of tlust / Sometimes / It doesn't matter two / A question of time / Stripped / Here is the house / World full of nothing / Dressed in black / New dress. (cd+=) – But not tonight / Breathing in fumes / Black day.
Apr 86. (7") **A QUESTION OF LUST. / CHRISTMAS ISLAND** [28] [ ]
(12"+=) – (versions) / It doesn't matter / People are people (live).
(free c-s. w/7") – ('A' Flood mix) / If you want (live) / Shame (live) / Blasphemous rumours (live).
Aug 86. (7") **A QUESTION OF TIME. / BLACK CELEBRATION** [17] [ ]
(12") – ('A'+'B'diff.mixes) – More than a party (live).
(12"+=) – Stripped (live) / Something to do (live).
Apr 87. (7") **STRANGELOVE. / PIMPF** [16] [76]
(12"+=) – ('A'mix).
(12"++=)(cd-s++=) – Agent orange.
Aug 87. (7") **NEVER LET ME DOWN AGAIN. / TREASURE LITTLE PLEASURE** [22] [63]
(c-s+=) – ('A' aggro mix).
(12"+=)(cd-s+=) – ('A'+'B'mixes) / To have and to hold (Spanish taster).
Sep 87. (lp)(d-c)(cd)(clear-lp) **MUSIC FOR THE MASSES** [10] [35]
– Never let me down again / The things you said / Strangelove / Sacred / Little 15 / Behind the wheel / I want you now / To have to hold / Nothing / Pimpf. *(cd+=)* – Agent orange / Never let me down again (aggro mix) / To have and to hold (Spanish) / Pleasure the treasure (glitter mix). *(d-c+=)* – BLACK CELEBRATION (album)
Dec 87. (7") **BEHIND THE WHEEL. / ROUTE 66** [21] [61]
(12") – ('A'+'B' versions).
(cd-s++=) – ('A'-lp version).
Jan 88. (7") **BEHIND THE WHEEL. / (part 2)** [-] [ ]
Mar 88. (7") **STRANGELOVE. / NOTHING** [-] [ ]
May 88. (7"import) **LITTLE 15. / ?** [60] [ ]
Feb 89. (7") **EVERYTHING COUNTS (live). / NOTHING (live)** [22] [ ]
(12"+=) – Sacred (live) / A question of lust (live).
(10") – ('A' absolute mix) / ('B' US mix)/ ('A'-1983 mix)
(12")(cd-s) – ('A'+'B' diff.mixes) – Strangelove (remix).
Mar 89. (d-lp)(d-c)(d-cd) **101 (live)** [5] [45]
– Pimpf / Behind the wheel / Strangelove / Sacred * / Something to do / Blasphemous rumours / Stripped / Somebody / Things you said / Black generation / Shake the disease / Nothing * / Pleasure little treasure / People are people / A question of time / Never let me down again / A question of lust * / Master and servant / Just can't get enough / Everything counts *. *(c+=*)(cd+=*)*
Aug 89. (7")(US-c-s) **PERSONAL JESUS. / DANGEROUS** [13] [28] Dec 89
(12"+=)(c-s+=)(3"cd-s+=) – ('A'acoustic mix).
Feb 90. (7") **NOTHING. / ('A' instrumental)** [-] [ ]
Feb 90. (7")(c-s) **ENJOY THE SILENCE. / MEMPHISTO** [6] [8] Apr 90
(12"+=)(cd-s+=) – ('A'bassline) ('A'harmonium) ('A'Rikki Tavi) mixes.
Mar 90. (cd)(c)(lp) **VIOLATOR** [2] [7]
– World in my eyes / Sweetest perfection / Personal Jesus / Halo / Waiting for the night / Enjoy the silence / Policy of truth / Blue dress / Clean.
May 90. (7")(c-s) **POLICY OF TRUTH. / KALEID (remix)** [16] [15] Aug 90
(12"+=)(cd-s+=) – ('A'-Pavlov's dub mix).
Sep 90. (7")(12")(cd-s) **WORLD IN MY EYES. / HAPPIEST GIRL / SEA OF SIN** [17] [52] Nov 90
(12") – (first 2 tracks) / ('A'remix).
(c-s+=)(cd-s+=) – Meaning of love / Somebody.

— In Nov 91.(re-iss.all singles on cd-s.3 ltd.box sets of 6)

Feb 93. (7")(c-s) **I FEEL YOU. / ONE CARESS** [8] [37]
(12"+=)(cd-s+=) – ('A'throb mix) / ('A'Babylon mix).
(12")(cd-s) – ('A'side) / ('A'swamp mix) / ('A'-Renegade Soundwave mix) / ('A'-Helmut mix).
Mar 93. (cd)(c)(lp) **SONGS OF FAITH AND DEVOTION** [1] [1]
– I feel you / Walking in my shoes / Condemnation / Mercy in you / Judas / In your room / Get right with me / Rush / One caress / Higher love.
May 93. (c-s)(cd-s) **WALKING IN MY SHOES. / MY JOY** [14] [69]
Sep 93. (c-ep)(12"ep) **CONDEMNATION. / PERSONAL JESUS (live) / ENJOY THE SILENCE (live) / HALO (live)** [9] [ ]
(cd-s) – ('A'Paris mix) / Death's door (jazz mix) / Rush (spiritual mix) / Rush (amylnitrate mix).
(12") – ('A'side) / Rush.
Dec 93. (cd)(c)(lp) **SONGS OF FAITH AND DEVOTION LIVE . . . (live)** [ ] [ ]
– (see last album)
Jan 94. (c-s)(cd-s) **IN YOUR ROOM / ('A'mixes) / HIGHER LOVE (adrenaline mix)** [8] [ ]
(cd-s)(12") – ('A'side) / ('A'mixes) / Never let me down again / Death's door.
(cd-s)(12") – ('A'side) / Policy of truth / World in my eyes / Fly on the windscreen.

— ANDREW FLETCHER departed to take over groups' business affairs.

— On the 17th August '95, GAHAN was thought by the music press, to have attempted suicide by cutting at his wrists after his wife left him. His record company however said this had been an accident and was over-hyped by the media.

. . . Jan – Jun '96 stop press . . .

— GAHAN is currently being treated for his drug problems and has been charged by US police for drug offences. They are recording an album.

MARTIN L. GORE

Mute Sire

Jun 89. (m-lp)(c)(cd) **COUNTERFEIT** [51] [ ]
– Smile in the crowd / Never turn your back on Mother Earth / Gone / Motherless child / Compulsion / In a manner of speaking.

DEREK & THE DOMINOES (see under ⇒ CLAPTON, Eric)

DESERT ROSE BAND (see under ⇒ BYRDS)

DEVO

Formed: Akron, Ohio, USA ... Sep'76 by 2 sets of brothers MOTHERSBAUGH and CASALE. From the early 70''s, they had been known as The DE-EVOLUTION BAND. Released 2 singles on own indie label 'Booji Boy', which became licensed to 'Stiff' UK in 1977. The following year, they signed to 'Warners'US & 'Virgin'UK, where they had Top 20 debut album inspiringly titled 'Q: ARE WE NOT MEN? A: WE ARE DEVO!'. Broke the US pop charts in 1980, when 'WHIP IT' made No.14. • **Style:** Comic strip, quirky new wave futurists, who experimented with electronic melody and intelligent pop-rock. Extreme dress sense brought a little light humour back into late 70's pop, and contrasted with the more serious German outfit KRAFTWERK. • **Songwriters:** JERRY & MARK wrote most of material, except the second best ever version of SATISFACTION (Rolling Stones) / ARE U EXPERIENCED (Jimi Hendrix) / WORKING IN A COALMINE (Lee Dorsey). • **Trivia:** In 1982, DEVO had contributed services to choreographer TONI BASIL on her debut solo album 'WORD OF MOUTH'. In the late 70's, MARK had appeared on HUGH CORNWALL (of The STRANGLERS) and ROBERT WILLIAMS collaboration 'Nosferatu'.

Recommended: HOT POTATOES: THE BEST OF DEVO (*8)

BOB MOTHERSBAUGH – vocals, guitar / **MARK MOTHERSBAUGH** – keyboards, synthesisers / **BOB CASALE** – guitar / **JERRY CASALE** – bass, vocals / **ALAN MYERS** – drums repl. JIM MOTHERSBAUGH

Stiff | Booji Boy

Feb 78. (7") **MONGOLOID. / JOCKO HOMO** | 62 | | Dec 76

Apr 78. (7")(12") **(I CAN'T GET ME NO) SATISFACTION. / SLOPPY (I SAW MY BABY GETTING)** | 41 | | Jul 77

Stiff | not issued

Jul 78. (7"clear)(7"lemon) **BE STIFF. / SOCIAL FOOLS** | 71 | |

Virgin | Warners

Aug 78. (7")(12")(7"grey) **COME BACK JONEE. / SOCIAL FOOLS** | 60 | - |

Sep 78. (lp)(c) **Q: ARE WE NOT MEN? A: WE ARE DEVO!** | 12 | 78 |
– Uncontrollable urge / (I can't get no) Satisfaction / Praying hands / Space junk / Mongoloid / Jocko homo / Too much paranoias / Gut feeling – (slap your mammy) / Come back Jonee / Sloppy (I saw my baby getting) / Shrivel-up. *(re-iss.Mar84) (also on pic-lp, w/free flexi-7")*

Sep 78. (7") **(I CAN'T GET NO) SATISFACTION. / UNCONTROLLABLE URGE** | - | |

Nov 78. (7") **COME BACK JONEE. / PRAYING HANDS** | - | |

Jun 79. (7") **THE DAY ME BABY GAVE ME A SURPRIZE. / PENETRATION IN THE CENTREFOLD** | | |

Jun 79. (lp)(c) **DUTY NOW FOR THE FUTURE** | 49 | 73 |
– Devo corporate anthem / Clockout / Timing X / Wiggly world / Blockhead / Strange pursuit / S.I.B. (Swelling Itching Brain) / Triumph of the will / The day my baby gave me a surprize / Pink pussycat / Secret agent man / Smart patrol – Mr. DNA / Red eye. *(re-iss.Mar84)*

Jul 79. (7") **SECRET AGENT MAN. / RED EYE** | - | |

Aug 79. (7") **SECRET AGENT MAN. / 500 BAWLS** | | - |

May 80. (7") **GIRL U WANT. / MR. B'S BALLROOM** | - | |

May 80. (7") **GIRL U WANT. / TURN AROUND** | | - |

May 80. (lp)(c) **FREEDOM OF CHOICE** | 47 | 22 |
– Girl u want / It's not right / Whip it / Snowball / Ton o' luv / Freedom of choice / Gates of steel / Cold war / Don't you know / That's Pep! / Mr.B's ballroom / Planet Earth. *(re-iss.Mar84)*

Nov 80. (7") **WHIP IT. / TURN AROUND** | 51 | 14 |

Feb 81. (7") **FREEDOM OF CHOICE. / SNOWBALL** | - | |

May 81. (7") **GATES OF STEEL. / BE STIFF (live)** | - | |

May 81. (m-lp)(c) **DEVO LIVE (live)** | | 49 | Apr 81
– Freedom of choice (theme song) / Whip it / Girl u want / Gates of steel / Be stiff / Planet Earth.

Aug 81. (7") **THROUGH BEING COOL. / GOING UNDER** | - | |

Aug 81. (7") **THROUGH BEING COOL. / RACE OF DOOM** | | - |

Aug 81. (lp)(c) **NEW TRADITIONALISTS** | 50 | 24 |
– Through being cool / Jerkin' back 'n' forth / Pity you / Soft things / Going under / Race of doom / Love without anger / The super thing / Beautiful world / Enough said. *(re-iss.Aug88)*

Oct 81. (7") **WORKING IN A COALMINE. / PLANET EARTH** | - | |

Oct 81. (7") **WORKING IN A COALMINE. / ENOUGH SAID** | | - |
(above iss. US on 'Asylum')

Nov 81. (7") **BEAUTIFUL WORLD. / ENOUGH SAID** | - | |

Jan 82. (7") **BEAUTIFUL WORLD. / THE SUPER THING** | | - |

Mar 82. (7") **JERKIN' BACK 'N' FORTH. / MECHA MANIA BOY** | - | |

Oct 82. (7")(US-12") **PEEK-A-BOO. / FIND OUT** | | |

Oct 82. (lp)(c) **OH NO! IT'S DEVO!** | | 47 |
– Time out for fun / Peek-a-boo / Out of synch / Explosions / That's good / Patterns / Big mess / Speed racer / What I must do / I desire / Deep sleep. *(re-iss.Aug88)*

Jan 83. (7") **THAT'S GOOD. / WHAT MUST I DO** | - | |

M.C.A. | Warners

Jun 83. (7")(12") **THEME FROM 'DOCTOR DETROIT'. / KING OF SOUL** | | 59 |

Warners | Warners

Oct 84. (7") **ARE YOU EXPERIENCED?. / GROWING PAINS** | - | |

Oct 84. (lp)(c) **SHOUT!** | | 83 |
– Shout / The satisfied mind / Don't rescue me / The 4th dimension / C'mon / Here to go / Jurisdiction of love / Puppet boy / Please please / Are you experienced?.

Mar 85. (7") **SHOUT. / C'MON** | | |
(d7"+=) – Mongloid / Jocko homo.

—— **DAVID KENDRICK** – drums, repl. MYERS.

Enigma | Enigma

Jul 88. (lp)(c)(cd) **TOTAL DEVO** | | | Jun 88
– Baby doll / Disco dancer / Some things never change / Plain truth / Happy guy / Don't be cruel / I'd cry if you died / Agitated / Man turned inside out / Blow up. *(re-iss.cd Mar95 on 'Restless')*

Oct 90. (7") **POST-POST MODERN MAN. / WHIP IT (live)** | | |
(12"+=) – ('A'-ultra post mix).
(cd-s++=) – Baby doll (mix).

Oct 90. (cd)(c)(lp) **SMOOTH NOODLE MAPS** | | |
– Stuck in a loop / Post-post modern man / When we do it / Spin the wheel / Morning dew / A chance is gonna cum / The big picture / Pink jazz trancers / Devo has feelings too / Jimmy / Danghaus. *(re-iss.cd Mar95 on 'Restless')*

– compilations etc. –

Jan 79. Stiff; (m-lp) **BE STIFF** (1st 3 singles 'A'&'B') | | - |

May 83. Virgin; (12"ep) **COME BACK JONEE. / WHIP IT / + 2** | | - |

Aug 87. Warners; (cd) **E-Z LISTENING DISC** | - | - |

Jul 89. Virgin; (d-lp)(cd) **NOW IT CAN BE TOLD** | | - |
(re-iss.cd Mar95 on 'Restless')

Jun 93. Virgin; (cd) **Q: ARE WE NOT MEN? A: WE ARE DEVO / DEVO LIVE** | | |

Jun 93. Virgin; (cd) **DUTY NOW FOR THE FUTURE / NEW TRADITIONALISTS** | | |

Jun 93. Virgin; (cd) **OH NO! IT'S DEVO / FREEDOM OF CHOICE** | | |

Sep 93. Virgin; (cd)(c) **HOT POTATOES: THE BEST OF DEVO** | | |
– Jocko homo / Mongoloid / Satisfaction (I can't get me no) / Whip it / Girl u want / Freedom of choice / Peek-a-boo / Thru being cool / That's good / Working in a coalmine / Devo corporate anthem / Be stiff / Gates of steel / Come back Jonee / Secret agent man / The day my baby gave me a surprise / Beautiful world / Big mess / Whip it (HMS & M remix).

Oct 90. Fan Club /US= Rykodisc; (cd)(lp) **HARD CORE DEVO** (demos 74-77) | | - |
(re-iss.c Mar94 on 'Rykodisc')

Dec 91. Rykodisc; (cd) **HARDCORE DEVO VOLUME 2: 1974-1977** | | |
(re-iss.c Mar94 on 'Rykodisc')

Sep 92. Rykodisc; (cd) **LIVE: THE MONGOLOID YEARS (live)** | | |

Oct 94. Virgin; (3xcd-box) **THE COMPACT COLLECTION** | | |

DEXY'S MIDNIGHT RUNNERS

Formed: Birmingham, England ... Jul'78 by ex-KILLJOYS members KEVIN ROWLAND and AL ARCHER. Named themselves after a frequently used pep-pill Dexerine. In 1979, new (ex-CLASH) manager Bernie Rhodes, obtained deal with 'Parlophone' records, and they scraped into the Top 40 with 'DANCE STANCE'. The following year, they became the darlings of the music press, after 'GENO' hit top spot. • **Style:** Initial image inspired from 'Mean Streets' film (i.e. New York dockers). Influenced by mid-60's brassy soul scene & GENO WASHINGTON whom they attributed on said No.1. In 1982, they took diverse new direction in acquiring scruffy dungareed attire to accompany gypsy-folk pop music. • **Songwriters:** All penned by ROWLAND, except BURNING DOWN THE WALLS OF HEARTACHE (Johnny Johnson & The Bandwagon) / ONE WAY LOVE (Russell-Meade) / SOUL FINGER (?) / JACKIE WILSON SAID (Van Morrison). • **Trivia:** In 1986, 'BECAUSE OF YOU', was used on TV sit-com 'Brush Strokes'.

Recommended: THE VERY BEST OF DEXY'S MIDNIGHT RUNNERS (*8)

KEVIN ROWLAND – vocals, guitar (b.17 Aug'53, Wolverhampton, England) (ex-KILLJOYS, as **KEVIN ROLAND) / AL ARCHER** – guitar, vocals (ex-KILLJOYS) / **PETE SAUNDERS** – keyboards / **PETE WILLIAMS** – bass, vocals / **JIMMY PATTERSON** – trombone / **J.B. BLYTE** – tenor, saxophone / **STEVE 'BABYFACE' SPOONER** – alto sax /

ANDY 'STOKER' GROWCOTT – drums repl. BOBBY JUNIOR

Parlophone not issued

Nov 79. (7") **DANCE STANCE. / I'M JUST LOOKING** 40 -

— **MICK TALBOT** – keyboards (ex-MERTON PARKAS) repl. SAUNDERS.

Mar 80. (7") **GENO. / BREAKING DOWN THE WALLS OF HEARTACHE** 1 -

Jun 80. (7") **THERE THERE MY DEAR. / THE HORSE** 7 -

Jul 80. (lp)(c) **SEARCHING FOR THE YOUNG SOUL REBELS** 6 -
– Burn it down / Tell me when my light turns green / The teams that meet in caffs / I'm just looking / Geno / Seven days too long / I couldn't help it if I tried / Thankfully not living in Yorkshire, it doesn't apply / Keep it / Love (pt.1) / There, there my dear. *(re-iss.1982 on 'Fame')*

Nov 80. (7") **KEEP IT. / ONE WAY LOVE** -

Mar 81. (7") **PLAN B. / SOUL FINGER** 58 -

— **ROWLAND and PATTERSON** recruited new guys **BILLY ADAMS** – guitar / **MICKEY BILLINGHAM** – keyboards / **PAUL SPEARE** – tenor sax / **BRIAN MAURICE** – alto sax / **SEB SHELTON** – drums (ex-SECRET AFFAIR) / **STEVE WYNNE** – bass (replaced ARCHER, GROWCOTT and TALBOT who formed BUREAU)

Mercury Mercury

Jun 81. (7") **SHOW ME. / SOON** 16

Nov 81. (7") **LIARS A TO E. / . . . AND YES, WE MUST REMAIN THE WILDHEARTED OUTSIDERS**

— Kept **ADAMS, SHELTON, PATTERSON** and **GIORGIO KILKENNY** – bass repl. WYNNE.

DEXY'S MIDNIGHT RUNNERS & EMERALD EXPRESS

added **HELEN O'HARA** – violin, vocals repl. BILLINGHAM / **STEVE BRENNAN** – violin / **ROGER MacDUFF** – violin

Mar 82. (7") **THE CELTIC SOUL BROTHERS. / LOVE (part.2)** 45

Jun 82. (7") **COME ON EILEEN. / DUBIOUS** 1 1 Jan 83
(12"+=) – Liars A to E (remix).

Jul 82. (lp)(c) **TOO-RYE-AY** 2 14 Feb 83
– The Celtic soul brothers / Let's make this precious / All in all / Jackie Wilson said (I'm in Heaven when you smile) / Old / Plan B – I'll show you / Liars A to E / Until I believe in my soul / Come on Eileen. *(cd-iss.Jan83)*

KEVIN ROWLAND & DEXY'S MIDNIGHT RUNNERS

PATTERSON left Jun82, MAURICE & SPEARE left Jul82.

Sep 82. (7") **JACKIE WILSON SAID. / LET'S MAKE THIS PRECIOUS** 5
(12"+=) – TSOP.

Nov 82. (7") **LET'S GET THIS STRAIGHT FROM THE START. / OLD (live)** 17
(12"+=) – Respect (live).

Mar 83. (7") **THE CELTIC SOUL BROTHERS. / REMINISCE (pt.1)** 20 86
(12"+=) – Show me.

DEXY'S MIDNIGHT RUNNERS

again. Line-up **ROWLAND, O'HARA & ADAMS / JIMMY PATTERSON** – trombone (returned) + new part-time sessioners / **NICKY GATFIELD** – saxophone / **JULIAN LITTMAN** – mandolin / **JOHN EDWARDS** – bass / **TOMMY EVANS** – steel guitar / **TIM DANCY** – drums / **ROBERT NOBLE** – keyboards, synthe / and special guest star **VINCENT CRANE** – piano (ex-ATOMIC ROOSTER)

Sep 85. (lp)(c)(cd) **DON'T STAND ME DOWN** 22
– The occasional flicker / This is what she's like / Knowledge of beauty / One of those things / Reminisce (pt.2) / Listen to this / The waltz. *(cd+=)* – This is what's she's like (instrumental).

Nov 85. (7") **THIS IS WHAT SHE'S LIKE. / ('A'instrumental)**
(12"+=) – Reminisce (part 1).
(10") – ('A'side) / Marguerita time.
(d12"+=) – ('A'+'B' versions).

Oct 86. (7") **BECAUSE OF YOU. / KATHLEEN MAVOUREEN** 13
(12"+=) – Sometimes theme.

– compilations, others, etc. –

Feb 83. E.M.I.; (7") **DANCE STANCE. / THERE THERE MY DEAR**

Mar 83. E.M.I.; (lp)(c) **GENO** 79
(re-iss.Oct87, cd-iss.Jun88 on 'Fame')

Mar 90. Old Gold; (7") **COME ON EILEEN. / JACKIE WILSON SAID** -

Sep 92. Old Gold; (cd-s) **GENO / THERE THERE MY DEAR / DANCE STANCE** -

Jun 91. Mercury; (cd)(c)(lp) **THE VERY BEST OF DEXY'S MIDNIGHT RUNNERS** 12
– Come on Eileen / Jackie Wilson said (i'm in heaven when you smile) / Let's get this straight (from the start) / Because of you / Show me / The celtic soul brothers (more, please, thank you) / Liars a to e / One way love / Old / Geno / There there my dear / Breakin' down the walls of heartache / Dance stance / Plan b / Keep it / I'm just looking / Soon / This is what she's like / Soul finger. (cd+=) – (5 extra tracks) *(re-iss.Jul92)*

Jun 91. Mercury; (7") **COME ON EILEEN. / BECAUSE OF YOU** -
(12"+=)(cd-s+=) – Let's get this straight (from the start).

May 93. Spectrum; (cd)(c) **BECAUSE OF YOU** -

Nov 93. Windsong; (cd) **BBC RADIO 1 LIVE IN CONCERT – NEWCASTLE (live)** -

ul 95. Nighttracks; (cd) **1980-1982 – THE RADIO SESSIONS** -

KEVIN ROWLAND

Mercury Mercury

Apr 88. (7") **WALK AWAY. / EVEN WHEN I HOLD YOU**
(12"+=) – ('A' version) / The way you look tonight.
(cd-s+=) – The way you look tonight / Because of you.

Jun 88. (lp)(c)(cd) **THE WANDERER**
– Young man / Walk away / You'll be the one for me / Heartaches by the number / I am a wanderer / Tonight / When you walk alone / Age can't wither you / I want / Remember me.

Jul 88. (7") **TONIGHT. / KEVIN ROWLAND'S BAND**
(12"+=) – Come on Eileen.

Oct 88. (7") **YOUNG MAN. / ONE WAY TICKET TO PALOOKAHVILLE**
(12"+=) – Jackie Wilson said (I'm in Heaven when you smile).
(cd-s+=) – Show me.

Bruce DICKINSON

Born: 7 Aug'58, Sheffield, England. Vocalist BRUCE BRUCE had cut his teeth in heavyweights SAMSON between 1978-1981. They released 2 albums 'HEAD ON' (1980) and 'SHOCK TACTICS', before he opted to join IRON MAIDEN. Now using his real surname, he became Britain's top heavy voxman, which helped boost all albums over the next 11 years to UK Top 3. Early in 1990 while still an IRON MAIDEN member, he unleashed his debut solo outing 'TATTOOED MILLIONAIRE'. While a little lighter and more commercial, it still gathered enough hard-rock support, even when re-hashing classic MOTT THE HOOPLE number 'ALL THE YOUNG DUDES'. Surprisingly he opted to leave IRON MAIDEN in 1993 and released second hit album the following year.

Recommended: BALLS TO PICASSO (*5)

solo, with **JANICK GERS** – guitar, co-composer / **FABIO DEL RIO** – drums (ex-JAGGED EDGE)

E.M.I. Columbia

Apr 90. (7")(c-s)(7"sha-pic-d) **TATTOOED MILLIONAIRE. / BALLAD OF MUTT** 18
(12"+=)(cd-s+=) – Winds of change.

May 90. (cd)(c)(lp) **TATTOOED MILLIONAIRE** 14 100
– Son of a gun / Tattooed millionaire / Born in '58 / Hell on wheels / Gypsy road / Dive! dive! dive! / All the young dudes / Lickin' the gun / Zulu Lulu / No lies.

Jun 90. (7")(c-s)(7"sha-pic-d) **ALL THE YOUNG DUDES. / DARKNESS BE MY FRIEND** 23
(12"+=)(cd-s+=) – Sin city.

Aug 90. (7")(c-s) **DIVE! DIVE! DIVE!. / RIDING WITH THE ANGELS (live)** 45
(12"+=)(cd-s+=)(12"pic-d+=) – Sin city / Black night.

Mar 91. (7")(c-s) **BORN IN '58. / TATTOOED MILLIONAIRE (live)**
(12"+=)(cd-s+=) – Son of a gun (live).

— feature backing from gangstas TRIBE OF GYPSIES.

May 94. (7"clear) **TEARS OF THE DRAGON. / FIRE CHILD** 28
(7"pic-d) – ('A'side) / Elvis has left the building.
(cd-s+=) – Breeding house / No way out . . .to be continued.
(cd-s+=) – Winds of change / Spirit of joy.

Jun 94. (cd)(c)(lp) **BALLS TO PICASSO** 21
– Cyclops / Hell no / Gods of war / 1000 points of light / Laughing in the hiding bush / Change of heart / Shoot all the clowns / Fire / Sacred cowboy / Tears of the dragon.

Sep 94. (7") **SHOOT ALL THE CLOWNS. / OVER AND OUT** 37
(cd-s) – ('A'side) / Tibet / Tears of the dragon: The first bit . . .
(cd-s) – ('A'side) / Cadillac gas mask / No way out – continued.
(12") – ('A'side) / Laughing in the hiding bush (live) / The post alternative Seattle fallout (live).

Castle Rykodisc

Mar 95. (cd)(c) **ALIVE IN STUDIO A (live)**
– Surrender to the city / She's the one that I adore / Wasted / D F dogs / The shipyard song / The past is another country.

. . . Jan – Jun '96 stop press . . .

Raw Power not issued

Mar 96. (cd)(c)(lp) **SKINKWORKS** 41

Apr 96. (single) **BACK FROM THE BREEZE** 68 -

DIFFORD & TILBROOK (see under ⇒ SQUEEZE)

DIGA RHYTHM BAND (see under ⇒ GRATEFUL DEAD)

Steve DIGGLE (see under ⇒ BUZZCOCKS)

DILLARD & CLARK (see under ⇒ BYRDS)

DINOSAUR JR.

Formed: Amherst, Massachusetts, USA . . . 1983 by J.MASCIS. After brief spell recording for US indie labels, they finally made it big in the 90s, landing contract for 'WEA' subsidiaries; Blanco Y Negro (UK) / Sire (US). • **Style:** Punk / hard-core rock, with flowing melodic psychedelia, not unlike HUSKER DU or MEAT PUPPETS, with MASCIS definitely influenced by NEIL YOUNG. • **Songwriters:** MASCIS wrote all, except JUST LIKE HEAVEN (Cure) / LOTTA LOVE (Neil Young) / QUICKSAND (David Bowie) / I FEEL A WHOLE LOT BETTER (Byrds) / GOIN' BLIND (Kiss) / HOT BURRITO 2 (Gram Parsons). • **Trivia:** In Jun'91, MASCIS as drummer, splintered with Boston satanic hard-core group UPSIDE DOWN CROSS, who made one self-titled album Autumn '91 on 'Taang!'. He also wrote songs and made a cameo appearance in the 1992 film 'Gas, Food, Lodging'.

Recommended: BUG (*7) / YOU'RE LIVING ALL OVER ME (*6) / GREEN MIND (*7) / WHERE YOU BEEN? (*7).

LOU BARLOW – guitar / **J.MASCIS** – drums / **CHARLIE NAKAJIMA** – vox / **SCOTT HELLAND** – bass

DEEP WOUND

not issued Radiobeat

Dec 83. (7"ep) **I SAW IT** [-] [ ]
– I saw it / Sisters / In my room / Don't need / Lou's anxiety song / Video prick / Sick of fun / Deep wound / Dead babies.

—— **J.MASCIS** – vocals, guitar, percussion / **LOU BARLOW** – bass, ukelele, vocals

DINOSAUR

added **MURPH** (b.PATRICK MURPHY) – drums (ex-ALL WHITE JURY)

not issued Homestead

Jun 85. (lp) **DINOSAUR** [-] [ ]
– Forget the swan / Cats in a bowl / The leper / Does it float / Pointless / Repulsion / Gargoyle / Several lips / Mountain man / Quest / Bulbs of passion,

Mar 86. (7") **REPULSION. / BULBS OF PASSION** [-] [ ]

DINOSAUR JR.

S.S.T. S.S.T.

Mar 87. (12"ep) **DINOSAUR JR.** [-] [ ]
– Little fury things / In a jar / Show me the way. *(cd-ep iss.Dec88)*

Jul 87. (m-lp)(c) **YOU'RE LIVING ALL OVER ME** [ ] [ ]
– Little fury things / Kracked / Sludgefeast / The lung / Raisans / Tarpit / In a jar / Lose / Poledo / Show me the way. *(cd-iss.Oct95)*

Blast First Blast First

Sep 88. (7") **FREAK SCENE. / KEEP THE GLOVE** [ ] [ ]
(US-iss.7"/7"green)

Oct 88. (lp)(c)(cd) **BUG** [ ] [ ]
– Freak scene / No bones / They always come / Yeah we know / Let it ride / Pond song / Budge / The post / Don't.

—— **DONNA BIDDELL** – bass (ex-SCREAMING TREES) repl. BARLOW

Apr 89. (7")(12"one-sided)(cd-s) **JUST LIKE HEAVEN / THROW DOWN / CHUNKS** [78] [ ] Feb 90
(US version 7"+=/7"green+=/12"ep+=/cd-ep+= Freak scene / Keep the glove)

—— BARLOW was sacked Jun'89, at the same time DONNA left. They were repl. by **DON FLEMING** – guitar + **JAY SPIEGEL** – drums (both B.A.L.L.)

not issued Sub Pop

Jun 90. (7")(7"purple) **THE WAGON. / BETTER THAN GONE** [-] [ ]

—— In Oct 90, J.MASCIS and other ex-DINOSAUR JR member FLEMING + SPIEGEL, made an album 'RAKE' as VELVET MONKEYS (aka B.A.L.L. + friends).

Blanco Y Negro Sire

Jan 91. (7")(c-s) **THE WAGON. / THE LITTLE BABY** [49] [ ]
(12"+=)(cd-s+=) – Pebbles and weeds / Quicksand.

Feb 91. (cd)(c)(lp) **GREEN MIND** [36] [ ]
– The wagon / Puke and cry / Blowing it – I live for that look / Flying cloud / How'd you pin that one on me / Water / Muck / Thumb / Green mind.

Aug 91. (7")(c-s) **WHATEVER'S COOL WITH ME. / SIDEWAYS** [ ] [ ]
(12"+=)(cd-s+=) – Thumb (live) / Keep the glove (live).

—— **MASCIS + MURPH** introduced new member **MIKE JOHNSON** – bass

Nov 92. (7") **GET ME. / HOT BURRITO 2** [44] [ ]
(12"+=)(c-s+=)(cd-s+=) – Qwest (live).

Jan 93. (7") **START CHOPPIN'. / TURNIP FARM** [20] [ ]
(12"+=)(cd-s+=)(10"pic-d+=) – Forget it.

Feb 93. (cd)(c)(lp) **WHERE YOU BEEN?** [10] [50]
– Out there / Start choppin' / What else is new? / On the way / Not the same / Get me / Drawerings / Hide / Goin' home / I ain't sayin'.

Jun 93. (7")(12")(c-s) **OUT THERE. / KEEBLIN' (live) / KRACKED (live)** [44] [ ]
(10"+=) – Post.
(cd-s++=) – Quest (live).
(cd-s) – ('A'side) / Get me / Severed lips / Thumb (radio sessions).

Aug 94. (7")(c-s)(10"etched)(cd-ep) **FEEL THE PAIN / GET OUT OF THIS / REPULSION (acoustic)** [25] [ ]

Sep 94. (cd)(c)(lp) **WITHOUT A SOUND** [24] [44]
– Feel the pain / I don't think so / Yeah right / Outta hand / Grab it / Even you / Mind glow / Get out of this / On the brink / Seemed like the thing to do / Over your shoulder.

Feb 95. (7"green)(c-s) **I DON'T THINK SO. / GET ME (live)** [67] [ ]
(cd-s+=) – What else is new? / Sludge.

. . . Jan – Jun '96 stop press . . .

MIKE JOHNSON

East West East West

Apr 96. (cd)(c) **YEAR OF MONDAYS** [ ] [ ]

J. MASCIS

WEA WEA

May 96. (cd)(c) **J. MASCIS** [ ] [ ]

DIO

Formed: By American RONNIE JAMES DIO, Oct'82 after basing himself in London, England. He recruited Irishman VIVIAN CAMPBELL and 2 Englishmen JIMMY BAIN and VINNY APPICE (brother of CARMINE). DIO's previous expreience, stretched back to the 1962, when he ran his own school group RONNIE & THE PROPHETS, who managed to issue a number of singles starting with 'LOVE PAINS. / OOH POO PAH DOO for 'Atlantic US'. In 1967, RONNIE and his cousin DAVID FEINSTEIN formed The ELECTRIC ELVES, who in the early 70's, became ELF. In 1972, they signed to 'Purple' records, and soon supported label boss's DEEP PURPLE. They made a couple of well-received albums, before he and most of others, took off in April 1975, to join RITCHIE BLACKMORE'S RAINBOW. In May'79, RONNIE took the place of OZZY OSBOURNE in BLACK SABBATH, and stayed with them until he formed own DIO group. Became successful albums orientated band throughout the 80's and early 90's. • **Style:** With dynamic vocal range, he obviously carried on where RAINBOW left off, portraying his anthemic tunes, to mystical themes backed with tight heavy metal backing. • **Songwriters:** DIO compositions, although he wrote material in ELF with MICKEY SOULE. • **Trivia:** RONNIE was also a fair player of the piano and bass in his early years.

Recommended: DIAMONDS – THE BEST OF DIO (*5)

RONNIE JAMES DIO (b.RONALD PADAVONA, 10 Jul'47, Portsmouth, New Hampshire, USA, raised Portland, NY) – vocals (ex-ELF, ex-RAINBOW, ex-BLACK SABBATH) / **VIVIAN CAMPBELL** – guitar (ex-SWEET SAVAGE) / **JIMMY BAIN** – bass (ex-RAINBOW, ex-WILD HORSES) / **VINNIE APPICE** – drums (ex-BLACK SABBATH) / **CLAUDE SCHNELL** – keyboards

Vertigo Warners

Jun 83. (lp)(c) **HOLY DIVER** [13] [56]
– Stand up and shout / Holy diver / Gypsy / Caught in the middle / Don't talk to strangers / Straight through the heart / Invisible / Rainbow in the dark / Shame on the night. *(re-iss.Mar88)*

Aug 83. (7") **HOLY DIVER. / EVIL EYES** [72] [ ]
(12"+=) – Don't talk to strangers.

Oct 83. (7") **RAINBOW IN THE DARK. / STAND UP AND SHOUT (live)** [46] [ ]
(12"+=) – Straight through the heart.

Oct 83. (7") **RAINBOW IN THE DARK. / GYPSY** [-] [ ]

Jul 84. (7") **MYSTERY. / I SPEED AT NIGHT** [-] [ ]

Jul 84. (lp)(c) **THE LAST IN LINE** [4] [23]
– We rock / The last in line / Breathless / I speed at night / One night in the

city / Evil eyes / Mystery / Eat your heart out / Egypt (the chains are on). *(cd-iss. 1985)(re-iss.cd Mar93 on 'Polygram')*

Jul 84. (7") **WE ROCK. / HOLY DIVER (live)** 42
(12"+=) – Shame on the night / Rainbow in the dark.

Sep 84. (7")(7"pic-d) **MYSTERY. / EAT YOUR HEART OUT** 34
(12"+=) – Don't talk to strangers.

Aug 85. (7") **ROCK'N'ROLL CHILDREN. / SACRED HEART**
(12"+=) – Last in line (live) / We rock (live).

Aug 85. (lp)(c)(cd) **SACRED HEART** 4 29
– King of rock'n'roll / Sacred heart / Another lie / Hungry for heaven / Rock'n 'roll children / Like the beat of a heart / Just another day / Fallen angels / Shoot shoot. *(re-iss.cd Mar93 on 'Polygram')*

Oct 85. (7")(7"sha-pic-d) **HUNGRY FOR HEAVEN. / KING OF ROCK'N'ROLL** 72
(12"+=) – ?

May 86. (7")(7"pic-d) **HIDING (FROM) THE RAINBOW. / HUNGRY FOR HEAVEN** 56
(d7"+=)(12"+=)(12"pic-d+=) – Shame on the night / Egypt (the chains are on).

—— **CRAIG GOLDIE** – guitar (in the studio) repl. CAMPBELL

Jun 86. (m-lp)(c) **INTERMISSION (live except *)** 22 70
– King of rock'n'roll / Rainbow in the dark / Sacred heart / Time to burn* / Rock'n'roll children / We rock. *(re-iss.cd Mar93 on 'Polygram')*

Jul 87. (7") **I COULD HAVE BEEN A DREAMER. / NIGHT PEOPLE** 69
(12"+=) – Sunset superman.

Aug 87. (lp)(c)(cd) **DREAM EVIL** 8 43
– Night people / Dream evil / Sunset superman / All the fools sailed away / Naked in the rain / Over love / I could have been a dreamer / Faces in the window / When a woman cries.

Aug 87. (7") **I COULD HAVE BEEN A DREAMER. / OVER LOVE** -

—— **DIO** recruited entire new line-up; **ROWAN ROBERTSON** (b.1971, Cambridge, England) – guitar repl. GOLDIE / **JENS JOHANSSON** (b.Sweden) – keyboards repl. SCHNELL / **TEDDY COOK** (b.New York, USA) – bass repl. BAIN / **SIMON WRIGHT** (b.19 Jun'63, England) – drums (ex-AC/DC) repl. APPICE

May 90. (cd)(c)(lp) **LOCK UP THE WOLVES** 28 61
– Wild one / Born on the sun / Hey angel / Between two hearts / Night music / Lock up the wolves / Evil on Queen street / Walk on water / Twisted / My eyes. *(cd+=)* – Why are they watching me.

Jun 90. (7") **HEY ANGEL. / WALK ON WATER**
(12"+=) – Rock'n'roll children / Mystery.
(cd-s++=) – We rock.
(12"+=) – We rock / Why are they watching me.

Mar 92. (cd)(c)(lp) **DIAMONDS – THE BEST OF DIO** (compilation)
– Holy Diver / Rainbow In The Dark / Don't Talk To Strangers / We Rock / The Last In Line / Rock 'n' Roll Children / Sacred Heart / Hungry For Heaven / Hide In The Rainbow / Dream Evil / Wild One / Lock Up The Wolves

Oct 93. (cd)(c)(lp) **STRANGE HIGHWAYS**
– Jesus, Mary & the holy ghost / Fire head / Strange highways / Hollywood black / Evilution / Pain / One foot in the grave / Give her the gun / Blood from a stone / Here's to you / Bring down the rain. *(re-iss.cd Apr95)*

– early material below –

ELECTRIC ELVES

RONNIE JAMES DIO – vocals, bass / **DAVE FEINSTEIN** – guitar / **DOUG THALER** – keyboards / **GARY DRISCOLL** – drums / **NICK PANTAS** – guitar

M.G.M. M.G.M.

Dec 67. (7") **HEY LOOK ME OVER. / IT PAYS TO ADVERTISE**

The ELVES

Decca ?

Sep 69. (7") **IN DIFFERENT CIRCLES. / SHE'S NOT THE SAME**

M.C.A. ?

Feb 70. (7") **AMBER VELVET. / WEST VIRGINIA**

—— Mid'70, all were involved in a car crash, PANTAS was killed and THALER hospitalised for a year.

ELF

were formed mid'71, by DIO, THALER (now guitar), **FEINSTEIN, DRISCOLL** and **MICKEY LEE SOULE** – keyboards, guitar

Epic Epic

Aug 72. (lp)(c) **ELF**
– Hoochie coochie lady / First avenue never more / I'm coming back for you / Sit down honey / Dixie Lee junction / Love me like a woman / Gambler gambler. *(re-iss.Sep86 on 'CBS')In Jul93, 'ELF' was issued on cd, by 'Sony Europe'.*

Sep 72. (7") **HOOCHIE KOOCHIE LADY. / FIRST AVENUE**

—— Early'73, moved to England. Added **CRAIG GRUBER** – bass STEVE EDWARDS – guitar replaced FEINSTEIN

Purple M.G.M.

Mar 74. (lp)(c) **CAROLINA COUNTRY BALL (US-title; L.A.59)**
– Carolina country ball / L.A.59 / Ain't it all amusing / Happy / Anmorte New Orleans / Rockin' chair rock'n'roll blues / Rainbow / Do the same thing / Blanche. *(re-iss.Aug84 on 'Safari')*

Apr 74. (7") **LA. 59. / AIN'T IT ALL AMUSING**

1975. (7") **SITTING IN A DREAM** ("RONNIE DIO & GUESTS") / ('B' by JOHN LAWTON) -

—— Added **MARK NAUSEEF** – percussion (ex-VELVET UNDERGROUND)

M.G.M. M.G.M.

Jun 75. (lp)(c) **TRYING TO BURN THE SUN**
– Black swan water / Prentice wood / When she smiles / Good time music / Liberty road / Shotgun boogie / Wonderworld / Streetwalker. *(re-iss.Aug84 on 'Safari')*

—— Apr'75. NAUSEEF joined GILLAN then THIN LIZZY. The rest with DIO joined (RITCHIE BLACKMORE'S) RAINBOW. DIO joined BLACK SABBATH in 1979.

– compilations, others, etc. –

May 87. Safari; (cd) **THE GARGANTIAN ELF ALBUM**
– (1974 + 1975 albums, minus a few tracks)

DIRE STRAITS

Formed: Deptford, London, England . . . mid-77 by ex-teacher and journalist MARK KNOPFLER, brother DAVID and JOHN ILLSLEY. In Oct'77, Radio 1 DJ Charlie Gillett gave their demo an airing, and soon A&R man John Stainze found and signed them to 'Vertigo' records. In May78, their debut single 'SULTANS OF SWING' missed chart, but eponymous album made the UK 40, after great live reviews and a major signing to 'Warners' in the States. After a sell-out US tour the single re-gained momentum again early the following year, re-peaking at US No.4 & UK 8. This enormously re-actified debut album sales, which shot it up to cross-Atlantic million selling Top 5 placings. BOB DYLAN invited MARK KNOPFLER to augment him on his 'Slow Train Coming' album of 1979. Meanwhile DIRE STRAITS were becoming worldwide rock stars, and by 1985 had one of the biggest selling albums of all-time, 'BROTHERS IN ARMS'. • **Style:** MARK was certainly influenced by laid back rock legends such as BOB DYLAN or JJ CALE. But DIRE STRAITS and virtuso guitarist MARK KNOPFLER were certainly treading most of their own ground all through the 80's. • **Songwriters:** KNOPFLER compositions, except when he formed a sort of TRAVELING WILBURYS style band The NOTTING HILLBILLIES, who based music on country folk-roots and covered FEEL LIKE GOING HOME (Charlie Rich). • **Trivia:** MARK penned 'PRIVATE DANCER' for TINA TURNER in 1983, and also produced to name but a few; 'Infidels' for BOB DYLAN and 'Knife' for AZTEC CAMERA.

Recommended: MONEY FOR NOTHING (*8).

MARK KNOPFLER (b.12 Aug'49, Glasgow, Scotland) – vocals, lead guitar / **DAVID KNOPFLER** (b.1951) – guitar / **JOHN ILLSLEY** (b.24 Jun'49, Leicester, England) – bass / **PICK WITHERS** – drums

Vertigo Warners

May 78. (7") **SULTANS OF SWING. / EASTBOUND TRAIN**
(re-iss.Jan79, hit UK No.8 + US No.4) (re-iss. 12" – Jan 83)

Jun 78. (lp)(c) **DIRE STRAITS** 5 2 Oct 78
– Down to the waterline / Water of love / Setting me up / Six blade knife / Southbound train / Sultans of swing / Wild West End / Lions / In the gallery. *(cd-iss.1987)(re-iss.cd+c May93)*

Jul 79. (7") **LADY WRITER. / WHERE DO YOU THINK YOU'RE GOING?** 45

Aug 79. (lp)(c) **COMMUNIQUE** 5 11 Jun 79
– Once upon a time in the west / News / Where do you think you're going? / Communique / Lady writer / Angel of mercy / Portobello belle / Single-handed sailor / Follow me home. *(cd-iss.1987)(re-iss.cd+c May93)*

Oct 79. (7") **ONCE UPON A TIME IN THE WEST. / NEWS** -

—— **HAL LINDES** (b.30 Jun'53, Monterey, California, USA) – guitar repl. DAVID who later went solo, also added **ROY BITTAN** – keyboards / (ex-E-STREET BAND BRUCE SPRINGSTEEN).

Oct 80. (lp)(c) **MAKING MOVIES** 4 19
– Tunnel of love / Romeo and Juliet / Skateaway / Expresso love / Hand in hand / Solid rock / Les boys. *(master deition Apr82) (cd-iss.1987)(re-iss.cd+c May93)*

Nov 80. (7") **ROMEO AND JULIET / SOLID ROCK** 8

Dec 80. (7") **SKATEAWAY. / SOLID ROCK** - 58

Mar 81. (7") **SKATEAWAY. / EXPRESSO LOVE** 37 -

Sep 81. (7") **TUNNEL OF LOVE. / TUNNEL OF LOVE (part 2)** 54

—— **ALAN CLARK** (b. 5 Mar'52, Durham, England) – keyboards repl ROY.

Aug 82. (7")(10") **PRIVATE INVESTIGATIONS. / BADGES, POSTERS, STICKERS, T-SHIRTS** 2 [ ]

Sep 82. (lp)(c)(cd) **LOVE OVER GOLD** 1 19
– Telegraph road / Private investigations / Industrial disease / Love over gold / It never rains / If I had you / Twisting by the pool / Two young lovers / Badges, posters, stickers, T-shirts. *(re-iss.cd+c May93)*

Nov 82. (7") **INDUSTRIAL DISEASE. / BADGES, POSTERS, STICKERS, T-SHIRT** - 75

Jan 83. (7"m)(12"m) **TWISTING BY THE POOL. / TWO YOUNG LOVERS / IF I HAD YOU** 14 53
(above iss.US Mar83 as m-lp, += Badges, Posters, Stickers, T-shirts)

—— **IOMAR HAKIM** – drums, percussion repl. PICK / above was replaced by **TERRY WILLIAMS** – drums ex-MAN, ex-MOTORS, ex-ROCKPILE. / (both played on album below alongside **MARK, JOHN, HAL** and **ALAN).**

Feb 84. (10")(12") **LOVE OVER GOLD (live). / SOLID GOLD (live)** 50 [ ]

Mar 84. (d-lp)(c)(cd) **ALCHEMY – LIVE** 3 46
– Once upon a time in the west / Romeo and Juliet / Expresso love / Private investigations / Sultans of swing / Two young lovers / Tunnel of love / Telegraph road / Solid rock / Going home (theme from "Local Hero"). *(c+=)(cd+=)* – Love over gold (live). *(re-iss.cd.1988)*

—— added **GUY FLETCHER** – keyboards / also **JACK SONNI** – guitar (on tour)

Apr 85. (7")(10")(12") **SO FAR AWAY. / WALK OF LIFE** 20 -

May 85. (lp)(c)(cd) **BROTHERS IN ARMS** 1 1
– So far away / Money for nothing / Walk of life / Your latest trick / Why worry? / Ride across the river / The man's too strong / One world / Money for nothing / Brothers in arms. *(c+=)(cd+=)* – So far away / Money for nothing / Your latest trick / Why worry? (extended versions). *(also available oblong pic-d)*

Jun 85. (7")(10")(12")(7"pic-d) **MONEY FOR NOTHING. / LOVE OVER GOLD (live)** 4 1

Oct 85. (7") **WALK OF LIFE. / ONE WORLD** - 7

Oct 85. (7")(10") **BROTHERS IN ARMS. / GOING HOME (live)** 16 [ ]
(12"+=) – Why worry.
(d7"++=)(ltd-cd-s++=) – ('A'version).

Jan 86. (7") **WALK OF LIFE. / TWO YOUNG LOVERS (live)** 2 -
(12"+=) – Sultans of swing.
(d7"++=) – Eastbound train (live).

Feb 86. (7") **SO FAR AWAY. / IF I HAD YOU** - 19

Apr 86. (7") **YOUR LATEST TRICK. / IRISH BOY** 26 [ ]
(12"+=) – The long road.

Oct 88. (lp)(c)(cd) **MONEY FOR NOTHING** (compilation) 1 62
– Sultans of swing / Down to the waterline / Portobello belle (live) / Twisting by the pool / Tunnel of love / Romeo and Juliet / Where do you think you're going? / Walk of life / Private investigations / Telegraph Road (live) / Money for nothing / Brothers in arms.

Nov 88. (7") **SULTANS OF SWING (re-issue). / PORTOBELLO BELLE** 62 [ ]
(12"+=)(cd-s+=) – Romeo and Juliet / Money for nothing.

Aug 91. (7")(c-s) **CALLING ELVIS. / IRON HAND** 21 [ ]
(12"+=)(cd-s+=) – Millionaire blues.

Sep 91. (cd)(c)(lp) **ON EVERY STREET** 1 12
– Calling Elvis / On every street / When it comes to you / Fade to black / The bug / You and your friend / Heavy fuel / Iron hand / Ticket to Heaven / My parties / Planet of New Orleans / How long.

Oct 91. (7") **HEAVY FUEL. / PLANET OF NEW ORLEANS** 55 [ ]
(12"+=)(cd-s+=) – Kingdom come.

Feb 92. (7")(c-s) **ON EVERY STREET. / ROMEO AND JULIET** 42 [ ]
(cd-s+=) – Private investigations / Sultans of swing.

Jun 92. (7")(c-s) **THE BUG. / TWISTING BY THE POOL** 67 [ ]
(cd-s+=) – ('A'version) ???

—— added touring band 91-93 **DANNY CUMMINGS** – percussion / **PHIL PALMER** – guitar / **PAUL FRANKLIN** – pedal steel / **CHRIS WHITE** – sax, flute / **CHRIS WHITTEN** – drums

May 93. (cd)(c)(lp) **ON THE NIGHT (live)** 4 [ ]
– Calling Elvis / Walk of life / Heavy fuel / Romeo & Juliet / Your latest trick / Private investigations / On every street / You and your friend / Money for nothing / Brothers in arms.

May 93. (12"ep)(c-ep)(cd-ep) **ENCORES LIVE EP (live)** 31 [ ]
– Your latest trick / The bug / Solid rock / Local hero (wild theme).

Oct93; MARK was credited on HANK MARVIN's single 'Wonderful Land'.

compilations, etc.

Jul 95. Windsong; (cd)(c)(lp) **LIVE AT THE BBC (live)** 71 -

MARK KNOPFLER

(first with **CLARK, LINDES** plus **MIKE BRECKER** – sax)

Vertigo Warners

Feb 83. (7")(12") **GOING HOME. / SMOOCHING** 56 [ ]

Apr 83. (lp)(c) **MUSIC FROM THE FILM SOUNDTRACK 'LOCAL HERO'** 14 [ ]
– The rocks and the water / Wild theme / Freeway flyer / Boomtown / The way it always starts / The rocks and the thunder / The ceilidh and the northern lights / The mist covered mountains / The ceilidh: Louis' favourite Billy's tune / Whistle theme / Smooching / The rocks and the thunder / Going home (theme from "Local Hero"). *(cd-iss.Jun89)*

Jul 84. (12") **COMFORT (THEME FROM COMFORT AND JOY. / FISTFUL OF ICE-CREAM** [ ] [ ]

Sep 84. (7")(12") **LONG ROAD. / IRISH BOY** [ ] [ ]

Oct 84. (lp)(c)(cd) **CAL (MUSIC FROM THE FILM)** 65 [ ]
– Irish boy / The road / Waiting for her / Irish love / A secret place / Where will you go? / Father and son / Meeting under the trees / Potato picking / in a secret place / Fear and hatred / Love and guilt / The long road.

Oct 86. (7")(12") **GOING HOME. / WILD THEME** [ ] [ ]
(cd-s+=) – Comfort (theme from Comfort And Joy).
(re-iss.7"/c-s Oct 93)

Nov 87. (lp)(c)(cd) **MUSIC FROM THE FILM SOUNDTRACK 'THE PRINCESS BRIDE'** [ ] [ ]
– Once upon a time . . . storybook love / I will never love again / Florin dance / Morning ride / The friends' song / The cliffs of insanity / The sword fight / Guide my sword / The fireswamp and the rodents of unusual size / Revenge / A happy ending / Storybook love.

Mar 88. (7") **STORYBOOK LOVE. / THE FRIENDS SONG** [ ] [ ]
(c-s+=)(cd-s+=) – ('A'version) / Once upon a time.

Nov 89. (lp)(c)(cd) **LAST EXIT TO BROOKLYN (Soundtrack)** [ ] [ ]
– Last exit to Brooklyn / Victims / Think fast / A love idea / Tralala / Riot / The

reckoning / As low as it gets / Last exit to Brooklyn -finale

NOTTING HILLBILLIES

MARK KNOPFLER – guitar, vocals, producer / **GUY FLETCHER** – guitar, vocals, producer / **BRENDAN CROKER** – guitar, vocals / **STEVE PHILLIPS** – guitar, vocals / with **PAUL FRANKLIN** – pedal steel guitar

Vertigo Warners

Feb 90. (7")(c-s) **YOUR OWN SWEET WAY. / BEWILDERED**
(12"+=)(cd-s+=) – That's where I belong.

Mar 90. (cd)(c)(lp) **MISSING . . . PRESUMED HAVING A GOOD TIME** 2 52
– Railroad worksong / Bewildered / Your own sweet way / Run me down / One way gal / Blues stay away from me / Will you miss me / Please baby / Weapon of prayer / That's where I belong / Feel like going home.

Apr 90. (7")(c-s) **FEEL LIKE GOING HOME. / LONESOME WIND BLUES**
(12"+=)(cd-s+=) – One way gal.

Jun 90. (7")(c-s) **WILL YOU MISS ME. / THAT'S WHERE I BELONG**
(12"+=)(cd-s+=) – Lonesome wind blues.

CHET ATKINS & MARK KNOPFLER

C.B.S. Columbia

Oct 90. (7") **POOR BOY BLUES. / ?**

Nov 90. (cd)(c)(lp) **NECK AND NECK** 41
– Poor boy blues / Sweet dreams / There'll be some changes made / Just one time / So soft / Your goodbye / Yakety axe / Tahitian skies / Tears / I'll see you in my dreams / The next time I'm in town. *(re-iss.cd/c May93)*

. . . Jan – Jun '96 stop press . . .

MARK KNOPFLER

Vertigo Warners

Mar 96. (single) **DARLING PRETTY** 33
Apr 96. (cd)(c) **GOLDEN HEART** 9
May 96. (single) **CANNIBAL** 42

JOHN ILLSLEY

Vertigo Warners

Jun 84. (7")(12") **NEVER TOLD A SOUL. / HYPNOTISED**

Jun 84. (lp)(c)(cd) **NEVER TOLD A SOUL**
– Boy with Chinese eyes / The night cafe / Never told a soul / Jimmy on the central line / Northern land / Another alibi / Let the river flow.

May 88. (7") **I WANT TO SEE THE MOON. / WORDS**
(12"+=)(cd-s+=) – The world is made of glass.

May 88. (lp)(c)(cd) **GLASS**
– High stakes / I want to see the Moon / Papermen / All I want is you / The world is full of glass / Red turns to blue / Let's dance / She wants everything / Star for now.

DISCO 2000 (see under ⇒ KLF)

DIVINE COMEDY

*** NEW ENTRY ***

Formed: Enniskillen & Londonderry, N. Ireland . . .1990 by NEIL HANNON and two others. Debut produced by SEAN O'NEILL of THAT PETROL EMOTION. Half a decade later, HANNON (DIVINE COMEDY) had their first success with the album 'CASANOVA'. • **Style:** HANNON is a romantic eccentric and son of the bishop of Cloghes. Influenced by SCOTT WALKER or MICHAEL NYMAN. • **Songwriters:** HANNON. • **Trivia:** The PROMENADE album featured comedian SEAN HUGHES. Came to light in 1994 when instrumental 'SONGS OF LOVE' was used on the Channel 4 Irish comedy 'Father Ted'.

Recommended: CASANOVA (*8)

NEIL HANNON (b. 7 Nov'70) – vocals, guitar / + 2

Setanta not issued

Aug 90. (m-lp) **FANFARE FOR THE COMIC MUSE** -

Nov 91. (12"ep) **TIMEWATCH. / JERUSALEM / THE RISE AND FALL** -

Feb 92. (12"ep) **EUROPOP. / NEW WAVE / INTIFADA / MONITOR** -
(cd-ep+=) – TIMEWATCH EP.

Jul 93. (7"ep)(12"ep)(cd-ep) **LUCY. / THE POP SINGER'S FEAR OF THE POLLEN COUNT / I WAS BORN YESTERDAY** -

Aug 93. (cd)(lp) **LIBERATION** -
– Festive road / Death of a supernaturalist / Bernice bobs her hair / I was born yesterday / Your daddy's car / Europop / Timewatching / The singer's fear of the pollen count / Queen of the south / Victoria Falls / Three sisters / Europe by train / Lucy.

Oct 93. (7"pic-d-ep) **INDULGENCE No.1** -
– Untitled melody / Hate my way / Europe by train.

Mar 94. (cd)(c)(lp) **PROMENADE** -
– Bath / Going downhill / The booklovers / A seafood song / Geronimo / Don't look down / When the lights go out all over Europe / The summerhouse / Neptune's daughter / A drinking song / Ten seconds to midnight / Tonight we fly.

Aug 94. (7"ep) **INDULGENCE No.2** -

— now one-man band NEIL HANNON

Apr 96. (cd)(c)(lp) **CASANOVA** 71
– Something for the weekend / Becoming more like Alfie / Middle class heroes / In and out of Paris and London / Charge / Songs of love / The frog princess / A woman of the world / Through a long and sleepless night / Theme from Casanova / The dogs and the horses.

Jun 96. (c-s) **SOMETHING FOR THE WEEKEND / SONGS OF LOVE (theme from 'Father Ted')** 14
(cd-s+=) – Birds of Paradise farm / Love is lighter than air.

DODGY

Formed: Hounslow, London, England . . .early 1990 as a trio. With DJ CHRIS SLADE, they set up The Dodgy Club in the summer, where they gained local support. Did first national tour in September '91 termed the 'Word Of Mouth' tour, as they didn't know where they were playing until their fans phoned up prospective promoters and venues. A year later, they were snapped up by 'A&M', who released 2 quickfire singles in Spring '93. • **Style:** Pop-rock; The BEATLES and SQUEEZE rolled into one. • **Songwriters:** Basic trio, except I CAN'T MAKE IT (Small Faces). • **Trivia:** Guests on second album were ROB LORD – keyboards / CAROLINE LAVELLE + SONIA SLANY – strings. It was produced by HUGH JONES.

Recommended: THE DODGY ALBUM (*7) / HOMEGROWN (*6) / FREE PEACE SWEET (*8)

NIGEL CLARK – vocals, bass / **ANDY MILLER** – lead guitar, vocals / **MATHEW PRIEST** – drums, vocals, percussion

Bostin' not issued

Sep 91. (12") **SUMMER FAYRE. / ST.LUCIA** -

Nov 91. (7") **EAST WAY. / SEEMS LIKE A BAD DAY** -
(cd-s+=) – Groove song (St.Lucia demo) / Smeasy way.

Apr 92. (7"white)(7")(12")(12"white) **THE BLACK AND WHITE SINGLE-black side: JUNGLE DARK DANCE BATH / ELEVATORS GOIN' UP (WORTH THE BLOOD). / white side: 4am NOCTURNAL / WATCH THE SUN GO DOWN (THE ELEPHANT)** -
(cd-s+=) – D-Club (versions).

— added 4th member **CHRIS SLADE** – DJ, keyboards

A & M A & M

Mar 93. (7")(c-s) **WATER UNDER THE BRIDGE. / IT'S BEEN SO LONG**
(12"+=)(cd-s+=) – She wants my loving / Valuable fool.

Apr 93. (7")(c-s) **LOVEBIRDS. / BIG BROWN MOON** 65
(12"+=)(cd-s+=) – Sylvia's bedroom / Smashed up in a flat.

Jun 93. (cd)(c)(lp) **THE DODGY ALBUM** 75
– Water under the bridge / I need another / Lovebirds / Satisfied / Grand old English oak tree / Stand by yourself / As my time goes by / Never again / Cold tea / We're not going to take this anymore.

Jun 93. (7"mustard-ep)(c-ep) **I NEED ANOTHER. / IF I FALL / HENDRE DHU** 67
(12"ep+=)(cd-ep+=) – Never again (campfire version).

Oct 93. (12"ep)(cd-ep) **HOMEGROWN E.P.**
– Don't go back (to the beaten track) / Home grown / Let's wait till we get there.

— now without CHRIS and back to trio

Jul 94. (7"ep)(c-ep) **THE MELOD-E.P.: MELODIES HAUNT YOU. / THE SNAKE** 53
(10"+=) – Don't go back (to the beaten track).
(cd-s++=) – Summer fayre.

Sep 94. (7"blue)(c-s) **STAYING OUT FOR THE SUMMER. / LOVEBIRDS (original)** 38
(cd-s+=) As time goes by (demo) / Back to life.
(cd-s) ('A'side) / A summer's day in mid-January / Don't you think / Colour me with paints.

Oct 94. (cd)(c)(lp) **HOMEGROWN** 43

– Staying out for the summer / Melodies haunt you / So let me go far / Crossroads / One day / We are together / Whole lot easier / Making the most of / Waiting for the day / What have I done wrong? / Grassman. *(re-iss.Jun95, hit No.28)*

Dec 94. (c-s) **SO LET ME GO FAR. / DON'T GET LOW, DON'T GET LOW (U.K.R.I.P.)** [30] [ ]
(12"+=)(cd-s+=) – The elephant / So let me wobble jah.
(cd-s) – ('A'side) / I need another (live) / Satisfied (live) / Melodies haunt you (live).

— below featured The KICK HORNS

Feb 95. (7"pic-d)(c-s) **MAKING THE MOST OF. / FAISONS AU MIEUX (YES, IT'S IN FRENCH)** [22] [ ]
(cd-s+=) – The Ludlow sessions part 1: Spent all my time running / All the time in the world.
(cd-s) – ('A'extended) / The Ludlow sessions part 2: Watch out watcha doin' / This is ours / (Get off your) High horse.

May 95. (c-s) **STAYING OUT FOR THE SUMMER (mixed up in 95) / SATISFIED (live)** [19] [ ]
(cd-s) – ('A'side) / (Your love keeps lifting me) Higher and higher / Crossroads (live) / Melodies haunt you (live).
(cd-s) – ('A'side) / Waiting for the day (live) / One day (live) / (Get off your) High horse (live).

. . . Jan – Jun '96 stop press . . .

May 96. (single) **IN A ROOM** [12] [ ]
Jun 96. (cd)(c)(lp) **FREE PEACE SWEET** [7] [ ]

DOG EAT DOG

*** NEW ENTRY ***

Formed: New York, USA . . .1993 by 5-piece below. The EP 'WARRANT' was issued that year, but the following year's 'ALL BORO KINGS' saw them using producer JASON CORSARO. • **Style:** Anthemic thrash rap; hot on the heels of RED HOT CHILI PEPPERS, RAGE AGAINST THE MACHINE, CYPRESS HILL or BIOHAZARD. • **Songwriters:** Group.

Recommended: ALL BORO KINGS (*6)

JOHN CONNOR -vocals / **DAN NASTASI** -guitar, vocals / **SEAN KILKENNY** -guitar / **DAVE NEABORE** -bass / **DAVID MALTBY** -drums

Road-runner / Road-runner

Aug 93. (cd-ep) **WARRANT** [ ] [ ]
– It's like that / Dog eat dog / World keeps spinnin' / In the dog house / Psychorama / In the dog house (dog pound remix).

Jun 94. (cd) **ALL BORO KINGS** [ ] [ ]
– If these are good times / Think / No fronts / Pull my finger / Who's the king / Strip song / Queen / In the dog house / Funnel king / What comes around / It's like that / Dog eat dog / World keeps spinnin' / No fronts.

Sep 94. (cd-s) **IF THESE ARE THE GOOD TIMES / NO FRONTS / MORE BEER / WHY DOES IT HURT WHEN I PEE?** [ ] [ ]

Mar 95. (cd-s) **WHO'S THE KING / PULL MY FINGER OUT (live)** [ ] [ ]
(cd-s) – ('A'side) / Think (live) / Dog eat dog (live).

Aug 95 (cd-s) **NO FRONTS: THE REMIXES** [64] [ ]
– (Jam Master Jay's main mix) / (Clean Greene mix).
(cd-s+=) – (Psycho Les Pass mix) / (Jam Master Jay's TV mix).
(12"+=) – (Not Pearl Jame mix) / (Jam Master Jay's TV mix).
(re-iss.Jan96, hit UK No.9)

— **BRANDON FINDLAY** -drums repl.MALTBY

— **MARK DE BACKER** – guitar + **SCOTT MUELLER** -sax repl.NASTASI

DOLPHIN BROTHERS (see under ⇒ JAPAN)

DOME (see under ⇒ WIRE)

DONOVAN

Born: DONOVAN PHILIP LEITCH, 10 May'46, Maryhill, Glasgow, Scotland. At age 10, his family had moved to Hatfield, England. In 1964, while playing small gigs in Southend, he was noticed by Geoff Stephens and Peter Eden, who became his managers. Late 1964, while playing 3 consecutive weeks on 'Ready Steady Go!' pop show, he signed to 'Pye'. His debut single 'CATCH THE WIND', released the same time as DYLAN's 'The Times They Are A-Changin'', broke him into the UK Top 5, and later reached No.23 in the US, where he also had burgeoning career. • **Style:** Initially Britain's answer to BOB DYLAN, who retained folk/pop roots which progressed into flower-power in 1966. Dressed himself in denim cap and jeans which led to beatnik/hippie tag. A peace loving anti-war activist, guided in the studio by enigmatic producer MICKIE MOST. In 1968, he was yet another star (i.e.The BEATLES), to seek the inspiration and transcendental meditation of the Maharishi Mahesi Yogi. In 1971, he recorded a double album of children's songs 'H.M.S. DONOVAN', which led to a critical backlash from the music press. After a 3-year exile in Ireland due to tax purposes, he set up home in California 1974, with wife Linda Lawrence and daughters Astrella and Oriole. He has 2 other children to American ENID; DONOVAN LEITHCH JNR. (star of film 'Gas, Food, Lodging') and IONE SKYE, although the latter is said nt to bother too much about her famous father. • **Songwriters:** Self-penned except, UNIVERSAL SOLDIER (Buffy Sainte-Marie) / LONDON TOWN (Tim Harding) / REMEMBER THE ALAMO (Jane Bowes) / CAR CAR (Woody Guthrie) / GOLDWATCH BLUES (Mick Softley) / DONNA DONNA (Kevess-Secunda-Secanta-Schwartz-Zeitlin) / OH DEED I DO+ DO YOU HEAR ME NOW (Bert Jansch) / CIRCUS OF SOUR (Paul Bernath) / LITTLE TIN SOLDIER (Shawn Phillips / LORD OF THE DANCE (Sydney Carter) / ROCK'N'ROLL WITH ME (David Bowie-Warren Peace) / MY SONG IS TRUE (Darell Adams) / NO MAN'S LAND (Eric Bogle) / WIND IN THE WILLOWS (Eddie Hardin) / NEWEST BATH GUIDE + MOIRA McCAVENDISH (John Betjeman) / THE SENSITIVE KIND (J. J. Cale) / traditional:- KEEP ON TRUCKIN' + YOU'RE GONNA NEED SOMEBODY + CANDY MAN + THE STAR + COULTER'S CANDY + HENRY MARTIN + THE HEIGHTS OF ALMA + YOUNG BUT GROWING + STEALIN'. He also put music to words/poetry by; William Shakespeare (UNDER THE GREENWOOD TREE) / Gypsy Dave (A SUNNY DAY) / Lewis Carroll (WALRUS AND THE CARPENTER + JABBERWOCKY) / Thora Stowell (THE SELLER OF STARS + THE LITTLE WHITE ROAD) / Fifida Wolfe (LOST TIME) / Lucy Diamond (THE ROAD) / Agnes Herbertson (THINGS TO WEAR) / Edward Lear (THE OWL AND THE PUSSYCAT) / Eugene Field (WYNKEN, BLYNKEN AND NOD) / W. B. Yeats (THE SONG OF WANDERING AENGUS) / Natalie Joan (A FUNNY MAN) / Thomas Hood (QUEEN MAB) / Astella Leitch (MEE MEE I LOVE YOU) / Warwick Embury (ONE NIGHT IN TIME) / Note; HURLEY GURLEY MAN originally had a verse by GEORGE HARRISON but this was not recorded and he only added this for live appearences. • **Trivia:** Sang co-lead on title track from ALICE COOPER's 1973 lp 'Billion Dollar Babies'.

Recommended: GREATEST HITS AND MORE (*8)

DONOVAN – vocals, acoustic guitar, harmonica with **BRIAN LOCKING** – bass / **SKIP ALLEN** – drums / **GYPSY DAVE** (b. DAVID MILLS) – kazoo, etc.

P.Y.E. / Hickory

Mar 65. (7") **CATCH THE WIND. / WHY DO YOU TREAT ME LIKE YOU DO** [4] [23] Apr 65
May 65. (7") **COLOURS. / TO SING FOR YOU** [4] [61] Jun 65
May 65. (lp) **WHAT'S BIN DID AND WHAT'S BIN HID** [3] [30]
– Josie / Catch the wind / Remember the Alamo / Cuttin' out / Car car * (riding in my car) / Keep on truckin' / Goldwatch blues / To sing for you / You're gonna need somebody on your bond / Tangerine puppet / Donna Donna * / Ramblin' boy *(re-iss.Jul68 on 'Marble Arch' omiting *)*
Sep 65. (7") **UNIVERSAL SOLDIER. / DO YOU HEAR ME** [-] [53]
Sep 65. (7"ep) **THE UNIVERSAL SOLDIER EP** [13] [-]
– Universal soldier* / The ballad of a crystal man / Do you hear me now* / The war drags on.
Oct 65. (lp) **FAIRY TALE** [20] [85] Dec 65
– Colours * / I'll try for the Sun / Sunny Goodge street / Oh deed I do / Circus of sour / The summer day reflection song / Candy man / Jersey Thursday / Belated forgiveness plea / Ballad of a crystal man / Little tin soldier * / Ballad of Geraldine. *(re-iss.Mar69 on 'Marble Arch' omitting *) (re-iss.cd+c.Feb91 on 'Castle')*
Nov 65. (7") **TURQUOISE. / HEY GYP (DIG THE SLOWNESS)** [30] [-]
Nov 65. (7") **YOU'RE GONNA NEED SOMEBODY ON YOUR BOND. / THE LITTLE TIN SOLDIER** [ ] [ ]
Jan 66. (7") **I'LL TRY FOR THE SUN. / TURQUOISE** [-] [ ]
Feb 66. (7") **JOSIE. / LITTLE TIN SOLDIER** [ ] [-]
Apr 66. (7") **REMEMBER THE ALAMO. / THE BALLAD OF A CRYSTAL MAN** [ ] [-]

— **DONOVAN** plus **JOHN CAMERON** – piano, harpsicord / **HAROLD McNAIR** – flute

P.Y.E. / Epic

Jul 66. (7") **SUNSHINE SUPERMAN. / THE TRIP** [2] [1] Jun 66
Sep 66. (lp) **SUNSHINE SUPERMAN** [-] [11]
– Sunshine Superman / Legend of a girl child Linda / The observation / Guinevere / Celeste / Writer in the Sun / Season of the witch / Hampstead incident / Sand and foam / Young girl blues / Three kingfishers / Bert's blues. *(UK-iss.Feb91 on 'BGO')(re-iss.cd+c Sep93 on 'Remember')*

Nov 66. (7") **MELLOW YELLOW. / SUNNY SOUTH KENSINGTON** [-] [2]
Jan 67. (7") **EPISTLE TO DIPPY. / PREACHIN' LOVE** [-] [19]
Feb 67. (7") **MELLOW YELLOW. / PREACHIN' LOVE** [8] [-]
Feb 67. (lp) **MELLOW YELLOW** [-] [14]
– Mellow yellow / Writer in the Sun / Sand and foam / The observation / Bleak city woman / House of Jansch / Young girl blues / Museum / Hampstead incident / Sunny South Kensington. *(cd-iss.Oct93 on 'Sony Europe')*
Jun 67. (lp) **SUNSHINE SUPERMAN** [25] [-]
-(compilation of last 2 US albums)
Oct 67. (7") **THERE IS A MOUNTAIN. / SAND AND FOAM** [8] [11] Sep 67

— **DONOVAN** retained **HAROLD** and in came **TONY CARR** – percussion / **CANDY JOHN CARR** – bongos **CLIFF BARTON** – bass / **KEITH WEBB** – drums / **MIKE O' NEIL** – keyboards / **MIKE CARR** – vibraphone / **ERIC LEESE** – electric guitar

Dec 67. (7") **WEAR YOUR LOVE LIKE HEAVEN. / OH GOSH** [-] [23]
Dec 67. (lp) **WEAR YOUR LOVE LIKE HEAVEN** [-] [60]
– Wear your love like Heaven / Mad John's escape / Skip-a-long Sam / Sun / There was a time / Oh gosh / Little boy in corduroy / Under the greenwood tree / The land of doesn't have to be / Someone's singing / Song of the naturalist's wife / The enchanted gypsy.

— **KEN BALDOCK** – bass repl. BARTON, LEESE, WEBB, O'NEIL + MIKE CARR.

Dec 67. (lp) **FOR LITTLE ONES** [-] [ ]
– Voyage into the golden screen / Isle of Islay / The mandolin man and his secret / Lay of the last tinker / The tinker and the crab / Widow with shawl (a portrait) / The lullaby of spring / The magpie / Starfish-on-the-toast / Epistle to Derroll.
Feb 68. (7") **JENNIFER JUNIPER. / POOR COW** [5] [26]
Apr 68. (d-lp-box) **A GIFT FROM A FLOWER TO A GARDEN** [13] [19]
(contains 2 US Dec67 albums boxed) *(cd-iss.Jul 93 on 'B.G.O.')*
May 68. (7") **HURDY GURDY MAN. / TEEN ANGEL** [4] [5]
Sep 68. (lp) **DONOVAN IN CONCERT (live)** [ ] [18] Jul68
– Isle of Islay / Young girl blues / There is a mountain / Poor cow / Celeste / The fat angel / Guinevere / Widow with shawl (a portrait) / Preachin' love / The lullaby of Spring / Writer in the Sun / Rules and regulations / Pebble and the man / Mellow yellow. *(re-iss.+c+cd.May91 on 'BGO') (cd-iss.Nov94 on 'Start')*
Oct 68. (7") **LALENA. / AYE, MY LOVE** [-] [33]
Oct 68. (lp) **HURDY GURDY MAN** [-] [20]
– Jennifer Juniper / Hurdy gurdy man / Hi, it's been a long time / Peregrine / The entertaining of a shy girl / Tangier / As I recall it / Get thy bearings / West Indian lady / Teas / The river song / The Sun is a very magic fellow / A sunny day.
Nov 68. (7") **ATLANTIS. / I LOVE MY SHIRT** [23] [-]
Feb 69. (7") **ATLANTIS. / TO SUSAN ON THE WEST COAST WAITING** [-] [7]
[35]

DONOVAN with The JEFF BECK GROUP

(**JEFF BECK** – guitar)
Jun 69. (7") **GOO GOO BARABAJAGAL (LOVE IS HOT). / BED WITH ME** [12] [-]
Sep 69. (7") **GOO GOO BARABAJAGAL (LOVE IS HOT). / TRUDI** [-] [36]
Sep 69. (lp) **BARABAJAGAL** [-] [ ]
– Barabajagal / Superlungs my supergirl / I love my shirt / The love song / To Susan on the West Coast waiting / Atlantis / Trudi / Pamela Jo / Happiness runs. *(cd-iss.Oct93 on 'Sony Europe')*

DONOVAN AND THE OPEN ROAD

with **JOHN CARR** – drums, vocals / **MIKE THOMPSON** – bass, vocals / **MIKE O'NEILL** – piano

Dawn Epic
Sep 70. (lp) **OPEN ROAD** [30] [16] Jul 70
– Changes / Song for John / Curry land / Joe Bean's theme / People used to / Celtic rock / Riki tiki tavi / Clara clairvoyant / Roots of oak / Season of farewell / Poke at the Pope / New Year's resovolution.
Sep 70. (7") **RIKI TIKI TAVI. / ROOTS OF OAK** [ ] [55]

DONOVAN WITH DANNY THOMPSON

(DANNY – double bass)
Dec 70. (7") **CELIA OF THE SEALS. / MR.WIND** [ ] [-]

DONOVAN

was now solo again.
Feb 71. (7") **CELIA OF THE SEAS. / THE SONG OF THE WANDERING AENGUS** [-] [84]
Jul 71. (d-lp) **H.M.S. DONOVAN** [ ] [ ]
– The walrus and the carpenter / Jabberwocky / The seller of the stars / Lost time / The little white road / The star / Coulter's candy / The road / Things to wear / The owl and the pussycat / Homesickness / Fishes in love / Mr.Wind / Wynken, Bylnken and Nod / Celia of the seas / The pee song / The voyage to the Moon / The unicorn / Lord of dance / Little Ben / Can ye dance / In an old fashioned picture book / The song of the wandering Aengus / A funny man / Lord of the reedy river / Henry Martin / Queen Mab / La moor.

— with guests **CHRIS SPEDDING** – guitar / **JOHN 'RABBIT' BUNDRICK** – keyboards / **JIM HORN** – bass / **COZY POWELL** – drums

Epic Epic
Mar 73. (lp)(c) **COSMIC WHEELS** [15] [ ]
– Cosmic wheels / Earth sign man / Sleep / / Maria Magenta / Wild witch lady / Sleep / The music makers / The intergallactic laxative / I like you / Only the blues / Appearances. *(cd-iss.Sep94 on 'Rewind')*
Apr 73. (7") **I LIKE YOU. / EARTH SIGN MAN** [ ] [66]
Jun 73. (7") **MARIA MAGENTA. / THE INTERGALLACTIC LAXATIVE** [ ] [ ]

— now with **STEVE MARRIOT, PETER FRAMPTON** and **NICKY HOPKINS**

Nov 73. (7") **SAILING HOMEWARD. / LAZY DAZE** [-] [ ]
Dec 73. (lp)(c) **ESSENCE TO ESSENCE** [ ] [ ]
– Operating manual for spaceship Earth / Lazy daze / Life goes on / There is an ocean / Dignity of man / Yellow star / Divine daze of deathless delight / Boy for every girl / Saint Valentine's angel / Life is a merry-go-round / Sailing homeward.
Jan 74. (7") **SAILING HOMEWARD. / YELLOW STAR** [-] [ ]

— Mainly used session musicians from now on.

Sep 74. (7") **ROCK'N'ROLL WITH ME. / THE DIVINE DAZE OF DEATHLESS DELIGHT** [ ] [ ] Nov 74
Nov 74. (lp)(c) **7-TEASE** [ ] [ ]
– Rock and roll souljer / Your broken heart / Salvation stomp / The ordinary family / Ride-a-mile / Sadness / Moon rok / Love of my life / The voice of protest / How silly / The great song of the sky / The quest.
Jan 75. (7") **ROCK AND ROLL SOULJER. / HOW SILLY** [-] [ ]
Feb 75. (7") **ROCK AND ROLL SOULJER. / LOVE OF MY LIFE** [ ] [-]
Jun 76. (lp)(c) **SLOW DOWN WORLD** [ ] [ ]
– Dark-eyed blue jean angel / Cryin' shame / The mountain / Children of the world / My love is true (love song) / A well known has-been / Black widow / Slow down world / Liberation rag.
Jun 76. (7") **A WELL-KNOWN HAS-BEEN. / DARK EYED BLUE JEAN ANGEL** [-] [ ]

Rak Arista
Aug 77. (7") **DARE TO BE DIFFERENT. / THE INTERNATIONAL MAN** [-] [ ]
Oct 77. (lp)(c) **DONOVAN** [ ] [ ]
– Brave new world / Local boy chops wood / Kalifornia kids / International man / Lady of the stars / Dare to be different / Mijah's dance / The light / Astral angel.
Nov 77. (7") **THE LIGHT. / THE INTERNATIONAL MAN** [ ] [-]
Feb 78. (7") **DARE TO BE DIFFERENT. / SING MY SONG** [ ] [-]

— (note:- on above US singles [Jan 73, Jan 75, Jun 76, Aug 77] the 'B' side was mono version on 'A').

not issued R.A.
Aug 80. (lp) **NEUTRONICA** [-] [-] Germ.
– Shipwreck / Only to be expected / Comin' to you / No hunger / Neutron / Mee Mee I love you / The heights of Alma / No man's land / We are one / Madrigalinda / Harmony.

— with **DANNY THOMPSON** – double bass / **JOHN STEPHENS** – drums / **TONY ROBERTS** – multi-wind instruments / and his 9 year-old daughter **ASTELLA** – dual vocals

Luggage- RCA not issued
Oct 81. (lp)(c) **LOVE IS ONLY FEELING** [ ] [-]
– Lady of the flowers / Lover o lover / The actor / Half Moon bay / The hills of Tuscany / Lay down Lassie / She / Johnny Tuff / Love is only feeling / Marjorie Margerine.
Oct 81. (7") **LAY DOWN LASSIE. / LOVE IS ONLY FEELING** [ ] [-]

R.C.A. Allegiance
Jan 84. (lp)(c) **LADY OF THE STARS** [ ] [ ]
– Lady of the stars / I love you baby / Seasons of the witch / Bye bye girl / Every reason / Boy for every girl / Local boy chops wood / Sunshine superman / Til I see you again / Living for the lovelight.

After nearly 7 years in the wilderness, he returned on new label

Permanent Permanent
Nov 90. (cd)(c)(lp) **DONOVAN RISING** [ ] [ ]
– Jennifer Juniper / Catch the wind / The hurdy gurdy man / Sunshine superman / Sadness / Universal soldier / Cosmic wheels / Atlantis / Wear your love like heaven / Colours / To Susan on the west coast waiting / Young girl blues / Young but growing / Stealing / Sailing homeward / Love will find a way / Lalena.

— He had also credited on The SINGING CORNER's (Nov90) single version of his JENNIFER JUNIPER.

Silhouette not issued
Apr 92. (7"m) **NEW BATH GUIDE / MOIRA McCAVENDISH / BROTHER SUN, SISTER MOON** [ ] [-]

– compilations, others, etc. –

Dec 65. Pye; (7"ep) **COLOURS** [ ] [-]
– Catch the wind / Why do you treat me like you do / Colours / To sing for you.
Mar 66. Pye; (7"ep) **DONOVAN VOL.1** [ ] [-]
– Sunny Goodge Street / Oh deed I do / Jersey Thursday / Hey Gyp (dig the slowness).
Jul 66. Hickory; (7") **HEY GYP (DIG THE SLOWNESS). / THE WAR DRAGS ON** [-] [ ]
Oct 66. Hickory; (7") **SUNNY GOODGE STREET. / SUMMER DAY REFLECTION SONG** [-] [ ]
Sep 66. Hickory; (lp) **THE REAL DONOVAN** [-] [96]
Feb 68. Pye; (7"ep) **CATCH THE WIND** [ ] [-]
– Catch the wind / Remember the Alamo / Josie / Rambling Rose.
Apr 68. Hickory; (lp) **LIKE IT IS, WAS AND EVERMORE SHALL BE** [-] [ ]
1968. Hickory; (7") **DO YOU HEAR ME NOW. / WHY DO YOU TREAT ME LIKE YOU DO** [-] [ ]
Aug 68. Pye; (7"ep) **HURDY GURDY DONOVAN** [ ] [-]
– Jennifer juniper / Hurdy gurdy man / Mellow yellow / There is a mountain. *(re-iss.Nov71)*
Jan 69. Hickory; (7") **CATCH THE WIND. / UNIVERSAL SOLDIER** [-] [ ]
Mar 69. Pye/ US= Epic; (lp) **DONOVAN'S GREATEST HITS** [ ] [4]
(re-iss.1973) (re-iss.Sep79 on 'CBS-Embassy') (cd-iss.Aug90 on 'Epic')
1973. Pye/ US= Epic; (4xlp-set) **FOUR SHADES OF DONOVAN / OPEN ROAD / DONOVAN'S GREATEST HITS/ / H.M.S. DONOVAN** [ ] [ ]
Nov 77. Pye; (d-lp) **THE DONOVAN FILE** [ ] [-]
1978. Epic; (7") **SUNSHINE SUPERMAN. / MELLOW YELLOW** [-] [ ]
Jul 78. Epic; (7") **COLOURS. / UNIVERSAL SOLDIER** [-] [ ]
Oct 67. Marble Arch; (lp) **UNIVERSAL SOLDIER** [5] [-]
(re-iss.Feb83 on 'Spot')
1969. Marble Arch; (lp)(c) **THE WORLD OF DONOVAN** [ ] [-]
Mar 69. United Artists; (lp) **IF IT'S TUESDAY IT MUST BE BELGUIM (Soundtrack)** [ ] [ ]
Oct 70. Janus; (7") **COLURS. / JOSIE** [-] [ ]
Oct 70. Janus; (7") **CATCH THE WIND. / WHY DO YOU TREAT ME LIKE YOU DO** [-] [ ]
Oct 70. Janus; (7") **CANDY MAN. / HEY GYP (DIG THE SLOWNESS)** [-] [ ]
Nov 70. Janus; (d-lp) **DONOVAN P.LEITCH** (early work) [-] [ ]
1971. Golden Hour; (lp)(c) **THE GOLDEN HOUR OF DONOVAN** [ ] [-]
Nov 69. Hickory; (lp) **THE BEST OF DONOVAN** [-] [ ]
1971. Hallmark; (lp)(c) **CATCH THE WIND** [ ] [-]
(re-iss.Apr86 on 'Castle')
1972. Hallmark; (lp) **COLOURS** [ ] [-]
(re-iss.+cd.Oct87 on 'P.R.T.')
1972. Memory Lane; (7") **SUNSHINE SUPERMAN. / MELLOW YELLOW** [-] [ ]
1972. Memory Lane; (7") **JENNIFER JUNIPER. / HURDY GURDY MAN** [-] [ ]
Jul 80. Flashback; (7"ep) **EP** [ ] [-]
– Catch the wind / Turquoise / Colours / Universal soldier.
Oct 81. P.R.T.; (lp)(c) **SPOTLIGHT ON DONOVAN** [ ] [-]
Jul 83. P.R.T.; (10"lp) **MINSTREL BOY** [ ] [-]
Jul 82. Old Gold; (7") **CATCH THE WIND. / COLOURS** [ ] [-]
Feb 85. E.M.I.; (7") **MELLOW YELLOW. / SUNSHINE SUPERMAN** [ ] [-]
Aug 89. E.M.I.; (7") **SUNSHINE SUPERMAN. / JENNIFER JUNIPER** [ ] [-]
('A'extended-12"+=) – Wear your love like Heaven.
(cd-s++=) – Mellow yellow.
Sep 89. E.M.I.; (lp)(c)(cd) **GREATEST HITS AND MORE** [ ] [-]
– Sunshine Superman / Wear your love like Heaven / Jennifer Juniper / Barabajagal (love is hot) / Hurdy gurdy man / Epistle to Dippy / To Susan on the West Coast waiting / Catch the wind / Mellow yellow / There is a mountain / Happiness runs / Season of the witch / Colours / Superlungs-My Supergirl / Lalena / Atlantis.
(cd+=) – Preachin' love / Poor cow / Teen angel / Aye my love.
Feb 91. E.M.I.; (d-cd)(d-c)(d-lp) **THE TRIP** (1964-1968 material) [ ] [ ]
Nov 94. E.M.I.; (4xcd-box) **ORIGINALS** [ ] [ ]
Oct 90. See For Miles; (lp)(c)(cd) **THE EP COLLECTION** [ ] [-]
Mar 91. Gulf Peace Team; (7") **UNIVERSAL SOLDIER. / CATCH THE WIND** [ ] [ ]
(12"+=) I'll try for the sun.
Jun 91. Mammoth; (cd)(c) **THE HITS** [ ] [-]
Dec 93. Disky; (cd) **GOLD: GREATEST HITS** [ ] [-]
May 94. Magnum; (cd) **COLOURS** [ ] [-]
Jul 94. Success; (cd)(c) **JOSIE** [ ] [-]
Jul 94. Success; (cd)(c) **TILL I SEE YOU AGAIN** [ ] [-]
Jan 95. Spectrum; (cd) **UNIVERSAL SOLDIER** [ ] [-]
Dec 95. Javelin; (cd) **SUNSHINE SUPERMAN** [ ] [-]

DOOBIE BROTHERS

Formed: San Jose, California, USA ... 1970 as PUD, by JOHN HARTMAN, TOM JOHNSTON and DAVE SHOGREN. In 1971, they signed to 'Warner Bros.' and released unsuccessful eponymous Ted Templeton produced album. Their second album 'TOULOUSE STREET', gave them their first gold disc, with cut from it 'LISTEN TO THE MUSIC', nearly hitting US Top 10 in 1972. • **Style:** Typical West Coast soft-rock outfit with boogie feel, described as an easy-listening ALLMANS. They blended together a fine harmonious (near gospel) backing, with funky soulful rock. In 1978, their sound had encompassed aspects of dance beat AOR. • **Songwriters:** JOHNSTON or SIMMONS penned until MICHAEL McDONALD contributed on his 1975 arrival. JESUS IS JUST ALRIGHT (Byrds) / TAKE ME IN YOUR ARMS (Holland-Dozier-Holland) / LITTLE DARLIN' (I NEED YOU) (Marvin Gaye) / etc. WHAT A FOOL BELIEVES was co-written by McDONALD and KENNY LOGGINS. • **Trivia:** They took the name 'DOOBIE' from the slang for a joint.

Recommended: LISTEN TO THE MUSIC – THE VERY BEST OF THE DOOBIES (*7) / THE BEST OF THE DOOBIES, VOL.II (1981 compilation lp)

TOM JOHNSTON (b. Visalia, California, USA) – vocals, guitar / **PAT SIMMONS** (b.23 Jan'50, Aberdeen, Washington, USA) – guitar, vocals / **DAVE SHOGREN** (b. San Francisco, California, USA) – bass / **JOHN HARTMAN** (b.13 Mar'50, Falls Church, Virginia, USA) – drums

Warners Warners

Apr 71. (lp)(c) **THE DOOBIE BROTHERS** [ ] [ ]
– Nobody / Slippery St. Paul / Greenwood creek / It won't be right / Travellin' man / Feelin' down farther / The master / rowin' a litle each day / Beehive state / Closer every day / Chicago. *(re-iss.Jul87) (cd-iss.May95)*
Apr 71. (7") **NOBODY. / SLIPPERY ST. PAUL** [-] [ ]
Jul 71. (7") **TRAVELIN' MAN. / FEELIN' DOWN FARTHER** [-] [ ]
Sep 71. (7") **BEEHIVE STATE. / CLOSER EVERY DAY** [-] [ ]

—— **TIRAN PORTER** (b. Los Angeles) – bass, vocals repl. SHOGREN.
added 2nd drummer **MICHAEL HOSSACK** (b.18 Sep'50, Paterson, New York, USA)

Jul 72. (lp)(c) **TOULOUSE STREET** [ ] [21]
– Listen to the music / Don't start me talkin' / Mamaloi / Toulouse Street / Rockin' down the highway / Jesus is just alright / White sun / Cotton mouth / Disciple / Snake man. *(quad-lp 1976) (cd-iss.Jul88)(cd-iss.May93)*
Aug 72. (7") **LISTEN TO THE MUSIC. / TOULOUSE STREET** [29] [11]
Dec 72. (7") **JESUS IS JUST ALRIGHT. / ROCKIN' DOWN THE HIGHWAY** [ ] [35]
Mar 73. (lp)(c) **THE CAPTAIN AND ME** [ ] [7]
– Natural thing / Long time runnin' / China Grove / Dark-eyed Cajun woman / Clear as the driven snow / Without you / South city midnight lady / Evil woman / Busted down around O'Connelly corners / Ukiah / The captain and me. *(cd-iss.Oct87 & Feb95)*
Apr 73. (7") **LONG TRAIN RUNNIN'. / WITHOUT YOU** [ ] [8]
Aug 73. (7") **CHINA GROVE. / EVIL WOMAN** [ ] [15]

—— **KEITH KNUDSON** (b.18 Oct'52, Ames, Iowa) – drums (ex-MANDELBAUM) repl. HOSSACK / added **BILL PAYNE** – keyboards (ex-LITTLE FEAT)

Feb 74. (lp)(c) **WHAT WERE ONCE VICES ARE NOW HABITS** [19] [4]
– Song to see you through / Spirit / Pursuit on 53rd street / Black water / Eyes of silver / Road angel / You just can't stop it / Tell me what you want / Down in the track / Another park, another Sunday / Flying cloud. *(quad-lp US 1976) (cd-iss.Jul88)(cd-iss.May93)*
Apr 74. (7") **ANOTHER PARK, ANOTHER SUNDAY. / BLACK WATER** [ ] [32]
Jul 74. (7") **EYES OF SILVER. / YOU JUST CAN'T STOP IT** [ ] [52]
Oct 74. (7") **FLYING CLOUD. / NOBODY** [ ] [58] B-side
Dec 74. (7") **BLACK WATER. / SONG TO SEE YOU THROUGH** [ ] [1]

—— **JEFF BAXTER** (b.13 Dec'48, Washington DC) – guitar (ex-STEELY DAN) repl. PAYNE who rejoined LITTLE FEAT.

Apr 75. (lp)(c) **STAMPEDE** [14] [4]
– Sweet Maxine / Neal's fandango / Texas lullaby / Music man / Slat key sequel rag / Take me in your arms / I cheat the hangman / Precis / Rainy day crossroad blues / I've been workin' on you / Double dealin' four flusher. *(cd-iss.Jun89)(cd-iss.May93)*
Apr 75. (7") **TAKE ME IN YOUR ARMS. / SLAT KEY SEQUEL RAG** [29] [ ]
Jul 75. (7") **SWEET MAXINE. / DOUBLE DEALIN' FOUR FLUSHER** [ ] [40]
Nov 75. (7") **I CHEAT THE HANGMAN. / MUSIC MAN** [ ] [60]

— **MICHAEL McDONALD** (b.1952, St.Louis, Missouri) – keyboards, vocals (ex-STEELY DAN) repl. JOHNSTON who fell ill.

Mar 76. (lp)(c) **TAKIN' IT TO THE STREETS** [42] [8]
– Wheels of fortune / Takin' it to the streets / 8th Avenue shuffle / Losin' end / Rio / For someone special / It keeps you runnin' / Turn it loose / Carry me away. *(cd-iss.Jun89)*

Mar 76. (7") **TAKIN' IT TO THE STREETS. / FOR SOMEONE SPECIAL** [ ] [13]

Aug 76. (7") **WHEELS OF FORTUNE. / SLAT KEY SEQUEL RAG** [ ] [87]

Nov 76. (7") **IT KEEPS YOU RUNNIN'. / TURN IT LOOSE** [ ] [37]

— **TOM JOHNSTON** returned but left again early '77 to go solo.

Jul 77. (7") **LITTLE DARLING (I NEED YOU). / LOSING END** [ ] [48]

Aug 77. (lp)(c) **LIVIN' ON THE FAULT LINE** [25] [10]
– You're made that way / Echoes of love / Little darling (I need you) / You belong to me / Livin' on the fault line / Nothin' but a heartache / Chinatown / There's a light / Need a lady / Larry the logger two-step. *(cd-iss.Jun89)*

Sep 77. (7") **ECHOES OF LOVE. / THERE'S A LIGHT** [ ] [66]

Mar 78. (7") **LIVIN' ON THE FAULT LINE. / NOTHIN' BUT A HEARTACHE** [-] [ ]

Dec 78. (lp)(c) **MINUTE BY MINUTE** [ ] [1]
– Sweet feelin' / Open your eyes / Dependin' on you / Here to love you / Minute by minute / You never change / What a fool believes / Steamer lane breakdown / How do the fools survive? / Don't stop to watch the wheels. *(cd-iss. 1988 & Feb95)*

Jan 79. (7"+12") **WHAT A FOOL BELIEVES. / DON'T STOP TO WATCH THE WHEELS** [31] [1]

Apr 79. (7") **MINUTE BY MINUTE. / SWEET FEELIN'** [-] [14]

Apr 79. (7") **MINUTE BY MINUTE. / HOW DO THE FOOLS SURVIVE?** [ ] [-]

Jul 79. (7") **DEPENDIN' ON YOU. / HOW DO THE FOOLS SURVIVE?** [ ] [25]

Aug 79. (7") **OPEN YOUR EYES. / STEAMER LANE BREAKDOWN** [ ] [ ]

— **JOHN McFEE** (b.18 Nov'53, Santa Cruz, California) – guitar, vocals repl. BAXTER / **CHET McCRACKEN** (b.17 Jul'52, Seattle, Washington) – drums, vibes (ex-session man) repl. HARTMAN / added **CORNELIUS BUMPUS** (b.13 Jan'52) – keys, sax (ex-MOBY GRAPE) / (now septet alongside **SIMMONS, McDONALD, PORTER and KNUDSEN**).

Aug 80. (7") **REAL LOVE. / THANK YOU LOVE** [ ] [5]

Oct 80. (lp)(c) **ONE STEP CLOSER** [53] [3]
– Dedicate this heart / Real love / No stoppin' us now / Thank you love / One step closer / Keep this train a-rollin' / Just in time / South bay strut / One by one.

Nov 80. (7") **ONE STEP CLOSER. / SOUTH BAY STRUT** [ ] [24]

Dec 80. (7") **WYNKEN, BLYNKEN AND NOD. / IN HARMONY** [ ] [76]

— (above credited w/ KATE + SIMON TAYLOR)

Jan 81. (7") **KEEP THIS TRAIN A-ROLLIN'. / JUST IN TIME** [ ] [62]

— **WILLIE WEEKS** – bass repl. PORTER.

They split Mar82, recorded final concert album Sep82.

Jun 83. (d-lp)(d-c) **THE DOOBIE BROTHERS FAREWELL TOUR (live)** [ ] [79]
– Slippery St. Paul / Takin it to the streets / Jesus is just alright / Minute by minute / Can't let it get away / Listen to the music / Echoes of love / What a fool believes / Black water / You belong to me / Slat key sequel rag / Streamer lane breakdown / South city / Midnight lady / Olana / Don't start me to talking / Long train runnin' / China grove. *(re-iss.Aug84)*

Jul 83. (7") **YOU BELONG TO ME. / SOUTH CITY MIDNIGHT LADY** [ ] [79]

— By this time MICHAEL McDONALD had gone solo, as did PATRICK SIMMONS. **DOOBIE BROTHERS** reformed mid'88. (JOHNSTON, HARTMAN, SIMMONS, PORTER) plus **MICHAEL HOSSACKS** – drums / **BOBBY LAKIND** – percussion

Capitol Capitol

Jul 89. (lp)(c)(cd) **CYCLES** [ ] [17] Jun 89
– The doctor / One chain (don't make no prison) / Take me to the highway / South of the border / Time is here and gone / Need a little taste of love / I can read your mind / Wrong number / Tonight I'm coming through (the border) / Too high a price.

Jul 89. (7") **THE DOCTOR. / TOO HIGH A PRICE** [73] [9] May 89
(12"+=)(cd-s+=) – Anything for love.

Sep 89. (7") **NEED A LITTLE TASTE OF LOVE. / I CAN READ YOUR MIND** [ ] [45] Aug 89
(12"+=)(cd-s+=) – The doctor.

Apr 91. (cd)(c)(lp) **BROTHERHOOD** [ ] [82]
– Something you said / Is love enough / Dangerous / Our love / Divided highway / Under the spell / Excited / This train I'm on / Showdown / Rollin' on.

– compilations etc. –

Nov 76. Warners; (lp)(c) **THE BEST OF THE DOOBIES** [ ] [5]
– China Grove / Long train runnin' / Takin' it to the streets / Listen to the music / Black water / Rockin' down the highway / Jesus is just alright / It keeps you runnin' / South city midnight lady / Take me in your arms (rock me a little while) / Without you. *(cd-iss.1988)*

Nov 81. Warners; (lp)(c) **THE BEST OF THE DOOBIES VOL.2** [ ] [39]
– Little darlin' / Echoes of love / You belong to me / One step closer / What a fool believes / Dependin' on you / Here to love you / One by one / Real love / Minute by minute.

Jan 82. Warners; (7") **HERE TO LOVE YOU. / WYNKEN, BLYNKEN AND NOD** [ ] [65]

1984. Warners; (d-c) **TAKIN' IT TO THE STREETS. / LIVIN' ON THE FAULT LINE** [ ] [ ]

Jan 87. Warners; (7") **WHAT A FOOL BELIEVES. / MINUTE BY MINUTE** [57] [ ]
(12"+=) – Real love.

May 93. Warners; (cd)(c) **LISTEN TO THE MUSIC – THE VERY BEST OF THE DOOBIE BROTHERS** [ ] [ ]
(re-iss. May 94)

Nov 93. Warners; (7")(c-s) **LONG TRAIN RUNNIN'. / ('A'mix)** [7] [ ]
(12"+=)(cd-s+=) – ('A' mix).

Apr 94. Warners; (7")(c-s) **LISTEN TO THE MUSIC ('94 remix). / ('A'mix)** [37] [ ]
(12"+=)(cd-s+=) – ('A'remixes by MOTIV8 / RAMP . . . / DEVELOPMENT CORPORATION)

Mar 86. Old Gold; (7") **LISTEN TO THE MUSIC. / WHAT A FOOL BELIEVES** [ ] [-]

May 93. F.N.A.C.; (cd) **INTRODUCING . . .** [ ] [-]

— JOHN HARTMAN who was a reserve fireman /policeman, was refused promotion by his home state court, due to his alleged drug-taking past.

PATRICK SIMMONS

Elektra Elektra

Mar 83. (7") **SO WRONG. / IF YOU WANT A LITTLE LOVE** [ ] [30]

Apr 83. (lp)(c) **ARCADE** [ ] [52]
– Out on the streets / So wrong / Don't make me do it / Why you givin' up / Too long / Knocking at your door / If you want a little love / Have you seen her / Sue sad / Dream about me.

Jun 83. (7") **DON'T MAKE ME DO IT. / SUE SAD** [-] [75]

DOORS

Formed: Los Angeles, California, USA . . . July 1965 by RAY MANZAREK and JIM MORRISON. In 1966 after some personnel changes, they soon settled with JOHN DENSMORE and ROBBIE KREIGER, to become The DOORS. They were released from a 'Columbia' recording contract, when ARTHUR LEE (of LOVE), recommended them to his 'Elektra' label boss Jac Holzman. Early in 1967, their eponymous debut lp was issued, and soon climbed to US No.2, after an edited version of 'LIGHT MY FIRE' hit No.1 in Jul'67. This classic lp contained an extremely disturbing 11 minute gem 'THE END' (which was later used on the 1979 Francis Ford Coppola film 'Apocalypse Now'). After another US Top 3 album at the end of '67, things looked bleak as MORRISON's drink and drugs antics were increasing. He was arrested many times on stage and off, mostly for lewd simulation of sexual acts and indecent exposure. In the late summer of '68, they were top of the US charts again with 45 'HELLO I LOVE YOU' and lp 'WAITING FOR THE SUN'. More controversy was aroused when in Nov'69, MORRISON was accused of interfering with a stewardess while a flight was in progress. He was later acquitted, but the following year, he was given 8 months hard labour, etc., after being found guilty of indecent exposure and profanity. He was freed on appeal, but moved to Paris in March '71, where he was to be found dead in his bathtub on the 3rd July 1971. Speculation was rife at the time, but it seemed he died from a drugs/drink induced heart attack. He was also buried in Paris, his grave becoming a shrine to all but his parents, who disowned him in '67. Two months prior to his death, The DOORS had issued their 6th studio US Top 10 album 'L.A.WOMAN'. It was a remarkable return to form, and featured a superb title track and 2 classic US Top 20 hits, 'LOVE HER MADLY' & 'RIDERS ON THE STORM'. The others continued as a trio for the next 2 years, but sadly the public refused to acknowledge them as the real DOORS. • **Style:** Theatrical rock and blues, which diversified dramatically from organ orientated rock'n'roll to experimental but classic pop. MORRISON's stage energy and sexual aura although controversial, was group's forte. Many groups have copied, but few have sustained any lasting god-like credibility. • **Songwriters:** MORRISON – words/poetry (under the influence of explorative narcotics), Group/MANZAREK compositions. Covered; ALABAMA SONG (Brecht-Weill) / BACK DOOR MAN (Howlin' Wolf) / WHO DO YOU LOVE (Bo Diddley) / CRAWLING KING SNAKE (John Lee Hooker) / LITTLE RED ROOSTER (Willie Dixon). • **Trivia:** In 1968, they featured on a UK TV documentary 'The Doors Are Open', which was later issued on video. In

Lizard King

1991, Oliver Stone released a feature film 'THE DOORS', with Val Kilmer playing the role of MORRISON.

Recommended: THE DOORS (*10) / STRANGE DAYS (*8) / ABSOLUTELY LIVE (*7) / L.A. WOMAN (*9) / WEIRD SCENES INSIDE THE GOLDMINE (*8).

JIM MORRISON (b. 8 Dec'43, Melbourne, Florida, USA) – vocals / **RAY MANZAREK** (b.12 Feb'35, Chicago, Illinois, USA) – keyboards, bass pedal / **ROBBIE KRIEGER** (b. 8 Jan'46, Los Angeles, California, USA) – guitar / **JOHN DENSMORE** (b. 1 Dec'45, Los Angeles, California, USA) – drums / also guest **DOUG LABAHN** – bass (of CLEAR LIGHT)

Elektra Elektra

Feb 67. (7") **BREAK ON THROUGH (TO THE OTHER SIDE). / END OF THE NIGHT** [ ] [ ] Jan 67

Mar 67. (lp) **THE DOORS** [ ] [1] Mar 67
– Break on through (to the other side) / Soul kitchen / The crystal ship / Twentieth century fox / Alabama song (whiskey song) / Light my fire / Back door man / I looked at you / End of the night / Take it as it comes / The end. *(re-iss.+c.Nov71) (cd-iss.Jan84 & Feb89) (re-iss.Apr91 hit UK No.43)*

May 67. (7") **ALABAMA SONG (WHISKEY BAR). / TAKE IT AS IT COMES** [ ] [ ]

Jul 67. (7") **LIGHT MY FIRE (edit). / THE CRYSTAL SHIP** [49] [1] Jun 67
(re-iss.Jul71)

Sep 67. (7") **PEOPLE ARE STRANGE. / UNHAPPY GIRL** [ ] [12]

Dec 67. (lp) **STRANGE DAYS** [ ] [3] Nov 67
– Strange days / You're lost little girl / Love me two times / Unhappy girl / Horse latitudes / Moonlight drive / People are strange / My eyes have seen you / I can't see your face in my mind / When the music's over. *(re-iss.+c.Nov71) (cd-iss.Jan86 & Feb89)*

Dec 67. (7") **LOVE ME TWO TIMES. / MOONLIGHT DRIVE** [ ] [25]

Apr 68. (7") **THE UNKNOWN SOLDIER. / WE COULD BE SO GOOD TOGETHER** [ ] [39] Mar 68

Aug 68. (7") **HELLO I LOVE YOU. / LOVE STREET** [15] [1] Jul 68

—— **LEROY VINEGAR** – acoustic bass repl. LABAHN

Sep 68. (lp) **WAITING FOR THE SUN** [16] [1] Aug 68
– Hello I love you / Love street / Not to touch the Earth / Summer's almost gone / Wintertime love / The unknown soldier / Spanish caravan / My wild love / We could be so good together / Yes, the river flows / Five to one. *(re-iss.+c.Nov71) (cd-iss.Jan86 & Feb89)*

Dec 68. (7") **TOUCH ME. / WILD CHILD** [ ] [3]

May 69. (7") **WISHFUL SINFUL. / WHO SCARED YOU** [ ] [44] Mar 69

Aug 69. (7") **TELL ALL THE PEOPLE. / EASY RIDE** [ ] [57] Jun 69

Sep 69. (lp) **THE SOFT PARADE** [ ] [6] Aug 69
– Tell all the people / Touch me / Shaman's blues / Do it / Easy ride / Wild child / Runnin' blue / Wishful sinful / The soft parade. *(re-iss.+c.Nov71) (cd-iss.Feb89)*

Sep 69. (7") **RUNNIN' BLUE. / DO IT** [-] [64]

—— guest **LONNIE MACK** – bass repl. LABAHN

Apr 70. (7") **YOU MAKE ME REAL. / ROADHOUSE BLUES** [-] [50]

Apr 70. (7") **YOU MAKE ME REAL. / THE SPY** [ ] [-]

Apr 70. (lp)(c) **MORRISON HOTEL / HARD ROCK CAFE** [12] [4] Mar 70
– Land ho! / The spy / Queen of the highway / Indian summer / Maggie McGill / Roadhouse blues / Waiting for the sun / You make me real / Peace frog / Blue Sunday / Ship of fools. *(re-iss.+c.Nov71) (cd-iss.Apr86 & Feb89)*

Jul 70. (7") **ROADHOUSE BLUES. / BLUE SUNDAY** [ ] [-]

Sep 70. (d-lp)(c) **ABSOLUTELY LIVE (live)** [69] [8] Aug 70
– Who do you love medley: Alabama song – Back door man – Love hides – Five to one / Build me a woman / When the music's over / Close to you / Universal mind / Break on through (to the other side) / The celebration of the lizard / Soul kitchen. *(re-iss.Nov71) (d-cd-iss.Mar87)*

Oct 70. (7") **UNIVERSAL MIND. / THE ICEWAGON FLEW** [-] [ ]

—— guest **JERRY SCHEFF** – bass repl. MACK

May 71. (7") **LOVE HER MADLY. / (YOU NEED MEAT) DON'T GO NO FURTHER** [ ] [11] Apr 71

Jun 71. (lp)(c) **L.A. WOMAN** [26] [9] May 71
– The changeling / Love her madly / Been down so long / Cars hiss by my window / L.A. woman / L'America / Hyacinth house / Crawling KIng Snake / The wasp (Texas radio and the big beat) / Riders on the storm. *(re-iss.+cd.1984) (cd-iss.Feb89) (re-iss.Apr91)*

Jul 71. (7") **RIDERS ON THE STORM (edit). / THE CHANGELING** [22] [14]

—— **RAY** – vocals, ROBBIE and JOHN carried on when JIM MORRISON died 3rd Jul'71 of a mysterious heart attack. The trio continued (MANZAREK now on vox). Used guest session bassmen **WILLIE RUFF, WOLFGANG MERTZ** and **JACK CONRAD**

Nov 71. (7") **TIGHTROPE RIDE. / VARIETY IS THE SPICE OF LIFE** [ ] [71]

Dec 71. (lp)(c) **OTHER VOICES** [ ] [31] Nov 71
– In the eye of the sun / Variety is the spice of life / Ships w.sails / Tightrope ride / Down on the farm / I'm horny, I'm stoned / Wandering musician / Hang on to your life

May 72. (7") **SHIP W. SAILS. / IN THE EYE OF THE SUN** [ ] [ ]

—— bass sessions **J. CONRAD, CHARLES LARKEY, LEE SKLAR and CHRIS ETHRIDGE.**

Aug 72. (7") **GET UP AND DANCE. / TREE TRUNKS** [ ] [ ]

Sep 72. (lp)(c) **FULL CIRCLE** [ ] [68]
– Get up and dance / Four billion souls / Verdilac / Hardwod floor / Good rockin' / The mosquito / The piano bird / It slipped my mind / The Peking King and the New York Queen.

Sep 72. (7") **THE MOSQUITO. / IT SLIPPED MY MIND** [-] [85]

Dec 72. (7") **THE PIANO BIRD. / GOOD ROCKIN'** [-] [ ]

—— They finally split 1973. MANZAREK went solo and KRUGER & DENSMORE formed The BUTTS BAND. With JESS RODEN as lead singer / **PHILIP CHEN** – bass / **ROY DAVIS** – keyboards, they made 2 albums for ~'Blue Thumb' records; 'THE BUTTS BAND' (1974) / **'HEAR AND NOW'** (1975).

– compilations, etc. –

Note; All on 'Elektra' until mentioned.

Mar 71. (lp)(c) **13** [ ] [25] Dec 70

Mar 72. (d-lp)(c) **WEIRD SCENES INSIDE THE GOLDMINE** [50] [55]
– Break on through (to the other side) / Strange days / Shaman's blues / Love street / Peace frog / Blue Sunday / The wasp (Texas radio and the big beat) / End of the night / Love her madly / Ship of fools / The spy / The end / Take it as it comes / Running blue / L.A. woman / Five to one / Who scared you? / Don't go no further / Riders on the storm / Maggie McGill / Horse latitudes / When the music's over.

Oct 74. (lp)(c) **THE BEST OF THE DOORS** [ ] [ ]

Feb 76. (7") **RIDERS ON THE STORM. / L.A. WOMAN** [33] [ ]

Sep 76. (7") **LIGHT MY FIRE. / THE UNKNOWN SOLDIER** [ ] [ ]

Sep 76. (7") **LOVE HER MADLY. / TOUCH ME** [ ] [ ]

Jan 79. (d7") **LOVE ME TWO TIMES. / HELLO I LOVE YOU / GHOST SONG / ROADHOUSE BLUES** [ ] [ ]

Jan 79. (7") **ROADHOUSE BLUES. / AN AMERICAN PRAYER** [-] [ ]

Jan 80. (12") **THE END. / (b-side 'Delta' not by The DOORS.)** [ ] [ ]

Oct 80. (lp)(c) **GREATEST HITS** [ ] [17]
(cd-iss.Oct95)

Oct 80. (7") **PEOPLE ARE STRANGE. / NOT TO TOUCH THE EARTH** [-] [ ]

Aug 82. (d-c) **THE SOFT PARADE / AN AMERICAN PRAYER** [ ] [ ]

Oct 83. (12") **GLORIA (live). / LOVE ME TWO TIMES (live)** [ ] [71]

Oct 83. (lp)(c) **ALIVE SHE CRIED (live)** [36] [23]
– Gloria / Light my fire / You make me real / The wasp (Texas radio and the big beat) / Love me two times / Little red rooster / Moonlight drive. *(cd-iss.Jul84)*

Oct 83. (7") **GLORIA (live). / MOONLIGHT DRIVE (live)** [-] [ ]

Jun 85. (lp)(c) **CLASSICS** [ ] [ ]

Nov 85. (d-lp)(c)(cd) **BEST OF THE DOORS** (diff.to '74 version) [ ] [ ]
– Break on through (to the other side) / Light my fire / The crystal ship / People are strange / Strange days / Love me two times / Five to one / Waiting for the Sun / Spanish caravan / When the music's over / Hello, I love you / Roadhouse blues / L.A. woman / Riders on the storm / Touch me / Love her madly / The unknown soldier / The end. (cd+=) – Alabama song (whiskey bar). *(re-iss.Apr91 hit UK No.17 & US No.32)*

Jun 87. (m-lp)(c)(cd) **LIVE AT THE HOLLYWOOD BOWL (live)** [ ] [ ]
– Wake up / Light my fire / The unknown soldier / A little game / The hill dwellers / Spanish caravan.

Mar 91. (cd)(c)(lp) **THE DOORS: A FILM BY OLIVER STONE - MUSIC FROM THE ORIGINAL SOUNDTRACK** [11] [8]

Apr 91. (7")(c-s) **BREAK ON THROUGH. / LOVE STREET** [64] [ ]
(12"+=)(cd-s+=) – Hello I love you / Touch me.

May 91. (7") **LIGHT MY FIRE (edit). / PEOPLE ARE STRANGE** [7] [ ]
(12"+=)(cd-s+=) – Soul kitchen.

May 91. (d-cd)(d-c)(t-lp) **THE DOORS: IN CONCERT (live)** [24] [50]

Jul 91. (7")(c-s) **RIDERS ON THE STORM. / LOVE ME TWO TIMES (live)** [68] [ ]
(12"+=)(cd-s+=) – Roadhouse blues (live).

Sep 85. Old Gold; (7") **RIDERS ON THE STORM. / LIGHT MY FIRE** [ ] [-]

Jun 95. Elektra; (c-s) **THE GHOST SONG. ("JIM MORRISON & THE DOORS") / (interview)** [ ] [ ]
(cd-s+=) – Love me two times / Roadhouse blues (live).

JIM MORRISON

poetry with sparse musical accompaniment-

Elektra Elektra

Nov 78. (lp) **AN AMERICAN PRAYER** (recorded 8 Nov '70) [ ] [54]
– Awake / Ghost song / Dawn's highway / Newborn awakening / To come of age / Black polished chrome / Latino chrome / Angels and sailors / Stoned immaculate / The poet's dreams / The movie / Curses invocations / World on fire / American night / Roadhouse blues / Lament / The hitchhiker / An American prayer. *(re-iss.cd/c/lp May95)*

DRAIN (see under ⇒ BUTTHOLE SURFERS)

NICK DRAKE

Born: 19 Jun'48, Burma. By mid'50's, his family moved to Tamworth-in-Ardon then Stratford, England. Discovered by ASHLEY HUTCHINGS (Fairport Convention) who after seeing him gig in Cambridge, where he was at college, got him signed to 'Island'. From then on his work was heralded by critics, but commercial success never came, setting NICK off into a depression which led to his untimely death in '74. He did however leave behind at least one great classic album in 1970, 'BRYTER LAYTER'. • **Style:** Broody melancholic melodies, that were at first compared with ASTRAL WEEKS (Van Morrison), but later with more jazz feel. He quit gigging around the early 70's, and the 6'3" genius opted out from the music world. **Songwriters:** All work penned by himself. • **Trivia:** His sister Gabrielle was semi-successful TV actress in the 70's/80's, noteably on 'Crossroads' soap.

Recommended: BRYTER LAYTER (*9) / FIVE LEAVES LEFT (*7) / PINK MOON (*5)

NICK DRAKE – vocals, guitar, piano with **RICHARD THOMPSON** – guitar / **DANNY THOMPSON** – double bass / **PAUL HARRIS** – keyboards / **CLAIRE LOWTHER** and **ROCKY DZIDZORNU,** plus 15-piece orchestra.

Island | Antilles

Sep 69. (lp) **FIVE LEAVES LEFT** [ ] [-] 1976
– Time has told me / River man / Three hours / Day is done / Way to blue / Cello song / The thoughts of Mary Jane / Man in a shed / Fruit tree / Saturday sun. *(c-iss.1974) (re-iss.+cd.Feb87) (re-cd.May89)*

— retained **RICHARD** bringing in other (FAIRPORT CONVENTION members: **DAVE PEGG** – / **DAVE MATTACKS** – . Also sessioned **PAUL HARRIS, RAY WARLEIGH, CHRIS McGREGOR.**

Nov 70. (lp) **BRYTER LAYTER** [ ] [-] 1977
– Introduction / Hazey Jane II / At the chime of a city clock / One of these things first / Hazey Jane I / Bryter layter / Fly / Poor boy / Northern sky / Sunday. *(c-iss.1974) (re-iss.+cd.May87 + Oct89)*

— **NICK DRAKE** – vocals, guitar (totally solo)

Feb 72. (lp) **PINK MOON** [ ] [-]
– Pink moon / Place to be / Road / Which will / Horn / Things behind the sun / Know / Parasite / Ride / Harvest breed / From the morning / Voice from the mountain / Rider on the wheel / Black eyed dog / Hanging on a star. *(c-iss.1974) (cd-iss.Apr90)*

He had put down some tracks for new album, when in 25 Nov'74 he overdosed on medication/drugs. Questionable coroner's verdict was 'Death by suicide'.

– compilations, others, etc. –

1972. Antilees; (lp) **NICK DRAKE** (69-70 material) [-] [ ]
Apr 79. Island; (3xlp-box) **FRUIT TREE – THE COMPLETE RECORDED WORKS** [ ] [ ]
(contains all 3 albums)
May 85. Island; (lp)(c) **HEAVEN IN A WILD FLOWER** [ ] [ ]
(cd-iss.Apr90)
Aug 86. Hannibal/ US= Rykodisc; (4xlp-box)(US-4xcd-box) **FRUIT TREE** [ ] [ ]
(all 3 lp's, plus TIME OF NO REPLY rec.1973) *(cd-iss.Dec91)* (all.+=) – Fruit tree / Fly / Man in a shed / Thoughts of Mary Jane.
Jan 87. Hannibal/ US= Rykodisc; (lp) **TIME OF NO REPLY** [ ] [ ]
(c+cd-iss.May89)
Jun 94. Island; (cd)(c) **WAY TO BLUE – AN INTRODUCTION TO NICK DRAKE** [ ] [ ]

DR. DRE (see under ⇒ N.W.A.)

DREADZONE

Formed: London, England . . .1992 by GREG ROBERTS and TIM BRAN. Were a surprise signing to major indie 'Creation', where they released debut '360°'. After appearing on the bill at many rave concerts, they signed to 'Virgin' and album chart debutted with 'SECOND LIGHT'. From it came the catchy Top 20 hit 'LITTLE BRITAIN', now used on TV sports features. • **Style:** Thumping bassy trance-dub. Described unfairly in the NME as sea shanty techno. Use samples from B-movies / cult film. • **Songwriters:** Group or ROBERTS. • **Trivia:** Appeared in the dance tent at 1995's 'T In The Park' in Hamilton, Scotland.

Recommended: 360° (*5) / SECOND LIGHT (*6)

GREG ROBERTS -drums (ex-SCREAMING TARGET, ex-BIG AUDIO DYNAMITE) / **TIM BRAN** -samples, keyboards, etc

Creation | not issued

May 93. (12"ep)(cd-ep) **THE WARNING / AFRICA. / NO JUSTICE NO PEACE (the Warning remix) / HEART OF DARKNESS (Africa remix)** [ ] [-]
Jul 93. (12")(cd-s) **THE GOOD, THE BAD AND THE DREAD** [ ] [-]
– mixes; (part one, the good) / (part two, the bad) / (part three, the dread) / (a fistful of dub).
Oct 93. (cd)(c)(lp) **360°** [ ] [-]
– House of Dread / L.O.V.E. / Chinese ghost story / The good, the bad and the Dread / The warning / Dream on / Far encounter / Skeleton at the feast / Rastafarout.

CanCan | not issued

Feb 94. (12") **SOUNDS FROM THE HOUSE OF DREAD (remixes)** [ ] [-]

— added **LEO WILLIAMS** -bass (ex-BIG AUDIO DYNAMITE)

Totem | not issued

Oct 94. (m-cd)(m-lp) **PERFORMANCE, DREADZONE** [ ] [-]
– Africa / House of Dread / Far encounter / Dream on / The warning.
Oct 94. (12"ep)(cd-ep) **FIGHT THE POWER. / (Drum club mix) / (DJ Evolution) / (Dread Zone dub)** [ ] [-]

In 1994, they mixed TRANS-GLOBAL UNDERGROUND for 'Lookee Here' EP.

Virgin | Virgin

Apr 95. (c-ep)(12"ep)(cd-ep) **ZION YOUTH. / ('A'-Underworld mix) / ('A'-Dan Donovan mix) / ('A'-Digidub mix)** [49] [ ]
Jun 95. (cd)(c)(d-lp) **SECOND LIGHT** [37] [ ]
– Life, love & unity / Litle Britain / A Canterbury tale / Captain Dread / Cave of angels / Zion youth / One way / Shining path / Out of Heaven.
Jul 95. (c-s) **CAPTAIN DREAD / ('A'-Zexos free troupe mix)** [49] [ ]
(12"+=)(cd-s+=) – ('A'-Walk the plank mix) / ('A'-X-Press 2 mix).
(cd-s++=) – ('A'-Zexos citizen mix) / Epilogue.
Sep 95. (12"ep)(cd-ep) **MAXIMUM EP** [56] [ ]
– Fight the power / One way / Maximum.
Dec 95. (c-s) **LITTLE BRITAIN / ('A'vocal mix)** [20] [ ]
(12"+=)(cd-s+=) – ('A'-Eon mix) / ('A'-Black Star Liner mix) / ('A'-More Rockers mix).

. . . Jan – Jun '96 stop press . . .

Mar 96. (single) **LIFE LOVE & UNITY** [56] [ ]

DREAM (see under ⇒ EXTREME)

DRUGSTORE

Formed: London-based, England . . .1992 by Brazilian born ISOBEL MONTEIRO and L.A. born MIKE CHYLINSKI. They were joined a year later by DARREN ROBINSON. Two singles on 'Honey' 1 for 'Rough Trade', were followed by a signing for 'Go! Discs' in 1994. Eponymous debut in Spring of '95, just missed out on a UK Top 30 placing. • **Style:** Smokey-voxed female fronted alternative rock outfit. MAZZY STAR like. • **Songwriters:** MONTEIRO main writer/ some with group except SHE DON'T USE JELLY (Flaming Lips) / TEENAGE KICKS (Undertones).

Recommended: DRUGSTORE (*6)

ISOBEL MONTEIRO -vocals, bass/ **DARON ROBINSON** -guitar / **MIKE CHYLINSKI** -drums

Honey | not issued

1994. (7") **ALIVE. /** [ ] [-]

Honey – Go! Discs | Go! Discs

Sep 94. (7") **STARCROSSED. / ACCELERATE** [ ] [-]
(10"+=)(cd-s+=) – Fader.
Dec 94. (7") **NECTARINE. / ANAESTHASIA** [ ] [-]
(10"+=)(cd-s+=) – She don't use jelly.
Mar 95. (7") **SOLITARY PARTY GROOVER. / ELECTRIC LIGHT / STARCROSSED (demo)** [ ] [ ]
(12")(cd-s) – (first 2 tracks) / Get inside my head / Spacegirl.
Apr 95. (cd)(c)(lp) **DRUGSTORE** [31] [ ]
– Speaker 12 / Favourite sinner / Alive / Solitary party groover / If / Devil / Saturday sunset / Fader / Super glider / Baby astrolab / Gravity / Nectarine / Accelerate. (lp w/free 7")(cd w/free cd-s) SOLITARY PARTY GROOVER (acoustic). / BABY ASTROLAB (acoustic)
May 95. (7") **FADER. / REBOUND / UNDER THE MOON** [72] [ ]
(12")(cd-s) – ('A'side) / French devil / Slide / Sugar sugar.
Oct 95. (7"ep)(cd-ep) **INJECTION / HEART OF HONEY. / SHE DON'T USE JELLY (electric version) / GRAVITY (Terry Edwards mix)** [ ] [ ]

Bill DRUMMOND (see under ⇒ KLF)

DUBSTAR

Formed: Sheffield, England . . .1994 by ex-JOANS members; WILKIE and HILLIER, who soon met with SARAH BLACKWOOD. With help from manager Graham Robinson, they secured a deal with Parlophone outlet 'Food' (home to BLUR). In June 1995, they had debut chart appearance with 'STARS' and grew to be an alternative pop favourite of '95. • Style: Dreamy experimental Euro-pop lying somewhere between SAINT ETIENNE and The PET SHOP BOYS. • Songwriters: Group. • Trivia: Produced by STEPHEN HAGUE.

Recommended: DISGRACEFUL (*7)

SARAH BLACKWOOD -vocals / **CHRIS WILKIE** -guitar / **STEVE HILLIER** -programmer

		Food	???
Jun 95.	(c-s) **STARS / ('A'mixes)**	40	
Sep 95.	(c-s)(cd-s)(12") **ANYWHERE / DON'T BLAME ME**	37	
Oct 95.	(cd)(c)(lp) **DISGRACEFUL**	33	

– Stars / Anywhere / Just a girl she said / Elevator song / The day I see you again / Week in week out / Not so manic now / opdorian / Not once not ever / St. Swithin's Day / Disgraceful.

Dec 95.	(c-s) **NOT SO MANIC NOW / IF IT ISN'T YOU**	18	

(cd-s+=) – Song No.9 / Certain sadness.

. . . Jan – Jun '96 stop press . . .

Mar 96.	(single) **STARS**	15	
May 96.	(single) **ELEVATOR SONG**		

DUET EMMO (see under ⇒ WIRE)

DUKES OF STRATOSPHEAR (see under ⇒ XTC)

DURAN DURAN

Formed: Birmingham, England ... 1978 by NICK RHODES, JOHN TAYLOR, STEPHEN DUFFY and clarinetist SIMON COLLEY. They took group name from a character in the 60's sci-fi/fantasy film 'Barbarella'. In 1979, ANDY WICKETT and ROGER TAYLOR replaced DUFFY and COLLEY respectively (the former going on to have successful pop solo career). Soon a new guitarist was added to take the place of brief newcomer JOHN CURTIS. In April 1980, they recruited new vocalist SIMON LE BON to complete the line-up, after WICKETT had left late 1979. Their first UK tour supporting HAZEL O'CONNOR, was rewarded late 1980 when 'E.M.I.' signed them up. Their debut 45 in 1981, broke them into the UK Top 20, where they became resident throughout the 80's and 90's. • **Style:** Latched onto the 'new romantic' boom period in the early 80's. Their electronic dance sound and photogenic looks helped sell to a new video age audience. Progressed to a more adult rock based synth sound with each new album release. • **Songwriters:** LE BON – lyrics / RHODES – music. Covered; MAKE ME SMILE (Steve Harley & Cockney Rebel) / WHITE LINES (Grandmaster Flash) / I WANNA TAKE YOU HIGHER (Sly & The Family Stone) / PERFECT DAY (Lou Reed) / WATCHING THE DETECTIVES (Elvis Costello) / LAY LADY LAY (Bob Dylan) / 911 IS A JOKE (Public Enemy) / SUCCESS (Iggy Pop) / CRYSTAL SHIP (Doors) / BALL OF CONFUSION (Temptations) / THANK YOU (Led Zeppelin). POWER STATION covered GET IT ON (T.Rex). • **Trivia:** SIMON LE BON married top-model Yasmin Parvanah on 27 Dec'85. In mid-84, other two ROGER and NICK had also married cosmopolitan models.

Recommended: DECADE (*8).

(1980) **SIMON LE BON** (b.27 Oct'58, Bushley, Hertfordshire, England) – vocals / **ANDY TAYLOR** (b.16 Feb'61, Newcastle, England) – guitar / **NICK RHODES** (b. NICHOLAS BATES, 8 Jun'62) – keyboards / **JOHN TAYLOR** (b.20 Jul'60, Solihull, England) – bass / **ROGER TAYLOR** (b.26 Apr'60) – drums.

		E.M.I.	Harvest
Jan 81.	(7") **PLANET EARTH. / LATE BAR**	12	

(12"+=) – Planet earth (night version). *(re-iss.Aug83 7+12")*

Apr 81.	(7")(12") **CARELESS MEMORIES. / KHANDA**	37	

(re-iss.Aug83 7"/12" (+=) – Fame.

Jun 81.	(lp)(c) **DURAN DURAN**	3	10 Feb 83

– Girls on film / Planet Earth / Anyone out there / To the shore / Careless memories / (Waiting for the) Night boat / Sound of thunder / Friends of mine / Tel Aviv. *(re-iss.Aug83) (cd-iss.Oct84) (re-iss.Sep87 on 'Fame') (re-iss.d-cd Jan94)*

Jul 81.	(7") **GIRLS ON FILM. / FASTER THAN LIGHT**	5	

(12"+=) – ('A' instrumental). *(re-iss.Aug83, 7"/12")*

Nov 81.	(7") **MY OWN WAY. / LIKE AN ANGEL**	14	

(12"+=) – ('A'night version) *(re-iss.Aug83, 7"/12")*

May 82.	(7")(12") **HUNGRY LIKE THE WOLF. / CARELESS MEMORIES (live)**	5	3 Jan 83

(re-iss.Aug83, 7"/12")

		E.M.I.	Capitol
May 82.	(lp)(c) **RIO**	2	6 Jan 83

– Rio / My own way / Lonely in your nightmare / Hungry like the wolf / Hold back the rain / New religion / Last chance on the stairway / Save a prayer / The chauffeur. *(re-iss.Aug83) (cd-iss.Jan84) (re-iss.+cd.Mar90)(re-iss.cd+c Sep93 on 'Parlophone')*

Aug 82.	(7")(12") **SAVE A PRAYER. / HOLD BACK THE RAIN (remix)**	2	16 Feb 85

(re-iss.Aug83, 7+12")

Sep 82.	(m-lp; on 'Harvest-US) **CARNIVAL**	-	98

– My own way / Hold back the rain / Girls on film / Hungry like the wolf.

Nov 82.	(7") **RIO. / THE CHAUFFEUR (BLUE SILVER)**	9	14 Mar 83

(12") – ('A'side) / Rio / (pt.2) / My own way. *(re-iss.Aug83 7+12")*

Mar 83.	(7")(12") **IS THERE SOMETHING I SHOULD KNOW. / FAITH IN THIS COLOUR**	1	4 May 83

(re-iss.Aug83 7"/12")

Oct 83.	(7") **UNION OF THE SNAKE. / SECRET OKTOBER**	3	3

(12"+=) – ('A' monkey remix).

Nov 83.	(lp)(c) **SEVEN AND THE RAGGED TIGER**	1	8

– The reflex / New Moon on Monday / (I'm looking for) Cracks in the pavement / I take the dice / Of crime and passion / Union of the snake / Shadows on your side / Tiger tiger / The seventh stranger. *(cd-iss.Mar84) (re-iss.+cd.Aug88 on 'Fame') (re-iss.cd+c Sep93)*

Jan 84.	(7")(12") **NEW MOON ON MONDAY. / TIGER TIGER**	9	10
Apr 84.	(7")(12")(12"pic-d) **THE REFLEX. / MAKE ME SMILE (COME UP AND SEE ME) (live)**	1	1

		Parlophone	Capitol
Oct 84.	(7")(12") **THE WILD BOYS. / (I'M LOOKING FOR) CRACKS IN THE PAVEMENT**	2	2
Nov 84.	(lp)(c)(cd) **ARENA (live)**	6	4

– Is there something I should know / Hungry like the wolf / New religion / Save a prayer / The wild boys / The seventh stranger / The chauffeur / Union of the snake / Planet Earth / Careless memories. *(re-iss.+cd.Oct89 on 'Fame')*

May 85.	(7")(12")(7"white) **A VIEW TO A KILL. / ('A' instrumental)**	2	1

— After taking time off for own solo projects (see below) only 3 returned. **SIMON, NICK** and **JOHN.** (ANDY went solo). (ROGER quits music)

		E.M.I.	Capitol
Oct 86.	(7")(12") **NOTORIOUS. / WINTER MARCHES ON**	7	2

(c-s+=) – ('A' extra mix).

Nov 86.	(lp)(c)(cd) **NOTORIOUS**	16	12

– Notorious / American science / Skin trade / A matter of feeling / Hold me / Vertigo (do the demolition) / So misled / Meet el Presidente / Winter marches on / Proposition.

Feb 87.	(7")(12")(c-s) **SKIN TRADE. / WE NEED YOU**	22	39
Apr 87.	(7")(12") **MEET EL PRESIDENTE. / VERTIGO (DO THE DEMOLITION)**	24	70

(cd-s+=) – Meet el Beat.

— added **WARREN CUCCURULLO** – guitar (ex-FRANK ZAPPA, ex-MISSING PERSONS) / **STEVE FERRONE** – drums (ex-BRIAN AUGER, ex-AVERAGE WHITE BAND) (both on last lp

Sep 88.	(7") **I DON'T WANT YOUR LOVE. / ('A' instrumental)**	14	4

(12"+=)(cd-s+=) – ('A'version).

Oct 88.	(lp)(c)(cd) **BIG THING**	15	24

– Big thing / I don't want your love / All she wants is / Too late Marlene / Drug (it's just a state of mind) / Do you believe in shame? / Palomino / Interlude one / Land / Flute interlude / The edge of America / Lake shore driving. *(re-iss.+cd.Mar90)(re-iss.cd+c Sep93 on 'Parlophone')*

Dec 88.	(7") **ALL SHE WANTS IS. / I BELIEVE**		22

(12"+=) – ('A'-US mix) / All you need to know.
(cd-s+=) – Skin trade.

Apr 89.	(7")(7"pic-d) **DO YOU BELIEVE IN SHAME?. / KRUSH BROTHERS (l.s.d. mix)**	30	72

(12"+=) – Palomino (edit) / Drugs (it's just a state of mind).
(10"+=) – Notorious (live).
(3"cd-s+=) – God.

Nov 89.	(lp)(c)(cd) **DECADE**	5	67

– Planet Earth / Girls on film / Hungry like the wolf / Rio / Save a prayer / Is there something I should know / Union of the snake / The reflex / Wild boys / A view to a kill / Notorious / Skin trade / I don't want your love / All she wants is.

Dec 89.	(7") **BURNING THE GROUND. / DECADENCE**	31	

(12"+=)(cd-s+=) – ('B' extended).

— **STERLING CAMPBELL** – drums repl. FERRONE

		Parlophone	Capitol
Jul 90.	(7") **VIOLENCE OF SUMMER (LOVE' TAKING OVER). / ('A'mix)**	20	64

(12"+=) – ('A'extended).
(cd-s+=) – Throb.

Aug 90.	(cd)(c)(lp) **LIBERTY**	8	46

– Violence of summer (love's taking over) / Liberty / Hothead / Serious / All along the water / My Antartica / Read my lips / First impression / Can you deal with it / Venice drowning / Downtown. *(re-iss.cd+cSep93)*

Nov 90.	(7")(c-s) **SERIOUS. / YOU BAD AZIZI**	48	

(12"+=)(cd-s+=) – Water babies.

Jan 93.	(7")(c-s)(7"pic-d) **ORDINARY WORLD. / MY ANTARTICA**	6	3

(cd-s+=) – Save a prayer / Skin trade.

(cd-s) – ('A'side) / The reflex / Hungry like the wolf / Girls on film.

Feb 93. (cd)(c)(lp) **DURAN DURAN** 4 7
– Too much / Information / Ordinary world / Love voodoo / Drowning man / Shotgun / Come undone / Breath after breath / UMF / Home of the above / Femme fatale / Shelter / To whom it may concern.

Mar 93. (7")(c-s) **COME UNDONE. / ORDINARY WORLD (acoustic)** 13 7
(cd-s+=) – ('A'mixes).
(cd-s) – ('A'side) / ('A'version) / Rio / Is there something I should know / A view to a kill.

Aug 93. (c-s)(12") **TOO MUCH INFORMATION. / COME UNDONE (live)** 35 45
(12"+=) – Come undone (12"mix Coming together) / Notorious (live).
(cd-s) – ('A'side) / Drowning man.

Mar 95. (7")(c-s) **PERFECT DAY. / FEMME FATALE (alt.mix)** 28
(cd-s+=) – Make me smile (come up and see me) / Perfect day (acoustic).
(cd-s) – ('A'side) / Love voodoo / Needle and the damage done / 911 is a joke (alternative mix).

Mar 95. (cd)(c) **THANK YOU** 12 19
– White lines / I wanna take you higher / Perfect day / Watching the detectives / Lay lady lay / 911 is a joke / Success / Crystal ship / Ball of confusion / Thank you / Drive by / I wanna take you higher again.

below actually featured GRANDMASTER FLASH

Jun 95. (c-s) **WHITE LINES (DON'T DO IT) / SAVE A PRAYER / NONE OF THE ABOVE (Drizabone mix)** 17
(cd-s+=) – Ordinary world (acoustic).
(12") – ('A'side) / ('A'-Junior Vasquez mix) / ('A'-Oakland fonk mix) / ('A'-70's club mix).

The POWER STATION

(ANDY and JOHN TAYLOR) / **ROBERT PALMER** – vocals (solo artist see under own listing) / **TONY THOMPSON** – drums (ex-CHIC)

E.M.I. Capitol

Mar 85. (7")(7"pic-d) **SOME LIKE IT HOT. / THE HEAT IS ON** 14 6
(12"+=)(12"pic-d+=) – ('A'extended).

Apr 85. (lp)(c) **THE POWER STATION** 12 6
– Some like it hot / Murderess / Lonely tonight / Communication / Get it on (bang a gong) / Go to zero / Harvest for the world / Still in your heart. *(re-iss.cd+c Aug93 on 'Parlophone')*

May 85. (7")(12") **GET IT ON. / GO TO ZERO** 22 9

Nov 85. (7")(12") **COMMUNICATION. / MURDERESS** 75 34

—— **MICHAEL DES BARNES** – vocals repl.PALMER on tour.

JOHN TAYLOR

Mar 86. (7")(12") **I DO WHAT I DO (theme from 9 1/2 weeks). / JAZZ** 42 23

ARCADIA

(SIMON LE BON – vocals / **NICK RHODES** – keyboards / **ROGER TAYLOR** – drums) with session people

Oct 85. (7") **ELECTION DAY. / SHE'S MOODY AND SHE'S MEAN AND SHE'S RESTLESS** 7 6
(12"+=) – (2 -'A' mixes).

Dec 85. (lp)(c)(cd) **SO RED THE ROSE** 30 23
– Election day / Keep me in the dark / Goodbye is forever / The flame / Missing / Rose Arcana / The promise / El Diablo / Lady Ice. *(re-iss.cd+c Aug93 on 'Parlophone')*

Dec 85. (7") **GOODBYE IS FOREVER. / MISSING** - 33

Feb 86. (7") **THE PROMISE. / ROSE ARCANE** 37
(12"+=) – ('A' extended).

Jul 86. (7") **THE FLAME. / FLAME AGAIN** 58
(12"+=) – Election day.

Ian DURY

Born: 12 May'42, Upminster, Essex, England. At age 7 he became partially crippled from contracting polio. In 1970, he was employed as a teacher / lecturer at Canterbury College. The following year, he formed KILBURN & THE HIGH ROADS, who embarked on pub/college circuit in London. After 1 album in the mid-70's and many line-up changes, they disbanded, leaving DURY and manager DAVE ROBINSON to create solo deal for DURY. Signing to Jake Riviera's new indie label 'Stiff', he soon raced up album charts in 1977 with the new wave favourite 'NEW BOOTS AND PANTIES!'. • **Style:** DURY's articulate patter and intelligent lyrics, fused well with funky/jerky group backing, that diversed between rock'n'roll and disco. He also developed many areas of Cockney rhyme-slang into rude but clever lyrics. • **Songwriters:** DURY – words / JANKEL – music, until his departure from The BLOCKHEADS. • **Trivia:** After he semi-retired in the mid-80's, he started acting career in films:- NUMBER ONE (1985) / PIRATES (1986) / HEARTS OF FIRE (1987), and TV plays:- KING OF THE GHETTOS (1986) / TALK OF THE DEVIL (1986) / NIGHT MOVES (1987). His other work on TV was mainly on commercials, etc.

Recommended: NEW BOOTS AND PANTIES (*8) / SEX AND DRUGS AND ROCK AND ROLL (*7).

KILBURN & THE HIGH ROADS

IAN DURY – vocals / **KEITH LUCAS** – guitar / **DAVEY PAYNE** – sax / **CHARLIE SINCLAIR** – bass repl. HUMPHREY OCEAN who had repl. CHARLIE HART / **LOUIS LAROSE** then **GEORGE BUTLER** – drums

Early 1974, recorded lp for 'Raft', which was shelved after 'Warners' took over label. It was later issued by them in Oct'78 as 'WOTABUNCH', after DURY was top of the charts.

—— (mid-74) **DAVID ROHOMAN** – drums repl. BUTLER / **ROD MELVIN** – piano repl. HARDY

Dawn-Pye not issued

Nov 74. (7") **ROUGH KIDS. / BILLY BENTLEY** -

Feb 75. (7") **CRIPPLED WITH NERVES. / HUFFETY PUFF** -

Jun 75. (lp) **HANDSOME** -
– The roadette song / Pam's mood / Crippled with nerves / Broken skin / Upminster kid / Patience / Father / Thank you mum / Rough kids / The badger and the rabbit / The mumble rumble and the cocktail rock / The call up. *(re-iss.+c.Nov85 on 'Flashback')*

—— Disbanded mid-75, although IAN gigged at times with a new line-up as IAN DURY & THE KILBURNS. KEITH LUCAS was later to become NICK CASH and form 999.

There were also other KILBURN material re-released after DURY's success.

IAN DURY

– vocals solo with **CHAZ JANKEL** – guitar, keys (ex-BYZANTIUM) plus session men that became The BLOCKHEADS (see below)

Stiff Stiff

Aug 77. (7")(7"orange) **SEX AND DRUGS AND ROCK AND ROLL. / RAZZLE IN MY POCKET** -

Sep 77. (lp)(c)(gold-lp) **NEW BOOTS AND PANTIES** 5 Apr 78
– Sweet Gene Vincent / ake up and make love with me / I'm partial to your abracadabra / My old man / Billericay Dickie / Clevor Trever / If I was with a woman / Plainstow Patricia / Blockheads / Blackmail man. *(re-iss.+cd.Sep86 on 'Demon')* (cd+=) – (interview). *(re-iss.cd May95 on 'Disky')*

Nov 77. (7") **SWEET GENE VINCENT. / YOU'RE MORE THAN FAIR** -

IAN DURY AND THE BLOCKHEADS

with **JANKEL** plus **NORMAN WATT-ROY** – bass (ex-LOVING AWARENESS, ex-GLENCOE) / **CHARLEY CHARLES** – drums (ex-LOVING AWARENESS, ex-GLENCOE) / **MICKEY GALLAGHER** – keyboards (ex-LOVING AWARENESS, ex-FRAMPTON'S CAMEL) / **JOHN TURNBULL** – guitar (ex-LOVING AWARENESS) / **DAVEY PAYNE** – saxophone (ex-WRECKLESS ERIC)

Apr 78. (7")(12") **WHAT A WASTE. / WAKE UP AND MAKE LOVE WITH ME** 11
(re-iss. 1981)

Nov 78. (7") **HIT ME WITH YOUR RHYTHM STICK. (as "Ian & THE BLOCKHEADS" one-off) / THERE AIN'T HALF BEEN SOME CLEVER BASTARDS** 1

May 79. (lp)(c) **DO IT YOURSELF** 2 Jul 79
– Inbetweenies / Quiet / Don't ask me / Sink my boats / Waiting for your taxi / This is what we find / Uneasy sunny hotsy totsy / Mischief / Dance of the screamers / Lullaby for Francies. *(re-iss.+cd.Feb90 on 'Demon') (re-iss.cd May95 on 'Disky')*

Jul 79. (7")(12") **REASONS TO CHEERFUL (pt.3). / COMMON AS MUCK** 3

Aug 80. (7")(12") **I WANT TO BE STRAIGHT. / THAT'S NOT ALL HE WANTS** 22

—— **WILKO JOHNSON** – guitar (ex-DR. FEELGOOD, solo artist) repl. JANKEL who went solo

Oct 80. (7") **SUEPERMAN'S BIG SISTER. / FUNKY ADA** 51
(12"+=) – You'll see glimpses.

Nov 80. (lp)(c) **LAUGHTER** 48 Jan 81
– Sueperman's big sister / Pardon / Delusions of grandeur / Yes and no (Paula) / Dance of the crackpots / Over the points / (Take your elbow out of the soup you're sitting on the chicken) / Uncoolohol / Hey, hey, take me away / Manic depression / Oh, Mr. Peanut / Fucking Ada. *(cd-iss.May95 on 'Disky')*

—— IAN DURY now brought in the services of rhythm boys **SLY & ROBBIE** plus **JANKEL + TYRONE DOWNIE** – keyboards.

Polydor Polydor

Aug 81. (7")(12") **SPASTICUS AUSTICIOUS. / ('A'instrumental)**

Sep 81. (lp)(c) **LORD UPMINSTER** [53] [ ]
– Funky disco pops / Red letter / Girls watching / Wait for me / The body song / Lonely town / Trust is a must / Spasticus austicious. *(re-iss.+cd.Dec89 on 'Great Expectations')*

IAN DURY & THE MUSIC STUDENTS

with many musicians incl. **JANKEL, PAYNE + RAY COOPER**

Polydor Polydor

Nov 83. (7")(12") **REALLY GLAD YOU CAME. / INSPIRATION** [ ] [ ]
Jan 84. (lp)(c) **4,000 WEEKS HOLIDAY** [54] [ ]
– (You're my) Inspiration / Friends / Tell your daddy / Peter the painter / Ban the bomb / Percy the poet / Very personal / Take me to the cleaners / The man with no face / Really glad you came. *(re-iss.+cd.Dec89 on 'Great Expectations')*
Feb 84. (7") **VERY PERSONAL. / BAN THE BOMB** [ ] [ ]
(12"+=) – The sky's the limit.

IAN DURY

solo, with **PAYNE, GALLAGHER, COOPER** plus **STEVE WHITE** – drums / **MICHAEL McEVOY** – bass, synth / **MERLIN RHYS-JONES** – guitar / **FRANCES RUFELLE** – vocals / etc.

E.M.I. not issued

Oct 89. (7")(7"pic-d) **PROFOUNDLY IN LOVE WITH PANDORA (theme from 'ADRIAN MOLE' TV series). / EUGENIUS (YOU'RE A GENIUS)** [45] [-]

WEA WEA

Oct 89. (7") **APPLES. / BYLINE BROWN** [ ] [ ]
Oct 89. (lp)(c)(cd) **APPLES** [ ] [ ]
– Apples / Love is all / Byline Browne / Bit of kit / Game on / Looking for Harry / England's glory / Bus driver's prayer / P.C.Honey / The right people / All those who say okay / Riding the outskirts of fantasy.

In Sep90 he reforms IAN DURY & THE BLOCKHEADS for two reunion gigs. Credited to

IAN DURY

Demon not issued

Oct 92. (cd)(c) **THE BUS DRIVERS PRAYER & OTHER STORIES** [ ] [-]
– That's enough of that / Bill Haley's last words / Poor Joey / Quick quick slow / Fly in the ointment / O'Donegal / Poo-poo in the prawn / Ave a word / London talking / D'orine the cow / Your horoscope / No such thing as love / Two old dogs without a name / Bus driver's prayer.

– compilations etc. –

Nov 81. Stiff; (lp)(c) **JUKE BOX DURIES** [ ] [ ]
(re-iss.Sep82 as 'GREATEST HITS' on 'Fame') (cd-iss.May95 on 'Disky')
May 85. Stiff; (7") **HIT ME WITH YOUR RHYTHM STICK (Paul Hardcastle mix). / SEX AND DRUGS AND ROCK AND ROLL** [55] [ ]
(12"+=) – Reasons to be cheerful / Wake up and make love to me (Paul Hardcastle mix).
Apr 87. Demon; (lp)(c)(cd) **SEX AND DRUGS AND ROCK AND ROLL** [ ] [ ]
– Hit me with your rhythm stick / I want to be straight / There ain't half been some clever bastards / What a waste! / Common as muck / Reasons to be cheerful part 3 / Sex and drugs and rock and roll / Superman's big sister / Razzle in my pocket / You're more than fair / Inbetweenies / You'll see glimpses.
Apr 91. Demon; (cd)(c)(lp) **WARTS'N'AUDIENCE (live)** [ ] [ ]
Aug 91. Demon; (cd)(c)(lp) **IAN DURY & THE BLOCKHEADS** [ ] [-]
1991. Demon; (cd-set) **NEW BOOTS AND PANTIES / DO IT YOURSELF / SEX AND DRUGS AND ROCK AND ROLL** [ ] [-]
Jul 91. Flying; (7")(c-s) **HIT ME WITH YOUR RHYTHM STICK '91 (The Flying Remix Version) / HIT ME WITH YOUR RHYTHM STICK** [73] [-]
(12"+=)(cd-s+=)
Nov 94. Repertoire; (cd) **THE BEST OF IAN DURY** [ ] [-]

— The BLOCKHEADS also released their own singles and lp early 80's.

Bob DYLAN

Born: ROBERT ALLAN ZIMMERMAN, 24 May'41, Duluth, Minnesota, USA. In 1960, he left his local university and changed name to BOB DYLAN. He also began trek to New York, where he played first gig supporting JOHN LEE HOOKER on 11 Apr'61 at Gerde's Folk City. Soon after this, he enjoyed harmonica session work for folk songstress Caroline Hester. Her employers 'Columbia' records, through John Hammond Snr., signed him Oct'61. His eponymous debut album in 1962, gained sparse attention, although his live work created critical appraisal. In 1963 he unleashed 'THE FREEWHEELIN' BOB DYLAN', and after PETER, PAUL & MARY lifted a million seller from it 'BLOWIN' IN THE WIND', it gained enough respect to give him US Top 30 album. In 1965, at the peak of his career, the album was to make the top spot in the UK. Many up and coming and already established artists were successfully covering his material (see below). • **Style:** Idolized folk legend WOODY GUTHRIE who was to die 3 Sep'67 of a paralyzing hereditary disease. In 1966, DYLAN stunned folk purists, by employing an electric band The HAWKS (later The BAND) to augment his live and studio work. (A year earlier, he had introduced electric sound with band on half of No.1 album 'BRINGING IT ALL BACK HOME'.) After a motorcycle accident later in '66, he sustained severe neck injuries and retired for 2 years. This was of course after laying down tracks for legendary double lp 'BLONDE ON BLONDE'. He returned with slight change of vocal chords to release more country-rock orientated music. In the mid-70's, he returned with two harder edged rock classics 'BLOOD ON THE TRACKS' & 'DESIRE', which gave him needed regained credibility from critics and buying public alike. From 1979 and throughout the 80's, his work mellowed into more spiritual themes, due to his new-found Christianity. • **Songwriters:** 99% DYLAN compositions except, HOUSE OF THE RISING SUN + IN MY TIME OF DYIN' (trad.) / TAKE A MESSAGE TO MARY (Everly Brothers) / THE BOXER (Simon & Garfunkel) / EARLY MORNIN' RAIN (Gordon Lightfoot) / A FOOL SUCH AS I + CAN'T HELP FALLING IN LOVE (hits; Elvis Presley) / BIG YELLOW TAXI (Joni Mitchell) / MR.BOJANGLES (Jerry Jeff Walker) / LET'S STICK TOGETHER (Wilbert Harrison) / SPANISH IS THE LOVING TONGUE + SHENANDOAH (trad.) / ANGELS FLYING TOO CLOSE TO THE GROUND (Willie Nelson) / etc. **Writing credits/hits:** BLOWIN' IN THE WIND + DON'T THINK TWICE, IT'S ALRIGHT (Peter, Paul & Mary; 1963) / ALL I REALLY WANT TO DO (Cher; 1965) / IT AIN'T ME BABE (Turtles; 1965) / MR.TAMBOURINE MAN + ALL I REALLY WANT TO DO + MY BACK PAGES (Byrds; 1965-1967) / IT'S ALL OVER NOW, BABY BLUE + FAREWELL ANGELINA (Joan Baez; 1965) / IF YOU GOTTA GO, GO NOW + JUST LIKE A WOMAN + MIGHTY QUINN (Manfred Mann; 1965/66/68) / TOO MUCH OF NOTHING (Peter, Paul & Mary; 1967) / THIS WHEEL'S ON FIRE (Julie Driscoll, Brian Auger & The Trinity; 1968) / ALL ALONG THE WATCHTOWER (Jimi Hendrix; 1968) / IF NOT FOR YOU (Olivia Newton-John; 1971) / A HARD RAIN'S A-GONNA FALL (Bryan Ferry; 1973) / KNOCKIN' ON HEAVEN'S DOOR (Eric Clapton; 1975 / Guns'n'Roses; 1992) / I'LL BE YOUR BABY TONIGHT (UB40 & Robert Palmer; 1990) / & some minor hits. **Filmography:** DON'T LOOK BACK (1965 documentary) / EAT THE DOCUMENTARY (1971 docu-film) / PAT GARRETT & BILLY THE KID (1973) / RENALDO AND CLARA (1978) / HEARTS OF FIRE (1987). • **Trivia:** On the 22 Nov'65, BOB married Sara Lowndes, but she divorced him in 1977. (Band members in discography are selectful.)

Recommended: DESIRE (*10) / BLOOD ON THE TRACKS (*9) / BLONDE ON BLONDE (*10) / THE FREEWHEELIN' BOB DYLAN (*9) / BRINGING IT ALL BACK HOME (*9) / ANOTHER SIDE OF BOB DYLAN (*7) / THE TIMES THEY ARE A-CHANGIN' (*7) / HIGHWAY 61 REVISITED (*10) / MORE BOB DYLAN'S GREATEST HITS (*7) / BOB DYLAN (*5) / GREATEST HITS (*10) / JOHN WESLEY HARDING (*5) / NASHVILLE SKYLINE (*5) / SELF PORTRAIT (*4) / NEW MORNING (*3) . PAT GARRETT AND BILLY THE KID (*3) / PLANET WAVES (*6) / DYLAN (*3) / BEFORE THE FLOOD (*7) / THE BASEMENT TAPES (*7) / HARD RAIN (*6) / STREET LEGAL onwards *5s and under.

BOB DYLAN – vocals, guitar, harmonica

C.B.S. Columbia

Mar 62. (7") **MIXED UP CONFUSION. / CORRINA CORRINA** [-] [ ]
Jun 62. (lp) **BOB DYLAN** [ ] [ ] Mar 62
– She's no good / Talkin' New York / In my time of dyin' / Man of constant sorrow / Fixin' to die blues / Pretty Peggy-o / Highway 51 blues / Gospel plow / Baby, let me follow you down / House of the risin' sun / Freight train blues / Song to Woody / See that grave is kept clean. *(re-dist.May65, hit No.13) (re-iss.+c.Mar81) (cd-iss.Nov89)*

— added musicians **HOWARD COLLINS** – guitar / **GEORGE BARNES** – bass / **HERB LOVELL** – drums / **LEONARD GASKIN** – bass / etc.

Nov 63. (lp) **THE FREEWHEELIN' BOB DYLAN** [16] [22] May 63
– Blowin' in the wind / Girl from the North Country / Masters of war / Down the highway / Bob Dylan's blues / A hard rains a-gonna fall / Don't think twice, it's all right / Bob Dylan's dream / Oxford Town / / Talking World War III blues / Corrina, Corina / Honey, just allow me one more chance / I shall be free. *(re-dist.Apr65, hitNo.1) (re-iss.+c.Mar81) (cd-iss.Nov89)*
Jun 64. (lp) **THE TIMES THEY ARE A-CHANGING** [20] [20] Mar 64
– The times they are a-changin' / Ballad of Hollis Brown / With God on our side / One too many mornings / North country blues / Only a pawn in their

game / Boots of Spanish leather / When the ship comes in / The lonesome death of Hattie Carroll / Restless farewell. *(re-dist.Apr65, hit No.4) (re-iss.+c.Mar81) (cd-iss.Nov89)*

Nov 64. (lp) **ANOTHER SIDE OF BOB DYLAN** 8 | 43 Sep 64
– All I really want to do / Black crow blues / Spanish Harlem incident / Chimes of freedom / I shall be free No.10 / To Ramona / Motorpsycho nitemare / I don't believe you / To Ramona / Ballad in plain D / It ain't me babe. *(re-iss.+c.Mar81) (cd-iss.Nov89)*

Mar 65. (7") **THE TIMES THEY ARE A-CHANGING. / HONEY, JUST ALLOW ME ONE MORE CHANCE** 9 | □

— with **BOBBY GREGG** – drums / **JOHN SEBASTIAN** – bass / **BRUCE LANGHORNE** – guitar

Apr 65. (7") **SUBTERRANEAN HOMESICK BLUES. / SHE BELONGS TO ME** 9 | □

May 65. (lp) **BRINGING IT ALL BACK HOME** 1 | 6 Mar 65
– Subterranean homesick blues / She belongs to me / Maggie's farm / Love minus zero – No limit / Outlaw blues / On the road again / Bob Dylan's 115th dream / Mr. Tambourine man / Gates of Eden / It's alright, ma (I'm only bleeding) / It's all over now, baby blue. *(re-iss.+c.Jul83) (cd-iss.Jul89 as 'SUBTERRANEAN HOMESICK BLUES')*

Jun 65. (7") **MAGGIE'S FARM. / ON THE ROAD AGAIN** 22 | -

— now with **AL KOOPER** – organ / **PAUL BUTTERFIELD** – guitar / **PAUL GRIFFIN** – keys / **CHARLIE McCOY** – guitar / **RUSS SAVAKUS** – bass /

Aug 65. (7") **LIKE A ROLLING STONE. / GATES OF EDEN** 4 | 2 Jul 65

Sep 65. (lp) **HIGHWAY 61 REVISITED** 4 | 3 Aug 65
– Like a rolling stone / Tombstone blues / It takes a lot to laugh, it takes a train to cry / From a Buick 6 / Ballad of a thin man / Queen Jane approximately / Highway 61 revisited / Just like Tom Thumb's blues / Desolation row. *(re-iss.+c.Dec85) (cd-iss.Nov89)*

Oct 65. (7") **POSITIVELY 4TH STREET. / FROM A BUICK 6** 8 | 7 Sep 65

Jan 66. (7") **CAN YOU PLEASE CRAWL OUT YOUR WIN-DOW. / HIGHWAY 61 REVISITED** 17 | 58 Nov 65

Apr 66. (7") **ONE OF US MUST KNOW (SOONER OR LATER). / QUEEN JANE APPROXIMATELY** 33 | □ Feb 66

— Now augmented by members of The **BAND:- ROBBIE ROBERTSON** – guitar / **RICHARD MANUEL** – keyboards / **LEVON HELM** – drums / **RICK DANKO** – bass / **GARTH HUDSON** – keyboards plus also **KENNY BUTTREY** – drums

May 66. (7") **RAINY DAY WOMEN NOS.12 & 35. / PLEDGING MY TIME** 7 | 2 Apr 66

Jul 66. (7") **I WANT YOU. / JUST LIKE TOM THUMB'S BLUES (live)** 16 | 20 Jun 66

Aug 66. (d-lp) **BLONDE ON BLONDE** 3 | 9 May 66
– Rainy day women # 12 & 35 / Pledging my love / Visions of Johanna / One of us must know (sooner or later) / Most likely you go your way (and I'll go mine) / Temporary like Achilles / Absolutely sweet Marie / 4th time around / Obviously 5 believers / I want you / Stuck inside of Mobile with the Memphis blues again / Leopard-skin pill-box hat / Just like a woman / Sad eyed lady of the lowlands. *(re-iss.+d-c.May82) (cd-iss.Jul87 + Jun89 + Feb95)*

Sep 66. (7") **JUST LIKE A WOMAN. / OBVIOUSLY 5 BELIEVERS** - | 33

Jan 67. (lp) **GREATEST HITS** (US diff.tracks) 6 | 10 Dec 66
– Blowin' in the wind / It ain't me babe / The times they are a-changin' / Mr.Tambourine man / She belongs to me / It's all over now, baby blue / Subterranean homesick blues / One of us must know (sooner or later) / Like a rolling stone / Just like a woman / Rainy day women Nos. 12 & 35. *(re-iss.Mar88, hit UK 99) (cd-iss.Nov89) (cd+c-iss.Feb91 on 'Columbia') (re-iss.cd Oct94 as 'BEST OF . . .')*

May 67. (7") **LEOPARD SKIN PILL-BOX HAT. / MOST LIKELY YOU GO YOUR WAY (AND I'LL GO MINE)** □ | 81 Mar 67

— now with **BUTTREY, McCOY** and **PETE DRAKE** – sitar, guitar

Feb 68. (lp) **JOHN WESLEY HARDING** 1 | 2
– John Wesley Harding / As I went out one morning / I dreamed I saw St. Augustine / All along the watchtower / The ballad of Frankie Lee and Judas Priest / Drifter's escape / Dear landlord / I am a lonesome hobo / I pity the poor immigrant / The wicked messenger / Down along the cove / I'll be your baby tonight. *(c-iss.1969) (cd-iss.Nov89)*

— next featured **CHARLIE DANIELS** – bass, guitar / **etc.**

May 69. (7") **I THREW IT ALL AWAY. / DRIFTER'S ESCAPE** 30 | 85

May 69. (lp)(c) **NASHVILLE SKYLINE** 1 | 3
– Girl from the North country (with JOHNNY CASH) / Nashville skyline rag / To be alone with you / I threw it all away / Pegy Day / Lady lady lay / One more night / Tell me that it isn't true / Country pie / Tonight I'll be staying here with you. *(re-iss.May87) (cd-iss.Jan86) (quad-lp 1970's)*

Sep 69. (7") **LAY LADY LAY. / PEGGY DAY** 5 | 7 Jul 69

Dec 69. (7") **TONIGHT I'LL BE STAYING HERE WITH YOU. / COUNTRY PIE** □ | 50 Oct 69

Jul 70. (dlp,d-c) **SELF PORTRAIT** 1 | 4
– All the tired horses / Alberta #1 / I forgot more than you'll ever know / Days of 49 / Early mornin' rain / In search of little Sadie / Let it be me / Little Sadie / Woogie boogie / Belle isle / Living the blues / Like a rolling stone (version) / Copper kettle (the pale moonlight) / Gotta travel on / Blue Moon / The boxer / The mighty Quinn (Quinn, the eskimo) / Take me as I am / Take a message to Mary / It hurts me too / Minstrel boy / She belongs to me / Wigwam / Alberta #2. *(re-iss.Sep87) (cd+c-iss.Feb91 on 'Columbia')*

Jul 70. (7") **WIGWAM. / COPPER KETTLE (THE PALE MOONLIGHT)** □ | 41

Nov 70. (lp)(c) **NEW MORNING** 1 | 7
– If not for you / Day of the locusts / Time passes slowly / Went to see the gypsy / Winterlude / If dogs ran free / New morning / Sign on the window / One more weekend / The man in me / Three angels / Father of the night. *(re-iss.Sep83) (cd+c-iss.Feb91 on 'Columbia') (re-iss.cd+c Feb94 on 'Columbia')*

Mar 71. (7") **IF NOT FOR YOU. / NEW MORNING** □ | □

Jun 71. (7") **WATCHING THE RIVER FLOW. / SPANISH IS THE LOVING TONGUE** 24 | 41

Dec 71. (7") **GEORGE JACKSON (Acoustic). / GEORGE JACKSON (big band version)** □ | 33

Dec 71. (d-lp)(d-c) **MORE BOB DYLAN GREATEST HITS** 12 | 14
– Watching the river flow / Don't think twice, it's alright / Lay lady lay / Stuck inside Mobile with the Memphis blues again / I'll be your baby tonight / All I really want to do / My back pages / Maggie's farm / Tonight I'll be staying here with you / Positively 4th Street / All along the watchtower / The mighty Quinn (Quinn, the eskimo) / Just like Tom Thumb's blues / A hard rain's a-gonna fall / If not for you / New morning / Tomorrow is a long time / When I paint my masterpiece / I shall be released / You ain't goin' nowhere / Down in the flood. (US-title BOB DYLAN'S GREATEST HITS, VOL.II) *(cd-iss.Oct87) (cd-re-iss.Aug92 on 'Columbia')(re-iss.cd+cMar93 on 'Columbia')*

Sep 73. (lp)(c) **PAT GARRETT AND BILLY THE KID (Soundtrack)** 29 | 16
– Mmain title theme / Cantina theme (working for the law) / Billy 1 / Bunkhouse theme / River theme / Turkey chase / Knockin' on Heaven's door / Final theme / Billy 4 / Billy 7. *(re-iss.Mar82) (cd+c-iss.Feb91 on 'Columbia')*

Sep 73. (7") **KNOCKIN' ON HEAVEN'S DOOR. / TURKEY CHASE** 14 | 12

Nov 73. (lp)(c) **DYLAN** (recorded 1970) □ | 17
– Lily of the west / Can't help falling in love / Sarah Jane / The ballad of Ira Hayes / Mr. Bojangles / Mary Ann / Big yellow taxi / A fool such as I / Spanish is the loving tongue. *(re-iss.Mar83) (cd+c-iss.Feb91 on 'Columbia')*

Jan 74. (7") **A FOOL SUCH AS I. / LILY OF THE WEST** □ | 55

Island | Asylum

Feb 74. (lp)(c) **PLANET WAVES** 7 | 1
– On a night like this / Going going gone / Tough mama / Hazel / Something there is about you / Forever young / Dirge / You angel you / Never say goodbye / Wedding song. *(re-iss.Sep82) (cd-iss.Nov89 on 'CBS' + Jun88 on 'Collector's Choice')(quad-lp US 1970's)*

Feb 74. (7") **ON A NIGHT LIKE THIS. / YOU ANGEL YOU** □ | -

Feb 74. (7") **ON A NIGHT LIKE THIS. / FOREVER YOUNG** □ | -

Apr 74. (7") **SOMETHING THERE IS ABOUT YOU. / GOING GOING GONE** - | □

Asylum | Asylum

Jul 74. (d-lp)(d-c) **BEFORE THE FLOOD (live) ("BOB DYLAN / The BAND")** 8 | 3
– Most likely you go your way (and I'll go mine) / Lay lady lay / Rainy day women #12 & 35 / Knockin' on Heaven's door / It ain't me babe / The ballad of a thin man / Up on Cripple Creek * / I shall be released / Endless highway * / The night they drove old Dixie down * / Stage fright * / Don't think twice, it's all right / Just like a woman / It's alright ma (I'm only bleeding) / The shape I'm in * / When you awake * / The weight * / All along the watchtower / Highway 61 revisited / Like a rolling stone / Blowin' in the wind. (* tracks by The BAND) *(re-iss.Sep82) (cd-iss.Jul87 + Nov89)*
The BAND had been his backing group from the mid '60's.

Aug 74. (7") **MOST LIKELY YOU GO YOUR WAY (AND I'LL GO MINE) (live). / SATGE FRIGHT (The BAND live)** - | 66

Nov 74. (7") **ALL ALONG THE WATCHTOWER (live). / IT AIN'T ME BABE (live)** - | □

C.B.S. | Columbia

Feb 75. (lp)(c) **BLOOD ON THE TRACKS** 4 | 1
– Tangled up in blue / Simple twist of fate / You're a big girl now / Idiot wind / You're gonna make me lonesome when you go / Meet me in the morning / Lily, Rosemary and the Jack of Hearts / If you see her, say hello / Shelter from the storm / Buckets of rain. *(re-iss.May82) (cd-iss.Dec85)(re-iss.cd+cSep93 on 'Columbia')*

Mar 75. (7") **TANGLED UP IN BLUE. / IF YOU SEE HER, SAY HELLO** - | 31

Jul 75. (d-lp)(d-c) **THE BASEMENT TAPES** (recorded 1967) 8 | 7
– Odds and ends / Orange juice blues (blues for breakfast) / Million dollar bash / Yazoo street scandal / Goin' to Acapulco / Katie's been gone / Lo and behold / Bessie Smith / Clothes line saga / Apple suckling tree / Please Mrs.Henry / Tears of rage / Too much of nothing / Yea! heavy and a bottle of wine / Ain't no more Cane / Crash on the levee (down in the flood) / Ruben Remus / Tiny Montgomery / You ain't goin' nowhere / Don't ya tell Henry / Nothing was delivered / Open the doors, Homer / Long distance operator. *(cd-iss.Nov89)*

Oct 75. (7") **MILLION DOLLAR BASH. / TEARS OF RAGE** □ | □

— next featured **EMMYLOU HARRIS** – vocals / **SCARLET RIVIERA** – violin / **RONNE BLAKELY** – vocals / **HOWIE WYTHE** – drums / **ROB STONER** – bass / **STEVEN SOLES** – guitar

Jan 76. (7") **HURRICANE (part 1). / HURRICANE (full version)** 43 | 33 Dec 75

Jan 76. (lp)(c) **DESIRE** 3 | 1
– Hurricane / Isis / Mozambique / One more cup of coffee / Oh, sister / Joey / Romance in Durango / Black diamond bay / Sara. *(re-iss.Apr85) (cd-iss.Jul87 +*

Jun89) (quad-lp rel.1976)

Apr 76. (7") **MOZAMBIQUE. / OH, SISTER** [ ] [54]

— His HARD RAIN tour added **MICK RONSON** – guitar / **DAVID MANSFIELD** – keys

Sep 76. (lp)(c) **HARD RAIN (live)** [3] [17]
– Maggie's farm / One too many mornings / Stuck inside of Mobile with the Memphis blues again / Lay lady lay / Shelter from the storm / You're a big girl now / I threw it all away / Idiot wind. *(re-iss.Apr83) (cd-iss.Nov89)*

Feb 77. (7") **RITA MAY. / STUCK INSIDE OF MOBILE WITH THE MEMPHIS BLUES AGAIN (live)** [ ] [ ]

May 78. (7")(12") **BABY STOP CRYING. / NEW PONY** [13] [ ]

Jun 78. (lp)(c) **STREET-LEGAL** [2] [11]
– Changing of the guards / New pony / No time to think / Baby stop crying / Is your love in vain / Senor (tales of Yankee power) / True love tends to forget / We better talk this over / Where are you tonight (journey through dark heat). *(cd-iss.Mar86 & May95 +c)*

Oct 78. (7")(12") **IS YOUR LOVE IN VAIN. / WE BETTER TALK THIS OVER** [56] [ ]

Dec 78. (7") **CHANGING OF THE GUARDS. / SENOR (TALES OF YANKEE POWER)** [ ] [ ]

1978. (7"ep) **4 SONGS FROM "RENALDO AND CLARA"** [-] [ ]
– People get ready / Never let me go / Isis / It ain't me babe.

May 79. (d-lp)(d-c) **BOB DYLAN AT BUDOKAN (live)** [4] [13]
– Mr.Tambourine man / Shelter from the storm / Love minus zero – No limit / Ballad of a thin man / Don't think twice, it's all right / Maggie's farm / One more cup of coffee / Like a rolling stone / I shall be released / Oh sister / Is your love in vain? / Going going gone / Blowin' in the wind / Just like a woman / Simple twist of fate / All along the watchtower / I want you / All I really want to do / Knockin' on Heaven's door / It's alright ma (I'm only bleeding) / Forever young / The times they are a-changin'. *(cd-iss.Jul87)(re-iss.d-cd+d-c Apr93 on 'Columbia')*

Jun 79. (7") **FOREVER YOUNG (live). / ALL ALONG THE WATCHTOWER (live)** [ ] [-]

Aug 79. (7") **PRECIOUS ANGEL. / TROUBLE IN MIND** [ ] [-]

Aug 79. (lp)(c) **SLOW TRAIN COMING** [2] [3]
– Gotta serve somebody / Precious angel / I believe in you / Slow train / Gonna change my way of thinking / Do right to me baby (do unto others) / When you gonna wake up / Man gave names to all the animals / When he returns. *(re-iss.Nov85, cd-Mar86 +Apr89)*

Sep 79. (7") **GOTTA SERVE SOMEBODY. / TROUBLE IN MIND** [-] [24]

Oct 79. (7") **MAN GAVE NAMES TO ALL THE ANIMALS. / WHEN HE RETURNS** [ ] [-]

Jan 80. (7") **MAN GAVE NAMES TO THE ANIMALS. / WHEN YOU GONNA WAKE UP** [-] [ ]

Jan 80. (7") **GOTTA SERVE SOMEBODY. / GONNA CHANGE MY WAY OF THINKING** [ ] [-]

Mar 80. (7") **SLOW TRAIN. / DO RIGHT TO ME BABY (DO UNTO OTHERS)** [-] [ ]

May 80. (7") **SOLID ROCK. / COVENANT WOMAN** [-] [ ]

Jun 80. (lp)(c) **SAVED** [3] [24]
– A satisfied mind / Saved / Covenant woman / What can I do for you? / Solid rock / Pressing on / In the garden / Saving Grace / Are you ready. *(cd+c-iss.Feb91 on 'Columbia')(re-iss.cd+c Mar93 on 'Columbia')*

Jun 80. (7") **SAVED. / ARE YOU READY** [ ] [ ]

Jun 81. (7") **HEART OF MINE. / THE GROOM'S STILL WAITING AT THE ALTAR** [-] [ ]

Jul 81. (7") **HEART OF MINE. / LET IT BE ME** [ ] [-]

Aug 81. (lp)(c) **SHOT OF LOVE** [6] [33]
– Shot of love / Heart of mine / Property of Jesus / Lenny Bruce / Watered down love / Dead man, dead man / In the summertime / Trouble / Every grain of sand. *(cd+c-iss.Feb91 on 'Columbia' +=)*– The groom's still waiting at the altar. *(re-iss.cd Jun94 on 'Sony Europe')*

Sep 81. (7") **LENNY BRUCE. / DEAD MAN, DEAD MAN** [ ] [ ]

Oct 83. (7") **UNION SUNDOWN. / I AND I** [ ] [ ]

Nov 83. (lp)(c) **INFIDELS** [9] [20]
– Jokerman / Sweetheart like you / Neighbourhood bully / License to kill / Man of peace / Union sundown / I and I / Don't fall apart on me tonight. *(cd-iss.Jul87) (re-iss.+cd.Dec89)*

Dec 83. (7") **SWEETHEART LIKE YOU. / UNION SUNDOWN** [-] [55]

May 84. (7") **JOKERMAN. / ISIS** [-] [ ]

Jun 84. (7") **JOKERMAN. / LICENSE TO KILL** [ ] [-]

Dec 84. (lp)(c)(cd) **REAL LIVE (live)** [54] [ ]
– Highway 61 revisited / Maggie's farm / I and I / License to kill / It ain't me babe / Tangled up in blue / Masters of war / Ballad of a thin man / Girl from the North country / Tombstone blues. *(cd+c-iss.Feb91 on 'Columbia')*

Jan 85. (7") **HIGHWAY 61 REVISITED (live). / IT AIN'T ME BABE (live)** [ ] [ ]

Jun 85. (7") **TIGHT CONNECTION TO MY HEART. / WE'D BETTER TALK THIS OVER** [ ] [ ]

Jun 85. (lp)(c)(cd) **EMPIRE BURLESQUE** [11] [33]
– Tight connection to my heart (has anybody seen my love) / Seeing the real you at last / I'll remember you / Clean cut kid / Never gonna be the same again / Trust yourself / Emotionally yours / When the night comes falling from the sky / Something's burning, baby / Dark eyes. *(re-cd.1988) (cd+c-iss.Feb91 on 'Columbia')*

Aug 85. (7")(12") **WHEN THE NIGHT COMES FALLING FROM THE SKY. / DARK EYES** [ ] [-]

— Apr86, was credited next on TOM PETTY ⇒ single BAND OF THE HAND.

Oct 85. (7") **WHEN THE NIGHT COMES FALLING FROM THE SKY. / EMOTIONALLY YOURS** [-] [ ]

Jul 86. (lp)(c)(cd) **KNOCKED OUT LOADED** [35] [53]
– You wanna ramble / They killed him / Driftin' too far from shore / Precious memories / Maybe someday / Brownsville girl / Got my mind made up / Under your spell. *(cd+c-iss.Feb91 on 'Columbia')(re-iss.cd+c Mar93 on 'Columbia')*

Oct 86. (7") **THE USUAL. / GOT MY MIND MADE UP** [ ] [ ]
(12"+=) – They killed him.

Jun 88. (lp)(c)(cd) **DOWN IN THE GROOVE** [32] [61]
– Let's stick together / When did you leave Heaven? / Sally Sue Brown / Death is not the end / Had a dream about you, baby / Ugliest girl in the world / Silvio / Ninety miles an hour (down a dead end street) / Shenandoah / Rank strangers to me.

Jul 88. (7") **SILVIO. / WHEN DID YOU LEAVE HEAVEN?** [ ] [ ]
(12"+=) – Driftin' too far from shore. (US; b-side)

Later in 1988 onwards he was also part of supergroup TRAVELLING WILBURYS

Feb 89. (lp)(c)(cd) **DYLAN & THE DEAD (live) ("BOB DYLAN & GRATEFUL DEAD")** rec. Summer '87 [38] [37]
– Slow train / I want you / Gotta serve somebody / Queen Jane approximately / Joey / All along the watchtower / Knockin' on Heaven's door. *(re-iss.cd+c May94 on 'Columbia')*

Sep 89. (lp)(c)(cd) **OH MERCY** [6] [30]
– Political world / Where teardrops fall / Everything is broken / Ring them bells / Man in the long black coat / Most of the time / What good am I? / Disease of conceit / What was it you wanted / Shooting star.

Oct 89. (7") **EVERYTHING IS BROKEN. / DEAD MAN, DEAD MAN** [-] [ ]

Oct 89. (7") **EVERYTHING IS BROKEN. / DEATH IS NOT THE END** [ ] [-]
(12") – ('A'side) / Dead man, dead man / I want you (live)
(cd-s) – ('A'side) / Where the teardrops fall / Dead man, dead man / Ugliest girl in the world.

Feb 90. (7") **POLITICAL WORLD. / RING THEM BELLS** [ ] [ ]
(12"+=)(cd-s+=) – Silvio / All along the watchtower (live).
(cd-s) – ('A'side) /Caribbean wind / You're a big girl now / It's all over now, baby blue.

Sep 90. (cd)(c)(lp) **UNDER THE RED SKY** [13] [38]
– Wiggle wiggle / Under the red sky / Unbelievable / Born in time / TV talkin' time / 10,000 men / 2x2 / God knows / Handy Dandy / Cat's in the well.

Sep 90. (7") **UNBELIEVABLE. / 10,000 MEN** [ ] [ ]
(cd-s+=) – In the summertime / Jokerman.

Feb 91. (7")(c-s) **SERIES OF DREAMS. / SEVEN CURSES** [ ] [ ]
(cd-s+=) – Tangled up in blue / Like a rolling stone.

— totally solo DYLAN

Columbia Columbia

Nov 92. (cd)(c)(lp) **GOOD AS I BEEN TO YOU** [18] [51]
– Frankie & Albert / Jim Jones / Blackjack Davey / Canadee-i-o / Sittin' on top of the world / Little Maggie / Hard times / Step it up and go / Tomorrow night / Arthur McBride / You're gonna quit me / Diamond Joe / Froggie went a courtin'.

In Aug93, a host of artists released a live tribute d-cd,d-c 'ANNIVERSARY CONCERT', which hit US No.30. Below all traditional tunes.

Nov 93. (cd)(c) **WORLD GONE WRONG** [35] [70]
– World gone wrong / Ragged and dirty / Love Henry / Blood in my eyes / Delia / Broke down engine / Two soldiers / Stack A Lee / Jack A Roe / Love pilgrim.

— with **TONY GARNIER** -bass / **JOHN JACKSON** -guitar / **BUCKY BAXTER** -pedal steel, dobro / **WINSTON WATSON** -drums / **BRENDAN O'BRIEN** -hammond organ

Apr 95. (cd)(c)(lp) **MTV UNPLUGGED** [10] [23]
– Tombstone blues / Shooting star / All along the watchtower / The times they are a-changin' / John Brown / Desolation row / Rainy day women £ 12 & 35 / Love minus zero – No limit / Dignity / Knockin' on Heaven's door / Like a rolling stone / With God on our side.

May 95. (c-s) **DIGNITY / JOHN BROWN** [33] [ ]
(cd-s+=) – It ain't me babe (live).
(cd-s) – ('A'side) / A hard rain's a-gonna fall.

– compilations, others, etc. –

Apr 66. C.B.S.; (7"ep) **ONE TOO MANY MORNINGS** [ ] [-]
– One too many mornings / Spanish Harlem incident / Oxford town / She belongs to me.

Jun 66. C.B.S.; (7"ep) **DON'T THINK TWICE IT'S ALRIGHT** [ ] [-]
– Don't think twice it's alright / Blowin' in the wind / Corrina, Corrina / When the ship comes.

Oct 66. C.B.S.; (7"ep) **MR.TAMBOURINE MAN** [ ] [-]
– Mr.Tambourine man / Subterranean homesick blues / It's all over now, baby blue.

Mar 73. C.B.S.; (7") **JUST LIKE A WOMAN. / I WANT YOU** [ ] [ ]

Feb 76. C.B.S.; (7") **LAY LADY LAY. / I THREW IT ALL AWAY** [ ] [ ]
(re-iss.Feb79)

Nov 85. C.B.S./ US= Columbia; (5xlp-box)(3xc-box)(3xcd-box) **BIOGRAPH** [ ] [33]

— (above contains 16 unreleased tracks)

		UK	US
1988.	C.B.S.; (d-c) **DESIRE / BLOOD ON THE TRACKS**		-
Apr 91.	Columbia; (3xcd)(3xc)(6xlp) **THE BOOTLEG SERIES VOLUMES 1-3 (RARE & UNRELEASED) 1961-1991**	32	49
Aug 92.	Columbia; (d-cd) **HIGHWAY 61 REVISITED / JOHN WESLEY HARDING**		
Oct 93.	Columbia; (3xcd-box) **BLONDE ON BLONDE / JOHN WESLEY HARDING / SELF PORTRAIT**		
Oct 83.	Go Int.; (lp)(c) **HISTORICAL ARCHIVES VOL.1**		
Oct 83.	Go Int.; (lp)(c) **HISTORICAL ARCHIVES VOL.2**		
Sep 87.	Compact Collection; (cd) **THE GASLIGHT TAPES**		
1988.	Joker; (lp) **THE BEST OF BOB DYLAN**		-
May 88.	Big Time; (lp)(c) **BLOWIN' IN THE WIND**		-
May 88.	Big Time; (lp)(c) **DON'T THINK TWICE, IT'S ALRIGHT**		-
Nov 94.	Columbia; (cd)(c)(d-lp) **GREATEST HITS VOLUME III**		

– Tangled up in blue / Changing the guards / The groom's still waiting at the altar / Hurricane / Forever young / Jokerman / Dignity / Silvio / Ring them bells / Gotta serve somebody / Series of dream / Brownsville girl / Under the red sky / Knockin' on Heaven's door.

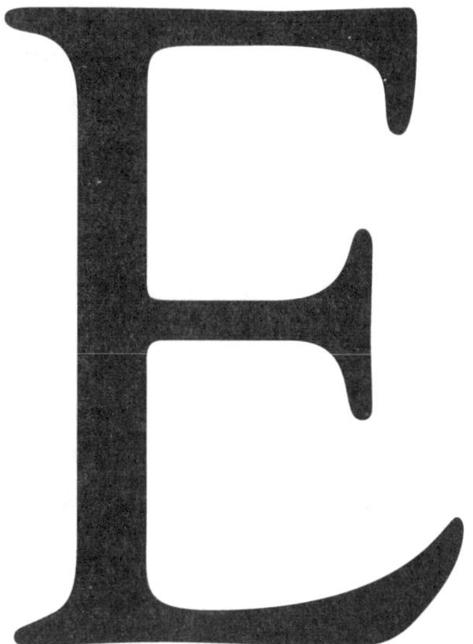

EAGLES

Formed: Los Angeles, California, USA . . . 1972, by FREY and HENLEY. Signed to 'Asylum' records that year, and soon issued eponymous debut album which hit US Top 30. By 1975, they had become America's top rock-pop band when album and single ONE OF THESE NIGHTS shot to top slot. The following year (1976) saw them release their classic all-time great HOTEL CALIFORNIA. For another 4 years, they enjoyed an unrivalled reign as easy-listening FM rock stars, until they split. All continued solo, with most success stemming from HENLEY and FREY. HENLEY's career was set back somewhat in Nov'80, when a 16 year-old female was found naked and drugged in his Californian home. He was fined and ordered to attend a drug counselling scheme. The next year, he recorded debut album with DANNY KORTCHMAR and GREG LADANYI, but this lay dormant until late 1982. In the meantime, he was credited on US Top 10 single by STEVIE NICKS 'Leather And Lace'. His debut album titled 'I CAN'T STAND STILL', hit US Top 30, helped by an appropriately titled Top 3 single 'DIRTY LAUNDRY'. In '84, he moved to 'Geffen' label, and secured cross-Atlantic Top 20 single 'THE BOYS OF SUMMER' & album 'BUILDING THE PERFECT BEAST'. FREY first dueted on STEVIE NICKS (Fleetwood Mac) early '82 hit single 'Leather And Lace'. That same year, still contracted to 'Asylum' records, he issued US Top 40 album 'NO FUN ALOUD'. In 1984, his next Top 40 album 'THE ALLNIGHTER', which prompted NBC TV to feature 'SMUGGLER'S BLUES' and FREY, on their 'Miami Vice' cop series. This gave him a cross-Atlantic Top 30 hit in 1985, and was proceeded by another hit song from the series 'YOU BELONG TO THE CITY'. After a quiet 2 years, FREY returned to business, with 1988's 'SOUL SEARCHIN' album. • **Style:** West-coast country AOR rock, that hardened up somewhat with the entry of JOE WALSH in '76. • **Songwriters:** All took turns writing. Covered; OL'55 (Tom Waits) / TAKE IT EASY (co-written by FREY and Jackson Browne) / PLEASE COME HOME FOR CHRISTMAS (Charles Brown). HENLEY covered EVERYBODY KNOWS (Leonard Cohen). • **Trivia:** HOTEL CALIFORNIA track won a Grammy award in 1977. A few years later, FREY, HENLEY and WALSH appeared on RANDY NEWMAN's 'Little Criminals'. In 1990, FREY was honoured by the Rock'n'charity foundation for his work to prevent against AIDS and cancer.

Recommended: THEIR GREATEST HITS 1971-1975 (*9) / ONE OF THESE NIGHTS (*8) / HOTEL CALIFORNIA (*8).

GLEN FREY (b. 6 Nov'48, Detroit, Michigan, USA) – guitar, vocals (ex-LINDA RONSTADT Band, ex-LONGBRANCH PENWHISTLE) / **BERNIE LEADON** (b.19 Jul'47, Minneapolis, Minnesota, USA) – guitar, vocals (ex-LINDA RONSTADT Band, ex-FLYING BURRITO BROTHERS) / **RANDY MEISNER** (b. 8 Mar'47, Scottsbluff, Nebraska, USA) – bass, vocals (ex-LINDA RONSTADT Band, ex-POCO, ex-RICK NELSON) / **DON HENLEY** (b.22 Jul'47, Gilmer, Texas, USA) – drums, vocals (ex-LINDA RONSTADT Band, ex-SHILOH)

		Asylum	Asylum	
Jun 72.	(7") **TAKE IT EASY. / GET YOU IN THE MOOD**		12	May 72
Sep 72.	(7") **WITCHY WOMAN. / EARLY BIRD**		9	
Oct 72.	(lp)(c) **EAGLES**		22	Jun 72
	– Take it easy / Witchy woman / Chug all night / Most of us are sad / Nightingale / Train leaves here this morning / Take the Devil / Early bird / Peaceful easy feeling / Tryin'. *(re-iss.Jun76) (cd-iss.Feb87 + 1989)*			
Dec 72.	(7") **PEACEFUL EASY FEELING. / TRYIN'**	-	22	
Feb 73.	(7") **TRYIN'. / CHUG ALL NIGHT**			
Apr 73.	(lp)(c) **DESPERADO**		41	
	– Doolin-Dalton / Twenty-one / Out of control / Tequila sunrise / Desperado / Certain kind of fool / Outlaw man / Saturday night / Bitter creek. *(re-iss.Aug75, hit UK No.39) (re-iss.Jun76) (cd-iss.1989)*			
Jul 73.	(7") **TEQUILA SUNRISE. / TWENTY-ONE**		64	Jun 73
Oct 73.	(7") **OUTLAW MAN. / CERTAIN KIND OF FOOL**		59	Sep 73

—— added **DON FELDER** (b.21 Sep'47, Topanga, California, USA) – guitar, vocals (ex-FLOW)

Date	Release	UK	US	
Apr 74.	(lp)(c) **ON THE BORDER**	28	17	
	– Already gone / You never cry like a lover / Midnight flyer / My man / On the border / James Dean / Ol' 55 / Is it true / Good day in Hell / Best of my love. *(re-iss.Jun76) (quad-lp 1977) (cd-iss.1989)*			
Apr 74.	(7") **ALREADY GONE. / IS IT TRUE**	-	32	
May 74.	(7") **JAMES DEAN. / IS IT TRUE**		77	
Jul 74.	(7") **ALREADY GONE. / OL' 55**		-	
Sep 74.	(7") **JAMES DEAN. / GOOD DAY IN HELL**	-		
Nov 74.	(7") **BEST OF MY LOVE. / OL' 55**	-	1	
Dec 74.	(7") **BEST OF MY LOVE. / MIDNIGHT FLYER**		-	
May 75.	(7"m) **MY MAN. / TAKE IT EASY / TEQUILA SUNRISE**		-	
Jun 75.	(lp)(c) **ONE OF THESE NIGHTS**	8	1	
	– One of these nights / Too many hands / Hollywood waltz / Journey of the sorceror / Lyin' eyes / Take it to the limit / Visions / After the thrill is gone / I wish you peace. *(re-iss.Jun76) (quad-lp 1977) (cd-iss.1989)*			
Jun 75.	(7") **ONE OF THESE NIGHTS. / VISIONS**	23	1	May 75
Sep 75.	(7") **LYIN' EYES. / TOO MANY HANDS**	-	2	
Oct 75.	(7") **LYIN' EYES. / JAMES DEAN**	23	-	
Dec 75.	(7") **TAKE IT TO THE LIMIT. / AFTER THE THRILL IS GONE**	-	4	
Feb 76.	(7") **TAKE IT TO THE LIMIT. / TOO MANY HANDS**	12	-	
Feb 76.	(lp)(c) **THEIR GREATEST HITS 1971-1975 (compilation)**	2	1	
	– Take it easy / Witchy woman / Lyin' eyes / Already gone / Desperado / One of these nights / Tequila sunrise / Take it to the limit / Peaceful easy feeling / Best of my love. *(cd-iss.May87)*			

—— **JOE WALSH** (b.20 Nov'47, Wichita, Kansas, USA) – guitar, vocals (ex-Solo artist, ex-JAMES GANG),repl. LEADON who formed own duo band

Date	Release	UK	US	
Dec 76.	(lp)(c) **HOTEL CALIFORNIA**	2	1	
	– Hotel California / New kid in town / Life in the fast lane / Wasted time / Wasted time (reprise) / Victim of love / Pretty maids all in a row / Try and love again / The last resort. *(cd-iss.May87) (re-iss.Jun91)*			
Jan 77.	(7") **NEW KID IN TOWN. / VICTIM OF LOVE**	20	1	Dec 76
Apr 77.	(7") **HOTEL CALIFORNIA. / PRETTY MAIDS ALL IN A ROW**	8	1	Feb 77
Jun 77.	(7") **LIFE IN THE FAST LANE. / THE LAST RESORT**		11	May 77

—— **TIMOTHY B. SCHMIT** (b.30 Oct'47, Sacramento, California, USA) – bass, vocals (ex-POCO) repl. MEISNER who went solo.

(SCHMIT now alongside FREY, HENLEY, WALSH and FELDER)

Date	Release	UK	US
Dec 78.	(7") **PLEASE COME HOME FOR CHRISTMAS. / FUNKY NEW YEAR**	30	18

—— added p/t **JOE VITALE** – keyboards

Date	Release	UK	US
Sep 79.	(7") **HEARTACHE TONIGHT. / TEENAGE JAIL**	40	1
Sep 79.	(lp)(c) **THE LONG RUN**	4	1
	– The long run / I can't tell you why / In the city / The disco strangler / King of Hollywood / Heartache tonight / Those shoes / Teenage jail / The Greeks don't want no freaks / The sad cafe. *(cd-iss.1986)*		
Nov 79.	(7") **THE LONG RUN. / THE DISCO STRANGLER**	66	8
Jan 80.	(7") **I CAN'T TELL YOU WHY. / THE GREEKS DON'T WANT NO FREAKS**		8
May 80.	(7") **THE SAD CAFE. / THOSE SHOES**		
Nov 80.	(d-lp)(d-c) **THE EAGLES LIVE (live)**	24	6
	– Hotel California / Heartache tonight / I can't tell you why / The long run / New kid in town / Life's been good / Seven bridges road / Wasted time / Take it to the limit / Doolin-Dalton / Desperado / Saturday night / All night long / Life in the fast lane / Take it easy. *(d-cd-iss.Feb93)*		
Dec 80.	(7") **SEVEN BRIDGES ROAD (live). / THE LONG RUN (live)**	-	21
Jan 81.	(7") **TAKE IT TO THE LIMIT (live). / SEVEN BRIDGES ROAD (live) / TAKE IT EASY (live)**		

		not issued	Full Moon
Mar 81.	(7") **I CAN'T TELL YOU WHY. / AMBROSIA OUTSIDE**	-	

—— By this time they had all mutually agreed to disband. All five went on to individual solo careers.

– more compilations etc. –

Note; All releases on 'Asylum' until mentioned.

Sep 76. (7") **TAKE IT EASY. / WITCHY WOMAN** [ ] [ ]
Sep 76. (7") **PEACEFUL EASY FEELING. / OL'55** [ ] [ ]
Sep 76. (7") **TEQUILA SUNRISE. / ON THE BORDER** [ ] [ ]
Oct 82. (lp)(c) **EAGLES GREATEST HITS - VOL.2** [ ] [52]
– Hotel California / Heartache tonight / Life in the fast lane / Seven bridges road / The sad cafe / I can't tell you why / New kid in town / The long run / Victim of love / After the thrill is gone.
Oct 83. (d-c) **DESPERADO / ONE OF THESE NIGHTS** [ ] [ ]
Nov 83. (d-c) **HOTEL CALIFORNIA / THE LONG RUN** [ ] [ ]
May 85. (lp)(c)(cd) **THE BEST OF THE EAGLES** [10] [ ]
– Tequila sunrise / Lyin' eyes / Take it to the limit / Hotel California / Life in the fast lane / Heartache tonight / The long run / Take it easy / Peaceful easy feeling / Desperado / Best of my love / One of these nights / New kid in town. *(re-iss.Aug88 hit UK No.8)*
Jun 88. (7") **HOTEL CALIFORNIA. / PRETTY MAIDS ALL IN A ROW** [ ] [ ]
(12"+=) – The sad cafe.
(cd-s++=) – Hotel California (live).
Jun 89. (cd-ep) **TAKE IT EASY / ONE OF THESE NIGHTS / DESPERADO / LYIN' EYES** [ ] [ ]
Jan 91. (cd)(c)(lp) **BEST OF EAGLES** [ ] [ ]
Jul 94. (cd)(c) **THE VERY BEST OF EAGLES** [5] [ ]
Sep 85. Old Gold; (7") **TAKE IT TO THE LIMIT. / BEST OF MY LOVE** [ ] [-]
Sep 85. Old Gold; (7") **HOTEL CALIFORNIA. / DESPERADO** [ ] [-]
Oct 85. Old Gold; (7") **LYIN' EYES. / ONE OF THESE NIGHTS** [ ] [-]

Don HENLEY

Asylum Asylum

Aug 82. (lp)(c) **I CAN'T STAND STILL** [ ] [24]
– I can't stand still / You better hang up / Long way home / Nobody's business / Talking to the Moon / Dirty laundry / Johnny can't read / Them and us / La Eile / Lilah / The uncloudy day. *(cd-iss.1988)*
Sep 82. (7") **JOHNNY CAN'T READ. / LONG WAY HOME** [ ] [42] Aug 82
Dec 82. (7") **DIRTY LAUNDRY. / LILAH** [59] [3] Oct 82
(12"+=) – Them and us. *(re-iss.Jun85)*
Jan 83. (7") **I CAN'T STAND STILL. / THEM AND US** [-] [48]
May 83. (7") **THE UNCLOUDED DAY. / LONG WAY HOME** [ ] [ ]
(12"+=) – I can't stand still.
Jul 83 (7") **NOBODY'S BUSINESS. / LONG WAY HOME** [-] [ ]

Geffen Geffen

Dec 84. (7") **THE BOYS OF SUMMER. / A MONTH OF SUNDAYS** [12] [5] Nov 84
Feb 85. (lp)(c) **BUILDING THE PERFECT BEAST** [14] [13] Dec 84
– The boys of summer / You can't make love / Man with a mission / You're not drinking enough / Not enough love in the world / Building the perfect beast / All she wants to do is dance / Sunset grill / Drivin' with your eyes closed / Land of the living. *(cd+=)* – A month of Sundays. *(re-iss.Sep86) (cd-iss.Feb87 & 1988) (re-iss.+cd.Jan91 & Mar95)*
Apr 85. (7") **SUNSET GRILL. / BUILDING THE PERFECT BEAST** [ ] [-]
Jun 85. (7") **ALL SHE WANTS TO DO IS DANCE. / BUILDING THE PERFECT BEAST** [ ] [9] Feb 85
Jul 85. (7") **NOT ENOUGH LOVE IN THE WORLD. / MAN WITH A MISSION** [ ] [34] May 85
Aug 85. (7") **SUNSET GRILL. / MAN WITH A MISSION** [-] [22]

— His basic back-up consisted of **DANNY KORTCHMAR** – guitar, keyboards / **STAN LYNCH** – drums / **PINO PALLADINO** – bass / **JAI WINDING** – keyboards / **MIKE CAMPBELL** –

Jun 89. (lp)(c)(cd) **THE END OF THE INNOCENCE** [17] [8]
– The end of the innocence / How bad do you want it? / I will not go quietly / The last worthless evening / New York minute / Shangri-la / Little tin god / Gimme what you got / If dirt were dollars / The heart of the matter. *(re-iss.+cd.Jan91 & Oct95)*
Jul 89. (7") **THE END OF THE INNOCENCE. / IF DIRT WERE DOLLARS** [48] [8] Jun 89
(12"+=)(cd-s+=) – The boys of summer.
Oct 89. (7")(c-s) **NEW YORK MINUTE. / GIMME WHAT YOU GOT** [ ] [48] Nov 90
(10"+=)(12"+=)(cd-s+=) – Sunset grill (live).
Oct 89. (7") **THE LAST WORTHLESS EVENING. / GIMME WHAT YOU GOT** [-] [21]
Feb 90. (7")(c-s) **THE LAST WORTHLESS EVENING. / ALL SHE WANTS TO DO IS DANCE** [ ] [-]
(12"+=) – You can't make love.
(cd-s++=) – ('A'version).
Feb 90. (c-s) **THE HEART OF THE MATTER. / LITTLE TIN GOD** [-] [21]
Jul 90. (c-s) **HOW BAD DO YOU WANT IT?. / ?** [-] [48]

— In Sep 92, HENLEY charted US No.2 / UK No.22 with SOMETIMES LOVE JUST AIN'T ENOUGH.

— In Mar'93, DON featured on TRISH YEARWOOD's single 'Walkaway Joe'.

Nov 95. (cd)(c) **ACTUAL MILES: HENLEY'S GREATEST HITS** [ ] [48]
(compilation + 2 new *)
– Dirty laundry / The boys of summer / All she wants to do is dance / Not enough love in the world / Sunset grill / The end of the innocence / The last worthless evening / New York minute / The heart of the matter / The garden of Allah * / You don't know me at all *. *(cd+=)*– I get the message.

Glenn FREY

Asylum Asylum

Jun 82. (lp)(c) **NO FUN ALOUD** [ ] [32]
– I found somebody / The one you love / Party town / I volunteer / I've been born again / Sea cruise / That girl / All those lies / She can't let go / Don't give up.
Jul 82. (7") **I FOUND SOMEONE. / SHE CAN'T LET GO** [ ] [31] Jun 82
Oct 82. (7") **THE ONE YOU LOVE. / ALL THOSE LIES** [-] [15]
Jan 83. (7") **ALL THOSE LIES. / THAT GIRL** [-] [41]

M.C.A. M.C.A.

Jul 84. (lp)(c) **THE ALLNIGHTER** [ ] [37]
– The allnighter / Sexy girl / I got love / Somebody else / Lover's moon / Smuggler's blues / Let's go home / Better in the U.S.A. / The heat is on / New love. *(re-act.Jun85 reached UK No.31) (cd-iss.Aug89)*
Aug 84. (7") **SEXY GIRL. / BETTER IN THE U.S.A.** [ ] [20]
Oct 84. (7") **THE ALLNIGHTER. / SMUGGLER'S BLUES** [-] [54]
Nov 84. (7") **SMUGGLER'S BLUES. / NEW LOVE** [ ] [12] Apr 85
Jan 85. (7")(12") **THE HEAT IS ON. / ('B'side by Harold Faltermeyer)** [12] [2] Dec 84

— Above was used for the film 'Beverly Hills Cop', starring Eddie Murphy.

— Below was issued on 'BBC' records in Britain only.

Jun 85. (7") **SMUGGLER'S BLUES. / NEW LOVE** [22] [-]
(12"+=) – Living in darkness.
Jul 85. (7") **SEXY GIRL. / BETTER IN THE U.S.A.** [ ] [-]
(12"+=) – The heat is on (dub) / New love.
Sep 85. (7") **YOU BELONG TO THE CITY. / SMUGGLER'S BLUES** [-] [2]
Oct 85. (7") **YOU BELONG TO THE CITY. / I GOT LOVE** [ ] [2] Sep 85
(12"+=) – ('A' version).
Sep 88. (7") **TRUE LOVE. / WORKING MAN** [ ] [13] Aug 88
(12"+=)(cd-s+=) – The heat is on.
Oct 88. (lp)(c)(cd) **SOUL SEARCHING** [ ] [36] Aug 88
– Soul searchin' / Livin' right / True love / I did it for your love / Working man / Two hearts / Some kind of blue / Can't put out this fire / Let's pretend we're still in love / It's your life.
Jan 89. (7") **SOUL SEARCHIN'. / IT'S COLD DOWN HERE** [ ] [ ]
(12"+=)(cd-s+=) – True love.
Mar 89. (7") **LIVIN' RIGHT. / SOUL SEARCHIN'** [-] [90]
May 89. (7") **TWO HEARTS. / SOME KIND OF BLUE** [-] [ ]

— Now writes with keyboard player **JAY OLIVER** or **JACK TEMPCHIN**

Apr 91. (c-s) **PART OF ME, PART OF YOU. /** [-] [55]

— (above taken from the film 'Thelma And Louise')

Jul 92. (7")(c-s) **I'VE GOT MINE. / PART OF ME, PART OF YOU** [ ] [91]
(cd-s+=) – A walk in the dark. (US; b-side)
Aug 92. (cd)(c)(lp) **STRANGE WEATHER** [ ] [ ]
– Silent spring / Long hot summer / Strange weather / Agua tranquillo / Love in the 21st century / He took advantage / River of dreams / Before the ship goes down / I've got mine / Rising sun / Brave new world / Delicious / A walk in the dark / Big life / Part of me, part of you.
Sep 92. (7") **RIVER OF DREAMS. / HE TOOK ADVANTAGE** [-] [ ]
May 93. (cd)(c) **LIVE (live)** [ ] [ ]
– Peaceful easy feeling / New kid in town / The one you love / Wild mountain thyme / Strange weather / I've got mine / Lyin' eyes -Take it easy (medley) / River of dreams / True love / Love in the 21st century / Smuggler's blues / The heat is on / Heartache tonight / Desperado.
Apr 95. (cd) **SOLO CONNECTION** [ ] [ ]
-

EAGLES

re-formed **HENLEY/ FREY/ WALSH/ FELDER + SCHMIDT**

Geffen Geffen

Nov 94. (cd)(c) **HELL FREEZES OVER** [28] [1]
– Get over it / Love will keep us alive / The girl from yesterday / Learn to be still / Tequila sunrise / Hotel California / Wasted time / Pretty maids all in a row / I can't tell you why / New York minute / The last resort / Take it easy / In the city / Life in the fast lane / Desperado.
Nov 94. (c-s)(cd-s) **GET OVER IT. / ?** [-] [31]

Steve EARLE

Born: 17 Jan'55, Fort Monroe, Virginia, USA but moved to Schertz, Texas, then Nashville. In 1981 he went solo and after one-off single on US indie, signed to 'Epic'. Gained hard reputation and with his DUKES signed worldwide to 'M.C.A.' in 1986. • **Style:** Country rock'n'roll with a social conscience that was influenced by SPRINGSTEEN or MELLENCAMP. • **Songwriters:** Himself except covers THE DEVIL'S RIGHT HAND MAN (Waylon Jennings) / DEAD FLOWERS (Rolling Stones) / TECUNSEH VALLEY (Steve Van Zandt) / RIVERS OF BABYLON (trad.) / etc. MARIA McKEE (ex-LONE JUSTICE) co-wrote 2 songs on his 1990 album. • **Trivia:** Late 1987 EARLE was attacked by policeman LONNIE ALLEN, but was sentenced to probation himself.

Recommended: COPPERHEAD ROAD (*6)

STEVE EARLE – vocals, guitar + sessions

not issued L.S.I.

1982. (7"ep) **PINK AND BLACK** [-] [ ]

not issued Epic

Aug 83. (7") **NOTHING BUT YOU. / CONTINENTAL TRAILWAY BLUES** [-] [ ]
Feb 84. (7") **SQUEEZE ME IN. / THE DEVIL'S RIGHT HAND** [-] [ ]
Jun 84. (7") **WHAT'LL YOU DO ABOUT ME. / CRY MYSELF TO SLEEP** [-] [ ]
Oct 84. (7") **A LITTLE BIT IN LOVE. / THE CRUSH** [-] [ ]

— (a couple more 45's were released Stateside, not known yet) **STEVE EARLE** – vocals, guitar (with The **DUKES**) **BUCKY BAXTER** – steel guitar, vocals / **RICHARD BENNETT** – guitars / **KEN MOORE** – organ, synthesizers, vocals / **HARRY STINSON** – drums, vocals / **EMORY GORDY JR.** – bass, mand plus **JOHN JARVIS** – piano / **STEVE NATHAN** – synth. / **PAUL FRANKLIN** – pedal steel

M.C.A. M.C.A.

Aug 86. (7") **SOMEDAY. / GUITAR TOWN** [ ] [ ]
Aug 86. (lp)(c) **GUITAR TOWN** [ ] [89]
– Guitar town / Goodbye's all we've got left / Hillbilly highway / Good ol' boy (gettin' tough) / My old friend the blues / Someday / Think it over / Fearless heart / Little rock'n'roller / Down the road. *(cd-iss.Apr87 / Jan90 +=) – Good ol' boy (gettin' tough) (live).*
Feb 87. (7") **SOMEDAY. / GUITAR TOWN** [ ] [ ]
(12"+=) – Good ol' boy (gettin' tough).
(cd-s++=) – Goodbye's all we've got.

— credited on sleeve to "STEVE EARLE & THE DUKES" (EARLE, BAXTER, MOORE, STINSON plus **RENO KING** – bass / **MIKE McADAM** – guitars. Others included **BENNETT, GORDY JR. / JARVIS** and **K-MEAUX BOUDIN** – accordion

Apr 87. (7") **FEARLESS HEART. / LITTLE ROCK'N'ROLLER** [ ] [ ]
(12"+=) – ('A'long version).
Apr 87. (lp)(c)(cd) **EXIT 'O'** [77] [90]
– Nowhere road / Sweel little '66' / No.29 / Angry young man / San Antonio girl / The rain came down / I ain't ever satisfied / The week of living dangerously / I love you too much / It's all up to you.
May 87. (7")(12") **I AIN'T EVER SATISFIED. / NOWHERE ROAD** [ ] [ ]
Nov 87. (d7") **THE RAIN CAME DOWN. / GUITAR TOWN (live)/ / I LOVE YOU TOO MUCH (live). / No.29 (live)** [ ] [ ]
Jun 88. (7") **I AIN'T EVER SATISFIED. / MY OLD FRIEND THE BLUES** [ ] [ ]
(12"+=) – I love you too much.

M.C.A. Uni

Sep 88. (7") **COPPERHEAD ROAD. / LITTLE SISTER** [45] [ ]
(12"+=) – No.29.
(cd-s+=) – San Antonio girl / I ain't ever satisfied.
Oct 88. (lp)(c)(cd) **COPPERHEAD ROAD** [44] [56]
– Copperhead road / Snake oil / Back to the wall / You belong to me / Devil's right hand / Johnny come lately / Even when I'm blue / Waiting on you / Once you love / Nothing but a child. *(re-iss.cd+cAug93)*
Dec 88. (7") **JOHNNY COME LATELY. / NOTHING BUT A CHILD** [75] [ ]
(12"+=) – Nebraska (live).
(cd-s++=) – Copperhead Road (live).
Feb 89. (7") **BACK TO THE WALL (edit). / SNAKE OIL** [ ] [ ]
(12"+=)(cd-s+=) – State trooper.

STEVE EARLE AND THE DUKES

He retained **BAXTER, MOORE** and p/t **JARVIS.** Newcomers = **ZIP GIBSON** – guitar, vocals / **KELLY LEONEY** – bass, vocals / **CRAIG WRIGHT** – drums. plus **PATRICK EARLE** – percussion and other guests

May 90. (7") **THE OTHER KIND. / WEST NASHVILLE BOOGIE** [ ] [ ]
(12"+=)(cd-s+=) – Guitar town (live) / Dead flowers (live).
Jun 90. (cd)(c)(lp) **THE HARD WAY** [22] [100]
– The other kind / Promise you anything / Hopeless romantics / Esmeralda's Hollywood / This highway's mine (roadmaster) / Billy Austin / Justice in Ontario / Have mercy / Country girl / When the people find out / Regular guy / Close your eyes / West Nashville boogie.
Sep 90. (7")(c-s) **JUSTICE IN ONTARIO. / THIS HIGHWAY'S MINE (ROADMASTER)** [ ] [ ]
(12"+=)(cd-s+=) – Copperhead road (live) / I ain't ever satisfied (live).

— **STACEY EARLE-MIMS** – b.vocals, acoustic percussion repl. JARVIS

Sep 91. (cd)(c)(d-lp) **SHUT UP AND DIE LIKE AN AVIATOR (live)** [62] [ ]
– Good ol' boy (gettin' tough) / Devil's right hand / I ain't ever satisfied / Someday / West Nashville boogie / Snake oil / Blue yodel #9 / The other kind / Billy Austin / Copperhead road / Fearless heart / Guitar town / I love you too much / The rain came down / She's about a mover / Dead flowers.

— EARLE was dropped by record label, after being busted for heroin possession. He was sentenced to a year in prison and to attend a rehab centre. He was released in 1994 and was straight back to recording.

— with PETER ROWAN / NORMAN BLAKE / ROY HUSKEY + EMMYLOU HARRIS

TranatlanticWinter Har

Jul 95. (cd)(c) **TRAIN a COMIN'** [ ] [ ]
– Mystery train part II / Hometown blues / Sometimes she forgets / Mercenary song / Goodbye / Tom Ames' prayer / Nothin' without you / Angel is the Devil / I'm looking through you / Northern winds / Ben McCulloch / Rivers of Babylon / Tecumseh Valley.

. . . Jan – Jun '96 stop press . . .

— with The V-ROYS

Mar 96. (cd)(c) **I FEEL ALRIGHT** [44] [ ]
Apr 96. (single) **FEEL ALRIGHT** [ ] [ ]
Jun 96. (single) **JOHNNY TOO BAD** [ ] [ ]

- compilations etc. -

Jul 87. Epic; (lp)(c) **EARLY TRACKS** [ ] [ ] Oct 86
– Nothin' but you / If you need a fool / Continental trailway blues / Open up your door / Breakdown lane / Squeeze me in / Annie, is tonight the night / My baby worships me / Cadillac / Devil's right hand. *(cd-iss.Jul91 on 'Pickwick') (was to have been released '83 as 'CADILLAC')*
Oct 93. Pickwick; (cd)(c) **THIS HIGHWAY'S MINE** [ ] [ ]

Elliott EASTON (see under ⇒ CARS)

EAT STATIC (see under ⇒ OZRIC TENTACLES)

EAZY-E (see under ⇒ N.W.A.)

ECHO AND THE BUNNYMEN

Formed: Liverpool, England ... Autumn 1978 by McCULLOCH, SERGEANT and PATTINSON. McCULLOCH had once been in The CRUCIAL THREE alongside JULIAN COPE and PETE WYLIE. McCULLOCH and COPE formed A SHALLOW MADNESS, and together they co-wrote 'READ IT IN BOOKS' (the b-side of debut single 'PICTURES ON MY WALL'). The BUNNYMEN, complete with drum machine ECHO, released this one-off for local 'Zoo' label, before signing to 'W.E.A.' subsidiary 'Korova' late in '79. By the following year, they'd had a Top 10 album and were soon breaking into singles chart. • **Style:** Very much DOORS influenced, but with fresher up-tempo appeal, that was very much part of a new Merseyside-based sound of the early 80's. • **Songwriters:** Mainly group compositions except PEOPLE ARE STRANGE (Doors) / PAINT IT BLACK (Rolling Stones) / ALL YOU NEED IS LOVE (Beatles) / FRICTION (Television) / RUN RUN RUN (Velvet Underground) / SHIP OF FOOLS (John Cale). McCULLOCH covered: SEPTEMBER SONG (Kurt Weill) / RETURN TO SENDER (Elvis Presley) / LOVER, LOVER, LOVER (Leonard Cohen). • **Trivia:** DAVE BALFE (of DALEK I LOVE YOU) played keyboards on their first JOHN PEEL session in August 1979.

Recommended: CROCODILES (*9) / HEAVEN UP HERE (*9) / SONGS TO LEARN AND SING (*9) / PORCUPINE (*7) / OCEAN RAIN (*7) / ECHO & THE BUNNYMEN (*5) / CANDLELAND (Ian McCulloch) (*6).

IAN McCULLOCH (b. 5 May'59) – vocals, guitar (ex-CRUCIAL THREE) **WILL SERGEANT** (b.12 Apr'58) – lead guitar / **LES PATTINSON** (b.18 Apr'58) – bass (& 'ECHO' a drum machine)

Zoo not issued

Mar 79. (7") **PICTURES ON MY WALL. / READ IT IN BOOKS** [ ] [-]
(re-iss.Mar91 on 'Document')

— **PETE DE FREITAS** (b. 2 Aug'61, Port Of Spain, Trinidad) – drums repl. 'ECHO'

Korova Sire

Apr 80. (7") **RESCUE. / SIMPLE STUFF** [62] [-]
(12"+=) – Pride.
Jul 80. (lp)(c) **CROCODILES** [17] [ ]

– Going up / Stars are stars / Pride / Monkeys / Crocodiles / Rescue / Villier's terrace / Pictures on my wall / All that jazz / Happy death men. *(re-iss.Dec80 + below) (re-iss.+cd.1989 on 'WEA')* (free-7" w/a) – **DO IT CLEAN. / READ IT IN BOOKS**

Sep 80. (7") **THE PUPPET. / DO IT CLEAN** [ ] [ ]

Apr 81. (12"ep) **SHINE SO HARD (live)** [37] [ ]
– Crocodiles / All that jazz / Over the wall / Zimbo (All my colours).

May 81. (lp)(c) **HEAVEN UP HERE** [10] [ ]
– Show of strength / With a hip / Over the wall / It was a pleasure / A promise / Heaven up here / The disease / All my colours / No dark things / Turquoise days / All I want. *(cd-iss.Jul88 on 'WEA')*

Jul 81. (7")(12") **A PROMISE. / BROKE MY NECK** [49] [ ]

May 82. (7") **THE BACK OF LOVE. / THE SUBJECT** [19] [ ]
(12"+=) – Fuel.

Jan 83. (7") **THE CUTTER. / WAY OUT** [8] [8]
(12"+=) – Zimbo.
(c-s) – ('A'side) / Villier's terrace / Ashes to ashes / Monkeys / Read it in books.

Jan 83. (lp)(c) **PORCUPINE** [2] [ ]
– The cutter / The back of love / My white devil / Clay / Porcupine / Heads will roll / Ripeness / Higher hell / Gods will be gods / In bluer skies. (free ltd.c-s w/a) – 'JOHN PEEL SESSIONS' (see below Nov88 version) *(re-iss.+cd.Jul88 on 'WEA')*

Feb 83. (7") **THE CUTTER. / GODS WILL BE GODS** [-] [ ]

Jul 83. (7") **NEVER STOP. / HEADS WILL ROLL** [15] [ ]
('A'disco 12"+=) – The original cutter (A drop in the ocean).

Jan 84. (7") **THE KILLING MOON. / DO IT CLEAN** [9] [ ]
(12"+=) – ('A'extended).

Jan 84. (m-lp) **ECHO AND THE BUNNYMEN** [-] [ ]
– Back of love / Never stop / Rescue / The cutter / Do it clean.

Apr 84. (lp)(c)(cd) **OCEAN RAIN** [4] [87] Jun 84
– Silver / Nocturnal me / Crystal days / The yo yo man / Thorn of crowns / The killing moon / Seven seas / My kingdom / Ocean rain.

Apr 84. (7") **SILVER. / ANGELS AND DEVILS** [3] [ ]
(12"+=) – Silver (Tidal wave).

Jun 84. (7") **SEVEN SEAS. / ALL YOU NEED IS LOVE** [16] [ ]
(12"+=)(d7"+=) – Killing Moon / Starts and stars (acoustic) / Villier's terrace (acoustic).

Oct 85. (7")(7"pic-d) **BRING ON THE DANCING HORSES. / OVER MY SHOULDER** [21] [ ]
(extended 12"+=) – Beds, bugs and ballyhoo.
(d7"+=) – Villier's terrace / Monkeys.

Nov 85. (lp)(c)(cd) **SONGS TO LEARN AND SING** (compilation) [6] [ ]
– Rescue / The puppet / Do it clean / The promise / The back of love / The cutter / Never stop / The killing moon / Silver / Seven seas / Bring on the dancing horses. (c/cd+=) – Pride / Simple stuff / Read it in books / Angels and devils. (free ltd.c-s w/ same extra tracks)

— (Feb86) temp. **MARK FOX** – drums (ex-HAIRCUT 100) repl. DE FREITAS until return Sep'86.

WEA Sire

Jun 87. (7") **THE GAME. / SHIP OF FOOLS** [28] [ ]
(12"+=) – Lost And Found.

Jul 87. (lp)(c)(cd) **ECHO AND THE BUNNYMEN** [4] [51]
– The game / Over you / Bedbugs and ballyhoo / All in your mind / Bombers bay / Lips like sugar / Lost and found / New direction / Blue blue ocean / Satellite / All my life. *(re-iss.cd Nov94)*

Jul 87. (7") **LIPS LIKE SUGAR. / ROLLERCOASTER** [36] [ ]
(12"+=) – People are strange.

Feb 88. (7")(c-s) **PEOPLE ARE STRANGE. / RUN RUN RUN** [29] [ ]
(12"+=) – Paint it black / Friction. *(re-iss.Feb91 on 'East-West' hit No.34)*

— They split some unofficial time in '88. Re-formed after McCULLOCH went solo. PETE DE FREITAS joined SEX GODS. He died in motorcycle accident 14 Jun '89.

— **SERGEANT** and **PATTINSON** reformed group early 1990, with newcomers **NOEL BURKE** – vocals / **JACK BROCKMAN** – keyboards / **DAMON REECE** – drums

Korova not issued

Oct 90. (7")(c-s) **ENLIGHTEN ME. / LADY, DON'T FALL BACKWARDS** [ ] [ ]
(12"+=)(cd-s+=) – ('A'extended).

Nov 90. (cd)(c)(lp) **REVERBERATION** [ ] [ ]
– Freaks dwell / Cut and dried / Revilment / Flaming red / Salvatore / Fine thing / Gone, gone, gone / Enlighten me / King of your castle / Senseless / Thick skinned world. (cd+=) – False goodbyes.

Euphoric not issued

Oct 91. (12"ep)(cd-ep) **PROVE ME WRONG. / FINE THING / REVERBERATION** [ ] [-]

Mar 92. (12")(cd-s) **INSIDE ME, INSIDE YOU. / WIGGED OUT WORLD** [ ] [-]

— The BUNNYMEN disbanded soon after the above and LES joined TERRY HALL'S backing group.

– compilations etc. –

Strange Fruit / not issued

Nov 88. Strange Fruit; (12"ep)(c-ep)(cd-ep) **THE PEEL SESSIONS (15.8.79)** [ ] [-]
– Read it in books / Stars are stars / I bagsy yours / Villier's terrace. *(re-iss.cd-ep Dec94)*

Jul 90. Old Gold; (7") **THE CUTTER. / THE BACK OF LOVE** [ ] [-]

Jul 90. Old Gold; (7") **THE KILLING MOON. / SEVEN SEAS** [ ] [-]

Nov 91. Windsong; (cd) **BBC RADIO 1 LIVE IN CONCERT (live)** [ ] [-]

Mar 93. Pickwick; (cd)(c) **THE CUTTER** [ ] [-]
(re-iss.Sep95 on 'Warners')

Ian McCULLOCH

IAN McCULLOCH – vocals while still a member of The BUNNYMEN

Korova / not issued

Nov 84. (7")(10") **SEPTEMBER SONG. / COCKLES AND MUSCLES** [51] [-]
(12"+=) – ('A'extended).

—— Now solo his back-up came from **RAY SHULMAN** – keyboards, programmer, bass, producer / plus guests **MICHAEL JOBSON** – bass / **BORIS WILLIAMS** – drums / **OLLE REMO** – drum programmer / **LIZ FRASER** – vox (of COCTEAU TWINS)

W.E.A. / Sire

Aug 89. (7")(c-s) **PROUD TO FALL. / POTS OF GOLD** [51] [ ]
(12") – ('A' side) / ('A'extended) / The dead end (long version).
(cd-s++=) – ('A'version).
(12") ('A' side / Everything is real / The circle game.

Sep 89. (lp)(c)(cd) **CANDLELAND** [18] [ ]
– The flickering wall / The white hotel / Proud to fall / The cape / Candleland / Horse's head / Faith and healing / I know you well / In bloom / Start again.

Nov 89. (7")(c-s) **FAITH AND HEALING (remix). / TOAD** [ ] [ ]
(12"+=) – Fear of the known.
(cd-s++=) Rocket ship.
(12") – ('A' side) / Fear of the known / Rocket ship.

Apr 90. (7")(c-s) **CANDLELAND (THE SECOND COMING). / THE WORLD IS FLAT** [75] [ ]
(12"+=)(cd-s+=) – Big days / Wassailing in the night.

His backing band from late '89, were The PRODIGAL SONS (**MIKE MOONEY** – guitar / **JOHN McEVOY** – r.guitar, keys / **EDGAR SUMMERTIME** – bass / **STEVE HUMPHRIES** – drums)

East West / East West

Feb 92. (7")(c-s) **LOVER, LOVER, LOVER. / WHITE HOTEL (acoustic) / THE GROUND BELOW** [47] [ ]
(12"+=) – ('A'-Indian dawn mix).
(cd-s++=) – Vibor blue (acoustic).

Apr 92. (cd)(c)(lp) **MYSTERIOSO** [46] [ ]
– Mayreal world / Close your eyes / Dug for love / Honeydrip / Damnation / Lover, lover, lover / Webbed / Pomegranate / Vibor blue / Heaven's gate / In my head.

Apr 92. (7")(c-s) **DUG FOR LOVE. / DAMNATION (live)** [ ] [ ]
(12"+=)(cd-s+=) – Do it clean / Pomegranite / In my head (all live).

WILL SERGEANT

Jul 82. Korova; (7") **FAVOURITE BRANCHES. / (b-side by RAVI SHANKER & BILL LOVELADY)** [ ] [-]

Mar 82. 92 Happy Customers; (lp) **THEMES FOR GRIND** [ ] [ ]

ELECTRAFIXION

—— **IAN McCULLOCH** – vocals, guitar / **WILL SERGEANT** – guitar / **LEON DE SYLVA** – bass / **TONY McGUIGAN** – drums

W.E.A. / Warners

Nov 94. (12"ep)(c-ep)(cd-ep) **THE ZEPHYR EP** [47] [ ]
– Zephyr / Burned / Mirrorball / Rain on me.

Sep 95. (7"red-ep)(c-ep)(12"ep)(cd-ep) **LOWDOWN / HOLY GRAIL. / LAND OF THE DYING SUN / RAZORS EDGE** [54] [ ]

Sep 95. (cd)(c) **BURNED** [38] [ ]
– Feel my pulse / Sister pain / Lowdown / Timebomb / Zephyr / Never / Too far gone / Mirrorball / Who's been sleeping in my head? / Hit by something / Bed of nails.

Oct 95. (c-s) **NEVER / NOT OF THIS WORLD** [58] [ ]
(cd-s+=) – Subway train / Lowdown (rest of the trash mix).
(cd-s) – ('A'side) / Lowdown / Work it on out / Never (Utah Saints blizzard on mix) / Sister pain.

. . . Jan – Jun '96 stop press . . .

Mar 96. (single) **SISTER PAIN** [27] [ ]

ECHOBELLY

Formed: London, England by Anglo-Asian SONYA aged 27. In 1994, toured in the States with fan MORRISSEY; the injured GLENN was replaced by Curve's DEBBIE SMITH. • **Style:** Like BLONDIE vox on a SMITHS-type backing. • **Songwriters:** MADDEN / JOHANSSON.

Recommended: EVERYONE'S GOT ONE (*5)

SONYA AURORA MADAN – vocals / **GLENN JOHANSSON** – guitar / **ALEX KEYSER** – bass, piano / **ANDY HENDERSON** – drums

Pande-monium / not issued

Nov 93. (12"ep)(cd-ep) **BELLYACHE** [ ] [-]
– Give her a gun / Call me names / England swings.

Jan 94. (12"ep)(cd-ep) **BELLYACHE / SLEEPING HITLER. / GIVE HER A GUN / I DON'T BELONG HERE** [ ] [ ]
(re-iss.May94)

Fauve-Rhythm King / not issued

Mar 94. (7")(c-s) **INSOMNIAC. / TALENT** [47] [ ]
(12"+=) – ('A'mix).
(cd-s+=) – Centipede.

—— added **DEBBIE SMITH** – guitar noise

Jun 94. (7")(c-s) **I CAN'T IMAGINE THE WORLD WITHOUT ME. / VENUS WHEEL** [39] [ ]
(12"+=)(cd-s+=) – Sober.

Aug 94. (cd)(c)(lp) **EVERYONE'S GOT ONE** [8] [ ]
– Today tomorrow sometime never / Father, ruler, king, computer / Give her a gun / I can't imagine the world without me / Bellyache / Taste of you / Insomniac / Call me names / Close . . .but / Cold feet warm heart / Scream.

Oct 94. (7")(12")(c-s) **CLOSE . . .BUT. / SO LA DI DA** [59] [ ]
(cd-s+=) – I can't image the world without me (live) / Cold feet warm heart (live).

Aug 95. (7")(c-s) **GREAT THINGS. / HERE COMES THE SCENE** [13] [ ]
(cd-s+=) – God's guest list / On turn off.
(cd-s) – ('A'side) / On turn on / Bunty / One after 5 a.m.

Sep 95. (cd)(c)(lp) **ON** [4] [ ]
– Oar fiction / King of the kerb / Great things / Natural animal / Go away / Pantyhose and roses / Something hot in a cold country / Four letter word / Nobody like you / In the year / Dark therapy / Worms an angels.

Oct 95. (c-s) **KING OF THE KERB / CAR FICTION (French)** [25] [ ]
(cd-s+=) – On turn on (acoustic) / Natural animal (acoustic).
(cd-s) – ('A'live) / I can't imagine the world without me (live) / Insomniac (live) / Great things (live).

. . . Jan – Jun '96 stop press . . .

Feb 96. (single) **DARK THERAPY** [20] [ ]

The EDGE (see under ⇒ U2)

Graeme EDGE (see under ⇒ MOODY BLUES)

808 STATE

Formed: Manchester, England . . . 1987 by PRICE and MASSEY. All met while working next to, and frequenting MARTIN PRICE's 'Eastern Bloc' record shop. After 2 albums on indie label 'Creed', they signed to 'Island' off-shoot 'ZTT' in 1989. Their first single PACIFIC STATE (co-written with A GUY CALLED GERALD) breeched UK Top 10, and began onslaught into Europe. • **Style:** Techno-dance rave-rock using sampling, sparse anthemic vocals, once described as TANGERINE DREAM on speed. • **Songwriters:** Group compositions, except ONE IN TEN (UB40). • **Trivia:** Composed theme tune in 1990 for TV pop/chat programme 'The Word'. Remixed many, including QUINCY JONES!?! (mid 91).

Recommended: EX:EL (*7).

GRAHAM MASSEY (b. 4 Aug'60) – prog., saxophone, engineer (ex-BITING TONGUES) / **MARTIN PRICE** (b.26 Mar'55) – programming, keyboards

Creed / not issued

Sep 88. (lp) **NEWBUILD** [ ] [-]

Nov 88. (12") **LET YOURSELF GO (303 mix). / LET YOURSELF GO (D50 mix) / DEEPVILLE** [ ] [-]

—— **ANDREW BARKER** – DJ, drum prog., keys + **DARREN PARTINGTON** – DJ, drum prog., replaced GERALD SIMPSON who formed solo project A GUY CALLED GERALD.

Jul 89. (m-lp) **QUADRASTATE** [ ] [-]
– Pacific state / 106 / State ritual / Disco state / Fire cracker / State to state.

Z.T.T. / Tommy Boy

Oct 89. (7")(c-s) **PACIFIC STATE. / ('A' version)** [10] [ ]

(12"+=) – Pacific 707 / Pacific 202.
Dec 89. (12"+=)(cd-s+=) **PACIFIC STATE (9 minute version). / COBRA BORA (6 minutes)**
Dec 89. (lp)(c)(cd) **90** 57
– Magical dream / Ancodia / Cobra bora / Pacific 202 / Donkey doctor / Sunrise / 808080808 / The fat shadow (pointy head mix). (US-title 'UTD.STATE '90').
Mar 90. (12"ep)(cd-ep) **THE EXTENDED PLEASURE OF DANCE** 56
– Cobra bora (call the cops mix) / Cubik / Ancodia (deep nittater funky beat mix)
Oct 90. (7")(c-s) **CUBIK. / OLYMPIC (mix)** 10
(12"+=)(cd-s+=) – ('A' Pan-Am mix) / ('B' Eir bass mix).
Feb 91. (7")(c-s) **IN YER FACE. / LEO LEO** 9
(12"+=)(cd-s+=) – ('A'version) / ('B'mixes).

— next featured **BJORK** (Sugarcubes) – vocals (*)

Mar 91. (cd)(c)(lp)(2xlp-on 45 r.p.m.) **EX: EL** 4
– San Francisco / Spanish heart / Leo Leo / Qwart * / Nephatiti / Lift / Ooops * / Empire / In yer face / Cubik / Lambrusco cowboy / Techno ball. (cd+=) – Olympic.
Apr 91. (7")(c-s) **OOOPS. / THE SKI FAMILY** 42
(12"+=)(cd-s+=) – 808091 (live).
(12") – (2 'A'mixes).
Aug 91. (7")(c-s) **LIFT. / OPEN YOUR MIND** 38
(12"+=)(cd-s+=) – ('A'open version) / ('B'sound galore mixes).

— MARTIN PRICE departed Oct'91.

In Feb'92, they collaborated with DAVID BOWIE on a version of 'SOUND AND VISION'. Below single as "808 STATE featuring BJORK".

Aug 92. (7")(c-s) **TIME BOMB. / NIMBUS**
('A'-Fon mix) (12"+=)(cd-s+=) – Reaper repo (short mix) / Reaper repo.
Nov 92. (7")(c-s) **ONE IN TEN 808. / ('A'vocal)** 17
(12"+=) – ('A'-fast Fon mix) / ('A'-forceable lobotomy mix).
(cd-s++=) – ('A'instrumental).
Jan 93. (7")(c-s) **PLAN 9. / OLYMPIC '93 (The word mix)** 50
('A'choki galaxy mix-12"+=) – ('A'guitars on fire mix).
(cd-s++=) – Bbambi (the April showers mix).
Feb 93. (cd)(c)(lp) **GORGEOUS** 17
– Plan 9 / Moses / Contrique / 10 X 10 / Timebomb / One in ten / Europa / Orbit / Black morpheus / Southern cross / Nimbus / Colony.
Jun 93. (c-s) **10 X 10 (radio mix). / LA LUZ (chunky funky mix)** 67
(12"+=) – ('A'black eye mix) / ('A'trace mix).
('A'hit man's club-10"+=) – ('A'instrumental).
(cd-s) – (3 'A'mixes above) / ('A'rockathon mix) / ('A'vox mix) / ('A'beats mix) / ('A'hit man's acapella mix).
Aug 94. (12")(c-s)(cd-s) **BOMBADIN. / MARATHON** 67

. . . Jan – Jun '96 stop press . . .

Jun 96. (single) **BOND** 57
Jun 96. (cd)(c)(lp) **DON SOLARIS**

MC TUNES Versus 808 STATE

(MC =NICHOLAS LOCKETT – English rapper)

May 90. (7")(c-s) **THE ONLY RHYME THAT BITES. / ('A'version)** 10
(12"+=)(cd-s+=) – (other versions).
Sep 90. (7")(c-s) **TUNES THAT SPLIT THE ATOM. / DANCE YOURSELF TO DEATH** 18
(12"+=) – (other versions)
(cd-s++=) – (1 extra version).
Oct 90. (cd)(c)(lp) **NORTH AT IT'S HEIGHT** 26
– The only rhyme that bites / This ain't no fantasy / Dance yourself to death / Own worst enemy / The north at it's heights / Tunes splits the atom / Mancunian blues / The sequel / Primary rhyming / Dub at it's heights.

MC TUNES also released own single Nov90.- PRIMARY RISING

EGGMAN (see under ⇒ BOO RADLEYS)

Mark EITZEL (see under ⇒ AMERICAN MUSIC CLUB)

ELASTICA

Formed: London, England ... Oct'92 by JUSTINE, who had been an embryonic member of SUEDE with then boyfriend BRETT ANDERSON. Signed for new 'Deceptive' label in 1993 and collected critical acclaim from music press for their debut 45 'STUTTER'. Their follow-up 'LINE UP' early '94 stretched them into the UK Top 20 and made US labels take note. The 'Geffen' label soon took up the option for worldwide sales as all awaited 1995's tip for the top and their first album. • **Style:** New wave of the new wave featuring fuzzgun WIRE-like guitars. However this blatant plagiarism didn't go without notice, when they had to settle out of court with WIRE, for the use of 'Three Girl Rhumba' riff on 'CONNECTION' hit. Soon after this The STRANGLERS were paid out for 'No More Heroes' backing on another hit 'WAKING UP'. However bassist JEAN-JAQUES BURNEL is said to be a great fan. • **Songwriters:** FRISCHMANN lyrics / group compositions. • **Trivia:** In 1993-96, JUSTINE was the girlfriend of DAMON ALBARN (Blur). As DAN ABNORMAL (anagram) he played keyboards on their debut album and with them on Top Of The Pops.

Recommended: ELASTICA (*9)

JUSTINE FRISCHMANN (b.1968, Twickenham) – vocals, rhythm guitar (ex-SUEDE) / **DONNA MATTHEWS** (b. Newport, Wales) – vocals, guitar / **ANNIE HOLLAND** (b.Brighton, England) – bass / **JUSTIN WELCH** (b. Nuneaton, England) – drums (ex-SUEDE)

Deceptive Sub Pop
Oct 93. (7") **STUTTER. / PUSSYCAT** Aug94
Jan 94. (7") **LINE UP. / VASELINE** 20
(12"+=)(cd-s+=) – Rockunroll / Annie (John Peel sessions).

Deceptive Geffen
Oct 94. (7")(c-s) **CONNECTION. / SEE THAT ANIMAL** 17 53 Feb95
(12"+=)(cd-s+=) – Blue (demo) / Spastica.
Feb 95. (7")(c-s) **WAKING UP. / GLORIA** 13
(12"+=)(cd-s+=) – Car wash / Brighton rock.
Mar 95. (cd)(c)(lp) **ELASTICA** 1 66 Apr95
– Line up / Annie / Connection / Car song / Smile / Hold me now / S.O.F.T. / Indian song / Blue / All-nighter / Waking up / 2:1 / Vaseline / Never here / Stutter.

— In Jul'95, they guested on 'Sub Pop' 4x7"box-set 'HELTER SHELTER'.

Jun 95. (10"gold-ep) **STUTTER / ROCKUNROLL. / 2:1 (1 F.M. evening session) / ANNIE (John Peel session)** - 67

— ANNIE departed in August.

ELECTRAFIXION (see under ⇒ ECHO & THE BUNNYMEN)

ELECTRIC LIGHT ORCHESTRA

Formed: Birmingham, England ... 1968 by ROY WOOD, as alternative/idea to his other group The MOVE, who were drifting into slight cabaret circuit band. In 1969, he offered close friend JEFF LYNNE a place in The MOVE, but he declined, waiting until ROY came up with E.L.O. in 1971. The two outfits co-existed at this time, and the ELO debut finally hit the shops later that year. Highly regarded by the critics, it didn't hit No.32 until single '10538 OVERTURE', made the Top 10 in August 1972. WOOD soon departed ELO and The MOVE to form glam/flash rockers WIZZARD, which left JEFF LYNNE as the main man. The new line-up rejuvenated a past Chuck Berry classic 'ROLL OVER BEETHOVEN' to the heights of the Top 10. By the mid-70's, they had signed a new deal with 'Jet', where they took off to become massive international band. In the early 90's, an ELO PART II should have never been, as JEFF LYNNE had by now gone solo releasing hit album 'ARMCHAIR THEATER'. • **Style:** Creative BEATLES influenced rock-pop outfit, who relied heavily on string-laden themes, and a romanticised lyrical future. • **Songwriters:** JEFF LYNNE compositions (bar debut). Covered DO YA (Move). In the 90's, TROYER, HAYCOCK, BEVAN, etc, co-wrote songs after the departure of JEFF LYNNE. • **Trivia:** JEFF LYNNE also produced DAVE EDMUNDS (1981-84) / BRIAN WILSON (1988) / TOM PETTY (1989) / etc.

Recommended: OUT OF THE BLUE (*7) / THE GREATEST HITS (*8) / FACE THE MUSIC (*6) / A NEW WORLD RECORD (*6)

ROY WOOD (b. 8 Nov'46) – cello, vocals, multi (ex-The MOVE) / **JEFF LYNNE** (b.30 Dec'47) – vocals guitar (ex-The MOVE, ex-IDLE RACE) / **BEV BEVAN** (b. BEVERLEY, 24 Nov'46) – **drums, vocals**(ex-The MOVE) / **RICHARD TANDY** – bass, keyboards, vocals(ex-BALLS, ex-UGLYS) / **BILL HUNT** – keyboards, French horn / **WILF GIBSON** – violin / **HUGH McDOWELL** – cello / **ANDY CRAIG** – cello

Harvest United Art
Dec 71. (lp)(c) **THE ELECTRIC LIGHT ORCHESTRA** 32
– 10538 overture / Look at me now / Nellie takes her bow / The battle of Marston Moor (July 2nd, 1644) / First movement (jumpin' biz) / Mr.Radio / Manhattan rumble (49th Street massacre) / Queen of the hours / Whisper in the night. *(re-iss.Nov83 on 'Fame') (quad-lp 1972)*
Jul 72. (7") **10538 OVERTURE. / FIRST MOVEMENT (JUMPIN' BIZ)** 9 -
Sep 72. (7") **10538 OVERTURE. / THE BATTLE OF MARSTON MOOR (JULY 2ND, 1644)** -

— **MIKE EDWARDS** – cello repl. ROY WOOD who formed WIZZARD (Also went solo) / **MICHAEL DE ALBUQUERQUE** – bass repl. HUNT and

McDOWELL who joined WIZZARD / **COLIN WALKER** – cello repl. ANDY CRAIG

Jan 73. (7") **ROLL OVER BEETHOVEN. / QUEEN OF THE HOURS** [6] [42] Apr 73

Feb 73. (lp)(c) **E.L.O. 2** [35] [62]
– In old England town (boogie £2) / Momma / Roll over Beethoven / From the sun to the world (boogie £1) / Kuiama. *(re-iss.May82 on 'Fame')*

Sep 73. (7") **SHOWDOWN. / IN OLD ENGLAND TOWN (BOOGIE £2)** [12] [53] Nov 73
(US re-iss.Jul76)

—— **MIK KAMINSKI** – violin repl. GIBSON / **HUGH McDOWELL** – cello returned to repl. WALKER (Above 2 in septet with **LYNNE, BEVAN, TANDY, WALKER ALBUQUERQUE** and **EDWARDS.**

Warners / United Art

Dec 73. (lp)(c) **ON THE THIRD DAY** [ ] [52]
– Ocean breakup – King of the universe / Daybreaker / Bluebird is dead / Oh no, not Susan / New world rising / Ocean breakup (reprise) / Showdown / Daybreaker / Ma-Ma-Ma belle / Dreaming of 4000 / In the hall of the Mountain King. *(re-iss.1976 on 'Jet') (clear-lp iss.1978) (re-iss.'76 on 'Jet' & '78 clear vinyl)*

Mar 74. (7") **MA-MA-MA BELLE. / CAN'T FIND THE TITLE** [22] [-]

Mar 74. (lp) **THE NIGHT THE LIGHT WENT OUT IN LONG BEACH (live)** [-] [ ]
– Daybreaker / Showdown / Daytripper / 10538 overture / Mik's solo / Orange blossom special / Medley: In the hall of the mountain king – Great balls of fire / Roll over Beethoven. *(UK-iss.Nov85)*

Apr 74. (7") **DAYBREAKER (live). / MA-MA-MA BELLE (live)** [-] [87]

Jun 74. (7") **CAN'T GET IT OUT OF MY HEAD. / ILLUSIONS IN G MAJOR** [ ] [9] Dec 74

Oct 74. (lp)(c) **ELDORADO – A SYMPHONY BY THE ELECTRIC LIGHT ORCHESTRA** [ ] [16]
– Eldorado – overture / Can't get it out of my head / Boy blue / Larendo tornado / Poor boy (the greenwood) / Mister Kingdom / Nobody's child / Illusions in G major / Eldorado – finale. *(re-iss.'76 on 'Jet' & '78 yellow vinyl)*

Nov 74. (7") **ELDORADO. / BOY BLUE** [-] [ ]

—— **KELLY GROUCUTT** – bass, vocals repl. ALBUQUERQUE / **MELVYN GALE** – cello repl. EDWARDS

Jet / United Art

Oct 75. (lp)(c) **FACE THE MUSIC** [ ] [8]
– Fire on high / Waterfall / Evil woman / Night rider / Poker / Strange magic / Down home town / One summer dream. *(re-iss.'78 green vinyl) (re-iss.Jun85 on 'Epic') (re-iss.cd Mar94 on 'Sony Collectors') (re-iss.cd on 'Columbia')*

Dec 75. (7") **EVIL WOMAN. / 10538 OVERTURE (live)** [10] [10] Nov 75

Mar 76. (7") **NIGHT RIDER. / DAYBREAKER** [ ] [-]

Mar 76. (7") **STRANGE MAGIC. / NEW WORLD RECORD** [-] [14]

Jun 76. (7") **STRANGE MAGIC. / SHOWDOWN (live)** [38] [-]

Jul 76. (7") **SHOWDOWN (live). / DAYBREAKER (live)** [-] [59]

Oct 76. (7")(7"blue)(12"blue) **LIVIN' THING. / FIRE ON HIGH** [4] [-]

Oct 76. (7") **LIVIN' THING. / MA-MA-MA BELLE** [-] [13]

Nov 76. (lp)(c) **A NEW WORLD RECORD** [6] [5] Oct 76
– Tightrope / Telephone line / Rockaria! / Mission (a new world record) / So fine / Livin' thing / Above the clouds / Do ya / Shangri-la. *(re-iss.1978 on red-vinyl) (re-iss.Nov84 on 'Epic', cd-iss.Mar87) (re-iss.Aug88 on 'Jet', cd-iss.Apr89) (re-iss.+cd.Sep89 on 'Pickwick')*

Jan 77. (7") **DO YA. / NIGHTRIDER** [-] [24]

Feb 77. (7") **ROCKARIA!. / POKER** [9] [ ]
(re-iss.May78)

May 77. (7") **TELEPHONE LINE. / CALL BOY** [8] [-]
(re-iss.May78)

Jun 77. (7") **TELEPHONE LINE. / POOR BOY (THE GREENWOOD)** [-] [7]

Oct 77. (7") **TURN TO STONE. / MISTER KINGDOM** [18] [13] Nov 77
(re-iss.May78)

Nov 77. (d-lp)(d-c) **OUT OF THE BLUE** [4] [4]
– Turn to stone / It's over / Sweet talkin' woman / Across the border / Night in the city / Starlight / Jungle / Believe me now / Steppin' out / Standing in the rain / Summer and lightning / Mr. Blue Sky / Sweet is the night / The whale / Wild west hero / Birmingham Blues. *(re-iss.blue-lp 1978) (re-iss.+cd.May87 & Jun91 on 'Epic')*

Jan 78. (7")(7"blue) **MR. BLUE SKY. / ONE SUMMER DREAM** [6] [35] Jun 78
(re-iss.May78)

Feb 78. (7") **SWEET TALKIN' WOMAN. / FIRE ON HIGH** [-] [17]

Jun 78. (7")(12"yellow) **WILD WEST HERO. / ELDORADO** [6] [ ]

Oct 78. (7") **IT'S OVER. / THE WHALE** [-] [75]

Sep 78. (7")(7"mauve)(12"mauve) **SWEET TALKING WOMAN. / BLUEBIRD IS DEAD** [6] [17] Feb 78

May 79. (7")(12"white) **SHINE A LITTLE LOVE. / JUNGLE** [6] [8]

Jun 79. (lp)(c) **DISCOVERY** [1] [5]
– Shine a little love / Confusion / Need her love / The diary of Horace Wimp / Last train to London / Midnight blue / On the run / Wishing / Don't bring me down. *(re-iss.+cd.Nov86 & Jun91 on 'Epic')*

Jul 79. (7") **THE DIARY OF HORACE WIMP. / DOWN HOME TOWN** [6] [ ]

Aug 79. (7")(12") **DON'T BRING ME DOWN. / DREAMING OF 4000** [3] [4]

Oct 79. (7") **CONFUSION. / POKER** [-] [37]

Nov 79. (7") **CONFUSION. / LAST TRAIN TO LONDON** [8] [-]

Jan 80. (7") **LAST TRAIN TO LONDON. / DOWN HOME TOWN** [-] [39]

—— Now trimmed basic quartet of **LYNNE, BEVAN, TANDY** and **GROUCUTT** (KAMINSKI formed VIOLINSKI) (McDOWELL and GALE also departed). For below album / singles they shared billing with OLIVIA NEWTON JOHN (ONJ) (E.L.O. tracks (***) / ELO and ONJ tracks (**) / ONJ tracks (*).

May 80. (7") **I'M ALIVE (***). / DRUM DREAMS (***)** [2] [16]

Jun 80. (7")(10"pink) **XANADU (**). / FOOL COUNTRY (*)** [1] [ ]

Jun 80. (7") **XANADU (*). / (other track by GENE KELLY & OLIVIA NEWTON JOHN)** [-] [8]

Jul 80. (lp)(c) **XANADU (film Soundtrack)** [2] [4]
– Xanadu ** / I'm alive (***) / All over the world (***) / etc

Jul 80. (7")(10"blue) **ALL OVER THE WORLD**(***). / **MIDNIGHT BLUE** (***) [11] [ ]

Jul 80. (7") **ALL OVER THE WORLD (***). / DRUM DREAMS (***)** [-] [ ]

Nov 80. (7") **DON'T WALK AWAY** (***). / **ACROSS THE BORDER** (***) [21] [-]

E.L.O

Jul 81. (7") **HOLD ON TIGHT. / WHEN TIME STOOD STILL** [4] [10]

Aug 81. (lp)(c) **TIME** [1] [16]
– Prologue / Twilight / Yours truly, 2095 / Ticket to the Moon / The way life's meant to be / Another heart breaks / Rain is falling / From the end of the world / The lights go down / Here is the news / 21st century man / Hold on tight / Epilogue. *(re-iss.+cd.Feb88) (c+cd.re-iss.Jun91)*

Oct 81. (7") **TWILIGHT. / JULIE DON'T LIVE HERE** [30] [33]

Dec 81. (7")(12"pic-d) **TICKET TO THE MOON. / HERE IS THE NEWS** [24] [-]

Jan 82. (7") **RAIN IS FALLING. / ANOTHER HEART BREAKS** [-] [ ]

Mar 82. (7") **THE WAY LIFE'S MEANT TO BE . / WISHING** [ ] [ ]

Jun 83. (7")(12") **ROCK'N'ROLL IS KING. / AFTER ALL** [13] [19]

Jun 83. (lp)(c)(cd) **SECRET MESSAGES** [4] [36]
– Secret messages / Loser gone wild / Bluebird / Take me on and on / Four little diamonds / Stranger / Danger ahead / Letter from Spain / Train of gold / Rock'n'roll is king. *(cd-iss.May87)* (cd+=) – Time after time. *(c/cd.re-iss.Jun91, re-iss.cd+c.Mar93)*

Aug 83. (7")(7"pic-d) **SECRET MESSAGES. / BUILDINGS HAVE EYES** [48] [36]

Oct 83. (7")(12") **FOUR LITTLE DIAMONDS. / LETTER FROM SPAIN** [ ] [86] Sep 83

Jan 84. (7") **STRANGER. / TRAIN OF GOLD** [-] [ ]

ELECTRIC LIGHT ORCHESTRA

After a brief spell in BLACK SABBATH, **BEVAN** rejoined ELO with others **JEFF LYNNE** and the returning **MICK KAMINSKI**

Epic / C.B.S.

Feb 86. (7")(12") **CALLING AMERICA. / CAUGHT IN A TRAP** [28] [18] Jan 86

Mar 86. (lp)(c) **BALANCE OF POWER** [9] [49] Feb 86
– Heaven only knows / So serious / Getting to the point / Secret lives / Is it alright? / Sorrow about to fall / Without someone / Calling America / Endless lies / Send it. *(cd-iss.May87) (c+cd.re-iss.Jun91)(re-iss.cd/c.Mar93)*

Apr 86. (7") **SO SERIOUS. / A MATTER OF FACT** [ ] [-]
(12"+=) – ('A' alternative mix).

May 86. (7") **SO SERIOUS. / ENDLESS LIES** [-] [ ]

Jul 86. (7")(12") **GETTING TO THE POINT. / SECRET LIVES** [ ] [ ]

—— continued without LYNNE! who went solo and joined TRAVELING WILBURYS

ELECTRIC LIGHT ORCHESTRA PART II

now with **BEVAN, KAMINSKI, McDOWELL, GROUCUTT, LOUIS CLARK, PETE HAYCOCK** – vocals (ex-CLIMAX BLUES BAND) / session **NEIL LOCKWOOD, ERIC TROYER.**

Telstar / not issued

Apr 91. (7")(c-s) **HONEST MAN. / LOVE FOR SALE** [60] [ ]
(12"+=)(cd-s+=) – ('A'extended).

May 91. (cd)(c)(lp) **PART II** [34] [ ]
– Hello / Honest man / Every night / Once upon a time / Heartbreaker / Thousand eyes / For the love of a woman / Kiss me red / Heart of hearts / Easy street.

—— **ERIC TROYER + PHIL BATES** – guitar, vocals repl. HAYCOCK (now solo again)

Ultrapop / Ultrapop

Aug 94. (c-s)(cd-s) **POWER OF A MILLION LIGHTS. / ?** [ ] [-]

Oct 94. (cd)(c) **MOMENT OF TRUTH** [ ] [ ]

– Moment of truth (overture) / Breakin' down the walls / Power of a million lights / Interlude / One more tomorrow / Don't wanna / Voices / Interlude 2 / Vixen / The fox / Love or money / Blue violin / Whiskey girls / Interlude / Twist of the knife / So glad you said goodbye / Underture / The leaving.

Oct 94. (c-s)(cd-s) **BREAKIN' DOWN THE WALLS. / ?** [ ] [-]

– compilations etc. –

Note; All 'Harvest' releases were issued on 'United Artists' US.

Oct 74. Harvest; (lp)(c) **SHOWDOWN** [ ] [ ]

Apr 77. Harvest; (lp)(c) **THE LIGHT SHINES ON** [ ] [ ]

Mar 79. Harvest; (lp)(c) **THE LIGHT SHINES ON (VOL.2)** [ ] [ ]

Apr 86. Harvest; (lp)(c)(cd) **FIRST MOVEMENT** [ ] [ ]

Note; All 'Jet' releases were issued on 'United Artists' US.

Jun 76. Jet; (lp)(c) **OLE ELO** [ ] [32]

Dec 78. Jet; (7"ep) **E.L.O. EP** [34] [ ]
– Can't get it out of my head / Strange magic / Evil woman / Ma-ma-ma-belle.

Dec 78. Jet; (3xlp-box) **THREE LIGHT YEARS** [38] [ ]
(first 3 albums boxed)

Nov 79. Jet; (lp)(c) **ELO'S GREATEST HITS** [7] [30]
(re-iss.Jan87 on 'Epic', cd-iss. 1986)

1980. Jet; (4xlp-box) **FOUR LIGHT YEARS** [ ] [ ]
(first 4 albums boxed)

1988. Jet; (cd) **A PERFECT WORLD OF MUSIC** [ ] [-]

Dec 92. Epic; (3xcd-box) **ELDORADO / A NEW WORLD RECORD / OUT OF THE BLUE** [ ] [-]
(re-iss.cd+c Jun94)

May 84. Old Gold; (7") **ROLL OVER BEETHOVEN. / 10538 OVERTURE** [ ] [-]

May 88. Arcade; (cd) **ALL OVER THE WORLD** [ ] [-]

Dec 89. Telstar; (lp)(c)(cd) **THE GREATEST HITS** [13] [-]
-Evil woman / Livin' thing / Can't get it out of my head / Showdown / Turn to stone / Rockaria! / Sweet talkin' woman / Telephone line / Ma ma ma belle / Strange magic / Mr blue sky *(re-iss.Oct90 as 'THE VERY BEST OF THE ELECTRIC LIGHT ORCHESTRA', hit 28)*

Aug 91. E.M.I.; (cd)(c)(d-lp) **EARLY ELO** [ ] [ ]
– (first 2 albums, plus bonus tracks)

Jun 93. Sony Europe; (cd) **THE DEFINITIVE COLLECTION** [ ] [-]

Jun 94. Dino; (cd)(c) **THE VERY BEST OF THE ELECTRIC LIGHT ORCHESTRA** [4] [-]

Jul 94. Legacy; (3xcd-box) **AFTERGLOW** [ ] [-]

Oct 94. Epic; (cd) **THE BEST VOLUME 1** [ ] [ ]

Oct 94. Epic; (cd) **THE BEST VOLUME 2** [ ] [ ]

Oct 94. Epic; (3xcd-box) **TIME / SECRET MESSAGES / DISCOVERY** [ ] [ ]

JEFF LYNNE

(solo, while a ELO member)

Jet / Jet

Jul 77. (7")(12") **DOIN' THAT CRAZY THING. / GOIN' DOWN TO RIO** [ ] [ ]

not issued / Epic

Aug 84. (7") **VIDEO. / SOONER OR LATER** [-] [ ]
(above from the film 'Electric Dreams')

BEV BEVAN

Jet / not issued

May 76. (7") **LET THERE BE DRUMS. / HEAVY HEAD** [ ] [-]

ELECTRONIC (see under ⇒ NEW ORDER)

ELF / (ELECTRIC ELVES) (see under ⇒ DIO)

E.L.O. (see under ⇒ ELECTRIC LIGHT ORCHESTRA)

EMERSON LAKE & PALMER

Formed: London, England . . . mid-1970. Soon signed to 'Island' records, after featuring on the Isle Of Wight festival 29 Aug'70. Their eponymous debut later in the year, made the UK/US Top 20, with 1971 follow-up hitting Top spot in UK. Early singles were issued at this time, but only in America where they were signed to 'Atlantic' subsidiary 'Cotillion'. In 1977, an edited version of FANFARE FOR THE COMMON MAN nearly gave them a surprise UK No.1. This however was to mark the end of ELP, at least commercially. They re-formed in '86, with the P of the band taken up by new veteran drummer COZY POWELL. The original group re-formed again in 1991, but were found floundering on past glories with 'BLACK MOON' album in '92. • **Style:** Techno-rock supergroup with considerable musical ability appreciated in most polls, although they were accused of flashy over-indulgence. Their concept pieces, although slightly mechanical, revived their classical inhibitions in the progressive rock world. • **Songwriters:** GREG LAKE compositions / PETE SINFIELD words. Covered complete PICTURES AT AN EXHIBITION (Mussorgsky) / NUT ROCKER (Tchaikovsky) / JERUSALEM (trad.hymn) / FANFARE FOR THE COMMON MAN (Aaron Copeland / PETER GUNN (Henry Mancini). KEITH EMERSON solo:- HONKY TONK TRAIN BLUES (Meade Lux Lewis). • **Trivia:** 'Manticore' their label formed in 1973, also signed PETE SINFIELD, P.F.M. and LITTLE RICHARD!

Recommended: TRILOGY (*8) / BRAIN SALAD SURGERY (*8)

KEITH EMERSON (b. 2 Nov'44) – keyboards (ex-NICE, ex-GARY FARR & THE T-BONES / **GREG LAKE** (b.10 Nov'48) – vocals, guitar, bass (ex-KING CRIMSON) / **CARL PALMER** (b.20 Mar'47) – drums, percussion (ex-ATOMIC ROOSTER, ex-CRAZY WORLD OF ARTHUR BROWN)

Island / Cotillion

Nov 70. (lp)(c) **EMERSON LAKE & PALMER** [4] [18]
– The barbarian / Take a pebble / Knife edge / The three fates:- Clotho – Lachesis – Acropus / Tank / Lucky man. *(re-iss.'74 on 'Manticore') (cd-iss.1988 on 'WEA')(re-iss.cd Dec93 on 'Victory')*

Mar 71. (7") **LUCKY MAN. / KNIFE EDGE** [-] [48]
(US re-iss.Jan73 hit No.51)

Jun 71. (lp)(c) **TARKUS** [1] [9]
– Tarkus:- Eruption – Stones of years – Iconoclast – The mass – Manticore – Battlefield – Aquatarkus – (conclusion) / Jeremy Bender / Bitches crystal / The only way / Infinite space / A time and a place / Are you ready Eddy?. *(re-iss.'74 on 'Manticore') (cd-iss.Sep89 on 'WEA') (re-iss.cd Dec93 on 'Victory')*

Sep 71. (7") **STONES OF YEARS. / A TIME AND A PLACE** [-] [ ]

Nov 71. (lp)(c) **PICTURES AT AN EXHIBITION** [2] [10]
– Promenade: The gnome – Promenade – The sage – The old castle – Blues variation – Promenade / The hut of Baba Yaga – The curse of Baba Yaga – The hut of Baba Yaga – The great gates of Kiev – Nutrocker. *(re-iss '74 on 'Manticore') (cd-iss.1988 on 'Cotillion' & Sep89 on 'WEA')(re-iss. Dec93 on 'Victory')*

Mar 72. (7") **NUTROCKER. / THE GREAT GATES OF KIEV** [-] [70]

Jul 72. (lp)(c) **TRILOGY** [2] [5]
– The endless enigma (part 1) – Fugue – The endless enigma (part 2) / From the beginning / The sheriff / Hoedown / Trilogy / Living sin / Abaddon's bolero. *(re-iss.'74 on 'Manticore') (cd-iss.Jun89 on 'Atlantic')(re-iss.cd Dec93 on 'Victory')*

Aug 72. (7") **FROM THE BEGINNING. / LIVING SIN** [-] [39]

Manticore / Manticore

Dec 73. (lp)(c) **BRAIN SALAD SURGERY** [2] [11]
– Jerusalem / Toccata / Still . . .you turn me on / Benny the bouncer / Karn evil 9. 1st impression -part 1 & 2 – 2nd impression – 3rd impression. *(cd-iss.Jun89 on 'WEA') (re-iss.cd Dec93 on 'Victory')*

Dec 73. (7") **JERUSALEM. / WHEN THE APPLE BLOSSOM BLOOMS IN THE WINDMILLS OF YOUR MIND, I'LL BE YOUR VALENTINE** [ ] [ ]

Aug 74. (t-lp)(d-c) **WELCOME BACK MY FRIENDS TO THE SHOW THAT NEVER ENDS – LADIES AND GENTLEMEN . . . EMERSON, LAKE & PALMER (live)** [5] [4]
– Howdown / Jerusalem / Toccata / Tarkus:- Eruption – Stones of years – Iconoclaust – The mass – Manticore – Battlefield – Epitaph – Aquatarkus – (conclusion) / Take a pebble – Piano improvisations – Take a pebble (conclusion) / Jeremy Bender / The sheriff / Karn evil 9. 1st impression – 2nd impression – 3rd impression. *(re-iss.cd Dec93 on 'Victory')*

– solo projects –

GREG LAKE

Nov 75. (7") **I BELIEVE IN FATHER CHRISTMAS. / HUMBUG** [2] [ ]
(re-iss.Nov82 hit 72 & Dec83 hit 65)

KEITH EMERSON

with **KENDALL STUBBS** – bass / **FRANK SCULLY** – drums

Apr 76. (7") **HONKY TONK TRAIN BLUES. / BARREL HOUSE SHAKE DOWN** [21] [ ]

EMERSON, LAKE & PALMER

Atlantic / Atlantic

Mar 77. (d-lp)(d-c) **WORKS 1** [9] [12]
– Piano concerto No.1 – 1st movement: Allegro giojoso / 2nd movement: Andante molto cantabile / 3rd movement: Toccata con fuoco / Lend your love to me tonight / C'est la vie / Hallowed by thy name / Nobody loves you like I do / Closer to believing / The enemy God dances with the black spirits / L.A. nights / New Orleans / Bach: Two part invention in D minor / Food for your soul /

Tank / Fanfare for the common man / Pirates. *(cd-iss.Jun89)(re-iss.d-cd Dec93 on 'Victory')*

Jun 77. (7")(12") **FANFARE FOR THE COMMON MAN (edit). / BRAIN SALAD SURGERY** [2] [ ]

Aug 77. (7") **C'EST LA VIE (as "GREG LAKE" solo). / JEREMY BENDER** [ ] [ ]

Nov 77. (lp)(c) **WORKS 2** (compilation of rare and demo work) [20] [37]
– Tiger in a spotlight / When the apple blossoms bloom in the windmills of your mind I'll be your valentine / Bullfrog / Brain salad surgery / Barrelhouse shakedown / Watching over you / So far to fall / Maple leaf rag / I believe in Father Christmas / Close but not touching / Honky tonk train blues / Show me the way to go home. *(cd-iss.Jun89) (re-iss.cd Dec93 on 'Victory')*

Jan 78. (7") **WATCHING OVER YOU ("GREG LAKE" solo). / HALLOWED BE THY NAME** [ ] [ ]

Nov 78. (lp)(c) **LOVE BEACH** [48] [55]
– All I want is you / Love beach / Taste of my love / The gambler / For you / Canario / Memoirs of an officer and a gentleman – Prologue -The education of a gentleman / Love at first sight / Letters from the front / Honourable company. *(cd-iss.Jun89) (re-iss.cd Dec93 on 'Victory')*

Nov 78. (7") **ALL I WANT IS YOU. / TIGER IN A SPOTLIGHT** [ ] [ ]

— (disbanded Dec78)

KEITH EMERSON

(solo)

Atlantic Atlantic

Sep 80. (7") **TAXI RIDE. / MATER TENEBARUM** [ ] [ ]

Atlantic Cinevox

Dec 80. (lp) **INFERNO (Soundtrack)** [ ] [ ]
– Inferno / Rose's descent into a cellar / The taxi ride / The library / Sarah in the library vaults / Bookbinder's delight / Rose leaves the apartment / Rose gets it / Elisa's story / A cat attic attack / Kazanian's tarantella / Mark's discovery / Matter tenebarum / Inferno (finals) / Ices, cigarettes, etc. *(re-iss.Mar90 on 'Silva Screen')*

— added **NEIL SYMONETTE** – drums / **TRISTAN FRY** – percussion / **GREG BOWEN** – trumpet / **JEROME RICHARDSON** – sax / **PAULETTE McWILLIAMS** – vocals

M.C.A. Backstreet

Apr 81. (7") **I'M A MAN. / NIGHTHAWKS** [ ] [ ]

Apr 81. (lp) **NIGHTHAWKS (Soundtrack)** [ ] [ ]
– Nighthawks – main title theme / Mean stalkin' / The bust / Nighthawking / The chase / I'm a man / The chopper / tramway / I'm comin' in / Face to face / The flight of the hawk.

Red Bus not issued

Dec 83. (7") **UP THE ELEPHANT AND ROUND THE CASTLE. / ('A'version)** [ ] [-]

Chord not issued

Mar 85. (lp) **ARMAGEDDON** [ ] [-]
– Theme from Floi / Joe and Micheko / Children of the light / Funny's skate state / Zamedy stomp / Challenge of the psonic fighters. *(re-iss.Feb87)*

— **MOTT** – guitar / **DICK MORRISSEY + ANDREW BRENNAN + PETE KING** – saxophone

Apr 85. (cd) **HONKY** [ ] [-]
– Hello sailor / Bach before the mast / Salt cay / Green ice / Intro-juicing / Big horn breakdown / Yancey special / Rum-a-thing / Jesus loves me. *(lp-iss.Mar86)*

— Some with **DOREEN CHANTER** – vocals / **MIKE SEBBAGE** – vocals / **TOM NICOL + DEREK WILSON** – drums / **MICHAEL SHEPPARD** – bass, guitar, co-producer

May 86. (lp)(cd) **MURDEROCK** [ ] [-]
– Murderock / Tonight is your night / Streets to blame / Not so innocent / Prelude to Candice / Don't go in the shower / Coffee time / Candice / New York dash / Tonight is not your night / The spill one.

— next with The National Philharmonic Orchestra, plus **BRAD DELP, L.HELM.**

Oct 86. (lp)(cd) **BEST REVENGE (Film Soundtrack) (by "KEITH EMERSON & JOHN COLEMAN")** [ ] [ ]
– Dream runner / The runner / Wha 'dya mean / Straight between the eyes / Orchestral suite to "Best Revenge" / Playing for keeps (main title theme).

Priority not issued

Nov 88. (lp)(c)(cd) **EMERSON – THE CHRISTMAS ALBUM** [ ] [ ]
(cd-iss.Jun93 on 'A.M.P.') (re-iss.cd Dec95 on 'Amp')

Emerson not issued

Dec 88. (7") **WE THREE KINGS OF ORIENT ARE. / CAPTAIN STARSHIP HOPKINS** [ ] [-]

– (KEITH EMERSON) compilations etc. –

Feb 87. Chord; (d-lp) **ARMAGEDDON. / CHINA FREE FALL (with "DEREK AUSTIN")** [ ] [ ]

Oct 88. Chord; (lp)(cd) **THE KEITH EMERSON COLLECTION** [ ] [ ]

Dec 95. Amp; (cd-s) **TROIKA (THE CHRISTMAS SINGLE). /** [ ] [-]

GREG LAKE BAND

GREG LAKE – vocals, guitar, bass with **TOMMY EYRE** – keyboards / **GARY MOORE** – guitar (ex-solo artist ex-THIN LIZZY ex-COLOSSEUM) / **TRISTRAM MARGETTS** – bass / **TED McKENNA** – drums (ex-SENSATIONAL ALEX HARVEY BAND)

Chrysalis Chrysalis

Sep 81. (7") **LOVE YOU TOO MUCH. / SOMEONE** [ ] [ ]

Oct 81. (lp)(c) **GREG LAKE** [62] [62]
– Nuclear attack / Love you too much / It hurts / One before you go / Loving goodbye / Retribution drive / Black and blue / Let me love you once / The lies / For those who dare.

Dec 81. (7") **LET ME LOVE YOU ONCE. /** [-] [48]

Feb 82. (7") **IT HURTS. / RETRIBUTION DRIVE** [ ] [ ]

E.M.I. not issued

Jul 83. (lp)(c) **MANOEUVRES** [ ] [ ]
– Manoeuvres / Too young to love / Paralysed / A woman like you / I don't want to lose your love tonight / It's you, you've got to believe / Famous last words / Slave to love / Haunted / I don't know why I still love you.

— LAKE joined ASIA with PALMER

P.M.

CARL PALMER with **TODD COCHRAN** – keyboards / **BARRY FINNERTY** – guitar, vocals / **JOHN NITZINGER** – guitar, vocals / **ERIK SCOTT** – bass, vocals

Ariol Ariola

May 80. (lp)(c) **1 P.M.** [ ] [ ]
– Dynamite / You've got me rockin' / Green velvet splendour / Dreamers / Go on carry on / D'ya go all the way / Go for it / Madeleine / You're too much / Children of the air age.

Apr 80. (7") **YOU GOT ME ROCKIN'. / GO FOR IT** [ ] [ ]

Jul 80. (7") **DYNAMITE. / D'YA GO ALL THE WAY** [ ] [ ]

— (Jan81) PALMER joined ASIA.

EMERSON, LAKE & POWELL

are the new set up **COZY POWELL** – drums, (ex-solo artist, ex-RAINBOW, etc.)

Polydor Polydor

Jul 86. (lp)(c)(cd) **EMERSON, LAKE & POWELL** [35] [23] Jun 86
– Mars, the bringer of war / The score / Learning to fly / Touch and go / Miracle / Love blind / Step aside / Lay down your guns.

Jul 86. (7") **TOUCH AND GO. / LEARNING TO FLY** [ ] [60] Jun 86
(12"+=) – The locomotion.

1986. (7") **LAY DOWN YOUR GUNS. / ?** [-] [ ]

— (1987 originals reformed but disbanded Oct87)

3

was unit formed by **EMERSON, PALMER** and American **ROBERT BERRY** – vocals (ex-HUSH)

Geffen Geffen

Feb 88. (lp)(c)(cd) **TO THE POWER OF THREE** [ ] [ ]
– Talkin' about / Lover to lover / Chains / Desde la vida / Eight miles high / Runaway / You do or you don't / On my way home.

Feb 88. (7") **TALKIN' ABOUT. / LA VISTA** [-] [ ]

EMERSON, LAKE & PALMER

re-formed 1992.

Victory Victory

Apr 92. (cd)(c)(lp) **BLACK MOON** [ ] [78]
– Black Moon / Paper blood / Affairs of the heart / Romeo and Juliet / Farewell to arms / Changing states / Burning bridges / Close to home / Better days / Footprints in the snow.

May 92. (7") **BLACK HOLE. / MILES IZ DEAD** [ ] [ ]
(12")(cd-s) – ('A'side) / ('A'version) / A blade of grass.

London London

Nov 92. (7")(c-s) **AFFAIRS OF THE HEART. / BETTER DAYS** [ ] [ ]
(cd-s+=) – A blade of grass / Black moon.

Feb 93. (cd)(c) **LIVE AT THE ROYAL ALBERT HALL (live)** [ ] [ ]
– 1st impression part 2 / Tarkus: Eruption – Stones of years – Iconoclast / Knife edge / Paper blood / Romeo & Juliet / Creole dance / Still . . . you turn me on / Lucky man / Black moon / The pirates / Finale / Fanfare for the common man / America / Blue rondo A la Turk

Sep 94. (cd)(c) **IN THE HOT SEAT** [ ] [ ]
– Hand of truth / Daddy / One by one / Heart on ice / Thin line / Man in the long black coat / Change / Give me a reason to stay / Gone too soon / Street war. *(cd+=)* – Pictures at an exhibition: a) Promenade- b) The gnome- c) Promenaded) The sage- e) The hut of Baba Yaga- f) The great gates of Kiev.

– compilations, others, etc. –

Oct 79. Atlantic; (lp)(c) **EMERSON, LAKE & PALMER IN CONCERT (live 1978)** [ ] [73]

– (introductory fanfare) / Peter Gunn / Tiger in a spotlight / C'est la vie / The enemy god dances with the black spirits / Knife edge / Piano concerto No.1 / Pictures at an exhibition.

Dec 79. Atlantic; (7") **PETER GUNN (live). / KNIFE EDGE (live)** [ ] [ ]

Nov 80. Atlantic; (lp)(c) **THE BEST OF EMERSON, LAKE & PALMER** [ ] [ ]

– Hoedown / Lucky man / Karn evil 9 / Trilogy / Fanfare for the common man / Still . . .you turn me on / Tiger in a spotlight / Jerusalem / Peter Gunn. *(cd-iss.1983)*

Jul 92. Atlantic; (cd)(c)(lp) **THE ATLANTIC YEARS** [ ] [ ]

Dec 93. Victory; (4xcd-box) **THE RETURN OF THE MANTICORE** [ ] [ ]

Dec 93. Victory; (d-cd) **WORKS LIVE (live)** [ ] [ ]

EMF

Formed: Forest of Dean, Gloucestershire, England . . . early 1990 by the older Oxford graduate IAN DENCH (23) and 4 other teenagers (19). After 4th gig, they were found by ABBO (ex-UK DECAY) and his girlfriend LINDA who got them signed to 'E.M.I.' sub. 'Parlophone' Mar90. Debut single, UNBELIEVABLE broke into UK Top 3, and in '91 they set about taking both sides of the Atlantic by storm. • **Style:** Similar to JESUS JONES or a high speed DEPECHE MODE. • **Songwriters:** Group compositions except LOW SPARK OF THE HIGH HEELED BOYS (Traffic) / SHADDAP YOU, FACE (Joe Dolce) / I'M A BELIEVER (Monkees). • **Trivia:** EMF stands for ECSTASY MOTHER FUCKERS.

Recommended: SCHUBERT DIP (*5) / STIGMA (*7)

JAMES ATKIN – vocals / **IAN DENCH** – guitar, keyboards (ex-APPLE MOSAIC) / **DERRY BROWNSON** – samples, percussion (ex-LAC's) / **ZAC FOLEY** – bass (ex-IUC's) / **MARK DE CLOEDT** – drums (ex-ZU) / plus **MILF** – DJ scratcher

Parlophone E.M.I.

Oct 90. (7")(c-s) **UNBELIEVABLE. / EMF (live)** [3] [1] Feb91

(12"+=)(cd-s+=) – ('A' Sin City sex mix).

Jan 91. (7")(c-s) **I BELIEVE. / WHEN YOU'RE MINE** [6] [ ]

(12"+=)(cd-s+=) Unbelievable (funk mix).

Apr 91. (7")(c-s) **CHILDREN. / STRANGE BREW (live remix)** [19] [ ]

(12"+=) – Children (mix).

(cd-s++=) – Children – Battle for the minds of North Amerika.

(7"ep+=) – (live versions)

May 91. (cd)(c)(lp) **SCHUBERT DIP** [3] [12]

– Children / Long summer days / When you're mine / Travelling not running / I believe / Unbelievable / Girl of an age / Admit it / Lies / Long time. *(re-iss.cd+c Mar94)*

Aug 91. (7")(c-s) **LIES. / HEAD THE BALL** [28] [21]

(12"+=)(cd-s+=) – ('A'mix).

Apr 92. (7"ep) **UNEXPLAINED** [18] [ ]

– Getting through / Far from me / The same.

(12"ep+=)(cd-ep+=) – Search and destroy.

Sep 92. (7")(c-s) **THEY'RE HERE. / PHANTASMAGORIC** [29] [ ]

(12"+=) – ('A'remix).

(cd-s+=) – Low spark of the high heeled boys.

Sep 92. (cd)(c)(lp) **STIGMA** [19] [ ]

– They're here / Arizona / It's you that leaves me dry / Never know / Blue highs / Inside / Getting through / She bleeds / Dog / The light that burns twice as bright . . .

Nov 92. (cd-ep) **IT'S YOU (3 Butch Vig mixes) / DOF (Foetus mix)** [23] [ ]

(cd-ep) – It's you (Orbital mix) / The light that burns twice as bright . . . (mix) / They're here (mix).

Feb 95. (c-s) **PERFECT DAY / ANGEL** [27] [ ]

(cd-s+=) – I won't give into you / Kill for you (lo-fi mix).

(12"+=) – ('A'-Temple of boom remix) / ('A'-Chris & James epic).

(cd-s) – ('A'side) / ('A'-Chris & James mix) / ('A'-Black One mix) / ('A'-Toytown mix).

Mar 95. (cd)(c) **CHA CHA CHA** [30] [ ]

– Perfect day / La plage / The day I was born / Secrets / Shining / Bring me down / Skin / Slouch / Bleeding you dry / Patterns / When will you come / West of the Cox / Ballad o' the bishop / Glass smash Jack.

Apr 95. (c-s) **BLEEDING YOU DRY / TOO MUCH / EASY / PERFECT DAY (acoustic)** [ ] [ ]

(cd-s) – (first 3 tracks) / Shining (acoustic).

(cd-s) – ('A'side) / I pushed the boat out so far it sank / Patterns (acoustic).

Jun 95. (7")(c-s) **I'M A BELIEVER. ("EMF with REEVES & MORTIMER") / AT LEAST WE'VE GOT OUR GUITARS** [3] [-]

(cd-s) – ('A'side) / At this stage I couldn't say / ('A'-Unbelievable mix) / La plage (mix).

Oct 95. (c-s) **AFRO KING / UNBELIEVABLE** [51] [ ]

(cd-s+=) – Children / I believe.

(cd-s) – ('A'side) / Too much / Easy / Bring me down.

Brian ENO

Born: BRIAN PETER GEORGE ST.JOHN LE BAPTISTE DE LA SALLE ENO, 15 May'48, Suffolk, England. After leaving art school, where he fronted heavy group MAXWELL DEMON, he joined ROXY MUSIC in 1971. After contributing greatly to their image and sound on albums 'ROXY MUSIC' & 'FOR YOUR PLEASURE', he left them, due to dispute over new pop-rock direction. His first post-ROXY venture was '(NO PUSSYFOOTING)' in 1973 with ROBERT FRIPP (of KING CRIMSON). This was nothing more than extreme experimentation of synth-electronics and treated guitar. However it did provide art lovers, with a photo-shot of ENO & FRIPP in a multi-mirrored room. His first solo work in early 1974 'HERE COME THE WARM JETS', disappointed the critics, who gave it the thumbs down, bar one gem 'BABY'S ON FIRE'. He released 2 more greatly improved efforts for 'Island', before he formed own label in '75 appropriately titled 'Obscure'. Preceeding this in a fit of depression, he joined The WINKIES for a short tour Feb-Mar74, but departed after being diagnosed with a collapsed lung. Recovered to find himself, on an 'Island records' concert bill on '1st JUNE, 1974', alongside stablemates KEVIN AYERS, NICO and JOHN CALE. The following year, he was hit by a car, which caused slight, but not lasting brain damage. In the late 70's & 80's, he concentrated more on specialist albums, collaborations, soundtracks and production work (see below). • **Style:** The balding genius once described himself as a non-musician, who just turned dials and switches. Technically brilliant ambient experimentalist, whose new obscure musak is possibly a direct link to what listeners will appreciate in the 21st century. (Martin the prophet!? – ed). • **Songwriters:** All composed by ENO. • **Trivia:** His 1977 song 'KING'S LEAD HAT' was in fact an anagram of TALKING HEADS. In the mid-80's, his work was featured on an BBC2 'Arena Special', and included paintings by RUSSELL MILLS, and 'ANOTHER GREEN WORLD' title track, which had become the programme's theme tune. ENO has also done session and production work for JOHN CALE (1974-75), ROBERT WYATT (1975), ROBERT CALVERT (1975), DAVID BOWIE (1977) / DEVO (1978) / TALKING HEADS (1978-80) / U2 (1985-91 with Daniel Lanois) / etc.

Recommended: DESERT ISLAND SELECTION (*7) / HERE COME THE WARM JETS (*6) / ANOTHER GREEN WORLD (*9) / TAKING TIGER MOUNTAIN BY STRATEGY (*7) / NERVE NET (*6) / MY LIFE IN THE BUSH OF GHOSTS (*8) with DAVID BYRNE / APOLLO (*8) / WRONG WAY UP (*7) with JOHN CALE.

FRIPP & ENO

ROBERT FRIPP – guitar of KING CRIMSON / **BRIAN ENO** – synthesizers, instruments

Island-Help Antilles

Nov 73. (lp) **(NO PUSSYFOOTING)** [ ] [ ]

– The heavenly music corporation / Swastika girls. *(re-iss.Oct77 on 'Polydor', re-iss.Jan87 on 'EG')*

ENO

now solo with guest session people, including ROXY MUSIC musicians and ROBERT FRIPP, CHRIS SPEDDING, PAUL RUDOLPH and others.

Island Island

Jan 74. (lp)(c) **HERE COME THE WARM JETS** [26] [ ]

– Needles in the camel's eye / The paw paw Negro blowtorch / Baby's on fire / Cindy tells me / Driving me backwards / On some faraway beach / Black rank / Dead finks don't talk / Some of them are old / Here come the warm jets. *(re-iss.Mar77 on 'Polydor', re-iss.'87 on 'EG')*

Mar 74. (7") **SEVEN DEADLY FINNS. / LATER ON** [ ] [ ]

— guests incl. PORTSMOUTH SINFONIA ORCHESTRA, PHIL COLLINS – drums / etc.

Nov 74. (lp)(c) **TAKING TIGER MOUNTAIN (BY STRATEGY)** [ ] [ ]

– Burning airlines give you so much more / Back in Judy's jungle / The fat lady of Limbourg / Mother whale eyeless / The great pretender / Third uncle / Put a straw under baby / The truth wheel / China my China / Taking tiger mountain. *(re-iss.Mar77 on 'Polydor') (re-iss.Jan87 on 'EG')*

Aug 75. (7") **THE LION SLEEPS TONIGHT. /** [-] [ ]

— now with **FRIPP** (3) / **COLLINS** (3) / **JOHN CALE** – viola (2) / **PAUL RUDOPLH** (3) / **PERCY JONES** – bass (3) / **ROD MELVIN** – piano (3) / **BRIAN TURRINGTON** – bass, piano (1)

Sep 75. (lp)(c) **ANOTHER GREEN WORLD** [ ] [ ]

– Sky saw / Over Fire Island / St. Elmo's fire / In dark trees / The big ship / I'll come running / Another green world / Sombre reptiles / Little fishes / Golden hours / Becalmed / Zawinul – Lava / Everything merges with the night. *(re-iss.Mar77 on 'Polydor', re-iss.+cd Jan87 on 'EG')*

	Obscure	Antilles
Nov 75. (lp)(c) **DISCREET MUSIC**		

– Discreet music 1 & 2 / Three Variations on canon in D major; a) Fullness of wind – b) French catalogues – c) Brutal ardour.

FRIPP & ENO

collaborate again.

	Help-Island	not issued
Dec 75. (lp)(c) **EVENING STAR**		-

– Wind on water / Evening star / Evensong / Wind on wind / An index of metals. *(re-iss.Oct77 on 'Polydor') (re-iss.+cd Jan87 on 'EG')*

— For the next couple of years he worked with 801 (PHIL MANZANERA's band). He also produced his own 'Obscure' label, discovering people including PENGUIN CAFE ORCHESTRA, MICHAEL NYMAN, MAX EASTLEY & DAVID TOOP, HAROLD BUDD plus JAN STEELE / JOHN CAGE. More commercially he also played on and produced 1977 albums by DAVID BOWIE, TALKING HEADS, ULTRAVOX.

BRIAN ENO

solo once more

	Polydor	Island
Dec 77. (lp)(c) **BEFORE AND AFTER SCIENCE**		

– No one receiving / Backwater / Kurt's rejoiner / Energy fools the magician / King's lead hat / Here he comes / Julie with . . . / By this river / Through hollow lands / Spider and I.

Jan 78. (7") **KING'S LEAD HAT. / R.A.F. ('B'side credited to "ENO & SNATCH")**		
Sep 78. (lp)(c) **MUSIC FOR FILMS**	55	

– M386 / Aragon / From the same hill / Inland sea / Two rapid formations / Slow water / Sparrowfall 1 / Sparrowfall 2 / Sparrowfall 3 / Quartz / Events in dense fog / There is nobody / A measured room / Patrolling wire borders / Task force / Alternative 3 / Strange light / Final sunset. *(re-iss.+cd Jan87 on 'EG')*

	Ambient-EG	P.V.C.
Mar 79. (lp)(c) **AMBIENT 1: MUSIC FOR AIRPORTS**		

– Side 1 / Side 2. *(re-iss.+cd Jan87 on 'EG')*

HAROLD BUDD & BRIAN ENO

(BUDD – piano)

	Ambient	E.G.
Apr 80. (lp)(c) **AMBIENT 2: THE PLATEAUX OF MIRROR**		

– First light / Steal away / The plateau of mirror / Above Chiangmai / An arc of doves / Not yet remembered / The chill air / Among fields of crystal / Wind in lonely fences / Failing light. *(re-iss Jan87 on 'EG')*

JON HASSELL & BRIAN ENO

(HASSELL – trumpet)

	Editions	E.G.
Apr 80. (lp) **FOURTH WORLD VOL.1: POSSIBLE MUSICS**		

– Chemistry / Delta rain dream / Griot (over contageous magic) / Ba-Benzele / Rising thermal 14 degrees 16n, 32 degrees 28e / Charm (over Borundi cloud). *(re-iss Jan87 on 'EG')*

BRIAN ENO & DAVID BYRNE

BYRNE of TALKING HEADS

	EG	Sire
Feb 81. (lp)(c) **MY LIFE IN THE BUSH OF GHOSTS**	29	44

– America is waiting / Mea culpa / Regiment / Help me somebody / The Jezebel spirit / Qu'ran / Moonlight in glory / The carrier / A secret life / Come with us / Mountain of needles. *(re-iss Jan87 on 'EG')*

May 81. (7") **THE JEZEBEL SPIRIT. / REGIMENT**		

(12"+=) – Very very hungry (Qu'ran).

BRIAN ENO

	Editions-EG	Sire
Mar 82. (lp)(c) **AMBIENT (4): ON LAND**	93	

– Lizard point / The lost day / Tal coat / Shadow / Lantern marsh / Unfamiliar wind / A clearing / Dunwich Beach, Autumn 1960. *(re-iss Jan87 on 'EG')*

BRIAN ENO with DANIEL LANOIS & ROGER ENO

	E.G.	Sire
Jul 83. (lp)(c) **APOLLO: ATMOSPHERES & SOUNDTRACKS**		

– Under stars / The secret place / Matta / Signals / An ending (ascent) / Under stars II / Drift / Silver morning / Deep blue day / Weightless / Always returning / Stars. *(re-iss.+cd Jan87 on 'EG')*

HAROLD BUDD & BRIAN ENO with DANIEL LANOIS

	Editions-EG	Sire
Aug 84. (lp)(c) **THE PEARL**		

– Late October / A stream with bright fish / The silver ball / Against the sky / Lost in the humming air / Dark-eyed sister / Their memories / The pearl / Foreshadowed / An echo of night / Still return. *(re-iss.+cd Jan87)*

ENO

	E.G.	Sire
Oct 85. (cd) **THURSDAY AFTERNOON**		

– Thursday afternoon. *(1 track only)*

MICHAEL BROOK with BRIAN ENO & DANIELS LANOIS

	Editions-EG	Sire
Aug 85. (lp)(c) **HYBRID**		

– Hybrid / Distant village / Mimosa / Pond life / Ocean motion / Midday / Earth floor / Vacant.

ROGER ENO with BRIAN ENO

did guest appearance

	Editions-EG	Sire
Aug 85. (lp)(c) **VOICES**		

– A place in the wilderness / The day after / At the water's edge / Grey promenade / A paler sky / Through the blue / Evening tango / Recalling winter / Voices / The old dance / Reflections on I.K.B. *(re-iss Jan87)*

ENO / CALE

(collaboration **JOHN CALE** – vocals, multi-)with **ROBERT AHWAI** – rhythm guitar / **DARYL JOHNSON** – bass / **NEIL CATCHPOLE** – violin / **RONALD JONES** – drums, tabla / **DAVE YOUNG** – guitars, bass

	Land	Sire
Oct 90. (cd)(c)(lp) **WRONG WAY UP**		

– Lay my love / One word / In the backroom / Empty frame / Cordoba / Spinning away / Footsteps / Been there done that / Crime in the desert / The river.

Nov 90. (12"ep)(cd-ep) **ONE WORLD. / GRANDFATHER'S HOUSE / PALAQUIN**		-

BRIAN ENO

	Opal-WEA	Opal-WEA
Jul 92. (7") **FRACTIAL ZOOM. / ('A'-Moby mix)**		

(12"+=) – (4 mixes).
(cd-s++=) – (another mix) / The roil, the choke.

Sep 92. (cd)(c)(lp) **NERVE NET**	70	

– Fractial zoom / Wire shock / What actually happened? / Pierre in mist / My squelchy life / Decentre / Juju space jazz / The roil, the choke / Ali click / Distributing being / Web.

Oct 92. (7") **ALI CLICK (Beirut mix). / ('A'rural mix)**		

(12"+=) – ('A'-Markus Draws + Grid mix).
(cd-s) – ('A'side) / (++=) – ('A'trance long darkly mad mix) / ('A'trance instrumental).

Nov 92. (cd)(c) **THE SHUTOV ASSEMBLY**		

– (music inspired by Moscow painter Sergei Shutov)

Around the same time as above, he lectured at Sadler's Wells, and is the brunt of NME jokes as Professor Eno.

	All Saints	not iss?
Jun 93. (cd) **:NEROLI:**		-

-:Neroli:.

— Above long piece of music, was used in hospitals for childbirth!

— Sep 94; he was credited on JAMES' ltd.album 'WAH WAH'.

BRIAN ENO / JAH WOBBLE

	All Saints	not issued
Oct 95. (cd)(c)(lp) **SPINNER**	71	-

– Where we lived / Like organza / Steam / Garden recalled / Marine radio / Unusual balance / Space diary 1 / Spinner / Transmitter and trumpet / Left where it fell.

– (ENO) compilations, others, etc. –

1982. E.G.; (d-c) **NO PUSSYFOOTIN' + EVENING STAR ("FRIPP & ENO")**		-
Nov 83. E.G.; (10xlp-box) **WORKING BACKWARDS 1983-1973**		

– (first 9 lp's, plus MUSIC FOR FILMS VOL.2 / + RARITIES m-lp:- Seven deadly finns / The lion sleeps tonight / Strong flashes of light / More volts / Mist rhythm)

Mar 86. E.G.; (lp)(c) **MORE BLANK THAN FRANK**

Jan 87. E.G.; (cd) **DESERT ISLAND SELECTION**

– Here he comes / Everything merges with the night / I'll come running (edit) / On some faraway beach (edit) / Spirits drifting / Back in Judy's jungle / St Elmo's fire / No one receiving / Julie with . . . / Taking tiger mountain (edit).

Jan 87. E.G.; (lp)(c) **MUSIC FOR FILMS 2**

– The dove / Roman twilight / Matta / Dawn, marshland / Climate study / The secret place / An ending (ascent) / Always returning 1 / Signals / Under stars / Drift / Study / Approaching Taidu / Always returning 2.

Mar 89. E.G.; (cd-s) **ANOTHER GREEN WORLD / DOVER BEACH / DEEP BLUE DAY / 2-1** | -

Dec 89. E.G.; (t-lp)(t-c)(t-cd) **ISLAND VARIOUS ARTISTS** | -

– (with other artists / ANOTHER GREEN WORLD / BEFORE AND AFTER SCIENCE / APOLLO)

Nov 93. Virgin; (3xcd-box) **BRIAN ENO (collaborations)**

Nov 93. Virgin; (3xcd-box) **BRIAN ENO 2 (collaborations)**

Feb 94. Venture; (cd)(c) **THE ESSENTIAL FRIPP AND ENO**

Oct 94. Virgin; (3xcd-box) **THE COMPACT COLLECTION**

ENO contributed 2 tracks on live lp 'JUNE 1st, 1974' with KEVIN AYERS, NICO and JOHN CALE. He also with brother ROGER and DANIEL LANOIS provided one track to DUNE film (1984).

CLUSTER & ENO

CLUSTER (see below members), had released several German albums in 70's on 'Sky'.

May 78. (lp) **CLUSTER AND ENO** | -

Mar 79. (lp) **AFTER THE HEAT** (ENO, MOEBIUS & ROEDELIUS) | -

Apr 84. (lp)(cd) **BEGEGNUNGEN** (ENO, MOEBIUS, ROEDILIUS & PLANK) | -

1985. (lp)(cd) **BEGEGNUNGEN II** (ENO, MOEBIUS, ROEDILIUS & PLANK) | -

Jan 86. (lp) **OLD LAND** (CLUSTER AND ENO) | -

JOHN ENTWISTLE (see under ⇒ WHO)

ENYA

Born: EITHNE NI BHRAONAIN, 17 May '61, Gweadore, County Donegal, Ireland. Classically a trained pianist, she went solo, after 2 appearances in the early 80's on her family's (CLANNAD) album 'FUAIM'. Her first solo project in 1985, was an 'Island' records film soundtrack 'THE FROG PRINCE'. The following year, she was commissioned by the BBC, to write the TV score to documentary 'THE CELTS'. Its minor success, and the rise of CLANNAD, enabled 'WEA' records in 1988 to give her record deal. Her first single for the label 'ORINOCO FLOW', became surprise UK No.1 later in October. • **Style:** Beautiful vocalist with atmospheric and dreamy landscapes that cannot be pigeonholed into pop or rock. • **Songwriters:** ENYA pens songs and collaborates with her backing musicians ROMA and NICKY RYAN (her producer from 1988). • **Trivia:** Her father LED BRENNAN was a member of showband SLIEVE FOY BAND.

Recommended: WATERMARK (*7) / SHEPHERD MOONS (*6).

ENYA – vocals, keyboards, percussion (ex-CLANNAD)

Island | not issued

Oct 85. (lp)(c) **THE FROG PRINCE** | -

B.B.C. | not issued

Feb 87. (lp)(c) **THE CELTS** (recorded 1980) 69 | -

– The Celts / Aldebaran / I want tomorrow / March of the Celts / Deireadh on tuath / The Sun in the stream / To go beyond (1) / Epona / Fairytale / Epona Triad: St. Patrick Cu Chulainn-oisin / Boadicea / Bard dance / Dan y dur / To go beyond (II). *(re-iss.Dec88 as 'ENYA') ('THE CELTS' re-iss.+cd.Nov92 on 'WEA', hit UK No.10, extra track 'Portrait (out of the blue)').*

Feb 87. (7") **I WANT TOMORROW. / THE CELTS THEME**

(12"+=)(cd-s+=) – To Go Beyond I + II. *(re-iss.Nov88)*

W.E.A. | Geffen

Sep 88. (lp)(c)(cd) **WATERMARK** 5 | 25 Mar 89

– Watermark / Cursum perficio / On your shore / Storms in Africa / Exile / Miss Clare remembers / Orinoco flow / Evening falls / River / The longships / Na laetha geal m'oige / Storms in Africa (part II). *(re-iss.Oct91 hit No.44, Jul92-No.43)*

Oct 88. (7") **ORINOCO FLOW. / OUT OF THE BLUE** 1 | 24 Feb 89

(12"+=) – Smaotin.

Dec 88. (7") **EVENING FALLS. / OICHE CHIUN (SILENT NIGHT)** 20

(12"+=)(cd-s+=) – Morning glory.

Feb 89. (7") **STORMS IN AFRICA (pt.II)./STORMS IN AFRICA** 41

(12"+=)(3"cd-s+=) – The Celts / Aldebaran. *(re-dist.May89)*

May 91. (7")(c-s) **EXILE. / ON YOUR SHORE**

(12"+=)(cd-s+=) – Watermark / River.

W.E.A. | Reprise

Oct 91. (7") **CARIBBEAN BLUE. / ORINOCO FLOW** 13 | 79 Feb92

(cd-s+=) – Angels.

(cd-s++=) – As baile / Oriel window.

—— album guests **ROMA RYAN** – percussion / **STEVE SIDWELL** – cornet / **NICKY RYAN** and **ANDY DUNCAN** – perc. / **LIAM O'FLIONN** – vulcan pipes / **ROY JEWITT** – clarinet

Nov 91. (cd)(c)(lp) **SHEPHERD MOONS** 1 | 17

– Shepherd moons / Caribbean blue / How can I keep from singing? / Ebudae / Angeles / No holly for Miss Quinn / Book of days / Evacuee / Lothlorien / Marble halls / Afer Ventus / Smaonte . . .

Dec 91. (7") **HOW CAN I KEEP FROM SINGING?. / ORCHE CHIUN (SILENT NIGHT)** 13

(12"+=)(cd-s+=) – 'S Fagain mo baile.

Jul 92. (7") **BOOK OF DAYS. / AS BAILE** 10

(cd-s) – ('A'side) / Watermark / On your shoe / Exile.

Nov 92. (7")(c-s) **THE CELTS. / OFCHE CHIUN** 29

(cd-s+=) – S'fagain mobhaile.

Nov 95. (7")(c-s)(cd-s) **ANYWHERE IS. / BOADICEA** 7

(cd-s+=) – Oriel window.

(cd-s) – ('A'side) / Book of days / Caribbean blue / Orinoco flow.

Nov 95. (cd)(c) **THE MEMORY OF TREES** 5 | 9

– The memory of trees / Anywhere is / Pax deorum / Athair ar neamh / From where I am / China roses / Hope has a place / Tea-house moon / Once you had gold / La sonadora / On my way home.

Melissa ETHERIDGE

Born: 1961, Leavenworth, Kansas, USA. Studied guitar at Boston's Berklee College Of Music, before being found playing live at Long Beach, California (where she now lives) by CHRIS BLACKWELL of 'Island' records. Her eponymous debut album released in 1988, made headway with growing audience. It finally hit US Top 30 a year later and was nominated for a Grammy. • **Style:** Soft-rock blonde with vox similar to BONNIE TYLER, although looking a touch LITA FORD of late. • **Songwriters:** Self penned except a few each album with co-producer and bass player KEVIN McCORMICK. • **Trivia:** After writing for 'Weeds' film in 1988, she provided backing vox for DON HENLEY's 'New York Minute'. BONO of U2 guested on her second album 'BRAVE AND CRAZY'.

Recommended: NEVER ENOUGH (*6)

MELISSA ETHERIDGE – vocals, guitar, piano / **KEVIN McCORMICK** – bass / **CRAIG KRAMPF** – drums, percussion / **WADDY WACHTEL + JOHNNY LEE SCHELL** – guitars / **SCOTT THURSTON + WALLY BADAROU** – keyboards

Island | Island

Apr 88. (7") **SIMILIAR FEATURES. / I WANT YOU**

(12"+=)(cd-s+=) – Don't you need.

May 88. (lp)(c)(cd) **MELISSA ETHERIDGE** | 22

– Similiar features / Chrome plated heart / Like the way I do / Precious pain / Don't you need / The late September dogs / Occasionally / Watching you / Bring me some water / I want you.

Jun 88. (7") **DON'T YOU NEED. / PRECIOUS PAIN**

(12"+=) – ('A'live).

(cd-s++=) – Similiar features.

Feb 89. (7") **BRING ME SOME WATER. / OCCASIONALLY**

(12"+=)(cd-s+=) – I want you.

Mar 89. (7") **SIMILAR FEATURES. / BRING ME SOME WATER** - | 94

—— **MAURICIO FRITZ LEWAK** – drums + **BERNIE LARSEN** – guitar repl. SCHELL + BADAROU

Jul 89. (7") **NO SOUVENIRS. / ('A'live)** | 95

(12"+=)(cd-s+=) – Brave and crazy (live).

Sep 89. (lp)(c)(cd) **BRAVE AND CRAZY** 63 | 22 Aug89

– No souvenirs / Brave and crazy / You used to love to dance / The angels / You can sleep while I drive / Testify / Let me go / My back door / Skin deep / Royal Station 4-16.

Nov 89. (7") **THE ANGELS. / ('A'live)**

(12"+=)(cd-s+=) – Chrome plated heart. *(re-iss.May90)*

1990. (7") **YOU CAN SLEEP WHILE I DRIVE. / THE LATE SEPTEMBER DOGS (live)**

(12"+=) – ('A'live).

—— **STEUART SMITH + MARK GOLDENBERG** – guitars repl. LARSEN + WACHTEL

1992. (7")(c-s) **DANCE WITHOUT SLEEPING. / AIN'T IT HEAVY**

(12"+=)(cd-s+=) – Similiar features.

Apr 92. (cd)(c)(lp) **NEVER ENOUGH** 56 | 21

– Ain't it heavy / 2001 / Dance without sleeping / Place your hand / Must be crazy for me / Meet me in the back / The boy feels strange / Keep it precious /

The letting go / It's for you.

Apr 92. (7") **AIN'T IT HEAVY. / THE BOYS FEEL STRANGE** □ □
(12"+=)(cd-s+=) – Royal Station 4-16 (live).

Jul 92. (7")(c-s) **2001. / ('A'remix)** □ □
(12"+=) – Meet me in the back / Testify.
(cd-s+=) – Meet me in the back / ('A'-12"remix).

Oct 93. (cd)(c)(lp) **YES I AM** □ 15
– I'm the only one / If I wanted to / Come to my window / Silent legacy / I will never be the same / All American girl / Yes I am / Resist / Ruins / Talking to my angel. *(re-iss.Apr94)*

Nov 93. (c-s) **I'M THE ONLY ONE. / ('A'version)** □ 8
(12"+=)(cd-s+=) – Yes I am.

Apr 94. (c-ep)(cd-ep) **COME TO MY WINDOW / AIN'T IT HEAVY / THE LETTING GO / I'M THE ONLY ONE** □ 22

Feb 95. (c-s)(cd-s) **IF I WANTED TO / LIKE HIS . . .** - 16

Oct 95. (c-s) **YOUR LITTLE SECRET / ALL AMERICAN GIRL** □ □
(cd-s+=) – Bring me some water / Skin deep.

Nov 95. (cd)(c) **YOUR LITTLE SECRET** □ 6
– Your little secret / I really like you / Nowhere to go / An unusual kiss / I want to come over / All the way to Heaven / I could have been you / Shriner's Park / Change / This war is over.

. . . Jan – Jun '96 stop press . . .

Feb 96. (single) **I WANT TO COME OVER** - 22

EURYTHMICS

Formed: By LENNOX and STEWART in London, England . . . where they met in 1976. They formed The CATCH in 1977 with PETE COOMBES, but by 1979 they had evolved into The TOURISTS. They signed to 'Logo' records, and scored Top 10 hits with some fine pop singles (i.e.'I ONLY WANT TO BE WITH YOU' & 'SO GOOD TO BE BACK HOME'), before breaking with COOMBES late in 1980. The duo, now The EURYTHMICS became live-in lovers, and after a flop Conny Plank produced debut album 'IN THE GARDEN', they registered in the 1983 charts with No.2 single 'SWEET DREAMS'. They went on to hit No.1 in the States, and secured a regular place in both charts throughout the 80's until they split in 1990. In 1992 ANNIE LENNOX went solo, and disappointed no-one with her appropriately titled album 'ANNIE LENNOX – DIVA', which later received Best Album award. • **Style:** Innovative pop-rock, that shifted between electronic dance-rock and melancholy romantic pop. ANNIE became the queen chameleon of video, changing visually with each new acting out portrayal. In 1985, she acted (approx. 10 lines) alongside Al Pacino and Donald Sutherland in the flop film 'Revolution'. • **Songwriters:** COOMBES penned songs in The TOURISTS, except I ONLY WANT TO BE WITH YOU (Dusty Springfield). DAVE and ANNIE wrote together in The EURYTHMICS. Now a solo writer, ANNIE LENNOX covered KEEP YOUNG AND BEAUTIFUL (Al Dubin-Harry Warren) / FEEL THE NEED (Detroit Emeralds) / RIVER DEEP MOUNTAIN HIGH (Phil Spector) / DON'T LET ME DOWN (Beatles) / NO MORE "I LOVE YOU'S" (The Lover Speaks) / TAKE ME TO THE RIVER (Al Green) / A WHITER SHADE OF PALE (Procol Harum) / DON'T LET IT BRING YOU DOWN (Neil Young) / TRAIN IN VAIN (Clash) / I CAN'T GET NEXT TO YOU (Strong-Whitfield) / DOWNTOWN LIGHTS (Blue Nile) / THE THIN BLUE LINE BETWEEN LOVE AND HATE (Pretenders; hit) / WAITING IN VAIN (Bob Marley) / SOMETHING SO RIGHT (Paul Simon) / LADIES OF THE CANYON (Joni Mitchell) / I'M ALWAYS TOUCHED BY YOUR PRESENCE DEAR (Blondie). DAVE STEWART's VEGAS covered SHE (Charles Aznavour). • **Trivia:** In Mar'84 ANNIE, now not involved intimately with DAVE, married German Hare Krishna RADHA RAMAR, but this only lasted 6 months. She married again in the late 80's?, and gave birth to first child in Spring 1993. On 1st of August, DAVE married SHAKESPEAR'S SISTER & ex-BANANARAMA singer SIOBHAN FAHEY. He has also produced many artists including FEARGAL SHARKEY, MARIA McKEE, DARYL HALL, BOB GELDOF, BOB DYLAN. TOM PETTY, MICK JAGGER, BORIS GREBENSHIKOV (Russian rocker) and LONDONBEAT.

Recommended: EURYTHMICS GREATEST HITS (*8). ANNIE LENNOX solo:- ANNIE LENNOX – DIVA (*7).

The CATCH

ANNIE LENNOX (b. 25 Dec'54, Aberdeen, Scotland) – vocals, keyboards, flute / **DAVE STEWART** (b. 9 Sep'52, Sunderland, England) – guitar, keyboards, etc. (ex-LONGDANCER) / **PETE COOMBES** – guitar, vocals

Logo / not issued

Nov 77. (7") **BORDERLINE. / BLACK BLOOD** □ -

TOURISTS

adding **EDDY CHIN** – bass / **JIM TOOMEY** – drums

Logo / R.C.A.

May 79. (7") **BLIND AMONG THE FLOWERS. / HE WHO LAUGHS LAST LAUGHS LONGEST** 52 □
(d7"+=) – The golden lamp / Wrecked

Jun 79. (lp)(c) **THE TOURISTS** 72 □
– Blind among the flowers / Save me / Fool's paradise / Can't stop laughing / Don't get left behind / Another English day / Deadly kiss / Ain't no room / The loneliest man in the world / Useless duration of time / He who laughs last laughs longest / Just like you. *(re-iss.Jun81 on 'R.C.A.')*

Aug 79. (7")(7"pic-d) **THE LONELIEST MAN IN THE WORLD. / DON'T GET LEFT BEHIND** 32 □

Oct 79. (lp)(c) **REALITY EFFECT** 23 □
– It doesn't have to be this way / I only want to be with you / In the morning / All life's tragedies / Everywhere you look / So good to be back home / Nothing to do / Circular fever / In my mind / Something in the air tonight / Summers night.

Oct 79. (7") **I ONLY WANT TO BE WITH YOU. / SUMMER NIGHT** 4 83 Apr 80

Jan 80. (7") **SO GOOD TO BE BACK HOME. / CIRCULAR SAW** 6 □

R.C.A. / R.C.A.

Sep 80. (7") **DON'T SAY I TOLD YOU SO. / STRANGE SKY** 40 □

Oct 80. (lp)(c) **LUMINOUS BASEMENT** 75 □
– Walls and foundations / Don't say I told you so / Week days / So you want to go away now / One step nearer the edge / Angels and demons / Talk to me / Round round blues / Let's take a walk / Time drags so slow / I'm going to change my mind. *(free-7"yellow-w/a)* **FROM THE MIDDLE ROOM. / INTO THE FUTURE**

— After The TOURISTS split late '80.

EURYTHMICS

were formed by **ANNIE LENNOX** and **DAVE STEWART** with guests **ROBERT GORL** and **GABI DELGADO** of D.A.F. / **JAKI LIEBEZEIT** – percussion and **HOLGER CZUKAY** – bass (both ex-CAN)

R.C.A. / R.C.A.

Jun 81. (7")(12") **NEVER GONNA CRY AGAIN. / LE SINISTRE** 63 □

Aug 81. (7") **BELINDA. / HEARTBEAT, HEARTBEAT** □ □

Oct 81. (lp)(c) **IN THE GARDEN** □ □
– English summer / Belinda / Take me to your heart / She's invisible now / Your time will come / Caveman head / Never gonna cry again / All the young (people of today) / Sing sing / Revenge. *(re-iss.Mar84) (cd-iss.Jan87 & Sep91)*

— **ANNIE** and **DAVE** now augmented with synthesisers, also guests **CLEM BURKE** – drums (ex-BLONDIE, who later joined RAMONES in '87)

Mar 82. (7") **THIS IS THE HOUSE. / HOME IS WHERE THE HEART IS** □ □
(12") – ('A'side) / Take me to your heart (live) / 4-4 In leather (live) / Never gonna cry again (live) / Your time will come (live).

Jun 82. (7") **THE WALK. / STEP ON THE BEAST / THE WALK (pt.2)** □ □
(12") – The walk (pt.1 & 2) / -Invisible hands / Dr.Trash.

Sep 82. (7")(7"pic-d) **LOVE IS A STRANGER. / MONKEY MONKEY** 54 □
(12"+=) – Let's just close our eyes. *(re-iss.Apr83 reached no.6, US re-iss.Sep83 reached 23)*

Jan 83. (7")(7"pic-d) **SWEET DREAMS (ARE MADE OF THIS). / I COULD GIVE YOU (A MIRROR)** 2 1 May 83
(12"+=) – Baby's gone blue.

Feb 83. (lp)(c)(pic-lp) **SWEET DREAMS (ARE MADE OF THIS)** 3 15 May 83
– Sweet dreams (are made of this) / Jennifer / This city never sleeps / This is the house / Somebody told me / The walk / I've got an angel / Love is a stranger / Wrap it up / I could give you (a mirror). *(re-iss.Aug84) (cd-iss.Jan84 & re-iss.Oct87)*

Jul 83. (7")(7"pic-d) **WHO'S THAT GIRL. / YOU TAKE SOME LENTILS . . . AND YOU TAKE SOME RICE** 3 -
(12"+=) – A.B.C. (freeform).

Oct 83. (7")(7"pic-d) **RIGHT BY YOUR SIDE. / ('A'party mix)** 10 29 Jul 84
(12"+=) – ('A'&'B' special mix) / Plus something else.
(free-c-s.with 7") – Intro speech / Step on the beast / Invisible hands / Angel (dub) / Satellite of love.

— **ANNIE** and **DAVE** were augmented on album by **CLEM** – drums plus **DICK CUTHELL** – brass MARTIN DOBSON – horns / **DEAN GARCIA** – bass(above 3 also went on tour adding) **VIC MARTIN** – synthesizers / **PETE PHIPPS** – drums / and backing singers **GILL O'DONOVAN, SUZIE O'LISZT and MAGGIE RYDER**

Nov 83. (lp)(c) **TOUCH** 1 7 Jan 84
– Here comes the rain again / Regrets / Right by your side / Cool blue / Who's that girl? / The first cut / Aqua / No fear, no hurt, no pain (no broken hearts) / Paint a rumour. *(cd-iss.Sep84) (re-iss.+cd.Sep89) (also iss.pic-lp)*

Jan 84. (7")(7"pic-d) **HERE COMES THE RAIN AGAIN. / PAINT A RUMOUR** 8 4

(12"+=) – This city never sleeps (live).

Apr 84. (7") **WHO'S THAT GIRL?. / AQUA** [-] [21]

Jun 84. (m-lp)(c)(cd) **TOUCH DANCE** (remixes) [31] [ ]
– The first cut (instrumental) / Cool blue (instrumental) / Paint a rumour (instrumental) / The first cut / Cool blue / Paint a rumour / Regrets. *(cd-iss.Dec91)*

Virgin R.C.A.

Oct 84. (7") **SEXCRIME (NINETEEN EIGHTY-FOUR). / I DID IT JUST THE SAME** [4] [81]
(12")(12"pic-d) – ('A'extended).

Nov 84. (lp)(c)(cd) **1984 – FOR THE LOVE OF BIG BROTHER (soundtrack)** [23] [93]
– I did it just the same / Julia / Sexcrime (nineteen eighty-four) / Doubleplusgood / For the love of big brother / Ministry of love / Winston's diary / Room 101 / Greetings from a dead man. *(re-iss.Jan88) (cd-iss.Apr89 & Dec95)*

Jan 85. (7")(7"pic-d) **JULIA. / MINISTRY OF LOVE** [44] [ ]
(12"+=) – ('A'extended).

R.C.A. R.C.A.

Apr 85. (7")(12")(12"red)(12"yellow)(12"blue) **WOULD I LIE TO YOU? / HERE COMES THAT SINKING FEELING** [11] [5]
(also available on d7"red / blue / or yellow)

May 85. (lp)(c)(cd) **BE YOURSELF TONIGHT** [3] [9]
– It's alright (baby's coming back) / Would I lie to you / There must be an angel (playing with my heart) / I love you like a ball and chain / Sisters are doin' it for themselves / Conditioned soul / Adrian / Here comes that sinking feeling / Better to have lost in love (than never to have loved at all). *(re-iss.+cd.May90)*

Jun 85. (7") **THERE MUST BE AN ANGEL (PLAYING WITH MY HEART). / GROWN UP GIRLS** [1] [22]
(12"+=) – ('A'dance mix).

Oct 85. (7")(12") **SISTERS ARE DOIN' IT FOR THEMSELVES. ("EURYTHMICS & ARETHA FRANKLIN") / I LOVE YOU LIKE A BALL AND CHAIN** [9] [18]

Jan 86. (7") **IT'S ALRIGHT (BABY'S COMING BACK). / CONDITIONED SOUL** [12] [78]
(12"+=) – Tous les garcons et les filles.

Jun 86. (7") **WHEN TOMORROW COMES. / TAKE YOUR PAIN AWAY** [30] [ ]
(12"+=) – ('A'orchestral).

Jul 86. (lp)(c)(cd) **REVENGE** [3] [12]
– Let's go / Take your pain away / A little of you / Thorn in my side / In this town / I remember you / Missionary man / The last time / When tomorrow comes / The miracle of love.

Aug 86. (7") **THORN IN MY SIDE. / IN THIS TOWN** [5] [68] Oct 86
(12"+=) – ('A'extended).

Aug 86. (7")(12") **MISSIONARY MAN. / TAKE YOUR PAIN AWAY** [-] [14]

Nov 86. (7")(7"pic-d) **THE MIRACLE OF LOVE. / WHEN TOMORROW COMES (live)** [23] [ ]
(12"+=) – Who's that girl (live).
(12"pic-d+=) – Don't ask me why.

Feb 87. (7") **MISSIONARY MAN. / THE LAST TIME (live)** [31] [-]
(12"+=) – ('A'extended).

Oct 87. (7") **BEETHOVEN (I LOVE TO LISTEN TO). / HEAVEN** [25] [ ]
(10"+=)(12"+=)(cd-s+=) – ('A'dance mix).

Nov 87. (lp)(c)(cd) **SAVAGE** [7] [41]
– Beethoven (I love to listen to) / I've got a lover (back in Japan) / Do you want to break up? / You have placed a chill in my heart / Shame / Savage / I need a man / Put the blame on me / Heaven / Wide eyed girl / I need you / Brand new day. *(re-iss.cd May93)*

Dec 87. (7") **SHAME. / I'VE GOT A LOVER (BACK IN JAPAN)** [41] [ ]
(12"+=) – ('A'dance mix).
(cd-s+=) – There must be an angel (playing with my heart).

Dec 87. (7") **I NEED A MAN. / HEAVEN** [-] [46]

Mar 88. (7") **I NEED A MAN. / I NEED YOU** [26] [-]
(12"+=) – ('A'macho mix).
(cd-s++=) – Missionary man (live).
(10"+=) – There must be an angel (playing with my heart).
(7"m+=) – I need a man (live).

May 88. (7") **YOU HAVE PLACED A CHILL IN MY HEART. / ('A'acoustic mix)** [16] [64]
(12"+=) – ('A'dance).
(cd-s++=) – Do you want to break up / Here comes the rain again (live).

In Oct'88, ANNIE was credited on AL GREEN ⇒ single PUT A LITTLE LOVE IN YOUR HEART

R.C.A. Arista

Aug 89. (7")(c-s) **REVIVAL. / PRECIOUS** [26] [ ]
(12"+=)(cd-s+=) – ('A'extended-ET dance mix).

Sep 89. (lp)(c)(cd) **WE TOO ARE ONE** [1] [34]
– We two are one / The King and Queen of America / (My my) Baby's gonna cry / Don't ask me why / Angel / Revival / You hurt me (and I hate you) / Sylvia / How long? / When the day goes down. *(re-iss.cd Jun94)*

Oct 89. (7")(c-s) **DON'T ASK ME WHY. / RICH GIRL** [25] [40] Sep 89
(12"+=)(cd-s+=)(12"pic-d+=) – Sylvia.
(12"+=)(cd-s+=) – ('A'version) / When the day goes down.

Jan 90. (7")(c-s) **KING AND QUEEN OF AMERICA (remix). / SEE NO EVIL** [29] [ ]
(12") – ('A'dance mix) / ('B'side) / ('A'dub mix).
(12"+=)(cd-s+=) – There must be an angel (playin' with my heart) (live) / I love you like a ball and chain (live).
(12"++=)(cd-s++=) – ('A'dub mix).

Apr 90. (7")(c-s) **ANGEL. / ANGEL (choir version)** [23] [-]
(12"+=)(cd-s+=) – Missionary man (acoustic).
(12") – ('A'remix) / Sweet dreams (are made of this) mix

Apr 90. (c-s) **ANGEL / PRECIOUS** [-] [ ]

Jun 90. (c-s) **(MY MY) BABY'S GONNA CRY / ('A'acoustic)** [-] [ ]

—— Disbanded after last album.

– compilations, others, etc. –

Nov 88. Virgin; (3"cd-ep)(5"cd-ep) **SEXCRIME (1984 extended mix) / JULIA (extended) / I DID IT JUST THE SAME** [ ] [ ]

Mar 89. R.C.A.; (3"cd-ep) **SWEET DREAMS (ARE MADE OF THIS) / I COULD GIVE YOU (A MIRROR) / HERE COMES THE RAIN AGAIN / PAINT A RUMOUR** [ ] [ ]

Mar 91. R.C.A.; (cd)(c)(lp) **EURYTHMICS' GREATEST HITS** [1] [72]
– Love is a stranger / Sweet dreams (are made of this) / Who's that girl? / Right by your side / Here comes the rain again / There must be an angel (playing with my heart) / Sisters are doin' it for themselves / It's alright (baby's coming back) / When tomorrow comes / You have placed a chill in my heart / Sexcrime (nineteen eighty-four) / Thorn in my side Don't ask me why. *(cd/c+=)* – Miracle of love / Angel / Would I lie to you? / Missionary man / I need a man.

Mar 91. R.C.A.; (7")(c-s) **LOVE IS A STRANGER. / JULIA** [46] [ ]
(12"+=)(cd-s+=) – ('A'obsession mix) / There must be an angel (playin' with my heart).
(12") – ('A'diff.mix) / ('A'instrumental) / ('A'-Coldcut mix).

Nov 91. R.C.A.; (7")(c-s) **SWEET DREAMS (ARE MADE OF THIS) '91. / KING AND QUEEN OF AMERICA** [48] [ ]
(12") – ('A'side) / ('A'house mix) / ('A'nightmare mix) / ('A'hot remix).
(cd-s) – ('A'side) / Beethoven (I love to listen to) / Shame / This city never sleeps.

Nov 93. R.C.A.; (d-cd)(d-c) **EURYTHMICS LIVE 1983-1989 (live)** [22] [ ]
– Never gonna cry again / Love is a stranger / Sweet dreams (are made of this) / This city never sleeps / Somebody told me / Who's that girl? / Right by your side / Here comes the rain again / Sex crime / I love you like a ball and chain / There must be an angel (playing with my heart) / Thorn in my side / Let's go / Missionary man / The last time / Miracle of love / I need a man / We two are one / (My my) Baby's gonna cry / Don't ask me why / Angel. *(cd includes free 7 track EP) (re-iss.Oct95)*

Apr 95. R.C.A.; (cd) **BE YOURSELF TONIGHT / REVENGE** [ ] [-]

ANNIE LENNOX

in 1992 with **STEPHEN LIPSON** – guitars, prog., keyboards / **PETER-JOHN VITTESE** – keyboards, prog., recorder / **MARIUS DE VRIES** – prog., keys/ also **LOUIS JARDIM** – percussion / **ED SHEARMUR** – piano / **KEITH LeBLANC** – drums / **DOUG WIMBUSH** – bass / **KENJI JAMMER** – guitar / **STEVE JANSON** – drum pro / **DAVE DeFRIES** – trumpet / **GAVON WRIGHT** – violin / **PAUL MOORE** – keyboards (co-writer on 1)

R.C.A. Arista

Mar 92. (7")(c-s) **WHY. / PRIMITIVE** [5] [34]
(12"+=//+cd-s+=) – Keep young and beautiful./ / ('A'instrumental).

Apr 92. (cd)(c)(lp) **ANNIE LENNOX – DIVA** [1] [27]
– Why / Walking on broken glass / Precious / Legend in my living room / Cold / Money can't buy it / Little bird / Primitive / Stay by me / The gift.

May 92. (7")(c-s) **PRECIOUS. / ('A'version)** [23] [ ]
(cd-s+=) – Step by step / Why.

Aug 92. (7")(c-s)(cd-s) **WALKING ON BROKEN GLASS. / LEGEND IN MY LIVING ROOM** [8] [14]
(12"+=)(cd-s+=) – Don't let me down.

Oct 92. (7")(c-s) **COLD. / ('A'live)** [26] [ ]
(c-s+=) – River deep mountain high / You have placed a chill in my heart.
(cd-s) – ('A'side) / Why / The gift / Walking on broken glass.
(cd-s) – ('A'side) / It's alright / Here comes the rain again / You have placed a chill in my heart.

Feb 93. (7")(c-s)(12")(cd-s) **LITTLE BIRD. / LOVE SONG FOR A VAMPIRE** [3] [49]
(cd-s+=)/ /(cd-s+=)/ /(cd-s+=) – Feel the need (live). / / River deep mountain high (live). / / Don't let me down (live).

—— with **STEPHEN LIPSON** -programmer, guitar, keyboards, bass

Feb 95. (7")(c-s) **NO MORE I LOVE YOU'S. / LADIES OF THE CANYON** [2] [23]
(cd-s+=) – Love song for a vampire.
(cd-s) – ('A'side) / Why (acoustic) / Cold (acoustic) / Walking on broken glass (acoustic).

Mar 95. (cd)(c)(lp) **MEDUSA** [1] [11]
– No more "I love you's" / Take me to the river / A whiter shade of pale / Don't let it bring you down / Train in vain / I can't get next to you / Downtown lights / The thin line between love and hate / Waiting in vain / Something so right. *(re-iss.d-cd Dec95 w/ free 'LIVE IN CENTRAL PARK')*

May 95. (c-s) **A WHITER SHADE OF PALE / HEAVEN** [16] [ ]
(cd-s+=) – I'm always touched by your presence dear / Love song for a vampire.
(cd-s) – ('A'side) / Don't let it bring you down / You have placed a chill in my

heart / Here comes the rain again.

Sep 95. (12")(c-s)(cd-s) **WAITING IN VAIN. / NO MORE "I LOVE YOU'S"** [31] [ ]
(cd-s+=) – Train in vain.
(cd-s+=) – (interview) / ('A'-Strong body mix).
(cd-s) – ('A'side) / ('A'-Strong body mix) / ('A'-Howie B mix).
(cd-s) – ('A'side) / Train in vain (3 mixes).

(below feat.PAUL SIMON)

Nov 95. (c-s)(cd-s) **SOMETHING SO RIGHT / SWEET DREAMS (ARE MADE OF THIS)** [44] [ ]
(cd-s+=) – Who's that girl / I love you like a ball and chain.
(cd-s) – ('A'side) / Waiting in vain live) / Something so right (live) / Money can't buy it.

— as DAVID A. STEWART he recorded single 'AVENUE D' with ETTA JAMES (May89)

DAVID A. STEWART & CANDY DULFER

(CANDY solo artist and ex-PRINCE)

Anxious-RCA / R.C.A.

Feb 90. (7")(c-s) **LILY WAS HERE. / LILY ROBS THE BANK** [7] [11] Apr 91
(12"+=)(cd-s+=) – ('A'space centre medical unit mix).

Apr 90. (cd)(c)(lp) **LILY WAS HERE (Soundtrack)** [35] [ ]
– Lily was here / The pink building / Lily robs the bank / Toyshop robbery / Toys on the sidewalk / The good hotel / Second chance / Here comes the rain again / Alone in the city / Toyshop (part one) / The coffin / Teletype / Inside the pink building / Percussion jam / Peaches / Lily was here (reprise).

DAVID A. STEWART

R.C.A. / R.C.A.

Oct 91. (cd)(c)(lp) **JUTE CITY** (BBC Soundtrack) [ ] [ ]
– Jute City / Dead planets / Last love / In Duncan's arms / Black wedding / Jute City revisited / Contaminated / See no evil / Jigula / The lords theme / Hats off to Hector / Deep waters / Dark wells.

Oct 91. (7")(c-s) **JUTE CITY. / JUTE CITY (Caroline's mix)** [ ] [ ]
(cd-s+=) – Dead planet / Black wedding.
(12") – ('A'remix) / (above extra 2).

DAVE STEWART AND THE SPIRITUAL COWBOYS

with **IZZY MAE DOORITE** – guitar, vocals / **WILD MONDO** – keyboards, vocals / **CHRISTOPHER D.JAMES** – bass, vocals / **MARTIN O'DALE** – drumwarp, vocals / **ZAC BARTEL** – drum prog. / **JOHN TEXAS TURNBULL** – electric bow semi-acoustic

R.C.A. / R.C.A.

Aug 90. (7")(c-s) **JACK TALKING. / SUICIDE SID** [69] [ ]
(12"+=)(cd-s+=) – Love calculator.

Sep 90. (cd)(c)(lp) **DAVE STEWART AND THE SPIRITUAL COWBOYS** [38] [ ]
– Soul years / King of the hypocrites / Diamond avenue / This little town / On fire / Heaven and Earth / Love shines / Party town / Mr.Reed / Fashion bomb / Jack talking / Hey Johnny / The Devil's just been using you / Spiritual love.

Oct 90. (7")(12")(c-s) **LOVE SHINES. / MARIANNE** [ ] [-]
(10"+=)/ /(cd-s+=) – Instant karma (live). / / Victim of fate.

Feb 91. (c-s) **PARTY TOWN (party on down mix). / PARTY TOWN (politico mix)** [-] [ ]
(cd-s+=) Love calculator. / Suicidal Sid

May 91. (c-s) **LOVE SHINES. / INSTANT KARMA** [-] [ ]

Sep 91. (7")(c-s) **CROWN OF MADNESS. / FRUSTRATION** [ ] [ ]
(12"+=)(cd-s+=) – If that's love.
(cd-s) – ('A'side) / Honest (live) / On fire (live) / Motorcycle mystics (live).

Oct 91. (cd)(c)(lp) **HONEST** [ ] [ ]
-Honest / Whole wide world / Count of madness / Out of reach / You've lost / Fool's parradise / Motorcycle mystery / Impossible / Here we go again / Here she comes / Fade away / Cat with a tale / R U satisfied

Nov 91. (7")(c-s) **OUT OF REACH. / DAY OF THE DEAD** [ ] [ ]
(12"+=)(cd-s+=) – The ballad of Michael Pain.

— DAVE STEWART teamed up with TERRY HALL to form VEGAS.

DAVE STEWART

with **BOOTSY COLLINS** – bass, space bass / **BERNIE WORRELL** – keyboards / **JEROME 'BIG FOOT' BRAILEY** – drums + guests **LAURIE ANDERSON** (electric violin, vox on 'Kinky Sweetheart') / **LOU REED** (guitar solo on 'You Talk a lot' w /saxophone **DAVE SANBORN**) / **CARLY SIMON** (argumented w/**SANBORN;** last track) / **TERRY DISLEY** – keyboards

East West / Warners

Aug 94. (c-s)(cd-s) **HEART OF STONE / PEACE IN WARTIME / COAL NIGHTS** [36] [ ]
(12"+=)(cd-s+=) – Sure is Pure (remixes).

Sep 94. (cd)(c) **GREETINGS FROM THE GUTTER** [ ] [ ]
– Heart of stone / Greetings from the gutter / Jealousy / St.Valentine's day / Kinky sweetheart / Damien save me / Crazy sister / You talk a lot / Tragedy Street / Chelsea lovers / Oh no, not you again.

Apr 95. (c-s) **JEALOUSY / BLIND LEADING THE BLIND** [ ] [ ]
(cd-s+=) – Tragedy Street.

Oct 95. (c-s) **SECRET / ('A'-SPS vocal mix)** [ ] [ ]
(cd-s+=) – Kinky sweetheart.
(12"+=) – ('A'-Posterity mix) / ('A'-SPS mad club mix).

EVERLAST (see under ⇒ HOUSE OF PAIN)

EVER READY CALL (see under ⇒ BYRDS)

EVERYTHING BUT THE GIRL

Formed: Hull, England ... mid 1982 by ex-Hull university graduates TRACEY THORN and BEN WATT. They had both recorded solo for indie label 'Cherry Red', before venturing in 1983 onto 'WEA' subsidiary 'Blanco Y Negro' run by Geoff Travis & Mike Alway. They immediately struck gold, with 'EACH AND EVERY ONE', making the UK Top 30. It's parent album 'EDEN', was their first of 5 to hit or nearly hit, the UK Top 20. These were obviously helped to do so, by the large experienced ensemble of musicians the duo employed. • **Style:** Publicly shy melancholy duo, who blended together light jazz, folk and agitpop. Their influences ranged from COLE PORTER to the modern day JOHN MARTYN. 1995 saw a significant development in their sound as they became more dance-orientated. The results were astonishing – Top 3 success on both sides of the Atlantic with the Todd Terry remix of 'MISSING'. It looks set to continue in 1996 with the highly acclaimed and commerically successful follow-up single + album 'WALKING WOUNDED'. • **Songwriters:** Most written by duo or individually, except the covers; NIGHT AND DAY (Cole Porter) / I DON'T WANT TO TALK ABOUT IT (c.Danny Whitten, of Crazy Horse; Rod Stewart hit) / KID (Pretenders) / ALFIE (hit; Cilla Black) / DOWNTOWN TRAIN (Tom Waits) / I FALL TO PIECES (Patsy Cline) / TAKE ME (Womack And Womack) / ON MY MIND (?) / NO PLACE LIKE HOME (from 'Wizard Of Oz') / LOVE IS STRANGE (Everly Brothers) / TOUGHER THAN THE REST (Bruce Springsteen) / TIME AFTER TIME (Cyndi Lauper) / ALISON (Elvis Costello) / MY HEAD IS MY ONLY HOUSE UNLESS IT RAINS (Captain Beefheart) / THESE DAYS (Jackson Browne). TRACEY THORN solo:- FEMME FATALE (Velvet Underground). • **Trivia:** EVERYTHING BUT THE GIRL was the name of a local second hand store in Hull.

Recommended: HOME MOVIES (*7)

BEN WATT

solo releases

Cherry Red / not issued

Jun 81. (7") **CAN'T. / AUBADE / TOWER OF SILENCE** [ ] [-]

Apr 82. (12"ep) **SUMMER INTO WINTER (by "BEN WATT & ROBERT WYATT")** [ ] [-]
– Walter and John / Aquamarine / Slipping slowly / Another conversation with myself / A girl in winter.

Feb 83. (7") **SOME THINGS DON'T MATTER. / ON BOX HILL** [ ] [-]

Feb 83. (lp)(c) **NORTH MARINE DRIVE** [ ] [-]
– On Boxhill / Some things don't matter / Lucky one / Empty bottles / North marine drive / Waiting like mad / Thirst for knowledge / Long time no sea / You're gonna make me lonesome when you go. *(cd-iss.Jul93)*

TRACEY THORN

solo releases

Cherry Red / not issued

Aug 82. (m-lp) **A DISTANT SHORE** [ ] [-]
– Smalltown girl / Simply couldn't care / Seascape / Femme fatale / Dreamy / Plain sailing / New opened eyes / Too happy. *(re-iss.+cd+c.Aug93)*

Dec 82. (7") **PLAIN SAILING. / GOODBYE JOE** [ ] [-]

EVERYTHING BUT THE GIRL

TRACEY THORN (b.26 Sep'62) – vocals, guitar (ex-MARINE GIRLS, ex-solo) / **BEN WATT** (b. 6 Dec'62) – vocals, guitar, piano (ex-solo artist)

Jun 82. (7"m)(12"m) **NIGHT AND DAY. / FEELING DIZZY / ON MY MIND** [ ] [-]
(re-iss.12"/cd-s/7"-Jul93)

— with **SIMON BOOTH** – guitar (of WORKING WEEK, ex-WEEKEND) / **CHUCHO MERCHAN** – double bass / **CHARLES HAYWARD** – drums / **BOSCO DE OLIVEIRA** – percuss / **PETER KING** – alto saxophone / **NIGEL NASH** – tenor saxophone / **DICK PEARCE** – flugel trumpet

Blanco Y Negro | Sire

Apr 84. (7") **EACH AND EVERY ONE. / LAUGH YOU OUT THE HOUSE** [28] [ ]
(12"+=) – Never have been worse.

Jun 84. (lp)(c) **EDEN** [14] [ ]
– Each and every one / Bittersweet / Tender blue / Another bridge / The spice of life / The dustbowl / Crabwalk / Even so / Frost and fire / Fascination / I must confess / Soft touch. *(US-title EVERYTHING BUT THE GIRL)*

Jul 84. (7") **MINE. / EASY AS SIN** [58] [ ]
(12"+=) – Gun coloured love.

Sep 84. (7") **NATIVE LAND. / RIVER BED DRY** [73] [ ]
(12"+=) – Don't you go.

— now with **NEIL SCOTT** – guitars / **PHIL MOXHAM** – bass (ex-The GIST ex-YOUNG MARBLE GIANTS) / **JUNE MILES KINGSTON** – drums, vocals (ex-MODETTES, ex-FUN BOY THREE) and the wind section above

Mar 85. (7") **WHEN ALL'S WELL. / HEAVEN HELP ME** [ ] [ ]
(12"+=) – Kid.

Apr 85. (lp)(c)(cd) **LOVE NOT MONEY** [10] [ ]
– When all's well / Uglt little dreams / Shoot me down / Are you trying to be funny / Sean / Ballad of the times / Anytown / This love (not for sale) / Trouble and strife / Angel. *(c+=)* – Heaven help me / Kid.

May 85. (7") **ANGEL. / PIGEONS IN THE ATTIC ROOM / CHARMLESS CALLOW WAYS** [ ] [ ]
(12"+=) – Easy as sin.

— now **BEN** and **TRACEY** used new session people below plus an orchestra **CARA TIVEY** – keyboards / **MICKEY HARRIS** – bass / **PETER KING** – alto sax / **ROBERT PETERS** – drums (ex-DANGEROUS GIRLS)

Jul 86 (7") **COME ON HOME. / DRAINING THE BAR** [44] [ ]
(12"+=) – I fall to pieces / ('A' version).

Aug 86. (lp)(c)(cd) **BABY THE STARS SHINE BRIGHT** [22] [ ]
– Come on home / Don't leave me behind / A country mile / Cross my heart / Don't let the teardrops rust your shining heart / Careless / Sugar Finney / Come hell or high water / Fighting talk / Little Hitler.

Sep 86. (7") **DON'T LEAVE ME BEHIND. / ALFIE** [72] [-]
(12"+=) – Where's the playground Suzie.

Feb 87. (7") **DON'T LEAVE ME BEHIND. / DRAINING THE BAR** [-] [ ]

— **BEN and TRACEY** now with **PETER KING / IAN FRASER** – tenor saxophone / **STEVE PEARCE** – bass / **JAMES McMILLAN** – trumpet / **DAMON BUTCHER** – piano, synth.

Feb 88. (7") **THESE EARLY DAYS. / DYED IN THE GRAIN** [75] [ ]
(12"+=) – No place like home.
(12"+=) – ('A' demo) / Another day another dollar.

Mar 88. (lp)(c)(cd) **IDLEWILD** [13] [ ]
– Love is here where I live / These early days / I always was your girl / Oxford Street / The night I heard Caruso sing / Goodbye Sunday / Shadow on a harvest moon / Blue moon rose / Tears all over town / Lonesome for a place I know / Apron strings. *(re-iss.Jul88 +=)* – I don't wanna talk about it. *(re-iss.cd Nov94)*

Mar 88. (7") **I ALWAYS WAS YOUR GIRL. / HANG OUT THE FLAGS** [ ] [ ]
(12"+=) – Home from home.
(cd-s++=) – Almost blue.

Jun 88. (7") **I DON'T WANNA TALK ABOUT IT. / OXFORD STREET** [3] [ ]
(12"+=) – ('A' instrumental) / Shadow on a harvest moon.
(cd-s+=) – Come on home.

Sep 88. (7") **LOVE IS WHERE I LIVE. / LIVING ON A HONEYCOMB** [ ] [ ]
(12"+=) – Each and every one / How about me.

Dec 88. (7")(12") **THESE EARLY DAYS (remix). / DYED IN THE GRAIN** [ ] [ ]
(cd-s+=) – No place like home / Another day another dollar.

— duo now with **OMAR HAKIM** – drums / **JOHN PATITUCCI** – bass / **LARRY WILLIAMS** – synth.prog., piano / **LENNY CASTRO** – percussion / **MICHAEL LANDAU** – guitar / etc.

Jan 90. (7")(c-s) **DRIVING. / ME AND BOBBY D** [54] [ ]
(12"+=) – Easy as sin / I don't want to talk about it.
(cd-s+=) – ('A'version) / Downtown train.

Feb 90. (cd)(c)(lp) **THE LANGUAGE OF LIFE** [10] [77]
– Driving / Get back together / Meet me in the morning / Take me / Me and Bobby D / The language of life / Imagining America / My baby don't love me / Letting love go / The road. *(re-iss.cd Feb95)*

Mar 90. (7")(c-s) **TAKE ME. / DRIVING (acoustic)** [ ] [ ]
(12"+=)(cd-s+=) – ('A'remix).

1991. (cd) **ACOUSTIC** [-] [ ]

— now with **GEOFF GISCOYNE and STEVE PEARCE** – bass / **DICK OATTS** – saxophone / **RALPH SALMINS** – drums, percussion

Aug 91. (7") **OLD FRIENDS. / APRON STRINGS (live)** [ ] [ ]
(cd-s+=) – Politics aside (instrumental) / Back to the old house (live).

Sep 91. (cd)(c)(lp) **WORLDWIDE** [29] [ ]
– Old friends / Understanding / You lift me up / Talk to me like the sea / British summertime / Twin cities / Frozen river / One place / Politics aside / Boxing and pop music / Feel alright. *(re-iss.cd Feb95)*

Nov 91. (7") **TWIN CITIES. / MEET ME IN THE MORNING (live)** [ ] [ ]
(12"+=)(cd-s+=) – ('A'acapella) / Mine.

Feb 92. (7"ep)(12"ep)(c-ep)(cd-ep) **THE COVERS EP** [13] [ ]
– Love is strange / Tougher than the rest / Time after time / Alison.

Apr 93. (7")(c-s) **THE ONLY LIVING BOY IN NEW YORK. / BIRDS / HORSES IN THE ROOM** [42] [ ]
(12"+=)(cd-s+=) – Gabriel / Horses in the room.

May 93. (cd)(c)(lp) **HOME MOVIES – THE BEST OF EVERYTHING BUT THE GIRL** (compilation) [5] [ ]
– Each and every one / Another bridge / Fascination / Native land / Come on home / Cross my heart / Apron strings / I don't want to talk about it / The night I heard Caruso sing / Driving / Imagining America / Understanding / Twin cities / Love is strange / I didn't know I was looking for love / The only living boy in New York.

Jun 93. (7"ep)(c-ep)(cd-ep) **I DIDN'T KNOW I WAS LOOKING FOR LOVE. / MY HEAD IS MY ONLY HOUSE UNLESS IT RAINS / POLITICAL SCIENCE / A PIECE OF MY MIND** [72] [ ]

— with **DAVE MATTACKS** – drums / **DANNY THOMPSON** – double bass (both ex-FAIRPORT CONVENTION) / **MARTIN DITCHAM** – percussion / (guests) **RICHARD THOMPSON** – guitar / **PETER KING** – alto sax / **KATE ST.JOHN** – cor anglais

May 94. (7"ep)(c-ep)(cd-ep) **THE ROLLERCOASTER EP** [65] [ ]
– Rollercoaster / Straight back to you / Lights of Te Touan / I didn't know I was looking for love (demo).

Jun 94. (cd)(c)(lp) **AMPLIFIED HEART** [20] [ ]
– Rollercoaster / Troubled mind / I don't understand anything / Walking to you / Get me / Missing / Two star / We walk the same line / 25th December / Disenchanted. *(re-iss.cd/c Nov95, hit US 46)*

Aug 94. (c-ep)(cd-ep) **MISSING / EACH & EVERY ONE (live) / I DON'T WANT TO TALK ABOUT IT (live) / THESE DAYS (live)** [69] [ ]
(12"ep)(cd-ep) – ('A'side) / ('A'-Chris & James remix) / ('A'-Little Joey remix) / ('A'-Ultramarine remix).

Aug 95. (c-ep)(cd-ep) **MISSING – THE LIVE EP (live)** [69] [ ]
– Missing / Each and every one (live) / I don't want to talk about it (live) / These days (live).
(12")(cd-s) THE REMIX EP – ('A'-Chris & James full on club mix) / ('A'-Little Joey remix) / ('A'-Ultramarine mix.

Oct 95. (c-s) **MISSING (Todd Terry club mix) / ('A'-Amplified Heart album mix)** [3] [2]
(cd-s+=) – ('A'-radio edit) / ('A'-Rockin' blue mix) / ('A'-Chris & James full on club mix) / ('A'-Todd Terry's piece).
(12") – (all above except 'B'side).

. . . Jan – Jun '96 stop press . . .

Virgin | Virgin

Apr 96. (single) **WALKING WOUNDED** [6] [ ]
May 96. (cd)(c)(lp) **WALKING WOUNDED** [4] [37]
Jun 96. (single) **WRONG** [8] [68]

EXPLORERS (see under ⇒ ROXY MUSIC)

EXTREME

Formed: Boston, Massachusetts, USA . . . 1988 initially as The DREAM. Soon became EXTREME signing to A&M in 1987 through A&R man Bryan Huttenhower. Cracked charts early in '91, when single MORE THAN WORDS hit US No.1. In 1992, they paid tribute to recently deceased by playing QUEEN numbers at his benefit concert. • **Style:** Heavy ballad rock similar to CHEAP TRICK with danceable appeal and image. Initially influenced by QUEEN and KISS. • **Songwriters:** BETTENCOURT (also producer) and CHERONE. Cover on record LOVE OF MY LIFE (Queen), STRUTTER (Kiss). • **Trivia:** Unlike others of their genre, they were pro-Christian.

Recommended: PORNOGRAFFITTI (*5) / III SIDES TO EVERY STORY (*6)

THE DREAM

GARY CHERONE (b.26 Jul'61, Malden, Massachusetts) – vocals / **NUNO BETTENCOURT** (b.20 Sep'66, Azores, Portugal) – guitar, keyboards, vocals / **PAT BADGER** (b.22 Jul'67, Boston) – bass, vocals / **PAUL GEARY** (b.24 Jul'61, Medford, Massachusetts) – drums, percussion

not issued | Toppe

1985. (lp) **THE DREAM** [-] [ ]
-Take your time / The tender touch / Makes no sense / All over again / Tipsy on the brink of love / You / Here is the love / Desires / Suzanne / Wonderful world / Last Monday.

EXTREME

		A&M	A&M	
Mar 89.	(lp)(c)(cd) **EXTREME** – Little girls / Wind me up / Kid ego / Watching, waiting / Mutha (don't wanna go to school today) / Teachers pet / Big boys don't cry / Smoke signals / Flesh'n'blood / Rock a bye bye. *(cd+=)* – (1 track).		80	
Apr 89.	(7") **KID EGO. / FLESH'N'BLOOD** (12"+=) – Smoke signals. *(US; b-side)*			
May 91.	(7")(c-s) **GET THE FUNK OUT. / LIL' JACK HORNY** (12"+=) – Little girls (edit). (12"pic-d+=) – Nice place to visit. (cd-s+=) – Mutha (don't wanna go to school today).	19		
Jun 89.	(7") **TEACHER'S PET. / MUTHA (DON'T WANNA GO TO SCHOOL TODAY)**	-		
Feb 91.	(7") **MORE THAN WORDS. / GET THE FUNK OUT**	-	1	
May 91.	(cd)(c)(lp) **PORNOGRAFFITTI** – Decadence dance / Li'l Jack Horny / When I'm president / Get the funk out / More than words / Money (in God we trust) / It ('s a monster) / Pornograffitti / When I first missed you / Suzi (wants her all day what?) / He-man woman hater / Song for love. *(originally released UK Sep90)*	12	10	Aug 90
Jul 91.	(7")(c-s) **MORE THAN WORDS. / NICE PLACE TO VISIT** (cd-s+=) – Little girls. (12"++=) – Mutha (don't wanna go to school today).	2	-	
Aug 91.	(7")(c-s) **HOLE HEARTED. / SUZI (WANTS HER ALL DAY WHAT?)**	-	4	
Sep 91.	(7") **DECADENCE DANCE. / MONEY (IN GOD WE TRUST)** (12"+=)(cd-s+=) – ('A'version) / More than words (acapella with congas).	36		Mar 91
Nov 91.	(7")(c-s) **HOLE HEARTED. / GET THE FUNK OUT (remix)** (12"box+=)(cd-s+=) – Suzi (wants her all day what?) / Sex'n'love.	12	-	
Apr 92.	(7")(12")(c-s)(cd-s) **SONG FOR LOVE. / LOVE OF MY LIFE (feat. BRIAN MAY)**	12		
Aug 92.	(7")(c-s) **REST IN PEACE. / PEACEMAKER DIE** (etched-12"+=) – ('A'album version). (cd-s++=) – Monica.	13	96	
Sep 92.	(cd)(c)(d-lp) **III SIDES TO EVERY STORY** – Warheads / Rest in peace / Politicalamity / Color me blind / Cupid's dead / Peacemaker die/ / Seven Sundays / Tragic comic / Our father / Stop the world / God isn't dead/ / Everything under the Sun (I) Rise'n shine / (II) Am I ever gonna change / (III) Who cares?	2	10	
Nov 92.	(7")(c-s) **STOP THE WORLD. / CHRISTMAS TIME AGAIN** (12"+=) – Warheads. (cd-s++=) – Don't leave me alone.	22	95	
Jan 93.	(7"etched) **TRAGIC COMIC. / HOLEHEARTED (horn mix)** (12"pic-d+=)(cd-s+=) – ('A'version) / Rise'n'shine (acoustic). (cd-s) – ('A'side) / Help! / When I'm president (live).	15		
Feb 95.	(cd)(c) **WAITING FOR THE PUNCHLINE** – There is no God / Cynical / Tell me something I don't know / Hip today / Naked / Midnight express / Leave me alone / No respect / Evilangelist / Shadow boxing / Unconditionally / Fair-weather friend.	10	40	
Mar 95.	(7"sha-pic-d) **HIP TODAY. / THERE IS NO GOD** (cd-s+=) – Better off dead / Kid ego (live). (cd-s+=) – Never been funked / When I'm president (live) / Strutter. (12") – ('A'side) / Wind me up (1987 demo).	44		
Jul 95.	(c-s) **UNCONDITIONALLY /** (cd-s) –			

– compilations, etc. –

Oct 93.	A&M; (cd) **EXTREME / PORNOGRAFFITTI**			

FACES (see under ⇒ SMALL FACES)

Donald FAGEN (see under ⇒ STEELY DAN)

FAIRPORT CONVENTION

Formed: Muswell Hill, London, England . . . mid-1967 by THOMPSON, NICOL, HUTCHINGS, DYBLE and original drummer SHAUN FRATER. By the end of the year, FRATER was ousted by LAMBLE, and after a debut 45 for 'Polydor', they added IAN MATTHEWS. This new sextet with Joe Boyd on production, made 1968 eponymous debut lp, but after its release, JUDY left and was replaced by SANDY DENNY. They signed to 'Island' at the same time, and issued 2nd lp 'WHAT WE DID ON OUR HOLIDAYS', which was the last to feature MATTHEWS. He was soon at UK No.1 in 1970, with his SOUTHERN COMFORT version of 'Woodstock'. After the completion of their 3rd lp 'UNHALFBRICKING' and while on tour, tragedy struck on 14 May'69, when MARTIN LAMBLE was killed when their tour van crashed. With the help of their Top 30 French version 'SI TU DOIS PARTIR' of a Dylan song, their 3rd lp was the first of 4 consecutive UK Top 20 sellers. They continued with various personnel during the next 2 decades. • **Style:** Initially Britain's answer to US West Coast folk-rock, they moved into more traditional folk sounds in the 70's, which influenced many others to follow suit. • **Songwriters:** Mainly group compositions, with numerous renditions of traditional English folk tunes. Other writers:- IF I HAD A RIBBON BOW (Maxine Sullivan) / NOTTAMUN TOWN + SHE MOVED THROUGH THE FAIR + loads more (trad.) / MILLION DOLLAR BASH + SI TU DOIS PARTIR (IF YOU GOTTA GO, GO NOW – Bob Dylan) / etc. The 1972 lp as The BUNCH, was full of covers. • **Trivia:** In 1970, their 'B'side 'SIR B.McKENZIE'S DAUGHTER, etc . . . ' got into The Guinness Book Of Records, for having longest song title ever.

Recommended: THE HISTORY OF FAIRPORT CONVENTION (*8).

RICHARD THOMPSON (b. 3 Apr'49, London, England) – guitar, vocals / **SIMON NICOL** (b.13 Oct'50) – guitar, vocals / **JUDY DYBLE** (b. 1948) **vocals, autoharp / ASHLEY HUTCHINGS** (b.Jan'45) – bass / **MARTIN LAMBLE** (b.Aug'49) – drums repl. SHAUN FRATER

Polydor | Cotillion

Nov 67. (7") **IF I HAD A RIBBON BOW. / IF (STOMP)** [ ] [ ]

— added **IAN MATTHEWS** (b.IAN McDONALD, 16 Jun'46, Scunthorpe, England) – vocals (ex-PYRAMIDS)

Jun 68. (lp) **FAIRPORT CONVENTION** [ ] [ ]
– Time will show the wiser / I don't know where I stand / If (stomp) / Decameron / Jack O'Diamonds / Portfolio / Chelsea morning / Sun shade / The lobster / It's alright ma, it's only witchcraft / One sure thing / M1 breakdown. *(re-iss.Jul75)*

— **SANDY DENNY** (b. 6 Jan'41) – vocals (ex-STRAWBS, etc) repl. JUDY who joined GILES, GILES and FRIPP

Island | A&M

Nov 68. (7") **MEET ON THE LEDGE. / THROWAWAY STREET PUZZLE** [ ] [-]

Jan 69. (lp) **WHAT WE DID ON OUR HOLIDAYS** [ ] [-]
– Fotheringay / Mr. Lacey / Book song / The Lord is in his place / No man's land / I'll keep it with mine / Eastern rain / Mr. Lacey / Nottamun town / Tale in hard time / She moves through the fair / Meet on the ledge / End of a holiday. *(re-iss.May89 on 'Carthage') (cd-iss.Feb90)*

1969. (7") **FOTHERINGAY. / I'LL KEEP IT WITH MINE** [-] [ ]

— Trimmed to a quintet when IAN formed MATTHEW'S SOUTHERN COMFORT

Jul 69. (7") **SI TU DOIS PARTIR. / GENESIS HALL** [21] [ ]

Jul 69. (lp)(c) **UNHALFBRICKING** [12] [ ]
– Genesis Hall / Si tu dois partir / Autopsy / A sailor's life / Cajun woman / Who knows where the time goes / Percy's song / Million dollar bash. *(re-iss.May89 on 'Carthage') (cd-iss.Nov89)*

— **DAVE MATTACKS** (b.Mar'48, London) – drums repl. MARTIN LAMBLE who died 14 May'69 in tour bus crash / also added **DAVE SWARBRICK** (b. 5 Apr'41, London) – fiddle, vocals

Dec 69. (lp)(c) **LIEGE & LIEF** [17] [ ]
– Come all ye / Reynardine / Matty Groves / Farewell farewell / The deserter / The lark in the morning / Tamlin / Crazy man Michael / Rakish Paddy / Foxhunters jigs / Toss the feathers. *(re-iss.+cd.Sep86)*

— **DAVE PEGG** (b. 2 Nov'47, Birmingham, England) – bass, vocals (ex-UGLYS) repl HUTCHINGS who joined STEELEYE SPAN (**PEGG** now in quintet with **THOMPSON, NICOL, MATTACKS** and **SWARBRICK** because SANDY DENNY also departed to form FOTHERINGAY)

Jul 70. (lp)(c) **FULL HOUSE** [13] [ ]
– Walk awhile / Dirty linen / Sloth / Sir Patrick Spens / Flatback caper / Doctor of physick / Flowers of the forest. *(re-iss.Jul87 on 'Hannibal', + cd-iss.Jan92)*

Oct 70. (7") **NOW BE THANKFUL. / SIR B. McKENZIE'S DAUGHTER'S LAMENT FOR THE 77th MOUNTED LANCERS' RETREAT FROM THE STRAITS OF LOCH KOMBE IN THE YEAR OF OUR LORD 1727, ON THE LAIRD OF KINLEAKIE** [ ] [ ]

— Now a quartet when RICHARD THOMPSON left to go solo

Jun 71. (7") **THE JOURNEYMAN'S GRACE. / THE WORLD HAS SURELY LOST IT'S HEAD** [-] [ ]

Jun 71. (lp)(c) **ANGEL DELIGHT** [8] [ ]
– Lord Marlborough / Sir William Gower / Bridge over the River Ash / Wizard of the worldly game / The journeyman's grace / Angel delight / Banks of the sweet primroses / Instrumental medley:- Cuckoo's nest – Hardiman the fiddler – Papa stoor / The bonny black hare / Sickness and diseases. *(cd-iss.Mar93)*

Sep 71. (7") **JOHN LEE. / THE TIME IS NEAR** [ ] [ ]

Nov 71. (lp)(c) **BABBACOMBE LEE** [ ] [ ]
– John Babbacombe Lee: (John's reflection of his boyhood / His struggle with his family / Then the happiest period of his life, the Navy / Returning reluctantly to his job after being invalided out of the service / And the senseless murder of his mistress and the three attempts to hang him – Hanging song).

— **ROGER HILL** – guitar, vocals repl. NICOL who joined ALBION COUNTRY BAND / **TOM FARNAL** – drums repl. MATTACKS who joined ALBION COUNTRY BAND

— In Jun72, **DAVID REA** – guitar repl. ROGER HILL until Aug72 when **MATTACKS** returned to repl. FARNALL / **TREVOR LUCAS** (b.Dec'43, Melbourne, Australia) – guitar, vocals (ex-FOTHERINGAY) repl. REA / **adding JERRY DONAHUE** (b.24 Sep'46, New York City, USA) – guitar, vocals (ex-FOTHERINGAY)

Mar 73. (7") **ROSIE. / KNIGHTS OF THE ROAD** [ ] [ ]

Mar 73. (lp)(c) **ROSIE** [ ] [ ]
– Rosie / Matthew, Mark, Luke and John / Knights of the road / Peggy's pub / The plainsman / Hungarian rhapsodie / My girl / Me with you / The hen's march through the midden & the four-poster bed / Furs and feathers.

Oct 73. (lp)(c) **NINE** [ ] [ ]
– The Hexamshire lass / Polly on the shore / The brilliancy medley and Cherokee shuffle / To Althea from prison / Tokyo / Bring 'em down / Big William / Pleasure and pain / Possibly Parsons Green.

— added the returning **SANDY DENNY** – vocals (who had had solo career)

Oct 74. (lp)(c) **LIVE CONVENTION (live)** [ ] [-]
– Matty Groves / Rosie / Fiddlestix / John the gun / Something you got / Sloth / Dirty linen / Down in the flood / Sir B. MacKenzie . . .

— **PAUL WARREN** – drums repl. MATTACKS who rejoined ALBION DANCE BAND

— **BRUCE ROWLANDS** – drums (ex-RONNIE LANE, ex-JOE COCKER) repl. WARREN

Island | Island

Jul 75. (7") **WHITE DRESS. / TEARS** [ ] [-]

Jul 75. (lp)(c) **RISING FOR THE MOON** [52] [ ]
– Rising for the Moon / Restless / White dress / Let it go / Stranger to himself / What is true? / Iron lion / Dawn / After halloween / Night-time girl / One more chance.

— FAIRPORT Basic trio **SWARBRICK, PEGG** and **ROWLANDS** recruited new folks **DAN AR BRAS** – guitar repl. SANDY DENNY who went solo again. (She later died of a brain haemorrage on 21 Apr78 after falling down her stairs) **BOB BRADY** – piano (ex-WIZZARD) repl. LUCAS who became producer. **ROGER BURRIDGE** – mandolin, fiddle repl. DONAHUE who became session man

Island / Antilles

May 76. (lp)(c) **GOTTLE O'GEER (as "FAIRPORT")**
– When first into this country / Our band / Lay me down easy / Cropedy capers / The frog up the pump / Don't be late / Sandy's song / Come and get it / Limey's lament.

— **FAIRPORT CONVENTION** again because founder member **SIMON NICOL** – guitar returned to repl. BRADY, BRAS and BURRIDGE

Vertigo / not issued

Feb 77. (lp)(c) **THE BONNY BUNCH OF ROSES** [-]
– James O'Donnell's jig / The Eynsham poacher / Adieu adieu / The bonny bunch of roses / The poor ditching boy / General Taylor / Run Johnny run / The last waltz / Royal Selection No.13. *(re-iss.+cd.Oct88 on 'Woodworm')*

May 78. (lp)(c) **TIPPLERS TALES** [-]
– Ye mariner's all / Three drunken maidens / Jack O'rion / Reynard the fox / Lady of pleasure / Bankruptured / The widow of Westmorland / The hair of the dogma / As bitme / John Barleycorn. *(re-iss.+cd.1989 on 'B.G.O.')*

Simon's / not issued

Oct 79. (7") **RUBBER BAND. / BONNY BLACK HARE** [-]
Nov 79. (lp) **FAREWELL FAREWELL (live)** [-]
– Matty Groves / Orange blossom special / John Lee / Bridge over the River Ash / Sir Patrick Spens / Mr.Lacey / Walk awhile / Bonny black hare / Journeyman's grace / Meet on the ledge. *(re-iss.cd+c Jun94 on 'Terrapin Truckin')*

Wood-worm / Varrick

1982. (lp) **MOAT ON THE LEDGE – LIVE AT BROUGHTON CASTLE 1981 (live)** [-]
– Walk awhile / Country pie / Rosie / Matty Groves / Both sides now / Poor Will and the hangman / The brilliancy medley – Cherokee shuffle / Woman or man / High school confidential.

— **DAVE MATTACKS and DAVE PEGG** returned to repl. SWARBRICK and ROWLAND **NICOL** also recruited sessioners **MARTIN ALLCOCK** (b. 5 Jan'57, Manchester, England) – strings / **RIC SAUNDERS** – violin (ex-SOFT MACHINE)

Wood-worm / Rounder

Aug 85. (lp)(c)(cd) **GLADYS LEAP** 1988
– How many times / Bird from the mountain / Honour and praise / The hiring fair / Instrumental medley '85: The riverhead – Glady's leap – The wise maid / My feet are set for dancing / Wat Tyler / Head in a sack. *(cd-iss.Mar93)*

1986. (lp)(c) **EXPLETIVE DELIGHTED** [-]
– Medley; The Rutland reel – Sack the juggler / Medley; The cat on the mixer – Three left feet / Bankruptured / Portmeirion / James O'Donnell's jig / Expletive delighted / Sigh beg sigh mor / Innstuck / The gas almost works / Hanks for the memory; Shazam – Pipeline – Apache – Peter Gunn. *(cd-iss.Mar93)*

— now 7-piece of **ALLCOCK, SAUNDERS, PEGG, MATTACKS, NICOL, DONAHUE** and **RICHARD THOMPSON**

New Routes / not issued

Jan 89. (lp)(c)(cd) **RED AND GOLD** [74] [-]
– Set me up / The noise club / Red and gold / The beggars song / The battle / Dark eyed Molly / The rose hip / Summer before the war / Open the door Richard. *(re-iss.cd Dec95 on 'HTD')*

Dec 90. (cd)(c)(lp) **THE FIVE SEASONS** [-]
– Cloudy beats: medley – Cup of tea! – A loaf of bread – Miss Monahan's / All your beauty / Sock in it / Gold / Ginnie / Mock Morris '90:- The green man – The cropedy badger – Molly on the jetty / Medley:- The card song – Shuffle the pack – The wounded whale.

— **NICOL, ALLCOCK, PEGG, MATTACKS + SAUNDERS**

Wood-worm / not issued

Jan 95. (cd)(c) **JEWEL IN THE CROWN**
– Jewel in the crown / Slip jigs and reels / A surfeit of lampreys / Kind of fortune / Diamonds and gold / The naked highwayman / The islands / The youngest daughter / London Danny / Summer in December / Travelling by steam / (Travel by steam) / She's like the swallow / Red tide / Home is where the heart is / Closing time.

– compilations etc. –

Nov 72. Island/ US= A&M; (d-lp)(c) **THE HISTORY OF FAIRPORT CONVENTION**
– Meet on the ledge / Fotheringay / Mr.Lacey / Book song / Sailor's life / Si tu dois partir / Who knows where the time goes / Matty Groves / Crazy man Michael / Now be thankful (medley) / Walk awhile / Sloth / The bonny black hare / Angel delight / Bridge over the river Ash / John Lee / Breakfast in Mayfair / Hanging song / The hen's march through the midden / The four-poster bed. *(re-iss.+cd.Jul91. omits 2 tracks)*

1976. A&M; (lp) **FAIRPORT CHRONICLES** [-]
May 87. Island; (7") **MEET ON THE LEDGE. / SIGH BEG SIGH MORE**
(12"+=) – John Barleycorn.
Nov 87. Island; (lp)(c)(cd) **IN REAL TIME**
Apr 88. Island; (cd) **THE BEST OF FAIRPORT CONVENTION**
Jul 70. Polydor; (7") **IF (STOMP). / CHELSEA MORNING**

Dec 76. Help-Island/ US= Antilees; (lp) **LIVE AT THE L.A. TROUBADOUR 1970 (live)**
(re-iss.Jan87 as HOUSE FULL on 'Hannibal', + cd-iss.Jan92)
Sep 84. Woodworm; (c) **THE AIRING CUPBOARD TAPES** [-]
1992. Woodworm; (cd) **THE WOODWORM YEARS** [-]
Sep 87. Hannibal; (lp)(c) **HEYDAY (BBC sessions '68-'69)** [-]

The BUNCH

TREVOR LUCAS (his idea), **SANDY DENNY, RICHARD THOMPSON, ASHLEY HUTCHINGS, DAVE MATTACKS** and session people

Island / A&M

Apr 72. (lp) **ROCK ON**
– That'll be the day / Love's made a fool of you / When will I be loved / Willie and the hand jive / Learning the game / My girl in the month of May / Don't be cruel / The locomotion / Jambalaya (on the bayou) / Sweet little rock'n'roller / Nadine / Crazy arms. *(7"flexi w/a)* **-LET THERE BE DRUMS (1 sided)** *(re-iss.+c May88 on 'Carthage')*
Apr 72. (7") **WHEN WILL I BE LOVED. / WILLIE AND THE HAND JIVE**

Marianne FAITHFULL

Born: 29 Dec'46, Hampstead, London, England. Daughter of a university lecturer and an Austrian baroness, who had sent her to St.Joseph's convent school in Reading, Berkshire. While attending a London party with artist boyfriend John Dunbar in 1964, she was snapped up by (ROLLING STONES manager) ANDREW LOOG OLDHAM, who signed her to 'Decca' records. Her debut 45 'AS TEARS GO BY', soon made the UK Top 10 and US Top 30. She flopped with follow-up, but had another Top 10 hit early in '65 with 'COME AND STAY WITH ME'. This was followed by 2 simultaneously issued lp's 'COME MY WAY' & 'MARIANNE FAITHFULL', which both hit UK Top 20. In Nov'65, she gave birth to son Nicholas, but separated from Dunbar. Later that year, she began much-publicised affair with MICK JAGGER, after allegedly bedding the other 3! (except WATTS). She was busted for drugs with JAGGER and The STONES on many occasions, with the couple visiting Maharishi Yogi in '68. At this time, she also began acting; 'The Three Sisters' (Chekhov play) & on film 'Girl On A Motorcycle' with Alain Delon. In late 1968, she miscarried with JAGGER's baby, and 6 months later, both were arrested in their London home for possession of marijuana. In mid-69, while on the set of film 'Ned Kelly' alongside JAGGER, she was found in a coma, after an overdose of barbituates (100+ Tuinal). She was dropped from the film and went into hospital for heroin addiction and depression. In 1970, after a season playing Ophelia in 'Hamlet' alongside Nicol Williamson, her suspected suicide bids were reported by press, as was her divorce from Dunbar and split with JAGGER. After 5 years, in the wilderness, she returned on 'Nems' in 1975 with single 'DREAMING MY DREAMS'. After 2 albums for label, she signed to 'Island' in 1979 and had returned to Top 50 with 'THE BALLAD OF LUCY JORDAN'. On 23 Nov'79, she married BEN BRIERLY of punk rock band The VIBRATORS, but her future was always marred by drug intake. In 1987 still surprisingly contracted to 'Island' and now living in Cambridge, Massachusetts, USA with new husband writer Girgio Della, she issued album 'STRANGE WEATHER'. The next year, she was deported from the States, but settled in Ireland. • **Style:** Light-folk singer, whose pop stardom, might have been bigger, but for her drug addiction. In 1978, she moved into C&W, with little acclaim. A year later though she was the leather-clad punk mistress diva when she sang the explicit 'WHY DYA DO IT' from classy 'BROKEN ENGLISH' album. • **Songwriters:** Penned some herself with MARK but she mostly covered others; AS TEARS GO BY + SISTER MORPHINE (music; M.Jagger) / BLOWIN' IN THE WIND + I'LL BE YOUR BABY TONIGHT (Bob Dylan) / GREENSLEEVES + HOUSE OF THE RISING SUN + SCARBOROUGH FAIR (trad.) / COME AND STAY WITH ME (Jackie DeShannon) / GREEN ARE YOUR EYES (Bert Jansch) / THE LAST THING ON MY MIND (Tom Paxton) / THE FIRST TIME EVER I SAW YOUR FACE (Ewan MacColl) / SALLY FREE AND EASY (. . . Tannery) / COCKLESHELLS (. . . Taylor) / THIS LITTLE BIRD (John D.Loudermilk) / SUNNY GOODGE STREET + THE MOST OF WHAT IS LEAST (Donovan) / YESTERDAY (Beatles) / SOMETHING BETTER (Goffin-King) / IS THIS WHAT I GET FOR LOVING YOU (Ronettes) / THE BALLAD OF LUCY JORDAN (Stel Silverstein) / DREAMING MY DREAMS (Waylon Jennings) / WORKING CLASS HERO (John Lennon) / STRANGE WEATHER (Tom Waits) / MADAME GEORGE (Van Morrison) / GHOST DANCE (Patti Smith), etc. In 1979, she began writing partnership with guitarist BARRY REYNOLDS. • **Trivia:** In 1967, she provides guest appearance & backing vocals for The BEATLES on their 'All You Need Is Love' 45 & TV video.

Recommended: THE VERY BEST OF MARIANNE FAITHFULL (*7) / BROKEN ENGLISH (*7).

MARIANNE FAITHFULL – vocals (with session people)

Decca | London

Jul 64. (7") **AS TEARS GO BY. / GREENSLEEVES** 9 | 22 Sep 64
Oct 64. (7") **BLOWING IN THE WIND. / THE HOUSE OF THE RISING SUN**
Feb 65. (7") **COME AND STAY WITH ME. / WHAT HAVE I DONE WRONG** 4 | 26 Jan 65
Apr 65. (7") **THIS LITTLE BIRD. / MORNING SUN** 6 | 32 Jun 65
May 65. (lp) **COME MY WAY** 12 | -
– Come my way / Jabberwock / Portland town / House of the rising sun / Spanish is a loving tongue / Fare thee well / Lonesome traveller / Down in the Salley garden / Mary Ann / Full fathom five / Four strong winds / Black girl / Once I had a sweetheart / Bells of freedom. *(re-iss.+cd.Sep91 on 'Deram' +=)* – Blowin' in the wind / Et maintenant (what now my love) / That's right baby / Sister Morphine.
May 65. (lp) **MARIANNE FAITHFULL** 15 | 12
– Come and stay with me / They will never leave you *(UK-only)* / / What have they done to the rain / In my time of sorrow / What have I done wrong / I'm a loser / As tears go by / If I never get to love you / Time takes time / He'll come back to me / Paris bells / Plasir d'amour. *(re-iss.Aug84) (re-iss.1988 on 'Castle' cd-iss.Jun89 w/ extra +=)* – Can't you hear my heartbeat? / Downtown.
Jul 65. (7") **SUMMER NIGHTS. / THE SHA LA LA SONG** 10 | 24 Aug 65
Oct 65. (7") **YESTERDAY. / OH LOOK AROUND YOU** 36
Nov 66. (7") **GO AWAY FROM MY WORLD. / ?** - | 89
Dec 65. (lp) **GO AWAY FROM MY WORLD** - | 81
– Go away from my world / Yesterday / Come my way / Last thing on my mind / How should true love / Wild mountain time / Summer nights / Mary Ann / Scarborough Fair / Lullabye / North country maid / Sally free and easy.
Apr 66. (lp) **NORTH COUNTRY MAID** | -
– Green are your eyes / Scarborough fair / Cockleshells / The last thing on my mind / The first time ever I saw your face / Sally free and easy / Sunny Goodge Street / How should your true love know / She moved through the fair / North country maid / Lullaby / Wild mountain thyme. *(cd-iss.1992, with +=)* – The most of what is least / Come my way / Mary Ann.
May 66. (7") **TOMORROW'S CALLING. / THAT'S RIGHT BABY**
Jul 66. (7") **COUNTING. / I'D LIKE TO DIAL YOUR NUMBER**
Nov 66. (lp) **FAITHFULL FOREVER** - |
– Counting / Tomorrow's calling / The first time / With you in mind / In the night time / Ne me quitte pas (love theme from Umbrellas of Cherbourg) / Monday Monday / Some other Spring / That's right baby / Lucky girl / I'm the sky / I have a love.
Feb 67. (7") **IS THIS WHAT I GET FOR LOVING YOU. / TOMORROW'S CALLING** 43
Feb 67. (lp) **LOVE IN A MIST** | -
– Yesterday / You can't go where the roses go / Our love has gone / Don't make promises / In the night time / This little bird / Ne me quite pas / Counting / Reason to believe / Conquillage / With you in mind / Young girl blues / Good guy / I love a love. *(cd-iss.Oct88 +=)* – Rosie, Rosie.
Feb 69. (7") **SOMETHING BETTER. / SISTER MORPHINE**

—— She retired from music business, and when she and MICK JAGGER broke up, attempted to commit suicide many times. She had period of hospitalisation, due to increasing heroin addiction early in the 70's. By Autumn 1975, she had recovered and was back in the studio.

NEMS | not issued

Nov 75. (7") **DREAMIN' MY DREAMS. / LADY MADELAINE** | -
Sep 76. (7") **ALL I WANNA DO IN MY LIFE. / WRONG ROAD AGAIN** | -
Jan 77. (lp)(c) **DREAMIN' MY DREAMS** | -
– Fairy tale hero / This time / I'm not Lisa / he way you want me to be / Wrong road again / All I wanna do in life / I'm looking for blue eyes / Somebody loves you / Vanilla O'lay / Dreamin' my dreams / Lady Madelaine / Sweet little sixteen.

—— She was now backed by **The GREASE BAND**

Mar 78. (lp)(c) **FAITHLESS** | -
– Dreamin' my dreams / Vanilla O'Lay / Wait for me down by the river / I'll be your baby tonight / Lady Madelaine / All I wanna do in life / The way you want me to be / Wrong road again / This was the day (Nashville) / This time / I'm not Lisa / Honky tonk angels. *(re-iss.+cd.Apr89)*

—— now with **BARRY REYNOLDS** – guitar, co-producer / **STEVE YORK** – bass / **TERRY STANNARD** – drums / **JOE HAVETY** – keys / etc.

Island | Island

Oct 79. (7") **THE BALLAD OF LUCY JORDAN. / BRAIN DRAIN** 48
Oct 79. (lp)(c) **BROKEN ENGLISH** 57 | 82
– Broken English / Witches song / Brain drain / Guilt / The ballad of Lucy Jordan / What's the hurry / Working class hero / Why d'ya do it?. *(re-iss.Sep86) (re-iss.lp Jan94 + May94)*
Jan 80. (7") **BROKEN ENGLISH. / BRAIN DRAIN**
Jan 80. (7") **BROKEN ENGLISH. / WHAT'S THE HURRY** | -
Oct 81. (7") **INTRIGUE. / FOR BEAUTY'S SAKE**
Oct 81. (lp)(c) **DANGEROUS ACQUAINTANCES** 45
– Sweetheart / Intrigue / Easy in the city / Strange one / Tenderness / For beautie's sake / So sad / Eye communication / Truth bitter truth. *(cd-iss.May95)*
Nov 81. (7") **SWEETHEART. / OVER HERE** | -
Jan 82. (7") **SWEETHEART. / FOR BEAUTIE'S SAKE** - |
May 82. (7")(12") **BROKEN ENGLISH. / SISTER MORPHINE**

—— **BEN BRIERLEY + MIKEY CHUNG** – guitar repl. MAVETY **FERNANDO SAUNDERS** – bass + **WALLY BADAROU** – keyboards repl. YORK

Feb 83. (lp)(c) **A CHILD'S ADVENTURE** 99
– Times Square / The blue millionaire / Falling from grace / Morning come / Ashes in my hand / Running for our lives / Ireland / She's got a problem. *(re-iss.Apr87) (cd-iss.May95)*
Mar 83. (7") **RUINING OF OUR LIVES. / SHE'S GOT A PROBLEM**

—— now w/ **many on session, incl. SAUNDERS.**

Jun 87. (7") **AS TEARS GO BY. / TROUBLE IN MIND (THE RETURN)**
(12"+=) – This hawk el Gavian.
Jul 87. (lp)(c)(cd) **STRANGE WEATHER** 78
– Stranger intro / Boulevard of broken dreams / I ain't goin' down to the well no more / Yesterdays / Sign of judgement / Strange weather / Love, life and money / I'll keep it with mine / Hello stranger / Penthouse serenade / As tears go by / A stranger on Earth.

—— now with **BARRY REYNOLDS** – guitar / **MARC RIBOT / LEW SOLOFF / GARTH HUDSON**

May 90. (cd)(c)(lp) **BLAZING AWAY (live + 1 studio)**
– Les prisons du roi / Guilt / Sister morphine / Why d'ya do it? / The ballad of Lucy Jordan / Blazing away / Broken English / Strange weather / Working class hero / As tears go by / When I find my life / Times Square / She moved through the fair. *(re-iss.cd May95)*
Sep 94. (cd)(c) **FAITHFULL – A COLLECTION OF HER BEST RECORDINGS (compilation)**
– Broken English / The ballad of Lucy Jordan / Working class hero / Guilt / Why d'ya do it? / Ghost dance / Trouble in mind (the return) / Times Square (live) / Strange weather / She / As tears go by.

—— below from a VAN MORRISON tribute album on 'Exile-Polydor' / 'M.C.A.'

Sep 94. (c-s) **MADAME GEORGE. / ('b'side by Brian Kennedy)**
(cd-s+=) – (other by Brian Kennedy + Shana Morrison).

—— below with composer ANGELO BADALEMENTI

Apr 95. (cd)(c) **A SECRET LIFE**
– Prologue / Sleep / Love in the afternoon / Flaming September / She / Bored by dreams / Losing / The wedding / The stars line up / Epilogue.

– compilations, others, etc. –

May 65. Decca; (7"ep) **MARIANNE FAITHFULL** | -
– Go away from my world / The most of what is least / El main tenant (what now my love) / The sha la la song.
Feb 69. Decca; (lp) **THE WORLD OF MARIANNE FAITHFULL** | -
Apr 69. London; (lp) **MARIANNE FAITHFULL'S GREATEST HITS** (same tracks as above) - |
Jul 80. Decca; (7") **AS TEARS GO BY. / COME AND STAY WITH ME** | -
(re-iss.Oct83 on 'Old Gold')
Feb 81. Decca; (lp)(c) **AS TEARS GO BY** | -
Mar 84. Decca; (lp)(c) **SUMMER NIGHTS** | -
Nov 85. Castle; (d-lp)(c)(cd) **RICH KID BLUES** | -
Mar 87. London; (cd) **THE VERY BEST OF MARIANNE FAITHFULL** | -
– As tears go by / Come and stay with me / Scarborough Fair / Monday, Monday / Yesterday / The last thing on my mind / What have they done to the rain / This little bird / Something better / In my time of sorrow / Is this what I get for loving you? / Tomorrow's calling / Reason to believe / Sister Morphine / Go away from my world / Summer nights *(lp/c.iss.Jun87 + Sep87)*
Oct 87. Hannibal; (lp) **HEYDAY** (BBC sessions 1968-69) | -
Oct 93. Spectrum; (cd)(c) **THIS LITTLE BIRD** | -

FAITH NO MORE

Formed: Los Angeles & San Francisco, California, USA . . . 1980 by MOSELEY and GOULD, although they only started gigging 1982. In 1985, they issued eponymous debut lp on local indie 'Mordam' label. Early in 1987, they moved on to 'Slash' records, who unleashed 'INTRODUCE YOURSELF'. In 1988, due to musical differences and off-beat stage humour, MOSELEY was discharged from band. By the end of the year, he was succeeded by 20 year-old MIKE PATTON. Their 1989 album 'THE REAL THING', went cross-Atlantic Top 30, and hosted a string of hits, the best and biggest being 'EPIC'. • **Style:** Funk-metal rap with diverse heavy image similar in vein to RED HOT CHILI PEPPERS or DAN REED

NETWORK. • **Songwriters:** Group compositions (PATTON took over lyric duties from MOSELEY in 1989). Covered WAR PIGS (Black Sabbath) / THE RIGHT STUFF (Edwin Starr) / MIDNIGHT COWBOY (John Barry) / MALPRACTICE (sampled: Kronos Quartet No.8) / LET'S LYNCH THE LANDLORD (Dead Kennedys) / I'M EASY (Commodores) / I STARTED A JOKE (Bee Gees) / GREENFIELDS (Gilykson-Dehr-Miller). • **Trivia:** Their 1987 album was produced by MATT WALLACE and STEVE BERLIN (of LOS LOBOS).

Recommended: ANGEL DUST (*9) / THE REAL THING (*8) / INTRODUCE YOURSELF (*7).

CHUCK MOSELEY – vocals / **BILLY GOULD** (b.24 Apr'63) – bass / **RODDY BOTTUM** (b. 1 Jul'63) – keyboards / **JIM MARTIN** (b.21 Jul'61) – guitar / **MIKE BORDIN** (b.27 Nov'62) – drums

not issued / Mordam

1985. (lp) **FAITH NO MORE** [-] [ ]
– We care a lot / The jungle / Mark Bowen / Jim / Why do you bother / Greed / Pills for breakfast / As the worm turns / Arabian disco / New beginnings. *(iss.UK Feb88 as 'WE CARE A LOT')*

Slash-London / Slash

Oct 87. (lp)(c)(cd) **INTRODUCE YOURSELF** [ ] [ ]
– Faster disco / Anne's song / Introduce yourself / Chinese arithmetic / Death march / We care a lot / R'n'r / Crab song / Blood / Spirit.

Jan 88. (7") **WE CARE A LOT. / SPIRIT** [53] [ ]
(12"+=) – Chinese Arithmetic (radio mix).

Apr 88. (7")(12")(7"pic-d) **ANNE'S SONG (remix). / GREED** [ ] [ ]

— **MIKE PATTON** (b.27 Jan'68) – vocals (ex-MR. BUNGLE) repl. CHUCK who later (1991) joined BAD BRAINS

Jul 89. (lp)(c) **THE REAL THING** [30] [11]
– From out of nowhere / Epic / Falling to pieces / Surprise, you're dead / Zombie eaters / The real thing / Underwater love / The morning after / Woodpecker from Mars. (cd+=) – Edge of the world / War pigs. *(re-iss.Sep92)*

Oct 89. (7") **FROM OUT OF NOWHERE. / COWBOY SONG** [ ] [ ]
(12"+=) – The grave.

Jan 90. (7")(7"sha-pic-d) **EPIC. / WAR PIGS (live)** [37] [ ]
(12"+=)(cd-s+=) – Chinese arithmetic.
(7"m+=) – Surprise you're dead (live).

Apr 90. (c-s) **FROM OUT OF NOWHERE. / WOODPECKER FROM MARS (live)** [23] [ ]
(7"m+=) – Epic (live).
(12"+=)(cd-s+=)(12"pic-d+=) – The real thing (Live).

Jul 90. (7") **FALLING TO PIECES. / WE CARE A LOT (live)** [41] [92] Nov 90
(7"m+=)(c-s+=) – Underwater love (live).
(12"+=)(cd-s+=) – From out of nowhere.

Sep 90. (7"sha-pic-d) **EPIC. / FALLING TO PIECES (live)** [25] [9] Jun 90
(7"m+=)(c-s+=) – Epic (live).
(12"++=)(cd-s++=) – As the worm turns.

Feb 91. (cd)(c)(m-lp) **LIVE AT BRIXTON ACADEMY (live)** [20] [-]
– Falling to pieces / The real thing / Pump up the jam / Epic / War pigs / From out of nowhere / We care a lot / The right stuff / Zombie eaters / Edge of the world. (cd/c+=) – The grade / The cowboy song.

Slash-London / Slash-Reprise

May 92. (7")(c-s)(7"colrd) **MIDLIFE CRISIS. / JIZZLOBER / CRACK HITLER** [10] [ ]
(12"pic-d+=)(pic-cd-s+=) – Midnight cowboy.

Jun 92. (cd)(c)(lp) **ANGEL DUST** [2] [10]
– Land of sunshine / Caffeine / Midlife crisis / RV / Smaller and smaller / Everything's ruined / Malpractise / Kindergarten / Be aggressive / A small victory / Crack Hitler / Jizzlober / Midnight cowboy. (lp +free-12"ep 'MIDLIFE CRISIS (remix)' / (2). *(re-iss.Feb93)* (+=) I'm easy.

Jul 92. (7") **A SMALL VICTORY. / LET'S LYNCH THE LANDLORD** [29] [ ]
(12"+=)(12"pic-d+=) – Malpractise.
(cd-s++=) – ('A'full version).

Sep 92. (12"ep)(cd-ep) **A SMALL VICTORY (Youth remix) / R-EVOLUTION 23 (full Moon mix) / SUNDOWN (mix) / SUNDOWN (instrumental).** [ ] [-]

Nov 92. (7")(c-s) **EVERYTHING'S RUINED. / MIDLIFE CRISIS (live)** [28] [ ]
(cd-s+=) – Land of sunshine (live).
(cd-s) – ('A'side) / Edge of the world (live) / RV (live).

Jan 93. (7")(12")(cd-s) **I'M EASY. / BE AGGRESSIVE** [3] [58]

Oct 93. (12"ep)(cd-ep) **ANOTHER BODY MURDERED. ("FAITH NO MORE / BOO-YA TRIBE") / Just Another Victim (by "HELMET / HOUSE OF PAIN")** [26] [ ]

— (above from the film 'Judgement Day')

Mar 95. (7")(c-s) **DIGGING THE GRAVE. / UGLY IN THE MORNING** [16] [ ]
(12"blue+=) – Absolute zero / Get out.
(cd-s+=) – Absolute zero / Cuckoo for Caca.
(cd-s) – ('A'side) / I started a joke / Greenfields.

Mar 95. (cd)(c)(lp)(5x7"box) **KING FOR A DAY - FOOL FOR A LIFETIME** [5] [31]
– Get out / Ricochet / Evidence / The great art of making enemies / Star A.D. / Cuckoo for Caca / Caralho Voador / Ugly in the morning / Digging the grave / Take this bottle / King for a day / What a day / The last to know / Just a man. (7"box-set feat. interviews).

May 95. (c-s) **RICOCHET / SPANISH EYES** [27] [ ]
(cd-s+=) – I wanna f**k myself.
(cd-s) – ('A'side) / Midlife crisis (live) / Epic (live) / We care a lot (live).

Jul 95. (c-s) **EVIDENCE / EASY (live)** [32] [ ]
(cd-s+=) – Digging the grave (live) / From out of nowhere (live).
(cd-s) – ('A'side) / Das schutzenfest / (interview).

MR.BUNGLE

PATTON also still a member of

Slash / Slash

Sep 91. (cd)(c)(lp) **MR.BUNGLE** [57] [ ]
– Quote unquote / Slowly growing deaf / Squeeze me macaroni / Carousel / Egg / Stubb (a dub) / The girls of porn / Love is a fist / Dead goon.

... Jan – Jun '96 stop press ...

Jan 96. (cd)(c) **DISCO VOLANTE** [ ] [ ]

FALL

Formed: Salford, Manchester, England ... Dec'76 by MARK E.SMITH, MARTIN BRAMAH and TONY FRIEL. After 1977 session on The John Peel Radio 1 show, they were signed to indie label 'Step Forward'. Their debut release 'BINGO-MASTERS BREAK-OUT! EP', was issued in Jun78, and was soon followed by Bob Sargeant produced first studio lp 'LIVE AT THE WITCH TRIALS'. Advanced steadily throughout the next decade, and had first taste of commercial success, when album 'BEND SINISTER' hit UK Top 40. • **Style:** Repetitive and uncompromising punk rock, that progressed experimentally incorporating rockabilly, alternative rock and poetic punk. MARK E.SMITH became unlikely cult figure in the 80's, fusing his sharp acid-tongue screach with CAN-like backing from ever-changing group personnel. • **Songwriters:** All lyrics by MARK E. and music by MARK E. & various group members, especially SCANLON or wife of 5 years BRIX E. Started doing covers from 1986:- ROLLIN' DANY (Gene Vincent) / THERE'S A GHOST IN MY HOUSE (R.Dean Taylor) / VICTORIA (Kinks) / MR. PHARMACIST (Other Half) / JERUSALEM (William Blake) / POPCORN DOUBLE FEATURE (Searchers) / WHITE LIGHTNING (Big Bopper) / A DAY IN THE LIFE (Beatles) / LEGEND OF XANADU (Dave Dee, Beaky, Mick and Tich) / TELEPHONE THING (Cold Cut) / BLACK MONK THEME (Monks) / JUST WAITING (Hank Williams) / LOST IN MUSIC (Sister Sledge) / I'M GOING TO SPAIN (S. Bent) / WHY ARE PEOPLE GRUDGEFUL? (Lee Perry – unknown) / SHUT UP! (Monks) / JUNK MAN (McFree) / WAR (Blegvad-Moore) / I'M NOT SATISFIED (Frank Zappa) / ROADHOUSE (John Barry). • **Trivia:** MARK's ex-wife BRIX appeared on new boyfriend NIGEL KENNEDY's 1991 'This Is Your Life'. His classical violin virtuoso, had featured on album 'BEND SINISTER'?. MARK E. featured on TACKHEAD b-side of 'Dangerous Sex' in mid 1990, alongside ADRIAN SHERWOOD and GARY CLAIL. Just previous to this, he had a solo track 'ERROR-ORROR I' for Various Artists compilation 'HOME'.

Recommended: THIS NATION'S SAVING GRACE (*9) / BEND SINISTER (*8) / LIVE AT THE WITCH TRIALS (*9) / EXTRICATE (*8) / SHIFT-WORK (*8) / THE WONDERFUL AND FRIGHTENING WORLD OF ... (*8) / DRAGNET (*8) / PERVERTED BY LANGUAGE (*8) / I AM KURIOUS ORANJ (*8) / THE FRENZ EXPERIMENT (*7) / HEX ENDUCTION HOUR (*7) / THE FALL LIVE (*7) / GROTESQUE (*7) / SLATES (*6) / ROOM TO LIVE (*6) / MIDDLE CLASS REVOLT (*6) / CODE : SELFISH (*5) / SEMINAL LIVE (*4) / CELEBRAL CAUSTIC (*6) / THE LIGHT USER SYNDROME (*7)

MARK E. SMITH (b. 5 Mar'57) – vocals / **TONY FRIEL** – bass / **MARTIN BRAMAH** – guitar / **UNA BAINES** – electric piano / **KARL BURNS** – drums

Step Forward / I.R.S.

Jun 78. (7"ep) **BINGO-MASTERS BREAK-OUT!** [ ] [-]
– Psycho Mafia / Bingo-Master / Repitition.

— **MARC RILEY** – bass repl. (ERIC and JOHNNIE BROWN) who had repl. FRIEL (He formed The PASSAGE) / **YVONNE PAWLETT** – keyboards repl. BAINES who formed BLUE ORCHIDS

Nov 78. (7") **IT'S THE NEW THING. / VARIOUS TIMES** [ ] [-]

Jan 79. (lp) **LIVE AT THE WITCH TRIALS** [ ] [ ]

– Frightened / Crap rap 2 – Like to blow / Rebellious jukebox / No Xmas for John Quays / Mother-sister! / Industrial estate / Underground medecin / Two steps back / Live at the Witch Trials / Futures and pasts / Music scene.

— **MARK E.** (now sole founder), **RILEY** (now guitar) and **PAWLETT** recruited **STEVE HANLEY** (b. 1959, Dublin, Ireland) – bass repl. BRAMAH who also joined BLUE ORCHIDS / **MIKE LEIGH** – drums repl. BURNS who also joine The PASSAGE and P.I.L.

Jul 79. (7") **ROWCHE RUMBLE. / IN MY AREA** ☐ -

— **CRAIG SCANLON** – guitar (RILEY now guitar, keyboards) repl. PAWLETT

Oct 79. (lp) **DRAGNET** ☐ ☐
– Psykick dancehall / A figure walks / Printhead / Dice man / Before the Moon falls / Your heart out / Muzorewi's daughter / Flat of angles / Choc-stock / Spectre vs. rector / Put away. *(re-iss.+cd.Dec90 on 'I.R.S.')*

Jan 80. (7") **FIERY JACK. / SECOND DARK AGE / PSYKICK DANCEHALL II** ☐ -

Rough Trade not issued

May 80. (lp) **THE FALL LIVE – TOTALE'S TURNS (IT'S NOW OR NEVER) (live)** ☐ -
– (intro) – Fiery Jack / Rowche rumble / Muzorewi's daughter / In my area / Choc-stock / Spectre vs. rector 2 / Cary Grant's wedding / That man / New puritan / No Xmas for John Quays. *(cd-iss.Nov92 on 'Dojo')*

— **PAUL HANLEY** – drums repl. LEIGH

Jun 80. (7") **HOW I WROTE ELASTIC MAN. / CITY HOBGOBLINS** ☐ -

Sep 80. (7") **TOTALLY WIRED. / PUTTA BLOCK** ☐ -

— **KAY CARROLL** their manager augmented p/t on backing vocals, kazoo

Nov 80. (lp) **GROTESQUE (AFTER THE GRAMME)** ☐ ☐
– Pay your rates / English scheme / New face in Hell / C'n'c Smithering / The container drivers / Impression of J. Temperance / In the park / W.M.C. – Blob 59 / Gramme Friday / The N.W.R.A. *(re-iss.cd Sep93 on 'Castle')*

Apr 81. (10"m-lp) **SLATES** ☐ -
– Middle mass / An older lover etc. / Prole art threat / Fit and working again / Slates, slags, etc. / Leave the capitol.

— **KARL BURNS** – drums returned now alongside **SMITH, RILEY, SCANLON, S & P HANLEY**

Kamera not issued

Nov 81. (7") **LIE DREAM OF A CASINO SOUL. / FANTASTIC LIFE** ☐ ☐

Mar 82. (lp) **HEX ENDUCTION HOUR** 71 -
– The classical / Jaw-bone and the air-rifle / Hip priest / Fortress – Deer park / Mere psued mag. ed / Winter / Winter 2 / Just step s'ways / Who makes the Nazis? / Iceland / And this day. *(re-iss.1987 on 'Line', cd-iss.Sep89)*

Apr 82. (7") **LOOK KNOW. / I'M INTO C.B.** ☐ -

Nov 82. (lp) **ROOM TO LIVE** ☐ -
– Joker hysterical face / Marquee cha-cha / Hard life in the country / Room to live / Detective instinct / Solicitor in studio / Papal visit. *(re-iss.Oct87 on 'Line')*

— Reverted to quintet when RILEY left to form MARC RILEY & THE CREEPERS (note that their manager and p/t member KAY CARROLL also departed)

Rough Trade not issued

Jun 83. (7") **THE MAN WHOSE HEAD EXPANDED. / LUDD GANG** ☐ -

Oct 83. (d7") **KICKER CONSPIRACY. // WINGS / CONTAINER DRIVERS (live) / NEW PURITANS (live)** ☐ -

— added **LAURA-ELISE** (now BRIX E. SMITH) (b.USA) – guitar, vocals (ex-BANDA DRATSING) P. HANLEY added keyboards and BURNS added lead bass to their repertoire

Dec 83. (lp)(c) **PERVERTED BY LANGUAGE** ☐ -
– Eat y'self fitter / Neighbourhood of infinity / Garden / Hotel Bloedel / I feel voxish / Tempo house / Hexen definitive / strife knot. *(re-iss.Oct87 on 'Line', cd-iss.Sep89)* (cd+=) – Oh! brother / God-box / C.R.E.E.P. / Pat-trip dispenser. *(re-iss.cd.Sep93 on 'Castle')*

Begger's Banquet P.V.C.

Jun 84. (7") **OH BROTHER. / GOD-BOX** ☐ -
(12"+=) – ('A' instrumental).

Aug 84. (7")(7"pic-d) **C.R.E.E.P. / PAT-TRIP DISPENSER** ☐ -
(12"+=)(12"green+=) – ('A'extended).

— added **GAVIN FRIDAY** – some vocals (of VIRGIN PRUNES) (on next 2 releases)

Sep 84. (lp)(c) **THE WONDERFUL AND FRIGHTENING WORLD OF . . .** 62 ☐
– Lay of the land / 2 x 4 / Copped it / Elves / Slang king / Bug day / Stephen song / Craigness / Disney's dream debased. *(re-iss.+cd.Jul88)* (cd+=) – Oh! brother / Draygo's guilt / God-box / Clear off! / C.R.E.E.P. / Pat-trip dispenser / No bulbs.

Oct 84. (12"ep) **CALL FOR ESCAPE ROUTE** ☐ -
– Draygo's Guilt / No bulbs / Clear Off!. (with free-7") **NO BULBS 3. / SLANG KING**

— **SIMON ROGERS** – bass, keyboards repl. P. HANLEY (he cont. with KISS THE BLADE) (GAVIN returned to VIRGIN PRUNES and S. HANLEY took a holiday)

Jul 85. (7") **COULDN'T GET AHEAD. / ROLLIN' DANY** ☐ ☐
(12"+=) – Petty (thief) lout.

— **STEVE HANLEY** returned to join **MARK E., BRIX, CRAIG, KARL and SIMON**

Sep 85. (lp)(c) **THIS NATION'S SAVING GRACE** 54 ☐
– Mansion / Bombast / Barmy / What you need / Spoilt Victorian child / L.A. / Out of the quantifier / My new house / Paintwork / I am Damo Suzuki / To nkroachment: yarbles. *(re-iss.+cd.Feb90 +=)* – Vixen / Couldn't get ahead / Pretty (thief) lout / Rollin' Dany / Cruiser's creek.

Oct 85. (7") **CRUISER'S CREEK. / L.A.** ☐ ☐
(12"+=) – Vixen.

Jul 86. (7") **LIVING TOO LATE. / HOT AFTER-SHAVE BOP** ☐ ☐
(12"+=) – Living too long.

— **JOHN S. WOOLSTENCROFT** – drums (ex-WEEDS) repl. BURNS who formed THIRST

Sep 86. (7") **MR. PHARMICIST. / LUCIFER OVER LANCASHIRE** 75 ☐

(12"+=) – Auto-tech pilot.
Oct 86. (lp)(c)(cd) **BEND SINISTER** [36] [ ]
– R.O.D. / Dktr. Faustus / Shoulder pads £1 / Mr. Pharmicist / Gross chapel – British grenadiers / U.S. 80's-90's / Terry Waite sez / Bournemouth runner / Riddler / Shoulder pads £2. *(cd-iss.Jan88 +=)* – Living too late / Auto-tech pilot.
Nov 86. (7") **HEY! LUCIANI. / ENTITLED** [59] [ ]
(12"+=) – Shoulder pads.
Apr 87. (7") **THERE'S A GHOST IN MY HOUSE. / HAF FOUND, BORMAN** [30] [ ]
(12"+=)(c-s+=) – Sleepdebt / Snatches / Mark'll sink us.

— added **MARSHA SCHOFIELD** – keyboards, vocals of ADULT NET, (ex BANDA DRATSING)

Oct 87. (7")(7"pic-d) **HIT THE NORTH. / Pt.2** [57] [ ]
(12"+=) – Australians in Europe.
(cd-s+=) – Northerns in Europe / (Hit the north versions).

— reverted back to sextet of **MARK E., BRIX, CRAIG, JOHN S., STEVE** and **MARSHA** when **SIMON** became their producer & studio guitarist only

Jan 88. (7") **VICTORIA. / TUFF LIFE BOOGIE** [35] [ ]
(12"+=) – Guest informant / Twister.
Mar 88. (lp)(c)(cd) **THE FRENZ EXPERIMENT** [19] [ ]
– Frenz / Carry bag man / Get a hotel / Victoria / Athlete cured / In these times / The steak place / Bremen nacht / Guest informant (excerpt) / Oswald defence lawyer. *(c/cd+=)* – Tuff life boogie / Guest informant / Twister / There's a ghost in my house / Hit the north (part 1).

Below album was a MICHAEL CLARK and company ballet, first premiered in Amsterdam 11 Jun'88. Dancer MICHAEL had been a long-time fan and friend.

Oct 88. (lp)(c)(cd) **I AM KURIOUS, ORANJ** [54] [ ]
– New big prinz / Overture from 'I Am Curious, Orange' / Dog is life – Jerusalem / Wrong place, right time / Guide me soft * / C.D. win fall 2088 ad / Yes, o yes / Van plague? / Bad news girl / Cab it up! / Last nacht * / Big new priest *. *(c/cd+= *)*
Nov 88. (d7"ep)(d3"cd-ep) **JERUSALEM / ACID PRIEST 2088. / BIG NEW PRINZ / WRONG PLACE, RIGHT TIME** [59] [ ]
Jun 89. (7") **CAB IT UP. / DEAD BEAT DESCENDENT (out take from ballet** [ ] [ ]
(12"+=) – Kurious oranj (live) / Hit the north (live).
Jun 89. (lp)(c)(cd) **SEMINAL LIVE (some studio)** [40] [ ]
– Dead beat descendant / Pinball machine / H.O.W. / Squid law / Mollusc in Tyrol / 2 x 4 / Elf prefix – L.A. / Victoria / Pay your rates / Cruiser's creek. *(c/cd+=)* – Kurious oranj / Hit the north / In these times / Frenz.

— **MARTIN BRAMAH** – guitar returned to repl. BRIX E. who continued with ADULT NET.

Cog Sinister-Fontana | Fontana

Jan 90. (7")(c-s) **TELEPHONE THING. / BRITISH PEOPLE IN HOT WEATHER** [58] [ ]
(12"+=)(cd-s+=) – Telephone (dub).
Feb 90. (cd)(c)(lp) **EXTRICATE** [31] [ ]
– Sing! Harpy / I'm Frank / Bill is dead / Black monk theme part 1 / Popcorn double feature / Telephone thing / Hilary / Chicago, now! / The littlest rebel / British people in hot weather / And therein. (c+cd+=) – Arms control poseur / Black monk theme part II / Extricate.
Mar 90. (7") **POPCORN DOUBLE FEATURE. / BUTTERFLIES 4 BRAINS** [ ] [ ]
(12"+=) – Arms control poseur.
(12"+=)(cd-s+=) – Zandra / Black monk theme part II.

— trimmed to basic quartet of **MARK E, CRAIG, STEVE and JOHN.**

Aug 90. (7") **WHITE LIGHTNING. / BLOOD OUTTA STONE** [56] [ ]
(12"+=) – Zagreb.
(12"ep)(cd-ep) – THE DREDGER EP (++=) – Life just bounces.
Dec 90. (7") **HIGH TENSION LINE. / XMAS WITH SIMON** [ ] [ ]
(12"+=)(cd-s+=) – Don't take the pizza.

— added guest **KENNY BRADY** – violin

Apr 91. (cd)(c)(lp) **SHIFT-WORK** [17] [ ]
– EARTH'S IMPOSSIBLE DAY :-So what about it? / Idiot joy showland / Edinburgh man / Pittsville direkt / The book of lies / High tension line / The war against intelligence/ / NOTEBOOKS OUT PLAGLARISTS :-Shift-work / You haven't found it yet / The mixer / White lightning / A lot of wind / Rose / Sinister waltz.

— **DAVID BUSH** – keyboards, machines repl. BRADY

Mar 92. (7") **FREE RANGE. / EVERYTHING HURTZ** [40] [ ]
(12"+=)(pic-cd-s+=) – Dangerous / Return.
Mar 92. (cd)(c)(lp) **CODE: SELFISH** [21] [ ]
– The Birmingham school of business school / Free range / Return / Time enough at last / Everything hurtz / Immorality / Two-face! / Jusy waiting / So-called dangerous / Gentlemen's agreement / Married, 2 kids / Crew filth. *(re-iss.cd Aug93)*
Jun 92. (12"ep)(cd-ep) **ED'S BABE / PUMPKIN HEAD XSCAPES / THE KNIGHT, THE DEVIL AND DEATH / ARID'S AL'S DREAM / FREE RANGER** [ ] [ ]

Permanent-Cog Sinister | Permanent

Apr 93. (7") **WHY ARE PEOPLE GRUDGEFUL?. / GLAM-RACKET** [43] [ ]
(12"+=)(cd-s+=) – The Re-Mixer / Lost In Music
Apr 93. (cd)(c)(lp) **THE INFOTAINMENT SCAN** [9] [ ]
– Ladybird (green grass) / Lost in music / Glam-racket / I'm going to Spain / It's a curse / Paranoia man in cheap sh*t room / Service / The league of bald-headed men / A past gone mad / Light fireworks / League Moon monkey mix. (cd+=) – Why are people grudgeful?.

— added the returning **KARL BURNS** – percussion(now 6-piece yet again)

Dec 93. (d-cd-ep)(d12"ep) **BEHIND THE COUNTER EP** [75] [ ]
– Behind the counter / War / M5 / Happy holiday / Cab driver / (1).

— Feb 94; MARK guested for INSPIRAL CARPETS on their single 'I Want You'.

Apr 94. (10"clear-ep)(12"ep)(cd-ep) **15 WAYS. / HEY! STUDENT / THE $500 BOTTLE OF WINE** [65] [ ]
May 94. (cd)(c)(lp) **MIDDLE CLASS REVOLT (aka THE VAPOURISATION OF REALITY** [48] [ ]
– 15 ways / The reckoning / Behind the counter / M5£1 / Surmount all obstacles / Middle class revolt! / You're not up to much / Symbol of Mordgan / Hey! student / Junk man / The $500 bottle of wine / City dweller / War / Shut up!.

— added on tour the returning **BRIX SMITH**

Feb 95. (cd)(c)(lp) **CEREBRAL CAUSTIC** [67] [-]
– The joke / Don't call me darling / Rainmaster / Feeling numb / Pearl city / Life just bounces / I'm not satisfied / The aphid / Bonkers in Phoenix / One day / North west fashion show / Pine leaves.
Aug 95. (d-cd)(d-c)(d-lp) **THE TWENTY-SEVEN POINTS (live)** [ ] [-]
– Mollusc in Tyrol / Return / Lady bird (green grass) / Idiot – Walk-out / Ten points / Idiot – Walk-out / Big new prinz / Intro: Roadhouse / The joke / ME's jokes – The British people in hot weather / Free range / Hi-tension line / The league of the bald headed men / Glam racket: Star / Lost in music / Mr. Pharmacist / Cloud of black / Paranoia man in cheap shit room / Bounces / Outro / Passable / Glasgow advice / Middle class revolt: Simon, Dave and John / Bill is dead / Strychnine / War! / Noel's chemical effluence / Three points – Up too much.

. . . Jan – Jun '96 stop press . . .

— added **JULIA NAGLE** – keyboards / **LUCY RIMMER** – backing vocals / + returning **BRIX**

Jet | not issued

Feb 96. (single) **THE CHISELERS** [60] [-]

— MARK E. worked with DOSE on their single 'PLUG MYSELF IN', released on Pete Waterman's new label 'Coliseum'!

Jun 96. (cd)(c)(lp) **THE LIGHT USER SYNDROME** [54] [-]

– compilations, etc. –

Sep 81. Step Forward; (lp) **77-EARLY YEARS-79** [ ] [-]
Mar 82. Chaos; (c) **LIVE AT ACKLAM HALL, LONDON 1980** [ ] [-]
Nov 82. Cottage; (lp) **A PART OF AMERICA THEREIN** [-] [ ]
Nov 83. Kamera; (7") **MARQUEE CHA-CHA. / ROOM TO LIVE/ / (PAPAL VISIT orig. 'B')** [ ] [-]
Mar 85. Situation 2; (lp)(c) **HIP PRIESTS AND KAMERADS** (81-82 material) [ ] [-]
(c+=) – (has 4 extra tracks) *(cd-iss.Mar88 += same 4) (re-iss.cd Sep95 on 'Beggar's Banquet')*
May 87. Strange Fruit; (12"ep) **THE PEEL SESSIONS** (28.11.78) [ ] [-]
– Put away / No Xmas for John Quay / Like to blow / Mess of my.
Mar 93. Strange Fruit; (12"ep) **KIMBLE** [ ] [-]
– Kimble / C'n'c hassle schmuk / Spoilt Victorian child / Words of expectation.
Nov 87. Cog Sinister; (lp)(c)(cd) **IN PALACE OF SWORDS REVERSED (80-83)** [ ] [-]
Sep 90. Cog Sinister; (cd)(c)(lp) **458489** ('A'sides; 1984-89) [47] [ ]
– Oh! brother / C.R.E.E.P. / No bulbs 3 / Rollin' Dany / Couldn't get ahead / Cruiser's creek / L.A. / Living too late / Hit the north (part 1) / Mr.Pharmacist / Hey! Luciani / There's a ghost in my house / Victoria / Big new prinz / Wrong place, right time No.2 / Jerusalem / Dead beat descendant. // God-box / Pat-trip dispenser / Slang king 2 / Draygo's guilt / Clear off! / No bulbs / Petty thief lout / Vixen / Hot aftershave bop / Living too long / Lucifer over Lancashire / Auto tech pilot / Entitled / Shoulder pads £1 / Sleep debt snatches / Mark'll sink us / Haf found Bormann / Australians in Europe / Northerns in Europe / Hit the north (part 2) / Guest informant / Tuff life boogie / Twister / Acid priest 2088 / Cab it up.
Dec 90. Cog Sinister; (cd)(c)(d-lp) **458489** (B'sides; 1984-89) [ ] [ ]
-God-box / Pat-trip dispenser / Slang king 2 / Draygo's guilt / Clear off! / No bulbs / Petty thief lout / Vixen / Hot aftershave bop / Living too long / Lucifer over Lancashire / Auto tech pilot / Entitled / Shoulder pads £1 / Sleep debt snatches / Mark'll sink us / Haf found Bormann / Australians in Europe / Northerns in Europe / Hit the north (part 2) / Guest informant / Tuff life boogie / Twister / Acid priest 2088 / Cab it up. *(cd+=)* Bremen nache run out / Mark'll sink us (live) / Kurious oranj.
Apr 93. Castle; (cd)(c) **THE COLLECTION** [ ] [-]
Aug 93. Windsong; (cd) **BBC RADIO 1 LIVE IN CONCERT** [ ] [-]

. . Jan-Jun'96 stop press compilations . . .

Feb 96. Receiver; (cd) **SINISTER WALTZ** [ ] [-]
Apr 96. Receiver; (cd) **FIEND WITH A VIOLIN** [ ] [-]
Apr 96. Receiver; (cd) **OSWALD DEFENCE LAWYER** [ ] [-]

FAMILY

Formed: Leicester, England . . . 1967 by WHITNEY, CHAPMAN, KING and GRECH. The 4 originally stemmed from The FARINAS, who were on the go for 5 years, and who issued 'Fontana' 45 in Aug'64; 'YOU'D BETTER STOP. / I LIKE IT LIKE THAT'. As FAMILY, they moved to London, and made their debut at The Royal Albert Hall in Jul'67 supporting TIM HARDIN. After a one-off 7" vinyl debut for 'Liberty', they signed to 'Reprise' in 1968. Their DAVE MASON & JIMMY MILLER produced first lp 'MUSIC FROM A DOLL'S HOUSE', made the UK Top 40. Their next 5 lp's, all hit Top 20, and they also ventured into singles chart with classics 'NO MULE'S FOOL', 'STRANGE BAND', 'IN MY OWN TIME' & 'BURLESQUE'. • **Style:** Excellent progressive power-rock outfit, fronted by the manic 'frog-in-throat', but prolific voxist ROGER CHAPMAN. Their last album 'IT'S ONLY A MOVIE' (1973), saw a divertion to more commercial good-time rock, although it suffered undeserved critical panning. • **Songwriters:** CHAPMAN-WHITNEY penned most of material, except ROGER CHAPMAN solo covers LET'S SPEND THE NIGHT TOGETHER (Rolling Stones) / I'M YOUR HOOCHIE COOCHIE MAN + THAT SAME THING (Willie Dixon) / KEEP A KNOCKIN' (Little Richard) / I'M A KING BEE (Sam Moore) / STONE FREE (Jimi Hendrix) / LOVE LETTERS IN THE SAND (Pat Boone?) / SLOW DOWN (Hank Williams) / BUSTED LOOSE (Paul Brady) / KEEP FORGETTING (Leiber-Stoller) / TALKING ABOUT YOU (Chuck Berry). • **Trivia:** In 1968, their exploits on tour, were given light in Jenny Fabian's obscure novel 'Groupie'.

Recommended: THE BEST OF FAMILY (*9) / MUSIC IN A DOLL'S HOUSE (*7) / ENTERTAINMENT (*6) / A SONG FOR ME (*6) / FEARLESS (*6) / BANDSTAND (5) / THE BEST OF STREETWALKERS (*5) / KICK IT BACK (*4) (ROGER CHAPMAN).

ROGER CHAPMAN (b. 8 Apr'44, Leicester, England) – vocals / **CHARLIE WHITNEY** (b. 4 Jun'44, Leicester) – guitar, vocals / **JIM KING** – saxophone, flute / **RIC GRECH** (b. 1 Nov'46, Bordeaux, France) – bass / **HARRY OVENALL** – drums

Liberty | not issued

Sep 67. (7") **SCENE THROUGH THE EYE OF A LENS. / GYPSY WOMAN** [ ] [-]

— **ROB TOWNSEND** (b. 7 Jul'47) – drums repl. HARRY

Reprise | Reprise

Jun 68. (7") **ME AND MY FRIEND. / HEY MR. POLICEMAN** [ ] [ ]

Jul 68. (7") **OLD SONGS NEW SONGS. / HEY MR. POLICEMAN** [-] [ ]

Jul 68. (lp) **MUSIC IN A DOLL'S HOUSE** [35] [ ]
– The chase / Mellowing grey / Never like this / Me and my friend / Variation on a theme of Hey Mr. Policeman / Winter / Old songs new songs / Variation on a theme of the breeze / Hey Mr. Policeman / See through windows / Variation on a theme of me and my friend / Peace of mind / Voyage / The breeze / 3 x time. *(re-iss.+cd.Sep87 on 'See For Miles')*

Nov 68. (7") **SECOND GENERATION WOMAN. / HOME TOWN** [ ] [ ]

Mar 69. (lp) **ENTERTAINMENT** [6] [ ]
– The weaver's answer / Observations from a hill / Hung up down / Summer '67 / How-hi-the-li / Second generation woman / From past archives / Dim / Processions / Face in the crowd / Emotions. *(re-iss.+cd.Sep87 on 'See For Miles')*

— **JOHN WEIDER** (b.21 Apr'47) – bass, violin (ex-ERIC BURDON & ANIMALS) repl. GRECH who joined BLIND FAITH

Oct 69. (7") **NO MULE'S FOOL. / GOOD FRIEND OF MINE** [29] [ ]

— **POLI PALMER** (b. JOHN, 25 May'43) – keyboards, vibes (ex-ECLECTION) repl. KING who joined RING OF TRUTH

Jan 70. (lp)(c) **A SONG FOR ME** [4] [ ]
– Drowned in wine / Some poor soul / Love is a sleeper / Stop for the traffic (through the heart of me) / Wheels / Song for sinking lovers / Hey let it rock / The cat and the rat / 93's ok J. / A song for me. *(re-iss.+cd.Nov88 on 'See For Miles')*

Apr 70. (7") **TODAY. / SONG FOR SINKING LOVERS** [ ] [ ]

Aug 70. (7"m) **STRANGE BAND. / THE WEAVER'S ANSWER / HUNG UP DOWN** [11] [ ]

Reprise | United A..

Nov 70. (lp)(c) **ANYWAY . . .** (half live) [7] [ ]
– Good news bad news / Holding the compass / Strange band / Willow tree / Part of the load / Anyway / Normans / Lives and Ladies. *(re-iss.+cd.Nov88 on 'See For Miles') (re-iss.cd May94 on 'Castle')*

Mar 71. (lp)(c) **OLD SONGS NEW SONGS** (compilation remixed) [ ] [ ]
– Hung up down / Today / Observations from a hill / Good friend of mine / Drowned in wine / Peace of mind / Home town / The cat and the rat / No mule's fool / See through windows / The weaver's answer.

Jun 71. (7") **IN MY OWN TIME. / SEASONS** [4] [ ]

— **JOHN WETTON** (b.12 Jul'49, Derby, England) – bass, vocals (ex-MOGUL THRASH) repl. WEIDER who joined STUD

Oct 71. (lp)(c) **FEARLESS** [14] [ ]
– Between blue and me / Sat'd'y barfly / Larf and sing / Spanish tide / Save some for thee / Take your partners / Children / Crinkly grin / Blind / Burning bridges. *(re-iss.+cd Nov88 on 'See For Miles') (re-iss.cd May94 on 'Castle')*

Sep 72. (7") **BURLESQUE. / THE ROCKIN' R'S** [13] [ ]

Sep 72. (lp)(c) **BANDSTAND** [15] [ ]
– Burlesque / Bolero babe / Coronation / Dark eyes / Broken nose / My friend the sun / Glove / Ready to go / Top of the hill. *(re-iss.+cd.Nov88 on 'See For Miles') (cd-iss.Mar94 on 'Castle')*

Jan 73. (7") **MY FRIEND THE SUN. / GLOVE** [ ] [ ]

— CHAPMAN, WHITNEY and TOWNSEND were joined by **JIM CREGAN** – bass, guitar (ex-STUD) repl. WETTON who joined KING CRIMSON / **TONY ASHTON** (b. 1 Mar'46, Blackburn, England) – keyboards (ex-ASHTON, GARDNER and DYKE) repl. PALMER

Raft | United Art

Apr 73. (7") **BOOM BOOM. / STOP THIS CAR** [ ] [ ]

Sep 73. (7") **SWEET DESIREE. / DRINK TO YOU** [ ] [ ]

Sep 73. (lp)(c) **IT'S ONLY A MOVIE** [30] [ ]
– It's only a movie / Leroy / Buffet tea for two / Boom bang / Boots 'n' roots / Banger / Sweet Desiree / Suspicion / Check out.

— They split late '73 with TOWNSEND joining MEDICINE HEAD and CREGAN went to COCKNEY REBEL, ASHTON went into production. ROGER and CHARLIE formed CHAPMAN / WHITNEY STREETWALKERS

– compilations, others, etc. –

Note; All below releases on 'Reprise' issued in US 'United Artists'

Sep 74. Reprise; (lp)(c) **THE BEST OF FAMILY** [ ] [ ]
– Burlesque / My friend the Sun / The chase / Old songs, new songs / Part of the load / In my own time / It's only a movie / Sweet desiree / Sat'd'y barfly / Children / No mule's fool / The weaver's answer. *(re-iss.+cd.Nov91 on 'See For Miles', with extra tracks)(re-iss.cd+cApr93 on 'Castle')*

Nov 74. Reprise; (7") **MY FRIEND THE SUN. / BURLESQUE** [ ] [ ]

May 78. Reprise; (7"ep) **BURLESQUE. / IN MY OWN TIME / THE WEAVER'S ANSWER** [ ] [ ]

Oct 81. Rebecca; (lp) **RISE** [ ] [-]

Jan 82. Rebecca; (7") **BURLESQUE. / MY FRIEND THE SUN** [ ] [-]

Nov 88. Strange Fruit; (12"ep)(cd-ep) **THE PEEL SESSIONS (8.5.73)** [ ] [-]

Aug 89. That's Original; (d-lp)(c)(cd) **IT'S ONLY A MOVIE / FEARLESS** [ ] [-]

Nov 92. Castle; (cd) **A's & B's** [ ] [-]

Mar 93. Dutch East India; (cd) **THE PEEL SESSIONS** [ ] [-]

STREETWALKERS

ROGER CHAPMAN – vocals / **CHARLIE WHITNEY** – guitar / **BOBBY TENCH** – guitar, vocals (ex-JEFF BECK) / **PHILIP CHEN** – bass / **TIM HINKLEY** – keyboards / **MEL COLLINS** – saxophone, flute / **IAN WALLACE** – drums (both ex-KING CRIMSON)

Reprise | Mercury

May 74. (lp)(c) **STREETWALKERS** [ ] [ ]
– Parisienne high heels / Roxianna / Systematic stealth / Call ya / Creature feature / Sue and Betty Jean / Showbiz Joe / Just four men / Tokyo rose / Hangman.

Jun 74. (7") **ROXIANNA. / CRACK** [ ] [ ]

— **JON PLOTEL** – bass (ex-CASABLANCA) repl. CHEN & HINKLEY (to sessions) / **NICKO McBAIN** – drums repl. WALLACE & COLLINS (to ALVIN LEE ⇒ TEN YEARS AFTER)

Vertigo | Mercury

Oct 75. (lp)(c) **DOWNTOWN FLYERS** [ ] [ ]
– Downtown flyers / Toenail draggin' / Raingame / Miller / Crawfish / Walking on waters / Gypsy moon / Burn it down / Ace o'spades.

Oct 75. (7") **RAINGAME. / MILLER** [ ] [ ]

May 76. (red-lp)(c) **RED CARD** [16] [ ]
– Run for cover / Me an' me horse an' me rum / Crazy charade / Daddy rolling stone / Roll up, roll up / Between us / Shotgun messiah / Decadence code.

Jun 76. (7") **DADDY ROLLING STONE. / HOLE IN YOUR POCKET** [ ] [ ]

— **CHAPMAN, WHITNEY + TENCH** were joined by **MICKY FEAT** – bass / **DAVID DOWLE** – drums / **BRIAN JOHNSON** – keyboards (**McBAIN** joined **PAT TRAVERS** and later **IRON MAIDEN**)

Jan 77. (lp)(c) **VICIOUS BUT FAIR** [ ] [ ]
– Mama was mad / Chili con carne / Dice man / But you're beautiful / Can't come in / Belle star / Sam (maybe he can come to some arrangement) / Cross time woman. *(cd-iss.Aug92 on 'See For Miles' ' . . . PLUS' +=)*– Downtown flyers / Gypsy Moon / Crawfish / Raingame / Crazy charade / Shotgun Messiah / Decadence code / Daddy rolling stone.

Dec 77. (lp)(c) **LIVE (live)** [ ] [ ]
– Chilli con carne / Crazy charade / Walking on waters / Dice man / My friend the Sun / Toenail draggin' / Mama was mad / Me an' me horse an' me rum / Run for cover / Burlesque / Can't come in.

— Had already split, TENCH and FEAT joined VAN MORRISON. JOHNSON and DOWLE joined DAVID COVERDALE'S WHITESNAKE.

– (STREETWALKERS) compilations, etc. –

Dec 90. Phonogram; (cd) **THE BEST OF STREETWALKERS** [ ] [-]
Jun 94. Windsong; (cd) **BBC RADIO 1 LIVE IN CONCERT** [ ] [-]

ROGER CHAPMAN

went solo, augmented by MICKEY JUPP

Arista Arista

Mar 79. (lp)(c) **CHAPPO** [ ] [ ]
– Midnite child / Moth to a flame / Keep forgettin' / Shape of things / Face of stone / Who pulled the nite down / Always gotta pay in the end / Hang on to a dream / Pills / Don't give up. *(re-iss.+cd.1988 on 'Maze') (cd-iss.Jul92 on 'Castle')*

Acrobat not issued

Mar 79. (7") **MIDNITE CHILD. / MOTH TO A FLAME** [ ] [-]
May 79. (7") **WHO PULLED THE NIGHT DOWN. / SHORTLIST** [ ] [-]
Jul 79. (7") **LET'S SPEND THE NIGHT TOGETHER. / SHAPE OF THINGS** [ ] [-]
Dec 79. (lp)(c) **LIVE IN HAMBURG (live w/ The SHORTLIST)** [ ] [-]
– Moth to a flame / Keep forgettin' / Midnite child / Who pulled the nite down / Talking about you / Shortlist / Can't get in / Keep a knockin' / I'm your hoochie coochie man / Let's spend the night together. *(re-iss.+cd.1988 on 'Maze') (cd-iss.Dec92 on 'Castle')*

B.B.C. not issued

Oct 80. (7") **SPEAK FOR YOURSELF. / SWEET VANILLA** [ ] [-]

— with **PALMER / HINKLEY / WHITEHORN**

Kamera not issued

Sep 80. (lp)(c) **MAIL ORDER MAGIC** [ ] [-]
– Unknown soldier (can't get to Heaven) / He was, she was / Barman / Right to go / Duelling man / Making the same mistake / Another little hurt / Mail order magic / Higher ground / Ground floor. *(re-iss.+cd.1988 on 'Maze') (cd-iss.Dec92 on 'Castle')*

Polydor not issued

Dec 81. (lp)(c) **HYENAS ONLY LAUGH FOR FUN** [ ] [-]
– Prisoner / Hyenas only laugh for fun / Killing time / Want's nothing chained / The long goodbye / Blood and sand / Common touch / Goodbye (reprise) / Hearts on the floor / Step up – Take a bow / Jukebox mama.
Oct 82. (d-lp)(c) **HE WAS SHE WAS YOU WAS WE WAS (live)** [ ] [-]
– Higher ground / Ducking down / Making the same mistake / Blood and sand / Medley:- I'm a king bee – That same thing – Face of stone / Hyeanas only laugh for fun / Prisoner / Medley:- Slow down – Common touch / Jukebox mama No.3 / He was, she was / Stone free / Bitches brew / Unknown soldier. *(re-iss.+cd.1988 on 'Maze') (re-iss.cd Apr94 on 'Castle')*
Mar 83. (lp)(c) **MANGO CRAZY** [ ] [-]
– Mango crazy / Toys: Do you? / I read your file / Los dos Bailadores / Blues breaker / Turn it up loud / Let me down / Hunt the man / Rivers run dry / I really can't go straight / Room service / Hegoshegoyougoamigo. *(re-iss.+cd.1988 on 'Maze') (cd-iss.Dec92 on 'Castle')*

(CHAPMAN provided vocals for MIKE OLDFIELD on single 'Shadow On The Wall')

Apr 84. (7") **HOW HOW HOW. / HOLD THAT TIDE BACK** [ ] [-]

R.C.A. not issued

May 85. (lp)(c)(cd) **THE SHADOW KNOWS** [ ] [-]
– Busted loose / Leader of men / Ready to roll / I think of you now / The shadow knows / How how how / Only love is in the red / Sweet vanilla / I'm a good boy now. *(re-iss.cd Mar94 on 'Castle')*
1986. (lp)(c)(cd) **ZIPPER** [ ] [-]
– Zipper / Running with the flame / On do die day / Never love a rolling stone / Let the beat get heavy / It's never too late to do-ron-ron / Woman of destiny / Hoodoo me up.
1987. (lp)(c) **TECHNO-PRISONERS** [ ] [-]
– The drum / Wild again / Techno-prisoner / Black forest / We will touch again / Run for your love / Slap bang in the middle / Who's been sleeping in my bed / Ball of confusion. *(re-iss.cd Mar94 on 'Castle')*
1989. (lp)(c)(cd) **WALKING THE CAT** [ ] [-]
– Kick it back / Son of Red Moon / Stranger than strange / Just a step away (let's go) / The fool / Walking the cat / J & D / Come the dark night / Hands off / Jivin' / Saturday night kick back.

Maze not issued

Nov 89. (m-lp) **LIVE IN BERLIN (live)** [ ] [-]
– Shadow on the wall / Let me down / How how how / Mango crazy. *(cd-iss.Dec92 on 'Castle')*

Castle not issued

1992. (cd) **KICK IT BACK** [ ] [-]
– Walking the cat / Cops in shades / House behind the Sun / Chicken fingers / Kick it back / Son of red Moon / Someone else's clothes / Hideaway / Toys: Do you? / Hot night to rhumba / Stranger than strange / Just a step away (let's go) / Jesus and the Devil.

FANATICS (see under ⇒ OCEAN COLOUR SCENE)

FARM

Formed: Liverpool, England . . . early '83 by PETE HOOTEN and STEVE GRIMES. Appeared on BBC2 TV's 'Oxford Road Show', and met MADNESS man SUGGS McPHERSON, who produced their 1984 debut 45 'HEARTS AND MINDS'. Struggled early on and suffered tragedy when drummer ANDY McVANN died in a car crash late '86. Things got decidedly better, when they started own label 'Produce' in 1990. Their first single that year 'STEPPING STONE', hit No.56, and was followed by 2 classy UK Top 10 hits 'GROOVY TRAIN' & 'ALL TOGETHER NOW'. • **Style:** At first influenced by brassy DEXY's or REDSKINS sound, but opted in the late 80's for new rave/dance scene. • **Songwriters:** All written by HOOTEN-GRIMES, except covers of STEPPING STONE (hit; Monkees) / DON'T YOU WANT ME (Human League) / SHAKE SOME ACTION (Flamin' Groovies). • **Miscellaneous:** In 1990, their live technician RAY TOOMEY, was jailed for 30 months for his part in the Risley remand centre rooftop protest.

Recommended: SPARTACUS (*7).

PETE HOOTEN (b.28 Sep'62) – vocals / **STEVE GRIMES** (b. 4 Jun'62) – guitar / **JOHN MELVIN** – guitar / **PHILIP STRONGMAN** – bass / **ANDY McVANN** – drums / plus **TONY EVANS** – trombone / **GEORGE MAHER** – trumpet / **STEVE 'SNOWY' LEVY** – saxophone / **and occasional live JOE MUSKER** – percussion

Skysaw not issued

Nov 84. (12"ep) **HEARTS AND MINDS. / ('A'dub version) / INFORMATION MAN / SAME OLD STORY** [ ] [-]

Admirality not issued

Nov 85. (7") **STEPS OF EMOTION. / MEMORIES** [ ] [-]
(12") – ('A'side) / Power over me / No man's land / Better / Living for tomorrow.

Fire not issued

Sep 86. (7") **SOME PEOPLE. / STANDING TOGETHER** [ ] [-]
(12"+=) – Sign of the times / The Moroccan.
Oct 86. (lp) **PASTURES OLD AND NEW** [ ] [-]
– Hearts and minds / Information man / Same old story / Hearts and minds (dub) / Steps of emotion / Power over me / No man's land / Better / Worn out sayings / Some people / Little old wine drinker me. *(comp. of Radio 1 sessions) (re-iss.Aug89)*

— (early '87) **MICK HANRATTY** – drums (on tour) repl. ANDY McVANN who died in a crash Dec86. Late 1987; **ROY BOULTER** (b. 2 Jul'64) – drums repl. HANRATTY and the horn section /**KEITH MULLEN** (DR. KEITH LOVE) (b.Bootle) – guitar repl. MELVIN / **CARL HUNTER** (b.14 Apr'65, Bootle, England) – bass repl. PHILLIP

— (early '89) **HOOTEN, GRIMES, HUNTER, MULLEN, and BOULTER** added **BEN LEACH** (b. 2 May'69) – keyboards

Foresight not issued

Jul 89. (7") **BODY AND SOUL. / COLONELS AND HEROES** [ ] [-]
(12"+=) – Stuck on you.

Produce Sire

Apr 90. (12")(7") **STEPPING STONE. / FAMILY OF MAN** [58] [-]
Sep 90. (7") **GROOVY TRAIN. / ('A' 3:30 a.m. mix)** [6] [41] Aug 91
(12"+=)(cd-s+=) – ('A'bottle mix).
Nov 90. (7")(c-s) **ALL TOGETHER NOW. (featuring PETE WYLIE) / ('A' Terry Farley mix)** [4] [ ]
(12"+=)(cd-s+=) – ('A'Rocky & Diesel mix).

— added guest backing vocalist **PAULA DAVID**

Mar 91. (cd)(c)(lp) **SPARTACUS** [1] [ ]
– Hearts and minds / How long / Sweet inspiration / Groovy train / Higher and higher / Don't let me down / Family of man / Tell the story / Very emotional / All together now. *(initial copies, incl.free remix lp)*
Apr 91. (7")(c-s) **DON'T LET ME DOWN. / ('A' Terry Farley mix)** [36] [ ]
(12"+=)(cd-s+=) – ('A'-Rocky & Diesel mix).
Aug 91. (7")(c-s) **MIND. / STEPPING STONE** [31] [ ]
(12"+=)(cd-s+=) – ('A'new mix).
Dec 91. (7") **LOVE SEE NO COLOUR (Suggs mix). / ('A' Noel Watson mix)** [58] [ ]
(d12"+=)(cd-s+=) – (6 other remixes).

— In October 1991, KEITH MULLEN was attacked and stabbed needing over 80 stitches. 'ALL TOGETHER NOW' is used by The Labour Party in their General election campaign.

End Product-Sony Sony

Jun 92. (7")(c-s) **RISING SUN. / CREEPERS** [48] [ ]
(12"+=)(cd-s+=) – ('A'-Mark Saunders mix) / ('A'-Steve Spiro mix).
Oct 92. (7")(c-s) **DON'T YOU WANT ME. / OBVIOUSLY** [18] [ ]
(cd-s+=) – Groovy train (US mix).
Dec 92. (7")(c-s) **LOVE SEE NO COLOUR. / ALL TOGETHER NOW** [35] [ ]
(12"+=) – Anytown / (other 'A'side).

(cd-s) – ('A'side) / ('A'original) / Rain / Don't you want me (mixes).

Produce | not issued

Feb 93. (5x12"box)(cd-box-ep) **STEPPING STONE. / ALL TOGETHER NOW (mix)/ / GROOVY TRAIN. / (mix)/ / ALL TOGETHER NOW. / (mix)/ / MIND. / (mix)/ / DON'T LET ME DOWN. / (mix)/ /** [ ] [-]

Sire-Reprise | Sire-Reprise

Jul 94. (7")(c-s) **MESSIAH. / ONE MORE FOOL** [ ] [ ]
(cd-s+=) – Somewhere (acoustic) / Love made up my mind.

Aug 94. (cd)(c) **HULLABALOO** [ ] [ ]
– Messiah / Shake some action / Comfort / The man who cried / Hateful / Golden vision / To the ages / All American world / Distant voices / Echoes.

Mark FARNER (see under ⇒ GRAND FUNK RAILROAD)

Bryan FERRY (see under ⇒ ROXY MUSIC)

FFWD (see under ⇒ ORB)

Tim FINN / FINN (see under ⇒ CROWDED HOUSE)

FIRM (see under ⇒ LED ZEPPELIN)

FISH

Born: DEREK WILLIAM DICK, 25 Apr'58, Dalkeith, Lothian, Scotland. After leaving MARILLION in Sep'88, he released debut single 'STATE OF MIND', a year later. This hit UK Top 40, as did his early 1990 follow-up 'BIG WEDGE'. A Top 5 album 'VIGIL IN A WILDERNESS OF MIRRORS' was soon in chart, and he continued further fruitful activities on 'Polydor'. He had now moved back to Scotland, after living in London. • **Style:** FISH sported a more commercial guitar-based sound, although his vox always was indebted to PETER GABRIEL. • **Songwriters:** He co-wrote most of material with MICKEY SIMMONDS. He covered; THE FAITH HEALER (Sensational Alex Harvey Band). In early 1993, he released full covers album with tracks: QUESTION (Moody Blues) / BOSTON TEA PARTY (Sensational Alex Harvey Band) / FEARLESS (Pink Floyd) / APEMAN (Kinks) / HOLD YOUR HEAD UP (Argent) / SOLD (Sandy Denny) / I KNOW WHAT I LIKE (Genesis) / JEEPSTER (T.Rex) / FIVE YEARS (David Bowie) / ROADHOUSE BLUES (Doors). • **Trivia:** October '86, FISH was credited on TONY BANKS (Genesis) single 'Short Cut To Nowhere'.

Recommended: VIGIL IN A WILDERNESS OF MIRRORS (*6).

FISH – vocals (ex-MARILLION) with guest musicians on debut album **FRANK USHER** – guitar / **HAL LINDES** – guitar / **MICKEY SIMMONDS** – keyboards / **JOHN GIBLIN** – bass / **MARK BRZEZICKI** – drums / **CAROL KENYON** – backing vocals / plus **LUIS JARDIM** – percussion / **JANICK GERS** – guitar

E.M.I. | E.M.I.

Oct 89. (7")(c-s) **STATE OF MIND. / THE VOYEUR (I LIKE TO WATCH)** [32] [ ]
(12"+=)(cd-s+=) – ('A'version).

Dec 89. (7")(c-s) **BIG WEDGE. / JACK AND JILL** [25] [ ]
(12"+=)(cd-s+=)(12"pic-d+=) – Faith healer (live).

Feb 90. (cd)(c)(lp)(pic-lp) **VIGIL IN A WILDERNESS OF MIRRORS** [5] [ ]
– Vigil / Big wedge / State of mind / The company / A gentleman's excuse me / The voyeur (I like to watch) / Family business / View from the hill / Cliche.

Mar 90. (7")(c-s)(7"sha-pic-d)(7"red) **A GENTLEMAN'S EXCUSE ME. / WHIPLASH** [30] [ ]
(12"+=)(cd-s+=)(12"pic-d+=) – ('A'demo version).

— retained SIMMONDS and USHER, and brought in **ROBIN BOULT** – lead guitar, vocals / **DAVID PATON** – bass / **ETHAN JOHNS** – drums, perc. / guest drummer **TED McKENNA**

Polydor | Polydor

Sep 91. (7") **INTERNAL EXILE. / CARNIVAL MAN** [37] [ ]
(12"+=)(12"pic-d+=) – ('A' karaoke mix).
(cd-s++=) – ('A'other mix).

Oct 91. (cd)(c)(lp) **INTERNAL EXILE** [21] [ ]
– Shadowplay / Credo / Just good friends (close) / Favourite stranger / Lucky / Dear friend / Tongues / Internal exile. *(re-iss.cd Apr95)*

Dec 91. (7")(c-s) **CREDO. / POET'S MOON** [38] [ ]
(12"+=)(cd-s+=) – ('A'mix).
(12"+=) – (2 'A'versions) / Tongues (demo).

Jun 92. (7")(c-s) **SOMETHING IN THE AIR. / DEAR FRIEND** [51] [ ]
(12"+=) – ('A'-Teddy bear mix).
(cd-s++=) – ('A'radio mix).
(cd-s) – ('A'&'B'diff.mixes) / Credo / Shadowplay.

— **FOSTER PATTERSON** – keyboards, vocals repl. SIMMONS / **KEVIN WILKINSON** – drums, percussion repl. JOHNS.

Jan 93. (cd)(c)(lp) **SONGS FROM THE MIRROR** (covers) [46] [ ]
– Question / Boston tea party / Fearless / Apeman / Hold your head up / Solo / I know what I like / Jeepster / Five years. *(re-iss.cd Apr95)*

Dick Bros | not issued

Mar 94. (d-cd) **SUSHI (live)** [ ] [-]
– Fearless / Big wedge / Boston tea party / Credo / Family business / View from a hill / He knows you know / She chameleon / Kayleigh / White Russian / The company / / Just good friends / Jeepster / Hold your head up / Lucky / Internal exile / Cliche / Last straw / Poets Moon / 5 years.

Apr 94. (c-s)('A'ext-12"pic-d) **LADY LET IT LIE / OUT OF MY LIFE. / BLACK CANAL** [46] [ ]
(cd-s) – ('A'extended) / ('B'live) / Emperors song (live) / Just good friends.

May 94. (cd)(c)(pic-lp)(d-lp) **SUITS** [18] [ ]
– 1470 / Lady let it lie / Emperor's song / Fortunes of war / Somebody special / No dummy / Pipeline / Jumpsuit city / Bandwagon / Raw meat.

Sep 94. (cd-ep) **FORTUNES OF WAR (edit) / SOMEBODY SPECIAL (live) / STATE OF MIND (live) / LUCKY (Live)** [67] [ ]
(cd-ep) – ('A'live) / Warm wet circles / Jumpsuit city / The company (all live).
(cd-ep) – ('A'acoustic) / Kayleigh (live) / Internal exile (live) / Just good friends (acoustic).
(cd-ep) – ('A'acoustic) / Sugar mice (live) / Dear friend (live) / Lady let it lie (acoustic).

— Above 4-cd single (nearly 90 mins.) (can be fitted in together as 1 package.

Aug 95. (c-s) **JUST GOOD FRIENDS. ("FISH featuring SAM BROWN") / SOMEBODY SPECIAL** [63] [ ]
(cd-s+=) – State of mind.
(cd-s) – ('A'side) / Raw meat (live) / Roadhouse blues (live).

Sep 95. (cd)(c) **YIN** (THE BEST OF FISH & '95 remixes) [58] [-]
– Incommunicado / Family business / Just good friends / Pipeline / Institution waltz / Tongues / Favourite stranger / Boston tea party / Raw meat / Time & a word / Company / Incubus / Solo.

Sep 95. (cd)(c) **YANG** (THE BEST OF FISH & '95 remixes) [52] [-]
– Lucky / Big wedge / Lady let it lie / Lavender / Credo / A gentleman's excuse me / Kayleigh / State of mind / Somebody special / Sugar mice / Punch & Judy / Internal exile / Fortunes of war.

FLAG OF CONVENIENCE / F. O. C. (see under ⇒ BUZZCOCKS)

FLAMING LIPS

Formed: Oklahoma City, USA . . . early 80's by COYNE brothers WAYNE and MARK, who reputedly stole instruments from church hall. Received their break in 1985, when 'Enigma' took them onto books. Signed to 'Warners' in 1992, and the following 2 years appeared at the Reading Festivals. • **Style:** Avant-garde psychedelic BARRETT /FLOYD inspired, whose barrage of sound was described as JAMC meeting BLACK FLAG or DEAD KENNEDYS. • **Songwriters:** Coyne-English-Ivins except; SUMMERTIME BLUES (Eddie Cochran) / WHAT'S SO FUNNY 'BOUT PEACE, LOVE & UNDERSTANDING (Brinsley Schwarz) / STRYCHNINE (Sonics).

Recommended: TELEPATHIC SURGERY (*6)

MARK COYNE – vocals / **WAYNE COYNE** – guitar / **MICHAEL IVINS** – bass / **RICHARD ENGLISH** – drums

not issued | L.S.D.

1985. (7"green-ep) **THE FLAMING LIPS E.P.** [ ] [ ]
– Bag full of thoughts / Out for a walk / Garden of eyes – Forever is a long time / Scratching the door / My own planet. *(re-iss.1986 red-ep) (re-iss.1987 +c-ep on 'Pink Dust')*

— **WAYNE** now on vox, when MARK departed

Nov 86. (lp)(cd) **HEAR IT IS** [ ] [ ]
– With you / Unplugged / Trains, brains and rain / Jesus shootin' heroin / Just like before / She is death / Charles Manson blues / Man from Pakistan / Godzilla flick / Staring at sound – With you.
(cd+=) – Summertime blues / FLAMING LIPS E.P.

Nov 87. (lp)(cd)(clear-lp) **OH MY GAWD!!!** [-] [ ]

Feb 89. (lp)(c)(cd) **TELEPATHIC SURGERY** [ ] [ ]
– Drug machine / Michael time to wake up / Miracle on 42nd Street / UFO story / Shaved gorilla / Begs and achin' / Right now / Hare Krishna stomp wagon / Chrome plated suicide / Redneck school of technology / Spontaneous combustion of John / The last drop of morning dew.

— **JONATHAN PONEMANN** – guitar + **JOHN DONAHUE** – guitar

Glitterhouse / Sub Pop

Jun 89. (7"m) **STRYCHNINE / DRUG MACHINE. / (WHAT'S SO FUNNY ABOUT) PEACE, LOVE AND UNDERSTANDING** [ ] [ ] Jan89

— **NATHAN ROBERTS** – drums repl. ENGLISH

City Slang / Sub Pop

Jan 91. (12"ep) **UNCONSCIOUSLY SCREAMING E.P.** [ ] [ ]
–

Feb 91. (cd)(c)(lp)(pink-lp) **IN A PRIEST DRIVEN AMBULANCE** [ ] [ ]
– Shine on sweet Jesus – Jesus song No.5 / Unconsciously screaming / Rainin' babies / Take Meta Mars / Five stop Mother Superior rain / Stand in line / God walks among us now / Jesus song No.6 / There you are / Jesus song No.7 / Mountain song / Wonderful world.

Warners / Warners

Aug 92. (cd)(c)(lp) **HIT TO DEATH IN THE MAJOR HEAD** [ ] [ ]
– Talkin' about the deathporn immorality (everyone wants to live forever) / Hit me like you did the first time / The Sun / Felt good to burn / Gingerale afternoon (the astrology of a Saturday) / Halloween on the Barbary Coast / The magician vs. the headache / You have to be joking (autopsy of the Devil's brain) / Frogs / Hold your head. *(re-iss.Apr95)*

— **RONALD JONES** – guitar repl. JOHN who joined MERCURY REV

— **STEVEN DROZD** – drums repl. NATHAN

Jun 93. (cd)(c)(lp) **TRANSMISSIONS FROM THE SATELLITE HEART** [ ] [ ]
– Turn it on / Pilot can at the queer of God / Oh my pregnant head (labia in the sunlight) / She don't use jelly / Chewin' the apple of your eye / Superhumans / Be my head / Moth in the incubator / Plastic Jesus / When yer twenty-two / Slow nerve action.

Aug 94. (7")(c-s) **SHE DON'T USE JELLY. / TURN IT ON (bluegrass version)** [ ] [55]
(cd-s+=) – Translucent egg.
(cd-s) – ('A'side) / The process / Moth in the incubator.

Sep 95. (cd)(c)(lp) **CLOUDS TASTE METALLIC** [ ] [ ]
– The abandoned hospital ship / Psychiatric explorations of the fetus with needles / Placebo headwood / This here giraffe / Brainville / Guy who lost a headache and accidentally saves the world / When you smile / Kim's watermelon gun / They punctured my yolk / Lightning strikes the postman / Christmas at the zoo / Evil will prevail / Bad days (aurally excited version).

Dec 95. (c-s) **BAD DAYS / GIRL WITH HAIR LIKE AN EXPLOSION** [ ] [ ]
(cd-s+=) – She don't use jelly / Giraffe (demo).
(cd-s) – ('A'side) / Ice drummer / When you smiled I lost my only idea / Put the water bug in the policeman's ear.

. . . Jan – Jun '96 stop press . . .

Feb 96. (single) **THIS HERE GIRAFFE** [72] [ ]

— above format included worlds first ever shaped cd.

FLEETWOOD MAC

Formed: London, England . . . July 1967, by MICK FLEETWOOD, PETER GREEN and BOB BRUNNING. They quickly inducted JEREMY SPENCER and made live debut at prestigeous Windsor Jazz & Blues Festival on 12 Aug'67. They replaced BRUNNING with another ex-BLUESBREAKERS member JOHN McVIE, and signed to 'Blue Horizon'. Billed at first as PETER GREEN'S FLEETWOOD MAC, they flopped late '67 with first 45 'I BELIEVE MY TIME AIN'T LONG'. Around the same time, they became in-house band for blues artists like OTIS SPANN and DUSTER BENNETT. Early in '68, their debut lp 'PETER GREEN'S FLEETWOOD MAC', hit the Top 5, and was soon pursued by Top 40 singles 'BLACK MAGIC WOMAN' & 'NEED YOUR LOVE SO BAD'. Their 2nd lp 'MR. WONDERFUL', also cracked the UK Top 10, and was followed by million-selling UK No.1 instrumental 'ALBATROSS'. Out of contract, they signed one-off deal with 'Immediate', who issued another Top 3 gem 'MAN OF THE WORLD' early '69. In the Autumn, yet another classic 'OH WELL' (in 2 parts), hit No.2 for new label 'Reprise', and at the same time lp 'THEN PLAY ON' made UK Top 10. On Apr'70, GREEN departed group, due to increasing state of mental health. He left behind another haunting Top 10 single 'THE GREEN MANALISHI', which showed his deep lyrical attitude at the time. Without him, the group failed to emulate earlier success, and had rough period until the mid-70's. Newcomers LINDSEY BUCKINGHAM and STEVIE NICKS, came into the fold alongside CHRISTINE McVIE (member and wife of JOHN McVIE since Aug'70) and MICK FLEETWOOD. Early in 1976 now residents of California, USA, they had 3 US Top 20 hits, and a self-titled album, that eventually rose to the top that year. Their much anticipated 1977 follow-up 'RUMOURS' surpassed its predecessor, topping both US & UK charts, before going on to sell over 15 million copies. Although the McVIE's separation quickly followed, the break-up of BUCKINGHAM and NICKS sealed the band's fate. The group, however, continued to be massive attraction for the rest of the 70's & 80's. All had own solo sideline, with the beautiful STEVIE being the most prolific in the 80's until her departure. • **Style:** Pioneers of the white blues boom of the late 60's, they progressed into sophisticated husband-wife AOR team, ready-made for FM radio. • **Songwriters:** GREEN compositions, except early covers; NEED YOUR LOVE SO BAD (Little Willie John) / NO PLACE TO GO (Howlin' Wolf) / DUST MY BROOM (Robert Johnson) / etc. • **Trivia:** Late 1973, their manager Clifford Davis, put together a bogus FLEETWOOD MAC, which resulted in a legal court battle, in which they won. The bogus group became STRETCH, and had a late '75 UK Top 20 hit with 'Why Did You Do It'.

Recommended: GREATEST HITS (*9 1971) / RUMOURS (*8) / FLEETWOOD MAC'S GREATEST HITS (*9 1988).

JEREMY SPENCER (b. 4 Jul'48, Hartlepool, England) – guitar, vocals / **PETER GREEN** (b. PETER GREENBAUM, 29 Oct'49) – guitar, vocals (ex-JOHN MAYALL'S BLUESBREAKERS, ex-SHOTGUN EXPRESS) / **MICK FLEETWOOD** (b.24 Jun'42) – drums (ex-JOHN MAYALL'S BLUESBREAKERS) / **JOHN McVIE** (b.26 Nov'45) – bass (ex-JOHN MAYALL'S BLUESBREAKERS) repl. BOB BRUNNING who formed SUNFLOWER BLUES BAND after recording B-side)

Blue Horizon / Epic

Nov 67. (7") **I BELIEVE MY TIME AIN'T LONG. / RAMBLING PONY** [ ] [-]

Feb 68. (lp) **(PETER GREEN'S) FLEETWOOD MAC** [4] [ ]
– My heart beat like a hammer / Merry go round / Long grey mare / Shake your moneymaker / Looking for somebody / No place to go / My baby's good to me / I love another woman / Cold black night / The world keep on turning / Got to move. *(re-iss.Oct73 on 'CBS/Embasssy' & Jul77 on 'CBS') (cd-iss.May88 on 'Line')(cd-iss.Nov93 on 'B.G.O.')*

Mar 68. (7") **BLACK MAGIC WOMAN. / THE SUN IS SHINING** [37] [-]

Apr 68. (7") **BLACK MAGIC WOMAN. / LONE GREY MARE** [-] [ ]

Jul 68. (7") **NEED YOUR LOVE SO BAD. / STOP MESSIN' ROUND** [31] [-]

Aug 68. (lp) **MR. WONDERFUL** [10] [-]
– Stop messin' round / Coming home / Rollin' man / Dust my broom / Love that burns / Doctor Brown / Need your love tonight / If you be my baby / Evenin' boogie / Lazy poker blues / I've lost my baby / Trying so hard to forget. *(re-iss.+c,cd.Nov89 on 'Essential')*

— added **DANNY KIRWAN** (b.13 Mar'50) – guitar, vocals (ex-BOILERHOUSE)

Nov 68. (7") **ALBATROSS. / JIGSAW PUZZLE BLUES** [1] [-]

Feb 69. (lp) **ENGLISH ROSE** [-] [ ]
– Stop messin' round / Jigsaw puzzle blues / Doctor Brown / Something inside of me / Evenin' boogie / Love that burns / Black magic woman / I've lost my baby / One sunny day / Without you / Coming home / Albatross.

Immediate / not issued

Apr 69. (7") **MAN OF THE WORLD. / SOMEBODY'S GONNA GET THEIR HEAD KICKED IN TONIGHT (B-side by "EARL VINCE & THE VINCENTS")** [2] [-]

Reprise / Reprise

Sep 69. (7") **OH WELL (Pt.1). / OH WELL (Pt.2)** [2] [55] Jan 70

— (note that SPENCER, for some reason did not play on the below album)

Sep 69. (lp) **THEN PLAY ON** [6] [ ]
– Coming your way / Closing my eyes / Showbiz blues / Underway / Oh well / Although the sun is shining / Rattlesnake shake / Searching for Madge / Fighting for Madge / Closing my eyes / When you say / One sunny day / Although the sun is shining / Like crying / Before the beginning. *(re-iss.Apr77)*

Oct 69. (7") **COMING YOUR WAY. / RATTLESNAKE SHAKE** [-] [ ]

May 70. (7") **THE GREEN MANALISHI (WITH THE TWO PRONGED CROWN). / WORLD IN HARMONY** [10] [ ]

— Now a quartet of **FLEETWOOD, McVIE, SPENCER and KIRWAN** when GREEN went solo

Sep 70. (lp)(c) **KILN HOUSE** [39] [69]
– This is the rock / Station man / Blood on the floor / Hi ho silver / Jewel eyed Judy / Buddy's song / Earl Grey / One together / Tell me all the things you do / Mission bell. *(re-iss.cd.Feb93 on 'Warners')*

Jan 71. (7") **JEWEL EYED LADY. / STATION MAN** [-] [ ]

— added **CHRISTINE** (PERFECT) **McVIE** – keyboards, vocals (ex-CHICKEN SHACK) (she had already guested on 'MR. WONDERFUL' album)

Mar 71. (7") **DRAGONFLY. / PURPLE DANCER** [ ] [ ]

— **BOB WELCH** (b.31 Jul'46, California, USA) – guitar, vocals (ex-HEAD WEST) repl. SPENCER who formed CHILDREN OF GOD

Sep 71. (lp)(c) **FUTURE GAMES** [ ] [91]
– Women of 1000 years / Morning rain / What a shame / Future games / Sands of time / Sometimes / Lay it all down / Show me a smile. *(re-iss.Apr77)*

Sep 71. (7") **SANDS OF TIME. / LAY IT ALL DOWN** [-] [ ]

Apr 72. (lp)(c) **BARE TREES** [ ] [70]
– Child of mine / The ghost / Homeward bound / Sunny side of Heaven / Bare trees / Sentimental lady / Danny's chant / Spare me a little of your love / Dust / Thoughts on a grey day. *(re-iss.Apr77)*

Aug 72. (7") **SENTIMENTAL LADY. / SUNNY SIDE OF HEAVEN** [-] [ ]

— **DAVE WALKER** – vocals (ex-SAVOY BROWN) repl. KIRWAN who went solo / added **BOB WESTON** – guitar, vocals (ex-LONG JOHN BALDRY) (above two now with FLEETWOOD, J. McVIE, C. McVIE and WELCH)

May 73. (7") **REMEMBER ME. / DISSATISFIED** [-]
May 73. (lp) **PENGUIN** [ ] [49] Apr 73
– Remember me / Bright fire / Dissatisfied / (I'm a) Road runner / The derelict / Revelation / Did you ever love me / Night watch / Caught in the rain. *(re-iss.Apr77)*
Jun 73. (7") **DID YOU EVER LOVE ME. / THE DERELICT** [ ] [-]
Jun 73. (7") **DID YOU EVER LOVE ME. / REVELATION** [-] [ ]

— Reverted to a quintet when WALKER departed forming HUNGRY FIGHTER

Jan 74. (lp)(c) **MYSTERY TO ME** [ ] [67] Nov 73
– Emerald eyes / Believe me / Just crazy love / Hypnotised / Forever / Keep on going / The city / Miles away / Somebody / The way I feel / Good things come to those who wait / Why. *(re-iss.Apr77) (re-iss.cd.Feb93 on 'Warners')*

— Trimmed to quartet when WESTON also left

Mar 74. (7") **FOR YOUR LOVE. / HYPNOTISED** [ ] [ ]
Sep 74. (lp)(c) **HEROES ARE HARD TO FIND** [ ] [34]
– Heroes are hard to find / Coming home / Angel / The Bermuda Triangle / Come a little bit closer / She's changing me / Bad loser / Silver heels / Prove your love / Born enchanter / Safe harbour. *(re-iss.cd.Feb93 on 'Warners')*
Feb 75. (7") **HEROES ARE HARD TO FIND. / BORN ENCHANTER** [ ] [ ]

— **LINDSEY BUCKINGHAM** (b. 3 Oct'47. Palo Alto, USA) – guitar, vocals (as below; ex-BUCKINGHAM-NICKS) repl. WELCH / added **STEVIE NICKS** (b.26 May'48, Phoenix, Arizona, USA) – vocals

Aug 75. (lp)(c)(white-lp) **FLEETWOOD MAC** [ ] [1]
– Monday morning / Warm ways / Blue letter / Rhiannon / Over my head / Crystal / Say you love me / Landslide / World turning / Sugar daddy / I'm so afraid. *(reached UK No.23 Nov76) (cd-iss.Dec85) (re-iss.cd Sep94 on 'Rewind')*
Oct 75. (7") **WARM WAYS. / BLUE LETTER** [ ] [ ]
Feb 76. (7") **OVER MY HEAD. / I'M SO AFRAID** [ ] [20] Nov 75
Apr 76. (7"m) **RHIANNON. / WILL YOU EVER WIN / SUGAR DADDY** [ ] [11] Mar 76
(re-iss.Feb78 reached UK-No.46)
Sep 76. (7") **SAY YOU LOVE ME. / MONDAY MORNING** [40] [11] Jul 76

Warners Warners

Jan 77. (7") **GO YOUR OWN WAY. / SILVER SPRINGS** [38] [10]
Feb 77. (lp)(c) **RUMOURS** [1] [1]
– Second hand news / Dreams / Never going back again / Don't stop / Go your own way / Songbird / The chain / You make loving fun / I don't want to know / Oh daddy / Gold dust woman. *(re-iss.Jun88) (cd-iss.Dec83)*
Apr 77. (7") **DON'T STOP. / GOLD DUST WOMAN** [32] [3] Jul77
Jun 77. (7") **DREAMS. / SONGBIRD** [24] [1] Apr 77
Sep 77. (7") **YOU MAKE LOVING FUN. / NEVER GOING BACK AGAIN** [45] [-]
Oct 77. (7") **YOU MAKE LOVING FUN. / GOLD DUST WOMAN** [-] [9]
Mar 79. (7") **THINK ABOUT ME. / SAVE ME A PLACE** [-] [20]
Sep 79. (7") **TUSK. / NEVER MAKE ME CRY** [6] [8]
Oct 79. (d-lp)(c) **TUSK** [1] [4]
– Over & over / The ledge / Think about me / Save me a place / Sara / What makes you think you're the one / That's all for everyone / Not that funny / Sisters of the Moon / Angel / That's enough for me / Brown eyes / Never make me cry / I know I'm not wrong / Honey hi / Beautiful child / Walk a thin line / Tusk / Never forget. *(cd-iss.Mar87)*
Dec 79. (7") **SARA. / THAT'S ENOUGH FOR ME** [37] [7]
Feb 80. (7") **NOT THAT FUNNY. / SAVE ME A PLACE** [ ] [ ]
Mar 80. (7") **THINK ABOUT ME. / HONEY HI** [ ] [-]
Mar 80. (7") **THINK ABOUT ME. / SAVE ME A PLACE** [-] [20]
Jun 80. (7") **SISTERS OF THE MOON. / WALK A THIN LINE** [-] [86]
Nov 80. (d-lp)(c) **FLEETWOOD MAC LIVE (live)** [31] [14]
– Monday morning / Say you love me / Dreams / Oh well / Over & over / Sara / Not that funny / Never going back again / Landslide / Fireflies / Over my head / Rhiannon / Don't let me down again / One more night / Go your own way / Don't stop / I'm so afraid / The farmer's daughter. *(cd-iss.May88 on 'Commander')*
Jan 81. (7") **FIREFLIES. / OVER MY HEAD** [-] [60]
Feb 81. (7") **THE FARMER'S DAUGHTER (live). / DREAMS (live)** [ ] [-]
Mar 81. (7") **THE FARMER'S DAUGHTER (live). / MONDAY MORNING (live)** [-]
Jul 82. (7") **HOLD ME. / EYES OF THE WORLD** [ ] [4] Jun 82
Jul 82. (lp)(c) **MIRAGE** [5] [1]
– Love in store / Can't go back / That's alright / Book of love / Gypsy / Only over you / Empire state / Straight back / Hold me / Oh Diane / Eyes of the world / Wish you were here. *(cd-iss.Dec83 + 1989)*
Sep 82. (7") **GYPSY. / COOL CLEAN WATER** [46] [12]
Nov 82. (7") **LOVE IN STORE. / CAN'T GO BACK** [-] [22]
Dec 82. (7")(7"pic-d) **OH DIANE. / ONLY OVER YOU** [9] [-]
(12"+=) – The chain.
Feb 83. (7") **OH DIANE. / THAT'S ALRIGHT** [-] [ ]
Apr 83. (7") **CAN'T GO BACK. / THAT'S ALRIGHT** [ ] [ ]
(12"+=) – Rhiannon / Tusk.

Mar 87. (7") **BIG LOVE. / YOU AND I (Pt.1)** [9] [5]
(12"+=)(12"pic-d) – ('A'extended).
(d7"+=) – The chain / Go your own way.
Apr 87. (lp)(c)(cd) **TANGO IN THE NIGHT** [1] [7]
– Big love / Seven wonders / Everywhere / Caroline / Tango in the night / Mystified / Little lies / Family man / Welcome to the room . . . Sara / Isn't it midnight / When I see you again / You and I, part II.
Jun 87. (7") **SEVEN WONDERS. / BOOK OF MIRACLES** [56] [19]
(12"+=)(12"pic-d+=) – ('A'dub).
Aug 87. (7") **LITTLE LIES. / RICKY** [5] [4]
(12"+=)(c-s+=)(12"pic-d+=) – ('A'dub).
Nov 87. (7") **FAMILY MAN. / DOWN ENDLESS STREET** [54] [90] Mar 88
(12") – ('A'side) / You and I (Pt.2) / Family party.
Feb 88. (7") **EVERYWHERE. / WHEN I SEE YOU AGAIN** [4] [14] Nov 87
(12"+=) – ('A'version) / ('A'dub).
Jun 88. (7")(12") **ISN'T IT MIDNIGHT. / MYSTIFIED** [60] [ ]
(3"cd-s+=) – Say you love me / Gypsy.
Nov 88. (7")(12") **AS LONG AS YOU FOLLOW. / OH WELL (live)** [66] [43]
(cd-s+=) – Gold dust woman.
Nov 88. (lp)(c)(cd) **FLEETWOOD MAC'S GREATEST HITS** (compilation) [3] [14]
– As long as you follow / No questions asked / Rhiannon / Don't stop / Go your own way / Hold me / Everywhere / Gypsy / Say you love me / Dreams / Little lies / Sara / Tusk. *(cd+c+=)* – Oh Diane / Big love / You making loving fun / Seven wonders.
Feb 89. (7") **HOLD ME. / NO QUESTIONS ASKED** [ ] [ ]
(12"+=)(cd-s+=) – I loved another woman (live).

— (Jul88) When BUCKINGHAM departed, he was repl. by **RICK VITO** – guitar / **BILLY BURNETT** – guitar

Feb 90. (7") **THE SKIES THE LIMIT. / THE SECOND TIME** [-] [ ]
Apr 90. (7") **SAVE ME. / I LOVED ANOTHER WOMAN (live)** [53] [33]
(12"+=)(cd-s+=) – Everywhere (live).
Apr 90. (cd)(c)(lp) **BEHIND THE MASK** [1] [18]
– The skies the limit / In the back of my mind / Do you know / Save me / Affairs of the heart / When the Sun goes down / Behind the mask / Stand on the rock / Hard feelings / Freedom / When it comes to love / The second time. *(re-iss.cd Feb95)*
Aug 90. (7")(c-s) **IN THE BACK OF MY MIND. / LIZARD PEOPLE** [58] [ ]
(12") – ('A'side) / Little lies (live) / The chain (live).
(cd-s) (all 4 tracks).
Nov 90. (7")(c-s) **SKIES THE LIMIT. / LIZARD PEOPLE** [ ] [ ]
(12")(cd-s) – ('A'side) / Little lies (live) / The chain (live).

— STEVIE NICKS left to go solo, and CHRISTINE departed due to MICK's new book allegations.

— **MICK FLEETWOOD, JOHN McVIE, CHRISTINE McVIE + BILLY BURNETTE** added **DAVE MASON** -vocals, guitars (ex-TRAFFIC, ex-solo artist)/ **BEKKA BRAMLETT** -vocals (daughter of DELANEY & BONNIE)

Oct 95. (cd)(c) **TIME** [47] [ ]
– Talkin' to my heart / Hollywood (some other kind of town) / Blow by blow / Winds of change / I do / Nothing without you / Dreamin' the dream / Sooner or later / I wonder why / Nights in Estoril / I got it in for you / All over again / These strange times.

– compilations etc. –

Note all 'Blue Horizon' releases were on 'Epic' US.
Jul 69. Blue Horizon; (7") **NEED YOUR LOVE SO BAD. / NO PLACE TO GO** [32] [ ]
Aug 69. Blue Horizon; (lp)(c) **PIOUS BIRD OF GOOD OMEN** [18] [ ]
– Need your love so bad / Coming home / Rambling pony / The big boat / I believe my time ain't long / The sun is shing / Albatross / Black magic woman / Just the blues / Jigsaw puzzle blues / Looking for somebody / Stop messin' around. *(re-iss.Jun81 on 'CBS') (cd-iss.Jun95 on 'Rewind')*
Dec 69. Blue Horizon; (d-lp) **BLUES JAM AT CHESS (-with other artists)** [ ] [ ]
– *(re-iss.d-cd.Oct93 on 'Sony Europe')*
Oct 71. Epic; (d-lp) **BLACK MAGIC WOMAN** [-] [ ]
(UK-iss.Feb80 on 'C.B.S.')
Note all CBS releases were on 'Epic' US.
May 71. C.B.S.; (lp) **THE ORIGINAL FLEETWOOD MAC BEFORE THE SPLIT** [ ] [ ]
(re-iss.+c/cd.Jun90 on 'Castle')
Nov 71. C.B.S.; (lp)(c) **GREATEST HITS** [36] [ ]
– The green Manalishi (with the two-pronged crown) / Oh well (part 1 & 2) / Shake your moneymaker / Need your love so bad / Rattlesnake shake / Dragonfly / Black magic woman / Albatross / Man of the world / Stop messin' around / Love that burns. *(re-iss.cd Dec94 on 'Columbia')*
Mar 72. C.B.S.; (7") **ALBATROSS. / I NEED YOUR LOVE SO BAD** [2] [ ]
(re-iss.Feb78)
Aug 73. C.B.S.; (7") **BLACK MAGIC WOMAN. / STOP MESSIN' ROUND** [ ] [ ]
1974. Epic; (d-lp) **ENGLISH ROSE** (incl.extra rare tracks) [-] [ ]

Jun 75. C.B.S.; (d-lp)(d-c) **THE ORIGINAL FLEETWOOD MAC / ENGLISH ROSE** [ ] [ ]
(re-iss.Jun76) (re-iss.cd May94 on 'Castle')
Mar 77. C.B.S.; (lp)(c) **VINTAGE YEARS** [ ] [ ]
(re-iss.May82 as THE HISTORY OF FLEETWOOD MAC)
Aug 77. C.B.S.; (lp)(c) **ALBATROSS (1 side by 'CHRISTINE PERFECT')** [ ] [ ]
(re-iss.+cd.Feb91 on 'Columbia')
Sep 78. C.B.S.; (lp)(c) **MAN OF THE WORLD** [ ] [ ]
Feb 89. C.B.S.; (7") **ALBATROSS. / MAN OF THE WORLD** [ ] [-]
(12"+=)(cd-s+=) – Black magic woman / Love that burns.
Jul 71. Blue Horizon; (d-lp) **FLEETWOOD MAC IN CHICAGO (rec. Jan69) (live)** [ ] [ ]
Mar 73. Reprise; (7") **THE GREEN MANALISHI. / OH WELL (Pt.1)** [ ] [ ]
1978. Reprise; (lp)(c) **THE BEST OF FLEETWOOD MAC** [ ] [ ]
Oct 75. D.J.M.; (7") **MAN OF THE WORLD. / SECOND CHAPTER ('B' side 'DANNY KIRWAN')** [ ] [ ]
(re-iss.Feb76 on 'Epic')
Jun 79. Flyover; (lp)(c) **FLEETWOOD MAC** [ ] [ ]
Nov 86. Thunderbolt; (lp)(c)(cd) **LONDON LIVE '68 (live)** [ ] [ ]
Jul 87. Castle; (d-lp)(c)(cd) **THE COLLECTION** [ ] [-]
Apr 89. Castle; (lp)(c)(cd) **THE BLUES COLLECTION** [ ] [-]
1988. Varrick; (lp)(c) **JUMPING AT SHADOWS** [-] [ ]
May 88. Mainline; (lp)(c)(cd) **GREATEST HITS LIVE (live)** [ ] [ ]
(re-iss.Dec89 on 'Commander')
Dec 89. Mainline; (lp)(c)(cd) **OH WELL** [ ] [-]
Oct 82. Warners; (d-c) **RUMOURS / FLEETWOOD MAC** [ ] [ ]
Nov 92. Warners; (4xcd)(4xc) **25 YEARS – THE CHAIN** [ ] [ ]
Jan 93. Warners; (7"ep)(c-ep)(cd-ep) **LOVE SHINES. / THE CHAIN (alternate mix) / ISN'T IT MIDNIGHT (alternate mix)** [ ] [ ]
Jan 85. Shanghai; (lp)(c) **LIVE IN BOSTON (live)** [ ] [-]
(re-iss.May88 on 'Line', cd-iss.Oct89 on 'Castle')
Aug 85. Shanghai; (d-lp)(c) **CERULEAN** [ ] [-]
Oct 85. Shanghai; (cd) **RATTLESNAKE SHAKE** [ ] [-]
Sep 85. Old Gold; (7") **MAN OF THE WORLD. / ('B'side by Humble Pie)** [ ] [-]
Nov 89. Pickwick; (lp)(c)(cd) **LOOKING BACK AT FLEETWOOD MAC** [ ] [-]
Feb 91. Essential; (3xcd)(5xlp) **THE ORIGINAL FLEETWOOD MAC: THE BLUES YEARS** [ ] [ ]
(re-iss.May93 on 'Castle')
Jun 91. Elite; (cd)(c) **LIKE IT THIS WAY** [ ] [-]
(re-iss.Sep93)
Jun 92. Sunflower; (cd) **LIVE AT THE MARQUEE (live by "PETER GREEN'S FLEETWOOD MAC")** [ ] [-]
Sep 92. Dojo; (cd) **THE EARLY YEARS ("PETER GREEN'S FLEETWOOD MAC")** [ ] [-]
Jul 94. Success; (cd)(c) **LIVE (live)** [ ] [-]
Jun 95. Savanna; (cd)(c) **LIVE** [ ] [-]
Sep 95. Essential; (d-cd)(d-c) **LIVE AT THE BBC** [48] [-]

MICK FLEETWOOD

R.C.A. R.C.A.

Jun 81. (lp)(c) **THE VISITOR** [ ] [43]
– Rattlesnake shake / You weren't in love / O'Niamali / Super brains / Don't be sorry (just be happy) / Walk a thin line / Not fade away / Cassiopeia surrender / The visitor / Amelle (come on show me your heart).
Aug 81. (7") **YOU WEREN'T IN LOVE. / AMELLE (COME ON SHOW ME YOUR HEART)** [ ] [ ]

ZOO

— **MICK FLEETWOOD** with **BILLY BURNETTE** -guitar, vocals / **STEVE ROSS** -guitar, vocals / **GEORGE HAWKINS** -bass, keyboards, vocals + **CHRISTINE + LINDSEY + TODD SHARP** (main writer in '92)

Nov 83. (lp)(c) **I'M NOT ME** [ ] [ ]
– Angel come home / You might need somebody / I want you back / Tonight / I'm not me / State of the art / I give / This love / Put me right / Just because / Tear it up.
Oct 83. (7") **I WANT YOU BACK. / PUT ME RIGHT** [ ] [ ]
Feb 84. (7") **ANGEL COME HOME. / I GIVE** [-] [ ]

Capricorn Capricorn

Jun 92. (cd)(c) **SHAKIN' THE CAGE** [ ] [ ]
– Reach out / God created woman / Night life / Shakin' the cage / Voodoo / How does it feel / The night and you / Takin' it out to the people / Breakin' up / In your hands.

CHRISTINE PERFECT

solo with **DANNY KIRWAN** and **JOHN McVIE** plus **CHRIS HARDING** – drums / **TONY TOPHAM** – guitar / **MARTIN DUNSFORD** – guitar and RICK HAYWARD – guitar

Blue Horizon Sire

Oct 69. (7") **WHEN YOU SAY. / NO ROAD IS THE RIGHT ROAD** [ ] [ ]
Mar 70. (7") **I'D RATHER GO BLIND. / CLOSE TO ME** [-] [ ]
Apr 70. (7") **I'M TOO FAR GONE. / CLOSE TO ME** [ ] [-]
Jun 70. (lp) **CHRISTINE PERFECT** [ ] [ ]
– Crazy 'bout you / I'm on my way / Let me go (leave me alone) / Wait and see / Close to me / I'd rather go blind / I want you / When you say / And that's saying a lot / No road is the right road / For you / I'm too far gone (to turn around) / I want you. *(re-iss.'82 on 'CBS') (re-iss.Oct93 on 'B.G.O.') (re-iss.Aug76 as 'THE LEGENDARY CHRISTINE PERFECT ALBUM' on 'Sire' US)*

C.B.S. C.B.S.

1974. (7") **I'D RATHER GO BLIND. / SAD CLOWN** [ ] [ ]

CHRISTINE McVIE

with **TODD SHARP** -guitar / **GEORGE HAWKINS** -bass, vocals / **STEVE FERRONE** -drums, percussion / + guests **LINDSEY, MICK + STEVE WINWOOD, ERIC CLAPTON, EDDY QUINTELA + RAY COOPER**

Warners Warners

Jan 84. (7"pic-d)(12"pic-d) **GOT A HOLD ON ME. / WHO'S DREAMING THIS DREAM** [ ] [10]
Feb 84. (lp)(c)(cd) **CHRISTINE McVIE** [58] [26]
– Love will show us how / The challenge / One in a million / So excited / Ask anybody / Got a hold on me / Who's dreaming this dream / I'm the one / Keeping secrets / The smile I live for.
May 84. (7") **LOVE WILL SHOW US HOW. / THE CHALLENGE** [ ] [30]
Jul 84. (7") **I'M THE ONE. / THE CHALLENGE** [-] [ ]

BUCKINGHAM-NICKS

duo (recorded before MAC members) **with TOM MONCREIFF** – bass / **GARY HODGES and BOB GEARY** – drums

Polydor Polydor

Apr 74. (7") **DON'T LET ME DOWN AGAIN. / RACES ARE RUN** [ ] [ ]
Jun 76. (7") **DON'T LET ME DOWN AGAIN. / CRYSTAL** [ ] [ ]
Feb 77. (lp) **BUCKINGHAM NICKS** [ ] [ ] 1973
– Crying in the night / Stephanie / Without a leg to stand on / Crystal / Long distance winner / Don't let me down again / Django / Races are run / Lola / Frozen love.
Mar 77 (7") **CRYING IN THE NIGHT. / STEPHANIE** [-] [ ]

LINDSEY BUCKINGHAM

solo with MICK FLEETWOOD and CHRISTINE McVIE as guests

Mercury Asylum

Nov 81. (lp)(c) **LAW AND ORDER** [ ] [32]
– Bwana / Trouble / Mary Lee Jones / I'll tell you now / It was I / September song / Shadow of the west / That's how we do it in L.A. / Johnny Stew / Love from here, love from there / A satisfied mind. *(cd-iss. 1984)*
Dec 81. (7") **TROUBLE. / THAT'S HOW WE DO IT IN L.A.** [31] [-]
Dec 81. (7") **TROUBLE. / MARY LEE JONES** [-] [9]
Feb 82. (7") **IT WAS I. / LOVE FROM HERE, LOVE FROM THERE** [-] [ ]
Mar 82. (7") **THE VISITOR. / A SATISFIED MIND** [ ] [-]
May 82. (7") **MARY LEE JONES. / SEPTEMBER SONG** [ ] [43]
Jul 83. (7") **HOLIDAY ROAD. / MARY LEE JONES** [ ] [ ]
— (above from film 'Vacation')

Mercury Elektra

Aug 84. (lp)(c)(cd) **GO INSANE** [ ] [45]
– I want you / Go insane / Slow dancing / I must go / Play in the rain (part 1 & 2) / Loving cup / Bang the drum / D.W. suite.
Sep 84. (7")(12") **GO INSANE. / PLAY IN THE RAIN** [ ] [23]
Dec 84. (7") **SLOW DANCING. / D.W. SUITE** [ ] [ ]
— Left FLEETWOOD MAC in '87 + released 1992 album 'OUT OF THE CRADLE'.

FLUKE

Formed: Beaconsfield, Buckinghamshire, England . . .mid 1989 by trio of MIKE BRYANT, MICHAEL TOURNIER and JONATHAN FUGLER. They emerged with white label 12" 'THUMPER!', before creating a stir with dancehall favourite 'JONI', which sampled her 'BIG YELLOW TAXI' single. In 1990, after a debut gig at a 'Boy's Own' label rave, they signed to major indie 'Creation'. Early the following year saw the release of their first album 'THE TECHNO ROSE OF BLIGHTY', which paved the way for a major signing to Virgin subsidiary 'Circa'. In 1993, their 3rd album nearly made UK Top 40 lists. • **Style:** Electronic dance pop/rock similar to the CABS or YELLO. • **Songwriters:** Group – sampled many including TALK TALK's 'Life's What You Make It'/ STEVE HILLAGE's 'Hello Dawn'/ BILL NELSON's 'When Your Dream Of Perfect Beauty Comes True'/ etc. • **Trivia:** Have been house remixers for TEARS FOR FEARS, TALK TALK, WORLD OF TWIST, etc.

Recommended: SIX WHEELS ON MY WAGON (*7) / OTO (*6)

MIKE BRYANT (b. 1 May'60, High Wycombe) -synthesizer/ **MICHAEL TOURNIER** (b.24 May'63, High Wycombe) -synthesizer/ **JONATHAN FUGLER** (b.13 Oct'2, St.Austell, Cornwall, England) -synthesizer

white label / not issued

Sep 89. (12") **THUMPER! (mixes)** [-] [-]

Taxi / not issued

May 90. (12") **JONI (mixes)** [ ] [-]

Creation / not issued

Oct 90. (7") **PHILLY. / TAXI** [ ] [-]
(12")(cd-s) – ('A'side) / ('A'-amorphous mix) / ('A'-Jamoeba mix) / ('A'-Jameteur mix).

Feb 91. (cd(c)(lp) **THE TECHNO ROSE OF BLIGHTY** [ ] [-]
– Philly / Glorious / Cool hand Fluke / Joni / Easy peasy / Phin / Jig / Taxi / Coolest.

Circa / Circa

Nov 91. (12"ep)(cd-ep) **THE BELLS. / (other mixes)** [ ] [-]

Nov 91. (12"ep)(cd-ep)(c-ep) **OUT (IN ESSENCE)** [ ] [ ]
– Pan Am into Philly / Pearls of wisdom / The bells:- Heresy – Garden of Blighty.

— added **JULIAN NUGENT** -synthesizer

Mar 93. (12"ep)(cd-ep) **SLID (glid). / (4 other mixes; No guitars / Glidub / PDFMIX / Scat and sax frenzy mix)** [59] [ ]

Jun 93. (12"ep)(c-ep) **ELECTRIC GUITAR (vibrochamp). / ('A'-superhound mix) / ('A'-headstock mix)** [58] [ ]
(cd-ep+=) – ('A'-sunburst mix) / ('A'-hot tube mix).

Sep 93. (7"ep)(c-ep) **GROOVY FEELING (Toni Bell's single scoop) / ('A'-Make mine a 99 mix) / ('A'-Nutty chip cornet mix)** [45] [ ]
(12"ep+=)(cd-ep+=) – ('A'-Lolly gobble choc bomb) / ('A'-screwball mix).

Oct 93. (cd)(c)(lp) **SIX WHEELS ON MY WAGON** [41] [ ]
– Groovy feeling – Make mine a 99 / Letters / Glidub / Electric guitar – Humbucker / Top of the world / Slid – PDFMONE / Slow motion / Spacey (Catch 22 dub) / Astrosapiens / Oh yeah / Eko / Life support. (cd w/free cd) THE TECHNO ROSE OF BLIGHTY

Apr 94. (c-ep)(cd-ep) **BUBBLE (speakbubble). / ('A'-stuntbubble mix) / ('A'-burstbubble mix)** [37] [ ]
(12"+=) – ('A'-Braillbubble mix).

Jul 95. (12"ep)(cd-ep) **BULLET / ('A'-Dust Brothers (US) mix) / ('A-Empirion mix) / ('A'-Atlas space odyssey mix)** [23] [ ]
(cd-ep+=) – ('A'-Bullion mix) / ('A'-percussion cap mix) / ('A'-cannonball mix) / ('A'-bitter mix).

Aug 95. (cd)(c)(lp) **OTO** [44] [ ]
– Bullet / Tosh / Cut / Freak / Wobbler / Squirt / O.K. / Setback.

Nov 95. (12"ep) **TOSH / (mixes; gosh / mosh / cosh / posh)** [32] [ ]
(cd-s) – ('A'mixes; Nosh / Dosh / Josh / Shriekbackwash).
(12") – ('A'mixes; Mosh / Gosh / Nosh / Dosh).

compilations, etc –

Dec 95. Strange Fruit; (cd-ep) **THE PEEL SESSIONS** [ ] [-]
– Thumper / Taxi / Jig / Our definition of jazz / The bells / The allotment of Blighty / Time keeper.

John FOGERTY (see under ⇒ CREEDENCE CLEARWATER REVIVAL)

FOLK IMPLOSION (see under ⇒ SEBADOH)

FOO FIGHTERS (see under ⇒ NIRVANA)

FOREIGNER

Formed: New York, USA . . . early 1976 by English expatriots JONES, McDONALD and ELLIOTT, who linked up with New Yorkans GRAMM, GREENWOOD and GAGLIARI. After a year in the studio, they unleashed eponymous debut lp for 'Atlantic'. Although it did not chart in the UK, it hit Top 5 in the States. This was boosted by 2 hit cuts from it, 'FEELS LIKE THE FIRST TIME' & 'COLD AS ICE'. They remained constant hitmakers during the next several years, peaking early in 1985 with cross-Atlantic No.1 single 'I WANT TO KNOW WHAT LOVE IS'. • **Style:** Radio FM aimed AOR band, with leanings to hard-rock empire. • **Songwriters:** JONES penned some with GRAMM, until his 1987 departure. • **Trivia:** Saxist JUNIOR WALKER guested on their 1981 single 'URGENT', which with its parent album '4', was produced by THOMAS DOLBY & ROBERT 'MUTT' LANGE.

Recommended: GREATEST HITS (*6).

LOU GRAMM (b. 2 May'50, Rochester, New York) – vocals (ex-BLACK SHEEP) / **MICK JONES** (b.27 Dec'47, London, England) – guitar (ex-SPOOKY TOOTH) / **IAN McDONALD** (b.25 Jun'46, London) – guitar, keyboards (ex-KING CRIMSON) / **AL GREENWOOD** (b. New York) – keyboards / **ED GAGLIARI** (b.13 Feb'52, New York) – bass (ex-STORM) / **DENNIS ELLIOTT** (b.18 Aug'50, London) – drums (ex-IAN HUNTER BAND)

Atlantic / Atlantic

Apr 77. (7") **FEELS LIKE THE FIRST TIME. / WOMAN OH WOMAN** [39] [4] Mar 77

Apr 77. (lp)(c) **FOREIGNER** [ ] [4] Mar 77
– Feels like the first time / Cold as ice / Starrider / Headknocker / The damage is done / Long, long way from home / Woman oh woman / At war with the world / Fool for the anyway / I need you. *(cd-iss.1988 & Oct95)*

Jul 77. (7")(7"clear) **COLD AS ICE. / I NEED YOU** [24] [6]

Dec 77. (7") **LONG, LONG WAY FROM HOME. / THE DAMAGE IS DONE** [-] [20]

Apr 78. (7"m) **LONG, LONG WAY FROM HOME. / FEELS LIKE THE FIRST TIME / COLD AS ICE** [ ] [-]

Aug 78. (lp)(c) **DOUBLE VISION** [32] [3] Jul 78
– Back where you belong / Blue morning, blue day / Double vision / Hot blooded / I have waited so long / Lonely children / Spellbinder / Tramontane / You're all I am. *(cd-iss.1988 & Oct95)*

Oct 78. (7")(7"red) **HOT BLOODED. / TRAMONTANE** [42] [3] Jun 78

Jan 79. (7")(7"pic-d) **BLUE MORNING, BLUE DAY. / I HAVE WAITED SO LONG** [45] [15]

Jul 79. (7") **DOUBLE VISION. / LONELY CHILDREN** [ ] [2] Sep 78

— **RICK WILLS** – bass (ex-ROXY MUSIC, ex-SMALL FACES) repl. AL (joined SPYS)

Sep 79. (7") **DIRTY WHITE BOY. / REV ON THE RED LINE** [ ] [12]

Sep 79. (lp)(c) **HEAD GAMES** [ ] [5]
– Dirty white boy / Love on the telephone / Women / I'll get even with you / Seventeen / Head games / The modern day / Blinded by science / Do what you like / Rev on the red line. *(cd-iss.Nov85) (re-iss.cd Feb93 on 'Atco') (re-iss.cd Oct95)*

Feb 80. (7") **HEAD GAMES. / DO WHAT YOU LIKE** [ ] [14] Nov79

Apr 80. (7") **WOMEN. / THE MODERN DAY** [ ] [41] Feb 80

Sep 80. (7") **I'LL GET EVEN WITH YOU. / BLINDED BY SCIENCE** [ ] [ ]

— Trimmed to quartet, when GAGLIARI and McDONALD leave.

Jul 81. (7") **URGENT. / GIRL ON THE MOON** [54] [4] Jun 81

Jul 81. (lp)(c) **4** [5] [1]
– Night life / Juke box hero / Break it up / Waiting for a girl like you / Luanne / Urgent / I'm gonna win / Woman in black / Urgent / Girl on the Moon / Don't let go. *(cd-iss.1988 & Oct95)*

Sep 81. (7") **JUKE BOX HERO. / I'M GONNA WIN** [48] [26] Feb 82

Oct 81. (7") **WAITING FOR A GIRL LIKE YOU. / I'M GONNA WIN** [-] [2]

Nov 81. (7"m) **WAITING FOR A GIRL LIKE YOU. / FEELS LIKE THE FIRST TIME / COLD AS ICE** [8] [-]

Mar 82. (7") **DON'T LET GO. / FOOL FOR YOU ANYWAY** [ ] [ ]

Apr 82. (7") **BREAK IT UP. / LUANNE** [-] [26]

Apr 82. (7") **URGENT. / HEAD GAMES (live)** [45] [-]
(12") – ('A'side) / Hot Blooded (live).

Jul 82. (7") **LUANNE. / FOOL FOR YOU ANYWAY** [-] [75]

Dec 82. (lp)(c)(cd) **RECORDS (THE BEST OF . . .)** (compilation) [58] [10]
– Cold as ice / Double vision / Head games / Waiting for a girl like you / Feels like the first time / Urgent / Dirty white boy / Jukebox hero / Long, long way from home / Hot blooded. *(re-iss.cd Oct95)*

Nov 84. (7")(7"sha-pic-d) **I WANT TO KNOW WHAT LOVE IS. / STREET THUNDER** [1] [1]
(12"+=) – Urgent.

Dec 84. (lp)(c)(cd) **AGENT PROVOCATEUR** [1] [4] Nov 84
– Tooth and nail / That was yesterday / I want to know what love is / Growing up the hard way / Reaction to action / Stranger in my own house / A love in vain / Down on love / Two different worlds / She's too tough. *(re-iss.cd Oct95)*

Mar 85. (7") **THAT WAS YESTERDAY (remix). / TWO DIFFERENT WORLDS** [28] [12]
(12"+=) – ('A'orchestral version).

May 85. (7") **REACTION TO ACTION. / SHE'S TOO TOUGH** [-] [54]

Aug 85. (7") **DOWN ON LOVE. / GROWING UP THE HARD WAY** [-] [54]

— LOU GRAMM left to go solo.

Jul 87. (7") **SAY YOU WILL. / A NIGHT TO REMEMBER** [71] [6] Nov 87

(12"+=)(cd-s+=) – Hot blooded (live).
Dec 87. (lp)(c)(cd) **INSIDE INFORMATION** 64 15
– Heart turns to stone / Can't wait / Say you will / I don't want to live without you / Counting every minute / Inside information / The beat of my heart / Face to face / Out of the blue / A night to remember.
May 88. (7") **I DON'T WANT TO LIVE WITHOUT YOU. / FACE TO FACE** [ ] 5 Mar 88
(12"+=) – ('A'extended).
(cd-s++=) – Urgent.
Jul 88. (7") **HEART TURNS TO STONE. / COUNTING EVERY MINUTE** - 56

— (1990) added **JOHNNY EDWARDS** – vocals to join **JONES + THOMAS**
Jun 91. (7")(c-s) **LOWDOWN AND DIRTY. / FLESH WOUND** [ ] [ ]
(12"+=)(cd-s+=) – No hiding place.
Jul 91. (cd)(c)(lp) **UNUSUAL HEAT** 56 [ ]
– Only Heaven knows / Lowdown and dirty / I'll fight for you / Moment of truth / Mountain of love / Ready for the rain / When the night comes down / Safe in my heart / No hiding place / Flesh wound / Unusual heat. *(cd-iss.Nov93)*
Aug 91. (7")(c-s) **I'LL FIGHT FOR YOU / MOMENT OF TRUTH** [ ] [ ]
(12"+=)(cd-s+=) – Dirty white boy (live).

Arista Arista
Oct 94. (7")(c-s) **WHITE LIE. / UNDER THE GUN** 58 [ ]
(cd-s+=) – ('A'mixes).
Nov 94. (cd)(c) **MR. MOONLIGHT** 59 [ ]
–
Mar 95. (c-s) **UNTIL THE END OF TIME / HAND ON MY HEART** [ ] 42
(cd-s+=) – ('A'mix).

– compilations, others, etc. –

Nov 88. Atlantic; (7") **JUST WANNA HOLD. / YOU ARE MY FRIEND** - [ ]
Jun 85. Atlantic; (7") **COLD AS ICE (remix). / REACTION TO ACTION** 64 [ ]
(12"+=) – Head games (live).
(d7"++=) – Hot blooded (live).
Apr 92. Atlantic; (cd)(c)(lp) **GREATEST HITS** 19 [ ]
– Feels like the first time / Cold as ice / Starrider / Hot blooded / Blue morning, blue day / Double vision / Dirty white boy / Women / Head games / Juke Box hero / Waiting for a girl like you / Urgent / That was yesterday / I want to know what love is / Say you will / I don't want to live without you. *(re-iss Dec 92 as 'THE VERY BEST AND BEYOND')*
Apr 92. Atlantic; (7")(c-s) **WAITING FOR A GIRL LIKE YOU. / COLD AS ICE** [ ] [ ]
(12"+=)(cd-s+=) – That was yesterday / Feels like the first time.
Dec 93. Atlantic; (cd)(c) **CLASSIC HITS LIVE (live)** [ ] [ ]

MICK JONES

Atlantic Atlantic
Nov 88. (7") **JUST WANNA HOLD. / YOU ARE MY FRIEND** - [ ]
Jan 89. (7") **EVERYTHING THAT COMES AROUND. / THE WRONG SIDE OF THE LAW** [ ] [ ]
(12"+=) – ('A'extended).
Aug 89. (lp)(c)(cd) **MICK JONES** [ ] [ ]
– Just wanna hold / Save me tonight / That's the way my love is / The wrong side of the law / 4 wheels turnin' / Everything that comes around / You are my friend / Danielle / Write tonight / Johnny (part 1).

Robert FORSTER (see under ⇒ GO-BETWEENS)

FOTHERINGAY (see under ⇒ FAIRPORT CONVENTION)

4 NON BLONDES

Formed: San Francisco, California, USA . . . 1990 by LINDA PERRY, etc. After signing to 'Atlantic' off-shoot label 'Intercord', they smashed the US Top 20 with classic 'WHAT'S UP' single, which also broke them into Top 3 in Britain. • **Style:** Loud and eccentric looking 3 girl / 1 guy hard-edged rock outfit, with sense of political lyrical awareness. PERRY's paint-stripping vox was described as the female equivalent of AXL ROSE. • **Songwriters:** PERRY or group penned.

Recommended: BIGGER, BETTER, FASTER, MORE! (*5).

LINDA PERRY – vocals / **ROGER ROCHA** – guitar repl. LOUIS METOYER after 1st lp / **CHRISTA HILLHOUSE** – bass, vocals / **DAWN RICHARDSON** – drums / and 1 track guests

Interscope Interscope
Jun 93. (7")(c-s) **WHAT'S UP. / THE TRAIN** 2 14 Apr 93
(cd-s+=) – ('A'mixes).
Jun 93. (cd)(c) **BIGGER, BETTER, FASTER, MORE!** 4 14 May 93
– Train / Superfly / What's up / Pleasantly blue / Morphine & chocolate / Spaceman / Old Mr. Heffer / Calling all the people / Dear Mr. President / Drifting / No place like home.
Oct 93. (7")(c-s) **SPACEMAN. / STRANGE** 53 [ ]
(12"+=)(cd-s+=) – What's up (remix or piano version).
Dec 93. (7")(c-s) **DEAR MR.PRESIDENT. / SUPERFLY** [ ] [ ]
(cd-s+=) – Drifting.

— In Aug 94, 'WHAT'S UP' was ripped off by charting dance / pop terrorist DJ MIKO.

FRANKIE GOES TO HOLLYWOOD

Formed: Liverpool, England . . . Aug'80, initially as HOLLYCAUST by HOLLY JOHNSON, who had issued 2 solo singles 'YANKEE ROSE' & 'HOBO JOE', after being part of BIG IN JAPAN. Taking name from a headline concerning singer FRANKIE VAUGHAN going into the movies, they embarked on TV exposure late 1982. After a session on the David Jensen Radio 1 show, they were included on the Channel 4's 'The Tube', demoing 'RELAX'. This led to 'ZTT' (Zang Tumb Tumm) label, run by PAUL MORLEY and TREVOR HORN (ex-BUGGLES) signing them Autumn 1983. With HORN on clever production, the song 'RELAX', soon climbed to the top in the UK, helped by another Radio 1 DJ Mike Read, getting it banned for its risque lyrics. In Jun'84, with RELAX still in the chart, the follow-up 'TWO TRIBES', went straight to No.1, and gave a new lease of life to RELAX, which re-ran up to No.2, while TWO TRIBES was still at the top. Their debut double-lp in Oct'84 'WELCOME TO THE PLEASURE DOME', also hit peak position, as did their 3rd consecutive No.1 single 'THE POWER OF LOVE'. A feat only previously achieved by another Merseyside group GERRY & THE PACEMAKERS. Their 4th 45 in 1985, spoiled the run, when it stalled at No.2. The group returned late Summer 1986 with Top 5 single 'RAGE HARD', but with a poor review of their Top 5 album 'LIVERPOOL', they faded commercially into decline. HOLLY JOHNSON was back with a solo contract on 'M.C.A.', and had 2 UK Top 5 hits 'LOVE TRAIN' & 'AMERICANOS', which previewed his No.1 album 'BLAST'. • **Style:** Well-produced power-disco rock outfit, whose controversial gay M&S sex themes, were provided by leather clad HOLLY and boyfriend/dancer PAUL RUTHERFORD. • **Songwriters:** All group compositions except; FERRY ACROSS THE MERSEY (Gerry & The Pacemakers) / BORN TO RUN (Bruce Springsteen) / WAR (Edwin Starr) / SUFFRAGETTE CITY (David Bowie) / GET IT ON (T.Rex) / SAN JOSE (Bacharach-David). HOLLY solo covered; LOVE ME TENDER (Elvis Presley). ACROSS THE UNIVERSE was not The BEATLES original. • **Trivia:** The 'TWO TRIBES' video, which contained Ronald Reagan & Chernenko lookalikes, fighting in a ring, was directed by GODLEY & CREME. In mid-1990, HOLLY was asked by friend RICHARD O'BRIEN, to act as FRANK 'N' FURTER in the 'Rocky Horror Picture Show'.

Recommended: WELCOME TO THE PLEASURE DOME (*7).

HOLLY JOHNSON (b. WILLIAM JOHNSON, 9 Feb'60, Khartoum, Sudan) – vocals (ex-solo artist, ex-BIG IN JAPAN) / **PAUL RUTHERFORD** (b. 8 Dec'59) – vocals (ex-SPITFIRE BOYS) / **BRIAN NASH** (b.20 Mar'63) – guitar repl. GED O'TOOLE / **MARK O'TOOLE** (b. 6 Jan'64) – bass / **PETER GILL** (b. 8 Mar'64) – drums

ZTT-Island Island
Oct 83. (7")(7"pic-d) **RELAX. / ONE SEPTEMBER MORNING** 1 67 Mar 84
(12")(12"pic-d) – ('A'version) / Ferry across the Mersey.
(c-ep) – "Relax's Greatest Bits" – (various mixes).
Jun 84. (7")(7"pic-d) **TWO TRIBES. / ONE FEBRUARY MORNING** 1 43 Oct 84
(12")(12"pic-d) – ('A'version) / War (hide yourself).
(12"pic-d) – (all 3 tracks above)
(c-ep) – "Two Tribes (Keep The Peace)" – (various mixes).
Oct 84. (d-lp)(c)(cd)(d-pic-lp) **WELCOME TO THE PLEASURE DOME** 1 33
– Well . . . / The world is my oyster / Snatch of fury / Welcome to the pleasure dome / Relax / War / Two tribes / Ferry / Born to run / San Jose / Wish the lads were here (inc. 'Ballad of 32') / Black night white light / The only star in Heaven / The power of love / Bang . . . *(re-iss.cd+c May94 & Feb95)*
Nov 84. (7")(7"pic-d) **THE POWER OF LOVE. / THE WORLD IS MY OYSTER** 1 [ ]
(12"+=)(c-s+=)(12"pic-d+=) – Trapped and scrapped / Holier than thou.
(12"ep+=) – Pleasurefix / Starfix.

Mar 85. (7")(7"sha-pic-d) **WELCOME TO THE PLEASURE DOME. / HAPPY HI / GET IT ON** [2] [48]
(12"++=) – Relax (International).
(12"+=)(12"sha-pic-d+=) – Born to run (live).
Aug 86. (7") **RAGE HARD. / (DON'T LOSE WHAT'S LEFT) OF YOUR LITTLE MIND** [4] [ ]
(12"+=//+12"+=) – Suffragette City/ / Roadhouse blues.
(cd-s+=) – (above 2 tracks)
Sep 86. (lp)(c)(cd) **LIVERPOOL** [5] [88]
– Warriors of the wasteland / Rage hard / Kill the pain / Maximum joy / Watching the wildlife / Lunar bay / For Heaven's sake / Is anybody out there?. *(re-iss. 1989 on 'Island') (re-iss.cd+c May94)*
Nov 86. (7") **WARRIORS OF THE WASTELAND. / WARRIORS (instrumental)** [19] [ ]
(12"+=)(c-s+=)(cd-s+=) – Warriors (lots of different mixes).
Feb 87. (7") **WATCHING THE WILDLIFE. / THE WAVES** [28] [ ]
(12"+=) – Wildlife (Bit 3 & 4).
(c-s+=)(cd-s+=) – (various mixes, etc).

— They split after legal contractual problems. RUTHERFORD went solo,

– compilations, etc. –

Sep 93. Z.T.T.-Island; (7")(c-s) **RELAX. / ('A'mix)** [5] [ ]
(12"+=)(cd-s+=) – ('A'mixes).
Oct 93. Z.T.T.-Island; (cd)(c)(lp) **BANG! . . . THE GREATEST HITS OF . . .** [4] [ ]
– Relax / Two tribes / War / Ferry / Warriors of the wasteland / For Heaven's sake / The world is my oyster / Welcome to the Pleasure dome / Watching the wildlife / Born to run / Rage hard / The power of love / Bang . . . *(re-iss.cd+c Jun94)*
Nov 93. Z.T.T.-Island; (7")(c-s) **WELCOME TO THE PLEASURE DOME. / ('A'mix)** [18] [ ]
(12"+=)(cd-s+=) – ('A'mixes).
Dec 93. Z.T.T.-Island; (7")(c-s) **THE POWER OF LOVE. / ('A'mix)** [10] [ ]
(cd-s+=) – Rage hard (original DJ mix) / Holier than thou.
Feb 94. Z.T.T.-Island; (7")(c-s) **TWO TRIBES (Fluke's minimix). / ('A'mix)** [16] [ ]
(12"+=)(cd-s+=) – ('A'mixes).
May 94. Z.T.T.-Island; (cd)(c)(lp) **RELOAD** – THE WHOLE 12 [ ] [ ]
In Spring of '93, HOLLY revealed he had HIV positive (AIDS).

HOLLY JOHNSON

had earlier returned to a solo career.

M.C.A. M.C.A.

Jan 89. (7")(c-s) **LOVE TRAIN. / MURDER IN PARADISE** [4] [ ]
(12"+=)(cd-s+=) – ('A'mix).
Mar 89. (7")(c-s) **AMERICANOS. / ('A'dub version)** [4] [ ]
(12"+=)(cd-s+=) – ('A' liberty mix).
Apr 89. (lp)(c)(cd) **BLAST** [1] [ ]
– Atomic city / Heaven's here / Americanos / Deep in love / S.U.C.C.E.S.S. / Love train / Got it made / Love will come / Perfume / Feel good.
Jun 89. (7")(c-s) **ATOMIC CITY. / BEAT THE SYSTEM** [18] [ ]
(12"+=)(cd-s+=) – ('A'extended).
Sep 89. (7")(c-s)(7"pic-d) **HEAVEN'S HERE. / HALLELUJAH** [62] [ ]
(12"+=)(cd-s+=) – ('A'version).
Jul 90. (cd)(c)(lp) **HALLELUJAH, THE REMIX ALBUM** (BLAST remixed) [ ] [-]
Nov 90. (7")(12")(c-s) **WHERE HAS THE LOVE GONE? / PERFUME** [73] [ ]
(cd-s+=) – ('A'version).
Mar 91. (7")(c-s) **ACROSS THE UNIVERSE. / FUNKY PARADISE** [ ] [ ]
(12"+=)(cd-s+=) – ('A'-Space a-go-go mix).
May 91. (cd)(c)(lp) **DREAMS THAT MONEY CAN'T BUY** [ ] [ ]
– Across the universe / When the party's over / The people want to dance / I need your love / Boyfriend '65 / Where has love gone? / Penny arcade / Do it for love / You're a hit / The great love story.
Aug 91. (7")(c-s) **PEOPLE WANT TO DANCE. / ('A'-Apollo 440 mix)** [ ] [ ]
(12"+=)(cd-s+=) – Love train (anxious big beat version).

Club Tool not issued

Sep 94. (12"ep)(cd-ep) **LEGENDARY CHILDREN (ALL OF THEM QUEER). / (4-'A'mixes)** [ ] [-]

HOLLY

early solo

Eric's not issued

Dec 79. (7"m) **YANKEE ROSE. / TREASURE ISLAND / DESPERATE DAN** [ ] [-]
1980. (7") **HOBO JOE. / STARS OF THE BARS** [ ] [-]

FREE

Formed: London, England ... Spring 1968, by KOSSOFF, KIRKE, RODGERS and FRASER. They were spotted at their first gig by white blues artist ALEXIS KORNER, who named them FREE, and introduced them to Chris Blackwell of 'Island'. They signed to label, and released 'TONS OF SOBS', by the end of year. In 1969, after supporting a US tour of BLIND FAITH, they broke UK Top lists with self-titled lp. In mid-1970, they stormed the charts with classic 'ALL RIGHT NOW', which hit both UK & US Top 5's. Its full version was available on UK Top3 / US Top 20 album 'FIRE AND WATER', which was followed by disappointing 'HIGHWAY' & 'FREE LIVE!', before their split May'71. After 9 months of other projects, noteably lp 'KOSSOFF, KIRKE, TETSU & RABBIT', they re-formed original line-up early '72, They struck back with Top 20 hit 'LITTLE BIT OF LOVE', taken from parent Top 10 album 'FREE AT LAST'. After another UK Top 10 hit 45 ('WISHING WELL') & album ('HEARTBREAKER'), they decided to announce split mid-73. • **Style:** Heavy-blues outfit, who came out of the shadow of CREAM, and gained own reputation for hard-edged rock'n'blues. Their basic riffs, were transported powerfully and sometimes melancholy by frontman RODGERS. • **Songwriters:** Group compositions, except some blues standards. Covered THE HUNTER (Albert King). • **Trivia:** Early in 1991, after being used on a chewing gum UK TV ad, 'ALL RIGHT NOW', hit the Top 10, as does compilation cd.

Recommended: THE BEST OF FREE – ALL RIGHT NOW (1991 compilation cd).

PAUL RODGERS (b.12 Dec'49, Middlesbrough, England) – vocals (ex-BROWN SUGAR) / **PAUL KOSSOFF** (b.14 Sep'50, Hampstead, London) – guitar (ex-BLACK CAT BONES) / **SIMON KIRKE** (b.28 Jul'49, Shrewsbury, England) – drums (ex-BLACK CAT BONES) / **ANDY FRASER** (b. 7 Aug'52, Shropshire, England) – bass (ex-JOHN MAYALL'S BLUESBREAKERS)

Island A & M

Nov 68. (lp) **TONS OF SOBS** [ ] [ ] Aug 69
– Over the green hills (part 1) / Worry / Walk in my shadow / Wild Indian woman / Goin' down slow / I'm a mover / The hunter / Moonshine / Sweet tooth / Over the green hills (part 2). *(cd-iss.Jun88)*
Mar 69. (7") **I'M A MOVER. / WORRY** [-] [ ]
Mar 69. (7") **BROAD DAYLIGHT. / THE WORM** [ ] [ ]
Jul 69. (7") **I'LL BE CREEPIN'. / SUGAR FOR MR. MORRISON** [ ] [-]
Aug 69. (7") **I'LL BE CREEPIN'. / MOUTHFUL OF GRASS** [-] [ ]
Oct 69. (lp)(c) **FREE** [22] [ ]
– I'll be creepin' / Songs of yesterday / Lying in the sunshine / Trouble on double time / Mouthful of grass / Woman / Free me / Broad daylight / Mourning sad morning. *(cd-iss.Jun88)*
May 70. (7") **ALL RIGHT NOW. / MOUTHFUL OF GRASS** [2] [4]
(re-iss.Jul73 hit UK No.15)
Jun 70. (lp)(c) **FIRE AND WATER** [2] [17] Aug 70
– Oh I wept / Remember / Heavy load / Fire and water / Mr.Big / Don't say you love me / All right now. *(re-iss.+cd.Sep86, cd-iss.Apr90) (re-iss.lp Jan94 + May94)*
Nov 70. (7") **THE STEALER. / LYING IN THE SUNSHINE** [ ] [-]
Nov 70. (7") **THE STEALER. / BROAD DAYLIGHT** [-] [49]
Dec 70. (lp)(c) **HIGHWAY** [41] [ ] Feb 71
– The highway song / The stealer / On my way / Be my friend / Sunny day / Ride on pony / Love you so / Bodie / Soon I will be gone. *(cd-iss.Jun88)*
Jan 71. (7") **THE HIGHWAY SONG. / LOVE YOU SO** [-] [ ]
Mar 71. (7") **I'LL BE CREEPIN'. / MR. BIG** [-] [ ]
Apr 71. (7") **MY BROTHER JAKE. / ONLY MY SOUL** [4] [ ]
Jun 71. (lp)(c) **FREE LIVE! (live)** [4] [89] Aug 71
– All right now / I'm a mover / Be my friend / Fire and water / Ride on pony / Mr. Big / The hunter / Get where I belong (studio). *(cd-iss.Jun88)*

— They had already split May71. FRASER formed TOBY. RODGERS formed PEACE.

KOSSOFF, KIRKE, TETSU & RABBIT

were formed by the other two plus **TETSU YAMAUCHI** (b.21 Oct'47, Fukuoka, Japan)- bass / **JOHN 'RABBIT' BUNDRICK** – keyboards, vocals / and guest **B.J. COLE** – steel guitar

Nov 71. (lp) **KOSSOFF, KIRKE, TETSU & RABBIT** [ ] [ ]
– Blue grass / Sammy's alright / Just for the box / Colours / Hold on / Yellow house / Dying fire / Fool's life / Anna / I'm on the run. *(cd-iss.Aug 91) (re-iss.cd May95 on 'Repertoire')*

FREE

re-formed originals Feb72 (**RODGERS, KOSSOFF, FRASER** and **KIRKE**)
May 72. (7") **LITTLE BIT OF LOVE. / SAIL ON** [13] [ ]
Jun 72. (lp)(c) **FREE AT LAST** [9] [69]
– Catch a train / Soldier boy / Magic ship / Sail on / Travelin' man / Little bit of

love / Guardian of the universe / Child / Goodbye. *(cd-iss.Jun88 & Feb90)*

— **TETSU YAMAUCHI** – bass(see above) repl. FRASER who joined SHARKS added **JOHN 'RABBIT' BUNDRICK** – keyboards (see above) **RODGERS** – also guitar

Dec 72. (7") **WISHING WELL. / LET ME SHOW YOU** [7] [ ]

Jan 73. (lp)(c) **HEARTBREAKER** [9] [47]
– Wishing well / Come together in the morning / Travellin' in style / Heartbreaker / Muddy water / Common mortal man / Easy on my soul / Seven angels. *(cd-iss.Jun88 & Feb90)*

Mar 73. (7") **TRAVELLIN' IN STYLE. / EASY ON MY SOUL** [ ] [ ]

— **WENDELL RICHARDSON** – guitar of OSIBISA, on UK & US tour early '73) repl. KOSSOFF who formed BACK STREET CRAWLER. He died in his sleep 19 Mar'76, after years of drug abuse. FREE split early '73. RABBIT went solo before joining (KOSSOFF's) CRAWLER. TETSU joined The FACES. RODGERS and KIRKE formed BAD COMPANY.

- compilations, etc. -

Island / A & M

Mar 74. Island/ US= A&M; (d-lp)(c) **THE FREE STORY** [2] [ ]

Apr 75. A&M; (lp)(c) **THE BEST OF FREE** [-] [ ]

Nov 76. Island; (lp)(c) **FREE AND EASY, ROUGH AND READY** [ ] [ ]

Nov 76. Island/ US= A&M; (7") **THE HUNTER. / WORRY** [ ] [ ]

Feb 78. Island/ US= A&M; (7"ep) **THE FREE EP** [11] [ ]
– All right now / My brother Jake / Wishing well. *(re-iss.Oct82 as 12"pic-d, hit 57)*

Oct 82. Island/ US= A&M; (lp)(c) **COMPLETELY FREE** [ ] [ ]

May 85. Island; (7")(12") **WISHING WELL. / WOMAN** [ ] [ ]

Feb 91. Island; (7")(c-s) **ALL RIGHT NOW. / I'M A MOVER** [8] [ ]
(12"+=)(cd-s+=) – Get where I belong.

Feb 91. Island; (cd)(c)(lp) **ALL RIGHT NOW – THE BEST OF FREE** [9] [ ]
– Wishing well / All right now / Be my friend / Fire and water / Travellin' in style / The hunter / Sail on / My brother Jake / Little bit of love / Come together in the morning / Mr.Big / The stealer / Travelling man / Don't say you love me.

Apr 91. Island; (7")(c-s) **MY BROTHER JAKE (remix). / WISHING WELL (remix)** [ ] [ ]
(12"+=)(cd-s+=) – The stealer (extended) / Only my soul (extended).

PAUL KOSSOFF

with all of FREE as guests; plus **TREVOR BURTON** – bass / **ALAN WHITE** – drums

Island / Island

Dec 73. (lp)(c) **BACK STREET CRAWLER** [ ] [ ]
– Tuesday morning / I'm ready / Time away / Molten gold / Back street crawler. *(re-iss.Apr87, cd-iss.Feb90) (cd-iss.Jul92 & May95 on 'Repertoire')*

BACK STREET CRAWLER

KOSSOFF – lead guitar with **TERRY WILSON-SLESSER** – vocals / **TERRY WILSON** – bass / **TONY BRAUNAGEL** – drums / **MIKE MONTGOMERY** – keyboards / plus **PETER VAN DER PUIJE** – sax / **EDDIE QUANSAH** – horns / **GEORGE LEE LARNYOH** – flute, saxes

Atlantic / Atco

Aug 75. (lp)(c) **THE BAND PLAYS ON** [ ] [ ]
– Who do women / New York, New York stealing my way / Survivor / It's a long way down to the top / All the girls are crazy / Jason blue / Train song / Rock & roll junkie / The band plays on.

— **GEOFF WHITEHORN** – guitar repl. wind section

May 76. (lp)(c) **2ND STREET** [ ] [ ]
– Selfish lover / Blue soul / Stop doing what you're doing / Raging river / Some kind of happy / Sweet beauty / Just for you / On your life / Leaves the wind.

— Tragedy had already struck when on 19th March '76 KOSSOFF died in his sleep, suffering from drug abuse.

— The rest carried on as CRAWLER and released 4 singles as well as 2 albums on 'Epic'; 'CRAWLER' (1977) & 'SNAKE, RATTLE & ROLL' (1978).

- compilations, etc -

Oct 77. D.J.M.; (d-lp) **KOSS** (1974 /75) [ ] [ ]
(re-iss.Aug83 on 'Street Tunes', cd-iss.Jul87)

May 83. Street Tunes; (lp) **THE HUNTER** (1969-75) [ ] [-]

Aug 83. Strret Tunes; (lp) **LEAVES IN THE WIND** (1975 /76) [ ] [-]

Sep 83. Street Tunes; (lp) **CROYDON** – JUNE 15th 1975 (live) [ ] [-]
(cd-iss.May95 on 'Repertoire')

Nov 83. Street Tunes; (c) **MR.BIG** [ ] [-]

Apr 86. Island; (lp)(c) **BLUE SOUL** [ ] [-]

May 94. Island; (cd) **MOLTEN GOLD** [ ] [-]

Ace FREHLEY (see under ⇒ KISS)

FREUR (see under ⇒ UNDERWORLD)

Glenn FREY (see under ⇒ EAGLES)

Robert FRIPP (see under ⇒ KING CRIMSON)

Edgar FROESE (see uner ⇒ TANGERINE DREAM)

FUTURE SOUND OF LONDON

Formed: London, England . . . 1991 by HUMANOID techno Manchester dance duo GARY COCKBAIN & BRIAN DOUGANS. They had a UK Top 20 hit late in 1988 with 'STAKKER HUMANOID'. Spawned other projects SEMI REAL, YAGE, METROPOLIS + ART SCIENCE TECHNOLOGY before 'Virgin' signed the duo as FUTURE SOUND OF LONDON in '92. • **Style:** Modern ambient conceptual soundscapes of gothic beauty, reminiscent of early TANGERINE DREAM. Could be dubbed The PREHISTORIC SOUND OF GERMANY? • **Songwriters:** DOUGANS / COCKBAIN except FLAK; co-written w / ROBERT FRIPP plus WILLIAMS / GROSSART / THOMPSON / NIGHTINGALE. OMNIPRESENCE co-wriiten with KLAUS SCHULZE. • **Trivia:** Augmented on NOMAD's single 'Your Love Has Lifted Me', SYLVIAN-FRIPP's album 'Darshan' and APOLLO 440's 'Liquid Cool'.

Recommended: ACCELERATOR (*7) / LIFEFORMS (*8)

HUMANOID

GARRY COCKBAIN (b. Bedford, England) – keyboards / **BRIAN DOUGANS** (b.Scotland) – keyboards

Westside / not issued

Oct 88. (7") **STAKKER HUMANOID. / (part 2)** [6] [-]
(12"+=) – ('A'-open mix).
(re-iss.12"+cd-ep 8 mixes Jul92 on 'Jumpin' & Pumpin'', hit No.40)

— (note 7"+c-s+cd-s; original part 2 was repl. by 'A'-Smart Systems remix).

Apr 89. (7")(12") **SLAM. / BASS INVADERS** [54] [-]
(12"+=)(cd-s+=) – ('A'dub mix) / ('A'hip house version).

Aug 89. (7") **TONIGHT. / ?** [ ] [-]
(12"+=)(cd-s+=) –

Oct 89. (lp)(c)(cd) **GLOBAL** [ ] [ ]
–

Apr 90. (12"ep) **THE DEEP (3 mixes). / CRY BABY** [ ] [-]

The duo then formed SMART SYSTEMS, before re-grouping as . . .

FUTURE SOUND OF LONDON

same line-up as above.

Jumpin' & Pumpin' / not issued

Feb 92. (12"ep) **PAPUA NEW GUINEA (Dali mix) / ('A'dumb child of a Q mix) / ('A'-Qube mix)** [22] [ ]
(12"ep)(c-ep)(cd-ep) – (the remixes by Andy Weatherall & Graham Massey). *(re-iss.May95)*

Jun 92. (cd)(c) **ACCELERATOR** [75] [ ]
– Expander / Stolen documents / While others cry / Calcium / It's not my problem / Papau New Guinea / Moscow / 1 in 8 / Pulse state / Central industrial. *(re-iss.Aug94)*

— above featured **BASIL CLARKE** – vocals (ex-YARGO)

1992. (12"ep) **EXPANDER (remix). / MOSCOW (remix) / CENTRAL INDUSTRIAL (remix)** [ ] [ ]
(cd-ep+=) – ('A'radio remix). *(re-iss.Jul94, hit 72)*

AMORPHOUS ANDROGYNOUS

Virgin / Virgin

Jun 93. (cd)(lp) **TALES OF EPHIDRINA** [ ] [ ]
– Swab / Mountain goat / In mind / Ephidrina / Auto pimp / Pod room / Fat cat.

Aug 93. (12"ep)(cd-ep) **ENVIRONMENTS** [ ] [ ]

FUTURE SOUND OF LONDON

Virgin / Virgin

Oct 93. (12")(c-s) **CASCADE. / ('A'-parts 2-5)** [ ] [ ]
(cd-s+=) – ('A'-short form mix).

May 94. (d-cd)(c)(d-lp) **LIFEFORMS** [6] [ ]
– Cascade / Ill flower / Flak / Bird wings / Dead skin cells / Lifeforms / Eggshell / Among myselves / / Domain / Spineless jelly / Interstat / Vertical pig / Cerebral /

Life form ends / Vit / Omnipresence / Room 208 / Elaborate burn / Little brother.

Aug 94. (7") **LIFEFORMS. / ('A'alternative mix)** 14
(12"+=)(c-s+=)(cd-s+=) – ('A'-paths 1-7).

— (above featured LIZ FRASER (of COCTEAU TWINS) on vocals)

Dec 94. (cd)(c)(d-lp) **I.S.D.N.** 62
– Just a f***in' idiot / Far out son of lung and the ramblings of a madman / Appendage / Slider / Smokin' Japanese babe / You're creeping me out / Eyes-pop-skin-explodes-everybody's dead / It's my mind that works / Dirty shadows / Tired of bugs / Egypt / Are they fighting us? / Hot knives. *(re-iss.Jun95 with 3 new remixed tracks, hit No.44)*

— (In 1994, they were also at time abbreviated to F.S.O.L.)

May 95. (12"ep)(c-ep)(cd-ep) **FAR OUT SON OF LUNG AND THE RAMBLINGS OF A MADMAN. /** 22
– Ramblings of a madman / Snake hips / Smokin' Japanese babe / Amoeba.

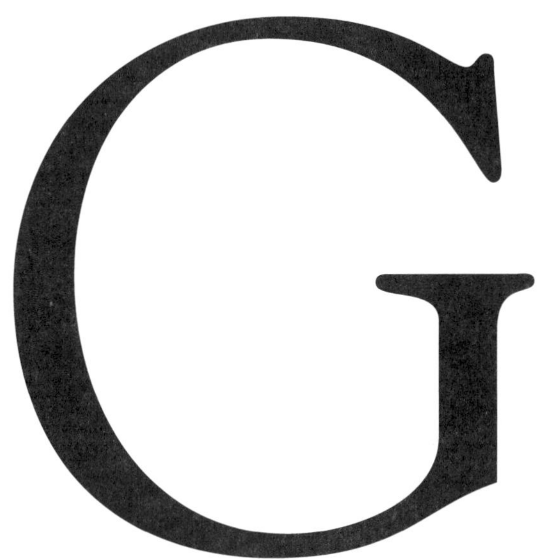

Peter GABRIEL

Born: 13 May'50, Cobham, Surrey, England. After 8 years as leader of GENESIS, he left in May'75 to go solo, although he didn't venture into the studio for over a year. Early in '77, he released first solo album, which was produced by Bob Ezrin, and this hit UK Top 10. A cut from it 'SOLISBURY HILL', also made Top 20, but its follow-up 'MODERN LOVE' failed. In Summer of '78, he issued second Top 10 album, also titled 'PETER GABRIEL', but produced by ROBERT FRIPP (ex-KING CRIMSON). In 1980, he had a Top 10 single 'GAMES WITHOUT FRONTIERS', which previewed No.1 third album, produced by Steve Lillywhite. He continued as a major artist throughout the 80's and early 90's. • **Style:** Adventurous rock performer, whose enigmatic personality always shined through into music. He experimentated with African rhythms, pop/rock music and more recently film soundtracks (i.e. 'BIRDY' & 'PASSION – MUSIC FOR THE LAST TEMPTATION OF CHRIST'). • **Songwriters:** Self-composed except; STRAWBERRY FIELDS FOREVER (Beatles) / SUZANNE (Leonard Cohen). • **Trivia:** In 1982, he co-wrote & produced 'Animals Have More Fun' for JIMMY PURSEY (ex-SHAM 69). Early in 1987, he won 'Best Video Award' for his revolutionary 'claymation' video single 'SLEDGEHAMMER'. He has also guested for ROBBIE ROBERTSON (1987 album) & JONI MITCHELL (1991 album).

Recommended: SHAKIN' THE TREE: SIXTEEN GOLDEN GREATS (*9).

PETER GABRIEL – vocals, keyboards (ex-GENESIS, ex-GARDEN WALL) with **TONY LEVIN** – bass / **STEVE HUNTER** – guitar / **LARRY FAST** – keyboards / **JIMMY MAELEN** – percussion / **ALAN SCHWARTZBERG** – drums / **ROBERT FRIPP** – guitar

Charisma | Atco

Feb 77. (lp)(c) **PETER GABRIEL** [7] [38]
– Moribund the burgermeister / Solisbury Hill / Modern love / Excuse me / Humdrum / Slowburn / Waiting for the big one / Down the Dolce Vita / Here comes the flood. *(cd-iss.May83 + re-iss.+cd.Aug88)*

Mar 77. (7") **SOLISBURY HILL. / MORIBUND THE BURGERMEISTER** [13] [68]

Jun 77. (7") **MODERN LOVE. / SLOWBURN** [ ] [ ]

— now with **FRIPP,** plus **JERRY MAROTTA** – drums / **ROY BITTAN** – piano / **SID McGINNIS** – guitar / **BAYETE** – keyboards

May 78. (7") **D.I.Y.. / PERSPECTIVE** [ ] [-]
(12") – ('A'remix) / Mother of violence / Me and my teddy bear.

Charisma | Atlantic

Jun 78. (lp)(c) **PETER GABRIEL** [10] [45]
– On the air / D.I.Y. / Mother of violence / A wonderful day in a one-way world / White shadow / Indigo / Animal magic / Exposure / Flotsam and jetsam / Perspective / Home sweet home. *(re-iss.Mar84) (cd-iss.May87)*

Jun 78. (7") **D.I.Y. / MOTHER OF VIOLENCE** [-] [ ]

Charisma | Mercury

Feb 80. (7"m) **GAMES WITHOUT FRONTIERS. / THE START / I DON'T REMEMBER** [4] [48] Aug 80

May 80. (7") **NO SELF CONTROL. / LEAD A NORMAL LIFE** [33] [ ]

— now with **FRIPP, LEVIN + MAROTTA** plus guests **PHIL COLLINS** – drums / **KATE BUSH + PAUL WELLER** – vocals

May 80. (lp)(c) **PETER GABRIEL** [1] [22]
– Intruder / No self control / Start / I don't remember / Family snapshot / And through the wire / Not one of us / Lead a normal life / Biko. *(re-iss.Sep83) (cd-iss.May87)*

Aug 80. (7")(12") **BIKO. / SHOSHOLOZA / JETZ KOMMT DIE FLUT** [38] [ ]

— guests on next incl. **DAVID LORD** – synthesizers, co-producer / **JOHN ELLIS** – guitar / + some of last line-up

Charisma | Geffen

Sep 82. (lp)(c) **PETER GABRIEL** [6] [28]
– The rhythm of the heat / San Jacinto / I have the touch / The family and the fishing net / Shock the monkey / Lay your hands on me / Wallflower / Kiss of life. *(US title 'SECURITY'; and on a sticker) (re-iss.Sep83) (cd-iss.1986)*

Sep 82. (7")(12") **SHOCK THE MONKEY. / SOFT DOG** [58] [29]
(7"pic-d) – ('A'side) / ('B'instrumental).

Dec 82. (7") **I HAVE THE TOUCH. / ACROSS THE RIVER** [ ] [ ]

Jun 83. (d-lp)(c) **PETER GABRIEL PLAYS LIVE (live)** [8] [44]
– The rhythm of the heat / I have the touch / Not one of us / Family snapshot / D.I.Y. / The family and the fishing net / Intruder / I go swimming / San Jacinto / Solisbury Hill / No self control / I don't remember / Shock the monkey / Humdrum / On the air / Biko. *(re-iss.Jun83) (cd-iss.Jun85 + 1988; omits 4 tracks).*

Jun 83. (7") **I DON'T REMEMBER (live). / SOLISBURY HILL (live)** [62] [ ]
(12"+=) – Kiss of life (live). (free-12"w/ 12") – GAMES WITHOUT FRONTIERS (live). / SCHNAPPSCHUSS

Virgin | Geffen

Nov 83. (7") **SOLISBURY HILL (live). / I GO SWIMMING (live)** [-] [84]

May 84. (7") **WALK THROUGH THE FIRE. / THE RACE** [69] [ ]
(12"+=) – I have the touch (remix).

Mar 85. (lp)(c)(cd) **BIRDY – MUSIC FROM THE FILM (soundtrack)** [51] [ ]
– At night / Floating dogs / Quiet and alone / Close up / Slow water / Dressing the wound / Birdy's flight / Slow marimbas / The heat / Sketchpad with trumpet and voice / Under lock and key / Powerhouse at the foot of the mountain. *(re-iss.Apr90)*

— with **MAROTTA, LEVIN** plus **DANIEL LANOIS** – guitar, co-producer / **MANU KATCHE** – percussion / **YOUSSOU N'DOUR + KATE BUSH** – guest vocals / **STEWART COPELAND** – drums **/etc.**

Apr 86. (7") **SLEDGEHAMMER. / JOHN HAS A HEADACHE** [4] [1]
('A'dance-12"+=) – I have the touch ('85 remix).
(12"++=)(c-s++=) – Biko.
(12"+=) – Don't break this rhythm. *(US; b-side)*

May 86. (lp)(c)(cd) **SO** [1] [2]
– Red rain / Sledgehammer / Don't give up / That voice again / In your eyes / Mercy street / Big time / We do what we're told. (cd+=) – This is the picture (excellent birds).

Sep 86. (7") **IN YOUR EYES. / ('A'-Special mix)** [-] [26]
(re-iss.Jun89 on 'WTG' US, reached 41)

Oct 86. (7") **DON'T GIVE UP. (by "PETER GABRIEL & KATE BUSH") / IN YOUR EYES** [9] [-]

Jan 87. (7") **BIG TIME. / WE DO WHAT WE'RE TOLD** [-] [8]

Mar 87. (7") **BIG TIME. / CURTAINS** [13] [-]
(12"+=) – ('A'extended).
(c-s) – ('A'extended) / ('B'side) / Across the river / No self control. *(re-iss.3"cd-s.1989)*

Mar 87. (7") **DON'T GIVE UP ("PETER GABRIEL & KATE BUSH"). / CURTAINS** [-] [72]

Jun 87. (7") **RED RAIN. / GAGA** [46] [ ]
(12"+=)(c-s+=) – Walk through the fire.

Jan 88. (7")(12")(c-s) **BIKO (live). / NO MORE APARTEID** [49] [-]
(cd-s+=) – I have the touch ('85 remix).

— In May 89, PETER ws credited with YOUSSOU N'DOUR on minor hit single 'SHAKIN THE TREE'.

Real World | Geffen

Jun 89. (d-lp)(c)(cd) **PASSION (Soundtrack film 'The Last Temptation Of Christ')** [29] [60]
– The feeling begins / Gethsemane / Of these, hope / Lazarus raised / Of these, hope – reprise / In doubt / A different drum / Zaar / Troubled / Open* / Before night falls / With this love / Sandstorm / Stigmata** / Passion / With this love – choir / Wall of breath / The promise of shadows / Disturbed / It is accomplished / Bread and wine. *(*= with SHANKAR) (**= with MAHMOUD TABRIZI ZADEH)*

Sep 92. (7")(c-s) **DIGGING IN THE DIRT. / QUIET STEAM** [24] [52]
(cd-s+=)/ /(cd-s++=) – ('A'instrumental). / / Bashi-bazouk.

Oct 92. (cd)(c)(lp) **US** [2] [2]
– Come talk to me / Love to be loved / Blood of Eden / Steam / Digging in the dirt / Fourteen black paintings / Kiss that frog / Secret world.

Jan 93. (7")(c-s) **STEAM. / ('A'-Carter . . . mix)** [10] [32] Nov 92
(cd-s) – ('A' mix) / Games without frontiers (mix) / (2 'A' extended + dub mix or Games (other mix)

Mar 93. (7")(c-s) **BLOOD OF EDEN. / MERCY STREET** [43] [ ]
(cd-s+=) – ('A'-special mix)
(cd-s+=) – Sledgehammer.

Sep 93. (7")(c-s) **KISS THAT FROG. / ('A' mindblender mix)** [46] [ ]
(cd-s+=) – Digging in the dirt.
(cd-s+=) – Across the river / Shaking the tree (Bottrill remix).

— Below single, another from 'Philadelphia' film on 'Epic' records.

Jun 94. (7")(c-s) **LOVE TOWN. / LOVE TO BE LOVED** [49] [ ]
(cd-s+=) – Different drum.

— live with **TONY LEVIN** – bass, vocals / **DAVID RHODES** – guitar, vocals / **MANU KATCHE** – drums / **PAULA COLE** – vocals / **JEAN CLAUDE NAIMRO** – keyboards, vocals / **RAVI SHANKAR** – violin, vocals / **LEVON MINASSIAN** – doudouk

Aug 94. (c-s) **SECRET WORLD (live). / COME TALK TO ME** [39] [ ]
(cd-ep) – ('A'live) / Red rain (live) / San Jacinto (live) / Mercy Street (live).

Sep 94. (d-cd)(d-c) **SECRET WORLD LIVE (live)** [10] [23]
– Come talk to me / Steam / Across the river / Slow marimbas / Shaking the tree / Red rain / Blood of Eden / Kiss that frog / Washing of the water / Solisbury Hill / Digging in the dirt / Sledgehammer / Secret world / Don't give up / In your eyes.

– compilations, etc. –

1988. Virgin; (3"cd-ep) **SOLISBURY HILL / MORIBUND THE BURGERMEISTER / SOLISBURY HILL (live)** [ ] [ ]
(re-iss.Apr90)

Oct 90. Virgin; (3xcd-box) **PETER GABRIEL 1 / 2 / 3** [ ] [ ]

Nov 90. Virgin/ US= Geffen; (cd)(c)(lp) **SHAKING THE TREE – SIXTEEN GOLDEN GREATS** [11] [48]
-Solisbury Hill / I don't remember / Sledgehammer / Family snapshot / Mercy Street / Shaking the tree / Don't give up / Here comes the flood / Games without frontiers / Shock the monkey / Big time / Biko.
(cd+c+=) – San Juanito / Red rain / I have the touch / Zaar.

Dec 90. Virgin; (7")(c-s) **SOLISBURY HILL. / SHAKING THE TREE (by "PETER GABRIEL & YOUSSOU N'DOUR")** [57] [ ]
(12"+=)(cd-s+=) – Games without frontiers.

Mar 83. Charisma; (d-c) **PETER GABRIEL 1 / PETER GABRIEL 2** [ ] [-]

Jan 83. Old Gold; (7") **SOLISBURY HILL. / GAMES WITHOUT FRONTIERS** [ ] [-]

Rory GALLAGHER

Born: 2 Mar'49, Ballyshannon, Donegal, Ireland. After playing in various school bands in Cork, he formed The FONTANA SHOWBAND, who soon became The IMPACT. In 1965, they secured residencies in Hamburg, mostly playing CHUCK BERRY songs. In 1966, he formed TASTE with NORMAN DAMERY and ERIC KITTERINGHAM, but they departed 2 years later, and were replaced by CHARLIE McCRACKEN and JOHN WILSON. After a debut lp failed to breakthrough, they hit UK Top20 in 1970 with 'ON THE BOARDS'. However they soon disbanded and GALLAGHER went solo. His first lp was self-titled, and made UK Top40 lists. He progressed the following year, when 'LIVE IN EUROPE' lp hit Top 10. He and his always accomplished sidekicks, scored a few more successes, and persevered with rock industry into the 90's. • **Style:** The gentle man of rock and blues, described as the people's guitarist, due to his unconformist rock star look (i.e. lumberjack shirt, jeans and ruffled hair). Renowned for his heavy bouts of seroius drinking. His inspirations stemmed from B.B. KING, FREDDIE KING, ALBERT KING, etc. • **Songwriters:** GALLAGHER penned many new blues numbers, incorporating past standards; SUGAR MAMA + DON'T START ME TALKING (Sonny Boy Williamson) / I'M MOVING ON (Hank Snow) / I TAKE WHAT I WANT (Hayes-Porter-Hedges) / ALL AROUND MAN (Davenport) / OUT ON THE WESTERN PLAINS (Leadbelly) / RIDE ON RED, RIDE ON (Levy-Glover-Reid) / I WONDER WHO (. . . Boyle) / AS THE CROW FLIES (Josh White) / JUST A LITTLE BIT (Dexter Gordon) / MESSING WITH THE KID (Julie London) / PISTOL SLAPPER BLUES (. . . Allen) / etc. • **Trivia:** VINCENT CRANE of ATOMIC ROOSTER guested on RORY's debut lp in '71. GALLAGHER also sessioned on albums by MUDDY WATERS (London Sessions) / JERRY LEE LEWIS (London Sessions) / LONNIE DONEGAN (Putting On The Style) / etc.

Recommended: THE BEST OF RORY GALLAGHER & TASTE (*6) / IRISH TOUR '74 (*7)

TASTE

RORY GALLAGHER – vocals, guitar / **CHARLIE McCRACKEN** (b.26 Jun'48) – bass repl. ERIC KITTERINGHAM / **JOHN WILSON** (b. 3 Dec'47) – drums (ex-THEM) repl. NORMAN DAMERY

Major Minor — not issued

Apr 68. (7") **BLISTER ON THE MOON. / BORN ON THE WRONG SIDE OF TIME** [ ] [-]
(re-iss.Jul70)

Polydor — Atco

Mar 69. (7") **BORN ON THE WRONG SIDE OF TIME. / SAME OLD STORY** [ ] [-]

Apr 69. (lp) **TASTE** [ ] [ ]
– Blister on the moon / Leaving blues / Sugar mama / Hail / Born on the wrong side of time / Dual carriageway of pain / Same old story / Hail / Catfish / I'm moving on. *(re-iss.'79) (cd-iss.Aug92)*

Jan 70. (lp) **ON THE BOARDS** [18] [ ]
– What's going on / Railway & gun / It's happened before, it'll happen again / If the day was any longer / Morning sun / Eat my words / On the boards / If I don't sing I'll cry / See here / I'll remember. *(cd-iss.Apr94)*

Feb 71. (lp) **LIVE TASTE (live)** [ ] [-]
– Sugar mama / Gamblin' blues / I feel so good (Pt.1 & 2) / Catfish / Same old story. *(cd-iss.Apr94)*

— GALLAGHER went solo. The other two formed STUD. McCRACKEN also joined SPENCER DAVIS GROUP

RORY GALLAGHER

solo – vocals, guitar with **GERRY MacAVOY** – bass (ex-DEEP JOY) / **WILGAR CAMPBELL** – drums (ex-METHOD)

Polydor — Atlantic

May 71. (lp)(c) **RORY GALLAGHER** [32] [ ]
– Laundromat / Just the smile / I fall apart / Wave myself goodbye / Hands up / Sinner boy / For the last time / It's you / I'm not surprised / Can't believe it's true. *(re-iss.'79 on 'Chrysalis')*

Jun 71. (7"m) **IT'S YOU. / JUST THE SMILE / SINNER BOY** [ ] [ ]

Nov 71. (lp)(c) **DEUCE** [39] [ ]
– Used to be / I'm not awake yet / Don't know where I'm going / Maybe I will / Whole lot of people / In your town / Out of my mind / Should've learn't my lesson / There's a light / Crest of a wave. *(re-iss.'79 on 'Chrysalis')*

Polydor — Polydor

May 72. (lp)(c) **LIVE! IN EUROPE (live)** [9] [ ]
– Messin' with the kid / Laundromat / I could've had religion / Pistol slapper blues / Going to my home town / Bullfrog blues / In your town. *(re-iss.'79 on 'Chrysalis')*

— **ROD DE'ATH** – drums (ex-KILLING FLOOR) repl. CAMPBELL / added **LOU MARTIN** – keyboards, mandolin (ex-KILLING FLOOR)

Feb 73. (lp)(c) **BLUEPRINT** [12] [ ]
– Walk on hot coals / Daughter of the Everglades / Banker's blues / Hands off / Race the breeze / The seventh son of a seventh son / Unmilitary two-step / If I had a reason. *(re-iss.'79 on 'Chrysalis') (cd-iss.Jan94)*

Aug 73. (lp)(c) **TATTOO** [32] [ ]
– Tattoo'd lady / Cradle rock / 20:20 vision / They don't make them like you anymore / Livin' like a trucker / Sleep on a clothes-line / A million miles away / Admit it. *(re-iss.'79 on 'Chrysalis') (cd-iss.Jan94)*

Jul 74. (d-lp)(c) **IRISH TOUR '74 (live)** [36] [ ]
– Cradle rock / I wonder who (who's gonn be your sweet man) / Tattoo'd lady / Too much alcohol / As the crow flies / A million miles away / Walk on hot coals / Who's that coming / Back on my (stompin' ground) / Just a little bit. *(re-iss.'79 on 'Chrysalis') (re-iss.+d-cd May88 on 'Demon')*

Chrysalis — Chrysalis

Oct 75. (lp)(c) **AGAINST THE GRAIN** [ ] [ ]
– Let me in / Cross me off your list / Ain't too good / Souped up Ford / Bought and sold / I take what I want / Lost at sea / All around man / Out on the western plain / At the bottom. *(re-iss.+cd.May91 on 'Castle')*

Nov 75. (7") **SOUPED UP FORD. / I TAKE WHAT I WANT** [ ] [ ]

Oct 76. (lp)(c) **CALLING CARD** [32] [ ]
– Do you read me / Country mile / Moonchild / Calling card / I'll admit you're gone / Secret agent / Jacknife beat / Edged in blue / Barley and grape rag. *(re-iss.+cd Jun91 on 'Essential') (cd re-iss.Mar94)*

— **TED McKENNA** – drums (ex-SENSATIONAL ALEX HARVEY BAND) repl.DE'ATH and MARTIN (to RAMROD)

Oct 76. (lp)(c) **PHOTO FINISH** [ ] [ ]
– Shin kicker / Brute force and ignorance / Cruise on out / Cloak and dagger / Overnight bag / Shadow play / The Mississippi sheiks / The last of the indepenents / Fuel to the fire.

Jan 79. (7"m) **SHADOW PLAY. / SOUPED UP FORD / BRUTE FORCE AND IGNORANCE** [ ] [ ]

Aug 79. (7")(7"colrd) **PHILBY. / HELLCAT / COUNTRY MILE** [ ] [ ]

Sep 79. (lp)(c) **TOP PRIORITY** [56] [ ]
– Follow me / Philby / Wayward child / Keychain / At the depot / Bad penny / Just hit town / Off the handle / Public enemy No.1. *(re-iss.+cd May88 on 'Demon')*

Aug 80. (7")(7"colrd) **WAYWARD CHILD (live). / KEYCHAIN** [ ] [ ]

Sep 80. (lp)(c) **STAGE STRUCK (live)** [40] [ ]
– Shin kicker / Wayward child / Brute force and ignorance / Moonchild / Follow me / Bought and sold / The last of the independents / Shadow play.

1980. (7") **HELLCAT. / NOTHIN' BUT THE DEVIL** [ ] [ ]

— (May81) **GALLAGHER** with **McAVOY** brought in **BRENDAN O'NEILL** – drums repl. McKENNA who joined GREG LAKE BAND then MSG

Apr 82. (lp)(c) **JINX** [68] [ ]
– Signals / The Devil made me do it / Double vision / Easy come, easy go / Big guns / Jinxed / Bourbon / Ride on Red, ride on / Loose talk. *(re-iss.+cd May88*

on 'Demon')
Jun 82. (7") **BIG GUNS. / THE DEVIL MADE ME DO IT**
1983. (10"ep) **SHADOWPLAY / BRUTE FORCE AND IGNORANCE. / MOONCHILD / SOUPED UP FORD** [ ] [-]

Capo-Demon / Intercord

Jul 87. (lp)(c)(cd) **DEFENDER** [ ] [-]
– Kickback city / Loanshark blues / Continental O.P. / I ain't no saint / Failsafe day / Road to Hell / Doing time / Smear campaign / Don't start me talkin' / Seven days. *(c+cd+=) – (below free 7") (free-7".w/a)* – **SEEMS TO ME. / NO PEACE FOR THE WICKED**

— guests **MARK FELTHAM** – harmonica / **LOU MARTIN** – piano / **JOHN EARL** – saxes. / **GERAINT WATKINS** – accordion / **JOHN COOKE** – keyboards / **RAY BEAVIS** – tenor sax. / **DICK HANSON** – trumpet.

Jun 90. (cd)(c)(lp) **FRESH EVIDENCE**
– 'Kid' gloves / The king of Zydeco (to: Clifton Chenier) / Middle name / Alexis / Empire state express / Ghost blues / Heaven's gate / The loop / Walkin' wounded / Slumming angel. *(re-iss.cd Oct92 on 'Essential')*

— On the 14th June 1995, RORY died after complications from a liver transplant operation.

- compilations etc. -

1974. Emerald/ US= Gem; (c) **IN THE BEGINNING (VOCAL AND GUITAR)** (rec.'67)
Aug 72. Polydor; (lp) **LIVE AT THE ISLE OF WIGHT (live)** [41] [-] *(cd-iss.Aug92)*
Feb 75. Polydor; (lp)(c) **SINNER . . . AND SAINT** (1971 material) [-] [ ]
1977. Polydor; (lp) **TASTE** [ ] [-]
Oct 82. Polydor; (7"ep)(12"ep) **BLISTER ON THE MOON / SUGAR MAMA / CATFISH / ON THE BOARD** [ ] [-]
Feb 76. Polydor; (lp)(c) **THE STORY SO FAR**
Feb 88. Razor; (cd) **THE BEST OF RORY GALLAGHER & TASTE** [ ] [-]
– Blister on the Moon / Hail / Born on the wrong side of time / Dual carriageway pain / Same old story / On the boards / See here / I'll remember / Sugar mama (live) / Sinner boy (live) / I feel so good (live) / Catfish / I'm movin' on / What's going on / Ralway and gun / Morning Sun / Eat my words.
May 89. Castle; (d-lp)(cd) **LIVE! IN EUROPE / STAGE STRUCK** [ ] [-]
Jul 89. Castle; (d-lp)(cd) **TATTOO / BLUEPRINT** [ ] [-]
1991. Demon; (4xcd-box) **RORY GALLAGHER** [ ] [-]
– IRISH TOUR '74 / DEFENDER / TOP PRIORITY / JINX
Jun 92. Demon; (cd)(c)(lp) **EDGED IN BLUE** [ ] [-]
Nov 92. Essential; (3xcd-box) **G-MEN: BOOTLEG SERIES VOLUME ONE** [ ] [-]

GALLIANO

Formed: South London, England . . . late 80's by ROB GALLAGHER (GALLIANO) and friends CONSTANTINE and SPRY. Their early gigs were augmented by former STYLE COUNCIL musicians MICK TALBOT (who also became their producer) and STEVE WHITE. They soon were picked up by Giles Peterson's 'Talkin' Loud' label, who released debut single 'WELCOME TO THE STORY' late 1990. • **Style:** Hippy jazz-soul with rap and influenced by The LAST POETS. • **Songwriters:** GALLAGHER-ROBERTSON-WEIR except LONG TIME GONE (Crosby, Stills & Nash). • **Trivia:** They also featured on QUIET BOYS single 'Let The Good Times Roll'.

Recommended: A JOYFUL NOISE UNTO THE CREATOR (*6) / THE PLOT THICKENS (*7)

ROB GALLAGHER – vocals / **BROTHER CONSTANTINE** (b. WEIR) – vocals / **BROTHER SPRY** (CRISPIN ROBERTSON) – piano with many on session incl. TALBOT & WHITE

Talkin Loud / Talkin' Loud

Nov 90. (7") **WELCOME TO THE STORY. / MOTHER NATURE**
(cd-s+=) – ('A'peace mix) / ('A'dub mix).
(12") – (3 'A'mixes).
Feb 91. (7") **NOTHING HAS CHANGED. / ('A'mix)**
(12"+=)(cd-s+=) – Little ghetto boy (remix) / Cheesy little cheese (instrumental).
Mar 91. (cd)(c)(lp) **IN PURSUIT OF THE 13th NOTE**
– Leg in the sea of history / Welcome to the story / Coming on strong / Sweet you like your favourite gears / Cemetary of drums / Five sons of the mother / Storm clouds gather / Nothing has changed / 57th minute of the 23rd hour / Power and glory / Stoned again / Reviewing the situation / Little ghetto boy. (c+=) – Me my mike my lyrics / Love bomb.
(cd++=) – Power and glory (live jazz mix) / Welcome to the story (summer breeze mix).
May 91. (7") **POWER AND GLORY (livin' mix). / ('A'-G-Funk edit)**
(12") – ('A'side) / ('A'-dirty claw Mick Talbot instrumental remix) / Stoned again.
(cd-s) – (all 4 tracks).
Oct 91. (7") **JUS' REACH. / ('A'-Easy nuh star mix)**
(12"+=)(cd-s+=) – ('A'instrumental).
(12") – (4-'A'mixes).

— added **SNAITH** – keyboards + 5th member **STEVE** – dancer

May 92. (7")(cd-s) **SKUNK FUNK (Marco Nelson mix). / ('A'-Andy Weatherall mix)** [41] [ ]
(12") – ('A'cabin fever mix) / ('A'dub mix) / ('A'soldier mix).
Jun 92. (cd)(c) **A JOYFUL NOISE UNTO THE CREATOR** [28] [ ]
– Grounation (part 1) / Jus' reach / Skunk funk / Earth boots / Phantom / Jazz? / New world order / So much confusion / Totally together / Golden flower / Prince of peace / Grounation (part 2).

— above featured vocalists – **CARLEEN ANDERSON, VALERIE ETIENNE + OMAR**

Jul 92. (12")(cd-s) **PRINCE OF PEACE. / TALES OF THE G / GOLDEN FLOWER (featuring OMAR)** [47] [ ]
Sep 92. (12")(cd-s) **JUS' REACH RECYCLED. / HUNGRY LIKE A BABY / FROM THE NORTH, THE SOUTH, THE EAST AND THE WEST** [66] [ ]
(cd-ep; live) – Jus' reach / Skunk funk / New world order / Vibe anthem.

— (now full-time) **VALERIE ETIENNE** – vocals repl. CONSTANTINE

May 94. (12")(c-s)(cd-s) **LONG TIME GONE (extended & palm skin productions remix) / WHAT COLOUR OUR FLAG (parts 1 & 2)** [15] [ ]
(12"+=//cd-s++=) – Rivers. / / Scratching.
(cd-s+=) – Bloodlines.
May 94. (cd)(c) **THE PLOT THICKENS** [7] [ ]
– Was this the time / Blood lines / Rise and fall / Twyford Down / What colour our flag (part 1) / Cold wind / Long time gone / Believe / Do you hear / Travels the road / Better all the time / Little one.
Jul 94. (c-s) **TWYFORD DOWN. / KOH PHAN GHAN** [37] [ ]
(cd-s+=) – The homecoming.
(12") – (3-'A'mixes) / The return.
(cd-s) – (5-'A'mixes).
Dec 94. (cd)(d-lp) **A THICKER PLOT – THE REMIXES** [ ] [-]

GARBAGE

Formed: Wisconsin, USA . . .1994 by DUKE ERIKSON, STEVE MARKER and BUTCH VIG. The latter had found fame in production work for greats like NIRVANA, SONIC YOUTH, SMASHING PUMPKINS, NINE INCH NAILS and U2, before coming across Edinburgh born SHIRLEY MANSON fronting ANGEL FISH on MTV. They contributed the track 'Vow' on a 'Volume' various compilation and this ended up as their limited edition debut 45 in 1995. By that years' summer, they had signed to Geffen's 'Almo Sounds' (UK 'Mushroom') records, which helped them break into UK Top 50 with 'SUBHUMAN'. • **Style:** Grungeful but melodic alternative rock outfit. • **Songwriters:** Group, except a CLASH 'Train In Vain' sample on 'STUPID GIRL'.

Recommended: GARBAGE (*8)

SHIRLEY MANSON -vocals, guitar (ex-GOODBYE MR MACKENZIE) / **STEVE MARKER** -guitar, samples, loops / DUKE ERIKSON -guitar, keyboards, bass / **BUTCH VIG** -drums, loops, efx

Discordant / AlmoSounds

Mar 95. (7") **VOW. / VOW (TORN APART)** [ ] [97] Jun95

Mushroom / AlmoSounds

Aug 95. (7") **SUBHUMAN. / £1 CRUSH** [50] [ ]
(cd-s+=) – Vow.
Sep 95. (7")(c-s)(cd-s) **ONLY HAPPY WHEN IT RAINS. / GIRL DON'T COME / SLEEP** [29] [55] Mar 96
Oct 95. (cd)(c)(d-lp)(boxed-7") **GARBAGE** [6] [29] Mar 96
– Supervixen / Queer / Only happy when it rains / As Heaven is wide / Not my idea / Stroke of luck / Vow / Stupid girl / Dog new tricks / My lover's box / Fix me now / Milk.
Nov 95. (7") **QUEER. / QUEER (Adrian Sherwood remix)** [13] [ ]
(silver-cd-s+=) – Trip my wire / ('A'-Martin Gore, Paul Freeguard and Jones remix).
(cd-s) – ('A'side) / Butterfly collector / ('A'-Rabbit in the Moon remix) / ('A'-Danny Saber remix).

. . . Jan – Jun '96 stop press . . .

Mar 96. (single) **STUPID GIRL** [4] [ ]

Jerry GARCIA (see under ⇒ GRATEFUL DEAD)

Art GARFUNKEL (see under ⇒ SIMON & GARFUNKEL)

Bob GELDOF (see under ⇒ BOOMTOWN RATS)

GENE

Formed: London, England ... summer 1993 by MARTIN and 3 ex-members of SPIN. Debutted with 'FOR THE DEAD' in the Spring of '94. They and their label 'Costermonger' were then picked up by 'Polydor', who issued Top 60 single 'BE MY LIGHT . . . '. Broke through big time in '95, when the 'OLYMPIAN' album went Top 10 UK. • **Style:** Influenced by The SMITHS or The STONES. • **Songwriters:** Group penned except DON'T LET ME DOWN (Beatles).

Recommended: OLYMPIAN (*7)

MARTIN ROSSITER (b.Cardiff, Wales) – vocals, keyboards / **STEVE MASON** – guitars / **KEVIN MILES** – bass / **MATT JAMES** – drums, percussion

		Coster-monger	not issued
Apr 94.	(7") **FOR THE DEAD. / CHILD'S BODY**		-
		Costermonger-Polydor	Polydor
Aug 94.	(7")(c-s) **BE MY LIGHT, BE MY GUIDE. / THIS IS NOT A CRIME**	54	-
	(cd-s+=) – I can't help myself.		
Oct 94.	(7")(c-s)(cd-s) **SLEEP WELL TONIGHT. / SICK, SOBER AND SORRY / HER FIFTEEN YEARS**	36	-
Feb 95.	(cd-s) **HAUNTED BY YOU / HOW MUCH FOR LOVE**	32	
	(7"+=)(c-s+=)(cd-s+=) – Do you want to hear it from me.		
Mar 95.	(cd)(c)(lp) **OLYMPIAN**	8	
	– Haunted by you / Your love, it lies / Truth, rest your head / A car that sped / Left-handed / London, can you wait? / To the city / Still can't find the phone / Sleep well tonight / Olympian / We'll find our own way.		
Jun 95.	(7") **BE MY LIGHT, BE MY GUIDE. / I CAN'T HELP MYSELF**		
	(above on 'Sub Pop' UK & feat. on 'HELTER SHELTER' box-set)		
Jul 95.	(cd-s) **OLYMPIAN / I CAN'T DECIDE IF SHE REALLY LOVES ME**	18	
	(7"+=)(c-s+=)(cd-s+=) – To see the lights / Don't let me down.		
	(cd-s++=) – Don't let me down.		
	. . . Jan – Jun '96 stop press . . .		
Jan 96.	(single re-issue) **FOR THE DEAD**	14	
Jan 96.	(cd)(c)(d-lp) **TO SEE THE LIGHTS** (compilation of rare, live & bootleg material)	11	

GENERATION X

Formed: London, England ... late 1976 by BILLY IDOL and TONY JAMES, whom had cut their teeth in embryonic CHELSEA group. After a few gigs at The ROXY in London, they were snapped up to 'Chrysalis' in 1977. Their debut 45 'YOUR GENERATION', gave them first entry into UK Top40, and an appearance on Top Of The Pops. • **Style:** Anthem riled punk-rock pop, fronted by the energetic lip curling blonde frontman BILLY IDOL. • **Songwriters:** IDOL-JAMES penned except; GIMME SOME TRUTH (John Lennon) / SHAKIN' ALL OVER (Johnny Kidd & The Pirates). • **Trivia:** IAN HUNTER (ex-MOTT THE HOOPLE) produced 1979 album 'VALLEY OF THE DOLLS', and took over from earlier producer MARTIN RUSHENT.

Recommended: PERFECT HITS (*7).

BILLY IDOL (b. WILLIAM BROAD, 30 Nov'55, Middlesex, England) – vocals (ex-CHELSEA, ex-INFANTS) / **BOB 'Derwood' ANDREWS** – guitar / **TONY JAMES** – bass, vocals (ex-CHELSEA, ex-INFANTS) / **MARK LAFF** – drums (ex-SUBWAY SECT) repl. JOHN TOWE (ex-CHELSEA, ex-INFANTS) who joined ALTERNATIVE TV then ADVERTS, etc

		Chrysalis	Chrysalis
Sep 77.	(7") **YOUR GENERATION. / DAY BY DAY**	36	
Dec 77.	(7") **WILD YOUTH. / WILD DUB / (ltd. mispress=) NO NO NO**		
Mar 78.	(7") **READY STEADY GO. / NO NO NO**	47	
Mar 78.	(lp)(c) **GENERATION X**	29	
	– From the heart / One hundred punks / Listen / Ready steady go / Kleenex / Promises promises / Day by day / The invisible man / Kiss me deadly / Too personal / Youth, youth, youth. *(cd-iss.1986) (re-iss.cd Mar94)*		
Jan 79.	(7")(7"red)(7"pink)(7"orange)(7"yellow) **KING ROCKER. / GIMME SOME TRUTH**	11	
Jan 79.	(lp)(c) **VALLEY OF THE DOLLS**	51	
	– Running with the boss sound / Night of the Cadillacs / Paradise west / Friday's angels / King rocker / Valley of the dolls / English dream / Love like fire / Paradise west / The prime of Kenny Silvers. *(cd-iss.1986)*		
Mar 79.	(7")(7"brown) **VALLEY OF THE DOLLS. / SHAKIN' ALL OVER**	23	
Jun 79.	(7")(7"pink) **FRIDAY'S ANGELS. / TRYING FOR KICKS / THIS HEAT**	62	

— **TERRY CHIMES** – drums (ex-CLASH, ex-COWBOYS INTERNATIONAL) repl. LAFF / **JAMES STEPHENSON** – guitar (ex-CHELSEA) repl. 'DERWOOD' (later to WESTWORLD) (above 2 now with **IDOL** and **T. JAMES**)

GEN X

		Chrysalis	Chrysalis
Sep 80.	(7") **DANCING WITH MYSELF. / UGLY RASH**	62	
	(12"+=) – Loopy dub / What do you want		
Jan 81.	(lp)(c) **KISS ME DEADLY**		
	– Dancing with myself / Untouchables / Happy people / Heaven's inside / Triumph / Revenge / Stars look down / What do you want / Oh mother.		
Jan 81.	(7"ep)(12"ep)(7"clear-ep) **DANCING WITH MYSELF / UNTOUCHABLES / KING ROCKER / ROCK ON.**	60	

— Band split early '81. BILLY IDOL went solo. CHIMES rejoined The CLASH, TONY JAMES later formed SIGUE SIGUE SPUTNIK. STEPHENSON later joined GENE LOVES JEZEBEL, then The CULT.

– compilations etc. –

Nov 85.	Chrysalis; (lp)(c) **THE BEST OF GENERATION X**		
Oct 91.	Chrysalis; (cd)(c)(lp) **PERFECT HITS (1975-81)**		
	– Dancing with myself / Your generation / Ready steady go / The untouchables / Day by day / Wild youth / Wild dub / One hundred punks / King rocker / Kiss me deadly / Gimme some truth / New order / English dream / Triumph / Youth, youth, youth.		
Feb 87.	Old Gold; (7") **KING ROCKER. / VALLEY OF THE DOLLS**		-
Jun 87.	M.B.C.; (lp) **THE ORIGINAL GENERATION X**		-
Jun 87.	M.B.C.; (lp) **GENERATION X LIVE (live)**		-

GENESIS

Formed: Godalming, Surrey, England ... early 1967 by Charterhouse public school boys PETER GABRIEL and TONY BANKS, both ex-The GARDEN WALL. They teamed up with former members of The ANON; MICHAEL RUTHERFORD, ANTHONY PHILLIPS and CHRIS STEWART. Still at school, they signed to 'Decca', having sent demos to solo artist and producer JONATHAN KING. Their first 2 singles flopped, as did 1969 lp 'FROM GENESIS TO REVELATION', which sold only around 500 copies. Early in 1970, they were seen live by TONY STRATTON-SMITH, who became their manager after signing them to his 'Charisma' label. Their lp 'TRESPASS' failed to breakthrough, although it contained live favourite and edited 45 'THE KNIFE'. After its release, they found new members PHIL COLLINS and STEVE HACKETT, who replaced recent additions JOHN MAYHEW and ANTHONY PHILLIPS. Late in '71, they unleashed 'NURSERY CRYME', which featured another 2 gems 'THE MUSICAL BOX' & 'THE RETURN OF THE GIANT HOGWEED'. It was also the brief debut on lead vox for COLLINS, who sang on the track 'FOR ABSENT FRIENDS'. A year later with many gigs behind them, they had first taste of chart success, when 'FOXTROT' hit the UK Top 20. This contained the excellent concept piece 'SUPPER'S READY', which lasted all of 23 minutes. In 1973, a live album of their best work so far, hit the Top 10, as did their studio follow-up 'SELLING ENGLAND BY THE POUND'. This enclosed another beaut 'THE BATTLE OF EPPING FOREST', plus another COLLINS sung song 'MORE FOOL ME'. Lifted from it was a near Top20 hit 45 'I KNOW WHAT I LIKE (IN YOUR WARDROBE)'. Late in 1974, they again made Top 10, with concept double album 'THE LAMB LIES DOWN ON BROADWAY', which was first US Top 50 entry and part of worldwide live show. Shortly after last concert in May'75, GABRIEL left for a solo career, and COLLINS stepped in for vocal duties. Surprisingly this did not harm commercial appeal of group, when they returned in 1976 with Top 3 album 'A TRICK OF THE TAIL'. His drum-stool was filled for live gigs by experienced BILL BRUFORD, then CHESTER THOMPSON, who appeared on 1977 double album 'SECONDS OUT'. This was also the last album to feature STEVE HACKETT, who also left for lucrative solo venture. In 1978, their next album, appropriately titled ' . . . AND THEN THERE WERE THREE' (COLLINS, BANKS & RUTHERFORD), hit No.3 and also climbed into US Top 20. The 80's became even more fruitful for the band, hitting top spot in the UK with each album release. They also amassed a number of hit singles on both sides of the Atlantic. During this era, PHIL COLLINS (who had sidelined drumming attributes, in own BRAND X group) scored a number of easier-listening hit singles and albums. He also re-launched his acting career (as a teenager, he was 'The Artful Dodger' in West End production of 'Oliver'), starring on TV series 'Miami Vice' and films 'RISKY BUSINESS', 'BUSTER' & 'HOOK'. He had also sessioned for over 100 groups/artists, including ENO, JOHN CALE and ARGENT. His later production work included; FRIDA (Abba) / ADAM & THE ANTS, HOWARD JONES and ERIC CLAPTON to name but a few. TONY BANKS also released solo work, as did MIKE RUTHERFORD, who also chose a pop outlet in MIKE + THE MECHANICS. • **Style:** Early GENESIS moved through pop/rock like MOODY BLUES sound, to progressive theatrical act, fronted by the bizarre extrovert PETER GABRIEL. After his untimely departure, group were not too dissimilar, although in recent years, they have mellowed with age. Although many PHIL COLLINS' pop fans might disagree, their best work definitely sprouted from the 70's. Ask any old MARILLION fan, especially their one-time singer FISH. • **Songwriters:** GABRIEL lyrics and group compositions. From 1978, the trio collaborated on all work. PHIL COLLINS covered; YOU CAN'T HURRY LOVE (Supremes) / SEPARATE LIVES (Stephen Bishop) / TWO HEARTS (co-with Lamont Dozier) / GROOVY KIND OF LOVE (Mindbenders) / ALWAYS (Irving Berlin) and a few more. MIKE + THE MECHANICS covered YOU'VE REALLY GOT A HOLD ON ME (Smokey Robinson & The Miracles) / I BELIEVE (WHEN I FALL IN LOVE IT WILL BE FOREVER) (Stevie Wonder & Syreeta). • **Miscellaneous:** COLLINS divorced wife in '78, and married Jill Taverman on 4 Aug'84. He guested on 1985 'LIVE AID' concert and played drums behind LED ZEPPELIN re-union of ROBERT PLANT and JIMMY PAGE.

Recommended: NURSERY CRYME (*8) / TRESPASS (*5) / FOXTROT (*9) / GENESIS LIVE (*6) / SELLING ENGLAND BY THE POUND (*8) / THE LAMB LIES DOWN ON BROADWAY (*7) / A TRICK OF THE TAIL (*6) / WIND & WUTHERING (*6) / . . . AND THEN THERE WERE THREE (*6) / DUKE (*6) / INVISIBLE TOUCH (*5).

PETER GABRIEL (b.13 May'50, London, England) – vocals / **TONY BANKS** (b.27 Mar'51, East Heathly, Sussex, England) – keyboards, vocals / **ANTHONY PHILLIPS** – guitar, vocals / **MICHAEL RUTHERFORD** (b. 2 Oct'50, Guildford, Surrey, England) – bass, guitar / **CHRIS STEWART** – drums

Decca | Parrot

Feb 68. (7") **THE SILENT SUN. / THAT'S ME** [ ] [ ]
May 68. (7") **A WINTER'S TALE. / ONE-EYED HOUND** [ ] [-]

—— **JOHN SILVER** – drums repl. CHRIS

Mar 69. (lp) **FROM GENESIS TO REVELATION** [ ] [ ]
– Where the sour turns to sweet / In the beginning / Fireside song / The serpent / Am I very wrong? / In the wilderness / The conqueror / In hiding / One day / Window / In limbo / The silent sun / A place to call my own. *(re-iss.'74 as 'IN THE BEGINNING') (re-iss.cd+c Oct93 on 'Music Club')*
Jun 69. (7") **WHERE THE SOUR TURNS TO SWEET. / IN HIDING** [ ] [-]

—— (Jul69) **JOHN MAYHEW** – drums repl. JOHN SILVER

Charisma | Impulse

Oct 70. (lp)(c) **TRESPASS** [ ] [ ]
– Looking for someone / White mountain / Visions of angels / Stagnation / Dusk / The knife. *(re-iss.Mar84, hit 98) (re-iss.Mar86, cd-iss.Jun88) (re-iss.'74 in US on 'A.B.C.') (cd re-iss.Aug94 on 'Virgin')*
Jun 71. (7") **THE KNIFE (Pt.1). / THE KNIFE (Pt.2)** [ ] [-]

—— (Dec70) **GABRIEL, BANKS and RUTHERFORD** recruit new members **PHIL COLLINS** (b.31 Jan'51, Chiswick, London, England) – drums, vocals (ex-FLAMING YOUTH) repl. MAYHEW / **STEVE HACKETT** (b.12 Feb'50, London) – guitar (ex-QUIET WORLD) repl. ANTHONY PHILLIPS who went solo

Charisma | Charisma

Nov 71. (lp)(c) **NURSERY CRYME** [ ] [ ]
– The musical box / For absent friends / The fountain of Salmacis / Seven stones / Harold the barrel / Harlequin / The return of the giant hogweed. *(hit UK No.39 May74) (re-iss.Mar84 on 'Virgin', hit 68) (cd-iss.Sep85) (cd re-iss.Aug94 on 'Virgin')*
May 72. (7") **HAPPY THE MAN. / SEVEN STONES** [ ] [ ]
Oct 72. (lp)(c) **FOXTROT** [12] [ ]
– Get 'em out by Friday / Time-table / Watcher of the skies / Can-utility and the coastliners / Horizon / Supper's ready; (i) Lover's leap, (ii) The guaranteed eternal sanctuary man, (iii) Ikhaton and Itsacon and their band of merry men, (iv) How dare I be so beautiful, (v) Willow farm, (vi) Apocalypse in 9/8 co-starring the delicious talents of Gabble Ratchet, (vii) As sure as eggs is eggs (aching men's feets). *(re-iss.Sep83 on 'Virgin') (cd-iss.Jul86) (cd re-iss.Aug94 on 'Virgin')*
Feb 73. (7") **WATCHER OF THE SKIES. / WILLOW FARM** [-] [ ]
Jul 73. (lp)(c) **GENESIS LIVE (live)** [9] [ ]
– Watcher of the skies / Get 'em out by Friday / The return of the giant hogweed / The musical box / The knife. *(re-iss.Frb86 on 'Virgin') (cd-iss.Jul87) (cd re-iss.Aug94 on 'Virgin')*
Oct 73. (lp)(c) **SELLING ENGLAND BY THE POUND** [3] [70]
– Dancing in the moonlight knight / I know what I like (in your wardrobe) / Firth of fifth / More fool me / The battle of Epping Forest / After the ordeal / The cinema show / Aisle of plenty. *(re-iss.Oct86 on 'Virgin') (cd-iss.Feb86) (cd re-iss.Aug94 on 'Virgin')*
Mar 74. (7") **I KNOW WHAT I LIKE (IN YOUR WARDROBE). / TWILIGHT ALEHOUSE** [21] [ ]

Charisma | Atco

Nov 74. (d-lp)(d-c) **THE LAMB LIES DOWN ON BROADWAY** [10] [41]
– The lamb lies down on Broadway / Fly on a windshield / Broadway melody of 1974 / Cuckoo cocoon / In the cage / The grand parade of lifeless packaging / Back in N.Y.C. / Hairless heart / Counting out time / Carpet crawlers / The chamber of 32 doors / / Lilywhite Lilith / The waiting room / Anyway / Here comes the supernatural anaesthetist / The lamia / Silent sorrow in empty boats / The colony of Slippermen (The arrival – A visit to the doktor – Raven) / Ravine / The light dies down on Broadway / Riding the scree / it. *(re-iss.Sep83 on 'Virgin') (d-cd-iss.Feb86) (cd re-iss.Aug94 on 'Virgin')*
Nov 74. (7") **COUNTING OUT TIME. / RIDING THE SCREE** [ ] [-]
1974. (7") **THE LAMB LIES DOWN ON BROADWAY. / COUNTING OUT TIME** [-] [ ]
Apr 75. (7") **CARPET CRAWLERS. / THE WAITING ROOM (evil jam)** [ ] [-]

—— Now just a quartet when PETER GABRIEL left to go solo.

Feb 76. (lp)(c) **A TRICK OF THE TAIL** [3] [31]
– Dance on a volcano / Entangled / Squonk / Mad mad Moon / Robbery, assault and battery / Ripples / A trick of the tail / Los endos. *(re-iss.+cd.Sep83 on 'Virgin') (cd re-iss.Oct94)*
Mar 76. (7") **A TRICK OF THE TAIL. / RIPPLES** [ ] [-]
Mar 76. (7") **RIPPLES. / ENTANGLED** [-] [ ]
Jan 77. (lp)(c) **WIND AND WUTHERING** [7] [26]
– Eleventh Earl of Mar / One for the vine / Your own special way / Wot gorilla? / All in a mouse's night / Blood on the rooftops / Unquiet slumbers for the sleepers . . .In that quiet Earth / Afterglow. *(re-iss.Sep83 on 'Virgin') (re-iss.Apr90) (cd-iss.Apr86) (cd re-iss.Oct94)*
Feb 77. (7") **YOUR OWN SPECIAL WAY. / IT'S YOURSELF** [43] [-]
Feb 77. (7") **YOUR OWN SPECIAL WAY. / . . .IN THAT QUIET EARTH** [-] [62]
May 77. (7"ep) **SPOT THE PIGEON** [14] [ ]
– Match of the day / Inside and out / Pigeons. *(cd-ep iss.1988 on 'Virgin')*

—— added **BILL BRUFORD** – drums (ex-YES, ex-KING CRIMSON) **CHESTER THOMPSON** – drums (ex-FRANK ZAPPA) they were both used on live album below, with CHESTER augmenting on tours.

Oct 77. (d-lp)(d-c) **SECONDS OUT (live)** [4] [47]
– Sqounk / Carpet crawlers / Robbery, assault and battery / Afterglow / Firth of fifth / I know what I like (in your wardrobe) / The lamb lies down on Broadway / The musical box / Supper's ready / The cinema show / Dance on a volcano / Los endos. *(re-iss.Sep83 on 'Virgin', d-cd.iss.Nov85) (cd re-iss.Oct94)*

—— (Jun77) Now a trio of **COLLINS, BANKS & RUTHERFORD** when STEVE HACKETT continued solo career.

Charisma | Atlantic

Mar 78. (7") **FOLLOW YOU FOLLOW ME. / BALLAD OF BIG** [7] [-]
Mar 78. (7") **FOLLOW YOU FOLLOW ME. / INSIDE AND OUT** [-] [23]
Apr 78. (lp)(c) **. . .AND THEN THERE WERE THREE** [3] [14]
– Down and out / Undertow / Ballad of big / Snowbound / Burning rope / Deep in the motherlode / Many too many / Scene from a night's dream / Say it's alright Joe / The lady lies / Follow you follow me. *(re-iss.Sep83 on 'Virgin') (cd-iss.mid'83) (c+cd.re-iss.Aug91) (cd re-iss.Oct94)*
Jun 78. (7") **MANY TOO MANY. / THE DAY THE LIGHT WENT OUT IN VANCOUVER** [43] [ ]
Jul 78. (7") **SCENE FROM A NIGHT'S DREAM. / DEEP IN THE MOTHERLODE** [-] [ ]
Mar 80. (7") **TURN IT ON AGAIN. / BEHIND THE LINES (part 2)** [8] [-]
Mar 80. (lp)(c) **DUKE** [1] [11]
– Behind the lines / Duchess / Guide vocal / Man of our time / Misunderstanding / Heathaze / Turn it on again / Alone tonight / Cul-de-sac / Please don't ask / Duke's end / Duke's travels. *(re-iss.Sep83 on 'Virgin') (cd-iss.Apr85) (c+cd-re-iss.Mar91) (cd re-iss.Oct94)*
May 80. (7") **DUCHESS. / OPEN DOOR** [46] [ ]
May 80. (7") **MISUNDERSTANDING. / BEHIND THE LINES** [-] [14]
Sep 80. (7") **TURN IT ON AGAIN. / EVIDENCE OF AUTUMN** [-] [58]
Sep 80. (7") **MISUNDERSTANDING. / EVIDENCE OF AUTUMN** [42] [-]
Aug 81. (7") **ABACAB. / ANOTHER RECORD** [9] [-]
Sep 81. (lp)(c) **ABACAB** [1] [7]
– Abacab / No reply at all / Me and Sarah Jane / Kep it dark / Dodo / Lurker / Who dunnit? / Man on the corner / Like it or not / Another record. *(cd-iss.Sep83 & Apr85) (c+cd.re-iss.Mar91) (cd re-iss.Oct94)*
Oct 81. (7") **KEEP IT DARK. / NAMINANU** [33] [-]
(12"+=) – Abacab (long version).

Oct 81. (7") **NO REPLY AT ALL. / HEAVEN LOVE MY LIFE** [-] [29]
Jan 82. (7") **ABACAB. / WHO DUNNIT?** [-] [26]
May 82. (7") **PAPERLATE. / YOU MIGHT RECALL** [-] [32]
Mar 82. (7") **MAN IN THE CORNER. / SUBMARINE** [41] [40]
May 82. (7"ep)**3" X 3"** [10] [-]
– Paperlate / You might recall / Me and Virgil.
Jun 82. (d-lp)(c) **THREE SIDES LIVE (live except ***)** [2] [10]
– Turn it on again / Dodo / Abacab / Behind the lines / Duchess / Me and Sarah Jane / Follow you follow me / Misunderstanding / In the cage / Afterglow / One for the vine * / Fountain of Salmacis * / Watcher of the skies * / It * / Paperlate *** / You might recall *** / Me and Virgil *** / Evidence of Autumn *** / Open door *** / You might recall II ***. *(cd-iss.Apr85 & 1988) (US-cd.repl.* w/ The cinema show + The colony of Slippermen) (cd re-iss.Oct94)*

Virgin Atco
Aug 83. (7")(12") **MAMA. / IT'S GONNA GET BETTER** [4] [73]
(cd-ep.iss.Jun88 with extended versions)
Oct 83. (lp)(c)(cd) **GENESIS** [1] [9]
– Mama / That's all / Home by the sea / Second home by the sea / Illegal alien / Taking it all too hard / Just a job to do / Silver rainbow / It's gonna get better. *(re-iss.Jul87)*
Nov 83. (7") **THAT'S ALL. / TAKING IT ALL TOO HARD** [16] [-]
(12"+=) – Firth of fifth (live).
Nov 83. (7") **THAT'S ALL. / SECOND HOME BY THE SEA** [-] [6]
Feb 84. (7")(7"sha-pic-d) **ILLEGAL ALIEN. / TURN IT ON AGAIN (live)** [46] [44]
(12"+=) – ('A'extended).
Jun 84. (7") **TAKING IT ALL TOO HARD. / SILVER RAINBOW** [-] [50]
May 86. (7")(7"clear) **INVISIBLE TOUCH. / THE LAST DOMINO** [15] [1]
(12"+=) – ('A'extended).
Jun 86. (lp)(c)(cd) **INVISIBLE TOUCH** [1] [3]
– Invisible touch / Tonight, tonight, tonight / Land of confusion / In too deep / Anything she does / Domino:- In the glow of the night – The last domino / Throwing it all away / The Brazilian. *(pic-lp+cd.Dec88)*
Aug 86. (7")(12") **IN TOO DEEP. / DO THE NEUROTIC** [19] [-]
Aug 86. (7") **THROWING IT ALL AWAY. / DO THE NEUROTIC** [-] [4]
Nov 86. (7") **LAND OF CONFUSION. / FEED FIRE WITH THE FIRE** [16] [4] Oct 86
(12"+=)/ /(cd-s++=) – Do the neurotic. / / ('A'extended).
Mar 87. (7")(12") **TONIGHT, TONIGHT, TONIGHT. / IN THE GLOW OF THE NIGHT** [ ] [3] Feb 87
(12"+=)(cd-s+=) – Paperlate / ('A'remix).
Apr 87. (7") **IN TOO DEEP. / I'D RATHER BE WITH YOU** [-] [3]
Jun 87. (7") **THROWING IT ALL AWAY. / I'D RATHER BE WITH YOU** [ ] [-]
(12"+=)(c-s+=) – Invisible touch (live).
Oct 91. (7")(c-s) **NO SON OF MINE. / LIVING FOREVER** [6] [13]
(12"+=)(c-s+=)(cd-s+=) – Invisible touch (live).
Nov 91. (cd)(c)(d-lp) **WE CAN'T DANCE** [1] [4]
– No son of mine / Jesus he knows me / Driving the last spike / I can't dance / Never a time / Dreaming while you sleep / Tell me why / Living forever / Hold on my heart / Way of the world / Since I lost you / Fading lights.
Jan 92. (7")(c-s) **I CAN'T DANCE. / ON THE SHORELINE** [7] [7]
(cd-s+=) – In too deep (live) / That's all (live).
(cd-s+=) – ('A'sex mix).
Apr 92. (7")(c-s) **HOLD ON MY HEART. / WAY OF THE WORLD** [16] [12]
(cd-s+=)/ /(cd-s+=) – Your own special way./ / Home by the sea.
Jul 92. (7")(c-s) **JESUS HE KNOWS ME. / HEARTS OF FIRE** [20] [23]
(cd-s+=)/ /(cd-s+=) – I can't dance (mix)./ / Land of confusion.
Nov 92. (cd)(c)(d-lp) **THE WAY WE WALK VOLUME 1: THE SHORTS (live)** [3] [35]
– Land of confusion / No son of mine / Jesus he knows me / Throwing it all away / I can't dance / Mama / Hold on my heart / That's all / In too deep / Tonight, tonight, tonight / Invisible touch.
Nov 92. (7")(c-s) **INVISIBLE TOUCH (live). / ABACAB** [7] [-]
(cd-s+=) – The Brazilian.
Nov 92. (c-s) **NEVER A TIME. / ?** [-] [21]
Jan 93. (cd)(c)(lp) **LIVE / THE WAY WE WALK VOLUME 2: THE LONGS (live)** [1] [ ]
– Old medley: Dance on a volcano – Lamb lies down on Broadway – The musical box – Firth of fifth – I know what I like . . . / Driving the fast spike / Domino: part I – In the glow of the night, part II – The last domino / Home by the sea – Second home by the sea / Drum duet.
Feb 93. (7")(c-s) **TELL ME WHY. / DREAMING WHILE YOU SLEEP** [40] [ ]
(cd-s+=) – Tonight, tonight, tonight.

– compilations etc. –

May 74. Charisma; (d-lp-box) **TRESPASS / NURSERY CRYME** [ ] [-]
May 74. Charisma; (d-lp-box) **FOXTROT / SELLING ENGLAND..** [ ] [-]
Mar 83. Charisma; (d-c) **FOXTROT / TRESPASS** [ ] [-]
May 76. Decca; (lp)(c) **ROCK ROOTS** (debut +early 45's) [ ] [-]
1976. Buddah; (d-lp) **THE BEST – GENESIS** (early) [-] [ ]
Mar 87. London; (cd) **AND THE WORLD WAS** (early) [ ] [-]
Oct 87. Razor; (lp)(c)(cd) **THE SOUR TURNS TO SWEET** [ ] [-]
(re-iss.Jul91)
Jun 88. Old Gold; (7") **FOLLOW YOU FOLLOW ME. / A TRICK OF THE TAIL** [ ] [-]
Jun 88. Old Gold; (7") **I KNOW WHAT I LIKE (IN YOUR WARDROBE). / COUNTING OUT TIME** [ ] [-]
Nov 90. Virgin; (pic-cd-box) **GENESIS CD COLLECTORS EDITION** [ ] [ ]
– (TRESPASS / NURSERY CRYME / FOXTROT)

—— **PHIL COLLINS** with **BRAND X** (alongside **ROBIN LUMLEY** – keyboards / **JOHN GOODSALL** – bass / **PERCY JONES** – bass / **MORRIS PERT** – percussion / **etc.)** albums **UNORTHODOX BEHAVOIR** (Jun76) / **MOROCCAN ROLL** (Apr77 hit UK No.37) / **LIVESTOCK** (Nov77) / **MASQUES** (1978) / **PRODUCT** (Sep79) / **DO THEY HURT?** (May80) / **IS THERE ANYTHING ABOUT** (Sep82, without Phil) **.** (all re-iss.on cd)

—— Compilation cd Dec92 **'THE PLOT THINS – A HISTORY OF BRAND X'** on 'Virgin'.

PHIL COLLINS

Virgin Atlantic
Jan 81. (7") **IN THE AIR TONIGHT. / THE ROOF IS LEAKING** [2] [19] May 81
Feb 81. (lp)(c) **FACE VALUE** [1] [7]
– In the air tonight / This must be love / Behind the lines / The roof is leaking / Droned / Hand in hand / I missed again / You know what I mean / I'm not moving / If leaving me is easy / Tomorrow never knows / Thunder and lightning. *(cd-iss.Jun88)*
Mar 81. (7")(12") **I MISSED AGAIN. / I'M NOT MOVING** [14] [19]
May 81. (7") **IF LEAVING ME IS EASY. / DRAWING BOARD** [17] [ ]
Oct 82. (7")(7"pic-d) **THRU THESE WALLS. / DO YOU KNOW, DO YOU CARE** [56] [ ]
Nov 82. (lp)(c) **HELLO I MUST BE GOING!** [2] [8]
– I don't care anymore / I cannot believe it's true / Like China / Do you know, do you care? / You can't hurry love / It don't matter to me / Thru these walls / Don't let him steal your love away / The west side / Why can't it wait 'til morning. *(cd-iss.Jun88) (re-iss.Jun91 hit UK No.48)*
Nov 82. (7")(7"pic-d) **YOU CAN'T HURRY LOVE. / I CANNOT BELIEVE IT'S TRUE** [1] [-]
(12"+=) – Oddball.
Nov 82. (7") **YOU CAN'T HURRY LOVE. / DO YOU KNOW, DO YOU CARE** [-] [10]
Mar 83. (7") **DON'T LET HIM STEAL YOUR HEART AWAY. / THUNDER AND LIGHTNING** [45] [ ]
(12") – ('A'side) / And so to F.
Feb 83. (7") **I DON'T CARE ANYMORE. / THE WEST SIDE** [-] [39]
May 83. (7") **WHY CAN'T IT WAIT 'TIL MORNING. / LIKE CHINA** [ ] [-]
May 83. (7") **I CANNOT BELIEVE IT'S TRUE. / THRU THESE WALLS** [-] [79]
Feb 84. (7") **AGAINST ALL ODDS. / (b-side by Larry Carlton)** [-] [1]
Mar 84. (7")(7"pic-d) **AGAINST ALL ODDS (TAKE A LOOK AT ME NOW). / MAKING A BIG MISTAKE ('B' side by MIKE RUTHERFORD)** [2] [-]
(above from the film of the same name)
1984. (7") **WALK THROUGH THE FIRE. / MAKING A BIG MISTAKE** [-] [ ]
Jan 85. (7") **SUSSUDIO. / THE MAN WITH THE HORN** [12] [1] Apr 85
(12"+=)(12"sha-pic-d+=) – ('A'extended).
Feb 85. (lp)(c)(cd) **NO JACKET REQUIRED** [1] [1]
– Sussudio / Only you know and I know / Long long way to go / Don't want to know / One more night / Don't lose my number / Who said I would / Doesn't anybody stay together anymore? / Inside out / Take me home. (cd+=) – We said hello, goodbye.
Feb 85. (7") **ONE MORE NIGHT. / THE MAN WITH THE HORN** [-] [1]

Mar85 saw him duet with **PHIL BAILEY (ex-EARTH, WIND & FIRE)** on single **EASY LOVER** which hit UK No.1 & US No.2 (Nov84)

Apr 85. (7")(12")(7"pic-d) **ONE MORE NIGHT. / I LIKE THE WAY** [4] [-]
Apr 85. (7") **SUSSIDIO. / I LIKE THE WAY** [-] [1]
Jul 85. (7") **TAKE ME HOME. / WE SAID HELLO, GOODBYE** [19] [-]
(12"+=) – ('A'extended).
(d7"+=) – Against all odds / Making a big mistake.
Jul 85. (7") **DON'T LOSE MY NUMBER. / WE SAID HELLO GOODBYE** [-] [4]
Oct 85. (7") **SEPARATE LIVES ("PHIL COLLINS & MARILYN MARTIN"). / I DON'T WANNA KNOW** [-] [1]
Nov 85. (7")(12")(7"white)(7"-2-interlocking pic-discs) **SEPARATE LIVES. (by "PHIL COLLINS & MARILYN MARTIN") / ONLY YOU KNOW AND I KNOW** [4] [-]
Mar 86. (7") **TAKE ME HOME. / ONLY YOU AND I KNOW** [-] [7]
Aug 88. (7")(12") **A GROOVY KIND OF LOVE. / BIG NOISE** [1] [1]
(cd-s+=) – Will you still be waiting.

—— (above & below singles were from the film 'BUSTER', in which he starred and contributed some tracks to soundtrack released Sep88)

Nov 88. (7") **TWO HEARTS. / THE ROBBERY (excerpt)** [6] [1]
(12"+=)(cd-s+=) – ('B'extended).

Nov 89. (7")(12") **ANOTHER DAY IN PARADISE. / HEAT ON THE STREET** [2] [1]
(c-s+=)(cd-s+=) – Saturday night and Sunday morning.

Nov 89. (lp)(c)(cd) **. . . BUT SERIOUSLY** [1] [1]
– Hang in long enough / That's just the way it is / Do you remember? / Something happened on the way to Heaven / Colours / I wish it would rain down / Another day in Paradise / Heat on the street / All of my life / Saturday night and Sunday morning / Father to son / Find a way to my heart.

Jan 90. (7") **I WISH IT WOULD RAIN DOWN. / HOMELESS (ANOTHER DAY IN PARADISE) (demo)** [7] [-]
(12"+=)(cd-s+=) – You've been in love (that little bit too long). (US; b-side)

Jan 90. (7") **I WISH IT WOULD RAIN DOWN. / YOU'VE BEEN IN LOVE** [-] [3]

Apr 90. (7") **DO YOU REMEMBER. / I WISH IT WOULD RAIN DOWN** [-] [4]

Apr 90. (7")(c-s) **SOMETHING HAPPENED ON THE WAY TO HEAVEN. / I WISH IT WOULD RAIN DOWN (live)** [15] [-]
(12"+=)(cd-s+=) – ('A'remix).

Jul 90. (7")(c-s) **THAT'S JUST THE WAY IT IS. / BROADWAY CHORUS (SOMETHING HAPPENED ON THE WAY TO HEAVEN)** [26] [ ]
(12"+=)(cd-s+=) – In the air tonight (extended).

Aug 90. (7") **SOMETHING HAPPENED ON THE WAY TO HEAVEN. / LIONEL** [-] [4]

Sep 90. (7")(c-s) **HANG IN LONG ENOUGH. / AROUND THE WORLD IN 80 PRESETS** [34] [-]
(cd-s+=) – ('A'dub) / That's how I feel.
(cd-s+=) – ('A'-12"mix).
(12") – ('A'side) / ('A'dub) / ('A'-12"mix).

Nov 90. (c-s) **HANG IN LONG ENOUGH. / SEPARATE LIVES** [-] [23]

— live with **LELAND SKLAR** – bass / **CHESTER THOMPSON** – drums / **DARYL STUERMER** – guitar / **BRAD COLE** – keyboards / **BRIDGETTE BRYANT, ARNOLD McCULLER and FRED WHITE** – backing vocals. plus **DON MYRICK** – alto sax / **LUI LUI** – trombone / **RAHMLEE MICHAEL DAVIS** – trumpet / **HARRY KIM** – trumpet.

Nov 90. (cd)(c)(lp) **SERIOUS HITS LIVE! (live)** [2] [11]
– Something happened on the way to Heaven / Against all odds (take a look at me now) / Who said I would / One more night / Don't lose my number / Another day in Paradise / Do you remember / Separate lives / In the air tonight / You can't hurry love / Two hearts / Sussidio / Groovy kind of love / Easy lover / Take me home.

Nov 90. (7")(c-s) **DO YOU REMEMBER (live). / AGAINST THE ODDS (live)** [57] [-]
(12"+=) – Doesn't anyone stay together anymore (live).
(cd-s++=) – The roof is leaking.

Feb 91. (c-s) **WHO SAID I WOULD (live). / ?** [-] [73]

In May 93, PAUL was credited on DAVID CROSBY'S Top 50 hit 'Hero'.

Oct 93. (7")(c-s) **BOTH SIDES OF THE STORY. / ALWAYS** [7] [25]
(cd-s+=) Both sides of the demo.
(cd-s++=) Rad Dudeski.

Nov 93. (cd)(c)(lp) **BOTH SIDES** [1] [13]
– Both sides of the story / Can't turn back the years / Everyday / I've forgotten everything / We're sons of our fathers / Can't find my way / Survivors / We fly so close / There's a place for us / We wait and wonder / Please come out tonight

Jan 94. (7")(c-s) **EVERYDAY. / DON'T CALL ME ASHLEY** [15] [24]
(cd-s+=) – ('A'demo).
(cd-s+=) – Doesn't anybody stay together anymore (live).

Apr 94. (7")(c-s) **WE WAIT AND WE WONDER. / HERO** [45] [ ]
(cd-s+=) – For a friend.
(cd-s) – ('A'side) / Take me with you / Stevie's blues – There's a place for us (instrumental).

– his compilations, others, etc. –

Jan 88. Virgin; (cd)(US-lp)(US-cd) **12 INCHERS** [ ] [ ]
– (12" remixed extended versions of 6 hits)

Jun 88. Vigin; (7") **IN THE AIR TONIGHT ('88 remix). / I MISSED AGAIN** [4] [ ]
(12"+=)(cd-s+=) – ('A'extended).

TONY BANKS

Charisma Charisma

Oct 79. (7") **FOR A WHILE. / FROM THE UNDERTOW** [ ] [ ]

Oct 79. (lp)(c) **A CURIOUS FEELING** [21] [ ]
– From the undertow / Lucky me / The lie / After the lie / A curious feeling / Forever morning / You / Somebody else's dream / The waters of Lethe / For a while / In the dark. *(re-iss.Oct86) (cd-iss.1988)*

Jul 80. (7") **FOR A WHILE. / A CURIOUS FEELING** [ ] [ ]

Apr 83. (7")(12") **THIS IS LOVE. / CHARM** [ ] [ ]

— May83, he released single and film soundtrack THE WICKED LADY on 'Atlantic'

Jun 83. (lp)(c) **THE FUGUTIVE** [50] [ ]
– This is love / Man of spells / And the wheels keep turning / Say you'll never leave me / Thirty three's / By you / At the edge of night / Charm / Moving under.

Aug 83. (7") **AND THE WHEELS KEEP TURNING. / K.2.** [ ] [ ]
(12"+=) – Sometime never.

Sep 85. (7"ep) **'TONY BANKS' (with JIM DIAMOND and TOYAH)** [ ] [ ]
– Red wing (instrumental) / You call this victory / Line of symmetry.

Oct 86. (7") **SHORT CUT TO NOWHERE. (by "FISH & TONY BANKS") / SMILIN JACK CASEY** [ ] [ ]
(12"+=) – K.2.

Jul 87. (cd) **SOUNDTRACKS ('Quicksilver' // 'Lorca And The Outlaws')** [ ] [ ]
– Short cut to nowhere / Smilin' Jack Casey / Quicksilver suite: Rebirth – Gypsy – Final chase // You call this victory / Lion of symmetry / Redwing suite: Redwing – Lorca – Kid and Detective Droid – Lift off – Death of Abby. *(lp/c.Nov89)*

BANKSTATEMENT

TONY BANKS with friends, etc.

Virgin Atlantic

Jul 89. (7") **THROWBACK. / THURSDAY THE 12th** [ ] [ ]
(12"+=) – This is love.

Aug 89. (lp)(c)(cd) **BANKSTATEMENT** [ ] [ ]
– Throwback / I'll be waiting / Queen of darkness / That night / Raincloud / he border / Big man / A house needs a roof / The more I hide it. *(cd+=)* – Diamonds aren't so bad / Thursday the 12th.

Oct 89. (7") **I'LL BE WAITING. / DIAMONDS AREN'T SO BAD** [ ] [ ]
(12"+=)(cd-s+=) – And the wheels keep turning.

TONY BANKS

solo, with guest vocals **ANDY TAYLOR, FISH, JAYNEY KLIMEK**

May 91. (7")(c-s) **I WANNA CHANGE THE SCORE. / HERO FOR AN HOUR** [ ] [ ]
(12"+=) – Big man (BANKSTATEMENT).
(cd-s++=) – The waters of Lethe.

Jun 91. (cd)(c)(lp) **STILL** [ ] [ ]
– Red day on blue street / Angel face / The gift / Still it takes me by surprise / Hero for an hour / I wanna change the score / Water out of wine / Another murder of a day / Back to back / The final curtain.

MIKE RUTHERFORD

Charisma Passport

Jan 80. (7") **WORKING IN LINE. / COMPRESSION** [ ] [-]

Feb 80. (lp)(c) **SMALLCREEP'S DAY** [13] [ ]
– Smallcreep's day: Between the tick and the tock – Working in line – After hours – Cats and rats in the neighbourhood – Smallcreep alone – Out into the daylight – At the end of the day / Moonshine / Time and time again / Romani / Every road / Overnight job. *(re-iss.Oct86) (cd-iss.Jun89)*

Mar 80. (7") **WORKING IN LINE. / MOONSHINE** [-] [ ]

Jul 80. (7") **TIME AND TIME AGAIN. / AT THE END OF THE DAY** [ ] [-]

W.E.A. Atlantic

Aug 82. (7") **HALFWAY THERE. / A DAY TO REMEMBER** [ ] [ ] Nov 82

Aug 82. (7") **A DAY TO REMEMBER. / MAXINE** [-] [ ]

Sep 82. (lp)(c) **ACTING VERY STRANGE** [23] [ ]
– Acting very strange / A day to remember / Maxine / Halfway there / Who's fooling who / Couldn't get arrested / I don't wanna know / Hideaway.

Oct 82. (7")(12") **ACTING VERY STRANGE. / COULDN'T GET ARRESTED** [ ] [-]

Jan 83. (7") **HIDEAWAY. / CALYPSO** [ ] [-]

MIKE + THE MECHANICS

RUTHERFORD with **PAUL CARRACK** – vocals, keyboards (ex-ACE, ex-SQUEEZE, ex-Solo artist) / **PAUL YOUNG** – vocals (ex-SAD CAFE) / **PETER VAN HOOKE** – drums / **ADRIAN LEE** – keys

WEA Atlantic

Oct 85. (lp)(c) **MIKE + THE MECHANICS** [78] [26]
– Silent running (on dangerous ground) / All I need is a miracle / Par Avion / Hanging by a thread / I get the feeling / Take the reins / You are the one / A call to arms / Taken in. *(cd-iss.Jul86)*

Nov 85. (7") **SILENT RUNNING (ON DANGEROUS GROUND). / PAR AVION** [-] [6]

Feb 86. (7") **SILENT RUNNING (ON DANGEROUS GROUND). / I GET THE FEELING** [21] [-]
(12"+=) – Too far gone.

May 86. (7")(12") **ALL I NEED IS A MIRACLE. / YOU ARE THE ONE** [53] [5] Mar 86
(12"+=) – A call to arms.

Jun 86. (7") **TAKEN IN. / A CALL TO ARMS** [-] [32]

— added **TIM RENWICK** – guitar (ex-SUTHERLAND BROTHERS & QUIV-

ER, etc.)

Nov 88. (7")(12") **NOBODY'S PERFECT. / NOBODY KNOWS** [ ] [63]
(cd-s+=) – All I need is a miracle.

Nov 88. (lp)(c)(cd) **THE LIVING YEARS** [2] [13]
– Nobody's perfect / The living years / Seeing is believing / Nobody knows / Poor boy down / Blame / Don't / Black and blue / Beautiful day / Why me?.

Feb 89. (7") **THE LIVING YEARS. / TOO MANY FRIENDS** [2] [1] Jan 89
(12"+=)(cd-s+=) – I get the feeling (live).

Apr 89. (7") **NOBODY KNOWS. / WHY ME?** [ ] [ ]
(12"+=)(cd-s+=)(c-s+=) – The living years / ('A'edit).

Apr 89. (c-s) **SEEING IS BELIEVING. /** [-] [62]

Mar 91. (7")(12")(c-s)(cd-s) **WORD OF MOUTH. / LET'S PRETEND IT DIDN'T HAPPEN** [13] [78]
(cd-s+=) – Taken in (live).

Apr 91. (cd)(c)(lp) **WORD OF MOUTH** [11] [ ]
– Get up / Word of mouth / A time and place / Yesterday, today, tomorrow / The way you look at me / Everybody gets a second chance / Stop baby / My crime of passion / Let's pretend it didn't happen / Before (the next heartache falls).

May 91. (7")(c-s) **A TIME AND A PLACE. / GET UP** [58] [ ]
(12"+=)(cd-s+=) – I think I've got the message.
(cd-s) – ('A'side) (++=) – My crime of passion (acoustic).

Sep 91. (7")(c-s) **STOP BABY. / GET UP** [ ] [ ]
(cd-s+=) – Before the heartache falls.

Feb 92. (7")(c-s) **EVERYBODY GETS A SECOND CHANCE. / THE WAY YOU LOOK AT ME** [56] [ ]
(cd-s+=) – At the end of the day (MIKE RUTHERFORD).

— now without RENWICK, who was repl. by guests **B.A. ROBERTSON / GARY WALLIS / WIX + CLEM CLEMPSON**

Feb 95. (7")(c-s) **OVER MY SHOULDER. / SOMETHING TO BELIEVE IN** [12] [ ]
(cd-s+=) – Always the last to know.
(cd-s+=) – Word of mouth / ('A'version).

Mar 95. (cd)(c) **BEGGAR ON A BEACH OF GOLD** [9] [ ]
– Beggar on a beach of gold / Another cup of coffee / You've really got a hold on me / Mea culpa / Over my shoulder / Someone always hates someone / The ghost of sex and you / Web of lies / Plain & simple / Something to believe in / A house of many rooms / I believe (when I fall in love it will be forever) / Going going . . .home.

Jun 95. (c-s)(cd-s) **BEGGAR ON A BEACH OF GOLD / HELP ME / NOBODY TOLD ME** [33] [ ]
(cd-s) – ('A'side) / Boys at the front / Little boy / ('A'acoustic).

Aug 95. (c-s) **ANOTHER CUP OF COFFEE / YOU NEVER CHANGE** [65] [ ]
(cd-s+=) – You don't know what love is.
(cd-s) – ('A'side) / Everyday hurts / How long.

. . . Jan – Jun '96 stop press . . .

Feb 96. (single) **ALL I NEED IS A MIRACLE '96 (remix)** [27] [ ]
Mar 96. (cd)(c) **HITS** (compilation) [3] [ ]

GENIUS / GZA (see under ⇒ WU-TANG CLAN)

Lowell GEORGE (see under ⇒ LITTLE FEAT)

G-FORCE (see under ⇒ MOORE, Gary)

GILBERT & LEWIS (see under ⇒ WIRE)

GILES, GILES & FRIPP (see under ⇒ KING CRIMSON)

GILLAN (see under ⇒ DEEP PURPLE)

David GILMOUR (see under ⇒ PINK FLOYD)

GIN BLOSSOMS

Formed: Tempe, Arizona, USA . . . early 90's by (see below). In 1992, they signed to 'A&M', who issued debut 'NEW MISERABLE EXPERIENCE'. Although slow to get off the mark, it soon shot into Stateside Top 30, helped by 2 memorable major hit singles in 1993; 'HEY JEALOUSY' and 'FOUND OUT ABOUT YOU'. However tragedy struck when 32 year-old DOUG HOPKINS committed suicide on 5 Dec'93. • **Style:** Country-orientated rock outfit similar to of course The BYRDS or The EAGLES. • **Songwriters:** Mostly HOPKINS or VALENZUELA / WILSON; except CHRISTINE SIXTEEN (Kiss). • **Trivia:** Produced by JOHN HAMPTON (ex-Replacements).

Recommended: NEW MISERABLE EXPERIENCE (*5)

ROBIN WILSON – vocals, acoustic guitar / **JESSE VALENZUELA** – guitar, vocals / **DOUG HOPKINS** – guitars / **BILL LEEN** – bass / **PHILLIP RHODES** – drums, percussion

A&M A&M

Nov 92. (cd)(c) **NEW MISERABLE EXPERIENCE** [ ] [30]
– Lost horizons / Hey jealousy / Mrs. Rita / Until I fall away / Hold me down / Cajun song / Hands are tied / Found out about you / Allison Road / 29 / Pieces of the night / Cheatin'. *(re-iss.Sep93 on 'Fontana', hit UK No.53 early '94) (re-iss.May94)*

Fontana A&M

Aug 93. (c-ep)(cd-ep) **HEY JEALOUSY / KELI RICHARDS / COLD RIVER DICK / KRISTINE IRENE** [ ] [25] Jul93

Oct 93. (12"colrd)(c-s)(cd-s) **MRS.RITA. / SOUL DEEP / HEART AWAY** [ ] [ ]

Jan 94. (7"ep)(c-ep) **HEY JEALOUSY / COLD RIVER DICK. / KRISTINE IRENE / KELI RICHARDS** [24] [-]
(cd-ep) – ('A'side) / Cajun song / Just south of nowhere / Angels tonight.
(9"ep) – ('A' side) / Keli Richards / Cajun song.

— **SCOTT JOHNSON** – guitars repl. HOPKINS who killed himself 5 Dec'93

Apr 94. (7")(c-s) **FOUND OUT ABOUT YOU. / HEY JEALOUSY (live)** [40] [25] Nov93
(cd-s+=) – Hands are tied (live) / 29 (live) / Fulsome Prison (live).
(cd-s+=) – Hold me down (live) / Mrs.Rita (live).

. . . Jan – Jun '96 stop press . . .

Jan 96. (single) **TIL I HEAR IT FROM YOU / FOLLOW YOU DOWN** [-] [9]
Jan 96. (single) **TIL I HEAR IT FROM YOU** [39] [-]
Feb 96. (cd)(c) **CONGRATULATIONS I'M SORRY** [42] [10]
Apr 96. (single) **FOLLOW YOU DOWN** [ ] [-]

GLOVE (see under ⇒ SIOUXSIE AND THE BANSHEES)

Roger GLOVER (see under ⇒ DEEP PURPLE)

GO-BETWEENS

Formed: Brisbane, Australia . . . 1978 by FORSTER and McLENNAN. After two local Australian singles, they moved to Britain in 1980 to record one 45 for Scottish label 'Postcard'. Soon settled in London, after signing to top indie label 'Rough Trade'. They had already in 1982 released debut lp 'SEND ME A LULLABY', which was followed a year later by 'BEFORE HOLLYWOOD'. The rest of the 80's, was spent adding new members, and trying to penetrate unwielding charts. • **Style:** Described early on as an antipodean TALKING HEADS, although their inspiration stemmed from BOB DYLAN or The VELVET UNDERGROUND. Their well-balanced romantic sound, was always nicely blended with heavy subject material. • **Songwriters:** All compositions by FORSTER and McLENNAN, with LINDY MORRISON contributing some. McLENNAN covered BALLAD OF EASY RIDER (Byrds). • **Trivia:** In 1991, FORSTER and McLENNAN did support slot to LLOYD COLE on a Toronto gig, which prompted GO-BETWEENS reformation rumours.

Recommended: THE GO-BETWEENS 1979-1990 (*9) / WATERSHED (*7; E. W. McLENNAN).

GRANT McLENNAN (b.12 Feb'58) – vocals, lead guitar, bass / **ROB FORSTER** (b.29 Jun'57) – guitar, vocals / **DENNIS CANTWELL** – drums

Abel not issued

Oct 78. (7") **LEE REMICK. / KAREN** [-] [-] Aussie

— added **TIM MUSTAFA** – drums + **MALCOLM KELLY** – organ to repl. CANTWELL

Oct 79. (7") **PEOPLE SAY. / DON'T LET HIM COME BACK** [-] [-]
(above 2 first released UK as 12"ep Nov86 on 'Situation 2')

— **LINDY MORRISON** (b. 2 Nov'51) – drums (ex-ZERO) repl. TIM + MALCOLM

Postcard not issued

Nov 80. (7") **I NEED TWO HEADS. / STOP BEFORE YOU SAY IT** [ ] [-]

Missing L. not issued

Jul 81. (7") **YOUR TURN, MY TURN. / WORLD WEARY** [-] [-] Aussie

Rough Trade not issued

Jun 82. (lp) **SEND ME A LULLABY** [ ] [-]
– Your turn, my turn / One thing can hold us / Eight pictures / People know / The girls have moved / Midnight to neon / Ride / Caress / All about strength / Hold your horses / It could be anyone / Arrow in a bow. *(released Australia Nov81 on 'Missing Link')*

Jul 82. (7") **BY CHANCE. / HAMMER THE HAMMER** [ ] [-]

— added **ROBERT VICKERS** (b.25 Nov'59) – bass

Feb 83. (7") **CATTLE AND CANE. / HEAVEN SAYS** [ ] [-]
Sep 83. (lp)(c) **BEFORE HOLLYWOOD** [ ] [-]
– A bad debt follows you / Two steps step out / Before Hollywood / Dusty in here /

Ask / Cattle and cane / By chance / As long as that / On my block / That way.
Oct 83. (7") **MAN O' SAND TO GIRL O' SEA. / THIS GIRL BLACK GIRL** [ ] [-]

Sire Sire

Jul 84. (7") **PART COMPANY. / JUST A KING IN MIRRORS** [ ] [-]
(12"+=) – Newton told me.
Sep 84. (lp)(c) **SPRING HILL FAIR** [ ] [-]
– Bachelor kisses / Five words / The old way out / You've never lived / Part company / Slow slow music / Draining the pool for you / River of money / Unkind and unwise / Man o' sand girl o' sea.
Sep 84. (7") **BACHELOR KISSES. / RARE BREED** [ ] [-]
(12"+=) – Unkind and unwise (instrumental).

Beggar's B Beggar's B

Feb 86. (7") **SPRING RAIN. / LIFE AT HAND** [ ] [-]
(12"+=) – Little Joe.
Mar 86. (lp)(c)(cd) **LIBERTY BELLE AND THE BLACK DIAMOND EXPRESS** [ ] [ ]
– Spring rain / The ghost and the black hat / The wrong road / To reach me / Twin layers of lightning / In the core of the flame / Head full of steam / Palm Sunday (on board the S.S.Within) / Apology accepted. *(re-iss.+cd.Feb89)*
May 86. (7") **HEAD FULL OF STEAM. / DON'T LET HIM COME BACK** [ ] [-]
(12"+=) – The wrong road.

— added **AMANDA BROWN** (b.17 Nov'65) – keyboards, violin, guitar, oboe

Feb 87. (7") **RIGHT HERE. / WHEN PEOPLE ARE DEAD** [ ] [-]
(12"+=) – Don't call me gone.
(d7"++=) – A little romance (live).
May 87. (7") **CUT IT OUT. / TIME IN DESERT** [ ] [-]
(12"+=) – Doo wop in 'A'.
Jun 87. (lp)(c)(cd) **TALLULAH** [91] [ ]
– Right here / You tell me / Someone else's wife / I just get caught out / Cut it out / The house that Jack Kerouac built / Bye bye pride / Spirit of a vampyre / The Clarke sisters / Hope then strife. *(re-iss.+cd.Feb90)*
Aug 87. (7") **BYE BYE PRIDE. / THE HOUSE THAT JACK KEROUAC BUILT** [ ] [-]

— **JOHN WILSTEED** (b.13 Feb'57) – bass repl. VICKERS

Beggar's B Capitol

Jul 88. (7") **STREETS OF YOUR TOWN. / WAIT UNTIL JUNE** [ ] [ ]
(12"+=) – Casanova's last words.
(cd-s++=) – Spring rain / Right here.
Aug 88. (lp)(c)(cd) **16 LOVERS LANE** [81] [ ]
– Love goes on / Quiet heart / Love is a sign / You can't say no forever / The Devil's eye / Streets of your town / Clouds / Was there anything I could do? / I'm alright / Dive for your memory.
Oct 88. (7") **WAS THERE ANYTHING I COULD DO. / ROCK'N'ROLL FRIEND** [ ] [-]
(12"+=) – Mexican postcard.
(cd-s++=) – Bye bye pride.

— Split 31 Dec'89. FORSTER and McLENNAN went solo. The latter also being part of JACK FROST with STEVE KILBEY of The CHURCH. AMANDA formed CLEOPATRA WONG.

– compilations, others, etc. –

Mar 90. Beggar's Banquet; (cd)(c)(d-lp) **THE GO-BETWEENS 1979-1990** [ ] [ ]
– Hammer the hammer / I need two heads / Cattle and cane / When people are dead / Man o' sand to girl o' sea / Bachelor kisses / People say / Draining the pool for you / World weary / Spring rain / Rock and roll friend / Dusty in here / The Clarke sisters / Right here / Second-hand furniture / Bye bye pride / This girl, black girl / The house that Jack Kerouac built / Don't call me gone / Streets of our own town / Love is a sign / You won't find it again. *(c+=)(d-lp+=)* – Karen / 8 pictures / The sound of rain / The wrong road / Mexican postcard.
Oct 89. Strange Fruit; (12"ep)(cd-ep) **THE PEEL SESSIONS** [ ] [-]
– The power that I have now / Second hand furniture / Fire woods / Rare breed.
Feb 85. Missing Link Australia; (lp) **VERY QUICK ON THE EYE BRISBANE 1981 (demo)** [-] [-]
1985. Pacific-Jem; (lp)(c) **METAL AND SHELLS** [-] [ ]

TUFF MONKS

(original GO-BETWEENS + BIRTHDAY PARTY members)
Oct 83. Au Go-Go Australia; (7") **AFTER THE FIREWORKS. / AFTER, AFTER THE FIREWORKS** [-] [-]

ROBERT FORSTER

(solo, with MICK HARVEY – producer)

Beggar's B. Beggar's B.

Sep 90. (7") **BABY STONES. / ?** [ ] [-]
(12"+=)(cd-s+=) – ?
Oct 90. (cd)(c)(lp) **DANGER IN THE PAST** [ ] [ ]
– Baby stones / The river people / Leave here satisfied / Heart out to tender / Is this what you call change / Dear black dream / Danger in the past / I've been looking for somebody / Justice.
Apr 93. (cd)(c) **CALLING FROM A COUNTRY PHONE** [ ] [ ]
– Atlanta lie low / 121 / The circle / Falling star / I want to be quiet / Cats life / Girl to a world / Drop / Beyond theit law / Forever & time. *(re-iss.cd Sep95)*

— with **JOHN KEANE** – guitars, banjos, keyboards, bass, etc / **JOEL MORRIS** – drums / **STEVE VENZ** – bass / **ANDY CARLSON** – guitars, mandolin / **TIM WHITE & BILL HOLMES** – porga & piano / **DWIGHT MANNING** – oboe / **SYD STRAW** – backing vocals

Jul 94. (cd-ep) **25-41 / 3 a.m. / FREDDIE FENDER / DANGER IN THE PAST (live)** [ ] [ ]
Aug 94. (cd)(c) **I HAD A NEW YORK GIRLFRIEND** [ ] [ ]
– Nature's way / Broken hearted people / Echo beach / Tell me that it isn't true / 2541 / Anytime / Locked away / Look out loves comes tomorrow / Alone / Bird / Frisco depot / 3 a.m. *(re-iss.cd Sep95)*

— FORSTER covered; NATURE'S WAY (Spirit) / BROKEN HEARTED PEOPLE (. . .Clarke) / ECHO BEACH (Martha & The Muffins) / TELL ME THAT IT ISN'T TRUE (Bob Dylan) / 2541 (Bob Mould) / ANYTIME (. . .Nelson) / LOCKED AWAY (Richards-Jordan) / LOOK OUT HERE COMES TOMORROW (Neil Diamond) / ALONE (Kelly-Steinberg) / BIRD (. . .Hansoms) / FRISCO DEPOT (. . .Newbury) / 3 A.M. (Anderson-Todd).

G.W. McLENNAN

Beggar's B. Beggar's B.

Mar 91. (12"ep)(cd-ep) **WHEN WORD GET AROUND / BLACK MULE / SHE'S SO STRANGE / THE MAN WHO DIED IN RAPTURE** [ ] [ ]
May 91. (7") **EASY COME EASY GO. / MAKING IT RIGHT FOR HER** [ ] [-]
(12"+=)(cd-s+=) – Stones for you.
Jun 91. (cd)(c)(lp) **WATERSHED** [ ] [ ]
– When word get around / Haven't I been a fool / Haunted house / Stones for you / Easy come easy go / Black mule / Rory the weeks back on / You can't have everything / Sally's revolution / Broadway bride / Just get that straight / Dream about tomorrow.
Jan 93. (cd-ep) **FINGERS / WHOSE SIDE ARE YOU ON / WHAT WENT WRONG** [ ] [ ]
Feb 93. (cd-ep) **LIGHTING FIRES / DARK SIDE OF TOWN / IF I SHOULD FALL BEHIND** [ ] [ ]
Mar 93. (cd)(c) **FIREBOY** [ ] [ ]
– Lighting fires / Surround me / One million miles from here / The dark side of town / Things will change / The pawnbroker / Whose side are you on? / Fingers / Signs of life / The day my eyes Came back / Bathe (in the water) / When I close my eyes / Riddle in the rain. *(re-iss.cd Sep95)*
Aug 94. (cd-ep) **DON'T YOU CRY / COMING UP FOR AIR / GIRL IN A BERET / PUT YOU DOWN / NO PEACE IN THE PALACE / THAT'S THAT** [ ] [ ]
Nov 94. (d-cd)(c) **HORSEBREAKER STAR** [ ] [ ]
– Simone & Perry / Ice in Heaven / What went wrong / Race day rag / Don't you cry for me no more / Put you down / Late afternoon in early August / Coming up for air / Ballad of Easy Rider / Open invitation / Open my eyes / From my lips / / Dropping you / Hot water / Keep my word / Do your own thing / That's that / If I was a girl / Head over heels / Girl in a beret / All her songs / No peace in the palace / I'll call you wild / Horsebreaker star. *(re-iss.d-cd Sep95)*
Jun 95. (cd-ep) **SIMONE & PERRY / DON'T YOU CRY FOR ME NO MORE / BALLAD OF EASY RIDER / WHAT WENT WRONG (original)** [ ] [ ]

GOLDIE

Born: 1966, Manchester, England. Lived in Miami in the late 80's, where he built up skills of graffiti artistry. Soon after he moved back to Britain to collaborate with Mancunian (A GUY CALLED) GERALD (famous for his 'Voodoo Ray' 45). They collaborated on single 'ENERGY'. / 'THE RENO'. After a few singles with his METALHEADZ outfit, GOLDIE made impact in 1995 when his 'TIMELESS' album hit UK Top 10 (a favourite of the NME). • **Style:** A hybrid of ambient jazz jungle beats and inner-city symphonies of bassy dub sounds. Obtained the GOLDIE motif, due to his gold designer molars. • **Songwriters:** Himself. Collaborated in 1994/5 with MEL GAYNOR (of-SIMPLE MINDS).

Recommended: TIMELESS (*9)

GOLDIE (b.1967) – vocals (with METALHEADZ)

Reinforced not issued

1992. (12"ep) **KILLERMUFFIN EP** [ ] [-]
1993. (12"ep)(c-ep)(cd-ep) **TERMINATOR (original) / KEMISTRY / KNOWLEDGE / SINISTER** [ ] [-]
1993. (12"ep) ENFORCERS / [ ] [-]

ffrr London

Nov 94. (12")(c-s)(cd-s) **INNER CITY LIFE / ('A'mixes)** 49
(12") – ('A'mixes; Roni Size / Nookie remix).
(above as GOLDIE PRESENTS METALHEADS)
Mar 95. (c-s)(cd-s) **TIMELESS / INNER CITY LIFE**
Jul 95. (d-cd)(d-c)(d-lp) **TIMELESS** 7
– Timeless / Saint Angel / State of mind / This is a bad / Sea of tears / Jah the seventh / State of rage (sensual V.I.P. mix) / Still life / Angel / Adrift / Kemistry / You & me. (d-lp+=) (2 other mixes).
Aug 95. (12")(c-s) **ANGEL. / SAINT ANGEL / YOU AND ME (THE BEAUTY – THE BEAST)** 41
(cd-s+=) – Angel (Peshay back from Narm mix).
Nov 95. (c-s) **INNER CITY LIFE / ('A'-Peshay mix)** 39
(cd-s+=) – Kemistry (Doc Scott mix).
(cd-s) – ('A'radio mix) / ('A'extended) / ('A'-4 Hero part 1 mix) / ('A'-Roni Size instrumental).
— now the boyfriend of the Icelandic pixie BJORK.

GOLLIWOGS (see under ⇒ CREEDENCE CLEARWATER REVIVAL)

Martin L. GORE (see under ⇒ DEPECHE MODE)

GRADUATE (see under ⇒ TEARS FOR FEARS)

GRAND FUNK RAILROAD

Formed: Michigan, USA ... 1964 as TERRY KNIGHT & THE PACK, who quickly scored US Top 50 hit 'I (WHO HAVE NOTHING)'. KNIGHT became manager in 1969, after FARNER and BREWER became GRAND FUNK RAILROAD. They signed to 'Capitol', after appearing at Atlanta Pop Festival in mid'69, and hit immediately with Top 30 lp 'ON TIME', which featured hit 45 'TIME MACHINE'. In Mar'72 after several more hits, they fired KNIGHT and brought in new manager John Eastman (brother-in-law of PAUL McCARTNEY). They continued to be big attraction until they split in 1976. • **Style:** Loud heavy-metal outfit, who broke BEATLES' box-office records in 1971 after selling out New York's Shea Stadium. • **Songwriters:** Group compositions except: THE LOCOMOTION (Little Eva) / WE'VE GOTTA GET OUT OF THIS PLACE (Animals) / GIMME SHELTER (Rolling Stones) / etc. • **Trivia:** TODD RUNDGREN produced their 1973 album 'WE'RE AN AMERICAN BAND'.

Recommended: THE COLLECTION (*6).

TERRY KNIGHT & THE PACK

TERRY KNIGHT (b. RICHARD KNAPP) – vocals / **MARK FARNER** (b. 29 Sep'48) – vocals, bass (guitar from 1969) / **DONALD BREWER** (b. 3 Sep'48) – drums (ex-JAZZ MASTERS)

not iss. A & M

1965. (7") **YOU LIE. / THE KIDS WILL BE THE SAME** -

Cameo Parkway Lucky 11

1966. (7") **I'VE BEEN TOLD. / HOW MUCH MORE** -
1966. (7") **YOU'RE A BETTER MAN THAN I. / I GOT LOVE** -
1966. (7") **LOVIN' KIND. / LADY JANE** -
1966. (7") **WHAT'S ON YOUR MIND. / A CHANGE ON THE WAY** -
Nov 66. (lp) **TERRY KNIGHT & THE PACK** -
-Numbers / What's on your mind / Where do you go / You're a better man than I / Lovin' kind / The shut-in / Got love / A change on the way / Lady Jane / Sleep talkin' / I've been told / I (who have nothing).
Jan 67. (7") **I (WHO HAVE NOTHING). / NUMBERS** 46
Apr 67. (7") **THIS PRECIOUS TIME. / LOVE, LOVE, LOVE, LOVE, LOVE** -
Jul 67. (7") **ONE MONKEY DON'T STOP NO SHOW. /** -

MARK FARNER & DON BREWER

not issued Lucky 11

1968. (7") **WE GOTTA HAVE LOVE. / DOES IT MATTER TO YOU GIRL** -

GRAND FUNK RAILROAD

KNIGHT became their manager. Added **MEL SCHACHER** (b. 3 Apr'51) – bass (ex-? AND THE MYSTERIANS)

Capitol Capitol

Sep 69. (7") **TIME MACHINE. / HIGH ON A HORSE** - 48
Sep 69. (lp) **ON TIME** 27
– Are you ready / Anybody's answer / Time machine / High on a horse / T.N.U.C. / Into the sun / Heartbreaker / Call yourself a man / Can't be too long / Ups and down.
Nov 69. (7") **MR. LIMOUSINE DRIVER. / HIGH FALOOTIN' WOMAN** - 97
Jan 70. (lp)(c) **GRAND FUNK** 11
– Got this thing on the move / Please don't worry / High falootin' woman / Mr. Limousine driver / In need / Winter and my soul / Paranoid / Inside looking out.
Mar 70. (7") **HEARTBREAKER. / PLEASE DON'T WORRY** 72 Jan 70
Jun 70. (7") **NOTHING IS THE SAME. / SIN'S A GOOD MAN'S BROTHER** -
Jul 70. (lp)(c) **CLOSER TO HOME** 6
– Sin's a good man's brother / Aimless lady / Nothing is the same / Mean mistreater / Get it together / I don't have to sing the blues / Hooked on love / I'm your captain.
Oct 70. (7") **CLOSER TO HOME. / AIMLESS LADY** 22 Aug 70
Dec 70. (7") **MEAN MISTREATER. / MARK SAYS ALRIGHT** - 47
Jan 71. (d-lp)(c) **LIVE ALBUM (live)** 5 Nov 70
– (introduction) / Are you ready / Paranoid / In need / Heartbreaker / Inside looking out / Words of wisdom / Meam mistreater / Mark says alright / T.N.U.C. / Into the sun.
Jan 71. (7") **INSIDE LOOKING OUT. / PARANOID** 40
Apr 71. (7") **FEELIN' ALRIGHT. / I WANT FREEDOM** 54
Apr 71. (lp)(c) **SURVIVAL** 6
– Country road / All you've got is money / Comfort me / Feelin' alright / I want freedom / I can feel him in the morning / Gimme shelter.
Jul 71. (7") **GIMME SHELTER. / I CAN FEEL HIM IN THE MORNING** - 61
Jul 71. (7"m) **I CAN FEEL HIM IN THE MORNING. / ARE YOU READY / MEAN MISTREATER** -
Sep 71. (7") **GIMME SHELTER. / COUNTRY ROAD** Aug 71
Dec 71. (7") **PEOPLE, LET'S STOP THE WAR. / SAVE THE LAND**
Jan 72. (lp)(c) **E PLURIBUS FUNK** 5 Nov 71
– Footstompin' music / People, let's stop the war / Upsetter / I come tumblin' / Save the land / No lies / Loneliness.
Mar 72. (7") **FOOTSTOMPIN' MUSIC. / I COME TUMBLIN'** 29 Jan 72
May 72. (7") **UPSETTER. / NO LIES** 73 Apr 72
Nov 72. (7") **ROCK'N'ROLL SOUL. / FLIGHT OF THE PHOENIX** 29 Sep 72
Jan 73. (lp)(c) **PHOENIX** 7 Oct 72
– Flight of the Phoenix / Trying to get away / Someone / She got to move me / Rain keeps fallin' / I just gotta know / So you won't have to die / Freedom is for children / Gotta find me a better day / Rock & roll soul.

GRAND FUNK

Aug 73. (7")(7"US-pic-d) **WE'RE AN AMERICAN BAND. / CREEPIN'** 1 Jul 73
Aug 73. (lp)(c) **WE'RE AN AMERICAN BAND** 2
– We're an American band / Stop / Lookin' back / Creepin' / Black lycurice / The railroad / Ain't got nobody / Walk like a man / Loneliest rider.
Nov 73. (7") **WALK LIKE A MAN. / RAILROAD** 19
added **CRAIG FROST – keyboards**
May 74. (7") **THE LOCOMOTION. / DESTITUTE & LOSIN'** 1 Mar 74
Jun 74. (lp)(c) **SHININ' ON** 5 Mar 74
– Shinin' on / To get back in / The locomotion / Carry me through / Please me / Mr.Pretty boy / Gettin' over you / Little Johnny Hooker.
Jul 74. (7") **SHININ' ON. / MR.PRETTY BOY** 11
— reverted back to trio.
Dec 74. (lp)(c) **ALL THE GIRLS IN THE WORLD BEWARE!!!** 10
– Responsibility / Runnin' life / Look at granny run run / Memories / All the girls in the world beware / Wild / Good and evil / Bad time / Some kind of wonderful.
Feb 75. (7") **SOME KIND OF WONDERFUL. / WILD** 3 Dec74
Mar 75. (7") **BAD TIME. / GOOD AND EVIL** 4

GRAND FUNK RAILROAD

Dec 75. (d-lp)(c) **CAUGHT IN THE ACT (live)** 21 Sep75
– Footstompin' music / Rock'n'roll soul / Closer to home / Some kind of wonderful / Heartbreaker / Shinin' on / The locomotion / Black licorice / The railroad / We're an American band / T.N.U.C. / Inside looking out / Gimme shelter.
Dec 75. (7") **TAKE ME. / GENEVIEVE** - 53
Mar 76. (7") **SALLY. / LOVE IS DYIN'** - 69
Apr 76. (lp)(c) **BORN TO DIE** 47 Jan 76
– Born to die / Duss / Sally / I fell for your love / Talk to the people / Take me / Genevieve / Love is dying / Politician / Good things.

EMI Inter. M.C.A.

Aug 76. (7") **CAN YOU DO IT. / 1976** 45
Aug 76. (lp)(c) **GOOD SINGIN' GOOD PLAYIN'** 52
– Just couldn't wait / Can you do it / Pass it around / Don't let 'em take your gun / Miss my baby / Big buns / Out to get you / Crossfire / 1976 / Release your love / Goin' for the pastor.
Jan 77. (7") **PASS IT AROUND. / DON'T LET 'EM TAKE YOUR GUN** -
Jan 77. (7") **JUST COULDN'T WAIT. / OUT TO GET YOU** -

— Disbanded when the rest formed FLINT.

MARK FARNER BAND

went solo. **FARNER** was joined by **DENNIS BELLINGER** – bass / **ANDY NEWMARK** – drums

Atlantic Atlantic

Nov 77. (7") **YOU AND ME BABY. / SECOND CHANCE TO DANCE** [-]
Jan 78. (lp)(c) **MARK FARNER**
– Dear Miss Lucy / Street fight / Easy breezes / Social disaster / He let me love / You and me baby / Second chance to dance / Lorraine / Lady luck / Ban the man.
Nov 78. (7") **WHEN A MAN LOVES A WOMAN. / IF IT TOOK ALL DAY** [-]
Jan 79. (lp)(c) **NO FRILLS** [-]
Feb 79. (7") **JUST ONE LOOK. / CRYSTAL EYES** [-]

GRAND FUNK

re-formed with **FARNER, BREWER & DENNIS BELLINGER** – bass, vocals.(FROST had joined BOB SEGER.)

Full Moon Full Moon

Nov 81. (7") **Y-O-U. / TESTIFY** [-]
Jan 82. (lp)(c) **GRAND FUNK LIVES** Oct 81
– Good times / Queen bee / Testify / Can't be with you tonight / No reason why / We gotta get out of this place / Y.O.U. / Stuck in the middle / Greed of man / Wait for me.
Feb 82. (7") **STUCK IN THE MIDDLE. / NO REASON WHY** [-]
Jan 83. (lp)(c) **WHAT'S FUNK?**
– Rock'n'roll American style / Nowhere to run / Innocent / Still waitin' / Borderline / El Salvador / It's a man's world / I'm so true / Don't lie to me / Life in Outer Space.

— Disbanded again after appearing on 'Heavy Metal' soundtrack. BREWER joined BOB SEGER'S SILVER BULLET BAND. FARNER went solo again in 1988 releasing album 'JUST ANOTHER INJUSTICE' for 'Frontline'.

– compilations, others, etc. –

May 72. Capitol; (d-lp)(c) **MARK, DON & MEL 1969-1971** [17]
Oct 72. Capitol; (lp)(c) **MARK, DON AND TERRY 1966-67** [-]
Nov 76. Capitol; (lp)(c) **GRAND FUNK HITS** [-]
Apr 91. Capitol; (cd)(lp) **CAPITOL COLLECTORS**
– Time machine / Heartbreaker / Inside looking out / Medley / Closer to home / I'm your captain / Mean mistreater / Feelin' alright / Gimme shelter / Footstompin' music / Rock & roll soul / We're an American band / Walk like a man / The Loco-motion / Shinin' on / Some kind of wonderful / Bad time.
Sep 91. Rhino; (cd) **MORE OF THE BEST**
Jun 92. Castle; (cd)(c) **THE COLLECTION** [-]
– The locomotion / Gimme shelter / Inside looking out / Closer to home / I'm your captain / We're an American band / Into the Sun / Loneliness / Paranoid / Walk like a man / Shinin' on / Creepin' / Sally.

GRANT LEE BUFFALO

Formed: North Hollywood, California, USA ... 1992 by namesake GRANT LEE PHILLIPS. Released their debut 'FUZZY' the next year to deserved critical acclaim, although it was 1994's that broke them into commercial success. • **Style:** Hard-edged country rock, with a similarity to The WATERBOYS. • **Songwriters:** PHILLIPS penned except covers BURNING LOVE (hit; Elvis Presley). • **Trivia:** Their debut was a favourite of MICHAEL STIPE (R.E.M.).

Recommended: FUZZY (*8) / MIGHTY JOE MOON (*7)

GRANT LEE PHILLIPS – vocals, guitars / **PAUL KIMBLE** – bass, piano, vocals, producer / **JOEY PETERS** – drums, percussion

Slash-London Slash

Jun 93. (cd)(c)(lp) **FUZZY** [74]
– The shining hour / Jupiter and teardrop / Fuzzy / Wish you well / The hook / Soft wolf tread / Stars n' stripes / Dixie drug store / America snoring / Grace / You just have to be crazy.
Aug 93. (7")(c-s)(cd-s) **AMERICA SNORING. / WISH YOU WELL**
(12"+=)(cd-s+=) – The hook / Burning love.
Sep 93. (7")(c-s) **FUZZY. / STARS & STRIPES**
(12"+=)(cd-s+=) – Dixie drugstore (ju ju mix) / I will take him.
Nov 93. (12"ep)(cd-ep) **BUFFALONDON EP**
– Jupiter and teardrop / Wish you well / Soft wolf tread / The shining hour.
Sep 94. (cd)(c)(lp) **MIGHTY JOE MOON** [24]
– Lone star song / Mockingbirds / It's the life / Sing along / Mighty Joe Moon / Demon called Deception / Lady Godiva and me / Drag / Last days of Tecumseh / Happiness / Honey don't think / Side by side / Rock of ages.
Oct 94. (cd-ep) **MOCKINGBIRDS / ORPHEUS. / GOODNIGHT JOHN DEE**
(12"ep+=) – (first 3 tracks) / Let go of my hand.
(cd-ep) – (first track) / Let go of my hand / We're coming down.

... Jan – Jun '96 stop press ...

May 96. (single) **HOMESPUN**
Jun 96. (cd)(c)(lp) **COPPEROPOLIS** [34]

GRATEFUL DEAD

Formed: San Francisco, California, USA ... 1965 by JERRY GARCIA, who had spent 9 months of 1959 in the army, before finding ROBERT HUNTER and forming The THUNDER MOUNTAIN TUB THUMPERS. JERRY went onto make demos in 1963 as duo JERRY & SARAH GARCIA. As The WARLOCKS in 1965 (GARCIA, WEIR, PIGPEN, LESH and KREUTZMANN), became friends with 'One Flew Over The Cuckoo's Nest' author KEN KESEY, who introduced them to L.S.D. in his commune. By the end of '65, they had become GRATEFUL DEAD and toured California alongside JEFFERSON AIRPLANE. In 1966, they issued one-off 45 'DON'T EASE ME IN' for 'Fantasy' off-shoot label 'Scorpio', which led to 'Warners' giving them break early '67. Their eponymous debut soon broke the US Top 75, although they had to wait another 3 years for breakthrough into US Top 30 with 'WORKINGMAN'S DEAD'. In 1992, they were still survivors loved by most Americans and some other countries, even Britain. Sadly, JERRY GARCIA died on the 9th August 1995 of a heart attack after his arteries clogged up. • **Style:** Psychedelic hippie band who did concerts averaging 3 hours, and who verged on experimental harmonising country-tinged rock. • **Songwriters:** Most by HUNTER-GARCIA or WEIR, LESH and some by others, including JOHN BARLOW. Covered; GOOD MORNING LITTLE SCHOOLGIRL (Don & Bob) / NEW MINGLEWOOD BLUES + SAMSON AND DELILAH (trad.) / JOHNNY B.GOODE (Chuck Berry) / NOT FADE AWAY (Buddy Holly) / ME AND BOBBY McGEE (Kris Kristofferson) / BIG BOSS MAN (Bo Diddley) / DANCING IN THE STREET (Martha & The Vandellas) / STAGGER LEE (Lloyd Price) / LITTLE RED ROOSTER (Willie Dixon) / DEAR MR.FANTASY (Traffic) / WALKIN' BLUES (Robert Johnson) / NEXT TIME YOU SEE ME (Junior Parker) / etc. • **Trivia:** An edited 'DARK STAR', was used as theme in the US 70's series of 'Twilight Zone'.

Recommended: LIVE DEAD (*6) / WORKINGMAN'S DEAD (*6) WHAT A LONG STRANGE TRIP IT'S BEEN (*8).

JERRY GARCIA (b. JEROME JOHN GARCIA, 1 Aug'42) – vocals, lead guitar / **BOB WEIR** (b. ROBERT HALL, 6 Oct'47) – rhythm guitar / **RON 'PIGPEN' McKERNAN** (b. 8 Sep'45) – keyboards, vocals, mouth harp / **PHIL LESH** (b. PHILIP CHAPMAN, 15 Mar'40, Berkeley, Calif.,USA) – bass / **BILL KREUTZMANN** (b. 7 Apr'46, Palo Alto, Calif.) – drums (DAN MORGAN left before recording)

not issued Scorpio

Jun 66. (7") **DON'T EASE ME IN. / STEALIN'** [-]

Warners Warners

Feb 67. (7") **THE GOLDEN ROAD (TO UNLIMITED DEVOTION). / CREAM PUFF WAR** [-]
Dec 67. (lp) **THE GRATEFUL DEAD** [73] Feb 67
– The golden road (to unlimited devotion) / Cold rain and snow / Good morning little schoolgirl / Beat it on down / Sitting on top of the world / Cream puff war / Morning dew / New, new Minglewood blues / Viola Lee blues. *(re-iss.Mar87 on 'Edsel') (cd-iss.Jul88 on 'Atlantic') (cd-iss.Feb93) (re-iss.cd Oct95)*

— added **TOM CONSTANTEN** – keyboards / **MICKEY HART** – percussion and returning lyricist **ROBERT HUNTER**

Oct 68. (7") **BORN CROSS-EYED. / DARK STAR**
Nov 68. (lp) **ANTHEM OF THE SUN** [87] Aug 68
– That's it for other one:- Cryptical envelopment – Quadlibet for tender feet – The faster we go, the rounder we get – We leave the castle / New potato caboose / Born cross-eyed / Alligator / Caution (do not stop on the tracks). *(re-iss.Jul71) (c+cd-iss.1989 on 'WEA')*
Oct 69. (lp) **AOXOMOXOA** [73] Jun 69
– St. Stephen / Dupree's diamond blues / Rosemary / Doin' the rag / Mountains of the Moon / China cat sunflower / What's become of the baby / Cosmic Charlie. *(re-iss.Jul71 & Jan77) (c+cd-iss.1989 on 'WEA')*
Oct 69. (7") **DUPREE'S DIAMOND BLUES. / COSMIC CHARLIE** [-]
Feb 70. (d-lp) **LIVE / DEAD (live in the studio)** [64] Dec 69
– Dark star / Death don't have no mercy / Feedback / And we bid you goodnight / St. Stephen / The eleven / Turn on your love light. *(re-iss.Jul71)*

— **DAVID NELSON** – accoustic guitar repl. CONSTANTEN / added guest **JOHN DAWSON** – guitar, vocals (on some)

— above pairing also formed off-shoot band The NEW RIDERS OF THE PURPLE SAGE, who initially toured as support to DEAD, with GARCIA in their ranks.

DARK STAR
JERRY GARCIA

Sep 70. (lp) **WORKINGMAN'S DEAD** [ ] [27] Jun 70
– Uncle John's band / High time / Dire wolf / New speedway boogie / Cumberland blues / Black Peter / Easy wind / Casey Jones. *(re-iss.Jul71) (re-iss.+cd.1989)*

Aug 70. (7") **UNCLE JOHN'S BAND. / NEW SPEEDWAY BOOGIE** [ ] [69]

— added guest **DAVID TORBERT** – bass (1)

Dec 70. (lp)(c) **AMERICAN BEAUTY** [ ] [30]
– Box of rain / Friend of the Devil / Sugar magnolia / Operator / Candyman / Ripple / Brokedown palace / Till the morning comes / Attics of my life / Truckin'. *(re-iss.Jul71 & Jan77) (c+cd-iss.1989 on 'WEA')*

Jan 71. (7") **TRUCKIN'. / RIPPLE** [-] [64]

— Now **GARCIA, WEIR, LESH, KREUTZMANN** and **'PIGPEN'** with new members **MERL SAUNDERS** – keyboards (repl. PIGPEN for a while when he was ill) all guests had departed, incl. HART and NELSON.

Oct 71. (d-lp) **GRATEFUL DEAD** (SKULL-FUCK & ROSES) (live) [ ] [25]
– Bertha / Mama tried / Big railroad blues / Playing in the band / The other one / Me & my uncle / Big boss man / Me & Bobby McGhee / Johnny B. Goode / Wharf rat / Not fade away / Goin' down road feeling bad. *(cd-iss.1988)*

Jan 72. (7") **JOHNNY B. GOODE. / SO FINE (by 'Elvin Bishop')** [-] [ ]

Apr 72. (7") **ONE MORE SATURDAY NIGHT. (by "GRATEFUL DEAD with BOBBY ACE" (aka BOB WEIR) / CASSIDY** (U.S.) / **BERTHA** (U.K.) [ ] [ ]

— added on tour **KEITH GODCHAUX** (b.14 Jul'48) – keyboards (ex-DAVE MASON band) and **DONNA GODCHAUX** – vocals (They both repl. SAUNDERS)

Dec 72. (t-lp) **EUROPE '72 (live)** [ ] [24] Nov 72
– Cumberland blues / He's gone / One more Saturday night / Jack Straw / You win again / China cat sunflower / I know you rider / Brown-eyed woman / Hurts me too / Ramble on Rose / Sugar magnolia / Mr. Charlie / Tennessee Jed / Truckin' / (epilog) / (prelude) / (Walk me out in the) Morning dew. *(cd-iss.Oct95)*

Dec 72. (7") **SUGAR MAGNOLIA (live). / MR. CHARLIE (live)** [-] [91]

— Now just basic 4 of **GARCIA, WEIR, LESH, KREUTZMANN** and both **GODCHAUX'S.** ('PIGPEN' sadly died 8 May'73 after a long and threatening bout of illness) note that ROBERT HUNTER was still writing their lyrics, next 2 albums also included ten or more session people.

Warners Grateful D

Jul 73. (lp)(c) **WAKE OF THE FLOOD** [ ] [18] Oct 73
– Mississippi half-step uptown toodeloo / Let me sing your blues away / Row Jimmy / Stella blue / Here comes sunshine / Eyes of the world / Weather Report suite (part 1; Prelude – part 2; Let it grow). *(re-iss.Apr89) (cd-iss.Feb90)*

Nov 73. (7") **LET ME SING YOUR BLUES AWAY. / HERE COMES SUNSHINE** [ ] [ ]

Jan 74. (7") **EYES OF THE WORLD. / WEATHER REPORT SUITE (part 1; PRELUDE)** [-] [ ]

Jul 74. (lp)(c) **FROM THE MARS HOTEL** [47] [16]
– Scarlet begonias / Ship of fools / Pride of Cucamonga / Loose Lucy / U.S. blues / Unbroken chain / China doll / Money money. *(re-iss.+cd.Mar89)*

Aug 74. (7") **U.S. BLUES. / LOOSE LUCY** [-] [ ]

— added the returning **MICKEY HART** – percussion

United Art Grateful D

Oct 75. (lp)(c) **BLUES FOR ALLAH** [45] [12] Sep 75
– Help on the way / Slipknot / Franklin's tower / King Solomon's marbles / Stronger than dirt or milkin' the turkey / The music never stopped / Crazy fingers / Sage & spirit / Blues for Allah / Sand castles & glass camels / Unusual occurances in the desert. *(re-iss.+cd.Mar89) (cd-iss.Feb90)*

Oct 75. (7") **THE MUSIC NEVER STOPPED. / HELP IS ON THE WAY** [-] [81]

Jun 76. (d-lp)(c) **STEAL YOUR FACE (live)** [42] [56]
– The promised land / Cold rain and snow / Around and around / Stella blue / Mississippi half-step uptown toodeloo / Ship of fools / Beat it down the line / Big river / Black-throated wind / U.S. blues / El Paso / Sugaree / It must have been the roses / Casey Jones. *(re-iss.+cd.Mar89) (cd-iss.Feb90)*

Arista Arista

Aug 77. (lp)(c) **TERRAPIN STATION** [ ] [28]
– Estimated prophet / Samson and Delilah / Passenger / Dancing in the street / Sunrise / Terrapin station. *(re-iss.Jan87) (cd-iss.1988 on 'Ariola')*

Oct 77. (12") **DANCING IN THE STREET. / TERRAPIN STATION** [ ] [ ]

Feb 78. (7") **PASSENGER. / TERRAPIN STATION** [-] [ ]

Dec 78. (lp)(c) **SHAKEDOWN STREET** [ ] [41]
– Good lovin' / France / Shakedown street / Serangetti / Fire on the mountain / I need a miracle / From the heart of me / Stagger Lee / New, new Minglewood blues / If I had the world to give. *(cd-iss.Jun91)*

Dec 78. (7") **GOOD LOVIN'. / STAGGER LEE** [ ] [ ]

Mar 79. (7") **SHAKEDOWN STREET. / FRANCE** [-] [ ]

— **BRENT MYDLAND** (b. 1953) – keyboards repl. both GODCHAUX'S (KEITH was killed in car crash 23 Jul'80)

May 80. (lp)(c) **GO TO HEAVEN** [ ] [23]
– Far from home / Althea / Feel like a stranger / Alabama getaway / Don't ease me in / Easy to love you / Lost sailor / Saint of circumstance.

Jun 80. (7") **ALABAMA GETAWAY. / FAR FROM ME** [-] [68]

Jan 81. (7") **DON'T EASE ME IN. / FAR FROM ME** [-] [ ]

Apr 81. (d-lp)(d-c) **RECKONING (live)** (all line-ups) [ ] [43]
– Dire wolf / The race is on / Oh babe it ain't no lie / It must have been the roses / Dark hollow / China doll / Been all around the world / Monkey and the engineer / Jack-a-roe / Deep Elam blues / Cassidy / To lay me down / Rosalie McFall / On the road again / Bird song / Ripple.

Sep 81. (d-lp)(d-c) **DEAD SET (live)** [ ] [29]
– Samson and Delilah / Friend of the Devil / New, new Minglewood blues / Deal / Candyman / Little red rooster / Loser / Passenger / Feel like a stranger / Franklin's tower / Fire on the mountain / Rhythm devils / Greatest story ever told / Brokedown palace.

Sep 87. (7")(12")(7"pic-d) **TOUCH OF GREY. / MY BROTHER ESAU** [ ] [9] Jul 87

Oct 87. (lp)(c)(cd) **IN THE DARK** [57] [6] Jul 87
– Touch of grey / Hell in a bucket / When push comes to shove / West L.A. fadeaway / Tons of steel / Throwing stones / Black muddy river.

Nov 87. (7") **THROWING STONES. / ('A'version)** [-] [ ]

— Late '87, they recorded live album 'DYLAN AND THE DEAD' with BOB DYLAN, which was released early 1989, and hit US No.37.

Nov 89. (lp)(c)(cd) **BUILT TO LAST** [ ] [27]
– Foolish heart / Just a little light / Built to last / Blow away / Standing on the Moon / Victim or the crime / We can run / Picasso moon / I will take you home.

Nov 89. (7") **FOOLISH HEART. / WE CAN RUN** [-] [ ]

Oct 90. (d-cd)(d-c)(t-lp) **WITHOUT A NET (live)** [ ] [43]
– Feel like a stranger / Mississippi half-step uptown toodeloo / Walkin' blues / Althea / Cassidy / Let it grow / China cat sunflower – I know you rider / Looks like rain / Eyes of the world / Victim or the crime / Help on the way – Slipknot! – Franklin's tower / Bird song / One more Saturday night / Dear Mr. Fantasy.

— BRETT MYDLAND died 26 Jul'90 of a drug overdose. Replaced by **VINCE WELNICK** – keyboards (ex-TUBES, ex-TODD RUNDGREN)

– compilations etc. –

Below releases on 'Polydor' issued on 'Sunflower' US.

Nov 70. Polydor; (lp) **VINTAGE DEAD (live '66)** [ ] [ ] Oct 71

Jul 71. Polydor; (lp) **HISTORIC DEAD (rare '66)** [ ] [ ] Jun 71

Sep 73. Warners/ US= Grateful Dead; (lp) **HISTORY OF THE DEAD – BEAR'S CHOICE (live rarities)** [ ] [60] Jul 73

Mar 74. Warners/ US= Grateful Dead; (lp)(c) **SKELETONS FROM THE CLOSET** [ ] [75]
(re-iss.+cd.Oct86 on 'Thunderbolt')

Feb 77. United Artists/ US= Grateful Dead; (d-lp)(d-c) **WAKE OF THE FLOOD / FROM MARS HOTEL** [ ] [ ]

Feb 78. Warners/ US= Grateful Dead; (d-lp)(d-c) **WHAT A LONG STRANGE TRIP IT'S BEEN: THE BEST OF GRATEFUL DEAD** [ ] [ ] Nov 77
– New, new Minglewood blues / Cosmic Charlie / Truckin' / Black Peter / Born cross-eyed / Ripple / Doin' that rag / Dark star / High time / New speedway boogie / St. Stephen / Jack Straw / Me & my uncle / Tennessee Jed / Cumberland blues / Playing in the band / Brown-eyed woman / Ramble on Rose.

— All below on 'Grateful Dead' records, unless otherwise mentioned.

Jun 91. (d-cd)(d-c)(t-lp) **ONE FROM THE VAULT** (live 13 Aug'75, Great American Music Hall, San Francisco) [ ] [ ] May 91
– (introduction) / Help on the way / Franklin's tower / Music never stopped / It must have been the roses / Eyes of the world – drums / King Solomon's marbles / Around and around / Sugaree / Big river / Crazy fingers – drums / The other one / Sage and spirit / Goin' down the road feeling bad / U.S. blues / Blues for Allah.

Jan 92. (cd) **INFRARED ROSES (live)** [ ] [ ]
– Crowd sculpture / Parallelogram / Little Nemo in Lightland / Riverside rhapsody / Post-modern highrise table top stomp / Infrared roses / Silver apples of the Moon / Speaking in swords / Magnesium night light / Sparrow hawk row / River of nine sorrows / Apollo at the Ritz.

Aug 92. (d-cd) **TWO FROM THE VAULT** (live 23/24 Aug'68, Shrine Auditorium, L.A.) [ ] [ ] May 92
– Good morning little schoolgirl / Dark star / St. Stephen / The eleven / Death don't have no mercy / The other one / New potato caboose / Turn on your lovelight / Morning dew.

Dec 93. Grateful Dead; (d-cd) **DICK'S PICK** [ ] [ ]
– Here comes sunshine / Big river / Mississippi half-step uptown toodeloo / Weather report suite (Prelude – part 1, Let it grow – part 2) / Big railroad blues / Playing in the band / He's gone / Truckin' / Nobody's fault but mine / Jam / The other one / Jam / Stella blue / Around and around.

Jan 94. Dare International; (cd)(c) **RISEN FROM THE VAULTS** [ ] [ ]

Jun 95. Grateful Dead; (cd) **DICK'S PICKS VOLUME 2** [ ] [ ]
– ark star / Jam / Sugar magnolia / St. Stephen / Not fade away / Going down the road feeling bad / Not fade away.

Oct 95. Grateful Dead; (d-cd)(d-c) **HUNDRED YEAR HALL** (live 26th April 1972, Jahrhundert Halle, Frankfurt) [ ] [26]
– Bertha / Me & my uncle / The next time you see me / China cat sunflower / I know you rider / Jack Straw / Big railroad blues / Playing in the band / Turn on your love light / Going down the road feeling bad / One more Saturday night / Truckin' / Cryptical envelopment / Comes a time / Sugar magnolia.

JERRY GARCIA

solo used session men from the DEAD plus others

C.B.S. Douglas

Jul 71. (lp) **HOOTEROLL (by "JERRY GARCIA & HOWARD WALES")**
– South side strut / A trip to what next / Up from the desert / DC-502 / One a.m. approach / Uncle Martin's / Da bird song. *(cd-iss.Oct87 & Jun92 on 'Rykodisc')*
(below also by duo above)

Jan 72. (7") **SOUTH SIDE STRUT. / UNCLE MARTIN'S** -

Warners Warners

Jan 72. (lp)(c) **GARCIA** (aka 'THE WHEEL') 35
– Deal / Bird song / Sugaree / Loser / Late for supper / Spiderdawg / Eep hour / To lay me down / An odd little place / The wheel. *(re-iss.+c+cd.Feb89 on 'Grateful Dead')*

1973. (7") **SUGAREE. / EEP HOUR** -

1973. (7") **THE WHEEL. / DEAL** -

not issued Fantasy

1973. (lp) **LIVE AT THE KEYSTONE (live)** -

Round Round

Jun 74. (lp) **GARCIA (II)** 49
– Let it rock / When the hunter gets captured by the game / That's what love will make us do / Russian lullabye / Turn on the bright lights / He ain't give you none / What goes around / Let's spend the night together / Mississippi moon / Midnight town. *(re-iss.+c+cd.Apr89 as 'COMPLIMENTS OF . . . ')*

Jul 74. (7") **LET IT ROCK. / MIDNIGHT TOWN** -

— OLD & IN THE WAY:- **GARCIA, DAVID GRISMAN, PETER ROWAN, JOHN KAHN, VASSAR CLEMENTS**

Mar 75. (lp) **OLD AND IN THE WAY** -
– Pig in a pen / Midnight moonlight / Old and in the way / Knockin' on your door / The hobo song / Panama red / Wild horses / Kissimmee kid / White dove / Land of the Navajo. *(re-iss. Feb 85 on 'Sugarhill')*

United Art Round

Feb 76. (lp) **REFLECTIONS** 42
– Might as well / Mission in the rain / They love each other / I'll take a melody / It must have been the roses / Tore up over you / Catfish John / Comes a time. *(re-iss.+cd.Feb89 on 'Grateful Dead')*

Arista Arista

Apr 78. (lp)(c) **CAT UNDER THE STARS (as "JERRY GARCIA BAND")**
– Rubin and Cherise / Love in the afternoon / Palm Sunday / Cats under the stars / Rhapsody in red / Rain / Down home / Gomorrah.

Nov 82. (lp)(c) **RUN FOR THE ROSES**
– Run for the roses / I saw her standing there / Without love / Midnight getaway / Leave the little girl alone / Valerie / Knockin' on Heaven's door.

Grateful D Grateful D

Mar 89. (lp)(c)(cd) **ALMOST ACOUSTIC ("JERRY GARCIA ACOUSTIC BAND")**
– Swing low, sweet chariot / Deep Elam blues / Blue yodel £9 (standing on the corner) / Spike driver blues / I've been all around this world / I'm here to get my baby out of jail / I'm troubled / Oh, the wind and the rain / The girl at the Crossroads bar / Oh babe it ain't no lie / Casey Jones / Diamond Joe / Gone home / Ripple.

— with **JOHN KAHN** – bass / **DAVID KEMPER** – drums / **MARVIN SEALS** – keyboards / and backing vocalists **JACKIE LA BRANCH** and **GLORIA JONES**

Sep 91. (cd)(c)(lp) **JERRY GARCIA BAND (live)** 97
– The way you do the things you do / Waiting for a miracle / Simple twist of fate / Get out of my life / My sister and brothers / I shall be released / Dear Prudence / Deal / Stop that train / Senor (tales of Yankee power) / Evangeline / The night they drove old Dixie down / Don't let go / That lucky old Sun / Tangled up in blue.

BOB WEIR

solo, with DEAD session men

Warners Warners

Jun 72. (lp) **ACE**
– The greatest story ever told / Black-throated wind / Walk in the sunshine / Playing in the band / Looks like rain / Mexicali blues / One more Saturday night / Cassidy. *(re-iss.+c+cd.Apr89 on 'Grateful Dead')*

KINGFISH

with **BOB WEIR** and **DAVE TORBERT** plus DEAD and other sessioners

United Art Grateful Dead

Apr 76. (lp) **KINGFISH** 50 Mar 76
– Lazy lightnin' / Supplication / Wild northland / Asia minor / Home to Dixie / Jump for joy / Goodbye yer honor / Big iron / This time / Hypnotize / Bye and bye. *(re-iss.+cd.Nov89 on 'Grateful Dead') (cd-iss.Jun93)*

United Art Jet

Jun'77. (lp) **LIVE 'N' KICKIN'** (live, BOB appears rarely) May 77
– Goodbye yer honor / Juke / Mule skinner blues / I hear you knockin' / Hypnotize / Jump for joy / Overnight bag / Jump back / Shake and fingerpop / Around and around. *(re-iss.Feb79 on 'Jet')*

Nov 77. (7") **GOODBYE YER HONOR. / JUMP FOR JOY / I HEAR YOU KNOCKIN'**

— BOB left KINGFISH before they released another album 'TRIDENT' in '78 on 'Jet' US.

BOB WEIR

continued solo career as well as returning to the DEAD

Arista Arista

1977. (7") **I'LL BE DOGGONE. / SHADE OF GREY** -

Feb 78. (7") **BOMBS AWAY. / EASY TO SLIP** -

Apr 78. (lp)(c) **HEAVEN HELP THE FOOL** 69 Feb 78
– Easy to slip / I'll be doggone / Wrong way / Heaven help the fool / Shade of grey / This time forever / Salt Lake City / Bombs away.

— **"BOBBY & THE MIDNITES"BOB WEIR** – vocals, guitar / **BILLY COBHAM** – drums, vocals / **BOBBY COCHRAN** – guitar / **ALPHONSO JOHNSON** – bass / **BRENT MYLAND** – keyboards / **MATTHEW KELLY** – harmonica

1981. (lp)(c) **BOBBY AND THE MIDNITES** -
– Book of rules / Me without you / Josephine / Fly away / Carry me / Festival.

— **DAVE GARLAND** – keyboards, synths + **KENNY GRADNEY** – bass, vocals repl. JOHNSON, MYLAND + JOHNSON

C.B.S. Columbia

Dec 84. (lp)(c) **WHERE THE BEAT MEETS THE STREET**
– (I want to live in) America / Where the beat meets the street / She's gonna win your heart / Ain't that peculiar / Lifeguard / Rock in the 80's / Lifeline / Falling / Thunder and lightning / Gloria Monday.

SEASTONES

PHIL LESH with **NED LAGIN**, plus DEAD session men and others

not issued Round

1975. (lp) **SEASTONES** -

MICKEY HART

Warners Warners

Oct 72. (lp)(c) **ROLLING THUNDER**
– Rolling thunder – Shoestone invocation / The main ten (playing in the band) / Fletcher Carnaby / The chase (progress) / Blind John / Young man / Deep wide and frequent / Pump song / Granma's cookies / Hangin' on. *(re-iss.Mar89 on 'Grateful Dead')*

1974. (7") **BLIND JOHN. / THE PUMP SONG** -

Celestial.. not issued

1983. (lp) **YAMANTAKA** - - Germ'y
– Yamantaka (parts 1-7) / The revolving mask of Yamantaka.

Rykodisc Rykodisc

1989. (lp)(cd) **DAFOS (w/ AIRTO + PURIN)**
– Dry sands of the desert / Ice of the north / Reunion (1, 2, 3) / Saudacao popular / Psychopomp / Subterranean caves of Kronos / The gates of Dafos / Passage. *re-iss.Nov 94)*

1990. (lp)(cd) **MUSIC TO BE BORN BY**
– Music to be born by.

Mar 91. (cd) **AT THE EDGE**

Nov 94. (cd) **PLANET DRUM**

DIGA RHYTHM BAND

MICKEY HART – drums, plus 10 percussionists

United Art Grateful D

1976. (lp) **DIGA**
– Razooli / Happiness is drumming / Tal Mala / Sweet sixteen / Magnificent sevens. *(cd+c-iss.1992 on 'Rykodisc')*

RHYTHM DEVILS

with HART, LESH and KREUTZMANN plus more percussionist

not issued Passport

1980. (lp) **RHYTHM DEVILS PLAY RIVER MUSIC** -
– Compound / Trenches / Street gang / The beast / Steps / Tar / Lance / Cave / Napalm for breakfast / Hell's bells. *(re-iss.+c Mar 89 on 'Rykodisc')*

ROBERT HUNTER

solo with numerous session people incl. GRATEFUL DEAD folk

not issued Round

1974. (lp) **TALES OF THE GREAT RUM RUNNERS** -
– Lady simplicity / That train / Dry dusty road / I heard you singing / Rum runners / Children's lament / Maybe she's a bluebird / Boys in the barroom / It must have been the roses / Arizona lightning / Standing at your door / Mad / Keys to the rain. *(re-iss.+cd.May89 on 'Grateful Dead')*

1974. (7") **RUM RUNNERS. / IT MUST HAVE BEEN THE ROSES** -

1975. (lp) **TIGER ROSE** -
– Tiger rose / One thing to try / Rose of Sharon / Wild Bill / Dance a hole / Cruel

white water / Over the hills / Last flash of rock'n'roll / Yellow Moon / Ariel. *(re-iss.+cd.May89 on 'Grateful Dead')*

Dark Star Dark Star

1981. (lp) **JACK O'ROSES**
– Box of rain / Book of Daniel / Friend of the Devil / etc.

Relix Relix

1982. (lp) **PROMONTORY RIDER** (74-75 rare material) -
1984. (lp)(cd) **AMAGAMALIN STREET**
– Roseanne / Amagamalin Street / Gypsy parlor ight / Rambling ghost / Ithaca / Don't be deceived / Taking Maggie home / Out of the city / Better bad luck / Streetwise / Where did you go / 13 roses. *(re-iss. 1990+Jun 93)*

Aug 86. (lp) **ROCK COLUMBIA**
– Eva / End of the road / I never see you / Aim at the heart / Kick it on down / What'll you raise? / Who, baby who? / Rock Columbia. *(cd-iss.Jun93)*

Mar 89. (lp) **LIBERTY** 1987
– Liberty / Cry down the years / Bone alley / Black shamrock / The song goes on / Do deny / Worried song / Come and get it / When a man loves a woman.

Rykodisc Rykodisc

Jan 94. (cd) **SENTINEL**
Mar 94. (cd) **A BOX OF RAIN**

KEITH & DONNA

with GARCIA plus more sessioners

not issued Relix

1975. (lp) **KEITH AND DONNA GODCHAUX** -
– River deep, mountain high / Sweet baby / Woman make you / When you start to move / Showboat / My love for you / Farewell Jack / Who was John / Every song I sing.

— also 'SAMPLER FOR DEAD HEADS' m-lp's featuring various solo material.

GREEN DAY

Formed: Rodeo, nr. Berkeley, California, USA ... early 90's out of The SWEET CHILDREN by BILLY JOE and MIKE. When TRE COOL replaced BILLY JOE's sister ANA on drums, they became GREEN DAY. Their debut lp '39/ SMOOTH' was recorded in under 24 hours. Their third album 'DOOKIE' (their first for 'Reprise') was a surprise US smash in 1994 due to college /MTV favourite 'BASKET CASE'. • **Style:** Retro punk-rock for Americans (& now Brits!) who missed out on BUZZCOCKS, DICKIES, RAMONES, and even earlier 60's pop outfit MONKEES. • **Songwriters:** Lyrics; BILLY JOE, group songs except TIRED OF WAITING FOR YOU (Kinks). DIRNT guested on The SCREAMING WEASEL album 'How to Make Enemies And Irritate People'. BILLIE JOE was also a member of PINHEAD GUNPOWDER who released an album 'Jump Salty' plus a few EP's, also for 'Lookout'.

Recommended: DOOKIE (*8)

BILLY JOE ARMSTRONG (b.1972) – vocals, guitar / **MIKE PRITCHARD** (b.1972) – bass, vocals / **TRE COOL** (b.1972) – drums

not issued Lookout

1989. (7"ep) **1000 HOURS EP** -
– 1000 hours / Dry ice / Only of you / The one I want.
1990. (7"ep) **SLAPPY EP** -
– Paper lanterns / Why do you want him? / 409 in your coffeemaker / Knowledge.
1990. (lp) **39/ SMOOTH** -
– At the library / Don't leave me / I was there / Disappearing boy / Green day / Going to Pasalacgua / 16 / Road to exceptance / Rest / The judge's daughter / Paper lanterns / Why do you want him? / 409 in your coffeemaker / Knowledge / 1000 hours / Dry ice / Only of you / The one I want / I want to be alone. *(re-iss.+cd.Nov91) (UK-iss.Sep94 as '1,039/ SMOOTHED OUT SLAPPY HOURS' on 'Lookout')*

Dec 91. (lp) **KERPLUNK!** -
– 2000 light years away / One for the razorbacks / Welcome to Paradise / Christie Road / Private ale / Dominated love slave / One of my lies / 80 / Android / No one knows / Who wrote Holden Caulfield? / Words I might have ate. *(UK-iss.+cd.Sep94, on 'Lookout')* (cd+=) Sweet children / Best thing in town / Strangeland / My generation. (by SWEET CHILDREN and released US 1990 on 'Skene')

Reprise Reprise

Feb 94. (cd)(c) **DOOKIE** 2
– Burnout / Having a blast / Chump / Longview / Welcome to Paradise / Pulling teeth / Basket case / She / Sassafras roots / When I come around / Coming clean / Emenius sleepus / In the end / F.O.D. (cd+=) (hidden track). *(re-iss.Jun94 + Nov94 on green-lp, hit UK No.35/ early '95 hit 13)*

Jun 94. (7")(c-s) **LONGVIEW. / ON THE WAGON**
(10")(cd-s) – ('A'side) / Going to Pasalaqua / F.O.D. (live) / Christy Road (live).

Aug 94. (7"green)(c-s) **BASKET CASE. / TIRED OF WAITING FOR YOU** 55
(cd-s+=) – On the wagon / 409 in your coffeemaker.

Oct 94. (12"green)(c-s)(cd-s) **WELCOME TO PARADISE. / CHUMP (live) / EMENIUS SLEEPUS** 20

Jan 95. (7"green)(c-s) **BASKET CASE. / 2,000 LIGHT YEARS AWAY (live)** 7
(cd-s+=) – Burnout (live) / Longview (live).

Mar 95. (7")(c-s) **LONGVIEW. / WELCOME TO PARADISE (live)** 30
(cd-s+=) – One of my lies (live).

May 95. (7"pic-d)(c-s) **WHEN I COME AROUND. / SHE (live)** 27
(cd-s+=) – Coming clean (live).

Sep 95. (7"red)(c-s) **GEEK STINK BREATH. / I WANNA BE ON T.V.** 16
(cd-s+=) – Don't wanna fall in love.

Oct 95. (cd)(c)(lp) **INSOMNIAC** 8 2
– Armatage Shanks / Brat / Stuck with me / Geek stink breath / No pride / Bab's Uvula who? / 86 / Panic song / Stuart and the Ave. / Brain stew / Jaded / Westbound sign / Tight wad hill / Walking contradiction.

Dec 95. (c-s) **STUCK WITH ME / WHEN I COME AROUND (live)** 24
(cd-s+=) – Jaded (live).
(cd-s) – ('A'side) / Dominated love slave (live) / Chump (live).

... Jan – Jun '96 stop press ...

Jun 96. (single) **BRAIN STEW / JADED** 28

Dave GREENFIELD & J. J. BURNEL (see under ⇒ STRANGLERS)

GREEN RIVER (see under ⇒ PEARL JAM)

GRID

Formed: based London, England ... Spring 1990, by DAVE BALL, and University graduate RICHARD NORRIS, after meeting in Ibiza about 9 months earlier. They signed to 'East West', and issued Top 60 breakthrough 'FLOATATION'. Both had already signed to 'WEA' in 1988, writings ads for Wow-Ball, T.S.B. and Shell-Oil. Also remixed some tracks for ART OF NOISE, SOFT CELL (remixes obviously), ERASURE, HAPPY MONDAYS, JESUS LOVES YOU, WORLD OF TWIST and The BHUNDU BOYS. • **Style:** Ambient club dance outfit like KRAFTWERK and CAN fused with soul, but influenced by PINK FLOYD's 'Dark Side Of The Moon' era. • **Songwriters:** The duo penned all. • **Trivia:** NORRIS was a former employee at 'Bam Caruso' record label. The GRID guested on comedian VIC REEVES (& MORTIMER)'s version of 'Abide With Me'.

Recommended: EVOLVER (*7)

DAVE BALL – keyboards, synthesizers (ex-SOFT CELL) / **RICHARD NORRIS** – DJ, vocals, keyboards, synthesizers, guitar (ex-PSYCHIC TV) with **SACHA REBECCA SOUTER** – vocals / **COBALT STARGAZER** (of ZODIAC MINDWARP) / **JULIAN STRINGLE** – clarinet / **ANDY MURRAY** – slide guitar / **GUY BARKER** – trumpet / etc

East West East West

Jun 90. (7")(c-s)(12")(cd-s) **FLOATATION (Andrew Weatherall remix). / ('A'-Richard Norris mix)** 60

Sep 90. (7")(c-s)(cd-s) **A BEAT CALLED LOVE. / ('A'original studio)** 64
(12"+=) – Floatation (Olimax and DJ Shapps remix).
(cd-s) – ('A'side) / ('A'club mix) / ('A'dub mix).

Oct 90. (cd)(c)(lp) **ELECTRIC HEAD**
– One giant step / Interference / Are you receiving / Islamatron / The traffic / Driving instructor / A beat called love / The first stroke / Central locking / Intergalactica / Beautiful & profound / This must be Heaven / Machine delay / Doctor Celine / Typical Waterloo sunset / Strange electric Sun / Floatation. (cd+c+=) – Virtual.

— In Nov 90, they remix STEX (a soul trio, which featured JOHNNY MARR), on their single 'Still Feel The Rain'. A month later, they and TIMOTHY LEARY (yes! that 60's hippy who sanctioned the drug culture 'Tune In, Tune On, Drop Out') issued white label 12" 'ORIGINS OF DANCE'.

Virgin Virgin

Sep 91. (12")(cd-s) **BOOM! (freestyle mix). / ('A'-707 mix) / Bonus BOOM! beats**

Jul 92. (12")(c-s)(cd-s) **FIGURE OF EIGHT. / ('A'mixes)** 50
(12") – ('A'remixes by Todd Terry).

Sep 92. (12")(cd-s) **HEARTBEAT. / BOOM! (space cadet mix)** 72

— next feat. guests **ROBERT FRIPP** – guitar / **COBALT STARGAZER + ZOD** (of ZODIAC MINDWARP) / **RUN RA / DIETER MEIER** – keyboards (of YELLO) / **P.P. ARNOLD** – vocals

Oct 92. (cd)(c)(lp) **FOUR FIVE SIX**
– Face the Sun / Ice machine / Crystal clear / Aquarium / Instrument / Heartbeat / Oh six one / Figure of eight / Boom! / Leave your body / Fire engine red.

Mar 93. (12") **CRYSTAL CLEAR. / ('A'mix)** 27
(c-s+=)(cd-s+=) – (4 more 'A'mixes).

DeConstruction DeConstruction?

Oct 93. (7")(c-s) **TEXAS COWBOYS. / RISE** 21

(12"+=)//(cd-s++=) – ('A'mix). / / Cheerleader song.
May 94. (c-s) **SWAMP THING. / ('A'mix)** [3]
(12"+=)//(cd-s++=) – ('A'mix). / / ('A'other mix).
Sep 94. (12")(c-s)(cd-s) **ROLLERCOASTER. / ('A'-Justin Robertson mix) / ('A'-Global Communication mix)** [19]
Sep 94. (cd)(c)(lp) **EVOLVER** [14]
– Wake up / Rollercoaster / Swamp thing / Throb / Rise / Shades of sleep / Higher peaks / Texas cowboys / Spin cycle / Golden dawn.
Nov 94. (c-s) **TEXAS COWBOYS. / ('A'mix)** [17]
(12"+=) – (2 more 'A'mixes).
(cd-s++=) – (2 more 'A'mixes; now 6 in total).
Sep 95. (c-s) **DIABLO / ('A'-Acapulco mix)** [32]
(12") – ('A'side) / ('A'-Atomic bidet mix) / ('A'-Devil rides out mix) / ('A'-Devil dubs out mix).
(cd-s) – (all 5 mixes).
Sep 95. (cd)(c)(d-lp) **MUSIC FOR DANCING** (remixes) [67]
– Floatation (the subsonic Grid mix) / Crystal clear (456 mix) / Boom! (freestyle mix) / Figure of 8 (tribal trance mix) / Rollercoaster (nemesis mix) / Texas cowboys (ricochet mix) / Swamp thing (southern comfort mix) / Crystal clear (prankster prophet mix) / Figure of 8 (Todd's master dub) / Diablo (the Devil rides out mix) / Rollercoaster (the yellow submarine re-take).

GRIN (see under ⇒ LOFGREN, Nils)

GUN

Formed: Glasgow, Scotland . . . 1986 by BABY STAFFORD and MARK RANKIN. Were originally called HAIRSPRAY TO HEAVEN then PHOBIA, before opting simply for GUN. Late 1987, they signed to 'A&M', and soon made UK Top 50 lists with debut 1989 album 'TAKING ON THE WORLD'. • **Style:** Hard'n'heavy rock act, influenced by AEROSMITH or BON JOVI. • **Songwriters:** RANKIN-GIZZI-GIZZI except; LET'S GO CRAZY (Prince) / DON'T BELIEVE A WORD (Thin Lizzy) / WORD UP (Cameo) / CHILDREN OF THE REVOLUTION (T.Rex) / SUFFRAGETTE CITY (David Bowie) / PANIC (Smiths) / KILLING IN THE NAME (Rage Against The Machine) / SO LONELY (Police) / ARE YOU GONNA GO MY WAY (Lenny Kravitz). • **Trivia:** SHARLEEN SPITERI of TEXAS guested on their debut album.

Recommended: TAKING ON THE WORLD (*7).

MARK RANKIN – vocals / **BABY STAFFORD** – guitar / **GUILIANO GIZZI** – guitar / **DANTE GIZZI** – bass / **SCOTT SHIELDS** – drums

A & M A & M
May 89. (lp)(c)(cd) **TAKING ON THE WORLD** [44]
– Better days / The feeling within / Inside out / Shame on you / Money (everybody loves her) / Taking on the world / Shame / Can't get any lower / Something to believe in / Girls in love / I will be waiting. *(re-iss.cd Mar95)*
Jun 89. (7") **BETTER DAYS. / WHEN YOU LOVE SOMEBODY** [33]
(12"+=)(cd-s+=) – Coming home.
Aug 89. (7") **MONEY (EVERYBODY LOVES HER). / PRIME TIME** [73]
(12"+=)(cd-s+=) – Dance.
Oct 89. (7")(c-s)(7"pic-d) **INSIDE OUT. / BACK TO WHERE WE STARTED** [57]
(12"+=)(cd-s+=) – Where do we go?
Jan 90. (7") **TAKING ON THE WORLD. / DON'T BELIEVE A WORD** [50]
(12"+=)(cd-s+=) – Better days (extended).
Jun 90. (7")(c-s) **SHAME ON YOU. / BETTER DAYS (live)** [33]
(12"+=)(cd-s+=) – Money (everybody loves her).

— **ALEX DICKSON** – guitar repl. BABY STAFFORD

Mar 92. (7")(c-s) **STEAL YOUR FIRE. / DON'T BLAME ME** [24]
(12"+=)(cd-s+=) – Burning down the house / Reach out for love.
Apr 92. (7")(c-s) **HIGHER GROUND. / RUN** [48]
(12"+=)(pic-cd-s+=) – One desire.
Apr 92. (cd)(c)(lp) **GALLUS** [14]
– Steal your fire / Money to burn / Long road / Welcome to the real world / Higher ground / Borrowed time / Freedom / Won't break down / Reach out for love / Watching the world go by. *(re-iss.cd/c Mar95)*
Jun 92. (7")(c-s) **WELCOME TO THE REAL WORLD. / STEAL YOUR FIRE (live)** [43]
(12"pic-d+=) – Standing in your shadow.
(cd-s+=) – Better days / Shame on you (acoustic).

— **MARK KERR** – drums repl. SHIELDS + DICKSON

Jul 94. (12")(c-s) **WORD UP. / ('A'mixes)** [8]
(cd-s) – ('A'side) / Stay forever / The man I used to be / Stranger.
Aug 94. (cd)(c)(lp) **SWAGGER** [5]
– Stand in line / Find my way / Word up / Don't say it's over / The only one / Something worthwhile / Seems like I'm losing you / Crying over you / One reason / Vicious heart.
Sep 94. (7")(c-s) **DON'T SAY IT'S OVER. / MONEY** [19]
(cd-s) – ('A'side) / Steal your fire / Better days / Shame on you.
Feb 95. (c-s) **THE ONLY ONE / WORD UP (mix) / WORD UP (Tinman remix)** [29]
(12"+=) – Inside out – So lonely.
(cd-s++=) – Time.
(cd-s) – ('A'side) / Killing in the name / Panic / Are you gonna go my way.
Apr 95. (cd-ep) **SOMETHING WORTHWHILE / SUFFRAGETTE CITY / CHILDREN OF THE REVOLUTION / WORD UP** [39]
(cd-ep) – ('A'side) / One reason / ('A'-Mac attack mix) / ('A'-Priory mix).
(12"pic-d-ep) – ('A'side) / ('A'-Mac attack mix) / ('A'-King Dong mix) / ('A'-Breakdown mix).

GUN CLUB

Formed: Los Angeles, California, USA . . . 1980 by ex 'Splash' magazine editor JEFFREY LEE PIERCE and KID CONGO. They changed name from CREEPING DEATH, at the request of KEITH MORRIS of CIRCLE JERKS. In 1981, they unearthed debut lp 'FIRE OF LOVE', which was issued by own 'Ruby' label, and produced by CHRIS D. (Of FLEASHEATERS). It saw light in UK on 'Beggar's Banquet', and prompted CHRIS STEIN's (Blondie) label 'Animal' label to sign them in '82. A couple of promising lp's followed, but after PIERCE's solo jaunt and group reformation in the mid-80's, they drifted to UK indie scene. In '87, they signed to soon-to-be defunct 'Red Rhino', and regained credibility with ROBIN GUTHRIE (Cocteau Twins) who produced album 'MOTHER JUNO'. • **Style:** Bluesy punk rock, in the mould of contemporaries The CRAMPS. • **Trivia:** The howling J.L.PIERCE was once head of the BLONDIE fan club, thus his association with STEIN. • **Songwriters:** PIERCE except; PREACHIN' THE BLUES + COOL DRINK OF WATER (Robert Johnson) / RUN THROUGH THE JUNGLE (Creedence Clearwater Revival) / etc.

Recommended: FIRE OF LOVE (*7) / MIAMI (*6) / MOTHER JUNO (*6)

JEFFREY LEE PIERCE (b. 1961) – vocals, guitar / **WARD DOTSON** – lead guitar repl. KID CONGO POWERS who joined The CRAMPS / **ROB RITTER** – bass / **TERRY GRAHAM** – drums (ex-BAGS)

Beggar's B. Ruby
May 82. (lp)(c) **FIRE OF LOVE** [ ] [ ] Dec 81
– Goodbye Johnny / Preachin' the blues / Jack on fire / She's like heroin to me / Ghost on the highway / Black train / Sex beat / Free spirit / Promise me / Cool drink of water / For the love of Ivy. *(re-iss.blue-lp.Jan86 on 'New Rose')*
Jul 82. (7") **SEX BEAT. / GHOST ON THE HIGHWAY**

Chrysalis Animal
Aug 82. (7") **WALKING WITH THE BEAST. / FIRE OF LOVE**
Sep 82. (lp)(c) **MIAMI**
– A devil in the woods / Carry home / Run through the jungle / Brothers and sisters / Texas serenade / Watermelon man / Like calling up thunder / Bad Indian / Fire of love / John Hardy / Sleeping in Blood city / Mother of Earth.

— **KID CONGO POWERS** (b.BRIAN TRISTIAN) – guitar returned to repl. RITTER + DOTSON (latter formed PONTIAC BROTHERS)

Feb 84. A.B.C.; (lp)(c) **THE BIRTH, THE DEATH, THE GHOST (live 1983)** [ ] [-]
– Bo Diddley's a gunslinger / Railroad Bill / Seven miles with the Devil / Preachin' the blues / Goodbye Johnny / Black train / Walking with the beast / Bad mood / Not that much / Going down the red river / Willie Brown / Field Holler / Sex beat.

— **PIERCE** recruited new members
JIM DUCKWORTH – lead guitar (ex-TAV FALCO'S PANTHER BURNS) repl. KID CONGO who later formed FUR BIBLE / **DEE POP** – drum (ex-BUSH TETRAS) repl. TERRY GRAHAM

Apr 83. (7") **DEATH PARTY. / HOUSE OF HIGHLAND AVENUE / THE LIE**
(12+=) – Light of the world / Come back Jim.

— added **PATRICIA MORRISON** – bass

Jun 84. (lp)(c) **THE LAS VEGAS STORY**
– The Las Vegas story / Walking with the beast / Eternally is here / The stranger in our town / My dreams / The creator was a master plan / My man's gone now / Bad America / Moonlight hotel / Give up the Sun.

— Split late 1984. PATRICIA joined FUR BIBLE and later went to SISTERS OF MERCY

JEFFREY LEE PIERCE

went solo with **MURRAY MITCHELL** – guitar / **JOHN McKENZIE** – bass / **ANDY ANDERSON** – drums

Statik not issued
Apr 85. (lp)(c) **WILDWEED** [ ] [-]
– Love and desperation / Sex killer / Cleopatra dreams on / From temptation to

you / Sensitivity / Hey Juana / Love Circus / Wildweed / From temptation to you / The midnight promise. *(cd-iss Jun 89 +=)* – The Fertility Goddess / Portrait of an artist in Hell / Love & Desperation (long) / Chris and Maggie meet Blind Willie McTell at . . .

— **PIERCE** brought in **HIROMI** – guitar / **DEAN DENNIS** – bass / **NICK SANDERSON** – drums (both ex-CLOCKDVA)

Aug 85. (7") **LOVE AND DESPERATION. / THE FERTILITY GODDESS** [ ] [-]
(12"+=) – Portrait of an artist in Hell.

Nov 85. (12"ep) **FLAMINGO (part 1 & 2). / GET AWAY / FIRE / NO MORE FIRE / LOVE AND DESPERATION** [ ] [-]

GUN CLUB

were reformed by **PIERCE, KID CONGO** and **SANDERSON plus ROMI MORI** – bass

Red Rhino / Solid

Oct 87. (lp)(c)(cd) **MOTHER JUNO** [ ] [ ]
– Breaking hands / Araby / Hearts / My cousin Kim / Port of souls / Bill Bailey / Thunderhead / Lupita screams / Yellow eyes.

Mar 88. (12"m) **BREAKING HANDS. / CRABDANCE / NOBODY'S CITY** [ ] [-]

— split again, KID CONGO went solo, but last line-up soon reformed.

Fire / Solid

Sep 90. (12"ep)(cd-ep) **THE GREAT DIVIDE. / CRABDANCE / ST JOHN'S DIVINE (part 2)** [ ] [-]

Oct 90. (cd)(c)(lp) **PASTORAL HIDE AND SEEK** [ ] [ ]
– Humanesque / The straits of love and hate / Emily's changed / I hear your heart singing / St.John's divine / The great divide / Another country's young / Flowing / Temptation and I.

New Rose / Solid

Oct 91. (cd)(d-lp) **DIVINITY (3 live / 4 studio)** [ ] [-] France
– Sorrow knows / Richard Speck / Keys to the kingdom / Black hole / Yellow eyes (live) / Hearts (live) / Fire of love (live). (cd+=) – St.John's divine

– compilations etc. –

Oct 84. Lolita; (lp) **SEX BEAT '81 (live)** [-] [ ]

Jul 85. Dojo; (lp) **TWO SIDES OF THE BEAST** [ ] [-]
(re-iss.Apr86)

Nov 85. Eva; (lp) **LOVE SUPREME (live '82)** [-] [ ]

Dec 85. Roadrunner; (lp) **DANCE KALINDA BOOM (live)** [ ] [-]

May 89. New Rose; (cd-ep) **SEX BEAT / FOR THE LOVE OF IVY / BLACK TRAIN** [-] [-]

Aug 92 Triple X; (cd)**IN EXILE** [ ] [ ]

1992 Solid; (cd) **AHMED'S WILD DREAM (live)** [ ] [ ]

JEFFREY LEE PIERCE

May 92. Solid; (cd) **RAMBLIN' JEFFREY LEE & CYPRESS GROVE WITH WILLIE LOVE** [ ] [ ]
– Goin' down / Pony blues / Future blues / Long long gone / Bad luck and trouble / Alabama blues / Good times / Stranger in my heart / Go tell the mountain / Moanin' in the moonlight / Hardtime / Killin' floor blues

. . . Jan – Jun '96 stop press . . .

— On 31st March '96, reformed heroin addict JEFFREY LEE PIERCE, died of a blood clot to the brain.

GUNS'N'ROSES

Formed: Los Angeles, California, USA . . . early 1985 by AXL ROSE, IZZY STRADLIN and moonlighting L.A.GUNS member TRACII GUNS, who was soon to return to said outfit. The new GUNS'N'ROSES were soon found by SLASH, DUFF and STEVE, who begin 'hell' tour of the US. In the summer of '86, they unleashed debut recording, a 7"ep entitled 'LIVE ?!*' LIKE A SUICIDE', which quickly sold its limited 10,000 copies. It was soon issued by 'Geffen', who had just recently signed them. After failing with debut single 'IT'S SO EASY' in Jul'87, they released debut album 'APPETITE FOR DESTRUCTION', which caused controversy due to its robot/rape sleeve cover. With constant tours between US and UK going great, it made steady progress on its way to US No.1 a year later! (it made UK No.5 a year after that!). This was aided by a US chart topping hit single 'SWEET CHILD O' MINE'. Hit singles taken from the album, continued to roll out, and they finally released official long-playing follow up in Sep'91. It came out as 2 double-lp's 'USE YOUR ILLUSION I' & 'USE YOUR ILLUSION II', which contained over 2 hours of new material. • **Style:** Raw heavy-metal rock, that exploded with menacing power, through the bleeding, always feeling vox of AXL, and the razor-sharp guitar-licks of SLASH. They balanced this with an acoustic ballad side, that diversed away from AXL's acidic voice, which was slated by his offendees; the blacks and gays. The group have always maintained their love of drink and drugs throughout turbulent and at times violent career. • **Songwriters:** All written by AXL except; MAMA KIN (Aerosmith) / NICE BOYS DON'T PLAY ROCK'N'ROLL (Rose Tattoo) / WHOLE LOTTA ROSIE (Ac-Dc) / KNOCKIN' ON HEAVEN'S DOOR (Bob Dylan) / LIVE AND LET DIE (Paul McCartney & Wings). Punk covers album; SINCE I DON'T HAVE YOU (Skyliners) / NEW ROSE (Damned) / DOWN ON THE FARM (UK Subs) / HUMAN BEING (New York Dolls) / RAW POWER (Iggy & The Stooges) / AIN'T IT FUN (Dead Boys) / BUICK MAKANE (T.Rex) / HAIR OF THE DOG (Nazareth) / ATTITUDE (Misfits) / BLACK LEATHER (Sex Pistols) / YOU CAN'T PUT YOUR ARMS AROUND A MEMORY (Johnny Thunders) / I DON'T CARE ABOUT YOU (Fear) / WHAT'S YOUR GAME! (Charles Manson, yes that one!). McKAGAN covered CRACKED ACTOR (David Bowie) • **Trivia:** On 28 Apr'90, AXL was married to ERIN, daughter of DON EVERLY (Brothers), but a couple of months later, they counterfiled for divorce. BAILEY was AXL's step-father's surname, and he found out real surname ROSE in the 80's.

Recommended: APPETITE FOR DESTRUCTION (*8) / G'N'R LIES (*5) / USE YOUR ILLUSION I (*7) / USE YOUR ILLUSION II (*6).

W. AXL ROSE (b. WILLIAM BAILEY, 6 Feb'62, Lafayette, Indiana, USA) – vocals / **SLASH** (b. SAUL HUDSON, 23 Jul'65, Stoke-On-Trent, England) – lead guitar / **IZZY STRADLIN** (b.JEFFREY ISBELL, 8 Apr'62) – guitar / **DUFF McKAGAN** (b. MICHAEL, 5 Feb'64, Seattle) – bass / **STEVE ADLER** (b.22 Jan'65, Ohio) – drums repl. ROB to L.A. GUNS again.

not issued / Uzi Suicide

Aug 86. (7"ep) **LIVE ?!*' LIKE A SUICIDE** [-] [ ]
– Mama kin / Reckless life / Move to the city / Nice boys (don't play rock'n'roll). *(US re-iss.Jan87 on 'Geffen')*

Geffen / Geffen

Jun 87. (7") **IT'S SO EASY. / MR. BROWNSTONE** [ ] [ ]
(12"+=)(12"pic-d+=) – Shadow of your love / Move to the city.

Aug 87. (lp)(c)(cd) **APPETITE FOR DESTRUCTION** [68] [1]
– Welcome to the jungle / It's so easy / Nightrain / Out ta get me / Mr. Brownstone / Paradise city / My Michelle / Think about you / Sweet child o' mine / You're crazy / Anything goes / Rocket queen. *(peaked UK-No.5 in 1989) (re-iss.Nov90) (re-iss.cd/c Oct95)*

Sep 87. (7") **WELCOME TO THE JUNGLE. / WHOLE LOTTA ROSIE (live)** [67] [ ]
(12"+=)(12"pic-d+=) – It's so easy (live) / Knockin' on Heaven's door (live).

Aug 88. (7") **SWEET CHILD O' MINE. / OUT TA GET ME** [24] [1] Jun 88
(12"+=) – Rocket queen.

Oct 88. (7") **WELCOME TO THE JUNGLE. / NIGHTRAIN** [24] [7]
(12"+=)(12"pic-d+=) – You're crazy. *(re-iss.Apr89)*

Dec 88. (lp)(c)(cd) **G'N'R LIES (live)** [22] [2]
– Reckless life / Nice boys (don't play rock'n'roll) / Move to the city / Mama kin / Patience / I used to love her / You're crazy / One in a million. *(re-iss.Nov90) (re-iss.cd/c Oct95)*

Mar 89. (7")(7"sha-clear)(7"white pic-d) **PARADISE CITY. / I USED TO LOVE HER** [6] [5] Jan 89
(12"+=) – Anything goes.
(c-s+=)(cd-s+=) – Sweet child o'mine.

May 89. (7")(12") **SWEET CHILD O'MINE. / OUT TO GET ME (live)** [6] [-]
(3"cd-s+=) – Whole lotta Rosie (live) / It's so easy (live).

Jun 89. (7")(c-s) **PATIENCE. / ROCKET QUEEN** [10] [4] Apr89
(12"+=)(3"cd-s+=) – (Axl Rose interview).

Aug 89. (7")(c-s)(7"sha-pic-d) **NIGHTTRAIN. / RECKLESS LIFE** [17] [ ] Jul 89
(12"+=)(cd-s+=) – Knockin' on Heaven's door (live '87).

— (Aug90) **MATT SORUM** – drums (ex-CULT) repl. ADAM MARPLES (ex-SEA HAGS) who repl. ADLER due to bouts of drunkeness.

Jul 91. (7")(12")(c-s)(cd-s)(12"clear-pic-d) **YOU COULD BE MINE. / CIVIL WAR** [3] [29]

Sep 91. (cd)(c)(d-lp) **USE YOUR ILLUSION I** [2] [2]
– Right next door to Hell / Dust'n'bones / Live and let die / Don't cry (original) / Perfect crime / You ain't the first / Bad obsession / Back off bitch / Double talkin' jive / November rain / The garden / Garden of Eden / Don't damn me / Bad apples / Dead horse / Coma.

Sep 91. (cd)(c)(d-lp) **USE YOUR ILLUSION II** [1] [1]
– Civil war / 14 years / Yesterdays / Knockin' on Heaven's door / Get in the ring / Shotgun blues / Breakdown / Pretty tied up / Locomotive / So fine / Estranged / You could be mine / Don't cry (alt.lyrics) / My world.

Sep 91. (7") **DON'T CRY (original). / DON'T CRY (alt.lyrics)** [8] [10]
(12"+=)(cd-s+=) – ('A'demo).

Dec 91. (7")(12")(c-s) **LIVE AND LET DIE. / ('A' live)** [5] [33]
(cd-s+=) – Shadow of your love.

— (Sep91) **DAVID NAVARRO** – guitar (of JANE'S ADDICTION) repl. IZZY who walked out on tour. **GILBY CLARKE** – guitar finally repl. IZZY who went solo

Feb 92. (7")(c-s) **NOVEMBER RAIN. / SWEET CHILD O'MINE (live)** [4] [3] Jun 92

SLASH
BORN TO BE AMERICAN

(12"+=)(pic-cd-s+=) – Patience.

May 92. (7")(12")(c-s)(cd-s) **KNOCKIN' ON HEAVEN'S DOOR (live '92 at Freddie Mercury tribute). / ('A'studio)** [2] [ ]

Oct 92. (7")(c-s) **YESTERDAYS. / NOVEMBER RAIN** [8] [ ]
(12"pic-d+=) – ('A'live version) / Knockin' on Heaven's door (live 87)

May 93. (cd-ep) **CIVIL WAR EP** [11] [ ]
– Civil war / Garden of Eden / Dead horse / (interview with Slash).

Nov 93. (c-s) **AIN'T IT FUN. / DOWN ON THE FARM** [9] [ ]
(cd-s+=) – Attitude.

Nov 93. (cd)(c)(lp) **THE SPAGHETTI INCIDENT** [2] [4]
– Since I don't have you / New rose / Down on the farm / Human being / Raw power / Ain't it fun / Buick Makane / Hair of the dog / Attitude / Black leather / You can't put your arms around a memory / I don't care about you / What's your game!.

May 94. (7"colrd)(c-s) **SINCE I DON'T HAVE YOU. / YOU CAN'T PUT YOUR ARMS AROUND A MEMORY** [10] [69]
(cd-s+=) – Human being.
(cd-s) – ('A'side) / Sweet child o' mine / Estranged.

— **PAUL HUGE** – guitar repl. GILBY who was sacked and had already went solo

Jan 95. (7") **SYMPATHY FOR THE DEVIL. / LIVE AND LET DIE** [9] [55]
(7")(c-s)(cd-s) – ('A'side) / Escape to Paris.

SLASH'S SNAKEPIT

— with **MATT + GILBY/ + ERIC DOVER** -vocals (ex-JELLYFISH)/ **MIKE INEZ** -bass (of ALICE IN CHAINS)

Geffen Geffen

Feb 95. (cd)(c)(lp) **IT'S FIVE O'CLOCK SOMEWHERE** [15] [70]
– Neither can I / Dime store rock / Beggars and hangers-on / Good to be alive / What do you want to be / Monkey chow / Soma city ward / Jizz da pit / Lower / Take it away / Doin' fine / Be the ball / I hate everybody (but you) / Back and forth again.

DUFF McKAGAN

DUFF McKAGAN – vocals, guitar (ex-GUNS'N'ROSES) with **TED ANDREADIS + DIZZY REED** – keyboards / **WEST ARKEEN** – lead guitar (co-wrote 'Man In The Meadow') / plus other guests **SLASH** – lead guitar / **MATT SORUM** – drums (co-wrote 'F@*ked Up Beyond Belief'), **GILBY CLARKE** – guitars (co-wrote '10 Years'), **JOIE MASTROKALOS** – b.vocals (co-wrote 'Just Not There'), **DOC NEWMAN** – vocals (+ co-wrote 'F@*k You'), **SNAKE, SEBASTIAN BACH, LENNY KRAVITZ + JEFF BECK**

Geffen Geffen

Oct 93. (cd)(c)(lp) **BELIEVE IN ME** [27] [ ]
– Believe in me / I love you / Man in the meadow / (F@*ked up) Beyond belief / Could it be U / Just not there / Punk rock song / The majority / 10 years / Swamp song / Trouble / F@*k you / Lonely tonite.

Nov 93. (cd-s) **BELIEVE IN ME. / BAMBI / CRACKED ACTOR** [ ] [ ]

GILBY CLARKE

Virgin America Virgin

Jul 94. (cd)(c) **PAWNSHOP GUITARS** [39] [ ]
– Cure me . . .or kill me . . . / Black / Tijuana jail / Skin and bones / Johanna's chopper / Let's get lost / Pawn shop guitar / Dead flowers / Jail guitar doors / Hunting dogs / Shut up.

— Covered: DEAD FLOWERS (Rolling Stones) / JAIL GUITAR DOORS (Clash).

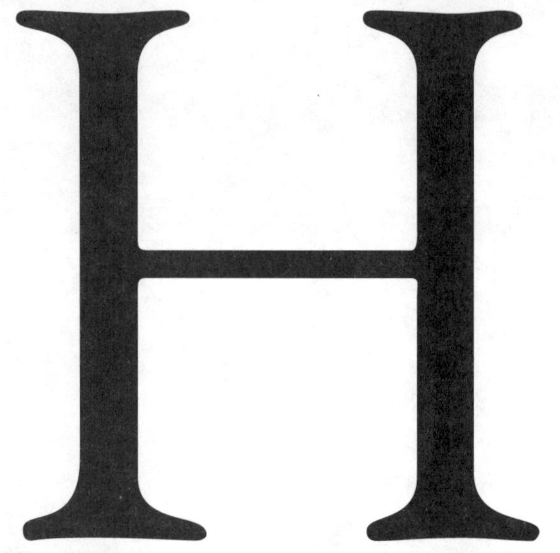

Daryl HALL & John OATES

Formed: Philadelphia, USA . . . 1972 by the duo, who signed to 'Atlantic', due to their work with band GULLIVER. They had originally met in 1967, while attending local Temple University. HALL had classical training as a boy, and progressed to doo-wop groups while also featuring on a single recorded by future producer KENNY GAMBLE & THE ROMEOS. He then sessioned for many including THE TEMPTONES and SMOKEY ROBINSON, before forming GULLIVER with TIM MOORE, TOM SELLERS and JIM HELMER. They released 1 self-titled lp in 1969 for 'Elektra', before being joined by OATES. They broke up before OATES could provide them with any songs. The duos debut lp 'WHOLE OATS', was produced by Arif Mardin, and was followed in 1974 by 'ABANDONED LUNCHEONETTE'. After moving to New York, the album hit US Top 40, helped by their Top 60 single 'SHE'S GONE'. Their 3rd album 'WAR BABIES' produced by TODD RUNDGREN, failed to provoke much interest and the duo were dropped by Atlantic. They then signed to 'RCA' in 1975, and issued eponymous 4th album, which eventually climbed into US Top 20 in 1976. It contained their first entry into US Top 5 'SARA SMILE', which provoked last label to re-issue 'SHE'S GONE' to hit US Top 10 and UK Top 50. Early in 1977, they made first of 6 US chart toppers with 'RICH GIRL'. • **Style:** White soul-rock / R&B duo, with one excursion into heavier field in '74's 'WAR BABIES'. • **Songwriters:** HALL-OATES except; YOU'VE LOST THAT LOVIN' FEELIN' (Righteous Brothers) / THE WAY YOU DO THE THINGS YOU DO – MY GIRL (Temptations) / CAN'T HELP FALLING IN LOVE (Elvis Presley) / LOVE TRAIN (O'JAYS) / etc. They co-wrote some songs with SARA and JANNA ALLEN. HALL covered; WRITTEN IN STONE (J.Allen-S.Dubin-K.Savigar) / ME AND MRS.JONES (Billy Paul). • **Trivia:** ROBERT FRIPP (of KING CRIMSON) produced HALL's solo outing 'SACRED SONGS'.

Recommended: THE BEST OF HALL & OATES – LOOKING BACK (*6).

DARYL HALL (b.DARYL HOHL, 11 Oct'48, Pottstown, Philadelphia) – vocals, keys (ex-TEMPTONES, ex-solo artist, ex-CELLAR DOR, ex-EXECUTIVE SUITE, ex-GULLIVER) / **JOHN OATES** (b. 7 Apr'49, New York, USA) – vocals, guitar (ex-MASTERS) with various personnel session players.

Atlantic | Atlantic

Sep 72. (7") **GOODNIGHT AND GOOD MORNING. / ALL OUR LOVE (as "WHOLE OATS")** [-] [ ]

Nov 72. (lp)(c) **WHOLE OATS** [-] [ ]
– I'm sorry / All our love / Georgie / Fall in Philadelphia / Water wheel / Lazy man / Good night & good morning / They needed each other / Southeast city window / Thank you for . . . / Lily (are you happy).*(UK-iss.Sep76) (cd-iss.Feb93)*

Nov 72. (7") **I'M SORRY. / LILY (ARE YOU HAPPY)** [-] [ ]

Jan 74. (lp)(c) **ABANDONED LUNCHEONETTE** [ ] [ ]
– I'm just a kid / Laughing boy / She's gone / Las Vegas turnaround / Had I known you better then / Lady rain / When the morning comes / Abandoned luncheonette / Everytime I look at you. *(US re-iss.Oct76, hit No.33) (cd-iss.Jun93)*

Jan 74. (7") **LAS VEGAS TURNAROUND. / I'M JUST A KID** [ ] [ ]

Feb 74. (7") **SHE'S GONE. / I'M JUST A KID** [-] [60]
(re-iss. US Jul'76, hit No.7)

Jul 74. (7") **WHEN THE MORNING COMES. / LADY RAIN** [ ] [ ]

Sep 74. (7") **SHE'S GONE. / ABANDONED LUNCHEONETTE** [ ] [-]

Nov 74. (lp)(c) **WAR BABIES** [ ] [86] Oct 74
– Can't stop the music (he played it much too long) / Is it a star / Beanie G and the rose tattoo / You're much too soon / 70's scenario / War baby son of Zorro / I'm watching you (a mutant romance) / Better watch your back / Screaming through December / Johnny Gone and the "C" eaters.

Nov 74. (7") **CAN'T STOP THE MUSIC (HE PLAYED IT MUCH TOO LONG). / 70'S SCENARIO** [-] [ ]

R.C.A. | R.C.A.

Sep 75. (lp)(c) **DARYL HALL & JOHN OATES** [56] [17]
– Camelia / Sara smile / Alone too long / Out of me, out of you / Nothing at all / Gino (the manager) / (You know) It doesn't matter anymore / Ennui on the mountain / Grounds for separation / Soldering. *(re-iss.Apr80)*

Sep 75. (7") **CAMELIA. / ENNUI ON THE MOUNTAIN** [ ] [ ]

Nov 75. (7") **ALONE TOO LONG. / NOTHING AT ALL** [-] [ ]

Jan 76. (7") **SARA SMILE. / SOLDERING** [ ] [4]

May 76. (7") **GINO (THE MANAGER). / SOLDERING** [ ] [-]

Sep 76. (lp)(c) **BIGGER THAN BOTH OF US** [25] [13] Aug 76
– Back together again / Rich girl / Crazy eyes / Do what you want, be what you are / Kerry / London luck and love / Room to breathe / You'll never learn / Falling.

Nov 76. (7") **DO WHAT YOU WANT, BE WHAT YOU ARE. / YOU'LL NEVER LEARN** [ ] [39] Oct 76

Nov 76. (7") **RICH GIRL. / YOU'LL NEVER LEARN** [ ] [-]

Late in '76 DARYL duetted with RUTH COPELAND on single 'Heaven'.

Jan 77. (7") **RICH GIRL. / LONDON LUCK & LOVE** [-] [1]

May 77. (7") **BACK TOGETHER AGAIN. / ROOM TO BREATHE** [-] [28]

May 77. (7") **BACK TOGETHER AGAIN. / ENNUI ON THE MOUNTAIN** [ ] [-]

Oct 77. (lp)(c) **BEAUTY ON A BACK STREET** [40] [30] Sep77
– Don't change / Why do lovers (break each other's heart?) / You must be good for something / The emptyness / Love hurts (love heals) / Bigger than both of us / Bad habits and infections / Winged bull / The girl who used to be. *(re-iss.Jul84)*

Oct 77. (7") **WHY DO LOVERS (BREAK EACH OTHER'S HEART?). / THE GIRL WHO USED TO BE** [ ] [73]

Jan 78. (7") **DON'T CHANGE. / THE EMPTYNESS** [-] [ ]

—— **CHARLES DE CHANT** – saxophone, keyboards, perc. repl. TOM SCOTT / **KENNY PASSARELLI** – bass repl. LEE SKLAR & SCOTT EDWARDS / **ROGER POPE** – drums repl. JEFF PORCARO / **CALEB QUAYE** – lead guitar / **DAVID KENT** – keyboards repl. other sessioners.

Jun 78. (lp)(c) **LIVE TIME (live)** [ ] [42] May 78
– Rich girl / The emptyness / Do what you want, be what you are / I'm just a kid / Sara smile / Abandoned luncheonette / Room to breathe. *(re-iss.Jun83)*

Aug 78. (7") **IT'S A LAUGH. / SERIOUS MATTER** [-] [20]

Sep 78. (7") **THE LAST TIME. / SERIOUS MATTER** [ ] [-]

Sep 78. (lp)(c) **ALONG THE RED LEDGE** [ ] [27]
– It's a laugh / Melody for a memory / The last time / I don't wanna lose you / Have I been away too long / Alley katz / Don't blame it on love / Serious matter / Pleasure beach / August day. *(re-iss.Jun83)*

Jan 79. (7") **I DON'T WANNA LOSE YOU. / AUGUST DAY** [ ] [42] Dec 78

—— They retained **DECHANT, PASSARELLI** (on next only), and brought in **TOM 'T-Bone' WOLK** – bass, synthe / **G.E.SMITH** – guitar / **MICKEY CURRY** – drums

Nov 79. (7") **PORTABLE RADIO. / NUMBER ONE** [ ] [-]

Nov 79. (lp)(c) **X-STATIC** [ ] [33] Oct 79
– The woman comes and goes / Wait for me / Portable radio / All you want is Heaven / Who said the world was fair / Running from Paradise / Number one / Bebop – Drop / Hallofon / Intravino.

May 80. (7") **WAIT FOR ME. / NO BRAIN NO PAIN** [-] [18] Oct 79

May 80. (7") **WHO SAID THE WORLD WAS FAIR. / ALL YOU WANT IS HEAVEN** [-] [ ]

Jun 80. (7") **RUNNING FROM PARADISE. / BEBOP – DROP** [41] [-]

Jul 80. (7") **HOW DOES IT FEEL TO BE BACK. / UNITED STATE** [-] [30]

Aug 80. (lp)(c) **VOICES** [ ] [17]
– How does it feel to be back / Big kids / United state / Hard to be in love with you / Kiss on my list / Gotta lotta nerve (perfect perfect) / You've lost that lovin' feelin' / You make my dreams / Everytime you go away / Africa / Diddy doo wop (I hear the voices). *(re-iss.Sep81) (re-iss.+cd.Oct87)*

Sep 80. (7") **YOU'VE LOST THAT LOVIN' FEELIN' / DIDDY DOO WOP (I HEAR THE VOICES)** [-] [12]

Sep 80. (7") **YOU'VE LOST THAT LOVIN' FEELIN'. / UNITED STATE** [55] [-]

Nov 80. (7") **KISS ON MY LIST. / AFRICA** [33] [1] Jan 81

Jun 81. (7") **YOU MAKE MY DREAMS. / GOTTA LOTTA NERVE (PERFECT PERFECT)** [ ] [5] Apr 81

Sep 81. (7")(12") **PRIVATE EYES. / TELL ME WHAT YOU WANT** [ ] [1] Aug 81
(UK re-iss.Mar82, hit No.32)

Sep 81. (lp)(c) **PRIVATE EYES** [8] [5]

– Private eyes / Loking for a good gun / I can't go for that (no can do) / Mama a mano / Did it in a minute / Head above water / Tell me what you want / Friday let me down / Ungaurded minute / Your imagination / Some men. *(re-iss.1984) (re-iss.+cd.Oct87)*

Jan 82. (7")(12") **I CAN'T GO FOR THAT (NO CAN DO). / UNGUARDED MINUTE** 8 1 Nov 81

Mar 82. (7") **DID IT IN A MINUTE. / HEAD ABOVE WATER** - 9

Jun 82. (7")(12") **YOUR IMAGINATION. / SARA SMILE** 33

Oct 82. (7")(12") **MANEATER. / DELAYED REACTION** 6 1

Oct 82. (lp)(c) **H2O** 24 3

– Maneater / Crime pays / One on one / Art of heartbreak / Open all night / Family man / Italian girls / Guessing games / Delayed reaction / At tension / Go solo. *(re-iss.+cd.Oct87)*

Jan 83. (7")(12") **ONE ON ONE. / ART OF HEARTBREAK** 63 7

(US 12") – ('A'club) / I can't go for that (no can do) (extended).

Apr 83. (7") **FAMILY MAN. / CRIME PAYS** 15 6

(7"+=)(12"+=) – Open All Night. *(US B-side)*

Sep 83. (7") **SAY IT ISN'T SO. / KISS ON MY LIST** - 2

Oct 83. (7")(12") **SAY IT ISN'T SO. / DID IT IN A MINUTE** 69 -

Oct 83. (lp)(c)(cd) **ROCK'N SOUL, PART 1** (compilation) 16 7

– Sara smile / She's gone / Rich girl / Kiss on my list / You make my dreams / Private eyes / I can't go for that (no can do) / Maneater / One on one / Wait for me (live) / Adult education / Say it isn't so.

Feb 84. (7") **ADULT EDUCATION. / MANEATER** - 8

Feb 84. (7") **ADULT EDUCATION. / SAY IT ISN'T SO** 63 -

(12"+=) – I can't go for that (no can do).

Oct 84. (7")(12") **OUT OF TOUCH. / COLD DARK AND YESTERDAY** 48 1 Sep 84

Oct 84. (lp)(c)(cd) **BIG BAM BOOM** 28 5

– Going thru the motions / Cold dark and yesterday / All American girl / Possession obsession / Dance on your knees / Out of touch / Method of modern love / Bank on your love / Some things are better left unsaid

Jan 85. (7")(12") **METHOD OF MODERN LOVE. / BANK ON YOUR LOVE** 21 5 Dec 84

(d7"+=) – I can't go for that (live) / Maneater (live).

Mar 85. (7") **SOME THINGS ARE BETTER LEFT UNSAID. / ALL AMERICAN GIRL** - 18

May 85. (7") **OUT OF TOUCH (remix). / DANCE ON YOUR KNEES** 62 -

(12"+=) – Everytime you go away.

May 85. (7") **POSSESSION OBSESSION. / DANCE ON YOUR KNEES** - 30

Sep 85. (7")(12") **A NITE AT THE APOLLO LIVE! (live medley: - THE WAY YOU DO THE THINGS YOU DO - MY GIRL). / ADULT EDUCATION** 58 20 Aug 85

— (above and below credited DAVID RUFFIN & EDDIE KENDRICKS; ex-Temptations)

Sep 85. (lp)(c)(cd) **LIVE AT THE APOLLO (WITH DAVID RUFFIN & EDDIE KENDRICKS)** 32 21

– Get ready – Ain't too proud to beg – The way you do the things you do – My girl / When something is wrong with my baby / Everytime you go away / I can't go for that (no can do) / One by one / Possession obsession / Adult education. *(cd-iss.Sep93)*

In 1986 split for a while, HALL made solo album. See further below.

Arista Arista

Apr 88. (7")(12") **EVERYTHING YOUR HEART DESIRES. / REAL LOVE** 3

Jun 88. (lp)(c)(cd) **OOH YEAH!** 52 24 May 88

– Downtown life / Everything your heart desires / I'm in pieces / Missed opportunity / Talking all night / Rockability / Rocket to God / Soul love / ReaLove / Keep on pushin' love.

Jul 88. (7") **MISSED OPPORTUNITY. / SOUL LOVE** - 29

Sep 88. (7") **DOWNTOWN LIFE. / ('A'urban mix)** - 31

Sep 90. (7") **SO CLOSE. / ('A'unplugged)** 69 11

(cd-s+=) – She's gone (live) / Can't help falling in love.

Nov 90. (cd)(c)(lp) **CHANGE OF SEASON** 44 61 Oct 90

– So close / Starting all over again / Sometimes a mind changes / Change of season / I ain't gonna take it this time / Everywhere I look / Give it up (old habits) / Don't hold back your love / Halfway there / Only love / Heavy rain / So close – unplugged.

Dec 90. (c-s) **DON'T HOLD BACK YOUR LOVE. / CHANGE OF SEASON** - 41

Jan 91. (7")(c-s) **EVERYWHERE I LOOK. / I CAN'T GO FOR THAT (NO CAN DO) (remix)** 74 -

(12"+=)(cd-s+=) – Sometimes a mind changes.

Oct 91. (cd)(c)(lp) **LOOKING BACK - THE BEST OF DARYL HALL & JOHN OATES** (compilation) 9

– She's gone / Sara smile / Rich girl / You've lost that lovin' feelin' / Kiss on my list / Every time you go away / Private eyes / I can't go for that (no can do) / Maneater / One on one / Family man / Adult education / Out of touch / Method of modern love / Starting all over again. *(cd+)(c+=)* – Back together again / So close / Everything your heart desires.

- compilations, others -

Sep 76. Atlantic; (7"ep) **SHE'S GONE / WAR BABY SON OF ZORRO / LAZY MAN** 42 -

Jan 77. Atlantic; (7") **LAS VEGAS TURNAROUND. / HAD I KNOWN YOU BETTER THEN**

Feb 77. Atlantic; (lp)(c) **NO GOODBYES** 92

Apr 77. Atlantic; (7") **IT'S UNCANNY. / BEANIE G. & THE ROSE TATTOO** -

Jun 77. Atlantic; (7") **IT'S UNCANNY. / LILY (ARE YOU HAPPY)** - 80

Jul 81. Atlantic; (7") **SHE'S GONE. / WHEN THE MORNING COMES**

Apr 77. Chelsea; (lp)(c) **PAST TIMES BEHIND** (71-72)

1977. Chelsea; (7") **THE REASON WAY (with GULLIVER) / IF THAT'S WHAT MAKES YOU HAPPY (Hall & Oates)** -

May 82. RCA Gold; (7") **KISS ON MY LIST. / RUNNING FROM PARADISE** -

May 83. R.C.A.; (c-ep) **CASSETTE EP** -

– I can't go for that (no can do) / Maneater / Private eyes / Kiss on my list.

Jun 84. Magnum Force; (lp) **THE PROVIDER** -

Oct 85. Thunderbolt; (lp)(c) **REALLY SMOKIN'** -

Apr 86. Showcase; (lp)(c) **THE EARLY YEARS** -

Nov 86. Old Gold; (7") **MANEATER. / I CAN'T GO FOR THAT (NO CAN DO)** -

Oct 92. Old Gold; (cd-ep) **I CAN'T GO FOR THAT (NO CAN DO) / PRIVATE EYES / KISS IS ON MY LIST** -

Oct 92. Old Gold; (cd-ep) **MANEATER / FAMILY MAN / METHOD OF MODERN LOVE** -

Nov 86. Meteor; (lp)(c)(cd) **20 CLASSIC TRACKS** -

1988. Big Time; (lp)(c)(cd) **FIRST SESSIONS**

Feb 94. Javelin; (cd)(c) **SPOTLIGHT ON HALL & OATES** -

Sep 94. Prestige; (cd) **A LOT OF CHANGES COMIN'** -

Feb 95. B.A.M.; (cd) **PEARLS OF THE PAST** -

Oct 95. R.C.A.; (cd) **ROCK'N'SOUL PART 2 (GREATEST HITS)** -

DARYL HALL

not issued Parallex

1968. (7") **A LONELY GIRL / VICKY, VICKY** -

not issued Amy

1968. (7") **THE PRINCESS & THE SOLDIER./ (Part 2)**

R.C.A. R.C.A.

Apr 80. (lp)(c) **SACRED SONGS** (rec.1977) 58

– Sacred songs / Something in 4/4 time / Babs and Babs / Urban landscape / NYNCY / The farther away (I am) / Why was it so easy / Don't leave me alone with her / Survive / Without tears. *(re-iss.Jul84)*

Apr 80. (7") **SACRED SONGS. / SOMETHING IN 4-4 TIME** -

Jul 86. (7")(12") **DREAMTIME. / LET IT OUT** 28 5

Aug 86. (lp)(c)(cd) **THREE HEARTS IN THE HAPPY ENDING MACHINE** 26 29

– Dreamtime / Only a vision / I wasn't born yesterday / Someone like you / Next stop / For you / Foolish pride / Right as rain / Let it out / What's going to happen to us. *(re-iss.May88)*

Oct 86. (7") **FOOLISH PRIDE. / WHAT'S GOING TO HAPPEN TO US** - 33

Nov 86. (7") **I WASN'T BORN YESTERDAY. / WHAT'S GONNA HAPPEN TO US**

(12"+=) – Dreamtime.

Jan 87. (7") **SOMEONE LIKE YOU. / ('A' sax solo version)** - 57

— writes with **PETER LORD MORELAND** – keyboards / **V. JEFFREY SMITH** – synth.bass / **ALAN GORRIE** – bass / other musicians **TOMMY EYRE** – keyboards / **MEL WESSON** – programming / **TREVOR MURRELL** – drums / **BOB BITSAND** – bass / **MYLES BOULD** – percussion

Epic Epic

Sep 93. (7")(c-s) **I'M IN A PHILLY MOOD (Edit) / MONEY CHANGES EVERYTHING** 59 82

(cd-s+=) – I've finally seen the light.

(cd-s) – ('A'side) / Love T.K.O. (live) / Me and Mrs.Jones (live). *(re-iss.Mar94 hit UK 52)*

Oct 93. (cd)(c)(lp) **SOUL ALONE** 57

– Power of seduction / This time / Love revelation / I'm in a Philly mood / Borderline / Stop loving me, stop loving you / Help me find a way to your heart / Send me / Wildfire / Money changes everything / Written in stone. *(re-dist. Jan94)*

Jan 94. (c-s) **STOP LOVING ME, STOP LOVING YOU. / MONEY CHANGES EVERYTHING** 30

(12"+=)(cd-s+=) – (4 more 'A'mixes).

May 94. (7")(c-s) **HELP ME FIND A WAY TO YOUR HEART. / POWER OF SEDUCTION** 70

(cd-s+=) – Stop loving me, stop loving you (live) / I'm in a Philly mood (live).

— Below on 'Mercury' & the theme from USA soccer World Cup Finals.

Jun 94. (7"pic-d)(c-s)(cd-s) **GLORYLAND. ("DARYL HALL & SOUNDS OF BLACKNESS") / ('A'mixes)** 36

Aug 94. (c-s) **WILDFIRE. / THIS TIME**
(cd-s+=) – ('A'extended).

— DARYL surfaced again when credited in May95 on DUSTY SPRINGFIELD's UK Top50 hit single 'WHEREVER WOULD I BE'.

GULLIVER

with **DARYL HALL**

Elektra Elektra

1969. (7") **EVERY DAY'S A LOVELY DAY / ANGELINA** -

1970. (lp) **GULLIVER**
– Everyday's a lovely day / I'm really smokin' / Christine / Rose come home / Enough -Over the mountain / Angelina / Flogene / Lemon road / Seventy / Truly good song.

1970. (7") **A TRULY GOOD SONG. /EVERY DAY'S A LOVELY DAY**

Peter HAMMILL
(see under ⇒ VAN DER GRAAF GENERATOR)

HAPPY MONDAYS

Formed: Salford, Manchester, England . . . 1984 by brothers SHAUN and PAUL RYDER. In 1985 helped by A&R man and producer Mike Pickering, they signed contract with Tony Wilson's 'Factory' records, and issued debut 12" 'FORTY-FIVE'. Soon became darlings of NME and indie chart scene after release of first lp in 1987 'SQUIRREL AND G-MAN . . . '. In late '89, they scored first top 20 hit with 'HALLELUJAH'. The following year, they had 2 Top 5 hits 'STEP ON' & 'KINKY AFRO', which premiered Top 5 album 'PILLS 'N' THRILLS & BELLYACHES'. • **Style:** Inovators and pioneers of the Manchester rave scene, that created a new breed of danceable rock. SHAUN's at times hoarse vox, was squeeky but nonetheless effective. The drug scene was also part of SHAUN and BEZ's outgoing culture, as was appearing alongside naked female models in a 1991 issue of Penthouse'. • **Songwriters:** Group compositions except; DESMOND (Ob-la-di Ob-la-da; Beatles) / LAZYITIS (Ticket To Ride; Beatles) / STEP ON + TOKOLOSHE MAN (John Kongos) / KINKY AFRO (similar to 'Lady Marmalade'; LaBelle). • **Trivia:** Produced by JOHN CALE in 1987 and The TOM TOM CLUB duo in 1992.

Recommended: SQUIRREL AND G-MAN TWENTY FOUR HOUR PARTY . . . (*8) / BUMMED (*8) / PILLS N' THRILLS AND BELLYACHES (*9) / YES PLEASE (*6).

SHAUN RYDER (b.23 Aug'62) – vocals / **PAUL RYDER** (b.24 Apr'64) – bass / **MARK DAY** (b.29 Dec'61) – guitar / **PAUL DAVIS** (b. 7 Mar'66) – keyboards / **GARY 'GAZ' WHELAN** (b.12 Feb'66) – drums

Factory RoughTrade

Sep 85. (12"ep) **FORTY-FIVE EP** -
– Delightful / This feeling / Oasis.

— added **MARK 'Bez' BERRY** (b.18 Apr'64) – percussion, dancer

Jun 86. (7") **FREAKY DANCIN'. / THE EGG** -
(12") – ('A'extended) / ('A'live).

Mar 87. (12") **TART TART. / LITTLE MATCHSTICK OWEN'S RAP** -

Apr 87. (lp)(c) **SQUIRREL AND G-MAN TWENTY-FOUR HOUR PARTY PEOPLE PLASTIC FACE CARNT SMILE (WHITE OUT)** -
– Kuff dam / Tart tart / 'Enery / Russell / Olive oil / Weekends / Little matchstick Owen / Oasis / Desmond * / Cob 20. *(cd-iss.Mar90 +=) – Little matchstick Owen's rap. (re-iss.Sep87, re-iss.Nov88, * repl. by* '24 hour party people') (re-iss.cd/c Sep95 on 'London')

Oct 87. (7") **24 HOUR PARTY PEOPLE. / YAHOO** -
(12"+=) – ('A'extended) / Wah wah (think tank).

Nov 88. (7") **WROTE FOR LUCK. / BOOM** -
(cd-s+=) – ('A'dance mix) / ('A'club mix).
(12") – (all above 3 tracks minus 'Boom').

Nov 88. (lp)(c)(cd)(dat) **BUMMED** -
– Country song / Moving in with / Mad Cyril / Fat lady wrestlers / Performance / Brain dead / Wrote for luck / Bring a friend / Do it better / Lazyitis. *(reached 59 UK chart Jan90) (re-iss.cd/c Sep95 on 'London')*

May 89. (7")(12") **LAZYITIS (ONE ARMED BOXER). / MAD CYRIL (HELLO GIRLS)** 85 -

— (above featured 50's pop star KARL DENVER – backing vocals) *(re-iss.May90 hit No.46)*

1989. (7"clear)(12"clear) **MAD CYRIL. / DO IT BETTER** -

Sep 89. (7")(12") **WFL (Vince Clarke mix). / WFL (THINK ABOUT THE FUTURE** 68 -
(cd-s+=) – ('A'&'B'extended) / Lazyitis (the one armed boxer).

Nov 89. (7"ep)(12"ep) **RAVE ON MADCHESTER EP** 19 -
– Hallelujah / Holy ghost / Clap your hands / Rave on.

Nov 89. (7")(c-s) **HALLELUJAH (MaColl mix). / HALLELUJAH (in out mix)** -
(12"+=)(cd-s+=) – ('A'club mix) / Rave on (club mix).
(cd-ep)(m-lp) – (all the above)(+=) WFL (Think about the future).

— added guest **ROWETA** – backing vocals to repl. other guest KIRSTY MacCOLL

Factory Elektra

Mar 90. (7")(12") **STEP ON (stuff it in mix). / ('A'-one louder mix)** 5 57 Jan 91
(c-s+=)(cd-s+=) – ('A'twistin' my melons mix).

Oct 90. (7")(12")(c-s) **KINKY AFRO. / KINKY AFRO (live)** 5
(cd-s+=) – ('A'radio edit).

Nov 90. (cd)(c)(lp) **PILLS'N THRILLS AND BELLYACHES** 4 89
– Kinky Afro / God's cop / Donovan / Grandbag's funeral / Loose fit / Dennis & Lois / Bob's your uncle / Step on / Holiday / Harmony. *(re-iss.cd/c Sep95 on 'London')*

Feb 91. (7")(12")(c-s) **LOOSE FIT (edit). / BOB'S YOUR UNCLE (edit)** 17
(cd-s+=) – Kinky Afro (Euro mix).

Sep 91. (cd)(c)(d-lp) **LIVE (live BABY BIG HEAD Bootleg album)** 21
– Hallelujah / Donovan / Kinky Afro / Clap your hands / Loose fit / Holiday / Rave on / E / Tokoloshe man / Dennis and Lois / God's cop / Step on / W.F.L. *(d-lp+=)(c+=)* – Bob's your uncle. *(re-iss.cd/c Sep95 on 'London')*

Nov 91. (12") **JUDGE FUDGE. / TOKOLOSHE MAN** 24
(cd-s+=) – ('A'version).

Sep 92. (7")(c-s) **STINKIN' THINKIN'. / ('A'boys own mix)** 31
(12"+=)(cd-s+=) – ('A'-Terry Farley mix) / Baby bighead.

Oct 92. (cd)(c)(lp) **. . . YES PLEASE!** 14
– Stinkin' thinkin' / Monkey in the family / Sunshine & love / Dustman / Angel / Cut 'em loose Bruce / Theme from Netto / Love child / Total Ringo / Cowboy Dave. *(re-iss.cd/c Sep95 on 'London')*

Nov 92. (7")(c-s) **SUNSHINE & LOVE. / STAYING ALIVE (mix) / 24 HOUR PARTY PEOPLE (remix)** 62
(12"+=)(cd-s+=) – ('A'dance mix).

— They disbanded early '93, with SHAUN and other two briefly forming The MONDAYS, which evolved into BLACK GRAPE.

– compilations, others, etc. –

May 90. Strange Fruit; (12"ep)(c-ep)(cd-ep) **THE PEEL SESSIONS (1989)** -
– Tart tart / Mad Cyril / Do it better. *(cd-ep re-iss.Feb92)*

Nov 91. Strange Fruit; (cd-ep) **THE PEEL SESSIONS (1986)** -
– Freaky dancin' / Kuff dam / Olive Oil / Cob 20.

Oct 95. London; (cd)(c) **LOADS** 41
– Step on / W.F.L. / Kinky Afro / Hallelujah – MacColl mix / Mad Cyril / Lazyitis / Tokoloshe man / Loose fit / Bob's yer uncle / Judge fudge / Stinkin' thinkin' / Sunshine & love / Angel / Tart tart / Kuff dam / 24 hour party people. (some cd's w/free cd+=) **LOADS MORE** -Lazyitis (one armed boxer mix) / W.F.L. (Perfecto mix) / Bob's yer uncle (Perfecto mix) / Loose fit (Perfecto mix) / Hallelujah (Deadstock mix) / Freaky dancing / Delightful.

HARDLINE (see under ⇒ JOURNEY)

George HARRISON

Born: 25 Feb'43, Wavertree, Liverpool, England. In late 1968, he was the first BEATLE to release a solo lp 'WONDERWALL MUSIC', but it flopped in UK. He soon released on own 'Zapple' label, another instrumental lp 'ELECTRONIC SOUND', which used moog synthesizer for first time. When the BEATLES officially split in 1969, he took solo activities more seriously, bringing in famous session people to augment 1970 triple album 'ALL THINGS MUST PASS'. It hit No.1 in the US and was quickly followed by cross-Atlantic chart topping 45 'MY SWEET LORD'. The song was claimed by Bright Tunes (owners of songwriter Ronnie Mack's estate) that it plagiarised their CHIFFONS song 'HE'S SO FINE'. 5 years later, the court gave 6-figure royalties to the plaintiffs. In 1972, he released another triple, this time live album 'CONCERT FOR BANGLA DESH'. After another successful album 'LIVING IN THE MATERIAL WORLD', he formed own label 'Dark Horse' in 1974. It soon issued his own releases, as well as new signings RAVI SHANKAR and SPLINTER. He continued to be major star, all but hiccup flop 1982 album 'GONE TROPPO'. He returned in 1987 with Top 10 album 'CLOUD NINE', with him also joining the ranks of veteran supergroup TRAVELING WILBURYS. • **Style:** Multi-talented rock-pop star, with eastern Indian leanings. • **Songwriters:**

Self-penned except; I'D HAVE YOU ANYTIME + IF NOT FOR YOU (co-written with Bob Dylan) / BYE BYE LOVE (Everly Brothers) / I DON'T WANT TO DO IT (Bob Dylan) / GOT MY MIND SET ON YOU (James Ray) / ROLL OVER BEETHOVEN (Chuck Berry) / etc. • **Trivia:** He and his wife PATTI were divorced in Jun'77, after her much publicised affair with ERIC CLAPTON. From 1979, he founded own 'Homemade' film productions, which released 80's movies 'Life Of Brian', 'The Long Good Friday', 'Time Bandits', 'The Missionary', 'Mona Lisa', 'A Private Function', 'Water', and 'Shanghai Surprise'.

Recommended: ALL THINGS MUST PASS (*8) / THE BEST OF GEORGE HARRISON (*7) / THE BEST OF DARK HORSE 1976-89 (*6)

GEORGE HARRISON – instruments (no vocals) (of-BEATLES)

Apple Apple

Nov 68. (lp) **WONDERWALL MUSIC (Soundtrack)** [ ] [49]
– Microbes / Red lady too / Tabla and Pavajak / In the park / Drilling a hole / Guru Vandana / Greasy legs / Ski-ing / Gat Kirwani / Dream scene / Party Seacombe / Love scene / Crying / Cowboy music / Fantasy sequins / On the bed / Glass box / Wonderwall to be here / Singing om. *(cd-iss.Jun92)*

— **GEORGE** – moog synthesizer (no vocals)

Zapple Zapple

May 69. (lp) **ELECTRONIC SOUND** [ ] [ ]
– Under the Mersey wall / No time or space.

— He became in-house 'Apple' producer, before gigging with DELANEY & BONNIE late 1969. The BEATLES break-up, and he went solo again with vocals, etc. with **DEREK & THE DOMINOES** (Eric Clapton and his band) / **BADFINGER / BILLY PRESTON** – keyboards / **RINGO STARR, GINGER BAKER** – drums / etc.

Apple Apple

Nov 70. (t-lp) **ALL THINGS MUST PASS** [4] [1]
– I'd have you anytime / My sweet Lord / Wah-wah / Isn't it a pity / What is life / If not for you / Behind that locked door / Let it down / Run of the mill / Beware of darkness / Apple scruffs / Ballad of Frankie Crisp (let it roll) / Awaiting on you all / All things must pass / I dig love / Art of dying / Isn't it a pity / Hear me Lord / Out of the blue / It's Johnny's birthday / Plug me in / I remember Jeep / Thanks for the pepperoni. *(d-cd.iss.May87 on 'E.M.I.')*

Nov 70. (7") **MY SWEET LORD. / ISN'T IT A PITY** [-] [1]

Jan 71. (7") **MY SWEET LORD. / WHAT IS LIFE** [1] [-]
(re-iss.Nov76)

Feb 71. (7") **WHAT IS LIFE. / APPLE SCRUFFS** [-] [10]

Jul 71. (7") **BANGLA-DESH. / DEEP BLUE** [10] [23]

In Jan72, He with other artists released live triple album CONCERT FOR BANGLA-DESH which hit UK No.1 & US No.2. (d-cd-iss.Aug91)

— **GEORGE** now with various session people

May 73. (7") **GIVE ME LOVE (GIVE ME PEACE ON EARTH). / MISS O'DELL** [8] [1]

Jun 73. (lp)(c) **LIVING IN THE MATERIAL WORLD** [2] [1]
– Give me love (give me peace on earth) / Sue me, sue you blues / The light that has lighted the world / Don't let me wait too long / Who can see it / Living in the material world / The Lord loves the one (that loves the Lord) / Be here now / Try some buy some / The day the world gets 'round / That is all. *(cd-iss.Jan92 on 'E.M.I.')*

Dec 74. (7") **DING DONG; DING DONG. / I DON'T CARE ANYMORE** [38] [36] Jan 75

Dec 74. (lp)(c) **DARK HORSE** [ ] [4]
– Hari's on tour (express) / Simply shady / So sad / Bye bye love / Maya love / Ding dong; ding dong / Dark horse / Far East man / Is it he (Jai Sri Krishna). *(re-iss.Dec80 on 'M.f.P.') (cd-iss.Jan92 on 'E.M.I.')*

Feb 75. (7") **DARK HORSE. / HARI'S ON TOUR (EXPRESS)** [ ] [15] Nov 74

Sep 75. (7") **YOU. / WORLD OF STONE** [38] [20]

Oct 75. (lp)(c) **EXTRA TEXTURE (READ ALL ABOUT IT)** [16] [8]
– The answer's at the end / This guitar (can't keep from crying) / You / Ooh baby (you know that I love you) / World of stone / A bit more of you / Can't stop thinking about you / Tired of midnight blue / Grey cloudy lies / His name is legs (ladies & gentlemen). *(cd-iss.Jan92 on 'E.M.I.')*

Feb 76. (7") **THIS GUITAR (CAN'T KEEP FROM CRYING). / MAYA LOVE** [ ] [ ]

Oct 76. (lp)(c) **THE BEST OF GEORGE HARRISON** [ ] [31]
– Something (BEATLES) / If I needed someone (BEATLES) / Here comes the sun (BEATLES) / Taxman (BEATLES) / Think for yourself (BEATLES) / While my guitar gently weeps (BEATLES) / For you blue (BEATLES) / My sweet Lord / Give me love (give me peace on Earth) / You / Bangla-Desh / Dark horse / What is life. *(re-iss.Oct81 on 'MFP') (cd-iss.May87 on 'Parlophone')*

Dark Horse Dark Horse

Nov 76. (7") **THIS SONG. / LEARNING HOW TO LOVE YOU** [ ] [25]

Nov 76. (lp)(c) **THIRTY-THREE AND A THIRD** [35] [11]
– Woman don't you cry for me / Dear one / Beautiful girl / This song / See yourself / It's what you value / True love / Pure Smokey / Crackerbox palace / Learning how to love you. *(cd-iss.Jan92 on 'E.M.I.')*

Jan 77. (7") **CRACKERBOX PALACE. / LEARNING HOW TO LOVE YOU** [-] [19]

Feb 77. (7") **TRUE LOVE. / PURE SMOKEY** [ ] [-]

Jun 77. (7") **IT'S WHAT YOU VALUE. / WOMAN DON'T YOU CRY FOR ME** [ ] [-]

Feb 79. (7") **BLOW AWAY. / SOFT-HEARTED HANA** [-] [16]

Feb 79. (7") **BLOW AWAY. / SOFT TOUCH** [51] [-]

Feb 79. (lp)(c) **GEORGE HARRISON** [39] [14]
– Love comes to everyone / Not guilty / Here comes the moon / Soft- hearted Hana / Blow away / Faster / Your love is forever / Dark sweet lady / Soft touch / If you believe. *(cd-iss.Jan92 on 'E.M.I.')*

Apr 79. (7") **LOVE COMES TO EVERYONE. / SOFT-HEARTED HANA** [ ] [-]

Apr 79. (7") **LOVE COMES TO EVERYONE. / SOFT TOUCH** [-] [ ]

Jul 79. (7")(7"pic-d) **FASTER. / YOUR LOVE IS FOREVER** [ ] [-]

May 81. (7") **ALL THOSE YEARS AGO. / WRITING'S ON THE WALL** [13] [2]

Jun 81. (lp)(c) **SOMEWHERE IN ENGLAND** [13] [11]
– Blood from a clone / Unconsciousness rules / Life itself / All those years ago / Batlimore oriole / Teardrops / That which I have lost / Writing's on the wall / Hong Kong blues / Save the world. *(re-iss.Jul88) (cd-iss.Jan92 on 'E.M.I.')*

Jul 81. (7") **TEARDROPS. / SAVE THE WORLD** [ ] [ ]

Oct 82. (7") **WAKE UP MY LOVE. / GREECE** [ ] [53]

Nov 82. (lp)(c) **GONE TROPPO** [ ] [ ]
– Wake up my love / That's the way it goes / I really love you / Greece / Gone troppo / Mystical one / Unknown delight / Baby don't run away / Dream away / Circles. *(re-iss.Jul88) (cd-iss.Jan92 on 'E.M.I.')*

Jan 83. (7") **I REALLY LOVE YOU. / CIRCLES** [-] [ ]

— Took long time off from solo career to establish his film production work. Returned after nearly five years with new session people.

Sep 87. (lp)(c)(cd) **CLOUD NINE** [10] [8] Nov 87
– Cloud 9 / That's what it takes / Fish on the sand / Just for today / This is love / When we was fab / Devil's radio / Someplace else / Wreck of the Hesperus / Breath away from Heaven / Got my mind set on you.

Oct 87. (7") **GOT MY MIND SET ON YOU. / LAY HIS HEAD** [2] [1]
(12"+=)(12"pic-d+=) – ('A'extended).

Feb 88. (7") **WHEN WE WAS FAB. / ZIGZAG** [25] [23]
(12"+=)(12"pic-d+=)(3"cd-s+=) – That's the way it goes (remix) / ('A'mix).

Jun 88. (7") **THIS IS LOVE. / BREATH AWAY FROM HEAVEN** [55] [ ]
(12"+=) – All those wasted years ago.
(3"cd-s++=) – Hong Kong blues.

— Later in 1988, HARRISON teamed up with BOB DYLAN, ROY ORBISON, JEFF LYNNE and TOM PETTY in The TRAVELLING WILBURYS. He also continued solo work below.

Oct 89. (lp)(c)(cd) **THE BEST OF DARK HORSE (1976-1989)** (compilation) [ ] [ ]
– Poor little girl / Blow away / That's the way it goes / Cockamamie business / Wake up my love / Life itself / Got my mind set on you / Here comes the Moon / Gone troppo / When we was fab / Love comes to everyone / All those years ago / Cheer down. *(c+cd+=)* – Crackerbox Palace.

Nov 89. (7")(c-s) **CHEER DOWN. / POOR LITTLE GIRL** [ ] [-]
(12"+=)(cd-s+=) – Crackerbox palace.

Jul 92. (cd)(c)(d-lp) **LIVE IN JAPAN (live with ERIC CLAPTON AND BAND)** [ ] [ ]
– I want to tell you / Old brown shoe / Taxman / Give me love (give me peace on Earth) / If I needed someone / Something / What is life / Dark horse / Piggies / Got my mind set on you / Cloud nine / Here comes the Sun / My sweet Lord / All those years ago / Cheer down / Devil's radio / Isn't it a pity / While my guitar gently weeps / Roll over Beethoven.

– compilations etc. –

Oct 82. Dark Horse; (d-c) **THIRTY-THREE AND A THIRD / GEORGE HARRISON** [ ] [ ]

Jerry HARRISON (see under ⇒ TALKING HEADS)

Deborah / Debbie HARRY (see under ⇒ BLONDIE)

Grant HART (see under ⇒ HUSKER DU)

Mickey HART (see under ⇒ GRATEFUL DEAD)

Alex HARVEY

Born: 5 Feb'35, The Gorbals, Glasgow, Scotland. After loads of jobs from the early 50's, he played in various skiffle groups. After winning a local talent contest in 1956, he was dubbed 'The TOMMY STEELE Of Scotland'. In 1959, his BIG SOUL BAND backed touring American stars EDDIE COCHRAN and GENE VINCENT. They soon made their way to Germany, where they played many gigs and soon signed to 'Polydor'. They recorded a few lp's, and several 45's (some solo), before he joined the crew of the 'Hair' musical in London's West End. In 1972, he returned to Scotland and found TEAR GAS, who were just about to disband after 2 poorly received lp's. They became The SENSATIONAL ALEX HARVEY BAND, and released, after nationwide tours and signature for 'Vertigo', their debut album 'FRAMED'. Late in '73, he issued the near excellent 'NEXT . . . ', and should have scored with edited cut and fan favourite 'THE FAITH HEALER'. In Oct'74, they secured first UK Top 20 album with 'THE IMPOSSIBLE DREAM', which was followed by a Top 10 album in 1975, and a marvellous Top 10 single rendition of 'DELILAH'. They peaked for another year, but found it difficult to maintain success, with advent of punk. Sadly no longer in the limelight, ALEX died of a heart attack in Belguim on 4th Feb'82. • **Style:** HARVEY's solo R&B roots, were abandoned in the 70's, for more theatrical and comic book rock'n'roll. His buchaneer attitude and attire, was a visionary plus, only matched by his clown-like guitarist ZAL CLEMINSON. • **Songwriters:** Most by himsef and HUGH McKENNA, with additions from either ZAL or D.BATCHELOR. Covered; FRAMED (Leiber-Stoller) / I JUST WANT TO MAKE LOVE TO YOU (Willie Dixon) / NEXT (Jacques Brel) / GIDDY-UP-A-DING-DONG (Freddie Bell & The Bellboys) / THE IMPOSSIBLE DREAM (?) / RIVER OF LOVE (?) / TOMORROW BELONGS TO ME (German national anthem) / DELILAH (hit; Tom Jones) / CHEEK TO CHEEK (Irving Berlin) / LOVE STORY (Jethro Tull) / CRAZY HORSES (Osmonds) / SCHOOL'S OUT (Alice Cooper) / RUNAWAY (Del Shannon) / GOODNIGHT IRENE (Leadbelly) / SHAKIN' ALL OVER (Johnny Kidd) / etc. • **Trivia:** His 'LOCH NESS' lp, released unusually on 'K-Tel', featured only interviews from sightings of the monster.

Recommended: THE COLLECTION (*8). / NEXT . . . (*9)

ALEX HARVEY & HIS SOUL BAND

ALEX – vocals / **RICKY BARNES** – saxophone, vocals / **ISOBEL BOND** – vocals / **GIBSON KEMP** – drums / **IAN HINDS** – organ / **BILL PATRICK** – guitar

Polydor / not issued

Jan 64. (7") **I JUST WANNA MAKE LOVE TO YOU. / LET THE GOOD TIMES ROLL** [ ] [-]

Mar 64. (lp) **ALEX HARVEY AND HIS SOUL BAND (live)** [ ] [-]
– Framed / I ain't worrying baby / Backwater blues / Let the good times roll / Going home / I've got my mojo working / Teensville U.S.A. / New Orleans / Bo Diddley is a gunslinger / When I grow too old to rock / Evil hearted man / I just wanna make love to you / The blind man / Reeling and rocking. *(re-iss.Oct87 Germany)*

Jun 64. (7") **GOT MY MOJO WORKING. / I AIN'T WORRIED BABY** [ ] [-]

— ALEX HARVEY brought in new soul band, (his brother **LES HARVEY** – guitar / **BOBBY THOMPSON** – bass / **GILSON KEMP** – drums)

Jul 65. (7") **AIN'T THAT JUST TOO BAD. / MY KIND OF LOVE** [ ] [-]

Nov 65. (lp) **THE BLUES** [ ] [-]
– Trouble in mind / Honey bee / I learned about woman / Danger zone / The riddle song / Waltzing Matilda / The blues / The big rock candy mountain / The Michegan massacre / No peace / Nobody knows you when you're down and out / St.James infirmary / Strange fruit / Kisses sweeter than wine / Good God almighty.

ALEX HARVEY

solo with session musicians.

Fontana / not iss.

Sep 65. (7") **AGENT O-O-SOUL. / GO AWAY BABY** [ ] [-]

Nov 66. (7") **WORK SONG. / I CAN'T DO WITHOUT YOUR LOVE** [ ] [-]

— HARVEY now backed by **GIANT MOTH:- JIM CONDRON** – guitar, bass / **MOX** – flute / **GEORGE BUTLER** – drums

Decca / not issued

Jul 67. (7") **THE SUNDAY SONG. / HORIZONS** [ ] [-]

Sep 67. (7") **MAYBE SOMEDAY. / CURTAINS FOR MY BABY** [ ] [-]

— with band ROCK WORKSHOP which incl. brother LES and loads of others.

Fontana / not issued

Oct 69. (lp) **ROMAN WALL BLUES** [ ] [-]
– Midnight Moses / Hello L.A., bye bye Birmingham / Broken hearted fairytale / Donna / Roman wall blues / Jumping Jack Flash / Hammer song / Let my bluebird sing / Maxine / Down at Bart's place / Candy.

Nov 69. (7") **MIDNIGHT MOSES. / ROMAN WALL BLUES** [ ] [-]

— ALEX then formed his trio (**IAN ELLIS** – bass, ex-CLOUDS, **DAVE DUFORT** – drums) This was broken up after the death, by stage electrocution, of his brother LES, who had been part of STONE THE CROWS since '69 (Aug72) **ALEX** recruited a whole band

— **TEAR GAS** who had already made two albums – Nov70 'PIGGY GO BETTER' on 'Famous', without the McKENNA brothers. Aug71. 'TEAR GAS' on 'Regal Zono.', with all the members below of –

The SENSATIONAL ALEX HARVEY BAND

(ALEX – vocals, guitar) / **ZAL CLEMINSON** (b. 4 May'49) – guitar, vocals / **CHRIS GLEN** (b. 6 Nov'50) – bass / **HUGH McKENNA** (b.28 Nov'49) – keyboards / **TED McKENNA** (b.10 Mar'50) – drums

Vertigo / Vertigo

Oct 72. (7") **JUNGLE JENNY. / BUFF'S BAR BLUES** [ ] [-]

Dec 72. (lp)(c) **FRAMED** [ ] [ ]
– Framed / Hammer song / Midnight Moses / Isobel Goudie (part 1 – My lady of the night, part 2 – Coitus interruptus, part 3 – The virgin and the hunter) / Buff's bar blues / I just want to make love to you / Hole in her stocking / There's no lights on the Christmas tree, mother, they're burning big Louie tonight / St. Anthony. *(re-iss.Mar79 on 'Mountain', re-iss.+cd '84 on 'Samurai', cd-iss+=)* – Smouldering / Chase it into the night.

Dec 72. (7") **THERE'S NO LIGHTS ON THE CHRISTMAS TREE, MOTHER, THEY'RE BURNING BIG LOUIE TONIGHT. / HARP** [ ] [-]

Nov 73. (lp)(c) **NEXT . . .** [ ] [ ]
– Swampsnake / Gang bang / The faith healer / Giddy up a ding dong / Next / Vambo marble eye / The last of the teenage idols (part I-III). *(re-iss.Mar79 on 'Mountain', re-iss.Mar82 on 'Fame', cd-iss.Jul86 on 'Samurai')*

Feb 74. (7") **THE FAITH HEALER (edit). / ST. ANTHONY** [ ] [-]

Feb 74. (7") **SWAMPSNAKE. / GANG BANG** [-] [-]

Aug 74. (7") **SERGEANT FURY. / GANG BANG** [ ] [-]

Sep 74. (7") **SERGEANT FURY. / TOMAHAWK KID** [-] [ ]

Sep 74. (lp)(c) **THE IMPOSSIBLE DREAM** [16] [ ]
– The hot city symphony; (part 1 – Vambo, part 2 – Man in the Jar) / River of love / Long hair music / Sergeant Fury / Weights made of lead / Money honey – The impossible dream / Tomahawk kid / Anthem. *(re-iss.Mar79 on 'Mountain', re-iss.+cd Jul86 on 'Samurai')*

Nov 74. (7") **ANTHEM. / ('A'version)** [ ] [-]

Apr 75. (lp)(c) **TOMORROW BELONGS TO ME** [9] [ ]
– Action strasse / Snake bite / Soul in chains / The tale of the giant stoneater / Ribs and balls / Give my compliments to the chef / Sharks teeth / Ribs and balls / Shake that thing / Tomorrow belongs to me / To be continued . . . *(re-iss.+cd Jul86 on 'Samurai', cd-iss+=)* – Big boy / Pick it up and kick it.

Vertigo / Atlantic

Jul 75. (7") **DELILAH (live). / SOUL IN CHAINS (live)** [7] [ ]

Sep 75. (lp)(c) **THE SENSATIONAL ALEX HARVEY BAND "LIVE" (live)** [14] [100]
– Fanfare (justly, skillfully, magnanimously) / The faith healer / Tomahawk kid / Vambo / Give my compliments to the chef / Delilah / Framed. *(re-iss.+cd Jul86 on 'Samurai', cd-iss+=)* – I wanna have you back / Jungle Jenny / Runaway / Love story / School's Out. *(re-iss.Apr86 on 'Sahara', re-iss.Oct86 on 'Fame')*

Vertigo / Vertigo

Nov 75. (7") **GAMBLIN' BAR ROOM BLUES. / SHAKE THAT THING** [38] [-]

Mar 76. (7") **RUNAWAY. / SNAKE BITE** [ ] [-]

Mar 76. (lp)(c) **PENTHOUSE TAPES** [14] [ ]
– I wanna have you back / Jungle Jenny / Runaway / Love story / School's out / Goodnight Irene / Say you're mine / Gamblin' bar room blues / Crazy horses / Cheek to cheek. *(re-iss.Mar79 on 'Mountain', re-iss.Nov84 on 'Sahara', re-iss.+cd Jul86 on 'Samurai')*

Mountain / Mountain

May 76. (7") **BOSTON TEA PARTY. / SULTAN'S CHOICE** [13] [ ]

Jul 76. (lp)(c) **SAHB STORIES** [11] [ ]
– Boston Tea Party / Sultan's choice / $25 for a massage / Dogs of war / Dance to your daddy / Amos Moses / Jungle rub out / Sirocco.

Aug 76. (7") **AMOS MOSES. / SATCHEL AND THE SCALP HUNTER** [ ] [ ]

SAHB WITHOUT ALEX

all 4 members without ALEX HARVEY (HUGH – vocals)

Jan 77. (lp)(c) **FOURPLAY** [ ] [ ]
– Smouldering / Chase it into the night / Shake your way to Heaven / Outer boogie / Big boy / Pick it up and kick it / Love you for a lifetime / Too much American pie. *(re-iss.Nov84 on 'Sahara')*

Jan 77. (7") **PICK IT UP AND KICK IT. / SMOULDERING** [ ] [-]

— **ALEX HARVEY** released in Apr 77 solo narrative lp PRESENTS THE LOCH NESS MONSTER on 'K-Tel'.

The SENSATIONAL ALEX HARVEY BAND

reformed **HARVEY, CLEMINSON, T.McKENNA and GLEN** recruited **TOMMY EYRE** – keyboards repl. HUGH

Mountain / Mountain

Aug 77. (7") **MRS. BLACKHOUSE. / ENGINE ROOM BOOGIE** [ ] [-]

Mar 78. (lp)(c) **ROCK DRILL** [ ] [ ]
– The rock drill suite: Rock drill – The dolphins – Rock and roll – King Kong /

Booids / Who murdered sex / Nightmare city / Water beastie / Mrs. Blackhouse. *(re-iss.Nov84 on 'Sahara')*

— (had already split late '77) CHRIS and TED joined ZAL in his own named band. ZAL later joined NAZARETH. TED later joined RORY GALLAGHER and then GREG LAKE BAND. TED and CHRIS later joined MICHAEL SCHENKER GROUP.

ALEX HARVEY BAND

with **TOMMY EYRE** – keyboards / **MATTHEW CANG** – guitar / **GORDON SELLAR** – bass / **SIMON CHATTERTON** – drums

R.C.A. | not issued

Oct 79. (7") **SHAKIN' ALL OVER. / WAKE UP DAVIS** [ ] [-]
Nov 79. (lp)(c) **THE MAFIA STOLE MY GUITAR** [ ] [-]
– Don's delight / Back in the depot / Wait for me mama / The Mafia stole my guitar / Shakin' all over / The whalers (thar she blows) / Oh Sparticus / Just a gigolo / I ain't got nobody. *(re-iss.+cd.Sep91 on 'Demon')*
May 80. (7") **BIG TREE SMALL AXE. / THE WHALERS (THAR SHE BLOWS)** [ ] [-]

ALEX HARVEY died of a heart attack 4th Feb'82 while in Belguim.

– his posthumous releases –

Nov 83. Power Supply; (7") **THE POET AND I. /** [ ] [ ]
Nov 83. Power Supply; (lp)(c) **SOLDIER ON THE WALL** [ ] [-]

– other SAHB compilations, etc. –

May 77. Vertigo; (lp)(c) **BIG HITS AND CLOSE SHAVES** [ ] [ ]
(re-iss.Apr79 on 'Mountain')
Nov 92. Vertigo; (cd)(c) **ALL SENSATIONS** [ ] [-]
Jun 77. Vertigo; (7") **CHEEK TO CHEEK. / JUNGLE JENNY** [ ] [-]
Jul 80. Mountain; (lp)(c) **COLLECTOR'S ITEMS** [ ] [-]
Jul 80. Mountain; (7"m) **DELILAH (live). / BOSTON TEA PARTY / THE FAITH HEALER** [ ] [-]
Aug 82. R.C.A.; (d-lp)(d-c) **THE BEST OF THE SENSATIONAL ALEX HARVEY BAND** [ ] [ ]
– Next / Framed / The faith healer / Tomahawk kid / The hot city symphony; part 1 – Vambo, part 2 – Man in the jar / Sergeant Fury / The tale of the giant stoneater / Action strasse / Delilah / Weights made of lead / Boston Tea Party / Anthem / Runaway / Crazy horses / Big tree small axe / The Mafia stole my guitar / Gang bang / Tomorrow belongs to me. *(re-iss.May84)*
Nov 85. Sahara; (lp) **LEGEND** [ ] [-]
(cd-iss.1986 on 'Samurai')
Jan 86. Sahara; (c) **ANTHOLOGY** [ ] [-]
Apr 86. Aura; (c) **DOCUMENT** [ ] [-]
Sep 86. Castle; (d-lp)(cd) **THE COLLECTION** [ ] [-]
– $25 for a massage / The tale of the giant stoneater / Action strasse / Gang bang / Next / Give my compliments to the chef / Framed / Tomorrow belongs to me / Dance to your daddy / Sgt.Fury / Sultan's choice / Delilah (live) / Soul in chains / The faith healer / Boston tea party / Vambo (part 1) / Dogs of war / There's no lights on the Christmas tree mother, they're burning big Louie tonight / Giddy up a ding dong.
Jul 87. K-Tel; (lp)(c)(cd) **THE BEST OF THE SENSATIONAL ALEX HARVEY BAND** [ ] [-]
– Delilah / The faith healer / Framed / Sergeant Fury / Jungle rub out / Love story / School's out / Boston Tea Party / Gamblin' bar room blues / Next / The man in the jar / Snake bite / Give my compliments to the chef / Cheek to cheek.
Sep 87. Start; (lp)(c)(cd) **PORTRAIT** [ ] [-]
Feb 91. Music Club; (cd)(c) **THE BEST OF S.A.H.B.** [ ] [-]
Oct 91. Windsong; (lp) **LIVE IN CONCERT (live)** [ ] [-]
Nov 94. Windsong; (cd) **LIVE ON THE TEST** [ ] [-]
Jul 94. Success; (cd)(c) **THE BEST OF THE SENSATIONAL ALEX HARVEY BAND** [ ] [-]
Sep 94. Spectrum; (cd)(c) **DELILAH** [ ] [-]

PJ HARVEY

Formed: Yeovil, England . . . 1991 by POLLY JEAN HARVEY, who had just left Bristol-based covers band The AUTOMATIC DILAMINI. They made 3 singles; 'THE CRAZY SUPPER EP', 'I DON'T KNOW YOU BUT . . .' & 'ME AND MY CONSCIENCE', plus album 'THE D IS FOR DRUM' (on 'Idea') during 1986 + 87. PJ HARVEY soon became top self-financed indie band, which led to a near Top 10 success in 1992 with debut Steve Albini (ex-BIG BLACK) produced album 'DRY' (as was next). • **Style:** Uncompromising feminist rock act, led by sculptor POLLY. • **Songwriters:** POLLY, and covers; HIGHWAY 61 (Bob Dylan) / DADDY (Willie Dixon). • **Trivia:** POLLY guested for GRAPE on their 'Baby In A Plastic Bag' single, and also for The FAMILY CAT.

Recommended: DRY (*9) / RID OF ME (*8) / TO BRING YOU MY LOVE (*9)

POLLY HARVEY – vocals, guitar / **STEPHEN VAUGHAN** – bass / **ROB ELLIS** – drums, vocals

Too Pure | not issued

Oct 91. (12")(cd-s) **DRESS. / WATER / DRY** [ ] [-]
(re-iss.Mar92)
Feb 92. (12"ep)(cd-ep) **SHEELA-NA-GOIG. / HAIR / JOE** [69] [-]
Mar 92. (cd)(c)(lp) **DRY** [11] [ ]
– Oh my lover / O Stella / Dress / Victory / Happy and bleeding / Sheela-na-gig / Hair / Joe / Plants and rags / Fountain water, (w/ free demos cd + lp)

Island | Island

Apr 93. (7"ep)(12"ep)(c-ep)(cd-ep) **50 FT. QUEENIE. / REELING / MAN SIZED (demo)** [27] [ ]
Apr 93. (cd)(c)(lp) **RID OF ME** [3] [ ]
– Rid of me / Missed / Legs / Rub till it bleeds / Hook / Man-size sextet / Highway '61 revisited / 50ft. Queenie / Yuri-G / Man-size / Dry / Me-Jane / Snake / Ecstasy
Jul 93. (12"ep)(cd-ep) **MAN-SIZE. / WANG DANG DOODLE / DADDY** [42] [ ]

— drummer ROB ELLIS departed after above.

Oct 93. (cd)(c)(lp) **4-TRACK DEMOS (demos)** [19] [ ]
– Rid of me / Legs / Reeling / Snake / Hook / 50ft Queenie / Driving / Ecstasy / Hardly wait / Rub 'til it bleeds / Easy / M-bike / Yuri-G / Goodnight.
Feb 95. (7"ep)(12"ep)(cd-ep) **DOWN BY THE WATER. / LYING IN THE SUN / SOMEBODY'S DOWN, SOMEBODY'S NAME** [38] [ ]
Feb 95. (cd)(c)(lp) **TO BRING YOU MY LOVE** [12] [40]
– To bring you my love / Meet ze monsta / Working for the man / C'mon Billy / Teclo / Long snake moan / Down by the water / I think I'm a mother / Send his love to me / The dancer. *(re-iss.d-cd Dec95 w/ extra B-sides)*
Jul 95. (12") **C'MON BILLY. / DARLING BE THERE / MANIAC** [29] [ ]
(cd-s+=) – One time too many.
Oct 95. (7"pic-d)(cd-s) **SEND HIS LOVE TO ME / HOOK (live) / WATER (live)** [34] [ ]
(cd-s) – Longtime coming (evening session version) / Harder.

. . . Jan – Jun '96 stop press . . .

— Enjoyed more chart success on duet with NICK CAVE; 'Henry Lee' single released early '96.

HATER (see under ⇒ SOUNDGARDEN)

HAWKWIND

Formed: London, England . . . mid-69 as GROUP X, by ex-FAMOUS CURE members DAVE BROCK and MICK SLATTERY, who were joined by NIK TURNER, TERRY OLLIS, DIK MIK and JOHN HARRISON. They soon became HAWKWIND ZOO, but SLATTERY opted out, for gypsy lifestyle in Ireland, after they signed to 'United Art' late '69. Now as HAWKWIND and after many free concerts (mostly at open-air festivals) they released eponymous debut late summer 1970. With a few personnel changes (which always seemed to be always part of story), they unleashed second album 'IN SEARCH OF SPACE', which gave them initial entry into UK Top 20. The following summer (1972), they smashed the Top 3 with classic 45 'SILVER MACHINE'. It had previously featured on a live 'GREASY TRUCKERS' PARTY' lp, which had them on 1 side only, and a various artists 'GLASTONBURY FAYRE' album. The success of the single, secured them Top 20 placings, on all 4 of their future lp's for 'UA'. In 1976, they signed to 'Charisma', and still found many friends in the buying public. They were still going strong in 1992, but with only DAVE BROCK, the sole originator surviving in a trio with ALAN DAVEY and RICHARD CHADWICK. • **Style:** Drug-loving commune hippies, who mixed heavy psychedelia with electronic space rock music. • **Songwriters:** Mostly by BROCK or CALVERT until latter's departure. ALAN DAVEY finally replaced his writing assets. Other various personnel over the years, also took part in writing. Psi-fi writer MICHAEL MOORCOCK provided them with some words and vox, during mid-70's. • **Trivia:** They formed own 'Flicknife' records to accomodate legion of 'Hawkfans' (their ever-wanting loyal fan club).

Recommended: IN SEARCH OF SPACE (*8) / SPACE RITUAL (*8) / WARRIOR ON THE EDGE OF TIME (*6) / STASIS – THE U.A. YEARS 1971-1975 (*7)

DAVE BROCK – vocals, guitar / **NIK TURNER** – vocals, saxophone / **HUW-LLOYD LANGTON** – guitar repl. MICK SLATTERY (Oct69, when as HAWKWIND ZOO) **JOHN HARRISON** – bass / **TERRY OLLIS** – drums / **DIK MIK** (b. S.McMANUS) – electronics engineer, synthesizers

Liberty | United A..

Jul 70. (7") **HURRY ON SUNDOWN. / MIRROR OF ILLUSION** [ ] [ ]
Aug 70. (lp)(c) **HAWKWIND** [ ] [ ]

– Hurry on sundown / The reason is / Be yourself / Paranoia (part 1 & 2) / Seeing it as you really are / Mirror of illusion. *(re-iss.Sep75 on 'Sunset') (re-iss.Feb84 on 'E.M.I.' hit 75) (re-iss.Feb80 as 'ROCKFILE') (cd-iss.Feb94 on 'Repertoire')*

— (Sep70) **THOMAS CRIMBLE** – bass repl. JOHN HARRISON / **DEL DETTMAR** – synthesizer repl. LANGTON (partway through next album)

— (May71) **DAVE ANDERSON** – bass (ex-AMON DUUL II) repl. CRIMBLE On stage they also added on vocals **BOB CALVERT** (b.South Africa) – poet, vocals, **MICHAEL MOORCOCK** – sci-fi writer and **STACIA** – exotic dancer

United Art United Art

Oct 71. (lp)(c) **IN SEARCH OF SPACE** [18] [ ]
– You shouldn't do that / You know you're only dreaming / Master of the universe / We took the wrong step years ago / Adjust me / Children of the sun. *(re-iss.Jan81 on 'Liberty') (re-iss.Jun85 on 'Liberty-EMI') (cd-iss.May89 & Dec95 on 'Fame')*

— (Sep71) **LEMMY** – bass, vocals repl. ANDERSON

— (Jan72) **SIMON KING** – drums (ex-OPAL BUTTERFLY) repl. OLLIS (group now **KING, LEMMY, BROCK, TURNER, DIK MIK, DETTMAR, CALVERT, STACIA** and p/t **MOORCOCK**)

Jun 72. (7") **SILVER MACHINE. / SEVEN BY SEVEN** [3] [ ]
(re-iss.'76) (Oct78 reached No.34) (re-iss.+12"+7"pic-d.Dec82 hit 67)

Nov 72. (lp)(c) **DOREMI FASOL LATIDO** [14] [ ]
– Brainstorm / Space is deep / Down through the night / One change / Lord of light / Time we left this world today / The watcher. *(re-iss.1979)(re-iss.Jun85 on 'Liberty-EMI') (US cd-iss.Jul91 on 'One Way')*

May 73. (d-lp)(d-c) **SPACE RITUAL – RECORDED LIVE IN LIVERPOOL AND LONDON (live)** [9] [ ]
– Earth calling / Born to go / Down through the night / The awakening / Lord of light / The black corridor / Space is deep / Electronic No.1 / Orgone accumulator / Upside down / 10 seconds of forever / Brainstorm / 7 by 7 / Sonic attack / Time we left this world today / Master of the universe / Welcome to the future. *(re-iss.1979)*

Aug 73. (7") **URBAN GUERILLA. / BRAINBOX POLLUTION** [39] [ ]

— Now a trim sex/septet when DIK MIK and CALVERT departed. The latter going solo. (Apr74) **SIMON HOUSE** – keyboards, synthesizers, violin (ex-THIRD EAR BAND. ex-HIGH TIDE) repl. DETTMAR who emigrated to Canada

Aug 74. (7") **PSYCHEDELIC WARLORDS (DISAPPEAR IN SMOKE). / IT'S SO EASY** [ ] [ ]

Sep 74. (lp)(c) **HALL OF THE MOUNTAIN GRILL** [16] [ ]
– Psychedelic warlords (disappear in smoke) / Wind of change / D-rider / Web weaver / You'd better believe it / Hall of the mountain grill / Lost Johnnie / Wind of change / Goat willow / Paradox. *(re-iss.Jan81 on 'Liberty') (re-iss.Jun85 on 'Liberty-EMI') (re-iss.Sep85 on 'Fame', cd-iss.May89 & Dec95)*

— added **ALAN POWELL** – 2nd drums (ex-STACKRIDGE, ex-CHICKEN SHACK, etc)

Charisma Atco

Mar 75. (7") **KINGS OF SPEED. / MOTORHEAD** [ ] [ ]

May 75. (lp)(c) **WARRIOR ON THE EDGE OF TIME** [13] [ ]
– Assault and battery – part one / The golden void – part two / The wizard blew his horn / Opa-Loka / The demented man / Magnu / Standing at the edge / Spiral galaxy 28948 / Warriors / Dying seas / Kings of speed. *(re-iss.1979)(re-iss.Jan81 + Jun85 on 'Liberty-EMI')*

— **PAUL RUDOLPH** – bass (ex-PINK FAIRIES) repl. LEMMY who formed MOTORHEAD **BOB CALVERT** – vocals returned, STACIA the dancer left to get married. **CALVERT** and **RUDOLPH** now with **BROCK, TURNER, KING, HOUSE** and **POWELL**. note also that MOORCOCK left to form his DEEP FIX

Charisma Charisma

Jul 76. (7") **KERB CRAWLER. / HONKY DORKY** [ ] [-]

Aug 76. (lp)(c) **ASTOUNDING SOUNDS AND AMAZING MUSIC** [33] [-]
– Reefer madness / Steppenwolf / City of lagoons / The aubergine that ate Rangoon / Kerb crawler / Kadu flyer / Chronoglide skyway. *(re-iss.1983)(cd-iss.Apr89 on 'Virgin')*

Jan 77. (7") **BACK ON THE STREETS. / THE DREAM OF ISIS** [ ] [ ]

— **ADRIAN SHAW** – bass TURNER who formed SPHINX then INNER CITY BLUES

Jun 77. (lp)(c) **QUARK, STRANGENESS AND CHARM** [30] [-]
– Spirit of the age / Damnation alley / Fable of a failed race / Quark, strangeness and charm / Hassan I Sah Ba / The forge of Vulcan / Days of the underground / Iron dream. *(re-iss.Oct86) (cd-iss.Apr89)*

Jul 77. (7") **QUARK, STRANGENESS AND CHARM. / THE FORGE OF VULCAN** [ ] [-]

— **PAUL HAYLES** – keyboards repl. HOUSE who joined DAVID BOWIE on tour

HAWKLORDS

BROCK and **CALVERT** recruiting new members **STEVE SWINDELLS** – keyboards (ex-STRING DRIVEN THING, ex-PILOT) / **HARVEY BAINBRIDGE** – bass / **MARTIN GRIFFIN** – drums

Oct 78. (lp)(c) **25 YEARS ON** [48] [-]
– Psi-power / Free fall / Automotion / 25 years / Flying doctor / The only ones / The dead dreams of the cold war kid / The age of the micro man. *(re-iss.Aug82) (cd-iss.Apr89 on 'Virgin')*

Oct 78. (7") **PSI-POWER. / DEATH TRAP** [ ] [-]

Dec 78. (7") **PSI-POWER. / ('A'extended)** [-] [ ]

HAWKWIND

recorded '78 by **BROCK, TURNER, SHAW, KING** and **HAYLES**

Mar 79. (7") **25 YEARS ON. / PXR 5** [ ] [ ]
(12"grey+=) – Only the dead dreams of the cold war kid.

May 79. (lp)(c) **PXR 5** [59] [ ]
– Death trap / Jack of shadows / Uncle Sam's on Mars / Infinity / Life form / Robot / High rise / PXR 5. *(re-iss.Mar84) (cd-iss.Apr89 on 'Virgin')*

— **HAWKWIND** in 1979 were **SIMON KING** – drums returned from QUASAR, to repl. GRIFFITHS in Dec78 (CALVERT left to go solo). **TIM BLAKE** – keyboards (ex-GONG)repl. SWINDELLS who went solo, added **HUW-LLOYD LANGTON** – guitar who returned from QUASAR, band now – **BROCK, LANGTON, BAINBRIDGE, KING** and **BLAKE**

Bronze not issued

Jul 80. (lp)(c) **LIVE 1979 (live)** [15] [ ]
– Shot down in the night / Motorway city / Spirit of the age / Brainstorm / Lighthouse / Master of the universe / Silver machine.

Jul 80. (7") **SHOT DOWN IN THE NIGHT (live). / URBAN GUERILLA (live)** [59] [-]

— **GINGER BAKER** – drums (ex-CREAM, ex-BLIND FAITH, ex-AIRFORCE etc) repl. KING who teamed up with SWINDELLS

Nov 80. (7") **WHO'S GONNA WIN THE WAR. / NU-CLEAR TOYS** [ ] [ ]

Nov 80. (blue-lp)(c) **LEVITATION** [21] [ ]
– Levitation / Motorway city / Psychosis / World of tiers / Prelude / Who's gonna win the war / Space chase / The 5th second forever / Dust of time. *(re-iss.+cd.Jul87 on 'Castle')*

— **MARTIN GRIFFIN** – drums returned to repl. BAKER / **KEITH HALE** – keyboards repl. BLAKE

R.C.A. not issued

Oct 81. (7") **ANGELS OF DEATH. / TRANS-DIMENSIONAL** [ ] [-]

Oct 81. (lp)(c) **SONIC ATTACK** [19] [-]
– Sonic attack / Rocky paths / Psychosonia / Virgin of the world / Angels of death / Living on the edge / Coded language / Disintigration / Streets of fear / Lost chances.

May 82. (lp)(c) **CHURCH OF HAWKWIND** [26] [-]
– Angel voices / Nuclear drive / Star cannibal / The phenomena of luminosity / Fall of Earth city / The church / The joker at the gate / Some people never die / Light specific data / Experiment with destiny / The last Messiah / Looking in the future. *(cd-iss.Jun94 on 'Dojo')*

— **NIK TURNER** – vocals, saxophone returned to repl. HALE

Aug 82. (7") **SILVER MACHINE (remix). / PSYCHEDELIC WARLORDS (remix)** [ ] [-]

Oct 82. (lp)(c) **CHOOSE YOUR MASQUES** [29] [-]
– Choose your masques / Dream worker / Arrival in Utopia / Silver machine / Void city / Solitary mind games / Fahrenheit 451 / The scan / Waiting for tomorrow.

Flicknife not issued

Oct 83. (lp)(c) **ZONES** (live, with other 80's line-ups) [57] [-]
– Zones / Dangerous vision / Running through the back brain / The island / Motorway city / Utopia 84 / Society alliance / Sonic attack / Dream worker / Brainstorm. *(re-iss.Mar84 on pic-lp)*

Oct 83. (7") **MOTORWAY CITY (live). / MASTER OF THE UNIVERSE (live)** [ ] [-]

Jan 84. (7") **NIGHT OF THE HAWKS. / GREEN FINNED DEMON** [ ] [-]
(12"ep) **THE EARTH RITUAL PREVIEW** (+=) – Dream dancers / Dragons + fables.

Nov 84. (lp)(c) **THIS IS HAWKWIND, DO NOT PANIC** [ ] [-]
– Psi power / Levitation / Circles / Space chase / Death trap / Angels of death / Shot down in the night / Stonehenge decoded / Watching the grass grow.

— **ALAN DAVEY** – bass, vocals repl. BAINBRIDGE and TURNER / **CLIVE DEAMER** – drums repl. GRIFFIN

Nov 85. (lp)(c)(cd) **CHRONICLE OF THE BLACK SWORD** [65] [-]
– Song of the swords / Shade gate / Sea king / Pulsing cavern / Elric the enchanter / Needle gun / Zarozinia / Demise / Sleep of a thousand tears / Chaos army / Horn of destiny. *(cd-iss.w / 3 extra tracks)*

Nov 85. (7") **NEEDLE GUN. / ARIOCH** [ ] [-]
(12"+=) – Song of the swords.

Mar 86. (7") **ZAROZINIA. / ASSAULT AND BATTERY** [ ] [-]
(12"+=) – Sleep of a thousand tears.

— **HAWKWIND** are now **BROCK**, as DR. HASBEEN – vocals, guitar, keys, synthesizers, **LANGTON, DAVEY, BAINBRIDGE** now vocals, keyboards, synthesizer and **DANNY THOMPSON** – drums, percussion, vocals

G.W.R. Road-runner

May 88. (lp)(c)(cd) **THE XENON CODEX** [79] [ ] 1989
– The war I survived / Wastelands of sleep / Neon skyline / Lost chronicles / Tides / Heads / Heads / Mutation zone / E.M.C. / Sword of the east / Good evening.

(US-iss. on pic-d)

— **BROCK, BAINBRIDGE, DAVEY** plus **SIMON HOUSE, RICHARD CHADWICK & BRIDGETT WISHART**

Oct 90. (cd)(c)(lp) **SPACE BANDITS** [70] [-]
– Images / Black elk speaks / Wings / Out of the shadows / Realms / Ship of dreams / TV suicide.

Essential not issued

May 92. (cd)(c)(d-lp) **ELECTRIC TEEPEE** [53] [-]
– L.S.D. / Blue shift / Death of war / The secret agent / Garden pests / Space dust / Snake dance / Mask of the morning / Rites of Netherworld / Don't understand / Sadness runs deep / Right to decide / Going to Hawaii / Electric teepee. *(re-iss.Jul95 on 'Dojo')*

Oct 93. (cd)(c)(lp) **IT'S THE BUSINESS OF THE FUTURE TO BE DANGEROUS** [75] [ ]
– It's the business of the future to be dangerous / Space is their (Palestine) / Tibet is not China (pt.1 & 2) / Let barking dogs lie / Wave upon wave / Letting in the past / The camera that could lie / 3 or 4 erections during the course of the night / Technotropic zone exists / Give me shelter / Avante.

Emergency not issued

Sep 94. (12"ep)(cd-ep) **QUARK, STRANGENESS & CHARM / UNCLE SAM'S ON MARS / BLACK SUN** [ ] [-]

Sep 94. (cd)(d-lp) **THE BUSINESS TRIP** [ ] [-]
– Altair / Quark strangeness and charm / LSD / The camera that would lie / Green finned demon / Do that / The day a wall came down / Berlin axis / Void of golden light / Right stuff / Wastelands / The dream goes on / Right to decide / The dream has ended / The future / Terra mystica.

Sep 95. (12"ep)(cd-ep) **AREA S.4.** [ ] [-]
– Alien / Sputnik Stan / Medley: Death trap – Wastelands of sleep – Dream has . . ..

Oct 95. (cd)(lp) **ALIEN 4** [ ] [-]
– Abducted / Alien (I am) / Reject your human touch / Blue skin / Beam me up / Vega / Xenonorph / Journey / Sputnik Stan / Kapal / Festivals / Deah trap / Wastelands / Are you losing your mind.

. . . Jan – Jun '96 stop press . . .

May 96. (cd)(lp) **LOVE IN SPACE (live October 1995)** [ ] [-]

– compilations, etc. –

1973. United Artists; (d7") **HURRY ON SUNDOWN. / MASTER OF THE UNIVERSE/ / SILVER MACHINE. / ORGONE ACCUMULATOR** [-] [ ]

Apr 76. United Artists; (lp)(c) **ROADHAWKS (live in the 70's)** [34] [ ]
– Hurry on sundown / Paranoia / You shouldn't do that / Silver machine / Urban guerilla / Space is deep / Wind of change / The golden void. *(re-iss.Apr84 on 'Fame')*

Feb 77. United Artists; (lp)(c) **MASTERS OF THE UNIVERSE** [ ] [ ]
(re-iss.May82 on 'Fame', re-iss.+cd Jun87 & Dec95) (re-iss.+cd.1991 on 'Marble Arch') (re-iss.cd+c Jul94 on 'Success')

Sep 80. Charisma; (lp)(c) **REPEAT PERFORMANCE** [ ] [-]

Mar 83. Charisma; (d-c) **QUARK, STRANGENESS & CHARM / PXR 5** [ ] [-]
(re-iss.'88)

May 81. Flicknife; (12"ep) **HURRY ON SUNDOWN. / KINGS OF SPEED / SWEET MISTRESS OF PAIN** [ ] [-]
(re-iss.Dec83)

Jul 81. Flicknife; (7")(12") **MOTORHEAD. / VALIUM TEN** [ ] [-]
(re-iss.12" Oct82)

Nov 81. Flicknife; (12") **OVER THE TOP. / FREEFALL / DEATH TRAP (by "SONIC ASSASSINS")** [ ] [-]

Mar 82. Flicknife; (lp)(c) **FRIENDS & RELATIONS** (1/2 live '77-78, 1/2 studio '82) [ ] [-]
(re-iss.Nov83) (re-iss.cd+c Nov94 on 'Emporio')

Jun 82. Flicknife; (7") **WHO'S GONNA WIN THE WAR. / TIME OFF (as "HAWKLORDS")** [ ] [-]

Feb 83. Flicknife; (7") **HURRY ON SUNDOWN. / LORD OF THE HORNETS / DODGEM DUKE** [ ] [-]

1983. Flicknife; (lp) **TWICE UPON A TIME: HAWKWIND FRIENDS AND RELATIONS VOL.2** [ ] [-]

Jun 84. Flicknife; (10"m-lp) **INDEPENDENTS DAY** [ ] [-]
(re-iss.Nov88 on 'Thunderbolt')

Feb 85. Flicknife; (lp)(c) **HAWKWIND, FRIENDS AND RELATIONS VOL.3** [ ] [-]
(c-iss.with VOL.1 on reverse / other c-iss.with VOL.2 on reverse)

Jul 86. Flicknife; (7") **MOTORHEAD. / HURRY ON SUNDOWN** [ ] [-]

Nov 86. Flicknife; (lp)(c) **INDEPENDENTS DAY VOL.2** [ ] [-]

Apr 87. Flicknife; (lp)(c) **CUT AND INTAKES** [ ] [-]
(cd+=) – (2 extra tracks).

Oct 87. Flicknife; (3xbox-pic-lp's/+lp) **OFFICIAL PICTURE LOGBOOK** [ ] [-]
– ('STONEHENGE' / 'BLACK SWORD' / 'OUT & INTAKE' / '(interview)' lp *(cd-iss.Nov94 on 'Dojo')*)

Nov 88. Flicknife; (cd) **ZONES / STONEHENGE** [ ] [-]

Dec 88. Flicknife; (d-lp)(c)(cd) **THE TRAVELLERS AND TRUST** [ ] [-]

Jul 83. Illuminated; (d-lp) **TEXT OF FESTIVAL (live '70-72)** [ ] [-]
(1-lp re-iss.Feb85 as 'IN THE BEGINNING') (re-iss.Dec88 on 'Thunderbolt', cd-iss.first 3 sides)

Nov 84. A.P.K.; (d-lp)(d-c) **SPACE RITUAL 2 (live)** [ ] [-]
(cd-iss.1987)

Jul 85. Demi Monde; (lp) **HAWKWIND '73** [ ] [-]
(cd-iss.'87 on 'Castle')

Feb 85. Demi Monde; (lp) **BRING ME THE HEAD OF YURI GAGARIN** (live '73 Empire Pool) [ ] [-]
(cd-iss.Nov92)

Jul 85. Dojo; (lp) **70-73** [ ] [-]

May 85. Mausoleum; (lp) **UTOPIA 84** [ ] [-]

Nov 85. Mausleum; (lp) **WELCOME TO THE FUTURE** [ ] [-]

Nov 85. Obsession; (lp) **RIDICULE** [ ] [-]
(re-iss.of disc 2 of 'SPACE RITUAL') (re-iss.1990)

Samurai not issued

Nov 85. Samurai; (lp) **ANTHOLOGY – HAWKWIND VOL.1** [ ] [-]
(cd+=) – Silver machine. *(re-iss.pic-lp.Nov86 as 'APPROVED HISTORY OF . . . ')(re-iss.Apr90 as 'ACID DAZE 1' on 'Receiver')*

Mar 86. Samurai; (lp)(c)(cd) **ANTHOLOGY – HAWKWIND VOL. 2** [ ] [-]
(cd-iss.1986 extra 4 tracks) (re-iss.Apr90 as 'ACID DAZE 2' on 'Receiver')

May 86. Samurai; (7")(7"sha-pic-d) **SILVER MACHINE. / MAGNU** [ ] [-]
(12"+=) – Angels of death.

Jul 86. Samurai; (lp) **ANTHOLOGY – HAWKWIND VOL.3** [ ] [-]
(re-iss.Apr90 as 'ACID DAZE 3' on 'Receiver')

Jul 86. Hawkfan; (lp) **HAWKFAN 12** [ ] [-]

Sep 86. Castle; (d-lp)(d-c) **THE COLLECTION (PTS.1 & 2)** [ ] [-]
(cd-iss.Dec86 omits some tracks

Dec 88. Castle; (d-lp)(d-cd) **LEVITATION / HAWKWIND LIVE** [ ] [-]

Jun 87. R.C.A.; (lp)(c) **ANGELS OF DEATH** [ ] [-]

Sep 87. Start; (lp)(c)(cd) **BRITISH TRIBAL MUSIC** [ ] [-]

Dec 87. Thunderbolt; (lp)(c)(cd) **EARLY DAZE THE BEST OF . . .** [ ] [-]

Sep 88. Vigin; (cd) **SPIRIT OF THE AGE** [ ] [-]
(re-iss.+c.Oct91 on 'Elite')(re-iss cd, Sep 93)

May 89. Powerhouse; (lp)(c)(cd) **NIGHT OF THE HAWKS** [ ] [-]
(cd-iss. has 3 extra tracks)

Mar 89. Avanti; (cd) **IRONSTRIKE** [ ] [-]

May 89. Legacy; (lp) **LIVE CHRONICLES** [ ] [-]

1990. Action Replay; (cd)(c) **BEST AND THE REST OF HAWKWIND** [ ] [-]

Mar 90. Receiver; (2xcd-box)(3xlp-box) **ACID DAZE (re-issue)** [ ] [-]
(3 VOLUMES re-iss.cd Jul93)

Dec 90. Receiver; (12"blue-ep) **THE EARLY YEARS LIVE** [ ] [-]
– Silver machine / Spirit of the age / Urban guerilla / Born to go.

May 90. E.M.I.; (cd)(c)(lp) **STASIS, THE U.A. YEARS 1971-1975** [ ] [-]
– Urban guerilla / Psychedelic warlords (disappear in smoke) / Brainbox pollution / 7 by 7 / Paradox / Silver machine / You'd better believe it / Lord of light / The black corridor (live) / Space is deep (live) / You shouldn't do that (live). *(re-iss.cd Dec95 on 'Fame')*

1990. Capitol; (c) **METAL CLASSICS 2: BEST OF HAWKWIND** [-] [ ]

1990. Knight; (cd)(c) **NIGHT RIDING** [ ] [-]

Jun 91. G.W.R.; (cd)(c)(lp) **PALACE SPRINGS** [ ] [-]
– (remixed tracks from 'WARRIORS . . . ' & 'XENON . . .)

Oct 91. Windsong; (cd)(c) **BBC RADIO 1 LIVE IN CONCERT (live)** [ ] [-]

Feb 92. Raw Fruit; (cd) **FRIDAY ROCK SHOW SESSIONS (live '86)** [ ] [-]

May 92. Essential; (3xcd-box) **ANTHOLOGY (re-issue)** [ ] [-]

Jun 92. Anagram; (cd)(c)(lp) **MIGHTY HAWKWIND CLASSICS 1980-1985** [ ] [-]

Jun 93. Real; (12"ep)(c-ep)(cd-ep) **SPIRIT OF THE AGE (The Solstice remixes)** [ ] [-]

Nov 93. Real; (12"ep)(cd-ep) **DECIDE YOUR FUTURE. / ?** [ ] [-]

Mar 94. Charly; (cd) **IN THE BEGINNING** [ ] [-]

Mar 94. Emergency Broadcast; (lp) **UNDISCLOSED FILES** [ ] [-]

Apr 94. Cleopatra; (cd) **LORD OF LIGHT** [ ] [-]

Apr 94. Cleopatra; (cd) **PSYCHEDELIC WARLORDS** [ ] [-]

Dec 94. Cyclops; (cd) **CALIFORNIA BRAINSTORM** [ ] [-]

Feb 95. Emergency Broadcast; (cd) **UNDISCLOSED FILES – ADDENDUM** [ ] [-]

Mar 95. Anagram; (cd) **THE RARITIES . . .** [ ] [-]

May 95. Spectrum; (cd) **SILVER MACHINE** [ ] [-]

Oct 95. Anagram; (cd) **INDEPENDENTS DAY VOLUMES 1 & 2** [ ] [-]

DAVE BROCK

Hawkfan not issued

Jun 83. (7") **ZONES / PROCESSED (as "DR.TECHNICAL & THE MACHINES")** [ ] [-]

Flicknife not issued

Sep 83. (7")(7"pic-d) **SOCIAL ALLIANCE. / RAPING ROBOTS IN THE STREET** [ ] [-]

Apr 86. (lp) **EARTHED TO THE GROUND** [ ] [-]

– Earth to the ground / Assassination / Green finned demon / Spirits / Sweet obsession / Oscillations / Machine dreams / Now is the winter of our discontent / On the case.

Apr 88. (lp)(c) **AGENT OF CHAOS ("DAVE BROCK & HIS AGENTS OF CHAOS")** [ ] [-]
– High tech cities / A day in the office / Hades deep / Words of a song / Heads / Nocturn / Wastelands of sleep / Empty dreams / Into the realms / Mountain in the sky. *(cd-iss.May89, with 1984 album minus 2 tracks)*

Emergency | not issued

Jul 95. (cd) **STRANGE TRIPS AND PIPE DREAMS** [ ] [-]
– Hearing aid test / White zone / UFO line / Space / Pipe dream / Self / Something's going on / Bosnia / Parasites are here on Earth / Gateway / It's never too late / La forge / Encounters.

HUW LLOYD-LANGTON GROUP

Flicknife | not issued

Jul 83. (7") **WIND OF CHANGE. / OUTSIDE THE LAW** [ ] [-]
Dec 83. (lp) **OUTSIDE THE LAW** [ ] [-]
– Outside the law / Five to four / Talk to you / Rocky paths / Space chase / Waiting for tomorrow / Mark of gain / Psychedelic warlords. (incl. 2 'Hawkwind' tracks). (free 7" w/a) – WORKING TIME. / I SEE YOU

Ultra Noise | not issued

Jul 84. (12") **DREAMS THAT FADE AWAY. / OUTSIDE THE LAW** [ ] [-]
Mar 85. (lp) **NIGHT AIR** [ ] [-]

Gas | not issued

Apr 86. (lp) **LIKE AN ARROW . . . (THROUGH THE HEART)** [ ] [-]

G W.R. | not issued

Aug 88. (lp)(c) **TIME SPACE AND LLG** [ ] [-]

He released other album in 1991 'ELEGY', after departure from HAWKWIND. In 1994 he issued 'RIVER RUN' for 'Allegro' records.

ROBERT CALVERT

United Art | United Art

May 74. (lp) **CAPTAIN LOCKHEED AND THE STARFIGHTERS** [ ] [ ]
– Franz Joseph Strauss / The aerospace inferno / Aircraft salesman / The widow maker / Test pilots / The right stuff / Board meeting / The song of the gremlin / Ground crew / Hero with a wing / Ground control to pilot / Ejection / Interview / I resign / The song of the gremlin (part 2) / Bier garten / Catch a falling starfighter (the gremlin). *(re-iss.+cd Jan87 on 'B.G.O.')*
Jun 74. (7") **CATCH A FALLING STARFIGHTER (THE GREMLIN). / EJECTION** [ ] [ ]

—— (above as "CAPTAIN LOCKHEED & THE STARFIGHTERS")

Sep 75. (lp) **LUCKY LIEF AND THE LONGSHIPS** [ ] [ ]
– Ship of fools / The lay of the surfers / Brave new world / Voyaging to inland / The making of Midgare / Moonshine in the mountains / Magical potion / Stormchant of the Skraelings / Volstead o vodeo do / Phase locked lopp / Ragna rock. *(cd-iss.Jan89 on 'BGO')*

Flicknife | not issued

1981. (7") **LORD OF THE HORNETS. / THE GREENFLY & THE ROSE** [ ] [-]

A-side | not issued

Sep 81. (m-lp) **HYPE (THE SONGS OF TOM MAHLER)** [ ] [-]
– Over my head / Ambitious / It's the same / Hanging out on the seafront / Sensitive / Evil rock / We like to be frightened / Teen ballad of Deano / Flight 105 / The luminous green glow of the dials of the dashboard (at night) / Greenfly and the rose / Lord of the hornets. *(cd-iss.Dec89 on 'See For Miles')*

Flicknife | not issued

Sep 84. (m-lp) **FREQ** [ ] [-]
– Ned Ludd / Acid rain / All the machines are quiet / Picket line / The cool courage of the bomb squad / Work song. *(cd-iss.Jun92 as 'FREQ REVISITED', with 2 extra) – Lord of the hornets / The greenfly and the rose.*
Apr 86. (lp) **TEST TUBE CONCEIVED** [ ] [-]
– Telekinesis / I hear voices / Fanfare for the perfect race / On line / Save them from the scientists / Fly on the wall / Thanks to the scientists / ? / In vitro / Breed / The rah rah band. *(cd-iss.Aug87 on 'Cd Label')*

On 14 Aug'88, ROBERT CALVERT died of a heart attack.

– (CALVERT) posthumous, etc. –

Clear | not issued

Aug 89. (lp) **ROBERT CALVERT AT THE QUEEN ELIZABETH HALL (live)** [ ] [-]
(re-iss.cd May93 on 'B.G.O.')

B.G.O | not issued

Oct 92. (cd) **BLUEPRINTS FROM THE CELLAR** [ ] [-]

MICHAEL MOORCOCK

(whilst a member of HAWKWIND)

United Art | United Art

May 75. (lp) **NEW WORLD'S FAIR** [ ] [ ]
(cd-iss.Jun95 on 'Dojo')

MICHAEL MOORCOCK & DEEP FIX

Flicknife | not issued

Dec 80. (7") **DODGEM DUDE. / STARCRUSHER** [ ] [-]
1982. (7"ltd.) **THE BROTHEL OF ROSENSTRASSE. / TIME CENTRE** [ ] [-]

He and label 'Cyborg' released in May92 a cass 'BROTHEL IN ROSENSTRASSE'.

NIK TURNER

("SPHYNX")with **TIM BLAKE & MIQUETTE GIRAUDY** – synthesizers / **MORRIS PERT & ALAN POWELL** – percussion / **MIKE HOWLETT** – bass / **STEVE HILLAGE** – guitar

Charisma | not issued

Jun 78. (lp) **XITINTODAY** [ ] [-]
– The awakening / Pyramid spell / Tha hall of double truth / Anabus Thoth / Horos, Isis & Nepthys.

—— ("INNER CITY UNIT") with **MICK STUPP** – drums / **BAZ MAGENTO** – bass / **DEAD FRED** – keyboards, vocals **TREN THOMAS** – guitar, vocals

Riddle | not issued

Oct 79. (7") **SOLITARY ASHTRAY. / SO TRY AS ID** [ ] [-]
1980. (lp) **PASS OUT (THE 360° PSYCHO DELERIA SOUND)** [ ] [-]
(cd-iss.Feb90 on 'Oldhitz', w/2 extra)
Jul 80. (7") **PARADISE BEACH. / AMYL NITRATE** [ ] [-]

—— **DON FERARI** – drums repl. STUPP / **RAY BURNS** (CAPTAIN SENSIBLE) – guitar repl. BAZ added **BILL BOSTON** – horns / **MAX WALL** – vocals

Avatar | not issued

May 81. (lp) **THE MAXIMUM EFFECT** [ ] [-]
Sep 81. (7"red) **BEER, BACCY, BINGO, BENIDORM. / IN THE MOOD (NUDE)** [ ] [-]
Feb 82. (7") **BONES OF ELVIS. / SID'S SONG** [ ] [-]

Flicknife | not issued

Jul 82. (lp)(c) **PUNKADELIA** [ ] [-]
– Watching the grass grow / Space invaders / God disco / Disco tango / Polythene / Cars eat with autoface / Gas money / Blue mine haggard robot / Alright on the flight / Bildeborg.

—— (not sure about this line-up)

Demi Monde | not issued

Dec 84. (lp) **NEW ANATOMY** [ ] [-]
– Young girls / Convoy / Beyond the stars / Help shark / Hectic electric / Birdland / Lonesome train / Forbidden planet / Stop the city / Doctor Strange / Wild hunt. *(cd-iss.Mar93 on 'Thunderb.')*

Flicknife | not issued

Sep 85. (lp) **THE PRESIDENT'S TAPES** [ ] [-]

Jettisound | not issued

Oct 85. (m-lp) **BLOOD AND BONES** [ ] [-]
– Blood and bones / Little black egg / Paint your windows white / Help sharks.

—— TURNER later issued 'PROPHETS OF TIME' in 1994 for 'Cleopatra'.

NIK TURNER / ROBERT CALVERT

Pompadour | not issued

1982. (lp) **ERSATZ** [ ] [-]

STEVE SWINDELLS

(80's with SIMON KING, HUW-LLOYD LANGTON, and NIC POTTER

R.C.A. | not issued

1974. (lp) **MESSAGES** [ ] [ ]
– Miles away again / Energy crisis / The Earl's Court case / Living in sin / I don't like eating meat / Shake up your soul / Surrender / I can't see where the light switch is / Messages from Heaven.

Atco | not issued

Oct 80. (7") **SHOT DOWN IN THE NIGHT. / IT'S ONLY ONE NIGHT IN YOUR LIFE** [ ] [-]
Oct 80. (lp) **FRESH BLOOD** [ ] [-]
– Turn it on, turn it off / Fresh blood / I feel alive / Is it over now / Low life Joe / Bitter and twisted / I don't wait on the stairs / Down on Love street / Figures of authority / Shot down in the night.
Dec 80. (7") **TURN IT ON, TURN IT OFF. / LOW LIFE JOE** [ ] [-]

TIM BLAKE

—— also had solo releases, mainly in France 1977 + 1978. CRYSTAL MACHINE lp + BLAKE'S NEW JERUSALEM lp on 'Egg' records. The later was issued UK Nov78 on 'Barclay Towers'. The cds were given light there in 1992 on 'Mantra' label. He issued 'MAGICK' cd in US 1991 on 'Voiceprint'.

ALAN DAVEY

Hawkfan — not issued

Oct 87. (d7") **THE ELF EP** [ ] [-]
– Solar jug / Cosmic dawn / Chinese whispers / Ode to a brass assassin / The switch (don't touch).

Isaac HAYES

Born: 20 Aug'42, Covington, Tennessee, USA. As a teenager he moved to Memphis, where he learned to play sax and piano. He was soon invited to session for the 'Stax' label. The following year, he formed writing partnership with DAVID PORTER, who went on to pen for 'Stax' artists OTIS REDDING, SAM & DAVE, EDDIE FLOYD, etc. After a dismal debut lp in 1968, his next 'HOT BUTTERED SOUL' gave him a US Top10 placing, gaining wide respect from critics for his venture into extended classics (noteably the 18-min.+ 'BY THE TIME I GET TO PHOENIX'). Late '71, his 'THEME FROM SHAFT' gave him international smash hit, reaching peak spot in the US. It's full version which won an Oscar, was from the (black detective) No.1 film soundtrack. After a couple more excursions into film scores, he left 'Enterprise-Stax', due to squabbles over non-payments. In 1975 he signed to 'A.B.C.', but after mediocre album sales and declaring bankruptcy in '77, he shifted to 'Polydor'. In the 80's, he became more interested in film acting, with sparse trips back into the studio. • **Style:** Sophisticated and sensuous soul singer, who breathed and orchestrated new life into black music. His sexy? macho (bare-chested) aura, made him dub himself The BLACK MOSES. He diversified into a more disco-orientated sound when he formed The ISAAC HAYES MOVEMENT in the mid-70's. He introduced soul-rap into his early work, years ahead of its commerciality in the late 70's. • **Songwriters:** HAYES wrote own work alongside covers; WALK ON BY (Bacharach-David) / BY THE TIME I GET TO PHOENIX (Jim Webb) / I STAND ACCUSED (Jerry Butler) / THE LOOK OF LOVE (Lesley Gore) / NEVER CAN SAY GOODBYE (Jackson 5) / YOU'VE LOST THAT LOVIN' FEELIN' (Righteous Brothers) / LET'S STAY TOGETHER (Al Green) / HEY GIRL (Freddie Scott) / FRAGILE (Sting) / LET'S GO OUT TONIGHT (Blue Nile) / etc. • **Trivia:** When HAYES was Stax writer with PORTER, he co-wrote SOUL MAN and HOLD ON, I'M COMIN and others for SAM & DAVE.

Recommended: ISAAC'S MOODS – THE BEST OF ISAAC HAYES (*8) / HOT BUTTERED SOUL (*9) / THE BEST OF SHAFT (*7) / BRANDED (*7)

ISAAC HAYES – vocals, keyboards, etc. with Stax session men **DUCK DUNN and AL JACKSON**

Stax — Enterprise

1968. (lp) **PRESENTING ISAAC HAYES** [ ] [ ]
– Precious, precious / When I fall in love / I just want to make love to me / Rock me baby / Going to Chicago blues / Misty / You don't know like I know.
– (re-iss.as 'IN THE BEGINNING' Mar72 on 'Atlantic')

1968. (7") **GOING TO CHICAGO BLUES. / PRECIOUS PRECIOUS** [-] [ ]

Oct 69. (lp) **HOT BUTTERED SOUL** [ ] [8] Jul 69
– Walk on by / Hyperbollesyllaciscesquelalymistc / One woman / By the time I get to Phoenix. *(re-iss.Aug74 + Aug81 + Nov87) (cd-iss.Jun91 on 'Stax-Ace')*

Sep 69. (7") **BY THE TIME I GET TO PHOENIX. / WALK** [ ] [37] Aug 69
ON BY [30]

Nov 69. (7") **THE MISTLETOE AND ME. / WINTER SNOW** [-] [ ]

May 70. (lp) **THE ISAAC HAYES MOVEMENT** [ ] [8] Apr 70
– I stand accused / One big unhappy family / I just don't know what to do with myself / Something. *(re-iss.Aug74) (re-iss.+cd.Feb90)*

Aug 70. (7") **I STAND ACCUSED. / I JUST DON'T KNOW WHAT TO DO WITH MYSELF** [ ] [42] Jul 70
(re-iss.US 1975)(other 45's from early to mid'70's were also re-iss.)

Dec 70. (lp) **TO BE CONTINUED** [ ] [11] Nov 70
– (monologue) / Ike's rap 1 / Our day will come / The look of love / Ike's mood – You've lost that lovin' feelin' / Runnin' out of fools. *(re-iss.Aug74 + Oct81) (cd-iss.Feb91 on 'Stax-Ace')*

Feb 71. (7") **THE LOOK OF LOVE. / IKE'S MOOD** [ ] [79]

May 71. (7") **NEVER CAN SAY GOODBYE. / I CAN'T HELP IT IF I'M STILL IN LOVE** [ ] [22]

Sep 71. (7") **YOU'VE LOST THAT LOVIN' FEELIN'. / OUR DAY WILL COME** [ ] [-]

Nov 71. (7") **THEME FROM SHAFT. / CAFE REGIO'S** [4] [1] Oct 71

Dec 71. (d-lp)(c) **SHAFT (Soundtrack)** [17] [1] Aug 71
– Theme from Shaft * / Bumpy's lament / Walk from Regio's / Ellie's love theme / Shaft's cab ride / Cafe Regio's / Early Sunday morning / Be yourself / A friend's place / Soulsville * / No name bar / Bumpy's blues / Shaft strikes again / Do your thing * / (the end theme). *(tracks *= have vocals)*

(above has background vocals by **HOT BUTTERED + SOUL**)

Feb 72. (d-lp)(c) **BLACK MOSES** [38] [10] Dec 71
– Never can say goodbye / (They long to be) Close to you / Nothing takes the place of you / Man's temptation / Part time love / Ike's rap – A brand new me / Going in circles / Gonna give you up / Ike's rap 2 – Help me love / Need to belong / Good love / Ike's rap 3 – Your love is so doggone good / For the good times / I'll never fall in love again. *(re-iss.Aug74) (re-iss.+cd.Sep90 on 'Stax-Ace')*

Mar 72. (7") **DO YOUR THING. / ELLIE'S LOVE THEME** [ ] [30] Feb 72

Apr 72. (7") **LET'S STAY TOGETHER. / AIN'T THAT LOVING YOU (FOR MORE REASONS THAN ONE)** [ ] [-]

Apr 72. (7") **LET'S STAY TOGETHER. / SOULSVILLE** [-] [48]

May 72. (7") **AIN'T THAT LOVING YOU (FOR MORE REASONS THAN ONE). ("ISAAC HAYES & DAVID PORTER") / BABY I'M A WANT YOU** [-] [ ]

Nov 72. (7") **THEME FROM THE MEN. / TYPE THANG** [ ] [38] Oct 72
(above was from US TV cop series 'The Men')

Jun 73. (d-lp)(c) **LIVE AT SAHARA TAHOE (live)** [ ] [14] May 73
– Theme from Shaft / The come on / Light my fire / Ike's rap / Never can say goodbye / Windows of the world / The look of love / Ellie's love theme / Use me / Do your thing / Theme from The Men / It's too late / Rock me baby / Stormy Monday blues / Type thang / The first time ever I saw your face / Ike's rap VI / Ain't no sunshine / Feelin' alright. *(re-iss.Aug74 + Nov86, cd-iss.Oct92)*

Nov 73. (lp)(c) **JOY** [ ] [16] Oct 73
– Joy / I love you that's all / A man will be a man / The feeling keeps on coming / I'm gonna make it (without you). *(re-iss.Aug74, cd-iss.Jun92)*

Nov 73. (7") **I DON'T WANT TO BE RIGHT. / ROLLING DOWN A MOUNTAINSIDE** [ ] [ ]

Dec 73. (7") **JOY (pt.1). / JOY (pt.2)** [ ] [30]

May 74. (7") **WONDERFUL. / SOMEONE MADE YOU FOR ME** [-] [71]

Jun 74. (lp)(c) **TOUGH GUYS (Soundtrack)** [ ] [ ]
– (title theme) / Randolph & Dearborn / The red rooster / Joe Bell / Hung up on my baby / Kidnapped / Run Fay run / Buns o'plenty / (the end theme).

Aug 74. (7") **TRUCK TURNER. / HUNG UP ON MY BABY** [ ] [ ]

Aug 74. (d-lp)(c) **TRUCK TURNER (Soundtrack)** [ ] [ ] Jul74
– Truck Turner / House of beauty / Blue's crib / Driving in the Sun / You're in my arms again / Give it to me / Drinking / Insurance company / Breakthrough / Now we're one / The duke / Dorinda's party / Pursuit of the pimpmobile / We need each other girl / A house full of girls / Hospital shootout / (end theme).

A.B.C. — H.B.S.

Jun 75. (lp)(c) **CHOCOLATE CHIP** [ ] [18]
– That loving feeling / Body language / Chocolate chip / Chocolate chip (instrumental) / I want to make love to you so bad / Come live with me / I can't turn around.

Jul 75. (7") **CHOCOLATE CHIP. / ('A'version)** [ ] [92]

Dec 75. (lp)(c) **DISCO CONNECTION (by "ISAAC HAYES MOVEMENT")** [-] [85]
– The first day of forever / St. Thomas Square / Vykkii / Disco connection / Disco shuffle / Choppers / After five / Aruba.

Feb 76. (7") **DISCO CONNECTION. / ST.THOMAS SQUARE** [10] [ ]
(12"of above re-iss.Aug77)

Feb 76. (lp)(c) **GROOVE A THON** [ ] [45]
– Groove-a-thon / Your loving is much too strong / Rock me easy baby / We've got a whole lot of love / Wish you were here / Make a little love to me.

Jun 76. (7") **ROCK ME EASY BABY. / ('A'instrumental)** [ ] [ ]

Aug 76. (lp)(c) **JUICY FRUIT (DISCO FREAK)** [ ] [ ] Jul 76
– Juicy fruit (disco freak) / Let's don't ever blow our thing / The storm is over / Music to make love by / Thank you love / Lady of the night / Love me or lose me.

Aug 76. (7") **JUICY FRUIT (DISCO FREAK). / (pt.2)** [ ] [ ]

Feb 77. (d-lp)(c) **A MAN AND A WOMAN ("ISAAC HAYES & DIONNE WARWICK")** [ ] [49]
– Unity / Just don't know what to do with myself / Walk on by / My love / The way I want to touch you – Have you never been mellow – Love will keep us together – I love music – This will be (an everlasting love) – That's the way I like it – Get down tonight / By the time I get to Phoenix / I say a little prayer / Then came you / Feelings / My eyes adored you / Body language / Can't hide love / Come love with me / Once you hit the road / Chocolate chip.

not issued — Stax

1977. (7") **FEEL LIKE MAKIN' LOVE. / (part 2)** [-] [ ]

Polydor — Polydor

Jan 78. (lp)(c) **NEW HORIZON** [ ] [78] Dec 77
– Stranger in Paradise / Moonlight lovin' / Don't take your love away / Out of the ghetto / It's heaven to me.

Jan 78. (7") **OUT OF THE GHETTO. / IT'S HEAVEN TO ME** [-] [ ]

May 78. (7") **MOONLIGHT LOVIN'. / IT'S HEAVEN TO ME** [ ] [ ]

Dec 78. (lp)(c) **FOR THE SAKE OF LOVE** [ ] [75] Nov 78
– Just the way you are / Believe in me / If we ever needed peace / Shaft II / Zeke the freak / Don't let me be lonely tonight.

Jan 79. (7")(12") **ZEKE THE FREAK. / IF WE EVER NEEDED PEACE** [ ] [ ]

Mar 79. (7") **JUST THE WAY YOU ARE. / (part 2)** [-] [ ]

(Later '79, he was credited with MILLIE JACKSON on 'Royal Rappin's' album, which hit US No.80)

—— Also issued 2 US singles with her on 'Polydor'; DO YOU WANNA MAKE LOVE / I CHANGED MY MIND / + YOU NEVER CROSS MY MIND / FEELS LIKE THE FIRST TIME

Nov 79. (lp)(c) **DON'T LET GO** [ ] [39] Sep 79
– Don't let go / What does it take / Few more kisses to go / Fever / Someone who will take the place of you.
Dec 79. (7")(12") **DON'T LET GO. / YOU CAN'T HOLD YOUR WOMAN** [ ] [18] Oct 79
Feb 80. (7") **FEW MORE KISSES TO GO. / WHAT DOES IT TAKE** [-] [ ]
May 80. (lp)(c) **AND ONCE AGAIN** [ ] [59]
– It's all in the game / Ike's rap VII – This time I'll be sweeter / I ain't ever / Wherever you are / Love has been good to us.
Jun 80. (7") **I AIN'T EVER. / LOVE HAS BEEN GOOD TO US** [ ] [ ]
Sep 80. (7") **IT'S ALL IN THE GAME. / WHEREVER YOU ARE** [-] [ ]
Sep 81. (7") **I'M GONNA MAKE ME LOVE YOU. / I'M SO PROUD** [-] [ ]
Sep 81. (lp)(c) **LIFETIME THING** [ ] [ ]
– I'm gonna make you love me / Three times a lady / Fugitive / Summer / I'm so proud / Lifetime thing.
Nov 81. (7") **LIFETIME THING. / FUGITIVE** [-] [ ]

—— Took time out to concentrate on spiraling acting career. He had previously acted in own soundtrack films, 'Truck Turner', etc. He also appeared in 'The Rockford Files' with DIONNE WARWICK in 1977. In 1981, he plays a baddie (what else!) in the film 'Escape From New York'. In 85-86, he cameod in TV for series 'The A-Team' + 'Hunter'.

(Returned in '86, plays everything)

C.B.S. Columbia

Dec 86. (7") **HEY GIRL. / IKE'S RAP VIII** [ ] [ ]
(12"+=) – Hey Fred (you need a sunbed).
Dec 86. (lp)(c) **U-TURN** [ ] [ ]
– If you want my lovin' (do me right) / Flash backs / You turn me on / Ike's rap VIII – Hey girl / Doesn't rain in London / Can't take my eyes off you / Thing for you / Thank God for love.
Mar 87. (7") **THING FOR YOU. / THANK GOD FOR LOVE** [-] [ ]
Jun 87. (7") **IF YOU WANT MY LOVIN' (DO ME RIGHT). / (part 2)** [-] [ ]
Jul 88. (lp)(c) **LOVE ATTACK** [-] [ ]
– Love attack / Let me be your everything / Showdown / Eye of the storm / Accused rap / I stand accused '88 / She's got a way / Foreplay rap / Love won't let me wait.
Jul 88. (7") **SHOWDOWN. / (part 2)** [-] [ ]
Dec 88. (7") **LET ME BE YOUR EVERYTHING. / CURIOUS** [-] [ ]

—— He once again appears in films (i.e. 'Counter Force' + 'The Sofia Conspiracy').

PointBlank Virgin

May 95. (cd)(c)(lp) **BRANDED** [ ] [ ]
– Ike's plea / Life's mood / Fragile / Life's mood II / Summer in the city / Let me love you / I'll do anything (to turn you on) / Thanks to the fool / Branded / Soulsville / Hyperbolicsyllabicsesquedalymistic.
Jun 95. (c-s)(12") **FRAGILE. / FRAGILE / BIRTH OF SHAFT** [ ] [ ]
(cd-s+=) – Let's go out tonight.

– compilations, others, etc. –

Below 'Stax' releases were issued on 'Enterprise' US.

Sep 75. Stax; (lp)(c) **THE BEST OF ISAAC HAYES** [ ] [ ]
Oct 75. Stax; (7") **GOOD LOVE 6-9969. / I'M GONNA HAVE TO TELL HER** [ ] [ ]
Nov 75. Stax; (lp)(c) **USE ME** [ ] [ ]
1977. Stax; (lp)(c)**MEMPHIS MOVEMENT** [ ] [ ]
1978. Stax; (lp)(c) **HOT BED** (rarities) [ ] [ ]
(cd-iss.Aug94)
1977. Stax; (7") **THEME FROM SHAFT. / DO YOUR THING** [ ] [ ]
Nov 77. Stax; (7") **THEME FROM SHAFT. / I DON'T WANT TO BE RIGHT** [ ] [ ]
Apr 78. Stax; (lp)(c) **THE ISAAC HAYES CHRONICLES** [ ] [ ]
Jan 80. Stax; (lp)(c) **LIGHT MY FIRE** [ ] [ ]
Nov 80. Stax; (d-lp)(c) **HIS GREATEST HITS** [ ] [ ]
Oct 81. Stax; (lp)(c) **THE BEST OF SHAFT** [ ] [ ]
(re-iss.Jun86)
Mar 82. Stax; (7") **THEME FROM SHAFT. / IF LOVING YOU IS WRONG** [ ] [-]
Apr 88. Stax; (lp)(c)(cd) **ISAAC'S MOODS – THE BEST OF ISAAC HAYES** [ ] [ ]
– Ike's mood / Soulsville / Joy (part 1) / If loving you is wrong I don't want to be right / Never can say goodbye / The theme from Shaft / Ike's rap VI / A brand new me / Do your thing / Walk on by / I stand accused. (cd+=) – Ike's rap I / Hyperbolic-syllabic-sesquedaly-mystic / Ike's rap III / Ike's rap II.
Aug 93. Stax; (d-cd) **TOUGH GUYS / TRUCK TURNER** [ ] [-]
Mar 76. Golden Hour; (lp)(c) **THE GOLDEN HOUR OF . . .** [ ] [-]
Sep 85. Old Gold; (7") **THEME FROM SHAFT. / NEVER CAN SAY GOODBYE** [ ] [-]
May 89. Southbound; (7") **THEME FROM SHAFT. / THEME FROM THE MEN** [ ] [ ]
(12"+=) – Theme from The Men / Type thang.
(cd-s++=) – Walk on by.
Mar 95. Connoisseur; (cd) **THE COLLECTION** [ ] [-]

Justin HAYWARD (see under ⇒ MOODY BLUES)

HEART

Formed: Vancouver, Canada . . . 1975 by sisters ANN and NANCY WILSON, who had evolved from Seattle groups The ARMY and WHITE HEART. In these line-ups were brothers ROGER and MIKE FISHER, the respective boyfriends of ANN and NANCY. The latter had arrived from solo-folk scene to replace MIKE, who became sound engineer, with group moving to Vancouver to avoid his draft papers. They were signed to local 'Mushroom' label by owner Shelley Siegal, and issued well-received debut lp 'DREAMBOAT ANNIE'. It gained a US release in Jun'76, and soon shot into Top 10, assisted by a couple of Top 50 hits, including Top 10'er 'CRAZY ON YOU'. They returned to Seattle late '76, and signed a new deal with 'CBS-Portrait', but Mushroom sued them for breach of contract. The new label issued 2nd album 'LITTLE QUEEN' in mid-77, and this also made Top 10. In 1978, a Seattle judge gave right to Mushroom to issue their out-takes album 'MAGAZINE', but allowed group to re-record it. Despite all this aggro, the album surprised most, even the band, by hitting Top 20. Later in 1978, their 4th album 'DOG AND BUTTERFLY' was another Top 20 success, although groups' love matches were now all but over. They continued the 80's as top act, peaking with 1985 US No.1 'THESE DREAMS'. • **Style:** Hard / soft-rock act, similar to JEFFERSON STARSHIP or (mid-70's) FLEETWOOD MAC, but with visual aspect from glamourous WILSON's. • **Songwriters:** ANN WILSON or group wrote most except; TELL IT LIKE IT IS (Aaron Neville) / I'M DOWN (Beatles) / LONG TALL SALLY (Little Richard) / UNCHAINED MELODY (hit; Righteous Brothers) / I'VE GOT THE MUSIC IN ME (Kiki Dee) / THESE DREAMS (Martin Page & Bernie Taupin) / ALONE (Billy Steinberg & Tom Kelly) / ALL I WANNA DO IS MAKE LOVE TO YOU (Mutt Lange) / etc. • **Trivia:** In 1967, ANN WILSON AND THE DAYBREAKS issued a couple of singles on 'Topaz'; STANDIN' WATCHIN' YOU. / WONDER HOW I MANAGED and THROUGH EYES AND GLASS. / I'M GONNA DRINK MY HURT AWAY.

Recommended: DREAMBOAT ANNIE (*7) / LITTLE QUEEN (*6) / HEART (*6) / BAD ANIMALS (*5).

ANN WILSON (b.19 Jun'51, San Diego, California, USA) – vocals, flute / **NANCY WILSON** (b.16 Mar'54, San Francisco, California) – guitar, vocals / **ROGER FISHER** – guitar / **STEVE FOSSEN** – bass with session keyboard player and drummer

Arista Mushroom

Sep 76. (7") **CRAZY ON YOU. / DREAMBOAT ANNIE** [-] [35]
Oct 76. (7") **MAGIC MAN. / HOW DEEP IT GOES** [ ] [9] Jul 76
Oct 76. (lp)(c)(US-pic-lp) **DREAMBOAT ANNIE** [36] [7] Apr 76
– Magic man / Dreamboat Annie (fantasy child) / Crazy on you / Soul of the sea / Dreamboat Annie / White lightning and wine (love me like music) / I'll be your song / Sing child / How deep it goes / Dreamboat Annie (reprise). *(re-iss.+cd Oct87 on 'Capitol')*
Feb 77. (7") **CRAZY ON YOU. / SOUL OF THE SEA** [ ] [-]
(re-iss.US Jan 78, hit US No.62)
Apr 77. (7") **DREAMBOAT ANNIE. / SING CHILD** [ ] [42] Dec 76

—— added **HOWARD LEESE** – keyboards, guitar (he appeared as guest on debut album) / **MICHAEL DEROSIER** – drums

Portrait Portrait

Jul 77. (lp)(c) **LITTLE QUEEN** [34] [9] May 77
– Barracuda / Love alive / Sylvan song / Dream of the archer / Kick it out / Little queen / Treat me well / Say hello / Cry to me / Go on cry. *(re-iss.Aug86, re-iss.+cd.May87) (cd-iss.Sep93 on 'Sony Collectors')*
Aug 77. (7") **BARRACUDA. / CRY TO ME** [ ] [11] May 77
Oct 77. (7") **KICK IT OUT. / LOVE ALIVE** [ ] [-]
Nov 77. (7") **LITTLE QUEEN. / TREAT ME WELL** [ ] [62]
Jan 78. (7") **KICK IT OUT. / GO ON CRY** [-] [79]

(The following few releases on 'Arista' UK & 'Mushroom' US were contractual)

Arista Mushroom

Sep 77. (7") **HEARTLESS. / JUST THE WINE** [-] [24]
Apr 78. (lp)(c)(US-pic-lp) **MAGAZINE** [ ] [17]
– Heartless / Devil delight / Just the wine / Without you / Magazine / Here song / Mother Earth blues / I've got the music in me (live). *(re-iss.+cd Oct87 on 'Capitol')*
May 78. (7") **HEARTLESS (version II). / HERE SONG** [ ] [-]
May 78. (7") **WITHOUT YOU. / HERE SONG** [-] [ ]
Jul 78. (7") **MAGAZINE. / DEVIL DELIGHT** [-] [ ]
Aug 78. (7") **MAGAZINE. / JUST THE WINE** [ ] [-]

Portrait Portrait

Oct 78. (7") **STRAIGHT ON. / LIGHTER TOUCH** [ ] [15] Sep 78
Jan 79. (lp)(c) **DOG & BUTTERFLY** [ ] [17] Oct 78
– Cook with fire / High time / Hijinx / Straight on / Lighter touch / Dog &

butterfly / Nada one / Mistral wind*(re-iss.Aug86, re-iss.+cd May87)*
Mar 79. (7") **DOG & BUTTERFLY. / MISTRAL WIND** [-] [34]

— Now a quartet when Nancy's boyfriend ROGER FISHER left the band

Epic Epic

Mar 80. (7") **EVEN IT UP. / PILOT** [ ] [34] Feb 80
Mar 80. (lp)(c) **BEBE LE STRANGE** [ ] [5]
– Bebe le strange / Down on me / Silver wheels / Break / Rockin' heaven down / Even it up / Strange night / Raised on you / Pilot / Sweet darlin'. *(re-iss.+cd '88) (re-iss.cd+c May93 on 'Sony Collectors')***LITTLE QUEEN** *(cd-iss.Sep93 on 'Sony Collectors')*
May 80. (7") **DOWN ON ME. / RAISED ON YOU** [-] [ ]
Jul 80. (7") **BEBE LE STRANGE. / SILVER WHEELS** [-] [ ]
Nov 80. (7") **TELL IT LIKE IT IS. / STRANGE EUPHORIA** [-] [8]
Jan 81. (7") **TELL IT LIKE IT IS. / BARRACUDA (live)** [ ] [-]
Mar 81. (lp)(c)(US-d-lp) **GREATEST HITS / LIVE** (half comp / half live) [ ] [13] Nov 80
– Tell it like it is / Barracuda / Straight on / Dog & butterfly / Even it up / Bebe le strange / Sweet darlin' / I'm down – Long tall Sally – Unchained melody / Rock and roll. *(re-iss.+cd Dec88)*
Mar 81. (7") **UNCHAINED MELODY (live). / MISTRAL WIND** [-] [83]
Jun 82. (7") **THIS MAN IS MINE. / AMERICA** [ ] [33] May 82
Jun 82. (lp)(c) **PRIVATE AUDITION** [77] [25]
– City's burning / Bright light girl / Perfect stranger / Private audition / Angels / This man is mine / The situation / Hey darlin' darlin' / One word / Fast times / America. *(re-iss.+cd Feb88) (re-iss.cd May94)*
Sep 82. (7") **PRIVATE AUDITION. / BRIGHT LIGHT GIRL** [-] [ ]

— **MARK ANDES** – bass (ex-SPIRIT, ex-JO JO GUNNE, ex-FIREFALL) repl. FOSSEN **DENNY CARMASSI** – drums (ex-MONTROSE, ex-SAMMY HAGAR, ex-GAMMA) repl. DEROSIER who formed ORION THE HUNTER

Aug 83. (7") **HOW CAN I REFUSE. / JOHNNY MOON** [-] [ ]
Sep 83. (lp)(c) **PASSIONWORKS** [ ] [39]
– How can I refuse / Blue guitar / Johnny Moon / Sleep alone / Together now / Allies / (Beat by) Jealousy / Heavy heart / Love mistake / Language of love / Ambush. *(re-iss.+cd Feb88)*
Sep 83. (12"m) **HOW CAN I REFUSE. / BARRACUDA / LITTLE QUEEN** [ ] [-]
Oct 83. (7") **ALLIES. / TOGETHER NOW** [-] [83]

— While HEART looked for new contract ANN WILSON teamed up in '84 with MIKE RENO of LOVERBOY on 7" ALMOST PARADISE from the film 'Footloose'.

Capitol Capitol

Jul 85. (7") **WHAT ABOUT LOVE?. / HEART OF DARKNESS** [ ] [10] May 85
Oct 85. (lp)(c)(cd) **HEART** [50] [1] Jul 85
– If looks could kill / What about love? / Never / These dreams / The wolf / All eyes / Nobody home / Nothin' at all / What he don't know / Shell shock. *(re-iss.cd Sep94)*
Oct 85. (7") **NEVER (remix). / SHELL SHOCK** [ ] [4] Sep 85
(12"+=) – ('A'extended).
Mar 86. (7") **THESE DREAMS. / IF LOOKS COULD KILL (live)** [62] [1] Jan 86
(12"+=) – Shell shock. *(US B-side)*
(d7"+=) – What about love? / Heart of darkness.
May 86. (7")(7"sha-pic-d) **NOTHIN' AT ALL (remix). / THE WOLF** [ ] [1] Apr 86
(12"+=) – ('A'extended).
Jul 86. (7") **IF LOOKS COULD KILL. / WHAT HE DON'T KNOW** [-] [54]
May 87. (7") **ALONE. / BARRACUDA** [3] [1]
(12"+=)(c-s+=) – Magic man (live).
May 87. (lp)(c)(cd) **BAD ANIMALS** [7] [5]
– Who will you run to / Alone / There's the girl / I want you so bad / Wait for the answer / Bad animals / You ain't so tough / Strangers of the heart / Easy target / RSVP. *(re-iss.cd Jul94)*
Aug 79. (7") **WHO WILL YOU RUN TO. / MAGIC MAN** [-] [ ]
Sep 87. (7")(7"pic-d) **WHO WILL YOU RUN TO. / NOBODY HOME** [30] [-]
(12"+=) – These dreams.
(cd-s++=) – ('A'rock mix).
Nov 87. (7") **THERE'S THE GIRL (remix). / BAD ANIMALS** [34] [12]
(12"+=) – ('A'extended).
(c-s+=)(cd-s++=) – Alone.
Jan 88. (7")(7"pic-d) **NEVER. / THESE DREAMS** [8] [-]
(12"+=) – ('A'extended) / ('B'version).
(cd-s+=) – Heart of darkness / If looks could kill (live).
(12"+=) – ('B'extended) / ('B'instrumental).
Feb 88. (7") **I WANT YOU SO BAD. / EASY TARGET** [-] [49]
May 88. (7")(7"pic-d) **WHAT ABOUT LOVE. / SHELL SHOCK** [14] [-]
(12"+=) – ('A'extended).
(cd-s+=) – Crazy on you / Dreamboat Annie.
Oct 88. (7") **NOTHIN' AT ALL (remix). / I'VE GOT THE MUSIC IN ME (live)** [38] [-]
(12"+=)(12"pic-d+=) – I want you so bad (extended version).
(cd-s++=) – Nothin' at all (extended remix).
Feb 89. (7") **SURRENDER TO ME. ("ANN WILSON & ROBIN ZANDER" of Cheap Trick). / TEQUILA DREAMS** [ ] [6]
(12"+=)(cd-s+=) – (other artist).
Dec 89. (7") **HERE IS CHRISTMAS. /** [-] [ ]
Mar 90. (7")(c-s) **ALL I WANNA DO IS MAKE LOVE TO YOU. / CALL OF THE WILD** [8] [2]
(12"+=)(12"clear+=)(12"pic-d+=)(cd-s+=) Cruel tears.
Apr 90. (cd)(c)(lp) **BRIGADE** [2] [3]
– Wild child / All I wanna do is make love to you / Secret / Tall, dark handsome stranger / I didn't want to need you / The night / Fallen from grace / Under the sky / Cruel nights / Stranded / Call of the wild / I want your world to turn / I love you. *(re-iss.cd+c Mar94)*
Jul 90. (7") **I DIDN'T WANT TO NEED YOU. / THE NIGHT** [47] [23] Jun 90
(12"+=)(c-s+=)(cd-s+=)(12"pic-d+=) – The will to love.
Nov 90. (7")(c-s) **STRANDED. / UNDER THE SKY** [60] [13] Sep 90
(12"+=)(cd-s+=)(12"pic-d+=) – I'll never stop loving you.
Feb 91. (7")(c-s) **SECRET. / I LOVE YOU** [ ] [ ]
(12"+=)(cd-s+=) – How can I refuse (live).
Sep 91. (cd)(c)(lp) **ROCK THE HOUSE (live)** [45] [ ]
– Wild child / Fallen from grace / Call of the wild / How can I refuse / Shell shock / Love alive / Under the sky / The night / Tall, dark, handsome stranger / If looks could kill / Who will you run to / You're the voice / The way back machine / Barracuda.
Sep 91. (7")(c-s) **YOU'RE THE VOICE (live). / CALL OF THE WILD (live)** [56] [ ]
(10"colrd+=)(cd-s+=) – Barracuda (live).

— In 1992, the WILSONS were in splinter groups FAUK HAUK and the LOVEMONGERS. The latter (which also included SUE ENNIS + FRANK COX) released a self-titled cd-ep on 'Capitol' w/tracks – Battle for evermore / Love of the common man / Papa was a rollin' stone / Crazy on you

Nov 93. (7"pic-d)(c-s) **WILL YOU BE THERE (IN THE MORNING). / THESE DREAMS (live)** [19] [39]
(cd-s) – ('A'side) / What about love? / Risin' suspicion / Who will you run to.
Nov 93. (cd)(c) **DESIRE WALKS ON** [32] [48]
– Desire / Black on black II / Back to Avalon / The woman in me / Rage / In walks the night / My crazy head / Ring them bells / Will you be there (in the morning) / Voodoo doll / Anything is possible / Avalon (reprise) / Desire walks on (UK+=) / La mujer que hay en mi / Te quedaras (en la manana).
Mar 94. (cd-s) **BACK TO AVALON / WILL YOU BE THERE (IN THE MORNING) / ALL I WANNA DO IS MAKE LOVE TO YOU** [ ] [ ]
Aug 95. (cd)(c) **THE ROAD HOME** [-] [87]

– compilations etc. –

Sep 87. Epic; (d-lp)(c) **HEART (THE BEST OF . . .)** [ ] [ ]
1991. Epic; (d-cd) **DOG & BUTTERFLY / LITTLE QUEEN** [ ] [-]
Nov 88. Capitol; (box-lp)(box-cd) **WITH LOVE FROM HEART (HEART & BAD ANIMALS)** [ ] [-]
(re-iss.box-cd.1990 as HEART BOX SET)
May 94. Columbia; (cd)(c) **GREATEST HITS** [ ] [ ]

ANN WILSON

solo from the film 'The Golden Child'
Jan 87. (7 + 12") **THE BEST MAN IN THE WORLD. / ('A' instrumental)** [-] [ ]

HEAVY STEREO

*** NEW ENTRY ***

Formed: London-based, England . . .1993 by GEM, PETE, NEIL and NICK. They signed to 'Food' records but remained recordless until they changed their name to HEAVY STEREO. Having moved from the home of BLUR ('Food') to the stable of OASIS ('Creation'), they hit Top 50 with mid-1995 debut 'SLEEP FREAK'. Two others repeated the hit formula as the fans awaited an album. • **Style:** Glam-rock devotees, influenced by BOLAN or even The SWEET. • **Songwriters:** ARCHER.

GEM (ARCHER) – vocals (ex-CONTENDERS, ex-WHIRLPOOL) / **PETE DOWNING** – guitar / **NEIL** – bass / **NICK JONES** – drums

Creation ???

Jul 95. (7"red)(c-s) **SLEEP FREAK. / MAGIC SPONGE** [46] [-]
(cd-s+=) – Pleasure dip.
Oct 95. (7"purple)(c-s) **SMILER. / CARTOON MOON** [46] [-]
(cd-s+=) – Wonder fools.
Feb 96. (7")(c-s) **CHINESE BURN. / WORM BRAIN** [45] [-]
(cd-s+=) – Big apple pie.

'Really, I'm just an actor – the only difference between me and those cats in Hollywood is that I write my own script.' Jimi H.

Jimi HENDRIX EXPERIENCE

Born: JOHNNY ALLEN HENDRIX, 27 Nov'42, Seattle, Washington, USA. Raised by part Cherokee Indian mother and black father, who at 3 changed his forenames to JAMES MARSHALL and bought him first guitar in the summer of '58. Due to him being left-handed, he turned it upside down and reversed the strings. JIMI soon taught himself by listening to blues and rock'n'roll artists such as ROBERT JOHNSON, MUDDY WATERS, B.B. KING and CHUCK BERRY. In the early 60's, he enlisted in the paratroopers, thus avoided draft into US army. He was discharged for medical reasons in 1962, when he was injured during jump. Two years later, he moved to New York and backed acts LITTLE RICHARD, The ISLEY BROTHERS, IKE & TINA TURNER. He soon struck up partnership with soul singer CURTIS KNIGHT, while also obtaining contract with Ed Chalpin. He is said to have written 'The Ballad Of Jimi' in 1965, after JIMI told him he would die in 1970! Early in 1966, JIMMY JAMES & THE BLUE FLAMES were born. With JIMI's reputation now spreading, he was seen by ex-ANIMALS bassman CHAS CHANDLER, who invited him to London. After auditions, they found a rhythm section of NOEL REDDING and MITCH MITCHELL, and smashed their way into UK Top 10 early '67 with 'Polydor' one-off 45 'HEY JOE'. Chandler then set up deal with Kit Lambert's new 'Track' label, and The JIMI HENDRIX EXPERIENCE exploded into place. Their first Hendrix-penned 45 'PURPLE HAZE', made UK Top 3, as did scintillating debut lp 'ARE YOU EXPERIENCED?' after their 3rd Top 10 single 'THE WIND CRIES MARY'. He was duly booked on the Monterey International Pop Festival bill, where he played a resounding version of 'WILD THING'. The next month of July, saw an weird support US tour with The MONKEES, leaving him and teenybop audiences baffled, but no doubt entertained for 7 nights. After another classic UK hit 'THE BURNING OF THE MIDNIGHT LAMP', he released 2nd lp 'AXIS: BOLD AS LOVE', which made Top 5 early '68, and was first to chart and hit Top 3 in his home U.S.A. In Autumn of '68, he revived and transformed BOB DYLAN's 'ALL ALONG THE WATCHTOWER', which broke into US Top 20 and UK 5. It was trailed by a superb UK Top 10 double-lp 'ELECTRIC LADYLAND', which went No.1 in US, and featured the now famous controversial naked women sleeve, which some shops sold in a brown cover!. In 1969, he was busted for drugs, which led to the split of his band who played together for last time on 29 June at Denver Pop Festival. REDDING had already FAT MATTRESS, but MITCHELL returned with other musicians BILLY COX and LARRY LEE. They played the Woodstock Festival 17-18 August '69, with excellent version of 'STAR SPANGLED BANNER' going down into folklore of rock music. To end the year, he was found not guilty of an earlier charge of heroin and marijuana possession. At the same time, he formed all-black outfit BAND OF GYPSYS, with COX and drummer BUDDY MILES. They released live lp 'BAND OF GYPSYS' in May'70 recorded at FILLMORE EAST, New Year's Eve/Day 1969/70. This hit Top 5 in the States, and due to court action, he paid ex-manager Ed Chalpin $1m in compensation and percentage of royalties. Tragically after a few more open-air festival concerts and some bad drugs trips, he died in London on 18th Sep'70. He was said to have left a phoned message to Chandler saying "I need help bad, man". The official cause of death, was an inhalation of vomit, due to barbiturate intoxication, which led to coroner's decision of an open verdict. • **Style:** Wild man of rock'n'roll, his well-crafted blues poems were always fused with "out of this world" guitar-virtuoso, never seen before or since! His gentlemanly vox, was always climaxed in concert, with heavy lead guitar complete with teeth-playing, feedback and setting fire to his Stratocaster. He virtually re-invented the electric guitar and still to many rock music buffs, the greatest axegrinder of all-time. Who knows what he might have become and progressed onto? • **Songwriters:** HENDRIX except other covers; HEY JOE (William Roberts) / JOHNNY B.GOODE (Chuck Berry) / GLORIA (Them) / SGT. PEPPER (Beatles) / HANG ON SLOOPY (McCoys) / TUTTI FRUTTI + LUCILLE (LIttle Richard) / BO DIDDLEY (Bo Diddley) / PETER GUNN (Henry Mancini) / HOOCHIE

COOCHIE MAN (Muddy Waters) / BLUE SUEDE SHOES (Carl Perkins) / etc. • **Trivia:** In Jan'69, he and band play live tribute of CREAM's 'Sunshine Of Your Love' on The LULU Show, much to annoyance of TV controllers.

Recommended: ARE YOU EXPERIENCED? (*10) / AXIS: AS BOLD AS LOVE (*9) / ELECTRIC LADYLAND (*10) / BAND OF GYPSYS (*8) / THE CRY OF LOVE (*7) / THE ULTIMATE EXPERIENCE (compilation *10)

JIMI HENDRIX – vocals, lead guitar (ex-CURTIS KNIGHT) with **NOEL REDDING** (b.DAVID REDDING, 25 Dec'45, Folkstone, Kent, England) – bass / **MITCH MITCHELL** (b.JOHN MITCHELL, 9 Jun'47, Ealing, London, England) – drums

		Polydor	Reprise	
Dec 66.	(7") **HEY JOE. / STONE FREE (credited "JIMI HENDRIX")**	6	-	

(re-iss.Jul84 on 'Old Gold')

		Track	Reprise	
Mar 67.	(7") **PURPLE HAZE. / 51ST ANNIVERSARY**	3	-	
Mar 67.	(7") **HEY JOE. / 51st ANNIVERSARY**	-		
May 67.	(7") **THE WIND CRIES MARY. / HIGHWAY CHILE**	6	-	
May 67.	(lp) **ARE YOU EXPERIENCED**	2	5	Aug 67

– Foxy lady / Manic depression / Red house / Can you see me / Love or confusion / I don't live today / May this be love / Fire / Third stone from the sun / Remember / Are you experienced. *(re-iss.+c Nov70, re-iss.Nov81+Sep85 on 'Polydor' re+cd Jun91)(re-iss.cd+c Oct93)*

Aug 67.	(7") **PURPLE HAZE. / THE WIND CRIES MARY**	-	65	
Aug 67.	(7") **BURNING OF THE MIDNIGHT LAMP. / THE STARS THAT PLAY WITH LAUGHING SAM'S DICE**	18	-	
Dec 67.	(7") **FOXY LADY. / HEY JOE**	-	67	
Dec 67.	(lp) **AXIS: BOLD AS LOVE**	5	3	Feb 68

– Experience / Up from the skies / Spanish castle magic / Wait until tomorrow / Ain't no telling / Little wing / If six was nine / You've got me floating / Castles made of sand / She's so fine / One rainy wish / Little Miss Lover / Bold as love. *(re-iss.+c.Nov70, re-iss.Aug83, cd-iss.1987, re-iss.+cd.Jul91 on 'Polydor')(re-iss.cd+c Oct93)*

Feb 68.	(7") **UP FROM THE SKIES. / ONE RAINY WISH**	-	82	
May 68.	(7") **FOXY LADY. / PURPLE HAZE**	-		

—— Jimi now brought in sessions **AL KOOPER** and **STEVE WINWOOD** – keyboards plus **JACK CASADY** – bass / **BUDDY MILES** – drums / (to repl.MITCHELL and REDDING)

Sep 68.	(7") **ALL ALONG THE WATCHTOWER. / CROSSTOWN TRAFFIC**	-	20	
Oct 68.	(7") **ALL ALONG THE WATCHTOWER. / LONG HOT SUMMER NIGHT**	5	-	
Nov 68.	(d-lp) **ELECTRIC LADYLAND**	6	1	Oct 68

– And the gods made love / (Have you ever been to) Electric Ladyland / Crosstown traffic / Voodoo chile / Rainy day, dream away / 1983 (a merman I should turn to be) / Moon, turn the tide . . .gently gently away / Little Miss Strange / Long hot summer night / Come on / Gypsy eyes / The burning of the midnight lamp / Still raining still dreaming / House burning down / All along the watchtower / Voodoo chile (slight return). *(re-iss.'69, re-iss.+d-c Jun73, re-iss.+d-cd Jan84 on 'Polydor', cd-iss.Jul91) (re-iss.cd+c Oct93)*

Apr 69.	(7") **CROSSTOWN TRAFFIC. / GYPSY EYES**	37	52	

JIMI HENDRIX

retained only **BUDDY MILES** and recruited **BILLY COX** – bass to repl. others

		Track	Capitol	
Apr 70.	(7") **STEPPING STONE. / IZABELLA**	-		
Jun 70.	(lp)(c) **BAND OF GYPSYS (live)**	6	5	Apr 70

– Who knows / Machine gun / Changes / Power of soul / Message to love / We gotta live together. *(re-iss.Jun73, re-iss.Aug83 on 'Polydor', re-iss.+cd May88) (cd-iss.Dec89, re-iss.+cd.Jul91)*

—— On 18th Sep'70 HENDRIX died of a drug overdose.

– compilations etc. –

Feb 68.	London/ US= Capitol; (lp) **GET THAT FEELING (live 1964, with 'CURTIS KNIGHT' as above)**	39	75
Nov 68.	London/ US= Capitol; (lp) **STRANGE THINGS**		

(re-iss.Apr86 on 'Showcase')

Note; All below 'Track' releases were issued on 'Reprise' US.

Sep 67.	Track; (7") **HOW WOULD YOU FEEL. / YOU DON'T WANT ME**		

Apr 68. Track; (lp) **SMASH HITS** | 4 | 6 | Jul 69
– Purple haze / Fire / The wind cries Mary / Can you see me / 51st anniversary / Hey Joe / Stone free / The stars that play with laughing Sam's dice / Manic depression / Highway chile / The burning of the midnight lamp / Foxy lady. *(re-iss.Jun73, re-iss.Aug83 on 'Polydor', cd-iss.Feb85)*
Oct 69. Track; (7") **(LET ME LIGHT YOUR) FIRE. / BURNING OF THE MIDNIGHT LAMP**
May 70. Track; (lp) **BACKTRACK:4 (shared with The WHO)**
May 70. Track; (lp) **BACKTRACK:8 (shared with The WHO)**

– posthumous albums / singles (some exploitation), etc. –

Oct 70. London/ US= Capitol; (7") **THE BALLAD OF JIMI. / GLOOMY MONDAY (with 'CURTIS KNIGHT')**
Sep 70. Track; (lp)(c) **MONTEREY INTERNATIONAL POP FESTIVAL (live soundtrack)** | - | 16
Oct 70. Track; (7"m) **VOODOO CHILE (SLIGHT RETURN). / HEY JOE / ALL ALONG THE WATCHTOWER** | 1 | -
Mar 71. Track; (lp)(c) **THE CRY OF LOVE** | 2 | 3
– Freedom / Drifting / Ezy rider / Night bird flying / My friend / Straight ahead / Astro man / Angel / In from the storm / Belly button window. *(re-iss.Jun73 & Sep85, cd-iss.Mar89, re-+cd.Jul91 on 'Polydor')(re-iss.cd+c Mar93)*
Apr 71. Track; (7") **NIGHT BIRD FLYING. / FREEDOM** | | -
Apr 71. Reprise; (7") **FREEDOM. / ANGEL** | - | 59
Oct 71. Reprise; (7") **DOLLY DAGGER. / STAR SPANGLED BANNER** | - | 74
Oct 71. Track; (7"ep) **GYPSY EYES. / REMEMBER / PURPLE HAZE / STONE FREE** | 35 |
Note; All below releases on 'Polydor' were issued on 'Reprise' US.
Nov 71. Polydor; (lp)(c) **JIMI HENDRIX AT THE ISLE OF WIGHT (live)** | 17 |
– Midnight lightning / Foxy lady / Lover man / Freedom / All along the watchtower / In from the storm. *(re-iss.Apr84, re+cd.Mar89 & Jul91) (re-iss.cd+c Mar93)*
Jan 72. Polydor; (lp)(c) **HENDRIX IN THE WEST (live)** | 7 | 12
– Johnny B.Goode / Lover man / Blue suede shoes / Voodoo chile (slight return) / The queen / Sergeant Pepper's lonely hearts club band / Little wing / Red house.
Jan 72. Reprise; (7") **JOHNNY BE GOODE. / LOVERMAN** | - |
Feb 72. Polydor; (7") **JOHNNY B. GOODE. / LITTLE WING** | 35 | -
May 72. Reprise; (7") **LITTLE WING. / THE WIND CRIES MARY** | - |
Nov 72. Polydor; (lp)(c) **WAR HEROES** | 23 | 48
– Bleeding heart / Highway chile / Tax free / Peter Gunn / Catastrophe / Stepping stone / Midnight / 3 little bears / Beginning / Izabella. *(re-iss.Aug83 on 'Polydor') (cd-iss.Mar89, & re-iss.+cd.Jul91) (re-iss.cd+c Mar93)*
Oct 73. Polydor; (d-lp)(c) **ARE YOU EXPERIENCED / AXIS: BOLD AS LOVE**
Feb 74. Polydor; (lp)(c) **LOOSE ENDS** | | -
– Come down hard on me / Blue suede shoes / Jam 292 / The stars that play with laughing Sam's dice / Drifter's escape / Hoochie koochie man / (Have you ever been to) Electric Ladyland. *(cd-iss.Mar89)*
Mar 75. Polydor; (lp) **JIMI HENDRIX 'Flashback'** | 35 |
Sep 75. Polydor; (lp)(c) **CRASH LANDING** | 35 | 5 | Mar 75
– Message to love / Somewhere over the rainbow / Crash landing / Coming down hard on me / Peace in Mississippi / With the power / Stone free again / Captain Coconut. *(re-iss.Mar85) (cd-iss.Mar89) (re-+cd.Jun91)(re-iss.cd+c Mar93)*
Nov 75. Polydor; (lp)(c) **MIDNIGHT LIGHTNING** | 46 | 43
– Trashman / Midnight lightning / Hear my train a-coming / Gypsy boy / Blue suede shoes / Machine gun / Once I had a woman / Beginnings. *(re-iss.+cd.Mar89)*
Oct 76. Polydor; (lp) **JIMI HENDRIX VOL.2 'Flashback'**
Jul 78. Polydor; (d-lp)(d-c) **THE ESSENTIAL JIMI HENDRIX** (with free one-sided 33rpm 7" **GLORIA.**
Jun 80. Polydor; (lp)(c) **NINE TO THE UNIVERSE**
Jun 80. Polydor; (lp)(c) **STONE FREE**
(re-iss.Nov83)
Sep 80. Polydor; (7") **VOODOO CHILE. / GLORIA**
Sep 80. Polydor; (6x7"-box) **6 SINGLES BOXED (1st 6)**
Sep 80. Polydor; (12xlp) **10th ANNIVERSARY BOXED SET**
Jan 81. Polydor; (lp)(c) **ESSENTIAL JIMI HENDRIX VOLUME 2** | | | Aug 79
Nov 81. Polydor; (12"ep) **ALL ALONG THE WATCHTOWER. / FOXY LADY / PURPLE HAZE / MANIC DEPRESSION**
Jun 82. Polydor; (lp)(c) **VOODOO CHILE**
(re-iss.Nov83)
Sep 82. Polydor; (12"ep) **VOODOO CHILE. / GIPSY EYES / HEY JOE / 3RD STONE FROM THE SUN**
Feb 83. Polydor; (d-lp)(c) **SINGLES ALBUM** | 77 |
Jun 83. Polydor; (d-c) **CRASH LANDING / MIDNIGHT LIGHTNING**
Nov 84. Polydor; (lp)(c)(cd) **KISS THE SKY**
(re-iss.+cd.Jun91)(re-iss.cd+c Mar93)
Feb 86. Polydor; (lp)(c)(cd) **JIMI PLAYS MONTEREY (live)**
(re-iss.+cd.Jun91) (re-iss.cd+c Mar93)
Jul 87. Polydor; (lp)(c)(cd) **LIVE AT WINTERLAND (live)**
(re-iss.+cd.Jun91)(re-iss.cd+c Mar93)
Jan 89. Polydor; (7") **PURPLE HAZE. / 51ST ANNIVERSARY**
(12"+=) – All along the watchtower.
(cd-s+=) – Hey Joe.
1989. Polydor; (4xcd-box) **BOXED SET**
-ARE YOU EXPERIENCED? / WAR HEROES / IN THE WEST / BAND OF GYPSIES
Mar 90. Polydor; (7") **CROSSTOWN TRAFFIC. / PURPLE HAZE** | 61 |
(12"+=) – All along the watchtower.
(cd-s++=) – Hey Joe.
1990. Polydor; (cd) **THE JIMI HENDRIX EXPERIENCE**
Oct 90. Polydor; (cd)(c)(lp) **CORNERSTONES (1967-1970, FOUR YEARS THAT CHANGED THE MUSIC)** | 5 |
– Hey Joe / Foxy lady / Purple haze / The wind cries Mary / Have you ever been to (Electric Ladyland) / Crosstown traffic / All along the watchtower / Voodoo chile (slight return) / Star spangled banner / Stepping stone / Room full of mirrors / Ezy rider / Freedom / Drifting / In from the storm / Angel. *(cd+c+=)* Fire (live) / Stone free (live).
Oct 90. Polydor; (7"m) **ALL ALONG THE WATCHTOWER. / VOODOO CHILE / HEY JOE** | 52 |
(12"+=)(c-s+=) – Crosstown traffic.
Feb 91. Polydor; (4xcd-box) **SESSIONS BOX – ARE YOU EXPERIENCED? / AXIS: BOLD AS LOVE / ELECTRIC LADYLAND / CRY OF LOVE**
Mar 91. Polydor; (4xcd-box) **FOOTLIGHTS**
-JIMI PLAYS MONTEREY / ISLE OF WIGHT / BAND OF GYPSIES / LIVE AT WINTERLAND
Feb 92. Polydor; (4xcd-box) **STAGES (live)**
– (Stockholm 5 Sep'67 / Paris 29 Jan'68 / San Diego 24 May'69 / Atlanta 4 Jul'70)
Jul 93. Polydor; (cd)(c) **THE ULTIMATE EXPERIENCE** | 28 | 72
– All along the watchtower / Purple haze / Hey Joe / The wind cries Mary / Angel / Voodoo chile (slight return) / Foxy lady / Burning of the midnight lamp / Highway chile / Crosstown traffic / Castles made of sand / Long hot summer night / Red house / Manic depression / Gypsy eyes / Little wing / Fire / Wait until tomorrow / Star spangled banner (live) / Wild thing (live). *(re-iss.Sep95)*
Nov 92. Polygram; (cd) **THE ULTIMATE COLLECTION** | 25 |
Feb 94. I.T.M.; (cd) **PURPLE HAZE IN WOODSTOCK (live)**
Apr 94. Pulsar; (3xcd) **GREATEST HITS** | | -
Apr 94. Polydor/ US= M.C.A.; (cd)(c) **BLUES** | 10 | 45
Aug 94. Polydor/ US= M.C.A.; (cd)(c) **WOODSTOCK (live)** | 32 | 37
May 94. Ramble Tamble; (cd) **LIVE AT THE 'SCENE' CLUB N.Y., N.Y. (live)** | | -
Aug 94. Charly; (cd) **BEFORE THE EXPERIENCE** | | -
Oct 94. Charly; (cd) **THE EARLY YEARS** | | -
Oct 70. R.C.A.; (7") **NO SUCH ANIMAL (Pt.1). / (Pt.2) (with 'CURTIS KNIGHT')**
Apr 71. Saga; (lp)(c) **JIMI HENDRIX**
1972. Saga; (lp) **JIMI HENDRIX AT HIS BEST VOL.1**
1972. Saga; (lp) **JIMI HENDRIX AT HIS BEST VOL.2**
1972. Saga; (lp) **JIMI HENDRIX AT HIS BEST VOL.3**
Apr 71. Hallmark; (lp) **THE ETERNAL FIRE OF JIMI HENDRIX (with 'CURTIS KNIGHT')**
1973. Hallmark; (lp) **THE WILD ONE (with 'CURTIS KNIGHT')**
Aug 71. Ember; (lp)(c) **EXPERIENCE** | 9 | -
– (opening jam) / Room full of mirrors / C-blues / Smashing of amps. *(re-iss.Sep79 on 'Bulldog', cd-iss.Jan87) (cd-iss.Mar95 on 'Nectar')*
1972. Ember; (lp)(c) **MORE EXPERIENCE** | | -
(re-iss.Sep79 & Jul82 on 'Bulldog')
Sep 73. Ember; (lp) **LOOKING BACK WITH JIMI HENDRIX**
Oct 73. Ember; (lp) **IN THE BEGINNING**
(re-iss.'84 on 'Premier')
1974. Ember; (lp) **FRIENDS FROM THE BEGINNING (with 'LITTLE RICHARD')**
(re-iss.Jan77)
Nov 71. Reprise; (lp)(c) **RAINBOW BRIDGE (soundtrack)** | 16 | 15 | Oct 71
– Dolly dagger / Earth blues / Pali gap / Room full of mirrors / Star spangled banner / Look over yonder / Hear my train a-comin' / Hey baby. *(cd-iss.Mar87)*
Jun 73. Reprise; (7") **HEAR MY TRAIN A-COMIN'. / ROCK ME BABY**
Jul 73. Reprise; (d-lp)(c) **SOUNDTRACK RECORDINGS FROM THE FILM 'JIMI'** | 37 |
Jun 82. Reprise; (7") **FIRE. / LITTLE WING** | - |
1972. M.F.P.; (lp) **WHAT'D I SAY** | | -
Sep 84. M.F.P.; (lp) **THE BIRTH OF SUCCESS** | | -
Nov 72. Enterprise; (lp) **RARE HENDRIX**
Dec 72. Enterprise; (lp) **JIMI HENDRIX IN SESSION**
1973. Enterprise; (lp) **HENDRIX '66**
1973. Boulevard; (lp) **JIMI HENDRIX 1964** | | -
Nov 75. D.J.M.; (lp)(c) **FOR REAL**
(re-iss.Feb82 on 'Audio Fidelity')
Aug 79. Bulldog/ US= Douglas; (lp) **GOLDEN PIECES OF JIMI HENDRIX**
(re-iss.Dec82)
Sep 79. Bulldog/ US= Douglas; (lp) **MORE ESSENTIAL**

Nov 80. Red Lightnin'; (lp) **WOKE UP THIS MORNING AND FOUND MYSELF DEAD** [ ] [-]
(cd-iss.Nov86) (pic-lp.Oct88)
Jun 81. Audio Fidelity; (lp)(c) **COSMIC TURNAROUND** [ ] [-]
Oct 81. Audio Fidelity; (4xlp) **THE GENIUS OF HENDRIX** [ ] [-]
Mar 82. Audio Fidelity; (lp) **HIGH, LIVE AND DIRTY** [ ] [-]
Oct 84. Audio Fidelity; (c) **JIMI HENDRIX VOL.1** [ ] [-]
Oct 84. Audio Fidelity; (c) **JIMI HENDRIX VOL.2** [ ] [-]
Oct 84. Audio Fidelity; (c) **JIMI HENDRIX VOL.3** [ ] [-]
Nov 81. Phoenix; (lp) **FREE SPIRIT** [ ] [ ]
(re-iss.Jun87 on 'Thunderb.')
Sep 82. Phoenix; (lp) **MOODS** [ ] [-]
Sep 82. Phoenix; (lp) **ROOTS OF HENDRIX** [ ] [-]
Aug 82. C.B.S./ US= Eprise; (d-lp)(c) **THE JIMI HENDRIX CONCERTS (live)** [16] [79]
– Fire / I don't live today / Red house / Stone free / Are you experienced? / Little wing / Voodoo chile (slight return) / Bleeding heart / Hey Joe / Wild thing / Hear my train a-comin'. *(re-iss.Sep84) (re-iss.+cd.Aug89 on 'Media Motion')*
Aug 82. C.B.S.; (7")(12") **FIRE (live). / ARE YOU EXPERIENCED (live)** [ ] [ ]
Oct 82. Dakota; (lp)(c) **THE BEST OF JIMI HENDRIX** [ ] [-]
Nov 83. Contour; (lp) **THE JIMI HENDRIX ALBUM** [ ] [-]
Jul 84. Old Gold; (7") **PURPLE HAZE. / THE WIND CRIES MARY** [ ] [-]
Jul 84. Old Gold; (7") **VOODOO CHILE (SLIGHT RETURN). / BURNING OF THE MIDNIGHT LAMP** [ ] [-]
Jul 84. Old Gold; (7") **ALL ALONG THE WATCHTOWER. / FOXY LADY** [ ] [-]
Jul 85. Topline; (lp)(c) **GANGSTER OF LOVE** [ ] [-]
Apr 86. Arcade; (lp)(c) **THE LEGEND** [ ] [-]
(re-iss.Dec88)
May 86. Sierra; (lp)(c) **REPLAY OF JIMI HENDRIX** [ ] [-]
Aug 86. Fame-EMI; (lp)(c) **JOHNNY B. GOODE** [ ] [-]
May 87. E.M.I.; (cd) **THE BEST OF JIMI HENDRIX** [ ] [-]
May 88. Big Time; (cd) **16 GREAT CLASSICS** [ ] [-]
Jun 88. Thunderbolt; (cd) **VOICES IN THE WIND** [ ] [-]
Apr 90. Thunderbolt; (cd)(c)(lp) **NIGHT LIFE** [ ] [-]
Nov 88. Strange Fruit; (12"ep) **THE PEEL SESSIONS** [ ] [ ]
– Radio One theme / Day tripper / Wait until tomorrow / Hear my train a'comin' / Spanish castle magic.
Feb 89. Castle/ US= Rykodisc; (d-lp)(c)(cd) **THE RADIO ONE SESSIONS** [30] [ ]
– Stone free / Radio one theme / Day tripper / Killing floor / Love or confusion / Catfish blues / Drivin' south / Wait until tomorrow / Hear my train a-comin' / Hound dog / Fire / Hoochie coochie man / Purple haze / Spanish castle magic / Hey Joe / Foxy lady / The burning of the midnight lamp.
Nov 89. Castle/ US= Rykodisc; (lp)(c)(cd) **LIVE AND UNRELEASED – THE RADIO SHOWS** [ ] [ ]
Feb 89. Koine; (cd) **JAM SESSIONS** [ ] [-]
Jan 90. Zeta; (cd) **THE LAST EXPERIENCE CONCERT (live)** [ ] [-]
Dec 90. Discussion; (pic-lp) **WELL I STAND NEXT TO A MOUNTAIN** [ ] [-]
Feb 91. Action Replay; (lp) **THE BEST & THE REST OF . . .** [ ] [-]
Dec 91. U.F.O.; (cd)(lp) **IN 1967 (free w/booklet)** [ ] [-]
Nov 92. East West; (7")(c-s) **THE WIND CRIES MARY. / FIRE** [ ] [ ]
(12"+=)(cd-s+=) – Foxy lady / May this be love
Dec 92. Univibes; (cd) **CALLING LONG DISTANCE** [ ] [-]
Apr 93. Deja Vu; (cd)(c) **THE GOLD COLLECTION** [ ] [-]
(re-iss.Jun95)
Apr 93. Pulsar; (cd) **HIS FINAL LIVE PERFORMANCE (live)** [ ] [-]
Sep 93. I.T.M.; (cd) **JIMI HENDRIX AT THE MONTEREY POP FESTIVAL, 1967 (live)** [ ] [-]
Dec 93. Entertainers; (cd) **FIRE** [ ] [-]
Jan 95. Collection; (cd) **THE COLLECTION** [ ] [-]
Mar 95. Top Masters; (cd) **THE EARLY JIMI HENDRIX** [ ] [-]
Apr 95. Muskateer; (cd)(c) **LIVE IN NEW YORK** [ ] [-]
Apr 95. Polydor; (cd)(c) **VOODOO SOUP** [ ] [66]
– The new rising sun / Belly button window / Stepping stone / Freedom / Angel / Room full of mirrors / Midnight / Night bird flying / Drifting / Ezy rider / Pali gap / Mesage to love / Peace in Mississippi / In from the storm.
May 95. Thunderbolt; (cd) **NIGHT LIFE** [ ] [-]
Jun 95. Receiver; (cd) **SUNSHINE OF YOUR LOVE** [ ] [-]
Aug 95. Voiceprint; (cd) **SUPERSESSION** [ ] [-]
Sep 95. Strawberry; (cd) **THE LAST EXPERIENCE** [ ] [-]
Nov 95. The Collection; (cd) **GREATEST HITS** [ ] [-]
. . . Jan – Jun '96 stop press . . .

— On April 5th, JIMI's girlfriend at the time of his death; MONIKA DANNEMAN, committed suicide (carbon monoxide poisoning). In her book ' The Inner Life Of Jimi Hendrix', she had recently broke an injunction, involving a libelous statement made to JIMI's other one-time girlfriend KATHY ETCHINGHAM.

Ken HENSLEY (see under ⇒ URIAH HEEP)

Kirsten HERSH (see under ⇒ THROWING MUSES)

HE SAID (see under ⇒ WIRE)

Steve HILLAGE

Born: 2 Aug'51, London, England. While at school he joined URIEL for six months early 1968. They became EGG after his departure to university, and made 2 albums in the early 70's. One of them, 'ARACHEZ' issued on 'Evoluton', is now worth over £200. In Spring 1971 he formed KHAN, and after one album in 1972, he played live with KEVIN AYERS BAND. In 1973, HILLAGE joined and then became leader of GONG, until his departure to a solo career in 1975 with girlfriend MIQUETTE GIRAUDY. Sticking with Richard Branson's 'Virgin' records, he gained semi-success with albums throughout the 70's. • **Style:** Experimental quasi-psychedelia that leant on the extreme avant-garde, mixed with sense of rock feel. • **Songwriters:** Himself, except NOT FADE AWAY (Buddy Holly) / HURDY GURDY MAN (Donovan) / IT'S ALL TOO MUCH + GETTING BETTER (Beatles). In SYSTEM & he co-writes w/ GIRAUDY. • **Trivia:** TODD RUNDGREN produced 2nd lp 'L'.

Recommended: LIVE HERALD (*7) / SYSTEM 7 (*6) / FISH RISING (*6)

KHAN

STEVE HILLAGE – guitar, vocals (ex-GONG, ex-URIEL, ex-KHAN) / **DICK HENNINGHAM** – organ (ex-ARTHUR BROWN) / **NICK GREENWODD** – bass (ex-ARTHUR BROWN) **/ ERIC PEACHEY** – drums

Deram / P.V.C.

May 72. (lp) **SPACE SHANTY** [ ] [-] 1978
– Space shanty / Stranded effervescent psychonovelty No.5 / Mixed up man of the mountains / Driving to Amsterdam / Stargazers / Hollow stone escape of the space pirates. *(re-iss.Feb77) (cd-iss 1991 on 'Mantra' FRANCE)*

— **DAVE STEWART** – organ (ex-EGG, ex-URIEL) repl. HENNINGHAM **/ NIGEL SMITH** – bass repl. GREENWOOD. (DAVE moved to HATFIELD + THE NORTH) Late 1972, HILLAGE joined KEVIN AYERS Band on tour. In 1973, he joined GONG making 3 lp's **FLYING TEAPOT** (1973), **ANGEL'S EYES** (1973), **YOU** (1974). He guested for EGG on their Nov74 album 'THE CIVIL SURFACE'.

STEVE HILLAGE

went solo with some GONG members.

Virgin / Atlantic

Apr 75. (lp)(c) **FISH RISING** [33] [ ]
– Solar musick suite:- (i) Sun song – (ii) Canterbury sunrise – (iii) Hiram afterglid meets the Dervish – (iv) Sun song (reprise) / Fish / Meditation of the snake / The salmon song:- (i) Salmon pool – (ii) Solomon's Atlantis – (iii) Swimming with the salmon – (iv) King of the fishes / Afterglid:- (i) Sun moon surfing – (ii) Great wave and the boat of Hermes – (iii) The silver ladder – (iv) Astral meadows – (v) The Lafta yoga song – (vi) Gliding – (vii) Golden vibe – the outglid. *(re-iss.Mar84) (cd-iss.Jun87)*

— Next used TODD RUNDGREN'S UTOPIA as backing with others.

Sep 76. (lp)(c) **L** [10] [ ]
– Hurdy gurdy man / Hurdy gurdy glissando / Electrick gypsies / Om nama Shivaya / Luna musick suite / It's all too much. *(re-iss.Mar84) (cd-iss.Jun87)*
Oct 76. (7") **IT'S ALL TOO MUCH. / SHIMMER** [ ] [ ]
Feb 77. (7") **HURDY GURDY MAN. / OM NAMA SHIVAYA** [ ] [ ]
Sep 77. (lp)(c) **MOTIVATION RADIO** [28] [ ]
– Mellow dawn / Motivation / Light in the sky / Radio / Wait one moment / Saucer surfing / Searching for the spark / Ovtave doctors / Not fade away (glide forever). *(re-iss.Mar84) (cd-iss.Jun88)*
Dec 77. (7") **NOT FADE AWAY (GLIDE FOREVER). / SAUCER SURFING** [ ] [ ]
Apr 78. (lp)(c)(green-lp) **GREEN** [30] [-]
– Sea nature / Ether ships / Musick of the trees / Palm trees (love guitar) / Unidentified (flying being) / U.F.O. over Paris / Leyliness to Glassdom / Crystal city / Activation meditation / The glorious om riff. *(re-iss.Mar84) (cd-iss.Jun90)*
May 78. (7") **GETTING BETTER. / PALM TREES (LOVE GUITAR)** [ ] [ ]
Feb 79. (d-lp)(c) **LIVE HERALD (live)** [54] [-]
– The salmon song / The Dervish riff / Castle in the clouds / Hurdy gurdy man / Light in the sky / Searching for the spark / Electrick gypsies / Radiom / Lunar musick suite / Meditation of the dragon / It's all too much / The golden vibe / Talking to the sun / 1988 aktivator / New age synthesis (unzipping the zype) / Healing feeling. *(cd-iss.Jun90, omits side 4)*
Apr 79. (lp)(c)(clear-lp) **RAINBOW DOME MUSICK** [52] [-]

– Garden of Paradise / Four ever rainbow. *(re-iss black vinyl 1984)*

Sep 79. (lp)(c) **OPEN** | 71 | - |
– Day after day / Getting in tune / Open / Definite activity / Don't dither, do it / The fire inside / Earthrise. *(re-iss.Mar84) (cd-iss.Jun90 as "OPEN FEATURING STUDIO HERALD")*

Nov 79. (7") **DON'T DITHER, DO IT. / GETTING IN TUNE**

—— Took time off for sessions, etc., until his return in 1982

Jan 83. (7")(12") **KAMIKAZE EYES. / BEFORE THE WORLD WAS MADE**

Feb 83. (lp)(c) **FOR TO NEXT** | 48 | - |
– These uncharted lands / Kamikaze eyes / Alone / Anthems for the blind / Bright future / Frame by frame / Waiting / Glory. *(free instrumental-lp w/a 'AND NOT OR')* – Before the storm / Red Admiral / Serotonin / And not or / Knights templar / Still golden. *(re-iss.Aug88) (cd-iss.Jul90 with free album) (cd-iss.Mar94)*

Apr 83. (7") **ALONE. / FRAME BY FRAME** | | - |
(12"+=) – Timelines.

—— HILLAGE went more into production for SIMPLE MINDS, ROBYN HITCHCOCK, etc. In the 90's, he guested with ALEX PATERSON in The ORB and founded own ambient group SYSTEM 7.

– compilations, others, etc. –

1979. Virgin; (12"pic-ep) **SIX PACK** | | - |
The salmon song / It's all too much / The golden vibe / Not fade away / Elektric gypsies / Radio.

1983 Aura; (lp) **AURA** | - | |

Aug 92. Windsong; (cd) **BBC RADIO 1 LIVE IN CONCERT (live)** | | - |

SYSTEM 7

STEVE HILLAGE – guitar / **with ALEX PATERSON** (Orb) / **YOUTH** / **DERRICK MAY** / **STEVE WADDINGTON** (Beloved) / **PAUL OAKENFIELD** / **MICK McNEIL** (ex-Simple Minds) / **MIQUETTE GIRAUDY** (ex-Gong) / **OLU ROWE** – vocals / **ZOE THRASH** (Orb) / **ANDY FALCONER** (engineer)

10-Virgin Virgin

Nov 90. (12"clear) **SUNBURST. / MIRACLE**

—— now w/ **ANIFF COUSINS** (Chapter and the Verse) / + **MONDAY MICHIRU** – vocals

Sep 91. (cd)(c)(d-lp) **SYSTEM 7**
– Sunburst / Freedom fighters / Habibi / Altitude / Bon humeur / Fractal liaison / Dog / Thunderdog / Listen / Strange quotations / Miracle / Over and out

Oct 91. (12")(cd-s) **HABIBI. / MIRACLE**

Feb 92. (7")(12")(c-s)(cd-s) **FREEDOM FIGHTERS** (Robin Hancock mixes)
(12"clear+=)(pic-cd-s) ('A' version)

Jun 92. (cd)(c) **ALTITUDES** (8 mixes)

Big Life Big Life

Feb 93. 12") **7:7 EXPANSION** | 39 | |
(12"ep)(cd-ep) – ('A' extended) / ('B' extended)

Feb 93. (cd)(c)(lp) **777** | 30 | |
– 7:7 expansion / A cool dry place / Desir (ghost mix) / On the seventh night / Sinbad / Ship of the desert / Fay deau deau.

Jul 93. (12"ep)(cd-ep) **SINBAD. / QUEST**

Oct 94. (12"ep) **SIRENES. / ('A'-Marshall Jefferson mix) / ('A'-Laurent Garnier mix) / Coltrane (water mix)**
(cd-ep+=) – Alpha wave / Gliding in two-tone curves (water edit).

Oct 94. (cd)(c)(lp) **POINT 3: THE FIRE ALBUM**
– Sirenes / Alpha wave (water edit) / Mysterious traveler / Coltrane (remix) / Radiate / Overview / Gliding on duo-tone curves / Jupiter! / Dr.Livingstone I pressume / Batukau.

Oct 94. (cd)(c) **POINT 3: THE WATER ALBUM**
–

Apr 95. (12"ep)(cd-ep) **ALPHA WAVE (lastikman acid house mix). / ('A'-Alpha mix) / ('A'-That sound mix)**

. . . Jan – Jun '96 stop press . . .

Jan 96. (single) **INTERSTATE**

Feb 96. (cd)(c) **POWER OF SEVEN**

Chris HILLMAN (see under ⇒ BYRDS)

HINDU LOVE GODS (see under ⇒ R.E.M.)

Robyn HITCHCOCK (see under ⇒ SOFT BOYS)

HOLE

Formed: Los Angeles, USA . . . late 1989 by COURTNEY LOVE and 6 foot 4 inch guitarist and Capitol records employee ERIC ERLANDSON. COURTNEY had played alongside JENIFER FINCH (L7) and KAT BJELLAND (Babes In Toyland), in a band called SUGAR BABY DOLL. Took their name HOLE from a line in Euripides' Medea. Placed an ad in local paper 'Flipside', and found a bassist and drummer. In Spring 1990, they released 'RAT BASTARD' EP, before moving to the Seattle area. Early the next year, 'Sub Pop' issued 'DICKNAIL' EP, before signing to 'Geffen', much to the dismay of MADONNA, who wanted her for 'Maverick'. Around the same time, her relationship with NIRVANA's KURT COBAIN, was being highlighted by music press. She had secretly married him in February '92, and soon gave birth to his child in August '92. 1993 saw their debut album 'PRETTY ON THE INSIDE' (produced by KIM GORDON and DON FLEMING) hit lower chart regions, and was voted album of the year by New York's Village Voice magazine. In Spring 1994, she celebrated a UK Top 20 album, but this was overshadowed by the tragic suicide of

KURT on 8th April. She was to hold a memorial on the 10th, and hailing everyone there to call him an asshole. More press coverage followed, and more so on 16th June, when their new bassist KRISTIN PFAFF was found dead in her bath. It was believed to be an accidental drug related death. • **Style:** Grunge-rock fronted by wild child COURTNEY. Similiarities to BABES IN TOYLAND, LYDIA LUNCH or SONIC YOUTH (co-produced 1991 by KIM GORDON and DON FLEMING) • **Songwriters:** Group; except STAR BELLY which sampled DREAMS (Fleetwood Mac) + INTO THE BLACK (Neil Young). Covered; DO IT CLEAN (Echo & The Bunnymen) / CREDIT IN THE STRAIGHT WORLD (Young Marble Giants) / HUNGRY LIKE THE WOLF (Duran Duran) / SEASON OF THE WITCH (Donovan) / HE HIT ME (IT FELT LIKE A KISS) (hit; Crystals). 'I THINK THAT I WOULD DIE' was co-written w / KAT BJELLAND (Babes In Toyland). • **Trivia:** After stints an an actress and a stripper, COURTNEY had a brief stint in FAITH NO MORE. In 1993, COURTNEY sued her doctor for allegedly disclosing her pregnancy details to the press.

Note: Not to be confused with band who released in the late 80's; OTHER TONGUES, OTHER FLESH (lp) and DYSKINSIA (12") both on 'Eyes Media'.

Recommended: PRETTY ON THE INSIDE (*8) / LIVE THROUGH THIS (*10).

COURTNEY LOVE – vocals, guitars / **ERIC ERLANDSON** – guitars / **JILL EMERY** – bass, vocals / **CAROLINE RUE** – drums

		not issued	Sympathy..	
Jul 90.	(7"white-ep) **RETARD GIRL. / PHONEBILL SONG / JOHNNIES IN THE BATHROOM**	-		
		not issued	Sub Pop	
Apr 91.	(7"grey)(7"green)(7"purple)(7"blue) **DICKNAIL. / BURNBLACK**	-		
		City Slang	Caroline	
Aug 91.	(12"ep)(cd-ep) **TEENAGE WHORE. / DROWN SODA / BURNBLACK**			
Oct 91.	(cd)(c)(lp)(red-lp) **PRETTY ON THE INSIDE** – Teenage whore / Babydoll / Garbadge man / Sassy / Goodsister – bad sister / Mrs. Jones / Berry / Loaded / Star belly / Pretty on the inside / Clouds. *(re-iss.Sep95)*	59		

— **LESLEY** – bass repl. JILL / **PATTY SCHEMEL** – drums repl. CAROLINE

		City Slang	D.G.C.	
Apr 93.	(7")(12")(c-s) **BEAUTIFUL SON. / 20 YEARS IN THE DAKOTA / OLD AGE** (cd-s+=) – Pale blue eyes (live).	54	-	

— **KRISTEN PFAFF** – bass, piano, vocals repl. LESLEY

Mar 94.	(7"pink) **MISS WORLD. / ROCK STAR (alternate mix)** (cd-s+=) – Do it clean (live).	64		
Apr 94.	(cd)(c)(lp)(white-lp) **LIVE THROUGH THIS** – Violet / Miss World / Plump / Asking for it / Jennifer's body / Doll parts / Credit in the straight world / Softer, softest / She walks on me / I think that I would die / Gutless / Rock star. *(re-iss.cd/c Apr95)*	13	52	

— KRISTEN was found dead in her bath 16th June 1994. COURTNEY, ERIC + PATTI continued and later recruited **MELISSA AUF DER MAUR** – bass

Apr 95.	(7") **DOLL PARTS. / THE VOID** (cd-s+=) – Hungry like the wolf. (cd-s) – ('A'side) / Credit in the straight world (live) / Plump (live) / I think that I would die (live).	16	58	Dec94
Jul 95.	(7"colrd)(c-s) **VIOLET. / HE HIT ME (IT FELT LIKE A KISS)** (cd-s+=) – Old age / Who's porno you burn (black). (7") – ('A'side) / Old age.	17		

— Back in the news again, COURTNEY was fined for assaulting BIKINI KILL's KATHLEEN HANNA.

. . . Jan – Jun '96 stop press . . .

— COURTNEY and PATTY take three security guards to court for assaulting them, while signing autographs close to the stage of a GREEN DAY concert at Lakefront Arena.

HOLY BARBARIANS (see under ⇒ CULT)

HONEYCRACK

*** NEW ENTRY ***

Formed: London, England ...1995 by CJ, WILLIE DOWLING and MARK McRAE. • **Style:** Melodic Brit-rock similar to TERRORVISION and METALLICA fused with The BEACH BOYS. • **Songwriters:** WD + CJ or MM. Cover HEY BULLDOG (Beatles). • **Trivia:** Produced by GIL NORTON.

Recommended: PROZAIC (*7)

CJ (CHRIS JAGDHAR) – vocals, guitar (ex-WILDHEARTS, ex-TATTOOED LOVE BOYS) / **WILLIE DOWLING** – bass / **MARK McRAE** - / +2

		Epic	Epic
Nov 95.	(7")(c-s) **SITTING AT HOME / IF I HAD A LIFE** (cd-s+=) – 5 minutes / Hey bulldog.	42	
Feb 96.	(7"yellow) **GO AWAY. / GUN** (cd-s+=) – Where do you come from? (cd-s) – ('A'side) / Sitting at home (live) / Powerless.	41	
May 96.	(7"blue) **KING OF MISERY. / GO AWAY (live)** (cd-s+=) – Paperman (live) / Hey bulldog (live). (cd-s) – ('A'side) / Mr. Ultra sheen / All gone wrong / Still dead (. . .and then there were three).	32	
May 96.	(cd)(c)(lp)(white-lp) **PROZAIC** – King of misery / No – please don't / Go away / Powerless / The genius is loose / Good good feeling / If I had a life / I hate myself and everybody else / Animals / Samantha Pope / Paperman / Sitting at home / Parasite.		

HONEYDRIPPERS (see under ⇒ LED ZEPPELIN)

HOOTIE & THE BLOWFISH

Formed: South Carolina, USA . . .1993 by DARIUS, etc (see below). Their debut single 'HOLD MY HAND' stormed America, as did multi-million selling No.1 album 'CRACKED REAR VIEW'. In Britain, they were lauded by the likes of TV/radio presenter Danny Baker, which I suppose helped gain growing reputation on Virgin FM safe rock music station. • **Style:** Corporate melodic MTV adult-orientated rock, with similar vox references of African-American DARIUS, to BRAD ROBERTS (Crash Test Dummies) or EDDIE VEDDER (Pearl Jam). • **Songwriters:** Group? • **Trivia:** DAVID CROSBY guested backing vox on the song 'HOLD MY HAND'.

Recommended CRACKED REAR VIEW (*7) / FAIRWEATHER JOHNSON (*6)

DARIUS RUCKER -vocals, acoustic guitar, percussion / **MARK BRYAN** -guitars, vocals, etc / **DEAN FELBER** -bass, clavinet, vocals / **JIM 'SONI' SONEFELD** -drums, vocals, piano, etc.

		Atlantic	Atlantic	
Feb 95.	(c-s) **HOLD MY HAND / I GO BLIND** (cd-s+=) – Running from an angel.	50	10	Sep94
Mar 95.	(cd)(c) **CRACKED REAR VIEW** – Hannah Jane / Hold my hand / Let her cry / Only wanna be with you / Running from an angel / I'm goin' home / Drowning / Time / Look away / Not even the trees / Goodbye.	12	1	Jun94
May 95.	(c-s) **LET HER CRY / FINE LINE** (cd-s+=) – Hannah Jane (live) / Where were you. (cd-s) – ('A'side) / Goodbye (live) / The ballad of John and Yoko (live) / Hold my hand (live).	75	9	
Aug 95.	(c-s) **ONLY WANNA BE WITH YOU / USE ME (live)** (cd-s) – ('A'live).		6	Jul95
Nov 95.	(c-s)(cd-s) **TIME /**	-	14	

. . . Jan – Jun '96 stop press . . .

Apr 96.	(single) **OLD MAN & ME (WHEN I GET TO HEAVEN)**	57	13
Apr 96.	(album) **FAIRWEATHER JOHNSON**	9	1

HOURGLASS (see under ⇒ ALLMAN BROTHERS BAND)

HOUSEMARTINS

Formed: Hull, England ... late 1983 by PAUL HEATON and STAN CULLIMORE. After local gigs, many of them for political causes (i.e.the miners & CND), they signed in '85 to Andy McDonald's new 'Go! Discs' label. With HUGH WHITAKER replacing LANG, their debut 45 'FLAG DAY' was released, but this flopped. In 1986, NORMAN COOK replaced KEY, and they made UK Top 60 with 'SHEEP'. Hot on its heels, was Top 3 single 'HAPPY HOUR' (complete with plasticine/animated video), and parent debut album 'LONDON 0 HULL 4'. By the end of the year, they had Christmas No.1 with acappella 'CARAVAN OF LOVE'. • **Style:** Like MADNESS or The UNDERTONES, fun pop – rock with meaning and lyrical intelligence. • **Songwriters:** Penned by HEATON-CULLIMORE except covers; HE AIN'T HEAVY, HE'S MY BROTHER (Hollies) / CARAVAN OF LOVE (Isley Jasper Isley). • **Trivia:** LONDON 0 HULL 4, stemmed from group's promotional hometown pride. They often described themselves as Hull's 4th best group. Who were better? RED GUITARS, EVERYTHING BUT THE GIRL and GARGOYLES?

Recommended: NOW THAT'S WHAT I CALL QUITE GOOD (*7).

PAUL HEATON (b. 9 May'62) – vocals / **STAN CULLIMORE** (b.IAN, 6 Apr'62) – guitar, vocals / **TED KEY** – bass / **HUGH WHITAKER** – drums repl. CHRIS LANG

Go! Discs / Elektra

Oct 85. (7") **FLAG DAY. / STAND AT EASE** [ ] [-]
(12"+=) – Coaltrain to Hatfield Main.

— **NORMAN COOK** (b.QUENTIN COOK, 31 Jul'63) – bass repl. TED KEY who formed GARGOYLES

Mar 86. (7")(7"pic-d) **SHEEP. / DROP DOWN DEAD** [54] [-]
(12"+=) – I'll be your shelter / Anxious / People get ready.
(d7"+=)(d12"+=) – Flag day / Stand at ease.

May 86. (7")(7"sha-pic-d) **HAPPY HOUR. / THE MIGHTY SHIP** [3] [ ] Sep 86
(12"+=) – Sitting on a fence / He ain't heavy, he's my brother.

Jun 86. (lp)(c)(cd) **LONDON 0 HULL 4** [3] [ ] Feb 87
– Happy hour / Get up off our knees / Flag day / Anxious / Reverends revenge / Sitting on a fence / Sheep / Over there / Think for a minute / We're not deep / Lean on me / Freedom. *(c+=)* – I'll be your shelter (just like a shelter) / (other 'B'sides) *(re-iss.cd+c.Oct92)*

Sep 86. (7")(7"sha-pic-d) **THINK FOR A MINUTE. / WHO NEEDS THE LIMELIGHT** [18] [ ]
(12"+=) – I smell winter / Joy joy joy / Rap around the clock.
(d7"+=) Sheep / Drop down dead.

Nov 86. (7")(7"sha-pic-d) **CARAVAN OF LOVE. / WHEN I FIRST MET JESUS** [1] [ ]
(12"+=) – We shall not be moved / So much in love / Heaven help us.
(d7"+=) – Flag day / Stand at ease.

Feb 87. (7") **FLAG DAY. / THE MIGHTY SHIP** [-] [ ]

— **DAVE HEMMINGHAM** – drums repl. WHITAKER who joined GARGOYLES full-time

May 87. (7") **FIVE GET OVER EXCITED. / REBEL WITHOUT THE AIRPLAY** [11] [ ]
(12"+=)(c-s+=) – So glad / Hopelessly devoted to them.

Aug 87. (7") **ME AND THE FARMER. / I BIT MY LIP** [15] [ ]
(12"+=)(c-s+=) – Step outside / He will find you out.

Sep 87. (lp)(c)(cd) **THE PEOPLE WHO GRINNED THEMSELVES TO DEATH** [9] [ ] Jan 88
– The people who grinned themselves to death / I can't put my finger on it / The light is always green / The world's on fire / Pirate aggro / We're not coming back / Me and the farmer / Five get over excited / Johannesburg / Bow down / You better be doubtful / Build. *(re-iss.cd+c.Oct92)*

Nov 87. (7") **BUILD. / PARIS IN FLAMES** [15] [ ]
(10"+=)(12"+=)(c-s+=)(cd-s+=) – Forwards and backwards / The light is always green.

Apr 88. (7") **THERE'S ALWAYS SOMETHING THERE TO REMIND ME. / GET UP OFF YOUR KNEES (live)** [35] [ ]
(12"+=)(cd-s+=) – Johannesburg (live) / Five get over excited (live).

Apr 88. (d-lp)(c)(cd) **NOW THAT'S WHAT I CALL QUITE GOOD** (compilation) [8] [ ]
– I smell winter / Bow down / Think for a minute / There is always something there to remind me / The mighty ship / Sheep / I'll be your shelter (just like a shelter) / Five get over excited / Everybody's the same / Build / Step outside / Flag day / Happy hour / You've got a friend / He ain't heavy, he's my brother / Freedom / The people who grinned themselves to death / Caravan of love / The light is always green / We're not deep / Me and the farmer / Lean on me.

— They had already decided to split up Jan88. NORMAN COOK developed several solo projects and the unashamedly commercial BEATS INTERNATIONAL. HEATON and HEMINGWAY formed The BEAUTIFUL SOUTH.

– compilations etc. –

Dec 86. Go! Discs; (7"-box) **CHRISTMAS SINGLES BOX** [84] [-]

HOUSE OF LOVE

Formed: Camberwell, London, England . . . 1986 by CHADWICK, BICKERS, GROOTIZEN and HEUKAMP. They quickly signed to Alan McGee's 'Creation' label, and unleashed classic debut 'SHINE ON', which became a John Peel favourite throughout 1987. The following year, they issued 2 more beauties 'CHRISTINE' & 'DESTROY THE HEART', which after a superb debut album, led to a contract on 'Fontana'. In 1989, they had first of several hits 'NEVER', which was pursued in the early 90's by UK Top 10 album 'FONTANA'. • **Style:** Inspired by 60's outfits VELVET UNDERGROUND, LOVE and The BYRDS. Progressed with similarities to the ONLY ONES, through 80's psychedelia and new breed rock. • **Songwriters:** CHADWICK penned except; I CAN'T STAND IT (Velvet Underground) / PINK FROST (Chills) / IT'S ALL TOO MUCH (Beatles) / STRANGE BREW (Cream) / ROCK YOUR BABY (George McCrae). • **Trivia:** Debut album was produced by PAT COLLIER (ex-Vibrators) and STEVE NUNN.

Recommended: THE HOUSE OF LOVE (*8) / FONTANA (*7).

GUY CHADWICK – vocals, guitar (ex-KINGDOMS) / **TERRY BICKERS** – guitar (ex-COLENSO PARADE) / **ANDREA HEUKAMP** (b.Germany) – guitar, vocals / **CHRIS GROOTHIZEN** (b.New Zealand) – bass / **PETE EVANS** – drums

Creation / Relativity

May 87. (12"m) **SHINE ON. / LOVE / FLOW** [ ] [-]

Sep 87. (12"m) **REAL ANIMAL. / PLASTIC / NOTHING TO ME** [ ] [-]

— Now a quartet when ANDREA returned to Germany

Apr 88. (7") **CHRISTINE. / LONELINESS IS A GUN** [ ] [-]
(12"+=) – The hill.

May 88. (lp)(c)(cd) **THE HOUSE OF LOVE** [ ] [ ]
– Christine / Hope / Road / Sulphur / Man to child / Salome / Love in a car / Happy / Fisherman's tale / Touch me. *(re-iss.cd+c Aug94)*

Aug 88. (7") **DESTROY THE HEART. / BLIND** [ ] [ ]
(12"+=) – Mr. Jo.

Fontana / Fontana

Apr 89.. (7") **NEVER. / SOFT AS FIRE** [41] [ ]
(12"+=)(cd-s+=) – Safe.

Nov 89. (7")(c-s) **I DON'T KNOW WHY I LOVE YOU. / SECRETS** [41] [ ]
(12"+=) – I can't stand it. (repl. on some 12") – The spy.
(cd-s++=) – Clothes. (above on some 7"b-side, repl. by) – Love II.

— **SIMON WALKER** – guitar (of DAVE HOWARD SINGERS) repl. BICKERS

Jan 90. (7") **SHINE ON (remix). / ALLERGY** [20] [ ]
(12"+=)(c-s+=) – Scratched inside.
(12"+=) – Rosalyn.
(cd-s+=) – Rough.

Feb 90. (cd)(c)(lp) **FONTANA** [8] [ ]
– Hannah / Shine on / Beatles and the Stones / Shake and crawl / Hedonist / I don't know why I love you / Never / Somebody's got to love you / In a room / Blind / 32nd floor / Se dest.

Mar 90. (7") **BEATLES AND THE STONES. / LOVE IV** [36] [ ]
(12"+=) – Phone.
(12"+=) – Cut the fool down.
(cd-s+=) – Marble.
(cd-s+=) – Phone (extended).
(12"+=)(cd-s+=) – Glorify me./ / Soft as fire.
(7"ltd.) – ('A'side) / Love IV / Love V.

Nov 90. (cd)(c)(lp) **SPY IN THE HOUSE OF LOVE** (rare material, etc.) [49] [ ]
– Safe / Marble / D song '89 / Scratched inside / Phone (full version) / Cut the fool down / Ray / Love II / Baby teen / Love III / Soft as fire / Love IV / No fire / Love V. *(re-iss.cd Aug94)*

— (Sep90) added returning **ANDREA HEUKAMP** – guitar, vocals

Oct 91. (7")(c-s) **THE GIRL WITH THE LONELIEST EYES. / PURPLE KILLER ROSE** [58] [ ]
(12"+=)(cd-s+=) – Tea in the Sun / Pink frost.

Apr 92. (7"ep) **FEEL / IT'S ALL TOO MUCH** [45] [ ]
(10"+=) – Let's talk about you / Strange brew.
(cd-s++=) – Real animal.

— During recording of following album, SIMON left. He was succeeded by album guests **ANDREA HEUKAMP** – guitar, vox / **WARNE LIVESEY** – guitar, keyboards, etc. / **CAROL KENYON** – vocals / **PANDIT DENESH** – tablas

Jun 92. (7") **YOU DON'T UNDERSTAND. / SWEET ANATOMY** [46] [ ]
(10"+=)(cd-s+=) – Kiss the mountain / Third generation liquid song.
(cd-s+=) – Destroy the heart / Blind / Mr.Jo.

Jul 92. (cd)(c)(lp) **BABE RAINBOW** [34] [ ]
– You don't understand / Crush me / Crue / High in your face / Fade away / Feel / The girl with the loneliest eyes / Burn down the world / Philly Phile / Yer eyes. *(re-iss.cd Aug94)*

Nov 92. (7") **CRUSH ME. / LOVE ME** [67] [ ]
(10"+=) – Last edition of love / Skin 2 phase 2.
(cd-s) – ('A'side) / Christine / Ladies is a gun / The hitch.

Jun 93. (cd)(c)(lp) **AUDIENCE WITH THE MIND** [38] [ ]
– Sweet Anatomy / Audience With The Mind / Haloes / Erosion / Call Me / Shining On / Portrait In Atlanta / Corridors / Hollow / All Night Long / Into The Tunnel / You've Got To Feel *(re-iss.cd+c Aug94)*

HOUSE OF PAIN

Formed: Woodland Hills, Los Angeles, California, USA . . . 1991 by solo artist EVERLAST, DANNY BOY and LETHAL DJ. By late 1992, their sexist words 'JUMP AROUND', were being sprayed on both sides of the Atlantic. • **Style:** Shamrock-touting hip hoppers, with degradation to women, their forte. Besides this, their screeching gangsta sound, went a long way to establish them as a top rap act of the early 90's. • **Songwriters:** Group penned, and partly produced by DJ MUGGS (Cypress Hill). Sampled HARLEM SHUFFLE (Bob Earl) / I COME TO YOU BABY (John Lee Hooker) • **Trivia:** DANNY BOY's preoccupation with his Irish ancestry, made him mark his body with a 'Sinn Fein' tattoo, although he admitted to being more influenced by actor Mickey Rourke, than the Irish political party.

Recommended: HOUSE OF PAIN (*7).

EVERLAST

w/**ICE-T** – vox / **BILAL BASHIR** – keyboards / **CLARENCE METHENY** – synth. / **JOHN BREYER** – guitar / **MIKE GREG** – sax

		Warners	Warners
1989.	(12") **SYNDICATION. / BUSTIN' LOOSE**	-	
Feb 90.	(cd)(c)(lp) **FOREVER EVERLAST** – Syndicate soldier / Speak no evil / Syndication (remix) / What is this? / The rhythm / I got the knack / On the edge / Fuck everyone / Goodbye / Pass it on / Never missin' a beat.		
Mar 90.	(12") **SYNDICATE SOLDIER. / NEVER MISSIN' A BEAT**	-	
Jun 90.	(c-s) **PAY THE PRICE. / I GOT THE KNACK**	-	

HOUSE OF PAIN

ERIC "EVERLAST" SCHRODY– vocals / **"DANNY BOY" O'CONNER** – vocals / **LEOR "DJ LETHAL" DiMANT** (b.Latvia) – turntable

		X.L.	Tom-my Boy
Sep 92.	(12")(cd-s) **JUMP AROUND (Master Mix) / HOUSE OF PAIN ANTHEM (Master Mix)**	32	3 Jun 92
Nov 92.	(cd)(c)(lp) **HOUSE OF PAIN** – Salutations / Jump around / Put your head out / Top o' the morning to ya / House and the rising sun / Shamrocks and shenanigans (boom shalock lock boom) / House of pain anthem / Danny boy, Danny boy / Guess who's back / Put on your shit kickers / Come and get some of this / Life goes on / One for the road / Feel it / All my love	73	14 Aug 92
Nov 92.	(12")(cd-s) **SHAMROCKS AND SHENANIGANS (BOOM SHALOCK LOCK BOOM)**		65
		Ruffness	Ruffness
May 93.	(12")(c-s)(cd-s) **JUMP AROUND (remix). / TOP O' THE MORNING TO YA (remix) / (other mixes of 'A'+'B')**	8	
May 93.	(c-s) **WHO'S THE MAN. /**	-	96
Oct 93.	(12")(c-s)(cd-s) **SHAMROCKS & SHENANIGANS. / WHO'S THE MAN**	23	

— EVERLAST was jailed at home for 3 months in Feb'94, for earlier carrying a weapon. 'IT AIN'T A CRIME' sampled UNDER THE BRIDGE (Red Hot Chili Peppers).

Jul 94.	(12")(c-s)(cd-s) **ON POINT (The Beatminerz mix). / ('A'-DJ Lethal mix)**	19	85
Jul 94.	(cd)(c)(d-lp) **SAME AS IT EVER WAS** – Back from the dead / I'm a swing it / All that / On point / Runnin' up on ya / Over the shit / Word is bond / Keep it comin' / Interlude / Same as it ever was / It ain't a crime / Where I'm from / Still got a lotta love / Who's the man / On point (lethal dose remix).	8	12
Oct 94.	(12")(c-s)(cd-s) **IT AIN'T A CRIME (madhouse remix). / LEGEND** (cd-s) – ('A'side) / Word is bond (Diamond D + Darkman remixes).	37	
Jun 95.	(12")(cd-s) **OVER THERE (I DON'T CARE). / JUMP AROUND (mastermix)** (cd-s+=) – Shamrocks and shenanigans / Top o' the morning to ya. (cd-s) – ('A'side) / Runnin' up on ya (versions incl. House of Pain vs. Kerbdog).	20	

Steve HOWE (see under ⇒ YES)

HUMAN LEAGUE

Formed: Sheffield, England ... Autumn 1977 by computer operators MARTYN WARE and IAN CRAIG-MARSH. As The FUTURE, with vocalist ADI NEWTON, they recruited former hospital porter PHIL OAKEY, who soon replaced ADI (later to CLOCKDVA). Now as HUMAN LEAGUE, the trio recorded demo, which was accepted by Edinburgh-based indie 'Fast', run by Bob Last. Their debut 45 'BEING BOILED', became NME single of the week in mid-78. They added ADRIAN WRIGHT on visuals and synths, and after a dire instrumental EP 'THE DIGNITY OF LABOUR', they signed to 'Virgin' in Apr'79. Their first 45 for the label 'I DON'T DEPEND ON YOU', was credited to The MEN, but their credibility was restored later that year, when 'EMPIRE STATE HUMAN', nearly gave them hit. This was duly followed by a debut album 'REPRODUCTION', which failed to produce early promise. In Spring 1980, they went into UK Top 60 with double 7"EP 'HOLIDAY '80', and Top 20 with album 'TRAVELOGUE'. In Oct'80, OAKEY and WRIGHT brought in teenage girls JOANNE and SUZANNE to replace WARE and CRAIG-MARSH who left to form HEAVEN 17. 12 months later, with new additions IAN BURDEN and JO CALLIS, they were at No.1 with both 'DARE' album, and 'DON'T YOU WANT ME' single, which also peaked at the top in the States. They continued to score on both sides of the Atlantic throughout the next decade. • **Style:** Initially an experimental industrial outfit, who manufactured themselves into top synth-pop group of the 80's. OAKEY's hair was always a main feature, as it was very long, only on one side!. • **Songwriters:** WARE and CRAIG-MARSH before their departure, and OAKEY and WRIGHT on all since early 80's. The 90's, featured OAKEY composing alongside new member NEIL SUTTON. Covered:- YOU'VE LOST THAT LOVIN' FEELIN' (Righteous Brothers) / ROCK'N'ROLL (Gary Glitter) / NIGHTCLUBBIN' (Iggy Pop) / ONLY AFTER DARK (Mick Ronson). • **Trivia:** MARTIN RUSHENT was their main producer, although JIMMY JAM & TERRY LEWIS worked with them in '86.

Recommended: GREATEST HITS (*8) / DARE (*8).

PHIL OAKEY (b. 2 Oct'55) – vocals / **IAN CRAIG-MARSH** (b.19 Nov'56) – synthesizers / **MARTYN WARE** (b.19 May'56) – synthesizers

		Fast	not issued
Jun 78.	(7") **BEING BOILED. / CIRCUS OF DEATH** *(re-iss.Jan82 reached No.6 UK)*		-

— added **ADRIAN WRIGHT** (b.30 Dec'56) – synthesizers, visuals

Apr 79.	(12"ep) **THE DIGNITY OF LABOUR** – (part 1 / part 2 / part 3 / part 4) *(contains free flexi)*		-
		Virgin	A & M
Jul 79.	(12") **I DON'T DEPEND ON YOU. ("The MEN") / CRUEL**		-
Sep 79.	(7") **EMPIRE STATE HUMAN. / INTRODUCING**		-
Oct 79.	(lp)(c) **REPRODUCTION** – Almost medieval / Circus of death / The path of least resistance / Blind youth / The word before last / Empire state human / Morale / You've lost that lovin' feelin' / Austerity / Girl one / Zero as a limit. *(re-iss.+cd.1987)*		-
Apr 80.	(7") **HOLIDAY '80** – Rock'n'roll / Being boiled / Nightclubbing / Dancevision. *(re-iss.Nov81 as 12"ep += Marianne. reached No.46)*	56	-
May 80.	(lp)(c) **TRAVELOGUE** – The black hit of space / Only after dark / Life kills / Dreams of leaving / Toyota city / Crow and a baby / The touchables / Gordon's Gin / Being boiled / WXJL tonight. *(re-iss.+cd.1987)*	16	-
Jun 80.	(7") **ONLY AFTER DARK. / TOYOTA CITY** (free 7" w/) – EMPIRE STATE HUMAN. / INTRODUCING	62	

— **JO CATHERALL** (b.18 Sep'62) **& SUSANNE SULLEY** (b.22 Mar'63) – b.vocals repl. WARE and MARSH who formed HEAVEN 17. also added **IAN BURDEN** (b.24 Dec'57) – bass, synthesizers

Feb 81.	(7") **BOYS AND GIRLS. / TOM BAKER**	48	
Apr 81.	(7") **THE SOUND OF THE CROWD.(as "HUMAN LEAGUE RED") / ('A' instrumental)** (12"+=) – Tom Baker / Boys and girls / Dancevision.	12	

— added **JO CALLIS** – guitar (ex-REZILLOS, ex-BOOTS FOR DANCING, ex-SHAKE)

Jul 81.	(7") **LOVE ACTION (I BELIEVE IN LOVE). / HARD TIMES** (12"+=) – ('A'&'B'instrumental). (with free 7"flexi) *(cd-ep.iss.Jun88, – the 4 12"tracks)*	3	Apr 82
Oct 81.	(7") **OPEN YOUR HEART.(as "HUMAN LEGUE BLUE") / NON-STOP** (12"+=) – ('A'&'B'instrumental).	6	
Oct 81.	(lp)(c)(pic-lp) **DARE** – Things that dreams are made of / Open your heart / The sound of the crowd / Darkness / Do or die / Get Carter / I am the law / Seconds / Love action (I believe in love) / Don't you want me. *(cd-iss.1987)*	1	3 Feb 82
Nov 81.	(7")(12") **DON'T YOU WANT ME. ("HUMAN LEAGUE 100") / SECONDS**	1	1 Feb 82
Jul 82.	(lp)(c) **LOVE AND DANCING ("LEAGUE UNLIMITED ORCHESTRA")** – (instrumental versions of "DARE" except) / Get Carter / Darkness.	6	
Aug 82.	(7") **THINGS THAT DREAMS ARE MADE OF. / ('A' instrumental)**	-	
Oct 82.	(7") **DON'T YOU WANT ME ("LEAGUE UNLIMITED ORCHESTRA"). / (part 2)**	-	
Nov 82.	(7")(12")(7"pic-d) **MIRROR MAN. / YOU REMIND ME OF GOLD**	2	-
Apr 83.	(7")(12") **(KEEP FEELING) FASCINATION. / TOTAL PANIC**	2	8 May 83
Jul 83.	(m-lp) **FASCINATION** (import, recent hits).	-	22
Sep 83.	(7") **MIRROR MAN. / NON-STOP**	-	30
Apr 84.	(7")(12") **THE LEBANON. / THIRTEEN**	11	64 Jul 84
May 84.	(lp)(c)(cd) **HYSTERIA** – I'm coming back / I love you too much / Rock me again and again and again and again and again and again / Louise / The Lebanon / Betrayed / The sign / So hurt / Life on your own / Don't you know I want you. *(cd-re-iss.Jul87) (re-iss.cd Mar94)*	3	62
Jun 84.	(7")(12") **LIFE ON YOUR OWN. / THE WORLD TONIGHT**	16	-
Aug 84.	(7") **DON'T YOU KNOW I WANT TO. / THIRTEEN**	-	

Oct 84. (7") **LOUISE. / THE WORLD TONIGHT** [-] [ ]
Nov 84. (7")(12")(7"pic-d) **LOUISE. / THE SIGN** [13] [-]

— Trimmed down to main trio of **PHIL, SUSANNE, JOANNE** plus **ADRIAN / JIM RUSSELL** – synthesizer repl. BURDEN and CALLIS

Aug 86. (7") **HUMAN. / ('A'instrumental)** [8] [1]
(12"+=) – ('A'extended) / ('A'acapella).
Sep 86. (lp)(c)(cd) **CRASH** [7] [24]
– Money / Swang / Human / Jam / Are you ever coming back? / I need your loving / Party / Love on the run / The real thing / Love is all that matters.
Nov 86. (7")(12") **I NEED YOUR LOVING. / ('A'version)** [72] [-]
Nov 86. (7") **I NEED YOUR LOVING. / ARE YOU EVER COMING BACK** [-] [44]
Jan 87. (7") **LOVE IS ALL THAT MATTERS. / ('A' instrumental)** [-] [ ]
Apr 87. (7") **ARE YOU EVER COMING BACK. / JAM** [-] [ ]
Oct 88. (7") **LOVE IS ALL THAT MATTERS. / I LOVE YOU TOO MUCH** [41] [ ]
(12"+=)(cd-s+=) – ('A'dub version).
Nov 88. (lp)(c)(cd) **GREATEST HITS** (compilation) [3] [ ]
– Mirror man / (Keep feeling) Fascination / The sound of the crowd / The Lebanon / Human / Together in electric dreams (PHIL OAKEY & GIORGIO MORODER) / Don't you want me? / Being boiled (re-boiled) / Love action (I believe in love) / Louise / Open your heart / Love is all that matters / Life on your own. *(re-iss.cd/c Nov95)*

— The basic trio, added **RUSSELL BENNETT** – guitar / **NEIL SUTTON** – keyboards

Aug 90. (7")(US-c-s) **HEART LIKE A WHEEL. / REBOUND** [29] [32] Sep 90
(12"+=)(cd-s+=) – ('A'extended).
(cd-s++=) – A doorway (dub mix).
Sep 90. (cd)(c)(lp) **ROMANTIC?** [24] [ ]
– Kiss the future / A doorway / Heart like a wheel / Men are dreamers / Mister Moon and Mister Sun / Soundtrack to a generation / Rebound / The stars are going out / Let's get together again / Get it right this time.
Nov 90. (7")(c-s) **SOUNDTRACK TO A GENERATION. / ('A'instrumental)** [ ] [ ]
(12"+=) – ('A'acappella version).
(cd-s++=) – ('A'dub version).

East West East West

Dec 94. (c-s) **TELL ME WHEN. / ('A'mix)** [6] [31] Mar95
(cd-s+=) – Kimi ni mune kyun / The bus to Crookes.
(12")(cd-s) – ('A'side) / ('A'-Overworld mix) / ('A'-Red Jerry mix) / ('A'-strictly blind dub mix).
Jan 95. (cd)(c) **OCTOPUS** [6] [ ]
– Tell me when / These are the days / One man in my heart / Words / Filling up with Heaven / House full of nothing / John Cleese; is he funny? / Never again / Cruel young lover.
Mar 95. (c-s)(cd-s) **ONE MAN IN MY HEART / THESE ARE THE DAYS (Ba ba mix)** [13] [ ]
(cd-s+=) – These are the days (sonic radiation) / ('A'version).
(12") – ('B'side) / ('B'-Symphone Ba Ba mix) / ('B'instrumental) / ('A'-T.O.E.C. unplugged).
Jun 95. (c-s)(cd-s) **FILLING UP WITH HEAVEN / JOHN CLEESE, IS HE FUNNY?** [36] [ ]
(cd-s) – ('A'side) / ('A'-Hardfloor mix) / ('A'-Neil McLellen mix).
Oct 95. (c-s) **DON'T YOU WANT ME (remix) / ('A'-Snap remix) / (2-'A'-Red Jerry mix)** [16] [ ]
(12") – ('A'-Snap remix extended) / ('A'-Red Jerry remix extended).
(cd-s) – (all 6-'A'versions).

. . . Jan – Jun '96 stop press . . .

Jan 96. (single) **STAY WITH ME TONIGHT** [40] [ ]

– compilations, etc. –

Oct 90. Virgin; (cd-box) **DARE / HYSTERIA / CRASH** [ ] [ ]

PHIL OAKEY & GIORGIO MORODER

– synthesizers

Virgin A & M

Sep 84. (7")(7"pic-d) **TOGETHER IN ELECTRIC DREAMS. / ('A'instrumental)** [3] [ ]
(12"+=) – ('A'extended).
Jun 85. (7")(12") **GOODBYE BAD TIMES. /('A' version)** [44] [ ]
Jul 85. (lp)(c)(cd) **CHROME** [52] [ ]
– Goodbye bad times / Together in electric dreams / Valerie / Why must the show go on / Be me lover now / Shake it up / Brand new lover / In transit / Now. *(cd-re-iss.Jun88)*
Aug 85. (7")(12") **BE MY LOVER NOW. / ('A' instrumental)** [ ] [ ]

HUMANOID

(see under ⇒ FUTURE SOUND OF LONDON)

Robert HUNTER

(see under ⇒ GRATEFUL DEAD)

HUSKER DU

Formed: Minneapolis, USA . . . 1978 by MOULD, HART and NORTON. In 1980-82, they issued a few 45's and a live lp 'LAND SPEED RECORD', which was on own label 'New Alliance'. After another lp on 'Reflex' in 1983, they shifted to BLACK FLAG's US indie label 'SST', and unleashed mini-lp 'METAL CIRCUS'. Three classic lp's 'ZEN ARCADE', 'NEW DAY RISING' & 'FLIP YOUR WIG' (1st was double) appeared between Autumn '84 & '85, before they were snapped up by 'Warners'. After 2 uncompromising sets 'CANDY APPLE GREY' & 'WAREHOUSE' in 1986, they argued and split up the next year. Solo projects by MOULD and HART appeared, but commercial success arrived in 1992, when BOB MOULD's band "SUGAR" signed to 'Creation' and made UK Top 10. • **Style:** Innovators of hardcore speed-metal, which in the mid-80's, became integrated with 2 or 3 minute rock gems. SUGAR were energy and melody fused together somewhere between NIRVANA and PIXIES. • **Songwriters:** MOULD-HART compositions except; SUNSHINE SUPERMAN (Donovan) / TICKET TO RIDE + SHE'S A WOMAN + HELTER SKELTER (Beatles) / EIGHT MILES HIGH (Byrds). NOVA MOB covered I JUST WANT TO MAKE LOVE TO YOU (Willie Dixon) / SHEENA IS A PUNK ROCKER (Ramones). Solo GRANT HART covered SIGNED D.C. (Love). • **Trivia:** HUSKER DU means; DO YOU REMEMBER in Swedish.

Recommended: NEW DAY RISING (*8) / FLIP YOUR WIG (*9) / ZEN ARCADE (*8) / CANDY APPLE GREY (*7) / WAREHOUSE (*7)

BOB MOULD (b.Lake Placid) – vocals, guitar, keyboards, percussion / **GRANT HART** – drums, keyboards, percussion, vocals / **GREG NORTON** – bass

not issued Reflex

1980. (7") **STATUES. / AMUSEMENT (live)** [-] [ ]

not issued New Allia..

Aug 81. (lp) **LAND SPEED RECORD (live)** [-] [ ]
– All tensed up / Don't try to call / I'm not interested / Big sky / Guns at my school / Push the button / Gilligan's Island / MTC / Don't have a life / Bricklayer / Tired of doing things / You're naive / Strange week / Do the bee / Ultracore / Let's go die / Data control. *(UK import mid-82 on 'Alt.Tent.') (UK rel.Nov88 on 'S.S.T.' & re-iss.cd/c/lp Oct95)*
1982. (7"m) **IN A FREE LAND. / WHAT DO I WANT? / M.I.C.** [-] [ ]

not issued Reflex

Jul 83. (lp) **EVERYTHING FALLS APART** [-] [ ]
– From the gut / Blah, blah, blah / Punch drunk / Bricklayer / Afraid of being wrong / Sunshine Superman / Signals from above / Everything falls apart / Wheels / Obnoxious / Gravity. *(cd-iss. May93 with extra tracks)*

S.S.T. S.S.T.

Dec 83. (m-lp) **METAL CIRCUS** [ ] [ ]
– Real world / Deadly skies / It's not funny anymore / Diane / First of the last calls / Lifeline / Out on a limb.
Apr 84. (7"colrd) **EIGHT MILES HIGH. / MASOCHISM WORLD** [ ] [ ]
(iss.cd-s.Dec88)
Sep 84. (d-lp) **ZEN ARCADE** [ ] [ ]
– Something I learned today / Broken home, broken heart / Never talking to you again / Chartered trips / Dreams reoccurring / Indecision time / Hare Krishna / Beyond the threshold / Pride / I'll never forget you / The biggest lie / What's going on / Masochism world / Standing by the sea / Somewhere / One step at a time / Pink turns to blue / Newest industry / Monday will never be the same / Whatever / The tooth fairy and the princess / Turn on the news / Reoccurring dreams. *(cd-iss.Oct87) (re-iss.cd/c/d-lp Oct95)*
Feb 85. (lp) **NEW DAY RISING** [ ] [ ]
– New day rising / Girl who lives on Heaven Hill / I apologize / Folklore / If I told you / Celebrated summer / Perfect example / Terms of psychic warfare / 59 times the pain / Powerline / Books about UFO's / I don't know what you're talking about / How to skin a cat / Watcha drinkin' / Plans I make. *(cd-iss.Oct87) (re-iss.cd/c/lp Oct95)*
Aug 85. (7") **MAKE NO SENSE AT ALL. / LOVE IS ALL AROUND (MARY'S THEME)** [ ] [ ]
Oct 85. (lp) **FLIP YOUR WIG** [ ] [ ]
– Flip your wig / Every everything / Makes no sense at all / Hate paper doll / Green eyes / Divide and conquer / Games / Find me / The baby song / Flexible flyer / Private plane / Keep hanging on / The wit and the wisdom / Don't know yet. *(cd-iss.Oct87) (re-iss.cd/c/lp Oct95)*

Warners Warners

Feb 86. (7") **DON'T WANT TO KNOW IF YOU ARE LONELY. / ALL WORK NO PLAY** [ ] [ ]
(12"+=) – Helter skelter (live).
Mar 86. (lp)(c) **CANDY APPLE GREY** [ ] [ ]
– Crystal / Don't want to know if you are lonely / I don't know for sure / Sorry somehow / Too far down / Hardly getting over it / Dead set on destruction / Eiffel Tower high / No promises have I made / All this I've done for you.
Sep 86. (7") **SORRY SOMEHOW. / ALL THIS I'VE DONE FOR YOU** [ ] [ ]

(d7+=)(12"+=) – Flexible flyer / Celebrated summer.
Jan 87. (7")(12") **COULD YOU BE THE ONE. / EVERYTIME**
Jan 87. (d-lp)(d-c) **WAREHOUSE: SONGS & STORIES** 72
– These important years / Charity, chastity, prudence and hope / Standing in the rain / Back from somewhere / Ice cold ice / You're a soldier / Could you be the one? / Too much spice / Friend, you've got to fall / Visionary / She floated away / Bed of nails / Tell you why tomorrow / It's not peculiar / Actual condition / No reservations / Turn it around / She's a woman (and now he is a man) / Up in the air / You can live at home.
Jun 87. (7")(12") **ICE COLD ICE. / GOTTA LETTA**

– compilations –

May 94. Warners; (cd)(c) **THE LIVING END (live)**
– New day rising / Heaven Hill / Standing in the rain / Back from somewhere / Ice cold ice / Everytime / Friend you're gonna fall / She floated away / From the gut / Target / It's not funny anymore / Hardly getting over it / Terms of psychic warfare / Powertime / Books about UFO's / Divide and conquer / Keep hangin' on / Celebrated summer / Now that you know me / Ain't no water in the well / What's goin' on / Data control / In a free land / Sheena is a punk rocker.

— Disbanded in 1987 after manager DAVID SAVOY Jr. committed suicide. GRANT HART went solo in '89, as did BOB MOULD. In 1992 he formed SUGAR.

GRANT HART

S.S.T. S.S.T.

Nov 89. (lp,cd) **INTOLERANCE**
– All of my senses / Now that you know me / The main / Roller risk / Fanfare in D major (come, come) / You're the victim / 2541 / Anything / She can see the angels coming / Reprise.
May 90. (12"ep)(cd-ep) **ALL OF MY SENSES. / THE MAIN (edit) / SIGNED D.C.**

World Ser. World Ser.

Dec 95. (cd) **ECCE HOMO**
–

NOVA MOB

(GRANT HART) & his group:- **TOM MERKL** – bass / **MICHAEL CRECO** – drums

Rough Trade Rough Trade

Feb 91. (cd)(c)(lp) **THE LAST DAYS OF POMPEII**
– Introduction / Woton / Getaway (gateway) in time / Admiral of the sea (79 a.d. version) / Wernher Von Braun / Space jazz / Where you grave land (next time you fall off of yo) / Over my head / Admiral of the sea / Persuaded / Lavender and grey / Medley:- The last days of Pompeii / Benediction.
Feb 91. (12"ep)(cd-ep) **ADMIRAL OF THE SEA (first avenue mix) / ('A' milk off mix) / THE LAST DAYS OF POMPEII (mix) / GETAWAY IN TIME (instrumental) / I JUST WANT TO MAKE LOVE TO YOU (live)**

— **MARK RELISH** – drums repl. CRECO

Southern Big Shoe

Jul 92. (cd-ep) **SHOT YOUR WAY TO FREEDOM / BALLAD NO. 19 / OH! TO BEHOLD / CHILDREN IN THE STREET**

— **HART** with **CHRIS HENSLER** – guitar / **TOM MERKL** – bass / **STEVE SUTHERLAND** – drums

World Service World Service

May 94. (cd)(lp) **NOVA MOB**
– Shoot your way to freedom / Puzzles / Buddy / See and feel and know / Little Miss Information / I won't be there anymore / Please don't ask / The sins of their sons / Beyond a reasonable doubt / I was afraid – Coda.
Sep 94. (cd-ep) **OLD EMPIRE / PLEASE DON'T ASK / LITTLE MISS INFORMATION / BEYOND A REASONABLE DOUBT**

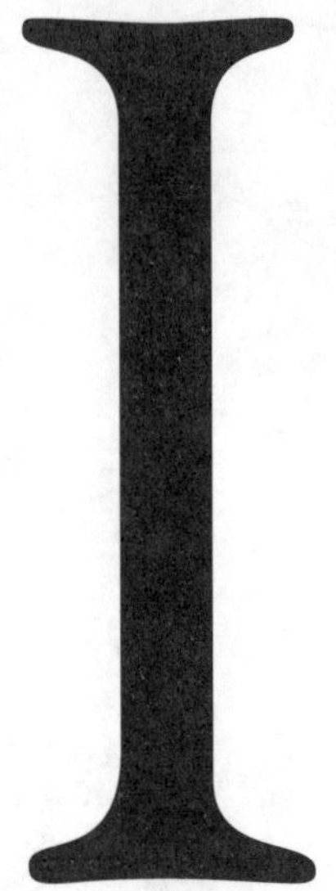

ICE CUBE

Born: OSHEA JACKSON, Jun'69, Crenshaw, Los Angeles, USA. Was a former leader of group N.W.A. (NIGGERS WITH ATTITUDE), who hit US Top 40 with album 'STRAIGHT OUTA COMPTON'. Departed from them due to verbal confrontations with himself and Jewish manager Jerry Hellen. ICE CUBE debuted in summer of 1990, with the politicised 'AMERIKKKA'S MOST WANTED'. By December '92, 'THE PREDATOR' had bolted straight in at No.1. • **Style:** Idealogical black rapper, with overtly sexist lyrics. Controversial for being anti-white power, anti-police, anti-media, anti- poverty, etc, etc. • **Songwriters:** Co-writes with SADLER or JINX. Sample The ISLEYS, JAMES BROWN, STEELY DAN and MICHAEL JACKSON, OHIO PLAYERS, PUBLIC ENEMY, DAS EFX, MOMENTS + GRANDMASTER FLASH. • **Trivia:** Starred and contributed to soundtracks for the films 'Boyz'n'the hood' and 'Trespass' (circa early 90's). In 1991, he co-wrote with JAMES BROWN and produced female hardcore rapper YO-YO on their 'East-West' debut US hit single 'You can't Play With My World'.

Recommended: AMERIKKKA'S MOST WANTED (*8) / THE PREDATOR (*7) / DEATH CERTIFICATE (*7)

ICE CUBE – vocals (with LENCH MOB)

4th & Bro. Priority

May 90. (7") **AMERIKKKA'S MOST WANTED. / ONCE UPON A TIME IN THE PROJECTS**
(12"+=)(cd-s+=) – ('A'&'B' instrumentals)

Jun 90. (cd)(c)(lp) **AMERIKKKA'S MOST WANTED** [48] [19] May 90
– Better off dead / The nigga ya love to hate / Amerikkka's most wanted / What they hittin' foe? / You can't fade me / JD's gaffilin' / Once upon a time in the projects / Turn off the radio / Endangered species (tales from the darkside) / A gangsta's fairytale / I'm only out for one thing / Get off my Dick and tell yo bitch to come here / The drive-by / Rollin' with the Lench Mob / Who's the Mack? / It's a man's world / The bomb.

Mar 91. (cd)(c)(m-lp) **KILL AT WILL** (above remixes) [66] [34] Dec 90
– Endangered species (tales from the darkside) / Jackin' for beats / Get off my Dick and tell yo bitch to come here / The product / Dead Homiez / JD's gaffilin (part 2) / I gotta say what up!!!.

Oct 91. (cd)(c)(lp) **DEATH CERTIFICATE** [2]
– The funeral / The wrong nigga to fuck wit / My summer vacation / Steady mobbin' / Robin Lench / Givin' up the nappy dug out / Look who's burnin' / A bird in the hand / Man's best friend / Alive on arrival / Death / The birth / I wanna kill Sam / Horny lil' devil / True to the game / Color blind / Doing dumb shit / Us. *(cd+=)* – No Vaseline / Black Korea.

Dec 91. (7")(cd-s) **STEADY MOBBIN?. / US**
(12"+=)(cd-s+=) – Dead Homrez / Endangered species (tales from the dark side) (remix).

Nov 92. (12")(cd-s) **WICKED. / WE HAD TO TEAR THIS MOTHAFUCKA UP / THE WRONG NIGGA TO FUCK WIT / ('A'instrumental)** [55]
(cd-s+=) – ('A'&'B' instrumental). *(re-iss.Sep93, hit UK 62)*

Nov 92. (cd)(c)(lp) **THE PREDATOR** [73] [1]
– (the first day of school intro) / When will they shoot? / (I'm scared) / Wicked / Now I gotta wet 'cha / The predator / It was a good day / We had to tear this mothafucka up / **** 'em / Dirty Mack / Don't trust 'em / Gangsta's fairytale 2 / Check yo self / Who's got the camera? / Integration / Say hi to the bad guy.

Mar 93. (c-s) **IT WAS A GOOD DAY. / AIN'T GONNA TAKE MY LIFE** [27] [15]
(12"+=)(cd-s+=) – ('A'&'B' instrumentals).

Jul 93. (c-s) **CHECK YO SELF. ("ICE CUBE feat. DAS EFX") / IT WAS A GOOD DAY (radio mix)** [36] [20]
(12"+=)(cd-s+=) – 24 with an L / ('A'version).
(cd-s+=) – It was a good day (instrumental) / Who got the camera.

Dec 93. (cd)(c)(lp) **LETHAL INJECTION** [52] [5]
– The shot / Really doe / Ghetto bird / You know how we do it / Cave bitch / Bop gun (one nation) / What can I do? / Lil ass gee / Make it ruff, make it smooth / Down for whatever / Enemy / When I get to heaven

Dec 93. (12") **REALLY DOE. / MY SKIN IS MY SKIN** [66] [54]
(cd-s+=) – ('A'&'B'mixes).

Mar 94. (7")(c-s) **YOU KNOW HOW WE DO IT. / 2 N THE MORNING** [41] [30]
(12"+=)(cd-s+=) – ('A'instrumental). *(re-entered UK No.46 Dec94)*

Aug 94. (7")(c-s) **BOP GUN (ONE NATION). / DOWN FOR WHATEVER** [22] [23]
(12"+=)(cd-s+=) – ('A'-MYR mix) / Ghetto bird (Dr.Jam's mix).

— Above single features GEORGE CLINTON (ex-PARLIAMENT), with snippets from his FUNKADELIC song 'One Nation Under A Groove'.

Dec 94. (cd)(c)(d-lp) **BOOTLEGS AND B-SIDES** (compilation) [19]
– Robin Hood (cause it ain't all good) / What can I do (remix) / 24 with an L / You know how we do it (remix) / 2 n the morning / Check yo self (remix) / You don't want to fuck with these (unreleased '93 shit) / Lil piss gee (eerie gumbo mix) / My skin is my sin / It was a good day (remix) / D'voidofpopniggafied – megamix.

Dec 94. (12")(c-s)(cd-s) **YOU KNOW HOW WE DO IT (remix). / D'VOIDOFPOPNIGGAFIED (megamix)**
(cd-s+=) – 2 n the morning (mixes).

ICE-T

Born: TRACEY MARROW, 1958, Newark, New Jersey, USA. Moved to South Central L.A. and took the name from the black exploitation writer ICEBERG SLIM. His first record 'THE COLDEST RAPPER' appeared in 1983, but this led to his contract being retained by WILLIE STRONG. In 1991, he starred as a cop in the film 'New Jack City'. He had earlier formed own label 'Rhyme Syndicate' in 1988, which was soon distributed by 'Sire'. • **Style:** Extreme and aggressive pro-black, anti-establishment rapper, who branched into hard – core rock for his 1992 project BODY COUNT, with co-writer ERNIE C. Also liked to show off near-naked wife Darlene to promote sales. • **Songwriters:** ICE-T except; BACK IN BLACK (Ac-Dc). • **Trivia:** Clashed with President George Bush & Colonel Oliver North, over his controversial hard-talking single 'COP KILLER'. In 1995, ICE-T presented a new show 'Baadaasss TV' for Channel 4 UK.

Recommended: BODY COUNT (*6) / O. G. ORIGINAL GANGSTER (*8) / POWER (*8).

ICE-T – vocals / w/**AFRIKA ISLAM** – synthesizers

Rhyme Synd. Sire Rhyme Synd. Sire

Jul 87. (12") **MAKE IT FUNKY. / SEX**

Jul 87. (lp)(c)(cd) **RHYME PAYS** [93]
– (intro) / Rhyme pays / 6 'n the mornin' / Make it funky / Somebody gotta do it (pimpin' ain't easy) / 409 / I love ladies / Sex / Pain / Squeeze the trigger.

Nov 87. (12") **SOMEBODY GOT DO IT (PIMPIN' AIN'T EASY). / OUR MOST REQUESTED RECORD**

Jun 88. (12")(c-s) **COLORS. / SQUEEZE THE TRIGGER** [-] [10]

Sep 88. (lp)(c)(cd) **POWER** [35]
– (intro) / Power / Drama / Heartbeat / The syndicate / Radio suckers / I'm your pusher / Personal / High rollers / Girls L.G.B.N.A.F. / Grand larceny / Soul on ice / (outro).

Nov 88. (7") **I'M YOUR PUSHER. / GIRLS L.G.B.N.A.F.** [-]
(12"+=) – ('A'instrumental) / ('A'acappella) / ('B'instrumental) / ('B'acappella).

Mar 89. (7") **HIGH ROLLERS. / THE HUNTED CHILD** [63]
(12"+=) – Power.

Sep 89. (7") **LETHAL WEAPON. / HEARTBEAT (remix)**
(12"+=)(cd-s+=) – ('A'instrumental).

Oct 89. (lp)(c)(cd) **THE ICEBERG: FREEDOM OF SPEECH ... JUST WATCH WHAT YOU SAY** [42] [37]
– (intro) / Shut up, be happy / The iceberg / Lethal weapon / You played yourself / Peel their caps back / The girl tried to kill me / Black'n'decker / Hit the deck / This one's for me / The hunted child / What ya wanna do? / Freedom of speech / My word is bond. *(re-iss.cd Feb95)*

— Guested on CURTIS MAYFIELD's re-make of classic 'Superfly'.

Feb 90. (7") **YOU PLAYED YOURSELF. / MY WORD IS BOND** — 64 |
(12"+=) – Freedom of speech (with HENDRIX sample) *(US b-side)*

Apr 90. (c-s) **WHAT DO YOU WANNA DO? / THE GIRL TRIED TO KILL ME** — - |

1990. (7")(12")(cd-s) **NEW JACK HUSTLER (NINO'S THEME) (Master Radio Version) / NEW JACK HUSTLER (NINO'S THEME) (Instrumental)** — | 67
(above US label 'Giant')

May 91. (7") **O.G. ORIGINAL GANGSTER. / BITCHES 2** — |
(12"+=)(cd-s+=) – Mind over matter / Midnight.

May 91. (cd)(c)(lp) **O.G. ORIGINAL GANGSTER** — 38 | 5
– Home of the bodybag / First impression / Ziplock / Mic contract / Mind over matter / New Jack hustler / Ed / Bitches 2 (incl. sample:- Dr. Funkenstein) / Straight up nigga / O.G. Original Gangster / The house / Evil E – what about sex? / Fly by / Midnight / Fried chicken / M.V.P.'s / Lifestyles of the rich and infamous / Body count / Prepared to die / Escape from the killing fields / Street killer / Pulse of the rhyme / The tower / Ya should killed me last year. *(re-iss.cd Feb95)*

BODY COUNT

ICE-T with **ERNIE C and D-ROC** – guitar / **MOOSEMAN** – bass / **BEATMASTER 'V'** – drums

Sire | Sire

Jan 92. (12")(cd-s) **COP KILLER. / (withdrawn)** — - |

Mar 92. (cd)(c)(lp) **BODY COUNT** — | 26
– Smoked pork / Body Count's in the house / New sports / Body count / A statistic / Bowels of the Devil / The real problem / KKK bitch / C note / Voodoo / The winner loses / There goes the neighborhood / Oprah / Evil Dick / Body Count anthem / Momma's gotta die tonight / Freedom of speech.

Jun 92. (12") **THERE GOES THE NEIGHBORHOOD. / KKK BITCH** — |

Sep 94. (cd)(c)(red-lp) **BORN DEAD** — 15 | 74
– Body M-F Count / Masters of revenge / Killin' floor / Necessary evil / Drive by / Last breath / Hey Joe / Shallow graves / Surviving the game / Who are you / Sweet lobotomy / Born dead.

Sep 94. (c-s) **BORN DEAD. / BODY COUNT'S IN THE HOUSE (live)** — 28 |
(12"pic-d+=) – ('A'live).
(cd-s+=) – Body M-F Count (live) / On with the Body Count (live).

Dec 94. (etched-10"pic-d) **NECESSARY EVIL / NECESSARY EVIL (Live) / BOWELS OF THE DEVIL (live)** — 45 |
(cd-s) – ('A'side) / Body Count anthem (live) / Drive by (live) / There goes the neighborhood (live).

— In Dec 94, ICE-T was credited with WHITFIELD CRANE (Ugly Kid Joe) on MOTORHEAD single 'Born To Raise Hell', hit UK No.47

ICE-T

Sire | Sire

Mar 93. (cd)(c)(lp) **HOME INVASION** — 15 | 14
– Warning / It's on / Ice MFT / Home invasion / G style / Addicted to danger / Question and answer / Watch the ice break / Race war / That's how I'm livin' / I ain't new ta this / Pimp behind the wheels (DJ Evil E the great) / Gotta lotta love / Hit the fan / Depths of Hell (featuring DADDY NITRO) / 99 problems (featuring BROTHER MARQUIS) / Funky Gripsta / Message to the soldier / Ain't a damn thing changed

Apr 93. (12"ep)(c-ep)(cd-ep) **I AIN'T NEW TA THIS. / MIXED UP / MIXED UP (instrumental)** — 62 |

Dec 93. (12"ep)(c-ep)(cd-ep) **THAT'S HOW I'M LIVIN'. / COLOURS – RICOCHET – NEW JACK HUSTLER (film excerpts)** — 21 |

Mar 94. (c-s)(12")(cd-s) **GOTTA LOTTA LOVE. / ('A'mixes) / excerpt from book 'The Ice Opinion (who gives a f***)'** — 24 |
(cd-s) – ('A'mix) / Addicted to danger / G style / Racewar (remixes).

. . . Jan – Jun '96 stop press . . .

May 96. (single) **I MUST STAND** — 41 |

May 96. (cd)(c)(lp) **VI – THE RETURN OF THE REAL** — 26 | 89

– compilations, etc. –

May 93. Warners; (cd)(c)(lp) **THE CLASSICS COLLECTION** — |

Apr 94. Warners; (cd)(d-lp) **HOME INVASION / THE LAST TEMPTATION OF ICE** — |

ICICLE WORKS

Formed: Liverpool, England . . . 1980 by IAN McNABB, CHRIS LAYHE and CHRIS SHARROCK. After initial cassingle on 'Probe' & a 45 on indie 'Troll Kitchen' label in 1982, they signed to 'Beggar's B.' the next year. Their 3rd single 'LOVE IS A WONDERFUL COLOUR' soon gave them a UK Top 20 entry, and was followed by a re-issue of 'BIRDS FLY (WHISPER TO A SCREAM)', which also broke into US Top 40. Their eponymous debut album also cracked the 40 there, having already made No.24 in UK. They continued to score with some quality releases, until their signature with 'Epic', led to a slide in their popularity and their split. • **Style:** Power-rock outfit, fronted by McNABB (complete with attached microphone gadget) sounding SCOTT WALKER-ish early on and loved by college circuit. • **Songwriters:** Mostly McNABB compositions except; SEA SONG (Robert Wyatt) / NATURE'S WAY (Spirit) / COLD TURKEY (John Lennon) / INTO THE MYSTIC (Van Morrison) / YOU AIN'T SEEN NOTHIN' YET (Bachman-Turner Overdrive) / SHOULD I STAY OR SHOULD I GO (Clash) / MR SOUL + FOR WHAT IT'S WORTH (Buffalo Springfield) / ROCK'N'ROLL (Led Zeppelin) / PRIVATE REVOLUTION (World Party) / ROADHOUSE BLUES (Doors). McNABB covered CAROLINE NO (Brian Wilson) / UNKNOWN LEGEND (Neil Young). • **Trivia:** In Aug'85, an off-shoot MELTING POT, were supposed to have had a single 'IT MAKES NO DIFFERENCE' issued.

Recommended: THE BEST OF THE ICICLE WORKS (*8) / HEAD LIKE A

ROCK (*8; IAN McNABB).

(ROBERT) **IAN McNABB** (b. 3 Nov'62) – vocals, guitar, keyboards / **CHRIS LAYHE** – bass, keyboards, vocals / **CHRIS SHARROCK** – drums, percussion

Probe / not issued

1981. (c-ep) **ASCENDING** [ ] [-]

Troll Kitchen / not issued

Oct 82. (7"m) **NIRVANA. / LOVE HUNT / SIROCCO** [ ] [-]

Situation 2 / not issued

Jun 83. (7") **BIRDS FLY (WHISPER TO A SCREAM). / REVERIE GIRL** [ ] [-]
(12"+=) – Gun boys.

Beggar's B. / Arista

Oct 83. (7")(7"pic-d) **LOVE IS A WONDERFUL COLOUR. / WATERLINE** [15] [ ]
(12"+=)(12"pic-d+=) – In the dance The Shamen led.
(d7"++=) – The Devil on horseback.

Mar 84. (7")(12") **BIRDS FLY (WHISPER TO A SCREAM). / IN THE CAULDRON OF LOVE** [53] [-]
(12"+=) – Scarecrow / Ragweed campaign.

Mar 84. (lp)(c) **THE ICICLE WORKS** [24] [40]
– Chop the tree / Love is a wonderful colour / Reaping the rich harvest / As the dragonfly flies / Lover's day / In the cauldron of love / Out of season / A factory in the desert / Birds fly (whisper to a scream) / Nirvana. *(re-iss.+cd.Jul88) (cd-iss.Jul86)*

Mar 84. (7") **BIRDS FLY (WHISPER TO A SCREAM). / IN THE DANCE THE SHAMEN LED** [-] [37]

Sep 84. (7") **HOLLOW HORSE. / THE AETHIEST** [ ] [ ]
(12"+=) – Nirvana (live).
(12"+=) – ('A'remix).

May 85. (7") **ALL THE DAUGHTERS (OF HER FATHER'S HOUSE). / A POCKETFUL OF NOTHING** [ ] [ ]
(12"+=) – Mr. Soul.

Jul 85. (7") **SEVEN HORSES. / SLINGSHOT** [ ] [ ]
(12") – ('A'-US version) / -Beggar's legacy.
(d7"++=) – Goin' back.

Sep 85. (lp)(c) **THE SMALL PRICE OF A BICYCLE** [55] [ ]
– Hollow horse / Perambulator / Seven horses / Rapids / Windfall / Assumed sundown / Saint's sojourn / All the daughter's (of her father's horse) / Book of reason / Conscience of kings. *(re-iss.+cd.Jan89)*

Oct 85. (7") **WHEN IT ALL COMES DOWN. / LET'S GO DOWN TO THE RIVER** [ ] [ ]
(12"+=) – Cold turkey.

Jun 86. (7") **UNDERSTANDING JANE. / I NEVER SAW MY HOMETOWN TILL I WENT ROUND THE WORLD** [52] [ ]
(d7"+=) – Hollow horses (live) / You ain't seen nothin' yet (live).
(12"+=) – Into the mystic.
(c-s+=) – Seven horses (live) / Perambulator (live) / Rapids (live).

Sep 86. (7")(c-s) **WHO DO YOU WANT FOR LOVE. / UNDERSTANDING JANE (live)** [54] [ ]
(d7"+=) – John Jeffrey Muir shopkeeper / Impossibly three lovers.
(12"+=) – Should I stay or should I go / Roadhouse blues.

Dec 86. (12"ep) **UP HERE IN THE NORTH OF ENGLAND. / SEA SONG / NATURE'S WAY / IT MAKES NO DIFFERENCE** (issued on 'Situation 2' UK-only) [ ] [ ]

Jan 87. (7") **EVANGELINE. / EVERYBODY LOVE TO PLAY THE FOOL** [53] [ ]
(12"+=) – Waiting in the wings.

Mar 87. (lp)(c) **IF YOU WANT TO DEFEAT YOUR ENEMY SING HIS SONG** [28] [ ]
– Hope springs eternal / Travelling chest / Sweet Thursday / Up here in the north of England / Who do you want for your love / When you were mine / Evangeline / Truck driver's lament / Understanding Jane / Walking with a mountain. *(c+=)* – Everybody loves to play the fool. *(cd++=)* – Don't let it rain on my parade / I never saw my hometown till went round the world / Into the mystic.

Nov 87. (7") **HIGH TIME. / BROKEN HEARTED FOOL** [ ] [ ]
(12"+=) – Private revolution (live) / Travelling light (live).

Feb 88. (7") **THE KISS OFF. / SURE THING** [ ] [ ]
(12"ep+=)(c-ep+=)(cd-ep+=) – THE NUMB EP – High time / Whipping boy.

Apr 88. (7"m) **LITTLE GIRL LOST. / TIN CAN / HOT PROPHET GOSPEL** [59] [ ]
(12"+=)(pic-cd-s+=) – One time.

May 88. (lp)(c)(cd) **BLIND** [40] [ ]
– (intro) Shit creek / Little girl lost / Starry blue-eyed wonder / One true love / Blind / Two two three / What do you want me to do? / Stood before Saint Peter / The kiss off / Here comes trouble / Walk a while with me.

Jun 88. (7") **HERE COMES TROUBLE. / STARRY BLUE-EYED WONDER** [ ] [ ]
(12"+=) – Rock'n'roll (live) / For what it's worth (live).

— **ZAK STARKEY** (son of RINGO) – drums repl. LAYHE SHARROCK who joined WILD SWANS+The LA'S / added **DAVE GREEN** – keyboards / **ROY CORKHILL** – bass (both ex-BLACK) /

— (1989) **IAN and ROY** brought in **DAVE BALDWIN** – keyboards / **MARK REVELL** – guitar, vocals / **PAUL BURGESS** – drums

Epic / Epic

Mar 90. (7")(12") **MOTORCYCLE RIDER. / TURN ANY CORNER** [73] [ ]
(cd-s+=) – Victoria's ghost.

May 90. (cd)(c)(lp) **PERMANENT DAMAGE** [ ] [ ]
– I still want you / Motorcycle rider / Melanie still hurts / Hope street rag / I think I'm gonna be OK / Baby don't burn / What she did to my mind / One good eye / Permanent damage / Woman on my mind / Looks like rain / Dumb angel.

May 90. (7") **MELANIE STILL HURTS. / WHEN THE CRYING'S DONE** [ ] [ ]
(12"+=) – Mickey's blue.
(7"ep++=)(cd-ep++=) – I dreamt I was a beautiful woman.

Jul 90. (7")(c-s) **I STILL WANT YOU. / I WANT THE GIRL** [ ] [ ]
(10"+=)(12"+=)(cd-s+=) – It's gonna rain forever / Sweet disposition.

— McNABB joined the WILD SWANS briefly.

– compilations, etc. –

Feb 86. Beggar's Banquet; (m-lp)(c) **SEVEN SINGLES DEEP** [52] [ ]
(re-iss.+cd Sep88, cd+=6 extra tracks)

Aug 92. Beggar's Banquet; (cd)(c) **THE BEST OF THE ICICLE WORKS** [60] [ ]
– Hollow horse (long version) / Love is a wonderful colour / Birds fly (whisper to a scream) / Understanding Jane ('92 version) / Shit creek / High time (acoustic) / Who do you want for your love? / Evangeline / Little girl lost / When it all comes down ('92 version) / Starry blue eyed wonder / Out of season / The kiss off / Up here in the North of England / Firepower / Blind. *(re-iss.cd Sep95)*

Aug 92. Beggar's Banquet; (7") **UNDERSTANDING JANE '92. / LITTLE GIRL LOST** [ ] [ ]
(12"+=) – When it all comes down '92 / Firepower.
(cd-s+=) – Solid ground / Like weather.

Nov 88. Nighttracks; (12"ep) **THE EVENING SHOW SESSIONS (14.11.82)** [ ] [ ]
– Birds fly (whisper to a scream) / Lover's day / Love hunt / As the dragonfly flies.

Jan 90. Strange Fruit; (7") **LOVE IS A WONDERFUL COLOUR. / BIRDS FLY (WHISPER TO A SCREAM)** [ ] [-]

Mar 94. Windsong; (cd) **BBC RADIO 1 LIVE IN CONCERT (live)** [ ] [-]

IAN McNABB

Way Cool / not issued

Jun 91. (12"ep) **GREAT DREAMS OF HEAVEN / UNKNOWN LEGEND. / I'M GAME / CAROLINE NO** [ ] [-]

This Way Up / not issued

Jan 93. (7") **IF LOVE WAS LIKE GUITARS. / TRAMS IN AMSTERDAM** [67] [-]
(12"+=)(cd-s+=) – Great dreams of Heaven

Jan 93. (cd)(c)(lp) **TRUTH AND BEAUTY** [51] [-]
– (I go) My own way / These are the days / Great dreams of Heaven / Truth and beauty / I'm game / If love was like guitars / Story of my life / That's why I believe / Trip with me / Make love to you / Presence of the one. *(re-iss.cd/c Apr95)*

Mar 93. (7")(c-s) **GREAT DREAMS OF HEAVEN. / UNKNOWN LEGEND** [ ] [ ]
(12"+=)(cd-s+=) – I'm game / Caroline no.

Sep 93. (10"ep)(cd-ep) **(I GO) MY OWN WAY / PLAY THE HAND THEY DEAL YOU / IF MY DADDY COULD SEE ME NOW / FOR YOU, ANGEL** [ ] [ ]

— with **RALPH MOLINA + BILLY TALBOT** (of NEIL YOUNG's CRAZY HORSE) + **MIKE 'TONE' HAMILTON** (of SMITHEREENS)

Jun 94. (12")(cd-s) **YOU MUST BE PREPARED TO DREAM. / THAT'S WHY THE DARKNESS EXISTS** [54] [ ]
(cd-s+=) – Sometimes I think about you / Woo yer.
(cd-s+=) – Love is a wonderful colour / When it all comes down (both acoustic).

Jul 94. (cd)(c) **HEAD LIKE A ROCK** [29] [ ]
– Fire inside my soul / You must be prepared to dream / Child inside a father / Still got the fever / Potency / Go into the light / As a life goes by / Sad strange solitary Catholic mystic / This time is forever / May you always.

Aug 94. (c-s) **GO INTO THE LIGHT. / TIME YOU WERE IN LOVE** [ ] [ ]
(12"+=)(cd-s+=) – For you angel.
(cd-s) – ('A'side) / I stood before St.Peter / Rock.

. . . Jan – Jun '96 stop press . . .

Apr 96. (single) **DON'T PUT YOUR SELL ON ME** [ ] [ ]
May 96. (cd)(c)(lp) **MERSEYBEAST** [30] [ ]
Jun 96. (single) **MERSEYBEAST** [74] [ ]

Billy IDOL

Born: WILLIAM BROAD, 30 Nov'55, Stanmore, Middlesex, England. After 4 years, fronting punk-pop band GENERATION X, he went solo in 1981

and moved to New York, where he met manager Bill Aucoin and producer Keith Forsey. He also enlisted American guitarist STEVE STEVENS and others to augment his first album 'DON'T STOP', which didn't receive a UK release. In 1982, he scored first US Top 30 hit with 'HOT IN THE CITY' single, which featured on eponymous Top 50 second album. After hit album 'REBEL YELL' in 1984, he became major star on both sides of the big lake. • **Style:** Hard-driving sexual rocker, whose lip sneer was reminiscent of CLIFF, and who was loved by teeny boppers to heavy-metal fans. • **Songwriters:** IDOL & STEVENS collaborated until 1990 when he wrote with WERNER. Covered; MONY MONY (Tommy James & The Shondells) / SHAKIN' ALL OVER (Johnny Kidd & The Pirates) / L.A. WOMAN (Doors) / HEROIN (Lou Reed) / MOTHER DAWN (McBrook – Youth). • **Trivia:** BILLY drove a Harley-Davison motorbike, which he loved to drive around the States. This was scuppered slightly on 6 Feb'90, when he suffered a broken leg and wrist in a crash. In mid 1988, his girlfriend Perry Lister, gave birth to his son.

Recommended: IDOL SONGS – 11 OF THE BEST (*7).

BILLY IDOL – vocals (ex-GENERATION X) with **STEVE STEVENS** – guitar / **PHIL FEIT** – bass / **STEVE MISSAL** – drums

Chrysalis Chrysalis

Sep 81. (7") **MONY MONY. / BABY TALK** [ ] [71] m-lp
(12"+=) – Dancing with myself / Untouchables. *(US-title 'DON'T STOP')*
Jul 82. (lp)(c) **BILLY IDOL** [ ] [45]
– Come on, come on / White wedding (part 1 & 2) / Hot in the city / Dead on arrival / Nobody's business / Love calling / Hole in the wall / Shooting stars / It's so cruel / Congo man. *(cd-iss.1986) (re-iss.cd+c Jul94)*
Aug 82. (7")(12")(7"pic-d) **HOT IN THE CITY. / DEAD ON ARRIVAL** [58] [23] Jul 82
Oct 82. (7")(12") **WHITE WEDDING. / HOLE IN THE WALL** [ ] [ ]
Sep 83. (7")(7"clear) **WHITE WEDDING. / HOT IN THE CITY** [ ] [36] May 83
(12"+=) – Love calling / Dancing with myself.
Jan 84. (lp)(c) **REBEL YELL** [36] [6] Nov 83
– Rebel yell / Daytime drama / Eyes without a face / Blue highway / Flesh for fantasy / Catch my fall / Crank call / (Do not) Stand in the shadows / The dead next door. *(re-iss.+cd Jan86) (re-iss.cd Mar94)*
Feb 84. (7")(7"square pic-d) **REBEL YELL. / CRANK CALL** [62] [46] Jan 84
(12"+=)(d7"+=) – White wedding.
Jun 84. (7") **EYES WITHOUT A FACE. / THE DEAD NEXT DOOR** [18] [4] May 84
(12"+=)(d7"+=)(12"pic-d+=) – Dancing with myself / Rebel yell.
Sep 84. (7") **FLESH FOR FANTASY. / BLUE HIGHWAY** [54] [29] Aug 84
(12"+=)(12"pic-d+=) – ('A'version).
Nov 84. (7") **CATCH MY FALL. /** [-] [50]
Jun 85. (7")(7"white) **WHITE WEDDING. / FLESH FOR FANTASY** [6] [-]
(12")(12"white)(12"pic-d)(7"clear) – ('A'shotgun mix) / ('A'mega-mix)
Sep 85. (7")(7"pic-d) **REBEL YELL. / (DO NOT) STAND IN THE SHADOWS (live)** [6] [ ]
(12"+=)(12"pic-d+=) – Blue highway.
Sep 86. (7")(7"colrd) **TO BE A LOVER. / ALL SUMMER SINGLE** [22] [6]
(12"+=)(12"pic-d+=) – ('A'version).
(d7"+=) – Mega-Idol-mix / White wedding.
Oct 86. (lp)(c)(cd) **WHIPLASH SMILE** [8] [6]
– Worlds forgotten boy / To be a lover / Soul standing by / Sweet sixteen / Man for all seasons / Don't need a gun / Beyond belief / Fatal charm / All summer single / One night, one chance. *(re-iss.cd+c. Mar93)*
Feb 87. (7")(7"colrd) **DON'T NEED A GUN. / FATAL CHARM** [26] [37] Jan 87
(12"+=)(12"pic-d+=) – ('A'version).
May 87. (7") **SWEET 16. / BEYOND BELIEF** [17] [20] Apr 87
(12"+=)(12"pic-d+=) – Rebel yell.
Sep 87. (7") **MONY MONY (live). / SHAKIN' ALL OVER (live)** [7] [1]
(12"+=) – ('A'version).

— now with **MARK YOUNGER-SMITH** – guitar, bass / **KEITH FORSEY** – drums, producer **VITO** and **PHIL SOUSSAN** – bass / **ARTHUR BARROW** – keyboards / **MIKE BAIRD** – drums

Apr 90. (7")(c-s) **CRADLE OF LOVE. / 311 MAN** [34] [2]
(cd-s+=) – ('A'extended) / Rob the cradle of love.
(12") – (as above) (except 7" b-side).
Apr 90. (cd)(c)(lp) **CHARMED LIFE** [15] [11]
– The loveless / Pumping on steel / Prodigal blues / L.A. woman / Trouble with the sweet stuff / Cradle of love / Mark of Caine / Endless sleep / Love unchained / The right way / License to thrill.
Jul 90. (7")(c-s) **L.A. WOMAN. / LICENSE TO THRILL** [70] [52]
(12"+=)(cd-s+=) – Love child.
Dec 90. (7")(c-s) **PRODIGAL BLUES. / MARK OF CAINE** [47] [ ]
(12"+=)(cd-s+=) – Flesh for fantasy.

— **IDOL** retained co-writer **YOUNGER-SMITH** + recruited **ROBIN HANCOCK** – keyboards, producer / **DOUG WIMBUSH** – bass / **JAMIE MAMOBERAC** – organ / **TAL BERGHAN** – drums

Jun 93. (7")(12") **SHOCK TO THE SYSTEM. / HEROIN (overloads mix) / HEROIN (durge trance dub)** [30] [ ]
(cd-s) – ('A'side) / Heroin (original) / Rebel yell.
(cd-s) – ('A'side) / Heroin (smack attack) / White wedding.
Jun 93. (cd)(c)(lp) **CYBERPUNK** [20] [48]
– Wasteland / Shock to the system / Tomorrow people / Adam in chains / Neuromancer / Power junkie / Love labours on / Heroin / Shangrila / Concrete kingdom / Venus / Then the night comes / Mother Dawn.
Sep 93. (7")(c-s) **ADAM IN CHAINS. / SHOCK TO THE SYSTEM** [ ] [ ]
(cd-s) – ('A'side) / Venus / Eyes without a face.

Fox-Arista Arista

Sep 94. (7")(c-s)(cd-s) **SPEED. / REBEL YELL (acoustic)** [47] [ ]

– compilations etc. –

Jul 85. Chrysalis; (lp)(c) **VITAL IDOL** (remixes) [7] [10] Oct 87
– White wedding (part 1 & 2) / Dancing with myself / Flesh for fantasy / Catch my fall / Mony Mony / Love calling (dub) / Hot in the city. *(cd-iss.1986)*
Jan 88. Chrysalis; (7") **HOT IN THE CITY. / CATCH MY FALL (remix)** [13] [48] Dec 87
(12"+=) – Soul standing by.
(cd-s++=) – Mony Mony.
Jun 88. Chrysalis; (lp)(c)(cd) **IDOL SONGS – 11 OF THE BEST** [2] [ ]
– Rebel yell / Hot in the city / White wedding / Eyes without a face / Catch my fall / Mony mony / To be a lover / Sweet sixteen / Flesh for fantasy / Don't need a gun / Dancing with myself.
Aug 88. Chrysalis; (7") **CATCH MY FALL. / ALL SUMMER SINGLE** [63] [-]
(12"+=)(cd-s+=) – ?

John ILLSLEY (see under ⇒ DIRE STRAITS)

INDIGO GIRLS

Formed: Decatur, Georgia, USA . . . 1986 by AMY RAY and EMILY SALIERS. Signed the dotted line 'Epic' in '87 and scored near US Top 20 album with eponymous second album, which featured R.E.M. and HOTHOUSE FLOWERS. • **Style:** Folksy apple-pie college duo, similar to British outfits EVERYTHING BUT THE GIRL or FAIRGROUND ATTRACTION, although obvously a litter deeper lyrically. • **Songwriters:** Either AMY or EMILY. • **Trivia:** 'CLOSER TO FINE' featured mandolin & backing vox by PETER O'TOOLE! of HOTHOUSE FLOWERS. In Sep'91, they participated with ELTON JOHN and many others on an AIDS charity walk, which raised over half a million dollars. Their 2nd & 3rd albums were produced by SCOTT LITT (of R.E.M. fame). PETER COLLINS took over the controls in 1992, and this album featured guest spots for DAVID CROSBY, JACKSON BROWNE & The ROCHES.

Recommended: INDIGO GIRLS (*6) / SWAMP OPHELIA (*6)

AMY RAY – vocals, guitars / **EMILY SALIERS** – vocals, acoustic guitar

not issued Columbia

1987. (lp)(c) **STRANGE FIRE** [-] [ ]
– Strange fire / Crazy game / Left me a fool / I don't wanna know / Hey Jesus / Get together / Walk away / Make it easier / You left it up to me / Land of Canaan. *(US re-iss.Nov89 on 'Epic')*

— now with **JAY DEE DAUGHERTY** – drums (ex-HOTHOUSE FLOWERS, ex-WATERBOYS, etc.) / **JOHN KEANE** – guitar, bass / **JOHN VAN TONGEREN** – keyboards / **KASIM SULTAN + DEDE VOGT** – bass / **PAULINHO DA COSTA** – percussion / **JAI WINDING** – piano

Epic Epic

Jun 89. (7") **CLOSER TO FINE. / COLD AS ICE** [-] [ ]
Jun 89. (7") **CLOSER TO FINE. / HISTORY OF US** [ ] [-]
(12"+=) – American tune / Mona Lisas and mad hatters.
(cd-s+=) – Center stage. *(re-iss. Oct89)*
Jul 89. (lp)(c)(cd) **INDIGO GIRLS** [ ] [22] Apr89
– Closer to fine / Secure yourself / Kid fears / Prince of darkness / Blood and fire / Tried to be true / Love's recovery / Land of Canaan / Center stage / History of us.
Sep 89. (7") **LAND OF CANAAN. / NEVER STOP** [-] [ ]
Feb 90. (7") **GET TOGETHER. / FINLANDIA** [-] [ ]

— now w / **DAUGHERTY / PETER BUCK** (of R.E.M.) / **SARA LEE** – bass (ex-GANG OF FOUR) / **MARY CHAPIN CARPENTER / KENNY ARONOFF / BENMONT TENCH / JIM KELTNER / PETER HOLSAPPLE / JOHN JENNINGS / DA COSTA / CHRIS McGUIRE / CRAIG EDWARDS** / etc.

Oct 90. (c-s) **HAMMER AND NAIL. / WELCOME (live)** [-] [ ]
Nov 90. (cd)(c)(lp) **NOMADS, INDIANS, SAINTS** [ ] [43] Oct90
– Hammer and nail / Welcome me / World falls / Southland in the springtime / 1,2,3 / Keeper of my heart / Watershed / Hand me downs / You and me of the 10,000 wars / Pushing the needle too far / The girl with the weight of the world in her hands.
1991. (cd) **BACK ON THE BUS (live)** [-] [ ]

— now w / **SARA LEE** – bass / **BUDGIE** – drums (of SIOUXSIE & THE BANSHEES) / **LISA GERMANO** – fiddle / **JERRY MAROTTA** – drums / **MARTIN**

McCARRICK – cello / **DONAL LUNNY** – bouziki, bodhran / **JENNINGS** – guitar / **WINDING** – piano

Jun 92. (cd)(c) **RITES OF PASSAGE** [ ] [21] May92
– Three hits / Galileo / Ghost / Joking / Jonas & Ezekial / Love will come to you / Romeo & Juliet / Virginia Woolf / Chicken man / Airplane / Nashville / Let it be me / Cedar tree.

Aug 92. (c-s)(cd-s) **GALILEO / GHOST / JOKING / LOVE WILL COME TO YOU / JONAS & EZEKIAL** [-] [89]

Oct 92. (7")(c-s) **GALILEO. / KID FEARS** [ ] [-]
(cd-s) – ('A'side) / Closer to fine / Tried to be true / Hammer and nail.

— Augmented by **SARA LEE** – bass (ex-GANG OF FOUR, etc.) / **JERRY MAROTTA** – drums / **JAMES HALL** – trumpet / **DANNY THOMPSON** – acoustic bass / **LISA GERMANO** – violin / **JOHN PAINTER** – flugel horn / **JANE SCARPANTONI** – cello / **MICHAEL LORANT** – drums, b.vocals

May 94. (cd-ep) **LEAST COMPLICATED / DEAD MAN'S HILL / MYSTERY / KID FEARS** [ ] [ ]

May 94. (cd)(c)(lp) **SWAMP OPHELIA** [66] [9]
– Fugitive / Least complicated / Language or the kiss / Reunion / Power of two / Touch me fall / The wood song / Mystery / Dead man's hill / Fare thee well / This train revised.

Jun 95. (c-ep)(cd-ep) **CLOSER TO FINE / ROCKIN' IN THE FREE WORLD** [ ] [ ]
(cd-s+=) – Dead man's hill (acoustic) / Mystery (acoustic).
(cd-s) – ('A'side) / Kid fears / All along the watchtower (live) / Let me a fool (live).

Jul 95. (cd)(c) **4.5 THE BEST OF THE INDIGO GIRLS** (compilation) [43] [ ]
– Joking / Hammer and nail / Kid fears / Galileo / Tried to be true / Power of love / Pushing the needle tto far / Reunion / Closer to fine / Three hits / Least complicated / Touch me fall / Love's recovery / Land of Canaan / Ghost.

Oct 95. (cd)(c) **1200 CURFEWS (live)** [-] [40]

INSPIRAL CARPETS

Formed: Manchester, England ... 1980 initially as The FURS, by schoolboy GRAHAM LAMBERT. He was joined in the mid-80's by STEPHEN HOLT, TONY WELSH and CHRIS GOODWIN. In 1986, as The INSPIRAL CARPETS, they replaced GOODWIN and WELSH, with CRAIG GILL, DAVE SWIFT and CLINT BOON. Early in '87, they recorded a version of 'GARAGE' for a 7" flexi-disc given free with 'Debris' magazine. After gigs supporting the WEDDING PRESENT, JAMES, STONES ROSES and The SHAMEN, they issued official debut 'PLANE CRASH EP in mid-'88 for indie 'Playtime' records. Early in 1989, they set up own 'Cow' label, after their distributers 'Red Rhino' went bust. At the same time, HOLT and SWIFT left to form The RAINKINGS, and were replaced by HINGLEY and WALSH. After a late 1988 recording 'TRAIN SURFING EP' was issued, they issued 808 STATE produced 'JOE' single/EP. Late 1989, they had first UK Top 50 entry with 'MOVE', which led to Daniel Miller of 'Mute' records giving them & 'Cow' a record deal. In April 1990, they broke into UK Top 20 with single 'THIS IS HOW IT FEELS', which aided their debut album 'LIFE' to reach Top 3. • **Style:** Heavy organ-orientated alternative-pop group, who lay somewhere between The DOORS and The FALL. • **Songwriters:** Group penned except; 96 TEARS (? & The Mysterians) / GIMME SHELTER (Rolling Stones) / TAINTED LOVE (Soft Cell) / PARANOID (Black Sabbath). • **Trivia:** To promote debut album, they employed the services of the Milk Marketing Board who ran a TV ad on their bottles. Early 1990, they penned 'THE 8.15 FROM MANCHESTER' (theme) from children's Saturday morning TV show.

Recommended: LIFE (*8) / THE BEAST INSIDE (*7).

GRAHAM LAMBERT – guitar / **STEPHEN HOLT** – vocals / **DAVE SWIFT** – bass repl. TONY WELSH / **CRAIG GILL** – drums repl. CHRIS GOODWIN who joined ASIA FIELDS (later BUZZCOCKS F.O.C. and The HIGH) / added **CLINT BOON** – organ, vocals

Playtime / not issued

Jul 88. (7"ltd.) **KEEP THE CIRCLE AROUND. / THEME FROM COW** [ ] [-]
(12"ep+=) **PLANE CRASH EP** – Seeds of doubt / Garage full of flowers / 96 tears.

Cow / not issued

Mar 89. (12"ep) **TRAIN SURFING** [ ] [-]
– Butterfly / Causeway / You can't take the truth / Greek wedding song.

— **TOM HINGLEY** – vocals (ex-TOO MUCH TEXAS) repl. HOLT who formed RAINKINGS **MARTIN WALSH** – bass (ex-NEXT STEP) repl. SWIFT who formed RAINKINGS

May 89. (12"ep) **JOE. / COMMERCIAL MIX / DIRECTING TRAFFIK / COMMERCIAL RAIN** [ ] [-]

Aug 89. (7") **FIND OUT WHY. / SO FAR** [ ] [-]
(12"+=)(cd-s+=) – Plane crash (live).

Oct 89. (7") **MOVE. / OUT OF TIME** [49] [-]
(12"+=)(cd-s+=) – Move in.

Cow-Mute / Sire

Mar 90. (7") **THIS IS HOW IT FEELS. / TUNE FOR A FAMILY** [14] [ ]
(12") – ('A'-Rob mix) / ('B'drum mix)
(cd-s) – ('A'radio mix) / Seeds of doubt.
(c-s) – ('A'radio mix) / Whiskey.

Apr 90. (cd)(c)(lp) **LIFE** [2] [ ]
– Real thing / Song for a family / This is how it feels / Directing traffik / Besides me / Many happy returns / Memories of you / She comes in the fall / Monkey on my back / Sun don't shine / Inside my head / Move * / Sackville. *(cd+= *) (US++=)* – Commercial rain / Weakness / Biggest mountain / I'll keep it in mind.

Jun 90. (7") **SHE COMES IN THE FALL. / SACKVILLE** [27] [ ]
(12"+=)(cd-s+=) – Continental reign (version).
(12"+=) – ('A'acapella version).

Nov 90. (7"ep)(12"ep) **ISLAND HEAD** [21] [ ]
– Biggest mountain / I'll keep it in mind / Weakness / Gold to . . .
(cd-ep+=) – Mountain sequence.

Mar 91. (7") **CARAVAN. / SKIDOO** [30] [ ]
(7")(12") – ('A'side) / ('B'possession mix)
(cd-s) – ('A'what noise rethink mix) / ('B'side)

Apr 91. (cd)(c)(lp) **THE BEAST INSIDE** [5] [ ]
– Caravan / Please be cruel / Born yesterday / Sleep well tonight / Grip / Beast inside / Niagara / Mermaid / Further away / Dreams are all we have.

Jun 91. (7")(c-s) **PLEASE BE CRUEL. / THE WIND IS CALLING YOUR NAME** [50] [ ]
(12"+=)(cd-s+=) – St.Kilda (version).

Feb 92. (7")(c-s) **DRAGGING ME DOWN. / I KNOW I'M LOSING YOU** [12] [ ]
(12"+=)(cd-s+=) – (2 other 'A'mixes).

May 92. (7") **TWO WORLDS COLLIDE. / BOOMERANG** [32] [ ]
(12"+=)(cd-s+=) – ('A'-Mike Pickering remix).

Sep 92. (7") **GENERATIONS. / ('A'remix)** [28] [ ]
(cd-s) – ('A'side) / She comes in the fall / Move / Directing traffik (all live).
(cd-s) – ('A'side) / Joe / Commercial rain / Butterfly (all live).

Oct 92. (cd)(c)(lp) **REVENGE OF THE GOLDFISH** [17] [ ]
– Generations / Saviour / Bitches brew / Smoking her clothes / Fire / Here comes the flood / Dragging me down / A little disappeared / Two worlds collide / Mystery / Rain song / Irresistable force.

Nov 92. (12"ep)(c-ep) **BITCHES BREW / TAINTED LOVE. / BITCHES BREW (Fortran 5 remix) / IRRESISTABLE FORCE (Fortran 5 mix)** [36] [ ]
(cd-ep+=) – Mermaid / Born yesterday / Sleep well tonight (all live).
(cd-ep+=) – Dragging me down / Smoking her clothes / Fire (all live).

Have now parted company with 'Cow' co-founder/manager Anthony Boggiano.

May 93. (7")(c-s) **HOW IT SHOULD BE. / IT'S ONLY A PAPER MOON** [49] [ ]
(12"+=)(cd-s+=) – I'm alive.

Jan 94. (7")(c-s) **SATURN 5. / PARTY IN THE SKY** [20] [ ]
(cd-s+=)(12"+=) – ('A'mixes).
(cd-s) – ('A'side) / Well of seven heads / Two cows / Going down.

Feb 94. (7")(c-s) **I WANT YOU. / I WANT YOU (feat. MARK E.SMITH)** [18] [ ]
(cd-s+=) – We can do everything / Inside of you.
(cd-s) – ('A'side) / Dragging me down / Party in the sky / Plutoman.

Mar 94. (cd)(c)(lp) **DEVIL HOPPING** [10] [ ]
– I want you / Party in the sky / Plutoman / Uniform / Lovegrove / Just Wednesday / Saturn 5 / All of this and more / The way the light falls / Half way there / Cobra / I don't want to go blind. *(w / free ltd-cd of 'BBC SESSIONS' or free ltd.red-10" lp)*

Apr 94. (7")(c-s)(cd-s) **UNIFORM. / PARANOID** [51] [ ]
(cd-s) – ('A'side) / Paranoid (Collapsed Lung mix).

Aug 95. (7"m) **JOE (acoustic). / SEEDS OF DOUBT / WHISKEY** [37] [ ]
(7"m) – Joe (live) / Sackville (live) / Saviour (live).
(cd-s) – ('A'side) / I want you / I'll keep it in mind / Tainted love.

Sep 95. (cd)(c)(d-lp) **THE SINGLES** (compilation) [17] [ ]
– Joe / Find out why / Move / This is how it feels / (extended) / She comes in the fall / Commercial reign / Sackville / Biggest mountain / Weakness / Caravan / Please be cruel / Dragging me down / Two worlds collide / Generations / Bitches brew / How it should be / Saturn 5 / I want you / Uniform.

— Had already been dropped from the 'Mute' roster late in 1994.

– compilations, etc. –

May 89. Cow; (c) **DEMO CASSETTE (ltd. edition)** [ ] [-]
– Keep the circle around / Seeds of doubt / Joe / Causeway / 26 / Inside my head / Sun don't shine / Theme from Cow / 96 tears / Butterfly / Garage full of flowers. *(rec.Dec87)*

Jul89. Strange Fruit; (12"ep)(cd-ep) **THE PEEL SESSIONS** [ ] [-]
– Out of time / Directing traffic / Keep the circle around / Gimme shelter.

Aug92. Strange Fruit; (cd)(10"lp) **PEEL SESSIONS** [ ] [-]

— also released import 7"colrd/12"colrd/pic-cd-s, GIMME SHELTER

INXS

Formed: Sydney, Australia ... 1977 as The FARRISS BROTHERS by TIM, ANDREW and JON, plus MICHAEL HUTCHENCE, KIRK PENGILLY and GARRY BEERS. After briefly moving to Perth in 1978, they returned the next year as INXS, and with a contract on 'Deluxe' through 'RCA'. They released 2 albums and several singles in the early 80's, before moving to 'WEA' Australia in '82. Their 3rd album 'SHABOOH SHOOBAH' became another Australian success, and led to a contract on 'Atco' in the US, where it made the Top 50. Early in 1983, they also signed to 'Mercury' in the UK, but debut 45 'DON'T CHANGE' flopped. With progress from 1985's 'LISTEN LIKE THIEVES' album, they became massive outfit late in 1987, with cross-Atlantic Top 10 album 'KICK'. Taken from it, were 4 US Top 10 singles including No.1 'NEED YOU TONIGHT', which also made No.2 a year later in UK. • **Style:** Sophisticated and complex rock-pop outfit, fronted by JIM MORRISON like HUTCHENCE, who was once boyfriend of Aussie pop star KYLIE MINOGUE. • **Songwriters:** Most by ANDREW FARRISS and HUTCHENCE, except some B-sides by TIM. Covered; THE LOVED ONE (The Loved One). • **Trivia:** In 1987, idol HUTCHENCE starred as a drug crazed punk in the Australian film 'Dogs In Space'. Two years later he appeared in 'Frankenstein Unbound'.

Recommended: INXS – THE GREATEST HITS (*8).

MICHAEL HUTCHENCE (b.12 Jan'60, Lain Cove, Sydney, Australia) – vocals / **ANDREW FARRISS** (b.27 Mar'59) – keyboards, guitar / **TIM FARRISS** (b.16 Aug'57) – guitar / **KIRK PENGILLY** (b. 4 Jul'58) – saxophone, guitar, vocals / **GARRY BEERS** (b.22 Jun'57) – bass, vocals / **JON FARRISS** (b.18 Aug'61) – drums

not issued | Deluxe

May 80. (7") **SIMPLE SIMON. / WE ARE ALL VEGETABLES** [-] [-] Aussie
Oct 80. (7") **JUST KEEP WALKING. / SCRATCH** [-] [-] Aussie
(UK-rel.Sep81 on 'RCA')
Oct 80. (lp) **INXS** [-] [-] Aussie
– On a bus / Doctor / Just keep walking / Learn to smile / Jumping in vain / Roller skating / Body language / Newsreel babies / Wishy washy. *(UK-iss.May89/Jul90 on 'Vertigo') (US-iss.Aug84 on 'Atco')*

not issued | Deluxe-RCA

Feb 81. (7") **THE LOVED ONE.** [-] [-] Aussie
1981. (7") **STAY YOUNG.** [-] [-] Aussie
1981. (7") **NIGHT OF REBELLION.** [-] [-] Aussie
Nov 81. (lp) **UNDERNEATH THE COLOURS** [-] [-] Aussie
– Stay young / Horizons / Big go-go / Underneath the colours / Fair weather ahead / Night of rebellion / What would you do / Follow / Barbarian / Just to learn again. *(UK-iss.Mar82 on 'RCA') (re-iss.+c.Jul89 on 'Vertigo')*

not issued | R.C.A.

1982. (7") **THE ORIGINAL SIN.** [-] [-] Aussie

not issued | Atco

Oct 82. (lp) **SHABOOH SHABOOH** [-] [46]
– The one thing / To look at you / Spy of love / Soul mistake / Here comes / Black and white / Golden playpen / Jan's song / Old world new world / Don't change. *(UK-iss.Jun87) (cd-iss.May90 on 'Mercury')*
1983. (7") **DON'T CHANGE. / GO WEST** [-] [-] Aussie

— from now on UK + US releases only, with US labels, etc. mentioned

Mercury | Atco

Mar 83. (7") **THE ONE THING. / PHANTOM OF THE OPERA** [-] [30]
Jun 83. (7") **DON'T CHANGE. / LONG IN TOOTH** [-] [80]
Jun 83. (7") **DON'T CHANGE. / YOU NEVER USED TO CRY** [ ] [ ]
(12"+=) – Golden playpen.
1983. (m-lp) **DEKADANCE** [-] [ ]
– Black and white / Here comes / The one thing / To look at you
Sep 83. (7") **THE ONE THING. / THE SAX THING** [ ] [-]
(12") – ('A'side) / Black and white.
(12") – ('A'side) (++=) – Here comes II.
Oct 83. (7") **TO LOOK AT YOU. / THE SAX THING** [-] [ ]
Feb 84. (7") **ORIGINAL SIN. / JAN'S SONG (live)** [ ] [-]
(12"+=) – To look at you (live) / ('A'extended version).
Apr 84. (7") **ORIGINAL SIN. / STAY YOUNG** [-] [58]
May 84. (lp)(c)(cd) **THE SWING** [ ] [52]
– Original sin / Melting in the sun / I send a message / Dancing on the jetty / The swing / Johnson's aeroplane / Love is (what I say) / Face the change / Burn for you / All the voices.

Philips | Atco

May 84. (7") **I SEND A MESSAGE. / MECHANICAL** [ ] [77] Jul 84
(12"+=) – ('A'longer version)
Oct 84. (7") **BURN FOR YOU. / JOHNSON'S AEROPLANE** [-] [ ]

Mercury | Atlantic

Nov 85. (lp)(c)(cd) **LISTEN LIKE THIEVES** [48] [11]
– What you need / Listen like thieves / Kiss the dirt (falling down the mountain) / Shine like it does / Good and bad times / Biting bullets / This time / Three sisters / Same direction / One x one / Red red sun. *(ltd. copies of the above cont. THE SWING album) (re-iss.cd/c Apr95)*
Feb 86. (7") **THIS TIME. / ORIGINAL SIN (ext.)** [ ] [81] Nov 85
(12"+d7"+=) – Burn for you / Dancing on the jetty.
Apr 86. (7") **WHAT YOU NEED. / SWEET AS SIN** [51] [5] Jan 86
(12"+=) – ('A' live) / The one thing.
(d12"++=) – Don't change / Johnson's aeroplane.
(c-s+=) – ('B' + 2 alt. versions) / This time / I'm over you.
Jun 86. (7")(7"sha-pic-d) **LISTEN LIKE THIEVES. / BEGOTTEN** [46] [54] May 86
(d7"+=) – One x one / Xs verbage.
(12"+=) – ('A' instrumental) / ('A' extended).
Aug 86. (7") **KISS THE DIRT (FALLING DOWN THE MOUNTAIN). / 6 KNOTS / THE ONE THING (live)** [54] [ ]
(12"+=) – Spy of love.
(d7"+=) – This time / Original sin.
Sep 87. (7") **NEED YOU TONIGHT. / I'M COMING (HOME)** [58] [1] Oct 87
(12"+=)(cd-s+=) – Mediate.
Nov 87. (lp)(c)(cd) **KICK** [9] [3]
– Guns in the sky / New sensation / Devil inside / Need you tonight / Mediate / The loved one / Wild life / Never tear us apart / Mystify / Kick / Calling all nations / Tiny daggers. *(pic-lp Dec88) (re-iss.Jul91 hit UK No.50)*
Nov 87. (7")(7"pic-d) **NEW SENSATION. / DO WOT YOU DO** [25] [-]
(12"+=) – Love is (what I say).
(12"+=)(c-s+=)(cd-s+=) – Same direction.
Feb 88. (7") **DEVIL INSIDE. / ON THE ROCKS** [47] [2]
(12"+=) – Devil inside (extended).
(cd-s+=) – What you need.
(10"+=) – Dancing on the jetty / Shine like it does.
May 88. (7") **NEW SENSATION. / GUNS IN THE SKY (kookaburra mix)** [-] [ ]
Jun 88. (7")(12") **NEVER TEAR US APART. / GUNS IN THE SKY (remix)** [24] [-]
(12"+=) – Burn for you / One world new world.
(cd-s+=) – Different world / This time.
(10"white+=) – Need you tonight / Listen like thieves.
Aug 88. (7") **NEVER TEAR US APART. / DIFFERENT WORLD** [-] [7]
Oct 88. (7") **NEED YOU TONIGHT. / MOVE ON** [2] [-]
(12"+=) – New sensation.
(12"+=) – Kiss the dirt / ('A' remix).
(cd-s+=) – Original sin / Don't change.
Mar 89. (7") **MYSTIFY. / DEVIL INSIDE** [14] [ ]
(12"+=) – Never tear us apart (live) / Shine like it does (live).
(cd-s+=) – Listen like thieves / What you need (remix).
Sep 90. (7") **SUICIDE BLONDE. / EVERYBODY WANTS U TONIGHT** [11] [9]
(12"+=)(cd-s+=) – ('A'milk mix).
Sep 90. (cd)(c)(lp) **X** [2] [5]
– Suicide blonde / Disappear / The stairs / Faith in each other / By my side / Lately / Who pays the price / Know the difference / Bitter tears / On my way / Hear that sound. *(re-iss.cd/c Apr95)*
Nov 90. (7") **DISAPPEAR. / MIDDLE EAST** [21] [8]
(12"+=)(cd-s+=) – What you need (Cold Cut force mix).
(12") – ('A'side) / Need you tonight (mix) / New sensation.
Mar 91. (7")(c-s) **BY MY SIDE. / THE OTHER SIDE** [42] [-]
(12"+=)(cd-s+=) – Faith in each other (live).
(cd-s++=) – Disappear (mix).
Jul 91. (7") **BITTER TEARS. / SOOTHE ME** [30] [46] Apr 91
(12"+=) – Disappear (mix) / ('A'tears are bitter mix) / ('A'other mix).
(cd-s+=) – Original sin / Listen like thieves (extended remixes).
Oct 91. (7")(12")(cd-ep) **SHINING STAR** [27] [ ]
– Shining star / Send a message (live) / Faith in each other (live) / Bitter tears (live).
Nov 91. (cd)(c)(lp) **LIVE BABY LIVE (live)** [8] [72]
– New sensation / Mystify / Never tear us apart / Need you tonight / Suicide blonde / By my side / Mediate / Hear that sound / The stairs / What you need / Shining star (studio).
Jul 92. (7")(12")(c-s)(cd-s)(7"pic-d) **HEAVEN SENT. / IT AIN'T EASY** [31] [-]
Aug 92. (c-s) **NOT ENOUGH TIME / ?.** [-] [28]
Aug 92. (cd)(c)(lp) **WELCOME TO WHEREVER YOU ARE** [1] [16]
– Questions / Heaven sent / Communication / Taste it / Not enough time / All around / Baby don't cry / Beautiful girl / Wishing well / Back on line / Strange desire / Men and women. *(re-iss.cd/c Apr95)*
Sep 92. (7")(c-s) **BABY DON'T CRY. / (Part 2)** [20] [ ]
(cd-s+=) – Ptar speaks / Question 8 (instrumental) / ('A'acappella mix).
Nov 92. (7")(c-s) **TASTE IT. / LIGHT THE PLANET** [21] [ ]
(cd-s+=) – Youth / Not enough time (mix).
Feb 93. (7")(c-s) **BEAUTIFUL GIRL. / IN MY LIVING ROOM / ASHTAR SPEAKS** [23] [46]
(cd-s) – ('A'side) / Strange desire.
(cd-s) – ('A'side) / Underneath my colours / Wishing well.
Oct 93. (7"-c-s) **THE GIFT. / BORN TO BE WILD** [11] [ ]
(cd-s) – ('A'side) / ('A'mix) / Heaven sent (live).
Nov 93. (cd)(c)(lp) **FULL MOON, DIRTY HEARTS** [3] [53]
– Days of rust / The gift / Make your peace / Time / I'm only looking / Please (you've got that . . .) / Full moon, dirty hearts / Freedom deep / Kill the pain / Cut your roses down / The messenger / Viking juice
Dec 93. (12")(c-s) **PLEASE (YOU GOT THAT . . .). ("INXS & RAY CHARLES") / ('A'mixes)** [50] [ ]

(cd-s) – ('A'side) / Freedom deep / Communication (live) / Taste it (live).

Oct 94. (7"red)(c-s) **THE STRANGEST PARTY (THESE ARE THE TIMES). / WISHING WELL** [15] [ ]
(cd-s+=) – ('A'mix) / Sing something.
(cd-s) – ('A'side) / Need you tonight (remix) / I'm only looking (remix).

Nov 94. (cd)(c)(lp) **INXS – THE GREATEST HITS** (compilation) [3] [ ]
– Mystify / Suicide blonde / Taste it / The strangest party (these are the times) / Need you tonight / Original sin / Heaven sent / Disappear / Never tear us apart / The gift / Devil inside / Beautiful girl / Deliver me / New sensation / What you need / Listen like thieves / Bitter tears / Baby don't cry.

— From mid 90's, HUTCHENCE and BOB GELDOF's estranged misses PAULA YATES starting living together. In 1996, she with the breat implants, had HUTCHENCE's baby with long silly Christian name (once again!).

– some other AUSTRALIA only releases –

Oct 83. WEA; (7")(12") **ORIGINAL SIN. / IN VAIN / JUST KEEP WALKING** [-] [-]

1984. WEA; (7")(12") **BURN FOR YOU. /** [-] [-]

1984. WEA; (7")(12") **DANCING ON THE JETTY. /** [-] [-]

MICHAEL HUTCHENCE also released below single

1987. WEA; (7") **ROOMS FOR THE MEMORY. / GOLFCOURSE** [-] [-]

MAX Q

(HUTCHENCE with **IAN 'OLLIE' OLSEN** duo named after his dog!)

Mercury / Atlantic

Sep 89. (7") **WAY OF THE WORLD. / ZERO 2-0** [ ] [ ]
(12"+=)(c-s+=)(cd-s+=) – Ghost of the year.

Oct 89. (lp)(c)(cd) **MAX Q** [69] [ ]
– Sometimes / Way of the world / Ghost of the year / Everything / Zero 2-0 / Soul engine / Buckethead / Monday night by satellite / Tight / Ot-ven-rot.

Feb 90. (7")(c-s) **SOMETIMES. / LOVE MAN** [53] [-]
(12"+=) – ('A'instrumental).
(12"+=)(cd-s+=) – ('A'-land of Oz mix) / ('A'rock home mix).

Feb 90. (7") **SOMETIMES. / GHOST OF THE YEAR** [-] [ ]

JIMMY BARNES & INXS

Atlantic / Atlantic

Jun 87. (7") **GOOD TIMES. / LAY DOWN THE LAW** [ ] [47]
(UK-iss.7"/12"/cd-s.Jan91, hit No.18)

IRONHORSE (see under ⇒ BACHMAN-TURNER OVERDRIVE)

IRON MAIDEN

Formed: Leytonstone, East London, England . . . mid 1976 by DI'ANNO, MURRAY, HARRIS and SAMPSON, who first gigged around mid-'77. In 1978, they recorded demo EP 'THE SOUNDHOUSE TAPES', which got to the ears of DJ Neal Kay, who set them on a 'Heavy Metal Crusade' tour at London's Music Machine. Late in 1979, they signed to 'EMI', and had first of personnel changes (see below). Their debut single 'RUNNING FREE', hit the shops and UK Top 40 early 1980, and was followed by a self-titled debut album, which made Top 5. They had further chart triumphs, but surpassed everything before, when in 1982 they recruited Sheffield vocalist BRUCE DICKINSON. He added his power to give them first Top 10 single 'RUN TO THE HILLS' & first No.1 album 'THE NUMBER OF THE BEAST'. They went from strength to strength and scored a run of 7 UK Top 3 albums, and 17 UK Top 30 singles. Not only this, but like metal rivals DEF LEPPARD, they had stormed America. • **Style:** Instigated from early 1980 tag 'The New Wave Of British Heavy Metal', although their identity spurred from occult lyrics. Sounded not far removed from 70's heavies URIAH HEEP. • **Songwriters:** All mostly HARRIS and group. In the 90's, HARRIS or DICKINSON + GERS. Covered; COMMUNICATION BREAKDOWN (Led Zeppelin) / KILL ME, CE SOIR (Golden Earring) / SPACE STATION No.5 (Montrose). DICKINSON solo re-hashed; ALL THE YOUNG DUDES (hit; Mott The Hoople). • **Trivia:** Derek Riggs became the groups' artistic designer and created 'EDDIE', an evil skeleton comic-strip character, who appeared on album sleeves, poster bills & theatrical stage shows. Banned in Chile for being interpreted as 'devils and satanists'.

Recommended: LIVE AFTER DEATH (*8) / FEAR OF THE DARK (*8) / NO PRAYER FOR THE DYING (*7) / SEVENTH SON OF A SEVENTH SON (*7).

PAUL DI'ANNO (b.17 May'59, Chingford, Essex, England) – vocals / **DAVE MURRAY** (b.23 Dec'58) – guitar / **STEVE HARRIS** (b.12 Mar'57) – bass, vocals / **DOUG SAMPSON** – drums

Rock Hard / not issued

Jan 79. (7"ep) **THE SOUNDHOUSE TAPES** [ ] [-]
– Invasion / Iron Maiden / Prowler.

— (Nov79) **CLIVE BURR** (b. 8 Mar'57) – drums repl. SAMPSON / **DENNIS STRATTON** (b. 9 Nov'54) – guitar repl. TONY PARSONS (brief stay)

E.M.I. / Harvest

Feb 80. (7") **RUNNING FREE. / BURNING AMBITION** [34] [ ]

Apr 80. (lp)(c) **IRON MAIDEN** [4] [ ]
– Prowler / Remember tomorrow / Running free / Phantom of the opera / Transylvania / Strange world / Charlotte the harlot / Iron maiden. *(re-iss.May85 on 'Fame' hit 71, cd-iss.Oct87) (re-iss.cd Jul94)*

May 80. (7"m) **SANCTUARY. / DRIFTER / I'VE GOT THE FIRE (live)** [29] [ ]

Oct 80. (7") **WOMEN IN UNIFORM. / INVASION** [35] [ ]
(12"+=) – Phantom of the opera (live).

— **ADRIAN SMITH** (b.27 Feb'57) – guitar (ex-URCHIN) repl. STRATTON who formed LIONHEART

Feb 81. (lp)(c) **KILLERS** [12] [78]
– The ides of march / Wrathchild / Murders of the Rue Morgue / Another life / Ghenghis Khan / Innocent exile / KIllers / Prodigal son / Purgatory / Drifter. *(re-iss.May85 & cd-iss.Oct87 on 'Fame') (re-iss.cd Jul94)*

Mar 81. (7")(c-s)(7"clear)(7"red) **TWILIGHT ZONE. / WRATH CHILD** [31] [ ]

Jun 81. (7") **PURGATORY. / GHENGIS KHAN** [52] [ ]

Sep 81. (7"ep)(12"ep) **MAIDEN JAPAN** [43] [89] m-lp
– Remember tomorrow / Killers / Running free / Innocent exile.

— **BRUCE DICKINSON** (b. 7 Aug'58, Sheffield, England) – vocals (ex-SAMSON) repl. DI'ANNO who formed LONE WOLF

Feb 82. (7")(7"pic-d) **RUN TO THE HILLS. / TOTAL ECLIPSE** [7] [ ]

Mar 82. (lp)(c) **THE NUMBER OF THE BEAST** [1] [33]
– Invaders / Children of the damned / The prisoner / 22 Acacia Avenue / The number of the beast / Run to the hills / Gangland / Hallowed be thy name. *(re-iss.May87) (also on pic-lp) (cd-iss.Jan87 & Apr88 on 'Fame') (re-iss.cd Jul94)*

Apr 82. (7")(7"red) **THE NUMBER OF THE BEAST. / REMEMBER TOMORROW** [18] [ ]

— now **HARRIS, MURRAY, DICKINSON** and **SMITH** were joined by **NICKO McBAIN** (b. MICHAEL, 5 Jun'54) – drums (ex-PAT TRAVERS, ex-TRUST, ex-STREETWALKERS) repl. BURR who joined STRATUS

E.M.I. / Capitol

Apr 83. (7")(12"pic-d) **FLIGHT OF ICARUS. / I'VE GOT THE FIRE** [11] [ ]

May 83. (lp)(c) **PIECE OF MIND** [3] [14]
– Where eagles dare / Revelation / Flight of Icarus / Die with your boots on / The trooper / Still life / Quest for fire / Sun and steel / To tame a land. *(cd-iss.Dec86 & Jun91) (re-iss.cd Jul94)*

Jun 83. (7")(7"sha-pic-d) **THE TROOPER. / CROSS-EYED MARY** [12] [-]

Aug 84. (7") **2 MINUTES TO MIDNIGHT. / RAINBOW'S GOLD** [11] [-]
(12"pic-d+=) – Mission from 'Arry.

Sep 84. (lp)(c)(cd) **POWERSLAVE** [2] [21]
– Aces high / 2 minutes to midnight / Losfer words (big 'orra) / Flash of the blade / The duellists / Back in the village / Powerslave / Rime of the ancient mariner. *(also on pic-lp) (re-iss.Jun91) (re-iss.cd Jul94)*

Oct 84. (7") **ACES HIGH. / KING OF TWILIGHT** [20] [-]
(12"+=)(12"pic-d+=) – The number of the beast (live).

Sep 85. (7") **RUNNING FREE (live). / SANCTUARY (live)** [19] [-]
(12"+=)(12"pic-d+=) – Murders in the Rue Morgue (live).

Oct 85. (d-lp)(c)(cd) **LIVE AFTER DEATH (live)** [2] [19]
– Aces high / 2 minutes to midnight / The trooper / Revelations / Flight of Icarus / The rime of the ancient mariner / Powerslave / The number of the beast / Hallowed be thy name / Iron maiden / Run to the hills / Running free. (d-lp+c+=) Wrathchild / 22 Acacia Avenue / Children of the damned / Die with your boots on / Phantom of the opera. *(re-iss.Jun91) (re-iss.cd Jul94)*

Nov 85. (7") **RUN TO THE HILLS (live). / PHANTOM OF THE OPERA (live)** [26] [-]
(12"+=)(12"pic-d+=) – Losfer words (The big 'Orra) (live).

Aug 86. (7")(7"sha-pic-d) **WASTED YEARS. / REACH OUT** [18] [-]
(12"+=) – The sheriff of Huddersfield.

Sep 86. (lp)(c)(cd) **SOMEWHERE IN TIME** [3] [11]
– Caught somewhere in time / Wasted years / Sea of madness / Heaven can wait / The loneliness of the long distance runner / Stranger in a strange land / Deja-vu / Alexander the Great. *(re-iss.Jun91) (re-iss.cd Jul94)*

Nov 86. (7") **STRANGER IN A STRANGE LAND. / THAT GIRL** [22] [-]
(12"+=)(12"pic-d+=) – Juanita.

Mar 88. (7")(7"sha-pic-d) **CAN I PLAY WITH MADNESS. / BLACK BART BLUES** [3] [ ]
(12"+=)(cd-s+=) – Massacre.

Apr 88. (lp)(c)(cd) **SEVENTH SON OF A SEVENTH SON** [1] [12]
– Moonchild / Infinite dreams / Can I play with madness / The evil that men do / Seventh son of a seventh son / The prophecy / The clairvoyant / Only the good die young. *(also on pic-lp) (re-iss.Jun91) (re-iss.cd Jul94)*

Aug 88. (7")(7"sha-pic-d) **THE EVIL THAT MEN DO. / PROWLER '88** [5] [ ]
(12"+=)(cd-s+=) – Charlotte the harlot '88.

Nov 88. (7")(7"clear)(7"sha-pic-d) **THE CLAIRVOYANT (live). / THE PRISONER (live)** [6] [ ]
(12"+=)(cd-s+=)(12"pic-d+=) – Heaven can wait (live).

Nov 89. (7")(7"sha-pic-d) **INFINITE DREAMS (live). / KILLERS (live)** [6] [ ]
(12"+=)(c-s+=)(cd-s+=)(12"etched+=) – Still life (live).

—— (Feb90) **JANICK GERS** – guitar (ex-GILLAN, ex-WHITE SPIRIT, etc.) repl. SMITH who formed A.S.A.P.

Sep 90. (7")(c-s) **HOLY SMOKE. / ALL IN YOUR MIND** [3] [ ]
(12"+=)(cd-s+=)(12"pic-d+=) – Kill me ce soir.

Oct 90. (cd)(c)(lp) **NO PRAYER FOR THE DYING** [2] [17]
– Tailgunner / Holy smoke / No prayer for the dying / Public enemy number one / Fake warning / The assassin / Run silent run deep / Hooks in you / Bring your daughter . . . to the slaughter / Mother Russia. *(re-iss.cd Jul94)*

Dec 90. (7")(c-s)(7"pic-d) **BRING YOUR DAUGHTER . . . TO THE SLAUGHTER. / I'M A MOVER** [1] [ ]
(12"+=)(cd-s+=)(12"pic-d+=) – Communication breakdown.

—— In Summer 1991, HARRIS and McBAIN back up tennis stars McENROE & CASH on their version of LED ZEPPELIN'S 'Rock And Roll'. In Mar'92, BRUCE DICKINSON was to feature on single with Rowan Atkinson's comic character 'MR.BEAN & SMEAR CAMPAIGN' on a version of an Alice Cooper song '(I Want To Be) Elected'.

Apr 92. (7") **BE QUICK OR BE DEAD. / NODDING DONKEY BLUES** [2] [ ]
(12"+=)(cd-s+=)(12"pic-d+=) – Space station No.5.

May 92. (cd)(c)(lp) **FEAR OF THE DARK** [1] [12]
– Be quick or be dead / From here to eternity / Afraid to shoot strangers / Fear is the key / Childhood's end / Wasting love / The fugitive / Chains of misery / The apparition / Judas be my guide / Weekend warrior / Fear of the dark. *(re-iss.cd Jul94)*

Jul 92. (7") **FROM HERE TO ETERNITY. / ROLL OVER VELLA** [21] [ ]
(12"+=)(cd-s+=) – No prayer for the dying.

Mar 93. (7")(7"sha-pic-d) **FEAR OF THE DARK (live). / TAILGUNNER (live)** [8] [ ]
(cd-s) – ('A'side) / Hooks in you (live) / Bring your daughter . . . to the slaughter (live).

Mar 93. (cd)(c)(lp) **A REAL LIVE ONE (live)** [3] [ ]
– Be quick or be dead / From here to eternity / Can I play with madness / Wasting love / Tailgunner / The evil that men do / Afraid to shoot strangers / Bring your daughter . . .to the slaughter / Heaven can wait / The clairvoyant / Fear of the dark.

—— DICKINSON had already announced he had departed from group to go solo in'94.

Oct 93. (7"red) **HALLOWED BE THY NAME (live). / WRATHCHILD (live)** [9] [ ]
(12"pic-d+=)(cd-s+=) – The trooper (live) / Wasted years (live).

Oct 93. (cd)(c)(lp) **A REAL DEAD ONE (live)** [12] [ ]
– The number of the beast / The trooper / Prowler / Transylvania / Remember tomorrow / Where eagles dare / Sanctuary / Running free / 2 minutes to midnight / Iron Maiden / Hallowed be thy name.

Nov 93. (cd)(c)(lp) **LIVE AT DONINGTON 1992 (live)** [23] [ ]
– Be quick or be dead / The number of the beast / Wrathchild / From here to eternity / Can I play with madness / Wasting love / Tailgunner / The evil that men do / Afraid to shoot strangers.

—— **BLAZE BAILEY** -vocals (ex-WOLFSBANE) finally repl.DICKINSON

Sep 95. (c-s) **MAN ON THE EDGE / THE EDGE OF DARKNESS** [10] [ ]
(12"pic-d+=) – I live my way.
(cd-s+=) – Judgement day / (Blaze Bailey interview part 1).
(cd-s+=) – Justice of the peace / (Blaze Bailey interview part 2).

Oct 95. (cd)(c)(clear-d-lp) **THE X FACTOR** [9] [ ]
– Sign of the cross / Lord of the flies / Man on the edge / Fortunes of war / Look for the truth / The aftermath / Judgement of Heaven / Blood on the world's hands / The edge of darkness / 2 a.m. / The unbeliever.

– compilations, others, etc. –

Feb 90. E.M.I.; (d12")(cd-ep) **RUNNING FREE / BURNING AMBITION / SANCTUARY / DRIFTER (live) / I'VE GOT THE FIRE (live) / Listen with Nicko (part 1)** [10] [ ]

Feb 90. E.M.I.; (d12")(cd-ep) **WOMEN IN UNIFORM / INVASION / PHANTOM OF THE OPERA / TWILIGHT ZONE / WRATHCHILD / Listen with Nicko (part 2)** [10] [ ]

Feb 90. E.M.I.; (d12")(cd-ep) **PURGATORY / GENGHIS KHAN / RUNNING FREE / REMEMBER TOMORROW / KILLERS / INNOCENT EXILE / Listen with Nicko (part 3)** [5] [ ]

Mar 90. E.M.I.; (d12")(cd-ep) **RUN TO THE HILLS / TOTAL ECLIPSE / THE NUMBER OF THE BEAST / REMEMBER TOMORROW (live) / Listen with Nicko (part 4)** [3] [ ]

Mar 90. E.M.I.; (d12")(cd-ep) **FLIGHT OF ICARUS / I'VE GOT THE FIRE / THE TROOPER / CROSS-EYED MARY / Listen with Nicko (part 5)** [7] [ ]

Mar 90. E.M.I.; (d12")(cd-ep) **2 MINUTES TO MIDNIGHT / RAINBOW'S GOLD / MISSION FROM 'ARRY / ACES HIGH / KING OF TWILIGHT / THE NUMBER OF THE BEAST (live) / Listen with Nicko (part 6)** [11] [ ]

Apr 90. E.M.I.; (d12")(cd-ep) **RUNNING FREE / MURDERS OF THE RUE MORGUE / RUN TO THE HILLS / PHANTOM OF THE OPERA / LOSFER WORDS (THE BIG 'ORRA) / Listen with Nicko (part 7)** [9] [ ]

Apr 90. E.M.I.; (d12")(cd-ep) **WASTED YEARS / REACH OUT / THE SHERIFF OF HUDDERSFIELD / STRANGER IN A STRANGE LAND / THAT GIRL / JUANITA / Listen with Nicko (part 8)** [9] [ ]

Apr 90. E.M.I.; (d12")(cd-ep) **CAN I PLAY WITH MADNESS / BLACK BART BLUES / MASSACRE / THE EVIL THAT MEN DO / PROWLER '88 / CHARLOTTE THE HARLOT '88 / Listen with Nicko (part 9)** [10] [ ]

Apr 90. E.M.I.; (d12")(cd-ep) **THE CLAIRVOYANT (live) / THE PRISONER (live) / HEAVEN CAN WAIT (live) / INFINITE DREAMS (live) / KILLERS (live) / STILL LIFE (live) / Listen with Nicko (part 10)** [11] [ ]

—— (all 10 releases above, basically hit peak number before crashing out of 50)

Aug 94. E.M.I.; (cd)(cd-vid) **MAIDEN ENGLAND (live)** [ ] [-]

NICKO McBRAIN

E.M.I. ?

Jul 91. (7") **RHYTHM OF THE BEAST. / BEEHIVE BOOGIE** [ ] [-]
(7"pic-d) – ('A'extended) / (McBrain damage interview).

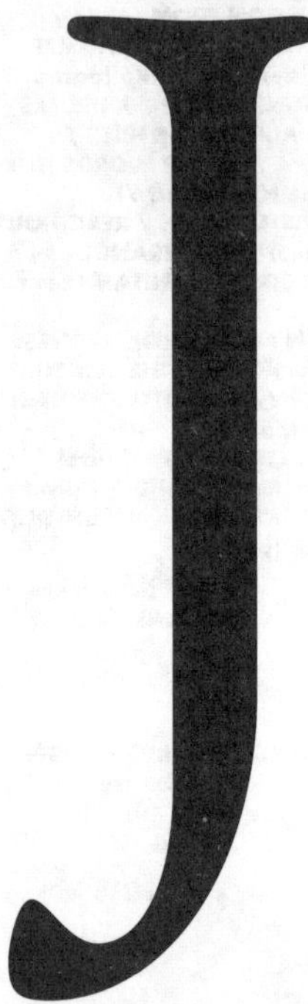

David J (see under ⇒ BAUHAUS)

JACK OFFICERS (see under ⇒ BUTTHOLE SURFERS)

Joe JACKSON

Born: 11 Aug'54, Burton-On-Trent, Staffordshire, England. Raised from a very early age in Gosport, near Portsmouth. He left school with top grade music honour and enrolled at The Royal College Of Music in 1973. After a spell in JOHNNY DANKWORTH's NATIONAL YOUTH JAZZ ORCHESTRA, he joined pub rock outfit ARMS & LEGS. They released 3 flop singles for 'MAM' between 1976-1977, before he quit. In 1977, he became musical director for 'Opportunity Knocks' (TV talent show, hosted by Hughie Green) winners COFFEE AND CREAM. The next year, he moved away from the cabaret scene and to London, to record own demo tape, which 'A&M''s David Kershenbaum approved of. He also produced first solo attempt, 'IS SHE REALLY GOING OUT WITH HIM?', but it took a re-issue of this 45 in Summer 1979 to break him into UK + US charts. Although he had several more UK hits, his appeal came mainly in the albums market. • **Style:** Progressed from ELVIS COSTELLO-like comparisons to a more sophisticated rock-pop, which incorporated many styles, including jazz, Latin-salsa and ballads. In 1982, he moved to New York, USA, after the bust-up of his marriage. • **Songwriters:** Self-penned, except his second jazz LOUIS JORDAN inspired album JUMPIN' JIVE, which contained covers of 40's & 50's CAB CALLOWAY / GLENN MILLER. JOE also went on to cover OH WELL (Fleetwood Mac) / MAKING PLANS FOR NIGEL (Xtc). • **Trivia:** He also produced The KEYS in '81, and reggae outfits RASSES and The TOASTERS.

Recommended: STEPPIN' OUT – THE VERY BEST OF JOE JACKSON (*6)

ARMS AND LEGS

JOE JACKSON – piano, violin, vocals, harmonica / **MARK ANDREWS** – vocals / **GRAHAM MABY** – bass

		M.A.M.	not issued
Apr 76.	(7") **JANICE. / SHE'LL SURPRISE YOU**		-
Aug 76.	(7") **HEAT OF THE NIGHT. / GOOD TIMES**		-
Feb 77.	(7") **IS THERE ANYMORE WINE. / SHE'LL SURPRISE YOU**		-

JOE JACKSON

solo – lead vocals, piano with backing band **GRAHAM MABY** – bass / **GARY SANFORD** – guitar / **DAVE HOUGHTON** – drums

Date	Release	A & M	A & M
Sep 78.	(7") **IS SHE REALLY GOING OUT WITH HIM?. / YOU GOT THE FEVER**		-
Jan 79.	(lp)(c) **LOOK SHARP!** – One more time / Sunday papers / Is she really going out with him? / Happy loving couples / Throw it away / Baby stick around / Look sharp! / Fools in love / (Do the) Instant mash / Pretty girls / Got the time. *(re-iss.Aug79 on white-lp re-iss.Mar82, re-iss.Jul85 on 'Hallmark') (cd-iss.Nov84 & re-iss.1988)*	40	20
Feb 79.	(7") **SUNDAY PAPERS. / LOOK SHARP!**		-
May 79.	(7") **IS SHE REALLY GOING OUT WITH HIM? / (DO THE) INSTANT MASH**	-	21
May79.	(7"white)(10"white) **ONE MORE TIME. / DON'T ASK ME**		-
Jul 79.	(7") **IS SHE REALLY GOING OUT WITH HIM?. / YOU GOT THE FEVER**	13	-
Aug 79.	(7") **IT'S DIFFERENT FOR GIRLS. / COME ON**	-	
Oct 79.	(7") **I'M THE MAN. / COME ON (live)**		
Oct 79.	(lp)(c)(5x7"box) **I'M THE MAN** – On your radio / Geraldine and John / Kinda kute / It's different for girls / I'm the man / The band wore blue shirts / Don't wanna be like that / Amateur hour / Get that girl / Friday. *(re-iss.+cd.1988)*	12	22
Dec 79.	(7") **IT'S DIFFERENT FOR GIRLS. / FRIDAY**	5	-
Mar 80.	(7") **KINDA KUTE. / GERALDINE AND JOHN**		-

JOE JACKSON BAND

Date	Release	A & M	A & M
Jun 80.	(7")(12") **THE HARDER THEY COME. / OUT OF STYLE / TILT**		-
Oct 80.	(7") **MAD AT YOU. / ENOUGH IS NOT ENOUGH**		-
Oct 80.	(lp)(c) **BEAT CRAZY** – Beat crazy / One to one / In every dream home (a nightmare) / The evil eye / Mad at you / Crime don't pay / Someone up there / Battleground / Biology / Pretty boys / Fit. *(cd-iss.1988) (re-iss.c. Jan93)*	42	41
Nov 80.	(7") **ONE TO ONE. / ENOUGH IS NOT ENOUGH**	-	
Jan 81.	(7") **BEAT CRAZY. / IS SHE REALLY GOING OUT WITH HIM?**		
Mar 81.	(7") **ONE TO ONE. / SOMEONE UP THERE**		

JOE JACKSON'S JUMPIN' JIVE

JOE retained **GRAHAM MABY** plus **PETE THOMAS** – sax / **RAUOL OLIVERA** – trumpet / **DAVE BITELI** – wind instr. NICK WELDON – piano / **LARRY TOLFREE** – drums / **NICK WELDON** – piano

Date	Release	A & M	A & M
Jun 81.	(7") **JUMPIN' JIVE. / KNOCK ME A KISS**	43	
Jun 81.	(lp)(c) **JOE JACKSON'S JUMPIN' JIVE** – Jumpin' with symphony Sid / Jack, you're dead / Is you or is you ain't my baby / We the cats will help ya / San Francisco fan / Five guys named Moe / Jumpin' jive / You run your mouth (and I'll run my business) / What's the use of getting sober (when you're gonna get drunk again) / You're my meat / Tuxedo junction / How long must I wait for you. *(cd-iss.1988) (re-iss.cd+c May93 on 'Spectrum')*	14	42
Aug 81.	(7") **JACK, YOU'RE DEAD. / FIVE GUYS NAMED MOE**		

JOE JACKSON

SUE HADJOPOULOS – percussion, vocals, flute, etc. repl. WELDON + horns

Date	Release	A & M	A & M
Jun 82.	(7")(7"pic-d) **REAL MEN. / CHINATOWN**		
Jun 82.	(lp)(c) **NIGHT AND DAY** – Another world / Chinatown / T.V. age / Target / Steppin' out / Breaking us in two / Cancer / Real men / A slow song. *(cd-iss.1983)*	3	4
Aug 82.	(7") **BREAKING US IN TWO. / EL BLANCO**		-
Aug 82.	(7") **STEPPIN' OUT. / CHINATOWN**	-	6
Oct 82.	(7")(12") **STEPPIN' OUT. / ANOTHER WORLD**	6	-
Jan 83.	(7") **BREAKING US IN TWO. / TARGET**	-	18
Feb 83.	(7") **BREAKING US IN TWO. / EL BLANCO** (12"+=) – T.V. age.	59	-
May 83.	(7") **A SLOW SONG. / REAL MEN**		
Jul 83.	(7") **ANOTHER WORLD. / ORTO MUNDO**	-	

—— added **JOY ASKEW** – synthesizers

Date	Release	A & M	A & M
Aug 83.	(7") **COSMOPOLITAN. / BREAKDOWN**		
Sep 83.	(lp)(c) **MIKE'S MURDER (soundtrack)** – Cosmopolitan / 1-2-3-go (this town's a fairground) / Laundromat Monday / Memphis / Moonlight / Zemeo / Breakdown / Moonlight theme.		64
Nov 83.	(7") **MEMPHIS. / BREAKDOWN**	-	85

—— retained only **MABY** and brought in **GARY BURKE** – drums / **VINNIE ZUMMO** – guitar / **ED ROYNESDAL** – keyboards, violin / **TONY AIELLO** – sax, flute / **MICHAEL MORREALE** – wind

Date	Release	A & M	A & M
Mar 84.	(lp)(c) **BODY AND SOUL** – The verdict / Cha cha loco / Not here, not now / You can't get what you want ('till you know what you want) / Go for it / Loisaida / Be my number two / Heart	14	20

of ice. *(cd-iss.Oct84)*

Apr 84. (7")(12") **HAPPY ENDING. / LOISAIDA** [58] [57] Jul 84

Jun 84. (7")(12") **BE MY NUMBER TWO. / HEART OF ICE** [70] [ ]
(7") – ('A'side) / Is she really going out with him?

Sep 84. (7") **YOU CAN'T GET WHAT YOU WANT ('TILL YOU KNOW WHAT YOU WANT). / CHA CHA LOCO** [ ] [15] Apr 84
(12"+=) – ('A' dub version).

—— **RICK FORD** – bass, guitar, vox repl. MABY, AIELLO, ROYNESDAL + MORREALE

Mar 86. (d-lp)(c)(cd) **BIG WORLD (live)** [41] [34]
– Wild west / Right and wrong / (It's a) Big world / Precious time / Tonight and forever / Shanghai sky / Fifty dollar love affair / We can't live together / Forty years / Survival / Soul kiss / The jet-set / Tango Atlantico / Hometown / Man in the street. *(not 4-sided d-lp, but 3-sided)*

Apr 86. (7") **RIGHT OR WRONG. / BREAKING US IN TWO (live)** [ ] [ ]
(12"+=) – I'm the man (live).

Jun 86. (7")(12") **HOME TOWN. / TANGO ATLANTICO** [ ] [ ]

Apr 87. (lp)(c)(cd) **WILL POWER** [ ] [ ]
– No Pasaran / Solitude / Will power / Nocturne / Symphony in one movement.

May 87. (7") **WILL POWER. / NOCTURNE** [-] [ ]

Apr 88. (7")(12") **JUMPIN' JIVE (live). / MEMPHIS (live)** [ ] [ ]

May 88. (d-lp)(c)(cd) **LIVE 1980/86 (live)** [66] [91]
– One to one / I'm the man / Beat crazy / Is she really going out with him? / Cancer / Don't wanna be like that / On your radio / Fools in love / Cancer / Is she really going out with him? (acappella version) / Look sharp! / Sunday papers / Real men / Is she really going out with him? (acoustic) / Memphis / A slow song / Be my number two / Breaking us in two / It's different for girls / You can't get what you want ('till you know what you want) / Jumpin' jive / Steppin' out.

Jun 88. (7") **LOOK SHARP (live). / MEMPHIS (live** [-] [ ]

Aug 88. (7") **(HE'S A) SHAPE IN A DRAPE. / SPEEDWAY** [ ] [ ]
(12"+=) – Sometime in Chicago.

Nov 88. (lp)(c)(cd) **TUCKER – A MAN AND HIS DREAMS (Soundtrack)** [ ] [ ]
– Captain of industry / Car of tomorrow / No chance blues / (He's a) Shape in a drape / Factory / Vera / It pays to advertise / Tiger rag / Showtime in Chicago / Loan bank loan blues / Speedway / Marilee / Hangin' in Howard Hughes' hangar / The toast of the town / Abe's blues / The trial / Freedom swing / Rhythm delivery.

—— Now with 10-piece line-up, **MABY, ZUMMO, BURKE, ASKEW, AIELLO, FORD, ROYNESDAL, HADJOPOULOS + TOM TEELEY** – guitar / **ANTHONY COX** – bass

Apr 89. (lp)(c)(cd) **BLAZE OF GLORY** [36] [61]
– Tomorrow's child / Me and you (against the world) / Down to London / Sentimental thing / Acropolis now / Blaze of glory / Rant and rave / Nineteen forever / The best I can do / Evil empire / Discipline / The uman touch.

May 89. (7") **NINETEEN FOREVER. / ACROPOLIS NOW (instrumental)** [ ] [ ]
(cd-s+=) – ('A'extended).

Oct 89. (7")(12") **DOWN TO LONDON. / YOU CAN'T GET WHAT YOU WANT (TIL YOU KNOW WHAT YOU WANT)** [ ] [ ]
(cd-s+=) – Sunday papers.

Aug 90. (7")(c-s) re-issue **STEPPIN' OUT. / SENTIMENTAL THING** [ ] [ ]
(cd-s+=) – It's a big worth.

Sep 90. (cd)(c)(lp) **STEPPIN' OUT – THE VERY BEST OF JOE JACKSON** (compilation) [7] [ ]
– Is she really going out with him? / Fools in love / I'm the man / It's different for girls / Beat crazy / Jumpin' jive / Breaking us in two / Steppin' out / Slow song (live) / You can't get what you want ('till you know what you want) / Be my number two / Right and wrong / Home town / Down to London / Nineteen forever.

Virgin Virgin

Apr 91. (7") **STRANGER THAN FICTION. / DROWNING** [ ] [ ]
(12"+=)(cd-s+=) – Different for girls (acoustic).

May 91. (cd)(c)(lp) **LAUGHTER AND LUST** [41] [ ]
– Obvious song / Goin' downtown / Stranger than fiction / Oh well / Jamie G / Hit single / It's all too much / When you're not around / The other me / Trying to cry / My house / The old songs / Drowning.

Oct 94. (cd)(c) **NIGHT MUSIC** [ ] [ ]
– Nocturne No.1 / Flying nocturne No.2 / Ever after / The man who wrote Danny Boy / Nocturne No.3 / Lullaby / Only the future / Nocturne No.4 / Sea of secrets.

– compilations, others, etc. –

Oct 93. A&M; (cd) **NIGHT AND DAY / LOOK SHARP** [ ] [-]

Mick JAGGER (see under ⇒ ROLLING STONES)

JAM

Formed: Woking, Surrey, England . . . late '73 by WELLER, FOXTON, BUCKLER and 4th member STEVE BROOKS – guitar. This quartet first gigged mid-74, and progressed in late 1976 to London's Marquee, 101 Club & Red Cow, but as a trio without BROOKS. Early in 1977 after many gigs, they were signed by A&R man Chris Parry to 'Polydor'. In Spring '77, their debut 'IN THE CITY' cracked the UK Top 40, and preceded by a month the Top 20 album of the same. They advanced greatly throughout the next 3 years, and had first of 4 UK No.1's early 1980 with 'GOING UNDERGROUND'. • **Style:** Mod revivalists, with power and energy of punk rock, but with mid-60's fashion (parkers, mohair suits, two-tone shoes & motor scooters). By 1982, their music had incorporated more of a soul sound, which led to WELLER taking off to form STYLE COUNCIL. • **Songwriters:** WELLER penned except; SWEET SOUL MUSIC (Arthur Conley) / BACK IN MY ARMS AGAIN (Holland-Dozier-Holland) / DAVID WATTS (Kinks) / MOVE ON UP (Curtis Mayfield). • **Trivia:** In Oct'81, WELLER started own record company 'Respond', and signed acts The QUESTIONS and TRACIE.

Recommended: SNAP (*10) / ALL MOD CONS (*8) / IN THE CITY (*5) / THIS IS THE MODERN WORLD (*5) / SETTING SONS (*7) / SOUND EFFECTS (*7) / THE GIFT (*6).

PAUL WELLER (b.JOHN WELLER, 25 May'58) – vocals, guitar / **BRUCE FOXTON** (b. 1 Sep'55) – bass, vocals / **RICK BUCKLER** (b.PAUL RICHARD BUCKLER, 6 Dec'55) – drums

Polydor Polydor

Apr 77. (7") **IN THE CITY. / TAKIN' MY LOVE** [40] [ ]
(re-iss.Apr80 hit No.40. re-iss.Jan83 hit No.47.)

May 77. (lp)(c) **IN THE CITY** [20] [ ]
– Art school I've changed my address / Slow down / I got by in time / Away from the numbers / Batman / In the city / Sounds from the street / Non stop dancing / Time for truth / Takin' my love / Bricks and mortar. *(re-iss.Aug83, hit 100) (re-iss.+cd.Jul90)*

Jul 77. (7") **ALL AROUND THE WORLD. / CARNABY STREET** [13] [-]
(re-iss.Apr80 hit No.43. re-iss.Jan83 hit No.38.)

Oct 77. (7"m) **THE MODERN WORLD. / SWEET SOUL MUSIC / BACK IN MY ARMS AGAIN / BRICKS AND MORTAR** [36] [-]
(re-iss.Apr80 hit No.52. re-iss.Jan83 hit No.51)

Nov 77. (lp)(c) **THIS IS THE MODERN WORLD** [22] [ ]
– The modern world / London traffic / Standards / Life from the window / The combine / Don't tell them you're sane / In the street today / London girl / I need you / Here comes the weekend / Tonight at noon / In the midnight hour. *(re-iss.Aug83) (re-iss.+cd.Jul90 & Sep95)*

Feb 78. (7") **I NEED YOU. / IN THE CITY** [-] [ ]

Mar 78. (7"m) **NEWS OF THE WORLD. / AUNTIES AND UNCLES / INNOCENT MAN** [27] [-]
(re-iss.Apr80 hit No.53) (re-iss.Jan83 hit No.39.)

Aug 78. (7") **DAVID WATTS. / 'A' BOMB IN WARDOUR STREET** [25] [-]
(re-iss.Apr80 hit No.54) (re-iss.Jan83 hit No.50)

Oct 78. (7") **DOWN IN THE TUBE-STATION AT MIDNIGHT. / SO BAD ABOUT US / THE NIGHT** [15] [-]
(re-iss.Apr80) (re-iss.Jan83 hit No.30)

Nov 78. (lp)(c) **ALL MOD CONS** [6] [ ]
– All mod cons / To be someone (didn't we have a nice time) / Mr. Clean / David Watts / English rose / In the crowd / Billy Hunt / It's too bad / Fly 3.18 / The place I love / 'A' bomb in Wardour Street / Down in the tube station at midnight. *(re-iss.Aug80) (re-iss.+cd.1989)*

Jan 79. (7") **DOWN IN THE TUBE STATION AT MIDNIGHT. / MR. CLEAN** [-] [ ]

Mar 79. (7") **STRANGE TOWN. / THE BUTTERFLY COLLECTOR** [15] [ ]
(re-iss.Apr80 hit No.44. (re-iss.Jan83 hit No.42.)

Aug 79. (7") **WHEN YOU'RE YOUNG. / SMITHERS-JONES** [17] [-]
(re-iss.Jan83 hit No.53)

Oct 79. (7") **THE ETON RIFLES. / SEE-SAW** [3] [-]
(re-iss.Jan83 hit No.54)

Nov 79. (lp)(c) **SETTING SONS** [4] [ ]
– Girl on the phone / Thick as thieves / Private hell / Little boy soldiers / Waste land / Burning sky / Smithers-Jones / Saturday's kids / The Eton rifles / Heat wave. *(re-iss.Aug83) (cd-iss.May88)*

Feb 80. (7") **GOING UNDERGROUND. / DREAMS OF CHILDREN** [1] [-]
(d7"+=) – The modern world / Away from the numbers / Tube-station. *(re-iss.Jan83 hit No.21.)*

Aug 80. (7") **START!. / LIZA RADLEY** [1] [-]
(re-iss.Jan83 hit 60)

Nov 80. (lp)(c) **SOUND AFFECTS** [2] [72]
– Pretty green / Monday / But I'm different now / Set the house ablaze / Start! / That's entertainment / Dreamtime / Man in the cornershop / Music for the last couple / Boy about town / Scrape away. *(re-iss.Aug83) (cd-iss.May88, re-iss.+cd.Apr90)*

Jan 81. (7") **THAT'S ENTERTAINMENT. / DOWN IN THE TUBE STATION AT MIDNIGHT** [21] [-]
(above 45, was actually issued on German import *'Metrognome') (re-iss.Jan83 on 'Polydor', hit 60)*

Eton Rifles

May 81. (7") **FUNERAL PYRE. / DISGUISES** [4] [ ]
(re-iss.Jan83)
Oct 81. (7") **ABSOLUTE BEGINNERS. / TALES FROM THE RIVERBANK** [4] [ ]
(re-iss.Jan83)
Dec 81. (m-lp) **THE JAM** [-] [ ]
– Absolute beginners / Funeral pyre / Liza Radley / Tales from the riverbank.
Feb 82. (7")(12") **TOWN CALLED MALICE. / PRECIOUS** [1] [ ]
(re-iss.Jan83 hit 73)
Mar 82. (lp)(c) **THE GIFT** [1] [82]
– Happy together / Ghosts / Precious / Just who is the 5 o'clock hero? / Trans-global express / Running on the spot / Circus / The planner's dream goes wrong / Carnation / Town called Malice / The gift. *re-iss.Aug83) (re-iss.+cd.Apr90)*
Jun 82. (7") **JUST WHO IS THE 5 O'CLOCK HERO?. / THE GREAT DEPRESSION** [6] [ ]
(12"+=) – War.
Sep 82. (7") **THE BITTEREST PILL. / PITY POOR ALFIE / FEVER** [2] [ ]
(US-iss. Nov 82 as 12"m-lp w/extra track)
Nov 82. (7") **BEAT SURRENDER. / SHOPPING** [1] [ ]
(d7"+=)(d12"+=) – Move on up / War / Stoned out of my mind.
(US-iss. Apr 83 as 12"m-lp)
Dec 82. (lp)(c) **DIG THE NEW BREED (live 77-82)** [2] [ ]
– In the city / All mod cons / To be someone / It's too bad / Start! / Big bird / Set the house ablaze / Ghosts / Standards / In the crowd / Going underground / Dreams of children / That's entertainment / Private hell. *(re-iss.Jun87) (re-iss.Jun90 & Sep95)*

—— They split late '82. WELLER formed The STYLE COUNCIL. FOXTON went solo. BUCKLER formed TIME UK before both formed SHARP.

– compilations, etc. –

Sep 80. Polydor; (d-lp)(d-c) **IN THE CITY / THIS IS THE MODERN WORLD** [ ] [ ]
(cd-iss.Jan90)
Jan 83. Polydor; (d-lp)(d-c) **SOUND AFFECTS / THE GIFT** [ ] [ ]
Feb 83. Polydor; (d-lp)(d-c) **ALL MOD CONS / SETTING SONS** [ ] [ ]
Oct 83. Polydor; (d-lp)(d-c) **SNAP** [2] [ ]
– In the city / Away from the numbers / All around the world / The modern world / News of the world / Billy Hunt / English Rose / Mr. Clean / David Watts / 'A' bomb in Wardour Street / Down in the tube station at midnight / Strange town / The butterfly collector / When you're young / Smithers-Jones / Thick as thieves / The Eton rifles / Going underground / Dreams of children / That's entertainment / Start! / Man in the cornershop / Funeral pyre / Absolute beginners / Tales from the riverbank / Town called Malice / Precious / The bitterest pill (I ever had to swallow) / Beat surrender. *(d-lp.w / free 7"ep)* **LIVE AT WEMBLEY (live)**– The great depression / But I'm different now / Move on up / Get yourself together. *(cd-iss.Sep84 cd-omits 8 tracks).*
Jun 91. Polydor; (7")(c-s) **THAT'S ENTERTAINMENT. / DOWN IN THE TUBE-STATION AT MIDNIGHT (live)** [57] [-]
(12"+=)(cd-s+=) – Town called Malice (live).
Jul 91. Polydor; (cd)(c)(lp) **GREATEST HITS** [2] [-]
Mar 92. Polydor; (7")(c-s) **THE DREAMS OF CHILDREN. / AWAY FROM THE NUMBERS (live)** [ ] [-]
(12"+=)(cd-s+=) – This is the modern world (live).
Apr 92. Polydor; (cd)(c)(lp) **EXTRAS** (available for Fan Club members) [-] [-]
Oct 93. Polydor; (cd)(c)(d-lp) **LIVE JAM (live)** [28] [ ]
– The modern world / Billy Hunt / Thick as thieves / Burning sky / Mr. Clean / Smithers-Jones / Little boy soldiers / The Eton Rifles / Away from the numbers / Down in the tube station at midnight / Strange town / When you're young / 'A' Bomb In Wardour Street / Pretty green / Boy about town / Man in the cornershop / David Watts / Funeral pyre / Move on up / Carnation / The butterfly collector / Precious / Town called Malice / Heatwave.
1989. Old Gold; (7") **BEAT SURRENDER. / THE BITTEREST PILL** [ ] [-]
Mar 90. Old Gold; (7") **TOWN CALLED MALICE. / ABSOLUTE BEGINNERS** [ ] [-]
Mar 90. Old Gold; (7") **GOING UNDERGROUND. / START!** [ ] [-]
Mar 90. Old Gold; (7") **THE ETON RIFLES. / DOWN IN THE TUBE-STATION AT MIDNIGHT** [ ] [-]
Sep 90. Strange Fruit; (12"ep)(cd-ep) **THE PEEL SESSIONS** [ ] [-]
– In the city / Art school / I've changed my address / The modern world.
Oct 92. Pickwick; (cd)(c) **WASTELAND** [ ] [-]
Sep 95. Polydor; (cd) **EXTRAS** [ ] [-]

JAMES

Formed: Manchester, England . . . 1982 by JIM GLENNIE, TIM BOOTH, LARRY GOTT and GAVAN WHELAN. In 1983 they signed to Tony Wilson's 'Factory' label, and issued debut 3-track 'JIMONE EP'. Soon loved by the music press, especially after their 2nd classic 45 'HYMN FROM A VILLAGE', topped the indie chart early in '85. They were soon snapped up by Seymour Stein's 'Sire', but financial difficulties after release of Lenny Kaye produced album 'STUTTER', led to them moving to WEA subsidiary 'Blanco Y Negro'. In 1990, after a change of personnel and a spell on 'Rough Trade', they had first Top 40 hit on 'Fontana' with 'HOW WAS IT FOR YOU?'. It was soon followed by a Top 20 album 'GOLD MOTHER', that when re-promoted early 1991 with No.2 hit 'SIT DOWN', also hit No.2. • **Style:** Sometimes erratic and unorthodox, intelligent rock band tinged with INCREDIBLE STRING BAND like folk, with the overtly accented TIM BOOTH their feature. • **Songwriters:** TIM BOOTH penned, except SUNDAY MORNING (Velvet Underground). • **Trivia:** In the 1990s, they were produced by BRIAN ENO, who also contributed musicianship.

Recommended: GOLD MOTHER (*8) / STUTTER (*6) / LAID (*7) / SEVEN (*8).

TIM BOOTH – vocals / **LARRY GOTT** (b.JAMES GOTT) – guitar / **JIM GLENNIE** – bass / **GAVAN WHELAN** – drums

Factory / not issued
Sep 83. (7") **JIMONE** [ ] [-]
– What's the world / Fire so close / Folklore.
Feb 85. (7") **JAMES II: HYMN FROM A VILLAGE. / IF THINGS WERE PERFECT** [ ] [-]
Jun 85. (12"ep) **VILLAGE FIRE** [ ] [-]
– (remixes of the above 5 tracks).

Sire / Warners
Feb 86. (7") **CHAIN MAIL. / HUP STRINGS** [ ] [-]
(12"+=) – ('A' extended) / Uprising.
Jun 86. (lp)(c) **STUTTER** [68] [-]
– Skullduggery / Scarecrow / So many ways / Just hip / Johnny Yen / Summer song / Really hard / Billy's shirts / Why so close / Withdrawn / Black hole. *(re-iss.+cd.Nov91)*
Jul 86. (7") **SO MANY WAYS. / WITHDRAWN** [ ] [-]
(12"+=) – Just hipper.

Blanco YN / Sire
Sep 87. (7") **YAHO. / MOSQUITO** [ ] [-]
(12"+=) – New nature / Left out of her will.
Mar 88. (7") **WHAT FOR. / ISLAND SWING** [ ] [-]
(12"+=)(c-s+=) – Not there.
May 88. (lp)(c)(cd) **STRIP MINE** [90] [ ]
– What for / Charlie Dance / Fairground / Are you ready / Yaho / Medieval / Not there / Riders / Vulture / Strip mining / Refrain. *(re-iss.Sep88) (re-iss.+cd.Jul91) (cd-iss.Feb95)*

Rough Trade / not issued
Mar 89. (lp)(c)(cd) **ONE MAN CLAPPING (live in Bath)** [ ] [-]
– Chain mail / Sandman (hup strings) / Whoops / Riders / Why so close / Leaking / Johnny Yen / Scarecrow / Are you ready / Really hard / Burned / Stutter. *(cd+=)* – Yaho.

—— **DAVE BAIGNTON-POWER** – drums repl. WHELAN, / added **SAUL DAVIS** – violin, percussion, guitar / **MARK HUNTER** – keyboards

Jun 89. (7") **SIT DOWN. / SKY IS FALLING** [ ] [-]
(12"+=)(cd-s+=) – Goin' away / Sound investment.

—— added **ANDY DIAGRAM** – trumpet (ex-PALE FOUNTAINS, ex-DIAGRAM BROS.)

Nov 89. (7") **COME HOME. / PROMISED LAND** [ ] [-]
('A'ext-12"+=)(cd-s+=) – Slow right down.

Fontana / Mercury
May 90. (7") **HOW WAS IT FOR YOU?. / WHOOPS (live)** [32] [ ]
(12") – ('A'side) / Hymn from a village (live) / Lazy.
(cd-s) – ('A'side) / Hymn from a village (live) / Undertaker.
(12") – ('A'different mix) / Lazy / Undertaker.
Jun 90. (cd)(c)(lp) **GOLD MOTHER** [16] [ ]
– Come home / Government walls / God only knows / You can tell how much suffering (on a face that's always smilimg) / How was it for you? / Crescendo / Hang on / Walking the ghost / Gold mother / Top of the world. *(re-iss.Apr91, hit No.2)* (tracks =repl. by) – Sit down / Lose control.
Jul 90. (7")(c-s) **COME HOME (flood mix). / DREAMING UP TOMORROW** [32] [ ]
(12") – ('A'side) / Stutter (live) / Fire away.
(cd-s) – ('A'side) / Gold mother (remix) / Fire away.
Nov 90. (7")(c-s) **LOSE CONTROL. / SUNDAY MORNING** [38] [ ]
(12"+=)(cd-s+=) – ('A'extended) / Out to get you.
Mar 91. (7")(c-s) **SIT DOWN. / ('A'live version)** [2] [ ]
(12"+=)(cd-s+=) – Tonight.
Nov 91. (7")(c-s) **SOUND. / ALL MY SONS** [9] [ ]
(12"+=)(cd-s+=) – ('A'full version) / Come home (Youth mix).
Jan 92. (7")(c-s) **BORN OF FRUSTRATION. / BE MY PRAYER** [13] [ ]
(12"+=)(cd-s+=) – Sound (mix).
Feb 92. (cd)(c)(lp) **SEVEN** [2] [ ]
– Born of frustration / Ring the bells / Sound / Bring a gun / Mother / Don't wait that long / Live a life of love / Heavens / Protect me / Seven. (cd/c+=) – Next lover.
Mar 92. (7")(c-s) **RING THE BELLS. / FIGHT** [37] [ ]
(12"+=)(cd-s+=) – The skunk weed skank / Come home (live dub version).
(12"++=) – Once a friend.
Jul 92. (7"ep)(c-ep)(cd-ep) **SEVEN** [46] [ ]
– Seven / Goalies ball / William Burroughs / Still alive.
Sep 93. (7")(c-s) **SOMETIMES. / AMERICA** [18] [ ]

(12"+=)(cd-s+=) – Building a charge.

Sep 93. (cd)(c)(lp) **LAID** [3] [64]
– Out to get you / Sometimes (Lester Piggott) / Dream thrum / One of the three / Say something / Five-o / P.S. / Everybody knows / Knuckle too far / Low, low / Laid / Lullaby / Skindiving. *(re-iss.Apr94)*

Nov 93. (7")(c-s) **LAID. / WAH WAH KITS** [25] [61]
(cd-s+=) – The lake / Seconds away.
(cd-s) – ('A'live) / Five-O / Say something / Sometimes.

Mar 94. (c-s) **JAM J. / SAY SOMETHING** [24] [ ]
(cd-s+=) – Assassin / ('B'new version).
(12") – ('A'side) / (James VS The Sabres Of Paradise – 33 mins of instrumental remix).

Sep 94. (cd)(c)(d-lp;ltd) **WAH WAH** (w / BRIAN ENO) [11] [ ]

. . . Jan – Jun '96 stop press . . .

BOOTH AND THE BAD ANGEL

— TIM BOOTH / ANGELO BADALAMENTI & BERNARD BUTLER (ex-Suede)

Fontana Mercury

Jun 96. (single) **I BELIEVE** [25] [ ]

— An album due out early July.

JAMIE WEDNESDAY (see under ⇒ CARTER THE UNSTOPPABLE SEX MACHINE)

JAMIROQUAI

Formed: Ealing, London based . . . from early 1991 by 22 year-old JAY K. After hitting minor placing with debut 'WHEN YOU GONNA LEARN?', they switched labels to 'Sony Soho Square', where they soon had Top 20 singles. Their debut album 'EMERGENCY ON PLANET EARTH', went straight to UK No.1, as they await to conquer America. • **Style:** Jazzy soulful dirty funk band, led by JAY K., whose green views and vox are not too dissimilar to STEVIE WONDER. • **Songwriters:** JAY and TOBY are main contributers. • **Trivia:** Pronounced JAM-EAR-OH-KWAI, they took name from a tribe of American Indians.

Recommended: EMERGENCY ON PLANET EARTH (*9).

JAY K – vocals / **TOBY SMITH** – keyboards / **NICK VAN GELDER** – drums / **STUART ZENDER** – bass / plus **KOFI KARIKARI** – percussion / **MAURIZIO RAVALIO** – percussion / **GLENN NIGHTINGALE + SIMON BARTHOLOMEW** – guitars / **D-ZIRE** – DJ / **GARY BARNACLE** – sax, flute / **JOHN THIRKELL** – trumpet, flugel horn / **RICHARD EDWARDS** – trombone / etc

Acid Jazz not iss.?

Oct 92. (12") **WHEN YOU GONNA LEARN?. / ('A'-Mark Nelson mix)** [52] [ ]
(re-iss. Feb93)

Sony Epic

Mar 93. (12")(c-s)(cd-s) **TOO YOUNG TO DIE. / ('A'mixes)** [10] [ ]

Jun 93. (12")(c-s)(cd-s) **BLOW YOUR MIND (PART 1) / HOOKED UP** [12] [ ]

Jun 93. (cd)(c)(lp) **EMERGENCY ON PLANET EARTH** [1] [ ]
– When you gonna learn (digeridoo) / Too young to die / Hooked up / If I like it, I do it / Music of the mind / Emergency on Planet Earth / Whatever it is, I just can't stop / Blow your mind / Revolution 1993 / Didgin' out.

Aug 93. (12")(c-s)(cd-s) **EMERGENCY ON PLANET EARTH. / IF I LIKE IT, I DO IT (MTV acoustic) / REVOLUTION 1993 (demo)** [32] [ ]

Sep 93. (12")(c-s)(cd-s) **WHEN YOU GONNA LEARN (Didgeridoo) / DIDGIN' OUT** [28] [ ]

Sep 94. (c-s) **SPACE COWBOY. / ('A'mix)** [17] [ ]
(12"+=)(cd-s+=) – Journey to Arnhem land / Kids.

Oct 94. (cd)(c)(d-lp) **THE RETURN OF THE SPACE COWBOY** [2] [ ]
– Just another story / Stillness in time / Half the man / Light years / Manifest destiny / The kids / Mr.Moon / Scam / Journey to Arnhemland / Morning glory / Space cowboy.

Nov 94. (c-s) **HALF THE MAN. / SPACE CLAV** [15] [ ]
(12"+=)(cd-s+=) – Emergency on Planet Earth (version).
(cd-s) – ('A'side) / Jamiroquai's Greatest Hits: When you gonna learn? / Too young to die / Blow your mind.

Feb 95. (c-s) **LIGHT YEARS / JOURNEY TO ARNHEMLAND (live)** [ ] [ ]
(ext.12"+=) – Light years (live).
(cd-d+=) – Scan / We gettin' down.

Jun 95. (c-s)(cd-s) **STILLNESS IN TIME / SPACE COWBOY (mix)** [9] [ ]
(12"+=)(cd-s+=) – Emergency on Planet Earth / Light years.

JANE'S ADDICTION

Formed: Los Angeles, California, USA . . . 1984 by Miami raised PENNY FARRELL. In 1988 after a self-financed eponymous debut on 'Triple XXX', they signed to 'Warner Bros.'. Their first product for them 'NOTHING'S SHOCKING', caused quite a stir, mainly due to its banned sleeve cover, depicting two naked females strapped to an electric chair. In 1990, their third album 'RITUAL DE LO HABITUAL', reached Top 40 on both sides of the Atlantic. • **Style:** Weird heavy rock outfit, who blend in ecletic folk & thrash. • **Songwriters:** Group penned, except SYMPATHY FOR THE DEVIL (Rolling Stones).

Recommended: RITUAL DE LO HABITUAL (*9) / NOTHING'S SHOCKING (*8) / PORNO FOR PYROS (*5) / GOOD GODS URGE (*6)

PENNY FARRELL (b.BERNSTEIN, New York, USA) – vocals / **DAVE NAVARRO** – guitar / **ERIC A's** – bass / **STEPHEN PERKINS** – drums

not issued Triple X

Aug 87. (lp) **JANE'S ADDICTION (live)** [-] [ ]
– Trip away / Whores / Pigs in Zen / 1% / I would for you / My time / Jane says / Rock'n'roll / Sympathy / Chip away. *(UK-iss.cd/c/lp.Dec90 on 'Warner Bros.') (re-iss.cd Aug95)*

Warners Warners

Dec 88. (lp)(c)(cd) **NOTHING'S SHOCKING** [ ] [ ] Sep 88
– Up the beach / Ocean size / Had a dad / Ted, just admit it . . . / Standing in the shower . . .thinking / Summertime rolls / Mountain song / Idiots rule / Jane says / Thank you boys. *(cd+=)*– Pigs in Zen.

Mar 89. (7") **MOUNTAIN SONG. / STANDING IN THE SHOWER . . . THINKING** [-] [ ]

May 89. (12"ep) **THE SHOCKING EP** [ ] [ ]
– Mountain song / Jane says / Had a dad (live).

— added guest **MORGAN** (a female) – violin

Aug 90. (cd)(c)(lp) **RITUAL DE LO HABITUAL** [37] [19]
– Stop / No one's leaving / Ain't no right / Obvious / Been caught stealing / Three days / Then she did . . . / Of course / Classic girl. *(re-iss.cd/c Feb95)*

Aug 90. (7")(c-s) **THREE DAYS. / (part 2)** [ ] [ ]
(12")(cd-s) – ('A'side) / I would for you (demo) / Jane says (demo).

Mar 91. (7") **BEEN CAUGHT STEALING. / HAD A DAD (demo)** [34] [ ]
(12"+=)(cd-s+=) – ('A'remix) / L.A. medley:- L.A. woman / Nausea / Lexicon devil.

May 91. (7")(c-s)(7"pic-d) **CLASSIC GIRL. / NO ONE'S LEAVING** [ ] [ ]
(12"+=)(cd-s+=) – Ain't no right.

— Had already disbanded when FARRELL looked liked heading into film acting. NAVARRO had briefly filled in for IZZY STRADLIN in GUNS'N'ROSES.

PORNO FOR PYROS

FARRELL + PERKINS with **PETER DiSTEFANO** – guitar / **MARTIN LENBLE** – bass (ex-THELONLUS MONSTER) / **DJ SKATEMASTER TATE** – keys, samples

Warners Warners

Apr 93. (cd)(c)(lp) **PORNO FOR PYROS** [13] [3]
– Sadness / Porno for pyros / Meija / Cursed female – cursed male / Pets / Badshit / Packin' / • 25 / Black girlfriend / Blood rag / Orgasm.

Jun 93. (7")(c-s) **PETS. / TONIGHT (from 'West Side Story')** [53] [67]
(12"pic-d+=)(cd-s+=) – Cursed female – cursed male (medley).

. . . Jan – Jun '96 stop press . . .

May 96. (cd)(c)(lp) **GOOD GODS URGE** [40] [20]

JAPAN

Formed: Catford / Lewisham, London, England . . . mid-70's by DAVID SYLVIAN, his brother STEVE JANSEN, MICK KARN and RICHARD BARBIERI. In 1977, they added second guitarist ROB DEAN, and won a talent competition run by 'Ariola-Hansa', who duly signed them. In the Spring of '78, they released debut album 'ADOLESCENT SEX', which was followed 6 months later by 'OBSCURE ALTERNATIVES'. In 1979, they scored a hit in of all places Japan, with Giorgio Moroder produced single 'LIFE IN TOKYO'. Early in 1980, they had first UK chart placing with 'QUIET LIFE'. Later that year, they moved to 'Virgin', and released Top 50 John Punter produced album 'GENTLEMEN TAKE POLAROIDS'. The next year, after 3 Top 50 hits in UK, they had Top 20 classic album 'TIN DRUM'. Early in 1982, their haunting Top 5 single 'GHOSTS', scored at the same time that their old label re-issued 'EUROPEAN SON'. They split soon after, but exploitation releases filled the charts for the next 18 months. All the band went on to other projects, with DAVID SYLVIAN having the greatest success. After a 1982 collaboration with RYUICHI SAKAMOTO, he released debut solo album 'BRILLIANT TREES' in 1984, which made UK Top 5. • **Style:** Initially influenced by ROXY MUSIC, they turned to disco and later melancholy atmospheric alternative rock. • **Songwriters:** SYLVIAN lyrics / group compositions except; DON'T RAIN ON MY PARADE (Rogers-Hammerstein) / AIN'T THAT PECULIAR (Marvin Gaye) / I SECOND THAT EMOTION (Smokey Robinson) / ALL TOMORROW'S PARTIES (Velvet Underground). • **Trivia:** MICK KARN whose solo work was reminiscent of ENO or BILL NELSON, went on to work as a sculptor. His piece 'TRIBAL DAWN' was used on Channel 4's arty TV programme 'Altered States'.

Recommended: EXORCISING GHOSTS (*9) / ASSEMBLAGE (*7) / TIN DRUM (*9) / GENTLEMEN TAKE POLAROIDS (*7). BRILLIANT TREES (*8; DAVID SYLVIAN) / GONE TO EARTH (*6; DAVID SYLVIAN) / TITLES (*7; MICK KARN).

DAVID SYLVIAN (b. DAVID BATT, 23 Feb'58) – vocals, guitar, keyboards / **RICHARD BARBIERI** (b.30 Nov'57) – keyboards, synthesizers / **ROB DEAN** – guitar, mandolin / **MICK KARN** (b. ANTHONY MICHAELIDES, 24 Jul'58) – bass, saxophone / **STEVE JANSEN** (b. STEVE BATT, 1 Dec'59) – drums, percussion

Ariola Ariola

Mar 78. (7") **DON'T RAIN ON MY PARADE. / STATELINE** [ ] [-]
Apr 78. (lp)(c) **ADOLESCENT SEX** [ ] [ ]
– Transmission / The unconventional / State line / Wish you were black / Performance / Lovers on Main Street / Don't rain on my parade / Suburban love / Adolescent sex / Communist China / Television. *(re-iss.Sep82) (re-iss.Sep84 on 'Fame') (cd-iss.1989 on 'Hansa')*
Aug 78. (7") **THE UNCONVENTIONAL. / ADOLESCENT SEX** [ ] [-]
Nov 78. (lp)(c) **OBSCURE ALTERNATIVES** [ ] [ ]
– Automatic gun / Rhodesia / Love is infectious / Sometimes I feel so low / Obscure alternatives / Deviation / Suburban Berlin / The tenant. *(re-iss.Sep82) (re-iss.Apr84 on 'Fame') (cd-iss.1989 on 'Hansa')*
Nov 78. (7")(7"blue) **SOMETIMES I FEEL SO LOW. / LOVE IS INFECTIOUS** [ ] [ ]
May 79. (7"red)(12"red) **LIFE IN TOKYO (part 1). / LIFE IN TOKYO (part 2)** [ ] [-]
Jul 79. (12") **LIFE IN TOKYO. / LOVE IS INFECTIOUS** [-] [ ]
Jan 80. (lp)(c) **QUIET LIFE** [53] [ ]
– Quiet life / Fall in love with me / Despair / In-vogue / Halloween / All tomorrow's parties / Alien / The other side of life. *(re-iss.Jul81) (re-iss.Sep82 on 'Fame') (cd-iss.1989 on 'Hansa')*
Feb 80. (7") **I SECOND THAT EMOTION. / QUIET LIFE** [ ] [-]

Virgin Virgin

Oct 80. (7") **GENTLEMEN TAKE POLAROIDS. / THE EXPERIENCE OF SWIMMING** [60] [ ]
(d7"+=) – The width of a room / Burning bridges.
Oct 80. (lp)(c) **GENTLEMEN TAKE POLAROIDS** [45] [ ]
– Gentlemen take polaroids / Swing / Some kind of fool / My new career / Methods of dance / Ain't that peculiar / Night porter / Taking islands in Africa. *(re-iss.+cd.Apr85) (cd-re-iss.Jun88)*

— Trimmed to quartet when ROB DEAN left, to later form ILLUSTRATED MAN

Apr 81. (7")(12") **THE ART OF PARTIES. / LIFE WITHOUT BUILDINGS** [48] [-]
Oct 81. (7")(12") **VISIONS OF CHINA. / TAKING ISLANDS IN AFRICA** [32] [-]
Nov 81. (lp)(c) **TIN DRUM** [12] [ ]
– The art of parties / Talking drum / Ghosts / Canton / Still life in mobile homes / Visions of China / Sons of pioneers / Cantonese boy. *(re-iss.+cd.Apr86)*
Jan 82. (7")(12") **GHOSTS. / THE ART OF PARTIES (version)** [5] [ ]
Feb 82. (7") **VISIONS OF CHINA. / CANTON** [-] [ ]
May 82. (d7")(12") **CANTONESE BOY. / BURNING BRIDGES // GENTLEMEN TAKE POLAROIDS / THE EXPERIENCE OF SWIMMING** [24] [ ]

— They had earlier in the year quietly branched out into new projects. DAVID SYLVIAN went solo after a brief collaboration with RYUICHI SAKAMOTO. MICK KARN went solo, had one-off single with MIDGE URE, then went into sessions before forming DALI'S CAR with PETE MURPHY in '84. BARBERI and JANSEN produced Swedes LUSTAN LAKEJER. The pair formed their own duo (The DOLPHIN BROTHERS) before joining DAVID SYLVIAN again.

- compilations, exploitation releases etc. -

Apr 81. Hansa-Ariola; (7")(12") **LIFE IN TOKYO. / EUROPEAN SON** [ ] [ ]
Aug 81. Hansa-Ariola; (7")(12") **QUIET LIFE. / A FOREIGN PLACE / FALL IN LOVE WITH ME** [19] [ ]
Sep 81. Hansa-Ariola; (lp)(c) **ASSEMBLAGE** [26] [ ]
– Adolescent sex / State line / Communist China / Rhodesia / Suburban Berlin / Life in Tokyo / European son / All tomorrow's parties / Quiet life / I second that emotion. *(cassette includes 12" extended versions) (re-iss.lp/c.Sep85 on 'Fame')*
Jan 82. Hansa-Ariola; (7")(12") **EUROPEAN SONG. / ALIEN** [31] [ ]
Jun 82. Hansa-Ariola; (7")(12") **I SECOND THAT EMOTION. / HALLOWEEN** [9] [ ]
Sep 82. Hansa-Ariola; (7")(12") **LIFE IN TOKYO. / THEME** [28] [ ]
Feb 83. Hansa-Ariola; (7")(12") **ALL TOMORROW'S PARTIES. / IN VOGUE** [38] [ ]
Aug 83. Hansa-Ariola; (d-c) **ADOLESCENT SEX / OBSCURE ALTERNATIVES** [ ] [-]
Dec 89. Hansa-Ariola; (lp)(c)(cd) **A SOUVENIR FROM JAPAN** [ ] [-]
Nov 82. Virgin; (7") **NIGHT PORTER. / AIN'T THAT PECULIAR** [29] [ ]
(12"+=) – Methods of dance.
May 83. Virgin; (7") **CANTON (live). / VISIONS OF CHINA (live)** [42] [ ]
Jun 83. Virgin; (d-lp)(c) **OIL ON CANVAS (live)** [5] [ ]
– Oil on canvas / Sons of pioneers / Gentlemen take polaroids / Swing / Cantonese boy / Visions of china / Ghosts / Voices raised in welcome, hands held in prayer / Night porter / Still life in mobile homes / Methods of dance / Quiet life / The art of parties / Canton / Temple of dawn. *(cd-iss. Apr85)*
Nov 84. Virgin; (d-lp)(c)(cd) **EXORCISING GHOSTS** [45] [ ]
– Methods of dance / Swing / Gentlemen take polaroids / Quiet life / A foreign place * / Night porter / My new career / The other side of life / Visions of China / Sons of pioneers * / Talking drum / The art of parties / Taking islands in Africa / Voices raised in welcome, hands held in prayer / Life without buildings / Ghosts. *(cd-omits *)*
Dec 84 Virgin; (7")**VISIONS OF CHINA / TAKING ISLANDS IN AFRICA** [ ] [ ]
(12"+=) – Swing
Jun 88. Virgin; (3"cd-ep) **GHOSTS / THE ART OF PARTIES / VISIONS OF CHINA** [ ] [ ]
Nov 88. Virgin; (3"cd-ep) **GENTLEMEN TAKE POLAROIDS / CANTONESE BOY / METHODS OF DANCE** [ ] [ ]
Sep 87. Old Gold; (7") **I SECOND THAT EMOTION. / ALL TOMORROW'S PARTIES** [ ] [-]
(12"+=) – Life in Tokyo.
Nov 87. Old Gold; (7") **QUIET LIFE. / LIFE IN TOKYO** [ ] [-]
Nov 88. Old Gold; (7") **GHOSTS. / CANTONESE BOY** [ ] [-]
Nov 92. Old Gold; (cd-ep) **I SECOND THAT EMOTION / QUIET LIFE / LIFE IN TOKYO** [ ] [-]
Oct 91. Receiver; (cd)(c)(lp) **THE OTHER SIDE OF JAPAN** [ ] [-]

SYLVIAN/SAKAMOTO

DAVID SYLVIAN – vocals, instruments (ex-JAPAN) / **RYUICHI SAKAMOTO** – synthesizers (ex-YELLOW MAGIC ORCHESTRA)

Virgin Virgin

Jun 82. (7") **BAMBOO HOUSES. / BAMBOO MUSIC** [30] [ ]
(12"+=) – ('A' & 'B' mixes).

DAVID SYLVIAN & RYUICHI SAKAMOTO

Jun 83. (7") **FORBIDDEN COLOURS. / THE SEED AND THE SOWER (by "RYUICHI SAKAMOTO")** [16] [ ]
(12"+=) – Last regrets.
(from the the film soundtrack 'Merry Christmas Mr.Lawrence')

- compilations etc. -

Aug 88. Virgin; (3"cd-ep)(5"cd-ep) **FORBIDDEN COLOURS. / BAMBOO HOUSES / BAMBOO MUSIC** [ ] [ ]

DAVID SYLVIAN

solo, – vocals, keyboards, guitar, percussion, with **RICHARD BARBIERI** and **STEVE JANSEN** (ex-JAPAN) / **RYUICHI SAKAMOTO** – synthesizers / **HOLGER CZUKAY** – tapes / **DANNY THOMPSON** – upright bass / **KENNY WHEELER** – horns

Virgin Virgin

May 84. (7")(12")(7"pic-d) **RED GUITAR. / FORBIDDEN COLOURS (version)** [17] [ ]
Jun 84. (lp)(c)(cd) **BRILLIANT TREES** [4] [ ]
– Pulling punches / The ink in the well / Nostalgia / Red guitar / Weathered wall / Backwaters / Brilliant trees. *(re-iss.Apr90)*
Aug 84. (7")(12") **THE INK IN THE WELL (remix). / WEATHERED WALL (instrumental)** [36] [ ]
Oct 84. (7") **PULLING PUNCHES. / BACKWATERS (remix)** [56] [ ]
(12"+=) – ('A'extended).

— now with **JOHN HASSELL** and **ROBERT FRIPP** – guitar / **HOLGER CZUKAY** – tapes / **KENNY WHEELER** – horns

Nov 85. (12"ep) **WORDS WITH THE SHAMEN** [72] [ ]
– Part 1:-Ancient evening / Part 2:-Incantation / Part 3:-Awakening. *(re-iss.as c.Dec85.***ALCHEMY (AN INDEX OF POSSIBILITIES)**(c+=) – Preparations for a journey / Steel cathedrals.

— with **ROBERT FRIPP** and **BILL NELSON** – guitar / **PHIL PALMER** – accoustic guitar / **MEL COLLINS** – soprano sax. / **KENNY WHEELER** – flugel horn

Jul 86. (7")(7"square pic-d) **TAKING THE VEIL. / ANSWERED PRAYERS** [53] [ ]

(12"+=) – Bird of prey vanishes into a bright blue sky.

Aug 86. (d-lp)(c)(cd) **GONE TO EARTH** [24] [ ]
– Taking the veil / Laughter and forgetting / Before the bullfight / Gone to earth / Wave / River man / Silver moon / The healing place / Answered prayers * / Where the railroad meets the sea / The wooden cross * / Silver moon over sleeping steeples * / Campfire: Coyote country * / A bird of prey vanishes into a blue cloudless sky * / Sunlight seen through the towering trees * / Upon this Earth. *(cd-omits tracks *)*

Sep 86. (7") **SILVER MOON. / GONE TO EARTH** [ ] [ ]
(12"+=) – Silver moon over sleeping steeples.

— DAVID was also credited on VIRGINIA ASTLEY's Feb87 'Some Small Hope'.

— now with **SAKAMOTO, PALMER, JANSEN** plus **DANNY CUMMINGS** – percussion / **DAVID TORN** – guitar / **DANNY THOMPSON** – d. bass / **MARK ISHAM** – trumpet

Oct 87. (lp)(c)(cd) **SECRETS OF THE BEEHIVE** [37] [ ]
– September / The boy with the gun / Maria / Orpheus / The Devil's own / When poets dreamed of angels / Mother and child / Let the happiness in / Waterfront.

Oct 87. (7") **LET THE HAPPINESS IN. / BLUE OF MOON** [66] [ ]
(12"+=) – Buoy (remix).

Apr 88. (7") **ORPHEUS. / THE DEVIL'S OWN** [ ] [ ]
(12"+=) – Mother and child.

— His touring band **JANSEN, BARBIERI, TORN, ISHAM** plus **IAN MAIDMAN** – bass, percussion / **ROBBY ALEDO** – guitar

DAVID SYLVIAN & HOLGER CZUKAY

with **JAKI LIEBEZEIT** – drums (ex-CAN)

Venture-Virgin | Venture

Mar 88. (lp)(c)(cd) **PLIGHT AND PREMONITION** [71] [ ]
– Plight (the spiralling of winter ghosts) / Premonition (giant empty iron vessel).

— with **LIEBEZEIT, MICHAEL KAROLI** – guitar / **MARKUS STOCKHAUSEN** – flugel horn / **MICHI** – vocals

Sep 89. (lp)(c)(cd) **FLUX AND MUTABILITY** [ ] [ ]
– Flux (a big, bright, colourful world) / Mutability ("a new beginning is in the offing").

DAVID SYLVIAN

Virgin | Virgin

Nov 89. (7") **POP SONG. / A BRIEF CONVERSATION ENDING IN DIVORCE** [ ] [ ]
(12"+=)/ /(cd-box-s+=) – ('A'remix). / / Stigma of childhood.

Nov 89. (5-cd-box) **WEATHERBOX** (all 3 solo albums + 1 extra). [ ] [ ]

SYLVIAN-SAKAMOTO

with **INGRID CHAVEZ**

Virgin | Virgin . . .

Jun 92. (7") **HEARTBEAT (TAINAI KAIKI II) RETURNING TO THE WOMB. / NUAGES** [58] [ ]
(cd-s+=) – The lost emperor.
(cd-s)- ('A' side) / Forbidden colours / Heartbeat.

MICK KARN

– vocals, bass, keyboards, synthesizers (ex-JAPAN) with session

Virgin | Virgin

Jun 82. (7")(12") **SENSITIVE. / THE SOUND OF WAVES** [ ] [ ]

Nov 82. (lp)(c) **TITLES** [74] [ ]
– Tribal dawn / Lost affections in a room / Passion in moisture / Weather the windmill / Saviour, are you with me / Trust me / Sensitive / Piper blue. *(re-iss.Aug88)*

— In Jun83, he teamed up with ULTRAVOX's MIDGE URE, on the single AFTER A FASHION which reached UK No.39. In 1984 KARN formed **DALI'S CAR** with **PETE MURPHY** (ex-BAUHAUS, see ⇒) and **PAUL VINCENT LAWFORD.**

MICK KARN returned solo '86.

Virgin | Virgin

Jan 87. (lp)(c)(cd) **DREAMS OF REASON PRODUCE MONSTERS** [89] [ ]
– First impression / Language of ritual / Buoy / Land / The three fates / When love walks in / Dreams of reason / Answer.

Jan 87. (7") **BUOY. ("MICK KARN featuring DAVID SYLVIAN"). / DREAMS OF REASON** [63] [ ]
(12"+=) – Language of ritual.

C.M.P. | not issued

Oct 93. (cd) **BESTIAL CLUSTER** [ ] [-]
– Bestial cluster / Back in the beginning / Beard in the letterbox / The drowning dream / The sad velvet breath of Summer & Winter / Saday, Maday / Liver and lungs / Bones of mud.

— with **RICHARD BARBIERI** – keyboards / **STEVE JANSEN** – drums / **DAVID TORN** – guitar / **DAVID LIEBMAN** – soprano sax

May 95. (cd) **THE TOOTH MOTHER** [ ] [-]
– Thundergirl mutation / Plaster the magic tongue / Lodge of skins / Gossip's cup / Feat funk / The tooth mother / Little less hope / There was not anything but nothing.

JANSEN / BARBIERI

JANSEN – vocals, etc / **BARBIERI** – keyboards, etc

Pan-East | not issued

Oct 86. (lp)(c)(cd) **WORLD IN A SMALL ROOM** [ ] [-]
(At same time JANSEN w/TAKAHASHI rel.7" STAY CLOSE. / BETSU-NI on 'Rime')

— The JAPAN duo now

The DOLPHIN BROTHERS

with **DAVID RHODES** – guitar / **DANNY THOMPSON** – ac. bass / **MATTHEW SELIGMAN + ROBERT BELL** – bass / **PHIL PALMER** – acoustic guitar / **MARTIN DITCHAM** – percussion

Virgin | Virgin?

Jun 87. (7")(12") **SHINING. / MY WINTER** [ ] [-]

Jul 87. (lp)(c) **CATCH THE FALL** [ ] [ ]
– Catch the fall / Shining / Second sight / Love that you need / Real life, real answers / Host to the holy / My winter / Pushing the river.

Aug 87. (7")(12") **SECOND SIGHT. / HOST TO THE HOLY** [ ] [-]

STEVE JANSEN & RICHARD BARBIERI

Venture | Virgin

Sep 91. (cd) **STORIES ACROSS BORDERS** [ ] [ ]
– Long tales, tall shadows / When things dream / Luman / The insomniac's bed / The night gives birth / Celebration 1988 remix (saw) / Nocturnal sightseeing / One more zombie.

Medium | not issued

Oct 95. (cd) **STONE TO FLESH** [ ] [-]
– Mother London / Sleepers awake / Ringing the bell backwards: Siren – Drift / Swim there / Closer than "I" / Everything ends in darkness.

— JAPAN reformed quartet in 1990, but as . . .

RAIN TREE CROW

Virgin | Virgin

Mar 91. (7")(c-s) **BLACK WATER. / RAIN TREE CROW / I DRINK TO FORGET** [62] [ ]
(12") – (1st + 3rd track) / Red Earth (as summertime ends).
(cd-s) – (all above 4).

Apr 91. (cd)(c)(lp) **RAIN TREE CROW** [24] [ ]
– Big wheels in Shanty town / Every colour you are / Rain tree crow / Red Earth (as summertime ends) / Rocket full of charge / Boat's for burning / New Moon Red Deer wallow / Black water / A reassuringly dull Sunday / Blackcrow hats shoe shine city.

DAVID SYLVIAN & ROBERT FRIPP

FRIPP – guitar (ex-KING CRIMSON & solo artist) / **TREY GUNN** – synthesizers, vocals, co-writer plus band **DAVID BOTTRILL** – synthesizers / **JERRY MAROTTA** – drums, percussion / **MARC ANDERSON** – percussion / **INGRID CHAVEZ** – backing vocals.

Virgin | Virgin

Jul 93. (cd)(c)(lp) **THE FIRST DAY** [21] [ ]
-God's monkey / Jean the birdman / Firepower / Brightness falls / 20th century dreaming (a shaman's song) / Darshan (the road to Graceland).

Aug 93. (c-ep)(cd-ep) **JEAN THE BIRDMAN / EARTHBOUND / STARBLIND / ENDGAME** [68] [ ]
(cd-ep) – ('A'side) / Tallow moon / Dark water / Gone to Earth.

Dec 93. (cd)(c)(lp) **DARSHAN (mixes)** [ ] [ ]

Sep 94. (cd) **DAMAGE (live)** [ ] [ ]
– Damage / God's monkey / Brightness falls / Every colour you are / Firepower / Gone to Earth / 20th century dreaming (a shaman's song) / Wave / Riverman / Darshan (the road to Graceland) / Blinding light of Heaven / The first day.

JANSEN, BARBIERI, KARN

Medium | not issued

Mar 94. (cd) **BEGINNING TO MELT** [ ] [-]
– Beginning to melt / The wilderness / March of the innocents / Human agie / Shipwrecks / Ego dance / The orange asylum.

Oct 94. (cd) **SEED** [ ] [-]
– Beginning to melt / In the black of desire / The insect tribe / Prey.

Jean-Michel JARRE

Born: 24 Aug'48, Lyon, France. In the late 60's, having played lead guitar for a few rock bands, he enrolled at Pierre Schaeffer's Musical Research

Group, studying ethnic music. His love of free-form conflicted with GMR, and he left to work in his own studio with new synthesizer. He released 3 lp's in France at the turn of the decade, but chose to write jingles for radio and TV, etc. In 1971 he had become youngest composer to appear at the Palais Garnier Opera House. In 1973, he composed soundtrack for film Les Granges Brulee'. In 1977 he was signed to 'Polydor', and issued 'OXYGENE', which was earlier released in France on 'Disques Motors'. The album soon rose to No.2 in the UK charts, helped by a surprise Top 5 single 'OXYGENE (part 4)'. Late in 1978, his next album 'EQUINOXE' hit No.11 and he continued to excel commercially throughout the 80's. • **Style:** Multi-layered electronic rock & pop musak, with concepts similar to MIKE OLDFIELD, but without the instrumentation. • **Songwriters:** Wrote all material. • **Trivia:** He married actress Charlotte Rampling, after meeting her at 1976 Cannes film festival. In 1983, he released 1 copy of an lp 'MUSIC FOR SUPERMARKETS', and after auctioning it for around £10,000, destroyed the master disc. In Apr'86, he set another record, when playing live to over one million people at Houston, Texas. Two and a half years later, he appeared in front of 3 million people at Docklands, London, on 2 seperate nights, due to earlier Newham Council objection. HANK MARVIN guitarist of The SHADOWS, featured on 'LONDON KID' hit single, which was even played by him at the concert.

Recommended: OXYGENE (*7) / EQUINOXE (*6) / IMAGES – THE BEST OF JEAN-MICHEL JARRE (*6).

JEAN-MICHEL JARRE – synthesizers, keyboards

not issued | EMI-Pathe

1969. (lp) **LA CAGE** - | - France
1971. (lp) **EROS MACHINE** - | -

not issued | Disques Motors

1972. (lp) **DESERTED PALACE** - | - France
1973. (7") **HYPNOSE. / DESERTED PALACE** - | -

Polydor | Polydor

Jul 77. (lp)(c) **OXYGENE** 2 | 78
– Oxygene (Parts 1 – 6). *(cd-iss.1983)*
Aug 77. (7") **OXYGENE (part 4). / OXYGENE (part 6)** 4
Dec 78. (lp)(c) **EQUINOXE** 11
– Equinoxe (Parts I – VIII). *(cd-iss.1983; re-iss.c.Jan93)*
Dec 78. (7") **EQUINOXE (part V). / EQUINOXE (part I)** 45
Jul 79. (7") **EQUINOXE (part IV remix). / EQUINOXE (part III)**
Jun 80. (7") **EQUINOXE (part VII) (live). / EQUINOXE (part VIII) (live)**
May 81. (lp)(c) **MAGNETIC FIELDS** 6 | 98
– Magnetic fields (parts 1 – 5) / The last rumba. *(cd-iss.1983)(re-iss.c. Jan93)*
Jun 81. (7") **MAGNETIC FIELDS (part 2 remix). / MAGNETIC FIELDS (part 1 excerpt)**
Nov 81. (7") **MAGNETIC FIELDS (part 4 remix). / MAGNETIC FIELDS (part 1 excerpt)**

— added **DOMINIQUE PERRIER + FREDERIC ROUSSEAU** – synthesizers / **ROGER RIZZITELLI** – percussion, drums

May 82. (d-lp)(d-c) **THE CONCERTS IN CHINA (live)** 6
– The overture / Arpegiator / Equinoxe IV / Fishing junks at sunset / Band in the rain / Equinoxe VII / Laser harp / Orient express / Magnetic fields I, III & IV / Night in Shanghai / The last rumba / Magnetic fields II Souvenir of China. *(cd-iss.1983) (re-iss.c. Jan93)*
May 82. (7") **ORIENT EXPRESS. / FISHING JUNKS AT SUNSET**
Nov 84. (lp)(c)(cd) **ZOOLOOK** 47
– Ethnicolour / Diva / Zoolook / Wooloomooloo / Zoolookologie / Blah-blah cafe / Ethnicolour II. *(cd+=)* – Zoolook (remix) / Zoolookologie (remix).

— retained **FREDERIC** and recruited **ADRIAN BELEW + IRA SIEGEL** – guitar / **MARCUS MILLER** – bass / **YOGI HORTON** – drums, percussion / **LAURIE ANDERSON** – vocals

Nov 84. (7")(12") **ZOOLOOK (remix). / WOOLOOMOOLOO**
(re-iss.Jan85 as 12") (+=) – (extra effects) / ('A'extended).
Mar 85. (7") **ZOOLOOKOLOGIE. / ETHNICOLOUR**
(12"+=) – ('A'extended remixed).
(d7"+=) – Oxygene (part 4) / Oxygene (part 6).

— w / **PERRIER / MICHEL GEISS** – synth / **JO HAMMER** – electro drums / **DAVID JARRE** – keyboards

Apr 86. (lp)(c)(cd) **RENDEZ-VOUZ** 9 | 52
– First rendez-vous / Second rendez-vous (part I / II / III / IV) / Third rendez-vous / Fourth rendez-vous / Fifth rendez-vous (part I / II / III) / Last rendez-vous – Ron's piece.
Aug 86. (7") **FOURTH RENDEZ-VOUS. / FIRST RENDEZ-VOUS** 65
(12") – ('A'side) / Rendez-vous (special + original mix) / Moon machine.

— with **GEISS** – synthesizers / **FRANCIS LIMBERT** – keyboards, synth. / **PASCAL LEBOURG** – keyboards, synth. / **SYLVIAN DURAND** – keyboards, synthesizers / **PERRIER** – keys, synth (HOUSTON only) / **CHRISTINE DURAND** – soprano / **HAMMER** – drums / **KIRK WHALUM** – sax / **GUY DELACROIX** – bass (LYON only) / **DINO LUMBROSO** – percussion (LYON only) / also used choirs & orchestra, etc.

Jul 87. (lp)(c)(cd) **IN CONCERT – LYON / HOUSTON (live)** 18
– Oxygene V / Ethnicolour / Magnetic fields I / Souvenir of China / Equinoxe 5 / Rendez-vous III / Rendez-vous II / Ron's piece / Rendez-vous IV.

— with **DOMINIQUE, MICHAEL, JO** and **GUY,** plus guests **SYLVIAN** – synth / & **HANK MARVIN** – guitar (of SHADOWS) on track – *

Aug 88. (lp)(c)(cd) **REVOLUTIONS** 3
– Industrial revolution: (overture – part 1 – part 2 – part 3) / London kid * / Revolutions / Tokyo kid / Computer weekend / September / The emigrant.
Oct 88. (7") **REVOLUTIONS. / INDUSTRIAL REVOLUTION 2** 52
(12"+=) – ('A'extended).
(cd-s++=) – ('A'mix).
Dec 88. (7")(c-s) **LONDON KID. / INDUSTRIAL REVOLUTION 3** 48
(12"+=)(cd-s+=) – Revolutions (remix).
Sep 89. (7") **OXYGENE IV (remix). / INDUSTRIAL REVOLUTION OVERTURE** 65
(12"+=) – ('A'live version).
(cd-s++=) – September.
Oct 89. (lp)(c)(cd) **JARRE LIVE (live)** 16
– Introduction (revolution) / Industrial revolution: (Overture – part I – part II – part III) / Magnetic fields II / Oxygene IV / Computer weekend / Revolutions / Rendez-vous IV / Rendez-vous II / The emigrant. *(cd+=)* – (2 extra).

— Retained **PERRIER and GEISS,** plus introduced The **AMACO RENEGADES** – steel drums / guests **GUY DELACROIX** – bass / **CHRISTOPHE DESCHAMPS** – drums

Jun 90. (cd)(c)(lp) **WAITING FOR COSTEAU**
– Calypso / Calypso (pt.2) / Calypso (pt.3, finale side) / Waiting for Costeau. *(cd+=)* – (extra music).
May 93.(cd)(c)(lp) **CHRONOLOGIE** 11
– (part.1 – part.4) / (part.5 – part.8).
Jun 93. (12")(c-s)(cd-s) **CHRONOLOGIE (part 4). / ('A'part)** 55
(re-mixed re-iss.Oct93, hit 56)
May 94. (cd)(c)(lp) **CHRONOLOGIE VI**
– (slam mix) / (slam mix 2) / (main mix) / (alternative mix) / (original mix).
Oct 95. (cd) **JARREMIX** (dance mixes compilation) | -

– compilations etc. –

1981. Polydor; (d-c) **OXYGENE / EQUINOXE** | -
Oct 83. Polydor; (lp)(c) **THE ESSENTIAL JEAN-MICHEL JARRE** 14
(cd-iss.Sep84)
Dec 87. Polydor; (3xcd-box) **CD BOX SET** (1st-3 lp's)
Oct 91. Polydor; (cd)(c)(lp) **IMAGES – THE BEST OF JEAN MICHEL JARRE** 16
– Oxygene 4 / Equinoxe 5 / Magnetic fields 2 / Oxygene 2 / Computer weekend / Equinoxe 4 / Band in the rain / Rendez-vous 2 / London kid / Ethnicolor 1 / Orient express / Calypso 1 / Calypso 3 (fin de siecle) / Rendez-vous 4 / Moon machine / Eldorado / Globe trotter.
Jan 93. Polydor; (cd)(c)(lp) **MUSIK AUS ZEIT UND RAUM**
Feb 88. Old Gold; (7") **OXYGENE (part IV). / EQUINOXE (part 5)** | -

JEFFERSON AIRPLANE

Formed: San Francisco, California, USA ... early 1965 by MARTY BALIN and PAUL KANTNER. They recruited others and signed to 'RCA' late '65, releasing debut 45 'IT'S NO SECRET' which flopped. In Sep66, their first lp ' ... TAKES OFF' was finally issued, although group went through major personnel changes. In came vocalist GRACE SLICK and SPENCER DRYDEN, who added extra needed power to second lp 'SURREALISTIC PILLOW'. In 1967 it soared up to No.3 in USA, and included 2 Top 10 singles 'SOMEBODY TO LOVE' & 'WHITE RABBIT' (the latter inspired by Lewis Carroll book 'Alice In Wonderland'). In Jul'68, the band bought headquarters at 2400 Fulton, San Franscisco and continued to score in the charts until their fragmentation in 1970. They had made an appearance in Aug'69, at the 'Woodstock' festival, with song 'VOLUNTEERS' being used in film. Live-in lovers SLICK and KANTNER produced daughter China in Jan71 and also released own lp in '71 'SUNFIGHTER'. A year earlier, KANTNER had formed initial aggregation of his JEFFERSON STARSHIP, releasing 'BLOWS AGAINST THE EMPIRE' lp. JEFFERSON AIRPLANE returned in 1971 without BALIN, but on own RCA distributed 'Grunt' label. Their album 'BARK' introduced a 54 year-old violinist PAPA JOHN CREACH to the fold, and nearly broke them back into US Top 10. In Mar'74, the group became JEFFERSON STARSHIP and soon added the returning MARTY BALIN for a US No.1 album 'RED OCTOPUS' in 1975, which included Top 3 single 'MIRACLES'. Remained in the limelight for the next 10 years, and when they changed name to STARSHIP (due to departure of KANTNER) in the mid-80's, they had 3 US top spots 'WE BUILT THIS CITY', 'SARA' & 'NOTHING'S GONNA STOP US NOW'. The latter, from the film 'Mannequin', also gave them a UK No.1 hit in 1987. • **Style:** Acid-rock blues & psychedelia outfit, whose drug-orientated epics were put aside in 1974 for AOR textures when JEFFERSON STARSHIP came to be. Confusion was rife in the late 80's, when STARSHIP were competing with re-formed JEFFERSON AIRPLANE. • **Songwriters:** KANTNER or BALIN, plus SLICK, who initially brought in 2 songs (first 2 Top 10's in 1967) written with husband at the time JERRY SLICK and brother-in-law DARBY SLICK.

Recommended: SURREALISTIC PILLOW (*8) / AFTER BATHING AT BAXTER'S (*7) / CROWN OF CREATION (*7) / VOLUNTEERS (*6) GREATEST HITS (TEN YEARS AND CHANGE 1979-1991) (STARSHIP *6).

MARTY BALIN (b.30 Jan'42, Cincinnati, Ohio, USA) – vocals, guitar (ex-solo) / **PAUL KANTNER** (b.12 Mar'42, San Franscisco) – guitar, vocals / **JORMA KAUKONEN** (b.23 Dec'40, Washington DC) – lead guitar / **SIGNE TOLY ANDERSON** – vocals / **JACK CASADY** – bass repl. BOB HARVEY / **SKIP SPENCE** – drums (ex-QUICKSILVER MESSENGER SERVICE) repl. JERRY PELOQUIN

R.C.A. R.C.A.

Feb 66. (7") **IT'S NO SECRET. / RUNNIN' ROUND THIS TABLE** [-] [ ]

1966. (7") **COME UP THE YEARS. / BLUES FROM AN AEROPLANE** [-] [ ]

Sep 66. (lp) **JEFFERSON AIRPLANE TAKES OFF** [-] [ ]
– Blues from an airplane / Let me in / It's no secret / Bringing me down / Tobacco road / Coming up the years / Run around / Let's get together / Don't slip away / Chauffeur blues / And I like it. *(UK rel.Oct71, re-iss.Jun74)*

1966. (7") **BRINGING ME DOWN. / LET ME IN** [-] [ ]

—— **GRACE SLICK** (b.GRACE WING, 30 Oct'39, Chicago, Illinois) – vocals (ex-GREAT SOCIETY) repl. SIGNE who left to look after her baby / **SPENCER DRYDEN** (b. 7 Apr'38, New York) – drums (ex-PEANUT BUTTER CONSPIRACY, ex-ASHES) repl. SKIP who formed MOBY GRAPE

Dec 66. (7") **MY BEST FRIEND. / HOW DO YOU FEEL** [-] [ ]

Sep 67. (lp) **SURREALISTIC PILLOW** [ ] [3] Feb 67
– She has funny cars / Somebody to love / My best friend / Today / Comin' back to me / How do you feel / 3/5 mile in 10 seconds / D.C.B.A. – 25 / Embryonic journey / White rabbit / Plastic fantastic lover. *(UK-rel.differed tracks) (cd-iss.Sep84 & Oct87)*

May 67. (7") **SOMEBODY TO LOVE. / SHE HAS FUNNY CARS** [ ] [5] Feb 67

Sep 67. (7") **WHITE RABBIT. / PLASTIC FANTASTIC LOVER** [ ] [8] Jun 67

Nov 67. (7") **THE BALLAD OF YOU AND ME AND POONEIL. / TWO HEADS** [ ] [42] Sep 67

Jun 68. (lp) **AFTER BATHING AT BAXTER'S** [ ] [17] Dec 67
– (Streetmasse): / The ballad of you and me and Pooneil – A small package of value will come to you, shortly – Young girl Sunday blues / (The war is over): / Martha – Wild thyme / (Hymn to an older generation): / The last wall of the castle – Rejoyce / How sweet it is:- Watch her ride – Spare chaynge / Shizoforest love suite: Two heads – Won't you try – Saturday afternoon.

Jan 68. (7") **WATCH HER RIDE. / MARTHA** [-] [1] Dec 67

Jun 68. (7") **GREASY HEART. / SHARE A LITTLE JOKE** [ ] [98] Mar 68

Sep 68. (7") **IF YOU FEEL. / LIKE CHINA BREAKING** [ ] [-]

Oct 68. (7") **CROWN OF CREATION. / TRIAD** [-] [64]

Dec 68. (lp) **CROWN OF CREATION** [ ] [6] Sep 68
– Lather / In time / Triad / Star track / Share a little joke / Chushingura / If you feel / Crown of creation / Ice cream Phoenix / Greasy heart / The house at Pooh Corner. *(re-iss.Oct85) cd-iss.Jun88)*

Jun 69. (lp) **BLESS IT'S POINTED LITTLE HEAD (live)** [38] [17] Feb 69
– Clergy / 3/5 of a mile in 10 seconds / Somebody to love / Fat angel / Rock me baby / The other side of this life / It's no secret / Plastic fantastic lover / Turn out the lights / Bear melt.

1969. (7") **PLASTIC FANTASTIC LOVER (live). / THE OTHER SIDE OF THIS LIFE (live)** [-] [ ]

Feb 70. (lp) **VOLUNTEERS** [34] [13] Nov 69
– We can be together / Good shepherd / The farm / Hey Frederick / Turn my life down / Wooden ships / Eskimo blue day / A song for all seasons / Meadowlands / Volunteers. *(re-iss.Oct85)*

Mar 70. (7") **VOLUNTEERS. / WE CAN BE TOGETHER** [ ] [65] Nov 69

—— **JOEY COVINGTON** – drums repl. DRYDEN who joined NEW RIDERS OF THE PURPLE SAGE (above new with **SLICK, CASADY, BALIN** and **KAUKONEN)** (note also DRYDEN played on below 'A' side)

Aug 70. (7") **MEXICO. / HAVE YOU SEEN THE SAUCERS?** [ ] [ ]

—— At this time various mambers, mainly KAUKONEN and CASADY side lined HOT TUNA. PAUL KANTNER then recorded album with what was then p/t JEFFERSON STARSHIP (see further below and his late '71 co-credit with GRACE SLICK

—— **PAPA JOHN CREACH** (b.28 May 1917, Beaver Falls, Pennsylvania) – violin (of HOT TUNA) finally repl. BALIN who left earlier.

Grunt Grunt

Oct 71. (lp)(c) **BARK** [42] [11] Sep 71
– When the Earth moves again / Feel so good / Crazy Miranda / Pretty as you feel / Wild turkey / Law man / Rock and roll island / Third week in Chelsea / Never argue with a German if you're tired or European song / Thunk / War movie. *(re-iss.Jul84)*

Oct 71. (7") **PRETTY AS YOU FEEL. / WILD TURKEY** [ ] [60]

—— **JOHN BARBATA** – drums (ex-CROSBY & NASH ex-TURTLES) repl. JOEY

Jun 72. (lp)(c) **LONG JOHN SILVER** [30] [20]
– Long John Silver / Aerie (gang of eagles) / Twilight double leader / Milk train / Son of Jesus / Easter? / Trial by fire / Alexander the medium / Eat starch mom.

Sep 72. (7") **LONG JOHN SILVER. / MILK TRAIN** [ ] [ ]

1972. (7") **TWILIGHT DOUBLE DEALER. / TRIAL BY FIRE** [-] [ ]

—— **DAVID FREIBERG** – vocals (ex-QUICKSILVER MESSENGER SERVICE) (They made last album recorded between 71-72)

Apr 73. (lp)(c) **30 SECONDS OVER WINTERLAND (live)** [ ] [52]
– Have you seen the saucers / Feel so good / Crown of creation / When the Earth moves again / Milk train / Trial by fire / Twilight double leader. *(re-iss.Oct85)*

—— Now non-recoding quintet of SLICK, KANTNER, FREIBERG, BARBATA and CREACH. CASADY and KAUKONEN made HOT TUNA their full-time band.

PAUL KANTNER & JEFFERSON STARSHIP

with JERRY GARCIA, DAVID CROSBY, GRAHAM NASH, MICKEY HART

R.C.A. Grunt

Apr 71. (lp) **(IT'S A FRESH WIND THAT) BLOWS AGAINST THE NORTH** [ ] [20] Nov 70
– Mau mau (Amerikon) / The baby tree / Let's go together / A child is coming / Sunrise / Hijack / Home / Have you seen the stars tonite / X-M / Starship.

PAUL KANTNER & GRACE SLICK

Grunt Grunt

Dec 71. (lp) **SUNFIGHTER** [ ] [89]
– Silver spoon / Diana (part 1) / Sunfighter / Titanic / Look at the wood / When I was a boy I watched the wolves / Million / China / Earth mother / Diana (part 2) / Universal Copernican mumbles / Holding together. *(re-iss.+cd.Apr89 on 'Essential')*

—— KANTNER later released a US only album 'THE PLANET EARTH ROCK AND ROLL ORCHESTRA iss.Aug83. After leaving JEFFERSON STARSHIP he formed KBC with BALIN and CASADY. (ex-JEFFERSON members). They released a single and album early '83.

PAUL KANTNER, GRACE SLICK, DAVID FREIBERG

with guests **JORMA KAUKONEN** – guitar / **JACK CASADY** – bass / **CHAQUICO** – guitar / **JERRY GARCIA** ('Grateful Dead') / **DAVID CROSBY** ('Crosby, Stills & Nash')

Grunt Grunt

May 73. (lp) **BARON VON TOLBOOTH AND THE CHROME NUN** [ ] [ ]
– Ballad of the chrome nun / Fat / Flowers of the night / Walkin' / Your mind has left your body / Across the board / Harp tree lament / White boy (transcaucasian airmachine blues) / Fishman / Sketches of China.

Jun 73. (7") **BALLAD OF THE CHROME NUN. / SKETCHES OF CHINA** [-] [ ]

JEFFERSON STARSHIP

(new name re-formed)**SLICK, KANTNER, FREIBERG, CREACH** and **BARBATA** recruited **CRAIG CHAQUICO** (b.26 Sep'54) – guitar (ex-STEELWIND)repl. JORMA / **PETE SEARS** – bass, keyboards, vocals repl. PETER KAUKONEN who had repl. JACK

Grunt-RCA Grunt-RCA

Nov 74. (7") **RIDE THE TIGER. / DEVIL'S SON** [-] [84]

Dec 74. (lp) **DRAGONFLY** [ ] [11] Oct 74
– Ride the tiger / That's for sure / Be young you / Caroline / Devil's den / Come to life / All fly away / Hyperdrive.

1975. (7") **BE YOUNG YOU. / CAROLINE** [-] [ ]

—— added the returning **MARTY BALIN** – vocals, guitar

Jul 75. (lp)(c) **RED OCTOPUS** [ ] [1]
– Fast buck Freddie / Miracles / Git fiddler / Al Garimasu (there is love) / Sweeter than honey / Play on love / Tumblin' / I want to see another world / Sandalphon / There will be love. *(re-iss.Feb81, re-iss.Oct84 on 'RCA Int.')(re-iss.Jun86 on 'Fame') (cd-iss.Oct87)*

Sep 75. (7") **MIRACLES. / AL GARIMASU (THERE IS LOVE)** [ ] [3] Aug 75

Nov 75. (7") **PLAY ON LOVE. / I WANT TO SEE ANOTHER WORLD** [-] [49]

—— Trimmed to sextet when PAPA JOHN CREACH went solo. GRACE SLICK also left

Jul 76. (lp)(c) **SPITFIRE** [30] [3]
– Hot water / Big city / Switchblade / Cruisin' / Love lovely love / St. Charles / Dance with the dragon / St. Charles / With your love / Song to the sun / Ozymandias / Don't let it rain.

Aug 76. (7") **WITH YOUR LOVE. / SWITCHBLADE** [ ] [12] Jul 76

Nov 76. (7") **ST.CHARLES. / LOVE LOVELY LOVE** [-] [64]

Feb 78. (7") **COUNT ON ME. / SHOW YOURSELF** [ ] [8]

Mar 78. (lp)(c) **EARTH** [ ] [5]

– Love too good / Count on me / Take your time / Crazy feelin' / Skateboard / Fire / Show yourself / All nite long.

Jun 78. (7") **RUNAWAY. / HOT WATER** [ ] [12] May 78
Aug 78. (7") **CRAZY FEELIN' / LOVE TOO GOOD** [-] [54]
Nov 78. (7")(12") **LIGHT THE SKY ON FIRE. / HYPERDRIVE** [-] [66]

— **MICKEY THOMAS** – vocals (ex-ELVIN BISHOP) repl. BALIN who went solo / **AYNSLEY DUNBAR** – drums (ex-JOURNEY ex-KGB) repl. BARBATA (above 2 joining **KANTNER, FREIBERG, CHAQUICO** and **SEARS) / GRACE SLICK** also guested uncredited on the next album (she joined full-time Feb81.)

Jan 80. (7") **JANE. / FREEDOM AT ZERO POINT** [21] [14] Nov 79
Jan 80. (lp) **FREEDOM AT ZERO POINT** [22] [10] Nov 79
– Girl with hungry eyes / Freedom at Zero Point / Fadiing lady night / Lightning Rose / Things to come / Just the same / Rock music / Awakening / Jane. *(re-iss.Sep81 on 'RCA') (re-iss.Jun89, cd-iss.Feb90)*
Apr 80. (7") **GIRL WITH THE HUNGRY EYES. / JUST THE SAME** [ ] [55]
Jun 80. (7") **ROCK MUSIC. / LIGHTNING ROSE** [-] [ ]

R.C.A. Grunt

May 81. (7")(12") **FIND YOUR WAY BACK. / MODERN TIMES** [ ] [29] Apr 81
Jun 81. (lp) **MODERN TIMES** [ ] [26] Apr 81
– Find your way back / Stranger / Wild eyes / Save your love / Modern times / Mary / Free / Alien / Stairway to Cleveland. *(re-iss.Sep81)*
Jul 81. (7") **STRANGER. / FREE** [-] [48]
Oct 81. (7")(12") **SAVE YOUR LOVE. / WILD EYES** [-] [ ]
Oct 82. (7") **BE MY LADY. / OUT OF CONTROL** [-] [28]
Feb 83. (lp)(c) **WINDS OF CHANGE** [ ] [26] Oct 82
– Winds of change / Keep on dreamin' / Be my lady / I will stay / Out of control / Can't find love / Black widow / I came back from the jaws of the dragon / Quit wasting time. *(re-iss.+cd.Oct84)*
Jan 83. (7") **WINDS OF CHANGE. / BLACK WIDOW** [-] [38]
Apr 83. (7") **CAN'T FIND LOVE. / I WILL STAY** [-] [ ]

— **DON BALDWIN** – drums (ex-ELVIN BISHOP BAND) repl. DUNBAR

Jun 84. (7") **NO WAY OUT. / ROSE GOES TO YALE** [ ] [ ] May 84
(12"+=) – Be my lady.
Jun 84. (lp)(c)(cd) **NUCLEAR FURNITURE** [ ] [28]
– Layin' it on the line / No way out / Sorry me, sorry you / Live and let live / Connection / Nuclear furniture / Rose goes to Vale / Magician / Assassin / Shining in the moonlight / Showdown / Champion.
Sep 84 (7") **LAYIN' IT ON THE LINE. / SHOWDOWN** [-] [66]

STARSHIP

was the name they were allowed to use after KANTNER left. Now **GRACE SLICK, MICKEY THOMAS, CRAIG CHAQUICO, PETE SEARS** and **DON BALDWIN**

Oct 85. (7")(12") **WE BUILT THIS CITY. / PRIVATE ROOM** [12] [1] Sep 85
Nov 85. (lp)(c)(cd) **KNEE DEEP IN THE HOOPLA** [ ] [7] Oct 85
– We built this city / Sara / Tomorrow doesn't matter tonight / Rock myself to sleep / Desperate heart / Private room / Before I go / Hearts of the world (will understand) / Love rusts. *(re-iss.+cd.Sep89)*
Jan 86. (7") **SARA. / HEARTS OF THE WORLD (WILL UNDERSTAND)** [ ] [1] Dec 85
(12"+=) – Jane.
May 86. (7") **TOMORROW DOESN'T MATTER TONIGHT. / LOVE RUSTS** [ ] [26] Apr 86
(12"+=) – No way out / Laying it on the line.
Jun 86. (7")(12") **BEFORE I GO. / CUT YOU DOWN** [-] [68]

— now w/out SEARS

Mar 87. (7") **NOTHING'S GONNA STOP US NOW. / LAYING IT ON THE LINE** [1] [1] Jan 87
(12"+=) – We built this city / Tomorrow doesn't matter tonight.
Jul 87. (lp)(c)(cd) **NO PROTECTION** [26] [12]
– Beat patrol / Nothing's gonna stop us now / It's not over ('til it's over) / Girls like you / Wings of a lie / The children / I don't know why / Transatlantic / Babylon / Set the night to music.
Aug 87. (7") **IT'S NOT OVER ('TIL IT'S OVER). / BABYLON** [ ] [9] Jun 87
(12"+=) – Jane / Sara. *(also on US cass.)*
Nov 87. (7") **BEAT PATROL. / GIRLS LIKE YOU** [ ] [46] Sep 87
Feb 88. (7") **SET THE NIGHT TO MUSIC. / I DON'T KNOW WHY** [-] [ ]
(12"+=) – ('A' dub version) / ('A' instrumental).

— STARSHIP in the 90's were: – **MICKEY THOMAS, DONNY BALDWIN, CRAIG CHAQUICO** plus **MARK MORGAN** – keyboards / **BRETT BLOOMFIELD** – bass.

Feb 89. (7") **WILD AGAIN. / LAYIN' IT ON THE LINE** [ ] [73] Dec 88
(12"+=) – Tutti Frutti.
Sep 89. (7")(c-s) **IT'S NOT ENOUGH. / LOVE AMONG THE CANNIBALS** [ ] [12] Aug 89
(12"+=) – Wild again.
(cd-s++=) – Nothing's gonna stop us now.
Sep 89. (lp)(c)(cd) **LOVE AMONG THE CANNIBALS** [ ] [64] Aug 89
– The burn / It's not enough / Trouble in mind / I didn't mean to stay all night / Send a message / Love among the cannibals / We dream in colour / Healing waters / Blaze of love / I'll be there. *(cd+=)–* Wild again.
Nov 89. (7")(c-s) **I DIDN'T MEAN TO STAY ALL NIGHT. / ?** [-] [75]
Apr 91. (c-s)(cd-s) **GOOD HEART. /** [-] [81]
Aug 91. (cd)(c)(lp) **GREATEST HITS (TEN YEARS AND CHANGE 1979-1991)** (compilation) [ ] [-]
– Jane / Find your way back / Stranger / No way out / Layin' it on the line / Don't lose any sleep / We built this city / Sara / Nothing's gonna stop us now / It's not over ('til it's over) / It's not enough / Good heart. *(re-iss.cd Oct95)*

JEFFERSON AIRPLANE

were reformed with **SLICK, KANTNER, KAUKONEN, CASADY and BALIN.** Augmented by **KENNY ARONOFF** – drums / **PETER KAUKONEN and RANDY JACKSON** – guitar (ex-ZEBRA)

Epic Epic

Oct 89. (lp)(c)(cd) **JEFFERSON AIRPLANE** [ ] [85]
– Planes / Solidarity / Summer of love / The wheel / True love / Now is the time / Panda / Freedom / Ice age / Madeleine Street / Common market madrigal / Upfront blues / Too many years.
Oct 89. (7") **SUMMER OF LOVE. / PANDA** [-] [ ]
Jan 90. (7") **TRUE LOVE. /** [-] [ ]

JEFFERSON STARSHIP

Essential Rykodisc

Jul 95. (cd)(c) **DEEP SPACE – VIRGIN SKY** [ ] [ ]
– Shadowlands / Ganja of love / Dark ages / I'm on fire / Papa John / Women who fly / Gold / The light / Crown of creation / Count on me / Miracles / Intro to lawman / Lawman / Wooden ships / Somebody to love / White rabbit.

– (AIRPLANE) compilations, etc.

Jun 70. RCA; (7") **WHITE RABBIT. / SOMEBODY TO LOVE** [ ] [ ]
Nov 70. RCA; (lp)(c) **THE WORST OF JEFFERSON AIRPLANE** [ ] [12]
(re-iss.Sep86 on 'Fame')
Dec 76. RCA; (d-lp) **FLIGHT LOG (1966-76 all work)** [ ] [37]
Apr 76. RCA; (7") **WHITE RABBIT. / SOMEBODY TO LOVE / CROWN OF CREATION** [ ] [ ]
(re-iss. as 12" Apr79 on 'RCA Gold') (re-iss.Nov86 on 'Old Gold')
Jul 80. RCA; (lp)(c) **THE BEST OF JEFFERSON AIRPLANE** [ ] [ ]
Aug 81. RCA; (d-lp) **ROCK GALAXY ('CROWN OF CREATION' & 'VOLUNTEERS')** [ ] [ ]
Jul 87 RCA; (d-lp)(c)(d-cd)**2400 FULTON STREET – AN ANTHOLOGY** [ ] [ ]
– It's no secret / Come up the years / My best friend / Somebody to love / Comin' back to me / Embryonic journey / She has funny cars / Plastic fantastic lover / Wild tyme / The ballad of you & me & Pooneil – A small package of value will come to you, shortly / White rabbit / Won't you try Saturday afternoon / Lather / We can be together / Crown of creation / Mexico / Wooden ships / Rejoyce / Volunteers / Pretty as you feel / Martha / Today / Third week in Chelsea. *(d-cd+=)–* Let's get together / Blues from an airplane / J.P.P. McStep B. Blues / Fat angel / Greasy heart / We can be together / Have you seen the saucers / Eat starch mom / Good shepherd / Eskimo blue day / The Levi commercials. *(re-iss.d-cd 1992)*
Nov 92. RCA; (3xcd-box) **JEFFERSON AIRPLANE LOVES YOU** [ ] [ ]
May 87. Ariola; (7") **WHITE RABBIT. / SOMEBODY TO LOVE** [ ] [ ]
(12"+=) – She has funny cars / Third week in Chelsea.
Oct 88. Castle; (d-lp)(c)(cd) **THE COLLECTION** [ ] [-]
(iss.US on cd Oct92)
May 90. Thunderbolt; (cd)(lp) **LIVE AT THE MONTEREY FESTIVAL (live)** [ ] [-]
Apr 74. Grunt; (lp) **EARLY FLIGHT (rare)** [ ] [ ]
Apr 93. Pulsar; (cd) **WOODSTOCK REVIVAL** [ ] [-]
Sep 93. Remember; (cd)(c) **WHITE RABBIT** [ ] [-]

– (STARSHIP) compilations etc. –

Mar 79. Grunt-RCA; (lp)(c) **GOLD** [ ] [20] Feb 79
(with free 7" **LIGHT THE SKY ON FIRE. / HYPERDRIVE)**
1979. Grunt-RCA; (7") **MIRACLES. / WITH YOUR LOVE** [-] [ ]
Nov 92. Old Gold; (cd-ep) **NOTHING'S GONNA STOP US NOW / WE BUILT THIS CITY / SARA** [ ] [-]

GRACE SLICK

solo, all featuring JEFFERSON's and session people

Grunt Grunt

Jan 74. (lp)(c) **MANHOLE** [ ] [ ]
– Jay / Theme from 'Manhole' / Come again? Toucan / It's only music / Better lying down / Epic (£38).

R.C.A. R.C.A.

May 80. (7") **SEASONS. / ANGEL OF NIGHT** [-] [ ]
May 80. (7") **DREAMS. / ANGEL OF NIGHT** [50] [-]
May 80. (lp)(c) **DREAMS** [28] [32]
– Dreams / El Diablo / Face to the wind / Angel of night / Seasons / Do it the hard way / Full Moon man / Let it go / Garden of man. *(re-iss.Sep81) (cd-iss.Sep91 on 'Great Expectations')*
Jul 80. (7")(12") **DREAMS. / DO IT THE HARD WAY** [-] [ ]
Feb 81. (7") **MISTREATER. / FULL MOON MAN** [ ] [ ]

Feb 81. (lp)(c) **WELCOME TO THE WRECKING BALL** [ ] [48]
– Wrecking ball / Mistreater / Shot in the dark / Round & round / Shooting star / Just a little love / Sea of love / Lines / Right kind / No more heroes. *(cd-iss.Sep91 on 'Great Expectations')*
Mar 84. (lp)(c) **SOFTWARE** [ ] [ ]
– Call it right call it wrong / Me and me / All the machines / Fox face / Through the window / It just won't stop / Habits / Rearrange my face / Bikini Atoll.
Mar 84. (7") **ALL THE MACHINES. / ('A'long version)** [-] [ ]
May 84. (7") **THROUGH THE WINDOWS. / HABITS** [-] [ ]

— In 1965, with GREAT SOCIETY, she released a single 'SOMEBODY TO LOVE'. / 'FREE ADVICE'; for 'North Beach' US. An album of these 1965/66 recordings was rel.Apr68 by 'Columbia'/'CBS' as 'CONSPICUOUS ONLY IN ITS ABSENCE'. Later in the year, another album 'HOW IT WAS' and single 'SALLY GO ROUND THE ROSES'. / 'DIDN'T THINK SO' were credited to GRACE SLICK & THE GREAT SOCIETY.

JENNIFERS (see under ⇒ SUPERGRASS)

JESUS & MARY CHAIN

Formed: East Kilbride, Scotland . . . 1983, by brothers WILLIAM and JIM REID. After local Glasgow gigs, they moved to Fulham in London, having signed for Alan McGhee's independent 'Creation' label in May'84. Their debut SLAUGHTER JOE produced 45 'UPSIDE DOWN', soon topped indie charts which led to WEA subsidiary label 'Blanco Y Negro' snapping them up early 1985. They hit the UK Top 50 with next single 'NEVER UNDERSTAND', and they were soon antagonising new audiences, when crashing gear after 20 minutes on set. Riots ensued at nearly every major gig, and more controversy arrived when the next 45's B-side 'JESUS SUCKS', was boycotted by pressing plant. With new B-side, the single 'YOU TRIP ME UP', hit only No.55, but was soon followed by another Top 50 hit in October 'JUST LIKE HONEY'. A month later they unleashed their debut album 'PSYCHOCANDY', and although this just failed to breach the UK Top 30, it was regarded by many (NME critics especially) as the album of the year. They hit the Top 20 in 1986 with next 45 'SOME CANDY TALKING', and scored first Top 10 single & album in '87 with 'APRIL SKIES' and 'DARKLANDS' respectively. • **Style:** Initially a noisy post-punk outfit who screeched with feedback. Described as VELVET UNDERGROUND meeting The SEX PISTOLS, they soon mellowed at times into romantic garage type rock. • **Songwriters:** All written by JIM and WILLIAM except; VEGETABLE MAN (Syd Barrett) / SURFIN' USA (Beach Boys) / WHO DO YOU LOVE (Bo Diddley) / MY GIRL (Temptations) / MUSHROOM (Can) / GUITAR MAN (Jerry Lee Hubbard) / TOWER OF SONG (Leonard Cohen) / LITTLE RED ROOSTER (Willie Dixon) / (I CAN'T GET NO) SATISFACTION (Rolling Stones) / REVERBERATION (13th Floor Elevators) / GHOST OF A SMILE (Pogues) / ALPHABET CITY (Prince) / NEW KIND OF KICK (Cramps). • **Trivia:** Their 1986 single 'SOME CANDY TALKING' was banned by Radio 1 DJ Mike Smith, due to its drug references. The following year in the States, they were banned from a chart show due to their blasphemous name. Although yet not overwhelming, their success in the US, have made albums reach between 100 & 200. In 1989 they produced and featured on The SUGARCUBES '89 version of hit 'Birthday'.

Recommended: PSYCHOCANDY (*10) / DARKLANDS (*8) / AUTOMATIC (*7) / HONEY'S DEAD (*8) / BARBED WIRE KISSES (*7).

JIM REID (b.1961) – vox, guitar / **WILLIAM REID** (b.1958) – guitar, vox / **MURRAY DALGLISH** – drums (bass tom & snare) / **DOUGLAS HART** – bass

Creation / not issued

Nov 84. (7") **UPSIDE DOWN. / VEGETABLE MAN** [ ] [-]
(12"+=) – ('A' demo).

— **BOBBY GILLESPIE** – drums (ex-WAKE, of PRIMAL SCREAM) repl. DALGLISH who formed BABY'S GOT A GUN

Blanco YN / Reprise

Feb 85. (7") **NEVER UNDERSTAND. / SUCK** [47] [ ]
(12"+=) – Ambition.
Jun 85. (7") **YOU TRIP ME UP. / JUST OUT OF REACH** [55] [ ]
(12"+=) – Boyfriend's dead.
Oct 85. (7") **JUST LIKE HONEY. / HEAD** [45] [ ]
(12"+=) – Just like honey (demo) / Cracked.
(d7"+=) – ('A'demo) / Inside me.
Nov 85. (lp)(c) **PSYCHOCANDY** [31] [ ]
– Just like honey / The living end / Taste the floor / Hardest walk / Cut dead / In a hole / Taste of Cindy / Never understand / It's so hard / Inside me / Sowing seeds / My little underground / You trip me up / Something's wrong. *(cd-iss.Apr86 +=)–* Some candy talking.

— **JOHN LODER** – drums (on stage when BOBBY was unavailable)
Jul 86. (7") **SOME CANDY TALKING. / PSYCHO CANDY / HIT** [13] [ ]
(12"+=) – Taste of Cindy.
(d7"+=) – Cut dead / You trip me up / Some candy talking / Psycho candy (all four tracks accoustic versions).

— now basic trio of **JIM, WILLIAM** and **DOUGLAS** brought in **JOHN MOORE** – drums repl. GILLESPIE (who was busy with PRIMAL SCREAM) / **JAMES PINKER** – drums (ex-DEAD CAN DANCE) repl. MOORE now on guitar
Apr 87. (7") **APRIL SKIES. / KILL SURF CITY** [8] [ ]
(12"+=) – Who do you love.
(d7"+=) – Mushroom / Bo Diddley is Jesus.
Aug 87. (7") **HAPPY WHEN IT RAINS. / EVERYTHING IS ALRIGHT WHEN YOU'RE DOWN** [25] [ ]
(12"+=) – Happy place / F-Hole.
(10"+=) – ('A' version) / Shake.

— trimmed to basic duo of REID brothers.
Sep 87. (lp)(c)(cd) **DARKLANDS** [5] [ ]
– Darklands / Deep one perfect morning / Happy when it rains / Down on me / Nine million rainy days / April skies / Fall / Cherry came too / On the wall / About you. *(re-iss.cd Nov94)*
Oct 87. (7") **DARKLANDS. / RIDER / ON THE WALL (demo)** [33] [ ]
(12"+=) – Surfin' U.S.A.
(10"+=)(cd-s+=) – Here it comes again.

— **DAVE EVANS** – rhythm guitar repl. MOORE who formed EXPRESSWAY
Mar 88. (7") **SIDEWALKING. / TASTE OF CINDY (live)** [30] [ ]
(12"+=) – ('A' extended) / April skies (live).
(cd-s++=) – Chilled to the bone.
Apr 88. (lp)(c)(cd) **BARBED WIRE KISSES** (part compilation) [9] [ ]
– Kill Surf City / Head / Rider / Hit / Don't ever change / Just out of reach / Happy place / Psychocandy / Sidewalking / Who do you love / Surfin' USA / Everything's alright when you're down / Upside down / Taste of Cindy / Swing / On the wall. *(c+cd+=)–* Cracked / Here it comes again / Mushroom / Bo Diddley is Jesus.
Nov 88. (7") **KILL SURF CITY. / SURFIN' USA (summer mix)** [-] [ ]

— Basically REID brothers, HART and EVANS. (added **RICHARD THOMAS** – drums) / **BEN LURIE** – rhythm guitar repl. EVANS
Sep 89. (7") **BLUES FROM A GUN. / SHIMMER** [32] [-]
(10"+=) – Break me down / Penetration.
(12"+=)(c-s+=) – Penetration / Subway.
(3"cd-s+=) – Penetration / My girl
Oct 89. (lp)(c)(cd) **AUTOMATIC** [11] [ ]
– Here comes Alice / Coast to coast / Blues from a gun / Between planets / UV ray / Her way of praying / Head on / Take it / Halfway to crazy / Gimme hell.
Nov 89. (7") **HEAD ON. / IN THE BLACK** [57] [-]
(7") – ('A'side) / DEVIANT SLICE (or) I'M GLAD I NEVER
(12"+=)(cd-s+=) – Terminal beach.
Mar 90. (7") **HEAD ON. / PENETRATION** [-] [ ]
Aug 90. (7") **ROLLER COASTER. / SILVER BLADE** [46] [ ]
(12"+=) – Tower of song.
(7"ep++=)(cd-ep++=) – Low-life.

— Trimmed again, when THOMAS joined RENEGADE SOUNDWAVE on U.S.tour. HART became video director. The **REID** brothers and **BEN** recruited **MATTHEW PARKIN** – bass + **BARRY BLACKER** – drums (ex-STARLINGS)
Feb 92. (7") **REVERENCE. / HEAT** [10] [ ]
(12"+=)(cd-s+=) – ('A'radio remix) / Guitar man.
Mar 92. (cd)(c)(lp) **HONEY'S DEAD** [14] [ ]
– Reverence / Teenage lust / Far gone and out / Almost gold / Sugar Ray / Tumbledown / Catchfire / Good for my soul / Rollercoaster / I can't get enough / Sundown / Frequency.
Apr 92. (7") **FAR GONE AND OUT. / WHY'D DO YOU WANT ME** [23] [ ]
(12"+=)(cd-s+=) – Sometimes you just can't get enough.
Jun 92. (7") **ALMOST GOLD. / TEENAGE LUST (acoustic)** [41] [ ]
(12"+=) – Honey's dead.
(gold-cd-s+=) – Reverberation (doubt) / Don't come down.
Jun 93. (7"ep)(10"ep)(c-ep)(cd-ep) **SOUND OF SPEED EP** [30] [ ]
– Snakedriver / Something I can't have / White record release blues / Little red rooster.
Jul 93. (cd)(c)(lp) **THE SOUND OF SPEED** (part comp '88-'93) [15] [ ]
– Snakedriver / Reverence (radio mix) / Heat / Teenage lust (acoustic version) / Why'd you want me / Don't come down / Guitar man / Something I can't have / Sometimes / White record release blues / Shimmer / Penetration / My girl / Tower of song / Little red rooster / Break me down / Lowlife / Deviant slice / Reverberation / Sidewalking (extended version).

— next album feat. guest vox HOPE SANDOVAL (Mazzy Star) + SHANE McGOWAN.
Jul 94. (7") **SOMETIMES ALWAYS. / PERFECT CRIME** [22] [96]
(10"+=)(cd-s+=) – Little stars / Drop.
Aug 94. (cd)(c)(lp) **STONED AND DETRONED** [13] [98]
– Dirty water / Bullet lovers / Sometimes always / Come on / Between us / Hole / Never saw it coming / She / Wish I could / Save me / Till it shines / God help me / Girlfriend / Everybody I know / You've been a friend / These days / Feeling lucky.

Sep 94. (7")(c-s) **COME ON. / I'M IN WITH THE OUT-CROWD** 52
(cd-s+=) – New York City / Taking it away.
(cd-s) – ('A'side) / Ghost of a smile / Alphabet city / New kind of kick.
Jun 95. (12"ep)(c-ep)(cd-ep) **I LOVE ROCK'N'ROLL / BLEED ME / 33 1/3 / LOST STAR** 61

– compilations etc. –

Sep 91. Strange Fruit; (cd)(m-lp) **PEEL SESSIONS (1985-86)** -
Jun 94. Audioglobe; (cd+book) **LIVE (live)** -

ACID ANGELS

DOUGLAS HART, plus **JO HEAD** – vocals / **PHIL ERB** – computers / **PETER FOWLER** – videos

Product Inc. | not issued

Nov 88. (12") **SPEED SPEED ECSTACY. / TOP FUEL ELIMINATOR**

JESUS JONES

Formed: Bradford-Upon-Avon, Wiltshire, England ... late 1986 as CAMOUFLAGE, by MIKE, GEN and AL. In Aug'88 after moving to Wathamstow, London, they became JESUS JONES. They were soon snapped up by David Balfe's 'Food' label, through 'EMI. Early in '89, they released Craig Leon produced debut single 'INFO-FREAKO', which hit Top 50. Their 2 follow-ups 'NEVER ENOUGH' and 'BRING IT ON DOWN', also both hit the Top 50, and premiered the UK Top 40 album 'LIQUIDIZER'. Further success came in the early 90's, when album 'DOUBT' hit UK No.1 and US Top 30, after their single 'RIGHT HERE, RIGHT NOW' was a surprise No.2 smash there in '91. • **Style:** Sampled danceable punk-ish pop rock outfit influenced by skateboards, early SHAMEN, etc. • **Songwriters:** MIKE EDWARDS penned except; I DON'T WANT THAT KIND OF LOVE (Crazyhead) / VOODOO CHILE (Jimi Hendrix Experience). • **Trivia:** The song 'NEVER ENOUGH' was inspired by Woody Allen's film 'Stardust Memories'.

Recommended: LIQUIDIZER (*7) / DOUBT (*7).

MIKE EDWARDS – vocals / **JERRY DE BORG** – guitar / **AL JAWORSKI** (b.ALAN DOUGHTY) – bass / **BARRY D.** (b.IAIN BAKER) – keyboards, samplers / **GEN** (b.SIMON MATTHEWS) – drums

Food-EMI | S.B.K.

Feb 89. (7") **INFO-FREAKO. / BROKEN BONES** 42
(12"+=)(cd-s+=) – Info sicko.
(12") – ('A'side) / Info-psycho.
Jun 89. (7")(c-s) **NEVER ENOUGH. / WHAT'S GOING ON** 42
(12")(cd-s) – ('A'side) / -Enough – Never enough / It's the . . . ..that counts.
Sep 89. (7") **BRING IT ON DOWN. / CUT AND DRIED** 46
(12"+=) – Info sicko.
(cd-s++=) – None of the answers / Beat it down.
Oct 89. (lp)(c)(cd) **LIQUIDIZER** 32
– Move mountains / Never enough / The real world / All the answers / What's going on / Song 13 / Info-freako / Bring it on down / Too much to learn / What would you know? / Too much to learn / One for the money / Someone to blame.
Mar 90. (7")(c-s) **REAL REAL REAL. / DEAD PEOPLE'S LIVES** 19 | 4 May 91
(12"+=)(cd-s+=) – ('A'-12"mix) / Info freako.
(12") – ('A'side) / (above 2).
Sep 90. (7")(c-s) **RIGHT HERE RIGHT NOW. / MOVE ME / DAMN GOOD AT THIS** 31
(10"+=)(cd-s+=) – Are you satisfied.
(12") – ('A'side) / Are you satisfied / Move mountains (mix) / ('A'different mix).
Dec 90. (7")(c-s) **INTERNATIONAL BRIGHT YOUNG THING. / MARYLAND** 7
(12"+=) – ('A'mix).
(12"pic-d) – ('A'side) / Need to know / I.B.Y.T.
(cd-s) – (all 4 tracks above).
Feb 91. (cd)(c)(lp) **DOUBT** 1 | 25
– Trust me / Who? where? why? / International bright young thing / I'm burning / Right here right now / Real real real / Welcome back Victoria / Two and two / Stripped / Blissed. *(re-iss.cd+c Mar94)*
Feb 91. (7")(c-s) **WHO? WHERE? WHEN? (crisis mix). / CARICATURE** 21
(12"+=) – ('A'-12"mix).
(10"++=) – Kill today.
(cd-s+=) – ('A'versions).
Jul 91. (7")(c-s) **RIGHT HERE RIGHT NOW. / WELCOME BACK VICTORIA** 31 | 2 Apr 91
(12"+=)(cd-s+=) – Info psycho / Broken bones.
Jan 93. (7") **THE DEVIL YOU KNOW. / PHOENIX** 10
(12"+=)(cd-s+=) – What to know
Jan 93. (cd)(c)(lp) **PERVERSE** 6 | 59
– Zeroes and heroes / The Devil you know / Get a good thing / From love to war / Yellow brown / Magazine / The right decision / Your crusade / Don't believe it / Tongue tied / Spiral / Idiot stare.
Mar 93. (7")(c-s) **THE RIGHT DECISION. / STARTING FROM SCRATCH** 36
(12"+=)(cd-s+=) – ('A'mixes).
Jun 93. (c-s) **ZEROES AND HEROES. / MACHINE DRUG / ZEROES AND HEROES (mixes)** 30
(cd-s) – ('A'side) / Real real real (rhythm 2) / International bright young thing / Right here, right now.
(12") – ('A'side) / ('A'mixes).

– compilations, others, etc. –

Nov 89. Food; (7"ep) **FOOD CHRISTMAS** | -
– I don't want that kind of love. (others by CRAZYHEAD / DIESEL PARK WEST)

JESUS LIZARD

Formed: Austin, Texas, USA . . . late 80's by DAVID YOW and DAVID SIMS, who had just folded SCRATCH ACID. They found Chicago-born DENNISON and McNEILLY, and set up more rampaging tours from US to UK. After a few albums for 'Touch & Go', they were approached by 'Atlantic' in 1991. They refused a lucrative money-spinning deal and opted to stay as a US indie band. Remarkably after worldly tours, they broke through early in 1993 with the help from NIRVANA on a joint single. • **Style:** Psychotic apocalyptic cabaret fronted by the BUTTHOLE SURFERS, BIRTHDAY PARTY and IGGY POP influenced DAVID YOW. He was renowned for taking off from stage into the crowd, and at times getting lost, although remarkably still managing to sing!. • **Songwriters:** Group except WHEELCHAIR EPIDEMIC (Dicks). • **Trivia:** JESUS LIZARD were produced by STEVE ALBINI (ex-BIG BLACK, RAPEMAN).

Recommended: LIAR (*7) / SHOT (*7)

SCRATCH ACID

DAVID YOW – vocals, bass / **BRETT BRADFORD** – guitar, vocals / **DAVID WILLIAM SIMS** – bass, guitar / **REY WASHAM** – drums, piano

Fun-damental | Rabid Cat

Apr 86. (lp) **SCRATCH ACID**
– Cannibal / Greatest gift / Monsters / Owners lament / She said / Mess / El spectro / Lay screaming.
Jul 86. (m-lp) **JUST KEEP EATING**
– Crazy Dan / Eyeball / Big bone lick / Unlike a beast / Damned for all time / Ain't that love / Holes / Albino slug / Spit a kiss / Amicus / Cheese plug.
Mar 87. (lp) **BESERKER**
– Mary had a little drug problem / For crying out loud / Moron's moron / Skin drips / Thing is bliss / Flying houses.
— In 1988, YOW joined RAPEMAN alongside STEVE ALBINI (BIG BLACK). WESHAM joined TAD. One of the others formed The BIG BOYS.

– compilation –

Oct 91. Touch & Go; (cd)(lp) **THE GREATEST GIFT**

JESUS LIZARD

DAVID YOW – vocals / **DUANE DENISON** – guitar / **DAVID WILLIAM SIMS** – bass / **MAC McNEILLY** – drums

Touch & Go | Touch & Go

1989. (m-lp) **PURE**
– Blockbuster / Bloody Mary / Rabid pigs / Starlet / Happy bunny goes fluff fluff along. *(re-iss.Jul93)*
Feb 90. (7") **CHROME. / ?**
May 90. (cd)(c)(lp) **HEAD**
– One evening / S.D.B.J. / My own urine / If you had lips / 7 vs 8 / Pastoral / Waxeater / Good thing / Tight 'n shiny / Killer McHann. *(re-iss.+cd Jul93 incl. 'PURE')*
Nov 90. (7") **MOUTHBREAKER. / ?**
Jan 91. (cd)(lp) **GOAT**
– Then comes Dudley / Mouthbreaker / Nub / Monkey trick / Karpis / South mouth / Lady shoes / Rodeo in Joliet / Seasick. *(re-iss.Apr94)*
— In Apr'91, YOW featured for PIGFACE super techno-punks on 'GUB' album.
May 92. (7") **WHEELCHAIR EPIDEMIC. / DANCING NAKED LADIES**
Oct 92. (cd)(c)(lp) **LIAR**

– Boilermaker / Gladiator / The art of self-defence / Slave ship / Puss / Whirl / Rope / Perk / Zachariah / Dancing naked ladies.

Feb 93. (7") **PUSS. / (b-side by NIRVANA)** [12] [ ]

Jun 93. (cd)(lp) **SHOW** [-] [ ]
(imported into UK Jul 94 on 'Collision')

Sep 93. (12")(cd-s) **LASH. /** [ ] [ ]

Nov 93. (12")(cd-s) **FLY ON THE WALL. / WHITE HOLE** [ ] [ ]

Aug 94. (cd)(c)(lp) **DOWN (live)** [64] [ ]
– Fly on the wall / Mistletoe / Countless backs of sad losers / Queen for a day / The associate / Destroy before reading / Low rider / 50 cents / American BB / Horse / Din / Elegy / The best parts.

. . . Jan – Jun '96 stop press . . .

Parlophone Capitol

May 96. (cd)(c)(lp) **SHOT** [ ] [ ]

JETHRO TULL

Formed: London, England . . . late 1967 by Scots-born IAN ANDERSON and GLENN CORNICK, who had both been for 4 years in Blackpool band JOHN EVANS' SMASH, alongside school friends EVANS and JEFFREY HAMMOND-HAMMOND. IAN and GLENN brought in former McGREGORY'S ENGINE members MICK ABRAHAMS plus CLIVE BUNKER, and used an 18th Century name of an English agriculturist/inventor. It was often mistaken by the uninitiated, as the name of lead singer IAN ANDERSON. Early in 1968, through agents Terry Ellis & Chris Wright, 'MGM' issued debut single 'SUNSHINE DAY', but mistakenly they credited it to JETHRO TOE at the pressing plant. (It has since changed hands for over £50 at record fairs). On 29 Jun'68, after a residency at Marquee Club, they supported PINK FLOYD at a free rock concert at Hyde Park, London. Due to another enthusiastically received concert at Sunbury's Jazz & Blues Festival in August, they signed to 'Island'. By the end of the year, debut lp 'THIS WAS' cracked the UK Top 10, and even managed to make Top 75 in the US. Early in 1969, they played a few gigs with TONY IOMMI (future BLACK SABBATH) and DAVID O'LIST (of The NICE), to briefly deputize for the departing ABRAHAMS. In May '71 with new member MARTIN BARRE, they hit UK Top 3 with classic 'LIVING IN THE PAST' single, which was quickly followed by UK No.1 & US Top 20 album 'STAND UP'. They then signed to associate label 'Chrysalis', and scored 2 more UK Top 10 singles 'SWEET DREAM' & 'THE WITCHES PROMISE'. The group continued to burst into the UK & US, with nearly every album throughout the 70's, 80's & early 90's?. • **Style:** Initially blues orientated, they shifted into more progressive-rock field by the early 70's. ANDERSON's medieval vagrant-look and eccentric flute-playing, gave group its visual trademark. In 1972-73 their concept albums 'THICK AS A BRICK' & 'A PASSION PLAY', were originally panned by UK rock critics, although both survived this unfair onslaught, and both surprisingly hit No.1 in the States. • **Songwriters:** ANDERSON lyrics / group compositions, except BOUREE (J.S.Bach) / JOHN BARLEYCORN (trad.) / CAT'S SQUIRREL (Cream). • **Trivia:** ANDERSON still controls his trout-farming business in Northern Scotland. In 1974, he produced STEELEYE SPAN's 'Now We Are Six' album.

Recommended: AQUALUNG (*8) / A PASSION PLAY (*7) / LIVING IN THE PAST (*7) / THE VERY BEST OF JETHRO TULL (*8)

IAN ANDERSON (b.10 Aug'47, Edinburgh, Scotland) – vocals, flute / **GLENN CORNICK** (b.24 Apr'47, Barrow-in-Furness, England) – bass / **MICK ABRAHAMS** (b. 7 Apr'43, Luton) – guitar, vocals (ex-McGREGORY'S ENGINE) / **CLIVE BUNKER** (b.12 Dec'46) – drums (ex-McGREGORY'S ENGINE)

M.G.M. not issued

Mar 68. (7") **SUNSHINE DAY. / AEROPLANE (as "JETHRO TOE")** [ ] [-]

Island Reprise

Aug 68. (7")**SONG FOR JEFFREY. / ONE FOR JOHN GEE** [ ] [ ]

Oct 68. (lp)(c) **THIS WAS** [10] [62] Feb 69
– My Sunday feeling / Some day the sun won't shine for you / Beggar's farm / Move on alone / Serenade to a cuckoo / Dharma for one / It's breaking me up / Cat's squirrel / A song for Jeffrey / Round. *(re-iss.+c Jan74) (cd-iss.1986)*

Dec 68. (7") **LOVE STORY. / A CHRISTMAS SONG** [29] [ ]

Mar 69. (7") **LOVE STORY. / A SONG FOR JEFFREY** [-] [ ]

—— **MARTIN BARRIE** – guitar repl. MICK ABRAHAMS to BLODWYN PIG,

May 69. (7") **LIVING IN THE PAST. / DRIVING SONG** [3] [-]

Jul 69. (lp)(c) **STAND UP** [1] [20] Oct 69
– A new day yesterday / Jeffrey goes to Leicester Square / Bouree / Back to the family / Look into the sun / Nothing is easy / Fat man / We used to know / Reasons for waiting / For a thousand mothers. *(re-iss.Nov83 on 'Fame') (cd-iss.1986 & 1989)*

Chrysalis Reprise

Oct 69. (7") **SWEET DREAM. / SEVENTEEN** [9] [-]

Oct 69. (7") **SWEET DREAM. / REASONS FOR WAITING** [-] [ ]

Jan 70. (7") **THE WITCHES PROMISE. / TEACHER** [4] [ ]

—— augmented by **JOHN EVANS** – keyboards (he later joined full-time)

Apr 70. (lp)(c) **BENEFIT** [3] [11]
– With you there to help me / Nothing to say / Alive and well and living in / Son / For Michael Collins, Jeffrey and me / To cry you a song / A time for everything / Inside / Play in time / Sossity; you're a woman. *(cd-iss.Jun87)*

May 70. (7") **INSIDE. / ALIVE AND WELL AND LIVING IN** [ ] [-]

Jul 70. (7") **INSIDE. / A TIME FOR EVERYTHING** [-] [ ]

—— **JEFFREY HAMMOND-HAMMOND** – bass repl. CORNICK who formed WILD TURKEY

Mar 71. (lp)(c) **AQUALUNG** [4] [7] Apr 71
– Aqualung / Cross-eyed mary / Cheap day return / Mother goose / Wond'ring aloud / Up to me / My God / Hymn £43 / Slipstream / Locomotive breath / Wind-up. *(re-iss.Jan74, cd-iss.1988) (re-iss.cd Mar94)*

Jul 71. (7") **HYMN £43. / MOTHER GOOSE** [-] [91]

—— **ANDERSON, BARRE, HAMMOND-HAMMOND** and **EVAN** were joined by **BARRIEMORE BARLOW** – drums (ex-JOHN EVANS' SMASH) who repl. BUNKER who joined BLODWYN PIG

Sep 71. (7"ep) **LIFE IS A LONG SONG. / UP THE POOL / DR. BOGENBROOM / FOR LATER / NURSIE** [11] [-]

Oct 71. (7") **LOCOMOTIVE BREATH. / WIND** [-] [ ]

Chrysalis Reprise

Mar 72. (lp)(c) **THICK AS A BRICK** [5] [1] May 72
– Thick as a brick (side 1) / Thick as a brick (side 2). *(re-iss.Jan74, cd-iss.1986) (cd-re-Apr89 on 'Mobile Fidelity')*

Apr 72. (7") **THICK AS A BRICK (edit £1). / HYMN £43** [-] [ ]

Chrysalis Chrysalis

Jul 72. (d-lp)(d-c) **LIVING IN THE PAST** (live / studio comp) [8] [3] Nov 72
– By kind permission of / Dharma for one / Wond'ring again / Locomotive breath / Life is a long song / Up the pool / Dr.Bogenbroom / For later / Nursie / A song for Jeffrey / Love story / Christmas song / Teacher / Living in the past / Driving song / Bouree / Sweet dream / Singing all day / Teacher / The witches promise / Inside / Just trying to be. *(cd-iss.Oct87) (re-iss.cd+c Mar94)*

Oct 72. (7") **LIVING IN THE PAST. / ?** [-] [11]

May 73. (7") **A PASSION PLAY (edit £8). / A PASSION PLAY (edit £6)** [-] [80]

Jul 73. (lp)(c) **A PASSION PLAY** [13] [1]
– A passion play (part 1; including 'The story of the hare who lost his spectacles' part 1)- /- (part 2) / A passion play (part 2). *(cd-iss.Jan89)*

Aug 73. (7") **A PASSION PLAY (edit £9). / A PASSION PLAY (edit £10)** [-] [ ]

Oct 74. (7") **BUNGLE IN THE JUNGLE. / BACK DOOR ANGEL** [ ] [12]

Oct 74. (lp)(c) **WAR CHILD** [14] [2]
– War child / Queen and country / Ladies / Back-door angels / Sea lion / Skating away on the thin ice of a new day / Bungle in the jungle / Only solitaire / The third hooray / Two fingers.

Jan 74. (7") **SKATING AWAY ON THE THIN ICE OF A NEW DAY. / SEA LION** [-] [ ]

Sep 75. (lp)(c) **MINSTREL IN THE GALLERY** [20] [7]
– Minstrel in the gallery / Cold wind to Valhalla / Black satin dancer / Requiem / One white duck / 0x10 = Nothing at all – Baker St. Muse (including Pig-me and the whore – Nice little tune – Crash barrier waltzer – Mother England reverie) / Grace. *(cd-iss.1986)*

Oct 75. (7") **MINSTREL IN THE GALLERY. / SUMMER DAY SANDS** [ ] [79]

—— **JOHN GLASCOCK** – bass (ex-CHICKEN SHACK, ex-TOE FAT) repl. HAMMOND

Mar 76. (7") **TOO OLD TO ROCK'N'ROLL, TOO YOUNG TO DIE. / RAINBOW BLUES** [ ] [-]

Mar 76. (lp)(c) **TOO OLD TO ROCK'N'ROLL, TOO YOUNG TO DIE** [25] [14] May 76
– Quizz kid / Crazed institution / Salamander / Taxi grab / From a dead beat to an old greaser / Bad-eyed and loveless / Big dipper / Too old to rock'n'roll, too young to die / Pied piper / The chequered flag (dead or alive).

Apr 76. (7") **TOO OLD TO ROCK'N'ROLL, TOO YOUNG TO DIE. / BAD- EYED AND LOVELESS** [-] [ ]

—— added **DAVID PALMER** – keyboards (He had been their past orchestrator)

Nov 76. (7"ep) **RING OUT, SOLSTICE BELLS. / MARCH THE MAD SCIENTIST / A CHRISTMAS SONG / PAN DANCE** [28] [-]
(re-iss.Dec79)

Jan 77. (7") **THE WHISTLER. / STRIP CARTOON** [ ] [59] Apr 77

Feb 77. (lp)(c) **SONGS FROM THE WOOD** [13] [8]
– Songs from the wood / Jack-in-the-green / Cup of wonder / Hunting girl / Ring out, solstice bells / Velvet green / The whistler / Pibroch (cap in hand) / Fire at midnight. *(cd-iss.1986)*

Apr 78. (7") **MOTHS. / LIFE IS A LONG SONG** [ ] [-]

Apr 78. (lp)(c) **HEAVY HORSES** [20] [19]
– . . .And the mouse police never sleeps / Acres wild / No lullaby / Moths / Journeyman / Rover / One brown mouse / Heavy horses / Weathercock. *(cd-*

iss.1986)

Nov 78. (7")(7"white) **A STITCH IN TIME. / SWEET DREAM (live)** [ ] [-]

Nov 78. (d-lp)(c) **LIVE-BURSTING OUT** [17] [21] Oct 78
– No lullaby / Sweet dream / Skating away on the thin ice of a new day / Jack-in-the-green / One brown mouse / A new day yesterday / Flute solo improvisation – God rest ye merry gentlemen / Bouree / Songs from the wood / Thick as a brick / Hunting girl / Too old to rock'n'roll, too young to die / Conundrum / Cross-eyed Mary / Quatrain / Aqualung / Locomotive breath / The dambuster's march -medley. *(cd-iss.1990)*

Sep 79. (7") **NORTH SEA OIL. / ELEGY** [ ] [ ]

Sep 79. (lp)(c) **STORMWATCH** [27] [22]
– North Sea oil / Orion / Home / Dark ages / Warm sporran / Something's on the move / Old ghosts / Dun Ringill / Flying Dutchman / Elegy. *(cd-iss.Jan89)*

Nov 79. (7"ep) **HOME / RING OUT, SOLSTICE BELLS. / WARM SPORRAN / KING HENRY'S MADRIGAL** [ ] [-]

Nov 79. (7") **HOME. / WARM SPORRAN** [-] [ ]

— ANDERSON for what was supposed to be a solo album retained **BARRE** / plus new **DAVE PEGG** – bass (ex-FAIRPORT CONVENTION) repl. GLASCOCK who died. / **EDDIE JOBSON** – keyboards (ex-ROXY MUSIC, ex-CURVED AIR, etc) repl. EVANS and PALMER who took up session work / **MARK CRANEY** – drums repl. BARLOW who went solo.

Aug 80. (lp)(c) **"A"** [25] [30] Sep 80
– Crossfire / Fylingdale flyer / Working John, working Joe / Black Sunday / Protect and survive / Batteries not included / 4.W.D. (low ratio) / The Pine Marten's jig / And further on.

— **PETER JOHN VITESSE** – keyboards repl. JOBSON who went solo / **GERRY CONWAY** – drums (ex-STEELEYE SPAN) repl. CRANEY

Apr 82. (lp)(c) **BROADSWORD AND THE BEAST** [27] [19] May 82
– Beastie / Clasp / Fallen on hard times / Flying colours / Slow marching band / Broadsword / Pussy willow / Watching me watching you / Seal driver / Cheerio.

May 82. (7")(7"pic-d) **BROADSWORD. / FALLEN ON HARD TIMES** [ ] [-]

May 82. (7") **PUSSY WILLOW. / FALLEN ON HARD TIMES** [-] [ ]

— **DOANNE PERRY** – drums repl. CONWAY

Sep 84. (lp)(c)(cd) **UNDER WRAPS** [18] [76]
– Lap of luxury / Under wraps I / European legacy / Later that same evening / Saboteur / Radio free Moscow / Nobody's car / Heat / Under wraps II / Paperazzi / Apogee. *(c+=)(cd+=)*– Automatic engineering / Astronomy / Tundra / General crossing.

Sep 84. (7") **LAP OF LUXURY. / ASTRONOMY** [70] [ ]
(d7"+=)(12"+=) – Tundra / Automatic engineering.

Jun 86. (7") **CORONIACH. / JACK FROST AND THE HOODED CROW** [ ] [ ]
(12"+=) – Living in the past.

— **ANDERSON, BARRE, PEGG** and **PERRY** recruited new member **MARTIN ALLCOCK** – keyboards (ex-FAIRPORT CONVENTION) repl. VITESSE

Sep 87. (lp)(c)(cd) **CREST OF A KNAVE** [19] [32]
– Steel monkey / Farm on the freeway / Jump start / Said she was a dancer / Dogs in midwinter * / Budapest / Mountain men / The waking edge * / Raising steam. *(cd+= *)*

Oct 87. (7")(7"pic-d) **STEEL MONKEY. / DOWN AT THE END OF YOUR ROAD** [ ] [ ]
(12"+=)(c-s+=) – Too many too / I'm your gun.

Dec 87. (7")(7"pic-d) **SAID SHE WAS A DANCER. / DOGS IN MIDWINTER** [55] [ ]
(12"+=) – The waking edge.
(cd-s+=) – Down at the end of your road / Too many too.

Aug 89. (lp)(c)(cd) **ROCK ISLAND** [18] [56]
– Kissing Willie / The rattlesnake trail / Ears of tin / Undressed to kill / Rock Island / Heavy water / Another Christmas song / The whalers dues / Big Riff and Mando / Strange avenues.

Aug 89. (c-s) **KISSING WILLIE. / EARS OF TIN** [-] [ ]

Nov 89. (7") **ANOTHER CHRISTMAS SONG. / SOLSTICE BELLS** [ ] [ ]
(12"+=) – Jack Frost.
(cd-s) – ('A'side) / -A Christmas song (live) / Cheap day return (live) / Mother goose (live) / Locomotive breath (live).

— **ANDY GIDLINGS** – keyboards (3) / **MATT PEGG** – bass (3) / etc. repl. ALLCOCK

Aug 91. (7")(c-s) **THIS IS NOT LOVE. / NIGHT IN THE WILDERNESS** [ ] [ ]
(12"+=)(cd-s+=) – Jump start (live).

Sep 91. (cd)(c)(lp) **CATFISH RISING** [27] [88]
– This is not love / Occasional demons / Rocks on the road / Thinking round corners / Still loving you tonight / Doctor to my disease / Like a tall thin gin / Sparrow on the schoolyard wall / Roll yer own / Goldtipped boots, black jacket and tie. (free 12"ep) **WHEN JESUS CAME TO PLAY. / SLEEPING WITH THE DOG / WHITE INNOCENCE**

— **DAVID MATTACKS** – drums, percussion, keyboards repl. PERRY and guests

Mar 92. (7") **ROCKS ON THE ROAD. / JACK-A-LYNN** [47] [ ]
(cd-s+=)/ /(cd-s++=) – Mother goose./ / Bouree.
(c-s+=)(cd-s+=) – Tall thin god / Fat man.
(12"pic-d+=) – Aqualung / Locomotive breath.

Sep 92. (cd)(c)(d-lp) **A LITTLE LIGHT MUSIC (live in Europe '92)** [34] [ ]
– Someday the Sun won't shine for you / Living in the past / Life is a long song / Under wraps / Rocks on the road / Nursie / Too old to rock and roll, too young to die / One white duck / A new day yesterday / John Barleycorn / Look into the Sun / A Christmas song / From a dead beat to an old greaser / This is not love / Bouree / Pussy willow / Locomotive breath.

— **PERRY** returned to repl.MATTACKS. Bass playing was provided by **DAVE PEGG / STEVE BAILEY**

Sep 95. (cd)(c) **ROOTS TO BRANCHES** [20] [ ]
– Roots to branches / Rare and precious chain / Out of the noise / This free will / Wounded, old and reacherous / Dangerous veils / Beside myself / Valley / At last, forever / Stuck in the August rain / Another Harry's bar.

- compilations, others, etc. -

Jan 76. Chrysalis; (7") **LIVING IN THE PAST. / REQUIEM** [ ] [ ]

Jan 76. Chrysalis; (lp)(c) **M.U. – THE BEST OF JETHRO TULL** [44] [13]
– Teacher / Aqualung / Thick as a brick (edit £1) / Bungle in the jungle / Locomotive breath / Fat man / Living in the past / A passion play (£8) / Skating away on the thin ice of a new day / Rainbow blues / Nothing is easy. *(re-iss.+cd.Dec85)*

Feb 76. Chrysalis; (7") **LOCOMOTIVE BREATH. /** [-] [62]

Nov 77. Chrysalis; (lp)(c) **REPEAT – THE BEST OF JETHRO TULL VOL.2** [ ] [94]
– Minstrel in the gallery / Cross-eyed Mary / A new day yesterday / Bouree / Thick as a brick (edit £1) / War child / A passion play (edit £9) / To cry you a song / Too old to rock'n'roll, too young to die / Glory row. *(cd-iss.Apr86)*

Dec 82. Chrysalis; (d-c) **M.U. / REPEAT** [ ] [ ]

Oct 85. Chrysalis; (lp)(c)(cd) **ORIGINAL MASTERS** [63] [ ]

Jun 88. Chrysalis; (5xlp-box)(3xc-box)(3xcd-box) **20 YEARS OF JETHRO TULL** [78] [97]
– THE RADIO ARCHIVES:- A song for Jeffrey / Love story * / Fat man / Bouree / Stormy Monday blues * / A new day yesterday * / Cold wind to Valhalla / Minstrel in the gallery / Velvet green / Grace * / The clasp / / Pibroch (pee-break) – Black satin dancer (instrumental) * / Fallen on hard times // THE RARE TRACKS:- Jack Frost and the hooded crow / I'm your gun / Down at the end of your road / Coronach * / Summerday sands * / Too many too / March the mad scientist * / Pan dance / Strip cartoon / King Henry's madrigal / A stitch in time / 17 / One for John Gee / Aeroplane / Sunshine day // FLAWED GEMS:- Lick your fingers clean * / The Chateau Disaster Tapes: Scenario – Audition – No reheasal / Beltane / Crossword * / Saturation * / Jack-A-Lynn * / Motoreyes * / Blues instrumental (untitled) / Rhythm in gold // THE OTHER SIDES OF TULL:- Part of the machine * / Mayhem, maybe * / Overhang * / Kelpie * / Living in these hard times / Under wraps II * / Only solitaire / Cheap day return / Wond'ring aloud * / Dun Ringill * / Salamander / Moths / Nursie * / Life is a long song * / One white duck – 0x10 = Nothing at all // THE ESSENTIAL TULL:- Songs from the wood / Living in the past * / Teacher * / Aqualung * / Locomotive breath * / The witches promise * / Bungle in the jungle / Farm on the freeway / Thick as a brick / Sweet dream. *(re-iss.Aug88 as d-lp/d-c/d-cd; tracks *)*

Apr 93. Chrysalis; (4xcd-box) **25th ANNIVERSARY BOXED SET** [ ] [ ]
REMIXED (CLASSIC SONGS) / CARNEGIE HALL N.Y. (RECORDED LIVE NEW YORK CITY 1970) / THE BEACON'S BOTTOM (TAPES) / POT POURRI (LIVE ACROSS THE WORLD AND THROUGH THE YEARS)

May 93. Chrysalis; (7") **LIVING IN THE PAST. / HARD LINER** [32] [ ]
(12") – ('A'side) / ('A'mix).
(cd-s) – ('A'side) / Truck stop runner / Piece of cake / Man of principle.
(cd-s) – Living in the (slightly more recent) past / Silver river turning / Rosa on the factory floor / I don't want to be me.

May 93. Chrysalis; (d-cd)(d-c) **THE VERY BEST OF JETHRO TULL – THE ANNIVERSARY COLLECTION** [ ] [ ]
– A song for Jeffrey / Beggar's farm / A Christmas song / A new day yesterday / Bouree / Nothing is easy / Living in the past / To cry you a song / Teacher / Sweet dream / Cross-eyed Mary / Mother goose / Aqualung / Locomotive breath / Life is a long song / Thick as a brick (extract) / Skating away on the thin ice of a new day / Bungle in the jungle/ / Minstrel in the gallery / Too old to rock'n'roll / Songs from the wood / Jack in the green / The whistler / Heavy horses / Dun Ringill / Fylingdale flyer / Jack-a-Lynn / Pussy willow / Broadsword / Under wraps II / Steel monkey / Farm on the freeway / Jump start / Kissing Willie / This is not love.

Nov 93. Chrysalis; (d-cd) **NIGHTCAP – THE UNRELEASED MASTERS 1972-1991** [ ] [ ]
– CHATEAU D'ISASTER – First post / Animelee / Tiger Moon / Look at the animals / Law of the bungle part II / Left right / Solitaire / Critique oblique / Post last / Scenario / Audition / No rehearsal/ / UNRELEASED & RARE TRACKS – Paradise steakhouse / Sealion II / Piece of cake / Quartet / Silver river turning / Crew nights / The curse / Rosa on the factory floor / A small cigar / Man of principle / Commons brawl / No step / Drive on the young side of life / I don't want to be me / Broadford bazaar / Lights out / Truck stop runner / Hard liner.

Aug 87. Old Gold; (7") **LIVING IN THE PAST. / THE WITCHES' PROMISE** [ ] [-]

Jan 91. Raw Fruit; (cd)(c)(lp) **LIVE AT HAMMERSMITH 1984 (live)** [ ] [-]

Apr 95. Winsong; (cd) **IN CONCERT (live)** [ ] [-]

IAN ANDERSON

solo album augmented by **PETER JOHN VITESSE** – synth, keyboards

Chrysalis Chrysalis

Nov 83. (7") **FLY BY NIGHT. / END GAME** [ ] [ ]

Nov 83. (lp)(c) **WALK INTO LIGHT** [78] [ ]

– Fly by night / Made in England / Walk into light / Trains / End game / Black and white television / Toad in the hole / Looking for Eden / User-friendly / Different Germany.

Billy JOEL

Born: WILLIAM MARTIN JOEL, 9 May'49, The Bronx, New York, USA. In 1965 he played piano in first group The ECHOES, having been a welter-weight boxing champ for local Hicksville, Long Island boys' club. In 1967 he joined The HASSLES who signed to 'United Art' and released 2 lp's, after initial SAM & DAVE cover version 45 'YOU GOT ME HUMMIN''. In 1969, JOEL became a rock critic for 'Changes' art-magazine and formed own hard-rock duo ATTILA with JON SMALL. They issued one 1970 album for 'Epic', before disbanding. JOEL then suffered bout of depression and entered Meadowbrook mental hospital, with psychiatric problems. In 1971 he was back in circulation to sign a solo contract with Family Productions' Artie Ripp (alledgedly known as 'Ripp-off' to his employees, due to his large percentage of artist royalties). JOEL's debut lp 'COLD SPRING HARBOR' was soon issued but, due to mixing fault, was pressed at the wrong speed!! Embarrassingly for JOEL, who had been well-received by live audiences, it hit shops without being corrected, and it made him sound slightly Chipmunk-ish. He moved to Los Angeles, and soon married ex-wife of JON SMALL; Elizabeth Weber. In 1973, he got deserved break with 'Columbia', after his 'CAPTAIN JACK' track was played on FM radio. The following year, his acclaimed 2nd lp 'PIANO MAN' made US Top 30, as did its title track. He went from strength to strenth from then on, becoming major US star during next 15 or so years. In 1989, he had his 3rd US No.1 with 'WE DIDN'T START THE FIRE', which was taken from top album 'STORM FRONT'. **Style & Songwriters:** Influenced in early teens by BEETHOVEN and The BEATLES, he went on to write own story-telling ballads or uptempo rock'n'roll numbers, which were similar to The FOUR SEASONS or DION. Covered: BACK IN THE USSR (Beatles) / THE TIMES THEY ARE A CHANGIN' (Bob Dylan) / LIGHT AS THE BREEZE (Leonard Cohen) / and a few more. • **Trivia:** Divorced from his wife in Jul'82, he soon married supermodel and star of his 'UPTOWN GIRL' promo video; Christine Brinkley. In 1989, he fired his manager ex-brother-in-law Frank Weber, after an audit of the accounts showed nearly $100 million missing. The following year, JOEL was awarded $2 million by the courts, and a countersuit by Weber for $30 million was thrown out.

Recommended: THE STRANGER (*8) / GREATEST HITS VOLUMES 1&2 (*7)

The HASSLES

BILLY JOEL – piano / **JOHN DIZEK** – vocals / **RICHARD McKENNAR** – guitar / **HOWARD BLAUVELT** – bass / **JONATHAN SMALL** – drums

		United Art	United Art	
1968.	(7") **YOU GOT ME HUMMIN'. / I'M THINKIN'**			
1968.	(7") **EVERY STEP I TAKE (EVERY MOVE I MAKE). / I HEAR VOICES**	-		

—— Released 2 lp's 'THE HASSLES' and 'HOUR OF THE WOLF' in US.

1968.	(7") **4 O' CLOCK IN THE MORNING. / LET ME BRING YOU SUNSHINE**	-		
1969.	(7") **NIGHT AFTER DAY. / COUNTRY BOY**	-		
1969.	(7") **GREAT BALLS OF FIRE. / TRAVELIN' BAND**	-		

ATTILA

was formed by JOEL and SMALL.

		not issued	Epic	
1970.	(lp) **ATTILA**	-		

– Wonder woman / California flash / Revenge is sweet / Amplifier fire: part 1 – Godzilla, part 2 – March of the Huns / Rollin' home / Tear this castle down / Holy Moses / Brain invasion. *(cd-iss.Apr93 on 'Sony Europe')*

BILLY JOEL

went solo, and many session people

		Philips	Family	
May 72.	(7") **SHE'S GOT A WAY. / EVERYBODY LOVE YOU NOW**			
Jun 72.	(lp)(c) **COLD SPRING HARBOUR**			Nov 71

– She's got a way / You can make me free / Everybody loves you now / Why Judy why / Falling of the rain / Turn around / You look so good to me / Tomorrow is today / Nocturne / Got to begin again. *(re-iss.& re-mixed Jan84 on 'CBS', hit 95 UK)*

Jan 73.	(7") **TOMORROW IS TODAY. / EVERYBODY LOVES YOU NOW**	-		
Apr 74.	(7") **THE BALLAD OF BILLY THE KID. / IF I ONLY HAD THE WORDS (TO TELL YOU)**			

—— Stage band around this time were **DON EVANS** – guitar / **PAT McDONALD** – bass / **TOM WHITEHORSE** – steel guitar, banjo / **RHYS CLARK** – drums

		C.B.S.	Columbia	
Jun 74.	(7") **WORSE COMES TO THE WORST. / SOMEWHERE ALONG THE LINE**	-	80	
Aug 74.	(7") **TRAVELIN' PRAYER. / AIN'T NO CRIME**	-	77	
Apr 75.	(lp)(c) **PIANO MAN**		27	Nov 73

– Travelin' prayer / Piano man / Ain't no crime / You're my home / The ballad of Billy The Kid / Worse comes to the worst / Stop in Nevada / If I only had the words (to tell you) / Somewhere along the line / Captain Jack. *(re-iss.Mar81, re-iss.Jun84, hit 98 UK) (cd-iss.Sep85 & Apr89) (also US iss.quad)*

—— (above should have been released May74 by 'Philips' but withdrawn)

Nov 74.	(7") **THE ENTERTAINER. / THE MEXICAN CONNECTION**	-	34	
Apr 75.	(7") **PIANO MAN. / YOU'RE MY HOME**		25	Feb 74
Sep 75.	(7") **IF I ONLY HAD THE WORDS (TO TELL YOU). / STOP IN NEVADA**		-	
Jul 75.	(lp)(c) **STREETLIFE SERENADE**		35	Nov 74

– Streetlife serenader / Los Angelenos / The great suburban showdown / Root beer rag / Roberta / Last of the big time spenders / Weekend song / Souvenir / The Mexican connection. *(re-iss.Jul78, re-iss.Mar81) (cd-iss.Mar87) (re-iss.cd+c May94 on 'Columbia')*

—— band now incl. **NIGEL OLSSON + DEE MURRAY** (both ex-ELTON JOHN)

Jul 76.	(lp)(c) **TURNSTILES**			Jun 76

– Say goodbye to Hollywood / Summer, Highland falls / All you wanna do is dance / New York state of mind / James / Prelude / Angry young man / I've loved these days / Miami 2017 (seen the lights go on Broadway). *(re-iss.Nov81) (cd-iss.Mar87) (c+cd-iss.Nov89 on 'Pickwick') (re-iss.cd Sep93 'Sony Collectors')*

Jul 76.	(7") **SUMMER, HIGHLAND FALLS. / JAMES**	-		
Oct 76.	(7") **I'VE LOVED THESE DAYS. / SAY GOODBYE TO HOLLYWOOD**	-		
Nov 76.	(7") **SAY GOODBYE TO HOLLYWOOD. / STOP IN NEVADA** *(re-iss.Feb77)*			
Sep 77.	(7") **MOVIN' OUT (ANTHONY'S SONG). / SHE'S ALWAYS A WOMAN**	-		
Dec 77.	(lp)(c) **THE STRANGER**	25	2	Oct 77

– Movin' out (Anthony's song) / The stranger / Just the way you are / Scenes from an Italian restaurant / Vienna / Only the good die young / She's always a woman / Get it right the first time / Everybody has a dream. *(re-iss.Nov80 & May87) (cd-iss.Dec85 & Jun89)*

Jan 78.	(7") **JUST THE WAY YOU ARE. / GET IT RIGHT THE FIRST TIME** *(re-iss.May82)*	19	3	Nov 77
Mar 78.	(7") **MOVIN' OUT (ANTHONY'S SONG). / EVERYBODY HAS A DREAM**	-	17	
Apr 78.	(7") **SHE'S ALWAYS A WOMAN. / EVERYBODY HAS A DREAM**		-	
May 78.	(7") **ONLY THE GOOD DIE YOUNG. / GET IT RIGHT THE FIRST TIME**	-	24	
Jun 78.	(7") **MOVIN' OUT (ANTHONY'S SONG). / VIENNA**	35	-	
Aug 78.	(7") **SHE'S ALWAYS A WOMAN. / VIENNA**	-	17	
Nov 78.	(lp)(c) **52nd STREET**	10	1	Oct 78

– Big shot / Honesty / My life / Zanzibar / Stiletto / Rosalind's eyes / Half a mile away / Until the night / 52nd Street. *(re-iss.Nov85, cd-iss.Nov87) (re-iss.cd/c Mar93 + Feb95 on 'Columbia')*

Nov 78.	(7") **MY LIFE. / 52nd STREET**	12	3	
Feb 79.	(7") **BIG SHOT. / ROOT BEER BAG**	-	14	
Mar 79.	(7") **UNTIL THE NIGHT. / ROOT BEER RAG**	50	-	
Jun 79.	(7") **HONESTY. / THE MEXICAN CONNECTION**		24	Apr 79
Feb 80.	(7") **SOUVENIR. / ALL FOR LENYA**	-		
Mar 80.	(lp)(c) **GLASS HOUSES**	9	1	

– You may be right / Sometimes a fantasy / Don't ask me why / It's still rock'n'roll to me / All for Lenya / I don't want to be alone / Sleeping with the television on / C'Etait toi (you were the one) / Close to the borderline / Through the long night. *(re-iss.+cd.Nov86) (cd-iss.Mar91) (re-iss.cd+c May94 on 'Columbia')*

Mar 80.	(7") **ALL FOR LEYNA. / CLOSE TO THE BORDERLINE**	40	-	
Mar 80.	(7") **YOU MAY BE RIGHT. / CLOSE TO THE BORDERLINE**	-	7	
May 80.	(7") **YOU MAY BE RIGHT. / THROUGH THE LONG NIGHT**		-	
Jul 80.	(7") **IT'S STILL ROCK'N'ROLL TO ME. / THROUGH THE LONG NIGHT**	14	1	May 80
Oct 80.	(7") **DON'T ASK ME WHY. / C'ETAIT TOI (YOU WERE THE ONE)**		19	Aug 80
Oct 80.	(7") **SOMETIMES A FANTASY. / ALL FOR LEYNA**	-	36	
Jan 81.	(7") **SOMETIMES A FANTASY. / SLEEPING WITH THE TELEVISION ON**		-	
Sep 81.	(7") **SAY GOODBYE TO HOLLYWOOD (live). / SUMMER, HIGHLAND FALLS (live)**		17	
Sep 81.	(lp)(c) **SONGS IN THE ATTIC (live)**	57	8	

– Miami 2017 (seen the lights go out on Broadway) / Summer, Highland Falls / Streetlife serenader / Los Angelenos / She's got a way / Everybody loves you now / Say goodbye to Hollywood / Captain Jack / You're my home / The ballad of Billy The Kid / I've loved these days. *(re-iss.Nov83, cd-iss.May87 & Jun89) (re-iss.cd Jan94 on 'Sony Europe')*

Nov 81. (7") **YOU'RE MY HOME (live). / THE BALLAD OF BILLY THE KID (live)** [ ] [-]
Jan 82. (7") **SHE'S GOT A WAY (live). / THE BALLAD OF BILLY THE KID (live)** [ ] [23] Nov 81
Sep 82. (7") **PRESSURE. / LAURA** [ ] [20]
Sep 82. (lp)(c) **THE NYLON CURTAIN** [27] [7]
– Allentown / Laura / Pressure / Goodnight Saigon / She's right on time / A room on your own / Surprises / Scandinavian skies / Pressure / Where's the orchestra. *(cd-iss.Jan83) (lp re-iss.Mar88)*
Nov 82. (7") **ALLENTOWN. / ELVIS PRESLEY BOULEVARD** [ ] [17]
Feb 83. (7") **GOODNIGHT SAIGON. / WHERE'S THE ORCHESTRA** [ ] [-]
Feb 83. (7") **GOODNIGHT SAIGON. / A ROOM OF OUR OWN** [-] [56]
Aug 83. (7") **TELL HER ABOUT IT. / EASY MONEY** [ ] [1] Jul 83
Sep 83. (lp)(c) **AN INNOCENT MAN** [2] [4] Aug 83
– Easy money / An innocent man / The longest time / This night / Tell her about it / Uptown girl / Careless talk / Christie Lee / Leave a tender moment alone / Keeping the faith. *(cd-iss.Aug84)*
Oct 83. (7") **UPTOWN GIRL. / CARELESS TALK** [1] [3] Sep 83
(12"+=) – Just the way you are / It's still rock'n'roll to me.
Dec 83. (7") **TELL HER ABOUT IT. / EASY MONEY** [4] [-]
(12"+=) – You got me hummin' (live).
Dec 83. (7") **AN INNOCENT MAN. / I'LL CRY INSTEAD** [-] [10]
Feb 84. (7") **AN INNOCENT MAN. / YOU'RE MY HOME (live)** [8] [ ]
(12"+=) – She's always a woman / Until the night.
Apr 84. (7") **THE LONGEST TIME. / CHRISTIE LEE** [25] [14] Mar 84
(12"+=) – Captain Jack (live) / The ballad of Billy the kid (live).
Jun 84. (7") **LEAVE A TENDER MOMENT ALONE. / GOODNIGHT SAIGON** [29] [-]
(12"+=) – Movin' out (Anthony's song) / Big shot / You may be right.
Jul 84. (7") **LEAVE A TENDER MOMENT ALONE. / THIS NIGHT** [-] [27]
Nov 84. (7") **THIS NIGHT. / I'LL CRY INSTEAD (live)** [ ] [ ]
Jan 85. (7") **KEEPING THE FAITH. / SHE'S RIGHT ON TIME** [-] [18]

—— featured on the 'USA for AFRICA' single 'WE ARE THE WORLD'.

Jun 85. (7") **YOU'RE ONLY HUMAN. / SURPRISES** [ ] [9]
(12"+=) – Keeping the faith / Scenes from an Italian restaurant.
Oct 85. (7") **THE NIGHT IS STILL YOUNG. / SUMMER, HIGHLAND FALLS** [ ] [34]
Jul 86. (7") **MODERN WOMAN. / SLEEPING WITH THE TELEVISION ON** [ ] [10] Jun 86
(d7"+=) – Uptown girl / All for love.
(12"+=) – The night is still young / You're only human.
Aug 86. (lp)(c)(cd) **THE BRIDGE** [38] [7]
– Running on ice / This is the time / A matter of trust / Modern woman / Baby grand (w/ RAY CHARLES) / Big man on Mulberry Street / Temptation / Code of silence (w/ CYNDI LAUPER) / Getting closer. *(re-iss.Oct89) (re-iss.cd+c Feb94 on 'Columbia')*
Sep 86. (7") **A MATTER OF TRUST. / GETTING CLOSER** [52] [10] Aug 86
(12"+=) – An innocent man / Tell her about it.
Nov 86. (7") **THIS IS THE TIME. / CODE OF SILENCE** [-] [18] Dec 86
Mar 87. (7") **BABY GRAND. / BIG MAN ON MULBERRY STREET** [-] [75]
Nov 87. (d-lp)(c)(cd) **KOHYEPT – LIVE IN LENINGRAD (live)** [92] [38]
– Odoya / Angry young man / Honesty / Goodnight Saigon / Stiletto / Big man on Mulberry Street / Baby grand / An innocent man / Allentown / A matter of trust / Only the good die young / Sometimes a fantasy / Uptown girl / Big shot / Back in the U.S.S.R. / The times they are a-changin'.
Nov 87. (7") **BACK IN THE U.S.S.R. (live). / BIG SHOT (live)** [ ] [ ]
(12"+=)(cd-s+=) – A matter of trust (live) / The times they are a-changin' (live).
Feb 88. (7") **THE TIMES THEY ARE A-CHANGIN' (live). / BACK IN THE U.S.S.R. (live)** [-] [ ]

—— new band **MINDY JOSTIN** – rhythm guitar, violin, harp / **DAVID BROWN** – guitar / **MARK RIVIERA** – sax / **LIBERTY DeVITO** – drums / **SCHUYLER DEALE** – bass / **JEFF JACOBS** – synthesizers / **CRYSTAL TALIEFERO** – vocals, percussion

Sep 89. (7")(c-s) **WE DIDN'T START THE FIRE. / HOUSE OF BLUE LIGHT** [7] [1] Oct 89
(12"+=)(cd-s+=) – Just the way you are.
Oct 89. (lp)(c)(cd) **STORM FRONT** [5] [1]
– That's not her style / We didn't start the fire / The downeaster "Alexa" / I go to extremes / Shameless / Storm front / Leningrad / State of Grace / When in Rome / And so it goes.
Dec 89. (7")(c-s) **LENINGRAD. /** [53] [-]
(12"+=)(cd-s+=) –
Mar 90. (7")(c-s) **I GO TO EXTREMES. / WHEN IN ROME** [70] [6] Jan 90
(12"+=)(cd-s+=) – Uptown girl / All for Leyna.
(c-ep+=) – Prelude / Angry young man / Tell her about it / Leave a tender moment alone.
May 90. (7")(c-s) **DOWNCASTER ALEXA. / AND SO IT GOES / STREETLIFE SERENADE** [ ] [ ]
(12"+=) – I've loved these days / An innocent man.
(pic-cd-s+=) – Say goodbye to Hollywood / Allentown / Only the good die young.
Oct 90. (7"ep)(cd-ep) **THAT'S NOT HER STYLE / WE DIDN'T START THE FIRE / UNTIL THE NIGHT / JUST THE WAY YOU ARE** [ ] [ ] Jul 90
Sep 90. (c-s) **THAT'S NOT HER STYLE. / AND SO IT GOES** [-] [ ]
Oct 90. (c-s) **AND SO IT GOES. / THE DOWNEASTER ALEXA / SHAMELESS / STATES OF GRACE** [-] [37]
Jan 91. (c-s) **SHAMELESS. / STORM FRONT (live)** [-] [ ]

—— (below from film 'Honeymoon In Las Vegas' on 'Epic records')

Aug 92. (7")(c-s) **ALL SHOOK UP. / ('b' side by Ricky Van Shelton)** [27] [92]
(cd-s+=) – other artist

other musicians; **DAN KORTCHMAR, TOMMY BYRNES, LESLIE WEST** – guitar / **T.H. STEVENS, LONNIE HILLER** – bass / **STEVE JORDAN, ZACHARY ALFORD, LIBERTY DeVITTO** – drums.

Jul 93. (7")(c-s) **THE RIVER OF DREAMS. / NO MAN'S LAND** [3] [3]
(cd-s+=) The great wall of China
Aug 93. (cd)(c)(lp) **RIVER OF DREAMS** [3] [1]
– No man's land / The great wall of China / Blonde over blue / A minor variation / Shades of grey / All about soul / Lullabye (goodnight, my angel) / The river of dreams / Two thousand years / Famous last words.
Oct 93. (c-s) **ALL ABOUT SOUL (Radio Edit) / YOU PICKED A REAL BAD TIME** [32] [29]
Feb 94. (7")(c-s) **NO MAN'S ISLAND. / SHADES OF GREY (live)** [50] [ ]
(cd-s+=) – ('A'mix).
Mar 94. (c-s)(cd-s) **LULLABY (GOODNIGHT MY ANGEL) /** [-] [77]

– compilations etc. –

Note; All 'CBS' releases were issued on US counterpart 'Columbia'.

Oct 79. CBS; (3-lp-box) **3-LP BOX SET** [ ] [ ]
– 'TURNSTILES' / 'THE STRANGER' / '52nd STREET'. *(re-iss.Oct80)*
Feb 83. CBS; (7"ep) **GREATEST ORIGINAL HITS** [ ] [ ]
– Just the way you are / Movin' out (Anthony's song) / My life / She's a woman. *(c-iss.Aug82)*
Jul 84. CBS; (7") **JUST THE WAY YOU ARE. / MY LIFE** [ ] [ ]
Jul 85. CBS; (d-lp)(c)(cd) **GREATEST HITS VOL.1 & VOL.2** [7] [6]
– Piano man / Say goodbye to Hollywood / New York state of mind / The stranger / Just the way you are / Movin' out (Anthony's song) / Only the good die young / She's always a woman / My life / Big shot / Honesty / You may be right / It's still rock and roll to me / Pressure / Allentown / Goodnight Saigon / Tell her about it / Uptown girl / The longest time / You're only human (second wind) / The night is still young.
Feb 86. CBS; (7") **SHE'S ALWAYS A WOMAN. / JUST THE WAY YOU ARE** [53] [-]
Jul 87. CBS; (d-lp) **THE STRANGER / AN INNOCENT MAN** [ ] [ ]
1988. CBS; (d-c) **PIANO MAN / STREETLIFE SERENADE** [ ] [ ]
Aug 88. CBS; (3"cd-ep) **IT'S STILL ROCK'N'ROLL TO ME. / JUST THE WAY YOU ARE** [-] [ ]
Nov 91. CBS; (4xcd)(4xc) **THE BILLY JOEL SOUVENIR** [ ] [ ]
– (GREATEST HITS VOL.1 & 2 / STORM FRONT / LIVE AT THE YANKEE STADIUM plus 50 minute interview)
Sep 92. Columbia; (d-cd) **THE BRIDGE / GLASS HOUSES** [ ] [ ]
Mar 93. Columbia; (d-cd) **AN INNOCENT MAN / THE STRANGER** [ ] [ ]
(re-iss.Feb95)
1980. Columbia; (7") **DOWN IN THE BOONDOCKS. / 21ST CENTURY MAN** [-] [ ]
Apr 86. Showcase; (lp)(c) **CALIFORNIA FLASH** [ ] [-]

David JOHANSEN (see under ⇒ NEW YORK DOLLS)

Elton JOHN

Born: REGINALD KENNETH DWIGHT, 25 Mar'47, Pinner, Middlesex, England. After learning piano at an early age, he attained scholarship from Royal Academy Of Music. In the early 60's, he joined BLUESOLOGY, and by 1965 wrote first 45 'COME BACK BABY' for 'Fontana'. They toured in the UK as back-up to American acts (i.e. MAJOR LANCE, The BLUE BELLES with PATTI LaBELLE, etc). Late in 1966, the band were joined by 5 others including singer LONG JOHN BALDRY, who virtually took over show, much to the dislike of the young REG DWIGHT. In 1967, he left BLUESOLOGY and auditioned for 'Liberty', but after failure he found other writer BERNIE TAUPIN (b.22 May'50, Lincolnshire). They wrote LONG JOHN BALDRY's 'B'side 'Lord You Made The Night Too Long', for his UK No.1 'Let The Heartaches Begin'. DWIGHT of course became ELTON

JOHN, taking names from BLUESOLOGY members ELTON DEAN and LONG JOHN BALDRY. In 1968, ELTON and BERNIE joined the Dick James Music Publishing (later D.J.M.) stable, and earned around £10 a week each. With CALEB QUAYE (ex-BLUESOLOGY) on production, ELTON released debut solo single 'I'VE BEEN LOVING YOU TOO LONG' for 'Philips'. Early in '69, he gained needed airplay for 'LADY SAMANTHA', but when this failed, he tried to join KING CRIMSON, but to no avail. The pair now wrote a song for Eurovision song contest 'I CAN'T GO ON LIVING WITHOUT YOU', which was heard but rejected by LULU for eventual winner 'Boom Bang A Bang'. Early in 1969, ELTON signed to 'DJM', and flopped with both 45 'IT'S ME THAT YOU NEED' & lp 'EMPTY SKY'. To make ends meet, ELTON played on HOLLIES 'He Ain't Heavy . . . ' session, and worked for budget labels 'Pickwick' & 'MFP', on some pop covers. In 1970 after more HOLLIES sessions, he released 'BORDER SONG', which when picked up by 'Uni', broke into US Top 100. His eponymous 2nd lp that year hit Top 5 there, and resurrected in the UK made No.11 early 1971. This was mainly brought on by his first UK Top 10 hit 'YOUR SONG', which also peaked into US Top 10. An lp 'TUMBLEWEED CONNECTION' not containing the song, and released late 1970, was the first of many UK & US Top 10 lp's. In 1972, he scored a massive hit with 'ROCKET MAN', and after another summer hit 'HONKY CAT', he had first of 6 US No.1's with 'CROCODILE ROCK'. It took another 18 years for ELTON to clock up first UK solo top spot with 'SACRIFICE', although his duet with KIKI DEE on 'DON'T GO BREAKING MY HEART' made it in 1976. • **Style:** Flashy but talented showman, described early on as 'The Liberace of Rock'. His elaborate over-the-top costumes, and numerous spectacles, slightly detracted from his more serious ballads. In the late 80's, after his 3-year marriage to Renate Blauer had ended in divorce, he turned to alcohol and pills, but happily announced on TV, he was tee-total in 1992. • **Songwriters:** ELTON co-wrote with BERNIE TAUPIN on lyrics for most of career, although between mid-1978 & 1982, co-wrote with lyricist GARY OSBOURNE. ELTON also covered; MY BABY LEFT ME (?) / GET BACK + LUCY IN THE SKY WITH DIAMONDS + I SAW HER STANDING THERE (Beatles; on which ELTON did duet with JOHN LENNON) / PINBALL WIZARD (Who; from the film 'Tommy', in which he featured) / JOHNNY B.GOODE (Chuck Berry) / WHERE HAVE ALL THE GOOD TIMES GONE (Kinks) / I HEARD IT THROUGH THE GRAPEVINE (hit; Marvin Gaye) / I'M YOUR MAN (Leonard Cohen) / etc. • **Trivia:** He was chairman of Watford Football Club between Nov'73 to early 90's, and is still an honourary president. Early in 1986 after a long court battle, he and TAUPIN were given £5 million in back royalties from Dick James' publishers. In Oct'88, ELTON was awarded one million pounds damages after The Sun printed false and libelous stories concerning his sex life.

Recommended: GOODBYE YELLOW BRICK ROAD (*9) / DON'T SHOOT ME I'M ONLY THE PIANO PLAYER (*8) / ELTON JOHN (*8) / BLUE MOVES (*7) / THE VERY BEST OF ELTON JOHN (*8)

BLUESOLOGY

REG DWIGHT – vocals, piano / **STUART BROWN** – guitar, vocals / **REX BISHOP** – bass / **MICK INKPEN** – drums

Fontana / not issued

Jul 65. (7") **COME BACK BABY. / TIME'S GETTING TOUGHER THAN TOUGH** [ ] [-]

Feb 66. (7") **MR.FRANTIC. / EVERYDAT (I HAVE THE BLUES)** [ ] [-]

— added **LONG JOHN BALDRY** – vocals / **CALEB QUAYE** – guitar / **ELTON DEAN** – sax / **PETE GAVIN, NEIL HUBBARD + MARK CHARIG** – wind

Polydor / not iss

Oct 67. (7") **SINCE I FOUND YOU BABY. / JUST A LITTLE BIT** [ ] [-]

ELTON JOHN

(solo) – vocals, piano with session people, incl.**NIGEL OLSSON** (note most of BLUESOLOGY later joined SOFT MACHINE)

Philips / Congress

Mar 68. (7") **I'VE BEEN LOVING YOU TOO LONG. / HERE'S TO THE NEXT TIME** [ ] [-]

Jan 69. (7") **LADY SAMANTHA. / ALL ACROSS THE HEAVENS** [ ] [-]

1969. (7") **LADY SAMANTHA. / IT'S ME THAT YOU NEED** [-] [ ]

1969. (7") **BORDER SONG. / BAD SIDE OF THE MOON** [-] [ ]

— In 1969, ELTON was part of BREAD & BEER BAND, who issued 1 'Decca' single 'THE DICK BARTON THEME. / BREAKDOWN BLUES. (re-iss.1972)

D.J.M. / Uni

May 69. (7") **IT'S ME THAT YOU NEED. / JUST LIKE STRANGE RAIN** [ ] [-]

Jun 69. (lp) **EMPTY SKY** [ ] [ ]
– Empty sky / Valhala / Western Ford gateway / Hymn 2000 / Lady what's tomorrow / Sails / The scaffold / Skyline pigeon / Gulliver – Hay chewed – Reprise. *(re-iss.Nov76, re-iss.May81, US-re-iss.Jan75 reached No.6) (re-iss.+cd.May87 & May95 on 'Rocket')*

— now with band **NIGEL OLSSON** (b.10 Feb'49, Merseyside) – drums / **DEE MURRAY** (b.DAVID MURRAY OATES, 3 Apr'46, Southgate, London) – bass / **CALEB QUAYE** – guitar (ex-BLUESOLOGY)

Mar 70. (7") **BORDER SONG. / BAD SIDE OF THE MOON** [ ] [92] Jul 70

Apr 70. (lp)(c) **ELTON JOHN** [11] [4] Sep 70
– Your song / I need you to turn to / Take me to the pilot / No shoestrings on Louise / First episode at Heinton / Sixty years on / Border song / Greatest discovery / The cage / The king must die. *(re-iss.Nov76, re-iss.May81) (re-iss.+cd Apr87 & May95 on 'Rocket')*

Jun 70. (7") **ROCK AND ROLL MADONNA. / GREY SEAL** [ ] [-]

Oct 70. (lp)(c) **TUMBLEWEED CONNECTION** [6] [5] Jan 71
– Ballad of well-known gun / Come down in time / Country comfort / Son of your father / My father's gun / Where to now St. Peter / Love song / Amoreena / Talking old soldiers / Burn down the mission. *(re-iss.Nov76, re-iss.May81) (re-iss.+cd Apr87 & May95 on 'Rocket')*

Nov 70. (7") **YOUR SONG. / TAKE ME TO THE PILOT** [-] [8]

Jan 71. (7") **YOUR SONG. / INTO THE OLD MAN'S SHOES** [7] [-]

Apr 71. (7") **FRIENDS. / HONEY ROLL** [ ] [34] Mar 71

Apr 71. (lp)(c) **17.11.70 THE ELTON JOHN LIVE ALBUM** [20] [11] May 71
– Take me to the pilot / Honky tonk women / Sixty years on / Can I put you on / Bad side of the Moon / Burn down the mission: My baby left me – Get back. *(re-iss.Mar78 on 'Hallmark') (cd-iss.Sep95 on 'Rocket')*

Nov 71. (lp)(c) **MADMAN ACROSS THE WATER** [41] [8]
– Tiny dancer / Levon / Razor face / Madman across the water / Indian sunset / Holiday inn / Rotten Peaches / All the nasties / Goodbye. *(reached No.41 May72, re-iss.Nov76, re-iss.May81, re-iss.+cd Apr87 & Aug95 on 'Rocket')*

Dec 71. (7") **LEVON. / GOODBYE** [-] [24]

Feb 72. (7") **TINY DANCER. / RAZOR FACE** [-] [41]

— **DAVEY JOHNSTONE** (b. 6 May'51, Edinburgh, Scotland) – guitar (ex-MAGNA CARTA) repl. QUAYE. Added **RAY COOPER** – percussion

Apr 72. (7"m) **ROCKET MAN. / HOLIDAY INN / GOODBYE** [2] [-]

May 72. (7") **ROCKET MAN. / SUZIE (DREAMS)** [-] [6]

May 72. (lp)(c) **HONKY CHATEAU** [2] [1] Jun 72
– Honky cat / Mellow / I think I'm going to kill myself / Susie (dramas) / Rocket man / Salvation / Slave / Amy / Mona Lisas and mad hatters / Hercules. *(re-iss.Nov76, re-iss.May81) (re-iss.Apr87 & Aug95 on 'Rocket')*

Aug 72. (7"m) **HONKY CAT. / LADY SAMANTHA / IT'S ME THAT YOU NEED** [31] [-]

Aug 72. (7") **HONKY CAT. / SLAVE** [-] [8]

D.J.M. / M.C.A.

Oct 72. (7") **CROCODILE ROCK. / ELDERBERRY WINE** [5] [1] Dec 72

Jan 73. (7") **DANIEL. / SKYLINE PIGEON** [4] [2] Apr 73

Feb 73. (lp)(c) **DON'T SHOOT ME I'M ONLY THE PIANO PLAYER** [1] [1]
– Daniel / Teacher I need you / Elderberry wine / Blues for my baby and me / Midnight creeper / Have mercy on the criminal / I'm going to be a teenage idol / Texan love song / Crocodile rock / High flying bird. *(re-iss.Nov76, re-iss.May81) (re-iss.+cd Apr87 & May95 on 'Rocket')*

Jun 73. (7"m) **SATURDAY NIGHT'S ALRIGHT FOR FIGHTING. / JACK RABBIT / WHEN YOU'RE READY (WE'LL GO STEADY AGAIN)** [7] [12] Jul 73

Sep 73. (7") **GOODBYE YELLOW BRICK ROAD. / SCREW YOU** [6] [-]

Oct 73. (7") **GOODBYE YELLOW BRICK ROAD. / YOUNG MAN'S BLUES** [-] [2]

Oct 73. (d-lp)(d-c) **GOODBYE YELLOW BRICK ROAD** [1] [1]
– Funeral for a friend / Love lies bleeding / Bennie and the jets / Candle in the wind / Goodbye yellow brick road / This song has no title / Grey seal / Jamaica jerk off / I've seen that movie too / Sweet painted lady / The ballad of Danny Bailey (1909-34) / Dirty little girl / All the girls love Alice / Your sister can't twist (but she can rock'n'roll) / Saturday night's alright for fighting / Roy Rogers / Social disease / Harmony. *(re-iss.Nov76) (re-iss.+cd.Nov87 & May95 on 'Rocket')*

Nov 73. (7") **STEP INTO CHRISTMAS. / HO! HO! HO! WHO'D BE A TURKEY AT CHRISTMAS** [24] [ ]

Feb 74. (7") **BENNY AND THE JETS. / HARMONY** [-] [1]

Feb 74. (7") **CANDLE IN THE WIND. / BENNIE AND THE JETS** [11] [-]

May 74. (7") **DON'T LET THE SUN GO DOWN ON ME. / SICK CITY** [16] [2] Jun 74

Jun 74. (lp)(c) **CARIBOU** [1] [1]
– The bitch is back / Pinky / Grimsby / Dixie Lily / Solar prestige a gammon / You're so static / I've seen the saucers / Stinker / Don't let the sun go down on me / Ticking. *(re-iss.Nov76 & May81) (re-iss.+cd.Nov87 & May95 on 'Rocket')*

Sep 74. (7") **THE BITCH IS BACK. / COLD HIGHWAY** [15] [4]

Nov 74. (7") **LUCY IN THE SKY WITH DIAMONDS. / ONE DAY AT A TIME** [10] [1]

Feb 75. (7") **PHILADELPHIA FREEDOM. (as "ELTON JOHN'S BAND") / I SAW HER STANDING THERE (w/ JOHN LENNON)** [12] [1]

May 75. (lp)(c) **CAPTAIN FANTASTIC AND THE BROWN DIRT COWBOY** [2] [1]

– Captain Fantastic and the brown dirt cowboy / Tower of Babel / Bitter fingers / Tell me when the whistle blows / Someone saved my life tonight / (Gotta get a) Meal ticket / Better off dead / Writing / We fall in love sometimes / Curtains. *(re-iss.Nov76, re-iss.pic-disc '78, re-iss.May81) (re-iss.+cd. Nov87 & Aug95 on 'Rocket')*

Jun 75. (7") **SOMEONE SAVED MY LIFE TONIGHT. / HOUSE OF CARDS** [22] [4]

—— ELTON now w/ others, after firing MURRAY and OLSSON (to BILLY JOEL)

Sep 75. (7") **ISLAND GIRL. / SUGAR ON THE FLOOR** [14] [1]

Nov 75. (lp)(c) **ROCK OF THE WESTIES** [5] [1]
– Medley: Yell help – Wednesday night – Ugly / Dan Dare (pilot of the future) / Island girl / Grow some funk of your own / I feel like a bullet (in the gun of Robert Ford) / Street kids / Hard luck story / Billy Bones and the white bird. *(re-iss.Nov76, re-iss.May81) (re-iss.+cd.Nov87 & Aug95 on 'Rocket')*

Jan 76. (7") **GROW SOME FUNK OF YOUR OWN. / I FEEL LIKE A BULLET (IN THE GUN OF ROBERT FORD)** [ ] [14]

Mar 76. (7") **PINBALL WIZARD. / HARMONY** [7] [-]

May 76. (lp)(c) **HERE AND THERE (live)** [6] [4]
– Skyline pigeon / Border song / Honky cat / Love song / Crocodile rock / Funeral for a friend / Love lies bleeding / Rocket man / Bennie and the jets / Take me to the pilot. *(re-iss.Nov76, re-iss.Sep78 as 'LONDON AND NEW YORK' on 'Hallmark') (cd-iss.Sep95)*

Rocket — M.C.A.

Jun 76. (7") **DON'T GO BREAKING MY HEART. ("ELTON JOHN & KIKI DEE") / SNOW QUEEN** [1] [1]

Oct 76. (d-lp)(c) **BLUE MOVES** [3] [3]
– Your starter for . . . / Tonight / One horse town / Chameleon / Boogie pilgrim / Cage the songbird / Crazy water / Shoulder holster / Sorry seems to be the hardest word / Out of the blue / Between seventeen and twenty / The wide-eyed and laughing / Someone's final song / Where's the shoorah / If there's a God in Heaven (what's he waiting for) / Idol / Theme from a non-existant TV series / Bite your lip (get up and dance!). *(re-iss.Sep84) (cd-iss.Jun89)*

Oct 76. (7") **SORRY SEEMS TO BE THE HARDEST WORD. / SHOULDER HOLSTER** [11] [6]

Feb 77. (7") **BITE YOUR LIP (GET UP AND DANCE!). / CHAMELEON** [-] [28]

Feb 77. (7") **CRAZY WATER. / CHAMELEON** [27] [ ]

May 77. (7")(12") **BITE YOUR LIP (GET UP AND DANCE!). / CHICAGO** [28] [-]

Apr 78. (7") **EGO. / FLINTSTONE BOY** [34] [34]

Oct 78. (7") **PART-TIME LOVE. / I CRY AT NIGHT** [15] [22]

Oct 78. (lp)(c) **A SINGLE MAN** [8] [15]
– Shine on through / Return to Paradise / I don't care / Big dipper / Georgia / It ain't gonna be easy / Part-time love / Georgia / Shooting star / Madness / Reverie / Song for Guy. *(re-iss.+cd.Jun83)*

Dec 78. (7") **SONG FOR GUY. / LOVESICK** [4] [ ]

May 79. (7") **ARE YOU READY FOR LOVE (part 1). / (part 2)** [42] [51] (m-lp)
(12"+=) – Three way love affair / Mama can't buy you love.

Above was named in the US 'THE THOM BELL SESSIONS' recorded 1977.

Jun 79. (7") **MAMA CAN'T BUY YOU LOVE. / THREE WAY LOVE AFFAIR** [-] [9]

Sep 79. (7") **VICTIM OF LOVE. / STRANGERS** [ ] [31]

Oct 79. (lp)(c) **VICTIM OF LOVE** [41] [35]
– Johnny B. Goode / Warm love in a cold climate / Born bad / Thunder in the night / Spotlight / Street boogie / Born Bad / Victim of love. *(re-iss.Jul84)*

Dec 79. (7") **JOHNNY B. GOODE. / GEORGIA** [-] [ ]

Dec 79. (7")(12") **JOHNNY B. GOODE. / THUNDER IN THE NIGHT** [ ] [-]

May 80. (7") **LITTLE JEANNIE. / CONQUER THE SUN** [33] [3]

May 80. (lp)(c) **21 AT 33** [12] [13]
– Chasing the crown / Little Jeannie / Sartorial eloquence / Two rooms at the end of the world / White lady, white powder / Dear God / Never gonna fall in love again / Take me back / Give me the love. *(re-iss.+cd.Jul84) (cd-iss.Jun88)*

Aug 80. (7") **SARTORIAL ELOQUENCE. / WHITE MAN DANCER; CARTIER** [44] [39]

Nov 80. (7") **DEAR GOD. / TACTICS** [ ] [ ]
(d7") – Steal away child / Love so cold.

Rocket — Geffen

May 81. (7") **NOBODY WINS. / FOOLS IN FASHION** [42] [21]

May 81. (lp)(c) **THE FOX** [12] [21]
– Breaking down barriers / Heart in the right place / Just like Belgium / Nobody wins / Fascist faces / Carla etude / Fanfare / Chloe / Heels of the wind / Elton's song / The fox. *(re-iss.+cd.Jul84)*

Jul 81. (7") **JUST LIKE BELGIUM. / CAN'T GET OVER LOSING YOU** [ ] [-]

Jul 81. (7") **CHLOE. / TORTURED** [-] [34]

Mar 82. (7") **BLUE EYES. / HEY PAPA LEGBA** [8] [12] Jul 82

Apr 82. (lp)(c) **JUMP UP!** [13] [17]
– Dear John / Spiteful child / Ball and chain / Legal boys / I am your robot / Blue eyes / Empty garden /Princess / Where have all the good times gone? / All quiet on the western front. *(cd-iss.1983)*

May 82. (7")(7"pic-d) **EMPTY GARDEN. / TAKE ME DOWN TO THE OCEAN** [51] [13] Mar 82

Sep 82. (7") **PRINCESS. / THE RETREAT** [ ] [-]

Nov 82. (7") **ALL QUIET ON THE WESTERN FRONT. / WHERE HAVE ALL THE GOOD TIMES GONE?** [ ] [-]

Nov 82. (7") **BALL AND CHAIN. / WHERE HAVE ALL THE GOOD TIMES GONE?** [-] [ ]

Apr 83. (7") **I GUESS THAT'S WHY THEY CALL IT THE BLUES. / LORD CHOC ICE GOES MENTAL** [5] [-]

May 83. (7") **I'M STILL STANDING. / LOVE SO COLD** [-] [12]

Jun 83. (lp)(c)(cd) **TOO LOW FOR ZERO** [7] [25]
– Cold at Christmas / I'm still standing / Too low for zero / Religion / I guess that's why they call it the blues / Crystal / Kiss the bride / Whipping boy / Saint / One more arrow.

Jul 83. (7")(12")(7"sha-pic-d) **I'M STILL STANDING. / EARN WHILE YOU LEARN** [4] [-]

Aug 83. (7") **KISS THE BRIDE. / LORD CHOC ICE GOES MENTAL** [-] [25]

Oct 83. (7")(12") **KISS THE BRIDE. / DREAMBOAT** [20] [-]

Oct 83. (7") **I GUESS THAT'S WHY THEY CALL IT HTE BLUES. / THE RETREAT** [-] [4]
(d7"+=) – Ego / Song for Guy.

Dec 83. (7") **COLD AT CHRISTMAS. / CRYSTAL** [33] [ ]
(d7"+=) – Don't go breaking my heart / Snow queen.

May 84. (7")(12")(7"sha-pic-d) **SAD SONGS (SAY SO MUCH). / SIMPLE MAN** [7] [5]

Jun 84. (lp)(c)(cd) **BREAKING HEARTS** [2] [20]
– Restless / Slow down Georgie (she's poison) / Who wears these shoes? / Breaking hearts (ain't what it used to be) / Li'l fridgerator / Passengers / In neon / Burning bridges / Did he shoot her? / Sad songs (say so much).

Aug 84. (7")(12") **PASSENGERS (remix). / LONELY BOY** [5] [ ]

Sep 84. (7") **WHO WEARS THESE SHOES? / LONELY EYES** [-] [16]

Oct 84. (7") **WHO WEARS THESE SHOES? / TORTURED** [50] [-]
(12"+=) – I heard it through the grapevine.

Nov 84. (7") **IN NEON. / TACTICS** [-] [38]

Feb 85. (7") **BREAKING HEARTS (AIN'T WHAT IT USED TO BE). / IN NEON** [59] [38] Nov 84

Jun 85. (7") **ACT OF WAR (part 1). ("ELTON JOHN & MILLIE JACKSON") / (part 2)** [32] [ ]
(12"+=) – (part 3) / (part 4).

Sep 85. (7") **NIKITA. / THE MAN WHO NEVER DIED** [3] [-]
(12"+=)(d7"+=) – Sorry seems to be the hardest word (live) / I'm still standing (live).

Oct 85. (7") **WRAP HER UP. / THE MAN WHO NEVER DIED** [-] [ ]

Nov 85. (lp)(c)(cd) **ICE ON FIRE** [3] [48]
– Wrap her up / Satellite / Tell me what the papers say / Candy by the pound / Shoot down the Moon / This town / Cry to heaven / Soul glove / Nikita / Too young. *(c+=)(cd+=)–* Act of war (with MILLIE JACKSON).

Nov 85. (7")(7"sha-pic-d) **WRAP HER UP. / RESTLESS (live)** [12] [ ]
(12"+=) – ('A' extended).
(d12"+=) – Nikita / The man who never died.

Jan 86. (7") **NIKITA. / RESTLESS** [-] [7]

Feb 86. (7") **CRY TO HEAVEN. / CANDY BY THE POUND** [47] [ ]
(12"+=)/ /(d7"++=) – Rock'n'roll medley./ / Your song.

Sep 86. (7") **HEARTACHES ALL OVER THE WORLD. / HIGHLANDER** [45] [55]
(12"+=) – ('A'version).
(d7"+=) – Passengers / I'm still standing.

Nov 86. (lp)(c)(cd) **LEATHER JACKETS** [24] [91]
– Leather jackets / Hoop of fire / Go it alone / Don't trust that woman / Gypsy heart / Slow rivers / Heartache all over the world / Angeline / Memory of love / Paris / I fall apart.

Nov 86. (7") **SLOW RIVERS. ("ELTON JOHN & CLIFF RICHARD") / BILLY AND THE KIDS** [44] [ ]
(12"+=) – Lord of the flies.
(c-s+=) – Nikita / Blue eyes / I guess that's why they call it the blues

Rocket — M.C.A.

Jun 87. (7") **YOUR SONG (live). / DON'T LET THE SUN GO DOWN ON ME (live)** [ ] [ ]
(12"+=) – I need you to turn to / The greatest discovery.

Sep 87. (d-lp)(c)(cd) **LIVE IN AUSTRALIA (live)** [43] [24] Dec 87
– Sixty years on / I need you to turn to / The greatest discovery / Tonight / Sorry seems to be the hardest word / The king must die / Take me to the pilot / Tiny dancer / Have mercy on the criminal / Madman across the water / Candle in the wind / Burn down the mission / Your song / Don't let the Sun go down on me.

Dec 87. (7")(7"pic-d) **CANDLE IN THE WIND (live). / SORRY SEEMS TO BE THE HARDEST WORD (live)** [5] [6] Nov 87
(12"+=)(c-s+=)(cd-s+=) – Your song (live) / Don't let the sun go down on me (live).

Mar 88. (7") **TONIGHT. / TAKE ME TO THE PILOT** [-] [ ]

May 88. (7")(12") **I DON'T WANT TO GO ON WITH YOU LIKE THAT. / ROPE AROUND A FOOL** [30] [2] Jun 88
(12"+=)/ /(cd-s+=) – ('A'version)/ / ('A'-Shep Pettibone mix).

Jun 88. (lp)(c)(cd) **REG STRIKES BACK** [18] [16]
– Town of plenty / A word in Spanish / Mona Lisas and mad hatters (part 2) / I

don't want to go on with you like that / Japanese hands / Goodbye Marlon Brando / The camera never lies / Heavy traffic / Poor cow / Since God invented girls.

Sep 88. (7") **TOWN OF PLENTY. / WHIPPING BOY** [74] [ ]
(12"+=) – My baby's a saint.
(cd-s++=) – I guess that's why they call it the blues.

Nov 88. (7") **A WORD IN SPANISH. / HEAVY TRAFFIC** [ ] [19] Sep88
(12"+=) – Live in Australia medley: Song for Guy – I guess that's why they call it the blues – Blue eyes.
(cd-s++=) – Daniel.

— In Apr89, he was credited on 'THROUGH THE STORM' UK No.41 / No.16 single with ARETHA FRANKLIN.

Aug 89. (7")(c-s) **HEALING HANDS. / DANCING IN THE END ZONE** [45] [13]
(12"+=)(cd-s+=) – ('A'version).

Sep 89. (lp)(c)(cd) **SLEEPING WITH THE PAST** [1] [23]
– Durban deep / Healing hands / Whispers / Club at the end of the street / Sleeping with the past / Stone's throw from hurtin' / Sacrifice / I never knew her name / Amazes me / Blue avenue. *(re-dist. May90, No.1).*

Oct 89. (7")(c-s) **SACRIFICE. / LOVE IS A CANNIBAL** [55] [18] Jan 90
(12"+=)(cd-s+=) – Durban deep.

Apr 90. (7") **CLUB AT THEN END OF THE STREET. / SACRIFICE** [-] [28]

Jun 90. (7")(c-s) **SACRIFICE. / HEALING HANDS** [1] [-]
(12"+=)(cd-s+=) – Durban deep.

Aug 90. (7")(c-s) **CLUB AT THE END OF THE STREET. / WHISPERS** [47] [-]
(12"+=) – I don't wanna go on with you like that.
(cd-s+=) – Give peace a chance.

Oct 90. (7")(c-s) **YOU GOTTA LOVE SOMEONE. / MEDICINE MAN** [33] [43] Nov 90
(12"+=)(cd-s+=) – ('B'-Adamski version).

Nov 90. (7")(c-s) **EASIER TO WALK AWAY. / SWEAR I HEARD THE NIGHT TALKING** [63] [ ]
(12"+=)(cd-s+=) – Made for me.

— 45 year-old DEE MURRAY died of a heart attack, after suffering from cancer

May 92. (7")(c-s) **THE ONE. / SUIT OF WOLVES** [10] [9]
(cd-s+=) – Fat boys and ugly girls.

Jun 92. (cd)(c)(lp) **THE ONE** [2] [8]
– Simple life / The one / Sweat it out / Runaway train / Whitewash county / The North / When a woman doesn't want you / Emily / On dark street / Understanding women / The last song.

Jul 92. (7")(c-s) **RUNAWAY TRAIN. ("ELTON JOHN & ERIC CLAPTON") / UNDERSTANDING WOMEN** [31] [ ]
(cd-s+=) – Made for me.
(cd-s) – ('A'side) / Through the storm (with ARETHA FRANKLIN) / Don't let the Sun go down on me (with GEORGE MICHAEL) / Slow rivers (with CLIFF).

Oct 92. (7")(c-s) **THE LAST SONG. / THE MAN WHO NEVER DIED / SONG FOR GUY** [21] [23]
(cd-s) – ('A'side) / Are you ready / Three way love affair / Mama can't buy you love.

May 93. (7")(c-s) **SIMPLE LIFE. / THE LAST SONG** [44] [30] Feb 93
(cd-s+=) – The north.

Nov 93. (7")(c-s) **TRUE LOVE. ("ELTON JOHN & KIKI DEE") / THE SHOW MUST GO ON** [2] [56]
(cd-s+=) -- Runaway train.
(cd-s) – ('A'side) / Wrap her up / That's what friends are for / Act of war.

Nov 93. (cd)(c)(d-lp) **DUETS** (w/ whoever in brackets) [5] [25]
– Teardrops (k.d.LANG) / When I think about love (I think about you) (P.M.DAWN) / The power (LITTLE RICHARD) / Shakey ground (DON HENLEY) / True love (KIKI DEE) / If you were me (CHRIS REA) / A woman's needs (TAMMY WYNETTE) / Don't let the Sun go down on me (GEORGE MICHAEL) / Old friend (NIK KERSHAW) / Go on and on (GLADYS KNIGHT) / Don't go breaking my heart (RuPAUL) / Ain't nothing like the real thing (MARCELLA DETROIT) / I'm your puppet (PAUL YOUNG) / Love letters (BONNIE RAITT) / Born to lose (LEONARD COHEN) / Duets for one (ELTON JOHN solo).

Feb 94. (7")(c-s) **DON'T GO BREAKING MY HEART. ("ELTON JOHN & RuPAUL") / DONNER POUR DONNER** [7] [92]
(cd-s+=) – A woman's needs.
(cd-s) – ('A'side) / ('A'mixes).

— In May 94, he & MARCELLA DETROIT (ex-SHAKESPEAR'S SISTER) hit UK No.24 with 'AIN'T NOTHIN' LIKE THE REAL THING'.

Jun 94. (7")(c-s) **CAN YOU FEEL THE LOVE TONIGHT?. / ('A'mix)** [14] [4] May94
(cd-s+=) – Hakuna Matata / Under the stars.

Sep 94. (c-s) **CIRCLE OF LIFE. / ('A'mix)** [11] [18]
(cd-s+=)(pic-cd-s+=) – I just can't wait to be king / This land.

— with **GUY BABYLON** -keyboards/ **BOB BIRCH** -bass/ **DAVEY JOHNSTONE** -guitar, mandolin, banjo/ **CHARLIE MORGAN** -drums/ **RAY COOPER** -percusion

Feb 95. (c-s) **BELIEVE / SORRY SEEMS TO BE THE HARDEST WORD (live)** [15] [13]
(cd-s+=) – Believe (live).
(cd-s) – ('A'side) / The one / The last song.

Mar 95. (cd)(c)(lp) **MADE IN ENGLAND** [3] [13]
– Believe / Made in England / House / Cold / Pain / Belfast / Latitude / Please / Man / Lies / Blessed.

May 95. (cd-s) **MADE IN ENGLAND / DANIEL (live)** [18] [52]
(c-s+=) – Can you feel the love tonight.
(cd-s+=) – Your song / Don't let the sun go down on me.
(cd-s) – ('A'side) / Whatever gets you thru the night / Lucy in the sky with diamonds / I saw her standing there.

Oct 95. (c-s)(cd-s) **BLESSED / LATITUDE** [ ] [34]
(cd-s) – ('A'side) / Made in England (mixes).
(cd-s) – ('A'side) / Honky cat (live) / Take me to the pilot (live) / The bitch is back (live).

Nov 95. (cd)(c) **LOVE SONGS** (compilation) [7] [ ]
– Sacrifice / Candle in the wind / I guess that's why they call it the blues / Don't let the sun go down on me (with GEORGE MICHAEL) / Sorry seems to be the hardest word / Blue eyes / Daniel / Nikita / Your song / The one / Someone saved my life tonight / True love (with KIKI DEE) / Can you feel the love tonight / Circle of life / Blessed / Please / Song for Guy.

. . . Jan – Jun '96 stop press . . .

Jan 96. (single) **PLEASE** [33] [ ]

– compilations, exploitation releases, etc. –

Apr 71. Paramount; (lp) **FRIENDS (soundtrack)** [ ] [36]
(re-iss. on 'Anchor')

Note; All 'DJM' releases were issued on 'MCA' in the US.

Nov 74. DJM; (lp)(c) **ELTON JOHN'S GREATEST HITS** [1] [1]
– Your song / Daniel / Honky cat / Goodbye yellow brick road / Saturday night's alright for fighting / Rocket man / Candle in the wind / Don't let the Sun go down on me / Border song / Crocodile rock / The bitch is back / Lucy in the sky with diamonds / Sorry seems to be the hardest word / Don't go breaking my heart / Someone saved my life tonight / Philadelphia freedom / Island girl / Grow somw funk of your own / Benny & the jets / Pinball wizard. *(re-iss.Nov76) (cd-iss.Oct84)*

Sep 76. DJM; (7") **BENNIE AND THE JETS. / ROCK AND ROLL MADONNA** [37] [-]

May 77. DJM; (7"ep) **FOUR FROM FOUR EYES** [ ] [ ]
– Your song / Rocket man / Saturday night's alright for fighting / Whenever you're ready (we'll go steady again).

Sep 77. DJM; (lp)(c) **GREATEST HITS VOL.2** [6] [21]

Sep 78. DJM; (12"ep) **FUNERAL FOR A FRIEND; LOVE LIES BLEEDING / CURTAINS / WE ALL FALL IN LOVE SOMETIMES** [ ] [ ]
(re-iss.'88)

Sep 78. DJM; (12x7"-box) **THE ELTON JOHN SINGLES COLLECTION** [ ] [ ]
(also available separately as below)

Sep 78. DJM; (7") **LADY SAMANTHA. / SKYLINE PIGEON** [ ] [ ]

Sep 78. DJM; (7") **YOUR SONG. / BORDER SONG** [ ] [ ]

Sep 78. DJM; (7") **HONKY CAT. / SIXTY YEARS ON** [ ] [ ]

Sep 78. DJM; (7") **CROCODILE ROCK. / COUNTRY COMFORT** [ ] [ ]

Sep 78. DJM; (7") **ROCKET MAN. / DANIEL** [ ] [ ]

Sep 78. DJM; (7") **GOODBYE YELLOW BRICK ROAD. / SWEET PAINTED LADY** [ ] [ ]

Sep 78. DJM; (7") **DON'T LET THE SUN GO DOWN ON ME. / SOMEONE SAVED MY LIFE** [ ] [ ]

Sep 78. DJM; (7") **CANDLE IN THE WIND. / I FEEL LIKE A BULLET (. . .** [ ] [ ]

Sep 78. DJM; (7") **THE BITCH IS BACK. / GROW SOME FUNK OF YOUR OWN** [ ] [ ]

Sep 78. DJM; (7") **ISLAND GIRL. / SATURDAY NIGHT'S ALRIGHT FOR FIGHTING** [ ] [ ]

Sep 78. DJM; (7") **PHILADELPHIA FREEDOM. / BENNIE AND THE JETS** [ ] [ ]

Sep 78. DJM; (7") **PINBALL WIZARD. / BENNIE AND THE JETS** [ ] [ ]

Feb 79. Pickwick; (d-lp)(d-c) **THE ELTON JOHN LIVE COLLECTION** [ ] [ ]
(live albums Apr71 + May76) *(re-iss. Nov88 as 'THE COLLECTION')*

Aug 79. DJM; (5xlp-box) **ELTON JOHN** [ ] [ ]
(originally released in US contains 'EARLY YEARS', 'ELTON ROCKS', 'MOODS', 'SINGLES' & 'CLASSICS')

Oct 80. DJM; (lp)(c) **LADY SAMANTHA** (rare 'B's) [56] [ ]

Nov 80. DJM; (7") **HARMONY. / MONA LISA AND THE MAD HATTERS** [ ] [ ]

Mar 81. DJM; (7") **I SAW HER STANDING THERE. / WHATEVER GETS YOU THROUGH THE NIGHT / LUCY IN THE SKY WITH DIAMONDS (with JOHN LENNON)** [30] [ ]

1988. DJM; (d-c) **ROCK OF THE WESTIES / ELTON JOHN'S GREATEST HITS** [ ] [ ]

1988. DJM; (d-c) **EMPTY SKY / GREATEST HITS VOL.2** [ ] [ ]

1988. DJM; (d-c) **CAPTAIN FANTASTIC AND THE BROWN DIRT COWBOY / ELTON JOHN** [ ] [ ]

1988. DJM; (d-c) **DON'T SHOOT ME I'M ONLY THE PIANO PLAYER / TUMBLEWEED CONNECTION** [ ] [ ]

1988. DJM; (d-c) **GREATEST HITS / ROCK OF THE WESTIES** [ ] [ ]

1988. DJM; (7") **LUCY IN THE SKY WITH DIAMONDS. / ONE DAY AT A TIME** [ ] [ ]

1988. DJM; (7") **CANDLE IN THE WIND. / BENNIE AND THE JETS** [ ] [ ]
1988. DJM; (7") **YOUR SONG. / INTO THE OLD MAN'S SHOES** [ ] [ ]
Note; All 'Rocket' releases were issued on 'MCA' in the US.
Apr 77. Rocket; (7") **THE GOALDIGGER SONG. / (spoken)** [ ] [ ]
Mar 81. Rocket; (7") **DON'T GO BREAKING MY HEART. / SNOW QUEEN 7** [-]
Oct 90. Rocket; (cd)(c)(d-lp) **THE VERY BEST OF ELTON JOHN** [1] [ ]
– Your song / Rocket man / Crocodile rock / Daniel / Goodbye yellow brick road / Saturday night's alright for fighting / Candle in the wind / Don't let the Sun go down on me / Lucy in the sky with diamonds / Philadelphia freedom / Someone saved my life tonight / Don't go breaking my heart / Bennie and the jets / Sorry seems to be the hardest word / Song for Guy / Part time love / Blue eyes / I guess that's why they call it the blues / I'm still standing / Kiss the bride / Sad songs / Passengers / Nikita / Sacrifice / You gotta love someone. *(cd+c+=)* – Pinball wizard / The bitch is back / I don't wanna go on with you like that / Easier to walk away. *(re-iss.Nov91 hit UK No.29)*
Feb 91. Rocket; (7")(c-s) **DON'T LET THE SUN GO DOWN ON ME. / SONG FOR GUY** [ ] [ ]
(12"+=)(cd-s+=) – Sorry seems to be the hardest word.
Nov 91. MCA; (cd-box)(c-box) **TO BE CONTINUED . . .** [ ] [82]
Sep 87. Geffen; (cd)(c)(lp) **ELTON JOHN'S GREATEST HITS, VOLUME III, 1979-1987** [?] [84]
Jan 78. St.Michael; (lp) **CANDLE IN THE WIND (ltd)** [ ] [ ]
Oct 80. K-Tel; (lp)(c) **THE VERY BEST OF ELTON JOHN** [24] [-]
Sep 81. Hallmark; (lp)(c) **THE ALBUM** [ ] [ ]
Nov 82. T.V.; (lp)(c) **LOVE SONGS** [ ] [ ]
Jun 83. Everest; (lp)(c) **THE NEW COLLECTION** [ ] [ ]
Jun 83. Everest; (lp)(c) **THE NEW COLLECTION VOL.2** [ ] [ ]
1983. Cambra; (d-c) **ELTON JOHN (hits)** [ ] [ ]
May 84. Cambra; (d-c) **SEASONS . . . THE EARLY LOVE SONGS** [ ] [-]
Oct 84. DJM; (cd) **THE SUPERIOR SOUND OF . . .** [ ] [ ]
Jun 88. Old Gold; (7") **DON'T GO BREAKING MY HEART. / I GOT THE MUSIC IN ME (Kiki Dee)** [ ] [ ]
Feb 88. Old Gold; (7") **NIKITA. / I'M STILL STANDING** [ ] [ ]
Jun 88. Old Gold; (7") **SONG FOR GUY. / BLUE EYES** [ ] [ ]
1988. Starr; (cd) **BIGGEST** [ ] [-]

— below, a guest spot w/**KIKI DEE.**

Apr 81. Ariola; (7") **LOVING YOU IS SWEETER THAN EVER. / 24 HOURS** [ ] [ ]
May 87. CBS/ US= Epic; (7") **FLAMES OF PARADISE. / CALL ON ME** [ ] [36]
above JENNIFER RUSH & ELTON JOHN single
Mar 94. Spectrum; (cd)(c) **ROCK & ROLL MADONNA** [ ] [-]
Feb 95. D.J.; (cd-s) **UNITED WE STAND / NEANDERTHAL MAN** [ ] [-]
(above credited to REG DWIGHT) (early recordings)
Apr 95. RPM; (cd) **CHARTBUSTERS ARE GO** [ ] [-]

JOHNNY & THE SELF-ABUSERS (see under ⇒ SIMPLE MINDS)

Holly JOHNSON (see under ⇒ FRANKIE GOES TO HOLLYWOOD)

Matt JOHNSON (see under ⇒ THE THE)

Mike JOHNSON (see under ⇒ DINOSAUR JR)

JON & VANGELIS (see under ⇒ VANGELIS)

Mick JONES (see under ⇒ FOREIGNER)

Janis JOPLIN

Born: 19 Jan'43, Port Arthur, Texas, USA. In the early 60's, she hitched to California and San Francisco, where she sang in WALLER CREEK BOYS trio alongside future 13th FLOOR ELEVATORS member R.POWELL ST.JOHN. In 1963, she sang alongside JORMA KAUKONEN (later JEFFERSON AIRPLANE) at local night spots. In 1966, after nearly giving up singing and her hippy drug life to marry, she returned to Texas, where she briefly rehearsed with 13th FLOOR ELEVATORS. That same year, she again ventured to San Francisco, but this time she joined BIG BROTHER & THE HOLDING COMPANY (see ⇒). They made 2 lp's, the second of which 'CHEAP THRILLS', stayed at US No.1 for 8 weeks. When they temporary folded late in '68, she went solo, although her alcohol and drug abuse was becoming more apparent. After 3 major concerts at London's Royal Albert Hall, Newport Festival and New Orleans pop festival, she unleashed 1969 solo debut 'I GOT DEM OL' KOSMIC BLUES AGAIN', which made US Top 5. In May'70, she formed her new backing group The FULL-TILT BOOGIE BAND, and they began working on an album in Autumn 1970. However before it was completed, on 4 Oct'70, JANIS was found dead at her Hollywood apartment. The coroner's verdict said it was due to an accidental overdose she took at a party. Early in 1971, her last recordings 'PEARL' were issued, and they topped the US charts for 9 weeks, and gave her first dent into UK Top 50. She also scored a US No.1 single with a great version of KRIS KRISTOFFERSON's 'ME AND BOBBY McGEE'. But for her death, she would probably have become greatest female singer of all-time. • **Style:** Powerful 3 octave vocalist, with the capacity to roust any standard or rock tune into her own. • **Songwriters:** She used many outside writers, including JERRY RAGAVOY, and covered; PIECE OF MY HEART (hit; Erma Franklin) / MAYBE (Chantells) / TO LOVE SOMEBODY (Bee Gees) / etc. • **Trivia:** In 1979, a film 'The Rose' was released based on her life, and featuring BETTE MIDLER in her role.

Recommended: JANIS JOPLIN'S GREATEST HITS (*8)

JANIS JOPLIN – vocals (ex-BIG BROTHER & THE HOLDING COMPANY) / **SAM ANDREW** – guitar (ex-BIG BROTHER & THE HOLDING COMPANY) / others in her KOZMIC BLUES BAND were **BRAD CAMPBELL** (aka KEITH CHERRY) – bass / **TERRY CLEMENTS** – saxophone / **RICHARD KERMODE** – organ repl. BILL KING (Feb69) / **LONNIE CASTILLE** – drums repl. ROY MARKOWITZ (Apr69) / **TERRY HENSLEY** – trumpet repl. MARCUS DOUBLEDAY (Apr69) / added **SNOOKY FLOWERS** – saxophone (Feb69)

— (Jul69) **JOHN TILL** – guitar, vocals repl. SAM ANDREW / **MAURY BAKER** – drums repl. CASTILLE / **DAVE WOODWARD** – trumpet repl. GASCA who repl. HENSLEY

C.B.S. Columbia

Oct 69. (lp) **I GOT DEM OL' KOZMIC BLUES AGAIN MAMA!** [ ] [5]
– Try (just a little bit harder) / Maybe / One good man / As good as you've been to this world / To love somebody / Kozmic blues / Little girl blue / Work me, Lord. *(re-iss.+c.1983) (cd-iss.Jan91)*
Nov 69. (7") **KOZMIC BLUES. / LITTLE GIRL BLUE** [ ] [41]
1970. (7") **TRY (JUST A LITTLE BIT HARDER). / ONE GOOD MAN** [-] [ ]
1970. (7") **MAYBE. / WORK ME, LORD** [-] [ ]

JANIS JOPLIN & THE FULL TILT BOOGIE BAND

She retained **CAMPBELL** and **TILL** / added **RICHARD BELL** – piano / **KEN PEARSON** – organ / **CLARK PIERSON** – drums/ On the 4th Oct70, JANIS died of a drug overdose. She had just recorded below lp

Jan 71. (lp)(c) **PEARL** [50] [1]
– Move over / Cry baby / A woman left lonely / Half Moon / Buried alive in the blues / My baby / Me and Bobby McGee / Mercedes Benz / Trust me / Get it while you can. *(contains 2 instrumentals. re-iss.Jan84) (also as quad-lp) (cd-iss. Jan91)*
Jan 71. (7") **ME AND BOBBY McGEE. / HALF MOON** [ ] [1]
May 71. (7") **CRY BABY. / MERCEDES BENZ** [ ] [42]
Sep 71. (7") **GET IT WHILE YOU CAN. / MOVE OVER** [-] [78]

– other posthumous JANIS JOPLIN releases –

Note; Below were issued on 'CBS' UK/ 'Columbia' US until stated.
Oct 71. (7"ep) **MOVE OVER. / TRY (JUST A LITTLE BIT HARDER) / PIECE OF MY HEART** [ ] [ ]
Jul 72. (d-lp)(c) **JANIS JOPLIN IN CONCERT (live)** [30] [4] May 72
– Down on me / Bye, bye baby / All is loneliness / Piece of my heart / Road block / Flower in the sun / Summertime / Ego rock / Half moon / Kozmic blues / Move over / Try (just a little bit harder) / Get it while you can / Ball and chain. *(half with 'BIG BROTHER & etc..', half with 'FULL TILT')*
Jul 72. (7") **DOWN ON ME (live). / BYE, BYE BABY (live)** [ ] [91]
Jul 73. (lp)(c) **JANIS JOPLIN'S GREATEST HITS** [ ] [37]
– Piece of my heart / Summertime / Try (just a little bit harder) / Cry baby / Me and Bobby McGee / Down on me / Get it while you can / Bye, bye baby / Move over / Ball and chain. *(re-iss. +cd 1992 on 'Sony')*
May 75. (d-lp)(d-c) **JANIS (soundtrack)** [ ] [54]
(includes rare 1963-65 material)
Mar 76. (7") **PIECE OF MY HEART. / KOZMIC BLUES** [ ] [-]
Jul 80. (d-lp)(d-c) **ANTHOLOGY** [ ] [ ]
Feb 82. (lp)(c) **FAREWELL SONG** [ ] [ ]
Nov 84. (d-c) **PEARL / CHEAP THRILLS** [ ] [ ]
(some of the above posthumous releases were recorded with 'BIG BROTHER & etc.')
Sep 92. Sony; (d-cd) **PEARL / I GOT DEM OL' KOZMIC BLUES AGAIN** [ ] [ ]
Sep 93. I.T.M.; (cd) **LIVE AT WOODSTOCK, 1969 (live)** [ ] [ ]
Jan 94. Legacy; (3xcd) **JANIS** [ ] [ ]
Dec 94. Columbia; (cd) **THE BEST** [ ] [ ]
Apr 95. Legacy; (cd) **18 ESSENTIAL SONGS** [ ] [-]

JOURNEY

Formed: San Francisco, California, USA ... early 1973 originally as The GOLDEN GATE BRIDGE by NEAL SCHON, GEORGE TICKNER, ROSS VALORY and PRAIRIE PRINCE. Due to manager Walter Herbert auditioning through a radio station for a group name, they came up with JOURNEY. They added GREGG ROLIE and replaced TUBES-bound PRAIRIE PRINCE, with English-born AYNSLEY DUNBAR. Late in 1974, they gained contract on 'Columbia', and soon issued eponymous US Top 200 lp. Early in 1976 & 1977, they dented the Top 100 with albums 'LOOK INTO THE FUTURE' and 'NEXT'. In Oct'77, they brought in new voxist STEVE PERRY, who brought them much needed venom and a US Top 30 album 'INFINITY' in 1978. After a 1979 Top 20 album 'EVOLUTION', they soared in the 80's, to become one of America's top bands. • **Style:** They switched from jazz-rock in the mid-70's to pomp AOR in the late 70's & 80's. • **Songwriters:** SCHON-ROLIE penned most? • **Trivia:** They made their live debut on 31st Dec'73, in front of over 10,000 people at San Francisco's 'Wonderland' venue. A couple of JOURNEY tracks, featured on the 1980 & 1981 film soundtracks of 'Caddyshack' & 'Heavy Metal'.

Recommended: ESCAPE (*7) / THE BEST OF JOURNEY (*7).

NEAL SCHON (b.27 Feb'54, San Mateo) – lead guitar, vocals (ex-SANTANA) / **GREGG ROLIE** (b.1948) – vocals, keyboards (ex-SANTANA) / **GEORGE TICKNER** – guitar, vocals / **ROSS VALORY** (b. 2 Feb'49) – bass, vocals (ex-STEVE MILLER BAND) / **AYNSLEY DUNBAR** (b.1946, Liverpool, England) – drums (ex-FRANK ZAPPA, ex-JOHN MAYALL, ex-JEFF BECK) repl. PRAIRIE PRINCE who joined The TUBES.

		C.B.S.	Columbia
Apr 75.	(lp)(c) **JOURNEY** – Of a lifetime / In the morning day / Kohoutek / To play some music / Topaz / In my lonely feeling – Conversations / Mystery mountain. *(cd-iss.Oct93 on 'Sony Collectors') (cd-iss.Oct94 on 'Rewind')*		
Jun 75.	(7") **TO PLAY SOME MUSIC. / TOPAZ**	-	
—	(Apr75) reverted to a quartet when TICKNER departed		
Jan 76.	(lp)(c) **LOOK INTO THE FUTURE** – On a Saturday nite / It's all too much / Anyway / She makes me (feel alright) / You're on your own / Look into the future / Midnight dreamer / I'm gonna leave		100

you. *(re-iss.Mar82)*
Mar 76. (7") **ON A SATURDAY NIGHT. / TO PLAY SOME MUSIC** [-] [ ]
Jul 76. (7") **SHE MAKES ME (FEEL ALRIGHT). / IT'S ALL TOO MUCH** [-] [ ]
Feb 77. (7") **SPACEMAN. / NICKEL AND DIME** [-] [ ]
Feb 77. (lp)(c) **NEXT** [ ] [85]
– Spaceman / People / I would find you / Here we are / Hustler / Next / Nickel & dime / Karma.

— (Jun77) added **ROBERT FLEISCHMAN** – lead vocals

— (Oct77) **STEVE PERRY** (b.22 Jan'53) – lead vocals repl. FLEISCHMAN
May 78. (lp)(c) **INFINITY** [ ] [21] Feb 78
– Lights / Feeling that way / Anytime / La do da / Patiently / Wheel in the sky / Somethin' to hide / Winds of March / Can do / Opened the door. *(cd-iss.!)*
Apr 78. (7") **WHEEL IN THE SKY. / CAN DO** [ ] [57]
Jun 78. (7") **ANYTIME. / CAN DO** [-] [83]
Aug 78. (7") **LIGHTS. / OPEN THE DOOR** [ ] [-]
Aug 78. (7") **LIGHTS. / SOMETHIN' TO HIDE** [-] [68]

— (Nov78) **STEVE SMITH** – drums repl. DUNBAR who joined JEFFERSON STARSHIP (above now alongside SCHON, ROLIE, PERRY and VALORY)
Apr 79. (lp)(c) **EVOLUTION** [100] [20]
– Sweet and simple / Just the same way / Do you recall / City of angels / Lovin', touchin', squeezin' / Daydream / When you're alone (it ain't easy) / Lady luck / Too late / Lovin' you is easy / Majestic. *(re-iss.Jul83) (cd-iss.Oct93 on 'Sony Europe')*
Apr 79. (7") **JUST THE SAME WAY. / SOMETHIN' TO HIDE** [-] [58]
Sep 79. (7") **LOVIN', TOUCHIN', SQUEEZIN'. / DAYDREAM** [ ] [16] Jul 79
Dec 79. (7") **TOO LATE. / DO YOU RECALL** [-] [70]
Feb 80. (7") **ANY WAY YOU WANT IT. / WHEN YOU'RE ALONE (IT AIN'T EASY)** [-] [23]
Mar 80. (lp)(c) **DEPARTURE** [ ] [8]
– Any way you want it / Walks like a lady / Someday soon / People and places / Precious time / Where were you / I'm cryin' / Line of fire / Departure / Good morning girl / Stay awhile / Homemade love. *(re-iss.Feb86) (cd-iss.Oct93 on 'Sony Europe')*
Sep 80. (7") **ANY WAY YOU WANT IT. / DO YOU RECALL** [ ] [-]
May 80. (7") **WALKS LIKE A LADY. / PEOPLE AND PLACES** [-] [ ]
Aug 80. (7") **GOOD MORNING GIRL. / STAY AWHILE** [ ] [55]
Feb 81. (d-lp)(c) **CAPTURED (live)** [ ] [9]
– Majestic / Where were you / Just the same way / Line of fire / Lights / Stay awhile / Too late / Dixie highway / Feeling that way / Anytime / Do you recall / Walks like a lady / La do da / Lovin', touchin', squeezin' / Wheel in the sky / Any way you want it / The party's over (hopelessly in love). *(re-iss.+cd.Sep87)*
Mar 81. (7") **THE PARTY'S OVER (HOPELESSLY IN LOVE) (live). / WHEEL IN THE SKY (live)** [ ] [34] Feb 81

— (Apr81) **JONATHAN CAIN** (b.26 Feb'50, Chicago, Illinois) – keyboards, guitar, vocals (ex-BABYS) repl. ROLIE who went solo, and later formed The STORM with VALORY and SMITH
Aug 81. (lp)(c) **ESCAPE** [32] [1]
– Don't stop believin' / Stone in love / Who's crying now / Keep on runnin' / Still they ride / Escape / Lay it down / Dead or alive / Mother, father / Open arms. *(re-iss.Feb88)*
Jul 81. (7") **WHO'S CRYING NOW. / MOTHER, FATHER** [-] [4]
Aug 81. (7")(12") **WHO'S CRYING NOW. / ESCAPE** [ ] [4] Jul 81
Dec 81. (7")(12")(12"pic-d) **DON'T STOP BELIEVIN'. / NATURAL THING** [62] [9] Oct 81
Apr 82. (7") **OPEN ARMS. / LITTLE GIRL** [ ] [2] Jan 82
May 82. (7") **STILL THEY RIDE. / RAZA DEL SOL** [-] [19]
Aug 82. (7") **WHO'S CRYING NOW. / DON'T STOP BELIEVIN'** [46] [-]
(12") – ('A'side) / THE JOURNEY STORY (14 best snips).
Oct 82. (7") **STONE IN LOVE. / ONLY SOLUTIONS** [ ] [ ]
Feb 83. (lp)(c) **FRONTIERS** [6] [2]
– Separate ways (worlds apart) / Send her my love / Chain reaction / After the fall / Faithfully / Edge of the blade / Troubled child / Back talk / Frontiers / Rubicon. *(re-iss.cd Jun94 on 'Sony Europe')*
Feb 83. (7")(12") **SEPARATE WAYS (WORLDS APART). / FRONTIERS** [ ] [8]
Apr 83. (7") **FAITHFULLY. / FRONTIERS** [-] [12]
Apr 83. (7") **FAITHFULLY. / EDGE OF THE BLADE** [-] [-]
Jul 83. (7") **AFTER THE FALL. / OTHER SOLUTIONS** [-] [23]
Jul 83. (7") **AFTER THE FALL. / RUBICON** [ ] [-]
(12"+=) – Any way you want me / Don't stop believin'.
Sep 83. (7") **SEND HER MY LOVE. / CHAIN REACTION** [-] [ ]

— (the band take on some solo projects, see further below)
Feb 85. (7") **ONLY THE YOUNG. / ('B' side by Sammy Hagar)** [ ] [9] Jan 85
(above songs fron the film 'Vision Quest')

— **PERRY, SCHON and CAIN** regrouped and added **RANDY JACKSON** – bass (ex-ZEBRA) / **LARRIE LONDIN** – drums
Apr 86. (7") **BE GOOD TO YOURSELF. / ONLY THE YOUNG** [ ] [9]
(12"+=) – Any way you want it / Stone in love.
(d7"+=) – After the fall / Rubicon.
May 86. (lp)(c)(cd) **RAISED ON RADIO** [22] [4]
– Girl can't help it / Positive touch / Suzanne / Be good to yourself / Once you love somebody / Happy to give / Raised on radio / I'll be alright without you / It could have been you / The eyes of a woman / Why can't this night go on forever. *(re-iss.cd+c.Apr91 on 'Columbia')*
Jul 86. (7") **SUZANNE. / ASK THE LONELY** [ ] [17] Jun 86
(12"+=) – Raised on radio.

— (Aug86) **MIKE BAIRD** – drums repl. LONDIN
Oct 86. (7") **GIRL CAN'T HELP IT. / IT COULD HAVE BEEN YOU** [ ] [17] Aug 86
Jan 87. (7") **I'LL BE ALRIGHT WITHOUT YOU. / THE EYES OF A WOMAN** [ ] [14] Dec 86
Apr 87. (7") **WHY CAN'T THIS NIGHT GO ON FOREVER. / POSITIVE TOUCH** [-] [60]

— split early '87. CAIN and VALORY joined MICHAEL BOLTON. SCHON joined BAD ENGLISH in '89, then HARDLINE in '92 with ROLIE and SMITH.

– compilations, others, etc. –

All below on 'CBS' were issued on 'Columbia' US.
Sep 80. CBS; (t-lp) **IN THE BEGINNING** (first 3 albums) [ ] [ ] Jan 80
(re-iss.Aug84)
Dec 82. CBS; (c-ep) **CASSETTE EP** [ ] [ ]
– Don't stop believing / Who's crying now / Open arms / Lovin' touchin' squeezin'.
Feb 83. CBS; (d-c) **INFINITY / NEXT** [ ] [ ]
Aug 87. CBS; (d-lp)(d-c) **FRONTIERS / ESCAPE** [ ] [ ]
Dec 88. CBS; (lp)(c)(cd) **GREATEST HITS** [ ] [10]
– Only the young / Don't stop believin' / Wheel in the sky / Faithfully / I'll be alright with you / Any way you want it / Ask the lonely / Who's crying now / Separate ways (worlds apart) / Lights / Lovin', touchin', squeezin' / Open arms / Girl can't help it / Send her my love / Be good to yourself.
Mar 92. Columbia; (cd)(c) **JOURNEY – THE BALLADS** [ ] [ ]
Dec 92. Columbia; (t-cd)(t-c) **TIME 3** [ ] [90]
Jan 93. Columbia; (c-s)(cd-s) **LIGHTS. /** [-] [74]
Jan 89. Old Gold; (7") **WHO'S CRYING NOW. / OPEN ARMS** [ ] [ ]
(12"+=)(cd-s+=) – Suzanne / Don't stop believing.

NEAL SCHON / JAN HAMMER

collaboration with HAMMER – keyboards (solo)

C.B.S. Columbia
Nov 81. (lp)(c) **UNTOLD PASSION (instrumental)** [ ] [ ] Oct 81
– Wasting time / I'm talking to you / The ride / I'm down / Arc / It's alright / Hooked on love / On the beach / Untold passion.
Feb 83. (lp)(c) **HERE TO STAY** [ ] [ ]
– No more lies / Don't stay away / (You think you're) So hot / Turnaround / Self defence / Long time / Time again / Sticks and stones / Peace of mind / Covered by midnight.

— **NEAL SCHON** collaborated next (May84) on album 'THROUGH THE FIRE' with **SAMMY HAGAR, KENNY AARONSON & MIKE SHRIEVE.**

STEVE PERRY

C.B.S. Columbia
May 84. (7") **OH SHERRIE. / DON'T TELL ME WHY YOU'RE LEAVING** [ ] [3] Mar 84
May 84. (lp)(c) **STREET TALK** [ ] [12] Apr 84
– Oh Sherrie / I believe / Go away / Foolish heart / It's only love / She's mine / You should be happy / Running alone / Captured by the moment / Strung out.
Jul 84. (7") **SHE'S MINE. / YOU SHOULD BE HAPPY** [ ] [21] Jun 84
Sep 84. (7") **STRUNG OUT. /** [ ] [40]
Jan 85. (7") **FOOLISH HEART. / IT'S ONLY LOVE** [ ] [18] Nov 84

— STEVE PERRY released solo recordings between 88-89. In Aug94, 'Columbia' issued the album 'FOR THE LOVE OF STRANGE MEDICINE' hit UK 64.

The STORM

(**ROLIE** – vox, keys / **ROSS VALORY** – bass / **STEVE SMITH** – drums) with **KEVIN CHALFONT** – vocals (ex-707) / **JOSH RAMOS** – guitar (ex-LE MANS)

East West Interscope
Nov 91. (cd)(c)(lp) **THE STORM** [ ] [ ]
– You got me waiting / I've got a lot to learn about love / In the raw / You're gonna miss me / Call me / Show me the way / I want you back / Still loving you / Touch and go / Gimme love / Take me away / Can't live without your love.
Sep 91. (7")(c-s) **I'VE GOT A LOT TO LEARN ABOUT LOVE. / ?** [ ] [26]
(12"+=)(cd-s+=) – ?

HARDLINE

NEIL SCHON – lead guitar, vocals / **JOHNNY SCHON** – vocals / **JOEY GIOELLI** – guitar / **TODD JENSEN** – bass (ex-DAVID LEE ROTH) / **DEAN CASTRONOVO** – drums (ex-BAD ENGLISH)

M.C.A. M.C.A.

May 92. (cd)(c)(lp) **DOUBLE ECLIPSE** [ ] [ ]
– Life's a bitch / Doctor love / Red car / Change of heart / Everything / Taking me down / Hot Cheri / Bad taste / Can't find my way / I'll be there / 31-91 / In the hands of time.

Jun 92. (c-s) **CAN'T FIND MY WAY / HOT CHERIE / TAKIN' ME DOWN / I'LL BE THERE** [-] [ ]

JOY DIVISION

Formed: Salford, Manchester, England . . . mid'77 as The STIFF KITTENS, then WARSAW by IAN CURTIS, BERNARD ALBRECHT, PETER HOOK and STEPHEN MORRIS. By late '77 they became JOY DIVISION, and after an indie EP in 1978, signed to Tony Wilson's new 'Factory' records. They recorded a track 'AT A LATER DATE' for 10" 'Virgin' Various Artists lp 'Short Circuit: Live At The Electric Circus', before featuring on double compilation 'Factory' artists EP 'A Factory Sample', with tracks 'GLASS' & 'DIGITAL'. In mid'79, another 2 tracks 'AUTO-SUGGESTION' & 'FROM SAFETY TO WHERE', surfaced on 'Fast' records compilation EP 'Earcom 2'. Having earlier been given a longer termed contract by 'Factory' through manager Rob Gretton, they unleashed the excellent Martin Hannett produced lp 'UNKNOWN PLEASURES'. It's well documented the now rich and famous TONY WILSON (TV presenter), put his life savings of over £8,000 into band's lp expenses. It soon topped the indie charts, and was pursued by classic debut 45 'TRANSMISSION'. With a new lp in the can, and a free flexi-7" in the shops, IAN an epileptic suffered illness which cancelled several gigs. Tragically on the 18 May 1980, IAN CURTIS hanged himself after his depression caused by his recent marriage break-up. A month later, they were to have first UK Top 20 with superb 'LOVE WILL TEAR US APART'. It was soon followed by UK Top 10 lp 'CLOSER', which might have, who knows, made it in the States, where they were heading 3 days after IAN's death. With the remaining members becoming the massive NEW ORDER, many exploitation releases later hit chart. • **Style:** Alternative underground rock band, fronted by the manic, glossy-eyed IAN CURTIS, whose deep melancholy sound was reminiscent of JIM MORRISON but without the female fan adulation. • **Songwriters:** Group compositions except; SISTER RAY (Velvet Underground). • **Trivia:** Their name JOY DIVISION, was taken from Nazi concentration camp book 'House Of Dolls'. Obviously, they ran into a little media trouble, who unfairly branded them little Adolfs.

Recommended: UNKNOWN PLEASURES (*10) / CLOSER (*10) / SUBSTANCE (*9) / STILL (*8).

IAN CURTIS (b.1957, Macclesfield, England) – vocals / **BERNARD ALBRECHT** (b.BERNARD DICKEN, 4 Jan'56) – guitar, vocals / **PETER HOOK** (b.13 Feb'56) – bass / **STEPHEN MORRIS** (b.28 Oct'57, Macclesfield) – drums

Anonymous not issued

Jun 78. (12"ep) **AN IDEAL FOR LIVING** [ ] [-]
– An ideal for living / Warsaw / Leaders of men / No love lost / Failures. *(7"on 'Enigma', re-iss.1985 as 'THE IDEAL BEGINNING')*

Factory not issued

Aug 79. (lp) **UNKNOWN PLEASURES** [ ] [-]
– Disorder / Day of the lords / Candidate / Insight / New dawn fades / She's lost control / Shadowplay / Wilderness / Interzone / I remember nothing. *(re-dist.Jul80, hit No.71) (re-iss.Jul82, c-iss.Nov84, cd-iss.Apr86)(re-iss.cd+lp Jul93 on 'Centredate')*

Oct 79. (7")(12") **TRANSMISSION. / NOVELTY** [ ] [-]

Apr 80. (free 7"flexi) **KOMAKINO. / INCUBATION** [-] [-]

Jun 80. (7") **LOVE WILL TEAR US APART. / THESE DAYS** [13] [-]
(12"+=) – ('A' version). *(re-iss.Oct83, hit UK No.19)*

Jul 80. (lp) **CLOSER** [6] [-]
– Heart and soul / 24 hours / The eternal / Decades / Atrocity exhibition / Isolation / Passover / Colony / Means to an end. *(re-iss.+c.Jul82) (cd-iss.Apr86) (re-iss.cd+c Jul93 on 'Centredate')*

— After another fit of depression, IAN CURTIS hanged himself 18th May 1980. The others became NEW ORDER ⇒ .

– compilations & other posthumous releases etc. –

Sep 80. Factory Benelux; (12") **ATMOSPHERE. / SHE'S LOST CONTROL** [ ] [-]
(above was first released Mar80 in France with 'B' side 'DEAD SOULS')

Apr 81. Factory; (7"flexi) **KOMAKINO. / INCUBATION / THEN AGAIN** [ ] [-]

Oct 81. Factory; (d-lp) **STILL (rare & live)** [5] [-]
– Exercise one / Ice age / The sound of music / Glass / The only mistake / Walked in line / The kill / Something must break / Dead souls / Sister Ray / Ceremony / Shadowplay / Means to an end / Passover / New dawn fades / Transmission / Disorder / Isolation / Decades / Digital. *(re-iss.+c.Dec86, cd-iss.Mar90) (re-iss.cd+c Jul93 on 'Centredate')*

Jun 88. Factory; (7") **ATMOSPHERE. / THE ONLY MISTAKE** [34] [-]
(12"+=) – The sound of music / Transmission.
(cd-s+=) – Love will tear us apart.

Jul 88. Factory; (lp)(c) **SUBSTANCE** (The best of..) [7] [ ]
– She's lost control / Dead souls / Atmosphere / Love will tear us apart / Warsaw / Leaders of men / Digital / Transmission / Auto-suggestion. (cd+=) – (7 extra tracks). *(re-iss.cd+c Jul93 on 'Centredate')*

Jun 95. London; (c-s) **LOVE WILL TEAR US APART (radio version) / ('A'-original version)** [19] [ ]
(12"+=)(cd-s+=) – These days / Transmission.

Jun 95. London; (cd)(c)(d-lp) **PERMANENT: JOY DIVISION 1995 (remixes)** [16] [ ]
– Love will tear us apart / Transmission / She's lost control / Shadow play / Day of the lords / Isolation / Passover / Heart and soul / 24 hours / These days / Novelty / Dead souls / The only mistake / Something must break / Atmosphere / Love will tear us apart (permanent mix).

Nov 86. Strange Fruit; (12"ep) **THE PEEL SESSIONS (31.1.79)** [ ] [-]
– Exercise one / Insight / She's lost control / Transmission. *(cd-ep.iss.Jul88)*

Sep 87. Strange Fruit; (12"ep)**THE PEEL SESSIONS 2 (26.11.79)** [ ] [-]
– Love will tear us apart / 24 hours / Colony / The sound of music. *(cd-ep.iss.Jul88)*

Sep 90. Strange Fruit; (cd)(lp) **THE PEEL SESSIONS** (above 2) [ ] [-]

JUDAS PRIEST

Formed: Birmingham, England . . . 1969 by KK DOWNING and IAN HILL. In 1971, they recruited singer ROB HALFORD and drummer JOHN HINCH. 3 years later, after a few hundred gigs behind them, they brought in other guitarist GLENN TIPTON and signed to 'Decca' off-shoot 'Gull'. They released in 1974, a Roger Bain produced lp 'ROCKA ROLLA', and surfaced again in '76 with the excellent 'SAD WINGS OF DESTINY'. After a resounding appearance at the Reading Festival, they signed to 'CBS' early '77, and soon had a UK Top 30 album 'SIN AFTER SIN', produced by ROGER GLOVER (ex-Deep Purple). In the 80's, they became worldwide success with Top 20 lp's on both sides of the lake. • **Style:** Demonic heavy-metal act, fronted by leather-clad HALFORD. • **Songwriters:** TIPTON, HALFORD & DOWNING on most, except covers; DIAMONDS AND RUST (Joan Baez) / BETTER BY YOU, BETTER BY ME (Spooky Tooth) / THE GREEN MANALISHI (Fleetwood Mac) / JOHNNY B.GOODE (Chuck Berry). • **Trivia:** Their name was taken from the DYLAN track 'Frankie Lee & Judas Priest'. • **Miscellaneous:** Late in 1985, two of their fans shot themselves while listening to a track off the 'STAINED CLASS' album. A year later, the parents of the boys, sued the group and 'CBS', saying the album had sublimal Satanic messages in the lyrics, forcing the boys to commit suicide. This fiasco finally got to court in Jul'90, when the judge ruled against the dead boys' parents, although he did fine 'CBS' a 5-figure sum for withholding master tapes!!?

Recommended: SAD WINGS OF DESTINY (*8) / SIN AFTER SIN (*7) / THE COLLECTION (*7). STAINED CLASS is recommended to anyone who can't easily get a gun, a bazooka, a tank or any tacticle nuclear weapon to harm themselves with.

ROB HALFORD (b.25 Aug'51) – vocals repl. ALAN ATKINS / **KK DOWNING** (b.KENNETH) – guitars / **GLENN TIPTON** (b.25 Oct'48) – guitar, vocals / **IAN HILL** – bass / **JOHN HINCH** – drums repl. JOHN ELLIS

Gull-Decca Janus

Aug 74. (7") **ROCKA ROLLA. / NEVER SATISFIED** [ ] [-]

Sep 74. (lp) **ROCKA ROLLA** [ ] [-]
– One for the road / Rocka rolla / Winter / Deep freeze / Winter retreat / Cheater / Never satisfied / Run of the mill / Dying to meet you / Caviar and meths. *(re-iss.Sep77) (re-iss.Nov85 on 'Fame') (cd-iss.Nov87 on 'Line') (US-release Oct82 on 'Visa') (cd-iss.Mar93 on 'Repertoire')*

— **ALAN MOORE** – drums (who had been 1971 member) returned to repl. HINCH

Mar 76. (7") **THE RIPPER. / ISLAND OF DOMINATION** [ ] [ ]
(re-iss.12".Aug80)

Apr 76. (lp)(c) **SAD WINGS OF DESTINY** [ ] [ ]
– Prelude / Tyrant / Genocide / Epitaph / Island of domination / Victim of changes / The ripper / Epitaph / Dreamer deceiver. *(re-iss.Sep77) (cd-iss.Nov87 on 'Line') (re-iss.cd May95 on 'Repertoire')*

— **SIMON PHILLIPS** – drums repl. MOORE

C.B.S. Columbia

Apr 77. (7") **DIAMONDS AND RUST. / DISSIDENT AGGRESSOR** [ ] [-]

Apr 77. (lp)(c) **SIN AFTER SIN** [23] [ ]
– Sinner / Diamonds and rust / Starbreaker / Last rose of summer / Let us prey / Call for the priest / Raw deal / Here come the tears / Dissident aggressor. *(re-iss.Mar81) (re-iss.cd.Nov93 on 'Sony Collectors')*

— **LES BINKS** – drums repl. PHILLIPS

Jan 78. (7") **BETTER BY YOU, BETTER BY ME. / INVADER** [ ] [-]
Feb 78. (lp)(c) **STAINED CLASS** [27] [ ]
– Exciter / White heat, red hot / Better by you, better by me / Stained class / Invader / Saints in Hell / Savage / Beyond the realms of death / Heroes end. *(re-iss.Nov81) (cd+c re-iss.May91 on 'Columbia')*
Sep 78. (7") **EVENING STAR. / STARBREAKER** [ ] [-]
Nov 78. (lp)(c) **KILLING MACHINE** (US-title 'HELL BENT FOR LEATHER') [32] [ ]
– Delivering the goods / Rock forever / Evening star / Hell bent for leather / Take on the world / Burnin' up / Killing machine / Running wild / Before the dawn / Evil fantasies. *(re-iss.red-lp.Sep82)*
Oct 78. (7") **BEFORE THE DAWN. / ROCK FOREVER** [ ] [ ]
Jan 79. (7") **TAKE ON THE WORLD. / STARBREAKER** [ ] [14]
(re-iss.May82)
Apr 79. (7") **EVENING STAR. / BEYOND THE REALMS OF DEATH** [53] [ ]
(12"+=)(12"clear+=) – The green Manalishi.
May 78. (7") **ROCK FOREVER. / THE GREEN MANAZISHI (WITH THE TWO-PRONGED CROWN)** [-] [ ]
Sep 79. (lp)(c) **UNLEASHED IN THE EAST (live)** [10] [70]
– Exciter / Running wild / Sinner / The ripper / The green manalishi (with the two-pronged crown) / Diamonds and rust / Victim of changes / Genocide / Tyrant. *(free 7"w.a.)* **ROCK FOREVER / HELL BENT FOR LEATHER. / BEYOND THE REALMS OF DEATH** *(cd-iss.1988) (re-iss.cd May94 on 'Columbia')*
Dec 79. (7") **DIAMONDS AND RUST (live). / STARBREAKER (live)** [-] [ ]

—— **DAVE HOLLAND** – drums repl. BINKS

Mar 80. (7") **LIVING AFTER MIDNIGHT. / DELIVERING THE GOODS** [12] [ ]
Apr 80. (lp)(c) **BRITISH STEEL** [4] [34]
– Breaking the law / Rapid fire / Metal gods / Grinder / United / Living after midnight / You don't have to be old to be wise / The rage / Steeler. *(re-iss.+cd.Jan84) (re-iss.cd Jun94 on 'Sony')*
May 80. (7") **LIVING AFTER MIDNIGHT. / METAL GODS** [-] [-]
May 80. (7") **BREAKING THE LAW. / METAL GODS** [12] [ ]
Aug 80. (7") **UNITED. / GRINDER** [26] [ ]
(re-iss.Apr82)
Feb 81. (7") **DON'T GO. / SOLAR ANGELS** [51] [ ]
Feb 81. (7") **HEADING OUT TO THE HIGHWAY. / ROCK FOREVER** [-] [ ]
Feb 81. (lp)(c) **POINT OF ENTRY** [14] [39]
– Heading out to the highway / Don't go / Hot rockin' / Turning circles / Desert plains / Solar angels / You say yes / All the way / Troubleshooter / On the run.
Apr 81. (7") **HOT ROCKIN' / BREAKING THE LAW (live)** [60] [ ]
(12") – ('A'side) / Steeler / You don't have to be old to be wise.
Jul 82. (lp)(c) **SCREAMING FOR VENGEANCE** [11] [17]
– The hellion / Electric eye / Riding on the wind / Bloodstone / (Take these) Chains / Pain and pleasure / Screaming for vengeance / You've got another thing comin' / Fever / Devil's child. *(re-iss.Feb86)*
Aug 82. (7")(7"pic-d) **YOU'VE GOT ANOTHER THING COMIN'. / EXCITER (live)** [66] [-]
Oct 82. (7") **YOU'VE GOT ANOTHER THING COMIN'. / DIAMONDS AND RUST** [-] [67]
Oct 82. (7") **(TAKE THESE) CHAINS. / JUDAS PRIEST AUDIO FILE** [ ] [ ]
Jan 84. (7") **FREEWHEEL BURNING. / BREAKING THE LAW** [42] [-]
(12"+=) – You've got another thing comin'.
Jan 84. (lp)(c)(cd) **DEFENDERS OF THE FAITH** [19] [18]
– Freewheel burning / Jawbreaker / Rock hard ride free / The sentinel / Love bites / Eat me alive / Some heads are gonna roll / Night comes down / Heavy duty / Defenders of the faith.
Feb 84. (7") **SOME HEADS ARE GONNA ROLL. / BREAKING THE LAW (live)** [-] [-]
Mar 84. (7") **SOME HEADS ARE GONNA ROLL. / THE GREEN MANALISHI (WITH THE TWO-PRONGED CROWN)** [ ] [ ]
(12"+=) – Jailbreaker.
Apr 84. (7") **JAWBREAKER. / LOVE BITES** [-] [ ]
Apr 86. (lp)(c)(cd) **TURBO** [33] [17]
– Turbo lover / Locked in / Private property / Parental guidance / Rock you all around the world / Out in the cold / Wild night, hot and crazy days / Hot for love / Reckless. *(re-iss.Feb89)*
Apr 86. (7") **TURBO LOVER. / HOT FOR LOVE** [ ] [-]
May 86. (7") **LOCKED IN. / RECKLESS** [ ] [-]
('A'ext-12"+=) – Desert plains (live) / Freewheel burning (live).
May 86. (7") **LOCKED IN. / HOT FOR LOVE** [-] [ ]
Aug 86. (7") **TURBO LOVER. / RESTLESS** [-] [ ]
Nov 86. (7") **PARENTAL GUIDANCE. / ROCK YOU AROUND THE WORLD** [-] [ ]
Jun 87. (d-lp)(c)(cd) **PRIEST . . . LIVE (live)** [47] [38]
– Out in the cold / Heading out to the highway / Metal gods / Breaking the law / Love bites / Some heads are gonna roll / The sentinel / Private property / Rock you all around the world / Electric eye / Turbo lover / Freewheel burning / Parental guidance / Living after midnight / You've got another thing comin'.

Atlantic Columbia
Apr 88. (7") **JOHNNY B.GOODE. / ROCK AROUND THE WORLD** [64] [ ]
(12"+=) – Turbo lover.
May 88. (lp)(c)(cd) **RAM IT DOWN** [24] [31]
– Ram it down / Heavy metal / Love zone / Come and get it / Hard as iron / Blood red skies / I'm a rocker / Johnny B. Goode / Love you to death / Monsters of rock.

—— **SCOTT TRAVIS** – drums (ex-RACER-X) repl. HOLLAND

C.B.S. Columbia
Sep 90. (7")(c-s) **PAINKILLER. / UNITED** [74] [ ]
(12"+=)(cd-s+=) – Better by you, better than me.
Sep 90. (cd)(c)(lp) **PAINKILLER** [24] [26]
– Painkiller / Hell patrol / All guns blazing / Leather rebel / Metal meltdown / Night crawler / Between the hammer and the anvil / A touch of evil / Battle hymn (instrumental) / One shot at glory.

Columbia Columbia
Mar 91. (7")(c-s)(7"sha-pic-d) **A TOUCH OF EVIL. / BETWEEN THE HAMMER AND THE ANVIL** [58] [ ]
(12"+=)(cd-s+=) – You've got another thing comin' (live).

—— In Oct'92, HALFORD left after already forming FLIGHT in 1991.

Apr 93. (7")(c-s) **NIGHT CRAWLER (Edit) / BREAKING THE LAW** [63] [ ]
(cd-s+=) – Living After MIdnight
Apr 93. (d-cd)(d-c)(t-lp) **METAL WORKS '73-'93** (compilation) [37] [ ]
– The hellion / Electric eye / Victim of changes / Painkiller / Eat me alive / Devil's child / Dissident agrressor / Delivering the goods / Exciter / Breaking the law / Hell bent for leather / Blood red skies / Metal gods / Before the dawn / Turbo lover / Ram it down / Metal meltdown/ / Screaming for vengeance / You've got another thing comin' / Beyond the realms of death / Solar angels / Bloodstone / Desert plains / Wild nights, hot & crazy days / Heading out to the highway / Living after midnight / A touch of evil / The rage / Night comes down / Sinner / Freewheel burning / Night crawler.

– more compilations, others, etc. –

Feb 78. Gull; (lp)(pic-lp) **THE BEST OF JUDAS PRIEST** (early work) [ ] [-]
(cd-iss.May87, 2 extra tracks)
1979. Gull; (7") **THE RIPPER. / VICTIMS OF CHANGE** [ ] [-]
(12"+=) – Never satisfied.
Jun 83. Gull; (12"m) **TYRANT. / ROCKA ROLLA / GENOCIDE** [ ] [-]
Jan 83. CBS; (c-ep) **CASSETTE EP** [ ] [-]
– Breaking the law / Living after midnight / Take on the world / United.
Aug 83. CBS; (d-c) **SIN AFTER SIN / STAINED GLASS** [ ] [ ]
Sep 83. Scoop; (7"ep)(c-ep) **6 TRACK HITS** [ ] [-]
– Sinner / Exciter / Hell bent for leather / The ripper / Hot rockin' / The green manalishi.
Aug 86. Shanghai; (lp)(pic-lp) **JUDAS PRIEST** [ ] [-]
Feb 89. Old Gold; (7") **LIVING AFTER MIDNIGHT. / BREAKING THE LAW** [ ] [-]
May 89. Castle; (lp)(c)(cd) **THE COLLECTION** [ ] [-]
– (first two albums)
Mar 93. Columbia; (3xcd-box) **BRITISH STEEL / SCREAMING FOR VENGEANCE / STAINED GLASS** [ ] [ ]
Jul 95. Connoisseur; (cd) **HERO, HERO** [ ] [-]

JUSTIFIED ANCIENTS OF MUMU (see under ⇒ KLF)

KANSAS

Formed: Topeka, Kansas, USA . . . 1970 initially as WHITE CLOVER, by LIVGREN, HOPE and EHART. They brought in other 3 (see below) and became KANSAS during 1972. Two years later after constant touring, they signed to 'Kirshner' and hit US Top 200 with self-titled lp. In 1977, they had classic near US Top 10 smash with 'CARRY ON WAYWARD SON', from the Jeff Glixman produced Top 5 album 'LEFTOVERTURE'. Became major attractions for the next decade, until 1988 album 'IN THE SPIRIT OF THINGS' failed to make Top 100. • **Style:** Progressive hard-rock act, with harmonies and sound similar to BOSTON or STYX. • **Songwriters:** Mostly LIVGREN compositions. • **Trivia:** In 1977, STEVE WALSH guested vox on STEVE HACKETT album 'Please Don't Touch'.

Recommended: THE BEST OF KANSAS (*6)

STEVE WALSH (b.1951, St.Joseph) – vocals, keyboards, synthesizer / **KERRY LIVGREN** (b.18 Sep'49) – guitar, piano, synthesizer / **ROBBY STEINHARDT** (b.1951, Mississippi) – violin / **RICH WILLIAMS** (b.1951) – guitar / **DAVE HOPE** (b. 7 Oct'49) – bass / **PHIL EHART** (b.1951) – drums

Kirshner Kirshner

Nov 74. (7") **CAN I TELL YOU. / THE PILGRIMAGE** [-] [ ]
Feb 75. (7") **BRINGING IT ALL BACK. / LONELY WIND** [-] [ ]
Apr 75. (lp)(c) **KANSAS** [ ] [ ] Jun 74
– Can I tell you / Bringing it back / Lonely wind / Belexes / Journey from Mariabronn / The pilgrimage / Apercu / Death of Mother Nature suite. *(cd-iss.Oct93 on 'Sony Europe')*
Apr 75. (7") **SONG FOR AMERICA. / (part 2)** [-] [ ]
Aug 75. (lp)(c) **SONG FOR AMERICA** [ ] [57] Mar 75
– Down the road / Song for America / Lamplight symphony / Lonely street / The Devil game / Incomudro – hymn to the Atman.
Feb 76. (7") **IT TAKES A WOMAN'S LOVE (TO MAKE A MAN). / IT'S YOU** [-] [ ]
May 76. (lp)(c) **MASQUE** [ ] [70] Dec 75
– It takes a woman's love (to make a man) / Two cents worth / Icarus – borne on wings of steel / All the world / Child of innocence / It's you / Mysteries and mayhem / The pinnacle.
Dec 76. (lp)(c) **LEFTOVERTURE** [ ] [5] Nov 76
– Carry on wayward son / The wall / What's on my mind / Miracles out of nowhere / Opus insert / Questions of my childhood / Cheyenne anthem / Magnus opus: Father Padilla meets the gnat – Howling at the Moon – Man overboard – Industry on parade – Release the beavers – Gnat attack.
Jan 77. (7") **CARRY ON WAYWARD SON. / QUESTIONS OF MY CHILDHOOD** [-] [11]
May 77. (7") **WHAT'S ON MY MIND. / LONELY STREET** [-] [ ]
Nov 77. (lp)(c)(US-pic-lp) **POINT OF KNOW RETURN** [ ] [4] Oct 77
– Point of know return / Paradox / The spider / Portrait (he knew) / Closet chronicles / Lightning's hand / Dust in the wind / Sparks of the tempest / Nobody's home / Hopelessly human.
Dec 77. (7") **POINT OF KNOW RETURN. / CLOSET CHRONICLES** [ ] [28] Oct 77
Mar 78. (7") **DUST IN THE WIND. / PARADOX** [ ] [6] Jan78
Jun 78. (7") **CARRY ON WAYWARD SON. / QUESTIONS OF MY CHILDHOOD** [51] [-]
Jun 78. (7") **PORTRAIT (HE KNEW). / LIGHTNING'S HAND** [-] [64]
Dec 78. (d-lp)(c) **TWO FOR THE SHOW (live)** [ ] [32] Nov78
– Songs for America / Point of know return / Paradox / Icarus – borne on wings of steel / Portrait (he knew) / Carry on wayward son / Journey from Mariabronn / Dust in the wind / Lonely wind / Mysteries and mayhem / Lamplight symphony / The wall / Closet chronicles / Magnum opus: Father Padilla meets the gnat – Howling at the Moon – Man overboard – Industry on parade / Release the beavers – Gnat attack.
Jan 79. (7") **LONELY WIND. / SONG FOR AMERICA (live)** [-] [60]
Jun 79. (7") **PEOPLE OF THE SOUTH WIND. / STAY OUT OF TROUBLE** [ ] [23]
Jul 79. (lp)(c) **MONOLITH** [ ] [10] May 79
– On the other side / People of the south wind / Angels have fallen / How my soul cries out for you / A glimpse of home / Away from you / Stay out of trouble / Reason to be.
Sep 79. (7") **REASON TO BE. / HOW MY SOUL CRIES OUT FOR YOU** [-] [52]
Sep 80. (7") **HOLD ON. / DON'T OPEN YOUR EYES** [-] [40]
Oct 80. (lp)(c) **AUDIO-VISIONS** [ ] [26] Sep 80
– Relentless / Anything for you / Hold on / Loner / Curtain of iron / Got to rock on / Don't open your eyes / No one together / No room for a stranger / Back door.
Dec 80. (7") **GOT TO ROCK ON. / NO ROOM FOR A STRANGER** [-] [76]

—— **JOHN ELEFANTE** (b.1958, New York, USA) – vocals, keyboards repl. WALSH who continued on recent solo work.

Jul 82. (7") **PLAY THE GAME TONIGHT. / PLAY ON** [ ] [17] May 82
Jul 82. (lp)(c) **VINYL CONFESSIONS** [ ] [16] Jun 82
– Play the game tonight / Right away / Fair exchange / Chasing shadows / Diamonds and pearls / Face it / Windows / Borderline / Play on / Crossfire.
Aug 82. (7") **RIGHT AWAY. / WINDOWS** [-] [73]

—— now w/out STEINHARDT

Epic CBS Assoc.

Aug 83. (7") **FIGHT FIRE WITH FIRE. / INCIDENT ON A BRIDGE** [-] [58]
Sep 83. (lp)(c) **DRASTIC MEASURES** [ ] [41]
– Fight fire with fire / Everybody's my friend / Mainstream / Andi / Going through the motions / Get rich / Don't take your love away / End of the age / Incident on a bridge.
Sep 83. (7") **FIGHT FIRE WITH FIRE. / CARRY ON WAYWARD SON / DUST IN THE WIND** [ ] [-]
Nov 83. (7") **EVERYBODY'S MY FRIEND. / END OF THE AGE** [-] [ ]

—— Disbanded late 1983. Re-formed 1986 but without LIVGREN, HOPE & ELEFANTE. Past members **EHART & WILLIAMS** brought back **STEVE WALSH.** They recruited **STEVE MORSE** – guitar (ex-DIXIE DREGS) / **BILLY GREER** – bass (ex-STREETS)

M.C.A. M.C.A.

Dec 86. (lp)(c)(cd) **POWER** [ ] [35] Nov 86
– Silhouettes in disguise / Power / All I wanted / Secret service / We're not alone anymore / Musicatto / Taking in the view / Three pretenders / Tomb 19 / Can't cry anymore.
Jan 87. (7")(12") **ALL I WANTED. / WE'RE NOT ALONE ANYMORE** [ ] [19] Oct 86
Feb 87. (7") **POWER. / TOMB 19** [-] [84]
Apr 87. (7") **CAN'T CRY ANYMORE. / THREE PRETENDERS** [-] [ ]
Oct 88. (lp)(c)(cd) **IN THE SPIRIT OF THINGS** [ ] [ ]
– Ghosts / One big sky / Inside of me / One man, one heart * / House on fire / Once in a lifetime * / Stand beside me / I counted on love * / The preacher / Rainmaker / T.O. Witcher * / Bells of Saint James. *(cd+= *)*
Nov 88. (7") **STAND BESIDE ME. / HOUSE ON FIRE** [-] [ ]

—— In 1991, they added **DAVID RAGSDALE** – violin

—— **WALSH / LIVGREN / EHART / RAGSDALE**

Jul 93. Now & Then; (cd) **LIVE AT THE WHISKY (live)** [ ] [ ]

Essential Rykodisc

Jul 95. (cd)(c) **FREAKS OF NATURE** [ ] [ ]
– I can fly / Desperate times / Hope once again / Black fathom four / Under the knife / Need / Freaks of nature / Cold grey morning / Peaceful and warm.

– compilations, others –

Sep 84. Epic/ US= CBS Assoc; (lp)(c) **THE BEST OF KANSAS** [ ] [ ]
– Carry on wayward son / The point of know return / Fight fire / No one together / Play the game tonight / The wall. *(cd-iss. Nov85)*
Jul 94. Legacy; (d-cd) **THE KANSAS BOXED SET** [ ] [ ]

STEVE WALSH

solo, with some KANSAS members.

not issued Kirshner

Mar 80. (lp) **SCHEMER-DREAMER** [-] [ ]
– Schemer-dreamer (that's all right) / Get too far / So many nights / You think you

got it made / Every step of the way / Just how does it feel / Wait until tomorrow.

Mar 80. (7") **SCHEMER-DREAMER (THAT' ALL RIGHT). / JUST HOW DOES IT FEEL** [-] [ ]

Jun 80. (7") **EVERY STEP OF THE WAY. / YOU THINK YOU GOT IT MADE** [-] [ ]

After his KANSAS departure early '81, WALSH formed STREETS with **MIKE SLAMER** – guitar (ex-CITY BOY) / **BILLY GREER** – bass / **TIM GEHRT** – drums. Released 2 albums for 'Atlantic' between 1983 & 1985; STREETS & CRIMES IN MIND.

KERRY LIVGREN

solo, with KANSAS members.

not issued / Kirshner

Oct 80. (lp) **SEEDS OF CHANGE** [-] [ ]
– Just one way / Mask of the great deceiver / How can you live / Whiskey seed / To live for the king / Down to the core / Ground zero.

Oct 80. (7") **MASK OF THE GREAT DECEIVER. / TO LIVE FOR THE KING** [-] [ ]

— After he left KANSAS in 1982, he made 4 more albums, mostly religious. He also formed Christian band AD in 1984.

Paul KANTER & Grace SLICK (see under ⇒ JEFFERSON AIRPLANE)

Mick KARN (see under ⇒ JAPAN)

John KAY (see under ⇒ STEPPENWOLF)

KHAN (see under ⇒ HILLAGE, Steve)

KILBURN & THE HIGH ROADS (see under ⇒ DURY, Ian)

KILLING JOKE

Formed: London, England ... 1979 by JAZ COLEMAN and PAUL FERGUSON, who soon moved to Cheltenham. After supporting the likes of JOY DIVISION and The RUTS, they signed to 'Island-EG', and started own label 'Malicious Damage'. After a number of singles received airplay on John Peel show, they unleashed classic eponymous debut lp in Autumn of 1980. This dented the UK Top 40, and paved the way for future chart ventures. • **Style:** A hybrid of angst punk-metal, experimental rock with occult lyrics, fronted by the extreme clown-faced showman JAZ. **Songwriters:** COLEMAN and group compositions. • **Trivia:** YOUTH's departure early in '82, was due to JAZ and GEORDIE's disappearance on tour in Iceland.

Recommended: KILLING JOKE (*9) / FIRE DANCES (*7) / LAUGH, I NEARLY BOUGHT ONE (*8) / WHAT'S THIS FOR (*6) / DEMOCRACY (*6)

JAZ COLEMAN (b. Egypt) – vocals, keyboards / **GEORDIE** (WALKER) – guitar, synthesizers / **YOUTH** (b. MARTIN GLOVER, 27 Dec'60, Africa) – bass, vocals (ex-RAGE) / **PAUL FERGUSON** – drums

Malicious Damage / not issued

Oct 79. (10"m) **ARE YOU RECEIVING ME. / TURN TO RED / NERVOUS SYSTEM** [ ] [-]

Island / not issued

Nov 79. (7") **NERVOUS SYSTEM. / TURN TO RED** [ ] [-]
(12"+=) – Almost red / Are you receiving me.

Malicious Damage / not issued

Mar 80. (7") **WARDANCE. / PSYCHE** [ ] [-]

Malicious Damage-EG / not issued

Sep 80. (7") **REQUIEM. / CHANGE** [ ] [-]
(12"+=) – Requiem 434 / Change (version).

Oct 80. (lp)(c) **KILLING JOKE** [39] [-]
– Requiem / Wardance / Tomorrow's world / Bloodsport / The wait / Complications / S.O. 36 / Primitive. *(re-iss.+cd Jan87)*

May 81. (7") **FOLLOW THE LEADERS. / TENSION** [55] [-]
(10"+=)(12"+=) – ('A'dub).

Jun 81. (lp)(c) **WHAT'S THIS FOR . . .!** [42] [-]
– The fall of Because / Tension / Unspeakable / Butcher / Follow the leaders / Madness / Who told you how? / Exit. *(re-iss.+cd Jan87)*

E.G. / Virgin

Mar 82. (7") **EMPIRE SONG. / BRILLIANT** [43] [-]

— **GUY PRATT** – bass repl. YOUTH who formed BRILLIANT

Apr 82. (lp)(c) **REVELATIONS** [12] [-]
– The hum / Empire song / We have joy / Chop-chop / The Pandys are coming / Chapter III / Have a nice day / Land of milk and honey / Good samaritan / Dregs. *(re-iss.+cd Jan87)*

Jun 82. (7") **CHOP-CHOP. / GOOD SAMARITAN** [ ] [-]

Oct 82. (7") **BIRDS OF A FEATHER. / FLOCK THE B-SIDE** [64] [-]
(12"+=) – Sun goes down.

Nov 82. (10"m-lp) **HA – KILLING JOKE LIVE (live)** [66] [-]
– Psyche / Sun goes down / The Pandys are coming / Take take take / Unspeakable / Wardance.

— **PAUL RAVEN** – bass (ex-NEON HEARTS) repl. PRATT who joined ICEHOUSE

Jun 83. (7") **LET'S ALL GO (TO THE FIRE DANCES). / DOMINATOR** [51] [-]
(12"+=) – The fall of Because (live).

Jul 83. (lp)(c) **FIRE DANCES** [29] [ ]
– The gathering / Fun and games / Rejuvenation / Frenzy / Harlequin / Feast of blaze / Song and dance / Dominator / Let's all go (to the fire dances) / Lust almighty. *(re-iss.+cd Jan87)*

Oct 83. (7") **ME OR YOU?. / WILFUL DAYS** [57] [-]
(10"+=)(12"+=) – Feast of blaze.
(d7"++=) – ('A'side again).

Mar 84. (7") **EIGHTIES. / ('A'-The coming mix)** [60] [-]
(12"+=) – ('A'dance mix).

Jun 84. (7") **A NEW DAY. / DANCE DAY** [56] [-]
(12"+=) – ('A'dub).

Jan 85. (7") **LOVE LIKE BLOOD. / BLUE FEATHER** [16] [-]
(12"+=) – ('A'instrumental).
(d7"+=) – ('A'-Gestalt mix).

Feb 85. (lp)(c) **NIGHT TIME** [11] [ ]
– Night time / Darkness before dawn / Love like blood / Kings and queens / Tabazan / Multitudes / Europe / Eighties. *(re-iss.+cd Jan87)*

Mar 85. (7") **KINGS AND QUEENS. / THE MADDING CROWD** [58] [ ]
(12"+=) – ('A'-Royal mix).
(12"+=) – ('A'-Knave mix).

Aug 86. (7") **ADORATIONS. / EXILE** [42] [-]
(12"+=) – Ecstacy.
(d7"++=) – ('A'instrumental).

Oct 86. (7") **SANITY. / GOODBYE TO THE VILLAGE** [70] [-]
(12"+=) – Victory.
(free c-s with-7"+=) – Wardance.

Nov 86. (lp)(c)(cd) **BRIGHTER THAN A THOUSAND SUNS** [54] [ ]
– Adorations / Sanity / Chessboards / Twilight of the mortal / Love of the masses / A southern sky / Wintergardens / Rubicon. *(c+=)(cd+=)–* Goodbye to the village / Victory.

Apr 88. (7") **AMERICA. / JIHAD** [ ] [-]
(12"+=) – ('A'extended).
(cd-s+=) – Change.

Jun 88. (lp)(c)(cd) **OUTSIDE THE GATE** [92] [ ]
– America / My love of this land / Stay one jump ahead / Unto the ends of the Earth / The calling / Obsession / Tiahuanaco / Outside the gate. *(cd+=)–* America (extended) / Stay one jump ahead (extended).

Jul 88. (7") **MY LOVE OF THIS LAND. / DARKNESS BEFORE DAWN** [ ] [-]
(12"+=) – Follow the leaders (dub) / Psyche.
(10"+=) – Follow the leaders (dub) / Sun goes down.

— **JAZ** and **GEORDIE** brought in new members **MARTIN ATKINS** – drums (ex-PUBLIC IMAGE LTD.) repl. FERGUSON / **TAFF** – bass repl. ANDY ROURKE (ex-SMITHS) who had repl. RAVEN. Early 1990, **JAZ COLEMAN** teamed up with **ANNE DUDLEY**(see; ART OF NOISE)

— **KILLING JOKE** reformed (**JAZ, GEORDIE, MARTIN & PAUL**)

Noise Int. / Noise Int.

Nov 90. (cd)(c)(lp) **EXTREMITIES, DIRT AND VARIOUS REPRESSED EMOTIONS** [ ] [-]
– Money is not our god / Age of greed / Beautiful dead / Extremities / Inside the termite mound / Intravenus / Solitude / North of the border / Slipstream / Kalijuga struggle.

Jan 91. (12")(cd-s) **MONEY IS NOT OUR GOD. / NORTH OF THE BORDER** [ ] [-]

Invisible / not issued

Jul 93. (d-lp) **THE COURTHOLD TALKS** [ ] [-]
– (spoken word with JAZ, GEORDIE & JAFF SCANTLEBURY on percussion)

Butterfly-Big Life

Mar 94. (10"ep)(cd-ep) **EXORCISM. / ('A'live) / ('A'-German mix) / WHITEOUT(ugly mix) / ANOTHER CULT GOES DOWN (mix) / ('A'-bictonic revenge mix)** [ ] [-]

Apr 94. (7"clear)(c-s) **MILLENNIUM. / ('A'-Cybersank remix)** [34] [ ]
(12"+=)(cd-s+=) – ('A'-Drum Club remix) / ('A'Juno Reactor remix).

Jul 94. (12")(c-s)(cd-s) **PANDEMONIUM. / ('A'mix)** [28] [ ]
(cd-s) – ('A'side) / Requiem (Kris Weston & Greg Hunter remix).

Jul 94. (cd)(c)(d-lp) **PANDEMONIUM** [16] [ ]
– Pandemonium / Exorcism / Millenium / Communion / Black Moon / Labyrinth / Jana / Whiteout / Pleasures of the flesh / Mathematics of chaos.

— Re-united originals **JAZ COLEMAN / GEORDIE + YOUTH**

Jan 95. (cd-ep) **JANA (Youth remix) / JANA (Dragonfly mix) / LOVE LIKE BLOOD (live) / WHITEOUT** 54
(12"ep)(cd-ep+=) – Jana (live) / Wardance (live) / Exorcism (live) / Kings and queens (live).

... Jan – Jun '96 stop press ...

Mar 96. (single) **DEMOCRACY** 39
Apr 96. (cd)(c)(lp) **DEMOCRACY** 71

– compilations, others, etc. –

Sep 92. Virgin; (12")(c-s) **CHANGE. / REQUIEM**
(cd-s) – ('A'spiral tribe mix). / ('B'trash Greg Hunter mix).
(cd-s) – ('A'-Youth mix). / ('B'-Youth mix).

Oct 92. (cd)(c)(lp) **LAUGH, I NEARLY BOUGHT ONE**
– Turn to red / Psyche / Requiem / Wardance / Follow the leaders / Unspeakable / Butcher / Exit / The hum / Empire song / Chop-chop / The Sun goes down / Eighties / Darkness before dawn / Love like blood / Wintergardens / Age of greed.

May 95 Virgin; (cd) **WILFUL DAYS** (remixes) -

Oct 95. Windsong; (cd) **BBC LIVE IN CONCERT (live)** -

KING CRIMSON

Formed: Bournemouth, England ... summer 1967 by ROBERT FRIPP, plus brothers MIKE and PETE GILES, who formed soft-rock trio GILES, GILES & FRIPP. After signing to 'Deram' early in '68, and adding couple IAN McDONALD and JUDY DYBLE, they issued flop lp 'THE CHEERFUL INSANITY OF ... ' in Sep'68. With IAN now replacing PETE, the trio soon became KING CRIMSON, and added new vocalist GREG LAKE, who debuted at The Speakeasy on 9th Apr'69. 3 months later, they supported The ROLLING STONES at Hyde Park's free concert, which attracted 'Island' label. In Oct'69, they unleashed 'IN THE COURT OF THE CRIMSON KING', a masterful debut lp which made UK Top 5 and US Top 30. During the early 70's, they were in turmoil once more, when more group members departed, leaving FRIPP and lyricist and road manager PETE SINFIELD to work things out. Eventually with augmentation from session men and departees, they recorded 1970 follow-up lp 'IN THE WAKE OF POSEIDON'. An aggregation of KING CRIMSON members had earlier in March, played on 'Top Of The Pops' with weird 'CAT FOOD' 45. FRIPP and group went through more upheavals, but with astounding album successes, until they split late 1974. FRIPP had already been prolific session man for VAN DER GRAAF GENERATOR plus ENO. With the latter he was co-credited on 2 experimental budget lp's 'NO PUSSYFOOTIN'' (1973) & 'EVENING STAR' (1975). He then moved to New York and worked with PETER GABRIEL on his first 3 albums, BOWIE on 'Heroes' & BLONDIE. In 1979, FRIPP released debut solo album 'EXPOSURE', which featured many of said friends handling vocals (see below). The next year, his instrumental set 'GOD SAVE THE QUEEN / UNDER HEAVY MANNERS', was followed by his short-lived project/band LEAGUE OF GENTLEMEN. In 1981, he re-formed KING CRIMSON with BILL BRUFORD, ADRIAN BELEW & TONY LEVIN. They made 3 more fruitful albums, before they too left FRIPP to ponder solo pastures. Between 1982-84, FRIPP had collaborated on 2 albums 'I ADVANCE MASKED' & 'BEWITCHED', with ANDY SUMMERS (ex-POLICE). • **Style:** Progressive neo-classical rock outfit, whose initial MOODY BLUES' mellotron-sound was swopped for the distinctive self-indulgence master of guitar FRIPP. In the early 70's, they advanced with jazz-rock tinted fusion, and in the 80's a more modern, solid & basic approach with many directions. FRIPP solo often experimented with his electronics, which were dubbed in the early 80's as 'Frippertronics'. • **Songwriters:** FRIPP music, lyrics as said. BELEW collaborated in the 80's. • **Trivia:** In the mid-80's, FRIPP married singer / actress TOYAH WILLCOX, and even collaborated with her on an album 'THE LADY OR THE TIGER' (1987).

Recommended: IN THE COURT OF THE CRIMSON KING (*9) / IN THE WAKE OF POSEIDON (*6) / LIZARD (*6) / ISLANDS (*7) / LARK'S TONGUE'S IN ASPIC (*8) / RED (*8) / STARLESS & BIBLE BLACK (*8) / FRAME BY FRAME – THE CONCISE ... (*9) / NETWORK (*7).

GILES, GILES & FRIPP

PETE GILES – bass / **MICHAEL GILES** (b.1942)– drums / **ROBERT FRIPP** (b. May'46, Wimbourne, Dorset, England)– guitar

Deram | not issued

Jun 68. (7") **ONE IN A MILLION. / NEWLY WEDS** -

— added **IAN McDONALD** (b.25 Jun'46, London) – keyboards / and guest **JUDY DYBLE** – vocals (ex-FAIRPORT CONVENTION) also featured as did KING CRIMSON lyricist **PETE SINFIELD**

Sep 68. (lp) **THE CHEERFUL INSANITY OF GILES, GILES & FRIPP** -
– The Saga of Rodney Toady / One in a million / Just George / Thursday morning / North meadow / Call tomorrow / Newly weds / Digging my lawn / Suite No.1 / Little children / The crukster / How do you know / The sun is shining / Brudite eyes / Elephant song. *(re-iss.Apr82)*

— IAN now on vocals (JUDY left to join TRADER HORNE)

Sep 68. (7") **THURSDAY MORNING. / ELEPHANT SONG** -

KING CRIMSON

ROBERT, IAN & MIKE recruited **GREG LAKE** (b.10 Nov'48) – vocals, bass (ex-GODS)

Island | Atlantic

Oct 69. (7") **THE COURT OF THE CRIMSON KING. / (Pt.2)** — 80 Dec 69
Oct 69. (lp)(c) **IN THE COURT OF THE CRIMSON KING** 5 — 28 Dec 69
– 21st century schizoid man (including; Mirrors) / I talk to the wind / Epitaph (including; March for no reason – Tomorrow and tomorrow) / Moonchild (including; The dream – The illusion) / The court of the Crimson King (including; The return of the fire witch – The dance of the puppets). *(re-iss.Mar77 on 'Polydor', cd-May83) (re-iss.+cd.Jan87 on 'EG')*

— **PETE GILES** – bass (ex-GILES, GILES & FRIPP) repl. IAN who with MIKE had formed McDONALD & GILES. IAN later formed FOREIGNER. MIKE appeared below. Added **KEITH TIPPET** – piano (other two were FRIPP & LAKE)

Mar 70. (7") **CAT FOOD. / GROON**

— added **MEL COLLINS** – saxophone (ex-CIRCUS) / plus guest on 1 track **GORDON HASKELL** – vocals

May 70. (lp)(c) **IN THE WAKE OF POSEIDON** 4 — 31 Sep 70
– Peace – a beginning / Pictures of a city (including; 42nd at Treadmill) / Cadence and cascade / In the wake of Poseidon (including; Libra's theme) / Peace – a theme / Cat food / The Devil's triangle: Merday morn – Hand of Sceiron – Garden of worm / Peace – an end. *(re-iss.Mar77 on 'Polydor') (re-iss.+cd.Jan87 on 'EG')*

— **GORDON HASKELL** (now full-time) repl. GREG who formed EMERSON, LAKE & PALMER (earlier). FRIPP had also retained **MEL COLLINS. / ANDY McCULLOCH** – drums repl. MIKE

Dec 70. (lp)(c) **LIZARD** 30
– Cirkus (including; Entry of the chameleons) / Indoor games / Happy family / Lady of the dancing water / Lizard suite: Prince Rupert awakes – Bolero-The peacock's tale – The battle of glass tears; (a) Dawn song – (b) Last skirmish – (c) Prince Rupert's lament / Big top. *(re-iss.Apr77 on 'Polydor') (re-iss.+cd.Jan87 on 'EG')*

— **BOZ BURRELL** – vocals, bass repl. HASKELL who went solo / **IAN WALLACE** – drums repl. McCULLOCH who joined GREENSLADE

Dec 71. (lp)(c) **ISLANDS** 30 — 76
– Formentera lady / The sailor's tale / Letters / (prelude) / Song of the gulls – Islands / Ladies of the road. *(re-iss.Apr77 on 'Polydor') (re-iss.+cd.Jan87 on 'EG')*

Island-Help | Antilees

Jun 72. (lp) **EARTHBOUND (live)**
– 21st century schizoid man / Peoria / The sailor's tale / Earthbound / Groon. *(re-iss.Oct77 on 'Polydor') (re-iss.Apr82 on 'EG')*

— FRIPP was sole survivor (lyricist PETE SINFIELD left early '72, to go into production for ROXY MUSIC's debut and be lyricist for Italiand P.F.M.) / **JOHN WETTON** – vocals, bass (ex-FAMILY) repl. BOZ who formed BAD COMPANY / **BILL BRUFORD** – drums (ex-YES) repl. WALLACE who joined STREETWALKERS / **DAVID CROSS** – violin, flute repl. COLLINS who later joined CAMEL + sessions / added **JAMIE MUIR** – percussion and new lyricist **RICHARD PALMER-JAMES**

Island | Atlantic

Mar 73. (lp)(c) **LARKS' TONGUES IN ASPIC** 20 — 61
– Larks' tongues in aspic (part one) / Book of Saturday / Exiles / Easy money / The talking drum / Larks' tongues in aspic (part two). *(re-iss.Apr77 on 'Polydor')(re-iss.+cd.Jan87 on 'EG')*

— Reverted to a quartet when JAMIE became a Tibetan monk

Feb 74. (7") **THE NIGHT WATCH. / THE GREAT DECEIVER**
Feb 74. (lp)(c) **STARLESS AND BIBLE BLACK** 28 — 64
– The great deceiver / Lament / We'll let you know / The night watch / Trio / The mincer / Starless and bible black / Trio / Fracture. *(re-iss.Apr77 on 'Polydor') (re-iss.+cd.Jan87 on 'EG')*

— now just basically a trio of FRIPP, WETTON and BRUFORD with old guests **MEL COLLINS, IAN McDONALD** and the departing **CROSS** augmenting on a track

Oct 74. (lp)(c) **RED** 45 — 66
– Red / Fallen angel / One more red nightmare / Providence / Starless. *(re-iss.Apr77 on 'Polydor') (re-iss.+cd.Jan87 on 'EG')*

— Split just before last album. Next live album was recorded with DAVID CROSS

Apr 75. (lp)(c) **U.S.A. (live)**
– Larks' tongues in aspic (part II) / Lament / Exiles / Asbury park / Easy money / 21st century schizoid man. *(re-iss.Dec79 on 'Polydor')*

— JOHN WETTON joined BRIAN FERRY, then URIAH HEEP and later ASIA etc. As above BILL BRUFORD went solo and formed UK, after GONG stints.

ROBERT FRIPP

solo adding keyboards and a number of friends **PETER GABRIEL, PETER HAMILL & DARYL HALL** on vox, plus **PHIL COLLINS, BARRY ANDREWS, TONY LEVIN & MICHAEL NARADA WALDEN** – other instruments

E.G. Polydor

Apr 79. (lp)(c) **EXPOSURE** [71] [79]
– (prelude) / You burn me up I'm a cigarette / Breathless / Disengage / North star / Chicago / NY3 / Mary / Exposure / Haaaden two / Urban landscape / I may not have had enough of me but I've had enough of you / (first inaugural address to the J.A.C.E. Sherborne House) / Water music I / Here comes the flood / Water music II / Postscript. *(re-iss.Jul85 & Jan87)*

Mar 80. (lp)(c) **GOD SAVE THE QUEEN / UNDER HEAVY MANNERS (instrumental)** [ ] [ ]
– Under heavy manners / The zero of the signified / Red two scorer / God save the Queen / 1983. *(re-iss.Jan87)*

Apr 81. (lp) **LET THE POWER FALL (FRIPPERTRONICS)** [ ] [ ]
– 1984 / 1985 / 1986 / 1987 / 1988 / 1989. *(re-iss.+cd.Jan87)*

LEAGUE OF GENTLEMEN

FRIPP retained **BARRY ANDREWS** adding **SARA LEE** – bass (ex-JANE AIRE) / **JOHNNY TOOBAD** – drums

E. G. Polydor

Dec 80. (7")**HEPTAPARAPARSHINOKH / MARRIAGEMUZIC** [ ] [-]

Mar 81. (lp)(c) **LEAGUE OF GENTLEMEN (instrumental)** [ ] [ ]
– Indiscreet / Inductive recurrance / Minor man / Heptaparaparshinokh / Dislocated / Pareto optimum 1 / Eye needles / Indiscreet II / Pareto optimum 2 / Cognitive dissonance / H.G. Wells / Trap / Ochre / Indiscreet III.

Mar 81. (7") **DISLOCATED. / 1984** [ ] [ ]

KING CRIMSON

FRIPP along with past member BRUFORD recruits newcomers **ADRIAN BELEW** – guitar, vocals (ex-TOM TOM CLUB) / **TONY LEVIN** – bass (ex-session man including PETER GABRIEL)

E.G. Warners

Sep 81. (lp)(c) **DISCIPLINE** [41] [45]
– Elephant talk / Frame by frame / Matte Kudasai / Indiscipline / ThelaHun ginjeet / The sheltering sky / Discipline. *(re-iss.+cd.Jan87) (re-iss.Jun88)*

Nov 81. (7") **MATTE KUDASAI. / ELEPHANT TALK** [ ] [-]

Jun 82. (lp)(c) **BEAT** [39] [52]
– Neal and Jack and me / Heartbeat / Sartori in Tangier / Waiting man / Neurotica / Two hands / The howler / Requiem. *(cd-iss.Apr84) (re-iss.+cd.Jan87)*

Jun 82. (7") **HEARTBEAT. / REQUIEM (excerpt)** [ ] [ ]

Feb 84. (7") **SLEEPLESS. / NUAGES** [ ] [ ]
(12") – ('A'side) / ('A'instrumental & dance vesions).

Mar 84. (lp)(c)(cd) **THREE OF A PERFECT PAIR** [30] [58]
– Three of a perfect pair / Model man / Sleepless / Man with an open heart / Nuages (that which passes, passes like clouds) / Industry / Dig me / No warning / Lark's tongues in aspic (part three). *(re-iss.Jan87)*

— FRIPP disbanded KING CRIMSON project for a decade.

– compilations, others, etc. –

Feb 76. Island/ US= Atlantic; (d-lp)(c) **A YOUNG PERSON'S GUIDE TO KING CRIMSON** [ ] [ ]
– Epitaph (including; (a) March for no reason – (b) Tomorrow and tomorrow / Cadence and cascade / Ladies of the road / I talk to the wind / Red / Starless / The night watch / Book of Saturday / Peace – a beginning / Cat food / Groon / Coda from Larks' tongue's in aspic part 2 / Moonchild; (a) Mirrors – (b) The illusion / Trio / The court of the crimson king (including; (a) The return of the fire witch – (b) Dance of the puppets / 21st century schizoid man. *(re-iss.Mar77 on 'Polydor', cd-iss.1986 on 'E.G.')*

Feb 76. Island; (7") **21ST CENTURY SCHIZOID MAN. / EPITAPH** [ ] [ ]

Dec 80. Polydor; (d-lp) **IN THE COURT OF THE CRIMSON KING / LARKS' TONGUES IN ASPIC** [ ] [-]

Dec 86. E.G.; (cd)(d-lp)(d-c) **THE COMPACT KING CRIMSON** [ ] [ ]

Dec 89. E.G.; (3xlp)(3xc)(3xcd) **IN THE COURT OF THE CRIMSON KING / LARK'S TONGUES IN ASPIC / DISCIPLINE** [ ] [-]

(above 3 albums were packaged with other 'Island' artists)

1991. E.G.; (cd-ep) **HEARTBEAT – ABBRIEVIATED KING CRIMSON** [ ] [-]
– The King Crimson barber shop – 21st century schizoid man – Court of the crimson king – Elephant talk – Matte Kudesai – Heartbeat (edit).

Dec 91. Virgin; (cd) **FRAME BY FRAME: THE ESSENTIAL KING CRIMSON** [ ] [-]

Sep 93. Virgin; (cd)(c) **SLEEPLESS: THE CONCISE KING CRIMSON** [ ] [ ]
– 21st century schizoid man / Epitaph / In the court of the crimson king / Cat food / Ladies of the road / Starless (abridged) / Red / Fallen angel / Elephant talk / Frame by frame / Matte Kudasai / Heartbeat / Three of a perfect pair / Sleepless.

Dec 93. Virgin; (3xcd-box) **IN THE COURT OF THE CRIMSON KING / IN THE WAKE OF POSEIDON / LIZARD** [ ] [-]

ROBERT FRIPP / LEAGUE OF GENTLEMEN

E.G. E.G.

1985. (lp)(c) **GOD SAVE THE KING** [ ] [ ]
– God save the King / Under heavy manners / Heptaparparshinokh / Inductive resonance / Cognitive dissonance / Dislocated / HG Wells / Eye needles / Trap.

Nov 86. (lp)(c)(cd) **ROBERT FRIPP AND THE LEAGUE OF CRAFTY GUITARISTS: LIVE! (live)** [ ] [ ]
– Guitar craft theme 1: Invocation / Tight muscle party at Love Beach / The chords that bind / Guitar craft theme 3: Eye of the needle / All or nothing II / Guitar craft theme 2: Aspiration / All or nothing I / Circulation / A fearful symmetry / The new world / Crafty march.

— Late 1988, FRIPP / FRIPP (TOYAH) toured augmented by **TREY GUNN** – stick bass / **PAUL BEAVIS** – percussion, drums

— In mid'93, ROBERT FRIPP collaborated with ex-JAPAN singer DAVID SYLVIAN on near UK Top 20 album 'THE FIRST DAY'.

— In Aug'94, FRIPP was part of FFWD alongside THOMAS FEHLYN, KRIS WESTON + Dr.ALEX PATTERSON of The ORB. In Sep'94, FRIPP again teamed up with DAVID SYLVIAN on album 'DAMAGE'.

KING CRIMSON

— **FRIPP / BRUFORD / BELEW / LEVIN / GUNN / MASTELOTTO**

Discipline Virgin

Dec 94. (cd)(c) **VROOOM** [ ] [ ]
– Vrooom / Sex, sleep, eat, drink, dream / Cage / Thrak / When I say stop, continue / One time.

Apr 95. (cd)(c) **THRAK** [58] [83]
– Vrooom / Coda: Marine 475 / Dinosaur / Walking on air / B'boom / Thrak / Inner garden I / People / Radio I / One time / Radio II / Inner garden II / Sex, sleep, eat, drink, dream / Vrooom vrooom / Vrooom vrooom coda.

Aug 95. (d-cd) **B'BOOM: OFFICIAL SOUNDTRACK – LIVE IN ARGENTINA (live** [ ] [-]
– Vrooom / Frame by frame / Sex, sleep, eat, drink, dream / Red / One time / B'boom / Thrak / Improv – Two sticks / Elephant talk / Indiscipline // Vrooom vrooom / Matte Kudesai / The talking drum / Lark's tongues in aspic (part 2) / Heartbeat / Sleepless / People / B'boom / Thrak.

ROBERT FRIPP

Discipline Virgin

Nov 94. (cd) **THE BRIDGE BETWEEN (w/ his STRING QUARTET)** [ ] [ ]
–

Feb 95. (cd) **1999 -SOUNDSCAPES -LIVE IN ARGENTINA (live)1999 (part one) / 2000 / 2001 / Interlude / 2002.** [ ] [-]

Sep 95. (cd) **1995 SOUNDSCAPES – VOLUME TWO – LIVE IN CALIFORNIA (live)** [ ] [-]
– The cathedral of tears / First light / Midnight blue / Reflection 1 / Second light / A blessing of tears / Returning I / Returning II.

Oct 95. (cd) **INTERGALACTIC BOOGIE EXPRESS – LIVE IN EUROPE 1991** (live with The LEAGUE OF CRAFTY GUITARISTS) [ ] [-]
– A Connecticut Yankee in the court of King Arthur / Rhythm of the universe / Lark's hrak / Circulation 1 / Intergalactic boogie express / G force / Eye of the needle / Corrente / Driving force / Groove penetration / Flying home / Circulation II / Fireplace / Fragments of skylab / Asturias / Prelude circulation / Cheeseballs / Prelude in c minor / Wabash cannonball / Fractal Jazn / Ashesis.

– FRIPP compilations, etc. –

Jan 87. E.G.; (m-lp)(c) **NETWORK** [ ] [ ]
– North star / (i) Water music 1 (ii) Here comes the flood / God save the king / Under heavy manners.

KINGFISH (see under ⇒ GRATEFUL DEAD)

KINKS

Formed: Muswell Hill, London, England . . . 1963 by brothers RAY and DAVE DAVIES, who found QUAIFE from The RAVENS. With help from managers Robert Wace and Grenville Collins, they met Larry Page who gave them name KINKS late '63. He also arranged demos, which were soon heard by American SHEL TALMY, who got them signed to 'Pye' early '64. Two singles flopped, but third 'YOU REALLY GOT ME' stormed into

No.1 in the UK, and soon broke into US Top 10. A top selling eponymous lp followed, as did a series of Top 10 sixties singles, including two more UK No.1's 'TIRED OF WAITING FOR YOU' & 'SUNNY AFTERNOON'. After 2 big hits in 1970; 'LOLA' & 'APEMAN', they struggled on new label 'RCA', from then on. It was different in the States, where they progressed commercially again from 1975's 'SOAP OPERA' album. • **Style:** Fashionable R&B beat-pop outfit, whose teenage anthems, drifted more into concept theories by 1968. They developed into a more US mainstream rock act in the 80's, with RAY never quite forgetting his Englishness. • **Songwriters:** RAY DAVIES wrote all of work, except covers; TOO MUCH MONKEY BUSINESS (Chuck Berry) / GOT LOVE IF YOU WANT IT (Slim Harpo) / MILK COW BLUES (Elvis Presley) / etc. • **Trivia:** RAY produced 1969 lp 'Turtle Soup' for The TURTLES. He was married 12 Dec'64 to Rasa Dicpetri, but divorced later (see KINKS biography by Johnny Rogan). In 1981 he divorced second wife Yvonne. (RAY had for 3 years a relationship with CHRISSIE HYNDE of The PRETENDERS.) She gave him daughter Natalie on Feb'83, although they separated when she started dating JIM KERR (of SIMPLE MINDS). In 1986, RAY appeared in the film musical 'Absolute Beginners'.

Recommended: FACE TO FACE (*8) / VILLAGE GREEN PRESERVATION SOCIETY (*8) / THE ULTIMATE COLLECTION (*9) / COME DANCING WITH THE KINKS – THE BEST OF . . . 1977-1986 (*7).

RAY DAVIES (b.21 Jun'44) – vocals, guitar / **DAVE DAVIES** (b. 3 Feb'47) – guitar, vocals / **PETER QUAIFE** (b.31 Dec'43, Tavistock, Devon) – bass with session drummers

Pye Cameo

Mar 64. (7") **LONG TALL SHORTY. / I TOOK MY BABY HOME** [ ] [ ] Apr 64
(US re-iss.Nov64)

May 64. (7") **YOU STILL WANT ME. / YOU REALLY GOT ME** [ ] [-]

Pye Reprise

Aug 64. (7") **YOU REALLY GOT ME. / IT'S ALRIGHT** [1] [7] Sep 64

—— **MICK AVORY** (b.15 Feb'44) – drums was now used although he joined 9 months previous.

Oct 64. (lp) **THE KINKS** (US-title 'YOU REALLY GOT ME') [3] [29] Dec64
– Beautiful Delilah / So mystifying / Just can't go to sleep / Long tall Shorty / You really got me / Cadillac / Bald headed woman / Revenge / Too much monkey business / Revenge / I've been driving on Bald mountain / Stop your sobbing / Got love if you want it. *(UK re-as.May80 on 'P.R.T.', c+cd.Oct87) (cd-iss.Dec89 on 'Castle')*

Oct 64. (7") **ALL DAY AND ALL OF THE NIGHT. / I GOTTA MOVE** [2] [7] Dec 64
(re-iss 7" pic-d Oct 84 on 'PRT') (re-iss 7" Jan 88)

Jan 65. (7") **TIRED OF WAITING FOR YOU. / COME ON NOW** [1] [6] Mar 65

Mar 65. (lp) **KINDA KINKS** [3] [60]
– Look for me baby / Got my feet on the ground / Nothin' in the world can stop me worryin' 'bout that girl / Naggin' woman / Wonder where my baby is tonight / Tired of waiting for you / Dancing in the street / Don't ever change / Come on now / So long / You shouldn't be sad / Something better beginning. *(re-iss.+c.May80 on 'P.R.T.', c+cd.Oct87) (cd-iss.Dec89 on 'Castle')*

Mar 65. (lp) **KINKS-SIZE** [-] [13]
– Tired of waiting for you / Louie Louie / I've got that feeling / Revenge / I gotta move / Things are getting better / I gotta go now / I'm a lover not a fighter / Come on now / All day and all of the night.

Mar 65. (7") **EVERYBODY'S GONNA BE HAPPY. / WHO'LL BE THE NEXT IN LINE** [11] [34] Aug 65b

May 65. (7") **SET ME FREE. / I NEED YOU** [9] [23] Jun 65

Jul 65. (7") **SEE MY FRIEND. / NEVER MET A GIRL LIKE YOU BEFORE** [10] [ ]

Nov 65. (7") **TILL THE END OF THE DAY. / WHERE HAVE ALL THE GOOD TIMES GONE** [6] [50] Mar 66

Nov 65. (lp) **THE KINK KONTROVERSY** [9] [95] Apr 66
– Milk cow blues / Ring the bells / Gotta get the first plane home / When I see that girl of mine / Till the end of the day / The world keeps going round / I'm on the island / Where have all the good times gone / It's too late / What's in store for me / You can't win. *(re-iss.May80 on 'P.R.T.', c+cd.Oct87) (cd-iss.Dec89 on 'Castle')*

Dec 65. (lp) **KINKS KINKDOM** [-] [13]
– Well respected man / Such a shame / Wait 'til the summer comes along / Naggin' woman / Who'll be the next in line / Don't you fret / I need you / It's all right / Louie Louie.

Dec 65. (7") **A WELL RESPECTED MAN. / MILK COW BLUES** [-] [13]

Feb 66. (7") **DEDICATED FOLLOWER OF FASHION. / SITTING ON MY SOFA** [4] [36] May 66

—— **JOHN DALTON** – bass deputised on tour for QUAIFE while injured

Jun 66. (7") **SUNNY AFTERNOON. / I'M NOT LIKE EVERYBODY ELSE** [1] [14] Aug 66

—— **JOHN DALTON** sessioned on songs between 66-69, QUAIFE's photo on covers

Oct 66. (lp) **FACE TO FACE** [12] [ ]
– Party line / Rosy won't you please come home / Dandy / Too much on my mind / Session man / Rainy day in June / House in the country / Sunny afternoon / Holiday in Waikiki / Most exclusive residence for sale / Fancy / Little Miss Queen of Darkness / You're looking fine / I'll remember. *(re-iss.Jun80 on 'P.R.T.', c+cd.Oct87) (cd-iss.Dec89 on 'Castle')*

Nov 66. (7") **DEAD END STREET. / BIG BLACK SMOKE** [5] [73] Jan 67

May 67. (7") **WATERLOO SUNSET. / TWO SISTERS** [-] [ ]

May 67. (7") **WATERLOO SUNSET. / ACT NICE AND GENTLE** [2] [ ]

May 67. (lp) **LIVE AT KELVIN HALL (live in Glasgow)** (US-title 'THE LIVE KINKS') [ ] [ ]
– Till the end of the day / I'm on an island / You really got me / All day and all of the night / A well respected man / You're looking fine / Sunny afternoon / Dandy / Come on now / Milk cow blues – Batman theme – Tired of waiting for you. *(re-iss.Aug80 on 'P.R.T.', c+cd.Sep87) (cd-iss.Dec89 on 'Castle')*

Jun 67. (7") **MR. PLEASANT. / HARRY RAG** [-] [80]

Oct 67. (lp) **SOMETHING ELSE BY THE KINKS** [35] [ ]
– David Watts / Death of a clown / Two sisters / No return / Harry Rag / Tin soldier man / Situation vacant / Love me till the sun shines / Lazy old sun / Afternoon tea / Funny face / End of the season / Waterloo sunset. *(re-iss.Feb81 on 'P.R.T.', c+cd.Sep87) (cd-iss.Dec89 on 'Castle')*

Oct 67. (7") **AUTUMN ALMANAC. / MR. PLEASANT** [3] [ ]

—— (above UK 'B'side was US 'A'side)

Apr 68. (7") **WONDERBOY. / POLLY** [37] [ ]

Jul 68. (7") **DAYS. / SHE'S GOT EVERYTHING** [12] [ ]

Jul 68. (lp) **THE KINKS ARE THE VILLAGE GREEN PRESERVATION SOCIETY** [ ] [ ]
– Village green preservation society / Do you remember Walter / Picture book / Johnny Thunder / The last of the steam powered trains / Big sky / Sitting by the riverside / Animal farm / Village green / Starstruck / Phenomenal cat / All my friends were there / Wicked Annabella / Monica / People take pictures of each other. *(re-iss.Feb81 on 'P.R.T.', re-iss.Nov85, cd-iss.Sep87)*

Apr 69. (7") **PLASTIC MAN. / KING KONG** [31] [ ]

Apr 69. (7") **STARSTRUCK. / PICTURE BOOK** [-] [ ]

—— **JOHN DALTON** (b.21 May'43) – bass officially repl. QUAIFE

Jun 69. (7") **WALTER. / VILLAGE GREEN PRESERVATION SOCIETY** [-] [ ]

Jun 69. (7") **DRIVIN'. / MINDLESS CHILD OF MOTHERHOOD** [ ] [-]

Sep 69. (7") **SHANGRI-LA. / THIS MAN HE WEEPS TONIGHT** [ ] [-]

Oct 69. (lp) **ARTHUR (OR THE DECLINE AND FALL OF THE BRITISH EMPIRE** [ ] [ ]
– Victoria / Yes sir, no sir / Some mother's son / Brainwashed / Australia / Shangri-la / Mr. Churchill says / She bought a hat like Princess Marina / Young and innocent days / Nothing to say / Arthur. *(re-iss.1974) (re-iss.Oct87 on 'P.R.T.'+cd.) (cd-iss.Dec89 on 'Castle')*

Dec 69. (7") **VICTORIA. / MR. CHURCHILL SAYS** [33] [-]

Jan 70. (7") **VICTORIA. / BRAINWASHED** [-] [62]

Jun 70. (7") **LOLA. / BERKELEY MEWS** [2] [-]

Aug 70. (7") **LOLA. / MINDLESS CHILD OF MOTHERHOOD** [-] [9]

Nov 70. (lp)(c) **LOLA VERSUS POWERMAN & THE MONEYGOROUND, PART ONE** [ ] [35]
– The contenders / Strangers / Denmark Street / Get back in line / Lola / Top of the pops / The moneygoround / This time tomorrow / A long way from home / Rats / Apeman / Powerman / Got to be free. *(re-iss.Oct74 on 'Golden Hour')*

Nov 70. (7") **APEMAN. / RATS** [5] [45] Jan 71

Mar 71. (lp)(c) **(SOUNDTRACK FROM THE FILM) "PERCY"** [ ]
– God's children / Lola / The way love used to be / Completely / Running round town / Moments / Animals in the zoo / Just friends / Helga / Willesden Green / God's children – end.

Apr 71. (7"ep) **GOD'S CHILDREN. / THE WAY LOVE USED TO BE / DREAMS / MOMENTS** [ ] [-]

Qpr 71. (7") **GOD'S CHILDREN. / THE WAY LOVE USED TO BE** [-] [ ]

—— added **JOHN GOSLING** – keyboards (he guested on 'LOLA' album), plus **LAURIE BROWN** – trumpet / **JOHN BEECHAM** – trombone / **ALAN HOLMES** – saxophone recruited from The MIKE COTTON SOUND. The three became full-time members '73, adding to **R. DAVIES, D. DAVIES, AVORY and DALTON**

R.C.A. R.C.A.

Nov 71. (lp)(c) **MUSWELL HILLBILLIES** [ ] [100]
– 20th century man / Acute schizophrenia paranoia blues / Holiday / Skin and bone / Alcohol / Complicated life / Here come the people in the grey / Have a cuppa tea / Holloway jail / Oklahoma U.S.A. / Uncle son / Muswell hillbilly.

May 72. (7") **SUPERSONIC ROCKET SHIP. / YOU DON'T KNOW MY NAME** [16] [ ]

Jun 72. (7") **20th CENTURY MAN. / SKIN AND BONE** [-] [ ]

Aug 72. (d-lp)(c) **EVERYBODY'S IN SHOWBIZ** [ ] [70]
– Here comes yet another day / Maximum consumption / Unreal reality / Hot potatoes / Sitting in my hotel / You don't know my name / Supersonic rocket ship / Look a little on the sunny side / Celluloid heroes / Motorway. *(live-lp)* **EVERYBODY'S A STAR (live)** – Top of the pops / Brainwashed / Mr. Wonderful / Acute schizophrenia paranoia blues / Holiday / Muswell Hillbilly / Alcohol / Banana boat song / Skin and bone / Baby face / Lola.

Nov 72. (7") **CELLULOID HEROES. / HOT POTATOES** [ ] [ ]

Jun 73. (7") **SCRAPHEAD CITY. / ONE OF THE SURVIVORS** [-] [ ]

Jun 73. (7") **SITTING IN THE MIDDAY SUN. / ONE OF THE SURVIVORS** [ ] [ ]

Sep 73. (7") **SWEET LADY GENEVIEVE. / SITTING IN MY HOTEL** [ ] [ ]

Dec 73. (d-lp)(c) **PRESERVATION ACT I** [ ] [ ]

– Morning song / Daylight / Sweet Lady Genevieve / There's a change in the weather / Where are they now / One of the survivors / Cricket / I am your man / Here comes Flash / Sitting in the midday Sun / Demolution.

—— note: next 45 only contained **RAY & DAVE DAVIES**, before full 5 + 3 again

Apr 74. (7") **MIRROR OF LOVE. / CRICKET** [ ] [-]
Jun 74. (d-lp)(c) **PRESERVATION ACT II** [ ] [ ]
– (announcement) / Introduction to solution / When a solution comes / Money talks / (announcement) / Shepherds of the nation / Scum of the Earth / Secondhand car spiv / He's evil / Mirror of love / (announcement) / Nobody gives / Oh where oh where is love? / Flash's dream / Flash's confession / Nothing lasts forever / (announcement) / Artificial man / Scrapheap city / (announcement) / Salvation Road.
Jul 74. (7") **MIRROR OF LOVE. / HE'S EVIL** [-] [ ]
Oct 74. (7") **HOLIDAY ROMANCE. / SHEPHERDS OF THE NATION** [ ] [-]
Oct 74. (7") **PRESERVATION. / SALVATION** [-] [ ]
Apr 75. (7") **ORDINARY PEOPLE. / STAR MAKER** [-] [ ]
Apr 75. (7") **DUCKS ON THE WALL. / RUSH HOUR BLUES** [ ] [-]
May 75. (lp)(c) **SOAP OPERA** [ ] [51]
– Everybody's a star (starmaker) / Ordinary people / Rush hour blues / Nine to five / When work is over / Have another drink / Underneath the neon sign / Holiday romance / You make it all worth while / Ducks on the wall / Face in the crowd / You can't stop the music. *(re-iss.Jul84)*
May 75. (7") **YOU CAN'T STOP THE MUSIC. / HAVE ANOTHER DRINK** [ ] [-]
Nov 75. (lp)(c) **SCHOOLBOYS IN DISGRACE** [ ] [45]
– Schooldays / Jack the idiot dunce / Education / The first time we fall in love / I'm in disgrace / Headmaster / The hard way / The last assembly / No more looking back / (finale).
Nov 75 (7") **THE HARD WAY. / I'M IN DISGRACE** [-] [ ]
Jan 76. (7"m) **NO MORE LOOKING BACK. / JACK THE IDIOT DUNCE / THE HARD WAY** [ ] [-]

—— Now down to basic 5-piece after the 3 brass section members departed

Arista Arista

Feb 77. (lp)(c) **SLEEPWALKER** [ ] [21]
– Life on the road / Mr. Big man / Sleepwalker / Brother / Juke box music / Sleepless night / Stormy sky / Full moon / Life goes on.
Mar 77. (7") **SLEEPWALKER. / FULL MOON** [ ] [48]
Jun 77. (7") **JUKE BOX MUSIC. / SLEEPLESS NIGHT** [ ] [-]
Jun 77. (7") **JUKE BOX MUSIC. / LIFE GOES ON** [-] [ ]

—— **ANDY PYLE** – bass (ex-BLODWYN PIG, ex-SAVOY BROWN, etc) repl. DALTON

Dec 77. (7") **FATHER CHRISTMAS. / PRINCE OF THE PUNKS** [ ] [ ]
May 78. (lp)(c) **MISFITS** [ ] [40]
– Misfits / Hay fever / Live life / Rock'n'roll fantasy / In a foreign land / Permanent waves / Black Messiah / Out of the wardrobe / Trust your heart / Get up.
May 78. (7") **ROCK'N'ROLL FANTASY. / ARTIFICIAL LIGHT** [ ] [30] Jul 78
Jul 78. (7") **LIVE LIFE. / IN A FOREIGN LAND** [ ] [-]
Jul 78. (7") **LIVE LIFE. / BLACK MESSIAH** [-] [ ]
Sep 78. (7") **BLACK MESSIAH. / MISFITS** [ ] [-]

—— RAY DAVIES, DAVE DAVIES and MICK AVORY recruited new members **GORDON EDWARDS** – keyboards (ex-PRETTY THINGS) repl. GOSLING (formed NETWORK) / **JIM RODFORD** – bass (ex-ARGENT, ex-PHOENIX) repl. PYLE (formed NETWORK)

Jan 79. (7")(12") **(WISH I COULD FLY LIKE) SUPERMAN. / LOW BUDGET** [ ] [-]

—— **IAN GIBBON** – keyboards repl. EDWARDS

Apr 79. (7") **(WISH I COULD FLY LIKE) SUPERMAN. / PARTY LINE** [-] [41]
Sep 79. (7") **MOVING PICTURES. / IN A SPACE** [ ] [-]
Sep 79. (lp)(c) **LOW BUDGET** [ ] [11] Jul 79
– Attitude / Catch me now I'm falling / Pressure / National health / (I wish I could fly like) Superman / Low budget / In a space / Little bit of emotion / Gallon of gas / Misery / Moving pictures. *(cd-iss.Apr88)*
Sep 79. (7") **GALLON OF GAS. / LOW BUDGET** [-] [ ]
Nov 79. (7") **CATCH ME NOW I'M FALLING. / LOW BUDGET** [-] [ ]
Nov 79. (7") **PRESSURE. / NATIONAL HEALTH** [ ] [-]
Jul 80. (d-lp)(c) **ONE FOR THE ROAD (live)** [ ] [14] Jun 80
– The hard way / Catch me now I'm falling / Where have all the good times gone / Lola / Pressure / All day and all of the night / 20th century man / Misfits / Prince of the punks / Stop your sobbing / Low budget / Attitude / (Wish I could fly like) Superman / National health / Till the end of the day / Celluloid heroes / You really got me / Victoria / David Watts.
Jul 80. (7"ep) **WHERE HAVE ALL THE GOOD TIMES GONE (live)** [ ] [-]
– Where have all the good times gone / Victoria / Attitude / David Watts.
Aug 80. (7") **LOLA (live). / CELLULOID HEROES (live)** [-] [81]
Oct 80. (7") **YOU REALLY GOT ME (live). / ATTITUDE (live)** [-] [ ]
Jun 81. (lp)(c) **GIVE THE PEOPLE WHAT THEY WANT** [ ] [15]
– Around the dial / Give the people what they wnt / Killer's eyes / Predictable / Add it up / Destroyer / Yo-yo / Back to front / Art lover / A little bit of abuse / Better things.
Jun 81. (7") **BETTER THINGS. / MASSIVE REDUCTIONS** [46] [-]
(d7"+=) – Lola / David Watts.

Oct 81. (7")(7"pic-d) **PREDICTABLE. / BACK TO FRONT** [ ] [ ]
Oct 81. (7") **DESTROYER. / BACK TO FRONT** [-] [85]
Nov 81. (7") **BETTER THINGS. / YO-YO** [-] [92]
Jun 83. (lp)(c) **STATE OF CONFUSION** [ ] [12]
– State of confusion / Definite maybe / Labour of love / Come dancing / Property / Don't forget to dance / Young Conservatives / Heart of gold / Cliches of the world (B movie) / Bernadette. *(cd-iss.1988 on 'Ariola')*
Jul 83. (7")(12") **COME DANCING. / NOISE** [12] [6] May 83
Aug 83. (7") **DON'T FORGET TO DANCE. / YOUNG CONSERVATIVES** [-] [29]
Sep 83. (7")(12") **DON'T FORGET TO DANCE. / BERNADETTE** [58] [-]
Mar 84. (7") **STATE OF CONFUSION. / HEART OF GOLD** [ ] [ ]
(12"+=) – 20th century man (live) / Lola (live).
Jul 84. (7") **GOOD DAY. / TOO HOT** [ ] [ ]
(12"+=) – Superman / Don't forget to dance.
Nov 84. (lp)(c) **WORD OF MOUTH** [ ] [57]
– Do it again / Word of mouth / Good day / Living on a thin line / Sold me out / Massive reductions / Guilty / Too hot / Missing persons / Summer's gone / Going solo. *(cd-iss.Jun88 on 'Ariola')*
Apr 85. (7") **DO IT AGAIN. / GUILTY** [ ] [41] Dec 84
(12"+=) – Summer's gone.
Apr 85. (7") **SUMMER'S GONE. / GOING SOLO** [-] [ ]

—— Returned to original line-up of **RAY, DAVE + MICK,** plus sessioners. (RODFORD and GIBBONS departed).

London M.C.A.

Nov 86. (7") **ROCK'N'ROLL CITIES. / WELCOME TO SLEAZY TOWN** [-] [ ]
Nov 86. (lp)(c)(cd) **THINK VISUAL** [ ] [81]
– Working at the factory / Lost and found / Repetition / Welcome to Sleazy Town / The video shop / Rock'n'roll cities / How are you / Think visual / Natural gift / Killing time / When you were a child.
Dec 86. (7") **HOW ARE YOU. / KILLING TIME** [ ] [-]
(12"+=) – Welcome to Sleazy town.
Mar 87. (7") **LOST AND FOUND. / KILLING TIME** [ ] [ ]
(12"+=) – (Ray Davies interview).
May 87. (7") **HOW ARE YOU. / WORKING AT THE FACTORY** [-] [ ]
Feb 88. (7") **THE ROAD. / ART LOVER** [ ] [ ]
(12"+=) – Come dancing. / ('A' version).
May 88. (lp)(c)(cd) **THE ROAD (live / studio *)** [ ] [ ]
– The road * / Destroyer / Apeman / Come dancing / Art lover / Cliches of the world (B-movie) / Living on a thin line / Lost and found / It * / Around the dial / Give the people what they want.
Feb 89. (7") **DOWN ALL THE DAYS (TILL 1992). / YOU REALLY GOT ME (live)** [ ] [ ]
(12"+=)(cd-s+=) – Entertainment. *(re-dist.Sep89)*

—— **BOB HENRIT** – drums repl. AVORY / added **MARK HALEY** – keyboards, vocals

Oct 89. (lp)(c)(cd) **UK JIVE** [ ] [ ]
– Aggravation / How do I get close / UK jive / Now and then / What are we doing / Entertainment / War is over / Down all the days (till 1992) / Loony balloon / Dear Margaret. *(c++)(cd+=)–* Bright lights / Perfect strangers. *(re-iss.Apr91)*
Feb 90. (7") **HOW DO I GET CLOSE. / DOWN ALL THE DAYS (TILL 1992)** [ ] [ ]
(12"+=)(cd-s+=) – War is over. *(US 7" b-side)*

Columbia Columbia

Mar 93. (cd)(c) **PHOBIA** [ ] [ ]
– Opening / Wall of fire / Drift away / Still searching / Phobia / Only a dream / Don't / Babies / Over the edge / Surviving / It's alright (don't think about it) / The informer / Hatred (a duet) / Somebody stole my car / Close to the wire / Scattered. (cd+=) – Did ya.
Jul 93. (cd-s) **SCATTERED. / HATRED (A DUET) / DAYS** [ ] [ ]
Nov 93. (7")(cd-s) **ONLY A DREAM (Radio Version) / SOMEBODY STOLE MY CAR / BABIES** [ ] [ ]

Konk Konk

Oct 94. (cd)(c)(lp) **TO THE BONE (live)** [ ] [ ]
– All day and all of the nigt / Apeman / Tired of waiting for you / See my friend / Death of a clown / Waterloo sunset / Muswell hillbillies / Better things / Don't forget to dance / Autumn almanac / Sunny afternoon / Dedicated follower of fashion / You really got me.
Oct 94. (cd-ep) **WATERLOO SUNSET E.P. (live)** [ ] [ ]
– Waterloo sunset / You really got me / Elevator man / On the outside.

– compilations etc. –

Nov 64. Pye; (7"ep) **KINGSIZE SESSION** [ ] [ ]
– I've gotta go now / I've got that feeling / Things are getting better / Louie Louie.
Jan 65. Pye; (7"ep) **KINGSIZE HITS** [ ] [ ]
– You really got me / It's alright / All day and all of the night / I gotta move.
Sep 65. Pye; (7"ep) **KWYET KINKS** [ ] [ ]
– Wait till the summer / Such a shame / A well respected man / Don't you fret.
Jul 66. Pye; (7"ep) **DEDICATED KINKS** [ ] [ ]
– Dedicated follower of fashion / Till the end of the day / See my friend / Set me free.
Aug 66. Reprise; (lp) **THE KINKS GREATEST HITS** [-] [9]
Apr 68. Pye; (7"ep) **SOMETHING ELSE** [ ] [ ]
– David Watts / Two sisters / Lazy old Sun / Situation.

Feb 70.	Pye/ US= Reprise; (d-lp)(c) **THE KINKS**		
Aug 71.	Pye; (7"ep) **YOU REALLY GOT ME. / WONDERBOY / SET ME FREE / LONG TALL SALLY**		
Oct 71.	Pye; (lp)(c) **THE GOLDEN HOUR OF THE KINKS** *(re-iss.Oct74) ((cd+c.Apr91 on 'Knight')*	21	
Apr 72.	Reprise; (lp)(c) **THE KINKS KRONICLES**	-	94
Feb 73.	Reprise; (lp)(c) **THE GREAT LOST KINKS ALBUM**	-	
Nov 73.	Pye; (7") **WHERE HAVE ALL THE GOOD TIMES GONE. / LOLA**		
May 75.	Pye; (7") **SUNNY AFTERNOON/. SITTING ON MY SOFA**		
May 77.	Pye; (12"ep) **LOLA / SUNNY AFTERNOON. / WATERLOO SUNSET / DEDICATED FOLLOWER OF FASHION**		-
Nov 77.	Pye; (d-lp)(c) **THE KINKS FILE**		-
Nov 78.	Pye; (7"ep) **EP** – Long tall Shorty / I took my baby home / You still want me / You do something to me.		-
Apr 79.	Pye; (7") **YOU REALLY GOT ME. / ALL DAY AND ALL OF THE NIGHT** *(re-iss.Feb80) (re-iss Jun 84 on 'Old Gold')*		
Mar 80.	Pye; (7") **DEDICATED FOLLOWER OF FASHION. / WATERLOO SUNSET** *(re-iss.Mar82 on 'Old Gold')*		
Jun 80.	Pye; (7"ep) **WATERLOO SUNSET / DAVID WATTS. / A WELL RESPECTED MAN / STOP YOUR SOBBIN'**		-
1980.	Pye; (d-lp)(d-c) **SPOTLIGHT ON THE KINKS**		-
Oct 78.	Pye-Ronco; (d-lp)(c) **THE KINKS 20 GOLDEN GREATS**	19	
Jun 66.	Marble Arch; (lp) **WELL RESPECTED KINKS**	5	
Sep 67.	Marble Arch; (lp) **SUNNY AFTERNOON**	9	
Jun 76.	RCA; (lp)(c) **CELLULOID HEROES – THE KINKS GREATEST**		
Jul 80.	Pickwick; (lp)(c) **THE KINKS COLLECTION**		-
Aug 89.	Pickwick; (lp)(c)(cd) **THE BEST OF THE KINKS – 1964-66**		-
Aug 91.	Pickwick; (cd)(c) **THE BEST OF THE KINKS 1966-67**		-
Jun 82.	P.R.T.; (c) **100 MINUTES OF . . .**		-
Feb 83.	P.R.T.; (7") **SUNNY AFTERNOON. / TIRED OF WAITING FOR YOU**		-
Apr 83.	P.R.T.; (lp)(c) **SHAPE OF THINGS TO COME**		-
Jul 83.	P.R.T.; (lp)(c) **CANDY FROM MR. DANDY**		-
Oct 83.	P.R.T.; (lp)(c) **KINKS' GREATEST HITS – DEAD END STREET**	96	-
Oct 83.	P.R.T.; (7")(7"pic-d) **YOU REALLY GOT ME. / MISTY WATER** (12"pic-d+=) – All day and all of the night.	47	-
Oct 84.	P.R.T.; (lp)(c)(cd) **THE KINKS GREATEST HITS**		-
Nov 84.	P.R.T.; (lp)(c) **KOLLECTABLES**		-
Nov 84.	P.R.T.; (lp)(c) **KOVERS**		-
Nov 84.	P.R.T.; (box-c) **THE KINKS BOX SET**		-
Mar 86.	P.R.T.; (7") **DEDICATED FOLLOWER OF FASHION. / AUTUMN ALMANAC** *(re-iss. 7"pic-d. Mar 88)*		-
Oct 87.	P.R.T.; (lp)(c) **HIT SINGLES**		-
Sep 87.	P.R.T.; (d-lp)(c) **THE KINKS ARE WELL RESPECTED MEN**		-
Mar 86.	Old Gold; (7") **LOLA. / APEMAN**		-
Mar 86.	Old Gold; (7") **SUNNY AFTERNOON. / TIRED OF WAITING FOR YOU** *(re-iss. Jul 87 on 7"pic-d 'PRT')*		-
Nov 88.	Old Gold; (cd-ep) **YOU REALLY GOT ME / ALL DAY AND ALL OF THE NIGHT / TIRED OF WAITING FOR YOU**		-
Feb 89.	Old Gold; (cd-ep) **WATERLOO SUNSET / SUNNY AFTERNOON / LOLA**		-
Nov 85.	Castle; (d-lp)(c) **THE COLLECTION** *(cd-iss.1988 & Jul92 on 'BMG-RCA')*		
Sep 89.	Castle; (lp)(c)(cd) **THE ULTIMATE COLLECTION** – You really got me / All day and all of the night / Tired of waiting for you / Everybody's gonna be happy / Set me free / Till the end of the day / Dedicated follower of fashion / Sunny afternoon / Dead end street / Waterloo sunset / Autumn almanac / Wonder boy / Days / Plastic man / Victoria / Lola / Apeman / David Watts / Where have all the good times gone / Well respected man / I'm not like everybody else / End of the season / Death of a clown (DAVE DAVIES) / Suzannah's still alive (DAVE DAVIES).	35	-
Dec 85.	Starblend; (d-lp)(c)(cd) **BACKTRACKIN' – THE DEFINITIVE COLLECTION**		-
Apr 89.	Legacy; (c)(cd) **C90 COLLECTOR**		-
Sep 91.	Rhino; (d-cd) **PRESERVATION (A PLAY IN TWO ACTS)**		-
Feb 92.	See For MIles; (cd)(c)(lp) **THE EP COLLECTION VOL.2**		-
Sep 93.	Polygram TV; (cd)(c) **THE DEFINITIVE COLLECTION – THE KINKS' GREATEST HITS**	18	
Dec 93.	Disky; (cd) **GOLD: GREATEST HITS**		-
May 94.	BR Music; (cd)(c) **GREATEST HITS**		-
Jul 94.	Success; (cd)(c) **YOU REALLY GOT ME**		-
Aug 94.	Spectrum; (cd)(c) **YOU REALLY GOT ME**		-
Feb 95.	Essential; (cd) **REMASTERED**		-
Aug 95.	Spectrum; (cd) **LOLA**		-

DAVE DAVIES

		Pye	Reprise
Jul 67.	(7") **DEATH OF A CLOWN. / LOVE ME TILL THE SUN SHINES**	3	
Nov 67.	(7") **SUSANNAH'S STILL ALIVE. / FUNNY FACE**	21	
Aug 68.	(7") **LINCOLN COUNTY. / THERE IS NO LOVE WITHOUT LIFE**		
Jan 69.	(7") **HOLD MY HAND. / CREEPING JEAN**		
		R.C.A.	**R.C.A.**
Sep 80.	(7") **IMAGINATION'S REAL. / WILD MAN**	-	
Sep 80.	(lp)(c) **AFLI-3603 (UK) / PL-13603 (US)** – Where do you come from / Doing the best for you / Move over / Visionary dreamer / Nothin' more to lose / Imagination real / In you I believe / See the beast / Run / The world is changing hands.	-	42 Jul 80
Nov 80.	(7") **DOING THE BEST FOR YOU. / NOTHING MORE TO LOSE**	-	
Dec 80.	(7") **DOING THE BEST FOR YOU. / WILD MAN**		-
Oct 81.	(lp)(c) **GLAMOUR** – Is this the only way / Reveal yourself / World of our own / Two serious / Glamour / 7th channel / Body / Eastern eyes / Body.		Jul 81
		Warners	**Warners**
Sep 83.	(lp)(c) **CHOSEN PEOPLE** – Mean disposition / Love gets you / Take one more / True story / Danger zone / Tapes / Freedom lies / Fire burning / Cold winter / Matter of decision / Is it any wonder / Charity / Chosen people.		Aug 83
Sep 83.	(7") **LOVE GETS YOU. / ONE NIGHT WITH YOU**	-	
Nov 83.	(7") **MEAN DISPOSITION. / COLD WINTER**	-	

– DAVE DAVIES compilations etc. –

Apr 68.	Pye; (7"ep) **DAVE DAVIES HITS**		
Aug 82.	Old Gold; (7") **DEATH OF A CLOWN. / SUZANNAH'S STILL ALIVE**		-
Feb 88.	P.R.T.; (lp)(c) **DAVE DAVIES – THE ALBUM THAT NEVER WAS** – (1960's singles)		-
Jul 92.	Mau Mau; (cd) **DAVE DAVIES / GLAMOUR**		-

RAY DAVIES

		not issued	R.C.A.
1984.	(lp) **RETURN TO WATERLOO** (withdrawn)	-	
	(below from film 'Absolute Beginners')	**Virgin**	**Virgin**
May 86.	(7")(12") **QUIET LIFE. / VOICES IN THE DARK**		

KISS

Formed: New York, USA . . . late '71 by ex-WICKED LESTER members GENE SIMMONS and PAUL STANLEY, who recruited ACE FREHLEY and PETER CRISS. After a year of touring in '73, they signed to 'Casablanca', and hit US Top 100 with eponymous lp early '74. After another Top 100 success at the end of '74, they scored with first of many US Top 40 albums 'DRESSED TO KILL' in 1975. • **Style:** Heavy riffed glam-rockers, with explosive stage shows their forte. Their comic-book image and facial character make-up led to a legion of young fans copying them, that is, until they were 'UNMASKED' on album in 1980. Their following album, THE ELDER, was dismissed by loyal supporters, for having concept inclinations. For the rest of the 80's, they were back to early hard-rock anthems and ballads of sex and violence. KISS' favourite haunts have been Detroit and Japan, where they have amassed tremendous KISS army. • **Songwriters:** Most by STANLEY or SIMMONS, with some ballads by CRISS. Covered; THEN (S)HE KISSED ME (Crystals) / GOD GAVE ROCK'N'ROLL TO YOU (Argent). MICHAEL BOLTON co-wrote with STANLEY their minor hit ballad 'FOREVER'. GENE SIMMONS solo covered; WHEN YOU WISH UPON A STAR (Judy Garland). • **Trivia:** BOB EZRIN produced 'DESTROYER' & 'THE ELDER'. First live double and several studio lp's from EDDIE KRAMER. In 1977, Marvel Comics started a KISS feature series in their monthly mag. In 1984, SIMMONS starred as a villain in the film 'Runaway' alongside Tom Selleck. Two years later 'The Bat-Winged Vampire' featured in films 'Never Too Young To Die', 'Trick Or Treat' & 'Wanted Dead Or Alive'. In 1994, a tribute album 'KISS MY ASS' was released by 'Mercury'. It featured star cover

versions by LENNY KRAVITZ, GARTH BROOKS, ANTHRAX, GIN BLOSSOMS, TOAD THE WET SPROCKET, SHANDI's ADDICTION, DINOSAUR JR., EXTREME, LEMONHEADS, etc.

Recommended: ALIVE! (*8) / SMASHES, THRASHES AND HITS (*7).

GENE SIMMONS (b.GENE KLEIN, 25 Aug'50, Haifa, Israel) – vocals, bass / **PAUL STANLEY** (b.STANLEY EISEN, 20 Jan'50, Queens, NY) – guitar, vocals / **ACE FREHLEY** (b.PAUL FREHLEY, 22 Apr'51, The Bronx, NY) – lead guitar, vocals / **PETER CRISS** (b.PETER CRISSCOULA, 27 Dec'47, Brooklyn, NY) – drums, vocals.

Casablanca Casablanca

Feb 74. (7") **NOTHIN' TO LOSE. / LOVE THEME FROM KISS** [-] [ ]
Feb 74. (lp) **KISS** [-] [87]
– Strutter / Nothin' to lose / Firehouse / Cold gin / Let me know / Kissin' time / Love theme from Kiss / Deuce / 100,000 years / Black diamond. *(UK-iss.Feb75, re-iss.May77 red vinyl, re-iss.+c Feb82, cd-iss Aug88)*
May 74. (7") **KISSIN' TIME. / NOTHIN' TO LOSE** [-] [83]
Aug 74. (7") **STRUTTER. / 100,000 YEARS** [-] [ ]
Nov 74. (lp) **HOTTER THAN HELL** [-] [100]
– Got to choose / Parasite / Goin' blind / Hotter than Hell / Let me go, rock'n roll / All the way / Watchin' you / Mainline / Comin' home / Strange ways. *(UK-iss.May77 red vinyl, re-iss.+c Feb82, re-iss.+cd Aug88)*
Jan 75. (7") **NOTHIN' TO LOSE. / LOVE THEME FROM KISS** [ ] [ ]
Mar 75. (7") **LET ME GO ROCK'N'ROLL. / HOTTER THAN HELL** [-] [ ]
Mar 75. (lp)(c) **DRESSED TO KILL** [ ] [32]
– Room service / Two timer / Ladies in waiting / Getaway / Rock bottom / C'mon and love me / Anything for my baby / She / Love her all I can / Rock and roll all nite. *(UK-iss.Aug75, re-iss.May77 red vinyl, re-iss.+c Feb82, re-iss.+cd Aug88)*
May 75. (7") **ROCK AND ROLL ALL NITE. / GETAWAY** [-] [68]
Jun 75. (7") **ROCK AND ROLL ALL NITE. / ANYTHING FOR MY BABY** [ ] [-]
Oct 75. (7") **C'MON AND LOVE ME. / GETAWAY** [-] [ ]
Oct 75. (d-lp)(d-c) **ALIVE! (live)** [49] [9]
– Deuce / Strutter / Got to choose / Hotter than Hell / Firehouse / Nothin' to lose / C'mon and love me / Parasite / She / Watchin' you / 100,000 years / Black diamond / Rock bottom / Cold gin / Rock and roll all nite / Let me go rock 'n roll. *(UK-iss.Jun76, re-iss.May77 red vinyl, re-iss.+c Sep84, re-iss.+cd May89)*
Dec 75. (7") **ROCK AND ROLL ALL NITE (live). / ('A' new studio mix)** [ ] [12] Nov 75
Apr 76. (7") **SHOUT IT OUT LOUD. / SWEET PAIN** [ ] [31] Mar 76
May 76. (lp)(c) **DESTROYER** [22] [11] Mar 76
– Detroit rock city / King of the night time world / God of thunder / Great expectations / Flaming youth / Sweet pain / Shout it out loud / Beth / Do you love me. *(re-iss.May77 red vinyl, re-iss.+c Feb82, re-iss.+cd May89)*
Jun 76. (7") **FLAMING YOUTH. / GOD OF THUNDER** [-] [74]
Aug 76. (7") **BETH. / DETROIT ROCK CITY** [-] [7]
Jul 76. (7") **BETH. / GOD OF THUNDER** [-] [-]
Nov 76. (lp)(c) **ROCK AND ROLL OVER** [ ] [11]
– See you in your dreams / Love 'em and leave 'em / Hard luck woman / Makin' love / Take me / I want you / Calling Dr. Love / Baby driver / Ladies room / Mr. Speed. *(re-iss.Feb77 red vinyl, re-iss.Feb82, re-iss.+cd May89) (re-iss.cd Jan93 on 'Vertigo')*
Dec 76. (7") **HARD LUCK WOMAN. / MR. SPEED** [-] [15]
May 77. (7"m) **HARD LUCK WOMAN. / CALLING DR. LOVE / BETH** [ ] [-]
Jun 77. (7") **CALLING DR. LOVE. / TAKE ME** [ ] [16] Mar 77
Jun 77. (lp)(c) **LOVE GUN** [ ] [4]
-Love gun / Got love for sale / Tomorrow and tonight / Christine sixteen / Almost human / Plaster caster / Shock me / The she kised me / I stole your love / Hooligan. *(UK-iss red vinyl, re-iss.Feb82, re-iss.Jul84, cd-iss.Aug88 US) (cd-iss.Jan93 on 'Vertigo')*
Jul 77. (7") **CHRISTINE SIXTEEN. / SHOCK ME** [-] [25]
Aug 77. (7"m) **THEN SHE KISSED ME. / HOOLIGAN / FLAMING YOUTH** [ ] [-]
Sep 77. (7") **LOVE GUN. / HOOLIGAN** [-] [61]
Nov 77. (d-lp)(d-c) **KISS ALIVE II** [60] [7]
– Detroit rock city / King of the night time world / Ladies room / Makin' love / Love gun / Calling Dr. Love / Christine sixteen / Shock me / Hard luck woman / Tomorrow and tonight / I stole your love / Beth / God of thunder / I want you / Shout it loud / All American man / Rockin' in the U.S.A. / Larger than life / Rocket ride / Any way you want it. *(re-iss.Feb82, cd-iss.May89)*
Jan 78. (7") **SHOUT IT OUT LOUD (live). / NOTHIN' TO LOSE (live)** [-] [54]
Feb 78. (7") **ROCKET RIDE. / TOMORROW AND TONIGHT** [-] [39]
Mar 78. (7") **ROCKET RIDE. / LOVE GUN (live)** [ ] [-]
(12"+=) – Detroit rock city (live).

— Took time to do solo projects (all on label below)

GENE SIMMONS

Casablanca Casablanca

Sep 78. (lp) **GENE SIMMONS** [-] [22]
– Radioactive / Burning up with fever / See you tonite / Tunnel of love / True confessions / Living in sin / Always near you / Nowhere to hide / Man of 1,000 faces / Mr. Make Believe / See you in your dreams / When you wish upon a star. *(re-iss.'87 in +pic-lp Europe) (cd-iss.Nov91)*
Jan 79. (7") **RADIOACTIVE. / WHEN YOU WISH UPON A STAR** [41] [ ]

PAUL STANLEY

Sep 78. (lp)**PAUL STANLEY** [-] [40]
– Tonight you belong to me / Move on / Ain't quite right / Wouldn't you like to know / Take me away (together as one) / It's alright / Hold me touch me (think of me when we're apart) / Love in chains / Goodbye. *(re-iss.'87 +pic-lp in Europe) (cd-iss.Nov91)*
Feb 79. (7") **HOLD ME TOUCH ME. / GOODBYE** [ ] [ ]

ACE FREHLEY

Sep 78. (lp)**ACE FREHLEY** [-] [26]
– Rip it out / Speedin' back to my baby / Snowblind / Ozone / What's on your mind / New York groove / I'm in need of love / Wiped out / Fractured mirror. *(re-iss.+pic-lp 1987 in Europe) (cd-iss.Nov91)*
Nov 78. (7")(7"blue) **NEW YORK GROOVE. / SNOW BLIND** [ ] [13]

PETER CRISS

Sep 78. (lp) **PETER CRISS** [-] [43]
– I'm gonna love you / You matter to me / Tossin' and turnin' / Don't you let me down / That's the kind of sugar papa likes / Easy thing / Rock me, baby / Kiss the girl goodbye / Hooked on rock'n'roll / I can't stop the rain. *(re-iss.'87 +pic-lp in Europe) (cd-iss.Nov91) (re-iss.cd+red-lp+book Aug94 on 'Megarock')*
Dec 78. (7") **DON'T YOU LET ME DOWN. / HOOKED ON ROCK AND ROLL** [-] [ ]
Feb 79. (7") **HOOKED ON ROCK AND ROLL. / YOU MATTER TO ME** [ ] [ ]

KISS

returned to studio

Casablanca Casablanca

Jun 79. (7") **I WAS MADE FOR LOVIN' YOU. / HARD TIMES** [50] [11] May 79
(12") – ('A'side) / Charisma.
Jun 79. (lp)(c) **DYNASTY** [50] [9]
– Charisma / Dirty livin' / Hard times / I was made for lovin' you / Magic touch / Save your love / Sure know something / X-ray eyes / 2,000 man. *(re-iss.Oct83, cd-iss.'88 US import) (cd-iss.Jan93 on 'Vertigo')*
Aug 79. (7") **SURE KNOW SOMETHING. / DIRTY LIVIN'** [ ] [47]
Feb 80. (7"m) **2,000 MAN. / I WAS MADE FOR LOVIN' YOU / SURE KNOW SOMETHING** [ ] [-]

Mercury Casablanca

Jun 80. (7") **SHANDI. / SHE'S SO EUROPEAN** [-] [47]
Jun 80. (7") **TALK TO ME. / SHE'S SO EUROPEAN** [ ] [-]
Jun 80. (lp)(c) **KISS UNMASKED** [48] [35]
– Easy as it seems / Is that you? / Naked city / Shandi / She's so European / Talk to me / Tomorrow / Torpedo girl / Two sides of the coin / What makes the world go 'round / You're all that I want. *(cd-iss.Dec89)*
Aug 80. (7") **WHAT MAKES THE WORLD GO 'ROUND. / NAKED CITY** [ ] [-]
Aug 80. (7") **TOMORROW. / NAKED CITY** [-] [ ]

— (May80) **ERIC CARR** (b.12 Jul'50) – drums, producer repl. CRISS who went solo (early 80's albums; OUT OF CONTROL / LET ME ROCK YOU)

Nov 81. (lp)(c) **MUSIC FROM THE ELDER** [51] [75]
– Just a boy / Odyssey / Only you / Under the rose / Darl light / A world without heroes / The oath / Mr. Blackwell / Escape from the island. *(cd-iss.Jun89) (cd-iss.Jun94 on 'Sony . . . ')*
Nov 81. (7") **A WORLD WITHOUT HEROES. / DARK LIGHT** [-] [56]
Jan 82. (7")(7"pic-d) **A WORLD WITHOUT HEROES. / MR. BLACKWELL** [55] [-]

— **VINNIE VINCENT** (b.VINCENT CUSANO) – guitar repl. BOB KULICK who had repl. FREHLEY who formed own band.

Casablanca Casablanca

Oct 82. (7") **DANGER. / I LOVE IT LOUD** [-] [ ]
Oct 82. (7") **KILLER. / I LOVE IT LOUD** [ ] [-]
(12"+=) – I was made for lovin' you.
Oct 82. (lp)(c) **CREATURES OF THE NIGHT** [22] [45]
– Creatures of the night / Saint and sinner / Keep me comin' / Rock and roll Hell / Danger / I love it loud / I still love you / Killer / ar machine. *(re-iss.+cd Aug88) (re-iss.cd Jan93 on 'Vertigo')*
Mar 83. (7")(12") **CREATURES OF THE NIGHT. / ROCK AND ROLL ALL NIGHT (live)** [34] [-]
(12"+=) – War machine.

Vertigo Mercury

Oct 83. (7") **LICK IT UP. / DANCE ALL OVER YOUR FACE** [-] [66]
Oct 83. (7")(7"sha-pic-d) **LICK IT UP. / NOT FOR THE INNOCENT** [34] [-]
(12"+=) – I still love you.

Oct 83. (lp)(c) **LICK IT UP** [7] [24]
– Exciter / Not for the innocent / Lick it up / Young and wasted / Gimme more / All Hell's breakin' loose / A million to one / Fits like a glove / Dance all over your face / And on the 8th day. *(re-iss.+cd Dec89 on 'Mercury')*
Jan 84. (7") **ALL HELL'S BREAKIN' LOOSE. / YOUNG AND WASTED** [-] [ ]

— **MARK** (NORTON) **ST.JOHN** – guitar repl. VINCENT who formed his INVASION

Sep 84. (7") **HEAVEN'S ON FIRE. / LONELY IS THE HUNTER** [43] [49]
(12"+=) – All Hell's breakin' loose.
Sep 84. (lp)(c) **ANIMALIZE** [11] [19]
– I've had enough (into the fire) / Heaven's on fire / Burn bitch burn / Get all you can take / Lonely is the hunter / Under the gun / Thrills in the night / While the city sleeps / Murder in high-heels. *(re-iss.+cd Dec89 on 'Mercury') (re-iss.cd Jan93)*
Nov 84. (7") **THRILLS IN THE NIGHT. / BURN BITCH BURN** [-] [ ]

— **BRUCE KULICK** – guitar repl. MARK who became ill

Oct 85. (lp)(c)(cd) **ASYLUM** [12] [20]
– King of the mountain / Any way you slice it / Who wants to be lonely / Trial by fire / I'm alive / Love's a deadly weapon / Tears are falling / Secretly cruel / Radar for love / Uh! All night. *(re-iss.+cd Dec89 on 'Mercury') (re-iss.cd Jan93)*
Oct 85. (7") **TEARS ARE FALLING. / HEAVEN'S ON FIRE (live)** [57] [51]
(12"+=) – Any way you slice it (US b-side).
Sep 87. (7") **CRAZY CRAZY NIGHTS. / NO, NO, NO** [4] [65]
(12"+=) – Lick it up / Uh! All night.
(12"pic-d+=) – Heaven's on fire / Tears are falling.
Oct 87. (lp)(c)(cd) **CRAZY NIGHTS** [4] [18]
– Crazy crazy nights / I'll fight Hell to hold you / Bang bang you / No, no, no / Hell on high water / My way / When your walls come down / Reasons to live / Good girl gone bad / Turn on the night / Thief in the night. *(cd-iss.Feb91)*
Dec 87. (7") **REASON TO LIVE. / THIEF IN THE NIGHT** [33] [64]
(c-s+=) – Who wants to be lonely.
(12"++=) – Thrills in the night.
(12"pic-d++=) – Secretly cruel.
(cd-s+=) – Tears are falling / Crazy crazy nights.
Feb 88. (7") **TURN ON THE NIGHT. / HELL OR HIGH WATER** [41] [ ]
(12"+=)(12"pic-d+=) – King of the mountain / Any way you slice it.
(cd-s+=) – Heaven's on fire / I love it loud.
Oct 89. (7")(c-s)(7"red) **HIDE YOUR HEART. / BETRAYED** [59] [66]
(12"+=)(cd-s+=) – Boomerang.
(10"pic-d) – ('A'side) / Lick it up / Heaven's on fire.
Oct 89. (lp)(c)(cd) **HOT IN THE SHADE** [35] [29]
– Rise to it / Betrayed / Hide your heart / Prisoner of love / Read my body / Love's a slap in the face / Forever / Silver spoon / Cadillac dreams / King of hearts / The street giveth and the street taketh away / You love me to hate you / Somewhere between Heaven and Hell / Little Caesar / Boomerang.
Mar 90. (7") **FOREVER. / THE STREET GIVETH AND THE STREET TAKETH AWAY** [65] [8] Feb 90
(12"+=) – Deuce (demo) / Strutter (demo).
(12") – ('A'side) / All American man / Shandi / The Oath.
(cd-s) – ('A'side) / Creatures of the night / Lick it up / Heaven's on fire.
Jun 90. (7")(c-s) **RISE TO IT. / SILVER SPOON** [-] [81]

— In May'91, ERIC CARR underwent open heart surgery. He was admitted to hospital again but they found malignant cancer growth. He died 24th Nov'91. In Jan'92, KISS hit UK No.4 with 'GOD GAVE ROCK'N'ROLL TO YOU II' from the film 'Bill & Ted's Bogus Journey'. On the same single issued on 'Interscope' were tracks by 'KINGS X' & 'SLAUGHTER'.

May 92. (7")(c-s) **UNHOLY. / GOD GAVE ROCK'N'ROLL TO YOU II** [26] [ ]
(12"+=)(cd-s+=)(12"pic-d+=) – Partners in crime / Deva / Strutter (demos).
May 92. (cd)(c)(lp) **REVENGE** [10] [6]
– Unholy / Take it off / Tough love / Spit / God gave rock'n'roll to you II / Domino / Heart of chrome / Thou shalt not / Every time I look at you / Paralysed / I just wanna / Carr jam 1981.
May 93. (cd)(c) **KISS ALIVE III (live)** [24] [9]
– Creatures of the night / Deuce / I just wanna / Unholy / Heaven's on fire / Watchin' you / Domino / I was made for lovin' you / I still love you / Rock'n'roll all nite / Lick it up (featuring BOBBY WOMACK) / Take it off / I love it loud / Detroit rock city / God gave rock'n'roll to you / Star spangled banner.

. . . Jan – Jun '96 stop press . . .

Mar 96. (cd)(c)(lp) **MTV UNPLUGGED (live)** [74] [15]

– compilations etc. –

Aug 76. Casablanca; (t-lp) **THE ORIGINALS** (first 3 albums) [ ] [ ]
May 78. Casablanca; (d-lp)(d-c) **DOUBLE PLATINUM** [ ] [24]
(re-iss.Feb82 & May85, cd-iss.Jun87)
Jun 78. Casablanca; (7") **ROCK AND ROLL ALL NITE. / C'MON AND LOVE ME** [ ] [-]
Jan 81. Casablanca; (lp) **THE BEST OF THE SOLO ALBUMS** [-] [ ]
Jun 82. Casablanca; (lp)(c) **KILLERS** [42] [-]
Nov 88. Mercury; (7") **LET'S PUT THE 'X'. / CALLING DR. LOVE** [-] [97]
Nov 88. Vertigo/ US= Mercury; (lp)(c)(cd) **SMASHES, THRASHES AND HITS** [62] [21]
– Let's put the X in sex / Crazy crazy nights / (You make me) Rock hard / Love gun / Detroit rock city / I love it loud / Deuce / Lick it up / Heaven's on fire / Strutter / Beth / Tears are falling / I was made for lovin' you / Rock and roll all nite / Shout it out loud.
Oct 88. Vertigo; (5"vid-cd) **CRAZY CRAZY NIGHTS. / NO, NO, NO / WHEN YOUR WALLS COME DOWN / THIEF IN THE NIGHT** [ ] [-]
1989. Mercury; (7") **BETH. / HARD LUCK WOMAN** [-] [ ]
1989. Mercury; (7") **ROCK AND ROLL ALL NITE. / I WAS MADE FOR LOVIN' YOU** [-] [ ]
Sep 89. Vertigo; (5"vid-cd) **LICK IT UP. / DANCE ALL OVER YOUR FACE / GIMME MORE / FITS LIKE A GLOVE** [ ] [-]
Sep 89. Vertigo; (5"vid-cd) **TEARS ARE FALLING. / ANY WAY YOU SLICE IT / WHO WANTS TO BE LONELY / SECRETLY CRUEL** [ ] [-]

— (all lp's were released as pic-lp's in Europe).

KLF

Formed: KOPYRIGHT LIBERATION FRONT. Based; London, England . . . 1986 by BILL DRUMMOND and JIM CAUTY. BILL DRUMMOND had been the owner of 'Zoo' records, who signed up TEARDROP EXPLODES and ECHO & THE BUNNYMEN, with the latter being his first major managerial experience. Calling themselves JUSTIFIED ANCIENTS OF MU MU, the KLF issued a number of limited edition 45's, which sold well in the indie shops on their own label. In the summer of '88, they surprised many when hitting UK No.1 with TIMELORDS 'Dr.Who theme / Rock And Roll Part 2 – Gary Glitter theme'. They then spread their name as KLF, and soon mastered the charts with 1990 anthems 'WHAT TIME IS LOVE' and the answer '3 A.M. ETERNAL'. The latter hit UK No.1 early 1991, as did the album 'THE WHITE ROOM', as they stormed across America. • **Style:** Experimental dance power-rock samplers, both appealing to underground and pop fans alike. • **Songwriters:** Pen own material, with a host of lenders from ABBA, The BBC, GARY GLITTER, PETULA CLARK, BEATLES and STEVIE WONDER, to mention a few. • **Trivia:** Their 9th official release was a book entitled 'The Manuel Of How To Have A Number One The Easy Way'.

Recommended: SHAG TIMES (*6) / THE WHITE ROOM (*8).

JUSTIFIED ANCIENTS OF MU MU

(aka J.A.M.M.s) **KING BOY D** (aka BILL DRUMMOND) (b.WILLIAM BUTTERWORTH, 29 Apr'53, S.Africa, raised Clydebank, Scotland) – synths (ex-BIG IN JAPAN, ex-LORI & CHAMELEONS) / **ROCKMAN ROCK** (aka JIM CAUTY) (b.1957) – synthesizers (ex-BRILLIANT, etc.)

K.L.F. not issued

May 87. (12") **ALL YOU NEED IS LOVE. / BABY, YOU'RE A RICH MAN** [ ] [ ]
(7"+=) – ('A' me ru con mix) (above ltd-5,000).
Jun 87. (lp) **1987 WHAT THE FUCK IS GOING ON** [ ] [ ]
Sep 87. (12") **WHITNEY JOINS THE JAMS. /** (1 sided) [ ] [-] SCOT
Nov 87. (12") **1987 – THE EDITS** (excerpts from above album) [ ] [-]
Dec 87. (12") **DOWNTOWN. / ('A'version)** [ ] [-]
Feb 88. (lp) **WHO KILLED THE JAMMS** [ ] [ ]
– The candy store / The candy man / Disaster fund collection / King boy's dream / The porpoise song / The Prestwich prophet's grin / Burn the bastards.
Mar 88. (12") **BURN THE BASTARDS. / BURN THE BEAT / THE PORPOISE SONG** [ ] [ ]

The TIMELORDS

KLF TVT

May 88. (7")(7"sha-pic-d)**DOCTORIN' THE TARDIS. / ('A'version)** [1] [66] Dec 88
(12"+=) – ('A'-with Gary Glitter).
(cd-s+=) – ('A'club version).

K.L.F.

Jun 88. (12")**WHAT TIME IS LOVE?. /** ('A'trance) [ ] [ ]
(re-iss.Jun89 – ('A' (primal remix)). / ('A' techno) / ('A' original)
Jul 89. (7") **KYLIE SAID TO JASON. / KYLIE SAID TRANCE** [ ] [ ]
(12"+=)(cd-s+=) – Madrugaral eternal.
Oct 89. (lp)(cd) **WHAT TIME IS LOVE?** [ ] [ ]
– What time is love? (original) / Relax your body / What time is love? (Italian) / Heartbeat / No limit (dance mix) / What time is love? (live at the Land of Oz).
Dec 89. (7") **LAST TRAIN FROM TRANCENTRAL./(withdrawn)** [ ] [ ]

— added **MAXINE HARVEY** – vocals

		KLF	Arista
Jul 90.	(12") **WHAT TIME IS LOVE? (live at Transcentral). / ('A' wanderful) or ('A' Technogat mix)**	5	

(cd-s+=) – ('A'Trance mix).
(d-c-s) – (all 3 mixes above).

Aug 90.	(12") **3 A.M. ETERNAL (live at SSL). / ETERNAL (GUNS OF MU MU)**	1	5 Jun 91

(cd-s+=)(d-c-s+=) – Break for love.

Mar 91.	(cd)(c)(lp) **THE WHITE ROOM**	3	39

– What time is love? / Make it rain / 3 a.m. eternal (live at the S.S.L.) / Church of the KLF / Last train to Transcentral / Build a fire / The white room / No more tears / Justified and ancient.

Apr 91.	(7") **LAST TRAIN TO TRANSCENTRAL. / THE IRON HORSE**	2	
Oct 91.	(c-s) **WHAT TIME IS LOVE? / BUILD A FIRE**	-	57

(12"+=) – Live from the Lost Continent.
(cd-s++=) – ('A' Pure trance version '89).

JUSTIFIED ANCIENTS OF MU MU

Oct 91.	(7")(12")(c-s)**IT'S GRIM UP NORTH. / (part 2)**	10	

(cd-s+=) – Jerusalem on the Moors.

Nov 91.	(7") **JUSTIFIED AND ANCIENT (STAND BY THE JAMMS). / ('A' original version)**	2	11 Jan 92

(12"+=)(cd-s+=) – Let them eat ice-cream / Make mine a 99 / All bound for Mu Mu land (with MAXINE).

(above 'A'side credited THE FIRST LADY OF COUNTRY: MISS TAMMY WYNETTE)

Jan 92.	(7")(c-s) **P.O. 3 A.M. ETERNAL / ('A'guns of MuMu mix)**		

(12"+=)(cd-s+=) – ('A'diff.versions).

KLF

Feb 92.	(7")(c-s)**AMERICA:- WHAT TIME IS LOVE?. / AMERICA NO MORE**	4	

(12"+=)(cd-s+=) – (other 'A'mixes).

		Discipline	not issued
Dec93.	(12") **3 A.M. ETERNAL. ("EXTREME NOISE TERROR & KLF") / 3AM Eternal (Christmas Top Of The Pops 1991)**		-

– compilations, etc. –

Jan 89.	KLF; (d-lp)(cd) **SHAG TIMES**		

– All you need is love / Don't take five (take what you want) / Whitney joins the JAMS / Downtown / Candyman / Burn the bastards / Doctorin' the tardis / 114 BPM / 90 BPM / 118 BPM / 125 BPM / 120 BPM / 118 BPM / 120 BPM (all releases, from all aliases)

Jan 90.	KLF; (cd)(lp) **CHILL OUT**		-

BILL DRUMMOND

		Creation	not issued
Nov 86.	(lp) **THE MANAGER**		

– True to the trail / Ballad for a sex god / Julian Cope is dead / I want that girl / Going back / Queen of the south / I believe in rock'n'roll / Married man / I'm the king of joy / Son of a preacher man / Such a parcel of rogues in a nation. *(re-iss.+cd.Sep90)*

Mar 87.	(12") **KING OF JOY. / THE MANAGER**		

DISCO 2000

(aka DRUMMOND)

		D2000	not issued
Apr 88.	(12") **I GOTTA CD. / I LOVE DISCO 2000**		-
Apr 88.	(12") **ONE LOVE NATION. / ('A'edit) / ('A'instrumental)**		-
Jan 89.	(7") **UPTIGHT (EVERYTHING'S ALRIGHT – edit). / MR.HOTTY LOVES YOU (edit)**		-

(12") – ('A'discorama mix) / ('B'side)

— JIM CAUTY released eponymous album under **SPACE** banner mid-1990 on 'Space-Rough Trade'.

Terry KNIGHT & THE PACK (see under ⇒ GRAND FUNK RAILROAD)

Mark KNOPFLER (see under ⇒ DIRE STRAITS)

Paul KOSSOFF (see under ⇒ FREE)

KRAFTWERK

Formed: Dusseldorf, Germany . . . 1969 as ORGANISATION by RALF HUTTER, FLORIAN SCHNEIDER and 3 others (see below). After one Conrad Plank produced lp 'TONE FLOAT' for 'RCA' in 1970, the pair broke away to form KRAFTWERK (German for POWERPLANT), with KLAUS DINGER and THOMAS HOMANN. After one lp for 'Philips', RALF & FLORIAN became KRAFTWERK and released 1973 album of their names as title for #096Vertigo'. In 1974, they added KLAUS ROEDER & WOLFGANG FLUR, and issued their magnus-opus 'AUTOBAHN'. This UK & US Top 5 album contained a 22 minute title track, which edited into 3 minutes, also became hit. The next album 'RADIO ACTIVITY' (which was also now issued on own 'Kling Klang' label in Germany), disappointed most and failed to secure a Top 50 placing. In 1978, they were back in the UK Top 10 at least, with excellent return to form 'THE MAN MACHINE'. In the early 80's, they enjoyed another hit album 'COMPUTER WORLD', and a run of UK hit singles, one of which 'THE MODEL' (from 1978 lp) made top spot. Sparodic recording followed with only 1 album of new material being released in the next decade. • **Style:** Robotic electronic rock act, with minimalist synth-tunes at times being twidled by their dummies. Were more inspirational than contemporaries TANGERINE DREAM, and were a major influence to ULTRAVOX!, GARY NUMAN, DAVID BOWIE '77, JEAN-MICHEL JARRE, SIMPLE MINDS, OMD, etc. • **Songwriters:** RALF & FLORIAN. • **Trivia:** They have been sampled by many including AFRIKA BAMBAATAA in 1983 on single 'Planet Rock'.

Recommended: AUTOBAHN (*7) / RADIOACTIVITY (*4) / TRANS-EUROPE EXPRESS (*8) / THE MAN MACHINE (*8) / COMPUTER WORLD (*6)

ORGANISATION

RALF HUTTER (b.1946, Krefeld, Germany)– electric organ, strings / **FLORIAN SCHNEIDER-ESLEBEN** (b.1947, Dusseldorf)– flute, echo unit, strings / **BUTCH HAUF** – bass, percussion / **FRED MONICKS** – drums / **BASIL HAMMOND** – percussion, vocals

		R.C.A.	not issued
1970.	(lp) **TONE FLOAT**		- GERM

– Tone float / Milk float / Silver forest / Rhythm salad / Noitasinagro.

KRAFTWERK

HUTTER + SCHNEIDER with KLAUS DINGER – guitar, keyboards / **THOMAS HOMANN** – percussion

		not issued	Philips
1971.	(lp) **KRAFTWERK (HIGHRAIL)**	-	- Germ'y

– Ruckzuck / Stratowargius / Megaherz / Vom Himmel hoch.

— **HUTTER** and **SCHNEIDER** trimmed to a duo. (DINGER and HOMANN formed NEU!)

1972.	(lp) **KRAFTWERK II (VAR)**	-	- Germ'y

– Klingklang / Atem / Strom / Spule 4 / Wellenlange / Harmonika.

		Vertigo	Vertigo
1972.	(d-lp) **KRAFTWERK** (2 German lp's combined)		-
Nov 73.	(lp)(c) **RALF AND FLORIAN**		Sep 75

– Elektrisches roulette (Electric roulette) / Tongebirge (Mountain of sound) / Kristallo (Crystals) / Heimatklange (The bells of home) / Tanzmusik (Dance music) / Ananas symphonie (Pineapple symphony).

— added **KLAUS ROEDER** – violin, guitar / **WOLFGANG FLUR** – percussion

Nov 74.	(lp)(c) **AUTOBAHN**	4	5

– Autobahn / Kometenmelodie 1 & 2 (Comet melody) / Mitternacht (Midnight) / Morgenspaziergang (Morning walk). *(re-iss.Mar82 & Jun85 on 'EMI' hit 61 UK, cd-iss.Jun87) (re-iss.Jun83)*

Feb 75.	(7") **AUTOBAHN. / KOMETENMELODIE**	11	-
Feb 75.	(7") **AUTOBAHN. / MORGENSPAZIERGANG**	-	25
Jul 75.	(7") **KOMETENMELODIE. / MITTERNACHT**	-	
Jul 75.	(7") **KOMETENMELODIE 2. / KRISTALLO**		-

— Oct75, **KARL BARTOS** – percussion repl. ROEDER

		Capitol	Capitol
Nov 75.	(lp)(c) **RADIO-ACTIVITY**		

– Geiger counter / Radio-activity / Radioland / Airwaves / (intermission) / News / The voice of energy / Antenna / Radio stars / Uran / Transistor / Ohm sweet ohm. *(re-iss.Jun84 on 'Fame/Capitol') (re-iss.+cd.Jun87) (re-iss.cd Apr94 on 'Cleopatra') (cd-iss.Apr95 on 'EMI')*

Feb 76.	(7") **RADIO-ACTIVITY. / ANTENNA**		
Apr 77.	(lp)(c) **TRANS-EUROPE EXPRESS**		

– Europe endless / The hall of mirrors / Showroom dummies / Trans-Europe express / Metal on metal / Franz Schubert / Endless endless. *(reached No.49 Feb82, re-iss.'85, re-iss.Jun86 on 'Fame')(cd-iss.May87) (re-iss.cd Apr94 on 'Cleopatra')*

Apr 77.	(7") **TRANS-EUROPE EXPRESS. / EUROPE ENDLESS**		-
Jun 77.	(7") **TRANS EUROPE EXPRESS. / FRANZ SCHUBERT**	-	67
Aug 77.	(7") **SHOWROOM DUMMIES. / EUROPE EXPRESS**		

May 78. (lp)(c) **THE MAN MACHINE** [9] [ ]
– The robots / Spacelab / Metropolis / The model / Neon lights / The man machine. *(re-iss.+cd Jul88 on 'Fame') (re-iss.cd Apr94 on 'Cleopatra') (cd-iss.Apr95 on 'EMI')*
May 78. (7") **THE ROBOTS (edit). / SPACELAB** [ ] [ ]
Jun 78. (7") **NEON LIGHTS. / THE ROBOTS** [-] [ ]
Sep 78. (12"m) **SHOWROOM DUMMIES. / EUROPE ENDLESS / SPACELAB** [ ] [-]
Sep 78. (7"luminous)(12"luminous) **NEON LIGHTS. / TRANS-EUROPE EXPRESS / THE MODEL** [53] [ ]

E.M.I. Warners

Apr 81. (7")(12")(US-7"green) **POCKET CALCULATOR. / DENTAKU** [39] [ ]
(c-s) – ('A'extended version) / Numbers.
May 81. (lp)(c) **COMPUTER-WORLD** [15] [72]
– Pocket calculator / Numbers / Computer-world / Computer love / Home computer / It's more fun to compute. *(cd-iss.Apr95 on EMI')*
Jun 81. (7")(12") **COMPUTER LOVE. / THE MODEL** [36] [-]
(above double 'A'-side, flipped over Dec81 reached No.1.*(re-1983)*
Jun 81. (7") **COMPUTER LOVE. / NUMBERS** [-] [ ]
Feb 82. (7")(12") **SHOWROOM DUMMIES. / NUMBERS** [25] [ ]
Jul 83. (7") **TOUR DE FRANCE. / TOUR DE FRANCE (instrumental)** [22] [ ]
(12"+=)(c-s+=) – ('A'&'B' versions). *(re-iss.+ remixed 7+12" Aug84, reached No.24, 12" had all versions)*
Aug 83. (lp)(c) **TECHNO POP** (cancelled) [-] [-]
Oct 86. (7")(12") **MUSIQUE NON STOP. / MUSIQUE NON STOP (version)** [ ] [ ]
Nov 86. (lp)(c)(cd) **ELECTRIC CAFE** [58] [ ]
– Boom boom tschak / Techno pop / Musique non stop / The telephone call / Sex object / Techno pop / Electric cafe.
Feb 87. (7") **THE TELEPHONE CALL. / DER TELEFON ANRUF** [ ] [ ]
(12"+=) – Housephone.

— **FRITZ HIJBERT** repl. WOLFGANG FLUR
May 91. (7")(c-s) **THE ROBOTS (remixed). / ('A'version)** [20] [ ]
(12"+=)(cd-s+=) – Robotronix / ('A'version).
Jun 91. (cd)(c)(d-lp) **THE MIX** ('91 remixes) [15] [ ]
– The robots / Computer love / Pocket calculator / Dentaku / Autobahn / Radioactivity / Trans Europe express / Abzug / Metal on metal / Homecomputer / Musique non stop.
Oct 91. (7")(c-s) **RADIOACTIVITY (remix). / ('A'orbit remix)** [43] [ ]
(12"+=)(cd-s+=) – ('A'remixes extended).

— In Jul'91, BARTOS and FLUR formed own project ELEKTRIC.

– compilations, others, imports –

1975. Philips; (d-lp) **DOPPELALBUM** [-] [-]
Oct 75. Vertigo; (lp)(c) **EXCELLER 8** [ ] [ ]
Oct 80. Vertigo Germany; (7") **AUTOBAHN. / ('B'by BEGGAR'S OPERA)** [-] [-]
Apr 81. Vertigo; (lp)(c) **ELEKTRO KINETIC** [ ] [ ]
May 81. Vertigo; (7") **KOMETENMELODIE 2. / VON HIMMEL HOCH** [ ] [ ]
1976. Fontana Germany; (lp) **POP LIONS** [-] [-]
May 84. Old Gold; (7") **THE MODEL. / COMPUTER LOVE** [ ] [-]

— (In the States, there was also comp.lp 'THE ROBOTS' on 'Capitol')
Apr 94. Cleopatra; (cd) **SHOWROOM DUMMIES** [ ] [-]
Apr 94. Cleopatra; (cd) **THE MODEL** [ ] [-]

Lenny KRAVITZ

Born: 26 May'64, New York, USA, son of a Russian Jew and black Bahamian actress. As a teenager, they moved to Los Angeles, where he joined local boys' choir and learned himself to play guitar and piano. In 1987, he formed own one-man band ROMEO BLUE, and married 'Cosby Show' actress Lisa Bonet in Nov'87. For the next 2 years, he recorded demos which were soon heard by Henry Hirsch, who recommended them to 'Virgin'. By the time they signed him, LENNY had divorced (1988) and befriended new circle of friends like SEAN LENNON and his mother YOKO ONO. In Oct'89, after many arguments with record company over use of production, etc., he finally released debut album and single 'LET LOVE RULE'. The album notched up sales of half a million copies in the US, and eventually reached Top 60 in the UK. In 1990, the title track became first Top 40 success in Britain, and tempted MADONNA into asking him and INGRID CHAVEZ to write her controversial 'Justify My Love' single. Later that year, he also appeared in Liverpool at YOKO ONO's tribute to her late husband JOHN LENNON. Early in '92, after a Top 10 album 'MAMA SAID', LENNY settled out of court royalties to INGRID CHAVEZ. • **Style:** Late 60's influenced heavy soul-rock artist, reminiscent of JIMI HENDRIX, CURTIS MAYFIELD and LED ZEPPELIN. His psychedelic-pop image, leant more from 80's star PRINCE, while definitely filling the gap in the 90's for the musically vacationing TERENCE TRENT D'ARBY. • **Songwriters:** Writes and plays in studio all instruments, and covers; COLD TURKEY + GIVE PEACE A CHANCE (John Lennon) / IF SIX WAS NINE (Jimi Hendrix / DEUCE (Kiss). • **Trivia:** SLASH of GUNS'N'ROSES played guitar on 2 tracks from 'MAMA SAID'.

Recommended: MAMA SAID (*8) / LET LOVE RULE (*7) / ARE YOU GONNA GO MY WAY (*7).

LENNY KRAVITZ – vocals, guitar, piano, bass, drums with a few on session / **HENRY HIRSCH** – keyboards / **KARL DENSON** – sax / +guests.

Virgin America Virgin

Oct 89. (7") **LET LOVE RULE. / EMPTY HANDS** [ ] [89]
(12"+=)(cd-s+=) – Blues for Sister Someone / Flower child.
Nov 89. (lp)(c)(cd) **LET LOVE RULE** [56] [61] Jan 90
– Sitting on top of the world / Let love rule / Freedom train / My precious love / I build this garden for us / Fear / Does anybody out there even care / Mr. Cab driver / Rosemary / Be. *(c+=)*– Blues for Sister Someone / Flower child. *(cd++=)*– Empty hands. *(re-dist.May90.hit UK No.56)*
Jan 90. (7")(c-s) **I BUILD THIS GARDEN FOR US. / FLOWER CHILD** [81] [ ]
(12"+=)(cd-s+=) – Fear.
May 90. (7")(c-s) **MR. CAB DRIVER. / BLUES FOR SISTER SOMEONE (live) / DOES ANYBODY OUT THERE EVEN CARE (live)** [58] [ ]
(12"+=) – (first 2 tracks) / Rosemary (live).
(10"++=) – (first 2 tracks) / Let love rule (live).
Jul 90. (7")(c-s) **LET LOVE RULE. / COLD TURKEY (live)** [39] [ ]
(12"+=) – Flower child (live).
(cd-s+=) – My precious love (live).
(10") – ('A'side) / My precious love (live) / If six was nine (live).
Mar 91. (7")(c-s) **ALWAYS ON THE RUN. / ('A'instrumental)** [41] [ ]
(12"box+=) – Light skin girl from London.
(cd-s++=) – Butterfly.
Apr 91. (cd)(c)(lp) **MAMA SAID** [8] [39]
– Fields of joy / Always on the run / Stand by my woman / It ain't over 'til it's over / More than anything in this world / What goes around comes around / The difference is why / Stop draggin' around / Flowers for Zoe / Fields of joy (reprise) / All I ever wanted / When the morning turns to night / What the . . . . are we saying? / Butterfly.
May 91. (7")(c-s) **IT AIN'T OVER 'TIL IT'S OVER. / THE DIFFERENCE IS WHY** [11] [2]
(12"+=)(cd-s+=) – I'll be around.
(12"pic-d) – ('A'side) / (interview).
Sep 91. (7")(c-s) **STAND BY MY WOMAN. / FLOWERS FOR ZOE** [55] [76]
(12"+=) – Stop dragging around (live).
(cd-s+=) – What the . . .. are we saying / Always on the run (both live)

— with **CRAIG ROSS** – electric guitar (co-writes, some music) / **TONY BRETT** – bass / **MICHAEL HUNTER** – flugel horn
Feb 93. (7")(c-s) **ARE YOU GONNA GO MY WAY. / MY LOVE** [4] [ ]
(cd-s) – ('A' side) Always on the run / It ain't over 'til it's over / Let love rule.
Mar 93. (cd)(c)(lp) **ARE YOU GONNA GO MY WAY** [1] [12]
– Are you gonna go my way / Believe / Come on and love me / Heaven help / Just be a woman / Is there any love in your heart / Black girl / My love / Sugar / Sister / Eleutheria.
May 93. (7")(c-s) **BELIEVE. / FOR THE FIRST TIME** [30] [60]
(10"pic-d+=)(cd-s+=) – ('A'acoustic) / Sitar (acoustic).
Aug 93. (7")(c-s) **HEAVEN HELP. / ELEUTHERIA** [21] [-]
(cd-s+=) – Ascension / Brother.
Nov 93. (7"pic-d)(12") **IS THERE ANY LOVE IN YOUR HEART. / ALWAYS ON THE RUN (live)** [52] [ ]
(cd+=) – What goes around comes around (live) / Freedom train (live).
Mar 94. (c-s)(cd-s) **HEAVEN HELP. / SPINNING AROUND OVER YOU** [-] [80]
Aug 95. (7")(c-s) **ROCK AND ROLL IS DEAD. / ANOTHER LIFE** [22] [75]
(10"+=)(cd-s+=) – Confused / Is it me or is it you.
Sep 95. (cd)(c)(lp) **CIRCUS** [5] [10]
– Rock and roll is dead / Circus / Beyond the 7th sky / Tunnel vision / Can't get you off my mind / Magdalene / God is love / Thin ice / Don't go and put a bullet in your head / In my life today / The resurrection.
Dec 95. (c-s) **CIRCUS / ('A'acoustic)** [54] [ ]
(10"+=)(cd-s+=) – Tunnel vision (live) / Are you gonna go my way (live).

. . . Jan – Jun '96 stop press . . .

Feb 96. (single) **CAN'T GET YOU OFF MY MIND** [54] [62]

KUKL (see under ⇒ BJORK)

KULA SHAKER

*** NEW ENTRY ***

Formed: Highgate, London, England . . .mid 90's out of mods The KAYS by CRISPIAN MILLS. Played down the fact his mother was famous English actress HAYLEY MILLS (daughter of SIR JOHN MILLS). In the late 80's, CRISPIAN and ALONZA BEVIN set up school group LOVELY LADS, who became The OBJECTS. In 1995 after jointly winning 'In The City' new band competition and a Glastonbury appearance, KULA SHAKER signed to 'Columbia', through A&R man Ronnie Gurr. Debuted at Xmas with limited edition single 'TATTVA'. After a Top 40 breakthrough in April '96, it became a Top 5 smash in June. • **Style:** Glam retro psychedelic outfit influenced by 13th FLOOR ELEVATORS. • **Songwriters:** MILLS or some by group. • **Trivia:** Produced by JOHN LECKIE.

CRISPIAN MILLS – vocals, guitar / **ALONZA BEVIN** – bass, vocals / **JAY DARLINGTON** – keyboards / **PAUL WINTER-HART** – drums

		Columbia	Columbia
Dec 95.	(ltd-cd-s) **TATTVA / HOLLOW MAN (part 2)**		-
Apr 96.	(7")(c-s) **GRATEFUL WHEN YOU'RE DEAD. / JERRY WAS THERE / ANOTHER LIFE**	35	
	(cd-s+=) – Under the hammer.		
Jun 96.	(7") **TATTVA. / TATTVA ON ST. GEORGE'S DAY / DANCE IN YOUR SHADOW**	4	
	(cd-s) – (first & third tracks) / Moonshine / Tattva (lucky 13).		
	(cd-s) – (second & third tracks) / Red balloon (Vishnu's eyes).		

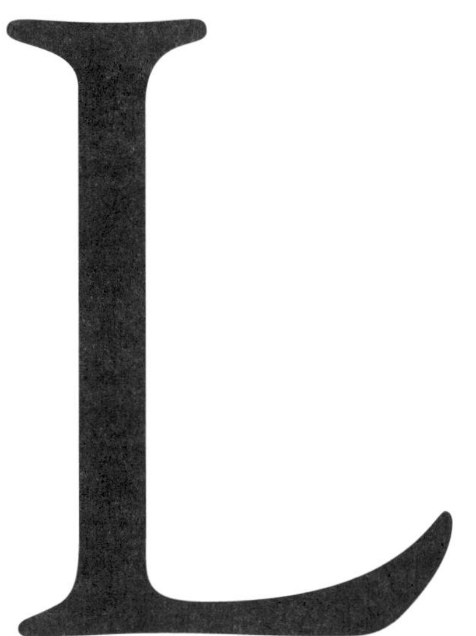

Greg LAKE (see under ⇒ EMERSON, LAKE & PALMER)

Robert LAMM (see under ⇒ CHICAGO)

Jerry LANDIS (see under ⇒ SIMON & GARFUNKEL)

LARD (see under ⇒ DEAD KENNEDYS)

LA'S

Formed: Liverpool, England . . . 1986 by LEE MAVERS, etc. They signed to 'Go! Discs' in 1987, and released a single a year, until eponymous debut album in 1990. It scraped into the UK Top 30, helped by a new version of 'THERE SHE GOES' hitting Top 20. • **Style:** Influenced from 60's garage to The TROGGS or R.E.M. • **Songwriters:** LEE MAVERS penned. • **Trivia:** Steve Lilywhite produced them in 1990.

Recommended: THE LA'S (*8).

LEE MAVERS (b. 2 Aug'62) – vocals, guitar / **JOHN BYRNE** – guitar / **JOHN POWER** (b.14 Sep'67) – bass / **PAUL HEMMINGS** – guitar / **JOHN TIMSON** – drums

		Go! Discs	London
Oct 87.	(7") **WAY OUT. / ENDLESS**		
	(12"+=) – Knock me down.		
	(12"++=) – Liberty ship (demo) / Freedom song (demo).		
—	**CHRIS SHARROCK** – drums (ex-ICICLE WORKS) repl. TIMSON		
Nov 88.	(7") **THERE SHE GOES. / COME IN COME OUT**	59	
	(12"+=)(cd-s+=) – Who knows / Man I'm only human.		
	(7"ep+=) – Who knows / Way out.		
May 89.	(7") **TIMELESS MELODY. / CLEAN PROPHET**	57	
	(12"+=)(cd-s+=) – Knock me down. *(re-iss.Sep90, hit 57)*		
	(10"+=) – All by myself / There she goes.		
—	**NEIL MAVERS** (b. 8 Jul'71) – drums repl. SHARROCK / **JAMES JOYCE** (b.23 Sep'70) – bass repl. POWER who formed The CAST / added **CAMMY** (b.PETER JAMES CAMELL, 30 Jun'67) – guitar (ex-MARSHMALLOW)		
Oct 90.	(cd)(c)(lp) **THE LA'S**	30	
	– Son of a gun / I can't stop / Timeless melody / Liberty ship / There she goes / Doledrum / Feelin' / Way out / I.O.U. / Freedom song / Failure / Looking glass.		
Oct 90.	(7")(c-s) **THERE SHE GOES (new version). / FREEDOM SONG**	13	49 Jun 91
	(12"+=)(cd-s+=) – All by myself.		
Feb 91.	(7"ep)(c-ep) **FEELIN' 91 / I.O.U. / ('A'alternative) / DOLEDRUM**	43	
	(12"ep+=)(cd-ep+=) – Liberty ship. (repl. 3rd track above.)		

LAW (see under ⇒ RODGERS, Paul)

LEAGUE OF GENTLEMEN (see under ⇒ KING CRIMSON)

Paul LEARY (see under ⇒ BUTTHOLE SURFERS)

LED ZEPPELIN

Formed: London, England . . . mid-68 out of The NEW YARDBIRDS by JIMMY PAGE, JOHN PAUL JONES and ROBERT PLANT. They soon found another former session man JOHN BONHAM, who arrived in time for live debut, 15 Oct'68 at Surrey University. They had chosen group name through KEITH MOON's often said phrase "going down like a lead zeppelin". With manager PETER GRANT at the helm, they secured a worldwide deal on 'Atlantic'. Early in 1969, they unleashed eponymous debut, which due to growing reputation, hit cross-Atlantic Top 10. Later in the year 'LED ZEPPELIN II' plants itself into both top spots, with a lifted cut 'WHOLE LOTTA LOVE' making US Top 5. As with all their US singles, it was thought better by Peter Grant not to issue any 45's in Britain, although they were readily available in import shops. They topped each chart with every album release, until the untimely death on 25 Sep'80 of JOHN BONHAM. In 1982, PAGE and PLANT went solo, but re-united in 1984 as The HONEYDRIPPERS. PLANT continued to be the more successful of the two, having mostly hit albums during the next decade. Sadly, PETER GRANT died of a heart attack on 21st Nov'95. • **Style:** Greatest heavy-metal band of all-time, who re-arranged the blues into own distinctive sound, based around PLANT's power-vox and PAGE's climatic guitar epics, that also showed a folkier acoustic side on some songs. • **Songwriters:** PAGE + PLANT wrote nearly all with some help from JONES and/or BONHAM. They also covered; I CAN'T QUIT YOU BABY (Otis Rush) / YOU SHOOK ME (Willie Dixon) / BRING IT ON HOME (Sonny Boy Williamson) / GALLOW'S POLE + HATS OFF TO HARPER (trad.) / etc. JIMMY PAGE covered; HUMMINGBIRD (B.B.King). The HONEYDRIPPERS;- SEA OF LOVE (Phil Phillips with the Twilights). ROBERT PLANT: LET'S HAVE A PARTY (Elvis Presley) / IF I WERE A CARPENTER (Robert Plant). • **Trivia:** SANDY DENNY featured on track 'BATTLE OF EVERMORE' from 1971's symbol album. The previous year, C.C.S. (aka. ALEXIS KORNER) had a Top 10 hit with 'WHOLE LOTTA LOVE'. In 1985, with PHIL COLLINS on drums, LED ZEPPELIN played LIVE AID. JOHN BONHAM's drumming son JASON formed his band BONHAM in the late 80's. Around the same time, a kitsch mickey-take outfit DREAD ZEPPELIN, hit the music scene, playing reggae versions of group's classics. In 1992, Australian 60's hitmaker and TV personality ROLF HARRIS charts, but destroys top college favourite 'STAIRWAY TO HEAVEN'. It was even worse than 1985's FAR CORPORATION version, which also hit UK Top 10. **Early work:** As well as session work with many (THEM, etc.), JIMMY PAGE released solo single in Mar'65 'SHE JUST SATIFIES' / 'KEEP MOVIN'' for 'Fontana'. He had earlier played on 45's by NEIL CHRISTIAN & THE CRUSADERS, plus CARTER-LEWIS & THE SOUTHERNERS. JOHN PAUL JONES played in The TONY MEEHAN COMBO, before issuing solo 45 in Apr'64 'A FOGGY DAY IN VIETNAM' / 'BAJA', for 'Pye' label. ROBERT PLANT had been part of LISTEN, who released one single for 'CBS' in Nov'66; 'YOU'D BETTER RUN' / 'EVERYBODY'S GOTTA SAY'. He stayed with label for 2 solo releases in Mar'67; 'OUR SONG' / 'LAUGHIN' CRYIN' LAUGHIN'', & Jul'67 'LONG TIME COMIN'' / 'I'VE GOT A SECRET'. He then teamed up that year with BONHAM, to form Birmingham based group BAND OF JOY. All these rare singles now fetch upwards of £100.

Recommended: LED ZEPPELIN (*8) / LED ZEPPELIN II (*9) / LED ZEPPELIN III (*9) / UNTITLED (LED ZEPPELIN IV) (*9) / HOUSES OF THE HOLY (*8) / PHYSICAL GRAFFITI (*9) / PRESENCE (*6) / THE SONG REMAINS THE SAME (*7) / IN THROUGH THE OUT DOOR (*7) / REMASTERS (*10). ROBERT PLANT solo: PICTURES AT ELEVEN (*6) / PRINCIPLES OF MOMENT (*6) / MAGIC NIRVANA (*7) / FATE OF NATIONS (*6) / JIMMY PAGE solo: OUTRIDER (*6).

ROBERT PLANT (b.20 Aug'48, West Bromwich, England) – vocals (ex-LISTEN) / **JIMMY PAGE** (b. 9 Jan'44, Heston, England) – lead guitars (ex-YARDBIRDS) / **JOHN PAUL JONES** (b.JOHN BALDWIN, 3 Jun'46, Sidcup, Kent, England) – bass / **JOHN BONHAM** (b.31 May'48, Bromwich, England) – drums

		Atlantic	Atlantic
Mar 69.	(lp)(c) **LED ZEPPELIN**	6	10 Feb 69
	– Good times bad times / Babe I'm gonna leave you / You shook me / Dazed and confused / Your time is gonna come / Black mountain side / Communication		

breakdown / You shook me / I can't quit you baby / How many more times. *(cd-iss.Jan87) (re-iss.cd+c Jul94)*

Mar 69. (7") **GOOD TIMES BAD TIMES. / COMMUNICATION BREAKDOWN** - 80

Oct 69. (lp)(c) **LED ZEPPELIN II** 1 1

– Whole lotta love / What is and what should never be / The lemon song / Thank you / Heartbreaker / Livin' lovin' maid (she's just a woman) / Ramble on / Moby Dick / Bring it on home. *(cd-iss.Jan87) (re-iss.cd+c Jul94)*

Nov 69. (7") **WHOLE LOTTA LOVE. / LIVIN' LOVIN' MAID (SHE'S JUST A WOMAN)** - 4 / 65

Oct 70. (lp)(c) **LED ZEPPELIN III** 1 1

– Immigrant song / Friends / Celebration day / Since I've been loving you / Out on the tiles / Gallow's pole / Tangerine / That's the way / Bron-y-aur stomp / Hats off to (Roy) Harper. *(cd-iss.Jan87)*

Nov 70. (7") **IMMIGRANT SONG. / HEY HEY WHAT CAN I DO** - 16

Nov 71. (lp)(c) **(UNTITLED – 4 SYMBOLS)** 1 2

– Black dog / Rock and roll / The battle of Evermore / Stairway to Heaven / Misty mountain hop / Four sticks / Goin' to California / When the levee breaks. *(lilac-lp Nov78) (cd-iss.Jul83) (re-iss.cd+c Jul94)*

Dec 71. (7") **BLACK DOG. / MISTY MOUNTAIN HOP** - 15

Mar 72. (7") **ROCK AND ROLL. / FOUR STICKS** - 47

Apr 73. (lp)(c) **HOUSES OF THE HOLY** 1 1

– The song remains the same / The rain song / Over the hills and far away / The crunge / Dancing days / D'yer maker / No quarter / The ocean. *(cd-iss.Jan87) (re-iss.cd+c Jul94)*

Jun 73. (7") **OVER THE HILLS AND FAR AWAY. / DANCING DAYS** [-] [51]

Oct 73. (7") **D'YER MAKER. / THE CRUNGE** [-] [20]

Swan Song Swan Song

Mar 75. (d-lp)(d-c) **PHYSICAL GRAFFITI** [1] [1]
– Custard pie / The rover / In my time of dying / Houses of the holy / Trampled underfoot / Kashmir / In the light / Bron-y-aur / Down by the seaside / Ten years gone / Night flight / The wanton song / Boogie with Stu / Black country woman / Sick again. *(d-cd-iss.Jan87)*

Mar 75. (7") **TRAMPLED UNDERFOOT. / BLACK COUNTRY WOMAN** [-] [38]

Apr 76. (lp)(c) **PRESENCE** [1] [1]
– Achilles last stand / For your life / Royal Orleans / Nobody's fault but mine / Candy store rock / Hots for nowhere / Tea for one. *(cd-iss.Jun87)*

May 76. (7") **CANDY STORE ROCK. / ROYAL ORLEANS** [-] [ ]

Oct 76. (d-lp)(d-c) **THE SONG REMAINS THE SAME (live)** [1] [2]
– Rock and roll / Celebration day / The song remains the same / The rain song / Dazed and confused / No quarter / Stairway to Heaven / Moby Dick / Whole lotta love. *(d-cd-iss.Feb87)*

— Above was also a film from concerts at Madison Square Gardens in 1973. It featured some dream sequences / fantasies of each member.

Aug 79. (lp)(c) **IN THROUGH THE OUT DOOR** [1] [1]
– In the evening / South bound Saurez / Fool in the rain / Hot dog / Carouselambra / All my love / I'm gonna crawl. *(cd-iss.Jan87) (re-iss.cd+c Oct94 on 'Atlantic')*

Dec 79. (7") **FOOL IN THE RAIN. / HOT DOG** [-] [21]

— Disbanded when JOHN BONHAM died after a drinking session 25 Sep'80.

– compilations, others, etc. –

Nov 82. Swan Song; (lp)(c) **CODA (demos from 68-79)** [4] [6] Dec 82
– We're gonna groove / Poor Tom / I can't quit you baby / Walter's walk / Ozone baby / Darlene / Bonzo's Montreaux / Walter's walk / Wearing and tearing.

Oct 90. Swan Song; (4xcd)(4xc)(6xlp) **LED ZEPPELIN** [48] [18]

Nov 90. Swan Song; (d-cd)(d-c)(t-lp) **REMASTERS** [10] [47] Mar 92
– Communication breakdown / Babe I'm gonna leave you / Good times bad times / Dazed and confused / Whole lotta love / Heartbreaker / Ramble on / Immigrant song / Celebration day / Since I've been loving you / Black dog / Rock and roll / The battle of Evermore / Misty mountain hop / Stairway to Heaven / The song remains the same / The rain song / D'yer maker / No quarter / Houses of the holy / Kashmir / Trampled underfoot / Nobody's fault but mine / Achilles last stand / All my love / In the evening.

Sep 93. Atlantic; (10xcd-box) **LED ZEPPELIN BOXED SET II** [56] [87]

Oct 93. Atlantic; (d-cd)(d-c) **REMASTERS 2** [ ] [ ]

— JOHN PAUL JONES went on to become a top producer. In 1992, he contributed string arrangements to R.E.M.'s classic album 'Automatic For The People'. ROBERT PLANT went solo and teamed up with JIMMY PAGE in The HONEYDRIPPERS. PAGE also went solo and formed The FIRM.

In Aug 94; JOHN PAUL JONES turned up on an unusual collaboration (single 'Do You Take This Man') between himself and loud punk-opera diva DIAMANDA GALAS.

ROBERT PLANT

with **BOBBIE BLUNT** – guitar / **JEZZ WOODRUFFE** – keyboards / **PAUL MARTINEZ** – bass / **COZY POWELL** – drums / guest **PHIL COLLINS** – drums, perc.

Swan Song Swan Song

Jul 82. (lp)(c) **PICTURES AT ELEVEN** [2] [5]
– Burning down one side / Moonlight in Samosa / Pledge pin / Slow dancer / Worse that Detroit / Fat lip / Like I've been gone / Mystery title. *(cd-iss.1986)*

Sep 82. (7")(12") **BURNING DOWN ONE SIDE. / MOONLIGHT IN SAMOSA** [ ] [44]

Nov 82. (7") **PLEDGE PIN. /** [-] [74]

— **RITCHIE HAYWARD** – drums (ex-LITTLE FEAT) repl. COZY / added **BOB MAYO** – keyboards, guitar

W.E.A. Atlantic

Jul 83. (lp)(c) **THE PRINCIPLE OF MOMENTS** [7] [8]
– Other arms / In the mood / Messin' with the Mekon / Wreckless love / Thru with the two-step / Horizontal departure / Stranger here . . .than over there / Big log. *(cd-iss.1984)*

Jul 83. (7") **BIG LOG. / MESSIN' WITH THE MEKON** [11] [-]
(12"+=) – Stranger here . . . than over there.

Sep 83. (7") **BIG LOG. / FAR POSY** [-] [20]

Nov 83. (7") **IN THE MOOD. / HORIZONTAL DEPARTURE** [-] [39]

Jan 84. (7") **IN THE MOOD. / PLEDGE PIN (live)** [ ] [-]
(12"+=) – Horizontal departure.

Es Paranza Es Paranza

May 85. (7")(12") **PINK AND BLACK. / TROUBLE YOUR MONEY** [ ] [ ]

May 85. (7") **LITTLE BY LITTLE. / TROUBLE YOUR MONEY** [-] [36]

May 85. (lp)(c)(cd) **SHAKEN 'N' STIRRED** [19] [20]
– Hip to hoo / Kallalou Kallalou / Too loud / Trouble your money / Pink and black / Little by little / Doo doo a do do / Easily led / Sixes and sevens.

Jul 85. (7") **TOO LOUD. / KALLALOU KALLALOU** [-] [ ]

Aug 85. (7") **LITTLE BY LITTLE. / DOO DOO A DO DO** [ ] [-]
(12"+=) – Easily led.

— now with **DOUG BOYLE** – guitars / **PHIL SCRAGG** – bass / **PHIL JOHNSTONE** – keys, co-writer / **JIMMY PAGE** – guitar 2 / **CHRIS BLACKWELL** – drums, perc. / **MARIE PIERRE, TONI HALLIDAY and KIRSTY MacCOLL** – backing vocals

Jan 88. (7")(12") **HEAVEN KNOWS. / WALKING TOWARDS PARADISE** [33] [ ]
(cd-s+=) – Big log.

Feb 88. (lp)(c)(cd) **NOW AND ZEN** [10] [6]
– Heaven knows / Dance on my own / Tall cool one / The way I feel / Helen of Troy / Billy's revenge / Ship of fools / Why / White, clean and neat. *(cd+=)*– Walking towards Paradise.

Apr 88. (7")(12") **TALL COOL ONE. / WHITE, CLEAN AND NEAT** [ ] [25]
(cd-s+=) – ('A' extended version) / Little by little.

Aug 88. (7") **SHIP OF FOOLS. / HELEN OF TROY** [ ] [-]
(12"+=) – Heaven Knows (live).
(cd-s+=) – Dimples (live).

Aug 88. (7") **SHIP OF FOOLS. / BILLY'S REVENGE** [-] [84]

— **PAT THORPE** – drums repl. BLACKWELL who became ill.

— now with **BLACKWELL, CHARLIE JONES, JOHNSTONE and BOYLE**

Mar 90. (cd)(c)(lp) **MANIC NIRVANA** [15] [ ]
– Hurting kind (I've got my eyes on you) / Big love / S S S & Q / I cried / She said / Nirvana / The dye on the highway / Your ma said you cried in your sleep last night / Anniversary / Liars dance / Watching you.

Apr 90. (7")(c-s) **HURTING KIND (I'VE GOT MY EYES ON YOU). / OOMPAH (WATERY BINT)** [45] [46] Mar 90
(12"+=) – I cried / One love.
(cd-s+=) – Don't look back / One love.

Jun 90. (7")(c-s) **YOUR MA SAID YOU CRIED IN YOUR SLEEP LAST NIGHT. / SHE SAID** [ ] [ ]
(12")(cd-s) – ('A'side) / ('A'version) / One love.

— with **KEVIN SCOTT MACMICHAEL** – guitar / **PHIL JOHNSTONE** – electric piano / **CHARLIE JONES** – bass / **MICHAEL LEE** – drums / **CHRIS HUGHES** – drums, co-producer / plus guests **FRANCIS DUNNERY, MAIRE BRENNAN, NIGEL KENNEDY + RICHARD THOMPSON**

Es Paranza Es Paranza

Apr 93. (7")(c-s) **29 PALMS. / 21 YEARS** [21] [ ]
(cd-s+=) – Dark Moon.
(cd-s++=) – Whole lotta love (you need love).

May 93. (cd)(c)(lp) **FATE OF NATIONS** [6] [ ]
– Calling to you / Down to the sea / Come into my life / I believe / 29 palms / Memory song (hello, hello) / If I were a carpenter / Colours of a shade / Promised land / The greatest gift / Great spirit / Network news.

Jun 93. (7")(c-s) **I BELIEVE. / GREAT SPIRIT (acoustic mix)** [ ] [ ]
(cd-s+=) – Hey Jayne.
(12"pic-d++=) – Whole lotta love (you need love).

Aug 93. (c-s) **CALLING TO YOU. / NAKED IF I WANT TO** [ ] [ ]
(12"+=)(cd-s+=) – 8.05.

Dec 93. (7")(c-s) **IF I WERE A CARPENTER. / SHIP OF FOOLS (live)** [ ] [ ]
(cd-s) – ('A'side) / I believe (live) / Tall cool one (live).

JIMMY PAGE

solo with **CHRIS FARLOWE** – vocals / **DAVE LAWSON + DAVID SINCLAIR WHITTAKER + GORDON EDWARDS** – piano / **DAVE PATON** – bass / **DAVE MATTACKS** – drums

Swan Song Swan Song

Feb 82. (lp)(c) **DEATH WISH II (Soundtrack)** [40] [50]
– Who's to blame / The chase / City sirens / A jam sandwich / Of Carole's theme / The release / Hotelrats and photostats / A shadow in the sky / Jill's theme / Prelude / Big band, sax & violence / Hypnotizing ways (oh mamma).

— In 1985, PAGE collaborated with friend ROY HARPER on dual album 'WHATEVER HAPPENED TO JUGULA', which hit UK Top 50.

— now guest vocals – **JOHN MILES, ROBERT PLANT, CHRIS FARLOWE JASON BONHAM** – drums / **DURBAN LEVERDE** – bass / **FELIX KRISH, TONY FRANKLIN, BARRYMORE BARLOW** – drums

Geffen Geffen

Jun 88 (lp)(c)(cd) **OUTRIDER** [27] [26]
– Wasting my time / Wanna make love / The only one / Writes of winter / Hummingbird / Liquid mercury / Emerald eyes / Prison blues / Blues anthem (if I cannot have your love). *(re-cd+c.Aug91)*

Jun 88. (7") **WASTING MY TIME. / WRITES OF WINTER** [ ] [ ]

– other recordings, etc –

Jan 82. Charly; (lp) **JAM SESSION** (rec.1964 with SONNY BOY WILLIAMSON & BRIAN AUGER) [ ] [-]
– Don't send me no flowers / I see a man downstairs / She was so dumb / The goat / Walking / Little girl, how old are you / It'a a bloody life / Getting out of town.

— below featured on session; **JOHN PAUL JONES / ALBERT LEE / NICKY HOPKINS**

+ **CLEM CATTINI**

Sep 84. Thunderbolt; (lp)(c)(cd) **NO INTRODUCTION NECCESSARY** [ ] [-]
– Lovin' up a storm / Everything I do is wrong / Think it over / Boll Weevil song / Livin' lovin' wreck / One long kiss / Dixie friend / Down the line / Fabulous / Breathless / Rave on / Lonely weekends / Burn up. *(re-iss.cd May93)*

— below from early 70's featuring; **JOHN BONHAM / JEFF BECK + NICKY HOPKINS**

May 85. Thunderbolt; (lp)(c)(cd) **SMOKE AND FIRE** [ ] [-]
– Wailing sounds / 'Cause I love you / Flashing lights / Gutty guitar / Would you believe / Smoke and fire / Thumping beat / Union Jack car / One for you baby / L-O-N-D-O-N / Brightest lights / Baby come back.

— below featured him in session with:- JET HARRIS & TONY MEEHAN / MICKIE MOST / DAVE BERRY / The FIRST GEAR / MICKEY FINN / solo / etc.

Jan 90. Archive; (cd)(lp) **JAMES PATRICK PAGE SESSION MAN VOLUME 1** [ ] [-]
Jul 90. Archive; (cd)(lp) **JAMES PATRICK PAGE SESSION MAN VOLUME 2** [ ] [-]
Aug 92. Sony; (cd)(c)(lp) **JIMMY'S BACK PAGES: THE EARLY YEARS** [ ] [ ]

HONEYDRIPPERS

ROBERT PLANT – vocals / **JIMMY PAGE** – guitar / **JEFF BECK** – guitar (also solo artist) / **NILE RODGERS** – producer, etc.

Es Paranza Es Paranza

Oct 84. (7") **SEA OF LOVE. / I GET A THRILL** [-] [3]
Nov 84. (m-lp)(c) **VOLUME 1** [56] [4] Oct 84
– I get a thrill / Sea of love / I got a woman / Young boy blues / Rockin' at midnight. *(re-iss.cd Feb93)*
Jan 85. (7") **SEA OF LOVE. / ROCKIN' AT MIDNIGHT** [56] [-]
Mar 85. (7") **ROCKIN' AT MIDNIGHT. / YOUNG BOY BLUES** [-] [25]

THE FIRM

JIMMY PAGE – guitar / **PAUL RODGERS** – vocals (ex-FREE, ex-BAD COMPANY) / **TONY FRANKLIN** – bass, keys / **CHRIS SLADE** – drums (ex-MANFRED MANN'S EARTH BAND)

Atlantic Atlantic

Feb 85. (lp)(c)(cd) **THE FIRM** [15] [17]
– Closer / Make or break / Someone to love / Radioactive / You've lost that lovin' feeling / Money can't buy satisfaction / Satisfaction guarenteed / Midnight moonlight.
Feb 85. (7")(7"sha-pic-d) **RADIOACTIVE. / TOGETHER** [ ] [28]
(12"+=) – City sirens / Live in peace.
Apr 85. (7") **SATISFACTION GUARENTEED. / CLOSER** [-] [73]
Apr 86. (lp)(c)(cd) **MEAN BUSINESS** [46] [22] Feb 86
– Fortune hunter / Cadillac / All the King's horses / Live in peace / Tear down the walls / Dreaming / Free to live / Spirit of love.
Apr 86. (7") **ALL THE KING'S HORSES. / FORTUNE HUNTER** [ ] [61]
Jun 86. (7") **LIVE IN PEACE. / FREE TO LIVE** [-] [ ]

— In 1993, JIMMY collaborated with DAVID COVERDALE to make one hit album 'COVERDALE • PAGE'.

JIMMY PAGE & ROBERT PLANT

with **CHARLIE JONES** – bass, percussion / **PORL THOMPSON** – guitar, banjo / **MICHAEL LEE** – drums, percussion / **NAJMA AKHTAR** – vocals / **JOE SUTHERLAND** – mandolin, bodhran / **NIGEL EASTON** – hurdy gurdy / **ED SHEARMUR** – hammond organ & orchestral arrangements for (large) English + Egyptian Ensemble + London Metropolitan Orchestra

Fontana Fontana

Nov 94. (cd)(c)(d-lp) **NO QUARTER – UNLEDDED** [7] [4]
– Nobody's fault but mine / Thank you / No quarter / Friends / Yallah / City don't cry / Since I've been loving you / The battle of Evermore / Wonderful one / Wah wah / That's the way / Gallow's pole / Four sticks / Kashmir.
Dec 94. (cd-s) **GALLOW'S POLE / CITY DON'T CRY / THE RAIN SONG** [35] [ ]
(cd-s) – ('A'side) / Four sticks / What should never be.

Arthur LEE (see under ⇒ LOVE)

LEFTFIELD

Formed: London, England ... 1990 by ex-teacher of English NEIL BARNES and PAUL DALEY, whom also founded indie dance label 'Hard Hands' after first 2 singles. The first of these 'NOT FORGOTTEN', used sample /snippets from the film 'Mississippi Burning'. In the summer of 1993, they teamed up vocalist JOHN LYDON (of PUBLIC IMAGE LTD), to record with great secrecy their track 'OPEN UP' (LYDON chants 'Burn Hollywood Burn'). His record label 'Virgin' finally let them release it in November that year and it soon shot into UK Top 20, aided by its controversial video which coincidentally was released same time as the Californian fires. • **Style:** Dance orientated experimentalists, who broke new ground with each release. • **Songwriters:** The duo and samples. • **Trivia:** Their label 'Hard Hands' run by manager LISA HORRAN, also included acts VINYL BLAIR, DELTA LADY, DEE PATTEN and SCOTT HARRIS.

Recommended: LEFT-ISM (*8)

— **NEIL BARNES** – DJ, percussion, synthesizers / **PAUL DALEY** – samples (ex-A MAN CALLED ADAM)

Outer Rhythm not issued

Mar 90. (12") **NOT FORGOTTEN. / PATELL'S ON THE CASE / ('A'version)** [ ] [-]

Rhythm King not issued

Feb 91. (12")(cd-s) **MORE THAN I KNOW. / NOT FORGOTTEN** [ ] [-]

Hard Hands Hard Hands

Aug 92. (12"ltd.) **RELEASE THE PRESSURE. / ('A'mixes)** [ ] [-]
Nov 92. (12"ltd.) **SONG OF LIFE. / ('A'mixes)** [59] [-]
Dec 92. (cd) **BACKLOG** (compilation of above) [ ] [-]

Below single credited to "LEFTFIELD / LYDON" (vocals= LYDON of PUBLIC IMAGE LTD.)

Nov 93. (7") **OPEN UP (radio edit). / ('A'instrumental)** [13] [ ]
(12"+=)(cd-s+=) – ('A'vocal 12" mix) / ('A'-Dervish overdrive mix) / ('A'-Andrew Weatherall mix) / ('A'-Dust Brothers mix).
Jan 95. (d-cd)(c)(d-lp)(3x12") **LEFT-ISM** [3] [ ]
– Release the pressure / Afro-left / Melt / Song of life ('95 remix) / Original / Black flute / Space shanty / Inspection (check one) / Storm 3000 / Half past dub *(3x12"only)* / Open up / 21st century poem.

below as "LEFTFIELD/ HALLIDAY" feat. TONI HALLIDAY -vocals (ex-CURVE)

Mar 95. (c-ep)(cd-ep) **ORIGINAL / ('A'live mix) / ('A'jam mix) / FILTER FISH** [18] [-]
(12"ep) – ('A'-Drift version) -repl.'A'live.

below featured DJUM DJUM

Jul 95. (12"ep)(c-ep)(cd-ep) **AFRO-LEFT EP** [22] [ ]
– Afro left / Afro ride / Afro sol / Afro central.

. . . Jan – Jun '96 stop press . . .

Jan 96. (single) **RELEASE THE PRESSURE** [13] [ ]

LEMONHEADS

Formed: Boston, Massachusetts, USA . . . 1983 by DANDO who had come from middle-class upbringing, but whose parents divorced when he was 12. In March 86, they were joined by another school-friend; jazz-bassist JESSE PORETZ. After releases on 'Taang!', they finally hit the big time in 1992 after earlier signing to 'Atlantic', and mellowing during a stay in Australia. • **Style:** Moved from hardcore rock outfit similar to DINOSAUR JR, PIXIES, HUSKER DU, REPLACEMENTS to more jangly melodic zany rock. • **Songwriters:** DANDO is main pensmith, although DELLY or MADDOX were contributors early on. Covered; I AM A RABBIT (Proud Scum) / HEY JOE + AMAZING GRACE (trad.) / MOD LANG (Big Star) / LUKA (Suzanne Vega) / DIFFERENT DRUM (Michael Nesmith) / BRASS BUTTONS (Gram Parsons) / STRANGE (Patsy Cline) / YOUR HOME IS WHERE YOU ARE HAPPY (C. MANSON / PLASTER CASTER (Kiss) / SKULLS (Misfits) / GONNA GET ALONG WITHOUT YA NOW ('50s) / STEP BY STEP (New Kids On The Block) / FRANK MILLS (from 'Hair' musical) / KITCHEN (Hummingbirds) / MRS.ROBINSON (Simon & Garfunkel) / MISS OTIS REGRETS (Cole Porter). • **Trivia:** DANDO and JOHN STROHM appeared on BLAKE BABIES lp 'Slow Learners'.

Recommended: IT'S A SHAME ABOUT RAY (*8) / COME ON FEEL THE LEMONHEADS (*9) / LICK (*7).

EVAN DANDO – vocals, guitar + some drums / **JESSE PERETZ** – bass / **BEN DEILY** – guitar, + some drums.

not issued Armory Arms/ Huh Bag

Jul. 86. (7"ep) **LAUGHING ALL THE WAY TO THE CLEANERS** [-] [ ]
– Glad I don't know / I like to / I am a rabbit / So I fucked up.

— added **DOUG TRACHTON** – drums

Jun 87. (lp)(c) **HATE YOUR FRIENDS** [-] [ ]
– I don't wanna / 394 / Nothing time / Second change / Sneakyville / Amazing Grace / Belt / Hate your friends / Don't tell yourself it's ok / Uhhh / Fed up /

Rat velvet. *(UK-iss. May88 on 'World Service') (US-cd 1989+=)* – Glad I don't know / I like to / I am a rabbit / So I fucked up / Ever / Sad girl / Buried alive / Gotta stop. *(re-iss.cd Mar93 with 5 extra tracks including 'Laughing all the way. . .')*

— **EVAN,** on bass, also joined BLAKE BABIES in 1988, whose punk image wasn't suitable at the time, alongside girlfriend JULIANNA HATFIELD. **JOHN STROHM** – drums (ex-BLAKE BABIES) repl. DOUG.

World Service / Taang!

Sep 88. (lp)(c) **CREATOR** [ ] [ ]
– Burying ground / Sunday / Clang bang clang / Out / Your home is where you're happy / Falling / Die right now / Two weeks in another town / Plaster caster / Come to my window / Take her down / Postcard / Live without. *(US-cd 1989 +=)*– Luka (live) / Interview / Mallo cup. *(re-iss.Sep92 on 'Taang!', with 6 extra live tracks included) (re-iss.cd Mar93 with all re-issued tracks + 2 acoustic)*

— **COREY LOOG BRENNAN**– guitar (ex-BULLET LAVOLTA) repl. JOHN STROHM

Apr 89. (7"colrd) **LUKA / STRANGE / MAD** [ ] [-]
(re-iss. 7"/12"/cd-s Apr93)

Apr 89. (lp)(c)(cd) **LICK** [ ] [-]
– Mallo cup / Glad I don't know / 7 powers / A circle of one / Cazzo di ferro / Anyway / Luka / Come back D.A. / I am a rabbit / Sad girl / Ever. *(US-cd+=)* Strange / MAD. *(re-iss.cd Mar93 = Mad / Strange)*

— **MARK "BUDOLA"** – drums, toured until he checked out mid '89. (COREY also left to concentrate on his PhD.

Roughneck / Roughneck

Jun 90. (7") **DIFFERENT DRUM. / PAINT** [ ] [ ]
(12"+=)(cd-s+=) – Ride with me. *(re-iss.12"+cd-s.Feb93)*

Atlantic / Atlantic

Jun 90. (cd-ep) **FAVOURITE SPANISH DISHES EP** [-] [ ]
– Different drum / Paint / Ride with me / Skulls / Step by step.

— **DAVID RYAN** b. 20 Oct '64, Fort Wayne, Indiana – drums repl. DEILY

Aug 90. (cd)(c)(lp) **LOVEY** [ ] [ ]
– Ballarat / Half the time / Year of the cat / Ride with me / Li'l seed / Stove / Come downstairs / Left for dead / Brass buttons / (The) Door. *(UK-iss. Oct91)(re-iss.cd,c,lp Nov93)*

— In Sep. 90, **DANDO** recruited **BEN DAUGHTY** – drums (ex-SQUIRREL BAIT) repl. RYAN / **BYRON HOAGLAND -bass** (ex-FANCY PANTS) repl. PERETZ.

Sep 91. (7") **GONNA GET ALONG WITHOUT YA NOW. / HALF THE TIME** [ ] [ ]
(12"ep+=) **PATIENCE AND PRUDENCE**: Stove (remix) / Step by step.

— **DANDO, RYAN + JULIANA HATFIELD** – bass, vocals (ex BLAKE BABIES)

Jul 92. (cd)(c)(lp) **IT'S A SHAME ABOUT RAY** [69] [68]
– Rockin' stroll / Confetti / Rudderless / My drug buddy / The turnpike down / Bit part / Alison's starting to happen / Hannah and Gaby / Kitchen / Ceiling fan in my spoon / Frank Mills. *(album will hit UK No.33 Jan'93) (re-iss.Feb95)*

Oct 92. (7")(c-s) **IT'S A SHAME ABOUT RAY. / SHAKEY GROUND** [70] [ ]
(10"+=)(cd-s+=) – Dawn can't decide / The turnpike down.

Nov 92. (7")(c-s) **MRS.ROBINSON. / BEING AROUND** [19] [ ]
(10"+=)(cd-s+=) – Divan / Into your arms.

— 1993 line-up: **DANDO, RYAN, NIC DALTON** (b. 6 Jun '66, Australia) although she did provide b.vox for 1993 releases. – bass HATFIELD formed own trio)

Jan 93. (7")(c-s) **CONFETTI (remix). / MY DRUG BUDDY** [44] [ ]
(10"+=)(cd-s+=) – Ride with me (live) / Confetti (acoustic).

Mar 93. (c-s) **IT'S A SHAME ABOUT RAY. / ALISON'S STARTING TO HAPPEN** [31] [ ]
(cd-s) – Different drum (Evan acoustic) / Stove (Evan acoustic).
(10"+=) Different drum (acoustic) / Rockin' stroll (live).
(cd-s) – ('A'side) / Confetti / Mallo cup / Rudderless (all 4 live).

Oct 93. (7")(c-s) **INTO YOUR ARMS. / MISS OTIS REGRETS** [14] [67]
(10"+=)(cd-s+=) – Little black egg / Learning the game.

Oct 93. (cd)(c)(lp) **COME ON FEEL THE LEMONHEADS** [5] [56]
– The great big no / Into your arms / It's about time / Down about it / Paid to smile / Big gay heart / Style / Rest assured / Dawn can't decide / I'll do it anyway / Rick James style / Being around / Favourite T / You can take it with you / The jello fund. *(lp+=)* Miss Otis regrets.

Nov 93. (7")(c-s) **IT'S ABOUT TIME. / RICK JAMES ACOUSTIC STYLE** [57] [ ]
(10"+=)(cd-s+=) – Big gay heart (demo) / Down about it (acoustic).

(above 'A' side was written about JULIANA. I'LL DO IT ANYWAY for BELINDA CARLISLE)

May 94. (10"ep)(c-ep)(cd-ep) **BIG GAY HEART. / DEEP BOTTOM COVE / HE'S ON THE BEACH / FAVORITE T (live in session)** [55] [ ]

— Offending lyrics to above 'A'side, were changed; with Stroke & Brick.

— DALTON departed Sep 94

— **MURPH** -drums (ex-DINOSAUR JR) repl.RYAN

- compilations, etc. -

1990. Taang!; (cd) **CREATE YOUR FRIENDS** [-] [ ]
– HATE YOUR FRIENDS / CREATOR / LAUGHING E.P.

LEMON INTERRUPT (see under ⇒ UNDERWORLD)

John LENNON

Born: 9 Oct'40, Liverpool, England. While still a member of The BEATLES late 1968, he teamed up with his new girlfriend at the time YOKO ONO, to issue controversial 'UNFINISHED MUSIC NO.1: TWO VIRGINS', which displayed a self-taken full-frontal photo of both on lp sleeve. This was sold in brown paper wrapping, to save embarrassment to customer and retailer!. During Spring next year, its follow-up 'UNFINISHED MUSIC NO.2: LIFE WITH THE LIONS', hit the shops and continued anti-commercial free-form, mainly recorded on small cassette. Now divorced from wife CYNTHIA, JOHN had already married YOKO on 20 Mar'69, and even changed by deed poll, his middle name from WINSTON to ONO. After the LENNONS completed an 8-day peace protest, while publicly lying/sitting in a hotel bed, they released PLASTIC ONO BAND's debut 45 'GIVE PEACE A CHANCE'. This gave JOHN his first non-BEATLES hit, when it rose to UK Top 3 and US Top 20. Later that year 'COLD TURKEY' (a drug withdrawal song), also gave him a Top 30 smash on both sides of the Atlantic. Late 1969, he unveiled 2 albums, one another avant-garde collaboration with YOKO; 'THE WEDDING ALBUM', and the other a more standard commercial product THE PLASTIC ONO BAND 'LIVE IN TORONTO 1969', which breached US Top 10. They also scored with another UK/US Top 5 hit 'INSTANT KARMA', which was produced by PHIL SPECTOR early 1970. In May that year, The BEATLES officially split just prior to another No.1 album 'LET IT BE'. JOHN then concentrated completely on solo career with The PLASTIC ONO BAND and returned to the chart with late 1970 album 'JOHN LENNON: PLASTIC ONO BAND', which was followed by another Top 20 anthem 'POWER TO THE PEOPLE'. On 3rd Sep'71, he went to New York to live with YOKO, and subsequently never returned to UK. A month later, his classic album 'IMAGINE', was a No.1 in both US & UK, with its US-only released title track hitting No.3. He failed in a bid to have US-only Christmas hit with 'HAPPY XMAS WAR IS OVER), although this reached Top 5 a year later in '72. During the next 3 years in which he released 3 albums, he fought to stay in the US, after being ordered by immigration authorities to leave. In this time, he also went through drinking bouts, while temporarily splitting from YOKO. On 9 Oct'75, YOKO gave birth to their first child (together) SEAN, and LENNON went into retirement to look after him in their Manhattan apartment. He left behind a charting greatest hits 'SHAVED FISH', and soon was to receive his green-card, allowing him to permanently reside in US. However, he returned to studio in 1980, with David Geffen offering to release an album on his label. In November, 'DOUBLE FANTASY' was unleashed, and this soon topped both album charts. There was also a return to the singles chart, when appropriately title '(JUST LIKE) STARTING OVER' made Top 10. Tragically on 8th December 1980, JOHN was shot 5 times by so-called fan/mental case Mark Chapman, outside the LENNON's apartment block. He died shortly afterwards at Roosevelt hospital. Not surprisingly his previous 45, climbed back up the charts and peaked at No.1, with also a re-issue of 'IMAGINE' following it there early 1981. His killer was sent to a mental institution for the rest of his life, and we can only ponder on what 40-year-old JOHN might have achieved in the 80's & 90's. • **Style:** Much revered genius, who attempted to alienate pop industry by non-conventional musics. A peaceful man, whose outbursts and human faults, seemed to be portrayed wickedly by media, especially in his BEATLES days. His love of YOKO was undoubtably his turning point, finding both himself and the world around him a happier place to live. His music with all its facets, showed a poetic beauty and untouched romance, although other songs exploded into frenetic rock anthems of anti-war and anti-government feelings. • **Songwriters:** LENNON, except covers album ROCK'N'ROLL which contained;- BE-BOP-A-LULA (Gene Vincent) / STAND BY ME (Ben E.King) / PEGGY SUE (Buddy Holly) / AIN'T THAT A SHAME (Fats Domino) / SWEET LITTLE SIXTEEN + YOU CAN'T CATCH ME (Chuck Berry) / BONY MORONIE (Larry Williams) / BRING IT HOME TO ME + SEND ME SOME LOVIN' (Sam Cooke) / JUST BECAUSE (Lloyd Price) / YA YA (Lee Dorsey) / RIP IT UP + SLIPPIN' AND SLIDIN' + READY TEDDY (Little Richard) / DO YOU WANT TO DANCE (Bobby Freeman). • **Trivia:** In 1967, JOHN acted in the film 'How I Won The War', and also appeared in many zany films with The BEATLES. In 1975, he co-wrote 'Fame' with DAVID BOWIE, which hit US No.1. His son from his first marriage JULIAN, is currently enjoying chart status, and SEAN has also began to sing at benefits, etc.

Recommended: IMAGINE (*8) / MIND GAMES (*7) / THE JOHN LENNON COLLECTION (*9).

JOHN LENNON & YOKO ONO

JOHN LENNON – vocals, guitar, etc. / **YOKO ONO** (b.18 Feb'33, Tokyo, Japan) – wind, vocals

		Apple	Apple
Nov 68.	(lp) **UNFINISHED MUSIC NO.1: TWO VIRGINS**		

– Section 1, 2, 3, 4, 5, 6 / Side 2. *(cd-iss.Jan93 on'Rock Classics')*

		Zapple	Zapple
May 69.	(lp) **UNFINISHED MUSIC NO.2: LIFE WITH THE LIONS (1/2 live)**		

– Cambridge 1969 / No bed for Beatle John / Baby's heartbeat / Two minutes silence / Radio play.

The PLASTIC ONO BAND

		Apple	Apple
Jul 69.	(7") **GIVE PEACE A CHANCE. / REMEMBER LOVE** *(re-iss.Jan81, reached UK No.33)*	2	14
Oct 69.	(7") **COLD TURKEY. / DON'T WORRY KYOKO**	14	30 Dec 69

— JOHN and YOKO hired the following musicians **ERIC CLAPTON** – guitar (ex-YARDBIRDS, ex-CREAM, ex-BLUESBREAKERS) / **KLAUS VOORMAN** – bass (ex-MANFRED MANN) / **ALAN WHITE** – drums

Dec 69.	(lp) **THE PLASTIC ONO BAND – LIVE PEACE IN TORONTO 1969 (live 13 Sep'69)**		10 Jan 70

– Blue Suede shoes / Money (that's what I want) / Dizzy Miss Lizzy / Yer blues / Cold turkey / Give peace a chance / Don't worry Kyoko / John John (let's hope for peace).

Dec 69.	(lp) **WEDDING ALBUM** (as "JOHN ONO LENNON & YOKO ONO LENNON")		

– John and Yoko / Amsterdam.

LENNON / ONO & THE PLASTIC ONO BAND

Feb 70.	(7") **INSTANT KARMA!. / WHO HAS SEEN THE WIND (Yoko Ono)**	5	3

JOHN LENNON & THE PLASTIC ONO BAND

The **LENNONs** retained only **KLAUS / RINGO STARR** – drums (ex-BEATLES) repl. WHITE who later joined YES

Dec 70.	(lp)(c) **JOHN LENNON: PLASTIC ONO BAND**	11	6

– Mother / Hold on / I found out / Working class hero / Isolation / Remember / Love / Well well well / Look at me / God / My mummy's dead. *(re-iss.Jul84 on 'Fame', cd-iss.Dec94) (cd-iss.Apr88 on 'EMI')*

Dec 70.	(7") **MOTHER. / WHY (Yoko Ono)**	-	43

— next single also credited with **YOKO ONO**

Mar 71.	(7") **POWER TO THE PEOPLE. / OPEN YOUR BOX**	7	-
Mar 71.	(7") **POWER TO THE PEOPLE. / TOUCH ME (Yoko Ono)**	-	11
Oct 71.	(lp)(c) **IMAGINE**	1	1 Sep 71

– Imagine / Crippled inside / Jealous guy / It's so hard / I don't want to be a soldier / Give me some truth / Oh my love / How do you sleep? / How? / Oh Yoko!. *(also on quad-lp Jun72) (cd-iss.May87 on 'Parlophone')*

Oct 71.	(7") **IMAGINE. / IT'S SO HARD**	-	3
May 72.	(7") **WOMAN IS THE NIGGER OF THE WORLD. / SISTERS, OH SISTERS (Yoko Ono)**	-	57

JOHN & YOKO / PLASTIC ONO BAND

with ELEPHANT'S MEMORY & FLUX / INVISIBLE STRINGS and lots of guests including **FRANK ZAPPA, ERIC CLAPTON,** etc.

Sep 72.	(d-lp)(d-c) **SOMETIME IN NEW YORK CITY (live)**	11	48

– Woman is the nigger of the world / Sisters o sisters / Attica state / Born in a prison / New York City / Sunday bloody Sunday / The luck of the Irish / John Sinclair / Angela / We're all water / (w/ CAST OF THOUSANDS); Cold turkey / Don't worry Kyoko / (w/ The MOTHERS); Jamrag / Scumbag / Au. *(re-iss.Feb86 on 'Parlophone')*

— Next single credited as **JOHN & YOKO / PLASTIC ONO BAND** with **The HARLEM COMMUNITY CHOIR**

Nov 72.	(7")(7"green) **HAPPY XMAS (WAR IS OVER). / LISTEN THE SNOW IS FALLING**	4	Nov 71

(re-iss.Dec74 reached No.48, re-iss.Dec80 – No.2, re-iss.Dec81 – No.28, re-iss.Dec82, hit 56)

JOHN LENNON

Nov 73.	(7")**MIND GAMES. / MEAT CITY**	26	18
Nov 73.	(lp)(c) **MIND GAMES ("JOHN LENNON & PLASTIC U.F.ONO BAND")**	13	9

– Mind games / Tight a $ / Aisumasen (I'm sorry) / One day (at a time) / Bring on the Lucie (Freeda people) / Nutopian international anthem / Intuition / Out of the blue / Only people / I know (I know) / You are here / Meat city. *(re-iss.Oct80 on 'MFP') (cd-iss.Aug87 on 'Parlophone')*

Oct 74.	(7") **WHATEVER GETS YOU THRU THE NIGHT. (as "JOHN LENNON & THE PLASTIC ONO NUCLEAR BAND featuring ELTON JOHN") / BEEF JERKY**	36	1 Sep 74
Oct 74.	(lp)(c) **WALLS AND BRIDGES**	6	1

– Going down on love / Whatever gets you thru the night / Old dirt road / What you got / Bless you / £9 dream / Surprise surprise (sweet bird of Paradise) / Steel and glass / Beef jerky / Nobody loves you (when you're down and out) / Ya-ya / Scared. *(re-iss.Jan85 on 'Parlophone', cd-iss.Jul87)*

Jan 75.	(7") **£9 DREAM. / WHAT YOU GOT**	23	9
Feb 75.	(lp)(c) **ROCK'N'ROLL**	6	6

– Be-bop-a-lula / Stand by me / Medley: Rip it up – Ready Teddy / You can't catch me / Ain't that a shame / Do you want to dance / Sweet little sixteen / Slippin' and slidin' / Peggy Sue / Medley: Bring it on home to me – Send me some lovin' / Ya ya / Just because. *(re-iss.Nov81 on 'MFP') (cd-iss.Jul87 on 'Parlophone')*

Apr 75.	(7") **STAND BY ME. / MOVE OVER MS. L** *(re-iss.Apr81)*	30	20 Mar 75
Oct 75.	(7") **IMAGINE. / WORKING CLASS HERO** *(re-iss.Dec80 reached UK No.1)*	6	
Nov 75.	(lp)(c) **SHAVED FISH** (compilation)	8	12

– Give peace a chance / Cold turkey / Instant karma / Power to the people / Mother / Woman is the nigger of the world / Imagine / Whatever gets you thru the night / Mind games / £9 dream / Happy Xmas (war is over) / Give peace a chance (reprise). *(cd-iss May 87 on 'E.M.I.')*

— JOHN was also credited on a few singles by ELTON JOHN – Feb75 'I Saw Her Standing There' which was also realeased Mar81 with 2 other. In Jul71 a rare single 'GOD SAVE US'/'DO THE OZ' was released by him and Plastic Ono Band backing 'BILL ELLIOT AND THE ELASTIC OZ BAND'

JOHN LENNON & YOKO ONO

returned after a long break

		Geffen	Geffen
Oct 80.	(7") **(JUST LIKE) STARTING OVER. / KISS KISS KISS (Yoko Ono)**	1	1
Nov 80.	(lp)(c) **DOUBLE FANTASY**	1	1

– (Just like) Starting over / Every man has a woman who loves him (YOKO ONO) / Clean up time / Give me something (YOKO ONO) / I'm losing you / I'm moving on (YOKO ONO) / Beautiful boy (darling boy) / Watching the wheels / I'm your angel (YOKO ONO) / Dear Yoko / Beautiful boys (YOKO ONO) / Kiss kiss kiss (YOKO ONO) / Woman / Hard times are over (YOKO ONO). *(re-iss.+cd.Jan89 on 'Capitol')*

Jan 81.	(7") **WOMAN. / BEAUTIFUL BOYS (Yoko Ono)**	1	2
Mar 81.	(7") **WATCHING THE WHEELS. / I'M YOUR ANGEL (Yoko Ono)**	30	10

— His last two singles were released after his untimely murder 8 Dec80.

JOHN & YOKO

had recorded one more album prior to his death.

		Polydor	Polydor
Jan 84.	(7") **NOBODY TOLD ME. / O SANITY**	6	5
Jan 84.	(lp)(c)(cd)(pic-lp) **MILK AND HONEY**	3	11

– I'm stepping out / Sleepless night (YOKO ONO) / I don't wanna face it / Don't be scared (YOKO ONO) / Nobody told me / O'sanity (YOKO ONO) / Borrowed time / Your hands (YOKO ONO) / (Forgive me) My little flower princess / Let me count the ways (YOKO ONO) / Grow old with me / You're the one (YOKO ONO).

Dec 83.	(lp)(c) **A HEART PLAY: UNFINISHED DIALOGUE** (interview with Playboy)		
Mar 84.	(7") **BORROWED TIME. / YOUR HANDS (Yoko Ono)** (12"+=) – Never say goodbye.	32	
Jul 84.	(7") **I'M STEPPING OUT. / SLEEPLESS NIGHT (Yoko Ono)** (12"+=) – Loneliness.		55
Nov 84.	(7") **EVERY MAN HAS A WOMAN WHO LOVES HIM. / IT'S ALRIGHT** (above from various compilation 'B'-side by his son SEAN ONO LENNON)		

– posthumous exploitation releases etc. –

Jun 81.	Apple; (8xlp-box) **JOHN LENNON (BOXED)** (All lp's from LIVE PEACE – SHAVED FISH)		

– Give peace a chance / Instant karma / Power to the people / Whatever gets you thru the night / 9 dream / Mind games / Love / Happy Xmas (war is over) / Imagine / Jealous guy / Stand by me / Starting over / Woman / I'm losing you /

Beautiful boy, darling boy / Watching the wheel / Dear Yoko. (cd+=) – Move over Miss L. / Cold turkey.
Nov 82. EMI/ US= Geffen; (lp)(c) **THE JOHN LENNON COLLECTION** [1] [33]
(re-iss. Jun 85, cd-iss. Oct 89; 2 extra tracks)
Oct 90. EMI/ US= Geffen; (cd-box) **LENNON** [ ] [ ]
Note; Below 'Parlophone' UK /'Capitol' US, until stated.
Nov 82. (7") **LOVE. / GIVE ME SOME TRUTH** [41] [ ]
Nov 85. (7") **JEALOUS GUY / GOING DOWN ON LOVE** [65] [ ]
(12"+=) – Oh Yoko!
Feb 86. (lp)(c)(cd) **LIVE IN NEW YORK CITY (live)** [55] [41]
Nov 86. (lp)(c)(cd) **MENLOVE AVE.** (sessions 74-75) [ ] [ ]
– Here we go again / Rock'n'roll people / Angel baby / Since my baby left me / To know her is to love her / Steel and glass / Scared / Old dirt road / Nobody loves you (when you're down and out).
Aug 87. (cd) **LIVE JAM** (half of SOMETIME lp) [ ] [ ]
Oct 88. (lp)(c)(cd) **IMAGINE** (Music from the Motion Picture; with some songs by The BEATLES) [64] [31]
– Real love / Twist and shout / Help! / In my life / Strawberry fields forever / A day in the life / Revolution / The ballad of John & Yoko / Julia / Don't let me down / Give peace a chance / How? / Imagine (rehearsal / God / Mother / Stand by me / Jealous guy / Woman / Beautiful boy (darling boy) / (Just like) Starting over / Imagine.
Nov 88. (7")(7"pic-d) **IMAGINE. / JEALOUS GUY** [45] [80] B-side
(12"+=)(12"pic-d+=) – Happy Xmas (war is over).
(cd-s+=) – Give peace a chance.
Mar 84. Old Gold; (7") **GIVE PEACE A CHANCE. / COLD TURKEY** [ ] [-]
May 87. Antar; (7") **TWO MINUTES SILENCE. / TWO MINUTES SILENCE (dub!)** [ ] [ ]

Annie LENNOX (see under ⇒ EURYTHMICS)

LEVELLERS

Formed: Brighton, England, early 1988, and after heavy touring and some indie singles, they released album for French label 'Musidisc'. In 1991, after signing to 'China', they made UK Top 20 with album 'LEVELLING THE LAND'. • **Style:** New-age group mixing hippie travellers folk with angst theme-rock. • **Songwriters:** Group compositions except; THE DEVIL WENT DOWN TO GEORGIA (Charlie Daniels Band) / TWO HOURS (McDermott). • **Trivia:** The FENCE had one single in May 87 on 'Flag'; FROZEN WATER. / EXIT.

Recommended: LEVELLING THE LAND (*8) / WEAPON CALLED THE WORD (*7) / LEVELLERS (*6).

MARK CHADWICK – vocals, guitar, banjo (ex-FENCE) / **JEREMY CUNNINGHAM** – bass, bazouki / **CHARLIE HEATHER** – drums / **JON SEVINK** – violin (ex-FENCE) / **ALAN MILES** – vocals, guitar, mandolin, harmonica.

H A G — not issued
May 89. (12"ep) **CARRY ME** [ ] [-]
– Carry me / What's in the way / The lasy days of winter / England my home /
Oct 89. (12"ep) **OUTSIDE INSIDE. / HARD FIGHT / I HAVE NO ANSWERS / BARREL OF A GUN** [ ] [-]

Musicdisc — not issued
Apr 90. (7") **WORLD FREAK SHOW. / BARREL OF A GUN (acoustic)** [ ] [-]
(12"+=) What you know. *(re-iss.Jan92)*
Apr 90. (cd)(c)(lp) **WEAPON CALLED THE WORD** [ ] [-]
– World freak show / Carry me / Outside-inside / Together all the way / Barrel of a gun / Three friends / I have no answers / No change / Blind faith / The ballad of Robbie Jones / England my home / What you know.
Oct 90. (7") **TOGETHER ALL THE WAY. / THREE FRIENDS (re-mix) (Arfa mix short version)** [ ] [-]
(12"+=) – Cardboard box city / Social security

— **SIMON FRIEND** – guitars, vocals repl. ALAN.

China — Elektra
Sep 91. (7")(c-s) **ONE WAY. / HARD FIGHT (acoustic) / THE LAST DAYS OF WINTER** [51] [ ]
(12"+=)(cd-s+=) – ('A'mix) / The Devil went down to Georgia.
Oct 91. (cd)(c)(lp) **LEVELLING THE LAND** [14] [ ]
– One way / The game / The boatman / The liberty song / Far from home / Sell out / Another man's cause / The road / The riverflow / Battle of the beanfield. *(re-iss.Jun92 hit No.22)*
Nov 91. (7")(c-s) **FAR FROM HOME. / WORLD FREAK SHOW (live)** [71] [ ]
(12"+=)(cd-s+=) – Outside inside / The boatman / Three friends (all live).
May 92. (10"pic-d-ep)(12"ep)(c-ep)(cd-ep) **15 YEARS** [11] [ ]
– 15 years / Dance before the storm / River flow (live) / Plastic Jeezus.
(In May'93 'LEVELLING THE LAND' returned to finally hit UK No.40 by Sep 93)
Jun 93. (c-s) **BELARUSE. / SUBVERT (live) / BELARUSE RETURN** [12] [ ]
(12"+=)(cd-s+=) – Is this art.
Sep 93. (cd)(c)(lp) **LEVELLERS** [2] [ ]
– Warning / 100 years of solitude / The likes of you and I / Is this art? / Dirty Davey / This garden / Broken circles / Julie / The player / Belaruse.
Oct 93. (7"pic-d)(c-s) **THIS GARDEN. / LIFE (acoustic)** [12] [ ]
(12"+=)(cd-s+=) – ('A'Marcus Dravs remix) / ('A'-Banco De Gaia remix).
May 94. (7"clear-ep)(c-ep)(10"pic-d-ep)(cd-ep) **THE JULIE EP** [17] [ ]
– Julie (new version) / English civil war / Warning (live) / 100 years of solitude / The lowlands of Holland.
Jul 95. (7"pic-d) **HOPE ST. / LEAVE THIS TOWN** [12] [ ]
(7"pic-d) – ('A'side) / Miles away.
(cd-s++=)(c-s++=) – Busking on Hope Street.
Aug 95. (cd)(c)(lp) **ZEITGEIST** [1] [ ]
– Hope St. / The fear / Exodus / Maid of the river / Saturday to Sunday / 4.am / Forgotten ground / Fantasy / P.C. Keen / Just the one / Haven't made it / Leave this town / Men-an-tol.
Oct 95. (7")(c-s)(cd-s) **FANTASY. / SARA'S BEACH / SEARCHLIGHTS (extended)** [16] [ ]

— (below featured JOE STRUMMER (ex-CLASH) on piano)
Dec 95. (7"ep)(c-ep)(cd-ep) **JUST THE ONE / A PROMISE. / YOUR 'OUSE / DRINKING FOR ENGLAND** [12] [ ]

– compilations, etc.

Mar 93. China; (cd)(c)(lp) **SEE NOTHING, HEAR NOTHING, DO SOMETHING** (early) [ ] [ ]

LEVON & THE HAWKS (see under ⇒ BAND)

LFO

*** NEW ENTRY ***

Formed: Sheffield, England . . .1990 by MARK BELL and JEZ VARLEY. After two hit singles 'LFO' and 'WE ARE BACK', they received many plaudits for excellent 'FREQUENCIES' album. Early in 1992, they played rave gig at 'La Grande Arche de la Defence' in Paris. Went to Germany soon after to record with KRAFTWERK and remixed YELLOW MAGIC ORCHESTRA. They started recording follow-up album 'ADVANCE' in 1993, but its release gets delayed many times. A single, 'TIED UP', did reach the shops late 1994, but its length stops it charting. The album finally makes its appearance early '96, three years late, but worthy of another near Top 40 position. • **Style:** Described as The STONE ROSES of techno, although influences lay in KRAFTWERK or YMO. • **Songwriters:** Duo; except on debut with WILLIAMS. • **Trivia:** Also had solo outings; JEZ as G-MAN and MARK as FAWN, COUNTERPOINT or CLARK. Remixed many others including SABRES OF PARADISE (Tow Truck) / RADIOHEAD (Planet Telex) / BIOSPHERE, ART OF NOISE and AFRIKA BAMBAATAA's re-working of classic 'Planet Rock'.

Recommended: FREQUENCIES (*8) / ADVANCE (*7)

MARK BELL (b. 1972) – electronics / **JEZ VARLEY** (b. 1972) – electronics / augmented live by WILD PLANET: **SIMON HARTLEY + RITCHIE BROOK**

Warp — Tommy Boy
Jul 90. (7") **L.F.O. / TRACK 4** [12] [-]
(12"+=) – Probe (the Cuba edit).
(cd-s++=) – Mentok 1.
Jun 91. (7")(12") **WE ARE BACK. / NURTURE** [47] [-]
(cd-s+=) – We are back (remix) / Push.
Jul 91. (cd)(c)(d-lp) **FREQUENCIES** [42] [-]
– Intro / L.F.O. / Simon from Sydney / Nurture / Freeze / We are back / Tan ta ra / You have to understand / El ef oh! / Love is the message / Mentok 1 / Think a moment. *(cd+=)(c+=)–* Groovy distortion / Track 14.
Jan 92. (12"ep)(cd-ep) **WHAT IS HOUSE** [62] [-]
– Tan ta ra / Mashed potato / What is house / Syndrome.

— MARK BELL joined FEEDBACK (aka WILD PLANET) for a single 'I'm for Real'.
Nov 94. (d12")(d-cd-s) **TIED UP (Spiritualized Electric Mainline remix). / NURTURE** [ ] [-]
Jan 96. (cd)(c)(d-lp) **ADVANCE** [44] [ ]
– Advance / Shut down / Loch Ness / Goodnight Vienna / Tied up / Them / Ultra schall / Shove piggy shove / Psychodelik / Jason Vorhees / Forever / Kombat drinking.

Jaki LIEBZEIT (see under ⇒ CAN)

LIGHTNING SEEDS

Formed: By IAN BROUDIE, 4 Aug'58, Liverpool, England. He had been an integral part of BIG IN JAPAN (Autumn 77-78), before joining The SECRETS and then London-based band ORIGINAL MIRRORS late '78. They cut one eponymous lp early 1980 for 'Mercury', but he left to go into production work. He was chosen by ECHO & THE BUNNYMEN, The WAH!, The FALL and ICICLE WORKS, amongst many to want his services. He helped form The CARE in 1983, with ex-WILD SWANS leader PAUL SIMPSON, but they disbanded after around a year and 3 singles. BROUDIE re-surfaced in 1989, when he and a few session people formed The LIGHTNING SEEDS. They signed to new label 'Ghetto', and immediately scored with debut 45 'PURE'. This and its parent album 'CLOUDCUCKOOLAND', surprised many by also making US lists in '91. • **Style:** One-man alternative rock-pop studio act, similar to NEW ORDER, PET SHOP BOYS or FRAZIER CHORUS. • **Songwriters:** BROUDIE obviously, except SOMETHING IN THE AIR (Thunderclap Newman) / HANG ON TO A DREAM (Tim Hardin). LUCKY YOU + FEELING LAZY + MY BEST DAY were co-written & sung w / TERRY HALL + IAN McNABB + ALISON MOYET respectively. The track OPEN GOALS sampled; LOOK KA PY PY (Meters). • **Trivia:** The track 'PERSUASION' featured IAN McCULLOCH (ex-ECHO & THE BUNNYMEN). He has also produced NORTHSIDE, PRIMITIVES and TERRY HALL.

Recommended: CLOUDCUCKOOLAND (*7) / PURE (*8).

IAN BROUDIE – vocals, keyboards, guitar / with **PETER COYLE + PAUL SIMPSON** (ex-LOTUS EATERS + WILD SWANS)

		Ghetto	M.C.A.
Jun 89.	(7")(c-s) **PURE. / FOOLS**	16	31 Apr 90
	(12"+=) – God help them.		
	(cd-s++=) – All I want.		
Oct 89.	(7") **JOY. / FRENZY**		
	(12"+=)(cd-s+=) – Control The Flame.		
	(US cd-ep+=) Hang on to a dream.		
Jan 90.	(cd)(c)(lp) **CLOUDCUCKOOLAND**	51	46
	– All I want / Bound in a nutshell / Pure / Sweet dreams / The nearly man / Joy / Love explosion / Don't let go / Control the flame / The price / Fools / Frenzy. *(c+=)(cd+=)*– God help them.		
Feb 90.	(7") **SWEET DREAMS. /** (withdrawn)		
Apr 90.	(7")(c-s) **ALL I WANT. / PERSUASION**		
	(12"+=)(cd-s+=) – ('A'extended).		
		Virgin	M.C.A.
Mar 92.	(7")(c-s) **THE LIFE OF RILEY. / SOMETHING IN THE AIR**	28	98
	(12"+=)(cd-s+=) – Marooned.		
	(US c-s) ('A' side) / excerpts: Blowing bubbles – Sense – A cool place.		
Apr 92.	(cd)(c)(lp) **SENSE**	53	
	– Sense / The life of Riley / Blowing bubbles / Cool place / Where flowers fade / A smal slice of Heaven / Tingle tangle / Happy / Marooned / Tracking up, looking down.		
May 92.	(7")(c-s) **SENSE. / FLAMING SWORD**	31	-
	(12"+=)(cd-s+=) – The life of Riley (remix) / Hang on to a dream.		
Apr 92.	(c-s) **SENSE. / TINGLE TANGLE**	-	
	(cd-s) ('A' side) / The life of Riley / Flaming sword / Lucifer Sam.		

—— **BROUDIE** added **SIMON ROGERS** – instruments, co-producer / **CLIVE LAYTON** – Hammond organ / **MARINA VAN RODY** – vocals (Why Why Why). The live band **BROUDIE** – vocals, guitar / **w / ALI KANE** – keyboards / **MARTIN CAMPBELL** – bass / **CHRIS SHARROCK** – drums

		Epic	Epic
Aug 94.	(c-s) **LUCKY YOU. / ('A'lunar mix)**	43	
	(12")(cd-s) – ('A'hard luck mix) / ('A'lucky devil mix) / ('A'lunar cabaret mix).		

—— Above was co-written w / **TERRY HALL**. They are now best known for contributing football theme to Match of the Day's 'Goal Of The Month'. ALISON MOYET wrote a track for the next album.

Sep 94.	(cd)(c)(lp) **JOLLIFICATION**	13	
	– Perfect / Lucky you / Open goals / Change / Why why why / Marvellous / Feeling lazy / My best day / Punch & Judy / Telling tales.		
Jan 95.	(7")(c-s) **CHANGE. / SAY YOU WILL**	13	
	(cd-s+=) – Dust.		
	(cd-s) – ('A'side) / The life of Riley (inst.) / Lucky you (live).		
Apr 95.	(c-s) **MARVELLOUS / LUCIFER SAM**	24	
	(cd-s+=) – I met you.		
	(cd-s) – ('A'side) / ('A'mix) / All I want.		
Jul 95.	(c-s) **PERFECT / PERFECT (acoustic)**	18	
	(cd-s+=) – Howl / Blowing bubbles (extended remix).		
	(cd-s) – ('A'side) / Change (live) / Flaming sword (live).		
Oct 95.	(c-s) **LUCKY YOU / LUCKY YOU (Lunar mix)**	15	
	(cd-s) – ('A'side) / Life of Riley (live) / Pure (live) / Here today (live).		

. . . Jan – Jun '96 stop press . . .

Feb 96.	(single) **READY OR NOT**	20	
May 96.	(cd)(c)(lp) **PURE LIGHTNING SEEDS** (compilation)	27	
May 96.	(single) **THREE LIONS (The Official Song Of The England Football Team) (by "BADDIEL & SKINNER & LIGHTNING SEEDS")**	1	-

LIONROCK

*** NEW ENTRY ***

Formed: Manchester, England . . .1992 by JUSTIN ROBERTSON. He had been a student at Manchester University and worked at Eastern Bloc Records. He became a DJ and soon mixed many including DUM DUM GIRL (Talk Talk) / BIRTHDAY + MOTORCRASH (Sugarcubes) / FOREVERGREEN (Fini Tribe) / CARAVAN + SKIDOO (Inspiral Carpets) / SUNSHINE AND LOVE (Happy Mondays) / also The FALL, GRID, BJORK and ERASURE. LIONROCK's eponymous debut single, gave them first of Top 75 entries. They returned in 1996 with much-acclaimed 'AN INSTINCT FOR DETECTION'. • **Style:** Dub rock rave outfit. • **Songwriters:** ROBERTSON; some w/ STAGG then BRAITHWAITE.

Recommended: AN INSTINCT FOR DETECTION (*8)

JUSTIN ROBERTSON (b. 1968) – keyboards, guitar, bass / **MARK STAGG** – keyboards

		Deconstruc	???
Nov 92.	(12"ep)(cd-ep) **LION ROCK (mixes; Most Excellent / Roots and Culture / A Trumpet Jambouree in Edinburgh / Adubtastic jambouree in Edinburgh)**	63	-
May 93.	(12"ep)(c-ep)(cd-ep) **PACKET OF PEACE (mixes; Prankster Sound System / No More Fucking Trumpets / Instrumental)**	32	-
Sep 93.	(c-s) **CARNIVAL (Are You Willing To Testify mix) / THE GUIDE**	34	-
	(cd-s+=) – ('A'-As Dawn Approaches mix) / ('A'-Pranksters Mardi Gras mix).		
Aug 94.	(12"ep) **TRIPWIRE (theme from Moral Sense). / (mixes; Prankster's Piha Stomp / Prankster's Sound Track / Exploding Plastic Reconstruction)**	44	-
	(cd-ep+=) – ('A'radio mix).		

—— Disbanded briefly in 1994. In April '94, JUSTIN ROBERTSON MEETS PETER PERFECT on 'fineflex' single 'ANTHILL'. He/they then toured with PRIMAL SCREAM.

—— STAGG replaced by **MC BUZZ B (BRAITHWAITE)** – vocals / **ROGER LYONS** – synth, bass, keyboards

Apr 96.	(12") **STRENGTH AT YER HEAD. / WELCOME TO VIOLENCE / CLAPER BEATS**	33	
	(cd-s+=) – Packet of peace (Chemical Brothers mix) / Packet of peace (Jeff Mills werk mix).		
Apr 96.	(cd)(c)(3x12"lp) **AN INSTINCT FOR DETECTION**	30	
	– Morning will come when I'm not ready / Straight at yer head / Peace repackaged / Death Valley clapperboard / Fire up the shoeshaw / Don't die foolish / Depth / Snapshot on Pollard Street / The guide / Number nine / Bag of biros / Wilmslow Road.		

LITTLE ANGELS

Formed: Scarborough, England . . . May'87. In 1984, TOBY & MARK were in school band as ZEUS. Just over a year later, with BRUCE, they form MR.THRUD. To end 1985, they found JIM. They were spotted in Sep 86, by manager to be KEVIN NIXON. They changed group name in Feb'87. They were briefly Mr.THRUD, with JEPSON, PLUNKETT, HOPPER and the DICKINSON brothers. They soon issued an EP on a label run by their managers, adding these tracks later in the year to 'TOO POSH TO MOSH' mini-lp. In 1988, they signed to 'Polydor', and supported YWNGIE MALMSTEEN and CINDERELLA on US and UK tours, before issuing single '90° IN THE SHADE'. Their first taste of major chart action, was provided early in 1990 when 'KICKIN' UP DUST' hit UK Top 50. This was soon bettered by Top 40 'RADICAL YOUR LOVER' and near Top 20 hit 'SHE'S A LITTLE ANGEL'. After early 1991 UK Top 20 album 'YOUNG GODS', everything turned to gold, with America beckoning them for greater heights. • **Style:** Heavy rock combo, blending aggressive and American acoustic sound, fronted by ROBERT PLANT lookalike JEPSON.

• **Songwriters:** Mostly group compositions or JEPSON and collaborations with DESMOND CHILD or JIM VALLANCE in the early 90's. Covers:- TIE YOUR MOTHER DOWN (Queen) / BROKEN WINGS OF AN ANGEL (Hugh Cornwall) / FORTUNATE SON (Creedence Clearwater Revival) / RADICAL YOUR LOVER (co-with; Dan Reed) / BABYLON'S BURNING (Ruts) / OH WELL (Fleetwood Mac) / FUNK 49 (James Gang) / TIRED OF WAITING FOR YOU (Kinks) / WON'T GET FOOLED AGAIN (Who) / JAILHOUSE ROCK (Elvis Presley) / THE MIGHTY QUINN (Bob Dylan) / Feb 92 German single cover; FIRST CUT IS THE DEEPEST (Cat Stevens). • **Trivia:** Their 1991 work was produced by James 'Jimbo' Barton & Andy Julian Paul. In late '87, they featured on Channel 4 TV programe 'Famous For 15 Minutes'.

Recommended: LITTLE OF THE PAST (*7).

TOBY JEPSON – vocals, acoustic guitar / **BRUCE JOHN DICKINSON** – guitars, banjo / **JIMMY DICKINSON** – keyboards, vocals / **MARK PLUNKETT** – bass, vocals / **DAVE HOPPER** – drums

Man-agement | not issued

Jul 87. (12"ep) **THE '87 EP** [ ] [-]
– Bad or just no good / Better than the rest / Burning me / Reach for me.

Powerstation | not issued

Nov 87. (m-lp) **TOO POSH TO MOSH** [ ] [-]
– (1st EP tracks) / Too posh to mosh / No more whiskey / Down in the night. *(re-iss.cd,c,lp Jun94 on 'Essential', w / 3 extra '94 remix tracks 'Reach For Me', 'Bad Or Just No Good' & 'Burning Me' ; hit UK No.18)*

—— **MICHAEL LEE** – drums, percussion (ex-HOLOSAIDE) repl. HOPPER

Polydor | Polydor

Nov 88. (7")(7"pic-d) **90° IN THE SHADE. / ENGLAND ROCKS (live)** [ ] [ ]
(12"+=) – Big bad world.

Feb 89. (7") **SHE'S A LITTLE ANGEL. / BETTER THAN THE REST** [74] [ ]
(12"ep+=)(c-ep+=)(cd-ep+=) **THE BIG BAD EP** – Don't waste my time / Sex in cars.

Sep 89. (7") **DO YOU WANNA RIOT. / MOVE IN SLOW** [ ] [ ]
(12"+=)(cd-s+=) – Some kind of alien (live).
(10"++=) – Snatch (edited highlights of below lp).

Nov 89. (lp)(c)(cd) **DON'T PREY FOR ME** [ ] [ ]
– Do you wanna riot / Kick hard / Big bad world / Kickin' up dust / Don't prey for me / Broken wings of an angel / Bitter and twisted / Promises / When I get out of here / No solution / She's a little angel. *(c+=)*– Pleasure pyre. *(cd+=)*– Radical your lover (version) / Broken wings of an angel (version). *(re-dist.Jun90)*

Nov 89. (7")(c-s) **DON'T PREY FOR ME. / RADICAL YOUR LOVER** [ ] [ ]
(12"+=) – What do you want.
(cd-s++=) – ('A'extended).

Feb 90. (7") **KICKIN' UP DUST. / ('A'live)** [46] [ ]
(12"+=) – Big bad world (Nashville version).
(cd-s+=) – Pleasure pyre (live) / Kick hard (live).
(12"pic-d+=) – When I get out of here (live) / Kick hard (live) / Sex in cars (live).

Apr 90. (7")(c-s) **RADICAL YOUR LOVER. / DON'T LOVE YOU NO MORE** [34] [ ]
(12"pic-d-ep+=)(12"ep+=)(cd-ep+=) **GET RADICAL EP** – ('A'adult remix) / Promises (live).

Jul 90. (7")(c-s) **SHE'S A LITTLE ANGEL. / DOWN ON MY KNEES** [21] [ ]
(12") – ('A'side) / ('A'-Voodoo mix).
(12") – ('A'side) / ('A'-club) / When I get out of here.
(other 7") – ('A'side) / Sex in cars (live).

Jan 91. (7")(c-s) **BONEYARD. / FORTUNATE SON** [33] [ ]
(12"+=) – ('A'mix).
(12"++=) – Sweet love sedation.
(12"pic-d+=) – Jump the gun / ('A'album mix).

Feb 91. (cd)(c)(lp) **YOUNG GODS** [17] [ ]
– Back door man / Boneyard / Young gods (stand up, stand up) / I ain't gonna cry / The wildside of life / Product of the working class / That's my kinda life / Juvenile offender / Love is a gun / Sweet love sedation / Smoke in my eyes / Natural born fighter / Feels like the world has come undone (featuring the angel's anthem). *(re-iss.cd Apr95)*

Mar 91. (7")(c-s) **PRODUCT OF THE WORKING CLASS. / REVIVAL** [40] [ ]
(12"+=) – Take it off. (cd-s++=) – Might like you better.
(12"+=) – ('A'hot mix).

May 91. (7")(c-s) **YOUNG GODS. / GO AS YOU PLEASE** [34] [ ]
(cd-s+=) – Bad imitation.
(12"+=) – Frantic.

Jul 91. (7") **I AIN'T GONNA CRY. / BABYLON'S BURNING** [26] [ ]
(12"+=) – Funk 49.
(12"++=)(cd-s++=) – Oh well.

—— **MARK 'Rich' RICHARDSON** – drums repl. LEE

Nov 92. (7")(c-s) **TOO MUCH TOO YOUNG. / THE FIRST CUT IS THE DEEPEST** [22] [ ]
(12"+=)(cd-s+=) – 90° In The Shade / Young Gods

Jan 93. (7") **WOMANKIND. / SCHIZOPHRENIA BLUES** [12] [ ]
(12"+=)(cd-s+=) – ?

Jan 93. (cd)(c)(lp) **JAM** [1] [ ]
– The way that I live / Too much too young / Splendid isolation / Soapbox / S.T.W. / Don't confuse sex with love / Womankind / Eyes wide open / The colour of love / I was not wrong / Sail away / Tired of waiting for you (so tired) / S.T.W. (reprise), (with ltd.live cd+lp + extra tracks 1-side of c) **LIVE JAM** – She's a little angel / Product of the working class (grooved & jammed) / I ain't gonna cry / Boneyard 1993 (featuring Big Dave Kemp) / Don't prey for me (extended version) / Won't get fooled again. *(re-iss.cd Apr95)*

Apr 93. (7")(c-s) **SOAPBOX (remix). / I GOT THE SHAKES** [33] [ ]
(cd-s+=) – Womankind (live) / Too much too young (live).
(cd-s) – ('A'side) / Young gods (live) / Jailhouse rock (live) / I ain't gonna cry (live).

Sep 93. (12")(c-s) **SAIL AWAY. / I AIN'T GONNA CRY (live) / SOAPBOX (live)** [45] [ ]
(cd-s) – ('A'side) / The mighty Quinn / This ain't the way it's supposed to be.

Sony | Sony

Mar 94. (c-s)(12")(cd-s) **TEN MILES HIGH. / I WANNA BE LOVED BY YOU** [18] [ ]

Apr 94. (cd)(c)(lp) **LITTLE OF THE PAST** (compilation) [20] [ ]
– She's a little angel / Too much too young / Radical your lover / Womankind / Boneyard / Kickin' up dust / I ain't gonna cry / Sail away / Young gods / Ninety in the shade / Product of the working class / Soapbox / The first cut is the deepest / Ten miles high / I wanna be loved by you / Don't pray for me.

—— now w/out **JIMMY + BRUCE DICKINSON**, who formed b.l.o.w.

LITTLE FEAT

Formed: Los Angeles, California, USA … late 1969, by ex-FRANK ZAPPA stalwarts LOWELL GEORGE and ROY ESTRADA, who found BILL PAYNE and RICHIE HAYWARD. They signed to 'Warners' in 1970, and finally issued acclaimed eponymous debut later that year. It featured guest appearances from RY COODER and SNEAKY PETE KLEINOW, and was produced by RUSS TITELMAN. In 1974 after 2 more well-received commercial flops, they hit big with US Top 40 album 'FEATS DON'T FAIL ME NOW'. For the rest of the decade, they scored on both sides of the Atlantic, until their split and the untimely death of LOWELL GEORGE on 29th Jun'79. • **Style:** Classy country funk & boogie band, who drifted into milder stuff by the late 70's & late 80's on their re-union. • **Songwriters:** GEORGE penned most, until 1977 when his contribution was minimum. Covered; HOW MANY MORE YEARS (Howlin' Wolf) / ON YOUR WAY DOWN (Allen Toussaint) / etc. LOWELL solo:- EASY MONEY (Rickie Lee Jones) / + a few more. • **Trivia:** Their name was given to them by JIMMY CARL BLACK of FRANK ZAPPA's MOTHERS OF INVENTION, who joked about LOWELL's shoe size. ROBERT PALMER was once touted as a 1973 replacement for LOWELL, until their reformation. LOWELL produced GRATEFUL DEAD on their 'Shakedown Street' album, and sessioned for ROBERT PALMER 'Sneaking Sally … ', VAN DYKE PARKS 'Discover America' and JOHN CALE 'Paris 1919'.

Recommended: SAILIN' SHOES (*8) / FEATS DON'T FAIL ME NOW (*8) / THE LAST RECORD ALBUM (*8) / AS TIME GOES BY – THE BEST OF … (*9)

LOWELL GEORGE (b.13 Apr'45) – vocals, guitar (ex-MOTHERS OF INVENTION/**ZAPPA**) / **ROY ESTRADA** (b. Santa Ana) – bass, vocals (ex-MOTHERS OF INVENTION/ZAPPA) / **BILL PAYNE** (b.12 Mar'49, Waco, Texas) – keys, vocals (ex-FRATERNITY OF MAN) / **RICHIE HAYWARD** – drums (ex-FRATERNITY OF MAN)

Warners | Warners

May 70. (7") **STRAWBERRY FLATS. / HAMBURGER MIDNIGHT** [-] [ ]

Nov 70. (lp)(c) **LITTLE FEAT** [ ] [ ]
– Snakes on everything / Strawberry flats / Truck stop girl / Brides of Jesus / Willin' / Hamburger midnight; (a) Forty four blues, (b) How many more years / Crack in your door / I've been the one / Takin' my time / Crazy Captain Gunboat Willie. *(re-iss.Jan75)*

May 72. (lp)(c) **SAILIN' SHOES** [ ] [ ]
– Easy to slip / Cold cold cold / Trouble / Tripe face boogie / Willin' / Apolitical blues / Sailin' shoes / Teenage nervous breakdown / Got no shadows / Cat fever / Texas rose cafe. *(cd-iss.1988)*

—— **KENNY GRADNEY** (b. New Orleans) – bass (ex-DELANEY AND BONNY) repl. ESTRADA who joined CAPTAIN BEEFHEART & HIS MAGIC BAND / added **PAUL BARRERE** (b. 3 Jul'48, Burbank, California) – guitar, vocals / **SAM CLAYTON** – congas / **BONNIE BRAMLETT** – guest vocals

Nov 72. (7") **DIXIE CHICKEN. / LAFAYETTE RAILROAD** [-] [ ]

Feb 73. (lp)(c) **DIXIE CHICKEN** [ ] [ ]
– Dixie chicken / Two trains / Roll um easy / On your way down / Kiss it off / Fool yourself / Walkin' all night / Fat man in the bathtub / Juliette / Lafayette railroad. *(cd-iss.Jul88)*

—— Band split for 6 months (Oct '73-May '74). BILL joined DOOBIE BROTHERS and others, mainly LOWELL went into sessions. The sextet re-formed May74

Jul 74. (7") **OH ATLANTA. / DOWN THE ROAD** [-] [ ]
Sep 74. (7") **SPANISH MOON. / DOWN THE ROAD** [-] [ ]
Sep 74. (lp)(c) **FEATS DON'T FAIL ME NOW** [ ] [36]
– Rock and roll doctor / Cold cold cold / Tripe face boogie / The fan / Oh Atlanta / Skin it back / Down the road / Spanish moon / Down the road / Feats don't fail me now. *(cd-iss.Jan89)*
Nov 75. (lp)(c) **THE LAST RECORD ALBUM** [36] [36]
– Romance dance / All that you dream / Long distance love / Day or night / One love / Down below the borderline / Somebody's leavin' / Mercenary territory. *(cd-iss.Jul88)*
Feb 76. (7") **LONG DISTANCE LOVE. / ROMANCE DANCE** [ ] [ ] Oct 75
Feb 76. (7") **ALL THAT YOU DREAM. / ONE LOVE** [-] [ ]
May 77. (lp)(c) **TIME LOVES A HERO** [8] [34]
– Time loves a hero / Hi roller / New elhi freight train / Old folks boogie / Red streamliner / Keepin' up with the Joneses / Rocket in my pocket / Missin' you / Day at the dog races. *(cd-iss.Jul88)*
Jun 77. (7") **TIME LOVES A HERO. / SAILIN' SHOES** [-] [ ]
Jul 77. (7") **TIME LOVES A HERO. / ROCKET IN MY POCKET** [ ] [-]
Mar 78. (d-lp)(d-c) **WAITING FOR COLUMBUS (live)** [43] [18]
– Join the band / Fat man in the bathtub / All that you dream / Oh Atlanta / Old folks boogie / Time loves a hero / Day or night / Mercenary territory / Spanish moon / Dixie chicken / Tripe face boogie / Rocket in my pocket / Don't bogart that joint / Willin' / Apolitical blues / Sailin' shoes / Feats don't fail me now.
Jul 78. (7") **WILLIN' (live). / OH ATLANTA (live)** [-] [ ]
Oct 79. (lp)(c) **DOWN ON THE FARM** [46] [29]
– Down on the farm / Six feet of snow / Perfect imperfection / Kokomo / Be one now / Straight from the heart / Front page news / Wake up dreaming / Feel the groove. *(cd-iss.Jul88)*

— The had by this time split (Apr79). BARRERE and CLAYTON joined NICOLETTE LARSON. BARRERE went solo '83 and released 'ON MY OWN TWO FEET'. The others went into sessions.

– compilations, etc. –

Feb 75. Warners; (7") **DIXIE CHICKEN. / OH ATLANTA** [ ] [ ]
Oct 75. Warners; (d-lp) **TWO ORIGINALS OF . . . (LITTLE FEAT / DIXIE CHICKEN)** [ ] [ ]
Aug 81. Warners; (d-lp)(d-c) **HOY-HOY!** (remixes of rare material) [76] [39]
– Rocket in my pocket / Rock and roll doctor / Skin it back / Easy to slip / Red streamliner / Lonesome whistle / Front page news / The fan / Forty-four blues / Teenage nervous breakdown (live) / Framed / Strawberry flats / Gringo / Over the edge / Two trains / China white / All that you dream / Feats don't fail me now.
Aug 81. Warners; (7") **EASY TO SLIP. / FRONT PAGE NEWS** [-] [ ]
Oct 81. Warners; (7") **GRINGO. / STRAWBERRY FLATS** [-] [ ]
Aug 86. Warners; (lp)(c)(cd) **THE BEST OF LITTLE FEAT – AS TIME GOES BY** [ ] [ ]
– Dixie chicken / Willin' / Rock and roll doctor / Trouble / Sailin' shoes / Spanish Moon / Feats don't fail me now / All that you dream / Long distance love / Mercenary territory / Old folks boogie / Twenty million dollars.

LOWELL GEORGE

– solo (vocals, guitar) with **FRED TACKETT** – guitar / **EDDIE ZIP** – keyboards,vocals / **PETER WASNER** – keyboards / **JERRY JUMONVILLE** – saxophone / **LEE THORNBERG** – trumpet / **MAXINE DIXON** – b. vocals / **ARMANDO COMPION** – bass / **DON HEFFINGTON** – drums

Warners Warners

Apr 79. (7") **WHAT DO YOU WANT THE GIRL TO DO. / 20 MILLION THINGS** [-] [ ]
Apr 79. (lp)(c) **THANKS, I'LL EAT IT HERE** [ ] [71]
– What do you want the girl to do / Honest man / Two trains / Can't stand the rain / Cheek to cheek / Easy money / 20 million things / Find a river / Himmler's ring.
Jul 79. (7") **CHEEK TO CHEEK. / HONEST MAN** [ ] [ ]

— Tragically LOWELL died 29th June '79 of a drug induced heart attack. He had gigged the night before.

LITTLE FEAT

re-formed 1988. (**ESTRADA, PAYNE, HAYWARD & FRED TACKETT**) plus **CRAIG FULLER** – vocals (ex-PURE PRAIRIE LEAGUE)

Warners Warners

Jul 88. (lp)(c)(cd) **LET IT ROLL** [ ] [36]
– Hate to lose your lovin' / One clear moment / Cajun girl / Hangin' on to the good times / Listen to your heart / Let it roll / Long time till I get over you / Business as usual / Changin' luck / Voices on the wind. *(re-iss.cd Feb95)*
Jul 88. (7") **HATE TO LOSE YOUR LOVIN'. / CAJUN GIRL** [-] [ ]
Sep 88. (7") **ONE CLEAR MOMENT. / CHANGIN' LUCK** [-] [ ]
Nov 88. (7") **LET IT ROLL. / ?** [ ] [ ]
Apr 90. (cd)(c)(lp) **REPRESENTING THE MAMBO** [ ] [45]
– Texas twister / Daily grind / Representing the mambo / Woman in love / Rad gumbo / Teenage warrior / That's her, she's mine / Feelin's all gone / Those feet'll steer ya wrong sometimes / The ingenue / Silver screen. *(re-iss.cd Feb95)*

— added **MARTIN KIBBEE** – bass (ex-FRATERNITY OF MAN) / **& SAM CLAYTON** – percussion

Morgan Creek Morgan Creek

Oct 91. (cd)(c)(lp) **SHAKE ME UP** [ ] [ ]
– Spider's blues (might need it sometime) / Shake me up / Things happen / Mojo haiku / Loved and lied to / Don't try so hard / Boom boy car / Fast & furious / Livin' on dreams / Clownin' / Down in flames.

Zoo Zoo

Jun 95. (cd)(c)(lp) **AIN'T HAD ENOUGH FUN** [ ] [ ]
– Drivin' blind / Blue jean blues / Cadillac hotel / Romance without finance / Big bang theory / Cajun rage / Heaven's where you find it / Borderline blues / All that you can stand / Rock and roll every night / Shakeytown / Ain't had enough fun / That's a pretty good love.

LIVE

Formed: York, Pennsylvania, USA . . . early 90's by (see below). Signed to 'MCA' subsidiary 'Radioactive', where they unleashed debut album 'MENTAL JEWELRY'. • **Style:** Guitar-laden grunge-rock in the mould of PEARL JAM fused with GREEN ON RED. • **Songwriters:** Group penned. • **Trivia:** Produced by JERRY HARRISON (ex-Talking Heads).

Recommended: THROWING COPPER (*7)

ED KOWALCZYK – vocals / **CHAD TAYLOR** – guitar / **PATRICK DALHEIMER** – bass / **CHAD GRACEY** – drums

Radio-active Radio-active

Jan 92. (7") **PAIN LIES ON THE RIVERSIDE. / HEAVEN WORE A SKIRT** [-] [ ]
Apr 92. (cd)(c)(lp) **MENTAL JEWELRY** [ ] [73] Jan92
– Pain lies on the riverside / Operation spirit (the tyranny of tradition) / The beauty of Gray / Brothers unaware / Tired of me / Mirror song / Waterboy / Take my anthem / You are the world / Good pain / Mother Earth is a vicious crowd / 10,000 years (peace is now).
Apr 92. (cd-ep) **OPERATION SPIRIT (THE TYRANNY OF TRADITION) (live) / THE BEAUTY OF GRAY (live) / GOOD PAIN / LIES ON THE RIVERSIDE (live)** [-] [ ]
Jun 92. (7") **OPERATION SPIRIT. / HEAVEN WORE A SKIRT** [ ] [ ]
(12"+=)(cd-s+=) – Negation / Good pain.
Sep 94. (c-s)(cd-s) **SELLING THE DRAMA. / ('A'acoustic) / WHITE DISCUSSION** [ ] [43] Jun94
Oct 94. (cd)(c)(lp) **THROWING COPPER** [37] [1] May94
– The dam at Otter Creek / Selling the drama / I alone / Iris / Lightning crashes / Top / All over you / S*** towne / T.B.D. / Stage / Waitress / Pillar of Davidson / White discussion.
Feb 95. (7"clear)(c-s) **I ALONE. / PAIN LIES ON THE RIVERSIDE** [48] [ ]
(cd-s+=) – ('A'mix).
Jun 95. (c-s) **SELLING THE DRAMA / THE DAN AT OTTER CREEK** [30] [ ]
(cd-s+=) – ('A'acoustic).
Sep 95. (c-s) **ALL OVER YOU / SHIT TOWNE** [48] [ ]
(cd-s+=) – ('A'live at Glastonbury).
(cd-s) – ('A'side) / Waitress (live) / Iris (live at Glastonbury).

. . . Jan – Jun '96 stop press . . .

Jan 96. (single) **LIGHTNING CRASHES** [33] [ ]

LIVING COLOUR

Formed: New York, USA . . . 1984 by English-born VERNON REID and 2 others. In 1986, COREY GLOVER and WILL CALHOUN joined, with MUZZ being added in 1987. They guested on MICK JAGGER's 'Primitive Cool' album, which led him to produce a demo for them. Later that year, they obtained deal with 'Epic', and released 'VIVID' album in Spring '88. With a re-issue of single 'CULT OF PERSONALITY' hitting US Top 20 in 1989, it revived album to make Top 10. • **Style:** Politico outfit, described as black rock avengers, who brought back memories of HENDRIX, heavy psychedelia and deep soulful blues. • **Songwriters:** VERNON penned except; SHOULD I STAY OR SHOULD I GO (Clash) / FINAL SOLUTION (Pere Ubu) / MEMORIES CAN'T WAIT (Talking Heads) / BURNING OF THE MIDNIGHT LAMP (Jimi Hendrix) / TALKING LOUD AND SAYING NOTHING (James Brown) / LOVE AND HAPPINESS (Al Green) / SUNSHINE OF YOUR LOVE (Cream). • **Trivia:** COREY played a smart-assed soldier in the Vietnam film 'Platoon'. REID also guested for KEITH RICHARDS on his album 'Talk Is Cheap'.

Recommended: VIVID (*7) / TIME'S UP (*7) / STAIN (*6).

COREY GLOVER – vocals / **VERNON REID** – guitar / **MUZZ SKILLINGS** – bass / **WILLIAM CALHOUN** – drums

Epic Epic

May 88. (7")(7"pic-d) **MIDDLE MAN. / DESPERATE PEOPLE** [ ] [ ]
(12"+=)(cd-s+=) – Funny vibe.

May 88. (lp)(c)(cd) **VIVID** [ ] [6]
– Cult of personality / I want to know / Middle man / Desperate people / Open letter (to a landlord) / Funny vibe / Memories can't wait / Broken hearts / Glamour boys / What's your favourite colour / Which way to America? *(US hit May89)*

Jul 88. (7")(7"pic-d) **GLAMOUR BOYS. / WHICH WAY TO AMERICA?** [ ] [ ]
(12"+=)(cd-s+=) – Middle man / Rap track (conversation with LIVING COLOUR)

Sep 88. (7")**CULT OF PERSONALITY. / OPEN LETTER (TO A LANDLORD)** [ ] [ ]
(12"+=)(cd-s+=) – Middle Man (live).

Dec 88. (7")**OPEN LETTER (TO A LANDLORD). / CULT OF PERSONALITY (live)** [ ] [82] Jul 89
(12"+=)(cd-s+=) – Talkin' 'bout a revolution (live). (US; b-side)

Mar 89. (7") **CULT OF PERSONALITY. / FUNNY VIBE** [-] [13]

Apr 89. (7") **CULT OF PERSONALITY. / SHOULD I STAY OR SHOULD I GO** [ ] [-]
(12"+=)(cd-s+=) – What's your favourite colour.

Oct 89. (7") **GLAMOUR BOYS (remix). / CULT OF PERSONALITY (live)** [ ] [31] Aug 89
(12"+=) – Memories can't wait.
(cd-s++=) – I want to know.
(d7"+=) – Middle man / Open letter (to a landlord).

Oct 89. (7") **FUNNY VIBE. / ('A' instrumental)** [-] [ ]

Aug 90. (7") **TYPE. / SHOULD I STAY OR SHOULD I GO** [-] [ ]

Aug 90. (7") **TYPE. / FINAL SOLUTION** [75] [-]
(12"+=)(cd-s+=) – Should I stay or should I go / Middle man (live).

Sep 90. (cd)(c)(lp) **TIME'S UP** [20] [13]
– Time's up / History lesson / Pride / Love rears its ugly head / New Jack theme / Someone like you / Elvis is dead / Type / Information overload / Undercover of darkness / Olozy I / Fight the fight / Tag team partners / Solace of you / This is the life. *(cd+=)*– Final solution (live) / Middle man (live) / Love rears its ugly head (soul power mix).

Jan 91. (7")(c-s)(7"sha-pic-d) **LOVE REARS IT'S UGLY HEAD. / ('A'soul power mix)** [12] [ ]
(12"+=) – Type (remix).
(cd-s+=)(pic-cd+=) – ('A'version) / Love and happiness.

May 91. (c-s)(cd-s) **SOLACE OF YOU / SOMEONE LIKE YOU** [-] [ ]

May 91. (7")(c-s) **SOLACE OF YOU. / NEW JACK THEME** [33] [-]
(12"+=) – Elvis is dead (mix).
(cd-s+=) – ('A'live) / Type (live) / Information overload (live) / Desperate people (live).

Jul 91. (7"ep)(12"ep)(cd-ep) **BURNING OF THE MIDNIGHT LAMP / MEMORIES CAN'T WAIT / TALKING LOUD AND SAYING NOTHING** [ ] [ ]

Aug 91. (cd) **BISCUITS (live)** [-] [ ]
– Burning of the midnight lamp / Memories can't wait (live) / Talking loud and saying nothing / Desperate people (live) / Money talks / Love and happiness.

Oct 91. (7")(7"pic-d) **THE CULT OF PERSONALITY. / LOVE REARS IT'S UGLY HEAD (live)** [67] [ ]
(12"+=) – ('A'live) / Pride (live).
(cd-s+=) – Talkin' loud and saying nothing / Burning of the midnight lamp.

— MUZZ SKILLINGS departed Nov'91, and was replaced (Jun92) by **DOUG WIMBUSH** – bass (ex-TACKHEAD)

Feb 93. (7") **LEAVE IT ALONE. / 17 DAYS** [34] [ ]
(cd-s+=)(12"pic-d+=) – T.V. News / Hemp (Full Version)

Feb 93. (cd)(c)(lp) **STAIN** [19] [26]
– Go away / Ignorance is bliss / Leave it alone / B1 / Mind your own business / Auslander / Never satisfied / Nothingness / Postman / W.T.F.F. / This little pig / Hemp / Wal / T.V. news / Love rears its ugly head (live)

Apr 93. (7"pic-d) **AUSLANDER (Remix) / AUSLANDER (Dublander Mix)** [53] [ ]
(12"colrd+=)(pic-cd-s+=) – Auslander (Radio Days Mix) / New Jack theme.

May 93. (7"colrd) **NOTHINGLESS. / 17 DAYS** [ ] [ ]
(cd-s+=) – ('A'remix) / ('A'acoustic mix).

Aug 94. (c-ep) **SUNSHINE OF YOUR LOVE / AUSLANDER (overload mix) / ('A'-Adrian Sherwood & S.McDonald mix)** [ ] [ ]
(cd-ep) – (first 2 tracks) / ('A'remix) / Love rears its ugly head (extended).

— They disbanded after poor sales early 1995.

Nov 95. (cd)(c) **PRIDE – THE GREATEST HITS** (compilation) [ ] [ ]
– Pride / Release the pressure / Sacred ground / Visions / Love rears it's ugly head (soul power remix) / These are happy times / Memories can't wait / Cult of personality / Funny vibe / WTFF / Glamour boys / Open letter (to a landlord) / Solace of you / Nothingless / Type / Time's up / What's your favourite colour? (theme song).

Richard LLOYD (see under ⇒ TELEVISION)

Huw LLOYD-LANGTON (see under ⇒ HAWKWIND)

John LODGE (see under ⇒ MOODY BLUES)

Nils LOFGREN

Born: 21 Jun'51, Chicago, USA. Raised in Maryland, Washington DC with Italian/Swedish parents. In 1969, he formed PAUL DOWELL & THE DOLPHIN, but after two flop 45's, he broke them up to start GRIN. While building up their live reputation, he sessioned for NEIL YOUNG & CRAZY HORSE on 'After The Goldrush'. CRAZY HORSE also employed him the following year as part writer and session man on their brilliant eponymous debut. Meanwhile GRIN had signed to 'Spindizzy' who gained distribution from 'Columbia'. Their debut lp, issued late summer '71, only scraped the US Top 200, as did their follow-ups '1 + 1' and 'ALL OUT' (the latter added NILS' younger brother TOM). In 1973, they signed to 'A&M' but soon split after NILS joined NEIL YOUNG & CRAZY HORSE for tour work late '73. By Mar'74 he went solo again, re-signing for 'A&M'. By 1976, he and his solo band were reaching Top40 on both sides of the Atlantic. In 1984, after guesting on NEIL YOUNG's 'Trans' album, he joined BRUCE SPRINGSTEEN's E-STREET SHUFFLE. He continued to work parallel projects together, also fitting in a RINGO STARR ALL-STAR BAND tour in 1990. • **Style:** Highly praised cool-in-the shades rock guitarist, who progressed from cult youth following, to gain disencing adult audience. • **Songwriters:** Self-penned except covers; FOR YOUR LOVE (Yardbirds) / ANYTIME AT ALL (Beatles) / IT'S ALL OVER NOW (Valentinos) / etc. • **Trivia:** 'KEITH DON'T GO' was about 'Glimmer Twin' idol KEITH RICHARDS.

Recommended: THE BEST OF NILS LOFGREN – DON'T WALK (*7)

PAUL DOWELL & THE DOLPHIN

NILS LOFGREN – lead guitar, keyboards, / and **BOB GORDON** (b.1951, Oklahoma)– bass, vocals / unknown drummer

not issued Sire

1969. (7") **THE LAST TIME I SAW YOU. / IT'S BETTER TO KNOW YOU** [-] [ ]

GRIN

(NILS + BOB)plus **BOB BERBERICH** (b.1949, Maryland)– drums (ex-REEKERS)

Epic Spindizzy

Jul 71. (7") **WE ALL SUNG TOGETHER. / SEE WHAT A LOVE CAN DO** [ ] [ ] Oct 70

Aug 71. (lp) **GRIN** [ ] [ ] Jun 71
– Like rain / See what a love can do / Everybody's missin' the sun / 18 faced lover / Outlaw / We all sung together / If I were a song / Take you to the movies tonight / Direction / Pioneer Mary / Open wide / I had too much (Miss Dazi). *(re-iss.1975 on 'Spindizzy')*

Sep 71. (7") **EVERYBODY'S MISSIN' THE SUN. / 18 FACED LOVER** [ ] [ ]

Jan 72. (7") **WHITE LIES. / ?** [-] [75]

Jan 72. (lp) **1 + 1** [ ] [ ]
– White lies / Please don't hide / Slippery fingers / Moon tears / End unkind / Sometimes / Lost a number / Hi, hello home / Just a poem / Soft fun. *(re-iss.1975 on 'Spindizzy')*

— added **TOM LOFGREN** – rhythm guitar

Mar 73. (lp)(c) **ALL OUT** [ ] [ ]
– That letter / Heavy Chevy / Don't be long / Love again / She ain't right / Love or else / Ain't love nice / Hard on fire / All out / Rusty gun. *(cd-iss.Oct94)*

Apr 73. (7") **AIN'T LOVE NICE. / LOVE OR ELSE** [ ] [ ]

A & M A & M

Nov 73. (lp)(c) **GONE CRAZY** [ ] [ ]
– You're the weight / Boy and girl / What about me / One more time / True thrill / Beggar's day / Nightmare / Believe / Ain't for free. *(re-iss.Jan76)*

Feb 74. (7") **YOU'RE THE WEIGHT. / BEGGAR'S DAY** [-] [ ]

He joined NEIL YOUNG & CRAZY HORSE (Aug73-Mar74, on 'Tonight's The Night')

– (GRIN) compilations, others, etc. –

C.B.S. Columbia

Jun 76. (d-lp) **GRIN FEATURING NILS LOFGREN** [ ] [ ]

– ('GRIN' & '1 + 1' albums)
Jun 76. (7") **SOFT FUN. / SLIPPERY FINGERS**
Oct 79. (lp)(c) **THE BEST OF NILS LOFGREN AND GRIN**
(re-iss.Feb86)

NILS LOFGREN

with **WORNELL JONES** – bass / **AYNSLEY DUNBAR** – drums

A & M | A & M

Apr 75. (lp)(c) **NILS LOFGREN** — Mar 75
– Be good tonight / Back it up / One more Saturday night / If I say it, it's so / I don't want to know / Keith don't go (ode to the Glimmer twin) / Can't buy a break / Duty / The sun hasn't set on this boy yet / Rock and roll crook / Two by two / Goin' back.
Jun 75. (7") **BACK IT UP. / IF I SAY IT, IT'S SO**
Nov 75. (7") **I DON'T WANT TO KNOW. / ONE MORE SATURDAY NIGHT**
Jan 76. (ltd.lp) **BACK IT UP** (live radio show)

— added **TOM LOFGREN** – rhythm guitar, vocals (ex-GRIN)

Mar 76. (lp)(c) **CRY TOUGH** — 8 | 32
– Cry tough / It's not a crime / Incidentally . . . it's over / For your love / Share a little / Mud in your eye / Can't get closer (WCGC) / You lit a fire / Jailbait. *(re-iss.Jul83 on 'Fame') (re-iss.1988)*
May 76. (7") **CRY TOUGH. / SHARE A LITTLE**
Aug 76. (7") **IT'S NOT A CRIME. / SHARE A LITTLE**

— **ANDY NEWMARK** – drums repl. ZACK

— added **PATRICK HENDERSON** – keyboards

Mar 77. (lp)(c) **I CAME TO DANCE** — 30 | 36
– I came to dance / Rock me at home / Home is where your hurt is / Code of the road / Happy ending kids / Goin' south / To be a dreamer / Jealous gun / Happy.
May 77. (7") **I CAME TO DANCE. / CODE OF THE ROAD**

— **DAVID PLATSHON** -drums repl. NEWMARK

Oct 77. (d-lp)(c) **NIGHT AFTER NIGHT (live)** — 38 | 44
– Take you to the movies / Back it up / Keith don't go (ode to the Glimmer twin) / Like rain / Cry tough / It's not a crime / Goin' back / You're the weight / Beggars day / Moon tears / Code of the road / Rock and roll crook / Goin' south / Incidentally . . . it's over / I came to dance.

— now used mainly session people except TOM (on next only)

Jun 79. (lp)(c) **NILS** — | 54
– No mercy / I'll cry tomorrow / Baltimore / Shine silently / Steal away / Kool skool / A fool like me / I found her / You're so easy.
Jul 79. (7") **NO MERCY. / KOOL SKOOL** — - |
Jul 79. (7")(7"colrd) **SHINE SILENTLY. / KOOL SKOOL** — | -
Sep 79. (7") **SHINE SILENTLY. / BALTIMORE** — - |
Oct 79. (7") **NO MERCY. / A FOOL LIKE ME** — | -

Backstreet-MCA | Backstreet-MCA

Sep 81. (lp)(c) **NIGHTS FADE AWAY** — 50 | 99
– Nights fade away / I go to pieces / Empty heart / Don't touch me / Dirty money / Sailor boy / Anytime at all / Ancient history / Streets again / In motion. *(re-iss.Feb84 on 'M.C.A.')*
Sep 81. (7") **NIGHT FADES AWAY. / ANCIENT HISTORY** — - |
Sep 81. (7") **NIGHTS FADE AWAY. / ANYTIME AT ALL** — | -
Nov 81. (7") **I GO TO PIECES. / ANCIENT HISTORY**
Aug 83. (lp)(c) **WONDERLAND**
– Across the tracks / Into the night / It's all over now / I wait for now / Daddy dream / Wonderland / Room without love / Confident girl / Lonesome ranger / Everybody wants / Deadline. *(re-iss.Jun87)*
Oct 83. (7") **ACROSS THE TRACKS. / DADDY DREAM**

— Split his own band to join BRUCE SPRINGSTEEN & THE E-STREET SHUFFLE between 1984-1985. He returned to solo work, bringing back **NEWMARK + JONES** plus **TOMMY MANDELS + T. LAVITZ** – synthesizers

Towerbell | Columbia

May 85. (7") **SECRETS IN THE STREET. / FROM THE HEART** — 53 |
(12"+=) – ('A'extended).
(d7"+=) – Message / Little bit of time.
Jun 85. (lp)(c) **FLIP** — 36 |
– Flip ya flip / Secrets in the street / From the heart / Delivery night / King of the rock / Sweet midnight / New holes in old shoes / Dreams die hard / Big tears fall. *(cd-iss.Dec92 on 'Castle')*
Aug 85. (7") **FLIP YA FLIP. / NEW HOLES IN OLD SHOES** — | -
(12"+=) – ('A'extended).
(12"pic-d) – ('A'side) / Message (11 minute).
Aug 85. (7") **FLIP YA FLIP. / DELIVERY NIGHT** — - |
Nov 85. (7") **DELIVERY NIGHT. / DREAMS DIE HARD**
(12") – ('A'side) / Keith don't go (live).
Jan 86. (7") **SECRETS IN THE STREET. / FROM THE HEART** — | -
(d7"+=) – Message / Little bit of time.

— Live band = **JONES, TOM LOFGREN, STEWART SMITH, JOHNNY 'BEE' BADANJEK**

Mar 86. (d-lp)(c) **CODE OF THE ROAD (live)** — 86 |
– Beggars day / Secrets in the street / Across the tracks / Delivery night / Cry tough / Dreams die hard / Believe / The sun hasn't set on this boy yet / Code of the road / Moon tears / Back it up / Like rain / Sweet midnight / No mercy / Anytime at all / New holes in old shoes / Keith don't go / Shine silently / I came to dance. *(cd-iss.Dec92 on 'Castle')*
Mar 86. (7") **ANYTIME AT ALL (live). / NEW HOLES IN OLD SHOES (live)**

— He decided to re-join BRUCE SPRINGSTEEN, mainly for stage work. Returned in '91 with main band **SCOTT THURSTON** – keyboards / **ANDY NEWMARK** – drums / **KEVIN McCORMICK** – bass, keyboards, percussion / **+ LEVON HELM** – harmonica, vocals

Essential | Rykodisc

May 91. (cd)(c)(lp) **SILVER LINING** — 61 | — Mar91
– Silver lining / Valentine / Walkin' nerve / Live each day / Sticks and stones / Trouble's back / Little bit of time / Bein' angry / Gun and run / Girl in motion.
1991. (cd-s) **VALENTINE / ('A'-album version) / ('A'-original)**
1991. (cd-s) **WALKIN' NERVE / KEITH DON'T GO**
Jul 92. (cd)(c)(lp) **CROOKED LINE**
– A child could tell / Blue skies / Misery / You / Shot at you / Crooked line / Walk on me / Someday / New kind of freedom / Just a little / Drunken driver / I'll fight for you.

Permanent | Rykodisc

Oct 94. (d-cd) **EVERY BREATH** (feat. LOU GRAMM)
–

— next with **ANDY NEWMARK** -drums / **ROGER GREENAWALT** -bass, percussion, samples / **MICHAEL MATOUSEK** -production coordinator

Essential | Rykodisc

Oct 95. (cd)(c) **DAMAGED GOODS**
– Damaged goods / Only five minutes / Alone / Trip to Mars / Here for you / Black books / Setting Sun / Life / Heavy hats / In the room / Nothin's fallin' / Don't be late for yesterday.

– compilations, others, etc. –

Apr 82. A&M; (lp)(c) **A RHYTHM ROMANCE** — 100 |
Apr 82. A&M; (7") **SHINE SILENTLY. / KEITH DON'T GO (ODE TO THE GLIMMER TWIN)**
Jun 85. A&M; (7") **SHINE SILENTLY. / I CAME TO DANCE**
(12"+=) – No mercy.
Jun 90. Connoisseur; (cd)(c)(d-lp) **THE BEST OF NILS LOFGREN – DON'T WALK . . . ROCK** — | -
– Moon tears (live) / Back it up / Keith don't go (ode to the Glimmer twin) / The sun hasn't set on this boy yet / Goin' back / Cry tough / Jailbait / Can't get closer (WCGC) / Mud in your eye / I came to dance / To be a dreamer / No mercy / Steal away / Baltimore / Shine silently / Secrets in the street / Flip ya flip / Delivery night / Anytime at all (live).
Jun 94. Windsong; (cd) **LIVE ON THE TEST (live)** — | -
May 95. Spectrum; (cd) **SHINE SILENTLY** — | -
Jul 95. Raven; cd) **SOFT FUN, TOUGH TEARS 1971-79** — | -

LONGPIGS

*** NEW ENTRY ***

Formed: Sheffield, England . . .1993 by quartet below. A car crash involving the band, left CRISPIN in a coma and two others injured. They had signed to 'Elektra' UK and were stopped recording and playing live for two years until lawyer John Stratham bailed them out. They found a new contract with 'Mother' and soon broke into Top 75 with second single 'SHE SAID'. After three more between October '95 & April '96, it re-charted into the Top 20. • **Style:** Aggressive rock act inspired by AUTEURS, RADIOHEAD or R.E.M. • **Songwriters:** HUNT, and a few by HAWLEY + group. • **Trivia:** Produced by GIL NORTON.

Recommended: THE SUN IS OFTEN OUT (*8)

CRISPIN HUNT – vocals, guitar / **RICHARD HAWLEY** – guitar, vocals / **SIMON STAFFORD** – bass, piano / **DEE BOYLE** – drums (ex-CHAKK)

Mother | Mother

Mar 95. (7")(cd-s) **HAPPY AGAIN. / SALLY DANCES** — | -
Jul 95. (7")(c-s) **SHE SAID. / TAKE IT ALL** — 67 |
(cd-s+=) – Devoted / Juicy.
Oct 95. (7"red)(c-s) **JESUS CHRIST. / SWEETNESS** — 61 |
(cd-s+=) – Vagina song / Whiteness.
Feb 96. (7")(c-s) **FAR. / BLAH BLAH BLAH** — 37 |
(cd-s+=) – Amateur dramatics / Far (Sheffield version).
Apr 96. (7"ep)(c-ep)(cd-ep) **ON & ON / YOUR FACE. / DOZEN WICKED WORDS / SLEEP** — 16 |
May 96. (cd)(c)(lp) **THE SUN IS OFTEN OUT** — 26 |
– Lost myself / She said / Far / On and on / Happy again / All hype / Sally dances / Jesus Christ / Dozen wicked words / Elvis / Over our bodies.

Jun 96. (7")(cd-s) **SHE SAID. / FLARE IS METEOR** | 16 |
(c-s+=)(cd-s+=) – Soap opera credo / Tendresse.
(cd-s) – ('A'side) / I lost myself / Far / On and on.

Jon LORD (see under ⇒ DEEP PURPLE)

LOVE

Formed: Los Angeles, California, USA . . . early '65 originally as The GRASS ROOTS, by ARTHUR LEE and former BYRDS roadie BRYAN MacLEAN. When another band of that name made the US charts, they became LOVE, and soon signed to Jac Holzman's 'Elektra' records. In 1966, with their debut 45 'MY LITTLE RED BOOK' nearly hitting US Top 50, they also scored Top 60 eponymous lp. It was soon pursued by their first and only major hit '7 AND 7 IS', as group went through first of many personnel changes by end of the year. Early in 1967, they re-emerged with classic 'DA CAPO' lp, which contained a near 20 minute track 'REVELATION' alongside some other 3 minute beauts. The next year, they matched it with another gem 'FOREVER CHANGES', which contained 2 pieces of excellence 'ALONE AGAIN OR' & 'ANDMOREAGAIN', and which made the UK Top 30, but not the US Top 150! (These albums are still being sought out by cult collectors, despite receiving a cd re-issue in the late 80's.) In Aug'68, ARTHUR LEE sacked the rest of the group "cause they couldn't cut it", and recruited entire new line-up to make future lp's. Not surprisingly, LEE was left to pursue a solo career in 1972, although he resurrected another LOVE in 1974. After various other re-unions in the late 70's, LEE released a self-titled solo effort in 1981, before going AWOL again. Just recently in the early 90's with renewed LOVE interest, LEE re-formed group for a re-union album. • **Style:** Psychedelic & twee soulful R&B outfit, headed by the HENDRIX-like ARTHUR LEE, who shaped a soft melodic rock alongside more powerful electrifying songs. • **Songwriters:** ARTHUR LEE or BRYAN MacLEAN until latter's departure in 1967. Covered; HEY JOE (trad.) / MY LITTLE RED BOOK (Bacharach-David). • **Trivia:** In 1970, LEE was about to project idea BAND AID (not the charity), with STEVE WINWOOD and JIMI HENDRIX (but the latter died on Sep'70). In 1973, he recorded lp 'BLACK BEAUTY' for 'Buffalo' records, but this was shelved, although bootlegs did appear.

Recommended: DA CAPO (*8) / FOREVER CHANGES (*9).

ARTHUR LEE (b.1945, Memphis) – vocals, guitar (ex-LAG'S, ex-AMERICAN FOUR) / **BRYAN MacLEAN** (b.1947, Los Angeles) – guitar, vocals / **JOHN ECHOLS** (b.1945, Memphis) – lead guitar (ex-LAG'S) / **KEN FORSSI** (b.1943, Cleveland) – bass (ex-SURFARIS) / **ALBAN 'SNOOPY' PFISTERER** (b.1947, Switzerland) – drums repl. DON CONKA

London | Elektra

Mar 66. (7") **MY LITTLE RED BOOK. / A MESSAGE TO PRETTY** | - | 52
Jun 66. (7") **HEY JOE. / MY LITTLE RED BOOK** | - |
Sep 66. (7") **7 AND 7 IS. / No.14** | | 33 Aug 66

Elektra | Elektra

Sep 66. (lp) **LOVE** | | 57 Jul 66
– My little red book / A message to Pretty / Softly to me / Emotions / Gazing / Signed D.C. / Mushroom clouds / Can't explain / My flash on you / No matter what you do / You I'll be following / Hey Joe / Coloured bells falling / And more. *(re-iss.+cJan72) (re-iss.Feb87 on 'Edsel') (cd-iss.Feb93 & Dec93)*

— added **MICHAEL STUART** – drums ('SNOOPY' now on keyboards), / and **TJAY CANTRELLI** – saxophone

Dec 66. (7") **SHE COMES IN COLOURS. / ORANGE SKIES** | | -
Feb 67. (lp) **DA CAPO** | | 80
– Stephanie knows who / Orange skies / Que vida / 7 and 7 is / The castle / She comes in colors / Revelation. *(re-iss.+cJan72) (re-iss.May81) (cd-iss.1989 on 'WEA')*
Mar 67. (7") **QUE VIDA (edit). / HEY JOE** | - |
Sep 67. (7") **THE CASTLE. / SOFTLY TO ME** | | -

— Reverted to a quintet when 'SNOOPY' and TJAY left. (latter to DOMINIC TROIANO)

Jan 68. (7") **ALONE AGAIN OR. / A HOUSE IS NOT A MOTEL** | - |
Jan 68. (7") **ALONE AGAIN OR. / BUMMER IN THE SUMMER** | | -
(re-iss.Sep70, hit US No.99)
Feb 68. (lp) **FOREVER CHANGES** | 24 | Jan 68
– Alone again or / A house is not a motel / The Daily planet / Andmoreagain / Old man / The red telephone / Between Clark and Hilldale / Live and let live / Good honor man / Everything like this / Bummer in the summer / You set the scene. *(re-iss.+cJan72) (re-iss.Jan84) (cd-iss.Jul88 on 'WEA')*
Mar 68. (7") **ANDMOREAGAIN. / THE DAILY PLANET** | | -

— ARTHUR LEE dismissed others and recruited new people below **JAY DONELLAN** (LEWIS) – guitar / **JIM HOBSON** – keyboards / **FRANK FAYAD** – bass / **GEORGE SURANOVICH** – drums

Sep 68. (7") **YOUR MIND AND WE BELONG TOGETHER. / LAUGHING STOCK** | |

— Augmented by **PAUL MARTIN** and **GARY ROWLES** – guitar plus **DRACKEN THEAKER** – keyboards (ex-CRAZY WORLD OF ARTHUR BROWN)

Nov 69. (lp) **FOUR SAIL** | | Sep 69
– August / Your friend and mine – Neil's song / I'm with you / Good times / Singing cowboy / Dream / Robert Montgomery / Nothing / Talking in my sleep / Always see your face. *(re-iss.+cJan72) (re-iss.Nov87 on 'Thunderb.', cd-iss.Jun88)*
Mar 70. (7") **I'M WITH YOU. / ROBERT MONTGOMERY** | | -

Harvest | Blue Thumb

May 70. (d-lp)(c) **OUT HERE** | 29 | Dec 69
– I'll pray for you / Abalony / Signed D.C. / Listen to my song / I'm down / Stand out / Discharged / Doggone / I still wonder / Love is more than words or better late than never / Nice to be / Car lights on in the day time blues / Run to the top / Willow willow / Instra-mental / You are something / Gather round. *(re-iss.Jul88 as 1-lp on 'Big Beat') (cd-iss.Jul90)*
May 70. (7") **I'LL PRAY FOR YOU (edit). / STAND OUT** | - |
Nov 70. (7") **KEEP ON SHINING (edit). / THE EVERLASTING FIRST** | |

— **GARY ROWLES** now full time , repl. JAY

Jan 71. (lp) **FALSE START** | | Dec 70
– The everlasting first / Flying / Gimi a little break / Stand out / Keep on shining / Anytime / Slick Dick / Love is coming / Feel daddy feel good / Ride that vibration. *(cd-iss.Sep91 & Jul92 on 'B.G.O.')*
Mar 71. (7") **STAND OUT. / DOGGONE** | | -

ARTHUR LEE with BAND AID

a solo venture retaining **FAYAD** and new men **CHARLES KARP** – guitar / **CRAIG TARWATER** – guitar / **CLARENCE McDONALD** – keyboards / **DON PONCHA** – drums / and guest **DAVID HULL** – extra bass

A & M | A & M

Aug 72. (lp) **VINDICTIVE** | |
– Sad song / You can save up to 50% / Love jumped through my window / Find somebody / He said she said / Everytime I look up / Everybody's gotta live / He knows a lot of good women / You want change for your re-run / Hamburger breath stinkfinger / Ol' morgue mouth / Busted feet.
Aug 72. (7") **EVERYBODY'S GOT TO LIVE. / LOVE JUMPED THROUGH MY WINDOW** | - |
Nov 72. (7") **SAD SONG. / YOU WANT TO CHANGE FOR YOUR RE-RUN** | - |

— ARTHUR re-formed

LOVE

recruiting **MELVIN WHITTINGTON** and **JOHN STERLING** – guitar / **SHERWOOD AKUNA** and **ROBERT ROZENO** – bass / **JOE BLOCKER** – drums

R.S.O. | R.S.O.

Jan 75. (7") **TIME IS LIKE A RIVER. / YOU SAID YOU WOULD** | | Dec 74
Jan 75. (lp)(c) **REEL TO REAL** | |
– Time is like a river / Stop the music / Who are you? / Good old fashioned love / Which witch is which / With a little energy / Singing cowboy / Be thankful for what you got / You said you would / Busted feet / Everybody's gotta live.
1975. (7") **YOU SAID YOU WOULD (edit). / GOOD OLD FASHIONED DREAM** | - |

ARTHUR LEE

solo again, using loads of session people

Da Capo | not issued

1977. (7"ep) **I DO WONDER / JUST US. / DO YOU KNOW THE SECRET? / HAPPY YOU** | | -

Beggar's B. | Rhino

Jul 81. (lp) **ARTHUR LEE** | | -
– One / I do wonder / Just us / Happy you / Do you know the secret / One and one / Seven and seven is / Mr. Lee / Bend down / Stay away from evil / Many rivers to cross.

— LOVE re-formed in Autumn '91, with **ARTHUR LEE, DON CONKA, SHUGGIE OTIS** – guitar / **MELLAN WHITTINGTON** – guitar / **SHERWOOD AKUNA** – bass. Credited to

ARTHUR LEE

New Rose | not issued

May 92. (cd)(lp) **ARTHUR LEE AND LOVE** | |

– LOVE compilations etc. –

Aug 70. Elektra; (7") **ALONE AGAIN OR. / GOOD TIMES** | - |

Jul 73. Elektra; (7") **ALONE AGAIN OR. / ANDMOREAGAIN** [ ] [-]
(re-iss.Apr84 on 'Edsel')

Dec 70. Elektra; (lp)(c) **LOVE REVISITED** [ ] [ ] Sep 70
(re-iss.+c.Jan72)

Feb 73. Elektra; (lp)(c) **LOVE MASTERS** [ ] [ ]
– My little red book / Signed D.C. / Hey Joe / 7 and 7 is / Stephanie knows who / Orange skies / Que vida / The castle / She comes in colours / Laughing stock / Your mind / And we belong together / Old man / The Daily Planet / A house is not a motel / Andmoreagain / Alone again or.

Sep 76. Elektra; (7") **ALONE AGAIN OR. / THE CASTLE** [ ] [ ]

1980. Rhino; (lp) **THE BEST OF LOVE** [-] [ ]

1981. Rhino; (pic-lp) **LOVE LIVE (live)** [-] [ ]

1986. Rhino; (lp) **GOLDEN ARCHIVE** [-] [ ]

1982. M.C.A.; (lp)(c) **STUDIO / LIVE** [ ] [ ]

Mike LOVE / CELEBRATION (see under ⇒ BEACH BOYS)

L7

Formed: Los Angeles, California, USA ... 1986 by SPARKS and GARDNER. Move east to Chicago to sign for the now-famous indie label 'Sub Pop' in 1989, after an eponymous album for 'Epitaph'. They cracked the charts in 1992, when on 'Slash' they hit with near Top 20 classic 'PRETEND WE'RE DEAD'. • **Style:** All-girl grunge metal outfit influenced by METALLICA or NIRVANA. • **Songwriters:** Group or SPARKS penned. • **Trivia:** In Nov92, DONITA caused controversy on UK TV pop programme 'The Word', after dropping her jeans on stage, revealing that she didn't wear knickers.

Recommended: BRICKS ARE HEAVY (*8).

DONITA SPARKS (b.Chicago) – vox, guitar / **SUZI GARDNER** – guitar, vocals / **JENNIFER FINCH** – bass, vocals repl. ? / **ANNE ANDERSON** (b.Chicago) – drums

Epitaph / Epitaph

Dec 88. (lp) **L7** [-] [ ]
– Bite the wax tadpole / Cat o' nine tails / Metal stampede / Let's rock / Uncle Bob / Snake handler / Runnin' from the law / Cool out / It's not you / I drink / Ms.45.

—— **DEE PLAKAS** – drums repl. ANNE

not issued / Sub Pop

Jan 90. (7")(7"green) **SHOVE. / PACKIN' A ROD** [-] [ ]

Glitter... / Sub Pop

Nov 90. (12"ep)(12"purple-ep) **SMELL THE MAGIC** [ ] [ ] Aug 90
– Shove / Til the wheels fall off / Fast'n'frightening / (Right on) Thru / Deathwish / Broomstick. (cd-ep+=) – Packin' a rod / Just like me / American society.

Slash / London

Mar 92. (7")(c-s)(7"red) **PRETEND WE''RE DEAD. / SHIT LIST** [21] [ ]
(12"+=)(cd-s+=) – Lopsided head / Mr.Integrity.

Apr 92. (cd)(c)(lp) **BRICKS ARE HEAVY** [24] [ ]
– Wargasm / Scrap / Pretend we're dead / Diet pill / Everglade / Slide / One more thing / Mr.Integrity / Monster / Shit list / This ain't pleasure.

May 92. (7")(c-s)(7"colour) **EVERGLADE. / FREAK MAGNET** [27] [ ]
– (12"+=)(cd-s+=) – Scrap.

Sep 92. (7")(c-s) **MONSTER. / USED TO LOVE HIM** [33] [ ]
(12"+=)(cd-s+=) – Diet pill.

Nov 92. (7")(c-s) **PRETEND WE'RE DEAD. / FAST'N'FRIGHTENING (live)** [50] [ ]
(cd-s+=) – (Right on) Thru / Shove / Shit list / Diet pill.

—— Band will appear as CAMEL LIPS group in the film 'SERIAL MOM'.

Jun 94. (7"colrd)(12"colrd) **ANDRES. / BOMB** [34] [ ]
(cd-s+=) – (KRXT radio interview).

Jul 94. (cd)(c)(lp) **HUNGRY FOR STINK** [26] [ ]
– Andres / Baggage / Can I run / The bomb / Questioning my sanity / Riding with a movie star / Stuck here again / Fuel my fire / Freak magnet / She has eyes / Shirley / Talk box.

Steve LUKATHER (see under ⇒ TOTO)

LUSH

Formed: Camberwell, London, England ... Oct'88 by girls MIKI and EMMA, plus lads STEVE and CHRIS. After supports slots to DARLING BUDS, etc, they signed to top independent label '4.a.d.' in 1989. Their first release 'SCAR', paved way for 1990 minor hits produced by Robin Guthrie (of COCTEAU TWINS). • **Style:** Alternative rock, both melodic and lazy in harmony, and not unlike The COCTEAUS or MY BLOODY VALENTINE. • **Songwriters:** MIKI and EMMA, except HEY HEY HELEN (Abba) / FALLIN' IN LOVE (Dennis Wilson) / OUTDOOR MINER (Wire) / LOVE AT FIRST SIGHT (Young Marble Giants). • **Trivia:** In 1990, they all posed topless although artisticly painted for an NME cover shot.

Recommended: SPOOKY (*8) / GALA (*7) / SPLIT (*6) / LOVELIFE (*8).

MIKI BERENYI – vocals, guitar / **EMMA ANDERSON** – guitar, vocals / **STEVE RIPPON** – bass / **CHRIS ACLAND** – drums

4 a.d. / Relativity

Oct 89. (m-lp)(c)(cd) **SCAR** [ ] [ ]
– Thoughtforms / Baby talk / Scarlet / Bitter / Second sight / Etheriel / Hey hey Helen / Scarlet.

Feb 90. (12"ep)(c-ep)(cd-ep) **MAD LOVE EP** [55] [ ]
– De luxe / Leaves me cold / Downer / Thoughtforms.

Oct 90. (7"ep)(c-ep)(cd-ep) **SWEETNESS AND LIGHT. / SUNBATHING / BREEZE** [47] [ ]

Dec 90. (cd)(c)(lp) **GALA** [ ] [ ]
– Sweetness and light / Sunbathing / Breeze / De luxe / Leaves me cold / Downer / Thoughtforms / Baby talk / Thoughtforms / Scarlet / Bitter / Second light / Etheriel / Hey hey Helen / Scarlet.

Sep 91. (7")(c-s) **NOTHING NATURAL. / GOD'S GIFT** [43] [ ]
(12"ep)(cd-ep) – 'BLACK SPRING EP'(+=) – Monochrome / Fallin' in love.

Dec 91. (10"ep)(12"ep)(c-ep)(cd-ep) **FOR LOVE / OUTDOOR MINER. / STARLUST / ASTRONAUT** [35] [ ]

—— Although on above + below recording RIPPON had left Oct'91.

4ad / 4ad-Reprise

Jan 92. (cd)(c)(lp) **[SPOOKY]** [7] [ ]
– Stray / Nothing natural / Tiny smiles / Covert / Ocean / For love / Superblast! / Untogether / Fantasy / Take / Laura / Monochrome.

—— **RIPPON** was replaced by **PHIL KING** – bass (ex-SEE SEE RIDER, ex-APPLE BOUTIQUE, ex-FELT)

May 94. (7"ep)(12"ep)(cd-ep) **HYPOCRITE / LOVE AT FIRST SIGHT. / CAT'S CHORUS / UNDERTOW** [52] [ ]

May 94. (7"ep)(12"ep)(cd-ep) **THE DESIRE LINES / GIRL'S WORLD. / WHITE WOOD / LOVELIFE** [60] [ ]

Jun 94. (cd)(c)(lp) **SPLIT** [19] [ ]
– Light from a dead star / Kiss chase / Blackout / Hypocrite / Lovelife / Desire lines / The invisible man / Undertow / Never-never / Lit up / Stardust / When I die.

... Jan – Jun '96 stop press ...

Jan 96. (single) **SINGLE GIRL** [21] [ ]

Feb 96. (single) **LADYKILLERS** [22] [ ]

Mar 96. (cd)(c)(clear-lp) **LOVELIFE** [8] [ ]

—— JARVIS COCKER features vocals with MIKI on the track 'Ciao'. They also covered on a b-side 'I WANNA BE YOUR BOYFRIEND (Rubinoos).

Phil LYNOTT (see under ⇒ THIN LIZZY)

LYNYRD SKYNYRD

Formed: Jacksonville, Florida, USA ... 1966 initially as MY BACKYARD, by RONNIE VAN ZANT, GARY ROSSINGTON, ALLEN COLLINS, BOB BURNS and bassist LARRY JUNSTROM. They quickly became The NOBLE FIVE, but abandoned this title when they chose ex-school gym coach LEONARD SKINNER's name. To avoid legal action, they became LYNYRD SKYNYRD and issued late 60's limited single 'NEED ALL MY FRIENDS' for local 'Shade Tree' label. After local tours and another single release in 1971, they signed to 'MCA', after turning down Phil Walden's 'Capricorn'. They finally released debut album 'PRONOUNCED LEH-NERD SKIN-HERD' late 1973, which was produced (as was their future 2), by the man who spotted them; AL KOOPER (ex-BLUES PROJECT). This made US Top 30, due to airplay for its DUANE ALLMAN epic tribute track 'FREE BIRD'. Late the following year, they had Top 10 US hit with 'SWEET HOME ALABAMA' (a slight at NEIL YOUNG), which was lifted from US Top 15 album 'SECOND HELPING'. Became major attractions at home and in Britain, and had just released 6th album 'STREET SURVIVORS', when tragedy struck. On 20th Oct'77 while in between gigs, their chartered plane ran out of fuel and crashed into a swamp in McComb, Mississippi. All on board were seriously injured, but VAN ZANT, STEVE and sister CASSIE GAINES, plus roadie DEAN KILPATRICK were killed. Immediately afterwards the cover-shot of lp 'STREET SURVIVORS' was withdrawn, as it had flames apparently sprouting from group's heads. The remaining 4 (ROSSINGTON, COLLINS, POWELL & WILKESON) re-grouped in 1979 with 3 new members, and became the near equally profitable ROSSINGTON-COLLINS BAND. In 1987, the surviving LYNYRD SKYNYRD members re-formed, although this had little commercial impact, even after release of 1991 album. • **Style:** Southern hard rock'n'boogie, triple-guitar playing outfit, inspired by The ALLMAN BROTHERS and FREE. • **Songwriters:** Bulk by VAN ZANT + COLLINS or VAN ZANT + GAINES after '75. When they re-formed in '87, ROSSINGTON, KING and the new VAN ZANDT contributed all. Covered; HONKY TONK NIGHT TIME MAN (Merle Haggard) / SAME OLD BLUES + CALL ME THE BREEZE (J.J. Cale) / CROSSROADS (Robert Johnson) / etc. • **Trivia:** RONNIE's little brother DONNIE formed similiarly boogiefied • 38 SPECIAL.

Recommended: FREEBIRD – THE VERY BEST OF . . .(*8)

RONNIE VAN ZANT (b.15 Jan'49) – vocals / **GARY ROSSINGTON** – guitar / **ALLEN COLLINS** – guitar / **GREG WALKER** (or) **LEON WILKESON** – bass / **RICKY MEDLOCKE** (or) **BOB BURNS** – drums

not issued Shade Tree

1971. (7") **I'VE BEEN YOUR FOOL. / GOTTA GO** [-] [ ]
(UK iss. Oct82 on 'Me'.)

— **ED KING** – bass (ex-STRAWBERRY ALARM CLOCK) repl. LEON & GREG / added **BILLY POWELL** – piano (RICKY MEDLOCKE had now formed BLACKFOOT, after contributing vox + drums on 2 tracks 'White Dove' & 'The Seasons')

M.C.A. M.C.A.

Nov 73. (7") **GIMME THREE STEPS. / MR. BANKER** [-] [ ]
Jan 74. (lp)(c) **PRONOUNCED LEH-NERD SKIN-NERD** [ ] [ ] Nov 73
– I ain't the one / Tuesday's gone / Gimme three steps / Simple man / Things goin' on / Tuesday's gone / Mississippi kid / oison whiskey / Free bird. *(re-iss.Jun84, cd-iss. Jul88) (was US hit No.27 in Feb75)*

— added returning **LEON WILKESON** – bass (ED KING now 3rd guitarist)

May 74. (7") **DON'T ASK ME NO QUESTIONS. / TAKE YOUR TIME** [ ] [ ] Jan 74
Oct 74. (lp)(c) **SECOND HELPING** [ ] [12] May 74
– Sweet home Alabama / I need you / Don't ask me questions / Workin' for MCA / The ballad of Curtis Loew / Swamp music / The needle and the spoon / Call me the breeze. *(re-iss.1983, cd-iss.Aug89) (re-iss.Oct87 on 'Fame')*
Oct 74. (7") **SWEET HOME ALABAMA. / TAKE YOUR TIME** [ ] [8] Jul 74
Nov 74. (7") **FREE BIRD (edit). / DOWN SOUTH JUKIN'** [-] [19]
(UK-iss.Jan77)

— (Dec74) **ARTIMUS PYLE** – drums repl. BURNS

May 75. (lp)(c) **NUTHIN' FANCY** [43] [9] Apr 75
– Saturday night special / Cheatin' woman / Railroad song / I'm a country boy / On the hunt / Am I losin' / Made in the shade / Whiskey rock-a-roller. *(re-iss.1983, cd-iss.Aug87)*
Jul 75. (7") **SATURDAY NIGHT SPECIAL. / MADE IN THE SHADE** [ ] [27] May 75

— Reverted to six-piece, when ED KING departed. / Added backing vocalists **CASSIE GAINES, LESLIE HAWKINS & JO JO BILLINGSLEY**

Feb 76. (7") **DOUBLE TROUBLE. / ROLL GYPSY ROLL** [ ] [80]
Mar 76. (lp)(c) **GIMME BACK MY BULLETS** [34] [20] Feb 76
– Gimme back my bullets / Every mother's son / Trust / I got the same old blues / Double trouble / Roll gypsy roll / Searching / Cry for the bad man / All I can do is write about it. *(re-iss.Feb82)*
Jun 76. (7") **GIMME BACK MY BULLETS. / ALL I CAN DO IS WRITE ABOUT IT** [-] [ ]

— added **STEVE GAINES** – 3rd guitar (ex-SMOKEHOUSE)

Oct 76. (7") **TRAVELIN' MAN (live). / GIMME THREE STEPS (live)** [-] [ ]
Oct 76. (d-lp)(d-c) **ONE MORE FOR THE ROAD (live)** [17] [9] Sep 76
– Workin' for MCA / I ain't the one / Searching / Tuesday's gone / Saturday night special / Travelin' man / Whiskey rock-a-roller / Sweet home Alabama / Gimme three steps / Call me he breeze / T for Texas / The needle and the spoon / Crossroads / Free bird. *(US cd-iss. 1991 with edited applause)*
Dec 76. (7") **FREE BIRD (live). / SEARCHING (live)** [-] [38]
Oct 77. (lp)(c) **STREET SURVIVORS** [13] [5]
– What's your name / That smell / One more time / I know a little / You got that right / I never dreamed / Honky tonk night time man / Ain't no good life. *(re-iss.Jul82)*

— On 20th Oct'77, a few days after release of above album, the band's tour plane crashed. RONNIE VAN ZANT, STEVE & CASSIE GAINES plus roadie DEAN KILPATRICK were all killed. The remainder all suffered other injuries, but will recover. ARTIMUS went solo, the rest became ROSSINGTON-COLLINS BAND.

Jan 78. (7") **WHAT'S YOUR NAME. / I KNOW A LITTLE** [ ] [13] Dec 77
Mar 78. (7") **YOU GOT THAT RIGHT. / AIN'T NO GOOD LIFE** [-] [69]

ROSSINGTON-COLLINS BAND

formed 1979 by **GARY & ALLEN** with **BILLY POWELL** – keyboards / **LEON WILKESON** – bass / **DALE KRANTZ** – vocals / **BARRY HAREWOOD** – guitars, slide / **DEREK HASS** – drums, percussion

M.C.A. M.C.A.

Jul 80. (lp)(c) **ANYTIME, ANYPLACE, ANYWHERE** [ ] [13]
– Prime time / Three times as bad / Don't misunderstand me / Misery loves company / One good man / Opportunity / Getaway / Winners and losers / Sometimes you can put it out. *(re-iss.1983)*
Aug 80. (7") **DON'T MISUNDERSTAND ME. / WINNERS AND LOSERS** [ ] [55]
Oct 80. (7") **GETAWAY. / SOMETIMES YOU CAN PUT IT OUT** [-] [ ]
Oct 80. (7") **ONE GOOD MAN. / MISERY LOVES COMPANY** [ ] [-]
Jun 81. (7") **GOTTA GET IT STRAIGHT. / DON'T STOP ME NOW** [-] [ ]
Oct 81. (lp)(c) **THIS IS THE WAY** [ ] [24]
– Gotta get it straight / Teshawana / Gonna miss it when it's gone / Pine box / Fancy ideas / Don't stop me now / Seems like every day / I'm free today / Next phone call / Means nothing to you.
Oct 81. (7")(12") **TESHAWANA. / GONNA MISS IT WHEN IT'S GONE** [ ] [ ]

ROSSINGTON

with **GARY** & his wife **DALE** with **HASS** – drums / **JAY JOHNSON** – guitar / **TIM LINDSAY** – bass

Atlantic Atlantic

Nov 86. (lp)(c) **RETURNED TO THE SCENE OF THE CRIME** [-] [ ]
– Turn it up / Honest hearts / God luck to you / Wounded again / Waiting in the shadows / Dangerous love / Can you forget about my love / Returned to the scene of the crime / Are you leaving me / Path less chosen.
Nov 86. (7") **TURN IT UP. / PATH LESS CHOSEN** [-] [ ]

The ROSSINGTON BAND

with **TIM LINDSEY** – bass / **TIM SHARPTON** – keyboards / **RONNIE EADES** – sax / **MITCH RIGER** – drums

M.C.A. M.C.A.

Jul 88. (lp)(c)(cd) **LOVE YOUR MAN** [ ] [ ]
– Losin' control / Welcome me home / Call it love / Holdin' my own / Rock on / Love your man / Stay with me / Nowhere to run / Say it from the heart / I don't want to leave you.

ALLEN COLLINS BAND

with **COLLINS, HAREWOOD, POWELL, WILKESON, HESS,** plus **JIMMY DOUGHERTY** – vocals / **RANDALL HALL** – guitar

M.C.A. M.C.A.

1983. (lp)(c) **HERE THERE AND BACK** [-] [ ]
– Just trouble / One known soldier / Hangin' judge / Time after time / This ride's on me / Ready to move / Chapter one / Commitments / Everything you need.

— After spell in prison, POWELL joined Christian band VISION. Also in 1986, ALLEN COLLINS was involved in a car crash which killed his girlfriend, and paralized himself from the waist down. On the 23rd Jan'90 he died of pneumonia.

LYNYRD SKYNYRD

re-formed Autumn 1987, (ROSSINGTON, POWELL, PYLE, WILKESON, KING plus **DALE KRANTZ ROSSINGTON, RANDALL HALL** and **JOHNNY VAN ZANT.)**

M.C.A. M.C.A.

Apr 88. (d-lp)(c)(cd) **SOUTHERN BY THE GRACE OF GOD (live)** [ ] [68]
– (intro) / Workin' for MCA / That smell / I know a little / Comin' home / You got that right / What's your name / Gimme back my bullets / Swamp music / Call me the breeze / Dixie – Sweet home Alabama / Free bird.

— **LYNYRD SKYNYRD** re-formed again in 1991. **ROSSINGTON, KING** and **HALL** – guitars / **JOHNNY VAN ZANT** – vocals / **POWELL** – keyboards / **WILKESON** – bass / **PYLE** – percussion, drums / **CUSTER** – drums, percussion

Atlantic Atlantic

Jun 91. (cd)(c)(lp) **LYNYRD SKYNYRD 1991** [ ] [64]
– Smokestack lightning / Keeping the faith / Southern women / Pure & simple / I've seen enough / Backstreet crawler / Good thing / Money man / It's a killer / Mama (afraid to say goodbye) / End of the road. *(re-iss.cd Feb95)*

— extended members **JERRY JONES** – bass, guitar / **DALE KRANTZ-ROSSINGTON** – backing vocals repl. ARTIMUS PYLE

Mar 93. (cd)(c) **THE LAST REBEL** [ ] [64]
– Good lovin's hard to find / One thing / Can't take that away / Best things in life / The last rebel / Outta Hell in my Dodge / Kiss your freedom goodbye / South of Heaven / Love don't always come easy / Born to run. *(re-iss.cd Feb95)*

– compilations, others, etc. –

All 'MCA' unless stated.

Aug 76. (7"m) **FREE BIRD. / SWEET HOME ALABAMA / DOUBLE TROUBLE** [31] [-]
(re-iss.Dec79 hit No.43, re-iss.May82 hit No.21, re-iss.12" +12"pic-d. Dec83)
Oct 78. (lp)(c) **SKYNYRD'S FIRST AND LAST** (rec.1970-72) [50] [15] Sep 78
– Down south jukin' / Preacher's daughter / White dove / Was I right or wrong /

Lend a helpin' hand / Wino / Comin' home / The seasons / Things goin' on. *(re-iss.Aug81)*

Oct 78. (7") **DOWN SOUTH JUKIN'. / WINO** | - | |

Oct 78. (7"ep) **DOWN SOUTH JUKIN' / THAT SMELL. / LEND A HELPIN' HAND / CALL ME THE BREEZE** | | - |

Jan 80. (d-lp)(d-c) **GOLD AND PLATINUM** | 49 | 12 Dec 79

– Down south jukin' / Saturday night special / Gimme three steps / What's your name / You got that right / Gimme back my bullets / Sweet home Alabama / Free bird / That smell / On the hunt / I ain't the one / Whiskey rock-a-roller / Simple man / I know a little / Tuesday's gone / Comin' home. *(re-iss.Jul82)*

Apr 82. (d-c) **PRONOUNCED LEH-NERD SKIN-NERD / SECOND HELPING** | | - |

Nov 82. (lp)(c) **THE BEST OF THE REST** | - | |

Sep 86. (d-c)**NUTHIN' FANCY / GIVE ME BACK MY BULLETS** | | |

1987. (7") **WHEN YOU GOT GOOD FRIENDS. / TRUCK DRIVIN' MAN** | - | |

Nov 87. (lp)(c)(cd) **LEGEND (rare live)** | | 41 Oct 87

– Georgia peaches / When you got good friends / Sweet little Missy / Four walls of Ralford / Simple man / Truck drivin' man / One in the sun / Mr. Banker / Take your time.

Apr 89. (lp)(c)(cd) **SKYNYRD'S INNYRDS** | | |

Feb 92. (3xcd)(3xc)(3xlp) **THE DEFINITIVE LYNYRD SKYNYRD COLLECTION** | | |

Jul 84. Old Gold; (7") **FREE BIRD. / SWEET HOME ALABAMA** | | - |

(re-iss.7"/12".Jan89 on 'M.C.A.')

Mar 87. Raw Power; (d-lp)(c) **ANTHOLOGY** | | - |

Mar 94. Nectar; (cd)(c) **FREEBIRD – THE VERY BEST** | | - |

– Saturday night special / Whiskey rock & roller / Workin' for MCA / I ain't the one / Sweet home Alabama / Ballad of Curtis Loew / Tuesday's gone / Gimme 3 steps / The needle & the spoon / Free bird / Call me the breeze / What's your name / Swamp music / Gimme back my bullets / That smell / You got that right.

Sep 94. MCA; (cd)(c) **STREET SURVIVORS / FIRST AND LAST** | | |

Aug 95. Old Gold; (cd-s) **FREE BIRD / SWEET HOME ALABAMA** | | - |

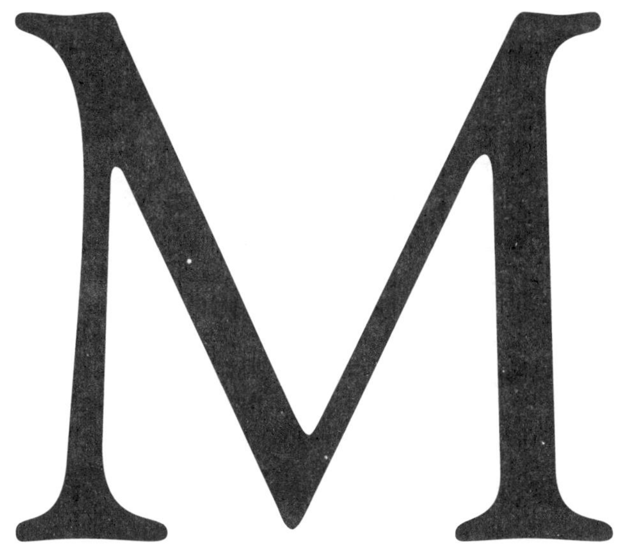

Shane MacGOWAN & THE POPES

Formed: King's Cross area, London, England . . . early 1994 by ex-NIPPLE ERECTORS (1978), ex-NIPS (1978-81) & ex-POGUES (1983-1991) frontman SHANE (b.25 Dec'57, Kent, England). Late in 1992, he teamed up with friend NICK CAVE on an inerpretation of 'What A Wonderful World'. His new outfit were a hit immediately, after POGUEY-like uptempo single 'CHURCH OF THE HOLY SPOOK' broke the Top 75. • **Style:** Due to MacGOWAN's presence, they were gladly welcomed as the new POGUES in 1994, when the real POGUES were absent from recording studio. • **Songwriters:** MacGOWAN except HER FATHER DIDN'T LIKE ME ANYWAY (Gerry Rafferty) / CRACKLIN' ROSIE (Neil Diamond) / THE RISING OF THE MOON + NANCY WHISKEY (trad.). • **Trivia:** Actor JOHNNY DEPP played guitar on their Top Of The Pops debut. Their /his debut album also featured guest appearances from ex-POGUES; SPIDER and FINER, plus DUBLINERS musician /friend BARNEY McKENNA. 'VICTORIA' was written about his recent writer girlfriend VICTORIA CLARKE. MacGOWAN is still a reader & fan of writer JAMES JOYCE and Spanish poet LORCA.

Recommended: THE SNAKE (*8)

SHANE McGOWAN – vocals (ex-POGUES, ex-NIPS) / **PAUL McGUINNESS** – guitar / **BERNIE FRANCE** – bass / **DANNY POPE** – drums / **TOM NcMANAMON** – banjo

		Z.T.T.	Warners
Sep 94.	(7")(c-s) **THE CHURCH OF THE HOLY SPOOK. / RAKE AT THE GATES OF HELL** (cd-s+=) – King of the bop / Nancy Whiskey.	74	
Oct 94.	(c-s) **THAT WOMAN'S GOT ME DRINKING. / HER FATHER DIDN'T LIKE ME ANYWAY** (12"+=)(cd-s+=) – Roddy McCorley / Minstrel boy.	34	
Oct 94.	(cd)(c)(lp) **THE SNAKE** – The church of the holy spook / That woman's got me drinking / The song with no name / Aisling / I'll be your handbag / Her father didn't like me anyway / A Mexican funeral in Paris / The snake with the eyes of Garnet / Donegal express / Victoria / The rising of the Moon / Bring down the lamp. *(re-iss.cd/c Jun95)* – Haunted (with SINEAD O'CONNOR) / You're the one (with MAIRE BRENNAN) / Cracklin' Rosie / Bring down the . . .	37	
Dec 94.	(c-s) **THE SONG WITH NO NAME. / NANCY WHISKEY** (12"+=)(cd-s+=) – Cracklin' Rosie.		
Apr 95.	(c-s) **HAUNTED. ("SHANE MacGOWAN & SINEAD O'CONNOR") / THE SONG WITH NO NAME** (cd-s+=)(12"+=) – Bring down the . . . / Cracklin' Rosie.	30	
Jun 95.	(c-s) **YOU'RE THE ONE. ("SHANE MacGOWAN & MAIRE BRENNAN") / AISLING** (cd-s) – Victoria.		

. . . Jan – Jun '96 stop press . . .

Apr 96.	(single) **MY WAY**	29	

MACHINE HEAD

Formed: Oakland, California, USA . . .mid '92 by (see below). In 1994, they unleashed what was to become one of Kerrang magazine favourite albums; 'BURN MY EYES'. • **Style:** Hard-metal similar to BIOHAZARD or ANTHRAX. • **Songwriters:** Group (FLYNN – lyrics) except 1 by POISON IDEA and CRO-MAGS.

Recommended: BURN MY EYES (*8)

ROBB FLYNN – vocals, guitar (ex-VIOLENCE) / **LOGAN MADER** – guitar / **ADAM DUCE** – bass / **CHRIS KONTOS** -drums

		Road-runner	Road-runner
Aug 94.	(cd)(c)(lp) **BURN MY EYES** – Davidian / Old / A thousand lies / None but my own / The rage to overcome / Death church / A nation on fire / Blood for blood / I'm your god now / Real eyes, realize, real lies / Block.	25	
Oct 94.	(12") **INFECTED. / PROTOPLAN** *(re-iss.Jun95)*		
May 95.	(10"pic-d-ep) **OLD / A NATION ON FIRE (demo) / REAL LIES – FUCK IT ALL (demo) / OLD (demo)** (cd-ep) – ('A'side) / Davidian (live) / Hard times (live) / Death church (demo). (cd-s) – ('A'side) / Death church (convent mix) / Old (eve of apocalypse mix) / The rage to overcome.	43	
Aug 95.	(10"pic-d) **DEATH CHURCH. / A NATION ON FIRE (demo)** (cd-s+=) – Fuck it all (demo) / Old (demo). (cd-s) – ('A'side) / Old (mix) / The rage to overcome (demo).		

Andy MACKAY (see under ⇒ ROXY MUSIC)

MAD SEASON (see under ⇒ ALICE IN CHAINS)

MANIC STREET PREACHERS

Formed: Blackwood, Gwent, South Wales . . . 1988 by JAMES DEAN BRADFIELD and cousin SEAN MOORE. They quickly found former school friends RICHEY and NICKY, and set about recording self-financed debut 45 'SUICIDE ALLEY'. After another indie 45 in 1990, they signed to 'Heavenly', where they had 2 minor UK hits. In summer of '91, after being snapped up by 'Columbia', they had first entry into the Top 40 with 'STAY BEAUTIFUL'. Darlings of the music press, they soon had Top 20 debut double lp 'GENERATION TERRORISTS' early '92. • **Style:** Talented heavy/punk outfit, taking influences from The CLASH, The ALARM or GUNS'N'ROSES. • **Songwriters:** NICKY + RICHEY lyrics, SEAN & JAMES music. Covered; IT'S SO EASY (Guns'n'Roses) / UNDER MY WHEELS (Alice Cooper) / SUICIDE IS PAINLESS (Theme from 'Mash') / CHARLES WINDSOR (McCarthy) / THE DROWNERS (Suede) / STAY WITH ME (Faces) / WROTE FOR LUCK (Happy Mondays) / RAINDROPS KEEP FALLING ON MY HEAD (Bacharach-David). • **Trivia:** LITTLE BABY NOTHING featured porn star Traci Lords on guest vocals.

Recommended: GENERATION TERRORISTS (*8) / GOLD AGAINST THE SOUL (*9) / THE HOLY BIBLE (*8) / EVERYTHING MUST GO (*9).

JAMES DEAN BRADFIELD (b.21 Feb'69) – vocals, guitar / **RICHEY EDWARDS** (b.27 Dec'69) – rhythm guitar / **NICKY WIRE** (b.JONES) – bass / **SEAN MOORE** (b.30 Jul'70) – drums

		S.B.S.	not issued
Aug 89.	(7") **SUICIDE ALLEY. / TENNESSEE (I FEEL SO LOW)**		-
		Damaged Goods	**not issued**
Jun 90.	(12"ep) **NEW ART RIOT** – New art riot / Stip it down / Last exit on yesterday / Teenage 20-20. *(re-iss.12"pink/cd-ep.Dec91) (re-iss.12"/cd-ep Jul93)*		-
		Heavenly	**not issued**
Jan 91.	(12"ep)(cd-ep) **MOTOWN JUNK. / SORROW 16 / WE HER MAJESTY'S PRISONERS**	92	-
May 91.	(7") **YOU LOVE US. / SPECTATORS OF SUICIDE** (12"+=)(cd-s+=) – Starlover / Strip it down (live).	62	-
		Columbia	**Columbia**
Jul 91.	(7") **STAY BEAUTIFUL. / R.P. McMURPHY** (12"+=)(cd-s+=) – Soul contamination. (US-cd-ep+=) – Motown junk / Sorrow 16 / Star lover.	40	
Nov 91.	(7") **LOVE'S SWEET EXILE. / REPEAT** (12"+=)(cd-s+=) – Democracy coma. (12"ltd.++=) – Stay beautiful (live).	26	
Jan 92.	(7") **YOU LOVE US. / A VISION OF DEAD DESIRE**	16	

(12"+=) – It's so easy.
(cd-s++=) – We want majesty's prisoners.

Feb 92. (cd)(d-c)(d-lp)(pic-d-lp) **GENERATION TERRORISTS** [13] [ ]
– Slash'n'burn / Nat West-Barclays-Midland-Lloyds / Born to end / Motorcycle emptiness / You love us / Love's sweet exile / Little baby nothing / Repeat (stars and stripes) / Tennessee / Another invented disease / Stay beautiful / So dead / Repeat (UK) / Spectators of suicide / Damn dog / Crucifix kiss / Methadone pretty / Condemned to rock'n'roll.

Mar 92. (7")(c-s) **SLASH'N'BURN. / AIN'T GOING DOWN** [20] [ ]
(12"+=) – Motown junk.
(cd-s++=) – ('A'version).

Jun 92. (7")(c-s) **MOTORCYCLE EMPTINESS. / BORED OUT OF MY MIND** [17] [ ]
(12"pic-d+=) – Under my wheels.
(cd-s++=) – Crucifix kiss (live).

Sep 92. (7")(cd-s) **SUICIDE IS PAINLESS (Mash mix). / ('b'side by 'Fatima Mansions' – Everything I Do (I Do It For You)** [7] [ ]

Nov 92. (7") **LITTLE BABY NOTHING. / SUICIDE ALLEY** [29] [ ]
(12"+=)(cd-s+=) – Yankee drawl / Never want again.

Jun 93. (c-s) **FROM DESPAIR TO WHERE. / HIBERNATION** [25] [ ]
(12"+=) – Spectators of suicide (Heavenly version).
(cd-s+=) – Star lover (Heavenly version).

Jun 93. (cd)(c)(lp) **GOLD AGAINST THE SOUL** [8] [ ]
– Sleepflower / From despair to where / La tristesse durera (scream to a sigh) / Yourself / Life becoming a landslide / Drug drug druggy / Roses in the hospital / Nostalgic pushead / Symphony of tourette / Gold against the soul.

Jul 93. (7")(c-s) **LA TRISTESSE DURERA (SCREAM TO A SIGH). / PATRICK BATEMAN** [22] [ ]
(12"+=) – Repeat (live) / Tennessee.
(cd-s+=) – What's my name (live) / Slash'n'burn (live).

Sep 93. (7")(c-s) **ROSES IN THE HOSPITAL. / US AGAINST YOU / DONKEY** [15] [ ]
(cd-s+=) – Wrote for luck.
(12") – ('A'side) / (5-'A' mixes).

Jan 94. (c-s) **LIFE BECOMING A LANDSLIDE EP** [36] [ ]
– Landslide / Comfort comes.
(12"+=) – Are mothers saints.
(cd-s++=) – Charles Windsor.

Jun 94. (7")(c-s)(10")(cd-s) **FASTER. / P.C.P.** [16] [ ]

Aug 94. (10")(c-s) **REVOL. / TOO COLD HERE** [22] [ ]
(cd-s+=) – You love us (original Heavenly version) / Love's sweet exile (live).
(cd-s) – ('A'side) / (3 live at Glastonbury tracks).

— RICHEY booked himself into a health clinic, after wasting himself down to 5 stone.

Aug 94. (cd)(c)(pic-lp) **THE HOLY BIBLE** [6] [ ]
– Yes / Ifwhiteamericatoldthetruthforonedayit'sworldwouldfallapart / Of walking abortion / She is suffering / Archives of pain / Revol / 4st 7lb / Mausoleum / Faster / This is yesterday / Die in the summertime / The intense humming of evil / P.C.P.

Oct 94. (10")(c-s) **SHE IS SUFFERING. / LOVE TORN US UNDER (acoustic)** [25] [ ]
(cd-s+=) – The drowners / Stay with me (both live w/ BERNARD BUTLER).
(cd-s) – ('A'side) / La tristesse durera (scream to a sigh) / Faster (Dust Brothers remixes).

— RICHEY was now fully recuperated . . . but on 1st Feb '95, he went AWOL again after walking out of London's Embassy Hotel at 7 that morning. Two weeks later, his car was found abandoned and after police frog search the Severn, it was believed he might be dead. By the end of 1995, with RICHEY still missing, the group carried on as a trio.

— Meantime, BRADFIELD produced the debut of hits to be NORTHERN UPROAR.

. . . Jan – Jun '96 stop press . . .

Apr 96. (single) **A DESIGN FOR LIFE** [2] [ ]
May 96. (cd)(c)(lp) **EVERYTHING MUST GO** [2] [ ]

Aimee MANN

Born: Boston, Massachusetts, USA. From 1984-89, she fronted local pop-rock group 'TIL TUESDAY, who had large US hit with 'VOICES CARRY'. They disbanded due to corporate record label pressures. She returned in 1993, with a debut solo release, that was lawded by many especially fan ELVIS COSTELLO. • **Style:** Her eclectic pop was quite close to PRETENDERS. • **Songwriters:** JULES SHEAR wrote for 'TIL TUESDAY, AIMEE co-wrote her solo album with ELVIS COSTELLO. Five years previous, he had guested on 'TIL TUESDAY's final album. • **Trivia:** 'TIL TUESDAY were produced by RHETT DAVIES apart from debut which was MIKE THORNE. In 1987, she guested on RUSH's hit single 'Time Stand Still'.

Recommended: WHATEVER (*7) / I'M WITH STUPID (*6)

'TIL TUESDAY

AIMEE MANN – vocals, bass / **ROBERT HOLMES** – guitar, vocals / **JOEY PESCE** – synthesizers, piano, vocals / **MICHAEL HAUSMANN** – drums, percussion

Epic Epic

Apr 85. (7") **VOICES CARRY. / ARE YOU SERIOUS** [ ] [8]

Jun 85. (lp)(c) **VOICES CARRY** [ ] [19] Apr85
– Love in a vacuum / Looking over my shoulder / I could get used to this / No more crying / Voices carry / Winning the war / You know the rest / Maybe Monday / Don't watch me bleed / Sleep. *(cd-iss.1988)*

Aug 85. (7") **LOOKING OVER MY SHOULDER. / DON'T WATCH ME BLEED** [-] [61]

Oct 85. (7") **LOVE IN A VACUUM. / NO MORE CRYING** [-] [ ]

Jan 87. (lp)(c)(cd) **WELCOME HOME** [ ] [49] Oct86
– What about love / Coming up close / On Sunday / Will she just fall down / David denies / Lover's day / Have mercy / Sleeping and walking / Angels never call / No one is watching you now.

Feb 87. (7") **WHAT ABOUT LOVE. / WILL SHE JUST FALL DOWN** [ ] [26] Sep86
– ('A'extended-12"+=) – Voices carry.

Apr 87. (7") **COMING UP CLOSE. / ANGELS NEVER CALL** [-] [59]

— **MICHAEL MONTES** – keyboards / + sessioners **MARCUS MILLER** – bass / **HAERYUNG SHIN** – violin / **PETER ABRAMS** – French horn / **MIKE DENNEEN** – keyboards repl. PESCE

Jan 89. (7") **(BELIEVED YOU WERE) LUCKY. / LIMITS TO LOVE** [ ] [95]
(12"+=)(cd-s+=) – Voices carry / What about love.

Mar 89. (lp)(c)(cd) **EVERYTHING'S DIFFERENT NOW** [ ] [ ] Nov88
– Everything's different now / R.I.P. in Heaven / Why must I / J for Jules / (Believed you were) Lucky / Limits to love / Long gone (buddy) / The other end (of the telescope) / Crash and burn / How can you give up.

Jul 89. (7") **R. I. P. IN HEAVEN. / HOW CAN YOU GIVE UP** [-] [ ]

— Disbanded after above album.

AIMEE MANN

solo with **DAVE GREGORY** – guitar (of XTC)

Imago Imago

Aug 93. (7")(c-s) **I SHOULD'VE KNOWN. / JIMMY HOFFA JOKES** [55] [ ]
(cd-s+=) – Jacob Marley's chains.

Sep 93. (cd)(c)(lp) **WHATEVER** [39] [ ]
– I should've known / Fifty years after the fair / 4th of July / Could've been anyone / Put me on top / Stupid thing / Say anything / Jacob Marley's chain / Mr. Harris / I could hurt you now / I know there's a word / I've had it / Way back when.

Nov 93. (7")(c-s) **STUPID THING. / I'VE HAD IT** [47] [ ]
(cd-s) – ('A'side) / Baby blue / Telescope / Say anything.
(cd-s) – ('A'side) / Put me on top / 4th of July / I should've known (all live).

Feb 94. (7")(c-s) **I SHOULD'VE KNOWN. / TRUTH ON MY SIDE** [45] [ ]
(cd-s+=) – Fifty years after the fair / Put on some speed.
(10") – ('A'side) / 4th July / Stupid thing / The other end (of the telescope).

— with **JON BRION** -guitars, drums, co-writer (some) / **JOHN SANDS -drums / guests BERNARD BUTLER** (co-writer SUGARCOATED) / **GLENN TILBROOK + CHRIS DIFFORD / JULIANA HATFIELD / MICHAEL PENN**

Geffen Geffen

Jan 95. (c-s)(cd-s) **THAT'S JUST WHAT YOU ARE /** [-] [93]

Nov 95. (cd)(c) **I'M WITH STUPID** [51] [82]
– Long shot / Choice in the matter / Sugarcoated / You could make a killing / Superball / Amateur / All over now / Par for the course / You're with stupid now / That's just what you are / Frankenstein / Ray / It's not safe.

. . . Jan – Jun '96 stop press . . .

Apr 96. (single) **LONG SHOT** [ ] [ ]

Manfred MANN

Formed: as MANFRED MANN, the group, London, England . . . late '62, initially as The MANN-HUGG BLUES BAND, by namesake MANFRED MANN and MIKE HUGG. They recruited DAVE RICHMOND, PAUL JONES and MIKE VICKERS, and played local gigs which attracted EMI's subsidiary label 'HMV' to sign them. Early 1964 after 2 flops, they had first chart success, with UK Top 5 single '5-4-3-2-1'. They continued to storm charts throughout the 60's, and hit UK top spot 3 times with 'DOO WAH DIDDY DIDDY', 'PRETTY FLAMINGO' & 'THE MIGHTY QUINN'. In 1969, MANN and HUGG wrote commercial jingles for Michelen and Ski yogurt, before forming MANFRED MANN CHAPTER THREE. They made a couple of lp's for 'Vertigo', but soon reverted to original name in '71. The following year, they re-emerged without HUGG, in the more adventurous MANFRED MANN'S EARTH BAND. They struggled initially, although they had 3 fine UK Top 10 singles in the 70's 'JOYBRINGER', 'BLINDED BY THE LIGHT' & 'DAVY'S ON THE ROAD AGAIN'. Continued to surface during the 80's, and had a Top 30 US single 'THE RUNNER'. • **Style:** R&B pop group, excelled by JONES' harmonica playing until '66. In the 70's, the EARTH BAND were a more heavy synth-band, although they did not disregard hit-making cover versions. • **Songwriters:** MANN-HUGG until latter's departure in '71. Covered; DOO WAH DIDDY DIDDY (Exciters) / SHA LA LA (Shirelles) / OH NO NOT MY BABY (Goffin-King) / SMOKESTACK LIGHTNING (Howlin' Wolf) / MY LITTLE RED BOOK (Bacharach-David) / WITH GOD ON OUR SIDE + IF YOU GOTTA GO, GO NOW + JUST LIKE A WOMAN + THE MIGHTY QUINN + PLEASE, MRS.HENRY + others (Bob Dylan) / SWEET PEA (Tommy Roe) / SO LONG DAD + LIVING WITHOUT YOU (Randy Newman) / MY NAME IS JACK (John Simon) / etc. His EARTH BAND covered JOYBRINGER (adapt. Gustav Holst 'The Planets') / FATHER OF DAY, FATHER OF NIGHT + YOU, ANGEL YOU (Bob Dylan) / SPIRIT IN THE NIGHT + BLINDED BY THE LIGHT + FOR YOU (Bruce Springsteen) / DON'T KILL IT CAROL (Mike Heron) / REDEPTION SONG (Bob Marley) / DO ANYTHING YOU WANNA DO (Eddie & The Hot Rods) / GOING UNDERGROUND (Jam) / BANQUET (Joni Mitchell) / etc. • **Trivia:** MIKE HUGG wrote 'SHAPES OF THINGS' in 1966 for fellow R&B hitmakers The YARDBIRDS. MANFRED guested Moog synthsizer on URIAH HEEP's 1971 album 'Look At Yourself'. 'GLORIFIED MAGNIFIED' track was used for the theme to Radio 1's 'Sound Of The 70's'.

Recommended: AGES OF MANN (22 CLASSICS OF THE 60s) (*8) / 20 YEARS OF MANFRED MANN'S EARTH BAND (*6).

MANFRED MANN (b.MICHAEL LUBOWITZ, 21 Oct'40, Johannesburg, S.Africa) – keys / **PAUL JONES** (b.PAUL POND, 24 Feb'42, Portsmouth, England) – vocals, harmonica / **MIKE VICKERS** (b.18 Apr'41, Southampton, England) – guitar / **DAVE RICHMOND** – bass / **MIKE HUGG** (b.11 Aug'42, Andover, England) – drums

H.M.V. Prestige

Jul 63. (7") **WHY SHOULD WE NOT. / BROTHER JACK** [ ] [-]
Oct 63. (7") **COCK-A-HOOP. / NOW YOU'RE NEEDING ME** [ ] [-]

— **TOM McGUINESS** (b. 2 Dec'41, Wimbledon, London, England) – bass (ex-ROOSTERS) repl. RICHMOND

Jan 64. (7") **5-4-3-2-1. / WITHOUT YOU** [5] [ ] Mar 64

H.M.V. Ascot

Apr 64. (7") **HUBBLE BUBBLE TOIL AND TROUBLE. / I'M YOUR KINGPIN** [11] [ ]
Jul 64. (7") **DOO WAH DIDDY DIDDY. / WHAT YOU GONNA DO** [1] [1] Aug 64
(re-iss.Oct82)
Sep 64. (lp) **THE FIVE FACES OF MANFRED MANN** [3] [ ] Feb 65
– Smokestack lightning / Don't ask me what I say / It's gonna work out fine / Sack of wool / What you gonna do / I'm your kingpin / Hoochie coochie / Down the road apiece / I've got my mojo working / Mr. Analles / Untie me / Bring it to Jerome / Without you / You've got to take it.
Oct 64. (7") **SHA LA LA. / JOHN HARDY** [3] [12] Nov 64
Nov 64. (lp) **MANFRED MANN ALBUM** [-] [35]
– (singles compilation)
– (* tracks I'm your kingpin , Mr.Anello & You've got to take it were repl. by Do wah diddy diddy on US version)
Jan 65. (7") **COME TOMORROW. / WHAT DID I DO WRONG** [4] [50] Feb 65
Apr 65. (7") **OH NO NOT MY BABY. / WHAT AM I DOING WRONG** [11] [ ]
Apr 65. (7") **POISON IVY. / I CAN'T BELIEVE WHAT YOU SAY** [-] [ ]
Jun 65. (7") **MY LITTLE BOOK. / WHAT AM I DOING WRONG** [-] [-]
Jul 65. (lp) **MY LITTLE RED BOOK OF WINNERS** [-] [ ]
– My little red book / Oh no, not my baby / What am I to do / One in the middle / You gave me somebody to love / You're for me / Poison Ivy / Without you / Brother Jack / Love like yours / I can't believe what you say / With God on your side.
Sep 65. (7") **IF YOU GOTTA GO, GO NOW. / STAY AROUND** [2] [-]
Sep 65. (lp) **MANN MADE** [7] [ ]
– Since I don't have you / You're for me / Look away / L.S.D. / The abominable snowman / Watch your step / The way you do the things you do / Stormy Monday blues / Hi lili hi lo / I really do believe / Bear Hugg / You don't know me / I'll make it up to you. *(re-iss.Nov69 on 'Starline')*
Oct 65. (7") **IF YOU GOTTA GO, GO NOW. / THE ONE IN THE MIDDLE** [-] [ ]
Jan 66. (7") **HI LILI, HI LO. / SHE NEEDS COMPANY** [-] [ ]

— (PETE BURFORD and DAVID HYDE deputised for VICKERS on tour until) / **JACK BRUCE** – bass (ex-JOHN MAYALL, ex-GRAHAM BOND) repl. VICKERS added / **LYN DOBSON** – saxophone / **HENRY LOWTHER** – trumpet (McGUINESS now guitar)

H.M.V. United Art

Apr 66. (7") **PRETTY FLAMINGO. / YOU'RE STANDING BY** [1] [29] Jul 66

— **MANN, HUGG** and **McGUINESS** added new members **MIKE D'ABO** (b. 1 Mar'44, England) – vocals (ex-BAND OF ANGELS) repl. JONES who went solo, etc. / **KLAUS VOORMAN** (b.29 Apr'42, Berlin, W.Germany) – bass repl. JACK BRUCE who formed CREAM.

Jun 66. (7") **YOU GAVE ME SOMEBODY TO LOVE. / POISON IVY** [36] [ ]

Fontana United Art.

Jul 66. (7") **JUST LIKE A WOMAN. / I WANNA BE RIGHT** [10] [-]
Oct 66. (7") **SEMI-DETACHED SUBURBAN MR. JAMES. / MORNING AFTER THE PARTY** [2] [ ]
Oct 66. (lp) **AS IS** (US title 'PRETTY FLAMINGO') [22] [ ]
– Trouble and tea/ A now and then thing / Each other's company / Box office draw / Dealer dealer / Morning after the party / Another kind of music / As long as I have lovin' / Autumn leaves / Superstitious guy / You're my girl / Just like a woman.
Mar 67. (7") **HA HA SAID THE CLOWN. / FEELING SO GOOD** [4] [ ]
May 67. (7") **SWEET PEA. / ONE WAY** [36] [ ]
Sep 67. (7") **SO LONG DAD. / FUNNIEST GIG** [ ] [ ]
Jan 68. (lp) **UP THE JUNCTION (Soundtrack)** [ ] [-]
– Up the junction (vocal) / Sing songs of love / Walking around up the junction (instrumental) / Love theme (instrumental) / Up the junction (vocal & instrumental) / Just for me / Love theme (instrumental) / Sheila's dance / Belgravia / Wailing horn / I need your love / Up the junction (vocal). *(re-iss.1970)*

Fontana Mercury

Jan 68. (7") **THE MIGHTY QUINN. / BY REQUEST EDWIN GARVEY** [1] [10]
Mar 68. (7") **UP THE JUNCTION. / SLEEPY HOLLOW** [ ] [ ]
Jun 68. (lp) **MIGHTY GARVEY** (US 'THE MIGHTY QUINN') [ ] [ ]
– Happy families / No better no worse / Each and every day / Country dancing / It's so easy falling / Happy families / Mighty Quinn / Big Betty / The vicar's daughter / Every day another hair turns grey / Cubist town / Ha! ha! said the clown / Harry the one-man band / Happy families.
Jun 68. (7") **MY NAME IS JACK. / THERE IS A MAN** [8] [ ]
Dec 68. (7") **FOX ON THE RUN. / TOO MANY PEOPLE** [5] [97]
May 69. (7") **RAGAMUFFIN MAN. / A 'B' SIDE** [8] [ ]

— split mid 69. TOM formed McGUINESS FLINT. D'ABO went solo, and VOORMAN joined The PLASTIC ONO BAND (see JOHN LENNON)

MANFRED MANN CHAPTER THREE

MANFRED retained **MIKE HUGG now** – vocals, electric piano. Recruited **BRIAN HUGG** – guitar / **STEVE YORK** – bass plus session singers, drummers and wind section.

Vertigo Polydor

Nov 69. (lp) **MANFRED MANN CHAPTER THREE** [ ] [ ]
– Travelling lady / Snakeskin garter / Konekuf / Sometimes / Devil woman / Time / One way glass / Mister you're a better man than I / Ain't it sad / A study in inaccuracy / Where am I going. *(cd-iss.Feb94 on 'Cohesion')*
Mar 70. (7") **SNAKESKIN GARTER. / SOMETIMES** [-] [ ]

— on session **CHRIS SLADE** – drums (alongside others)

Sep 70. (7") **HAPPY BEING ME. / DEVIL WOMAN** [ ] [ ]
Oct 70. (lp) **CHAPTER THREE, VOLUME TWO** [ ] [-]
– Lady Ace / I ain't laughing / Poor sad Sue / Jump before you think / It's good to be alive / Happy being me / Virginia. *(cd-iss.Feb94 on 'Cohesion')*

MANFRED MANN'S EARTH BAND

His new band now featured **CHRIS SLADE** – drums (now a full time member) / **MICK ROGERS** – vocals, guitar repl. MIKE HUGG / **COLIN PATTENDEN** – bass repl. STEVE YORK and BRIAN HUGG

Philips Polydor

Jun 71. (7") **LIVING WITHOUT YOU. / TRIBUTE** [ ] [69] Jan 72
Sep 71. (7") **PLEASE MRS. HENRY. / PRAYER** [ ] [ ]
Feb 72. (lp) **MANFRED MANN'S EARTH BAND** [ ] [ ]
– California coastline / Captain Bobby Stout / Sloth / Living without you / Tribute / Please Mrs. Henry / Jump sturdy / Prayer / Part time man / I'm up and leaving. *(re-iss.Apr77 & 1981 on 'Bronze') (cd-iss.Jan91 on 'Cohesion')*
Mar 72. (7") **PART TIME MAN. / I'M UP AND LEAVING** [-] [ ]
Sep 72. (lp) **GLORIFIED MAGNIFIED** [ ] [ ]
– Meat / Look around / One way glass / I'm gonna have you all / Down home / Our friend George / Ashes to the wind / It's all over now, baby blue / Glorified magnified. *(re-iss.Apr77 & 1981 on 'Bronze') (cd-iss.Dec93 on 'Cohesion')*
Nov 72. (7") **MEAT. / GLORIFIED MAGNIFIED** [ ] [ ]
Feb 73. (7") **IT'S ALL OVER NOW, BABY BLUE. / ASHES TO THE WIND** [-] [ ]

Vertigo Polydor

Apr 73. (7") **GET YOUR ROCKS OFF ("EARTH BAND"). / SADJOY** [ ] [-]
Jun 73. (lp) **MESSIN'** (US-title 'GET YOUR ROCKS OFF') [ ] [ ]
– Buddah / Messin' / Cloudy eyes / Get your rocks off / Sadjoy / Black and blue / Mardi Gras day. *(re-iss.Apr77 & 1981 on 'Bronze') (cd-iss.Jan91 on 'Cohesion')*

Jun 73. (7") **MARDI GRAS DAY. / SADJOY** [-] [ ]
Aug 73. (7") **GET YOUR ROCKS OFF. / ASHES TO THE WIND** [-] [ ]
Aug 73. (7") **JOYBRINGER. / CAN'T EAT MEAT** [9] [ ]
Sep 73. (7") **JOYBRINGER. / CLOUDY EYES** [-] [ ]

Bronze Polydor

Nov 73. (lp)(c) **SOLAR FIRE** [ ] [96]
– Father of night, in the beginning / Pluto the dog / Solar fire / Saturn (Mercury) / Earth the circle (pts.1 & 2). *(re-iss.Apr77 & 1981) (re-iss.Nov87 on 'Legacy') (cd-iss.Jan91 on 'Cohesion')*
Mar 74. (7") **FATHER OF DAY, FATHER OF NIGHT. / SOLAR FIRE 2** [ ] [ ]

Bronze Warners

Oct 74. (7") **BE NOT TOO HARD. / EARTH HYMN (part 2a)** [ ] [ ]
Oct 74. (lp)(c) **THE GOOD EARTH** [ ] [ ]
– Give me the good earth / Launching place / I'll be gone / Earth hymn (pts.1 & 2) / Sky high / Be not too hard. *(re-iss.Apr77 + 1981) (cd-iss.Dec93 on 'Cohesion')*
Jul 75. (7") **SPIRITS IN THE NIGHT. / AS ABOVE SO BELOW (part 2)** [ ] [97] Mar 76
Aug 75. (lp)(c) **NIGHTINGALES AND BOMBERS** [ ] [ ]
– Spirits in the night / Countdown / Time is right / Crossfade / Visionary mountains / Nightingales and bombers / Fat Nelly / As above so below. *(re-iss.Apr77 + 1981) (cd-iss.Jan91 on 'Cohesion')*

— **CHRIS THOMPSON** – vocals repl. ROGERS who later formed AVIATOR / added **DAVE FLETT** – guitar

Aug 76. (7") **BLINDED BY THE LIGHT. / STARBIRD No.2** [6] [1]
Aug 76. (lp)(c) **THE ROARING SILENCE** [10] [10]
– Blinded by the light / Singing the dolphin through / Waiter, there's a yawn in my ear / The road to Babylon / This side of Paradise / Starbird / Questions. *(re-iss.Apr77 + 1981) (re-iss.Nov87 on 'Legacy') (cd-iss.Jan91 on 'Cohesion')*
Nov 76. (7") **QUESTIONS. / WAITER, THERE'S A YAWN IN MY EAR No.2** [ ] [-]
Dec 76. (7") **QUESTIONS. / SPIRITS IN THE NIGHT** [-] [ ]

— **PAT KING** – bass (ex-SHANGHAI, etc.) repl. PATTENDEN (to TERRA NOVA)

Nov 77. (7") **CALIFORNIA. / CHICAGO INSTITUTE** [ ] [-]
Feb 78. (lp)(c) **WATCH** [33] [83]
– Circles / Drowning on dry land / Fish soup / California / Chicago institute / Davy's on the road again / Martha's madman / The mighty Quinn. *(re-iss.1981) (re-iss.Nov87 on 'Legacy') (cd-iss.Jan91 on 'Cohesion')*
Mar 78. (7") **THE MIGHTY QUINN. / TINY** [ ] [-]
Apr 78. (7") **DAVY'S ON THE ROAD AGAIN. / BOUILLABAISE** [6] [ ] Sep 78
Jul 78. (7") **CALIFORNIA. / BOUILLABAISE** [-] [ ]

— After a short split, MANN reformed band retaining **THOMPSON + KING / STEVE WALLER** – guitar (ex-GONZALES) repl. FLETT / **GEOFF BRITTON** – drums (ex-EAST OF EDEN, ex-WINGS, ex-ROUGH DIAMOND, ex-CHAMPION) repl. CHRIS SLADE who joined URIAH HEEP. He later joined The FIRM (see; LED ZEPPELIN.)

Feb 79. (7") **YOU ANGEL YOU. / OUT IN THE DISTANCE** [54] [-]
Mar 79. (lp)(c) **ANGEL STATION** [30] [ ]
– Don't kill it Carol / You angel you / Hollywood town / Belle of the Earth / Platform end / Angels at my gate / You are I am / Waiting for the rain / Resurrection. *(re-iss.1981) (re-iss.Nov87 on 'Legacy') (cd-iss.Jan91 on 'Cohesion')*
May 79. (7") **YOU ANGEL YOU. / BELLE OF THE EARTH** [-] [58]
Jun 79. (7")(7"pic-d) **DON'T KILL IT CAROL. / BLINDED BY THE LIGHT** [45] [ ]

— **JOHN LINGWOOD** – drums repl. BRITTON who became ill. / guests included **PETER MARSH, WILLY FINLAYSON.** (vocals – **CHRIS THOMPSON**)

Oct 80. (lp)(c) **CHANCE** [ ] [87]
– Lies (through the 80's) / On the run / For you / Adolescent dream / Fritz the blank / Stranded / This is your heart / No guarentee / Heart on the street. *(re-iss.1981) (cd-iss.Jan91 on 'Cohesion')*
Nov 80. (7") **LIES (THROUGH THE 80'S). / ADOLESCENT DREAM** [ ] [ ] Jun 81
Jan 81. (7") **FOR YOU. / A FOOL I AM** [ ] [ ]

— **MATT IRVING** – bass (ex-DREAM POLICE, ex-BABYS, ex-LONGDANCER) repl. KING

Nov 81. (7") **I (WHO HAVE NOTHING). / MAN IN JAM** [ ] [-]

Bronze Arista

Feb 82. (7")(12") **EYES OF NOSTRADAMUS. / HOLIDAY'S END** [ ] [-]
Jun 82. (7")(12") **REDEMPTION SONG (NO KWAZULU). / WARDREAM** [ ] [-]
Nov 82. (7") **TRIBAL STATISTICS. / WHERE DO THEY SEND THEM** [ ] [-]
Jan 83. (lp)(c) **SOMEWHERE IN AFRIKA** [87] [40] Mar 84
– Tribal statistics / Eyes of Nostradamus / Third world service / Demolition man / Brothers and sisters of Azania:- (a) Afrika suite – (b) Brothers and sisters of Afrika – (c) To ban Tustan – (d) Koze Kobenini (how long must we wait?) / Lalela / Redemption song (no Kwazulu) / Somewhere in Afrika. *(re-iss.Nov87 on 'Legacy') (cd-iss.Jan91 on 'Cohesion')*
Jan 83. (7") **DEMOLITION MAN. / IT'S STILL THE SAME** [ ] [-]
Feb 84. (7") **DAVY'S ON THE ROAD AGAIN (live). / THE MIGHTY QUINN (live)** [ ] [-]
(12"+=) – Don't kill it Carol (live).
Feb 84. (lp)(c) **BUDAPEST (live)** [ ] [ ]
– Spirits in the night / Demolition man / For you / Davy's on the road again / Lies (through the 80's) / Blinded by the light / Redemption song (no Kwazulu) / The mighty Quinn. *(cd-iss.Jan91 on 'Cohesion')*

— **MICK RODGERS** – vocals, guitar returned to repl. WALLER (MANN, THOMPSON, LINGWOOD) also still in band. (IRVING left to join LORDS OF THE NEW CHURCH. He later joined PAUL YOUNG band).

Jan 84. (7") **(THE) RUNNER. / NO TRANSKEI** [ ] [-]
(12"+=) – Lies (through the 80's).
Jan 84. (7") **(THE) RUNNER. / WHERE DO THEY SEND THEM** [-] [22]
JUn 84. (7") **REBEL. / FIGURES ON A PAGE** [-] [-]

10-Virgin Virgin

Mar 86. (7")(12") **DO ANYTHING YOU WANNA DO. / CROSSFIRE** [ ] [ ]
May 86. (7")(12") **GOING UNDERGROUND. / I SHALL BE RESCUED** [ ] [ ]
Jun 86. (lp)(c)(cd) **CRIMINAL TANGO** [ ] [ ]
– Going underground / Who are the mystery kids / Banquet / Killer on the loose / Do anything you wanna do / Rescue / You got me through the heart / Hey bulldog / Crossfire.

— **MAGGIE RYDER** – vocals repl. CHRIS THOMPSON who went solo (guests incl.**FRANK MEAD** – saxophone / **DENNY NEWMAN** – bass, vocals on 1)

Oct 87. (7")(12") **GERONIMO'S CADILLAC. / TWO FRIENDS** [ ] [ ]
Nov 87. (lp)(c)(cd) **MASQUE** [ ] [ ]
– Joybringer (from 'Jupiter') / Billies orno bounce (including Billies bounce) / What you give is what you get (start) / Rivers run dry / Planets schmanets / Geronimo's Cadillac / Sister Billies bounce (including Sister Sadie & Billies bounce) / Telegram to Monica / A couple of mates (from 'Mars' & 'Saturn') / Neptune *Icebringer) / The hymn (from 'Jupiter') / We're going wrong.

– compilations, others, etc. –

Jun 77. Bronze/ US= Warners; (7") **SPIRITS IN THE NIGHT. / ROAD TO BABYLON** [ ] [40]
Jul 77. Vertigo/ US= Warners; (lp)(c) **MANFRED MANN'S EARTH BAND 1971-73** [ ] [ ]
Oct 90. Cohesion; (7") **DAVY'S ON THE ROAD AGAIN. / BLINDED BY THE LIGHT** [ ] [-]
Jan 91. Cohesion; (cd) **20 YEARS OF MANFRED MANN'S EARTH BAND 1971-1991** [ ] [-]
– Blinded by the light / California / Joybringer / Tribal statistics / Somewhere in Africa / Davy's on the road again / You angel you / The runner / Questions / The mighty Quinn / Angels at the gate / For you / Demolition man.
Nov 92. (10xcd-box)(10xlp-box) **MANFRED MANN'S EARTH BAND** [ ] [ ]
– (albums from 1972-1986) (free-12"+=) – ?

– (MANFRED MANN) compilations etc. –

H.M.V. Ascot

Apr 64. H.M.V.; (7"ep) **MANFRED MANN'S COCK-A-HOOP WITH 5-4-3-2-1** [ ] [-]
– Cock-a-hoop / 5-4-3-2-1 / Why should we not / Without you.
Dec 64. H.M.V.; (7"ep) **GROOVING WITH MANFRED MANN** [ ] [-]
– Do wah diddy diddy / etc.
Jul 65. H.M.V.; (7"ep) **ONE IN THE MIDDLE** [6] [-]
– With God on our side / Watermelon man / What am I to do / One in the middle.
Sep 65. H.M.V.; (7"ep) **NO LIVING WITHOUT YOU** [ ] [-]
– Let's go and get stoned / I put a spell on you / Tired of trying / (1).
Apr 66. H.M.V.; (7"ep) **MACHINES** [ ] [-]
– She needs company / Machines / Tennessee waltz / When will I be loved.
Jun 66. H.M.V.; (7"ep) **INSTRUMENTAL ASYLUM** [ ] [-]
Sep 66. H.M.V./ US= Ascot; (lp) **MANN MADE HITS** [11] [-]
Oct 66. H.M.V.; (7"ep) **AS WAS** [ ] [-]
Dec 66. H.M.V.; (lp) **SOUL OF MANN** (instrumentals) [40] [ ]
(re-iss.Jul86 on 'See For Miles')
Jan 67. Ascot; (7") **MY LITTLE RED BOOK. / I CAN'T BELIEVE WHAT YOU SAY** [-] [ ]
Aug 83. E.M.I.; (d-lp)(c) **THE FIVE FACES OF MANFRED MANN / MANN MADE** [ ] [-]
Dec 66. Fontana; (7"ep) **INSTRUMENTAL ASSASSINATION** [ ] [-]
– Wild thing / With a girl like you / Sunny / Get away.
Mar 68. Fontana; (lp) **WHAT A MANN** [ ] [-]
1988. Fontana; (lp) **HIT RECORDS 1966-69** [ ] [-]
Nov 71. Philips; (lp) **THIS IS MANFRED MANN** [ ] [-]
Jul 77. Philips; (7"ep) **HA! HA! SAID THE CLOWN / THE MIGHTY QUINN. / SEMI-DETACHED SUBURBAN MR.JAMES / A 'B' SIDE** [ ] [ ]
1971. M.F.P.; (lp) **GREATEST HITS OF MANFRED MANN** [ ] [-]
Dec 93. M.F.P.; (cd)(c) **THE BEST OF MANFRED MANN 1964-1966** [ ] [-]
Jul 76. Sonic; (lp) **MANNERISMS** [ ] [-]
Jul 77. Nutt-EMI; (lp)(c) **THE BEST OF MANFRED MANN** [ ] [-]
Aug 77. E.M.I.; (7") **PRETTY FLAMINGO. / THE ONE IN THE MIDDLE / GOT MY MOJO WORKING** [ ] [-]

Sep 79. E.M.I.; (d-lp)(c) **SEMI-DETACHED SUBURBAN** [9] [-]
– Do wah diidy diddy / 5-4-3-2-1 / Sha la la / Hubble bubble, toil and trouble / Hi lili hi lo / One in the middle / Got my mojo working / With God on our side / Come tomorrow / If you gotta go, go now / Pretty flamingo / Semi-detached suburban Mr.James / There's no living without your loving / Just like a woman / Oh no not my baby / Ha ha said the clown / My name is Jack / Fox on the run / Ragamuffin man / Mighty Quinn.
Feb 86. E.M.I.; (lp)(c) **THE SINGLES ALBUM** [ ] [-]
(cd-iss. 1987 as 'THE SINGLES PLUS', cont.+ tracks)
Jun 93. E.M.I.; (cd) **THE BEST OF THE EMI YEARS** [ ] [ ]
May 82. E.M.I.; (lp)(c) **THE R&B YEARS** [ ] [-]
(re-iss.Nov86)
Jun 89. E.M.I.; (lp)(cd) **THE EP COLLECTION** [ ] [-]
(re-iss.cd Nov94)
Jun 82. Old Gold; (7") **THE MIGHTY QUINN. / BY REQUEST EDWIN GARVEY** [ ] [-]
Oct 82. Old Gold; (7") **PRETTY FLAMINGO. / 5-4-3-2-1** [ ] [-]
(above flipped over + re-iss.May84 on 'EMI')
Apr 87. Old Gold; (7") **PRETTY FLAMINGO. / COME TOMORROW** [ ] [-]
Sep 92. Old Gold; (cd-ep) **PRETTY FLAMINGO / IF YOU GOTTA GO, GO NOW / COME TOMORROW** [ ] [-]
Jul 90. Castle; (cd)(d-lp) **THE COLLECTION** [ ] [-]
Jan 93. Polygram TV; (cd)(c)(lp) **AGES OF MANN (22 CLASSICS OF THE 60's)** [23] [-]
(re-iss.cd/c Sep95)
Aug 94. Arcade; (cd)(c) **THE VERY BEST OF MANFRED MANN'S EARTH BAND** [69] [-]

MANSUN

*** NEW ENTRY ***

Formed: Chester, England . . .1995 by PAUL DRAPER and co, originally as MANSON. After one single 'TAKE IT EASY CHICKEN', their name caused a rumpus with the notorious CHARLES MANSON's legal people. They claimed their name was taken from a VERVE b-side 'A MAN CALLED SUN', so to avoid action, they shortened this to MANSUN. Late that year, they progressed to 'Parlophone', having been signed by Keith Wozencroft. Two UK Top 40 hits appeared as 'ONE' & 'TWO' in 1996. • **Style:** Scuzzy baggy-rockers similar to CHARLATANS, VERVE or OASIS with hip-hop. • **Songwriters:** DRAPER.

Recommended: MANSUN – ONE + MANSUN – TWO (awaiting debut album)

PAUL DRAPER – vocals / **CHAD** – guitar / **STOVE** – bass / **THE HIB** – drums / **MARK** – beatbox

Regal / not issued

Sep 95. (7") **TAKE IT EASY CHICKEN. / ('A'version)** [ ] [-]
Dec 95. (7"colrd) **SKIN UP PIN UP. / FLOURELLA** [ ] [-]

— early '96, MARK suddenly departed

Parlophone / Capitol

Mar 96. (7"ep)(c-ep)(cd-ep) **MANSUN – ONE** [37] [ ]
– Egg shaped Fred / Ski jump nose / Lemonade secret drinker / Thief.
Jun 96. (7"ep)(c-ep)(cd-ep) **MANSUN – TWO** [32] [ ]
– Take it easy chicken / Drastic sturgeon / The greatest pain / Moronica.

— Lost another member, when THE HIB quit.

Phil MANZANERA / 801 (see under ⇒ ROXY MUSIC)

MARILLION

Formed: Aylesbury, Buckinghamshire, England . . . late '78 initially as SILMARILLION by MICK POINTER and DOUG IRVINE. They took name from J.R.Tolkien novel, but soon shortened it to MARILLION a year later. By this time, they had added STEVE ROTHERY and BRIAN JELLIMAN. After IRVINE departed in late '80, they found Scotsman FISH and also DIZ MINNITT. In Nov'81 & Mar'82 they (FISH, POINTER & ROTHERY) secured last steady members Irishman MARK KELLY plus PETE TREWAVAS, and built up even larger following. In the summer of '82, they were finally snapped up by 'EMI', who issued 'MARKET SQUARE HEROES', which dented UK Top 60. Surprisingly they were voted early in '83, the best newcomer in Sounds magazine. Around the same time, they hit the Top 40 with single 'HE KNOWS, YOU KNOW', from parent debut Top 10 album 'SCRIPT FOR A JESTER'S TEAR'. They continued the rest of the 80's, with more hit 45's and Top 10 studio albums, one of which 'MISPLACED CHILDHOOD' hit UK No.1. • **Style:** Until the arrival of FISH, their early gigs were instrumental. Their progressive keyboard-orientated sound, was heavily influenced by GENESIS, and fulfilled vocally by PETER GABRIEL (Genesis) soundalike FISH. • **Songwriters:** FISH words, group compositions. In 1989, HOGARTH (a virtual PETER GABRIEL clone; sound and looks!) took over FISH mantle. Covered; SYMPATHY (Rare Bird). • **Trivia:** Their first 2 albums were produced by Nick Tauber, the 4th by Chris Kimsey. Their fan club 'The Web' was initiated in 1981, and included Radio 1 DJ Tommy Vance.

Recommended: SCRIPT FOR A JESTER'S TEAR (*7) / FUGAZI (*7) / MISPLACED CHILDHOOD (*6) / A SINGLES COLLECTION 1982-1992 (*8)

FISH (b.DEREK WILLIAM DICK, 25 Apr'58, Dalkeith, Scotland) – vocals / **MARK KELLY** (b. 9 Apr'61, Dublin, Eire) – keyboards repl. BRIAN JELLIMAN / **MICK POINTER** (b.22 Jul'56) – drums / **STEVE ROTHERY** (b.25 Nov'59) – guitar / **PETER TREWAVAS** (b.15 Jan'59) – bass repl. DOUG IRVINE

E.M.I. / Capitol

Oct 82. (7") **MARKET SQUARE HEROES. / THREE BOATS DOWN FROM THE CANDY** [60] [-]
(12"+=)(12"pic-d+=) – Grendel. *(12" re-iss.Apr83, hit 53)*
Jan 83. (7")(12") **HE KNOWS, YOU KNOW. / CHARTING THE SINGLE** [35] [-]
Mar 83. (lp)(c) **SCRIPT FOR A JESTER'S TEAR** [7] [ ]
– Script for a jester's tear / He knows, you know / The web / Garden party / Chelsea Monday / Forgotten sons. *(pic-lp Jun84) (cd-iss.Feb87) (re-iss.May90 on 'Fame')*
Jun 83. (7")(7"sha-pic-d) **GARDEN PARTY. / MARGARET** [16] [-]
(12"+=) – Charting the single (live).

— **ANDY WARD** – drums (ex-CAMEL) replaced POINTER / **IAN MOSLEY** (b.16 Jun'53) – drums (ex-STEVE HACKETT, ex-CURVED AIR) repl. WARD

Jan 84. (7")(12")(12"pic-d) **PUNCH AND JUDY. / MARKET SQUARE HEROES / THREE BOATS DOWN FROM THE CANDY** [29] [-]
Mar 84. (lp)(c)(cd)(pic-lp) **FUGAZI** [5] [ ]
– Assassing / Punch and Judy / Jigsaw / Emerald lies / She chameleon / Incubus / Fugazi. *(re-iss.+cd.May88 on 'Fame')*
Apr 84. (7") **ASSASSING. / CINDERELLA SEARCH** [22] [-]
(12"+=)(12"pic-d+=) – ('A'&'B'extended).
Nov 84. (m-lp)(c)(cd) **REAL TO REEL (live)** [8] [ ]
– Assassing / Incubus / Cinderella search / Forgotten sons / Garden party / Market square heroes. *(c/cd+=)*– Emerald lies. *(re-iss.Nov85 on 'Fame', cd-re-iss.Oct87)*
May 85. (7")(7"pic-d) **KAYLEIGH. / LADY NINJA** [2] [-]
(12"+=)(12"pic-d+=) – ('A'&'B'extended).
Jun 85. (lp)(c)(cd)(pic-lp) **MISPLACED CHILDHOOD** [1] [47]
– The pseudo silk kimono / Kayleigh / Lavender / Bitter suite – Heart of Lothian / Waterhole (expresso bongo) / Lords of the backstage / Blind curve / Childhood's end? / White feather. *(re-iss.1991 on 'Fame')*
Jun 85. (7") **KAYLEIGH. / HEART OF LOTHIAN** [-] [74]
Aug 85. (7") **LAVENDER. / FREAKS** [5] [ ]
(12"+=)(12"pic-d+=) – ('A'version).
Nov 85. (7") **HEART OF LOTHIAN. / CHELSEA MONDAY (live)** [29] [-]
(12"+=)(12"pic-d+=) – ('A'version).

In early 1986, FISH teamed up with TONY BANKS (GENESIS) on a single.

Dec 85. (7") **HEART OF LOTHIAN. / LADY NINJA** [-] [ ]
May 87. (7") **INCOMMUNICADO. / GOING UNDER** [6] [ ]
(12"+=)(cd-s+=) – ('A'version).
Jun 87. (lp)(c)(cd)(pic-lp) **CLUTCHING AT STRAWS** [2] [ ]
– Hotel hobbies / Warm wet circles / That time of the night (the short straw) / Going under * / Just for the record / White Russian / Incommunicado / Torch song / Slainte Mhath / Sugar mice / The last straw. *(cd+= *) (re-iss.1989)*
Jul 87. (7")(7"pic-d) **SUGAR MICE. / TUX ON** [22] [ ]
(12"+=)(12"pic-d+=) – ('A'version).
Oct 87. (7") **WARM WET CIRCLES. / WHITE RUSSIAN (live)** [22] [ ]
(cd-s+=) – Incommunicado (live).
(12"++=)(12"pic-d++=) – Up On Top Of A Rainbow.
Nov 88. (d-lp)(c)(d-cd) **THE THIEVING MAGPIE (live)** [25] [ ]
– (intro) / La gazza ladra / Slainte mhath / He knows, you know / Chelsea Monday / Freaks / Jigsaw / Punch and Judy / Sugar mice / Fugazi / Script for a jester's tear / Incommunicado / White Russian / Misplaced childhood part 1:- Pseudo silk kimono – Kayleigh – Lavender – Bitter suite – Heart of Lothian. *(d-cd+=)*– Misplaced childhood part 2:- Waterhole (expresso bongo) – Lords of the backstage – Blind curve – Childhood's end? – White feather.
Nov 88. (7")(7"pic-d) **FREAKS (live). / KAYLEIGH (live)** [24] [ ]
(12"+=)(cd-s+=) – Childhood's end (live) / White feather (live).

— **STEVE HOGARTH** – vocals (ex-HOW WE LIVE, ex-EUROPEANS, ex-LAST CALL) finally repl. FISH. (He left to go solo Sep'88).

Aug 89. (7") **HOOKS IN YOU. / AFTER ME** [30] [ ]
(12"+=)(c-s+=)(cd-s+=)(12"pic-d+=) – ('A'meaty mix).
Sep 89. (lp)(c)(cd) **SEASON'S END** [7] [ ]
– King of sunset town / Easter / The uninvited guest / Season's end / Holloway girl / Berlin / After me / Hooks in you / The space. (c+cd+=) – After me.

Nov 89. (7")(7"pic-d) **THE UNINVITED GUEST. / THE BELL IN THE SEA** [53] [ ]
(12"+=)(c-s+=)(cd-s+=) – ('A'version).

Mar 90. (7")(c-s)(7"pic-d) **EASTER. / THE RELEASE** [34] [ ]
(12"+=)(cd-s+=) – ('A'version) / The uninvited guest.

Jun 91. (7")(c-s) **COVER MY EYES (PAIN AND HEAVEN). / HOW CAN IT HURT** [34] [ ]
(12"+=)(cd-s+=) – The party.

Jul 91. (cd)(c)(lp) **HOLIDAYS IN EDEN** [7] [ ]
– Splintered heart / Cover my eyes (pain and Heaven) / The party / No one can / Holidays in Eden / Dry land / Waiting to happen / This town / The rakes progress / 100 nights.

Jul 91. (7")(c-s)(7"box) **NO ONE CAN. / A COLLECTION** [33] [ ]
(cd-s+=) – Splintered heart (live).

Sep 91. (7") **DRY LAND. / HOLLOWAY GIRL / AFTER ME** [34] [ ]
(12"+=) – Substitute.
(10"+=) – Waiting to happen.
(10"clear+=)(cd-s+=) – Easter / Sugar mice.
(12"pic-d+=) – King of Sunset town.

May 92. (7") **SYMPATHY. / KAYLEIGH (live)** [17] [ ]
(12"pic-d+=)(cd-s+=) – Dry land (live).
(cd-s+=) – Walk on water.

Jun 92. (cd)(c)(lp) **A SINGLES COLLECTION 1982-1992** [27] [ ]
(compilation)
– Cover my eyes (pain & Heaven) / Kayleigh / Easter / Warm wet circles / Uninvited guest / Assassing / Hooks in you / Garden party / No one can / Incommunicado / Dry land / Lavender / I will walk on water / Sympathy.

Jul 92. (7")(c-s) **NO ONE CAN. / A COLLECTION** [26] [ ]
(cd-s+=) – Splintered heart.

Feb 94. (cd)(c)(lp) **BRAVE** [10] [ ]
– Bridge / Living with the big lie / Runaway / Goodbye to all that (i) Wave (ii) Mad (iii) The opium den (iv) The slide (v) Standing in the swing / Hard as love / The hollow man / Alone again in the lap of luxury (i) Now wash your hands / Paper lies / Brave / The great escape (i) The last of you (ii) Fallin' from the Moon / Made again.

Mar 94. (7")(c-s) **THE HOLLOW MAN. / BRAVE** [30] [ ]
(cd-s+=) – Marouatte jam.
(cd-s) – ('A'side) / The last of you – Falling from the Moon (the great escape) / Winter trees.

Apr 94. (c-s) **ALONE AGAIN IN THE LAP OF LUXURY. / LIVING WITH THE BIG LIE (live)** [53] [ ]
(12"+=) – The space (live).
(cd-s+=) – River (live) / Bridge (live).
(cd-s) – ('A'side) / Cover my eyes / Slainte Mhath / Uninvited guest (all live).

Jun 95. (c-s)(cd-s) **BEAUTIFUL / AFRAID OF SUNRISE / ICON** [29] [ ]
(cd-s) – ('A'side) / Live forever / Great escape (demo) / Hard as love (demo).

Jun 95. (cd)(c)(lp) **AFRAID OF SUNLIGHT** [16] [ ]
– Gazpacho / Cannibal surf babe / Beautiful / Afraid of sunrise / Out of this world / Afraid of sunlight / Beyond you / King.

. . . Jan – Jun '96 stop press . . .

Mar 96. (d-cd)(d-c) **MADE AGAIN (live)** [37] [ ]

– other compilations etc. –

Jan 88. EMI; (cd)(lp) **B SIDES THEMSELVES (rare flips)** [64] [ ]
Dec 85. Capitol; (m-lp) **BRIEF ENCOUNTER (live & 'B'sides)** [-] [ ]
Nov 95. EMI; (3xcd-box) **SCRIFT FOR A JESTER'S TEAR / FUGAZI / MISPLACED CHILDHOOD** [ ] [-]

MARION

*** NEW ENTRY ***

Formed: Macclesfield, Manchester, England ...1992 by HARDING, GRANTHAM and CUNNINGHAM. One-off 1994 debut for 'Rough Trade', led to 'London' taking over the reins. Went from strength to strength throughout 1995, which led to Top 10 success with first album 'THIS WORLD AND BODY'. • **Style:** A young fusion of SMITHS and U2. • **Songwriters:** Group. • **Trivia:** Produced by STEPHEN STREET, then AL CLAY from late '95.

Recommended: THIS WORLD AND BODY (*7)

JAMIE HARDING (b.1975) -vocals / **ANTHONY GRANTHAM** -guitar / **PHIL CUNNINGHAM** -guitar / **JULIAN PHILLIPS** -bass / **MURAD MOUSSA** -drums

RoughTrade / not issued

May 94. (7") **VIOLENT MEN. / TOYS FOR BOYS** [ ] [-]
(cd-s+=) – Today and tonight.

London / London

Feb 95. (7") **SLEEP./ FATHER'S DAY** [53] [ ]
(12"+=)(cd-s+=) – Moving fast.

Apr 95. (7")(c-s) **TOYS FOR BOYS. / DOWN THE MIDDLE WITH YOU** [57] [ ]
(cd-s+=) – Changed for the same.

— **NICK GILBERT** -bass repl.PHILLIPS who joined ELECTRAFIXION

Oct 95. (7"yellow)(c-s) **LET'S ALL GO TOGETHER. / LATE GATE SHOW** [37] [ ]
(cd-s+=) – The only way (live).

Jan 96. (7")(c-s) **TIME. / CHANCE** [29] [ ]
(cd-s+=) – Let's all go together.

Feb 96. (cd)(c)(lp) **THIS WORLD AND BODY** [10] [ ]
– Fallen through / Sleep / Let's all go together / Wait / The only way / I stopped dancing / All for love / Toys for boys / Time / Vanessa / Your body lies / My children. *(lp w/ free 7")*– VIOLENT MEN

Mar 96. (7")(cd-s) **SLEEP (remix). / VIOLENT MEN** [17] [ ]
(cd-ep) – ('A'acoustic) / Wait (acoustic) / Time (acoustic).

MARK FOUR (see under ⇒ CREATION)

Bob MARLEY

Born: ROBERT NESTA MARLEY, 2 Feb'45, Rhoden Hall, St.Ann's, Jamaica, the son of an English sailor/captain and a Jamaican woman. In the early 60's, like most other Jamaicans (except older calypso fans), he became influenced by ska, and went to Leslie Kong's studio to record 'JUDGE NOT'. In 1964, after another solo 45, he formed The WAILIN' WAILERS, alongside PETER TOSH, BUNNY WAILER LIVINGSTONE, JUNIOR BRAITHWAITE and BEVERLEY KELSO. Their first 45 'SIMMER DOWN', sold well in homeland, promting Chris Blackwell to take note. On 10 Feb'66, he married RITA, and left for America to visit his mother. The following year, he was back in Jamaica to set up own 'Wailin' Soul' label with JOHNNY NASH. BOB re-united with The WAILERS again, and they issued numerous 45's during this period, which gained export to Britain. They became Rastafarians in 1969, and teamed up with 'Tuff Gong' producer LEE 'Scratch' PERRY, who issued WAILERS debut lp 'SOUL REBEL' in 1970. In 1972, after JOHNNY NASH had taken 'STIR IT UP' into UK Top 20, The WAILERS signed to Blackwell's 'Island' label. Two lp's were issued in '73 'CATCH A FIRE' & 'BURNIN'', before TOSH and BUNNY WAILER decided on own solo careers. In 1975, BOB MARLEY & THE (new) WAILERS released exceptional 'NATTY DREAD', which contained studio version of live smash hit 'NO WOMAN NO CRY'. MARLEY then enjoyed commercial worldwide superstar status for the next 5 years until his tragic death from cancer on 11 May'81. He had survived an attempt on his life on 6 Dec'76, when gunmen broke into his Kingston home, shooting and injuring him, his wife and manager Don Taylor. • **Style:** Rastafarian reggae giant, who drifted through ska and soul in the 60's, before finding and helping pioneer accessible roots reggae in the 70's. • **Songwriters:** Self-penned with other WAILERS until their departure in '74. • **Trivia:** On 6 Aug'81, a Sunsplash Reggae Festival was dedicated to BOB and was attended by over 20,000 fans, as well as his children The MELODY MAKERS. • **Trivia:** On 17 Apr'87, ex-WAILER CARLTON BARRETT is shot dead outside his Kingston home. The following month, the remaining WAILERS oust RITA as executor of MARLEY's will, calling for an investigation to his estate. On 11 Sep'87, PETER TOSH was murdered by burglars to his home.

Recommended: CATCH A FIRE (*9) / BURNIN' (*9) / NATTY DREAD (*10) / RASTAMAN VIBRATION (*7) / EXODUS (*9) / KAYA (*9) / UPRISING (*7) / LEGEND (*8) / SURVIVAL (*10)

ROBERT MARLEY

Island / not issued

Dec 62. (7") **JUDGE NOT (UNLESS YOU JUDGE YOURSELF). / DO YOU STILL LOVE ME?** [ ] [-]
1963. (7") **ONE CUP OF COFFEE. /('B'by "Ernest Ranglin")** [ ] [-]

The WAILERS

were formed by **MARLEY** (-vocals, +later guitar) plus **PETER TOSH** (b.WINSTON HUBERT McINTOSH, 19 Oct'44) – vocals, +later guitar / **BUNNY LIVINGSTONE** (b.NEVILLE O'RILEY, 10 Apr'47) – vocals, percussion / **JUNIOR BRAITHWAITE** – vocals / **BEVERLEY KELSO** – vocals / plus occasionally **RITA MARLEY** (b.ALPHARITA CONSTANTIA ANDERSON) – backing vocals / Instruments by SOUL BROTHERS then SKATELITES

Ska Beat / not issued

Jan 65. (7") **SIMMER DOWN. ("WAILIN' WAILERS") / I DON'T NEED YOUR LOVE** [ ] [-]

— Released in Jamaica earlier, UK in batches?

Island / not issued

Mar 65. (7") **IT HURTS TO BE ALONE. / MR.TALKATIVE** [ ] [-]
Apr 65. (7") **PLAYBOY. / YOUR LOVE** [ ] [-]

— added **CHERRY SMITH** – backing vocals

May 65. (7") **HOOT NANNY ROLL.(by "Peter Tosh") / DO YOU REMEMBER (by "BOB MARLEY")** [ ] [-]
May 65. (7") **HOOLIGAN. / MAGA DOG** [ ] [-]
Jun 65. (7") **SHAME AND SCANDAL. (by "PETER TOSH & THE WAILERS") / THE JERK** [ ] [-]
Jun 65. (7") **DON'T EVER LEAVE ME. / DONNA** [ ] [-]
Dec 65. (7") **WHAT'S NEW PUSSYCAT. / WHERE WILL I FIND** [ ] [-]
Mar 66. (7") **JUMBIE JAMBOUREE. /('B'by "Skatelites")** [ ] [-]
Apr 66. (7") **PUT IT ON (FEEL THE SPIRIT). / LOVE WON'T BE MINE** [ ] [-]
Aug 65. (7") **LONESOME FEELINGS. / THERE SHE GOES** [ ] [-]
1965. (7") **I MADE A MISTAKE. /('B'by "SOUL BROTHERS")** [ ] [-]

— (above 'A'side probaby by The "WAILIN' RUDEBOYS")

1966. (7") **LOVE AND AFFECTION. / TEENAGER IN LOVE** [ ] [-]
1966. (7") **AND I LOVE HER. / DO IT RIGHT** [ ] [-]
1966. (7") **LONESOME TRACK. / SINNER MAN** [ ] [-]

— (below might be without MARLEY)

Rio / not issued

1966. (7") **DANCING SHOES. / DON'T LOOK BACK** [ ] [-]

— MARLEY left Feb'66, to marry RITA but soon returned. CHERRY also left. LIVINGSTONE was imprisoned in 1966.

Doctor Bird / not issued

1966. (7") **RUDE BOY. /('B' by "Roland Al & The Soul Brothers")** [ ] [-]
1966. (7") **GOOD GOOD RUDIE. /('B' by "City Slickers")** [ ] [-]
Nov 66. (7") **RASTA PUT IT ON. /('B' by "Roland Al & The Soul Brothers")** [ ] [-]
(re-iss.Apr67 on 'Island')

— (below iss.JAMAICA on 'Rocksteady')

1967. (7") **NICE TIME. / HYPOCRITE** [ ] [-]

— (below 2 without MARLEY)

Island / not issued

Nov 66. (7") **HE WHO FEELS IT KNOWS IT. / SUNDAY MORNING** [ ] [-]
Dec 66. (7") **LET HIM GO (RUDE BOY GOT BAIL). / SINNER MAN** [ ] [-]
Apr 67. (7") **I NEED YOU. /('B' by "Ken Boothe")** [ ] [-]

— Now a trio of **MARLEY, TOSH & BUNNY.** (KELSO and BRAITHWAITE departed)

Apr 67. (7") **BEND DOWN LOW. / FREEDOM TOWN** [ ] [-]
Apr 67. (7") **I AM THE TOUGHEST. ("Peter Tosh & The Wailers") /('B' by "Marcia Griffiths")** [ ] [-]

Studio One / not issued

1967. (7") **I STAND PREDOMINANT. / ('B' by 'Norma Fraser')** [ ] [-]

Trojan / not issued

Oct 68. (7") **STIR IT UP. / THIS TRAIN** [ ] [-]

Bamboo / not issued

1970. (7") **JAILHOUSE. /('B' by "JOHN HOLT")** [ ] [-]

Escort / not issued

1970. (7") **RUN FOR COVER. / TO THE RESCUE** [ ] [-]

BOB MARLEY & THE WAILERS

added **ASTON BARRETT** (b.22 Nov'46, KIngston, Jamaica) – bass / **CARLTON BARRETT** (b.17 Dec'50, Kingston) – drums

Upsetter / Shelter

1970. (7") **MY CUP. / SON OF THUNDER (by "LEE PERRY & THE WAILERS")** [ ] [-]
1970. (7") **VERSION OF CUP.(by "WAILERS") /('B' by "Upsetters")** [ ] [-]
Dec 70. (7") **DUPPY CONQUEROR. /('B'by "UPSETTERS")** [ ] [-]
Jan 71. (7") **MR.BROWN. /('B'by "Upsetters")** [ ] [-]
Feb 71. (7") **KAYA. / ('A'version by "Upsetters")** [ ] [-]
Feb 71. (7") **SMALL AXE. / ALL IN ONE** [ ] [-]
1971. (7") **DREAMLAND ("WAILERS"). /('B'by "Upsetters")** [ ] [-]
1971. (7") **MORE AXE. /('B'by "Upsetters")** [ ] [-]
1971. (7") **PICTURE ON THE WALL.(by "Ras Dawkins & The Wailers") /('B'by "Upsetters")** [ ] [-]

Trojan / not issued

Sep 70. (7") **SOUL SHAKEDOWN PARTY. /('B'by "Beverley All-Stars")** [ ] [-]
Dec 70. (lp) **SOUL REBEL** [ ] [-]
– There she goes / Put it on / How many times / Mellow mood / Changes are / Hammer / Tell me / Touch me / Treat you right / Soul rebel. *(re-iss.+c.Sep81 on 'New Cross') (re-iss.Jun84 on 'Blue Moon') (re-iss.Apr90 on 'Action Replay') (cd-iss.Jan90 on 'Receiver')*

Jackpot / not issued

1971. (7") **MR.CHATTERBOX. / WALK THROUGH THE WORLD** [ ] [-]

Punch / not issued

1971. (7") **MORE AXE. /('B'by "Dave Berber")** [ ] [-]
1971. (7") **DOWN DRESSER ("WAILERS"). /('B'by "Junior Byles")**
1972. (7") **SCREW FACE. / FACE MAN** [ ] [-]

Bullet / not issued

1971. (7") **SOULTOWN. / LET THE SUN SHINE ON ME** [ ] [-]
1971. (7") **LICK SAMBA. / SAMBA** [ ] [-]

Summit / not issued

1971. (7") **STOP THE TRAIN. / CAUTION** [ ] [-]
1971. (7") **FREEDOM TRAIN. / ?** [ ] [ ]

Green Door / Tuff Gong

1971. (7") **LIVELY UP YOURSELF. /('B'by "Tommy McCook")** [ ] [-] JAMAI
Nov 71. (7") **TRENCHTOWN ROCK. / GROOVING KINGDOM** [ ] [-]
1972. (7") **GUAVA JELLY. / REDDER THAN RED** [ ] [-]

— (below was 1968 demo)

C.B.S. / not issued

May 72. (7") **REGGAE ON BROADWAY. / OH LORD I GOT TO GET THERE** [ ] [-]

Trojan / not issued

Sep 72. (7") **KEEP ON MOVING. / AFRICAN HERBSMAN** [ ] [-]
1972. (lp) **AFRICAN HERBSMAN** [ ] [-]
– Lively up yourself / Small axe / Duppy conqueror / African herbsman / Trenchtown rock / Keep on moving / Fussing and fighting / Stand alone / All in one / Don't rock the boat / Put it on / Sun is shining / Kaya / Riding high / 400 years / Brain washing. *(re-iss.+c.1981 & Jul84) (re-iss.Nov83 on 'Fame') (cd-iss. Jun88) (cd-iss.Mar94 on 'Trojan')*

The WAILERS

Blue Mountain / Island

Jan 73. (7") **BABY WE'VE GOT A DATE (ROCK IT BABY). / STOP THAT TRAIN** [ ] [ ]

Island / Island

Apr 73. (lp)(c) **CATCH A FIRE** [ ] [ ]
– Concrete jungle / Slave driver / 400 years / Stop that train / Baby we've got a date (rock it baby) / Stir it up / Kinky reggae / No more trouble / Midnight ravers. *(re-iss.Oct86) (re-iss.+cd.Jun90 on 'Tuff Gong')*

Jun 73. (7") **CONCRETE JUNGLE. / REINCARNATION SOUL** [ ] [-]
Jul 73. (7") **CONCRETE JUNGLE. / NO MORE TROUBLE** [-] [ ]
Sep 73. (7") **GET UP, STAND UP. / SLAVE DRIVER** [ ] [ ]
Nov 73. (lp)(c) **BURNIN'** [ ] [ ]
– Get up, stand up / Hallelujah time / I shot the sheriff / Burnin' and lootin' / Put it on / Small axe / Pass it on / Duppy conqueror / One foundation / Rastaman chant. *(re-iss.Mar87) (re-iss.+cd.Jun90 on 'Tuff Gong')*

Feb 74. (7") **I SHOT THE SHERIFF. / PUT IT ON** [-] [ ]

— added **The I-THREES** (female backers **JUDY MOWAT, MARCIA GRIFFITHS**, and **RITA**). They replaced PETER TOSH and BUNNY WAILER who both went solo.

BOB MARLEY & THE WAILERS

MARLEY, ASTON and **BARRETT** added **EARL LINDO** – keyboards / **BERNARD HARVEY** – keyboards / **AL ANDERSON** – guitar.

May 75. (lp)(c) **NATTY DREAD** (in Oct75 hit) [43] [92]
– Lively up yourself / No woman no cry / Them belly full (but we hungry) / Rebel music (3 o'clock road block) / So jah seh / Natty dread / Bend down low / Talkin' blues / Revolution. *(re-iss.May87) (re-iss.+cd.Jun90 on 'Tuff Gong')*

Jun 75. (7") **NATTY DREAD. / SO JAH SEH** [ ] [-]
Jun 75. (7") **LIVELY UP YOURSELF. / SO JAH SEH** [-] [ ]

— **TYRONE DOWNIE** – keyboards repl. HARVEY / **ALVIN 'SHECO' PATTERSON** – percussion repl. LINDO / added **JULIAN 'JUNIOR' MURVIN** – guitar

Aug 75. (7") **NO WOMAN NO CRY (live). / KINKY REGGAE** [22] [ ]
Dec 75. (lp)(c) **LIVE! (live)** [38] [90]
– Trenchtown rock / Burnin' and lootin' / Them belly full (but we hungry) / Lively up yourself / No woman no cry / I shot the sheriff / Get up, stand up. *(re-iss.Jul81 + Sep86.as 'LIVE AT THE LYCEUM', cd-iss.Jan87) (re-iss.cd+c.Nov90 on 'Tuff Gong')*

Jan 76. (7") **JAH LIVE. / CONCRETE JUNGLE (live)** [ ] [ ]
Apr 76. (7") **JOHNNY WAS (WOMAN HANG HER HEAD AND CRY). / CRY TO ME** [ ] [ ]
Apr 76. (lp)(c) **RASTAMAN VIBRATION** [15] [8]
– Positive vibration / Roots, rock, reggae / Johnny was / Cry to me / Want more / Crazy baldhead / Who the cap fit / Night shift / War / Rat race. *(re-iss.+cd.Apr87) (re-iss.cd+c.Nov90 on 'Tuff Gong')*

Jun 76. (7") **ROOTS ROCK REGGAE. / STIR IT UP** [ ] [-]
Jun 76. (7") **ROOTS ROCK REGGAE. / CRY TO ME** [-] [51]

Nov 76. (7") **WHO THE CAP FITS** [-] [ ]
May 77. (lp)(c) **EXODUS** [8] [20] Jun 77
– Natural mystic / So much things to say / Guiltiness / The heathen / Exodus / Jamming / Waiting in vain / Turn your lights down low / Three little birds / One love – People get ready. *(re-iss.+cd.Mar87) (re-iss.cd+c.Nov90 on 'Tuff Gong')*
Jun 77. (7") **EXODUS. / EXODUS (dub)** [14] [ ]
Aug 77. (7") **WAITING IN VAIN. / ROOTS** [27] [ ]
Dec 77. (7") **JAMMING. / PUNKY REGGAE PARTY** [9] [ ]
—— added the returning **EARL 'WIRE' LINDO** – keyboards
Feb 78. (7") **IS THIS LOVE. / CRISIS (version)** [9] [ ]
(re-iss.as 12"-Jun81)
Mar 78. (lp)(c) **KAYA** [4] [50]
– Easy shanking / Kaya / The sun is shining / Is this love / Satisfy my soul / She's gone / Misty morning / Crisis / Running away / Time will tell. *(re-iss.+cd.Feb87) (re-iss.cd+c.Nov90 on 'Tuff Gong')*
May 78. (7") **SATISFY MY SOUL. / SMILE JAMAICA** [21] [ ]
Dec 78. (d-lp)(c) **BABYLON BY BUS (live)** [40] [ ]
– Positive vibration / Punky reggae party / Exodus / Stir it up / Rat race / Concrete jungle / Kinky reggae / Lively up yourself / Rebel music (3 o'clock road block) / War / No more trouble / Is this love / The heathen / Jamming. *(re-iss.+cd.Feb87) (re-iss.cd+c.Nov90 on 'Tuff Gong')*
Jan 79. (7") **STIR IT UP (live). / RAT RACE (live)** [ ] [-]
(12") – ('A'side) / War (live) / No more trouble (live).
Jul 79. (7") **WAKE UP AND LIVE. / (part 2)** [-] [ ]
Sep 79. (7") **SO MUCH TROUBLE IN THE WORLD. / ('A'instrumental)** [56] [ ]
Oct 79. (lp)(c) **SURVIVAL** [20] [70]
– Wake up and live / Top rankin' / Ambush in the night / Babylon system / Survival / Ride Natty ride / One drop / So much trouble in the world / Zimbabwe / Africa unite. *(re-iss.+cd.Mar87) (re-iss.cd+c.Nov90 on 'Tuff Gong')*
Nov 79. (7") **ONE DROP. / KAYA** [-] [ ]
Nov 79. (7") **SURVIVAL. / WAKE UP AND LIVE** [ ] [-]
Mar 80. (7") **ZIMBABWE. / SURVIVAL** [ ] [-]
(12") – ('A'side) / Africa unite / Wake up and live.
May 80. (7") **COULD YOU BE LOVED. / ONE DROP** [5] [ ]
(12"+=) – Ride natty ride. *(US; b-side)*
Jun 80. (lp)(c) **UPRISING** [6] [45]
– Coming in from the cold / Real situation / Bad card / We and them / Work / Zion train / Pimper's paradise / Could you be loved / Forever loving Jah / Redemption song. *(cd-iss.Feb87) (re-iss.cd+c.Nov90 on 'Tuff Gong')*
Aug 80. (7") **THREE LITTLE BIRDS. / EVERY NEED GOT AN EGO FEED** [17] [ ]
Oct 80. (7")(12") **REDEMPTION SONG. / ('A'band version)** [ ] [ ]
—— In Oct'80, BOB MARLEY was diagnosed with lung cancer. He died on 11 May'81.

– compilations, others, etc. –

1974. Trojan; (7") **SOUL SHAKEDOWN PARTY. / CAUTION** [ ] [-]
Jul 74. Trojan; (lp)(c) **RASTA REVOLUTION** [ ] [-]
(re-iss.1981 + Jul84) (cd-iss.Jun88) (re-iss.Jul85 on 'Fame') (cd-iss.Mar94)
Aug 74. Trojan; (7") **MR.BROWN. / ('A'version)** [ ] [-]
1976. Trojan; (7") **MR.BROWN. / TRENCHTOWN ROCK** [ ] [-]
Jun 81. Trojan; (7") **THANK YOU LORD. / WISDOM** [ ] [-]
Oct 83. Trojan; (7") **SOUL SHAKEDOWN PARTY. / CAUTION** [ ] [-]
('A'-disco 12") – Keep on skanking.
Jan 84. Trojan; (lp)(c) **IN THE BEGINNING** [ ] [-]
(cd-iss.Jun88) (cd-iss.Mar94 on 'Trojan')
Jun 88. Trojan; (d-lp)(d-c)(d-cd) **SOUL REVOLUTION 1 & 2** [ ] [-]
(d-cd+d-c Mar94 on 'Trojan')
Jun 89. Trojan; (cd) **SOUL REVOLUTION / RHYTHM ALBUM** [ ] [-]
May 91. Trojan; (cd-box)(lp-box) **IN MEMORIAM** [ ] [-]
Jul 77. Epic; (lp)(c) **BIRTH OF A LEGEND VOL.1 (featuring PETER TOSH)** [ ] [-]
(re-iss.Jun80 + Nov81) (cd-iss.Jun91 on 'Pickwick')
Sep 77. Embassy; (lp)(c) **EARLY MUSIC** [ ] [-]
(re-iss.Nov81 on 'C.B.S.')
Oct 79. Hammer; (lp)(c) **BOB MARLEY & THE WAILERS** [ ] [-]
Oct 79. Psycho; (lp)(c) **IN THE BEGINNING** [ ] [-]
(re-iss.Jul84, cd-iss.Jun88 on 'Trojan')
Mar 81. Hallmark; (lp)(c) **BOB MARLEY & THE WAILERS WITH PETER TOSH** [ ] [-]
(re-iss.1981 on 'SS International')
1981. Accord; (lp) **JAMAICAN STORM** [ ] [-]
Sep 81. Warners/ US= Cotillion; (lp)(c) **CHANCES ARE** [ ] [-]
Sep 81. Warners/ US= Cotillion; (7")(12") **REGGAE ON BROADWAY. / GONNA GET YOU** [ ] [-]
Nov 81. Warners/ US= Cotillion; (7") **CHANCES ARE. /** [-] [ ]
Jun 81. Island; (12") **NO WOMAN NO CRY (live). / JAMMING** [8] [ ]
Mar 82. Island; (7") **NATURAL MYSTIC. / CARRY ON BEYOND** [ ] [-]
1982. Island; (9xlp-box) **BOB MARLEY – THE BOXED SET** [ ] [-]
1982. Island; (lp)(c) **COUNTRYMAN (Soundtrack,** w/8 MARLEY songs**)** [ ] [-]
Apr 83. Island; (7")(12") **BUFFALO SOLDIER. / BUFFALO (dub)** [4] [ ]
May 83. Island; (lp)(c) **CONFRONTATION** [5] [55]
– Chant down Babylon / Buffalo soldier / Jump Nyabinghi / Mix up, mix up / Give thanks and praises / Blackman redemption / Trenchtown / Stiff neked fools / I know / Rastaman live up!. *(re-iss.Mar87) (cd-iss.1988 on 'Mango') (re-iss.cd+c Jun90 on 'Tuff Gong')*
Apr 84. Island; (7") **ONE LOVE. / PEOPLE GET READY** [5] [ ]
(12"+=)(12"pic-d+=) – Keep on moving / So much trouble.
May 84. Island; (lp)(c) **LEGEND** [1] [54]
– Is this love / Jamming / No woman no cry / Stir it up / Get up, stand up / Satisfy my soul / I shot the sheriff / One love / People get ready / Buffalo soldier / Exodus / Redemption song / Could you be loved / Want more. *(cd-iss.Aug85) (cd re-iss.May91 on 'Tuff Gong' hit UK No.11, Mar92 No.18 / Jul92 No.25)*
Jun 84. Island; (7") **WAITING IN VAIN. / BLACK MAN REDEMPTION** [31] [ ]
(12"+=) – Marley mix-up.
Aug 84. Island; (7") **IS THIS LOVE. / BLACK MAN REDEPTION** [-] [ ]
Nov 84. Island; (7")(7"pic-d) **COULD YOU BE LOVED. / NO WOMAN NO CRY** [71] [ ]
(12"+=) – Jamming / Coming in from the cold.
Apr 85. Island; (lp)(c) **REGGAE GREATS** [ ] [-]
Jun 85. Island; (7")(12")(c-s) **THREE LITTLE BIRDS. / ('A'dub version)** [ ] [-]
Jun 86. Island; (lp)(c)(cd) **REBEL MUSIC** [54] [ ]
(re-iss.cd+c Jun90 on 'Tuff Gong')
Oct 83. C.B.S.; (d-c) **BIRTH OF A LEGEND / EARLY MUSIC** [ ] [-]
May 84. Breakaway; (lp)(c)(pic-lp) **THE ESSENTIAL** [ ] [-]
Jun 84. Happy Bird; (d-lp)(c) **25 GREATEST HITS** [ ] [-]
Nov 84. Topline; (lp)(c) **MELLOW MOOD** [ ] [-]
(cd-iss.Apr87)
Dec 84. Premier; (lp) **ONE LOVE** [ ] [-]
(cd-iss.1987, c-iss.1988, lp re-iss.Feb90 on 'Pickwick')
Feb 87. Premier; (lp)(c) **LIVELY UP YOURSELF** [ ] [-]
(cd-iss.Jun93 on 'Prestige')
Feb 85. Sierra; (lp)(c) **REPLAY ON BOB MARLEY** [ ] [-]
Feb 85. Cambra; (d-lp)(d-c) **ETERNAL** [ ] [-]
Aug 85. Daddy Kool; (12") **RAINBOW COUNTRY. /('B'by "PABLO & THE UPSETTERS")** [ ] [-]
Jan 86. Daddy Kool; (12") **NATURAL MYSTIC. / ('A'version)** [ ] [-]
Apr 86. Showcase; (lp)(c) **PUT IT ON** [ ] [-]
Apr 86. Castle; (d-lp)(c) **THE COLLECTION** [ ] [-]
(cd-iss.1988)
Nov 86. Blue Moon; (lp)(c) **ROOTS** *(cd-iss.1988)* [ ] [-]
Dec 88. Blue Moon; (cd) **ROOTS VOL.2** [ ] [-]
Jan 89. Blue Moon; (lp)(cd) **ONE LOVE / ROOTS VOL.2** [ ] [-]
Feb 87. Konnexion; (lp) **THE LEE PERRY SESSIONS** [ ] [-]
May 88. Streetlife; (lp)(c)(cd) **GREATEST HITS** [ ] [-]
Sep 88. Pickwick; (cd-ep) **REACTION / I GOTTA KEEP ON MOVING / PUT IT ON** [ ] [-]
Feb 87. Arena; (lp)(c) **THE CLASSIC YEARS** [ ] [-]
Nov 88. Arena; (cd-ep) **CLASSIC (w / TOOTS)** [ ] [-]
Jul 87. Intertape; (cd) **BOB MARLEY** [ ] [-]
May 88. Black Tulip; (lp)(c) **20 GREATEST HITS** [ ] [-]
1990. Connoisseur; (lp)(c)(cd) **THE BEST OF BOB MARLEY (1968-72)** [ ] [-]
Mar 91. Tuff Gong; (cd)(c)(lp) **TALKIN' BLUES** [ ] [-]
– (radio sessions 1973 + interviews 1975)
May 91. Tuff Gong; (7")(c-s) **ONE LOVE – PEOPLE GET READY. / SO MUCH TROUBLE IN THE WORLD** [42] [-]
(12"+=)(cd-s+=) **('A'extended) / Keep on moving.**
Sep 92. Tuff Gong; (7")(c-s) **IRON ZION LION ('74 track). / COULD YOU BE LOVED** [5] [ ]
(12")(cd-s) – ('A'side) / Smile Jamaica / Three little birds.
Sep 92. Tuff Gong; (4xcd-box)(4xc-box) **SONGS OF FREEDOM** [10] [86]
– (discovered demos, by wife Rita)
(re-iss.May93 as 8-lp box)
Nov 92. Tuff Gong; (7")(c-s) **WHY SHOULD I (Bone Remix Edit). / (Kindread Spirit Edit)** [42] [ ]
(cd-s+=) – Exodus (rebel the remix)
Apr 91. Rohit; (cd)(c)(lp) **ALL THE HITS** [ ] [-]
Aug 91. Entity; (cd)(c) **SAGA** [ ] [-]
Sep 91. Music Coll..; (cd)(c) **THE VERY BEST OF THE EARLY YEARS 1968-74** [ ] [-]
Feb 93. Charly; (cd) **TREAT HER RIGHT** [ ] [-]
Nov 93. Charly; (cd) **THE LEE PERRY SESSIONS** [ ] [-]
Nov 93. Charly; (cd) **RIDING HIGH** [ ] [-]
Mar 94. Charly; (cd) **RAINBOW COUNTRY** [ ] [-]
Sep 93. Trojan; (4xlp-box) **THE EARLY YEARS 1969-1973** [ ] [-]
Mar 94. Trojan; (cd)(c) **IN MEMORIAM** [ ] [-]
Sep 93. Laserlight; (d-cd) **BOB MARLEY** [ ] [-]
Feb 94. Studio One; (lp) **THE WAILING WAILERS ("WAILERS")** [ ] [-]
Jun 94. Sony; (cd) **THE BIRTH OF A LEGEND (with PETER TOSH)** [ ] [-]
Jul 94. Success; (cd)(c) **KEEP ON MOVING** [ ] [-]
Jul 94. Success; (cd)(c) **SOUL REBEL** [ ] [-]
Jul 94. Success; (cd)(c) **DON'T ROCK MY BOAT** [ ] [-]
Jul 94. Success; (cd)(c) **SOUL SHAKEDOWN PARTY** [ ] [-]

Jan 95. Reggae Best; (cd) **SOUL CAPTIVE** [ ] [-]
Feb 95. More Music; (cd) **POWER** [ ] [-]
Feb 95. B.A.M.; (cd) **PEARLS OF THE PAST** [ ] [-]
Feb 95. B.A.M.; (cd) **PEARLS OF THE PAST VOLUME 2** [ ] [-]
May 95. Tuff Gong; (c-s) **KEEP ON MOVING. / PIMPER'S PARADISE** [17] [ ]
(12+=)(cd-s+=) – ('A'mixes).
May 95. Tuff Gong; (cd)(c)(lp) **NATURAL MYSTIC** [5] [67]
May 95. Heartbeat; (cd)(c) **SIMMER DOWN AT STUDIO ONE** [ ] [-]
May 95. Heartbeat; (cd)(c) **THE WAILING WAILERS AT STUDIO ONE** [ ] [-]
Jul 95. A&A; (cd) **LEGEND IN SAX** [ ] [-]
Aug 95. Sony Europe; (cd) **GOLD COLLECTION** [ ] [-]
Dec 95. Columbia; (cd)(c) **EARLY COLLECTION** [ ] [-]

. . . Jan – Jun '96 stop press . . .

Jun 96. Tuff Gong; (single) **WHAT GOES AROUND COMES AROUND** [42] [ ]

— His son ZIGGY MARLEY (real name DAVID) & The MELODY MAKERS (other sons & daughters; STEPHEN, CEDELLA and SHARON) signed to EMI USA in 1986 and released album 'KEY WORLD'. In 1988, with producers TOM TOM CLUB (TINA WEXMOUTH and CHRIS FRANTZ of TALKING HEADS), they signed to 'Virgin' and had US No.23 hit album 'CONSCIOUS PARTY'. A single from it 'TOMORROW PEOPLE' made no.39 there mid-'88. A year later, the album 'ONE BRIGHT DAY' gave them last US chart appearance, hitting No.26.

J. MASCIS (see under ⇒ DINOSAUR JR)

Nick MASON (see under ⇒ PINK FLOYD)

MASSIVE ATTACK

Formed: Bristol, England . . . 1988 by 3-D, MUSHROOM and DADDY G. Founded own label 'Wild Bunch', which was snapped up by Virgin subsidiary 'Circa' late in 1990. Their second single 'UNFINISHED SYMPATHY' although suffering undignified name change (to MASSIVE) due to Gulf War. This was quickly followed up by what was quickly to become a classic album 'BLUE LINES', which made UK Top 20 lists. • **Style:** Classical dance /hip hop & dub reggae trio revered by music press and public alike. • **Songwriters:** Group except; BE THANKFUL FOR WHAT YOU'VE GOT (William DeVaughn) / LIGHT MY FIRE (Doors). Sampled JAMES BROWN, PIECES OF A DREAM, YOUNG HOLT TRIO. • **Trivia:** Remixed PETER GABRIEL, LES NEGRESSES VERTES.

Recommended: BLUE LINES (*10) / PROTECTION (*9) / NO PROTECTION (*8; MASSIVE ATTACK V MAD PROFESSOR)

3d (b. DEL NAJA) – vocals / **MUSHROOM** (b. A.VOWLES) – keyboards / **DADDY G.** (b. MARSHALL) – keyboards

Warners Warners

Jul 88. (12") **ANY LOVE. / ('A'mix)** [ ] [ ]

— w / **SHARA NELSON** – vocals / **NELLEE HOOPER** – programmer / arranger

Wild Bunch-Circa Virgin

Nov 90. (7")(c-s) **DAYDREAMING. / ('A'instrumental)** [ ] [ ]
(12"+=)(cd-s+=) – Any love (2).
(12") – ('A'-luv it mix) / ('A'-Brixton bass mix) / ('A'-luv it dub).
Feb 91. (7")(c-s) **UNFINISHED SYMPATHY. / ('A'-Nellee Hooper mix)** [13] [ ]
(12")(cd-s) – ('A'side) / ('A'-Paul Oakenfold mix) / ('A'-P.O. instrumental) / ('A'instrumental).

— (above single as "MASSIVE") Below also featured **HORACE ANDY** – vox

Apr 91. (cd)(c)(2x12"lp) **BLUE LINES** [13] [ ]
– Safe from harm / One love / Blue lines / Be thankful for what you've got / Five man army / Unfinished sympathy / Daydreaming / Lately / Hymn of the big wheel.
May 91. (7") **SAFE FROM HARM. / ('A'version)** [25] [ ]
(cd-s+=) – ('A'-Perfecto mix).
(12") – ('A'-Perfecto mix) / ('A'dub mix) / ('A'instrumental).
Feb 92. (7"ep)(12"ep)(cd-ep) **MASSIVE ATTACK** [27] [ ]
– Hymn of the big wheel / Home of the whale / Be thankful / Any love.

— now w / **TRACEY THORN** (Everything But The Girl) / **NICOLETTE / TRICKY + HORACE ANDY** – vocals. **CRAIG ARMSTRONG** – piano / **CHESTER KAMEN** – guitar / **ROB MERRIL** – drums

Sep 94. (cd)(c)(lp) **PROTECTION** [4] [ ]
– Protection / Karmacoma / Three / Weather storm / Spying glass / Better things / Eurochild / Sly / Heat miser / Light my fire (live).
Oct 94. (c-ep)(cd-ep) **SLY / ('A'mix by UNDERDOG) / ('A'-Mad Professor mix) / ('A'-Tim Simenon mix)** [24] [ ]
(12"ep+=)(cd-ep+=) – (extra 'A'mix).
Jan 95. (7") **PROTECTION. ("MASSIVE ATTACK with TRACEY THORN") / ('A'-J.Sw!ft mix)** [14] [ ]
(cd-s+=) – ('A'-Radiation for the nation mix).
(c-s++=) – ('A'-Eno mix).
(12"+++=) – ('A'-Mad Professor mix).
(cd-s) – ('A'-Underdog dust mix) / Three (Don T's house of fortune mix).
Feb 95. (cd)(c)(lp) **NO PROTECTION** ("MASSIVE ATTACK v MAD PROFESSOR") [ ] [ ]
– Radiation ruling the nation (Protection) / Bumper ball dub (Karmacoma) / Trinity dub (Three) / Cool monsoon (Weather storm) / Eternal feedback ((Sly) / Moving dub (Better things) / I spy (Spying glass) / Backward sucking (Heat miser).
Mar 95. (12"ep) **KARMACOMA. / ('A'-Napoli trip mix) / ('A'-Unkle mix) / BLACKSMITH – DAYDREAMING** [28] [ ]
(cd-ep+=) – ('A'-Portishead experience mix) / ('A'-Bumper ball mix).
(c-ep++=)(cd-ep++=) – ('A'-Portishead mix).

Dave MATTHEWS BAND

*** NEW ENTRY ***

Formed: Charlottesville, Virginia, USA . . .1991/92 by South African born MATTHEWS. Released a few rare items, before signing to 'RCA' late '93. Their debut for the label 'UNDER THE TABLE AND DREAMING' soon climbed up the US Top 20, selling three million copies in the process. • **Style:** Multi-racial acoustic rock with jam-packed jazzy feel. • **Songwriters:** MATTHEWS except several with band. • **Trivia:** Produced by STEVE LILLYWHITE.

Recommended: UNDER THE TABLE AND DREAMING (*8) / CRASH (*7)

DAVE MATTHEWS – vocals, guitar / **CARTER BEAUFORD / LeROI MOORE / FULLARTON**

R.C.A. R.C.A.

Mar 95. (cd)(c) **UNDER THE TABLE AND DREAMING** [ ] [11] Jul94
– The best of what's around / What would you say / Satellite / Rhyme and reason / Typical situation / Dancing Nancies / Ants marching / Lover lay down / Jimi thing / Warehouse / Pay for what you get / No.34.

— FULLARTON replaced by **BOYD TINSLEY** – fiddle / **STEFAN LESSARD**

Jun 96. (7") **TOO MUCH. / JIMI THING (acoustic)** [ ] [ ]
(cd-s+=) – Ants marching.
Jul 96. (cd)(c) **CRASH** [ ] [2] May 96
– So much to say / Two step / Crash into me / Too much / No.34 / Say goodbye / Drive in drive out / Let you down / Lie in our graves / Cry freedom / Tripping Billies / Proudest monkeys.

MAX Q (see under ⇒ INXS)

Brian MAY (see under ⇒ QUEEN)

Phil MAY & The FALLEN ANGELS (see under ⇒ PRETTY THINGS)

John MAYALL

Born: 29 Nov'33, Macclesfield, Cheshire, England. Early in 1963 after forming Manchester based outfit The BLUES SYNDICATE, he moved to London on the suggestion of ALEXIS KORNER. There he founded The BLUESBREAKERS, with ever-changing personnel including stalwart JOHN McVIE. They signed to 'Decca' Spring '64, and released 1 single 'CRAWLING UP A HILL', before MAYALL recruited HUGHIE FLINT and ROGER DEAN to replace MARTIN HART and BERNIE WATSON. This quartet lasted a year and issued (live at Klook's Kleek) debut lp 'JOHN MAYALL PLAYS JOHN MAYALL', and a single. In Apr'65, they substituted DEAN, with ex-YARDBIRDS guitar hero ERIC CLAPTON, and issued 2 more 45's. After some of group (CLAPTON and McVIE) took a vacation, they were back late '65, doing one-nighters and to record in the Spring of '66 the legendary 'BLUESBREAKERS' lp. Released in July and crediting JOHN MAYALL WITH ERIC CLAPTON, it soon raced into UK Top 10. At the same time CLAPTON quit to form CREAM, and was replaced by PETER GREEN. In Sep' 66, AYNSLEY DUNBAR moved in, after FLINT was ousted. This new line-up also hit Top 10 with lp 'A HARD ROAD' early '67, before drummer MICK FLEETWOOD joined. When all 3 of his band (FLEETWOOD, McVIE & GREEN) got together as FLEETWOOD MAC in Sep'67, MAYALL recruited entire new line-up on yet another Top 10 lp 'CRUSADE'. MAYALL continued to change personnel, although it didn't affect album chart appearances until late 1971's 'MEMORIES'. In his ranks between 1967-1971, were future stars KEEF HARTLEY (solo), MICK TAYLOR (Rolling Stones), CHRIS MERCER (Juicy Lucy), ANDY FRASER (Free) / DICK HECKSTALL-SMITH, TONY REEVES & JON HISEMAN (Colosseum), COLIN ALLEN & STEVE THOMPSON (Stone The Crows). • **Style:** Raw blues bandleader who developed with time into jazz & roots blues outfit. • **Songwriters:** Self-penned alongside covers; MY BABY IS SWEETER (Willie Dixon) / DOUBLE TROUBLE (Otis Rush) / ALL YOUR LOVE (Dixon-Rush) / BERNARD JENKINS (Eric Clapton) / + DOUBLE CROSS (w/ Clapton) / DUST MY BLUES (Elmore James) / THE SUPERNATURAL (Peter Green) / SO MANY ROADS (. . . Paul) / LOOKING BACK (Johnny Guitar Watson) / ALL MY LIFE (. . . Robinson) / RIPIN' ON THE L & N (Barley Hampton) / IT HURTS ME TOO (. . . London) / OH, PRETTY WOMAN (Big Joe Williams) / MAN OF STONE (. . . Kirkland) / NIGHT TRAIN (?) / LUCILLE (Little Richard) / PARCHMAN FARM (Jerry Allison) / STEPPIN' OUT (. . . Bracken) / etc. • **Trivia:** Another great young guitarist WALTER TROUT became member in 1984, and subsequently departed for his own solo career in the late 80's.

Recommended: THE COLLECTION (*7) / BLUESBREAKERS (*8).

BLUESBREAKERS

JOHN MAYALL – vocals, keyboards, harmonica, guitar(ex-BLUES SYNDICATE) / **BERNIE WATSON** – guitar repl. JOHN GILBEY who had repl. SAMMY PROSSER / **JOHN McVIE** – bass repl. PETE BURFORD who had repl. RICKY BROWN / **MARTIN HART** – drums repl. PETER WARD who had repl. KEITH ROBERTSON (note previous drummers early 1963 =BRIAN MYALL after SAM STONE.)

JOHN MAYALL'S BLUESBREAKERS

Decca / not issued

Apr 64. (7") **CRAWLING UP A HILL. / MR.JAMES** [ ] [-]

— MAYALL retained only McVIE, and recruited **ROGER DEAN** – guitar replaced WATSON **HUGHIE FLINT** – drums (ex-BLUES SYNDICATE) repl. HART

Feb 65. (7") **CROCODILE WALK. / BLUES CITY SHAKEDOWN** [ ] [-]

Mar 65. (lp) **JOHN MAYALL PLAYS JOHN MAYALL (live at Klook's Kleek)** [ ] [-]
– Crawling up a hill / I wanna teach you everything / When I'm gone / I need your love / The hoot owl / R&B time; Night train – Lucille / Crocodile walk / What's the matter with you / Doreen / Runaway / Heartache / Chicago line. *(cd-iss. Jun 88 on 'London')*

— **ERIC CLAPTON** – guitar, vocals (ex-YARDBIRDS) repl. DEAN

Immediate / Immediate

Oct 65. (7") **I'M YOUR WITCHDOCTOR. / TELEPHONE BLUES** [ ] [ ]

— (a month earlier CLAPTON departed to join The GONADS.) (he was repl. by ?) **JACK BRUCE** – bass (ex-GRAHAM BOND ORGANISATION) repl. McVIE

— MAYALL's band were now FLINT, McVIE and CLAPTON again. (BRUCE joined MANFRED MANN)

Decca / London

Jul 66. (lp) **BLUESBREAKERS (as "JOHN MAYALL WITH ERIC CLAPTON")** [6] [ ]
– All your love / Hideaway / Little girl / Another man / Double crossin' time / What'd I say / Key to love / Parchman farm / Have you heard / Ramblin' on my mind; (a) Steppin' out – (b) It ain't right. *(re-iss.1983) (cd-iss.Feb89)*

Sep 66. (7") **KEY TO LOVE. / PARCHMAN FARM** [ ] [ ]

Nov 66. (7") **ALL YOUR LOVE. / HIDEAWAY** [-] [ ]

— (Jul66) **PETER GREEN** – guitar(on above b-side) repl. CLAPTON who formed CREAM

— (Sep66) **AYNSLEY DUNBAR** – drums (ex-MOJOS) repl. FLINT who later formed McGUINNESS FLINT

Oct 66. (7") **LOOKING BACK. / SO MANY ROADS** [ ] [-]

Oct 66. (7") **SITTING IN THE RAIN. / OUT OF REACH** [ ] [ ]

Feb 67. (lp) **A HARD ROAD** [10] [ ]
– A hard road / It's over / You don't love me / The stumble / Another kinda love / Hit the highway / Leaping Christine / Dust my blues / There's always work / The same way / The super natural / Top of the hill / Someday after a while (you'll be sorry) / Living alone.

Mar 67. (7") **CURLY. / RUBBER DUCK** [ ] [ ]
(above credited to **"The BLUESBREAKERS"**)

— next ep was a collaboration with PAUL B of BUTTERFIELD BLUES BAND.

Apr 67. (7"ep) **JOHN MAYALL'S BLUESBREAKERS WITH PAUL BUTTERFIELD** [ ] [ ]

— **MICK FLEETWOOD** – drums repl. MICKEY WALLER who had repl. DUNBAR (to JEFF BECK GROUP) (others still in band MAYALL, GREEN and McVIE.)

Apr 67. (7") **DOUBLE TROUBLE. / IT HURTS ME TOO** [ ] [ ]

— added **TERRY EDMONDS** – rhythm guitar(for Jun67 only before he joined FERRIS WHEEL) / **MICK TAYLOR** – guitar, vocals (ex-GODS) repl. PETER who formed FLEETWOOD MAC / **KEEF HARTLEY** – drums (ex-ARTWOODS) repl. MICK who formed FLEETWOOD MAC / added **CHRIS MERCER** and **RIP KANT** – saxophones

Sep 67. (lp) **CRUSADE** [8] [ ]
– Oh pretty woman / Stand back baby / My time after a while / Snowy wood / Man of stone / Tears in my eyes / Driving sideways / The death of J.B. Lenoir / I can't quit you baby / Streamline / Me and my woman / Checkin' up on my baby.

— **MAYALL** retained **TAYLOR, HARTLEY** and **MERCER,** bringing in **PAUL WILLIAMS** – bass (ex-ZOOT MONEY) repl. McVIE who also joined FLEETWOOD MAC / **DICK HECKSTALL-SMITH** – saxophone (ex-GRAHAM BOND) repl. KANT / added **HENRY LOWTHER** – trumpet

Sep 67. (7") **SUSPICIONS (part 1). / SUSPICIONS (part 2)** [ ] [-]

Sep 67. (7") **SUSPICIONS. / OH PRETTY WOMAN** [-] [ ]

— **KEITH TILLMAN** – bass repl. WILLIAMS

Dec 67. (7") **JENNY. / PICTURES ON THE WALL** [ ] [ ]

Jan 68. (lp) **DIARY OF A BAND** (live interviews & chat) [27] [ ] Feb 70
– Blood on the night / (chat; Edmonton cooks Ferry Inn) / I can't quit you baby / (Keef Hartley interview x2) / Anzio Annie / (John Mayall interview x2) / Snowy wood / The lesson / My own fault / God save the queen.

Jan 68. (lp) **DIARY OF A BAND (Volume 2)** (live interviews & chat) [28] [ ] May 71
– (Gimme some lovin') / The train / Crying shame / (chat); local boy makes good / Help me / Blues in Bb / Soul of a short fat man. *(US title 'JOHN MAYALL LIVE IN EUROPE')*

Feb 68. (7") **BROKEN WINGS. / SONNY BOY BLUE** [-] [ ]

— **TONY REEVES** – bass repl. ANDY FRASER (to FREE) who had repl. TILLMAN / **JON HISEMAN** – drums (ex-GRAHAM BOND, ex-GEORGIE FAME) repl. HARTLEY (to solo)

Jun 68. (lp) **BARE WIRES (JOHN MAYALL'S BLUESBREAKERS)** [3] [59]
– Where did I belong / I start walking / Open up a new door / Fire / I know now / Look in the mirror / I'm a stranger / Hartley quits / No reply / Killing time / She's too young / Sandy. *(cd-iss. Jun 88 on 'London')*

Jun 68. (7") **NO REPLY. / SHE'S TOO YOUNG** [ ] [ ]

— **MAYALL** only retained **MICK TAYLOR / COLIN ALLEN** – drums (ex-ZOOT MONEY) repl. HISEMAN who formed COLOSSEUM / **STEVE THOMPSON** – bass repl. REEVES. (he & HECKSTALL-SMITH also formed above) (also note MERCER left going into sessions and LOWTHER joined KEEF HARLEY BAND)

Nov 68. (7") **THE BEAR. / 2401** [ ] [ ]

Dec 68. (lp) **BLUES FROM LAUREL CANYON** [33] [68]
– Vacation / Walking on sunset / Laurel Canyon home / 2401 / Ready to ride / Medicine man / Somebody's acting like a child / The bear / Miss James / First time alone / Long gone midnight / Fly tomorrow. *(cd-iss.Dec89)*

Dec 68. (7") **WALKING ON SUNSET. / LIVING ALONE** [-] [ ]

JOHN MAYALL

(his new band played without a drummer) **DUSTER BENNETT** – guitar, vocals repl. TAYLOR who joined ROLLING STONES / **JON MARK** – guitar / **JOHNNY ALMOND** – saxophone repl. ALLEN who joined STONE THE CROWS / (after below lp **ALEX DMOCHOWSKI** – bass repl. THOMPSON who joined STONE THE CROWS)

Polydor / Polydor

Oct 69. (lp) **THE TURNING POINT (live 1969)** [11] [32] Sep 69
– The laws must change / Saw mill Gulch road / I'm gonna fight for you J.B. / So hard to share / California / Thoughts about Roxanne / California / Room to move. *(re-iss.May82) (cd-iss.1992 on 'BGO')*

Oct 69. (7") **DON'T WASTE MY TIME. / DON'T PICK A FLOWER** [ ] [81]

Jan 70. (7") **ROOM TO MOVE. / SAW MILL GULCH ROAD** [-] [ ]

— **LARRY TAYLOR** – bass deputised for the ill THOMPSON. (DMOCHOWSKI tour)

Mar 70. (lp) **EMPTY ROOMS** [9] [33]
– Don't waste my time / Plan your revolution / Don't pick a flower / Something new / People cling together / Waiting for the right time / Thinking of my woman / Counting the days / When I go / Many miles apart / To a princess / Lying in my bed. *(re-iss.Aug74)*

May 70. (7") **THINKING OF MY WOMAN. / PLAN YOUR REVOLUTION** [ ] [-]

— MAYALL's completely new band of US musicians **HARVEY MANDEL** – guitar (ex-CANNED HEAT) repl. MARK who formed MARK-ALMOND / **DON 'SUGURCANE' HARRIS** – vocals (ex-FRANK ZAPPA) repl. ALMOND (as above) / **LARRY TAYLOR** – bass finally repl. DMOCHOWSKI

Dec 70. (lp)(c) **U.S.A. UNION** [50] [22] Oct 70
– Nature's disappearing / You must be crazy / Night flyer / Off the road / Possessive emotions / Where did my legs go / Took the car / Crying / My pretty girl / Deep blue sea.

Jan 71. (7") **NATURE'S DISAPPEARING. / MY PRETTY GIRL** [-] [ ]

— Next reunified MAYALL with nearly all old BLUESBREAKERS + new US musicians.

Jun 71. (d-lp) **BACK TO THE ROOTS** [31] [52] Apr 71
– Prisons on the road / My children / Accidental suicide / Groupie girl / Blue fox / Home again / Television eye / Marriage madness / Looking at tomorrow / Dream with me / Full speed ahead / Mr. Censor man / Force of nature / Boogie Albert / Goodbye December / Unanswered questions / Devil's tricks / Travelling.

— MAYALL retained only LARRY TAYLOR and recruited **JERRY McGEE** – guitar (ex-VENTURES) to replace MANDEL (who formed own band) and HARRIS

Nov 71. (lp)(c) **MEMORIES**
– Memories / Wish I knew a woman / Back from Korea / Home in a tree / Seperate ways / The fighting line / Grandad / The city / Nobody cares / Play the harp.

Feb 72. (7") **NOBODY CARES. / PLAY THE HARP** [-]

— **MAYALL** and **TAYLOR** brought in a drummer! – **RON SELICO / plus FREDDY ROBINSON** – guitar to repl. McGEE / added **BLUE MITCHELL** – trumpet / **CLIFFORD SOLOMON** – saxophone

May 72. (lp)(c) **JAZZ BLUES FUSION (live)** [64]
– Country road / Mess around / Good time boogie / Change your ways / Dry throat / Exercise in c-major for harmonica, bass and shufflers / Got to be this way. *(re-iss.1974)*

— **VICTOR GASKIN** – bass repl. LARRY / **KEEF HARTLEY** – drums returned to repl. RON

— added on next **CHARLES OWEN** -flute / **FRED JACKSON + ERNIE WATTS** - saxophones

Jan 73. (lp)(c) **MOVING ON** Oct 72
– (a brief introduction by Bill Cosby) / Worried mind / Keep our country green / Christmas 71 / Things go wrong / Do it / Moving on / Red sky / Reasons / High pressure living.

Jan 73. (7") **MOVING ON. / KEEP OUR COUNTRY GREEN** [-]

Nov 73. (d-lp) **TEN YEARS ARE GONE** Nov 73
– Ten years are gone / Driving till the break of day / Drifting / Better pass you by / California campground / Undecided / Good looking stranger / I still care / Don't hang me up / (introduction) / Sitting here thinking / Harmonica free form / Burning Sun / Dark of the night.

Nov 74. (7") **GASOLINE BLUES. / BRAND NEW BAND** [-]

Dec 74. (lp)(c) **THE LATEST EDITION**
– Gasoline blues / Perfect peace / Going to take my time / Deep down feelings / Troubled times / The pusher man / One of the few / Love song / Little kitchen / A crazy game.

Feb 75. (7") **LET ME GIVE. / PASSING THROUGH** [-]

— MAYALL brought back **LARRY TAYLOR** and **SUGERCANE HARRIS** plus new members **DEE McKINNIE** – vocals / **RICK VITO** – guitar / **JAY SPELL** – keyboards / **SOKO / RICHARDSON** – drums

A.B.C. Blue Thumb

Mar 75. (lp)(c) **NEW YEAR, NEW BAND, NEW COMPANY**
– Sitting on the outside / Can't get home / Step in the sun / To match the wind / Sweet Scorpio / Driving on / Taxman blues / So much to do / My train time / Respectively yours.

Apr 75. (7") **STEP IN THE SUN. / AL GOLDSTEIN BLUES** [-]

— **MAYALL** now totally solo.

Nov 75. (lp)(c) **TIME EXPIRED, NOTICE TO APPEAR**
– Lil boogie in the afternoon / Mess of love / That love / The boy most likely to succeed / Who's next who's now / Hail to the man who lives alone / There will be a way / Just knowing you is a pleasure / A hard day's night / Oldtime blues.

— His following albums feature session musicians.

Apr 76. (lp)(c) **A BANQUET OF BLUES**
– Sunshine / You can't put me down / I got somebody / Turn me loose / Seven days too long / Table top girl / Lady / Fantasyland.

Apr 77. (lp)(c) **LOTS OF PEOPLE** (live)
– (spoken introduction by Red Holloway) / Changes in the wind / Burning down / Play the harp / A helping hand / I got to get down with you / He's a travelling man / Seperate ways / Room to move.

— now with **JAMES QUILL SMITH** – vocals, guitar / **STEVE THOMPSON** – bass / **SOKO RICHARDSON** – drums / and a brass section

Feb 78. (lp)(c) **A HARD CORE PACKAGE** [-]
– Rock and roll hobo / Do I please you / Disconnected line / An old sweet picture / The last time / Make up your mind / Arizona bound / Now and then / Goodnight dreams / Give me a chance.

— now with loads of session people.

D.J.M. D.J.M.

May 79. (lp)(c) **BOTTOM LINE**
– Bottom line / Dreamboat / Desert flower / I'm gonna do it / Revival / Game of love / Celebration / Come with me.

Jul 79. (7") **BOTTOM LINE. / DREAMBOAT**

Dec 79. (lp)(c) **NO MORE INTERVIEWS**
– Hard going up / A bigger slice of pie / Falling / Take me home tonight / Sweet honey bee / Stars in the night / Consideration / Gypsy lady / Wild new lover.

— now with **SMITH, RICHARDSON + KEVIN McCORMICK** – bass / **MAGGIE PARKER** – vox

May 81. (lp)(c) **ROAD SHOW BLUES**
– Why worry / Road show / Mama talk to your daughter / A big man / Lost and gone / Mexico City / John Lee boogie / Reaching for a mountain / Baby what you want me to do. *(re-iss.+cd Jun88 on 'Thunderbolt')*

Jun 81. (7") **JOHN LEE BOOGIE. / WHY WORRY. / MAMA TALK TO YOUR DAUGHTER**

— **MAYALL'S** new line-up featured **COCO MONTAYA + WALTER TROUT** – guitar / **BOBY HAYES** – bass / **JOE YUELE** – drums

P.R.T. GNP Cres..

May 86. (lp)(c) **BEHIND THE IRON CURTAIN** (rec.1984) 1985
– Somebody's acting like a child / Rolling with the blues / The laws must change / Parchman farm / Have you heard / Fly tomorrow / Steppin' out. *(cd-iss.Dec95 on 'GNP Crescendo')*

— After couple of years out of the studio he returned Spring '87. with famous guests **MICK TAYLOR, JOHN McVIE,** etc.

Charly Entente

Dec 88. (lp)(c) **CHICAGO LINE**
– Chicago line / Gimme one more day / One life to live / The last time / Dream about the blues / Fascination lover / Cold blooded woman / The dirty dozen / Tears came rollin' down / Life in the jungle.

Island Island

Jun 90. (lp)(c)(cd) **A SENSE OF PLACE**
– I want to go / Congo square / Send me down to Vicksburg / Without her / Sensitive kind / Jacksboro highway / Let's work together / I can't complain / Black cat moon / Sugarcane / All my life. *(re-iss.cd Mar93)*

(above contained a number of covers)

Silvertone Silvertone

Apr 93. (cd)(c)(lp) **WAKE UP CALL** [61]
– Mail order mystics / Maydell / I could cry / Wake up call / Loaded dice / Undercover agent for the blues / Light the fuse / Anything I can see / Nature's disappearing / I'm a sucker for love / Not at home / Ain't that lovin' you baby.

– compilations, exploitation, etc. –

Aug 66. Purdah; (7") **LONELY HEARTS. / BERNARD JENKINS** [-]

Jun 67. Ace Of Hearts; (lp) **RAW BLUES** [-]

Nov 67. Ace Of Clubs; (lp) **THE BLUES ALONE** (nearly all instruments himself) [24] [-]
– Brand new start / Please don't tell / Down the line / Sonny Boy blow / Marsha's mood / No more tears / Catch that train / Cancelling out / Harp man / Brown sugar / Broken wings / Don't kick me. *(cd-iss. Jun 88 on 'London')*

Aug 69. Decca/ US= London; (lp) **LOOKING BACK** [14] [79]
– Mr.James / Blues city shakedown / They call it stormy Monday / So many roads / Looking back / Sitting in the rain / It hurts me too / Double trouble / Suspicions (part 2) / Jenny / Picture on the wall. *(cd-iss. Jan 89 on 'London')*

Jan 70. Decca; (lp)(c) **THE WORLD OF JOHN MAYALL** [-]

Feb 70. Decca/ US= London; (lp) **THE DIARY OF A BAND (live 1967)** [93]

Apr 71. Decca; (lp)(c) **THE WORLD OF JOHN MAYALL VOL.2** [-]

1978. Decca; (lp)(c) **BLUES ROOTS** [-]

Oct 78. Decca; (7") **CROCODILE WALK. / SITTING IN THE RAIN** [-]

Apr 83. Decca; (lp)(c) **PRIMAL SOLOS** [-]
(cd-iss.Feb89)

Oct 83. Decca;; (lp)(c) **THE JOHN MAYALL STORY VOL.1** [-]

Oct 83. Decca; (lp)(c) **THE JOHN MAYALL STORY VOL.2** [-]

Aug 84. Decca; (d-c) **STORMY MONDAY** [-]

Oct 71. London; (lp)(c) **THRU THE YEARS** [-]
(cd-iss.Jan91 on 'Deram')

Feb 73. London; (d-lp) **DOWN THE LINE** [-]
– (60's demos & 'JOHN MAYALL PLAYS JOHN MAYALL' lp)

Oct 71. Polydor; (lp)(c) **BEYOND THE TURNING POINT** [-]

Apr 76. Polydor; (lp)(c) **JOHN MAYALL** [-]

Nov 80. Polydor; (lp)(c) **GREATEST HITS** [-]

Apr 84. Polydor; (lp)(c) **ROOM TO MOVE**
(re-iss.cd Mar93)

Feb 82. M.C.A.; (lp)(c) **LAST OF THE BRITISH BLUES** [-]

Apr 86. Castle; (d-lp)(c)(cd) **THE COLLECTION** [-]
– Key to love / Hideaway / Ramblin' on my mind / All your love / They call it stormy Monday / Hoochie coochie man / Crocodile walk (1st version) / Crawling up a hill / Marsha's mood / Sonny Boy blow / Looking back / A hard road / The supernatural / You don't love me / Leaping Christine / Suspicions (part 2) / Picture on the wall / The death of J.B. / Lenoir / Sandy / The bear / Walking the sunset / Fly tomorrow.

Apr 86. Charly; (lp) **SOME OF MY BEST FRIENDS ARE BLUES** [-]

1992. Charly; (cd)(c) **LIFE IN THE JUNGLE** (rec. '84) [-]

Jun 88. Knight; (c) **NIGHTRIDING** [-]

Jun 91. Elite; (cd)(c) **WAITING FOR THE RIGHT TIME** [-]

Apr 93. Pulsar; (cd) **A BIG MAN** [-]

Jul 93. Deram; (cd) **LONDON BLUES 1964-1969** [-]

Jul 94. Success; (cd)(c) **WHY WORRY** [-]

Sep 94. Spectrum; (cd)(c) **STORMY MONDAY** [-]

Curtis MAYFIELD

Born: 3 Jun'42, Chicago, USA. Goes went in 1970, after 13 years a major part of The IMPRESSIONS ⇒ . Having formed his own 'Curtom' label two years previous, his debut solo release 'CURTIS', gave him US Top 20 status. From it, edited versions of '(DON'T WORRY) IF THERE'S A HELL . . . ' & 'MOVE ON UP' broke him into the US & UK Pop 30 respectively. After a live double album consisting of solo and Impressions songs, he issued third Top 40 album 'ROOTS' late '71. He was then commissioned to score 'Shaft' inspired 'SUPERFLY' film soundtrack, and this gave him his first and only No.1. It also contained two US Top 10 hits, including the superb title track. By the mid-70's though, his worked failed to appeal to mass audiences. • **Style:** Exponent of hard black political soul music in the early 70's. He transferred his creativity to number of soundtracks and heavy disco themes in the mid-late 70's. This included production work for GLADYS KNIGHT & THE PIPS / The STAPLE SINGERS and ARETHA FRANKLIN. • **Songwriters:** Writes own material, except TONIGHT'S THE NIGHT (Neil Young) / etc. • **Trivia:** His 1973 US TV special 'CURTIS IN CHICAGO' featured guest appearances by past and present IMPRESSIONS' members JERRY BUTLER and GENE CHANDLER.

Recommended: SUPERFLY (*9) / A MAN LIKE CURTIS – THE BEST OF (*8)

CURTIS MAYFIELD – vocals, guitar, keyboards + live band

		Buddah	Curtom	
Nov 70.	(7") **(DON'T WORRY) IF THERE'S A HELL BELOW WE'RE ALL GOING TO GO. / THE MAKINGS OF YOU**		29	
Feb 71.	(lp)(c) **CURTIS** – (Don't worry) If there's a Hell below we're all going to go / The other side of town / The makings of you / We the people who are darker than blue / Move on up / Miss Black America / Wild and free / Give it up. *(re-iss.Oct74) (re-iss.Jun76 on 'Curtom') (cd-iss.Nov93 on 'Movieplay Gold')*		19	Oct 70
May 71.	(7") **GIVE IT UP. / BEAUTIFUL BROTHER OF MINE**	-		
Jun 71.	(7"m) **MOVE ON UP. / GIVE IT UP / BEAUTIFUL BROTHER OF MINE**	12	-	
Aug 71.	(d-lp) **CURTIS – LIVE (live)** – Mighty mighty (spade and Whitey) / I plan to stay a believer / We're a winner (rap) / We've only just begun / Check out your mind / People get ready / Stare and stare / Gypsy woman / The makings of you / We the people who are darker than blue / (Don't worry) If there's a Hell below we're all going to go / Stone junkie. *(re-iss.Oct74) (re-iss.Jun76 on 'Curtom')*		21	May 71
Sep 71.	(7") **MIGHTY MIGHTY (SPADE AND WHITEY) (live). /**	-		
Nov 71.	(7") **WE GOT TO HAVE PEACE. / PEOPLE GET READY**		-	
Dec 71.	(7") **GET DOWN. / WE'RE A WINNER**	-	69	
Jan 72.	(lp)(c) **ROOTS** – Get down / Keep on keeping on / Underground / We got to have peace / Beautiful brother of mine / Now you're gone / Love to keep you in my mind. *(re-iss.Oct74) (re-iss.Jun76 on 'Curtom') (cd-iss.Nov93 on 'Movieplay Gold')*		40	Nov 71
Feb 72.	(7") **WE GOT TO HAVE PEACE. / WE'RE A WINNER**	-		
Apr 72.	(7") **BEAUTIFUL BROTHER OF MINE. / LOVE TO KEEP YOU IN MY MIND**	-		
May 72.	(7") **KEEP ON KEEPING ON. / STONE JUNKIE**		-	
JUn 72.	(7") **MOVE ON UP. / UNDERGROUND**	-		
Sep 72.	(7") **FREDDIE'S DEAD. / UNDERGROUND**		4	Aug 72
Nov 72.	(lp)(c) **SUPERFLY (Soundtrack)** – Little child runnin' wild / Freddie's dead / Give me your love / No thing on me (cocaine song) / Superfly / Pusherman / Junkie chase / Eddie you should know / Think. *(re-iss.Nov74) (re-iss.Aug79 on 'RSO') (re-iss.+cd.Jun88 on 'Ichiban') (cd-iss.Nov93 on 'Movieplay Gold')*	26	1	Aug 72
Nov 72.	(7") **SUPERFLY. / UNDERGROUND**	-	8	
Feb 73.	(7") **SUPERFLY. / GIVE ME YOUR LOVE**		-	
Jul 73.	(7") **FUTURE SHOCK. / THE OTHER SIDE OF TOWN**	-	39	
Sep 73.	(lp)(c) **BACK TO THE WORLD** -Back to the world / Future shock / Right on for the darkness / If I were only a child again / Can't say nothin' / Keep on trippin' / Future song (love of a good woman, love of a good man). *(re-iss.Oct74) (re-iss.Jun76 on 'Curtom') (cd-iss.Nov93 on 'Movieplay Gold')*		16	Jun 73
Oct 73.	(7") **BACK TO THE WORLD. / OTHER SIDE OF TOWN**			
Oct 73.	(7") **IF I WERE ONLY A CHILD AGAIN. / THINK**	-	71	
Jan 74.	(7") **CAN'T SAY NOTHIN'. / FUTURE SHOCK**	-	88	
Mar 74.	(lp)(c) **CURTIS IN CHICAGO (TV Soundtrack)** – Superfly / For your precious love / I'm so proud / Once in my life (IMPRESSIONS) / Preacher man (IMPRESSIONS) / Duke of Earl (GENE CHANDLER) / Love oh love (LEROY HUTSON) / Amen. *(cd-iss.Oct94 on 'Charly')*			Nov 73
Aug 74.	(lp)(c) **SWEET EXORCIST** – Ain't got time / Sweet exorcist / To be invisible / Power to the people / Kung Fu / Suffer / Make me believe in you. *(re-iss.Aug76 on 'Curtom') (cd-iss.Oct94 on 'Charly')*		39	May 74
Aug 74.	(7") **KUNG FU. / RIGHT ON FOR THE DARKNESS**		40	Jun 74
Oct 74.	(7") **SWEET EXORCIST. / SUFFER**	-		
Jan 75.	(lp)(c) **GOT TO FIND A WAY** – Love me (right in the pocket) / So you don't love me / A prayer / Mother's son / Cannot find a way / Ain't no love lost. *(cd-iss.Oct94 on 'Charly')*		76	Nov 74
Mar 75.	(7") **MOTHER'S SON. / LOVE ME RIGHT IN THE POCKET**			
Jun 75.	(7") **STASH THAT BUTT, SUCKER. / ZANZIBAR**	-		

(above single issued on 'Columbia')

—— His band from this period onwards **GARY THOMPSON** – guitar / **RICH TUFO** – keyboards / **LUCKY SCOTT** – bass / **QUINTON JOSEPH** – drums

Aug 75.	(lp)(c) **THERE'S NO PLACE LIKE AMERICA TODAY** – Billy Jack / When seasons change / So in love / Jesus / Blue Monday people / Hard times / Love to the people.			Jun 75
Sep 75.	(7") **SO IN LOVE. / HARD TIMES**	-	67	
Jul 76.	(7") **ONLY YOU BABE. / LOVE TO THE PEOPLE**	-		
Jul 76.	(lp)(c) **GIVE, GET, TAKE AND HAVE** – In your arms again / This love is sweet / P.S. I love you / Party night / Get a little bit (give, get, take and have) / Soul music / Only you babe / Mr. Welfare you.			
Sep 76.	(7") **PARTY NIGHT. / P.S. I LOVE YOU**	-		

		Curtom	Curtom	
Mar 77.	(7") **SHOW ME LOVE. / JUST WANT TO BE WITH YOU**	-		
Mar 77.	(lp)(c) **NEVER SAY YOU CAN'T SURVIVE** – Show me love / Just want to be with you / When we're alone / Never say you can't survive / I'm gonna win your love / All night long / When you used to be mine / Sparkle. *(cd-iss.Oct94 on 'Charly')*			
Nov 77.	(7") **DO DO WAP IS STRONG IN HERE. / NEED SOMEONE TO LOVE**	-		
Feb 78.	(lp)(c) **SHORT EYES (Soundtrack)** – Do do wap is strong in here / Back against the wall / Need someone to love / A heavy dupe / Short eyes / Break it down / Another fool in love / Father confessor.			Nov 77
Jul 78.	(7") **YOU ARE, YOU ARE. / GET A LITLE BIT (GIVE, GET, TAKE AND HAVE)**	-		
Sep 78.	(7") **DO IT ALL NIGHT. / PARTY PARTY**	-		
Oct 78.	(lp)(c) **DO IT ALL NIGHT** – Do it all night / No goodbyes / Party party / Keeps me loving you / In love, in love, in love / You are, you are. *(cd-iss.Oct94 on 'Charly')*	-		
Nov 78.	(12") **NO GOODBYES. / PARTY PARTY**	65	-	
Dec 78.	(7") **IN LOVE, IN LOVE, IN LOVE. / KEEPS ME LOVING YOU**	-		

—— With various session people

		R.S.O.	R.S.O.	
Mar 79.	(7") **THIS YEAR. / ('A'instrumental)**			
Sep 79.	(lp)(c) **HEARTBEAT** – Tell me, tell me (how ya like to be loved) / What is my woman for? / Between you baby and me / Victory / Over the hump / You better stop / You're so good to me / Heartbeat.		42	Aug 79

—— Next single & album credited vocalist LINDA CLIFFORD.

Aug 79.	(7") **BETWEEN YOU BABY AND ME. / YOU'RE SO GOOD TO ME**			
Jun 80.	(lp)(c) **THE RIGHT COMBINATION** – Rock to your socks / The right combination / I'm so proud / Ain't no love lost / It's lovin' time / Love's sweet sensation / Between you baby and me.			
Sep 80.	(lp)(c) **SOMETHING TO BELIEVE IN** – Something to believe in / Love me love me now / Never let me go / Tripping out / People never give up / It's alright / Never stop loving me. *(re-iss.+cd.Oct89 on 'Curtom')*			Jul 80
Oct 80.	(7") **IT'S ALRIGHT. / SUPERFLY**		-	

		not issued	Boardwalk
1981.	(lp) **LOVE IS THE PLACE** – She don't let nobody (but me) / Toot an' toot an' toot / Baby doll / Love is the place / Just ease my mind / You mean everything to me / You get all my love / Come free your people,	-	
1981.	(7") **SHE DON'T LET NOBODY (BUT ME). / YOU GET ALL MY LOVE**	-	
1981.	(7") **COME FREE YOUR PEOPLE. / TOOT AN' TOOT AN' TOOT**	-	

		Epic	Boardwalk	
Oct 82.	(7") **HEY BABY (GIVE IT ALL TO ME). / SUMMER HOT**	-		
Mar 83.	(lp)(c) **HONESTY** – Hey baby (give it all to me) / Still within your heart / Dirty laundry / Nobody but you / If you need me / What you gawn do? / Summer hot.			Oct 82
Mar 83.	(7") **DIRTY LAUNDRY. / NOBODY BUT YOU**	-		

		not issued	C.R.C.
Sep 85.	(lp)(c) **WE COME IN PEACE WITH A MESSAGE OF LOVE** *– (UK-iss.cd/c/lp.Feb91 on 'Curtom')*	-	

Date	Release	98.6	98.6
Nov 86.	(7")(12") **BABY IT'S YOU. / BREAKIN' IN THE STREETS**		

—— (In mid'87 he was credited on BLOW MONKEYS single 'Celebrate The Day'.)

Date	Release	Capitol	Capitol
1987.	(lp)(c) **LIVE IN LOS ANGELES (live)** *– (withdrawn?)*		

Date	Release	Ichiban	Ichiban
Jun 88.	(lp)(c)(cd) **LIVE IN EUROPE (live)** – (intro) / Freddie's dead / We gotta have peace / People get ready / Move on up /		

Back to the world / Gypsy woman / Pusher man / We've only just begun / When seasons change / (Don't worry) If there's a Hell below we're all going to go.

Jul 88. (12") **MOVE ON UP (live). / LITTLE CHILD RUNNIN' WILD (live)**

Curtom | Arista

May 89. (7") **HE'S A FLY GUY. (w/ FISHBONE) / ('A'instrumental)** -

May 89. (7") **I MO GIT U SUCKA. / HE'S A FLY GUY**
(12"+=)(cd-s+=) – ('A'extended).

Feb 90. (7")(12") **HOMELESS. / PEOPLE NEVER GIVE UP**

Mar 90. (cd)(c)(lp) **TAKE IT TO THE STREET**
– Homeless / Got to be real / Do be down / Who was that lady / On and on / He's a fly guy / Don't push / I mo git u sucka.

Jun 90. (7") **DO BE DOWN. / GOT TO BE REAL**
(12"+=) – ('A'extended) / ('A'radio version).

— A terrible accident occurred in September 1990 as CURTIS prepared for a gig. A high wind brought down a lighting scaffold which struck him and left him paralysed permanently from the neck downwards.

Capitol | Capitol

Sep 90. (7") **SUPERFLY 1990. / SUPERFLY 1990 (Fly edit mix)** 48
(12"+=)(cd-s+=) – ('A'diff.mix) (featured ICE-T)

– compilations, others, etc. –

Nov 74. Buddah/ US= Curtom; (lp)(c) **MOVE ON UP – THE BEST OF CURTIS MAYFIELD**

Nov 74. Buddah/ US= Curtom; (7") **MOVE ON UP. / GIVE IT UP**

Jan 83. P.R.T.; (7") **MOVE ON UP. /('B'by 'Melba Moore')** -

Feb 90. Essential; (cd)(c)(lp) **PEOPLE GET READY (live At Ronnie Scott's)** -

Nov 92. Music Collection; (cd) **A MAN LIKE CURTIS – THE BEST OF . . .** -
– Move on up / Superfly / (Don't worry) If there's a Hell below we're all gonna go / You are, you are / Give me your love / Never stop loving me / Tripping out / Soul music / This year / Ain't no love lost / Pusherman / Freddie's dead / Do do wop is strong in here / Hard times / In your arms again (shake it) / So in love.

Sep 93. Traditional Line; (cd) **HARD TIMES** -

Jan 94. Windsong; (cd) **BBC RADIO 1 LIVE IN CONCERT** -

Mar 94. Charly; (cd) **GET DOWN TO THE FUNKY GROOVE** -

Aug 94. Charly; (cd) **GROOVE ON UP** -

Nov 94. Charly; (cd) **TRIPPING OUT** -

Apr 94. Movieplay Gold; (cd) **LIVE! (live)** -

May 94. Laserlight; (cd)(c) **CURTIS MAYFIELD** -

— CURTIS also collaborated on other Film Soundtracks. 'CLAUDINE' in Aug74 with GLADYS KNIGHT & THE PIPS, 'LET'S DO IT AGAIN' in Sep76 with STAPLE SINGERS and 'SPARKLE' Oct76 with ARETHA FRANKLIN.

MAZZY STAR

Formed: Santa Monica, Los Angeles, California, USA . . . .early 90's by duo DAVID ROBACK and HOPE SANDOVAL. In 1993, their second album 'SO TONIGHT . . . ' cracked the US Top 50, and paved the way for hit single 'FADE INTO YOU'. • **Style:** Part acoustic psychedelic /folky rock outfit, with dreamy soft-VELVETS side. • **Songwriters:** SANDOVAL / ROBACK except; BLUE FLOWER (Slapp Happy) / I'M GONNA BAKE MY BISCUIT (McCoy) / I'M SAILIN' (Lawler) / FIVE STRING SERENADE (. . . Lee) / GIVE YOU MY LOVIN' (. . . Gomez). • **Trivia:** HOPE SANDOVAL guested on The JESUS & MARY CHAIN's 1994 single 'SOMETIMES ALWAYS'.

Recommended: SO TONIGHT THAT I MIGHT SEE (*8) / SHE HANGS BRIGHTLY (*8)

HOPE SANDOVAL – vocals, guitar / **DAVID ROBACK** – guitar (ex-RAIN PARADE, ex-RAINY DAY, ex-OPAL) /

Rough Trade | Rough Trade

Apr 90. (cd)(c)(lp) **SHE HANGS BRIGHTLY**
– Halah / Blue flower / Ride it on / She hangs brightly / I'm sailin' / Give you my lovin' / Be my angel / Taste of blood / Ghost highway / Free / Before I sleep. *(re-iss.May93 + Sep94 on 'Capitol')*

Capitol | Capitol

Oct 93. (cd)(c)(lp) **SO TONIGHT THAT I MIGHT SEE** 68 | 36
– Fade into you / Bells ring / Mary of silence / Five string serenade / Blue light / She's my baby / Unreflected / Wasted / Into dust / So tonight that I might see. *(re-iss.Jun94)*

Aug 94. (cd-s) **FADE INTO YOU / BLUE FLOWER / I'M GONNA BAKE MY BISCUIT** 48 | 44
(10") – ('A'side) / Five string serenade / Under my car / Bells ring (acoustic).

— The track 'TELL ME NOW' featured in the film 'Batman Forever' and the was on B-side of U2's 'Hold Me, Kiss Me, Kill Me!'.

McALMONT & BUTLER

Formed: Croydon, London, England . . .early 1995, by ex-THIEVES singer DAVID McALMONT and ex-SUEDE guitarist BERNARD BUTLER. McALMONT was raised by his mother in Norfolk until when he was 11, divorced she to him and his sister Guyana. He returned to London in 1992 and soon formed The THIEVES, who split after 3 singles (2 for Virgin's 'Hut' label). Their unreleased album finally surfaced Autumn '94 as his own eponymous debut. Also re-actified an earlier THIEVES flop 'EITHER'. • **Style:** Black and open homosexual McALMONT (he of the Danny La Rue influence), was described as Britain's answer to TERENCE TRENT D'ARBY. Although many likened him to AL GREEN or even LIZ FRASER of The COCTEAU TWINS!. • **Songwriters:** Partnership except YOU'LL LOSE A GOOD THING (Ozen-Meaux).

Recommended: THE SOUND OF McALMONT & BUTLER (*7)

THIEVES

DAVID McALMONT -vocals / **SAUL FREEMAN** – guitar / + 2 earlier members

Nursery | not issued

Nov 92. (12") **THROUGH THE DOOR. / PLACED ASIDE / THE SAME** -

Hut-Virgin | Caroline

Sep 93. (7")(c-s) **UNWORTHY. / THE NIGHT** -
(12"+=)(cd-s+=) – They hide / ('A'version).

Mar 94. (c-s) **EITHER /** -
(cd-s+=) –

McALMONT

DAVID McALMONT -vocals (with BERNARD, etc.)

Hut | Caroline

Sep 94. (cd)(c)(lp) **McALMONT**
– Either / Not wiser / Unworthy / Misunderstood / Is it raining? / Conversation / He loves you / Worn away / It's always this way / My grey boy / They hide. *(cd had ltd.bonus cd) (re-iss.Jan 95)*

Dec 94. (7") **EITHER. / YOU MADE ME**
(12"+=)(cd-s+=) – As if I'd known (live) / Either (mix).

On the 19th June '95, he made available for one day a cdep 'SATURDAY (GAY PRIDE EP). The tracks were:- Saturday / Fort James / My grey boy.

McALMONT & BUTLER

Hut | Caroline

May 95. (c-s) **YES / DON'T CALL IT SOUL** 8
(cd-s+=) – How about you?.
(cd-s) – ('A'side) / What's the excuse this time? / Disappointment.

Oct 95. (c-s) **YOU DO / TONIGHT** 17
(cd-s+=) – You'll lose a good thing.
(cd-s) – The debitor / Although.

Nov 95. (cd)(c)(lp) **THE SOUND OF McALMONT & BUTLER** 33
– Yes / What's the excuse this time? / The right thing / Although / Don't call it soul / Disappointment / The debitor / How about you? / Tonight / You'll lose a good thing / You do.

McAULEY-SCHENKER GROUP (see under ⇒ SCHENKER, Michael)

Nicko McBRAIN (see under ⇒ IRON MAIDEN) (see under ⇒ IRON MAIDEN)

Dan McCAFFERTY (see under ⇒ NAZARETH)

Paul McCARTNEY

Born: JAMES PAUL McCARTNEY, 18 Jun'42, Liverpool, England. Major part of The BEATLES in the 60's, he and JOHN LENNON were easily the greatest contemporary writing partnership of the 20th Cent. They officially split on 11 Apr'70, having just prior to issuing last recordings 'LET IT BE', (which was also name of docu-film, telling the last days of the fab four). Released 3 weeks earlier was McCARTNEY's first solo outing 'McCARTNEY', which included backing from wife LINDA (married 12 Mar'69). It topped the American charts, but was held off UK No.1 by SIMON & GARFUNKEL's 'Bridge Over Troubled Water'. The next year, he hit cross-Atlantic Top 5 with debut 45 'ANOTHER DAY', and then took unusual step of co-billing wife LINDA on subsequent album 'RAM'. This reversed chart positions of its predecessor, and encased US-only 45 'UNCLE ALBERT – ADMIRAL HALSEY', which hit No.1. Later in '71, he launched WINGS, which included LINDA, DENNY LAINE and DENNY SEIWELL. They hit critical low, with 'WILDLIFE' lp, which was followed by controversial and radio banned hit single 'GIVE IRELAND BACK TO THE IRISH'. Annoyed at its ban, WINGS then put music to nursery rhyme 'MARY HAD A LITTLE LAMB', which made UK Top 10 although losing much credibility. The McCARTNEYs then underwent a series of drug busts, and another this time silly BBC ban on next hit 'HI HI HI'. In Spring '73, PAUL McCARTNEY & WINGS hit US top with single 'MY LOVE', and album 'RED ROSE SPEEDWAY'. In 1974, they/he surpassed all before when album 'BAND ON THE RUN' hit the top and sold over 6 million copies during its 2 year plus stay in both UK & US charts. In 1975 wings continued to soar, until PAUL McCARTNEY reverted to even more fruitful solo career late '79. In 1977, they had massive selling UK No.1 for 9 weeks 'MULL OF KINTYRE', and he with STEVIE WONDER called for racial harmony in 1982, with cross-Atlantic No.1 'EBONY & IVORY'. • **Style:** Evergreen pop-rock superstar, talented singer & multi-instrumentalist with ability to write clever love songs, etc. with ease. • **Songwriters:** 99% by PAUL, except some with group. Covered; MONY MONY (Tommy James & The Shandells) / GO NOW (Moody Blues) / RUDOLPH THE RED-NOSED REINDEER (Christmas trad.) / KANSAS CITY (Wilbert Harrison) / MATCHBOX (Carl Perkins) / TWENTY FLIGHT ROCK (Eddie Cochran) / LAWDY MISS CLAWDY + IT'S NOW OR NEVER + BLUE MOON OF KENTUCKY (Elvis Presley) / BE-BOP – A-LULA (Gene Vincent) / BACK ON MY FEET (co-with Elvis Costello) / HI-HEEL SNEAKERS (Tommy Tucker) / GIVE PEACE A CHANCE (John Lennon) / AIN'T THAT A SHAME (Fats Domino) / etc., and many past BEATLES songs live. • **Trivia:** The 'BAND ON THE RUN' album sleeve featured the group being caught escaping alongside celebrities; Michael Parkinson, Kenny Lynch, James Coburn, Clement Freud, Christopher Lee & John Conteh.

Recommended: BAND ON THE RUN (*8) / ALL THE BEST (*7) / McCARTNEY (*6) / RAM (*7) / WILD LIFE (*5) / RED ROSE SPEEDWAY (*5)

PAUL McCARTNEY

– vocals, bass, guitar, keyboards, drums (ex-BEATLES) with **LINDA McCARTNEY** (b. LINDA EASTMAN, 24 Sep'42, Scarsdale, New York, USA) – backing vocals

Apple Apple

Apr 70. (lp)(c) **McCARTNEY** 2 1

– The lovely Linda / That would be something / Valentine day / Every night / Hot as sun / Glasses / Junk / Man we was lonely / Momma miss America / Teddy boy / Singalong junk / Maybe I'm amazed / Kreen-Akrove. *(re-iss.+cd.May84 on 'Fame') (re-iss.cd+c Jun93)*

Feb 71. (7") **ANOTHER DAY. / OH WOMAN OH WHY** 2 5

PAUL AND LINDA McCARTNEY

PAUL – vocals, guitar, bass / **LINDA** – keyboards, backing vocals, percussion / added **DENNY SEIWELL** – drums, vocals (plus various session people)

May 71. (lp)(c) **RAM** 1 2

– Too many people / Three legs / Ram on / Dear boy / Uncle Albert – Admiral Halsey / Smile away / Heart of the country / Monkberry moon delight / Eat at home / Long-haired lady / Ram on / The back seat of my car. *(re-iss.Jan85 on 'Parlophone') (re-iss.cd+c Jun93)*

Aug 71. (7") **THE BACK SEAT OF MY CAR. / HEART OF THE COUNTRY** 39 -

Aug 71. (7") **UNCLE ALBERT – ADMIRAL HALSEY. / TOO MANY PEOPLE** - 1

WINGS

was the group the above trio formed; adding **DENNY LAINE** – guitar, vocals (ex-MOODY BLUES, ex-UGLYS, ex-BALLS, etc.)

Dec 71. (lp)(c) **WILD LIFE** 8 10

– Mumbo / Bip bop / Love is strange / Wild life / Some people never know / I am your singer / Tomorrow / Dear friend. *(re-iss.+cd.Apr84 on 'Fame', cd+=)* – Mary had a little lamb / Little woman love / Oh woman, oh why. *(re-iss.cd+c Jun93)*

— added **HENRY McCULLOCH** – guitar, vocals (ex-JOE COCKER, etc.)

Feb 72. (7") **GIVE IRELAND BACK TO THE IRISH. / ('A'version)** 16 21 Mar 72

May 72. (7") **MARY HAD A LITTLE LAMB. / LITTLE WOMAN LOVE** 9 28 Jun 72

Dec 72. (7") **C MOON. / HI HI HI** 5 10

(above flipped over in the States)

PAUL McCARTNEY AND WINGS

Mar 73. (7") **MY LOVE. / THE MESS (live)** 9 1 Apr 73

May 73. (lp)(c) **RED ROSE SPEEDWAY** 5 1

– Big barn bed / My love / Get on the right thing / One more kiss / Little lamb dragonfly / Single pigeon / When the night / Hold me tight – Lazy dynamite – Hands of love – Power cut / Loup (1st Indian on the Moon). *(re-iss.+cd.Jan85 on 'Parlophone', cd+=)*– The mess (live) / I lie around / Country dreamer. *(re-iss. +cd ct 87 on 'Fame') (re-iss.cd+c Jun93)*

Jun 73. (7") **LIVE AND LET DIE. (as "WINGS") / I LIE AROUND** 9 2 Jul 73

— **PAUL & LINDA** plus **DENNY LAINE.** (McCULLOCH went solo, SEIWELL to sessions)

Oct 73. (7") **HELEN WHEELS. / COUNTRY DREAMER** 12 10 Nov 73

Dec 73. (lp)(c) **BAND ON THE RUN** 1 1

– Band on the run / Jet / Bluebird / Mrs. Vanderbilt / Let me roll it / Mamunia / No words / Picasso's last words (drink to me) / Nineteen hundred and eighty-five. *(re-iss.+cd.Jan85 on 'Parlophone', cd+=)*– Helen wheels. *(re-iss.cd+c Jun93) (US-pic-lp 1978)*

Feb 74. (7") **JET. / LET ME ROLL IT** 7 7

Apr 74. (7") **BAND ON THE RUN. / 1985** - 1

Jun 74. (7") **BAND ON THE RUN. / ZOO GANG** 3 -

— added **JIMMY McCULLOCH** (b. 4 Jun'53) – guitar, vocals (ex-THUNDERCLAP NEWMAN, ex-STONE THE CROWS) + **GEOFF BRITTON** – drums (ex-EAST OF EDEN)

Nov 74. (7") **JUNIOR'S FARM. / SALLY G** 16 3 / 17

WINGS

JOE ENGLISH (b. Rochester, New York) – drums (ex-JAM FACTORY) repl. BRITTON who joined CHAMPION

Capitol Capitol

May 75. (7") **LISTEN TO WHAT THE MAN SAID. / LOVE IN SONG** 6 1

Jun 75. (lp)(c) **VENUS AND MARS** 1 1

– Venus and Mars rock show / Love in song / You gave me the answer / Magneto and Titanium man / Letting go / Venus and Mars (reprise) / Spirits of ancient Egypt / Medicine jar / Call me back again / Listen to what the man said / Treat her gently – lonely old people / Crossroads theme. *(re-iss.+cd.1985 on 'Parlophone')* (cd+=) – Zoogang / My carnival / Lunch box – odd socks. *(re-iss.+cd Nov 88 on 'Fame') (re-iss.cd+c Jun93)*

Sep 75. (7") **LETTING GO. / YOU GAVE ME THE ANSWER** 41 39

Nov 75. (7") **VENUS AND MARS ROCK SHOW. / MAGNETO AND TITANIUM MAN** 12

E.M.I. Capitol

Apr 76. (lp)(c) **WINGS AT THE SPEED OF SOUND** 2 1

– Let 'em in / The note you never wrote / She's my baby / Beware my love / Wino junko / Silly love songs / Cook of the house / Time to hide / Must do something about it / San Ferry Anne / Warm and beautiful. *(re-iss 1985, cd-iss.Jul89 on 'Parlophone') (re-iss.+cd.Oct89 on 'Fame') (re-iss.cd+c Jun93)*

May 76. (7") **SILLY LOVE SONGS. / COOK OF THE HOUSE** 2 1 Apr 76

Jul 76. (7") **LET 'EM IN. / BEWARE MY LOVE** 2 3

Jan 77. (t-lp)(d-c) **WINGS OVER AMERICA (live)** 8 1 Dec 76

– Venus and Mars rock show / Jet / Let me roll it / Spirits of ancient Egypt / Medicine jar / Maybe I'm amazed / Call me back again / Lady Madonna / The long and winding road / Live and let die / Picasso's last words (drink to me) / Richard Cory / Bluebird / I've just seen a face / Yesterday / You gave me the answer / Magnet and Titanium man / Go now / My love / Listen to what the man said / Let 'em in / Time to hide / Silly love songs / Beware my love / Letting go / Band on the run / Hi hi hi / Soily. *(d-cd-iss. May 87)*

Feb 77. (7") **MAYBE I'M AMAZED (live). / SOILY (live)** 28 10

— cut to trio of **PAUL, LINDA** and **DENNY** when JIMMY joined SMALL FACES, and JOE joined SEA LEVEL (ex-ALLMANS).

Capitol Capitol

Nov 77. (7")(7"blue) **MULL OF KINTYRE. / GIRLS SCHOOL** 1 33

(Above flipped over in the States)

— added **STEVE HOLLY** – drums (on session but joined f/t Jul'78)

Parlophone Capitol

Mar 78. (7") **WITH A LITTLE LUCK. / CUFF LINK: BACKWARDS TRAVELLER** 5 1

Apr 78. (lp)(c) **LONDON TOWN** 4 2

– London town / Cafe on the Left Bank / I'm carrying / Backwards traveller – Cuff link / Children children / Girlfriend / I've had enough / With a little luck / Famous groupies / Deliver your children / Name and address / Don't let it bring you down / Morse Moose and the Grey Goose. *(re-iss.1985) (re-iss.+cd.Aug89 on 'Fame') (re-iss.cd+c Jun93)*

Jun 78. (7") **I'VE HAD ENOUGH. / DELIVER YOUR CHILDREN** 42 25

Aug 78. (7") **LONDON TOWN. / I'M CARRYING** 60 39

Nov 78. (lp)(c) **WINGS GREATEST** 5 29

– Another day / Silly love songs / Live and let die / Junior's farm / With a little luck / Band on the run / Uncle Albert – Admiral Halsey / Hi hi hi / Let 'em in / My love / Mull of Kintyre. *(re-iss.+cd.1985) (re-iss.cd+c Aug93)*

— added **LAURENCE JUBER** – guitar, vocals

Parlophone Columbia

Mar 79. (7")(12") **GOODNIGHT TONIGHT. / DAYTIME NIGHTIME SUFFERING** [5] [5]
Jun 79. (7") **OLD SIAM, SIR. / SPIN IT ON** [35] [-]
Jun 79. (7") **GETTING CLOSER. / SPIN IT ON** [-] [20]
Jun 79. (lp)(c) **BACK TO THE EGG** [6] [8]
– Reception / Getting closer / We're open tonight / Spin it on / Again and again and again / Old Siam, sir / Arrow through me / Rockestra theme / To you / After the ball – Million miles / Winter rose – Love awake / The broadcast / So glad to see you here / Baby's request. *(US promo pic-lp became worth $1,000) (re-iss.+cd Jul 89) (re-iss.cd+c Aug93)*
Aug 79. (7") **GETTING CLOSER. / BABY'S REQUEST** [60] [-]
Sep 79. (7") **ARROW THROUGH ME. / OLD SIAM, SIR** [-] [29]

PAUL McCARTNEY

went solo, augmented by LINDA plus session people

Parlophone Columbia

Nov 79. (7") **WONDERFUL CHRISTMASTIME. / RUDOLPH THE RED-NOSED REINDEER** [6] [ ]
(re-iss. Nov '83 US)
Apr 80. (7") **COMING UP. / COMING UP (live) / LUNCH BOX – ODD SOX** [2] [1]
May 80. (lp)(c) **McCARTNEY II** [1] [3]
– Coming up / Temporary secretary / On the way / Waterfalls / Nobody knows / Front parlour / Summer's day song / Frozen Jap / Bogey music / Darkroom / One of these days. *(re-iss.+cd.Sep87 on 'Fame' cd+=)–* Secret friend / Check my machine. *(re-iss.cd+c Aug93)*
Jun 80. (7") **WATERFALLS. / CHECK MY MACHINE** [9] [ ]
Sep 80. (12") **TEMPORARY SECRETARY. / SECRET FRIEND** [ ] [ ]
Apr 82. (7") **EBONY AND IVORY.(as "PAUL McCARTNEY & STEVIE WONDER") / RAINCLOUDS** [1] [1]
(12"+=) – ('A'solo version).
Apr 82. (lp)(c) **TUG OF WAR** [1] [1]
– Tug of war / Take it away / Somebody who cares / What's that you're doing? / Here today / Ballroom dancing / The pound is sinking / Wanderlust / Get it / Be what you see / Dress me up as a robber / Ebony and ivory. *(cd-iss.1985) (re-iss.+cd.Nov88 on 'Fame') (re-iss.cd+c Aug93)*
Jun 82. (12"m) **TAKE IT AWAY. / I'LL GIVE YOU A RING / DRESS ME UP AS A ROBBER** [15] [10]
Sep 82. (7") **TUG OF WAR. / GET IT** [53] [53]
— (In Oct82, duetted w /MICHAEL JACKSON on duet 'THE GIRL IS MINE' Top 10)
Oct 83. (7") **SAY SAY SAY. (as "PAUL McCARTNEY & MICHAEL JACKSON") / ODE TO KOALA BEAR** [2] [1]
(12"+=) – ('A' instrumental).
Nov 83. (lp)(c)(cd) **PIPES OF PEACE** [4] [15]
– Pipes of peace / Say say say / The other me / Keep under cover / So bad / The man / Sweetest little show / Average person / Hey hey / Tug of peace / Through our love. *(re-iss.cd+c Aug93)*
Dec 83. (7") **PIPES OF PEACE. / SO BAD** [1] [ ]
(flipped over US May'84, hit No. 23)
Sep 84. (7") **NO MORE LONELY NIGHTS. / ('A' extended)** [2] [6]
(12"+=)(12"pic-d+=) – Silly love songs.
Oct 84. (d-lp)(c)(cd) **GIVE MY REGARDS TO BROAD STREET – ORIGINAL SOUND TRACK** [1] [21]
– No more lonely nights (ballad) / Good day sunshine / Corridor music / Yesterday / Here, there and everywhere / Wanderlust / Ballroom dancing / Silly love songs (reprise) / Not such a bad boy / No values / No more lonely nights (reprise) / For no one / Eleanor Rigby – Eleanor's dream / The long and winding road / No more lonely nights (play out version). *(re-iss.cd+c Aug93)*
Nov 84. (7")(7"pic-d) **WE ALL STAND TOGETHER.(as "PAUL McCARTNEY & THE FROG CHORUS") / ('A' humming version)** [3] [ ]
(re-iss.Dec85 reached No.34 UK)

Parlophone Capitol

Nov 85. (7")(7"pic-d) **SPIES LIKE US. / MY CARNIVAL** [16] [7]
(12"+=)(12"pic-d+=) – ('A' party mix).
Jul 86. (7") **PRESS. / IT'S NOT TRUE** [25] [21]
(12"+=) – Hanglide. / ('A' dub).
(10"++=) – ('A'version).
Sep 86. (lp)(c)(cd) **PRESS TO PLAY** [8] [30]
– Stranglehold / Good times coming – Feel the sun / Talk more talk / Footprints / Only love remains / Press / Pretty little head / Move over busker / Angry / However absurd. *(cd+=)–* Write away / It's not true / Tough on a tightrope. *(re-iss.cd+c Aug93)*
Oct 86. (7") **PRETTY LITTLE HEAD. / WRITE AWAY** [ ] [-]
(12"+c-s+=) – Angry.
Nov 86. (7") **STRANGLEHOLD. / ANGRY (remix)** [-] [81]
Dec 86. (7")(12") **ONLY LOVE REMAINS. / TOUGH ON A TIGHTROPE** [34] [ ]
Nov 87. (7") **ONCE UPON A LONG AGO. / BACK ON MY FEET** [10] [ ]
(12"+=) – Midnight special / Don't get around much anymore.
(12"extra+=) – Lawdy Miss Clawdy / Kansas City.
(cd-s+=) – Don't get around much anymore / Kansas City.
Nov 87. (lp)(c)(cd) **ALL THE BEST** (compilation) [2] [62]
– Coming up / Ebony and ivory (w/ STEVIE WONDER) / Listen to what the man said / No more lonely nights / Silly love songs / Let 'em in / C Moon / Pipes of peace / Live and let die / Another day / Maybe I'm amazed / Goodnight tonight / Once upon a long time ago / Say say say / With a little luck / My love / We all stand together / Mull of Kintyre / Jet / Band on the run. *(US slightly different tracks)*
— now with **LINDA / WIX** (PAUL WICKENS) – keyboards / **CHRIS WHITTEN** – drums / **ROBBIE McINTOSH** – guitar / **HAMISH STUART** – guitar, bass (ex-AVERAGE WHITE BAND)
May 89. (7") **MY BRAVE FACE. / FLYING TO MY HOME** [18] [25]
(12"+=)(c-s+=)(cd-s+=) – I'm gonna be a wheel someday / Ain't that a shame.
Jun 89. (lp)(c)(cd) **FLOWERS IN THE DIRT** [1] [21]
– My brave face / Rough ride / You want her too / Distractions / We got married / Put it there / Figure of eight / This one / Don't be careless love / That day is done / How many people / Motor of love. *(cd+=)–* Ou est le soleil. *(re-iss.lp,cd.Nov89, as 'FLOWERS . . . WORLD TOUR PACK', w/free 7" PARTY PARTY free 3" cd-s.w/cd version) (re-iss.cd+c Aug93)*
Jul 89. (7")(c-s) **THIS ONE. / THE FIRST STONE** [18] [94]
(12"+=)(cd-s+=) – I wanna cry / I'm in love again.
Nov 89. (7")(c-s) **FIGURE OF EIGHT. / OU EST LE SOLEIL** [42] [92]
(12"+=) – ('B'dub mix).
(3"cd-s+=) – Rough ride.
(12") – ('A'side) / This one (club mix).
(cd-s) – ('A'side) / Long and winding road / Loveliest thing.
Feb 90. (7")(c-s) **PUT IT THERE. / MAMA'S LITTLE GIRL** [32] [ ]
(12"+=)(cd-s+=) – Same time next year.
Oct 90. (7")(c-s) **BIRTHDAY (live). / GOOD DAY SUNSHINE (live)** [29] [ ]
(12"+=)(cd-s+=) – P.S. I love you (live) / Let 'em in (live).
Nov 90. (d-cd)(d-c)(t-lp) **TRIPPING THE LIVE FANTASTIC (live)** [17] [26]
– Figure of eight / Jet / Rough ride / Got to get you into my life / Band on the run / Birthday / Ebony and ivory / we got married / Inner city madness / Maybe I'm amazed / The long and winding road / Cracking up / Fool on the hill / Sgt. Pepper's lonely hearts club band / Can't buy me love / Matchbox / Put it there / Together / Things we said today / Eleanor Rigby / This one / My brave face / I saw her standing there / Back in the USSR / Twenty flight rock / Coming up / Sally / Let it be / Ain't that a shame / Live and let die / If I were not upon the stage / Hey Jude / Yesterday / Get back / Golden slumbers – Carry that weight – The end / Don't let the Sun catch you crying.
Dec 90. (7") **ALL MY TRIALS (live). / C MOON (live)** [35] [ ]
(12"+=) – Mull of Kintyre / Put it there.
(cd-s+=) – Live medley:- Strawberry fields forever / Help / Give peace a chance.
— **BLAIR CUNNINGHAM** – drums (ex-LLOYD COLE) repl. WHITTEN
Jun 91. (cd)(c)(lp) **UNPLUGGED – THE OFFICIAL BOOTLEG** [7] [14]
– Be-bop-a-lula / I lost my little girl / Here there and everywhere / Blue Moon of Kentucky / We can work it out / San Francisco Bay blues / I've just seen a face / Every night / She's a woman / Hi-heel sneakers / And I love her / That would be something / Blackbird / Ain't no sunshine / Good rockin' tonight / Singing the blues / Junk. *(re-cd+c.Aug91 as 'CHOBA B CCCP', hit UK 63) (re-iss.Sep94)*?? same
Jan 93. (7")(c-s) **HOPE OF DELIVERANCE. / DELIVERANCE (dub)** [18] [83]
(12")(cd-s) – ('A'side) / Big boys bickering / Long leather coat / Kicked around no more.
Feb 93. (cd)(c)(lp) **OFF THE GROUND** [5] [17]
– Off the ground / Looking for changes / Hope of deliverance / Mistress and maid / I owe it all to you / Biker like an icon / Peace in the neighbourhood / Golden Earth girl / The lovers that never were / Get out of my way / Winedark open sea / C'mon people.
Feb 93. (7")(c-s) **C'MON PEOPLE. / I CAN'T IMAGINE** [41] [ ]
(cd-s+=) – Down to the river / Keep coming back to love.
(cd-s) – ('A'side) / Deliverance / Deliverance (dub).
Nov 93. (cd)(c)(lp) **PAUL IS LIVE! (live)** [34] [78]
– Drive my car / Let me roll it / Looking for changes / Peace in the neighbourhood / All my loving / Robbie's bit / Good rocking tonight / We can work it out / Hope of deliverance / Michelle / Biker like an icon / Here there and everywhere / My love / Magical mystery tour / C'mon people / Lady Madonna / Paperback writer / Penny Lane / Live and let die / Kansas City / Welcome to Soundcheck / Hotel in Benidorm / I wanna be your man / A fine day.
— In 1995, PAUL had his biggest hit in a long time (No.19), when he was part of The SMOKIN' MOJO FILTERS ('Come Together') alongside PAUL WELLER and NOEL GALLAGHER (Oasis).

– compilations, etc. –

Feb 81. EMI/ US= Capitol; (lp)(c) **McCARTNEY INTERVIEW** [34] [ ]

– under an alias (various connections) –

The **COUNTRY HAMS** featuring PAUL's brother MIKE McGEAR (ex-SCAFFOLD)
Oct 74. E.M.I.; (7") **WALKING IN THE PARK WITH ELOISE. / BRIDGE OVER THE RIVER SUITE** [ ] [ ]
— **PERCY 'THRILLS' THRILLINGTON**

Apr 77. E.M.I.; (7") **UNCLE ALBERT, ADMIRAL HALSEY. / EAST AT HOME** ☐ ☐

— next by **SUZI AND THE RED STRIPES** LINDA McCARTNEY's band.

Aug 79. A&M/ US= Epic; (7")(7"yellow) **SEASIDE WOMAN. / B SIDE TO SEASIDE** ☐ 59 Jun 77
(re-iss.+12" Jul80)

— PAUL had also guested on numerous singles and albums. DENNY LAINE has also had solo career, but with no commercial success.

Ian McCULLOCH (see under ⇒ ECHO & THE BUNNYMEN)

MC5

Formed: Detroit, Michigan, USA ... 1965 by TYNER, SMITH and KRAMER. After 2 limited singles releases, MC5 (MOTOR CITY FIVE) signed contract with 'Elektra' mid'68, helped by local DJ John Sinclair. Their controversial lp 'KICK OUT THE JAMS' (live late Oct'68) hit the shops on May'69. Its original uncensored version contained the line 'Kick Out The Jams, Motherfuckers!', with the offending word later supplanted with new '... Brothers And Sisters' on later copies. It had by this time dented the US Top 30, although they moved to 'Atlantic' in 1970 for another excellent lp 'BACK IN THE USA'. John Sinclair was sentenced to 10 years in the early 70's for a minor dope charge, but served only 2 of them after appeal. • **Style:** Pioneering political punk-rock activists, who competed with STOOGES. **Songwriters:** Group compositions, except; I CAN ONLY GIVE YOU EVERYTHING (Them) / TUTTI FRUTTI (Little Richard). • **Trivia:** JON LANDAU (now manager of SPRINGSTEEN), produced their 2nd lp.

Recommended: KICK OUT THE JAMS (*9) / BACK IN THE USA (*8).

ROB TYNER – vocals, harmonica / **WAYNE KRAMER** (b.30 Apr'48, Detroit, USA) – guitar, vocals, keyboards / **FRED 'SONIC' SMITH** – guitar / **MICHAEL DAVIS** – bass / **DENNIS THOMPSON** – drums

not issued / A.M.G.

1966. (7") **I CAN ONLY GIVE YOU EVERYTHING. / I JUST DON'T KNOW** - ☐

not issued / A2.

Mar 68. (7") **LOOKING AT YOU. / BORDERLINE** - ☐

— added 6th member **Brother J.C.CRAWFORD** – rapper / narrative

Elektra / Elektra

May 69. (7") **KICK OUT THE JAMS. / MOTOR CITY IS BURNING** ☐ 82 Mar 69

May 69. (lp) **KICK OUT THE JAMS** ☐ 30 Mar 69
– Ramblin' rose / Kick out the jams / Come together / Rocker reducer No.62 / Borderline / Motor city is burning / I want you right now / Starship. *(re-iss.May77.) (re-iss.+cd.Nov91) (re-iss.cd+c Mar93 on 'Pickwick') (re-iss.cd/c Sep95 on 'Warners')*

1969. (7") **RAMBLIN' ROSE. / BORDERLINE** ☐ -

Atlantic / Atlantic

Oct 70. (7") **TONIGHT. / LOOKING AT YOU** - ☐

Nov 70. (lp)(c) **BACK IN THE U.S.A.** ☐ ☐ Feb 70
– Tutti frutti / Tonight / Teenage list / Looking at you / Let me try / High school / Call me animal / The American ruse / Shakin' Street / The human being lawnmower / Back in the U.S.A. *(re-iss.Feb77.) (cd-iss.May93 on 'Rhino-Atlantic')*

1970. (7") **SHAKIN' STREET. / THE AMERICAN RUSE** - ☐

Oct 71. (lp)(c) **HIGH TIME** ☐ ☐
– Sister Anne / Baby won't ya / Miss X / Gotta keep movin' / Future – Now / Poison / Over nnd over / Skunk (sonically speaking). *(cd-iss.May93 on 'Rhino-Atlantic')*

— (split early '72 when DAVIS departed) THOMPSON, SMITH and DAVIS formed short-lived ASCENSION. FRED SMITH married PATTI SMITH and later formed SONIC'S RENDEZVOUS BAND. TYNER was credited on HOT RODS single, late'77. (see ⇒ EDDIE & THE HOT RODS.

– compilations, etc. –

1969. A.M.G.; (7") **I CAN ONLY GIVE YOU EVERYTHING. / ONE OF THE GUYS** - ☐

Jul 83. R.O.I.R.; (c) **BABES IN ARMS** - ☐
(cd-iss.Apr90 & Dec92 on 'Danceteria')

Nov 94. Alive; (cd)(10"lp) **POWER TRIP** ☐ ☐

May 94. Receiver; (cd) **BACK TO COME** ☐ -

Nov 94. Receiver; (cd) **LOOKING AT YOU** ☐ -

Feb 95. Alive; (10"lp) **AMERICAN RUSE** ☐ -

Feb 95. Skydog; (cd) **THUNDER EXPRESS – ONE DAY IN THE STUDIO** ☐ -

Mar 95. Alive; (10"lp) **ICE PICK SLIM** ☐ -

Sep 95. Alive; (10"lp) **LOOKING AT YOU** ☐ -

WAYNE KRAMER

went solo after spending 5 years in prison for cocaine dealing.

Stiff-Chiswick / not issued

Oct 77. (7") **RAMBLIN' ROSE. / GET SOME** ☐ -

Radar / not issued

1979. (7") **THE HARDER THEY COME. / EAST SIDE GIRL** ☐ -

not issued / Pure&Easy

1983. (7") **NEGATIVE GIRLS. / STREET WARFARE** - ☐

WAYNE KRAMER'S GANG WAR

were formed in 1980 with **JOHNNY THUNDERS** – vocals

Zodiac / not issued

1987. (7"ep) **GANG WAR (live at Max's May 1980)** ☐ -

— Their self-titled lp was issued by same label in May 1990. WAYNE joined the DEVIANTS in 1984 for their album HUMAN GARBAGE.

WAYNE KRAMER'S DEATH TONGUE

not issued / Curio

1987. (7") **SPIKE HEELS. / ?** - ☐

Apr 92. (cd) **DEATH TONGUE** ☐ ☐

— (WAYNE played late 80's with DAS DAMEN and G.G. ALLIN)
In Sep'91, ROB TYNER was found dead after suffering heart attack. He was 46.

WAYNE KRAMER

Epitaph / Epitaph

Dec 94. (cd)(c)(lp) **THE HARD STUFF** ☐ ☐
... Jan – Jun '96 stop press ...

Feb 96. (cd)(lp) **DANGEROUS MADNESS** ☐ ☐

— Actually, MC5 are about to reform with KRAMER, DAVIS + THOMSON

Roger McGUINN (see under ⇒ BYRDS)

G. W. McLENNAN (see under ⇒ GO-BETWEENS)

Ian McNABB (see under ⇒ ICICLE WORKS)

MC REN (see under ⇒ N.W.A.)

Christine McVIE (see under ⇒ FLEETWOOD MAC)

MEAT LOAF

Born: MARVIN LEE ADAY, 27 Sep'48, Dallas, Texas, USA. In 1966 he moved to Los Angeles and formed psychedelic-rock outfit POPCORN BLIZZARD, who opened for The WHO, AMBOY DUKES and The STOOGES, before disbanding early 1969. That year, he successfully auditioned for the 'Hair' musical, where he met female soul singer STONEY. In 1970, they made a self-titled lp together for 'Rare Earth', but he soon re-joined 'Hair' tour in Cleveland. Later in '72, he took the role of Buddha in the musical 'Rainbow'. Early in '74, he starred in JIM STEINMAN's Broadway musical 'More Than You Deserve'. The following year, he acted/sang in Richard O'Brien's Broadway musical 'The ROCKY HORROR PICTURE SHOW', which was soon made into a film with MEAT LOAF taking his part of EDDIE. He and STEINMAN went on to tour with comedy show 'National Lampoon', with MEAT LOAF playing the part of a priest in 'Rockabye Hamlet'. Also in 1976, he sang on TED NUGENT's 'Free For All' album. Early in 1977, he got together again with STEINMAN in New York, to start work on 'NEVERLAND' project. They signed to 'RCA', but moved stables after it was clear the label didn't want producer TODD RUNDGREN. Later in '77, MEAT LOAF and crew switched to 'Cleveland International', and gained promotion from 'Epic'. Late in 1977, they unleashed the project as 'BAT OUT OF HELL', and with heavy tours, it made US Top 20, also hitting UK Top 10. For the next 8 years, it featured on chart, selling millions in the process. In the late 70's, MEAT LOAF went through throat problems, but starred the following year in film 'Roadie', alongside DEBBIE HARRY & BLONDIE. In 1981, impatient with waiting on MEAT LOAF's recovery, STEINMAN released

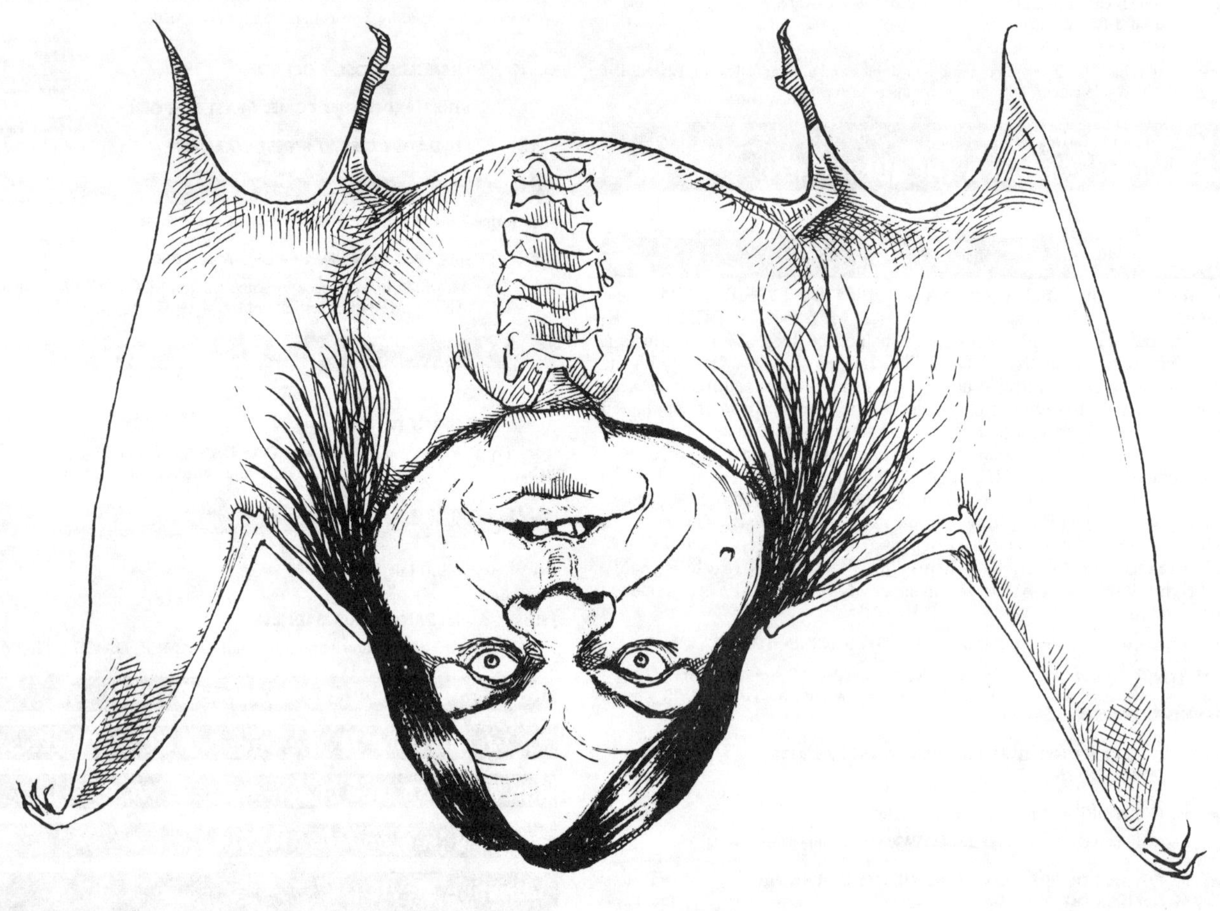

'BAD FOR GOOD' album which was intended for ML. The long-awaited follow-up 'DEAD RINGER FOR LOVE' was issued 4 months later, and although it hit UK No.1, it only managed to scrape into US Top 50. For the rest of the 80's, MEAT LOAF's activities lay mainly in Britain, where he soon became widely known celebrity. In 1993, he was back at the top again on both sides of the Atlantic, with 'BAT OUT OF HELL II'. This re-united him with STEINMAN, and provided him with first multi-selling No.1 'I WOULD DO ANYTHING FOR YOU (BUT I WOULDN'T DO THAT)'. • **Style:** 20-stone anthemic rocker, whose large vox range on 'BAT OUT OF HELL', is or should be part of everybody's collection. • **Songwriters:** JIM STEINMAN wrote everything, until he went solo after 1981 work. MEATLOAF then co-wrote w/ PAUL CHRISTIE + others in 1983. P. JACOBS + S. DURKEE took the bulk of the load in 1984 + STEINMAN was 'BACK INTO HELL' for 1993's 'BAT OUT OF HELL II'. Veteran pensmith DIANE WARREN took up most of the work for his mid-90's album. Covered; MARTHA (Tom Waits) / OH WHAT A BEAUTIFUL MORNING (Rogers-Hammerstein) / WHERE ANGELS SING (Davis) / WHATEVER HAPPENED TO SATURDAY NIGHT (O'Brien). • **Trivia:** His nickname MEAT LOAF, was given to him after he trod on the toes of his school coach. In 1967, POPCORN BLIZZARD issued 7" ONCE UPON A TIME. / HERO on 'Magenta'.

Recommended: BAT OUT OF HELL (*9) / HITS OUT OF HELL (*7).

STONEY AND MEAT LOAF

STONEY – vocals,(who later joined BOB SEGER).

		Rare Earth	Rare Earth
Apr 71.	(7") **WHAT YOU SEE IS WHAT YOU GET. / LADY OF MINE**	-	
Jun 71.	(7") **IT TAKES ALL KINDS OF PEOPLE. / THE WAY YOU DO THE THINGS YOU DO**		-
May 71.	(7") **WHAT YOU SEE IS WHAT YOU GET. / THE WAY YOU DO THE THINGS YOU DO**	-	71
Oct 71.	(lp) **FEATURING STONEY AND MEAT LOAF**	-	

– Jimmy Bell / She waits by the window / It takes all kind of people / Stone heart / Who is the leader of the people / What you see is what you get / Kiss me again / Sunshine (where's Heaven) / Jessica White / Lady be mine / Everything under the sun. *(re-iss. as 'FEATURING STONEY AND MEAT LOAF', Mar79 on 'Prodigal') (re-iss.1986 on 'Motown') (UK-iss. Oct 72)*

— Returned to feature in the musical 'Hair' (plus see above biography).

MEAT LOAF

		Ode	Ode
1973.	(7") **CLAP YOUR HANDS AND STAMP YOUR FEET. / STAND BY ME** (not released until 75)		
		not iss.	R.S.O.
1974	(7") **MORE THAN YOU DESERVE / PRESENCE OF THE LORD**	-	

— **MEAT LOAF** – vocals / **JIM STEINMAN** – composer, keyboards, percussion / **TODD RUNDGREN** – multi- / **ROY BITTAN** – piano, keyboards / **MAX WEINBERG** – drums / **KASIM SULTAN** – bass / **ROGER POWELL** – synth. / **ELLEN FOLEY + RORY DODD** – back.vox

Epic | Cleveland-Epic

Jan 78. (lp)(c) **BAT OUT OF HELL** 9 14 Oct 77
– Bat out of Hell / You took the words right out of my mouth / Heaven can wait / All reved up with no place to go / Two out of three ain't bad / Paradise by the dashboard light:- Let me sleep on it – I'll be praying for the end of time / For crying out loud. *(cd-iss.1983) (pic-lp 1978) (re-iss.Jul91, hit UK No.14, re-entered Jan92, peaked again at No.24-Jul92) (returned to hit UK No.19 Autumn 1993)*

Apr 78. (7") **YOU TOOK THE WORDS RIGHT OUT OF MY MOUTH. / FOR CRYING OUT LOUD** 33 39 Nov 78

Jul 78. (7") **TWO OUT OF THREE AIN'T BAD. / FOR CRYING OUT LOUD** 32 11 Mar 78

Sep 78. (7") **PARADISE BY THE DASHBOARD LIGHT. / ALL REVED UP WITH NO PLACE TO GO** 39 Mar 78

Jan 79. (ext-7"red)(ext-12"red) **BAT OUT OF HELL. / HEAVEN CAN WAIT** 15
(re-iss.Apr81)

— MEAT LOAF now brought in many session people, including **CHER** on title track.

Sep 81. (lp)(c)(pic-lp) **DEAD RINGER** 1 45
– Peel out / I'm gonna love her for both of us / More than you deserve / I'll kill you if you don't come back / Read 'em and weep / Nocturnal pleasure / Dead ringer for love / Everything is permitted. *(re-iss.Nov85) (cd-iss.Nov87)*

Sep 81. (7") **I'M GONNA LOVE HER FOR BOTH OF US. / EVERYTHING IS PERMITTED** 62 84

Nov 81. (7")(7"pic-d) **DEAD RINGER FOR LOVE. / MORE THAN YOU DESERVE** 5
(re-iss.Aug88)

Mar 82. (7") **READ 'EM AND WEEP. / EVERYTHING IS PERMITTED**
(12"+=) – (interview disc).

1982. (12"ep-clear) **MEAT LOAF IN EUROPE '82 (live)** -
– Two out of three ain't bad / You took the words . . . / I'm gonna love you. / Dead ringer for love.

May 83. (lp)(c) **MIDNIGHT AT THE LOST AND FOUND** 7
– Razor's edge / Midnight at the lost and found / Wolf at your door / Keep driving / The promised land / You never can be too sure about the girl / Priscilla / Don't you look at me like that / If you really want to / Fallen angel. *(cd-iss.Jan87)*

May 83. (7")(7"pic-d) **IF YOU REALLY WANT TO. / KEEP DRIVING** 59
(12"+=)(12"pic-d+=) – Lost love.

Jul 83. (7")(7"pic-d) **RAZOR'S EDGE. / YOU NEVER CAN BE TOO SURE ABOUT THE GIRL**
(12"+=) Don't look at me like that

Sep 83. (7") **MIDNIGHT AT THE LOST AND FOUND. / FALLEN ANGEL** 17
(d7"+=)(12"+=)(12"pic-d+=) – Bat out of Hell (live) / Dead ringer for love (live).

Jan 84. (7") **RAZOR'S EDGE. / PARADISE BY THE DASHBOARD LIGHT** 41
(12"+=) – Read 'em and weep.

Arista R.C.A.

Sep 84. (7")(7"sha-pic-d) **MODERN GIRL. / TAKE A NUMBER** 17
(12"+=)(12"pic-d+=) – ('A'extended).

Nov 84. (lp)(c)(cd) **BAD ATTITUDE** 8 74
– Bad attitude / Modern girl / Nowhere fast / Surf's up / Piece of the action / Jumpin' the gun / Cheatin' in your dreams / Don't leave your mark on me / Sailor to a siren. *(re-iss.May86 on 'Fame') (cd re-iss.Jun88)*

Nov 84. (7")(7"sha-pic-d) **NOWHERE FAST. / CLAP YOUR HANDS** 67
(ext-12"+=) – Stand by me.
(d7"+=) – Bat out of Hell (live) / Modern Girl (US mix).
(d12") – (all 5 tracks)

Mar 85. (7")(7"sha-pic-d) **PIECE OF THE ACTION. / SAILOR TO A SIREN** 47
(12"+=) – Bad attitude.

Aug 86. (7")(7"sha-pic-d) **ROCK'N'ROLL MERCENARIES. / REVOLUTIONS PER MINUTE** 31
(12"+=)(12"sha-pic-d+=) – ('A'extended). ('A'featured JOHN PARR)

Sep 86. (lp)(c)(cd) **BLIND BEFORE I STOP** 28
– Execution day / Rock'n'roll mercenaries / Getting away with murder / One more kiss / Night of the soft parade / Blind before I stop / Burning down / Standing on the outside / Masculine / Man and a woman / Special girl / Rock'n'roll hero.

Nov 86. (7")(7"sha-pic-d) **GETTING AWAY WITH MURDER. / ROCK'N'ROLL HERO**
(12"+=) – Scot free (remix).

Feb 87. (7")(12") **BLIND BEFORE I STOP. / EXECUTION DAY**
(12"+=) – Dead ringer for love / Paradise by the dashboard light (live).

Apr 87. (7") **SPECIAL GIRL. / ONE MORE KISS**
(12"+=)(cd-s+=) – Dead ringer for love (live) / Paradise by the dashboard light (live).

Oct 87. (7") **BAT OUT OF HELL (live). / MAN AND A WOMAN**
(12"+=) – ('A'full version).

Nov 87. (lp)(c)(cd) **LIVE AT WEMBLEY (live)** 60
– Blind before I stop / Rock'n'roll mercenaries / You took the words right out of mouth / Midnight at the lost and found / Modern girl / Paradise by the dashboard light / Two out of three ain't bad / Bat out of Hell. *(cd+=)–* Masculine / Rock'n'roll medley: Johnny B. Goode – Slow down – Jailhouse rock – Blue suede shoes.

— MEAT LOAF became more involved with the media / television interviews, etc. Revitalised interest in 'ROCKY HORROR PICTURE SHOW' also brought him renewed limelight which enabled his past solo work to hit charts.

— **MRS LOUD** – female vocal / **ROY BITTAN & BILL PAYNE** – piano / **TIM PIERCE & EDDIE MARTINEZ** – guitar / **KENNY ARONOFF & RICK MAROTTA & BRIAN MEAGHER & JIMMY BRALOWER** – drums / **STEVE BUSLOWE** – bass / **PAT THRALL** – guitar solo / **LENNY PICKETT** – sax / **JEFF BOVA** – synth. & prog. / **etc.**

Virgin M.C.A.

Sep 93. (cd)(c)(lp) **BAT OUT OF HELL II: BACK INTO HELL** 1 1
– I'd do anything for love (but I won't do that) / Life is a lemon and I want my money back / Rock and roll dreams come through / It just won't quit / Out of the frying pan (and into the fire) / Objects in the rear view mirror may appear closer than they are / Wasted youth / Everything louder than everything else / Good girls go to heaven (bad girls go everywhere) / Back into Hell / Lost boys and golden girls. *(ltd.pic-lp Dec93) (re-iss.Nov95)*

Oct 93. (7")(c-s) **I'D DO ANYTHING FOR LOVE (BUT I WON'T DO THAT). / BACK INTO HELL** 1 1 Sep 93
(cd-s+=) – Everything louder than everything else.
(cd-s) – ('A'side) / You took the words right out of my mouth (live NYC) / Bat out of hell (live NYC).

Feb 94. (7"pic-d)(c-s) **ROCK'N'ROLL DREAMS COME THROUGH. / WASTED YOUTH** 11 13 Jan94
(cd-s+=) – I'd do anything for love (but I won't do that) (live).
(cd-s) – ('A'side) / Heaven can wait (live) / Paradise by the dashboard light (live).

Apr 94. (7")(c-s)(cd-s) **OBJECTS IN THE REAR VIEW MIRROR MAY APPEAR CLOSER THAN YOU THINK. / ROCK AND ROLL DREAMS COME THROUGH (live)** 26 38
(cd-s+=) – All revved up (live) / Two out of three ain't bad (live).

Oct 95. (7")(c-s) **I'D LIE FOR YOU (AND THAT'S THE TRUTH). / I'D DO ANYTHING FOR LOVE (BUT I WON'T DO THAT)** 2 13
(cd-s+=) – Whatever happened to Saturday night.
(cd-s) – ('A'-Fountain Head mix) / Oh, what a beautiful mornin' / Runnin' for the red light (I gotta life).

Oct 95. (cd)(c)(d-lp) **WELCOME TO THE NEIGHBOURHOOD** 3 17 Nov95
– When the rubber meets the road / I'd lie for you (and that's the truth) / Original sin / 45 seconds of ecstacy / Runnin' for the red light (I gotta life) / Fiesta de las Almas Perdidas / Left in the dark / Not a dry eye in the house / Amnesty is granted / If this is the last kiss (let's make it last all night) / Martha / Where angels sing.

. . . Jan – Jun '96 stop press . . .

Jan 96. (single) **NOT A DRY EYE IN THE HOUSE** 7 82

Apr 96. (single) **RUNNIN' FOR THE RED LIGHT (I GOTTA LIFE)** 21

– compilations, others, etc. –

Aug 82. Epic; (c-ep) **GREATEST ORIGINAL HITS** -
– Bat out of Hell / Read 'em and weep / Dead ringer for love / I'm gonna love her for both of us. *(7"ep iss.Mar83, re-iss.Sep86)*

Jan 85. Epic; (lp)(c)(cd) **HITS OUT OF HELL** 2
– Bat out of Hell / Read 'em and weep / Midnight at the lost and found / Two out of three ain't bad / Dead ringer for love / Modern girl / I'm gonna love her for both of us / You took the words right out of my mouth (hot summer night) / Razor's edge / Paradise by the dashboard light.

Jun 91. Epic; (7")(c-s) **DEAD RINGER FOR LOVE. / HEAVEN CAN WAIT** 53
(12"+=)(cd-s+=) – Bat out of Hell.

Oct 91. Epic; (7") **TWO OUT OF THREE AIN'T BAD. / I'M GONNA LOVE HER FOR BOTH OF US** 69
(12"+=)(cd-s+=) – Midnight at the lost and found. *(re-iss.Jun92)*

Mar 93. Epic; (cd)(c) **THE 12" MIXES**

Dec 93. Epic; (12"pic-d-ep)(c-ep)(pic-cd-ep) **BAT OUT OF HELL / READ 'EM AND WEEP. / OUT OF THE FRYING PAN (AND INTO THE FIRE) / ROCK AND ROLL DREAMS COME THROUGH (Jim Steinman)** 8

Oct 94. Epic; (cd) **THE BEST**

Oct 94. Epic; (cd) **THE BEST (w/ BONNIE TYLER)**

Feb 86. Old Gold; (7") **BAT OUT OF HELL. / DEAD RINGER FOR LOVE** -
(re-iss.Jan88)

Feb 89. Old Gold; (7") **YOU TOOK THE WORDS RIGHT OUT OF MY MOUTH. / MIDNIGHT AT THE LOST AND FOUND** -

Nov 89. Arista; (lp)(c) **PRIME CUTS**

Nov 89. Telstar; (lp)(c)(cd) **HEAVEN AND HELL** -
(above was shared album with BONNIE TYLER on 1 side)
(re-iss.cd-c.May93 & Dec95 on 'Columbia')

May 94. Pickwick; (cd)(c) **ROCK'N'ROLL HERO** -
(re-iss.Jul95)

Oct 94. Pure Music; (cd)(c)(lp) **ALIVE IN HELL (live)** 33
– (tracks on 'LIVE AT WEMBLEY' album) + (studio tracks;-) Piece of the action / Bad attitude / Surf's up.

Feb 95. Epic; (d-cd) **DEAD RINGER / MIDNIGHT AT THE LOST AND FOUND** -

Apr 95. Arista; (cd) **BLIND BEFORE I STOP / BAD ATTITUDE** | | -

MEAT PUPPETS

Formed: Tempe, Phoenix, Arizona, USA . . . 1980 by brothers CURT and CRIS KIRKWOOD. They were soon snapped up by rising US indie label 'SST' in 1981, after a debut on own label. 13 years later, they had finally made headway (well at least in America) with Top 75 album 'TOO HIGH TO DIE'. • **Style:** Mystical psychedelia short-fusing hardcore punk rock and the country-boy slurr of CRIS. • **Songwriters:** Most by CURT, some with CRIS or DERRICK. Covered TUMBLIN' TUMBLEWEEDS (Bob Nolan). • **Trivia:** On 18 Nov'93, CURT & CRIS guested with NIRVANA's on an unplugged MTV spot. The tracks they performed were 'PLATEAU', 'OH ME' & 'LAKE OF FIRE'.

Recommended: UP ON THE SUN (*8) / MONSTERS (*9) / TOO HIGH TO DIE (*7) / FORBIDDEN PLACES (*6)

CURT KIRKWOOD – guitar, vocals / **CRIS KIRKWOOD** – vocals, bass, rhythm guitar / **DERRICK BOSTROM** – drums

not issued / World Invitation

Sep 81. (7"ep) **IN A CAR / BIG HOUSE. / DOLFIN FIELD / OUT IN THE GARDINER / FOREIGN LAWNS** - |
(cd-ep iss.Nov88 on 'S.S.T.')

S.S.T. / S.S.T.

Jan 82. (lp) **MEAT PUPPETS I** - |
– Reward / Love offering / Blue green god / Walking boss / Melons rising / Saturday morning / Our friends / Tumblin' tumbleweeds / Milo, Sorghum and maize / Meat puppets / Playing dead / Litterbox / Electromud / The goldmine. *(re-iss.+cd+c early 90's)*

Apr 84. (lp) **MEAT PUPPETS II**
– Split myself in two / Magic toy missing / Lost plateau / Aurora Borealis / We are here / Climbing / New gods / Oh, me / Lake on fire / I'm a mindless idiot / The whistling song. *(re-iss.+cd+c early 90's)*

Apr 85. (lp) **UP ON THE SUN**
– Up on the Sun / Maiden's milk / Away / Animal kingdom / Hot pink / Swimming ground / Bucket head / Too real / Enchanted pork fist / Seal whales / Two rivers / Creator. *(cd-iss.Sep87, and re-iss.+cd+c early 90's)*

Aug 86. (m-lp) **OUT MY WAY**
– She's hot / Out my way / Other kinds of love / Not swimming ground / Mountain line / Good golly Miss Molly. *(re-iss.+cd+c.Sep87)*

Apr 87. (lp)(c)(cd) **MIRAGE**
– Get on down / Love your children forever / Liquery / Confusion fog / Look at the rain / I am a machine / Quit it / Beauty / etc.****

Oct 87. (lp)(c)(cd) **HEUVOS**
– Paradise / Look at the rain / Bad love / Sexy music / Crazy / Fruit / Automatic mojo / Dry rain / I can't be counted on at all.

Oct 87. (12") **I CAN'T BE COUNTED ON AT ALL. / PARADISE**

Oct 89. (lp)(c)(cd) **MONSTERS**
– Attacked by monsters / Light / Meltdown / In love / The void / Touchdown king / Party till the world obeys / Flight of the fire weasel / Strings on your heart / Like being alive.

Nov 90. (cd)(d-lp) **NO STRINGS ATTACHED** (compilation)
– Big house / In a car / Tumblin' tumbleweeds / Reward / The whistling song / New gods / Lost / Lake of fire / Split myself in two / Up on the Sun / Swimming ground / Maiden's milk / Bucket head / Out my way / Confusion fog / I am a machine / Quit it / Beauty / Look at the rain / I can't be counted on at all / Automatic mojo / Meltdown / Like being alive / Attacked by monsters.

London / London

Nov 91. (cd)(c)(lp) **FORBIDDEN PLACES**
– Sam / Nail it down / This day / Open wide / Another Moon / That's how it goes / Whirlpool / Popskull / No longer gone / Forbidden places / Six gallon pie.

Mar 94. (cd)(c)(lp) **TOO HIGH TO DIE** | 62
– Violet eyes / Never to be found / We don't exist / Severed goddess head / Flaming heart / Shine / Backwater / Roof with a hole / Station / Things / Why / Evil love / Comin' down / Lake of fire.

Jul 94. (c-s)(cd-s) **BACKWATER. / ?** | 47

Oct 95. (cd)(c) **NO JOKE!**
– Scum / Nothing / Head / Taste of the sun / Vampires / Predator / Poison arrow / Eyeball / For free / Cobbler / Inflamable / Sweet ammonia / Chemical garden.

MEGA CITY FOUR

Formed: Farnborough, England . . . early 1987 by CHRIS JONES and ex-CAPRICORN members GERRY BRYANT and brothers WIZ and DANNY BROWN. After a number of local indie hits mostly for 'Decoy', they signed to 'Big Life' Jun'91. Hit the UK Top 50 in 1992, when 'SEBASTAPOL RD.' album made No.41. • **Style:** Uptempo melodic punk combo, similar to BUZZCOCKS and friends The SENSELESS THINGS. • **Songwriters:** WIZ. Covered; DON'T WAN'T TO KNOW IF YOU ARE LONELY (Husker Du). • **Trivia:** Took their name from a comic book hero Judge Dredd.

Recommended: TRANZOPHOBIA (*8) / SEBASTAPOL RD (*7) / WHO CARES WINS (*7).

DARREN 'WIZ' BROWN – vocals, guitar / **DANNY BROWN** – guitar / **GERRY BRYANT** – bass / **CHRIS JONES** – drums (ex-EXIT EAST) repl. MARTIN

Primitive / not issued

Mar 88. (7"ltd.) **MILES APART. / RUNNING IN DARKNESS** | -
(re-iss.Jun88 on 'Mega City')

Decoy / not issued

Nov 88. (7") **DISTANT RELATIVES. / CLEAR BLUE SKY** | -

Feb 89. (7") **LESS THAN SENSELESS. / DANCING DAYS ARE OVER** | -

May 89. (lp)(cd) **TRANZOPHOBIA** 67 | -
– Start / Pride and prejudice / Severe attack of the truth / Paper tiger / January / Twenty one again / On another planet / Things I never said / New years day / Occupation / Alternative arrangements / Promise / What you've got / Stupid way to die.

Oct 89. (7") **AWKWARD KID. / CRADLE** | -

Mar 90. (7"ep)(12"ep) **FINISH / SEVERANCE. / THANX / SQUARE THROUGH A CIRCLE** | -

Sep 90. (cd)(c)(lp) **WHO CARES WINS** | -
– Who cares? / Static interference / Rose coloured / Grudge / Me not you / Messenger / Violet / Rail / Mistook / Open / Revolution / No such place as home / Storms to come / Balance.

Big Life / Chrysalis

Sep 91. (7"ep)(12"ep)(cd-ep)(7"green-ep) **WORDS THAT SAY / UNTOUCHABLE. / LIPSCAY / MANSION** 66 | -
(re-iss 12"ep/cd-ep Aug93)

Jan 92. (7"red-ep)(12"ep)(cd-ep) **STOP / DESERT. / BACK TO ZERO / OVERLAP** 36 |
(live-7"ep) – Stop / Revolution / Who cares / Finish.
(re-iss. 7"ep/12"ep/cd-ep Aug93)

Feb 92. (cd)(c)(lp) **SEBASTOPOL RD** 41 |
– Ticket collector / Scared of cats / Callous / Peripheral / Anne Bancroft / Prague / Clown / Props / What's up / Vague / Stop / Wasting my breath. *(re-iss.Sep93)*

May 92. (7")(12")(cd-s) **SHIVERING SAND. / EVERYBODY LOVES YOU / DISTURBED** 35 |
(live-7"ep) – Shivering sand / Words that say / Callous / Don't want to know if you are lonely. *(re-iss.7"ep/12"ep/cd-ep Aug93)*

Nov 92. (cd)(c)(lp) **INSPIRINGLY TITLED (THE LIVE ALBUM) (live)**
– Who cares / Finish / Thanx / Shivering sand / Props / Messenger / Stop / Revolution / Words that say / Callous / Lipscar / Peripheral / Clown / Open / What've you've got / Don't want to know if you are lonely. *(re-iss.Sep93)*

Apr 93. (7"ep)(10"ep)(c-ep)(cd-ep) **IRON SKY. / ON THE EDGE / SOMETIMES** 48 |

May 93. (cd)(c)(lp) **MAGIC BULLETS** 57 |
– Perfect circle / Drown / Rain man / Toys / Iron sky / So / Enemy skies / Wallflower / President / Shadow / Underdog / Greener / Speck.

Jul 93. (7")(c-s) **WALLFLOWER. / INAMORATA** 69 |
(12"+=)(cd-s+=)(cd-s+=) – Wilderness.

Fire / not issued

Sep 95. (cd-s) **SKIDDING / STAY DEAD / LAZERGAZE**

Nov 95. (7") **SUPERSTAR. / CHRYSANTH**

. . . Jan – Jun '96 stop press . . .

Jan 96. (single) **ANDROID DREAMS**

Mar 96. (cd)(lp) **SOULSCRAPER**

– compilations, others, etc. –

Apr 91. Decoy; (cd)(c)(lp) **TERRIBLY SORRY BOB** (all singles 1987-Mar90) | -

Nov 93. Strange Fruit; (cd) **THE PEEL SESSIONS** | -

MEGADETH

Formed: San Franscisco, California, USA . . . 1983 by ex-METALLICA guitarist DAVE MUSTAINE alongside DAVE ELLEFSON, POLAND and SAMUELSON. They were given deal with 'Combat' records, who issued in 1985 their debut lp 'KILLING IS MY BUSINESS . . . AND BUSINESS IS GOOD'. They were soon snapped up by 'Capitol', who issued their next album 'PEACE SELLS . . . BUT WHO'S BUYING' late 1986. They commercially progressed with each release, culminating with 1992 US & UK Top 5 album 'COUNTDOWN TO EXTINCTION'. • **Style:** Aggressive thrash speed-metal outfit lying somewhere between heavy & punk-rock.

• **Songwriters:** MUSTAINE penned most except; THESE BOOTS ARE MADE FOR WALKING (hit; Nancy Sinatra) / ANARCHY IN THE UK; which featured STEVE JONES (Sex Pistols) / NO MORE MR.NICE GUY (Alice Cooper). • **Trivia:** Wildman MUSTAINE went into seclusion after heroin abuse in the late 80's.

Recommended: KILLING IS MY BUSINESS ... AND BUSINESS IS GOOD (*8) / RUST IN PEACE (*7) / COUNTDOWN TO EXTINCTION (*6).

DAVE MUSTAINE – vocals, lead guitar (ex-METALLICA) / **CHRIS POLAND** – guitar / **DAVE ELLEFSON** (b.12 Nov'64) – bass / **GAR SAMUELSON** – drums

M.F.N. / Combat

Jun 85. (lp)(c) **KILLING IS MY BUSINESS ... AND BUSINESS IS GOOD** [ ] [ ]
– Last rites / Killing in my business . . .and business is good / The skull beneath the skin / Boots / Rattlehead / Chosen ones / Looking down the cross / Mechanix. *(re-iss as d-lp May88, cd-iss.Aug87)*

— POLAND was replaced by MIKE ALBERT (ex-KING CRIMSON) briefly until his return.

Capitol / Capitol

Nov 86. (lp)(c)(cd) **PEACE SELLS ... BUT WHO'S BUYING?** [ ] [76]
– Wake up dead / The conjuring / Peace sells / Devils island / Good mourning – Black Friday / Bad omen / I ain't superstitious / My last words. *(cd-iss.Sep88, also on pic-d) (re-iss.cd+c Jul94 on 'Capitol')*

Nov 87. (7")(7"pic-d) **WAKE UP DEAD. / BLACK FRIDAY (live)** [65] [ ]
(12"+=) – Devil's island (live).

— **CHUCK BEHLER** – drums replaced SAMUELSON / **JEFF YOUNG**– guitar repl. JAY REYNOLDS who had briefly repl. POLAND.

Feb 88. (7")(7"pic-d) **ANARCHY IN THE U.K.. / LIAR** [45] [ ]
(12"+=) – 502.

Mar 88. (lp)(c)(cd)(pic-lp) **SO FAR ... SO GOOD ... SO WHAT!** [18] [28] Jan 88
– Into the lungs of Hell / Set the world afire / Anarchy in the U.K. / Mary Jane / 502 / In my darkest hour / Liar / Hook in mouth.

May 88. (7")(7"pic-d) **MARY JANE. / HOOK IN MOUTH** [46] [ ]
(12"+=) – My last words.

— Late '88, YOUNG joined BROKEN SILENCE and BEHLER joined BLACK & WHITE.

Nov 89. (7")(c-s)(7"pic-d) **NO MORE MR. NICE GUY. / DIFFERENT BREED** [13] [ ]
(12"+=)(cd-s+=) – Demon bell (the ballad of Horace Pinker).

— (Mar90) **MUSTAINE + ELLEFSON** bring in new members **MARTY FRIEDMAN** – guitar (ex-CACOPHONY) / **NICK MENZA** – drums

Sep 90. (7")(c-s) **HOLY WARS ... THE PUNISHMENT DUE. / LUCRETIA** [24] [ ]
(12"+=)(cd-s+=) – Information

Oct 90. (cd)(c)(lp) **RUST IN PEACE** [8] [23]
– Holy wars . . . the punishment due / Hangar 18 / Take no prisoners / Five magics / Poison was the cure / Lucretia / Tornado of souls / Dawn patrol / Rust in peace . . . Polaris. *(re-iss.cd+c Sep94)*

Mar 91. (7")(7"sha-pic-d) **HANGAR 18. / THE CONJURING (live)** [26] [ ]
(cd-s+=) – ('A'live) / Hook in mouth (live).

Jun 92. (7") **SYMPHONY OF DESTRUCTION. / PEACE SELLS (live)** [15] [71] Oct 92
(12"+=)(cd-s+=) – God to Hell / Breakpoint.
(7"pic-d) – ('A'side) / In my darkest hour (live).

Jul 92. (cd)(c)(lp) **COUNTDOWN TO EXTINCTION** [5] [2]
– Skin o' my teeth / Symphony of destruction / Architecture of aggression / Foreclosure of a dream / Sweating bullets / This was my life / Countdown to extinction / High speed dirt / Psychotron / Captive honour / Ashes in your mouth.

Oct 92. (7")(c-s)(7"pic-d) **SKIN O' MY TEETH. / HOLY WARS ... THE PUNISHMENT DUE (General Norman Schwarzkopf)** [13] [ ]
(cd-s+=) – ('A'version) / Lucretia.
(10"+=) – High speed drill / (Dave Mustaine interview).

Mar 93. (7")(c-s) **SWEATING BULLETS. / ASHES IN YOUR MOUTH (live)** [26] [ ]
(12")(cd-s) – ('A'side) / Countdown to extinction (live '92) / Symphony of destruction (gristle mix) / Symphony of destruction (live).

Oct 94. (cd)(c)(blue-lp) **YOUTHANASIA** [6] [4]
– Reckoning day / Train of consequences / Addicted to chaos / A tout le monde / Elysian fields / The killing road / Blood of heroes / Family tree / Youthanasia / I thought I knew it all / Black curtains / Victory. *(re-iss.Aug95 cd/c w/ free album; HIDDEN TREASURES, hit UK No.28 + US No.90)*

Dec 94. (7")(12") **TRAIN OF CONSEQUENCES. / CROWN OF WORMS** [22] [ ]
(12"+=) – Holy wars . . . the punishment due (live).
(cd-s) – ('A'side) / Peace sells . . . but who's buying (live) / Anarchy in the UK (live).

John (Cougar) MELLENCAMP

Born: 7 Oct '51, Seymour, Indiana, USA. After graduating from high school, where he played in 2 bands; CREPE SOUL and SNAKEPIT BANANA BARN. He left home in 1970 and moved to Valonia, where he married Priscilla. In the early 70's, he formed glam-rock outfit TRASH, alongside LARRY CRANE. In the mid 70's, he graduated from university, but separated from wife and child. At the same time he made a demo, and sent it to Tony DeFries, who gave him a deal with MainMan productions & 'MCA' records. In 1976 as JOHN COUGAR, his debut lp 'CHESTNUT STREET INCIDENT' was issued, but after parting with management, he moved to Bloomington. After another lp, 'THE KID INSIDE', he shifted to ROD STEWART's 'Riva' records, who released UK-only lp 'A BIOGRAPHY'. Most of the tracks re-surfaced the next year in lp 'JOHN COUGAR', which also included his first US top 30 entry 'I NEED A LOVER'. In the early 80's, he scored more hits, but surpassed all before when 45's 'HURTS SO GOOD' & 'JACK AND DIANE', hit US No.2 & 1 respectively. They were the main feature on his 1982 No.1 album 'AMERICAN FOOL', which also cracked the 40 in UK. For the rest of the 80's, all his lp's went US Top 10, and mostly all 45's went Top 10 or 20. • **Style:** SPRINGSTEEN sounding rocker, who finally broke away from tag, after the brilliant 1989 lp 'BIG DADDY'. • **Songwriters:** Penned most himself, with collaborations mainly stemming from CRANE. Covered; KICKS (Paul Revere & The Raiders) / JAILHOUSE ROCK (Elvis Presley) / OH PRETTY WOMAN (Roy Orbison) / DO YOU BELIEVE IN MAGIC (Lovin' Spoonful) / UNDER THE BOARDWALK (Drifters) / etc. • **Trivia:** Due to his height, he produced under the alias of The LITTLE BASTARD. His work in this field has included; MITCH RYDER (Never Kick A Sleeping Dog) / BLASTERS (Hard Line) / WILD NIGHT (Van Morrison). STEVE CROPPER (ex-BOOKER T. & THE MG'S) produced his 1980 lp 'NOTHING MATTERS AND WHAT IF IT DID'. In 1988, he became a grandfather, when his 18 year-old daughter Michelle had a baby. In 1990, he starred in the film 'Falling from Grace'.

Recommended: AMERICAN FOOL (*6) / SCARECROW (*7) / THE LONESOME JUBILEE (*7) / BIG DADDY (*8).

JOHN COUGAR

– vocals, guitar

not issued / M.C.A.

1976. (lp) **CHESTNUT STREET INCIDENT** [-] [ ]
– American dream / Oh pretty woman / Jailhouse rock / Dream killin' town / Supergirl / Chestnut street revisited / Good girls / Do you believe in magic / Twentieth century fox / Sad lady. *(UK-rel.Oct84 on 'Mainman') (re-iss.lp,c,cd.Apr86 on 'Castle')*

— his band **TIGER FORCE** were **LARRY CRANE** – guitars / **TOM WINCE** – keys / **DAVID PARMAN** – bass, guitar, violin, percussion / **TERENCE SALSA** – drums, perc. / **WAYNE HALL** – saxophone, flute, percussion

1977. (lp)(c) **THE KID INSIDE** [-] [ ]
– Kid inside / Take what you want / Cheap shot / Side-walks and street lights / R.Gang / American son / Gearhead / Young genocides / Too young to live / Survive. *(UK-iss.May86 on 'Castle', cd-iss. Nov 86)*

not issued / Gulcher

1977. (7"ep) **U.S. MALE** [-] [ ]
– 2000 a.d. / Lou-ser / Hot man / Kicks.

Riva / Riva

Mar 78. (7") **I NEED A LOVER. / BORN RECKLESS** [ ] [-]

Mar 78. (lp)(c) **A BIOGRAPHY** [ ] [-]
– Born reckless / Factory / Night slumming / Taxi dancer / I need a lover / Alley of the angels / High "C" Cherie / Where the side walk ends / Let them run your lives / Goodnight.

Jun 78. (7") **FACTORY. / ALLEY OF THE ANGELS** [ ] [-]

Jun 79. (7")(7"pic-d) **MIAMI. / DO YOU THINK THAT'S FAIR** [ ] [-]

Jul 79. (lp)(c) **JOHN COUGAR** [ ] [64]
– A little night dancin' / Small Paradise / Great mid-west / Miami / Take home pay / Sugar Marie / Welcome to Chinatown / Pray for me / Do you think that's fair / Taxi dancer. *(re-iss.Jun88 on 'Mercury', cd-iss.Jan86)*

Sep 79. (7") **I NEED A LOVER. / ELCOME TO CHINATOWN** [-] [28]

Oct 79. (7") **TAXI DANCER. / SMALL PARADISE** [ ] [ ]

Feb 80. (7") **SMALL PARADISE. / SUGAR MARIE** [-] [87]

Apr 80. (7") **PRAY FOR ME. / A LITTLE NIGHT DANCIN'** [-] [ ]

Sep 80. (7") **THIS TIME. / DON'T UNDERSTAND ME** [ ] [27]

Jan 81. (7") **AIN'T EVEN DONE WITH THE NIGHT. / MAKE ME FEEL** [-] [17]

Feb 81. (lp)(c) **NOTHIN' MATTERS, & WHAT IF IT DID?** [ ] [37] Sep 80
– Hot night in a cold town / Ain't even done with the night / Don't understand me / This time / Make me feel / To M.G. (wherever she may be) / Tonight / Wild angel / Cheap shot. *(cd-iss.Jan87)*

Feb 81. (7") **HOT NIGHT IN A COLD TOWN. / TONIGHT** [ ] [-]
May 81. (7") **AIN'T EVEN DONE WITH THE NIGHT. / TO M.G. WHEREVER SHE MAY BE** [ ] [-]

— his live band consisted of **LARRY CRANE** – guitar, vocals / **MIKE WANCHIC** – guitar, vocals / **TOBY MYERS** – bass, vocals / **KENNY ARONOFF** – drums, vocals

May 82. (7") **HURTS SO GOOD. / CLOSE ENOUGH** [ ] [2] Apr 82
Jul 82. (7") **JACK & DIANE. / CAN YOU TAKE IT** [-] [1]
Nov 82. (lp)(c) **AMERICAN FOOL** [37] [1] May 82
– Hurts so good / Jack & Diane / Hand to hold on to / Danger list / Can you take it / Thundering hearts / China girl / Close enough / Weakest moments. *(re-iss.Sep85 on 'Mercury', cd-iss.Jan85 + 1988)*
Sep 82. (7") **JACK & DIANE. / DANGER LIST** [25] [-]
(12"+=) – Need a lover.
Nov 82. (7") **HAND TO HOLD ON TO. / SMALL PARADISE** [-] [3]
Jan 83. (7")(12")(7"pic-d) **HAND TO HOLD ON TO. / HURTS SO GOOD** [ ] [-]

JOHN COUGAR MELLENCAMP

Nov 83. (7")(12") **CRUMBLIN' DOWN. / GOLDEN GATES** [ ] [9] Oct 83
Dec 83. (7") **PINK HOUSES. / SERIOUS BUSINESS** [-] [8]
Feb 84. (lp)(c)(cd) **UH-HUH!** [92] [9] Oct 83
– Crumblin' down / Pink houses / Authority song / Warmer place to sleep / Jackie O / Play guitar / Serious business / Lovin' mother fo ya / Golden Gates.
Feb 84. (7") **AUTHORITY SONG. / HURTS SO GOOD** [ ] [ ]
(12"+=) – Thundering hearts.
Mar 84. (7") **AUTHORITY SONG. / PINK HOUSES (acoustic)** [-] [15]
Jun 84. (7") **PINK HOUSES. / WARMER PLACE TO SLEEP** [ ] [-]

— added **JOHN CASCELLA** – keyboards plus others on session

Oct 85. (7")(12") **LONELY OL' NIGHT. / JACK & DIANE** [ ] [6] Aug 85
Nov 85. (lp)(c)(cd) **SCARECROW** [ ] [2] Sep 85
– Rain on the scarecrow / Grandma's theme / Small town / Minutes to memories / Lonely ol' night / The face of the nation / Justice and independence / Between a laugh and a tear / Rumbleseat / You've got to stand for somethin' / R.O.C.K. in the U.S.A. *(c+=)(cd+=)–* The kind of fella I am.
Jan 86. (7")(12") **SMALL TOWN. / SMALL TOWN (acoustic)** [53] [6] Oct 85
(d7"+=) – Hurt so good / The kinda fella I am.
(d12"+=) – Pink houses / Small town (acoustic).
Apr 86. (7")(12") **R.O.C.K. IN THE U.S.A. / UNDER THE BOARDWALK** [67] [2] Jan 86
Apr 86. (7") **RAIN ON THE SCARECROW. / ?** [-] [21]
Jun 86. (7") **RUMBLESEAT. / ?** [-] [28]

— added **LISA GERMANO** – violin / **PAT PETERSON** – backing vocals, percussion.

Mercury Mercury

Sep 87. (7")(12") **PAPER IN FIRE. / NEVER TO OLD** [ ] [9] Aug 87
Sep 87. (lp)(c)(cd) **THE LONESOME JUBILEE** [31] [6]
– Paper in fire / Down and out in paradise / Check it out / Real life / Cherry bomb / We are the people / Empty hands / Hard times for an honest man / Hot dogs and hamburgers / Rooty toot toot.
Nov 87. (7") **CHERRY BOMB. / SHAMA LAMA DING DONG** [ ] [8] Oct87
(12"+=) – Under the boardwalk.
(cd-s++=) – Pretty ballerina.
Feb 88. (7") **CHECK IT OUT. / WE ARE THE PEOPLE** [ ] [14]
(12"+=) – Shama lama ding dong / Pretty ballerina.
(cd-s+=) – Check it out (live) / Pink houses (acoustic).
Jul 88. (7") **ROOTY TOOT TOOT. / CHECK IT OUT (live)** [ ] [61] May 88
(12"+=) – Pretty ballerina.
(cd-s+=) – Like home (acoustic).
Apr 89. (7")(12") **RAVE ON. / (other track by LITTLE RICHARD)** [-] [ ]

— (above from the film 'Cocktail' on 'Elektra' label)

— added **CRYSTAL TALIEFERO** – backing vocals, percussion

May 89. (lp)(c)(cd) **BIG DADDY** [25] [7]
– Big daddy of them all / To live / Martha say / Theo and weird Henry / Jackie Brown / Pop singer / Void in my heart / Mansions in Heaven / Sometimes a great notion / Country gentlemen / J.M.'s question. *(cd+=)–* Let it all hang out.
Jun 89. (7") **POP SINGER. / JM'S QUESTION** [ ] [15] Apr 89
(12"+=) – Like a rolling stone (live).
(cd-s++=) – Check it out (live).
Jul 89. (7") **JACKIE BROWN. / ?** [-] [48]

JOHN MELLENCAMP

Sep 91. (7") **GET A LEG UP. / WHENEVER WE WANTED** [ ] [14]
(12"+=)(cd-s+=) – Seventh son.
Oct 91. (cd)(c)(lp) **WHENEVER WE WANTED** [39] [17]
– Love and happiness / Now more than ever / I ain't ever satisfied / Get a leg up / Crazy ones / Last chance / They're so tough / Melting pot / Whenever we wanted / Again tonight. *(re-iss.cd Apr95)*
Jan 92. (7")(c-s) **LOVE AND HAPPINESS. / ('A'-LA rock dance mix)** [ ] [ ]
(12"+=)/ /(cd-s++=) – ('A'mix)./ / ('A'other mix).
Feb 92. (c-s) **AGAIN TONIGHT. / ?** [-] [36]
Apr 92. (7")(c-s) **NOW MORE THAN EVER. / LONELY OLD NIGHT** [ ] [ ]
(cd-s+=) – Small town / Pink houses.
(cd-s) – ('A'side) / Jack and Diane / Check it out / Martha say (all live).

— Mid'92, MELLENCAMP suffered nervous exhaustion and cancelled gigs when his bassist MYERS severed a big toe in a boating accident. On 14th Nov '92, also saw his keyboard player JOHN CASCELLA die. He was only 35, but still played on half of next album. He was replaced by **MALCOLM BURN** – organ, guitar, harmonica, synth.

— **DAVID GRISSOM** – guitars, mandolin, bass repl. CRANE

Sep 93. (cd)(c) **HUMAN WHEELS** [37] [7]
– When Jesus left Birmingham / Junior / Human Wheels / Beige to beige / Case 795 (the family) / Suzanne and the jewels / Sweet evening breeze / What if I came knocking / French shoes / To the river.
Oct 93. (c-s) **HUMAN WHEELS. / ?** [-] [48]

— now w / **WANCHIC, MYERS, ARONOFF, ME'SHELL NDEGECELLO** (bass, vocals), **GERMANO, PETERSON + ANDY YORK** – guitar

Jun 94. (cd)(c) **DANCE NAKED** [ ] [13]
– Dance naked / Brothers / When Margaret comes to town / Wild night / L.U.V. / Another sunny day 12 /25 / Too much to think about / The big jack / The breakout.
Aug 94. (7"white)(c-s) **WILD NIGHT. (w/ ME'SHELL NDEGEOCELLO) / HURTS SO GOOD** [34] [3] Jun94
(cd-s) – ('A'side) / Dance naked (live) / When Jesus left Birmingham / Small town (acoustic).
(cd-s) – ('A'side) / Jack and Diane / Pink houses / Rock in the U.S.A. (a salute to the 60's).

— Above 'A' shared vocal duties with MADONNA's 'Maverick' protegee ME'SHELL.

Nov 94. (c-s)(cd-s) **DANCE NAKED. / ?** [-] [41]

– compilations, etc. (JOHN COUGAR) –

Mar 86. Castle; (lp)(c)(cd) **THE COLLECTION** (early) [ ] [-]

MENSWEAR

Formed: Camden, London, England . . .1994 by quintet below. In 1995, they scored first of 3 major UK with WIRE sounding 'DAYDREAMER'. • **Style:** WIRE meets mods, although BLUR and a punky MONKEES come to mind. • **Songwriters:** Group penned. • **Trivia:** CHRIS GENTRY is the boy-friend of DONNA from ELASTICA.

Recommended: NUISANCE (*7)

JOHNNY DEAN – vocals / **CHRIS GENTRY** – guitar / **SIMON WHITE** – guitar / **STUART BLACK** -bass / **MATT EVERETT** -drums

Laurel not issued

Dec 94. (7") **DAYDREAMER. / I'LL MANAGE SOMEHOW** [ ] [-]
Apr 95. (7")(cd-s) **I'LL MANAGE SOMEHOW. / SECOND HAND** [49] [-]
Jun 95. (7")(c-s) **DAYDREAMER. / GENTLEMAN JIM** [14] [ ]
(cd-s+=) – Around you again.
Sep 95. (7")(c-s) **STARDUST. / DAYDREAMER (dub dreamer)** [16] [ ]
(cd-s+=) – Back in the bar / Satellite.
Oct 95. (cd)(c)(lp) **NUISANCE** [11] [ ]
– 125 West 3rd Street / I'll manage somehow / Sleeping in / Little Miss Pinpoint eyes / Daydreamer / Hollywood girl / Being brave / Around you again / The one / Stardust / Piece of me.
Nov 95. (7")(c-s) **SLEEPING IN. / SUNDAY DRIVER** [24] [ ]
(cd-s+=) – Now is the hour / 26 years.

. . . Jan – Jun '96 stop press . . .

Mar 96. (single) **BEING BRAVE** [10] [ ]

Natalie MERCHANT (see under ⇒ 10,000 MANIACS)

Freddie MERCURY (see under ⇒ QUEEN)

METALLICA

Formed: Norvale, California, USA . . . 1981 by ULRICH and HETFIELD. The former had earlier emigrated from Denmark, and enjoyed drumming on UK tour for English group DIAMOND HEAD. After recruiting shifting personnel, they moved to New Jersey early in '83, where they signed to John Zazula's 'Megaforce' label. Their debut lp 'KILL 'EM ALL', gained a licence deal with UK label 'Music For Nations'. Their 2nd lp 'RIDE

THE LIGHTNING', was the last for US label, and they soon moved to 'Elektra'. In 1986, they broke into major chart territory with album 'MASTER OF PUPPETS', and by 1991 had a cross-Atlantic No.1 with self-titled masterpiece. This contained no less than 5 hit singles, all of them gems. • **Style:** New breed of high-speed heavy metal, influenced initially by BLACK SABBATH and MOTORHEAD, but progressing into a more WISHBONE ASH sound, with bouts of thrash. • **Songwriters:** ULRICH-HETFIELD, bar; BLITZKREIG (Blitzkreig) / AM I EVIL + HELPLESS + THE PRINCE (Diamond Head) / CRASH COURSE IN BRAIN SURGERY + BREADFAN (Budgie) / THE SMALL HOURS (Holocaust) / STONE COLD CRAZY (Queen). • **Miscellaneous:** In Spring'92, they paid tribute to the late FREDDIE MERCURY, when appearing at his AIDS benefit concert at Wembley.

Recommended: METALLICA (*10) / . . . AND JUSTICE FOR ALL (*7) / MASTER OF PUPPETS (*8) / RIDE THE LIGHTNING (*8) / KILL 'EM ALL (*7).

JAMES HETFIELD (b. 3 Aug'63) – vocals, rhythm guitar (ex-OBSESSION, etc) / **LARS ULRICH** (b.26 Dec'63, Copenhagen, Denmark) – drums / with **LLOYD GRAND** – guitar

not issued Bootleg.US

Dec 81. (7") **LET IT LOOSE. / KILLING TIME** [-] [ ]

— (Jan82) **DAVE MUSTAINE** – lead guitar, co-writer / **RON McGOVNEY** – bass repl. GRAND (JEF WARNER also played guitar in 1982)

— (early '83) **KIRK HAMMETT** (b.18 Nov'62) – lead guitar (ex-EXODUS) repl. MUSTAINE who was fired due to drunkeness. He was soon to form rivals MEGADETH.

— **CLIFF BURTON** (b.10 Feb'62) – bass (ex-TRAUMA) replaced McGOVNEY

M.F.N. Megaforce

Jul 83. (lp)(c) **KILL 'EM ALL** [ ] [ ]
– Hit the lights / The four horsemen / Motorbreath / Jump in the fire / (Anesthesia) Pulling teeth / Whiplash / Phantom Lord / No remorse / Seek and destroy / Metal militia. *(re-iss.Aug86 on pic-lp) (cd-iss.Apr87) (re-iss.Nov89 on 'Vertigo')*

Jan 84. (12")(12"red) **JUMP IN THE FIRE. / SEEK AND DESTROY (live). / PHANTOM LORD** [ ] [ ]
(re-iss.Mar86 on 7"sha-pic-d) (re-iss.+cd+c.Feb90, with other EP below)

Jul 84. (lp)(c) **RIDE THE LIGHTNING** [87] [ ]
– Fight fire with fire / Ride the lightning / For whom the bell tolls Fade to black / Trapped under ice / Escape / Creeping death / The call of Ktulu. *(re-iss.Sep86 on cd+pic-d) (US.re-iss.Oct84 on 'Elektra' hit 100) (re-iss.Nov89 on 'Vertigo')*

M.F.N. Elektra

Nov 84. (12")(12"pic-d) **CREEPING DEATH. / AM I EVIL. / BLITZKRIEG** [ ] [ ]
(above re-iss.Jan87 in gold + blue vinyl) (re-iss.+cd+c.Feb90, w/Mar86)

Mar 86. (lp)(c)(cd) **MASTER OF PUPPETS** [41] [29]
– Battery / Master of puppets / The thing that should not be / Welcome home (sanitarium) / Disposable heroes / Leper messiah / Orion / Damage Inc. *(also iss.Dec87 as d-lp,pic-d) (re-iss.Nov89 on 'Vertigo')*

— **JASON NEWSTEAD** (b. 4 Mar'63) – bass (ex-FLOTSAM AND JETSAM) repl. CLIFF who was killed in tour bus crash 27 Sep'86

Vertigo Elektra

Aug 87. (12"ep) **$5.98 EP – GARAGE DAYS REVISITED** [27] [28]
– Helpless / The small hours / Crash course in brain surgery / Last caress / Green hell. *(US version incl. 'The Wait' and was also m-lp) (re-iss.+cd.May90)*

Sep 88. (7") **EYE OF THE BEHOLDER. / BREAD FAN** [-] [ ]

Sep 88. (7")(12") **HARVESTER OF SORROW. / BREADFAN. / THE PRINCE** [20] [ ]

Oct 88. (d-lp)(c)(cd) **. . .AND JUSTICE FOR ALL** [4] [6] Sep 88
– Blackened / . . .And justice for all / Eye of the beholder / One / The shortest straw / Harvester of sorrow / The frayed ends of sanity / To live is to die / Dyers eve.

Feb 89. (7")(3"cd-s) **ONE. / THE PRINCE** [-] [35]

Mar 89. (7") **ONE. / SEEK AND DESTROY (live)** [13] [-] Feb 89
(12"+=) – Creeping death (live) / For whom the bell tolls (live).
(10"+=)(cd-s+=) – Welcome home (sanitarium).

Jul 91. (7")(7"pic-d) **ENTER SANDMAN. / STONE COLD CRAZY** [5] [16]
(12"+=)(cd-s+=) – Holier than thou.

Aug 91. (cd)(c)(d-lp) **METALLICA** [1] [1]
– Enter sandman / Sad but true / Holier than thou / The unforgiven / Wherever I may roam / Don't tread on me / Through the never / Nothing else matters / Of wolf and man / The god that failed / My friend of misery / The struggle within.

Nov 91. (7")(7"pic-d) **THE UNFORGIVEN. / KILLING TIME** [15] [35]
(12"+=)(cd-s+=) – ('A'demo) / So what.

Apr 92. (7")(7"pic-d) **NOTHING ELSE MATTERS. / ENTER SANDMAN (live)** [6] [34] Oct 92
(12"+=)(cd-s+=) – Harvester of sorrow (live) / ('A'demo).
(cd-s+=) – Stone cold crazy (live).
(cd-s+=) – Sad but true (live).

— On tour only **JOHN MARSHALL (of METAL CHURCH)** repl. injured (burnt) HETFIELD

Oct 92. (7")(7"pic-d) **WHEREVER I MAY ROAM. / FADE TO BLACK (live)** [25] [82] Jul 92
(12"+=) – ('A'demo).
(12")(cd-s) – ('A'side) / Medley (live) / ('A'demo).

Feb 93. (7") **SAD BUT TRUE. / NOTHING ELSE MATTERS** [20] [98]
(12"+=)(cd-s+=) – Creeping death (live) / Sad but true (demo).
(cd-s+=) – Sad but true (live).

Dec 93. (cd)(c) **LIVE SHIT: BINGE & PURGE (live)** [54] [26]
(also issued d-cd + 3 videos + book)

. . . Jan – Jun '96 stop press . . .

May 96. (single) **UNTIL IT SLEEPS** [18] [10]

Jun 96. (cd)(c)(d-lp) **LOAD** [1] [1]

– compilations, others, etc. –

May 90. Vertigo; (6x12"box) **THE GOOD, THE BAD & THE LIVE** [56] [-]

Aug 87. Megaforce; (7"ep) **WHIPLASH EP** [-] [ ]

METHOD MAN (see under ⇒ WU-TANG CLAN)

MIKE + THE MECHANICS (see under ⇒ GENESIS)

Steve MILLER

Born: 5 Oct'43, Milwaukee, Wisconsin, USA, but raised in Dallas, Texas. After forming school band The MARKSMAN COMBO with BOZ SCAGGS, he played for bluesman JIMMY REED at a 1957 gig. In the early 60's, he and SCAGGS joined The ARDELLS, who with BEN SIDRAN became The FABULOUS NIGHT TRAIN. In 1964, after a brief spell in Denmark, he moved to Chicago, where he sessioned for MUDDY WATERS, HOWLIN' WOLF and PAUL BUTTERFIELD. The next year, he partnered BARRY GOLDBERG in group The WORLD WAR III BAND, who issued one-off 45 'THE MOTHER SONG' as The GOLDBERG-MILLER BAND. Late in 1966, he moved to San Franscisco and formed The MILLER BAND with JAMES 'Curly' COOKE, LONNIE TURNER and TIM DAVIS. In Spring of '67, they added JIM PETERMAN, and replaced COOKE with BOZ. After a June appearance at The Monterey Pop Festival, they soon signed to 'Capitol' records. Early in 1968, they recorded 3 songs for the 'Revolution' film soundtrack, which hit shops late '69. In Apr'68, their debut lp 'CHILDREN OF THE FUTURE' was issued and made No.134 on the US charts. Its mild success, was overshadowed by the follow-up 'SAILOR', which gave them first of many entries into US Top 30. In 1973, after a lean couple of years, they hit US No.1 with 45 'THE JOKER'. Although it became a classic in the UK, it failed to chart. That is until 1990, when it hit No.1 after it was given fresh exposure on Levi jeans TV ad. • **Style:** The gangster of love & rock moved from progressive electronic music in the late 60's, which shaped into harmonious laid back rock by '73. In 1987-88, he chose a fusion of blues-jazz covers on his 2 albums. • **Songwriters:** MILLER and BEN SIDRAN compositions, except covers on 87 & 88 albums. • **Trivia:** On '69 song 'MY DARK HOUR', PAUL McCARTNEY played bass under psuedonym MARK RAMON.

Recommended: THE BEST OF STEVE MILLER BAND 1968-1973 (*8) / FLY LIKE AN EAGLE (*8) / ABRACADABRA (*6).

GOLDBERG / MILLER BLUES BAND

BARRY GOLDBERG – keyboards / **STEVE MILLER** – guitar, vocals

not issued Epic

1965. (7") **THE MOTHER SONG. / MORE THAN SOUL** [-] [ ]

— Late 1966, the MILLER BAND evolved into

The STEVE MILLER BAND

STEVE MILLER – vocals, guitar / **LONNIE TURNER** – bass, vocals / **BOZ SCAGGS** – guitar / **JIM PETERMAN** – organ, vocals / **TIM DAVIS** – drums

Capitol Capitol

Apr 68. (7") **SITTING IN CIRCLES. / ROLL WITH IT** [ ] [ ]

Sep 68. (lp) **CHILDREN OF THE FUTURE** [ ] [ ] Apr 68
– Children of the future / Pushed me to it / You've got the power / In my first mind / The beauty of time is that it's snowing / Baby's callin' me home / Steppin' stone / Roll with it / Junior saw it happen / Fanny Mae / Key to the highway.

Oct 68. (7") **LIVING IN THE U.S.A. / QUICKSILVER GIRL** [ ] [94]

Jan 69. (lp) **SAILOR** [ ] [24] Oct 68
– Song for our ancestors / Dear Mary / My friend / Living in the U.S.A. / Quicksilver girls / Lucky man / Gangster of love / You're so fine / Overdrive / Dime-a-dance romance. *(re-iss.Nov83 on 'Fame', +cd.Apr91)*

— Trim to a trio of **MILLER, TURNER** and **DAVIS** with session men. (PETERMAN left just after SCAGGS who went solo) **BEN SIDRAN** – keyboards (joined briefly)

— (Mar69) **NICKY HOPKINS** – keyboards (ex-JEFF BECK GROUP) repl. SIDRAN

Sep 69. (lp) **BRAVE NEW WORLD** [ ] [22] Jun 69
– Brave new world / Space cowboy / Got love 'cause you need it / It's a midnight dream / Can't you hear daddy's heartbeat / Celebration song / Seasons / Kow kow calculator / My dark hour. *(re-iss.Feb84 on 'EMI')*

Jul 69. (7") **MY DARK HOUR. / SONG FOR OUR ANCESTORS** [ ] [ ]
Nov 69. (7") **LITTLE GIRL. / DON'T LET NOBODY TURN YOU AROUND** [ ] [ ]
Mar 70. (lp) **YOUR SAVING GRACE** [ ] [38] Nov 69
– Little girl / Just a passin' fancy in a midnite dream / Don't let nobody turn you around / Baby's house / Motherless children / The last wombat in Mecca / Feel so glad / Your saving grace. *(cd-iss.May91 on 'E.M.I.')*

— **BOBBY WINKLEMAN** – bass, vocals repl. TURNER and HOPKINS who joined QUICKSILVER MESSENGER SERVICE

Nov 70. (lp)(c) **NUMBER 5** [ ] [23] Jul 70
– Good morning / I love you / Going to the country / Hot chili / Tokin's / Going to Mexico / Steve Miller's midnight tango / Industrial military complex hex / Jackson-Kent blues / Never kill another man.

Sep 70. (7") **GOING TO THE COUNTRY. / NEVER KILL ANOTHER MAN** [ ] [69] Aug 70
Dec 70. (7") **GOING TO MEXICO. / STEVE MILLER'S MIDNIGHT TANGO** [-] [ ]

— **STEVE MILLER** recruited entire new band **ROSS VALORY** – bass, vocals repl. WINKLEMAN / **JACK KING** – drums, vocals repl. DAVIS who went solo

Sep 71. (7") **ROCK LOVE. / LET ME SERVE YOU** [-] [ ]
Nov 71. (lp)(c) **ROCK LOVE** [ ] [ ] Oct 71
– The gangster is back / Blues without blame / Love shock / Let me serve you / Rock love / Harbor lights / Deliverance.

— **GERALD JOHNSON** – bass, vocals repl. VALORY who later joined JOURNEY / added **DICKY THOMPSON** – keyboards / **ROGER ALAN CLARK** – 2nd drummer

May 72. (lp)(c) **RECALL THE BEGINNING . . . A JOURNEY FROM EDEN** [ ] [ ] Mar 72
– Welcome / Enter Maurice / High on you mama / Heal your heart / The sun is going down / Somebody somewhere help me / Love's riddle / Fandango / Nothing lasts / Journey from Eden.

May 72. (7") **FANDANGO. / LOVE'S RIDDLE** [-] [ ]

— (Mar72) **JOHN KING** – drums repl. JACK and ROGER / **LONNIE TURNER** – bass, vocals returned to repl. JOHNSON who joined BOZ SCAGGS

Oct 73. (7") **THE JOKER. / SOMETHING TO BELIEVE IN** [ ] [1]
Oct 73. (lp)(c) **THE JOKER** [ ] [2]
– Sugar babe / Mary Lou / Loving cup / Shu ba da du ma ma / Your cash ain't nothin' but trash / The joker / Lovin' cup / Come on into my kitchen / Evil / Something to believe in. *(re-iss.Oct80) (re-iss.Jan83 on 'EMI')*

Feb 74. (7") **YOUR CASH AIN'T NOTHIN' BUT TRASH. / EVIL** [-] [51]

— (May74) **STEVE MILLER** retired for a while, when THOMPSON and KING departed.

— (Jul75) **MILLER** retained **TURNER** and recruited for Knebworth festival **LES DUDEK** – guitar, vocals / **DOUG CLIFFORD** – drums (ex-CREEDENCE CLEARWATER REVIVAL)

— (1976) **GARY MALLABER** – drums repl. CLIFFORD and DUDEK

Mercury Capitol

May 76. (7") **TAKE THE MONEY AND RUN. / SWEET MARIE** [ ] [11]
May 76. (lp)(c) **FLY LIKE AN EAGLE** [11] [3]
– (Space intro) / Fly like an eagle / Wild mountain honey / Serenade / Dance, dance, dance / Mercury blues / Take the money and run / Rock'n'me / You send me / Blue odyssey / Sweet Maree / The window. *(re-iss.Nov84)*

Aug 76. (7") **ROCK'N'ME. / LIVING IN THE U.S.A.** [-] [1]
Aug 76. (7") **FLY LIKE AN EAGLE. / MERCURY BLUES** [-] [-]
Oct 76. (7") **ROCK'N'ME. / THE WINDOW** [11] [-]
Nov 76. (7") **FLY LIKE AN EAGLE. / LOVIN' CUP** [-] [2]
Jan 77. (7") **SERENADE. / DANCE DANCE DANCE** [ ] [-]

— (Oct76) added **DAVID DENNY** – guitar, vocals (ex-TERRY & THE PIRATES) / **BYRON ALLRED** – keyboards / **NORTON BUFFALO** – harmonica, vocals

Apr 77. (7") **JET AIRLINER. / BABES IN THE WOOD** [ ] [8]
May 77. (lp)(c) **BOOK OF DREAMS** [12] [2]
– Threshold / Jet airliner / Winter time / Swingtown / True fine love / Wish upon a star / Jungle love / Electro lux imbroglio / Sacrifice / The stake / My own space / Babes in the wood. *(re-iss.Jan85)*

Sep 77. (7") **JUNGLE LOVE. / WISH UPON A STAR** [ ] [23] Aug 77
Jan 78. (7") **SWINGTOWN. / WINTER TIME** [ ] [17] Oct 77

— trimmed to a quintet of **MILLER, MALLABER, ALLRED, DOUGLAS** and **BUFFALO**

Oct 81. (lp)(c) **CIRCLE OF LOVE** [ ] [26]
– Heart like a wheel / Get on home / Baby wanna dance / Cricle of love / Macho city.

Oct 81. (7") **HEART LIKE A WHEEL. / TRUE FINE LOVE** [-] [24]
Nov 81. (7") **HEART LIKE A WHEEL. / JET AIRLINER / THRESHOLD** [ ] [-]
Jan 82. (7") **CIRCLE OF LOVE. / (part 2)** [-] [55]
Feb 82. (7") **MACHO CITY. / FLY LIKE AN EAGLE** [ ] [-]

— **KENNY LEWIS** – guitar / **JOHN MASSARO** – guitar both repl. DOUGLAS

May 82. (7") **ABRACADABRA. / GIVE IT UP** [-] [1]
Jun 82. (7") **ABRACADABRA. / NEVER SAY NO** [2] [-]
(re-iss.Oct84)
Jun 82. (lp)(c) **ABRACADABRA** [10] [3]
– Keeps me wondering why / Abracadabra / Something special / Give it up / Never say no / Things I told you / Young girl's heart / Goodbye love / Cool magic / While I'm waiting. *(cd-iss.Jan83)*

Aug 82. (7") **KEEPS ME WONDERING WHY. / GET ON HOME** [52] [ ]
(12"+=) – Abracadabra.
Oct 82. (7") **GIVE IT UP. / ROCK'N'ME** [ ] [-]
Oct 82. (7") **COOL MAGIC. / YOUNG GIRL'S HEART** [-] [57]
Dec 82. (7") **GIVE IT UP. / HEART LIKE A WHEEL** [-] [60]
Mar 83. (7") **LIVING IN THE U.S.A. (live). / BUFFALO SERENADE** [-] [ ]
Apr 83. (lp)(c) **THE STEVE MILLER BAND LIVE! (live)** [79] [ ]
– Gangster of love / Rock'n'me / Living in the U.S.A. / Fly like an eagle / Jungle love / The joker / Mercury blues / Take the money and run / Abracadabra / Jet airliner. *(cd-iss.1988)* (cd+=) – Buffalo serenade.

Apr 83. (7") **TAKE THE MONEY AND RUN (live). / THE JOKER (live)** [ ] [ ]
(12"+=) – Buffalo serenade (live).

— Now without MASSARO

Oct 84. (7") **SHANGRI-LA. / CIRCLE OF LOVE** [ ] [57]
(12"+=) – Abracadabra.
Nov 84. (lp)(c)(cd) **ITALIAN X-RAYS** [ ] [ ]
– Radio 1 / Italian x-rays / Daybreak / Shangri-la / Who do you love / Harmony of the spheres 1 / Radio 2 / Bongo bongo / Out of the night / Golden opportunity / The Hollywood dream / One in a million / Harmony of the spheres 2.

Jan 85. (7") **BONGO BONGO. / GET ON HOME** [ ] [84]
Mar 85. (7") **ITALIAN X-RAYS. / WHO DO YOU LOVE** [-] [ ]

— **MILLER** with **MALLABER** and **BUFFALO** bring back **LES DUDEK** – guitar

Capitol Capitol

Jan 87. (lp)(c)(cd) **LIVING IN THE 20TH CENTURY** [ ] [65] Nov 86
– Nobody but you baby / I want to make the world turn around / Slinky / Living in the 20th century / Maelstrom / I wanna be loved / My babe / Big boss man / Caress me baby / Ain't that lovin' you baby / Behind the barn.

Mar 87. (7")(12") **I WANT TO MAKE THE WORLD TURN AROUND. / SLINKY** [ ] [97] Nov 86
Apr 87. (7") **NOBODY BUT YOU BABY. / MAELSTROM** [-] [ ]
Jun 87. (7") **I WANNA BE LOVED. / (part 2)** [-] [ ]

STEVE MILLER

solo with **BEN SIDRAN** – keyboards / **BILLY PATERSON** – bass / **GORDY KNUDTSON** – drums

Sep 88. (7")(12") **YA YA. / FILTHY McNASTY** [ ] [ ]
Sep 88. (lp)(c)(cd) **BORN 2 B BLUE** [ ] [ ]
– Zip-a-dee-doo-dah / Ya ya / God bless the child / Filthy McNasty / Born to be blue / Mary Ann / Just a little bit / When Sunny gets blue / Willow weep for me / Red top.

Polydor Sailor

Jul 93. (cd)(c) **WIDE RIVER** [ ] [85]
-Wide river / Midnight train / Blue eyes / Lost in your eyes / Perfect world / Horse and rider / Circle of ir / Conversation / Cry cry cyr / Stranger blues / Walks like a lady / All your love (I miss loving).

Jul 93. (c-s)(cd-s) **WIDE RIVER. /** [-] [64]
Aug 93. (7")(c-s) **WIDE RIVER. / STRANGER BLUES** [ ] [ ]

– compilations, etc. –

Feb 72. Capitol; (7"ep) **MY DARK HOUR. / SONG FOR OUR ANCESTORS / THE GANGSTER IS BACK** [ ] [ ]
Mar 73. Capitol; (lp)(c) **ANTHOLOGY** [ ] [56] Nov 72
1973. Capitol; (d-lp) **CHILDREN OF THE FUTURE / LIVING IN THE U.S.A.** [ ] [ ]
Jun 74. Capitol; (7") **LIVING IN THE U.S.A. / KOW KOW CALQULATOR** [ ] [49] May 74
Mar 77. Capitol; (lp)(c) **THE BEST OF THE STEVE MILLER BAND 1968-73** [ ] [ ]
– Living in the U.S.A. / I love you / Don't let nobody turn you around / Seasons / Shu ba da du ma ma ma / Kow kow calculator / The joker / Going to the country / My dark hour / Your saving grace / Celebration song / Space cowboy. *(re-iss May 82 on 'Fame') (re-iss. Aug 86 on 'E.M.I.') (re-iss.+cd.Sep90, hit UK No.34)* (cd+= 4 extra).

Jan 83. Capitol; (7") **THE JOKER. / MY DARK HOUR. / LIVING IN THE U.S.A.** [ ] [ ]
Aug 90. Capitol; (7")(c-s) **THE JOKER. / DON'T LET NOBODY TURN YOU AROUND** [1] [ ]
(12"+=) – Shu ba da du ma ma ma.
(cd-s++=) – Living in the U.S.A.
Oct 75. Capitol Vine; (lp)(c) **THE LEGEND** [ ] [-]
Oct 78. Capitol; (7") **THE JOKER. / THE STAKE** [ ] [ ]
Nov 78. Capitol; (lp)(c) **GREATEST HITS 1974-78** [ ] [18]

(re-iss.May88) (cd-iss. 1983)

May 87. Mercury; (lp)(c)(cd) **GREATEST HITS – A DECADE OF AMERICAN MUSIC (1976-1986)**

MINISTRY

Formed: Chicago, Illinois, USA . . . 1981 by ex-SPECIAL EFFECT member AL JOURGENSEN. He formed own 'Wax Trax' label, and issued debut 12" COLD LIFE in 1982. Ten years later, MINISTRY were deservedly in both US & UK Top 40 with 'PSALM 69' album. • **Style:** Experimental heavy electronic outfit run by JOURGENSEN. The REVOLTING COCKS were described as 'disco for psychopaths'. • **Songwriters:** REVOLTING COCKS covered LET'S GET PHYSICAL (Olivia Newton John) / DO YA THINK I'M SEXY? (Rod Stewart) / SUPERNAUT (1000 Komo DJs). • **Trivia:** JOURGENSEN was also a member of LARD, with DEAD KENNEDYS leader JELLO BIAFRA. Early '91, The REVOLTING COCKS shocked many when they performed on stage with 2 naked go-go dancers.

Recommended: PSALM 69: HOW TO SUCCEED AND HOW TO SUCK EGGS (*7) / FILTHPIG (*6)

AL JOURGENSEN – keyboards, guitar, synthesizers, vocals

Situation 2 / Wax Trax

Mar 82. (12"m) **COLD LIFE. / I'M FALLING / COLD LIFE (dub) / PRIMENTAL**

—— AL used musicians on next lp; **SHAY JONES** – vocals / **WALTER TURBETT** – guitar / **JOHN DAVIS** – keyboards / **ROBERT ROBERTS** – keyboards / **STEPHEN GEORGE** – drums / **MARTIN SORENSEN** – bass

Arista / Arista

Apr 83. (7") **REVENGE (YOU DID IT AGAIN). / SHE'S GOT A CAUSE** [-]

Jun 83. (7") **I WANTED TO TELL HER. / A WALK IN THE PARK**
(12"+=) – ('A'tongue tied mix).

Sep 83. (7")(12") **WORK FOR LOVE. / FOR LOVE (instrumental)**

Sep83. (lp)(c) **WORK FOR LOVE** (US title 'WITH SYMPATHY') [ ] [96] Jun 83
– Work for love / Do the Etawa / I wanted to tell her / Say you're sorry / Here we go / Effigy / Revenge / She's got a cause / Should have known better. *(cd-iss.1989 as 'WITH SYMPATHY'; the original US title, += 'What He Say')*

Nov 83. (7") **REVENGE (YOU DID IT AGAIN). / EFFIGY** [ ] [-]
(12"+=) – Work for love.

—— now basically AL solo.

Wax Trax / Wax Trax

Oct 85. (12") **NATURE OF LOVE. / ('A'cruelty mix)**

Sire / Sire

Apr 86. (lp)(c)(cd) **TWITCH**
– Just like you / We believe / All day remix / The angel / Over the shoulder / My possession / Where you at now? / Crash and burn / Twitch (version II). *(cd+=)*– Over the shoulder (mix) / Isle Of Man.

—— added partner **PAUL BARKER** – instruments (ex-FRONT 242)

1987. (lp)(c) **IN CASE YOU DIDN'T FEEL LIKE SHOWING UP (live)** [-]
– The missing / deity / So what / Burning inside / Seed / Stigmata. *(re-iss.cd Dec92)*

Jan 89. (lp)(c)(cd) **THE LAND OF RAPE AND HONEY** [ ] [ ] Nov 88
– Stigmata / The missing / Deity / Golden dawn / Destruction / The land of rape and honey / You know what you are / Flashback / Abortive. *(cd+=)*– Hizbollah / I prefer. *(re-iss.cd Dec92)*

Feb 90. (cd)(c)(lp) **THE MIND IS A TERRIBLE THING TO TASTE** [ ] [ ] Dec 89
– Thieves / Burning inside / Never believe / Cannibal song / Breathe / So what / Test / Faith collapsing / Dream song. *(re-iss.cd Dec92)*

—— next with guest **GIBBY HAYNES** (of BUTTHOLE SURFERS)

Apr 92. (7") **JESUS BUILT MY HOTROD. / TV SONG**
(12"+=)(cd-s+=) – ('A'red line-white line version).

Jul 92. (cd)(c)(10"lp) **PSALM 69: HOW TO SUCCEED AND HOW TO SUCK EGGS** [33] [27]
– N.W.O. / Just one fix / TV II / hero / Jesus built my hot rod / Scarecrow / Psalm 69 / Corrosion / Grace.

Jul 92. (7") **N.W.O. / F***ED (non lp version)** [49]
(12"+=)(cd-s+=) – ('A'extended dance mix).

W.E.A. / W.E.A.

Dec 95. (c-s) **THE FALL / RELOAD** [53]
(cd-s+=) – TV III.

. . . Jan – Jun '96 stop press . . .

Jan 96. (cd)(c)(lp) **FILTHPIG** [43] [19]

Feb 96. (single) **LAY LADY LAY**

—— a Bob Dylan cover

– compilation, others, etc. –

1985. Hot Trax; (lp) **12" INCH SINGLES 1981-1984** [-]

REVOLTING COCKS

AL's studio outfit, with FRONT 242 members; LUC and RICHARD 23. The latter was soon replaced CHRIS CONNELLY of FINI TRIBE.

Beauty &.. / Wax Trax

Feb 86. (12"m) **NO DEVOTION. / ATTACK SHIPS / ON FIRE**

Wax Trax / Wax Trax

Feb 87. (12") **YOU OFTEN FORGET. / ?**

—— AL with VAN ACKER + JONCKHEERE

1988. (lp)(cd) **BIG SEXY LAND**
– 38 / We shall change the world / Attack ships on fire / Big sexy land / Union carbide / TV mind / No devotion / Union carbide (Bhopal version). *(re-iss.Mar92 on 'Devotion')*

Jun 88. (d-lp,cd) **YOU GODAMNED SON OF A BITCH** (live + 2 studio)
– You Goddamned son of a bitch / Cattle grid / We shall cleanse the world / 38 / In the neck / You often forget / TV mind / Union carbide / Attack ships on fire / No devotion. *(re-iss.May92 on 'Devotion')*

Mar 89. (12") **STAINLESS STEEL PROVIDERS. / AT THE TOP**

—— **AL + PHIL** were also part of JELLO BIAFRA'S (Dead Kennedys) group LARD.
AL now with **BARKER, VAN ACKER, RIEFLIN + CONNELLY** – vocals.

May 90. (cd)(c)(lp) **BEERS, STEERS AND QUEERS**
– Beers, steers and queers / (Let's get) Physical / In the neck / Get down / Stainless steel providers / Can't sit still / Something wonderful / Razor's edge. *(cd+=)*– (Let's talk) Physical. *(re-iss.Feb92 on 'Devotion')*

May 90. (12") **(LET'S GET) PHYSICAL. / (LET'S TALK) PHYSICAL**

—— now without RIEFLIN

Apr 91. (12"ep)(cd-ep) **SUPERNAUT / BY "1000 HOMO DJ'S" / HEY ASSHOLE / APATHY / BETTER WAYS**

Sep 93. (12")(cd-s) **DA YA THINK I'M SEXY? / SERGIO GUITAR / WRONG (sexy mix)** [61]

Sep 93. (cd)(c)(lp) **LINGER FICKEN' GOOD . . . AND OTHER BARNYARD ODDITIES** [39]
– Gila copter / Creep / Mr.Lucky / Crackin' up / Sergio / Da ya think I'm sexy? / The rockabye / Butcher flower's woman / Dirt / Linger ficken' good . . . and other barnyard oddities.

Jun 94. (12")(cd-s) **CRACKIN' UP. / ('A'-amylnitrate mix) / GUACOPTER (version 2)** [ ] [-]

LEAD INTO GOLD

AL + PAUL with **WILD BILL RIEFLIN** This was BARKER's main outlet.

Devotion / Devotion

1992. (lp)(c) **AGE OF REASON**
– Age of reason / Unreason / Snake oil / A giant on Earth / Faster than light / Lunatic-genius / Sweet thirteen / Fell from Heaven.

MISSION

Formed: Leeds, England ... late 1985 by ex-SISTERS OF MERCY members WAYNE HUSSEY and CRAIG ADAMS. Originally planned to be The SISTERHOOD, and did some gigs, until ANDREW ELDRITCH wanted group name for himself. To save fuss, they became The MISSION, and signed to indie 'Chapter 22' on Mar'86. 2 months later, their debut single 'SERPENT'S KISS', breached the Top 75, with a Summer follow-up 'GARDEN OF DELIGHT' scraping the 50. To end the Summer, they signed to major 'Mercury', and cracked the Top 30 with 'STAY WITH ME', and parent debut Top 20 album 'GOD'S OWN MEDICINE'. Continued consecutive string of hit UK albums and singles, although their last of '92 'SHADES OF GREEN', only just managed to make No.49. • **Style:** Goth supergroup, fusing a mixture of acoustic and hard-rock deep metal. • **Songwriters:** HUSSEY penned, except LIKE A HURRICANE (Neil Young) / DANCING BAREFOOT (Patti Smith) / SHELTER FROM THE STORM (Bob Dylan) / OVER THE HILLS AND FAR AWAY (Led Zeppelin) / LOVE (John Lennon) / ATOMIC (Blondie). • **Trivia:** Were called The MISSION U.K. for the States. JOHN PAUL JONES (ex-LED ZEPPELIN) produced 2nd album 'CHILDREN'. In 1991, HUSSEY was ushered off James Whale's late night TV show, for being drunk and abusive to its ever-polite presenter!!

Recommended: SUM AND SUBSTANCE (*8)

WAYNE HUSSEY (b.26 May'59, Bristol, England) – vocals, guitar (ex-SISTERS OF MERCY, ex-DEAD OR ALIVE, ex-HAMBI & THE DANCE, ex-WALKIE

TALKIES) / **CRAIG ADAMS** – bass (ex-SISTERS OF MERCY, ex-EXPELAIRES) / **SIMON HINKLER** – guitar (ex-ARTERY) / **MICK BROWN** – drums (ex-RED LORRY YELLOW LORRY)

Chapter 22 not issued

May 86. (7") **SERPENT'S KISS. / WAKE (R.S.V.)** 70 -
(12"+=) – Naked and savage.
Jul 86. (7") **GARDEN OF DELIGHT. / LIKE A HURICANE** 50 -
(12"+=) – Over the hills and far away / The crystal ocean.
(12"+=) – Dancing barefoot / The crystal ocean.

Mercury Mercury

Oct 86. (7") **STAY WITH ME. / BLOOD BROTHER** 30
(12"+=) – Islands in a stream.
Nov 86. (lp)(c)(cd) **GODS OWN MEDICINE** 14
– Wasteland / Bridges burning / Garden of delight (hereafter) / Stay with me / Blood brother * / Let sleeping dogs lie / Sacrilege / Dance on glass / And the dance goes on / Severina / Love me to death / Island in a stream *. *(c+= *)(cd+= *)*
Jan 87. (7") **WASTELAND. / SHELTER FROM THE STORM** 11
(12"+=) – Dancing barefoot (live).
(12"+=) – 1969 / Wake (both live).
(d7") – 1969 (live) / Serpent's kiss (live).
Mar 87. (7") **SEVERINA. / TOMORROW NEVER KNOWS** 25
(12"+=) – Wishing well.

— **PETE TURNER** – bass took over on tour while ADAMS recovered from illness **CRAIG ADAMS** was soon back after a 4 month lay-off.

Jan 88. (7")(12") **TOWER OF STRENGTH. / FABIENNE / BREATHE (vocal)** 12
(12"+=)(c-s+=)(cd-s+=) – Dream on / Breathe (instrumental; repl. vocal=)
Mar 88. (lp)(c)(cd) **CHILDREN** 2
– Beyond the pale / A wing and a prayer / Fabienne * / Heaven on Earth / Tower of strength / Kingdom come / Breathe / Child's play / Shamera kye / Black mountain mist / Dream on * / Heat / Hymn (for America). *(c+=)(cd+=)*
Jul 88. (7") **BEYOND THE PALE. / TADEUSZ (1912-1988)** 32
(12"+=) – For ever more.
(cd-s+=) – Tower of strength (reprise).
(12"+=)(cd-s+=) – Love me to death (reprise).
Nov 88. (7") **KINGDOM COME. / CHILD'S PLAY (live)**
(12"+=) – The crystal ocean.
(12"++=)(cd-s++=) – Garden of delight (live).
(all formats on above single withdrawn)
Jan 90. (7")(c-s) **BUTTERFLY ON A WHEEL. / THE GRIP OF DISEASE** 12
(12"+=)(cd-s+=) – ('A'magni-octopus) / Kingdom come (forever and again).
Feb 90. (cd)(c)(lp) **CARVED IN SAND** 7
– Amelia / Into the blue / Butterfly on a wheel / Sea of love / Deliverance / Grapes of wrath / Belief / Paradise (will shine like the Moon) / Hungry as the hunter / Lovely.
Mar 90. (7")(c-s) **DELIVERANCE. / MR.PLEASANT** 27
(10"+=)(12"+=)(cd-s+=)(pic-cd-s+=) – Heaven sends us.
May 90. (7")(c-s) **INTO THE BLUE. / BIRD OF PARADISE** 32
(12"+=)(cd-s+=) – Divided we fall.

— **DAVID WOLFENDEN** – guitar (ex-RED LORRY YELLOW LORRY) repl. HINKLER.

— (Oct90) added **ETCH** – guitar (ex-GHOST DANCE)

Oct 90. (cd)(c)(lp) **GRAINS OF SAND** (out-takes) 28
– Hands across the ocean / The grip of disease / Divided we fall / Mercenary / Mr.Pleasant / Kingdom come (forever and again) / Heaven sends you / Sweet smile of a mystery / Love / Bird of passage.
(c+cd+=) – (2 extra acoustic tracks)
Nov 90. (7")(c-s) **HANDS ACROSS THE OCEAN. / AMELIA / LOVE** 28
(12"+=) – Amelia (live) / Tower of strength (mix) / Mercenary.
(cd-s+=) – Amelia (live) / Stay with me / Mercenary.

Vertigo Mercury

Apr 92. (7")(c-s) **NEVER AGAIN. / BEAUTIFUL CHAOS** 34
(12"+=)(cd-s+=) – ('A'-F1 mix) / ('A'-Zero G mix.
Jun 92. (cd)(c)(lp) **MASQUE** 23
– Never again / Shades of green (part II) / Even you may shine / Trail of scarlet / Spider and the fly / She conjures me wings / Sticks and stones / Like a child again / Who will love me tomorrow? / You make me breathe / From one Jesus to another / Until there's another sunrise. *(re-is.cd/c Aug94)*
Jun 92. (7")(c-s) **LIKE A CHILD AGAIN (remix). / ALL TANGLED UP IN YOU** 30
(12"+=)(cd-s+=) – ('A'-Mark Saunders remix) / Hush a bye baby (child again) (Joe Gibbs remix).
Oct 92. (7")(c-s) **SHADES OF GREEN. / YOU MAKE ME BREATHE** 49
(cd-s) – ('A'side) / Sticks and stones / Trail of scarlet / Spider and the fly.
(etched-12"+=) – ('A'mix).

— (Nov92) **MARK THWAITE** – guitar (ex-SPEAR OF DESTINY) repl. HINKLER + ADAMS. Note:- **RIC SAUNDERS** – violin (of FAIRPORT CONVENTION) on last lp.

Jan 94. (7") **TOWER OF STRENGTH (Youth remix). / WASTELAND** 33
(12"+=) – Serpent's kiss.
(cd-s) – ('A'mixes) / ('A'-East India Cairo mix) / Deliverance.
Feb 94. (cd)(c)(d-lp) **SUM AND SUBSTANCE** (compilation) 49
– Never again / Hands across the ocean / Shades of green / Like a child again / Into the blue / Deliverance / Tower of strength / Butterfly on a wheel / Kingdom come / Beyond the pale / Severina / Stay with me / Wasteland / Garden of delight / Like a hurricane / Serpent's kiss / Sour puss / Afterglow.
Mar 94. (7") **AFTERGLOW. / SOUR-PUSS** 53
(cd-s+=) – Cold as ice / Valentine.

Equator not issued

Oct 94. (7"ep)(12"ep)(c-ep)(cd-ep) **MISSION 1 EP**
– Raising Cain / Sway / Neverland.
Jan 95. (7"ep)(10"ep)(cd-ep) **SWOON / WHERE / WASTING AWAY / ('A'-Resurrection mix)** 73
Feb 95. (cd)(c) **NEVERLAND** 58
– Raising Cain / Sway / Lose myself / Swoon / Afterglow (reprise) / Stars don't shine without you / Celebration / Cry like a baby / Heaven knows / Swim with the dolphins / Neverland / Daddy's going to Heaven now.

. . . Jan – Jun '96 stop press . . .

Jun 96. (cd)(lp) **BLUE** 73

– compilations, others, etc. –

Jun 87. Chapter 22; (lp)(c) **THE FIRST CHAPTER** 35 -
(contains all 'Chapter 22' material)
Jul 94. Nighttracks; (cd)(lp) **SALAD DAZE** -

Joni MITCHELL

Born: ROBERTA JOAN ANDERSON, 7 Nov'43, Fort McLeod, Alberta, Canada. In 1964 she performed at the Mariposa Folk Festival in Ontario, and married CHUCK MITCHELL in Jun'65, but after they relocated to Detroit the next year, they divorced. She retained surname and moved to New York, where her songs were gradually recorded by others, mainly JUDY COLLINS('BOTH SIDES NOW' & 'MICHAEL FROM MOUNTAINS') and TOM RUSH('THE CIRCLE GAME'). Her self-titled DAVID CROSBY produced debut lp, came out in Summer of '68, and managed to only scrape into US Top 200. In August 1969 on the advice of David Geffen, she pulled out of WOODSTOCK free festival, and instead wrote classic song of that name. It was later a US hit for CROSBY, STILLS, NASH & YOUNG, and also a UK No.1 for MATTHEWS' SOUTHERN COMFORT. Her 2nd solo lp 'CLOUDS' broke through into US Top 40, after her non-appearance, and was her second of many classic albums of the 70's. Her '79 album 'MINGUS' was dedicated to jazz legend CHARLIE MINGUS, who she had recently worked with, but who died of Lou Gegrig's disease on 5 Jan'79. • **Style:** Undoubtedly the greatest female singer/songwriter of all-time. She eased her romantically inclined moods, through folk, jazz and sophisticated rock, and was / is the inspiration for many female rock-pop acts. • **Songwriters:** All self-penned except; TWISTED (Annie Ross) / WHY DO FOOLS FALL IN LOVE (Frankie Lymon) / BABY I DON'T CARE (hit; Elvis Presley) / SLOUCHING TOWARDS BETHLEHEM (poem; W.B.Yeats). • **Trivia:** Her excellent paintings, were mostly always featured as the album cover.

Recommended: JONI MITCHELL (*7) / CLOUDS (*7) / LADIES OF THE CANYON (*9) / BLUE (*7) / FOR THE ROSES (*7) / COURT AND SPARK (*7) / HEJIRA (*10) / THE HISSING OF SUMMER LAWNS (*7) / CHALK MARK IN A RAINSTORM (*7).

JONI MITCHELL – vocals, acoustic guitar, piano with **STEPHEN STILLS** – bass /

Reprise Reprise

Jun 68. (lp) **JONI MITCHELL** Mar 68
– I CAME TO THE CITY:- I had a king / Michael from the mountains / Night in the city / Marcie / Nathan la Freneer / OUT OF THE CITY AND DOWN TO THE SEASIDE:- Sisotowbell Lane / The dawntreader / The pirate of penance / Song to a seagull / Cactus tree. *(cd-iss.1987)*
Jul 68. (7") **NIGHT IN THE CITY. / I HAD A KING** -
Aug 69. (7") **CHELSEA MORNING. / BOTH SIDES NOW** -
(iss. US Jun '72)
Oct 69. (lp) **CLOUDS** 31 May 69
– Tin angel / Chelsea morning / I don't know where I stand / That song about the Midway / Roses blue / The gallery / I think I understand / Songs to ageing children come / The fiddle and the drum / Both sides now. *(re-iss.c+cd.1989 on 'WEA')*

— next guests **MILT HOLLAND** – percussion / **TERESSA ADAMS** – cello / **JIM HORN** – baritone sax / **PAUL HORN** – clarinet, flute

May 70. (lp)(c) **LADIES OF THE CANYON** 8 27 Apr 70
– Morning Morgantown / For free / Conversation / Ladies of the canyon / Willy / The arrangement / Rainy night house / The priest / Blue boy / Big yellow taxi / Woodstock / The circle game. *(cd-iss.Jul88)*

Jun 70. (7") **BIG YELLOW TAXI. / WOODSTOCK** [11] [67]

— with **STILLS + JAMES TAYLOR** – guitar / **SNEAKY PETE KLEINOW** – steel guitar / **RUSS KUNKEL** – drums / etc.

Jul 71. (lp)(c) **BLUE** [3] [15] Jun 71
– All I want / My old man / Little green / Carey / Blue / California / This flight tonight / River / A case of you / The last time I saw Richard. *(cd-iss.Jan87)*

Aug 71. (7") **CAREY. / THIS FLIGHT TONIGHT** [-] [93]
Aug 71. (7") **CAREY. / MY OLD MAN** [ ] [-]
Apr 72. (7") **CALIFORNIA. / A CASE OF YOU** [ ] [ ] Oct 71
Jul 72. (7") **CAREY. / BIG YELLOW TAXI** [-] [ ]

— Her band now **STILLS + NASH** (her recent boyfriend) + **KUNKEL / WILTON FELDER / JAMES BURTON** – guitar / **TOM SCOTT** – wind

Asylum Asylum

Nov 72. (7") **YOU TURN ME ON, I'M A RADIO. / URGE FOR GOING** [ ] [25]
Dec 72. (lp)(c) **FOR THE ROSES** [ ] [11] Nov 72
– Banquet / Cold blue steel and sweet fire / Barangrill / Lesson in survival / Let the wind carry me / For the roses / See you sometime / Electricity / You turn me on, I'm a radio / Blonde in the bleachers / Woman of heart and mind / Judgement of the Moon and stars (Ludwig's tune). *(cd-iss.Dec87 on 'WEA')*
Mar 73. (7") **COLD BLUE STEEL AND SWEET FIRE. / BLONDE IN THE BLEACHERS** [ ] [-]

— Retained **TOM SCOTT's L.A.EXPRESS** with new boyfriend **JOHN GUERIN** – drums / **WILTON FELDER** – bass / **LARRY CARLTON** – guitar / **CHUCK FINDLEY** – trumpet / **JOE SAMPLE** – keyboards / **ROBBIE ROBERTSON** – guitar

Jan 74. (7") **RAISED ON ROBBERY. / COURT AND SPARK** [ ] [65] Dec 73
Mar 74. (lp)(c) **COURT AND SPARK** [14] [2] Feb 74
– Court and spark / Help me / Free man in Paris / People's parties / The same situation / Car on a hill / Down to you / Just like this train / People's parties / Raised on robbery / Trouble child. *(re-iss.Jun76) (cd-iss.May83)*
Mar 74. (7") **HELP ME. / JUST LIKE THIS TRAIN** [-] [7]
Jul 74. (7") **FREE MAN IN PARIS. / PEOPLE'S PARTIES** [-] [ ]
Oct 74. (7") **FREE MAN IN PARIS. / CAR ON A HILL** [ ] [-]
Jan 75. (7") **BIG YELLOW TAXI (live). / RAINY NIGHT HOUSE (live)** [ ] [24] Dec 74
Jan 75. (d-lp)(c) **MILES OF AISLES** [34] [2] Nov 74
– You turn me on, I'm a radio / Big yellow taxi / Rainy night house / Woodstock / Cactus tree / Cold blue steel and sweet fire / Woman of heart and mind / A case of you / The circle game / People's parties / All I want / Real good for free / Both sides now / Carey / The last time I saw Richard / Jericho / Love or money. *(cd-iss.1989, omits some dialogue)*

— (above also with **TOM SCOTT & THE L.A.EXPRESS;- SCOTT / GUERIN** plus **ROBBEN FORD** – guitar / **LARRY NASH** – piano / **MAX BENNETT** – bass

Nov 75. (lp)(c) **THE HISSING OF SUMMER LAWNS** [14] [4]
– In France they kiss on Main Street / The jungle line / Edith and the kingpin / Don't interrupt the sorrow / Shades of Scarlett conquering The hissing of summer lawns / The boho dance / Harry's house – Centerpiece / Sweet bird / Shadows and light. *(cd-iss.Nov87 on 'WEA')*
Mar 76. (7") **IN FRANCE THEY KISS ON MAIN STREET. / BOHO DANCE** [ ] [66] Feb 76
Nov 76. (lp)(c) **HEJIRA** [11] [13]
– Coyote / Amelia / Furry sings the blues / A strange boy / Hejira / Song for Sharon / Black crow / Blue motel room / Refuge of the roads. *(cd-iss.Oct87 on 'WEA')*
Feb 77. (7") **COYOTE. / BLUE MOTEL ROOM** [ ] [ ]

— now with **JACO PASTORIUS** – bass / **GLENN FREY** – vocals / **WAYNE SHORTER** – sax / **J.D.SOUTHER + CHAKA KHAN** – both backing vocals

Dec 77. (d-lp)(d-c) **DON JUAN'S RECKLESS DAUGHTER** [20] [25]
– Overture – Cotton Avenue / Talk to me / Jericho / Paprika plains / Otis and Marlena / The tenth world / Dreamland / Don Juan's reckless daughter / Off night backstreet / The silky veils of Ardor. *(cd-iss.1988)*
Feb 78. (7") **OFF NIGHT BACKSTREET. / JERICHO** [ ] [-]
Feb 78. (7") **JERICHO. / DREAMLAND** [-] [ ]

— now with **STANLEY CLARKE** – bass / **GERRY MULLIGAN** - / **JOHN McLAUGHLIN** – guitar / **JAN HAMMER** – keyboards

Jun 79. (7") **THE DRY CLEANER FROM DES MOINES. / GOD MUST BE A BOOGIE MAN** [ ] [ ]
Jul 79. (lp)(c) **MINGUS** [24] [17] Jun 79
– Happy birthday 1975 (rap) / God must be a boogie man / Funeral (rap) / A chair in the sky / The wolf that lives in Lindsey / I's a muggin' (rap) / Sweet sucker dance / Coin in the pocket (rap) / Lucky (rap) / Goodbye pork pie hat.

— now with **PAT METHENY** – lead guitar / **JACO PASTORUS** – bass / **LYLE MAYS** – keys / **DON ALIAS** – drums / **MICHAEL BRECKER** – saxophone

Sep 80. (d-lp)(c) **SHADOWS AND LIGHT (live)** [63] [38]
– (introduction) / In France they kiss on Main Street / Edith and the kingpin / Coyote / Goodbye pork pie hat / The dry cleaner from Des Moines / Amelia / Pat's solo / Hejira / Black crow / Don's solo / Dreamland / Free man in Paris / (band introduction) / Furry sings the blues / Why do fools fall in love? / Shadows and light / God must be a boogie man / Woodstock.
Oct 80. (7") **WHY DO FOOLS FALL IN LOVE? (live). / BLACK CROW (live)** [ ] [ ]

x

— **LARRY KLEIN** – bass (she marries him Nov'82) / **LARRY WILLIAMS** – keyboards / **LARRY CARLTON / JOHN GUERIN / VICTOR FELDMAN /** etc.

Geffen Geffen

Nov 82. (7") **(YOU'RE SO SQUARE) BABY I DON'T CARE. / LOVE** [ ] [47]
Nov 82. (lp)(c) **WILD THINGS RUN FAST** [32] [25]
– Chinese cafe – Unchained melody / Wild things run fast / Ladies man / Moon at the window / Solid love / Be cool / (You're so square) Baby, I don't care / You dream flat tyres / Man to man / Underneath the streetlight / Love. *(cd-iss.Jul88)*
Feb 83. (7") **BE COOL. / UNDERNEATH THE STREETLIGHT** [-] [ ]
Feb 83. (7") **CHINESE CAFE. / LADIES MAN** [ ] [-]
Nov 85. (7") **GOOD FRIENDS. / SMOKIN' (EMPTY TRY ANOTHER)** [ ] [85]

— Above feat. guest duet **MICHAEL McDONALD**

— now with co-producer **THOMAS DOLBY** – synthesizers / etc.

Nov 85. (lp)(c) **DOG EAT DOG** [57] [63]
– Good friends / Fiction / Three great stimulants / Tax free / Smokin' (empty, try another) / Dog eat dog / Shiny toys / Ethiopia / Impossible dreamer / Lucky girl. *(re-iss.Oct87) (cd-iss.May86) (re-iss.cd+c Mar93)*
Apr 86. (7")(12") **SHINY TOYS. / THREE GREAT STIMULANTS** [ ] [ ]

— guests **THOMAS DOLBY, TOM PETTY, WILLIE NELSON, DON HENLEY, WENDY & LISA, BILLY IDOL, PETER GABRIEL, etc. KLEIN** co-produced, as was next

Mar 88. (lp)(c)(cd) **CHALK MARK IN A RAIN STORM** [26] [45]
– My secret place / Number one / Lakota / The tea leaf prophecy / Dancing clown / The beat of black wings / Snakes and ladders / The recurring dream / The bird that whistles. *(re-iss.Jan91) (re-iss.cd+c Mar93)*
Apr 88. (7") **MY SECRET PLACE. / LAKOTA** [-] [ ]
May 88. (7") **MY SECRET PLACE. / NUMBER ONE** [ ] [-]
(12"+=) – Chinese cafe / Good friends.
('A'featured **PETER GABRIEL**)

— retained **KLEIN** with band **VINNIE COLAIUTA** – drums / **ALEX ACUNA** – percussion / **WAYNE SHORTER** – saxophone / **BILL DILLON + MICHAEL LANDAU** – guitars

Mar 91. (cd)(c)(lp) **NIGHT RIDE HOME** [25] [41]
– Night ride home / Passion play (when all the slaves are free) / Cherokee Louise / The windfall (everything for nothing) / Slouching towards Bethlehem / Come in from the cold / Nothing can be done / The only joy in town / Ray's dad's cadillac / Two grey rooms.
Jul 91. (7") **COME IN FROM THE COLD. / RAY'S DAD'S CADILLAC** [ ] [ ]
(cd-s+=)(pic-cd-s+=) – ('A'extended).

Warners Warners

Oct 94. (cd)(c) **TURBULENT INDIGO** [53] [47]
– Sunny Sunday / Sex kills / The Magdalene laundries / Turbulent indigo / How do you stop / Last chance lost / Not to blame / Borderline / Yvette in English / The sire of sorrow (Job's sad song).
Nov 94. (c-s)(cd-s) **HOW DO YOU STOP / THE SIRE OF SORROW / MOON AT THE WINDOW** [ ] [ ]

– compilations, others, etc. –

May 74. Reprise; (7"ep) **CAREY / BOTH SIDES NOW. / BIG YELLOW TAXI / WOODSTOCK** [ ] [-]
Oct 82. Reprise; (d-c) **CLOUDS / BLUE** [ ] [-]
Jul 76. Asylum; (7") **YOU TURN ME ON, I'M A RADIO. / FREE MAN IN PARIS** [ ] [-]
Nov 83. Asylum; (d-c) **FOR THE ROSES / COURT AND SPARK** [ ] [-]

MOBY

Born: RICHARD MELVILLE HALL, 1967, New York, USA. After being raised by his middle-class mother, he joined hardcore outfit The VATICAN COMMANDOES, which led to him having a brief stint in similar FLIPPER. He didn't record anything with them and moved back to New York to become a DJ, making hardcore techno/dance records under the guise of BRAINSTORM and UHF3, etc. Became mixer for The PET SHOP BOYS, ERASURE and MICHAEL JACKSON, before and during his return into solo work in the early 90's. • **Style:** From dance to ambient/techno hardcore and grunge punk. • **Songwriters:** Himself and writes a few with singer MIMI GOESE 'Into The Blue' + 'When It's Cold I'd Like To Die'. Other singers on 1995 album; ROZZ MOREHEAD / MYIM ROSE / NICOLE ZARAY / KOOKIE BANTON / SAUNDRA WILLIAMS. Samples BADALAMENTI's 'Twin Peaks' on 'GO'. Covered NEW DAWN FADES (Joy Division). • **Trivia:** RICHARD is a Christian vegan. In 1992 he remixed JAM & SPOON's club smash 'STELLA', which had sampled his 'GO'. He also provided vox for RECOIL's 1992 album 'Bloodline'. MOBY also remixed B-52's, ESKIMOS AND EGYPT, LFO,

FORTRAN 5, ORBITAL, ENO, PET SHOP BOYS + The OTHER TWO.

Recommended: THE STORY SO FAR (*6) / EVERYTHING IS WRONG (*9)

MOBY – vocals, keyboards, etc.

		Outer Rhythm	not issued
Jul 91.	(12")(cd-s) **GO (analog mix). / ('A'night time mix)/ ('A'soundtrack mix)**	10	

(12") – ('A'side) / ('A'video aux w/ LYNCH & BADALAMENTI) / ('A'rain forest mix).
(cd-s) – ('A'side) / ('A'low spirit mix) / ('A'woodtick mix).

		Mute	Elektra?
Jun 93.	(c-s) **I FEEL IT. / THOUSAND**	38	

(12")(cd-s) – (3-'A'mixes).

Aug 93. (cd)(c)(lp) **THE STORY SO FAR** (rel.on 'Equator')
– Ah ah / I feel it / Everything / Help me to believe / Go (woodtick mix) / Yeah / Drop a beat (the new version) / Thousand / Slight return / Go (sublimal mix unedited version) / Stream. (cd+=) Mercy.

Sep 93. (c-s) **MOVE (YOU MAKE ME FEEL SO GOOD)./ ('A'disco threat mix)** [21]
(12")(cd-s) – ('A'side) / ('A'subversion) / ('A'xtra mix) / ('A'-MK-Blades mix).
(cd-s) – ('A'side) / All that I need is to be loved / Unloved symphony / Rainfalls and the sky shudders.
(12") – (last track repl.by;) Morning dove.

Oct 93. (cd)(c)(lp) **AMBIENT** (rel.on 'Equator')
– My beautiful blue sky / Heaven / Tongues / J Breas / Myopia / House of blue leaves / Bad days / Piano & string / Sound / Dog / 80 / Lean on me.

Nov 93. (12") **ALL THAT I NEED IS TO BE LOVED. / (3 other 'A'mixes)** [ ] [-]

May 94. (c-s) **HYMN -THIS IS MY DREAM (extended). / ALL THAT I NEED IS TO BE LOVED (H.O.S. mix)** [31]
(cd-s+=) – ('A'-European edit) / ('A'-Laurent Garnier mix).
(12") – ('A'extended) / ('A'-Laurent Garnier mix) / ('A'-Upriver mix)/ ('A'-Dirty hypo mix).
(cd-s) – Hymn (alternate quiet version 33 mins).

Sep 94. (c-s) **GO (woodtick mix). / ('A'-Low spirit mix)**
(12"+=) – ('A'-Voodoo chile mix).
(12"+=) – ('A'-Appathoski mix) / ('A'-Amphemetix mix).
(cd-s+=) – ('A'-Delirium mix).

Oct 94. (c-s) **FEELING SO REAL. / NEW DAWN FADES** [30]
(cd-s+=) – ('A'-Unashamed ecstatic piano mix) / ('A'-Old skool mix).
(cd-s) – ('A'-Westbam remix) / ('A'-Ray Keith remix) / ('A'dub mix) / Everytime you touch me (remix parts).
(12") – ('A'side) / (4-'A'versions from cd's above).

Feb 95. (c-s) **EVERYTIME YOU TOUCH ME / THE BLUE LIGHT OF THE UNDERWATER SUN** [28]
(cd-s+=) – ('A'-Beatmasters mix) / ('A'-competition winner; Jude Sebastian mix) / ('A'Freestyle mix).
(cd-s++=) – ('A'-Uplifting mix).
(12") – ('A'-Sound Factory mix) / ('A'-SF dub) / ('A'-Follow me mix) / ('A'-Tribal mix).

Mar 95. (cd)(c)(d-lp) **EVERYTHING IS WRONG** [21]
– Hymn / Feeling so real / All that I need is to be loved / Let's go free / Everytime you touch me / Bring back my happiness / What love? / First cool hive / Into the blue / Anthem / Everything is wrong / God moving over the face of the waters / When it's cold I'd like to die. *(cd w/free cd)* – Underwater (parts 1-5).

Jun 95. (c-s) **INTO THE BLUE / ('A'-Shining mix)** [34]
(cd-s+=) – ('A'-Summer night mix) / ('A'-Beastmasters mix).
(12")(cd-s) – (other various mixes).
(12")(cd-s) – ('A'-Beastmasters mix) / ('A'-Jnr Vasquez mix) / ('A'-Phil Kelsey mix) / ('A'-Jon Spencer Blues mix).

. . . Jan – Jun '96 stop press . . .

Jan 96. (cd)(c) **EVERYTHING IS WRONG – MIXED AND REMIXED** [25]

— The track 'GOD MOVING OVER THE FACE OF THE WATERS' was used for the Rover 400 TV commercial. Toyota had earlier sampled his 'GO'.

MODERN LOVERS (see under ⇒ RICHMAN, Jonathan)

MOODY BLUES

Formed: Birmingham, England . . . May'64 by DENNY LAINE (who had just dissolved his DIPLOMATS band), PINDER, THOMAS, WARWICK and EDGE. They signed with manager Tony Secunda, who soon secured them a deal with 'Decca' records. Their debut 45 'LOSE YOUR MONEY', bombed, but by early '65, they were at the top spot with 'GO NOW'. They tried desperately to emulate hit, and although they scored with a few minor ones, they disbanded in Oct'66. They quickly re-united a month later, after finding JUSTIN HAYWARD and JOHN LODGE to replace DENNY LAINE and recent member ROD CLARKE. Late in the summer of '67, they switched to 'Deram', and hit immediately with concept lp 'DAYS OF FUTURE PASSED'. A piece from it 'NIGHTS IN WHITE SATIN', became a massive seller and an all-time classic in the process. After a rare concert at Queen Elizabeth Hall, London, they issued follow-up concept 'IN SEARCH OF THE LOST CHORD'. Another massive seller, it was pursued by their first 1969 UK No.1 album 'ON THE THRESHOLD OF A DREAM'. Later in '69, they founded own label 'Threshold', and soon became one of the world's top groups of the early 70's. • **Style:** Moved from mid-60's HOLLIES-style pop outfit, to neo-classical rock group, with own identifiable Mellotron organ sound fused with orchestral backing. Influenced a new generation of near copyists (aka BARCLAY JAMES HARVEST and early KING CRIMSON, etc). • **Songwriters:** LAINE wrote most of material, until LODGE or HAYWARD took over late '66. Also covered; GO NOW (Bessie Banks) / I DON'T WANT TO GO ON WITHOUT YOU (Drifters) / IT AIN'T NECESSARILY SO (Gershwin) / TIME IS ON MY SIDE (Rolling Stones) / BYE BYE BIRD (Sonny Boy Williamson) / etc. • **Trivia:** 10cc produced 1975 BLUE JAYS (HAYWARD & LODGE)'s album.

Recommended: VOICES IN THE SKY – THE BEST OF... (*8)

DENNY LAINE (b.BRIAN HINES, 29 Oct'44) – vocals, guitar (ex-DIPLOMATS) / **MIKE PINDER** (b.12 Dec'41) – keyboards, vocals (ex-CREWCATS) / **RAY THOMAS** (b.29 Dec'42, Stourport, England) – flute, vocals, harmonica / **CLINT WARWICK** (b.CLINTON ECCLES, 25 Jun'40) – bass, vocals / **GRAHAM EDGE** (b.30 Mar'42) – drums (ex-GERRY LEVENE AND THE AVENGERS)

		Decca	London
Aug 64.	(7") **LOSE YOUR MONEY (BUT DON'T LOSE YOUR MIND). / STEAL YOUR HEART AWAY**		-
Nov 64.	(7") **GO NOW. / IT'S EASY CHILD**	1	-
Feb 65.	(7") **I DON'T WANT TO GO ON WITHOUT YOU. / TIME IS ON MY SIDE**	33	
Feb 65.	(7") **GO NOW. / LOSE YOUR MONEY (BUT DON'T LOSE YOUR MIND)**	-	10
May 65.	(7") **FROM THE BOTTOM OF MY HEART (I LOVE YOU). / AND MY BABY'S GONE**	22	93
Jul 65.	(lp) **THE MAGNIFICENT MOODIES** (US-title 'GO NOW – THE MOODY BLUES')		

– I'll go crazy / Something you got / Go now / Can't nobody love you / I don't mind / I've got a dream / Let me go / Stop! / Thank you baby / It ain't necessarily so / True story / Bye bye bird. *(re-iss.cd Jan93 on 'Polydor') (re-issued again Mar93 on 'Repertoire' +=)*– Steal your heart away / Lose your money (but don't lose your mind) / It's easy child / I don't want to go on without you (come back) / Time is on my side / From the bottom of my heart / And my baby's gone.

Oct 65.	(7") **EVERYDAY. / YOU DON'T (ALL THE TIME)**	44	
Mar 66.	(7") **STOP! / BYE BYE BIRD**	-	98

— (Jul66) **ROD CLARKE** – bass repl. WARWICK

Oct 66. (7") **BOULEVARD DE LA MADELAINE. / THIS IS MY HOUSE (BUT NOBODY CALLS)**

— (Nov66) **JUSTIN HAYWARD** (b.14 Oct'46, Swindon, England) – vocals, guitar (ex-solo artist) repl. DENNY who went solo (and later to WINGS) / **JOHN LODGE** (b.20 Jul'45) – bass, vocals (ex-EL RIOT & THE REBELS) repl. CLARKE

Jan 67. (7") **LIFE'S NOT LIFE. / HE CAN WIN**
(above withdrawn after a day)

May 67. (7") **FLY ME HIGH. / REALLY HAVEN'T GOT THE TIME**

Aug 67. (7") **LOVE AND BEAUTY. / LEAVE THIS MAN ALONE**

		Deram	Deram
Nov 67.	(7") **NIGHTS IN WHITE SATIN. / CITIES**	19	

(re-iss.Sep72 reached UK no.9 / US no.2, re-Mar76, re-Oct79 no.14 all on 'Deram')(re-Oct83,Jun88 'Old Gold')

Nov 67. (lp) **DAYS OF FUTURE PASSED** [27] [3] Apr 68
– The day begins / Dawn:- Dawn is a feeling / The morning:- Another morning / Lunch break:- Peak hour / The afternoon:- Forever afternoon (Tuesday) / Time to get away / Evening:- The sunset / Twilight time / The night:- Nights in white satin. *(re-iss.Sep72 hit No.3 US) (cd-iss.Nov84 on 'Decca')*

Jul 68.	(7") **TUESDAY AFTERNOON (FOREVER AFTERNOON). / ANOTHER MORNING**	-	24
Jul 68.	(7") **VOICES IN THE SKY. / DR. LIVINGSTONE, I PRESSUME**	23	
Jul 68.	(lp) **IN SEARCH OF THE LOST CHORD**	5	23 Sep 68

– Departure / Ride my see-saw / Dr. Livingstone, I pressume / House of four doors (part 1) / Legend of a mind / House of four doors (part 2) / Voices in the sky / The best way to travel / The actor / The word / Om. *(re-iss.Nov84) (cd-iss.1986 on 'London')*

Oct 68.	(7") **RIDE MY SEE-SAW. / VOICES IN THE SKY**	-	61
Nov 68.	(7") **RIDE MY SEE-SAW. / A SIMPLE GAME**	42	-
Apr 69.	(7") **NEVER COMES THE DAY. / SO DEEP WITHIN YOU**		91
Apr 69.	(lp) **ON THE THRESHOLD OF A DREAM**	1	20 May 69

– In the beginning / Lovely to see you / Dear diary / Send me no wine / To share our love / So deep within you / Never comes the day / Lazy day / Are you sitting comfortably / The dream / Have you heard (part 1) / The voyage / Have you heard (part 2). *(cd-iss.1986 on 'London')*

Threshold Threshold

Oct 69. (7") **WATCHING AND WAITING. / OUT AND IN** [ ] [-]
Nov 69. (lp)(c) **TO OUR CHILDREN'S CHILDREN'S CHILDREN** [2] [14] Jan70
– Higher and higher / Eyes of a child (part 1) / Floating / Eyes of a child (part 2) / I never thought I'd live to be a hundred / Beyond / Out and in / Gypsy / Eternity road / Candle of life / Sun is still shining / I never thought I'd live to be a million / Watching and waiting. *(cd-iss.Aug86 on 'London')*
Apr 70. (7") **QUESTION. / CANDLE OF LIFE** [2] [21]
(re-iss.Oct83 on 'Old Gold')
Aug 70. (lp)(c) **A QUESTION OF BALANCE** [1] [3] Sep 70
– Question / How is it (we are here) / And the tide rushes in / Don't you feel small / Tortoise and the hare / It's up to you / Minstrel's song / Dawning is the day / Melancholy man / The balance. *(cd-iss.Aug86 on 'London')*
Jul 71. (lp)(c) **EVERY GOOD BOY DESERVES FAVOUR** [1] [2] Aug 71
– Procession / The story in your eyes / Our guessing game / Emily's song / After you came / Riches more than these / Nice to be here / You can never go home / My song. *(cd-iss.Aug86 on 'London')*
Aug 71. (7") **THE STORY IN YOUR EYES. / MELANCHOLY MAN** [-] [23]
Apr 72. (7") **ISN'T LIFE STRANGE. / AFTER YOU CAME** [13] [29]
Nov 72. (lp)(c) **SEVENTH SOJOURN** [5] [1]
– Lost in a lost world / New horizons / For my lady / Isn't life strange / You and me / The land of make-believe / When you're a free man / I'm just a singer (in a rock'n'roll band). *(cd-iss.Sep86 on 'London')*
Jan 73. (7") **I'M JUST A SINGER (IN A ROCK'N'ROLL BAND). / FOR MY LADY** [36] [12]

—— Split early '73 but only for a 5 year trial period, releasing own solos released (2) compilations while they split

Nov 74. (d-lp)(d-c) **THIS IS THE MOODY BLUES** [14] [11]
– Question / The actor / The word / Eyes of a child / Dear diary / Legend of a mind / In the beginning / Lovely to see you / Never comes the day / Isn't life strange / The dream / Have you heard / Voyage / Ride my see-saw / Tuesday afternoon / And the tide rushes in / New horizons / Simple game / Watching and waiting / I'm just a singer (in a rock'n'roll band) / For my lady / Story in your eyes / Melancholy man / Nights in white satin. *(d-cd.iss.Aug89)*

Decca London

Apr 77. (d-lp)(d-c) **CAUGHT LIVE + 5** (live '69 +1 studio side) [ ] [26] Jun 77
– Gypsy / The sunset / Dr. Livingstone, I pressume / Never comes the day / Peak hour / Tuesday afternoon / Are you sitting comfortably / Have you heard (part 1) / The voyage / Have you heard (part 2) / Nights in white satin / Legend of a mind / Ride my see-saw / Gimme a little somethin' / Please think about it / Long summer day / King and Queen / What am I doing here.

—— Re-formed mid 1978. **(HAYWARD, LODGE, EDGE, PINDER** and **THOMAS)**

Decca London

Jun 78. (lp)(c) **OCTAVE** [6] [13]
– Steppin' in a slide zone / Under moonshine / Had to fall in love / I'll be level with you / Driftwood / Top rank suite / I'm your man / Survival / One step into the light / The day we meet again. *(cd-iss.Oct86) (re-iss.cd Jan93)*
Jul 78. (7") **STEPPIN' IN A SLIDE ZONE. / I'LL BE LEVEL WITH YOU** [ ] [39]
Oct 78. (7") **DRIFTWOOD. / I'M YOUR MAN** [ ] [59]

—— **PATRICK MORAZ** – keyboards (ex-YES, solo artist, ex-REFUGEE) repl. PINDER

Threshold Threshold

May 81. (lp)(c) **LONG DISTANCE VOYAGER** [7] [1] Jun 81
– The voice / Talking out of turn / Gemini dream / In my world / 22,000 days / Nervous / Painted smile / Reflection smile / Veteran cosmic rocker. *(cd-iss.Oct86)*
Jun 81. (7") **GEMINI DREAM. / PAINTED SMILE** [ ] [12]
Jul 81. (7") **THE VOICE. / 22,000 DAYS** [ ] [15]
Nov 81. (7")(7"pic-d) **TALKING OUT OF TURN. / VETERAN COSMIC ROCKER** [ ] [65]
Aug 83. (7")(12") **BLUE WORLD. / GOING NOWHERE** [35] [-]
Sep 83. (lp)(c)(cd) **THE PRESENT** [15] [26]
– Blue world / Meet me halfway / Sitting at the wheel / Going nowhere / Hole in the world / Under my feet / It's cold outside of your heart / Running water / I am / Sorry. *(cd re-iss. Apr91 on 'London')*
Sep 83. (7") **SITTING AT THE WHEEL. / GOING NOWHERE** [-] [27]
Oct 83. (7") **SITTING AT THE WHEEL. / SORRY** [ ] [-]
(12"+=) – Gemini dream.
Nov 83. (7") **BLUE WORLD. / SORRY** [-] [62]
Feb 84. (7") **UNDER MY FEET. / RUNNING WATER** [-] [ ]

Polydor Polydor

Mar 86. (7")(12") **YOUR WILDEST DREAM. / TALKIN' TALKIN'** [ ] [9] Apr 86
May 86. (lp)(c)(cd) **OTHER SIDE OF LIFE** [24] [9]
– Your wildest dreams / Talkin' talkin' / Rock'n'roll over you / I just don't care / Running out of love / The other side of life / The spirit / Slings and arrows / It may be a fire.
Aug 86. (7") **THE OTHER SIDE OF LIFE. / NIGHTS IN WHITE SATIN (live)** [ ] [58]
(12"+=) – The spirit. *(US; b-side)*
May 88. (7") **I KNOW YOU'RE OUT THERE SOMEWHERE. / MIRACLE** [52] [30]
(12"+=) – ('A'extended).
(cd-s+=) – Rock'n'roll over you (live).
Jun 88. (lp)(c)(cd) **SUR LA MER** [21] [38]
– I know you're out there somewhere / Want to be with you / River of endless love / No more lies / Here comes the weekend / Vintage wine / Breaking point / Miracle / Love is on the run / Deep.
Dec 88. (7") **NO MORE LIES. / RIVERS OF ENDLESS LOVE** [ ] [ ]
(12"+=) – The other side of life.
Jun 91. (7")(c-s) **SAY IT WITH LOVE. / LEAN ON ME (TONIGHT)** [ ] [ ]
(12"+=)(cd-s+=) – Highway.
Aug 91. (cd)(c)(lp) **KEYS OF THE KINGDOM** [54] [94]
– Say it with love / Bless the wings (that bring you back) / Is this Heaven? / Say what you mean (pt.1 & 2) / Lean on me (tonight) / Hope and pray / Shadows on the wall / Celtic sonant / Magic / Never blame the rainbows for the rain. *(re-iss.cd,c,lp Jan93)*
Mar 93. (cd)(c) **LIVE AT RED ROCKS (live)** [ ] [ ]
– Overture / Late lament / Tuesday afternoon (forever afternoon) / For my lady / Lean on me (tonight) / Lovely to see you / I know you're out there somewhere / The voice / Your wildest dreams / Isn't life strange / The other side of life / I'm just a singer (in a rock and roll band) / Nights in white satin / Question / Ride my see-saw.

– other compilations, etc. –

May 65. Decca; (7"ep) **THE MOODY BLUES** [ ] [-]
– Go now / Lose your money (but don't lose your mind) / Steal your heart away / I don't want to go on without you.
Nov 84. Threshold; (7") **THE VOICE. / GEMINI DREAM** [ ] [ ]
(12"+=) – Nights in white satin.
Nov 84. Threshold; (lp)(c)(cd) **VOICES IN THE SKY – THE BEST OF THE MOODY BLUES** [ ] [ ] Mar 85
– Ride my see-saw / Talking out of turn / Driftwood / Never comes the day / I'm just a singer (in a rock and roll band) / Gemini dream / The voice / After you came / Question / Veteran cosmic rocker / Isn't life strange / Nights in white satin. *(cd re-iss. Apr91)*
Oct 79. K-Tel; (lp)(c) **OUT OF THIS WORLD** [15] [-]
Sep 83. A.K.A.; (lp)(c) **GO NOW** [ ] [-]
Sep 85. Old Gold; (7") **GO NOW. / I DON'T WANT TO GO ON WITHOUT YOU** [ ] [-]
Sep 85. Castle; (d-lp)(c) **THE MOODY BLUES COLLECTION** [ ] [-]
(cd-iss.1986)
Sep 87. London; (cd) **PRELUDE** [ ] [-]
Nov 89. Polydor; (lp)(c)(cd) **GREATEST HITS** [71] [ ]
Sep 93. Threshold; (cd)(c) **GO NOW** [ ] [-]
Sep 94. Polydor; (5xcd-box) **THE TRAVELLER** [ ] [ ]

—— below: solo work, etc. they released during 5 year trial split.

JUSTIN HAYWARD & JOHN LODGE

Threshold Threshold

Apr 75. (7") **I DREAMED LAST NIGHT. / REMEMBER ME (MY FRIEND)** [ ] [ ]
Apr 75. (lp)(c) **BLUE JAYS** [4] [16] Mar 75
– This morning / Remember me (my friend) / My brother / You / Nights, winters, years / Saved by the music / I dreamed last night / Who are you now / Maybe / When you wake up. *(re-iss.Nov84) (cd-iss.1988 on 'London')*
Sep 75. (7") **BLUE GUITAR. / WHEN YOU WAKE UP** [8] [94]
(re-iss.1989 on 'Old Gold')

JUSTIN HAYWARD

Deram Deram

Jan 77. (7") **LAY IT ON ME. / SONGWRITER (part 2)** [-] [ ]
Jan 77. (7") **ONE LOVELY ROOM. / SONGWRITER (part 2)** [ ] [-]
Feb 77. (lp)(c) **SONGWRITER** [28] [37]
– Tightrope / Songwriter (pt.1 – vocal & pt.2 – instrumental) / Country girl / One lonely room / Lay it on me / Stage door / Raised on love / Doin' time / Nostradamus. *(cd-iss.Dec87)* (cd+=) – Music / Learning the game.
Apr 77. (7") **COUNTRY GIRL. / DOIN' TIME** [ ] [-]
Apr 77. (7") **COUNTRY GIRL. / SONGWRITER (part 2)** [-] [ ]
Jul 77. (7") **STAGE DOOR. / LAY IT ON ME** [ ] [ ]

—— Appeared on JEFF WAYNE'S 'WAR OF THE WORLDS' Various Artists Jun78 album Below 2 'A'singles credited to "JUSTIN HAYWARD".

C.B.S. Columbia

Jun 78. (7") **FOREVER AUTUMN. / THE FIGHTING MACHINE** [5] [ ]
(re-iss. Oct84 & Jan87 on 'Old Gold')
Aug 78. (7") **EVE OF THE WAR. / THE RED WEED** [36] [ ]

Decca Deram

Apr 79. (7") **MARIE. / HEART OF STEEL** [ ] [ ]
May 80. (7") **NIGHT FLIGHT. / SUITCASE** [ ] [ ]
Jul 80. (lp)(c) **NIGHT FLIGHT** [41] [ ]
– Night flight / Maybe it's just love / Crazy lovers / Penumbra moon / Nearer to you / Face in the crowd / Suitcase / It's not on / Bedtime stories. *(cd-iss.Jan89)*

Towerbell not issued

Aug 85. (7")(12") **SILVERBIRD. / TAKE YOUR CHANCES** [ ] [ ]
Sep 85. (lp)(c)(cd) **MOVING MOUNTAINS** [78] [ ]
– One again / Take your chances / Moving mountains / Silverbird / Is it just a game / Lost and found / Goodbye / Who knows / The best is yet to come.
Nov 85. (7") **THE BEST IS YET TO COME. / MARIE** [ ] [ ]

B.B.C. not issued

Jul 87. (7") **STAR COPS (IT WON'T BE LONG). / OUTER SPACE** [ ] [ ]

— next with guests **MIKE BATT** and **The LONDON PHILHARMONIC ORCHESTRA**

Trax not issued

Oct 89. (lp)(c)(cd) **CLASSIC BLUE** [47] [-]
– The racks of my tears / MacArthur Park / Blackbird / Vincent / God only knows / Bright eyes / A whiter shade of pale / Scarborough fair / Railway hotel / Man of the world / Forever autumn / As long as the Moon can shine / Stairway to Heaven.

JOHN LODGE

Decca London

Jan 77. (7") **SAY YOU LOVE ME. / NATURAL AVENUE** [ ] [ ]
Feb 77. (lp)(c) **NATURAL AVENUE** [38] [ ]
– (Introduction to Children of rock'n'roll) / Natural avenue / Summer breeze / Carry me / Who could change / Broken dreams, hard road / Piece of my heart / Rainbow / Say you love me / Children of rock'n'roll. *(cd-iss.May87 on 'London')*
Mar 77. (7") **CHILDREN OF ROCK'N'ROLL. / PIECE OF MY HEART** [ ] [-]
Jul 77. (7") **SUMMER BREEZE. / RAINBOW** [ ] [-]
Oct 80. (7") **STREET CAFE. / THREW IT ALL AWAY** [ ] [-]

GRAEME EDGE BAND

with **ADRIAN GURVITZ** – guitar, vocals, keyboards and **PAUL GURVITZ** – bass, vocals / **MICK GALLAGHER** – keys / plus sessioners

Threshold London

Jul 74. (7") **WE LIKE TO DO IT. / SHOTGUN** [ ] [ ]
Sep 75. (lp)(c) **KICK OFF YOUR MUDDY BOOTS** [ ] [ ]
– Bareback rider / In dreams / Lost in space / Have you ever wondered / My life's not wasted / The tunnel / Gew Janna women / Shotgun / Something we'd like to say. *(cd-iss.Aug89 on 'London')*
Nov 75. (7") **THE TUNNEL. / BAREBACK RIDER** [ ] [ ]

Decca London

Apr 77. (7") **EVERYBODY NEEDS SOMEBODY. / BE MY EYES** [ ] [-]
Apr 77. (lp)(c) **PARADISE BALLROOM** [ ] [ ]
– Paradise ballroom / Human / Everybody needs somebody / All is fair / Down down down In the night of the light / Caroline. *(cd-iss.Jan89 on 'London')*

RAY THOMAS

Threshold London

Jun 75. (7") **HIGH ABOVE MY HEAD. / LOVE IS THE KEY** [ ] [ ]
Jul 75. (lp)(c) **FROM MIGHTY OAKS** [23] [ ]
– From mighty oaks / Hey mama life / Play it again / Rock-abye baby blues / High above my head / Love's the key / You make me feel alright / Adam and I / I wish we could fly. *(cd-iss.Aug89 on 'London')*
Jun 76. (7") **ONE NIGHT STAND. / CAROUSEL** [ ] [ ]
Jun 76. (lp)(c) **HOPES, WISHES AND DREAMS** [ ] [ ]
– In your song / Friends / We need love / Within your eyes / One stand stand / Keep on searching / Didn't I / The last dream / Migration / Carousel. *(cd-iss.Jan89 on 'London')*

MICHAEL PINDER

Threshold London

Apr 76. (lp)(c) **THE PROMISE** [ ] [ ]
– Free as a dove / You'll make it through / I only want to love you / Someone to believe in / Carry on / Air / Message / The seed / The promise. *(cd-iss.Aug89 on 'London')*
May 76. (7") **CARRY ON. / I ONLY WANT TO LOVE YOU** [ ] [ ]

Keith MOON (see under ⇒ WHO)

Michael MOORCOCK (see under ⇒ HAWKWIND)

Gary MOORE

Born: 4 Apr'52, Belfast, N.Ireland. in the mid-60's, he formed school group GRANNY'S INTENTIONS, which included NOEL BRIDGEMAN on drums, before he went to SKID ROW in 1969. A year later, they recorded 'HONEST INJUN' for 'Deram', but this was without GARY and NOEL. GARY then did on stage guest work for DR.STRANGELY STRANGE and appeared on their 'Heavy Pettin'' lp in 1970. He left SKID ROW in 1971, after they released 'SKID' lp for 'C.B.S.'. In 1972, GARY formed own band GRINDING STONE, who released lp for 'CBS' in '73. In 1974, he joined THIN LIZZY, but left to join COLOSSEUM II in Spring '75. He returned to THIN LIZZY early '77 but left again only to return once more on a full-time basis Aug'78. This time, MOORE stayed long enough to be part of their UK Top 3 album 'BLACK ROSE (A ROCK LEGEND)'. Around the same time, Spring 1979, after releasing solo album 'BACK ON THE STREETS' early '79 for 'MCA', he hit UK Top 10 with single 'PARISIENNE WALKWAYS'. This featured THIN LIZZY frontman PHIL LYNOTT on vocals, and enjoyed the usual '93 charting remix. In 1980, GARY formed G-FORCE, but gave this up after joining The GREG LAKE BAND in 1981. In 1982, he signed another solo deal with 'Virgin', and breached the UK Top 30 with album 'CORRIDORS OF POWER'. Continued to go from strength to strength for the next decade. • **Style:** Initially influenced by JEFF BECK, GARY's guitar work shifted through blues, jazz-rock with COLOSSEUM II, heavy rock with G-FORCE, and returning to basic blues in the early 90's. • **Songwriters:** MOORE penned most, and covered; DON'T LET ME BE MISUNDERSTOOD (hit; Animals) / SHAPES OF THINGS (Yardbirds) / FRIDAY ON MY MIND (Easybeats) / DON'T YOU TO ME (Hudson Whittaker) / THE BLUES IS ALRIGHT (Milton Campbell) / KEY TO LOVE (John Mayall) / JUMPIN' AT SHADOWS (Duster Bennett) / etc. • **Trivia:** GARY sessioned also on 1975's 'Peter & The Wolf', and ANDREW LLOYD WEBBER's 1978 lp 'Variations'. In 1980, he was heard on ROD ARGENT's 'Moving Home' & COZY POWELL's 'Over The Top'. The CHIEFTAINS guested on his 'WILD FRONTIER' album.

Recommended: WILD FRONTIER (*6) / BALLADS AND BLUES 1982-1994 (*6)

GARY MOORE BAND

GARY MOORE – guitar, vocals (ex-SKID ROW) with **JAN SCHELHAAS** – keyboards (ex-NATIONAL HEAD BAND) / **JOHN CURTIS** – bass / **PEARCE KELLY** – drums / plus session man **PHILIP DONNELLY** – guitar

C.B.S. Peters

1973. (lp) **GRINDING STONE** [ ] [ ]
– Grinding stone / Time to heal / Sail across the mountain / The energy dance / Spirit / Boogie my way back home. *(re-iss.Nov85) (re-iss.+cd.Oct90 & Dec92)*

— In 1974 GARY joined THIN LIZZY ⇒ for 3 mths. May75 he joined COLOSSEUM II before returning to THIN LIZZY p/t for 5 mths early'77 and f/t Aug'78.

GARY MOORE

also started a new solo career at this time with friends **DON AIREY** – keyboards (of COLOSSEUM) / **JOHN MOLE** – bass / **SIMON PHILLIPS** – drums / plus THIN LIZZY'S – **PHIL LYNOTT** and **BRIAN DOWNEY**.

M.C.A. Jet

Dec 78. (7") **BACK ON THE STREETS. / TRACK NINE** [ ] [ ]
Jan 79. (lp) **BACK ON THE STREETS** [70] [ ]
– Back on the streets / Don't believe a word / Fanatical fascists / Flight of the snow moose / Hurricane / Song for Donna / What would you rather bee or wasp / Parisian walkways. *(re-iss.Aug81.)*
Apr 79. (7") **PARISIAN WALKWAYS. / FANATICAL FASCISTS** [8] [ ]

— (above 'A' featured **PHIL LYNOTT** – vocals – (of THIN LIZZY)

Oct 79. (7") **SPANISH GUITAR. / SPANISH GUITAR (instrumental)** [ ] [ ]

G-FORCE

GARY MOORE – vocals / **TONY NEWTON** – vocals / **WILLIE DEE** – keyboards, bass, vocals / **MARK NAUSEEF** – drums, percussion (ex-THIN LIZZY, ex-ELF, ex-IAN GILLAN BAND)

Jet Jet

Jun 80. (7") **HOT GOSSIP. / BECAUSE OF YOUR LOVE** [ ] [ ]
Jun 80. (lp)(pic-lp) **G-FORCE** [ ] [ ]
– You / White knuckles – Rockin' & rollin' / She's got you / I look at you / Because of your love / You kissed me sweetly / Hot gossip / The woman's in love / Dancin'. *(re-iss.Mar87) (re-iss.Feb91 on 'Castle')*
Aug 80. (7") **YOU. / TRUST YOUR LOVIN'** [ ] [ ]
Nov 80. (7") **WHITE KNUCKLES – ROCKIN' & ROLLIN'. / I LOOK AT YOU** [ ] [ ]

— In '81 and '83 he was part of the GREG LAKE BAND. Although he did continue solo career

GARY MOORE

with **CHARLIE HUHN** – vocals (ex-JACK LANCASTER) / **TOMMY EYRE** – keyboards (ex-GREG LAKE BAND) / **NEIL MURRAY** – bass (ex-WHITESNAKE) / **IAN PAICE** – drums (ex-WHITESNAKE, ex-DEEP PURPLE, ex-PAICE, ex-ASHTON & LORD)

Virgin Mirage

Sep 82. (7")(7"pic-d) **ALWAYS GONNA LOVE YOU. / COLD HEARTED** [ ] [ ]

Oct 82. (lp)(c) **CORRIDORS OF POWER** [30] [ ] Apr 83
– Don't take me for a loser / Always gonna love you / Wishing well / Gonna break my heart again / Falling in love with you / End of the world / Rockin' every night / Cold hearted / I can't wait until tomorrow. *(free live 7"ep)* – PARISIAN WALKWAYS / ROCKIN' EVERY NIGHT / BACK ON THE STREETS

— **JOHN SLOMAN** – vocals, keyboards repl. HUHN / **DON AIREY** – keyboards (see above) (ex-OZZY OSBOURNE) repl. EYRE

Feb 83. (7")(7"pic-d) **FALLING IN LOVE WITH YOU. / ('A'instrumental)** [ ] [-]
(12"+=) – Wishing well.

— GARY MOORE recruited new personnel after SLOMAN departed / **NEIL CARTER** – keyboards, guitar (ex-UFO, ex-WILD HORSES) repl. AIREY / **BOBBY CHOUINARD** – drums 1/2 repl. PAICE (he appeared on most of next 2 lp's) / on tour Mar 84 **CRAIG GRUBER** – bass (ex-BILLY SQUIER) 1/2 replaced MURRAY (he appeared on lp) (note that all: MURRAY, AIREY and PAICE rejoined past bands WHITESNAKE, OZZY OSBOURNE and DEEP PURPLE respectively.)

Ten-Virgin Mirage

Jan 84. (7")(7"sha-pic-d) **HOLD ON TO LOVE. / DEVIL IN HER HEART** [65] [-]
(12"+=) – Law of the jungle.

Feb 84. (lp)(c) **VICTIMS OF THE FUTURE** [12] [ ] May 84
– Victims of the future / Teenage idol / Shapes of things / Empty rooms / Murder in the skies / All I want / Hold on to love / Law of the jungle. *(cd-iss.Jun88)*

Mar 84. (7")(7"sha-pic-d) **SHAPES OF THINGS. / BLINDER** [ ] [-]
(12"+=) – (an interview with Alan Freeman).

Aug 84. (7") **EMPTY ROOMS. / NUCLEAR ATTACK (live)** [51] [-]
(12"+=) – ('A'extended version).
(d-12"+=) – Rockin' every night (live) / Empty rooms (live).

Aug 84. (7") **EMPTY ROOMS. / MURDER IN THE SKIES** [-] [ ]

Oct 84. (d-lp)(d-c)(d-cd) **WE WANT MOORE (live)** [32] [ ] Dec 84
– Murder in the skies / Shapes of things / Victims of the future / Cold hearted / End of the world / Back on the streets / So far away / Empty rooms / Don't take me for a loser / Rockin' and rollin'.

— **GLENN HUGHES** – bass (ex-DEEP PURPLE) repl. BOB DAISLEY who repl. GRUBER / **PAUL THOMPSON** (ex-ROXY MUSIC) and **TED McKENNA** (ex-SAHB) took over drums

May 85. (7")(7"sha-pic-d) **OUT IN THE FIELDS. ("GARY MOORE & PHIL LYNOTT") / MILITARY MAN** [5] [-]
(12"+=) – Still in love with you.
(d7"+=) – Stop messin' around (live).

Jul 85. (7") **EMPTY ROOMS. / OUT OF MY SYSTEM** [23] [-]
(12"+=) – Parisienne walkways (live) / Empty rooms (summer '85).
(d7"+=) – Parisienne walkways (live) / Murder in the skies (live).

Sep 85. (lp)(c)(pic-lp) **RUN FOR COVER** [12] [ ] Feb 86
– Run for cover / Reach for the sky / Military man / Empty rooms / Out in the fields / Nothing to lose / Once in a lifetime / All messed up / Listen to your heartbeat. *(cd-iss.Feb86, re-iss.1989, c+cd+=)* – Out of my system.

— **GARY** now used members of **The CHIEFTAINS.** Retained **CARTER + DAISLEY.**

Dec 86. (7")(7"sha-pic-d) **OVER THE HILLS AND FAR AWAY. / CRYING IN THE SHADOWS** [20] [-]
(d7"+=) – All messed up (live) / Out in the fields (live).
(12"+=) – All messed up (live) / ('A'version).

Feb 87. (7") **WILD FRONTIER. / RUN FOR COVER (live)** [35] [-]
(12"+=) – ('A'live) / ('A'extended).
(d7"+=) – Murder in the skies (live) / Wild frontier (live).
(cd-s+=) – Over the hills and far away / Empty rooms / Out in the fields / Shapes of things.

Mar 87. (lp)(c)(cd) **WILD FRONTIER** [8] [ ] May 87
– Over the hills and far away / Wild frontier / Take a little time / The loner / Friday on my mind / Strangers in the darkness / Thunder rising / Johnny boy. *(cd+=)* – Crying in the shadows / Over the hills and far away (12"version) / Wild frontier (12"version) *(re-iss.Sep87. WILD FRONTIER (SPECIAL EDITION) (incl.extra 12"ep) (re-iss.cd Jan89 & Apr90 on 'Virgin')*

Apr 87. (7")(7"pic-d) **FRIDAY ON MY MIND. / REACH FOR THE SKY (live)** [26] [-]
(12"+=) – ('A'version).
(cd-s+=) – Parisian walkways (live).

Aug 87. (7") **THE LONER. / JOHNNY BOY** [53] [-]
(12"+=) – ('A'live).
(c-s+=) – ('A'extended version).

Nov 87. (7") **TAKE A LITTLE TIME. / OUT IN THE FIELDS** [75] [-]
(d7"+=) – All messed up (live) / Thunder rising (live).

— brought back **COZY POWELL** – drums

Virgin Virgin

Jan 89. (7")(7"pic-d) **AFTER THE WAR. / THIS THING CALLED LOVE** [37] [ ]
(12"+=) – Over the hills and far away.
(cd-s+=) – Emerald / Thunder rising.

Jan 89. (lp)(c)(cd) **AFTER THE WAR** [23] [ ] Mar 89
– After the war / Speak for yourself / Livin' on dreams / Led clones / Running from the storm / This thing called love / Ready for love / Blood of emeralds. *(c+=)(cd+=)* – Dunlace (pt.1 & 2) / The messiah will come.

Mar 89. (7") **READY FOR LOVE. / WILD FRONTIER** [56] [-]
(12"+=)(cd-s+=) – The loner (live).

Apr 89. (7") **SPEAK FOR YOURSELF. / LED CLONES** [-] [ ]

— **CHRIS SLADE** – drums (ex-MANFRED MANN'S EARTH BAND, ex-FIRM) repl. COZY POWELL

Oct 89. (7") **LIVIN' ON DREAMS. / THE MESSIAH WILL COME AGAIN** [ ] [ ]

— His band were now **DON AIREY** – keyboards / **BOB DAISLEY + ANDY PYLE** – bass / **GRAHAM WALKER + BRIAN DOWNEY** – drums / **FRANK MEAD** – tenor sax / **NICK PAYN** – sax

Mar 90. (7")(c-s) **OH PRETTY WOMAN. / KING OF BLUES** [48] [ ]
(12"+=)(cd-s+=) – The stumble.

Mar 90. (cd)(c)(lp) **STILL GOT THE BLUES** [13] [83] Jun 90
– Moving on / Oh pretty woman / Walking by myself / Still got the blues (for you) / Texas street / All your love / Too tired / King of the blues / Midnight blues / As the years go passing by / That kind of woman / Stop messin' around.

May 90. (7")(c-s) **STILL GOT THE BLUES (FOR YOU). / LET ME WITH THE BLUES** [31] [97] Jan 91
(12"+=) – ('A'extended) / The sky is crying.
(cd-s++=) – Further on up the road / Mean cruel woman.

Aug 90. (7") **WALKING BY MYSELF. / STILL GOT THE BLUES (FOR YOU) (live)** [48] [ ]
(12"+=) – ('A'live).
(cd-s++=) – Still got the blues (live).

Dec 90. (7") **TOO TIRED ("GARY MOORE featuring ALBERT COLLINS"). / TEXAS STRUT** [71] [ ]
(12"+=) – ('A'live).
(cd-s) – ('A'side) / All your love (live) / The stumble.

— He featured on TRAVELLING WILBURYS single 'She's My Baby'.

— **WILL LEE + JOHNNY B.GAYDON** – bass repl. PYLE / **ANTON FIG** – drums repl. DOWNEY / **TOMMY EYRE** – keyboards repl. AIREY / added on horns **MARTIN DROVER, NICK PENTELOW, ANDREW LOVE + WAYNE JACKSON RICHARD MORGAN** – oboe / backing vocals -**CAROLE KENYON + LINDA TAYLOR**

Feb 92. (7") **COLD DAY IN HELL. ("GARY MOORE & THE MIDNIGHT BLUES BAND") / ALL TIME LOW** [24] [ ]
(cd-s+=) – Stormy Monday (live) / Woke up this morning.

Mar 92. (cd)(c)(lp) **AFTER HOURS** [4] [ ]
– Cold day in Hell / Don't lie to me (I get evil) / Story of the blues / Since I met you baby / Separate ways / Only fool in town / Key to love / Jumpin' at shadows / The blues is alright / The hurt inside / Nothing's the same.

May 92. (7")(c-s) **STORY OF THE BLUES. / MOVIN' ON DOWN THE ROAD** [40] [ ]
(cd-s+=) – King of the blues / Midnight blues (live).
(cd-s+=) – ('A'dry mix).

Jul 92. (7")(c-s) **SINCE I MET YOU BABY. ("GARY MOORE & B.B.KING") / THE HURT INSIDE** [59] [ ]
(cd-s+=) – ('A'mix) / Moving on (live) / Texas strut (live).
(cd-s+=) – Don't start me talking / Once in a blue mood (instrumental)

Oct 92. (7")(c-s) **SEPARATE WAYS. / ONLY FOOL IN TOWN** [59] [ ]
(12"+=)(cd-s+=) – Farther on up the road / Caledonia.
(cd-s+=) You don't love me / Stumble.

Apr 93. (7")(c-s) **PARISIENNE WALKWAYS (live '93). / STILL GOT THE BLUES** [32] [ ]
(cd-s+=) – Stop messin' around / You don't love me.
(cd-s) – ('A'side) / Since I met you baby (live with B.B.KING) / Key to love.

Pointblank Virgin

May 93. (cd)(c)(d-lp) **BLUES ALIVE** [8] [ ]
– Cold day in Hell / Walking by myself / Story of the blues / Oh pretty woman / Separate ways / Too tired / Still got the blues / Since I met you baby / The sky is crying / Further on up the road / King of the blues / Parisienne walkways / Jumpin' at shadows.

— In Jun 94, MOORE teamed up with JACK BRUCE + GINGER BAKER (ex-CREAM, and both solo artists) to form BBM. They had UK Top10 album 'AROUND THE NEXT DREAM' for 'Virgin' records.

Virgin Virgin

Nov 94. (cd)(c)(lp) **BALLADS AND BLUES 1982-1994** (compilation) [33] [ ]

below a tribute to PETER GREEN (ex-Fleetwood Mac) guitarist

May 95. (cd)(c)(lp) **BLUES FOR GREENY** [14] [ ]
– If you be my baby / Long grey mare / Merry go round / I loved another woman / Need your love so bad / The same way / The supernatural / Driftin' / Showbiz blues / Love that burns / Looking for somebody.

Jun 95. (7"ep)(12"ep)(cd-ep) **NEED YOUR LOVE SO BAD / THE SAME WAY (acoustic). / THE WORLD KEEPS ON TURNIN' (acoustic) / STOP MESSIN' AROUND (acoustic)** 48

– compilations, etc. –

Jun 84. Jet; (lp)(c) **DIRTY FINGERS**
(re-iss.1987 on 'Castle')
Jun 84. Jet; (7") **DON'T LET ME BE MISUNDERSTOOD. / SHE'S GOT YOU (live)**
1984. Jet; (lp) **LIVE AT THE MARQUEE (live)**
(re-Jun87 on 'Raw Power')
Oct 85. Raw Power; (lp)(c)(cd) **WHITE KNUCKLES** -
Sep 86. Raw Power; (d-lp)(d-c) **ANTHOLOGY** -
Jun 86. 10-Virgin; (lp)(c)(cd) **ROCKIN' EVERY NIGHT (live Japan)** 99
(re-iss.cd.Jun88)
Nov 87. M.C.A.; (lp)(c) **PARISIENNE WALKWAYS**
(cd-iss.May90)
Mar 88. Castle; (d-cd) **G-FORCE / LIVE AT THE MARQUEE**
Oct 90. Castle; (cd)(c)(lp) **THE COLLECTION** -
– Nuclear attack / White knuckles – Rockin' & rollin' / Grinding stone / Spirit / Run to your mama / Don't let me be misunderstood / Bad news / I look at you / She's got you / Back on the streets (live) / Hiroshima / Parisienne walkways (live) / Dancin' / Really gonna rock tonight / Dirty fingers.
Mar 91. Castle; (cd)(c)(lp) **LIVE AT THE MARQUEE (live)** -
Jun 90. Nightriding; (cd) **GOLDEN DECADE OF GARY MOORE** -
—— next when as SKID ROW
Sep 90. Essential; (cd)(c)(lp) **GARY MOORE, BRUSH SHIELDS, NOEL BRIDGEMAN** -
Sep 94. Spectrum; (cd)(c) **WALKWAYS** -

Alanis MORISSETTE

Born: 1975, Ottawa, Canada, to a French-Canadian father and Hungarian mother, who were both teachers. She began writing songs at age ten and became a regular on cable show 'You Can't Do That On Television'. Her first single was released at the same time, and by 16 she had made two disco/pop albums. She then headed for LA, where she hawked around her demo which was refused by nearly every major. In 1994, along came MADONNA, who duly signed her to 'Maverick'. The resulting album 'JAGGED LITTLE PILL' in 1995, was heralded by critics and public alike and soon went No.1 Stateside. It won 4 Grammys and a Brit award early '96. • **Style:** Evocative and emotional singer, with a confrontational approach to all life's subjects; especially love. • **Songwriters:** Writes all music with GLEN BALLARD, who also plays guitar and keyboards. • **Trivia:** Guests on her debut included FLEA (Red Hot Chilis) and DAVE NAVARRO (ex-Jane's Addiction)

Recommended: JAGGED LITTLE PILL (*9)

ALANIS MORISSETTE -vocals/ with **BENMONT TENCH** organ (ex-TOM PETTY) / **LANCE MORRISON** -bass / **MATT LAUG** -drums

Maverick Maverick

Jun 95. (cd)(c)(lp) **JAGGED LITTLE PILL** 1 1
– All I really want / You oughta know / Perfect / Hand in my pocket / Right through you / Forgiven / You learn / Head over feet / Mary Jane / Ironic / Not the doctor / Wake up.
Jul 95. (c-s) **YOU OUGHTA KNOW / ('A'-Jimmy The Saint version)** 22
(cd-s+=) – Perfect (acoustic) / Wake up.
Oct 95. (c-s) **HAND IN MY POCKET / HEAD OVER FEET (live)** 26
(cd-s+=) – Not the doctor (live).
(cd-s) – ('A'side) / Right through (live) / Foreign (live).

. . . Jan – Jun '96 stop press . . .

Feb 96. (single) **YOU LEARN** 24
Apr 96. (single) **IRONIC** 11 4 Mar 96

Van MORRISON

Born: GEORGE IVAN, 31 Aug'45, Belfast, N.Ireland. In the early 60's, he formed The MONARCHS, who evolved into THEM in 1963. With MORRISON at the helm, they had number of chart hits, namely 'HERE COMES THE NIGHT' & 'GLORIA', before he moved to New York early '67, to sign contract with Bert Berns of 'Bang' records. His debut 45 'BROWN-EYED GIRL', reached the US Top 10, but his partnership with BERNS came to an end when BERNS died of a heart attack late '67. After

a debut lp 'BLOWIN' YOUR MIND', MORRISON moved to Cambridge, Massachusetts and was snapped up by 'Warner Bros.', where he recorded in 2 days 'ASTRAL WEEKS' with producer Lewis Merenstein. Although its sales were only moderate, it became critics' seminal lp of the decade. His next album 'MOONDANCE' was another gem, but this got deserved commercial success, and hit both US & UK Top 40's. He continued to be major album orientated star of the 70's, 80's & 90's. His 1971 album 'TUPELO HONEY', was written for his wife Janet Planet, whom he divorced in '73. • **Style:** Magical and melancholy jazz-influenced songer/songwriter, whose lyrics explore a deep spiritual mood, mixed with joy and romanticism. • **Songwriters:** Self-penned except covers; CALEDONIA (Fleecie Moore) / HELP ME (Sonny Boy Williamson) / BRING IT HOME TO ME (Sam Cooke) / SANTA FE (co-written w / Jackie DeShannon) / LONELY AVENUE (Doc Pomus) / GOOD MORNING LITTLE SCHOOLGIRL (Soony Boy Williamson) / THE LONESOME ROAD (N.Shikret – G.Austin) / MOODY'S MOOD FOR LOVE (James Moody) / I'LL TAKE CARE OF YOU (Brook Benton) / BEFORE THE WORLD WAS MADE (W.B.Yeats / music; Kenny Craddock) / YOU DON'T KNOW ME (hit; Ray Charles) / I'LL NEVER BE FREE (Benjamin-Weiss) / THAT OLD BLACK MAGIC (hit; Sammy Davis Jnr). • **Trivia:** Early in the 70's, still having a love for the blues, he jammed with JOHN LEE HOOKER on 2 songs. They were to re-unite on stage late '89, singing 'Boom Boom' & 'It Serves You Right To Suffer'.

Recommended: ASTRAL WEEKS (*10) / MOONDANCE (*9) / TUPELO HONEY (*8) / VEEDON FLEECE (*7) / INARTICULATE SPEECH OF THE HEART

(*7) / AVALON SUNSET (*8) / THE BEST OF VAN MORRISON (*9) / ENLIGHTENMENT (*7)

VAN MORRISON – vocals, guitar, saxophone (ex-THEM) with loads of session persons.

London Bang

Jun 67. (7") **BROWN EYED GIRL. / GOODBYE BABY (BABY GOODBYE)** [ ] [10]
(re-iss Mar71 on 'President' & Apr74 on 'London' records)
Sep 67. (7") **RO RO ROSEY. / CHICK-A-BOO** [-] [ ]
Nov 67. (7") **SPANISH ROSE / MIDNIGHT ROSE** [-] [ ]
Feb 68. (lp) **BLOWIN' YOUR MIND** [ ] [ ] Sep 67
– Brown eyed girl / He ain't give you none / T.B. sheets / Spanish rose / Goodbye baby (baby goodbye) / Ro Ro Rosey / Who drove the red sports car? / Midnight special. *(cd-iss.Jul95 on 'Epic')*

— now with **LARRY FALLON** – conductor, arranger / **JAY BERLINER** – guitar / **RICHARD DAVIS** – bass / **CONNIE KAY** – drums / **JOHN PAYNE** – flute, sporano sax / **WARREN SMITH JR** – percussion, vibraphone

Warners Warners

Sep 69. (lp)(c) **ASTRAL WEEKS** [ ] [ ] Nov 68
– In the beginning: Astral weeks / Beside you / Sweet thing / Cypress avenue / Afterwards: Young lovers do / Madame George / Ballerina / Slim slow rider. *(re-iss.Aug 71) (cd-iss.May87, re-iss.1989)*

— now with **JOHN PLATANIA** – guitar / **JEFF LABES** – keys / **JACK SHROER** – sax / **GARY MALLABER** – drums / **JOHN KLINGBERG** – bass.

Mar 70. (lp)(c) **MOONDANCE** [32] [29]
– And it stoned me / Moondance / Crazy love / Into the mystic / Caravan / Come running / These dreams of you / Brand new day / Everyone / Glad tidings. *(re-iss.Aug 71) (cd-iss.Jan86)*
May 70. (7") **COME RUNNING. / CRAZY LOVE** [ ] [39] Apr 70
Dec 70. (lp)(c) **HIS BAND AND THE STREET CHOIR** [ ] [32] Nov 70
– Domino / Crazy face / I've been working / Call me up in Dreamland / I'll be your lover, too / Blue money / Virgo clowns / Gypsy queen / Sweet Janine / If I ever needed someone / Street choir. *(re-iss.Aug 71) (re-iss.cd Feb93)*
Dec 70. (7") **DOMINO. / SWEET JANINE** [ ] [9] Oct 70
(re-iss.Jul 71)
Feb 71. (7") **BLUE MONEY. / SWEET THING** [-] [23]
Apr 71. (7") **CALL ME UP IN DREAMLAND. / STREET CHOIR** [-] [95]

— now with **MALLABER, SHROER + BILL CHURCH** – bass / **RONNIE MONTROSE** – guitar / **RICK SCHLOSSER** – drums + **CONNIE KAY** – drums.

Sep 71. (7") **WILD NIGHT. / WHEN THAT EVENING SUN GOES DOWN** [-] [28]
Nov 71. (lp)(c) **TUPELO HONEY** [ ] [27] Oct 71
– Wild night / (Straight to your heart) Like a cannonball / Old old Woodstock / Starting a new life / You're my woman / Tupelo honey / I wonna roo you / When that evening sun goes down / Moonshine whiskey. *(re-iss.+cd. Aug89 on 'Polydor') (re-iss.cd+c Feb94 on 'Polydor')*
Dec 71. (7") **TUPELO HONEY. / STARTING A NEW LIFE** [-] [47]
Mar 72. (7") **(STRAIGHT TO YOUR HEART) LIKE A CANNONBALL. / OLD OLD WOODSTOCK** [-] [ ]

— **LEROY VINNEGAR** – bass repl. CHURCH (who later joined MONTROSE) / **ROY ELLIOT** – guitar + **MARK NAFTALIN** – piano repl. SCHOSSLER + MALLABER

Jul 72. (7") **JACKIE WILSON SAID (I'M IN HEAVEN WHEN YOU SMILE). / YOU'VE GOT THE POWER** [ ] [61]
Aug 72. (lp)(c) **SAINT DOMINIC'S PREVIEW** [ ] [15]
– Jackie Wilson said (I'm in Heaven when you smile) / Gypsy / I will be there / Listen to the lion / Saint Dominic's preview / Redwood tree / Almost Independance day. *(re-iss.1974) (re-iss.+cd.Aug89 on 'Polydor' cd-iss.Apr95)*
Oct 72. (7") **REDWOOD TREE. / SAINT DOMINIC'S PREVIEW** [-] [98]

— RONNIE now formed MONTROSE went through various session personnel: **DAVID HAYES** – bass and most of new band.

Jul 73. (7") **WARM LOVE. / I WILL BE THERE** [ ] [ ] Jun 73
Jul 73. (lp)(c) **HARD NOSE THE HIGHWAY** [22] [27]
– Snow in San Anselmo / Warm love / Hard nose the highway / Wild children / The great deception / Green / Autumn song / Purple heather. *(re-iss.+cd.Aug89 on 'Polydor', cd-iss.Apr95)*
Sep 73. (7") **GREEN. / WILD CHILDREN** [-] [ ]
Feb 74. (7") **AIN'T NOTHING YOU CAN DO. / WILD CHILDREN** [-] [ ]
Feb 74. (d-lp)(d-c) **IT'S TOO LATE TO STOP NOW (live)** [ ] [53]
– Ain't nothing you can do / Warm love / Into the mystic / These dreams of you / I believe to my soul / I've been working / Help me / Wild children / Domino / I just wanna make love to you / Bring it on home to me / Saint Dominic's preview / Take your hand out of my pocket / Listen to the lion / Here comes the night / Gloria / Caravan / Cypress Avenue. *(re-iss.+d-cd.Aug89 on 'Polydor', cd-iss.Apr95)*
May 74. (7") **CALDONIA (WHAT MAKES YOUR BIG HEAD HARD?). / WHAT'S UP, CRAZY PUP** [ ] [ ]
Oct 74. (lp)(c) **VEEDON FLEECE** [41] [53]
– Streets of Arklow / Country fair / Cul de sac / Linden Arden stole the highlights / Fair play / Bulbs / You don't pull no punches but you don't push the river / Comfort you / Come here my love / Who was that masked man. *(re-iss.+cd.Aug89 on 'Polydor', cd-iss.Apr95)*
Jul 74. (7") **BULBS. / CUL DE SAC** [-] [ ]
Nov 74. (7") **BULBS. / WHO WAS THAT MASKED MAN** [ ] [-]
Mar 77. (lp)(c) **A PERIOD OF TRANSITION** [23] [43]
– You gotta make it through the world / It fills you up / The eternal Kansas City / Joyous sound / Flamingoes fly / Heavy connection / Cold wind in August. *(re-iss.+cd.Aug89 on 'Polydor')*
Apr 77. (7") **THE ETERNAL KANSAS CITY. / JOYOUS SOUND** [ ] [-]
Jul 77. (7") **JOYOUS SOUND. / MECHANICAL BLISS** [ ] [ ]
Oct 77. (7") **COLD WIND IN AUGUST. / MOONDANCE** [-] [ ]

— **PETER VAN HOOKE** – drums / **HERBIE ARMSTRONG** – guitar etc

Oct 78. (lp)(c) **WAVELENGTH** [27] [28]
– Kingdom hall / Checkin' it out / Natalia / Venice U.S.A. / Lifetimes / Wavelength / Santa Fe / Beautiful obsession / Hungry for your love / Take it where you find it. *(re-iss.+cd.Aug89 on 'Polydor') (re-iss.cd+c Feb94 on 'Polydor')*
Oct 78. (7") **WAVELENGTH. / CHECKIN' IT OUT** [ ] [42]
Feb 79. (7") **NATALIA. / LIFETIMES** [ ] [ ]
Apr 79. (7") **CHECKIN' IT OUT. /** [-] [ ]

— now with **HOOKE, ARMSTRONG, HAYES / + MARK JORDAN** – keyboards / **MARK ISHAM** – trumpet / **PEE WEE ELLIS** – saxophone

Vertigo Warners

Aug 79. (lp)(c) **INTO THE MUSIC** [21] [43]
– Bright side of the road / Full force gale / Stepping out queen / Troubadours / Rolling hills / You make me feel so free / Angeliou / And the healing has begun / It's all in the game / You know what they're writing about. *(re-iss.+cd.May83 on 'Mercury') (re-iss.+cd.Aug89 on 'Polydor') (re-iss.cd+c Feb94 on 'Polydor')*
Sep 79. (7") **BRIGHT SIDE OF THE ROAD. / ROLLING HILLS** [63] [ ]
Dec 79. (7") **FULL FORCE GALE. / YOU MAKE ME FEEL SO FREE** [-] [ ]

— **JOHN ALLAIR** – keyboards + **MICK COX** – guitar repl. JORDAN + MARCUS

Mercury Warners

Sep 80. (lp)(c) **COMMON ONE** [53] [73]
– Haunts of ancient peace / Summertime in England / Satisfied / Wild honey / Spirit / When heart is open. *(re-iss.May83, cd-iss.1986) (re-iss.+cd.Aug89 on 'Polydor'; cd-iss.Apr95)*

— added **TOM DONLINGER** – drums

Feb 82. (lp)(c) **BEAUTIFUL VISION** [31] [44]
– Celtic Ray / Northern muse (solid sound) / Dweller on the threshold / Beautiful vision / She gives me religion / Cleaning windows / Vanlose stairway / Aryan mist / Scandinavia / Across the bridge where angels dwell / Scandinavia. *(cd-iss.1983) (re-iss.Mar85) (re-iss.+cd.Aug89 on 'Polydor') (re-iss.cd+c Feb94 on 'Polydor')*
Mar 82. (7") **CLEANING WINDOWS. / SCANDINAVIA** [-] [ ]
Mar 82. (7") **CLEANING WINDOWS. / IT'S ALL IN THE GAME** [ ] [-]
Jun 82. (7") **SCANDINAVIA. / DWELLER ON THE THRESHOLD** [ ] [ ]

— **CHRIS MICHIE** – guitar repl. COX

Feb 83. (7") **CRY FOR HOME. / SUMMERTIME IN ENGLAND (live)** [ ] [ ]
(12"+=) – All Saint's day.
Mar 83. (lp)(c)(cd) **INARTICULATE SPEECH OF THE HEART** [14] [ ]
– Higher than the world / Connswater / River of time / Celtic swing / Rave on, John Donne / Inarticulate speech of the heart No.1 / Irish heartbeat / The street only knew your name / Cry for home / Inarticulate speech of the heart No.2 / September night. *(re-iss.May86) (re-iss.+cd.Aug89 on 'Polydor') (re-iss.cd+c Feb94 on 'Polydor')*
May 83. (7") **CELTIC SWING. / MR. THOMAS** [ ] [ ]
(12"+=) – Rave on, John Donne.
Feb 84. (lp)(c)(cd) **LIVE AT THE GRAND OPERA HOUSE, BELFAST (live)** [47] [ ]
– (intro) / Into the music / Inarticulate seech of the heart / Dweller on the threshold / It's all in the game – You know what they're writing about / She gives me religion / Haunts of ancient peace / Full force gale / Beautiful vision / Vanlose stairway / Rave on, John Donne – Rave on (part 2) / Northern muse (solid ground) / Cleaning windows. *(re-iss.+cd.Aug89 on 'Polydor')*
Mar 84. (7") **DWELLER ON THE THRESHOLD (live). / NORTHERN MUSE (SOLID GROUND)** [ ] [ ]
Nov 84. (7") **A SENSE OF WONDER. / HAUNTS OF ANCIENT PEACE (live)** [ ] [ ]
Feb 85. (lp)(c)(cd) **A SENSE OF WONDER** [25] [61]
– Tore down a La Rimbaud / Ancient of days / Evening meditation / The master's eyes / What would I do / A sense of wonder / Boffyflow and Spike / If you only knew / Let the slave / A new kind of man. *(re-iss.+cd.May90 on 'Polydor', cd-iss.Apr95)*
Jul 86. (lp)(c)(cd) **NO GURU, NO METHOD, NO TEACHER** [27] [70]
– Got to go back / Oh the warm feeling / Foreign window / Town called Paradise / In the garden / Tir na nog / Here comes the night / Thanks for the information / One Irish rover / Ivory tower. *(re-iss.Sep91) (re-iss.cd/c Feb94 on 'Polydor')*
Aug 86. (7") **GOT TO GO BACK. / IN THE GARDEN** [ ] [ ]

— note: HOOKE + ISHAM left early '84 / **ELLIS + DONLINGER** in '85 / now new band

Sep 87. (lp)(c)(cd) **POETIC CHAMPIONS COMPOSE** [26] [90]
– Spanish steps / The mystery / Queen of the slipstream / I forgot that love existed / Sometimes I feel like a motherless child / Celtic excavation / Someone like you /

Alan Watts blues / Give me my rapture / Did ye get healed? / Allow me.

Sep 87. (7") **DID YE GET HEALED?. / ALAN WATTS BLUES** [ ] [ ]

Apr 88. (7") **QUEEN OF THE SLIPSTREAM. / SPANISH STEPS** [ ] [ ]

Jun 88. (lp)(c)(cd) **IRISH HEARTBEAT ("VAN MORRISON & THE CHIEFTAINS")** [18] [ ]
– Star of the County Down / Irish heartbeat / Ta mo chleamhnas deanta / Raglan road / She moved through the fair / I'll tell me ma / Carrickfergus / Celtic Ray / My lagan love / Marie's wedding.

Jun 88. (7") **I'LL TELL ME MA. / TA MO CHLEAMHNAS DEANTA** [ ] [ ]
(12"+=)(cd-s+=) – Carrickfergus.

Polydor Mercury

May 89. (lp)(c)(cd) **AVALON SUNSET** [13] [91]
– Whenever God shines his light / Contacting my angel / I'd love to write another love song / Have I told you lately (that I love you) / Coney Island / I'm tired Joey boy / When will I ever learn to live in God / Orangefield / Daring night / These are the days.

Jun 89. (7") **HAVE I TOLD YOU LATELY (THAT I LOVE YOU). / CONTACTING MY ANGEL** [74] [ ]
(12"+=) – Listen to the lion.
(cd-s+=) – Irish heartbeat.

Sep 89. (7")(12") **ORANGEFIELD. / THESE ARE THE DAYS** [ ] [ ]
(cd-s+=) – And the healing has begun.

Nov 89. (7")(c-s) **WHENEVER GOD SHINES HIS LIGHT. (by "VAN MORRISON & CLIFF RICHARD") / I'D LOVE TO WRITE ANOTHER LOVE SONG** [20] [ ]
(12"+=) – Cry for home.
(cd-s++=) – ('A'-lp version).

Feb 90. (7") **CONEY ISLAND. / HAVE I TOLD YOU LATELY (THAT I LOVE YOU)** [ ] [ ]
(12"+=) – A sense of wonder.
(c-s++=)(cd-s++=) – Spirit.

Sep 90. (7")(c-s) **REAL REAL GONE. / START ALL OVER AGAIN** [ ] [ ]
(12"+=)(cd-s+=) – Cleaning windows.

Oct 90. (cd)(c)(lp) **ENLIGHTENMENT** [5] [62]
– Real real gone / Enlightenment / So quiet in here / Avalon of the heart / See me through / Youth of 1,000 summers / In the days before rock'n'roll / Start all over again / She's a baby / Memories.

Nov 90. (7")(c-s) **IN THE DAYS BEFORE ROCK'N'ROLL. / I'D LOVE TO WRITE ANOTHER LOVE SONG** [ ] [ ]
(12"+=)(cd-s+=) – Coney Island.

Jan 91. (7") **ENLIGHTENMENT. / AVALON OF THE HEART** [ ] [ ]
(12"+=)(cd-s+=) – Jackie Wilson said.

(VAN is credited w / TOM JONES on his Mar91 single 'CARRYING A TORCH')

May 91. (7")(c-s) **I CAN'T STOP LOVING YOU. ("VAN MORRISON & CHIEFTAINS") / ALL SAINTS DAY** [ ] [ ]
(12"+=)(cd-s+=) – Carrying a torch. (w / "TOM JONES")

Aug 91. (7")(c-s) **WHY MUST I ALWAYS EXPLAIN?. / SO COMPLICATED** [ ] [ ]
(12"+=)(cd-s+=) – Enlightenment.

Sep 91. (d-cd)(d-c)(d-lp) **HYMNS OF THE SILENCE** [5] [99]
– Professional jealousy / I'm not feeling it anymore / Ordinary life / Some peace of mind / So complicated / I can't stop loving you / Why must I always explain? / Village idiot / See me through part II (just a closer walk with thee) / Take me back / By his Grace / All Saints day / Hymns to the silence / On Hyndford Street / Be thou my vision / Carrying a torch / Green mansions / Pagan streams / Quality Street / It must be you / I need your kind of loving.

May 93. (7")(c-s) **GLORIA. ("VAN MORRISON & JOHN LEE HOOKER") / IT MUST BE YOU (live)** [31] [ ]
(cd-s+=) – The healing has begun (live) / See me through (live).
(cd-s) – ('A'side) / Whenever God shines his light (live) / It fills you up (live) / The star of County Down (live).

Jun 93. (cd)(c)(lp) **TOO LONG IN EXILE** [4] [29]
– Too long in exile / Big time operators / Lonely avenue / Ball & chain / In the forest / Till we get the healing done / Gloria / Good morning little schoolgirl / Wasted years / The lonesome road / Moody's mood for love / Close enough for jazz / Before the world was made / I'll take care of you – Instrumental – Tell me what you want.

Apr 94. (d-cd)(d-c) **A NIGHT IN SAN FRANCISCO (live)** [8] [ ]
– Did ya get healed? / It's all in the game / Make it real one more time / I've been working / I forgot that love existed / Vanlose stairway / Trans-Euro train / Fool for you / You make me feel so real / Beautiful vision / See me through / Soldier of fortune / Thankyoufalettinmebemiseldagain / Ain't that lovin' you baby / Stormy Monday / Have you ever loved a woman / No rollin' blues / Help me / Good morning little schoolgirl / Tupelo honey / Moondance / My funny valentine / Jumpin' with Symphony Sid / It fills you up / I'll take care of you / It's a man's man's man's world / Lonely avenue / 4 o'clock in the morning / So quiet in here / That's where it's at / In the garden / You send me / Allegheny / Have I told you lately that I love you / Shakin' all over / Gloria.

Jun 95. (cd-s) **DAYS LIKE THIS / YO** [65] [ ]
(7"+=)(c-s+=)(cd-s+=) – I don't want to go on without you / That old black magic.

Jun 95. (cd)(c)(lp) **DAYS LIKE THIS** [5] [33]
– Perfect fit / Russian roulette / Rain check / You don't know me / No religion / Underlying depression / Songwriter / Days like this / I'll never be free / Melancholia / Ancient highway / In the afternoon.

Sep 95. (c-s) **PERFECT FIT / RAINCHECK** [ ] [ ]
(cd-s+=) – Cleaning windows.

Nov 95. (cd-s) **NO RELIGION / HAVE I TOLD YOU LATELY** [54] [ ]
(cd-s+=) – Whenever God shines his light / Gloria.
(cd-s) – ('A'side) / Days like this / Raincheck.

– compilations, others, etc. –

May 71. President/ US= Bang; (lp) **THE BEST OF VAN MORRISON** [ ] [ ] 1970
(nearly a re-iss of debut '67 lp)

Mar 74. London/ US= Bang; (lp) **T.B. SHEETS** [ ] [ ] Jan 74
(nearly a re-iss of debut '67 lp) *(re-iss. Sep 88 on 'Bellaphon')(re-iss.+cd.May91 on 'C.B.S.')*

Sep 77. Bang; (lp) **THIS IS WHERE I CAME IN** [ ] [ ]
(nearly a re-iss of debut '67 lp)

Oct 75. Warners; (d-lp) **TWO ORIGINALS OF VAN MORRISON** [ ] [ ]
(VAN MORRISON, HIS BAND AND STREET CHOIR / TUPELO HONEY)

Oct 77. Warners; (7") **MOONDANCE. / ?** [-] [92]

Oct 82. Warners; (d-c) **MOONDANCE / . . . HIS BAND AND STREET CHOIR** [ ] [-]

Mar 90. Polydor/ US= Mercury; (cd)(c)(lp) **THE BEST OF VAN MORRISON** [4] [41] May 90
– Bright side of the road / Gloria (THEM) / Moondance / Baby please don't go (THEM) / Have I told you lately / Brown eyed girl / Sweet thing / Warm love / Wonderful remark / Jackie Wilson said (I'm in Heaven when you smile) / Full force gale / And it stoned me / Here comes the night (THEM) / Domino / Did ye get healed / Wild night / Cleaning windows / Whenever God shines his light (w / CLIFF RICHARD). *(c+cd.iss.has extra tracks)*

Jul 90. Polydor; (7") **GLORIA. / RAVE ON** [ ] [ ]

Feb 93. Polydor; (cd)(c) **THE BEST OF VAN MORRISON VOLUME 2** [31] [ ]
– Real real gone / When will I ever learn to live in God / Sometimes I feel like a motherless child / In the garden / A sense of wonder / I'll tell me ma / Coney Island / Enlightenment / Rave on john Donne – Rave on part two live / Don't look back / It's all over now, baby blue / One Irish Rover / The mystery / Hymns to the silence / Evening meditation.

Jan 92. Moles; (c) **CUCHULAINN** (spoken word) [ ] [-]

Mar 92. Sony; (d-cd)(c) **BANG MASTERS** [ ] [-]

Jan 93. Movieplay Gold; (cd) **THE LOST TAPES VOLUME 1** [ ] [-]

Jan 93. Movieplay Gold; (cd) **THE LOST TAPES VOLUME 1** [ ] [-]

May 94. Charly; (cd) **PAYIN' DUES** [ ] [-]

Oct 95. Verve; (cd)(c)(lp) **HOW LONG HAS THIS BEEN GOING ON ("VAN MORRISON with GEORGIE FAME & FRIENDS") (live 3 May'95 at Ronnie Scott's)** [ ] [55] Jan96
– I will be there / The new symphony Sid / Early in the morning / Who can I turn to? / Sack o'woe / Moondance / Centerpiece / How long has this been going on? / Your mind is on vacation / All saint's day / Blues in the night / Don't worry about a thing / That's life / Heathrow shuffle.

MORRISSEY

Born: STEPHEN PATRICK MORRISSEY, 22 May'59, Manchester, England. Former SMITHS frontman, until his fall-out with their guitarist JOHNNY MARR in August 1987. The SMITHS had already progressed from top indie 'Rough Trade' to 'EMI', but as there was now no band, MORRISSEY's releases were switched to EMI's re-activated 'HMV'. His debut single 'SUEDEHEAD', was his first ever entry into UK Top 5, early in '88. It was hastily pursued by Top 3 album 'VIVA HATE', which brought in new band and producer STEPHEN STREET. From then on, MORRISSEY was a regular feature in the charts, and surprised many when 1991 album 'KILL UNCLE', nearly hit the US Top 50. • **Style:** Intellectual, overtly confident chanter, who was best described as 'The Oscar Wilde of Rock'. • **Songwriters:** Writes all lyrics, with music by STEPHEN STREET until 1991, when MARK NEVIN augmented. Producers now being CLIVE LANGER and ALAN WINSTANLEY. Covered; THAT'S ENTERTAINMENT (Jam) / SKIN STORM (Bradford). • **Trivia:** In the late 80's, he made a cameo appearance in Channel 4's 'Brookside' off-shoot 'South'. MICK RONSON (ex-BOWIE) produced 1992 album.

Recommended: VIVA HATE (*9) / KILL UNCLE (*8) / YOUR ARSENAL (*8) / VAUXHALL AND I (*9).

MORRISSEY – vocals (ex-SMITHS) with **STEPHEN STREET** – guitar, bass, producer, co-writer / **ANDREW PARESI** – drums / **VINI REILLY** – guitar, keyboards (of DURUTTI COLUMN)

H.M.V. Sire

Feb 88. (7") **SUEDEHEAD. / I KNOW VERY WELL HOW I GOT MY NAME** [5] [ ]
(12"+=) – Hairdresser on fire.
(c-s++=)(cd-s++=) – Oh well, I'll never learn.

Mar 88. (lp)(c)(cd) **VIVA HATE** | 2 | 48 |
– Alsatian cousin / Little man, what now? / Everyday is like Sunday / Bengali in platforms / Angel, angel, down we go together / Late night, Maudlin Street / Suedehead / Break up the family / The ordinary boys / I don't mind if you forget me / Dial-a-cliche / Margaret on the guillotine. *(re-iss.cd+c Mar94 on 'Parlophone')*

Jun 88. (7") **EVERYDAY IS LIKE SUNDAY. / DISAPPOINTED** | 9 | |
(12"+=) – Sister I'm a poet.
(c-s++=)(cd-s++=) – Will never marry.

— **MORRISSEY** only retained **STREET.** He brought in **NEIL TAYLOR** – guitar and re-united with (ex-SMITHS):- **CRAIG GANNON, ANDY ROURKE + MIKE JOYCE**

Feb 89. (7") **THE LAST OF THE FAMOUS INTERNATIONAL PLAYBOYS. / LUCKY LIPS** | 6 | |
(12"+=)(cd-s+=) – Michael's bones.

Apr 89. (7") **INTERESTING DRUG. / SUCH A LITTLE THING MAKES SUCH A BIG DIFFERENCE** | 9 | |
(12"+=)(c-s+=)(cd-s+=) – Sweet and tender hooligan (live).

— He brought in complete new line-up:- **KEVIN ARMSTRONG** – guitar / **MATTHEW SELIGMAN** – bass / **STEVE HOPKINS** – drums and returning **ANDREW**

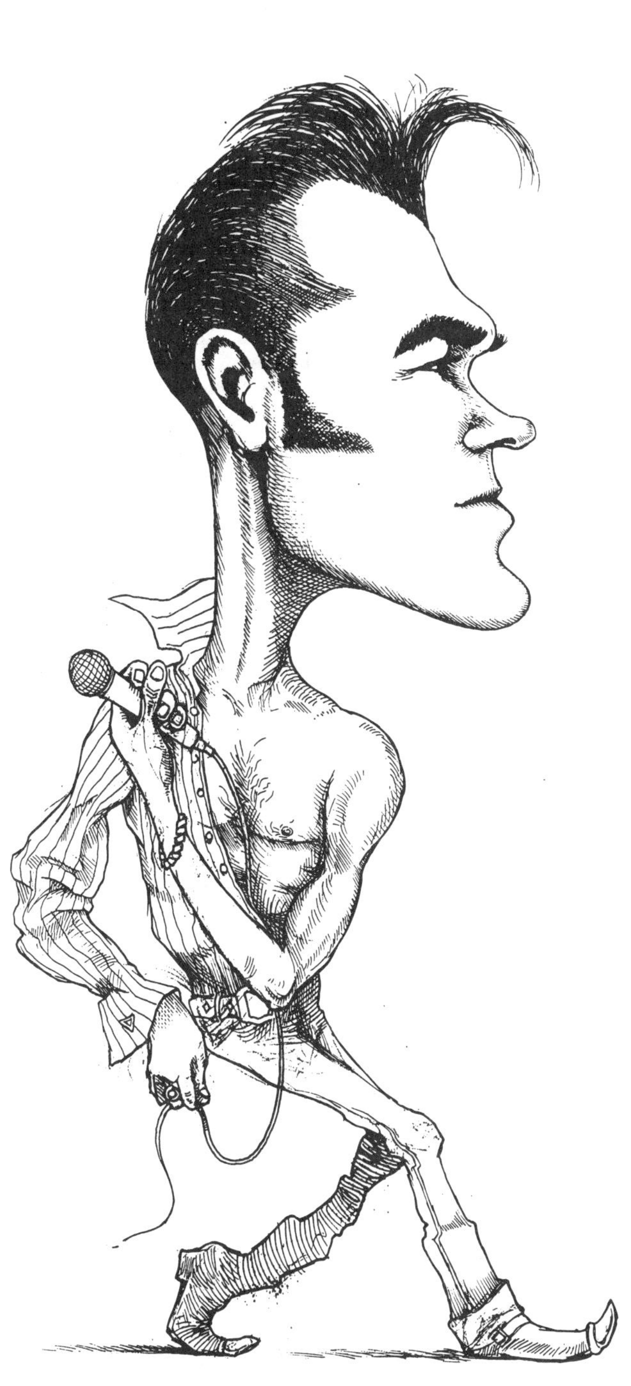

PARESI – keys

Nov 89. (7")(c-s) **OUIJA BOARD, OUIJA BOARD. / YES, I AM BLIND** [18] [ ]
(12"+=)(cd-s+=) – East west.

— **ANDY ROURKE** returned to repl. SELIGMAN + HOPKINS / added guest **MARY MARGARET O'HARA** – vocals (up & coming solo artist)

Apr 90. (7")(c-s) **NOVEMBER SPAWNED A MONSTER. / HE KNOWS I'D LOVE TO SEE HIM** [12] [ ]
(12"+=)(cd-s+=) – The girl least likely to.

Oct 90. (7")(c-s) **PICCADILLY PALAVARE. / GET OFF THE STAGE** [18] [ ]
(12"+=)(cd-s+=) – At amber.

Oct 90. (cd)(c)(lp) **BONA DRAG** (compilation of recent material) [9] [59]
– Piccadilly palavre / Interesting drug / November spawned a monster / Will never marry / Such a little thing makes such a big difference / The last of the famous international playboys / Ouija board, ouija board / Hairdresser on fire / Everyday is like Sunday / He knows I'd love to see him / Yes, I am blind / Lucky lisp / Suedehead / Disappointed. *(re-iss.cd/c Mar94 on 'Parlophone')*

— He now retained **ANDREW PARESI.** Newcomers were **BEDDERS** – bass (ex-MADNESS) / **MARK E.NEVIN** – guitars, co-composer (ex-FAIRGROUND ATTRACTION) plus **STEVE HEART + SEAMUS BEAGHAN** – keyboards / **NAWAZISH ALI KHAN** – violin

Feb 91. (7")(c-s) **OUR FRANK. / JOURNALISTS WHO LIE** [26] [ ]
(12"+=)(cd-s+=) – Tony the pony.

Feb 91. (cd)(c)(lp) **KILL UNCLE** [8] [52] Mar 91
– Our Frank / Asian rut / Sing your life / Mute witness / King Leer / Found found found / Driving your girlfriend home / The harsh truth of the camera eye / (I'm) The end of the family line / There's a place in Hell for me and my friends.

— His tour band Spring '91; **ALAIN WHYTE** – guitar / **GARY DAY** – bass / **BOZ BOORER** – guitar (ex-POLECATS) / **SPENCER COBRIN** – drums

Apr 91. (7")(c-s) **SING YOUR LIFE. / THAT'S ENTERTAINMENT** [33] [ ]
(12"+=)(cd-s+=) – The loop.

Jul 91. (7")(c-s) **PREGNANT FOR THE LAST TIME. / SKIN STORM** [25] [ ]
(12"+=)(cd-s+=) – Cosmic dancer (live) / Disappointed (live).

Oct 91. (7")(c-s) **MY LOVE LIFE. / I'VE CHANGED MY PLEA TO GUILTY** [29] [ ]
(12"+=)(cd-s+=) – There's a place in Hell for me and my friends.

late 91. (cd-ep) **MORRISEY AT KROQ (live)** [-] [ ]
– There's a place in Hell for my friends / My love life / Sing your life.

Apr 92. (7")(c-s) **WE HATE IT WHEN OUR FRIENDS BECOME SUCCESSFUL. / SUEDEHEAD** [17] [ ]
(12"+=) – Pregnant for the last time.
(cd-s+=) – I've changed my plea to guilty.

Jul 92. (7")(c-s) **YOU'RE THE ONE FOR ME, FATTY. / PASHERNATE LOVE** [19] [ ]
(12"+=)(cd-s+=) – There speaks a true friend.

Jul 92. (cd)(c)(lp) **YOUR ARSENAL** [4] [21]
– You're gonna need someone on your side / Glamorous glue / We'll let you know / The National Front disco / Certain people I know / We hate it when our friends become successful / You're the one for me, Fatty / Seasick, yet still docked / I know it's gonna happen someday / Tomorrow.

Aug 92. (12"ep)(cd-ep) **TOMORROW / LET THE RIGHT ONE SLIP IN / PAHERNATE LOVER** [-] [ ]

Nov 92. (7")(c-s) **CERTAIN PEOPLE I KNOW. / JACK THE RIPPER** [35] [ ]
(12"+=)(cd-s+=) – You've had her.

May 93. (cd)(c)(lp) **BEETHOVEN WAS DEAF (live)** [13] [ ]
– You're the one for me, Fatty / Certain people I know / National Front disco / November spawned a monster / Seasick, yet still docked / The loop / Sister I'm a poet / Jack the ripper / Such a little thing makes such a big difference / I know it's gonna happen someday / We'll let you know / Suedehead / He knows I'd love to see him / You're gonna need someone on your side / Glamorous glue / We hate it when our friends become successful. *(re-iss.cd+c Sep94)*

— **BOZ BOORER + ALAIN WHYTE** – guitars / **JONNY BRIDGEWOOD** – bass / **WOODIE TAYLOR** – drums

Parlophone / Sire

Mar 94. (7")(c-s) **THE MORE YOU IGNORE ME, THE CLOSER I GET. / USED TO BE A SWEET BOY** [8] [46]
(12"+=)(cd-s+=) – I'd love to.

Mar 94. (cd)(c)(lp) **VAUXHALL AND I** [1] [18]
– Now my heart is full / Spring-heeled Jim / Billy Budd / Hold on to your friends / The more you ignore me, the closer I get / Why don't you find out for yourself / I am hated for loving / Lifeguard sleeping, girl drowning / Used to be a sweet boy / The lazy sunbathers / Speedway.

Jun 94. (7")(c-s) **HOLD ON TO YOUR FRIENDS. / MOONRIVER** [47] [ ]
(12")(cd-s) – (extended versions).

Aug 94. (7")(c-s) **INTERLUDE. (w/ SIOUXSIE) / ('A'extended)** [25] [ ]
(12"+=)(cd-s+=) – ('A'mix).

Jan 95. (7")(c-s) **BOXERS. / HAVE-A-GO MERCHANT** [23] [ ]
(12"+=)(cd-s+=) – Whatever happens, I love you.

Feb 95. (cd)(c)(lp) **WORLD OF MORRISSEY** (part compilation) [15] [ ]
– Whatever happens, I love you / Billy Budd / Jack the ripper (live) / Have-a-go merchant / The loop / Sister I'm a poet (live) / You're the one for me, Fatty (live) / Boxers / Moon river (extended) / My love life / Certain people I know / The last of the famous international playboys / We'll let you know / Spring-heeled Jim.

— **SPENCER JAMES COBRIN** -drums repl.WOODIE

RCA Victor / RCA Victor

Aug 95. (7")(c-s) **DAGENHAM DAVE. / NOBODY LOVES US** [26] [ ]
(cd-s+=) – You must please remember.

Aug 95. (cd)(c)(lp) **SOUTHPAW GRAMMAR** [4] [66]
– The teachers are afraid of the pupils / Reader meet author / The boy racer / The operation / Dagenham Dave / Do your best and don't worry / Best friend on the payroll / Southpaw.

Nov 95. (7")(c-s) **THE BOY RACER. / LONDON (live)** [36] [ ]
(cd-s+=) – Billy Budd (live).
(cd-s) – Spring heeled Jim (live) / Why don't you find out for yourself (live).

Dec 95. (7")(c-s) **SUNNY. / BLACK-EYED SUSAN** [42] [ ]
(cd-s+=) – A swallow on my neck.

MOTHER LOVE BONE (see under ⇒ PEARL JAM)

MOTHERS (OF INVENTION) (see under ⇒ ZAPPA, Frank)

MOTLEY CRUE

Formed: Los Angeles, California, USA . . . early 1981 by NIKKI SIXX, etc (see below). In 1982, they issued lp 'TOO FAST FOR LOVE', on own US label 'Leathur'. This was re-issued the following year as their debut for 'Elektra'. Later in 1983, their 2nd album 'SHOUT AT THE DEVIL', which was produced by Tom Werman. After a nationwide tour supporting KISS, it hit the US Top 20. For the rest of the 80's, the band became one of top attractions and had a US No.1 album 'DR.FEELGOOD' in 1989. However on the 8 Dec'84, VINCE NEIL was involved in a serious accident while driving his car. A passenger NICK 'RAZZLE' DINGLEY was killed in the crash, and 2 others were injured. VINCE was ordered to pay $2• 5 million compensation and was sentenced to 20 days in jail, after being convicted of vehicle manslaughter. Early in 1988, MATTHEW TRIPPE sued the CRUE for royalties, alleging he masqueraded and wrote songs as NIKKI SIXX, while he recovered from a 1983 car crash. This was later proved to be false, although there is still much speculation on how SIXX's face was bloated on some mug pics. • **Style:** Theatrical and aggressive heavy-metal outfit, influenced by KISS or The TUBES. • **Songwriters:** All written by SIXX (in Dec'87 he was clinically dead for 2 minutes, after taking heroin). Covered; SMOKIN' IN THE BOYS ROOM (Brownsville Station) / HELTER SKELTER (Beatles) / JAILHOUSE ROCK (Leiber-Stoller). • **Trivia:** Late 1985, TOMMY LEE married actress Heather Lockear. On Dec'87, MICK married one-time PRINCE girlfriend VANITY (star of 'Purple Rain')?. In May'90, NIKKI was hitched to former Playboy centre-fold Brandi Brandt.

Recommended: DR. FEELGOOD (*7) / SHOUT AT THE DEVIL (*7) / DECADE OF DECADENCE (*8)

VINCE NEIL (b. VINCENT NEIL WHARTON, 8 Feb'61) – vocals (ex-ROCK CANDY) / **NIKKI SIXX** (b. FRANK FARRANO, 11 Dec'58, Seattle, DC) – bass (ex-LONDON) / **MICK MARS** (b. ROB DEAL, 4 Apr'55, Terre Haute, Indiana) – guitar / **TOMMY LEE** (b. 3 Oct'62, Athens, Greece) – drums (ex-SUITE 19)

not issued / Leathur

1981. (lp) **TOO FAST FOR LOVE** [-] [ ]
– Live wire / Public enemy No.1 / Take me to the top / Merry-go-round / Piece of your action / Starry eyes / Come on and dance / Too fast for love / On with the show. *(UK iss.Oct82 as 'MOTLEY CRUE' on 'Elektra') (US re-iss.Nov83 on 'Elektra') (cd-iss.Feb93 on 'Elektra')*

1982. (7") **TOAST OF THE TOWN. / STICK TO YOUR GUNS** [-] [ ]
(above a US gig freebie)

Elektra / Elektra

Sep 83. (lp)(c) **SHOUT AT THE DEVIL** [ ] [17]
– In the beginning / Shout at the Devil / Looks that kill / Bastard / Knock 'em dead, kid / Danger / Too young to fall in love / Helter skelter / Red hot / Ten seconds 'til love / God bless the children of the beast. *(cd-iss.Jan86)*

Jul 84. (7") **LOOKS THAT KILL. / PIECE OF THE ACTION** [ ] [54] Jan 84
(12"+=) – Live wire.

Oct 84. (7")(12") **TOO YOUNG TO FALL IN LOVE (remix). / TAKE ME TO THE TOP** [ ] [90] Jun 84

Jul 85. (lp)(c) **THEATRE OF PAIN** [36] [6]
– City boy blues / Smokin' in the boys' room / Louder than Hell / Keep your eye on the money / Home sweet home / Tonight (we need a lover) / Use it or lose it / Save our souls / Raise your hands to rock / Fight for your rights. *(cd-iss.Jul86)*

Aug 85. (7")(12") **SMOKIN' IN THE BOYS ROOM. / USE IT OR LOSE IT** 71 16 Jul 85
(US-12") – ('A'side) / Helter skelter / Piece of your action / Live wire.

Oct 85. (7") **HOME SWEET HOME. / RED HOT** - 89

Jan 86. (7")(7"pic-d) **SMOKIN' IN THE BOYS ROOM. / HOME SWEET HOME** 51 -
(12"+=) – Shout at the Devil.

Jun 87. (lp)(c)(cd) **GIRLS, GIRLS, GIRLS** 14 2
– Wild side / Girls, girls, girls / Dancing on glass / Bad bad boogie / Nona / Five years dead / All in the name of . . . / Sumthin' for nuthin' / You're all I need / Jailhouse rock (live).

Jul 87. (7") **GIRLS, GIRLS, GIRLS. / SUMTHIN' FOR NUTHIN'** 26 12 May 87
(12"+=)(12"pic-d+=) – Smokin' in the boys room.

Nov 87. (7") **WILD SIDE. / FIVE YEARS DEAD** -

Jan 88. (7") **YOU'RE ALL I NEED. / ALL IN THE NAME OF ROCK** - 83

Jan 88. (7') **YOU'RE ALL I NEED. / WILD SIDE** 23 -
(12"+=)(12"pic-d+=) – Home sweet home / Looks that kill.

Jul 88. (m-lp)(c)(cd) **HOME SWEET HOME** (RAW TRACKS) -
– Live wire / Piece of your action / Too young to fall in love / Knock 'em dead, kid / Home sweet home.

Sep 89. (lp)(c)(cd) **DR. FEELGOOD** 4 1
– Same ol' situation (S.O.S.) / Slice of your pie / Rattlesnake shake / Kickstart my heart / Without you / Don't go away mad (just go away) / She goes down / Sticky sweet / Time for a change / T.N.T. (Terror 'n' Tinseltown) / Dr. Feelgood.

Oct 89. (7")(c-s)(7"pic-d) **DR. FEELGOOD. / STICKY SWEET** 50 6 Sep 89
(12")(3"cd-s) – ('A'extended) / All in the name of rock.

Dec 89. (7")(c-s) **KICKSTART MY HEART. / SHE GOES DOWN** - 27

Feb 90. (7") **WITHOUT YOU. / SLICE OF YOUR LIFE** - 8

Apr 90. (7")(c-s)(7"pic-d) **WITHOUT YOU. / LIVE WIRE** 39 -
(12"+=)(cd-s+=) – Girls, girls, girls / All in the name of rock.

May 90. (c-s)(cd-s) **DON'T GO AWAY MAD (JUST GO AWAY). / ?** - 19

Aug 90. (c-s)(cd-s) **SAME OL' SITUATION (S.O.S.). / ?** - 78

Aug 91. (7")(c-s) **PRIMAL SCREAM. / DANCING ON GLASS** 32 63
(12"+=)(cd-s+=) – Red hot (live) / Dr.Feelgood (live).

Oct 91. (cd)(c)(lp) **DECADE OF DECADENCE** (compilation) 20 2
– Live wire / Piece of your action / Shout at the Devil / Looks that kill / Home sweet home / Smokin' in the boys room / Girls, girls, girls / Wild side / Dr. Feelgood / Kickstart my heart / Teaser / Rock'n'roll junkie / Primal scream / Angela / Anarchy in the UK.

Dec 91. (7") **HOME SWEET HOME ('91 remix). / YOU'RE ALL I NEED** 37 37 Nov 91
(12"+=)(cd-s+=)(12"pic-d+=) – Without you / ('A'original mix).

— Had already split temporarily Apr'91 to do own projects. The group parted company with VINCE NEIL, who went solo early 1992.

— **JOHN CORABI** – vocals (ex-SCREAM) repl. VINCE

Mar 94. (7"yellow) **HOOLIGAN'S HOLIDAY. / HYPNOTISED (demo)** 36
(12"+=)(cd-s+=) – ('A'mixes).

Mar 94. (cd)(c)(d-lp) **MOTLEY CRUE** 17 7
– Power to the music / Uncle Jack / Hooligan's holiday / Misunderstood / Loveshine / Poison apples / Hammered / 'Til death us do part / Welcome to the numb / Smoke the sky / Droppin' like flies / Driftaway.

MOTORHEAD

Formed: London, England . . . Jun'75 by LEMMY who had just been sacked from HAWKWIND for spending 5 days in a Canadian jail, following his arrest for a drug offence. After toying with the idea of name BASTARD, he opted for MOTORHEAD, named after a recent song he wrote for HAWKWIND. He recruited LARRY WALLIS – guitar, vocals (of PINK FAIRIES) and LUCAS FOX – drums, but by early 1976, they had been deposed by 'FAST' EDDIE CLARKE and PHIL 'ANIMAL' TAYLOR. The initial line-up, had recorded album 'ON PAROLE' for 'United Art', but label shelved it until exploiting their success in 1979. More bad luck ensued, when late '76, new 'Stiff' records, also withdrew their debut 45 'WHITE LINE FEVER' & 'LEAVIN' HERE', and they too gave it light in 1979. In Apr'77, they found solace in Ted Carroll's 'Chiswick', who 2 months later released eponymous single and lp. The latter made the UK Top 50, and prompted major 'Bronze' records to give them contract the next year. After a minor hit with cover 'LOUIE LOUIE', they went Top 40 in 1979 with 'OVERKILL' 45 and album. They grew with every subsequent release, peaking in 1981 with the live No.1 'NO SLEEP TIL HAMMERSMITH'. • **Style:** Hard-drinking, leather-clad, speed-metal rock outfit, whose loudness was their forte. • **Songwriters:** LEMMY or group penned except covers; LOUIE LOUIE (Kingsmen) / TRAIN KEPT A-ROLLIN' (Yardbirds) / PLEASE DON'T TOUCH (Johnny Kidd) / (I'M YOUR) HOOCHIE COOCHIE MAN (Willie Dixon) / CAT SCRATCH FEVER (Ted Nugent). • **Trivia:** In 1987, LEMMY appeared in the Comic Strip movie 'Eat The Rich'.

Recommended: NO SLEEP TIL HAMMERSMITH (*8) / NO REMORSE (*8).

LEMMY (b.IAN KILMISTER, 24 Dec'45, Stoke-On-Trent, England) – vocals, bass (ex-HAWKWIND, ex-OPAL BUTTERFLY, ex-SAM GOPAL'S DREAM, ROCKIN' VICKERS) / **PHIL 'ANIMAL' TAYLOR** (b.21 Sep'54, Chesterfield, England) – drums / **FAST EDDIE CLARKE** – guitar, vocals (ex-BLUE GOOSE, ex-CURTIS KNIGHT & ZEUS) (below withdrawn)

Stiff not issued

Dec 76. (7") **WHITE LINE FEVER. / LEAVING HERE** - -
(withdrawn but iss.Dec78 in 'Stiff' box set Nos.1-10)

Chiswick not issued

Jun 77. (7") **MOTORHEAD. / CITY KIDS** -
(re-iss.1979 diff.colrd 7") (re-iss.Feb82 in diff.colrd pic-d)

Aug 77. (lp)(c) **MOTORHEAD** 43 -
– Motorhead / Vibrator / Lost Johnny / Iron Horse – Born to lose / White line fever / Keepers on the road / The Watcher / Born to lose / Train kept a-rollin'. *(re-white-lp 1978) (re-iss.Sep81 on red / clear, cd-iss.1987 on 'Big Beat')* (re-iss.Feb91 on 'Big Beat')

Bronze not issued

Sep 78. (7") **LOUIE LOUIE. / TEAR YA DOWN** 68 -
(re-iss.Dec82)

Feb 79. (7") **OVERKILL. / TOO LATE, TOO LATE** 39 -
(re-iss.Dec82)

Mar 79. (lp)(c)(green-lp) **OVERKILL** 24 -
– Overkill / Stay clean / Pay your price / I'll be your sister / Capricorn / No class / Damage case / Tear ya down / Metropolis / Limb for limb. *(cd-iss.Jul87 on 'Legacy') (re-iss.+cd.May90 on 'Fame') (re-iss.+cd.Feb91 on 'Castle')*

Jun 79. (7") **NO CLASS. / LIKE A NIGHTMARE** 61 -
(re-iss.Dec82)

Oct 79. (lp)(c)(blue-lp) **BOMBER** 12 -
– Dead men tell no tales / Lawman / Sweet revenge / Sharpshooter / Poison / Stone dead forever / All the aces / Step down / Talking head / Bomber. *(cd-iss.Jul87 on 'Legacy') (re-iss.+cd.Apr91 on 'Castle')*

Nov 79. (7")(7"pic-d) **BOMBER. / OVER THE TOP** 34 -

Apr 80. (7"ep)(12"ep) **THE GOLDEN YEARS (live)** 8 -
– Dead men don't tell tales / Too late, too late / Leaving here / Stone dead forever. *(re-iss.Dec82)*

Bronze Mercury

Oct 80. (7")(12") **ACE OF SPADES. / DIRTY LOVE** 15
(re-iss.Dec82)

Oct 80. (lp)(c)(gold-lp) **ACE OF SPADES** 4
– Ace of spades / Bite the bullet / The chase is better than the catch / Dance / Fast and loose / Fire fire / The hammer / Jailbait / Live to win / Love me like a reptile / (We are) The road crew / Shoot you in the back. *(re-iss.Mar85) (cd-iss.Aug87 on 'Legacy')*

Feb 81. (7"ep) **ST.VALENTINE'S DAY MASSACRE (as "HEADGIRL")** 5
– Please don't touch (by MOTORHEAD & GIRLSCHOOL) / Bomber (by GIRLSCHOOL) / Emergency (by MOTORHEAD).

Jun 81. (lp)(c)(gold-lp) **NO SLEEP TIL HAMMERSMITH (live)** 1
– Ace of spades / Stay clean / Metropolis / The hammer / Iron horse / No class / Overkill / (We are) The road crew / Capricorn / Bomber / Motorhead. *(cd-iss.Aug87 on 'Legacy') (re-iss.+cd.Feb90 on 'Castle')*

Jul 81. (7")(7"pic-d) **MOTORHEAD (live). / OVER THE TOP (live)** 6

— below, one-off (MOTORHEAD and The NOLANS)

Nov 81. (7") **DON'T DO THAT ("YOUNG AND MOODY BAND"). / HOW CAN I HELP YOU TONIGHT**

Mar 82. (7")(7"red)(7"blue) **IRON FIST. / REMEMBER ME I'M WRONG** 29

Apr 82. (lp)(c) **IRON FIST** 6
– Iron fist / Heart of stone / I'm the doctor / Go to Hell / Loser / Sex and outrage / America / Shut it down / Speed freak / (Don't let 'em) Grind ya down / (Don't need) Religion / Bang to rights. *(re-iss.Mar87 +cd.on 'Castle')*

Sep 82. (7"m) **STAND BY YOUR MAN. (by "LEMMY & WENDY" O'WILLIAMS) / NO CLASS (By "PLAS-MATICS") / MASTERPLAN (by "MOTORHEAD")** -

— **BRIAN ROBERTSON** (b. 2 Feb'56, Clarkston, Scotland) – guitar, vocals (ex-THIN LIZZY, ex-WILD HORSES) repl. CLARKE who formed FASTWAY

May 83. (7") **I GOT MINE. / TURN YOU AROUND AGAIN** 46
(12"+=) – Tales of glory.

May 83. (lp)(c) **ANOTHER PERFECT DAY** 20 -
– Back at the funny farm / Shine / Dancing on your grave / Rock it / One track mind / Another perfect day / Marching off to war / I got mine / Tales of glory / Die you bastard. *(re-iss.+cd.Feb91 on 'Castle')*

Jul 83. (7") **SHINE. / (I'M YOUR) HOOCHIE COOCHIE MAN (live)** 59 -
(12"+=) – (Don't need) Religion.

— LEMMY with **PHIL CAMPBELL** (b. 7 May'61, Pontypridd, Wales) – guitar / **WURZEL** (b.MICHAEL BURSTON, 27 Oct'49, Cheltenham, England) – guitar both replace ROBERTSON who joined FRANKIE MILLER BAND / **PETE GILL**

(b.9 Jun'51, Sheffield, England) – drums (ex-SAXON) repl. TAYLOR

Aug 84. (7")(7"sha-pic-d) **KILLED BY DEATH. / UNDER THE KNIFE** 51 -
(12"+=) – ('B'version).

Sep 84. (d-lp)(d-c) **NO REMORSE** (compilation) 14
– Ace of spades / Motorhead / Jailbait / Stay clean / Killed by death / Bomber / Iron fist / Shine / Dancing on your grave / Metropolis / Snaggletooth / Overkill / Please don't touch / Stone dead forever / Like a nightmare / Emergency / Steal your face / Louie Louie / No class / Iron horse / (We are) The road crew / Leaving here / Locomotive. *(cd-iss.Dec86 on 'Castle') (cd contains 4 new tracks)*

— (couldn't record for a couple of years)

G.W.R. | GWR-Profile

Jun 86. (7") **DEAF FOREVER. / ON THE ROAD** 67
(12"+=) – Steal your face.

Jul 86. (lp)(c)(cd) **ORGASMATRON** 21 Nov 86
– Deaf forever / Nothing up my sleeve / Claw / Mean machine / Ain't my crime / Built for speed / Riding with the driver / Doctor Rock / Orgasmatron. *(pic-lp.Aug89)*

— **PHILTHY ANIMAL** – drums returned to repl. GILL

Aug 87. (lp)(c)(cd) **ROCK'N'ROLL** 43 Oct 87
– Rock'n'roll / Eat the rich / Blackheart / Stone deaf in the U.S.A. / The wolf / Traitor / Dogs / All for you / Boogeyman.

Nov 87. (7") **EAT THE RICH. / CRADLE TO GRAVE**
(12"+=) – Power.

Oct 88. (lp)(c)(cd) **NO SLEEP AT ALL (live)** 79
– Doctor Rock / Stay clean / Traitor / Metropolis / Dogs / Ace of spades / Eat the rich / Built for speed / Deaf forever / Just cos you got the power / Killed by death / Overkill.

Epic | W.T.G.

Jan 91. (7")(c-s)(7"sha-pic-d) **THE ONE TO SING THE BLUES. / DEAD MAN'S HAND** 45
(12"+=)(cd-s+=) – Eagle rock / Shut you down.

Jan 91. (cd)(c)(lp)(pic-lp)(pic-cd) **1916** 24
– The one to sing the blues / I'm so bad (baby I don't care) / No voices in the sky / Going to Brazil / Nightmare / The dreamtime / Love me forever / Angel city / Make my day / Ramones / Shut you down / 1916.

Aug 92. (cd)(c)(lp) **MARCH OR DIE** 60
– Stand / Cat scratch fever / Bad religion / Jack the ripper / I ain't no nice guy / Hellraiser / Asylum choir / Too good to be true / You better run / Name in vain / March or die.

Nov 92. (7"ep)(c-ep)(cd-ep) **'92 TOUR (live)** 63
– Hellraiser / You better run / Going to Brazil / Ramones.

Above 1st track co-written w / OZZY OSBOURNE.

not issued | ZYX

Nov 93. (cd)(c) **BASTARDS** -

Arista | Arista

Nov 94. (7")(12")(c-s)(cd-s) by MOTORHEAD with ICE-T & WHITFIELD CRANE) **BORN TO RAISE HELL. / ('A'mixes)** 49

Plastic H. | Plastic H.

Apr 95. (cd)(c)(lp) **SACRIFICE** -

– compilations, others, etc. –

Oct 79. United Artists; (lp)(c) **ON PAROLE** 65
(was to be have been released Dec75) *(re-iss.May82 on 'Fame', cd-iss.1986)*

Nov 80. Big Beat; (7"ep)(12"blue-ep)(12"pink)(12"orange) **BEER DRINKERS EP** 43
– Beer drinkers and Hell raisers / On parole / Instro / I'm your witchdoctor.

Mar 83. Big Beat; (lp)(c) **WHAT'S WORDS WORTH (live at the Roundhouse 18/2/78)** 71 -
(re-iss.Jan90)

Aug 82. Bronze; (d-c) **OVERKILL. / BOMBER**

Nov 84. Astan; (lp)(c) **RECORDED LIVE (live)**

Apr 86. Raw Power; (lp)(c) **ANTHOLOGY**
(cd-iss.Dec86)

Apr 86. Dojo; (lp)(c) **BORN TO LOSE**

Apr 88. That's Original; (cd) **OVERKILL / ANOTHER PERFECT DAY**

1988. Castle; (3"cd-ep) **MOTORHEAD / ACE OF SPADES / BOMBER / OVERKILL** -

Apr 90. Castle; (cd)(d-lp) **WELCOME TO THE BEAR TRAP** -

Apr 90. Castle; (cd)(d-lp) **BOMBER / ACE OF SPADES** -

Nov 93. Castle; (cd)(c)(lp) **ALL THE ACES** -

Nov 89. Receiver; (lp)(cd) **BLITZKREIG ON BIRMINGHAM LIVE '77 (live)** -

Jan 90. Receiver; (cd)(c)(lp) **DIRTY LOVE** -

Jul 90. Receiver; (cd)(c)(lp) **LOCK UP YOUR DAUGHTERS (live 1977)** -

Feb 92. Receiver; (cd)(c)(lp) **LIVE JAILBAIT (live)** -

Jun 93. Receiver; (4xcd-box) **MOTORHEAD BOX SET** -

Jul 90. Action Replay; (cd)(c) **THE BEST OF MOTORHEAD** -
(re-iss.Jul93)

Jul 93. Action Replay; (cd)(c) **BEST OF THE REST** -

Nov 90. Musidisc; (cd)(c)(lp) **THE BIRTHDAY PARTY (live '85)** -
(cd has 3 extra tracks)

Nov 90. Knight; (cd)(c)(lp) **FROM THE VAULTS** -

Jul 91. Essential; (3xcd-box) **MELTDOWN** -

Sep 92. Roadrunner; (cd)(c)(lp) **THE BEST OF MOTORHEAD** -

Mar 94. Roadrunner; (cd) **LIVE AT BRIXTON ACADEMY (live)** -

Apr 93. Tring; (cd)(c) **LIVE (live)** -

Aug 93. W.G.A.F.; (12")(c-s)(cd-s) **ACE OF SPADES (THE C.C.N.remix). /** 23 -

Jul 94. Success; (cd)(c) **GRIND YA DOWN** -

Aug 94. Spectrum; (cd)(c) **ACES HIGH** -

Sep 94. Cleopatra; (cd) **IRON FIST AND THE HORDES FROM HELL** -

May 95. Spectrum; (cd) **ULTIMATE METAL** -

Jul 95. Emporio; (cd)(c) **THE BEST OF MOTORHEAD** -

Jul 95. Griffin; (box-cd) **FISTFUL OF ACES – THE BEST OF MOTORHEAD** -

MOTT THE HOOPLE

Formed: Herefordshire, England ... Jun'69 by WATTS, GRIFFIN, ALLEN and RALPHS, who were part of The SHAKEDOWN SOUND, with singer STAN TIPPINS. In '69, with new manager and producer Guy Stevens placing ad in music paper, they found new singer IAN HUNTER, who had guested on 45 by CHARLIE WOLFE. They named themselves MOTT THE HOOPLE (after a recent novel by Willard Manus), and soon signed to Chris Blackwell's 'Island'. Their eponymous debut, gained minor chart placing, as did their 2 follow-ups in the early 70's. In 1972, after a brief split, they transferred to 'CBS', where they immediately made impact with Top 3 single 'ALL THE YOUNG DUDES'. This was written by for them by DAVID BOWIE after he encouraged them to re-form. For the next 2 years, they enjoyed fruitful period that ended late '74, with the exit of IAN HUNTER and recent member MICK RONSON. Without them, the group MOTT carried on, but with little success. • **Style:** BOB DYLAN influenced rock'n'rollers, fronted by FREDDIE MERCURY's good friend IAN HUNTER. • **Songwriters:** HUNTER or others wrote most except; YOU REALLY GOT ME (Kinks) / LAUGH AT ME (Sonny Bono) / ? (Sir Douglas Quintet) / KEEP A KNOCKIN' (Little Richard) / WHOLE LOTTA SHAKIN' GOIN' ON (Jerry Lee Lewis) / etc.

Recommended: THE BALLAD OF MOTT THE HOOPLE – A RETROSPECTIVE (*8)

IAN HUNTER (b. 3 Jun'46, Shrewsbury, England) – vocals, guitar, piano / **MICK RALPHS** (b.31 May'44, Hereford, Wales) – guitar, vocals / **VERDEN ALLEN** (b.26 May'44, Hereford) – organ / **OVEREND WATTS** (b.13 May'49, Birmingham, England) – bass, vocals / **DALE 'BUFFIN' GRIFFIN** (b.24 Oct'48, Hereford) – drums, vocals

Island | Atlantic

Oct 69. (7") **ROCK AND ROLL QUEEN. / ROAD TO BIRMINGHAM**

Nov 69. (lp) **MOTT THE HOOPLE** 66
– You really got me / At the crossroads / Laugh at me / Backsliding fearlessly / Rock and roll queen / Rabbit foot and Toby time / Half Moon Bay / Wrath and wroll. *(re-iss.+c.1974)*

Jan 70. (7") **ROCK AND ROLL QUEEN. / BACKSLIDING FEARLESSLY** -

Sep 70. (lp) **MAD SHADOWS** 48
– Thunderbuck ram / No wheels to ride / You are one of us / Walkin' with a mountain / I can feel / Threads of iron / When my mind's gone. *(re-iss.+c.1974)*

Feb 71. (lp) **WILD LIFE** 44
– Whisky woman / Angel of 8th avenue / Wrong side of the river / Waterloo / Lay down / It must be love / Original mixed-up lad / Home is where I want to be / Keep a knockin'. *(re-iss.+c.1974)*

Sep 71. (lp) **BRAIN CAPERS**
– Death maybe your Santa Claus / Darkness darkness / Your own backyard / Journey / Sweet Angeline / Wheel of the quivering meat conception / Second love / Moon upstairs. *(re-iss.+c.1974)*

Oct 71. (7") **MIDNIGHT LADY. / THE DEBT**

Dec 71. (7") **DOWNTOWN. / HOME IS WHERE I WANT TO BE**

C.B.S. | Columbia

Jul 72. (7") **ALL THE YOUNG DUDES. / ONE OF THE BOYS** 3 37

Sep 72. (lp)(c) **ALL THE YOUNG DUDES** 21 89 Nov 72
– Sweet Jane / Momma's little jewel / All the young dudes / Sucker / Jerkin' crocus / One of the boys / Soft ground / Ready for love – After lights / Sea diver. *(re-iss.1974)*

Jan 73. (7") **ONE OF THE BOYS. / SUCKER** - 96

Mar 73. (7") **SWEET JANE. / JERKIN' CROCUS** -

— **MICK BOLTON** – keyboards filled in for departing VERDEN who went solo

May 73. (7") **HONALOOCHIE BOOGIE. / ROSE** | 12 | –
Jul 73. (lp)(c) **MOTT** | 7 | 35 Aug 73
– All the way from Memphis / Whizz kid / Hymn for the dudes / Honaloochie boogie / Violence / Drivin' sister / Ballad of Mott The Hoople (March 26, 1972 – Zurich) / I'm a Cadillac – El Camino Dolo Roso / I wish I was your mother. *(cd-iss.Mar95 on 'Rewind')*
Aug 73. (7") **ALL THE WAY FROM MEMPHIS. / BALLAD OF MOTT THE HOOPLE (MARCH 26, 1972 - ZURICH)** | 10 | -
Sep 73. (7") **ALL THE WAY FROM MEMPHIS. / I WISH I WAS YOUR MOTHER** | - |

— **ARIEL BENDER** (b.LUTHER GROSVENOR) – guitar (ex-SPOOKY TOOTH) replaced RALPHS who joined BAD COMPANY / **MORGAN FISHER** – keyboards (ex-LOVE AFFAIR) repl. BOLTON (above 2 with HUNTER, WATTS and GRIFFIN.)

Nov 73. (7") **ROLL AWAY THE STONE. / WHERE DO YOU ALL COME FROM** | 8 | -
Mar 74. (7") **THE GOLDEN AGE OF ROCK'N'ROLL. / REST IN PEACE** | 16 | 96 Feb 74
Mar 74. (lp)(c) **THE HOOPLE** | 11 | 28 Apr 74
– The golden age of rock'n'roll / Marionette / Alice / Crash Street kids / Born late '58 / Trudi's song / Pearl 'n' Roy (England) / Through the looking glass / Roll away the stone.
Apr 74. (7") **ROLL AWAY THE STONE. / THROUGH THE LOOKING GLASS** | - |
Jun 74. (7") **FOXY FOXY. / TRUDI'S SONG** | 33 | -

— **BLUE WEAVER** – organ on tour (ex-AMEN CORNER)

Nov 74. (lp)(c) **LIVE** (live; Broadway-Nov73 / Hammersmith-May74) | 32 | 23
– All the way from Memphis / Sucker / Rest in peace / All the young dudes / Walkin' with a mountain / Sweet Angeline / Rose / Medley; (a) Jerkin' crokus – (b) One of the boys – (c) Rock and roll queen – (d) Get back – (e) Whole lotta shakin' goin' on – (f) Violence.

— **MICK RONSON** – guitar, vocals (Solo artist, ex-DAVID BOWIE; SPIDERS FROM MARS) repl. ARIEL who formed WIDOWMAKER

Oct 74. (7") **SATURDAY GIGS. / MEDLEY; JERKIN' CROCUS – SUCKER (live)** | 41 | -
Dec 74. (7") **ALL THE YOUNG DUDES (live). / ROSE** | - |

— Split Dec74. HUNTER and RONSON formed duo and went solo.

MOTT

(OVEREND, DALE and **MORGAN**) were joined by **NIGEL BENJAMIN** – vocals (ex-ROYCE) / **RAY MAJORS** – guitar (ex-HACKENSHACK)

C.B.S. | Columbia

Aug 75. (7") **MONTE CARLO. / SHOUT IT ALL OUT** | |
Sep 75. (lp)(c) **DRIVE ON** | 45 |
– By tonight / Monte Carlo / She does it / I'll tell you something / Stiff upper lip / Love now / Apologies / The great white wall / Here we are / It takes one to know one / I can show you how it is.
Oct 75. (7") **BY TONIGHT. / I CAN SHOW YOU HOW IT IS** | |
Feb 76. (7") **IT TAKES ONE TO KNOW ONE. / I'LL TELL YOU SOMETHING** | |
Jun 76. (lp)(c) **SHOUTING AND POINTING** | |
– Shouting and pointing / Collision course / Storm / Career (no such thing as rock'n'roll) / Hold on, you're crazy / See you again / Too short arms (I don't care) / Broadside outcasts / Good times.

– compilations, etc. –

Oct 72. Island/ US= Atlantic; (lp)(c) **ROCK'N'ROLL QUEEN** | | Jul 74
1980. Island; (lp)(c) **TWO MILES FROM HEAVEN** | | -
Jun 90. Island; (cd) **WALKING WITH A MOUNTAIN (BEST OF 1969-1972)** | |
– Rock'n'roll queen / At the crossroads / Thunderbuck ram / Whiskey woman / Waterflow / The Moon upstairs / Second love / The road to Birmingham / Black scorpio (mama's little jewel) / You really got me / Walking with a mountain / No wheels to ride / Keep a knockin' / Midnight lady / Death may be your Santa Claus / Darkness darkness / Growing man blues / Black hills.
Mar 76. CBS/ US= Columbia; (lp)(c) **GREATEST HITS** | |
– All the way from Memphis / Honaloochie boogie / Hymn for the dudes / Born late '58 / All the young dudes / Roll away the stone / Ballad of Mott The Hoople / Golden age of rock'n'roll / Foxy lady / Saturday gigs. *(re-iss.Jun81) (cd-iss.1989)*
Jul 84. CBS; (7") **ALL THE YOUNG DUDES. / HONALOOCHIE BOOGIE** | |
Jun 92. Columbia; (7")(c-s) **ALL THE YOUNG DUDES. / ONCE BITTEN TWICE SHY (IAN HUNTER)** | |
(cd-s+=) – Roll Away The Stone
Mar 81. Hallmark; (lp)(c) **ALL THE WAY FROM MEMPHIS** | |
Apr 83. Old Gold; (7") **ALL THE YOUNG DUDES. / ROLL AWAY THE STONE** | | -
1988. Castle; (d-lp)(c)(cd) **THE COLLECTION** | | -
Jun 93. See For Miles; (cd) **MOTT THE HOOPLE FEATURING STEVE HYAMS** | | -
Nov 93. Legacy; (d-cd) **THE BALLAD OF MOTT THE HOOPLE – A RETROSPECTIVE** | | -

— In Feb80, MOTT THE HOOPLE tracks were included on album SHADES OF IAN HUNTER – THE BALLAD OF IAN HUNTER & MOTT THE HOOPLE

BRITISH LIONS

MOTT + **JOHN FIDDLER** – vocals (ex-MEDICINE HEAD) repl. NIGEL who joined ENGLISH ASSASSINS

Vertigo | not issued

Feb 78. (7") **ONE MORE CHANCE TO RUN. / BOOSTER** | | -
Feb 78. (lp)(c) **BRITISH LIONS** | | -
– Big drift away / Booster / Break this fool / Eat the rich / Fork talking man / International heroes / My life in your hands / One more chance to run / Wild in the street.
Apr 78. (7") **INTERNATIONAL HEROES. / EAT THE RICH** | | -

Cherry Red | not issued

May 80. (lp) **TROUBLE WITH WOMEN** | | -
– Trouble with women / Any port in a storm / Lady don't fall backwards / High noon / Lay down your love / Waves of love / Electric chair / Won't you give him up.

— When they split MORGAN FISHER went solo. GRIFFIN and WATTS went into production incl. HANOI ROCKS.

MORGAN FISHER

solo.

Cherry Red | not issued

Sep 79. (7"ep) **GENEVE / ROLL AWAY THE STONE '78. / SLEEPER / LYDIA'S THEME** | | -

Bob MOULD (see under ⇒ HUSKER DU)

MR.BUNGLE (see under ⇒ FAITH NO MORE)

M.S.G. (see under ⇒ SCHENKER GROUP, Michael)

MUDHONEY

Formed: Seattle, USA . . . 1988 by ex-GREEN RIVER members MARK ARM and STEVE TURNER. They were soon joined by MATT LUKIN (ex-MELVINS) and DAN PETERS (ex-BUNDLES OF PISS). Signed to Bruce Pavitt's 'Sub Pop' label and issued UK debut 'TOUCH ME, I'M SICK' (later covered by SONIC YOUTH). Debut album 'SUPERFUZZ BIGMUFF' (named after TURNER's favourite effects pedals), failed to impress many, although success found them in 1991 with 'EVERY GOOD BOY DESERVES FUDGE'. The following year, they moved to 'Warners' and enjoyed another album UK chart entry with 'PIECE OF CAKE'. • **Style:** Garageland fuzz/thrash outfit, hot on the heels of The STOOGES, SONIC YOUTH or The HEARTBREAKERS. • **Songwriters:** ARM-TURNER? except; HATE THE POLICE (Dicks) / EVOLUTION (Spacemen 3) / OVER THE TOP (Motorhead) / PUMP IT UP (Elvis Costello). MARK ARM solo:- MASTERS OF WAR (Bob Dylan).

Recommended: EVERY GOOD BOY DESERVES FUDGE (*7).

MARK ARM – vocals, guitar / **STEVE TURNER** – guitar (both ex-GREEN RIVER) / **MATT LUKIN** – bass (ex-MELVINS) / **DAN PETERS** – drums

Glitterhouse | Sub Pop

Aug 88. (7")(7"brown) **TOUCH ME I'M SICK. / SWEET YOUNG THING AIN'T SWEET NO MORE** | |
Oct 88. (12"ep) **SUPERFUZZ BIGMUFF** | |
– No one has / If I think / In 'n' out of grace / Need / Chain that door / Mudride. *(re-iss.+cd-ep.Apr89)*
Jan 89. (7")(7"clear) **('A'side by 'Sonic Youth'). / TOUCH ME I'M SICK** | |
Jun 89. (7")(7"white)(12") **YOU GOT IT (KEEP IT OUTTA MY FACE). / BURN IT CLEAN / NEED (demo)** | |
(re-iss.May93)
Oct 89. (7")(7"purple)(12") **THIS GIFT. / BABY HELP ME FORGET / REVOLUTION** | |
(re-iss.May93)
Oct 89 (m-lp)(c)(cd) **MUDHONEY** | |
– This gift / Flat out f***ed / Get into yours / You got it / Magnolia caboose babyshit / Come to mind / Here comes sickness / Running loaded / The further I go / By her own hand / When tomorrow hits / Dead love.

Jun 90. (7")(7"pink) **YOU'RE GONE. / THORN / YOU MAKE ME DIE** [60] [ ]
(re-iss.Jun93)

Sub Pop — Sub Pop

Jul 91. (7")(12"grey) **LET IT SLIDE. / OUNCE OF DECEPTION / CHECKOUT TIME** [60] [ ]
(cd-s+=) – Paperback life / The money will roll right in.

Aug 91. (cd)(c)(lp) **EVERY GOOD BOY DESERVES FUDGE** [34] [ ]
– Generation genocide / Let it slide / Good enough / Something so clear / Thorn / Into the drink / Broken hands / Who you drivin' now / Move out / Shoot the Moon / Fuzzgun '91 / Poking around / Don't fade IV / Check out time.

— MARK + STEVE took up time in MONKEYWRENCH, and DAN joined SCREAMING TREES, after below album.

Warners — Reprise

Oct 92. (7")(c-s) **SUCK YOU DRY. / DECEPTION PASS** [65] [ ]
(12"+=)(cd-s+=) – Underride / Over the top.

Oct 92. (cd)(c)(lp) **PIECE OF CAKE** [39] [ ]
– No end in sight / Make it now / Suck you dry / Blinding Sun / Thirteenth floor opening / Youth body expression explosion / I'm spun / Take me there / Living wreck / Let me let you down / Ritzville / Acetone.

Oct 93. (cd)(c)(m-lp) **FIVE DOLLAR BOB'S MOCK COOTER STEW** [ ] [ ]
– In the blood / No song III / Between you and me kid / Six two one / Make it now again / Deception pass / Underide.

— In Apr'94, they released with JIMMIE DALE GILMOUR a 7"yellow and cd-s 'TONIGHT' for 'Sub Pop'.

Reprise — Reprise

Mar 95. (cd)(c)(lp) **MY BROTHER THE COW** [70] [ ]
– Judgement, rage, retribution and thyme / Generation spokesmodel / What moves the heart? / Today, is a good day / Into yer schtik / In my finest suit / F.D.K. (Fearless Doctor KIllers) / Orange ball-pen hammer / Crankcase blues / Execution style / Dissolve / 1995.

Apr 95. (7") **INTO YOUR SCHTIK. / YOU GIVE ME THE CREEPS** [ ] [ ]

— above single on 'Super Electro'

May 95. (7"colrd)(c-s) **GENERATION SPOKESMODEL. / NOT GOING DOWN THAT ROAD AGAIN** [ ] [ ]
(cd-s+=) – What moves the heart live) / Judgement, rage, retribution and thyme (live).

Amphetami. — Amphetami.

Aug 95. (7") **GOAT CHEESE. /** [ ] [ ]

– compilations, etc. –

Nov 89. Tupelo; (12"ep)(cd-ep) **BOILED BEEF AND ROTTING TEETH** [ ] [ ]

THE FREEWHEELIN' MARK ARM

Sub Pop — Sub Pop

Feb 91. (7")(7"red)(7"green) **MASTERS OF WAR. / MY LIFE WITH RICKETS** [ ] [ ] Dec 90

MONKEYWRENCH

— **MARK ARM / STEVE TURNER / TOM PRICE / TIM KERR / MARTIN BLAND**

Sub Pop — Sub Pop

1992. (7") **BOTTLE UP AND GO /** [ ] [ ]

Peter MURPHY (see under ⇒ BAUHAUS)

MY BLOODY VALENTINE

Formed: Dublin, Ireland ... 1984 by KEVIN SHIELDS and COLM CUSACK. Late that year, they went to Germany and recorded mini-lp 'THIS IS YOUR BLOODY VALENTINE', for small 'Tycoon' records. It was issued the next year, but only 50 copies seemed to emerge, which are now very rare. They moved to London and soon issued 'GEEK!' EP for 'Fever'. After more 45's for 'Kaleidoscope' then 'Lazy' (home of The PRIMITIVES), they were transferred to 'Creation' in 1988 by SLAUGHTER JOE FOSTER (ex-TV PERSONALITIES). They finally made the breakthrough in 1990, when the 'GLIDER' EP, nearly went Top 40 UK. • **Style:** Twangly fuzzy IGGYPOP-like beginnings, progressed into dreamy psychedelia and uncompromising rock, with a new complete concept and landscape of sound. • **Songwriters:** SHIELDS writes most of material, with words after 1987 by BILINDA. • **Trivia:** A track 'SUGAR' was given away free with 'The Catalogue' magazine of Feb '89.

Recommended: LOVELESS (*8) / ISN'T ANYTHING (*8) / ECSTASY AND WINE (*7).

KEVIN SHIELDS – guitar, vocals, occasional bass / **DAVE CONWAY** – vocals / **COLM CUSACK** (b. O'COISDIG) – drums / **TINA** – keyboards

Tycoon — not issued

1985. (m-lp) **THIS IS YOUR BLOODY VALENTINE** [-] [-] GERM
– Forever and again / Homelovin' guy / Don't cramp my style / Tiger in my tank / The love gang / Inferno / The last supper.

— **DEBBIE GOOGE** – bass repl. TINA

Fever — not issued

Apr 86. (12"ep) **GEEK!** [ ] [-]
– No place to go / Moonlight / Love machine / The sandman never sleeps.

Jun 86. (7") **NO PLACE TO GO. / MOONLIGHT** [ ] [-]

Kaleidoscope — not issued

Oct 86. (12"ep) **THE NEW RECORD BY MY BLOODY VALENTINE** [ ] [-]
– Lovelee sweet darlene / By the danger in your eyes / We're so beautiful / On another rainy Sunday.

Lazy — not issued

Feb 87. (7") **SUNNY SUNDAE SMILE. / PAINT A RAINBOW** [ ] [-]
(12"+=) – Kiss the eclipse / Sylvie's head.

— **BILINDA BUTCHER** – vocals, guitar repl. CONWAY

Nov 87. (m-lp) **ECSTASY** [ ] [-]
– (Please) Lose yourself in me / The things I miss / I don't need you / Clair / (You're) Safe in your sleep / She loves you no less / Strawberry wine / Lovelee sweet darlene.

Nov 87. (12") **STRAWBERRY WINE. / NEVER SAY GOODBYE / CAN I TOUCH YOU** [ ] [-]

Creation — not issued

Jul 88. (7") **YOU MADE ME REALISE. / SLOW** [ ] [-]
(12"+=) – Thorn / Cigarette in your bed / Drive it all over me. *(above 12" tracks re-iss.Mar90 as cd-ep)*

Oct 88. (7") **FEED ME WITH YOUR KISSES. / EMPTINESS INSIDE** [ ] [-]
(12"+=) – I believe / I need no trust. *(re-iss.Mar90 as cd-ep)*

Nov 88. (lp)(c)(cd) **ISN'T ANYTHING** [ ] [-]
– Soft as snow (but warm inside) / Lose my breath / Cupid come / (When you wake) You're still in a dream / No more sorry / All I need / Feed me with your kiss / Sue is fine / Several girls galore / You never should / Nothing much to lose / I can see it (but I can't feel it). *(free 7"w.a.)* – INSTRUMENTAL. / INSTRUMENTAL

Apr 90. (7"ep)(12"ep)(cd-ep) **GLIDER** [41] [-]
– Soon / Glider / Don't ask why / Off your face.

Feb 91. (7"ep)(12"ep)(cd-ep) **TREMOLO** [29] [ ]
– To here knows when / Swallow / Honey power / Moon song.

Apr 91. (cd)(c)(lp) **LOVELESS** [24] [ ]
– Only shallow / Loomer / Touched / To here knows when / When you sleep / I only said / Come in alone / Sometimes / Blown a wish / What you want / Soon.

Signed to 'Island' records in Oct'92.

– compilations, others, etc. –

Feb 89. Lazy; (lp)(c)(cd) **ECSTASY AND WINE** [ ] [-]
– Strawberry wine / Never say goodbye / Can I touch you / She loves you no less / The things I miss / I don't need you / Safe in your sleep / Clair / You've got nothing / Lose yourself in me.

. . . Jan – Jun '96 stop press . . .

— An album is finally due for 'Island' at the end of '96. Meanwhile they have recorded 'MAP REF 41 . . .' for a WIRE tribute album.

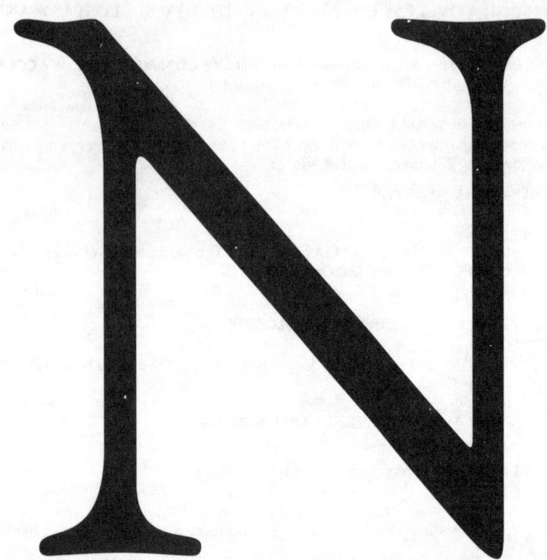

NAILBOMB (see under ⇒ SEPULTURA)

NAPALM DEATH

Formed: Ipswich, England . . . 1982 by DORRIAN and STEER. Finally made it onto vinyl (after a few John Peel sessions), on their own 'Earache' label. In 1987, they unveiled 'SCUM', a 27-track lp of song spurts. Were making headway into UK brains, when they split with surviving originals, and brought in some easier going Americans. • **Style:** Innovators of hardcore grindcrushing rock. A hybrid of death speed-metal and greasy haired punk. Their short abrupt ditties, were carcassed with inaudible vox, which virtually brain-washed their lemmingmania audience. In the 90's with changed line-up, they opted for a more longer-tuned heavy-metal song. • **Songwriters:** All written by DORRIAN (lyrics) and STEER (music!!), until their departure. • **Trivia:** Recorded the shortest track ever (1 second), for a free 7", given away with an 'Earache' sampler 'Grindcrusher'. SHANE EMBURY exchanged death threats with another teeth-grinding outfit SORE THROAT (mainly band member RICH MILITIA).

Recommended: DEATH BY MANIPULATION (*7)

LEE DORRIAN – vocals (also runs own label 'Rise Above') / **BILL STEER** – guitar (also of CARCASS) / **SHANE EMBURY** – bass (also drummer of UNSEEN TERROR) / **MICK HARRIS** – drums (also vocals of EXTREME NOISE TERROR) repl. FRANK HEALEY (other early drummer JUS of HEAD OF DAVID)

Earache | not issued

Jul 87. (lp) **SCUM** [ ] [-]
– Multinational corporations / Instinct of survival / The kill / Scum / Caught in a dream / Polluted minds / Sacrificied / Stage of power / Control / Born on your knees / Human garbage / You suffer / Life? / Prison without walls / Negative approach / Success? / Deceiver / C.S. / Parasites / Pseudo youth / Divine death / As the machine rolls on / Common enemy / Moral crusade / Stigmatized / M.A.D. / Dragnet. *(c-iss.May89) (re-iss.cd Sep94)*

Nov 88. (lp)(c)(cd) **FROM ENSLAVEMENT TO OBLITERATION** [ ] [-]
– Evolved as one / It's a man's world / Lueid fairytale / Private death / Impressions / Unchallenged hate / Uncertainty blurs the vision / Cock rock alienation / Retreat to nowhere / Think for a minute / Display to me . . . / From enslavement to obliteration / Blind to the truth / Social sterility / Emotional suffocation / Practise what you preach / Inconceivable / Worlds apart / Obstinate direction / Mentally murdered / Sometimes / Make way. *(pic-lp iss.Jul90) (re-iss.cd Sep94)*

Aug 89. (7") **MENTALLY MURDERED. / CAUSE AND EFFECT** [ ] [-]
(12"ep) **MENTALLY MURDERED EP** (+=) – Rise above / Missing link – Mentally murdered / Walls of confinement / Cause and effect – No manual effort.

— (Aug89) **MARK 'Barney' GREENWAY** – vocals (ex-BENEDICTION) repl. LEE (LEE was to join CATHEDRAL, another 'Earache' band) **MITCH HARRIS** (b.Las Vegas, USA) + **JESSE PINTADO** (b.Mexico) – guitars repl. BILL who went full-time with CARCASS)

Aug 90. (7") **SUFFER THE CHILDREN. / SIEGE OF POWER** [ ] [-]
(12"+=) – Harmony corruption.

Sep 90. (cd)(c)(lp) **HARMONY CORRUPTION** [67] [-]
– Vision conquest / If the truth be known / Inner incineration / Malicious intent / Unfit Earth / Circle of hypocrisy / Suffer the children / The chains that bind us / Mind snare / Extremity retained. (some w/free 12") *(re-iss.cd Sep94)*

May 91. (7") **MASS APPEAL MADNESS. / PRIDE ASSASSIN** [ ] [-]
(12"+=) – Unchallenged hate / Social sterility.

— MICK HARRIS was arrested for jewel shop robbery & he left to join SCORN. He was soon replaced by **DANNY HERARRA** – drums

May 92. (cd)(c)(lp) **UTOPIA BANISHED** [58] [-]
– Discordance / I abstain / Dementia access / Christening of the blind / The world keeps turning / Idiosyncratic / Arayanisus / Cause and effect / Judicial slime / Distorting the medium / Got time to kill / Upward and Uninterested / Exile / Awake (to a life of misery) / Contemptious. (free 4 track 7"ep). *(re-iss.cd Sep94)*

Jun 92. (12"ep)(cd-ep) **THE WORLD KEEPS TURNING. / A MEANS TO AN END / INSANITY EXCURSION** [ ] [-]

Jul 93. (7")(cd-s) **NAZI PUNKS FUCK OFF. / ARYANISMS / ('A' version) / CONTEMPTUOUS (xtreem mix)** [ ] [-]

(above a cover of a DEAD KENNEDYS single)

May 94. (cd)(c)(lp) **FEAR, EMPTINESS, DESPAIR** [ ] [-]
– Twist the knife (slowly) / Hung / Remain nameless / Plague rages / More than meets the eye / Primed time / State of mind / Armageddon X7 / Retching on the dirt / Fasting on deception / Throwaway.

Nov 95. (m-cd)(m-c)(10"m-lp) **GREED KILLING** [ ] [-]
– Greed killing / My own worst enemy / Self betrayal / Finer truths, white lies / Antibody / All links severed / Plague rages (live).

. . . Jan – Jun '96 stop press . . .

Jan 96. (cd)(c)(10"d-lp) **DIATRIBES** [73] [ ]

– compilations, others, etc. –

May 88. Strange Fruit; (12"ep) **THE PEEL SESSIONS** (13.9.87) [ ] [-]
– The kill / Prison without walls / Dead part one / Deceiver / Lucid fairytale / In extremis / Blind to the trash / Negative approach / Common enemy / Obstinate direction / Life? / You suffer (Part 2). *(re-iss.as d12"/c-ep/cd-ep.May89, cont. += Mar88 sessions)*

Feb 92. Earache; (cd)(lp) **DEATH BY MANIPULATION** [ ] [-]
(free cd-ep) *(re-iss.Oct92) (re-iss.cd Sep94)*

Graham NASH (see under ⇒ CROSBY, STILLS, NASH & YOUNG)

NAZARETH

Formed: Dunfermline, Scotland . . . 1969 by McCAFFERTY, AGNEW and SWEET. For a number of years they had toured Scotland as The SHADETTES, until the addition of CHARLTON in '69. In 1971, they turned pro and moved to London, where they gained deal with 'Pegasus'. After 2 albums in the early 70's, they careered into the UK Top 10 in 1973 with single 'BROKEN DOWN ANGEL'. For the next 2 years, they enjoyed fruitful period, helped by the services of producer ROGER GLOVER (ex-DEEP PURPLE). • **Style:** No frills, hard-rock outfit, fronted by mean-looking screecher McCAFFERTY. • **Songwriters:** Group penned, except SHAPES OF THINGS (Yardbirds) / DOWN HOME GIRL (Leiber-Stoller) / I WANT TO DO EVERYTHING FOR YOU (Joe Tex) / THIS FLIGHT TONIGHT (Joni Mitchell) / TEENAGE NERVOUS BREAKDOWN (Little Feat) / THE BALLAD OF HOLLIS BROWN (Bob Dylan) / MY WHITE BICYCLE (Tomorrow) / YOU'RE THE VIOLIN (Golden Earring) / WILD HONEY (Beach Boys) / SO YOU WANT TO BE A ROCK'N'ROLL STAR (Byrds) / I DON'T WANT TO GO ON WITHOUT YOU (Berns/Wexler) / LOVE HURTS (Boudleaux Bryant) / etc. DAN McCAFFERTY solo covered OUT OF TIME (Rolling Stones) / WHATCHA GONNA DO ABOUT IT (Small Faces) / etc. • **Trivia:** Also internationally known, especially in Canada and mosts parts of Europe.

Recommended: THE SINGLES COLLECTION (*8)

DAN McCAFFERTY – vocals / **MANNY CHARLTON** – guitar, vocals / **PETE AGNEW** (b.14 Sep'48) – bass / **DARRYL SWEET** – drums, percussion

Pegasus | Warners

Nov 71. (lp) **NAZARETH** [ ] [ ] Feb 73
– Witchdoctor woman / Dear John / Empty arms, empty heart / If I had a dream / Red light lady / Fat man / Country girl / Morning dew / King is dead. *(re-iss.Apr 74 on 'Mooncrest') (re-iss.Nov 75 on 'Mountain')*

Jan 72. (7") **DEAR JOHN. / FRIENDS** [ ] [-]

Jul 72. (7") **MORNING DEW. / SPINNING TOP** [ ] [-]

Jul 72. (7") **MORNING DEW. / DEAR JOHN** [-] [ ]

Jul 72. (lp) **EXERCISES** [ ] [ ] Nov 72
– Fool about you / Love now you're gone / Madelaine / Sad song / 1692 (Glencoe massacre) / I will not be led / Cat's eye, apple pie / In my time / Woke up this morning / Called her name. *(re-iss. Apr 74 on 'Mooncrest') (re-iss. Nov 75+ Apr 80 on 'Mountain') (re-iss.May85 on 'Sahara') (cd-iss.Feb91 on 'Castle')*

Sep 72. (7") **IF YOU SEE MY BABY. / HARD LIVING** [ ] [-]

Mooncrest A & M

Apr 73. (7") **BROKEN DOWN ANGEL. / WITCHDOCTOR WOMAN** [9] [-]

May 73. (lp)(c) **RAZAMANAZ** [11] [ ]
– Razamanaz / Alcatraz / Vigilante man / Woke up this morning / Night woman / Bad, bad boy / Sold my soul / Too bad, too sad / Broken down angel. *(re-iss. Nov75 + Apr80 on 'Mountain') (re-iss.Oct82 on 'NEMS') (re-iss.+cd.Dec89 on 'Castle')*

Jul 73. (7"m) **BAD, BAD BOY. / HARD LIVING / SPINNING TOP** [10] [-]

Sep 73. (7") **BROKEN DOWN ANGEL. / HARD LIVING** [-] [ ]

Oct 73. (7") **THIS FLIGHT TONIGHT. / CALLED HER NAME** [11] [-]

Nov 73. (lp)(c) **LOUD 'N' PROUD** [10] [ ]
– Go down fighting / Not faking it / Turn on your receiver / Teenage nervous breakdown / Freewheeler / This flight tonight / Child in the sun / The ballad of Hollis Brown. *(re-iss. Nov75 & Apr80 on 'Mountain') (re-iss.May85 on 'Sahara') (re-iss.+cd.Dec89 on 'Castle')*

Nov 73. (7") **BAD BAD BOY. / RAZAMANAZ** [-] [ ]

Feb 74. (7") **THIS FLIGHT TONIGHT. / GO DOWN FIGHTING** [-] [ ]

Mar 74. (7") **SHANGHAI'D IN SHANGHAI. / LOVE, NOW YOU'RE GONE** [41] [ ]

May 74. (lp)(c) **RAMPANT** [13] [ ]
– Silver dollar forger (parts 1 & 2) / Glad when you're gone / Loved and lost / Shanghai'd in Shanghai / Jet lag / Light my way / Sunshine / a) Shapes of things – b) Space safari. *(re-iss. Nov75+Apr80 on 'Mountain')*

Jul 74. (7") **SUNSHINE. / THIS FLIGHT TONIGHT** [-] [ ]

Nov 74. (7") **LOVE HURTS. / DOWN** [ ] [8] Nov 75

Mar 75. (7") **HAIR OF THE DOG. / TOO BAD, TOO SAD** [ ] [-]

Apr 75. (lp)(c) **HAIR OF THE DOG** [ ] [17]
– Hair of the dog / Miss Misery / Guilty * / Changin' times / Beggars day / Rose in the heather / Whiskey drinkin' woman / Please don't Judas me. *(In the US, track* repl. by 'Love hurts') (re-iss.Nov75 + Apr80 on 'Mountain') (re-iss.Oct82 on 'NEMS') (re-iss.May85 on 'Sahara')*

May 75. (7") **HAIR OF THE DOG. / LOVE HURTS** [-] [ ]

May 75. (7") **MY WHITE BICYCLE. / MISS MISERY** [14] [ ]

Mountain A & M

Oct 75. (7") **HOLY ROLLER. / RAILROAD BOY** [36] [-]

Nov 75. (lp)(c) **GREATEST HITS** (compilation) [54] [ ]
– Razamanaz / Holy roller / Shanghai'd in Shanghai / Love hurts / Turn on your receiver / Bad bad boy / This flight tonight / Broken down angel / Hair of the dog / Sunshine / My white bicycle / Woke up this morning *(re-iss.Apr80) (re-iss.Oct82 on 'NEMS') (re-iss.+cd. Apr89 on 'Castle')*

Feb 76. (7") **CARRY OUT FEELINGS. / LIFT THE LID** [ ] [ ]

Mar 76. (lp)(c) **CLOSE ENOUGH FOR ROCK'N'ROLL** [ ] [24]
– Telegram (part 1:- On your way / part 2:- So you want to be a rock'n'roll star / part 3:- Sound check / part 4:- Here we are again) / Vicki / Homesick again / Vancouver shakedown / Born under the wrong sign / Loretta / Carry out feelings / Lift the lid / You're the violin. *(re-iss.Apr80) (re-iss.May85 on 'Sierra') (cd-iss.Feb91 on 'Castle')*

Jun 76. (7") **YOU'RE THE VIOLIN. / LORETTA** [ ] [-]

Sep 76. (7") **LIFT THE LID. / LORETTA** [-] [ ]

Nov 76. (7") **I DON'T WANT TO GO ON WITHOUT YOU. / GOOD LOVE** [ ] [-]

Nov 76. (lp)(c) **PLAY 'N' THE GAME** [ ] [75]
– Somebody to roll / Down home girl / Flying / Waiting for the man / Born to love / I want to (do everything for you) / I don't want to go on without you / Wild honey / L.A. girls. *(cd-iss.Feb91 on 'Castle')*

Dec 76. (7") **I WANT TO (DO EVERYTHING FOR YOU). / BLACK CATS** [-] [ ]

Jan 77. (7") **SOMEBODY TO ROLL. / VANCOUVER SHAKEDOWN** [ ] [ ]

Feb 77. (7") **I DON'T WANT TO GO ON WITHOUT YOU. / I WANT TO DO (EVERYTHING FOR YOU)** [-] [ ]

Apr 77. (7") **SOMEBODY TO ROLL. / THIS FLIGHT TONIGHT** [-] [ ]

Jun 77. (lp)(c) **HOT TRACKS** (compilation) [-] [ ]

Sep 77. (7"ep) **HOT TRACKS** (compilation) [15] [ ]
– Love hurts / This flight tonight / Broken down angel / Hair of the dog. *(re-iss.1983 on pic-ep 'NEMS')*

Nov 77. (lp)(c) **EXPECT NO MERCY** [ ] [82]
– Expect no mercy / Gone dead train / Shot me down / Revenge is sweet / Gimme what's mine / Kentucky fried blues / New York broken toy / Busted / A place in your heart / All the king's horses. *(re-iss.May85 on 'Sierra')(cd-iss.Sep93 on 'Elite') (re-iss+cd. Jun 90 on 'Castle')*

Jan 78. (7"m) **GONE DEAD TRAIN. / GREENS / DESOLATION ROAD** [49] [-]

Apr 78. (7") **A PLACE IN YOUR HEART. / KENTUCKY FRIED BLUES** [70] [ ]

Apr 78. (7") **SHOT ME DOWN. / KENTUCKY FRIED BLUES** [-] [ ]

Jul 78. (7") **GONE DEAD TRAIN. / KENTUCKY FRIED BLUES** [-] [ ]

— added **ZAL CLEMINSON** – guitar, synth. (ex-SENSATIONAL ALEX HARVEY BAND)

Jan 79. (7") **MAY THE SUN SHINE. / EXPECT NO MERCY** [22] [ ]

Jan 79. (lp)(c) **NO MEAN CITY** [34] [88]
– Just to get into it / May the sun shine / Simple solution / Star / Claim to fame / Whatever you want babe / May the Sun shine / What's in it for me / No mean city. *(re-iss.May85 on 'Sahara') (re-iss. +cd May 91 on 'Castle')*

Apr 79. (7")(7"purple) **WHATEVER YOU WANT BABE. / TELEGRAM (PARTS 1, 2 & 3)** [ ] [ ]

Jul 79. (7") **STAR. / EXPECT NO MERCY** [-] [ ]

Jul 79. (7") **STAR. / BORN TO LOVE** [54] [-]

Jan 80. (7") **HOLIDAY. / SHIP OF DREAMS** [ ] [87]

Jan 80. (lp)(c) **MALICE IN WONDERLAND** [ ] [41]
– Holiday / Showdown at the border / Talkin' to one of the boys / Heart's grown cold / Fast cars / Big boy / Talkin' 'bout love / Fallen angel / Ship of dreams / Turning a new leaf. *(cd-iss.Feb91 on 'Castle')*

Apr 80. (7") **SHIP OF DREAMS. / HEARTS GROWN COLD** [-] [ ]

NEMS A & M

Dec 80. (d7") **NAZARETH LIVE (live)** [ ] [-]
– Hearts grown cold / Talkin' to one of the boys / Razamanaz / Hair of the dog.

— added **JOHN LOCKE** – keyboards (ex-SPIRIT)

Feb 81. (lp)(c) **THE FOOL CIRCLE** [60] [70]
– Dressed to kill / Another year / Moonlight eyes / Pop the Silo / Let me be your leader / We are the people / Every young man's dream / Little part of you / Cocaine (live) / Victoria. *(re-iss. +cd Feb91 on 'Castle')*

Mar 81. (7") **DRESSED TO KILL. / POP THE SILO** [ ] [ ]

— **BILLY RANKIN** – guitar (ex-SPIRIT) repl. ZAL who joined TANDOORI CASSETTE

Sep 81. (d-lp)(c) **SNAZ (live)** [78] [83]
– Telegram (part 1:- On your way – part 2:- So you want to be a rock'n'roll star – part 3:- Sound check) / Razamanaz / I want to (do everything for you) / This flight tonight / Beggars day / Every young man's dream / Heart's grown cold / Java blues / Cocaine / Big boy / So you want to be a rock'n'roll star / Holiday / Dressed to kill / Hair of the dog / Expect no mercy / Shape of things / Let me be your leader / Love hurts / Tush / Juicy Lucy / Morning dew. *(re-iss+cd. Jan 87 on 'Castle')*

Sep 81. (7") **MORNING DEW (live). / JUICY LUCY (live)** [ ] [ ]

Dec 81. (7") **HAIR OF THE DOG (live). / HOLIDAY (live)** [-] [ ]

Jun 82. (lp)(c) **2 x 5** [ ] [ ]
– Love will lead to madness / Boys in the band / You love another / Gatecrash / Games / Back to the trenches / Dream on / Lonely in the night / Preservation / Take the rap / Mexico. *(cd-iss.Feb91 on 'Castle')*

Jul 82. (7") **LOVE LEADS TO MADNESS. / TAKE THE RAP** [ ] [ ]

Aug 82. (7") **DREAM ON. / TAKE THE RAP** [-] [ ]

Jan 83. (7") **GAMES. / YOU LOVE ANOTHER** [ ] [-]

Jun 83. (7") **DREAM ON. / JUICY LUCY** [ ] [-]

Vertigo Capitol

Jun 83. (lp)(c) **SOUND ELIXIR** [ ] [ ]
– All nite radio / Milk and honey / Whippin' boy / Rain on the window / Backroom boys / Why don't you read the book / I ran / Rags to riches / Local still / Where are you now. *(re-iss.Jul85 on 'Sahara') (cd-iss.Feb91 on 'Castle')*

Sep 84. (lp)(c) **THE CATCH** [ ] [ ]
– Party down / Ruby Tuesday / Last exit Brooklyn / Moondance / Love of freedom / This month's Messiah / You don't believe in us / Sweetheart tree / Road to nowhere.

Sep 84. (7") **RUBY TUESDAY. / SWEETHEART TREE** [ ] [ ]
(12"+=) – This month's Messiah / Do you think about it.

1986. (lp)(c) **CINEMA** [-] [-] Europe
– Cinema / Juliet / Just another heartache / Other side of you / Hit the fan / One from the heart / Salty salty / White boy / A veterans song / Telegram / This flight tonight.

1989. (cd)(c)(lp) **SNAKES AND LADDERS** [-] [-] Europe
– We are animals / Lady luck / Hang on to a dream / Piece of my heart / Trouble / The key / Back to school / Girls / Donna – Get off that crack / See you, see you / Helpless.

— **BILLY RANKIN** – guitar now totally repl. CHARLTON

Mausoleum not issued

Nov 91. (cd)(c)(lp) **NO JIVE** [ ] [-]
– Hire and fire / Do you wanna play house / Right between the eyes / Every time it rains / Keeping our love alive / Thinkin' man's nightmare / Cover your heart / Lap of luxury / The Rowan tree / Tell me that you love me / Cry wolf. *(cd+=)* – This flight tonight.

Jan 92 (7")**EVERY TIME IT RAINS / THIS FLIGHT TONIGHT 1991** [ ] [-]
(12"+=)(cd-s+=) – Lap of Luxury.

Mar 92. (cd-ep) **TELL ME THAT YOU LOVE ME / RIGHT BETWEEN THE EYES / ROWAN TREE / TELL ME THAT YOU LOVE ME (extended)** [ ] [-]

– more compilations, others, etc. –

Jun 85. Sahara; (d-lp) **20 GREATEST HITS** [ ] [-]

Jan 89. Castle; (cd-ep)**THIS FLIGHT TONIGHT / BROKEN DOWN / ANGEL / LOVE HURTS / BAD BAD BOY** [ ] [-]

Jan 91. Castle; (cd)(c)(d-lp) **THE SINGLES COLLECTION** [ ] [-]
– Broken down angel / Bad, bad boy / This flight tonight / Shanghai'd in Shanghai / Love hurts / Hair of the dog / My white bicycle / Holy roller / Carry

out feelings / You're the violin / Somebody to roll / I don't want to go on without you / Gone dead train / A place in your heart / May the Sun shine / Star / Dressed to kill / Morning dew / Games / Love will lead to madness.

Dec 88. Raw Power; (lp)(c)(cd) **ANTHOLOGY** [ ] [-]
Jun 88. That's Original; (d-lp)(c)(cd) **RAMPANT / HAIR OF THE DOG** [ ] [-]
Oct 88. Old Gold; (7") **LOVE HURTS. / BAD BAD BOY** [ ] [-]
Oct 88. Old Gold; (7") **THIS FLIGHT TONIGHT. / BROKEN DOWN ANGEL** [ ] [-]
(above 4 tracks were also featured on a 'Special Edition' cd-ep)
Oct 91. Essential; (3xcd-box) **ANTHOLOGY** [ ] [-]
Nov 91. Windsor; (cd) **BBC RADIO 1 LIVE IN CONCERT** [ ] [-]
Dec 91. Dojo; (cd) **THE EARLY YEARS** [ ] [-]
Jun 93. Optima; (cd)(c) **ALIVE AND KICKING** [ ] [-]
Apr 93. Elite; (cd) **FROM THE VAULTS** [ ] [-]

DAN McCAFFERTY

with some members of NAZARETH and SAHB.

Mountain / A & M

Aug 75. (7") **OUT OF TIME. / CINNAMON GIRL** [41] [ ]
Oct 75. (lp)(c) **DAN McCAFFERTY** [ ] [ ]
– The honky tonk down stairs / Cinnamon girl / The great pretender / Boots of Spanish leather / Watcha gonna do about it / Out of time / You can't lie to a liar / Troubles / You got me hummin' / Stay with me baby. *(cd-iss.Jul94 on 'Sequel')*
Oct 75. (7") **WHAT'CHA GONNA DO ABOUT IT. / NIGHTINGALE** [ ] [ ]
Mar 78. (7") **STAY WITH ME, BABY. / OUT OF TIME / WHAT('CHA GONNA DO ABOUT IT** [ ] [-]
Aug 78. (7") **THE HONKY TONK DOWNSTAIRS. / TROUBLE** [ ] [-]
Aug 79. (7") **BOOTS OF SPANISH LEATHER. / WHAT('CHA GONNA DO ABOUT IT** [ ] [-]

—— with German musicians + **PETE AGNEW** – bass

Mercury / not issued

1987 (lp)(cd) **INTO THE RING** [-] [-] Germ'y
– Into the ring / Backstage pass / Starry eyes / My sunny island / For a car / Caledonia / Headin' for South America / The departure (instrumental) / Southern Cross / Where the ocean ends we'll find a new born land / Sally Mary / Island in the Sun / Albatross / The last ones will be the first after all / Reprise.
1987. (7") **STARRY EYES. / SUNNY ISLAND** [-] [-] Germ.
(12"+=)(cd-s+=) Where the ocean ends, we'll find a new born land.

NAZZ (see under ⇒ RUNDGREN, Todd)

NEARLY GOD (see under ⇒ TRICKY)

NED'S ATOMIC DUSTBIN

Formed: Stourbridge, W.Midlands, England ... Nov'87 by JOHN PENNEY, RAT, MATT CHESLIN, ALEX GRIFFIN and DAN WARTON. Surfaced on own 'Furtive' label in 1990, which after a few minor hits, was taken over by 'Sony'. Their debut album 'GOD FODDER', became their first to hit UK Top 5. • **Style:** Alternative pop-rock outfit, similar to WONDER STUFF or JESUS JONES. • **Songwriters:** Group compositions. • **Trivia:** Took their name from a character on BBC TV's 'Goon Show'.

Recommended: GOD FODDER (*8) / ARE YOU NORMAL (*7)

JONN PENNEY (b.17 Sep'68) – vocals / **RAT** (b.GARETH PRING, 8 Nov'70) – guitar / **ALEX GRIFFIN** (b.29 Aug'71) – bass / **MAT CHESLIN** (b.28 Nov'70) – bass / **DAN WARTON** (b.28 Jul'72) – drums

Furtive / not issued

Mar 90. (12"ep) **THE INGREDIENTS** [ ] [-]
– Aim / Plug me in / Grey cell green / Terminally groovy.

Chapter 22 / not issued

Jul 90. (7"ep)(12"ep)(cd-ep) **KILL YOUR TELEVISION** [53] [-]
– Kill your television / That's nice / Sentence / Kill your remix.
Oct 90. (7")(c-s) **UNTIL YOU FIND OUT. / FLEXIBLE HEAD** [51] [-]
(12"+=)(cd-s+=) – Bite.

Furtive - Sony / Columbia

Feb 91. (7")(c-s) **HAPPY. / TWENTY-THREE HOUR TOOTHACHE** [16] [ ]
(12"+=)(cd-s+=) – Aim (at the Civic live) / 45 second blunder.
Apr 91. (cd)(c)(lp) **GOD FODDER** [4] [91]
– Kill your television / Less than useful / Selfish / Grey cell green / Cut up throwing things / Capital letters / Happy / Your complex / Nothing like until you find out / You / What gives my son. *(re-iss.cd May95)*
Sep 91. (7") **TRUST. / FACELESS** [21] [ ]
(12"+=)(cd-s+=) – Titch.
(US-cd-ep++=) – Grey cell green / Until you find out (live).
Feb 92. (c-s) **GREY CELL GREEN. / TRUST** [-] [ ]
Apr 92. (cd-ep) **KILL YOUR TELEVISION. / TERMINALLY GROOVIE / SENTENCE / KILL YOUR REMIX** [-] [ ]

Furtive / Chaos

Oct 92. (7") **NOT SLEEPING AROUND. / CUT UP** [19] [ ]
(12"+=)(cd-s+=) – Scrawl.
(US c-s+=) – N. S. A. (NAD VS. NOX).
Oct 92. (cd)(c)(lp) **ARE YOU NORMAL?** [13] [ ]
– Suave and suffocated / Walking through syrup / Legoland / Swallowing air / Who goes first / Tantrum / Not sleeping around / You don't want to do that / Leg end in his own boots / Two and two made five / Fracture / Spring / Intact.
Nov 92. (7") **INTACT. / PROSTRATE** [36] [ ]
(10"+=) – NAD & NDX =Intact.
(12"+=)(cd-s+=) – Swiss legoland (live).
Mar 95. (c-s) **ALL I ASK OF MYSELF IS THAT I HOLD TOGETHER / CAPSIZE** [33] [ ]
(12"+=) – ('A'-Just together mix) / ('A'-No answer mix).
(cd-s++=) – ('A'-In control mix).
(cd-s+=) – Take me to the cleaners / Premonition (need to know mix).
Jul 95. (7") **STUCK. / A TEMPTED FATE** [64] [-]
(cd-s+=) – . . .To be right (acoustic) / ('A'acoustic).
(12") – ('A'side) / Premonition (as I thought mix) / Premonition (dirty caller mix).
Jul 95. (cd)(c)(lp) **BRAINBLOODVOLUME** [ ] [ ]
– All I ask of myself is that I hold together / Floote / Premonition / Talk me down / Borehole / Your only joke / Stuck / . . .To be right / I want it over / Traffic / Song eleven could take forever.

—— Disbanded October 1995.

– compilations, etc. –

Jan 91. R.T.D.Euro; (lp) **BITE** (imported) [72] [-]

Bill NELSON

Born: 18 Dec'48, Wakefield, Yorkshire, England. In the late 60's, after a job as government officer, he joined local groups GLOBAL VILLAGE TRUCKING COMPANY and GENTLE REVOLUTION. He then released an obscure and limited solo lp on own label. The album in 1971 'NORTHERN DREAM', found its way to Radio 1 DJ John Peel, who gave it night-time airplay. That year, NELSON formed BE-BOP DELUXE (see below), and after one single, signed to 'Harvest'. Their first album 'AXE VICTIM' in 1974, was followed by a tour supporting COCKNEY REBEL. In Aug'74, NELSON split band up, but quickly re-formed group with unhappy ex-REBELS. After a well-received album 'FUTURAMA', they followed it early next year, with a UK Top 30 hit single 'SHIPS IN THE NIGHT', from parent hit album 'SUNBURST FINISH'. They experienced a couple of years in the top flight, until NELSON decided to form other project RED NOISE. After a promising 1979 album, NELSON went solo, and hit Top 10 immediately with adventurous double-lp 'QUIT DREAMING AND GET ON THE BEAM'. For the rest of the 80's, NELSON packed in loads of albums, mostly released on his own obscure 'Cocteau' label. • **Style:** Gifted multi-instrumentalist and guitarist, who shifted from contemporary rock with BE-BOP DELUXE, to more experimental instrumental work. • **Songwriters:** All penned by NELSON. • **Trivia:** His younger brother IAN (of RED NOISE), also had minor hit with FIAT LUX.

Recommended: RAIDING THE DIVINE ARCHIVES (*8; BE BOP DELUXE) / SOUND ON SOUND (*7; RED NOISE) / QUIT DREAMING AND GET . . . (*9) CHIMERA (*7)

BILL NELSON

– vocals, lead guitar

1971 (lp) **NORTHERN DREAM** [ ] [-]
– Photograph (a beginning) / Everyone's hero / House of sand / End of the seasons / Rejoice / Love's a way / Northern dreamer (1957) / Bloo blooz / Sad fellings / See it through / Smiles / Chymepeace (an ending). *(re-iss.Feb81, Mar82 & Aug86 on 'Butt')*

BE-BOP DELUXE

was formed by **BILL NELSON** plus **IAN PARKIN** – rhythm guitar / **ROBERT BRYAN** – bass / **NICHOLAS CHATTERTON-DEW** – drums / **RICHARD BROWN** – keyboards

Smile / not issued

1973. (7") **TEENAGE ARCHANGEL. / JETS AT DAWN** [ ] [-]

—— became trio, when BROWN departed.

Harvest / Harvest

May 74. (7") **JET SILVER & THE DOLLS OF VENUS. / THIRD FLOOR HEAVEN** [ ] [-]

Jun 74. (lp)(c) **AXE VICTIM** [ ] [ ]
– Axe victim / Love is swift arrows / Jet Silver & the dolls of Venus / Third floor Heaven / Night creatures / Rocket cathedrals / Adventures in a Yorkshire landscape / Jets at dawn / No trains to Heaven / Darkness (l'immoralise). *(cd-iss.Feb91 with 3 extra)*

— Aug74, **NELSON** recruited entire new line-up **MILTON REAME-JAMES** – keyboards (ex-COCKNEY REBEL) repl. IAN / **PAUL AVRON JEFFRYS** – bass (ex-COCKNEY REBEL) repl. ROBERT / **SIMON FOX** – drums (ex-HACKENSHACK) repl. NICHOLAS

— (late 1974) **BILL** and **SIMON** were joined by **CHARLIE TUMAHAI** (b. New Zealand) – bass who repl. MILTON & PAUL

Feb 75. (7") **BETWEEN THE WORLDS. / LIGHTS** (withdrawn) [-] [-]
May 75. (lp)(c) **FUTURAMA** [ ] [ ]
– Stage whispers / Love with the madman / Maid in Heaven / Sister seagull / Sound track / Music in Dreamland / Jean Cocteau / Between the worlds / Swan song. *(cd-iss.Feb91)*
Jun 75. (7") **MAID IN HEAVEN. / LIGHTS** [ ] [-]
Jul 75. (7") **MAID IN HEAVEN. / SISTER SEAGULL** [-] [ ]

— added **ANDREW CLARKE** – keyboards

Jan 76. (7") **SHIPS IN THE NIGHT. / CRYING TO THE SKY** [23] [ ]
Jan 76. (lp)(c) **SUNBURST FINISH** [17] [96]
– Fair exchange / Heavenly homes / Ships in the night / Crying to the sky / Sleep that burns / Beauty secrets / Life in the air age / Like an old blues / Crystal gazing / Blazing apostles. *(re-iss.Mar82 on 'Fame') (re-iss.Jun86 on 'Revolver') (cd-iss.Feb91 with 3 extra tracks)*
Aug 76. (7") **THE KISS OF LIGHT. / SHINE** [ ] [ ]

— (above 'B'side as "FUNKY PHASER UNEARTHLY MERCHANDISE")

Sep 76. (lp)(c) **MODERN MUSIC** [12] [88]
– Orphans of Babylon / Twilight capers / Kiss of light / The bird charmer's destiny / The gold at the end of my rainbow / Bring back the spark / Modern music / Dancing in the moonlight / Honeymoon on Mars / Lost in the neon world / Dance of the Uncle Sam humanoids / Modern music / Forbidden lovers / Down on Terminal street / Make the music magic. *(cd-iss.Feb91 with 3 extra)*
Jul 77. (white-lp)(c) **LIVE IN THE AIR AGE (live)** [10] [65]
– Life in the air age / Ships in the night / Piece of mine / Fair exchange / Mill street junction / Adventures in a Yorkshire landscape / Blazing apostles. (free-7"ep) **SHINE. / SISTER SEAGULL / MAID IN HEAVEN** *(cd-iss.Feb91 with the 3 extra free tracks)*
Sep 77. (7") **JAPAN. / FUTURIST MANIFESTO** [ ] [ ]
Feb 78. (7") **PANIC IN THE WORLD. / BLUE AS A JEWEL** [ ] [ ]
Feb 78. (lp)(c) **DRASTIC PLASTIC** [22] [95]
– Electrical language / New precision / New mysteries / Surreal estate / Love in flames / Panic in the world / Dangerous stranger / Superenigmatix (lethal appliances for the home) / Islands of the dead / Visions of endless hopes / Possession / Islands of the dead. *(cd-iss.Feb91 with 3 extra)*
May 78. (7") **ELECTRICAL LANGUAGE. / SURREAL ESTATE** [ ] [ ]

— Disbanded Spring 1978. TUMAHAI joined The DUKES, SIMON joined JACK GREEN. CLARKE joined NICO's band.

– (BE – BOP DELUXE) compilations, others –

Oct 76. Harvest; (7"ep) **HOT VALVES** [36] [ ]
– Maid in Heaven / Blazing apostles / Jet Silver and the dolls of Venus / Bring back the spark.
1978. Harvest; (d-lp)(c) **THE BEST OF AND THE REST OF BE-BOP DELUXE** [ ] [ ]
(cd-iss.May90)
May 81. Harvest; (lp)(c) **THE SINGLES A & B** [ ] [-]
Sep 83. Harvest; (d-lp) **AXE VICTIM / FUTURAMA** [ ] [-]
Mar 87. Harvest; (lp)(c) **RAIDING THE DIVINE ARCHIVES** [ ] [-]
– Jet silver and the dolls of Venus / Adventures in a Yorkshire landscape / Maid in Heaven / Ships in the night / Life in the air age / Kiss of light / Sister seagull / Modern music / Japan / Panic in the world / Bring back the spark / Forbidden lovers / Electrical language. *(re-iss.+cd.Apr90 on 'EMI'+=)* – Fair exchange / Sleep that burns / Between the worlds / Music in Dreamland.
Feb 83. Cocteau; (12"ep) **ELECTRICAL LANGUAGE** [ ] [-]
– Electrical language / Panic in the world / Maid in Heaven. *(re-1985)*
Aug 83. Cocteau; (7") **PANIC IN THE WORLD. / MAID IN HEAVEN** [ ] [-]
May 84. EMI Gold; (7") **SHIPS IN THE NIGHT. / MAID IN HEAVEN** [ ] [-]
Aug 86. Dojo; (lp) **BOP TO THE NOISE** [ ] [-]
Sep 94. Windsong; (cd) **RADIOLAND – BBC RADIO 1 LIVE IN CONCERT (live)** [ ] [-]

BILL NELSON'S RED NOISE

BILL NELSON with **ANDREW CLARKE** – keyboards / **RICK FORD** – drums / **IAN NELSON** (brother) – saxophone / **STEVE PEER** – drums

Harvest Harvest

Feb 79. (7")(7"red) **FURNITURE MUSIC. / WONDERTOYS THAT LAST FOREVER / ACQUITTED BY MIRRORS** [59] [ ]
Feb 79. (lp)(c) **SOUND ON SOUND** [33] [ ]
– Don't touch me, I'm electric / For young moderns / Stop – go – stop / Furniture music / Radar in my heart / Stay young / Out of touch / A better home in the phantom zone / Substitute flesh / The atom age / Art – empire – industry / Revolt into style. *(re-iss.Nov85 on 'Cocteau')*
Apr 79. (7")(7"blue) **REVOLT INTO STYLE. / OUT OF TOUCH** [69] [ ]
(12") – ('A'side) / Stay young / Furniture music. *(re-iss.Aug83 on 'Cocteau')*

BILL NELSON

solo, with **TOM KELLICHAN** – drums / with sessioners

Cocteau not issued

Jun 80. (7"ep) **DO YOU DREAM IN COLOUR? / IDEAL HOMES. / INSTANTLY YOURS / ATOM MAN LOVES RADIUM GIRL** [52] [ ]

Crepescule not issued

Mar 81. (7") **ROOMS WITH BRITTLE VIEWS. / DADA GUITARS** [ ] [-]

Mercury Mercury

Mar 81. (7") **BANAL. / MR. MAGNETISN HIMSELF** [ ] [ ]
(12"+=) – Turn to fiction.
May 81. (lp)(c) **QUIT DREAMIMG AND GET ON THE BEAM** [7] [ ]
– Banal / Living in my limousine / Vertical games / Disposable / False alarms / Decline and fall / Life runs out like sand / A kind of loving / Do you dream in colour? / U.H.F. / Youth of nation on fire / Quit dreaming and get on the beam. *(cd-iss.Jul86 on 'Cocteau')* (cd+=) – White sound. (free-lp.w.a.) **SOUNDING THE RITUAL ECHO** – Annuciation / The ritual echo / Sleep / Near east / Emak bakia / My intricate image / Endless orchids / The heat in the room / Another willingly opened window / Vanishing parades / Glass fish (for the final aquarium) / Cubical domes / Ashes of roses / The shadow garden (opium). *(iss.on own.Jun85 on 'Cocteau')(cd-iss.on own.Sep89)*
Jun 81. (7") **YOUTH OF NATION ON FIRE. / BE MY DYNAMO** [73] [ ]
(d7"+=) – Rooms with brittle views / All my wives were iron.
Sep 81. (7") **LIVING IN MY LIMOUSINE. / BIRDS OF TIME** [ ] [ ]
(12"+=) – Love in the abstract.
Apr 82. (7") **EROS ARRIVING. / HAUNTING IN MY HEAD** [ ] [-]
(d7"+=) – Flesh / He and sleep were brothers.
Jun 82. (d-lp)(c) **THE LOVE THAT WHIRLS** [28] [ ]
– Empire of the senses / Hope for the heartbeat / Waiting for the voices / Private view / Eros arriving / Bride of Christ in Autumn / When your dream of perfect beauty comes true / Flaming desire / Portrait of Jan with flowers / Crystal escalator in the palace of God department store / Echo in her eyes / October man. *(re-iss.+cd.Jul86 on 'Cocteau', cd+=)* – Flesh / He and sleep were brothers.
Jul 82. (7")(12") **FLAMING DESIRE. / THE PASSION** [ ] [-]
May 83. (lp)(c) **CHIMERA** [30] [-]
– The real adventure / Acceleration / Every day feels like another new drug / Tender is the night / Glow world / Another day, another ray of hope. *(cd-iss.Sep87 on 'Cocteau', re-iss.Apr89)*

Cocteau Portrait

Aug 83. (7"m) **TOUCH AND GLOW. / DANCING IN THE WILD / LOVE WITHOUT FEAR** [ ] [-]
Dec 83. (m-lp) **SAVAGE GESTURES FOR CHARMS SAKE** [ ] [ ]
– The man in the exine suit / Watching my dream boat go down in flames / The meat room / Another happy thought (carved forever in your cortex) / Portrait of Jan with Moon and stars. *(re-iss.Feb85)*
Aug 84. (7") **ACCELERATION. / HARD FACTS FROM THE FICTION DEPARTMENT** [ ] [-]
(12"+=)(12"pic-d+=) – ('A'short version) / ('A'long version).
Oct 84. (lp) **VISTAMIX** [-] [ ]
– The real adventure / Flaming desire / Acceleration / Empire of the senses / Everyday feels like another new drug / Do you dream in color? / A kind of loving / Tender is the night / Glow world / Another day, another ray of hope.

Portrait Portrait

Mar 86. (7")(12") **WILDEST DREAMS. / SELF IMPERSONATION** [ ] [ ]
Apr 86. (lp)(c) **GETTING THE HOLY GHOST ACROSS** [91] [ ]
– Suvasini / Contemplation / Theology / Wildest dreams / Lost in your mystery / Rise like a fountain / Age of reason / Hidden flame / Because of you / Living for the spangled moment / Word for word / Illusions of you / Heart and soul / Finks and stooges of the spirit. *(cd-iss.1988 on 'C.B.S.')*

Cocteau Enigma

Jun 86. (lp) **CHAMBER OF DREAMS** [ ] [-]
– The blazing memory of innuendo / Into the luminous future / Dip in the swimming pool / Reactor / Tomorrowland (the threshold of 1947) / Listening to lizards / Endless torsion / My sublime perversion / Eros in Autumn / Sleeplessness / The latest skyline / Train of thought / Packs and fountains clouds and trees / Golden bough / Forever Orpheus / In arcadia / Sentimental / Autumn fires / Wild blue yonder. *(cd-iss.Aug89)*
Oct 86. (lp)(c) **SUMMER OF GOD'S PIANO** [ ] [-]
– Antennae two / N.B.C.97293 / The sleep of Hollywood / The celestial bridegroom / Under the red arch / Orient pearl / Sacrament / Falling blossoms / The difficulty of being / Zanoni / The Chinese nightingale / Soon September (another enchantment) / Rural shires / Perfido incanto / The lost years / The charm of transit / Night thoughts (twilight radio) / Wysteria / Swing / Snowfall / Real of dusk / Over ocean. *(cd-iss.Aug89)*
Jan 87. (lp)(c)(cd) **MAP OF DREAMS** [ ] [-]
– Legions of the endless night / Spinning creatures / At the gates of the singing garden / Heavenly message No.1, 2 & 3 / Fellini's picnic / Dark angel / Infernal regions / Dance of the fragrant woman / The alchemy of ecstasy / Aphrodite

adorned / The wheel of fortune and the hand of fate / Forked tongues, mixed blessings / Another tricky mission for the celestial pilot / Water of life (transfiguration).

May 87. (12") **SECRET CEREMONY (theme from 'BROND'). / WIPING A TEAR FROM THE ALLSEEING EYES** [ ] [-]

— (above by "SCALA" (BILL NELSON & DARYL RUNSWICK)

Nov 87. (d-lp)(c)(cd) **CHANCE ENCOUNTERS IN THE GARDEN OF LIGHT** [ ] [-]
– My dark demon / The dove consumed (the serpent slumbers) / Calling Heaven, calling Heaven overs / Path of return / Theurgia / Staircase to no place / Evocation of a radiant childhood / The kingdom of consequence / Divine raptures of a radiant childhood / Bright star (moonlight over the ocean blue) / A bird of the air shall earn the voice / Clothed in light amongst the stars / Hastening the chariot of my hearts desire / Transcendant conversation / West deep / The spirit cannot fail / Pilots of kite / Phantom gardens / The angel of hearth and home / Villefranche interior / Night tides / First memory / Azure extention / Radiant spires / Evening peal / Thremodia / Short drink for a certain fountain / Body of light / At the centre / Self-initiation / The word that became flesh / The hermetic garden / Revolving globes / The four square citadel / Orient of Memphis / Little daughters of light / Angel at the western window.

Sep 88. (lp)(c)(cd) **OPTIMISM (by "BILL NELSON ORCHESTRA ARCANA")** [ ] [ ]
– Exactly the way you want it / Why be lonely / Everyday is a better day / The receiver and the fountain pen / Welcome home Mr. Kane / This is true / Greeting a new day / The breath in my father's saxophone / Our lady of apparations / The whole city between us / Deva dance / Always looking forward to tomorrow / Profiles, hearts, stars / Alchemia.

Dec 88. (7") **LIFE IN YOUR HANDS. / DO YOU DREAM IN COLOUR** [ ] [-]
(12"+=) – Get out of that hole / Drean demon.

Aug 89. (lp)(cd) **PAVILLIONS OF THE HEART AND SOUL** [ ] [-]
– Gift of the August tide / Loving tongues / Blue nude / In the realms of bells / Your nebulous smile / The glance of a glittering stranger / Another kiss for your slender neck / The warmth of women's eyes / Seduction (ritual with roses) / Dreamed entrances / Four pieces for imaginary strings:- Herself with her shadow – The exquisite corpse – Ardent hands – Her laughing torso / Migrating angels / Les amoureaux / Meshes of the afternoon / Mountains of the heart / Willow silk / Tender encounters (states of grace) / Melancholia / The eternal female.

Aug 89. (lp)(cd) **CATALOGUE OF OBSESSIONS** [ ] [-]
– Sex party six / Tune in Tokyo / Promise of perfume / View from a balcony / Test of affection / Birds in two hemispheres / Wider windows for the walls / The boy pilots of Bangkok / Talk technique / Glass breakfast / Edge of tears / Erotikon.

Imaginary — not issued

Apr 91. (cd)(c) **LUMINOUS** [ ] [-]

1992. (cd) **BLUE MOONS AND LAUGHING GUITARS** [ ] [ ]

Resurgence — not issued

Feb 95. (cd) **CRIMSWORTH (FLOWERS STONES FOUNTAINS AND FLAMES)** [ ] [-]
– (part 1) / (part 2).

Nov 95. (cd) **CULTUREMIX WITH BILL NELSON** [ ] [-]

All Saints — not issued

Mar 95. (cd) **PRACTICALLY WIRED** [ ] [-]
– Roses and rocketships / Spinning planet / Thousand fountain island / Piano 45 / Pink buddha blues / Kid with cowboy tie / Royal ghosts / Her presence in flowers / Big noise in Twangtown / Tiny little thing / Wild blue cycle / Every moment infinite / Friends from Heaven / Eternal for Eniko.

– (BILL NELSON) compilations, specials, others –

Nov 81. Cocteau; (d-lp)(c) **DAS KABINET (OF DR.CAGLIARI)** [ ] [-]
– The asylum / Waltz / The fairground / Doctor Cagliari / Cesare the somnabulist / Murder / The funeral / The somnabulist and the children / The children / Cagliari disciplines Cesare / Cagliari opens the cabinet / Jane discovers Cesare / The attempted murder of Jane / The dream dance of Jane and the somnabulist / Escape over the rooftops / The unmasking / The shot / The cabinet closes.

1982. Cocteau; (lp)(c) **LA BELLE ET LA BETE (THE BEAUTY AND THE BEAST)** [ ] [-]
– Overture / The family / Sisters and Sedan chairs / In the forest of storms / The castle / The gates / The corridor / The great hall / Dreams (the merchant sleeps) / The rose and the beast / Magnificent (the white horse) / Beauty enters the castle / The door / The mirror / Candelabra and the gargoyles / Beauty and the beast / Transition No.1, 2 – The gift / The garden / Transitions No.3, 4 – The tragedy / Transitions No.5 – The enchanted glove / Tears as diamonds (the gift reverses) / The beast in solitude / Return of the magnificent / Transition No.6-The journey / The pavillion of Diana / Transformation No.1 & 2 / The final . . . *(above 2 albums re-iss.Jun85)*

Nov 82. Cocteau; (5x7"box) **PERMANENT FLAME** [ ] [-]

Jan 85. Cocteau; (4xlp-box) **TRIAL BY INTAMACY** [ ] [-]
– (DAS KABINET / BEAUTY & . . . / CHAMBER OF . . . / SUMMER OF . . .)

Feb 85. Cocteau; (d-lp)(cd) **THE TWO-FOLD ASPECT OF EVERYTHING** [-] [ ]

Jul 85. Cocteau; (7"pic-d) **ACCELERATION. / ('A'instrumental)** [ ] [-]

Sep 87. Cocteau; (d-cd) **CHIMERA / SAVAGE GESTURES FOR CHARMS SAKE** [ ] [-]

Sep 89. Cocteau; (d-lp)(c)(cd) **DUPLEX: THE BEST OF BILL NELSON** [ ] [-]
– Flaming desire / Acceleration (remix) / hope for the heartbeat (remix) / Here and now / Life in your hands / Glow world / The blazing memory of the innuendo / The angel at the western window / The man in the Rexine suit / Right then left / Half asleep in the hall of mirrors / Opening / Metaphysical jerks / Loving tongues / Radiant spires / Do you dream in clour / Living in my limousine (remix) / October man / Private view / Contemplation / Another day, another ray of hope / Another tricky mission / Portrait of Jan with flowers / Wiping a tear from the all-seeing eye / Secret ceremony (theme from 'Brond') / Broadcast news (from 'Right To Reply') / Loosening up with lady luck / The garden / Burning the groove of Satyre / Set me a seal upon thine heart.

Dec 89. Cocteau; (4xlp)(4xc)(4xcd) **DEMONSTRATIONS OF AFFECTION** (new) [ ] [-]

Aug 92. Magpie; (3xcd-box) **QUIT DREAMING AND GET ON THE BEAM / CHIMERA – SAVAGE GESTURES / THE LOVE THAT WHIRLS** [ ] [-]

Dec 95. Resurgence; (4xcd-box) **BOXED SET** [ ] [-]

Colin NEWMAN (see under ⇒ WIRE)

NEW MODEL ARMY

Formed: Bradford, England . . . 1980 by SLADE THE LEVELLER (aka JUSTIN SULLIVAN). After their own 45 'BITTERSWEET' on 'Quiet', they moved to bigger indie 'Abstract' in 1983, for a single and a mini-lp 'VENGEANCE'. Early in '85, they were given contract by 'EMI', who gave them free reign of output. Their first 45 for the label 'NO REST' / 'HEROIN', saw them banned by the IBA for the latter's subject matter. The Americans also initially banned them from arriving there, reputedly citing their lack of artistic quality. In 1985, their first full album 'NO REST FOR THE WICKED', went into the UK Top 30, thus rendering all banning efforts pointless. • **Style:** A blend of raw punk, protest and politics. • **Songwriters:** All written by SULLIVAN / HEATON. • **Trivia:** Their name was taken from Oliver Cromwell's forces in the 11th century English civil war. SULLIVAN and HEATON played back-up to the former's girlfriend poet JOOLZ on many stage shows.

Recommended: HISTORY THE SINGLES (*7) / VENGEANCE (*8)

SLADE THE LEVELLER (b. JUSTIN SULLIVAN, 1956) – vocals, guitar / **STUART MORROW** – bass / **ROBB HEATON** (b.1962) -drums

Quiet — not issued

May 83. (7") **BITTERSWEET. / BETCHA / TENSION** [ ] [-]
(w/free flexi-7") – FASHION / CAUSE.

Abstract — not issued

Nov 83. (7") **GREAT EXPECTATIONS. / WAITING** [ ] [-]
(re-iss.Feb90 on colour vinyl)

Apr 84. (m-lp) **VENGEANCE** [73] [-]
– Christian militia / Notice me / Smalltown England / A liberal education / Vengeance / Sex (the black angel) / Running / Spirit of the Falklands. *(c-iss.Nov85) (cd-iss.Jun87 +=)* – Great expectations / Waiting / The price / 1984 / No man's land. *(blue-lp iss.Nov87 w / 6xbox-set of 'Abstract' label records: 'SIX DISQUES BLEU')*

Oct 84. (7") **THE PRiCE. / 1984** [ ] [-]
(12"+=) – No man's land / Notice me / Great expectations.

E.M.I. — Capitol

Apr 85. (7")(c-s) **NO REST. / HEROIN** [28] [-]
(d12"+=) – Vengeance / The price / No greater love (all 3 live).

May 85. (lp)(c) **NO REST FOR THE WICKED** [22] [-]
– Frightened / Ambition / Grandmother's footsteps / Better than them / My country / No greater love / No rest / Young, gifted & skint / Drag it down / Shot 18 / The attack. *(re-iss.May88 on 'Fame', cd-iss.Jul89)*

Jun 85. (d7")(7"ep)(12"ep) **BETTER THAN THEM. / NO SENSE/ / ADRENELIN. / TRUST** [49] [-]

— **JASON 'MOOSE' HARRIS** repl. MORROW

Nov 85. (7") **BRAVE NEW WORLD. / R.I.P.** [57] [-]
(12"+=) – Brave new world 2.
(d12"+=) – Young, gifted & skint (live) / Sex (the black angel) (live)

Sep 86. (lp)(c) **THE GHOST OF CAIN** [45] [-]
– The hunt / Lights go out / 51st state / All of this / Poison street / Western dream / Love songs / Heroes / Ballad / Master race. *(re-iss.+cd Jul89)*

Oct 86. (7")(12") **51st STATE. / TEN COMMANDMENTS** [71] [-]
(d12"+=) – A liberal education / No rest / No man's land (all 3 live).

Feb 87. (7")(7"red) **POISON STREET. / COURAGE** [64] [-]
(12"+=) – ('A'extended version).
(d12"+=) – All of this (live) / My country (live).

Jun 87. (7"ep)(12"ep) **WHITE COATS / THE CHARGE. / CHINESE WHISPERS / MY COUNTRY** [50] [-]

Dec 88. (m-lp) **SEVEN SONGS** [-] [ ]
– My country (live) / Waiting / 51st state / The hunt (live) / White coats / The charge / Chinese whispers.

Jan 89. (7") **STUPID QUESTIONS. / NOTHING TOUCHES** [31] [ ]

(12") – ('A'extended) / Betcha (live).
(cd-s++=) – 51st state.

Feb 89. (lp)(c)(cd) **THUNDER AND CONSOLATION** [20] [ ]
– I love the world / Stupid questions / 225 / Inheritence / Green and grey / Ballad of Bodmin Pill / Family / Family life / Vagabonds / Archway towers. *(re-iss.Aug91 on 'Fame', cd+=)–* The charge / Chinese whispers / Nothing changes / White coats.

Feb 89. (7")(7"pic-d) **VAGABONDS. / DEAD EYE** [37] [ ]
(12"+=) – ('A'extended) / White coats (live).
(cd-s++=) – Lights go out (extended).

Jun 89. (7")(c-s)(7"pic-d) **GREEN AND GREY. / THE CHARGE (live)** [37] [ ]
(12") – ('A'side) / Family life (live) / 125 mph (live).
(cd-s+=) – Green and grey (live).

— **NELSON** – bass (ex-HIDING PLACE) repl. JASON

Aug 90. (7") **GET ME OUT. / PRISON** [34] [ ]
(10"+=) – ('A'extended) / Waiting (live).
(12"+=) – ('A'extended) / White coats (live).
(cd-s+=) – White coats (live) / Waiting (live).

Sep 90. (cd)(c)(lp) **IMPURITY** [23] [ ]
– Get me out / Space / Innocense / Purity / Whirlwind / Lust for power / Bury the hatchet / 11 years / Lurkstop / Before I get old / Vanity. (cd+=) – Marrakesh.

Oct 90. (7") **PURITY (IS A LIE). / CURSE** [61] [-]
(12"+=)(cd-s+=) – ('A'extended) / Vengeance (live).

May 91. (7")(c-s) **SPACE (live). / FAMILY LIFE** [39] [ ]
(12") – ('A'side) / No rest (live) / Stupid questions (live).
(cd-s) – ('A'side) / 225 (live) / Ambition (live).
(10") – ('A'side) / Bury the hatchet (live) / Stupid questions (live).

Jun 91. (cd)(c)(lp) **RAW MELODY MEN (live)** [43] [ ]
– Whirlwind / The charge / Space / Purity / White coats / Vagabonds / Get me out / Lib. fol / Better than them / Innocense / Love songs / Innhstaap / Archway towers / Smalltown England / Green & grey / The world. *(re-iss.cd+c Jun93 on 'Fame')*

Apr 92. (cd)(c)(lp) **HISTORY THE SINGLES 1985-91** (compilation) [ ] [ ]
– No rest / Better than them / Brave new world / 51st state / Poison street / White coats / Stupid questions / Vagabonds / Green and grey / Get me out / Purity / Space (live). *(incl.free 12")–* Far Better Thing / Higher Wall / Adrenalin (version) Luurstaap (acoustic). *(cd+c+=) – (2 extra tracks *)*

— Jun'92, JUSTIN was nearly killed when he was electrocuted on stage.

Epic Epic

Jan 93. (7") **HERE COMES THE WAR. / MODERN TIMES** [25] [ ]
(12"+=)(cd-s+=) – Ghost of your father.

Mar 93. (cd)(c)(lp) **THE LOVE OF HOPELESS CAUSES** [22] [ ]
– Here comes the war / Fate / Living in the rose / White light / Believe it / Understand U / My people / These words / Afternoon song / Bad old world.

Jul 93. (12"ep)(cd-ep) **THE BALLADS EP** [51] [ ]
– Living in a rose / Drummy B / Marry the sea / Sleepwalking.

– compilations, others, etc. –

Apr 88. Abstract; (m-lp)(cd) **RADIO SESSIONS (1983-1984 rare)** [ ] [-]
Dec 93. Windsong; (cd) **BBC RADIO 1 LIVE IN CONCERT (live)** [ ] [-]
Sep 94. E.M.I.; (cd) **B SIDES AND ABANDONED TRACKS** [ ] [-]
Oct 94. Abstract; (12"ep)(cd-ep) **VENGEANCE 1994. / ('A'-Zion Train mix) / ('A'-The Headman mix) / ('A'-Pressure Of Speech mix)** [ ] [-]
Jun 95. Abstract; (d-cd) **VENGEANCE / RADIO SESSIONS** [ ] [-]

NEW ORDER

Formed: Manchester, England ... Jun'80, after the death of JOY DIVISION frontman IAN CURTIS on 18 May'80. The remaining JOY DIVISION members ALBRECHT (now SUMNER), HOOK & MORRIS stayed with 'Factory' records, and played some gigs until Mar'81, when they issued debut 45 'CEREMONY'. This broke the Top 40, as did the Martin Hannett produced follow-up 'PROCESSION' / 'EVERYTHING'S GONE GREEN', which introduced 4th member GILLIAN GILBERT. Their first lp 'MOVEMENT', scraped into the UK Top 30 late in '81. By 1989, they had hit the UK No.1 for the first time with Stephen Hague co-produced album 'TECHNIQUE'. In between these in 1983, they had Top 10 for the first time with classic 12"only 45 'BLUE MONDAY', which also went down well on the US dancefloors. • **Style:** Sombre but infectious alternative rock outfit, who ventured into the techno-rock field after 1982. Their 1983 singles 'BLUE MONDAY' and 'CONFUSION', were produced by US dance producer ARTHUR BAKER, who also co-wrote the latter. He also collaborated on the 1984 follow-up 'THIEVES LIKE US'. • **Songwriters:** All group compositions except; TURN THE HEATER ON (Keith Hudson). • **Trivia:** In 1987, they contributed some tracks to the movie 'SALVATION'.

Recommended: POWER, CORRUPTION AND LIES (*9) / TECHNIQUE (*9) / MOVEMENT (*8) / SUBSTANCE 1980-1987 (*10) / LOW-LIFE (*8) / BROTHERHOOD (*8) / ELECTRONIC (*8; ELECTRONIC) / THE BEST OF NEW ORDER (*9).

BERNARD SUMNER (b.BERNARD DICKEN, 4 Jan'56) – vocals, guitar / **PETER HOOK** (b.13 Feb'56) – bass / **STEPHEN MORRIS** (b.28 Oct'57) – drums

Factory Streetwise

Mar 81. (7") **CEREMONY. / IN A LONELY PLACE** [34] [-]
(12"+=) – ('B'extended). *(12"w/re-recorded 'A'version re-iss.Jul81)*

— added **GILLIAN GILBERT** (b.27 Jan'61) – keyboards, synth., guitar

Sep 81. (7") **PROCESSION. / EVERYTHING'S GONE GREEN** [38] [-]
Nov 81. (lp) **MOVEMENT** [30] [-]
– Dreams never end / Truth / Senses / Chosen time / I.C.B. / The him / Doubts even here / Denial. *(re-iss.+c+cd.Nov86)(re-iss.cd+c Jul93 on 'Centredate')*

May 82. (7") **TEMPTATION. / HURT** [29] [-]
(12"+=) – ('A'&'B'extended).

Mar 83. (12") **BLUE MONDAY. / THE BEACH** [9] [ ]
(re-iss.Dec83)

May 83. (lp) **POWER, CORRUPTION AND LIES** [4] [ ]
– Your silent face / Ultraviolence / Ecstasy / Leave me alone / Age of consent / We all stand / The village / 5-8-6. *(c-iss.Nov84 +=)*
-Blue Monday / The beach. *(cd-iss.Nov86) (re-iss.cd+c Jul93 on 'Centredate')*

Jul 83. (12"ep) **CONFUSION. / CONFUSED BEATS / CONFUSION (instrumental & Rough mixes)** [12] [ ]

May 84. (12") **THIEVES LIKE US. / LONESOME TONIGHT** [18] [ ]

Factory Qwest

May 85. (7") **THE PERFECT KISS. / THE KISS OF DEATH** [46] [ ]
(12"+=) – Perfect pit (US mix). (US; b-side)

May 85. (lp)(c)(cd) **LOW-LIFE** [7] [94]
– Sooner than you think / Sub-culture / Face up / Love vigilantes / Elegia / The perfect kiss / This time of the night / Sunrise. *(c+=) – (3 extra tracks =last single). (re-iss.cd+c Jul93 on 'Centredate')*

Nov 85. (7")(12") **SUB-CULTURE. / DUB-CULTURE** [63] [-]
Mar 86. (7") **SHELLSHOCK (edit). / THIEVES LIKE US (instrumental)** [28] [-]
(12") – ('A'extended) / Shellshock (dub).

Sep 86. (7")(12") **STATE OF THE NATION. / SHAME OF THE NATION** [30] [-]

Oct 86. (lp)(c)(cd) **BROTHERHOOD** [9] [ ]
– Paradise / Weirdo / As it was when it was / Broken promise / Way of life / Bizarre love triangle / All day long / Angel dust / Every little counts. *(cd+=) –* State of the nation. *(re-iss.cd+c Jul93 on 'Centredate')*

Nov 86. (7")(12") **BIZARRE LOVE TRIANGLE. / BIZARRE DUB TRIANGLE** [56] [-]

Mar 87. (7") **BIZARRE LOVE TRIANGLE. / EVERY LITTLE COUNTS** [-] [ ]

Jul 87. (7")(12") **TRUE FAITH. / 1963** [4] [32]
(12"+=) – True dub.

Aug 87. (d-lp)(d-c)(d-cd) **SUBSTANCE (1980-1987)** (compilation) [3] [36]
– Ceremony / Everthing's gone green / Temptation / Blue Monday / Confusion / Thieves like us / Perfect kiss / Subculture / Shellshock / State of the nation / Bizarre love triangle / True faith.
(d-c+=)– Procession / Mesh / Hurt / In a lonely place / The beach / Confused / Murder / Lonesome tonight / Kiss of death / Shame of the nation / 1963. *(cd++=)–* Cries and whispers / Dub culture / Shellcock / Bizarre dub triangle. *(re-iss.cd+c Jul93 on 'Centredate', hit UK No.32)*

Dec 87. (7") **TOUCHED BY THE HAND OF GOD. / TOUCHED BY THE HAND OF DUB** [20] [-]
(12") – ('A'&'B'extended).
(cd-s) – ('A'extended) / Confusion (dub '87) / Temptation (original).

Mar 88. (7") **TOUCHED BY THE HAND OF GOD. / BLUE MONDAY 1988** [-] [ ]

Nov 88. (7") **FINE TIME. / DON'T DO IT** [11] [ ]
(12"+=) – Fine line.
(cd-s+=) – ('A'silk mix) / ('A'messed around mix).

Jan 89. (lp)(c)(cd)(dat) **TECHNIQUE** [1] [32]
– Fine time / All the way / Love less / Round & round / Guilty partner / Run / Mr. Disco / Vanishing point / Dream attack. *(re-iss.cd+c Jul93 on 'Centredate')*

Mar 89. (7") **ROUND & ROUND. / BEST AND MARSH** [21] [64]
(12") – ('A'&'B'extended).
(12"+=)(3"cd-s) – ('A'club mix) / ('A'Detroit mix) / ('B'extended).
(cd-s+=) – Vanishing point (instrumental 'Making Out' mix) / ('A'-12"mix).

Sep 89. (12"ep) **RUN 2 / RUN 2 (extended). / MTO / MTO (minus mix)** [49] [-]

May 90. (7")(12")(c-s) **WORLD IN MOTION. (as "ENGLAND / NEW ORDER") / THE B SIDE** [1] [-]
(cd-s+=) – ('A' no alla violenzia / ('A'subbuteo mix).
(12") – ('A'subbuteo mix) / ('A'subbuteo dub). / ('A' no alla violenzia mix) / ('A' Carabinieri mix).

— Around the late 80's/early 90's, all members splintered to do own projects

Centredate-London / Qwest

Apr 93. (7")(c-s) **REGRET ('A' mix)** [4] [28]
(cd-s+=) – ('A' Fire Isalnd mix) / ('A'-Junior's dub mix).
(12") – ('A'-Fire Island mix) / ('A'-Junior's dub mix) / (2-'A' Sabres mixes)

May 93. (cd)(c)(lp) **REPUBLIC** [1] [11]
– Regret / World / Ruined in a day / Spooky / Everyone everywhere / Young offender / Liar / Chemical / Times change / Special / Avalanche.

Jun 93. (7")(c-s) **RUINED IN A DAY. / VICIOUS CIRCLE (mix)** [22] [ ]
(cd-s+=)/ /(cd-s) – ('A'mixes)./ / ('A'mixes).
(12") – ('A'side) / World (the price of dub mix).

Aug 93. (c-s) **WORLD (THE PRICE OF LOVE). / ('A'mixes)** [13] [92]
(12"+=)(cd-s+=) ('A' perfecto + sexy club mixes)
(cd-s) – ('A' Brothers in rhythm mix) / ('A' dubstramental mix) / ('A' World in action mix) / ('A' pharmacy dub)

Dec 93. (12")(c-s)(cd-s) **SPOOKY. / (3 'A' mixes-magimix-minimix-moulimix)** [22] [ ]
(cd-s) – ('A' out of order mix) / ('A' stadium mix) / ('A'-in Heaven mix) / ('A'-Boo-dub mix) / ('A' stadium instrumental).

Nov 94. (7")(c-s) **TRUE FAITH '94. / ('A'-Perfecto mix)** [9] [ ]
(12"+=) – ('A'-sexy disco dub mix) / ('A'-TWA Gim Up North mix).
(cd-s++=) – ('A'radio mix).

Nov 94. (cd)(c)(d-lp) **? (THE BEST OF)** (compilation) [4] [78]
– True faith '94 / Bizarre love triangle '94 / 1963 / Regret / Fine time / The perfect kiss / Shellshock / Thieves like us / Vanishing point / Run (2) / Round and round '94 / World (price of love) / Ruined in a day / Touched by the hand of God / Blue Monday '88 / World in motion.

Jan 95. (c-s)(cd-s) **NINETEEN63 (Arthur Baker remix)./ ('A'-'94 album version)/ ('A'-Lionrock full throttle mix)/ ('A'-Joe T Venelli remix)** [21] [ ]
(12") – ('A'-Lionrock & Joe T mixes / True faith (Eschreamer mix)/ ('A'-Eschreamer dub).
(cd-s) – ('A'-Arthur Baker remix) / Let's go/ Spooky (Nightstripper mix)/ True faith '87 (Shep Pettibone mix).

Jul 95. (c-s) **BLUE MONDAY -95 / ('A'-original)** [17] [ ]
(12"+=)(cd-s+=) – ('A'-Hardfloor mix) / ('A'-Jam & Spoon mix).

Jul 95. (c-s)(cd-s) **BIZARRE LOVE TRIANGLE (new mix)** [-] [98]

Aug 95. (cd)(c) **THE REST OF NEW ORDER** (remixes, etc) [ ] [ ]

– other compilations, etc. –

Dec 81. Factory Benelux; (12"m) **EVERYTHING'S GONE GREEN (extended). / MESH / CRIES AND WHISPERS** [-] [-] Belg'm
(cd-ep iss.Jul90)

Nov 82. Factory Benelux; (m-lp) **NEW ORDER 1981-82** [-] [-] Belg'm

Jun 84. Factory Benelux; (12") **MURDER. / THIEVES LIKE US (instrumental)** [-] [-] Belg'm

Sep 86. Strange Fruit; (12"ep) **THE PEEL SESSIONS** (1.6.82) [54] [-]
– Turn the heater on / We all stand / 586 / Too late.
(c-ep.Jul87) (cd-ep Aug88)

Oct 87. Strange Fruit; (12"ep) **THE PEEL SESSIONS** (29.1.81) [ ] [-]
– Truth / Senses / I.C.B. / Dreams never end. *(cd-ep.May88)*

Mar 88. Factory/ US= Qwest; (7")(12") **BLUE MONDAY 1988. / THE BEACH** [3] [68]
(cd-s+=) – ('A'original).

Sep 90. Strange Fruit; (cd)(c)(m-lp) **THE PEEL SESSIONS** [ ] [-]
(above tracks)

Feb 92. Windsong; (cd)(c)(lp) **BBC RADIO 1 LIVE IN CONCERT (live Jun'87)** [33] [-]
– Touched by the hand of God / Temptation / True faith / Your silent face / Every second counts / Bizarre love triangle / Perfect kiss / Age of consent / Sister Ray.

—— In Mar'89, issued two 5"cd-videos of TRUE FAITH + BLUE MONDAY '88.

ELECTRONIC

BERNARD SUMNER – vocals, guitar / **JOHNNY MARR** – guitar (ex-SMITHS) + both programmers. also with **NEIL TENANT** – vocals (of PET SHOP BOYS)

Factory / Warners

Dec 89. (7")(c-s) **GETTING AWAY WITH IT. / LUCKY BAG** [12] [38]
(12"+=)(cd-s+=)/ /(12"ltd.+=) – ('A'extended)./ / ('A'extra mixes).

—— added further guests **CHRIS LOWE, DONALD JOHNSON, DAVID PALMER, DENISE JOHNSON, HELEN POWELL + ANDREW ROBINSON** (on same track)

Apr 91. (7")(c-s) **GET THE MESSAGE. / FREE WILL** [8] [ ]
(cd-s+=)/ /(12"+=) – ('A' DNA groove mix)./ / ('A' 2 other mixes).

May 91. (cd)(c)(lp) **ELECTRONIC** [2] [ ]
– Idiot country / Reality / Tighten up / The patience of a saint / Gangster / Soviet / Get the message / Try all you want / Some distant memory / Feel every beat

Sep 91. (7")(c-s) **FEEL EVERY BEAT. / LEAN TO THE INSIDE** [39] [ ]
(12"+=) – ('A'dub version).
(cd-s+=) – Second to none / ('A' DNA mix)

Next with NEIL TENANT again.

Parlophone / Warners

Jun 92. (7") **DISAPPOINTED. / IDIOT COUNTRY TWO** [6] [ ]
(12"+=)(cd-s+=) – ('A'-808 State mix) /('B'ultimatum mix).

. . . Jan – Jun '96 stop press . . .

Jun 96. (single) **FORBIDDEN CITY** [14] [ ]

REVENGE

PETER HOOK – bass with **DAVE HICKS** – words, vocals / **C.JONES**

Factory / Warners

Nov 89. (7") **REASONS. / JESUS I LOVE YOU** [ ] [ ]
(12"+=) – Love you 2.
(cd-s+=) – ('B'version) / Bleach boy.

May 90. (7")(c-s) **PINEAPPLE FACE. / 14K** [ ] [ ]
(12"+=) – ('A'-Revenge version).
(cd-s+=) – ('A'-Last Lunge version).

Jun 90. (cd)(c)(lp) **ONE TRUE PASSION** [ ] [ ]
– Pineapple face / Big bang / Lose the chrome / Slave / Bleachman / Surf Nazi / Fag hag / It's quiet.

Sep 90. (7") **(I'M NOT YOUR) SLAVE. / AMSTERDAM** [ ] [ ]
(12"+=)(cd-s+=) – ('A' II version) / Slave.

—— DAVE HICKS departed Apr'91, replaced by **POTTSY**

Dec 91. (12"ep)(cd-ep) **GUN WORLD PORN** [ ] [-]
– Deadbeat (remix) / Cloud nine / State of shock / Little pig.

The OTHER TWO

STEPHEN + GILLIAN

Parlophone / Warners

Oct 91. (7")(c-s) **TASTY FISH (Pascal mix). / ('A'mix)** [ ] [-]
(12"+=)(cd-s+=) – ('A'-almond slice mix).

London / London

Oct 93. (7")(c-s) **SELFISH. / SELFISH (that pop mix)** [46] [ ]
(12") (all 4 versions)
(cd-s+=) – ('A'-East Village vocal mix) / ('A'-Waterfront mix).

Nov 93. (cd)(c)(lp) **THE OTHER TWO AND YOU** [ ] [ ]
– Tasty fish / The greatest thing / Selfish / Movin' on / Ninth configuration / Feel this love / Spirit level / Night voice / Innocence.
(cd+=) Love it.

NEW POWER GENERATION (see under ⇒ PRINCE)

NEW YORK DOLLS

Formed: New York, USA ... Dec'71 by THUNDERS, JOHANSEN, MURCIA, KANE & RIVETS. In Mar'72, RIVETS left to form The BRATS, and was replaced by SYLVAIN. On 6 Nov'72, MURCIA died after drowning in his own bath (not to contrary belief from a drug overdose). He was soon superseded by NOLAN, as they signed to 'Mercury', Mar'73. Their TODD RUNDGREN produced eponymous debut album came out in the summer of '73, but sold moderately enough for a GEORGE MORTON produced 2nd, 'TOO MUCH TOO SOON' in 1974. Early the following year, they brought in Londoner MALCOLM McLAREN as manager, but it was clear their short trail was at an end. • **Style:** Comparisons drew on the ROLLING STONES, as JOHANSEN was a dead-ringer in voice and looks for MICK JAGGER. THUNDERS too, was similar to the other 'Glimmer Twin' KEITH RICHARDS. Their trashy transvestite attire, also was derived from The STONES (circa '66 'Have You Seen Your Mother . . . '). Their other sources of inspiration came from MC5, The PRETTY THINGS, PINK FAIRIES and The SHANGRI-LAS'S! Their double-axed guitar sound, although limited and punk-rock like, was effective nonetheless. • **Songwriters:** JOHANSEN with THUNDERS or SYLVAIN. Covered PILLS (Bo Diddley) / DON'T START ME TALKIN' (Sonny Boy Williamson) / SHOWDOWN (Archie Bell) / SOMETHIN' ELSE (Eddie Cochran) / etc. • **Trivia:** 2 songs 'PERSONALITY CRISIS' & 'WHO ARE THE MYSTERY GIRLS', appeared on the 1977 Various Artists compilation 'NEW WAVE'. **Johansen's filmography:** Married To The Mob + Scrooged.

Recommended: NEW YORK DOLLS (*8) / TOO MUCH TOO SOON (*7)

DAVID JOHANSEN (b. 9 Jan'50, Staten Island, New York) – vocals / **JOHNNY THUNDERS** (b.JOHN GENZALE, 15 Jul'54) – guitar, vocals / **SYLVAIN SYLVAIN** (b.SIL MIZRAHI) – guitar, vocals repl. RICK RIVETS / **ARTHUR KANE** (b. 3 Feb'51) – bass JERRY NOLAN (b. 7 May'51) – drums repl. BILLY MURCIA who died.

Mercury / Mercury

Jul 73. (7") **TRASH. / PERSONALITY CRISIS** [-] [ ]

Aug 73. (lp)(c) **NEW YORK DOLLS** [ ] [ ] Jul 73
– Personality crisis / Looking for a kiss / Vietnamese baby / Lonely planet boy / Frankenstein / Trash / Bad girl / Subway train / Pills / Private world / Jet boy.
(US re-iss.1984)

Nov 73. (7") **JET BOY JET GIRL. / VIETNAMESE BABY** [ ] [-]

Jul 74. (lp)(c) **TOO MUCH TOO SOON** [ ] [ ] May 74

– Babylon / Stranded in the jungle / Who are the mystery girls? / (There's gonna be a) Showdown / It's too late / Puss 'n' boots / Chatterbox / Bad detective / Don't start me talkin' / Human being. *(US re-iss.1984)*

Jul 74. (7") **STRANDED IN THE JUNGLE. / WHO ARE THE MYSTERY GIRLS?** [ ] [ ]

not issued — Fan Club

1974. (7"ep) **LOOKING FOR A KISS (live). / WHO ARE THE MYSTERY GIRLS? (live) / SOMETHIN' ELSE (live)** [-] [ ]

—— **PETER JORDAN** – bass (the roadie filled in on stage when KANE was drunk)

—— Disbanded mid 1975, after **BOBBY BLAIN** – keyboards repl. CHRIS ROBINSON who had repl. THUNDERS (he formed The HEARTBREAKERS with NOLAN). **TOMMY MACHINE** (was last drummer). The NEW YORK DOLLS reformed again with JOHANSEN and SYLVIAN but only toured until late '76. SYLVIAN later formed The CRIMINALS.

– compilations, others, etc. –

Jun 77. Mercury; (7"m) **JET BOY, JET GIRL. / BABYLON / WHO ARE THE MYSTERY GIRLS?** [ ] [-]

Jul 77. Mercury; (d-lp) **NEW YORK DOLLS / TOO MUCH TOO SOON** [ ] [-]
(re-iss.Apr89)

1985. Mercury; (lp) **NIGHT OF THE LIVING DOLLS** [-] [ ]

1983. R.O.I.R.; (c) **LIPSTICK KILLERS – MERCER ST.SESSIONS** [-] [ ]
(lp/cd. iss.May90 on 'Danceteria') (cd-iss.Feb95 on 'ROIR Europe')

Sep 82. Kamera; (12"ep) **PERSONALITY CRISIS / LOOKING FOR A KISS. / SUBWAY TRAIN / BAD GIRL** [ ] [-]
(re-iss.Feb86) (cd-ep re-iss.Jul90 on 'See For Miles')

1985. Antler; (7")(12"pic-d)(12"red) **PERSONALITY CRISIS. / SUBWAY TRAIN** [ ] [-]

1985. Antler; (7")(12"pic-d)(12"blue) **LOOKING FOR A KISS. / BAD GIRL** [ ] [-]

1986. Receiver; (lp) **AFTER THE STORM** [ ] [-]

Sep 84. Fan Club; (red-m-lp) **RED PATENT LEATHER (rec. 75)** [-] [-] France
– Girls / Downtown / Private love / Personality crisis / Pills / Something else / Daddy rollin' stone / Dizzy Miss Lizzy. *(cd-iss.Oct88) (cd-iss.Feb93 on 'Receiver')*

Oct 84. Fan Club; (7"white) **PILLS (live). / DOWN, DOWN, DOWN TOWN (live)** [-] [-]

Oct 94. Mercury; (cd) **ROCK'N'ROLL** [ ] [ ]

DAVID JOHANSEN

– vocals, keyboards with his group **STATEN ISLAND BOYS: THOMAS TRASK** – guitar / **JOHHNY RAO** – guitar / **BUZZ VERNO** – bass (ex-CHERRY VANILLA) / **FRANKI LA ROCKA** – drums (ex-CHERRY VANILLA)

Blue Sky — Blue Sky

Jul 78. (lp)(c) **DAVID JOHANSEN** [ ] [ ] May 78
– Funky but chic / Girls / Pain in my heart / Not that much / Donna / Cool metro / I'm a lover / Lonely tenement / Frenchette.

Sep 78. (7") **FUNKY BUT CHIC. / THE ROPE (THE LET GO SONG)** [ ] [ ]

Sep 79. (lp)(c) **IN STYLE** [ ] [ ]
– Melody / She / Big city / She knew she was falling in love / Swaheto woman / Justine / In style / You touched me too / Wreckless crazy / Flamingo road.

Sep 79. (7") **MELODY. / RECKLESS CRAZY** [-] [ ]

Mar 80. (7")(12") **SWAHETO WOMAN. / SHE KNEW SHE WAS FALLING IN LOVE** [ ] [ ] 1979

—— with new band **BLONDIE CHAPLIN** – guitar, vocals / **ERNIE BROOKS** – bass / **TOM MANDEL** – organ / **BOBBY BLAIN** – piano / **TONY MACHINE** – drums

Aug 81. (lp)(c) **HERE COMES THE NIGHT** [ ] [ ]
– She loves strangers / Bohemian love pad / You fool me / My obsession / Marquesa de Sade / Here comes the night / Suspicion / Party tonight / Havin' so much fun / Rollin' job / Heart of gold. *(cd-iss.Oct94 on 'Rewind')*

Sep 81. (7") **HERE COMES THE NIGHT. / SHE LOVES STRANGERS** [-] [ ]

Jun 82. (7") **BOHEMIAN LOVE PAD. / MEDLEY: WE GOTA GET OUT OF THIS PLACE – DON'T BRING ME DOWN (live)** [-] [ ]

1982. (lp) **LIVE IT UP** [-] [ ]
(cd-iss.Jan 94 on 'Legacy')

—— now with **JOE DELIA** – keyboards / **DAVID NELSON** – guitar / **BRETT CARTWRIGHT** – bass / **DENNIS McDERMOTT** – drums

10-Virgin — Passport

Feb 85. (lp)(c) **SWEET REVENGE** [ ] [ ]

Mar 85. (7")(12") **HEARD THE NEWS. / KING OF BABYLON** [ ] [ ]

BUSTER POINDEXTER & HIS BANSHEES OF BLUE

(aka DAVID JOHANSEN)

R.C.A. — R.C.A.

Jun 88. (7")(12") **HOT HOT HOT. / CANNIBAL** [ ] [45] Nov 87

Jul 88. (lp)(c)(cd) **BUSTER POINDEXTER** [ ] [90] Jan 88
– Smack dab in the middle / Bad boy / Hot hot hot / Are you lonely for me baby / Screwy music / Good morning judge / Oh me oh my (I'm a fool for you baby) / Whadaya want? / House of the rising sun / Cannibal / Heart of gold.

Jul 88. (7") **OH ME, OH MY (I'M A FOOL FOR YOU BABY). / CANNIBAL** [-] [ ]

Sep 88. (7") **HEART OF GOLD. / HIT THE ROAD JACK** [-] [ ]

1989. (7") **ALL NIGHT PARTY. / ('A'-hot mix)** [-] [ ]

1989. (7") **UNDER THE SEA. / DEBOURGE YOURSELF** [-] [ ]

Oct 94. Sequel-Rhino; (cd) **BUSTER'S HAPPY HOUR** [ ] [ ]

NICE

Formed: London, England ... Oct'67 by ex-GARY FARR & THE T-BONES members KEITH EMERSON and LEE JACKSON, who had just previously with DAVID O'LIST and BRIAN DAVISON, been back-up to British black soul singer P.P.ARNOLD. Being part of Andrew Loog Oldham's 'Immediate' label, they moved to different musical direction, and issued first 45 'THOUGHTS OF EMERLIST DAVJACK'. This flopped, as did its same titled debut lp containing their show-stopper 'RONDO', early in '68. In the summer, they surprised nearly everyone, when their re-indition of Leonard Bernstein's 'AMERICA' (from 'West Side Story'), nearly hit UK Top 20. It was banned in the States, however, when their promotional poster featured recently deceased Martin Luther King, Bobby and John F.Kennedy. At a concert at The Royal Albert Hall, they burned an American flag, which riled Bernstein enough to prevent the 45 being issued in the US. Although their next lp failed, their subsequent ones all went Top 5. • **Style:** Pioneers of classical-rock, they at times dislocated classic music, arranging new interpretations, around the keyboard-stabbing showman KEITH EMERSON. He also went on to become the greatest ivory-tinkler after forming EMERSON, LAKE & PALMER. • **Songwriters:** Group compositions, using first letters of forenames (aka 'EMERLIST DAVJACK' until O'LIST left in 1968). Covered AMERICA (Sondheim / Bernstein) / INTERMEZZO FROM KARELIA SUITE (Sibelius) / HANG ON TO A DREAM (Tim Hardin) / SHE BELONGS TO ME + MY BACK PAGES + COUNTRY PIE (Bob Dylan) / and other classical re-inditions.

Recommended: THE NICE COLLECTION (*8)

KEITH EMERSON (b. 2 Nov'44) – keyboards / **DAVID O'LIST** – guitar, vocals / **BRIAN DAVISON** (b.25 May'42, Leicester, England) – drums / **LEE JACKSON** (b. 8 Jan'43, Newcastle, England) – vocals, bass

Immediate — Immediate

Nov 67. (7") **THE THOUGHTS OF EMERLIST DAVJACK. / AZRIAL (ANGEL OF DEATH)** [ ] [ ]

Dec 67. (lp) **THE THOUGHTS OF EMERLIST DAVJACK** [ ] [ ]
– Flower king of flies / The thoughts of Emerlist Davjack / Bonnie K. / Rondo / War and peace / Tantalising Maggie / Dawn / The cry of Eugene / Angel of death / America: 1A (adapted from 'West Side Story') – 1B second amendment / The diamond hard apples of the Moon. *(re-iss.Jul 68) (re-iss.1978 on 'Charly') (cd-iss.1988 on 'Line') (cd-iss.1990's on 'Repertoire')*

Jun 68. (7") **AMERICA. / THE DIAMOND HARD APPLES OF THE MOON** [21] [ ]
(re-iss.Dec82)

—— now a trio, when O'LIST departed, later joining ROXY MUSIC

Dec 68. (lp) **ARS LONGA VITA BREVIS** [ ] [ ]
– Daddy, where did I come from? / Little Arabella / Happy Freuds / Intermezzo from Karelia / Don Edito el Gruva / Ars longa vita brevis – Prelude: 1st movement – Wakening ; 2nd movement – Realisation ; 3rd movement – Acceptance – Brandenburger ; 4th movement – Denial / Coda – Extention to the big note. *(cd-iss.1990's on 'Castle')*

Dec 68. (7") **BRANDENBURGER. / HAPPY FREUDS** [ ] [-]

Jul 69. (7") **SHE BELONGS TO ME. / ('A'version)** [ ] [-]

Aug 69. (lp) **THE NICE** [3] [ ]
– Azrael revisited / Hang on to a dream / Diary of an empty day / For example / Rondo 69 / She belongs to me. *(cd-iss.1990's on 'Repertoire')*

Charisma — Mercury

Jun 70. (lp)(c) **FIVE BRIDGES SUITE** [2] [ ]
– The five bridges suite:- Fantasia, 1st bridge – 2nd bridge – Choral, 3rd bridge – High level fugue, 4th bridge – Finale, 5th bridge / Intermezzo Karelia suite:- Pathetique, 'Symphony No.6. 3rd movement' / Country pie – Bach: Brandenburg concerto No.6 / One of those people. *(cd-iss.Feb91 on 'Virgin')*

Jul 70. (7") **COUNTRY PIE. / ONE OF THOSE PEOPLE** [ ] [ ]

—— Disbanded mid 1970. KEITH formed EMERSON, LAKE AND PALMER. LEE and BRIAN later surfaced as REFUGEE and made one eponymous album in 1974 for 'Charisma', which featured future YES man, PATRICK MORAZ.

– compilations, others, etc. –

Apr 71. Charisma/ US= Mercury; (lp)(c) **ELEGY (live)** [5] [ ]

– Hang on to a dream / My back pages / 3rd movement – Pathetique / America (from 'West Side Story'). *(cd-iss.Feb91 on 'Virgin') (cd-iss.Jun93 on 'Virgin' +=)* – Diamonds blue apples of the Moon / Dawn / Tantalising Maggie / The cry of Eugene / Daddy, where did I come from? / Aziral.

1972. Charisma/ US= Mercury; (lp)(c) **AUTUMN 67 SPRING 68** [ ] [ ]

Mar 83. Charisma; (d-c) **FIVE BRIDGES SUITE / AUTUMN 67 AND SPRING 68** [ ] [-]

Mar 76. Immediate; (lp) **AMOENI REDIVI** [ ] [-]

Jan 78. Immediate; (lp) **THE NICE GREATEST HITS** [ ] [-]

Dec 93. Immediate; (cd) **THE BEST OF THE NICE – AMERICA** [ ] [-]

Nov 85. Castle; (d-lp)(d-c)(cd) **THE NICE COLLECTION** [ ] [-]
– America 1A (adapted from 'West Side Story') – 1B Second amendment / Happy Freuds / The cry of Eugene / The thoughts of Emerlist Davjack / Rondo / Daddy, where did I come from? / Little Arabella / Intermezzo from Karelia / Hang on to a dream / The diamond hard apples of the Moon / Angel of death / Ars longa vita brevis – Prelude:- 1st movement – Wakening, 2nd movement – Realisation, 3rd movement – Acceptance, Brandenburger, 4th movement – Denial / Coda – Extention to the big note. *(re-iss.cd Apr94)*

Aug 87. Seal; (lp)(c) **THE 20th ANNIVERSARY OF THE NICE** [ ] [-]
(cd-iss.Apr88 on 'Bite Back')

Feb 72. Mercury; (d-lp) **KEITH EMERSON WITH THE NICE** [-] [ ]
(4th + 5th albums)
(cd-iss. 1988)

Mar 94. Laserlight; (cd)(c) **AMERICA** [ ] [-]

Nov 95. Charly; (3xcd-box) **THE IMMEDIATE YEARS** [ ] [-]

NINE INCH NAILS

Formed: San Francisco, California, USA . . . 1989 by REZNOR. Toured on the 'Lolla palooza' tour with JANE'S ADDICTION around the same time as they unleashed their debut album 'PRETTY HATE MACHINE'. • **Style:** Violent hard-core alternative metal influenced by KILLING JOKE and obsessed with Charles Manson. They smashed up gear and soaked electrical equipment on stage!!! • **Songwriters:** 'The Terminator' REZNOR penned except PHYSICAL YOU'RE SO (Adam Ant). • **Trivia:** REZNOR appeared in the 1987 film 'LIGHT OF DAY'. ALAN MOULDER is the mixing engineer.

Recommended: PRETTY HATE MACHINE (*7) / BROKEN (*7) / THE DOWNWARD SPIRAL (*8)

TRENT REZNOR – vocals, guitar / **JAMES WOOLEY** – keyboards / **RICHARD** – guitar / **CHRIS VRENNA** – drums

TVT-Island / Nothing-Interscope

Nov 90. (12"ep)(cd-ep) **DOWN IN IT (skin). / TERRIBLE LIE (mix) / DOWN IN IT (shred)** [ ] [ ]
(12"ep)(cd-ep) – (1st 2 tracks) / Down in it (demo)

Sep 91. (7")(10") **HEAD LIKE A HOLE. / ('A'copper mix)** [45] [ ]
(cd-s+=) – ('A'opal mix).

Sep 91. (cd)(c)(lp) **PRETTY HATE MACHINE** [67] [75] Nov 90
– Head like a hole / Terrible lie / Down in it / Sanctified / Something I can never have / Kinda I want to / Sin / That's what I get / The only time / Ringfinger.

Nov 91. (7") **SIN. / GET DOWN MAKE LOVE** [35] [ ]
(10"+=)(cd-s+=) – Sin (dub).

Sep 92. (cd)(c)(lp) **BROKEN** [18] [7]
– Pinion / Wish / Last / Help me I am in Hell / Happiness is slavery / Gave up. (free 7"+cd+=) – Physical (you're so) / Suck.

Nov 92. (cd)(c)(m-lp) **FIXED** (remixes) [ ] [ ]
– Gave up / Wish / Happiness is slavery / Throw this away / Fist fuck / Screaming slave.

—— Below controversially recorded at the house of the Charles Manson murders (some produced by /with FLOOD). Guests on 1 track each were **ADRIAN BELEW + DANNY LOHNER** – guitar / **CHRIS VRENNA + STEPHEN PERKINS + ANDY KUBISZEWSKI +** – drums (live:- **VRENNA, LOHNER, WOOLLEY + ROBIN FINCK**)

Mar 94. (cd)(c)(d-lp) **THE DOWNWARD SPIRAL** [9] [2]
– Mr.Self destruct / Piggy / Heresy / March of the pigs / Closer / Ruiner / The becoming / I do not want this / Big man with a gun / A warm place / Eraser / Reptile / The downward spiral / Hurt.

Mar 94. (etched-7") **MARCH OF THE PIGS. / A VIOLENT FLUID** [45] [59]
(9"+=) – All the pigs, all lined up / Underneath the skin.
(cd-s) – ('A'side) / Underneath the skin / Reptillian.
(cd-s+=) – All the pigs, all lined up / Big man with a gun.

Jun 94. (12")(cd-s) **CLOSER / CLOSER TO GOD / MARCH OF THE FUCKHEADS / HERESY (BLIND) / MEMORABILIA** [25] [41] Sep94
(cd-s) – ('A'side) – (deviation) – (further away) / ('A'original) / ('A'precursor) / ('A'internal).

May 95. (cd)(c) **FURTHER DOWN THE SPIRAL** (remixes) [ ] [23]
– Piggy (nothing can stop me) / The art of destruction (part one) / Self destruction (part three) / Heresy (version) / The downward spiral (the bottom) / Hurt / At the heart of it all / Ruiner (version) / Eraser (denial: realization) / Self destruction: final.

NIRVANA (US)

Formed: Aberdeen, Washington, USA . . . 1987 by KURT & CHRIS. Released debut 45 'LOVE BUZZ' on US indie label 'Sub Pop' in 1988, before finally issuing first lp 'BLEACH' in 1989. After a quiet following year, they returned in 1991 with a classic! 'NEVERMIND'. It soon raced up the US and UK charts, helped by the lifted track 'SMELLS LIKE TEEN SPIRIT', smashing the hit parade. • **Style:** A blend of punk Pixies, power GUNS'N'ROSES and even melody of R.E.M. Their "New-wave" grunge metal shifted music finally into the 90's. • **Songwriters:** COBAIN wrote late 80's work. In the 90's, the group were credited with COBAIN lyrics. Covers; LOVE BUZZ (Shocking Blue) / HERE SHE COMES NOW (Velvet Underground) / DO YOU LOVE ME? (Kiss) / TURNAROUND (Devo) / MOLLY'S LIPS + SON OF A GUN + JESUS WANTS ME FOR A SUNBEAM (Vaselines) / D7 (Wipers) / THE MAN WHO SOLD THE WORLD (David Bowie) / WHERE DID YOU SLEEP LAST NIGHT (Leadbelly). FOO FIGHTERS covered OZONE (Kiss). • **Trivia:** KURT married COURTNEY LOVE (of Hole) in Feb'92, who gave a him child in Aug'92.

Recommended: NEVERMIND (*10) / IN UTERO (*9) / BLEACH (*7) / UNPLUGGED IN NEW YORK (*9) / FOO FIGHTERS (*8; FOO FIGHTERS)

KURT COBAIN (b.20 Feb'67) – vocals, guitar / **CHRIS NOVOSELIC** (b.16 May'65) – bass / **CHAD CHANNING** – drums

Tupelo / Sub Pop

Oct 88. (7") **LOVE BUZZ. / BIG CHEESE** [-] [ ]

—— Early '89, added **JASON EVERMAN** – guitar Also guest drummer on 2 tracks **DALE CROVER**

Aug 89. (lp)(cd)(white-lp)(green-lp) **BLEACH** [ ] [ ] Jun 89
– Blew / Floyd the barber / About a girl / School / Paper cuts / Negative creep / Scoff / Swap meet / Mr.Moustache / Sifting / Big cheese. (cd+=) – Love buzz / Downer. *(US re-iss.Dec 91 hit 89) (re-iss.+cd+c.Feb92 on 'D.G.C.', hit UK No.33)* (c+=) – Big cheese. *(re-iss.cd/c Oct95 on 'Geffen')*

Dec 89. (12"ep)(cd-ep) **BLEW / LOVE BUZZ. / BEEN A SON / STAIN** [ ] [-]

—— **DAN PETERS** – drums (of MUDHONEY) repl. CHANNING (Apr90)

Jan 91. (7")(7"green) **SLIVER. / DIVE** [ ] [ ] Sep 90
(12"+=) – About a girl (live). *(US-iss.7"blue)*
(cd-s++=) – Spank thru (live).

Feb91. (7")(7"green) **MOLLY'S LIPS. / FLUID** [-] [ ]

not issued / Communion

Mar 91. (7"colrd) **HERE SHE COMES NOW. /('B'by "Melvins")** [-] [ ]

—— (Apr91 trio) **DAVID GROHL** (b.14 Jan'69) – drums, vocals (ex-SCREAM) repl. PETERS and EVERMAN, who joined MIND FUNK.

D.G.C. / D.G.C.

Sep 91. (cd)(c)(lp) **NEVERMIND** [7] [1]
– Smells like teen spirit / In bloom / Come as you are / Breed / Lithium / Polly / Territorial pissings / Drain you / Lounge act / Stay away / On a plain / Something in the way. *(cd+=)*– Endless nameless.

Oct 91. (7") **SMELLS LIKE TEEN SPIRIT. / EVEN IN HIS YOUTH** [-] [6]

Nov 91. (7")(c-s) **SMELLS LIKE TEEN SPIRIT. / DRAIN YOU** [7] [-]
(12"+=)/ /(12"pic-d+=) – Even in his youth./ / Aneurysm.
(cd-s+=) – Even in his youth / Aneurysm.

(above only issued in US on c-s/cd-s)

Mar 92. (7") **COME AS YOU ARE. / DRAIN YOU (live)** [-] [32]

Mar 92. (7")(c-s) **COME AS YOU ARE. / ENDLESS NAMELESS** [9] [-]
(12"+=)/ /(cd-s++=) – Drain you (live)./ / School (live).

Jul 92. (7")(c-s) **LITHIUM. / BEEN A SON (live)** [11] [ ]
(12"pic-d+=)/ /(cd-s++=) – Curmudgeons./ / D7.

Nov 92. (7")(c-s) **IN BLOOM. / POLLY** [28] [ ]
(cd-s+=)(12"pic-d+=) – Sliver (live)

Dec 92. (cd)(c)(lp) **INCESTICIDE** (rare material) [14] [39]
– Dive / Sliver / Stain / Been a son / Turnaround / Molly's lips / Son of a gun / (New wave) Polly / Beeswax / Downer / Mexican seafood / Hairspray queen / Aero zeppelin / Big long now / Aneurysm.

—— In Feb'93, NIRVANA's 'OH, THE GUILT' appeared on double'A'side with JESUS LIZARD's 'Puss'. Issued on 'Touch & Go' 7"blue +cd-s, it made UK No.12, and crashed out of the Top 60 the following week!.

—— GOODBYE MR MACKENZIE's BIG JOHN played guitar live for them in mid'93.

In Aug'93, KURT KOBAIN and WILLIAM S.BURROUGHS narrated 'The Priest, They Call Him By' on 10"lp,cd 'T.K.'.

Aug 93. (7")(c-s) **HEART-SHAPED BOX. / MARIGOLD** [5] [ ]
(12"+=)(cd-s+=) – Milk it.

Sep 93. (cd)(c)(lp)(clear-lp) **IN UTERO** [1] [1]

– Serve the servants / Scentless apprentice / Heart-shaped box / Rape me / Frances Farmer will have her revenge on Seattle / Dumb / Very ape / Milk it / Penny royal tea / Radio friendly unit shifter / Tourette's / All apologies / Gallons of rubbing alcohol flow through the strip.

Dec 93. (7")(c-s) **ALL APOLOGIES. / RAPE ME** [32] [ ]
(12"+=)(cd-s+=) – MV.

— On the 4th March '94, KURT overdosed while on holiday in Italy and went into a coma. A month later, on the 8th April he committed suicide, by shooting himself through the mouth. He was only 27, and this was certainly the biggest rock star death since JOHN LENNON. For more details see HOLE and the COURTNEY LOVE story.

— below album featured **LORI GOLDSTON** -cello + **MEAT PUPPETS' Curt & Cris Kirkwood** on 3rd, 4th & 5th last songs.

Nov 94. (cd)(c)(white-lp) **UNPLUGGED IN NEW YORK** (live acoustic) [1] [1]

– About a girl / Come as you are / Jesus doesn't want me for a sunbeam / Dumb / The man who sold the world / Pennyroyal tea / Polly / On a plain / Something in the way / Plateau / Oh me / Lake of fire / All apologies / Where did you sleep last night.

— GROHL (now vox, guitar) formed The FOO FIGHTERS, taking their name from the mysterious lights that were reported by fighter pilots during World War 2. He recruited ex-GERMS guitarist PAT SMEAR. Meanwhile NOVOSELIC formed the trio SWEET 75.

compilations, etc

Nov 95. Geffen; (6xcd-s) **6 CD SINGLE BOXED SET** [ ] [-]

FOO FIGHTERS

DAVE GROHL -vocals, guitar / **PAT SMEAR** -guitar (ex-GERMS) / **NATE MANDEL** -

bass / **WILLIAM GOLDSMITH** -drums (both of SUNNY DAY REAL ESTATE) -signed to 'Capitol' through below . . .

Date	Release	Rosswell	Rosswell
Jun 95.	(7") **THIS IS A CALL. / WINNEBAGO** (12"+=)(cd-s+=) – Podunk.	5	
Jun 95.	(cd)(c)(lp) **FOO FIGHTERS** – This is a call / I'll stick around / Big me / Alone and easy target / Good grief / Floaty / Weenie beenie / Oh, George / For all the cows / X-static / Watershed / Exhausted.	3	23
Sep 95.	(7"red)(c-s) **I'LL STICK AROUND. / HOW I MISS YOU** (12"+=)(cd-s+=) – Ozone.	18	
Nov 95.	(7"blue)(c-s) **FOR ALL THE COWS. / WATTERSHED (live)** (cd-s+=) – ('A'live at Reading).	28	
	. . . *Jan – Jun '96 stop press* . . .		
Mar 96.	(single) **BIG ME**	19	

—— cover on b-side; GAS CHAMBER (Angry Samoans).

NO DOUBT

*** NEW ENTRY ***

Formed: Orange County, California, USA . . .1987 by JOHN SPENCE, TOM DUMYNE, TONY KANAL and ADRIAN YOUNG. Tragedy struck a year later, when SPENCE committed suicide. They went underground for a while, but returned in the early 90's with new blonde bombshell GWEN STEFANI. After two albums for 'Trauma', they were licensed to 'Interscope' in 1995 and were soon having US Top 20 album 'TRAGIC KINGDOM'. • **Style:** Metallic ska-rock influenced by MADNESS, BAD BRAINS and KISS, with a CYNDI LAUPER lookalike thrown in. • **Songwriters:** STEFANI w/ others. • **Trivia:** GWEN hangs out with Scottish born GARBAGE singer SHIRLEY MANSON.

Recommended: TRAGIC KINGDOM (*7)

GWEN STEFANI – vocals / **TOM DUMYNE** – guitar / **TONY KANAL** – bass / **ADRIAN YOUNG** – drums

Date	Release	Interscope	Trauma
Jun 96.	(cd)(c) **TRAGIC KINGDOM** – Spiderwebs / Excuse me Mr. / Just a girl / Happy now? / Different people / Hey you / The climb / Sixteen / Sunday morning / Don't speak / You can do it / World go 'round / End it on this / Tragic kingdom.		11 Feb 96
Jun 96.	(c-s) **JUST A GIRL / DIFFERENT PEOPLE** (cd-s+=) – Open the gate.		23 Mar 96

NORTHERN UPROAR

*** NEW ENTRY ***

Formed: Manchester, England . . .1995 by Spanish born LEON, plus PK, JEFF and KEITH. Played Scotland's 'T In The Park' in the summer of '95 (returned the following year) and signed to 'Heavenly', immediately gate-crashing the Top 50 with JAMES DEAN BRADFORD (Manics) produced single 'ROLLERCOASTER'. 1996 started off with a Top 20 hit 'FROM A WINDOW'. • **Style:** Brash and cocky teenage fuzz-pop guitar band influenced by SMALL FACES, CLASH and friends OASIS. • **Songwriters:** Most by MEYA or with KELLY except MY MIND'S EYE (Small Faces) / I AM THE COSMOS (Chris Bell). • **Trivia:** LEON MEYA was called up for national service to the Spanish army although he only lived there for first five years!

Recommended: NORTHERN UPROAR (*6)

LEON MEYA – vocals, bass / **PK (PAUL KELLY)** – guitar / **JEFF FLETCHER**– guitar, vocals / **KEITH CHADWICK**– drums, piano

Date	Release	Heavenly	London
Oct 95.	(7")(c-s) **ROLLERCOASTER. / ROUGH BOYS** (cd-s+=) – Smooth geezer / Waiting on.	41	
Jan 96.	(7")(c-s) **FROM A WINDOW. / THIS MORNING** (cd-s++) – My mind's eye / Credibility.	17	
Apr 96.	(7"ep)(c-ep)(cd-ep) **LIVIN' IT UP / STONEFALL. / GOODBYE / IN MY WORLD**	24	
May 96.	(cd)(c)(lp) **NORTHERN UPROAR** – From a window / Rough boy / Town / Kicks / Breakthrough / Memories / Waiting on / Livin' it up / Head under water / Moods / Rollercoaster / Living in the red.	22	
Jun 96.	(7")(c-s) **TOWN. / KICKS (acoustic)** (cd-s+=) – Memories / I am the cosmos.	48	

Ted NUGENT

Born: 13 Dec'49, Detroit, Michegan, USA. In 1966, he formed garage-rock Chicago band The AMBOY DUKES, who quickly signed to 'Mainstream' US, releasing debut 'BABY PLEASE DON'T GO' in 1967. Their eponymous lp, early '68 broke into the Top 200, and by the Summer, the 45 'JOURNEY TO THE CENTER OF THE MIND', was in the US Top 20. Although they toured constantly in the US for the next couple of years, the band only managed minor chart placings. In 1971, they transgressed to TED NUGENT & THE AMBOY DUKES, who were snapped up by FRANK ZAPPA's 'Discreeet' label and unleashed 2 albums in the mid-70's, before dissolving. In 1975, NUGENT subscribed to a solo deal with 'Epic', and hit US Top 30 with eponymous Tom Werman produced debut early '76. His next album in 1977, 'FREE FOR ALL' (which featured MEAT LOAF) ventured further, and was first to earn him a Top 40 placing in UK. • **Style:** Controversial heavy-metal axeman, whose love of hunting animals and blood sports was well-publicised. A vehement non-drug taker, he sacked anyone in the band who dabbled with them. Early in 1978, he enscribed his name with a bowie knife on the arm of a fan! • **Songwriters:** NUGENT penned, except BABY PLEASE DON'T GO (hit; Them). The DAMN YANKEES credited TED, TOM & JACK. • **Trivia:** In 1973 while working on new record deal, he featured alongside other stars MIKE PINERA (Iron Butterfly), WAYNE KRAMER (MC5) and FRANK MARINO (Mahogany Rush), on 'battle of the guitarists' stage shows.

Note: There was another UK group called The AMBOY DUKES, and they released several singles on 'Polydor', around the mid 60's to '68.

Recommended: GREAT GONZOS (*8)

AMBOY DUKES

(UK = "AMERICAN AMBOY DUKES"). **TED NUGENT** – guitar, vox / plus **JOHN DRAKE** – vocals / **STEVE FARMER** – guitar / **BILL WHITE** – bass / **RICK LOBER** – keys / **DAVID PALMER** – drums

Date	Release	Fontana	Mainstream
1967.	(7") **BABY PLEASE DON'T GO. / PSALMS OF AFTERMATH**	-	
1967.	(7") **LET'S GO GET STONED. / IT'S NOT TRUE**		-
1968.	(lp) **THE AMBOY DUKES** – Baby please don't go / I feel free / Young love / Psalms of aftermath / Colors / Let's go get stoned / Down on Philips escalator / The lovely lady / Night time / It's not true / Gimme love. *(cd-iss.Dec92 on 'Repertoire' +=)*– J.B. special.		Jan 68

—— **RUSTY DAY** – vocals repl. DRAKE and FARMER / **ANDY SOLOMAN** – keyboards repl. LOBER **GREG ARAMA** – bass repl. WHITE

Date	Release	London	Mainstream
Jul 68.	(7") **JOURNEY TO THE CENTER OF THE MIND. / MISSISSIPPI MURDERER**		16
Aug 68.	(lp) **JOURNEY TO THE CENTER OF THE MIND** – Mississippi murderer / Surrender to your kings / Flight of the Byrd / Scottish tea / Dr. Slingshot / Journey to the center of the mind / Ivory castles / Why is a carrot more orange than an orange? / Missionary Mary / Death is life / Saint Philips friend / I'll prove I'm right / (Conclusion). *(cd-iss.Dec92 on 'Repertoire'+=)*– You talk sunshine, I breathe fire.		74
Oct 68.	(7") **SCOTTISH TEA. / YOU TALK SUNSHINE, I BREATHE FIRE**	-	
1969.	(lp) **MIGRATION** – Migration / Prodigal man / For his namesake / I'm not a juvenile delinquent / Good natured Emma / Inside the outside / Shades of green and grey / Curb your elephant / Loaded for bear. *(cd-iss.Dec92 on 'Repertoire'+=)*– Sobbin' in my mug of bear.		
1969.	(7") **PRODIGAL SON. / GOOD NATURED EMMA**	-	
1969.	(7") **MIGRATION. / FLIGHT OF THE BIRDS**	-	

Date	Release	Polydor	Polydor
Mar 70.	(lp) **MARRIAGE ON THE ROCKS – ROCK BOTTOM** – Marriage:- (a) Part 1 – Man / (b) Part 2 – Woman / (c) Part 3 – Music / Breast-fed 'gator (bait) / Get yer guns / Non-conformist wilderbeast man / Today's lesson / Children of the woods / Brain games of the yesteryear / The inexhaustable quest for the cosmic garbage (part 1 & 2) / (excerpt from Bartok).		

—— **NUGENT** brought in new members **BOB GRANGE** – bass / **KJ KNIGHT** – drums retaining also **ANDY SOLOMAN** (RUSTY DAY joined CACTUS)

TED NUGENT & THE AMBOY DUKES

Mar 71. (lp) **SURVIVAL OF THE FITTEST** (live) [ ] [ ]
– Survival of the fittest / Rattle my snake / Mr. Jones' hanging party / Papa's will / Slidin' on / Prodigal man.

— Disbanded in the early 70's, but in 1973 re-surfaced as

TED NUGENT'S AMBOY DUKES

with others **BOB GRANGE** – bass / **ANDY JEZOWSKI** – vocals / **GABRIEL MAGNO** – keyboards / **VIC MASTRIANNI** – drums

Discreet Discreet

Jun 74. (lp)(c) **CALL OF THE WILD** [ ] [ ]
– Call of the wild / Sweet revenge / Pony express / Ain't it the truth / Renegade / Rot gut / Below the belt / Cannon balls. *(re-iss.+cd.Oct89 on 'Edsel')*

Jun 74. (7") **SWEET REVENGE. / AIN'T IT THE TRUTH** [ ] [ ]

— **Rev.ATROCIOUS THEODOLIUS** – guitar, vocals repl. MAGNO

1975. (lp)(c) **TOOTH FANG & CLAW** [ ] [ ]
– No holds barred / Sacha / The great white buffalo / Maybelline / Free flight / Hibernation / Living in the woods / Lady luck.

— TED finally gave up AMBOY DUKES in 1975.

TED NUGENT

(solo) with **ROB GRANGE** – bass / **DEREK ST.HOLMES** – vocals, guitar (ex-SCOTT) / **CLIFF DAVIS** – drums / plus guests.

Epic Epic

Nov 75. (7") **MOTORCITY MADNESS. / WHERE HAVE YOU BEEN ALL MY LIFE** [-] [ ]

Mar 76. (lp)(c) **TED NUGENT** [56] [28] Nov 75
– Stranglehold / Stormtroopin' / Hey baby / Just what the doctor ordered / Snakeskin cowboy / Motor city madhouse / Where have you been all my life / You make me feel right at home / Queen of the forest. *(re-iss.Mar81)*

Mar 76. (7") **HEY BABY. / STORMTROOPIN'** [ ] [72]
(above poss.rel.UK Feb77)

Oct 76. (lp)(c) **FREE-FOR-ALL** [33] [24] Sep 76
– Dog eat dog / Free-for-all / Together / Hammerdown / Writing on the wall / Light my way / Street rats / I love you so I told you a lie / Turn it up. *(re-iss.Jan84)*

Nov 76. (7") **DOG EAT DOG. / LIGHT MY WAY** [-] [91]

Nov 76. (7") **DOG EAT DOG. / I LOVE YOU SO I TOLD YOU A LIE** [ ] [-]

Jan 77. (7") **FREE-FOR-ALL. / STREET RAGS** [-] [ ]

Jun 77. (lp)(c) **CAT SCRATCH FEVER** [28] [17]
– Cat scratch fever / Wang dang sweet poontang / Death by misadventure / Live it up / Home bound / Workin' hard, playin' hard / Sweet Sally / A thousand nights / Fist fightin' son of a gun / Out of control. *(cd-iss.Jun89)*

Jun 77. (7") **CAT SCRATCH FEVER. / WANG DANG SWEET POONTANG** [-] [ ]

Jul 77. (7") **CAT SCRATCH FEVER. / A THOUSAND NIGHTS** [ ] [-]

Feb 78. (7") **HOME BOUND. / DEATH BY MISADVENTURE** [ ] [70]

Feb 78. (d-lp)(c) **DOUBLE LIVE GONZO! (live)** [47] [13]
– Just what the doctor ordered / Wang dang sweet poontang / Cat scratch fever / Stormtroopin' / Hibernation / Motor city madhouse / Stranglehold / Gonzo / Baby please don't go / Yank me, crank me / Great white buffalo.

Mar 78. (7") **YANK ME, CRANK ME (live). / CAT SCRATCH FEVER (live)** [-] [58]

— **CHARLIE HUHN** – vocals, vocals repl. ST.HOLMES (to ST.PARADISE, etc) **DAVID HULL** – bass repl. BOB GRANGE (also to ST.PARADISE)

Nov 78. (lp)(c) **WEEKEND WARRIORS** [ ] [24]
– Tight spots / Weekend warriors / Need you bad / Smokescreen / Cruisin' / Name your poison / Venom soup / Good friends and a bottle of wine / I got the feelin' / One woman.

Dec 78. (7") **NEED YOU BAD. / I GOT THE FEELIN'** [-] [84]

— **WALTER MONAHAN** – bass repl. HULL

Jun 79. (lp)(c)(US-pic-lp) **STATE OF SHOCK** [ ] [18] May 79
– Alone / Bite down hard / I want to tell you / It doesn't matter / Paralyzed / Saddle sore / Satisfied / Snake charmer / State of shock / Take it or leave it.

Jun 79. (7") **I WANT TO TELL YOU. / BITE DOWN HARD** [-] [ ]

Jul 79. (7") **I WANT TO TELL YOU. / PARALYSED** [ ] [-]

May 80. (7")(12") **FLESH AND BLOOD. / MOTOR CITY MADHOUSE** [ ] [-]

Jun 80. (lp)(c) **SCREAM DREAM** [37] [13] May 80
– Wango tango / Scream dream / Hard as nails / I gotta move / Violent love / Flesh and blood / Spit it out / Come and get it / Terminus Eldorada / Don't cry.

Jul 80. (7") **WANGO TANGO. / SCREAM DREAM** [-] [86]

Feb 81. (7") **LAND OF A THOUSAND DANCES. / THE TNT OVERTURE** [-] [ ]

Apr 81. (lp)(c) **(INTENSITIES) IN 10 CITIES** [75] [51]
– Put up or shut up / Spontaneous combustion / My love is like a tire iron / Jailbait / I am a predator / Heads will roll / The flying lip lock / Land of a thousand dances / The TNT overture / I take no prisoners.

Dec 81. (lp)(c) **GREAT GONZOS! THE BEST OF TED NUGENT** (compilation) [ ] [ ]
– Cat scratch fever / Just what the doctor ordered / Free-for-all / Dog eat dog / Motor city madness / Paralysed / Stranglehold / Baby please don't go / Wango tango / Wang dang sweet poontang.

— **DEREK ST.HOLMES** – vocals returned from WHITFORD / ST.HOLMES to repl. HUHN / **DAVE KISWINEY** – bass repl. MONAGHAN / **CARMINE APPICE** – drums (ex-VANILLA FUDGE, ex-CACTUS, etc.) repl. DAVIS

Atlantic Atlantic

Aug 82. (lp)(c) **NUGENT** [ ] [51] Jul 82
– No, no, no / Bound and gagged / Habitual offender / Fightin' words / Good and ready / Ebony / Don't push me / Can't stop me now / We're gonna rock tonight / Tailgunner.

Sep 82. (7") **BOUND AND GAGGED. / HABITUAL OFFENDER** [-] [ ]

Nov 82. (7") **NO, NO, NO. / HABITUAL OFFENDER** [-] [ ]

— **NUGENT** recruited entire new band again! **BRIAN HOWE** – vocals / **ALAN ST.JOHN** – keyboards / **DOUG LABAHN** – bass / **BOBBY CHOUINARD** – drums

Feb 84. (lp)(c) **PENETRATOR** [ ] [56]
– Tied up in love / (Where do you) Draw the line / Knockin' at your door / Don't you want my love / Go down fighting / Thunder thighs / No man's land / Blame it on the night / Lean mean R&R machine / Take me home.

Feb 84. (7") **TIED UP IN LOVE. / LEAN MEAN R&R MACHINE** [ ] [-]

Apr 84 (7") **(WHERE DO YOU) DRAW THE LINE. / LEAN MEAN R&R MACHINE** [ ] [-]

— Took time out to appear in 'Miami Vice' US TV programme. He also played on charity single 'Stars' by aggregation 'HEAR'N AID' circa Spring 1986.

— **DAVE AMATO** – guitar, vocals repl. HOWE who joined BAD COMPANY / **RICKY PHILIPS** – bass (ex-BABYS) repl. LABAHN

Nov 86. (lp)(c)(cd) **LITTLE MISS DANGEROUS** [ ] [76] Mar 86
– High heels in motion / Strangers / Little Miss Dangerous / Savage dancer / Crazy ladies / When your body talks / My little red book / Take me away / Angry young man / Painkiller.

Apr 86. (7") **HIGH HEELS IN MOTION. / ANGRY YOUNG MAN** [-] [ ]

Jul 86. (7") **LITTLE MISS DANGEROUS. / ANGRY YOUNG MAN** [-] [ ]

— **NUGENT** re-recruited **DEREK ST.HOLMES** – vocals, guitar / **DAVE KISWINEY** – bass / plus new drummer -**PAT MARCHINO**

Feb 88. (lp)(c)(cd) **IF YOU CAN'T LICK 'EM ... LICK 'EM** [ ] [ ]
– Can't live with 'em / She drives me crazy / If you can't lick 'em . . . lick 'em / Skintight / Funlover / Spread your wings / The harder they come (the harder I get) / Separate the men from the boys, please / Bite the hand / That's the story of love.

DAMN YANKEES

TED NUGENT – guitar / **TOMMY SHAW** – vocals (ex-STYX) / **JACK BLADES** – bass (ex-NIGHT RANGER) / **MICHAEL CARTELLONE** – drums, non-s/writer

Warners Warners

Apr 90. (cd)(c)(lp) **DAMN YANKEES** [26] [13] Mar 90
– Coming of age / Bad reputation / Runaway / High enough / Damn Yankees / Come again / Mystified / Rock city / Tell me how you want it / Piledriver.

Apr 90. (c-s)(cd-s) **COMING OF AGE. / TELL ME HOW YOU WANT IT** [-] [60]

Jan 91. (7") **HIGH ENOUGH. / PILEDRIVER** [ ] [3] Oct 90
(12"+=)(cd-s+=) – Bonestripper.

Apr 91. (c-s) **COME AGAIN. / ('A' radio version)** [-] [50]

Aug 92. (cd)(c)(lp) **DON'T TREAD** [ ] [22]
– Don't tread on me / Fifteen minutes of fame / Where you goin' now / Dirty dog / Mister please / Silence is broken / Firefly / Someone to believe / This side of Hell / Double coyote / Uprising. *(re-iss.cd Feb95)*

Jan 93. (7")(c-s) **WHERE YOU GOIN' NOW. / THIS SIDE OF HELL** [ ] [20] Sep 92
(12"+=)(cd-s+=) – ('A'version).

Apr 93. (c-s)(cd-s) **SILENCE IS BROKEN. /** [-] [62]
(12"+=)(cd-s+=) – High enough (live) / ('A'live version).

Ted NUGENT

— returned w/ **ST.HOLMES / LUTZ**

Atlantic Atlantic

Dec 95. (cd)(c) **SPIRIT OF THE WILD** [ ] [86] May95
– Thighraceous / Wrong side of town / I shoot back / Tooth, fang and claw / Lovejacker / Fred bear / Primitive man / Hot or cold / Kiss my ass / Heart and soul / Spirit of the wild / Just do it like this.

– more compilations, others, etc. –

Feb 83. Epic; (d-c) **TED NUGENT / FREE FOR ALL** [ ] [-]

Sep 86. Raw Power; (d-lp)(d-c) **ANTHOLOGY** [ ] [-]
(re-iss.cd+c.Feb91 on 'Castle')

May 91. Thunderbolt; (cd)(c) **ON THE EDGE** [ ] [-]

Jun 93. Sony; (cd) **THE VERY BEST OF TED NUGENT** [ ] [ ]

May 94. Epic-Legacy; (d-cd)(d-c) **OUT OF CONTROL** [ ] [ ]

1975. Mainstream; (lp) **DR.SLINGSHOT (AMBOY DUKES)** [-] [ ]

Apr 75. Polydor; (d-lp) **JOURNEYS & MIGRATIONS (AMBOY DUKES)** [ ] [ ]
Jun 77. Polydor; (d-lp) **MARRIAGE ON THE ROCKS – ROCK BOTTOM / SURVIVAL OF THE FITTEST (AMBOY DUKES)** [ ] [ ]
1977. Warners; (d-lp) **TWO ORIGINALS OF . . . (AMBOY DUKES)** [ ] [ ]
– (CALL OF THE WILD & TOOTH, FANG & CLAW) albums

Gary NUMAN

Born: GARY WEBB, 8 Mar'58, Hammersmith, London, England. In 1977, he formed punk outfit MEAN STREET, who appeared on Various Artists live compilation 'Live At The Vortex'. To end the year, he set up TUBEWAY ARMY, which was basically his solo project, accompanied on live work by PAUL GARDINER and uncle GERALD LIDYARD. Their debut vinyl outing 'THAT'S TOO BAD', was issued by indie punk label 'Beggar's B.' early '78. Their eponymous debut lp, virtually went unnoticed, but things dramatically changed in Jun'79, when they/he had first No.1 with 'ARE FRIENDS ELECTRIC', spurred on by a stunning appearance on UK's 'Top Of The Pops'. Its parent album 'REPLICAS', also shot to the top in the same month. In August, he decided to release next '45 'CARS' as GARY NUMAN. This quickly shot to the top, as did yet another 1979 album 'THE PLEASURE PRINCIPLE'. The following year, he had a few Top 10 hits, and another No.1 lp 'TELEKON'. He continued throughout the 80's as mainly Top 50 artist. In 1984 he formed his own label 'Numa', to issue own product, plus brother JOHN's outfit HOHOKAM. • **Style:** NUMAN played futuristic-synth based rock-pop, and was a confessed plagiarist of BOWIE. NUMAN found his own clone-type fans, as BOWIE had ventured into other areas of rock and pop. • **Songwriters:** Wrote own material, with inspiration from psi-fi writers (i.e. WILLIAM S.BURROUGHS). Covered 1999 + U GOT THE LOOK (Prince). • **Trivia:** NUMAN appeared on ROBERT PALMER's 'Clues' album in 1980, and was part of initial off-shoot outfit DRAMATIS. In the early 80's, he took up flying planes, and bought own aircrafts (mainly warplanes).

Recommended: THE GARY NUMAN COLLECTION (*7) / THE PLEASURE PRINCIPLE (*6) / REPLICAS (*7; TUBEWAY ARMY)

TUBEWAY ARMY

GARY NUMAN – vocals, guitar, synthesizer, keyboards (ex-MEAN STREET) / **PAUL 'Scarlett' GARDINER** – bass / **GERALD 'Rael' LIDYARD** – drums

Beggars Banquet / not issued

Feb 78. (7") **THAT'S TOO BAD. / OH! DIDN'T I SAY** [ ] [-]
— **BARRY BENN** – drums repl. BOB SIMMONDS who had repl. LIDYARD / added **SEAN BURKE** – guitar
Jul 78. (7") **BOMBERS. / O.D. RECEIVER. / BLUE EYES** [ ] [-]
Aug 78. (lp)(c)(blue-lp) **TUBEWAY ARMY** [ ] [-]
– Listen to the sirens / My shadow in vain / The life machine / Friends / Something's in the house / Every day I die / Steal and you / My love is a liquid / Are you real / The dream police / Jo the waiter / Zero bass. *(re-iss.Aug79 reached No.14) (re-iss.May83 on 'Fame') (re-iss.Jul88)*
— **JESS LIDYARD** – drums returned to replace BARRY and SEAN
Mar 79. (7") **DOWN IN THE PARK. / DO YOU NEED THE SERVICE?** [ ] [-]
(12"+=) – I nearly married a human 2.

Beggars Banquet / Warners

May 79. (7")(7"pic-d)(US-7")(US-c-s) **ARE 'FRIENDS' ELECTRIC. / WE ARE SO FRAGILE?** [1] [ ]
Jun 79. (lp)(c) **REPLICAS** [1] [ ]
– Me I disconnect from you / Are 'friends' electric / The machman / Praying to the aliens / Down in the park / You are in my vision / Replicas / It must have been years / When the machines rock / I nearly married a human. *(re-iss.+cd.Sep88) (re-iss.cd/c Apr95 on 'Music Club')*

GARY NUMAN

solo retaining **PAUL GARDINER** – bass / **CEDRIC SHARPLEY** – drums / **CHRIS PAYNE** – synth, viola / **BILLY CURRIE** – keyboards.

Beggars Banquet / Atco

Aug 79. (7") **CARS. / ASYLUM** [1] [-]
Sep 79. (lp)(c) **THE PLEASURE PRINCIPLE** [1] [16] Jan 80
– Airplane / Metal / Complex / Films / M.E. / Tracks / Observer / Conversation / Cars / Engineers. *(re-iss.Sep88)*
Nov 79. (7") **COMPLEX. / BOMBERS (live)** [6] [ ]
(12"+=) – Me I disconnect from you (live).
Feb 80. (7") **CARS. / METAL** [-] [9]
— **DENNIS HAINES** – keyboards repl. CURRIE who returned to ULTRAVOX and VISAGE; added **RUSSELL BELL** – guitar (on tour) .
May 80. (7") **WE ARE GLASS. / TROIS GYMNPEDIES (1st MOVEMENT)** [5] [ ]
Aug 80. (7") **I DIE: YOU DIE. / DOWN IN THE PARK (piano version)** [6] [-]
Sep 80. (lp)(c) **TELEKON** [1] [64]
– This wreckage / The aircrash bureau / Telekon / Remind me to smile / Sleep by windows / I'm an agent / I dream of wires / Remember I was a vapour / Please push no more / The joy circuit. *(free-7"w.a.)* – REMEMBER I WAS A VAPOUR. / ON BROADWAY *(re-iss.Jul88)*
Sep 80. (7") **I DIE: YOU DIE. / SLEEP BY WINDOWS** [-] [ ]
Dec 80. (7") **REMIND ME TO SMILE. /** [-] [ ]
Dec 80. (7") **THIS WRECKAGE. / PHOTOGRAPH** [20] [ ]
Apr 81. (d-lp)(d-c) **LIVING ORNAMENTS 1979-1980 (live)** [2] [ ]
Apr 81. (lp)(c) **LIVING ORNAMENTS 1979** [47] [ ]
– Airplane / Cars / We are so fragile? / Films / Something's in the house / My shadow in vain / Conversation / The dream police / Metal. *(re-iss.1988)(both available as single lp)*
Apr 81. (lp)(c) **LIVING ORNAMENTS 1980** [39] [ ]
– This wreckage / I die: you die / M.E. / Everyday I die / Down in the park / Remind me to smile / The joy circuit / Tracks / Are 'friends' electric / We are glass. *(re-iss.1988)*
— GARY now recruited famous stars to replace BELL, SHARPLEY, HAINES and PAYNE. They became DRAMATIS. Jul'81 he guested on PAUL GARDINER single STORMTROOPER IN DRAG, which hit UK No.49. Next with The stars were **MICK KARN** – bass (of JAPAN) / **ROGER TAYLOR** – drums (of QUEEN) and **NASH THE SLASH** – violin (solo artist from Canada).
Aug 81. (7") **SHE'S GOT CLAWS. / I SING RAIN** [6] [ ]
(12"+=) – Exhibition.
Sep 81. (lp)(c) **DANCE** [3] [ ]
– Slowcar to China / Night talk / A subway called you / Cry the clock said / She's got claws / Crash / Boys like me / Stories / My brother's time / You are you are / Moral. *(re-iss.Jan89)*
Nov 81. (7") **LOVE NEEDS NO DISGUISE. (as "GARY NUMAN & DRAMATIS") / TAKE ME HOME** [33] [ ]
(12"+=) – Face to face.
— GARY NUMAN now used session people.
Feb 82. (7") **MUSIC FOR CHAMELEONS. / NOISE NOISE** [19] [ ]
(12") – ('A'extended) / Bridge? what bridge.
Jun 82. (7") **WE TAKE MYSTERY (TO BED). / THE IMAGE IS** [9] [ ]
(12") – ('A'extended) / ('A'early version).
Aug 82. (7") **WHITE BOYS AND HEROES. / WAR GAMES** [20] [ ]
(12") – ('A'extended) / Glitter and ash.
Sep 82. (lp)(c) **I, ASSASSIN** [8] [ ]
– White boys and heroes / War songs / A dream of Siam / Music for chameleons / This is my house / I, assassin / The 1930's rust / We take mystery (to bed). *(re-iss.Jan89)*
Aug 83. (7")(7"sha-pic-d) **WARRIORS. / MY CAR SLIDE (1)** [20] [ ]
(12") – ('A'extended) / My car slides (2).
Sep 83. (lp)(c) **WARRIORS** [12] [ ]
– Warriors / I am render / The iceman comes / This prison moon / My centurion / Sister surprise / The tick tock man / Love is like clock law / The rhythm of the evening. *(re-iss.Jan89)*
Oct 83. (7") **SISTER SUPRISE. / POETRY AND POWER** [32] [ ]
(12") – ('A'extended) / Letters.

Numa / Numa

Oct 84. (7")(7"sha-pic-d) **BERSERKER. / EMPTY BED, EMPTY HEART** [32] [ ]
(12"+=) – ('A'extended version).
Nov 84. (lp)(c) **BERSERKER** [45] [ ]
– Berserker / This is new love / The secret / My dying machine / Cold warning / Pump it up / The God film / A child with the ghost / The hunter. *(c+=) – (6 extra tracks). (cd-iss.Dec95)*
Dec 84. (7") **MY DYING MACHINE. / HERE I AM** [66] [ ]
(12") – ('A'extended) / She cries.
— next single on 'Polydor' by (SHARPE of SHAKATAK)
Feb 85. (7")(7"pic-d) **CHANGE YOUR MIND.(as "SHARPE & NUMAN") / REMIX, REMAKE, REMODEL** [17] [ ]
(12")(12"pic-d) – ('A'extended) / ('B'side) / Fools in a world of fire.
Apr 85. (d-lp)(c) **WHITE NOISE (live)** [29] [ ]
– (intro) / Berserker / Metal / Me, I disconnect from you / Remind me to smile / Sister surprise / Music for chameleons / The iceman comes / Cold warning / Down in the park / This prison moon / I die; you die / My dying machine / Cars / We take mystery (to bed) / We are glass / This is new love / My shadow in vain / Are 'friends' electric.
May 85. (7")(12")(12"blue)(12"white) **THE LIVE EP (live)** [27] [ ]
– Are 'friends' electric / Cars / We are glass / Beserker.
Jul 85. (7")(7"pic-d) **YOUR FASCINATION. / WE NEED IT** [46] [ ]
(12")(12"pic-d) – ('A'extended) / Anthem.
Sep 85. (7") **CALL OUT THE DOGS. / THIS SHIP COMES APART** [49] [ ]

(12") – ('A'extended) / No shelter.
Sep 85. (lp)(c)(cd)(pic-lp) **THE FURY** 24
– Call out the dogs / This disease / Your fascination / Miracles / The pleasure skin / Creatures / ricks / God only knows / Creatures / I still remember. *(c+)–* (all tracks extended).
Nov 85. (7")(7"red)(7"white) **MIRACLES. / THE FEAR** 49
(12")(12"red)(12"white+=) – ('A'&'B'extended).
Apr 86. (7")(7"pic-d) **THIS IS LOVE. / SURVIVAL** 28
(12")(12"pic-d) – ('A'extended). (all w/free 7"flexi)
(d12"+=) – Call out the dogs (extended) / No shelter / This ship comes apart.
Jun 86. (7")(7"pic-d) **I CAN'T STOP. / FACES** 27
(12") – ('A'extended). *(all w/free 7"flexi).*
(12"pic-d)/ /(10") – ('A' picture mix)./ / ('A'club mix).
Sep 86. (7")(7"pic-d) **NEW THING FROM LONDON TOWN. (as "SHARPE & NUMAN") / TIME TO DIE** 52
(12")(12"pic-d) – ('A'&'B'extended).
Oct 86. (lp)(c)(cd) **STRANGE CHARM** 59
–
Nov 86. (7")(7"pic-d) **I STILL REMEMBER (new version). / PUPPETS** 74
(12")(12"pic-d) – ('A'&'B'extended).

— Early in 1987, he teamed up with RADIO HEART (see below)

Aug 87. (7")(7"pic-d) **CARS (E-REG MODEL). / ARE FRIENDS ELECTRIC?** 16
(12")(c-s) – ('A'extended) / We are glass / I die: you die (US mix).
(12"+=) – ('A'extended) / ('A'motorway mix).
Sep 87. (d-lp)(c)(d-cd) **EXHIBITION** – (compilation) 43
– Me, I disconnect from you / That's too bad / My love is a liquid / Music for chameleons / We are glass / Bombers / Sister Surprise / Are 'friends' electric / I dream of wires / Complex / Noise noise / Warriors / Everyday I die / Cars / We take mystery to bed / I'm an agent / My centurion / Metal / You are in my vision / I die: you die / She's got claws / This wreckage / My shadow in vain / Down in the park / The iceman comes. *(d-cd += 11 tracks)*

SHARPE AND NUMAN

Polydor | Warners

Jan 88. (7")(7"pic-d)(7"white)(7"blue)(7"clear) **NO MORE LIES. / VOICES** 34
(12"+=)(12"pic-d+=) – ('A'extended).
(cd-s++=) – Change your mind.

GARY NUMAN

Illegal | I.R.S.

Sep 88. (7") **NEW ANGER. / I DON'T BELIEVE** 46
(12"+=)/ /(cd-s+=) – Children./ / Creatures / I can't stop.
Oct 88. (lp)(c)(cd) **METAL RHYTHM** 48
– Respect / Don't call my name / New anger / America / Hunger / Voix / Young heart / Cold metal rhythm / This is emotion. *(pic-lp iss.Mar89)*
Nov 88. (7")(7"pic-d) **AMERICA. / RESPECT (live)** 49
(12"+=) – New anger (live).
(cd-s++=) – Call out the dogs (live).

SHARPE & NUMAN

again with **ROGER ODELL** – drums / **TESSA MILES + LINDA TAYLOR** – backing vocals

Polydor | M.C.A.

May 89. (7")(7"pic-d) **I'M ON AUTOMATIC. / LOVE LIKE A GHOST** 44
(12") – ('A'extended) Voices / ('89 mix).
(7") – ('A'side) / No more lies (new version).
(cd-s+=) – (all 4 above).
Jun 89. (lp)(c)(cd) **AUTOMATIC** 59
– Change your mind / Turn off the world / No more lies / Breathe in emotion / Some new game / I'm on automatic / Rip it up / Welcome to love / Voices / Nightlife. *(cd+=)–* (2 extended mixes).

GARY NUMAN

solo with **RUSSELL BELL** – guitar / **CHRIS PAYNE** – keyboards, violin / **ADE ORANGE** – keyboards / **CEDRIC SHARPLY** – drums / **JOHN WEBB** – saxophone / **ANDY COUGHLAN** – bass / **VAL CHALMERS + EMMA CHALMER** – backing vocals

I.R.S. | I.R.S.

Oct 89. (lp)(c)(cd) **THE SKIN MECHANIC (live Sep88)** 55
– Survival / Respect / Call out the dogs / Cars / Hunger / Down in the park / New anger / Creatures / Are 'friends' electric / Young heart / We are glass / I die: you die.
Mar 91. (7")(c-s)(7"red) **HEART. / SHAME**
(12") – ('A'side) / Icehouse.
(cd-s) – ('A'side) / Tread careful.
(12") – ('A'side) / Are 'friends' electric.
Apr 91. (cd)(c)(lp) **OUTLAND** 39
– Confession / My world storm / Interval 1 / From Russia infected / Interval 2 / They whisper you / Dark Sunday / Heart / Devotion / Outland / Interval 3 / 1999 / Dream killer.
Sep 91. (7")(c-s) **EMOTION. / IN A GLASSHOUSE** 43
(12"+=) – Hanoi.
(cd-s++=) – ('A'diff.mix).
Mar 92. (7")(c-s) **THE SKIN GAME. / DARK MOUNTAIN** 68
(12"+=)(cd-s+=) – U got the look / ('A'digi mix).
Jul 92. (7") **MACHINE AND SOUL. / ('A'promo mix)** 72 | -
(cd-s+=) – 1999 / The hauntings.
(cd-s) ('A' side) / Soul protection (live) / Confession (live) / From Russia infected (live).
(12"+=) – Your fascination (live) / Outland (live) / Respect (live).
(cd-s+=) – Cry baby / Wonder eye.
Jul 92. (cd)(c)(lp) **MACHINE AND SOUL** 42
– Machine and soul / Generator / The skin game / Poison / I wonder / Emotion / Cry / U got the look / Love isolation. *(ext.cd re-iss.Sep93 on 'Numa')*

— Apr 94; He guested for GENERATOR on their version of 'ARE FRIENDS' ELECTRIC'.

— NUMAN & DADAGANG; Apr 94 12"/cd-s LIKE A REFUGEE (I WON'T CRY) on 'Record Label', re-iss.Aug 94 as GARY NUMAN & FRIENDS.

Numa | Numa

Aug 94. (d-cd)(d-c)(t-lp) **DREAM CORROSION** | -
Oct 94. (12")(cd-s) **A QUESTION OF FAITH**
Mar 95. (cd)(c)(lp) **SACRIFICE**
Mar 95. (12")(cd-s) **ABSOLUTION. / MAGIC (trick mix) / MAGIC (extended)** | -
Jun 95. (12"ep)(cd-ep) **DARK LIGHT LIVE E.P. (live)** | -
– Bleed / Everyday I die / The dream police / Listen to the sirens.
Jul 95. (d-cd)(c) **DARK LIGHT (live)**
– Pray / A question of faith / I dream of wires / Noise noise / Listen to the sirens / Everyday I die / Desire / Friens / Scar / Magic / Praying to the aliens / Replicas I / Mean street / Stormtrooper in drag / Dead liner / Bleed / The dream police / I die, you die / The hunter / Remind me to smile / Are friends "electric"? / Do you need the service? / Love and napalm / Jo the waiter / I'm an agent.
Nov 95. (cd)(c) **HUMAN** (with MICHAEL R. SMITH) | -

... Jan – Jun '96 stop press ...

Mar 96. (single re-issue) **CARS (premier mix)** 17
Mar 96. Premier; (cd)(c) **THE PREMIER HITS** (compilation) 21 | -

– compilations, etc. (TUBEWAY ARMY *)

Aug 79. Beggar's Banquet; (d7") * **THAT'S TOO BAD. / OH! I DIDN'T SAY/ / BOMBERS. / O.D. RECEIVER / BLUE EYES** | -
Apr 83. Beggar's Banquet; (12"ep) * **TUBEWAY ARMY '78 VOL.1** | -
– (same tracks as above +) Do you need the service? *(re-iss.1985 on 12"yellow)*
Sep 84. Beggar's Banquet; (lp)(c)(pic-lp) * **THE PLAN (by "TUBEWAY ARMY /GARY NUMAN)** 29 | -
(re-iss.1989)
1985. Beggar's Banquet; (12"red-ep) **TUBEWAY ARMY '78-'79 VOL.2** | -
– Fade out / 1930 / The crazies / Only a downstate / We have a technical.
1985. Beggar's Banquet; (12"blue-ep) **TUBEWAY ARMY '78-'79 VOL.3** | -
– The Monday troup / Crime of assikon / The life machine / A game called Echo / Random / Oceans.
Dec 87. Beggar's Banquet; (cd) * **REPLICAS / * THE PLAN** | -
(re-iss.d-cd Dec93)
Dec 87. Beggar's Banquet; (cd) * **TUBEWAY ARMY / DANCE** | -
(re-iss.d-cd Dec93)
Dec 87. Beggar's Banquet; (cd) **THE PLEASURE PRINCIPLE / WARRIORS**
(re-iss.d-cd Dec93)
Dec 87. Beggar's Banquet; (cd) **TELEKON / I, ASSASSIN**
(re-iss.d-cd Dec93)
(above series of cd's, omitted some tracks on each)
1990. Beggar's Banquet; (pic-cd-ep) **THE SELECTION** | -
– Cars('E' reg.model) / Down in the park / I die: you die / Are 'friends' electric? / We are glass / Music for chameleons.
Aug 93. Beggar's Banquet; (7")(c-s) **CARS. / ('A'mix)** 53
(12"sha-pic-d+=)(cd-s+=) – CARS ('93 SPRINT) / CARS (TOP GEAR)
Sep 93. Beggar's Banquet; (d-cd)(c) **THE BEST OF GARY NUMAN 1978-1983** 70 | -
Apr 81. Old Gold; (7") * **ARE 'FRIENDS' ELECTRIC. / DOWN IN THE PARK** | -
1990. Old Gold; (7") * **ARE FRIENDS ELECTRIC?. / I DID YOU** | -
1990. Old Gold; (7") **CARS. / WE ARE GLASS** | -
Nov 82. TV-Virgin; (lp)(c) **NEW MAN NUMAN – THE BEST OF GARY NUMAN** 45 | -
Aug 87. Strane Fruit; (12"ep)(c-ep) * **THE PEEL SESSIONS** | -
– Me I disconnect from you / Down in the park / I nearly married a human.
Dec 89. Strange Fruit; (m-lp)(cd) **DOUBLE PEEL SESSIONS** | -
Oct 89. Castle; (d-lp)(cd) **THE GARY NUMAN COLLECTION** | -

Dec 92. Connoisseur; (cd)(c) **DOCUMENT SERIES** [ ] [-]

— GARY has also contributed to other DRAMATIS recordings.

Jul 94. Receiver; (cd) **HERE I AM** [ ] [-]

RADIO HEART

with **DAVID + HUGH NICHOLSON**

G.F.M. not issued

Mar 87. (7")(7"sha-pic-d) **RADIO HEART. / ('A'instrumental)** [35] [ ]
(12"+=)(12"pic-d+=) – Mistasax version 2.

May 87. (7")(7"sha-pic-d) **LONDON TIMES. / RUMOUR** [48] [ ]
(12"+=) – ('A'extended).

Oct 87. (7") **ALL ACROSS THE NATION** [ ] [-]
(12"+=)/ /(cd-s+=) – ('A'extended)./ / ('A'instrumental).

Nov 87. (lp)(c)(cd) **RADIO HEART** [ ] [-]
– All across the nation / London times / Radio heart / Blue nights / Starlight jingles / Strange thing / I'm alone / Mad about the girl / Victim.

N.W.A.

Formed: NIGGAS WITH ATTITUDE, Los Angeles, California, USA . . . 1988 by (see below). Gathered local COMPTON momentum and angst when they unleashed debut anti-everything album 'STRAIGHT OUTTA COMPTON'. Mainman ICE CUBE departed for slightly more laid-back solo approach in 1990, but group went straight to No.1 slot with follow-up 'EFIL4ZAGGIN'. • **Style:** Rebelious and violent rapping gangstas, who spray a barrage of expletives to show their anger against racist peers. • **Songwriters:** Group penned plus samples. DR.DRE (a half-bro to WARREN G) sampled on 'NUTHIN' BUT A G THANG'; I Want'a Do Somethin' Freakey To You (Leon Haywood). Also on 'LET ME RIDE'; Mothership Connection (Parliament). His 1993 album also featured rapper SNOOP DOGGY DOGG. • **Trivia:** Album 'EFIL4ZAGGIN' is actually NIGGAZ4LIFE spelt backwards (as seen on sleeve).

Recommended: STRAIGHT OUTTA COMPTON (*9) / EFIL4ZAGGIN (*7) / THE CHRONIC (DR. DRE *7)

ICE CUBE (b. OSHEA JACKSON) – vocals (ex-C.I.A.) / **DR DRE** (b. ANDRE YOUNG) – vocals (also of WORLD CLASS WRECKIN' CREW) / **EAZY-E** (b. ERIC WRIGHT, 7 Sep'73) – vocals / **MC REN** (b. LORENZO PATTERSON) – vocals / **DJ YELLA** (b. ANTOINE CARRABY) – turntables

4th & Bro. Ruthless

Aug 89. (7") **EXPRESS YOURSELF. / STRAIGHT OUTTA COMPTON** [50] [ ]
(ext-12"+=)(cd-s+=) – ('A'bonus beats) / A bitch is a bitch. *(re-iss.May90, hit Uk 26)*

Aug 89. (lp)(c)(cd) **STRAIGHT OUTTA COMPTON** [41] [37]
– Straight outta Compton / Fu** the police / Gangsta gangsta / If it ain't ruff / Parental discretion iz advised / 8 ball (remix) / Something like that / Express yourself / Compton's in the house (remix) / I ain't tha 1 / Dopeman (remix) / Quiet on the set / Something to dance to.

Aug 90. (7") **GANGSTA, GANGSTA / IF IT AIN'T RUFF** [70] [ ]
(12"+=)(cd-s+=) – Dopeman (remix).

— now without ICE CUBE who was now solo.

Oct 90. (7") **100 MILES AND RUNNIN'. / REAL NIGGAZ** [38] [27] Aug90
(12")(cd-s) – ('A'side) / Just don't bite it / Sa prize (pt.2) / Kamurshoi.

Apr 91. (12")(cd-s) **F*** THE POLICE. / ('A'mixes)** [ ] [ ]

— (above written for RODNEY KING, who was the black motorist beat up by police. The court case instigated the race riots all around America.

Jun 91. (cd)(c)(lp) **EFIL4ZAGGIN** [25] [1]
– Prelude / Real niggaz don't die / Real niggaz 4 life / Protest / Appetite for destruction / Don't drink that wine / Alwayz into somethin' / Message to B.A. / Real niggaz / To kill a hooker / One less bitch / Findum, f***um and flee / Automobile / She swallowed it / I'd rather f*** you / Approach to danger / 1-900-2 Compton / The dayz of wayback.

Nov 91. (7") **ALWAYZ INTO SOMETHIN'. / EXPRESS YOURSELF** [60] [ ]
(12"+=)(cd-s+=) – Something 2 dance 2.

— Disbanded and all went solo.

EAZY-E

4th & Bro. Ruthless

Sep 89. (lp)(c)(cd) **EAZY-DUZ-IT** [ ] [41] Dec88
– (Prelude) Still talkin' / Nobody move / 2 Hard muthas (featuring MC REN) / Boyz-n-the-hood (remix) / Eazy-duz-it / We want Eazy / Eazy-er said than dunn / Radio / No more ?'s / Imma break it down / Eazy – Chapter 8, verse 10. *(re-iss.Jun91)*

Jan 93. (cd)(c) **5150 HOME FOR THA SICK** [ ] [70]

Oct 93. (cd)(c) **IT'S ON (DR.DRE 187 UM) KILLA** [ ] [5]
–

Jan 94. (c-s)(cd-s) **REAL MUTHAPHUCKIN' G'S. /** [-] [42]

— Early in 1995, EAZY-E featured on BONE THUGS N HARMONY's hit single 'Foe Tha Love Of'.

— EAZY-E died of AIDS on the 26th March 1995 after only being diagnosed HIV a month earlier.

Epic Epic

Dec 95. (c-s) **JUST TAH LET U KNOW / THE MUTHAPHU**IN' REAL** [30] [45]
(12"+=)(cd-s+=) – ('A'-Ruthless "G" mix) / ('A'-Ba-da-ba-do acappella mix).

. . . Jan – Jun '96 stop press . . .

Jan 96. (cd)(c) **ETERNAL E** (compilation) [ ] [84] Dec95

Virgin Virgin

Feb 96. (cd)(c) **STR8 OFF THA STREETZ OF MUTHAPH**IN – E.W. COMPTON** [66] [3]

MC REN

4th & Bro. Ruthless

Jul 92. (cd)(c) **KIZZ MY BLACK AZZ** [ ] [12]
– Check it out y'all / Behind the scenes / Hound dogz / Kiss my black azz / Right up my alley / Final frontier.

Nov 93. (cd)(c) **SHOCK OF THE HOUR** [ ] [22]
–

Nov 93. (c-s)(cd-s) **SAME OL' SHIT. / ?** [-] [90]

— Above sampled; LET'S GET IT ON (Marvin Gaye) / I GOT A GOOD THING (James Brown) / LAD DI DA DI (Doug E.Fresh).

. . . Jan – Jun '96 stop press . . .

Ruthless Ruthless

Apr 96. (cd)(c) **THE VILLAIN IN BLACK** [ ] [ ]

DR. DRE

Interscope Death Row

Feb 93. (cd)(c) **THE CHRONIC** [ ] [3]
– The chronic / Fuck wit Dre day (and everybody's celebrating) / Let me ride / The day the niggaz took over / Nuthin' but a "G" thang / Dreeez nuuuts / Bitches ain't shit / Lil' ghetto boy / A nigga witta gun / Rat-tat-tat-tat / The $20 sack pyramid / Lyrical gangbang / High powered / The doctor's office / Stranded on death row / The roach (the chronic outro).

Mar 93. (7") **NUTHIN' BUT A "G" THANG. / ('A'mix)** [ ] [2] Jan93
(club-12"+=) – ('A'-freestyle mix).

May 93. (7")(c-s) **DRE DAY. / ('A'-flavour mix)** [ ] [8]
(cd-s+=) – ('A'extended club) / ('A'-UK Flavour mix) / ('A'instrumental) / ('A'again).
(12") – (A+B) / (above 2) / Puffin' on blunts and drinkin' tanqueray.

Aug 93. (c-s)(cd-s)(12") **LET ME RIDE / ('A'mixes)** [ ] [34]

Jan 94. (12"ep) **NUTHIN' BUT A G THANG (club) / ('A'red-eye mix) / ('A'mix) / LET ME RIDE (remix)** [31] [ ]
(12") – (1st & 4th tracks) / Let me ride (extended club mix).
(cd-s) – (1st & 4th tracks) + their club mixes.

Aug 94. (7") **DRE DAY. / ('A'-UK radio mix)** [59] [ ]
(12"+=) – puffin' on blunts and drinkin' tanqueray.
(cd-s+=) – ('A'-radio remix) / ('A'instrumental) / ('A'-2 other mixes).

— In Sep'94, DR.DRE was convicted of battery (assault) and imprisoned for 8 months, although it seems likely he'll be out a lot sooner.

Interscope Triple X

Oct 94. (cd)(c) **CONCRETE ROOTS** [ ] [43]

— DR.DRE & ICE CUBE; below from the film 'Murder Was The Case'.

Mar 95. (c-s) **NATURAL BORN KILLAZ / THA DOGG POUND: What Would U Do?** [45] [ ]
(12"+=)(cd-s+=) – (2 'A'versions).

Virgin Priority

May 95. (c-s) **KEEP THEIR HEADS RINGIN'. / TAKE A HIT (mix)** [25] [10] Mar 95
(12"+=)(cd-s+=) – (other mixes).

above 'A' from the film 'Friday'.

. . . Jan – Jun '96 stop press . . .

Triple X Triple X

Jun 96. (cd)(c) **1ST ROUND KNOCKOUT** [-] [52]

DUBLIN
12 m →
MANCHESTER
←

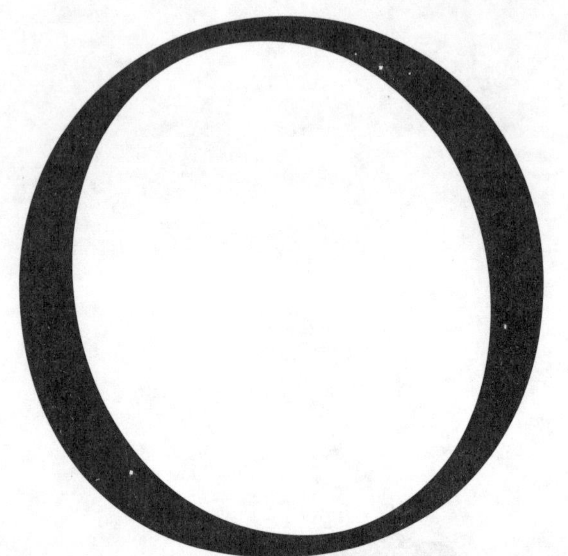

Phil OAKEY & Giorgio MORODER (see under ⇒ HUMAN LEAGUE)

OASIS

Formed: Manchester, England . . . summer 1992, by LIAM, BONEHEAD, PAUL & TONY. Initially called RAIN, they were soon joined by LIAM's older brother NOEL who was a roadie for The INSPIRAL CARPETS. After a year of rehearsals and occasional local gigs, they were signed by Creation's ALAN McGEE, who caught them playing at a Glasgow gig mid 1993. With plenty hype behind them, they secured a near UK Top 30 debut single with 'SUPERSONIC'. They went from strength to strength with each release and topped the album charts with 'DEFINITELY MAYBE' (most critics' choice for album of the year award). Certainly 1994 had belonged to this self-proclaimed 'best band in the world' and they even tried to knock popstarts EAST 17 off the Christmas No.1 slot with 'WHATEVER'. • **Style:** The BEATLES, The SEX PISTOLS and The SMITHS all rolled into one delicious and most exciting rock group since the aforementioned! • **Songwriters:** NOEL, except I AM THE WALRUS (Beatles) / FEELIN' LONELY by Noel (Small Faces). • **Trivia:** NOEL wrote 'SLIDE AWAY' on a Les Gibson guitar, which he bought from friend JOHNNY MARR (ex-Smiths) and which was once the property of PETE TOWNSHEND (The Who). LIAM has now an on-off relationship with PATSY KENSIT (singer/actress and estranged wife of Simple Minds voxman JIM KERR).

Recommended: DEFINITELY MAYBE (*10) / (WHAT'S THE STORY) MORNING GLORY? (*10)

LIAM GALLAGHER (b.21 Sep'72) – vocals / **NOEL GALLAGHER** (b.29 May'67) – guitar / **PAUL 'BONEHEAD' ARTHURS** (b.23 Jun'65) – guitar / **PAUL McGUIGAN** (b.19 May'71) – guitar / **TONY McCARROLL** – drums

		Creation	Creation	
Apr 94.	(7") **SUPERSONIC. / TAKE ME AWAY** (12"+=) – I will believe (live). (cd-s++=) – Columbia (demo).	31		
Jun 94.	(7")(c-s) **SHAKER MAKER. / D'YER WANNA BE A SPACEMAN?** (12"+=) – Alive (demo). (cd-s++=) – Bring it on down (live).	11		
Aug 94.	(7")(c-s) **LIVE FOREVER. / UP IN THE SKY (acoustic)** (12"+=) – Cloudburst. (cd-s++=) – Supersonic (live).	10		
Aug 94.	(cd)(c)(lp) **DEFINITELY MAYBE** – Rock'n'roll star / Shaker maker / Live forever / Up in the sky / Columbia / Supersonic / Bring it down / Cigarettes and alcohol / Digsy's dinner / Slide away / Married with children.(lp+=) – Sad song.	1	58	Jan95
Oct 94.	(7")(c-s) **CIGARETTES AND ALCOHOL. / I AM THE WALRUS (live)** (12"+=) – Fade away. (cd-s++=) – Listen up.	7		
Dec 94.	(7")(c-s) **WHATEVER. / (IT'S GOOD) TO BE FREE** (12"+=) – Slide away. (cd-s++=) – Half the world away.	3		

— After a punch-up McCARROLL left and was replaced by drummer **ALAN WHITE (b.26 May'72, London)** (ex-IDHA) and brother of STEVE WHITE (long-time sticksman with PAUL WELLER)

Apr 95.	(c-s) **SOME MIGHT SAY / TALK TONIGHT** (12"+=) – Acquiesce. (cd-s++=) – Headshrinker.	1		

— Their first 5 singles re-entered UK Top 60 in Jun'95. The next single lost the battle with rivals BLUR to the No.1 spot. It was a year of running verbal battles between them, although LIAM's arrogance and NOEL's songwriting abilities on next album, finally won over the public.

Aug 95.	(c-s) **ROLL WITH IT / IT'S BETTER, PEOPLE** (12"+=) – Rockin' chair. (cd-s+=) – Live forever (live).	2		
Oct 95.	(cd)(c)(lp) **(WHAT'S THE STORY) MORNING GLORY?** – Hello / Roll with it / Wonderwall / Don't look back in anger / Hey now! / Some might say / Cast no shadow / She's electric / Morning glory / Champagne supernova. (lp+=) Bonehead's bank holiday.	1	4	
Oct 95.	(c-s) **WONDERWALL / ROUND ARE WAY** (12"+=) – The swamp song. (cd-s+=) – The masterplan.	2	12	

— NOEL also part of one-off supergroup The SMOKIN' MOJO FILTERS alongside PAUL WELLER and PAUL McCARTNEY. They had Top 20 hit with 'COME TOGETHER'.

. . . Jan – Jun '96 stop press . . .

Feb 96.	(single) **DON'T LOOK BACK IN ANGER**	1		

— cover on b-side; CUM ON FEEL THE NOIZE (Slade). NOEL met up with great pensmith and fan! BURT BACHARACH, who wanted to do a collaboration. He also refused to accept his Ivor Novello award for best songwriter of the year, after he was told it would be shared with rivals BLUR.

Ric OCASEK (see under ⇒ CARS)

OCEAN COLOUR SCENE

*** NEW ENTRY ***

Formed: Moseley, Birmingham, England . . .mid-'89 out of The FANATICS, by SIMON FOWLER, DAMON MINCHELLA and OSCAR HARRISON. They had released one 45 for 'Chapter 22' label, before recruiting BOYS' guitarist STEVE CRADOCK. In the summer of 1990, OCS found manager JOHN MOSTYN, who signed them to his new !Phffft' stable. Debut 'SWAY', helped gain a joint venture with 'Phonogram' on next 45 'YESTERDAY TODAY'. This breeched the Top 50 in March '91, but '!Phffft' was sold during the recording of their JIMMY MILLER produced album. Now on Phonogram's 'Fontana', they're pushed into re-recording album. Early in 1992, the label re-issued 'SWAY', but this and its follow-up 'GIVING IT ALL AWAY' plummet. In April, the eponymous album was finally given light, but it's criticised for its over-cooked production. After another 45 bombed, they took rest of year to recover, and be freed from contract. They were aided by lawyer Michael Thomas, who got Fontana's DAVE BATES to waive a million owed by the band. They returned with a support to mate PAUL WELLER, and CRADOCK and FOWLER guested on his Autumn 1993 classic album 'WILDWOOD'. CRADOCK became an integral part of WELLER's band for the next year. Meanwhile in the summer of '94, OCEAN COLOUR SCENE supported OASIS and did a 'Fontana' tour of the U.S.A. supporting HOUSE OF LOVE and The CATHERINE WHEEL. In 1995, all group members played for WELLER at some point, with CRADOCK and MINCHELLA guesting on his No.1 album 'STANLEY ROAD'. The band recorded their long-awaited follow-up album, and signed to 'MCA'. Early in 1996 (with WELLER on organ), they had their first of many Top 20 hits with 'THE RIVERBOAT SONG' (later chosen for CHRIS EVANS' TFI Friday Show theme song). 'YOU'VE GOT IT BAD' fared even better, and was followed by a BRENDAN LYNCH produced album 'MOSELEY SHOALS' (name of own studio), which hit UK No.2. It featured WELLER on a few other tracks and he augmented on their 'Later With Jools Holland' spot. • **Style:** Shoe-gazing melodic white soul-rock outfit, influenced by The STONE ROSES and PRIMAL SCREAM. • **Songwriters:** FOWLER lyrics / group music; except DO YOURSELF A FAVOUR (Stevie Wonder & Syreeta).

Recommended: OCEAN COLOUR SCENE (*6) / MOSELEY SHOALS (*8)

FANATICS

SIMON FOWLER – vocals / **DAMON MINCHELLA** – bass / **PAUL WILKES** – guitar / **OSCAR HARRISON** – drums (ex- ECHO BASE) who repl. CAROLINE BULLOCK

Chapter 22 not issued

Mar 89. (12"ep) **SUBURBAN LOVE SONGS** [ ] [-]
– Suburban love songs / 1.2.3.4. / My brother Sarah / Tight rope.

OCEAN COLOUR SCENE

STEVE CRADOCK – guitar (ex- BOYS; late 80's mods) repl. WILKES

!Phffft not issued

Sep 90. (7") **SWAY. / TALK ON** [ ] [-]
(ext-12"+=)(ext-cd-s+=) – One of these days.

Mar 91. (7") **YESTERDAY TODAY. / ANOTHER GIRL'S NAME / FLY ME** [49] [ ]
(12"+=)(cd-s+=) – No one says.

Fontana not issued

Feb 92. (7")(c-s) **SWAY. / MY BROTHER SARAH** [ ] [-]
(12"+=)(cd-s+=) – Mona Lisa eyes / Bellechoux.

Apr 92. (7")(c-s) **GIVING IT ALL AWAY. / THIRD SHADE OF GREEN** [ ] [ ]
(12"+=)(cd-s+=) – Flowers / Don't play.

Apr 92. (cd)(c)(lp) **OCEAN COLOUR SCENE** [ ] [ ]
– Talk on / How about you / Giving it all away / Justine / Do yourself a favour / Third shade of green / Sway / Penny pinching rainy Heaven days / One of these days / Is she coming home / Blue deaf ocean / Reprise.

May 92. (7") **DO YOURSELF A FAVOUR. / THE SEVENTH FLOOR** [ ] [ ]
(12"+=)(cd-s+=) – Patsy in green / Suspended motion.

M.C.A. M.C.A.

Feb 96. (7")(c-s) **THE RIVERBOAT SONG. / SO SAD** [15] [ ]
(cd-s+=) – Charlie Brown says.

Apr 96. (c-s) **YOU'VE GOT IT BAD / ROBIN HOOD / I WANNA STAY ALIVE WITH YOU** [7] [ ]
(cd-s+=) – Huckleberry Grove.
(cd-s) – ('A'demo) / Here in my heart / Men of such opinion / Beautiful losers.

Apr 96. (cd)(c)(lp) **MOSELEY SHOALS** [2] [ ]
– The riverboat song / The day we caught the train / The circle / Lining your pockets / Fleeting mind / Forty past midnight / One for the road / It's my shadow / Policeman and pirates / Downstream / You've got it bad / Get away.

Jun 96. (c-s) **THE DAY WE CAUGHT THE TRAIN / THE CLOCK STRUCK 15 HOURS AGO** [4] [ ]
(cd-s+=) – I need a love song / Chicken bones and stones.
(cd-s) – ('A'acoustic) / Travellers tune / Justine.

Sinead O'CONNOR

Born: 12 Dec'66, Glenageary, Ireland. Raised in Dublin, her parents divorced when she was 8, and she was later put to a Dominican nun-run center for girls with behavioural problems. In 1985, after attending Dublin's College of Music, she joined local band TON TON MACOUTE, where she met boyfriend and future manager FACHTNA O'CEALLAIGH. In 1986, he arranged for her to guest on U2's The EDGE's soundtrack album 'Captive'. She was soon spotted by Nigel Grainge and Chris Hill of 'Ensign' records, who contracted her that year. In April the following year, she guested for stablemates WORLD PARTY (aka KARL WALLINGER) on album 'Private Revolution'. Two months later, she and new boyfriend / drummer John Reynolds, had a son, Jake. At the end of '87, she issued debut solo 45 'TROY', but this failed to sparkle commercially. Early the next year, she scored first Top 20 hit with 'MANDINKA', which re-actified sales of earlier released album 'THE LION AND THE COBRA'. Early in 1990, she unleashed the excellent PRINCE-penned 'NOTHING COMPARES 2 U', which hit Top spot on both sides of the Atlantic. It was quickly pursued by her second album 'I DO NOT WANT WHAT I HAVEN'T GOT', which also made No.1 in both UK & US. Throughout the rest of early 90's, she was surrounded by controversy for her outspoken views on abortion, religion, AIDS, etc, etc, etc (see further below). • **Style:** Shaven-headed, angel-faced nightingale, whose well intentioned public out-bursts have overshadowed her classy contributions to rock and pop. In 1992, she and her orchestra gave her a more BARBRA STREISAND feel, taking her further back to classic renditions of past standards. **The covers:** YOU DO SOMETHING TO ME + MY HEART BELONGS TO DADDY (Cole Porter) / SOMEONE TO WATCH OVER ME (Ira Gershwin) /DAMN YOUR EYES (Etta James) / SECRET LOVE (Doris Day) / ALL APOLOGIES (Nirvana). Her 1992 album was filled with covers originally sung by; WHY DONT YOU DO RIGHT? (Julie London; J.McCoy) / BEWITCHED, BOTHERED AND BEWILDERED (Ella Fitzgerald; L.Hart & R.Rodgers) / SECRET LOVE + BLACK COFFEE (Sarah Vaughan; F.Webster & S.Burke) / SUCCESS HAS MADE A FAILURE OF OUR HOME (Loretta Lynn; J.Mullins) / DON'T CRY FOR ME ARGENTINA (Elaine Page; Tim Rice & Andrew Lloyd Webber) / I WANT TO BE LOVED BY YOU (Marilyn Monroe; H.Stothart, H.Ruby & B.Kalmar) / GLOOMY SUNDAY (Billie Holiday; L.Javor, R.Seress & Lewis) / LOVE LETTERS (Alison Moyet; E.Heyman & V.Young) / HOW INSENSITIVE (Astrud Gilberto; V.de Morales, A.C.Jobim & Gimbel) / SCARLET RIBBONS (her mum & dad; J.Segal & E.Danzig). She co-writes w/COULTER or REYNOLDS and sample merchant TIM SIMENON for return 1994 album. Other covers; YOU MAKE ME FEEL SO REAL (Van Morrison) • **Miscellaneous:** She married John Reynolds in Mar'89, but soon split from him 18 months later. Early in 1991, she moved in to a house with long-time friend Ciara O'Flanagan.

Recommended: I DO NOT WANT WHAT I HAVEN'T GOT (*9) / THE LION AND THE COBRA (*7).

SINEAD O'CONNOR – vocals (ex-TON TON MACOUTE) / with **ENYA** + **MARCO PIRRONI**

Ensign Chrysalis

Oct 87. (7")(12") **TROY. / STILL LISTENING** [ ] [ ]

Nov 87. (lp)(c)(cd) **THE LION AND THE COBRA** [27] [36]
– Jackie / Mandinka / Jerusalem / Just like U said it would B / Never get old / Troy / I want your (hands on me) / Drink before the war / Just call me Joe. *(re-iss.Jan90 hit No.37)*

Dec 87. (7") **MANDINKA. / DRINK BEFORE THE WAR** [17] [ ]
(12"+=)/ /(12"+=) – ('A'dub mix)./ / ('A'remix).
(cd-s+=) – ('A'instrumental dub) / Still listening.

Apr 88. (7") **I WANT YOUR (HANDS ON ME). / JUST CALL ME JOE** [ ] [ ]

— ('B'side as "SINEAD O'CONNOR with MC LYTE")
(12"+=)(cd-s+=) – ('A'dance) / ('A'street).
(12"+=) – ('A'-2 different mixes).

Oct 88. (7") **JUMP IN THE RIVER. / NEVER GET OLD (live)** [ ] [ ]
(12"+=)(cd-s+=) – ('A'duet with KAREN FINLAY).

— Early 1989, she appeared on THE THE's album 'Mind Bomb', singing on 'Kingdom Of Rain'.

Ensign Ensign

Jan 90. (7") **NOTHING COMPARES 2 U. / JUMP IN THE RIVER** [1] [1] Ma4 90
(12"+=)(cd-s+=) – ('B'instrumental).

Mar 90. (cd)(c)(lp) **I DO NOT WANT WHAT I HAVEN'T GOT** [1] [1]
– Feel so different / I an stretched on your grave / Three babies / The Emperor's new clothes / Black boys in mopeds / Nothing compares 2 U / Jump in the river / You cause as much sorrow / The last day of our acquaintance / I do not want what I haven't got. *(re-iss.cd Mar94)*

Jul 90. (7") **THE EMPEROR'S NEW CLOTHES. / WHAT DO YOU WANT** [31] [60] Jun 90
(c-s+=) – I am stretched on your grave.
(12")(cd-s) – ('A'side remixed) / I am stretched on your grave (mix) / ('A'dub mix).

Oct 90. (7") **THREE BABIES. / DAMN YOUR EYES** [42] [ ]
(12"+=)(c-s+=)(cd-s+=) – Troy (live) / The value of ignorance.

May 91. (7") **MY SPECIAL CHILD. / NOTHING COMPARES 2 U (live)** [42] [ ]
(12"+=)(cd-s+=) – ('A'instrumental) / The Emperor's new clothes (live).
(12"+=)(c-s+=)(cd-s+=) – Standing on your grave.

Dec 91. (7")(cd-s) **SILENT NIGHT. / IRISH WAYS & IRISH LAWS (live)** [60] [ ]

— Early in 1991, she was the first ever person to refuse her Grammy for alternative 1990 album. She protested about anti-legalizing Irish abortion on TV and press. After earlier ripping a photo of Pope John Paul II on US Saturday Night Live, she was booed off-stage (Oct92) at a Bob Dylan tribute concert at Madison Square Garden. Due to crowd noise which drowned out backing band, she eventually sang unaccompanied a Bob Marley! song 'War'. She announced that month she was to retire, although thankfully she retracted press statements by late '92.

— now with **CHRIS PARKER** – drums / **DAVID FINCK** – bass / **RICHARD TEE** – piano / **IRA SIEGAL** – guitar / **DAVE LEBOLT** – synthesizer / plus a host of saxists, flautists, violinists, trumpeters & backing singers.

Sep 92. (cd-s) **SUCCESS HAS MADE A FAILURE OF OUR HOME / YOU DO SOMETHING TO ME / I WANT TO BE LOVED BY YOU** [18] [ ]
(cd-s) – (1st track) / Someone to watch over me / My heart belongs to daddy.

Sep 92. (cd)(c)(lp) **AM I NOT YOUR GIRL?** [6] [27]
– Why don't you do right? / Bewitched, bothered and bewildered / Secret love / Black coffee / Success has made a failure of our lives / Don't cry for me Argentina / I want to be loved by you / Gloomy Sunday / Love letters / How insensitive / Scarlet ribbons / Don't cry for me Argentina (inst.).

In Oct'92, she collaborated on MARXMAN single 'Ship Ahoy'.

Dec 92. (7")(c-s) **DON'T CRY FOR ME ARGENTINA. / AVE MARIA** [53] [ ]

(cd-s+=) – Scarlet ribbons.
(cd-s) – ('A'side) / Love letters / Scarlet ribbons.
In Jun'93, she was credited on WILLIE NELSON single 'Don't Give Up'.
Feb 94. (7")(c-s) **YOU MADE ME THE THIEF OF YOUR HEART. / THE FATHER AND HIS WIFE THE SPIRIT** [42] [ ]
(12"+=)(cd-s+=) – ('A'mixes).
(above single from film 'In The Name Of The Father'; on 'Island' records)

— now with **JOHN REYNOLDS** – drums / **PHIL COULTER** – piano / **DAVE CLAYTON** – keyboards / **MARCO PIRRONI + VAN GILLIANO** – guitar / **TIM SIMENON** etc.

Sep 94. (cd)(c)(lp) **UNIVERSAL MOTHER** [19] [37]
– Fire on Babylon / John I love you / My darling child / Am I human? / Red football / All apologies / A perfect Indian / Scorn not his simplicity / All babies / In this heart / Tiny grief song / Famine / Thank you for hearing me.
Nov 94. (12")(c-s)(cd-s) **THANK YOU FOR HEARING ME. / FIRE ON BABYLON (remix)** [13] [ ]
(cd-s) – ('A'side) / I believe in you / Streets of London / House of the rising Sun.

— In Apr'95, she duetted with SHANE MacGOWAN on his 'HAUNTED' hit.

Aug 95. (c-s)(cd-s) **FAMINE (extended) / FAMINE / ALL APOLOGIES** [51] [ ]
(12") – ('A'extended) / Fire On Babylon (M Beat remix).

OFFSPRING

Formed: Orange County, California, USA ... 1991 by DEXTER HOLLAND, etc. After one lp and a 45 as THE OFFSPRING, they quickly signed to other DIY label 'Epitaph' run by BRAD GUREWITZ (ex-BAD RELIGION's guitarist), where they unleashed follow-up album 'IGNITION'. However it wasn't until 1994 and their follow-up 'SMASH', that their breakthrough came to light. It went onto sell over a million copies in the States and was awaiting deserved recognition in the UK. • **Style:** Underground punk skatecore rock, hard on the heels of GREEN DAY, but more like BLACK FLAG. Fronted by the dreadlocked DEXTER. • **Songwriters:** HOLLAND most.

Recommended: SMASH (*8)

DEXTER HOLLAND – vocals, guitar / **NOODLES** (KEVIN WASSERMAN) – guitar / **GREG KRIESEL** – bass / **RON WELTY** – drums

not issued / Nitro
1989. (lp) **THE OFFSPRING** [-] [ ]
– Jennifer lost the war / Elders / Out on patrol / Crossroads / Demons / Beheaded / Tehran / A thousand days / Black ball / I'll be waiting / Kill the president. *(re-iss.cd/c Nov95 on 'Nitro')*

not issued / Plastic Head
1991. (7") **BAGHDAD. /** [-] [ ]

Epitaph / Epitaph
Oct 92. (cd)(c)(lp) **IGNITION** [ ] [ ]
– Session / We are one / Kick him when he's down / Take it like a man / Get it right / Dirty magic / Hypodermic / Burn it up / No hero / L.A.P.D. / Nothing from something / Forever and a day.
Sep 94. (cd)(c)(lp) **SMASH** [21] [4] Apr94
– Time to relax / Nitro (youth energy) / Bad habit / Gotta get away / Genocide / Something to believe in / Come out and play / Self esteem / It'll be a long time / Killboy powerhead / What happened to you / So alone / Not the one / Smash.
Sep 94. (c-s)(12")(cd-s) **COME OUT AND PLAY. / SESSION / ('A'acoustic)** [ ] [ ]
Feb 95. (7")(c-s)(12")(cd-s) **SELF ESTEEM. / JENNIFER LOST THE WAR / BURN IT UP** [37] [ ]

OutOfStep / Epitaph
Aug 95. (7")(c-s)(cd-s) **GOTTA GET AWAY. / SMASH** [43] [ ]

Mike OLDFIELD

Born: 15 May'53, Reading, Berkshire, England. Started playing guitar at age 7, and by 1968, had formed SALLYANGIE with sister SALLY. They signed to folk-orientated label 'Transatlantic', who issued lp 'CHILDREN OF THE SUN'. After releasing a single 'TWO SHIPS'. / 'COLOURS OF THE WORLD' in Sep69, they broke partnership to concentrate on other projects. After a spell in short-lived BAREFOOT, MIKE became bassist in Mar70 for KEVIN AYERS' band The WHOLE WORLD. He appeared on 2 of his albums 'SHOOTING AT THE MOON' & 'WHATEVERSHEBRINGSWESING' between 1971 & 1972, before they dissolved. Around this time, MIKE started work on his own solo project, which gained financial support in 1972 from Richard Branson's newly formed 'Virgin' label. The same year, MIKE also contributed session work for EDGAR BROUGHTON BAND and DAVID BEDFORD. The project 'TUBULAR BELLS', finally saw light of day in May73, and soon stirred critical acclaim from music press. A near 50-minute concept piece, played and overdubbed many times by now multi-instrumentalist MIKE, it went into UK Top 3 a year later. Helped by an unusual Top 10 single cut in the US that was used for the horror movie 'The Exorcist', it hit Top 3. In Sep'74, his follow-up 'HERGEST RIDGE', was complete, and this went straight to UK No.1. Critically lambasted by some critics as "Son of Tubular Bells", it only managed to hit No.87 in the States. OLDFIELD continued to surface with some work during the next couple of decades, but never quite regained earlier impact of the then and still now classic 'TUBULAR BELLS'. In 1992 (19 years after), 'WEA' records returned MIKE to UK No.1, with the almost identical but still appealling 'TUBULAR BELLS II'. • **Style:** Multi-talented introverted genius, with an over-the-top approach to his music, due to his move into more commercially based rock in the 80's. However his contribution to the 70's, in both classical and rock-pop fields, were only matched by PINK FLOYD in that era. 1975-1978, saw him even branch into African and folk-type origins on albums 'OMMADAWN' & 'INCANTATIONS'. Although he embarrassed his rock following by releasing mainly Christmassy hit 45's around same time. • **Songwriters:** Writes own material except; SAILOR'S HORNPIPE (trad.) / IN DULCE JUBILO (R.L. Pearsall) / WILLIAM TELL OVERTURE (Korsokov) / BLUE PETER (BBC copyright) / ARRIVAL (Abba) / WONDERFUL LAND (Shadows) / ETUDE (Franscisco Tarrega). In 1982, he was augmented in writing by group. • **Trivia:** In the mid-70's, MIKE also had time to session on albums by Virgin artists; DAVID BEDFORD (Star's End) / ROBERT WYATT (Rock Bottom) / TOM NEWMAN (Fine Old Tom). MIKE's sister SALLY also went on to have a UK Top 20 hit late '78 with 'MIRRORS'.

Recommended: TUBULAR BELLS (*10) / HERGEST RIDGE (*7) / OMMADAWN (*8) / INCANTATIONS (*8).

MIKE OLDFIELD – guitar, bass, everything (ex-KEVIN AYERS, ex-SALLYANGIE) with **TOM NEWMAN** – guitar / **JON FIELD** – flute / **STAN BROUGHTON** – drums / **LINDSAY COOPER** – wind. plus **VIVIAN STANSHALL** – narration (ex-BONZO DOG BAND)

Virgin / Virgin
May 73. (lp)(c) **TUBULAR BELLS** [1] [3] Nov 73
– Tubular bells (side 1) / Tubular bells (side 2). *(Finally hit UK No.1 in Oct74) (quad-lp iss.Jul74) (pic-lp Dec78) (cd-iss.Jun83 hit No.28)*
Feb 74. (7") **TUBULAR BELLS (edit). / TUBULAR BELLS (excerpt)** [-] [7]
Jun 74. (7") **MIKE OLDFIELD'S SINGLE (THEME FROM TUBULAR BELLS). / FROGGY WENT A-COURTIN'** [31] [-]

— now with **TERRY OLDFIELD** – wind / etc.

Sep 74. (lp)(c) **HERGEST RIDGE** [1] [87]
– Hergest ridge (side 1) / Hergest ridge (side 2). *(re-iss.+cd.Apr86)*
Jan 75. (lp)(c) **THE ORCHESTRAL TUBULAR BELLS (WITH THE ROYAL PHILHARMONIC ORCHESTRA)** [17] [ ]
– The orchestral Tubular Bells part 1 / The orchestral Tubular Bells part 2. (Rec.live Sep'74, conducted by DAVID BEDFORD, with MIKE OLDFIELD – guitar) *(cd-iss.Jul87) (re-iss.+cd.Sep89)*
Feb 75. (7") **DON ALFONSO. / IN DULCE JUBILO** [ ] [-]

— back-up were **JUBULA** (African musicians) / **PIERRE MOERLEN** (of GONG) / backing vocals by sister **SALLY OLDFIELD + CLODAGH SIMMONDS**

Nov 75. (lp)(c) **OMMADAWN** [4] [ ]
– Ommadawn (side 1) / Ommadawn (side 2). *(quad-lp Feb86) (cd-iss.1986)*
Nov 75. (7") **IN DULCE JUBILO. / ON HORSEBACK** [4] [-]
Nov 75. (7") **OMMADAWN (excerpt). / ON HORSEBACK** [-] [ ]
Oct 76. (7") **PORTSMOUTH. / SPEAK (THO' YOU ONLY SAY FAREWELL)** [3] [-]
Nov 76. (7") **PORTSMOUTH. / ALGIERS** [-] [ ]
Feb 77. (7") **WILLIAM TELL OVERTURE. / ALGIERS** [ ] [-]
Dec 77. (7") **THE CUCKOO SONG. / PIPE TUNE** [ ] [-]

— added from last album. (see most musicians from following live album)

Nov 78. (d-lp)(d-c) **INCANTATIONS** [14] [ ]
– Incantations (part 1) / Incantations (part 2) / Incantations (part 3) / Incantations (part 4). *(cd-iss.Feb87, omits 4 mins.of side 3)*
Apr 79. (7") **GUILTY. / INCANTATIONS (excerpt)** [22] [-]
(12"blue) – ('A'side) / Guilty (live).

— MIKE with **PIERRE MOERLEN** – drums, percussion / **RINGO McDONOUGH** – bodhran / **MIKE FRYE, BENOIT MOERLEN, DAVID BEDFORD** (also string arrangements) / **NICO RAMSDEN** – guitar / **PHIL BEER** – guitar, vocals / **PEKKA POHJOLA** – bass / **RAY GAY, RALPH IZEN, SIMO SALMINEN, COLIN MOORE** – trumpets / **SEBASTIAN BELL, CHRIS NICHOLLS** – flutes / **PETE LEMER, TIM CROSS** – keyboards / **MADDY PRIOR** – vocals / **JONATHAN KAHAN, DICK STUDT, BEN CRUFT, JANE PRYCE, LIZ EDWARDS, NICOLA HURTON** – violins / **VANESSA PARK, DAVID BUCKNALL, JESSICA FORD, NIGEL WARREN-GREEN** – cellos / **NICK WORTERS, JOE KIRBY** – bass / **DON McVAY, PAULINE MACK, DANNY**

DAGGERS, MELINDA DAGGERS, LIZ BUTLER, ROSS COHEN – vocals, plus 11 piece choir.

Aug 79. (d-lp)(d-c) **EXPOSED (live)** [16] [-]
– Incantations (parts 1 and 2) / Incantations (parts 3 and 4) / Tubular bells (part 1) / Tubular bells (part 2) / Guilty. *(also on quad) (d-cd-iss.Jul86)*

— Trimmed backing group down.

Nov 79. (7") **BLUE PETER. / WOODHENGE** [19] [-]
Dec 79. (lp)(c) **PLATINUM** [24] [-]
– Platinum:- Airborne – Platinum – Charleston North star – Platimun finale / Woodhenge / Sally / Punkadiddle / I got rhythm. *(cd-iss.1989)*

— next featured **PHIL COLLINS** – drums

Sep 80. (7") **ARRIVAL. / POLKA** [ ] [-]
Oct 80. (lp)(c) **QE2** [27] [-]
– Taurus I / Sheba / Conflict / Arrival / Wonderful land / Mirage / QE2 / Celt / Molly. *(cd-iss.1989)*
Nov 80. (7") **WONDERFUL LAND. / SHEBA** [ ] [-]
Dec 80. (d-lp)(d-c) **AIRBORN** [-] [ ]
– (see PLATINUM tracks, except 'Guilty' repl. -/ / Tubular bells live part 1 / Incantations (segue of 20+ mins. studio and live recordings)

— MIKE brought in **MAGGIE REILLY** – vocals (ex-CADO BELLE) / **TIM CROSS** – keys / **MORRIS PERT** – percussion, drums (ex-BRAND X) / **RICK FENN** – bass, guitar / **PIERRE MOERLEN** – drums, percussion returned to repl. MIKE FRYE / added **TIM RENWICK** – bass, guitar

Mar 82. (7")(7"pic-d) **FIVE MILES OUT. / LIVE PUNKADIDDLE** [43] [ ]
Mar 82. (lp)(c) **FIVE MILES OUT** [7] [ ]
– Taurus II / Family man / Orabidoo / Mount Teidi / Five miles out. *(cd-iss.1983) (re-iss.Apr90) (re-iss.cd+c Oct94 on 'Virgin-VIP')*
Jun 82. (7")(7"pic-d) **FAMILY MAN. / MOUNT TEIDI** [45] [ ]
Sep 82. (7")(7"pic-d) **MISTAKE. / (THE PEAK) WALDBERG** [ ] [ ]

— MIKE retained REILLY + MOERLEN. New members were **SIMON PHILLIPS** – drums / **PHIL SPALDING** – bass / **GRAEME PLEETH** – keyboards / **SIMON HOUSE** – violin

May 83. (7")(7"pic-d) **MOONLIGHT SHADOW. / RITE OF MAN** [4] [ ]
(12"+=) – ('A'extended).
May 83. (lp)(c)(cd) **CRISES** [6] [ ]
– Crises / Moonlight shadow / In high places / Foreign affair / Taurus III / Shadow on the wall *. (* vocals by **ROGER CHAPMAN, ex-FAMILY**) *(re-iss.cd+c May94 on 'Virgin-VIP')*
Sep 83. (7") **SHADOW ON THE WALL. / TAURUS III** [ ] [ ]
(12") – ('A'extended).
Jan 84. (7") **CRIME OF PASSION. / JUNGLE GARDENIA** [61] [ ]
(12") – ('A'extended).

— He retained **REILLY, PHILLIPS + SPALDING** – adding guitar / plus **BARRY PALMER** – vocals / **MICKEY SIMMONDS** – keyboards / **HAROLD ZUSCHRADER** – synth.

Jun 84. (7") **TO FRANCE. / IN THE POOL** [48] [ ]
(12"+=) – Bones.
Jul 84. (lp)(c)(cd) **DISCOVERY** [15] [ ]
– To France / Poison arrows / Crystal gazing / Tricks of the light / Discovery / Talk about your life / Saved by a bell / The lake.
Sep 84. (7") **TRICKS OF THE LIGHT. / APEMAN** [ ] [ ]
(12"+=) – ('A'instrumental).
Nov 84. (7") **ETUDE. / EVACUATION** [ ] [ ]
(12") – ('A' & 'B'extended).
Dec 84. (lp)(c)(cd) **THE KILLING FIELDS (Film Soundtrack)** [97] [ ]
– Pran's theme / Requiem for a city / Evacuation / Pran's theme 2 / Capture / Execution / Bad news / Pran's departure / Worksite / The year zero / Blood sucking / The year zero 2 / Pran's escape – The killing fields / The trek / The boy's burial – Pran sees the red cross / Good news / Etude. *(re-iss.Jun88)*

— **ANITA HEGERLAND + ALED JONES** – vocals repl. REILLY

Nov 85. (7") **PICTURES IN THE DARK. / LEGEND** [50] [ ]
('A'ext-12") – The trap.
Apr 86. (7")(7"sha-pic-d) **SHINE. / THE PATH** [ ] [ ]
('A'ext-12") – (as above)
May 87. (7") **IN HIGH PLACES. / POISON ARROWS** [ ] [-]
(12"+=) – Jungle Gardenia.

— vocalists – **JON ANDERSON / KEVIN AYERS / BONNIE TYLER**

Sep 87. (7") **ISLANDS. / THE WIND CHIMES (part one)** [ ] [ ]
(c-s+=)(cd-s+=)(12"+=) – When the night's on fire.
(12"='A'extended).
Oct 87. (lp)(c)(cd) **ISLANDS** [29] [ ]
– The wind chimes (parts 1 & 2) / Islands / Flying start / North point / Magic touch / The time has come. *(cd+=)– When the night's on fire.*
Nov 87. (7") **THE TIME HAS COME. / (Final extract from) THE WIND CHIMES** [ ] [-]
(12"+=) – ('A'original mix).
Nov 87. (7") **MAGIC TOUCH. / THE WIND CHIMES (part 1)** [-] [ ]
Feb 88. (7")(12") **FLYING START. / THE WIND CHIMES (part 2)** [ ] [ ]
Jul 89. (7") **EARTHMOVING. / BRIDGE TO PARADISE** [ ] [ ]
(12"+=)(cd-s+=) – ('A'disco mix).
Jul 89. (lp)(c)(cd) **EARTHMOVING** [30] [ ]
– Holy / Hostage / Far country / Innocent / Runaway son / See the light / Earthmoving / Blue night / Nothing but – Bridge to Paradise.
Oct 89. (7") **INNOCENT. / EARTHMOVING (club mix)** [ ] [ ]
(12"+=)(cd-s+=) – ('A'version).
Jun 90. (cd)(c)(lp) **AMAROK** [49] [ ]
– Amarok (part 1) / Amarok (part 2).

MICHAEL OLDFIELD

with **SIMON PHILLIPS** – drums / **DAVE LEVY** – bass / **MICKEY SIMMONDS** – keyboards / **ANDY LONGHURST** – keyboards / **COURTNEY PINE** – sax

Jan 91. (7")(12")(cd-s) **HEAVEN'S OPEN. / EXCERPT FROM AMAROK** [ ] [-]
Mar 91. (cd)(c)(lp) **HEAVEN'S OPEN** [ ] [ ]
– Make make / No dream / Mr.Shame / Gimme back / Heaven's open / Music from the balcony.

MIKE OLDFIELD

solo again playing most instruments, except some guests & a bagpipe band.

W.E.A. W.E.A.

Sep 92. (cd)(c)(lp) **TUBULAR BELLS II** [1] [ ]
– Sentinel / Dark star / Clear light / Blue saloon / Sunjammer / Red dawn / The bell / Weightless / The great pain / Sunset door / Tattoo / Altered state / Maya gold / Moonshine.
Sep 92. (7")(c-s)(cd-s) **SENTINEL (SINGLE RESTRUCTION). / EARLY STAGES** [10] [ ]
Dec 92. (7")(c-s) **TATTOO. / SILENT NIGHT / SENTINEL (live)** [33] [ ]
(cd-ep+=) – Live At Edinburgh Castle:- Moonshine / Reprise / Maya gold.
Apr 93. (7")(c-s) **THE BELL. / SENTINEL** [50] [ ]
(cd-s+=) – ('A' 3 mixes).
(cd-s) – (5 'A'mixes).
Nov 94. (cd)(c)(lp) **THE SONGS OF DISTANT EARTH** [24] [ ]
– In the beginning / Let there be light / Supernova / Magellan / First landing / Oceania / Only time will tell / Prayer for the Earth / Lament for Atlantis / The chamber / Hibernaculum / Tubular world / The shining ones / Crystal clear / The sunken forest / Ascension / A new beginning. *(re-iss.cd/c Oct95)*
Dec 94. (cd-s) **HIBERNACULUM. / MOONSHINE (mixes)** [47] [ ]
(c-s)(cd-s) – ('A'side) / The spectral Song of the boat men.
Aug 95. (cd-s) **LET THERE BE LIGHT (Indian Lake mix) / LET THERE BE LIGHT (BT's entropic dub)** [51] [ ]
(12") – ('A'-BT's pure luminescence remix) / ('A'-Hardfloor mix) / ('A'club mix).
(cd-s) – (above club mix) repl.by – ('A'-Ultraviolet mix).

- compilations, etc. -

Nov 76. Virgin; (4xlp-box) **BOXED** [22] [-]
– (TUBULAR BELLS / HERGEST RIDGE / OMMADAWN / + COLLABORATIONS (singles, etc.) *(re-iss.+4xc+4xcd. 1985) (cd-box re-iss.1990)*
Dec 78. Virgin; (7"ep)(12"ep) **TAKE 4** [72] [-]
– Portsmouth / In dulce jubilo / Wrekorder wrondo / Sailor's hornpipe.
Oct 85. Virgin; (d-lp)(c)(cd) **THE COMPLETE MIKE OLDFIELD** [36] [-]
– Arrival / In dulce jubilo / Portsmouth / Jungle gardenia / Guilty / Blue Peter / Waldberg (the peak) / Etude / Wonderful land / Moonlight shadow / Family man / Mistake / Five miles out / Crime of passion / To France / Shadow on the wall / Excerpt from Tubular Bells / Sheba / Mirage / Platinum / Mount Tiede / Excerpt from Ommadawn / Excerpt from Hergest Ridge / Excerpt from Incantations / Excerpt from Killing Fields.
Jun 88. Virgin; (3"cd-ep) **MOONLIGHT SHADOW (extended) / RITE OF MAN / TO FRANCE / JUNGLE GARDENIA** [ ] [-]
Jun 88. Virgin; (cd-video) **THE WIND CHIMES (Soundtrack 1986)** [ ] [-]
Dec 90. Virgin; (7")(c-s) **ETUDE. / GAKKAEN** [ ] [-]
(12"+=)(cd-s+=) – ('A'extended) (with "ONO GAGUKU KAI").

— (The above 'A'side was now used on TV ad for 'Nurofen'.)

Sep 93. Virgin; (cd)(c)(d-lp) **ELEMENTS: THE BEST OF MIKE OLDFIELD** [5] [ ]
– Tubular bells – opening hteme / Family man / Moonlight shadow / Heaven's open / Five miles out / To France / Foreign affair / In dulce jubilo / Shadow on the wall / Islands / Etude / Sentinel / Ommadawn – excerpt / Incantations part four – excerpt / Amarok – excerpt / Portsmouth.
Sep 93. Virgin; (4xcd-box) **ELEMENTS – MIKE OLDFIELD 1973-1991** [ ] [ ]
– (all TUBULAR BELLS & other album excerpts, plus singles to 1991)
Oct 93. Virgin; (7")(c-s) **MOONLIGHT SHADOW. / MOONLIGHT SHADOW (extended version)** [52] [ ]
(cd-s+=) – In The Pool (Instrumental) / Bones (Instrumental)
Nov 93. Virgin; (c-ep)(cd-ep) **THE MIKE OLDFIELD CHRISTMAS EP** [ ] [ ]
– In dulce jubilo / Portsmouth

OMD (see under ⇒ ORCHESTRAL MANOEUVRES IN THE DARK)

ORANGE JUICE (see under ⇒ COLLINS, Edwyn)

ORB

Formed: South London, England . . . 1989 by remix supremo and ex-KILLING JOKE roadie Dr.ALEX PATERSON. He took the name from a Woody Allen psi-fi film 'Sleepers' and found ex-BRILLIANT guitarist JIM CAUTY. They broke through in the early 90's when 'BLUE ROOM' hit UK Top 10. Their label 'Wau! Mr. Modo' had by now been taken over by 'Big Life'. • **Style:** Ambient electronic rave project, whose lengthy ep's & lp's, have graced the new dancefloors of the 90's, although influenced by TANGERINE DREAM or ENO. • **Songwriters:** Most by WESTON and PATERSON. • **Trivia:** The ORB have remixed many including 'Mute' label stars; DEPECHE MODE / ERASURE & WIRE. In 1992, caused upset in the Asian community when using their religious chant.

Recommended: UF ORB (*9) / ADVENTURES BEYOND THE ULTRAWORLD (*9)

ALEX PATERSON -synth, keyboards / with **JIM CAUTY**

Wau! Mr.Modo — not issued

May 89. (ltd.12"ep) **KISS (as "ROCKMAN ROCK & LX DEE")** [ ] [-]
– Kiss your love / Suck my kiss mix / The roof is on fire / Ambiorix mix.

Oct 89. (12") **A HUGE EVER GROWING PULSATING BRAIN THAT RULES FROM THE CENTRE OF THE ULTRAWORLD: LOVIN' YOU (Orbital mix). / ('A'bucket and spade mix) / WHY IS 6 SCARED OF 7?** [ ] [-]
(re-iss.+cd-ep.Jun90 on next new label, remixed Jul90)

In Nov90, they collaborated on STEVE HILLAGE's SYSTEM 7 release 'Sunburst'.

Big Life — Mercury

Nov 90. (7") **LITTLE FLUFFY CLOUDS. / ('A'ambient mix Mk.1)** [ ] [ ]
(dance mix-12"+=)(cd-s+=) – Into the fourth dimension (Essenes beyond..)

— CAUTY was replaced by **STEVE HILLAGE** – guitar (ex-Solo artist, ex-GONG) / **MIQUETTE GIRAUDY** (ex-GONG) + **ANDY FALCONER**

Apr 91. (d-cd)(d-c)(d-lp) **ADVENTURES BEYOND THE ULTRAWORLD** [29] [ ] Nov 91
– Little fluffy clouds / Earth (Gaia) / Supernova at the end of the universe / Back side of the Moon / Spanish castles in space / Perpetual dawn / Into the fourth dimension / Outlands / Star 6 & 7 8 9 / A huge ever growing pulsating brain that rules from the centre of the Ultraworld.

Jun 91. (7")(c-s) **PERPETUAL DAWN (SOLAR YOUTH). / STAR 6&789 (phase II)** [61] [ ]
(ext-12"+=)(cd-s+=) – ('A'ultrabass 1 mix).
(12"ep 'ORB IN DUB' Andy Weatherall ultrabass mixes += Towers Of Dub')

— In Nov91, SYSTEM 7 issued another release on '10-Virgin'; 'Miracle'.

Dec 91 (cd)(c)(lp) **THE AUBREY MIXES: THE ULTRAWORLD EXCURSIONS (deleted after 1 day)** [44] [ ]
-Little fluffy clouds / (Pal Joey mix) / Black side of the moon (Steve Hillage remix) / Spanish castles in Spain (Youth remix) / Outlands (Ready made remix) / A huge overgrowing pulsating brain (Jim Caldy & Dr. Alex Patterson remix).

— **PATERSON** now with **THRASH** – guitars? plus guests **YOUTH, STUART McMILLAN, GUY PRATT, JAH WOBBLE, STEVE HILLAGE, MIQUETTE GIRAUDY, THOMAS FEHLMANN, GREG HUNTER, ORDE MEIKLE, TOM GREEN, MARNEY PAX.**

Jun 92. (12"ep)(c-ep)(cd-ep) **THE BLUE ROOM** [8] [ ]
– The blue room (nearly 40 mins.)
(cd-ep+=) – The blue room (2 shorter 4 minute versions) / Towers of dub (mad professor mix).

Jul 92. (d-cd)(d-c)(t-lp) **UF ORB** [1] [ ]
– O.O.B.E. / U.F. Orb / Blue room / Towers of dub / Close encounters / Majestic / Sticky end.
– (free live lp at some shops 'Soundtrack To The Film: ADVENTURES BEYOND THE ULTRAWORLD: PATTERNS & TEXTURES')

Oct 92. (12"-box)(c-box)(d-cd-box) **ASSASSIN (the oasis of rhythms mix). / U.F.ORB (Bandalu mix)** [12] [ ]
(d-cd+=) – ('A'another live version mix).

Nov 93. (12"ep)(c-ep)(cd-ep) **LITTLE FLUFFY CLOUDS. / ('A'mixes)** [10] [ ]

Island — Island

Nov 93. (d-cd)(d-c)(d-lp) **LIVE 93 (live)** [23] [ ]
– Plateau / The valley / Oobe / Little fluffy clouds / Star 6, 7, 8 & 9 / Towers of dub / Spanish castles in space / The blue room / Perpetual dawn / Assassin / Outlands / Huge ever pulsating brain . . .

Jan 94. (12")(c-s)(cd-s) **PERPETUAL DAWN. / TOWERS OF DUB (ambient mix)** [18] [ ]
(12") – ('A'-Andy Weatherall mixes) / Towers of dub (ambient mix).

Jun 94. (cd)(c)(lp) **POMMEFRITZ** [6] [ ]
– Pommefritz / More gills less fishcakes / We're paste to be grill you / Banger'n'chips / Allers ist schoen / His immortal logness.

— now w /out KRIS WESTON, who was repl. (after 1995 recording by) **ANDREW HUGHES**

Mar 95. (cd)(c)(d-lp) **ORBUS TERRARUM** [20] [ ]
– Valley / Plateau / Oxbow lakes / Montagne d'or (der gute berg) / White river junction / Occidental / Slug dub.

May 95. (cd-s) **OXBOW LAKES / ('A'-Everglades mix)** [38] [ ]
(12") – ('A'-Everglades mix) / ('A'-Sabres No.1 mix).
(cd-s) – (3 tracks above).
(12") – ('A'-Carl Craig psychic pals family wealth plan mix). / ('A'-Evensong string arrangement mix).
(cd-s) – (all 5 mixes above).

. . .Jan-Jun'96 stop press compilation . . .

Apr 96. Strange Fruit; (cd)(lp) **THE PEEL SESSIONS** [ ] [-]

FFWD

aka **ROBERT FRIPP / THOMAS FEHLYN / KRIS WESTON / DR.ALEX PATTERSON**

Intermodo — Intermodo

Aug 94. (cd)(c)(d-lp) **FFWD** [48] [ ]
– Hidden / Lucky saddle / Drone / Hempire / Collosus / What time is clock / Can of bliss / Elauses / Meteor storm / Buckwheat and grits / Klangtest / Suess wie eine nuss.

– compilations, others, etc. –

Nov 91. Strange Fruit; (cd)(c)(lp) **THE PEEL SESSIONS** [ ] [-]

Feb 92. Strange Fruit; (cd-ep) **THE PEEL SESSIONS** [ ] [-]
– A huge ever growing brain that rules from the centre of the ultraworld.

APOLLO XI

DR. ALEX PATTERSON + guest **BEN WATKINS** (of SUNSONIC)

Wau! Mr. Modo — not issued

Feb 91. (12")(cd-s) **PEACE (IN THE MIDDLE EAST) /** [ ] [-]

ORBITAL

Formed: Seven Oaks, London, England . . . late 80's by brothers PHIL and PAUL HARTNOLL. Issued own label release, which gained attention of London's 'Ffrr' records, who duly signed them, unleashing revised debut 'CHIME'. They were soon starring on Top Of The Pops early 1991, when 'SATAN' (complete with BUTTHOLE SURFERS sample) nearly hit UK 30. • **Style:** Techno-electro sample duo, with KRAFTWERK-like keys backing pulsating infectious dance themes. • **Songwriters:** The duo, except noted samples; O EUCHARI (performed by Emily Van Evera). • **Trivia:** Vox on tracks 'SAD BUT TRUE' & 'ARE WE HERE?' by ALISON GOLDFRAPP.

Recommended: UNTITLED (ORBITAL 1) (*7) / UNTITLED (ORBITAL II) (*7) / SNIVILIZATION (*8) / IN SIDES (*9)

PHIL HARTNOLL – keyboards / **PAUL HARTNOLL** – keyboards

Oh-Zone — not issued

Dec 89. (12"ep) **CHIME. / DEEPER (full version)** [ ] [-]

Ffrr-London — Ffrr-London

Mar 90. (7")(ext.12") **CHIME. / DEEPER** [ ] [-]
(cd-ep+=) – ('A'version).
(12"ep) – ('A'-JZM remix) / ('A'-Bacardi mix)

Jul 90. (12"ep) **OMEN. / 2 DEEP / OPEN MIND** [ ] [-]
(cd-ep) – (1st & 3rd track) / ('A'edit)
(12"ep) – Omen: The chariot / The tower / Wheel of fortune / The fool.

Jan 91. (7") **SATAN. / BELFAST** [31] [-]
(12"ep+=)(cd-ep+=) – L.C.1.
(12"ep) – ('A'-rhyme & reason mix) / L.C.2 (outer limits mix) / Chime.

Aug 91. (12") **MIDNIGHT. / CHOICE** [ ] [-]
(12"ep) – Midnight (Sasha mix) / Choice (Orbital & Eye & I mix).
(cd-ep+=) – Analogue test Feb'90.

Sep 91. (cd)(c)(lp) **UNTITLED (ORBITAL 1)** [71] [ ]
– The moebius / Speed freak / Oolaa / Desert storm / Fahrenheit 303 / Steel cube idolatry / High rise / Chime (live) / Midnight (live) / Belfast / Macrohead.
(cd w /out last track, repl. by – I Think It's Disgusting
(c+=) – Untitled.

Feb 92. (12"ep) MUTATIONS (I): OOLAA (Joey Beltram remix) / OOLAA (Meat Beat Manifesto mix) / CHIME (Joey Beltram). / SPEED FREAK (Moby mix) [24] [-]

(12"ep) MUTATIONS (II): Chime (Ray Keith mix) / Chime (Crime remix) / Steel cube idolatory / Farenheit 303.
(cd-ep) Oolaa (Joey Beltram mix) / Chime (Ray Keith mix) / Speed freak / Fahrenheit 303.

Internal | Ffrr-London

Sep 92. (12"ep) **RADICCIO EP: THE NAKED AND THE DEAD. / SUNDAY** [37] [ ]
(cd-ep+=) – Halycon.
Apr 93. (12"ep) LUSH 3-1. / LUSH 3-2 / LUSH 3-3 (underworld) [ ] [-]
(12"ep) **LUSH 3-4 (Psychick Warriors Ov Gaia) / LUSH 3-5 (CJ Bollard).**
(cd-ep) **(all 5 tracks).**
Jun 93. (cd)(c)(lp) **UNTITLED (ORBITAL II)** [28] [-]
– Time becomes / Planet of the shapes / Lush 3-1 / Lush 3-2 / Impact (the Earth is burning) / Remind / Walk now . . . / Monday / Halycon + on + on / Input out.
Mar 94. (m-cd)(m-lp) **PEEL SESSION EP** [ ] [-]
– Lush (Euro-tunnel disaster '94) / Walk about / Semi detached / Attached.
(cd-ep) DIVERSIONS EP – Impact USA / Lush 3 (Euro-Tunnel disaster '94) / Walkabout / Lush 3-5 (CJ Bolland) / Lush 3-4 (Warrior drift) / Lush 3-4 (Underworld).
Aug 94. (cd)(c) **SNIVILIZATION** [4] [ ]
– Forever / I wish I had duck feet / Sad but true / Crash and carry / Science friction / Philosophy by numbers / Kein trink wasser / Quality seconds / Are we here? / Attached.
Sep 94. (12")(c-s)(cd-s) **ARE WE HERE? EP** [33] [ ]
– Are we here: Who are they? / Do they here? / They did it (mix) / What was that? / Criminal Justice Bill? / Industry standard?.

—— In May'95, they covered THERAPY?'s 'Belfast' on special cd-s which hit UK No.53. THERAPY? gave us interpretation of 'INNOCENT X'.

Aug 95. (d7"ep)(d12"ep)(cd-ep) **UNTITLED EP** [ ] [-]
-Times fly (slow) / Sad but new / Times fly (fast) / The tranquilizer.
(above was not eligible for UK chart position due to it's length)

. . . Jan – Jun '96 stop press . . .

Apr 96. (single) **THE BOX** [11] [ ]
Apr 96. (cd)(c)(3x12"lp) **IN SIDES** [5] [ ]

ORCHESTRAL MANOEUVRES IN THE DARK

Formed: West Kirby, Liverpool, England . . . Autumn 1978, initially as The ID, by McCLUSKEY and HUMPHREYS. After one-off indie single 'ELECTRICITY' for 'Factory', they signed to 'Virgin' subsidiary label 'Dindisc'. Early in 1980, they hit UK Top 75 with 'RED FRAME – WHITE LIGHT', which paved the way for eponymous parent album, which made Top 30. In the summer of 1980, they hit the Top 20 with 'MESSAGES' & 'ENOLA GAY' (the name of the plane which dropped the Hiroshima bomb). They remained in the chart limelight for the next decade plus. • **Style:** Electronic pop-rockers, influenced by KRAFTWERK, although they drifted into more mainstream sound, away from experimental period of the early 80's. • **Songwriters:** All material written by McCLUSKEY & HUMPHREYS, until latter's exit in '89. Covered; I'M WAITING FOR THE MAN (Velvet Underground) / NEON LIGHTS (Kraftwerk). • **Trivia:** An ID track 'JULIA'S SONG', appeared on an 'Open Eye' indie compilation lp 'Street To Street' in 1978.

Recommended: THE BEST OF O.M.D. (*8)

ANDREW McCLUSKEY (b.24 Jun'59, Wirral, England) – vocals, bass (ex-DALEK I) / **PAUL HUMPHRIES** (b.27 Feb'60, London, England) – keys, synths. (ex-The ID) with backing from computer 'Winston'.

Factory | not issued

May 79. (7") **ELECTRICITY. / ALMOST** [ ] [-]
(re-iss.Sep79 on 'Dindisc')

Dindisc | not issued

Feb 80. (7")(12") **RED FRAME – WHITE LIGHT. / I BETRAY MY FRIENDS** [67] [-]

—— guests **DAVID FAIRBURN** – guitar / **MALCOLM HOLMES** – drums / **MARTIN COOPER** – sax

Feb 80. (lp)(c) **ORCHESTRAL MANOEUVRES IN THE DARK** [27] [-]
– Bunker soldiers / Almost / Mystereality / Electricity / The Messerschmit twins / Messages / Julia's song / Red frame – white light / Dancing / Pretending to see the future. *(re-iss.Aug84 on 'Virgin') (cd-iss.Jul87)*
May 80. (7") **MESSAGES. / TAKING SIDES AGAIN** [13] [-]
(10") – ('A'extended) / Waiting for the man.

—— added **DAVID HUGHES** – keyboards (ex-DALEK I LOVE YOU, ex-SECRETS) and now f/t member **MALCOLM HOLMES** – drums (ex-CLIVE LANGER & THE BOXES, ex-ID)

Sep 80. (7")(12") **ENOLA GAY. / ANNEX** [8] [-]
Oct 80. (lp)(c) **ORGANISATION** [6] [-]
– Enola Gay / 2nd thought / VCL XI / Motion and heart / Statues / The misunderstanding / The more I see you / Promise / Stanlow. *(free 7"ep)*– INTRODUCING RADIOS / PROGRESS. / DISTANCE FADES BETWEEN US / WHEN I WAS SIX *(re-iss.Aug88 on 'Virgin') (cd-iss.Jul87)*

—— **MALCOLM COOPER** – saxophone, keyboards (ex-DALEK I LOVE YOU) repl. HUGHES

Dindisc | Epic

Aug 81. (7")(10") **SOUVENIR. / MOTION AND HEART (Amazon version) / SACRED HEART** [3] [-]
Oct 81. (7")(12") **JOAN OF ARC. / THE ROMANCE OF THE TELESCOPE (unfinished version)** [5] [ ]
Nov 81. (lp)(c) **ARCHITECTURE & MORALITY** [3] [ ]
– New stone age / She's leaving / Souvenir / Sealand / Joan Of Arc / Joan Of Arc (Maid of Orleans) / Architecture and morality / Georgia / The beginning and the end. *(cd-iss.1988 on 'Virgin') (re-iss.Apr90)*
Jan 82. (7")(12") **MAID OF ORLEANS (THE WALTZ JOAN OF ARC). / NAVIGATION** [4] [ ]
(12"+=) – Of all the things we've made. *(3" cd-s iss.Jun88)*
Jan 82. (7") **SOUVENIR. / NEW STONE AGE** [-] [ ]

Virgin | Epic-Virgin

Feb 83. (7")(12")(7"pic-d) **GENETIC ENGINEERING. / 4-NEU** [20] [-]
Mar 83. (lp)(c) **DAZZLE SHIPS** [5] [ ]
– Radio Prague / Genetic engineering / ABC auto-industry / Telegraph / This is Helena / International / Dazzle ships / The romance of the telescope / Silent running / Radio waves / Time zones / Of all the things we've made. *(re-iss.1987, cd-iss.1985)*
Apr 83. (7")(7"pic-d) **TELEGRAPH. / 66 AND FADING** [42] [-]
(12") – ('A'extended).
May 83. (7") **TELEGRAPH. / THIS IS HELENA** [-] [ ]

Virgin | A & M

Apr 84. (7")(7"pic-d) **LOCOMOTION. / HER BODY IN MY SOUL** [5] [ ] Nov 84
(12") – ('A'extended) / The avenue. *(3" cd-s iss.Jun88)*
May 84. (lp)(c) **JUNK CULTURE** [9] [ ] Nov 84
– Junk culture / Tesla girls / Locomotion / Apollo / Never turn away / Apollo / Love and violence / Hard day / All wrapped up / White trash / alking loud and clear. *(cd-iss.1986 & Mar90)*
Jun 84. (7")(7"pic-d) **TALKING LOUD AND CLEAR. / JULIA'S SONG** [11] [-]
(12") – ('A'&'B'extended).
Aug 84. (7")(c-s) **TESLA GIRLS. / TELEGRAPH (live)** [21] [-]
(12"+=) – Garden city.
Oct 84. (7")(7"pic-d) **NEVER TURN AWAY. / WRAP-UP** [70] [-]
(12") – ('A'extended) / Waiting for the man (live).
May 85. (7") **SO IN LOVE. / CONCRETE HANDS** [27] [26] Aug85
(12")(12"pic-d) – ('A'&'B'extended) / Maria Gallante.
(d12"++=) – White trash (live).
Jun 85. (lp)(c) **CRUSH** [13] [38] Jul 85
– So in love / Secret / Bloc bloc bloc / Women III / Crush / 88 seconds in Greensboro / The native daughters of the west / La femme accident / Hold you / The lights are going out. *(cd-iss.Jan86 & Mar90)*
Jul 85. (7") **SECRET. / DRIFT** [34] [-]
(12"+=) – ('A'extended).
(d12"+=) – Red frame – white light / I betray my friends.
Oct 85. (7")(7"sha-pic-d) **LA FEMME ACCIDENT. / FIREGUN** [42] [ ]
(12"+=) – ('A'extended).
(d12"++=) – Locomotion (live) / Enola Gay (live).
Nov 85. (7") **SECRET. / FIREGUN** [-] [63]
Mar 86. (7") **IF YOU LEAVE. / LA FEMME ACCIDENT** [-] [ ]
Apr 86. (7") **IF YOU LEAVE. / 88 SECONDS IN GREENSBORO** [48] [-]
(12") – ('A'extended) / Locomotion (live).

—— added The **WEIR BROTHERS** (NEIL & GRAHAM) (had guested on earlier songs)

Aug 86. (7")(7"pic-d) **(FOREVER) LIVE AND DIE. / THIS TOWN** [11] [19]
(12"+=) – ('A'extended).
Sep 86. (lp)(c)(cd) **THE PACIFIC AGE** [15] [47]
– Stay (the black rose and the universal wheel) / (Forever) Live and die / The Pacific age / The dead girls / Shame / Southern / Flame of hope / Goddess of love / We love you / Watch us fall. *(re-iss.Mar90)*
Nov 86. (7") **WE LOVE YOU. / WE LOVE YOU (dub)** [54] [ ]
(12"+=) – ('A'extended).
(d7"+=) – If you leave / 88 seconds on Greensboro.
(free c-s w7"+=) – Souvenir / Electricity / Enola Gay / Joan of Arc.
Apr 87. (7") **SHAME (re-recorded). / GODDESS OF LOVE** [52] [ ]
(12"+=) – ('B're-recorded version).
(cd-s+=) – (Forever) Live and die / Messages.
Jan 88. (7") **DREAMING. / SATELLITE** [50] [16] Feb 88
(12")(12"pic-d) – ('A'extended) / Gravity never failed.
(cd-s++=)(3"cd-s++=) – Dreaming. *(re-dist.Jun88, hit 60)*
(10") – ('A'side) / ('A'William Orbit mix) / Messages / Secret.
Feb 88. (lp)(c)(cd)(pic-cd) **IN THE DARK – THE BEST OF O.M.D.** (compilation) [2] [46]
– Electricity / Messages / Enola Gay / Souvenir / Joan of Arc / Maid of Orleans

(Joan Of Arc waltz) / Talking loud and clear / Tesla girls / Locomotion / So in love / Secret / If you leave / (Forever) Live and die / Dreaming. *(cd+=)–* Telegraph / We love you (12"version) / La femme accident (12"version) / Genetic engineering.

OMD

ANDY McCLUSKEY now sole survivor after others left 1989. HUMPHREYS formed The LISTENING POOL in the early 90's. / added **STUART BOYLE** – guitar plus additional 8 vocalists.

Mar 91. (7")(c-s) **SAILING ON THE SEVEN SEAS. / BURNING** [3] [ ]
(12") – ('A'extended) / Floating on the seven seas.
(cd-s) – ('A'extended) / Dancing on the seven seas / Big town.
(cd-s) – ('A'side) / Floating on the seven seas / Dancing on the seaven seas (Larrabee mix) / Sugartax.

May 91. (cd)(c)(lp) **SUGAR TAX** [3] [ ]
– Sailing on the seven seas / Pandora's box / Then you turn away / Speed of light / Was it something I said / Big town / Call my name / Apollo XI / Walking on air / Walk tall / Neon lights / All that glitters.

Jun 91. (7")(c-s) **PANDORA'S BOX. / ALL SHE WANTS IS EVERYTHING** [7] [ ]
(cd-s+=) – ('A'constant pressure mix) / ('A'diesel fingers mix).
(12")/ /(cd-s) – (2 'A'mixes)./ / (3 'A'mixes).

Sep 91. (7")(c-s) **THEN YOU TURN AWAY. / SUGAR TAX** [50] [ ]
(cd-s+=) – Area / ('A'inforce repeat mix).
(cd-s) – ('A'side) / ('A'repeat mix) / Sailing on the seven seas / Vox humana.

Nov 91. (7")(c-s) **CALL MY NAME. / WALK TALL** [50] [ ]
(12") – ('A'side) / Brides of Frankenstein.
(cd-s++=) – ('A'side) / ('A'version) / Brides . . . (dub).

May 93. (7")(c-s) **STAND ABOVE ME. / CAN I BELIEVE YOU** [21] [ ]
(cd-s+=) – ('A' transcendental mix) / ('A' hynofunk mix).
(12") – ('A'side) / ('A'transcendental mix) / ('A'-10 minute version)

Jun 93. (cd)(c)(lp) **LIBERATOR** [14] [ ]
– Stand above me / Everyday / King of stone / Dollar girl / Dream of me (based on Love's theme) / Sunday morning / Agnus Dei / Love and hate you / Heaven is / Best years of our lives / Christine / Only tears.

Jul 93. (7")(c-s) **DREAM OF ME (BASED ON LOVE'S THEME). / ('A' mix)** [24] [ ]
(cd-s+=) – Strange sensations / The place you fear the most.
(cd-s) ('A' side) / Enola Gay / Dreaming / Call my name

Sep 93. (7")(c-s) **EVERYDAY. / ELECTRICITY (live)** [59] [ ]
(cd-s+=) – Walk tall (live) / Locomotion (live).

– other compilations, etc. –

May 84. Epic; (lp) **ORCHESTRAL MANOEUVRES IN THE DARK** [-] [ ]
– (compilation of first 2 albums)

Feb 89. Old Gold; (7") **ENOLA GAY. / ELECTRICITY** [ ] [-]

Mar 89. Old Gold; (12") **SOUVENIR (extended). / TALKING LOUD AND CLEAR (ext.)** [ ] [-]

Feb 89. Virgin/ US= A&M; (12") **BRIDES OF FRANKENSTEIN (OMD megaremixes: LOCOMOTION / SO IN LOVE / SECRET / IF YOU LEAVE / WE LOVE YOU)** [-] [ ]

Nov 90. Virgin; (3xpic-cd-box) **CD BOXED SET** [ ] [-]
– (first 3 albums)

Sep 94. Virgin; (cd)(c) **THE BEST OF OMD** [69] [ ]

ORGANISATION (see under ⇒ KRAFTWERK)

Benjamin ORR (see under ⇒ CARS)

Joan OSBORNE

*** NEW ENTRY ***

Born: 1962, Anchorage, Kentucky, USA. She dropped out of Louisville College in 1988, and went to New York where she sang in blues clubs, including BILLIE HOLLIDAY's 'God Bless The Child'. In 1992, she and her new band released live album on 'Womanly Hips', a label formed by her manager at the time PAUL RISELLI. The HOOTERS guitarist ROB HYMAN saw a live performance and phoned producer RICH CHERTOFF, who worked for 'Polygram'. In 1995, she appeared on Mercury off-shoot 'Blue Gorilla'. The classy single 'ONE OF US', soon became US Top 5 and was nominated for a Grammy early in '96. It was lifted from her US Top 10 album 'RELISH', which also did the same in Britain. • **Style:** Kooky angst-ridden songstress like a hick version of PJ HARVEY fused with TORI AMOS or ALANIS MORISSETTE. Her songs covered most subjects including religion, sex, degradation of society, etc. • **Songwriters:** She co-writes with her group and ex-HOOTERS guitarist ERIC BAZILIAN, who solely penned 'ONE OF US'. Covers; MAN IN THE LONG BLACK COAT (Bob Dylan) / HELP ME (Sonny Boy Williamson). Sample CAPTAIN BEEFHEART (Right Hand Man) and T.REX.

Recommended: RELISH (*7)

JOAN OSBORNE – vocals / **ERIC BAZILIAN** – guitar / **MARK EGAN** – bass / **ANDY KRAVITZ** – drums (of CYPRESS HILL, URGE OVERKILL) / **ROB HYMAN** – organ, synth.

Mercury / BlueGorilla

Feb 96. (c-s) **ONE OF US / ('A'edit)** [6] [4] Nov 95
(cd-s) – ('A'side) / Dracula Moon / Crazy baby (live).

Mar 96. (cd)(c) **RELISH** [5] [9] Dec 95
– St. Teresa / Man in the long black coat / Right hand man / Pensacola / Dracula Moon / One of us / Ladder / Spider web / Let's just get naked / Help me / Crazy baby / Lumina.

Jun 96. (c-s) **ST. TERESA / LUMINA** [33] [ ] Apr 96
(cd-s+=) – Spider web / ('A'edit).
(cd-s) – ('A'side) / Help me / One of us / ('A'edit).

Ozzy OSBOURNE

Born: JOHN MICHAEL OSBOURNE, 3 Dec'48, Aston, Birmingham, England. After 11 years as frontman for BLACK SABBATH, he formed own BLIZZARD OF OZZ in 1980. They signed to Don Arden's 'Jet', and released self-titled album, which hit UK Top 10 & US No.21. Their next album 'DIARY OF A MADMAN' in 1981, credited to OZZY solo, also went into cross-Atlantic Top 20. For the rest of the 80's, OZZY became renowned for his upsetting stage shows, where he used to bite the heads off doves, bats, etc. • **Miscellaneous:** He divorced wife Thelma in 1981, and married Don Arden's daughter Sharon on 4 Jul'82, who became his manager. Ozzy was always a hard drinker and drug user, although she forced him to attend the Betty Ford Clinic in 1984. He was taken to court a few times around the mid-80's, for people committing suicide while listening to his music, mainly citing the track 'SUICIDE SOLUTION'. • **Style:** Aleister Crowley influenced heavy-metal, lyrically evil, but taken seriously?. OZZY's screach was well-matched for this near SABBATH-like sound. • **Songwriters:** OZZY lyrics, RHOADS music, until his tour bus / plane-crash death on 19 Mar'82. In 1982, the group recorded a live album 'TALK OF THE DEVIL', full of BLACK SABBATH covers. OZZY later collaborated with BOB DAISLEY. • **Trivia:** In 1987, he played a bible-punching preacher in the film 'Trick Or Treat'.

Recommended: NO MORE TEARS (*7) / DIARY OF A MADMAN (*7) / OZZY OSBOURNE'S BLIZZARD OF OZZ (*6) / THE ULTIMATE SIN (*6).

OZZY OSBOURNE'S BLIZZARD OF OZZ

OZZY OSBOURNE – vocals (ex-BLACK SABBATH) / **RANDY RHOADS** – guitar (ex-QUIET RIOT) / **LEE KERSLAKE** – drums (ex-URIAH HEEP) / **BOB DAISLEY** – bass (ex-RAINBOW, ex-CHICKEN SHACK) / **DON AVERY** – keyboards

Jet / Jet-CBS

Sep 80. (7") **CRAZY TRAIN. / YOU LOOKING AT ME LOOKING AT YOU** [49] [-]

Sep 80. (lp)(c) **OZZY OSBOURNE'S BLIZZARD OF OZZ** [7] [21] Mar81
– I don't know / Crazy train / Goodbye to romance / Dee / Suicide solution / Mr. Crowley / No bone movies / Revelation (Mother Earth) / Steal away (the night). *(re-iss.Nov87 on 'Epic', cd-iss.on 'Jet' & Nov95 on 'Epic')*

Nov 80. (7") **MR.CROWLEY. / YOU SAID IT ALL** [46] [-]
(12"+=) – Suicide solution.

Feb 81. (7") **CRAZY TRAIN. / STEAL AWAY (THE NIGHT)** [-] [ ]

OZZY OSBOURNE

(same line-up, except AVERY)

Oct 81. (lp)(c) **DIARY OF A MADMAN** [14] [16]
– Over the mountain / Flying high again / You can't kill rock and roll / Believer / Little dolls / Tonight / S.A.T.O. / Diary of a madman. *(cd-iss.May87) (re-iss.+cd.Apr91 & Nov95 on 'Epic')*

Nov 81. (7") **OVER THE MOUNTAIN. / I DON'T KNOW** [ ] [-]

— (Nov81) **RUDY SARZO** – bass (ex-QUIET RIOT) repl. DAISLEY (to URIAH HEEP) **TOMMY ALDRIDGE** – drums (ex-BLACK OAK ARKANSAS, etc) repl. KERSLAKE

— (Apr'82) **BRAD GILLIS** – guitar (of NIGHT RANGER) repl. RANDY RHOADS who was killed in a light aeroplane crash on 19th Mar'82.

Nov 82. (d-lp)(d-c) **TALK OF THE DEVIL** (live at Ritz Club, NY) [21] [14]
– Symptom of the universe / Snowblind / Black sabbath / Fairies wear boots / War pigs / The wizard / N.I.B. / Sweet leaf / Never say die / Sabbath bloody sabbath / Iron man / Children of the grave / Paranoid. *(cd-iss.Jan89 omits dialogue) (re-iss.complete cd+c.Jul91 on 'Castle') (re-iss.cd Nov95 on 'Epic')*

Dec 82. (7")(7"pic-d) **SYMPTOM OF THE UNIVERSE (live). / N.I.B. (live)** [ ] [-]

(12"+=) – Iron man – Children of the grave (live).
Feb 83. (7") **NEVER SAY DIE (live). / PARANOID (live)** [-] [ ]

— (Dec82) **JAKE E.LEE** (b.JAKEY LOU WILLIAMS, San Diego, California, USA) – guitar (ex-RATT) repl. GILLIS who returned to NIGHT RANGER / **DON COSTA** – bass repl. PETE WAY (ex-UFO) who had deputised for the departing RUDY SARZO who had returned to QUIET RIOT. (He later joined WHITESNAKE)

— **OZZY, JAKE E + TOMMY** re-recruit **BOB DAISLEY** to repl. COSTA

Epic / CBS Assoc.

Nov 83. (7") **BARK AT THE MOON. / SPIDERS** [-] [ ]
Nov 83. (7") **BARK AT THE MOON. / ONE UP ON THE B-SIDE** [21] [ ]
(12"+=)(12"silver+=)(12"pic-d+=) – Slow down.
Dec 83. (lp)(c) **BARK AT THE MOON** [24] [19]
– Rock'n'roll rebel / Bark at the Moon / You're no different / Now you see it (now you don't) / Forever / So tired / Waiting for darkness / Spiders. *(re-iss.Apr86, cd-iss.Oct88 & Nov95)*
Mar 84. (7") **SO TIRED. / FOREVER (live)** [ ] [ ]
(12"+=)(d7"+=) – Waiting for darkness / Paranoid (live).

— ALDRIDGE was briefly replaced (Mar-May84) on tour by CARMINE APPICE.

May 84. (7") **SO TIRED. / BARK AT THE MOON (live)** [20] [ ]
(12"+=)(12"gold+=) – Waiting for darkness (live) / Suicide solution (live) / Paranoid (live).

— **PHIL SOUSSAN** – bass repl. DAISLEY / **RANDY CASTILLO** – drums (ex-LITA FORD BAND) repl. ALDRIDGE

Jan 86. (7")(12") **SHOT IN THE DARK. / ROCK'N'ROLL REBEL** [20] [-]
Feb 86. (lp)(c) **THE ULTIMATE SIN** [8] [6]
– Lightning strikes / Killer of giants / Thank God for the bomb / Never / Shot in the dark / The ultimate sin / Secret loser / Never know why / Fool like you. *(cd-iss.Jul86 & Feb89 & Nov95) (pic-lp Aug86)*
Mar 86. (7") **SHOT IN THE DARK. / YOU SAID IT ALL** [-] [69]
Jul 86. (7")(12") **THE ULTIMATE SIN. / LIGHTNING STRIKES** [72] [ ]

— (Aug88) **ZAKK WILDE** (b.ZACH ADAMS, 14 Jan'66) – guitar repl. JAKE who formed BADLANDS. / **DAISLEY** returned to repl. SOUSSAN (to BILLY IDOL) / added **JOHN SINCLAIR** – keyboards

Oct 88. (lp)(c)(cd) **NO REST FOR THE WICKED** [23] [13]
– Miracle man / Devil's daughter / Crazy babies / Breaking all the rules / Bloodbath in Paradise / Fire in the sky / Tattooed dancer / The demon alcohol. *(cd+=)– Hero. (re-iss.cd+c Jun94 & Nov95)*
Oct 88. (7")(7"pic-d) **MIRACLE MAN. / CRAZY BABIES** [ ] [-]
(12"+=)(cd-s+=) – The liar.
Dec 88. (7") **MIRACLE MAN. / MAN YOU SAID IT ALL** [-] [ ]
Feb 89. (7") **CRAZY BABIES. / THE DEMON ALCOHOL** [-] [ ]

— Earlier in the year OZZY had accompanied LITA FORD on 45 'CLOSE MY EYES FOREVER'. In Apr'89, it was to reach UK/US Top50.

— **TERRY 'GEEZER' BUTLER** – bass was used for tour work late 1988.

Feb 90. (cd)(c)(lp) **JUST SAY OZZY (live)** [69] [58]
– Miracle man / Bloodbath in Paradise / Shot in the dark / Tattooed dancer / Sweet leaf / War pigs. *(re-iss.cd Nov95)*

— In the late 80's, OZZY retired to his Buckinghamshire mansion with his manager/wife Sharon Arden and 3 kids. He had also kicked his alcohol addiction.

Returned 1991 after being cleared of causing death of fan. See last studio line-up. Augmented also by **MICHAEL INEZ** – bass, inspiration repl. BUTLER

Sep 91. (7") **NO MORE TEARS. / S.I.N.** [32] [71]
(12"+=)(c-s+=)(cd-s+=)(12"pic-d+=) – Party with the animals.
Oct 91. (cd)(c)(lp) **NO MORE TEARS** [17] [7]
– Mr.Tinkertrain / I don't want to change the world / Mama, I'm coming home / Desire / S.I.N. / Hellraiser / Time after time / Zombie stomp / A.V.H. / Road to nowhere. *(re-iss.cd Nov95)*
Nov 91. (7") **MAMA, I'M COMING HOME. / DON'T BLAME ME** [46] [28] Feb 92
(12"+=) – I don't know / Crazy train.
(cd-s+=) – (Steve Wright interview)
(12"+=) – Time after time / Goodbye to romance.
(US-cd-ep+=) Party with the animals.
Jun 93. (d-cd) **LIVE & LOUD (live)** [ ] [22]
– Intro / Paranoid / I don't want to change the world / Desire / Mr.Crowley / I don't know / Road to nowhere / Flying high again / Guitar solo / Suicide solution / Goodbye to romance / Shot in the dark / No more tears / Miracle man / Drum solo / War pigs / Bark at the Moon / Mama, I'm coming home / Crazy train / Black sabbath / Changes. *(re-iss.Nov95)*
Jun 93. (12")(cd-s) **CHANGES (live). / CHANGES / NO MORE TEARS / DESIRE** [ ] [ ]
Oct 95. (cd)(c)(lp) **OZZMOSIS** [22] [4]
– Perry Mason / I just want you / Ghost behind my eyes / Thunder underground / See you on the other side / Tomorrow / Denial / My little man / Mr. Jekyll doesn't hide / Old L.A. tonight.
Nov 95. (7"pic-d) **PERRY MASON. / LIVING WITH THE ENEMY** [23] [ ]
(cd-s+=) – The whole world's falling down.
(cd-s) – ('A'side) / No more tears / I don't want to change the world / Flying high again.

– compilations, others, etc. –

May 87. Epic/ US= CBS; (d-lp)(c)(cd) **TRIBUTE (live)** [13] [6]
– I don't know / Crazy train / Revelation (Mother Earth) / Believer / Mr.Crowley / Flying high again / No bone movies / Steal away (the night) / Suicide solution / Iron man – Children of the grave / Goodbye to romance / Paranoid / Dee. *(cd-omits studio track 'Dee') (re-iss.cd+c Apr93 & Nov95 on 'Epic')*
(Album + 45 were recorded 1981 with the deceased RANDY RHOADS)
Jun 87. Epic/ US= CBS; (7")(12") **CRAZY TRAIN (live). / CRAZY TRAIN** [ ] [ ]
Jul 88. Epic; (12"ep)(cd-ep) **THE ULTIMATE SIN / BARK AT THE MOON. / MR.CROWLEY / DIARY OF A MADMAN** [ ] [-]
Mar 93. Epic; (cd) **BARK AT THE MOON / BLIZZARD OF OZ** [ ] [ ]
Aug 90. Priority; (cd)(c)(lp) **TEN COMMANDMENTS** (rare) [-] [ ]

OTHER TWO (see under ⇒ NEW ORDER)

OZRIC TENTACLES

Formed: London, England . . . after meeting at Stonehenge in 1982. Brothers ED and ROLY WYNNE with the others, decamped to Trowbridge, Somerset in the early 90's, having issued second album (a double) 'ERPLAND' on managers' JOHN BENNETT own 'Dovetail' label. • **Style:** Psychedelic /progressive festival crusty band, who had similar inclinations to STEVE HILLAGE, CAMEL or HAWKWIND. • **Songwriters:** Group / or ED and JOIE. • **Trivia:** JOIE bet their record company that aliens!!! would land on Earth by the year 2000.

Recommended: STRANGEITUDE (*7) / JURASSIC SHIFT (*6) / ARBORESCENCE (*6)

ED WYNNE – guitar, synthesizers / **ROLY WYNNE** – bass / **JOIE 'OZROONICULATOR' HINTON** – synthesizers / **NICK 'TIG' VAN GELDER** – drums / **GAVIN GRIFFITHS** – guitar / added in 1983; **TOM BROOKES** – synthesizers / **PAUL HANKIN** – percussion

— In 1984, GRIFFITHS left to form ULLINATORS, and a year later BROOKES also left. HINTON sidelined with group ULLINATORS and OROONIES. Released cassette-only albums which I think were untitled.

— **MERV PEPLER** – drums, percussion repl. VAN GELDER

Demi-Monde / not issued

Feb 89. (lp) **PUNGENT EFFULGENT** [ ] [-]
– Dissolution (the clouds disperse) / 0-1 / Phalarn dawn / The domes of G'bal / Shaping the pelm / Ayurvedic / Kick muck / Agog in the ether / Wreltch. *(re-iss.+cd/c Mar91 on 'Dovetail')*

Dovetail / not issued

Nov 90. (cd)(d-lp) **ERPLAND** [ ] [-]
– Eternal wheel / Toltec spring / Tidal convergence / Sunscape / Mysticum Arabicola / Crackerblocks / The throbbe / Erpland / Valley of a thousand thoughts / Snakepit / Iscence / A gift of wings.
Jul 91. (12")(cd-s) **SPLOOSH!. / LIVE THROBBE** [ ] [-]
Aug 91. (cd)(c)(lp) **STRANGEITUDE** [70] [-]
– White rhino tea / Sploosh / Saucers / Strangeitude / Bizzare bazaar / Space between your ears. (cd+=) – Live Throbbe.

— **STEVE EVERETT** – synthesizers repl. BROOKES

— added **MARCUS CARCUS** – percussion / **JOHN EGAN** – flute

Jan 92. (d-cd) **AFTERWISH** (compilation 1984-1991) [ ] [ ]
– Guzzard / Chinatype / The sacred turf / Og-ha-be / Thyroid / Omnidibectional Bhadba / Afterwish / Velmwend / Travelling the great circle / Secret names / Soda water / Fetch me the pongmaster / Zall! / Abul Hagag / It's a hup ho world / The dusty pouch / Thrashing breath texture / Floating seeds / Invisible carpet / The code for Chickendon / Kola b'pep / Mae Hong song / Symetricum / Jabular / Sliding and gliding.
Apr 92. (cd)(c)(d-lp) **LIVE UNDERSLUNKY (live)** [ ] [-]
– Dot thots / Og-ha-be / Erpland / White rhino tea / Bizzare bazaar / Sunscrape / Erpsongs / Snake pit / Kick muck / 0-1 / Ayurvedic.

— **ZIA** – bass repl. ROLY (late'92)

— (5-piece **ED, JOIE, JON, MERV + ZIA**)

Apr 93. (cd)(c)(lp) **JURASSIC SHIFT** [11] [-]
– Sun hair / Stretchy / Feng Shui / Jurassic shift / Pteranodon / Train oasis / Vita voom.
Jul 94. (cd)(c)(d-lp) **ARBORESCENCE** [18] [ ]
– Astro Cortez / Yog-bar-og / Arborescence / Al-salooq / Dance of the Loomi / Myriapod / There's a planet here / Shima Koto.

— JOIE + MERV were now EAT STATIC full-time. They had splintered as said outfit since summer '92.

Oct 95. (cd) **BECOME THE OTHER** [ ] [-]
– Og-ha-be / Shards of ice / Sniffing dog / Music to gargle at / Ethereal cereal / Atmosphear / Ulluvar gate / Tentacles of Erpmiad / Trees of eternity / Mescalito /

Odhanshan / Become the other / Gnuthlia / Sorry style / The Aun shuffle.

– compilations, etc. –

Nov 93. Dovetail; (6xcd-box) **VITAMIN ENHANCED** [ ] [-]
Feb 94. Dovetail; (cd) **ERPSONGS** [ ] [-]
Feb 94. Dovetail; (cd) **TANTRIC OBSTACLES** [ ] [-]
Feb 94. Dovetail; (cd) **LIVE ETHEREAL CEREAL** [ ] [-]
Feb 94. Dovetail; (cd) **THERE IS NOTHING** [ ] [-]
Feb 94. Dovetail; (cd) **SLIDING GLIDING WORDS** [ ] [-]
Feb 94. Dovetail; (cd) **THE BITS BETWEEN THE BITS** [ ] [-]
(all 6 above re-iss.Mar94)

EAT STATIC

JOIE + MERV + STEVE

Alien — not issued

1992. (c) **PREPARE YOUR SPIRIT** [ ] [-]
– Hallucinate / Fudge / Wormlips / Instinct / Eat-Static / Destroy / Raga / Almost human / Om machine / Cyper-funk / The watcher / Higher-state / Woman is life / Medicine wheel / Fourt dimension.

Nov 92. (12"ep)(cd-ep) **ALMOST HUMAN / FOURTH DIMENSION. / PUPAE (THE LOCUST SONG) / MOTHER PLANET** [ ] [-]

Ultimate-Planet Dog — not issued

May 93. (cd)(c)(lp) **ABDUCTION** [62] [-]
– Prana / Gulf breeze / Kalika / Splitting world / Kinetic flow / Forgotten rites / Abduction / Intruder / Xenomorph / Inner peace.

Nov 93. (12"ep)(cd-ep) **LOST IN TIME. / GULF BREEZE / THE BRAIN** [ ] [-]
Mar 94. (12"ep)(cd-ep) **GULF BREEZE (remix). / ('A'-Ashoshashoz mix) / ('A'cat mix)** [ ] [-]
Jun 94. (cd)(c)(lp) **IMPLANT** [13] [ ]
– Implant.
Jul 94. (1 track; 12"ep/cd-ep) **SURVIVORS** [ ] [-]
Mar 95. (12"ep)(d12"ep)(c-ep)(cd-ep) **EPSYLON EP** [ ] [-]
– Epsylon / Dionsyiac / Peeou / Undulattice.

. . . Jan – Jun '96 stop press . . .

Feb 96. (single) **BONY INCUS EP** [ ] [-]

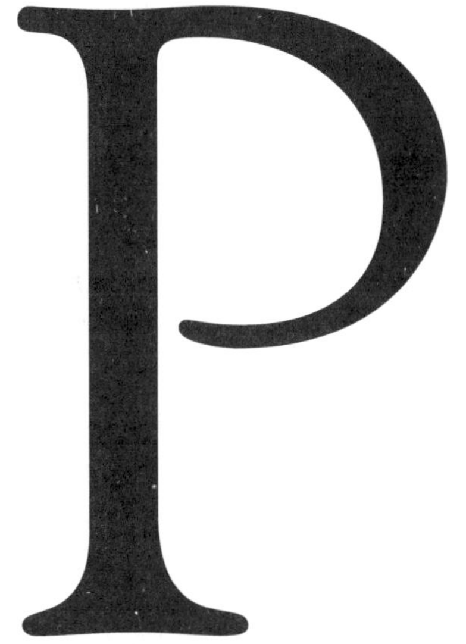

Jimmy PAGE (see under ⇒ LED ZEPPELIN)

PAICE, ASHTON & LORD (see under ⇒ DEEP PURPLE)

Robert PALMER

Born: ALAN ROBERT PALMER, 19 Jan'49, Batley, Yorkshire, England. From the age of 3, lived with family in Malta, due to father being in the services. In 1969 after being in semi-pro group MANDRAKE PADDLE STEAMER, he moved to London. He joined ALAN BOWN SET, replacing solo bound JESS RODEN. Late that year, he featured on 'Deram' 45 'GYPSY GIRL'. The following year, he joined jazz-rockers DADA, who also had on their eponymous 'Atco' album debut, singer ELKIE BROOKS. In 1971, they evolved into VINEGAR JOE, but after 3 poor selling albums for 'Island' (VINEGAR JOE / ROCK'N'ROLL GYPSIES + SIX-STAR GENERAL), they split-up Mar'74. After nearly replacing LOWELL GEORGE in LITTLE FEAT, PALMER was retained by 'Island'. His first album release 'SNEAKING SALLY . . . ', failed in the UK, but sales in the US, nearly made it crack the Top 100. The next year, he flitted to New York with his wife. After his follow-up album 'PRESSURE DROP', and support slot on LITTLE FEAT tour, he again relocated, this time to Nassau, Bahamas. After making inroads into Transatlantic charts in the mid-70's, he broke through in the US with 1978 singles 'EVERY KINDA PEOPLE' & 'BAD CASE OF LOVING YOU (DOCTOR, DOCTOR)'. He gained deserved commercial leap in the early 80's, with album 'CLUES'. In 1985, he teamed up with DURAN DURAN members to become The POWER STATION. They scored with a few hits including 'SOME LIKE IT HOT'. In 1987, now as an accomplished worldwide artist, he emigrated to Lugano, Switzerland, although he and his wife also stayed in Milan, Italy. • **Style:** BRYAN FERRY like in image/smart attire. His use of stunning female filled videos also drew attention to American AOR reggae beat/disco leanings. • **Songwriters:** PALMER penned, except SNEAKING SALLY THROUGH THE ALLEY + FROM A WHISPER TO A SCREAM (Allen Toussaint) / PRESSURE DROP (Lee Perry) / EVERY KINDA PEOPLE (Andy Fraser) / YOU REALLY GOT ME (Kinks) / JEALOUS + THE SILVER GUN (Alan Powell) / YOU ARE IN MY SYSTEM (System) / CAN WE STILL BE FRIENDS (Todd Rundgren) / SOME GUYS HAVE ALL THE LUCK (Persuaders) / BAD CASE OF LOVING YOU (Moon Martin) / I DIDN'T MEAN TO TURN YOU ON (hit; Cherrelle) / EARLY IN THE MORNING (Gap Band) / I'LL BE YOUR BABY TONIGHT (Bob Dylan) / MERCY MERCY ME (THE ECOLOGY) – I WANT YOU (Marvin Gaye) / WITCHCRAFT (hit; Frank Sinatra) / GIRL U WANT (Devo) / RESPECT YOURSELF (Staple Singers) / etc. • **Trivia:** GARY NUMAN featured on his 1980 'CLUES' album. PALMER produced The COMSAT ANGELS, DESMOND DEKKER and PETER BAUMANN.

Recommended: ADDICTIONS VOL.1 (*7) / ADDICTIONS 2 (*5).

ROBERT PALMER – vocals with various session people

		Island	Island
Sep 74.	(lp)(c) **SNEAKIN' SALLY THROUGH THE ALLEY**		May 75
	– Sailing shoes / Hey Julia / Sneakin' Sally through the alley / Through it all there's you / Get outside / Blackmail / How much fun / From a whisper to a scream / Through it all there's you. *(re-iss.Jan87, cd-iss.Aug89)*		
Nov 74.	(7") **SNEAKIN' SALLY THROUGH THE ALLEY. / EPIDEMIC**	-	
Oct 75.	(7") **WHICH OF US IS THE FOOL. / GET OUTSIDE**		
Feb 76.	(7") **GIMME AN INCH. / PRESSURE DROP**		
Mar 76.	(lp)(c) **PRESSURE DROP**		Nov 75
	– Give me an inch / Work to make it work / Back in my arms / Riverboat / Pressure drop / Here with you tonight / Trouble / Fine time / Which of us is the fool. *(re-iss.Jan87, cd-iss.Apr87 + Aug89)*		
Oct 76.	(7") **MAN SMART, WOMAN SMARTER. / FROM A WHISPER TO A SCREAM**		-
Oct 76.	(lp)(c) **SOME PEOPLE CAN DO WHAT THEY LIKE**	46	68
	– One lost look / Keep in touch / Man smart, woman smarter / Spanish moon / Have mercy / Gotta get a grip on you (part II) / What can you bring me / Hard head / Off the bone / Some people can do what they like.		
Oct 76.	(7") **MAN SMART, WOMAN SMARTER. / KEEP IN TOUCH**	-	63
Mar 77.	(7") **SOME PEOPLE CAN DO WHAT THEY LIKE. / ONE LOST LOOK**	-	
Jan 78.	(lp)(c) **DOUBLE FUN**		45 Mar 78
	– Every kinda people / Best of both worlds / Come over / Where can it go / Night people / Love can run faster / You overwhelm me / You really got me / You're gonna get what's coming. *(re-iss.Jan87, cd-iss.Nov87 + Aug89)*		
Mar 78.	(7") **EVERY KINDA PEOPLE. / HOW MUCH FUN**	-	16
Mar 78.	(7") **EVERY KINDA PEOPLE. / KEEP IN TOUCH**	53	-
May 78.	(7") **COME OVER. / YOU OVERWHELM ME**	-	
Jun 78.	(7") **BEST OF BOTH WORLDS. / ('A'dub version)**		
	(12"+=) – Pressure drop.		
May 79.	(7") **BAD CASE OF LOVIN' YOU (DOCTOR, DOCTOR). / LOVE CAN RUN FASTER**	61	14 Jul 79
Jun 79.	(lp)(c) **SECRETS**	54	19 Jul 79
	– Bad case of loving you (doctor, doctor) / Too good to be true / Can we still be friends / In walks love again / Mean old world / Love stop / Jealous / Under suspicion / Woman you're wonderful / What's it take / Remember to remember. *(re-iss.Jan87, cd-iss.1988 + Aug89)*		
Jul 78.	(7") **YOU'RE GONNA GET WHAT'S COMING. / WHERE CAN IT GO**	-	
Aug 79.	(7") **JEALOUS. / WOMAN YOU'RE WONDERFUL**		-
Sep 79.	(7") **JEALOUS. / IN WALKS LOVE AGAIN**	-	
Nov 79.	(7") **CAN WE STILL BE FRIENDS. / BACK IN MY ARMS**	-	
Dec 79.	(7") **CAN WE STILL BE FRIENDS. / REMEMBER TO REMEMBER**	-	52
Aug 80.	(7") **JOHNNY AND MARY. / STYLE KILLS**	-	
Aug 80.	(7") **JOHNNY AND MARY. / WHAT'S IT TAKE**	44	-
	(12"+=) – Remember to remember.		
Aug 80.	(lp)(c) **CLUES**	31	59 Oct 80
	– Looking for clues / Sulky girl / Johnny and Mary / What do you care / I dream of wires / Woke up laughing / Not a second time / Found you now. *(re-iss.+cd.Jan87, cd-iss.Jan89)*		
Oct 80.	(7") **LOOKING FOR CLUES. / WOKE UP LAUGHING**	-	
Nov 80.	(7") **LOOKING FOR CLUES. / IN WALKS LOVE AGAIN**	33	-
	(12") – ('A'side) / Good care of you / Style kills.		
Jun 81.	(7") **NOT A SECOND TIME. / WOKE UP LAUGHING**		
Jan 82.	(7")(7"pic-d) **SOME GUYS HAVE ALL THE LUCK. / TOO GOOD TO BE TRUE**	16	
	(12")(12"pic-d) – ('A'side) / Style kills / Si Chatouillieux / What do you care.		
Mar 82.	(lp)(c) **MAYBE IT'S LIVE (live)**	32	May 82
	– Sneakin' Sally through the alley / What's it take / Best of both worlds / Every kinda people / Bad case of loving you (doctor, doctor) / Some guys have all the luck / Style kills / Si Chatouillieaux / Maybe it's you / What do you care. *(cd+c.-iss.Apr91) (re-iss.cd+cMay93 on 'Spectrum')*		
Nov 82.	(7")(7"pic-d) **PRIDE. / PRIDE (instrumental)**		
	(12") – ('A'side) / Parade of the obliterators.		
Mar 83.	(7")(12") **YOU ARE IN MY SYSTEM. / DEADLINE**	53	78 Jun 83
Apr 83.	(lp)(c) **PRIDE**	37	
	– Pride / Deadline / Want you more / Dance for me / You are in my system / It's not difficult / Say you will / You can have it (take my heart) / What you waiting for / The silver gun. *(re-iss.+cd.Jan87, cd-iss.Jun89)*		
Jun 83.	(7")(12")(7"pic-d) **YOU CAN HAVE IT (TAKE MY HEART). / THE SILVER GUN**	66	

— From early '85, PALMER became lead singer of DURAN DURAN off-shoot band The POWER STATION. Their eponymous lp, hit both UK + US Top 20's, and spawned a few hits 'SOME LIKE IT HOT', 'GET IT ON' & 'COMMUNICATION'. (see DURAN DURAN ⇒).

Oct 85.	(7") **DISCIPLINE OF LOVE. / DANCE FOR ME**		82

(12"+=) – Woke up laughing.
Nov 85. (lp)(c)(cd) **RIPTIDE** [5] [8]
– Riptide / Hyperactive / Addicted to love / Trick bag / Get it through your heart / I didn't mean to turn you on / Flesh wound / Discipline of love / Riptide (reprise). *(cd-iss.1988) (re-iss.+cd.Apr91)*
Dec 85. (7") **RIPTIDE. / BACK IN MY ARMS** [ ] [ ]
(12") – ('A'side) / No not much (live) / Trick bag (live)
(d7"++=) – (12"tracks) / Johnny and Mary.
Feb 86. (7") **ADDICTED TO LOVE. / LET'S FALL IN LOVE TONIGHT** [-] [1]
Apr 86. (7")(12") **ADDICTED TO LOVE. / REMEMBER TO REMEMBER** [5] [-]
(7"sha-pic-d) – ('A'side) / More.
May 86. (7") **HYPERACTIVE. / WOKE UP LAUGHING** [-] [33]
Jun 86. (7")(12") **I DIDN'T MEAN TO TURN YOU ON. / GET IT THROUGH YOUR HEART** [9] [2] Aug 86
(d7"+=) – You are in my system / Johnny and Mary.
Oct 86. (7")(12") **DISCIPLINE OF LOVE. / DANCE FOR ME** [68] [-]
(12"+=) – Riptide (medley).
(d7"+=) – Remember to remember / Addicted to love.
Mar 88. (7") **SWEET LIES. / WANT YOU MORE** [ ] [94]
(12"+=) – Riptide.
(cd-s++=) – ('A'extended).

E.M.I. Manhattan

Jun 88. (7")(7"pic-d) **SIMPLY IRRESISTABLE. / NOVA** [44] [2]
(12"+=)(cd-s+=) – ('A'extended version) / ('A'instrumental).
Jun 88. (lp)(c)(cd) **HEAVY NOVA** [17] [13]
– Simply irresistable / More than ever / Change his ways / Disturbing behaviour / Early in the morning / It could happen to you / She makes my day / It could happen to you / Tell me I'm not dreaming / Between us / Casting a spell. *(re-iss.cd+c Mar94)*
Oct 88. (7") **SHE MAKES MY DAY. / DISTURBING BEHAVIOUR** [6] [ ]
(12"+=)(cd-s+=) – Simply irresistable (extended).
Oct 88. (7") **EARLY IN THE MORNING. / ?** [-] [19]
May 89. (7")(7"pic-d) **CHANGE HIS WAYS. / MORE THAN EVER** [28] [ ]
(12") – (2 diff.mixes).
(cd-s++=) – She makes my day.
Jun 89. (7") **TELL ME I'M NOT DREAMING. / ?** [-] [60]
Aug 89. (7")(c-s) **IT COULD HAPPEN TO YOU. / CHANGE HIS WAYS** [71] [ ]
(12"+=) – Early in the morning (get up mix).
(cd-s++=) – Casting a spell.

E.M.I. E.M.I.

Oct 90. (7")(c-s) **I'LL BE YOUR BABY TONIGHT. ("ROBERT PALMER & UB40") / DEEP END** [6] [ ]
(12"+=)(cd-s+=) – ('A'version).
Nov 90. (cd)(c)(d-lp) **DON'T EXPLAIN** [9] [88]
– Your mother should have told you / Light-years / You can't get enough of a good thing / Dreams to remember / You're amazing / Mess around / Happiness / History / I'll be your baby tonight / Housework / Mercy mercy me – I want you / Don't explain / Aeroplane / People will say we're in love / Not a word / Top 40 / You're so desirable / You're my thrill. *(re-iss.cd+c Sep94)*
Nov 90. (c-s) **YOU'RE AMAZING. / ?** [-] [28]
Dec 90. (7")(c-s) **MERCY MERCY ME (THE ECOLOGY) – I WANT YOU. / OH YEAH** [9] [16] Feb 91
(12"+=)(cd-s+=) – (2 'A'&'B'versions).
Apr 91. (7")(c-s) **HAPPINESS. / ALL SHOOK UP** [ ] [ ]
(12"+=)(cd-s+=) – ('A'extended).
Jun 91. (7")(c-s) **DREAMS TO REMEMBER. / MESS AROUND** [68] [ ]
(12"+=) – Happiness.
(cd-s+=) – Mercy mercy me / I want you.
Oct 92. (7")(c-s) **WITCHCRAFT. / CHANCE** [50] [ ]
(cd-s) – ('A'side) / She makes my day / Mercy mercy me – I want you.
Oct 92. (cd)(c)(d-lp) **RIDIN' HIGH** [32] [ ]
– Love me or leave me / (Love is) The tender trap / You're my thrill / Want you more / Baby it's cold outside / Aeroplane / Witchcraft / What a little moonlight can do / Don't explain / Chance / Goody goody / Do nothin' till you hear from me / Honeysuckle rose / No not much / Ridin' high / Hard head.
(above featured many 40's + 50's covers)
Jul 94. (7")(c-s) **GIRL U WANT. / NO FUSS** [57] [ ]
(cd-s+=) – ('A'mixes).
Aug 94. (7")(c-s) **KNOW BY NOW. / MERCY MERCY ME –** I WANT YOU [25] [ ]
(cd-s+=) – Simply irrestible.
(cd-s) – ('A'side) / ('A'mixes) / In the stars / She makes my day.
Sep 94. (cd)(c)(lp) **HONEY** [25] [ ]
– Honey A / Honey B / You're mine / Know by now / Nobody but you / Love takes time / Honeymoon / You blow me away / Close to the edge / Closer to the edge / Girl u want / Wham bam boogie / Big trouble / Dreams come true.
Dec 94. (7")(c-s) **YOU BLOW ME AWAY. / SIMPLY IRRESISTABLE** [38] [ ]
(cd-s) – ('A'side) / No control / ('A'mix) / Know by now.
(cd-s) – ('A'side) / ('A'mixes) / Change his ways.
Sep 95. (c-s) **RESPECT YOURSELF / YOU BLOW ME AWAY** [45] [ ]
(cd-s+=) – Girl u want / Race to the end of the set medley:- Bad case of loving you (doctor, doctor) – Simply irrisistible – Some guys have all the luck – I didn't mean to turn you on – Looking for clues – Addicted to love – You are in my system – Know by now – Some like it hot – I want you – Every kinda people.
(cd-s) – ('A'side) / Get it on (45 mix) / Some like it hot (7"mix) / Respect yourself (FX mix).
Oct 95. (cd)(c) **THE VERY BEST OF ROBERT PALMER** (compilation) [4] [ ]
– Addicted to love / Bad case of loving you (doctor, doctor) / Simply irresistable / Get it on (POWER STATION) / Some guys have all the luck / I didn't mean to turn you on / Looking for clues / You are in my system / Some like it hot (POWER STATION) / Respect yourself / I'll be your baby tonight (w/ UB40) / Johnny & Mary / She makes my day / Know by now / Every kinda people / Mercy mercy me – I want you (medley).

– compilations, others, etc. –

Nov 89. Island; (7") **BAD CASE OF LOVING YOU (DOCTOR, DOCTOR). / SWEET LIES** [ ] [ ]
(12"+=)(cd-s+=) – What's it take.
Nov 89. Island; (lp)(c)(cd) **ADDICTIONS VOL.1** [7] [79]
– Bad case of loving you (doctor, doctor) / Pride / Addicted to love / Sweet lies / Woke up laughing / Looking for clues / Some guys have all the luck / Some like it hot (POWER STATION) / What's it take? / Every kinda people / Johnny & Mary / Simply irritible / Style kills.
Feb 92. Island; (7")(12")(c-s)(cd-s) **EVERY KINDA PEOPLE. / ('A'radio mix)** [43] [ ]
Mar 92. Island; (cd)(c)(lp) **ADDICTIONS VOL.2** [12] [ ]
– Remember to remember / Sneakin' Sally through the alley / Maybe it's you / You are in my system / I didn't mean to turn you on / Can we still be friends / Man smart, woman smarter / Too good to be true / Every kinda people / She makes my day / Best of both worlds / Give me an inch / You're gonna get what's coming / I dream of wires / The silver gun.
Jun 92. Island; (7")(c-s)(cd-s) **YOU ARE IN MY SYSTEM. / YOU'RE GONNA GET WHAT'S COMING / TOO GOOD TO BE TRUE** [ ] [ ]
Jul 87. See For Miles; (lp)(c) **THE EARLY YEARS** [ ] [-]
– (above featured before solo work with The ALAN BOWN SET)
Nov 95. Island; (d-cd) **ADDICTIONS VOL.1 & 2** [ ] [ ]

PANTERA

Formed: Texas, USA . . . 1981 by TERRY GLAZE, DARRELL ABBOTT, (brother) VINCE ABBOTT and REX ROCKER. After 4 albums on own homegrown 'Metal Magic' (and recommendation from ROB HALFORD of JUDAS PRIEST), they switched to 'Atco' for the 90's. • **Style:** Power groove heavy-metal similar to KISS, which progressed into anthemic grindcore NAPALM DEATH sound by the 90's. • **Songwriters:** Group, except PLANET CARAVAN (Black Sabbath) / THE BADGE (Poison Idea). • **Trivia:** Means PANTHER in Spanish. In the late 80's, DARRELL turned down the chance to join MEGADETH.

Recommended: A VULGAR DISPLAY OF POWER (*6)

TERRY GLAZE – vocals, guitar / **DARRELL ABBOTT** – guitar / **REX ROCKER** – bass / **VINCE ABBOTT** – drums

not issued Metal Magic

1983. (lp) **METAL MAGIC** [-] [ ]
– Ride my rocket / I'll be alright / Tell me if you want it / Latest lover / Biggest part of me / Metal magic / Widowmaker / Nothin' on (but the radio) / Sad lover / Rock out!.

— GLAZE became TERRENCE LEE, DARRELL prefixed the word DIMEBAG and VINCE was now VINNIE PAUL.

1984. (lp) **PROJECTS IN THE JUNGLE** [-] [ ]
– All over tonite / Out for blood / Blue lite turnin' red / Like fire / In over my head / Projects in the jungle / Heavy metal rules! / Heartbeat away / Killers / Takin' my life.
1985. (lp) **I AM THE NIGHT** [-] [ ]
– Hot and heavy / I am the night / Onward we rock! / D.S.G.S.T.S.T.S.M. / Daughters of the queen / Down below / Come-on eyes / Right on the edge / Valhalla / Forever tonight.

— **PHILIP ANSELMO** – vocals repl. TERRY

May 88. (lp) **POWER METAL** [-] [ ]
– Rock the world / Power metal / We'll meet again / Over and out / Proud to be loud / Down below / Death trap / Hard ride / Burnnn! / P.S.T. 88.

Atco Atco

Jul 90. (cd)(c)(lp) **COWBOYS FROM HELL** [ ] [ ]
– Cowboys from Hell / Primal concrete sledge / Psycho holiday / Heresy / Cemetery gates / Domination / Shattered / Clash with reality / Medicine man / Message in blood / The sleep / The art of shredding.
Feb 92. (cd)(c)(lp) **A VULGAR DISPLAY OF POWER** [64] [44]
– Mouth for war / A new level / Walk / F**king hostile / This love / Rise / No good (attack the radical) / Live in a hole / Regular people (conceit) / By demons

be driven / Hollow.

Oct 92. (7")(c-s) **MOUTH FOR WAR. / RISE** — 73 | —
(cd-s+=) – Cowboys from Hell / Heresy.
(12") – ('A'side) / ('A'-superloud mix) / Domination / Primal concrete sledge.

Feb 93. (12"m) **WALK. / COWBOYS FROM HELL / PSYCHO HOLIDAY (live)** — 34 | —
(cd-ep) – ('A'side) / Fucking hostile / By demons be driven.
(cd-ep) – ('A'side) / No good (attack the radical)/ A new level / Walk (extended).
(cd-ep) – ('A'side) / ('A'remixes by Jim 'Foetus' Thirlwell).

East West | Atco

Mar 94. (12")(cd-s) **I'M BROKEN. / SLAUGHTERED** — 19 | —
(cd-s+=) – Domination (live) / Primal concrete sledge.
(cd-s) – ('A'side) / Cowboys from Hell (live) / Psycho holiday (live).
(12") – ('A'side) / Walk (cervical edit) / Fuckin' hostile.

Mar 94. (cd)(c)(lp) **FAR BEYOND DRIVEN** — 3 | 1
– Strength beyond strength / Becoming / 5 minutes alone / I'm broken / Good friends and a bottle of pills / Hard lines, sunken cheeks / Slaughtered / 25 years / Shedding skin / Use my third arm / Throes of rejection / Planet Caravan.

May 94. (7"white) **5 MINUTES ALONE. / THE BADGE** — — | —

Oct 94. (12") **PLANET CARAVAN. / COWBOYS FROM HELL / HERESAY** — 26 | —
(cd-s) – ('A'side) / The badge / New level / Becoming.
(cd-s) – ('A'side) / Domination / Hollow.

. . . Jan – Jun '96 stop press . . .

May 96. (cd)(c)(lp) **THE GREAT SOUTHERN TRENDKILL** — 17 | 4

PARADISE LOST

Formed: Halifax, England . . .1988. Took their name from poet Milton. Debutted early in 1990 with 'IN DUB' single. Finally found fortune in 1995, when their 5th album 'DRACONIAN TIMES' briefly hit the UK Top 20. • **Style:** Initially a death-metal band in mould of OBITUARY or NAPALM DEATH. Evolved with slower songs, into a fusion of METALLICA and SISTERS OF MERCY. • **Songwriters:** McINTOSH-HOLMES except DEATH WALKS BEHIND YOU (Atomic Rooster) / WALK AWAY (Sisters Of Mercy). • **Trivia:** Produced by SIMON EFFEMEY.

Recommended: GOTHIC (*7) / DRACONIAN TIMES (*8)

NICK HOLMES -vocals / **GREGOR McINTOSH** -lead guitar / **AARON AEDY** -guitars / **STEHEN EDMONDSON** -bass / **MATT ARCHER** -drums, percussion

Peaceville | Rough Trade

Apr 90. (12") **IN DUB** — — | -
– Rotting misery (doom dub) / Breeding fear (demolition dub).

Apr 90. (cd)(c)(lp) **LOST PARADISE** — — | -
– Intro / Deadly inner sense / Paradise lost / Our saviour / Rotting misery / Frozen illusion / Breeding fear / Lost Paradise. (cd+=) – Internal torment II. *(re-iss.cd Apr95)*

Apr 91. (cd)(c)(lp) **GOTHIC** — — | —
– Gothic / Dead emotion / Shattered / Rapture / Eternal / Falling forever / Angel tears / Silent / The painless / Desolate.

1992. (cd-ep) **GOTHIC EP** — — | -
– Gothic / IN DUB (tracks) / The painless (mix). *(re-iss.Jul94)*

M.F.N. | M.F.N.

Jun 92. (cd)(c)(lp) **SHADES OF GOD** — — | —
– Mortals watch the day / Crying for eternity / Embraced / Daylight torn / Pity the sadness / No forgiveness / Your hand in mine / As I die / The word made flesh.

Oct 92. (12"ep)(cd-ep) **AS I DIE / RAPE OF VIRTUE. / DEATH WALKS BEHIND YOU / ETERNAL (live)** — — | —

Sep 93. (cd)(c)(d-lp) **ICON** — — | —
– Embers fire / Remembrance / Forging sympathy / Joys of the emptiness / Dying freedom / Widow / Colossal rains / Weeping words / Poison / True belief / Shallow seasons / Christendom / Deus miseratur.

Feb 94. (12"ep)(cd-ep) **SEALS THE SENSE** — — | —
– Embers fire / Sweetness / True belief / Your hand in mine (live).

— now without ARCHER

May 95. (12"ep)(c-ep)(cd-ep) **LAST TIME. / WALK AWAY / LAID TO WASTE / MASTER OF MISRULE** — 60 | —

Jun 95. (cd)(c)(lp)(pic-lp) **DRACONIAN TIMES** — 16 | —
– Enchantment / Hallowed land / The last time / Forever failure / Once solemn / Shadowkings / Elusive cure / Yearn for change / Shades of God / Hands of reason / I see your face / Jaded.

Oct 95. (12"ep)(c-ep)(cd-ep) **FOREVER FAILURE. / ANOTHER DESIRE / FEAR** — 66 | —

PARAMOUNTS (see under ⇒ PROCOL HARUM)

Andy PARTRIDGE (see under ⇒ XTC)

PASSENGERS (see under ⇒ U2)

PAVEMENT

Formed: Stockton, North California, USA . . . 1989 by GARY YOUNG and STEVEN MALKMUS. Only part-time they released a number of US 7" singles, before record companies fell at their feet in 1992. Two years later they had first outing into UK Top 20 with album 'CROOKED RAIN CROOKED RAIN'. • **Style:** Quirky, chaotic avant-garde rock, similar to early FALL, PIXIES, The VELVET UNDERGROUND or KING CRIMSON!. • **Songwriters:** MALKMUS. • **Trivia:** MALMUS produced early 90's album 'Eyes Wide Smile' for FAITH OVER REASON. BOB and STEVEN played on SILVER JEW's (David Berman) album 'Starlite Walter'.

Recommended: SLANTED AND ENCHANTED (*7) / WESTING (BY MUSKET & SEXTANT) (*8) / CROOKED RAIN CROOKED RAIN (*7) / WOWEE ZOWEE (*8)

STEVEN MALKMUS – vocals, guitar

not issued | Treble Kicker

1989. (7"ep) **SLAY TRACKS 1933-1969** — - | —
– You're killing me / Box elder / Maybe maybe / She believes / Price yeah!.

— added **GARY YOUNG** (b.1953, Stockton) – drums

not issued | Drag City

1990. (7"ep) **DEMOLITION PLOT J-7** — - | —
– Forklift / Spizzle trunk / Recorder grot / Internal K-dart / Perfect depth / Recorder grot (rally).

— (Aug90) added **BOB NASTANOVICH** – drums

1991. (10"m-lp) **PERFECT SOUND FOREVER** — - | —
– Heckler spray / From now on /Angel carver blues – Mellow jazz docent / Drive by fader / Debris slide / Home / Krell vid-user.

— (mid '91) added **MARK IBOLD** (b. New York) – bass

Jan 92. (7"ep) **SUMMER BABE (Winter version) / MERCY: THE LAUNDROMAT. / BAPTISS BLACKTICK / MY FIRST MINE / MY RADIO** — - | —

— added **SCOTT KANNBERG** – guitar, vocals (ex-SPIRAL STAIRS)

Big Cat | Matador

Mar 92. (cd)(c) **SLANTED AND ENCHANTED** — 72 | —
– Summer babe (winter version) / Trigger cut – Wounded – Kite at: 17 / No life singed her / In a mouth of a desert / Conduit for sale / Chesleys little wrists / Loretta's scars / Here / Two states / Perfume-V / Fame throwa / Jackals, false grails – The lonesome era / Our singer / Zurich is stained.

Jul 92. (7"ep)(12"ep)(cd-ep) **TRIGGER CUT. / SUE ME JACK / SO STARK (YOU'RE A SKYSCRAPER)** — — | —

Nov 92. (12"ep)(cd-ep) **WATERY, DOMESTIC EP** — 58 | —
– Brick wall / Sick profile / Annual report / Fear the Panzers.
(12"pic-d) – Texas never whispers / Frontwards / Feed 'em to the (Linden) lions / Shoot the singer (1 sick verse).

Mar 93. (cd)(c)(lp) **WESTING (BY MUSKET & SEXTANT)** (all first 4 US ep material) — 30 | —

STEVE WEST – drums repl. GARY YOUNG – solo (single; 'PLANET MAN' 94)

Jan 94. (7") **CUT YOUR HAIR. / CAMERA** — 52 | —
(12"+=)(cd-s+=) – Stare.

Feb 94. (cd)(c)(lp) **CROOKED RAIN CROOKED RAIN** — 15 | —
– Silence kit / Elevate me later / Stop breathin / Cut your hair / Newark wilder / Unfair / Gold sound Z / 5-4 = unity / Range life / Heaven is a truck / Hit the plane down / Fillmore jive.

Jul 94. (7") **GOLD SOUNDZ. / KNEELING BUS** — — | —
(12"+=)(cd-s+=) – Strings of Nashville / The exit theory.

line-up= **S.M. JENKINS/ MARK IBOLD/ ROBERT NASTANOVICH/ STEVE WEST/ SPIRAL STAIRS/ FATAH RUARK**

Jan 95. (7") **RANGE LIFE. / COOLIN' BY SOUND** — — | —
(12"+=)(cd-s+=) – Raft.

Mar 95. (7")(12") **RATTLED BY THE RUSH. / FALSE SKORPION / EASILY FOOLED** — — | —
(cd-s+=) – Brink of the clouds.

Apr 95. (cd)(c)(3-sided-d-lp) **WOWEE ZOWEE!** — 18 | —
– We dance / Rattled by the rush / Black out / Brinx job / Grounded / Serpentine pad / Motion suggests / Father to a sister of thought / Extradition / Best friends arm / Grave architecture / At & t / Flux = rad / Fight this generation / Kennel district / Pueblo / Half a canyon / Western homes.

Jun 95. (7"ep)(12"ep)(cd-ep) **FATHER TO A SISTER OF THOUGHT. / KRIS KRAFT / MUSSLE ROCK (IS A HORSE IN TRANSITION)** — — | —

. . . Jan – Jun '96 stop press . . .

Jan 96. (single) **GIVE IT A DAY** — — | —

PEARL JAM

Formed: Seattle, USA . . . 1991 by ex-GREEN RIVER members AMENT and GOSSARD. Their debut album 'TEN', soon smashed its way into the US Top 10. • **Style:** Moved through grunge-metal with GREEN RIVER to more late 60's type DOORS, STOOGES or MC5, which gave credibility in the alternative and heavy circuit. Competed from 1992 with NIRVANA and SOUNDGARDEN. • **Songwriters:** VEDDER wrote lyrics / GOSSARD and AMENT the songs. GREEN RIVER covered QUEEN BITCH (David Bowie). • **Trivia:** Their album 'TEN' was named after the number of basketball player Mookie Blaylock, where they also took group title.

Recommended: TEN (*9) / VS (*8) / VITALOGY (*7) / MOTHER LOVE BONE (*8).

GREEN RIVER

MARK ARM – vocals / **STEVE TURNER** – guitar / **STONE GOSSARD** – guitar / **JEFF AMENT** – bass / **ALEX VINCENT** – drums

		not issued	Homestead
Sep 85.	(12"ep) **COME ON DOWN** – New god / Swallow my pride / Ride of your life / Corner of my eye / Tunnel of love. *(cd-iss.May94)*	-	

— **BRUCE FAIRWEATHER** – guitar repl. TURNER who later joined MUDHONEY

		not issued	I.P.C.
Nov 86.	(7"green) **TOGETHER WE'LL NEVER. / AIN'T NOTHIN' TO DO**	-	

		Glitterhouse	Sup Pop
Jun 87.	(12"ep) **DRY AS A BONE** – Unwind / Baby takes / This town / PCC / Ozzie. *(UK-iss.Mar91 on 'Tupelo') (cd-iss.May94)*	-	
Feb 88.	(12"ep) **REHAB DOLL** (c-ep+=) – Queen bitch. *(US re-iss.c+cd-lp Jul88 as 'DRY AS A BONE'/'REHAB DOLL')*		May 88

— MARK ARM formed MUDHONEY ⇒ .

MOTHER LOVE BONE

formed by **AMENT, GOSSARD + FAIRWEATHER** plus **ANDREW WOOD** (b.1966) – vocals (ex-MALFUNKSHUN) / **GREG GILMORE** – drums

		Polydor	Stardog
1989.	(m-lp) **SHINE** – Thru fade away / Midshaker meltdown / Halfass monkey boy / Medley:- Chloe dancer / Lady Godiva blues.	-	
Jul 90.	(cd)(c)(lp) **APPLE** – This is Shangri-la / Stardog champion / Holy roller / Bone China / Come bite the apple / Stargazer / Heartshine / Captain hi-top / Man of golden words / Mr.Danny boy / Capricorn sister / Crown of thorns. *(above 2 re-iss.as 'STAR DOG CHAMPION' cd Sep92 on 'Polydor', hit US No.77)*		Mar 90

— ANDREW WOOD died 19 Mar'90 after heroin overdose. AMENT and GOSSARD paid tribute to him by teaming with SOUNDGARDEN ⇒ members in off-shoot TEMPLE OF THE DOG. After this project was completed,

PEARL JAM

AMENT + GOSSARD with **EDDIE VEDDER** – vocals / **MIKE McCREADY** – lead guitar / **DAVE ABBRUZZESE** – drums repl. DAVE KRUZON

		Epic	Epic
Feb 92.	(cd)(c)(lp)(pic-lp) **TEN** – Once / Even flow / Alive / Why go / Black / Jeremy / Oceans / Porch / Garden / Deep / Release. *(re-dist.Dec92, will still be in US Top 10)* (re-cd+=) – Alive (live) / Wash / Dirty Frank.	18	2 Dec 91
Feb 92.	(7")(c-s)(7"white) **ALIVE. / WASH** (12"+=)(pic-cd-s+=) – Once.	16	
Apr 92.	(7")(c-s) **EVEN FLOW (remix). / OCEANS** (12"white+=)(cd-pic-s+=) – Dirty Frank.	27	
Sep 92.	(7"white)(c-s) **JEREMY. / ALIVE (live)** (12"pic-d+=) – Footsteps (live). (pic-cd-s+=) – Yellow Ledbetter.	15	
Oct 93.	(cd)(c)(lp) **VS** – Go / Animal / Daughter / Glorified G / Dissident / W.M.A. / Blood / Rear view mirror / Rats / Elderly woman behind the counter in a small town / Leash / Indifference.	2	1
Oct 93.	(12"ep)(cd-ep) **GO. / ALONE / ELDERLY WOMAN BEHIND THE COUNTER IN A SMALL TOWN (acoustic)** (free c-s+=) – Animal (live).		
Dec 93.	(7"red)(c-s) **DAUGHTER. / BLOOD (live)** (12"+=)(cd-s+=) – Yellow leadbetter (live).	18	
May 94.	(7")(c-s) **DISSIDENT. / REARVIEWMIRROR (live)** (cd-s+=) – Release / Even flow (versions). (cd-s) – ('A'side) / Deep / Even flow / Why go (versions).	14	

— ABBRUZZESE departed and was repl. after below album by **JACK IRONS** (ex-RED HOT CHILI PEPPERS)

Nov 94.	(7")(c-s) **SPIN THE BLACK CIRCLE. / TREMOR CHRIST**	10	18
Nov 94.	(cd)(c)(d-lp) **VITALOGY** – Last exit / Spin the black circle / Not for you / Tremor Christ / Nothingman / Whipping / Pry, to / Corduroy / Bugs / Satan's bed / Better man / Aye davanita / Immortality / Stupid mop.	6	1

— McCREADY now also moonlighted for MAD SEASON (see under ALICE IN CHAINS) due to lead singer being LAYNE STALEY. Meanwhile, STONE GOSSARD set up own record label 'Loosegroove' and signed MALFUNKSHUN, DEVILHEAD, WEAPON OF CHOICE, BRAD and PROSE AND CONCEPTS.

Feb 95.	(7"colrd)(c-s)(cd-s) **NOT FOR YOU. / OUT OF MY MIND (live)**	34	
Jul 95.	(c-s)(cd-s) **JEREMY / YELLOW LEDBETTER**	-	79
Dec 95.	(7")(cd-s) **MERKINBALL** – I got I.D. / Long road. (both rec. w/ NEIL YOUNG)	25	7

. . . Jan – Jun '96 stop press . . .

Jan 96.	(cd-s) **DAUGHTER / YELLOW LEDBETTER**	-	97

PERE UBU

Formed: Akron & Cleveland, Ohio, USA . . . Sep'75 by DAVID THOMAS (aka CROCUS BEHEMOTH; his alter-ego). They formed own 'Hearthan' label, and released 4 rare and brilliant 45's, before debuting on 12" in 1977 with classic lp 'THE MODERN DANCE'. The next year, they signed to major 'Chrysalis' label, and brought out another creative 'DUB HOUSING' album. Became mainly a cult band for the next decade or so, remarkably never gaining any chart success, even after a 1988 comeback album 'THE TENEMENT YEARS'. • **Style:** Underground avant-garde synth. orientated rock'n'roll outfit, capturing a collective array of influences from CAPTAIN BEEFHEART, CAN or ROXY MUSIC. The large-framed eccentric DAVID THOMAS, never quite appealed commercially, although music press and night time Radio 1 DJ John Peel, gave them acolade and deserved airplay. • **Songwriters:** All group compositions, except MIRROR MAN (Captain Beefheart) / DOWN BY THE RIVER (Neil Young) / LIKE A ROLLING STONE (Bob Dylan). THOMAS collaborated with others on solo work. • **Trivia:** The name PERE UBU, was taken from the French writer Alfred Jarry's book.

Recommended: TERMINAL TOWER: AN ARCHIVAL COLLECTION (*9) / THE MODERN DANCE (*9) / DUB HOUSING (*7) / NEW PICNIC TIME (*7) / CLOUDLAND (*6). DAVID THOMAS & THE PEDESTRIANS:- THE SOUND OF THE SAND . . . (*5).

DAVID THOMAS – vocals / **PETER LAUGHNER** – guitar / **TIM WRIGHT** – bass, guitar / **TOM HERMAN** – guitar, bass / **R.SCOTT KRAUSE** – drums / **ALLEN RAVENSTINE** – synthesizer

		not issued	Hearthan
Dec 75.	(7"ltd) **30 SECONDS OVER TOKYO. / HEART OF DARKNESS**	-	

— **DAVE TAYLOR** – synthesizer repl. RAVENSTINE

Mar 76.	(7"ltd) **FINAL SOLUTION. / CLOUD 149**	-	

— **ALLEN RAVELSTINE** – synthesizer returned to repl. TAYLOR / **ALAN GREENBLATT** – guitar repl. LAUGHNER who formed FRICTION (he died Jun77) .

— **TONY MAIMONE** – bass, piano repl. WRIGHT who joined DNA. (GREENBLATT left too) (were now a quintet with **THOMAS, HERMAN, KRAUSE MAIMONE** and **RAVELSTINE**) .

Nov 76.	(7"ltd) **STREET WAVES. / MY DARK AGES**	-	
Aug 77.	(7"ltd) **UNTITLED (aka THE MODERN DANCE). / HEAVEN**	-	

		not issued	Blank
Jan 78.	(lp) **THE MODERN DANCE** – Non-alignment pact / The modern dance / Laughing / Street waves / Chinese radiation / Life stinks / Real world / Over my head / Sentimental journey / Humor me. *(UK-iss.+re-US-iss.Apr78 on 'Mercury') (UK re-iss.Jan81 on 'Rough Trade') (re-iss.+cd+c.Feb88 on 'Fontana' ltd)*	-	

		Chrysalis	Chrysalis
Nov 78.	(lp)(c) **DUB HOUSING** – Navy / On the surface / Dub housing / Cagliari's mirror / Thriller / I will wait / Drinking wine Spodyody / Ubu dance party / Blow daddy-o / Codex. *(cd-iss.Mar89 on 'Rough Trade')*		
Sep 79.	(lp)(c) **NEW PICNIC TIME** – One less worry / Make hay / Goodbye / The voice of the sand / Jehovah's kingdom comes / Have shoes will walk / 49 guitars and 1 girl / A small dark cloud / Small was fast / All the dogs are barking. *(cd-iss.Mar89 on 'Rough Trade')*		

Oct 79. (7") **THE FABULOUS SEQUEL (HAVE SHOES WILL WALK). / HUMOR ME (live). / THE BOOK IS ON THE TABLE**

— **MAYO THOMPSON** – guitar (ex-RED CRAYOLA) repl. HERMAN who went solo

Rough Trade not issued

Sep 80. (lp) **THE ART OF WALKING**
– Go / Rhapsody in pink / Arabia * / Miles * / Misery goats / Loop / Rounder / Birdies / Lost in art / Horses / Crush this horn. *(re-iss.1981 * tracks became 'Arabian nights' & 'Tribute to Miles') (cd-iss.Apr89 tracks as re-issue)*

Feb81. (7") **NOT HAPPY. / LONESOME COWBOY DAVE**

— added **ANTON FIER** – drums, percussion (ex-FEELIES) / guest **EDDIE THORNTON** – trumpet

Jun 82. (lp) **SONG OF THE BAILING MAN**
– The long walk home / Use of a dog / Petrified / Stormy weather / West Side story / Thoughts that go by steam / Big Ed's used farms / A day such as this / The vulgar boatman bird / My hat / Horns are a dilemma. *(cd-iss.Apr89)*

— Split mid'82. MAYO returned to RED CRAYOLA (which also incl. most UBU's) **KRAUSE** and **MAIMONE** formed HOME AND GARDEN, (see below for more).

DAVID THOMAS

had already gone solo.

Rough Trade Recommended

1981. (12") **VOCAL PERFORMANCES. /** | | -

DAVID THOMAS & THE PEDESTRIANS

included **THOMPSON, KRAUSE, FIER & RAVENSTINE** plus **CHRIS CUTLER** – drums / **JOHN GREAVES** – bass (both ex-HENRY COW) / **PHILIP MOXHAM** – multi (ex-YOUNG MARBLE GIANTS) / **RICHARD THOMPSON** – guitar

Jan 82. (lp) **THE SOUND OF THE SAND AND OTHER SONGS OF THE PEDESTRIANS**
– The birds are good ideas / Yiki Tiki / The crickets in the flats / Sound of the sand / The new atom mine / Big dreams / Happy to see you / Crush this horn – part 2 / Confuse did / Sloop John B. / Man's best friend.

Oct 82. (7") **PETRIFIED. / ?** - |

— next 1 credited to back. group HIS LEGS:- **CHRIS CUTLER & LINDSAY COOPER** – bassoon (ex-MIKE OLDFIELD) Issued on 'Recommended' US.

Feb 83. (lp) **WINTER COMES HOME (live Munich, 1982)**
– A day such as this / Winter comes home / West side story / Sunset / Stormy weather / Poetic license / Rhapsody in pink / Dinosaurs like me / Petrified / Bones in action / Contrasted views of the archaeopterix

— added **RICHARD THOMPSON** etc. (CUTLER, COOPER)

Dec 83. (lp) **VARIATIONS ON A THEME** - |
– A day at the Botanical Gardens / Pedestrians walk / Bird town / The egg and I / Who is it / Song of hoe / Hurry back / The ram / Semaphore.

— **TONY MAIMONE** – bass repl. GREAVES who joined The FLYING LIZARDS

May 85. (lp) **MORE PLACES FOREVER**
– Through the magnifying glass / Enthusiastic / Big breezy day / About true friends / Whale head king / Song of the bailing man / The farmer's wife / New broom.

DAVID THOMAS & THE WOODEN BIRDS

(**DAVID** retained **MAIMONE** and **CUTLER**) brought in **RAVENSTINE** again. (**DAVID HILD** – accordion of LOS LOBOS guested)

Apr 86. (lp) **MONSTER WALKS THE WINTER LAKE**
– My theory of similtanious similtude – Red tin bus / What happened to me / Monster walks the winter lake / Bicycle / Coffee train / My town / Monster Magge king of the seas / Monster thinks about the good days / What happened to us.

— **JIM JONES** – guitar was added

Mar 87. (lp) **BLAME THE MESSENGER**
– The long rain / My town / King Knut / A fact about trains / When love is uneven / Storm breaks / Having time / Velikovsky / The two-step.

PERE UBU

(**THOMAS, RAVENSTINE, MAIMONE, CUTLER, JONES** and **KRAUSE**)

Fontana Fontana

Mar 88. (lp)(c)(cd) **THE TENEMENT YEARS**
– Something's gotta give / George had a hat / Talk to me / Busman's honeymoon / Say goodbye / Universal vibration / Miss you / Dream the Moon / Rhythm kind / The hollow Earth / We have the technology.

Jul 88. (7") **WE HAVE THE TECHNOLOGY. / THE B-SIDE**
(12"+=)(cd-s-ltd.+=) – The postman drove a caddy / ('A'diff.mix).

— **ERIC DREW FELDMAN** – drums (ex-CAPTAIN BEEFHEART) repl. RAVENSTINE + CUTLER

Mar 89. (7") **WAITING FOR MARY (WHAT ARE WE DOING HERE?). / WINE DARK SPARKS**
(12"+=)(cd-s+=) – Flat.

May 89. (lp)(c)(cd) **CLOUDLAND**
– Breath / Bus called happiness / Race the sun / Waiting for Mary / Cry / Flat * / Ice cream truck / Lost nation road / Monday night / Pushin' / The wire * / The waltz. *(cd+= *)*

Jun 89. (7") **LOVE LOVE LOVE. / FEDORA SATELLITE**
(cd-s+=) – Say goodbye.
(12") – ('A'side) / (2 diff.'A'mixes).

Oct 89. (7") **BREATH. / BANG THE DRUM**
(12"+=) – Over my head (live) / Universal initiation (live).
(cd-s+=) – Humor me (live).

Mar 91. (7")(c-s) **I HEAR THEY SMOKE THE BARBEQUE. / INVISIBLE MAN**
(12"+=)(cd-s+=) – Around the fire.

May 91. (cd)(c)(lp) **WORLD'S IN COLLISION**
– Oh Catherine / I hear they smoke the barbeque / Turpentine / Goodnight Irene / Mirror man / Cry cry / World's in collision / Life of Riley / Over the Moon / Don't look back / Playback / Nobody knows / Winter in the Netherlands.

May 91. (7") **OH CATHERINE. / LIKE A ROLLING STONE**
(12"+=)(cd-s+=) – Down by the river.

Jan 93. (cd)(c)(lp) **THE STORY OF MY LIFE**
– Wasted / Come home / Louisiana train wreck / Fedora satellite II / Heartbreak garage / Postcard / Kathleen / Honey Moon / Sleep walk / The story of my life / Last will and testament.

— **THOMAS / KRAUSS / JONES / TEMPLE / YELLIN**

Cooking V. ???

Aug 95. (cd) **RAY GUN SUITCASE**
– Folly of youth / Electricity / Beach Boys / Turquoise fins / Vacuum in my head / Memphis / Three things / Horse / Don't worry / Ray gun suitcase / Surfer girl / Red sky / Montana / My friend is a stooge for the media priests / Down by the river II.

Nov 95. (cd-ep) **FOLLY OF YOUTH / BALL 'N' CHAIN (jam) / DOWN BY THE RIVER II (demo) / MEMPHIS (demo)**

– (PERE UBU) compilations, others, etc. –

Apr 78. Radar; (12"ep) **DATAPANIK IN THE YEAR ZERO (remixes)**
– Heart of darkness / 30 seconds over Tokyo / Cloud 149 / Untitled / Heaven.

Jun 80. Rough Trade; (7") **FINAL SOLUTION. / MY DARK AGES**

May 81. Rough Trade; (lp) **390° OF SIMULATED STEREO – UBU LIVE: VOLUME 1 (live 76-79)**
– Can't believe it / Over my head / Sentimental journey / 30 seconds over Tokyo / Humor me / Rea world / My dark ages / Street waves / Laughing / Non-alignment pact / Heart of darkness / The modern dance. *(cd-iss.Apr89)*

Nov 85. Rough Trade; (lp) **TERMINAL TOWER: AN ARCHIVAL COLLECTION**
– (early 'Hearthan' sides + rare)

Mar 89. Rough Trade; (cd) **ONE MAN DRIVES WHILE THE OTHER MAN SCREAMS – LIVE VOL.2: PERE UBU ON TOUR**

Nov 95. Cooking Vinyl; (4x7"box) **(the 4 'Hearthan' 45's)** | -

Nov 95. Movieplay Gold; (d-cd) **MODERN DANCE / TERMINAL TOWER** | -

Steve PERRY (see under ⇒ JOURNEY)

Mike PETERS (see under ⇒ ALARM)

Tom PETTY

Born: 20 Oct'53, Gainesville, Florida, USA. In 1968, he formed school band The SUNDOWNERS, who later became The EPICS. In 1971, they evolved into MUDCRUTCH who also had in their ranks MIKE CAMPBELL – guitar, TOMMY LEADON (brother of EAGLES man BERNIE) – lead guitar & RANDALL MARSH – drums. They made demo tape, which was heard by Denny Cordell's 'Shelter' records, who signed band in 1975. They released a single 'DEPOT STREET', and recorded an album which did not see the light of day due to their demise. PETTY was retained by Shelter in 1976, and he instigated The HEARTBREAKERS, with CAMPBELL and TENCH, plus RON BLAIR, STAN LYNCH and JEFF JOURARD. The latter soon left to form The MOTELS with brother Marty. Late '76 the album 'TOM PETTY & THE HEARTBREAKERS' was released, but it initially flopped until it is resurrected by well-received tour of US in summer of '77. They had already hit UK Top 40, with 2 classic singles 'ANYTHING THAT'S ROCK'N'ROLL' & 'AMERICAN GIRL'. In May78, their first US Top 40 hit 'BREAKDOWN', was used on the movie 'FM'. Two months later their second album 'YOU'RE GONNA GET IT', hit both US & UK Top 40. A year on, PETTY filed for bankruptcy owing more than half a million dollars, due to Shelter being sold to 'ABC' and then 'MCA', who sued him for breach of contract. Luckily they came to an agreement, when MCA decided to put band on their Danny Bramson run 'Backstreet' label. Their first output late 1979 'DAMN THE TORPEDOES', sold only moderately in the UK, but smashed into the US Top 3, due to lifted Top 10 cut 'DON'T DO ME LIKE THAT'. • **Style:** Influenced by the early BYRDS, but soon became embodiment of US mainstream rock. • **Songwriters:** PETTY wrote material, except; SO YOU WANT TO BE A ROCK'N'ROLL STAR (Byrds) / NEEDLES AND PINS (Searchers) /FEEL A WHOLE LOT BETTER (Byrds) / SOMETHING IN THE AIR (Thunderclap Newman). • **Trivia:** In 1983, PETTY produced DEL SHANNON's 'Drop Down And Get Me', with backing from The HEARTBREAKERS. In 1985, PETTY co-produced album 'SOUTHERN ACCENTS' with Jimmy Iovine and Eurythmics guitarist Dave Stewart.

Recommended: GREATEST HITS (*9) / DAMN THE TORPEDOES (*8) / FULL MOON FEVER (*7) / TOM PETTY & THE HEARTBREAKERS (*6)

TOM PETTY AND THE HEARTBREAKERS

TOM PETTY – vocals, guitar (ex-MUDCRUTCH) / **MIKE CAMPBELL** (b. 1 Feb'54, Panama City, Florida) – guitar (ex-MUDCRUTCH) / **BELMONT TENCH** (b. 7 Sep'54, Gainesville) – keyboards (ex-MUDCRUTCH) / **RON BLAIR** (b.16 Sep'52, Macon, Georgia, USA) – bass / **STAN LYNCH** (b.21 May'55, Gainsville) – drums

		Island	Shelter
Jan 77.	(7") **BREAKDOWN. / THE WILD ONE, FOREVER**	-	
Feb 77.	(7") **AMERICAN GIRL. / THE WILD ONE, FOREVER**		-
May 77.	(lp)(c) **TOM PETTY AND THE HEARTBREAKERS** – Rockin' around (with you) / Breakdown / Hometown blues / The wild one, forever / Anything that's rock'n'roll / Strangered in the night / Fooled again (I don't like it) / Mystery man / Luna / American girl. *(cd-iss.Jul87 on 'MCA')*	24	55
May 77.	(7") **AMERICAN GIRL. / FOOLED AGAIN (I DON'T LIKE IT)**	-	
Jun 77.	(7")(12") **ANYTHING THAT'S ROCK'N'ROLL. / FOOLED AGAIN (I DON'T LIKE IT)**	36	
Jul 77.	(7")(12") **AMERICAN GIRL. / LUNA**	40	-
Oct 77.	(7") **BREAKDOWN. / FOOL AGAIN (I DON'T LIKE IT)**	-	40
May 78.	(lp)(c) **YOU'RE GONNA GET IT** – When the time comes / You're gonna get it / Hurt / Magnolia / Too much ain't enough / I need to know / Listen to her heart / No second thoughts / Restless / Baby's a rock'n'roller. *(cd-iss.Jun88 on 'MCA')*	34	23
Jun 78.	(7")(12")**I NEED TO KNOW. / NO SECOND THOUGHTS**		41
Sep 78.	(7")(12")**LISTEN TO HER HEART. / I DON'T KNOW WHAT TO SAY TO YOU**		59
		M.C.A.	Backstreet
Nov 79.	(lp)(c) **DAMN THE TORPEDOES** – Refugee / Here comes my girl / Even the losers / Century city / Don't do me like that / Shadows of a doubt (a complex kind) / What are you doin' in my life? / Louisiana rain / You tell me. *(re-iss,+cd.Oct87, cd-iss.Jul88 + 89)*	57	2
Nov 79.	(7") **HERE COMES MY GIRL. / DON'T BRING ME DOWN** (12"+=) – Casa Dega.		59 Apr 80
Feb 80.	(7")(7"pic-d) **REFUGEE. / IT'S RAINING AGAIN**		15 Jan 80
Jul 80.	(7") **DON'T DO ME LIKE THAT. / CENTURY CITY** (d7"+=) – Somethin' else / Stories we can tell.		10 Nov 79

— **DONALD DUNN** – bass replaced RON BLAIR

Apr 81.	(7") **THE WAITING. / NIGHTWATCHMAN**		19
May 81.	(lp)(c) **HARD PROMISES** – The waiting / A woman in love (it's not me) / Nightwatchman / Something big / King's road / Letting you go / A thing about you / Insider / The criminal kind / You can still change your mind. *(re-iss.+cd.May86, re-cd.1988)*	32	5
Jul 81.	(7") **A WOMAN IN LOVE (IT'S NOT ME). / GATOR ON THE LAWN**		79

— PETTY and his band then were credited with backing STEVIE NICKS of FLEETWOOD MAC on a single 'Stop Draggin' My Heart Around' Aug81 hit US No.3.

Jul 82.	(7") **REFUGEE. / THE INSIDER ("with STEVIE NICKS")**		

— **HOWARD EPSTEIN** – bass repl. DUNN

Nov 82.	(7") **YOU GOT LUCKY. / BETWEEN TWO WORLDS**		20
Nov 82.	(lp)(c) **LONG AFTER DARK** – A one story town / You got lucky / Deliver me / Change of heart / Finding out / We stand a chance / Straight into darkness / The same old you / Between two worlds / A wasted life. *(re-iss.May86, cd-iss.Oct87)*	45	9
Dec 82.	(7") **STRAIGHT INTO DARKNESS. / HEARTBREAKERS BEACH PARTY**		
Apr 83.	(7") **CHANGE OF HEART. / HEARTBREAKERS BEACH PARTY**		21 Feb 83
Apr 85.	(7")(12") **DON'T COME AROUND HERE NO MORE. / TRAILER**	50	13 Mar 85
Apr 85.	(lp)(c) **SOUTHERN ACCENTS** – Rebels / It ain't nothin' to me / Don't come around here no more / Southern accents / Make it better (forget about me) / Spike / Dogs on the run / Mary's new car / The best of everything. *(cd-iss.1986)*	23	7
Jun 85.	(7") **MAKE IT BETTER (FORGET ABOUT ME). / CRACKING UP** (12") – ('A'side) / ('A'instrumental).		54
Aug 85.	(7") **REBELS. / SOUTHERN ACCENTS (live)**	-	74
Jan 86.	(d-lp)(d-c) **PACK UP THE PLANTATION (live)** – So you want to be a rock'n'roll star / Needles and pins / The waiting / Breakdown / American girl / It ain't nothin' to me / Insider / Rockin' around (with you) / Refugee / I need to know * / Southern accents / Rebels / Don't bring me down / You got lucky * / Shout / The stories we can tell. *(cd-iss.Oct87, omits *)*		22 Dec 85
Jan 86.	(7") **NEEDLES AND PINS (live). / SPIKE (live)**	-	37
Feb 86.	(7") **SO WANT TO BE A ROCK'N'ROLL STAR (live). / AMERICAN GIRL (live)** (12"+=) – Spike (live).		-
Aug 86.	(7")(12") **BAND OF THE HAND. ("with BOB DYLAN") / THEME FROM 'JOE'S DEATH'**		
Apr 87.	(7") **JAMMIN' ME. / LET ME UP (I'VE HAD ENOUGH)** (12"+=) – Make that connection.		18
Apr 87.	(lp)(c)(cd) **LET ME UP (I'VE HAD ENOUGH)** – Jammin' me / Runaway trains / The damage you've done / It'll all work out / My life – Your world / Think about me / All mixed up / A self made man / Ain't love strange / How many more days / Let me up (I've had enough).	59	20
Sep 87.	(7") **ALL MIXED UP. / LET ME UP (I'VE HAD ENOUGH)** (12"+=) – Little bit of soul.		
Nov 87.	(7") **THINK ABOUT ME. / MY LIFE – YOUR WORLD** (12"+=) – The damage you've done.		

In 1988, before he went solo, TOM PETTY teamed up with BOB DYLAN, GEORGE HARRISON, JEFF LYNNE and ROY ORBISON in The TRAVELLING WILBURYS (see ⇒)

TOM PETTY

solo with **JEFF LYNNE** – guitar, bass keyboards, vocals, co-writer / **MIKE CAMPBELL** – guitar, bass mandolin, keyboards, co-writer / **PHIL JONES** – drums, percussion / +guests **GEORGE HARRISON, ROY ORBISON, BENMONT TENCH, JIM KELTNER, HOWIE EPSTIEN, KELSEY CAMPBELL.**

		M.C.A.	M.C.A.
Apr 89.	(7") **I WON'T BACK DOWN. / THE APARTMENT SONG** (12"+=)(cd-s+=) – Don't treat me like a stranger.	28	12
Jun 89.	(lp)(c)(cd) **FULL MOON FEVER** – Free fallin' / I won't back down / Love is a long road / A face in the crowd / Runnin' down a dream / Feel a whole lot better / Yer so bad / Depending on you / The apartment song / Alright for now / A mind with a heart of it's own / Zombie zoo.	8	3 May 89
Aug 89.	(7")(c-s) **RUNNIN' DOWN A DREAM. / ALRIGHT FOR NOW** (12"+=)(cd-s+=) – Down the line.	55	23 Jul 89
Nov 89.	(7") **FREE FALLIN'. / DOWN THE LINE**	-	7
Nov 89.	(7") **FREE FALLIN'. / LOVE IS A LONG ROAD** (12"+=)(cd-s+=) – ('A'live version).	64	-
Feb 90.	(c-s) **A FACE IN THE CROWD. / A MIND WITH A HEART OF ITS OWN**	-	46

TOM PETTY AND THE HEARTBREAKERS

(originals reformed)

		M.C.A.	M.C.A.
Jun 91.	(7")(c-s) **LEARNING TO FLY. / TOO GOOD TO BE TRUE** (12"+=)(cd-s+=) – Baby's a rock'n'roller / I need to know.	46	28
Jul 91.	(cd)(c)(lp) **INTO THE GREAT WIDE OPEN** – Learning to fly / Into the great wide open / Two gunslingers / The dark of the Sun / All or nothin' / All the wrong reasons / Too good to be true / Out in the cold / You and I will meet again / Makin' some noise / Built to last.	3	13
Aug 91.	(7")(c-s) **INTO THE GREAT WIDE OPEN. / MAKIN' SOME NOISE** (cd-s+=) – Strangered in the night / Listen to her heart.		92 Nov 91
Jan 92.	(7")(c-s) **KING'S HIGHWAY. / I WON'T BACK DOWN** (cd-s+=) – Into the great wide open / Learning to fly.		
Mar 92.	(7")(c-s) **TOO GOOD TO BE TRUE. / THE DARK SIDE OF THE SUN** (cd-s+=) – Hurt / Don't come around here no more. (cd-s+=) – Psychotic reaction / I'm tired / Lonely.	34	
Oct 93.	(7")(c-s) **SOMETHING IN THE AIR. / THE WAITING** (cd-s+=) – American girl.	53	
Nov 93.	(cd)(c)(lp) **GREATEST HITS** (compilation) – American girl / Breakdown / Anything that's rock'n'roll / Listen to her heart / I need to know / Refugee / Don't do me like that / Even the losers / Here comes my girl / The waiting / You got lucky / Don't come around here no more / I won't back down / Runnin' down a dream / Free fallin' / Learning to fly / Into the great wide open / Jane's last dance / Something in the air.	10	8

Feb 94.	(c-s) **MARY JANE'S LAST DANCE. / KING'S HIGHWAY (live)** (cd-s+=) – Make that connection (live) / Take out some insurance (live). (cd-s) – ('A'side) / Casa dega / Gator on the lawn / Down the line.	52	14
		Warners	Warners
Oct 94.	(c-s) **YOU DON'T KNOW HOW IT FEELS. / HOUSE IN THE WOODS** (cd-s+=) – Girl on L.S.D.		13
Nov 94.	(cd)(c)(lp) **WILDFLOWERS** – Wildflowers / You don't know how it feels / Time to move on / You wreck me / It's good to be king / Only a broken heart / Honey bee / Don't fade on me Hard on me / Cabin down below / To find a friend / A higher place / House in the woods / Crawling back to you / Wake up time.	36	8
Feb 95.	(c-s) **YOU WRECK ME / CABIN DOWN BELOW (acoustic)** (cd-s+=) – Only a broken heart.		
May 95.	(c-s)(cds) **IT'S GOOD TO BE KING /**	-	68

– compilations, others, etc. –

Sep 84.	MCA; (d-c) **DAMN THE TORPEDOES. / HARD PROMISES**		-
Apr 86.	MCA; (12"ep) **REFUGEE / DON'T DO ME LIKE THAT. / HERE COMES MY GIRL / THE WAITING**		
Nov 95.	MCA; (cd) **PLAYBACK**		

PIL (see under ⇒ PUBLIC IMAGE LTD.)

Michael PINDER (see under ⇒ MOODY BLUES)

PINK FLOYD

Formed: London, England . . . 1965 by WATERS, WRIGHT and MASON, initially as The SCREAMING ABDABS, with 3 others CLIVE METCALFE – bass, KEITH NOBLE and JULIETTE GALE on vocals. They were dismissed, after finding SYD BARRETT and becoming PINK FLOYD (the name taken from bluesman PINK ANDERSON and the FLOYD district council). In Mar'66, they became regulars at London's Marquee club, where their Sunday afternoon gigs were described as "spontaneous underground". Having played the UFO club late in 1966, they were surprisingly signed to EMI's 'Columbia' early 1967, helped by new management team of Peter Jenner and Andrew King. FLOYD's debut outing 'ARNOLD LAYNE' (about a transvestite washing-line thief), was not banned by the BBC and managed a UK Top 20 spot. Their follow-up 'SEE EMILY PLAY', hit UK No.6, and preceeded their debut Top 10 classic lp 'THE PIPER AT THE GATES OF DAWN'. Their 3rd 45 'APPLES AND ORANGES' (another not featured on debut lp) flopped late in 1967 and BARRETT started to suffer bad LSD (drug) trips. Early in 1968, DAVE GILMOUR an old school friend of SYD's, was added for live gigs to augment the spaced out BARRETT. In April '68, BARRETT was asked to leave group, and he retreated to a life of reclusiveness in Cambridge home. After another flop 45 'IT WOULD BE SO NICE', they unleashed their second lp 'A SAUCERFUL OF SECRETS', which again hit the UK Top 10. On 29 June, they played first free concert at London's Hyde Park, alongside JETHRO TULL and ROY HARPER. They finished the year, with another flop single 'POINT ME TO THE SKY', which was their last one in the UK for 11 years. They now concentrated on albums, with disappointing Barbet Schroeder soundtrack 'MORE' being last Top tenner for 'Columbia'. They now moved to EMI's new 'Harvest' label, and issued part live/part solo 'UMMA GUMMA' double album to end 1969. A year later, they achieved first No.1 album, with 'ATOM HEART MOTHER', which contained the excellent title track on one side, with trumpeter RON GEESIN given co-credit. He was to collaborate with ROGER WATERS the same year, on a soundtrack for the Roy Battersby documentary film 'THE BODY'. On the 15th May'71, they played at a Crystal Palace Garden Party, and introduced a new piece of music 'RETURN TO THE SUN OF NOTHING', which in 6 months time, became 'ECHOES', and took up one side of their UK Top 3 album 'MEDDLE'. In 1972, they were used on another Schroeder film 'LA VALLEE', which recorded in France became Top 10 album 'OBSCURED BY CLOUDS', and although disappointing many die hard FLOYD fans, hit the Top 50 in the States. The same year, the group premiered own Italian-made music film 'LIVE AT POMPEII', at Edinburgh Theater. In March 1973, after its spectacular January showing at the Planetarium, the masterpiece 'DARK SIDE OF THE MOON' was unveiled. A concept piece taking a year of meticulous crafting, which dealt with lunacy, depression and death. It hit No.1 in the US, and No.2 in the UK, also amassing over 10 million sales, while staying in the chart for nearly 300 weeks. It became regarded by many as the greatest album of all time, and gave new meaning to stereo headphones. They returned to London's Earl's Court for a spectacular laser show, which featured albums' all-girl backing singers The BLACKBERRIES. In 1974, they did benefit gig raising £10,000 for their recently disabled friend ROBERT WYATT. In the same year, NICK MASON also produced his 'Rock Bottom' album. In the summer of '75, their stupendous Knebworth Festival concert, previewed another best selling album 'WISH YOU WERE HERE', which went straight to No.1 on both sides of the Atlantic. Late in 1976, they lost their 40 foot inflatable pig on their Top 3 to be 'ANIMALS' album sleeve shot. The Civil Aviation Authority was alerted to warn pilots of the danger, but it was never found. In 1978, DAVID GILMOUR and RICHARD WRIGHT released own solo project albums, and MASON also produced The DAMNED (late '77) and STEVE HILLAGE ('Green' lp). FLOYD returned late 1979, with a new ROGER WATERS written concept double lp 'THE WALL', which lifted a Christmas No.1 single 'ANOTHER BRICK IN THE WALL (PART II)'. The next couple of years were spent making it into a film, which was directed by Alan Parker and issued in 1982, with BOB GELDOF playing the main character Pink. WRIGHT had already quarrelled with WATERS and left in 1980. In Spring 1983, they/WATERS issued follow-up album 'THE FINAL CUT' which hit UK No.1 but was found too depressing, and called by critics as a poor "son of The Wall". The year ended with WATERS departing to go solo, leaving GILMOUR and MASON to fight him in court for the use of the PINK FLOYD name. In 1984, GILMOUR released another solo album 'ABOUT FACE', which was followed a year later by a NICK MASON / RICK FENN album 'PROFILES'. In 1987, after WRIGHT returned to boost live shows (which helped them win court battle with WATERS), PINK FLOYD returned with Transatlantic Top 3 album 'A MOMENTARY LAPSE OF REASON'. A live double album followed a year later, but this was first album not to hit UK + US Top 10. • **Style:** Psychedelic rock outfit, who progressed into more experimental and percussive sound after the departure of SYD. • **Songwriters:** BARRETT wrote nearly all of compositions, until he left after writing 'JUGBAND BLUES' for A SAUCERFUL OF SECRETS album. WATERS and sometimes WRIGHT, took over writing credits. By the late 70's, WATERS had virtually taken full control, until he left. • **Trivia:** MASON also made a 30 minute autobiographical film 'Life Could Be A Dream' with his other outlet, racing driving, the main feature. In 1995, GILMOUR featured on JOHN 'RABBIT' BUNDRICK's ambient album 'Dream Jungle'.

Recommended: THE DARK SIDE OF THE MOON (*10) / MEDDLE (*9) / THE PIPER AT THE GATES OF DAWN (*9) / WISH YOU WERE HERE (*10) / THE WALL (*8) / ATOM HEART MOTHER (*8) / ANIMALS (*8) / A SAUCERFUL OF SECRETS (*8) / UMMA GUMMA (*8) / THE DELICATE SOUND OF THUNDER (*7) / THE DIVISION BELL (*7).

SYD BARRETT (b.ROGER KEITH BARRETT, 6 Jan'46) – vocals, guitar / **RICHARD WRIGHT** (b.28 Jul'45, London) – keyboards / **ROGER WATERS** (b.GEORGE WATERS, 9 Sep'44) – bass, vocals, percussion / **NICK MASON** (b.27 Jan'45, Birmingham, England) – drums, percussion

		Columbia	Tower
Mar 67.	(7") **ARNOLD LAYNE. / CANDY AND THE CURRENT BUN**	20	
Jun 67.	(7") **SEE EMILY PLAY. / THE SCARECROW**	6	
Aug 67.	(lp) **THE PIPER AT THE GATES OF DAWN** – Astronomy domine / Lucifer Sam / Matilda mother / Flaming / Pow R. Toc H. / Take up thy stethoscope and walk / Interstellar overdrive / The gnome / Chapter 24 / Scarecrow / Bike. *(re-iss.May83 on 'Fame') (cd-iss.Feb87 on 'EMI') (re-iss.cd+c Oct94 on 'EMI')*	6	-
Nov 67.	(lp) **PINK FLOYD** (nearly as above)	-	
Nov 67.	(7") **APPLES AND ORANGES. / PAINTBOX**		-
Jan 68.	(7") **FLAMING. / THE GNOME**	-	

— added **DAVID GILMOUR** – guitar who soon repl. BARRETT who later went solo.

Apr 68.	(7") **IT WOULD BE SO NICE. / JULIA DREAM**		
Jun 68.	(lp) **A SAUCERFUL OF SECRETS** – Let there be more light / Remember a day / Set the controls for the heart of the sun / Corporal Clegg / A saucerful of secrets / See saw / Jugband blues. *(re-iss.May83 on 'Fame') (cd-iss.Feb87 on 'EMI') (re-iss.cd+c Jul94 on 'EMI')*	9	
Jul 68.	(7") **LET THERE BE MORE LIGHT. / REMEMBER A DAY**	-	
Dec 68.	(7") **POINT ME TO THE SKY. / CAREFUL WITH THAT AXE, EUGENE**		-
Jul 69.	(lp)(c) **MORE (Film Soundtrack)** – Cirrus minor / The Nile song / Crying song / Up the khyber / Green is the colour / Cymbaline / Party sequence / Main theme / Ibiza bar / More blues / Quicksilver / A Spanish piece / Dramatic theme. *(cd-iss.Apr87)*	9	

Harvest Harvest

Nov 69. (d-lp)(d-c) **UMMA GUMMA** (live */ others solo) [5] [74]
– Astronomy domine * / Careful with that axe, Eugene * / Set the control for the heart of the sun * / A saucerful of secrets * / RICHARD WRIGHT:- Sysyphus (parts 1-4) / ROGER WATERS:- Grantchester Meadows / Several species of small furry animals gathered together in a cave and grooving with a pict / DAVID GILMOUR: – The narrow way (parts 1-3) / NICK MASON:- The Grand Vizier's garden party – part 1; Entrance – part 2; Entertainment / part 3; Exit. *(re-iss.Dec79 on 'EMI', d-cd-iss.Mar87) (re-iss.d-cd,d-c Oct94 on 'EMI')*

Oct 70. (lp)(c) **ATOM HEART MOTHER** [1] [55]
– Atom heart mother; (a) Father's shout – (b) Breast milky – (c) Mother fore – (d) Funky dung – (e) Mind your throats please – (f) Remergence / If / Summer '68 / Fat old Sun / Alan's psychedlic breakfast / Rise and shine / Sunny side up / Morning glory. *(quad-lp 1973) (cd-iss.Mar87) (re-iss.cd+c Oct94 on 'EMI')*

— (above featured **RON GEESIN** – horns, co-writer)

Nov 71. (lp)(c) **MEDDLE** [3] [70]
– One of these days / A pillow of winds / Fearless (interpolating 'You'll never walk alone') / San Tropez / Seamus / Echoes. *(re-iss.Nov83 on 'Fame') (cd-iss.Aug84) (cd-iss. Apr89 on 'Mobile Fidelity') (re-iss.cd+c Aug94 on 'EMI')*

Dec 71. (7") **ONE OF THESE DAYS. / FEARLESS** [-] [ ]

Jun 72. (lp)(c) **OBSCURED BY CLOUDS** [6] [46]
– Obscured by clouds / When you're in / Burning bridges / The gold it's in the . . . / Wots . . . uh the deal / Mudmen / Childhood's end / Free four / Stay / Absolute curtains. *(cd-iss.Apr87 on 'EMI')*

Jul 72. (7") **FREE FOUR. / STAY** [-] [ ]

Mar 73. (lp)(c) **THE DARK SIDE OF THE MOON** [2] [1]
– Speak to me / Breathe / On the run / Time / The great gig in the sky / Money / Us and them / Any colour you like / Brain damage / Eclipse. *(cd-iss.Aug84) (re-iss.cdMar93, hit UK No.4) (re-iss.cd+c. Jul94 on 'EMI') (also on quad-lp + US pic-lp)*

May 73. (7") **MONEY. / ANY COLOUR YOU LIKE** [-] [13]

Harvest Columbia

Sep 75. (lp)(c)(quad-lp) **WISH YOU WERE HERE** [1] [1]
– Shine on you crazy diamond (parts 1-5) / Welcome to the machine / Have a cigar / Wish you were here / Shine on you crazy diamond (parts 6-9). *(cd-iss.Aug84) (re-iss.cd+c Jul94 on 'EMI')*

Oct 75. (7") **HAVE A CIGAR. / SHINE ON YOU CRAZY DIAMOND (excerpt)** [-] [ ]

Jan 77. (lp)(c) **ANIMALS** [2] [3] Feb 77
– Pigs on the wing (part 1) / Dogs / Pigs (three different ones) / Sheep / Pigs on the wing (part 2). *(cd-iss.Jul86) (re-iss.cd+c Jul94 on 'EMI')*

Nov 79. (7") **ANOTHER BRICK IN THE WALL (PART 2). / ONE OF MY TURNS** [1] [1] Jan 80

Dec 79. (d-lp)(c) **THE WALL** [3] [1]
– In the flesh / The thin ice / The happiest days of our lives / Another brick in the wall (part 2) / Mother / Goodbye blue sky / Empty spaces / Young lust / One of my turns / Don't leave me now / Another brick in the wall (part 3) / Goodbye cruel world / Hey you / Is there anybody out there? / Nobody home / Vera / Comfortably numb / The show must go on / Run like hell / Waiting for the worms / Stop / The trial / Outside the wall. *(cd-iss.Sep84) (re-iss.UK & US Jul90) (re-iss.cd+c Oct94 on 'EMI')*

Apr 80. (7") **RUN LIKE HELL. / DON'T LEAVE ME NOW** [-] [53]

Jun 80. (7") **COMFORTABLY NUMB. / HEY YOU** [-] [ ]

Jul 82. (d-lp) **SOUNDTRACK FROM THE FILM 'THE WALL'** [ ] [ ]
– (tracks from above + new singles)

Aug 82. (7") **WHEN THE TIGERS BROKE FREE. / BRING THE BOYS BACK HOME** [39] [ ]

— Now just main trio **WATERS, GILMOUR, MASON.**(WRIGHT left to form ZEE) guests on lp were **ANDY BROWN** – organ, **RAY COOPER** – perc., **MICHAEL KAMEN** – piano, **RALPH RAVENSCROFT** – saxophone.

Mar 83. (lp)(c) **THE FINAL CUT** [1] [6]
– The post war dream / Your possible pasts / One of the few / The hero's return / The gunners dream / Paranoid eyes / Get your filthy hands off my desert / The Fletcher memorial home / Southampton dock / The final cut / Not now John / Two suns in the sunset. *(cd-iss.Jul86) (re-iss.cd+c Oct94 on 'EMI')*

May 83. (7") **NOT NOW JOHN. / THE HERO'S RETURN (pt.1)** [30] [ ]
(12"+=) – The hero's return (part 2).

— **MASON** and **GILMOUR** recruited new members below to replace WATERS who went solo. **TIM RENWICK** – guitar (ex-SUTHERLAND BROTHERS & QUIVER, ex-TV SMITH) / **GUY PRATT** – bass (ex-KILLING JOKE, ex-ICEHOUSE) / **SCOTT PAGE** – saxophone.**RICK WRIGHT** – keyboards also returned p/t.

E.M.I. Columbia

Sep 87. (lp)(c)(cd) **A MOMENTARY LAPSE OF REASON** [3] [3]
– Signs of life / Learning to fly / The dogs of war / One slip / On the turning away / Yet another movie / Round and around / A new machine (part 1) / Terminal frost / A new machine (part 2) / Sorrow.

Sep 87. (cd-ep) **LEARNING TO FLY (edit) / ONE SLIP (edit) / TERMINAL FROST (lp version) / TERMINAL FROST (DYOL version)** [ ] [70]

Dec 87. (7") **ON THE TURNING AWAY. / RUN LIKE HELL (live)** [55] [ ]
(12"+=)(cd-s+=) – ('A'live).

Jun 88. (7") **ONE SLIP. / TERMINAL FROST** [50] [ ]
(12"+=)(cd-s+=) – Dogs of war (live).

Nov 88. (d-lp)(d-c)(d-cd) **THE DELICATE SOUND OF THUNDER (live)** [11] [11]
– Shine on you crazy diamond / Learning to fly / Yet another movie / Round and around / Sorrow / The dogs of war / On the turning away / One of these days / Time / Wish you were here / Us and them * / Money / Another brick in the wall (part 2) / Comfortably numb / Run like hell. *(d-cd+= *)*

— with **GILMOUR, MASON + WRIGHT** plus **GUY PRATT / TIM RENWICK / BOB EZRIN** – keyboards, percussion / **DICK PARRY** – tenor sax / **GARY WALLIS** – percussion / **JON CARIN** – programming + add.keyboards / + backing vocalists

Apr 94. (cd)(c)(lp) **THE DIVISION BELL** [1] [1]
– Cluster one / What do you want from me / Poles apart / Marooned / A great day for freedom / Wearing the inside out / Take it back / Coming back to life / Keep talking / Lost for words / High hopes.

May 94. (7"colrd)(c-s) **TAKE IT BACK. / ('A'mix)** [23] [73]
(cd-s+=) – Astronomy Domine (live).

Oct 94. (7")(c-s) **HIGH HOPES. / KEEP TALKING** [26] [ ]
(12"+=)(cd-s+=) – One of these days.

Jun 95. (d-cd)(d-c)(q-lp)(video) **PULSE (live)** [1] [1]
– Shine on you crazy diamond / Astronomy domine / What do you want from me / Learning to fly / Keep talking / Coming back to life / Hey you / A great day for freedom / Sorrow / High hopes / Another brick in the wall (part 2) / One of these days *[not on cd]* / Speak to me / Breathe / On the run / Time / The great gig in the sky / Money / Us and them / Any colour you like / Brain damage / Eclipse / Wish you were here / Comfortably numb / Run like hell.

– compilations, etc. –

May 71. Starline/ US= Harvest; (lp) **RELICS** – (early 45's and rare) [32] [ ]
(re-iss.Oct78 on 'MFP')

Jan 74. Harvest; (d-lp)(c) **A NICE PAIR** (re-issue of first 2 lps) [21] [36] Dec 73

Nov 81. Harvest/ US= Columbia; (lp)(c) **A COLLECTION OF GREAT DANCE SONGS** (remixes) [37] [31]
– One of these days / Money / Another brick in the wall (part 2) / Wish you were here / Shine on you crazy diamond / Sheep.
(re-iss.85 on 'Fame') (cd-iss.Nov88)

Nov 81. Harvest; (7") **MONEY. / LET THERE BE MORE LIGHT** [ ] [-]

1979. Harvest; (11xlp-box) **THE FIRST XI (67-77)** (boxed lp's) [ ] [ ]

Jun 83. Capitol; (lp)(c) **WORKS (68-73)** [-] [68]

Nov 92. EMI/ US= Columbia; (7xcd)(7xc)(7xlp) **SHINE ON** [ ] [ ]
– (A SAUCERFUL OF SECRETS – MOMENTARY LAPSE . . . + rare singles)

Nov 93. See For Miles; (cd) **TONITE LET'S ALL MAKE LOVE IN LONDON . . . PLUS** [ ] [-]

Nov 95. See For Miles; (cd) **LONDON '66-'67** [ ] [-]

DAVID GILMOUR

solo with **MICK WEAVER** – keyboards / **RICK WILLIS** – bass / **JOHN WILLIE WILSON** – drums

Harvest Columbia

Jun 78. (lp)(c) **DAVID GILMOUR** [17] [29]
– Mihalis / There's no way out of it / Cry from the street / So far away / Short and sweet / Raise my rent / No way / Deafinitely / I can't breathe anymore. *(re-iss.1983 on 'Fame')*

Jun 78. (7") **THERE'S NO WAY OUT OF IT. / DEAFINATELY** [ ] [ ]

— Now with various sessioners incl.STEVE WINWOOD, JEFF PORCARO & JON LORD

Feb 84. (7")(12") **BLUE LIGHT. / CRUISE** [ ] [62]

Mar 84. (lp)(c)(cd) **ABOUT FACE** [21] [32]
– Until we sleep / Murder / Love on the air / Blue light / Out of the blue / All lovers are deranged / You know I'm right / Cruise / Let's get metaphysical / Near the end. *(re-iss.Mar87 on 'Fame')*

May 84. (7")(7"pic-d) **LOVE ON THE AIR. / LET'S GET METAPHYSICAL** [ ] [ ]

RICHARD WRIGHT

solo with **SNOWY WHITE** – guitar / **MEL COLLINS** – saxophone / **LARRY STEELE** – bass / **REG ISADORE** – drums

Harvest Columbia

Sep 78. (lp)(c) **WET DREAM** [ ] [ ]
– Medterranean c / Against the odds / Cat cruise / Summer elegy / Waves / Holiday / Mad Yannis dance / Drop in from the top / Pink's song / Funky deux.

— In 1984, he formed ZEE duo, and still appeared with FLOYD later in the 80's..

ZEE

RICHARD WRIGHT / DAVE HARRIS – guitar, vocals, keyboards, synth (ex-FASHION)

Harvest Columbia

Apr 84. (7")(12") **CONFUSION. / EYES OF A GYPSY** [ ] [ ]

Apr 84. (lp) **IDENTITY** [ ] [ ]
– Confusion / Voices / Private person / Strange rhythm / Cuts like a diamond / By touching / How do you do it / Seems we are dreaming.

NICK MASON

solo with **CARLA BLEY** and **ROBERT WYATT**

Harvest Columbia

May 81. (lp)(c) **FICTITIOUS SPORTS** ☐ ☐
– Can't get my motor to start / I was wrong / Siam / Hot river / Boo to you too / Do ya / Wervin' / I'm a mineralist.

NICK MASON with RICK FENN

Harvest Columbia

Aug 85. (lp)(c) **PROFILES** ☐ ☐
– Malta / Lie for a lie / Rhoda / Profiles (part 1 & 2) / Israel / And the address / Mumbo jumbo / Zip code / Black ice / At the end of the day / Profiles (part 3).
Sep 85. (7") **LIE FOR A LIE. / AND THE ADDRESS** ☐ ☐
(12"+=) – Mumbo jumbo.

PIXIES

Formed: Boston, Massachusetts, USA ... 1986 by L.A.born BLACK FRANCIS. Alongside fellow Bostonians THROWING MUSES, they were a surprise signing for Ivo's UK indie label '4 a.d.'. Their first vinyl outing 'COME ON PILGRIM', came out late '87, receiving plaudets from NME and Radio 1 DJ John Peel. By 1989, they had first UK Top 10 album 'DOOLITTLE'. • **Style:** Alternative hard-rock band, moving from underground PERE UBU/HUSKER DU type sound to more accessible IGGY POP influenced punk. • **Songwriters:** BLACK FRANCIS penned except; WINTERLONG + I'VE BEEN WAITING FOR YOU (Neil Young) / EVIL HEARTED YOU (Yardbirds) / HEAD ON (Jesus & Mary Chain) / CECELIA ANN (Surftones) / BORN IN CHICAGO (Paul Butterfield's Blues Band). • **Trivia:** STEVE ALBINI (Big Black) produced 1988 album, with GIL NORTON producing further material. In the 90's, KIM moved to Ohio and JOEY to Los Angeles.

Recommended: SURFER ROSA (*8) / DOOLITTLE (*9) / BOSSANOVA (*8) / TROMPE LE MONDE (*9) / FRANK BLACK (*8).

BLACK FRANCIS (b.CHARLES MICHAEL KITRIDGE THOMPSON IV) – vocals, guitar / **JERRY SANTIAGO** – lead guitar / **KIM DEAL** (Mrs.JOHN MURPHY) – bass, vocals / **DAVE LOVERING** – drums

4.a.d. Elektra

Oct 87. (m-lp)(c) **COME ON PILGRIM** ☐ -
– Caribou / Vamos / Islade encounter / Ed is dead / The holiday song / Nimrod's son / I've been tried / Levitate me.
Mar 88. (lp)(c)(cd) **SURFER ROSA** ☐ -
– Bone machine / Break my body / Something against you / Broken face / Gigantic / River Euphrates / Where is my mind? / Cactus / Tony's theme / Oh my golly! / Vamos / I'm amazed / Brick is red. *(cd+=)* – COME ON PILGRIM (m-lp)
Aug 88. (12"ep)(cd-ep) **GIGANTIC. / RIVER EUPHRATES. / VAMOS. / IN HEAVEN (LADY IN THE RADIATOR SONG)** ☐ -
Mar 89. (7") **MONKEY GONE TO HEAVEN. / MANTA RAY** 60 ☐
(12"+=)(cd-s+=) – Weird at my school / Dancing the manta ray.
Apr 89. (lp)(c)(cd) **DOOLITLE** 8 98
– Debaser / Tame / Wave of mutilation / I bleed / There goes my gun / Here comes your man / Dead / Monkey gone to Heaven / La la love / Mr. Grieves / Crakity Jones / 13 baby / Silver / Hey / Gouge away.
Jun 89. (7") **HERE COMES YOUR MAN. / INTO THE WHITE** 54 ☐
(12"+=)(cd-s+=) – Wave of mutilation / Bailey's walk.

— KIM DEAL was also part of amalgamation The BREEDERS (see: THROWING MUSES ⇒)

Jul 90. (7")(c-s) **VELOURIA. / I'VE BEEN WAITING FOR YOU** 28 ☐
(12"+=)(cd-s+=) – Make believe / The thing.
Aug 90. (cd)(c)(lp) **BOSSANOVA** 3 70
– Cecilia Ann / Rock music / Velouria / Allison / Is she weird / Ana / All over the world / Dig for fire / Down to the wall / The happening / Blown away / Hang fire / Stormy weather / Havalina.
Oct 90. (7")(c-s) **DIG FOR FIRE. / VELVETY (instrumental)** 62 ☐
(12"+=)(cd-s+=) – Santo / Winterlong.
May 91. (7") **PLANET OF SOUND. / BUILD HIGH** 27 ☐
(12"+=)(c-s+=)(cd-s+=) – Evil hearted you / Theme from Narc.
Sep 91. (cd)(c)(lp) **TROMPE LE MONDE** 7 92
– Trompe de Monde / Planet of sound / Alec Eiffel / The sad punk / Head on / U-mass / Palace of the brine / Letter to Memphis / Bird dream Of the Olympus mons / Space (I believe in) / Subbacultha / Distance equals rate times time / Lovely day / Motorway to Roswell / The Navajo know.

— Disbanded late in '92, with BLACK FRANCIS going solo as FRANK BLACK.

FRANK BLACK

With **ERIC DREW FELDMAN** – bass, keyboards, synthetics (ex-CAPTAIN BEEFHEART) / **NICK VINCENT** – drums, percussion / + extra guitars **SANTIAGO, MORRIS TEPPER + DAVID SARDY.**

4 a.d. Elektra

Mar 93. (cd)(c)(lp) **FRANK BLACK** 9 ☐
– Los Angeles / I heard Ramona sing / Hang on to your ego / Fu Manchu / Places named after numbers / Czar / Old black dawning / Ten percenter / Brackish boy / Two spaces / Tossed (instrumental version) / Parry the wind high, low / Adda Lee / Every time I go around here / Don't ya rile 'em.
Apr 93. (7")(c-s) **HANG ON TO YOUR EGO. / THE BALLAD OF JOHNNY HORTON** ☐ ☐
(12"+=)(cd-s+=) – Surf epic.

— same trio augmented by **SANTIAGO, TEPPER + LYLE WORKMAN** – guitars

May 94. (7") **HEADACHE. / ('A'mix)** 53 ☐
(10")(cd-s) – ('A'side) / Men in black / At the end of the world / Oddball.
(cd-s) – ('A'side) / Hate me / This is where I belong / Amnesia.
May 94. (cd)(c)(d-lp) **TEENAGER OF THE YEAR** 21 ☐
– Whatever happened to Pong? / Thalassocracy / (I want to live on an) Abstract plain / Calistan / The vanishing spies / Speedy Marie / Headache / Sir Rockaby / Freedom rock / Two reelers / Fiddle riddle / Ole Mulholland / Fazer eyes / I could stay here forever / The hostess with the mostess / Superabound / Big red / Space is gonna do me good / White noise maker / Pure denizen of the citizens band / Bad, wicked world / Pie in the sky.

— FRANK BLACK had earlier in the year teamed up with ex-SEX PISTOL; GLEN MATLOCK to form tribute band FRANK BLACK & THE STAX PISTOLS.

... Jan – Jun '96 stop press ...

Epic Columbia

Jan 96. (single) **MEN IN BLACK** 37 ☐

— b-side covers JUST A LITTLE (Beau Brummels) / RE-MAKE, RE-MODEL (Roxy Music).

Jan 96. (cd)(c) **THE CULT OF RAY** 39 ☐

PLACEBO

*** NEW ENTRY ***

Formed: South London, England ...1994 by BRIAN MOLKO and STEFAN OLSDAL, who had gone to same school in Luxembourg. They met again in a London tube having spent their recent years in the States and Sweden respectively. By 1995, both found Swiss drummer ROBERT SCHULTZBERG and the trio became joint winners of the 'In The City' bands competition. Late '95, they shared a one-off single with SOUP on 'Fierce Panda'. Another one-off for 'Deceptive' and tours with ASH, BUSH and WHALE, helped secure loads of dosh for signing with Virgin 'Hut' subsidiary 'Elevator'. In the summer of '96, they dented UK Top 40 with eponymous debut. • **Style:** Dark but melodic alternative unit, like NIRVANA fused with JOY DIVISION, fronted by GEDDY LEE (Rush) or DAVID SURKAMP (Pavlov's Dog). • **Songwriters:** Group. • **Trivia:** About to play in July '96, Scotland's (now Britain's) top festival 'T In The Park'.

Recommended: PLACEBO (*9)

BRIAN MOLKO – vocals, guitars, bass / **STEFAN OLSDAL** – bass, guitars, keyboards / **ROBERT SCHULTZBERG** – drums, percussion, didgeridoo

Fierce Pan not issued

Nov 95. (7") **BRUISE PRISTINE. / (Soup: 'Meltdown')** ☐ -

Deceptive not issued

Feb 96. (7")(cd-s) **COME HOME. / DROWNING BY NUMBERS / OXYGEN THIEF** ☐ -

Elevator Hut

Jun 96. (7") **36 DEGREES. / DARK GLOBE** ☐ ☐
(cd-s+=) – Hare Krishna.
Jun 96. (cd)(c) **PLACEBO** 40 ☐
– Come home / Teenage angst / Bionic / 36 degrees / Hang on to you IQ / Nancy boy / I know / Bruise pristine / Lady of the flowers / Swallow.

Robert PLANT (see under ⇒ LED ZEPPELIN)

PLASTIC ONO BAND (see under ⇒ LENNON, John)

P.M. (see under ⇒ EMERSON, LAKE & PALMER)

POGUES

Formed: North London, England ... late 1983 by Tipperary raised MacGOWAN, STACEY and FINER. Originally calling themselves POGUE MAHONE (Gaelic for 'kiss my arse'), they added drinking buddies RANKEN and FEARNLEY, plus female singer / bassist CAIT O'RIORDAN. In Spring 1984, they formed own self-named label, and issued 'DARK STREETS OF LONDON', which received an official BBC radio ban, after they found out what their name meant. A month later they secured a deal with 'Stiff', and became The POGUES. Their debut album 'RED ROSES FOR ME' produced by Stan Brennan, broke into the UK Top 100, as they acquired growing support from live audiences around the country. In Apr'85, they released 45 'A PAIR OF BROWN EYES' which was produced by ELVIS COSTELLO, who stayed on for their Top 20 album 'RUM, SODOMY & THE LASH'. On the 16th May'86, COSTELLO married CAIT, and she left them in Nov'86 after writing Top 50 hit 'HAUNTED' for the Alex Cox film 'SID & NANCY'. Around the same time, the group played 'The McMahon Gang' in Cox's movie 'Straight To Hell'. They met ex-CLASH singer JOE STRUMMER on the set, and he even temporarily deputised for the absent MacGOWAN on early 1988 US tour. This period also saw them peak at No.3 in the album charts with 'IF I SHOULD FALL FROM GRACE WITH GOD', which parented the No.2 Christmas 1987 hit 'FAIRY TALE OF NEW YORK', which featured solo artist KIRSTY MacCOLL on dual vox with SHANE. • **Style:** Pioneers of a new wave of Celtic punk-folk. A cross between The DUBLINERS (who they jointly hit the Top 10 with in 1987's version of 'THE IRISH ROVER') and The CLASH. MacGOWAN was/is a renowned heavy drinker, with a spacious set of front teeth and an uncompromising on/off stage appeal. • **Songwriters:** Group compositions, except; THE BAND PLAYED WALTZING MATILDA (Eric Bogle) / DIRTY OLD TOWN (Ewan MacColl) / WILD ROVER + MADRA RUM (trad.) / THE IRISH ROVER (Dubliners) / MAGGIE MAY (Rod Stewart) / HONKY TONK WOMAN (Rolling Stones) / WHISKEY IN THE JAR (Thin Lizzy) / MISS OTIS REGRETS (Cole Porter) / GOT A LOT O' LIVIN' TO DO (Elvis Presley) / HOW COME (Ronnie Lane) / WHEN THE SHIP COMES IN (Bob Dylan). FINER became main writer in the mid-90's with others contributed some material. • **Trivia:** FEARNLEY married actress Danielle Von Zerneck on 7th Oct'89. In the early '90s, they supplied the soundtarack for TV play 'A MAN YOU DON'T MEET EVERY DAY'. The song 'Fiesta' is used on Vauxhall-Tigra TV ad, after rights were sold from 1988 album.

Recommended: RED ROSES FOR ME (*8) / RUM, SODOMY & THE LASH (*9) / IF I SHOULD FALL FROM GRACE WITH GOD (*8) / PEACE AND LOVE (*6) / HELL'S DITCH (*6) / WAITING FOR HERB (*5) / POGUE MAHONE (*5) / THE BEST OF THE POGUES (*9) / THE BEST OF THE REST OF THE POGUES (*7)

SHANE MacGOWAN (b.25 Dec'57, Kent, England) – vocals, guitar (ex-NIPS) / **JAMES FEARNLEY** (b.10 Oct'54, Manchester, England) – accordion (ex-NIPS) / **SPIDER STACEY** (b.PETER, 14 Dec'58, Eastbourne, UK) – tin whistle (ex-NIPS) / **JEM FINER** (b.JEREMY, 29 Jul'55, Dublin, Ireland) – banjo / **CAIT O'RIORDAN** – bass, vocals / **ANDREW RANKEN** (b.13 Nov'53, London) – drums

Pogue Mahone — not issued

May 84. (7") **DARK STREETS OF LONDON.(as "POGUE MAHONE") / THE BAND PLAYED WALTZING MATILDA** — -
(soon re-iss.Jun84 on 'Stiff' by **"The POGUES"** their new adopted name)

Stiff — not issued

Sep 84. (lp)(c) **RED ROSES FOR ME** — 89 — -
– Transmetropolitan / The battle of Brisbane / The auld triangle / Waxie's dargle / Boys from the county Hell / Sea shanty / Dark streets of London / Streams of whiskey / Poor daddy / Dingle regatta / Greenland whale fisheries / Down in the ground where the dead men go / Kitty. *(cd-iss.May87) (re-iss.Jan89 on 'WEA')*

Oct 84. (7") **BOYS FROM THE COUNTY HELL. / REPEAL OF THE LICENSING LAWS** — -

Mar 85. (7")(7"pic-d) **A PAIR OF BROWN EYES. / WHISKEY YOU'RE THE DEVIL** — 72 — -
(12"+=) – Muirshin Durkin.

— added p/t **PHIL CHEVRON** (b.RYAN, 17 Jun'57, Dublin) – guitar, producer (ex-RADIATORS FROM SPACE)

Jun 85. (7")(7"pic-d)(7"green) **SALLY MacLENNANE. / WILD ROVER** — 51 — -
(12"+=) – The leaving of Liverpool.

Aug 85. (lp)(c)(cd) **RUM, SODOMY & THE LASH** — 13 — -
– The sick bed of Cuchulainn / The old main drag / Wild cats of Kilkenny / I'm a man you don't meet every day / A pair of brown eyes / Sally MacLennane / Dirty old town / Jesse James / Navigator / Billy's bones / The gentleman soldier / And the band played waltzing Matilda. *(cd+=)* – A pistol for Paddy Garcia. *(re-iss.Jan89 on 'WEA')*

Aug 85. (7")(7"pic-d) **DIRTY OLD TOWN. / A PISTOL FOR PADDY GARCIA** — 62 — -
(12"+=) – The parting glass.

Feb 86. (7"ep)(12"ep)(c-ep)(7"pic-ep) **POGUETRY IN MOTION** — 29 — -
– A rainy night in Soho / The body of an American / London girl / Planxty Noel Hill.

M.C.A. — M.C.A.

Aug 86. (7") **HAUNTED. / JUNK THEME** — 42
(12"+=) – Hot-dogs with everything.

— (above single from the motion picture 'Sid & Nancy')

— **DARRYL HUNT** (b. 4 May'50, Bournemouth, England) – bass (ex-PRIDE O' THE CROSS) replaced CAIT

Stiff — not issued

Mar 87. (7") **THE IRISH ROVER. (as "POGUES & The DUBLINERS") / THE RARE OLD MOUNTAIN DEW** — 8
(12"+=) – The Dubliners fancy.

— added **TERRY WOODS** (now 8-piece)

Pogue Mahone-EMI — Island

Nov 87. (7") **FAIRYTALE OF NEW YORK. ("POGUES featuring KIRSTY MacCOLL) / BATTLE MARCH MEDLEY** — 2
(12"+=)(c-s+=)(cd-s+=) – Shanne Bradley.

Jan 88. (lp)(c)(cd) **IF I SHOULD FALL FROM GRACE WITH GOD** — — 88
– If I should fall from grace with God / Turkish song of the damned / Bottle of smoke / Fairytale of New York (featuring KIRSTY MacCOLL) / Metropolis / Thousands are sailing / Fiesta / Medley:- The recruiting sergeant – The rocky road to Dublin – Galway races / Streets of Sorrow – Birmingham Six / Lullaby of London / Sit down by the fire / The broad majestic Shannon / Worms. *(cd+=)* – South Australia / The battle march medley. *(re-iss.Jan89 on 'WEA')*

Feb 88. (7") **IF I SHOULD FALL FROM GRACE WITH GOD. / SALLY MacLENNANE (live)** — 58
(7"ep)(12"red-ep)(cd-ep+=) – A pair of brown eyes / Dirty old town (both live).

Jul 88. (7") **FIESTA. / SKETCHES OF SPAIN** — 24
(12"+=)(cd-s+=) – South Australia.

Dec 88. (7") **YEAH YEAH YEAH YEAH YEAH. / LIMERICK'S RAKE** — 43
(12"+=)(cd-s+=) – Honky tonk women.

WEA — WEA

Jun 89. (7")(c-s) **MISTY MORNING ALBERT BRIDGE. / COTTONFIELDS** — 41
(12"+=)/ /(cd-s+=) – Young Ned of the hill./ / Train of love.

Jul 89. (lp)(c)(cd) **PEACE AND LOVE** — 5
– White City / Young Ned of the hill / Misty morning, Albert Bridge / Cotton fields / Blue heaven / Down all the days / U.S.A. / Lorelei / Gartloney rats / Boat train / Tombstone / Night train to Lorca / London you're a lady / Gridlock.

Aug 89. (7")(c-s) **WHITE CITY. / EVERYMAN IS A KING**
(12")(cd-s) – ('A'side) / Maggie May / Star of the County Down.

May 90. (7")(c-s) **JACK'S HEROES. ("POGUES & THE DUBLINERS") / WHISKEY IN THE JAR** — 63
(12"+=)(cd-s+=) – ('B'extended). *('A'side used by Eire in World Cup)*

Aug 90. (7") **SUMMER IN SIAM. / BASTARD LANDLORD** — 64
(12"+=)(cd-s+=) – Hell's ditch (instrumental) / The Irish rover.

Sep 90. (cd)(c)(lp) **HELL'S DITCH** — 12
– The sunnyside of the street / Sayonara / The ghost of a smile / Hell's ditch / Lorca's novena / Summer in Siam / Rain street / Rainbow man / The wake of the Medusa / House of the gods / Five green onions and Jean / Maidria Rua / Six to go.

Apr 91. (cd-s) **SAYONARA / CURSE OF LOVE / INFINITY** — -

Sep 91. (7") **A RAINY NIGHT IN SOHO (remix). / SQUID OUT OF WATER** — 67
(12"+=)/ /(cd-ep+=) – Infinity./ / POGUETRY IN MOTION (ep).

Sep 91. (cd)(c)(lp) **THE BEST OF THE POGUES** (compilation) — 11
– Fairytale of New York / Sally MacLennane / Dirty old town / The Irish rover / A pair of brown eyes / Streams of whiskey / A rainy night in Soho / Fiesta / Rain street / Misty morning, Albert Bridge / White City / Thousand are sailing / The broad majestic Shannon / The body of an American.

Dec 91. (7") **FAIRYTALE OF NEW YORK. / FIESTA** — 36
(12"+=)(cd-s+=) – A pair of brown eyes / Sick bed of Cuchulainn / Maggie May.

— p/t JOE STRUMMER is deposed by member SPIDER who takes over vox.

May 92. (7")(c-s) **HONKY TONK WOMAN. / CURSE OF LOVE** — 56
(12"+=)/ /(cd-s+=) – Infinity./ / The parting glass.

Jun 92. (cd)(c)(lp) **THE BEST OF THE REST OF THE POGUES** (compilation out-takes)
– If I should fall from grace with God / The sick bed of Cuchulainn / The old main drag / Boys from the County Hell / Young Ned of the hill / Dark streets of London / The auld triangle / Repeal of the licensing laws / Yeah yeah yeah yeah yeah / London girl / Honky tonk women / Summer in Siam / Turkish song of the damned / Lullaby of London / The sunnyside of the street / Hell's ditch.

— (Sep91) **SHANE McGOWAN** left when his health deteriorated. **JOE STRUMMER** (ex-CLASH) deputised for him on tour.

— added 8th member & producer **MICHAEL BROOK** – infinite guitar

W.E.A. W.E.A.

Aug 93. (7")(c-s) **TUESDAY MORNING. / FIRST DAY OF FOREVER** [18] [ ]
(cd-s+=) – Turkish song of the damned (live).
(cd-s) – ('A'side) / London calling / I fought the law (both live with JOE STRUMMER).

Sep 93. (cd)(c)(lp) **WAITING FOR HERB** [20] [ ]
– Tuesday morning / Smell of petroleum / Haunting / Once upon a time / Sitting on top of the world / Drunken boat / Big city / Girl from the Wadi Hammamat / Modern world / Pachinko / My baby's gone / Small hours.

Jan 94. (7")(c-s) **ONCE UPON A TIME. / TRAIN KEPT ROLLING ON** [66] [ ]
(12"+=)(cd-s+=) – Tuesday morning / Paris St.Germain.

—— FEARNEY and WOODS departed, apparently due to the brief Christmas come-back of SHANE McGOWAN.

—— **SPIDER / JEM / DARRYL + RANKEN** added **JAMIE CLARKE** -banjo / **JAMES McNALLY** -accordion, uilleann pipes / **DAVID COULTER** -mandolin, tambourine

Sep 95. (7"colrd)(c-s) **HOW COME. / EYES OF AN ANGEL** [ ] [ ]
(cd-s+=) – Tuesday morning (live) / Big city (live).

Oct 95. (cd)(c)(lp) **POGUE MAHONE** [ ] [ ]
– How come / Living in a world without her / When the ship comes in / Anniversary / Amadie / Love you 'till the end / Bright lights / Oretown / Pont Mirabeau / Tosspint / Four o'clock in the morning / Where that love's been gone / The Sun and the Moon.

– other special POGUES releases, etc. –

Nov 90. Chrysalis; (7")(c-s) **MISS OTIS REGRETS. (by "KIRSTY MacCOLL") / JUST ONE OF THOSE THINGS (by "The POGUES")** [ ] [ ]
(12"+=)(cd-s+=) (song by "Aztec Camera", all 3 songs on 'Chrysalis' Cole Porter tribute album 'Red, White & Blue').

Buster POINDEXTER (see under ⇒ NEW YORK DOLLS)

POISON

Formed: Harrisburg, Pennsylvania, USA . . . Mar'84 by former SPECTRES members MICHAELS and ROCKETT. In 1985, they moved to Los Angeles, where they signed to 'Enigma' records which was licensed to 'Capitol'. Their first album 'LOOK WHAT THE CAT DRAGGED IN', was first of many albums to hit the Top 3. Early in 1989, they had massive selling US No.1 with single 'EVERY ROSE HAS ITS THORN'. • **Style:** Glamourous heavy/soft metal outfit, similar to GUNS'N' ROSES, but with the bleached hair look, except DALL. • **Songwriters:** MICHAELS – DEVILLE penned, except YOUR MAMA DON'T DANCE (Loggins & Messina). • **Trivia:** Late in 1990, BRETT co-wrote and produced girlfriend SUSIE HATTON's debut lp.

Recommended: LOOK WHAT THE CAT DRAGGED IN (*6) / OPEN UP AND SAY . . . AAH! (*6).

BRET MICHAELS (b.15 Mar'?, Pittsburgh, Pennsylvania) – vocals / **C.C.DEVILLE** – lead guitar (ex-SCREAMING MIMI) repl. SLASH to GUNS'N'ROSES / **BOBBY DALL** (b. 2 Nov'?, Florida) – bass / **RIKKI ROCKETT** (b. 8 Aug'61, Mechanicsburg, Pennsylvania) – drums

M.F.N. Capitol

Oct 86. (lp)(c)(pic-lp) **LOOK WHAT THE CAT DRAGGED IN** [ ] [3] Jul 86
– Cry tough / I want action / I won't forget you / Play dirty / Look what the cat dragged in / Talk dirty to me / Want some, need some / Blame it on you / £1 bad boy / Let me go to the show. *(re-iss.lp/c/pic-lp/cd.Apr89) (re-iss.cd+c Jul94)*

May 87. (7") **TALK DIRTY TO ME. / WANT SOME, NEED SOME** [67] [9] Mar 87
(12"+=)(12"pic-d+=) – (interview).

Jun 87. (7") **I WANT ACTION. / PLAY DIRTY** [-] [50]

Aug 87. (7") **CRY TOUGH. / LOOK WHAT THE CAT DRAGGED IN** [ ] [ ]
(12"+=)(12"pic-d+=) – ('A'-US mix). *(re-iss.Apr89)*

Capitol Enigma

Sep 87. (7") **I WON'T FORGET YOU. / BLAME IT ON YOU** [-] [13]

Apr 88. (7") **NOTHIN' BUT A GOOD TIME. / LOOK BUT YOU CAN'T TOUCH** [35] [6]
(12"+=) – Livin' for a minute.

May 88. (lp)(c)(cd)(pic-lp)(pic-cd) **OPEN UP AND SAY . . .AAH!** [23] [2]
– Love on the rocks / Nothin' but a good time / Back to the rocking horse / Good love / Tearin' down the walls / Look but you can't touch / Fallen angel / Every rose has its thorn / Your mama can't dance / Bad to be good. *(re-iss.cd+c Mar94)*

Oct 88. (7") **FALLEN ANGEL. / BAD TO BE GOOD** [59] [12] Jul 88
(12"+=)(12"pic-d+=) – (interview).

Oct 88. (7") **EVERY ROSE HAS ITS THORN. / LIVING FOR THE MINUTE** [-] [1]

Jan 89. (7")(7"sha-pic-d) **EVERY ROSE HAS ITS THORN. / BACK TO THE ROCKING HORSE** [13] [-]
(12"+=)(cd-s+=) – Gotta face the hangman.

Apr 89. (7")(7"green) **YOUR MAMA DON'T DANCE. / TEARIN' DOWN THE WALLS** [13] [10] Feb 89
(12"+=)(cd-s+=)(12"green+=) – Love on the rocks.

Jul 89. (7")(c-s) **NOTHIN' BUT A GOOD TIME. / LIVIN' FOR THE MINUTE** [48] [-]
(12"+=)(cd-s+=)(12"pic-d+=) – Look what the cat dragged in (live).

Jun 90. (7")(c-s) **UNSKINNY BOP. / SWAMP JUICE (SOUL-O)** [15] [3]
(12"+=)(cd-s+=)(12"pic-d+=) – Valley of lost souls / Poor boy blues.

Jul 90. (cd)(c)(lp) **FLESH & BLOOD** [3] [2]
– Strange days of Uncle Jack / Valley of lost souls / Unskinny bop / (Flesh and blood) Sacrifice / Swamp juice (soul-o) / Let it play / Life goes on / Come Hell or high water / Ride the wind / Don't give up an inch / Something to believe in / Ball and chain / Life loves a tragedy / Poor boy blues. *(re-iss.cd Sep94)*

Oct 90. (7")(c-s) **SOMETHING TO BELIEVE IN. / BALLS AND CHAIN** [ ] [4]
(12"+=) – Look what the cat dragged in / Your mama don't dance / Every rose has its thorn.
(10"yellow+=)(cd-s+=) – (Bret Michaels interview).

Jan 91. (c-s)(12") **RIDE THE WIND. / ?** [-] [38]

Apr 91. (c-s)(12") **LIFE GOES ON. / ?** [-] [35]

Nov 91. (7")(7"clear) **SO TELL ME WHY. / GUITAR SOLO** [25] [ ]
(12"+=)(cd-s+=) – Unskinny bop (live) / Ride the wind (live).
(12"+=)(cd-s+=) – Only time will tell / No more Lookin' back (poison jazz)

Nov 91. (cd)(c)(d-lp) **SWALLOW THIS LIVE** (live / +studio tracks *) [52] [51]
– Intro / Look what the dragged in / Look but you can't touch / Good love / I want action / Something to believe in / Poor boy blues / Unskinny bop / Every rose has its thorn / Fallen angel / Your mama don't dance / Nothin' but a good time / Talk dirty to me / So tell me why* / Souls on fire* / Only time will tell* / No more lookin' back (poison jazz).

—— (Nov91) DeVILLE left, and was replaced by **RICKIE KOTZEN** (Jun92)

Feb 93. (7")(c-s) **STAND. / STAND (CHR edit)** [25] [50] Jan 93
(cd-s) – ('A'side) / Native tongue / Scream / Whip comes down / ('A'lp version).

Feb 93. (cd)(c)(lp) **NATIVE TONGUE** [20] [16]
– Native tongue / THe scream / Stand / Stay alive / Until you suffer some (Fire and ice) / Body talk / Bring it home / 7 days over you / Richie's acoustic thang / Ain't that the truth / Theatre of the soul / Strike up the band / Ride child ride / Blind faith / Bastard son of a thousand blues.

Apr 93. (7"pic-d)(c-s) **UNTIL YOU SUFFER SOME (FIRE AND ICE). / STAND (acoustic)** [32] [ ]
(cd-s+=) – Bastard son of a thousand blues / ('A'mix).
(12"colrd+=) – Strike up the band / ('A'mix).

POLICE

Formed: London, England based . . . early 1977 by COPELAND, STING and PADOVANI. In May'77, they released debut 45 'FALL OUT' for Miles Copeland's (Stewart's brother) indie label 'Illegal'. Immediately after this, they were invited by GONG member MIKE HOWLETT to join veteran guitarist ANDY SUMMERS in live band STRONTIUM 90. When PADOVANI left in August, SUMMERS decided to join. They first sessioned on German artist EBERHARD SCHOENER's 'Video Flashback' album. Early 1978, while recording debut album, they were seen with new dyed blonde look for a Wrigley's Spearmint Gum TV ad. After a support slot on a SPIRIT tour, they signed to 'A&M'. Their first 'A&M' 45, 'ROXANNE' was well-received but fails to hit chart. Their follow-up 'CAN'T STAND LOSING YOU' broke into the 50, and helped debut album 'OUTLANDOS D'AMOUR', sell well. With a re-release of 'ROXANNE' in Apr'79 which hit UK No.12, it eventually climbed into the Top 10. In the US, the single also peaked at 32, and a revived 'CAN'T STAND LOSING YOU', hit the Top 3 in Britain. By Autumn of '79, they were at No.1 with both single 'MESSAGE IN A BOTTLE' and album 'REGGATTA DE BLANC' (aka WHITE REGGAE). For the next half a decade they became worldwide superstars, until their unofficial split around mid-80's. • **Style:** New wave / reggae rock band with a social comment and an aspiration for experimentation. (see also; STING ⇒). • **Songwriters:** Mainly STING compositions, with some by or with either COPELAND or SUMMERS. STING also wrote lyrics. • **Trivia:** NIGEL GRAY produced or co-produced 70's albums. HUGH PADGHAM co-produced 'GHOST IN THE MACHINE'.

Recommended: EVERY BREATH YOU TAKE – THE SINGLES (*9) / OUTLANDOS D'AMOUR (*8) / REGGATTA DE BLANC (*7) / ZENYATTA MONDATTA (*7) / GHOST IN THE MACHINE (*7) / SYNCHRONICITY (*9)

STING (b.GORDON SUMNER, 2 Oct'51, Wallsend, England) – vocals, bass (ex-LAST EXIT) / **HENRY PADOVANI** (b. Corsica) – guitar, vocals / **STEWART COPELAND**

(b.19 Jul'52, Egypt) – drums, vocals (ex-CURVED AIR)

Illegal — not issued

May 77. (7") **FALL OUT. / NOTHING ACHIEVING** [ ] [-]
(re-iss.Dec79 reached UK No.47)

— **ANDY SUMMERS** (b.ANDREW SOMERS, 31 Dec'42, Lanc., England) – guitar (ex-KEVIN AYERS, ex-KEVIN COYNE, ex-ERIC BURDON, ex-SOFT MACHINE) soon repl. HENRY (after brief spell as 4-piece) left to form his FLYING PADOVANI BROTHERS

A & M — A & M

Apr 78. (7")(12") **ROXANNE. / PEANUTS** [ ] [-]
(re-iss.Apr79 reached UK No.12)

Aug 78. (7")(7"sha-pic-d)(7"in most colours) **CAN'T STAND LOSING YOU. / DEAD END JOB** [42] [-]
(re-iss.Jun79 hit UK No.2)

Oct 78. (lp)(c)(blue-lp) **OUTLANDOS D'AMOUR** [ ] [23] Feb 79
– Next to you / So lonely / Roxanne / Hole in my life / Peanuts / Can't stand losing you / Truth hits everybody / Born in the 50's / Be my girl – Sally / Masoko tanga. *(resurrected Apr79 made No.6) (cd-iss.1983 + Aug91)*

Oct 78. (7") **SO LONELY. / NO TIME THIS TIME** [ ] [ ]
(re-iss.Feb80 made No.6)

Jan 79. (7") **ROXANNE. / DEAD END JOB** [-] [32]

Apr 79. (7") **CAN'T STAND LOSING YOU. / NO TIME THIS TIME** [-] [ ]

Sep 79. (7")(7"green)(7"sha-pic-d) **MESSAGE IN A BOTTLE. / LANDLORD** [1] [74] Nov 79

Oct 79. (lp)(c)(2x10") **REGGATTA DE BLANC** [1] [25]
– Message in a bottle / Reggata de blanc / It's alright for you / Bring on the night / Deathwish / Walking on the Moon / On any other day / The bed's too big without you / Contact / Does everyone stare / No time this time. *(cd-iss.1983)*

Nov 79. (7")(12") **WALKING ON THE MOON. / VISIONS OF THE NIGHT** [1] [-]

Jan 80. (7") **BRING ON THE NIGHT. / VISIONS OF THE NIGHT** [-] [ ]

Sep 80. (7")(7"sha-pic-d) **DON'T STAND SO CLOSE TO ME. / FRIENDS** [1] [-]

Oct 80. (lp)(c) **ZENYATTA MONDATTA** [1] [5]
– Don't stand so close to me / Driven to tears / When the world is running down, you make the best of what's still around / Canary in a coalmine / Voices in my head / Bombs away / De do do do, de da da da / Behind my camel / Man in a suitcase / Shadows in the rain / The other way of stopping. *(re-iss.+cd.Sep86)*

Oct 80. (7") **DE DO DO DO, DE DA DA DA. / FRIENDS** [-] [10]

Dec 80. (7")(7"pic-d) **DE DO DO DO, DE DA DA DA. / A SERMON** [5] [-]

Feb 81. (7") **DON'T STAND SO CLOSE TO ME. / A SERMON** [-] [10]

Sep 81. (7") **INVISIBLE SUN. / SHAMELLE** [2] [ ]

Sep 81. (7") **EVERY LITTLE THING SHE DOES IS MAGIC. / SHAMBELLE** [-] [3]

Oct 81. (lp)(c) **GHOST IN THE MACHINE** [1] [2]
– Spirits in the material world / Every little thing she does is magic / Invisible sun / Hungry for love / emolition man / Too much information / Rehumanize yourself / One world (not three) / Omega man / Darkness / Omega man / Secret journey / Darkness. *(cd-iss.1983)*

Oct 81. (7")(7"pic-d) **EVERY LITTLE THING SHE DOES IS MAGIC. / FLEXIBLE STRATEGIES** [1] [-]

Dec 81. (7") **SPIRITS IN THE MATERIAL WORLD. / LOW LIFE** [12] [-]

Jan 82. (7") **SPIRITS IN THE MATERIAL WORLD. / FLEXIBLE STRATEGIES** [-] [11]

Apr 82. (7") **SECRET JOURNEY. / DARKNESS** [-] [46]

May 83. (7")(7"pic-d) **EVERY BREATH YOU TAKE. / MURDER BY NUMBERS** [1] [1]
(d-7"+=) – Truth hits everybody / Man in a suitcase.

Jun 83. (lp)(c)(cd) **SYNCHRONICITY** [1] [1]
– Synchronicity / alking in your footsteps / O my God / Mother / Miss Gradenko / Synchronicity II / Every breath you take / King of pain / Wrapped around your finger / Tea in the sahara. *(c+cd+=)* – Murder by numbers. *(re-iss.cd+c Mar93)*

Jul 83. (7")(7"pic-d-x3) **WRAPPED AROUND YOUR FINGER. / SOMEONE TO TALK TO** [7] [-]
(12"+=) – Message in a bottle / I burn for Mary.

Aug 83. (7") **KING OF PAIN. / SOMEONE TO TALK TO** [-] [3]

Oct 83. (7")(12") **SYNCHRONICITY II. / ONCE UPON A DAYDREAM** [17] [16] Nov 83

Jan 84. (7")(12") **KING OF PAIN. / TEA IN THE SAHARA** [17] [-]

Jan 84. (7") **WRAPPED AROUND YOUR FINGER. / TEA IN THE SAHARA** [-] [8]

— Split up although not officially, until 1986. All members went solo.

– compilations, etc. –

Jun 80. A&M; (6x7"box) **SIX PACK** [17] [ ]
– (first 5 – A&M singles re-issued in blue vinyl, plus added 45 below) **THE BED'S TOO BIG WITHOUT YOU. / TRUTH HITS EVERYBODY**

Sep 86. A&M; (7")(12") **DON'T STAND SO CLOSE TO ME '86. / (live version)** [24] [46]

Nov 86. A&M; (lp)(c)(cd) **EVERY BREATH YOU TAKE – THE SINGLES** [1] [7]
– Roxanne / Can't stand losing you / Message in a bottle / Walking on the Moon / Don't stand so close to me '86 / De do do do, de da da da / Every little thing she does is magic / Invisible Sun / Spirits in the material world / Every breath you take / King of pain / Wrapped around your finger. *(c/cd+=)* – So lonely. *(re-iss.UK Mar92 hit No.31)*

Nov 86. A&M; (7")(12") **ROXANNE '86. / SYNCHRONICITY II** [ ] [7]

Jan 87. A&M; (7") **WALKING ON THE MOON. / MESSAGE IN A BOTTLE** [-] [ ]

Apr 88. A&M; (3"cd-ep) **COMPACT HITS** [ ] [ ]
– Roxanne / Can't stand losing you / Canary in a coalmine / Bed's too big without you.

Jun 89. A&M; (d-c) **REGATTA DE BLANC / SYNCHRONICITY** [ ] [-]

Oct 92. A&M; (cd)(c)(lp) **THE POLICE: GREATEST HITS (like above)** [10] [ ]

Oct 93 A&M; (cd)(c) **MESSAGE IN A BOX: THE COMPLETE RECORDINGS** [-] [79]

May 95. A&M; (7"sha-pic-d)(12") **CAN'T STAND LOSING YOU (live). / VOICES IN MY HEAD (mix)** [27] [ ]
(cd-s+=) – Roxanne live).
(d12") – Voices in my head (8 remixes).

May 95. A&M; (d-cd)(d-c)(d-lp) **THE POLICE LIVE! (live)** [25] [86]
– Next to you / So lonely / Truth hits everybody / Walking on the Moon / Hole in my life / Fall out / Bring on the night / Message in a bottle / The bed's too big without you / Peanuts / Roxanne / Can't stand losing you / Landlord / Born in the 50's / Be my girl – Sally / Synchronicity I / Synchronicity II / Walking in your footsteps / Message in a bottle / O my God / De do do do, de da da da / Wrapped around your finger / Tea in the Sahara / Spirits in the material world / King of pain / Don't stand so close to me / Every breathe you take / Roxanne / Can't stand losing you / So lonely.

KLARK KENT

Pseudonym used by **STEWART COPELAND**.

Kryptone — not issued

May 78. (7"green) **DON'T CARE. / THRILLS / OFFICE GIRLS** [ ] [ ]
(re-iss.Jul78 on green vinyl 'A&M', hit No.48)

Nov 78. (7"green) **TOO KOOL TO KALYPSO. / THEME FROM KINETIC RITUAL** [ ] [ ]

A & M — A & M

May 80. (7"green) **AWAY FROM HOME. / OFFICE TALK** [ ] [ ]

Jul 80. (10"green-lp) **KLARK KENT** (compilation) [ ] [ ]

Aug 80. (7"green) **RICH IN A DITCH. / GRANDELINQUENT** [ ] [ ]

STEWART COPELAND

A & M — A & M

Jan 84. (7") **DON'T BOX ME IN. (by "STEWART COPELAND & STAN RIDGWAY") / DRAMA AT HOME** [ ] [ ]

Jan 84. (lp)(c) **RUMBLE FISH (Soundtrack)** [ ] [ ]
– Don't box me in / Tulsa tango / Our mother is alive / Party at someone's else place / Biff gets stomped by Rusty James / Brothers on wheels / Weat Tulsa story / Tulsa rags / Father on the stairs / Hostile bridge to Benny's / Your mother is not crazy / Personal midget – Clain's ballroom / Motorboy's fate.

— Soundtrack also feat. vocals of ex-WALL OF VOODOO man STAN RIDGWAY.

Apr 85. (7") **KOTEJA. (by "STEWART COPELAND & RAY LEMA") / GONG ROCK** [ ] [ ]

— Next featured numerous African musicians.

May 85. (lp)(c) **THE RHYTHMATIST** [ ] [ ]
– Koteja (oh Bolilla) / Brazzaville / Liberte / Coco / Kemba / amburu sunset / Gong rock / Franco / Serengeti / Long walk / African dream. *(cd-iss.1988)*

I.R.S. — I.R.S.

Aug 86. (7"w/ ADAM ANT) **OUT OF BOUNDS. / ('A' solo)** [-] [ ]

Aug 86. (7")(12") **LOVE LESSONS. (by "STEWART COPELAND & DEREK HOLT") / AMY (SILENT MOVIES)** [ ] [-]

— DEREK HOLT from CLIMAX BLUES BAND.

M.C.A. — M.C.A.

Nov 87. (7") **THE EQUALIZER (from US TV series). / ('A'instrumental)** [ ] [ ]
(12"+=) – Love lessons.

Dec 87. (lp)(c)(cd) **THE EQUALIZER (AND OTHER CLIFF-HANGERS)** [ ] [ ]
– Lurking solo / Music box / Screaming Lord Cole and the Commanches / The Equalizer busy equalizing / Green fingers (ten thumbs) / Archie David in overtime / Tancred ballet / Dark ships / Flowership quintet / Rag pole dance.

— COPELAND went on to writes scores for films 'Talk Radio', 'Wall Street', 'First Power', etc. The first were combined on cd for US release on 'Varese Sarabande'. He has since went on to form ANIMAL LOGIC with bassist STANLEY CLARKE ⇒ and vocalist DEBORAH HOLLAND. They made one eponymous album in 1989. He also in 1988 composed an opera 'Holy Blood And Crescent

Moon', for The CLEVELAND OPERATIC SOCIETY.

ANDY SUMMERS / ROBERT FRIPP

FRIPP – guitar, synths (of KING CRIMSON)

A & M A & M

Oct 82. (lp)(c) **I ADVANCE MASKED**
– I advance masked / Under bridges of silence / China, yellow leader / In the cloud forest / New marimba / Girl on a swing / Hardy country / Truth of skies / Painting and dance / Still point / Lakeland, Aquarelle / Steven on seven / Stultified. *(cd-iss.1986 on 'E.G.')*

Oct 82. (7") **I ADVANCE MASKED. / HARDY COUNTRY**

Sep 84. (lp)(c) **BEWITCHED**
– Parade / What kind of man reads Playboy? / Begin the day / Train / Bewitched / Maquillage / Guide / Forgotten steps / Image and likeness. *(cd-iss.1988)*

Sep 84. (7") **PARADE. / TRAIN**
(12"+=) – Hardy country.

Dec 84. (7") **2010. / TO HELL AND BACK** -

ANDY SUMMERS

now solo, augmented by **DAVID HENTSCEL** – keyboards, drum programmes / **NAN VERNON** – vocals and **MICHAEL G.FISHER.**

M.C.A. M.C.A.

Jul 87. (lp)(c)(cd) **XYZ**
– Love is the strangest way / How many days / Almost there / Eyes of a stranger / The change / Scary voices / Nowhere / XYZ / The only road / Hold me.

Jul 87. (7")(12") **LOVE IS THE STRANGEST WAY. / XYZ**

— now with **PAUL McCANDLESS / DOUG LUNN / KURT WORTMAN / JIMMY HASLIP**

not issued Private . . .

Apr 89. (lp)(c)(cd) **THE GOLDEN WIRE** -
– A piece of time / The golden wire / Earthly pleasures / Imagine you / Vigango / Blues for snake / The island of silk / Journey through blue regions / Piya tose / Rain forest in Manhattan / A thousand stones.

Oct 89. (lp)(c)(cd) **MYSTERIOUS BARRICADE** -
– Red balloon / Mysterious barricades / When that day comes / Train song / Luna / Satyric dancer / Shiny sea / Emperor's last straw / Rain / Tomorrow / In praise of shadows / The lost marbles / How can I forget.

— **ANDY SUMMERS w / JOHN ETHERIDGE** iss UK-cd 'INVISIBLE THREADS' on 'Inak' Jan 94.

Iggy POP

Born: JAMES JEWEL OSTERBURG, 21 Apr'47, Muskegan, Ann Arbor, Michegan, USA. Son of an English father and American mother, he joined The IGUANAS as a drummer in 1964. They issued a cover of Bo Diddley's 'MONA', which was limited to a 1,000 copies sold at gigs. In 1965, he became IGGY POP and joined The PRIME MOVERS, with bassist RON ASHETON, but they folded and IGGY moved to Chicago. In 1967, he returned to Michegan and formed The (PSYCHEDELIC) STOOGES, with RON and his drummer brother SCOTT. They were soon joined by DAVE ALEXANDER, and IGGY made celluloid debut on avant-garde film 'Francois De Moniere' with girlfriend NICO. In 1968, the band gigged more constantly, and on 1 occasion, IGGY was charged with indecent exposure. In 1969, A&R man Danny Fields while looking to sign MC5, signed The STOOGES to 'Elektra', with a $25,000 advance. Their eponymous debut, produced by JOHN CALE (another VELVET UNDERGROUND connection), nearly broke into the US Top 100. It proved later to be ahead of its time, with gems such as; NO FUN (later rec.'77 by punks SEX PISTOLS) / 1969 (later rec.'83 by goths SISTERS OF MERCY). After another semi-clasic lp in 1970, they disbanded due to dissentions in line-up and drug related circumstances. He moved to Florida, where he became a greenkeeper while taking up golf. In 1972, he met DAVID BOWIE and his manager TONY DeFRIES, who persuaded IGGY & THE STOOGES to sign to a MainMan management deal, leading to 'CBS' contract. After one album 'RAW POWER', they folded again citing drugs as cause. In 1975, IGGY checked in to a psychiatric institute weaning himself off heroin. His only true friend BOWIE, who regularly visited him in hospital, invited him to appear on his 'LOW' lp. He signed to 'RCA' (home of BOWIE) in 1977, and issued BOWIE produced debut solo album 'THE IDIOT', which due to recent 'New wave' explosion, broke into the UK Top 30 and US Top 75. It contained first BOWIE-POP collaboration 'CHINA GIRL', which was later a smash hit for BOWIE. His 2nd solo release 'LUST FOR LIFE' (also produced by BOWIE in '77), was another gem and deservedly again reached UK Top 30. In 1979, IGGY moved to 'Arista' records, and shifted through various famous personnel (see discography), but found commercial appeal leaving him behind. Until, that is, in 1987, when his revival of a 1957 Johnny O'Keefe hit 'REAL WILD CHILD', cracked the UK Top 10. • **Style:** Proclaimed 'The Godfather of Punk', he pioneered in the 60's what was to burgeon in the 70's. Psychotic gravel-voxed contortionist, whose early stage shows saw him slash his chest with a razor. He finally recovered in the mid-80's from drug addiction. • **Songwriters:** IGGY and STOOGES. In 1977 he collaborated with BOWIE, and 1986 with ex-SEX PISTOLS guitarist; STEVE JONES. Others covered; SOMETHING WILD (John Hiatt) / LIVIN' ON THE EDGE OF THE NIGHT (Rifkin / Rackin) / LOUIE LOUIE (Kingsmen). • **Trivia:** In 1987, he made a cameo appearance in the pool film 'The Color Of Money'. In 1990, his film & TV work included 'Cry Baby', 'Shannon's Deal', Tales From The Crypt' & 'Miami Vice'. In 1991, he starred in the opera 'The Manson Family'.

Recommended: THE STOOGES (*8) / FUN HOUSE (*9) / RAW POWER (*7) / THE IDIOT (*9) / LUST FOR LIFE (*9) / BLAH-BLAH-BLAH (*7) / INSTINCT (*8) / BRICK BY BRICK (*7).

STOOGES

IGGY POP – vocals / **RON ASHETON** – guitar / **DAVE ALEXANDER** – bass / **SCOTT ASHETON** – drums

Elektra Elektra

Sep 69. (lp) **THE STOOGES** Aug 69
– 1969 / I wanna be your dog / We will fall / No fun / Real cool time / Ann / Not right / Little doll. *(re-iss.Mar77) (US cd-iss.1988)(cd-iss.Nov93)*

Oct 69. (7") **I WANNA BE YOUR DOG. / 1969** -

— added guests **STEVE MACKAY** – saxophone / **BILL CHEATHAM** – 2nd guitar

Dec 70. (lp) **FUN HOUSE**
– Down on the street / Loose / T.V. eye / Dirt / I feel alright (1970) / Fun house / L.A. blues. *(re-iss.Mar77) (US cd-iss.1988)(cd-iss.Nov93)*

Dec 70. (7") **I FEEL ALRIGHT (1970). / DOWN ON THE STREET** -

— Break-up in 1972. Soon **IGGY** re-formed with **SCOTT** and **RON** (now bass) .

IGGY AND THE STOOGES

JAMES WILLIAMSON – guitar repl. DAVE

C.B.S. Columbia

May 73. (lp)(c) **RAW POWER**
– Search and destroy / Gimme danger / Hard to beat * / Penetration / Raw power / I need somebody / Shake appeal / Death trip. *(re-iss.May77 on 'CBS-Embassy', hit UK No.44,* *track repl. by – Your pretty face is going to Hell. *(re-iss.Nov81) (US cd-iss.1988 on 'Columbia') (UK cd-iss.May89 on 'Essential') (cd-iss.all tracks) (re-iss.cd+c May94 on 'Columbia').*

Jun 73. (7") **SEARCH AND DESTROY. / PENETRATION** -

— added **SCOTT THURSTON** – keyboards (on last 1974 tour, before disbanding) The ASHETONS formed The NEW ORDER (US version), with RON moving on to DESTROY ALL MONSTERS who had three 45's for UK label 'Cherry Red' in the late 70's.

– compilations, other, etc. –

(* = as "IGGY & THE STOOGES")

1976. Visa; (white-d-lp) * **METALLIC KO** -
(re-iss.+cd.May88 on 'Skydog') (cd-iss.Sep94 on 'Skydog')

1977. Bomp; (7"ep) * **I'M SICK OF YOU. / TIGHT PANTS / SCENE OF THE CRIME** -

1977. Bomp; (7"ep) * **JESUS LOVES THE STOOGES ("IGGY POP & JAMES WILLIAMSON")** -
– Jesus loves the Stooges / Consolation prizes / Johanna *(re-iss. 10" ep. Nov 94)*

1977. Skydog France; (7") **I GOT NOTHIN'. / GIMME DANGER** - -
(12"+=) – Heavy liquid.

1977. Siamese; (7") **I GOT A RIGHT. / GIMME SOME SKIN** -
(UK-iss.Dec95 on 'Bomp')

Feb 78. Radar/ US= Bomp; (lp) **KILL CITY (as "IGGY POP with James Williamson")**
– Sell your love / Kill city / I got nothin' / Beyond the law / Johanna / Night theme / Night theme reprise / Master charge / No sense of crime / Lucky monkeys / Consolation prizes. *(re-iss.! on 'Elektra') (cd-iss.Feb89 on 'Line') (cd-iss.Jan93) (re-iss.10" lp Feb95 on 'Bomp')*

Apr 78. Radar/ US= Bomp; (7") **KILL CITY. / I GOT NOTHIN'**

Aug 80. Elektra; (lp)(c) **NO FUN** (1969-70 best of THE STOOGES)

1983. Invasion; (lp) **I GOT A RIGHT** -

Dec 87. Fan Club; (lp) **RUBBER LEGS** -

Feb 95. Bomp; (10"lp) **ROUGH POWER** -

— Also in France 1988 on 'Revenge' records, a number of releases were issued.

'LUST FOR LIFE'

GIMME DANGER (12") / **OPEN UP AND BLEED** (cd) / **DEATH TRAP** (pic-lp) / **LIVE AT THE WHISKEY A-GO-GO**(lp) / **THE STOOGES**(12"ep) / **SHE CREATURES OF HOLLYWOOD HILLS**

IGGY POP

had already went solo, augmented by **DAVID BOWIE** – producer, keyboards / **RICKY GARDINER** – guitar / **TONY SALES** – bass / **HUNT SALES** – drums (latter 2; ex-TODD RUNDGREN) / guest **CARLOS ALOMAR** – guitar

R.C.A. R.C.A.

Feb 77. (7") **SISTER MIDNIGHT. / BABY** [-] [ ]
Mar 77. (lp)(c) **THE IDIOT** [30] [72]
– Sister midnight / Nightclubbing / Fun time / Baby / China girls / Dum dum boys / Tiny girls / Mass production. *(re-iss.+cd.Apr90 on 'Virgin')*
May 77. (7") **CHINA GIRL. / BABY** [ ] [ ]

— **STACEY HEYDON** – guitar / **SCOTT THURSTON** – keys repl. BOWIE + ALOMAR

Sep 77. (lp)(c) **LUST FOR LIFE** [28] [ ]
– Lust for life / Sixteen / Some weird sin / The passenger / Tonight / Success / Turn blue / Neighbourhood threat / Fall in love with me. *(re-iss.1984) (re-iss.+cd.Apr90 on 'Virgin')*
Oct 77. (7") **SUCCESS. / THE PASSENGER** [ ] [ ]

— **IGGY** retained **THURSTON**, and recruited **SCOTT ASHETON** – drums / **FRED 'SONIC' SMITH** – guitar (ex-MC5) / **GARY RAMUSSEN** – bass (The SALES bros.later to BOWIE's TIN MACHINE)

Apr 78. (7") **I GOT A RIGHT (live). / SIXTEEN (live)** [ ] [ ]
May 78. (lp)(c) **TV EYE (live 1977)** [ ] [ ]
– T.V. eye / Funtime / Sixteen / I got a right / Lust for life / Dirt / Nightclubbing / I wanna be your dog. *(cd-iss.Jul94 on 'Virgin')*

— **IGGY / THURSTON** now with **JAMES WILLIAMSON** – guitar, producer / **JACKIE CLARKE** – bass (ex-IKE & TINA TURNER) / **KLAUS KREUGER** – drums (ex-TANGERINE DREAM) / **JOHN HORDEN** – saxophone

Arista Arista

Apr 79. (lp)(c) **NEW VALUES** [60] [ ]
– Tell me a story / New values / Girls / I'm bored / Don't look down / The endless sea / Five foot one / How do ya fix a broken part / Angel / Curiosity / African man / Billy is a runaway. *(re-iss.Mar87)*
May 79. (7") **I'M BORED. / AFRICAN MAN** [ ] [ ]
Jul 79. (7")(7"pic-d) **FIVE FOOT ONE. / PRETTY FLAMINGO** [ ] [ ]

— **IGGY / KREUGER** recruited **IVAN KRAL** – guitar (ex-PATTI SMITH) / **PAT MORAN** – guitar / **GLEN MATLOCK** – bass (ex-SEX PISTOLS, ex-RICH KIDS) / **BARRY ANDREWS** – keyboards (ex-XTC, ex-LEAGUE OF GENTLEMEN) (THURSTON formed The MOTELS)

Jan 80. (lp)(c) **SOLDIER** [62] [ ]
– Knockin' 'em down (in the city) / I'm a conservative / I snub you / Get up and get out / Ambition / Take care of me / I need more / Loco mosquito / Mr.Dynamite / Play it safe / Dog food. *(US re-iss.Oct87) (UK re-iss.+cd.Apr91)*
Jan 80. (7") **LOCO MOSQUITO. / TAKE CARE OF ME** [ ] [ ]

— **IGGY / KRAL** now with **ROB DuPREY** – guitar / **MICHAEL PAGE** – bass / **DOUGLAS BROWNE** – drums (BARRY ANDREWS formed SHRIEKBACK)

May 81. (7") **BANG BANG. / SEA OF LOVE** [ ] [ ]
Jun 81. (lp)(c) **PARTY** [ ] [ ]
– Pleasure / Rock and roll party / Eggs on plate / Sincerity / Houston is hot tonight / Pumpin' for Jill / Happy man / Bang bang / Sea of love / Time won't let me. *(re-iss.Jan87) (cd-iss.Sep89 on 'RCA')*

— **IGGY / DuPREY** found new people **CHRIS STEIN** – guitar, producer (ex-BLONDIE) / **CLEM BURKE** – drums (ex-BLONDIE)

Animal-Chrysalis Animal

Aug 82. (7") **RUN LIKE A VILLAIN. / PLATONIC** [ ] [ ]
Sep 82. (lp)(c) **ZOMBIE BIRDHOUSE** [ ] [ ]
– Run like a villain / The villagers / Angry hills / Life of work / The ballad of Cookie McBride / Ordinary bummer / Eat to be eaten / Bulldozer / Platonic / The horse song / Watching the news / Street crazies.

— In 1984, he sang the title song on Alex Cox's movie 'REPO MAN'. For the same director, he appeared in the 1985 film 'SID & NANCY' about SID VICIOUS.

— **IGGY** now with **ERDAL KIZILCAY** – drums, bass, synthesizers / **KEVIN ARMSTRONG** – guitar / **BOWIE + STEVE JONES** (guest writers)

A & M A & M

Sep 86. (7") **CRY FOR LOVE. / WINNERS & LOSERS** [ ] [ ]
Oct 86. (lp)(c)(cd) **BLAH-BLAH-BLAH** [43] [75]
– Real wild child (wild one) / Baby, it can't fail / Shades / Fire girl / Isolation / Cry for love / Blah-blah-blah / Hideaway / Winners and losers. (cd+=) Little Miss Emperor. *(re-cd-iss.1989)*
Nov 86. (7")(12") **REAL WILD CHILD (WILD ONE). / LITTLE MISS EMPEROR** [10] [ ]
Feb 87. (7") **SHADES. / BABY IT CAN'T FAIL** [ ] [ ]
(12"+=) – Cry for love.
Apr 87. (7")(12") **FIRE GIRL. / BLAH-BLAH-BLAH (live)** [ ] [ ]
Jun 87. (7") **ISOLATION. / HIDEAWAY** [ ] [ ]
(12"+=) – Fire girl (remix).

— IGGY now with **STEVE JONES** – guitar / **PAUL GARRISTO** – drums (ex-PSYCHEDELIC FURS) / **SEAMUS BEAGHEN** – keyboards / **LEIGH FOXX** – bass

Jul 88. (lp)(c)(cd) **INSTINCT** [61] [ ]
– Cold metal / High on you / Strong girl / Tom tom / Easy rider / Power & freedom / Lowdown / Tuff baby / Squarehead.
Aug 88. (7") **COLD METAL. / INSTINCT** [ ] [ ]
(12"+=)(12"pic-d+=) – Tuff baby.
Nov 88. (7") **HIGH ON YOU. / SQUAREHEAD** [ ] [ ]
(12"+=) – Tuff baby (remix).

— **ALVIN GIBBS** – guitar (ex-UK SUBS) repl. STEVE JONES (continued solo) / **ANDY McCOY** – bass (ex-HANOI ROCKS) repl. FOXX (to DEBORAH HARRY)

Nov 88. (lp)(c)(cd) **LIVE AT THE CHANNEL (live 17.9.88)** [-] [ ]

— now with **SLASH** – guitar / **DUFF McKAGAN** – bass (both of GUNS'N'ROSES) / **KENNY ARONOFF** – drums

Virgin America Virgin America

Jan 90. (7")(c-s) **LIVIN' ON THE EDGE OF THE NIGHT. / THE PASSENGER** [51] [ ]
(12"+=)(cd-s+=)(12"pic-d+=) – Nightclubbing / China girl.
Jun 90. (7")(c-s) **HOME. / LUST FOR LIFE** [ ] [ ]
(12"+=)(cd-s+=) – Pussy power / Funtime.
Jul 90. (cd)(c)(lp) **BRICK BY BRICK** [50] [90]
– Home / Main street eyes / I won't crap out / Candy / Butt town / The undefeated / Moonlight lady / Something wild / Neon forest / Stormy night / Pussy power / My baby wants to rock & roll / Brick by brick / Livin' on the edge of the night.

— (below 'A'side feat. **KATE PIERSON – vox (of B-52's)**

Dec 90. (7")(c-s) **CANDY. / PUSSY POWER (acoustic demo)** [67] [28] Nov 90
(12")(cd-s) – ('A'side) / The undefeated / Butt town (acoustic demo).
(10"+=)(cd-s+=) – My baby wants to rock'n'roll (acoustic demos).

— Oct 90, IGGY dueted with DEBORAH HARRY on UK Top 50 single 'DID YOU EVAH')

— with **LARRY MULLINS** (U2) – drums, percussion / **HAL CRAGIN** – bass / **ERIC SCHERMERHORN** – guitar plus guests **MALCOLM BURN** – guitars, etc

Aug 93. (7"ep)(12"ep)(c-ep)(cd-ep) **THE WILD AMERICA EP** [63] [ ]
– Wild America / Credit card / Come back tomorrow / My angel.
Sep 93. (cd)(c)(d-lp) **AMERICAN CAESAR** [43] [ ]
– Character / Wild America / Mixin' the colors / Jealousy / Hate / It's our love / Plastic & concrete / F***in' alone / Highway song / Beside you / Sickness / Boogie boy / Perforation / Problems / Social life / Louie Louie / Caesar / Girls of N.Y
May 94. (10"ep) **BESIDE YOU / EVIL CALIFORNIA. / POEM (live) / FUCKIN' ALONE** [47] [ ]
(cd-s) – ('A'side) / Les amants / Louie Louie (live) / ('A'acoustic).

. . . Jan – Jun '96 stop press . . .

Feb 96. (cd)(c)(lp) **NAUGHTY LITTLE DOGGIE** [ ] [ ]

— He's soon to be featured in the film 'The Crow II'. Rumours are rife that he will re-form The STOOGES with RON and SCOTT, early in '97.

– his compilations, etc. –

May 82. RCA; (7") **THE PASSENGER. / NIGHTCLUBBING** [ ] [-]
Sep 84. RCA; (lp)(c) **CHOICE CUTS** [ ] [-]
Apr 88. A&M; (cd-ep) **COMPACT HITS** [ ] [-]
– Real wild child (the wild one) / Isolation / Cry for love / Shades.
Jun 93. Revenge; (cd) **LIVE NYC RITZ '86 (live)** [ ] [-]
Aug 93. Revenge; (cd)(c) **SUCK ON THIS!** [ ] [-]
Aug 95. Skydog; (cd) **WE ARE NOT TALKING ABOUT COMMERCIAL SHIT** [ ] [-]
Aug 95. Skydog; (cd) **WAKE UP SUCKERS** [ ] [-]

POP WILL EAT ITSELF

Formed: Stourbridge, Midlands, England . . . early 1985 initially as WILD AND WONDERING, by CLINT, ADAM and GRAHAM, out of the ashes of EDEN. After a ROLLING STONES inspired EP '2000 LIGHT ALES FROM HOME', they became POP WILL EAT ITSELF, early '86. The PWEI debut 'POPPIES SAY GRRRR . . . EP', was originally sold at a Dudley gig, but when given more DIY copies were in the shops, it became NME single of the week, and playlisted on night time Radio 1. In the summer of '86, they signed to Craig Jennings' indie 'Chapter 22' label, and after a few more releases, he became their manager. After becoming resident in the indie charts for the next years, they finally shifted to major 'RCA', with their first hit 'CAN U DIG IT', breaking into the 40 early 1989. • **Style:** Grebo pop-rock gurus, who were a hybrid of heavy punk (aka KILLING JOKE) and psychedelia, fused with samples and over-the-top sexist lyrics (aka 'BEAVER PATROL'). • **Songwriters:** Group compositions except; LOVE MISSILE F1-11 (Sigue Sigue Sputnik) / LIKE AN ANGEL (Mighty Lemon Drops) / ORGONE ACCUMULATOR (Hawkwind) / EVERYTHING

THAT RISES (Eno) / ROCK-A-HULA BABY (Elvis Presley). • **Trivia:** MILES and MALCOLM of The WONDER STUFF co-wrote and guested on W&W 1986 debut.

Recommended: BOX FRENZY (*8) / NOW FOR A FEAST (*7) / THIS IS THE DAY (*7).

WILD & WONDERING

CLINT MARSELL – vocals, guitar / **ADAM MOLE** – guitar, keyboards / **GRAHAM CRABB** – drums / **RICHARD MARCH** – bass

Iguana not issued

Feb 86. (12"ep) **2000 LIGHT ALES FROM HOME** [ ] [-]
– Dust me down / Stand by me / Real cool time / Interlong / Apple tree (pt.1 & 2).

POP WILL EAT ITSELF

Desperate not issued

May 86. (12"ep) **POPPIES SAY GRRRR . . . EP** [ ] [-]
– (see below Aug86 for the 5 tracks).

Jun 86. (7") **THERE'S A PSYCOPATH IN MY SOUP. / CANDIOSES** [ ] [-]

Chapter 22 not issued

Aug 86. (7") **I'M SNIFFING WITH YOU-HOO. / SICK LITTLE GIRL** [ ] [-]
(12"+=) – Mesmerised / There's a psychopath in my soup / Candioses.

Oct 86. (7"ep)(12"ep) **POPPIECOCK** [ ] [-]
– Oh Grebo I think I love you / Black country chainsaw massacre manogamy / Titanic clown / B-b-breakdown. (12"ep incl. – May86 ep).

Jan 87. (7") **SWEET SWEET PIE. / THE DEVIL INSIDE** [ ] [-]
(12"+=) – Runaround.

May 87. (7") **LOVE MISSILE F1-11 (remix). / ORGONE ACCUMULATOR** [ ] [-]
THE COVERS EP (12"+=) – Like an angel / Everything that rises.
(12"+=) – ('A'designer Grebo mix). repl. 'Like an angel'.

Sep 87. (7")(7"pink)(7"clear) **BEAVER PATROL. / BUBBLES** [ ] [-]
(12"+=) – Oh Grebo I think I love you (new version).
(12"+=) – Ugly.

Oct 87. (lp)(c)(cd) **BOX FRENZY** [ ] [-]
– Grebo guru / Beaver patrol / Let's get ugly / U.B.L.U.D. / Inside you / Evelyn / There is no love between us anymore / She's surreal / Intergalactic love mission / Love missile F1-11 / Hit the hi-tech groove / Razorblade kisses.

Jan 88. (7")(7"pic-d) **THERE IS NO LOVE BETWEEN US ANYMORE. / PICNIC IN THE SKY** [66] [-]
(12"+=) – On the razor's edge / Kiss that girl.

Jul 88. (7") **DEF CON ONE. / INSIDE YOU** [63] [-]
(12"+=) – She's surreal / ('A'remix).
(12"+=)(cd-s+=) – Hi-tech groove (live) / She's surreal (live).

Dec 88. (lp)(c)(cd) **NOW FOR A FEAST** (compilation) [ ] [-]
– Black country chainstore massacre / Monogamy / Oh Grebo I think I love you / Titanic clown / B-B-B Breakdown / Sweet sweet pie / Like an angel / I'm sniffin' with you hoo / Sick little girl / Mesmerized / There's a psychopath in my soup / Candyiosis / The devil inside / Orgone accumulator.

R.C.A. R.C.A.

Jan 89. (7")(7"orange)(7"green) **CAN U DIG IT. / POISON TO THE MIND** [38] [ ]
(cd-s+=) – Radio PWEI (acapella) / ('A'-12"version).
(12"++=) – The fuses have been lit.

Apr 89. (7")(7"pic-d) **WISE UP! SUCKER. / ORGYONE STIMULATOR** [41] [ ]
(12"+=)(c-s+=)(cd-s+=) – ('A'remix) / Can u dig it (riffs mix).
(10") – ('A'side) / ('A'-2 other versions).

May 89. (lp)(c)(cd) **THIS IS THE DAY, THIS IS THE HOUR, THIS IS THIS** [24] [ ]
– PWEI is a four letter word / Preaching to the peverted / Wise up! sucker / Sixteen different flavours of Hell / Inject me / Can u dig it? / The fuses have been lit / Poison to the mind / Def con one / Radio PWEI / Shortwave transmission on up to the minuteman / Satellite ecstatica / Now now James, we're busy / Wake up! time to die . . . *(cd+=)*– Wise up sucker (mix). *re-iss.cd Nov93)*

Aug 89. (7"ep)(12"ep)(c-ep)(cd-ep)(7"sha-pic-d-ep) **VERY METAL NOISE POLLUTION EP** [45] [ ]
– Pweization / 92 degrees f / Def con one (remix) / Preaching to the converted.

May 90. (7")(c-s) **TOUCHED BY THE HAND OF CICCIOLINA. / THE INCREDI-BULL MIX** [28] [ ]
(12"+=) – ('A'extra time mix).
(cd-s) – ('A'extra time mix). / ('A' Diva mix) / ('A' Renegade Sound..)
(12") – ('A' Diva futura mix). / ('A' Renegade Soundwave mix).

Oct 90. (7")(c-s) **DANCE OF THE MAD BASTARDS. / PREACHING TO THE PERVERTED PWEI VS. THE MORAL MAJORITY** [32] [ ]
(12"ep+=)(cd-ep+=) – ('A'other mix).

Oct 90. (cd)(c)(lp) **THE POP WILL EAT ITSELF CURE FOR SANITY** [33] [ ]
– Incredible PWEI vs. The Moral Majority / Dance of the mad bastards / 88 seconds... and still counting / X, Y and Zee / City Zen radio 1990-2000 FM / Dr.Nightmares medication time / Touched by the hand of Cicciolina / 1000 x no! / Psycho sexual / Axe of men / Another man's rhubarb / Medicine man speaks with forked tongue / Nightmare at 20,000 feet / Very metal noise pollution / 92 degrees F (the 3rd degree) / Lived in splendour, died in chaos / The beat that refused to die. *(re-iss.+pic-lp.May91)(re-iss.cd Nov93)*

Jan 91. (7")(c-s) **X, Y AND ZEE. / AXE OF MEN** [15] [ ]
(12"box+=) – Psychosexual.
(12"+=)(cd-s+=) – ('A'intergalactic mix) / ('A'sensory amp mix).

May 91. (7")(c-s) **92 f. / INCREDIBLE PWEI VS. DIRTY HARRY** [23] [ ]
(10"+=)(12"+=)(cd-s+=) – Another man's rhubarb.

May 92. (7")(c-s) **ARMADROME. / EAT ME DRINK ME LOVE ME KILL ME** [17] [ ]
(12"+=) – Dread alert in the karmadrome / Eat me drink me dub me kill me.
(cd-s) – ('A'side) / PWEI-zation (original metal noise pollution).
(12"pic-d+=) – PWEI-zation (original . . .) / Eat me drink me dub . . .

Aug 92. (7")(c-s) **BULLETPROOF. / ('A'-On-U-Sound mix)** [24] [ ]
(cd-s+=)(12"pic-d+=) – Good from far, far from good.
(12") – ('A'-mile high mix) / ('A'-no half measures mix).

Sep 92. (cd)(c)(lp) **THE LOOKS OF THE LIFESTYLE** [15] [ ]
– England's finest / Eat me, drink me, love me, kill me / Mother / Get the girl, kill the baddies! / I've always been a coward baby / Spoken drug song / Karmadrome / Urban futuristic (son of South Central) / Pretty pretty / I was a teenage grandad / Harry Dean Stanton / Bulletproof. *(re-iss.re-iss.cd Nov93)*

—— added 5th member **FUZZ** – drums

Jan 93. (7")(c-s) **GET THE GIRL! KILL THE BADDIES!. / ('A' Adrian Sherwood mix)** [9] [ ]
(12"+=)(cd-s+=) – ('A' black country & western mix) or ('A'boilerhouse mix)
(cd-s) – ('A'side) / Urban futuristic (live) / Can u dig it? (live) / Wise up! sucker! (live).

Feb 93. (cd)(c)(lp) **WEIRDS, BARS AND GRILLS (live)** [44] [ ]
– England's finest / Eat me drink me love me kill me / Get the girl, kill the baddies!! / Wise up! sucker / 88 seconds and counting / Karmadrome / Token drug song mother / Preaching to the perverted / Axe of men / Nightmare at 20,000 feet / Always been a coward / Can U dig it / Bullet proof / Urban futuristic / There is no love between us anymore / Def con one. (cd/c+=) – Harry Dean Stanton teenage grandad.

Oct 93. (cd)(c)(lp) **16 DIFFERENT FLAVOURS OF HELL** (compilation) [73] [ ]
– Def con one / Wise up! sucker / Can U dig it / Touched by the hand of Cicciolina (extra time mix) / Dance of the mad / X Y and Zee (sunshine mix) / 92 degrees (boilerhouse The Birth mix) / Karmadrome / Bullet proof / Get the girl kill the baddies / Another man's rhubarb / Rockahula baby / Wise up sucker / Cicciolina (Renegade Soundwave mix). (cd=) Preaching to the perverted (remix) / Eat me drink me love me kill me / PWElzatin.

Infectious ???

Oct 93. (12"ep)(c-ep)(cd-ep) **R.S.V.P. / FAMILUS HORRIBILUS** [27] [ ]
(cd-ep+=) – ('B' remixes) / ('B' live)
(12"ep+=)(cd-ep+=) – ('A'side) / ('B'-higher later space mix agency vocal).

Feb 94. (7")(c-s)(cd-s)(7"pic-d) **ICH BIN EIN AUSLANDER. ("POP WILL EAT ITSELF & FUN-DA-MENTAL") / CP1£2** [28] [-]
(12"+=)(cd-s+=) – ('A'-Fun-Da-Mental instrumental) / ('A'-Fun-Da-Mental extra).
(12"+=) – ('A'-drone ranger mix) / Intense.

Aug 94. (7"colrd) **EVERYTHING'S COOL?. / LET IT FLOW** [23] [ ]
(7"colrd) – ('A'side) / WILD WEST
(cd-s) – ('A'side) / ('A'-Youth remix) / R.S.V.P. (Fluke mix).
(cd-s) – ('A'side) / Ich bin ein Auslander (live) / Familus horribilus (live) / R.S.V.P. (live).

Sep 94. (cd)(c)(lp) **DOS DEDOS MIS AMIGOS** [11] [ ]
– Ich bin ein Auslander / Kick to kill / Familus horribilus / Underbelly / Fatman / Home / Cape connection / Menofeathereaper / Everything's cool / R.S.V.P. / Babylon.

Mar 95. (d-cd)(d-c)(d-lp) **TWO FINGERS MY FRIENDS!** (remixes) [25] [ ]
– Ich bin ein Auslander (Fun-Da-Mental) / Kick to kill (Jim Foetus seersucker mix) / Familus horribilus (mega web 2) / Underbelly (Renegade Soundwave blackout mix) / Fatman (Hoodlum Priest Fatboy mix) / Home (Orb sweet sin and salvation mix) / Cape Connection (Transglobal Underground Cossack in UFO encounter mix) / Menofearthereaper (concrete no fee, no fear mix) / Everything's cool (safe as milk mix) / R.S.V.P. (made in Japan, live at the Budokan double live Gonzo F mix) / Babylon (Loop Guru Babylon a dub fire mix) // Ich bin ein Auslander (Die Krupps mix) / Familus horribilus (Hia Nyg vocal mix) / Cape Connection (golden claw versus clock and dagger mix) / Intense / C.P.I. £2 / Cape Connection (TGV aliens, bodacious aliens mix) / Everything's cool (Dragonfly mix) / RSVP (Fluke lunch mix) / Cape Connection (Secret Knowledge transfered up mix) / Underbelly (The Drum Club bugsong mix).

. . . Jan – Jun '96 stop press . . .

—— CRABB left to pursue own career. He formed The BUZZARD and other project The Golden Claw Music.

PORNO FOR PYROS
(see under ⇒ JANE'S ADDICTION)

PORTISHEAD

Formed: Bristol, England . . . 1993 by duo GEOFF BARLOW and BETH GIBBONS. Signed to 'Chrysalis – Go! Discs' off-shoot 'Go Beat' and created quite a stir in 1994, with the release of their critically acclaimed debut album 'DUMMY'. This is currently breaking new chart ground and the UK Top 10. • **Style:** Melancholy cool jazz soul, chameleoned somewhere between a pastel SADE / SINEAD / BILLE HOLIDAY, fellow scratch Bristolites MASSIVE ATTACK and 60's spy-film soundtracks. In fact they also released a film 'TO KILL A DEAD MAN'. • **Songwriters:** BARROW-GIBBONS, but most with UTLEY. Sample; MORE MISSION IMPOSSIBLE (Lalo Schifrin) / SPIN IT JIG (Smokey Brooks) / ELEGANT PEOPLE (Weather Report) / MAGIC MOUNTAIN (War) / I'LL NEVER FALL IN LOVE AGAIN (Johnnie Ray; at slow speed!) / ISAAC MOODS (Isaac Hayes). • **Trivia:** Have remixed for the likes of DEPECHE MODE (In Your Room) / RIDE (I Don't Know Where It Comes From) / GRAVEDIGGAZ (Nowhere To Run).

Recommended: DUMMY (*10)

BETH GIBBONS – vocals / **GEOFF BARLOW** (b.1971) – programming, synthesizer with **ADRIAN UTLEY** – guitar, bass / **CLIVE DEAMER** – drums / **DAVE McDONALD** – nose flute / **RICHARD NEWELL** – drum programme / **NEIL SOLMAN** – synthesizers, organ / **ANDY HAGUE** – trumpet

Go Beat | Go! Discs

Jun 94. (c-s)(cd-s) **NUMB / NUMBED IN MOSCOW** [ ] [ ]
(12"+=)(cd-s+=) – Revenge of the numbed / Numb: Earth under / Extra numb.
(cd-s++=) – A tribute to Monk and Cantella.

Aug 94. (c-s)(cd-s) **SOUR TIMES / SOUR SOUR TIMES** [57] [ ]
(12"+=)(cd-s+=) – Lot more / Sheared times.
(cd-s++=) – Airbus reconstruction.
(cd-s) – ('A'side) / It's a fire / Pedestal / Theme from 'To Kill A Dead Man'.
(re-iss.Apr95, hit UK No.13/ issued US hit 53)

Aug 94. (cd)(c) **DUMMY** [2] [79] Jan 95
– Mysterons / Sour times / Strangers / It could be sweet / Wandering star / Numb / Roads / Pedestal / Biscuit / Glory box.

Oct 94. (c-s)(cd-s) **GLORY BOX / ('A'version)** [13] [ ]
(12"+=)(cd-s+=) – ('A'versions).

. . . Jan – Jun '96 stop press . . .

— BARROW guested on EARTHLING's 1996 minor hit album 'Radar'.

POWER STATION (see under ⇒ DURAN DURAN)

PRESIDENTS OF THE UNITED STATES OF AMERICA

*** NEW ENTRY ***

Formed: Santa Monica, California, USA . . .late 1993 by long-time friends CHRIS BALLEW, JASON FINN and DAVE DEDERER. Signed to 'Columbia' in 1995 and by the end of the year their eponymous debut was Top 30. • **Style:** Unusual fun funk, pop punk band, like fusing The CARS with DEVO. • **Songwriters:** BALLEW and group except KICK OUT THE JAMS (MC5) / WE ARE NOT GOING TO MAKE IT (Ben Reiser). • **Trivia:** PEACHES video was directed by ROMAN COPPOLA, son of FRANCIS FORD COPPOLA.

Recommended: PRESIDENTS OF THE UNITED STATES OF AMERICA (*6)

CHRIS BALLEW – vocals, two-string basitar / **DAVE DEDERER** – three-string guitbass, vocals (ex- LOVE BATTERY) / **JASON FINN** – drums, vocals

Columbia | Columbia

Oct 95. (cd)(c)(lp) **PRESIDENTS OF THE UNITED STATES OF AMERICA** [14] [6] Sep 95
– Kitty / Feather pluckn / Lump / Stranger / Boll Weevil / Peaches / Dune buggy / We are not going to make it / Kick out the jams / Body / Back porch / Candy / Naked and famous. *(re-iss.yellow-lp Apr96, w/ 2 extra) (cd+=)* – Dune buggy / Kick / Peaches / Lump / Back porch (versions).

Dec 95. (7"pic-d)(c-s) **LUMP. / WAKE UP** [15] [ ]
(cd-s+=) – Carolyn's bootie / Candy's cigarette.

Apr 96. (7"pic)(c-s) **PEACHES. / CONFUSION** [8] [29] Feb 96
(cd-s) – ('A'side) / Feather pluckn (live) / Boll Weevil (live) / Dune buggy (live).

PRETENDERS

Formed: London, England . . . Mar'78 by American CHRISSIE HYNDE, with Hereford based musicians; HONEYMAN-SCOTT, FARNDON and MACKLEDUFF. HYNDE's past had included spending the early 70's at Kent State University, before moving to London in 1973 to become an NME journalist. In 1974, she relocated to Paris to join The FRENCHIES, where she met CHRIS SPEDDING. He invited her to sing backing vocals on his 1977 released lp 'HURT'. Prior to this, she had returned to homeland Ohio in 1975 to join R&B group JACK RABBIT. A year later, she came back to London to form The BERK BROTHERS (DAVE & FRED), before they replaced her with JOHNNY MOPED. In Aug'77, she cut a demo tape for Dave Hill's new 'Real' records, who asked her to form a band; The PRETENDERS. Early in '79, their first 45 'STOP YOUR SOBBING', produced by NICK LOWE and written by Kinks' RAY DAVIES (her future beau, common-law husband, they were refused a marriage certificate by registrar annoyed by their arguing), and father of her child Natalie). They began the 80's, hitting the UK top spot with 'BRASS IN POCKET' and a No.1 eponymous album, which was first of many top sellers throughout the decade. Tragedy struck the band twice between 1982 and 1983, when HONEYMAN-SCOTT then the already departed FARNDON, both overdosed on heroin. • **Style:** New wave / power pop, smoothed down by the sultry goddess of rock'n'roll CHRISSIE HYNDE. • **Songwriters:** Group compositions, except as said plus; MAY THIS BE LOVE (Jimi Hendrix) / IF THERE WAS A MAN (co-w/ John Barry) / NOT A SECOND TIME (Beatles) / CREEP (Radiohead). • **Trivia:** After her relationship ended with DAVIES in 1984, she quickly married JIM KERR (Simple Minds) on the 5th May'85. They split in the 80's, after she gave birth to another child. She caused controversy in June '89, when she attended a Greenpeace Rainbow Warriors press conference, and told of how she (a staunch vegetarian) once firebombed McDonalds burger shop. The day after, one of their shops in Milton Keynes was firebombed and CHRISSIE was asked / told to sign a retracting statement, or be taken to court.

Recommended: THE SINGLES (*8) / PRETENDERS (*8) / PRETENDERS II (*7)

CHRISSIE HYNDE (b. 7 Sep'51, Akron, Ohio, USA) – vocals, guitar / **JAMES HONEYMAN-SCOTT** (b. 4 Nov'57) – guitar, keyboards (ex-CHEEKS) / **PETE FARNDON** (b.1953, Hereford, Wales) – bass / **GERRY MACKLEDUFF** – drums

Real | Sire

Jan 79. (7") **STOP YOUR SOBBING. / THE WAIT** [34] [-]

— **MARTIN CHAMBERS** (b. 4 Sep'51) – drums repl. GERRY

Jun 79. (7") **KID. / TATTOOED LOVE BOYS** [33] [ ] Jul 80

Nov 79. (7") **BRASS IN POCKET. / SWINGING LONDON** [1] [-]
(12"+=) – Nervous but shy. *(c-ep iss.Apr81) ?*

Jan 80. (lp)(c) **PRETENDERS** [1] [9]
– Precious / The phone call / Up the neck / Tattooed love boys / Space invader / The wait / Stop your sobbing / Kid / Private life / Brass in pocket / Lovers of today / Mystery achievement. *(cd-iss.1983)*

Feb 80. (7") **BRASS IN POCKET. / SPACE INVADER** [-] [14]

Apr 80. (7") **TALK OF THE TOWN. / CUBAN SLIDE AND SLIDE** [8] [ ]

May 80. (7") **STOP YOUR SOBBING. / PHONE CALL** [-] [65]

Feb 81. (7") **MESSAGE OF LOVE. / PORCELAIN** [11] [27] Apr 81
(7"ep+=) – Talk of the town / Cuban slide and slide.

Aug 81. (lp)(c) **PRETENDERS II** [7] [10]
– The adultress / Bad boys get spanked / Message of love / I go to sleep / Birds of Paradise / Talk of the town / Pack it up / Waste not, want not / Day after day / Jealous dogs / Waste not want not / English rose / Louie Louie. *(cd-iss.Nov86)*

Aug 81. (7") **LOUIE LOUIE. / IN THE STICKS** [-] [ ]

Aug 81. (7") **DAY AFTER DAY. / IN THE STICKS** [45] [ ]
(12"+=) – The adultress.
(7"ep+=)(c-ep+=) – Stop your sobbing / Kid.

Nov 81. (7") **I GO TO SLEEP. / THE ENGLISH ROSE** [7] [ ]
(12"+=) – Waste not, want not. *(US; b-side)*

— (Sep82) **BILLY BREMNER** – guitar (ex-NICK LOWE, ex-DAVE EDMUNDS' ROCKPILE) repl. HONEYMAN-SCOTT who died of drug overdose 16 Jun'82 / **TONY BUTLER** – bass (of BIG COUNTRY) repl. FARNDON (died o.d. 14 Apr'83)

Sep 82. (7") **BACK ON THE CHAIN GANG. / (part 2)** [17] [5] Dec 82
(12"+=) – My city was gone. *(US; b-side)*

— (Feb83) **HYNDE** and **CHAMBERS** brought in new members **ROBBIE McINTOSH** (25 Oct'57) – guitar (ex-MANFRED MANN'S EARTH BAND, ex-NIGHT) repl. BREMNER who rejoined NICK LOWE etc. / **MALCOLM FOSTER** (b.13 Jan'56) – bass repl. BUTLER who rejoined BIG COUNTRY.

Nov 83. (7") **2000 MILES. / THE LAW IS THE LAW** [15] [-]
('A'fast or slow versioned 12"+=) – Money (live).

Nov 83. (7") **MIDDLE OF THE ROAD. / 2,000 MILES** [-] [19]

Jan 84. (lp)(c)(cd) **LEARNING TO CRAWL** [11] [5]

– Middle of the road / Back on the chain gang / Time the avenger / Watching the clothes / Show me / Thumbelina / My city was gone / Thin line between love and hate / I hurt you / 2000 miles.

Feb 84. (7")(12") **MIDDLE OF THE ROAD. / WATCHING THE CLOTHES** — -

—— added **PAUL CARRACK** – keyboards (ex-ACE, ex-ROXY MUSIC, ex-solo artist)

Mar 84. (7") **SHOW ME. / FAST OR SLOW (THE LAW IS THE LAW)** - 28

Apr 84. (7") **THIN LINE BETWEEN LOVE AND HATE. / TIME THE AVENGER** 49 83 Jun 84
(12"+=) – Bad boys get spanked.

—— Sep 85, CHRISSIE HYNDE guests on UB40's 'I Got You Babe' which hits No.1. Three years later the same team hit no.6 with 'Breakfast In Bed'. **PRETENDERS** regroup with **HYNDE, McINTOSH** and **TIM STEVENS** – bass / **BLAIR CUNNINGHAM** – drums (ex-HAIRCUT 100) repl. CHAMBERS (on some) and **BERNIE WORRELL** – keyboards

W.E.A. Warners

Sep 86. (7") **DON'T GET ME WRONG. / DANCE** 10 10
(12"+=) – ('A'extended).

Oct 86. (lp)(c)(cd) **GET CLOSE** 6 25
– My baby / When I change my life / Light of the Moon / Dance * / Tradition of love / Don't get me wrong / I remember you / How much did you get for your soul / Chill factor / Hymn to her / Room full of mirrors. *(c+cd+= *)*

Nov 86. (7") **HYMN TO HER. / ROOM FULL OF MIRRORS** 8
(12"+=) – Stop your sobbing (demo).

Feb 87. (7") **MY BABY. / ROOM FULL OF MIRRORS** - 64

Mar 87. (7") **MY BABY. / TRADITION OF LOVE (remix)** -
(12"+=) – Thumbelina.
(7"ep+=) – Private life / Middle of the road.

Apr 87. (7") **HYMN TO HER. / TRADITION OF LOVE** -

Aug 87. (7") **IF THERE WAS A MAN. (as "PRETENDERS 007") / WHERE HAS EVERYBODY GONE** 49
(12"+=) – Into Vienna. (US; b-side)

Oct 87. (lp)(c)(cd) **THE SINGLES** (compilation) 6 69
– Stop your sobbing / Kid / Brass in pocket / Talk of the town / I go to sleep / Day after day / Message of love / Back on the chain gang / Middle of the road / 2000 miles / Show me / Thin line between love and hate / Don't get me wrong / Hymn to her / My baby / I got you babe (w / UB40) / What you gonna do about it.

Oct 87. (7") **KID (remix). / STOP YOUR SOBBING (original)**
(12"+=)(cd-s+=) – ('B' 1978 demo) / What you gonna do about it ('87 remix)

Jun'88, she guested again with UB40 on hit single 'BREAKFAST IN BED'.

—— added guest **JOHNNY MARR** – guitar (ex-SMITHS) repl. McINTOSH

Apr 89. (7")(12")(3"cd-s) **WINDOWS OF THE WORLD. / 1969**

—— (above from the film '1969', a one-off on label 'Polydor')

—— now virtually **CHRISSIE** solo, augmented by **BLAIR CUNNINGHAM** – drums / **BILLY BREMNER + DOMINIC MILLER** – guitar / **JOHN McKENZIE** – bass / plus others

May 90. (7")(c-s) **NEVER DO THAT. / NOT A SECOND TIME**
(12"+=) – The wait.
(cd-s++=) – Spirit of life.

May 90. (cd)(c)(lp) **PACKED!** 19 48
– Never do that / Let's make a pact / Millionaires / May this be love / No guarentee / When will I see you / Sense of purpose / Downtown (Akron) / How do I miss you / Hold a candle to this / Criminal. *(re-iss.cd Nov94)*

Oct 90. (7") **SENSE OF PURPOSE. / SPIRIT OF LIFE**
(12"+=) – Brass in pocket.
(cd-s++=) – Not a second time.

—— Oct 91, CHRISSIE's vox was credited on single 'SPIRITUAL HIGH', by MOOD SWINGS. It finally hit UK no. 47 early '93.

—— She wrote most with B.STEINBERG + T.KELLY. Covered; FOREVER YOUNG (Bob Dylan).

—— **CHRISSIE** + main band **MARTIN CHAMBERS** – drums / **ADAM SEYMOUR** – guitar / **ANDY HOBSON** – bass

Apr 94. (7")(c-s) **I'LL STAND BY YOU. / REBEL ROCK ME** 10 16 Aug94
(cd-s+=) – Bold as love.
(cd-s) – ('A'side) / Message of love / Brass in pocket / Don't get me wrong.

May 94. (cd)(c) **LAST OF THE INDEPENDENTS** 8 41
– Hollywood perfume / Night in my veins / Money talk / 977 / Revolution / All my dreams / I'll stand by you / I'm a mother / Tequila / Every mother's son / Rebel rock me / Love colours / Forever young.

Jun 94. (7")(c-s) **NIGHT IN MY VEINS. / BAD BOYS GET SPANKED** 25 72
(cd-s+=) – My city was gone / Tattooed love boys.

Oct 94. (7")(c-s) **977. / I'LL STAND BY YOU (live)** 66
(cd-s+=) – Hollywood perfume (live) / Kid (live).
(cd-s) – ('A'side) / Back on the chain gang (live) / Night in my veins (live) / Precious (live).

Sep 95. (c-s) **KID (acoustic) / THE ISLE OF VIEW (acoustic)** 73
(cd-s+=) – Creep (acoustic).

Oct 95. (cd)(c) **THE ISLE OF VIEW (live acoustic)** 23 100
– Sense of purpose / Chill factor / Private life / Back on the chain gang / Kid / I hurt you / Criminal / Brass in pocket / 2000 miles / Hymn to her / Lovers of today / The phone call / I go to sleep / Revolution. (cd+=) – The Isle of View.

Nov 95. (c-s) **2000 MILES (acoustic) / TEQUILA**
(cd-s+=) – Happy Christmas / Night in my veins.

– compilations –

Jul 94. Warners; (cd)(c) **DON'T GET ME WRONG** -
(re-iss.Sep95)

PRETTY THINGS

Formed: Dartford, Kent, England ... 1963 by DICK TAYLOR and PHIL MAY. DICK had once been a member of LITTLE BOY BLUE & THE BLUE BOYS, which was an embryonic version of The ROLLING STONES. Taking their name from a BO DIDDLEY song, they soon signed to 'Fontana', employing management team of Bryan Morrison and James Duncan, the latter of whom, wrote 1964 debut Top 50 hit 'ROSALYN'. Their follow-up 'DON'T BRING ME DOWN', dented the UK Top 10, and preceeded their eponymous Top 10 debut album early '65. Unlike The STONES, the hits dried up in 1967, and they moved to 'Columbia' records, who released first rock opera album 'S.F.SORROW' which flopped late in '68. They struggled on relentlessly, moving on to 'Harvest' in 1970 and LED ZEPPELIN's 'Swan Song' in '74. • **Style:** Rougher looking than even The STONES, their pure roots R&B sound, relied on black American blues artists of the 50's, for much inspiration and music. In 1968, they broke away from R&B to try underground psychedelic scene. • **Songwriters:** Most by PHIL MAY, except covers; PRETTY THING + ROADRUNNER + MONA (Bo Diddley) / CRY TO ME (Bert Berns) / A HOUSE IN THE COUNTRY (Ray Davies; Kinks) / REELIN' AND ROCKIN' (Chuck Berry) / I'M A KING BEE (Muddy Waters) / SHAKIN' ALL OVER (Johnny Kidd & The Pirates) / etc. • **Trivia:** Made cameo appearances in the films 'What's Good For The Goose' (1969 w / Norman Wisdom) and 'The Monster Squad' (1980 w / Vincent Price). They were given tribute by BOWIE in 1973, when he covered their first 2 hits on his 'PIN-UPS' album.

Recommended: THE PRETTY THINGS (*7) / S.F.SORROW (*7) / PARACHUTE (*6) / THE THINGS (*7).

PHIL MAY (b. 9 Nov'44, Kent, England) – vocals / **DICK TAYLOR** (28 Jan'43) – lead guitar (ex-LITTLE BOY BLUE & THE BLUE BOYS) / **BRIAN PENDLETON** (b.13 Apr'44, Wolverhampton, England) – rhythm guitar / **JOHN STAX** (b.JOHN FULLEGAR, 6 Apr'44) – bass / **VIV PRINCE** (b. 9 Aug'44, Loughborough, Leicestershire, England) – drums(PETE KITLEY then VIV ANDREWS sessioned on 1st-2 45's)

Fontana Fontana

Jun 64. (7") **ROSALYN. / BIG BOSS MAN** 41 Oct 64

Oct 64. (7") **DON'T BRING ME DOWN. / WE'LL BE TOGETHER** 10 Jan 65

Feb 65. (7") **HONEY I NEED. / I CAN NEVER SAY** 13

Mar 65. (lp) **THE PRETTY THINGS** 6
– Roadrunner / Judgement day / 13 Chester street / Honey I need / Big city / Unkown blues / Mama, keep your big mouth shut / Oh baby doll / She's fine she's mine / Don't you lie to me / The Moon is rising / Pretty thing. *(re-iss.1967 on 'Wing') (cd-iss. Jul 90)*

Jul 65. (7") **CRY TO ME. / JUDGEMENT DAY** 28

Dec 65. (7") **MIDNIGHT TO SIX MAN. / CAN'T STAND THE PAIN** 46

Dec 65. (lp) **GET THE PICTURE**
– Get the picture / You don't believe me / We'll play house / Can't stand the pain / Rainin' in my heart / Buzz the jerk / London town / You'll never do it to me baby / Cry to me / I had a dream / Gonna find me a substitute / I want your love. *(re-iss.Mar84, cd-iss.Jul90)*

—— **SKIP ALAN** (b.ALAN SKIPPER, 11 Jun'44) – drums repl. PRINCE on some

Fontana Blue Thumb

Apr 66. (7") **COME SEE ME. / L.S.D.** 43

Jul 66. (7") **A HOUSE IN THE COUNTRY. / ME NEEDING YOU** 50

Dec 66. (7") **PROGRESS. / BUZZ IN THE JERK**

Apr 67. (7") **CHILDREN. / MY TIME**

May 67. (lp) **EMOTIONS** -
– Death of a socialite / Children / The Sun / There will never be another day / House of ten / Out in the night / One long glance / Growing in my mind / Photographer / Bright lights of the city / Tripping / My time / A house in the country / Me needing you / Progress. *(re-iss.Apr91)*

—— **PHIL** and **DICK** were left to recruit new members **JOHN POVEY** (b.20 Aug'44) – keyboards, vocals (ex-FENMEN) repl. PENDLETON / **WALLY ALLEN** – bass, vocals (ex-FENMEN) repl. SKIP / **MITCH MITCHELL** – (session) drums repl. SKIP

Columbia Rare Earth

Nov 67. (7") **DEFLECTING GREY. / MR. EVASION** -

— **BOBBIE GRAHAM** – drums (also on session) repl. MITCHELL

Feb 68. (7") **TALKIN ABOUT THE GOOD TIMES. / WALKING THROUGH MY DREAMS** [ ] [-]

— **JOHN 'TWINK' ADLER** – percussion, vocals (ex-TOMORROW, etc) repl. GRAHAM

Nov 68. (7") **PRIVATE SORROW. / BALLROOM BURNING** [ ] [ ]

Dec 68. (lp) **S.F. SORROW** [ ] [ ] Feb 70
– S.F. sorrow / Bracelets of fingers / She says good morning / Private sorrow / Balloon burning / Death / Baron Saturday / I see you / The journey / Well of destiny / Trust / Old man going / Lonliest person. *(cd-iss. Apr 91)*

— **SKIP ALAN** – drums, vocals (returned from SUNSHINE) repl. TWINK who joined PINK FAIRIES (new one joining MAY, POVEY and ALLEN plus below) **VICTOR UNITT** – guitar, vocals (ex-EDGAR BROUGHTON) repl. TAYLOR (⇒ producer)

Harvest / Rare Earth

Apr 70. (7") **THE GOOD MR.SQUARE. / BLUE SERGE BLUES** [ ] [ ]

Jun 70. (lp)(c) **PARACHUTE** [43] [ ]
– Parachute / Scene 1: The good Mr. Square, she was tall, she was high / Rare Earth / In the square, the letter, rain / Miss Fay regrets / Cries from the midnight circus / Grass / Sickle clowns / She's a lover / What's the use. *(re-iss.+cd.Sep88 on 'Edsel')*

— **PETER TOLSON** (b.10 Sep'51, Bishops Stortford, England) – guitar, vocals (ex-EIRE APPARANT) repl. UNITT (who returned to EDGAR BROUGHTON BAND)

Oct 70. (7") **OCTOBER 26. / COLD STONE** [ ] [ ]

May 71. (7"m) **STONE HEARTED MAMA. / SUMMERTIME / CIRCUS MIND** [ ] [ ]

— **STUART BROOKS** – bass, vocals repl. WALLY who went into producing

Warners / Warners

Dec 72. (lp)(c) **FREEWAY MADNESS** [ ] [ ]
– Love is good / Havana bound / Peter / Rip off train / Over the Moon / Religion's dead / Country road / All night sailor / Onion soup / Another bowl?.

Jan 73. (7") **OVER THE MOON. / HAVANA BOUND** [ ] [ ]

— added **GORDON EDWARDS** (b.26 Dec'46, Southport, England) – keyboards (to **MAY, ALAN, POVEY, TOLSON and BROOKS)**

Swan Song / Swan Song

Oct 74. (lp)(c) **SILK TORPEDO** [ ] [ ]
– Dream / Joey / Maybe you tried / Atlanta / L.A.N.T.A. / Is it only love / Come home / Bridge of God / Singapore silk torpedo / Belfast cowboy / Bruise in the sky.

Jan 75. (7") **JOEY. / IS IT ONLY LOVE** [ ] [ ]

Jun 75. (7") **I'M KEEPING. / ATLANTA** [ ] [ ]

— **JACK GREEN** (b.12 Mar'51, Glasgow, Scotland) – bass, vocals (also as EDWARDS, ex-SUNSHINE) repl. BROOKS

Sep 75. (7") **JOEY. / COME HOME MOMMA** [ ] [ ]

Feb 76. (7") **SAD EYE . / REMEMBER THAT BOY** [ ] [-]

Apr 76. (7") **REMEMBER THAT DAY. / IT ISN'T ROCK 'N' ROLL** [-] [ ]

May 76. (lp)(c) **SAVAGE EYE** [ ] [ ] Feb 76
– Under the volcano / My song / Sad eye / Remember that boy / It isn't rock'n' roll / I'm keeping / It's been so long / Drowned man / Theme for Michelle.

May 76. (7") **TONIGHT. / IT ISN'T ROCK'N'ROLL** [ ] [-]

— Last original PHIL MAY went solo augmented by the FALLEN ANGELS (see below). POVEY also departed leaving only 4 (SKIP, PETER, JACK and GORDON) calling themselves METROPOLIS between mid '76-late'77. JACK also joined T.REX and GORDON went to The KINKS.

PHIL MAY & THE FALLEN ANGELS

with **MICKEY FINN** – guitar (ex-T.REX) / **BILL LOVELADY** – guitar / **BRIAN JOHNSTON** – keyboards (ex-STREETWALKERS) / **WALL ALLEN** – bass / **CHICO GREENWOOD** – drums / etc.

Philips / not issued

1978. (lp) **PHIL MAY & THE FALLEN ANGELS** [-] [-] Holl.
– Fallen angels / California / 13 floor suicide / Dance again / Shine on baby / My good friend / Cold wind / I keep on / Dogs of war / Girl like you. *(UK-iss.1982, re-iss.Feb85)*

PRETTY THINGS

re-formed ex-members in 1980. (**PHIL MAY, DICK TAYLOR, JOHN POVEY, PETER TOLSON, WALLY ALLEN** and **SKIP SLAN)**

Warners. / Warners

Aug 80. (lp)(c) **CROSS TALK** [ ] [ ]
– I'm calling / Edge of the night / Sea of blue / Office love / Lost that girl / Bitter end / Falling again / It's so hard / She don't / No future.

Aug 80. (7") **I'M CALLING. / SEA OF BLUE** [ ] [ ]

— Disbanded 1981. Reformed briefly as

ZAC ZOLAR AND ELECTRIC BANANA

Butt / not issued

1984. (7") **TAKE ME HOME. / JAMES MARSHALL** [ ] [-]

— (above appeared on 'Minder' TV series) *(re-iss.Aug86 on 'Shanghai')*

PRETTY THINGS

reformed by **MAY + TAYLOR** in 1984. Now with **JOE SHAW** – guitar / **DAVE WINTOUR** – bass / **KEVIN FLANAGAN** – saxophone / **JOHN CLARKE** – drums

Big Beat / not issued

Aug 84. (lp) **LIVE AT THE HEARTBREAK HOTEL (live)** [ ] [-]
– Big boss man / Midnight to six man / I'm a king bee / Honey I need / Shakin' all over / Rosalyn / Roadrunner / Mama keep your big mouth shut / Raining in my heart / Reelin' and rockin' / Don't bring me down / Mona.

— **ROLF TER VELD** -bass + **BERTRAM ENGEL** -drums (ex-UDO LINDENBERG, ex-PANIKORCHESTER) repl.WINTOUR, FLANAGAN + CLARKE

In-Akustik / not issued

Jun 88. (cd) **OUT OF THE ISLAND** [ ] [-]
– Cry to me / Baby doll / She's fine, she's mine / Get the picture / Havana bound / Can't stop / Loneliest person / L.S.D. / Private sorrow / The Moon is rising / Big city / Cause and effect / Well known blues / You don't believe me / Judement day. *(re-iss.May95)*

— **MAY + TAYLOR** again reformed them in 1989, with new **GLEN MATLOCK** – bass, vocals (ex-SEX PISTOLS, ex-RICH KIDS) / **FRANK HOLLAND** – guitar, keyboards / **BOBBY WEBB** – keyboards, vocals / **MARK ST.JOHN** – drums, bass, vocals

Trax / not issued

Sep 89. (7") **EVE OF DESTRUCTION. / GOIN' DOWNHILL** [ ] [-]
(12"+=) – Can't stop.

— (on tour) **STEVE BROWNING** – bass repl. MATLOCK

— Re-formed again in 1991, with **PHIL MAY / DICK TAYLOR** (ex-MEKONS) / **JIMMY McCARTY** (ex-YARDBIRDS) / **RICHARD HITE** (ex-CANNED HEAT)

PRETTY THINGS & THE YARDBIRD BLUES BAND

Superbluesgroup / collab with ex-YARDBIRDS and plenty covers

Demon / not issued

Oct 91. (cd) **CHICAGO BLUES TAPE 1991** [ ] [-]
– Can't judge the book / Down in the bottom / Hush hush / Can't hold out / Spoonful / She fooled me / Time is on my side / Scratch my back / Long tall Shorty / Diddley daddy / Ain't got you / Caress my baby / Here's my picture / Chain of fools / Don't start crying now.

Feb 94. (cd) **WINE, WOMEN & WHISKEY** [ ] [-]
– Wine, women and whiskey / Sure look good to me / No questions / The amble / It's all over now / Bad boy / Spoonful (bare bones remix) / French champagne / My back scratcher / Can't hold out (big city remix) / Diddley daddy (street corner remix) / I'm cryin' / Gettin' all wet.

PRETTY THINGS 'N MATES (WITH MATTHEW FISHER)

featuring a plethora of famous cover versions

Kingdom / not issued

May 94. (cd) **A WHITER SHADE OF DIRTY WATER** [ ] [-]
– He's waitin' / Strychnine / Pushing too hard / Kicks / Candy / Louie, Louie / 96 tears / Let's talk about girls / Sometimes good guys don't wear black / I'm a man / Red river rock / Midnight to 6 man '93.

PRETTY THINGS

not issued / Medicine

1994. (7") **HAVANA BOUND. / RELIGION'S DEAD** [-] [ ]

— re-formed again 1995, **MAY, TAYLOR, POVEY, ALEN, ALAN + HOLLAND**

Fragile / not issued

Oct 95. (d-cd) **UNREPENTANT – BLOODY BUT UNBOWED** [ ] [-]
–

– compilations, others, etc. –

Dec 64. Fontana; (7"ep) **PRETTY THINGS** [ ] [-]

Aug 65. Fontana; (7"ep) **RAINING IN MY HEART** [ ] [-]

Jan 66. Fontana; (7"ep) **ON FILM** [ ] [-]

Jun 69. Fontana; (7") **ROSALYN. / DON'T BRING ME DOWN** [ ] [-]

1968. Phonogram; (lp) **GREATEST HITS** [ ] [-]
(cd-iss.1991 on 'Carnaby')

Jun 75. Harvest/ US= Rare Earth; (d-lp) **REAL PRETTY:- S.F. SORROW / PARACHUTE** [ ] [ ] 1976

Jul 77. Harvest; (lp) **SINGLES A's & B's** [ ] [-]

May 86. Harvest; (lp)(c) **CRIES FROM THE MIDNIGHT CIRCUS** (1968-1971) [ ] [-]

1976. Sire; (d-lp) **THE VINTAGE YEARS** [-] [ ]

1979. Butt; (lp) **ELECTRIC BANANA – THE SEVENTIES** [ ] [-]

(recordings 1973-78 / + from 'De Wolfe' label of late 60's)
Film music lp's:- 1967; ELECTRIC BANANA/ 1968; MORE ELECTRIC BANANA/ 1969; EVEN MORE ELECTRIC BANANA/ 1973; HOT LICKS/ 1978; THE RETURN OF THE ELECTRIC BANANA.

Mar 82. See For Miles; (lp)(c) **THE PRETTY THINGS 1967-1971** [ ] [-]
(cd-iss.Oct89)
Jul 82. Old Gold; (7") **DON'T BRING ME DOWN. / HONEY I NEED** [ ] [-]
Jun 84. Edsel; (lp) **LET ME HEAR THE CHOIR SING** [ ] [-]
Feb 86. Bam Caruso; (lp) **CLOSED RESTAURANT BLUES** [ ] [-]
Apr 92. Band Of Joy; (cd) **ON AIR** [ ] [-]
Mar 94. Spectrum; (cd)(c) **MIDNIGHT TO 6** [ ] [-]

PRIMAL SCREAM

Formed: Glasgow, Scotland . . . mid'84 by JESUS & MARY CHAIN drummer BOBBY GILLESPIE. Signed to up and coming indie label 'Creation' early '85, and made 2 singles there, which led to GILLESPIE leaving J&MC. After spending 1987 on WEA subsidiary label 'Elevation', they returned to 'Creation'. They finally hit the UK Top 20 singles chart with 'LOADED', in the early 90's. • **Style:** Influenced by 60's flower-power scene, which evolved into indie disco by the early 90's. • **Songwriters:** GILLESPIE, YOUNG and BEATTIE, until the latter's replacement by INNES. Covered CARRY ME HOME (Dennis Wilson) / UNDERSTANDING (Small Faces). • **Trivia:** In 1991, they re-located to Tennessee, USA, recording highly acclaimed album 'SCREAMADELICA' in the process.

Recommended: SCREAMADELICA (*10) / PRIMAL SCREAM (*8) / GIVE OUT BUT DON'T GIVE UP (*7).

BOBBY GILLESPIE (b.22 Jun'64) – vocals (ex-WAKE) (also drummer of JESUS & MARY CHAIN) / **JIM BEATTIE** – guitar / **ROBERT YOUNG** – bass / **TOM McGURK** – drums / **MARTIN ST.JOHN** – tambourine

Creation / not issued

May 85. (7") **ALL FALL DOWN. / IT HAPPENS** [ ] [-]

— added **PAUL HARTE** – rhythm guitar (GILLESPIE left JESUS & MARY)

Apr 86. (7") **CRYSTAL CRESCENT. / VELOCITY GIRL** [ ] [-]
(12"+=) – Spirea X.

— **STUART MAY** – rhythm guitar (ex-SUBMARINES) repl. HARTE (Dec86) / **ANDREW INNES** – rhythm guitar (of REVOLVING PAINT DREAM) repl. MAY / Guest drummers **PHIL KING** (studio) + **DAVE MORGAN** (tour) repl. McGURK

Elevation / not issued

Jun 87. (7") **GENTLE TUESDAY. / BLACK STAR CARNIVAL** [ ] [-]
(12"+=) – I'm gonna make you mine.
Sep 87. (7") **IMPERIAL. / STAR FRUIT SURF RIDER** [ ] [-]
(12"+=) – So sad about us / Imperial (demo).
Oct 87. (lp)(c) **SONIC FLOWER GROOVE** [62] [ ]
– Gentle Tuesday / Treasure trip / May the sun shine bright for you / Sonic sister love / Silent spring / Imperial / Love you / Leaves / Aftermath / We go down slowly. *(re-iss.Jul91)*

— (Jun87) **GAVIN SKINNER** – drums repl. ST.JOHN

— (Feb88) Now a trio **GILLESPIE, YOUNG + INNES** augmented by **JIM NAVAJO** – guitar. (BEATTIE formed SPIREA X, and SKINNER also left)

— (Feb89) added **HENRY OLSEN** – bass (ex-NICO) / **PHILIP 'TOBY' TOMANOV** – drums (ex-NICO, ex-DURUTTI COLUMN, ex-BLUE ORCHIDS)

Creation / Sire

Jul 89. (7") **IVY, IVY, IVY. / YOU'RE JUST TOO DARK TO CARE** [ ] [ ]
(12"+=)(cd-s+=) – I got you split wide open over me.
Sep 89. (lp)(c)(cd) **PRIMAL SCREAM** [ ] [ ]
– Ivy, Ivy, Ivy / You're just dead skin to me / She power / You're just too dark to care / I'm losing more than I'll ever have / Gimme gimme teenage head / Lone star girl / Kill the king / Sweet pretty thing / Jesus can't save me. *(free 7"ltd.)* – SPLIT WIDE OPEN (demo). / LONE STAR GIRL (demo)

— Trimmed to a trio again (**GILLESPIE, YOUNG + INNES**)

Feb 90. (7") **LOADED. / I'M LOSING MORE THAN I'LL EVER HAVE** [16] [ ]
(12")(cd-s) – ('A'-Terry Farley extended remix) / Rambling Rose (live).
Jul 90. (7") **COME TOGETHER (Terry Farley remix). / COME TOGETHER (Andrew Weatherall mix)** [26] [ ]
(12"+=)(cd-s+=) – ('A'extended).
Jun 91. (7")(12") **HIGHER THAN THE SUN. / ('A' American mix)** [40] [ ]
(cd-s+=) – Higher than the Orb.

— guest spot on above 'A' by **JAH WOBBLE** – bass

Aug 91. (7")(12") **DON'T FIGHT IT, FEEL IT. / ('A'scat mix)** [41] [ ]
(cd-s+=) – ('A'extended version).
('A'vocals **DENISE JOHNSON**)
Sep 91. (cd)(c)(d-lp) **SCREAMADELICA** [8] [ ]
– Movin' on up / Slip inside this house / Don't fight it, feel it / Higher than the Sun / Inner flight / Come together / Loaded / Damaged / I'm comin' down / Higher than the Sun (a dub symphony in two parts) / Shine like stars.
Jan 92. (7"ep)(c-ep) **DIXIE NARCO** [11] [ ]
– Movin' on up / Carry me home / Screamadelica.
(12"ep+=)(cd-ep+=) – Stone my soul.

— In Jan'94, MARTIN DUFFY was stabbed in Memphis, although he recovered.

— Line-up:- **GILLESPIE, YOUNG, INNES, DUFFY + DAVID HOOD + DENISE JOHNSON** + guest **GEORGE CLINTON** – vocals

Mar 94. (7")(c-s) **ROCKS. / FUNKY JAM** [7] [ ]
(12")(cd-s) – ('A'side) / Funky jam (hot ass mix) / Funky jam (club).
Apr 94. (cd)(c)(lp) **GIVE OUT BUT DON'T GIVE UP** [2] [ ]
– Jailbird / Rocks / (I'm gonna) Cry myself blind / Funky jam / Big jet plane / Free / Call on me / Struttin' / Sad and blue / Give out but don't give up / I'll be there for you.
Jun 94. (7")(c-s) **JAILBIRD. / ('A'-Dust Brothers mix)** [29] [ ]
(12"+=) – ('A'-Toxic Trio stay free mix) / ('A'-Weatherall dub chapter 3 mix).
(cd-s++=) – ('A'-Sweeney 2 mix).
Nov 94. (7")(c-s) **(I'M GONNA) CRY MYSELF BLIND (George Drakoulias mix). / ROCKS (live)** [51] [ ]
(cd-s+=) – I'm losing more than I'll ever have (live) / Struttin' (back in our minds) (Brendan Lynch remix).
(10") – ('A'side) / Struttin' (back in our minds) (Brendan Lynch remix) / Give out but don't give up (Portishead remix) / Rockers dub (Kris Needs mix).

. . . Jan – Jun '96 stop press . . .

PRIMAL SCREAM, IRVINE WELSH & ON-U-SOUND

Jun 96. (single) **THE BIG MAN AND THE SCREAM TEAM MEET THE BARMY ARMY UPTOWN** [17] [ ]

PRIMUS

Formed: Bay Area, San Francisco, USA . . . mid-80's by LEE CLAYPOOL and TODD HUTH initially as PRIMATE until the late 80's. During the early 90's, they were regular guests of MTV, while signing big time to 'Interscope'. • **Style:** Psychedelic and experimental polka /thrash-funk, trio similar to a very bassy RED HOT CHILI PEPPERS, but with weird humour staccato-snorkle vox of CLAYPOOL whose sound could fuse elements of TALKING HEADS, VERY THINGS or STUMP. • **Songwriters:** CLAYPOOL except; MAKING PLANS FOR NIGEL (XTC). • **Trivia:** TOM WAITS guests on their 1991 album.

Recommended: SAILING THE SEAS OF CHEESE (*8) / PORK SODA (*9)

LEE CLAYPOOL – vocals, bass / LARRY LALONDE – guitar repl. TODD HUTH who joined BLIND ILLUSION / **JAY LANE** – drums, repl. drum machine

not issued / Prawnsong

1989. (lp) **SUCK ON THIS (live)** [ ] [ ]
– John the fisherman / Groundhog's day / The heckler / Pressman / Jelikit / Tommy the cat / Pudding time / Harold of the rocks / Frizzle fry. *(UK-iss.cd+c Mar92 on 'Interscope-Atlantic')*

— **TIM 'HERB' ALEXANDER** – drums repl. JAY who joined SAUSAGE

Virgin / Caroline

Jul 90. (cd)(c)(lp) **FRIZZLE FRY** [ ] [ ]
– To defy the laws of tradition / Ground hog's day / Too many puppies / Mr.Know-it-all / Frizzle fry / John the fisherman / You can't kill Michael Malloy / The toys go winding down / Pudding time / Sathington Willoby / Spaghetti western / Harold of the rocks / To defy.

Atlantic / Interscope

May 91. (cd)(c)(lp) **SAILING THE SEAS OF CHEESE** [ ] [ ]
– Seas of cheese / Here come the bastards / Sgt. Baker / American life / Jerry was a race car driver / Eleven / Is it luck? / Grandad's lil ditty / Tommy the cat / Sathington waltz / Those damned blue collar tweekers / Fish on / Los bastardos. *(re-iss.Feb95)*
Jun 92. (7"ep)(cd-ep) **CHEESY EP 1 (US title 'MISCELLANEOUS DEBRIS')** [ ] [ ]
– Making plans for Nigel / Tommy the cat / Tippy toes / Have a cigar.
(cd-s'CHEESY 2') – (1st 2 tracks) / Sinister exaggerator / Intruder.

Interscope / Interscope

May 93. (cd)(c)(lp) **PORK SODA** [56] [7]
– Pork chop's little ditty / My name is mud / Welcome to this world / Bob / D.M.V. / The ol' Diamondback sturgeon (Fisherman's chronicles, part 3) / Nature boy / Wounded Knee / Pork soda / The pressman / Mr.Krinkle / The air is getting slippery / Hamburger train / Pork chop's little ditty / Hail Santa.
Jun 95. (cd)(c) **TALES FROM THE PUNCHBOWL** [ ] [8]
– Professor Nutbutter's house of treats / Mrs. Blaileen / Wynona's big brown beaver / Southbound pachydern / Space farm / Year of the parrot / Hellbound 17

1/2 (theme from) / Glass sandwich / Del Davis tree farm / De Anza jig / On the tweak again / Over the electric grapevine / Captain Shiner.

PRINCE

Born: PRINCE ROGERS NELSON, 7 Jun'58, Minneapolis, Minnesota, USA. Named so after his father's jazz band The PRINCE ROGER TRIO, who featured his mother Mattie on vocals. When his parents divorced, he was taken to a JAMES BROWN concert in 1968 (an experience to influence his future solo work), by his stepfather. In 1970, he absconded from home to sleep rough while also finding father. He taught him guitar, and was eventually adopted by the ANDERSON family, whose son ANDRE (later ANDRE CYMONE) became friend. At this time, PRINCE learnt numerous other instruments and found he had writing ability. In 1972, he was invited to play in cousin CHARLES SMITH's junior high school band GRAND CENTRAL. The following year, they became CHAMPAGNE, with PRINCE becoming leader after SMITH was replaced by MORRIS DAY. In 1976, he sessioned guitar for Sound 80 studios' PEPE WILLIE. At this time he made a demo for producer Chris Moon, who also taught him studio skills. In 1977, PRINCE landed a solo deal with 'Warners', which gave him control of production, etc. The following year, his debut 'FOR YOU' was finally released and started the steady road to superstardom. In the late 70's, he had first US Top 30 album with 'PRINCE', which contained a near Top 10 single 'I WANNA BE YOUR LOVER' and a future No.1 for CHAKA KHAN; 'I FEEL FOR YOU'. By the mid-80's, PRINCE had become one of the world's top stars, especially after near biographical film 'PURPLE RAIN' and its soundtrack, smashed into No.1 spot. At this time, he also formed own record company 'Paisley P.', to issue not just his records, but also for friends The FAMILY, SHEILA E., GEORGE CLINTON, etc. In 1988, he mysteriously recalled his 'BLACK ALBUM' from its German pressing plant, and shelved album although many copies were bootlegged. • **Style:** Moved from R&B disco-funk multi-instrumentalist to experimental pop-rock artist, whose erotic sexy stage routines were likened to JAMES BROWN or MICHAEL JACKSON. • **Songwriters:** Prolific pensmith writing, unusually for the 80's, an album a year. He also wrote songs under pseudonyms CAMILLE, JAMIE STARR, CHRISTOPHER, etc., and has written hits especially for SHEENA EASTON (Sugar Walls) and BANGLES (Manic Monday). Note: WENDY AND LISA wrote 'MOUNTAINS' before departing for own duo. • **Trivia:** In 1988, his sister TYKA NELSON signed for 'Chrysalis', and issued poor selling album. **Filmography:** PURPLE RAIN (1984) / UNDER THE CHERRY MOON (1986) / GRAFFITI BRIDGE (1990). He also wrote score for BATMAN (1989).

Recommended: SIGN 'O' THE TIMES (*9) / PARADE (*8) / LOVESEXY (*8) / 1999 (*8) / PURPLE RAIN (*8) / DIAMONDS AND PEARLS (*8) / THE HITS 1 (*9) / THE HITS 2 (*9) / SYMBOL (*8) / MUSIC FROM GRAFITTI BRIDGE (*8).

PRINCE – vocals, multi-instrumentalist, synthesizers, producer, everything

Warners Warners

Oct 78. (lp)(c) **FOR YOU** [-] [ ]
– For you / In love / Soft and wet / Crazy you / Just as long as we're together / Baby / My love is forever / So blue / I'm yours. *(UK-iss.Sep86, cd-iss. Oct87)*

Nov 78. (7") **SOFT AND WET. / SO BLUE** [-] [92]

Jan 79. (7") **JUST AS LONG AS WE'RE TOGETHER. / IN LOVE** [-] [ ]

—— **PRINCE** – vocals, guitar live back-ups **DEZ DICKERSON** – guitar / **GAYLE CHAPMAN** – keyboards / **ANDRE CYMONE** – bass / **MATT FINK** – keyboards / **BOBBY Z** – drums

Nov 79. (7") **I WANNA BE YOUR LOVER. / MY LOVE IS FOREVER** [-] [11]

Dec 79. (7")(12") **I WANNA BE YOUR LOVER. / JUST AS LONG AS WE'RE TOGETHER** [41] [-] Nov 79

Jan 80. (lp)(c) **PRINCE** [ ] [22] Oct 79
– I wanna be your lover / Why you wanna treat me so bad? / Sexy dancer / When we're dancing close and slow / With you / Bambi / Still waiting / I feel for you / It's gonna be lonely.

Feb 80. (7") **WHY YOU WANNA TREAT ME SO BAD?. / BAD** [-] [ ]

—— (Feb80) live **LISA COLEMAN** – keyboards repl. GAYLE

Apr 80. (7")(12") **SEXY DANCER. / BAMBI** [ ] [-]

May 80. (7") **STILL WAITING. / BAMBI** [-] [ ]

Sep 80. (7") **UPTOWN. / CRAZY YOU** [-] [ ]

Oct 80. (lp)(c) **DIRTY MIND** [ ] [45]
– Dirty mind / When you were mine / Do it all night / Gotta broken heart again / Uptown / Head / Sister / Party up. *((re-iss.1989) (cd-iss.Dec85)*

Nov 80. (7") **DIRTY MIND. / WHEN WE'RE DANCING CLOSE AND SLOW** [-] [ ]

Mar 81. (7")(12") **DO IT ALL NIGHT. / HEAD** [ ] [-]

Jun 81. (7") **GOTTA STOP (MESSIN' ABOUT). / UPTOWN (live)** [ ] [-]
(12"+=) – Head (live).
(12") – ('A'side) / I wanna be your lover (live).

—— (mid'81) live **BROWN MARK** – bass repl. ANDRE who ventured solo

Oct 81. (7")(12") **CONTROVERSY. / WHEN YOU WERE MINE** [ ] [70]

Nov 81. (lp)(c) **CONTROVERSY** [ ] [21]
– Controversy / Sexuality / Do me, baby / Private joy / Ronnie talk to Russia / Let's work / Annie Christian / Jack u off. *(cd-iss.1984)*

Apr 82. (7")(12") **LET'S WORK. / RONNIE TALK TO RUSSIA** [ ] [-]

Jun 82. (7") **DO ME, BABY. / PRIVATE JOY** [-] [ ]

PRINCE & THE REVOLUTION

live **WENDY MELVOIN** – guitar repl. DEE

Jan 83. (7") **1999. / HOW COME U DON'T CALL ME ANYMORE** [25] [44] Oct 82
(free c-s w/7") – 1999 / Controversy. / Dirty mind / Sexuality.
(12"+=) – D.M.S.R. *(US re-dist.Jun83 hit No.12)*

Feb 83. (lp)(c) **1999** [ ] [26]
– 1999 / Little red Corvette / Delirious / Let's pretend we're married / D.M.S.R. * / Delirious / Automatic / Something in the water / Free / Lady cab driver / All the critics love u in New York / International lover. *(re-iss.Nov83 as d-lp/d-c, hit UK No.30 in Sep84 +cd.omits *)*

Feb 83. (7") **LITTLE RED CORVETTE. / ALL THE CRITICS LOVE U IN NEW YORK** [-] [6]

Apr 83. (7") **LET'S PRETEND WE'RE MARRIED. / IRRESISTIBLE BITCH** [-] [52]

Apr 83. (7") **LITTLE RED CORVETTE. / LADY CAB DRIVER** [54] [-]
(12") – ('A'extended) / Automatic lover / International lover.

Sep 83. (7") **DELIRIUS. / HORNY TOAD** [-] [8]

Sep 83. (7")(12") **LET'S PRETEND WE'RE MARRIED. / ALL THE CRITICS LOVE U IN NEW YORK** [ ] [-]

Nov 83. (7") **LITTLE RED CORVETTE. / HORNY TOAD** [66] [ ]
('A'extended-12"+=) – D.M.S.R.

Jun 84. (7")(12") **WHEN DOVES CRY. / 17 DAYS** [4] [1] May84
(d12"+=)(c-s+=) – 1999 / D.M.S.R.

Jul 84. (lp)(c)(cd)(purple-lp) **PURPLE RAIN** (Music From The Motion Picture) [7] [1]
– Let's go crazy / Take me with u / The beautiful ones / Computer blue / Darling Nikki / When doves cry / I would die 4 U / Baby I'm a star / Purple rain. (US-iss.as d-lp, w / += tracks by The TIME + APOLLONIA 6) *(re-iss.Jan92 hit UK No.59) (re-iss.cd/c Feb95)*

Jul 84. (7") **LET'S GO CRAZY. / EROTIC CITY** [-] [1]

Sep 84. (7")(7"sha-pic-d) **PURPLE RAIN. / GOD** [8] [2]
(12") – ('A'side) / ('A'vocal + instrumental).

Nov 84. (7") **I WOULD DIE 4 U. / ANOTHER LONELY CHRISTMAS** [58] [8]
(12"+=)/ /(12") – Free./ / ('A'&'B' US remixes).

Jan 85. (7")(12") **1999. / LITTLE RED CORVETTE** [2] [-]
(free c-s w/7"+=) – 1999 / Uptown / Controversy / D.M.S.R. / Sexy dancer.

Feb 85. (7") **LET'S GO CRAZY. / TAKE ME WITH U** [7] [-]
('A'extended-12"+=) – Erotic city.

Feb 85. (7") **TAKE ME WITH U. / BABY I'M A STAR** [-] [25]

—— added live **SHEILA E.** (b.ESCOVEDO) – percussion, vocals / **ERIC LEEDS** – saxophone

Paisley P. Paisley P.

Apr 85. (lp)(c)(cd) **AROUND THE WORLD IN A DAY** [5] [1]
– Around the world in a day / Paisley Park / Condition of the heart / Raspberry beret / Tambourine / America / Pop life / The ladder / Temptation.

May 85. (7")(7"sha-pic-d) **PAISLEY PARK. / SHE'S ALWAYS IN MY HAIR** [18] [2]
(12"+=)/ /(12"++=) – ('A'extended)./ / ('B'extended).

May 85. (7") **RASPBERRY BERET. / SHE'S ALWAYS IN MY HAIR** [-] [2]

Jul 85. (7") **RASPBERRY BERET. / HELLO** [25] [-]

Jul 85. (7") **POP LIFE. / HELLO** [-] [7]
(12") – ('A'&'B'extended remixes).

Oct 85. (7") **AMERICA. / GIRL** [-] [46]

Oct 85. (7")('A'ext-12") **POP LIFE. / GIRL** [60] [-]

Feb 86. (7")(7"pic-d)('A'ext-12") **KISS. / LOVE OR MONEY** [6] [1]

Apr 86. (lp)(c)(cd)(pic-lp) **PARADE (Music from the film 'Under The Cherry Moon')** [4] [3]
– Christopher Tracey's parade / New position / I wonder u / Under the cherry moon / Girls and boys / Life can be so nice / Venus de Milo / Mountains / Do u lie / Kiss / Anotherloverholdenyohead / Sometimes it snows in April.

May 86. (7") **MOUNTAINS. / ALEXA DE PARIS** [45] [23]
(10"white)(12") – ('A'&'B'extended).

Aug 86. (7")(7"sha-pic-d) **GIRLS AND BOYS (edit). / UNDER THE CHERRY MOON** [11] [ ]
(12"+=) – Erotic city.
(d7"+=) – She's always in my hair / 17 days.

Oct 86. (7") **ANOTHERLOVERHOLDENYOHEAD. / GIRLS AND BOYS** [-] [63]

Oct 86. (7") **ANOTHERLOVERHOLDENYOHEAD. / I WANNA BE YOUR LOVER** [36] [-]

SLAVE

('A'ext-12")(12"pic-d) – (same tracks).
(d7"+=) – Mountains / Alexa de Paris.

PRINCE

solo, without WENDY & LISA who formed own duo. He retained live **FINK, LEEDS & SHEILA E.** adding **MICO WEAVER** – guitar / **BONI BOYER** – keyboards / **LEVI STEACER JR.** – bass / **CAT GLOVER** – dancer, vocals

Mar 87. (7") **SIGN 'O' THE TIMES. / LA LA LA LA HE HE HE HE** [10] [3]
(12")(12"pic-d) – ('A'&'B'extended).

Mar 87. (d-lp)(c)(cd) **SIGN 'O' THE TIMES** [4] [6]
– Sign 'o' the times / Play in the sunshine / Housequake / Ballad of Dorothy Parker / It / Starfish and coffee / Slow love / Hot thing / Forever in my life / U got the look / If I was your girlfriend / Strange relationship / I could never take the place of your man / The cross / It's gonna be a beautiful night / Adore.

Jun 87. (7")(c-s)(7"peach)(ext-12")(ext.12"pic-d) **IF I WAS YOUR GIRLFRIEND. / SHOCKADELICA** [20] [ ] May 87

— (next 'A'side featured backing vocals by ex-Scots solo artist SHEENA EASTON now living in California with all her well-invested millions!)

Aug 87. (7")(c-s) **U GOT THE LOOK. / HOUSEQUAKE** [11] [2] Jul 87
('B'ext-12"+=)(12"pic-d+=) – ('A'long version).

Nov 87. (7")(c-s) **I COULD NEVER TAKE THE PLACE OF YOUR MAN. / HOT THING** [29] [10]
(12"+=)(12"pic-d+=) – ('B'extended).

Feb 88. (7") **HOT THING. /** [-] [63]

Apr 88. (7")(c-s) **ALPHABET ST. / THIS IS NOT MUSIC, THIS IS A TRIP** [9] [8]
(12")(cd-s) – ('A'&'B'extended).

May 88. (lp)(c)(cd) **LOVESEXY** [1] [11]
– I no / Alphabet St. / Glam slam / Anna Stesia / Dance on / Lovesexy / When 2 r in love / I wish U Heaven / Positivity. *(re-iss.cd/c Feb95)*

Jul 88. (7")(12") **GLAM SLAM. / ESCAPE** [29] [ ]
(cd-s+=) – Escape (free yo mind from this rat race).

Oct 88. (7") **I WISH U HEAVEN. / SCARLET PUSSY (by 'Camille')** [24] [ ]
(12"+=)(cd-s+=) – ('A' pts.2 & 3).

Jun 89. (7")(c-s)('A'ext-12")(c-s)(cd-s)(3"cd-s)(12"pic-d) **BATDANCE. / 200 BALLOONS** [2] [1]
(12"+=) – ('A'batmix) / ('B'side) / ('A' Vicki Vale mix).

Jun 89. (lp)(c)(cd)(pic-lp) **BATMAN** [1] [1]
– The future / Electric chair / The arms of Orion / Partyman / Vicki waiting / Trust / Lemon crush / Scandalous / Batdance. *(re-iss.cd/c Feb95)*

Aug 89. (7")(c-s)('A'remix-12")('A'ext-12") **PARTYMAN. / FEEL U UP** [14] [18]
(12"pic-d)(cd-s) – ('A'video mix). / ('B'long stroke mix)

Oct 89. (7")(c-s) **THE ARMS OF ORION. ("PRINCE & SHEENA EASTON") / I LUV U IN ME** [27] [36]
(12"+=)(cd-s+=)(12"pic-d+=) – ('A'extended).

— live **PATRICE RUSHDEN** – keyboards (solo artist) repl. BOYER + GLOVER / **MICHAEL BLAND** – drums repl. SHEILA E. / **CANDY DULFER** – saxophone repl. LEEDS

Jul 90. (7")(c-s) **THIEVES IN THE TEMPLE. / (Part 2)** [7] [6]
(12")(cd-s)(12"pic-d) – ('A'side) / ('A'remix) / ('A'dub version).

Aug 90. (cd)(c)(d-lp) **MUSIC FROM GRAFFITI BRIDGE (soundtrack)** [1] [6]
– Can't stop this feeling I got / New power generation / The question of U / Elephants and flowers / Joy in repetition / Tick, tock, bang / Thieves in the temple. *(also other tracks by 'The TIMES' etc.)*

Oct 90. (7")(c-s) **NEW POWER GENERATION. / (Part 2)** [26] [64]
(12"+=)(cd-s+=)(12"pic-d+=) – Melody cool (extended remix).

PRINCE & THE NEW POWER GENERATION

with **LEVI SEACER JR.** – guitar, vox / **TOMMY BARBARELLA** – keys, synths / **SONNY T.** – bass, vox / **ROSIE GAINES** – co-vocals, organ, synths / **MICHAEL B.** – drums / **TONY M.** – rap/vox / **KIRKY JOHNSON** – perc., vox / **DAMON DICKSON** – perc., vox.

Aug 91. (7")(c-s) **GETT OFF (remix). / HORNY PONY** [4] [21]
(12"+=)/ /(cd-s+=) – ('A'thrust mix)./ / ('A'purple pump mix).
(above: as a m-lp, its US import hit UK chart! at No.33)

Sep 91. (7")(c-s) **CREAM. / HORNY PONY** [15] [1]
(12"+=)(cd-s+=) – Gangster glam.

Sep 91. (cd)(c)(d-lp) **DIAMONDS AND PEARLS** [2] [3]
– Thunder / Daddy pop / Diamonds and pearls / Cream / Strollin' / Willing and able / Gett off / Walk don't walk / Jughead / Money don't matter 2 night / Push / Insatiable / Live 4 love. *(re-iss.cd/c Feb95)*

Nov 91. (7") **DIAMONDS AND PEARLS. / LAST DANCE** [25] [4]
(cd-s+=) – 2 the wire (Grammy instrumental) / Do you dance (remix).

Dec 91. (c-s) **INSATIABLE. / I LOVE YOU IN ME** [-] [77]

Mar 92. (7")(c-s)(cd-s) **MONEY DON'T MATTER 2 NIGHT. / CALL THE LAW** [19] [23]
(12"+=) – Push.

Jun 92. (7")(c-s) **THUNDER. / VIOLET THE ORGAN DRIVER** [28] [ ]
(12"+=)(cd-s+=)(12"pic-d+=) – Gett off (thrust dub).

— **MAYTE** – vocals repl. ROSIE

Jul 92. (7")(c-s) **SEXY M.F. / STROLLIN'** [4] [66]
(12"+=)(cd-s+=) – Daddy Pop.

Sep 92. (7")(c-s) **MY NAME IS PRINCE. / 2 WHOM IT MAY CONCERN** [7] [36]
(12"+=)/ /(cd-s++=) – Sexy mutha./ / ('A'extra mix).

Nov 92. (12")(cd-s) **MY NAME IS PRINCE (remixes). / (other mixes)** [51] [ ]

Oct 92. (cd)(c)(d-lp) **(SYMBOL)** [1] [5]
– My name is Prince / Sexy MF / Love 2 the 9's / The morning papers / The Max / Segue / Blue light / I wanna melt with U / Sweet baby / The continental / Dawn U / Arrogance / The flow / 7 / And God created woman / 3 chains o' gold / Segue / The sacrifice of Victor.

Nov 92. (7")(c-s) **7. / 7 (mix)** [27] [7]
(cd-s+=) – ('A'other mixes).

Mar 93. (7")(c-s) **THE MORNING PAPERS. / LIVE FOR LOVE** [52] [44]
(cd-s+=) – Love 2 the 9's.

Sep 93. (cd)(c)(d-lp) **THE HITS 1** (compilation) [5] [46]
– When doves cry / Pop life / Soft and wet / I feel for you / Why you wanna treat me so bad? / When you were mine / Uptown / Let's go crazy / 1999 / I could never take the place of your man / Nothing compares 2 U / Adore / Pink cashmere / Alphabet St. / Sign 'o' the times / Thieves in the temple / Diamonds and pearls / 7.

Sep 93. (cd)(c)(d-lp) **THE HITS 2** (compilation) [5] [54]
– Controversy / Dirty mind / I wanna be your lover / Head / Do me, baby / Delirious / Little red Corvette / I would die 4 U / Raspberry beret / If I was your girlfriend / Kiss / Peach / U got the look / Sexy M.F. / Gett off / Cream / Pope / Purple rain.

Sep 93. (3xcd)(3xc) **THE HITS / THE B-SIDES** [4] [19]
– (all of above plus corresponding 'B'sides)
+ Hello / 200 ballooons / Escape / Gotta stop (messin' about) / Horny toad / Feel u up / Girl / I love u in me / Erotic city / Shockadelica / Irresistable bitch / Scarlet pussy / La, la, la, he, he, hee / She's always in my hair / 17 days / How come u don't call me anymore / Another lonely Christmas / God / Tears in your eyes / Power fantastic.

Sep 93. (c-s) **PINK CASHMERE. / ?** [-] [50]

Oct 93. (7")(c-s) **PEACH. / WISH U HEAVEN** [14] [-]
(cd-s+=) – Girls & boys / My name is Prince.
(cd-s) – ('A'side) / Money don't matter 2 nite / Partyman / Mountains.

Dec 93. (7"pic-d)(c-s) **CONTROVERSY. / THE FUTURE** [5] [-]
(cd-s) – ('A'side) / The future (remix) / Glam slam / D.M.S.R.
(cd-s) – ('A'side) / Paisley Park / Anotherloverholenyohead / New power generation.

Mar 94. (7")(c-s) **THE MOST BEAUTIFUL GIRL IN THE WORLD. / BEAUTIFUL** [1] [3]
(12"+=)(cd-s+=) – ('A'mixes).

May 94. (cd)(c)(m-lp) **THE BEAUTIFUL EXPERIENCE** [18] [92]
– (7 versions of last single)

— Musicians: **PRINCE / MICHAEL B. / SONNY T. / TOMMY BARBARELLA / MR.HAYES / MAYLE**

Aug 94. (cd)(c)(lp) **COME** [1] [15]
– Come / Space / Pheromone / Loose! / Papa / Race / Dark / Solo / Letitgo / Orgasm.

Aug 94. (7"pic-d+c-s) **LETITGO. / SOLO** [30] [31]
(cd-s+=) – Alexa de Paris / Pope.

Mar 95. (cd-ep) **PURPLE MEDLEY / PURPLE MEDLEY (extended)/ PURPLE MEDLEY (Kirk J's B-side remix)** [33] [84]

NEW POWER GENERATION

Due to contractual problems with Warners (only allowed 1 album a year), PRINCE (aka SLAVE/ VICTOR/ THE ARTIST FORMERLY KNOWN AS . . ./TORA TORA) took to wearing a mask on stage, etc (or was it him?)

N.P.G. N.P.G.

Mar 95. (7"ep)(c-ep)(12"ep)(cd-ep) **GET WILD / BEAUTIFUL GIRL (sax version) / HALLUCINATION RAIN** [ ] [ ]

Apr 95. (cd)(c)(lp) **EXODUS** [11] [ ]
– N.P.G. operator intro / Get wild / Segue / DJ gets jumped / New power soul / DJ seduces Sonny / Segue / Count the days / The good life / Cherry, Cherry / Segue / Return of the bump squad / Mashed potato girl intro / Segue / Big fun / New power day / Segue / Hallucination rain / N.P.G. bum rush the ship / The exodus has begun / Outro.

Aug 95. (c-s) **THE GOOD LIFE /** [29] [ ]
(cd-s)(12") –

Oct 95. (c-s) **COUNT THE DAYS /** [ ] [ ]
(cd-s) –

PRINCE (symbol)

or T.A.F.K.A.P. (The Artist Formerly Known As PRINCE)

Warner-NPG Warner-NPG

Sep 95. (c-s) **EYE HATE U /** [20] [12]
(cd-s) –

Sep 95. (cd)(c)(lp) **THE GOLD EXPERIENCE** [4] [6]

– P control / npq operator / Endorphinmachine / Shhh / We march / npq operator / The most beautiful girl in the world / Dolphin / npq operator / Now / npq operator / 319 / npq operator / Shy / Billy Jack bitch / Eye hate u / npq operator / Gold.

Nov 95. (c-s) **GOLD / ROCK AND ROLL IS ALIVE! (AND IT LIVES IN MINNEAPOLIS)** 10 58
(cd-s+=) – Eye hate U (extended remix).

. . . Jan – Jun '96 stop press . . .

— In Apr 96, he wrote music for the film soundtrack 'GIRL 6' hit US 75

— Has handed in his official notice to quit the 'Warners' company and given them their three due albums.

- compilations, others, etc. -

Oct 88. WEA; (cd-s) **WHEN DOVES CRY / PURPLE RAIN**
Oct 88. WEA; (cd-s) **LET'S GO CRAZY (extended) / TAKE ME WITH U**
Oct 88. WEA; (cd-s) **LITTLE RED CORVETTE (dance mix) / 1999 (extended)**
Oct 88. WEA; (cd-s) **KISS / GIRLS AND BOYS / UNDER THE CHERRY MOON**
Nov 94. Warners; (cd)(c) **THE BLACK ALBUM** (finally released!) 36 47
– Le grind / Cindy C. / Dead on it / When 2 R in love / Bob George / Superfunkycalifragisexy / 2 nigs united for West Compton / Rockhard in a funky place.

PROCOL HARUM

Formed: Southend, Essex, England ... 1959 as The PARAMOUNTS, by five schoolboys; BOB SCOTT – vocals / GARY BROOKER – keyboards / ROBIN TROWER – guitar / CHRIS COPPING – bass / MICK BROWNLEE – drums. They played a number of local gigs, and GARY soon took over vocal chores, when SCOTT didn't turn up. In 1962, they left school and acquired manager Peter Martin. The following year with a few personnel changes, they signed to EMI's 'Parlophone' label, and soon hit the UK Top 40 with Coasters R&B cover 'POISON IVY'. Their follow-up of Thurston Harris's 'LITTLE BITTY PRETTY ONE', failed to emulate debut, and after a few more covers, they folded late summer '66. Note other covers:- I FEEL GOOD ALL OVER (Drifters) / I'M THE ONE WHO LOVES YOU (Major Lance) / BAD BLOOD (Coasters) / BLUE RIBBONS (Jackie DeShannon) / CUTTIN' IN (Johnny Guitar Watson) / YOU'VE NEVER HAD IT SO GOOD (P.F.Sloan). In 1967, BROOKER and lyricist KEITH REID, advertised in the Melody Maker for musicians, and soon settled with FISHER, ROYER, KNIGHTS and HARRISON. They became PROCOL HARUM (taking name from Latin "procul" meaning "far from these things"), and with help from producer Denny Cordell, unleashed mesmeric debut 45 'A WHITER SHADE OF PALE' for 'Deram'. It soon sold over half a million copies in the UK and stayed at No.1 for 6 weeks. With pressures to tour, ROYER and HARRISON departed from group, and were deposed by former PARAMOUNTS; TROWER and WILSON. Later in 1967, they moved with producer CORDELL, to 'Regal Zono.', and had another smash hit 'HOMBURG'. In 1969, the band line-up was same as The PARAMOUNTS of 1963, having brought back COPPING to replace management bound FISHER and KNIGHTS. In the 70's PROCOL HARUM continued to have album success, more so in the States and Canada. • **Style:** Gothic pop-rock outfit, who were never quite unpigeonholed from classical rock tag, although bluesy sounding BROOKER tried hard to disperse this. Mystical surreal lyrics were provided by non-playing member KEITH REID, until 1975. • **Songwriters:** BROOKER wrote music, except; A WHITER SHADE OF PALE (adapted from J.S.Bach's 'Suite No.3 in D Major (Air On The G String) / I KEEP FORGETTING (Leiber & Stoller; producers of 1975 lp) / EIGHT DAYS A WEEK (Beatles). • **Trivia:** CHRIS THOMAS produced their 3 albums in the early 70's.

Recommended: THE COLLECTION (*8) / BROKEN BARRICADES (*7).

PARAMOUNTS

GARY BROOKER (b.29 May'45) – vocals, keyboards / **ROBIN TROWER** (b. 9 Mar'45) – guitar / **DIZ DERRICK** – bass repl. CHRIS COPPING who went to Leicester University (Sep63) / **B.J. WILSON** (b.18 Mar'47) – drums repl. MICK BROWNLEE (Jan63).

Parlophone not issued

Dec 63. (7") **POISON IVY. / I FEEL GOOD ALL OVER** 35 -
Feb 64. (7") **LITTLE BIT PRETTY ONE. / A CERTAIN GIRL** -
Mar 64. (7"ep) **THE PARAMOUNTS** (see above 4 tracks) -
Jun 64. (7") **I'M THE ONE WHO LOVES YOU. / IT WON'T BE LONG** -
Nov 64. (7") **BAD BLOOD. / DO I** -
Mar 65. (7") **BLUE RIBBONS. / CUTTIN' IN** -
Oct 65. (7") **YOU'VE NEVER HAD IT SO GOOD. / DON'T YA LIKE MA LOVE** -

PROCOL HARUM

BROOKER with also **MATTHEW FISHER** (b. 7 Mar'46) – organ (ex-SCREAMING LORD SUTCH) / **RAY ROYER** (b. 8 Oct'45) – guitar / **DAVE KNIGHTS** (b.28 Jun'45) – bass / **BOBBY HARRISON** (b.28 Jun'43) – drums / **KEITH REID** (b.10 Oct'46) – lyrics

Deram Deram

May 67. (7") **A WHITER SHADE OF PALE. / LIME STREET BLUES** 1 5
(re-iss. US Jan 73 on 'A&M')

— **ROBIN TROWER** – guitar (ex-PARAMOUNTS) repl. ROYER who formed FREEDOM / **B.J. WILSON** – drums (ex-PARAMOUNTS) repl. HARRISON who also formed FREEDOM

Regal Zono. A & M

Sep 67. (7") **HOMBURG. / GOOD CAPTAIN CLACK** 6 34
(re-iss.Oct75 on 'Cube')

Dec 67. (lp) **PROCOL HARUM** (US-version w/the 2 single tracks) 47 Sep 67
– A whiter shade of pale / Conquistador / She wandered through the garden fence / Something following me / Mabel / Cerdes (outside the gate of) / Homburg / Christmas camel / Kaleidoscope / Salad days / Good Captain Clack / Repent Walpurgis. *(re-iss.+c.May85 as 'A WHITER SHADE OF PALE' on 'Sierra')*

Apr 68. (7") **QUITE RIGHTLY SO. / IN THE WEE SMALL HOURS OF SIXPENCE** 50

Dec 68. (lp) **SHINE ON BRIGHTLY** 24 Oct 68
– Quite rightly so / Shine on brightly / Skip softly (my moonbeams) / Wish me well / Rambling on / Magdalene (my regal zonophone) / In held twas I:- a) Glimpses of Nirvana – (b) Twas tea-time at the circus – (c) In the Autumn of my madness – (d) Look to your soul – (e) Grand finale. *re-iss.+c+cd Sep 85 on 'Sierra')*

May 69. (lp) **A SALTY DOG** 27 32
– A salty dog / The milk of human kindness / Too much between us / The Devil came from Arkansas / Boredom / Juicy John Pink / Wreck of the Hesperus / All this and more / Crucifiction Lane / Pilgrim's progress. *(re-iss. 1971 on 'MFP')(re-iss.+c+cd May85 on 'Sierra') (cd-iss.1986 on 'Mobile Fidelity')*

Jun 69. (7") **A SALTY DOG. / LONG GONE CREEK** 44 -
Jul 69. (7") **THE DEVIL CAME FROM KANSAS. / BOREDOM** -

— **CHRIS COPPING** – organ, bass (ex-PARAMOUNTS) repl. FISHER + KNIGHTS

Jun 70. (7") **WHISKEY TRAIN. / ABOUT TO DIE** -
Jun 70. (lp)(c) **HOME** 49 34
– Whiskey train / Dead man's dream / Still there'll be more / Nothing that I didn't know / About to die / Barnyard story / Piggy pig pig / Whaling stories / Your own choice. *(re-iss.+cd.Apr89 on 'Castle')*

Chrysalis A & M

Jun 71. (lp)(c) **BROKEN BARRICADES** 42 32 May 71
– Simple sister / Broken barricades / Memorial drive / Luskus Delph / Power failure / Song for a dreamer / Playmate of the mouth / Poor Mohammed. *(re-iss.1974)*

Jun 71. (7") **BROKEN BARRICADES. / POWER FAILURE** -
Oct 71. (7") **SIMPLE SISTER. / SONG FOR A DREAMER** -

— **DAVE BALL** (b.30 Mar'50) – guitar repl. ROBIN TROWER (later solo) / added **ALAN CARTWRIGHT** (b.10 Oct'45) – bass (to **BROOKER, COPPING, WILSON, REID + BALL)**

Apr 72. (lp)(c) **PROCOL HARUM IN CONCERT WITH THE EDMUNTON SYMPHONY ORCHESTRA (live)** 48 5
– Conquistador / Whaling stories / A salty dog / All this and more / In held 'twas I; a) Glimpses of Nirvana – (b) 'Twas teatime at the circus – (c) In the Autumn of my madness – (d) I know if I'd been wiser – (e) Grand finales. *(re-iss.1974) (re-iss.c+cd Aug 86)*

May 72. (7") **CONQUISTADOR (live). / A SALTY DOG (live)** - 16
Jul 72. (7") **CONQUISTADOR (live). / LUSKUS DELPH** 22 -

Chrysalis Chrysalis

Mar 73. (lp)(c) **GRAND HOTEL** 21
– Grand hotel / Toujours l'amour / A rum tale / T.V. Ceaser / Souvenir of London / Bringing home the bacon / Robert's box / For licorice John / Fires (which burnt brightly) / Robert's box.

Apr 73. (7") **ROBERT'S BOX. / A RUM TALE** -
Apr 73. (7") **BRINGING HOME THE BACON. / TOUJOURS L'AMOUR** -
Aug 73. (7") **GRAND HOTEL. / FIRE'S (WHICH BURNT BRIGHTLY)** -
Aug 73. (7") **SOUVENIR OF LONDON. / TOUJOURS L'AMOUR** -

— **MICK GRABHAM** – guitar (ex-PLASTIC PENNY, ex-COCHISE) repl. BALL to BEDLAM

Apr 74. (lp)(c) **EXOTIC BIRDS AND FRUIT** 86
– Nothing but the truth / Beyond the pale / As strong as Samson / The idol / The thin edge of the wedge / Monsieur R. Monde / Fresh fruit / Butterfly boys / New lamps for old.

Apr 74. (7") **NOTHING BUT THE TRUTH. / DRUNK AGAIN** [ ] [ ]
Jul 75. (7") **PANDORA'S BOX. / THE PIPER'S TUNE** [16] [ ]
Aug 75. (lp)(c) **PROCOL'S NINTH** [41] [52]
– Pandora's box / Fools gold / Taking the time / The unquiet zone / The final thrust / I keep forgetting / Without a doubt / The piper's tune / Typewriter torment / Eight days a week.
Oct 75. (7") **THE FINAL THRUST. / TAKING THE TIME** [ ] [-]
Jan 76. (7") **AS STRONG AS SAMSON. / THE UNQUIET ZONE** [ ] [-]

— **PETE SOLLEY** – keyboards (ex-ARTHUR BROWN, ex-SNAFU, ex-CHRIS FARLOWE) repl. CARTWRIGHT (COPPING now bass only)

Feb 77. (7") **WIZARD MAN. / BACKGAMMON** [ ] [-]
Mar 77. (lp)(c) **SOMETHING MAGIC** [ ] [ ]
– Something magic / Skating on thin ice / Wizard man / The mark of the claw / Strangers in space / The worm and the tree.
Mar 77. (7") **WIZARD MAN. / SOMETHING MAGIC** [-] [ ]

— Disbanded mid-77. WILSON joined JOE COCKER. GRABHAM to MICKEY JUPP. GARY BROOKER joined ERIC CLAPTON band and went solo. PROCOL HARUM reformed Oct'91, TIM RENWICK instead of TROWER.

– compilations, others, etc. –

1971. Fly; (lp) **THE BEST OF PROCOL HARUM** [ ] [-]
(US-iss.Oct 73 on 'A&M')
Apr 72. Magnifly; (7"m) **A WHITER SHADE OF PALE. / HOMBURG / A SALTY DOG** [13] [-]
Apr 72. Cube; (d-lp)(d-c) **PROCOL HARUM – A WHITER SHADE OF PALE / A SALTY DOG** [26] [-]
(re-iss.Jan75, Mar78, Oct81)
Mar 78. Cube; (7") **A WHITER SHADE OF PALE. / CONQUISTADOR** [ ] [ ]
(re-iss.12"white-Mar79) (re-iss.7"-Aug82 on 'Dakota')
Mar 78. Cube; (d-lp)(d-c) **SHINE ON BRIGHTLY / HOME** [ ] [-]
Oct 81. Cube; (d-lp)(c) **THE PLATINUM COLLECTION** [ ] [-]
Jun 83. Cube; (7") **A WHITER SHADE OF PALE. / HOMBURG** [ ] [-]
(12"+=) – Conquistador.
Mar 76. Decca; (lp) **ROCK ROOTS** [ ] [-]
May 78. Hallmark; (lp)(c) **PROCOL HARUM'S GREATEST HITS** [ ] [-]
Aug 78. Chrysalis; (7") **CONQUISTADOR. / A SALTY DOG** [ ] [-]
Aug 78. E.M.I.; (7"ep) **THE PARAMOUNTS** [ ] [-]
-Poison Ivy / I feel glad all over / Blue ribbons / Cuttin' in.
1981. E.M.I.; (cd)(c)(lp) **PORTFOLIO** [ ] [-]
Apr 82. Ace; (lp) **PROCOL HARUM** (67-69) [ ] [-]
Aug 82. Dakota; (7") **HOMBURG. / A SALTY DOG** [ ] [-]
Oct 82. Dakota; (lp)(c) **PROCOL HARUM** (67-70) [ ] [-]
Oct 84. Sierra; (d-lp)(c) **OFF THE RECORD WITH PROCOL HARUM** [ ] [-]
Apr 86. Castle; (d-lp)(d-c)(cd) **THE COLLECTION** [ ] [-]
– A whiter shade of pale / Homburg / Too much between us / A salty dog / The Devil came back from Kansas / Whaling stories / Good Captain Clack / All this and more / Quite rightly so / Shine on brightly / Grand hotel / Bringing home the bacon / Toujours l'armour / Broken barricades / Power failure / Conquistador (live) / Nothing but the truth / Butterfly boys / Pandora's box / Simple sister.
Mar 88. Castle; (d-lp)(c)(cd) **SHINE ON BRIGHTLY. / A SALTY DOG** [ ] [-]
Mar 88. Castle; (cd-ep) **A WHITER SHADE OF PALE / HOMBURG / CONQUISTADOR / A SALTY DOG** [ ] [-]
Feb 92. Castle; (cd-box) **PROCOL HARUM** [ ] [-]
Feb 87. Old Gold; (7") **CONQUISTADOR. / PANDORA'S BOX** [ ] [-]
Jun 88. Old Gold; (7") **A WHITER SHADE OF PALE. / HOMBURG** [ ] [-]
Jul 88. Knight; (lp)(c)(cd) **NIGHTRIDING** [ ] [-]
Dec 88. Fun; (lp)(c)(cd) **20 GREATEST HITS** [ ] [-]
Apr 83. Edsel; (lp) **WHITER SHADES OF R'N'B (PARAMOUNTS)** [ ] [-]
(cd-iss. Aug 87 + Sep 91)
Jun 88. A&M; (cd) **CLASSICS** [ ] [-]
Jun 92. Dojo; (cd) **THE EARLY YEARS** [ ] [-]
Oct 94. Disky; (cd) **PROCOL HARUM** [ ] [-]
Jul 95. Essential; (cd-ep) **A WHITER SHADE OF PALE / A SALTY DOG / REPENT WALPURGIS** [ ] [-]
Sep 95. Essential; (cd)(c) **THE BEST OF PROCOL HARUM** [ ] [-]

GARY BROOKER

Chrysalis Chrysalis

Apr 79. (7") **SAVANNAH. / S.S. BLUES** [ ] [ ]
May 79. (lp)(c) **NO MORE FEAR OF FLYING** [ ] [ ]
– Savannah / Pilot / (No more) Fear of flying / Get up and dance / Give me something to remember / Say it ain't so Joe / Old Manhattan melodies / Angelina / Let me in / Switchboard Susan.
Aug 79. (7")(7"pic-d) **SAY IT AIN'T SO JOE. / ANGELINA** [ ] [ ]
Apr 80. (7") **LEAVE THE CANDLE. / CHASING THE CHOP** [ ] [ ]

Mercury Mercury

May 81. (7") **HOMELOVIN'. / CHASING THE CHOP** [ ] [ ]
Feb 82. (lp)(c) **LEAD ME TO THE WATER** [ ] [ ]
– Mineral man / Another way / Hang on Rose / Home loving / The cycle (let it flow) / Lead me to the water / The angler / Low flying birds / Sympathy for the hard of hearing.
Mar 82. (7") **THE CYCLE (LET IT FLOW). / BADLANDS** [ ] [ ]
Nov 84. (7") **THE LONG GOODBYE. / TRICK OF THE LIGHT** [ ] [ ]
Apr 85. (7") **TWO FOOLS IN LOVE. / SUMMER NIGHTS** [ ] [ ]
Sep 85. (lp)(c) **ECHOES IN THE NIGHT** [ ] [ ]
– Count me out / Two fools in love / Echoes in the night / Ghost train / Mr. Blue day / Saw the fire / The long goodbye / Hear what you're saying / Missing person / Trick of the night.

GARY was still a member of ERIC CLAPTON's band.

PROCOL HARUM

re-formed in 1991. **BROOKER** – vocals, piano / **KEITH REID** – words / **ROBIN TROWER** – lead guitar / **MATTHEW FISHER** – hammond organ / with guests **DAVE BRONZE** – bass / **MARK BRZEZICKI** – drums / **JERRY STEVENSON** – mandolin, guitar.

B.M.G. B.M.G.

Feb 92. (cd)(c)(lp) **THE PRODIGAL STRANGER** [ ] [ ]
– The truth won't fade away / Holding on / Man with a mission / (You can't) Turn back the page / One more time / A dream in ev'ry home / The hand that rocks the cradle / The king of hearts / All our dreams are sold / Perpetual motion / Learn to fly / The pursuit of happiness.

PRODIGY

Formed: London, England . . . early 90's by LIAM HOWLETT. Signed to 'X.L.' and scored UK Top 3 hit, with 2nd single 'CHARLY' (LIAM's cats name). Deservedly topped the UK charts in 1994 with album 'MUSIC FOR THE JILTED GENERATION'. • **Style:** Hardcore techno punk rock /dance outfit, conjuring images of KRAFTWERK at 100 mph, although with a harder danceable edge (very danceable!). • **Songwriters:** HOWLETT except samples of BABY D ('Casanova') on 'BREAK & ENTER', and KELLY CHARLES on 'YOU'RE NO GOOD FOR ME'. 'FULL THROTTLE' is also reminiscent of JOAN ARMATRADING's 'Me Myself I'. • **Trivia:** POP WILL EAT ITSELF co-wrote and featured on the track 'THEIR LAW'. 'CHARLY' sampled from TV ad, which featured a cartoon cat telling children not to talk to strangers!!!

Recommended: EXPERIENCE (*7) / MUSIC FOR THE JILTED GENERATION (*9)

LIAM HOWLETT – keyboards / **MC MAXIM REALITY** – rapper-vox / **LEEROY THORNHILL + KEITH FLINT** – dancers

X.L. Elektra

Mar 91. (12"ep) **WHAT EVIL LURKS / WE GONNA ROCK. / ANDROID / EVERYBODY IN THE PLACE** [ ] [-]
Aug 91. (7")(c-s) **CHARLY. / CHARLY (original mix)** [3] [-]
(12"+=)(cd-s+=) – Pandemonium / Your love.
Dec 91. (7")(c-s) **EVERYBODY IN THE PLACE. / G-FORCE (ENERGY FLOW)** [2] [-]
(12"+=) – Crazy man / Rip up the sound system.
(cd-s++=) – ('A'remix).
Feb 92. (c-ep+cd-ep) **CHARLY (Beltram says mix) / CHARLY (alley cat mix) / EVERYBODY IN THE PLACE (dance hall version) / EVERYBODY IN THE PLACE (fairground mix) / YOUR LOVE (the original excursion) / G-FORCE (Part 1)** [-] [ ]
Sep 92. (7")(c-s) **FIRE. / JERICHO (original mix)** [11] [-]
(12"+=)(cd-s+=) – Fire (sunrise version) / Jericho (genaside II remix).
Oct 92. (c-ep)(cd-ep) **FIRE (edit) / JERICHO (original version) / FIRE (sunrise version) / JERICHO (genaside II remix) / PANDEMONIUM** [-] [ ]
Oct 92. (cd)(c)(lp) **EXPERIENCE** [12] [ ]
– Jericho / Music reach (1,2,3,4) / Wind it up / Your love (remix) / Hyperspeed (G-Force part 2) / Charly (trip into drum and bass version) / Out of space / Everybody in the place (155 and rising) / Weather experience / Fire (sunrise version) / Ruff in the jungle bizness / Death of the Prodigy dancers (live).
Nov 92. (7")(c-s) **OUT OF SPACE (remix). / RUFF IN THE JUNGLE BIZNESS (uplifting vibes remix)** [5] [-]
(12"+=)(cd-s+=) – ('A'techno underworld remix) / Music reach (1,2,3,4) (live).
Dec 92. (c-ep)(cd-ep) **OUT OF SPACE (edit) / OUT OF SPACE (techno underworld remix) / UT OF SPACE (millenium mix) / OUT OF SPACE (celestial bodies mix) / RUFF IN THE JUNGLE BIZNESS (uplifting vibes remix) / JERICHO (live)** [-] [ ]
Apr 93. (7")(c-s) **WIND IT UP (REWOUND). / WE ARE THE RUFFEST** [7] [ ]

(12"+=) – Weather experience (remix).
(cd-s++=) – ('A'edit).

May 93. (c-ep)(cd-ep) **WIND IT UP (the rewound edit) / WIND IT UP (tightly wound) / WIND IT UP (forward wind) / WIND IT UP (unwind) / WE ARE THE RUFFEST / WEATHER EXPERIENCE (top buzz remix) / WIND IT UP (bonus beats)** [-] [ ]

Oct 93. (12"ep)(c-ep)(cd-ep) **ONE LOVE / RHYTHM OF LIFE (original mix) / FULL THROTTLE (original mix) / ONE LOVE (Johny L remix)** [8] [ ]

May 94. (12")(c-s) **NO GOOD (START THE DANCE) / NO GOOD (bad for you mix) / NO GOOD (CJ Bolland's museum mix)** [4] [ ]
(cd-s+=) – No Good (original mix).

— below album with **PHIL BENT** – flute / **LANCE RIDDLER** – guitar

X.L. Mute

Jul 94. (cd)(c)(d-lp) **MUSIC FOR THE JILTED GENERATION** [1] [-] Mar95
– Intro / Break & enter / Their law (featuring POP WILL EAT ITSELF) / Full throttle / Voodoo people / Speedway (theme from 'Fastlane') / The heat (the energy) / Poison / No good (start the dance) / One love (edit) – The narcotic suite / 3 kilos / Skylined / Claustrophobic sting.

Sep 94. (12"ep)(cd-ep) **VOODOO PEOPLE (original mix) / VOODOO PEOPLE (Dust Brothers mix) / VOODOO PEOPLE** (12"= Haiti Island mix / cd= edit) / GOA (THE HEAT, THE ENERGY PART 2) [13] [ ]

Mar 95. (c-s) **POISON ('95) / ('A'-Rat Poison mix) / SCIENIDE** [15] [ ]
(12"+=)(cd-s+=) – ('A'-Environmental science dub mix).

. . . Jan – Jun '96 stop press . . .

Mar 96. (single) **FIRESTARTER** [1] [ ]

— All singles re-issued Apr96 hitting Top75

PROFESSIONALS (see under ⇒ SEX PISTOLS)

PUBLIC ENEMY

Formed: New York, USA . . . 1984 by CHUCK D and co-producer & future co-manager WILLIAM SHOCKLEE, who mixed some tapes for co-(as said) BILL STEPNEY. In 1986, 'Def Jam' owner Rick Rubin, signed CHUCK D and others (see below). Their debut self-titled single, hit the shops early in '87. By the end of the year, their 3rd single 'REBEL WITHOUT A PAUSE', cracked the UK Top 40. In 1990, they at last crossed over from R&B charts to mainstream US Top 10 with album 'FEAR OF A BLACK PLANET'. • **Style:** Groundbreaking + highly politicized pro-black urban rappers/samplers, who remonstrated white authoritarianism with violent anthemic lyrics, on and off record. • **Songwriters:** CHUCK D, with managers SHOCKLEE and STEPNEY, taking mostly samples from JAMES BROWN. • **Trivia:** PROFESSOR GRIFF (whose father was killed by the Ku Klux Klan when he was a boy), was sacked from the band in mid-89, after allegedly making an anti-Semetic statement to Washington Times.

Recommended: YO! BUM RUSH THE SHOW (*9) / IT TAKES A NATION OF MILLIONS TO HOLD US BACK (*10) / FEAR OF A BLACK PLANET (*10) / APOCALYPSE 91 . . .THE ENEMY STRIKES BACK (*8)

CHUCK D (b.CARLTON RIDENHOUR, 1960) – vocals / **FLAVOR FLAV** (b.WILLIAM DRAYTON) – multi-instrumentalist, classically trained pianist / **TERMINATOR X** (b.NORMAN RODGERS) – DJ / **PROFESSOR GRIFF** (b.RICHARD GRIFFIN) – vocals / plus part-time **JAMES ALLEN + JAMES NORMAN**
(Please note they never released a 7" in US)

Def Jam Def Jam

Mar 87. (7") **PUBLIC ENEMY No.1. / TIMEBOMB** [ ] [ ]
(12"+=) – Son of public enemy No.1 ('A'instrumental version).

Apr 87. (lp)(c)(cd) **YO! BUM RUSH THE SHOW** [ ] [ ]
– You're gonna get yours / Sophisticated bitch / Miuzi weighs a ton / Timebomb / Too much posse / Rightstarter (message to a black man) / Public enemy No.1 / M.P.E. / Yo! bum rush the show / Raise the roof / Megablast / Terminator X speaks with his hands. *(re-iss.cd+c Sep93 & Jul95)*

Jun 87. (7") **YOU'RE GONNA GET YOURS. / MUIZI WEIGHS A TON** [ ] [ ]
(12"+=) – ('A'dub) / ('A' terminator X mix) / Rebel without a pause.

Nov 87. (7") **REBEL WITHOUT A PAUSE (vocal). / ('A'instrumental)** [37] [-]
(12"+=)(cd-s+=) – Terminator X speaks with his hands / Sophisticated bitch.

Dec 87. (12") **ARE YOU MY WOMAN? (by "The BLACK FLAMES") / BRING THE NOISE** [-] [ ]
(12"+=) – ('A'noise version) / ('A'a cappella mix).

Jan 88. (7") **BRING THE NOISE. / SOPHISTICATED BITCH** [32] [-]
(12"+=) – ('A'noise version) / ('A'accapella version).

Jun 88. (7") **DON'T BELIEVE THE HYPE. / PROPHETS OF RAGE** [18] [ ]
(12"+=) – Rhythm & the rebel (accapella) / ('B'power version).
(cd-s+=) – Bring the noise / ('B'power version).

Jul 88. (lp)(c)(cd) **IT TAKES A NATION OF MILLIONS TO HOLD US BACK** [8] [42]
– Countdown to armageddon / Bring the noise / Don't believe the hype / Cold lampin' with Flavor / Terminator X to the edge of panic / Mind terrorist / Louder than a bomb / Caught, can we get a witness? / Show 'em whatcha got / She watch Channel Zero?! / Night of the living baseheads / Black steel in the hour of chaos / Security of the first world / Rebel without a pause / Prophets of rage / Party for your right to fight. *(re-iss.cd Jul95)*

Oct 88. (7") **NIGHT OF THE LIVING BASEHEADS. / TERMINATOR X TO THE EDGE OF PANIC (or) ('A' instrumental version)** [63] [ ]
(12"+=)/ /(cd-s+=) – (all 3) / / ('A'anti-high blood . . . mix).
(US-12"+=) – Cold lampin' with Flavor.

1989. (12") **BLACK STEEL IN THE HOUR OF CHAOS (radio version) / ('A' instrumental). / TOO MUCH POSSE / CAUGHT, CAN I GET A WITNESS (dub mix) / B-SIDE WINS AGAIN** [-] [ ]

Jun 89. (7")(c-s) **FIGHT THE POWER. / ('A'version)** [29] [ ]
('A'ext-12"+=)(cd-s+=) – ('A'Flavor meets Spike Lee mix).

— (above was issued in the States on a one-off 'Motown' deal).

Jan 90. (7")(c-s) **WELCOME TO THE TERRORDOME. / ('A'terromental version)** [18] [ ]
(12"+=) – Black steel in the hour of chaos.
(cd-s+=) – Terrorbeat.

— Trimmed when PROFESSOR GRIFF left permanently to go solo. He soon released debut 'PAWNS IN THE GAME' with his LAST ASIATIC DISCIPLES. A year later he followed this with second album 'KAD'S II WIZ *7* DOME'.

Apr 90. (7")(c-s) **911 IS A JOKE. / REVOLUTIONARY GENERATION** [41] [ ]
(12"+=)(cd-s+=) – ('A'&'B'instrumentals).
(12") – ('A'side) / Son of Public Enemy / Bring the noise / Rebel without a pause.

Apr 90. (cd)(c)(lp) **FEAR OF A BLACK PLANET** [4] [10]
– Contract on the world love jam / Brothers gonna work it out / 911 is a joke / Incident at 66.6 FM / Welcome to the terrordome / Meet the G that killed me / Pollywanacraka / Anti-nigger machine / Burn Hollywood burn / Power to the people / Who stole the soul / Fear of a black planet / Revolutionary generation / Can't do nuttin' for ya man / Reggae Jax / Leave this off your fuckin' charts / B side wins again / War at 33 1/3 / Final count of the collision between us and the damned. *(re-iss.cd Jul95)*

Jun 90. (7")(c-s) **BROTHERS GONNA WORK IT OUT (remix). / WAR AT 33 1/3** [46] [ ]
(12"+=) – Bring the noise (no noise instrumental) / ('B'instrumental).
(cd-s+=) – Anti-nigger machine / Don't believe the hype.

Oct 90. (7")(c-s) **CAN'T DO NUTTIN' FOR YA MAN. / ('A'version)** [53] [ ]
(12"+=)(cd-s+=) – ('A'full rub mix).
(12") – ('A'version) / Get the f . . . out of Dodge (uncensured) / Powersave / Burn Hollywood burn.

— added **SISTER SOULJAH** – vocals

— (May91) FLAVOR FLAV served 30 days in jail for an earlier incident in which he hit the mother of his 3 children Karen Ross.

— Jun91, teamed up with ANTHRAX on a hit single version of 'BRING THE NOISE'.

Sep 91. (7")(c-s) **CAN'T TRUSS IT (new bootleg mix). / ('A'radio mix)** [22] [50]
(cd-s+=) – Move (censored radio mix).
(12"++=) – ('A'instrumental).

Oct 91. (cd)(c)(d-lp) **APOCALYPSE 91 . . .THE ENEMY STRIKES BACK** [8] [4]
– Lost at birth / Rebirth / Night train / Can't truss it / I don't wanna be called yo niga / How to kill a radio consultant / By the time I get to Arizona / Move! / 1 million bottlebags / More news at 11 / Shut 'em down / A letter to the New York post / Get the f . . . outta Dodge / Bring the noise (w/ ANTHRAX). *(re-iss.cd Jul95)*

Jan 92. (7")(c-s) **SHUT 'EM DOWN (remix). / BY THE TIME I GET TO ARIZONA** [21] [ ]
(12"+=)(cd-s+=)(12"pic-d+=) – ('A'rock mixx instrumental) / ('A'bald beat acapella) / ('B'side dubbed).

Mar 92. (7")(c-s) **NIGHT TRAIN (mixx). / MORE NEWS AT 11 (mixx)** [55] [ ]
(12"+=)(cd-s+=)(12"pic-d+=) – ('A'funk mixx) / ('A'instrumental mixx).

Sep 92. (cd)(c)(d-lp) **GREATEST MISSES DON'T MISS IT** [14] [13]
– Tie goes to the runner / Hitt da road Jack / Get off my back / Air hoodlum got ta do what I gotta do / Hazy shade of criminal megablast (remix) / Louder than a bomb (telephone groove) / How to kill a radio consultant (DJ check chillout..) / Who stole the soul (mixx) / Party for your right to fight (metromix) / You're gonna get yours (version). (cd+=) – Shut 'em down (live in the UK). *(re-iss.cd Jul95)*

— PROFESSOR GRIFF, TERMINATOR X, and newcomer SISTER SOULJAH all had own releases for various labels from 1990 onwards.

FLAVOR FLAV was charged late '93, for drunkenly attempting to shoot his neighbour, after he allegedly thought his wife was committing adultery.

Aug 94. (12"ep)(c-ep)(cd-ep) **GIVE IT UP. / ('A'-main version) / ('A'-bedlam instrumental)** 18 33 Jul94
(cd-s+=) – Live and undrugged (part 2) / Harry Allen interactive highway / Bedlam instrumental.

Aug 94. (cd)(c) **MUSE SICK-N-HOUR MESS AGE** 12 14
– Whole lotta love / Theatrical / Give it up / What side you on? / Body count / Stop in the name / What kind of power we got? / So watcha gone do now? / White Heaven – black Hell / Race against time / Used to call it dope / Aintnuthin' buttersong / Live & undrugged parts I & II / I ain't madd at all / Death of carjacka / I stand accused / Gold complexx / Hitler day / Harry Allen superhighway.

Nov 94. (12"ep)(cd-ep) **I STAND ACCUSED / WHAT KIND OF POWER WE GOT**
(cd-s+=) – I stand accused (Sleek'sschool of self-defence mix) / Mao Tse Tung.

— On 26th May'95, FLAVOR was jailed for drug possession. He was sent to a rehab centre and given three years probation. While in Italy in July, he broke his leg in a motorcycle accident.

Jul 95. (c-s) **SO WHATCHA GONNA DO NOW? / BLACK STEEL IN THE HOUR OF CHAOS** 50
(12"+=)(cd-s+=) – ('A'-Drive by s**t mix) / ('A'-Drive by inst.).

- compilations, etc. -

Mar 93. Def Jam; (cd)(c) **THE 12" MIXES**

PUBLIC IMAGE LTD.

Formed: London, England . . . Jul'78 by ex-SEX PISTOLS singer JOHNNY ROTTEN who reverted to his real name JOHN LYDON. He recruited local friends KEITH LEVENE, JAH WOBBLE and Canadian JIM WALKER, and re-signed to 'Virgin'. Their near self-titled debut 45, which was wrapped in a mock-newspaper cover, reached the UK Top 10 late 1978, and preceeded an eponymous Top 30 album. A year later, they issued 'METAL BOX 1', which was packaged as three 12" 45's inside a metal box. It reached No.18, and when re-issued in normal format 2 months later, even managed a Top 50 placing. LYDON and various line-ups continued to score in the charts, but things slowed down in 1983, when he moved to New York. That year, he had also starred alongside Harvey Keitel in the film 'Out Of Order' (US title 'Cop Killer'). • **Style:** LYDON quickly abandoned initial punk rock sound, for more Eastern influenced experimental alternative rock. His cynical yet poignant attitude, had been both a commercial asset and a put off for many, but no one can deny his phenomanal contribution to rock, both in the PISTOLS and PIL. • **Songwriters:** LYDON and PIL compositions. • **Trivia:** On 13 Feb'80, LYDON's home was raided by police, who found virtually nothing. 8 months later in Ireland, he was arrested for assault. He was sentenced to 3 months imprisonment, but was acquited on appeal.

Recommended: PUBLIC IMAGE (*9) / METAL BOX 1 (*10) / GREATEST HITS – SO FAR (*9).

JOHN LYDON (b.31 Jan'56, Finsbury Park, London) – vocals (ex-SEX PISTOLS) / **KEITH LEVENE** – guitar (ex-CLASH) / **JAH WOBBLE** (b.JOHN WORDLE) – bass / **JIM WALKER** – drums (ex-FURIES) (most singles just credit "PIL")

Virgin Island

Oct 78. (7") **PUBLIC IMAGE. / THE COWBOY SONG** 9

Dec 78. (lp)(c) **PUBLIC IMAGE** 22
– Theme / Religion I / Religion II / Annalisa / Public image / Low life / Attack / Fodderstompf. *(re-iss.Apr86) (cd-iss.Oct86)*

— **DAVE CROWE** – drums repl. WALKER who joined The PACK (with KIRK BRANDON) added **JEANNETTE LEE** – keyboards, synthesizer

Jun 79. (7") **DEATH DISCO. / NO BIRDS DO SING** 20
(12") – ('A'extended) / Megamix (Fodderstompf remixed).

Sep 79. (7")('A'ext-12") **MEMORIES. / ANOTHER** 60

Nov 79. (3x12"lp-box) **METAL BOX 1** 18
– Albatross / Memories / Swan lake/ / Poptones / Careering / No birds / Graveyard / / The suit / Bad baby / Socialist – Chant – Radio 4. *(cd-iss.Jun90) (re-iss.Jan80 as d-lp/c- 'SECOND EDITION', hit No.46) (cd-iss.Jun87)*

— **RICHARD DUDANSKI** – drums (ex-101'ERS, ex-BASEMENT 5) repl. CROWE (above had joined during Apr-Sep'79) (below French titles of above songs)

Nov 80. (lp)(c) **PARIS AU PRINTEMPS (live 'PARIS IN THE SPRING')** 61
– Theme / Psalmodie (Chant) / Precipitamment (Careering) / Sale bebe (Bad baby) / La vie ignoble (Low life) / Attaque (Attack) / Timbres de pop (Poptones). *(re-iss.Mar84)*

— (Jul80) Trimmed to a quartet when JAH WOBBLE went solo. / **MARTIN ATKINS** (b. 3 Aug'59, Coventry, England) (aka BRIAN BRAIN) – drums repl. DUDANSKI who joined RAINCOATS. (ATKINS was sacked Jul80, most of drums by LYDON and LEVENE). ('B'side recorded 1978)

Virgin Warner

Mar 81. (7") **FLOWERS OF ROMANCE. / HOME IS WHERE THE HEART IS** 24
(12"+=) – ('A'instrumental).

Apr 81. (lp)(c) **FLOWERS OF ROMANCE** 11
– Four enclosed walls / Track 8 / Phenagen / Flowers of romance / Under the house / Hymie's him / Banging the door / Go back / Francis massacre. *(re-iss. Mar84, cd-iss.Apr90) (cd-iss.Mar94)*

— **KEN LOCKIE** – keyboards (ex-COWBOYS INTERNATIONAL, ex-Solo) repl. LEE / added (May82) **MARTIN ATKINS** – drums / **PETE JONES** – bass

Aug 83. (7") **THIS IS NOT A LOVE SONG. / PUBLIC IMAGE** 5
(12"+=) – Blue water / ('A'remix). *(cd-ep iss.Jun88)*

— LYDON + ATKINS were joined by US session people from New Jersey; **JOSEPH GUIDA** -guitar / **TOM ZVONCHECK** -keyboards / **LOUIE BERNARDI** – bass

Sep 83. (2xm-lp)(c) **LIVE IN TOKYO (live)** 28
– Annalisa / Religion / Low life / Solitaire / Flowers of romance / This is not a love song / Death disco / Bad life / Banging the door / Under the house. *(cd-iss.1986)*

May 84. (7")('A'ext-12") **BAD LIFE. / QUESTION MARK** 71

Jul 84. (lp)(c) **THIS IS WHAT YOU WANT . . . THIS IS WHAT YOU GET** 56
– Bad life / This is not a love song / Solitaire / Tie me to the length of that / The pardon / Where are you? / 1981 / The order of death. *(re-iss.1986, cd-iss.Apr90)* (US-iss.Aug84 as 'COMMERCIAL ZONE' by "KEITH LEVENE & PIL").

— Disbanded mid'84, but reformed by LYDON late '85 with on session **STEVE VAI** – guitar (ex-ALCATRAZZ) / **RYUICHI SAKAMOTO** – keys (ex-YELLOW MAGIC ORCHESTRA) / **GINGER BAKER** (ex-CREAM, etc) / **TONY WILLIAMS** (ex-MILES DAVIES, etc) / **RAVI SHANKER** – violin

Virgin Elektra

Jan 86. (7")(12") **SINGLE ('RISE'). / ('A'instrumental)** 11

Feb 86. (lp)(c)(cd) **ALBUM (CASSETTE / COMPACT DISC)** 14
– FFF / Rise / Fishing / Round / Bags / Home / Ease. *(re-iss.1989)*

Apr 86. (7") **HOME. / ROUND** 75
(12"+=) – ('A'-lp version).
(d7"+=) – Rise / ('A'instrumental).

— (Feb86) **LYDON** recruited **LU EDMUNDS** – guitar, keys (ex-DAMNED, ex-MEKONS) / **JOHN McGEOGH** – guitar (of ARMOURY SHOW, ex-SIOUXSIE & THE BANSHEES) / **ALAN DIAS** – bass / **BRUCE SMITH** – drums (ex-RIP, RIG & PANIC, ex-SLITS, ex-POP GROUP)

Virgin Virgin

Aug 87. (7") **SEATTLE. / SELFISH RUBBISH** 47
(12"+=)(c-s+=) – The suit.

Sep 87. (lp)(c)(cd) **HAPPY?** 40
– Seattle / Rules and regulations / The body / Save me / Hard times / Open and revolving / Angry / Fat chance hotel.

Oct 87. (7") **THE BODY. / RELIGION (new version)**
(12"+=) – Angry.
(12") – ('A'extended remix). / ('A'-US remix) / Angry.

— trimmed to a quartet when EDMUNDS dispersed.

Apr 89. (7") **DISAPPOINTED. / SAME OLD STORY** 38
('A'ext-12"+=)(12"pic-d+=)(3"cd-s+=) – ('A'version).

Jun 89. (lp)(c)(cd) **9** 36
– Happy / Disappointed / Warrior / U.S.L.S. 1 / Sand castles in the snow / Worry / Brave new world / Like that / Same old story / Armada.

Jul 89. (7") **WARRIOR (edit). / U.S.L.S. 1**
('A'extended-12"+=) – ('A'instrumental).
(3"cd-s+=) – ('A'extended).
(12") – ('A'-Dave Dorrell remix). / ('A'instrumental)

Oct 90. (7")(c-s) **DON'T ASK ME. / RULES AND REGULATIONS** 22
(12") – ('A'extended) / Warrior (remix).
(cd-s+=) – Warrior (original).

Oct 90. (cd)(c)(lp) **GREATEST HITS – SO FAR** (compilation) 20
– Public image / Death disco / Memories / Careering / Flowers of romance / This is not a love song / Rise / Home / The body / Rules and regulations / Disappointed / Warrior / Don't ask me / Seattle.

— **MIKE JOYCE** – drums (ex-SMITHS, ex-BUZZCOCKS) repl. BRUCE

P.I.L.

Feb 92. (7")**CRUEL. / LOVE HOPE** 49
(cd-s+=)/ /(10"+=) – Rise (live) / Home (live)./ / Happy (live).

Feb 92. (cd)(c)(lp) **THAT WHAT IS NOT** 46
– Acid drops / Lucks up / Cruel / God / Covered / Love hope / Unfairground / Think tank / Emperor / Good things.

— In Nov'93, LYDON was credited on acclaimed dance hit & UK No.19 'Open Up' by LEFTFIELD / LYDON on 'Hard Hands' records.

— Stop press:- Early '96, JOHN LYDON (ROTTEN) re-grouped with The SEX PISTOLS for summer tours in Britain, Europe and America.

PULP

Formed: Sheffield, England ... 1981 originally as ARABACUS PULP by JARVIS COCKER. In the mid-80's after release of 'IT' debut mini-lp, JARVIS was confined to a wheel-chair for a year, after falling from a window. They were releasing material for 'Fire' around this time and finally released first full album 'FREAKS' in 1987. Most of the band moved to London in the late 80's and it wasn't long before the enigmatic JARVIS and crew were on the roster of 'Island' and in chartland. • **Style:** A fusion between LEONARD COHEN and The FALL in their early days to mid-80's; MONOCHROME SET, ULTRAVOX! (John Foxx era). Later with fashion (aka Bri-Nylon, glitter-boots, early 70's), COCKER was to become a star on the same scale as BRETT ANDERSON (Suede) and LAWRENCE (ex-Felt; now Denim). • **Songwriters:** COCKER + SIMON HINKLER collaborated on debut. COCKER, SENIOR, C.DOYLE, MANSELL penned, until 90's when COCKER was main contributor. • **Trivia:** COCKER and MACKAY directed videos for TINDERSTICKS and The APHEX TWIN.

— **Note:** Not to be confused with other band fronted by ANDY BEAN + PAUL BURNELL, who released in 1979; LOW FLYING AIRCRAFT single.

Recommended: HIS 'N' HERS (*9) / DIFFERENT CLASS (*9) / MASTERS OF THE UNIVERSE (*7)

JARVIS COCKER (b. Sep'62) – vocals, guitar, piano / **SIMON HINKLER** – keyboards, vocals repl. PETER DALTON / **PETER BOAM** – bass repl. JAMIE PINCHBECK who had repl. DAVID LOCKWOOD / **DAVID HINKLER** – keyboards, trombone / **GARY WILSON** – drums (of ARTERY) repl. WAYNE FURNISS who had repl. JIMMY SELLERS who had repl. MARK SWIFT
plus guests **SASKIA COCKER + GILL TAYLOR** – b.vox / **TIMM ALLCARD** – keyboards.

Red Rhino — not issued

Apr 83. (m-lp) **IT** [ ] [-]
– My lighthouse / Wishful thinking / Joking aside / Boats and trains / Blue girls / Love love / In many ways. *(cd-iss.Mar94 on 'Cherry Red')* (cd+=) – Looking for life / Everybody's problem / There was. *(re-iss.cd Dec94 on 'Fire')* (cd+=) – Looking for life.

May 83. (7") **MY LIGHTHOUSE (remix). / LOOKING FOR LIFE** [ ] [-]

Sep 83. (7") **EVERYBODY'S PROBLEM. / THERE WAS** [ ] [-]

— **RUSSELL SENIOR** – guitar, violin, vocals repl. DAVID
CANDIDA DOYLE – keyboards, vocals repl. SIMON who joined ARTERY then the MISSION)

— **MAGNUS DOYLE** – drums repl. GARY, SASKIA, GILL + TIMM

— **PETER MANSELL** – bass repl. BOAM

Fire — not issued

Nov 85. (12"ep) **LITTLE GIRL AND OTHER PIECES** [ ] [-]
– Little girl (with blue eyes) / Simultaneous / Blue glow / The will to power. *(re-iss.Oct91)*

Jun 86. (12"ep) **DOGS ARE EVERYWHERE / THE MARK OF THE DEVIL. / 97 LOVERS / ABORIGINE / GOODNIGHT** [ ] [-]
(re-iss.Oct91)

Jan 87. (7")(ext-12") **THEY SUFFOCATE AT NIGHT. / TUNNEL** [ ] [-]

Mar 87. (7")(12") **MASTER OF THE UNIVERSE (sanitised version). / MANON / SILENCE** [ ] [-]
(re-iss.Oct91)

May 87. (lp) **FREAKS** [ ] [-]
– Fairground / I want you / Being followed home / Master of the universe / Life must be so wonderful / There's no emotion / Anorexic beauty / The never ending story / Don't you know / They suffocate at night. *(cd-iss.Apr93)*

— **STEPHEN MACKAY** – bass repl. STEPHEN HAVENLAND who had repl. PETER

— **NICHOLAS BANKS** – drums, percussion repl. MAGNUS

Sep 90. (12"ep) **MY LEGENDARY GIRLFRIEND. / IS THIS HOUSE? / THIS HOUSE IS CONDEMNED** [ ] [-]
(re-iss.Oct91)

Aug 91. (12"ep)(cd-ep) **COUNTDOWN. / DEATH GOES TO THE DISCO / COUNTDOWN (edit)** [ ] [-]
(re-iss.Oct91)

Oct 91. (cd)(c)(lp) **SEPARATIONS** [ ] [-]
– Love is blind / Don't you want me anymore / She's dead / Separations / Down by the river / Countdown / My legendary girlfriend / Death II / This house is condemned. *(re-iss.Jun92)*

Gift — not issued

May 92. (12"ep)(cd-ep) **O.U. (GONE GONE) / SPACE / O.U. (GONE GONE) (radio edit)** [ ] [-]

Oct 92. (12"ep)(cd-ep) **BABIES. / STYLOROC (NIGHTS OF SUBURBIA) / SHEFFIELD** – SEX CITY [ ] [-]

Feb 93. (12"ep)(cd-ep) **RAZZAMATAZZ. / MEDLEY (abridged)** [ ] [-]

Island — Island

Oct93. (cd)(c)(lp) **INTRO** – THE GIFT RECORDINGS [ ] [-]
– Space / Ou (gone gone) / Babies / Styloroc (nights of suburbia) / Razzamatazz / Sheffield-Sex city / Medley of stacks: Inside Susan (a story in 3 songs) Stacks – Inside Susan – 59 Lyndhurst Grove.

Nov 93. (7") **LIPGLOSS. / YOU'RE A NIGHTMARE** [50] [ ]
(12"+=)(cd-s+=) – Deep fried in Kelvin.

Mar 94. (7")(c-s) **DO YOU REMEMBER THE FIRST TIME?. / STREET LITES** [33] [ ]
(12"+=)(cd-s+=) – Babysitter.

Apr 94. (cd)(c)(lp) **HIS'N'HERS** [9] [ ]
– Joyriders / Lipgloss / Acrylic afternoons / Have you seen her lately? / She's a lady / Happy endings / Do you remember the first time? / Pink glove / Someone like the Moon / David's last summer.(cd,c+=) – Babies (remix).

May 94. (7"ep)(12"ep)(cd-ep) **THE SISTERS EP** [19] [ ]
– Babies / Your sister's clothes / Seconds / His'n'hers.

May 95. (c-s)(cd-s) **COMMON PEOPLE / UNDERWEAR** [2] [ ]
(cd-s) – ('A'side) / Razzmatazz (acoustic) / Dogs are everywhere (acoustic) / Joyriders (acoustic).

— Below second side (double A) caused controversy with tabloids and parents, due to it's mis-use of drugs in JARVIS's lyrics. JARVIS was to become the hero to most and villain to the few early in 1996 at a certain awards ceremony (skinny J.C. vs. St.MICHAEL & the bouncers; who won – you decide).

Sep 95. (c-s) **MIS-SHAPES / SORTED FOR E'S AND WIZZ** [2] [ ]
(cd-s+=) P.T.A. (Parent Teacher Association) / Common people (live at Glastonbury).
(cd-s+=) – Common people (Motiv8 mix).

Oct 95. (cd)(c)(lp) **DIFFERENT CLASS** [1] [ ]
– Mis-shapes / Pencil skirt / Common people / I spy / Disco 2000 / Live bed show / Something changed / Sorted out for E's and wizz / F.E.E.L.I.N.G.S.C.A.L.L.E.D.L.O.V.E. / Underwear / Monday morning / Bar Italia.

Nov 95. (c-s) **DISCO 2000 / ('A'mix)** [7] [ ]
(cd-s+=) – Ansaphone / Live bed show (extended).
(cd-s+=) – ('A'-Motiv8 discoid mixes).

... Jan – Jun '96 stop press ...

Mar 96. (single) **SOMETHING CHANGED** [10] [ ]

– compilations, etc. –

Jun 94. Fire; (cd)(c)(lp) **MASTERS OF THE UNIVERSE** (1985-86 singles) [ ] [-]
– Little girl (with blue eyes) / Simultaneous / Blue glow / The will to power / Dogs are everywhere / The mark of the Devil / 97 lovers / Aborigine / Goodnight / They suffocate at night / Tunnel / Master of the universe (sanitised version) / Manon.

. . .Jan-Jun'96 stop press compilations . . .

Mar 96. Nectar; (cd) **COUNTDOWN 1992-1983** [10] [-]

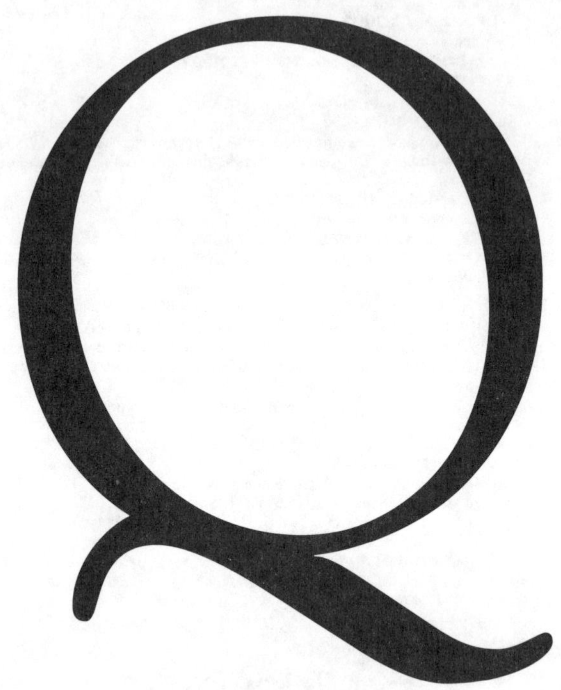

QUEEN

Formed: London, England . . . early 1971 by MAY, TAYLOR, MERCURY and DEACON. MAY had left school in 1963, with 10 O-levels and joined teenage group The OTHERS, who issued one single 'OH YEAH' for 'Fontana' in 1965. He & TAYLOR formed as SMILE in 1969 and released 45 'EARTH. / STEP ON ME' for 'Mercury US'. After spending most of 1972 in the studio, QUEEN signed to 'EMI' after sending demo tape through engineer John Anthony. In April 1973, they played The Marquee in London, but prior to any QUEEN release, FREDDIE MERCURY (as LARRY LUREX) issued a one-off 45 in Jun'73 for 'EMI'; I CAN HEAR MUSIC. / GOIN' BACK, (the former an old BEACH BOYS number). A month later, QUEEN unleashed similtaneously their eponymous Roy Thomas-Baker produced debut album, and single 'KEEP YOURSELF ALIVE'. In Nov'73, they supported friends to be MOTT THE HOOPLE, and early next year dented the UK Top 10 with 'SEVEN SEAS OF RHYE'. This was quickly followed by 'QUEEN II', which managed a Top 5 placing, thus rendering 'Elektra' records, to give them chance in the States. Became top group by Christmas 1975, when the near 6-minute epic 'BOHEMIAN RHAPSODY', made UK No.1 for record breaking 9 weeks. It was obviously helped by a masterful video, made for just £5,000, and a pioneer of the video-promo age. QUEEN went on to have over 35 Top 50 UK hits over the next 15 years. Tragically FREDDIE MERCURY was to die of AIDS on 23 Nov'91, after just announcing he had the dreaded disease the day before. • **Style:** Initially a LED ZEPPELIN influenced hard-rock act. The flamboyant FREDDIE MERCURY used large range of vox styles (falsetto or aggressive) for tremendous live sets, although it was largely known that he was a shy bi-sexual in real life. MAY also quiet off-stage, used new coin-pick and own custom made guitars to produce own unique sound. • **Songwriters:** Group or individual compositions. MAY covered: SINCE YOU'VE BEEN GONE (Rainbow; c.Russ Ballard). Note: In QUEEN, MAY wrote most of songs, except some by either MERCURY or group. MERCURY covered: THE GREAT PRETENDER (Platters). The CROSS covered FOXY LADY (Jimi Hendrix) and MAY did ROLLIN' OVER (Small Faces). • **Trivia:** In 1987, MAY began relationship with 'Eastenders' actress Anita Dobson. He also produced a few of her solo singles, and sessioned for LIVING IN A BOX.

Recommended: QUEEN (*7) / QUEEN II (*6) / SHEER HEART ATTACK (*7) / QUEEN'S GREATEST HITS (*9) / GREATEST HITS II (*8).

FREDDIE MERCURY (b.FREDERICK BULSARA, 5 Sep'46, Zanzibar, Africa. In 1959, he moved with family to Feltham, Middlesex, England) – vocals, piano / **BRIAN MAY** (b.19 Jul'47, Twickenham, Middlesex) – guitar, vocals, keyboards / **ROGER MEDDOWS-TAYLOR** (b.26 Jul'49, King's Lynn, England) – drums, vocals / **JOHN DEACON** (b.19 Aug'51, Leicester, England) – bass, vocals

E.M.I. | Elektra

Jul 73. (7") **KEEP YOURSELF ALIVE. / SON AND DAUGHTER**

Jul 73. (lp)(c) **QUEEN** (hit chart Mar74-) 24 | 83 Oct 73
– Keep yourself alive / Doing all right / Great King Rat / My fairy king / Liar / The night comes down / Modern times rock'n'roll / Son and daughter / Jesus / Seven seas of rhye. *(US-only last track) (re-iss.Aug82 on 'Fame') (cd-iss.May88 on 'Fame') (US cd-iss.Jun91 on 'Hollywood', +=)–* Mad the swine, keep yourself alive (long lost retake) / Liar (1991 remix) *(re-iss.cd+c Apr94 on 'Parlophone')*

Nov 73. (7") **LIAR. / DOING ALL RIGHT** -

Feb 74. (7") **SEVEN SEAS OF RHYE. / SEE WHAT A FOOL I'VE BEEN** 10
(re-iss.Nov88 as 3" cd-s, += Funny how love is)

Mar 74. (lp)(c) **QUEEN II** 5 | 49 May 74
– Procession / Father to son / White queen (as it began) / Some day one day / The loser in the end / Ogre battle / The fairy feller's master-stroke / Nevermore / The march of the black queen / Funny how love is / Seven seas of rhye. *(re-iss.Apr84 on 'Fame', cd-iss.Nov86 + May88) (US cd-iss.Oct91 on 'Hollywood', +=)–* See what a fool I've been / Ogre battle – 1991 remix / Seven seas of rhye – 1991 remix. *(re-iss.cd+c Apr94 on 'Parlophone')*

Oct 74. (7") **KILLER QUEEN. / FLICK OF THE WRIST** 2 | 12 Feb 75
(re-iss.Nov88 as 3" cd-s, += Brighton rock)

Nov 74. (lp)(c)(red-lp) **SHEER HEART ATTACK** 2 | 12 Dec 74
– Brighton rock / Killer Queen / Tenement funster / Flick of the wrist / Lily of the valley / Now I'm here / In the lap of the gods / Stone cold crazy / Dear friends / Misfire / Bring back that Leroy Brown / She makes me (stormtrooper in stilettos) / In the lap of the gods (revisited). *(re-iss.1985, cd-iss.Jun88) (US cd-iss.Nov88 on 'Hollywood', +=)–* Stone cold sober – 1991 remix) *(re-iss.cd+c Aug93)*

Jan 75. (7") **NOW I'M HERE. / LILY OF THE VALLEY** 11 | -

Apr 75. (7") **LILY OF THE VALLEY. / KEEP YOURSELF ALIVE** - |

Nov 75. (7") **BOHEMIAN RHAPSODY. / I'M IN LOVE WITH MY CAR** 1 | 9 Dec 75
(re-iss.Nov88 as 3" cd-s, += You're my best friend)

Dec 75. (lp)(c) **A NIGHT AT THE OPERA** 1 | 4
– Death on two legs (dedicated to . . .) / Lazing on a Sunday afternoon / I'm in love with my car / You're my best friend / '39 / Sweet lady / Seaside rendezvous / The prophet's song / Love of my life / Good company / Bohemian rhapsody / God save the Queen. *(re-iss.1985, cd-iss.Jun88) (US cd-iss.Aug91 on 'Hollywood', +=)–* I'm in love with my car – 1991 remix / You're my best friend – 1991 remix. *(re-iss.cd+c Aug93)*

Jun 76. (7") **YOU'RE MY BEST FRIEND. / '39** 7 | 16 May 76

Nov 76. (7") **SOMEBODY TO LOVE. / WHITE MAN** 2 | 13
(re-iss.Nov88 as 3" cd-s, += Tie your mother down)

Dec 76. (lp)(c) **A DAY AT THE RACES** 1 | 5 Jan 77
– Tie your mother down / You take my breath away / Long away / The millionaire waltz / You and I / Somebody to love / White man / Good old fashioned lover boy / Drowse / Teo Torriate (let us cling together). *(re-iss.1984, cd-iss.Jun88) (US cd-iss.Mar91 on 'Hollywood', +=)–* Tie your mother down – remix / Somebody to love – remix.

Mar 77. (7") **TIE YOUR MOTHER DOWN. / YOU AND I** 31 | -

Mar 77. (7") **TIE YOUR MOTHER DOWN. / DROWSE** - | 49

May 77. (7"ep) **QUEEN'S FIRST EP** 17 | -
– Good old fashioned lover boy / Death on two legs / White Queen (as it began) / Tenement funster. *(re-iss.Nov88 as 3" cd-ep)*

Jun 77. (7") **LONG AWAY. / YOU AND I** - |

Oct 77. (7") **WE ARE THE CHAMPIONS. / WE WILL ROCK YOU** 2 | 4
(re-iss.Nov88 as 3" cd-s, += Fat bottomed girls)

Nov 77. (lp)(c) **NEWS OF THE WORLD** 4 | 3
– We will rock you / We are the champions / Sheer heart attack / All dead, all dead / Spread your wings / Fight from the inside / Get down make love / Sleeping on the sidewalk / Who needs you / It's late / My melancholy blues. *(re-iss.1985, cd-iss.Jun88) (US cd-iss.Mar91 on 'Hollywood', +=)–* We will rock you – 1991 remix.

Feb 78. (7") **SPREAD YOUR WINGS. / SHEER HEART ATTACK** 34 | -

Apr 78. (7") **IT'S LATE. / SHEER HEART ATTACK** - | 74

Oct 78. (7") **BICYCLE RACE. / FAT BOTTOMED GIRLS** 11 | 24 Nov 78

Nov 78. (lp)(c) **JAZZ** 2 | 6
– Mustapha / Fat bottomed girls / Jealousy / Bicycle race / If you can't beat them / Let me entertain you / Dead on time / In only seven days / Dreamer's ball / Fun it / Leaving home ain't easy / Don't stop me now / More of that jazz. *(re-iss. 1985, cd-iss.Jun88) (US cd-iss.Jun91 on 'Hollywood', +=)–* Fat bottomed girls – 1991 remix / Bicycle race – 1991 remix. *(re-iss.cd+c Feb94 on 'Parlophone')*

Feb 79. (7") **DON'T STOP ME NOW. / IN ONLY SEVEN DAYS** 9 | -

Feb 79. (7") **DON'T STOP ME NOW. / MORE OF THAT JAZZ** - | 86

Apr 79. (7") **JEALOUSY. / FUN IT** - |

Jun 79. (d-lp)(c) **LIVE KILLERS (live)** 3 | 16
– We will rock you / Let me entertain you / Death on two legs (dedicated to . . .) /

Killer Queen / Bicycle race / I'm in love with my car / Get down, make love / You're my best friend / Now I'm here / Dreamer's ball / '39 / Keep yourself alive / Don't stop me now / Spread your wings / Brighton rock / Bohemian rhapsody / Tie your mother down / Sheer heart attack / We will rock you / We are the champions / God save the Queen. *(re-iss.1985, cd-iss.Jun88) (US cd-iss.Nov88 on 'Hollywood') (re-iss.cd+c Apr94 on 'Parlophone')*

Jul 79. (7") **LOVE OF MY LIFE (live). / NOW I'M HERE (live)** [63] [-]

Aug 79. (7") **WE WILL ROCK YOU (live). / LET ME ENTERTAIN YOU (live)** [-] [ ]

Oct 79. (7") **CRAZY LITTLE THING CALLED LOVE. / WE WILL ROCK YOU (live)** [2] [-]

Dec 79. (7") **CRAZY LTTLE THING CALLED LOVE. / SPREAD YOUR WINGS** [-] [1]

Feb 80. (7") **SAVE ME. / LET ME ENTERTAIN YOU (live)** [11] [-]

Jun 80. (7") **PLAY THE GAME. / HUMAN BODY** [14] [42]

Jul 80. (lp)(c) **THE GAME** [1] [1]

– Play the game / Dragon attack / Another one bites the dust / Need your loving tonight / Crazy little thing called love / Rock it (prime jive) / Don't try suicide / Sail away sweet sister / Coming soon / Save me. *(re-iss.1985, cd-iss.Jun88) (US cd-iss.Jun91 on 'Hollywood', +=)–* Dragon attack – 1991 remix. *(re-iss.cd+c Feb94 on 'Parlophone')*

Aug 80. (7") **ANOTHER ONE BITES THE DUST. / DRAGON ATTACK** [7] [-]

Aug 80. (7") **ANOTHER ONE BITES THE DUST. / DON'T TRY SUICIDE** [-] [1]

(re-iss.Nov88 as 3" cd-s, += Las Palabras de amor)

Oct 80. (7") **NEED YOUR LOVING TONIGHT. / ROCK IT (PRIME JIVE)** [-] [44]

Nov 80. (7") **FLASH. / FOOTBALL FIGHT** [10] [42] Jan 81

Dec 80. (lp)(c) **FLASH GORDON (Soundtrack)** [10] [23]

– Flash's theme / In the space capsule (the love theme) / Ming's theme (in the court of Ming the merciless) / The ring (hypnotic seduction of Dale) / Football fight / In the death cell (love theme reprise) / Execution of Flash / The kiss (Aura resurrects Flash) / Arboria (planet of the tree men) / Escape from the swamp / Flash to the rescue / Vultan's theme (attack of the hawk men) / Battle theme / The wedding march / The marriage of Dale and Ming (and Flash approaching) / Flash's theme reprise (victory celebrations) / The hero. *(re-iss. 1985, cd-iss.Jun88) (US cd-iss.Aug91 on 'Hollywood', +=)–* Flash – 1991 remix. *(re-iss.cd+c Apr94 on 'Parlophone')*

Nov 81. (lp)(c) **QUEEN'S GREATEST HITS** (compilation) [1] [14]

– Bohemian rhapsody / Another one bites the dust / Killer queen / Fat bottomed girls / Bicycle race / You're my best friend / Don't stop me now / Save me *(repl. on US-version by 'Keep Yourself Alive' + 'Under Pressure')* / Crazy little thing called love / Now I'm here / Good old-fashioned lover boy / Play the game / Flash / Seven seas of Rhye / We will rock you / We are the champions / Somebody to love. *(re-iss.Aug84) (re-iss.Dec91 on 'Parlophone', hit UK 7) (re-iss.cd+c Jun94 on 'Parlophone')*

Nov 81. (7") **UNDER PRESSURE. ("QUEEN and DAVID BOWIE") / SOUL BROTHER** [1] [29]

(re-iss.Nov88 as 3" cd-s, += Body language)

Apr 82. (7") **BODY LANGUAGE. / LIFE IS REAL (SONG FOR LENNON)** [25] [11]

May 82. (lp)(c) **HOT SPACE** [4] [22]

– Staying power / Dancer / Back chat / Body language / Action this day / Put out the fire / Life is real (song for Lennon) / Calling all girls / Las Palabras de amor / Cool cat / Under pressure. *(cd-iss.Jun88) (re-is.+cd.Aug89 on 'Fame') (US cd-iss.Mar91 on 'Hollywood', += Body language – 1991 remix) (re-iss.cd+c Feb94 on 'Parlophone')*

Jun 82. (7") **LAS PALABRAS DE AMOR. / COOL CAT** [17] [-]

Jul 82. (7") **CALLING ALL GIRLS. / PUT OUT THE FIRE** [-] [60]

Aug 82. (7")(12") **BACKCHAT. / STAYING POWER** [40] [ ]

E.M.I. Capitol

Jan 84. (7") **RADIO GA-GA (edit). / I GO CRAZY** [2] [16]

('A'ext-12") – ('A'dub version). *(re-iss.Nov88 as 3" cd-s += Hammer to fall +7"tracks)*

Mar 84. (lp)(c)(cd) **THE WORKS** [2] [23]

– Radio Ga-ga / Tear it up / It's a hard life / Man on the prowl / Machines (or back to humans) / I want to break free / Keep passing the open windows / Hammer to fall / Is his he world we created?. *(re-US cd-iss.Dec91 on 'Hollywood', +=)–* Radio Ga Ga (12"mix) / I want to break free (12"mix) / I go crazy) (re-iss.cd+c Feb94 on 'Parlophone')

Apr 84. (7")(12") **I WANT TO BREAK FREE (remix). / MACHINES (OR BACK TO HUMANS)** [3] [45]

(re-iss.Nov88 as 3" cd-s, += It's a hard life)

Jul 84. (7")(12"pic-d) **IT'S A HARD LIFE. / IS THIS THE WORLD WE CREATED?** [6] [72]

(12"+=) – ('A'extended remix).

Sep 84. (7") **HAMMER TO FALL (edit). / TEAR IT UP** [13] [ ]

(12") – ('A'headbangers mix).

Dec 84. (7") **THANK GOD IT'S CHRISTMAS. / MAN ON THE PROWL / KEEP PASSING OPEN WINDOWS** [21] [-]

(12") – ('B'side extended).

note:- In the mid 80's and earlier, each individual had also launched solo ⇒

Nov 85. (7")('A'ext-12") **ONE VISION. / BLURRED VISION** [7] [61]

Feb 86. (7") **PRINCESS OF THE UNIVERSE. / A DOZEN RED ROSES FOR MY DARLING** [-] [ ]

Mar 86. (7") **A KIND OF MAGIC. / A DOZEN RED ROSES FOR MY DARLING** [3] [42] Jun 86

('A'ext-12")(12"pic-d) – (as above) *(re-iss.Nov88 as 3" cd-s, += One vision)*

May 86. (lp)(c)(cd) **A KIND OF MAGIC** [1] [46]

– One vision / A kind of magic / One year of love / Pain is so close to pleasure / Friends will be friends / Who wants to live forever / Gimme the prize / Don't lose your head / Princes of the universe. *(cd+=)–* A kind of 'A kind of magic – Friends will be friends – Who wants to live forever). *(re-US cd-iss. Jun91 on 'Hollywood', +=)–* Forever, One vision.

Jun 86. (7")(7"pic-d) **FRIENDS WILL BE FRIENDS. / SEVEN SEAS OF RHYE** [14] [-]

(12"+=) – ('A'extended mix).

Jul 86. (7") **DON'T LOSE YOUR HEAD. / PAIN IS SO CLOSE TO PLEASURE** [-] [ ]

Sep 86. (7") **WHO WANTS TO LIVE FOREVER (edit). / KILLER QUEEN** [24] [-]

(12"+=) – ('A'lp version) / Forever.

Dec 86. (d-lp)(c)(cd) **LIVE MAGIC (live)** [3] [ ]

-- One vision / Tie your mother down / I want to break free / Hammer to fall / Seven seas of rhye / We are the champions / Another one bites the dust / Is this the world we created? / Bohemian rhasody / Radio Ga Ga / Friends will be friends / We will rock you / Under pressure / A kind of music / God save the Queen. *(re-iss.Dec91 on 'Parlophone', hit UK No.51)*

— During this lull in QUEEN activity, FREDDIE MERCURY had released some solo singles and collaborated with MONTSERRAT CABALLE. TAYLOR had formed The CROSS ⇒

Apr 89. (7")(c-s) **I WANT IT ALL. / HANG ON IN THERE** [3] [50]

(12"+=)(cd-s+=) – ('A'album version).

May 89. (lp)(c)(cd) **THE MIRACLE** [1] [24]

– Party / Khashoggis ship / The miracle / I want it all / The invisible man / Breakthru / Rain must fall / Scandal / Was it all worth it / My baby does me. *(cd+=)–* Hang on in there / Chinese torture / The invisible man (ext). *(re-US cd-iss.Oct91 on 'Hollywood', ++= Scandal – 12"mix)*

Jun 89. (7")(c-s)(7"sha-pic-d) **BREAKTHRU. / STEALIN'** [7] [ ]

(12"+=)(cd-s+=) – ('A'extended).

Aug 89. (7")(c-s)(7"clear) **INVISIBLE MAN. / HIJACK MY HEART** [12] [ ]

(12"+=)(cd-s+=)(12"clear+=) – ('A'extended).

Oct 89. (7")(c-s) **SCANDAL. / MY LIFE HAS BEEN SAVED** [25] [ ]

(12"+=)(cd-s+=) – ('A'extended).

Dec 89. (7")(c-s) **THE MIRACLE. / STONE COLD CRAZY (live)** [21] [ ]

(12"+=)(cd-s+=) – My melancholy blues (live '77).

Parlophone Hollywood

Jan 91. (7")(c-s) **INNUENDO. / BIJOU** [1] [ ]

(12"+=)(cd-s+=)(12"pic-d+=) – Under pressure (extended).

Feb 91. (cd)(c)(lp) **INNUENDO** [1] [30]

– Innuendo / I'm going slightly mad / Headlong / I can't live with you / Don't try so hard / Ride the wild wind / All God's people / These are the days of our lives / Delilah / Hit man / Bijou / The show must go on. *(re-hit.34 Dec91)*

Mar 91. (7")(c-s)(7"sha-pic-d) **I'M GOING SLIGHTLY MAD. / HIT MAN** [22] [ ]

(12"+=)(cd-s+=) – Lost opportunity.

May 91. (7")(c-s) **HEADLONG. / ALL GOD'S PEOPLE** [14] [ ]

(12"+=)(cd-s+=)(12"pic-d+=) – Mad the swine.

Sep 91. (7")(c-s) **THE SHOW MUST GO ON. / KEEP YOURSELF ALIVE** [16] [ ]

(12"+=) – (Queen talks – interview). (cd-s++=) – Body language.

(cd-s) – ('A'side) / Now I'm here / Fat bottomed girls / Los Palabras de amor.

Oct 91. (cd)(c)(d-lp) **GREATEST HITS II** (compilation) (US title 'CLASSIC QUEEN') [1] [4]

– A kind of magic / Under pressure / Radio Ga Ga / I want it all / I want to break free / Innuendo / It's a hard life / Breakthru / Who wants to live forever / Headlong / The miracle / I'm going slightly mad / The invisible man / Hammer to fall / Friends will be friends / The show must go on / One vision. *(hit UK No.29 in May93)* (US-version +=)– Bohemian rhapsody / Stone cold crazy / One year of love / Tie your mother down / These are the days of our lives / Keep yourself alive.

— On the 23 Nov'91, FREDDIE lost his 2 year silent battle against AIDS. The previous day, it was announced in the news. The rumours had now ended.

Dec 91. (7")(12")(c-s)(cd-s) **BOHEMIAN RHAPSODY. / THESE ARE THE DAYS OF OUR LIVES** [1] [2]

Jun 92. (c-s)(cd-s) **WE WILL ROCK YOU. / WE ARE THE CHAMPIONS** [-] [52]

Sep 92. (cd)(c) **GREATEST HITS** [-] [11]

Apr 93. (7"ep)(c-ep)(cd-ep) **FIVE LIVE EP ("GEORGE MICHAEL / QUEEN")** [1] [46] album

– Somebody to love / Medley: Killer / Papa was a rollin' stone / These are the days of our lives (with LISA STANSFIELD) / Calling you.

(cd-s) – ('A'side) / Medley: Killer / Papa was a rollin' stone (with PM DAWN).

(12"+=) – Medley: Killer / Papa was a rollin' stone – instrumental.

— (In the US, the EP's main track 'SOMEBODY TO LOVE', hit No.30)

— In Feb95, FREDDIE and BRIAN featured on EDDIE HOWELL's re-issued 1977 single 'THE MAN FROM MANHATTAN'.

Oct 95. (c-s) **HEAVEN FOR EVERYONE / IT'S A BEAUTIFUL DAY** [2] [ ]

(cd-s+=) – ('A'-lp version).
(cd-s) – ('A'sie) / Keep yourself alive / Seven seas of rhye / Killer queen.

Nov 95. (cd)(c)(lp) **MADE IN HEAVEN** [1] [58]
– It's a beautiful day / Made in Heaven / Let me live / Mother love / My life has been saved / I was born to love you / Heaven for everyone / Too much love will kill you / You don't fool me / A winter's tale / It's a beautiful day (reprise) / Yeh / Track 13.

Dec 95. (7")(c-s) **A WINTER'S TALE. / THANK GOD IT'S CHRISTMAS** [6] [ ]
(cd-s+=) – Rock in Rio blues.
(cd-s) – ('A'side) / Now I'm here / You're my best friend / Somebody to love.

. . . Jan – Jun '96 stop press . . .

Feb 96. (single) **TOO MUCH LOVE WILL KILL YOU** [15] [ ]
Jun 96. (single) **LET ME LIVE** [9] [ ]

– more compilations, etc. –

Dec 85. EMI/ US= Capitol; (14xlp-box) **THE COMPLETE WORKS** [ ] [ ]
Nov 88. EMI; (3"cd-s) **CRAZY LITTLE THING CALLED LOVE / SPREAD YOUR WINGS / FLASH** [ ] [-]
Dec 89. Band Of Joy; (lp)(c)(cd) **QUEEN AT THE BEEB (live)** [67] [-]
Jun 92. Parlophone/ US= Hollywood; (cd) **QUEEN: LIVE AT WEMBLEY (live)** [2] [53]
– (above was originally issued UK on video)
Oct 94. Parlophone; (d-cd)(d-c) **GREATEST HITS 1 & 2** [37] [ ]
Dec 95. EMI; (cd-box) **ULTIMATE QUEEN** [ ] [ ]

FREDDIE MERCURY

C.B.S. / Columbia

Sep 84. (7")(7"pic-d)('A'ext-12") **LOVE KILLS. / ROT WANG'S PARTY** [10] [69]
(above from film 'Metropolis' & co-written w / Georgio Moroder)
Apr 85. (7")('A'ext-12") **I WAS BORN TO LOVE YOU. / STOP ALL THE FIGHTING** [11] [ ]
(d7"+=) – Love kills (extended) / Stop all the fighting (extended).
May 85. (lp)(c)(cd) **MR. BAD GUY** [6] [ ]
– Let's turn it on * / Made in Heaven / I was born to love you * / Foolin' around / Mr. Bad guy / Man made Paradise / There must be more to life than this / Living on my own * / Your kind of lover / My love is dangerous / Love me like there's no tomorrow. *(c+cd+=)*– (* extended tracks).
Jul 85. (7")(7"sha-pic-d) **MADE IN HEAVEN (remix). / SHE BLOWS HOT AND COLD** [57] [-]
('A'&'B'extended-12") – (also 'A'side version).
Sep 85. (7") **LIVING ON MY OWN. / MY LOVE IS DANGEROUS** [50] [-]
(12") – ('A'&'B'extended).
Oct 85. (7") **LIVING ON MY OWN. / SHE BLOWS HOT AND COLD** [-] [ ]
Nov 85. (7") **LOVE ME LIKE THERE IS NO TOMORROW. / LET'S TURN IT ON** [ ] [-]
(12") – ('A'&'B'extended).
(below from Dave Clark musical 'Time')

E.M.I. / not issued

May 86. (7")(ext-12") **TIME. / TIME (instrumental)** [ ] [ ]

Parlophone / Capitol

Feb 87. (7")(7"sha-pic-d) **THE GREAT PRETENDER. / EXERCISES IN FREE LOVE** [4] [ ]
(12"+=) – ('A'extended).

FREDDIE MERCURY with MONTSERRAT CABALLE

(female Spanish opera star)

Polydor / Polydor?

Oct 87. (7") **BARCELONA. / EXERCISES IN FREE LOVE** (her version) [8] [ ]
(12"+=)(c-s+=)(cd-s+=)(12"pic-d+=) – ('A'extended version).
Oct 88. (lp)(c)(cd) **BARCELONA** [25] [ ]
– Barcelona / La Japonaise / The fallen priest / Ensueno / The golden boy / Guide me home / How can I go on / Overture piccante. *(re-iss.Aug92, hit UK No.15)*
Oct 88. (7") **THE GOLDEN BOY. / THE FALLEN PRIEST** [ ] [ ]
(12"+=)(cd-s+=) – ('A'instrumental).
Jan 89. (7")(7"pic-d) **HOW CAN I GO ON. / OVERTURE PICCANTE** [ ] [ ]
(12"+=)(cd-s+=) – Guide me home.

– (FREDDIE MERCURY) compilations, others, etc. –

Jul 92. Polydor; (7")(c-s)(cd-s) **BARCELONA. / EXCERCISES IN FREE LOVE** [2] [ ]
(12"+=) – ('A'extended).
Oct 92. Polydor; (7")(c-s) **HOW CAN I GO ON. / THE GOLDEN BOY** [ ] [ ]
(cd-s+=) – The fallen priest.
(12"+=)(cd-s+=) – Guide me home / Overture paccante.
Nov 92. Parlophone/ US= Maverick; (cd)(c)(lp) **THE FREDDIE MERCURY ALBUM** [4] [ ]
– The great pretender / Foolin' around / Time / Your kind of love / Exercises in free love / In my defence / Mr.Bad guy / Let's turn it on / Living on my own / Love kills / Barcelona (w / MONSERRAT CABALLE). *(re-iss.Jul93, hit UK No.13)*
Dec 92. Parlophone; (7")(c-s) **IN MY DEFENCE. / LOVE KILLS (original)** [8] [ ]
(cd-s+=) – Mr.Bad guy / Living on my own (mix).
Jan 93. Parlophone; (7")(c-s) **THE GREAT PRETENDER. / STOP ALL THE FIGHTING** [29] [ ]
(cd-s+=) – Exercises in free love / ('A'malouf mix).
Jul 93. (7")(12")(c-s)(cd-s) **LIVING ON MY OWN. / ('A'mixes)** [1] [ ]

BRIAN MAY & FRIENDS

with **EDDIE VAN HALEN** – guitar / **PHIL CHEN** – bass / **FRED MANDEL** – keyboards / **ALAN GRATZER** – drums etc.

E.M.I. / Capitol

Oct 83. (7") **STARFLEET. / SON OF STARFLEET** [65] [-]
Oct 83. (7") **STARFLEET. / STARFLEET (extended)** [-] [ ]
Oct 83. (m-lp)(c) **STARFLEET PROJECT** [35] [ ]
– Starfleet / Let me out / Bluesbreaker.

BRIAN MAY

E.M.I. / Capitol

Sep 89. (7") **WHO WANTS TO LIVE FOREVER.** (by **"IAN MEESON & BELINDA GHILETT") /** ('A'instrumental) [ ] [-]
(12"+=)(cd-s+=) – ('A'version by LOUISA MAY – original demo).

Parlophone / Capitol

Nov 91. (7")(c-s) **DRIVEN BY YOU. / JUST ONE LIFE (DEDICATED TO THE MEMORY OF PHILIP SAYER)** [6] [ ]
(cd-s+=) – ('B'guitar version) / ('A' Ford ad 1:30 version).
Sep 92. (7") **TOO MUCH LOVE WILL KILL YOU. / I'M SCARED** [5] [ ]
(cd-s+=) – ('A'guitar version) / Driven by you (feat. COZY POWELL + NEIL MURRAY).
Oct 92. (cd)(c)(lp) **BACK TO THE LIGHT** [6] [ ]
– The dark / Back to the light / Love token / Resurrection / Too much love will kill you / Driven by you / Nothin' but blue / I'm scared / Last horizon / Let your heart rule your head / Just one life / Rollin' over.

—— In Oct'92, BRIAN featured on HANK MARVIN's (Shadows) version of QUEEN's song 'WE ARE THE CHAMPIONS'.

Nov 92. (7") **BACK TO THE LIGHT. / NOTHING BUT BLUE (guitar version)** [19] [ ]
(cd-s+=) – Blues breaker. (cd-s+=) – Star fleet / Let me out.
Jun 93. (c-s) **RESURRECTION. ("BRIAN MAY with COZY POWELL") / LOVE TOKEN** [23] [ ]
(cd-s+=)(12"pic-d+=) – Too much love will kill you (live).
(cd-s) – ('A'side) / Driven by you (two) / Back to the light (live) / Tie your mother down (live).
Dec 93. (7")(c-s) **LAST HORIZON. / LET YOUR HEART RULE YOUR HEAD** [51] [ ]
(cd-s) – ('A'side) / ('A'live) / We will rock you (live) / ('A'lp mix).

The BRIAN MAY BAND

MAY – vox, guitar with **COZY POWELL** – drums / **NEIL MURRAY** – bass / **SPIKE EDNEY** – keyboards / **JAMIE MOSES** – guitar, vocals / **CATHY PORTER + SHELLEY PRESTON** – vox

Feb 94. (cd)(c)(d-lp) **LIVE AT THE BRIXTON ACADEMY (live London, 15th June 1993)** [20] [ ]
– Back to the light / Driven by you / Tie your mother down / Love token / Headlong / Love of my life / 39 – Let your heart rule your head / Too much love will kill you / Since you've been gone / Now I'm here / Guitar extravagance / Resurrection / Last horizon / We will rock you / Hammer to fall.

his compilations, etc

Dec 95. Javelin; (cd) **THEMES AND DREAMS** [ ] [-]
Dec 95. Koch; (cd-s) **BLACK WHITE HOUSE** [ ] [-]

ROGER TAYLOR

E.M.I. / Elektra

Aug 77. (7") **I WANNA TESTIFY. / TURN ON THE T.V.** [ ] [-]
Apr 81. (7") **FUTURE MANAGEMENT. / LAUGH OR CRY** [49] [-]
Apr 81. (lp)(c) **FUN IN SPACE** [18] [ ]
– No violins / Laugh or cry / Future management / Let's get crazy / My country I & II / Good times are now / Magic is loose / Interlude in Constantinople / Airheads / Fun in space.
Apr 81. (7") **LET'S GET CRAZY. / LAUGH OR CRY** [-] [ ]
Jun 81. (7") **MY COUNTRY (edit). / FUN IN SPACE** [ ] [-]

		E.M.I.	Capitol
Jun 84.	(7")(12") **MAN ON FIRE. / KILLING TIME**	66	-
Jul 84.	(lp)(c) **STRANGE FRONTIER** – Strange frontier / Beautiful dreams / Man on fire / Racing in the street / Masters of war / Killing time / Abandon fire / Young love / It's an illusion / I cry for you (love, hope & confusion).	30	
Aug 84.	(7") **STRANGE FRONTIER. / I CRY FOR YOU (remix)** ('A'&'B'extended-12"+=) – Two sharp pencils.		-

The CROSS

ROGER with **PETER NOONE** – bass / **CLAYTON MOSS** – guitar / **SPIKE EDNEY** – keyboards / **JOSH MacRAE** – drums

		Virgin	Virgin
Sep 87.	(7") **COWBOYS AND INDIANS. / LOVE LIES BLEEDING** (12"+=)(c-s+=) – ('A'extended).	74	
Jan 88.	(7") **SHOVE IT. / ROUGH JUSTICE** (12"+=) – ('A'metropolis mix). (cd-s++=) – Cowboys and Indians.		
Jan 88.	(lp)(c)(cd) **SHOVE IT** – Shove it / Heaven for everyone / Love on a tightrope (like an animal) / Cowboys and Indians / Stand up for love / Love lies bleeding (she was a wicked, wily waitress) / Contact. (cd+=) – Rough justice – 2nd shelf mix.	58	
Mar 88.	(7") **HEAVEN FOR EVERYONE. / LOVE ON A TIGHTROPE (LIKE AN ANIMAL)** (12"+=) – Contact.		
Jul 88.	(7") **MANIPULATOR. / STAND UP FOR LOVE** (12"+=) – ('A'extended).		
Apr 90.	(7") **POWER TO LOVE. / PASSION FOR TRASH** (12"+=)(cd-s+=) – ('A'extended).		
May 90.	(cd)(c)(lp) **MAD, BAD AND DANGEROUS TO KNOW** – On top of the world ma / Liar / Closer to you / Breakdown / Penetration guru / Power to love / Sister blue / Better things / Old men (lay down) / Final destination. (cd+=) – Foxy lady.		

ROGER TAYLOR

with **JASON FALLOON** – guitars / **PHIL SPALDING** – bass / **MIKE CROSSLEY** – piano, keyboards / **CATHERINE PORTER** – backing vocals / **JOSHUA J. MacRAE** – programming

		Parlophone	Capitol
Apr 94.	(7")(c-s) **NAZIS 1994. / ('A'radio mix)** (12"red+=) – ('A'extended) / ('A'big science mix). (cd-s++=) – ('A'kick mix) / ('A'-Schindler's extended mix).	22	
Sep 94.	(cd)(c) **HAPPINESS?** – Nazis 1994 / Happiness / Revelations / Touch the sky / Foreign sand / Freedom train / You had to be there / The key / Everybody hurts sometime / Loneliness . . . / Dear Mr.Murdoch / Old friends.	22	

— Below featured a Japanese classically trained drummer, pianist & co-composer **YOSHIKI** plus **JIM CREGAN** – guitars / **PHIL CHEN** – bass / **DICK MARX** – strings arr.

Sep 94.	(7"colrd)(c-s) **FOREIGN SAND. ("ROGER TAYLOR & YOSHIKI") / ('A'mix)** (12"pic-d+=)(cd-s+=) – You had to be there / Final destination.	26	
Nov 94.	(7") **HAPPINESS. / RIDE THE WILD WIND (live)** (12") – ('A'side) / Dear Mr.Murdoch / Everybody hurts sometime (live) / Old friends (live). (cd-s) – ('A'side) / Loneliness / Dear Mr.Murdoch / I want to break free (live).	32	

The IMMORTALS

— **JOHN DEACON** played bass on their (May86 'M.C.A.'(7")(12") **NO TURNING BACK. / ('A'mix)**from the film 'Biggles'.

QUEENSRYCHE

Formed: Bellevue, Seattle, Washington, USA . . . 1980 initially as THE MOB by high school friends (see line-up). After releasing debut EP on Diana Harris' '206' label in '83, they signed to 'EMI America', and re-issued it. Made commercial headway for the rest of the 80's, and finally cracked the US & UK market in the early 90's, with Top 20 album 'EMPIRE'. • **Style:** Heavy techno rockers whose 1988 concept album 'OPERATION: MINDCRIME', was inspired by the psi-fi writer George Orwell. It also featured Michael Kamen who arranged string and choir. • **Trivia:** Peter Collins produced this album JAMES GUTHRIE their debut + NEIL KERNON the follow-up. PAMELA MOORE was guest singer on 'SUITE SISTER MARY'. • **Songwriters:** DeGARMO or TATE / WILSON except; SCARBOROUGH FAIR – CANTICLE (Simon & Garfunkel) / GONNA GET CLOSE TO YOU (Lisa Diabello).

Recommended: OPERATION: MINDCRIME (*8) / EMPIRE (*7).

GEOFF TATE (b.14 Jan'59) – vocals / **CHRIS DeGARMO** (b.14 Jun'63) – guitar / **MICHAEL WILTON** (b.23 Feb'62) – guitar / **EDDIE JACKSON** (b.29 Jan'61) – bass / **SCOTT ROCKENFIELD** (b.15 Jun'50) – drums

		EMI Amer..	EMI Amer..
Sep 83.	(12"ep) **QUEENSRYCHE** – Queen of the Reich / Nightrider / Blinded / The lady wore black.		
Sep 84.	(7") **TAKE HOLD OF THE FLAME. / NIGHTRIDER**		
Sep 84.	(lp)(c) **THE WARNING** – The warning / En force / Deliverance / No sanctuary / N.M. 156 / Take hold of the flame / Before the storm / Child of fire / Roads to madness. *(cd-iss.Mar87) (cd+c.re-iss.Aug91) (re-iss.cd Oct94)*		61
Jul 86.	(lp)(c)(cd) **RAGE FOR ORDER** – Walk in the shadows / I dream in infrared / The whisper / Gonna get close to you / The killing words / Surgical strike / Neue regel / Chemical youth (we are rebellion) / London / Screaming in digital / I will remember. *(cd+c.re-iss.Aug91) (re-iss.cd Oct94)*	66	47
Aug 86.	(7") **GONNA GET CLOSE TO YOU. / PROPHECY** (d7"+=) – Queen of the Reich / Deliverance.		
		Manhattan	Manhattan
May 88.	(lp)(c)(cd) **OPERATION: MINDCRIME** – I remember now / Anarchy-X / Revolution calling / Operation: Mindcrime / Speak / Spreading the disease / The mission / The needle lies / Suite Sister Mary / Electric requiem / Breaking the silence / I don't believe in love / Waiting for 22 / My empty room / Eyes of a stranger. *(re-iss.cd Oct94)*	58	50
Oct 88.	(10"ep) **OVERSEEING THE OPERATION. / EXCERPTS FROM OPERATION MINDCRIME: SUITE SISTER MARY – I Remember Now / Revolution Calling / Operation: Mindcrime / Breaking The Silence / Eyes Of A Stranger.**		
Apr 89.	(7") **EYES OF A STRANGER. / QUEEN OF THE REICH** (12"+=) – Walk in the shadows / Take hold of the flame. (cd-s+=) – Prophecy / Take hold of the flame.	59	
		E.M.I. USA	Manhattan
Sep 90.	(7")(7"sha-pic-d) **EMPIRE. / SCARBOROUGH FAIR – CANTICLE** (12"+=)(cd-s+=) – Prophecy.	61	
Sep 90.	(cd)(c)(d-lp) **EMPIRE** – Best I can do / The thin line / Jet city woman / Della Brown / Another rainy night (without you) / Empire / Resistance / Silent lucidity / Hand on heart / One and only / Anybody listening? *(re-iss.cd Oct94)*	13	7
Apr 91.	(7")(c-s) **SILENT LUCIDITY. / THE MISSION (live)** (12"+=) – Eyes of a stranger. (cd-s++=) – Della Brown.	34	9 Mar 91
Jun 91.	(7")(c-s) **BEST I CAN DO. / I DREAM IN INFRARED (acoustic)** (10"+=) – Prophecy. (12"++=)(cd-s++=) – ('A'radio edit).	36	
Aug 91.	(7")(c-s) **JET CITY WOMAN. / EMPIRE (live)** (12"+=) – Walk in the shadows (live). (cd-s) ('A' side) / Queen of The Reich. / Walk in the shadows (live)	39	
Nov 91.	(cd)(c) **OPERATION: LIVECRIME (live)**	-	38
Aug 92.	(7")(c-s) **SILENT LUCIDITY. / I DON'T BELIEVE IN LOVE** (live) (12") – Last time in Paris / Take hold of the fame. (cd-s) ('A' side) / Eyes of a stranger (live) / Operation: Mindcrime. (cd-s) ('A' side) / Suite Sister Mary (live) / Last time in Paris.	18	
Oct 94.	(cd)(c)(lp) **PROMISED LAND** – 9:28 a.m. / I am I / Damaged / Out of mind / Bridge / Promised land / Disconnected / Lady Jane / My global mind / One more time / Someone else?.	13	3
Jan 95.	(12"gold) **I AM I. / REAL WORLD / SOMEONE ELSE?** (cd-s+=) – Dirty li'l secret.	40	
Mar 95.	(7"pic-d)(c-s) **BRIDGE. / THE KILLING WORDS (live)** (cd-s+=) – The lady wore black (live) / Damaged (live). (cd-s) – ('A'side) / Silent lucidity (live) / My empty room (live) / Real world (live).	40	

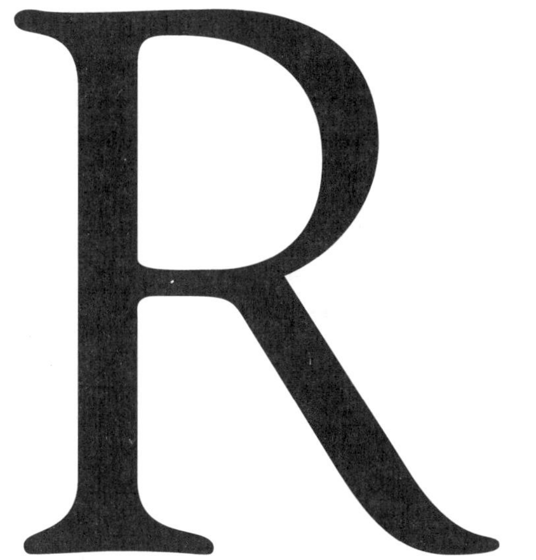

RADIOHEAD

Formed: Oxford, England . . . 1988 by YORKE, etc. Quickly found contract on 'Parlophone / Capitol', and ventured to the US in 1992, where their debut album 'PABLO HONEY', was selling like hotcakes, due to playlisting on MTV. By the end of the year, they were the toast of Britain as well, after their 'CREEP' single hit the Top 10. • **Style:** Grunge guitar punk-rock lying somewhere between U2, NIRVANA or The ONLY ONES, although YORKE's image is certainly his own. • **Songwriters:** YORKE lyrics / group music. • **Trivia:** NME readers voted them in Top 10 bands of '92!, after hearing only singles.

Recommended: PABLO HONEY (*8) / THE BENDS (*9)

THOM YORKE – vocals, guitar / **ED O'BRIEN** – guitar, vocals / **JON GREENWOOD** – guitar / **COLIN GREENWOOD** – bass / **PHIL SELWAY** – drums

		Parlophone	Capitol
May 92.	(12"ep)(c-ep)(cd-ep) **PROVE YOURSELF / STUPID CAR. / YOU / THINKING ABOUT YOU**		
Sep 92.	(12"ep)(c-ep)(cd-ep) **CREEP / LURCEE. / INSIDE MY HEAD / MILLION DOLLAR QUESTION**		
Feb 93.	(12"ep)(c-ep)(cd-ep) **ANYONE CAN PLAY GUITAR. / COKE BABIES / FAITHLESS, THE WONDER BOY**	32	
Feb 93.	(cd)(c)(lp) **PABLO HONEY** – You / Creep / How do you? / Stop whispering / Thinking about you / Anyone can play guitar / Ripcord / Vegetable / Prove yourself / I can't / Lurgee / Blow out.	25	32 Jun 93
May 93.	(12"ep)(c-ep)(cd-ep) **POP IS DEAD / BANANA CO. (live). / CREEP (live) / RIPCORD (live)**	42	
Sep 93.	(7"clear-ep)(c-ep)(cd-ep) **CREEP / YES I AM. / BLOW OUT (remix) / INSIDE MY HEAD (live)** (12"ep) – ('A'side) / Vegetable (live) / Killer cars (live) / You (live).	7	34 Jun 93
Oct 94.	(12"ep)(c-ep) **MY IRON LUNG E.P.** – Lewis (mistreated) / The trickster / Punchdrunk lovesick singalong. (cd-s) – (2nd + 3rd tracks) / Lozenger of love. (cd-s) – (1st track) / Permanent daylight / You never wash up after yourself.	24	
Mar 95.	(c-s) **HIGH & DRY. / PLANET TELEX** (cd-s+=) – Maquiladora / Planet Telex (hexidecimal mix). (cd-s+=) – Killer cars / (Planet Telex (L.F.O. JD mix). (12") – Planet Telex (hexidecimal mix) / Planet Telex (L.F.O. JD mix) / Planet Telex (hexidecimal dub) / High & dry.	17	78 Mar 96
Mar 95.	(cd)(c)(lp) **THE BENDS** – Planet Telex / The bends / High & dry / Fake plastic trees / Bones (nice dream) / Just / My iron lung / Bulletproof . . .I wish I was / Black star / Sulk / Street spirit (fade out).	6	88
May 95.	(c-s)(cd-s) **FAKE PLASTIC TREES / INDIA RUBBER / HOW CAN YOU BE SURE?** (cd-s) – ('A'side) / ('A'acoustic) / Bulletproof..I wish I was (acoustic) / Street spirit (fade out) (acoustic).	20	
Aug 95.	(c-s)(cd-s) **JUST / PLANET TELEX (Karma Sunra mix) / KILLER CARS (mogadon mix)** (cd-s) – ('A'side) / Bones (live) / Planet Telex (live) / Anyone can play guitar (live).	19	

. . . Jan – Jun '96 stop press . . .

Jan 96.	(single) **STREET SPIRIT (FADE OUT)**	5	

RADIO HEART (see under ⇒ NUMAN, Gary)

RAGE AGAINST THE MACHINE

Formed: Los Angeles, California, USA . . . 1992 by ZACK and TOM. In 1992 they signed to 'Epic', and due to early '93 appearance on 'The Word', soared into UK charts with riotous classic 'KILLING IN THE NAME'. With their eponymous debut album, making inroads into US charts, they made dramatic entrance in Philadelphia. In front of a 14,000 audience, they walked onto a stage naked with PMRC (Parents Music Resource Committee) written across their chests. This was to protest against the birthplace of American censorship. • **Style:** Multi-racial non-conformist heavy-rock rappers, against the hypocritical money power-whores of their homeland. • **Songwriters:** ROCHA lyrics / group music. • **Trivia:** TOM's father was part of the Mau Maus (Kenyan guerrillas) who fought to end British colonialism there. His uncle JOMO KENYATTA was imprisoned during this period, but went on to become the first Kenyan president. ZACK's father was a Spanish muralist and political activist in L.A.

Recommended: RAGE AGAINST THE MACHINE (*8) / EVIL EMPIRE (*6).

ZACK DE LA ROCHA (b.1971) – vocals / **TOM MORELLO** (b.1965) – guitar / **TIMMY C.** – bass / **BRAD WILK** – drums

		Epic	Epic
Feb 93.	(7")(12"white)(cd-s) **KILLING IN THE NAME. / CLEAR THE LANE / DARKNESS OF GREED**	25	
Feb 93.	(cd)(c)(lp) **RAGE AGAINST THE MACHINE** – Bombtrack / Killing in the name / Take the power back / Bullet in your head / Know your enemy / Wake up / Fistful of steel / Township rebellion / Freedom.	17	45
Apr 93.	(7")(12")(cd-s) **BULLET IN THE HEAD. / BULLET IN THE HEAD (remix)** – Bullet in the head / Settle for nothing.	16	
Sep 93.	(7") **BOMBTRACK. / BOMBTRACK** (12"+=)(cd-s+=) – ('A'version).	37	

. . . Jan – Jun '96 stop press . . .

Apr 96.	(single) **BULLS ON PARADE**	8	
Apr 96.	(cd)(c)(lp) **EVIL EMPIRE**	4	1

RAINBOW (see under ⇒ DEEP PURPLE)

RAIN TREE CROW (see under ⇒ JAPAN)

Bonnie RAITT

Born: 8 Nov'49, Burbank, California, USA. Daughter of Broadway musical star of ('Oklahoma', 'Carousel' & 'Kiss Me Kate') JOHN RAITT, who was a Quaker. In 1967 she relocated to Radcliffe College in Massachusetts, until 1969 when she moved to Cambridge in Boston with boyfriend/manager Dick Waterman. By the early 70's, she was enjoying underground status mostly at The Gaslite in New York. The following year, she was snapped up by to 'Warners' who released eponymous debut. After a follow-up in 1972, she moved back to Los Angeles and released John Hall (of band Orleans) produced album 'TAKIN' MY TIME', which was her first to crack the US Top 100. • **Style:** White country blues singer who mixed contemporary ballads with basic Dixieland R&B. Her constant touring in the early 70's, finally paid off late by the next decade, when 'NICK OF TIME' album reached US No.1. • **Songwriters:** Wrote some herself, but covered many including WALKING BLUES (Robert Johnson) / UNDER THE FALLING SKY (Jackson Browne) / LOVE HAS NO PRIDE + CRY LIKE A RAINSTORM (Eric Kaz) / GUILTY (Randy Newman) / WHAT IS SUCCESS (Allen Toussaint) / WOMEN BE WISE (Wallace-Beach) / LOVE ME LIKE A MAN (. . . Smither) / ANGELS FROM MONTGOMERY (John Prine) / MY FIRST NIGHT ALONE WITH YOU (. . . Vassey) / SUGAR MAMA (McClinton-Clark) / LOUISE (Paul Siebel) / NO WAY TO TREAT A LADY (Bryan Adams) / RUNAWAY (Del Shannon) / THE GLOW (. . . Hildebrand) / BUILT TO MAKE ME LEAVE HOME (. . . Randle) / WITH YA, WON'T CHAS (. . . Schell) / YOUR GOOD THING (Hayes-Porter) / YOUR GONNA GET WHAT'S COMING (Robert Palmer) / TRUE LOVE IS HARD TO FIND (Toots & The Maytals) / GOIN' WILD

FOR YOU BABY (Snow-Batteau) / BURNING DOWN THE HOUSE (Talking Heads) / etc. In 1989 most were written by JOHN HIATT and others including SOMETHING TO TALK ABOUT (S.Eikhardt) / I CAN'T MAKE YOU LOVE ME (Reid / Shamblin). • **Trivia:** Her album NICK OF TIME won a Grammy in 1990 for Best Female Performance. On 28 Apr'91, she married actor Michael O'Keefe.

Recommended: THE BONNIE RAITT COLLECTION (*7)

BONNIE RAITT – vocals, guitar, steel guitar / **FREEBO** – bass / **A.C.REID** – tenor sax / etc.

Warners Warners

Nov 71. (lp)(c) **BONNIE RAITT** [ ] [ ]
– Bluebird revisited / I'm a mighty tight woman / Thank you / Finest lovin' man / Any day woman / Big road / Walking blues / Danger heartbreak dead ahead / Since I fell for you / I ain't blue / Woman be wise. *(re-iss.Jun76)*

Dec 71. (7") **BLUEBEARD. / WOMAN BE WISE** [-] [ ]

Nov 72. (lp)(c) **GIVE IT UP** [ ] [ ] Oct 72
– Give it up or let me go / Nothing seems to matter / I know / If you gotta make a fool of somebody / Love me like a man / Stayed too long at the fair / Under the falling sky / You got to know how / You told me baby / Love has no pride. *(re-iss.Jun76)*

Dec 72. (7") **STAYED TOO LONG AT THE FAIR. / UNDER THE FALLING SKY** [ ] [ ]

— now on session **LOWELL GEORGE / BILL PAYNE / JIM KELTNER + TAJ MAHAL**

Oct 73. (7") **YOU'VE BEEN IN LOVE TOO LONG. / EVERY-BODY'S CRYIN' MERCY** [-] [ ]

Nov 73. (lp)(c) **TAKIN' MY TIME** [ ] [87] Oct 73
– You've been in love too long / I gave my love a candle / Let me in / Everybody's cryin' mercy / Cry like a rainstorm / Wah she go do / I feel the same / I thought I was a child / Write me a few of your lines – Kokomo blues / Guilty. *(re-iss.Jun76) (cd-iss.Feb93)*

Oct 74. (7") **I GOT PLENTY. / YOU GOTTA BE READY FOR LOVE (IF YOU WANNA BE MINE)** [-] [ ]

Nov 74. (lp)(c) **STREETLIGHTS** [ ] [80] Oct 74
– That song about the Midway / Rainy day man / Angel from Montgomery / I got plenty / Streetlights / What is success / Ain't nobody home / Everything that touches you / Got you on my mind / You gotta be ready for love (if you wanna be mine). *(cd-iss.1989)*

Nov 75. (7") **MY FIRST NIGHT ALONE WITH YOU. / GOOD ENOUGH** [-] [ ]

Dec 75. (lp)(c) **HOME PLATE** [ ] [43] Oct 75
– What do you want the boy to do / Good enough / Run like a thief / Fool yourself / My first night alone with you / Walk out the front door / Sugar mama / Pleasin' each other / I'm blowin' away / Your sweet and shiny eyes.

May 76. (7") **WALK OUT THE FRONT DOOR. / RUN LIKE A THIEF** [-] [ ]

Jun 76. (7") **I'M BLOWIN' AWAY. / RUN LIKE A THIEF** [ ] [ ]

— In 1976, she duetted w/**GEOFF MULDAUR** on single 'WHEN YOU TOUCH ME THIS WAY' / SINCE I'VE BEEN WITH YOU BABE'.

— Her touring band were **WILL McFARLANE** – guitar / **JEFF LABES** – keyboards / **DENNIS WHITTED** – drums / **FREEBO** – bass (as always) + guests **MICHAEL McDONALD + J.D.SOUTHER** on guest backing vocals

Apr 77. (lp)(c) **SWEET FORGIVENESS** [ ] [25]
– Sweet forgiveness / Gamblin' man / Two lives / Runaway / About to make me leave home / Three time loser / My opening farewell / Takin' my time / Home / Louise. *(cd-iss.Feb93)*

May 77. (7") **RUNAWAY. / LOUISE** [-] [57]

May 77. (7") **RUNAWAY. / HOME** [ ] [-]

Aug 77. (7") **THREE TIME LOSER. / TWO LIVES** [-] [ ]

Aug 77. (7") **THREE TIME LOSER. / LOUISE** [ ] [-]

Nov 77. (7") **GAMBLIN' MAN. / ABOUT TO MAKE ME LEAVE HOME** [-] [ ]

Oct 79. (lp)(c) **THE GLOW** [ ] [30]
– I thank you / Your good thing (is about to end) / Sleep's dark and silent gate / The glow / Bye bye baby / The boy can't help it / (I could have been your) Best old friend / You're gonna get what's coming / (Goin') Wild for you baby. *(cd-iss.Feb93)*

Nov 79. (7") **YOU'RE GONNA GET WHAT'S COMING. / THE GLOW** [-] [73]

Mar 80. (7") **(I COULD HAVE BEEN YOUR) BEST OLD FRIEND. / (GOIN') WILD FOR YOU BABY** [-] [ ]

— In mid-80's, she released 'Asylum' 45; 'DON'T IT MAKE YOU WANNA DANCE'. At the same time she and J.D. SOUTHER issued 'ONCE IN A LIFETIME' / 'YOU'RE ONLY LONELY'.

— next feat. **The BUMP BAND** incl. **IAN McLAGAN** – keyboards (ex-SMALL FACES) / **JOHNNY LEE SCHELL** – guitar / **RAY O'HARA** – bass / **RICKY FATAAR** – drums

Feb 82. (7") **CAN'T GET ENOUGH. / KEEP THIS HEART IN MIND** [-] [ ]

Feb 82. (lp)(c) **GREEN LIGHT** [ ] [38]
– Keep this heart in mind / River of tears / Can't get enough / Me and the boys / I can't help myself / Willya wontcha / Let's keep it between us / Baby come back / Talk to me / Green light.

Apr 82. (7") **ME AND THE BOYS. / RIVER OF TEARS** [-] [ ]

Apr 82. (7") **ME AND THE BOYS. / KEEP THIS HEART IN MIND** [ ] [-]

— She semi-retired in 1982 to go through a period of drug rehabilitation and attend a form of alcoholics anonymous.

Sep 86. (lp)(c)(cd) **NINE LIVES** [ ] [ ] Aug 86
– No way to treat a lady / Runnin' back to me / Who but a fool / Crime of passion / All day, all night / Stand up to the night / Excited / Freezin' (for a little human love) / True love is hard to find / Angel.

Sep 86. (7") **NO WAY TO TREAT A LADY. / STAND UP TO THE NIGHT** [-] [ ]

Feb 87. (7") **CRIMES OF PASSION. / STAND UP TO THE NIGHT** [-] [ ]

— In Oct '88, she teamed up with DON WAS of WAS (NOT WAS) on 'A&M' single 'BABY MINE'. Their vocalists **SWEAT PEA ATKINSON + SIR HARRY BOWENS** plus guests **DAVID CROSBY & GRAHAM NASH, FATAAR & SCHELL, KIM WILSON,** etc.

Capitol Capitol

Apr 89. (lp)(c)(cd) **NICK OF TIME** [51] [1]
– Nick of time / A thing called love / Love letter / Cry on my shoulder / Real man / Nobody's girl / Have a heart / Too soon to tell / I will not be denied / I ain't gonna let you break my heart again / The road's my middle name. *(re-iss.Apr90)*

May 89. (7")(c-s) **NICK OF TIME. / THE ROAD'S MY MIDDLE NAME** [ ] [92] May 90
(12"+=)(cd-s+=) – I ain't gonna let you break my heart again. *(re-iss.Mar90)*

Mar 90. (7") **HAVE A HEART. / ?** [-] [49]

May 90. (7") **A THING CALLED LOVE. / NOBODY'S GIRL** [ ] [ ]
(12"+=)(cd-s+=) – The road's my middle name.

— next also feat. **HIATT,** plus **BRUCE HORNSBY + RICHARD THOMPSON**

Jul 91. (cd)(c)(lp) **LUCK OF THE DRAW** [38] [2]
– Something to talk about / Good man, good woman / I can't make you love me / Tangled and dark / Come to me / No business / One part of my lover / Not the only one / Papa come quick (Jody and Chico) / Slow ride / Luck of the draw / All at once.

Jul 91. (7")(c-s) **SOMETHING TO TALK ABOUT. / ONE PART OF MY LOVER** [ ] [5]
(12"+=) – I ain't gonna let you break my heart again.
(cd-s++=) – Nick of time. *(re-iss.Feb92)*

Aug 91. (7")(c-s) **NOT THE ONLY ONE. / COME TO ME** [ ] [34] Mar 92
(12"+=)(cd-s+=) – Papa come quick (Jody and Chico).

Dec 91. (7")(c-s) **I CAN'T MAKE YOU LOVE ME. / COME TO ME** [50] [18] Nov 91
(cd-s+=) – Tangled and dark.

Jun 92. (7") **GOOD MAN, GOOD WOMAN. / NICK OF TIME** [ ] [ ]
(cd-s+=) – Thing called love / One part be my lover.

Apr 94. (c-s) **LOVE SNEAKIN' UP ON YOU / NICK OF TIME / HELL TO PAY** [69] [19] Mar94
(cd-s+=) – Baby mine.

Apr 94. (cd)(c)(lp) **LONGING IN THEIR HEARTS** [26] [1] Mar94
– Love sneakin' up on you / Longing in their hearts / You / Cool, clear water / Circle dance / I sho do / Dimming of the day / Feeling of falling / Steal your heart away / Storm warning / Hell to pay / Shadow of doubt.

Jun 94. (c-s) **YOU. / I CAN'T MAKE YOU LOVE ME** [31] [92]
(cd-s+=) – I ain't gonna let you break my heart again / All at once.
(cd-s) – ('A'side) / This thing called love / Longing in their hearts / Good man, good woman.

May 95. (c-s) **YOU GOT IT / FEELING OF FALLING** [ ] [33] Feb 95
(cd-s+=) – Circle dance.

— (above single issued on 'Arista')

Nov 95. (c-s) **ROCK STEADY ("BONNIE RAITT & BRYAN ADAMS" live) / COME TO ME (live) / FEELING OF FALLING (live)** [50] [73]
(cd-s+=) – Thing called love (live with BRUCE HORNSBY).

Nov 95. (cd)(c) **ROAD TESTED (live)** [69] [44]
– Thing called love / Something to talk about / Never make your move too soon / Shake a little / Matters of the heart / Love me like a man / The Kokomo medley: Write me a few of your lines – Kokomo blues / My opening farewell / Dimming of the day / Longing in their hearts / Love sneakin' up on you / Burning down the house / I can't make you love me / I believe I'm in love / Rock steady / Angel from Montgomery.

– compilations, others, etc. –

Aug 90. Warners; (cd)(c)(lp) **THE BONNIE RAITT COLLECTION** [ ] [61] Jul 90
– Finest lovin' man / Give it up or let me go / Women be wise (live with SIPPIE WALLACE) / Under the falling sky / Love me like a man / Love has no pride / I feel the same / Guilty / Angel from Montgomery / What is success / My first night alone without you / Sugar mama / Louise / About to make me leave home / Runaway / The glow / (Goin') Wild for you baby / Willya wontcha / True love is hard to find / No way to treat a lady.

RAMONES

Formed: Forest Hills, New York, USA . . . Aug'74 as a trio by JOHNNY, JOEY and DEE DEE, who all took the working surname RAMONE. Began residency at The CBGB's with TOMMY being added to let JOEY sing. In June 1975, they failed an audition for RICK DERRINGER's 'Blue Sky' label in front of 20,000 fans at a JOHNNY WINTER concert. Later that year, their new manager Danny Fields, obtained a deal with up and coming new wave label 'Sire' run by Seymour Stein. They soon recorded Craig Leon produced eponymous debut lp. In mid-76, its release caused minor stir and nearly made the US Top 100. With the new wave scene now burgeoning in the UK, they arrived to play a tour supporting FLAMIN' GROOVIES. The following year 1977, saw their second album 'LEAVE HOME', break into the UK Top 50, with it being closely chased by a hit single 'SHEENA IS A PUNK ROCKER'. They continued to compete in the charts until in 1980, when they lost credibility and past fans, by breaking the UK Top 10 with a PHIL SPECTOR produced 'BABY I LOVE YOU'. • **Style:** Innovators of 70's punk rock, famous for their high-speed 2 minute buzz-saw classics about girls, solvent-abuse and sunny weather. Their usual cartoon punk image, 1-2-3-4 intro and 'Gabba Gabba Hey', was shelved in the 80's, for a more sedated 3-4 minute song (a RAMONES epic!). • **Songwriters:** DEE DEE and group, except; DO YOU WANNA DANCE (Bobby Freeman) / SURFIN' BIRD (Trashmen) / BABY I LOVE YOU (Ronettes; Phil Spector) / NEEDLES AND PINS (Searchers) / STREET FIGHTIN' MAN (Rolling Stones) / TAKE IT AS IT COMES (Doors) / etc. In '77, DEE DEE co-wrote 'CHINESE ROCKS' for The HEARTBREAKERS. • **Trivia:** The RAMONES featured in the films 'Blank Generation' (1976) & 'Rock'n'roll High School' (Roger Corman 1979).

Recommended: RAMONES (*9) / LEAVE HOME (*8) / ROCKET TO RUSSIA (*8) / RAMONES MANIA (*9).

JOEY RAMONE (b.JEFFREY HYMAN, 19 May'52) – vocals (was drummer) / **JOHNNY RAMONE** (b.JOHN CUMMINGS, 8 Oct'48, Long Island) – guitar, vocals / **DEE DEE RAMONE** (b.DOUGLAS COLVIN, 18 Sep'52, Fort Lee, VA) – bass, vocals / **TOMMY RAMONE** (b.TOMMY ERDELYI, 29 Jan'49, Budapest, Hungary) – drums

Sire / Sire

Jul 76. (lp) **RAMONES** [ ] [ ] May 76
– Blitzkreig bop / Beat on the brat / Judy is a punk / I wanna be your boyfriend / Chain saw / Now I wanna sniff some glue / I don't wanna go down to the basement / Loudmouth / Havana affair / Listen to my heart / 53rd & 3rd / Let's dance / I don't wanna walk around with you / Today your love, tomorrow the world. *(re-iss.Sep78) (US re-iss.Sep87)*

Jul 76. (7") **BLITZKREIG BOP. / HAVANA AFFAIR** [ ] [ ] May 76

Oct 76. (7"m) **I WANNA BE YOUR BOYFRIEND. / CALIFORNIA SUN (live) / I DON'T WANNA WALK AROUND WITH YOU (live)** [-] [ ]

Feb 77. (7"m) **I REMEMBER YOU. / CALIFORNIA SUN (live) / I DON'T WANNA WALK AROUND WITH YOU (live)** [ ] [ ]

Mar 77. (lp)(c) **LEAVE HOME** [45] [ ] Feb 77
– Glad to see you go / Gimme gimme shock treatment / I remember you / Oh oh I love her so / Babysitter * / Suzy is a headbanger / Pinhead / Now I wanna be a good boy / Swallow my pride / What's your game / California sun / Commando / You're gonna kill that girl / You should have never have opened that door / California sun. *(re-iss.Jun77 'Carbona Not Glue' replaced *; other re-iss's same) (re-iss.Sep78) (re-iss.Nov87 on 'Mau Mau')*

May 77. (7"m)(12"m) **SHEENA IS A PUNK ROCKER. / COMMANDO / I DON'T CARE** [22] [81]

Jul 77. (7"m) **SWALLOW MY PRIDE. / PINHEAD / LET'S DANCE (live)** [36] [ ] Mar 77

Nov 77. (7"m)(12"m) **ROCKAWAY BEACH. / TEENAGE LOBOTOMY / BEAT ON THE BRAT** [ ] [-]

Nov 77. (7") **ROCKAWAY BEACH. / LOCKET LOVE** [-] [66]

Dec 77. (lp)(c) **ROCKET TO RUSSIA** [60] [49] Nov 77
– Cretin hop / Rockaway beach / Here today, gone tomorrow / Locket love / I don't care / Sheena is a punk rocker / We're a happy family / Teenage lobotomy / Do you wanna dance? / I wanna be well / I can't give you anything / Ramona / Surfin' bird / Why is it always this way. *(re-iss.Sep78)*

Feb 78. (7") **DO YOU WANNA DANCE?. / BABYSITTER** [-] [86]

Mar 78. (7"m) **DO YOU WANNA DANCE?. / IT'S A LONG WAY BACK TO GERMANY / CRETIN HOP** [ ] [-]

— **MARKY RAMONE** (b.MARC BELL) – drums (ex-RICHARD HELL & THE VOID-OIDS, ex-DUST) repl. TOMMY who continued producing others.

Sep 78. (7")(7"yellow)(12"yellow)(12"red) **DON'T COME CLOSE. / I DON'T WANT YOU** [38] [ ]

Oct 78. (lp)(c)(yellow-lp) **ROAD TO RUIN** [32] [ ]
– I just want to have something to do / I wanted everything / Don't come close / I don't want you / Needles and pins / I'm against it / I wanna be sedated / Go mental / Questioningly / She's the one / Bad brain / It's a long way back.

Nov 78. (7") **NEEDLES AND PINS. / I WANTED EVERYTHING** [-] [ ]

Jan 79. (7") **SHE'S THE ONE. / I WANNA BE SEDATED** [ ] [ ]

May 79. (d-lp)(c) **IT'S ALIVE (live)** [27] [ ]
– Rockaway beach / Teenage lobotomy / Blitzkreig bop / I wanna be well / Glad to see you go / Gimme gimme shock treatment / You're gonna kill that girl / I don't care / Sheena is a punk rocker / Havana affair / Commando / Here today, gone tomorrow / Surfin' bird / Cretin hop / Listen to my heart / California sun / I don't wanna walk around with you / Pinhead / Do you wanna dance? / Chain saw / Today your love, tomorrow the world / Now I wanna be a good boy / Judy is a punk / Suzy is a headbanger / Let's dance / Oh oh I love her so / Now I wanna sniff some glue / We're a happy family. *(album features TOMMY on drums) (cd-iss.Nov93 on 'Warners')*

Sep 79. (7") **ROCK'N'ROLL HIGH SCHOOL. / I WANT YOU AROUND** [-] [ ]

Sep 79. (7") **ROCK'N'ROLL HIGH SCHOOL. / SHEENA IS A PUNK ROCKER (live) / ROCKAWAY BEACH (live)** [67] [-]

Jan 80. (lp)(c) **END OF THE CENTURY** [14] [44]
– Do you remember rock'n'roll radio? / I'm affected / Danny says / Chinese rock / The return of Jackie and Judy / Let's go / Baby I love you / I can't make it on time / This ain't Havana / Rock'n'roll high school / All the way / High risk insurance. *(US re-iss.May88) (re-iss.cd Mar94)*

Jan 80. (7") **BABY I LOVE YOU. / HIGH RISK INSURANCE** [8] [ ]

Apr 80. (7") **DO YOU REMEMBER ROCK'N'ROLL RADIO?. / LET'S GO** [-] [ ]

Apr 80. (7") **DO YOU REMEMBER ROCK'N'ROLL RADIO?. / I WANT YOU AROUND** [54] [-]

Jul 81. (7") **WE WANT THE AIRWAVES. / ALL'S QUIET ON THE EASTERN FRONT** [ ] [ ]

Jul 81. (lp)(c) **PLEASANT DREAMS** [ ] [58]
– We want the airwaves / All's quiet on the Eastern front / The KKK took my baby away / Don't go / You sound like you're sick / It's not my place / She's a sensation / 7-11 / You didn't mean anything to me / Come on now / This business is killing me / Sitting in my room. *(US re-iss.May88) (re-iss.cd Mar94)*

Oct 81. (7") **SHE'S A SENSATION. / ALL'S QUIET ON THE EASTERN FRONT** [ ] [ ]

May 83. (lp)(c) **SUBTERRANEAN JUNGLE** [ ] [83]
– Little bit o' soul / I need your love / Outsider / What'd ya do / Highest trails above / Somebody like me / Psycho therapy / Time has come today / My-my kind of girl / In the park / Time bomb / Everytime I eat vegetables It makes me think of you. *(re-iss.cd Mar94)*

Jun 83. (7") **TIME HAS COME TODAY. / PSYCHO THERAPY** [ ] [ ]
(12"+=) – Baby I love you / Don't come close.

— **RICKY RAMONE** (b.RICHARD BEAU) – drums (ex-VELVETEENS) repl. MARC

Beggar's B. / Sire

Nov 84. (7") **HOWLING AT THE MOON (SHA LA LA). / WART HOG** [-] [ ]

Jan 85. (lp)(c) **TOO TOUGH TO DIE** [63] [ ] Oct 84
– Mama's boy / I'm not afraid of life / Too young to die / Durango 95 / Wart hog / Danger zone / Chasing the night / Howling at the Moon (sha-la-la) / Daytime dilemma (dangers of love) / Planet Earth 1988 / Human kind / Endless vacation / No go.

Jan 85. (7") **HOWLING AT THE MOON (SHA-LA-LA). / SMASH YOU** [ ] [-]
(12"+=) – Street fighting man.

Mar 85. (d7")(12"pic-d) **CHASING THE NIGHT. / HOWLING AT THE MOON (SHA-LA-LA)/ / SMASH YOU. / STREET FIGHTING MAN** [ ] [ ]

Jun 85. (7") **BONZO GOES TO BITBURG. / DAYTIME DILEMMA (DANGERS OF LOVE)** [ ] [-]
(12"+=) – Go home Annie.

Apr 86. (7") **SOMETHING TO BELIEVE IN. / SOMEBODY PUT SOMETHING IN MY DRINK** [69] [ ]
(12"+=) – Can't say anything nice.

May 86. (lp)(c)(cd) **ANIMAL BOY** [38] [ ]
– Somebody put something in my drink / Animal boy / Love kills / Apeman hop / She belongs to me / Crummy stuff / My brain is hanging upside down (Bonzo goes to Bitburg) / She belongs to me / Mental hell / Eat that rat / Freak of nature / Hair of the dog / Something to believe in.

Jul 86. (7") **CRUMMY STUFF. / SHE BELONGS TO ME** [ ] [ ]
(12"+=)(12"red+=) – I don't want to live this life.

— **MARC RAMONE** – drums returned to repl. CLEM BURKE (ex-BLONDIE) who had repl. RICKY (above now with originals JOEY, DEE DEE and JOHNNY.)

Sep 87. (7") **A REAL COOL TIME. / INDIAN GIVER** [ ] [ ]
(12"+=) – Life goes on.

Sep 87. (lp)(c)(cd) **HALFWAY TO SANITY** [78] [ ]
– I wanna live / Bop 'til you drop / Garden of serenity / Weasel face / Go lil' Camaro go / I know better now / Death of me / I lost my mind / A real cool time / I'm not Jesus / Bye bye baby / Worm man. *(cd+=)–* Indian giver / Life goes on.

Nov 87. (7")(12") **I WANNA LIVE. / MERRY CHRISTMAS (I DON'T WANT TO FIGHT TONIGHT)** [ ] [ ]

Jun 88. (d-lp)(c)(cd) **RAMONES MANIA** (compilation) [ ] [ ]
– I wanna be sedated / Teenage lobotomy / Do you remember rock'n'roll radio? / Gimme gimme shock treatment / Beat on the brat / Sheena is a punk rocker /

I wanna live / Pinhead / Blitzkrieg bop / Cretin hop / Rockaway beach / Commando / I wanna be your boyfriend / Mama's boy / Bop 'til you drop / We're a happy family / Bonzo goes to Bitburg / The outsider / Psycho therapy / Wart hog / Animal boy / Needles and pins / Howlin' at the Moon / Somebody put something in my drink / We want the airwaves / Chinese rocks / I just want to have something to do / The KKK took my baby away / Indian giver / Rock'n'roll high school.

Chrysalis | Sire

Aug 89. (lp)(c)(cd) **BRAIN DRAIN** [75] [ ] Jun 89
– I believe in miracles / Zero zero UFO / Don't bust my chops / Punishment fits the crime / All screwed up / Palisades Park / Pet sematary / Learn to listen / Can't get you outta my mind / Ignorance is bliss / Come back, baby / Merry Christmas (I don't want to fight tonight). *(re-iss.cd+c Mar93)*

Sep 89. (7") **PET SEMATARY. / ALL SCREWED UP** [ ] [-]
(12"+=) – Zero zero UFO.

Sep 89. (7") **PET SEMATARY. / SHEENA IS A PUNK ROCKER** [-] [ ]

— **C.J.RAMONE** – bass repl. DEE DEE who became rap artist DEE DEE KING

Oct 91. (cd)(c)(d-lp) **LIVE LOCO (live)** [ ] [ ]
– The good, the bad and the ugly / Django 95 / Teenage lobotomy / Psycho therapy / Blitzkreig bop / Rock'n'roll radio / I believe in miracles / Gimme gimme shock treatment / Rock'n'roll high school / I wanna be sedated / The KKK took my baby away / I wanna live / Bonzo goes to Bitzburg / Too tough to die / Sheena is a punk rocker / Rockaway beach / Pet semetary / Don't bust my shape / Palisades park / Mama's boy / Animal boy / Wart hog / Surfin' bird / Cretin hop / I don't wanna walk around with you / Today your love, tomorrow the world / Pinhead / Somebody put something in my drink / Beat on the brat / Judy is a punk / Chinese rocks / Love kills / Ignorance is bliss.

Chrysalis | Radio-active

Sep 92. (cd)(c)(lp) **MONDO BIZARRO** [ ] [ ]
– Censorshit / The job that ate my brain / Poison heart / Anxiety / Strength to endure / It's gonna be alright / Take it as it comes / Main man / Tomorrow she goes away / I won't let it happen again / Cabbies on crack / Heidi is a heartache / Touring.

Oct 92. (7")(c-s)(7"yellow) **POISON HEART. / CENSORSHIT (live)** [69] [ ]
(12"+=) – Chinese rocks (live) / Sheena is a punk rocker (live).
(cd-s+=) – Rock and roll radio (live).

Dec 93. (cd)(c)(lp) **ACID EATERS** [ ] [ ]
– Journey to the center of the mind / Substitute / Out of time / The shape of things to come / Somebody to love / When I was young / 7 and 7 is / My back pages / Can't seem to make you mine / Have you ever seen the rain / I can't control myself / Surf city.

— Album of covers; SUBSTITUTE (Who) / I CAN'T CONTROL MYSELF (Troggs) / SURF CITY (Jan & Dean) / OUT OF TIME (Rolling Stones) / THE SHAPE OF THINGS TO COME (Headboys) / etc.

Jun 95. (cd)(c)(lp) **IL ADIOS AMIGOS!** [62] [ ]
– I don't want to grow up / I'm makin' monsters for my friends / It's not for me to know / The crusher / Life's a gas / Take the pain away / I love you / Cretin family / Have a nice day / Scattergun / Got a lot to say / She talks to rainbows / Born to die in Berlin.

. . . *Jan – Jun '96 stop press* . . .

— split after tour early 1996, although they had a brief reunion.

DEE DEE RAMONE

writes with **REY**

World Dom. | World Dom.

Jun 94. (cd)(lp) **I HATE FREAKS LIKE YOU** [ ] [ ]
– I'm making monsters for my friends / Don't look in my window / Chinese bitch / It's not for me to know / Runaway / All's quiet on the Eastern Front / I hate it / Life is like a little smart Alleck / I hate creeps like you / Trust me / Curse on me / I'm seeing strawberry's again / Lass mich in Fuhe / I'm making monsters for my friends.

– (RAMONES) compilations, others, etc. –

Aug 80. RSO; (7") **I WANNA BE SEDATED. / THE RETURN OF JACKIE AND JUDY** [ ] [ ]

— (above from Various Artists Film Soundtrack 'Rock'n'roll High School' also incl.Medley: Blitzkreig / Lobotomy / California / Pinhead / She's the one)

Nov 80. Sire; (7"ep) **MELTDOWN WITH THE RAMONES** [ ] [ ]
– I just wanna have something to do / Questioningly / I wanna be your boyfriend / Here today, gone tomorrow.

Sep 90. (cd)(c)(d-lp) **ALL THE STUFF (AND MORE)** [ ] [ ]
(demos 1976-1977, etc.)

Mar 93. Selfless; (lp) **THE SCREECHING WEASEL** [ ] [ ]

— JOEY also on "HOLLY & JOEY" 7" – 1982 'I Got You Babe' on 'Virgin'. In Aug88, JOHNNY teamed up with DEBBIE HARRY for 7" – 'Go Lil Camara Go'.

Lee RANALDO (see under ⇒ SONIC YOUTH)

Otis REDDING

Born: 9 Sep'41, Dawson, Georgia, USA. He left school in Macon and soon gigged with local R&B outfit JOHNNY JENKINS & THE PINETOPPERS. His/their first release in 1960 was SHOUT BAMALAMA on 'Confederate' label. The following year after OTIS married Zelda, they issued GETTIN' HIP on 'Alshire'. At this time he was only given vocal stints, due to his driving them to concerts. Early in 1962, another single LOVE TWIST was given light by 'Gerald' records. In Oct'62, with groups' recording sessions for 'Atlantic' now over, 2 solo songs were listened to by new 'Stax' subsidiary label 'Volt'. The 45 'B'side; THESE ARMS OF MINE became minor US hit mid 1963. By mutual agreement and special contract, 'Atlantic (aka Atco)' decided to let 'Volt' continue releasing 45's, etc. After a few minor hits, he broke through in summer '65 with near Top20 hit I'VE BEEN LOVING YOU TOO LONG. Chalked up several more cross-Atlantic hits, before tragically he and most of his back-up group The BAR-KEYS, were killed in a charter plane crash on 10 Dec'67. His postumously-released next single became regarded as his greatest. '(SITTIN' ON) THE DOCK OF THE BAY' became a million selling US No.1 also hitting Top3 in the UK. • **Style:** Progressed from being a LITTLE RICHARD copyist (in the early 60's), to being a classic soul balladeer. • **Songwriters:** Penned own material, except singles DOCK OF THE BAY (c. Steve Cropper) / MY GIRL (Temptations) / PAIN IN MY HEART (Irma Thomas) / SATISFACTION (Rolling Stones) / DAY TRIPPER (Beatles) / SHAKE! (Sam Cooke) / KNOCK ON WOOD (Eddie Floyd) / PAPA'S GOT A BRAND NEW BAG (James Brown) / A LOVER'S QUESTION (Clyde McPhatter) / AMEN (Impressions) / etc. • **Trivia:** Late in 1973, his son DEXTER issued single GOD BLESS. In the early 80's, he was joined by other son OTIS and their cousin MARK LOCKET who transpired as The REDDINGS. All on vocals and instruments, they released 2 albums THE AWAKENING and CLASS on the 'Believe' label.

Recommended: THE COLLECTION (*9)

OTIS REDDING – vocals solo with sessioners

London | Volt

Oct 62. (7") **THESE ARMS OF MINE. / HEY HEY BABY** [-] [85]

Jul 63. (7") **THAT'S WHAT MY HEART NEEDS. / MARY'S LITTLE LAMB** [-] [ ]

Nov 63. (7") **PAIN IN MY HEART. / SOMETHING IS WORRYING ME** [ ] [61]

— His backing included BOOKER T. & THE MG'S plus JOHNNY JENKINS.

Mar 64. (7") **COME TO ME. / DON'T LEAVE ME THIS WAY** [ ] [69]

Apr 64. (lp) **PAIN IN MY HEART** [-] [ ]
– Pain in my heart / The dog / Stand by me / Hey hey baby / You send me / I need your lovin' / Louie Louie / These arms of mine / Something is worrying me / Security / That's what my heart needs / Lucille. *(UK-iss.Apr67 on 'Atlantic', hit No.28) (cd-iss.Aug93)*

May 64. (7") **SECURITY. / WONDERFUL WORLD** [ ] [-]

Jun 64. (7") **SECURITY. / I WANT TO THANK YOU** [-] [97]

Oct 64. (7") **CHAINED AND BOUND. / YOUR ONE AND ONLY MAN** [-] [70]

Atlantic | Volt

Apr 65. (7") **MR.PITIFUL. / THAT'S HOW STRONG MY LOVE IS** [ ] [41]
[74] Feb 65

May 65. (7") **I'VE BEEN LOVING YOU TOO LONG (TO STOP NOW). / I'M DEPENDING ON YOU** [-] [21]

Aug 65. (7") **I'VE BEEN LOVING YOU TOO LONG. / RESPECT** [ ] [-]

Sep 65. (lp) **THE GREAT OTIS REDDING SINGS SOUL BALLADS** [ ] [ ] Mar 65
– That's how strong my love is / Chained and bound / A woman, a lover, a friend / Your one and only man / Nothing can change this love / It's too late / For your precious love / I want to thank you / Come to me / Home in your heart / Keep your arms around me / Mr. Pitiful. *(hit UK chart No.30, Apr66) (re-iss.Jun88 on 'Atco', cd-iss.Jul91) (cd-iss.May93)*

Sep 65. (7") **RESPECT. / OLE MAN TROUBLE** [-] [35]

Nov 65. (7") **MY GIRL. / DOWN IN THE VALLEY** [11] [-]

Nov 65. (7") **JUST ONE MORE DAY. / I CAN'T TURN YOU LOOSE** [-] [85]

Feb 66. (lp) **OTIS BLUE (OTIS REDDING SINGS SOUL)** [6] [75] Oct 65
– My girl / (I can't get no) Satisfaction / Respect / Shake! / I've been loving you too long / You don't miss your water / Rock me baby / Wonderful world / Down in the valley / Change gonna come / Ole man trouble. *(UK re-iss.Jan67, hit No.7) (re-iss.1974 + Dec83 +c) (cd-iss.Jun91 on 'Atco')*

Mar 66. (7") **(I CAN'T GET NO) SATISFACTION. / ANY OLE WAY** [33] [31]

Jul 66. (7") **MY LOVER'S PRAYER. / DON'T MESS WITH CUPID** [37] [61] Jun 66

Jul 66. (lp) **THE SOUL ALBUM** [22] [54] Apr 66
– Just one more day / It's growing / Cigarettes and coffee / Chain gang / Nobody knows you (when you're down and out) / Good to me / Scratch my back / Treat

her right / Everybody makes a mistake / Any ole way / 634-5789. *(cd-iss.Jul91 on 'Atco') (cd-iss.Jun93)*
Aug 66. (7") **I CAN'T TURN YOU LOOSE. / JUST ONE MORE DAY** [29] [-]
Nov 66. (7") **FA FA FA FA FA (SAD SONG). / GOOD TO ME** [23] [29] Sep 66
Jan 67. (lp) **OTIS REDDING'S DICTIONARY OF SOUL** [23] [73] Nov 66
– Fa-fa-fa-fa-fa (sad song) / I'm sick y'all / Tennessee waltz / Sweet Lorene / Try a little tenderness / Day tripper / My lover's prayer / She put the hurt on me / Ton of joy / You're still my baby / Hawg for you / Love have mercy. *(re-iss.Jun88, cd-iss.Jul91 on 'Atco') (cd-iss.Jun93)* (US-title 'COMPLETE AND UNBELIEVABLE . . . THE OTIS REDDING DICTIONARY OF SOUL')
Jan 67. (7") **TRY A LITTLE TENDERNESS. / I'M SICK Y'ALL** [46] [25] Dec 66
Mar 67. (7") **RESPECT. / THESE ARMS OF MINE** [ ] [-]
(re-iss.Feb72)

Stax Volt
Mar 67. (7") **DAY TRIPPER. / SHAKE!** [43] [-]
Apr 67. (7") **LET ME COME ON HOME. / I LOVE YOU MORE THAN WORDS CAN SAY** [48] [78] B-side
May 67. (7") **TRAMP. ("OTIS & CARLA THOMAS"). / TELL IT LIKE IT IS** [-] [26]
Jun 67. (7") **SHAKE (live). / 634-5789 (live)** [28] [-]
Jun 67. (7") **SHAKE. / YOU DON'T MISS YOUR WATER** [-] [ ]
— Some releases on 'Stax' now with CARLA THOMAS, daughter of singer RUFUS.
Jun 67. (lp) **KING AND QUEEN ("OTIS REDDING & CARLA THOMAS")** [18] [36] Apr 67
– Knock on wood / Let me be good to you / Tramp / Tell it like it is / When something is wrong with my baby / Lovey dovey / New Year's resolution / It takes two / Are you lonely for me baby / Bring it on home to me / Ooh Carla, Ooh Otis.
– *(re-iss.Jun88, cd-iss.Jul91 on 'Atco')*
Jul 67. (7") **TRAMP. ("OTIS REDDING & CARLA THOMAS") / OOH CARLA OOH OTIS** [18] [ ]
Aug 67. (7") **GLORY OF LOVE. / I'M COMING HOME** [ ] [60] Jul 67
Sep 67. (lp) **LIVE IN EUROPE (live)** [-] [32] Aug 67
– Respect / Can't turn you loose / I've been loving you too long / My girl / Shame / Satisfaction / Fa-fa-fa-fa-fa (sad song) / These arms of mine / Day tripper / Try a little tenderness. *(UK-iss.Mar68, hit No.2) (re-iss.Aug69 on 'Atco') (cd-iss.Aug93) (cd-iss.Feb95 & Sep95 on 'Warners')*
Oct 67. (7") **KNOCK ON WOOD. ("OTIS REDDING & CARLA THOMAS") / LET ME BE GOOD TO YOU** [35] [30] Aug 67
Nov 67. (7") **SATISFACTION. / I'VE BEEN LOVING YOU TOO LONG** [ ] [-]
— On 10th Dec'67, OTIS was killed in a plane crash (see biography)

– immediate postumous releases, etc. –

Dec 67. Volt; (lp)(c) **THE HISTORY OF OTIS REDDING** [2] [9]
(re-iss.1974 on 'Atlantic')
Below released on 'Volt'/ 'Stax' unless mentioned.
Feb 68. (7") **(SITTIN' ON) THE DOCK OF THE BAY. / MY SWEET LORENE** [3] [1] Jan 68
Mar 68. (7") **LOVEY DOVEY. ("OTIS REDDING & CARLA THOMAS") / NEW YEAR'S RESOLUTION** [ ] [68] Feb 68
May 68. (lp) **DOCK OF THE BAY** (late 1967 sessions) [1] [4] Mar 68
– The dock of the bay / Home in your heart / I want to thank you / Your one and only man / Nothing can change this love / It's too late / For your precious love / Keep your arms around me / Come to me / A woman, a lover, a friend / Chained and bound / That's how strong my love is. *(re-iss.Jul69 on 'Atco') (re-iss.Nov71)*
May 68. (7") **THE HAPPY SONG (DUM DUM). / OPEN THE DOOR** [24] [25] Apr 68
Below released on 'Atlantic' UK/ 'Atco' US unless mentioned.
Feb 68. (7") **MY GIRL. / MR.PITIFUL** [36] [ ]
(re-iss.1972, 1980 & Mar84)
Jul 68. (7") **HARD TO HANDLE. / AMEN** [15] [36] B-side
Aug 68. (lp) **THE IMMORTAL OTIS REDDING** [19] [58] Jul 68
(re-iss.Jan72 on 'Atco') (cd-iss.Aug93)
Sep 68. (7") **I'VE GOT DREAMS TO REMEMBER. / NOBODY'S FAULT BUT MINE** [ ] [41]
Oct 68. (7") **I'VE GOT DREAMS TO REMEMBER. / CHAMPAGNE AND WINE** [ ] [-]
Nov 68. (lp) **OTIS REDDING IN PERSON AT THE WHISKEY A GO-GO (live 1966)** [ ] [82]
– I can't turn you loose / Pain in my heart / Just one more day / Mr.Pitiful / (I can't get no) Satisfaction / I'm depending on you / Any ole way / These arms of mine / Papa's got a brand new bag / Respect. *(cd-iss.Dec94 & Sep95 on 'Warners')*
Dec 68. (7") **MERRY CHRISTMAS BABY. / WHITE CHRISTMAS** [ ] [ ]
Dec 68. (7") **PAPA'S GOT A BRAND NEW BAG (live). / DIRECT ME** [ ] [21] Nov 68
Below released on 'Atco' unless mentioned.
Mar 69. (7") **A LOVER'S QUESTION. / YOU MADE A MAN OUT OF ME** [ ] [48] Feb 69
Apr 69. (7") **WHEN SOMETHING IS WRONG WITH MY BABY (w/CARLA THOMAS) / OOH CARLA, OOH OTIS** [-] [ ]
May 69. (7") **LOVE MAN. / CAN'T TURN YOU LOOSE** [-] [72]
Jun 69. (7") **LOVE MAN. / THAT'S HOW STRONG MY LOVE IS** [43] [-]
Jun 69. (lp) **LOVE MAN** [ ] [46]
(re-iss.Nov71 on 'Atlantic') (cd-iss.Jul92 on 'Rhino')
Aug 69. (7") **FREE ME. / (YOUR LOVE HAS LIFTED ME) HIGHER AND HIGHER** [ ] [ ]
Feb 70. (7") **LOOK AT THE GIRL. / THAT'S A GOOD IDEA** [ ] [ ]
1970. (7") **DEMONSTRATION. / JOHNNY'S HEARTBREAK** [-] [ ]
1970. (7") **GIVE AWAY NONE OF MY LOVE. / SNATCH A LITTLE PIECE** [-] [ ]

– other compilations, etc. –

Feb 68. Marble Arch; (lp) **HERE COMES SOME SOUL FROM OTIS REDDING AND LITTLE JOE CURTIS (W / LITTLE JOE CURTIS)** [ ] [-]
Jun 68. Pye Int.; (7") **SHE'S ALRIGHT. / GAMA LAMA** [ ] [-]
— Above and below single rec.1959
Sep 69. Evolution; (7") **SHE'S ALRIGHT. / TUFF ENUFF** [ ] [-]
— In Sep70, shared live lp with JIMI HENDRIX (rec.Jun67) 'MONTEREY INTERNATIONAL POP FESTIVAL' on 'Reprise', hit US No.16.
Below releases on 'Atlantic' UK/ 'Atco' US unless mentioned.
Jul 70. (7") **WONDERFUL WORLD. / SECURITY** [ ] [-]
Jul 70. (7") **I LOVE YOU. / I NEED YOU** [ ] [-]
Jan 71. (lp) **TELL THE TRUTH** (rec.1967) [ ] [ ] Aug70
– Demonstration / Tell the truth / Out of sight / Give away none of my love / Wholesale love / I got the will / Johnny's heartbreak / Snatch a little piece / Slippin' and slidin' / The match game / A little time / Swingin' on a string. *(cd-iss.Jul92 on 'Rhino')*
Mar 71. (7") **I'VE BEEN LOVIN' YOU TOO LONG. / TRY A LITTLE TENDERNESS** [ ] [-]
Aug 71. (7"m) **(SITTIN' ON) THE DOCK OF THE BAY. / RESPECT / MR.PITIFUL** [ ] [-]
(re-iss.Jan72, 1974, Jul84)
Aug 71. (7") **MY GIRL. / GOOD TO ME** [-] [ ]
Nov 71. (7") **WHITE CHRISTMAS. / MERRY CHRISTMAS BABY** [ ] [ ]
Jan 73. (7"m) **(SITTIN' ON) THE DOCK OF THE BAY. / SATISFACTION / I CANT TURN YOU LOOSE** [ ] [-]
Feb 73. (7") **TRAMP. ("OTIS REDDING & CARLA THOMAS"). / KNOCK ON WOOD** [ ] [-]
Jul 73. (d-lp)(c) **THE BEST OF OTIS REDDING** [ ] [76] Sep 72
(cd-iss.Mar87)
Aug 73. (7") **MY GIRL. / HARD TO HANDLE** [ ] [-]
Jun 79. (lp)(c) **PURE OTIS** [ ] [ ]
Apr 80. (12") **I CAN'T TURN YOU LOOSE. / (SITTIN' ON) THE DOCK OF THE BAY** [ ] [-]
May 81. (lp)(c) **OTIS REDDING VOL.1** [ ] [ ]
Apr 82. (lp)(c) **RECORDED LIVE (live)** [ ] [ ]
Oct 84. (7") **(SITTIN' ON) THE DOCK OF THE BAY. / YOU DON'T MISS YOUR WATER** [ ] [-]
May 87. (7") **TRY A LITTLE TENDERNESS. / I'VE BEEN LOVING YOU TOO LONG** [ ] [-]
(12"+=) – Hard to handle.
Jul 87. (lp)(c)(cd) **DOCK OF THE BAY – THE DEFINITIVE COLLECTION** [ ] [ ]
(re-iss.cd+c.Aug93,hit UK No.50)
Dec 88. (lp)(c) **THE OTIS REDDING STORY** [ ] [ ]
Nov 93. Rhino; (4xcd-box) **THE DEFINITIVE OTIS REDDING** [ ] [ ]
May 94. Rhino; (7")(c-s) **(SITTIN' ON THE) DOCK OF THE BAY. / ?** [ ] [ ]
(cd-s+=) –
Aug 74. WEA; (lp) **STAR COLLECTION** [ ] [-]
Jul 84. WEA; (lp)(c) **THE BEST OF OTIS REDDING** [ ] [-]
Apr 85. Charly; (lp)(c) **COME TO ME** [ ] [-]
Jan 85. Old Gold; (7") **(SITTIN' ON) THE DOCK OF THE BAY. / MY GIRL** [ ] [-]
Apr 91. Knight; (cd)(c) **HEART AND SOUL OF OTIS REDDING** [ ] [-]
— (below from film 'The Commitments')
Aug 91. MCA; (7")(c-s) **TRY A LITTLE TENDERNESS. / I'VE BEEN LOVING YOU TOO LONG** [ ] [ ]
(12"+=)(cd-s+=) – ?
Sep 91. Traditional Line; (cd) **SOUL EXPLOSION** [ ] [-]
Sep 91. Traditional Line; (cd) **LIVE IN CONCERT 1965 (live)** [ ] [-]
Oct 91. Stax; (cd) **1000 VOLTS OF STAX** [ ] [ ]
Dec 91. Stax; (cd) **IT'S NOT JUST SENTIMENTAL** [ ] [ ]
May 93. Stax; (cd)(lp) **GOOD TO ME – RECORDED LIVE AT THE WHISKEY A-GO-GO** [ ] [ ]
Nov 92. East West; (7")(12")(c-s)(cd-s) **(SITTIN' ON) THE DOCK OF THE BAY. / SWEET LORRAINE** [ ] [ ]
Jul 92. Castle; (cd)(c) **THE COLLECTION** [ ] [-]

– My girl / Stand by me / Higher and higher / The happy song / I love you more than words can say / Amen / Fa-fa-fa-fa-fa (sad song) / I've been losing you too long / The glory of love / I've got dreams to remember / Love man / Free me / Papa's got a brand new bag / (Sittin' on) The dock of the bay.
Apr 94. That's Soul; (cd) **I'VE BEEN LOVIN' YOU TOO LONG** [ ] [-]
Feb 95. Atlantic; (cd)(c) **THE DOCK OF THE BAY** [54] [ ]

RED HOT CHILI PEPPERS

Formed: Los Angeles, California, USA . . . 1983 after 4 years as ANTHEM. The CHILIS (see below line-up), signed to 'EMI' stark naked, as part of a now famous publicity stunt. They were later to feature naked (all but one sock each strategically placed; you guessed where), on a photo shoot (on Beatles' ABBEY ROAD). Their eponymous debut in 1984 and FREAKIE STYLIE follow-up, saw light of day only in America, but by 1988, the band had begun to venture over the Atlantic, soon issuing 'UPLIFT MOFO PARTY PLAN'. By the early 90's, although depleted somewhat by the death of HILLEL SLOVAK, the group had become red hot property. • **Miscellaneous:** In Apr'90, KIEDIS was given a 60-day jail sentence for sexual battery and indecent exposure to a female student. • **Style:** A hybrid of jazzy funksters PARLIAMENT/FUNFADELIC and 70's punk, fused together with inspiration from JIMI HENDRIX, due to the fact FLEA often played his bass upside down, hanging feet up by a rope!!!. • **Songwriters:** Group compositions except; SUBTERANEAN HOMESICK BLUES (Bob Dylan) / HOLLYWOOD (AFRICA) (Meters) / FIRE + CASTLES MADE OF SAND (Jimi Hendrix) / HIGHER GROUND (Stevie Wonder) / IF YOU WANT ME TO STAY / Sly & Family Stone) / MOMMY WHERE'S DADDY (Frank Zappa) / THEY'RE RED HOT (Robert Johnson) / SEARCH AND DESTROY (Iggy Pop). **Producers:** ANDY GILL (Gang Of Four) produced debut, GEORGE CLINTON of PARLIAMENT produced the 1985 follow-up. In 1991, RICK RUBINS of Def Jam label, held the reins.

Recommended: WHAT HITS? (*8) / BLOOD SUGAR SEX MAGICK (*8) / ONE HOT MINUTE (*7) / MOTHER'S MILK (*7)

ANTHONY KIEDIS (ANTWAN THE SWAN) (b. Michegan) – vocals / **HILLEL SLOVAK** (b. Israel) – guitar / **MICHAEL 'Flea' BALZARY** (b. Melbourne, Australia) – bass / **JACK IRONS** (b. California) – drums

EMI America / EMI America

1984. (lp)(c) **THE RED HOT CHILI PEPPERS** [-] [ ]
– True me don't kill coyotes / Baby appeal / Buckle down / Get up and jump / Why don't you love me / Green heaven / Mommy where's daddy? / Out in L.A. / Police helicopter / You always sing / Grand pappy du plenty. *(UK-iss.+cd.Aug90) (re-iss.cd+c Jun93 on 'Fame')*

(Due to contractual reasons, SLOVAK and IRONS couldn't play on debut. They were deputised by session men **JACK SHERMAN** – guitar (ex-CAPTAIN BEEFHEART) / & **CLIFF MARTINEZ** – drums (ex-WEIRDOS, ex-TEENAGE JESUS & THE JERKS)

— **HILLEL SLOVAK** returned from (**WHAT IS THIS?**) to repl. SHERMAN guests included **MACEO PARKER + FRED WESLEY** (of FUNKADELIC / PARLIAMENT)

1985. (lp)(c) **FREAKY STYLIE** [-] [ ]
– Jungle man / Hollywood (Africa) / American ghost dance / If you want me to stay / Never mind / Freaky stylie / Blackeyed blonde / The brothers cup / Battle ship / Lovin' and touchin' / Catholic school girls rule / Sex rap / Thirty dirty birds / Yertle the turtle. *(UK-iss.+cd.Aug90) (re-iss.cd+c Dec94 on 'Fame')*
Aug 85. (7") **HOLLYWOOD (AFRICA). / NEVER MIND** [ ] [ ]
('A'remixed-12"+=) – ('A'dub version).

— **JACK IRONS** returned from **WHAT IS THIS?** to repl. MARTINEZ

Jan 88. (7") **FIGHT LIKE A BRAVE. / FIRE** [ ] [ ]
(12"+=)(12"pic-d+=) – ('A' mofo mix) / ('A'knucklehead mix).
Mar 88. (lp)(c)(cd) **UPLIFT MOFO PARTY PLAN** [ ] [ ] Nov 87
– Fight like a brave / Funky crime / Me and my friends / Backwoods / Skinny sweaty man / Behind the sun / Subterranean homesick blues / Special secret song inside / No chump love sucker / Walkin' on down the road / Love trilogy / Organic anti-beat box band.

— **ANTWAN & FLEA** (now adding trumpet) brought in new lads **JOHN FRUSCIANTE** – guitar repl. HILLEL who died (of heroin OD) 20 Jun'88. **CHAD SMITH** – drums repl. IRONS who later formed ELEVEN

EMI Manhattan / Manhattan

Aug 89. (7")(7"pic-d) **KNOCK ME DOWN. / PUNK ROCK CLASSIC / PRETTY LITTLE DITTY** [ ] [ ]
(12") – (first 2 -7"tracks) / Special secret song inside / Magic Johnson
(cd-s) – (first 2 -7"tracks) / Jungle man / Magic Johnson.
Aug 89. (lp)(c)(cd) **MOTHER'S MILK** [ ] [52]
– Good time boys / Higher ground / Subway to Venus / Magic Johnson / Nobody weird like me / Knock me down / Taste the pain / Stone cold bush / Fire / Pretty little ditty / Punk rock classic / Sexy Mexican maid / Johnny kick a hole in the sky.
Dec 89. (7") **HIGHER GROUND. / MILLIONAIRES AGAINST HUNGER** [55] [ ]
(12") – ('A' Munchkin mix) / ('A'dub mix) / Politician.
(12") – ('A' Munchkin mix)(++=) – Mommy where's daddy.
('A' Munchkin mix -cd-s+=) – Mommy where's daddy / Politician (mini rap).
Jun 90. (7")(c-s) **TASTE THE PAIN. / SHOW ME YOUR SOUL** [29] [ ]
(12"+=)(9"square-pic-d+=) – Castles made of sand (live).
(cd-s++=) – Never mind.
(remixed-12"+=) – If you want me to stay / Never mind.
Aug 90. (7")(c-s) **HIGHER GROUND. / FIGHT LIKE A BRAVE** [54] [ ]
(12"+=)(cd-s+=) – ('A'mix) / Out in L.A.
(cd-s+=) – Behind the Sun.

Warners / Warners

Sep 91. (cd)(c)(d-lp) **BLOOD SUGAR SEX MAGIK** [25] [3]
– The power of equality / If you have to ask / Breaking the girl / Funky monks / Suck my kiss / I could have lied / Mellowship slinky in B major / The righteous & the wicked / Give it away / Blood sugar sex magik / Under the bridge / Naked in the rain / Apache Rose peacock / The greeting song / My lovely man / Sir psycho sexy / They're red hot. *(re-iss.Mar92)*
Dec 91. (c-s) **GIVE IT AWAY. / ?** [-] [73]
(US re-iss.Jul92, hit No.73)
Mar 92. (7") **UNDER THE BRIDGE. / GIVE IT AWAY** [26] [2]
(12")(cd-s) – ('A'side) / Search and destroy / Soul to squeeze / Skiamikanico.

— (the last track also featured on 'Wayne's World' film/single)

— **ZANDER SCHLOSS** (THELONIUS MONSTER) – guiter, repl. FRUSCANTE

Jun 92. (c-s) **IF YOU HAVE TO ASK. / ?** [-] [ ]
Aug 92. (7") **BREAKING THE GIRL. / FELA'S COOK** [41] [ ]
(12"+=)(cd-s+=) – Suck my kiss (live) / I could have lied (live).

— (Aug92) **ERIC MARSHALL** – guitar (ex-MARSHALL LAW) repl. SCHLOSS

Aug 93. (c-s)(cd-s) **SOUL TO SQUEEZE. / ?** [-] [22]
Jan 94. (7")(c-s) **GIVE IT AWAY. / IF YOU HAVE TO ASK (remix)** [9] [-]
(cd-s+=) – Nobody weird like me (live).
(cd-s) – ('A'side) / Soul to squeeze.
Apr 94. (7"blue)(c-s) **UNDER THE BRIDGE. / SUCK MY KISS (live)** [13] [-]
(cd-s+=) – Sikamikanico / Search and destroy.
(cd-s) – ('A'side) / I could have lied / Sela's cock / Give it away.

— **DAVE NAVARRO** -guitar (ex-JANE'S ADDICTION) repl.MARSHALL

Aug 95. (c-s) **WARPED / PEA** [31] [ ]
(cd-s+=) – Melancholy maniacs.
Sep 95. (cd)(c)(lp) **ONE HOT MINUTE** [2] [4]
– Warped / Aeroplane / Deep kick / My friends / Coffee shop / Pea / One big mob / Walkabout / Tearjerker / One hot minute / Falling into grace / Shallow be thy name / Transcending.
Oct 95. (c-s) **MY FRIENDS / LET'S MAKE EVIL** [29] [ ]
(12"+=)(cd-s+=) – Coffee / Stretch.

. . . *Jan – Jun '96 stop press* . . .

Feb 96. (single) **AEROPLANE** [11] [ ]

– compilations, others, etc. –

May 88. EMI Manhattan; (7"ep) **THE ABBEY ROAD EP** [ ] [-]
– Backwoods / Hollywood (Africa) / True men don't kill coyotes.
(12"ep+=) – Catholic school girls rule.
Oct 92. EMI Manhattan; (cd)(c)(d-lp) **WHAT HITS?** [23] [22]
– Higher ground / Fight like a brave / Behind the Sun / Me & my friends / Backwoods / True men don't kill coyotes / Fire / Get up and jump / Knock me down / Under the bridge / Show me your soul / If you want me to stay / Hollywood / Jungle man / The brothers cup / Taste the pain / Catholic school girls rule / Johnny kick a hole in the sky.
Oct 94. Warners; (d-cd) **PLASMA SHAFT** (rare mixes/live) [ ] [ ]
Nov 94. EMI; (cd)(c)(lp) **OUT IN L.A.** (rare remixes, demos & live) [61] [82]
Nov 95. EMI; (3xcd-box) **THE RED HOT CHILI PEPPERS / FREAKY STYLIE / UPLIFT MOFO PARTY PLAN** [ ] [ ]

Lou REED

Born: LOUIS FIRBANK, 2 Mar'42, Freeport, Long Island, New York, USA. In 1958, he formed the JADES who released 2 singles written by him 'LEAVE HER FOR ME / SO BLUE' plus 'LEAVE HER FOR ME / BELINDA' for 'Time' and 'Dot' respectively. Late in '64 he joined the 'Pickwick' stable of writers and achieved local minor hit when The PRIMITIVES issued his 'The Ostrich / Sneaky Pete' 45. Later in the year, he became part leader of seminal supergroup The VELVET UNDERGROUND. He departed in Sep'70, and went solo after signing to 'RCA'. His eponymous debut in 1972 with Richard Robinson on production, scraped into The US Top 200 but gained nothing in renewed respect. The following year, helped by RCA stablemates/fans DAVID BOWIE and MICK RONSON, he unleashed 'TRANSFORMER', which gave him first major taste of triumph, when it reached Top 30 on both sides of the Atlantic. It was boosted by a superb single lifted from it 'WALK ON THE WILD SIDE', which also broke into each Top 20. His next album 'BERLIN', although unfairly panned by US critics, still managed a Top 10 placing in Britain. On reflection, its subject matter like suicide and child neglect, didn't help win any new friends. • **Style:** Cult experimental rock artist, whose socially aware narratively sung lyrics and extreme looks made him punk superstar of the 70's and 80's. In 1975, he shot himself in the foot, when releasing in the US, an experimental double album 'METAL MACHINE MUSIC', which consisted of ENO type unaccessible pieces of noise interrupted with feedback, screams, hums, etc. • **Songwriters:** REED compositions except, SEPTEMBER SONG (Kurt Weill) / SOUL MAN (Sam & Dave). In 1979 & 1980, he co-wrote with MICHAEL FORFARA plus other group members. The single 'CITY LIGHTS' was co-written with NILS LOFGREN. • **Trivia:** Surprisingly in 1973, WALK ON THE WILD SIDE was not banned from airplay. It contained lyrics 'giving head', which had been overlooked by unstreet-wise cred. radio producers. LOU has been married twice. The first to cocktail waitress Betty on 9 Jan'73, the second to Sylvia Morales on 14 Feb'80. He played guitar and composed 4 tracks on NICO'S 'Chelsea Girl' lp in 1967. Nine years later he produced NELSON SLATER'S 'Wild Angel' album, also contributing guitar, piano and vocals. In 1979 & 1981 he co-composed with NILS LOFGREN and KISS on their 'NILS' and 'THE ELDER' albums respectively. In the late 80's, he guested for RUBEN BLADES and his old friend MAUREEEN TUCKER. He was also backing vocalist on SIMPLE MINDS' 'This is Your Land' / DION'S 'King of The New York Streets' and TOM TOM CLUB'S version of 'Femme Fatale'.

Recommended: TRANSFORMER (*10) / BERLIN (*8) / RETRO (*8) / NEW YORK (*9) / MAGIC AND LOSS (*8) / SONGS FOR DRELLA (*7 / SET THE TWILIGHT REELING (*8)).

LOU REED – vocals, guitar (ex-VELVET UNDERGROUND) / with **STEVE HOWE** – guitar / **RICK WAKEMAN** – keyboards (both of YES) / **CLEM CATTINI** – drums (ex-TORNADOES)

R.C.A. R.C.A.

Jun 72. (7") **GOING DOWN. / I CAN'T STAND IT** [-] [ ]
Jul 72. (lp)(c) **LOU REED** [ ] [ ] May 72
– I can't stand it / Going down / Walk and talk it / Lisa says / Berlin / I love you / Wild child / Love makes you feel / Ride into the Sun / Ocean.
Aug 72. (7") **WALK AND TALK IT. / WILD CHILD** [ ] [ ]

— now with **MICK RONSON** – guitar / **HERBIE FLOWERS + KLAUS VOORMANN** – bass / **JOHN HALSEY + RITCHIE DHARMA + BARRY DE SOUZA** – drums / **RONNIE ROSS** – saxophone / **DAVID BOWIE** – backing vocals, producer

Nov 72. (lp)(c) **TRANSFORMER** [13] [29]
– Vicious / Andy's chest / Perfect day / Hangin' round / Walk on the wild side / Make up / Satellite of love / Wagon wheel / New York telephone conversation / I'm so free / Goodnight ladies. *(re-iss.Feb81, Jun82 hit 91, 1984, cd-iss.1985 + Oct87)*
Nov 72. (7") **WALK ON THE WILD SIDE. / PERFECT DAY** [10] [16]
(re-iss.May79.on'RCA Gold')
Feb 73. (7") **SATELLITE OF LOVE. / WALK AND TALK IT** [-] [ ]
Mar 73. (7") **SATELLITE OF LOVE. / VICIOUS** [ ] [-]
Apr 73. (7") **VICIOUS. / GOODNIGHT LADIES** [-] [ ]

— all new band **DICK WAGNER + STEVE HUNTER** – guitar (both ex-ALICE COOPER) / **STEVE WINWOOD** – keyboards / **JACK BRUCE** – bass / **AYNSLEY DUNBAR** – drums / etc.

Oct 73. (7") **HOW DO YOU THINK IT FEELS. /LADY DAY** [-] [ ]
Oct 73. (lp)(c) **BERLIN** [7] [98]
– Berlin / Lady day / Men of good fortune / Caroline says I / How do think it feels / Oh Jim / Caroline says II / The kids / The bed / Sad song. *(re-iss. Oct81, re-iss.+cd.Jun86)*
Feb 74. (7") **CAROLINE SAYS I. / CAROLINE SAYS II** [ ] [-]

— **PRAKASH JOHN** – bass (ex-ALICE COOPER) repl. TONY LEVIN / **JOSEF CHIROWSKY** – keyboards / **WHITNEY GLEN** – drums (ex-ALICE COOPER)

Mar 74. (lp)(c) **ROCK'N'ROLL ANIMAL (live)** [26] [45] Feb 74
– (intro) – Sweet Jane / Heroin / White light – white heat / Lady day / Rock and roll. *(re-iss.May81 + 1984, re-iss.+cd.Jun86)*
Apr 74. (7") **SWEET JANE (live). / LADY DAY (live)** [ ] [ ]

— **MICHAEL FORFARA** – keyboards repl. JOSEF

Aug 74. (7") **SALLY CAN'T DANCE. / VICIOUS** [-] [ ]
Sep 74. (lp)(c) **SALLY CAN'T DANCE** [ ] [10]
– Ride Sally ride / Animal language / Baby face / N.Y. stars / Kill your sons / Billy / Sally can't dance / Ennui. *(re-iss.Feb81 + 1984, cd-iss.Mar87 + Feb89)*
Oct 74. (7") **SALLY CAN'T DANCE. / ENNUI** [ ] [ ]
Mar 75. (lp)(c) **LOU REED LIVE (live)** [ ] [62]
– Walk on the wild side / I'm waiting for the man / Vicious / Oh Jim / Satellite of love / Sad song. *(re-iss.Feb81 + 1984, cd-iss.Mar87 + Feb90)*

— LOU now used synthesizer only.

Jul 75. (d-lp) **METAL MACHINE MUSIC – (THE AMINE B RING)** [-] [ ]
– Metal machine music A1 / A2 / A3 / A4. *(quad-lp also iss.) (re-iss.+cd.Mar91 on 'Great Expectations')*

— Band now featured **MICHAEL SUCHORSKY** – percussion / **BOB KULICK** – guitar / **BRUCE YAW** – bass

Jan 76. (lp)(c) **CONEY ISLAND BABY** [52] [41]
– Crazy feeling / Charley's girl / She's my best friend / Kicks / A gift / Oooh baby / Nobody's business / Coney Island baby. *(re-iss.Mar81 + 1984, cd-iss. Dec86)*
Mar 76. (7") **CHARLEY'S GIRL. / NOWHERE AT ALL** [ ] [-]
May 76. (7") **CRAZY FEELING. / NOWHERE AT ALL** [-] [ ]

Arista Arista

Nov 76. (lp)(c) **ROCK AND ROLL HEART** [ ] [64]
– I believe in love / Banging on my drum / Follow the leader / You wear it so well / Ladies pay / Rock and roll heart / Temporary thing.
Nov 76. (7") **I BELIEVE IN LOVE. / SENSELESSLY CRUEL** [-] [ ]
Apr 77. (7") **ROCK AND ROLL HEART. / SENSELESSLY CRUEL** [ ] [-]

— **STUART HEINRICH** – guitar, vocals repl. KULICK / **MARTY FOGEL** – saxophone repl. YAW

Apr 78. (lp)(c) **STREET HASSLE** [ ] [89]
– Gimme some good times / Dirt / Street hassle / I wanna be black / Real good time together / Shooting star / Leave me alone / Wait.
Apr 78. (12") **STREET HASSLE. / (same track)** [-] [ ]
Jul 78. (12"ep) **STREET HASSLE. / Waiting For The Man + Venus In Furs (by "The VELVET UNDERGROUND")** [ ] [-]

— **ELLARD BOLES** – bass, guitar repl. HEINRICH. (Below released 'RCA' UK)

Mar 79. (d-lp)(c) **LIVE – TAKE NO PRISONERS (live)** [ ] [ ] Nov 78
– Sweet Jane / I wanna be black / Satellite of love / Pale blue eyes / Berlin / I'm waiting for the man / Coney Island baby / Street hassle / Walk on the wild side / Leave me alone. *(US-iss.red or blue-lp)*

— **REED** now with **FORFARA, BOLES, SUCHORSKY, FOGEL** and **DON CHERRY** – trumpet

Oct 79. (lp)(c) **THE BELLS** [ ] [ ] May 79
– Stupid man / Disco mystic / I want to boogie with you / With you / Looking for love / City lights / All through the night / Families / The bells.
Jun 79. (7") **CITY LIGHTS. / I WANT TO BOOGIE WITH YOU** [-] [ ]
Oct 79. (7") **CITY LIGHTS. / SENSELESSLY CRUEL** [ ] [-]

— **CHUCK HAMMER** – synthesizer, guitar repl. FOGEL & CHERRY

May 80. (lp)(c) **GROWING UP IN PUBLIC** [ ] [ ] Apr 80
– How do you speak to an angel / My old man / Keep away / Growing up in public / Standing on ceremony / So alone / Love is here to stay / The power of positive drinking / Smiles / Think it over / Teach the gifted children.
Jun 80. (7") **THE POWER OF POSITIVE DRINKING. / GROWING UP IN PUBLIC** [-] [ ]

— **ROBERT QUINE** – guitar repl. HAMMER

R.C.A. R.C.A.

Mar 82. (lp)(c) **THE BLUE MASK** [ ] [ ] Feb 82
– My house / Women / Underneath the bottle / The gun / The blue mask / The gun / The heroine / Waves of fear / The day John Kennedy died / Heavenly arms.
Mar 83. (lp)(c) **LEGENDARY HEARTS** [ ] [ ] Dec 82
– Legendary hearts / Don't talk to me about work / Make up mind / Martial law / The last shot / Turn out the light / ow wow / Betrayed / Bottoming out / Home of the brave / Rooftop garden. *(re-iss.Oct86, re-iss.+cd.Apr91)*
Jan 84. (d-lp)(c) **LIVE IN ITALY (live)** [ ] [-]
– Sweet Jane / I'm waiting for the man / Martial law / atellite of love / Kill your sons / Betrayed / Sally can't dance / Waves of fear / Average guy / White light – white heat / Some kinda love / Sister Ray / Walk on the wild side / Heroin / Rock and roll.

— Line-up now **FERNANDO SAUNDERS** – bass, rhythm guitar / **FRED MAHER** – drums / **PETER WOOD** – piano, synthesizer, accordion / **L. SHANKER** – electric violin

Apr 84. (12") **MY RED JOY STICK. / ('A' remix)** [-] [ ]
May 84. (lp)(c) **NEW SENSATIONS** [92] [56]
– I love you, Suzanne / Endlessly jealous / My red joystick / Turn to me / New sensations / Doin' the things that we want to / What becomes a legend most / Fly into the Sun / High in the city / My friend George / Down at the arcade. *(cd-iss.Jul86)*
May 84. (7") **I LOVE YOU, SUZANNE. / VICIOUS** [ ] [-]
(12"+=) – Walk on the wild side.
Apr 86. (12") **THE ORIGINAL WRAPPER. / (2 'A' versions)** [-] [ ]
Apr 86. (lp)(c)(cd) **MISTRIAL** [69] [47]
– Mistrial / No money down / Outside / Don't hurt a woman / Video violence / Spit it out / The original wrapper / Mama's got a lover / I remember you / Tell it to your heart. *(re-iss.+cd.Oct88)*
Jun 86. (7") **NO MONEY DOWN. / DON'T HURT A WOMAN** [ ] [-]
(12"+=) – ('A'dub version).

— Next from the film 'Soul Man'.

A & M A & M

Jan 87. (7") **SOUL MAN. (by "LOU REED and SAM MOORE") / Sweet Sarah (by 'Tom Scott')** [30] [ ]
(US-12"+=) – My love is chemical.

— new band **MIKE RATHKE** – guitar / **ROB WASSERMAN** – bass / **FRED MAHER** –

drums / **MAUREEN TUCKER** – drums on 2 (ex-VELVET UNDERGROUND)

Sire Sire

Jan 89. (lp)(c)(cd) **NEW YORK** [14] [40]
– Romeo had Juliette / Halloween parade / Dirty Blvd. / Endless cycle / There is no time / The last great American whale / Beginning of a great adventure / Busload of faith / Sick of you / Hold on / Good evening Mr.Waldheim / Xmas in February / Strawman / Dime store mystery. *(re-iss.cd/c Feb95)*

Feb 89. (7") **ROMEO HAD JULIETTE. / BUSLOAD OF FAITH (live)** [-] [ ]

Feb 89. (7") **DIRTY BLVD. / THE LAST GREAT AMERICAN WHALE** [ ] [-]
(12"+=) – The room.

Apr 90. (cd)(c)(lp) **SONGS FOR DRELLA ("LOU REED - JOHN CALE")** [22] [ ]
– Smalltown / Open house / Style it takes / Work / Trouble with classicists / Starlight / Faces and names / Images / Slip away (a warning) / It wasn't me / I believe / Nobody but you / A dream / Forever changed / Hello it's me. *(re-iss.Feb91)*

—— (above re-united the two VELVET UNDERGROUND members, tributing the recently deceased ANDY WARHOL)

—— **MICHAEL BLAIR** – percussion, drums, vocas repl. MAHER

Jan 92. (cd)(c)(lp) **MAGIC AND LOSS** [6] [80]
– Dorita – the spirit / What's good – the thesis / Power and glory – the situation / Magician – internally / Sword of Damocles – eternally / Goodby mass – in a chapel bodily termination / Cremation – ashes to ashes / Dreamin' – escape / No chance – regret / Warrior king – revenge / Harry's circumcision – reverie gone astray / Gassed and stoked – loss / Power and glory part II – magic transformation / Magic and loss – the summation.

Mar 92. (7")(c-s) **WHAT'S GOOD. / THE ROOM** [ ] [ ]
(12"+=)(cd-s+=) – Mary's circumcision / A dream.

. . . Jan – Jun '96 stop press . . .

WEA WEA

Feb 96. (cd)(c)(lp) **SET THE TWILIGHT REELING** [26] [ ]

May 96. (single) **HOOKY WOOKY** [ ] [ ]

– compilations, others, etc. –

Below releases issued on 'RCA' unless mentioned.

Apr 77. (lp)(c) **WALK ON THE WILD SIDE – THE BEST OF LOU REED** *(cd-iss.Mar87)* [ ] [ ]

Jan 79. (lp)(c) **VICIOUS** [ ] [ ]

Aug 81. (lp) **ROCK GALAXY** [ ] [ ]

Aug 81. (7") **WALK ON THE WILD SIDE. / VICIOUS** [ ] [-]
(re-iss.Oct86 + Mar89 on 'Old Gold')

Sep 82. (lp)(c) **I CAN'T STAND IT** [ ] [ ]

May 86. (c) **MAGIC MOMENTS** [ ] [ ]

Feb 89. (3"cd-ep) **WALK ON THE WILD SIDE / PERFECT DAY / SATELLITE OF LOVE / VICIOUS** [ ] [ ]

Sep 89. (lp)(c)(cd) **RETRO** [29] [ ]
– Walk on the wild side / Satellite of love / I love you Suzanne / Wild child / How do you think it feels / Lady day / Coney Island baby / Sweet Jane (live) / Vicious / Sally can't dance / Berlin / Caroline says II / Kill your sons / White light – white heat (live). (cd+=) – I'm waiting for the man (VELVET UNDERGROUND) / Heroin (VELVET UNDERGROUND).

Dec 80. Arista; (d-lp)(c) **ROCK AND ROLL DIARY 1967-1980** [ ] [ ]
above featured 8 tracks by VU.

Sep 86. Fame; (lp)(c) **NEW YORK SUPERSTAR** [ ] [-]

Oct 85. A&M; (7") **SEPTEMBER SONG. / Oh Heavenly Action (by 'Mark Bingham with Johnny Adams & Aaron Neville')** [ ] [ ]

Mar 92. BMG; (3xcd)(3xc) **BETWEEN THOUGHT AND EXPRESSION** [ ] [ ]

Aug 92. Arista; (cd) **THE BELLS / GROWING UP IN PUBLIC** [ ] [ ]

REEF

Formed: London-based from Bath, England . . .1994. Hit the ears of the nation in 1995, when a Sony Minidisc TV commercial featured their song 'NAKED'. This became their second! Top 30 hit, although they shunned STILTSKIN-like now-made-it-through-TV-ad comparisons. • **Style:** Funky country blues fusing American-like sound of BLACK CROWES or LENNY KRAVITZ with LED ZEPPELIN. • **Songwriters:** Group or STRINGER?.

Recommended: REPLENISH (*6)

GARY STRINGER -vocals / **KENWYN HOUSE** -guitar / **JACK BESSANT** -bass / **DOMINIC GREENSMITH** -drums

S2 – Sony Sony

Apr 95. (c-s) **GOOD FEELING / WAKE** [24] [ ]
(cd-s+=) – End.
(12"pic-d+=) – Water over stone.

May 95. (7"colrd)(c-s) **NAKED. / CHOOSE TO LIVE** [11] [ ]
(cd-s+=) – Fade.

Jun 95. (cd)(c)(lp) **REPLENISH** [9] [ ]
– Feed me / Naked / Good feeling / Repulsive / Mellow / Together / Replenish / Choose to live / Comfort / Loose / End / Reprise.

Jul 95. (7"colrd)(c-s) **WEIRD. / ACOUSTIC ONE** [19] [ ]
(cd-s) – ('A'side) / Sunrise shakers / Together / End (live).

R.E.M.

Formed: Athens, Georgia, USA . . . Spring 1980 by STIPE and BUCK, who met MILLS and BERRY at a party. In 1981, through manager Jefferson Holt, they released debut Mitch Easter produced 45 'RADIO FREE EUROPE', which made its way the ears of 'IRS' label boss Miles Copeland, who signed them in 1982. He retained Easter for their mini-lp 'CHRONIC TOWN', which gained heavy praise by critics. In 1983 their full album debut 'MURMUR' (co-produced by Easter & Don Dixon), became college favourite and soon broke into the US Top 40. They progressed steadily, bettering each album throughout the 80's. They superseded all before them in the 90's, when albums 'OUT OF TIME' & 'AUTOMATIC FOR THE PEOPLE' both made trans-Atlantic No.1's. For me and millions of others, the greatest band to come out of America. • **Style:** Moved from underground 60's influenced rock, similar to CREEDENCE CLEARWATER REVIVAL or The BYRDS, to a more country/folk tinted rock, mixed with new psychedelia, sifted from remains of the new wave. Unusually they have not toured since the 'GREEN' tour of early '89, and they intended being a studio outfit until 1994 at least. • **Songwriters:** Group compositions except 'B'side covers; THERE SHE GOES AGAIN + PALE BLUE EYES + FEMME FATALE (Velvet Underground) / TOYS IN THE ATTIC (Aerosmith) / KING OF THE ROAD (Roger Miller) / CRAZY (Pylon) / AFTER HOURS (Lou Reed) / LOVE IS ALL AROUND (Troggs) / FIRST WE TAKE MANHATTAN (Leonard Cohen) / LAST DATE (Floyd Cramer) / TIGHTEN UP (Booker T. & The MG's) / SEE NO EVIL (Television) / ACADEMY EIGHT SONG (Mission of Burma) / SUMMERTIME (Gershwin) / BABY BABY (Vibrators) / WHERE"S CAPAIN KICK? (Spizz) / PARADE OF WOODEN SOLDIERS (Tchaikovsky) / MOON RIVER (Henry Mancini) / THE ARMS OF YOU (Robyn Hitchcock) / THE LION SLEEPS TONIGHT (Tokens) / DARK GLOBE (Syd Barrett). • **Trivia:** R.E.M. stands for Rapid Eye Movement. The great STIPE, has been acquaintance of 10,000 MANIACS' singer NATALIE MERCHANT. Their other albums were produced by Joe Boyd (1985) / Don Gehman (1986) / Scott Litt & group (1987-1990's).

Recommended: AUTOMATIC FOR THE PEOPLE (*10) / OUT OF TIME (*10) / GREEN (*9) / DOCUMENT (*8) / LIFE'S RICH PAGEANT (*8) / FABLES OF THE RECONSTRUCTION (*9) / RECKONING (*9) / MURMUR (*9) / DEAD LETTER OFFICE (*7) / THE BEST OF R.E.M. (*9) / MONSTER (*8).

MICHAEL STIPE (b. 4 Jan'60) – vocals / **PETER BUCK** (b. 6 Dec'56) – guitar / **MIKE MILLS** (b.17 Dec'58) – bass / **BILL BERRY** (b.31 Jul'58) – drums

not issued Hib-tone

Jul 81. (7") **RADIO FREE EUROPE. / SITTING BULL** [-] [ ]

I.R.S. I.R.S.

Aug 82. (m-lp) **CHRONIC TOWN** [-] [ ]
– Wolves, lower / 1,000,000 / Gardening at night / Stumble / Carnival of sorts (box cars).

Aug 83. (7") **RADIO FREE EUROPE. / THERE SHE GOES AGAIN** [ ] [78] Jul 83

Aug 83. (lp)(c) **MURMUR** [ ] [36] May 83
– Radio free Europe / Pilgrimage / Laughing / Talk about the passion / Moral kiosk / Perfect circle / Catapult / Sitting bull / 9-9 / Shaking through / We walk / West of the fields. *(re-iss.1986, cd-iss.1988 & Mar91)*

Nov 83. (7") **TALK ABOUT THE PASSION. / SHAKING THROUGH** [ ] [ ]
(12"+=) – Carnival of sorts (box cars) / 1,000,000.

Mar 84. (7") **SO. CENTRAL RAIN. / KING OF THE ROAD** [ ] [85] Jun 84
(12"+=) – Voice of Harold / Pale blue eyes.

Apr 84. (lp)(c) **RECKONING** [91] [27]
– Harborcoat / 7 Chinese Bros. / So. central rain (I'm sorry) / Pretty persuasion / Time after time (Annelise) / Second guessing / Letter never sent / Camera / (Don't go back to) Rockville / Little America. *(cd-iss.1988 & 1992 +=)*– Wind out (with Friends) / Pretty persuasion (live in studio) / White tornado (live in studio) / Tighten up / Moon river. *(re-iss.cd+c Oct94 on 'A&M')*

Jun 84. (7") **(DON'T GO BACK TO) ROCKVILLE. / WOLVES, LOWER** [ ] [ ]
(12"+=) – Gardening at night (live) / 9-9.

Jun 84. (7") **(DON'T GO BACK TO) ROCKVILLE. / CATAPULT (live)** [-] [ ]

Jul 85. (7") **CAN'T GET THERE FORM HERE. / BANDWAGON** [-] [ ] (extended 12"+=) Burning Hell.

Jul 85. (lp)(c) **FABLES OF THE RECONSTRUCTION – RECONSTRUCTION OF THE FABLES** 35 28 Jun 85
– Feeling gravitys pull / Maps and legends / Driver 8 / Life and how to live it / Old Man Kensey / Can't get there from here / Green grow the rushes / Kokoutek / Auctioneer (another engine) / Good advices / Wendell Gee. *(cd-iss. Apr87 + Jan90 +=)*– Crazy / Burning Hell / Bandwagon / Driver 8 (live) / Maps of legends (live).

Oct 85. (7") **DRIVER 8. / CRAZY** -

Oct 85. (7") **WENDELL GEE. / CRAZY**
(12"+=)/ /(d7"+=) – Driver 8./ / Ages of you / Burning down.

Aug 86. (7") **FALL ON ME. / ROTARY TEN** 94
(12"+=) – Toys in the attic.

Aug 86. (lp)(c)(cd) **LIFE'S RICH PAGEANT** 43 21
– Begin the begin / These days / Fall on me / Cuyahoga / Hyena / Underneath the bunker / The flowers of Guatemala / I believe / What if we give it away? / Just a touch / Swan swan H / Superman. *(re-iss.cd.1992)*

Mar 87. (7") **SUPERMAN. / WHITE TORNADO**
(12"+=) – Femme fatale.

Aug 87. (7") **IT'S THE END OF THE WORLD AS WE KNOW IT (AND I FEEL FINE). / (THIS ONE GOES OUT TO) THE ONE I LOVE (live)** 69 Jan 88

Oct 87. (lp)(c)(cd) **DOCUMENT** 28 10 Sep 87
– Finest worksong / Welcome to the occupation / Exhuming McCarthy / Disturbance at Heron House / Strange / It's the end of the world as we know it (and I feel fine) / The one I love / Fireplace / Lightnin' Hopkins / King of birds / Oddfellows local 151. *(re-iss.cd.1992)*

Nov 87. (7")(12") **THE ONE I LOVE. / LAST DATE (live)** 51 9
(cd-s+=) – Disturbance at the Heron House (live).

Jan 88. (7") **FINEST WORKSONG. / TIME AFTER TIME (live)** 50
(12"+=) – ('A'club mix).
(12"+=) – Red rain / S.central rain (live).
(cd-s+=) – It's the end of the world and we know it (and I feel fine).

Mar 88. (12") **FINEST WORKSONG (lengthy club mix). / ('A'mix) / TIME AFTER TIME, ETC** -

Warners Warners

Nov 88. (lp)(c)(cd) **GREEN** 27 12
– Pop song 89 / Get up / You are the everything / Stand / World leader pretend / The wrong child / Orange crush / Turn you inside – out / Hairshirt / I remember California / Untitled song.

Jan 89. (7") **STAND. / MEMPHIS TRAIN BLUES** 51 6
(12"+=)(cd-s+=) – Eleventh untitled song.

Mar 89. (7") **ORANGE CRUSH. / GHOST RIDERS** 28
(12"+=)(7"box+=)(3"cd-s+=) – Dark globe.

Jul 89. (7") **STAND. / POP SONG '89 (acoustic)** 48 86 B-side
(12"+=)(cd-s+=) – Skin tight (live).
(all above 7"singles were re-iss. in 4xbox Dec89)

Sep 89. (7") **GET UP. / FUNTIME** -

— R.E.M. toured early '91 as BINGO HAND JOB.

Feb 91. (7")(c-s) **LOSING MY RELIGION. / ROTARY ELEVEN** 19 4
(12"+=) – After hours (live).
(cd-s) – ('A'side) / Stand (live) / Turn you inside out (live) / World leader pretend (live).

Mar 91. (cd)(c)(lp) **OUT OF TIME** 1 1
– Radio song / Losing my religion / Low / Near wild Heaven / Endgame / Shiny happy people / Belong / Half a world away / Texarkana / Country feedback / Me in honey. *(re-entered UK chart Dec92, peaked 50)*
(the album feat. PETER HOLSAPPLE – guitar (ex-DB'S) / KRS-1 – rapper) MICHAEL STIPE released album with KRS-1 'CIVILIZATION VS.TECHNOLOGY' Oct91.

May 91. (7") **SHINY HAPPY PEOPLE. / FORTY SECOND SONG** 6 10 Jul 91
(12"+=)(cd-s+=) – Losing my religion (live acoustic version).
(cd-s) – ('A'side) / I remember California / Get up / Pop song '89 (live).
(above 'A'side feat. KATE PIERSON of The B-52'S)

Aug 91. (7") **NEAR WILD HEAVEN. / POP SONG '89** 27
(12"+=) – Half a world away (acoustic live).
(cd-s) – ('A'side) / Tom's diner (live) / Low (live) / Endgame (live).

Nov 91. (7") **RADIO SONG. / LOVE IS ALL AROUND** 28
(12"+=) – Shiny happy people (remix).
(cd-s+=) – You are the everything / Orange crush / Belong (all live).

Oct 92. (7")(c-s) **DRIVE. / IT'S A FREE WORLD BABY** 11 28
(cd-s+=) – World leader pretend / First we take Manhattan / Winged manual thorn.

Oct 92. (cd)(c)(lp) **AUTOMATIC FOR THE PEOPLE** 1 2
– Drive / Try not to breathe / The sidewinder sleeps tonight / Everybody hurts / New Orleans instrumental No.1 / Sweetness follows / Monty got a raw deal / Ignoreland / Star me kitten / Man on the Moon / Nightswimming / Find the river. *(re-hit UK No.1 Apr93)*

Nov 92. (7")(c-s) **MAN ON THE MOON. / TURN YOU INSIDE OUT** 18 30 Feb 93
(cd-s+=) – Fruity organ / New Orleans instrumental No.1.
(cd-s+=) – The arms of you.

Feb 93. (7")(c-s) **THE SIDEWINDER SLEEPS TONIGHT. / GET UP** 17
(cd-s) – ('A'side) / The lion sleeps tonight (live) / Fretless.
(cd-s) – ('A'side) / Star me kitten (demo) / Organ song.

Apr 93. (7")(c-s) **EVERYBODY HURTS. / POP SONG '89** 7 -
(cd-s) – ('A'side) / Dark globe / Chance (dub).
(cd-s) – ('A'side) / Mandolin strum / New Orleans instrumental No.1.

Jul 93. (7")(c-s) **NIGHTSWIMMING. / LOSING MY RELIGION (live)** 27
(cd-s+=)(one-sided-12"pic-d) – ('A'side) / World leader pretend / Low / Belong (all 3 live).

Aug 93. (12"orange) **EVERYBODY HURTS. / MANDOLIN STRUM / BELONG / ORANGE CRUSH (live)** - 29
(12"white)(12"blue)(cd-ep) – ('A'side) / Star me kitten (demo) / Losing my religion (live) / Organ song

Dec 93. (7")(c-s) **FIND THE RIVER. / EVERYBODY HURTS (live)** 54
(cd-s+=)/ /(cd-s+=) – World leader pretend (live)./ / Orange crush.

Sep 94. (7")(c-s) **WHAT'S THE FREQUENCY, KENNETH?. / ('A'instrumental)** 9 21
(cd-s) – ('A'side) / Monty got a raw deal (live) / Everybody hurts (live) / Man on the Moon (live).

Oct 94. (cd)(c)(lp) **MONSTER** 1 1
– What's the frequency, Kenneth? / Crush with eyeliner / King of comedy / I don't sleep I dream / Star 69 / Strange currencies / Tongue / Bang and blame / I took your name / Let me in / Circus envy / You.

Nov 94. (c-s) **BANG AND FLAME. / ('A'instrumental)** 15 19
(cd-s) – ('A'side) / Losing my religion (live) / Country feedback (live) / Begin the begin (live).

Jan 95. (7")(c-s) **CRUSH WITH EYELINER. / ('A'instrumental)** 23
(cd-s) – ('A'side) / Calendar bag / Fall on me (live) / Me in honey (live) / Finest worksong (live).

— On 1st March, 1995, BILL BERRY suffered a brain haemorrhage, after collapsing during a concert in Switzerland. Thankfully, he steadily recovered during the following few months.

Apr 95. (7")(c-s) **STRANGE CURRENCIES. / ('A'instrumental)** 9 47
(cd-s) – ('A'side) / Drive (live) / Funtime (live) / Radio free Europe (live).

Jul 95. (c-s) **TONGUE / ('A'instrumental)** 13
(cd-s) – ('A'side) / Bang and flame (live) / What's the frequency, Kenneth? (live) / I don't sleep, I dream (live).

– compilations, others, etc. –

May 87. IRS; (lp)(c)(cd) **DEAD LETTER OFFICE** ('B' sides, rarities, etc.) 60 52
– Crazy / There she goes again / Burning down / Voice of Harold / Burning Hell / White tornado / Toys in the attic / Windout / Ages of you / Pale blue eyes / Rotary ten / Bandwagon / Femme fatale / Walters theme / King of the road. *(re-iss.cd+c Oct94 on 'A&M')* (cd+=) – CHRONIC TOWN (tracks).

Oct 88. IRS; (lp)(c)(cd) **EPONYMOUS** 69

Oct 88. IRS; (7") **THE ONE I LOVE. / FALL ON ME** -
(12"+=)(cd-s+=) – So. central rain (I'm sorry).

Sep 91. IRS-MCA; (cd)(c)(lp) **THE BEST OF R.E.M.** 7
– Carnival of sorts / Radio free Europe / Perfect circle / Talk about the passion / So. central rain / (Don't go back to) Rockville / Pretty persuasion / Green grow the rushes / Can't get there from here / Driver 8 / Fall on me / I believe / Cuyahoga / The one I love / Finest worksong / It's the end of the world as we know it (and I feel fine).

Sep 91. IRS-MCA; (cd-s) **THE ONE I LOVE. / MAPS AND LEGENDS** 16
(cd-ep+=) – Driver 8 / Disturbance at the Heron House.

Dec 91. IRS-MCA; (7")(c-s) **IT'S THE END OF THE WORLD (AS WE KNOW IT). / RADIO FREE EUROPE** 39
(cd-s+=) – Time after time / Red rain / So.central rain (all live).

May 90. A&M; (c) **MURMUR / RECKONING**

— When MICHAEL STIPE went off guesting for others incl.GOLDEN PALOMINOS; others splintered off into . . .

HINDU LOVE GODS

not issued I.R.S.

Sep 85. (7") **NARRATOR. / GONNA HAVE A GOOD TIME TONIGHT** -

with **WARREN ZEVON** – vocals They guested on his late '89 album; SENTIMENTAL HYGIENE.

Reprise Giant

Nov 90. (7") **RASPBERRY BERET. / WANG DANG DOODLE**
(12"+=)(cd-s+=) – Mannish boy.

Nov 90. (cd)(c)(lp) **HINDU LOVE GODS**
– Walkin' blues / Travelin' riverside blues / Raspberry beret / Crosscut saw / Junco pardner / Mannish boy / Wang dang doodle / Battleship chains / I'm a one woman man / Vigilante man.
(all above HINDU songs were covers)

REO SPEEDWAGON

Formed: Champaign, Illinois, USA ... 1968 by DOUGHTY and GRATZER, who soon brought in RICHRATH, LUTTRELL and PHILBIN.

With help from manager Irving Azoff, they signed to 'Epic' records in 1971, and released eponymous debut. They built up national following, but only managed minor US chart placing until the late 70's, when their 9th album 'NINE LIVES', hit the Top 40. Eighteen months later they had dual US No.1's with single 'KEEP ON LOVING YOU' & lp 'HI INFIDELITY'. Continued to be major stars throughout the 80's. • **Style:** Faceless soft-rock ballad group (harder on stage), similar to JOURNEY, STYX, BOB SEGER or KANSAS. • **Songwriters:** RICHRATH until 1976 when CRONIN returned to co-write most. • **Trivia:** Took their name from a 1911 fire truck.

Recommended: A SECOND DECADE OF ROCK'N'ROLL 1981-1991 (*6) / A DECADE OF ROCK'N'ROLL 1970 TO 1980 (*6).

GARY RICHRATH (b.18 Oct'49, Peoria, Illinois) – lead guitar / **NEAL DOUGHTY** (b.29 Jul'46, Evanston, Illinois) – keyboards, organ / **ALAN GRATZER** (b. 9 Nov'48, Syracuse, New York) – drums / **TERRY LUTTRELL** – vocals / **GREGG PHILBIN** – bass

Epic Epic

Jan 72. (7") **PRISON WOMAN. / SOPHISTICATED LADY** [-] [ ]

Mar 72. (lp) **REO SPEEDWAGON** [ ] [ ] Dec 71
– Gypsy woman's passion / 157 Riverside Avenue / Anti-establishment man / Lay me down / Sophisticated lady / Five men were killed today / Prison women / Dead at last. *(re-iss.+c.Nov81) (re-iss.cd+c Jun93 on 'Sony Collectors')*

Apr 72. (7") **GYPSY WOMAN'S PASSION. / LAY ME DOWN** [-] [ ]

Jun 72. (7") **157 RIVERSIDE AVENUE. / FIVE MEN WERE KILLED TODAY** [ ] [ ]

— **KEVIN CRONIN** (b. 6 Oct'51, Evanston) – vocals, guitar repl. LUTTRELL

Apr 73. (lp) **R.E.O.T.W.O.** [ ] [ ] Dec 72
– Let me ride / How the story goes / Little Queenie / Being kind / Music man / Like you do / Flash tan queen / Golden country.

Apr 73. (7") **GOLDEN COUNTRY. / LITTLE QUEENIE** [-] [ ]

— **MIKE MURPHY** – vocals repl. CRONIN who became unrecorded solo artist.

Feb 74. (7") **RIDIN' THE NIGHT STORM. / WHISKEY NIGHT** [-] [ ]

Jun 74. (lp) **RIDIN' THE STORM OUT** [ ] [ ] Jan 74
– Ridin' the storm out / Whiskey night / Oh woman / Find my fortune / Open up / Movin' / Son of a poor man / Start a new life / It's everywhere / Without expression.

Jun 74. (7") **OPEN UP. / START A NEW LIFE** [-] [ ]

Apr 75. (lp) **LOST IN A DREAM** [ ] [98] Nov 74
– Give me a ride / Throw the chains away / Sky blues / You can fly / Lost in a dream / Down by the dam / Do your best / Wild as the western wind / They're on the road / I'm feeling good.

Apr 75. (7") **THROW THE CHAINS AWAY. / SKY BLUES** [-] [ ]

— **KEVIN CRONIN** returned to repl. MURPHY

Aug 75. (7") **OUT OF CONTROL. / RUNNING BLIND** [-] [ ]

Nov 75. (lp) **THIS TIME WE MEAN IT** [ ] [74] Jul 75
– Reelin' / Headed for a fall / River of life / Out of control / You better realise / Gambler / Candalera / Lies / Dance / Dream weaver.

Nov 75. (7") **HEADED FOR A FALL. / REELIN'** [-] [ ]

Jun 76. (7") **KEEP PUSHIN' / TONIGHT** [-] [ ]

Jul 76. (lp) **R.E.O.** [ ] [ ] Jun 76
– Keep pushin' / Any kind of love / Summer love / Our time is gonna come / Breakaway / Flying turkey trot / Tonight / Lightning.

Nov 76. (7") **FLYING TURKEY TROT. / KEEP PUSHIN'** [-] [ ]

May 77. (7") **RIDIN' THE STORM OUT (live). / BEING KIND (live)** [-] [94]

Aug 77. (d-lp) **REO SPEEDWAGON LIVE / YOU GET WHAT YOU PLAY FOR (live)** [ ] [72] Mar 77
– Like you do / Lay me down / Any kind of love / Being kind (can hurt someone sometimes) / Keep pushin' / (Only) A summer love / Son of a poor man / (I believe) Our time is gonna come / Flying turkey trot / Gary's guitar solo / 157 Riverside Avenue / Ridin' the storm out / Music man / Little Queenie / Golden country. *(re-iss.Aug87)*

Aug 77. (7") **FLYING TURKEY TROT (live). / KEEP PUSHIN' (live)** [-] [ ]

— **BRUCE HALL** (b. 3 May'53) – bass repl. PHILBIN

Jul 78. (lp)(c) **YOU CAN TUNE A PIANO, BUT YOU CAN'T TUNA FISH** [ ] [29] Apr 78
– Roll with the changes / Time for me to fly / Runnin' blind / Blazin' your own trail again / Sing to me / Lucky for you / Do you know where your woman is tonight / The unidentified flying tuna trot / Say you love me or say goodnight. *(re-iss.Sep82)*

Jun 78. (7") **ROLL WITH THE CHANGES. / THE UNIDENTIFIED FLYING TUNA TROT** [ ] [58] May 78

Jul 78. (7") **TIME FOR ME TO FLY. / RUNNIN' BLIND** [-] [56]

Jul 79. (7") **EASY MONEY. / I NEED YOU TONIGHT** [-] [ ]

Aug 79. (lp)(c) **NINE LIVES** [ ] [33]
– Heavy on your love / Drop it (an old disguise) / Only the strong survive / Easy money / Rock'n 'roll music / Take me / I need you tonight / Meet me on the mountain / Back on the road again.

Oct 79. (7") **ONLY THE STRONG SURVIVE / DROP IT (AN OLD DISGUISE)** [-] [ ]

Aug 80. (7") **ONLY THE STRONG SURVIVE. / MEET ME ON THE MOUNTAIN** [ ] [-]

Nov 80. (7") **KEEP ON LOVING YOU. / TIME FOR ME TO FLY** [-] [1]

Feb 81. (7") **KEEP ON LOVING YOU. / FOLLOW MY HEART** [7] [-]

Apr 81. (lp)(c) **HI INFIDELITY** [6] [1] Dec 80
– Don't let him go / Keep on loving you / Follow my heart / In your letter / Take it on the run / Tough guys / Out of season / Shakin' it loose / Someone tonight / I wish you were there. *(re-iss.Nov84)*

Jun 81. (7") **TAKE IT ON THE RUN. / SOMEONE TONIGHT** [19] [5] Mar 81

Jun 81. (7") **DON'T LET HIM GO. / I WISH YOU WERE THERE** [-] [24]

Sep 81. (7") **IN YOUR LETTER. / SHAKIN' IT LOOSE** [ ] [20] Aug 81

Jul 82. (7") **KEEP THE FIRE BURNIN'. / I'LL FOLLOW YOU** [ ] [7] Jun 82

Jul 82. (lp)(c) **GOOD TROUBLE** [29] [7]
– Keep the fire burnin' / Sweet time / Girl with the heart of gold / Every now and then / I'll follow you / The key / Back in my heart again / Let's bebop / Stillness of the night / Good trouble. *(re-iss.1986)*

Sep 82. (7") **SWEET TIME. / STILLNESS OF THE NIGHT** [ ] [26] Aug 82

Oct 82. (7") **THE KEY. / LET'S BEBOP** [ ] [ ]

Nov 84. (7") **I DO WANNA KNOW. / ROCK AND ROLL STAR** [ ] [29] Oct 82

Nov 84. (lp)(c)(cd) **WHEELS ARE TURNIN'** [ ] [7]
– I do wanna know / One lonely night / Thru the window / Rock and roll star / Live every moment / Can't fight this feeling / Gotta feel more / Break his spell / Wheels are turnin'.

Jan 85. (7") **CAN'T FIGHT THIS FEELING. / BREAK HIS SPELL** [-] [1]

Feb 85. (7") **CAN'T FIGHT THIS FEELING. / ROCK AND ROLL STAR** [16] [-]
(12"+=) – Keep on loving you.

May 85. (7") **ONE LONELY NIGHT. / WHEELS ARE TURNIN'** [ ] [19] Mar 85
(12"+=) – Take it on the run.

Jul 85. (7") **LIVE EVERY MOMENT. / GOTTA FEEL MORE** [ ] [34]

Nov 85. (7") **WHEREVER YOU'RE GOING. / SHAKIN' IT LOOSE** [ ] [ ]

Mar 87. (7") **THAT AIN'T LOVE. / ACCIDENTS CAN HAPPEN** [ ] [16] Jan 87

Apr 87. (lp)(c)(cd) **LIFE AS WE KNOW IT** [ ] [28] Feb 87
– New way to love / That ain't love / In my dreams / One too many girlfriends / Variety tonight / Screams and whispers / Can't get you out of my heart / Over the edge / Accidents can happen / Tired of getting nowhere.

May 87. (7") **VARIETY TONIGHT. / TIRED OF GETTING NOWHERE** [-] [60]

Oct 87. (7") **IN MY DREAMS. / OVER THE EDGE** [ ] [19] Jul 87

— **GRAHAM LEAR** – drums (ex-SANTANA) repl. GRATZER

Sep 88. (7") **HERE WITH ME. / WHEREVER YOU'RE GOIN' (IT'S ALRIGHT)** [ ] [20] Jun 88
(12"+=)(cd-s+=) – Keep on loving you / Take it on the run.

Nov 88. (7") **I DON'T WANT TO LOSE YOU. / ON THE ROAD AGAIN** [-] [ ]

— (Apr89) **MILES JOSEPH** – guitar (ex-PLAYER) repl. RICHRATH

— (1990) **CRONIN, DOUGHTY & HALL** brought in new members **DAVE AMATO** – lead guitar, vocals (ex-TED NUGENT) repl. MILES JOSEPH / **BRYAN HITT** – drums (ex-WANG CHUNG) repl. LEAR / added **JESSE HARMS** – keyboards, vocals (ex-JOHN HIATT, ex-RY COODER)

Aug 90. (7") **LIVE IT UP. / ALL HEAVEN BROKE LOOSE** [-] [ ]

Sep 90. (cd)(c)(lp) **THE EARTH, A SMALL MAN, HIS DOG AND A CHICKEN** [ ] [ ] Aug 90
– Love is a rock / The heart survives / Live it up / All Heaven broke loose / Love in the future / Half way / Love to hate / You won't see me / Can't lie to my heart / L.I.A.R. / Go for broke.

Oct 90. (7") **LOVE IS A ROCK. / GO FOR BROKE** [ ] [65]
(12"+=)(cd-s+=) – ?

Jan 91. (7") **L.I.A.R. / HALF WAY** [-] [ ]

– compilations, others, etc. –

Below releases on 'Epic' unless mentioned.

May 80. (7") **TIME FOR ME TO FLY. / LIGHTNING** [-] [77]

Jul 80. (d-lp)(d-c) **A DECADE OF ROCK'N'ROLL 1970 TO 1980** [ ] [55] Apr 80
– Sophisticated lady / Music man / Golden country / Son of a poor man / Lost in a dream / Reelin' / Keep pushin' / Our time is gonna come / Breakaway / Lightning / Like you do / Flying turkey trot / 157 Riverside Avenue / Ridin' the storm out / Roll with the changes / Time for me to fly / Say you love me or say goodnight / Only the strong survive / Back on the road again. *(re-iss.Jul82)*

Nov 85. (lp)(c) **BEST FOOT FORWARD – THE BEST OF REO SPEEDWAGON** [ ] [-]
(re-iss.+cd.Jan92)

Jun 88. (lp)(c)(cd) **THE HITS** [ ] [56]

Aug 88. (3"cd-s) **KEEP ON LOVIN' YOU. / TIME FOR ME TO FLY** [-] [ ]

Oct 91. (cd)(c)(lp) **A SECOND DECADE OF ROCK'N'ROLL 1981-1991** [ ] [ ]
– Don't let him go / Tough guys / Take it on the run / Shakin' it loose / Keep the fire burnin' / Roll with the changes / I do wanna know / Can't fight this feeling / Live every moment / That ain't love / One too many girlfriends / Variety tonight / Back on the road again / Keep on loving you '89 / Love is a rock / All Heavens broke loose / L.I.A.R. / Live it up.

Oct 94. (cd) **THE BEST** [ ] [ ]

Aug 84. Scoop; (7"ep)(c-ep) **6 TRACK HITS** [ ] [-]
– Only the strong survive / Meet me on the mountain / Shakin' it loose / In your letter / I need you tonight / Roll with the changes.
Feb 86. Old Gold; (7"ep) **KEEP ON LOVIN' YOU. / (2 other tracks by 'Journey' & 'Meat Loaf')** [ ] [-]

REPLACEMENTS

Formed: Minneapolis, Minnesota, USA . . . 1980 originally as The IMPEDIMENTS by the STINSON brothers plus WESTERBERG and MARS. After 3 well-received albums for US label 'Twin Tone', they moved to US based indie label 'Zippo', who found an outley in 'Demon' for 1984 lp 'LET IT BE'. In 1985, they transferred to major 'Sire' records, and made headway with album 'TIM'. • **Style:** Raw HUSKER DU type R&B/punk rock, whose courseness mellowed somewhat by tne mid 80's, when stage eccentric BOB departed (he often played guitar in the nude or in a dress). • **Songwriters:** Penned by WESTERBERG, except; I WILL DARE (Kiss) / ROUTE 66 (Nelson Riddle Orchestra) / 20TH CENTURY BOY (T-Rex) / HEY GOOD LOOKING (Bo Diddley) / CRUELLA DE VILLE (from '1001 Dalmations'). • **Trivia:** Were quoted after a tour as saying 'Better hours, 9 to 5; 9 at night to 5 in the morning, that is'. Their '87 single 'ALEX CHILTON', was dedicated to legendary BOX TOPS leader.

Recommended: BOINK!! (*8) / LET IT BE (*8) / TIM (*7).

PAUL WESTERBERG (b.31 Dec'60) – vocals, rhythm guitar / **BOB STINSON** (b.17 Dec'59) – lead guitar / **TOMMY STINSON** (b. 6 Oct'66, San Diego, California) – bass / **CHRIS MARS** (b.26 Apr'61) – drums

not issued / Twin Tone

1981. (lp) **SORRY MA, FORGOT TO TAKE OUT THE TRASH** [-] [ ]
– Takin' a ride / Careless / Customer / Hanging downtown / Kick your door down / Otto / I bought a headache / Rattlesnake / I hate music / Johnny's gonna die / Shiftless when idle / More cigarettes / Don't ask why / Something to do / I'm in trouble / Love you till Friday / Shut up / Raised in the city. *(UK-iss.Mar88 on 'What Goes On') (cd-iss.Apr93 on 'Roadrunner') (cd-iss.Mar95)*
1981. (7") **I'M IN TROUBLE. / IF ONLY YOU WERE LONELY** [-] [ ]
1982. (lp) **STINK** [-] [ ]
– Kids don't follow / Fuck school / Stuck in the middle / God damn job / White and lazy / Dope smokin' moron / Go / Gimme noise. *(UK-iss.Mar88 on 'What Goes On') (cd-iss.Apr93 on 'Roadrunner') (cd-iss.Mar95)*
1983. (lp) **HOOTENANNY** [-] [ ]
– Hootenanny / Run it / Color me impressed / Will power / Take me down to the hospital / Mr. Whirly / Within your reach / Buck hill / Lovelines / You lose / Hayday / Treatment bound. *(UK-iss.Mar88 on 'What Goes On') (cd-iss.Mar95)*
1984. (12") **I WILL DARE. / 20TH CENTURY BOY / HEY GOOD LOOKING (live)** [-] [ ]

Zippo / Twin Tone

Oct 84. (lp) **LET IT BE** [ ] [ ]
– I will dare / We're comin' out / Tommy gets his tonsels out / Black diamond / Androgynous / Unsatisfied / Seen your video / Gary's got a boner / Sixteen blue / Answering machine. *(cd-iss.Apr93 on 'Roadrunner') (cd-iss.Mar95)*

Sire / Sire

Nov 85. (lp)(c) **TIM** [ ] [ ]
– Hold my life / I'll buy / Kiss me on the bus / Dose of thunder / Waitress in the sky / Swingin' party / Bastards of young / Lay it down clown / Left of the dial / Litle mascara / Here comes a regular. *(cd-iss.Jul93)*
Mar 86. (7") **SWINGIN' PARTY. / LEFT OF THE DIAL** [ ] [ ]
May 86. (7") **KISS ME ON THE BUS. / LITTLE MASCARA** [ ] [ ]

—— **SLIM DUNLAP** – keyboards repl. BOB (he was to die 18th February 1995 of a drug overdose)

Apr 87. (lp)(c)(cd) **PLEASED TO MEET ME** [ ] [ ]
– I.O.U. / Alex Chilton / I don't know / Nightclub jitters / The ledge / Never mind / Valentine / Shooting dirty pool / Red red wine / Skyway / Can't hardly wait. *(re-iss.cd Jul93)*
Jun 87. (7") **ALEX CHILTON. / ELECTION DAY** [ ] [ ]
(12"+=) – Nightclub jitters / Route 66.
Jul 87. (7") **CAN'T HARDLY WAIT. / COOL WATER** [-] [ ]

—— **BOB STINSON** – guitar returned to repl. SLIM who went solo.

Jan 89. (lp)(c)(cd) **DON'T TELL A SOUL** [ ] [57]
– Talent show / Back to back / We'll inherit the Earth / Achin' to be / They're blind / Anywhere's better than here / Asking me lies / I won't / Rock'n'roll ghost / Darlin' one. *(re-iss.cd Jul93)*
Apr 89. (7") **I'LL BE YOU. / DATE TO CHURCH (with TOM WAITS)** [-] [51]

—— (Below w/guests **STEVE BERLIN / MICHAEL BLAIR / BELMONT TENCH / JOHN CALE /** etc.

Sep 90. (cd)(c)(lp) **ALL SHOOK DOWN** [ ] [69]
– Merry go round / One wink at a time / Nobody / Bent out of shape / Sadly beautiful / Someone takes the wheel / When it began / All shook down / Attitude / Happy town / Torture / My little problem / The lost. *(re-iss.cd Jul93 & Feb95)*

—— (Mar91) **STEVE FOLEY** – drums repl. MARS who went solo.

—— Disbanded 1992, TOMMY formed BASH & POP, who released album 'FRIDAY NIGHT IS KILLING ME'.

– compilations, others, etc. –

Apr 86. Glass; (m-lp)(c) **BOINK!!** [ ] [-]
-Color me impressed / White and lazy / Within your reach / If only you were lonely / Kids don't follow / Nowhere is my home / Take me down to the hospital / Go.

PAUL WESTERBERG

Sire / Warners

Jun 93. (cd)(c) **14 SONGS** [ ] [44]
– Knockin' on mine / First glimmer / World class fad / Runaway wind / Dice behind your shades / Even here we are / Silver naked ladies / A few minutes of silence / Someone I once knew / Black eyed Susan / things / Something is me / Mannequin shop / Down love.
Jul 93. (7")(c-s) **WORLD CLASS FAD. / SEEING HER** [ ] [ ]
(12")(cd-s) – ('A'side) / Men without ties / Down love.
Oct 93. (7")(c-s) **WORLD CLASS FAD. / CAN'T HARDLY WAIT (live)** [ ] [ ]
(cd-s+=) – Left of the dial / Another girl another planet (both live).
(cd-s) – ('A'side) / Waiting for somebody / Dyslexic heart / Answering machine (live).

. . . Jan – Jun '96 stop press . . .

Apr 96. (cd)(c) **EVENTUALLY** [ ] [50]

REVENGE (see under ⇒ NEW ORDER)

REVOLTING COCKS (see under ⇒ MINISTRY)

RHYTHM DEVILS (see under ⇒ GRATEFUL DEAD)

Keith RICHARDS (see under ⇒ ROLLING STONES)

Jonathan RICHMAN

Born: 16 May'51, Boston, Massachusetts, USA. After a period in the late 60's being a contributor for local music papers 'Vibrations' & 'Fusion', he formed first real MODERN LOVERS in 1971. With the help of producer KIM FOWLEY, they recorded successful demo for 'Warners' in 1972. The following year, the label shelved their JOHN CALE produced lp and soon dropped group. They split late in '74, but re-formed again 6 months later to record debut 7" 'ROADRUNNER' for 'United Art'. They then moved to West Coast label 'Beserkley', who bought the Warners tapes, and released the songs as an eponymous album in 1976. RICHMAN then recruited his new MODERN LOVERS, who finaly re-issued 'ROADRUNNER', which zoomed up to a near UK Top 10 placing in 1977. They followed this, with an unusual instrumental 'EGYPTIAN REGGAE', which dented the Top 5. • **Style:** New wave eccentric, who was likened to a minimalist LOU REED, but with a sense of tongue-in-cheek humour. • **Songwriters:** RICHMAN compositions. • **Trivia:** JOHN CALE (ex-Velvet Underground), went on to record his brilliant 'PABLO PICASSO'.

Recommended: 23 GREAT RECORDINGS (*8)

The MODERN LOVERS

were formed by **RICHMAN** – vocals, guitar / with **JERRY HARRISON** – keyboards, vocals / **ERNIE BROOKS** – bass, vocals / **DAVID ROBINSON** – drums (left Nov73 to DMZ, after recording debut)

United Art / United Art

Jun 75. (7") **ROADRUNNER (once). / IT WILL STAND** [ ] [ ]

Beserkley / Beserkley

Jul 76. (lp) **THE MODERN LOVERS** (1972 demos) [ ] [ ] 1975
– Roadrunner / Astral plane / Old world / Pablo Picasso / I'm straight / She cracked / Hospital / Someone I care about / Girlfriend / Modern world. *(re-iss.Nov87) (cd-iss.Nov89 on 'Rhino') (cd-iss.Dec92 on 'Rev-ola', 3 extra tracks)*

—— HARRISON (also to TALKING HEADS) and BROOKS joined ELLIOTT MURPHY.

JONATHAN RICHMAN & THE MODERN LOVERS

with also **LEROY RADCLIFFE** – guitar, vox / **GREG KERANEN** – bass, vox / **DAVID**

ROBINSON – drums

Oct 76. (lp) **JONATHAN RICHMAN & THE MODERN LOVERS** [-] [ ]
– Rockin' shopping center / Back in the U.S.A. / Important in your life / New England / Lonely financial zone / Hi dear / Abominable snowman in the market / Hey there little insect / Here comes the Martian Martians / Springtime / Amazing Grace. *(UK-iss.Oct77) (re-iss.Nov86, cd-iss.Mar89)*

Feb 77. (7") **NEW ENGLAND. / HERE COME THE MARTIAN MARTIANS** [-] [ ]

Jun 77. (7") **ROADRUNNER (once). / ROADRUNNER (twice)** [11] [-]
(re-iss.Jul82 on 'Old Gold')

Aug 77. (lp)(c) **ROCK'N'ROLL WITH THE MODERN LOVERS** [50] [ ]
– The sweeping wind (kwa ti feng) / Ice cream man / Rockin' rockin' leprechauns / Summer morning / Afternoon / Fly into the mystery / South American folk song / Roller coaster by the sea / Dodge veg-o-matic / Egyptian reggae / Coomyah / The wheels on the bus / Angels watching over you. *(re-iss.Nov87) (cd-iss.Mar93 on 'Rev-ola')*

Sep 77. (7") **EGYPTIAN REGGAE. / ROLLER COASTER BY THE SEA** [5] [ ]

The MODERN LOVERS

D.SHARPE – drums repl. ROBINSON / **ASA BREMNER** – bass repl. KERANEN

Jan 78. (7") **MORNING OF OUR LIVES (live). / ROADRUNNER (thrice)** [28] [ ]

Apr 78. (7") **NEW ENGLAND. / ASTRAL PLANE** [ ] [ ]

Jul 78. (7") **ABDUL & CLEOPATRA. ("JONATHAN RICHMAN & THE MODERN LOVERS") / OH CAROL** [ ] [ ]

Dec 78. (lp)(c) **THE MODERN LOVERS LIVE (live)** [ ] [ ]
– I'm a little airplane / Hey there little insect / Egyptian reggae / Ice cream man / I'm a little dinosaur / My little kookenhaken / South American folk song / New England / Morning of our lives. *(re-iss.Nov86)*

JONATHAN RICHMAN

is credited solo, but still uses same backers.

Dec 78. (7") **BUZZ BUZZ BUZZ. / HOSPITAL** [ ] [ ]

Feb 79. (lp)(c) **BACK IN YOUR LIFE** [ ] [ ]
– Abdul and Cleopatra / (She's gonna) Respect me / Lover please / Affection / Buz buzz buzz / Back in your life / Party in the woods tonight / My love is a flower (just beginning to bloom) / I'm nature's mosquito / Emaline / Lydia / I hear you calling me. *(US re-iss.Nov86)*

Mar 79. (7") **LYDIA. / IMPORTANT IN YOUR LIFE** [ ] [ ]

Jan 80. (lp)(c) **JONATHAN RICHMAN SONGBOOK – THE BEST OF . . .** – (compilation) [ ] [ ]

— JONATHAN retired in the late 70's, until 1982. Joining him were **KEN FORFIA** – keyboards / **BETH HARRINGTON** – guitar / **GREG KERANEN** – bass, vocals / **MICHAEL GUARDABASCIO** – drums, vocals / **ELLIE MARSHALL** – backing vocals

Rough Trade / Sire

Aug 84. (lp)(c) **JONATHAN SINGS** [ ] [ ]
– That summer feeling / This kind of music / The neighbors / Somebody to hold me / These conga drums / Stop this car / Not yet three / Give Paris one more chance / You're the one for me / When I'm walking.

Jun 85. (7") **THAT SUMMER FEELING. / THIS KIND OF MUSIC** [ ] [ ]
(12"+=) – The tag game.

JONATHAN RICHMAN & THE MODERN LOVERS

re-formed with **JONATHAN, ELLIE, MICHAEL** and newcomer **ANDY PALEY** – toy piano

Jun 85. (lp)(c) **ROCKIN' AND ROMANCE** [ ] [ ]
– The beach / My jeans / Bermuda / The U.F.O. man / Down in Bermuda / V. Van Gogh / Walter Johnson / I'm just beginning to live / The fenway / Chewing gum wrapper / The Baltimores / Up in the sky sometime / Now is better than before.

Aug 85. (7") **I'M JUST BEGINNING TO LIVE. / CIRCLE 1** [ ] [ ]
(12"+=) – Shirlin & Fahrad.

Feb 86. (lp)(c) **IT'S TIME FOR JONATHAN RICHMAN & THE MODERN LOVERS** [ ] [ ]
– It's you / Let's take a trip / This love of mine / Neon sign / Double chocolate malted / Just about seventeen / Corner store / The desert / Yo Jo Jo / When I dance / Shirlin & Fahrad / Ancient and long ago.

— **JONATHAN** recruited complete new line-up **BRENDAN TOTTEN** – guitar / **JOHNNY AVILA** – drums

Demon / Rounder

Feb 88. (lp)(cd) **MODERN LOVERS '88** [ ] [ ]
– Dancin' late at night / When Harpo played his harp / Gail loves me / New kind of neighborhood / African lady / I love hot nights / California desert party / Everything's gotta be right / Circle 1 / I have come out to play / The theme from 'Moulin Rouge'!.

JONATHAN RICHMAN

Special D. / Rounder

Aug 89. (lp)(c)(cd) **JONATHAN RICHMAN** [ ] [ ]
– Malagueno de Jojo / Action packed / Everyday clothes / Fender Stratocaster / Blue Moon / Closer / I eat with Gusto / Damn!! you bet / Miracles will start to happen / Sleepwalk / Que reste t'll de nos amours / A mistake today for me / Cerca.

— now with **TOM BRUMLEY** – guitar

Aug 90. (cd)(c)(lp) **JONATHAN GOES COUNTRY** [ ] [ ]
– Since she started to ride / Reno / You're the one for me / Your good girl's gonna go bad / I must be king / You're crazy for takin' the blues / Rodeo wind / Corner store / The neighbours / Men walks among us / I can't stay mad at you / Satisfied mind.

Cheree / Cheree

Nov 91. (cd)(lp) **HAVING A PARTY (live US tour)** [ ] [ ]
– The girl stands up to me now / Cappuccino bar / my career as a homewrecker / She doesn't laugh at my jokes / When she kisses me / They're not tryin' on the dance floor / At night / When I say wife / 1963 / Monologue about bermuda / Our swingin' pad / Just for fun

Rounder / Rounder

May 94. (cd) **¡JONATHAN, TE VAS A EMOCIONAR!** [ ] [ ]
– Pantomima de el amor Brujo / Harpo en su Harpa / No te oye / No mas por fun / Papel de chicle / Los vecinos / Compadrito corazon / Melodia tradicional Ecuadoriana / Shirin y Farad / Reno / Cerca / El U.F.O. man / Ahora es Mejor / Sabor A.Mi / Una Fuerza alla.

May 95. (cd)(c) **YOU MUST ASK THE HEART** [ ] [ ]
– To hide a little thought / The heart of Saturday night / Vampire girl / Just because I'm Irish / That's how I feel / Let her go into darkness / The rose / You must ask the heart / Nothing can change this love / Amorcito corazon / City vs. country / Walter Johnson / Nishi.

– other compilations, etc. –

Oct 81. Bomp; (lp) **THE ORIGINAL MODERN LOVERS** [-] [ ]
(UK-iss.Jun87 on 'Link')

Jul 82. Old Gold; (7") **EGYPTIAN REGGAE. / MORNING OF OUR LIVES (live)** [ ] [-]

1988. Rounder; (cd) **JONATHAN RICHMAN & BARRENCE WHITFIELD** [-] [ ]

Sep 90. Castle; (cd) **23 GREAT RECORDINGS** [ ] [-]
– Roadrunner / Dignified & old / Pablo Picasso / I'm straight / Astral plane / Girl friend / Government centre / New teller / It will stand / Morning of our lives / Abominable snowman in the market / Important in your life / My little kookenhaken / Dodge veg-o-matic / Lonely financial zone / Roller coaster by the sea / New England / Egyptian reggae / Ice cream man / Buzz buzz buzz / Abdul & Cleopatra / Roadrunner (twice).

Apr 94. Castle; (cd) **THE COLLECTION** [ ] [-]

Apr 95. Rounder; (cd) **PRECISE MODERN LOVERS ORDER** [ ] [-]

Jun 95. Nectar; (cd) **A PLEA FOR TENDERNESS** [ ] [-]

RIDE

Formed: Oxford, England . . . 1989 by Oxford University students (see below). Immediately signed to 'Creation' records, and stirred up enough support through tour to generate eponymous 1990 debut EP into the UK Top 75. It was quickly followed by 2 more Top 40 EP's, and a near UK Top 10 album 'NOWHERE'. • **Style:** Solemn and dreamy psychedelic rock band, taking influences from The BYRDS, STOOGES and The JESUS & MARY CHAIN. • **Songwriters:** Lyrics MARK or ANDY / group compositions except EIGHT MILES HIGH (Byrds) / THE MODEL (Kraftwerk) / HOW DOES IT FEEL TO FEEL (Creation) / THAT MAN (Small Faces). • **Trivia:** In 1991, they headlined the Slough Music Festival in front of over 8,000 fans.

Recommended: NOWHERE (*8) / GOING BLANK AGAIN (*8) / TARANTULA (*6).

MARK GARDENER – vocals, guitar / **ANDY BELL** – guitar, vocals / **STEPHAN QUERALT** – bass / **LAURENCE COLBERT** – drums

Creation / Creation

Jan 90. (12"ep)(cd-ep) **RIDE** [71] [-]
– Chelsea girl / Drive blind / Close my eyes / All I can see. *(re-iss.Oct90)*

Apr 90. (12"ep)(cd-ep) **PLAY** [32] [ ]
– Like a daydream / Silver / Furthest sense / Perfect time.

Oct 90. (7"ep) **FALL** [34] [ ]
– Dreams burn down / Taste / Here and now / Nowhere.

Jul 90. (cd)(c) **SMILE** (above tracks) [-] [ ]

Oct 90. (cd)(c)(lp) **NOWHERE** [11] [ ]
– Seagull / Kaleidoscope / Polar bear / Dreams burn down / In a different place / Decay / Paralysed / Vapour trail.
(cd+=) Taste / Here and now / Nowhere

Mar 91. (12"ep)(c-ep)(cd-ep) **TODAY FOREVER** [14] [ ]
– Unfamiliar / Sennen / Beneath / Today.

Feb 92. (12"ep)(c-ep)(cd-ep) **LEAVE THEM ALL BEHIND. / CHROME WAVES / GRASSHOPPER** [9] [ ]

Mar 92. (cd)(c)(2x12"lp) **GOING BLANK AGAIN** [5] [ ]
– Leave them all behind / Twisterella / Not fazed / Chrome waves / Mouse trap /

Time of her life / Cool your boots / Making Jusy smile / Time machine / OX4.
Apr 92. (12"ep)(c-ep)(cd-ep) **TWISTERELLA / GOING BLANK AGAIN. / HOWARD HUGHES / STAMPEDE** 36
Apr 94. (12"ep)(12"clear-ep)(cd-ep) **BIRDMAN / ROLLING THUNDER £2. / LET'S GET LOST / DON'T LET IT DIE** 38
Jun 94. (7")(c-s) **HOW DOES IT FEEL TO FEEL?. / CHELSEA GIRL** 58
(12")(cd-s) – ('A'side) / Walkabout / At the end of the universe.
Jun 94. (pic-cd)(c)(d-lp) **CARNIVAL OF LIGHT** 5
– Moonlight medicine / 1000 miles / From time to time / Natural grace / Only now / Birdman / Crown of creation / How does it feel to feel? / Endless road / Magical spring / Rolling thunder / I don't know where it comes from.
Sep 94. (c-s) **I DON'T KNOW WHERE IT COMES FROM. / TWISTERELLA** 46
(12")(cd-s) – ('A'side) / Drive blind / From time to time / How does it feel to feel (live w / The CREATION).
(cd-s) – ('A'-Apollo 11 mix) / Moonlight medicine (ride on the wire mix by Portishead) / A journey to the end of the universe (version).

. . . Jan – Jun '96 stop press . . .

— split early '96. MARK citing ANDY's near take over of vocal duties.
Feb 96. (single) **BLACK NITE CRASH** 67
Mar 96. (cd)(c)(lp) **TARANTULA** (available for only 1 week) 21

RIFF RAFF (see under ⇒ BRAGG ,Billy)

RIGOR MORTIS (see under ⇒ WHO)

Robbie ROBERTSON

Born: JAMIE ROBERTSON, 4 July 1944, Toronto, Canada. Was an integral part of the BAND ⇒ in the late 60s and 70s before going into acting work. He starred and wrote the score for 'CARNY' in 1980. He produced NEIL DIAMOND's album 'Beautiful Noise' in 1976. His first solo outing finally arrived in 1987 when 'Geffen' released his eponymous debut. Lifted from it was the deep 'SOMEWHERE DOWN THE CRAZY RIVER'. • **Songwriters:** Self-penned. • **Trivia:** Other film parts; 'The Coal Miner's Daughter' (1980) + 'The Right Stuff' (1983).

Recommended: ROBBIE ROBERTSON (*7)

ROBBIE ROBERTSON – vocals, guitar, keyboards / with **BILL DILLON** – guitar / **TONY LEVIN** – bass / **MANU KATCHE** – drums, percussion / **DANIAL LANOIS** – percussion, guitar, bass, co-producer / **PETER GABRIEL** – vocals / **U2 / GARTH HUDSON + RICK DANKO**, etc

Geffen Geffen

Oct 87. (7") **SHOWDOWN AT THE BIG SKY. / HELL'S HALF ACRE** -
Oct 87. (lp)(c)(cd) **ROBBIE ROBERTSON** 47 38
– Fallen angel / Showdown at the big sky / Broken arow / Sweet fire of love / American roulette / Somewhere down the crazy river / Hell's half acre / Sonny get caught in the moonlight / Testimony. *(re-iss.Jan91) (re-iss.cd Oct95)*
Oct 87. (7") **FALLEN ANGEL. / HELL'S HALF ACRE**
(12"+=) – Tailgate. *(re-iss.Sep88)*
Jun 88. (7") **SOMEWHERE DOWN THE CRAZY RIVER. / BROKEN ARROW** 15
(12"+=) – Tailgate.
Sep 91. (cd)(c)(lp) **STORYVILLE** 30 69
– Night parade / Hold back the dawn / Go back to your woods / Soap box preacher / Day of reckoning (burnin' for you) / What about now / Shake this town / Break in the rules / Resurrection / Sign of the rainbow. *(re-iss.cd Oct95)*

— now with **The RED ROAD ENSEMBLE**

Capitol Capitol

Oct 94. (cd)(c) **THE NATIVE AMERICANS**
– Coyote dance / Mahk tchi (heart of the people) / Ghost dance / The vanishing breed / It's a good day to die / Golden feather / Akua Tutu / Words of fire, deeds of blood / Cherokee morning song / Skinwalker / Ancestor song / Twisted hair.

ROCKET FROM THE CRYPT

*** NEW ENTRY ***

Formed: San Diego, California, USA . . .1990 by NICK EVANS and SPEEDO (JOHN REIS). Debut'd in 1991, with well-received 'PAINT AS A FRAGRANCE'. Winner of the NME Brats new band award in 1995. • **Style:** Retro rockers of speedball rock'n'roll fused with punk (DEAD BOYS or The SAINTS). Highlight is Vegas ELVIS lookalike SPEEDO. He was a member of hardcore band PITCHFORK and recently married ND's sister. • **Songwriters:** Group. • **Trivia:** In 1995, supported JAMES BROWN or SUN RA.

Recommended: SCREAM, DRACULA, SCREAM! (*8)

SPEEDO – vocals, guitar / **ND** – guitar / **PETEY X** – bass / **ATOM** – drums / **APOLLO 9** – saxophone / **JC 2000** – trumpet

Headhunter Headhunter

Mar 91. (cd)(lp) **PAINT AS A FRAGRANCE**
(re-iss.Mar93)

PlasticHead PlasticHead

Jan 93. (c-s)(cd-s) **BAD NINJA. /**
(re-iss.Apr 95 on 'Helter Skelter')
Jan 93. (cd)(lp) **CIRCA: NOW**
?????. (ep) **THE STATE OF THE ART IS ON FIRE**

Bacteria S not issued

May 94. (7") **BLOODY THIRSTY BUTCHERS. /**

Elemental Interscope

Oct 95. (m-lp) **HOT CHARITY**
– Pushed / Guilt free / Poison eye / My arrow's aim / Feathered friends / Cloud over Branson / Lorna Doom / Shucks / Pity yr paws.
Dec 95. (cd)(lp) **SCREAM, DRACULA, SCREAM!** 40
– Middle / Born in '69 / On a rope / Young livers / Drop out / Used / Ball lightning / Fat lip / Suit city / Heater hands / Misbeaten / Come see, come saw / Salt future / Burnt alive.
Jan 96. (7")(cd-s) **BORN IN '69. / CIAO PATSY** 68
Apr 96. (7") **YOUNG LIVERS. / BURNING ARMY MEN** 67
(cd-s+=) – Lumps.

compilations, etc.

1994. Elemental; (cd) **ALL SYSTEMS GO**

Paul RODGERS

Born: 17 Dec '49, Middlesborough, England. After fronting massive selling hard rockers FREE (1968-1973) + BAD COMPANY (1974-1982), he ventured solo. In 1983, he issued his debut album 'CUT LOOSE' for 'Atlantic'. Early in 1985, he teamed up with ex-LED ZEPPELIN members to form supergroup 'The FIRM'. Early in the 90s RODGERS teamed up with KENNY JONES to form the LAW. They released one-off eponymous album in 1991, before they went their separate ways. He returned to solo work in 1993, giving tribute to blues legend Muddy Waters.

Recommended: MUDDY WATERS BLUES (*6)

Atlantic Atlantic

Nov 83. (lp)(c) **CUT LOOSE**
– Fragile / Cut loose / Live in peace / Sweet sensation / Rising sun / Boogie mama / Morning after the night before / Northwinds / Superstar woman / Talking guitar blues.
Nov 83. (7") **CUT LOOSE / TALKING GUITAR BLUES**
Jan 84. (7") **MORNING AFTER THE NIGHT BEFORE. / NORTHWINDS** -

— Early in 1985, he joined The Firm (see under ⇒ LED ZEPPELIN). In the 90's he returned to the studio.

The LAW

RODGERS wrote some material w/ **BRYAN ADAMS / DAVID GILMORE / CHRIS REA.**
Covered: MISS YOU IN A HEARTBEAT (Def Leppard).
RODGERS – vocals / **KENNY JONES** – drums (ex-WHO, ex-SMALL FACES).

Atlantic Atco

Mar 91. (7") **LAYING DOWN THE LAW / TOUGH LOVE**
(12"+=)(cd-s+=) That's when you fall.
Apr 91. (cd)(c)(lp) **THE LAW** 61
– For a little ride / Miss you in a heartbeat / Stone cold / Come save me (Julianne) / Laying down the law / Nature of the beast / Stone / Anything for you / Best of my love / Missing you bad girl.

Paul RODGERS

(solo) with **JASON BONHAM** – drums / **PINO PALLADINO** – bass / **IAN HATTON** – rhythm guitar / plus **JIMMIE WOOD** – harmonica / **RONNIE FOSTER** – organ / **MARK T.WILLIAMS** – bass drum and guest lead guitarists on each of the 15 tracks; **BUDDY GUY / TREVOR RABIN / BRIAN SETZER / JEFF BECK / JEFF BECK / STEVE MILLER / TREVOR RABIN / DAVID GILMOUR / SLASH / GARY MOORE / BRIAN MAY / JEFF BECK / NEAL SCHON / RICHIE SAMBORA / NEAL SCHON**

Victory Victory

Jun 93. (cd)(c) **MUDDY WATERS BLUES: A TRIBUTE TO MUDDY WATERS** 9 91
– Muddy Water blues (acoustic version) / Louisiana blues / I can't be satisfied /

Rollin' stone / Good morning little school girl (part 1) / I'm your hoochie coochie man / She's alright / Standing around crying / The hunter / She moves me / I'm ready / I just want to make love to you / Born under a bad sign / Good morning little school girl (part 2) / Muddy Water blues (electric version). (free-cd 'THE HISTORY'; re-recordings of FREE and BAD COMPANY hits) – All right now / Wishing well / Fire & water / Bad company / Feel like making love / Can't get enough.

Album 'MUDDY WATER BLUES' songs stemming from MUDDY WATERS, RODGERS, SONNY BOY WILLIAMSON, WILLIE DIXON or BOOKER T.JONES.

Feb 94. (cd-ep) **MUDDY WATER BLUES / PURPLE HAZE / STONE FREE / LITTLE WING** 45 ☐

(cd-ep) ('A'side) / The hunter / Stone free / Nature of the beast.

— More covers; PURPLE HAZE + STONE FREE + LITTLE WING (Jimi Hendrix).

ROLLING STONES

Formed: London, England ... mid-1962 by JONES, JAGGER and RICHARDS. In May'63 they were signed by A&R man Dick Rowe for 'Decca', who had just rejected The BEATLES. (Decca slightly re-christened Keith as KEITH RICHARD, although he regained real name by the late 70's). Their debut single 'COME ON' nearly hit UK Top 20, although by the next year, they had first of many No.1's with 'IT'S ALL OVER NOW'. In 1965, they scored their first US No.1 with gem '(I CAN'T GET NO) SATISFACTION'. After The BEATLES disbanded in 1969, The STONES took over the mantle in the 70's as the hottest property in rock and popular music. **Style & Trivia:** R&B rebels from the early 60's, who progressed through controversial lyrically hard-edged rock, that never wained throughout 3 decades. Constantly in the press headlines for drug-taking/busts. Tragically JONES was to die 3 Jul'69, when drowning after a drink and drugs binge, He had left The STONES a month previously. JAGGER also an early drug taker, was more in the papers for his love-life. His 60's relationship with singer MARIANNE FAITHFULL ended in 1970. He met and married Nicaraguan model Bianca Rosa Perez-Mora on 12 May'71. They split in 1978, probably over Marsha Hunt's allegations that MICK was the father of her child. He later married ex-Bryan Ferry girlfriend Jerry Hall on 21 Nov'90 after a long relationship. JAGGER's film work included:- NED KELLY (1969) / PERFORMANCE (1970) / FITZCARALDO (1981). The other glimmer-twin RICHARDS, relationship with actress Anita Pallenberg ended and he later married Patti Hansen on 18 Dec'83. WYMAN's marriage since 1959 ended abruptly in the mid-80's. In 1988, his 2-year relationship with a 16 year-old Mandy Smith was revealed in The News Of The World Sunday tabloid. They married relatively quietly on 2 Jun'89, but controversially divorced in 1992, with now-famous Mandy sueing for a half million. • **Songwriters:** JAGGER-RICHARDS mostly except covers; NOT FADE AWAY (Buddy Holly) / ROUTE 66 (Nelson Riddle Orchestra) / I JUST WANT TO MAKE LOVE TO YOU (Willie Dixon) / HONEST I DO (Jimmy Reed) / I NEED YOU BABY (Bo Diddley) / POISON IVY (Coasters) / NOW I'VE GOT A WITNESS ... (Gene Pitney) / LITTLE BY LITTLE (Pitney / Spector) / COME ON + CAROL + YOU CAN'T CATCH ME + TALKIN' 'BOUT YOU + LITTLE QUEENIE + AROUND AND AROUND + BYE BYE JOHNNY (Chuck Berry) / CAN I GET A WITNESS (Holland-Dozier-Holland) / MONEY (Barrett Strong) / I WANNA BE YOUR MAN (Beatles) / LITTLE BY LITTLE (w/Spector) / YOU CAN MAKE IT IF YOU TRY (Gene Allison; hit) / WALKING THE DOG (Rufus Thomas) / SUSIE Q (Dale Hawkins) / UNDER THE BOARDWALK (Drifters) / I CAN'T BE SATISFIED + MANNISH BOY (Muddy Waters) / DOWN HOME GIRL (Jerry Butler) / IT'S ALL OVER NOW (Valentinos) / PAIN IN MY HEART + MY GIRL (Otis Redding) / EVERYBODY NEEDS SOMEBODY TO LOVE (Solomon Burke) / DOWN THE ROAD APIECE (?. Raye) / TIME IS ON MY SIDE (Irma Thomas) / SHE SAID YEAH (Jackson/Christy) / I DON'T KNOW WHY (Stevie Wonder) / MERCY, MERCY (Don Covay) / GOOD TIMES (Sam Cooke) / CRY TO ME (Betty Harris; hit) / HITCH HIKE (Marvin Gaye) / THAT'S HOW STRONG MY LOVE IS (?. Jamison) / OH BABY ... (?. Ozen) / PRODIGAL SON (Robert Wilkins) / YOU BETTER MOVE ON (Arthur Alexander) / LOVE IN VAIN (Robert Johnson; trad.) / AIN'T TOO PROUD TO BEG + JUST MY IMAGINATION (Temptations) / I'M A KING BEE + SHAKE YOUR HIPS (Slim Harpo) / CHERRY OH BABY (? reggae) / GOING TO A GO-GO (Smokey Robinson / Miracles) / HARLEM SHUFFLE (Bob & Earl) / TWENTY FLIGHT ROCK (Eddie Cochran) / etc. KEITH RICHARDS solo wrote with JORDAN. RONNIE WOOD covered TESTIFY (Parliaments) / AM I GROOVIN' YOU (Bert Berns) / SEVEN DAYS (Bob Dylan) / SHOW ME (J. Williams).

Recommended: EXILE ON MAIN ST. (*9) / ROLLED GOLD (*10) / MADE IN THE SHADE (*8) / BEGGAR'S BANQUET (*8) / STICKY FINGERS (*7) / LET IT BE (*9).

MICK JAGGER (b.26 Jul'43, Dartford, Kent, England) – vocals, harmonica / **KEITH RICHARDS** (b.18 Dec'43, Dartford) – rhythm guitar / **BRIAN JONES** (b.28 Feb'43, Cheltenham, England) – lead guitar / **CHARLIE WATTS** (b. 2 Jun'41, Islington, London) – drums (ex-BLUES INC.) / **BILL WYMAN** (b.WILLIAM PERKS, 24 Oct'36, Lewisham, London) – bass repl. DICK TAYLOR who later joined PRETTY THINGS / **IAN STEWART** – piano (was 6th member, pushed to the background by manager)

Decca London

Jun 63. (7") **COME ON. / I WANT TO BE LOVED** 21 -

Nov 63. (7") **I WANNA BE YOUR MAN. / STONED** 12 ☐ Jan 64

Feb 64. (7") **NOT FADE AWAY. / LITTLE BY LITTLE** 3 -

Mar 64. (7") **NOT FADE AWAY. / I WANNA BE YOUR MAN** - 48

Apr 64. (lp) **THE ROLLING STONES** 1 11 Jun 64

– (Get your kicks on) Route 66 / I just want to make love to you / Honest I do / I need you baby (Mona) / Now I've got a witness (like uncle Phil and uncle Gene) / Little by little / I'm a king bee / Carol / Tell me (you're coming back) / Can I get a witness / You can make it if you try / Walking the dog. *(US title 'ENGLAND'S NEWEST HITMAKERS – THE ROLLING STONES')*(+=) – Not fade away. / =Mona *(in the US) re-iss.+c+cd.Jul84 & Jun95 on 'London')*

Jun 64. (7") **IT'S ALL OVER NOW. / GOOD TIMES, BAD TIMES** 1 26 Aug 64

Jul 64. (7") **TELL ME (YOU'RE COMING BACK). / I JUST WANT TO MAKE LOVE TO YOU** - 24

Oct 64. (7") **TIME IS ON MY SIDE. / CONGRATULATIONS** - 6

Nov 64. (7") **LITTLE RED ROOSTER. / OFF THE HOOK** 1 -

Nov 64. (lp) **12 x 5** - 3

– Around and around / Confessin' the blues / Empty heart / Time is on my side / Good times bad times / It's all over now / 2120 South Michigan Avenue / Under the boardwalk / Congratulations / Grown up wrong / If you need me / Susie Q. *(UK-iss.+c+cd-Aug84 & Jun95 on 'London', as US cd-iss.!)*

Jan 65. (lp) **THE ROLLING STONES No.2** 1 -

– Everybody needs somebody to love / Down home girl / You can't catch me / Time is on my side / What a shame / Grown up wrong / Down the road apiece / Under the boardwalk / I can't be satisfied / Pain in my heart / Off the hook / Susie Q. *(re-iss.c+cd.1986)*

Jan 65. (7") **HEART OF STONE. / WHAT A SHAME** - 19

Feb 65. (7") **THE LAST TIME. / PLAY WITH FIRE** 1 9
96 Mar65

Mar 65. (lp) **THE ROLLING STONES NOW!** - 5

– Everybody needs somebody to love / Down home girl / You can't catch me / Heart of stone / I need you baby (Mona) / Down the road apiece / Off the hook / Pain in my heart / Oh baby (we got a good thing goin') / Little red rooster / Surprise surprise. *(UK-iss.+c+cd Aug88 + Jun95 on 'London')*

May 65. (7") **(I CAN'T GET NO) SATISFACTION. / THE SPIDER AND THE FLY** 1 -

Jun 65. (7") **(I CAN'T GET NO) SATISFACTION. / THE UNDER ASSISTANT WEST COAST MAN** - 1

Sep 65. (lp) **OUT OF OUR HEADS** 2 1 Aug 65

– She said yeah* / Mercy, mercy / Hitch hike / That's how strong my love is / Good times / Gotta get away* / Talkin' 'bout you* / Cry to me / Oh baby (we got a good thing going)* / Heart of stone / The under assistant west coast man / I'm free. (in the US; tracks above* were repl. by) – I'm alright (live) / (I can't get no) Satisfaction / Play with fire / The spider and the fly / One more try. *(re-iss.+c+cd.Jul84 & Jun95 on 'London')*

Sep 65. (7") **GET OFF OF MY CLOUD. / I'M FREE** - 1

Oct 65. (7") **GET OFF OF MY CLOUD. / THE SINGER NOT THE SONG** 1 -

Nov 65. (lp) **DECEMBER'S CHILDREN (AND EVERYBODY'S)** - 4

– She said yeah / Talkin' 'bout you / You better move on / Look what you've done / The singer not the song / Route 66 (live) / Get off of my cloud / I'm free / As tears go by / Gotta get away / Blue turns to grey / I'm movin' on (live). *(UK-iss.+c+cd.Aug88 & Jun95 on 'London')*

Dec 65. (7") **AS TEARS GO BY. / GOTTA GET AWAY** - 6

Feb 66. (7") **19th NERVOUS BREAKDOWN. / AS TEARS GO BY** 1 -

Feb 66. (7") **19th NERVOUS BREAKDOWN. / SAD DAY** - 2

Apr 66. (lp) **AFTERMATH** 1 2 Jul 66

– Mother's little helper / Stupid girl / Lady Jane / Under my thumb / Doncha bother me / Goin' home / Flight 505 / High and dry / Out of time / It's not easy / I am waiting / Take it or leave it / Think / What to do. (US version incl.) – Paint it black. *(re-iss.+c+cd.May85 & Jun95 on 'London')*

May 66. (7") **PAINT IT BLACK. / STUPID GIRL** - 1

May 66. (7") **PAINT IT BLACK. / LONG LONG WHILE** 1 -

Jul 66. (7") **MOTHER'S LITTLE HELPER. / LADY JANE** - 8
24

Sep 66. (7") **HAVE YOU SEEN YOUR MOTHER BABY, STANDING IN THE SHADOW?. / WHO'S DRIVING YOUR PLANE?** 5 9

Nov 66. (lp) **BIG HITS (HIGH TIDE AND GREEN GRASS)** 4 3 Apr 66

(compilation) – Have you seen your mother baby, standing in the shadows? / Paint it black / It's all over now / The last time / Heart of stone / Not fade away /

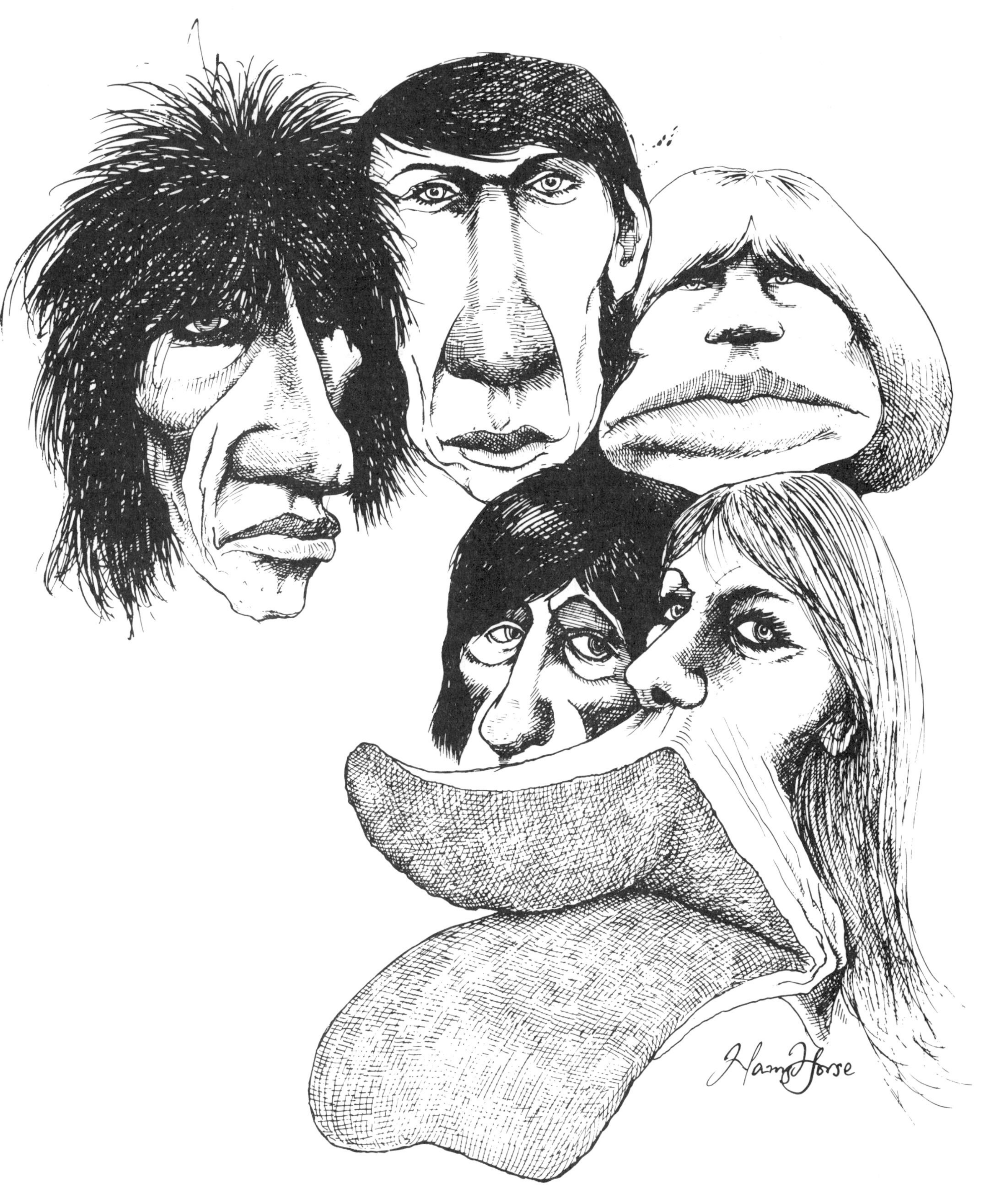

Come on / (I can't get no) Satisfaction / Get off my cloud / As tears go by / 19th nervous breakdown / Lady Jane / Time is on my side / Little red rooster. *(re-iss.+c+cd Jun95 on 'London')*

Dec 66. (lp) **GOT LIVE IF YOU WANT IT (live, Royal Albert Hall)** – 6
– Under my thumb / Get off of my cloud / Lady Jane / Not fade away / I've been loving you too long (to stop now) (studio) / Fortune teller (studio) / The last time / 19th nervous breakdown / Time is on my side / I'm alright / Have you seen your mother baby, standing in the shadow? / (I can't get no) Satisfaction. *(UK-iss.+c+cd.Aug88 & Jun95 on 'London', also in US on 'London')*

Jan 67. (7") **LET'S SPEND THE NIGHT TOGETHER. / RUBY TUESDAY** 3 55 / 1

Jan 67. (lp) **BETWEEN THE BUTTONS** 3 2 Feb 67
– Yesterday's papers / My obsession / Back street girl* / Connection / She smiled sweetly / Cool, calm and collected / All sold out / Please go home* / Who's been sleeping here? / Complicated / Miss Amanda Jones / Something happened to me yesterday. *(US version*; = tracks repl. by)*
– Let's spend the night together / Ruby Tuesday. *(cd-iss.Jan83) (re-iss.+c+cd.Apr85 + Jun95 on 'London') (re-iss.lp/cd. Dec91 on 'UFO' with free booklet)*

Jul 67. (lp) **FLOWERS** – 3
– (compilation of singles and out-takes) *(UK cd-iss.Aug88 & Jun95 on 'London')*

Aug 67. (7") **WE LOVE YOU. / DANDELION** 8 50 / 14

Nov 67. (7") **SHE'S A RAINBOW. / 2,000 LIGHT YEARS FROM HOME** – 25

Dec 67. (lp) **THEIR SATANIC MAJESTIES REQUEST** 3 2
– Sing this all together / Citadel / In another land / 2,000 man / Sing this all together (see what happens) / She's a rainbow / The lantern / Gomper / 2,000 light years from home / On with the show. *(re-iss.+c+cd.Feb86 + Jul90 + Jun95 on 'London')*

Dec 67. (7") **IN ANOTHER LAND. ("BILL WYMAN") / THE LANTERN** – 87

May 68. (7") **JUMPIN' JACK FLASH. / CHILD OF THE MOON** 1 3

Aug 68. (7") **STREET FIGHTING MAN. / NO EXPECTATIONS** – 48

Dec 68. (lp) **BEGGAR'S BANQUET** 3 5
– Sympathy for the Devil / No expectations / Dear doctor / Parachute woman / Jigsaw puzzle / Street fighting man / Prodigal son / Stray cat blues / Factory girl / Salt of the Earth. *(re-iss.+c+cd.Jul84 & JUn95 on 'London', +US-cd)*

—— (Jun69) **MICK TAYLOR** (b.17 Jan'48, Hertfordshire, England) – lead guitar (ex-JOHN MAYALL's BLUESBREAKERS) repl. BRIAN JONES who tragically after a bout of drink/drugs was found dead by his girlfriend on 3 Jul'69.

Jul 69. (7") **HONKY TONK WOMEN. / YOU CAN'T ALWAYS GET WHAT YOU WANT** 1 1

Sep 69. (lp)(c) **THROUGH THE PAST DARKLY (BIG HITS VOL.2)** 2 2
– Look what you've done / It's all over now / Confessin' the blues / One more try / As tears go by / The spider and the fly / My girl / Paint it black / If you need me / The last time / Blue turns to grey / Around and around. -(compilation of hits 1967-1969) *(re-iss.cd/c/lp Jun95 on 'London')*

(all UK singles so far were re-iss.Mar82).

Dec 69. (lp)(c) **LET IT BLEED** 1 3
– Gimme shelter / Love in vain / Country honk / Live with me / Let it bleed / Midnight rambler / You got the silver / Monkey man / You can't always get what you want. *(re-iss.+c+cd.Feb86 & Jun95 UK+US on 'London')*

(Mid-1970, MICK JAGGER finally appears as 'Ned Kelly' in the film of same.)

Sep 70. (lp)(c) **GET YER YA YA'S OUT** (live, New York, Nov'69) 1 6 Oct 69
– Jumpin' Jack Flash / Carol / Stray cat blues / Love in vain / Midnight rambler / Sympathy for the Devil / Live with me / Little Queenie / Honky tonk women. *(cd-iss.mid-80's & Jun95 on 'London')*

In 1970, MICK JAGGER starred in his second feature film 'Performance'.

Nov 70. (7") **MEMO FROM TURNER. (by "MICK JAGGER" from the film) / ('B'side by 'Jack Nitzsche')** 32

Apr 71. (lp)(c) **STONE AGE** (compilation) 4 –
– Look what you've done / It's all over now / Confessin' the blues / One more try / As tears go by / The spider and the fly / My girl / Paint it black / If you need me / The last time / Blue turns to grey / Around and around.

Rolling St. Rolling St.

Apr 71. (7"m) **BROWN SUGAR. / BITCH / LET IT ROCK** 2 1

Apr 71. (lp)(c) **STICKY FINGERS** 1 1
– Brown sugar / Sway / Wild horses / Can't you hear me knocking? / You gotta move / Bitch / I got the blues / Sister Morphine / Dead flowers / Moonlight mile. *(re-iss.Mar80 + Sep87) (re-iss.+cd.Nov89 on 'CBS' UK/US) (re-iss.cd Jun94 + c Aug94 on 'Virgin')*

Jun 71. (7") **WILD HORSES. / SWAY** – 28

Apr 72. (7") **TUMBLING DICE. / SWEET BLACK ANGEL** 5 7

Jun 72. (d-lp)(c) **EXILE ON MAIN ST.** 1 1
– Rocks off / Rip this joint / Shake your hips / Casino boogie / Tumbling dice / Sweet Virginia / Torn and frayed / Sweet black angel / Loving cup / Happy / Turd on the run / Ventilator blues / I just want to see his face / Let it loose / All down the line / Stop breaking down / Shine a light / Soul survivor. *(re-iss.Mar80 + Sep87) (re-iss.+cd.Nov89 on 'CBS' UK/US) (re-iss.cd+c Aug94 on 'Virgin')*

Jun 72. (7") **HAPPY. / ALL DOWN THE LINE** – 22

Aug 73. (7") **ANGIE. / SILVER TRAIN** 5 1

Sep 73. (lp)(c) **GOAT'S HEAD SOUP** 1 1
– Dancing with Mr.D / 100 years ago / Coming down again / Doo doo doo doo doo (heartbreaker) / Angie / Silver train / Hide your love / Winter / Can you hear the music / Star star. *(re-iss.Mar80 + Jan88) (re-iss.+cd.Nov89 on 'CBS' UK/US) (re-iss.cd+c Aug94 on 'Virgin')*

Jan 74. (7") **DOO DOO DOO DOO DOO (HEARTBREAKER). / DANCING WITH MR.D** – 15

Jul 74. (7") **IT'S ONLY ROCK'N'ROLL. / THROUGH THE LONELY NIGHTS** 10 16

Oct 74. (lp)(c) **IT'S ONLY ROCK'N'ROLL** 2 1
– If you can't rock me / Ain't too proud to beg / It's only rock'n'roll / Till the next goodbye / Time waits for no one / Luxury / Dance little sister / If you really want to be my friend / Short and curlies / Fingerprint file. *(re-iss.Mar80 + Jan88) (re-iss.+cd.Nov89 on 'CBS' UK/US) (re-iss.cd+c Aug94 on 'Virgin')*

Oct 74. (7") **AIN'T TOO PROUD TO BEG. / DANCE LITTLE SISTER** – 17

Jun 75. (lp)(c) **MADE IN THE SHADE** 14 6
– Brown sugar / Tumbling dice / Happy / Dance little sister / Wild horses / Angie / Bitch / It's only rock'n'roll (but I like it) / Doo doo doo doo (heartbreaker) / Rip this joint. *(re-iss.Mar80 + Mar88) (re-iss.+cd.Nov89 on 'CBS' UK/US)*

—— (Apr-Dec75) **RON WOOD** – lead guitar (ex-FACES, ex-CREATION, etc) repl. MICK TAYLOR who left Dec74 and later joined JACK BRUCE BAND

Apr 76. (7") **FOOL TO CRY. / CRAZY MAMA** 6 –

Apr 76. (7") **FOOL TO CRY. / HOT STUFF** – 10 / 49

May 76. (lp)(c) **BLACK AND BLUE** 2 1
– Hot stuff / The hand of fate / Cherry oh baby / Memory motel / Hey Negrita / Melody / Fool to cry / Crazy mama. *(re-iss.Mar80 + Jan88) (re-iss.+cd.Nov89 on 'CBS' UK/US) (re-iss.cd+c Aug94 on 'Virgin')*

Sep 77. (d-lp)(d-c) **LOVE YOU LIVE (live)** 3 5
– Fanfare for the common man / Honky tonk woman / If you can't rock me / Get off of my cloud / Happy / Hot stuff / Star star / Tumbling dice / Fingerprint file / You gotta me / You can't always get what you want / Mannish boy / Crackin' up / Little red rooster / Around and around / It's only rock'n'roll / Brown sugar / Jumpin' Jack Flash / Sympathy for the Devil. *(re-iss.Mar80 + Sep87) (re-iss. +d-cd.Nov89 on 'CBS' UK/US)*

May 78. (7"pink)(12"pink) **MISS YOU. / FARAWAY EYES** 3 1

Jun 78. (lp)(c) **SOME GIRLS** 2 1
– Miss you / When the whip comes down / Just my imagination / Some girls / Lies / Far away etes / Respectable / Before they make me run / Beast of burden / Shattered. *(re-iss.Sep87) (re-iss.+cd.Nov89 on 'CBS' UK/US) (re-iss.cd+c Aug94 on 'Virgin')*

Sep 78. (7") **BEAST OF BURDEN. / WHEN THE WHIP COMES DOWN** – 8

Sep 78. (7") **RESPECTABLE. / WHEN THE WHIP COMES DOWN** 23 –

Dec 78. (7") **SHATTERED. / EVERYTHING IS TURNING TO GOLD** – 31

Jun 80. (7") **EMOTIONAL RESCUE. / DOWN IN THE HOLE** 9 3

Jul 80. (lp)(c) **EMOTIONAL RESCUE** 1 1
– Dance (pt.1) / Summer romance / Send it to me / Let me go / Indian girl / Where the boys go / Down in the hole / Emotional rescue / She's so cold / All about you. *(re-iss.+cd.Nov89 on 'CBS' UK/US) (re-iss.cd+c Aug94 on 'Virgin')*

Sep 80. (7") **SHE'S SO COLD. / SEND IT TO ME** 33 26

Mar 81. (lp)(c) **SUCKING IN THE 70'S** (comp. + new) 15
– Shattered / Everything is turning to gold / Hot stuff / Time waits for no one / Fool to cry / Mannish boy / When the whip comes down (live) / I was a dancer (part 2) / Crazy mama / Beast of burden. *(re-iss.+cd.Nov89 on 'CBS' UK/US)*

Aug 81. (7") **START ME UP. / NO USE IN CRYING** 7 2

Sep 81. (lp)(c) **TATTOO YOU** 2 1
– Start me up / Hang fire / Slave / Little T & A / Black limousine / Neighbours / Worried about you / Tops / Heaven / No use in crying / Waiting on a friend. *(re-iss.+cd.Nov89 on 'CBS' UK/US) (re-iss.cd+c Aug94 on 'Virgin')*

Nov 81. (7") **WAITING ON A FRIEND. / LITTLE T & A** 50 13

Mar 82. (7") **HANG FIRE. / NEIGHBORS** – 20

Jun 82. (7") **GOING TO A GO-GO (live). / BEAST OF BURDEN (live)** 26 25

Jun 82. (lp)(c)(pic-lp) **STILL LIFE (AMERICAN CONCERTS 1981)** 4 5
– Under my thumb / Let's spend the night together / Shattered / Twenty flight rock / Going to a go-go / Let me go / Time is on my side / Just my imagination / Start me up / (I can't get no) Satisfaction / Take the A train / Star-spangled banner. *(re-iss.+cd.Nov89 on 'CBS' UK/US)*

Sep 82. (7") **TIME IS ON MY SIDE (live). / TWENTY FLIGHT ROCK (live)**
(12"+=) – Under my thumb (live).

Nov 83. (7") **UNDERCOVER OF THE NIGHT. / ALL THE WAY DOWN** 11 9
(12"+=) – Feel on baby (instrumental dub).

Nov 83. (lp)(c)(cd) **UNDERCOVER** 3 4
– Undercover of the night / She was hot / Tie you up / Wanna hold you / Feel on baby / Too much blood / Pretty beat up / Too tough / All the way down / It must be hell. *(re-iss.Apr86) (re-iss.all.Nov89 on 'CBS' UK/US) (re-iss.cd+c Aug94 on*

'Virgin')

Jan 84. (7") **SHE WAS HOT. / I THINK I'M GOING MAD** 42 44
(12"pic-d+=) – ('A'extended).

Jul 84. (lp)(c)(cd) **REWIND 1971-1984 (THE BEST OF THE ROLLING STONES)** (compilation) 23 86
– Brown sugar / Undercover of the night / Start me up / Tumbling dice / It's only rock'n'roll (but I like it) / She's so cold / Hang fire / Miss you / Beast of burden / Fool to cry / Waiting on a friend / Angie / Emotional rescue. (cd+= 2 extra) *(re-iss. all Nov89 on 'CBS' UK/US)*

— In 1984, JAGGER guested dual vocals w / MICHAEL JACKSON on The JACKSONS' 'State Of Shock'. He also recorded debut solo album 'She's The Boss', which was released 1985. Later mid'85, he appeared at LIVE AID with DAVID BOWIE duetting on (Martha & The Vandellas) song 'DANCING IN THE STREET'. When issued as a charity single, it made UK No.1 / US No.7 (see BOWIE ⇒).

— 12th Dec'85, IAN STEWART their long-serving 6th member died of a heart attack.

C.B.S. Columbia

Mar 86. (7") **HARLEM SHUFFLE. / HAD IT WITH YOU** 13 5
(12"+=)/ /(12"+=) – ('A'-London mix)./ / ('A'-New York mix).

Mar 86. (lp)(c)(cd) **DIRTY WORK** 4 4
– One hit (to the body) / Fight / Harlem shuffle / Hold back / Too rude / Winning ugly / Back to zero / Dirty work / Had it with you / Sleep tonight. *(re-iss.all.Nov89 on 'CBS' UK/US) (re-iss.cd+c Aug94 on 'Virgin')*

May 86. (7") **ONE HIT (TO THE BODY). / FIGHT** □ 28
(12") – ('A'London mix) / ('B'side)

— During this lull in group activity, JAGGER and RICHARDS ventured solo amidst rumours of disbandment. In 1989, they re-surfaced.

Aug 89. (7") **MIXED EMOTIONS. / FANCY MAN'S BLUES** 36 5
(12"+=)(c-s+=) – ('A'remixed version).
(cd-s+=) – Tumbling dice / Miss you.
(cd-s+=) – Shattered / Waiting on a friend.

Sep 89. (lp)(c)(cd) **STEEL WHEELS** 2 3
– Sad sad sad / Mixed emotions / Terrifying / Hold on to your hat / Hearts for sale / Blinded by love / Rock and a hard place / Can't be seen / Almost hear you sigh / Continental drift / Break the spell / Slipping away. *(cd re-iss.Dec92) (re-iss.cd+c Aug94 on 'Virgin')*

Nov 89. (7") **ROCK AND A HARD PLACE. / COOK COOK BLUES** 63 23
(12")(c-s) – ('A'dance mix) / ('A'dub mix) / ('B'side).
('A'mixed-cd-s+=) – Emotional rescue / Some girls.
(12") – ('A'side) / ('A'Michael Brauer mix) / ('A'dub).

Jun 90. (7") **ALMOST HEAR YOU SIGH. / BREAK THE SPELL** - 50

Jun 90. (7") **ALMOST HEAR YOU SIGH. / WISH I'D NEVER MET YOU** 31 -
(c-s+=) – Mixed emotions.
(cd-s+=) – Miss you / Waiting on a friend.
(12")(cd-s) – ('A'side) / Beast of burden / Angie / Fool to cry.

Aug 90. (7")(c-s) **TERRIFYING (remix). / ROCK AND A HARD PLACE (remix)** □ □
(cd-s+=) – ('A'-12"remix) / Harlem shuffle.
('A'diff.remix/'B'dance mixed 12"+=) – Harlem shuffle (London mix).
(cd-s) – ('A'side) / Start me up / Shattered / If you can't rock me.

Mar 91. (7")(c-s) **HIGH WIRE. / 2,000 LIGHT YEARS FROM HOME (live)** 29 57
(12"+=)(cd-s+=) – Sympathy for the Devil / I just want to make love to you (both live).
(cd-s+=) – Light my fire / Factory girl (both live).

Apr 91. (cd)(c)(lp) **FLASHPOINT (live)** 6 16
– Start me up / Sad sad girl / Miss you / Ruby Tuesday / Tou can't always get what you want / Factory girl / Little red rooster / Paint it black / Sympathy for the Devil / Brown sugar / Jumpin' Jack Flash / (I can't get no) Satisfaction / Sexdrive (studio) / High wire (studio). (cd+=) – Rock and a hard place / Can't be seen. *(cd re-iss.Dec92)*

May 91. (7")(c-s) **RUBY TUESDAY (live). / PLAY WITH FIRE (live)** 59 □
(12"+=)(cd-s+=) – You can't always get what you want / Rock and a hard place (both live).
(cd-s+=) – Harlem shuffle / Winning ugly VI (mix).

— In Nov'91, The STONES signed to 'Virgin', and BILL WYMAN soon quit.

Virgin Virgin

Nov 93. (cd)(c)(d-lp) **JUMP BACK: THE BEST OF THE ROLLING STONES 1971-1993** (compilation) 16 □
– Start me up / Brown sugar / Harlem shuffle / It's only rock'n'roll (but I like it) / Mixed emotions / Angie / Tumbling dice / Fool to cry / Rock and a hard place / Miss you / Hot stuff / Emotional rescue / Respectable / Beast of burden / Waiting on a friend / Wild horses / Bitch / Undercover of the night. *(re-iss.Oct94 & Jun95)*

— WYMAN replaced by sessioners **DARRYL JONES** – bass / **CHUCK LEAVELL** – piano

Virgin Virgin

Jul 94. (7")(c-s) **LOVE IS STRONG. / ('A'mix)** 14 93
(cd-s+=) – The storm / So strong.

Jul 94. (cd)(c)(d-lp) **VOODOO LOUNGE** 1 2
– Love is strong / You got me rocking / Sparks will fly / The worst / New faces / Moon is up / Out of tears / I go wild / Brand new car / Sweethearts together / Suck on the jugular / Blinded by rainbows / Baby break it down / Thru and thru. *(re-iss.Jun95)*

Oct 94. (7")(c-s) **YOU GOT ME ROCKING. / JUMP ON TOP OF ME** 23 □
(12"+=)(cd-s+=) – (2 'A'mixes).

Dec 94. (7")(c-s) **OUT OF TEARS. / I'M GONNA DRIVE** 38 60 Oct94
(cd-s+=)/-/(cd-s+=) – ('A'mix). / / Sparks will fly.

Jul 95. (7")(c-s) **I GO WILD. / ('A'-Scott Litt remix)** 29 □
(cd-s+=) – ('A'version) / ('A'-Luis Resto straight vocal mix).

Nov 95. (c-s) **LIKE A ROLLING STONE / BLACK LIMOUSINE / ALL DOWN THE LINE** 12 □
(cd-s+=) – ('A'edit).

Nov 95. (cd)(c)(d-lp) **STRIPPED (live)** 9 9
– Street fighting man / Like a rolling stone / Not fade away / Shine a light / The spider and the fly / I'm free / Wild horses / It let it bleed / Dead flowers / Slipping away / Angie / Love in vain / Sweet Virginia / Little baby.

– other compilations, etc. –

Below releases issued on 'Decca' UK/ 'Abkco' US unless mentioned.

Jan 64. (7"ep) **THE ROLLING STONES** □ -
– Bye bye Johnny / Money / You better move on / Poison Ivy. *(re-iss.Mar82) (12"ep-iss.Dec83)*

Aug 64. (7"ep) **5 X 5** □ -
– If you need me / Empty heart / 2120 South Michegan Avenue / Confessin' the blues / Around and around. *(re-iss.Mar82) (12"ep-iss.Dec83)*

Jun 65. (7"ep) **GOT LIVE IF YOU WANT IT (live)** □ -
– We want the Stones / Everybody needs somebody to love / Pain in my heart / Route 66 / I'm moving on / I'm alright. *(re-iss.Mar82) (12"ep-iss.Dec83)*

Jul 71. (7") **STREET FIGHTING MAN. / SURPRISE SURPRISE** 21 -

Aug 71. (lp)(c) **GIMME SHELTER** 19 -

Jan 72. (d-lp)(c) **HOT ROCKS 1964-1971** - 4
(UK cd-iss.1983 on 'Decca', re-iss.all Jul90) (US cd-iss.1989 on 'Abko') (hit UK 66 Oct93) (re-iss.cd/c/d-lp Jun95 on 'London')

Feb 72. (lp)(c) **MILESTONES** 14 -

Jun 72. (7") **EVERYBODY NEEDS SOMEBODY TO LOVE. / SURPRISE SURPRISE** □ -

Nov 72. (lp)(c) **ROCK'N'ROLLING STONES** 41 -

Dec 72. (lp)(c) **MORE HOT ROCKS (BIG HITS & FAZED COOKIES)** - 9
(UK re+cd-iss.Aug88 + Nov90 + Jun95 on 'London')

Apr 73. (7") **YOU CAN'T ALWAYS GET WHAT YOU WANT. / SAD DAY** □ 42

Oct 73. (lp)(c) **NO STONE UNTURNED** □ -

May 75. (7") **I DON'T KNOW WHY. / TRY A LITTLE HARDER** □ 42

Jun 75. (lp)(c) **METAMORPHISIS** (early demos) 45 8

Sep 75. (7") **OUT OF TIME. / JIVING SISTER FANNY** 45 81

Nov 75. (d-lp)(d-c) **ROLLED GOLD – (THE VERY BEST OF THE ROLLING STONES)** 7 -
– Come on / I wanna be your man / Not fade away / Carol / It's all over now / Little red rooster / Time is on my side / The last time / (I can't get no) Satisfaction / Get off my cloud / 19th nervous breakdown / As tears go by / Under my thumb / Lady Jane / Out of time / Paint it black / Have you seen your mother baby, standing in the shadows? / Let's spend the night together / Ruby Tuesday / Yesterday's papers / We love you / She's a rainbow / Jumpin' Jack Flash / Honky tonk women / Sympathy for the Devil / Street fighting man / Midnight rambler / Gimme shelter.

Apr 76. (7") **HONKY TONK WOMAN. / SYMPATHY FOR THE DEVIL** □ -
(re-iss.Mar82)

Oct 77. (lp)(c) **GET STONED** 13 -

Aug 80. (12x7"box) **BOXED SET SINGLES 1963-1969** □ □
COME ON. / I WANNA BE YOUR MAN // **IT'S ALL OVER NOW. / I WANT TO BE LOVED // (I CAN'T GET NO) SATISFACTION. / LITTLE BY LITTLE // NOT FADE AWAY. / LITTLE RED ROOSTER // THE LAST TIME. / PAINT IT BLACK // GET OFF OF MY CLOUD. / PLAY WITH FIRE // JUMPIN' JACK FLASH. / AS TEARS GO BY // 19th NERVOUS BREAKDOWN. / HAVE YOU SEEN YOUR MOTHER BABY, STANDING IN THE SHADOWS? // LET'S SPEND THE NIGHT TOGETHER. / YOU CAN'T ALWAYS GET WHAT YOU WANT // HONKY TONK WOMAN. / RUBY TUESDAY STREET FIGHTING MAN. / OUT OF TIME // SYMPATHY FOR THE DEVIL. / GIMME SHELTER**

Oct 80. (lp)(c) **SOLID ROCK** □ -

Nov 81. (lp)(c) **SLOW ROCKERS** □ -

Jan 86. (d-cd-box) **HOT ROCKS 1 & 2** □ - 1985

Sep 89. (d-lp)(d-c)(d-cd) **SINGLES COLLECTION: THE LONDON YEARS** - 91
(on 'Abkco' US) (re-iss.Jun95)

Jun 90. (7") **PAINT IT BLACK / HONKY TONK WOMAN** 61 -

Jan 74. Atlantic; (7") **BROWN SUGAR. / HAPPY / ROCKS OFF** □ -

May 79. Rolling Stones; (lp)(c) **TIME WAITS FOR NO ONE** □ -

Jul 82. Decca Holland; (lp)(c) **IN CONCERT (live)** 94 -

Jul 84. Rolling Stones; (7")(7"pic-d) **BROWN SUGAR. / BITCH** 58 -

Oct 82. K-Tel; (d-lp)(d-c) **THE STORY OF THE STONES** 24 -

Jul 90. Columbia; (cd) **COLLECTOR'S EDITION** □ -

Mar 92. Circus; (cd)(c)(lp)(video) **LIVE AT THE HOLLYWOOD PALLADIUM DECEMBER 15, 1988 (live)**

– solo releases –

MICK JAGGER

(see also other Nov70 ⇒)

C.B.S. Columbia

Feb 85. (7") **JUST ANOTHER NIGHT. / TURN THE GIRL LOOSE** 32 12
('A'extended-12"+=) – ('A'dub version).

Mar 85. (lp)(c)(cd) **SHE'S THE BOSS** 6 13
– Lonely at the top / Half a loaf / Hard woman / Lucky in love / Secrets / Just another night / She's the boss / Running out of luck / Turn the girl loose. *(re-iss.cd Aug95 on 'WEA')*

Apr 85. (7")(12") **LUCKY IN LOVE. / RUNNING OUT OF LUCK** – 38

Jul 86. (7") **RUTHLESS PEOPLE. / I'M RINGING** – 51

—— (above from the film 'Ruthless People', issued on 'Epic' records)

Aug 87. (7") **LET'S WORK. / CATCH US IF YOU CAN** 31 39
(12"+=) – ('A'dance mix).

Sep 87. (lp)(c)(cd) **PRIMITIVE COOL** 26 41
– Throwaway / Peace for the wicked / Say you will / Primitive cool / Kow Tow / Shoot off your mouth / Party doll / War baby. *(re-iss.cd Aug95 on 'WEA')*

Nov 87. (7")(7"pic-d) **THROWAWAY. / PEACE FOR THE WICKED** 67
('A'remixed-12"+=)(cd-s+=) – ('A'vocal dub mix).

Feb 88. (7") **SAY YOU WILL. / SHOOT OFF YOUR MOUTH** –

Atlantic Epic

Jan 93. (7")(c-s) **SWEET THING. / WANDERING SPIRIT** 24 84
(12"+=)(cd-s+=) – ('A'dub mix).

Feb 93. (cd)(c)(lp) **WANDERING SPIRIT** 12 11
– Wired all night / Sweet thing / Out of focus / Don't tear me up / Put me in the trash / Use me / Evening gown / Mother of a man / think / Wandering spirit / Hang on to me tonight / I've been lonely for so long / Angel in my heart / Handsome Molly. *(re-iss.cd Aug95 on 'WEA')*

Apr 93. (7")(c-s) **DON'T TEAR ME UP. / EVERYBODY KNOWS ABOUT MY GOOD THING**
(12"+=)(cd-s+=) – Sweet thing (funky guitar edit).

Jul 93. (7")(12")(c-s)(cd-s) **OUT OF FOCUS. / HIPGRASS**

KEITH RICHARDS

(covers 'A'side= Chuck Berry / 'B'= Jimmy Cliff)

Rolling St. Rolling St.

Nov 78. (7") **RUN RUDOLPH RUN. / THE HARDER THEY COME**

C.B.S. Virgin

Oct 88. (lp)(c)(cd) **TALK IS CHEAP** 37 24
– Talk is cheap / Take it so hard / Struggle / I could have stood you up / Make no mistake / You don't move me / It means a lot / Whip it up / How I wish / Rock awhile / Locked away. (re-iss.Sep90 on 'Virgin')

Oct 88. (7") **TAKE IT SO HARD. / I COULD HAVE STOOD YOU UP**
(12"+=)(cd-s+=) – It means a lot.

Apr 89. (7") **MAKE NO MISTAKE. / IT MEANS A LOT**
(12"+=)(cd-s+=) – ('A'extended).

Virgin Virgin

Nov 91. (cd)(c)(lp) **KEITH RICHARDS AND THE X-PENSIVE WINOS LIVE AT THE HOLLYWOOD, PALLADIUM, DECEMBER 15, 1988 (live)**
– Take it so hard / How I wish / I could have stood you up / Too rude / Make no mistake / Time is on my side / Big enough / Whip it up / Locked away / Struggle / Happy / Connection / Rockawhile.

Oct 92. (cd)(c)(lp) **MAIN OFFENDER** 45 99
– 999 / Wicked as it seems / Eileen / Words of wonder / Yap yap / Bodytalks / Hate it when you leave / Runnin' too deep / Will but you don't / Demon.

RICHARDS writes with JORDAN and some with WACHTEL.

BILL WYMAN

solo (see also 1967 R.S. releases)

Rolling St. Rolling St.

May 74. (lp)(c) **MONKEY GRIP** 39 99
– I wanna get me a gun / Crazy woman / Pussy / Mighty fine time / Monkey grip glue / What a blow / White lightnin' / I'll pull you thro' / It's a wonder. – *(US iss.quad !)*

Jun 74. (7") **MONKEY GRIP GLUE. / WHAT A BLOW**

Nov 74. (7") **WHITE LIGHTNIN'. / PUSSY**

Feb 76. (lp)(c) **STONE ALONE**
– A quarter to three / Gimme just one chance / Soul satisfying / Apache woman / Every sixty seconds / Get it on / Feet / Peanut butter time / Wime and wimmen / If you wanna be happy / What's the point / No more foolin'.

Apr 76. (7") **A QUARTER TO THREE. / SOUL SATISFYING**

Sep 76. (7") **APACHE WOMAN. / SOUL SATISFYING**

A & M A & M

Jul 81. (7") **(SI SI) JE SUIS UN ROCK STAR. / RIO DE JANEIRO** 14

Oct 81. (7") **COME BACK SUZANNE. / SEVENTEEN**

Mar 82. (7") **A NEW FASHION. / GIRLS** 37

Apr 82. (lp)(c)(pic-lp) **BILL WYMAN** 55
– Ride on baby / A new fashion / Nuclear reactions / Jump up / Come back Suzanne / (Si si) Je suis en rock star / Visions / Seventeen / Rio de Janeiro / Girls.

May 82. (7") **VISIONS. / NUCLEAR REACTION**

—— (next from film 'GREEN ICE' for which he provided the soundtrack)

Polydor Polydor

Jun 82. (7") **GREEN ICE THEME. / COULD HOPPERS**

—— BILL also recorded live jamming lp's with BUDDY GUY and JUNIOR WELLS. Alongside CHARLIE WATTS & FRIENDS, they released an album 'WILLIE & THE POOR BOYS' (May86). From it was taken single THESE ARMS OF MINE. / POOR BOY BOOGIE.

CHARLIE WATTS formed **ROCKET 88**, who released one eponymous lp Jan '81 on 'Atlantic'.

CHARLIE WATTS & FRIENDS

released lp (Dec86) on CBS **LIVE AT THE FULHAM TOWN HALL**.
In 1991, his quintet issued 10"lp,c,cd **FROM ONE CHARLIE** (which was on 'UFO Jazz').

RON WOOD

solo (74-75; while still with The FACES)

Warners Warners

Sep 74. (lp)(c) **I'VE GOT MY OWN ALBUM TO DO**
– I can feel the fire / Far east man / Mystifies me / Take a look at the guy / Act together / Am I grooving you / Shirley / Cancel everything / Sure the one you need / If you gotta make a fool of somebody / Crutch music. *(re-iss.Oct85 as 'CANCEL EVERYTHING' on 'Thunderbolt', cd-iss.Jun87, pic-lp iss.1989) (cd-iss.Sep94)*

Nov 74. (7") **I CAN FEEL THE FIRE. / BREATHE ON ME**

Jul 75. (lp)(c) **NOW LOOK**
– I got lost when I found you / Big bayou / Breathe on me / If you don't want my love for you / I can say she's alright / Caribbean boogie / Now look / Sweet baby of mine / I can't stand the rain / It's unholy / I got a feeling. *(re-iss. +cd.Nov87 on 'Thunderbolt', pic-lp iss.1989) (cd-iss.Sep94)*

Oct 75. (7") **IF YOU DON'T WANT MY LOVE. / I GOT A FEELING**

Jan 76. (7") **BIG BAYOU. / SWEET BABY MINE**

Atlantic Atlantic

Sep 76. (lp)(c) **MAHONEY'S LAST STAND ("RONNIE WOOD & RONNIE LANE")**
– Tonight's number / From the late to the early / Chicken wired / I'll fly away / Title one / Just for a momoent / Mons the blues / Car radio / Hay tumble / Wooly's thing / Rooster funeral. *(re-iss.+cd.Dec88 on 'Thunderbolt', pic-lp May89)*

C.B.S. Columbia

May 79. (lp)(c) **GIMME SOME NECK** 45
– Worry no more / Breaking my heart / Delia / Buried alive / Come to realise / Infekshun / Seven days / We all get old / F.U.C. her / Lost and lonely / Don't worry.

Aug 79. (7") **SEVEN DAYS. / COME TO REALISE**

Nov 81. (lp)(c) **1, 2, 3, 4**
– Fountain of love / 1, 2, 3, 4 / Outlaws / Down to the ground / Wind howlin' through / She never told me / Red eyes / Priceless / She was out there. *(re-iss.d-lp+d-cd.May90 on 'Castle', incl+= GIMME SOME NECK) (cd-iss.Apr93 on 'Sony Europe')*

—— Nov 90, had both his legs broken in a car accident.

RONNIE WOOD

w/ **BERNARD FOWLER** – vocals, co-producer / **JOHNNY LEE SCHELL** – guitars / **WAYNE P. SHEEKY** – drums / **SHAWN SOLOMON** – bass / **IAN McLAGEN** – keyboards / plus **CHUCK LEAVELL** – additional keyboards

Continuum Continuum

Aug 92. (cd-s) **SHOW ME. / BREATHE ON ME**

Mar 93. (cd-s) **SOMEBODY ELSE MIGHT (slidin' on this mix). / AIN'T ROCK & ROLL**

Sep 93. (12")(cd-s) **STAY WITH ME. / JOSEPHINE / SOMEBODY ELSE MIGHT (remix)**

Nov 93. (cd)(c) **SLIDE ON LIVE – PLUGGED IN AND STANDING (live)**
– Testify / Josephine / Pretty beat up / Am I groovin' you? / Flying / Breathe on me / Silicon grown / Seven days / Show me & show me (groove) / Ican feel the fire / Around the plinth / Gasoline alley / Traditional / Stay with me.

Henry ROLLINS

Born: HENRY GARFIELD, 13 Feb '61, Washington DC, USA. (see BLACK FLAG) After several albums released during the late 80's, he (ROLLINS BAND) broke through into UK charts 1992 with 'THE END OF THE SILENCE!' • **Style:** Aggressive but intelligent hard man of rock, playing hard core punk, curbed by anti-establishment talk/comedy gigs. • **Songwriters:** Writes own work except; EX-LION TAMER (Wire) / DO IT (Pink Fairies) / LET THERE BE ROCK (Ac-Dc) / FRANKLIN'S TOWER (Grateful Dead). • **Trivia:** A few lp's are spoken word/poetry and offensively straight to the point.

Recommended: END OF SILENCE (*7)

HENRY ROLLINS – vocals (ex-BLACK FLAG, ex-SOA) / with **CHRIS HASKETT** (b. Leeds, England) – guitar (ex-SURFIN' DAVE) / **BERNIE WANDEL** – bass / **MICK GREEN** – drums

Fun-damental | Fun-damental

Jul 87. (lp)(cd) **HOT ANIMAL MACHINE**
– Black and white / Followed around / Lost and found / There's a man outside / Crazy lover / A man and a woman / Hot animal machine 1 / Ghost rider / Move right in / Hot animal machine 2 / No one. *(re-iss.cd Mar94 on 'Intercord')*

Sep 87. (m-lp) **DRIVE BY SHOOTING (as "HENRIETTA ROLLINS & THE WIFE-BEATING CHILD HATERS")**
– Drive by shooting (watch out for that pig) / Ex-lion tamer / Hey Henriezza / Can you speak this? / I have come to kill you / Men are pigs.

HENRY ROLLINS BAND

retained **HASKETT** and recruited **ANDREW WEISS** – bass / **SIMEON CAIN** – drums

Sep 88. (lp)(cd) **LIFE TIME**
– Burned beyond recognition / What am I doing here / 1000 times blind / Lonely / Wreck-age / Gun in mouth blues / You look at you / If you're alive / Turned out. *(cd+=)*– What am I doing here? / Burned beyond recognition / Move right in / Hot animal machine 2. *(re-iss.cd Mar94 on 'Intercord')*

World Service | World Service

Mar 89. (lp) **OVER**
– *(cd-iss.+= Joyriding with Frank (30 minutes live))*

Nov 89. (lp)(cd) **HARD VOLUME**
– Hard / What have I got / I feel like this / Planet Joe / Love song / Turned inside out / Down and away / Joyriding with Frank. *(re-iss.cd Mar94 on 'Intercord')*

ROLLINS BAND

Touch & Go | Touch & Go

Nov 90. (cd)(lp) **TURNED ON (live '89)**
– Lonely / Do it / What have I got / Tearing / Out there / You didn't need / Hard // Followed around / Mask / Down & away / Turned inside out / The Dietmar song / Black & white / What do you do / Crazy lover.

HENRY ROLLINS & THE HARD-ONS

(Australian back-up)

Vinyl Sol. | Touch & Go

Jul 91. (12")(cd-s) **LET THERE BE ROCK. / CARRY ME DOWN**

ROLLINS BAND

retained same band.

Imago-RCA | Imago-RCA

Feb 92. (12") **LOW SELF OPINION. / LIE, LIE, LIE**

Feb 92. (cd)(c)(lp) **THE END OF SILENCE**
– The end of silence / Grip / Tearing / You didn't need / Almost real / Obscene / What do you do? / Blues jam / Another life / Just like you.

Aug 92. (7") **TEARING. / EARACHE IN MY EYE (live)** | 54
(12"+=)(cd-s+=) – (There'll be no) Next time / Ghost rider.

Jan 93. (2xcd-box,2xc-box) **BOXED LIFE**

— In early '94, he acted in the film 'The Chase', and was about to be seen in 'Johnny Mnemonic'.

— **MELVIN GIBBS** – bass repl. HASKINS who left in 1993.

Apr 94. (cd)(c)(clear-lp) **WEIGHT** | 22 | 33
– Disconnect / Fool / Icon / Civilized / Divine object of hatred / Liar / Step back / Wrong man / Volume 4 / Tired / Alien blueprint / Shine.

Aug 94. (7")(c-s) **LIAR. / DISCONNECT** | 27
(cd-s+=) – Right here too much / Nightsweat.

– others, imports, etc. –

Eksakt | not issued

Oct 87. Eksakt Dutch; (lp) **HENRY ROLLINS LIVE / GORE LIVE** | - | -

Dec 87. Texas Hotel; (lp) **BIG UGLY MOUTH (spoken word live Feb'87)** | -
(UK-cd-iss.Mar93)

Apr 89. Texas Hotel; (lp-box) **SWEAT BOX** | -
(UK-cd-iss.Mar93)

1989. Texas Hotel; (lp)(cd) **DO IT** | -
– Do it / Move light in / Next time / Joe is everything, everything is Joe / Black and white / Lost and found / Followed around / Wreck age / Lonely / Hot animal machine £1 / You look at you / Gun in mouth blues / Turned out / Thousand times blind / No one. *(re-iss.cd Mar94 on 'Intercord')*

1992. 1/4 Stick/ US= Touch & Go; (lp-box) **DEEP THROAT**

Mar 93. 1/4 Stick/ US= Touch & Go; (cd) **LIVE AT McCABES**

Mar 93. 1/4 Stick/ US= Touch & Go; (cd) **HUMAN BUTT**

Nov 94. Imago; (cd)(c) **HENRY: PORTRAIT OF A SINGER SINGER** (spoken word)

Nov 94. Imago; (cd)(c) **GET IN THE VAN** (life on the road with BLACK FLAG)

Ricky ROSS (see under ⇒ DEACON BLUE)

ROSSINGTON-COLLINS BAND (see under ⇒ LYNYRD SKYNYRD)

Kevin ROWLAND (see under ⇒ DEXY'S MIDNIGHT RUNNERS)

ROXY MUSIC

Formed: Newcastle, England . . . 1970 by art school graduate and teacher BRYAN FERRY with GRAHAM SIMPSON. Early in 1971, they invited ANDY MACKAY and electronic wizard BRIAN ENO, to join. They finally settled with debut album line – up a year later, when they added PHIL MANZANERA. Already signed to 'Island', they issued PETE SINFIELD (King Crimson lyricist) produced debut, which with airplay on John Peel's Radio 1 show, hit UK Top 10. In August '72, they broke into the singles chart with 'VIRGINIA PLAIN', regarded then and now, as an all-time classic. Their follow-up album 'FOR YOUR PLEASURE', made the Top 5, with their second 1973, giving them their first No.1. In the same year, ENO argued with FERRY, and departed for a solo career. FERRY too, also controlled a largely successful solo career side by side with ROXY. When they finally split in 1983, FERRY continued to hit the UK Top 30 with many releases. • **Style:** Moved through futurist experimental, but melodic rock to a more sophisticated rock-pop, highlighting the crooning of the smooth and image conscious FERRY. The inspiration for many 'New wave-futurist' bands of the 80's. • **Songwriters:** FERRY / MANZANERA with contributions from MACKAY and ENO until latter left. Covered IN THE MIDNIGHT HOUR (Wilson Pickett) / EIGHT MILES HIGH (Byrds) / JEALOUS GUY (John Lennon) / LIKE A HURRICANE (Neil Young). FERRY's solo covers:- A HARD RAIN'S A-GONNA FALL (Bob Dylan) / SYMPATHY FOR THE DEVIL (Rolling Stones) / DON'T EVER CHANGE (Crickets) / THESE FOOLISH THINGS (Cole Porter?) / PIECE OF MY HEART (hit; Janis Joplin) / I LOVE HOW YOU LOVE ME (Paris Sisters) / DON'T WORRY BABY (Beach Boys) / TRACKS OF MY TEARS (Miracles) / IT'S MY PARTY (Leslie Gore) / BABY I DON'T CARE (Leiber-Stoller) / WALK A MILE IN MY SHOES (Joe South) / THE IN-CROWD (Dobie Gray) / WHAT A WONDERFUL WORLD (Sam Cooke) / YOU ARE MY SUNSHINE (Ray Charles) / SMOKE GETS IN YOUR EYES (Platters) / HELP ME MAKE IT THROUGH THE NIGHT (Kris Kristofferson) / FINGERPOPPIN' (Hank Ballard) / FUNNY HOW TIME SLIPS AWAY (Jimmy Ellidge) / LET'S STICK TOGETHER (Wilbert Harrison) / THE PRICE OF LOVE (Everly Brothers) / IT'S ONLY LOVE (Barry White) / SHAME SHAME SHAME (Shirley & Company) / HEART ON MY SLEEVE (Gallagher & Lyle) / SHE'S LEAVING HOME + YOU WON'T SEE ME (Beatles) / WHEN SHE WALKS IN THE ROOM (Searchers) / TAKE ME TO THE RIVER (Al Green) / YOU DON'T KNOW (Sam & Dave) / PARTY DOLL (Buddy Knox) / FEEL THE NEED (Detroit Emeralds). Note:- JOHNNY MARR (ex-Smiths) co-wrote THE RIGHT STUFF with him. FERRY returned in 1993 with a covers album #096TAXI'. • **Trivia:** FERRY married model Lucy Helmore on 26 Jun'82, after a 70's relationship with Jerry Hall had finished. He was said to have turned down the Keith Forsey penned song 'DON'T YOU FORGET ABOUT ME', which was a No.1 for SIMPLE MINDS.

Recommended: ROXY MUSIC (*8) / FOR YOUR PLEASURE (*9) / STRANDED (*7) / COUNTRY LIFE (*6) / STREETLIFE (*8).

BRYAN FERRY (b.26 Sep'45, County Durham, England) – vocals, piano / **ANDY MACKAY** (b.23 Jul'46, London, England) – saxophone, oboe, wind inst. / (BRIAN) **ENO** (b.15 May'48, Woodbridge, Suffolk, England) – synthesizers-keys / **GRAHAM SIMPSON** – bass, vocals / **PHIL MANZANERA** (b.31 Jan'51, London) – guitar (ex-QUIET SUN) repl. DAVID O'LIST (ex-NICE) wo had repl. original ROGER BUNN (Jul'71). / **PAUL THOMPSON** (b.13 May'51, Jarrow, Northumberland, England) – drums repl. original DEXTER LLOYD (Jul71).

Island / Reprise

Jun 72. (lp)(c) **ROXY MUSIC** [10] [ ]
– Bitters end / The bob / Chance meeting / If there is something / Ladytron / Re-make/re-model / 2HB / Would you believe? / Sea brrezes. *(re-iss. Feb77 on 'Polydor') (re-iss.+cd.Jan87 on 'EG' +=)* – Virginia Plain. *(re-iss.cd+c.Sep91 on 'EG')*

— (May72) **RIK KENTON** – bass repl. SIMPSON

Aug 72. (7") **VIRGINIA PLAIN. / THE NUMBERER** [4] [ ]

— (Jan73) **JOHN PORTER** – bass repl. KENTON who went solo.

Island / Warners

Mar 73. (7") **PJAMARAMA. / THE PRIDE AND THE PAIN** [10] [ ]
Mar 73. (lp)(c) **FOR YOUR PLEASURE** [4] [ ]
– Do the strand / Beauty queen / Strictly confidential / Editions of you / In every dream home a heartache / The bogus man / Grey lagoons / For your pleasure. *(re-iss.Feb77 on 'Polydor') (re-iss.+cd.Jan87 cd+c.Sep91 on 'EG')*
Jul 73. (7") **DO THE STRAND. / EDITIONS OF YOU** [-] [ ]

— (Jul73) **EDDIE JOBSON** (b.28 Apr'55, Billingham, Teeside, England) – keyboards, violin (ex-CURVED AIR) repl. ENO who went solo.

ROXY MUSIC

session bassmen **JOHN GUSTAFSON** (studio) / **SAL MAIDA** (tour)repl. PORTER (other 5= **FERRY, MANZANERA, MACKAY, JOBSON & THOMPSON)**

Island / Atco

Nov 73. (7") **STREET LIFE. / HULA KULA** [9] [-]
Nov 73. (lp)(c) **STRANDED** [1] [ ]
– Street life / Just like you / Amazona / Psalm / Serenade / A song for Europe / Mother of pearl / Sunset. *(re-iss.Feb77 on 'Polydor') (re-iss.+cd.Jan87, cd+c. Sep91 on 'EG')*

— brought in **JOHN WETTON** – tour bass (ex-FAMILY, ex-KING CRIMSON, etc.) repl. MAIDA

Oct 74. (7") **ALL I WANT IS YOU. / YOUR APPLICATIONS FAILED** [12] [-]
Nov 74. (lp)(c) **COUNTRY LIFE** [3] [37] Jan 75
– The thrill of it all / Three and nine / All I want is you / Out of the blue / If it takes all night / Bitter-sweet / Triptych / Casanova / A really good time / Prairie rose. *(re-iss.Feb77 on 'Polydor') (re-iss.+cd.Jan87, cd+c.Sep91 on 'EG')*
Nov 74. (7") **THE THRILL OF IT ALL. / YOUR APPLICATIONS FAILED** [-] [ ]
Sep 75. (7") **LOVE IS THE DRUG. / SULTANESQUE** [2] [-]
Oct 75. (lp)(c) **SIREN** [4] [50]
– Love is the drug / End of the line / Sentimental fool / Whirlwind / She sells / Could it hapen to me / Both ends burning / Nightingale / Just another high. *(re-iss.Feb77 on 'Polydor') (re-iss.+cd.Jan87, cd+c.Sep91 on 'EG')*
Dec 75. (7") **BOTH ENDS BURNING. / FOR YOUR PLEASURE** [25] [ ]
Dec 75. (7") **LOVE IS THE DRUG. / BOTH ENDS BURNING** [-] [30]

— **RICK WILLS** – tour bass repl. WETTON who stayed on with FERRY (see below)

— Disbanded officially mid'76, leaving behind one more album

Jul 76. (lp)(c) **VIVA! ROXY MUSIC (live 1973-1975)** [6] [81]
– Out of the blue / Pjamarama / The bogus man / Chance meeting / Both ends burning / If there is something / In every dream home a heartache / Do the strand. *(re-iss.Feb77 on 'Polydor') (re-iss.+cd.Jan87, cd+c.Sep91 on 'EG')*

— After split ANDY MACKAY continued solo work, as did PHIL MANZANERA. EDDIE JOBSON joined FRANK ZAPPA.

BRYAN FERRY

also had simultaneous solo career. (same labels). He used various session people, including many members of ROXY MUSIC.

Sep 73. (7") **A HARD RAIN'S GONNA FALL. / 2HB** [4] [ ]
Oct 73. (lp)(c) **THESE FOOLISH THINGS** [5] [ ]
– A hard rain's a-gonna fall / River of salt / Don't ever change / Piece of my heart / Baby I don't care / It's my party / Don't worry baby / Sympathy for the Devil / Tracks of my tears / You won't see me / I love how you love me / Loving you is sweeter than ever / These foolish things. *(re-iss.+cd.Aug84 on 'Polydor') (re-iss.+cd.Jan87, cd+c.Sep91 on 'EG')*
May 74. (7") **THE IN-CROWD. / CHANCE MEETING** [13] [-]
Jul 74. (lp)(c) **ANOTHER TIME, ANOTHER PLACE** [4] [ ]
– The in-crowd / Smoke gets in your eyes / Walk a mile in my shoes / Funny how time slips away / You are my sunshine / (What a) Wonderful world / It ain't me babe / Fingerpoppin' / Help me make it through the night. *(re-iss.+cd.Aug84 on 'Polydor') (re-iss.+cd.Jan87, cd+c.Sep91 on 'EG')*
Aug 74. (7") **SMOKE GETS IN YOUR EYES. / ANOTHER TIME, ANOTHER PLACE** [17] [-]
Jun 75. (7") **YOU GO TO MY HEAD. / RE-MAKE RE-MODEL** [ ] [-]

— Solo again, with ex-ROXY MUSIC men **PAUL THOMPSON + JOHN WETTON**. Added **CHRIS SPEDDING** – guitar (ex-SHARKS)

Island / Atlantic

Jun 76. (7") **LET'S STICK TOGETHER. / SEA BREEZES** [4] [ ]
Aug 76. (7"ep) **EXTENDED PLAY** [7] [-]
– The price of love / Shame shame shame / Heart on my sleeve / It's only love.
Sep 76. (lp)(c) **LET'S STICK TOGETHER** [19] [ ]
– Let's stick together / Casanova / Sea breeze / Shame shame shame / 2HB / The price of love / Chance meeting / It's only love / You go to my head / Re-make/re-model / Heart on my sleeve. *(re-iss.+cd.Aug84 on 'Polydor') (re-iss.+cd.Jan87, cd+c.Sep91 on 'EG')*
Oct 76. (7") **HEART ON MY SLEEVE. / RE-MAKE/RE-MODEL** [-] [ ]

— added **PHIL MANZANERA** – guitar / **ANN ODELL** – keyboards / **MEL COLLINS** – sax/ plus many backing singers.

Polydor / Atlantic

Jan 77. (7") **THIS IS TOMORROW. / AS THE WORLD TURNS** [9] [ ]
Feb 77. (lp)(c) **IN YOUR MIND** [5] [ ]
– This is tomorrow / All night operator / One kiss / Love me madly again / Tokyo Joe / Party doll / Rock of ages / In your mind. *(re-iss.+cd.Jan87, cd+c.Sep91 on 'EG')*
Apr 77. (7") **TOKYO JOE. / SHE'S LEAVING HOME** [15] [-]
Jun 77. (7") **TOKYO JOE. / AS THE WORLD TURNS** [-] [ ]

— FERRY continued to use many different musicians, too many to mention.

Apr 78. (7") **WHAT GOES ON. / CASANOVA** [67] [ ]
Apr 78. (lp)(c) **THE BRIDE STRIPPED BARE** [13] [ ]
– Sign of the times / Can't let go / Hold on (I'm coming) / The same old blues / When she walks in the room / Take me to the river / What goes on / Carrickfergus / That's how strong my love is / This island Earth. *(re-iss.Jan87, cd+c.Sep91 on 'EG')*
Jul 78. (7") **SIGN OF THE TIMES. / FOUR LETTER LOVE** [37] [-]
Nov 78. (7") **SIGN OF THE TIMES. / CAN'T LET GO** [-] [ ]
Nov 78. (7") **CARRICKFERGUS. / WHEN SHE WALKS IN THE ROOM** [ ] [ ]

ROXY MUSIC

re-formed with **FERRY, MANZANERA, MACKAY, THOMPSON,** plus **PAUL CARRACK** – studio keyboards (ex-ACE) / **DAVID SKINNER** – tour keyboards / **GARY TIBBS** – bass (ex-VIBRATORS)

Polydor / Atco

Feb 79. (7") **TRASH. / TRASH 2** [40] [-]
Mar 79. (lp)(c)(pic-lp) **MANIFESTO** [7] [23]
– Manifesto / Trash / Angel eyes / Still falls the rain / Stronger through the years / Ain't that so / My little girl / ance away / Cry cry cry / Spin me round. *(re-iss.+cd.Jan87, cd+c.Sep91 on 'EG'+=)* – Angel eyes (12"disco version).
Apr 79. (7") **DANCE AWAY. / CRY CRY CRY** [2] [-]
Apr 79. (7") **DANCE AWAY. / TRASH 2** [-] [44]
Aug 79. (7")(disco-12") **ANGEL EYES. / MY LITTLE GIRL** [4] [ ]
May 80. (7") **OVER YOU. / MANIFESTO** [5] [-]
May 80. (lp)(c) **FLESH + BLOOD** [1] [35]
– In the midnight hour / Oh yeah (on the radio) / Same old scene / Flesh and blood / My only love / Over you / Eight miles high / Rain rain rain / No strange delight / Running wild. *(re-iss.+cd.Jan87, cd+c.Sep91 on 'EG')*
May 80. (7") **OVER YOU. / MY ONLY LOVE** [-] [80]
Jul 80. (7") **OH YEAH (ON THE RADIO). / SOUTH DOWNS** [5] [ ]
Nov 80. (7") **SAME OLD SCENE. / LOVER** [12] [-]
Dec 80. (7") **IN THE MIDNIGHT HOUR. /** [-] [ ]

— Earlier 1980, CARRACK joined SQUEEZE, and TIBBS joined ADAM & THE ANTS. Session men used at the time **NEIL HUBBARD** – guitar / **ALAN SPENNER** – bass / **ANDY NEWMARK** – drums repl. THOMPSON

Feb 81. (7") **JEALOUS GUY. / TO TURN YOU ON** [1] [ ]
Apr 82. (7") **MORE THAN THIS. / INDIA** [6] [-]
May 82. (lp)(c) **AVALON** [1] [53]
– More than this / The space between / India / While my heart is still beating / Main thing / Take a chance with me / Avalon / To turn you on / True to life / Tara. *(re-iss.+cd.Jan87 on 'EG')*
Jun 82. (7") **AVALON. / ALWAYS UNKNOWING** [13] [ ]
Sep 82. (7")(12") **TAKE A CHANCE WITH ME. / THE MAIN THING** [26] [-]
Sep 82. (7") **TAKE A CHANCE ON ME. / INDIA** [-] [ ]
Nov 82. (7") **MORE THAN THIS. / ALWAYS UNKNOWING** [-] [ ]

— added **GUY FLETCHER + JIMMY MAELEN** – keys / **MICHELLE COBBS + TAWATHA AGEE**

Mar 83. (m-lp)(c) **THE HIGH ROAD (live)** [26] [67]
– Can't let go / My only love / Like a hurricane / Jealous guy.

— Had already disbanded again late 1982. MANZANERA and MACKAY became The EXPLORERS, and FERRY went solo again (see further on).

BRYAN FERRY

solo again.

E.G. Warners

May 85. (7") **SLAVE TO LOVE. / VALENTINE (instrumental)** 10
(12"+=) – ('A'instrumental).
Jun 85. (lp)(c)(cd) **BOYS AND GIRLS** 1 63
– Sensation / Slave to love / Don't stop the dance / A wasteland / Windswept / The chosen one / Valentine / Stone woman / Boys and girls. *(re-iss.cd+c.Sep91)*
Aug 85. (7") **DON'T STOP THE DANCE. / NOCTURNE** 21
(12"+=) – Windswept (instrumental).
Nov 85. (7")(7"pic-d) **WINDSWEPT. / CRAZY LOVE** 46
(12"+=) – Feel the need / Broken wings.
Mar 86. (7") **IS YOUR LOVE STRONG ENOUGH. / WINDSWEPT (instrumental)** 22
(12"+=) – ('A'mix).
Jul 86. (7") **HELP ME. / BROKEN WINGS** -

EG-Virgin Reprise

Sep 87. (7")(12") **THE RIGHT STUFF. / ('A'instrumental)** 37
(c-s+=)(cd-s+=) – ('A'extended) / ('A'dub version).
Nov 87. (lp)(c)(cd) **BETE NOIRE** 9 63
– Limbo / Kiss and tell / New town / Day for night / Zamba / The right stuff / Seven deadly sins / The name of the game / Bete noire. *(cd-re-iss.Dec88)*
Feb 88. (7") **KISS AND TELL. / ZAMBA** 41 31
(12"+=)(cd-s+=) – ('A'&'B'remixes).
Jun 88. (7") **LIMBO (Latin mix). / BETE NOIRE (instrumental)**
(12"+=)(cd-s+=) – ('A'mix).
Feb 93. (7")(c-s) **I PUT A SPELL ON YOU. / THESE FOOLISH THINGS** 18
(cd-s+=) – Ladytron (live) / While my heart is still beating (live).
Mar 93. (cd)(c)(lp) **TAXI** 2 79
– I put a spell on you / Will you love me tomorrow / Answer me / Just one look / Rescue me / All tomorrow's parties / Girl of my best friend / Amazing Grace / Taxi / Because you're mine.
May 93. (7")(c-s) **WILL YOU LOVE ME TOMMOROW. / A HARD RAIN'S AGONNA FALL** 23
(cd-s+=) – A wasteland (live) / Windswept (live).
(cd-s) – ('A'side) / Crazy love / Feel the need / When she walks in the room.
Aug 93. (c-s) **GIRL OF MY BEST FRIEND /** 57
(cd-s) – Nocturne / Are you lonesome tonight? / Valentine.
(cd-s) – Let's stick together / Boys and girls (live) / The bogus man (live).

— now with a plethora of musicians **BRIAN ENO, PHIL MANZANERA, ANDY MACKAY, STEVE FERRONE, NEIL HUBBARD, NATHAN EAST, NILE RODGERS, ROBIN TROWER, GUY FLETCHER, PINO PALLADINO, CARLEEN ANDERSON, LUKE CRESSWELL, RHETT DAVIES, YANNICK ETIENNE, LUIS JARDIM, NEIL JASON, JHELISA, PAUL JOHNSON, CHESTER KAMEN, NAN KIDWELL, MIKE PAICE, MACEO PARKER, GUY PRATT, RICHARD T. NORRIS, STEVE SCALES, DAVID WILLIAMS, JEFF THALL + FONZI THORNTON**

Sep 94. (cd)(c) **MAMOUNA** 11 94
– Don't want to know / N.Y.C. / Your painted smile / Mamouna / The only face / The 39 steps / Which way to turn / Wildcat days / Gemini Moon / Chain reaction.
Oct 94. (7")(c-s) **YOUR PAINTED SMILE. / DON'T STOP THE DANCE**
(cd-s+=) – In every dream home a heartache (live) / Bete noire (live).
Feb 95. (7")(c-s) **MAMOUNA. / THE 39 STEPS (Brian Eno mix)** 57
(cd-s+=) – Jealous guy (live) / Slave to love (live).

– (FERRY) compilations, others, etc. –

Jun 88. EG; (3"cd-ep) **LET'S STICK TOGETHER / SHAME SHAME SHAME / CHANCE MEETING / SEA BREEZES** -
Oct 88. EG; (7") **LET'S STICK TOGETHER ('88 remix). / TRASH** 12
(12"+=) – Shame shame shame / Angel eyes.
(cd-s+=) – Casanova / Sign of the times.
Nov 88. EG/ US= Reprise; (lp)(c)(cd)(pic-lp) **THE ULTIMATE COLLECTION ("BRYAN FERRY & ROXY MUSIC")** 6
– Let's stick together ('88 remix) / The in-crowd / Angel eyes (ROXY MUSIC) / He'll have to go / Tokyo Joe / All I want is you (ROXY MUSIC) / Jealous guy (ROXY MUSIC) / The price of love / Don't stop the dance / Love is the drug (ROXY MUSIC) / This is tomorrow / Slave to love / Help me / Avalon (ROXY MUSIC) / Dance away (ROXY MUSIC).
Feb 89. EG; (7") **THE PRICE OF LOVE (R&B mix). / LOVER** 49
(12"+=) – Don't stop the dance (remix) / Nocturne.
(cd-s+=) – Don't stop the dance (remix) / Slave to love (remix).
Apr 89. EG; (7") **HE'LL HAVE TO GO. / CARRICKFERGUS** 63
(12") – ('A'side) / Windswept / Is your love strong enough.
(cd-s+=) – Take me to the river / Broken wings.
Dec 89. EG; (3xlp-box)(3xc-box)(3xcd-box) **THESE FOOLISH THINGS / LET'S STICK TOGETHER / BOYS AND GIRLS** (free w / Island Various Artists compilations) -
Oct 95. Virgin; (cd)(c)(d-lp) **MORE THAN THIS – THE BEST OF BRYAN FERRY & ROXY MUSIC** 15

– (ROXY MUSIC) compilations, etc. –

Oct 77. Polydor/ US= Atco; (7") **VIRGINIA PLAIN. / PJAMARAMA** 11
Nov 77. Polydor/ US= Atco; (lp)(c) **GREATEST HITS** 20
– Virginia Plain / Do the strand / All I want is you / Out of the blue / Pjamarama / Editions of you / Love is the drug / Mother of pearl / Song for Europe / Thrill of it all / Street life. *(re-iss.+cd.Jan87 on 'EG')*
Jan 78. Polydor; (7")(12") **DO THE STRAND. / EDITIONS OF YOU** -
Dec 81. EG; (7xlp-box) **BOXED SET** (all albums exc.'Viva') -
Nov 83. EG; (lp)(c)(cd) **THE ATLANTIC YEARS 1973-1980** 23
Apr 86. EG/ US= Reprise; (d-lp)(c)(cd) **STREETLIFE (as "BRYAN FERRY & ROXY MUSIC")** 1 100 Aug 89
– Virginia plain / A hard rain's a-gonna fall (BRYAN FERRY) / Pjamarama / Do the strand / These foolish things (BRYAN FERRY) / Street life / Let's stick together (BRYAN FERRY) / Smoke gets in your eyes (BRYAN FERRY) / Love is the drug / Sign of the times (BRYAN FERRY) / Dance away / Angel eyes / Oh yeah / Over you / Same old scene / The midnight hour / More than this / Avalon / Slave to love (BRYAN FERRY) / Jealous guy.
Jun 88. EG; (3"cd-ep) **JEALOUS GUY / LOVER / SOUTHDOWN**
Dec 89. EG; (3xlp)(3xc)(3xcd) **THE EARLY YEARS**
– (ROXY MUSIC / FOR YOUR PLEASURE / STRANDED albums)
Dec 89. EG; (3xlp)(3xc)(3xcd) **THE LATER YEARS**
– (MANIFESTO / FLESH AND BLOOD / AVALON albums)
Oct 90. EG; (cd)(c)(d-lp) **HEART STILL BEATIN' (live in France '82)**
Oct 90. EG; (7") **LOVE IS THE DRUG (live). / EDITIONS OF YOU (live)** -
(12"+=)(cd-s+=) – Do the strand (live).
Oct 94. EG; (3xcd-box) **THE COMPACT COLLECTION**
Nov 95. Virgin; (4xcd-box) **THE THRILL OF IT ALL – ROXY MUSIC 1972-1982**
Jan-Jun'96 stop press . . .
Apr 96. Virgin: (single) **LOVE IS THE DRUG (remix)** 33

ANDY MACKAY

Island not issued

Jun 74. (lp)(c) **IN SEARCH OF EDDIE RIFF** -
– The end of the world / Walking the whippet / What becomes of the broken-hearted / An die musik / The hour before dawn / Past, present and future * / Ride of the Valkyries / Summer Sun * / A four-legged friend *. *(re-iss.Feb77 on 'Polydor'* tracks* repl. by) – Wild weekend / Pyramid of night / Time regained / The long and winding road.
Aug 74. (7") **WILD WEEKEND. / WALKING THE WHIPPET** -

— In 1976-77, MACKAY wrote music for hit UK No.1 TV series 'ROCK FOLLIES'.

Bronze not issued

Oct 78. (lp)(c) **RESOLVING CONTRADICTIONS** -
– Iron blossom / Trumpets on the mountains / Off to work / Unreal city / The Loyang tractor factory / Rivers / Battersea Rise / Skill and sweat / The Ortolan bunting (a sparrow's fall) / The inexorable sequence / A song of friendship (the Renmin hotel) / Medley: Alloy blossom – Trumpets in the Sabu – Green and gold. *(re-iss.+cd.Nov90 on 'Expression')*
Oct 78. (7") **A SONG FOR FRIENDSHIP. / SKILL AND SWEAT** -

PHIL MANZANERA

Island Atco

May 75. (lp)(c) **DIAMOND HEAD** 40
– Frontera / Diamond head / Big day / The flex / Same time next week / Miss Shapiro / East of echo / Lagrima / Alma. *(re-iss.Mar77 on 'Polydor') (re-iss. 1980 on 'EG', cd-iss.1988)*

QUIET SUN

formed earlier by **MANZANERA, DAVE JARRETT** – keyboards / **BILL McCORMICK** – bass / **CHARLES HAYWARD** – drums

Help-Island Antilees

Aug 75. (lp)(c) **MAINSTREAM**
– Sol Caliente / Trumpets with motherhood / Trot / Rongwrong / Bargain classics / R.F.D. / Mummy was an asteroid, daddy was a small non-stick kitchen utensil. *(re-iss.Oct77 on 'Polydor') (re-iss.+cd.Jan87 on 'EG')*

801

featured **MANZANERA, McCORMICK, ENO** plus **LLOYD WATSON** – guitar / **FRANCIS MONKMAN** – piano, clarinet (ex-CURVED AIR) / **SIMON PHILLIPS** – drums

Island Polydor

Oct 76. (lp)(c) **801 LIVE (live)**
– Lagima / T.N.K. (Tomorrow Never Knows) / East of asteroid / Rongwrong / Sombre reptiles / Baby's on fire / Diamond head / Miss Shapiro / You really got

me / Third uncle. *(re-iss.Feb77 on 'Polydor') (re-iss.+cd.Jan87 on 'EG')*

— retained **McCORMICK**, and brought in **PAUL THOMPSON** – drums (ROXY MUSIC) **SIMON AINLEY** – guitar, vocals / **DAVID SKINNER** – keyboards, vocals / etc.

Polydor Polydor

Sep 77. (7") **FLIGHT 19. / CAR RHUMBA** [ ] [-]
Oct 77. (lp)(c) **LISTEN NOW!** [ ] [ ]
– Listen now / Flight 19 / Island / Law and order / ? Que ? / City of light / Initial speed / Postcard love / That falling feeling. *(re-iss.+cd.Jan87 on 'EG')*
Nov 77. (7") **FLIGHT 19. / INITIAL SPEED** [-] [ ]

PHIL MANZANERA

went solo again, using past QUIET SUN + 801 members.

Nov 78. (lp)(c) **K-SCOPE** [ ] [ ]
– K-scope / Remote control / Cuban crisis / Hot spot / Numbers / Slow motion T.V. / Gone flying / N-shift / Walking through Heaven's door / You are here.
Nov 78. (7") **REMOTE CONTROL. / K-SCOPE** [ ] [-]

E.G. not issued

Mar 82. (lp)(c) **PRIMITIVE GUITARS** [ ] [-]
– Criollo / Caracas / La nueva ola / Bogota / Ritmo de Los Angeles / Europe 70-1 / Impossible guitar / Europe 80-1. *(re-iss.Jan87 on 'Editions-EG')*
Apr 87. (lp)(c)(cd) **GUITARISSMO** (compilation) [ ] [-]
(cd-iss.3 extra tracks)

Expression not issued

May 90. (7") **A MILLION REASONS WHY. / SOUTHERN CROSS** [ ] [-]
(12"+=) – Blood brother.
Jun 90. (cd)(c)(lp) **SOUTHERN CROSS** [ ] [-]
– A million reasons why / Tambor / The great leveller / Astrud / Southern cross / Guantanemera / Rich and poor / Verde / Dr.Fidel / Venceremos.
May 95. Virgin; (cd) **THE MANZANERA COLLECTION** (compilation) [ ] [-]

The EXPLORERS

PHIL MANZANERA / ANDY MACKAY plus **JAMES WRAITH** – vocals (ex-FLYING TIGERS)

Virgin Virgin?

Jun 84. (7")(12") **LORELEI. / YOU GO UP IN SMOKE** [ ] [ ]
Oct 84. (7")(12") **FALLING FOR NIGHTLIFE. / CRACK THE WHIP** [ ] [ ]
Apr 85. (7") **TWO WORLDS APART. / IT ALWAYS RAINS IN PARADISE** [ ] [ ]
(12"+=) – Voodoo isle.
May 85. (lp)(c)(cd) **THE EXPLORERS** [ ] [ ]
– Ship of fools / Lorelei / Breath of life / Venus de Milo / Soul fantasy / Prussian blue / Two worlds apart / Robert Louis Stevenson / You go up in smoke.
Jun 85. (7")(12") **VENUS DE MILO. / ANOTHER LOST SOUL ON THE RUN** [ ] [ ]

PHIL MANZANERA & ANDY MACKAY

retained **WRAITH**

Expression not issued

Nov 90. (cd)(c)(lp) **MANZANERA & MACKAY** [ ] [-]
– Black gang chime / Free yourself / Built for speed / Many are the ways / I can be tender / Dreams of the East / Sacrosanct / Every kind of stone / Man with extraordinary ways / Safe in the arms of love / Forgotten man.

RTZ (see under ⇒ BOSTON)

Todd RUNDGREN

Born: 22 Jun'48, Upper Derby, Philadelphia, USA. In 1967, he and another ex-WOODY'S TRUCK STOP member CARSTEN VAN OSTEN formed The NAZZ, taking group name from a YARDBIRDS B-side. In 1968 after supporting The DOORS a year earlier, they signed to 'Screen Gems/Columbia'. Their eponymous debut album sold moderately, and RUNDGREN left band mid-69, after 2 more were completed. In 1970, he became an in-house producer for Albert Grossman's 'Bearsville', his first job being for The AMERICAN DREAM. Later in the year, he formed own band 'RUNT' (his nickname), and released RUNT, which fathered his first Top 20 hit 'WE GOTTA GET YOU A WOMAN'. After one more album, he decided to use his own name for further releases. In 1972, after taking over the production duties from GEORGE HARRISON on BADFINGER's 'Straight Up' lp, he unleashed a truly wonderful solo work 'SOMETHING/ANYTHING'. The double album reached US No.29, with a cut from it 'I SAW THE LIGHT' making the Top 20 US & a year later Top 40 in UK. He continued solo and production work, and even formed another outfit 'UTOPIA', to develop a more mystical lyrical side to his genius. • **Style:** Multi-talented rock star, progressing from NAZZ's metal psychedelia into solo experimentation that went from extreme avant-garde to pop/soul pastiche. • **Songwriters:** Phenomenal pensmith, although he did fit in a number of near perfect covers; DO YA (Move) / GOOD VIBRATIONS (Beach Boys) / LOVE OF THE COMMON MAN (from West Side Story?) / MOST LIKELY TO GO YOUR WAY (Bob Dylan) / TIN SOLDIER (Small Faces) / STRAWBERRY FIELDS FOREVER + RAIN (Beatles) / IF SIX WAS NINE (Jimi Hendrix) / HAPPENINGS TEN YEARS TIME AGO (Yardbirds) / etc? • **Trivia:** In 1983, TODD co-wrote the Top 20 hit 'KISSING WITH CONFIDENCE' for WILL POWERS (see under Carly SIMON). TODD's others major productions have included GRAND FUNK (1973) / HALL & OATES (1974) / MEAT LOAF (Bat Out Of Hell) / TOM ROBINSON (1978) / TUBES (1979) / PSYCHEDELIC FURS (1982) / etc. Note:- TODD has just released in 1992 a compilation album of his production work.

Recommended: SOMETHING / ANYTHING (*9) / INITIATION (*8) / THE COLLECTION (UTOPIA; *7) / THE EVER POPULAR TORTURED ARTIST (*7) / ANTHOLOGY (*8) / RA (*7)

NAZZ

TODD RUNDGREN – lead guitar, vocals, composer / **ROBERT 'Stewkey' ANTONI** (b.17 Nov'47, Rhode Island, USA) – vocals, piano / **CARSTEN VAN OSTEN** (b.24 Sep'46, New Jersey, USA) – bass, vocals / **THOM MOONEY** (b. 5 Jan'48, Pennsylvania, USA) – drums

Screen Gems Screen Gem

Sep 68. (7") **OPEN MY EYES. / HELLO IT'S ME** [ ] [71]
Oct 68. (lp) **NAZZ** [-] [ ]
– Back of your mind / Open my eyes / When I get my plane / If that's the way you feel / Hello it's me / Wildwood blues / She's going down / The lemming song / etc. *(US re-iss.Oct83 on 'Rhino')*
Apr 69. (7") **HELLO IT'S ME. / CROWDED** [ ] [66]
May 69. (lp)(red-lp) **NAZZ NAZZ** [-] [80]
– Forget all about it / Not wrong long / Rain rider / Gonna cry today / Meridian Leeward / Under the ice / Hang on Paul / Kiddie boy / Featherbedding lover / Letters don't count / A beautiful song. *(US re-iss.Oct83 on 'Rhino')*
May 69. (7") **UNDER THE ICE. / NOT WRONG LONG** [ ] [ ]
1970. (7") **SOME PEOPLE (or) KIDS. / MAGIC ME** [-] [ ]
Dec 70. (lp,green-lp) **NAZZ III** [-] [ ]
– You are my window / Old time lovemaking / Loosen up / Kicks / Take the hand / How can you call that beautiful / Only one winner / etc. *(US re-iss.Nov83 on 'Rhino')*

— Had already disbanded early 1970, after completion of III'rd album.

RUNT

was formed by **RUNDGREN** now on – lead vocals, guitar / **TONY SALES** – bass / **HUNT SALES** – drums

not issued Ampex

Nov 70. (7") **WE GOTTA GET YOU A WOMAN. / BABY LET'S SWING** [-] [20]
Dec 70. (lp) **RUNT** [-] [ ]
– Broke down and busted / Believe in me / We gotta get you a woman / Who's that man / Once burned / Devil's bite / I'm in the cliche / There are no words / Baby let's swing / The last thing you said / Don't tie my hands / Birthday carol. *(UK-iss.Apr72 on 'Bearsville') (US re-iss.Oct87 on 'Rhino') (re-iss.cd May93 on 'Rhino-Bearsville')*

— **N.D.SMART** – drums repl. HUNT who later joined IGGY POP then TIN MACHINE

May 71. (7") **BE NICE TO ME. / BROKE DOWN AND BUSTED** [-] [71]
May 71. (lp) **THE BALLAD OF TODD RUNDGREN** [-] [ ]
– Long flowing robe / The ballad / Bleeding / Wailing wall / The range war / Chain letter / A long time, a long way to go / Boat on the Charles / Be nice to me / Hope I'm around / Parole / Remember me. *(UK-iss.Apr72 on 'Bearsville') (US re-iss.Oct87 on 'Rhino') (re-iss.cd May93 on 'Rhino-Bearsville')*
Aug 71. (7") **A LONG TIME, A LONG WAY TO GO. / PAROLE** [-] [92]

TODD RUNDGREN

now completely solo except for one side of the d-lp which was frequented by session people.

Bearsville Bearsville

Mar 72. (d-lp) **SOMETHING / ANYTHING?** [ ] [29]
– I saw the light / It wouldn't have made any difference / Wolfman Jack / Cold morning light / It takes two to tango (this is for the girls) / Sweeter memories / (intro) Breathless / The night the carousel burned down / Saving grace / Marlene / Song of the Viking / I went to the mirror / Black Maria / One more day (one word) /

Couldn't I just tell you / Torch song / Little red lights / Dust in the wind / Piss Aaron / Hello it's me / Some folks is even whiter than me / You left me sore / Slut. *(US re-iss.Nov87 on 'Rhino') (d-cd-iss. Jul89 on 'Essential') (re-iss.cd Jun93 on 'Rhino-Bearsville')*

Mar 72. (7") **I SAW THE LIGHT. / BLACK MARIA** [-] [16]
Mar 72. (7") **I SAW THE LIGHT. / MARLENE** [ ] [-]
Jul 72. (7") **COULDN'T I JUST TELL YOU. / WOLFMAN JACK** [-] [93]
May 73. (7"m) **I SAW THE LIGHT. / BLACK MARIA / LONG FLOWING ROBE** *(re-iss.Nov76)* [36] [-]
Jun 73. (lp) **A WIZARD, A TRUE STAR** [ ] [86]
– International feel / Never never land / Tic tic tic it wear off / You need your head / Rock and roll pussy / Dogfight giggle / You don't have to camp around / Flamingo / Zen archer / Just another onionhead – Da da Dali / When the shit hits the fan – Sunset Blvd. / Le feel internacionale / Sometimes I don't know what to feel / Does anybody love you? / I'm so proud – Ooh ooh baby – La la means I love you – Cool jerk / Is it my name? / Just one victory. *(re-iss.Nov80 on 'Island') (re-iss.+cd.1987 on 'Castle') (re-iss.cd May93 on 'Rhino-Bearsville')*
Jul 73. (7") **SOMETIMES I DON'T KNOW WHAT TO FEEL. / DOES ANYONE LOVE YOU?** [-] [ ]
Oct 73. (7") **WE GOTTA GET YOU A WOMAN. / COULDN'T I JUST TELL YOU** [ ] [-]
Dec 73. (7") **HELLO IT'S ME. / COLD MORNING LIGHT** [ ] [5] Sep 73.

— He now used many musicians that were to appear as first UTOPIA incarnation

Mar 74. (d-lp) **TODD** [ ] [54]
– How about a little fanfare? / I hink you know / The spark of life / An elpee's worth of toons / A dream goes on forever / Lord Chancelor's nightmare song / Drunken blue rooster / The last ride / Everybody's going to Heaven / King Kong reggae / Number one lowest common denominator / Useless begging / Sidewalk cafe / Izzat love / Heavy metal kids / In and out of Chakras we go / Don't you ever learn / Sons of 1984. *(re-iss.+cd.Dec89 on 'Castle') (re-iss.cd May93 on 'Rhino-Bearsville')*
May 74. (7") **A DREAM GOES ON FOREVER. / HEAVY METAL KIDS** [ ] [69]

— **TODD** formed UTOPIA with **MOODY KLINGMAN** – keyboards / **RALPH SHUCKETT** – bass / **JOHN SIEGLER** – bass, cello / **M.FROG LABAT** – synthesizers

Nov 74. (lp)(c) **TODD RUNDGREN'S UTOPIA ("TODD RUNDGREN'S UTOPIA")** [ ] [34]
– Utopia (theme) / Freak parade / Freedom fighter / The ikon. *(re-iss.cd May93 on 'Rhino-Bearsville')*
Jun 75. (lp)(c) **INITIATION ("TODD RUNDGREN")** [ ] [86]
– Real man / Born to synthesize / The death of rock and roll / Eastern intrigue / Initiation / Fair warning / A treatise on cosmic fire (intro- Prana): (a) The fire of mind or solar fire – (b) The fire of spirit or electric fire – (c) The internal fire or fire by friction / (outro- Prana). *(re-iss.cd May93 on 'Rhino-Bearsville')*
Sep 75. (7") **REAL MAN. / PRANA ("TODD RUNDGREN")** [ ] [83]

— trimmed slightly when LABAT departed.

Oct 75. (lp)(c) **ANOTHER LIVE (live "TODD RUNDGREN'S UTOPIA")** [ ] [66]
– Another life / The wheel / The seven rays / (intro) – Mister Triscuts / West Side Story theme / Something's coming / Just one victory / Heavy metal kids / Do ya / Just one victory. *(re-iss.cd Aug93 on 'Rhino-Bearsville')*
Apr 76. (lp)(c) **FAITHFULL ("TODD RUNDGREN")** [ ] [54]
– Happenings ten years time ago / Good vibrations / Rain / Most likely you go your way and I'll go mine / If six was nine / Strawberry fields forever / Black and white / Love of the common man / When I pray / Cliche / The verb "to love" / Boogies (hamburger hell). *(re-iss.cd Jun93 on 'Rhino-Bearsville')*
Jun 76. (7") **GOOD VIBRATIONS. / LOVE OF THE COMMON MAN** [ ] [-]
Jun 76. (7") **GOOD VIBRATIONS. / WHEN I PRAY** [-] [34]
Nov 76. (7") **LOVE OF THE COMMON MAN. / BLACK AND WHITE** [-] [ ]

UTOPIA

with **TODD** now completely changed line-up into **ROGER POWELL** – keyboards (from late '75) / **JOHN 'Willie' WILCOX** – drums / **KASIM SULTON** – bass

Jan 77. (lp)(c) **RA** [27] [79]
– (overture) / Communion with the sun / Magig dragon theatre / Jealousy / Eternal love / Sunburst finish / Hiroshima / Singing and the glass guitar. *(re-iss.cd May93 on 'Rhino-Bearsville')*
Feb 77. (7") **COMMUNION WITH THE SUN. / SUNBURST FINISH** [ ] [ ]

— TODD played/produced 'BAT OUT OF HELL' album for MEAT LOAF, which included some UTOPIANS and was massive seller from 1978 onwards.

Sep 77. (lp)(c) **OOPS! WRONG PLANET** [59] [73]
– Trapped / Windows / Love in action / Crazy lady blue / Back on the street / Marriage of Heaven and Hell / The martyr / Abandon city / Gangrene / My angel / Rape of the young / Love is the answer. *(re-iss.cd Jun93 on 'Rhino-Bearsville')*
Oct 77. (7") **LOVE IS THE ANSWER. / THE MARRIAGE OF HEAVEN AND HELL** [ ] [ ]

TODD RUNDGREN

Apr 78. (lp)(c) **HERMIT OF MINK HOLLOW** [42] [36]
– All the children sing / Can we still be friends / Hurting for you / Too far gone / Onomatopoeia / Determination / Bread / Bag lady / You cried wolf / Lucky guy / Out of control / Fade away. *(re-iss.Nov80 on 'Island') (re-iss.cd May93 on 'Rhino-Bearsville')*
May 78. (7") **CAN WE STILL BE FRIENDS. / DETERMINATION** [ ] [29]
(some US copies had 'OUT OF CONTROL' on B-side)
Jul 78. (7") **YOU CRIED WOLF. / ONOMATOPOEIA** [-] [ ]
Nov 78. (7") **ALL THE CHILDREN SING. / BAG LADY** [ ] [ ]
Dec 78. (d-lp)(c) **BACK TO THE BARS (live)** [ ] [75]
– Real man / Love of the common man / The verb "to love" / Love in action / A dream goes on forever / Sometimes I just don't know what to think / The range war / Black and white / The last ride / Cliche / Don't you ever learn / Never never land / Black Maria / Zen archer / Medley: I'm so proud – Ooh ooh baby – La la means I love you / I saw the light / It wouldn't have made any difference / Eastern intrigue / Initiation / Couldn't I just tell you / Hello it's me. *(re-iss.cd Jun93 on 'Rhino-Bearsville')*
Feb 79. (7") **IT WOULDN'T HAVE MADE ANY DIFFERENCE. / DON'T YOU EVER LEARN** [-] [ ]

UTOPIA

Island Bearsville

Jan 80. (lp)(c) **ADVENTURES IN UTOPIA** [57] [32]
– The road to Utopia / You make me crazy / Second nature / Set me free / Caravan / Last of the new wave riders / Shot in the dark / The very last time / Love alone / Rock love. *(re-iss.cd May93 on 'Rhino-Bearsville')*
Mar 80. (7") **SET ME FREE. / THE UMBRELLA MAN** [ ] [27]
May 80. (7") **THE VERY LAST TIME. / LOVE ALONE** [-] [76]
Oct 80. (lp)(c) **DEFACE THE MUSIC** [ ] [65]
– I just want to touch you / Crystal ball / Where does the world go to hide / Silly boy / Alone / That's not right / Take it home / Hoi poloi / Life goes on / Feel too good / Always late / All smiles / Everybody else is wrong. *(re-iss.cd May93 on 'Rhino-Bearsville')*
Oct 80. (7") **SECOND NATURE. / YOU MAKE ME CRAZY** [-] [ ]
Nov 80. (7"ep) **I JUST WANT TO TOUCH YOU. / SILLY BOY / LIFE GOES ON / ALL SMILES** [ ] [-]
Dec 80. (7") **I JUST WANT TO TOUCH YOU. / ALWAYS LATE** [-] [ ]

TODD RUNDGREN

Feb 81. (7") **TIME HEALS. / TINY DEMONS** [-] [ ]
Feb 81. (lp)(c) **HEALING** [ ] [48]
– Healer / Pulse / Flesh / Golden goose / Compassion / Shine / Healing (part 1, 2 & 3). *(free-7"ltd.w.a.)*– TIME HEALS. / TINY DEMONS *(lp,c / re-iss.Dec81 on 'Avatar') (re-iss.cd May93 on 'Rhino-Bearsville')*
Jan 82. (7") **COMPASSION. / HEALING** [-] [ ]

UTOPIA

Avatar Bearsville

Mar 82. (lp)(c) **SWING TO THE RIGHT** [ ] [ ]
– Swing to the right / Lysistrata / The up / Junk rock (million monkeys) / Shinola / For the love of money / Last dollar on Earth / Fahrenheit 451 / Only human / One world.
Apr 82. (7") **ONE WORLD. / SPECIAL INTEREST** [-] [ ]
May 82. (7") **ONE WORLD. / JUNK ROCK (MILLION MONKEYS)** [ ] [-]
Jun 82. (7") **LYSISTRATA / JUNK ROCK (MILLION MONKEYS)** [-] [ ]
Nov 82. (7"ep) **TIME HEALS / TINY DEMONS / I SAW THE LIGHT / WHY CAN'T WE BE FRIENDS** [ ] [-]

Epic Network

Nov 82. (7") **FEET DON'T FAIL ME NOW. / FORGOTTEN BUT NOT GONE** [ ] [82]
Nov 82. (lp)(c) **UTOPIA** [ ] [84]
– Libertine / Bad little actress / Feet don't fail me now / Neck on up / Say yeah / Call it what you will / I'm looking at you but I'm talking to myself / Hammer in the heart / Burn three times / There goes my inspiration. *(w/ free UK+US m-lp)*– Princess of the universe / Infrared and ultraviolet / Forgotten but not gone / Private Heaven / Chapter and verse. *(re-iss.cd Aug93 on 'Rhino-Bearsville')*
Jan 83. (7") **HAMMER IN MY HEART. / I'M LOOKING AT YOU BUT I'M TALKING TO MYSELF** [-] [ ]

TODD RUNDGREN

Lamborghini Bearsville

Mar 83. (7") **BANG THE DRUM ALL DAY. / CHANT** [-] [63]
Aug 83. (lp)(c) **THE EVER POPULAR TORTURED ARTIST EFFECT** [ ] [66] Feb 83
– Hideaway / Influenza / Don't hurt yourself / There goes my baybay / Tin soldier / Emperor of the highway / Bang the drum all day / Drive / Chant. *(re-iss.cd Jun93 on 'Rhino-Bearsville')*
Aug 83. (7") **BANG THE DRUM ALL DAY. / DRIVE** [ ] [-]
Sep 83. (7") **HIDEAWAY. / EMPEROR OF THE HIGHWAY** [-] [ ]

UTOPIA

W.E.A. Passport

Apr 84. (lp)(c) **OBLIVION** [ ] [74]
– Itch in my brain / Love with a thinker / Bring me my longbow / If I didn't try / Too much water / Maybe I could change / Crybaby / Welcome to my revolution / Winston Smith takes it on the jaw / I will wait.

May 84. (7") **CRYBABY. / WINSTON SMITH TAKES IT ON THE JAW** [ ] [ ]

Jul 84. (7") **LOVE WITH A THINKER. / WELCOME TO MY REVOLUTION** [ ] [–]

Food For Thought Passport

Jun 85. (lp)(c) **P.O.V.** [ ] [ ] May 85
– Play this game / Style / Stand for something / Secret society / Zen machine / Mated / Wildlife / Mimi gets mad / Mystified / More light.

Jun 85. (7") **MATED. / MAN OF ACTION** [ ] [–]

Jun 85. (7") **MATED. / STAND FOR SOMETHING** [–] [ ]

— (Oct85) TODD is credited on duet with BONNIE TYLER on single 'LOVING YOU IS A DIRTY JOB'.

TODD RUNDGREN

W.E.A. Warners

Oct 85. (7") **SOMETHING TO FALL BACK ON. / LOCKJAW** [ ] [ ]
(UK-12"+=) – ('A'dance mix).

Nov 85. (lp)(c) **A CAPPELLA** [ ] [ ]
– Blue Orpheus / Johnee Jingo / Pretending to care / Hodja / Lost horizon / Something to fall back on / Miracle in the bazaar / Lockjaw / Honest work / Mighty love.

— Early in 1986, UTOPIA split and ROGER POWELL went solo. TODD returned to solo work in 1988 augmented by **ROSS VALORY** – bass (ex-JOURNEY) / **PRAIRIE PRINCE** – drums (ex-TUBES) (same label)

May 89. (lp)(c)(cd) **NEARLY HUMAN** [ ] [ ]
– The want of a nail / The waiting game / Parallel lines / Can't stop running / Unloved children / Fidelity / Feel it / Hawking / I love my life. *(cd+=)*– Two little Hitlers.

May 89. (7") **PARALLEL LINES. / I LOVE MY LIFE** [–] [ ]

Feb 91. (cd)(c)(lp) **SECOND WIND** [ ] [ ]
– Change myself / Love science / Who's sorry now / The smell of money / If I have to be alone / Love in disguise / Kindness / Public servant / Goya's eyes / Second wind.

Jun 93. (cd)(c) **REDUX '92: LIVE IN JAPAN (Utopia live)** [ ] [ ]

Sep 94. (d-cd) **NO WORLD ORDER – LITE** [ ] [ ]
– Worldwide epiphany / No world order / Worldwide epiphany / Day job / Property / Fascist Christ / Love thing / Time stood still / Proactivity / No world order / World epiphany / Time stood still / Love thing / Time stood still / World made flesh / Fever broke. (d-cd+=) – (10 different versions of above).

– compilations, others, etc. (UTOPIA =*) –

Feb 75. Bearsville; (7") **WOLFMAN JACK. / BREATHLESS** [ ] [ ]

Nov 87. Passport; (lp)(c)(cd) **TRIVIA *** [–] [ ]

Feb 88. Raw Power/ US= Rhino; (d-lp)(c)(cd) **ANTHOLOGY** [ ] [ ] 1989
– Can we still be friends / All the children sing / Too far gone / Sweet memories / It wouldn't have made any difference / Hello it's me / I saw the light / Just one victory / Love of the common man / The verb 'to love' / Sometimes I don't know what to feel / Couldn't I just tell you / Tiny demons / Initiation / Real man / A long time a long way to go / Long flowing robe / Compassion / We gotta get you a woman / A dream goes on forever / The last ride / Don't you ever learn / Bang the drum all day / Zen archer. *(cd-omits some+US diff. track listings) (re-iss.d-cd Aug93 on 'Rhino-Bearsville') (re-iss.cd Aug93 on 'Rhino-Bearsville')*

Mar 88. That's Original; (d-lp)(d-c)(d-cd) **RUNT / HERMIT OF MINK HOLLOW** [ ] [–]

Mar 88. That's Original; (d-lp)(d-c)(d-cd) **OOPS! SORRY WRONG PLANET * / ADVENTURES IN UTOPIA *** [ ] [–]

Jun 88. Castle; (d-lp)(d-c)(d-cd) **THE UTOPIA COLLECTION *** [ ] [–]
– Where does the world go to hide / Freedom fighters / All smiles / Lysistrata / Always late / Love in action / Rock love / Set me free / The seven rays / Traped / Swing to the right / One world / Heavy metal kids / The very last time / Crazy lady blue / Feel too good / Love alone / Love is the answer.

Sep 88. WEA; (3"cd-ep) **BANG THE DRUM ALL DAY / I SAW THE LIGHT / CAN WE STILL BE FRIENDS / ALL THE CHILDREN SING** [ ] [–]

Oct 88. Old Gold; (7") **I SAW THE LIGHT. / (other artist)** [ ] [–]

1989. Rhino; (lp) **THE BEST OF NAZZ** [–] [ ]

May 95. Rhino; (cd) **ANTHOLOGY *** [ ] [ ]

Apr 92. Rhino; (cd) **AN ELPEE'S WORTH OF PRODUCTIONS** (various) [ ] [–]

RUN DMC

Formed: Hollis, New York, USA . . . 1982 by SIMMONS, McDANIELS and MIZEL. In '83, SIMMONS' brother RUSSELL obtained deal with 'Profile' records, for whom they released acclaimed eponymous debut lp, which earned raps first gold disc. In 1985, they starred in first rap film 'Krush Groove', which was based on life story of RUSSELL, who had just become co-chairman of Rick Rubin's 'Def Jam' label. In 1986, their third album 'RAISING HELL' broke through to make US Top 3, and they soon became rappin' buddies with tour partners The BEASTIE BOYS. • **Style:** Fused a mixture of rap, sampling and heavy rock. • **Songwriters:** Group compositions, except WALK THIS WAY (Aerosmith) / MARY MARY (Mike Nesmith). • **Trivia:** In Mar'88, they lost legal battle with 'Profile', who had contracted them to 10 albums. This delayed and probably cancelled their much touted expensive movie 'TOUGHER THAN LEATHER'.

Recommended: RUN DMC'S GREATEST HITS TOGETHER FOREVER (*8) / RAISING HELL (*8)

JOSEPH 'Run' SIMMONS (b.'64) – vocals / **MC DARRYL 'D' McDANIELS** (b.'64) – vocals / **JASON MIZEL** (JAM-MASTER JAY) (b.'65) – DJ

4th & Bro. Profile

Jun 84. (lp) **RUN – D.M.C.** [–] [53]
– Hard times / Rock box / Jam-master Jay / Hollis Crew (krush-groove 2) / Sucker M.C.'s (krush-groove 1) / It's like that / Wake up / 30 days / Jay's game. *(UK-iss.+c.May85 on '4th & Broadway', re-iss.+cd.Apr91*

Jun 84. (7") **ROCK BOX. / ('A'vocal dub)** [ ] [ ]
(12"+=) – ('A'dub version).

Sep 84. (7") **30 DAYS. / ('A' instrumental)** [–] [ ]

Jan 85. (7") **HOLLIS CREW. / ('A' instrumental)** [–] [ ]

Feb 85. (lp)(c)(pic-lp) **KING OF ROCK** [ ] [52]
– Rock the house / King of rock / You talk too much / Jam-master jammin' / Roots, rap, reggae / Can you rock it like this / You're blind / It's not funny / Daryll and Joe (krush-groove 3). *(cd-iss.May88) (re-iss.+cd.Apr91)*

Mar 85. (7") **KING OF ROCK. / ROCK BOX (vocal)** [ ] [ ]
(12"+=) – ('A'instrumental).

Mar 86. (7") **YOU TALK TOO MUCH. / DARRYL AND JOE (KRUSH-GROOVE 3)** [ ] [ ]
(12"+=) – ('A'instrumental) / Sucker M.C.'s (krush-groove 1).

Apr 86. (7") **JAM-MASTER JAMMIN'. / (part 2)** [–] [ ]

May 86. (7") **CAN YOU ROCK IT LIKE THIS. / TOGETHER FOREVER** [–] [ ]

London Profile

Jun 86. (7") **MY ADIDAS. / PETER PIPER** [62] [ ]
(12"+=) – ('A'instrumental).

Jul 86. (lp)(c)(cd) **RAISING HELL** [41] [3] Jun 86
– Peter Piper / It's tricky / My Adidas / Walk this way / Is it live / Perfection / Hit it run / Raising Hell / You be illin' / Dumb girl / Son of Byford / Proud to be black.

Aug 86. (7") **WALK THIS WAY. ("RUN DMC featuring AEROSMITH"). / KING OF ROCK** [–] [4]

Aug 86. (7") **WALK THIS WAY. ("RUN DMC featuring AEROSMITH") / ('A' instrumental)** [8] [–]
(12"+=)(12"pic-d+=) – My Adidas.

Sep 86. (7") **KING OF ROCK. / JAM MASTER JAY** [ ] [–]
(12"+=) Rock box / Jay's game / You talk too much.

Feb 87. (7") **YOU BE ILLIN'. / HIT IT RUN** [42] [29] Oct 86
(12"+=) – ('A'instrumental).

May 87. (7") **IT'S TRICKY. / PROUD TO BE BLACK** [16] [57] Feb 87
(12"+=) – ('A'club tempo) / ('A'scratchapella) / ('A'reprise).

Sep 87. (7") **PETER PIPER. / MY ADIDAS** [ ] [–]
(12"+=) – Walk this way / King of rock.

Nov 87. (7") **XMAS IN HOLLIS. / PETER PIPER** [56] [–]
(12"+=) – My Adidas / Walk this way / King of rock.

Apr 88. (7") **RUN'S HOUSE. / BEATS TO THE RHYME** [37] [ ]
(12"+=)(cd-s+=) – ('A'&'B'instrumental).

Jun 88. (lp)(c)(cd) **TOUGHER THAN LEATHER** [13] [9]
– Run's house / Mary, Mary / They call us Run DMC / Beats to the rhyme / Radio station / Papa crazy / Tougher than leather / I'm not going out like that / How d'ya do it Dee? / Miss Elaine / Soul to rock and roll / Ragtime.

Aug 88. (7") **MARY, MARY. / RAISING HELL** [ ] [75] Jul 88
(12"+=) – ('A'instrumental).

M.C.A. M.C.A.

Aug 89. (7")(c-s) **GHOSTBUSTERS THEME II. / ('A'instrumental)** [65] [ ]
(12"+=)(cd-s+=) – Pause.

Profile Profile

Nov 90. (7")(c-s) **WHAT'S IT ALL ABOUT. / THE AVE** [48] [ ]
(12"+=) – ('A'&'B'instrumentals).
(cd-s+=) – ('A'instrumental) / ('A'version).

Dec 90. (cd)(c)(lp) **BACK FROM HELL** [–] [81]
– Back from hell / Bob your head / Livin' in the city / Sucker DJs / What's it all about / Word is born / Pause / Not just another groove / P upon a tree / Party time / Naughty / Kick the frama lama lama / Groove to the sound / Don't stop.

Mar 91. (7")(c-s) **FACES. / BACK FROM HELL (remix)** [ ] [ ]
(12"+=) – ('A'radio mix) / ('A'instrumental).
(cd-s) – (2 'A'versions see above) / (2 'B'versions).
(12") – (4 'A'mixes – 3 above).

Nov 91. (cd)(c)(lp) **RUN DMC GREATEST HITS TOGETHER FOREVER 1983-1991** (compilation) [ ] [ ]

– Sucker M.C.'s (krush groove 1) / Walk this way / Together forever (krush groove 4) (live at Hollis Park '84) / King of rock / Run's house / It's tricky / Pause / You be illin' / My Adidas / Here we go (live at The Funhouse) / Rock box / What's it all about / Hard times / Beats to the rhyme / Jam-master Jay / Peter Piper / It's like that / Christmas in Hollis.

— Earlier 1991, JOSEPH SIMMONS was charged with raping a 22-year female fan.

Mar 93. (12")(cd-s) **DOWN WITH THE KING. / ('A'mixes)** 69 21
(re-iss. Nov '93 UK)

May 93. (cd)(c)(lp) **DOWN WITH THE KING** 44 7
– Down with the king / C'mon everybody / Can I get it to yo / Hit 'em hard / To the maker / In the head / Ooh, what ya gonna do / Big Willie / Three little Indians / In the house / Kick it (can I get a witness) / Get open / What's next / Wreck shop / For ten years.

Jul 93. (12")(cd-s) **OOH, WHATCHA GONNA DO. / ('A'mixes)**

Apr 94. (12")(cd-s) **WHAT'S NEXT. / CAN I GET IT, YO / PIED PIPER**

compilations, etc

Nov 95. Profile; (10x12"box) **12" SINGLES BOX SET** -

RUNRIG

Formed: North Uist, Outer Hebrides, Scotland . . . 1973 as The RUN-RIG DANCE BAND, by brothers RORY and CALUM McDONALD plus BLAIR DOUGLAS. After many comings and goings throughout the next 6 years, RUNRIG issued debut album 'THE HIGHLAND CONNECTION' for own self-financed label 'Ridge'. After building up home support on the live front, and releasing 3 more albums during a 9 year period, they finally secured nationwide outlet when signing to 'Chrysalis'. Their first taste of success came in the late 80's, when album 'SEARCHLIGHT', nearly made the British Top 10. • **Style:** Traditional Celtic-rock outfit, who retained Gaelic roots and language throughout career. Described as a cross between BIG COUNTRY, The CHIEFTAINS or HORSLIPS. • **Songwriters:** McDONALD brothers / JONES write instrumental songs. Also play traditional songs. • **Trivia:** Due to religious beliefs, they never play live on a Sunday.

Recommended: ONCE IN A LIFETIME (*7).

DONNIE MUNRO (b. 2 Aug'53, Uig, Isle Of Skye, Scotland) – vocals / **RORY McDONALD** (b.RODERICK, 27 Jul'49, Dornoch, Scotland) – bass, vocals, acoustic guitar, accordion / **BLAIR DOUGLAS** – harmonica, organ (re-joined Jun78) / **CALUM McDONALD** (b.MALCOLM MORRISON McDONALD, 12 Nov'53, Lochmaddy, North Uist, Scotland) – drums, percussion

Neptune not issued

Apr 78. (c) **PLAY GAELIC** -
– Duisg mo run / Sguaban arbhair / Tillidh mi / Criogal cridhe / Nach neonach neiad a tha E / Sunndach / Air an traigh / De ni mi – pulp / An ros / Ceolan danasa / Chi'n geamhradh / Cum 'ur n'aire. *(lp-iss.Sep84) (re-iss.+c+cd.Jul95 as 'RUNRIG PLAY GAELIC – THE FIRST LEGENDARY RECORDINGS' on 'Lismor')*

— added **MALCOLM ELWYN JONES** (b.12 Jul'59, Inverness, Scotland) – guitar, bagpipes, mandolin to repl. BLAIR (who still guested later)

Ridge not issued

Oct 79. (lp)(c) **THE HIGHLAND CONNECTION** -
– Gamhna gealla / Mairi / What time? / Fichead bliadhna / Na luing air scoladh / Loch Lomond / Na h-vain a's t-earrach / Foghar nan Eilean / The twenty-five pounder / Going home / Morning tide / Cearcal a chuain. *(re-iss.Sep84 + Feb86) (cd-iss.Aug89)*

— added on tour '81, **RICHARD CHERNS** (b.England) – keyboards

Dec 82. (7") **LOCH LOMOND. / TUIREADH IAIN RUAIDH** 72 -

Aug 84. (7") **DANCE CALLED AMERICA. / NA H-UAIN A'S T-ERRACH** -
(12"+=) – Ribhinn o.

— added guests **BLAIR DOUGLAS / JOHN MARTIN** – cello / **RONNIE GERRARD** – fiddle

Sep 84. (lp)(c) **RECOVERY** -
– An toll dubh / Rubh nan cudaigean / 'Ic lain 'ic Sheimas / Recovery / Instrumental / 'S tu moIceanna – Nightfall in Marsco / Breakin' the chains / Fuaim a bhlair / Tir an airna / The old boys / Dust. *(re-iss.Feb86, c-iss.May88, cd-iss.Aug89)*

Nov 84. (7")(12") **SKYE. / HEY MANOU** -

— The 1984 singles were issued on 'Simple')

— **PETER WISHART** (b. 9 Mar'52, Dunfermline, Scotland) – keyboards, vocals (ex-BIG COUNTRY) repl. CHERNS / added **IAIN BAYNE** (b.22 Jan'60, St.Andrews, Scotland) – drums, percussion

Feb 86. (lp)(c) **HEARTLAND** -
– O cho mealdt / This darkest winter / Life line / Air a' chuain / Dance called America / The everlasting gun / Skye / Choc na feille / The wire / An ataireaachd Ard / The ferry / Tuireadh Iain ruaidh. *(cd-iss.1989)*

1986. (7") **THE WORK SONG. / THIS TIME OF YEAR** -

Nov 87. (7") **ALBA. / WORKER FOR THE WIND** -

Dec 87. (lp)(c)(cd) **THE CUTTER AND THE CLAN** -
– Alba / The cutter / Hearts of olden glory / Pride of the summer / Worker for the wind / Rocket to the Moon / The only rose / Protect and survive / Our Earth was once green / An ubhal as airde. *(re-iss.Jul88 on 'Chrysalis') (re-iss.cd Mar94) (re-iss.cd May95, hit No.45)*

Chrysalis Chrysalis?

Aug 88. (7") **PROTECT AND SURVIVE. / HEARTS OF OLDEN GLORY** -
(12"+=)(cd-s+=) – ('A'live).

Nov 88. (lp)(c)(cd) **ONCE IN A LIFETIME (live)** 61
– Dance called America / Protect and survive / Chi mi'n geamhradh / Rocket to the Moon / Going home / Choc na feille / Nightfall on Marsco / 'Stu mo Leannan / Skye / Loch Lomond / Hearts of olden glory.

Aug 89. (7")(c-s)(7"pic-d) **NEWS FROM HEAVEN. / SMALLTOWN**
(12"+=) – Chi min fir.
(12"pic-d+=)(cd-s+=) – The times they are a-changin'.

Sep 89. (lp)(c)(cd) **SEARCHLIGHT** 11
– News from Heaven / Every river / City of lights / Eirinn / Tir a'mhurain / World appeal / Tear down these walls / Only the brave / Siol ghoraidh / That final mile / Smalltown / Precious years.

Nov 89. (7")(c-s) **EVERY RIVER. / THIS TIME OF YEAR**
(12"+=)(cd-s+=) – Once our Earth was green.

Sep 90. (10"ep)(12"ep)(cd-ep) **CAPTURE THE HEART** 49
– Stepping down the glory road / Satellite flood / Harvest Moon / The apple came down.

Jun 91. (cd)(c)(lp) **THE BIG WHEEL** 4
– Headlights / Healer in your heart / Abhainn an t-sluaigh – The crowded river / Always the winner / This beautiful pain / An cuibhle mor – The big wheel / Edge of the world / Hearthammer / I'll keep coming home / Flower of the West.

Aug 91. (7")(c-s) **HEARTHAMMER. / BEAT THE DRUM** 25
(12")(cd-s) – ('A'side) / Loch Lomond (live) / Solus na madainn (live).
(7"ep+=) – Pride of the summer (live).

Nov 91. (7")(c-s) **FLOWER OF THE WEST (live). / CHI M'N GEAMHRADH** 43
(12"+=)(cd-s+=) – Ravenscraig / Harvest Moon (live).

Feb 93. (7")(7"blue)(c-s) **WONDERFUL. / APRIL COME SHE WILL** 29
(cd-s) – ('A'side) / Straidean na roinn Eorpa (Streets of Europe) / On the edge.

Mar 93. (cd)(c)(lp) **AMAZING THINGS** 2
– Amazing things / Wonderful / The greatest flame / Move a mountain / Pog aon oidhche earraich (A kiss one evening Spring) / Dream fields / Song of the Earth / Forever eyes of blue / Sraidean na roinn-earpa (Streets of Europe) / Canada / Ard (High) / On the edge.

Apr 93. (7")(c-s) **THE GREATEST FLAME. / SUILVAN** 36
(cd-s+=) – Saints of the soil / An t-lasgair (the fisherman).
(cd-s) – ('A'side) / The fisherman / Morning tide (re-recorded) / Chi m'in tir (I see the land).

Nov 94. (cd)(c)(lp) **TRANSMITTING LIVE (live)** 41
– Urlar / Ard / Edge of the world / The greatest flame / Harvest Moon / The wire / Precious years / Every river / Flower of the west / Only the brave / Alba / Pog aon oidche earraich (one kiss one Spring evening).

Dec 94. (12"ep)(c-ep)(cd-ep) **THIS TIME OF YEAR / WONDERFUL (live). / DREAM FIELDS (live) / I'LL KEEP COMING HOME (live) / THIS TIME OF YEAR (re-recorded)** 38 -

Apr 95. (7")(c-s)(cd-s) **AN UBHAL AS AIRDE (THE HIGHEST APPLE). / ABHAINN AN T-SLUIGH / THE GREATEST FLAME** 18
(cd-s+=) – Flower of the west.

Oct 95. (7")(c-s) **THINGS THAT ARE. / AN UBHAL AS AIRDE (THE HIGHEST APPLE)** 40
(cd-s+=) – Amazing things (remix) / That other landscape.

Nov 95. (cd)(c)(lp) **MARA** 24
– Day in a boat / Nothing but the sun / The mighty Atlantic / Things that are / Road and the river / Meadhan Oidhche air an Acairseid / The wedding / The dancing floor / Thairis air a ghleann / Lighthouse.

RUSH

Formed: Toronto, Canada . . . 1969 by LIFESON, LEE and RUTSEY. They toured local clubs, and by 1973 were supporting The NEW YORK DOLLS in their hometown. They released own financed eponymous Terry Brown produced debut album early '74, which was soon picked up by DJ Donna Halper, who sent a copy to 'Mercury' records. They signed the band for a 6-figure sum, and also re-released debut, which nearly made US Top 100. By 1976, they had built up large following, which enabled live double album 'ALL THE WORLD'S A STAGE' to creep into the 40. They grew from strenth to strength during next decade and a half, to stronger commercial triumphs in the UK. • **Style:** Spectacular sci-fi influenced heavy rock trio, who mixed ambitious concept pieces, with unique but complex lyrical content. They went into more sophisticated progressive rock during the 80's. • **Songwriters:** Group compositions / PEART lyrics from 1974 onwards. Covered NOT FADE AWAY (Buddy Holly). • **Trivia:** The concept album 2112, was based on the work by novelist and philosopher Ayn Rand. Early in 1982, GEDDY guests for BOB & DOUG McKENZIE (aka Rick Moranis & Dave Thomas) on their US Top 20 single 'Take Off'.

Recommended: ALL THE WORLD'S A STAGE (*9) / 2112 (*8) / CHRONICLES (*7).

GEDDY LEE (b.29 Jul'53, Willowdale, Toronto, Canada) – vocals, bass, keyboards / **ALEX LIFESON** (b.27 Aug'53, Fernie, British Columbia, Canada) – lead guitar / **JOHN RUTSEY** – drums

not issued — Moon

1973. (7") **NOT FADE AWAY. / YOU CAN'T FIGHT IT** [-] [ ]

Mercury — Mercury

Feb 75. (lp)(c) **RUSH** [ ] [ ] Jul 74
– Finding my way / Need some love / Take a friend / Here again / What you're doing / In the mood / Before and after / Working man. *(re-iss.Jun83, cd-iss.Apr87)*

— (Autumn '74) **NEIL PEART** (b.12 Sep'52, Hamilton, Ontario, Canada) – drums, vocals, lyrics repl. RUTSEY

Apr 75. (lp)(c) **FLY BY NIGHT** [ ] [ ] Feb 75
– Anthem / Best I can / Beneath, between and behind / By-Tor and the snowdog:- At the tobes of Hades – Across the styx – Of the battle – Epilogue / Fly by night / Making memories / Rivendell / In the end. *(re-iss.Jun83, cd-iss.Apr87)*

May 75. (7") **FLY BY NIGHT. / ANTHEM** (re-iss.Dec 77) [-] [ ]

Nov 75. (7") **BASTILLE DAY. / LAKESIDE PARK** [-] [ ]

Mar 76. (lp)(c) **CARESS OF STEEL** [ ] [ ] Oct 75
– Bastille day / The fountain of Lamneth: In the valley – Didacts and narpets – No one at the bridge – Panacea – Bacchus plateau – The fountain / I think I'm going bald / Lakeside Park / Necromancer:- Into the darkness – Under the shadow – Return of the prince. *(re-iss.Jun83, cd-iss.Apr87)*

Jun 76. (lp)(c) **2112** [61] [ ] Apr 76
– A passage to Bangkok / The twilight zone / Lessons / Tears / Something for nothing / 2112: (a) Overture – (b) The Temples of Syrinx – (c) Discovery – (d) Presentation – (e) Oracle – (f) The dream – (g) Soliliquy – (h) Grand finale. *(re-iss.Jan85, cd-iss.Apr87)*

Jun 76. (7") **LESSONS. / THE TWILIGHT ZONE** [-] [ ]

Mar 77. (d-lp)(d-c) **ALL THE WORLD'S A STAGE (live)** [ ] [40] Sep 76
– Anthem / Bastille day / By-Tor and the snowdog: At the tobes of Hades – Across the styx – Of the battle – Epilogue / Fly by night / In the mood / Lakeside park / Something for nothing / 2112: (a) Overture – (b) The Temples of Syrinx – (c) Discovery – (d) Presentation – (e) Oracle – (f) The dream – (g) Soliliquy – (h) Grand finale / What you're doing / Working man / Finding my way. *(re-iss.Sep84, cd-iss.Apr87)*

Dec 76. (7") **FLY BY NIGHT (live). / IN THE MOOD (live)** [-] [88]

Feb 77. (7") **THE TEMPLES OF SYRINX. / MAKING MEMORIES** [-] [ ]

Sep 77. (lp)(c) **A FAREWELL TO KINGS** [22] [33]
– A farewell to kings / Xanadu / Closer to the heart / Cinderella man / Madrigal / Cygnus X-1. *(cd-iss.Apr87)*

Nov 77. (7") **CLOSER TO THE HEART. / MADRIGAL** [-] [76]

Jan 78. (7"ep) **CLOSER TO THE HEART. / BASTILLE DAY / THE TEMPLES OF SYRINX** [36] [-]
(12"ep+=) – Anthem.

Nov 78. (lp)(c)(pic-lp) **HEMISPHERES** [14] [47]
– Cygnus X-1 Book 2; Hemispheres: Prelude – Apollo, bringer of wisdom – Dionysus, bringer of love – Armageddon, the battle of heart and mind – Cygnus, bringer of balance / Circumstances / The trees / La villa Strangiato. *(re-iss.Mar88, cd-iss.Apr87)*

Jan 79. (7") **CIRCUMSTANCES. / THE TREES** [-] [ ]

Jan 80. (lp)(c) **PERMANENT WAVES** [3] [4]
– The spirit of radio / Freewill / Jacob's ladder / Entre nous / Different strings / Natural science. *(cd-iss.Apr87)*

Feb 80. (7") **THE SPIRIT OF RADIO. / CIRCUMSTANCES** [-] [51]

Feb 80. (7") **THE SPIRIT OF RADIO. / THE TREES** [13] [-]
(12"+=) – Working man.

Apr 80. (7") **DIFFERENT STRINGS. / ENTRE NOUS** [-] [ ]

Feb 81. (7") **LIMELIGHT. / XYZ** [-] [55]

Feb 81. (lp)(c) **MOVING PICTURES** [3] [3]
– Tom Sawyer / Red Barchetta / XYZ / Limelight / The camera eye / Witch hunt (part III of fear) / Vital signs. *(cd-iss.1983)*

Mar 81. (7") **VITAL SIGNS. / IN THE MOOD** [41] [ ]
(12"+=) – A passage to Bangkok / Circumstances.

May 81. (7") **TOM SAWYER. / WITCH HUNT** [-] [ ]

Oct 81. (7") **FREEWILL (live). / CLOSER TO THE HEART (live)** [-] [ ]

Oct 81. (d-lp)(d-c) **EXIT . . . STAGE LEFT (live)** [6] [10]
– The spirit of radio / Red Barchetta / YYZ / A passage to Bangkok / Closer to the heart / Beneath, between and behind / Jacob's ladder / Broon's bane / The trees / Xanadu / Freewill / Tom Sawyer / La villa Strangiato. *(cd-iss.Apr87)*

Oct 81. (7") **TOM SAWYER (live). / A PASSAGE TO BANGKOK (live)** [25] [-]
(12"+=) – Red Barchetta (live).

Dec 81. (7") **CLOSER TO THE HEART (live). / THE TREES (live)** [ ] [69]

Aug 82. (7") **NEW WORLD MAN. / VITAL SIGNS (live)** [42] [21]
(12"+=) – Freewill (live).

Sep 82. (lp)(c) **SIGNALS** [3] [10]
– Subdivisions / The analog kid / Chemistry / Digital man / The weapon / New world man / Losing it / Countdown. *(cd-iss.1983)*

Oct 82. (7") **SUBDIVISIONS. / COUNTDOWN** [-] [ ]

Oct 82. (7")(7"pic-d) **SUBDIVISIONS. / RED BARCHETTA (live)** [53] [-]
(12"+=) – Jacob's ladder (live).

Apr 83. (7")(7"sha-pic-d) **COUNTDOWN. / NEW WORLD MAN** [36] [ ]
(12"+=) – The spirit of radio (live) / (interview excerpts).

Apr 84. (lp)(c)(cd) **GRACE UNDER PRESSURE** [5] [10]
– Distant early warning / After image / Red sector A / The enemy within / The body electric / Kid gloves / Red lenses / Between the wheels.

May 84. (7") **THE BODY ELECTRIC. / THE ANALOG KID** [56] [ ]
(12"+=)(10"red+=) – Distant early warning.

Oct 85. (7") **THE BIG MONEY. / TERRITORIES** [ ] [45]
(12"+=) – Red sector A.
(d7"+=) – Closer to the heart / The spirit of radio.
(7") – ('A'side). / Middletown dreams.

Nov 85. (lp)(c)(cd)(pic-lp) **POWER WINDOWS** [9] [10] Oct 85
– The big money / Grand designs / Manhattan project / Marathon / Territories / Middletown dreams / Emotion detector / Mystic rhythms.

Oct 87. (7") **TIME STAND STILL. / FORCE TEN** [41] [ ]
(12"pic-d+=) – The enemy within (live).
(12"++=) – Witch hunt (live).

Nov 87. (lp)(c)(cd) **HOLD YOUR FIRE** [10] [13] Sep 87
– Force ten / Time stand still / Open secrets / Second nature / Prime mover / Lock and key / Mission / Turn the page / Tai Shan / High water.

Mar 88. (7") **PRIME MOVER. / TAI SHAN** [ ] [ ]
(12"+=) – Open secrets.
(12"++=)(cd-s++=) – New world man (live).
(7"white) – ('A'side). / DISTANT EARLY WARNING (live)

Jan 89. (d-lp)(c)(cd) **A SHOW OF HANDS (live)** [12] [21]
– (intro) / The big money / Subdivisions / Marathon / Turn the page / Manhattan project / Mission / Distant early warning / Mystic rhythms / Witch hunt (part III of fear) / The rhythm method / Force ten / Time stand still / Red sector A / Closer to the heart.

Atlantic — Atlantic

Nov 89. (lp)(c)(cd) **PRESTO** [27] [16]
– Show don't tell / Chain lightning / The pass / War paint / Scars / Presto / Superconductor / Anagram (for Mongo) / Red tide / Hands over fist / Available light.

Jan 90. (7") **SHOW DON'T TELL. / ?** [-] [ ]

Sep 91. (cd)(c)(lp) **ROLL THE BONES** [10] [3]
– Dreamline / Bravado / Roll the bones / Face up / Where's my thing? (part IV 'Gangster Of Boats' trilogy) / The big wheel / Heresy / Ghost of a chance / Neurotica / You bet your life.

Feb 92. (7")(7"sha-pic-d) **ROLL THE BONES. / SHOW DON'T TELL** [49] [ ]
(cd-s+=) – (interviews) / Anagram.

Apr 92. (7")(c-s) **GHOST OF A CHANCE. / DREAMLINE** [ ] [ ]
(12"+=)(cd-s+=) – Chain lightning / Red tide.

Oct 93. (cd)(c)(lp) **COUNTERPARTS** [14] [2]
– Animate / Stick it out / Cut to the chase / Nobody's hero / Between Sun and Moon / Alien shore / The speed of love / Double agent / Leave that thing alone / Cold fire / Everyday glory.

– compilations, others, etc. –

May 78. Mercury; (t-lp)(d-c) **ARCHIVES** (first 3 lp's) [ ] [ ] Apr 78

1981. Mercury; (lp)(c)(pic-lp) **RUSH THROUGH TIME** [-] [ ]

Feb 88. Old Gold; (7") **THE SPIRIT OF RADIO. / CLOSER TO THE HEART** [ ] [-]

Sep 90. Vertigo/ US= Mercury; (d-cd)(d-c)(t-lp) **CHRONICLES** [42] [51]
– Finding my way / Working man / Fly by night / Anthem / Bastille day / Lakeside park / 2112: a) Overture, b) The temples of Syrinx / What you're doing (live) / A farewell to kings / Closer to the heart / The trees / La villa Strangiato / Freewill / The spirit of radio/ / Tom Sawyer / Red barchetta / Limelight / A passage to Bangkok (live) / Subdivisions / New world man / Distant early warning / Red sector A / The big money / Manhattan project / Force ten / Time stand still / Mystic rhythms (live) / Show don't tell.

. . . Jan – Jun '96 stop press . . .

VICTOR

ALEX LIFESON

East West — Atlantic

Jan 96. (cd)(c) **VICTOR** [ ] [99]

Mike RUTHERFORD (see under ⇒ GENESIS)

SAINT ETIENNE

Formed: North London, England . . . early 90's by BOB STANLEY and PETER WIGGS. Named themselves after French football team St Etienne, after once toying with idea REARDON (the snooker player). They signed to up-and-coming indie label 'Heavenly', where they quickly secured chart status. • **Style:** Psychedelic dance and dub outfit, fronted by the dreamy vox of SARAH CRACKNELL. • **Songwriters:** STANLEY-WIGGS except a few with CRACKNELL plus outside covers ONLY LOVE CAN BREAK YOUR HEART (Neil Young) / WHO DO YOU THINK YOU ARE (Scott-Dyer) / MY CHRISTMAS PRAYER (Billy Fury) / WESTERN WIND (trad.) / STRANGER IN PARADISE (hit; Tony Bennett) / IS IT TRUE (Marc Bolan) / HOW I LEARNED TO LOVE THE BOMB (TV Personalities). • **Trivia:** Sang a version of RIGHT SAID FRED's 'I'M TOO SEXY' on a 1992 'Heavenly' compilation ep.

Recommended: FOXBASE ALPHA (*8) / SO TOUGH (*7) / TIGER BAY (*6).

BOB STANLEY (b.Peterborough) – keyboards / **PETE WIGGS** – keyboards, synthesizers / **DONNA SAVAGE** – vocals

Heavenly ???

Jul 90. (7") **ONLY LOVE CAN BREAK YOUR HEART. / ('A'version)** [ ] [ ]
(12") – ('A'-Andy Weatherall mix) / The Official Saint Etiene world cup theme.

Sep 90. (7") **KISS AND MAKE UP. / SKY'S DEAD** [ ] [ ]
(cd-s+=) – ('A'extended).
(12") – (2-'A'mixes by Pete Helber incl. dub version).

— **SARAH CRACKNELL** – vocals repl. DONNA

May 91. (7") **NOTHING CAN STOP US. / SPEEDWELL** [54] [ ]
(12"+=)/ /(cd-s+=) – (2 'B'mixes) / 3-D tiger./ / ('A'instrumental).

Aug 91. (7") **ONLY LOVE CAN BREAK YOUR HEART. / FILTHY** [39] [97] Feb 92
(12"+=)(cd-s+=) – ('A'extended).
(cd-s) – ('A'side) / (2 half mixes by Andy Weatherall).

Oct 91. (cd)(c)(lp) **FOXBASE ALPHA** [34] [ ]
– This is Radio Etienne / Only love can break your heart / Wilson / Carnt sleep / Girl VII / Spring / She's the one / Stoned to say the least / Nothing can stop us / Etienne gonna die / London belongs to me / Like the swallow / Dilworth's theme.

May 92. (7")(c-s) **JOIN OUR CLUB. / PEOPLE GET REAL** [21] [ ]
(12"+=)(cd-s+=) – ('A'chemically friendly mix) / Scene '93.

Sep 92. (12"ep)(cd-ep) **AVENUE (club) / ('A'-Butlins mix) / ('A'marital mix) / ('A'-Venusian mix)** [40] [ ]
(12")(cd-s) – ('A'side) / Some place else / Paper / Johnny in the Echo cafe.

— added **IAN CATT** – guitar, programmer

Feb 93. (7")(c-s) **YOU'RE IN A BAD WAY. / CALIFORNIA SNOW STORY** [12] [ ]
(12"+=)(cd-s+=) – Archway people / Duke Duvet.

Mar 93. (cd)(c)(lp) **SO TOUGH** [7] [ ]
– Mario's cafe / Railway jam / Date with Spelman / Calico / Avenue / You're in a bad way / Memo to Pricey / Hobart paving / Leafhound / Clock milk / Conchita Martinez / No rainbows for me / Here come clown feet / Junk the morgue / Chicken soup. *(re-iss.Jun93 with free ltd.cd 'YOU NEED A MESS OF HELP TO STAND ALONE' compilation)* – Who do you think you are / Archway people / California snow storm / Kiss and make up / Duke duvet / Filthy / Join our club / Paper / Some place else / Speedwell.

May 93. (7")(c-s) **HOBART PAVING. / WHO DO YOU THINK YOU ARE** [23] [ ]
(cd-s+=) – Hobart Paving / Who Do You Think You Are

Dec 93. (7")(c-s) **I WAS BORN ON CHRISTMAS DAY. / MY CHRISTMAS PRAYER** [37] [ ]
(12"+=)(cd-s+=) – Snowplough / Peterloo.

(above 'A' featured dual vocals with TIM BURGESS of The CHARLATANS)

Dec 93. (cd)(c)(lp) **YOU NEED A MESS OF HELP TO STAND ALONE** [ ] [ ]
– (see last album)

Feb 94. (7")(c-s) **PALE MOVIE. / HIGHGATE ROAD INCIDENT** [28] [ ]
(12")(cd-s) – ('A'side) / ('A'-Stetorian dub) / ('A'-Secret Knowledge mix) / ('A'-Lemonentry mix).

Feb 94. (cd)(c)(lp) **TIGER BAY** [8] [ ]
– Urban clearway / Former lover / Hug my soul / Like a motorway / On the shore / Marble lions / Pale movie / Cool kids of death / Western wind / Tankerville / Western wind / Boy scouts of America.

May 94. (7")(c-s) **LIKE A MOTORWAY. / YOU KNOW I'LL MISS YOU WHEN YOU'RE GONE / SUSHI RIDER** [47] [ ]
(12")(cd-s) – ('A'side) / ('A'-Dust Brothers mix) / ('A'-David Holmes mix) / ('A'-Autechre mix).

Sep 94. (12"ep)(c-ep) **HUG MY SOUL / I BUY AMERICAN RECORDS / HATE YOUR DRUG** [32] [ ]
(cd-ep+=) – No, no, no.
(remixed-cd-ep) – ('A'side) / ('A'-Sure Is Pure) / ('A'-Motiv8) / ('A'-Juan 'Kinky' Hernandez) / ('A'-Secret Knowledge).

Oct 95. (c-s) **HE'S ON THE PHONE / ('A'-Motiv8 mix)** [11] [ ]
(cd-s) – ('A'-Motiv8 mix) / Cool kids of death (Underworld mix) / How I learned to love the bomb.
(cd-s) – ('A'side) / Groveley Road / Is it true / The process.

Nov 95. (cd)(c)(d-lp) **TOO YOUNG TO DIE – THE SINGLES** (compilation) [17] [ ]
– Only love can break your heart / Kiss and make up / Nothing can stop us / Join our club / People get real / Avenue / You're in a bad way / Who do you think you are / Hobart paving / I was born on Christmas day / Pale movie / Like a motorway / Hug my soul / He's on the phone. (cd+=) – (9 remixes).

. . .Jan-Jun'96 special release . . .

— next with French dance artist ETIENNE DAHO

Jan 96. Virgin; (m-cd) **RESERECTION** ("ST. ETIENNE DAHO") [50] [-]

SALAD

Formed: London, England . . .1992 by ex-MTV presenter and fashion model MARIJNE with her fellow ex-film student and boyfriend PAUL KENNEDY. After a few 45's in 1993, they signed to Island's new indie offshoot label 'Island Red' and soon made inroads into charts with classy singles 'ON A LEASH', 'YOUR MA', 'DRINK THE ELIXIR' and The Shangri-la's influenced 'MOTORBIKE TO HEAVEN'. All were included on their long-awaited UK Top 20 album 'DRINK ME' in 1995. • **Style:** Raw-edged alternative pop/rock, lying somewhere between ALL ABOUT EVE, The PRIMITIVES or BLONDIE. • **Songwriters:** KENNEDY, WAKEMAN or VAN DER VLUGT, except IT'S FOR YOU (Lennon-McCartney; hit Cilla Black).

Recommended: DRINK ME (*9)

MARIJNE VAN DER VLUGT -vocals, keyboards / **PAUL KENNEDY** -guitar, vocals / **PETE BROWN** -bass / **ROB WAKEMAN** -drums, samples

Waldorf not issued

Jun 93. (12"ep) **KENT EP** [ ] [-]
– Kent / The king of love / Heaven can wait / Mistress.

Oct 93. (12")(cd-s) **DIMINISHED CLOTHES. / CLEAR MY NAME / COME BACK TOMORROW** [ ] [-]

Island Red not issued

Apr 94. (7") **ON A LEASH. / WHAT DO YOU SAY ABOUT THAT?** [ ] [ ]
(12"+=)(cd-s+=) – Planet in the ocean / Problematique.

Jul 94. (7") **YOUR MA. / PLANK** [ ] [ ]
(12"+=)(cd-s+=) – Open.

Feb 95. (7")(c-s) **DRINK THE ELIXIR. / KISS MY LOVE** [66] [ ]
(12"+=)(cd-s+=) – Julius / Diminished clothes (live).

Apr 95. (7")(c-s) **MOTORBIKE TO HEAVEN. / DIARY HELL** [42] [ ]
(cd-s+=) – I am December.

May 95. (cd)(c)(lp) **DRINK ME** [16] [ ]
-Motorbike to Heaven / Drink the elixir / Granite statue / Machine of menace / Overhear me / Shepherds' isle / Muscleman / Your ma / Warmth of the hearth / Gertrude Campbell / Nothing happens / No.1's cooking / A man with a box / Insomnia.

Aug 95. (7")(c-s) **GRANITE STATUE. / IT'S FOR YOU** [50] [ ]

(cd-s+=) – Ici les amigos.
(cd-s) – ('A'side) / Rip goes love and lust / Roadsex.

Richie SAMBORA (see under ⇒ BON JOVI)

SANDKINGS (see under ⇒ BABYLON ZOO)

SANTANA

Formed: San Francisco, California, USA . . . Oct'66 as The SANTANA BLUES BAND by CARLOS SANTANA. In 1968 as SANTANA, they played concert at The Fillmore West. Later in the year, CARLOS guested on album 'THE LIVE ADVENTURES OF AL KOOPER and MIKE BLOOMFIELD', which brought him to the attention of 'Columbia' records. Their long-awaited eponymous debut lp late in '69, cracked the US Top 5 due to an August appearance at the now famous 'Woodstock' festival. Became massive group in the 70's, after 2 consecutive No.1 albums 'ABRAXAS' and 'SANTANA III'. • **Style:** Blues based Latin-American orientated rock, jazzily fused with percussive instrumentals mixed with CARLOS's clear guitar technique. • **Songwriters:** CARLOS penned with group except covers:- JIN-GO-LA-BA (Michael Babatunde Olatunji) / BLACK MAGIC WOMAN (Fleetwood Mac) / OYO COMO VA (c.Tito Puente) / GYPSY WOMAN (Curtis Mayfield) / PEACE ON EARTH (Alice Coltrane) / STORMY (Classics IV) / SHE'S NOT THERE (Zombies) / WELL ALL RIGHT (Buddy Holly) / ONE CHAIN (Four Tops) / WINNING (Russ Ballard) / THIRD STONE FROM THE SUN (Jimi Hendrix) / WHO'S THAT LADY (Isley Brothers) / FULL MOON (Paola Rustichelli) / RIGHT ON (Marvin Gaye) / I'VE BEEN TO THE MOUNTAIN TOP (. . . King) / etc. • **Trivia:** In 1973, CARLOS married Urmila, a Sri Chimnoy devotee. He also became highly religious and changed his name to DEVADIP, which means 'The Light Of The Lamp Supreme'. In the mid-70's, Bill Graham took over management of SANTANA. For all the lovers of anything, SANTANA, his brother JORGE (in Latin-rock band MALO) had success in Apr '72 with eponymous lp, which hit no. 14 US. A single lifted from it 'SALI VECITO' made no. 18. They went on to release 3 more 'Warner Bros.' albums; DOS (1972) / EVOLUTION (1973) + ASCENSION (1974).

Recommended: SANTANA (*7) / ABRAXAS (*8) / SANTANA III (*6) / CARAVANSERAI (*8) / VIVA! SANTANA (*8)

CARLOS SANTANA (b.20 Jul'47, Autlan de Navarro, Mexico. Raised in Tijuana then San Francisco, USA) – lead guitar / **GREGG ROLIE** – keyboards, vocals / **DAVID BROWN** – bass repl. GUS RODRIGUES (in 1967) / **MIKE SHRIEVE** – drums repl. BOB LIVINGSTONE (in '67). He had repl. ROD HARPER / **JOSE 'CHEPITO' AREAS** – perc. + **MIKE CARABELLO** – congas repl. TOM FRAZER – guitar

C.B.S. | Columbia

Oct 69. (7") **PERSUASION. / SAVOR** [ ] [ ] Sep 69
Oct 69. (7") **JIN-GO-LA-BA. / PERSUASION** [-] [56]
Nov 69. (lp)(c) **SANTANA** (UK re-dist.Mar70) [26] [4] Sep 69
– Waiting / Evil ways / Shades of time / Savor / Jingo / Persuasion / Treat / You just don't care / Soul sacrifice. *(re-iss.Mar81, cd-iss.May87 & May92)*
Jan 70. (7") **EVIL WAYS. / WAITING** [-] [9]
Apr 70. (7") **EVIL WAYS. / JINGO** [ ] [ ]
Nov 70. (lp)(c) **ABRAXAS** [7] [1] Sep 70
– Singing winds, crying beasts / Black magic woman – Gypsy queen / Oyo como va / Incident at Neshabur / Se a cabo / Mother's daughter / Samba pa ti / Hope you're feeling better / El Nicoya. *(re-iss.Mar81) (re-iss.+cd.Mar86)*
Dec 70. (7") **BLACK MAGIC WOMAN. / HOPE YOU'RE FEELING BETTER** [ ] [4] Nov 70
Mar 71. (7") **OYE COMO VA. / SAMBA PA TI** [ ] [13] Feb 71

—— added **NEIL SCHON** – guitar / **COKE ESCOVEDO** – percussion

Oct 71. (lp)(c) **SANTANA III** [6] [1]
– Batuka / No one to depend on / Taboo / Toussaint l'overture / Everybody's everything / Guajira / Everything's coming our way / Jungle strut / Para los rumberos. *(re-iss.Mar82, cd-iss.Mar87) (re-iss.cd+c Jun94 on 'Columbia')*
Nov 71. (7") **EVERYBODY'S EVERYTHING. / GUAJIRA** [ ] [12] Oct 71
Mar 72. (7") **NO ONE TO DEPEND ON. / TABOO** [ ] [36] Feb72
Jul 72. (lp)(c) **CARLOS SANTANA & BUDDY MILES LIVE (live) ("CARLOS SANTANA & BUDDY MILES")** [29] [8]
– Marbles / Lava / Evil ways / Faith interlude / Them changes / Free form funkafide filth. *(re-iss.Sep84)*
Oct 72. (7") **EVIL WAYS (live). / THEM CHANGES (live)** [ ] [84] Sep 72
(above was also credited to "CARLOS SANTANA & BUDDY MILES")

—— **ARMANDO PERAZA** – percussion repl. CARABELLO and ESCOVEDO / **TOM RUTLEY** – bass repl. BROWN

Nov 72. (lp)(c) **CARAVANSERAI** [6] [8]
– Eternal caravan of reincarnation / Waves within / Look up (to see what's coming down) / Just in time to see the sun / Song of the wind / All the love of the universe / Future primitive / Stone flower / La fuente del ritmo / Every step of the way. *(re-iss.Nov81, cd-iss.1988)*
Jan 73. (7") **LOOK UP (TO SEE WHAT'S COMING DOWN). / ALL THE LOVE OF THE UNIVERSE** [-] [ ]
Jul 73. (lp)(c) **LOVE DEVOTION SURRENDER ("CARLOS DEVADIP SANTANA AND MAHAVISHNU JOHN McLAUGHLIN")** [7] [14]
– A love supreme / Naima / The lie divine / Let us go into the house of the Lord / Meditation. *(re-iss.cd+c Jun94 on 'Columbia')*
(Above album feat. below newcomers (**RAUCH + LEWIS**) + **PERAZA, JAN HAMMER** – keyboards / **BILLY COBHAM** – drums / **LARRY YOUNG** – keyboards)

—— **CARLOS** retained **AREAS, PERAZA + SHRIEVE** and brought in newcomers **TOM COSTER** – keyboards, vocals repl. ROLIE who formed JOURNEY / **RICHARD KERMODE** – keyboards repl. SCHON who also formed JOURNEY / **DOUG RAUCH** – bass repl. RUTLEY / added **LEON THOMAS** – vocals / **JAMES MINGO LEWIS** – congas

Nov 73. (lp)(c) **WELCOME** [8] [25]
– Going home / Love, devotion and surrender / Samba de sausalito / When I look into your eyes / Yours is the light / Mother Africa / Light of life / Flame-sky / Welcome. *(re-iss.1984)*
Nov 73. (7") **WHEN I LOOK INTO YOUR EYES. / SAMBA DE SAUSALITO** [ ] [ ]
Sep 74. (lp)(c) **ILLUMINATIONS ("CARLOS SANTANA & ALICE COLTRANE")** [40] [79]
– Guru Sri Chimnoy aphorism / Angel of air – Angel of water / Bliss: The eternal now / Angel of sunlight / Illuminations. (**ALICE** – keyboards, etc.)

—— **GREG WALKER** – vocals + sessioners repl. KERMODE, LEWIS and THOMAS

Nov 74. (lp)(c) **BORBOLETTA** [18] [20]
– Spring manifestations / Canto de los flores / Life is anew / Give and take / One with the Sun / Aspirations / Practice what you preach / Mirage / Here and now / Flor de canela / Promise of a fisherman / Borboletta. *(re-iss.Nov83)(re-iss.cd Nov93 on 'Sony Collectors')*
Nov 74. (7") **PRACTICE WHAT YOU PREACH. / CANTO DE LOS FLORES** [ ] [ ]
Jan 75. (7") **MIRAGE. / FLOR DE CANELA** [ ] [ ]
Mar 75. (7") **GIVE AND TAKE. / LIFE IS ANEW** [-] [ ]
(Below triple album was issued initially in Japan 1973)
Dec 75. (t-lp) **LOTUS (live)** [ ] [ ]
– Meditation / Going home / A-1 funk / Every step of the way / Black magic woman – Gypsy queen / Oye como va / Yours is the light / Batuka / Xibaba (sheba-ba) / Savor / Stone flower / (introduction) / Castillos de arena (pt.1) / Waiting / Se a cabo / Samba pa ti / Toussaint l'overture / Incident at Neshabur. *(re-iss.d-c+d-cd.Dec90)*

—— **LEON NDUGU CHANCLER** – drums repl. SHRIEVE and AREAS / **IVORY STONE** – bass repl. RAUCH

Mar 76. (7") **EUROPA. / TAKE ME WITH YOU** [ ] [ ]
Apr 76. (lp)(c) **AMIGOS** [21] [10]
– Dance sister dance (baila mi Hermana) / Take me with you / Let me / Gitano / Tell me are you tired / Europa (Earth's cry, Heaven's smile) / Let it shine. *(re-iss.Jun84, cd-iss.Mar87 & Jun92)*
May 76. (7") **LET IT SHINE. / TELL ME ARE YOU TIRED** [ ] [77]
Aug 76. (7") **DANCE SISTER DANCE (BAILA MI HERMANA). / LET ME** [ ] [ ]

—— **JOSE AREAS** returned to repl. PERAZA / **PABLO TELEZ** – bass repl. STONE

Dec 76. (lp)(c) **FESTIVAL** [27] [27]
– Carnaval / Let the children play / Jugando / Carnival / Give me love / Verao Vermelho / Let the music set you free / Revelations / Reach up / The river / Try a little harder / Maria Caracoles.
Jan 77. (7") **REVELATIONS. / REACH UP** [ ] [-]
Jan 77. (7") **REVELATIONS. / GIVE ME LOVE** [-] [ ]
Mar 77. (7") **LET THE CHILDREN PLAY. / CARNAVAL** [ ] [ ]

—— Trimmed slightly when CHANCLER vacated

Sep 77. (7") **SHE'S NOT THERE. / ZULU** [11] [27]
Oct 77. (d-lp)(c) **MOONFLOWER (live + studio)** [7] [10]
– Dawn – Go within / Carnaval / Let the children play / Jugando / I'll be waiting / Zulu / Bahia / Black magic woman – Gypsy queen / Dance sister dance (baila mi Hermana) / Europa (Earth's cry, Heaven's smile) / She's not there / Flor de Luna (Moonflower) / Soul sacrifice / Heads, hands & feet / El Morocco / Transcendance / Savor / Toussaint l'overture. *(re-iss.Apr85, cd-iss.Apr89)*
Jan 78. (7") **BLACK MAGIC WOMAN (live). / TRANSCENDANCE** [ ] [-]
Jan 78. (7") **BLACK MAGIC WOMAN (live). / I'LL BE WAITING (live)** [-] [ ]
Aug 78. (7") **I'LL BE WAITING. ("CARLOS SANTANA") / FLOR DE LUNA (MOONFLOWER)** [ ] [ ]

—— **CARLOS** retained only **WALKER + COSTER** and introduced **ARMANDO PERAZA** returned to repl. AREAS / **DAVID MARGEN** – bass repl. TELLEZ / added **GRAHAM LEER** – drums / **CHRIS RHYME** – keyboards / **RAUL REKOW** – percussion / **CHRIS SOLBERG** – guitar, keyboards, vocals

Oct 78. (7") **WELL ALL RIGHT. / JERICHO** [-] [69]
Oct 78. (7") **WELL ALL RIGHT. / WHAM!** [53] [-]
(12"+=) – Life is a lady – Holiday.
Nov 78. (lp)(c) **INNER SECRETS** [17] [27]
– Dealer / Spanish rose / Well all right / One chain (don't make no prison) / Stormy / Open invitation / Wham! / The facts of love / Life is a lady – Holiday / Move on. *(cd-iss.Jun92)*
Jan 79. (7") **ONE CHAIN (DON'T MAKE NO PRISON). / MOVE ON** [ ] [-]
Jan 79. (7") **STORMY. / MOVE ON** [-] [32]
Mar 79. (lp)(c) **ONENESS: SILVER DREAMS, GOLDEN REALITY ("CARLOS SANTANA")** [55] [87]
– The chosen hour / Arise awake / Light versus darkness / Jim Jeannie / Transformation day / Victory / Silver dreams golden smiles / Cry of the wilderness / Guru's song / Oneness / Life is just a passing parade / Golden dawn / Free as the morning sun / Song for Devadip.
Apr 79. (7") **ONE CHAIN (DON'T MAKE NO PRISON). / LIFE IS A HOLIDAY** [-] [59]

— **ALEX LIGERTWOOD** – vocals (ex-BRIAN AUGER) repl. WALKER / **ALAN PASQUE** – keyboards, vocals repl. COSTER + RHYME

Oct 79. (7") **YOU KNOW THAT I LOVE YOU. / AQUA MARINE** [-] [35]
Oct 79. (lp)(c) **MARATHON** [28] [25]
– Marathon / Lightning in the sky / Aqua marine / You know that I love you / All I ever wanted / Stand up – Runnin' / Summer lady / Love / Stay / Hard times. *(cd-iss.May87)*
Feb 80. (7") **ALL I EVER WANTED. / LOVE** [57] [-]
Feb 80. (7") **ALL I EVER WANTED. / LIGHTNING IN THE SKY** [-] [ ]
Jun 80. (7") **AQUA MARINE. / STAND UP - RUNNIN'** [ ] [ ]
Sep 80. (d-lp)(d-c) **THE SWING OF DELIGHT ("CARLOS SANTANA")** [65] [65]
– Swapan tari / Love theme from 'Sparticus' / Phuler Matan / Song for my brother / Jharna kala / Gardenia / La Llave / Golden hours / Shere Khan, the tiger. *(this featured The MILES DAVIS QUINTET of the 60's)*

— added **ORESTES VILATO** – percussion / **RICHARD BAKER** – keyboards

Apr 81. (7") **WINNING. / BRIGHTEST STAR** [ ] [17]
Apr 81. (lp)(c) **ZEBOP!** [33] [9]
– Changes / E papa re / Primera invasion / Searchin' / Over and over / Winning / Tales of Kilimanjaro / The sensitive kind / American gypsy / I love you much too much / Brightest star / Hannibal. *(cd-iss.Dec85)*
Jun 81. (7") **CHANGES. / AMERICAN GYPSY** [ ] [ ]
Sep 81. (7") **THE SENSITIVE KIND. / AMERICAN GYPSY** [ ] [56] Aug 81
Jan 82. (7") **SEARCHIN'. / TALES OF KILIMANJARO** [-] [ ]

— **CARLOS** retained only **LEAR, MARGEN, BAKER + VILATO**

Aug 82. (lp)(c) **SHANGO** [35] [22]
– The Nile / Hold on / Night hunting time / Nowhere to run / Nueva York / Oxun / Body surfing / What does it take / Let me inside / Warrior / Shango. *(cd-iss.1988)*
Aug 82. (7") **HOLD ON. / OXUN** [-] [15]
Nov 82. (7") **NOWHERE TO RUN. / NUEVA YORK** [-] [66]

CARLOS SANTANA

solo again, featuring **WILLIE NELSON, BOOKER T.JONES & The FABULOUS THUNDERBIRDS.**

Apr 83. (7") **WATCH YOUR STEP. / TALES OF KILIMANJARO** [-] [ ]
Apr 83. (7") **WATCH YOUR STEP. / LIGHTNIN'** [ ] [-]
Apr 83. (lp)(c) **HAVANA MOON** [84] [31]
– Watch your step / Lightnin' / Who do you love / Mudbone / One with you / Ecuador / Tales of Kilimanjaro / Havana Moon / Daughter of the night / They all went to Mexico / Vereda tropical. *(cd-iss.May87) (cd re-iss.Jun88 on 'Collector's Choice')*
May 83. (7") **THEY ALL WENT TO MEXICO. / MUDBONE** [ ] [-]
Jun 83. (7") **HAVANA MOON. / LIGHTNIN'** [-] [ ]

SANTANA

CARLOS only retained **VILATO** plus sessioners

Mar 85. (7") **SAY IT AGAIN. / TOUCHDOWN RAIDERS** [ ] [46] Feb 85
(12"+=) – She's not there / ('A'instrumental).
Mar 85. (lp)(c) **BEYOND APPEARANCES** [58] [50]
– Breaking out / Written in sand / How long / Brotherhood / Spirit / Say it again / Who loves you / I'm the one who loves you / Touchdown raiders / Right now. *(re-iss.+cd.Mar86)*
May 85. (7") **HOW LONG. / RIGHT NOW** [ ] [-]
(12"+=) – She's not there.
May 85. (7") **I'M THE ONE WHO LOVES YOU. / RIGHT NOW** [-] [ ]

— **CARLOS** re-united **GREGG ROLIE, MIKE SHRIEVE, JOSE AREAS** +sessioners

Feb 87. (lp)(c)(cd) **FREEDOM** [ ] [95]
– Vera Cruz / She can't let go / Once it's gotcha / Love is you / Songs of freedom / Deeper, dig deeper / Praise / Mandela / Before we go / Victim of circumstance.
Feb 87. (7") **PRAISE. / LOVE IS YOU** [-] [ ]
May 87. (7")(12") **VERA CRUZ. / MANDELA** [ ] [ ]

— SANTANA touring band **ROLIE, CHESTER THOMPSON** – keyboards / **TOM COSTER** – synthesizers / **ALFONSO JOHNSON** – bass / **GRAHAM LEER** – drums / **BUDDY MILES** – vocals / **ARMANDO PERAZA, PAUL REKOW + ORESTES VILATO** – percussion

Nov 87. (lp)(c)(cd) **BLUES FOR SALVADOR ("CARLOS SANTANA")** [ ] [ ]
– Bailando / Aquatic park / Bella / I'm gone / 'Trane / Deeper, dig deeper / Mingus / Now that you know / Hannibal / Blues for Salvador.
(above featured mainly session people)

— **CARLOS** retained **THOMPSON + PERAZA,** plus recruited **BENNY RIETVELD** – bass / **ALEX LIGERTWOOD** – vocals, guitar / **WALFREDO REYES** – drums, timbales, perc with host of guests (over 15).

Jun 90. (cd)(c)(lp) **SPIRITS DANCING IN THE FLESH** [68] [85]
– Let there be light – Spirits dancing in the flesh / Gypsy woman / It's a jungle out there / Soweto (African libre) / Choose / Peace on Earth . . . Mother Earth . . . Third stone from the Sun / Full Moon / Who's that lady / Jin-go-la-ba / Goodness and mercy.
Jun 90. (7") **GYPSY WOMAN. / GOODNESS AND MERCY** [ ] [ ]
(12"+=)(cd-s+=) – Black magic woman / Oye como va / She's not there (live)

— Next with samples from MILES DAVIS and JOHN COLTRANE.

Polydor Polydor

Apr 92. (cd)(c)(d-lp) **MILAGRO** [ ] [ ]
– Medley:- Introduction by BILL GRAHAM – Milagro / Medley:- I've been to the mountain top – Somewhere in Heaven / Medley:- Saja – Right on / Your touch / Life is for living / Red prophet / Aqua que va ceer / Make somebody happy / Free all the people (South Africa) / Medley:- Gypsy – Grajoonca / We don't have to wait / Adios.
Nov 93. (cd)(c) **SACRED FIRE** (live in S. America) [ ] [ ]
– Angels all around us / Vive le Vada (life is for living) / Esperando / No one to depend on / Black magic woman – Gypsy queen / Oye como va / Samba pa ti / Guajira / Make somebody happy / Toussaint l'overture / Soul sacrifice / Don't try this at home / Europa / Jingo-la-ba.

— now with brother **JORGE** – guitar (ex-MALO)

Island Island

Sep 94. (cd)(c) **BROTHERS ("SANTANA BROTHERS")** [ ] [ ]
– Transmutation industrial / Thoughts / Luz amor y vida / En aranjouz con tu amour / Contigo / Blues Latino / La olaza / Brujo / The trip / Reflections / Morning in Marin.

– (SANTANA) compilations, others, etc. –

Below released on 'CBS/ Columbia' until mentioned otherwise.

Mar 73. (7") **OYE COMO VA. / BLACK MAGIC WOMAN** [ ] [ ]
(re-iss.Feb76)
Aug 74. (lp)(c) **SANTANA'S GREATEST HITS** [14] [17] Jul 74
(re-iss.Feb88, cd-iss.Jun87)
Sep 74. (7") **SAMBA PA TI. / INCIDENT AT NESHABUR** [27] [ ]
(re-iss.Feb79)
Oct 80. (t-lp) **BOX SET** (first 3 albums) [ ] [ ]
Jul 84. (7") **SHE'S NOT THERE. / SAMBA PA TI** [ ] [-]
(re-iss.Jan88 on 'Old Gold')
Oct 88. (t-lp)(d-c)(d-cd) **VIVA! SANTANA** (best + live) [ ] [ ]
– Everybody's everything / Black magic woman – Gypsy queen / Guajira / Jungle strut / Jingo / Ballin' / Bambara / Angel Negro / Incident at Neshabur / Just let the music speak / Super boogie – Hong Kong blues / Song of the wind / Abi cama / Vitalo / Paris finale / Brotherhood / Open invitation / Aqua marine / Dance, sisters, dance / Europa / Peraza I / She's not there / Bambele / Evil ways / Daughter of the night / Peraza II / Black magic woman – Gypsy woman (live) / Oyo como va / Persuasion / Soul sacrifice.
May 89. (3"cd-ep) **BLACK MAGIC WOMAN / SAMBA PA TI / OYE COMO VA / JIN-GO-LA-BA** [ ] [-]
Jun 92. (cd)(c)(lp) **THE BEST OF SANTANA** [ ] [ ]
Mar 93. Columbia; (cd) **SANTANA / ABRAXAS** [ ] [ ]
Feb 86. Old Gold; (12"ep) **SAMBA PA TI / JIN-GO-LA-BA. / SHE'S NOT THERE / EVIL WAYS** [ ] [-]
Oct 86. K-Tel; (lp)(c)(cd) **VIVA! SANTANA - THE VERY BEST OF SANTANA** [50] [-]
May 88. Arcade; (d-cd) **THE VERY BEST OF SANTANA - VOLUME 1 & 2** [ ] [-]
Jun 89. Thunderbolt; (lp)(cd) **PERSUASION** [ ] [-]
Jan 90. Thunderbolt; (cd)(lp) **LATIN TROPICAL** [ ] [-]
Jun 88. That's Orginal; (d-lp)(c)(d-cd) **WELCOME / CARLOS SANTANA & BUDDY MILES LIVE** [ ] [-]
Nov 93. Sony Collectors; (cd)(c) **SAMBA PA TI** [ ] [-]
(re-iss.cd Dec95 on 'Columbia')
Sep 93. Sony Collectors; (cd)(c) **SALSA, SAMBA & SANTANA** [ ] [-]
May 93. F.N.A.C.; (cd) **NINETEEN SIXTY EIGHT** [ ] [-]
Feb 94. Thunderbolt; (cd) **EVOLUTION** [ ] [-]
Mar 94. Charly; (cd) **SOUL SACRIFICE** [ ] [-]
Oct 94. Charly; (cd) **LATIN ROCK FUSIONS** [ ] [-]
Apr 94. Pulsar; (3xcd) **THE SUPER COLLECTION** [ ] [-]
Jul 94. Success; (cd)(c) **AS YEARS GO BY** [ ] [-]
Jul 94. Success; (cd)(c) **SANTANA JAM** [ ] [-]
Jul 94. Success; (cd)(c) **EVERY DAY I HAVE THE BLUES** [ ] [-]

Jul 94.	Success; (cd)(c) **WITH A LITTLE HELP FROM MY FRIENDS**		-
Oct 94.	Columbia; (cd) **THE BEST**		
Feb 95.	B.A.M.; (cd) **PEARLS OF THE PAST**		-
Apr 95.	Muskateer; (cd)(c) **THE EARLY YEARS**		-
Nov 95.	The Collection; (3xcd-box) **THE COLLECTION**		-

— Note: Most albums up to 1974, were also issued ! on quad-lp.

Joe SATRIANI

Born: Bay Area, San Francisco, USA. Raised in Carle Place, Long Island. After a time overseas, he formed The SQUARES in 1984. Played sessions on GREG KIHN's mid-80's album, before going solo in 1986 and releasing eponymous EP. • **Style:** New-age techno guitar-solo orientated rock. • **Songwriters:** Writes all his own work. • **Trivia:** Famous for having taught young guitarists STEVE VAI and Metallica's KIRK HAMMETT. He also guested on ALICE COOPER's 'Hey Stoopid' & SPINAL TAP's 'Break Like The Wind'.

Recommended: SURFING WITH THE ALIEN (*7) / FLYING IN A BLUE DREAM (*7)

JOE SATRIANI – guitar, bass, keyboards, percussion, etc. / with band **JEFF CAMPITELLI** – drums, percussion, DX / **JOHN CUNIBERTI** – percussion, vocals / **BONGO BOB SMITH** – electronics, drums / **JEFF KREEGER** – synth.

		F.F.Thought	Relativity	
1986.	(12"ep) **JOE SATRIANI**	-		
Feb 87.	(lp) **NOT OF THIS EARTH**			Nov 86

– Not of this Earth / The snake / Rubina / Memories / Brother John / The enigmatic / Driving at night / Hordes of locusts / New day / The headless horseman. *(c+cd-iss.Sep88)(re-iss.cd+c May93 on 'Relativity')*

— He was now joined by **STU HAMM** – bass / **JONATHAN MOVER** – drums

Nov 87.	(lp)(c)(cd) **SURFING WITH THE ALIEN**		29	

– Surfing with the alien / Ice 9 / Crushing day / Always with you, always with me / Satch boogie / Hill of the skull / Circles / Lords of Karma / Midnight / Echo. *(re-iss.cd+c May93 on 'Relativity')*

Jun 88.	(7") **ALWAYS WITH YOU, ALWAYS WITH ME. / SURFING WITH THE ALIEN**			
Dec 88.	(m-lp) **DREAMING £11**		42	

– The crush of love / Ice 9 / Memories (live) / Hordes of locusts (live). *(re-iss.cd-ep/c-ep May93 on 'Relativity')*

— SATRIANI now supplied vocals for 6 tracks & returned to original line-up.

Nov 89.	(lp)(c)(cd) **FLYING IN A BLUE DREAM**		23	

– Flying in a blue dream / The mystical potato head groove thing / Can't slow down / Headless / Strange / I believe / One big rush / Big bad Moon / The feeling / The phone call / Day at the beach (new rays from an ancient Sun) / Back to Shalla-bal / Ride / The forgotten (part one & two) / The bells of Lal (part one & two) / Into the light. *(re-iss.cd+c May93 on 'Relativity')*

Mar 90.	(7") **BIG BAD MOON. / DAY AT THE BEACH (NEW RAYS FROM AN ANCIENT SUN)**			1989

(12"+=)(cd-s+=) – ('A'extended).

Mar 91.	(7") **I BELIEVE. / FLYING IN A BLUE DREAM**			

(12"+=)(cd-s+=) – ('A'remix).

— Now with **ANDY JOHNS** on production, etc.

Aug 92.	(cd)(c)(lp) **THE EXTREMIST**	13	22	

– Friends / The extremist / War / Cryin' / Rubina's blue sky happiness / Summer song / Tears in the rain / Why / Motorcycle driver / New blues.

		Epic	Epic	
Feb 93.	(12"ep)(cd-ep) **THE SATCH EP**	53		

– The Extremist / Cryin' / Banana Mango / Crazy

Nov 93.	(2xcd)(2xc)(3xlp) **TIME MACHINE**	32	95	

– Time machine / The mighty turtle head / All alone (a.k.a. left alone) / Banana mango 11 / Thinking of you / Crazy / Speed of light / Baroque / Dweller of the threshold / Banana mango / Dreaming £11 / I am become death / Saying goodbye / Woodstock jam / Satch boogie / Summer song / Flying in a blue dream / Cryin' / The crush of love / Tears in the rain / Always with me, always with you / Big bad Moon / Surfing with the alien / Rubina / Circles / Drum solo / Lords of Karma / Echo.

Oct 95.	(cd)(c) **JOE SATRIANI**	21	51	

– Cool £9 / If / Down down down / Luminous flesh giants / SMF / Look my way / Home / Moroccan sunset / Killer bee bop / Slow down blues / (You're) My world / Sittin' 'round.

– compilations, etc. –

Oct 94.	Relativity; (3xcd-box) **NOT OF THIS EARTH / SURFING WITH THE ALIEN / FLYING IN A BLUE DREAM**		

SAW DOCTORS

Formed: Tuam, Galway, Ireland . . . late 70's by MORAN, CARTON, etc. Dropped their daytime jobs to support The WATERBOYS on UK tour. The following year, they released debut 45 'I USETA LOVE HER', which climbed to the top of the Irish charts. It stayed there for many a week, and became biggest seller ever a year later. After two more singles scored, their first album, poignantly titled 'IF THIS IS ROCK'N'ROLL I WANT MY OLD JOB BACK', made them stars. • **Style:** An unusual bunch, described as raggle-taggle showband with rock-pop attributions, or even folk-punk with pathos similar to POGUES or the early BEATLES. • **Songwriters:** Most by MORAN-CARTON except THE WEST'S AWAKE (trad). • **Trivia:** The 1991 track 'SING A POWERFUL SONG', was used on film '????' about the L.A. riots. Loved by MIKE SCOTT (Waterboys), who produced their debut 'N 17', before PHIL TENNANT took over.

Recommended: IF THIS IS ROCK'N'ROLL, I WANT MY OLD JOB BACK (*5)

JOHN 'TURPS' BURKE -mandolin, organ, guitars, vocals / **DAVY CARTON** – vocals, guitars / **LEO MORAN** – guitars, vocals, organ, etc / **TONY LAMBERT** – accordion, organ / **PEARSE 'BLACKIN' DOHERTY** – bass, vocals, piano, flute / guest **JOHN 'TANK' DONNELLY** – drums, percussion

		Solid	WEA	
1989.	(7") **n17. / ?**	-		IRE
Oct 90.	(7"m) **I USETA LOVE HER. / CAPTAIN JOE FIDDLE'S / I USED TO LOVER HER BLAZE X**		-	
May 91.	(cd)(c)(lp) **IF THIS IS ROCK'N'ROLL, I WANT MY OLD JOB BACK**	69		

– I useta lover / Only one girl / Why do I always want you / It won't be tonight / Irish poet / Sing a powerful song / Freedom fighters / That's what she said last night / Red Cortina / Presentation boarder / Don't let me down / £25 / What a day / n17 / I hope you meet again. *(re-iss.Dec93)(re-iss.cd+c Dec94 on 'Shamtown')*

Jul 91.	(7")(c-s) **N17. / N17 LIVE (including PADDY'S POEM)**			

(cd-s+=) – At least pretend.

Nov 91.	(7")(c-s) **THAT'S WHAT SHE SAID LAST NIGHT. / HAY WRAP: HAY WRAP – THE WEST'S AWAKE** – HAY WRAP			

(cd-s+=) – The trip to Tipp.

		W.E.A.	Warners	
Oct 92.	(cd)(c)(lp) **ALL THE WAY FROM TUAM**	33		

– Green and red of Mayo / You got me on the run / Pied piper / My heart is livin' in the sixties still / Hay wrap / Wake up sleeping / Midnight express / Broke my heart / Exhilarating sadness / All the way from Tuam / Music I love / Yvonne / Never mind the strangers. *(re-iss.Dec93)(re-iss.cd+c Dec94 on 'Shamtown')*

Feb 93.	(7")(c-s) **WAKE UP SLEEPING. / JOE WALL BROKE MY HEART**			

(cd-s+=) – Thank God it's a Tuesday / I hope you melt again.
(cd-s) – ('A'side) / Why do I always want you / What a day / N17 (all live).

— **ANTO THISTLETHWAITE** – saxophone, etc (ex-WATERBOYS, ex-solo artist 1993 album; AESOP WROTE . . .) repl. BURKE

May 94.	(7")(c-s) **TO WIN JUST ONCE. / ?**			

(cd-s+=) –

— Above the unofficial Irish World Cup theme.

— now without THISTLETWAITE who was now solo

		Shamtown	Warners	
Oct 94.	(c-ep)(cd-ep) **SMALL BIT OF LOVE / MICHAEL D. ROCKING IN THE DAIL / I'D LOVE TO KISS THE BANGLES / WHERE'S THE PARTY (live)**	24		

. . . Jan – Jun '96 stop press . . .

Jan 96.	(single) **WORLD OF GOOD**	15		
Feb 96.	(cd)(c) **SAME OUL' TOWN**	6		

SAXON

Formed: Barnsley, Yorkshire, England . . . 1977 by BIFF BYFORD and crew (see below), after initially calling themselves SON OF A BITCH. In 1978, they signed to French based label 'Carrere', where they finally hit big in 1980 with 2nd album 'WHEELS OF STEEL'. • **Style:** Under the banner of NWOBHM (New Wave Of British Heavy Metal), this leather-clad brigade, mixed their own blend of hard rock, fused with lyrical sword and sorcery. • **Songwriters:** Group compositions, except; S.O.S. (TOO BAD) (Saxon) / RIDE LIKE THE WIND (Christopher Cross). • **Trivia:** In 1981, they appeared at Castle Donnington's 'Monster Of Rock' festival.

Recommended: BACK ON THE STREETS (*7).

BIFF BYFORD (b.PETER BYFORD, 5 Jan'51) – vocals / **PAUL QUINN** – lead guitar / **GRAHAM OLIVER** – lead guitar / **STEVE DAWSON** – bass / **PETE GILL** – drums (ex-GLITTER BAND)

Carrere Carrere

Mar 79. (7") **STALLIONS OF THE HIGHWAY. / BIG TEASER** [ ] [ ]
May 79. (lp)(c) **SAXON** [ ] [ ]
– Rainbow theme / Frozen rainbow / Big teaser / Judgement day / Stallions of the highway / Backs to the wall / Still fit to boogie / Militia guard.
Jun 79. (7") **BIG TEASER. / STALLIONS OF THE HIGHWAY** [ ] [ ]
Nov 79. (7") **BACKS TO THE WALL. / MILITIA GUARD** [ ] [ ]
(re-iss.Jun80 on 'Atlantic', hit Uk 64)
Mar 80. (7") **WHEELS OF STEEL. / STAND UP AND BE COUNTED** [20] [ ]
Mar 80. (lp)(c) **WHEELS OF STEEL** [5] [ ]
– Motorcycle man / Stand up and be counted / 747 (strangers in the night) / Wheels of steel / Freeway mad / See the light shining / Street fighting gang / Suzi hold on / Machine gun. *(re-iss.Mar85)(re-iss.cd+c Jun93 on 'Optima')*
Jun 80. (7") **747 (STRANGERS IN THE NIGHT). / SEE THE LIGHT SHINING** [13] [ ]
Sep 80. (7") **SUZI HOLD ON. / JUDGEMENT DAY (live)** [ ] [ ]
Nov 80. (lp)(c) **STRONG ARM OF THE LAW** [11] [ ]
– Heavy metal thunder / To Hell and back again / Strong arm of the law / Taking your chances / 20,000 ft. / Hungry years / Sixth form girls / Dallas 1 p.m. *(re-iss.Dec84) (re-iss.May87 on 'Fame')*
Nov 80. (7")(12") **STRONG ARM OF THE LAW. / TAKING YOUR CHANCES** [63] [ ]
Apr 81. (7")(12")(7"pic-d) **AND THE BANDS PLAYED ON. / HUNGRY YEARS / HEAVY METAL THUNDER** [12] [ ]
Jul 81. (7") **NEVER SURRENDER. / 20,000 FT.** [18] [ ]
(d7"+=) – Bap-shoo-ap! (live) / Street fighting gang.
Sep 81. (lp)(c)(blue-lp) **DENIM AND LEATHER** [9] [ ]
– Princess of the night / Never surrender / Out of control / Rough and ready / Play it loud / And the bands played on / Midnight rider / Fire in the sky / Denim and leather. *(re-iss.+cd.May87 on 'Fame')*
Oct 81. (7") **PRINCESS OF THE NIGHT. / FIRE IN THE SKY** [57] [ ]

— **NIGEL GLOCKER** – drums (ex-TOYAH, etc.) repl. GILL who joined MOTORHEAD

May 82. (lp)(c)(pic-lp) **THE EAGLE HAS LANDED (live)** [ ] [ ]
– Motorcycle man / 747 (strangers in the night) / Princess of the night / Strong arm of the law / Heavy metal thunder / See the light shining / 20,000 ft. / Wheels of steel / Never surrender / Fire in the sky / Machine gun. *(re-iss.May86 on 'E.M.I.', cd-iss.Jul89)*
Mar 83. (lp)(c)(pic-lp) **POWER AND THE GLORY** [15] [ ]
– Power and the glory / Redline / Warrior / Nightmare / This town rocks / Watching the sky / Midas touch / The eagle has landed. *(re-iss.1986 on 'E.M.I.', cd-iss.Jul89)*
Apr 83. (7")(7"pic-d) **POWER AND THE GLORY. / SEE THE LIGHT SHINING** [32] [-]
(12"+=) – Denim and leather.
Jul 83. (7")(7"pic-d) **NIGHTMARE. / MIDAS TOUCH** [50] [-]
(12"+=) – 747 (strangers in the night).
Jan 84. (7")(12") **SAILING TO AMERICA. / A LITTLE BIT OF WHAT YOU FANCY** [ ] [-]
Feb 84. (lp)(c)(pic-lp) **CRUSADER** [18] [ ]
– (prelude) / Crusader / A little bit of what you fancy / Sailing to America / Set me free / Just let me rock / Bad boys (like to rock'n'roll) / Do it all for you / Rock city / Run for your lives. *(re-iss. Mar85, cd-iss.1986)*
Mar 84. (7")(12") **DO IT ALL FOR YOU. / JUST LET ME ROCK** [ ] [-]

Parlophone Capitol

Aug 85. (7")(7"sha-pic-d) **BACK ON THE STREETS. / LIVE FAST DIE YOUNG** [75] [ ]
(12"+=) ('A'extended version).
Sep 85. (lp)(c)(pic-lp) **INNOCENCE IS NO EXCUSE** [36] [ ]
– Rockin' again / Call of the wild / Back on the streets / The Devil rides out / Rock'n'roll gypsy / Broken heroes / Gonna shout / Everybody up / Raise some hell / Give it everything you've got.
Oct 85. (7") **ROCKIN' AGAIN. / KRAKATOA** [ ] [ ]
(12"+=) – Gonna shout (live).
Mar 86. (7")(7"pic-d) **ROCK'N'ROLL GYPSY. / KRAKATOA** [71] [ ]
(12"+=) – Medley: Heavy metal thunder – Stand up and be counted – Taking your chances – Warrior.

— **PAUL JOHNSON** – bass repl. DAWSON. (GLOCKER briefly joined G.T.R.)

E.M.I. Capitol

Aug 86. (7") **WAITING FOR THE NIGHT. / CHASE THE FADE** [66] [ ]
(12"+=) – ('A'extended).
Aug 86. (lp)(c)(cd) **ROCK THE NATIONS** [34] [ ]
– Rock the nations / Battle cry / Waiting for the night / We came here to rock / You ain't no angel / Running hot / Party 'til you puke / Empty promises / Northern lady.
Oct 86. (7")(12")(7"pic-d)(12"pic-d) **ROCK THE NATIONS. / 747 / AND THE BANDS PLAYED ON** [ ] [ ]
Jan 87. (7") **NORTHERN LADY. / EVERYBODY UP (live)** [ ] [ ]
(12"+=) – Dallas 1 p.m.

— **NIGEL DURHAM** – drums repl. GLOCKER

Feb 88. (7")(7"pic-d) **RIDE LIKE THE WIND. / RED ALERT** [52] [ ]
(12"+=) – Back on the streets (live).
(cd-s+=) – Rock the nations (live).
Mar 88. (lp)(c)(cd) **DESTINY** [49] [ ]
– Ride like the wind / Where the lightning strikes / I can't wait anymore / Calm before the storm / S.O.S. (too bad) / Song for Emma / For whom the bells toll / We are strong / Jericho siren / Red alert.
Apr 88. (7") **I CAN'T WAIT ANYMORE. / BROKEN HEROES (live)** [71] [ ]
(12"+=) – Gonna shout.

— **TIM NIBBS CARTER** – bass repl. JOHNSON.

M.F.N. Road-runner

Nov 89. (lp)(c)(cd) **ROCK'N'ROLL GYPSIES** (live '88 Hungary) [ ] [ ]
– Power and the glory / And the bands played on / Rock the nations / Dallas 1 p.m. / Broken heroes / Rock'n'roll gypsies / Northern lady / I can't wait anymore / This town rocks. *(cd+=)–* The eagle has landed / Just let me rock.

Virgin Int. Enigma

Jan 91. (cd)(c)(lp) **SOLID BALL OF ROCK** [ ] [ ]
– Solid ball of rock / Alter of the gods / Requiem (we will remember) / Lights in the sky / I just can't get enough / Baptism of fire / Ain't gonna take it / I'm on fire / Overture in b minor refugee / Bavarian beaver / Crash dive.
Mar 91. (7") **REQUIEM (WE WILL REMEMBER). / ALTAR OF THE GODS** [ ] [ ]
(12"+=)(cd-s+=) – Reeperbahn stomp.

Warhammer not issued

Apr 93. (12")(cd-s) **IRON WHEELS. / WHATEVER FREE** [ ] [-]

– compilations, others, etc. –

Jun 80. Atlantic; (7") **BIG TEASER. / RAINBOW THEME / FROZEN RAINBOW** [66] [-]
Apr 81. Atlantic; (7") **WHEELS OF STEEL. / 747 (STRANGERS IN THE NIGHT)** [ ] [-]
Jul 83. Carrere; (c-ep) **FLIPHITS** [ ] [-]
– 747 (strangers in the night) / And the bands played on / Never surrender / Princess of the night.
Dec 84. Carrere; (lp)(c) **GREATEST HITS – STRONG ARM METAL** [ ] [ ]
(re-iss.Jan86 on 'Parlophone', cd-iss.1988)
Oct 88. Castle; (d-lp)(c)(cd) **ANTHOLOGY** [ ] [-]
Jan 90. Connoisseur; (cd)(c)(d-lp) **BACK ON THE STREETS** [ ] [-]
– Power & the glory / Backs to the wall / Watching the sky / Never surrender / Princess of the night / Motorcycle man / 747 (Strangers in the night) / Wheels of steel / Nightmare / Back on the streets / Rock'n'roll gypsy / Broken heroes / Devil rides out / Party 'til you puke / Rock the nations / Waiting for the night / I can't wait anymore / We are the strong. (d-lp+=) – Midnight rider / Ride like the wind.
Mar 91. EMI; (cd)(c)(lp) **THE BEST OF SAXON** [ ] [-]
Oct 92. Old Gold; (cd-ep) **AND THE BAND PLAYED ON / 747 (AND THE BAND PLAYED ON) / NEVER SURRENDER** [ ] [-]
Aug 95. Smashing; (cd) **THE BEST OF SAXON** [ ] [-]

Michael SCHENKER GROUP

Born: 10 Jan'55, Savstedt, W.Germany. In 1971 he formed The SCORPIONS with brother RUDOLPH, but left in mid-73 to be part of English group UFO. He stayed there for 4 albums (PHENOMENON / FORCE IT / NO HEAVY PETTIN' / LIGHTS OUT), before returning in 1978 to Germany to re-join SCORPIONS. He guested on their 1979 album 'LOVEDRIVE', and featured in new live set-up, before moving on to form own outfit MICHAEL SCHENKER GROUP in 1980. He signed to 'Chrysalis' that year and surprisingly triumphed with UK Top 10 album. Continued to stir audiences, until he took break in the mid-80's. In 1988, MSG were based in L.A. • **Style:** Heavy rockers, in the mould of RAINBOW (70's style), with variations of axe-grinding by SCHENKER. • **Songwriters:** SCHENKER compositions. plus revived past SCORPIONS tracks. • **Trivia:** SCHENKER was also part of 1991 semi-supergroup CONTRABAND (see below). They covered Mott The Hoople's:- ALL THE WAY FROM MEMPHIS.

Recommended: PORTFOLIO (*6)

MICHAEL SCHENKER – lead guitar (ex-SCORPIONS, ex-UFO) / **GARY BARDEN** – vocals / **DON AIREY** – keyboards (ex-COLOSSEUM II) / **MO FOSTER** – bass / **SIMON PHILLIPS** – drums

Chrysalis Chrysalis

Aug 80. (lp)(c) **MICHAEL SCHENKER GROUP** [8] [100]
– Armed and ready / Cry for the nations / Victim of illusion / Bijou pleasurette / Feels like a good thing / Into the arena / Looking out from nowhere / Tales of mystery / Lost horizons. *(re-iss.Jun84 on 'Fame)*
Aug 80. (7")(7"colrd) **ARMED AND READY. / BIJOU PLEASURETTE** [53] [ ]
Oct 80. (7")(7"clear) **CRY FOR THE NATIONS. / INTO THE ARENA (live)** [56] [ ]

(12"+=) – Armed and ready (live).

— **PAUL RAYMOND** – keyboards (ex-UFO, etc.) repl. AIREY / **CHRIS GLEN** – bass (ex-SENSATIONAL ALEX HARVEY BAND) repl. FOSTER / **COZY POWELL** – drums (ex-RAINBOW, ex-Solo artist) repl. PHILLIPS

Aug 81. (7")(7"clear) **READY TO ROCK. / ATTACK OF THE MAD AXEMAN**

Sep 81. (lp)(c) **MSG** 14 81
– Are you ready to rock / Attack of the mad axeman / On and on / Let sleeping dogs lie / But I want more / Never trust a stranger / Looking for love / Secondary motion. *(cd-iss.May86)*

Feb 82. (d-lp)(d-c) **ONE NIGHT AT BUDOKAN (live)** 5
– Armed and ready / Cry for the nations / Attack of the mad axeman / But I want more / Victim of illusion / Into the arena / On and on / Never trust a stranger / Let sleeping dogs lie / Courvoisier concert / Lost horizon / Doctor doctor / Are you ready to rock.

— **GRAHAM BONNET** – vocals (ex-RAINBOW, ex-Solo) repl. BARDEN + RAYMOND / **TED McKENNA** – drums (ex-SENSATIONAL ALEX HARVEY BAND, ex-RORY GALLAGHER) repl. COZY who joined WHITESNAKE

Sep 82. (7")(7"clear)(7"pic-d) **DANCER. / GIRL FROM UPTOWN** 52
(12"+=) – ('A'extended).

Oct 82. (lp)(c)(pic-lp) **ASSAULT ATTACK** 19
– Assault attack / Rock you to the ground / Dancer / Samurai / Desert song / Broken promises / Searching for a reason / Ulcer.

— **GARY BARDEN** – vocals returned to repl. BONNET who went solo / added **DEREK ST.HOLMES** – keyboards (ex-TED NUGENT) (on tour **ANDY NYE** – keyboards)

Sep 83. (lp)(c)(pic-lp) **BUILT TO DESTROY** 23
– Rock my nights away / I'm gonna make you mine / The dogs of war / Systems failing / Captain Nemo / Still love that little devil / Red sky / Time waits (for no one) / Walk the stage. *(re-iss.1986)*

Jun 84. (lp)(c) **ROCK WILL NEVER DIE (live)** 24
– Captain Nemo / Rock my nights away / Are you ready to rock / Attack of the mad axeman / Into the arena / Rock will never die / Desert song / I'm gonna make you mine / Doctor, doctor.

— When CHRIS GLEN departed, most of others also folded.

McAULEY-SCHENKER GROUP

added **ROBIN McAULEY** (b.20 Jan'53, County Meath, Eire) – vox (ex-FAR CORPORATION) / **MITCH PERRY** – guitar / **ROCKY NEWTON** – bass / **BOBO SCHOPF** – drums

E.M.I. Capitol

Oct 87. (7") **GIMME YOUR LOVE. / ROCK TILL YOU'RE CRAZY**
(12"+=)(12"pic-d+=) – ('A'extended).

Oct 87. (lp)(c)(cd) **PERFECT TIMING** 65 95
– Gimme your love / Here today, gone tomorrow / Don't stop me now / No time for losers / Follow the night / Get out / Love is not a game / Time / I don't wanna lose / Rock 'til you're crazy.

Jan 88. (7")(12") **LOVE IS NOT A GAME. / GET OUT**

Apr 88. (7") **FOLLOW THE NIGHT. / DON'T STOP ME NOW** -

— **McAULEY & SCHENKER** now with **BOBO SCHOPF** – drums / **STEVE MANN** (b.9 Aug'56) – rhythm guitar / **ROCKY NEWMAN** (b.11 Sep'57) – bass (ex-LIONHEART)

Oct 89. (lp)(c)(cd) **SAVE YOURSELF** 92
– Save yourself / Bad boys / Anytime / Get down to bizness / I am your radio / Shadow of the night / What we need / There has to be another way / This is my heart / Destiny. *(cd+=)*– Take me back.

Apr 90. (7")(c-s) **ANYTIME. / WHAT WE NEED**
(12"+=)(12"pic-d+=)(cd-s+=) – ('A'-lp version).

— **SCHENKER** with **ROBIN McAULEY** – vocals / **JEFF PILSON** – bass (ex-DOKKEN) / **JAMES KOTTAK** – drums (ex-KINGDOM COME)

E.M.I. Impact

Feb 92. (12"ep)(cd-ep) **NEVER ENDING NIGHTMARE**

Feb 92. (cd)(c)(lp) **M.S.G. ("SCHENKER / McAULEY")**
– Eve / Paradise / When I'm gone / This broken heart / We believe in love / Crazy / Invincible / What happens to me / Lonely nights / This night is gonna last forever / Never ending nightmare.

– compilations, others, etc. –

Jun 87. Chrysalis; (d-lp)(c)(cd) **PORTFOLIO** -
– Doctor doctor (UFO) / Rock bottom (UFO) / Rock will never die / Armed and ready / Ready to rock / Assault attack / Ulcer / Attack of the mad axeman / I'm a loser / Reasons to love / Too hot to handle / Only you can rock me (UFO) / Lights out (UFO) / Arbory hill / Love drive (SCORPIONS) / Searching for a reason / Rock my nights away / Captain Nemo.

Jul 91. Castle; (cd)(lp) **THE COLLECTION** -

Nov 93. Windsong; (cd) **BBC RADIO 1 LIVE IN CONCERT (live)** -

Jun 94. Music Club; (cd)(c) **ARMED AND READY – THE BEST OF** -

Aug 95. Griffin; (d-cd) **ANTHOLOGY** -

CONTRABAND

MICHAEL SCHENKER – guitar / **RICHARD BLACK** – vocals (of-SHARK ISLAND) / **TRACII GUNS** – guitar (of-L.A.GUNS) / **SHARE PEDERSON** – bass (of-VIXEN) / **BOBBY BLOTZER** – drums (of-RATT)

E.M.I. Impact-EMI

Mar 91. (cd)(c)(lp) **CONTRABAND**
– All the way from Memphis / Kiss by kiss / Ultimate outrage / Bad for each other / Loud guitars, fast cars and wild, wild living / Good rockin' tonight / Stand / Tonight you're mine / Hang on to yourself.

Jul 91. (7")(c-s) **ALL THE WAY FROM MEMPHIS. / LOUD GUITARS, FAST CARS AND WILD, WILD LIVING** 65
(12"+=)(cd-s+=) – ('A'versions-3)
(12"+=) – ('A'-balls to the wall version).

Irwin SCHMIDT (see under ⇒ CAN)

Fred SCHNEIDER (see under ⇒ B-52's)

Neal SCHON & Joe HAMMER (see under ⇒ JOURNEY)

SCORPIONS

Formed: Hanover, W.Germany . . . 1971 by SCHENKER brothers and others (see below). Signed worldwide to 'RCA' in 1974, but didn't make big time until '79 when 'Harvest' took over. • **Style:** Initially a jazzy-hard rock outfit, that shifted into more basic heavy-rock, characterised by homeland accent. • **Songwriters:** SCHENKER / SCHENKER / MEINE wrote most. RAREBELL was co-credited when MICHAEL SCHENKER broke loose. Now mainly group compositions. • **Trivia:** Another heavy band to have colossal success in Japan.

Recommended: LOVEDRIVE (*8) / ANIMAL MAGNETISM (*6) / BLACKOUT (*7) / LOVE AT FIRST STING (*7) / THE BEST OF THE SCORPIONS (*7)

KLAUS MEINE (b.25 May'52) – vocals / **MICHAEL SCHENKER** – lead guitar / **RUDOLPH SCHENKER** (b.31 Aug'52) – guitar (ex-COPERNICUS) / **LOTHAR HEINBERG** – bass / **WOLFGANG ZIONY** – drums

Brain not issued

1973. (lp) **LONESOME CROW** - - Germ'y
– It all depends / Action / Lonesome crow / I'm goin' mad / Leave me / In search of the peace of mind / Inheritance. *(UK-iss.1979 on 'Logo-RCA') (pic-lp Nov82) (re-iss.Jul85 on 'Heavy Metal', cd-iss.1987) (re-iss.Oct86 on 'Razor', cd-iss. 1988) (re-iss.May80 as 'ACTION' on 'Logo-RCA') (re-iss.Nov77 as 'GOLD ROCK' on 'Brain') (re-iss.Aug74 as 'I'M GOIN' MAD & OTHERS' on 'Billingsgate')*

— (Jun73) **ULRICH ROTH** – lead guitar repl. MICHAEL who joined UFO / **JURGEN ROSENTHAL** – drums repl. WOLFGANG / **FRANCIS BUCHHOLZ** (b.19 Feb'50) – bass repl. LOTHAR

R.C.A. R.C.A.

Nov 74. (lp)(c) **FLY TO THE RAINBOW**
– Speedy's coming / They need a million / Drifting Sun / Fly, people, fly / This is my song / Fly away / Fly to the rainbow. *(re-iss.Oct85, cd-iss.Apr88)*

— (1975) **RUDY LENNERS** – drums repl. JURGENS

Mar 76. (lp)(c) **IN TRANCE**
– Dark lady / In trance / Life's like a river / Top of the bill / Living and dying / Robot man / Evening wind / Sun in my hand / Longing for fire / Night lights. *(re-iss.Jun83, cd-iss.Feb90)*

Nov 76. (7") **IN TRANCE. / NIGHT LIGHTS** -

Feb 77. (lp)(c) **VIRGIN KILLERS**
– Pictured life / Catch your train / In your park / Backstage queen / Virgin killer / Hell cat / Crying days / Polar nights / Yellow raven. *(cd-iss.Apr88)*

— **HERMAN RAREBELL** (b.18 Nov'53) – drums (ex-STEPPENWOLF) repl. RUDY

Apr 78. (lp)(c) **TAKEN BY FORCE**
– Steamrock fever / We'll burn the sky / I've got to be free / The riot of your time / The sails of Charon / Your light / He's a woman, she's a man / Born to touch your feelings. *(re-iss.Sep81) (re-iss.+cd.Oct88)*

Feb 79. (d-lp)(d-c) **THE TOKYO TAPES (live)**
– All night long / Pictured life / Backstage queen / Polar nights / In trance / We'll burn the sky / Surrender love / In search of the peace of mind / Fly to the rainbow. *(re-iss.1984, d-cd-iss.Nov88)*

— (Dec78) **MATHIAS JABS** (b.25 Oct'56) – lead guitar repl. ULRICH who formed ELECTRIC SUN. **MICHAEL SCHENKER** also guested on 3 tracks on next album, joining **KLAUS, RUDOLF, HERMAN, FRANCIS & MATHIAS**

Harvest Mercury

Mar 79. (7") **LOVING YOU SUNDAY MORNING. / COAST TO COAST** -

Apr 79. (lp)(c) **LOVEDRIVE** 36 55
– Loving you Sunday morning / Another piece of meat / Always somewhere /

Coast to coast / Can't get enough / Is there anybody there? / Lovedrive / Holiday. *(re-iss.Nov83 on 'Fame', cd-iss.Nov88)*

May 79. (7") **IS THERE ANYBODY THERE?. / ANOTHER PIECE OF MEAT** [39] [ ]

Aug 79. (7")(12") **LOVEDRIVE. / COAST TO COAST** [69] [ ]

Apr 80. (lp)(c) **ANIMAL MAGNETISM** [23] [52]
– Make it real / Don't make no promises (your body can't keep) / Hold me tight / 20th century man / Lady starlight / Fallin' in love / Only a man / The zoo / Animal magnetism. *(re-iss.+cd.May89 on 'Fame')*

Apr 80. (7") **LADY STARLIGHT. /** [-] [ ]

May 80. (7") **MAKE IT REAL. / DON'T MAKE NO PROMISES (YOUR BODY CAN'T KEEP)** [72] [ ]

Aug 80. (7") **THE ZOO. / HOLIDAY** [75] [ ]

— In 1981, MICHAEL SCHENKER briefly returned to repl. JABS while MEINE had throat surgery. Everything resumed as 1980 line-up re-appeared in 1982.

Mar 82. (lp)(c) **BLACKOUT** [11] [10]
– Blackout / Can't live without you / You give me all I need / Now! / No one like you / Dynamite / Arizona / China white / When the smoke is going down. *(re-iss.May85 on 'Fame') (re-iss.+cd.Nov88)*

Mar 82. (7")(7"pic-d) **NO ONE LIKE YOU. / NOW!** [64] [65] Jun 82

Jul 82. (7") **CAN'T LIVE WITHOUT YOU. / ALWAYS SOMEWHERE** [63] [ ]

Feb 84. (7") **ROCK YOU LIKE A HURRICANE. / COMING HOME** [ ] [25]

Mar 84. (lp)(c) **LOVE AT FIRST STING** [17] [6]
– Bad boys running wild / Rock you like a hurricane / I'm leaving you / Coming home / The same thrill / Big city nights / As soon as the good times roll / Crossfire / Still loving you. *(re-iss.Nov87) (re-iss.+cd.Aug89 on 'Fame')*

Aug 84. (7")(12")(12"pic-d) **BIG CITY NIGHTS. / BAD BOYS RUNNING WILD** [ ] [ ]

Mar 85. (7") **STILL LOVING YOU. / HOLIDAY** [ ] [64] Jun 84
(12"+=)(12"pic-d+=) – Big city nights.

Jun 85. (d-lp)(d-c) **WORLD WIDE LIVE (live)** [18] [14]
– Countdown / Coming home / Blackout / Bad boys running wild / Loving you Sunday morning / Make it real / Big city nights / Coast to coast / Holiday / Still loving you / Rock you like a hurricane / Can't live without you / Another piece of meast / Dynamite / The zoo / No one like you / Can't get enough (part 1: Six string sting – part 2: Can't get enough). *(d-cd.Feb86)*

Jun 85. (7") **NO ONE LIKE YOU (live). / THE ZOO (live)** [ ] [ ]

Apr 88. (lp)(c)(cd)(pic-lp) **SAVAGE AMUSEMENT** [18] [5]
– Don't stop at the top / Rhythm of love / Passion rules the game / Media overkill / Walking on the edge / We let it rock . . . you let it roll / Every minute every day / Love on the run / Believe in love.

May 88. (7")(7"pic-d) **RHYTHM OF LOVE. / WE LET IT ROCK . . . YOU LET IT ROLL** [59] [75]
(12"+=) – Love on the run (mix).

Aug 88. (7")(7"pic-d) **BELIEVE IN LOVE. / LOVE ON THE RUN** [ ] [ ]
(12"+=)(12"pic-d+=) – ('A' lp version).

Feb 89. (7")(7"pic-d) **PASSION RULES THE GAME. / EVERY MINUTE EVERY DAY** [74] [ ]
(12"+=)(12"pic-d+=) – Is there anybody there?
(cd-s++=) – ('A' other mix).

Vertigo Mercury

Nov 90. (cd)(c)(lp) **CRAZY WORLD** [ ] [21]
– Tease me please me / Don't believe her / Wind of change / To be with you in Heaven / Kicks after six / Send me an angel / Crazy world / Money and fame / Lust or love / Hit between the eyes / Restless nights. *(re-iss.Oct91, hit UK No.27)*

Dec 90. (7") **DON'T BELIEVE HER. / KICKS AFTER SIX** [ ] [ ]
(12"+=)(cd-s+=) – Big city nights / Holiday (live).

May 91. (7")(c-s)(7"red) **WIND OF CHANGE. / RESTLESS NIGHTS** [53] [4]
(12"+=) – Hit between the eyes / Blackout (live).
(cd-s+=) – To be with you in Heaven / Blackout (live). *(re-iss.Sep91, hit UK No.2 / US No.21)*

Nov 91. (7") **SEND ME AN ANGEL. / WIND OF CHANGE (Russian)** [27] [44]
(12"+=)(cd-s+=) – (2 live tracks).

— (May92) FRANCIS BUCHOLZ departed.

Sep 93. (cd)(c)(lp) **FACE THE HEAT** [51] [24]
– Alien nation / No pain, no gain / Someone to touch / Under the same sun / Unholy alliance / Woman / Hate to be nice / Taxman woman / Ship of fools / Nightmare Avenue / Lonely nights / Destin / Daddy's girl

Nov 93. (c-s) **UNDER THE SAME SUN. / SHIP OF FOOLS** [ ] [ ]
(12"+=) – Alien nation / Rubberfucker.
(cd-s+=) – Partners in crime.

Apr 95. (cd) **LIVE BITES (live)** [ ] [ ]
– Tease me, please me / Is there anybody there? / Rhythm of love / In trance / No pain, no gain / When the smoke is going down / Ave Maria no morro / Living for tomorrow / Concerto in V / Alien nation / Hit between the eyes / Crazy world / Wind of change / Heroes / Don't cry / White dove.

. . . Jan – Jun '96 stop press . . .

EastWest EastWest

May 96. (cd)(c)(lp) **PURE INSTINCT** [ ] [99]

– compilations, others, etc. –

Nov 79. RCA; (lp)(c) **THE BEST OF THE SCORPIONS** [ ] [ ]
– Steamrock fever / Pictured life / Robot man / Backstage queen / Speedy's coming / Hell-cat / He's a woman, she's a man / In trance / Dark lady / The sails of Charon / Virgin killer. *(re-iss.Sep81) (re-iss.+cd.Feb89)*

Apr 80. RCA; (12") **ALL NIGHT LONG. / ?** [ ] [-]

Jul 84. RCA; (lp)(c) **THE BEST OF THE SCORPIONS, VOL.2** [ ] [ ]
(re-iss.+cd Feb 90)

Feb 90. RCA; (cd) **HOT AND HEAVY** [ ] [ ]

Mar 90. RCA; (cd) **TAKE OFF** [ ] [ ]

Sep 93. RCA; (cd) **HOT AND HARD** [ ] [ ]

Nov 89. Harvest/ US= Mercury; (lp)(c)(cd) **BEST OF ROCKERS'N'BALLADS** [ ] [43]

Mar 90. Connoisseur; (cd) **HURRICANE ROCK** [ ] [-]

Apr 92. EMI; (cd)(c)(lp) **STILL LOVING YOU** [ ] [ ]

Mike SCOTT (see under ⇒ WATERBOYS)

Gil SCOTT-HERON

Born: 1 Apr'49, Chicago, Illinois, USA. Raised in Jackson, Tennessee, but later moved to New York, where he studied at Lincoln University. He met fellow poet BRIAN JACKSON, and had two novels 'The Vulture' & 'The Nigger Factory' published in 1970 and 72 respectively. This decade also started with him signing to Bob Thiele's 'Flying Dutchman' label, where he issued debut album of poetry 'SMALL TALK AT 125th AND LENNOX'. In 1975, he signed to 'Arista', where he cracked US Top 30 with lp 'THE FIRST MINUTE OF A NEW DAY'. • **Style:** Black political poet/rapper + pianist, who used highly original blend of jazz, blues reggae,latin and funk, with razor-sharp lyrics. • **Songwriters:** Collaborated with BRIAN JACKSON until 1978. Wrote own words and music from then on. Covered; INNER CITY BLUES (Marvin Gaye) and GRANDMA'S HANDS (Bill Withers). • **Trivia:** In the late fifties his Jamaican father, Gilbert St Elmo Heron, played professional football for Celtic and came to be known as the Black Arrow. GIL was the original voice-over for the "You know when you've been Tangoed" TV ad. LaBELLE covered his song 'THE REVOLUTION WILL NOT BE TELEVISED' in 1974.

Recommended: FREE WILL (*9) / PIECES OF A MAN (*8) / WINTER IN AMERICA (*10) / THE REVOLUTION WILL NOT BE TELEVISED (*9) / IT'S YOUR WORLD (*9) / REFLECTIONS (*7) / SPIRITS (*8)

GIL SCOTT-HERON – vocals, piano, guitar

Philips F.Dutchman

1972. (lp) **SMALL TALK AT 125th AND LENNOX** [-] [ ]
– (rap poems)

1972. (lp) **FREE WILL** [-] [ ]
– Free will / The middle of your day / The get out of the ghetto blues / Speed kills / Did you hear what they said? / The King Alfred Plan / No knock / Wiggy / Ain't no new thing / Bill Green is dead / Sex education: ghetto style / ...and then he wrote (Meditations)

— added **BRIAN JACKSON** – keyboards / **DANNY BOWENS** – bass / **BOB ADAMS** – drums

Apr 73. (lp) **PIECES OF A MAN** [ ] [ ]
– Lady Day and John Coltrane / When you are who you are / The revolution will not be televised / Home is where the hatred is / I think I'll call it morning / Save the children / The needle's eye / Pieces of a man / A sign of the ages / Or down you fall / The prisoner.

Apr 73. (7") **WHEN YOU ARE WHO YOU ARE. / LADY DAY AND JOHN COLTRANE** [ ] [ ]

RCA Flying Dutchman

Jul 75. (lp) **THE REVOLUTION WILL NOT BE TELEVISED** [ ] [-]
– The Revolution will not be televised / Sex education: ghetto style / The get out of the ghetto blues / No knock / Lady Day and John Coltrane / Pieces of a man / Home is where the hatred is / brother / Save the children / Did you hear what they said?
(cd-iss.May89 on 'Bluebird', += extra track)

not issued Strata East

1974. (lp) **WINTER IN AMERICA** [-] [ ]
– Peace go with you brother / Rivers of my father / A very precious time / Back home / The bottle / Song for Bobby Smith / Your Daddy loves you / H20 gate blues / Peace go with you brother

— next featured The MIDNIGHT BAND.

— **JOSEF BLOCKER + REGGIE BRISBANE** – drums repl. ADAMS

Arista Arista

Jul 75. (lp)(c) **THE FIRST MINUTE OF A NEW DAY (by "GIL SCOTT-HERON & BRIAN JACKSON")** [ ] [30] Jun 75

– Offering / The liberation song (red, black and green) / Must be something / Ain't no such thing as Superman / Pardon our analysis (we beg your pardon AMerica) / Winter in America / Guerilla / Western sunrise / Alluswe.

Jul 75. (7") **AIN'T NO SUCH THING AS SUPERMAN. / WE BEG YOUR PARDON AMERICA** [-] [ ]

Oct 75. (7") **(WHAT'S THE WORD) JOHANNESBURG. / FELL TOGETHER** [ ] [ ]

Jan 76. (lp)(c) **FROM SOUTH AFRICA TO SOUTH CAROLINA** [ ] [ ] Oct 75
– Johannesburg / A toast to the people / The summer of '42 / Beinnings (first minute of a new day) / South Carolina (Barnwell) / Essex / Fell together / A lovely day.

Nov 76. (lp)(c) **IT'S YOUR WORLD** (live) [ ] [ ]
– Seventeenth street / Tomorrow's trane (gospel trane) / Must be something / It's your world / New York City / The bottle / Possum Slim / Home is where the hatred is / Bicentennial blues / Sharing.

— **JOSEF BLOCKER + REGGIE BRISBANE** – drums repl. ADAMS

Dec 77. (lp)(c) **BRIDGES** [ ] [ ] Oct 77
– Hello Sunday! hello road! / Song of the wind / Racetrack in France / Vildgolia (deaf, dumb and blind) / Under the hammer / We almost lost Detroit / Tuskeegee No.626 / Delta man (where I'm coming from) / 95 South (all of the places we've been).

Dec 77. (7") **HELLO SUNDAY, HELLO ROAD. / THE BOTTLE (live)** [ ] [ ]

Dec 77. (7") **HELLO SUNDAY, HELLO ROAD. / SONG OF THE WIND** [-] [ ]

Mar 78. (7") **UNDER THE HAMMER. / RACETRACK IN FRANCE** [-] [ ]

— **GREG PHILLINGANES** – keyboards repl. BOWENS

Jul 78. (7") **ANGEL DUST. / THIRD WORLD REVOLUTION** [-] [ ]

Sep 78. (lp)(c) **SECRETS** [ ] [ ]
– Angel dust / Madison Avenue / Cane / Third world revolution / Better days ahead / Three miles down / Angola, Louisiana / Show bizness / A prayer for everybody / To be free.

Oct 78. (7") **SHOW BIZNESS. / BETTER DAYS AHEAD** [ ] [ ]

— retained only **JACKSON** + recruited **ED GRADY** – guitar / **KENNY POWELL** – drums / **GLEN TURNER** – keyboards / **CARL CORNWALL + VERNON JAMES** – tenor sax, flute / **KENNY SHEFFIELD** – trumpet

Feb 80. (lp)(c) **1980** [-] [ ]
– Shut 'um down / Alien / Willing / Corners / 1980 / Push comes to shove / Shah mot / Late last night. *(UK-iss.Jul85)*

Mar 80. (7")('A'ext-12") **SHUT 'EM DOWN. / BALTIMORE** [ ] [ ]

May 80. (7") **WILLIN'. /** [-] [ ]

Dec 80. (lp)(c) **REAL EYES** [ ] [ ]
– The train from Washington / Not needed / Waiting for the axe to fall / Combinations / A legend in his own mind / You could be my brother / The Klan / Your daddy loves you.

Dec 80. (7") **LEGEND IN HIS OWN MIND. /** [-] [ ]

Oct 81. (7") **STORM MUSIC. /** [-] [ ]

Dec 81. (lp)(c) **REFLECTIONS** [ ] [ ]
– Storm music / Grandma's hands / Is that jazz? / Morning thoughts / Inner city blues (poem – The siege of New Orleans) / Gun / B-movie.

Feb 82. (7") **STORM MUSIC. / B-MOVIE** [ ] [ ]
(12"+=) – Gun.

Sep 82. (7") **FAST LANE. / BLUE COLLAR** [-] [ ]

Sep 82. (lp)(c) **MOVING TARGET** [ ] [ ]
– Fast lane / Washington D.C. / No exit / Blue collar / Ready or not / Explanations / Black history – The word.

May 83. (7") **(WHAT'S THE WORD) JOHANNESBURG. / WAITING FOR THE AXE TO FALL** [ ] [ ]
(12"+=) – B-Movie (intro, poem, song).

Aug 84. (7") **RE-RON. / B-MOVIE** [ ] [ ]
(12") – Re-Ron (the missing brain mix). / B-Movie (intro, poem, song).

Sep 84. (lp)(c) **THE BEST OF GIL SCOTT-HERON** (compilation) [ ] [ ]
– The revolution will not be televised / The bottle / Winter in America / Ain't no such thing as Superman / Re-Ron / Shut 'em down / Angel dust / B-movie.

Nov 85. (7")(10") **WINTER IN AMERICA. / JOHANNESBURG** [ ] [ ]

— now with **ROBBIE GORDON** – bass, percussion / **RON HOLLOWAY** – saxophone

Essential Rykodisc

Mar 90. (7") **SPACE SHUTTLE (vocal). / ('A'original mix)** [ ] [ ]
(12"+=) – ('A'deep club mix) / Pieces of gold – medley.
(12"+=) – ('A'deep club dub) / War is very ugly.
(cd-s+=) – The bottle / Pieces of gold – medley.

Mar 90. (cd)(c)(d-lp) **THE TALES OF GIL SCOTT-HERON AND HIS AMNESIA EXPRESS (live)** [ ] [ ]
– Washington DC / Save the children / Angel dust / Gun / Blue collar / Amen (hold on to your dream) / Three miles down / The bottle.

Mother T.V.T.

Jul 94. (cd)(c) **SPIRITS** [ ] [ ]
– Message to the messengers / Spirits / Give her a call / Laly's song / Spirits past / The other side (parts 1-3) / Work for peace / Don't give up.

Mother Mother

Oct 94. (12")(cd-s) **DON'T GIVE UP. / MESSAGE TO THE MESSENGERS / THE BOTTLE (live)** [ ] [ ]

– others, etc. –

Jul 80. Inferno; (7")(12") **THE BOTTLE (drunken mix). / THE BOTTLE (sober mix)** [ ] [ ]
(re-iss.Jan 81 on 'Champagne')

— (above as "GIL SCOTT-HERON & BRIAN JACKSON")

1981. Audio Fidelity; (lp) **THE BOTTLE** (1973) [ ] [-]

Mar 88. Old Gold; (12"m) **THE BOTTLE. / JOHANNESBURG / WINTER IN AMERICA** [ ] [-]

Apr 94. Castle; (cd)(c) **MINISTRY OF INFORMATION (live)** [ ] [-]
– Winter in America / Alien / The bottle / Is that jazz / Washington DC / Gun / B-movie.

SEASTONES (see under ⇒ GRATEFUL DEAD)

SEBADOH

Formed: Boston, USA . . . 1989 by LOU BARLOW, former DINOSAUR JR. employee. After 2 albums in 1992 they finaly dented charts (UK) for 1993's 'BUBBLE AND SCRAPE'. • **Style:** NIRVANA + STOOGES-like eccentric alternative grunge rocker. • **Songwriters:** BARLOW and GAFFNEY (until latter repl. by FAY), some by LOWENSTEIN after 1992. Covered REJECT (Negros) / EVERYBODY'S BEEN BURNED (Byrds) / PINK MOON (Nick Drake) / NAIMA (John Coltrane?). FOLK IMPLOSION covered SCHOOL (Nirvana) / WON'T BACK DOWN (Tom Petty).

Recommended: BAKESALE (*8)

LOU BARLOW – vocals, guitar (ex-DINOSAUR JR) / **ERIC GAFFNEY** – drums

Homestead Homestead

Dec 89. (lp)(c) **THE FREED MAN** [ ] [ ]
–

1990. (lp) **WEED FORESTIN'** [ ] [ ]
(UK cd-iss of above 2 albums 'FREED WEED' in Nov92)

— added **JASON LOEWENSTEIN** – bass, guitar

Jul 91. (7") **GIMME INDIE ROCK** [-] [ ]

1991. (cd)(lp) **SEBADOH III** *(UK-iss.Jul94)* [-] [ ]

not issued Siltbreeze

1991. (7") **OVEN IS MY FRIEND. / ?** [-] [ ]

— In 1991, Sonic Life fanzine issued 'SPLIT WITH BIG STICK' for 'Blast First'.

not issued Vertical

1992. (7") **ASSHOLE** [-] [ ]

20 /20 Sub Pop

Aug 92. (cd)(m-lp) **ROCKIN' THE FOREST** [ ] [ ]
– Gimme indie rock / Ride the darker wave / It's so hard to fall in love / Cry sis / Really insane II / Vampire / Junk bands / Mind-held.

— Sep 92; split an EP release w/AZALIA SNAIL on 'Dark Beloved Cloud'.

Oct 92. (cd)(m-lp) **SEBADOH VS HELMET** [ ] [ ]
– Notsur dnuora selcric / Brand new love / Mean distance / . . . Burned / New worship / Good things, proud man / P.Moon / Cecilia chime in Melee / Soulmate. *(2 albums above issued in US together as 'SMASH YOUR HEAD ON THE PUNK ROCK')*

Domino Sub Pop

Mar 93. (7") **SOUL AND FIRE. / FANTASTIC DISASTER (amateur mix)** [ ] [ ]
(12"+=)(cd-s+=) – Emma get wild / Reject.

Apr 93. (cd)(lp) **BUBBLE AND SCRAPE** [63] [ ]
– Soul and fire / Two years two days / Telecosmic alchemy / Fantastic disaster / Happily divided / Sister / Cliche / Sacred attention / Elixir is Zog / Emma get wild / Sixteen / Homemade / Forced love / No way out / Bouquet for a siren / Think (let tomorrow be) / Flood.

Dec 93. (7") **REBOUND. / CAREFUL** [ ] [ ]
– (12"ep/cd-ep 'FOUR SONGS EP'+=) – Mar backlash / Not a friend / Foreground / Naima / 40203 / Mystery man / Drumstick jumble / Lime kiln.

— **BOB FAY** – drums repl. GAFFNEY who went solo (although still on below album)

Jul 94. (7")(cd-s) **SKULL. / PUNCHING MYSELF IN THE FACE REPEATEDLY, PUBLICLY / SING SOMETHING – PLATE O'HATRED** [ ] [ ]

Aug 94. (cd)(c)(lp) **BAKESALE** [40] [ ]
– License to confuse / Careful / Magnet's coil / Not a friend / Not too amused / Dreams / Skull / Got it / S. soup / Give up / Rebound / Mystery man / Temptation tide / Drama mine / Together or alone. *(ltd. w / free 7")*

Jun 95. (7")(cd-s) **NOT TOO AMUSED. / HANK WILLIAMS** [ ] [ ]

LOU BARLOW

not issued Sub Pop

1993. (7") **I AM NOT MOCKING YOU. /** [-] [ ]

LOU BARLOW AND HIS SENTRIDOH

not issued / Smells Like R.

1992. (7") **LOSERCORE. / REALLY INSANE** [-] [ ]

not issued / Little Bro.

1993. (7"ep) **THE MYSTERIOUS SENTRIDOH** [-] [ ]

LoFi

1994. (7"ep) **LOU BARLOW'S ACOUSTIC SENTRIDOH** [-] [ ] France

City Slang / Sub Pop

Jun 94. (cd)(d-lp) **A COLLECTION OF PREVIOUSLY RELEASED SONGS** (compilation) [ ] [ ]

FOLK IMPLOSION

LOU BARLOW + JOHN DAVIS

Chocolate / Drunken F.

1993. (c) **FOLK IMPLOSION** [-] [ ]
(5 tracks were featured in Sep94 on cd+10"m-lp 'TAKE A LOOK INSIDE THE FOLK IMPLOSION' om 'Tupelo-Communion' UK / 'Shrimper' US)

imported / Drunken F.

Aug 94. (7"ep) **WALK THRU THIS WORLD WITH THE FOLK IMPLOSION** [-] [ ]
– My head really hurts / End of the first side / Won't back down / School.

Communion / Com-munion

Sep 94. (cd)(lp) **TAKE A LOOK INSIDE** [ ] [ ]

. . . Jan – Jun '96 stop press . . .

Domino / Domino

Mar 96. (single) **DADDY NEVER UNDERSTOOD ("DELUXX FOLK IMPLOSION)** [ ] [ ]

London / London

May 96. (single) **NATURAL ONE** [45] [29] Dec 95

Bob SEGER

Born: 6 May'45, Ann Arbor, Michigan, USA; but raised in Detroit. In 1964 he joined (DOUG BROWN &) The OMENS contributing keyboards. He and the lead singer BROWN wrote their material, even managing a spoof of BARRY SADLER's 'The Ballad Of The Green Berets' under the "The BEACH BUMS" pseudonym early '66. The OMENS now became BOB SEGER & THE LAST HEARD, releasing a couple of 45's on local 'Hideout' label. Early in '68, Eddie Punch Andrews became manager and band were now billed as BOB SEGER SYSTEM gaining contract for 'Capitol'. In 1969, he had first US top 20 hit with 'RAMBLIN' GAMBLIN' MAN'. Commercially things dried up until 1976 + 1977 when with The SILVER BULLET BAND, he began to hit top 10 mainly in the US. Continued to have many hit albums and singles there, even in the 90's, when he returned after 4 year hiatus. • **Style:** 60's college rock band mould, until early 70's when he unsuccessfully tried out singer/troubadour image w / BRAND NEW MORNING lp. By the mid 70's, he had drifted into SPRINGSTEEN mould, although many could differentiate his gritty vocals. • **Songwriters:** SEGER wrote most except, RIVER DEEP MOUNTAIN HIGH + NUTBUSH CITY LIMITS (Ike & Tina Turner) / BO DIDDLEY (Bo Diddley) / IF I WERE A CARPENTER (Tim Hardin) / LOVE THE ONE YOU'RE WITH (Stephen Stills) / FORTUNATE SON (Creedence Clearwater Revival) / BLIND LOVE + 16 SHELLS FROM A 30.6 (Tom Waits) / SHE CAN'T DO ANYTHING WRONG (C. Davis-Richmond) / C'EST LA VIE (Chuck Berry) / etc. • **Trivia:** SEGER's songs have been covered by many including ROSALIE (Thin Lizzy) / GET OUT OF DENVER (Eddie & The Hot Rods) / WE'VE GOT TONITE (Kenny Rogers & Sheena Easton).

Recommended: GREATEST HITS (*8)

BOB SEGER & The LAST HEARD

BOB SEGER – vocas, guitar with **DAN HONAKER** – bass, guitar, vocals / **PEP PERRINE** – drums, vocals / **DOUG BROWN** – keyboards

not issued / Hideout

May 66. (7") **EAST SIDE STORY. / EAST SIDE SOUND** [-] [ ]

—— (Above & below 45's, were soon distributed by 'Cameo')

Jul 66. (7") **PERSECUTION SMITH. / CHAIN SMOKIN'** [-] [ ]

not issued / Cameo

Dec 66. (7") **SOCK IT TO ME, SANTA. / FLORIDA TIME** [-] [ ]
1967. (7") **VAGRANT WINTER. / VERY FEW** [-] [ ]
1967. (7") **HEAVY MUSIC (part 1). / HEAVY MUSIC (part 2)** [-] [ ]

BOB SEGER SYSTEM

repl BROWN who departed.

—— **BOB SCHULTZ** – keyboards, saxophone / **TONY NEME** – guitar, keyboards

Capitol / Capitol

Jan 68. (7") **2 + 2 = WHAT?. / DEATH ROW** [-] [ ]
Dec 68. (7") **RAMBLIN' GAMBLIN' MAN. / TALES OF LUCY BLUE** [ ] [17]
Jan 69. (lp) **RAMBLIN' GAMBLIN' MAN** [-] [62]
– Ramblin' gamblin' man / Tales of Lucy Blue / Ivory / Gone / Down home / Train man / White wall / Black eyed girl / 2 + 2 = what? / Doctor Fine / The lost song (love needs to be loved). *(UK-iss.Nov77) (re-iss.Jun81 on 'Greenlight')*
May 69. (7") **IVORY. / LOST SONG (LOVE NEEDS TO BE LOVED)** [-] [97]
Mar 70. (7") **LENNIE JOHNSON. / NOAH (or) OUT LOUD** [-] [ ]
Apr 70. (lp) **NOAH** [-] [ ]
Jun 70. (7") **INNERVENUS EYES. / LONELY MAN** [-] [ ]

BOB SEGER

now solo, after disbanding The SYSTEM. / added **DON WATSON** – keyboards to repl SCHULTZ + NEME

Oct 70. (7") **LUCIFER. / BIG RIVER** [ ] [84] Mar 70
Oct 70. (lp) **MONGREL** [-] [ ]
– Song to Rufus / Evil Edna / Highway child / Big river / Mongrel / Lucifer / Teachin' blues / Leavin' on my dream / Mongrel too / River deep mountain high. *(UK-iss.Nov77) (re-iss.Jun81 on 'Greenlight') (re-iss.Jul83 on 'Fame')*

—— now with **DAVE TEEGARDEN** – drums / **SKIP VANWINKLE KNAPE** – keyboards, bass / **MICHAEL BRUCE** – guitar

Nov 71. (lp) **BRAND NEW MORNING** [-] [ ]
Nov 71. (7") **LOOKIN' BACK. / HIGHWAY CHILD** [ ] [96]

Reprise / Palladium

Jul 72. (7") **IF I WERE A CARPENTER. / JESSE JAMES** [-] [76]
Aug 72. (lp)(c) **SMOKIN' O.P.'s** [ ] [ ] Jul 72
– Bo Diddley / Love the one you're with / If I were a carpenter / Hummingbird / Let it rock / Turn on your love light / Jesse James / Someday / Heavy music. *(re-iss.Apr80)*
Nov 72. (7") **TURN ON YOUR LOVE LIGHT. / BO DIDDLEY** [-] [ ]

—— SEGER's back-up back included **DICK SIMS** – keyboards / **TOM CARTMELL** – sax / **JAMIE OLDAKER** – drums / **SERGIO PASTORA** – percussion / **MARCY LEVY** – backing vocals

Mar 73. (lp)(c) **BACK IN '72** [ ] [ ]
– Midnight rider / So I wrote you a song / Stealer / Rosalie / Turn the page / Back in '72 / Neon sky / I've been working / I've got time.
Apr 73. (7") **ROSALIE. / NEON SKY** [-] [ ]
Nov 73. (7") **ROSALIE. / BACK IN '72** [ ] [-]

—— His band all left to join ERIC CLAPTON. Newcomers **KENNY BUTTREY** – drums / **RANDY MEYERS** – drums / **RICK MANSKA** – keyboards / **TOMMY COGBILL** – bass / + guitars.

Jun 74. (7") **NEED YA. / SEEN A LOT OF FLOORS** [-] [ ]
Jul 74. (lp)(c) **SEVEN / CONTRASTS** [ ] [ ]
– Get out of Denver / Long song comin' / Need ya / School teacher / Cross of gold / U.M.C. (Upper Middle Class) / Seen a lot of floors / 20 years from now / All your love. *(re-iss.Apr80) (re-iss.Jun81 on 'Greenlight')*
Aug 74. (7") **GET OUT OF DENVER. / LONG SONG COMIN'** [ ] [80]
Nov 74. (7") **U. M. C. (UPPER MIDDLE CLASS). . THIS OLD HOUSE** [-] [ ]

—— New line-up were **DREW ABBOTT** – guitar / **ROBIN ROBBINS** – keyboards / **CHRIS CAMPBELL** – bass / **ALTO REED** – saxophone / **CHARLIE ALLEN MARTIN** – drums

Capitol / Capitol

May 75. (7") **BEAUTIFUL LOSER. / FINE MEMORY** [-] [ ]
Aug 75. (lp)(c) **BEAUTIFUL LOSER** [ ] [ ] Apr 75
– Beautiful loser / Black night / Katmandu / Jody girl / Travellin' man / Momma / Nutbush city limits / Sailing nights / Fine memory. *(re-iss.Apr80)*
Aug 75. (7") **KATMANDU. / BLACK NIGHT** [ ] [43]
Nov 75. (7") **NUTBUSH CITY LIMITS. / TRAVELIN' MAN** [-] [ ]

BOB SEGER & THE SILVER BULLET BAND

Aug 76. (d-lp)(d-c) **LIVE BULLET (live Detroit)** [ ] [34] APr 76
– Nutbush city limits / Travellin' man / Beautiful loser / Jody girl / Lookin' back / Get out of Denver / Let it rock / I've been workin' / Turn the page / U.M.C. (Upper Middle Class) / Bo Diddley / Ramblin' gamblin' man / Heavy music / Katmandu. *(cd-iss.Feb95)*
Jun 76. (7") **NUTBUSH CITY LIMITS (live). / LOOKIN' BACK** [-] [69] May 76
Aug 76. (7") **TRAVELLIN' MAN (live). / BEAUTIFUL LOSER (live)** [ ] [ ]

—— Next 2 albums also credited The MUSCLE SHOALS RHYTHM SECTION on one side apiece. They were **DAVID HOOD** – bass / **ROGER HAWKINS** – drums / **BARRY BECKETT + JIMMY JOHNSON** – horns / **DOUG RILEY** – keyboards / **PETE CARR** – guitar / + **GLENN FREY**

Nov 76. (7") **MAINSTREET. / COME TO POPPA** [ ] [-]
Mar 77. (lp)(c) **NIGHT MOVES** [ ] [8] Nov 76
– Rock and roll never forgets / Night moves / The fire down below / Sunburst / Sunspot baby / Mainstreet / Come to poppa / Ship of fools / Mary Lou. *(re-iss. May82 on 'Fame') (cd-iss.Feb95)*
Mar 77. (7") **NIGHT MOVES. / SHIP OF FOOLS** [ ] [4] Dec76
Apr 77. (7") **MAINSTREET. / JODY GIRL** [-] [24]
Jul 77. (7") **ROCK AND ROLL NEVER FORGETS. / THE FIRE DOWN BELOW** [-] [41]
Sep 77. (7") **ROCK AND ROLL NEVER FORGETS. / SHIP OF FOOLS** [ ] [-]

— **DAVE TEEGARDEN** – drums (ex-STK) repl. CHARLIE (was paralysed from car crash)

May 78. (lp)(c)(silver-lp) **STRANGER IN TOWN** [31] [4]
– Hollywood nights / Still the same / Old time rock & roll / Till it shines / Feel like a number / Ain't got no money / We've got tonite / Brave strangers / The famous final scene. *(cd-iss.Feb95)*
May 78. (7") **STILL THE SAME. / FEEL LIKE A NUMBER** [ ] [4]
Jul 78. (7") **HOLLYWOOD NIGHTS. / BRAVE STRANGERS** [-] [ ]
Aug 78. (7")(7"silver) **HOLLYWOOD NIGHTS. / OLD TIME ROCK & ROLL** [42] [-]
Jan 79. (7") **WE'VE GOT TONITE. / AIN'T GOT NO MONEY** [41] [13] Oct 78
Mar 79. (7") **TILL IT SHINES. / BEAUTIFUL LOSER** [ ] [-]
(12"+=) – Get out of Denver.
Apr 79. (7") **OLD TIME ROCK & ROLL. / SUNSPOT BABY** [-] [28]
Mar 80. (7") **FIRE LAKE. / LONG TWIN SILVER LINE** [ ] [6] Feb 80
Mar 80. (lp)(c) **AGAINST THE WIND** [26] [1]
– The horizontal bop / You'll accomp'ny me / Her strut / No man's land / Long twin silver line / Against the wind / Good for me / Betty Lou's getting out tonight / Fire Lake / Shinin' brightly. *(cd-iss. 1986 & Feb95)*
May 80. (7") **AGAINST THE WIND. / NO MAN'S LAND** [ ] [5] Apr 80
Aug 80. (7") **YOU'LL ACCOMP'NY ME. / BETTY LOU'S GETTING OUT TONIGHT** [ ] [14] Jul 80
Oct 80. (7"m) **AGAINST THE WIND. / GET OUT OF DENVER / NUTBUSH CITY LIMITS** [ ] [-]
Nov 80. (7") **THE HORIZONTAL BOP. / HER STRUT** [-] [42]
Sep 81. (d-lp)(d-c) **NINE TONIGHT (live)** [24] [3]
– Nine tonight / Tryin' to live my life without you / You'll accomp'ny me / Hollywood nights / Old time rock & roll / Mainstreet / Against the wind / The fire down below / Her strut / Feel like a number / Fire Lake / Betty Lou's gettin' out tonight / We've got tonight / Night moves / Rock and roll never forgets / Let it rock. *(cd-iss.Feb95)*
Sep 81. (7") **TRYIN' TO LIVE MY LIFE WITHOUT YOU (live). / BRAVE STRANGERS (live)** [-] [5]
Oct 81. (7")(12") **HOLLYWOOD NIGHTS (live). / BRAVE STRANGERS (live)** [49] [-]
Dec 81. (7") **WE'VE GOT TONIGHT (live). / FEEL LIKE A NUMBER (live)** [60] [-]
(12"+=)(12"red+=) – Brave strangers (live).
Dec 81. (7") **FEEL LIKE A NUMBER (live). / HOLLYWOOD NIGHTS (live)** [-] [48]

— **SEGER** retained **CHRIS CAMPBELL + ALTO REED,** and recruited **ROY BITTAN** – keyboards (of BRUCE SPRINGSTEEN's E-STREET BAND) / **RUSS KUNKEL** – drums / **WADDY WACHTEL** – guitar / **CRAIG FROST** – keyboards (ex-GRAND FUNK RAILROAD)

Dec 82. (7") **SHAME ON THE MOON. / HOUSE BEHIND A HOUSE** [ ] [2]
Dec 82. (lp)(c) **THE DISTANCE** [45] [5]
– Even now / Makin' Thunderbirds / Boomtown blues / Shame on the Moon / Love's the last to know / Roll me away / House behind a house / Comin' home / Little victories. *(cd-iss.1983)*
Mar 83. (7") **EVEN NOW. / LITTLE VICTORIES** [73] [12]
(d7"+=) – We've got tonight / Brave strangers.
Jun 83. (7") **ROLL ME AWAY. / BOOMTOWN BLUES** [ ] [27] May 83
(below 'A'side was used on the film 'Teachers')
Jan 85. (7") **UNDERSTANDING. / EAST L.A.** [ ] [11] Nov 84
(12"+=) – We've got tonite.

— **DON BREWER** – drums (ex-GRAND FUNK RAILROAD) repl. KUNKEL

Mar 86. (7") **AMERICAN STORM. / FORTUNATE SON (live)** [ ] [13]
(12"+=) – Hollywood nights (live).
(d7"++=) – Hollywood nights.
Apr 86. (lp)(c)(cd) **LIKE A ROCK** [35] [3]
– American storm / Like a rock / Miami / The ring / Tightrope / The aftermath / Sometimes / It's you / Somewhere tonight. *(cd+=)*– Living inside my heart / Like a rock (edit) / Fortunate son (live).
Jul 86. (7") **LIKE A ROCK. / LIVING INSIDE MY HEART** [ ] [12] May 86
(12"+=) – Katmandu.
Aug 86. (7") **IT'S YOU. / THE AFTERMATH** [-] [52]
Nov 86. (7") **MIAMI. / SOMEWHERE TONIGHT** [-] [70]

— (below solo 45 from the 'Beverley Hills Cop II' film on 'M.C.A.')

Aug 87. (7")(12") **SHAKEDOWN. / THE AFTERMATH** [ ] [1] May87
Sep 91. (cd)(c)(lp) **THE FIRE INSIDE** [54] [7]
– Take a chance / The real love / Sightseeing / Real at the time / Always in my heart / The fire inside / Which way / New coat of paint / The mountain / The long way home / Blind love / She can't do anything wrong.
Sep 91. (7") **THE REAL LOVE. / WHICH WAY** [ ] [24] Aug 91
(12"+=) – The mountain.
(cd-s++=) – Hollywood nights.
Mar 92. (7")(c-s)(cd-s) **THE FIRE INSIDE. / THE REAL LOVE** [ ] [ ]
Jan 95. (7") **WE'VE GOT TONIGHT. / HOLLYWOOD NIGHTS** [22] [ ]
(c-s+=)(cd-s+=) – C'est la vie.
(cd-s) – ('A'side) / Night moves (live) / Nutbush city limits (live).
Feb 95. (cd)(c)(lp) **GREATEST HITS** (compilation) [6] [8] Nov94
– Roll me away / Night moves / Turn the page / You'll accomp'ny me / Hollywood nights / Still the same / Old time rock & roll / We've got tonight / Against the wind / Main street / The fire inside / Like a rock / C'est la vie / In your time.
Apr 95. (c-s) **NIGHT MOVES / EVEN NOW / WE'VE GOT TONIGHT (live)** [50] [ ]
(cd-s+=) – American storm.
(cd-s) – ('A'side) / Katmandu (live) / The fire down below / The famous final scene.
Jul 95. (c-s)(cd-s) **HOLLYWOOD NIGHTS / ROCK AND ROLL NEVER FORGETS / HOLLYWOOD NIGHTS (live)** [52] [ ]
(cd-s) – ('A'side) / Come to poppa / Fire lake.
Nov 95. (cd)(c) **IT'S A MYSTERY** [ ] [27]
– Rite of passage / Lock and load / By the river / Manhattan / I wonder / It's a mystery / Revisionism street / Golden boy / I can't save you, Angelene / 16 shells from a 30.6 / West of the Moon / Hands in the air.

. . . Jan – Jun '96 stop press . . .

Feb 96. (single) **LOCK AND LOAD** [57] [ ]

– compilations, others, etc. –

Jun 77. Reprise; (7"ep) **EXTENDED PLAY** [ ] [-]
– Get out of Denver / Back in '72 / Midnight rider / Rosalie.
Below releases on 'Capitol' unless mentioned.
Nov 77. (7"m) **TURN THE PAGE. / GET OUT OF DENVER (live) / HEAVY MUSIC (live)** [ ] [-]
Sep 83. (7") **OLD TIME ROCK & ROLL. / TILL IT SHINES** [-] [48]
Mar 84. (7") **OLD TIME ROCK & ROLL. / ROLL ME AWAY** [ ] [-]
(12"+=) – Makin' Thunderbirds.

SENSATIONAL ALEX HARVEY BAND
(see under ⇒ HARVEY, Alex)

SENSELESS THINGS

Formed: Twickenham, London, England ... late '86 by KEDS and NICHOLLS. A year later, they finally got to vinyl, after a session on the John Peel show. This flexi-7" was given free with a fanzine, and led to real debut for 'Red' records late 1988. Further indie 45's appeared, but things really took off in 1992, when on the major 'Epic' label, they smashed into UK Top 20 with 'EASY TO SMILE'. • **Style:** Thrashy amphetamine-rifled rock, lying somewhere between NIRVANA and The JAM!. • **Songwriters:** KEDS penned most, except; SHOPLIFTING (Slits) / BREAK IT AWAY (Perfect Daze) / APACHE (Shadows) / ANSWERING MACHINE (Replacements). • **Trivia:** BEN HARDING was once a clerk for the BBC.

Recommended: THE FIRST OF TOO MANY (*7)

MARK KEDS – vocals, guitar / **BEN HARDING** – lead guitar / **MORGAN NICHOLLS** – bass, guitar / **CASS BROWNE** – drums

Yo Jo Jo / not issued

Feb 88. (7"flexi) **I'M MOVING / LOW TIME / (ALL YOU'VE GOT TO DO IS) STAY TOGETHER** [ ] [-]

— (above was given free with 'Shy Like You' fanzine)

Red / not issued

Nov 88. (12"ep) **UP AND COMING** [ ] [-]
– Where the secret lies / I want to go back / I don't want to talk about it / You don't want me / When you let me down. *(re-iss.+cd-ep.Feb91)* (+=) – Girlfriend / Standing in the rain.

Way Cool / not issued

Mar 89. (7") **GIRLFRIEND. / STANDING IN THE RAIN** [ ] [-]
Oct 89. (7") **TOO MUCH KISSING. / TREVOR** [ ] [-]
Dec 89. (lp)(c)(cd) **POSTCARD C.V.** [ ] [-]
– Trevor / Come together / Sneaking kisses / Laura Lamona / Shoplifting / Drunk & soppy / Back to nowhere / Teenage / Someone in you / Too much kissing / Girlfriend / Standing in the rain. (cd+)(c+=) – UP AND COMING EP.

Decoy / not issued

May 90. (7") **IS IT TOO LATE?. / LEO** [ ] [-]
(12"+=)(cd-s+=) – Andi in a karmann / Ponyboy.
May 90. (cd)(m-lp) **IS IT TOO LATE?** [-] [-]
– Is it too late? / Leo / Andi is a karmann / Ponyboy / Celebrity / Tricia don't

belong. *(only for European export)*

Jul 90. (12"ep)(cd-ep) **CAN'T DO ANYTHING. / CAN'T EXPLAIN / TANGLED LINES** [ ] [-]
(re-issued 2 above in '92)

Epic / Epic

Jun 91. (7")(c-s) **EVERYBODY'S GONE. / MYSTERY TRAIN** [73] [-]
(12"+=)(cd-s+=) – I'm on black and white.

Sep 91. (7") **GOT IT AT THE DELMAR. / FISHING AT TESCOS** [50] [-]
(12"+=)(c-s+=)(cd-s+=) – Beat to Blondie / Can't remember.

Oct 91. (cd)(c)(lp) **THE FIRST OF TOO MANY** [66] [ ]
– Everybody's gone / Best friend / Ex teenager / It's cool to hang out with your ex / 19 blues / Should I feel it / Lip radio / In love again / Got it at the Delmar / American dad / Radio Spiteful / Chicken / Wrong number / Different tongues / Fishing at Tescos. *(re-iss.purple-lp Feb92)*

Dec 91. (7"pink)(c-s) **EASY TO SMILE. / HAZEL** [18] [ ]
(12"+=)(cd-s+=) – Mollylove.

Mar 92. (7"orange)(c-s) **HOLD IT DOWN. / CRUCIAL JUVENILIA** [19] [ ]
(12"+=)(pic-cd-s+=) – Splitting hairs.

Nov 92. (7")(c-s) **HOMOPHONIC ASSHOLE. / BODY BAG** [52] [ ]
(12"+=) – Just flirting.
(cd-s++=) – ('A' radio edit).

Feb 93. (7") **PRIMARY INSTINCT. / RUNAWAYS** [41] [ ]
(12"colrd+=)(cd-s+=) – Too much like I know you.

Mar 93. (cd)(c)(lp) **EMPIRE OF THE SENSELESS** [37] [ ]
– Homophobic asshole / Keepsake / Tempting Kate / Hold it down / Counting friends / Just one reason / Cruel Moon / Primary instinct / Rise (song for Dean & Gene) / Ice skating at the Milky Way / Say what you will / Runaways. *(re-iss.Jun93 which incl. 'POSTCARD CV')*

Jun 93. (7")(c-s) **TOO MUCH KISSING (remix). / KEEPSAKE / SAY WHAT YOU WILL (demo)** [69] [ ]
(cd-s) – (1st 2 tracks) / Cruel dub / ('A'original).

Oct 94. (7") **CHRISTINE KEELER. / HIGH ENOUGH** [56] [ ]
(12") – ('A'side) / Jerk / The revivalist / Can't go back.
(cd-s) – ('A'side) / Jerk / The revivalist / Driving on the right.

Jan 95. (7"colrd) **SOMETHING TO MISS. / 16.18.21** [61] [ ]
(12"+=)(cd-s+=) – Never haunted / Answering machine.

Feb 95. (cd)(c)(lp) **TAKING CARE OF BUSINESS** [ ] [ ]
– Christine Keeler / Something to miss / Page 3 valentine / Any which way / Marlene / Role models / Watching the pictures go / Scapegoats / 16.18.21 / Touch me on the heath / Wanted / Too late / Dead sun / The way to the drugstore.

— now without KEDS who joined WILDHEARTS for 2 months before going AWOL

– compilations, etc. –

Feb 94. Strange Fruit; (cd) **THE PEEL SESSIONS** [ ] [-]

SENSER

Formed: Wimbledon, London, England . . . late 1990 initially as a trio by NICK MICHAELSON, KERSTIN HAIGH and JAMES BARRETT. Added 4 others including dual singer; male HEITHAM AL-SAYED. Debut single 'EJECT' in 1993, was quickly followed by UK Top 50 single 'THE KEY'. • **Style:** Thrash-metal hip-hop rap, described as Britain's answer to RAGE AGAINST THE MACHINE. • **Songwriters:** Group except; SHE WATCH CHANNEL ZERO (Public Enemy). 'PEACE' was co-written w / TIM MORTON. • **Trivia:** Produced by HAGGIS.

Recommended: STACKED UP (*8)

HEITHAM AL-SAYED (b.1970, Riyadh, Saudi Arabia) – vocals, piano, bongos / **KERSTIN HAIGH** (b.1969, Balham, London) – vocals, flute / **NICK MICHAELSON** (b.1969, London) – guitar / **JAMES BARRETT** (b. 1970, London) – guitar / **ANDY CLINTON** (b. 1969, Buckinghamshire) – DJ / **HAGGIS** (b. 1966, Edinburgh, Scotland) – soundman, engineer / **JOHN MORGAN** (b.London, 1970) – drums

Ultimate / Ultimate?

Jun 93. (12")(cd-s) **EJECT / DON'T LOSE YOUR SOUL. / (other mixes)** [ ] [ ]

Sep 93. (7") **THE KEY. / NO COMPLY** [47] [ ]
(12"+=)(cd-s+=) – ('A'-radio mix) / ('A'-liquid lunch mix).

Mar 94. (7") **SWITCH. / CHANNEL ZERO** [ ] [ ]
(12"+=)(cd-s+=) – ('A'-Depth Charge mix) / Age of panic (Eat Static mix).

Apr 94. (cd)(c)(d-lp) **STACKED UP** [4] [ ]
– States of mind / The key / Switch / Age of panic / What's going on / One touch one bounch / Stubborn / Door game / Peanut game / Peace / Eject / No comply / Worth.

Jul 94. (c-s) **AGE OF PANIC. / LOOKING DOWN THE BARREL OF A GUN (live)** [52] [ ]
(12"+=)(cd-s+=) – ('A'-sick man mix).

SENTRIDOH (see under ⇒ SEBADOH)

SEPULTURA

Formed: Sao Paolo, Brazil . . . 1983 by brothers MAX and IGOR CAVELERA, who took the name SEPULTURA from the MOTORHEAD song 'Dancing On Your Grave'. (Sepultura =Grave; in Spanish). After a few releases on homeland label, they signed in 1986 to 'Roadrunner'. Fortunes changed in 1989, when GLORIA BUJNOWSKI took over management and then married MAX! Their 4th album for the label 'ARISE', surprised many by denting UK Top 40 in 1991. • **Style:** Heavy-metal thrash outfit, influenced by SLAYER and ANTHRAX. **Songwriters:** Group penned, except ORGASMATRON (Motorhead) / DRUG ME (Dead Kennedys) / SYMPTOM OF THE UNIVERSE (Black Sabbath) / THE HUNT (New Model Army) / CLENCHED FIST (Ratos De Porao). • **Trivia:** Drummer IGOR was 14 years old when he played on their 1984 debut release 'BEASTIAL DEVASTATION'.

Recommended: ARISE (*7) / ROOTS (*6)

MAX CAVELERA – vocals, guitar / **JAIRO T** -guitar/ **PAOLO JR.** – bass / **IGOR CAVELERA** – drums

Cogumelo Brazil / not issued

Nov 84. (m-lp) **BESTIAL DEVASTATION (shared with OVERDOSE)** [-] [-]
– Bestial devastation / Antichrist / Necromancer / Warriors of death.

Nov 85. (lp) **MORBID VISIONS** [-] [-]
– Morbid visions / Mayhem / Troops of doom / War / Crucifixion / Show me the wrath / Funeral rites / Empire of the damned / The curse. *(UK-iss.Apr89 on 'Shark') (UK iss.cd Nov 91 on 'Roadrunner' w/'BESTIAL DEVASTATION') (re-iss.cd/c/lp Apr94 & Aug95)*

— **ANDREAS KISSER** – lead guitar repl.JAIRO T

Roadracer / New Renaissance

Feb 87. (lp) **SCHIZOPHRENIA** [ ] [ ]
– Intro / From the past comes the storms / To the wall / Escape from the void / Inquisition symphony / Screams behind the shadows / Septic schizo / The abyss / R.I.P. (Rest In Peace). *(cd+c+=)* Troops of doom. *(re-iss.+cd.May88 on 'Shark') (re-iss.cd/c/lp Apr94 & Aug95)*

Roadrunner / Roadrunner

Apr 89. (lp)(c)(cd) **BENEATH THE REMAINS** [ ] [ ]
– Beneath the remains / Mass hypnosis / Inner self / Lobotomy / Sarcastic existence / Slaves of pain / Primitive future / Hungry / Stronger than hate. *(re-iss.cd/c/lp Apr94 & Aug95)*

Mar 91. (cd)(c)(lp) **ARISE** [40] [ ]
– Arise / Dead embryonic cells / Desperate cry / Murder / Subtraction / Altered states / Under siege (regnum Irae) / Meaningless movements / Infected voice. (pic-lp+=) – Orgasmatron. *(re-iss.cd/c/lp Apr94 & Aug95)*

Mar 91. (12"ep)(c-ep)(cd-ep) **UNDER SIEGE (REGNUM IRAE). / ORGASMATRON / TROOPS OF DOOM (re-recorded)** [ ] [ ]

Feb 92. (12"ep)(cd-ep) **ARISE. / TROOPS OF DOOM (live) / INNER SELF (live)** [ ] [ ]

Roadrunner / Epic

Sep 93. (7"pic-d)(c-s)(12")(cd-s) **TERRITORY. / POLIC!A / BIOTECH IS GODZILLA** [66] [ ]

Oct 93. (cd)(c)(lp)(ltd-cd) **CHAOS A.D.** [11] [32]
– Refuse-Resist / Territory / Slave new world / Amen / Kaiowas / Propaganda / Biotech is Godzilla / Nomad / We who are not as others / Manifest / The Hunt / Clenched fist *(re-iss.cd-tin Mar94 w/2 extra)*– Policia / Inhuman nature. *(re-iss.Aug95)*

Early in '94, MAX was arrested and fined for stamping on the Brazilian flag. He is said to have done it accidentally.

Feb 94. (7")(c-s)(12"purple)(cd-s) **REFUSE – RESIST. / INHUMAN NATURE / PROPAGANDA** [51] [ ]

May 94. (10"colrd-ep)(c-ep)(cd-ep)(12"ep) **SLAVE NEW WORLD. / CRUCIFICADOS PELO SYSTEMA / DRUG ME / ORGASMATRON (live)** [46] [ ]
(cd-s) – ('A'side) / Desperate cry.

. . . Jan – Jun '96 stop press . . .

Feb 96. (single) **ROOTS BLOODY ROOTS** [19] [ ]

Feb 96. (cd)(c)(lp) **ROOTS** [4] [27]

– compilations, others, etc. –

Nov 89. Shark; (cd) **MORBID VISIONS / CEASE TO EXIST** [ ] [-]

May 90. Shark; (cd) **SCHIZOPHRENIA / MORBID VISIONS** [ ] [-]

Sep 91. Roadrunner; (cd) **BEASTIAL DEVASTATION / MORBID VISIONS** [ ] [ ]

NAILBOMB

MAX CAVALERA + ALEX NEWPORT (of FUDGE TUNNEL)

		Road-runner	Roadracer
Mar 94.	(cd)(c)(lp) **POINT BLANK**	62	
	– Wasting away / Vai toma no cu / 24 hour bullshit / Guerillas / Blind and lost / Sum of your achievements / Cockroaches / For f***'s sake / World of shit / Exploitation / Religious cancer / Shit panata / Sick life. *(re-iss.Aug95)*		
Oct 95.	(cd)(c)(lp) **PROUD TO COMMIT COMMERCIAL SUICIDE**		

Will SERGEANT (see under ⇒ ECHO & THE BUNNYMEN)

SEX PISTOLS

Formed: London, England . . . Summer 1975 out of THE SWANKERS by COOK, JONES and MATLOCK, whom through their manager MALCOLM McLAREN, found the green-haired JOHN LYDON. He was re-named JOHNNY ROTTEN by JONES, who informed his farting rear-end 'You're rotten, you are'. After a few local gigs, they supported The 101'ers (JOE STRUMMER's band) in April '76. The rest of the year was spent causing havoc and controversy, which led to a £40,000 contract with 'EMI'. Their debut 45 'ANARCHY IN THE UK', having already shocked many on the 'So It Goes' pop TV show, was released Nov'76. It climbed into the Top 40, but after riotous appearances on the 'Today' show, in which they swore at interviewer Bill Grundy, they had single withdrawn from shops. They were also dropped by 'EMI', with label still honouring contract. In Feb'77, they fired MATLOCK, for being too nice, and brought in another violent and abusive character; SID VICIOUS. The next month they signed to 'A&M' for another six-figure sum, but due to protests from other A&M artists, they were dropped once again. Their follow-up single 'GOD SAVE THE QUEEN' had 25,000 copies pressed but it didn't hit the shops, until Richard Branson's 'Virgin' records took the reigns for a meagre £15,000 advance in May'77. It outsold its competing rivals for a No.1 spot, but due to its ban from airplay and major chainstores, it only unjustly reached No.2. Two more classics, 'PRETTY VACANT' & 'HOLIDAYS IN THE SUN', hit the Top 10, before debut album 'NEVER MIND THE BOLLOCKS, HERE'S THE SEX PISTOLS' controversially hit No.1, despite nearly contravening the 1889 indecent advertising act for the use of the word bollocks!. 1978 yet again started with more outrage, with US tours, COOK and JONES flying to Rio in Brazil to see train robber RONNIE BIGGS and JOHN LYDON leaving to form PUBLIC IMAGE LTD (see further below for more). • **Style:** The first punk-rock outfit to break into chart scene, due to their raw heavy R&B garage sound and anarchic attitude of frontman ROTTEN. Their influences ranged from The STOOGES to The NEW YORK DOLLS. • **Songwriters:** Group compositions, until COOK & JONES took over in 1978. They also covered; NO FUN (Stooges) / MY WAY (Paul Anka) / ROCK AROUND THE CLOCK (Bill Haley) / SOMETHIN' ELSE + C'MON EVERYBODY (Eddie Cochran) / JOHNNY B.GOODE (Chuck Berry) / STEPPING STONE (Boyce-Hart) / etc. • **Trivia:** In 1979, they took McLAREN to court for unpaid royalties. In 1986, the official receiver, through McLAREN paid a 7 figure out-of-court settlement to LYDON, JONES, COOK and SID's mother.

Recommended: NEVER MIND THE BOLLOCKS, HERE'S THE SEX PISTOLS (*10) / THE GREAT ROCK'N'ROLL SWINDLE (*8).

JOHNNY ROTTEN (b.JOHN LYDON, 31 Jan'56) – vocals / **STEVE JONES** (b. 3 Sep'55) – guitar / **GLEN MATLOCK** (b.27 Aug'56) – bass / **PAUL COOK** (b.20 Jul'56) – drums

		E.M.I.	not issued
Nov 76.	(7") **ANARCHY IN THE UK. / I WANNA BE ME**	38	-

—— (Feb77) **SID VICIOUS** (b.JOHN RITCHIE, 10 May'57) – bass, vocals (ex-SIOUXSIE & THE BANSHEES) repl. MATLOCK who soon formed RICH KIDS

(Mar77: They signed to 'A&M', but were soon paid off yet again. Some copies of next 45 filtered through and soon w/pic-cover became collector's items).

		Virgin	Warners
May 77.	(7") **GOD SAVE THE QUEEN. / DID YOU NO WRONG**	2	-

—— (above was banned by the BBC, and outsold the official No.1 at the time; Rod Stewart's 'I Don't Want To Talk About It'.)

Jul 77.	(7") **PRETTY VACANT. / NO FUN**	6	-
Oct 77.	(7") **HOLIDAYS IN THE SUN. / SATELLITE**	8	-
Nov 77.	(7") **PRETTY VACANT. / SUBMISSION**	-	
Nov 77.	(lp)(c) **NEVER MIND THE BOLLOCKS, HERE'S THE SEX PISTOLS**	1	106
	– Holidays in the sun / Bodies / No feelings / Liar / God save the Queen / Problems / Seventeen / Anarchy in the UK / Submission / Pretty vacant / New York / E.M.I. *(7" free w/some copies of above)*- **SUBMISSION** (one-sided). *(pic-lp 1979) (re-iss.+cd.Oct86)(re-iss.cd+c May93)*		

—— ROTTEN left, reverted to JOHN LYDON and created new band PUBLIC IMAGE LTD. His place was temporarily taken by **RONNIE BIGGS** (the Great Train Robber escapee now exiled in Brazil) 'A'-side vocals / **SID VICIOUS** – 'B'side vocals

Jun 78.	(7") **NO ONE IS INNOCENT. / MY WAY**	7	
	(some-12"+=) – (interview).		

—— On 11 Oct'78, SID was charged with the murder of girlfriend NANCY SPUNGEN. MALCOLM McLAREN/'Virgin' bailed him out, but he died 2 Feb'79 of drug overdose. The 1979/80 singles were all taken from THE GREAT ROCK'N'ROLL SWINDLE film.

Feb 79.	(7") **SOMETHING ELSE. / FRIGGIN' IN THE RIGGIN'**	3	
Mar 79.	(d-lp)(d-c) **THE GREAT ROCK'N'ROLL SWINDLE (Film Soundtrack)**	7	
	– God save the Queen symphony / Rock around the clock / Johnny B. Goode / Roadrunner / Black Arabs / Watcha gonna do about it (* on some) / Who killed Bambi? / Silly thing / Substitute / No lip / (I'm not your) Stepping stone / Lonely boy / Somethin' else / Anarchie pour le UK / Einmal war Belsen vortrefflich / No one is innocent / My way / C'mon everybody / E.M.I. / The great rock'n'roll swindle / You need hands / Friggin' in the riggin'. *(re-iss.1-lp May80) (d-cd iss.Jul86, re-iss.+d-cd.1989)(re-iss.cd+cMay93)*		
Apr 79.	(7") **SILLY THING. / WHO KILLED BAMBI?**	6	

—— (above 'A'vocals -**STEVE JONES**, 'B'vocals – **EDDIE TENPOLE TUDOR**) (below 'A'vocals – **SID VICIOUS**)

Jun 79.	(7") **C'MON EVERYBODY. / GOD SAVE THE QUEEN SYMPHONY / WATCHA GONNA DO ABOUT IT**	3	
Aug 79.	(lp)(c) **SOME PRODUCT: CARRI ON SEX PISTOLS**	6	-
	– The very name (the Sex Pistols) / From beyond the grave / Big tits across America / The complex world of Johnny Rotten / Sex Pistols will play / Is the Queen a moron / The fuckin' rotter.		
Oct 79.	(7") **THE GREAT ROCK'N'ROLL SWINDLE. / ROCK AROUND THE CLOCK**	21	
Dec 79.	(lp)(c) **SID SINGS ("SID VICIOUS")**	30	-
	– Born to lose / I wanna be your dog / Take a chance on me / (I'm not your) Stepping stone / My way / Belsen was a gas / Somethin' else / Chatterbox / Search and destroy / Chinese rocks / My way.		
Feb 80.	(lp)(c) **FLOGGIN' A DEAD HORSE**	23	
	– (singles compilation) *(re-iss.+cd.Apr86)*		
Jun 80.	(7") **(I'M NOT YOUR) STEPPING STONE. / PISTOLS PROPAGANDA**	21	-

—— COOK and JONES were now The PROFESSIONALS (see further below)

– more compilations, exploitation releases –

Note; on 'Virgin' until mentioned otherwise.

Dec 80.	(6x7"box) **PISTOLS PACK**		-
	– GOD SAVE THE QUEEN. / PRETTY VACANT / / HOLIDAYS IN THE SUN. / MY WAY / / SOMETHING ELSE. / SILLY THING / / C'MON EVERY-BODY. / THE GREAT ROCK'N'ROLL SWINDLE / / STEPPING STONE. / ANARCHY IN THE UK / / BLACK LEATHER. / HERE WE GO AGAIN		
	(below 45 credited EDDIE TENPOLE TUDOR)		
Sep 81.	(7") **WHO KILLED BAMBI?. / ROCK AROUND THE CLOCK**		-
1983.	(7") **ANARCHY IN THE UK. / NO FUN**		-
	(12"+=) – E.M.I. *(cd-ep-iss.Jun88)*		
1988.	(7") **GOD SAVE THE QUEEN. / DID YOU NO WRONG**		-
	(cd-s+=) – Don't give me no lip child.		
Sep 92.	(7")(c-s) **ANARCHY IN THE UK. / I WANNA BE ME**	33	
	(cd-s+=) – ('A'demo).		
Oct 92.	(d-cd)(c)(d-lp) **KISS THIS**	10	
	– Anarchy in the UK / God save the Queen / Pretty vacant / Holidays in ther Sun / I wanna be me / Did you no wrong / No fun / Satellite / Don't give me no lip child / (I'm not your) Stepping stone / Bodies / No feelings / Liar / Problems / Seventeen / Submission / New York / E.M.I. / My way / Silly thing / Live in Trondheim 21st July 1977:- Anarchy in the UK / I wanna be me / Seventeen / New York / E.M.I. / No fun / No feelings / Problems / God save the Queen.		
Nov 92.	(7") **PRETTY VACANT. / NO FEELINGS (demo)**	56	
	(cd-s+=) – E.M.I. (demo) / Satellite (demo).		
	(cd-s) – ('A'side) / Seventeen (demo) / Submission (demo) / Watcha gonna do about it.		
	(12"+=) – Satellite (demo) / Seventeen (demo).		
Jan 80.	Flyover; (lp) **THE BEST OF . . . AND WE DON'T CARE**		-
Jan 85.	Cherry Red; (7") **LAND OF HOPE AND GLORY. ("EX-PISTOLS") / FLOWERS OF ROMANSK**	69	-
Jan 85.	Chaos; (m-lp) **THE MINI-ALBUM**		-
	(re-iss.pic-lp Jan86) (re-iss.as 2-12"pic-d.Jan89 on 'Antler')		
Mar 87.	Chaos; (7")(7"yellow)(7"pink) **SUBMISSION. / NO FEELINGS**		-
	(12")(12"various colours) – ('A'side) / Anarchy in the UK.		
Jul 85.	Receiver; (lp) **ORIGINAL PISTOLS LIVE (live)**		-
	(re-iss.+pic-lp Jun86 on 'Demon', re-iss.+cd.Jan89) (re-iss.Dec86 on 'Dojo')		

(re-iss.May86 on 'Fame', cd-iss.Jul89)
Nov 85. Receiver; (lp) **WHERE WERE YOU IN '77** [ ] [-]
Dec 89. Receiver; (lp)(c)(cd) **NO FUTURE UK?** [ ] [-]
Jan 91. Receiver; (cd)(d-lp) **PRETTY VACANT** [ ] [-]
Aug 85. Konnexion; (lp) **LIVE WORLDWIDE (live)** [ ] [-]
Aug 85. Link; (lp) **LIVE AND LOUD (live)** [ ] [-]
(re-iss.Jun89)
Nov 85. Bondage; (lp)(pic-lp) **BEST OF SEX PISTOLS LIVE (live)** [ ] [-]
Nov 85. Hippy; (lp) **NEVER TRUST A HIPPY** [ ] [-]
Nov 85. '77 Records; (lp) **POWER OF THE PISTOLS** [ ] [-]
Feb 86. McDonald-Lydon; (lp) **THE LAST CONCERT ON EARTH (live)** [ ] [-]
Apr 86. McDonald-Lydon; (12") **ANARCHY IN THE UK (live). / FLOGGING A DEAD HORSE** [ ] [-]
Aug 86. McDonald-Lydon; (lp) **10th ANNIVERSARY ALBUM** [ ] [-]
Jan 87. McDonald-Lydon; (6xlp-box) **THE FILTH AND THE FURY** [ ] [-]
– FILTH & THE FURY / LAST SHOW ON EARTH / 10th ANNIVERSARY ALBUM / ITALIAN DOMOS / NO FUTURE USA / THE REAL SID & NANCY
Aug 86. Archive 4; (12"ep) **ANARCHY IN THE UK / I'M A LAZY SOD. / PRETTY VACANT / SUBSTITUTE** [ ] [-]
May 88. Restless; (lp)(cd) **BETTER LIVE THAN DEAD (live)** [-] [ ]
Jun 88. MBC; (lp)(cd) **IT SEEMED TO BE THE END UNTIL THE NEXT BEGINNING** [ ] [-]
Oct 88. Specific; (cd) **ANARCHY WORLDWIDE** [ ] [-]
Oct 88. Specific; (cd-ep) **CASH FOR CHAOS** [ ] [-]
Feb 90. Action Replay; (cd)(c) **THE BEST OF AND THE REST OF THE SEX PISTOLS** [ ] [-]
Jul 95. Dojo; (cd) **WANTED – THE GOODMAN TAPES** [ ] [-]

PROFESSIONALS

STEVE JONES – vocals, guitar / **PAUL COOK** – drums / **ANDY ALLEN** – guitar, vocals / **RAY McVEIGH** – guitar, vocals / **PAUL MYERS** – bass (ex-SUBWAY SECT)

Virgin — not issued

Jul 80. (7") **JUST ANOTHER DREAM. / ACTION MAN** [ ] [-]
Aug 80. (lp)(c) **THE PROFESSIONALS** [ ] [-]
– All the way / Are you? / Kick down the doors / Crescendo / Little boys in blue / Does anybody care / Kamikaze / 1-2-3 / Rockin' Mick.
Sep 80. (7"m) **1-2-3. / BABY I DON'T CARE / WHITE LIGHT, WHITE HEAT** [43] [-]
May 81. (7") **JOIN THE PROFESSIONALS. / HAS ANYBODY GOT AN ALIBI** [ ] [-]
Oct 81. (7") **THE MAGNIFICENT. / JUST ANOTHER DREAM** [ ] [-]
Nov 81. (lp)(c) **I DIDN'T SEE IT COMING** [ ] [-]
– The magnificent / Payola / Northern slide / Friday night square / Kick down the doors / Little boys / All the way / Crescendo / Madhouse / Too far to fall.

— PROFESSIONALS split early in '82 and COOK joined CHIEFS OF RELIEF. STEVE JONES joined IGGY POP and went solo in 1987 releasing 'MERCY'.

— — Stop press; the original SEX PISTOLS have re-formed at the back end of '95. Messrs LYDON, JONES, COOK + MATLOCK will tour summer '96.

. . . Jan – Jun '96 stop press . . .

— finally returned live on 24th June 1996, with packed out Finsbury Park concert. Embarked on their 'Filthy Lucre' tour soon after.

SHAMEN

Formed: Aberdeen, Scotland . . . 1984 as ALONE AGAIN OR (named after a LOVE track from '67) by COLIN ANGUS and McKENZIE brothers DEREK and KEITH. After 2 singles (1 for 'Polydor'; DREAM COME TRUE), they became The SHAMEN, and released mainly singles on own label 'Mouska' in 1986-87. In the late 80's, they signed to Derek Schulman's indie 'O. L. Indian' label, and soon secured UK chart placings by the early 90's. • **Style:** Shifted from psychedelic experimental rock in the mid-80's, to drug invoking rave-disco outfit during the 90's. Their No.1 single 'EBENEEZER GOODE', referred to the drug Ecstasy in the lyrics 'E's are good'. • **Songwriters:** All written by COLIN and DEREK, until latter's departure and replacement by the late WILL SINNOTT. ANGUS & WEST took over in '91. Covered; GRIM REAPER OF LOVE (Turtles) / FIRE ENGINE (13th Floor Elevators) / LONG GONE (Syd Barrett) / SWEET YOUNG THING (Monkees) / PURPLE HAZE (Jimi Hendrix). • **Trivia:** In Apr'88, they were dropped from a McEwans lager TV ad, because of their then anti-commercial approach.

Recommended: IN GORBACHEV WE TRUST (*7) / BOSS DRUM (*8) / EN-TACT (*9).

ALONE AGAIN OR

COLIN ANGUS (b.24 Aug'61) – keyboards / **DEREK McKENZIE** (b.27 Feb'64) – vocals, guitar / **KEITH McKENZIE** (b.30 Aug'61) – drums

All One — not issued

Dec 84. (7") **DRUM THE BEAT (IN MY SOUL). / SMARTER (edit)** [ ] [-]

Polydor — not issued

Mar 85. (7") **DREAM COME TRUE. / SMARTER THAN THE AVERAGE BEAR** [ ] [-]
(12") – ('A'&'B'-diff.versions) / Drum the beat (shall we dance?).

SHAMEN

added **ALISON MORRISON** – bass, keyboards

One Big Guitar — not issued

Apr 86. (12"ep) **THEY MAY BE RIGHT . . . BUT THEY'RE CERTAINLY WRONG** [ ] [-]
– Happy days / Velvet box / I don't like the way the world is turning.

— **PETER STEPHENSON** (b. 1 Mar,62, Ayrshire) – keyboards repl. ALISON

Mouska — not issued

Nov 86. (7"m) **YOUNG TILL YESTERDAY. / WORLD THEATRE / GOLDEN HAIR** [ ] [-]
(12"m) – (first 2 tracks) / Strange days dream / It's all around.
May 87. (7") **SOMETHING ABOUT YOU. / DO WHAT YOU WILL** [ ] [-]
(12"+=) – Grim reaper of love.
Jun 87. (lp)(c) **DROP** [ ] [-]
– Through with you / Something about you / Four letter girl / The other side / Passing away / Young till yesterday / Happy days / Where do you go / Through my window / I don't like the way the world is turning / World theatre / Velvet box. *(c+=)* – Do what you will. *(cd-iss.Nov88, +=)* – Strange days dream. *(re-iss.Jan92 on 'Mau Mau')*
Sep 87. (7") **CHRISTOPHER MAYHEW SAYS. / SHITTING ON BRITAIN** [ ] [-]
(12"+=) – Fire engine / Christopher Mayhew says a lot.

— **WILL SINNOTT** (b.23 Dec'60, Glasgow, Scotland) – bass repl. DEREK (COLIN now vocals, guitar)

Feb 88. (7") **KNATURE OF A GIRL. / HAPPY DAYS** [ ] [-]
(12"+=)(cd-s+=) – What's going down / Subknature of a girl.

Ediesta — not issued

Jun 88. (7") **JESUS LOVES AMERIKA. / DARKNESS IN ZION** [ ] [-]
(12"+=) – Do what you will.
(cd-s++=) – Sub knature dub.

— now a duo of **COLIN + WILL**

Desire — not issued

Nov 88. (12") **TRANSCENDENTAL.(as "The SHAMEN Vs. BAM BAM") / ('A'lounge mix)** [ ] [-]

Demon — not issued

Jan 89. (lp)(c)(cd) **IN GORBACHEV WE TRUST** [ ] [-]
– Synergy / Sweet young thing / Raspberry infundibulum / War prayer / Adam Strange / Jesus loves Amerika / Transcendental / Misinformation / Raptyouare / In Gorbachev we trust / (Fundamental). *(c+=)* – Resistance (once again). *(cd+=)* – Yellow cellaphane day / Mayhew speaks out.

added **SANDRA** – percussion

Moshka — not issued

Apr 89. (7") **YOU, ME & EVERYTHING. / RERAPTYOUARE** [ ] [-]
(12"+=)(cd-s+=) – Ed's bonus beats.
May 89. (10"m-lp)(c)(cd) **PHORWARD** [ ] [-]
– You, me & everything (else) / Splash 2 / Negation state / Reraptyouare / SDD 89 / Phorward. *(free 7")* – (The S&N Sessions) *(c+cd+=)* – (2 extra mixes of last single).

— **JOHN DELAFONS** – percussion repl. SANDRA

O. L. Indian — Epic

Nov 89. (12"ep)(cd-ep) **OMEGA AMICO / OMEGA A. / OMEGA PRE-MIX / PH 1** [ ] [-]
Mar 90. (7")(c-s) **PRO-GEN. / ('A'dub version)** [55] [-]
(12"+=) – Lightspan (Ben Chapman mix).
(c-s++=)(cd-s++=) – ('A'-Paul Oakenfield mix).
Sep 90. (7")(c-s) **MAKE IT MINE (PROGRESS). / ('A'evil Ed mix)** [42] [ ]
(12"+=)(cd-s+=) – Something wonderful / ('A'-Lenny D mix).
(12"+=) – Progen (Land of Oz mix) / ('A'other version).
Oct 90. (cd)(c)(2x12"lp) **EN-TACT** [31] [ ]
– Human N.R.G. / Progen (land of Oz) / Possible worlds / Omega amigo / Evil is even / Hypereal / Lightspan / Make it mine V 2.5 / Oxygen restriction / Here are my people (orbital delays expected). *(cd+=)* – *(extra tracks + mixes) (re-iss.Jul91, hit No.45)*
Mar 91. (7")(c-s) **HYPERREAL (William Orbit mix). / ('A'-lp version)** [29] [ ]
(12"+=)(cd-s+=) – ('A'dub or 'Meatbeat Manifesto' versions) / In the bag.
(12") – ('A' Meatbeat Manifesto mixes). / ('A'dub mix).

— (above featured **PLAVKA** (b. Poland) – vocals

On the 23 May'91, WILL drowned while on holiday in Ibiza. He was just 30.

Jul 91. (7")(c-s) **MOVE ANY MOUNTAIN – PROGEN '91. / ('A'well hung parliament mix)** [4] [38] Nov 91
(12"+=)//(cd-s+=) – (2 other mixes, diff.on each version).
Sep 91. (cd)(c)(lp) **PROGENCY** [23] [ ]
– Progency (8 versions).

— New line-up **COLIN** plus **MR.C** – vocals, rhythm / + **JHELSA ANDERSON** – backing vox (ex-SOUL FAMILY SENSATION) / **BOB BREEKS** – live keyboards / **GAVIN KNIGHT** – live drums / **RICHARD SHARPE** – occasional analogue

Jun 92. (7")(12") **L.S.I. (LOVE SEX INTELLIGENCE). / POSSIBLE WORLDS** [6] [ ]
(c-s+=)(cd-s+=) – Make it mine (Moby mix).
Aug 92. (7")(c-s) **EBENEEZER GOODE. / ('A'dub)** [1] [ ]
(12"+=)(cd-s+=) – ('A'mix) / L.S.I. (mix).
Oct 92. (cd)(c)(lp) **BOSS DRUM** [3] [ ]
– Boss drum / L.S.I.: Love Sex Intelligence / Space time / Librae solidi denari / Ebeneezer Goode (Beatmasters mix) / Comin' on / Phorever people / Fatman / Scientas / Re: evolution.
Oct 92. (7") **BOSS DRUM. / OMEGA AMIGO** [4] [ ]
(cd-s+=) – (3 'A'mixes).
(12"-2 diff.) – (5 'A'mixes either J.Robertson or Beatmasters).
(c-s++=) – ('A'-Steve Osbourne mixes & Youth).
Dec 92. (7"ep)(c-ep)(cd-ep) **PHOREVER PEOPLE. / ('A'dub + 'A'hypereal orbit mix)** [5] [ ]

— now with vocalist **VICTORIA WILSON-JAMES**

Aug 95. (7")(c-s) **DESTINATION ESCHATON (Beatmasters mix). / ('A'-Deep melodic mix)** [15] [ ]
(cd-s) – ('A'-Shamen acid: Escacid) / (2 'A'-Hardfloor mixes). / (cd-s) – (2 'A'-Basement Boys mixes) / (3 'A'-Beatmasters mixes).
Oct 95. (c-s) **TRANSAMAZONIA (Beatmasters mix) / ('A'-Visnadi mix) / ('A'-Watershed instrumental) / ('A'-LTJ Bukin mix)** [28] [ ]
(12"+=) – ('A'-Deep dish mix).
(cd-s) – (6 'A'mixes including; Alex Party Aguirre / Zion Train).
(cd-s+=) – ('A'-Nuv Idol mix).
Oct 95. (d-cd)(d-c)(d-lp) **AXIS MUTATIS** [27] [ ]
– Destination Eschaton / Transamazonia / Conquistador / Mauna Kea to Andromeda / Neptune / Prince of Popacatapertl / Heal the separation / Persephone's quest / Moment / Axis mundi / Eschaton omega (deep melodic techno). (d-lp w/other d-lp) – **ARBOR BONA / ARBOR MALA** – Asynptotic Escaton / Sefirotic axis (a)(b)(c) Formation (d) Action / Extraterrestrial / Deneter / Beneath the underworld / Xochipilis return / Rio Negro / Above the underworld / A moment in dub / Pizarro in Paradiso / West of the underworld / Anticipation Escaton (be ready for the storm) / Out in the styx.

... Jan – Jun '96 stop press ...

Feb 96. (single) **HEAL (THE SEPARATION)** [31] [ ]

– compilations, others, etc. –

Aug 88. Materiali Italy; (lp)(c)(cd) **STRANGE DAY DREAMS** [-] [-]
(re-iss.+cd.Oct91)(re-iss.all formats Jan93)
Dec 89. Communion; (m-lp)(cd) **WHAT'S GOING DOWN** [-] [ ]
Nov 93. Band Of Joy; (cd)(c)(lp) **ON AIR (live session)** [61] [-]

Feargal SHARKEY (see under ⇒ UNDERTONES)

SHARPE & NUMAN (see under ⇒ NUMAN, Gary)

SHED SEVEN

Formed: York, England . . . late 1991 by (see below). Signed to 'Polydor' late in '93 and with press adulation (NME, etc) they secured a near Top 75 hit with double-A side 'MARK' / 'CASINO GIRL'. In the summer of '94, they were on TOTP with high charting 'DOLPHIN'. • **Style:** Young indie-pop outfit like SUEDE, CHARLATANS, glam/mod. Singer WITTER has remarkable vox fusion lying somewhere between BRETT ANDERSON & ADAM ANT! • **Songwriters:** WITTER lyrics / group compositions. • **Trivia:** Said to have taken their group name, after it was revealed by ALAN the drummer that he lost his virginity in a shed aged only 7!. (eh!)

Recommended: CHANGE GIVER (*7) / A MAXIMUM HIGH (*8)

RICK WITTER – vocals / **PAUL BANKS** – guitar / **TOM GLADWIN** – bass / **ALAN LEACH** – drums

Polydor Polydor

Mar 94. (7"green)(c-s) **MARK. / CASINO GIRL** [77] [ ]
(12"+=)(cd-s+=) – Mobile 10.
Jun 94. (7")(c-s) **DOLPHIN. / IMMOBILITIES** [28] [ ]
(12"+=)(cd-s+=) – ('A'remix).
Aug 94. (7")(c-s) **SPEAKEASY. / AROUND YOUR HOUSE** [24] [ ]
(12"+=)(cd-s+=) – Your guess is as good as mine / Dolphin.
Sep 94. (cd)(c)(lp) **CHANGE GIVER** [16] [ ]
– Dirty soul / Speakeasy / Long time dead / Head and hands / Casino girl / Missing out / Dolphin / Stars in your eyes / Mark / Ocean pie / On an island with you.
Nov 94. (7")(c-s) **OCEAN PIE. / NEVER AGAIN** [33] [ ]
(12"+=)(cd-s+=) – Sleepeasy / Sensitive.
Apr 95. (7"green)(c-s) **WHERE HAVE YOU BEEN TONIGHT?. / SWING MY WAVE** [23] [ ]
(cd-s+=) – This is my house.

... Jan – Jun '96 stop press ...

Jan 96. (single) **GETTING BETTER** [14] [ ]
Mar 96. (single) **GOING FOR GOLD** [8] [ ]
Apr 96. (cd)(c)(lp) **A MAXIMUM HIGH** [8] [ ]
May 96. (single) **BULLY BOY** [22] [ ]

Pete SHELLEY (see under ⇒ BUZZCOCKS)

SILVERCHAIR

Formed: Australia . . .early 90's by schoolmates DANIEL, CHRIS and BEN. Made a huge impact in homeland with 1995 debut album 'FROGSTOMP', before repeating the formula ten-fold in the States. • **Style:** Teenage heavy-rock influenced by ROLLINS BAND, HELMET and BLACK SABBATH. • **Songwriters:** JOHNS-GILLIES.

Recommended: FROGSTOMP (*7)

DANIEL JOHNS -vocals, guitar / **CHRIS JOANNOU** -bass / **BEN GILLIES** -drums

Columbia Columbia

Jul 95. (12"ep) **PURE MASSACRE. / ACID RAIN / BLIND** [71] [ ]
(cd-ep+=) – Stoned.
Sep 95. (7")(c-s) **TOMORROW. / BLIND (live)** [59] [ ]
(cd-s) – ('A'side) / Leave me out / Undecided.
Sep 95. (cd)(c)(lp) **FROGSTOMP** [49] [9] Aug95
– Israel's son / Tomorrow / Faultline / Pure massacre / Shade / Blind / Leave me out / Suicidal dream / Madman / Undecided / Cicada / Findaway.

Patrick SIMMONDS (see under ⇒ DOOBIE BROTHERS)

Gene SIMMONS (see under ⇒ KISS)

SIMON AND GARFUNKEL

Formed: New York, USA . . . 1957 as TOM & JERRY by ART GARFUNKEL (b. ARTHUR GARFUNKEL, 5 Nov'41, Queens, New York) & PAUL SIMON (b.13 Oct'41, Newark, New Jersey). After a number of singles from 1958-1962, and PAUL's excursion into solo pseudonym territory, they finally teamed up together in 1964 as SIMON & GARFUNKEL. They signed to 'Columbia' that year, and issued debut lp 'WEDNESDAY MORNING 3 A.M.'. After it flopped, PAUL ventured to the UK, where he wrote 'HOMEWARD BOUND' on the Platform of Widnes railway station. It was included on his 1965 solo album ' . . . SONGBOOK'. In Oct'65, producer Tom Wilson decided to re-record 1964 track 'THE SOUNDS OF SILENCE' with electric backing, without informing the duo. Their protests were put aside, when the re-vamped track topped the US chart for 2 weeks early in '66. Pop trio The BACHELORS scored a Top 3 hit with it in Britain. S&G chose to issue 'HOMEWARD BOUND' as a duo, and this gave them worldwide smash. After a string of other hits, they were invited to supply music for the 1968 film 'THE GRADUATE' (which starred Dustin Hoffman & Anne Bancroft). In 1970, before their demise, they went into rock/pop history when 'BRIDGE OVER TROUBLED WATER' made UK + US No.1, staying in UK charts for over 300 weeks, and receiving a US grammy. The rest of the 70's saw ART going into acting and sparse solo work, while PAUL was the more successful having solo 70's Top 5 albums 'PAUL SIMON', 'THERE GOES . . . ' & 'STILL CRAZY AFTER ALL THESE YEARS'. In 1980, he signed a new deal with 'Warners'. His first venture was to write a soundtrack & script for his self-directed/acted movie 'ONE TRICK PONY'. After a disappointing follow-up in 1983, PAUL was back in the limelight in 1986 with a superb 'GRACELANDS' album, which featured South African dancers, musicians & singers. The following year, after being removed from anti-apartheid blacklists, it won a Grammy. • **Style:** Overly influenced by The EVERLY BROTHERS, although in the mid-60's, they caught on to burgeoning folk pop scene. Their clean-cut acoustic ballads were beautifully harmonised by both parties. In 1986, PAUL was inspired by African rhythms, etc on his album 'GRACELANDS'. • **Songwriters:** PAUL SIMON penned most. They covered THE TIMES THEY ARE A-CHANGIN' (Bob Dylan) / BYE BYE LOVE (Everly Brothers). PAUL SIMON covered GO TELL IT TO THE MOUNTAIN (trad). GARFUNKEL covered loads including ALL I KNOW (Jimmy Webb) / SECOND AVENUE (Tim Moore) / BREAKAWAY (Gallagher & Lyle) / I ONLY HAVE EYES FOR YOU (Flamingos) / WONDERFUL WORLD (Sam Cooke) / BRIGHT EYES (Mike Batt) / SINCE I DON'T HAVE YOU (Skyliners) / SO MUCH IN LOVE (Tymes) / MISS YOU NIGHTS (Cliff Richard) / WHEN A MAN LOVES A WOMAN (Percy Sledge) / RAG DOLL (Four Seasons) / etc. **ART's filmography:** CATCH 22 (1970 w/Alan Arkin) / CARNAL KNOWLEDGE (1971 w/Ann-Margret, Candice Bergen & Jack Nicholson) / BAD TIMING (1979 w/Teresa Russell) / ILLUSIONS (1980) / GOOD TO GO (1986) / MOTHER GOOSE ROCK'N'RHYME (1989 TV Disney musical with PAUL). Note PAUL cameod in the 1977 Woody Allen film 'Annie Hall'. • **Trivia:** PAUL's video for the 1986 single 'YOU CAN CALL ME AL' featured comic actor Chevy Chase. PAUL married long-time fiance and actress Carrie Fisher, on 16th May '83.

Recommended: THE DEFINITIVE SIMON & GARFUNKEL (*9). PAUL SIMON:- NEGOTIATIONS AND LOVE SONGS 1971-1986 (*8). ART GARFUNKEL:- THE ART GARFUNKEL ALBUM (*5).

TOM AND JERRY

(TOM = ART GARFUNKEL / JERRY = PAUL SIMON)

		not issued	Big
Dec 57.	(7") **HEY SCHOOLGIRL. / DANCIN' WILD** *(US re-iss.on 'King')*	-	49
1958.	(7") **OUR SONG. / TWO TEENAGERS**	-	
1959.	(7") **THAT'S MY STORY. / DON'T SAY GOODBYE** *(US re-iss.on 'Hunt')*	-	
1959.	(7") **BABY TALK. / TWO TEENAGERS** *(US re-iss.on 'Bell')*	-	
		not issued	**ABC Para..**
1960.	(7") **SURRENDER. / FIGHTING MAD**	-	
1960.	(7") **THAT'S MY STORY. / TIJUANA BLUES**	-	

TRUE TAYLOR

(aka PAUL SIMON)

		not issued	Big
1958.	(7") **TRUE OR FALSE. / TEENAGE FOOL**	-	

JERRY LANDIS

		not issued	M.G.M.
1959.	(7") **ANNA BELLE. / LONELINESS**	-	
		not issued	**Warwick**
1960.	(7") **JUST A BOY. / SHY**	-	
1960.	(7") **ID LIKE TO BE THE LIPSTICK ON YOUR COLLAR. / JUST A BOY**	-	
		not issued	**Amy**
Dec 62.	(7") **THE LONE TEEN RANGER. / LISA**	-	97

TICO & THE TRIUMPHS, PASSIONS

		not issued	Amy
1961.	(7") **PLAY ME A SAD SONG. / IT MEANS A LOT TO THEM**	-	
		not iss.	**Con-Am**
1961.	(7") **I'M LONELY. / I WISH I WEREN'T IN LOVE**	-	
		not iss.	**Amy**
Dec 61.	(7") **MOTORCYCLE. / I DON'T BELIEVE THEM**	-	99
1962.	(7") **EXPRESS TRAIN. / WILDFLOWER**	-	
1962.	(7") **CRY, LITTLE BOY, CRY. / GET UP & DO THE WONDER**	-	
1962.	(7") **CARDS OF LOVE. / NOISE**	-	

JERRY LANDIS (UK), PAUL KANE (US)

(different credits across the ocean)

		Oriole	Tribute
May 64.	(7") **HE WAS MY BROTHER. / CARLOS DOMINGUEZ**		

— ART also recorded 3 unknown US singles as ARTIE GARR.
In-between their re-united SIMON & GARFUNKEL debut & follow-up albums,

PAUL SIMON

released solo below.

		C.B.S.	Columbia
May 65.	(lp) **THE PAUL SIMON SONGBOOK** – I am a rock / Leaves that are green / A church is burning / April come she will / The sound of silence / Patterns / A most peculiar man / He was my brother / Kathy's song / The side of a hill / A simple desultory Philippic / Flowers never bend with the rainfall. *(cd-iss.Jan88)*		
Jul 65.	(7") **I AM A ROCK. / LEAVES THAT ARE GREEN**		

SIMON AND GARFUNKEL

both vocals, acoustic guitar

		C.B.S.	Columbia	
Oct 64.	(lp) **WEDNESDAY MORNING 3 A.M.** – You can tell the world / Last night I had the strangest dream / Bleecker Street / Sparrow / Benedictus / The sound of silence / He was my brother / Peggy-O / Go tell it to the mountain / The sun is burning / The times they are a-changin' / Wednesday morning 3 a.m. *(US re-dist.Jan66, hit No.30) (UK-iss.Nov68, hit No.24) (re-iss.+c+cd.Nov85)*	-		
Jul 65.	(7"ep) **SIMON AND GARFUNKEL** – Bleecker Street / Sparrow / Wednesday morning 3 a.m. / The sound of silence.			
Dec 65.	(7") **THE SOUND OF SILENCE. / WE'VE GOT A GROOVY THING GOIN'**		1	Nov 65
Mar 66.	(lp) **SOUND OF SILENCE** – The sound of silence / Leaves that are green / Blessed / Kathy's song / Somewhere they can't find me / Anji / Homeward bound / Richard Cory / A most peculiar man / April come she will / We've got a groovy thing goin' / I am a rock. *(re-iss.Mar81 hit UK 68, cd-iss.Dec85)*	13	21	Feb 66
Mar 66.	(7") **HOMEWARD BOUND. / LEAVES THAT ARE GREEN**	9	5	Feb 66
Jun 66.	(7") **I AM A ROCK. / FLOWERS NEVER BEND WITH THE RAINFALL** (7"ep+=) – The sound of silence / Blessed.	17	3	May 66
Sep 66.	(7") **THE DANGLING CONVERSATION. / THE BIG BRIGHT GREEN PLEASURE MACHINE**		25	Aug 66
Oct 66.	(lp) **PARSLEY, SAGE, ROSEMARY & THYME** – Dangling conversation / Scarborough fair – Canticle / Patterns / For Emily, whenever I may find her / The big bright green pleasure machine / A poem on the underground all / Cloudy / A simple desultory Philippic (or how I was Robert McNamara'd into submission) / The 59th Street Bridge song (feelin' groovy) / Flowers never bend with the rainfall / 7 o'clock news – Silent night / Parsley, sage, Rosemary and thyme. *(UK re-dist.Aug68, hit No.13) (re-iss.Mar81) (re-iss.+c+cd.Jul87 + Apr89)*		4	
Nov 66.	(7") **A HAZY SHADE OF WINTER. / FOR EMILY, WHENEVER I MAY FIND HER**		13	
Mar 67.	(7") **AT THE ZOO. / THE 59th STREET BRIDGE SONG (FEELIN' GROOVY)**		16	
Jun 67.	(7"ep) **FEELIN' GROOVY** – The 59th Street bridge song (feelin' groovy) / The big bright green pleasure machine / A hazy shade of winter / Homeward bound.		-	
Aug 67.	(7") **FAKIN' IT. / YOU DON'T KNOW WHERE YOUR INTEREST LIES**		23	Jul 67
Mar 68.	(7") **SCARBOROUGH FAIR; CANTICLE. / APRIL COME SHE WILL**		11	Feb 68
Jul 68.	(7") **MRS. ROBINSON. / OLD FRIENDS; BOOKENDS**	4	1	Apr 68
Jul 68.	(lp) **BOOKENDS** – Bookends theme / Save the life of my child / America / Overs / (voices of old people) – Old friends / Bookends / Fakin' it / Punky's dilemma / Mrs. Robinson / A hazy shade of winter / At the zoo. *(re-iss.+c.Nov82) (cd-iss. Dec 85)*	1	1	May 68
Oct 68.	(lp) **THE GRADUATE (Film Soundtrack; with tracks by DAVE GRUISIN *)** – The sound of silence / The singleman party foxtrot * / On the strip * / Sunporch cha-cha-cha * / Mrs.Robinson / A great effect * / Scarborough fair – Canticle / April come she will / Whew * / The folks * / The big bright green pleasure machine. *(re-iss.Feb84 + 1987, cd-iss.Dec85 + Apr89) (cd-iss.Apr91 on 'Sequel') (re-iss.cd+c Feb94 on 'Columbia')*	3	1	Mar 68
Dec 68.	(7"ep) **MRS. ROBINSON** – Mrs.Robinson / April come she will / Scarborough fair – Canticle / The sound of silence.	9	-	
Apr 69.	(7") **THE BOXER. / BABY DRIVER**	6	7	
Feb 70.	(7") **BRIDGE OVER TROUBLED WATER. / KEEP THE CUSTOMER SATISFIED** *(re-entered UK chart Aug70, at No.45) (re-iss.Feb78 + Jul84)*	1	1	
Feb 70.	(lp)(c) **BRIDGE OVER TROUBLED WATER** – Bridge over troubled water / El Condor Pasa / Cecilia / Keep the customer satisfied / So long, Frank Lloyd Wright / The boxer / Baby driver / The only living boy in New York / Why don't you write me / Bye bye love / Song for the asking. *(re-iss.on quad 1974) (cd-iss.Dec82) (re-iss.cd+c Sep93 & Feb95 & Dec95 on 'Columbia')*	1	1	
Apr 70.	(7") **CECILIA. / THE ONLY LIVING BOY IN NEW YORK**		4	
Sep 70.	(7") **EL CONDOR PASA. / WHY DON'T YOU WRITE ME**	-	18	

— Both went solo, after ART wanted to concentrate on acting career.

- compilations, exploitation releases, etc. -

1967. Allegro; (lp) **SIMON AND GARFUNKEL** [ ] [-]

Note; Released on 'CBS/ Columbia' unless otherwise mentioned.

Sep 70. (7") **THE SOUND OF SILENCE. / THE 59th STREET BRIDGE SONG** [ ] [-]

Jul 72. (lp)(c) **SIMON AND GARFUNKEL'S GREATEST HITS** [2] [5] Jun 72
– Mrs.Robinson / For Emily, wherever I may find her / The boxer / Feelin' groovy / The sound of silence / I am a rock / Scarborough fair (Canticle) / Homeward bound / Bridge over troubled water / America / Kathy's song / If I could / Bookends / Cecilia.

Sep 72. (7") **AMERICA. / FOR EMILY, WHENEVER I MAY FIND HER** [25] [97]

[53]

Apr 73. (7") **MRS. ROBINSON. / SCARBOROUGH FAIR; CANTICLE** [ ] [ ]

Mar 76. (7") **HOMEWARD BOUND. / THE SOUND OF SILENCE** [ ] [-]

Nov 81. (lp)(c) **THE SIMON AND GARFUNKEL COLLECTION** [4] [-]
– I am a rock / Homeward bound / America / 59th Street Bridge song / Wednesday morning 3 a.m. / El condor pasa / At the Zoo / Scarborough fair (Canticle) / The boxer / The sound of silence / Mrs.Robinson / Keep the customer satisfied / Song for the asking / Hazy shade of winter / Cecilia / Old friends / Bookends / Bridge over troubled water. *(cd-iss.Apr85 + 1988)*

Dec 81. (7") **HOMEWARD BOUND. / THE 59TH STREET BRIDGE SONG** [ ] [-]

— SIMON AND GARFUNKEL re-united for one-off concert 20 Dec'81.

Geffen Warners

Mar 82. (d-lp)(d-c) **THE CONCERT IN CENTRAL PARK (live)** [6] [6]
– Mrs. Robinson / Homeward bound / America / Scarborough fair / Me and Julio down by the schoolyard / Wake up little Susie / April come she will / Slip slidin' away / Still crazy after all these years / American tune / 50 ways to leave your lover / Late in the evening / Bridge over troubled water / A heart in New York / The 59th Street bridge song (feelin' groovy) / The sound of silence / Kodachrome / Old friends: bookends / Maybellene / The boxer. *(re-iss.+cd.May88)*

Mar 82. (7") **WAKE UP LITTLE SUSIE (live). / THE BOXER (live)** [ ] [-]

Mar 82. (7") **WAKE UP LITTLE SUSIE (live). / ME AND JULIO DOWN BY THE SCHOOLYARD (live)** [-] [27]

Jun 82. (7") **MRS. ROBINSON (live). / BRIDGE OVER TROUBLED WATER (live)** [ ] [ ]

- more compilations, etc. -

1988. CBS; (cd) **BRIDGE OVER TROUBLED WATER / PARSLEY, SAGE, ROSEMARY & SAGE** [ ] [ ]

May 88. Arcade; (cd) **COLLECTION** [ ] [-]

Nov 91. Sony-Columbia; (7")(c-s)(cd-s) **A HAZY SHADE OF WINTER. / SILENT NIGHT - SEVEN O'CLOCK NEWS (Medley)** [30] [ ]

Nov 91. Sony-Columbia; (cd)(c) **THE DEFINITIVE SIMON & GARFUNKEL** [8] [ ]
– Wednesday morning 3 a.m. / The sound of silence / Homeward bound / Cathy's song / I am a rock / For Emily wherever I may find her / Scarborough fair (canticle) / The 59th Street bridge song (feelin' groovy) / Seven o'clock news - Silent night / A hazy shade of winter / El Condor pasa (If I could) / Mrs.Robinson / America / At the zoo / Old friends / Bookends theme / Cecilia / The boxer / Bridge over troubled water / Song for the asking.

Feb 92. Sony-Columbia; (7") **THE BOXER. / CECILIA** [75] [ ]
(cd-ep+=)(cd-ep+=) –

Aug 92. Sony; (2xcd) **PARSLEY, SAGE, ROSEMARY & SAGE / BOOKENDS** [ ] [ ]

PAUL SIMON

(solo with session people)

C.B.S. Columbia

Feb 72. (7") **MOTHER AND CHILD REUNION. / PARANOIA BLUES** [5] [4]

Feb 72. (lp)(c) **PAUL SIMON** [1] [4]
– Mother and child reunion / Duncan / Everything put together falls apart / Run that body down / Armistice day / Me and Julio down by the schoolyard / Peace like a river / Papa hobo / Hobo's blues / Paranoia blues / Congratulations. *(re-iss. 1974 on quad) (re-iss.+cd.Dec87 on 'WEA')*

Apr 72. (7") **ME AND JULIO DOWN BY THE SCHOOLYARD. / CONGRATULATIONS** [15] [22]

Jul 72. (7") **DUNCAN. / RUN THAT BODY DOWN** [-] [52]

May 73. (lp)(c) **THERE GOES RHYMIN' SIMON** [4] [2]
– Kodachrome / Tenderness / Take me to the Mardi Gras / Something so right / One man's ceiling is another man's floor / American tune / Was a sunny day / Learn how to fall / St. Judy's comet / Loves me like a rock. *(re-iss.1974 on quad) (re-iss.+cd.Dec87 on 'WEA')*

May 73. (7") **KODACHROME. / TENDERNESS** [-] [2]

May 73. (7") **TAKE ME TO THE MARDI GRAS. / KODACHROME** [7] [-]

Sep 73. (7") **LOVES ME LIKE A ROCK. / LEARN HOW TO FALL** [39] [2] Aug 73

Feb 74. (7") **AMERICAN TUNE. / ONE MAN'S CEILING IS ANOTHER MAN'S FLOOR** [ ] [35] Nov 73

— Below in concert with URUBOMBA and The JESE DIXON SINGERS.

Mar 74. (lp)(c) **PAUL SIMON IN CONCERT / LIVE RHYMIN' (live)** [ ] [33]
– Jesus is the answer / The boxer / Duncan / El Condor pasa (if I could) / Me and Julio down by the schoolyard / American tune / Homeward bound / America / Mother and child reunion / Loves me like a rock / Bridge over troubled water / The sound of silence. *(re-iss.+cd.Dec87 on 'WEA')*

May 74. (7") **THE SOUND OF SILENCE (live). / MOTHER AND CHILD REUNION (live)** [ ] [ ]

Nov 74. (7") **SOMETHING SO RIGHT. / TENDERNESS** [ ] [ ]

Aug 75. (7") **GONE AT LAST (w/ PHOEBE SNOW). / TAKE ME TO THE MARDI GRAS** [-] [23]

Oct 75. (7") **GONE AT LAST. ("PAUL SIMON & PHOEBE SNOW with The JESSE DIXON SINGERS") / TENDERNESS** [ ] [-]

Oct 75. (lp)(c) **STILL CRAZY AFTER ALL THESE YEARS** [6] [1]
– Still crazy after all these years / My little town / I do it all for love / 50 ways to leave your lover / Night game / Gone at last / Some folks lives roll easy / Have a good time / You're kind / Silent eyes. *(re-iss.1976 on quad)(cd-iss.Dec85, re-iss.+cd.Dec87 on 'WEA')*

Oct 75. (7") **MY LITTLE TOWN ("SIMON & GARFUNKEL"). / RAG DOLL ("ART GARFUNKEL")** [-] [9]

Nov 75. (7"m) **MY LITTLE TOWN. ("SIMON AND GARFUNKEL") / RAG DOLL ("ART GARFUNKEL") / YOU'RE KIND** [ ] [-]

Dec 75. (7") **50 WAYS TO LEAVE YOUR LOVER. / SOME FOLKS LIVES ROLL EASY** [23] [1]

Apr 76. (7") **STILL CRAZY AFTER ALL THESE YEARS. / I DO IT FOR YOUR LOVE** [-] [40]

Apr 76. (7") **STILL CRAZY AFTER ALL THESE YEARS. / SILENT EYES** [ ] [-]

Nov 77. (7") **SLIP SLIDIN' AWAY. / SOMETHING SO RIGHT** [36] [5] Oct 77

Nov 77. (lp)(c) **GREATEST HITS, ETC.** (part compilation) [6] [18]
– Slip slidin' away / Stranded in a limousine / Still crazy after all these years / Have a good time / Duncan / Me and Julio down by the schoolyard / Something so right / Kodachrome / I do it for your love / 50 ways to leave your lover / American tune / Mother and child reunion / Loves me like a rock / Take me to the Mardi Gras. *(re-iss.+cd.Jan87, hit 73 UK)*

— See ART GARFUNKEL discography further on for other single

May 78. (7") **STRANDED IN A LIMOSINE. / HAVE A GOOD TIME** [ ] [ ]

Warners Warners

Aug 80. (lp)(c) **ONE-TRICK PONY** [17] [12]
– Late in the evening / That's why God made the movies / One-trick pony / How the heart approaches what it yearns / Oh, Marion / Ace in the hole / Nobody / God bless the absentee / Jonah / Long, long day. *(cd-iss.1987)*

Aug 80. (7") **LATE IN THE EVENING. / HOW THE HEART APPROACHES WHAT IT YEARNS** [58] [6]

Nov 80. (7") **ONE TRICK PONY. / LONG, LONG DAY** [ ] [40] Oct 80

Jan 81. (7") **OH, MARION. / GOD BLESS THE ABSENTEE** [ ] [ ]

— See ART GARFUNKEL discography again for duet A HEART IN NEW YORK single

Early '83, PAUL collaborated with RANDY NEWMAN on US No.51 single THE BLUES

Nov 83. (lp)(c)(cd) **HEARTS AND BONES** [34] [35]
– Allergies / Hearts and bones / When numbers get serious / Think too much (part 1) / Song about the Moon / Think too much (part 2) / Train in the distance / Renee and Georgette Margritte with the dog after the war / Cars are cars / The late great Johnny Ace.

Nov 83. (7") **ALLERGIES. / THINK TOO MUCH** [ ] [44]

Feb 84. (7") **SONG ABOUT THE MOON. / THINK TOO MUCH** [-] [ ]

Aug 86. (7")(12") **YOU CAN CALL ME AL. / GUMBOOTS** [4] [44]
(re-iss.Mar87 US, hit No.23)

Sep 86. (lp)(c)(cd) **GRACELAND** [1] [3]
– The boy in the bubble / Graceland / I know what I know / Gumboots / Diamonds on the sole of her shoes / You can call me Al / Under African skies / Homeless / Crazy love Vol.2 / That was your mother / All around the world of the myth of fingerprints.

Nov 86. (7") **THE BOY IN THE BUBBLE. / ('A'remix)** [33] [-]
(12"+=) – Hearts and bones.

Dec 86. (7") **GRACELAND. / HEARTS AND BONES** [-] [81]
(re-iss.US 1988)

Feb 87. (7") **THE BOY IN THE BUBBLE. / CRAZY LOVE VOL. 2** [-] [86]

Feb 87. (7")(12") **DIAMONDS ON THE SOLES OF HER SHOES. / ALL AROUND THE WORLD OF THE MYTH OF FINGERPRINTS** [ ] [ ] Apr 87

Apr 87. (7") **GRACELAND. / CRAZY LOVE VOL.2** [ ] [-]
(12"+=) – The late great Johny Ace.

Aug 87. (7") **UNDER AFRICAN SKIES. / I KNOW WHAT I KNOW** [ ] [ ]
(12"+=) – Homeless. (above w/LINDA RONSTADT)

Oct 90. (7") **THE OBVIOUS CHILD. / THE RHYTHM OF THE SAINTS** [15] [92]
(12"+=)/ /(cd-s++=) – You can call me Al./ / The boy in the bubble.

Oct 90. (cd)(c)(lp) **THE RHYTHM OF THE SAINTS** [1] [4]
– The obvious child / Can't run but / The coast / Proof / Further to fly / She moves

on / Born at the right time / The cool cool river / Spirit voices / The rhythm of the saints.

Feb 91. (7")(c-s) **PROOF. / THE OBVIOUS CHILD** [ ] [ ]
(12")(cd-s) – ('A'side) / The cool cool river / American tune.

Apr 91. (7") **BORN AT THE RIGHT TIME. / FURTHER TO FLY** [ ] [ ]
(12"+=) – You can call me Al.
(cd-s++=) – Me and Julio down by the schoolyard / 50 ways to leave your lover.

Nov 91. (cd)(c)(d-lp) **THE CONCERT IN THE PARK - AUGUST 15th 1991 (live)** [60] [ ]
-

– (PAUL SIMON) compilations, others, etc. –

Nov 88. CBS/ US= Columbia; (d-lp)(c)(cd) **NEGOTIATIONS AND LOVE SONGS** [17] [ ]
– Mother and child reunion / Me and Julio down by the schoolyard / Something so right / St.Judy's comet / Loves me like a rock / Have a good time / 50 ways to leave your lover / Still crazy after all these years / Late in the evening / Slip slidin' away / Hearts and bones / Train in the distance / Rene and Georgette Magritte with their dog after the war / Diamonds on the soles on her shoes / You can call me Al / Kodachrome. (d-lp+=) – Graceland.

Nov 88. CBS; (7") **MOTHER AND CHILD REUNION. / TRAIN IN THE DISTANCE** [ ] [ ]
(12"+=)(cd-s+=) – The boy in the bubble.

Feb 89. Venus; (c) **THE MAGIC OF PAUL SIMON** [ ] [-]

May 93. Royal; (cd)(c) **PAUL SIMON & FRIENDS** [ ] [-]

Sep 93. Warners; (3xcd) **1964-1993** [ ] [ ]

Sep 93. Warners; (cd)(c) **ANTHOLOGY** [ ] [ ]

ART GARFUNKEL

(solo with session people)

C.B.S. Columbia

Sep 73. (7") **ALL I KNOW. / MARY WAS AN ONLY CHILD** [ ] [9]

Oct 73. (lp)(c) **ANGEL CLARE** [14] [5] Sep 73
– Travelling boy / Down in the willow garden / I shall sing / Old man / Feuilles oh! – Do spacemen pass dead souls on their way to the Moon? / All I know / Woyaya / Mary was an only child / Barbara Allen / Another lullaby. *(also on quad-lp) (cd-iss.1988) (re-iss.Jul89 on 'Pickwick')*

Feb 74. (7") **I SHALL SING. / FEUILLES OH! - DO SPACEMEN PASS DEAD SOULS ON THEIR WAY TO THE MOON?** [ ] [38] Dec 73

Sep 74. (7") **SECOND AVENUE. / WOYAYA** [ ] [34]
(re-iss. UK Nov76)

—— (above 1973/74 releases as "GARFUNKEL")

Sep 75. (7") **I ONLY HAVE EYES FOR YOU. / LOOKING FOR THE RIGHT ONE** [1] [18] Aug 75

Oct 75. (lp)(c) **BREAKAWAY** [7] [7]
– I believe (when I fall in love it will be forever) / Rag doll / Breakaway / Disney girls / Waters of March / My little town / I only have eyes for you / Looking for the right one / 99 miles from L.A. / The same old tears on a new background. *(re-iss.Nov85, cd-iss.Ar86) (re-iss.+cd.Sep89 on 'Pickwick')(re-iss.cdSep93 on 'Sony Collectors')*

—— See PAUL SIMON section, for their hit duet MY LITTLE TOWN.

Dec 75. (7") **BREAKAWAY. / DISNEY GIRLS** [-] [ ]

Jan 76. (7") **BREAKAWAY. / THE SAME OLD TEARS ON A NEW BACKGROUND** [ ] [-]

May 76. (7") **I BELIEVE (WHEN I FALL IN LOVE IT WILL BE FOREVER). / WATERS OF MARCH** [ ] [ ]

Nov 77. (7") **CRYING IN MY SLEEP. / MR.SHUCK'N'JIVE** [ ] [ ]

Jan 78. (7") **(WHAT A) WONDERFUL WORLD. ("ART GARFUNKEL, PAUL SIMON & JAMES TAYLOR") / WOODEN PLANES** [ ] [17]

Feb 78. (lp)(c) **WATERMARK** [25] [19]
– Crying in my sleep / Marionette / Shine it on me / Watermark / Saturday suit / All my love's laughter / (What a) Wonderful world / Mr. Shuck 'n' jive / Paper chase / She moved through the fair / Someone else (1958) / Wooden planes. *(re-iss.Jan87) (cd-iss.Apr94 on 'Sony')*

Apr 78. (7") **MARIONETTE. / ALL MY LOVE'S LAUGHTER** [ ] [-]

Feb 79. (7") **BRIGHT EYES. / KEHAAR'S THEME** [1] [-]

(above from animated film 'Watership Down') *(re-iss.Jul84)*

Mar 79. (7") **AND I KNOW. / IN A LITTLE WHILE (I'LL BE ON MY WAY)** [-] [ ]

Apr 79. (lp)(c) **FATE FOR BREAKFAST** [2] [67]
– In a little while (I'll be on my way) / Since I don't have you / And I know / Sail on a rainbow / Miss you nights / Bright eyes / Finally a reason / Beyond the tears / Oh how happy / When someone doesn't want you / Take me away.

May 79. (7") **SINCE I DON'T HAVE YOU. / WHEN SOMEONE DOESN'T WANT YOU** [-] [53]

Jun 79. (7") **SINCE I DON'T HAVE YOU. / AND I KNOW** [38] [-]

Aug 79. (7") **BRIGHT EYES. / SAIL ON A RAINBOW** [-] [ ]

Aug 81. (7") **A HEART IN NEW YORK. ("ART GARFUNKEL & PAUL SIMON") / IS THIS LOVE** [ ] [66]

Sep 81. (lp)(c) **SCISSORS CUT** [51] [ ]
– Scissors cut / A heart in New York / Up in the world / Hang on in / So easy to begin / Can't turn my heart away / The French waltz / The romance / In cars / That's all I've got to say.

Oct 81. (7") **SCISSORS CUT. / SO EASY TO BEGIN** [ ] [-]

—— Late 1981, he had re-united with PAUL SIMON for live one-off album.

Oct 84. (7") **SOMETIME WHEN I'M DREAMING. / SCISSORS CUT** [ ] [-]

Nov 84. (lp)(c)(cd) **THE ART GARFUNKEL ALBUM** (compilation) [12] [-]
– Bright eyes / Break away / A heart in New York / I shall sing / 99 miles from L.A. / All I know / I only have eyes for you / Watermark / Sometimes when I'm dreaming / Travelin' boy / The same old tears on a new background / (What a) Wonderful world / I believe (when I fall in love it will be forever) / Scissors cut.

Nov 86. (7"w/AMY GRANT) **CAROL OF THE BIRDS. / THE DECREE** [-] [ ]

Dec 86. (lp)(c) **THE ANIMALS CHRISTMAS** [ ] [ ]
– The annunciation / The creatures of the field / Just a simple little tune / The decree / Incredible phat / The friendly beasts / The song of the camel / Words from an old Spanish carol / Carol of the birds / The frog / Herod / Wild geese.

Jan 88. (7") **SO MUCH IN LOVE. / KING OF TONGA** [-] [ ]

Feb 88. (7") **SO MUCH IN LOVE. / SLOW BREAKUP** [ ] [-]
(12"+=)(cd-s+=) – (What a) Wonderful world / I only have eyes for you.

Mar 88. (7") **THIS IS THE MOMENT. / SLOW BREAKUP** [-] [ ]

Mar 88. (lp)(c)(cd) **LEFTY** [ ] [ ]
– This is the moment / I have a love / So much in love / Slow breakup / Love is the only chain / When a man loves a woman / I wonder why / King of Tonga / If love takes you away / The promise.

May 88. (7") **WHEN A MAN LOVES A WOMAN. / KING OF TONGA** [ ] [-]

May 88. (7") **WHEN A MAN LOVES A WOMAN. / I HAVE A LOVE** [-] [ ]

Columbia Columbia

Nov 93. (cd)(c)(lp) **UP UNTIL NOW** [ ] [ ]
– Crying in the rain (w/ JAMES TAYLOR) / All I know / Just over the Brooklyn Bridge / The sound of silence / The breakup / Skywriter / The decree / It's all in the game / One less holiday / Since I don't have you / Two sleepy people / Why worry / All my love's daughter.

– (ART GARFUNKEL) compilation, etc. –

Oct 79. CBS; (3xlp-box) **ART GARFUNKEL** [ ] [ ]
(first 3 albums)

1984. Columbia; (7") **BRIGHT EYES. / THE ROMANCE** [-] [ ]

SIMPLE MINDS

Formed: Gorbals, Glasgow, Scotland, early 1978 after 4 members (KERR, BURCHILL, BARNWELL and McGEE) had left punk band JOHNNY & THE SELF-ABUSERS. In 1978, after taking group name from a line in a BOWIE song, SIMPLE MINDS gigged constantly at Glasgow's Mars Bar. They sent demo to record store owner BRUCE FINDLEY, who duly signed them to his independent Edinburgh label 'Zoom'. They were soon licensed to major 'Arista', after release of debut album, 'LIFE IN A DAY', scraped into the UK Top 30. In 1981, they transferred to 'Virgin' records and gained first Top 50 hit with 'LOVE SONG'. It was lifted from joint lp 'SONS AND FASCINATION' / 'SISTER FEELINGS CALL', which was produced by STEVE HILLAGE. In the mid-80's, they competed with U2 for stadium rock supremacy, while their albums 'SPARKLE IN THE RAIN' & 'ONCE UPON A TIME', hit No.1 in the UK. Between these, they also smashed the American charts with No.1 'DON'T YOU FORGET ABOUT ME'. (It's now cheapified on a UK TV ad for milk!). • **Style:** Initially a mix of experimental pop + rock, which progressed in the 80's to electro disco rock and sophisto-pop. • **Songwriters:** All group compositions or KERR-BURCHILL. Covered BIKO (Peter Gabriel) / SIGN O' THE TIMES (Prince) / DON'T YOU FORGET ABOUT ME (Keith Forsey-Steve Chiff). • **Trivia:** On the 5th May'84, JIM KERR married CHRISIE HYNDE of The PRETENDERS and settled in Queensferry. They divorced in the late 80's, and KERR soon married another singer and actress PATSY KENSIT. Needless to say, The MINDS have played both LIVE AID and MANDELA DAY concerts in 1985 and 1988 respectively.

Recommended: GLITTERING PRIZE 81-91 (*9) / CELEBRATION (*7) / EMPIRES AND DANCE (*8) / SONS AND FASCINATION (*8) / NEW GOLD DREAM (*8) / ONCE UPON A TIME (*7) / SPARKLE IN THE RAIN (*8) / LIFE IN A DAY (*7).

JOHNNY & THE SELF ABUSERS

JIM KERR (b. 9 Jul'59) – vocals / **CHARLIE BURCHILL** (b.27 Nov'59) – guitar / **DUNCAN BARNWELL** – guitar / **BRIAN McGEE** – drums / + 3 future CUBAN HEELS members.

Chiswick / not issued

Nov 77. (7") **SAINTS AND SINNERS. / DEAD VANDALS** [ ] [-]

SIMPLE MINDS

(KERR, BURCHILL, McGEE) recruited **MICK McNEILL** (b.20 Jul'58) – keyboards / **DEREK FORBES** (b.22 Jun'56) – bass

Zoom / not issued

Apr 79. (7") **LIFE IN A DAY. / SPECIAL VIEW** [62] [-]

Apr 79. (lp)(c) **LIFE IN A DAY** [30] [-]
– Someone / Life in a day / Sad affair / All for you / Pleasantly disurbed / No cure / Chelsea girl / Wasteland / Destiny / Murder story. *(re-iss.Oct82 + 1985 on 'Virgin', cd-iss.Jul86)*

Jun 79. (7") **CHELSEA GIRL. / GARDEN OF HATE** [ ] [-]

Arista / Arista

Nov 79. (lp)(c) **REAL TO REAL CACOPHONY** [ ] [ ]
– Real to real / Naked eye / Citizen (dance of youth) / Carnival (shelter in a suitcase) / Factory / Cacophony / Veldt / Premonition / Changeling / Film theme / Calling your name / Scar. *(re-iss.Oct82 + 1985 on 'Virgin', cd-iss.May88)*

Jan 80. (7") **CHANGELING. / PREMONITION (live)** [ ] [-]

Sep 80. (lp)(c) **EMPIRES AND DANCE** [41] [ ]
– I travel / Today I died again / Celebrate / This fear of gods / Capital city / Constantinople line / Twist-run-repulsion / Thirty frames a seconds / Kant-kino / Room. *(re-iss.Oct82 on 'Virgin', cd-iss.May88)*

Oct 80. (7") **I TRAVEL. / NEW WARM SKIN** [ ] [ ]
(free 7"blue flexi) – KALEIDOSCOPE. / FILM DUB THEME
(12") – ('A'side) / Film dub theme.

Feb 81. (7") **CELEBRATE. / CHANGELING (live)** [ ] [ ]
(12"+=) – I travel (live).

Virgin / A&M

May 81. (7")(12") **THE AMERICAN. / LEAGUE OF NATIONS** [59] [-]

— **KENNY HYSLOP** – drums (ex-SKIDS, ex-ZONES, ex-SLIK) repl. McGEE, who in 1994 became a songwriter for LES McKEOWN (ex-BAY CITY ROLLERS)

Aug 81. (7")(12") **LOVE SONG. / THE EARTH THAT YOU WALK UPON (instr.)** [47] [-]

Sep 81. (2xlp)(d-c) **SONS AND FASCINATION / SISTER FEELINGS CALL** [11] [ ]
– SONS AND FASCINATION – In trance as mission / Sweat in bullet / 70 cities as love brings the fall / Boys from Brazil / Love song / This Earth that you walk upon / Sons and fascination / Seeing out the angels. SISTER FEELINGS CALL – Theme for great cities * / The American / 20th Century promised land / Wonderful in young life / League of nations / Careful in career / Sound in 70 cities. *(iss.separately Oct81) (cd-iss.Apr86 + Apr90, omits*)*

Oct 81. (7") **SWEAT IN BULLET. / 20th CENTURY PROMISED LAND** [52] [-]
(d7"+=) – League of nations (live) / Premonition (live).
(12"+=) – League of nations (live) / In trance as mission (live).

Apr 82. (7") **PROMISED YOU A MIRACLE. / THEME FOR GREAT CITIES** [13] [-]
(12"+=) – Seeking out the angel (instrumental mix).

— **MIKE OGLETREE** – drums repl. HYSLOP who formed SET THE TONE

Aug 82. (7")(12") **GLITTERING PRIZE. / GLITTERING THEME** [16] [ ]

— **MEL GAYNOR** – drums (ex-sessions) repl. MIKE who joined FICTION FACTORY

Sep 82. (lp)(c) **NEW GOLD DREAM (81-82-83-84)** [3] [69] Jan 83
– Someone somewhere in summertime / Colours fly and the Catherine wheel / Promised you a miracle / Big sleep / Somebody up there likes you / New gold dream (81-82-83-84) / Glittering prize / Hunter and the hunted / King is white and in the crowd. *(cd-iss.Jul83) (iss.US on gold-lp)*

Nov 82. (7")(7"pic-d) **SOMEONE SOMEWHERE IN SUMMERTIME. / KING IS WHITE AND IN THE CROWD** [36] [ ]
(12"+=) – Soundtrack for every Heaven.

Nov 82. (7") **PROMISED YOU A MIRACLE. / THE AMERICAN** [-] [ ]

Nov 83. (7")(12") **WATERFRONT. / HUNTER AND THE HUNTED (live)** [13] [ ]

Jan 84. (7")(7"pic-d) **SPEED YOUR LOVE TO ME. / BASS LINE** [20] [ ]
(12"+=) – ('A'extended).

Feb 84. (lp)(c)(cd)(white-lp) **SPARKLE IN THE RAIN** [1] [64]
– Up on the catwalk / Book of brilliant things / Speed your love to me / Waterfront / East at Easter / White hot day / Street hassle / "C" Moon cry like a baby / The kick inside of me / Shake off the ghosts. *(re cd-iss.1986 + Mar91)*

Mar 84. (7")(7"pic-d) **UP ON THE CATWALK. / A BRASS BAND IN AFRICA** [27] [ ]
(12"+=) – ('B'other version).

Apr 85. (7")(7"sha-pic-d) **DON'T YOU (FORGET ABOUT ME). / A BRASS BAND IN AFRICA** [7] [1] Feb 85
(12"+=) – ('B'other version). *(cd-s iss.Jun88)*

— **KERR, BURCHILL, McNEILL + GAYNOR** brought in new member **JOHN GIBLING** – bass (ex-PETER GABRIEL sessions) to repl. FORBES

Oct 85. (7") **ALIVE AND KICKING. / ('A'instrumental)** [7] [3]
(12"+=) – Up on the catwalk (live). (US; b-side)

Oct 85. (lp)(c)(cd)(pic-lp) **ONCE UPON A TIME** [1] [10]
– Once upon a time / All the things she said / Ghost dancing / Alive and kicking / Oh jungleland / I wish you were here / Sanctify yourself / Come a long way.

Jan 86. (7") **SANCTIFY YOURSELF. / ('A'instrumental)** [10] [14]
(d7"+=) – Love song (live) / Street hassle (live).
(12") – ('A'mix). / ('A'dub instrumental)

Apr 86. (7") **ALL THE THINGS SHE SAID. / DON'T YOU (FORGET ABOUT ME)** [9] [28]
(12"+=) – Promised you a miracle (US mix).

Nov 86. (7") **GHOSTDANCING. / JUNGLELAND (instrumental)** [13] [ ]
(ext-12"+=)(cd-s+=) – ('A'instrumental) / ('B'mix).

May 87. (d-lp)(d-c)(d-cd) **LIVE IN THE CITY OF LIGHT (live)** [1] [96]
– Ghostdancing / Big sleep / Waterfront / Promised you a miracle / Someone somewhere in summertime / Oh jungleland / Alive and kicking / Don't you forget about me / Once upon a time / Book of brilliant things / East at Easter / Sanctify yourself / Love song / Sun City – Dance to the music / New gold dream (81-82-83-84).

Jun 87. (7")(10") **PROMISED YOU A MIRACLE (live). / BOOK OF BRILLIANT THINGS (live)** [19] [ ]
(12"+=)(c-s+=) – Glittering prize (live) / Celebrate (live).

— **KERR, BURCHILL + McNEILL** were basic trio, w/other 2 still sessioning.

Feb 89. (7") **BELFAST CHILD. / MANDELA DAY** [1] [ ]
(12"ep+=)(12"box-ep+=)(c-ep+=)(cd-ep+=) – BALLAD OF THE STREETS – Biko.

Apr 89. (7") **THIS IS YOUR LAND. / SATURDAY GIRL** [13] [ ]
(12"+=)(c-s+=)(3"cd-s+=) – Year of the dragon.

May 89. (lp)(c)(cd) **STREET FIGHTING YEARS** [1] [70]
– Soul crying out / Wall of love / This is your land / Take a step back / Kick it in / Let it all come down / Biko / Mandela day / Belfast child / Street fighting years. *(re-iss.box-lp+cd.Dec89, +=Interview)*

Jul 89. (7")(c-s) **KICK IT IN. / WATERFRONT ('89 mix)** [15] [ ]
(12"+=)/ /(12"+=)(cd-s+=) – ('A'mix)./ / Big sleep (live).

Dec 89. (7"ep)(12"ep)(c-ep)(cd-ep) **THE AMSTERDAM EP** [18] [ ]
– Let it all come down / Sign o' the times / Jerusalem.
(12"ep+=)(cd-ep+=) – Sign o' the times (mix).

— **KERR, BURCHILL + GAYNOR** brought in sessioners **MALCOLM FOSTER** – bass / **PETER JOHN VITESSE** – keyboards / **STEPHEN LIPSON** – bass, keyboards / **ANDY DUNCAN** – percussion / **GAVIN WRIGHT** – string leader / **LISA GERMANO** – violin

Mar 91. (7") **LET THERE BE LOVE. / GOODNIGHT** [6] [ ]
(12"+=) – Alive and kicking (live).
(cd-s++=) – East at Easter (live).

Apr 91. (cd)(c)(lp) **REAL LIFE** [2] [74]
– Real life / See the lights / Let there be love / Woman / Stand by love / African skies / Let the children speak / Ghostrider / Banging on the door / Travelling man / Rivers of ice / When two worlds collide.

May 91. (7")(c-s) **SEE THE LIGHTS. / THEME FOR GREAT CITIES ('91 edit)** [20] [40]
(12"+=)(cd-s+=) – Soul crying out (live).

Aug 91. (7")(c-s) **STAND BY LOVE. / KING IS WHITE AND IN THE CROWD (live)** [13] [ ]
(12"+=)(cd-s+=) – Let there be love (live).

Oct 91. (7")(c-s) **REAL LIFE. / SEE THE LIGHTS** [34] [ ]
('A'extended-12"+=) – Belfast child (extended).
(cd-s++=) – Ghostrider.

— **KERR + BURCHILL** with guests **MARK BROWNE, MALCOLM FOSTER, MARCUS MILLER + LANCE MORRISON -bass/ MARK SCHULMAN, TAL BERGMAN + VINNIE CALAITUTA -drums**

Jan 95. (7")(c-s) **SHE'S A RIVER. / E55 / ('A'mix)** [9] [52]
(cd-s+=) – Celtic strings.

Jan 95. (cd)(c)(lp) **GOOD NEWS FROM THE NEXT WORLD** [2] [87]
– She's a river / Night music / Hypnotised / Great leap forward / 7 deadly sins / And the band played on / My life / Criminal world / This time.

Mar 95. (7")(c-s) **HYPNOTISED. / £4** [18] [ ]
(cd-s+=) – ('A'-Tim Simenon extended remixes) / ('A'-Malfunction mix).
(cd-s) – ('A'side) / Up on the catwalk (live) / And the band played on (live) / She's a river (live).

– compilations, others, etc. –

Jan 82. Arista; (7") **I TRAVEL. / THIRTY FRAMES A SECOND (live)** [ ] [-]
(12"+=) – ('A'live).

Feb 82. Arista; (lp)(c) **CELEBRATION** [45] [ ]
(re-iss.Oct82 on 'Virgin', re-iss.+cd.Apr89)

Apr 83. Virgin; (12") **I TRAVEL (mix). / FILM THEME** [ ] [-]

Aug 90. Virgin; (5xcd-box-ep) **THEMES – VOLUME ONE** [ ] [ ]
– (Apr79 – LIFE IN A DAY – Apr82 – PROMISED YOU A MIRACLE singles)

Sep 90. Virgin; (5xcd-box-ep) **THEMES – VOLUME TWO** [ ] [ ]
– (Aug82 – GLITTERING PRIZE – Apr85 – DON'T YOU (FORGET ABOUT ME) singles)

Oct 90. Virgin; (5xcd-box-ep) **THEMES – VOLUME THREE** [ ] [ ]
– (Oct85 – ALIVE AND KICKING – Jun87 – PROMISED YOU A MIRACLE (live) singles)

Nov 90. Virgin; (5xcd-box-ep) **THEMES – VOLUME FOUR** [ ] [ ]
– (Feb89 – BELFAST CHILD, Dec 89 – THE AMSTERDAM EP)

Oct 92. Virgin; (7")(c-s) **LOVE SONG. / ALIVE AND KICKING** [6] [ ]
('A'&'B'ext-cd-s+=) – ('B'instrumental).

Oct 92. Virgin; (cd)(c)(lp) **GLITTERING PRIZE – SIMPLE MINDS 81-92** [1] [ ]
– Waterfront / Don't you (forget about me) / Alive and kicking / Sanctify yourself / Love song / Someone somewhere in summertime / See the lights / Belfast child / The American / All the things she said / Promised you a miracle / Ghostdancing / Speed your love to me / Glittering prize / Let there be love / Mandela Day.

SIOUXSIE & THE BANSHEES

Formed: London, England . . . Sep'76 by punkette SIOUXSIE SIOUX and STEVE SEVERIN. Throughout 1977, they toured constantly and signed to 'Track' records, who folded early 1978. Undeterred, they flitted to cousin label 'Polydor', who finally released debut 45 'HONG KONG GARDEN' in August '78. It raced up into the UK Top 10, and was soon followed by classic debut album 'THE SCREAM'. During the late 70's and throughout the 80's, the BANSHEES notched up a run of 20 consecutive Top 50 UK hits, not including 3 off-shoot CREATURES hits between 1981 and 83. • **Style:** Alternative punk-rock, that moved quickly into haunting cult rock that oozed sensuality and the imagery of SIOUXSIE. • **Songwriters:** All written by SIOUXSIE / SEVERIN except; HELTER SKELTER + DEAR PRUDENCE (Beatles) / 20th CENTURY BOY (T.Rex) / THE LORD'S PRAYER (trad.prayer re-arranged) / IL EST NE LE DIVIN ENFANT (French festive song) / ALL TOMORROW'S PARTIES (Velvet Underground). THROUGH THE LOOKING GLASS was a covers album containing THIS WHEEL'S ON FIRE (Bob Dylan) / THE PASSENGER (Iggy Pop) / YOU'RE LOST LITTLE GIRL (Doors) / GUN (John Cale) / THIS TOWN AIN'T BIG ENOUGH FOR THE BOTH OF US (Sparks) / SEA BREEZES (Roxy Music) / STRANGE FRUIT (Billie Holiday) / WALL OF MIRRORS (Kraftwerk) / LITTLE JOHNNY JEWEL (Television) / TRUST IN ME ('Jungle Book' animated film). CREATURES re-done RIGHT NOW (Mel Torme). • **Trivia:** SEVERIN produced ALTERED IMAGES debut 45 'Dead Pop Stars'. SIOUXSIE married BUDGIE May'91 after long relationship.

Recommended: THE SCREAM (*10) / JOIN HANDS (*8) / KALEIDOSCOPE (*7) / HYAENA (*8) / JU JU (*7) / ONCE UPON A TIME – THE SINGLES (*9) / TWICE UPON A TIME (*7) / A KISS IN THE DREAMHOUSE (*7).

SIOUXSIE SIOUX (b.SUSAN DALLION, 27 May'57) – vocals / **STEVEN SEVERIN** (b.STEVEN BAILEY, 1955) – bass / **JOHN McKAY** – guitar repl. PT FENTON who had repl. MARCO PIRRONI (who joined MODELS and later ADAM & THE ANTS) / **KENNY MORRIS** – drums repl. SID VICIOUS who later became bassman for SEX PISTOLS

Polydor Polydor

Aug 78. (7") **HONG KONG GARDEN. / VOICES** [7] [–]

Oct 78. (7") **HONG KONG GARDEN. / OVERGROUND** [–] [ ]

Nov 78. (lp)(c) **THE SCREAM** [12] [ ]
– Pure / Jigsaw feeling / Overground / Carcass / Helter skelter / Mirage / Metal postcard / Nicotine stain / Suburban relapse / Switch. *(cd-iss.Mar89 & Mar95 on 'Wonderland')*

Mar 79. (7") **THE STAIRCASE (MYSTERY). / 20th CENTURY BOY** [24] [–]

Jun 79. (7") **PLAYGROUND TWIST. / PULLED TO BITS** [28] [–]

Sep 79. (lp)(c) **JOIN HANDS** [13] [–]
– Poppy day / Regal zone / Placebo effect / Icon / Premature burial / Playground twist / Mother / Oh mein papa / The Lord's prayer. *(cd-iss.Mar89 & Mar95 on 'Wonderland')*

Sep 79. (7") **MITTAGEISEN (METAL POSTCARD). / LOVE IN A VOID** [47] [–]

— **BUDGIE** (b.PETER CLARK, 21 Aug'57, St.Helens, N.England) – drums (ex-SLITS, ex-PLANETS, ex-BIG IN JAPAN, etc.) repl. MORRIS who decamped / **JOHN McGEOGH** (b. 1955, Greenock, Scotland) – guitar (of MAGAZINE) finally repl. ROBERT SMITH (of The CURE) + JOHN CARRUTHERS who repl. disappearing McKAY

Mar 80. (7") **HAPPY HOUSE. / DROP DEAD** [17] [ ]

May 80. (7") **CHRISTINE. / EVE WHITE EVE BLACK** [24] [ ]

Aug 80. (lp)(c) **KALEIDOSCOPE** [5] [ ]
– Happy house / Tenant / Trophy / Hybrid / Lunar camel / Christine / Desert kisses / Red light / Paradise place / Skin. *(cd-iss.Mar89 & Mar95 on 'Wonderland')*

Nov 80. (7")('A'dance-12") **ISRAEL. / RED OVER WHITE** [41] [ ]

May 81. (7") **SPELLBOUND. / FOLLOW THE SUN** [22] [ ]
(12"+=) – Slap dash snap.

Jun 81. (lp)(c) **JU JU** [7] [ ]
– Spellbound / Into the light / Arabian knights / Halloween / Monitor / Night shift / Sin in my heart / Head cut / Voodoo dolly. *(cd-iss.Mar89 & Mar95 on 'Wonderland')*

Jul 81. (7") **ARABIAN KNIGHTS. / SUPERNATURAL THING** [32] [ ]
(12"+=) – Congo conga.

— In Sep81, SIOUXSIE & BUDGIE as The CREATURES hit Top 30 w / WILD THINGS EP.

Dec 81. (lp)(c) **ONCE UPON A TIME – THE SINGLES** [21] [ ]
– Hong Kong garden / Mirage / The staircase (mystery) / Playground twist / Happy house / Christine / Israel / Spellbound / Arabian knights / Fireworks. *(cd-iss.Mar89 & Mar95 on 'Wonderland')*

May 82. (7") **FIREWORKS. / COAL MIND** [22] [ ]
(12"+=) – We fall.

Sep 82. (7") **SLOWDIVE. / CANNIBAL ROSES** [41] [ ]
(12"+=) – Obsession II.

Nov 82. (lp)(c) **A KISS IN THE DREAMHOUSE** [11] [ ]
– Cascade / Green fingers / Obsession / She's a carnival / Circle / Melt! / Painted bird / Cocoon / Slowdive. *(cd-iss.Apr89 & Mar95 on 'Wonderland')*

Nov 82. (7") **MELT!. / IL EST NE LE DIVIN ENFANT** [49] [ ]
(12"+=) – A sleeping rain.

— **ROBERT SMITH** – guitar (of The CURE) returned part-time to repl. McGEOGH who later joined The ARMOURY SHOW.

— In 1983, SMITH and SEVERIN had also splintered into The GLOVE, with SIOUXSIE and BUDGIE re-uniting as The CREATURES (see further on).

Wonderland-Polydor Geffen

Sep 83. (7") **DEAR PRUDENCE. / TATTOO** [3] [ ]
(12"+=) – There's a planet in my kitchen.

Nov 83. (d-lp)(c) **NOCTURNE (live)** [29] [–]
– Intro – The rite of Spring / Israel / Dear Prudence / Paradise place / Melt! / Cascade / ulled to bits / Night shift / Sin in my heart / Slowdive / Painted bird / Happy house / Switch / Spellbound / Helter skelter / Eve white eve black / Voodoo dolly. *(cd-iss.Apr89 & Mar95)*

Mar 84. (7") **SWIMMING HORSES. / LET GO** [28] [–]
(12"+=) – The humming wires.

May 84. (7") **DAZZLE. / I PROMISE** [33] [–]
(12"+=) – Throw them to the lions / ('A'mix).

Jun 84. (lp)(c)(cd) **HYAENA** [15] [ ]
– Dazzle / We hunger / Take me back / Belladonna / Swimming horses / Bring me the head of the preacher man / Running town / Pointing bone / Blow the house down. *(re-iss.cd Mar95)*

— **JOHN CARRUTHERS** – guitar (ex-CLOCKDVA, ex-JEFFREY LEE PIERCE) returned to repl. SMITH who had CURE commitments.

Oct 84. (12"ep) **THE THORN (live)** [47] [–]
– Voices / Placebo effect / Red over white / Overground.

Oct 85. (7") **CITIES IN DUST. / AN EXECUTION** [21] [ ]
(12"+=) – Quarter drawing of the dog.

Feb 86. (7") **CANDYMAN. / LULLABY** [34] [–]
(12"+=) – Umbrella.

Apr 86. (lp)(c)(cd) **TINDERBOX** [13] [88]
– Candyman / The sweetest chill / This unrest / Cities in dust / Cannons / Partys fall / 92° / Lands End. *(cd+=)* – An execution / Quarter drawing of the dog / Lullaby / Umbrella / Candyman (extended). *(re-iss.cd Mar95)*

Jan 87. (7") **THIS WHEEL'S ON FIRE. / SHOOTING SUN** [14] [ ]
(12"+=) – Sleepwalking (on the high wire).

Feb 87. (lp)(c)(cd) **THROUGH THE LOOKING GLASS** [15] [ ]
– Hall of mirrors / Trust in me / This wheel's on fire / Strange fruit / This town ain't big enough for the both of us / You're lost little girl / The passenger / Gun / Sea breezes / Little Johnny Jewel. *(re-iss.cd Mar95)*

Mar 87. (7") **THE PASSENGER. / SHE'S CUCKOO** [41] [ ]
(12"+=) – Something blue.

— **JON KLEIN** – guitar (ex-SPECIMEN) repl. CARRUTHERS / added **MARTIN McCARRICK** – cello, keysboards (ex-MARC ALMOND, ex-The GLOVE) (to SIOUXSIE, SEVERIN, BUDGIE + KLEIN)

Jul 87. (7")(c-s)(7"pic-d) **SONG FROM THE EDGE OF THE WORLD. / THE WHOLE PRICE OF BLOOD** [59] [–]
(12"+=) – Mechanical eyes.

Jul 88. (7") **PEEK-A-BOO. / FALSE FACE** [16] [53]
(c-s+=)(cd-s+=)(vid-cd+=) – Catwalk / ('A'big suspender mix).
(12"+=) – ('A'-2 other mixes).

Sep 88. (lp)(c)(cd) **PEEPSHOW** [20] [68]
– Peek-a-boo / Killing jar / Scarecrow / Carousel / Burn-up / Ornaments of gold / Turn to stone / Rawhead and bloodybones / The last beat of my heart / Rhapsody. *(re-iss.cd Mar95)*

Sep 88. (7")(7"pic-d) **KILLING JAR. / SOMETHING WICKED (THIS WAY COMES)** [41] [ ]
(12"+=)(cd-s+=) – Are you still dying, darling.

Nov 88. (7") **THE LAST BEAT OF MY HEART. / EL DIABLO LOS MUERTOS** [44] [ ]
(12"+=) – Sunless.
(cd-s++=) – ('B'mix).

— In Autumn'89, The CREATURES issued singles and 'BOOMERANG' album.

May 91. (7")(c-s) **KISS THEM FOR ME. / RETURN** [32] [23]
('A'version-12"+=)(12"pic-d+=) – Staring back.
(cd-s++=) – ('A'side).

Jun 91. (cd)(c)(lp) **SUPERSTITION** [25] [65]
– Kiss them for me / Fear (of the unknown) / Cry / Drifter / Little sister /

Shadowtime / Silly thing / Got to get up / Silver waterfalls / Softly / The ghost in you. *(re-iss.cd Mar95)*
Jul 91. (7")(c-s) **SHADOWTIME. / SPIRAL TWIST** [57] [ ]
(12"+=)(cd-s+=) – Sea of light. / ('A'-eclipse mix).

— Below single from the film 'Batman Returns'.
Jul 92. (7")(c-s) **FACE TO FACE. / I COULD BE AGAIN** [21] [ ]
(cd-s+=) – ('A'-catatonic mix) / Hothead.
(12") – ('A'side) / ('A'-catatonic mix) / Hothead.
Oct 92. (cd)(c)(lp) **TWICE UPON A TIME – THE THING** [26] [ ]
– Fireworks / Slowdive / Melt / Dear Prudence / Swimming horses / Dazzle / Overground (from The Thorn) / Cities in dust / Candyman / This wheel's on fire / The passenger / Peek-a-boo / The killing jar / The last beat of my heart / Kiss them for me / Shadowtime / Fear (of the unknown) / Face to face. *(re-iss.cd Mar95)*

— In Aug 94, SIOUXSIE partnered MORRISSEY on his single 'INTERLUDE'.
Dec 94. (c-s) **O BABY. / OURSELVES** [34] [ ]
(cd-s+=) – ('A'-Manhattan mix).
(cd-s) – ('A'side) / Swimming horses (live) / All tomorrow's parties (live).
Jan 95. (cd)(c)(lp) **THE RAPTURE** [33] [ ]
– O baby / Tearing apart / Stargazer / Fall from grace / Not forgotten / Sick child / The lonely one / Falling down / Forever / The rapture / The double life / Love out me.
Feb 95. (7")(c-s) **STARGAZER. / HANG ME HIGH** [64] [ ]
(cd-s+=) – Black Sun.
(cd-s) – ('A'-Mambo sun) / ('A'-Planet queen mix) / ('A'-Mark Saunders mix).

. . . Jan – Jun '96 stop press . . .

— Split April 1996, although SIOUXSIE and BUDGIE will be recording a third album as The CREATURES. SEVERIN has written for the film 'Visions Of Ecstacy'.

– compilations, others, etc. –

Feb 87. Strange Fruit; (12"ep) **THE PEEL SESSIONS (29.11.77)** [ ] [-]
– Love in a void / Mirage / Suburban relapse / Metal postcard. *(c-ep iss. Jun87, cd-ep iss.Mar88)*
Feb 89. Strange Fruit; (12"ep)(cd-ep) **THE PEEL SESSIONS (Feb78)** [ ] [-]
– Hong Kong garden / Carcass / Helter skelter / Overground.
Apr 93. ZYX; (cd) **THE BEST OF THE CREATURES (CREATURES)** [ ] [-]

CREATURES

(SIOUXSIE & BUDGIE)

Polydor | not issued

Sep 81. (d7"ep) **WILD THINGS** [24] [-]
– Mad-eyed screamer / So unreal / But not them / Wild thing / Thumb.

Wonderland-Polydor | Geffen

May 83. (7") **MISS THE GIRL. / HOT SPRING IN THE SNOW** [21] [-]
May 83. (lp)(c) **FEAST** [17] [ ]
– Morning dawning / Inoa 'ole / Ice house / Dancing on glass / Gecko / Sky train / Festival of colours / Miss the girl / A strutting rooster / Flesh.
Jul 83. (7") **RIGHT NOW. / WEATHERCADE** [14] [-]
(12"+=) – Festival of colours.
Oct 89. (7") **STANDING THERE. / DIVIDED** [53] [-]
(10"+=)(12"+=)(cd-s+=) – Solar choir.
Nov 89. (lp)(c)(cd) **BOOMERANG** [ ] [ ]
– Standing there / Manchild / You! / Pity / Killing time / Willow / Pluto drive / Solar choir * / Speeding * / Fury eyes / Fruitman / Untiedundone * / Simoom * / Strolling wolf / Venus sands / Morriha. (*= extra tracks on cd)
Feb 90. (7")(c-s)(cd-s) **FURY EYES. / ABSTINENCE** [ ] [-]
(12") – ('A'side) / ('A'-2 dub + fever mixes).

The GLOVE

(SEVERIN & ROBERT SMITH) also incl. **MARTIN McCARRICK** – cello / **ANNE STEPHENSON + GINNY HEWES** – strings / **ANDY ANDERSON** – drums / (JEANETTE) **LANDRAY** – dual vocals w/**SMITH**

Wonderland-Polydor | Geffen

Aug 83. (7") **LIKE AN ANIMAL. / MOUTH TO MOUTH** [52] [-]
(12"+=) – Animal (club mix).
Aug 83. (lp)(c) **BLUE SUNSHINE** [35] [ ]
– Like an animal / Looking glass girl / Sex-eye-make-up / Mr. Alphabet says / A blues in drag / Punish me with kisses / This green city / Orgy / Perfect murder / Relax. *(re-iss.+cd.Sep90 +=)*– Mouth to mouth / The tightrope / Like an animal (club mix).
Nov 83. (7") **PUNISH ME WITH KISSES. / THE TIGHTROPE** [ ] [-]

SISTERS OF MERCY

Formed: Leeds, England . . . 1980 by ELDRITCH and MARX. Formed own indie 'Merciful' records in 1980, to release debut 'DAMAGE DONE'. After a tour supporting The BIRTHDAY PARTY and The PSYCHEDELIC FURS, they appeared on Leeds Futurama festival in the early 80's. In 1984, their label, received distribution from 'WEA' and they finally made UK Top 50 with 'BODY AND SOUL'. • **Style:** Atmospheric goth-punk outfit fronted by the deep, black-attired ELDRITCH. When PATRICIA MORRISON was added in 1986, it added glam to already heavy alternative disco-goth. • **Songwriters:** All ELDRITCH written, except period between 1983-85 when HUSSEY was writing partner. Covered:- EMMA (Hot Chocolate) / 1969 (Stooges) / GIMME SHELTER (Rolling Stones) / KNOCKIN' ON HEAVEN'S DOOR (Bob Dylan). In 1990, ELDRITCH co-wrote 'VISION THING' album with JIM STEINMAN. • **Trivia:** In 1982, they argued with stablemates The MARCH VIOLETS, who immediately left for new pastures 'Rebirth'.

Recommended: SOME GIRLS WANDER BY MISTAKE (*9) / FIRST AND LAST AND ALWAYS (*8) / FLOODLAND (*8) / VISION THING (*7). The SISTERHOOD:- GIFT (*7).

ANDREW ELDRITCH (b.ANDREW TAYLOR, 15 May'59, East Anglia, England) – vocals / **GARRY MARX** – guitar / + drum machine DOKTOR AVALANCHE

Merciful | not issued

1980. (7"m) **DAMAGE DONE. / WATCH / HOME OF THE HITMAN** [ ] [-]

— added **BEN GUNN** – guitar / **CRAIG ADAMS** – bass (ex-EXPELAIRES)

C.N.T. | not issued

Feb 82. (7") **BODY ELECTRIC. / ADRENOCHROME** [ ] [-]

Merciful | not issued

Nov 82. (7") **ALICE. / FLOORSHOW** [ ] [-]
Mar 83. (7") **ANACONDA. / PHANTOM** [ ] [-]
Apr 83. (12"ep) **ALICE. / FLOORSHOW / 1969 / PHANTOM** [ ] [-]
May 83. (12"ep) **THE REPTILE HOUSE** [ ] [-]
– Kiss the carpet / Lights / Valentine / Burn / Fix. *(re-iss.Apr94)*

— **WAYNE HUSSEY** – guitar (ex-DEAD OR ALIVE, ex-HAMBI & THE DANCE) repl. BEN
Oct 83. (7") **TEMPLE OF LOVE. / HEARTLAND** [ ] [-]
(12"+=) – Gimme shelter.

Merciful-WEA | Warners

Jun 84. (7") **BODY AND SOUL. (as "The SISTERS") / TRAIN** [46] [-]
(12"+=) – After hours / Body electric.
Oct 84. (7") **WALK AWAY. / POISON DOOR** [45] [-]
(above w/free 7"flexi) – Long Train.
(12"+=) – On the wire.
Feb 85. (7") **NO TIME TO CRY. / BLOOD MONEY** [63] [-]
(12"+=) – Bury me deep.
Mar 85. (lp)(c) **FIRST AND LAST AND ALWAYS** [14] [ ]
– Black planet / Walk away / No time to cry / A rock and a hard place / Marian / First and last and always / Possession / Nine while nine / Amphetamine logic / Some kind of stranger. *(cd-iss.Jul88) (re-iss.re-mastered.Jul92 on 'East West')*

— Disbanded mid'85 . . . GARRY MARX helped form GHOST DANCE. HUSSEY and ADAMS formed The MISSION after squabbles with ANDREW over use of group name.

— **ELDRITCH** with ever faithful drum machine adopted

The SISTERHOOD

recruited **PATRICIA MORRISON** (b.14 Jan'62) – bass, vocals (ex-FUR BIBLE, ex-GUN CLUB) **JAMES RAY** – guitar / **ALAN VEGA** – synthesizers (ex-SUICIDE) / **LUCAS FOX** – drums. (ELDRITCH moved to Berlin, Germany.)

Merciful | not issued

Feb 86. (7") **GIVING GROUND (remix). / GIVING GROUND (album version)** [ ] [-]
Jul 86. (lp)(c) **GIFT** [90] [-]
– Jihad / Colours / Giving ground / Finland red, Egypt white / Rain from Heaven. *(cd-iss.Sep89 & Jul94)*

The SISTERS OF MERCY

were again as **ELDRITCH** and **MORRISON** obtained rights to name. (drum machine)

Merciful-WEA | Elektra

Sep 87. (7") **THIS CORROSION. / TORCH** [7] [ ]
(c-s+=)/ /(12"+=)(cd-s+=) – ('A'version)./ / Colours.
Nov 87. (lp)(c)(cd) **FLOODLAND** [9] [ ]
– Dominion / Mother Russia / Flood I / Lucretia my reflection / 1959 / This corrosion / Flood II / Driven like the snow / Neverlan. *(c+=)*– Torch. *(cd-s++=)*– Colours.
Feb 88. (7") **DOMINION. / SANDSTORM / UNTITLED** [13] [-]
(d12"+=)/ /(c-s+=)(cd-s+=) – Emma./ / Ozy-Mandias.
May 88. (7") **LUCRETIA MY REFLECTION. / LONG TRAIN** [20] [ ]
(12"+=)(cd-s+=) – ('A'extended).

— (Feb90) **ELDRITCH** w/drum machine, recruited complete new line-up / **TONY JAMES** – bass, vocals (ex-SIGUE SIGUE SPUTNIK, ex-GENERATION X) / **ABDREAS BRUHN** – guitar / **TIM BRICHENO** – guitar (ex-ALL ABOUT EVE) / guests were **MAGGIE REILLY** – b.vocals (ex-MIKE OLDFIELD) / **JOHN PERRY** – guitar (ex-ONLY ONES)

Oct 90. (7")(c-s) **MORE. / YOU COULD BE THE ONE** [21] [ ]
(12"+=)(cd-s+=) – ('A'extended).

Oct 90. (cd)(c)(lp) **VISION THING** [11] [ ]
– Vision thing / Ribons / Destination Boulevard / Something fast / When you don't see me / Doctor Jeep / More / I was wrong.

Dec 90. (7") **DOCTOR JEEP. / KNOCKIN' ON HEAVEN'S DOOR (live)** [37] [ ]
(12"+=)(cd-s+=) – ('A'extended).
('A'ext-12") – Burn (live) / Amphetamine logic (live).

— (Oct91) **TONY JAMES** split from ELDRITCH amicably.

— Next featured vocals by **OFRA HAZA**

East West East West

Apr 92. (7") **TEMPLE OF LOVE (1992). / I WAS WRONG (American fade)** *(re-iss.Apr94)* [3] [ ]
('A'ext-12"+=) – Vision thing (Canadian club mix).
(cd-s+=) – When you don't see me (German release).

Apr 92. (cd)(c)(d-lp) **SOME GIRLS WANDER BY MISTAKE** [5] [ ]
(1980-1983 material)
– Alice / Floorshow / Phantom / 1969 / Kiss the carpet / Lights / Valentine / Fix / Burn / Kiss the carpet (reprise) / Temple of love / Heartland / Gimme shelter / Damage done / Watch / Home of the hitmen / Body electric / Adrenochrome / Anaconda.

— now just **ANDREW ELDRITCH** on own with guests

Aug 93. (7")(c-s) **UNDER THE GUN. / ALICE (1993)** [19] [ ]
(12"+=)(cd-s+=) – ('A'-Jutland mix).

Aug 93. (cd)(c)(d-lp) **GREATEST HITS VOLUME 1 – A SLIGHT CASE OF OVERBOMBING** (compilation) [14] [ ]
– Under the gun / Temple of love (1992) / Vision thing / Detonation boulevard / Doctor Jeep / More / Lucretia my reflection / Dominion – Mother / This corrosion / No time to cry / Walk away / Body and soul.

60 FT DOLLS

*** NEW ENTRY ***

Formed: Newport, Wales . . .1994 by RICHARD JOHN PARFITT, MIKE COLE and CARL BEVAN. Classic debut 45 'HAPPY SHOPPER' came courtesy of Swansea's 'Townhill'. Late 1995, they signed to 'Indolent', and charted early the next year with 'STAY'. • **Style:** Punky rock'n'roll or pop-art fusing The MANICS with The JAM or MOTT THE HOOPLE. • **Songwriters:** PARFITT or COLE or both. Covered; AFTERGLOW (Small Faces) / EVERYBODY'S GOT SOMETHING TO HIDE EXCEPT ME AND MY MONKEY (Beatles).

Recommended: THE BIG 3 (*7)

RICHARD JOHN PARFITT – vocals, guitar / **MIKE COLE** – vocals, bass / **CARL BEVAN** – drums

Townhill not issued

Jul 94. (7") **HAPPY SHOPPER. / LONDON BREEDS** [ ] [-]
(re-iss.Mar95)

RoughTrade not issued

May 95. (7") **WHITE KNUCKLE RIDE. / NO.1 PURE ALCOHOL** [ ] [-]
(cd-s+=) – Piss funk.

Indolent Geffen

Oct 95. (7")(cd-s) **PIG VALENTINE. / BRITISH RACING GREEN / YELLOW CANDLES** [ ] [ ] Dec 95

Jan 96. (7")(c-s) **STAY. / THE MAINDEE RUN** [48] [-]
(cd-s+=) – Rosalyn.

Apr 96. (7"colrd)(c-s) **TALK TO ME. / PONY RIDE** [37] [ ]
(cd-s+=) – Angel / Easy.

May 96. (cd)(c)(lp) **THE BIG 3** [36] [ ]
– New loafers / Talk to me / Stay / Hair / Happy shopper / The one / Good times / No.1 pure alcohol / Streamlined / Loser / Pig valentine / Terminal crash fear / Buzz.

SKID ROW

Formed: New Jersey, USA . . . late '86 by Canadian born BACH. Signed worldwide to 'Atlantic' in 1988, and soon released eponymous debut hit album. • **Style:** Hard-rock outfit influenced by KISS, DOKKEN, MOTLEY CRUE or even SEX PISTOLS. • **Songwriters:** BOLAN w/SNAKE + BACH or BOLAN w / AFFUSO + HILL. Covered C'MON AND LOVE ME (Kiss) / HOLIDAYS IN THE SUN (Sex Pistols) / WHAT YOU'RE DOING (Rush). • **Trivia:** Run by the same management team as BON JOVI.

Recommended: SKID ROW (*6) / SLAVE TO THE GRIND (*7).

SEBASTIAN BACH (b. BIERK, 3 Apr'68, Toronto) – vocals / **DAVE 'Snake' SABO** – guitar / **SCOTTI HILL** – guitar / **RACHEL BOLAN** – bass / **ROB AFFUSO** – drums

Atlantic Atlantic

Nov 89. (7")(7"sha-pic-d) **YOUTH GONE WILD. / SWEET LITTLE SISTER** [42] [99] Jun 89
(12"+=) – Makin' a mess (live).

Dec 89. (lp)(c)(cd) **SKID ROW** [30] [6] Feb 89
– Big guns / Sweet little sister / Can't stand the heartache / Piece of me / 18 and life / Rattlesnake shake / Youth gone wild / Here I am / Makin' a mess / I remember you / Midnight – Tornado. *(re-iss.cd/c Feb95 on 'Warners')*

Jan 90. (7"one-sided)(7"sha-pic-d) **18 AND LIFE. / MIDNIGHT TORNADO** [12] [4] Jul 89
(12"+=)(c-s+=)(cd-s+=) – Here I am (live).

Mar 90. (7")(c-s) **I REMEMBER YOU. / MAKIN' A MESS** [36] [6] Nov 89
(12"+=)(cd-s+=)/ /(10"+=) – Big guns./ / ('A'live).

East West Atlantic

Jun 91. (7")(7"sha-pic-d) **MONKEY BUSINESS. / SLAVE TO THE GRIND** [19] [ ]
(12"+=)(cd-s+=) – Riot act.

Jun 91. (cd)(c)(lp) **SLAVE TO THE GRIND** [5] [1]
– Monkey business / Slave to the grind / The threat / Quicksand Jesus / Psycho love / Get the fuck out / Lovin' on a chain gang / Creepshow / In a darkened room / Riot act / Mud kicker / Wasted time.

Sep 91. (7")(c-s) **SLAVE TO THE GRIND. / C'MON AND LOVE ME** [43] [ ]
(12") – ('A'side) / Creepshow / Beggar's day.
(cd-s++=) – (above 'B'side).

Nov 91. (7") **WASTED TIME. / HOLIDAYS IN THE SUN** [20] [88]
(12"+=) – What you're doing / Get the fuck out (live).
(cd-s+=) – Psycho love / Get the fuck out (live).
(12"pic-d) – ('A'side) / Psycho love.

Aug 92. (7")(c-s) **YOUTH GONE WILD. / DELIVERIN' THE GOODS** [22] [ ]
(12"+=)(cd-s+=) – Get the funk out / Psycho therapy.

Sep 92. (m-cd)(m-c) **B-SIDES OURSELVES** (as said) [-] [58]

Mar 95. (cd)(c)(lp) **SUBHUMAN RACE** [8] [35]
– My enemy / Firesign / Bonehead / Beat yourself blind / Eileen / Remains to be seen / Subhuman race / Frozen / Into another / Face against my soul / Medicine jar / Breakin' down / Ironwill.

Nov 95. (7"colrd) **BREAKIN' DOWN. / RIOT ACT (live)** [48] [ ]
(cd-s) – ('A'side) / Firesign (demo) / Slave to the grind (live) / Monkey business (live).
(cd-s) – ('A'side) / Frozen (demo) / Beat yourself blind (live) / Psychotherapy (live).

SKIN

Formed: London, England . . . 1991 briefly as TASTE, by MYKE GRAY (ex-JAGGED EDGE) and Welsh heavies KOUGAR. Early 1994, they scored first of 5 hits that year with 'SKIN UP' EP. • **Style:** Metal-pop /rock similar to WHITESNAKE with hard blues. • **Songwriters:** GRAY, some w/others, except HANGIN' ON THE TELEPHONE (Blondie) / PUMP IT UP (Elvis Costello). • **Trivia:** Produced by KEITH OLSEN.

Recommended: SKIN (*5)

NEVILLE MacDONALD – vocals (ex-KOOGA) / **MYKE GRAY** (b.12 May'68) – guitar (ex-JAGGED EDGE) / **ANDY ROBBINS** – bass, vocals / **DICKIE FLISZAR** – drums, vocals (ex-BRUCE DICKINSON)

Parlophone Capitol

Dec 93. (12"ep)(cd-ep) **SKIN UP EP** [67] [ ]
– Look but don't touch / Shine your light / Monkey.

Mar 94. (12"ep)(c-ep)(cd-ep) **HOUSE OF LOVE / GOOD TIME LOVIN'. / THIS PLANET'S ON FIRE / TAKE IT EASY** [45] [ ]

Apr 94. (c-s) **MONEY. / ALL I WANT / FUNKTIFIED** [18] [ ]
(cd-s) – (1st 2 tracks) / Unbelievable / Down down down.
(12"pic-d) – (1st & 3rd tracks) / Express yourself.
(cd-s) – (1st & 3rd tracks) / Express yourself / Unbelievable.

May 94. (cd)(c)(lp) **SKIN** [9] [ ]
– Money / Shine your light / House of love / Colourblind / Which are the tears / Look but don't touch / Nightsong / Tower of strength / Revolution / Raised on radio / Wings of an angel. *(re-iss.Oct94)*

Jul 94. (c-s) **TOWER OF STRENGTH. / LOOK BUT DON'T TOUCH (live) / UNBELIEVABLE (live)** [19] [ ]
(12"+=)(cd-s+=) – ('A'live).
(cd-s) – ('A'side) / Money (live) / Shine your light (live) / Colourblind (live).

Oct 94. (c-s) **LOOK BUT DON'T TOUCH. / HANGIN' ON THE TELEPHONE** [33] [ ]

(cd-s+=) – Should I stay or should I go / Dog eat dog.
(12"pic-d)(cd-s) – ('A'side) / Should I stay or should I go / Pump it up / Money.

May 95. (12"ep) **TAKE ME DOWN TO THE RIVER. / SPEED KING (live) / NEED YOUR LOVE SO BAD (live) / HOUSE OF LOVE (live)** [26] [ ]
(cd-s) – ('A'side) / Rock and roll (live) / Ain't talkin' 'bout love (live) / Rock candy (live).
(cd-s) – ('A'side) / Radar love (live) / Come together (live) / My generation (live).

. . . Jan – Jun '96 stop press . . .

Mar 96. (single) **HOW LUCKY YOU ARE** [32] [ ]
Apr 96. (cd)(c)(lp) **LUCKY** [38] [ ]
May 96. (single) **PERFECT DAY** [33] [ ]

SKUNK ANANSIE

Formed: London, England . . .1994 by aggressive shaven-headed black lesbian SKIN and guitarist ACE. Quickly made an impact on British audiences with three Top 50 singles and a Top 10 album in 1995. • **Style:** As said with anti-rascist overtones fused with blasting indie-metallic and punk rock. • **Songwriters:** SKIN – ARRAN.

Recommended: PARANOID & SUNBURNT (*7)

SKIN (DYER) -vocals / **ACE** (L.ARRAN) -guitar / **CASS** -bass / **ROBBIE** -drums

O. L. Indian ???

Mar 95. (c-s)(10"white) **SELLING JESUS. / THROUGH RAGE / YOU WANT IT ALL** [46] [ ]
(cd-s+=) – Skunk song.

Jun 95. (10"lime)(c-s) **I CAN DREAM. / AESTHETIC ANARCHIST / BLACK SKIN SEXUALITY** [41] [ ]
(cd-s+=) – Little baby Swastikkka.

—— **LOUIE** -drums repl.ROBBIE

Aug 95. (c-s) **CHARITY / I CAN DREAM (version)** [40] [ ]
(cd-s+=) – Punk by numbers.
(cd-s+=) – Kept my mouth shut.
(10"colrd) – ('A'side) / Used / Killer's war.

Sep 95. (cd)(c)(lp) **PARANOID & SUNBURNT** [8] [ ]
– Selling Jesus / Intellectualise my blackness / I can dream / Little baby swastikkka / All in the name of pity / Charity / It takes blood and guts / Weak / And here I stand (nigger rage) / 100 ways to be a good girl / Rise up.

. . . Jan – Jun '96 stop press . . .

Jan 96. (single) **WEAK** [20] [ ]
Apr 96. (single) **CHARITY** [20] [ ]

SLASH'S SNAKEPIT (see under ⇒ GUNS N' ROSES)

SLAUGHTER

Formed: USA . . . Sep'88 by MARK SLAUGHTER and DANA STRUM (both ex-VINNIE VINCENT'S INVASION). That year they stuck with past 'Chrysalis' label. Scored massive selling US Top 20 debut album in 1990 with 'STICK IT TO YA'. • **Style:** Heavy-metal, similar to KISS or BON JOVI, featuring the high-pitched vox of MARK. • **Songwriters:** MARK and DANA.

Recommended: STICK IT TO YA (*5).

MARK SLAUGHTER – vocals / **TIM KELLY** – guitar / **DANA STRUM** – bass / **BLAS ELIAS** – drums

Chrysalis Chrysalis

Apr 90. (cd)(c)(lp) **STICK IT TO YA** [ ] [18] Feb 90
– Eye to eye / Burnin' bridges / Up all night / Spend my life / Thinking of June / She wants more / Fly to the angels / Mad about you / That's not enough / You are the one / Give me your heart / Desperately / Loaded gun. *(cd+=)*– Fly to the angels (acoustic) / Wingin' it.

May 90. (7") **UP ALL NIGHT. / EYE TO EYE** [62] [27] Apr 90
(12"+=)(cd-s+=) – Stick it to ya (medley); Mad about you – Burning bridges – Fly to the angels.

Aug 90. (7")(c-s)(7"pic-d) **FLY TO THE ANGELS. / UP ALL NIGHT (live)** [55] [19]
(12"+=)(12"pic-d+=) – Loaded gun.
(cd-s++=) – ('A'acoustic version). *(re-iss.Jan91, hit UK No.55)*

Nov 90. (m-cd)(m-c)(m-lp) **STICK IT LIVE (live)** [-] [ ]
– Burnin' bridges / Eye to eye / Fly to the angels / Up all night / Loaded gun.

Dec 90. (c-s)(cd-s) **SPEND MY LIFE. / ?** [-] [39]

Mar 92. (cd)(c)(lp) **WILD LIFE** [64] [8]
– Reach for the sky / Out for love / The wild life / Days gone by / Dance for me baby / Times they change / Move to the music / Real love / Shake this place / Streets of broken hearts / Hold on / Do ya know. (cd+=) – Old man / Days gone by (acoustic version).

Aug 92. (c-s)(cd-s) **REAL LOVE. / ?** [-] [69]

S.P.V. ???

Jun 95. (cd) **FEAR NO EVIL** [ ] [ ]

SLAYER

Formed: Los Angeles, California, USA . . . late 1981 by ARAYA, HANNEMAN and former jazz drummer LOMBARDO. Following releases on indie labels, they agreed terms with 'Def American' in 1986. With Rick Rubin (co-owner of rap label 'Def Jam') producing 'REIGN IN BLOOD', they hit UK Top 50 and rose substantially in the States. The controversy over the track 'Angel Of Death', made 'Geffen' (UK distributers) pull out of agreement. 'London' records bailed them out in 1987, with new contract. It payed off, when their 1990 album 'SEASONS IN THE ABYSS' hit UK Top20 / US Top40. • **Style:** Heavy thrash-metal played with spitfire repitition and flavoured with grim occult lyrics. • **Songwriters:** ARAYA words / HANNEMAN music, also covering DISSIDENT AGGRESSOR (Judas Priest) / IN-A-GADDA-DA-VIDA (Iron Butterfly). • **Trivia:** Maiden track recording was on 'Metal Blade''s Various Artists gathering 'METAL MASSACRE II'.

Recommended: SOUTH OF HEAVEN (*7)

TOM ARAYA – vocals, bass / **JEFF HANNEMAN** – lead guitar / **KERRY KING** (b. 3 Jun'64) – lead guitar / **DAVE LOMBARDO** (b.16 Feb'54) – drums

M.F.N. Metal Blade

Jun 84. (lp) **SHOW NO MERCY** [ ] [ ]
– Evil has no boundaries / The antichrist / Die by the sword / Fight till death / Metalstorm – Face the slayer / Black magic / Tormentor / The final command / Crionics / Show no mercy. *(US re-iss.pic-lp Dec88)*

Roadrunner Metal Blade

Oct 84. (12"ep) **HAUNTING THE CHAPEL. / CHEMICAL WARFARE / CAPTOR OF SIN** [ ] [ ]
(re-iss.c-ep/cd-ep.Oct89)

Roadrunner Enigma

1984. (lp) **LIVE UNDEAD (live)** [ ] [ ]
– Black magic / Die by the sword / Captor of sin / The antichrist / Evil has no boundaries / Show no mercy / Aggressive perfector / Chemical warfare. *(re-iss.pic-lp/cd/lp Dec88) (US re-iss.Oct87)*

May 85. (lp) **HELL AWAITS** [ ] [ ]
– Hell awaits / Kill again / At dawn they sleep / Praise of death / Necrophiliac / Crypts of eternity / Hardening of the arteries. *(re-iss.c+d.Feb89)*

London Def Jam

Apr 87. (lp)(c)(cd)(pic-lp) **REIGN IN BLOOD** [47] [94] Nov 86
– Angel of death / Piece by piece / Necrophobic / Jesus saves / Altar of sacrifice / Criminally insane / Reborn / Epidemic / Post mortem / Raining blood.

May 87. (7") **CRIMINALLY INSANE. / AGGRESSIVE PERFECTER** [64] [ ]
(12"+=) – Post mortem.

Jun 88. (lp)(c)(cd) **SOUTH OF HEAVEN** [25] [57]
– South of Heaven / Silent scream / Live undead / Behind the crooked cross / Mandatory suicide / Ghosts of war / Cleanse the soul / Read between the lies / Dissident aggressor / Spill the blood.

Sep 88. (12")(7") **SOUTH OF HEAVEN. / ?** [ ] [ ]

Def Amer.. Def Amer..

Oct 90. (cd)(c)(lp) **SEASONS IN THE ABYSS** [18] [40]
– War ensemble / Blood red / Spirit in black / Expendable youth / Dead skin mask / Hallowed point / Skeletons of society / Temptation / Born of fire / Seasons in the abyss.

Def American Def American

Oct 91. (cd)(c)(d-lp) **DECADE OF AGGRESSION (live)** [29] [ ]
– Hell awaits / The anti-Christ / War ensemble / South of Heaven / Raining blood / Altar of sacrifice / Jesus saves / Dead skin mask / Seasons in the abyss / Mandatory suicide / Angel of death / Hallowed paint / Blood red / Die by the sword / Black magic / Captor of sin / Born of fire / Post mortem / Spirit in black / Expendable youth / Chemical warfare.

Oct 91. (7")(7"pic-d) **SEASONS IN THE ABYSS (live). / AGGRESSIVE PERFECTOR (live)** [51] [ ]
(12"+=) – Chemical warfare.
(cd-s+=)(12"pic-d+=) – ('A'-experimental).

—— (May92) **PAUL BOSTOPH** -drums repl.LOMBARDO

Oct 94. (cd)(c)(lp) **DIVINE INTERVENTION** [15] [8]
– Killing fields / Sex, murder, art / Fictional reality / Ditto head / Divine intervention / Circle of beliefs / SS III / Serenity in murder / Two-thirteen / Mind control.

Sep 95. (7"ep) **SERENITY IN MURDER / RAINING BLOOD. / DITTOHEAD / SOUTH OF HEAVEN** [ ] [ ]
(cd-s) – ('A'side) / At dawn they sleep / Dead skin mask / Divine intervention.
(cd-s) – ('A'side) / Angel of death / Mandatory suicide / War ensemble.

. . . Jan – Jun '96 stop press . . .

May 96. (cd)(c)(lp) **UNDISPUTED ATTITUDE** [31] [34]

SLEEPER

Formed: Ilford, Essex, England . . . 1993 by LOUISE and her boyfriend JOHN STEWART, who soon found ANDY McCLURE and DIID. Were indie successes of 1994 and were about to breakthrough into the pop charts early '95. • **Style:** On the same Wave as ELASTICA but with fuzzy WIRE guitars. • **Songwriters:** Most by WENER or some w/ STEWART. • **Trivia:** LOUISE had earlier attended Manchester Uni to study English and politics.

Recommended: SMART (*9) / THE IT GIRL (*5)

LOUISE WENER – vocals, guitar / **JOHN STEWART** – lead guitar / **DIID OSMAN** – bass / **ANDY MacCLURE** – drums, percussion

Indolent / not issued

Nov 93. (7"ep)(12"ep)(cd-ep) **ALICE IN VAIN. / HA HA YOU'RE DEAD / BIG NURSE** [ ] [-]

Feb 94. (7"ep)(cd-ep) **SWALLOW. / TWISTED / ONE GIRL DREAMING** [ ] [-]

May 94. (7"ep)(cd-ep) **DELICIOUS. / LADY LOVE YOUR COUNTRYSIDE / BEDSIDE MANNERS** [75] [-]
(12"ep+=) – Tatty.

Oct 94. (7"mail-order) **BUCKET AND SPADE (live)** [-] [-]
– Bedhead / Alice in vain / Swallow.

Jan 95. (7")(c-s) **INBETWEENER. / LITTLE ANNIE** [16] [ ]
(cd-s+=) – Disco Duncan.
(12"++=) – Bank.

Feb 95. (cd)(c)(lp) **SMART** [5] [ ]
– Inbetweener / Swallow / Delicious / Hunch / Amuse / Bedhead / Lady love your countryside / Vegas / Poor flying man / Alice in vain / Twisted / Pyrotechnician.

Mar 95. (7"blue)(c-s) **VEGAS. / HYMN TO HER** [33] [ ]
(12"pic-d)(cd-s+=) – It's wrong to breed / Close.

Sep 95. (7")(c-s)(cd-s) **WHAT DO I KNOW?. / PAINT ME / ROOM AT THE TOP** [14] [ ]
(cd-s) – ('A'side) / Vegas (live) / Amuse (live) / Disco Duncan (live).

. . . Jan – Jun '96 stop press . . .

Apr 96. (single) **SALE OF THE CENTURY** [10] [ ]

May 96. (cd)(c)(lp) **THE IT GIRL** [5] [ ]

Grace SLICK (see under ⇒ JEFFERSON AIRPLANE)

SLITS

Formed: London, England . . . early 1977 as foremost all-girl punk rock outfit (until BUDGIE joined that is). Supported The CLASH on Spring 1977 tour, but amazingly never secured a record deal until 1979 when 'Island' knocked on door. The 'Real' label (home of HEARTBREAKERS and PRETENDERS) were turned down the preceeding year. The two and a half year wait was over, when their vinyl debut (oddly not a 45! but the album CUT), controversially revealing on its sleeve the trio naked but coated with mud. This DENNIS BOVELL produced seminal classic album, scraped into the 30 and was astonishingly their commercial peak. The untitled follow-up jam/bootleg disaster saw to that. Anti-conventional attitudes were once more thrown away, when 'CBS' re-kindled aspirations for brief 'RETURN OF THE GIANT SLITS' lp. • **Style:** Anti-pro feminists who fused punk ideals/sounds with unorthodox tribal rhythm. • **Songwriters:** Group compositions, except I HEARD IT THROUGH THE GRAPEVINE (Marvin Gaye) / MAN NEXT DOOR (John Holt). • **Trivia:** Early 1978, they were sighted in the punk film 'JUBILEE'.

Recommended: CUT (*9) / RETURN OF THE GIANT (*7)

ARI UP (b.ARIANNA FOSTER) – vocals / **VIVIEN ALBERTINE** – guitar (ex-FLOWERS OF ROMANCE) repl. KATE KORUS to KLEENEX (Feb77) / **TESSA POLLITT** – bass repl. SUZI GUTSY who formed The FLICKS. / **PALM OLIVE** – drums (ex-FLOWERS OF ROMANCE) was repl. (Oct78) by **BUDGIE** (b.PETER CLARK) – percussion, drums (ex-BIG IN JAPAN, ex-SECRETS,etc)

Island / Antilles

Sep 79. (lp)(c) **CUT** [30] [ ]
– Instant hit / So tough / Spend spend spend / Shoplifting / FM / Newtown / Ping pong affair / Love and romance / Typical girls / Adventures close to home. *(cd-iss.Apr90)*

Sep 79. (7") **TYPICAL GIRLS. / I HEARD IT THROUGH THE GRAPEVINE** [60] [ ]
(12"+=) – Typical girls – brink style / Liebe and romance.

— **BRUCE SMITH** – drums (of POP GROUP) repl. BUDGIE to SIOUXSIE & BANSHEES jazz-trumpeter **DON CHERRY** guested

Y-Rough / not issued

Mar 80. (7") **IN THE BEGINNING THERE WAS RHYTHM. / ('B'by Pop Group)** [ ] [-]

May 80. (lp) **UNTITLED (Y3)** (bootleg demo jam) [ ] [-]
– A boring life / Slime / Or what it is / No.1 enemy / Once upon a time in a living room / Bongos on the lawn / Face place / Let's do the split / Mosquitos / Vaseline / No more rock and roll for you.

Jun 80. (7") **MAN NEXT DOOR. / MAN NEXT DOOR (dub)** [ ] [-]

— added guest **STEVE BERESFORD** – keyboards, guitar (of FLYING LIZARDS)

Human / not issued

Jun 81. (7")(12") **ANIMAL SPACE. / ANIMAL SPACIER** [ ] [-]

C.B.S. / Epic

Oct 81. (7") **EARTHBEAT. / BEGIN AGAIN RHYTHM** [ ] [-]
(12"+=) – Earthdub.

Oct 81. (12"m) **ANIMAL SPACE. / ANIMAL SPACE (dub) / IN THE BEGINNING** [-] [ ]

Oct 81. (lp)(c) **RETURN OF THE GIANT SLITS** [ ] [ ]
– Earthbeat / Or what it is? / Face place / Walkabout / Difficult fun / Animal space – Spacier / Improperly dressed / Life on Earth. *(free-7"w.a.)* – (INTERVIEW). / FACE DUB

Dec 81. (7") **EARTHBEAT. / OR WHAT IT IS?** [-] [ ]

— Parted ways early 1982. BRUCE joined RIP, RIG & PANIC. All except TESSA were part of colossus band NEW AGE STEPPERS.

– compilations, others, etc. –

Feb 87. Strange Fruit; (12"ep) **THE PEEL SESSIONS** (19.9.77) [ ] [-]
– Love and romance / Vindictive / Newtown / Shoplifting.

Dec 88. Strange Fruit; (m-lp)(c)(cd) **DOUBLE PEEL SESSIONS** [ ] [-]

SLY & THE FAMILY STONE

Formed: San Francisco, California, USA . . . 1966 initially as The STONERS by SLY STONE with brother FREDDIE, sister ROSEMARY and cousin LARRY GRAHAM. They soon became SLY & THE FAMILY STONE after gigging in local bars / clubs in Oakland. In 1967, they signed to 'Epic', and issued debut album 'A WHOLE NEW THING'. The following year, they broke through commercially with US Top 10 single 'DANCE TO THE MUSIC'. In 1969, they were given massive accolade, for their performance on the now famous 'Woodstock' festival. • **Style:** Pioneers of the psychedelic soul movement in 1967, which re-influenced older groups TEMPTATIONS and The ISLEY BROTHERS. One of the first inter-racial, inter-gender and inta-drugs outfits to emerge from the rock-soul world. • **Songwriters:** All by SLY and group except; I CAN'T TURN YOU LOOSE (Otis Redding)/ YOU REALLY GOT ME (Kinks). • **Trivia:** On 5 Jun'74, SLY married Kathy Silva on stage at Madison Square Garden. Two months earlier, she had given him first child Bubb Ali (all 3 pictured on album cover of SMALL TALK). She divorced SLY in '75, and he filed for bankruptcy early '76.

Recommended: STAND (*9) / THERE'S A RIOT GOIN' ON (*9) / TAKIN' YOU HIGHER – THE BEST OF (*8)

SLY STONE (b.SYLVESTER STEWART, 15 Mar'44, Dallas, Texas) – vox, guitar, keyboards (ex-SLY & THE MOJO MEN) / **FREDDIE STONE** (b.FREDDIE STEWART, 5 Jun'46, Dallas) – guitar / **CYNTHIA ROBINSON** (b.12 Jan'46) – trumpet / **ROSEMARY STONE** (b.ROSEMARY STEWART, 21 Mar'45) – vocals, piano / **LARRY GRAHAM** (b.14 Aug'46, Beaumont, Texas) – bass / **JERRY MARTINI** – saxophone / **GREG ERRICO** – drums

not iss. / Loadstone

1966. (7") **I AIN'T GOT NOBODY. / I CAN'T TURN YOU LOOSE** [-] [ ]

Columbia / Epic

1967. (lp) **A WHOLE NEW THING** [-] [ ]
– Underdog / If this room could talk / Run run run / Turn me loose / Let me hear it from you / Advice / I cannot make it / Trip to your heart / I hate to love her / Bad risk / That kind of person / Day.

1967. (7") **HIGHER. / UNDERDOG** [-] [ ]

Mar 68. (7") **DANCE TO THE MUSIC. / LET ME HEAR IT FROM YOU** [ ] [8] Jan 68

Direction / Epic

Jun 68. (7") **DANCE TO THE MUSIC. / LET ME HEAR IT FROM YOU** [7] [-]

Sep 68. (lp) **DANCE TO THE MUSIC** [ ] [ ] Apr 68
– Dance to the music / Higher / I ain't got nobody (for real) / Dance to the medley: Music is alive – Dance in – Music lover / Ride the rhythm / Color me true / Are you ready / Don't burn baby / I'll never fall in love again. *(re-iss.Oct73 on 'CBS-Embassy')*

Sep 68. (7") **M'LADY. / LIFE32** [93] [93] Jun 68

Jan 69. (lp) **M'LADY** (US-title 'LIFE') [ ] [ ] Nov68
– Dynamite! / Chicken / Plastic Jim / Fun / Into my own thing / Harmony / Life / Love city / I'm an animal / M'lady / Jane is a groupie.

Mar 69. (7") **EVERYDAY PEOPLE. / SING A SIMPLE SONG** [36] [1]
[89] Nov 68
(re-iss.1975 on 'Epic')

Jul 69. (lp) **STAND!** [ ] [13] Apr 69
– Stand! / Don't call me nigger, Whitey / I want to take you higher / Somebody's watching you / Sing a simple song / Everyday people / Sex machine / You can make it if you try. *(re-iss.cd Feb95)*

Aug 69. (7") **HOT FUN IN THE SUMMERTIME. / FUN** [ ] [2]

Oct 69. (7") **STAND!. / I WANT TO TAKE YOU HIGHER** [ ] [22]
[60] Apr 69
(re-iss.1975 on 'Epic')

Feb 70. (7") **THANK YOU (FALLETTINME BE MICE ELF AGIN). / EVERYBODY IS A STAR** [ ] [1] Dec 69

C.B.S. Epic

May 70. (7") **I WANT TO TAKE YOU HIGHER. / YOU CAN MAKE IT IF YOU TRY** [ ] [ ]

Jan 71. (lp)(c) **GREATEST HITS** (compilation) [ ] [2] Oct 70
– I want to take you higher / Everybody is a star / Stand / Life / Fun / You can make it if you try / Dance to the music / Everyday people / Hot fun in the summertime / M'lady / Sing a simple song / Thank you (falletinme be mice elf agin). *(re-iss.Mar81, cd-iss.Jun90) (quad-lp 1975)*

Epic Epic

Nov 71. (7") **FAMILY AFFAIR. / LUV 'N' HAIGHT** [15] [1] Oct 71

Jan 72. (lp)(c) **THERE'S A RIOT GOIN' ON** [31] [1] Nov 71
– Luv 'n' haight / Just like a baby / Poet / Family affair / Africa talks to you 'The Asphalt Jungle' / Brave & strong / (You caught me) Smilin' / Time / Spaced cowboy / Runnin' away / Thank you for talkin' to me Africa. (free ltd.12"w.a) *(re-iss.Feb86 on 'Edsel', cd-iss.Jan91) (re-iss.cd+c May94)*

Mar 72. (7") **RUNNIN' AWAY. / BRAVE & STRONG** [17] [23] Jan 72

Apr 72. (7") **(YOU CAUGHT ME) SMILIN'. / LUV 'N' HAIGHT** [-] [42]

— (Jan73) **RUSTEE ALLEN** – bass repl. LARRY (formed GRAHAM CENTRAL STATION) **ANDY NEWMARK** – drums repl. ERRICO. / added **PAT RICCO** – saxophone

Jun 73. (lp)(c) **FRESH** [ ] [7]
– In time / If you want me to stay / Let me have it all / Frisky / Thankful 'n' thoughtful / The skin I'm in / I don't know (satisfaction) / Keep on dancin' / Que sera sera / If it were left up to me / Babies makin' babies. *(re-iss.+cd.May87 on 'Edsel')*

Aug 73. (7") **IF YOU WANT ME TO STAY. / THANKFUL 'N' THOUGHTFUL** [ ] [12] Jun 73

Oct 73. (7") **FRISKY. / IF IT WERE LEFT UP TO ME** [-] [79]

Nov 73. (7") **QUE SERA SERA. / IF IT WERE LEFT UP TO ME** [ ] [-]

— **BILL LORDAN** – drums repl. NEWMARK who became session man

Jul 74. (lp)(c) **SMALL TALK** [ ] [15]
– Small talk / Say you will / Mother beautiful / Time for livin' / Can't strain my brain / Loose booty / Holdin' on / Wishful thinking / Better thee than me / Livin' while I'm livin' / This is love.

Jul 74. (7") **TIME FOR LIVIN'. / SMALL TALK** [ ] [32]

Jan 75. (7") **LOOSE BOOTY. / CAN'T STRAIN MY BRAIN** [ ] [84] Oct 84

— Discontinued for a while, as

SLY STONE

went solo (same label).

Oct 75. (lp)(c) **HIGH ON YOU** [ ] [45]
– I get high on you / Crossword puzzle / That's lovin' you / Who do you love / Green-eyed monster girl / Organize / Le lo li / My world / So good to me / Greed.

Oct 75. (7") **I GET HIGH ON YOU. / THAT'S LOVIN' YOU** [ ] [52] Sep 75

Dec 75. (7") **LE LO LI. / WHO DO YOU LOVE** [-] [ ]

Mar 76. (7") **CROSSWORD PUZZLE. / GREED** [-] [ ]

SLY & THE FAMILY STONE

reformed (same label)

Dec 76. (lp)(c) **HEARD YA MISSED ME, WELL I'M BACK** [ ] [ ]
– Heard ya missed me, well I'm back / What was I thinkin' / In my head / Sexy situation / Blessing in disguise / Everything in you / Mother is a hippie / Let's be together / The thing / Family again.

Feb 77. (7") **FAMILY AGAIN. / NOTHING LESS THAN HAPPINESS** [-] [ ]

Warners Warners

Sep 79. (7") **REMEMBER WHO YOU ARE. / SHEER ENERGY** [ ] [ ]

Oct 79. (lp)(c) **BACK ON THE RIGHT TRACK** [ ] [ ]
– Remember who you are / Back on the right track / If it's not addin' up . . . / The same thing (makes you laugh, makes you cry) / Shine it on / It takes all kinds / Who's to say / Sheer energy.

Dec 79. (7") **THE SAME THING (MAKES YOU LAUGH, MAKES YOU CRY). / WHO'S TO SAY** [-] [ ]

— In 1981, SLY guested on album 'THE ELECTRIC SPANKING OF WAR BABIES' by George Clinton's FUNKADELIC.

Mar 83. (lp)(c) **AIN'T BUT THE ONE WAY** [-] [ ]
– L.O.V.I.N.U. / One way / Ha ha, hee hee / Hobo Ken / Who in the funk do you think we are / You really got me / Sylvester / We can do it / High, y'all.

— In 1984, SLY joined BOBBY WOMACK on tour. He later guested on JESSE JOHNSON's 'A&M' US No.53 hit single 'Crazay' (Oct86).

SLY STONE

A & M A & M

Oct 86. (7") **EEK-A-BO-STATIK. / BLACK GIRLS (RAE DAWN CHONG)** [-] [ ]

Dec 86. (7"w/ MARTHA DAVIS) **STONE LOVE AND AFFECTION. / BLACK GIRLS** [-] [ ]

– (SLY & FAMILY . . .) compilations, others, etc. –

Mar 73. Epic; (7") **FAMILY AFFAIR. / DANCE TO THE MUSIC** [ ] [ ]

Feb 75. Epic; (7"ep) **DANCE TO THE MUSIC / COLOUR ME TRUE. / STAND! / RIDE THE RHYTHM** [ ] [ ]

May 75. Epic; (d-lp) **HIGH ENERGY** [ ] [ ]
– (A WHOLE NEW THING / LIFE)

1975. Epic; (7") **DANCE TO THE MUSIC. / LIFE** [ ] [ ]

1975. Epic; (7") **HOT FUN IN THE SUMMERTIME. / M'LADY** [ ] [ ]

1975. Epic; (7") **HOT FUN IN THE SUMMERTIME. / FUN** [-] [ ]

1975. Epic; (7") **FAMILY AFFAIR. / RUNNIN' AWAY** [ ] [ ]

1975. Epic; (7") **IF YOU WANT ME TO STAY. / FRISKY** [ ] [ ]

Jan 77. Epic; (7") **DANCE TO THE MUSIC. / I WANT TO TAKE YOU HIGHER** [ ] [-]

Mar 79. Epic; (7") **DANCE TO THE MUSIC. / STAND!** [ ] [-]

Nov 79. Epic; (7") **DANCE TO THE MUSIC. / SING A SIMPLE SONG** [ ] [ ]

Aug 80. Epic; (7") **DANCE TO THE MUSIC. / EVERYDAY PEOPLE** [ ] [ ]
(re-iss.Jul82 on 'Old Gold')

Mar 82. Epic; (d-lp)(d-c) **ANTHOLOGY** [ ] [ ]
(re-iss.Sep87)

Apr 85. Epic; (lp)(c)(cd) **DANCE TO THE MUSIC** [ ] [ ]

Sep 87. Epic; (7") **DANCE TO THE MUSIC. / FAMILY AFFAIR** [ ] [ ]
(12"+=) – Everyday people / Runnin' away.

Oct 94. Epic; (cd) **THE BEST** [ ] [ ]

1979. Sculpture; (lp) **RECORDED IN SAN FRANCISCO 1964-67** [ ] [-]

Jan 80. CBS; (lp) **TEN YEARS TOO SOON ("SLY STONE")** [ ] [ ]

Dec 91. CBS; (cd) **IN THE STILL OF THE NIGHT** [ ] [-]

Nov 91. Castle; (cd) **THE COLLECTION** [ ] [-]

1992 Sony; (cd)(c) **TAKIN' YOU HIGHER – THE BEST OF SLY & THE FAMILY STONE** [ ] [ ]
– Dance to the music / I want to take you higher / Family affair / Thank you (falletinme be mice elf agin) / I get high on you / Stand / M'lady / Skin I'm in / Everyday people / Sing a simple song / Hot fun in the summertime / Don't call me nigger, Whitey / Brave & strong / Life / Everybody is a star / If you want me to stay / (You caught me) Smilin' / Que sera sera / Running away / Family affair (remix).

Feb 94. Javelin; (cd)(c) **SPOTLIGHT ON SLY & THE FAMILY STONE** [ ] [-]

Mar 94. Charly; (cd) **REMEMBER WHO YOU ARE** [ ] [-]

Sep 94. Ace; (cd) **PRECIOUS STONE: IN THE STUDIO WITH SLY STONE** [ ] [-]

Dec 94. Prestige; (cd)(c) **EVERY DOG HAS IT'S DAY** [ ] [-]

Feb 95. B.A.M.; (cd) **PEARLS OF THE PAST ("SLY STONE & THE MOJO MEN")** [ ] [-]

— Thunderbolt records issued 2 albums of SLY STONE productions in Apr87 + Oct87 respectively, named 'DANCE TO THE MUSIC' & 'FAMILY AFFAIR'.

— **SLY STONE's** early US recordings under various pseudonyms (label in brackets)

STEWART BROTHERS

doo-wop outfit with brother FREDDIE and sister ROSE?

1959. (7") **THE RAT. / RA RA ROO** (Ensign)

1960. (7") **SLEEP ON THE PORCH. / YUM YUM YUM** (Keen)

LUKE STEWART

1961. (7") **A LONG TIME ALONE. / I'M JUST A FOOL** (Luke)

SYLVESTER STEWART

1961. (7") **A LONG TIME ALONE. / HELP ME WITH MY BROKEN HEART** (G&P)

The VISCANES

another doo-wop outfit.

1961. (7") **STOP WHAT YOU ARE DOING. / I GUESS I'LL BE** (Trop-po)
1961. (7") **YELLOW MOON. / UNCLE SAM NEEDS YOU** (V.P.M.)

SLY STEWART

1962. (7") **YELLOW MOON. / HEAVENLY ANGEL** (V.P.M.)
1963. (7") **I JUST LEARNED HOW TO SWIM. / SCAT SWIM** (Autumn)

SLY

1964. (7") **BUTTERMILK. / (part 2)** (Autumn)
1965. (7") **TEMPTATION WALK. / (part 2)** (Autumn)

— SLY at this time was producing Autumn acts The BEAU BRUMMELS, BOBBY FREEMAN and The MOJO MEN. He also became well-known local DJ for K-DIA.

SMALL FACES

Formed: East London, England ... mid '65 by LANE, JONES and WINSTON who quickly found lead singer and ex-child actor STEVE MARRIOTT. They soon signed to 'Decca' records, and released Top 20 hit 'WHATCHA GONNA DO ABOUT IT?'. The following year, they deposed The BEATLES' Eleanor Rigby at the top of charts with 'ALL OR NOTHING'. In 1968, they were No.1 in the album charts with concept 'OGDEN'S NUT GONE FLAKE', which was sleeved in a circle cover. Early in 1969, MARRIOTT departed from them, but they renewed band as The FACES with ex-JEFF BECK singer ROD STEWART. They quickly established themselves as UK/US top act after hitting big with 45 'STAY WITH ME'. The SMALL FACES re-united with MARRIOTT in 1977, but after 2 mediocre albums they finally folded. • **Style:** R&B mod outfit who branched out into pop psychedelia in 1967. The FACES were a high energy rock band, popular with live audiences, due to ROD STEWART's husky vox. • **Songwriters:** MARRIOTT and LANE except; WHATCHA GONNA DO ABOUT IT (Ian Samwell-Smith; their early producer) / SHA-LA-LA-LA-LEE (c.Kenny Lynch & Mort Schuman) / EVERY LITTLE BIT HURTS (Brenda Holloway) / TAKE THIS HURT OFF ME (Don Covay) / YOU'VE REALLY GOT A HOLD ON ME (Miracles) / etc. The FACES covered MAYBE I'M AMAZED (Paul McCartney) / I WISH IT WOULD RAIN (Temptations) / WICKED MESSENGER (Bob Dylan) / etc. • **Trivia:** The FACES had come together initially as supergroup QUIET MELON, which included ART WOOD, LONG JOHN BALDRY and JIMMY HOROWITZ.

Recommended: OGDEN'S NUT GONE FLAKE (*8) / THE ULTIMATE COLLECTION (*7) / The FACES:- SNAKES AND LADDERS – THE BEST OF THE FACES (*7)

STEVE MARRIOTT (b.30 Jan'47, Bow, London) – vocals, guitar (ex-solo artist) / **JIMMY WINSTON** (b.JAMES LANGWITH, 20 Apr'45, Stratford, London) – organ / **RONNIE LANE** (b. 1 Apr'45, Plaistow, London) – bass, vocals / **KENNEY JONES** (b.16 Sep'48, Stepney, London) – drums

		Decca	Press	
Aug 65.	(7") **WHATCHA GONNA DO ABOUT IT?. / WHAT'S A MATTER, BABY**	14		Jan66

— **IAN McLAGAN** (b.12 May'45) – keyboards repl. WINSTON who went solo

Nov 65.	(7") **I'VE GOT MINE. / IT'S TOO LATE**		-	
Jan 66.	(7") **SHA-LA-LA-LA-LEE. / GROW YOUR OWN**	3		Apr66
May 66.	(7") **HEY GIRL. / ALMOST GROWN**	10		Jul66
May 66.	(lp) **SMALL FACES**	3	-	

– Shake / Come on children / You better believe it / It's too late / One night stand / Whatcha gonna do about it? / Sorry she's mine / E to D / You need loving / Don't stop what you're doing / Own up / Sha-la-la-la-lee. *(cd-iss.Jul88 on 'London' +=)* – What's a matter baby / I've got mine / Grow your own / Almost grown.

		Decca	RCA Victor	
Aug 66.	(7") **ALL OR NOTHING. / UNDERSTANDING**	1		Sep66
Nov 66.	(7") **MY MIND'S EYE. / I CAN'T DANCE WITH YOU**	4		Dec66
Feb 67.	(7") **I CAN'T MAKE IT. / JUST PASSING**	26	-	
Apr 67.	(7") **PATTERNS. / E TO D**		-	
May 67.	(lp) **FROM THE BEGINNING** (out-takes, demos, etc)	17	-	

– Runaway / My mind's eye / Yesterday, today and tomorrow / That man / My way of giving / Hey girl / Tell me have you ever seen me? / Come back and take this hurt off me / All or nothing / Baby don't do it / Plum Nellie / Sha-la-la-la-lee / You really got a hold on me / Whatcha gonna do about it?. *(re-iss.Aug84) (cd-iss.Jan89 on 'London')*

		Immediate	Immediate	
Jun 67.	(7") **HERE COMES THE NICE. / TALK TO YOU**	12		
Jun 67.	(lp) **SMALL FACES**	12	-	

– Green circles / Become like you / Get yourself together / All our yesterdays / Talk to you / Show me the way / Up the wooden hills to Bedfordshire / Eddie's dreaming / (Tell me) Have you ever seen me / Something I want to tell you / Feeling lonely / Happy boys happy / Things are going to get better / My way of giving. *(cd-iss.May91 as 'GREEN CIRCLES (FIRST IMMEDIATE ALBUM)' on 'Sequel' +=)* Green circles (take 2) / Donkey rides, a penny, a glass / Have you ever seen me (take 2).

Aug 67.	(7") **ITCHYCOO PARK. / I'M ONLY DREAMING**	3	16	Nov 67
Nov 67.	(7") **TIN SOLDIER. / I FEEL MUCH BETTER**	9	73	Mar 68
Feb 68.	(lp) **THERE ARE BUT FOUR SMALL FACES**	-		

– Here comes the nice / All or nothing / Lazy Sunday / Sha-la-la-la-lee / Collibosher / The Autumn stone / Whatcha gonna do about it? / My mind's eye / Itchyco Park / Hey girl / The universal / Runaway / Call it something nice / I can't make it / Afterglow (of your love) / Tin soldier.

Apr 68.	(7") **LAZY SUNDAY. / ROLLIN' OVER**	2	
Jun 68.	(lp) **OGDENS NUT GONE FLAKE**	1	

– Ogden's nut gone flake / Afterglow (of your love) / Long agos and worlds apart / Rene / Son of a baker / Lazy Sunday / Happiness Stan / Rollin' over / The hungry intruder / The journey / Mad John / Happy days / Toy town. *(US re-iss. Mar 73 on 'Abkco') (re-iss.Mar80 on 'Virgin') (re-iss.+cd.Sep86) (re-iss.+cd.Oct86 on 'Castle', cd+=)–* Tin soldier (live).

Jul 68.	(7") **THE UNIVERSAL. / DONKEY RIDES, A PENNY, A GLASS**	16	
Nov 68.	(7") **THE JOURNEY. / MAD JOHN**	-	
Mar 69.	(7") **AFTERGLOW (OF YOUR LOVE). / WHAM BAM, THANK YOU MAM**	36	
Mar 69.	(d-lp) **THE AUTUMN STONE** (rarities, live, etc)		

– Here comes the nice / The Autumn stone / Collibosher / All or nothing / Red balloon / Lazy Sunday / Rollin' over / If I were a carpenter / Every litle bit hurts / My mind's eye / Tin soldier / Just assing / Call it something nice / I can't make it / Afterglow (of your love) / Sha-la-la-la-lee / The universal / Itchycoo Park / Hey girl / Wide eyed girl / On the wall / Whatcha gonn do about it / Wham bam thank you mam. *(re-iss.Jul84) (re-iss.lp/c/cd May86 on 'Castle')*

— Disbanded Mar'69. STEVE MARRIOTT formed HUMBLE PIE. The remaining formed . . .

The FACES

alongside **ROD STEWART** – vocals (also Solo artist, ex-JEFF BECK) / **RON WOOD** – guitar (ex-JEFF BECK GROUP, ex-CREATION)
(note: in the US, debut lp still credited to The SMALL FACES)

		Warners	Warners
Feb 70.	(7") **FLYING. / THREE BUTTON HAND ME DOWN**		-
Mar 70.	(lp)(c) **FIRST STEP**	45	

– Wicked messenger / Devotion / Shake, shudder, shiver / Stone / Around the plynth / Flying / Pineapple and the monkey / Nobody knows / Looking out the window / Three button hand me down. *(re-iss.Jul87 & Sep91 on 'Edsel') (cd-iss.Sep93)*

Mar 71.	(7") **HAD ME A REAL GOOD TIME. / REAR WHEEL SKID**		-
Mar 71.	(lp)(c) **LONG PLAYER**	31	29

– Bad 'n' ruin / Tell everyone / Sweet lady Mary / Richmond / Maybe I'm amazed / Had a real good time / On the beach / I feel so good / Jerusalem. *(cd-iss.Sep93)*

Apr 71.	(7") **MAYBE I'M AMAZED. / OH LORD I'M BROWNED OFF**	-	
Nov 71.	(7") **STAY WITH ME. / DEBRIS**	6	-
Nov 71.	(lp)(c) **A NOD'S AS GOD AS A WINK (TO A BLIND HORSE)**	2	6

– Miss Judy's farm / You're so rude / Love lives here / Last orders please / Stay with me / Debris / Memphis / Too bad / That's all I need. *(cd-iss.Sep93)*

Nov 71.	(7") **STAY WITH ME. / YOU'RE SO RUDE**	-	
Feb 73.	(7") **CINDY INCIDENTALLY. / SKEWIFF**	2	48
Apr 73.	(lp)(c) **OOH LA LA**	1	21

– Silicone grown / Cindy incidentally / Flags and banners / My fault / Borstal boys / Fly in the ointment / If I'm on the late side / Glad and sorry / Just another monkey / Ooh la la. *(cd-iss.Sep93)*

May 73.	(7") **OOH LA LA. / BORSTAL BOYS**	-	

— **TETSU YAMAUCHI** – bass (ex-FREE) repl. RONNIE LANE who went solo.

Nov 73.	(7") **POOL HALL RICHARD. / I WISH IT WOULD RAIN**	8	

ROD STEWART & THE FACES

due to ROD's solo successes.

Jan 74.	(lp)(c) **COAST TO COAST – OVERTURE FOR BEGINNERS (live)**	3	63

– It's all over now / Cut across Shorty / Too bad / Every picture tells a story / Angel / Stay with me / I wish it would rain / I'd rather go blind / Borstal boys / Amazing Grace / Jealous guy. *(cd-iss.Nov87)*

— (above featured ROD's song from solo career and was on 'Mercury')

Nov 74. (7") **YOU CAN MAKE ME DANCE SING OR ANYTHING. / AS LONG AS YOU TELL HIM** 12

— Late '75, crumbled again, as ROD STEWART enjoyed overwhelming solo stardom. RON WOOD went off to join The ROLLING STONES.

- (FACES) compilations, others, etc. -

Oct 75. Warners; (d-lp) **TWO ORIGINALS OF THE FACES** -
– (FIRST STEP / LONG PLAYER)

Apr 77. Riva; (lp)(c) **SNAKES AND LADDERS – THE BEST OF THE FACES** 24
– Pool hall Richard / Cindy incidentally / Ooh la la / Sweet Lady Mary / Flying / Pineapple and the monkey / You can make me dance, sing or anything / Had me a real good time / Stay with me / Miss Judy's farm / Silicone grown / That's all you need.

May 77. Riva; (7"ep) **THE FACES** 41
– Cindy incidentally / Stay with me / Memphis / You can make me dance, sing or anything.

Sep 80. Pickwick; (lp)(c) **THE FACES FEATURING ROD STEWART** -

Nov 92. Mercury; (cd)(c) **THE BEST OF ROD STEWART & THE FACES** 58 -

May 93. Spectrum; (cd)(c) **AMAZING GRACE (ROD STEWART & THE FACES)** -

SMALL FACES

were re-formed by **JONES, McLAGAN** + reinstated **MARRIOTT** incomer **RICKY WILLS** – bass (ex-Peter FRAMPTON'S CAMEL, ex-ROXY MUSIC, etc)

Atlantic Atlantic

Jul 77. (7") **LOOKIN' FOR A LOVE. / KO'D (BY LUV)**

Aug 77. (lp)(c) **PLAYMATES**
– High and happy / Never too late / Tonight / Say larvee / Find it / Lookin' for a love / Playmates / Drive in romance / This song's just for you / Smilin' in tune. *(cd-iss.Jun92 on 'Repertoire')*

— added on tour **JIMMY McCULLOCH** – guitar (of WINGS)

Jun 78. (7") **FILTHY RICH. / OVER TOO SOON**

Sep 78. (lp)(c) **78 IN THE SHADE**
– Over too soon / Too many crossroads / Let me down gently / Thinkin' about love / Stand by me (stand by you) / Brown man do / Soldier / Reel sour / You ain''t seen nothin' yet / Filthy rich. *(cd-iss.Nov93 on 'Repertoire')*

Nov 78. (7") **STAND BY ME (STAND BY YOU). / HUNGRY AND LOOKING**

— Disbanded again mid'78. KENNY JONES joined The WHO. MARRIOTT re-formed HUMBLE PIE. He was to tragically die in his Essex home after it went on fire 20 Apr'91.

- compilations, others, etc. -

1972. Pride; (7") **RUNAWAY./ SHAKE** -

Jul 72. Pride; (lp) **EARLY YEARS** -

1972. Pride; (lp) **THE HISTORY OF THE SMALL FACES** -

Jun 77. Decca; (lp) **ROCK ROOTS: THE SMALL FACES** -
('A'&'B'sides)

Sep 77. Decca; (7"m) **SHA-LA-LA-LA-LEE. / WHAT'CHA GONNA DO ABOUT IT / ALL OR NOTHING** -
(re-iss.Mar82)

Sep 79. Decca; (7"ep) **THE LONDON BOYS EP** -
– (shared EP w / DAVID BOWIE / DOBIE GRAY / +1)

Mar 81. Decca; (lp) **SHA-LA-LA-LA-LEE** -

Sep 81. Decca; (7") **SHA-LA-LA-LA-LEE. / ALL OR NOTHING** -
(re-iss.Oct83 on 'Old Gold')

Nov 75. Immediate; (7") **ITCHYCOO PARK. / MY MIND'S EYE** 9

1975. Immediate; (7") **LAZY SUNDAY./ THE AUTUMN STONE**
(re-iss.Sep81)

Mar 76. Immediate; (7") **LAZY SUNDAY. / (TELL ME) HAVE YOU EVER SEEN ME** 36

Jan 78. Immediate; (lp)(c) **GREATEST HITS** -

May 75. Sire; (d-lp) **VINTAGE YEARS -THE IMMEDIATE STORY VOL.2** -

1978. Charly; (lp) **LIVE UK 1969 (live)** -

May 80. New World; (lp) **THE SMALL FACES** (shared w / AMEN CORNER) -

Jul 80. Virgin; (lp)(c) **BIG HITS** -

Jul 80. Virgin; (7"m) **TIN SOLDIERS./ TIN SOLDIERS (live) / RENE (live)** -

Oct 80. Virgin; (lp) **FOR YOUR DELIGHT THE DARLINGS OF WAPPING WHARF LAUNDERETTE** -

Below released on 'Old Gold' unless otherwise stated.

Oct 83. (7") **ALL OR NOTHING. / MY MIND'S EYE** -

Jan 85. (7") **LAZY SUNDAY. / TIN SOLDIER** -

Jan 85. (7") **ITCHYCOO PARK. / HERE COMES THE NICE** -

Feb 89. (cd-ep) **ITCHYCOO PARK / LAZY SUNDAY / TIN SOLDIER** -

Nov 84. Astan; (lp) **GOLDEN HITS** -

Nov 85. Castle; (d-lp,c,cd) **SMALL FACES COLLECTION** -

May 88. Castle; (3"cd-ep); (Special Edition) **ITCHYCOO PARK / LAZY SUNDAY / ALL OR NOTHING (live)/ AUTUMN STONE** -

Apr 89. Castle; (lp)(c)(cd) **GREATEST HITS** -

May 90. Castle; (cd)(c)(lp) **THE ULTIMATE COLLECTION** -

Jun 86. Archive 4; (12"ep) **CLASSIC CUTS** -
– Itchycoo park / Lazy Sunday / Here comes the nice / Sha la la la lee.

Sep 86. Showcase; (lp)(c) **QUITE NATURALLY** -
(cd-iss.Dec87)

Jul 88. Knight; (c) **NIGHTRIDING** -

Jun 90. See For Miles; (cd)(c)(lp) **THE SINGLES A's & B's** -

May 93. Spectrum; (cd)(c) **IT'S ALL OR NOTHING** -

Sep 93. Laserlight; (cd)(c) **ITCHYCOO PARK** -

Mar 94. Laserlight; (cd)(c) **HERE COMES THE NICE** -

Apr 94. Disky; (cd-ep) **ITCHYCOO PARK / TIN SOLDIER / LAZY SUNDAY** -

Jul 95. Summit; (cd) **THE BEST OF THE SMALL FACES** -

Jul 95. Repertoire; (cd) **BOXED** -

Nov 95. Charly; (4xcd-box) **THE IMMEDIATE YEARS** -

. . .Jan-Jun'96 stop press compilation . . .

May 96. Deram; (d-cd)(d-c)(d-lp) **THE DECCA ANTHOLOGY 1965-1967** 66 -

S*M*A*S*H

Formed: Welwyn Garden City, Hertfordshire, England . . . early 90's as SMASH AT THE BLUES. In 1993, after controversial singles released on own label were lambasted by Tory councils, they signed to 'Hi-Rise', where their debut mini-album 'S*M*A*S*H SPRING 1994' hit UK Top 30. • **Style:** New wave of the new wave, anti-government punks inspired by The SEX PISTOLS, ANGELIC UPSTARTS and being on the dole. • **Songwriters:** ED and group. • **Trivia:** Played London's 100 Club late in 1993 alongside other NWOTNW hopefuls THESE ANIMAL MEN.

Recommended: SELF ABUSED (*6)

ED BORRIE – vocals, guitar / **SALVADOR ALESSI** – bass / **ROB HAIGH** – drums (ex-NIGHTMARE, ex-ASTRONAUTS)

Les Disques not issued

Jul 93. (7") **REAL SURREAL. / DRUGS AGAIN / REVISITED NO.3** -

Dec 93. (c-ep) **WHEELERS, DEALERS & CHRISTINE KEELERS** -
– Self-abused / Kill somebody / Altruism / Bang bang bang / (5 other tracks by THESE ANIMAL MEN)

Feb 94. (7")(7"pink)(7"red-one-sided) **LADY LOVE YOUR C***. / SHAME** -

Hi-Rise not issued

Mar 94. (m-cd)(m-c)(m-lp) **S*M*A*S*H SPRING 1994** 28 -
– Real surreal / Drugs again / Revisited No.3 / Lady love your c*** / Shame.

Jul 94. (12"ep)(c-ep)(cd-ep) **(I WANT TO) KILL SOMEBODY (Topper mix). / ('A'-Keith LeBlanc mix) / ('A'Gunshot headhunter mix) / ('A'-Bragg reshuffle mix)** 26

Sep 94. (cd)(c)(lp) **SELF ABUSED** 59
– Revisited No.5 / Barrabas / Oh ovary / Altruism / Reflections of you (remember me) / Self abused / Scream silent / Another love / Another shark in the deep end of my swimming pool / Real surreal / Dear Lou / Bang bang bang (granta 25) / Time / A.L.L.Y.C.

Nov 94. (7") **BARRABAS (PILOTED). / TURN ON THE WATER**

— (above single on 'Sub Pop')

Feb 95. (m-cd)(m-c)(m-lp) **ANOTHER LOVE** -
– Another love (Bobbit mix) / Petal buzz / You've got a friend who's a friend of mine / Reflections of you (live) / Time (live) / Self abused (live) / Another love (uncut).

. . . Jan – Jun '96 stop press . . .

Jan 96. (single) **REST OF MY LIFE** -

May 96. (single) **THE REST OF MY LIFE** -

— have now called it a day

SMASHING PUMPKINS

Formed: Chicago, Illinois, USA . . . 1986 by BILLY CORGAN (son of a jazz guitarist), JAMES IHA, female D'ARCY WRETZKY and JIMMY CHAMBERLAIN. After one 45 for local label, they moved on to 'Sub Pop' in 1990. Three years later now signed to Virgin subsidiary 'Hut', they made

Top 10 on both sides of the Atlantic with classic ground-breaking album 'SIAMESE DREAM'. • **Style:** Influenced by an acoustic LED ZEPPELIN fused with slices of 70's PINK FLOYD. CORGAN's croaky but effective vox was at its best on his pastel NIRVANA-like grunge classics (i.e. 'TODAY', 'DISARM', 'BULLET WITH BUTTERFLY WINGS', '1979' & 'TONIGHT, TONIGHT. • **Songwriters:** CORGAN, except several with IHA. Covered; A GIRL NAMED SANDOZ (Eric Burdon & The Animals) / LANDSLIDE (Fleetwood Mac) / DANCING IN THE MOONLIGHT (Thin Lizzy) / NEVER LET ME DOWN (Depeche Mode). • **Trivia:** Initially co-produced by BUTCH VIG (he of NIRVANA fame) and CORGAN. Album named after actress LILIAN GISH.

Recommended: GISH (*7) / SIAMESE DREAM (*9) / MELLON COLLIE AND THE INFINITE SADNESS (*10)

BILLY CORGAN (b.17 Mar'67) – vocals, guitar / **JAMES IHA** – guitar / **D'ARCY** – bass, vocals / **JIMMY CHAMBERLIN** – drums

		not issued	Potential
1989.	(7") **I AM ONE. / NOT WORTH ASKING**	-	
		Glitterhouse	**Sub Pop**
Dec 90.	(7")(7"pink) **TRISTESSA. / HONEY SPIDER** (12"+=) La Dolly Vita *(re-iss.12"-cd-s May93)*		
		Hut-Virgin	**Caroline**
Aug 91.	(12") **SIVA. / WINDOW PAINE**		
Feb 92.	(12"ep)(cd-ep) **LULL** – Rhinoceros / Blue / Slunk / Bye June (demo).		
Feb 92.	(cd)(c)(lp) **GISH** – I am one / Siva / Rhinoceros / Bury me / Crush / Suffer / Snail / Tristessa / Window paine / Daydream. *(re-iss.May94)*		Sep 91
Aug 92.	(12"ep)(cd-ep) **I AM ONE. / PLUME / STARLA** (10") – ('A'side) / Terrapin / Bullet train to Osaka.	73	
Jun 92.	(12"ep)(c-ep)(cd-ep) **THE PEEL SESSIONS** – Siva / Smiley / A girl named Sandoz.		-
		Hut-Virgin	**Virgin**
Jun 93.	(7"clear) **CHERUB ROCK. / PURR SNICKETY** (12"+=)(cd-s+=) Pissant/ French movie theme.	31	
Jul 93.	(cd)(c)(lp) **SIAMESE DREAM** – Cherub rock / Quiet / Today / Hummer / Rocket / Disarm / Soma / Geek U.S.A. / Mayonaise / Spaceboy / Silverfuck / Sweet sweet / Luna.	4	10
Sep 93.	(7")(c-s) **TODAY. / HELLO KITTY KAT** (12"+=)(cd-s+=) – Obscured	44	
Feb 94.	(7"purple) **DISARM. / SIAMESE DREAM** (12")(cd-s) – ('A'side) / Soothe (demo) / Blew away. (12") – ('A'side) / Dancing in the moonlight / Landslide.	11	
Oct 94.	(cd)(c)(lp) **PISCES ISCARIOT** (compilation of B-sides)		4
Dec 94.	(7") **ROCKET. / NEVER LET ME DOWN** – (4x7"box-set) **SIAMESE SINGLES** – (last 3 singles 1993-94 + above)		
Oct 95.	(c-s)(cd-s) **BULLET WITH BUTTERFLY WINGS / ...SAID SADLY**	20	25
Oct 95.	(d-cd)(d-c) **MELLON COLLIE AND THE INFINITE SADNESS** – DAWN TO DUSK:- Mellon Collie and the infinite sadness / Tonight, tonight / Jellybelly / Zero / Here is no why / Bullet with butterfly wings / To forgive / An ode to no one / Love / Cupid de Locke / Galapogos / Muzzle / Porcelina of the vast oceans / Take me down. // TWILIGHT TO STARLIGHT:- Where boys fear to tread / Bodies / Thirty-three / In the arms of sleep / 1979 / Tales of a scorched Earth / Thru the eyes of Ruby / Stumbleine / X.Y.U. / We only come out at night / Beautiful / Lily (my one and only) / By starlight / Farewell and goodnight.	4	1

... Jan – Jun '96 stop press ...

Jan 96.	(single) **1979**	16	12
Apr 96.	(re-issue; t-lp) **MELLON COLLIE ...** *(2 extra +=)*– Tonight reprise / Infinite sadness.		
May 96.	(m-cd)(m-c)(m-lp) **ZERO EP**	-	46
May 96.	(single) **TONIGHT, TONIGHT**	7	51 Jun 96

Patti SMITH

Born: 30 Dec'46, Chicago, Illinois, USA. She started to write for New York magazine 'Rock' in 1969, having earlier being shipped around by her family between Paris and London. In the early 70's, she began writing poetry full-time and met LENNY KAYE, who became her accompaniment at readings/gigs. In 1971, she scribed for 'Creem' mag, and soon developed professional musical partnership with playwright Sam Shepherd. By Christmas '72, she had 2 books of poetry 'Witt' & '7th Heaven', in the stores, and TODD RUNDGREN gave her credit on his 'A WIZARD A TRUE STAR' album, for nicknaming him 'Runt'. In 1974, she issued debut single 'HEY JOE' / 'PISS FACTORY' on a local label 'MER', which gained airplay when picked up by 'Sire' records. Early in 1975, she landed a contract with 'Arista', and by end of that year 'HORSES' was in the US Top 50. In 1978, she co-wrote 'BECAUSE THE NIGHT' with BRUCE SPRINGSTEEN, and this gave her a Top 10 hit, helping establish her return to the album charts. • **Style:** New wave/rock'n'roll poetess, influenced by JIM MORRISON and LOU REED. Her self-indulgence was forgotten in the late 70's, after 2 fine comeback albums. • **Songwriters:** Lyrics PATTI, some music KAYE. Covered HEY JOE (Jimi Hendrix) / LAND OF 1000 DANCES (Cannibal & The Headhunters) / MY GENERATION (The Who) / GLORIA (Them) / SO YOU WANNA BE A ROCK'N'ROLL STAR (Byrds) / 5-4-3-2-1 (Manfred Man) / DOWNTOWN TRAIN (Tom Waits). • **Trivia:** In 1974, she co-wrote with ex-boyfriend ALLEN LANIER, his groups' (BLUE OYSTER CULT) 'Career Of Evil'. Her albums were produced by JOHN CALE (1st) / JACK DOUGLAS (2nd) / JIMMY IOVINE (3rd) / TODD RUNDGREN (4th) / FRED SMITH and JIMMY IOVINE (1988). • **Miscellaneous:** Her career nearly ended abruptly in Jan'77, when she fell off stage at a concert in Tampa Bay, breaking a vertebrae in her neck.

Recommended: HORSES (*9) / EASTER (*7) / WAVE (*7)

PATTI SMITH – vocals, poetry / with **LENNY KAYE** – guitar / **RICHARD SOHL** – piano

		not issued	M.E.R.
Aug 74.	(7") **HEY JOE. / PISS FACTORY** *(UK-iss.Mar78 on 'Sire')*	-	

— added **IVAN KRAAL** – bass, guitar, piano / **JAY DAUGHERTY** – drums

		Arista	Arista
Dec 75.	(lp,c,silver+grey-lp) **HORSES** – Gloria / Redondo Beach / Birdland / Free monkey / Kimberley / Break it up / Land / Elegie. *(re-iss.+cd.Aug88)*		47
Apr 76.	(7") **GLORIA. / MY GENERATION** *(re-iss.12"-Sep77)*		
Oct 76.	(lp)(c) **RADIO ETHIOPIA** – Ask the angels / Ain't it strange / Poppies / Pissing in the river / Pumping (my heart) / Distant fingers / Radio Ethiopia / Abyssinia. *(re-iss.+cd.Aug88)*		

— Her tour featured **LEIGH FOXX** – bass repl. SOHL. Others augmenting at the time **ANDY PALEY** (ex-ELLIOT MURPHY) **+ BRUCE BRODY** – keyboards (ex-JOHN CALE)

PATTI SMITH GROUP

with **KAYE / KRAAL / DAUGHERTY / BRODY + SOHL**

Mar 78.	(7") **BECAUSE THE NIGHT. / GOD SPEED**	5	13
Mar 78.	(lp)(c) **EASTER** – Till victory / Space monkey / Because the night / Ghost dance / Babelogue / Rock'n'roll nigger / Privilege (set me free) / We three / 25th floor / High on rebellion / Easter. *(re-iss.Jan83 on 'Fame') (cd-iss.Aug88)*	16	20
Jun 78.	(7") **PRIVILEGE (SET ME FREE). / ASK THE ANGELS** (12"+=) – 25th floor (live) / Bablelogue (live).	72	

— **FRED 'Sonic' SMITH** – drums (ex-MC5) repl. DAUGHERTY to TOM VERLAINE

May 79.	(7") **FREDERICK. / FIRE OF UNKNOWN ORIGIN**	63	-
May 79.	(lp)(c) **WAVE** – Frederick / Dancing barefoot / Citizen ship / Hymn / Revenge / So you want to be a rock'n'roll star / Seven ways of going / Broken flag / Wave. *(re-iss.+cd.Aug88)*	41	18
Jun 79.	(7") **FREDERICK. / FREDERICK (live)**	-	90
Jul 79.	(7") **DANCING BAREFOOT. / FIVE, FOUR, THREE, TWO, ONE (live)**		-
Aug 79.	(7"m) **SO YOU WANT TO BE A ROCK 'N' ROLL STAR. / 5-4-3-2-1 / FIRE OF UNKNOWN ORIGIN**	-	
Sep 79.	(7") **SO YOU WANT TO BE A ROCK'N'ROLL STAR. / FREDERICK (live)**		-

— PATTI retired Mar'80 with her new husband FRED SMITH to bring up children. BRUCE BRODY was another to join ex-TELEVISION singer TOM VERLAINE's band.

PATTI SMITH

re-appeared in 1988 with still **SOHL, DAUGHERTY & SONIC**

		Fierce	Fierce
Feb 88.	(7"m) **BRIAN JONES. / STOCKINGED FEET / JESUS CHRIST ...**		
		Arista	**Arista**
Jul 88.	(7") **PEOPLE HAVE THE POWER. / WILD LEAVES** (12"+=)/ /(cd-s+=) – Where duty calls./ / ('A'-album version).		
Jul 88.	(lp)(c)(cd) **DREAM OF LIFE** – People have the power / Going under / Up there, down there / Paths that cross / Dream of life / Where duty calls / (I was) Looking for you / The Jackson song. *(re-iss.cd.Apr92)*	70	65

— RICHARD SOHL was to die from a cardiac arrest on 3 Jun'90. PATTI returned to reciting and recording her poetry in 1995.

... Jan – Jun '96 stop press ...

— returned with her original group and TOM VERLAINE, to record and release comeback album in July. It featured guest spots from BONO and MICHAEL STIPE.

– compilations, others, etc. –

Apr 83. Arista; (7") **BECAUSE THE NIGHT. / GLORIA** [ ] [-]
(12") – ('A'side) / Redondo beach / Dancing barefoot / Free money.
Jul 84. Old Gold; (7") **BECAUSE THE NIGHT. / GLORIA** [ ] [-]
Sep 91. RCA; (3xcd-box) **BOX SET** [ ] [ ]
– (RADIO ETHIOPIA / HORSES / WAVE albums)

SMITHS

Formed: Manchester, England . . . Nov'82 by MORRISSEY and MARR. MORRISSEY had recently had book 'James Dean Isn't Dead' published by Babylon, and had been UK president of The NEW YORK DOLLS fan club. Following rave reviews on debut UK tour, they signed one-off deal with 'Rough Trade' in March 1983, after turning down local 'Factory' records. Their first single 'HAND IN GLOVE', topped the indie charts, after being played on the nightly John Peel Radio 1 show. They turned down offers from major companies, to re-sign a long-term contract with 'Rough Trade'. To end 1983, they had first of many Top 30 hits with classic 'THIS CHARMING MAN'. Early in 1984, their eponymous debut album (John Porter taking over from Troy Tate on production) nearly hit No.1, and they were soon to become household names. • **Style:** Non-comformist alternative rock band, that featured superb guitarist MARR, and the extroverted Oscar Wilde of the pop/rock world MORRISSEY. • **Songwriters:** Lyrics – MORRISSEY / music – MARR, except HIS LATEST FLAME (Elvis Presley). • **Trivia:** HOW SOON IS NOW? was sampled in 1990 by duo SOHO on their hit 45 'Hippychick'.

Recommended: THE SMITHS (*10) / MEAT IS MURDER (*10) / THE QUEEN IS DEAD (*10) / HATFUL OF HOLLOW (*9) / THE WORLD WON'T LISTEN (*9) / STRANGEWAYS HERE WE COME (*9). / BEST . . . I (*10) / BEST II (*9)

MORRISSEY (b.STEPHEN PATRICK MORRISSEY, 22 May'59) – vocals (ex-NOSEBLEEDS) / **JOHNNY MARR** (b.JOHN MAHER, 31 Oct'63) – guitar, harmonica, mandolins, piano / **ANDY ROURKE** – bass / **MIKE JOYCE** (b. 1 Jun'63) – drums

Rough Trade / Sire

May 83. (7") **HAND IN GLOVE. / HANDSOME DEVIL** [ ] [-]
Nov 83. (7") **THIS CHARMING MAN. / JEANE** [25] [ ]
(12") – ('A'side) / Accept yourself / Wonderful woman.
Jan 84. (7") **WHAT DIFFERENCE DOES IT MAKE?. / BACK TO THE OLD HOUSE** [12] [ ]
(12"+=) – These things take time.
Feb 84. (lp)(c) **THE SMITHS** [2] [ ]
– Reel around the fountain / You've got everything now / Miserable lie / Pretty girls make graves / The hand that rocks the cradle / Still ill / Hand in glove / What difference does it make? / I don't owe you anything / Suffer little children. *(cd-iss.May87) (re-cd-iss.1989) (re-iss.cd/c/ltd-10" lp Nov93 on 'WEA')*
May 84. (7") **HEAVEN KNOWS I'M MISERABLE NOW. / SUFFER LITTLE CHILDREN** [10] [ ]
(12"+=) – Girl afraid.
Aug 84. (7") **WILLIAM, IT WAS REALLY NOTHING. / PLEASE PLEASE PLEASE LET ME GET WHAT I WANT** [17] [ ]
(12"+=) – How soon is now?.
Nov 84. (lp)(c) **HATFUL OF HOLLOW** (with BBC sessions *) [7] [ ]
– William, it was really nothing / What difference does it make? * / These things take time * / This charming man * / How soon is now? / Handsome devil * / Hand in glove / Still ill * / Heaven knows I'm miserable now / This night has opened my eyes * / You've got everything now * / Accept yourself * / Girl afraid / Back to the old house * / Reel around the fountain * / Please please please let me get what I want. *(cd-iss.May87) (re-iss.cd/c/ltd-d10" lp Nov93 on 'WEA')*
Jan 85. (7") **HOW SOON IS NOW?. / WELL I WONDER** [24] [-]
(12"+=) – Oscillate wildly.
Feb 85. (7") **HOW SOON IS NOW?. / THE HEADMASTER RITUAL** [-] [ ]
Feb 85. (lp)(c) **MEAT IS MURDER** [1] [ ]
– The headmaster ritual / Barbarism begins at home / Rusholme ruffians / I want the one I can't have / What she said / Nowhere fast / That joke isn't funny anymore / Nowhere fast / Well I wonder / Meat is murder. *(cd-iss.May87) (re-iss.cd/c/ltd-d10" lp Nov93 on 'WEA')*
Mar 85. (7") **SHAKESPEARE'S SISTER. / WHAT SHE SAID** [26] [ ]
(12"+=) – Stretch out and wait.
Jul 85. (7") **THAT JOKE ISN'T FUNNY ANYMORE. / MEAT IS MURDER (live)** [49] [ ]
(12"+=) – Nowhere fast / Shakespeare's siste / Stretch out and wait (all live).
Sep 85. (7") **THE BOY WITH THE THORN IN HIS SIDE. / ASLEEP** [23] [ ]
(12"+=) – Rubber ring.

— added **CRAIG GANNON** – guitar, bass (ex-AZTEC CAMERA, ex-BLUEBELLS)

May 86. (7") **BIGMOUTH STRIKES AGAIN. / MONEY CHANGES EVERYTHING** [26] [ ]
(12"+=) – Unloveable.
Jun 86. (lp)(c) **THE QUEEN IS DEAD** [2] [70]
– Frankly Mr. Shankly / I know it's over / Never had no one ever / Cemetery gates / Big mouth strikes again / Vicar in a tutu / There is a light that never goes out / Some girls are bigger than others / The queen is dead / The boy with the thorn in his side. *(cd-iss.May87) (re-iss.cd/c/ltd-d10" lp Nov93 on 'WEA')*
Jul 86. (7") **PANIC. / VICAR IN A TUTU** [11] [ ]
(12"+=) – The draize train.
Oct 86. (7") **ASK. / CEMETRY GATES** [14] [ ]
(12"+=)(c-s+=) – Golden lights. *(re-iss.Feb95 on 'Warners', hit No.62)*

— Reverted to a quartet, when GANNON left to join The CRADLE.

Feb 87. (7") **SHOPLIFTERS OF THE WORLD UNITE. / HALF A PERSON** [12] [ ]
(12"+=) – London.

— ('A'side on some 'YOU JUST HAVEN'T EARNED IT YET BABY')

Feb 87. (lp)(c)(cd) **THE WORLD WON'T LISTEN** (part compilation) [7] [ ]
– Panic / Ask / London / Big mouth strikes again / Shakespeare's sister / There is a light that never goes out / Shoplifters of the world unite / The boy with the thorn in his side / Asleep / Unloveable / Half a person / Stretch out and wait / That joke isn't funny anymore / Oscillate wildly / You just haven't earned it yet baby / Rubber ring. (c+=) – Money changes everything. *(re-iss.cd/c/ltd-d10" lp Nov93 on 'WEA')*
Apr 87. (7") **SHEILA TAKE A BOW. / IS IT REALLY SO STRANGE?** [10] [ ]
(12"+=) – Sweet and tender hooligan.
Aug 87. (7") **GIRLFRIEND IN A COMA. / WORK IS A FOUR-LETTER WORD** [13] [ ]
(12"+=)(c-s+=) – I keep mine hidden.
Sep 87. (lp)(c)(cd) **STRANGEWAYS HERE WE COME** [2] [55]
– A rush and a push and the land is ours / I started something I couldn't finish / Death of a disco dancer / Girlfriend in a coma / Stop me if you think you've heard this one before / Last night I dreamt that somebody loved me / Unhappy birthday / Paint a vulgar picture / Death at one's elbow / I won't share you. *(re-iss.cd/c/ltd-d10" lp Nov93 on 'WEA')*
Oct 87. (7") **STOP ME IF YOU THINK YOU'VE HEARD THIS ONE BEFORE. / I KEEP MINE HIDDEN** [-] [ ]
Nov 87. (7") **I STARTED SOMETHING I COULDN'T FINISH. / PRETTY GIRLS MAKE GRAVES** [23] [ ]
(12"+=) – Some girls are bigger than others (live).
(c-s++=) – What's the world (live).
Dec 87. (7") **LAST NIGHT I DREAMT THAT SOMEBODY LOVED ME. / NOWHERE FAST (BBC version)** [30] [ ]
(12"+=) – Rusholme Russians (BBC version).
(cd-s++=) – William, it was really nothing (BBC version).

— In August '87, although signed to 'EMI', they had already broken-up. Cited for reasons, were MARR's increasing session work for PRETENDERS, BRYAN FERRY, etc. ROURKE and JOYCE splintered with ADULT NET before joining MORRISSEY when he went solo.

– other compilations, etc. –

Note; on 'Rough Trade' UK / 'Sire' US, unless otherwise mentioned.

Jun 87. (d-lp)(d-c) **LOUDER THAN BOMBS** [38] [62] Apr 86
– Is it really so strange? / Sheila take a bow / Sweet and tender hooligan / Shoplifters of the world unite / Half a person / London / Panic / Girl afraid / Shakespeare's sister / William, it was really nothing / You just haven't earned it yet, baby / Golden lights / Ask / Heaven knows I'm miserable now / Unloveable / Asleep / Oscillate wildly / These things take time / Rubber ring / Back to the old house / Hand in glove / Stretch out and wait / This night has opened my eyes / Please, please, please, let me get what I want. *(re-iss.+cd.Nov88)*
Aug 88. (lp)(c)(cd)(dat) **RANK (live Oct'86)** [2] [77]
– The queen is dead / Panic / Vicar in a tutu / Ask / Rusholme ruffians / The boy with the thorn in his side / What she said / Is it really so strange? / Cemetry gates / London / I know it's over / The draize train / Still ill / Bigmouth strikes again / (Marie's the name) His latest flame – Take me back to dear old blighty. *(re-iss.cd/c/ltd-d10" lp Nov93 on 'WEA')*
Nov 88. (3"cd-ep) **THE HEADMASTER RITUAL / NOWHERE FAST (live) / MEAT IS MURDER (live) / STRETCH OUT AND WAIT (live)** [ ] [-]
Nov 88. (3"cd-ep) **BARBARISM BEGINS AT HOME / SHAKESPEARE'S SISTER / STRETCH OUT AND WAIT** [ ] [-]

— (Note:- 12"singles from Jan84 / May84 / Sep85 / Jul86 / Oct86 were issued on 3"cd-ep Nov88).

Oct 88. Strange Fruit; (12"ep)(cd-ep) **THE PEEL SESSIONS** (18.5.83) [ ] [-]
– What difference does it make? / Reel around the fountain / Miserable lie / Handsome devil.

Note; Below on 'WEA' UK/ 'Sire' US unless otherwise mentioned.

Jul 92. (7")(c-s) **THIS CHARMING MAN. / WONDERFUL WOMAN / ACCEPT YOURSELF** [8] [ ]

(cd-s+=) – Jeane.

Aug 92. (cd)(c)(lp) **BEST . . . 1** | 1 | |

– This charming man / William, it was really nothing / What difference does it make / Stop me if you think you've heard it before / Girlfriend in a coma / Half a person / Rubber ring / How soon is now? / Hand in glove / Shoplifters of the world unite / Sheila take a bow / Some girls are bigger than others / Panic / Please please please let me get what I want.

Sep 92. (7")(c-s) **HOW SOON IS NOW. / HAND IN GLOVE** | 16 | |

(cd-s+=) – The queen is dead / Handsome devil / I started something I couldn't finish.

(cd-s+=) – I know it's over / Suffer little children / Back to the old house.

Oct 92. (7")(c-s) **THERE IS A LIGHT THAT NEVER GOES OUT. / HANDSOME DEVIL (live)** | 25 | |

(cd-s+=) – I don't owe you anything / Hand in glove / Jeane.

(cd-s+=) – Money changes everything (live) / Some girls are bigger than others (live) / Hand in glove (live).

Nov 92. (cd)(c)(lp) **BEST II** | 29 | |

– The boy with a thorn in his side / The headmaster ritual / Heaven knows I'm miserable now / Ask / Osciliate wildly / Nowhere fast / Still ill / That joke isn't funny anymore / Shakespeare's sister / Girl afraid / Reel around the fountain / Last night I dreamt somebody loved me / There is a light that never goes out.

Mar 95. (cd)(c) **"SINGLES"** | 5 | |

– Hand in glove / This charming man / What difference does it make? / Heaven knows I'm miserable now / William, it was really nothing / How soon is now? / Shakespeare's sister / That joke isn't funny anymore / The boy with the thorn in his side / Bigmouth strikes again / Panic / Ask / Shoplifters of the world unite / Sheila take a bow / Girlfriend in a coma / I started something I couldn't finish / Last night I dreamt that somebody loved me / There is a light that never goes out.

SNOOP DOGGY DOGG

Born: CALVIN BROADUS, 1971, Long Beach, California, USA. Unleashed in 1993, when his debut DR.DRE (ex-N.W.A.) produced album 'DOGGYSTYLE' created furore amongst the moral majority in America. Once again this was hype that any up and coming controversial star needs and the album shot straight to No.1 with record sales for a debut. However before the time of its release (August '93) and after guesting on DR.DRE's 'Nuthin' But A G Thang', convicted teenage drug-dealer SNOOP was arrested, when a local hood was killed after shots were allegedly fired by his bodyguard MALIK out of SNOOP's car. SNOOP was released after being bailed for a $1m. Early in 1994, he hit London under a storm of protest, not least from tabloid press, including The Daily Star who headlined on the front page; 'KICK THIS EVIL BASTARD OUT!'. This only spurred the Brits to buy the album, especially after he was premiered on C4's 'The Word', complete with interview. • **Style:** Crude hard-core gangsta rapper, who portrays himself like a Doberman on heat. Music that broke the bounds of censorship and which was definitely not for the easily offended. • **Songwriters:** Himself and various samples. • **Trivia:** He was given his nickname by his mother!. Featured, as did DR.DRE and The DOGG POUND posse on film soundtrack 'Above The Rim'. Another mate of SNOOP's; WARREN G was also a massive hit in the summer of '94 with single 'REGULATE' from the album 'REGULATE . . . G FUNK ERA'.

Recommended: DOGGYSTYLE (*7)

with The DOGG POUND & The DRAMATICS plus **WARREN G / KURUPT / NANCY FLETCHER / DAT NIGGA DAZ / D.O.C. RBX / THE LADY OF RAGE / LIL HERSHEY LOC (MALIK) / NATE DOGG**

	Death Row-East West	Death Row-Interscope
Dec 93. (7")(c-s) **WHAT'S MY NAME. / ('A'club mix)**	20	8 Nov93

(12"+=)(cd-s+=) – ('A'explicit mix) / ('A'instrumental) / Who am I (what's my name?).

Dec 93. (cd)(c) **DOGGYSTYLE** | 38 | 1 Nov93

– Bathtub / G funk intro / Gin and juice / Tha shiznit / Lodi dodi / Murder was the case / Seria killa / Who am I (what's my name)? / For all my niggaz & bitches / Aint no fun (if the homies cant have none) / Doggy Dogg world / GZ and hustlas / Pump pump.

Feb 94. (c-s) **GIN AND JUICE. / ('A'-laid back mix)** | 39 | 8

(12"+=)(cd-s+=) – (2-'A'mixes).

Aug 94. (7")(c-s) **DOGGY DOGG WORLD. / ('A'-Perfecto mix)** | 32 | |

(12"+=)(cd-s+=) – ('A'-Dr.Dre mix) / ('A'-Perfecto x-rated mix).

— He is still to stand trial for murder 13 Jan'95. At the end of '94, he and 3 band members (RICHARD BROWN, DARRYL DANIEL + DELMAR ARNAUDE) were arrested and charged with possession of drugs. In Oct'95, SNOOP'S trial finally got underway, due to his attorney Johnnie Cochran being slightly busy with the O.J. Simpson case!.

— THA DOGG POUND album hit US No.1 in November '95.

. . . Jan – Jun '96 stop press . . .

— leader of tha dogg pound was cleared of murder and attempted manslaughter early '96. While on bail, he guested on 2 PAC's 'On Eyez on Me' album.

SOFT BOYS

Formed: Cambridge, England . . . 1976 by ROBYN HITCHCOCK, a one-time busker who had surfaced as The WORST FEARS, The BEETLES and MAUREEN & THE MEATPACKERS, etc. In 1977, one-time DENNIS AND THE EXPERTS members became The SOFT BOTS who issued debut release 'GIVE IT TO THE SOFT BOYS EP' on indie label 'Raw'. The following years saw them only actify cult interest. • **Style:** New wave rock, influenced by West Coast psychedelia, SYD BARRETT with tongue-in-cheek humour. • **Songwriters:** HITCHCOCK penned, some with REW.

Recommended: WADING THROUGH A VENTILATOR (*7) / ROBYN HITCHCOCK & THE EGYPTIANS :- INVISIBLE HITS (*7).

ROBYN HITCHCOCK (b. 3 Mar '52, East Grinstead, England) – vocals, guitar, bass / **ALAN DAVIS** – guitar / **ANDY METCALFE** – bass / **MORRIS WINDSOR** (aka OTIS FAGG) – drums

	Raw	not issued
Nov 77. (7"ep) **GIVE IT TO THE SOFT BOYS**		-

– Wading through a ventilator / The face of death / Hear my brane. *(re-iss.Oct79)*

— **KIMBERLEY REW** – guitar, harmonica, vocals repl. DAVIS

	Radar	not issued
May 78. (7") **(I WANT TO BE AN) ANGLEPOISE LAMP. / FAT MAN'S SON**		-

— In Oct79, 'Raw' quickly withdrew release of 45 'WHERE ARE THE PRAWNS'.

	Aura	not issued
Feb 80. (lp) **A CAN OF BEES**		-

– Give it to the soft boys / The pigworker / Human music / Leppo and the jooves / The rat's prayer / Do the chisel / Sandra's having her brain out / The return of the sacred crab / Cold turkey / Skool dinner blues / Wading through a ventilator. *(re-iss.Jun84 on 'Two Crabs') (cd-iss.Feb95 on 'Rhino' +=)* – Leppo and the jooves / Sandra's having her brain out / Skool dinner blues / Fatman's son / (I want to be an) Anglepoise lamp / Ugly Nora.

—— **MATTHEW SELIGMAN** – bass, keyboards (ex-SW9) repl. ANDY to FISH TURNED HUMAN

Armageddon Armageddon

Jun 80. (7"ep) **NEAR THE SOFT BOYS** [ ] [-]
– Kingdom of love / Vegetable man / Strange. *(re-iss.Jul82)*

Jul 80. (lp) **UNDERWATER MOONLIGHT** [ ] [-]
– I wanna destroy you / Kingdom of love / Positive vibrations / I got the job / Insanely jealous / Tonight / You'll have to go sideways / Old pervert / The queen of eyes / Underwater moonlight. *(cd-iss.Feb95 on 'Rhino' +=)* – Vegetable man / Strange / Only the stones remain / Where are the prawns / Dreams / Black snake diamond role / There's nobody like you / Song No.4.

Aug 80. (7") **I WANNA DESTROY YOU. / (I'M AN) OLD PERVERT (DISCO)** [ ] [-]
(re-iss.Jul81)

Oct 81. (7") **ONLY THE STONES REMAIN. / THE ASKING TREE** [ ] [ ]

Mar 82. (lp) **TWO HALVES FOR THE PRICE OF ONE** [ ] [ ]
– Only the stones remain / Where are the prawns / The bells of Rhymney / There's nobody like you / Innocent box / Black snake diamond role / Underwater moonlight / Astronomy domine / Outlaw blues / Mystery train. (Half of above lp / half-live) (US-title; ONLY THE STONES REMAIN; rel; Oct 81)

—— Disbanded in 1982, SELIGMAN who formed The THOMPSON TWINS

ROBYN HITCHCOCK

had already gone solo, using session people, including most ex-SOFT BOYS.

Armageddon not issued

Apr 81. (7") **THE MAN WHO INVENTED HIMSELF. / DANCING ON GOD'S THUMB** [ ] [-]
(free 7"flexi w.a.) **IT'S A MYSTIC TRIP. / GROOVING ON AN INNER PLANE**

May 81. (lp) **BLACK SNAKE DIAMOND ROLE** [ ] [-]
– The man who invented himself / Brenda's iron sledge / Do policemen sing? / The lizard / Meat / Acid bird / I watch the cars / Out of the picture / City of shame / Love. *(re-iss.May86 on 'Aftermath', cd-iss.1988) (cd-iss.Feb95 on 'Sequel' +=)* – Dancing on God's thumb / Happy the golden prince / I watch the cars / It was the night / Grooving on an inner plane.

—— now w / **SARA LEE** – bass / **ANTHONY THISTLETWAITE** – sax / **ROD JOHNSON** – drums repl. SELIGMAN to THOMAS DOLBY (REW who formed KATRINA & THE WAVES

Albion not issued

Mar 82. (7") **AMERICA. / IT WAS THE NIGHT / HOW DO YOU WORK THIS THING** [ ] [-]

Mar 82. (lp) **GROOVY DECAY** [ ] [-]
– Night ride to Trinidad / Fifty-two stations / Young people scream / The rain / America / The cars she used to drive / Grooving on an inner plane / St.Petersburg / When I was a kid / Midnight fish. *(re-iss.Dec85 on 'Midnight Music') (cd-iss.Nov89 on 'Line') (cd-iss.Feb95 as 'GRAVY DECO (THE COMPLETE GROOVY DECAY / DECOY SESSIONS)' on 'Sequel' + with extra mixes)*

May 83. (12") **NIGHT RIDE TO TRINIDAD. / KINGDOM OF LOVE / MIDNIGHT FISH** [ ] [-]

Midnight not issued

Nov 82. (7") **EATEN BY HER OWN DINNER. / DR. STICKY / LISTENING TO THE HIGSONS** [ ] [-]

Apr 83. (7") **HE'S A REPTILE. (by "SOFT BOYS") / SONG No.4** [ ] [-]

ROBYN HITCHCOCK

now w / **WINDSOR / METCALFE / + ROGER JACKSON** – keyboards

Midnight Slash

Aug 84. (lp) **I OFTEN DREAM OF TRAINS** [ ] [-]
– Nocturne / Uncorrected personality traits / Sounds great when you're dead / Flavour of night / This could be the day / Trams of old London / Furry green atom bowl / Heart full of leaves / Autumn is your last chance / I often dream of trains. *(cd-iss.Oct86) (cd-iss.Feb95 on 'Sequel')* (cd+=) – Ye sleeping knights of Jesus / Sometimes I wish I was a pretty girl / Cathedral / Mellow together / Winter love / The bones in the ground / My favourite buildings / I used to say I love you.

Nov 84. (12"m) **THE BELLS OF RHYMNEY / FALLING LEAVES. / WINTER LOVE / THE BONES IN THE GROUND** [ ] [-]

ROBIN HITCHCOCK & THE EGYPTIANS

same as solo line-up and same label

Mar 85. (lp) **FEGMANIA!** [ ] [ ]
– Egyptian cream / Another bubble / I'm only you / My wife and my dead wife / Goodnight I say / The man with the lightbulb head / Insect mother / Strawberry mind / Glass / The fly / Heaven. *(cd-iss.1986 +=)* – The bells of rhymney / Dwarfbeat / Some body. *(re-iss.Mar95 on 'Rhino-Sequel' +=)* – Egyptian cream (demo) / Heaven (live) / Insect mother (demo) / Egyptian cream (live) / The pit of souls: I) The plateau – II) The descent – III) The spinal dance – IV) Flight of the iron lung.

May 85. (12"m) **HEAVEN. / DWARFBEAT / SOME BODY** [ ] [-]

Midnight Relativity

Oct 85. (lp)(c) **GOTTA LET THIS HEN OUT (live)** [ ] [-]
– Sometimes I wish I was a pretty girl / Kingdom of love / Acid bird / The cars she used to drive / My wife and my dead wife / Brenda's iron sledge / The fly * / Only the stones remain * / Egyptian cream * / Leppo & the Jooves / America / Heaven / Listening to The Higsons / Face of death. *(cd-iss.Oct86; c/cd+= *) (re-iss.cd Mar95 on 'Rhino-Sequel')*

Feb 86. (12"ep) **BRENDA'S IRON SLEDGE (live). / ONLY THE STONES REMAIN (live) / PIT OF SOULS (parts 1-4)** [ ] [-]

Mar 86. (lp)(c)(pic-lp) **EXPLODING IN SILENCE** [ ] [ ]
– *(cd-iss.Dec86)*

Glass Fish Relativity

Sep 86. (7") **IF YOU WERE A PRIEST. / THE CRAWLING** [ ] [-]
(12"+=) – Tell me about your drugs / The can opener.

Sep 86. (lp)(cd) **ELEMENT OF LIGHT** [ ] [ ]
– If you were a priest / Winchester / Somewhere apart / Ted, Woody and Junior / The president / Raymond Chandler evening / Bass / Airscape / Never stop bleeding / Lady Waters & the hooded one / The black crow knows / The crawling / The leopard / Tell me about your drugs. *(re-iss.cd Mar95 on 'Rhino-Sequel' +=)* – The can opener / Raymond Chandler evening (demo) / President (demo) / If you were a priest (demo) / Airscape (live) / The leopard (demo).

Nov 86. (lp)(cd) **INVISIBLE HITCHCOCK** (compilation) [ ] [ ]
– All I wanna do is fall in love / Give me a spanner, Ralph / A skull, a suitcase, and a long red bottle of wine / It's a mystic trip / My favourite buildings / Falling leaves / Eaten by her own dinner / Pits of souls / Trash / Mr. Deadly / Star of hairs / Messages of dark / Vegetable friend / I got a message for you / Abandoned brain / Point it at gran / Let there be more darkness / Blues in A. *(re-iss.cd Mar95 on 'Rhino-Sequel' +=)* – Listening to the higsons / Dr. Sticky.

A & M A & M

Feb 88. (lp)(c)(cd) **GLOBE OF FROGS** [ ] [ ]
– Trapped flesh Mandela / Vibrating / Balloon man / Luminous rose / Sleeping with your devil mask on / Unsettled / Flesh number one / Chinese bones / A globe of frogs / Beatle Dennis / The shapes between us / Turn to animals.

Apr 88. (7") **GLOBE OF FROGS. / BALLOON MAN** [-] [ ]

—— still with **METCALFE + WINDSOR** + guest **PETER BUCK** – guitar (of R.E.M.)

Jul 89. (7") **MADONNA OF THE WASPS. / RULING CLASS** [-] [ ]
(12"+=)(cd-s+=) – Veins of the queen (royal mix) / Freeze (shatter mix).

Dec 89. (lp)(c)(cd) **QUEEN ELVIS** [-] [ ]
– Madonna of the wasps / The Devils coachman / Wax doll / Knife / Swirling / One long pair of eyes / Veins of the Queen / Freeze / Autumn sea / Superman. *(cd+=)* – Veins of the Queen (royal mix) / Freeze (shatter mix).

ROBIN HITCHCOCK

Go! Discs Twin Tone

Nov 90. (cd)(c)(lp) **EYE** [-] [ ]
– Cynthia mask / Certainly clickot / Queen Elvis / Flesh cartoons / Chinese water python / Executioner / Linctus House / Sweet ghosts of light / College of ice / Transparent lover / Beautiful girl / Raining twilight coast / Clean Steve / Agony of pleasure / Glass hotel / Satellite / Aquarium / Queen Elvis II. *(UK-cd-iss.Mar95 on 'Rhino-Sequel' +=)* – Raining twilight coast (demo) / Agony of pleasure (demo) / Queen Elvis III (demo).

Oct 91. (cd)(c)(lp) **PERSPEX ISLAND** [ ] [ ]
– Oceanside / So you think you're in love / Birds in perspex / Ultra unbelievable love / Vegetations and dines / Lysander / Child of the universe / She doesn't exist / Ride / If you go away / Earthly Paradise.

Jan 92. (7") **SO YOU THINK YOU'RE IN LOVE. / WATCH YOUR INTELLIGENCE** [ ] [ ]
(12"+=)(cd-s+=) – Dark green energy (featuring STIPE + BUCK of R.E.M.).

1993. (cd) **RESPECT** [-] [ ]
–

1994. (cd) **YOU & OBLIVION** [-] [ ]
– You've got / Don't you / Birdshead / She reached for a light / Victorian squid / Captain Dry / Mr. Rock I / August hair / Take your knife out of my back / Surgery / The dust / Polly on the shore / Aether / Fiend before the shrine / Nothing / Into it / Stranded in the future / Keeping still / September clones / Ghost ship / You & me / If I could look. *(UK-iss.1995 on 'Rhino-Sequel')*

Volume LV not issued

Feb 95. (7") **I SOMETHING YOU. / ZIPPER IN MY SPINE / MAN WITH A WOMAN'S SHADOW** [ ] [-]

– (SOFT BOYS) compilations –

Nov 83. Midnight Music; (lp) **INVISIBLE HITS** [ ] [-]
– Wey-wey-hep-uh-hole * / Have a heart Betty (I'm not fireproof) * / The asking tree / Muriel's hoof / The rout of the clones / Let me put it next to you / When I was a kid * / Rock & roll toilet * / Love poisoning * / Empty girl / Blues in the dark / He's a reptile. *(cd-iss.Feb95 on 'Rhino'' +=)* – (alt.takes of *)

Aug 85. De Laurean; (lp)(pic-lp) **WADING THROUGH A VENTILATOR** [ ] [-]

Oct 86. Midnight Music; (12"ep) **EATEN BY HER OWN DINNER / HAPPY THE GOLDEN PRINCE. / GROOVING ON AN INNER PLANE / MESSAGES OF DARK / THE ABANDONED BRAIN (all by "ROBYN HITCHCOCK")** -
Dec 87. Midnight Music; (lp) **LIVE AT PORTLAND ARMS** -
Sep 93. Rykodisc; (d-cd) **1976-81** -
Jul 94. Strange Roots; (cd) **THE KERSHAW SESSIONS** -

– (ROBYN HITCHCOCK) compilations, etc.

Mar 95. Rhino-Sequel; (cd) **RARE & UNRELEASED** -

SOFT CELL

Formed: Leeds, England . . . late 1979 by MARC ALMOND and DAVE BALL. With help from visual technician STEVEN GRIFFITHS, they embarked on studio and live work in 1980. After appearing on the now famous 'SOME BIZZARE ALBUM', with cut 'The Girl With The Patent Leather Face', they signed solo deal with said label. In 1981 their 2nd 45 for the label, 'TAINTED LOVE' made UK No.1 for 2 weeks. They continued to have string of hits up to their demise in 1984. MARC ALMOND, who had earlier splintered with his MARC & THE MAMBAS project, went solo and struggled to regain a top 20 placing, until early 1989, when GENE PITNEY provided old song and dual vox for the UK No.1 'SOMETHING'S GOTTEN HOLD OF MY HEART'. • **Style:** Northern electro-soul which fused sleazy sex with alternative disco rock-pop. ALMOND was always the brunt of slagging from the music press, for his extrovert homosexuality, which nearly made him retire for good during the mid-80's. • **Songwriters:** ALMOND lyrics / BALL music. SOFT CELL covered TAINTED LOVE (Gloria Jones; c.Ed Cobb) / WHERE DID OUR LOVE GO (Supremes) / HENDRIX MEDLEY (Jimi Hendrix). MARC & THE MAMBAS covered IF YOU GO AWAY + THE BULLS (Jacques Brel) / CAROLINE SAYS (Lou Reed) / TERRAPIN (Syd Barrett) / CATCH A FALLEN STAR (Perry Como). MARC ALMOND solo:- A WOMAN'S STORY (Cher) / A SALTY DOG (Procol Harum) / THE LITTLE WHITE CLOUD THAT CRIED (Johnnie Ray) / Album JACQUES (Jaques Brel). • **Trivia:** In 1983, DAVE BALL scored the music for Tennessee Williams' play 'Suddenly Last Summer'. In mid 1987, ALMOND guested and wrote on SALLY TIMMS' single 'This House Is A House Of Tears'.

Recommended: NON-STOP EROTIC CABARET (*9) / MEMORABILIA – THE SINGLES (*8) / MARC AND THE MAMBAS: – UNTITLED (*8) / MARC ALMOND:- THE SINGLES (1984-1987) (*7).

MARC ALMOND (b.PETER MARC ALMOND, 9 Jul'59, Southport) – vocals / **DAVE BALL** (b. 3 May'59, Blackpool, England) – keyboards, synthesizers, drum prog.

Big Frock — not issued

1980. (7"ep) **MUTANT MOMENTS** -
– Potential / L.O.V.E. feelings / Metro MRX / Frustration.

Some Bizzare — Sire

Mar 81. (7") **MEMORABILIA. / PERSUASION** -
(12"+=) – A man could get lost.
Jul 81. (7") **TAINTED LOVE. / WHERE DID OUR LOVE GO** 1 8 Jan 82
(12"+=) – ('A'version). *(UK re-iss.Jul82-hit 50, Jan85 – hit 43)*
Nov 81. (7") **BEDSITTER. / FACILITY GIRLS** 4
(12"+=) – ('A'extended version).

—— guests **CINDY ECSTACY** – b.vox / **DAVE TOFANI** – sax / **JOHN GATHELL** – trumpet

Dec 81. (lp)(c) **NON-STOP EROTIC CABARET** 5 22
– Frustration / Tainted love / Seedy films / Youth / Sex dwarf / Entertain me / Chips on my shoulder / Bedsitter / Secret life / Say hello, wave goodbye. *(cd-iss.1988 & May90 & Mar92 with extra tracks)*
Jan 82. (7") **SAY HELLO, WAVE GOODBYE. / FUN CITY** 3
(12"+=) – ('A'instrumental).
May 82. (7")(12") **TORCH. / INSECURE ME** 2

—— Duo carried on, without CINDY who later formed SIX SEE RED.

Jun 82. (m-lp)(c) **NON-STOP ECSTATIC DANCING** 6 57
– Memorabilia / Where did our love go / What! / A man could get lost / Chips on my shoulder * / Sex dwarf. *(US version repl.* w/)* – 'Insecure . . .me?') *(UK-cd-iss.Mar92)*
Aug 82. (7")(12") **WHAT!. / . . . SO** 3
Nov 82. (7") **WHERE THE HEART IS. / IT'S A MUG GAME** 21
(12"+=) – ('A'extended version).
Feb 83. (lp)(c) **THE ART OF FALLING APART** 5 84
– Forever the same / Where the heart is / Numbers / Heat / Kitchen sink drama / Baby doll / Loving you, hating me / The art of falling apart. *(12"ep w.a.+=)* **MARTIN. / HENDRIX MEDLEY: HEY JOE – PURPLE HAZE – VOODOO CHILE** *(re-iss.Nov87) (cd-iss.Mar92 with extra tracks)*
Feb 83. (7")(12") **NUMBERS. / BARRIERS** 25 -
Apr 83. (7") **HEAT. / IT'S A MUGS GAME** -
Sep 83. (7") **SOUL INSIDE. / YOU ONLY LIVE TWICE** 16
(12"+=) – Loving you, hating me / 007 theme.
(d7"+=) – Loving you, hating me / Her imagination.
Feb 84. (7") **DOWN IN THE SUBWAY. / DISEASE AND DESIRE** 24
(12"+=)(12"red+=)(12"gold+=) – Born to lose.
Mar 84. (lp)(c) **THIS LAST NIGHT . . . IN SODOM** 12
– Mr. Self destruct / Slave to this / Little rough rhinestone / Meet murder my angel / The best way to kill / L'Esqualita / Down in the subway / Surrender (to a stranger) / Soul inside / Where was your heart (when you needed it most). *(cd-iss.Aug84)*

—— Waved goodbye, just prior to above album.

– compilations, others, etc. –

Dec 86. Some Bizzare/ US= Sire; (lp)(c)(cd) **SOFT CELL – THE SINGLES** 58
Mar 91. Mercury; (7") **SAY HELLO, WAVE GOODBYE '91. / MEMORABILIA (Grid remix)** 38
(12"+=)(cd-s+=) – ('A'-Mendelsohn extended remix).
(cd-s) – ('A'side) / Numbers / Torch (12"version).
May 91. Mercury; (7")(c-s) **TAINTED LOVE ('91 remix). / ('A'other remix)** 5
(12"+=)(cd-s+=) – Where did our love go.
(cd-s+=) – Where the heart is / Loving you, hating me.
May 91. Mercury; (cd)(c)(lp) **MEMORABILIA – THE SINGLES** 8
– Memorabilia '91 / Tainted love / Bedsitter / Torch / What was the matter with Rachmaninov? / Say hello wave goodbye '91 / Where the heart is / I feel love / Tears run rings / A lover spurned / Something's gotten hold of my heart. (cd+=) – (Soul inside / Say hello wave goodbye (12"mix) / Waifs and strays (Grid twilight mix).
Mar 94. Spectrum; (cd)(c) **DOWN IN THE SUBWAY** -

—— In '82, ALMOND had already splintered with own band

MARC AND THE MAMBAS

with **ANNIE HOGAN** – piano / **TIM TAYLOR** – bass / **DAVE BALL** – multi instruments

Some Bizzare — not issued

Mar 82. (12"m) **SLEAZE (TAKE IT, SHAKE IT). / FUN CITY / TAKING IT SHAKING IT** -

—— guests on next 2 albums were **GENESIS P.ORRIDGE & MATT JOHNSON**

Sep 82. (lp)(c) **UNTITLED** 42 -
– Untitled / Empty eyes / Angels / Big Louise / Caroline says / Margaret / If you go away. *(free-12"ep.w.a+=)* – Terrapin / Twilights and lowlifes (street walking soundtrack) / Twilights and lowlifes.
Nov 82. (7") **BIG LOUISE. / EMPTY EYES** -
(12"+=) – The dirt behind the neon.
Jun 83. (7") **BLACK HEART. / YOUR AURA** 49 -
(12"+=) – Mamba.
Aug 83. (d-lp)(c) **TORMENT AND TOREROS** 28 -
– The animal in you / Narcissus / Gloomy Sunday / Vision / Your love is a lesson / The untouchable one / My little book of sorrows / In my room / First time / The bulls / Boss cat / Intro / Catch a fallen star / Beat out dat rhythm on a drum / A million manias / Torment / Black heart.
Nov 83. (12"m) **TORMENT / FIRST TIME. / YOU'LL NEVER SEE ME ON A SUNDAY / MAGAMILLIONMANIA-MULTIMANIAMIX** -

DAVE BALL

Some Bizzare — not issued

Nov 83. (lp)(c) **IN STRICT TEMPO** -
– Mirrors / Sincerity / Passion of a primitive / Strict tempo / Man in the man / Only time / Life of love / Rednecks / American stories.

—— After SOFT CELL divided, BALL formed The OTHER PEOPLE in 1984, with wife GINI and ANDY ASTLE. They issued one single 'HAVE A NICE DAY' on 'Arcadia'. In 1986, he was credited on 'DECODER' album alongside GENESIS P. & THE THE. Early in 1988, his new trio ENGLISH BOY ON THE LOVE RANCH issued 7+12"; THE MAN IN YOUR LIFE on French label 'New Rose'. BALL joined The GRID in the late 80's, and had degree of success under this project and on its production hits.

MARC ALMOND

meantime had went solo, augmented by **The WILLING SINNERS: ANNIE HOGAN** – piano / **BILLY McGEE** – bass / **RICHARD RILEY** – guitar / **STEPHEN HUMPHRIES** – drums / **MARTIN McCARRICK** – cello

Some Bizzare — Sire

May 84. (7")(10")(12") **THE BOY WHO CAME BACK. / JOEY DEMENTO** 52

Sep 84. (7") **YOU HAVE. / SPLIT UP** [57] [ ]
(10"+=)(12"+=) – Black mountain blues.

Oct 84. (lp)(c)(cd) **VERMINE IN ERMINE** [36] [ ]
– Shining sinners / Hell was a city / You have / Crime sublime / Gutter hearts / Ugly head / The boy who came back / Solo adultos / Tenderness is a weakness. *(c+cd+=)* – Pink shack blues / Split lip / Joey Demento.

Nov 84. (7") **TENDERNESS IS A WEAKNESS. / LOVE FOR SALE** [ ] [ ]
(10"+=) – Blues the heel.

— In Apr 85, he teamed up with BRONSKI BEAT on Top 3 version of I FEEL LOVE. Two months later, he featured anonymously on 12" SKIN as BURMOE BROTHERS.

Aug 85. (7") **STORIES OF JOHNNY. / BLOND BOY** [23] [ ]
(12"+=) – Take my heart.
(d7"++=) – Stories of Johnny (WESTMINSTER CITY SCHOOL CHOIR)

Sep 85. (lp)(c)(cd) **STORIES OF JOHNNY** [22] [ ]
– Traumas, traumas, traumas / Stories of Johnny / The house is haunted (by the echoes of your last goodbye) / Love letter / The flesh is willing / Always / Contempt / I who never / My candle burns / Love and little white lies. *(c+cd+=)* – Take my heart / Blond boy / ('A'version with WESTMINSTER C.S.)

Oct 85. (7")(12") **LOVE LETTER. / ('A'version)** [68] [ ]

Jan 86. (7") **THE HOUSE IS HAUNTED (BY THE ECHO OF YOUR LAST GOODBYE). / BROKEN BARRICADES** [55] [ ]
(12"+=)(d7"+=) – Burning boats / ('A'version).

May 86. (7") **A WOMAN'S STORY. / FOR ONE MOMENT** [41] [ ]
(10"pic-d-ep+=)(12"ep+=)(c-ep+=) – SOME SONGS TO TAKE TO THE TOMB EP – The heel / A salty dog / The plague / The little white cloud that cried / Just good friends.

Oct 86. (7") **RUBY RED. / I'M SICK OF YOU TASTING OF SOMEONE ELSE** [47] [ ]
(12"+=) – Anarcoma / Broken-hearted and beautiful / Jackal jackal.
(12") – Ruby red (extended dance mix). / Ruby red (instrumental)

Jan 87. (7") **MELANCHOLY ROSE. / GYP THE BLOOD** [71] [ ]
(12"+=) – World full of people / Black lullaby.
(d7+=) – Surabaya Johnny / Pirate Jenny.

Mar 87. (lp)(c)(cd) **MOTHER FIST AND HER FIVE DAUGHTERS** [40] [ ]
– Mother Fist / There is a bed / Saint Judy / The room below / Angel in her kiss / The hustler / Melancholy rose / Mr. Sad / The sea says / Champ / Ruby red / The river.

Mar 87. (7") **MOTHER FIST. / TWO SAILORS ON THE BEACH** [ ] [ ]
(12"+=) – The hustler.

Nov 87. (lp)(c)(cd) **THE SINGLES 1984-1987** (compilation) [ ] [ ]
– The boy who came back / You have / Tenderness is a weakness / Stories of Johnny / Love letters / The house is haunted / A woman's story / Ruby red / Melancholy rose / Mother Fist.

— He was now backed by LA MAGIA. (aka HOGAN, HUMPHRIES + McGEE)

Parlophone | Capitol

Aug 88. (7") **TEARS RUN RINGS. / EVERYTHING I WANT TO BE** [26] [67]
(12"+=)(cd-s+=) – ('A'extended).
(12"+=) – ('A'&'B'-different mixes).

Sep 88. (lp)(c)(cd) **THE STARS WE ARE** [41] [ ]
– The stars we are / These my dreams are true / Bitter sweet / Only the moment / Your kisses burn / Tears run rings / Something's gotten hold of my heart / The sensualist / She took my soul in Instanbul. *(c+cd+=)* – The frost comes tomorrow / Kept boy.

Oct 88. (7")(7"clear) **BITTER SWEET. / KING OF THE FOOLS** [40] [ ]
(12"+=)(cd-s+=) – Tears run rings (mix).

Jan 89. (7") **SOMETHING'S GOTTEN HOLD OF MY HEART. ("MARC ALMOND & GENE PITNEY") / ('A'-solo version)** [1] [ ]
(12"+=)(cd-s+=) – The frost comes tomorrow.

Mar 89. (7")(7"clear) **ONLY THE MOMENT. / REAL EVIL** [47] [ ]
(12"+=) – ('A'extended).
(cd-s+=) – She took my soul in Instanbul.

Feb 90. (7") **A LOVER SPURNED. / EXOTICA ROSE** [29] [ ]
(12"+=)(cd-s+=)(10"square-pic-d+=) – ('A'version).

May 90. (7")(c-s) **THE DESPERATE HOURS. / THE GAMBLER** [45] [ ]
(12"+=)(12"clear-pic-d+=)(cd-s+=)(pic-cd-s+=) – ('A'extended mix).

Jun 90. (cd)(c)(lp) **ENCHANTED** [52] [ ]
– Madame de la luna / Waifs and strays / The desperate hours / Toreador in the rain / Widow weeds / A lover spurned / Death's diary / Sea still sings / Carnival of life / Orpheus in red velvet.

Oct 90. (7") **WAIFS AND STRAYS. / OLD JACK'S CHARM** [ ] [ ]
(12"+=)/ /(cd-s+=) – ('A'mix)./ / City of nights.

— Wrote w/**DAVE BALL + NORRIS** (The GRID)

W.E.A. | W.E.A.

Sep 91. (7")(c-s) **JACKY. / DEEP NIGHT** [17] [ ]
(12"+=)/ /(cd-s+=) – ('A' alpine dub)./ / A love outgrown.
(12") – ('A'side) / ('A' Youth remixes).

Oct 91. (cd)(c)(lp) **TENEMENT SYMPHONY** [48] [ ]
– Meet me in my dream / Beautiful brutal thing / I've never seen your face / Vaudeville and burlesque / Champagne / Tenement symphony (i) Prelude (ii) Jacky (iii) What is love? (iv) Trois Chansons de Bilitis – extract (v) The days of Pearly Spencer (vi) My hand over my heart. *(re-entered UK chart 39; Apr92) (re-iss.cd Feb95)*

Dec 91. (7") **MY HAND OVER MY HEART. / DEADLY SERENADE** [33] [ ]
(12"+=)(cd-s+=) – Money for love (2 versions).

Apr 92. (7")(c-s) **THE DAYS OF PEARLY SPENCER. / BRUISES** [4] [ ]
(12"+=)(cd-s+=) – Dancing in a golden cage / Extract from 'Trois Chansons'.

— with **DAVE CLAYTON** – keyboards, musical director / **MARTIN WATKINS** – piano / **ANDY HAMILTON** – saxophone / **MICHELE DREES** – drums, perc. / **CRIS BONACCI** – guitars / **SHIRLEY LEWIS, ANNA ROSS & AILEEN McLAUGHLIN** – b.vox / **TENEMENT SYMPHONY ORCH.**

Mar 93. (7")(c-s) **WHAT MAKES A MAN A MAN (live). / TORCH (live)** [60] [ ]
(cd-s+=) – Stars we are (live) / Tainted love (live).
(cd-s) – ('A'side) / Vision (live) / Only the moment (live).

Apr 93. (cd)(c)(lp) **12 YEARS OF TEARS – LIVE AT THE ROYAL ALBERT HALL (live)** [ ] [ ]
– Tears run rings / Champagne / Bedsitter / Mr.Sad / There is a bed / Youth / If you go away / Jacky / Desperate hours / Waifs and strays / Something's gotten hold of my heart / What makes a man a man / Tainted love / Say hello wave goodbye.

Sep 93. (cd)(c)(lp) **ABSINTHE** [ ] [ ]
– Undress me / Abel and Cain / Lost Paradise / Secret child / Rue Des Blancs Manteaux / The slave / Remorse of the dead / Incestuous love / A man / My little lovers / In your bed / Yesterday when I was young.

Mercury | Mercury

Apr 95. (c-s) **ADORNED AND EXPLORED / LOVELESS WORLD** [25] [ ]
(cd-s+=) – The user.

Jul 95. (c-s) **THE IDOL / ('A'-Tin Tin Out mix)** [44] [ ]
(cd-s+=) – ('A'-Idolized mix) / ('A'-Tenage dream mix).
(cd-s) – ('A'-part 1) / Law of the night / Adorned and explored / Bedsitter.

Nov 95. (c-ep)(cd-ep) **CHILD STAR EP** [41] [ ]
– Child star / The edge of heartbreak / Christmas in Vegas / My guardian angel.
(cd-ep) – ('A'side) / We need jealousy (live) / The idol (live) / Out there (live).

. . . Jan – Jun '96 stop press . . .

Feb 96. (single) **OUT THERE** [ ] [ ]

Feb 96. (cd)(c) **FANTASTIC STAR** [54] [ ]

– more (MARC ALMOND) compilations, etc. –

Dec 89. Some Bizzare; (lp)(c)(cd) **JAQUES** (most rec.1986) [ ] [-]
– The Devil (okay) / If you need / The lockman / We must look / Alone / I'm coming / Litany for a return / If you go away / The town fell asleep / The bulls / (Never to be) Next / My death.

— (above a tribute to Belguin singer JAQUES BREL)

Sep 92. Virgin; (cd)(c)(d-lp) **A VIRGIN'S TALE VOL.1 (1985-1988)** [ ] [-]

Sep 92. Virgin; (cd)(c)(d-lp) **A VIRGIN'S TALE VOL.2 (1988-1991)** [ ] [ ]
(re-iss.both above Nov92 as d-cd)

SONIC BOOM (see under ⇒ SPACEMEN 3)

SONIC YOUTH

Formed: New York, USA ... early 1981 by THURSTON, LEE and KIM. After numerous releases on various US indie labels (noteably Glenn Branca's 'Neutral' records), they signed to 'Blast First'. Finally secured a major deal with 'DGC' (David Geffen Company) in the early 90's, and smashed into the UK Top 40 with album 'GOO'. • **Style:** Underground experimental punk outfit, similar in ideals to VELVET UNDERGROUND, but fused with garage. • **Songwriters:** MOORE / RANALDO / GORDON compositions, except I WANNA BE YOUR DOG (Stooges) / TICKET TO RIDE (Beatles) / BEAT ON THE BRAT (Ramones) / TOUCH ME, I'M SICK (Mudhoney) / COMPUTER AGE (Neil Young). Their off-shoot CICCONE YOUTH covered INTO THE GROOVE (Madonna) / ADDICTED TO LOVE (Robert Palmer) / IS IT MY BODY (Alice Cooper) / PERSONALITY CRISIS (New York Dolls) / CA PLANE POUR MOI (Plastic Bertrand). • **Trivia:** Early in 1989, they were featured on hour-long special TV documentary for Melvyn Bragg's 'The South Bank Show'.

Recommended: BAD MOON RISING (*8) / EVOL (*8) / SISTER (*9) / DAY-DREAM NATION (*9) / GOO (*9) / DIRTY (*8) / WASHING MACHINE (*8).

THURSTON MOORE – guitar / **KIM GORDON** – bass, vocals / **LEE RANALDO** – guitar, vocals repl. ANN DEMARIS / **RICHARD EDSON** – drums repl. DAVE KEAY

not issued | Neutral

Mar 82. (m-lp) **SONIC YOUTH (live)** [-] [ ]
– The burning spear / I dreamt I dreamed / She's not alone / I don't want to push it / The good and the bad. *(US + UK re-iss.+cd.Oct87 on 'S.S.T.')*

— **JIM SCLAVUNOS** – drums repl. EDSON

Feb 83. (lp) **CONFUSION IS SEX** [-] [ ]
– Inhuman / The world looks red / Confusion is next / Making the nature scene / Lee is free / (She's in a) Bad mood / Protect me you / Freezer burn / I wanna be your dog / Shaking Hell. *(US + UK re-iss.+cd.Oct87 on 'S.S.T.')*

— **BOB BERT** – drums repl. SCLAVUNOS (still featured on 2 tracks)

not issued Zensor

Oct 83. (m-lp) **KILL YR. IDOLS** [-] [ ] Germ'y
– Protect me you / Shaking Hell / Kill yr. idols / Brother James / Early American.

not issued Ecstatic..

1984. (c) **SONIC DEATH (SONIC YOUTH LIVE)** [-] [ ]
– Sonic Death Side 1 / Sonic Death Side 2
(cd-iss.Jul88 on 'Blast First')

Blast First Iridescene

Mar 85. (12"ep) **DEATH VALLEY '69. ("SONIC YOUTH & LYDIA LUNCH") / I DREAMT I DREAMED / INHUMAN / BROTHER JAMES / SATAN IS BORING** [ ] [ ] Dec 84

Mar 85. (lp)(c) **BAD MOON RISING** [ ] [ ]
– Intro / Brave men rule / Society is a hole / I love her all the time / Ghost bitch / I'm insane / Justice is might / Death valley '69. *(cd-iss.Nov86 +=)* – Satan is boring / Flower / Halloween.

Jan 86. (7")(12"yellow) **HALLOWEEN. / FLOWER** [-] [ ]
(above single issued US on 'Homestead')

Jan 86. (7") **FLOWER. / REWOLF** [ ] [-]
(12") – ('A'side) / Satan is boring (live).

May 86. (12") **HALLOWEEN II. / ('A'version)** [ ] [-]

— **STEVE SHELLEY** – drums repl. BOB BERT who joined PUSSY GALORE

May 86. (lp)(c) **EVOL** [ ] [ ]
– Green light / Star power / Secret girl / Tom Violence / Death to our friends / Shadow of a doubt / Marilyn Moore / In the kingdom / Madonna, Sean and me. *(cd-iss.Nov86,* (+=) – Bubblegum.

Jul 86. (7")(12") **STAR POWER. / BUBBLEGUM** [ ] [ ]

Nov 86. (7")(12") **INTO THE GROOVE(Y). / TUFF TITTY RAP** [ ] [ ]

— (above single as **"CICCONE YOUTH"**, adding **MIKE WATT** – bass (of FIREHOSE)

Jun 87. (lp)(c)(cd) **SISTER** [ ] [ ]
– White cross / (I got a) Catholic block / Hot wire my heart / Tuff gnarl / Kotton crown / Schizophrenia / Beauty lies in the eye / Stereo sanctity / Pipeline – killtime / PCH. *(cd+=)* – Master-Dik (original).

Jan 88. (12"ep) **MASTER-DIK.-** [ ] [ ]
– Beat on the brat / Under the influence of The Jesus And Mary Chain: Tick-et to ride.

Oct 88. (d-lp)(c)(cd) **DAYDREAM NATION** [99] [ ]
– Teenage riot / Silver rocket / The sprawl / 'Cross the breeze / Eric's trip / Total trash / Hey Joni / Providence / Candle? / Rain king / Kissability / Trilogy: The wonder – Hyperstation – Eliminator Jr.

— Late in '88, KIM teamed up with LYDIA LUNCH and SADIE MAE to form one-off project HARRY CREWS. Their live appearences were issued in Apr 90 as 'NAKED IN GARDEN HILLS' for 'Big Cat' UK + 'Widowspeak' US.

Jan 89. (lp)(c)(cd) **THE WHITEY ALBUM (as "CICCONE YOUTH")** [63] [ ]
– Needle-gun (silence) / G-force / Platoon II / Macbeth / Me & Jill / Hendrix Cosby / Burnin' up / Hi! everybody / Children of Satan / Third fig / Two cool rock chicks / Listening to Neu! / Addicted to love / Moby-Dik / March of the Ciccone robots / Making the nature scene / Tuff titty rap / Into the groovey.

Fierce Fierce

Feb 89. (12") **TOUCH ME, I'M SICK. / ('B'by 'Mudhoney')** [ ] [ ]

W.E.A. D.G.C.

Jun 90. (cd)(c)(lp) **GOO** [32] [96]
– Dirty boots / Tunic (song for Karen) / Mary-Christ / Kool thing / Mote / My friend Goo / Disappearer / Mildred Pierce / Cinderella's big score / Scooter + Jinx / Titanium expose. *(re-iss.Jun91 & Oct95 cd)*

Sep 90. (7")(c-s) **KOOL THING. / THAT'S ALL I KNOW (RIGHT NOW)** [ ] [ ]
(12"+=) – ('A'demo version).
(cd-s++=) – Dirty boots (rock & roll Heaven version).

— In Autumn '90, THURSTON was part of 'Rough Trade' supergroup VELVET MONKEYS.

D.G.C. D.G.C.

Apr 91. (cd)(c)(m-lp) **DIRTY BOOTS** (all live, except the title track) [69] [ ]
– Dirty boots / The bedroom / Cinderella's big scene / Eric's trip / White kross .

— Early in '92, THURSTON and STEVE also teamed up with RICHARD HELL's off-shoot group The DIM STARS.

Jun 92. (7") **100%. / CREME BRULEE** [28] [ ]
(12"+=)(10"orange+=) – Hendrix.
(cd-s++=) – Genetic.

Jul 92. (cd)(c)(d-lp) **DIRTY** [6] [83]
– 100% / Swimsuit issue / Theresa's sound-world / Drunken butterfly / Shoot / Wish fulfillment / Sugar Kane / Orange rolls, angel's spit / Youth against fascism / Nic fit / On the strip / Chapel Hill / JC / Purr / Creme brulee. *(d-lp+=)* – Stalker. *(re-iss.cd Oct95)*

Geffen Geffen

Oct 92. (7") **YOUTH AGAINST FASCISM. / PURR** [52] [ ]
(10"+=) – ('A'version).
(cd-s++=) – The destroyed room (radio version)

Apr 93. (7")(c-s) **SUGAR KANE. / THE END OF THE END OF THE UGLY** [26] [ ]
(10"blue+=)/ /(cd-s+=) – Is it my body./ / Personality crisis.

Apr 94. (c-s)(10"silver)(cd-s) **BULL IN THE HEATHER. / RAZORBLADE** [24] [ ]

May 94. (cd)(c)(blue-lp) **EXPERIMENTAL JET SET, TRASH AND NO STAR** [10] [34]
– Winner's blues / Bull in the heather / Starfield road / Skink / Self-obsessed and sexxee / Bone / Androgynous mind / Quest for the cup / Waist / Doctor's orders / Tokyo eye / In the mind of the bourgeois reader / Sweet shine.

— In Sep 94; 'A&M' released CARPENTERS tribute album, which contained their single 'SUPERSTAR'. It was combined with also another cover from REDD KROSS, and reached UK No.45.

— early '95, FREE KITTEN (aka KIM, JULIE CAFRITZ, MARK IBOLD + YOSHIMI) released album 'NICE ASS'.

Oct 95. (cd)(c)(d-lp) **WASHING MACHINE** [39] [58]
– Becuz / Junkie's promise / Saucer-like / Washing machine / Unwind / Little trouble girl / No queen blues / Panty lines / Becuz coda / Skip tracer / The diamond sea.

. . . Jan – Jun '96 stop press . . .

Apr 96. (single) **LITTLE TROUBLE GIRL** [ ] [ ]

– compilations, others, etc. –

Feb 88. Fierce; (7")(d7"etched-one-sided) **STICK ME DONNA MAGICK MOMMA. / MAKING THE NATURE SCENE (live)** [ ] [ ]

Feb 92. Sonic Death; (cd) **GOO DEMOS LIVE AT THE CONTINENTAL CLUB (live)** [ ] [ ]

Mar 95. Blast First; (cd)(c) **CONFUSION IS SEX / KILL YR IDOLS** [ ] [-]

Mar 95. Warners; (cd) **MADE IN THE U.S.A.** [ ] [-]

Apr 95. Blast First; (cd) **SCREAMING FIELDS OF SONIC LOVE** [ ] [ ]

LEE RANALDO

Blast First Blast First

Jul 87. (m-lp)(c) **FROM HERE ⇒ ETERNITY** [ ] [ ]
– Time stands still / Destruction site / Ouroboron / Slodrown / New groove loop / Florida flower / Hard left / Fuzz-locusts / To Mary / Lathe speaks / The resolution / King's egg.

THURSTON MOORE

May 95. (cd)(c)(d-lp;colrd 3-sides) **PSYCHIC HEARTS** [ ] [ ]
– Queen bee and her pals / Ono soul / Psychic hearts / Pretty bad / Patti Smith math scratch / Blues from beyond the grave / See-through play-mate / Hang out / Feathers / Tranquilizor / Staring statues / Cindy (rotten tanx) / Cherry's blues / Female cop / Elergy for all dead rock stars.

SOUL ASYLUM

Formed: Minneapolis, USA . . . 1983 by MURPHY and PIRNER. After releases on 'What Goes On', they signed to major 'A&M' in 1987. After 5 years on the label, they looked set to break through with album 'GRAVE DANCERS UNION'. • **Style:** Shifted from hard-core HUSKER DU metal to more easily accessible rock with vox similar to TOM PETTY. • **Songwriters:** Mostly PIRNER except covers; BARSTOOL BLUES (Neil Young) / SEXUAL HEALING (Marvin Gaye) / ARE FRIENDS ELECTRIC (Tubeway Army). • **Trivia:** DAVE PIRNER is now the beau of actress WYNONA RYDER.

Recommended: HANG TIME (*6) / GRAVE DANCERS UNION (*7).

DAVE PIRNER – vocals, guitar / **DAN MURPHY** – guitar, vocals / **KURT MUELLER**– bass / **GRANT YOUNG** – drums, percussion

not issued Twin Tone

Aug 84. (m-lp) **SAY WHAT YOU WILL** [-] [ ]
– Long day / Voodoo doll / Money talks / Stranger / Sick of that song / Walking / Happy / Black and blue / Religiavision. *(US re-iss.May89, +=* Dragging me down / Do you know / Spacehead / Broken glass / Masquerade.) *(UK-iss.cd.Mar93 as 'SAY WHAT YOU WILL CLARENCE . . . KARL SOLD THE TRUCK' on 'Roadrunner') (cd-iss.Mar95)*

Rough Trade Road-runner

Sep 86. (lp) **MADE TO BE BROKEN** [ ] [ ]
– Tied to the tracks / Ship of fools / Can't go back / Another world another day / Made to be broken / Never really been / Whoa / New feelings / Growing pain / Lone rider / Ain't that tough / Don't it (make your troubles seem small). *(cd-iss.Mar93 on 'Roadrunner'+=)*– Long way home) (cd-iss.Mar95)

Sep 86. (7") **TIED TO THE TRACKS. / ?** [-] [ ]

What Goes On / Road-runner

Mar 88. (lp) **WHILE YOU WERE OUT** [ ] [ ] 1987
– Freaks / Carry on / No man's land / Crashing down / The judge / Sun don't shine / Closer to the stars / Never too soon / Miracles mile / Lap of luxury / Passing sad daydream. *(cd-iss.Mar93 on 'Roadrunner') (cd-iss.Mar95)*

May 88. (m-lp) **CLAM DIP AND OTHER DELIGHTS** [ ] [ ] 1987
– Just plain evil / Chains / Secret no more / Artificial heart / P-9 / Take it to root. *(cd-iss.Mar93 on 'Roadrunner') (cd-iss.Mar95)*

— split but re-formed adding guest **CADD** – sax, piano.

A & M / A & M

Jun 88. (7")(12") **SOMETIME TO RETURN. / PUT THE BOOT IN** [ ] [ ]
(re-iss.Jun91, 12"+= Marionette)

Jun 88. (lp)(c)(cd) **HANG TIME** [ ] [ ]
– Down on up to me / Little too clean / Sometime to return / Cartoon / Beggars and choosers / Endless farewell / Standing in the doorway / Marionette / Ode / Jack of all trades / Twiddly dee / Heavy rotation. *(re-iss.cd+c.Sep93)*

Aug 88. (7") **CARTOON. / TWIDDLY DEE** [ ] [ ]
(12"+=) – Standing in the doorway.

Sep 90. (cd)(c)(lp) **SOUL ASYLUM & THE HORSE THEY RODE IN ON** [ ] [ ] 1988
– Spinnin' / Bitter pill / Veil of tears / Nice guys (don't get paid) / Something out of nothing / Gullible's travels / Brand new shine / Grounded / Don't be on your way / We / All the king's friends. *(re-iss.cd+c.Sep93)*

Jan 91. (7") **EASY STREET. / SPINNING** [ ] [ ]
(12"+=) – All the king's friends / Gullible's travels.

Columbia / Columbia

Oct 92. (cd)(c)(lp) **GRAVE DANCERS UNION** [ ] [11]
– Somebody to shove / Black gold / Runaway train / Keep it up / Homesick / Get on out / New world / April fool / Without a trace / Growing into you / 99% / The Sun maid. *(re-dist.Jul93, hit UK No.52) (UK No.27 early '94)*

Mar 93. (10"ep)(cd-ep) **BLACK GOLD / BLACK GOLD (live). / THE BREAK / 99%** [ ] [ ]

Jun 93. (c-s) **RUNAWAY TRAIN. / BLACK GOLD (live)** [37] [5]
(12"+=) – By the way / Never really been (live).
(cd-s++=) – Everybody loves a winner. (- Black Gold).
(above single returned into UK chart Nov93 to hit No.7)

Aug 93. (12"ep)(cd-ep) **SOMEBODY TO SHOVE / SOMEBODY TO SHOVE (live). / RUNAWAY TRAIN (live) / BY THE WAY (demo)** [34] [ ]
(c-ep) – ('A'side) / Black gold (live) / Runaway train (live).

Jan 94. (7")(c-s) **BLACK GOLD. / SOMEBODY TO SHOVE** [26] [ ]
(cd-s+=) – Closer to the stairs / Square root.
(cd-s+=) – Runaway train (live).

Mar 94. (7")(c-s) **SOMEBODY TO SHOVE. / BY THE WAY** [32] [ ]
(cd-s+=) – Stranger (unplugged) / Without a trace (live).
(cd-s++=) – ('A'mix).

Jun 95. (cd)(c) **LET YOUR DIM LIGHT SHINE** [22] [6]
– Misery / Shut down / To my own devices / Hopes up / Promises broken / Bittersweetheart / String of pearls / Crawl / Caged rat / Eyes of a child / Just like anyone / Tell me when / Nothing to write home about / I did my best.

Jul 95. (7"white)(c-s) **MISERY. / STRING OF PEARLS** [30] [20] Jun95
(cd-s+=) – Hope (demo) / I did my best.

Nov 95. (c-s) **JUST LIKE ANYONE / DO ANYTHING YOU WANNA DO (live)** [52] [ ]
(cd-s+=) – Get on out (live).
(cd-s) – ('A'side) / You'll live forever (demo) / Fearless leader (demo).

. . . Jan – Jun '96 stop press . . .

Feb 96. (single) **PROMISES BROKEN** [-] [63]

SOUNDGARDEN

Formed: Seattle, Washington, USA . . . 1984 by CORNELL, THAYIL and YAMAMOTO. After recruiting CAMERON in '86 and enjoying periods on US labels 'Sub Pop' & 'SST', they signed to 'A&M' in 1989. Their classic second album for the label 'BADMOTORFINGER' in 1991, cracked open the US charts and soon made inroads into UK ears. • **Style:** Hardcore-metal punk influenced by LED ZEPPELIN, BLACK SABBATH and KILLING JOKE, but inspired by a new metal generation of NIRVANA and the likes. • **Songwriters:** Most by CORNELL and group permutations. Covered SWALLOW MY PRIDE (Ramones) / FOPP (Ohio Players) / INTO THE VOID tune only (Black Sabbath) / BIG BOTTOM (Spinal Tap) / EAR-ACHE MY EYE (Cheech & Chong) / I CAN'T GIVE YOU ANYTHING (Ramones) / HOMOCIDAL SUICIDE (Budgie) / I DON'T CARE ABOUT YOU (Fear) / CAN YOU SEE ME (Jimi Hendrix) / COME TOGETHER (Beatles). • **Trivia:** LOUDER THAN LOVE was nominated for a Grammy in 1990.

Recommended: BADMOTORFINGER (*9) / ULTRAMEGA OK (*7) / LOUDER THAN LOVE (*8) / SUPERUNKNOWN (*9).

CHRIS CORNELL – vocals, guitar / **KIM THAYIL** – guitar / **HIRO YAMAMOTO** – bass / **MATT CAMERON** – drums

not issued / Sub Pop

Jun 87. (7"blue) **HUNTED DOWN. / NOTHING TO SAY** [-] [ ]

Oct 87. (12"ep)(orange-12"ep) **SCREAMING LIFE** [-] [ ]
– Hunted down / Entering / Tears to forget / Nothing to say / Little Joe / Hand of God.

Aug 88. (12"ep) **FOPP** [-] [ ]
– Fopp / Fopp (dub) / Kingdom of come / Swallow my pride. *(above 2 re-iss.! on cd/c)*

S.S.T. / S.S.T.

Nov 88. (m-lp)(c)(cd) **ULTRAMEGA OK** [ ] [ ]
– Flower / All your lies / 665 / Beyond the wheel / 667 / Mood for trouble / Circle of power / He didn't / Smokestack lightning / Nazi driver / Head injury / Incessant mace / One minute of silence. *(re-iss.cd/c/lp Oct95)*

May 89. (12")(c-s)(cd-s) **FLOWER. / HEAD INJURY / TOY BOX** [ ] [ ]

A & M / A & M

Sep 89. (lp)(c)(cd) **LOUDER THAN LOVE** [ ] [ ]
– Ugly truth / Hands all over / Gun / Power trip / Get on the snake / Full on Kevin's mom / Loud love / I awake / No wrong no right / Uncovered / Big dumb sex / Full on (reprise).

Apr 90. (10"ep)(cd-ep) **HANDS ALL OVER** [ ] [ ]
– Hands all over / Heretic / Come together / Big dumb sex.

Jul 90. (7"ep)(12"ep) **THE LOUD LOVE E.P.** [ ] [ ]
– Loud love / Fresh deadly roses / Big dumb sex (dub) / Get on the snake.

— **JASON EVERMAN** – bass (ex-NIRVANA) repl. HIRO

Sub Pop / Sub Pop

Oct 90. (7")(7"purple/green) **ROOM A THOUSAND YEARS WIDE. / H.I.V. BABY** [-] [ ]

— **BEN SHEPHERD** – bass repl. JASON

A & M / A & M

Oct 91. (cd)(c)(lp) **BADMOTORFINGER** [39] [39]
– Rusty cage / Outshined / Slaves & bulldozers / Jesus Christ pose / Face pollution / Somewhere / Searching with my good eye closed / Room a thousand years wide / Mind riot / Drawing flies / Holy water / New damage. *(hit +re-iss.Mar92)*

Mar 92. (7") **JESUS CHRIST POSE. / STRAY CAT BLUES** [30] [ ]
(12"+=)(cd-s+=) – Into the void (sealth).

Jun 92. (7")(7"pic-d) **RUSTY CAGE. / TOUCH ME** [41] [ ]
(12"+=)(cd-s+=) – Show me.
(cd-s+=) – Big bottom / Earache my eye.

Nov 92. (7") **OUTSHINED. / I CAN'T GIVE YOU ANYTHING** [50] [ ]
(12"+=)(cd-s+=) – Homocidal suicide.
(cd-s+=) – I don't care about you / Can't you see me.

Feb 94. (7"pic-d)(c-s) **SPOONMAN. / FRESH TENDRILS** [20] [ ]
(12"clear+=)(cd-s+=) – Cold bitch / Exit Stonehenge.

Mar 94. (cd)(c)(d-lp) **SUPERUNKNOWN** [4] [1]
– Let me drown / My wave / Fell on black days / Mailman / Superunknown / Head down / Black hole Sun / Spoonman / Limo wreck / The day I tried to live / Kickstand / Fresh tendrils / 4th of July / Half / Like suicide / She likes surprises.

Apr 94. (7"pic-d)(c-s) **THE DAY I TRIED TO LIVE. / LIKE SUICIDE (acoustic)** [42] [ ]
(12"etched+=)(cd-s+=) – Kickstand (live).

Aug 94. (7"pic-d)(c-s) **BLACK HOLE SUN. / BEYOND THE WHEEL (live) / FELL ON BLACK DAYS (live)** [12] [ ]
(pic-cd-s+=) – Birth ritual (demo).
(cd-s) – ('A'side) / My wave (live) / Jesus Christ pose (live) / Spoonman (remix).

Jan 95. (7"pic-d)(c-s) **FELL ON BLACK DAYS. / KYLE PETTY, SON OF RICHARD / MOTORCYCLE LOOP** [24] [ ]
(cd-s) – ('A'side) / Kyle Petty, son of Richard / Fell on black days (video version).
(cd-s) – ('A'side) / Girl u want / Fell on black days (early demo).

. . . Jan – Jun '96 stop press . . .

May 96. (single) **PRETTY NOOSE** [14] [ ]
May 96. (cd)(c)(lp) **DOWN ON THE UPSIDE** [7] [2]

– compilations, etc –

Oct 93. A&M; (cd) **LOUDER THAN LOUD / BADMOTORFINGER** [ ] [ ]
Oct 93. Sub Pop; (cd)(c) **SCREAMING LIFE / FOPP** [ ] [ ]

TEMPLE OF THE DOG

splinter-group feat. **CORNELL + CAMERON** plus **STONE GOSSARD / JEFF AMENT** (both ex-MOTHER LOVE BONE, future PEARL JAM)

A & M / A & M

Apr 91. (cd)(c)(lp) **TEMPLE OF THE DOG** [ ] [ ]
– Say hello to Heaven / Reach down / Hunger strike / Pushing forward back / Call me a dog / Times of trouble / Wooden Jesus / Your saviour / 4-walled world / All night thing. *(above album, finally made US No.5 mid'92)*

Oct 92. (7"pic-d)(c-s) **HUNGER STRIKE. / ALL NIGHT THING** [51] [ ]
(12"+=)(cd-s+=) – Your saviour.

HATER

MATT + BEN plus ?

A & M / A & M

Sep 93. (cd)(c)(lp) **HATER** [ ] [ ]
– Mona bone jakon / Who do I kill? / Tot finder / Lion and lamb / Roadside / Down undershoe / Circles / Putrid / Blistered / Sad McBain. *(re-iss.cd May95)*

not issued / Sub Pop

Sep 93 (7"imp) **CIRCLES / GENOCIDE** [-] [ ]

SOUTHERN DEATH CULT (see under ⇒ CULT)

SPACE

*** NEW ENTRY ***

Formed: Liverpool, England . . .1995 by quartet below. Debut 45 that year, saw them signed to 'Gut', where they had first chart entry 'NEIGHBOURHOOD'. The superb follow-up 'FEMALE OF THE SPECIES', surpassed this and hit UK Top 20 in mid '96. • **Style:** Basic but effective pop rock, reminiscent of BUZZCOCKS (sound and visually) or even JILTED JOHN (lyrically). Hints of glam or psychedelia. • **Songwriters:** SCOTT / GRIFFITHS. • **Trivia:** Use the same recording studio once shared by ECHO & THE BUNNYMEN and The TEARDROP EXPLODES.

JAMIE MURPHY – vocals, guitar / **TOMMY SCOTT** – vocals / **COLIN** - / **JAMES** –

HomeRecord / not issued

Oct 95. (7") **MONEY. / KILL ME** [ ] [-]
(cd-s+=) – ('A'club) / ('B'club).
(12") – ('A'-Lost in space remix) / ('A'-Still lost in space & safe bass mix) / ('A'-Space club mix) / ('A'-instrumental).

Gut / not issued

Mar 96. (c-s) **NEIGHBOURHOOD / REJECTS** [56] [-]
(cd-s+=) – Turn me on to spiders.
(12") – ('A'-Live it! club) / ('A'-Live it! instrumental club) / ('A'-Pissed up stomp) / ('A'-radio).

Jun 96. (c-s) **FEMALE OF THE SPECIES. / LOONEY TUNE** [14] [ ]
(12"+=)(cd-s+=) – ('A'radio) / Give me something.

SPACEMEN 3

Formed: Rugby, Warwickshire, England ... 1983 by KEMBER and PIERCE. Through their manager Gerald Palmer, they signed to 'Glass' early in 1986. Just as they were about to breakthrough in the early 90's, they splintered into 2 projects SONIC BOOM and SPIRITUALIZED. • **Style:** Psychedelic noise outfit, intertwined with melancholy bursts of beauty and experimentation. • **Songwriters:** KEMBER or PIERCE material until the 90's when KEMBER penned all. Covered; CHE + ROCK'N'ROLL IS KILLING MY LIFE (Suicide) / COME TOGETHER + STARSHIP (MC5) / MARY-ANNE (. . .Campbell) / ROLLER COASTER (13th Floor Elevators). SPIRITUALIZED covered; ANYWAY THAT YOU WANT ME (Troggs) / BORN NEVER ASKED (Laurie Anderson). • **Trivia:** In the early 90's, SPIRITUALIZED headlined at the ICA Rock Week sponsored by 'Irn Bru'.

Recommended: PLAYING WITH FIRE (*8) / LAZER GUIDED MELODIES (*9; SPIRITUALIZED) / PURE PHASE (*8; SPIRITUALIZED ELECTRIC MAINLINE)

SONIC BOOM (b.PETE KEMBER, 19 Nov'65) – vocals / **JASON PIERCE** (b.19 Nov'65) – guitar / **STEWART (ROSCO) ROSSWELL** – keyboards / **PETE (BASSMAN) BAINES** – bass

Glass / not issued

Jun 86. (lp) **SOUND OF CONFUSION** [ ] [-]
– Losing touch with my mind / Hey man / Roller coaster / Mary Anne / Little doll / 2:35 / O.D. catastrophe. *(re-iss.+cd.Sep89 on 'Fire')*

Dec 86. (12"m) **WALKIN' WITH JESUS (SOUND OF CONFUSION). / ROLLERCOASTER / FEEL SO GOOD** [ ] [-]

Jul 87. (12"ep) **TRANSPARENT RADIATION / ECSTASY SYMPHONY / TRANSPARENT RADIATION (FLASHBACK). / THINGS'LL NEVER BE THE SAME / STARSHIP** [ ] [-]

Aug 87. (lp)(c) **THE PERFECT PRESCRIPTION** [ ] [-]
– Take me to the other side / Walkin' with Jesus / Ode to street hassle / Ecstasy – Symphony / Feel so good / Things'll never be the same / Come down easy / Call the doctor / Soul 1 / That's just fine. *(re-iss.+cd.Dec89 on 'Fire')*

Mar 88. (7")(12") **TAKE ME TO THE OTHER SIDE. / SOUL 1 / THAT'S JUST FINE** [ ] [-]

— **WILLIE CARRUTHERS** – bass / **JON MATLOCK** – drums repl. ROSCO + BAINES who formed The DARKSIDE.

Fire / not issued

Nov 88. (7")(12") **REVOLUTION. / CHE** [ ] [-]
(cd-s+=) – May the circle be unbroken. *(re-iss.Oct91)*

Feb 89. (lp)(c)(cd) **PLAYING WITH FIRE** [ ] [-]
– Honey / Come down softly to my soul / How does it feel? / I believe it / Revolution / Let me down gently / So hot (wash away all my tears) / Suicide / Lord can you hear me. *(free-12"ep/cd-ep+=)* – Starship / Revolution / Suicide (live) / Repeater / Live intro theme (xtacy).

Jul 89. (7") **HYPNOTISED. / JUST TO SEE YOU SMILE HONEY (part 2)** [ ] [-]
(12"+=)(3"cd-s+=) – The world is dying. *(re-iss.Oct91)*
(free 7"flexi w.a) – EXTRACTS. / BARK PSYCHOSIS / FURY THINGS on 'Cheree' label.

Jan 91. (7") **BIG CITY. / DRIVE** [ ] [-]
(12"+=)(cd-s+=) – Big City (everybody I know can be found here).

Feb 91. (cd)(c)(lp) **RECURRING** [46] [-]
– Big city (everybody I know can be found here) / Just to see you smile (orchestral) / I love you / Set me free – I've got the key / Set me free (reprise) / Feel so bad (reprise) / Hypnotized / Sometimes / Feelin' just fine (head full of shit) / Billy Whizz – blue 1. (cd+=) When tomorrow hits / Why couldn't I see / Just to see you smile (instrumental) / Feel so sad (demo) / Drive.

May 91. (cd)(c)(lp) **PERFORMANCE** (live 1988 Holland) [ ] [-]
– Mary-Anne / Come together / Things'll never be the same / Take me to the other side / Roller coaster / Starship / Walkin' with Jesus.

— Had already folded Jun'90.

– compilations, etc. –

1991. Fierce; (cd)(d-lp) **DREAM WEAPON – ECSTASY IN SLOW MOTION** [ ] [-]
(re-iss.Nov95 on 'Space Age')

Nov 94. Bomp; (cd) **TAKING DRUGS TO MAKE MUSIC TO TAKE DRUGS TO** [ ] [-]

May 95. Sympathy For The . . . (cd)(lp) **FOR ALL FUCKED UP CHILDREN OF THE WORLD** [ ] [ ]

May 95. Bomp; (cd) **SPACEMEN ARE GO** [ ] [ ]

Nov 95. Space Age; (cd)(d-lp) **LIVE IN EUROPE 1989** [ ] [-]

SONIC BOOM

(PETE KEMBER solo with **WILLIE B. CARRUTHERS** and also **PHIL PARFITT + JO WIGGS** of PERFECT DISASTER)

Silvertone / not issued

Oct 89. (12") **ANGEL. / ANGEL (version) / HELP ME PLEASE** [ ] [-]

Feb 90. (cd)(c)(lp) **SPECTRUM** [65] [-]
– Pretty baby / If I should die / Lonely avenue / Help me please / Angel / Rock'n'roll is killing my life / You're the one. (free 10"w/lp) DRONE DREAM EP: OCTAVES. / TREMELOS.

Apr 91. (7" freebie gig) **(I LOVE YOU) TO THE MOON AND BACK. / CAPO WALTZ (live)** [-] [-]

. . . Jan – Jun '96 stop press . . .

— SONIC BOOM has now featured in group EAR.

SPECTRUM

KEMBER, CARRUTHERS, etc

Silvertone / Silvertone

Jun 92. (7")(12") **HOW YOU SATISFY ME. / DON'T GO (inst.2)** [ ] [-]
(12"clear+=)(cd-s+=) – My life spins around your every smile / Don't go (inst.1).

Jun 92. (cd)(c)(lp) **SOUL KISS (GLIDE DIVINE)** [ ] [-]
– How you satisfy me / Lord I don't even know my name / The drunk suite (overture) / Neon sigh / Waves wash over me / (I love you) To the Moon and back / My love for you never died away but my soul gave out and wit / Sweet running water / Touch the stars / Quicksilver glide divine / The drunk suite / Phase me out (gently). *(re-iss.cd/c Apr95)*

Sep 92. (7") **TRUE LOVE WILL FIND YOU IN THE END. / MY LIFE SPINS AROUND YOUR EVERY SMILE** [70] [-]
(12")(cd-s) – ('A' side) / To the moon and back / Waves wash over me.

Aug 93. (7") **INDIAN SUMMER. / BABY DON'T YOU WORRY (California lullabye)** [ ] [ ]
(12"+=)(cd-s+=) – It's alright / True love will find you in the end.

Apr 94. (12")(cd-s) **SKY ABOVE** [ ] [-]
above single issued on 'Sub Assertive Sounds'.

Nov 94. (cd)(lp) **HIGHS LOWS AND HEAVENLY BLOWS** [ ] [ ]
– Undo the taboo / Feedback / Then I just drifted away / Take your time / Soothe me / All night long / Don't pass me by / I know they say / Take me away.

SPIRITUALIZED

were 5-piece **JASON, WILL & JON** plus girlfriend **KATE RADLEY** – organ, keyboards, vocals / **MARK REFOY** – guitar, dulcimer

		Dedicated	not issued
Jun 90.	(12") **ANYWAY THAT YOU WANT ME. / STEP INTO THE BREEZE** (12"+=)(cd-s+=) – ('A'version) (12")('A'side) / ('A'parts 2-3) / ('A'demo)	75	-
Jun 91.	(7")(12")(cd-s) **FEEL SO SAD. / ('A'demos)**		-
Aug 91.	(7") **RUN. / I WANT YOU** (12"+=)(cd-s+=) Luminescent (stay with me) / Effervescent.	59	-
Nov 91.	(7") **WHY DON'T YOU SMILE NOW. / SWAY** (12"+=)(cd-s+=) – ('A'extended).		-
Apr 92.	(cd)(c)(2x12"lp) **LAZER GUIDED MELODIES** – You know it's true / If I were with her now / I want you / Run / Smiles / Step into the breeze / Symphony space / Take your time / Shine a light / Angel sigh / Sway / 200 bars. (free-7" at 'Chain With No Name' shops) ANY WAY THAT YOU WANT ME / WHY DON'T YOU SMILE NOW.	27	
Jul 92.	(7"red) **MEDICATION. / SMILES (Peel session)** (12"+=) – Feel so sad (Peel session) / Angel sigh. (cd-s++=) – Space (instrumental).	55	-
Jun 93.	(mail-order cd) **F***ED UP INSIDE**	-	-
Oct 93.	(7" **GOOD TIMES / LAY BACK IN THE SUN** (12"ep+=)(cd-ep+=) – Electric Mainline 1 + 2	49	

SPIRITUALIZED ELECTRIC MAINLINE

— **JASON + KATE RADLEY** -keyboards, vox/ **SEAN COOK** -synths/ plus **MARK REFOY** -guitar/ **JON MATTOCK** -percussion/ **LEON HUNT** -banjo/ **STEWART GORDON** -violin/ **THE BALANESCU QUARTET** -strings/ + others on wind instruments

Jan 95.	(cd-ep) **LET IT FLOW / DON'T GO / STAY WITH ME / DON'T GO / STAY WITH ME (THE INDIVIDUAL)** (cd-ep) – ('A'side) / Take good care of it / Things will never be the same / Clear rush. (cd-ep) – ('A'side) / Medication / Take your time / Smile. (3xbox-cd-ep)(10"ep) – (all above).	30	
Feb 95.	(cd)(c)(d-lp) **PURE PHASE** – Medication / The slide song / Electric phase / All of my tears / These blues / Let it flow / Take good care of it / Born never asked / Electric mainline / Lay back in the sun / Good times / Pure phase / Spread your wings / Feel like goin' home.	20	
Nov 95.	(cd-ep) **LAY BACK IN THE SUN / THE SLIDE SONG / SPREAD YOUR WINGS / LAY BACK IN THE SUN**		

— On Mar 92, HONEY TONGUES (aka MATTOCK + WIGGS) released lp 'NUDE NUDES' on 'Playtime'. *(re-iss.cd Oct93)*

SPARKLEHORSE

*** NEW ENTRY ***

Formed: Richmond, Virginia, USA ...1995 by former heroin addict MARK LINKOUS. Signed to 'Capitol' and supported stablemates RADIOHEAD in November '95, before releasing debut mouthful 'VIVADIXIESUBMARINETRANSMISSIONPLOT'. • **Style:** Lo-fi country rock with southern drawl, influenced by NEIL YOUNG, AFGHAN WHIGS or TOM WAITS. • **Songwriters:** LINKOUS.

Recommended: VIVADIXIESUBMARINETRANSMISSIONPLOT (*9)

MARK LINKOUS – vocals, guitar (ex-DANCING HOODS) / **SCOTT MINOR** - / **PAUL WATSON** - / **SCOTT FITZSIMMONS** –

		Parlophone	Capitol
Feb 96.	(7") **SOMEDAY I WILL TREAT YOU GOOD. / LONDON** (cd-s+=) – In the dry.		
Apr 96.	(7") **HAMMERING THE CRAMPS. / SPIRIT DITCH** (cd-s+=) – Dead opera star / Midget in a junkyard.		
May 96.	(cd)(c)(lp) **VIVADIXIESUBMARINETRANSMISSIONPLOT** – Homecoming queen / Weird sisters / 850 double pumper Holiday / Rainmaker / Spirit ditch / Tears on fresh fruit / Saturday / Cow / Little bastard choo choo / Hammering the cramps / Most beautiful widow in town / Heart of darkness / Ballad of a cold lost marble / Someday I will treat you good / Sad and beautiful world / Gasoline horseys.	58	Nov 95

SPARROW (see under ⇒ STEPPENWOLF)

SPECIALS

Formed: Coventry, Midlands, England ... 1978 by DAMMERS, GOULDING and GENTLEMAN. After a brief spell with CLASH manager Bernie Rhodes, DAMMERS formed own label '2-Tone' in 1979 to release debut 45 'GANGSTERS'. It picked up airplay on The John Peel Radio 1 Show, with it eventually cracking the Top 10. It sparked off a ska-revival that year, that showcased other splendid acts The SELECTER, MADNESS and The BEAT. The 2-Tone label was picked up by 'Chrysalis', and after another Top 10 hit 'MESSAGE TO YOU RUDY', they unleashed fantastic ELVIS COSTELLO produced eponymous album. • **Style:** As said, ska revivalists with a mission of social protest. Loved by rude boys, punks/new wavees and mods alike. • **Songwriters:** DAMMERS wrote most of work. Covered GANGSTERS (Prince Buster; 'Al Capone' song) / GUNS OF NAVARONE (Skatelites) / CONCRETE JUNGLE (Bob Marley) / LONG SHOT KICK DE BUCKET (Pioneers) / LIQUIDATOR (Harry J. All Stars) / MONKEY MAN (Maytals) / MAGGIE'S FARM (Bob Dylan) / SKINHEAD MOONSTOMP (Symarip). • **Trivia:** In 1984, DAMMERS wrote 'NELSON MANDELA', a song that called for the freedom of the jailed ANC South African leader. On 11 Jun'88, he organized MANDELA's 70th birthday benefit concert at Wembley Stadium, which featured artists EURYTHMICS, DIRE STRAITS, SIMPLE MINDS, STEVIE WONDER & TRACY CHAPMAN.

Recommended: THE SPECIALS (*8) / THE SPECIALS SINGLES (*9).

TERRY HALL (b.19 Mar'59) – vocals / **NEVILLE STAPLES** – vocals, percussion / **LYNVAL GOULDING** (b.24 Jul'51) – guitar, vocals / **JOHN BRADBURY** – drums / **JERRY DAMMERS** (b.GERALD DANKIN, 22 May'54, India) – keyboards / **RODDY RADIATION** (b.BYERS) – guitar / **HORACE GENTLEMAN** (b.PANTER) – bass

		2-Tone	not issued
Jul 79.	(7") **GANGSTERS. (as "The SPECIAL A.K.A.") / THE SELECTER (by "The SELECTER")**, the JOHN BRADBURY outfit)	6	-

— added (on some) guest **RICO RODRIQUEZ** – trombone

		2-Tone-Chrysalis	Chrysalis
Oct 79.	(7") **A MESSAGE TO YOU RUDY. / NITE CLUB**	10	
Oct 79.	(lp)(c) **SPECIALS** – A message to you Rudy / Do the dog / It's up to you / Nite club / Doesn't make it alright / Concrete jungle / Too hot / Monkey man / (Dawning of a) New era / Blank expression / Stupid marriage / Too much too young / Little bitch / You're wondering now. *(US-version w/)* – Gangsters. *(UK re-iss.Nov84 on 'Fame') (re-iss.cd Mar94)*	4	84
Jan 80.	(7"ep) **TOO MUCH TOO YOUNG – GUNS OF NAVARONE (live). / LONG SHOT KICK DE BUCKET – LIQUIDATOR – SKINHHEAD MOONSTOMP (live)**	1	
May 80.	(7") **RAT RACE. / RUDE BOYS OUTA JAIL**	5	
Sep 80.	(7") **STEREOTYPES (part 1). / INTERNATIONAL JET SET**	6	
Sep 80.	(lp)(c) **MORE SPECIALS** – Enjoy yourself (it's later than you think) / Man at C & A / Hey little rich girl / Do nothing / Pearl's cafe / Sock it to 'em J.B. / Stereotypes / Stereotypes (part 2) / Holiday fortnight / I can't stand it / International jet set / Enjoy yourself (reprise). *(free-7"w.a.)* **BEGGIN' TRYING NOT TO LIE. / RUDE BOYS OUTA JAIL (diff.mix)**	5	98
Jan 81.	(7") **DO NOTHING. / MAGGIE'S FARM**	4	
Jun 81.	(7")(12") **GHOST TOWN. / WHY / FRIDAY NIGHT, SATURDAY MORNING**	1	

— Only two originals (DAMMERS & BRADBURY) remained, as GOULDING, STAPLES & HALL formed The FUN BOY THREE. RADIATION formed TEARJERKERS. RICO went solo. All repl. by **RHODA DAKAR** – vocals + **NICKY SUMMERS** – bass (ex-BODYSNATCHERS) / **JOHN SHIPLEY** – guitar / **DICK CUTHELL** – saxophone

RHODA with The SPECIAL A.K.A.

(same label)

Jan 82.	(7") **THE BOILER. / THEME FROM THE BOILER**	35	-

The SPECIAL A.K.A.

HORACE PANTER – bass returned to repl. SUMMERS who joined The BELLE STARS / **STAN CAMPBELL** (b. 2 Jan'62) – vocals / **NICK PARKER** – violin repl. CUTHELL (same label)

Dec 82.	(7")(10") **WAR CRIMES (THE CRIME IS STILL THE SAME). / WAR CRIMES**		

— **RODDY RADIATION** – guitar returned with newcomer **EGIDIO NEWTON** – vox

Aug 83.	(7")(7"pic-d) **RACIST FRIEND. / BRIGHT LIGHTS**	60	

— **GARY McMANUS** – bass repl. PANTER who joined GENERAL PUBLIC guested on album **DICK CUTHELL** – cornet / **ANDY ADERINTO** – saxophone

Mar 84.	(7")(12") **NELSON MANDELA. / BREAK DOWN THE DOOR**	9	
Jun 84.	(lp)(c) **IN THE STUDIO** – Bright lights / Lonely crowd / House bound / War crimes / What I like most	34	

about you is your girlfriend / Night on the tiles / Nelso Mandela / War crimes / Rascist friend / Alcohol / Break down the door.

Aug 84. (7")(12") **WHAT I LIKE MOST ABOUT YOU IS YOUR GIRLFRIEND. / CAN'T GET A BREAK** [51] [ ]

— Folded late '84, STAN CAMPBELL went solo and BRADBURY formed The JB's ALL STARS. DAMMERS turned up on a charity single by STARVATION early 1985.

- compilations, others, etc. -

Dec 82. Chrysalis; (d-c) **SPECIALS / MORE SPECIALS** [ ] [-]
Jun 88. Chrysalis; (7")(12") **FREE NELSON MANDELA - 70th Birthday re-make). / ('A'original)** [ ] [-]
Aug 91. Chrysalis; (cd)(c)(lp) **THE SPECIALS SINGLES** [10] [ ]
– Gangsters / A message to you Rudy / Nite club / Too much too young – Guns of Navarone / Rat race / Rude boys outta jail / Stereotype / International jet set / Do nothing / Ghost town / Why? / Friday night, Saturday morning / Racist friend / Free Nelson Mandela / What I like most about you is your girlfriend.
Oct 91. Chrysalis; (7")(cd-s) **GHOST TOWN (REVISITED. / ('A'dub version)** [ ] [ ]
(12"+=) – Why / ('A'demo version).
Apr 92. Chrysalis; (cd)(c)(lp) **LIVE AT THE MOONLIGHT CLUB (live)** [ ] [-]
Feb 87. Strange Fruit; (12"ep) **THE PEEL SESSIONS** (23.5.79) [ ] [-]
– Gangsters / Too much too young / Concrete jungle / Monkey man.
Feb 87. Old Gold; (7") **TOO MUCH TOO YOUNG (live). / RAT RACE** [ ] [-]
Feb 87. Old Gold; (7") **GHOST TOWN. / RAT RACE** [ ] [-]
(re-iss.Mar90)
Apr 92. Receiver; (cd)(c)(lp) **TOO MUCH TOO YOUNG** [ ] [-]

— next shared with The SELECTER.

Dec 92. Windsong; (cd)(lp) **BBC RADIO 1 LIVE IN CONCERT (live)** [ ] [-]
Sep 93. 2-Tone; (12"ep)(c-ep)(cd-ep) **THE TWO-TONE EP ("Various Artists")** [30] [ ]
– Gangsters (SPECIAL AKA) / The Prince (MADNESS) / On my radio (SELECTER) / Tears of a clown (BEAT).

— In Oct'93, SPECIALS were credited on DESMOND DEKKER single 'Jamaica Sky'.

— re-form with **GOLDING, STAPLES + RADIATION** + featuring **SHEENA STAPLE + KENDELL**

. . . Jan – Jun '96 stop press . . .

Kuff-Virgin / Virgin

Jan 96. (single) **HYPOCRITE** [66] [ ]

— above a Bob Marley cover and below a Toots & The Maytals number.

Mar 96. (single) **PRESSURE DROP** [ ] [ ]
Apr 96. (cd) **TODAY'S SPECIALS** [ ] [ ]

SPECTRES (see under ⇒ STATUS QUO)

SPECTRUM (see under ⇒ SPACEMEN 3)

SPIDERS (see under ⇒ COOPER, Alice)

SPIN DOCTORS

Formed: New York, USA . . . 1991 by students at the New York New School Of Jazz. They were soon hitting the Top 10 in America with classy 'TWO PRINCES' single. • **Style:** Funky-metal likened to The ALLMAN BROTHERS or STEVE MILLER BAND. • **Songwriters:** Group penned except WOODSTOCK (Joni Mitchell). • **Trivia:** Produced by themselves plus PETER DENENBERG and FRANKIE LA ROCKA.

Recommended: POCKETFULL OF KRYPTONYTE (*6).

CHRIS BARRON – vocals / **ERIC SCHENKMAN** – guitar / **MARK WHITE** – bass / **AARON COMESS** – drums

Epic / Epic

Sep 92. (7") **LITTLE MISS CAN'T BE WRONG. / TWO PRINCES** [-] [ ]
Feb 93. (7")(c-s) **LITTLE MISS CAN'T BE WRONG. / WHAT TIME IS IT?** [ ] [-]
(cd-s+=) – Big fat funky booty – At this hour (live)
(re-iss. Jul 93, hit UK No. 23)
Mar 93. (cd)(c) **POCKET FULL OF KRYPTONYTE** [2] [3] Aug 92
– Jimmy Olsen's blues / What time is it? / Little Miss can't be wrong / forty or fifty / Refrigerator car / More than she knows / Two princes / Off my line / How could you want him (when you know you could have me?) / Shinbone alley – Hard to exist.*(released a year earlier in US)*
May 93. (7")(c-s) **TWO PRINCES. / OFF MY LINE** [3] [7] Jan 93
(cd-s) – ('A'side) / Yo mamas a pasama (live) / Little miss can't be wrong (live).
Sep 93. (7")(c-s) **JIMMY OLSEN'S BLUES. / AT THIS HOUR** [40] [78]
(cd-s+=) – Rosetta stone.
Nov 93. (7")(c-s) **WHAT TIME IS IT?. / ('A'live)** [56] [ ]
(cd-s+=) – Two princess (live) / Forty or fifty (live).
Dec 93. (cd)(c) **HOMEBELLY GROOVE (live)** [ ] [ ]
– What time is it? – Off my line / Freeway of the plains – Lady Kerosene / Yo baby / Little Miss can't be wrong / Shinbone alley / Refrigerator car / Sweet widow / Stepped on a crack / Yo mamas a pajama / Rosetta Stone.
Jun 94. (7"pic-d)(c-s) **CLEOPATRA'S CAT. / URANIUM CENTURY** [29] [84]
(cd-s+=) – Stop breaking down (live).
Jun 94. (cd)(c)(lp) **TURN IT UPSIDE DOWN** [3] [28]
– Big fat funky booty / You let your heart go too fast / Cleopatra's cat / Hungry Hamed's / Biscuit head / Indifference / Bags of dirt / Mary Jane / More than meets the ear / Laraby's gang / At this hour / Someday all this will be road / Beasts in the woods.
Jul 94. (7")(c-s) **YOU LET YOUR HEART GO TOO FAST. / PIECE OF GLASS** [66] [42]
(cd-s+=) – I can't.
Oct 94. (c-s) **MARY JANE / WOODSTOCK** [55] [ ]
(cd-s+=) – Hungry Hamed's.

— **ANTHONY KRIZAN** – guitar repl. ERIC

. . . Jan – Jun '96 stop press . . .

Jun 96. (single) **SHE USED TO BE MINE** [55] [ ]

SPIRIT

Formed: Los Angeles, California, USA . . . 1964 as The RED ROOSTERS by RANDY CALIFORNIA and his shaven-headed step-father ED CASSIDY. By late 1966, they became SPIRITS REBELLIOUS, but shortened to SPIRIT, with addition of other ex-RED ROOSTERS; JAY FERGUSON and MARK ANDES. Early in 1968, they signed to Lou Adler's 'Ode' records, which released eponymous debut soon after. The next year, they had first US Top 30 (and only) hit with drug-orientated 'I GOT A LINE ON YOU'. From 1970, they were haunted by numerous splits, and even a bogus SPIRIT!, which thought it could exist without RANDY + ED. • **Style:** Ecletic and progressive rock outfit, who diverted into psychedelia and the avant-garde. • **Songwriters:** CALIFORNIA and group, except YESTERDAY (Beatles) / HEY JOE (hit; Jimi Hendrix; c.William Roberts). CALIFORNIA covered solo:- MOTHER AND CHILD REUNION (Paul Simon) / RAIN + DAY TRIPPER (Beatles) / ALL ALONG THE WATCHTOWER (Bob Dylan) / WILD THING (Troggs). • **Trivia:** MARK ANDES played on BORIS PICKETT & THE CRYPT KICKER 5's hit single 'Monster Mash'. LED ZEPPELIN (Jimmy Page), must have listened to 1968 track 'TAURUS', before writing 'Stairway To Heaven'. Listen?

Recommended: TWELVE DREAMS OF DOCTOR SARDONICUS (*8) / THE BEST OF SPIRIT (*8) / POTATOLAND (*9)

RANDY CALIFORNIA (b.RANDY CRAIG WOLFE, 20 Feb'51, L.A., Calif) – guitar, vox / **JAY FERGUSON** (b.JOHN ARDEN FERGUSON, 10 May'47, Burnbank, Calif.) – vocals / **MARK ANDES** (b.19 Feb'48, Philadelphia) – bass (ex-YELLOW BALLOON, w /JAY) / **ED CASSIDY** (b. 4 May'31, Chicago) – drums (ex-NEW JAZZ TRIO) / **JOHN LOCKE** (b.25 Sep'53, L.A., Calif.) – keyboards (ex-NEW WORLD JAZZ CO.)

C.B.S. / Ode

Jun 68. (lp) **SPIRIT** [ ] [31] Jan 68
– Fresh garbage / Uncle Jack / Mechanical world / Taurus / Straight arrow / Topango windows / Gramophone man / Water woman / Great canyon fire in general / Elijah / Girl in your eyes. *(re-iss.Apr79 as 'THE FIRST OF . . . ' on 'CBS-Embassy') (re-iss.+c+cd.Apr89 on 'Edsel')*
Jun 68. (7") **UNCLE JACK. / MECHANICAL WORLD** [ ] [ ]
Feb 69. (7") **I GOT A LINE ON YOU. / SHE SMILED** [ ] [25] Dec 68
Apr 69. (lp) **THE FAMILY THAT PLAYS TOGETHER** [ ] [22] Jan 69
– I got a line on you / Poor Richard / Aren't you glad / It shall be / The drunkard / It's all the same / Dream within a dream / Jewish / So little to say / Silky Sam. *(US re-iss.Jul72) (re-iss.+c+cd.Mar86 on 'Edsel' +=)* – She smiles / Darlin' if, repl. track) *(cd-iss.Sep94 on 'Rewind')*
Aug 69. (7") **DARK EYED WOMAN. / ICE** [-] [ ]
Sep 69. (7") **DARK EYED WOMAN. / NEW DOPE AT TOWN** [ ] [ ]
Oct 69. (lp) **CLEAR SPIRIT** [ ] [55] Jul 69
– Dark eyed woman / Apple orchard / So little time to fly / Groundhog / Cold wind / Policeman's ball / Ice / Give a life, take a life / I'm truckin' / Clear / Caught / New dope in town. *(re-iss.+cd.Mar88 on 'Edsel')*
Jan 70. (7") **1984. / SWEET STELLA BABY** [ ] [69] Dec 69

Epic / Epic

Sep 70. (7") **ANIMAL ZOO. / RED LIGHT, ROLL ON** [ ] [97]
Oct 70. (7") **MR. SKIN. / NATURE'S WAY** [-] [92]
Dec 70. (7") **NATURE'S WAY. / SOLDIER** [ ] [-]

Feb 71. (lp) **TWELVE DREAMS OF DR. SARDONICUS** [ ] [63] Dec 70
– Nothing to hide / Nature's way / Animal zoo / Love has found a way / Why can't I be free / Mr. Skin / Space child / When I touch you / Sweet worm / Life has just begun / Morning will come / Soldier. *(re-iss.+c.Mar81) (re-iss.+c+cd.Apr89 on 'Edsel') (re-iss.cd+c May94)*
Mar 71. (7") **SOLDIER. / MR.SKIN** [ ] [-]

— (Dec70) **JOHN ARLISS** – bass repl. FERGUSON and ANDES who formed JO JO GUNNE (May71) **CASSIDY + LOCKE** recruited new men **AL STAEHELY** – bass (ex-PUMPKIN) / **J.CHRISTIAN** (b.CHRIS STAEHELY) – guitar repl. ARLISS + RANDY who went solo

May 72. (7") **CADILLAC COWBOYS. / DARKNESS** [ ] [ ]
Jun 72. (lp) **FEEDBACK** [ ] [63] Mar 72
– Chelsea girl / Cadillac / Cowboys / Puesta del scam / Ripe and ready / Darkness / Earth shaker / Mellow morning / Trancas fog-out / The witch.

— (Aug72) Now a totally 'bogus' SPIRIT, fronted by The STAEHELY brothers. **STU PERRY** – drums repl. CASSIDY (see further below), and LOCKE who went solo. An album 'STA-HAY-LEE', included CASSIDY and LOCKE surfaced in US later? CHRIS was another to join JO JO GUNNE. Regarded as the 'real SPIRIT'

RANDY CALIFORNIA

(solo!) with **TIM McGOVERN** – drums, vocals / **CHARLIE BUNDY** – bass, b.vox / **HENRY MANCKATITZ** (aka MITCH MITCHELL) – drums / **CLIT McTORIUS**(aka NOEL REDDING) – bass / guests **CASS STRANGE** (aka ED CASSIDY) – bass / **FUZZY KNIGHT** (aka ARRY WEISBER) – keyboards

Sep 72. (7") **WALKIN' THE DOG. / LIVE FOR THE DAY** [-] [ ]
Sep 72. (lp) **KAPTAIN KOPTER AND THE (FABULOUS) TWIRLY BIRDS** [ ] [ ]
– Downer / Devil / I don't want nobody / Day tripper / Mother and child reunion / Things yet to come / Rain / Rainbow. *(re-iss.+c.Jun80 on 'CBS') (re-iss. +c.Nov85 on 'Edsel'+=)* – Walkin' the dog / Live for the day. *(cd-iss.Aug93 on 'Edsel')*

— In 1973, CALIFORNIA attempted suicide by jumping off Chelsea Bridge.

SPIRIT

after a few other line-up's in 1974, settled with **CASSIDY, CALIFORNIA + MARK ANDES** who repl. FUZZY KNIGHT. **JOHN LOCKE** re-joined for short spell, until he went into sessions. Also ANDES (who joined FIREFALL) were repl. by **BARRY KEANE** – bass

Mercury Mercury

Jun 75. (d-lp)(d-c) **SPIRIT OF '76** [ ] [ ]
– America the beautiful / The times they are a-changin' / Victim of society / Lady of the lakes / Tampa man / Mounalo / What do I have / Sunrise / Walking the dog / Joker on the run / When? / Like a rolling stone / Once again / Feeling in time / Happy / Jack Bond (part 1) / Mr. Road / Thank you Lord / Urantia / Guide me / Veruska / Hey Joe / Jack Bond (part 2) / The star spangled banner. *(re-iss.May88 on 'Edsel') (cd-iss.Mar93)*
Aug 75. (7") **AMERICA THE BEAUTIFUL. / THE TIMES THEY ARE A-CHANGIN' / LADY OF THE LAKES** [-] [ ]

— added **MATT ANDES** – guitar (ex-JO JO GUNNE)

Oct 75. (lp)(c) **SON OF SPIRIT** [-] [ ]
– Holy man / Looking into darkness / Maybe you'll find / Don't go away / Family / Magic fairy princess / Circle / The other song / Yesterday / It's time now. *(UK-iss.+cd.May89 on 'Great Expectation')*
Oct 75. (7") **HOLY MAN. / LOOKING INTO DARKNESS** [-] [ ]
Jul 76. (lp) **FARTHER ALONG** [ ] [ ]
– Farther along / Atomic boogie / World eat world dog / Stoney night / Pineapple / Colossus / Mega star / Phoebe / Don't look up your door / Once with you / Diamond spirit / Nature's way.
Sep 76. (7") **FARTHER ALONG. / ATOMIC BOOGIE** [-] [ ]

— Now just a trio, when MARK re-joined FIREFALL and MATT & JOHN also left.

Apr 77. (lp)(c) **FUTURE GAMES (A MAGICAL KAHVANA DREAM)** [ ] [ ]
– CB talk / Stars are love / Kahouna dream / Brued my brain / Bionic unit / So happy now / All along the watchtower / Would you believe / Jack Bond speaks / Star Trek dreaming / Interlude XM / China doll / Hawaiian times / Gorn attack / Interlude 2001 / Detroit City / Freak out frog / The Romulan experiences / Monkey see, monkey do / Mt. Olympus / The journey of Nomad / Ending. *(re-iss.+cd.May89 on 'Great Expectations')*
May 77. (7") **ALL ALONG THE WATCHTOWER. / FARTHER ALONG** [ ] [ ]

— **LARRY KNIGHT** – bass returned to repl. KEENE

Illegal Potato

Dec 78. (7") **NATURE'S WAY (live). / STONE FREE (live)** [ ] [ ]
Jan 79. (lp) **SPIRIT LIVE** (live 11th Mar'78, Rainbow, London) [ ] [ ]
– Rock and roll planet / Nature's way / Animal zoo / 1984 / Looking down / It's all the same / I got a line on you / These are words / Hollywood dream.

— Disbanded yet again late 1978, RANDY formed own band with **STEVE LAURA** – bass / **JACK WILLOUGHBY** – drums.

SPIRIT

re-formed to re-record old unissued lost album below. **CALIFORNIA & CASSIDY** (alias KAPTAIN KOPTER & COMMANDER CASSIDY) enlisted **GEORGE VALUCK, JOHN LOCKE, MIKE BUNNELL + KARI NILE** – keys / **JEFF JARVIS, MIKE THORNBURGH + CHUCK SNYDER** – horns / **JOE GREEN** – strings

Beggar's B. Rhino

Apr 81. (lp)(c) **JOURNEY TO POTATOLAND** [40] [ ]
– We've got a lot to learn / Potatolandland theme / Open up your heart / Morning light / Potatoland prelude / Potatoland intro / Turn to the right / Donut house / Fish fry road / Information / My friend. *(re-iss.+cd+dat.1988 on 'Chord')*
Apr 81. (7") **WE'VE GOT A LOT TO LEARN. / FISH FRY ROAD** [ ] [ ]
Jun 81. (7") **TURN TO THE RIGHT. / POTATOLAND THEME** [ ] [ ]

— Band toured 1981:- **CALIFORNIA, CASSIDY, VALUCK + STEVE LAURA** (aka LIBERTY)

RANDY CALIFORNIA

solo including all present SPIRIT members and some past.

Apr 82. (lp)(c) **EURO AMERICAN** [ ] [ ]
– Easy love / Fearless leader / Five in the morning / Skull and crossbones / Breakout / Hand gun (toy guns) / This is the end / Mon ami / Rude reaction / Calling you / Wild thing. (free-7"w.a.) **SHATTERED DREAMS. / MAGIC WAND**
Apr 82. (7") **HAND GUNS (TOY GUNS). / THIS IS THE END** [ ] [ ]
Aug 82. (7") **ALL ALONG THE WATCHTOWER. / RADIO MAN** [ ] [ ]
(12"+=) – Breakout / Killer weed.

SPIRIT

originals re-formed re-recording material from that era.

Mercury Mercury

Jan 84. (7") **1984. / ELIJAH** [ ] [ ]
(12"+=) – I got a line on you.
Mar 84. (lp)(c)(cd) **THE THIRTEENTH DREAM** (remixes) [ ] [ ]
– Black satin nights / Mr. Skin / Mechanical world / Pick it up / All over the world / 1984 / Uncle Jack / Natures way / Fresh garbage / I got a line on you. *(c+=)* – Elijah.
Apr 84. (7")(6") **FRESH GARBAGE. / MR. SKIN** [ ] [ ]

RANDY CALIFORNIA

solo with live + studio **MIKE SHEPHERD** – bass / **NEIL MURRAY + ADRIAN LEE + NEAL DOUGHTY** – keyboards / **CURLY SMITH** – drums live: **SCOTT MONAHAN** – keys / **LES WARNER** – drums

Vertigo Mercury

May 85. (7") **RUN TO YOUR LOVER. / SECOND CHILD** [ ] [ ]
(12"+=) – Shane.
Jun 85. (lp)(c) **RESTLESS** [ ] [ ]
– Run to your lover / Restless nights / Second child / Jack Rabbit / Shane / One man's Heaven / Murphy's law / Camelot / Battle march of the overlords / Childhood's end.
Jun 85. (7") **JACK RABBIT. / SUPER CHILD** [ ] [ ]

Line not issued

1986. (lp) **SHATTERED DREAMS** [-] [-] Germ'y
– Hey Joe (live) / Shattered dreams / All along the watchtower / Don't bother me / Downer / Second child / Man at war / Killer weed / Hand guns (toy guns) / Radio man / Run to your lover.

— In Apr'89, RANDY appeared on Various Artists live d-lp,c,cd,video 'NIGHT OF THE GUITAR', which was on next label.

RANDY CALIFORNIA'S SPIRIT

gigged with various line-ups, until in 1989 settled with **RANDY, ED + SCOTT** plus **MIKE BUNNELL** – bass

I.R.S. I.R.S.

Jun 89. (7") **HARD LOVE. / THE PRISONER** [ ] [ ]
(12"+=) – Hey Joe.
Aug 89. (lp)(c)(cd) **RAPTURE IN THE CHAMBERS** [ ] [ ]
– Hard love / Love tonight / Thinking of / Rapture in the chambers / Mojo man / Contact / The prisoner / One track mind / Enchanted forest / Human sexuality / Shera, princess of power / End suite.

– compilations, others, etc. –

Apr 73. Epic; (7") **MR.SKIN. / NATURE'S WAY** [ ] [ ]
Aug 73. Epic; (d-lp) **SPIRIT. / CLEAR SPIRIT** [-] [ ]
Oct 73. Epic; (lp)(c) **THE BEST OF SPIRIT** [ ] [ ] Jul 73
(re-iss.Sep84, US re-iss.May89)
Dec 91. Columbia; (d-cd)(d-c) **TIME CIRCLE (1968-72)** [ ] [ ]
Jan 92. Castle; (cd)(c) **THE COLLECTION** [ ] [-]

SPIRITUALIZED (see under ⇒ SPACEMEN 3)

SPLIT ENZ (see under ⇒ CROWDED HOUSE)

Bruce SPRINGSTEEN

Born: 23 Sep'49, Freehold, New Jersey, USA. In 1969, he formed STEEL MILL, but they disbanded after 2 years, although 3 of them (VAN ZANDT, FEDERICKI + LOPEZ) soon became part of his 10-piece back-up band. In May'72, SPRINGSTEEN signed to 'Columbia' and set up recording debut album 'GREETINGS FROM ASBURY PARK, N.J.' with band. Released early '73, it originally sold poorly, as did his follow-up 'THE WILD, THE INNOCENT & THE E-STREET SHUFFLE'. After the latter's completion, he toured with backing band The E-STREET BAND, and gained enough renewed respect for his first two albums to both hit US Top 60 in mid-75. The much anticipated 3rd album 'BORN TO RUN', gave him breakthrough into superstardom, which stayed with him throughout the next 2 decades. • **Style:** Groomed by record co. as the next DYLAN, he moved into harder-edged rock'n'roll by the mid-70's and soon became known as 'The Boss'. After a very dissappointing 1982 folk/demo album 'NEBRASKA', he returned with the flag-waving multi-million selling 'BORN IN THE U.S.A.'. • **Songwriters:** All self-penned except; JERSEY GIRL (Tom Waits) / WAR (Edwin Starr) / SANTA CLAUS IS COMING TO TOWN (festive trad.) / VIVA LAS VEGAS (Elvis Presley) etc. • **Trivia:** SPRINGSTEEN produced 2 albums by GARY U.S.BONDS; DEDICATION (1981) / ON THE LINE (1982), which featured The BOSS's songs. He also provided songs for; SPIRIT IN THE NIGHT + BLINDED BY THE LIGHT for (Manfred Mann's Earth Band) / SANDY (Hollies) / FIRE (Robert Gordon) + (Pointer Sisters) / BECAUSE THE NIGHT (Patti Smith) / FOR YOU (Greg Kihn) / FROM SMALL THINGS (Dave Edmunds) / DANCING IN THE DARK (Big Daddy) / etc. On 13 May'85, BRUCE married model/actress Julianne Phillips, but she filed for divorce in August 1988, after seeing photographic newspaper evidence of a burgeoning relationship between BRUCE and backing singer PATTI SCIALFA. She had his child Evan James on 25 Jul'90.

Recommended: GREETINGS FROM ASBURY PARK, N.J. (*6) / THE WILD, THE INNOCENT & THE E-STREET SHUFFLE (*6) / BORN TO RUN (*9) / DARKNESS ON THE EDGE OF TOWN (*8) / THE RIVER (*7) / NEBRASKA (*7) / BORN IN THE U.S.A. (*8) / TUNNEL OF LOVE (*6) / HUMAN TOUCH (*5) / LUCKY TOWN (*5) / GHOST OF TOM JOAD (*6)

BRUCE SPRINGSTEEN – vocals, guitar / **DAVID SANCIOUS + DANNY FEDERICI** – keyboards / **GARRY TALLENT** – bass / **VINI LOPEZ** – drums / **CLARENCE CLEMENS** – saxophone / **STEVE VAN ZANDT** – lead guitar (left before recording of debut album)

C.B.S. / Columbia

Feb 73. (7") **BLINDED BY THE LIGHT. / ANGEL** [-] [ ]

Mar 73. (lp)(c) **GREETINGS FROM ASBURY PARK, N.J.** [ ] [ ] Jan73
– Blinded by the light / Growin' up / Mary Queen of Arkansas / Does this bus stop at 82nd Street / Lost in the flood / The angel / For you / / Spirit in the night / It's hard to be a saint in the city. *(hit No.60 in the US; Jul75) (UK re-iss.Nov82, re-iss.Jun85, hit No.41, cd-iss.1986)*

May 73. (7") **SPIRIT IN THE NIGHT. / FOR YOU** [-] [ ]

— For live appearances The BRUCE SPRINGSTEEN BAND now The E-STREET SHUFFLE. **ERNEST CARTER** – drums repl. LOPEZ

Feb 74. (lp)(c) **THE WILD, THE INNOCENT & THE E-STREET SHUFFLE** [ ] [ ] Nov 73
– The E-Street shuffle / 4th of July, Asbury Park (Sandy) / Kitty's back / Wild Billy's circus story / Incident on 57th Street / Rosalita (come out tonight) / New York City serenade. *(hit No.59 in the US; Jul75) (UK re-iss.Nov83, re-iss.Jun85, hit No.33, cd-iss.Apr89)*

— **ROY BITTAN** – piano / **MAX WEINBERG** – drums / and the returning **VAN ZANDT** repl. SANCIOUS and CARTER

Oct 75. (lp)(c) **BORN TO RUN** [17] [3] Sep 75
– Thunder road / Tenth Avenue freeze-out / Night / Backstreets / Born to run / She's the one / Meeting across the river / Jungleland. *(re-iss.Jan87 boxed w / free-7")* **BECAUSE THE NIGHT. / SSPIRIT IN THE NIGHT***(cd-iss.1983 + 1988)(re-iss.cdJun93)*

Oct 75. (7") **BORN TO RUN. / MEETING ACROSS THE RIVER** [ ] [23] Sep 75

Feb 76. (7") **TENTH AVENUE FREEZE-OUT. / SHE'S THE ONE** [ ] [83] Jan 76

Jun 78. (7") **PROVE IT ALL NIGHT. / FACTORY** [ ] [33]

Jun 78. (lp)(c)(US-pic-d) **DARKNESS ON THE EDGE OF TOWN** [16] [5]
– Badlands / Adam raised a Cain / Something in the street / Candy's room / Racing in the street / Promised land / Factory / Streets of fire / Prove it all night / Darkness on the edge of town. *(re-iss.+cd.Jul84)*

Jul 78. (7") **BADLANDS. / STREETS OF FIRE** [-] [42]

Jul 78. (7") **BADLANDS. / SOMETHING IN THE NIGHT** [ ] [-]

Oct 78. (7") **PROMISED LAND. / STREETS OF FIRE** [ ] [ ]

Oct 80. (d-lp)(d-c) **THE RIVER** [2] [1]
– The ties that bind / Sherry darling / Jackson cage / Two hearts / Independence day / Hungry heart / Out in the street / Crush on you / You can look (but you better not touch) / I wanna marry you / The river / Point blank / Cadillac ranch / I'm a rocker / Fade away / Stolen car / Ramrod / The price you pay / Drive all night / Wreck on the highway. *(d-cd-iss.1985) (re-iss.d-cd+d-c Oct94 on 'Columbia')*

Nov 80. (7") **HUNGRY HEART. / HELD UP WITHOUT A GUN** [44] [5]

Jan 81. (7") **FADE AWAY. / BE TRUE** [-] [20]

Feb 81. (7") **SHERRY DARLING. / BE TRUE** [ ] [ ]

May 81. (7") **THE RIVER. / INDEPENDENCE DAY** [35] [ ]
(12") – ('A'side) / Born to run / Rosalita.

Aug 81. (7") **CADILLAC RANCH. / WRECK ON THE HIGHWAY** [ ] [ ]

Sep 82. (lp)(c) **NEBRASKA** [3] [3]
– Nebraska / Atlantic City / Mansion on the hill / Johnny 99 / Highway patrolman / State trooper / Used cars / Open all night / My father's house / Reason to believe. *(re-iss.+cd.Feb89)*

Oct 82. (7") **ATLANTIC CITY. / MANSION ON THE HILL** [ ] [ ]

Nov 82. (7") **OPEN ALL NIGHT. / THE BIG PAYBACK** [ ] [ ]

— **NILS LOFGREN** – lead guitar (Solo artist) repl. VAN ZANDT to solo as LITTLE STEVEN / added **PATTI SCIALFA** – backing vox (ex-SOUTHSIDE JOHNNY)

May 84. (7")(12")(7"sha-pic-d) **DANCING IN THE DARK. / PINK CADILLAC** [28] [2]
(re-entered UK charts Jan85, hit No.4)

Jun 84. (lp)(c)(cd)(pic-lp) **BORN IN THE U.S.A.** [1] [1]
– Born in the U.S.A. / Cover me / Darlington County / Working on the highway / Downbound train / I'm on fire / No surrender / Bobby Jean / I'm goin' down / Glory days / Dancing in the dark / My hometown.

Sep 84. (7") **COVER ME. / JERSEY GIRL** [38] [7] Aug 84
(d7"+=) – Dancing in the dark / Pink Cadillac.
(12"+=) – Dancing in the dark (dub version).

Nov 84. (7") **BORN IN THE U.S.A. / SHUT OUT THE LIGHTS** [-] [9]

Jan 85. (7") **I'M ON FIRE. / JOHNNY BYE BYE** [-] [6]

Mar 85. (7")(7"sha-pic-d) **COVER ME. / JERSEY GIRL** [16] [-]
(12"+=) – Dancing in the dark (dub) / Shut out the light / Cover me (dub).

May 85. (7") **I'M ON FIRE. / BORN IN THE U.S.A. (mix)** [5] [-]
(12"+=) – Rosalita / Bye Bye Johnny.

Jul 85. (7")(12") **GLORY DAYS. / STAND ON IT** [17] [5] May 85

Aug 85. (7") **I'M GOIN' DOWN. / JANEY, DON'T YOU LOSE HEART** [-] [9]

Dec 85. (7")(12") **MY HOMETOWN. / SANTA CLAUS IS COMIN' TO TOWN** [9] [6]

Nov 86. (7") **WAR (live). / MERRY XMAS BABY** [18] [8]
(12"+=) – Incident on 57th Street.

Dec 86. (5xlp-box)(3xc-box)(3xcd-box) **LIVE 1977-1985 (live)** [4] [1] Nov 86
– Thunder road / Adam raised a Cain / Fire / Spirit in the night / 4th of July – Asbury Park (Sandy) / Paradise by the 'C' / Growin' up / It's hard to be a saint in the city / Backstreets / Rosalita (come out tonight) / Raise your hand / Hungry heart / Two hearts / Cadillac ranch / You can look (but you better not touch) / War / Candy's room / Badlands / Because the night / Independence day / Johnny 99 / Darkness on the edge of town / Racing in the street / Nebraska / This land is your land / Working on the highway / Reason to believe / Born in the U.S.A. / Seeds / The river / Born to run / Darlington County / Jersey girl / Bobby Jean / Cover me / My hometown / No surrender / I'm on fire / The promised land.

Jan 87. (7") **FIRE (live). / INCIDENT ON 57TH STREET** [-] [46]

Jan 87. (7")(12") **FIRE (live). / FOR YOU (live)** [54] [-]

May 87. (7") **BORN TO RUN (live). / JOHNNY 99 (live)** [16] [-]
(12"+=)/ /(d12"++=) – Seeds (live)./ / Because the night (live).
(cd-s+=) – Spirit in the night (live) / Seeds (live).

Sep 87. (7")(12") **BRILLIANT DISGUISE. / LUCKY MAN** [20] [5]

Oct 87. (lp)(c)(cd)(pic-lp)(pic-cd) **TUNNEL OF LOVE** [1] [1]
– Ain't got you / Tougher than the rest / All that Heaven will allow / Spare parts / Cautious man / Walk like a man / Tunnel of love / Two faces / Brilliant disguise / One step up / When you're alone / Valentine's day.

Dec 87. (7")(12")(7"sha-pic-d) **TUNNEL OF LOVE. / TWO FOR THE ROAD** [45] [9]
(cd-s+=) – Santa Claus is comin' to town.

Mar 88. (7") **ONE STEP UP. / ROULETTE** [ ] [13] Feb 88
(12"+=)(cd-s+=) – Lucky man.

Jun 88. (7") **TOUGHER THAN THE REST. / ROULETTE** [13] [ ]
(12"+=) – ('A'live) / Be true (live).
(cd-s+=) – Born to run (live).

Oct 88. (7")(12") **SPARE PARTS. / PINK CADILLAC** [32] [ ]
(cd-s+=) – ('A'live version) / Chimes of freedom.

— new band:- **SHANE FONTAYNE** – guitar / **ZACHERY ALFORD** – drums / **TOMMY SIMMS** – bass / **ROY BITTAN** – keyboards / **CRYSTAL TALIEFERO** – guitar, percussion, vocals / + backing vocalists.

Columbia / Columbia

Mar 92. (c-s) **HUMAN TOUCH. / BETTER DAYS** [-] [16]

Mar 92. (7")(c-s) **HUMAN TOUCH. / SOULS OF THE DEPARTED** [11] [-]
(12"+=)(cd-s+=)(pic-cd-d+=) – Long goodbye.

Mar 92. (cd)(c)(lp) **HUMAN TOUCH** [1] [2]
– Human touch / Soul driver / 57 channels (and nothin' on) / Cross my heart /

Gloria's eyes / With every wish / Roll of the dice / Real world / All or nothin' at al / Man's job / I wish I were blind / Long goodbye / Real man / Pony boy.

Mar 92. (cd)(c)(lp) **LUCKY TOWN** [2] [3]
– Better days / Lucky town / Local hero / If I should fall apart / Leap of faith / Big Muddy / Living proof / Book of dreams / Souls of the departed / My beautiful reward.

May 92. (7")(c-s) **BETTER DAYS. / TOUGHER THAN THE REST** [34] [ ]
(12"+=)(cd-s+=) – Part man, part monkey.

Jun 92. (7") **57 CHANNELS (AND NOTHIN' ON). / PART MAN, PART MONKEY** [-] [68]

Jul 92. (7")(c-s) **57 CHANNELS (AND NOTHIN' ON). / STAND ON IT** [32] [-]
(cd-s+=) – Janey don't you lose heart.

Oct 92. (7")(c-s) **LEAP OF FAITH. / ('A'version)** [46] [ ]
(cd-s+=) – Shut out the light / The big payback.
(cd-s) – ('A'side) / 30 days out.

Apr 93. (7")(c-s) **LUCKY TOWN (live). / ('A' version)** [48] [ ]
(cd-s+=) – Human touch (live)

Apr 93. (cd)(c)(lp) **IN CONCERT – MTV PLUGGED (live)** [4] [ ]
– Red headed woman / Better days / Atlantic city / Darkness on the edge of town / Man's job / Human touch / Lucky town / I wish I were blind / Thunder Road / Light of day / If I should fall behind / Living proof / My beautiful reward.

Wife PATTI had child on 5th Jan'94.

Below from the film 'Philadelphia', which won an Oscar for Tom Hanks.

Mar 94. (7")(12")(c-s) **STREETS OF PHILADELPHIA. / IF I SHOULD FALL BEHIND** [2] [9] Feb94
(cd-s+=) – Growing up (live) / The big Muddy (live).

Feb 95. (cd)(c) **GREATEST HITS** (compilation) [1] [1]
– Born to run / Thunder road / Badlands / The river / Hungry heart / Atlantic city / Dancing in the dark / Born in the U.S.A. / My hometown / Glory days / Brilliant disguise / Human touch / Better days / Streets of Philadelphia / Secret garden / Murder incorporated / Blood brothers / This hard land.

Apr 95. (c-s) **SECRET GARDEN / THUNDER ROAD (plugged version)** [44] [63]
(cd-s+=) – Murder incorporated.
(cd-s) – ('A'side) / Because the night / Pink Cadillac / 4th Of July, Asbury Park (Sandy).

Oct 95. (7"pic-d)(c-s) **HUNGRY HEART. / STREETS OF PHILADELPHIA** [28] [ ]
(cd-s+=) – ('A'-Berlin '95 version) / Thunder Road.

Nov 95. (cd)(c) **THE GHOST OF TOM JOAD** [16] [11]
– The ghost of Tom Joad / Straight time / Highway 29 / Youngstown / Sinaola cowboys / The line / Balboa Park / Dry lightning / The new timer / Across the border / Galveston Bay / The best was never good enough.

. . . Jan – Jun '96 stop press . . .

Apr 96. (single) **THE GHOST OF TOM JOAD** [26] [ ]

– compilations, others, etc. –

Nov 85. CBS; (lp-set) **BOXED SET 12" SINGLES** [ ] [ ]

1988. CBS; (d-cd) **NEBRASKA / BORN IN THE U.S.A.** [ ] [ ]

Mar 93. Columbia; (d-cd) **DARKNESS ON THE EDGE OF TOWN / NEBRASKA** [ ] [ ]
(re-iss.Feb95)

Jan 94. Dare Int.; (d-cd)(d-c)(d-lp) **PRODIGAL SON** [ ] [ ]

SQUEEZE

Formed: Deptford, South London, England ... Mar'74 by DIFFORD, TILBROOK and boogie pianist JOOLS HOLLAND. In 1976 they signed to 'BTM', but had debut 45 withdrawn. Afer releasing an indie EP, they transferred to major 'A&M' label late in '77. Early in 1978, they cracked the Top 20 with 'TAKE ME I'M YOURS', but this was surpassed the next year when they nearly hit No.1 twice with 'COOL FOR CATS' & 'UP THE JUNCTION'. • **Style:** Initially a pub rock / new wave outfit, who went into areas of pop, country, soul & AOR. • **Songwriters:** Mostly DIFFORD & TILBROOK compositions, and some by CARRACK who joined late 1980. Covered END OF THE CENTURY (Blur). • **Trivia:** JOOLS HOLLAND went on to become successful TV presenter, mainly for C4's 'The Tube', BBC2's 'Juke Box Jury', + most recently 'Later with Jools Holland'.

Recommended: ARGYBARGY (*7) / EAST SIDE STORY (*7) / GREATEST HITS (*8).

CHRIS DIFFORD (b. 4 Nov'54) – vocals, guitar / **GLENN TILBROOK** (b.31 Aug'57) – vocals, guitar / **JOOLS HOLLAND** (b.JULIAN, 24 Jan'58) – keyboards / **HARRY KAKOULI** – bass / **PAUL GUNN** – drums (below 45 withdrawn from release)

B.T.M. / not issued

Jan 77. (7") **TAKE ME I'M YOURS. / NO DISCO KID, NO** [-] [-]

— **GILSON LAVIS** (b.27 Jun'51) – drums (ex-MUSTARD) repl. GUNN

Deptford Fun City / not issued

Aug 77. (7"ep) **PACKET OF THREE** [ ] [-]
– Cat on a wall / Back track / Night ride. *(re-iss.12" Nov79)*

A & M / A & M

Feb 78. (7") **TAKE ME, I'M YOURS. / NIGHT NURSE** [19] [ ]

Mar 78. (lp)(c) **SQUEEZE** [ ] [ ]
– Sex master / Bang bang / Strong in reason / Wild sewerage tickles Brazil / Out of control / Take me, I'm yours / The call / Model / Remember what / First thing wrong / Hesitation (rool Britania) / Get smart. *(re-iss.Mar82)*

May 78. (7")(7"green) **BANG BANG. / ALL FED UP** [49] [-]

— **JOHN BENTLEY** (b.16 Apr'51) – bass repl. KAKOULI who went solo

Nov 78. (7") **GOODBYE GIRL. / SAINTS ALIVE** [63] [-]

Mar 79. (7")(12")(7"pink)(12"pink)(7"red) **COOL FOR CATS. / MODEL** [2] [ ]

Apr 79. (lp)(c) **COOL FOR CATS** [45] [ ]
– Slap and tickle / Revue / Touching me, touching you / It's not cricket / It's so dirty / The knack / Hop, skip and jump / Up the junction / Hard to find / Slightly drunk / Goodbye girl / Cool for cats. *(re-iss.Nov85, cd-iss.Mar91)*

May 79. (7")(7"lilac) **UP THE JUNCTION. / IT'S SO DIRTY** [2] [-]

Jun 79. (7") **SLIGHTLY DRUNK. / GOODBYE GIRL** [-] [ ]

Aug 79. (7")(7"red) **SLAP AND TICKLE. / ALL'S WELL** [24] [ ]

Nov 79. (7")(7"white) **CHRISTMAS DAY. / GOING CRAZY** [ ] [-]

Jan 80. (7")(7"clear) **ANOTHER NAIL IN MY HEART. / PRETTY THING** [17] [-]

Feb 80. (7") **IF I DIDN'T LOVE YOU. / PRETTY ONE** [-] [ ]

Feb 80. (lp)(c) **ARGYBARGY** [32] [71]
– Pulling mussels (from the shell) / Another nail in my heart / Seperate beds / Misadventure / I think I'm go go / Farfisa beat / Here comes that feeling / Vicky Verky / If I didn't love you / Wrong side of the Moon / There at the top.

Apr 80. (7")(7"red) **PULLING MUSSELS (FROM THE SHELL). / WHAT THE BUTLER SAW** [44] [-]

Jun 80. (7") **PULLING MUSSELS (FROM THE SHELL). / PRETTY ONE** [-] [ ]

Sep 80. (7") **ANOTHER NAIL IN MY HEART. / GOING CRAZY / WHAT THE BUTLER SAW** [-] [ ]
(re-iss. US Sep 82)

— **PAUL CARRACK** (b. Apr51, Sheffield) – keyboards (ex-ACE, ex-FRANKIE MILLER, ex-ROXY MUSIC) repl. JOOLS who formed his own MILLIONAIRES

Apr 81. (7") **IS THAT LOVE. / TRUST** [35] [ ]

May 81. (lp)(c) **EAST SIDE STORY** [19] [44]
– In quintessence / Someone else's heart / Tempted / Piccadilly / There's no tomorrow / A woman's world / Is that love / F-hole / Labelled with love / Someone else's bell / Mumbo jumbo / Vanity fair / Messed around. *(re-iss.Sep86, cd-iss.Jan87 & Mar91)*

Jul 81. (7") **TEMPTED. / YAP YAP YAP** [40] [-]

Jul 81. (7") **TEMPTED. / TRUST** [-] [49]
(free-5"w.a.) **ANOTHER NAIL IN MY HEART. / IF I DIDN'T LOVE YOU**

Sep 81. (7") **LABELLED WITH LOVE. / SQUABS ON FORTY FAB** [4] [ ]

Oct 81. (7") **MESSED AROUND. / YAP YAP YAP** [-] [ ]

— **DON SNOW** – keyboards (ex-VIBRATORS, ex-SINCEROS) repl. CARRACK (now solo)

Apr 82. (7")(7"pic-d) **BLACK COFFEE IN BED. / THE HUNT** [51] [ ] Jul 82

Apr 82. (12") **WHEN THE HANGOVER STRIKES. / I'VE RETURNED** [-] [ ]

May 82. (lp)(c) **SWEETS FROM A STRANGER** [37] [32]
– Out of touch / I can't hold on / Points of view / Stranger than the stranger on the shore / Onto the dance floor / When the hangover strikes / Black coffee in bed / I've returned / Tongue like a knife / His house her home / The very last dance / The elephant ride.

Jul 82. (7")(7"pic-d) **WHEN THE HANGOVER STRIKES. / THE ELEPHANT RIDE** [ ] [-]

Oct 82. (7") **ANNIE GET YOUR GUN. / SPANISH GUITAR** [43] [ ] Feb 83

Nov 82. (lp)(c) **THE SINGLES – 45 AND UNDER** (compilation) [3] [47]
– Take me I'm yours / Goodbye girl / Cool for cats / Up the junction / Slap and tickle / Another nail in my heart / Pulling mussels (from the shell) / Tempted / Is that love / Labelled with love / Black coffee in bed / Annie get your gun. *(cd-iss.Dec84, 1 diff. track)*

— Split at same time of compilation.

DIFFORD & TILBROOK

carried on as duo, augmented by **KEITH WILKINSON** – bass / other musicians

A & M / A & M

Jun 84. (7")(12") **LOVE'S CRASHING WAVES. / WITHIN THESE WALLS WITHOUT YOU** [57] [-]

Jun 84. (lp)(c) **DIFFORD & TILBROOK** [47] [55]
– Action speaks faster / Love's crashing waves / Picking up the pieces / On my mind tonight / Man for all seasons / Hope fell down / Wag-on train / You can't hurt the girl / Tears for attention / The apple tree.

Jun 84. (7") **WITHIN THESE WALLS. / PICKING UP THE PIECES** [-] [ ]

Oct 84. (7")(12") **HOPE FELL DOWN. / ACTION SPEAKS FASTER** [ ] [-]

SQUEEZE

reformed '78 line-up. -**KEITH WILKINSON** – bass (not HARRY)

A & M A & M

Jun 85. (7")(12") **LAST TIME FOREVER. / SUITE FROM FIVE STRANGERS** [45] [ ]

Aug 85. (lp)(c)(cd) **COSI FAN TUTTI FRUTTI** [31] [57]
– Big bang / By your side / King George Street / I learnt how to pray / Last time forever / No place like home / Heartbreakin' world / Hits of the year / Break my heart / I won't ever go drinking again.

Sep 85. (7") **HITS OF THE YEAR. / THE FORTNIGHT SAGA** [-] [ ]

Sep 85. (7") **NO PLACE LIKE HOME. / THE FORTNIGHT SAGA** [ ] [ ]
(12"+=) – Last time forever.

Nov 85. (7") **HEARTBREAKING WORLD. / BIG BANG** [ ] [ ]
(12"+=) – By your side (live) / Tempted (live) / Last time forever.

Apr 86. (7") **KING GEORGE STREET. / LOVE'S CRASHING WAVES (live)** [ ] [ ]
(12"+=) – Up the junction (live).

— added **ANDY METCALFE** – keyboards (ex-SOFT BOYS)

Aug 87. (7") **HOURGLASS. / WEDDING BELLS** [16] [15]
(12"+=) – Splitting into three.

Sep 87. (lp)(c)(cd) **BABYLON AND ON** [14] [36]
– Hourglass / Footprints / Tough love / The prisoner / 853-5937 / In today's room / Trust me to open my mouth / Striking matches / Cigarette of a single man / Who are you? / The waiting game / Some Americans.

Sep 87. (7") **TRUST ME TO OPEN MY MOUTH. / TAKE ME, I'M YOURS (live)** [72] [-]
(12"+=) – Black coffee in bed.

Nov 87. (7") **THE WAITING GAME. / LAST TIME FOREVER** [ ] [ ]
(12"+=) – The prisoner.

Dec 87. (7") **853-5937. / TAKE ME I'M YOURS (live)** [-] [32]

Jan 88. (7") **853-5937. / TOUGH LOVE** [ ] [-]
(12"+=) – ('A'bonus mix).

Apr 88. (7") **FOOTPRINTS. / BLACK COFFEE IN BED (live)** [-] [ ]

Jun 88. (7") **FOOTPRINTS. / STRIKING MATCHES – INSTANT BUFF** [ ] [-]
(12"+=) – In today's room.

— Reverted back to 5-piece when METCALFE departed.

Sep 89. (7") **IF IT'S LOVE. / FRANK'S HAG** [ ] [ ]
(12"+=)(cd-s+=) – Vanity fair.

Sep 89. (lp)(c)(cd) **FRANK** [58] [ ]
– Frank / If it's love / Peyton Place / Rose I said / Slaughtered, gutted and heartbroken / (This could be) The last time / She doesn't have to shave / Love circles / Melody hotel / Can of worms / Dr. Jazz / Is it too late.

Jan 90. (7") **LOVE CIRCLES. / RED LIGHT** [ ] [ ]
(12"+=)(cd-s+=) – Who's that.

— JOOLS left again to go solo and take up more TV work. In 1991 he was repl. by **MATT IRVING + STEVE NIEVE** – keyboards / **TONY BERG** – guitar, keyboards / **BRUCE HORNSBY** – accordion

Reprise Reprise

Jul 91. (7")(c-s) **SUNDAY STREET. / MAIDSTONE** [ ] [ ]
(12"+=)(cd-s+=) – Mood swings.

Aug 91. (cd)(c)(lp) **PLAY** [41] [ ]
– Satisfied / Crying in my sleep / Letting go / The day I get home / The truck / House of love / Cupid's toy / Gone to the dogs / Walk a straight line / Sunday street / Wicked and cruel / There is a voice. *(re-iss.cd Feb95)*

— **DIFFORD + TILBROOK + WILKINSON** plus returning **PAUL CARRACK** – keyboards / **PETE THOMAS** – drums

A & M A & M

Jul 93. (7")(c-s) **THIRD RAIL. / TAKE ME I'M YOURS (live)** [39] [ ]
(cd-s+=) – Cool for cats (live medley).
(cd-s) – ('A'side) / The truth (live) / Melody hotel (live) / Walk a straight line (live).

Sep 93. (7")(c-s) **SOME FANTASTIC PLACE. / JUMPING** [73] [ ]
(cd-s+=) – Dark saloons / Discipline.
(cd-s) – ('A'side) / Is that the time? / Don't be a stranger / Stark naked.

Sep 93. (cd)(c)(lp) **SOME FANTASTIC PLACE** [26] [ ]
– Everything in the world / Some fantastiv place / Third rail / Loving you tonight / It's over / Cold shoulder / Talk to him / Jolly comes home / Images of loving / True colours (the storm) / Pinocchio.

Oct 93. (7")(c-s) **LOVING YOU TONIGHT. / ('A'mix)** [ ] [ ]
(12"+=)(cd-s+=) – Tempted / Third rail.

Feb 94. (7")(c-s) **IT'S OVER. / IS THAT LOVE? (live)** [ ] [ ]
(cd-s+=) – Pulling mussels (from the shell) / Goodbye girl (live).

Aug 95. (c-s) **THIS SUMMER / GOODBYE GIRL (live)** [47] [ ]
(cd-s+=) – All the king's horses.
(cd-s) – ('A'side) / End of a century (live) / Periscope.

Nov 95. (c-ep)(cd-ep) **ELECTRIC TRAINS / CRACKER JACK / FIGHTING FOR PEACE / COLD SHOULDER (live)** [44] [ ]
(cd-ep) – ('A'side) / Some fantastic place / It's over / Hour glass.

Nov 95. (cd)(c) **RIDICULOUS** [50] [ ]
– Electric trains / Heaven knows / Grouch of the day / Walk away / This summer / Got to me / Long face / I want you / Daphne / Lost for words / Great escape / Temptation for love / Sound asleep / Fingertips.

. . . Jan – Jun '96 stop press . . .

Jun 96. (single) **HEAVEN KNOWS** [27] [ ]

– more compilations, etc. –

1981 A&M; (10"m-lp) **SIX SQUEEZE SONGS CRAMMED ONTO ONE TEN INCH RECORD** [-] [-]

Oct 83. Old Gold; (7") **TAKE ME, I'M YOURS. / UP THE JUNCTION** [ ] [-]

Sep 85. Old Gold; (7") **COOL FOR CATS. / LABELLED WITH LOVE** [ ] [-]

Mar 90. Deptford Fun City; (cd)(c)(d-lp) **ROUND AND A BOUT (live 1974-1989)** [50] [-]
– Footprints / Pulling mussels (from the shell) / Black coffee in bed / She doesn't have to shave / Is that love / Dr. Jazz / Up the junction / Slaughtered, gutted and heartbroken / Is it too late / Cool for cats / Take me, I'm yours / If it's love / Hourglass / Labelled with love / Annie get your gun / Boogie woogie country girl / Tempted. *(free 7"ep 'PACKET OF THREE').*

Apr 92. A&M; (7")(c-s) **COOL FOR CATS. / TRUST ME TO OPEN MY MOUTH** [62] [-]
(cd-s+=) – Squabs on forty fab (medley hits).

May 92. A&M; (cd)(c)(lp) **GREATEST HITS** [6] [ ]
– (as THE SINGLES 45 AND UNDER +) Take me, I'm yours / Goodbye girl / Cool for cats / Up the junction / Slap and tickle / Another nail in my heart / Pulling mussels (from the shell) / Tempted / Is that love / Labelled with love / Black coffee in bed / Annie get your gun / King George Street / Last time forever / No place like home / Hourglass / Trust me to open my mouth / Footprints / If it's love / Love circles.

Oct 93. A&M; (cd) **BABYLON AND ON / EAST SIDE STORY** [ ] [ ]

Chris SQUIRE (see under ⇒ YES)

Paul STANLEY (see under ⇒ KISS)

Ringo STARR

Born: RICHARD STARKEY, 7 Jul'40, Liverpool, England. The drummer of The BEATLES from Aug'62 to their final split in 1969. Early that year, he also appeared in the film 'Candy'. The next year he starred in 'The Magic Christian' film alongside Peter Sellers. This busy year also saw him release two solo albums; the George Martin produced covers lp 'SENTIMENTAL JOURNEY' and the Nashville recorded 'BEAUCOUPS OF BLUES'. He had his first major hit single in 1971, with 'IT DON'T COME EASY'. He also continued acting career throughout the 70's. **Filmography:** BLINDMAN (1971) / 200 MOTELS (1971 with Frank Zappa) / BORN TO BOOGIE (1972 T.Rex film he directed only) / THAT'LL BE THE DAY (1973) / LISZTOMANIA (1975) / SCOUSE THE MOUSE (1977) / PRINCESS DAISY (1983 TV mini-soap with Barbara) / THOMAS THE TANK ENGINE (1984-86; narrated children's TV) / GIVE MY REGARDS TO BROAD STREET (Paul McCartney's film 1984) / WATER (1985) / WILLIE AND THE POOR BOYS (1985 Bill Wyman video) / ALICE IN WONDERLAND (1985 TV). • **Style:** Pop rock legend whose patter and wit made up for his basic vocal talent. • **Songwriters:** As said above, wrote some himself and attempted covers YOU'RE SIXTEEN (Johnny Burnette) / ONLY YOU (Platters) / NO NO SONG (Hoyt Axton) / SNOOKEROO (elton John / Bernie Taupin) / IT'S ALL DOWN TO GOODNIGHT VIENNA (John Lennon) / HEY BABY (Bruce Channel). His 1978 album BAD BOY was another covers album. • **Miscellaneous:** In the early 80's, he met actress Barbara Bach, whom he married on 27 Apr'81. A year previous, they had survived a serious car crash.

Recommended: BLAST FROM THE PAST (*6).

RINGO STARR – vocals with session people

Apple Apple

Mar 70. (lp)(c) **SENTIMENTAL JOURNEY** [7] [22]
– Sentimental journey / Night and day / Whispering grass / Bye bye blackbird / I'm a fool to care / Stardust / Blue, turning grey over you / Love is a many splendoured thing / Dream / You always hurt the one you love / Have I told you lately that I love you / Let the rest of the world go by. *(cd-iss.May 95 on 'EMI')*

Sep 70. (lp)(c) **BEAUCOUPS OF BLUES** [ ] [65]
– Beaucoups of blues / Love don't last long / Fastest growing heartache in the west / Without her / Woman of the night / I'd be talking all the time / $15 draw / Wine, women and loud happy songs / I wouldn't have you any other way / Loser's

lounge / Waiting / Silent homecoming*(cd-iss.May95 on 'EMI')*

Nov 70. (7") **BEAUCOUPS OF BLUES. / COOCHY-COOCHY** | - | 87
Apr 71. (7") **IT DON'T COME EASY. / EARLY 1970** | 4 | 4
Mar 72. (7") **BACK OFF BOOGALOO. / BLINDMAN** | 2 | 9
Oct 73. (7") **PHOTOGRAPH. / DOWN AND OUT** | 8 | 1
Nov 73. (lp)(c) **RINGO** | 7 | 2
– You and me (babe) / I'm the greatest / Have you seen my baby / Photograph / Sunshine life for me / You're sixteen / Oh my my / Step lightly / Six o'clock * / Devil woman. *(US track *= extended) (re-iss.Nov80 on 'M.F.P.') (re-iss.+cd.Mar91 on 'EMI')*

Feb 74. (7") **YOU'RE SIXTEEN. / DEVIL WOMAN** | 4 | 8 Dec73
Mar 74. (7") **OH MY MY. / STEP LIGHTLY** | - | 5
Nov 74. (7") **ONLY YOU. / CALL ME** | 28 | 6
Nov 74. (lp)(c) **GOODNIGHT VIENNA** | 30 | 8
– It's all down to goodnight Vienna / Occapella / Oo-wee / Husbands and wives / Snookeroo / All by myself / Call me / No no song / Only you / Easy for me / Goodnight Vienna (reprise).

Feb 75. (7") **SNOOKEROO. / OO-WEE** | | -
Feb 75. (7") **NO NO SONG. / SNOOKEROO** | - | 3
Jun 75. (7") **IT'S ALL DOWN TO GOODNIGHT VIENNA. / OO-WEE** | - | 31
Dec 75. (lp)(c) **BLAST FROM YOUR PAST** (compilation) | | 30
– You're sixteen / No no song / It don't come easy / Photograph / Back off boogaloo / Only you / Beacoups of blues / Oh my my / Early 1970 / I'm the greatest.
(re-iss.Nov81 on 'M.F.P.') (cd-iss.1987 on 'E.M.I.')

Jan 76. (7") **OH MY MY. / NO NO SONG** | | -

Polydor | Atlantic

Sep 76. (7") **A DOSE OF ROCK'N'ROLL. / CRYIN'** | | 26
Sep 76. (lp)(c) **RINGO'S ROTOGRAVURE** | | 28
– A dose of rock'n'roll / Hey baby / Pure gold / Cryin' / You don't know me at all / Cookin' / I'll still love you / This be called a song / La brisas / Lady Gaye.

Nov 76. (7") **HEY BABY. / LADY GAYE** | | 74
Sep 77. (7") **DROWNING IN THE SEA OF LOVE. / GROWING** | - |
Sep 77. (7") **DROWNING IN THE SEA OF LOVE. / JUST A DREAM** | | -
Sep 77. (lp)(c) **RINGO THE 4th** | |
– Drowning in the sea of love / Tango all night / Wings / Gave it all up / Out on the streets / Can she do it like she dances / Sneaking Sally through the alley / It's no secret / Gypsies in flight / Simple love song.

Oct 77. (lp) **SCOUSE THE MOUSE** | |
– (8 children's songs)

Nov 77. (7") **WINGS. / JUST A DREAM** | - |
Apr 78. (lp)(c) **BAD BOY** | |
– Who needs a heart / Bad boy / Lipstick traces / Heart on my sleeve / Where did our love go / Hard times / Tonight / Monkey see monkey do / Old time relovin' / A man like me.

Jun 78. (7") **TONIGHT. / OLD TIME RELOVIN'** | |

not issued | Portrait

1980. (7") **OLD TIME RELOVIN'. / LIPSTICK TRACES (ON A CIGARETTE)** | - |
1980. (7") **HEART ON MY SLEEVE. / WHO NEEDS A HEART** | - |

— Released US single 'OKEY COKEY' with NILSSON as "COLONEL DOUG BOGIE")

R.C.A. | Boardwalk

Nov 81. (7") **WRACK MY BRAIN. / DRUMMING IS MY MADNESS** | | 38
Nov 81. (lp)(c) **STOP AND SMELL THE ROSES** | | 98
– Private property / Wrack my brain / Drumming is my madness / Attention / Stop and take the time to smell the roses / Dead giveaway / You belong to me / Sure to fall (in love with you) / Nice way / Back off boogaloo.

Feb 82. (7") **STOP AND TAKE TIME TO SMELL THE ROSES. / PRIVATE PROPERTY** | - |

Bellaphon | not issued

Jun 83. (7") **IN MY CAR. / AS FAR AS WE CAN GO** | - | - GERM

Boardwalk | not issued

Jun 83. (lp) **OLD WAVE** | - | -
– In my car / Hopeless / Alibi / Be my baby / She's about a mover / Keep forgettin' / Picture show life / As far as we can go / Everybody's in a hurry but me / I'm going down.

— Retired from solo work, guesting on ex-BEATLES' (PAUL McCARTNEY & GEORGE HARRISON solo). In '84, he narrated for children TV series 'Thomas The Tank Engine'. Returned to studio for 1990 album

RINGO STARR & HIS ALL-STAR BAND

DR.JOHN + BILLY PRESTON – keyboards / **NILS LOFGREN + JOE WALSH** – guitar / **RICK DANKO** – bass / **JIM KELTNER** – drums / **LEVON HELM** – perc. / **CLARENCE CLEMONS** – saxophone

R.C.A. | Arista

Nov 90. (cd)(c)(lp) **RINGO STARR AND HIS ALL-STARR BAND (live)** | |
– It don't come easy / The no-no song / Iko Iko / The weight / Shine silently / Honey don't / You're sixteen, you're beautifil, and you're mine / Quarter to three / Raining in my heart / Will it go round in circles / Life in the fast lane / Photograph.

May 92. (12") **WEIGHT OF THE WORLD. / AFTER ALL THESE YEARS** | 74 |

Rykodisc | Rykodisc

Oct 93. (cd)(c) **LIVE FROM MONTREUX (live)** | |
– Really serious introduction (QUINCY JONES & RINGO) / I'm the greatest (RINGO) / Don't go where the rain don't go (RINGO) / Desperado (JOE WALSH) / I can't tell you why (TIMOTHY B.SCHMIT) / Girls talk (DAVE EDMUNDS) / Weight of the world (RINGO) / Bang the drum all day (TODD RUNDGREN) / Walking nerve (NILS LOFGREN) / Black Maria (TODD RUNDGREN) / In the city (JOE WALSH) / American woman (BURTON CUMMINGS) / Boys (RINGO) / With a little help from my friends (RINGO).

– more compilations, etc. –

May 84. EMI Gold; (7") **IT DON'T COME EASY. / BACK OFF BOOGALOO** | | -
Feb 89. Rhino; (lp)(c)(cd) **STARRSTRUCK: RINGO'S BEST** | - |
(cd+=) – (4 tracks).

STARSHIP (see under ⇒ JEFFERSON AIRPLANE)

STATUS QUO

Formed: London, England ... 1962 as The SPECTRES by schoolboys ALAN LANCASTER, ALAN KEY, MIKE ROSSI (aka FRANCIS) and JESS JAWORSKI. They soon added JOHN COUGHLAN to replace BARRY SMITH, and by the mid-60's were playing residency at Butlin's holiday camp, where ROY LYNES took over from JESS. In Jul'66 they signed to 'Piccadilly' records, but failed with a debut 45, a Leiber & Stoller cover 'I (WHO HAVE NOTHING)'. They released 2 more flops, before they changed name in Mar'67 to The TRAFFIC JAM. After one 45, it was thought best to become STATUS QUO, after another group called TRAFFIC were hitting Top 10. In Oct'67, MIKE reverted name to FRANCIS and STATUS QUO added a second guitarist RICK PARFITT. Now re-signed on 'Pye' records, they unleashed first single 'PICTURES OF MATCHSTICK MEN', which gave them breakthrough into the UK Top 10, with it also hitting US No.12 (their only Top 50 hit). The following year, they were again in the Top 10 with 'ICE IN THE SUN'. After 2 more Top 30 hits in the early 70's, they moved to 'Vertigo' records (1972), and became top selling group of the 70's, which continued into the 80's. • **Style:** Moved from a late 60's pastiche psychedelic outfit, into a blues & boogie hard rock band from the early 70's onwards. The English answer to CANNED HEAT, also attired themselves in jeans and T-shirt, which they retained up to the 90's. Their 3-chord wonder barrage of rock'n'roll, has had few variations throughout their career Suffered critical onslaught, deservedly given to them after their 90's 'ANNIVERSARY WALTZ' pop medleys which made them sound more like CHAS & DAVE. • **Songwriters:** LANCASTER or ROSSI or PARFITT. In the early 70's, ROSSI and tour manager BOB YOUNG took over duties. Covered; SPICKS AND SPECKS (Bee Gees) / GREEN TAMBOURINE (Lemon Pipers) / SHEILA (Tommy Roe) / ICE IN THE SUN + ELIZABETH DREAMS + PARADISE FLAT + others (Marty Wilde – Ronnie Scott) / JUNIOR'S WAILING (Steamhammer) / DOWN THE DUSTPIPE (Carl Grossman) / THE PRICE OF LOVE (Everly Brothers) / ROADHOUSE BLUES (Doors) / WILD SIDE OF LIFE (Tommy Quickly) / ROCKIN' ALL OVER THE WORLD (John Fogerty) / THE WANDERER (Dion) / IN THE ARMY NOW (Bolland-Bolland) / RESTLESS (Jennifer Warnes) / WHEN YOU WALK IN THE ROOM (Jackie DeShannon) / etc. • **Trivia:** In 1985, the group with LANCASTER still in tow, played The LIVE AID Wembley concert.

Recommended: QUOTATIONS VOL.1 (THE EARLY YEARS) (*6) / 12 GOLD BARS (*7).

SPECTRES

MIKE ROSSI (b.FRANCIS, 29 Apr'49, Forest Hill, London) – vocals, guitar / **ROY LYNES** (b.25 Oct'43, Surrey, Kent) – organ, vocals repl. JESS JAWORSKI / **ALAN LANCASTER** (b. 7 Feb'49, Peckham, London) – bass, vocals / **JOHN COGHLAN** (b.19 Sep'46, Dulwich, London) – drums repl. BARRY SMITH

Piccadilly | not issued

Sep 66. (7") **I (WHO HAVE NOTHING). / NEIGHBOUR, NEIGHBOUR** | | -
Nov 66. (7") **HURDY GURDY MAN. / LATICA** | | -

— (above was not later covered by DONOVAN)

Feb 67. (7") **(WE AIN'T GOT) NOTHIN' YET. / I WANT IT** | | -

TRAFFIC JAM

Piccadilly | not issued

Jun 67. (7") **ALMOST THERE BUT NOT QUITE. / WAIT JUST A MINUTE** [ ] [-]

The STATUS QUO

added **RICK PARFITT** (b.RICHARD HARRISON, 12 Oct'48, Woking, Surrey) – guitar, vocals / MIKE now **FRANCIS ROSSI**

Pye | Cadet Con.

Nov 67. (7") **PICTURES OF MATCHSTICK MEN. / GENTLEMAN JOE'S SIDEWALK CAFE** [7] [12] May 68

Apr 68. (7") **BLACK VEILS OF MELONCHOLY. / TO BE FREE** [ ] [ ] Jul 69

Aug 68. (lp) **PICTURESQUE MATCHSTICKABLE MESSAGES FROM THE STATUS QUO** (US-title 'MESSAGES FROM THE STATUS QUO') [ ] [ ]
– Black veils of meloncholy / When my mind is not live / Ice in the Sun / Elizabeth dreams / Gentleman Joe's sidewalk cafe / Paradise flat / Technicolour dreams / Spicks and specks / Sheila / Sunny cellophane skies / Green tambourine / Pictures of matchstick men. *(re-iss.+c+cd.Oct87 on 'P.R.T.') (cd re-iss.Dec87 & Aug90 on 'Castle')*

Aug 68. (7") **ICE IN THE SUN. / WHEN MY MIND IS NOT ALIVE** [8] [70]

Feb 69. (7") **MAKE ME STAY A BIT LONGER. / AUNTIE NELLIE** [ ] [-]

Mar 69. (7") **TECHNICOLOR DREAMS. / SPICKS AND SPECKS** [-] [ ]

May 69. (7") **ARE YOU GROWING TIRED OF MY LOVE. / SO ENDS ANOTHER LIFE** [46] [-]

Sep 69. (lp)(c) **SPARE PARTS** [ ] [-]
– Face without a soul / You're just what I'm looking for / Mr.Mind detector / Antique Angelique / So ends another life / Are you growing tired of my love / Little Miss Nothing / Poor old man / The clown / Velvet curtains / When I awake / Nothing at all. *(re-iss.+cd.Oct87 on 'P.R.T.') (re-cd-iss.Aug90 on 'Castle')*

Oct 69. (7") **THE PRICE OF LOVE. / LITTLE MISS NOTHING** [ ] [ ]

Pye | Janus

Mar 70. (7") **DOWN THE DUSTPIPE. / FACE WITHOUT A SOUL** [12] [ ]

Sep 70. (lp)(c) **MA KELLY'S GREASY SPOON** [ ] [ ]
– Spinning wheel blues / Daughter / Everything / Shy fly / (April) Spring, Summer and Wednesdays / Junior's wailing / Lakky lady / Need your love / Lazy poker blues / Is it really me? – Gotta go home. *(re-iss.+cd.Oct87 on 'P.R.T.') (cd re-iss.Dec87 & Aug90 on 'Castle')*

STATUS QUO

now a quartet of **ROSSI, PARFITT, LANCASTER + COGHLAN** when LYNES departed.

Oct 70. (7") **IN MY CHAIR. / GERDUNDULA** [21] [ ]
(re-iss.Jun79)

Pye | Pye

Jun 71. (7") **TUNE TO THE MUSIC. / GOOD THINKING** [ ] [ ]

Dec 71. (lp)(c) **DOG OF TWO HEAD** [ ] [ ]
– Umleitung / Nanana / Something going on in my head / Mean girl / Nanana / Gerdundula / Railroad / Someone's learning / Nanana. *(re-iss.+cd. Oct87 on 'P.R.T.') (cd re-iss.Aug90 on 'Castle')*

Vertigo | A & M

Dec 72. (7") **PAPER PLANE. / SOFTER RIDE** [8] [-]

Jan 73. (lp)(c) **PILEDRIVER** [5] [ ]
– Don't waste my time / O baby / A year / Unspoken words / Big fat mama / Paper plane / All the reasons / Roadhouse blues. *(re-iss.May83, cd-iss.Feb91)*

May 73. (7") **DON'T WASTE MY TIME. / ALL THE REASONS** [-] [ ]

Jul 73. (7") **PAPER PLANE. / ALL THE REASONS** [-] [ ]

Sep 73. (7") **CAROLINE. / JOANNE** [5] [-]

Sep 73. (lp)(c) **HELLO!** [1] [ ]
– Roll over lay down / Claudie / A reason for living / Blue-eyed lady / Caroline / Softer ride / And it's better now / Forty-five hundred times. *(re-iss.May83, cd-iss.Feb91)*

Feb 74. (7") **CAROLINE. / SOFTER RIDE** [-] [ ]

Apr 74. (7") **BREAK THE RULES. / LONELY NIGHT** [8] [-]

May 74. (lp)(c) **QUO** [2] [ ]
– Backwater / Just take me / Break the rules / Drifting away / Don't think it matters / Fine fine fine / Lonely man / Slow train. *(re-iss.Aug83, cd-iss.Feb91)*

Vertigo | Capitol

Nov 74. (7") **DOWN DOWN. / NIGHT RIDE** [1] [ ]

Feb 75. (lp)(c) **ON THE LEVEL** [1] [ ]
– Little lady / Most of the time / I saw the light / Over and done / Night ride / Down down / Broken man / What to do / Where I am? / Bye bye Johnny. *(re-iss.Aug83, cd-iss.Feb91)*

May 75. (7"ep) **EXTENDED PLAY (live)** [9] [ ]
– Roll over lay down / Gerdundula / Junior's wailing.

Feb 76. (7") **RAIN. / YOU LOST YOUR LOVE** [7] [ ]

Mar 76. (lp)(c) **BLUE FOR YOU** (US title 'STATUS QUO') [1] [ ]
– Is there a better way? / Mad about the boy / Ring of a change / Blue for you / Rain / Rolling home / That's a fact / Ease your mind / Mystery song. *(re-iss.Dec83, cd see-compilations)*

Jul 76. (7") **MYSTERY SONG. / DRIFTING AWAY** [11] [ ]

Dec 76. (7") **WILD SIDE OF LIFE. / ALL THROUGH THE NIGHT** [9] [ ]

Mar 77. (d-lp)(d-c) **STATUS QUO LIVE! (live)** [3] [ ]
– Junior's wailing / Backwater / Just take me / Is there a better way? / In my chair / Little lady / Most of the time / Forty-five hundred times / Roll over lay down / Big fat mama / Caroline / Bye bye Johnny / Rain / Don't waste my time / Roadhouse blues. *(re-iss.Sep84)*

Oct 77. (7") **ROCKIN' ALL OVER THE WORLD. / RING OF A CHANGE** [3] [ ]

Nov 77. (lp)(c) **ROCKIN' ALL OVER THE WORLD** [5] [ ]
– Hard time / Can't give you more / Let's ride / Baby boy / You don't own me / Rockers rollin' / Rockin' all over the world / Who am I? / Too far gone / For you / Dirty water / Hold you back. *(re-iss.Aug85, cd-iss.Feb91)*

Aug 78. (7") **AGAIN AND AGAIN. / TOO FAR GONE** [13] [-]

Oct 78. (lp)(c) **IF YOU CAN'T STAND THE HEAT** [3] [-]
– Again and again / I'm giving up my worryin' / Gonna teach you to love me / Someone show me home / Long-legged Linda / Oh what a night / Accident prone / Stones / Let me fly / Like a good girl. *(cd-iss.see-compilations)*

Nov 78. (7") **ACCIDENT PRONE. / LET ME FLY** [36] [-]

Sep 79. (7") **WHATEVER YOU WANT. / HARD RIDE** [4] [-]

Oct 79. (lp)(c) **WHATEVER YOU WANT** [3] [-]
– Whatever you want / Shady lady / Who asked you / Your smiling face / Living on an island / Come rock with me / Rockin' on / Runaway / High flyer / Breaking away. *(cd-iss.see-compilations)*

Nov 79. (7") **LIVING ON AN ISLAND. / RUNAWAY** [16] [-]

Apr 80. (lp)(c) **12 GOLD BARS** (compilation) [3] [-]
– Rockin' all over the world / Down down / Caroline / Paper plane / Break the rules / Again and again / Mystery song / Roll over lay down / Rain / The wild side of life / Whatever you want / Living on an island. *(cd-iss.Nov84)*

Oct 80. (7") **WHAT YOU'RE PROPOSIN'. / A.B. BLUES** [2] [-]

Oct 80. (lp)(c) **JUST SUPPOSIN'** [4] [-]
– What you're proposin' / Run to mummy / Don't drive my car / Lies / Over the edge / The wild ones / Name of the game / Coming and going / Rock'n'roll. *(cd-iss.see-compilations)*

Dec 80. (7") **DON'T DRIVE MY CAR. / LIES** [11] [-]

Feb 81. (7") **SOMETHING 'BOUT YOU BABY I LIKE. / ENOUGH IS ENOUGH** [7] [-]

Mar 81. (lp)(c) **NEVER TOO LATE** [2] [-]
– Never too late / Something 'bout you baby I like / Take me away / Falling in falling out / Carol / Long ago / Mountain lady / Don't stop me now / Enough is enough / Riverside. *(cd-iss.Oct83, + see-compilations)*

Nov 81. (7"m) **ROCK'N'ROLL. / HOLD YOU BACK / BACKWATER** [8] [-]

— **PETE KIRCHNER** – drums (ex-ORIGINAL MIRRORS, ex-HONEYBUS, etc.) repl. COUGHLAN who formed PARTNERS IN CRIME

Mar 82. (7") **DEAR JOHN. / I WANT THE WORLD TO KNOW** [10] [-]

Apr 82. (lp)(c) **1+9+8+2** [1] [-]
– She don't fool me / Young pretender / Get out and walk / Jealousy / I love rock and roll / Resurrection / Dear John / Doesn't matter / I want the world to know / I should have known / Big man. *(cd-iss.Oct83, + see-compilations)*

Jun 82. (7") **SHE DON'T FOOL ME. / NEVER TOO LATE** [36] [-]

Oct 82. (7")(7"pic-d) **CAROLINE (live). / DIRTY WATER (live)** [13] [-]
(12"+=) – Down down (live).

Nov 82. (t-lp)(d-c) **FROM THE MAKERS OF . . .** (compilation & 2 lp-sides live) [4] [-]
– Pictures of matchstick men / Ice in the Sun / Down the dustpipe / In my chair / Junior's wailing / Mean girl / Gerdundula / Paper plane / Big fat mama / Roadhouse blues / Break the rules / Down down / Bye bye Johnny / Rain / Mystery song / Blue for you / Is there a better way / Again and again / Accident prone / The wild side of life / Living on an island / What you're proposing / Rock and roll / Something 'bout you baby I like / Dear John / Caroline / Roll over lay down / Backwater / Little lady / Don't drive my car / Whatever you want / Hold you back / Rockin' all over the world / Don't waste my time.

Sep 83. (7")(7"pic-d) **OL' RAG BLUES. / STAY THE NIGHT** [9] [-]
('A'extended-12"+=) – Whatever you want (live).

Oct 83. (lp)(c)(cd) **BACK TO BACK** [9] [-]
– A mess of the blues / Ol' rag blues / Can't be done / Too close to the ground / No contrast / Win or lose / Marguerita time / Your kind of love / Stay the night / Going down town tonight. *(cd re-iss. see-compilations)*

Oct 83. (7") **A MESS OF THE BLUES. / BIG MAN** [15] [-]
('A'extended-12"+=) – Young pretender.

Dec 83. (7")(7"pic-d) **MARGUERITA TIME. / RESURRECTION** [3] [-]
(d7"+=) – Caroline / Joanne.

May 84. (7") **GOING DOWN TOWN TONIGHT. / TOO CLOSE TO THE GROUND** [20] [-]

Oct 84. (7")(12")(7"pic-d)(12"clear) **THE WANDERER. / CAN'T BE DONE** [7] [-]

Nov 84. (d-lp)(c)(cd) **12 GOLD BARS VOL.2** (compilation) [12] [-]
– What you're proposing / Lies / Something 'bout you baby I like / Don't drive my car / Dear John / Rock and roll / Ol' rag blues / Mess of the blues / Marguerita time / Going down town tonight / The wanderer. (incl.VOL.1).

— **ROSSI + PARFITT** enlisted **ANDY BOWN** – keyboards (ex-HERD) (He was p/t member since 1974) / **JEFF RICH** – drums (ex-CLIMAX BLUES BAND) repl. KIRCHNER / **RHINO EDWARDS** (r.n.JOHN) – bass (ex-CLIMAX BLUES BAND) repl. LANCASTER

May 86. (7")(7"sha-pic-d) **ROLLIN' HOME. / LONELY** [9] [-]
(12"+=) – Keep me guessing.

Jul 86. (7") **RED SKY. / DON'T GIVE IT UP** [19] [-]

(12"+=) – The Milton Keynes medley (live).
(d7"+=) – Marguerita time.
Aug 86. (lp)(c)(cd) **IN THE ARMY NOW** | 7 | - |
– Rollin' home / Calling / In your eyes / Save me / In the army now / Dreamin' / End of the line / Invitation / Red sky / Speechless / Overdose.
Sep 86. (7")(7"pic-d) **IN THE ARMY NOW. / HEARTBURN** | 2 | - |
('A'military mix-12"+=) – Late last night.
(d7"+=) – Whatever you want / Rockin' all over the world.
Nov 86. (7") **DREAMIN'. / LONG-LEGGED GIRLS** | 15 | - |
('A'-wet mix-12"+=) – The Quo Christmas cake mix.
Mar 88. (7") **AIN'T COMPLAINING. / THAT'S ALRIGHT** | 19 | - |
('A'extended-12"+=) – Lean machine.
(cd-s++=) – In the army now (remix).
May 88. (7") **WHO GETS THE LOVE?. / HALLOWEEN** | 34 | - |
('A'extended-12"+=) – The reason for goodbye.
(cd-s++=) – The wanderer.
Jun 88. (lp)(c)(cd) **AIN'T COMPLAINING** | 12 | - |
– Ain't complaining / Everytime I think of you / One for the money / Another shipwreck / Don't mind if I do / I know you're leaving / Cross that bridge / Cream of the crop / The loving game / Who gets the love? / Burning bridges / Magic.
—— (Below single was a re-working of 'ROCKIN' ALL . . . ' for Sport Aid)
Aug 88. (7") **RUNNING ALL OVER THE WORLD. / MAGIC** | 17 | - |
(12"+=) – ('A'extended).
(cd-s++=) – Whatever you want.
Nov 88. (7") **BURNING BRIDGES (ON AND OFF AND ON AGAIN). / WHATEVER YOU WANT** | 5 | - |
(12"+=)(cd-s+=) – ('A'extended) / Marguerita time.
Oct 89. (7")(c-s) **NOT AT ALL. / GONE THRU THE SLIPS** | 50 | - |
(12"+=)(cd-s+=) – Every time I think of you.
Nov 89. (lp)(c)(cd) **PERFECT REMEDY** | 49 | - |
– Little dreamer / Not at all / Heart on hold / Perfect remedy / Address book / The power of rock / The way I am / Tommy's in love / Man overboard / Going down for the first time / Throw her a line / 1,000 years.
Dec 89. (7")(c-s)(7"pic-d) **LITTLE DREAMER. / ROTTEN TO THE BONE** | | - |
(12"+=)(cd-s+=) – Doing it all for you.
Oct 90. (7")(c-s)(7"silver) **THE ANNIVERSARY WALTZ – (PART 1). / THE POWER OF ROCK** | 2 | - |
(12"+=)(cd-s+=) – Perfect remedy.
Oct 90. (cd)(c)(lp) **ROCKIN' ALL OVER THE YEARS** (compilation) | 2 | - |
– Pictures of matchstick men / Ice in the Sun / Paper plane / Caroline / Break the rules / Down down / Roll over lay down / Rain / Wild side of life / Whatever you want / What you're proposing / Something 'bout you baby I like / Rock'n'roll / Dear John / Ol' rag blues / Marguerita time / The wanderer / Rollin' home / In the army now / Burning bridges / Anniversary waltz (part 1).
Dec 90. (7")(c-s) **THE ANNIVERSARY WALTZ – (PART 2). / DIRTY WATER (live)** | 16 | - |
(12"+=)(cd-s+=) – Pictures of matchstick men / Rock'n'roll music / Lover please / That'll be the day / Singing the blues.
Aug 91. (7")(c-s) **CAN'T GIVE YOU MORE. / DEAD IN THE WATER** | 37 | - |
(12"+=)(cd-s+=) – Mysteries from the ball.
Sep 91. (cd)(c)(lp) **ROCK 'TIL YOU DROP** | 10 | - |
– Like a zombie / All we really wanna do (Polly) / Fakin' the blues / One man band / Rock 'til you drop / Can't give you more / Warning shot / Let's work together / Bring it on home / No problems / Good sign / Tommy / Nothing comes easy / Fame or money / Price of love / Forty-five hundred times. *(re-iss.Feb93)*
Jan 92. (7")(c-s) **ROCK 'TIL YOU DROP. / Awards Medley:- CAROLINE – DOWN DOWN – WHATEVER YOU WANT – ROCKIN' ALL OVER THE WORLD** | 38 | - |
(12"+=)(cd-s+=) Forty-five hundred times.

	Polydor	Polydor

Oct 92. (7")(c-s)(cd-s) **ROADHOUSE BLUES MEDLEY (ANNIVERSARY WALTZ 25). / ('A'extended)** | 21 | |
(cd-s+=) – Don't drive my car.
Nov 92. (cd)(c)(d-lp) **LIVE ALIVE QUO (live)** | 37 | |
– Roadhouse medley:- Roadhouse blues -The wanderer -Marguerita time -Living on an island -Break the rules -Something 'bout you baby I like -The price of love -Roadhouse blues / Whatever you want / In the army now / Burning bridges / Rockin' all over the world / Caroline / Don't drive my car / Hold you back / Little lady. *(re-iss.cd Apr95)*
—— In May 94; their 'BURNING BRIDGES' tune, was used for Manchester United Football Squad's UK No.1 'Come On You Reds'.

	Polydor	M.C.A.

Jul 94. (7"colrd)(c-s) **I DIDN'T MEAN IT. / WHATEVER YOU WANT** | 21 | |
(cd-s+=) – Down down / Rockin' all over the world.
(cd-s) – ('A'side) / Survival.
(cd-ep) – ('A'side) / ('A'-hooligan version) / Survival / She knew too much.
Aug 94. (cd)(c)(lp) **THIRSTY WORK** | 13 | |
– Goin' nowhere / I didn't mean it / Confidence / Point of no return / Sail away / Like it or not / Soft in the head / Queenie / Lover of the human race / Sherri don't fail me now! / Rude awakening time / Back on my feet / Restless / Ciao ciao / Tango / Sorry.
Oct 94. (7"colrd)(c-s) **SHERRI DON'T FAIL ME NOW!. / BEAUTIFUL** | 38 | |
(cd-s+=) – In the army now.
(cd-s) – ('A'side) / Tossin' and turnin' / Down to you.
Nov 94. (7")(c-s)(cd-s) **RESTLESS (re-orchestrated). / AND I DO** | 39 | |

	PolygramTV	not issued

Oct 95. (7")(c-s) **WHEN YOU WALK IN THE ROOM. / TILTING AT THE MILL** | 34 | |
(cd-s+=) – ('A'version).
. . . Jan – Jun '96 stop press . . .
Feb 96. (single) **FUN FUN FUN** | 24 | - |
—— above a BEACH BOYS cover, with them guesting. Below album features all covers. They sue Radio One for not playing above hit on playlist after it charted. The QUO finally lose out in court and faces costs of over 50,000.
Feb 96. (cd)(c) **DON'T STOP** | 2 | |
Apr 96. (single) **DON'T STOP** | 35 | - |

– more compilations, etc. –

Dec 69. Marble Arch; (lp) **STATUS QUOTATIONS** | | - |
May 78. Marble Arch; (lp)(c) **STATUS QUO** | | - |
Mar 73. Pye; (7") **MEAN GIRL. / EVERYTHING** | 20 | |
May 73. Pye; (lp)(c) **THE BEST OF STATUS QUO** | 32 | |
– Down the dustpipe / Gerdundula / In my chair / Umleitung / Lakky lady / Daughter / Railroad / Tune to the music / April, Spring, Summer and Wednesdays / Mean girl / Spinning wheel blues. *(cd-iss.1986 on 'P.R.T.')*
Jul 73. Pye; (7") **GERDUNDULA. / LAKKY LADY** | | - |
Sep 76. Pye; (lp)(c) **THE REST OF STATUS QUO** | | - |
Jan 77. Pye; (lp)(c) **THE STATUS QUO FILE** | | - |
(re-iss.Sep79 on 'P.R.T.')
Apr 77. Pye; (12"ep) **DOWN THE DUSTPIPE / MEAN GIRL. / IN MY CHAIR / GERDUNDULA** | | - |
Oct 78. Pye; (7"yellow) **PICTURES OF MATCHSTICK MEN. / DOWN THE DUSTPIPE** | | - |
(re-iss.7"black Apr83 on 'Old Gold')
May 79. Pye; (7") **PICTURES OF MATCHSTICK MEN. / ICE IN THE SUN** | | - |
Jun 79. Pye; (lp)(c)(orange-lp) **JUST FOR THE RECORD** | | - |
Jun 73. Golden Hour; (lp)(c) **A GOLDEN HOUR OF . . .** | | - |
(c/cd-iss.Apr90 on 'Knight')
Oct 75. Golden Hour; (lp)(c) **DOWN THE DUSTPIPE** | 20 | - |
Apr 78. Hallmark; (lp)(c) **PICTURES OF MATCHSTICK MEN** | | - |
Aug 78. Pickwick; (d-lp)(d-c) **THE STATUS QUO COLLECTION** | | - |
Sep 80. Pickwick; (d-lp)(d-c) **STATUS QUO** | | - |
Jun 80. PRT; (d-lp)(d-c) **SPOTLIGHT ON . . .** | | - |
Oct 81. PRT; (10"lp)(c) **FRESH QUOTA** (rare) | 74 | - |
Jun 82. PRT; (c) **100 MINUTES OF . . .** | | - |
Oct 82. PRT; (lp)(c) **SPOTLIGHT ON . . . VOL.II** | | - |
Jul 83. PRT; (10"lp)(c) **WORKS** | | - |
Oct 85. PRT; (lp)(c) **NA NA NA** | | - |
Oct 87. PRT; (lp)(c)(cd) **QUOTATIONS VOL.1 – (THE EARLY YEARS)** | | - |
Oct 87. PRT; (lp)(c)(cd) **QUOTATIONS VOL.2 – (ALTERNATIVES)** | | - |
Sep 88. PRT; (lp)(c)(cd)(pic-lp) **FROM THE BEGINNING (1966-67)** | | - |
Apr 83. Contour; (lp)(c) **TO BE OR NOT TO BE** | | - |
(cd-iss.Apr91 on 'Pickwick')
1975. Starline; (lp) **ROCKIN' AROUND WITH** | | - |
Jul 82. Old Gold; (7") **MEAN GIRL. / IN MY CHAIR** | | - |
Sep 85. Old Gold; (7") **CAROLINE. / DOWN DOWN** | | - |
Nov 85. Old Gold; (7") **ROCKIN' ALL OVER THE WORLD. / PAPER PLANE** | | - |
(re-iss.Aug 89 + Sep 90)
Nov 85. Castle; (d-lp)(c) **THE COLLECTION** | | - |
(cd-iss.1988)
Apr 89. Legacy; (c)(cd) **C90 COLLECTOR** | | - |
Below 5 released on 'Vertigo'.
Jul 84. Dutch import; (lp) **LIVE AT THE N.E.C. (live)** | 83 | - |
Feb 91. (cd) **WHATEVER YOU WANT / JUST SUPPOSIN'** | | - |
Feb 91. (cd) **NEVER TOO LATE / BACK TO BACK** | | - |
Feb 91. (cd) **QUO / BLUE FOR YOU** | | - |
Feb 91. (cd) **IF YOU CAN'T STAND THE HEAT / 1+9+8+2** | | - |
May 93. Spectrum; (cd)(c) **A FEW BARS MORE** | | - |
Sep 94. Spectrum; (cd)(c) **IT'S ONLY ROCK'N'ROLL** | | - |
Jul 94. Success; (cd)(c) **ICE IN THE SUN** | | - |
Mar 95. Connoisseur; (cd) **THE OTHER SIDE OF STATUS QUO** | | - |
May 95. Spectrum; (cd)(c) **PICTURES OF MATCHSTICK MEN** | | - |
Jun 95. Savanna; (cd) **ICE IN THE SUN** | | - |

FRANCIS ROSSI & BERNARD FROST

Vertigo | not issued

Apr 85. (7")(ext-12") **MODERN ROMANCE (I WANT TO FALL IN LOVE AGAIN). / I WONDER WHY** [54] [-]
Oct 85. (7") **JEALOUSY. / WHERE ARE YOU NOW** [ ] [-]
('A'extended-12"+=) – That's all right.

STEELY DAN

Formed: New York, USA ... by DONALD FAGEN and WALTER BECKER initially as a writing partnership, after they left Bard's college in 1969. They recorded a soundtrack for the movie 'YOU GOTTA WALK IT LIKE YOU TALK IT', which starred Richard Pryor. In the early 70's, they joined JAY & THE AMERICANS, where they met producer GARY KATZ. When GARY was invited to be in-house producer for 'Dunhill-ABC', he secured a deal also for FAGEN and BECKER. In Jun'72, they added others (see below) and became STEELY DAN, taking name from the William Burroughs novel 'The Naked Lunch' describing a steam-powered dildo. Their debut album 'CAN'T BUY A THRILL' featuring the hit 45 'DO IT AGAIN', and this gave them their first of a string of Top 20 albums. • **Style:** Virtually a studio outlet, playing college loved laid back rock. They also added trad.jazz feel and clear production techniques that FM radio romantics loved. • **Songwriters:** BECKER-FAGEN except, EAST ST.LOUIS TOODLE-OO (Duke Ellington). • **Trivia:** In 1985, BECKER produced CHINA CRISIS' album 'Flaunt The Imperfection'. The duo teamed up yet again with KATZ when they sessioned on his 1987 production of ROSIE VELA's 1986 album 'ZAZU'. Scottish group DEACON BLUE, named themselves after a 1977 track of theirs 'DEACON BLUES'. **Recommended:** REELIN' IN THE YEARS – THE VERY BEST (*9).

DONALD FAGEN (b.10 Jan'48, Passaic, New Jersey, USA) – keyboards, vocals / **WALTER BECKER** (b.20 Feb'50, New York) – bass, vocals / **DAVID PALMER** – vocals (ex-MIDDLE CLASS) / **DENNY DIAS** – rhythm guitar / **JEFF BAXTER** – guitar (ex-HOLY MODAL ROUNDERS) / **JIM HODDER** – drums (ex-BEAD GAME)

Probe | A.B.C.

Sep 72. (7") **DALLAS. / SAIL THE WATERWAY** [ ] [ ]
Nov 72. (7") **DO IT AGAIN. / FIRE IN THE HOLE** [ ] [6]
(re-iss.Sep75 on 'ABC', hit UK No.39)
Dec 72. (lp)(c) **CAN'T BUY A THRILL** [ ] [17] Nov 72
– Do it again / Dirty work / Kings / Midnite cruiser / Only a fool would say that / Reeling in the years / Fire in the hole / Brooklyn (owes the charmer and me) / Change of the guard / Turn that heartbreak over again. *(re-iss.quad.Sep75 on 'ABC', hit UK No.38) (re-iss.1983 on 'MCA', cd-iss.Jul88)*
Mar 73. (7") **REELING IN THE YEARS. / ONLY A FOOL WOULD SAY THAT** [ ] [11]

— **BECKER & FAGEN** now on lead vocals, when PALMER left to BIG WHA-KOO.

Jul 73. (7") **SHOWBIZ KIDS. / RAZOR BOY** [ ] [61]
Jul 73. (lp)(c) **COUNTDOWN TO ECSTACY** [ ] [35]
– Bodhizattva / Razor boy / The Boston rag / Your gold teeth / Showbiz kids / My old school / Pearl of the quarter / King of the world. *(re-iss Jul83 on 'Fame') (re-iss.Feb82 on 'MCA', cd-iss.Jun88)*
Oct 73. (7") **MY OLD SCHOOL. / PEARL OF THE QUARTER** [ ] [63]
Mar 74. (lp)(c) **PRETZEL LOGIC** [37] [8]
– Rikki don't lose that number / Night by night / Any major dude / Barrytown / East St.Louis toodle-oo / Parker's bad / Thru with buzz / Pretzel logic / With a gun / Charlie Freak / Monkey in your soul. *(re-iss.quad.Oct74 on 'ABC') (re-iss.Feb84 on 'MCA', cd-iss.Aug88 + May90)*
May 74. (7") **RIKKI DON'T LOSE THAT NUMBER. / ANY MAJOR DUDE** [ ] [4]
(re-iss.Oct78 on 'ABC', hit UK 58 Mar79)
Oct 74. (7") **PRETZEL LOGIC. / THRU WITH BUZZ** [ ] [57]

— **MICHAEL McDONALD** – keyboards, vocals repl. BAXTER to DOOBIE BROTHERS / **JEFF PORCARO** – drums repl. HODDER

A.B.C. | A.B.C.

Apr 75. (lp)(c) **KATY LIED** [13] [13]
– Black Friday / Bad sneakers / Rose darling / Daddy don't live in that New York City no more / Doctor Wu / Everyone's gone to the movies / Your gold teeth II / Chain lightning / Any world (that I'm welcome to) / Throw back the little ones. *(re-iss Jun84 on 'MCA', cd-iss.Aug88)*
May 75. (7") **BLACK FRIDAY. / THROW BACK THE LITTLE ONES** [ ] [37]
Sep 75. (7") **BAD SNEAKERS. / CHAIN LIGHTNING** [ ] [ ]

— When McDONALD joined DOOBIE BROTHERS and PORCARO left later joining TOTO, **BECKER & FAGEN** employed session people incl. **DENNY DIAS** part-time

May 76. (lp)(c) **THE ROYAL SCAM** [11] [15]
– Kid Charlemagne / Caves of Altamira / Don't take me alive / Sign in stranger / The fez / Green earrings / Haitian divorce / Everything you did / The royal scam. *(re-iss.Sep82 on 'MCA', cd-iss.Jun88)*
May 76. (7") **KID CHARLEMAGNE. / GREEN EARRINGS** [ ] [82]
Sep 76. (7") **THE FEZ. / SIGN IN STRANGER** [-] [59]
Nov 76. (7") **HAITIAN DIVORCE. / SIGN IN STRANGER** [17] [-]
Sep 77. (lp)(c) **AJA** [5] [3]
– Black cow / Aja / Deacon blues / Peg / Home at last / I got the news / Josie.. *(re-iss.1983 on 'MCA', cd-iss.1985 & 1991)*
Nov 77. (7") **PEG. / I GOT THE NEWS** [ ] [11]
Apr 78. (7")(12") **DEACON BLUES. / HOME AT LAST** [ ] [19] Mar 78
Aug 78. (7") **JOSIE. / BLACK COW** [ ] [26]

— (Signed to new label earlier in the year)

M.C.A. | M.C.A.

Jul 78. (7") **FM (NO STATIC AT ALL). / FM (Reprise)** [49] [22] Jun 78
Nov 80. (lp)(c) **GAUCHO** [27] [9]
– Babylon sisters / Hey nineteen / Glamour profession / Gaucho / Time out of mind / My rival / Third world man. *(re-iss.Sep86, cd-iss.Jan85)*
Nov 80. (7") **HEY NINETEEN. / BODHISATTVA (live)** [ ] [10]
Mar 81. (7") **BABYLON SISTERS. / TIME OUT OF MIND** [ ] [-]
Mar 81. (7") **TIME OUT OF MIND. / BODHISATTVA** [-] [22]

Parted ways after 1980 album. FAGEN went solo and BECKER to production.

- compilations, others, etc. -

Jan 78. ABC; (12"ep) **+ FOUR** [ ] [-]
– Do it again / Haitian divorce / Dallas / Sail the waterway.
Nov 78. ABC; (d-lp)(c) **GREATEST HITS 1972-78** [41] [30]
(re-iss.Mar82 on 'MCA')
Apr 82. MCA; (d-c) **CAN'T BUY A THRILL / AJA** [ ] [-]
Jun 82. MCA; (lp)(c) **GOLD** [44] [ ]
(free-12"w.a) *(re-iss.+cd.Aug91)*
Jul 82. MCA; (7") **FM (NO STATIC AT ALL). / FM (REPRISE)** [ ] [ ]
(12"+=) – East St.Louis toodle-oo.
Oct 83. MCA; (d-c) **KATY LIED / THE ROYAL SCAM** [ ] [-]
Dec 83. MCA; (12"ep) **HAITIAN DIVORCE / DO IT AGAIN. / REELING IN THE YEARS / RIKKI DON'T LOSE THAT NUMBER** [ ] [-]
Sep 84. MCA; (d-c) **COUNTDOWN TO ECSTACY / PRETZEL LOGIC** [ ] [-]
Aug 85. MCA; (cd) **DECADE OF STEELY DAN – THE BEST OF STEELY DAN** [ ] [ ]
Oct 85. MCA; (lp)(c) **REELIN' IN THE YEARS – THE VERY BEST OF STEELY DAN** [43] [-]
– Do it again / Reelin' in the years / My old school / Bodhisattva / Show biz kids / Rikki don't lose that number / Pretzel logic / Black Friday / Bad sneakers / Doctor Wu / Haitian divorce / Kid Charlemagne / The fez / Peg / Josie / Deacon blues / Hey nineteen / Babylon sisters. *(re-iss. cd/c. Dec 92)*
Nov 85. MCA; (7") **REELING IN THE YEARS. / RIKKI DON'T LOSE THAT NUMBER** [ ] [ ]
Oct 87. MCA; (7") **RIKKI DON'T LOSE THAT NUMBER. / DO IT AGAIN** [ ] [ ]
Nov 93. MCA; (cd)(c) **REMASTERED – THE BEST OF STEELY DAN** [49] [ ]
Dec 93. MCA; (cd) **CITIZEN STEELY DAN** [ ] [ ]
Apr 83. Old Gold; (7") **DO IT AGAIN. / RIKKI DON'T LOSE THAT NUMBER** [ ] [-]
Oct 87. Telstar; (lp)(c)(cd) **DO IT AGAIN – THE VERY BEST OF STEELY DAN** [64] [-]
Apr 86. Showcase; (c) **SUN MOUNTAIN** (early demos) [ ] [-]
May 86. Bellaphon; (lp)(c) **BERRYTOWN** (demos) [-] [ ]
May 87. Thunderbolt; (lp)(c)(cd) **OLD REGIME** (early material) [ ] [-]
(re-iss.cd+c Mar94 on 'Prestige')
Apr 88. Thunderbolt; (lp)(cd) **STONE PIANO** (early material) [ ] [-]
Jun 94. Thunderbolt; (d-cd) **CATALYST** [ ] [-]
Jun 88. Castle; (d-lp) **BECKER AND FAGEN – THE COLLECTION** [ ] [-]
(early pre-STEELY DAN material)
Mar 78. Spark/ US= Visa; (lp) **YOU GOTTA WALK IT (Film Soundtrack)** [ ] [ ] 1971
Mar 84. Aero; (lp) **THE EARLY YEARS – WALTER BECKER & DONALD FAGEN** [-] [ ]
Sep 93. Remember; (cd)(c) **FOUNDERS OF STEELY DAN ("WALTER BECKER & DONALD FAGEN")** [ ] [-]
Feb 94. Javelin; (cd)(c) **SPOTLIGHT ON STEELY DAN** [ ] [-]
Feb 95. B.A.M.; (cd) **PEARLS OF THE PAST ("BECKER & FAGEN")** [ ] [-]

DONALD FAGEN

Warners | Warners

Oct 82. (lp)(c) **THE NIGHTFLY** [44] [11]
– New frontier / Walk between the raindrops / Maxine / Green flower street / The goodbye look / The nightfly / I.G.Y. (what a wonderful world). *(cd-iss.Jul88)*
Oct 82. (7") **I.G.Y. (WHAT A WONDERFUL WORLD). / WALK BETWEEN THE RAINDROPS** [ ] [26]
Jan 83. (7") **NEW FRONTIER. / MAXINE** [ ] [70]
(12"+=) – The goodbye look.

Apr 83. (7") **RUBY BABY. / WALK BETWEEN THE RAINDROPS** [ ] [-]
(below 'A'single from the film 'Bright Lights, Big City')
Apr 88. (7") **CENTURY'S END. / SHANGHAI CONFIDENTIAL (instrumental)** [ ] [83] Mar 88
(12"+=)(3"cd-s+=) – The nightfly / The goodbye look.

— with **WALTER BECKER** – bass, solo guitar, co-writer some / **GEORGE WADENIUS** – guitar / **PAUL GRIFFIN** – hamond organ / **LEROY CLOUDEN or CHRISTOPHER PARKER** – drums / **BASHIRI JOHNSON** – percussion / **RANDY BRECKER + others** – horns

Reprise Reprise
May 93. (cd)(c) **KAMAKIRIAD** [3] [10]
– Trans-island skyway / Countermoon / Springtime / Snowbound / Tomorrow's girls / Florida room / On the dunes / Teahouse on the tracks.
Jun 93. (7")(c-s) **TOMORROW'S GIRL. / SHANGHAI CONFIDENTIAL** [46] [ ]
(cd-s+=) – Confide in me.
Aug 93. (7")(c-s) **TRANS-ISLAND SKYWAY. / BIG NOISE, NEW YORK** [ ] [ ]
(cd-s+=) – Home at last (live).
Nov 93. (7")(c-s) **SNOWBOUND. / TRANS-ISLAND SKYWAY** [ ] [ ]
(cd-s+=) – ('A'mix).

WALTER BECKER

Giant Giant
Nov 94. (cd)(c) **ELEVEN TRACKS OF WHACK** [ ] [ ]
– Down in the bottom / Junkie girl / Surf and or die / Book of liars / Lucky Henry / Hard up case / Cringemaker / Girlfriend / My Waterloo / This moody bastard / Hat too flat.

STEELY DAN

duo re-formed for live appearances in the States.

Giant Giant
Oct 95. (cd)(c) **ALIVE IN AMERICA (live 1994)** [62] [40]
– Babylon sister / Green earrings / Bodhisattva / Reelin' in the years / Josie / Book of liars / Peg / Third World man / Kid Charlemagne / Sign in stranger / Aja.

STEPPENWOLF

Formed: Toronto, Canada . . . 1967 as blues band SPARROW by JOHN KAY and (see below). After one-off 45 for 'Columbia', they soon relocated to Los Angeles after a brief stay in New York. They met producer Gabriel Mekler, who gave them STEPPENWOLF name (after a Herman Hesse novel). They quickly signed to 'Dunhill' and recorded eponymous 1968 debut. That year's summer saw them hit US No.2 with classic biker's anthem 'BORN TO BE WILD', thus resurrecting albums' appeal which finally hit Top 10. The track was used on the 1969 film 'Easy Rider' alongside another from the debut; 'THE PUSHER'. Became one of America's top attractions, until they faded away mid-70's. • **Style:** Politically aware hard rock act, anti-war, anti-drugs, pro-rock'n'roll. • **Songwriters:** KAY written, except; THE PUSHER + SNOW BLIND FRIEND (Hoyt Axton) / SOOKIE SOOKIE (Don Covay) / BORN TO BE WILD (Dennis Edmonton; Jerry's brother) / I'M MOVIN' ON (Hank Snow) / HOOCHIE COOCHIE MAN (Muddy Waters). • **Trivia:** BORN TO BE WILD coined a new rock term in the their lyrics "heavy metal thunder". Early in 1969, they contributed some songs to another cult-ish film 'Candy'.

Recommended: GOLDEN GREATS (*8).

JOHN KAY (b.JOACHIM F.KRAULEDAT, 12 Apr'44, Tilsit, E.Germany) – vox, guitar / **MICHAEL MONARCH** (b. 5 Jul'50, Los Angeles, California, USA) – guitar / **GOLDY McJOHN** (b. 2 May'45) – organ / **RUSHTON MOREVE** (b.1948, Los Angeles) – bass / **JERRY EDMONTON** (b.24 Oct'46, Canada) – drums, vocals

The SPARROW

C.B.S. Columbia
1967. (7") **TOMORROW'S SHIP. / ISN'T IT STRANGE** [ ] [ ]
1967. (7") **GREEN BOTTLE LOVER. / DOWN GOES YOUR LOVE LIFE** [-] [ ]

JOHN KAY

1967. (7") **TWISTED. / SQUAREHEAD PEOPLE** [-] [ ]

STEPPENWOLF

JOHN RUSSELL MORGAN – bass repl. MOREVE. He was killed in car crash 1 Jul'81.

R.C.A. Dunhill
Nov 67. (7") **A GIRL I KNOW. / THE OSTRICH** [-] [ ]
Apr 68. (7") **SOOKIE SOOKIE. / TAKE WHAT YOU NEED** [ ] [ ] Jan 68

Stateside Dunhill
May 68. (lp) **STEPPENWOLF** [ ] [6] Jan 68
– Sookie Sookie / Everybody's next one / Berry rides again / Hoochie coochie man / Born to be wild / Your wall's too high / Desperation / The pusher / A girl I knew / Take what you need / The ostrich. *(hit UK No.59 Apr70) (re-iss.+cd.Jun87 on 'M.C.A.')*
Aug 68. (7") **BORN TO BE WILD. / EVERYBODY'S NEXT ONE** [-] [2] Jun 68
(above + below re-iss.in the UK May69 + Sep69, hit No.30 + 50)
Oct 68. (7") **MAGIC CARPET RIDE. / SOOKIE SOOKIE** [-] [3]
Jan 69. (lp) **STEPPENWOLF THE SECOND** [ ] [3] Nov 68
– Faster than the speed of life / Tighten up your wig / None of your doing / Spiritual fantasy / Don't step on the grass, Sam / 28 / Magic carpet ride / Disappointment / Number (unknown) / Lost and found by trial and error / Hodge, Podge strained through a Leslie / Resurrection / Reflections. *(re-iss.+cd.Jun87 on 'M.C.A.')*

— **LARRY BYROM** (b.27 Dec'48, USA) – guitar repl. MONARCH / **NICK ST.NICHOLAS** (b.28 Sep'43, Hamburg, W.Germany) – bass repl. RUSSELL

Feb 69. (7") **ROCK ME. / JUPITER CHILD** [ ] [10]
Jun 69. (lp) **AT YOUR BIRTHDAY PARTY** [ ] [7] Mar 69
– Don't cry / Chicken wolf / Lovely meter / Round and down / It's never too late / Sleeping dreaming / Jupiter child / She'll be better / Cat killer / Rock me / God fearing man / Mango juice / Happy birthday.
May 69. (7") **IT'S NEVER TOO LATE. / HAPPY BIRTHDAY** [-] [51]
Aug 69. (7") **MOVE OVER. / POWER PLAY** [-] [31]
Jan 70. (7") **MONSTER. / BERRY RIDES AGAIN** [-] [39]
Jan 70. (7") **MONSTER. / MOVE OVER** [ ] [-]
Jan 70. (lp)(c) **MONSTER** [43] [17] Nov 69
– Monster / Suicide / America / Draft resister / Power play / Move over / Fag / What would you do (if I did that to you) / From here to there eventually. *(cd-iss.Sep91 & Jul92 on 'B.G.O.')*
Mar 70. (7") **THE PUSHER (live). / YOUR WALL'S TOO HIGH (live)** [ ] [-]
Jun 70. (7") **HEY LAWDY MAMA (live). / TWISTED (live)** [ ] [35] Apr 70
Jun 70. (lp)(c) **STEPPENWOLF 'LIVE' (live)** [16] [7] Apr 70
– Sookie Sookie / Don't step on the grass, Sam / Tighten up your wig / Hey lawdy mama / Magic carpet ride / The pusher / Born to be wild / Monster / Draft resister / Power play / Corrina, Corrina / Twisted / From here to there eventually. *(re-iss.Oct74 on 'A.B.C.')*
Sep 70. (7") **SCREAMING NIGHT HOG. / SPIRITUAL FANTASY** [ ] [62] Aug 70

Probe Dunhill
Nov 70. (7") **WHO NEEDS YA. / EARSCHPLITTENLOUDENBOOMER** [ ] [54]
Nov 70. (lp)(c) **STEPPENWOLF 7** [ ] [19]
– Ball crusher / Forty days and forty nights / Fat Jack / Renegade / Foggy mental breakdown / Snow blind friend / Who needs ya / Earschplittenloudenboomer / Hippo stomp.
Mar 71. (7") **SNOW BLIND FRIEND. / HIPPO STOMP** [ ] [60]

— **KENT HENRY** – guitar repl. BYROM

— **GEORGE BIONDO** (b. 3 Sep'45, Brooklyn, New York) – bass repl. NICK

Jul 71. (7") **RIDE WITH ME. / FOR MADMEN ONLY** [ ] [52]
Oct 71. (7") **FOR LADIES ONLY. / SPARKLE EYES** [ ] [64]
Oct 71. (lp)(c) **FOR LADIES ONLY** [ ] [54]
– For ladies only / I'm asking / Snakes and chains / Tenderness / The night time's for you / Jadet strumpet / Sparkle eyes / Black pit / Ride with me / In hopes of a garden.

— Disbanded Feb'72, EDMUNTON and McJOHN formed MANBEAST.

JOHN KAY

went solo, augmented by **KENT HENRY + GEORGE BIONDO** plus **HUGH SULLIVAN** – keyboards / **PENTII WHITNEY GLEN** – drums / etc. (same label)

Apr 72. (lp)(c) **FORGOTTEN SONGS AND UNSUNG HEROES** [ ] [ ]
– Many a mile / Walk beside me / You win again / To be alive / Bold marauder / Two of a kind / Walking blues / Somebody / I'm moving on.
Apr 72. (7") **I'M MOVIN' ON. / WALK BESIDE ME** [-] [52]
Jul 72. (7") **YOU WIN AGAIN. / SOMEBODY** [-] [ ]
Jul 73. (7") **MOONSHINE. / NOBODY LIVES HERE ANYMORE** [-] [ ]
Jul 73. (lp)(c) **MY SPORTIN' LIFE** [ ] [ ]
– Moonshine / Nobody lives here anymore / Drift away / Heroes and devils / My sportin' life / Easy evil / Giles of the river / Dance to my song / Sing with the children.
Sep 73. (7") **EASY EVIL. / DANCE TO MY SONG** [ ] [ ]

STEPPENWOLF

re-formed (**KAY, McJOHN, EDMUNTON, BIONDO**) plus **BOBBY COCHRAN** – guitar repl. KENT (first and last with horn section)

C.B.S. Mums
Oct 74. (lp)(c) **SLOW FLUX** [ ] [47] Sep 74
– Gang war blues / Children of the night / Justice don't be slow / Get into the wind /

Jeraboah / Straight shootin' woman / Smokey factory blues / Morning blue / A fool's factory / Fishin' in the dark.

Oct 74. (7") **STRAIGHT SHOOTIN' WOMAN. / JUSTICE DON'T BE SLOW** [ ] [29] Sep 74

Jan 75. (7") **GET INTO THE WIND. / MORNING BLUE** [-] [ ]

Apr 75. (7") **SMOKEY FACTORY BLUES. / A FOOL'S FANTASY** [ ] [ ]

— **ANDY CHAPIN** – keyboards repl. McJOHN who went solo

Aug 75. (7") **CAROLINE (ARE YOU READY). / ANGEL DRAWERS** [ ] [ ]

Sep 75. (lp)(c) **HOUR OF THE WOLF** [ ] [ ]

– Caroline (are you ready for the outlaw world) / Annie, Annie over / Two for the love of one / Just for tonight / Hard rock road / Someone told a lie / Another's lifetime / Mr. Penny pincher.

— **WAYNE COOK** – keyboards repl. ANDY

Epic Epic

May 77. (lp)(c) **SKULLDUGGERY** [ ] [ ]

– Skullduggery / Roadrunner / Rock and roll song / Train of thought / Life is a gamble / Pass it on / Sleep / Lip service.

Dec 77. (lp)(c) **REBORN TO BE WILD** [ ] [ ]

– Straight shootin' woman / Hard rock road / Another's lifetime / Mr.Penny pincher / Smokey factory blues / Caroline / Get into the wind / Gang war blues / Children of night / Skullduggery.

— Disbanded yet again.

JOHN KAY

with **LARRY BYROM** – slide guitar / **MAC McANALLY** – guitar / **CLAYTON IVEY** – keyboards / **BOB WRAY** – bass / **ROGER CLARK** – drums

Mercury Mercury

Jun 78. (lp)(c) **ALL IN GOOD TIME** [ ] [ ]

– Give me some news I can use / The best is barely good enough / That's when I think of you / Ain't nobody home / Ain't nothin' like it used to be / Business is business / Show me how you'd like it done / Down in New Orleans / Say you will / Hey, I'm alright.

Jun 78. (7") **GIVE ME SOME NEWS I CAN USE. / BUSINESS IS BUSINESS** [ ] [-]

— In the early 80's, KAY and group toured as

JOHN KAY & STEPPENWOLF

with **MICHAEL PALMER** – guitar / **BRETT TUGGLE** – keyboards / **CHAD PERRY** – bass / **STEVEN PALMER** – drums

not issued Allegiance

Dec 81. (lp) **LIVE IN LONDON (live)** [-] [ ]

– Sookie Sookie / Give me news I can use / You / Hot night in a cold town / Ain't nothin' like it used to be / Magic carpet ride / Five finger discount / Hey lawdy mama / Business is business / Born to be wild / The pusher.

Dec 81. (7") **HOT TOME IN A COLD TOWN. /** [-] [ ]

— **WELTON GITE** – bass repl. CHAD / added **MICHAEL WILK** – keyboards

not issued CBS-Sony

1983. (lp)(cd) **WOLFTRACKS** [-] [ ]

– All I want is all you got / None of the above / You / Every man for himself / Five finger discount / Hold your head up / Hot night in a cold town / Down to earth / For rock'n'roll / The balance.

— now with **ROCKET RITCHOTTE** – guitar, vocals + **MICHAEL WILK** – keyboards, bass / **RON HURST** – drums, vocals. Finally issued new material 1988.

Disky Qwil

May 88. (lp)(c)(cd) **ROCK'N'ROLL REBELS** [ ] [ ] Sep 87

– Give me life / Rock'n'roll rebels / Hold on / Man on a mission / Everybody knows you / Rock steady / Replace the face / Turn out the lights / Give me news I can use / Rage.

I.R.S. I.R.S.

Aug 90. (cd)(c)(lp) **RISE & SHINE** [ ] [ ]

– Let's do it all / Time out / Do or die / Rise & shine / The wall / The daily blues / Keep rockin' / Rock'n'roll war / Sign on the line / We like it, we love it (we want more of it).

– compilations, others, etc. –

Jul 69. Stateside/ US= Dunhill; (lp) **EARLY STEPPENWOLF** [ ] [29]

– Power play / Howlin' for my baby / Goin' upstairs / Corina Corina / Tighten up your wig / The pusher. *(live material from 1967 recorded as The SPARROW)*

Mar 71. Probe/ US= Dunhill; (lp)(c) **STEPPENWOLF GOLD** [ ] [24]

– Born to be wild / It's never too late / Rock me / Hey lawdy mama / Move over / Who needs ya / Magic carpet ride / The pusher / Sookie Sookie / Jupiter's child / Screaming night hog. *(re-iss.Oct74 on 'ABC') (re-iss.Aug80 on 'MCA') (re-iss.Jan83 on 'Fame')*

Jul 72. Probe/ US= Dunhill; (lp)(c) **REST IN PEACE** [ ] [62] Jun 72

Mar 73. Probe/ US= Dunhill; (lp)(c) **16 GREATEST HITS** [ ] [ ] Feb 73

(re-iss.Oct74 on 'ABC')

Jun 80. MCA; (7") **BORN TO BE WILD. / THE PUSHER** [ ] [ ]

(re-iss.Apr83 on 'Old Gold')

Jul 85. MCA; (lp)(c) **GOLDEN GREATS** [ ] [ ]

– Born to be wild / Magic carpet ride / Rock me / Move over / Hey lawdy mama / It's never too late / Who needs you? / Monster / Snow blind friend / The pusher / Sookie sookie / Jupiter's child / Screaming dog night / Ride with me / For ladies only / Tenderness.

Apr 93. Movieplay; (cd) **BORN TO BE WILD** [ ] [-]

Jan 94. Legacy; (cd) **TIGHTEN UP YOUR WIG – THE BEST OF JOHN KAY & SPARROW** [ ] [ ]

STEREOLAB

Formed: South London, England ... early 1991 by ex-indie stalwards McCARTHY mainman TIM GANE and girlfriend LAETITIA SADIER. Formed own label 'Duophonic' and in 1993 signed in the States for 6 figure-sum to 'Elektra'. 1994 saw them unsurprisingly hit UK Top 20 with double album 'MARS AUDIAC QUINTET'. • **Style:** Indie electro-rock outfit influenced by minimalists VELVET UNDERGROUND, JOHN CAGE, NEU!, SPACEMEN 3 and The BEACH BOYS!. Lushishly fronted by NICO-like vox of LAETITIA (pronounced Le-ti-seaya). • **Songwriters:** GANE. • **Trivia:** Featured on Channel 4's TV show 'The Word' in 1993 promoting 'JENNY ONDIOLINE'.

Recommended: MARS AUDIAC QUINTET (*8) / TRANSIENT RANDOM ... (*8) / MUSIC FOR THE AMORPHOUS BODY STUDY CENTER (*8) / EMPEROR TOMATO KETCHUP (*8)

TIM GANE (b. 1966) – guitar, vox organ, guitar (ex-McCARTHY) / **LAETITIA SADIER** (b.1968, Paris, France) – vocals, vox organ, guitar, tambourine, moog / **REBECCA MORRIS** – vocals / **JOE DILWORTH** – drums (of TH' FAITH HEALERS)

Duophonic not issued

May 91. (10"ep-mail order) **SUPER 45** [ ] [-]

– The light (that will cease to fail) / Au grand jour / Brittle / Au grand jour!. *(first 2 tracks re-iss.Jun92 7"pink on 'Big Money Incorporated')*

— added **MARTIN KEAN** (b.New Zealand) – guitar (ex-CHILLS) / **RUSSELL YATES** – live guitar (of MOOSE). **MICK CONROY** (ex-MOOSE) was also a live member early '92.

Too Pure Slumberland

Sep 91. (10"ep) **SUPER ELECTRIC / HIGH EXPECTATION. / THE WAY WILL BE OPENING / CONTACT** [ ] [-]

Apr 92. (cd-ltd.) **SWITCHED ON** (compilation) [-] [ ]

– Super electric / Doubt / Au grand jour / The way will be opening / Brittle / Contract / Au grand jour / High expectation / The light that will cease to fail / Changer.

— GINA departed after above. (when did she join?)

May 92. (cd)(c)(lp) **PENG!** [ ] [-]

– Super falling star / Orgiastic / Peng! 33 / K-stars / Perversion / You little shits / The seeming and the meaning / Mellotron / Enivrez-vous / Stomach worm / Surrealchemist.

— added **MARY HANSEN** – vocals, tambourine, guitar / **ANDY RAMSAY** – percussion, vox organ, bazouki repl. DILWORTH

Sep 92. (10"ep)(10"clear-ep)(cd-ep) **LOW FI / (VAROOM!). / LAISSER-FAIRE / ELEKTRO (HE HELD THE WORLD IN HIS IRON GRIP)** [ ] [-]

— added **SEAN O'HAGAN** – vox organ, guitar (ex-MICRODISNEY, ex-HIGH LLAMAS)

Feb 93. (7")(7"pink) **JOHN CAGE BUBBLEGUM. / ELOGE D'EROS** [-] [ ]

— added **DUNCAN BROWN** – bass, guitar, vocals

Mar 93. (cd)(c)(m-lp) **THE GROUP PLAYED SPACE AGE BACHELOR PAD MUSIC** [ ] [-]

– Avant-garde M.O.R. / Space age bachelor pad music (mellow) / The groop play chord X / Space age bachelor pad music / Ronco symphony / We're not adult orientated / UHF-MFP / We're not adult orientated (new wave).

Duophonic Elektra

Aug 93. (10"ep)(cd-ep) **JENNY ONDIOLINE / FRUCTION / GOLDEN BALL / FRENCH DISCO** [75] [ ]

Sep 93. (cd)(c)(2xlp) **TRANSIENT RANDOM-NOISE BURSTS WITH ANNOUNCEMENTS** [62] [ ]

– Tone burst / Our trinitone blast / Pack yr romantic mind / I'm going out of my way / Golden ball / Pause / Jenny Ondioline / Analogue rock / Crest / Lock-groove lullaby.

Nov 93. (7") **FRENCH DISKO (new version). / JENNY ONDIOLINE** [ ] [-]

Jul 94. (7"ltd) **PING PONG. / MOOGIE WONDERLAND** [45] [ ]

(10"+=)(cd-s+=) – Pain et spectacles / Transcona (live).

Aug 94. (cd)(c)(d-lp) **MARS AUDIAC QUINTET** [16] [ ]

– Three-dee melodie / Wow and flutter / Transona five / Des etoiles electroniques / Ping pong / Anamorphose / Three longers later / Nihilist assault group / International colouring contest / The stars of our destination / Transporte sans bouger / L'enfer des formes / Outer accelerator / New orthophony / Fiery yellow. (free clear-7" w /d-lp + cd-s on cd) – Klang-tang / Ulaan batter.

Oct 94. (7")(10")(cd-s) **WOW AND FLUTTER. / HEAVY DENIM** [70] [ ]
Apr 95. (10"ep)(cd-ep) **AMORPHOUS BODY STUDY CENTRE** [59] [-]
– Pop quiz / The extension trip / How to explain your internal organs overnight / The brush descends the length / Melochord seventy five / Space moment.
Sep 95. (cd)(c)(colrd-d-lp) **REFRIED ECTOPLASM (SWITCHED ON – VOLUME 2)** (compilation on 'Duophonic Ultra High Frequency') [30] [-]

. . . Jan – Jun '96 stop press . . .

Feb 96. (single) **CYBELE'S REVERIE** [62] [ ]
Mar 96. (cd)(c)(d-lp) **EMPEROR TOMATO KETCHUP** [27] [ ]

– more very limited mail order only singles, etc. –

Nov 91. Duophonic; (7"clear)(7"colrd) **STUNNING DEBUT ALBUM: Doubt / Changer** [ ] [-]
Jul 92. Duophonic; (7"colrd) **HARMONIUM. / FARFISA** [ ] [-]
Oct 93. Clawfist; (10"ep) **CRUMB DUCK (with NURSE WITH WOUND)** [ ] [-]
– Animal or vegetable / Exploding head movie.
Oct 93. Sub Pop; (7"clear) **LE BOOB OSCILLATOR. / TEMPTER** [-] [ ]
Nov 93. Teenbeat; (7") **MOUNTAIN. / ('B'by Unrest)** [-] [ ]

STEREO MC'S

Formed: Clapham, London, England . . . 1985 by NICK HALLAM and ROB BIRCH. They shared a flat with others, but were given £7,000 to vacate it by property developers. They used the money to set up own label 'Gee Street', which gained backing by '4th & Bro.' in the US. After a number of 45's & a debut album '33-45-78', they toured the States, supporting The HAPPY MONDAYS. They gained first taste of chart action there, when single 'ELEVATE MY MIND' broke the 40. In 1992, they scored 2 UK Top 20 hits with 'CONNECTED' & 'STEP IT UP', and were on their way to superstardom early '93. • **Style:** Cybernetic multi-racial hip hop, fronted by ginger-haired ROB B. Their sound was/is similar to tour mates HAPPY MONDAYS mixed with LL COOL J. • **Songwriters:** BIRCH-HALLAM, except SALSA HOUSE (Richie Rich) / BLACK IS BLACK (Jungle Brothers) / DANCE 4 ME (Queen Lafitah). • **Trivia:** CESARE left amicably after first release.

Recommended: CONNECTED (*8).

ROB B (b.ROB BIRCH) – rapper / **THE HEAD** (b.NICK HALLAM) – DJ / **OWEN IF** (b.ROSSITER) – drums / with **CATH COFFEY** – backing vocals

4th & Bro. 4th & Bro.

Mar 88. (7")(12") **MOVE IT. / FEEL SO GOOD** [ ] [ ]
— above credited with **CESARE**, although he left soon after.
Oct 88. (7") **WHAT IS SOUL?. / ('A'-Rob B mix)** [ ] [ ]
(12"+=) – ('A'vocal mix) / ('A'instrumental) / ('A'accapella mix).
Jun 89. (7") **ON 33. / GEE STREET** [ ] [ ]
(10"+=)/ /(12"+=) – Non stop./ / ('A' DJ Mark the 45 King mix).
Jul 89. (lp)(c)(cd) **33-45-78** [ ] [ ]
– On 33 / Use it / Gee Street / Neighbourhood / Toe to toe / What is soul? / Use it (part 2) / Outta touch / Sunday 19th March / This ain't a love song / Ancient concept / On the mike / Back to the future.
Aug 89. (7") **LYRICAL MACHINE. / ON THE MIKE** [ ] [ ]
(12"+=) – Mechanical / Bring it on.
Sep 90. (7") **ELEVATE MY MIND. / SMOKIN' WITH THE MOTHERMAN (feat. Afrika)** [74] [39] May 91
(12"+=)(cd-s+=) – ('A' dub version).
Sep 90. (cd)(c)(lp) **SUPERNATURAL** [ ] [ ]
– I'm a believer / Scene of the crime / Declaration / Elevate my mind / Watcha gonna do / Two horse town / Ain't got nobody / Goin' back to my roots / Lost in music / Life on the line / The other side / Set me loose / What's the word / Early one morning. (cd+c+=) Smokin' with the motherman / Relentless. *(re-iss.cd+c Apr94 on 'Island')*
Mar 91. (7")(c-s) **LOST IN MUSIC (Ultimatum Remix). / EARLY ONE MORNING** [46] [ ]
(cd-s+=) – ('A' instrumental).
(12") – ('A'side) / ('A'-B.B.mix) / ('A'-B.B-instrumental).
— now a 6-piece, added **VERONICA + ANDREA** – backing vox
Sep 92. (7")(c-s) **CONNECTED. / FEVER** [18] [20] Mar 93
(cd-s+=) – ('A'-full version) / Disconnected.
Oct 92. (cd)(c)(lp) **CONNECTED** [2] [92]
– Connected / Ground level / Everything / Sketch / Fade away / All night long / Step it up / Playing with fire / Pressure / Chicken shake / Creation / The end.
Nov 92. (7")(c-s) **STEP IT UP. / ('A'mix)** [12] [58] Jun 93
(12"+=)(cd-s+=) – Lost in music (US mix).
Feb 93. (7")(c-s) **GROUND LEVEL. / EVERYTHING (EVERYTHING GROOVES pt.1)** [19] [ ]
(12"+=)(cd-s+=) – (B'mixes pt.2).
May 93. (7")(c-s) **CREATION. / ('A'ultimation mix)** [19] [ ]
(12"+=) – ('A'instrumental).
(cd-s+=) – All night long.

ST. ETIENNE (see under ⇒ SAINT ETIENNE)

Cat STEVENS

Born: STEVEN GEORGIOU, 21 Jul'47, Soho, London, England. Son of Greek restaurant owner and Swedish mother. While studying at Hammersmith college in 1966 he met Mike Hurst (ex-SPRINGFIELDS). He produced first single 'I LOVE MY DOG', after which CAT was signed by Tony Hall to new Decca subsidiary label 'Deram'. It reached the UK Top 30, but was surpassed the next year when follow-up 'MATTHEW AND SON' hit No.2. His songs were soon being covered by many, including P.P.ARNOLD (First Cut Is The Deepest) & TREMELOES (Here Comes My Baby). After a barren chart spell and recuperation from TB two years previous, he signed new deal with 'Island' in 1970 (A & M in America). He scored a comeback Top 10 hit with 'LADY D'ARBANVILLE', which lent on the production skills of ex-YARDBIRD Keith Relf. He stayed for the follow-up to 'MONA BONE JAKON', the 1970 classic album 'TEA FOR THE TILLERMAN'. CAT went on to become one of the biggest stars of the 70's until his retirement in 1979. He took up the Muslim faith and changed his name to Yusef Islam (see further on). • **Style:** Socially aware folk singer in the 60's, who progressed to classy rock-pop artist in the 70's, with hints of Eastern mysticism. • **Songwriters:** Self-penned except; MORNING HAS BROKEN (Eleanor Farjeon) / ANOTHER SATURDAY NIGHT (Sam Cooke). • **Trivia:** Other STEVENS' songs given new light were; WILD WORLD (Jimmy Cliff – 1970, Maxi Priest – 1988) / FIRST CUT IS THE DEEPEST (Rod Stewart) / PEACE TRAIN (10,000 Maniacs).

Recommended: THE VERY BEST OF CAT STEVENS (*9) / TEA FOR THE TILLERMAN (*8) / TEASER AND THE FIRECAT (*9).

CAT STEVENS – vocals, guitar, keyboards with orchestra

Deram Deram

Sep 66. (7") **I LOVE MY DOG. / PORTOBELLO ROAD** [28] [ ]
Dec 66. (7") **MATTHEW AND SON. / GRANNY** [2] [ ]
(re-iss.Aug81 on 'Decca')
Mar 67. (lp) **MATTHEW AND SON** [7] [ ]
– Matthew and son / I love my dog / Here comes my baby / Bring another bottle baby / Portobello road / I've found a love / I see a road / Baby get your head screwed on / Granny / When I speak to the flowers / The tramp / Come on and dance / Hummingbird / Lady. *(cd-iss.Jul 88 on 'London')*
Mar 67. (7") **I'M GONNA GET ME A GUN. / SCHOOL IS OUT** [6] [ ]
Jul 67. (7") **A BAD NIGHT. / THE LAUGHING APPLE** [20] [ ]
Dec 67. (7") **KITTY. / BLACKNESS OF THE NIGHT** [47] [ ]
Dec 67. (lp) **NEW MASTERS** [ ] [ ]
– Kitty / I'm so sleepy / Northern wind / The laughing apple / Smash your heart / Moonstone / The first cut is the deepest / I'm gonna be king / Ceylon city / Blackness of the night / Come on baby / I love them all. *(re-iss.Nov84) (cd-iss.Apr89 +=)* – Image of Hell / Lovely city / Here comes my wife / The view from the top / It's a supa dupa life / Where are you / A bad night.
Feb 68. (7") **LOVELY CITY. / IMAGE OF HELL** [ ] [ ]
— Around early 1968, CAT slowly recovered from tuberculosis.
Oct 68. (7") **HERE COMES MY WIFE. / IT'S A SUPA DUPA LIFE** [ ] [-]
Jun 69. (7") **WHERE ARE YOU. / THE VIEW FROM THE TOP** [ ] [-]
— recruits band **ALUN DAVIES** – guitar / **JOHN RYAN** – bass / **HARVEY BURNS** – drums

Island A & M

Jun 70. (7") **LADY D'ARBANVILLE. / TIME / FILL MY EYES** [8] [ ]
Jun 70. (lp)(c) **MONA BONE JAKON** [63] [ ]
– Lady D'Arbanville / Maybe you're right / Pop star / I think I see the light / Trouble / Mona bone Jakon / I wish, I wish / Katmandu / Time – Fill my eyes / Lilywhite. *(re-iss.1974 & Jan78)*
Nov 70. (lp)(c) **TEA FOR THE TILLERMAN** [20] [8] Feb 71
– Where do the children play / Hard headed woman / Wild world / Sad Lisa / Miles from nowhere / But I might die tonight / Longer boats / Into white / On the road to find out / Father and son / Tea for the tillerman. *(re-iss.1974 & Jan78, re-iss,+cd.Oct86) (re-iss.lp Jan94 + May94)*
Feb 71. (7") **WILD WORLD. / MILES FROM NOWHERE** [-] [11]
— **LARRY STEELE** – bass repl. RYAN
Jun 71. (7") **MOON SHADOW. / FATHER AND SON** [22] [30]
Sep 71. (7") **TUESDAY'S DEAD. / MILES FROM NOWHERE** [ ] [-]
Sep 71. (7") **PEACE TRAIN. / WHERE DO THE CHILDREN PLAY?** [-] [7]
Sep 71. (lp)(c) **TEASER AND THE FIRECAT** [3] [2]
– The wind / Ruby love / If I laugh / Changes IV / How can I tell you / Tuesday's

dead / Morning has broken / Bitterblue / Moon shadow / Peace train. *(re-iss.1974 & Jan78, re-iss.+cd.Oct86)*

— (below 'A'side featured **RICK WAKEMAN** – piano)

Dec 71. (7") **MORNING HAS BROKEN. / I WANT TO LIVE IN A WIGWAM** [9] [6] Mar 72

In Apr72, STEVENS contributed tracks to film 'Harold And Maude'.

— added **JEAN ROUSELL** – piano / **CAT** – some synthesizers repl. WAKEMAN. **ALAN JAMES** – bass repl. LARRY

Sep 72. (lp)(c) **CATCH BULL AT FOUR** [2] [1]
– Sitting / Boy with a moon and star on his head / Angel sea / Silent sunlight / Can't keep it in / 18th Avenue / Freezing steel / O Caritas / Sweet Scarlet / Ruins. *(re-iss.1974 & Jan78, re-iss.+cd.Oct86)*

Nov 72. (7") **CAN'T KEEP IT IN. / CRAB DANCE** [13] [-]
(re-iss.Jul81)

Nov 72. (7") **SITTING. / CRAB DANCE** [-] [16]

— CAT now became tax exile in Brazil and donated his extras to charity.

— now w / **ROUSSEL, DAVIS, LYNCH + CONWAY** plus loads of sessioners

Jul 73. (7") **THE HURT. / SILENT SUNLIGHT** [ ] [31]

Jul 73. (lp)(c) **FOREIGNER** [3] [3]
– Foreigner suite / The hurt / How many times / Later / 100 I dream. *(re-iss.quad.1974)*

— **BRUCE LYNCH** – bass repl. PAUL

Mar 74. (7") **OH VERY YOUNG. / 100 I DREAMS** [ ] [10]

Mar 74. (lp)(c) **BUDDAH AND THE CHOCOLATE BOX** [3] [2]
– Music / Oh very young / Sun – C79 / Ghost town / Jesus / Ready / King of trees / Bad penny / Home in the sky.

Aug 74. (7") **ANOTHER SATURDAY NIGHT. / HOME IN THE SKY** [19] [6]

Sep 74. (lp)(c) **SATURDAY NIGHT (live)** [-] [ ]
– Wild world / Oh very young / Sitting / Where do the children play / Lady D'Arbanville / Another Saturday night / Hard-headed woman / Peace train / Father & son / King of trees / A bad penny / Bitter blue.

Dec 74. (7") **READY. / I THINK I SEE THE LIGHT** [-] [26]

Jul 75. (7") **TWO FINE PEOPLE. / BAD PENNY** [ ] [33]

Jul 75. (lp)(c) **GREATEST HITS** (compilation) [2] [6]
– Wild world / Oh very young / Can't keep it in / Hard headed woman / Moonshadow / Two fine people / Peace train / Ready / Father and son / Sitting / Morning has broken / Another Saturday night. *(cd-iss. Mar 93)*

— now w / **ROUSSEL, DAVIS, LYNCH + CONWAY** plus loads of sessioners

Dec 75. (lp)(c) **NUMBERS** [ ] [13]
– Whistlestar / Novim's nightmare / Majik of majiks / Dry wood / Banapple gas / Land o' free love and goodbye / Jzero / Home / Nomad's anthem.

Mar 76. (7") **BANAPPLE GAS. / GHOST TOWN** [ ] [41] Feb 76

Mar 76. (7") **LAND O' FREE LOVE AND GOODBYE. / (I NEVER WANTED) TO BE A STAR** [-] [ ]

Apr 77. (lp)(c) **IZITSO** [18] [7]
– (Remember the days of the) Old schoolyard / Life / Killin' time / Kypros / Bonfire / To be a star / Crazy / Sweet Jamaica / Was Dog a doughnut / Child for a day.

Jun 77. (7") **(REMEMBER THE DAYS OF THE) OLD SCHOOLYARD. / DOVES** [44] [-]

Jun 77. (7") **(REMEMBER THE DAYS OF THE) OLD SCHOOLYARD. / LAND O' FREE LOVE AND GOODBYE** [-] [ ]

Nov 77. (7") **WAS DOG A DOUGHNUT. / SWEET JAMAICA** [-] [70]

Jan 79. (7") **BAD BRAKES. / NASCIMENTO** [-] [83]

Jan 79. (lp)(c) **BACK TO EARTH** [ ] [33] Dec 78
– Just another night / Daytime / Bad brakes / Randy / The artist / Last love song / Nascimento / Father / New York times / Never.

Feb 79. (7") **LAST LOVE SONG. / NASCIMENTO** [ ] [-]

Apr 79. (7") **RANDY. / NASCIMENTO** [-] [ ]

— He retired from the music scene, due to newfound Muslim religion. He changed his name to YUSEF ISLAM and married Fouzia Ali in Sep'79. They lived in London where he taught his faith to local school. In the late 80's, he was back in the limelight, when he condoned the Muslim assassination sanction against writer Salman Rushdie.

– more compilations, etc. –

1970. Decca; (lp)(c) **THE WORLD OF CAT STEVENS** [ ] [-]

Aug 81. Decca; (lp)(c) **THE FIRST CUT IS THE DEEPEST** [ ] [-]

Mar 71. Deram; (d-lp) **MATTHEW AND SON / NEW MASTERS** [-] [ ]
(UK-iss.May75 as 'VIEW FROM THE TOP')

Jan 72. Deram; (lp) **VERY YOUNG AND EARLY SONGS** [-] [94]

Nov 73. Deram; (7") **I LOVE MY DOG. / MATTHEW AND SON** [ ] [-]
(re-iss.Oct83)

Aug 80. Deram; (7"ep) **MATTHEW AND SON / I LOVE MY DOG. / A BAD NIGHT / I'M GONNA GET ME A GUN** [ ] [-]

Nov 89. Deram; (cd) **FIRST CUTS** [ ] [-]

Apr 86. Castle; (d-lp)(c) **THE COLLECTION** [ ] [-]

Apr 86. Spot; (c) **CAT STEVENS** [ ] [-]

Nov 83. Island; (7") **MORNING HAS BROKEN. / MOON SHADOW** [ ] [-]

Jan 85. Island/ US= A&M; (lp)(c) **FOOTSTEPS IN THE DARK – GREATEST HITS VOL. 2** [ ] [ ] Dec 84
(US version +=) – (3 extra tracks).

Feb 90. Island; (cd)(c)(lp) **THE VERY BEST OF CAT STEVENS** [ ] [ ]
– Where do the children play / Wild world / Tuesday's dead / Lady D'Arbanville / The first cut is the deepest / Oh very young / Rubylove / Morning has broken / Moonshadow / Matthew and son / Father and son / Can't keep it in / Hard headed woman / (Remember the days of the) Old school yard / I love my dog / Another Saturday night / Sad Lisa / Peace train.*(re-iss.Jul92)*

Apr 93. Pulsar; (cd) **WILD WORLD** [ ] [-]

Aug 93. Polygram TV; (cd)(c) **THE VERY BEST OF CAT STEVENS** [47] [-]
(different)

Sep 93. Spectrum; (cd)(c) **EARLY TAPES** [ ] [-]

Dave STEWART (see under ⇒ EURYTHMICS)

Rod STEWART

Born: RODERICK DAVID STEWART, 10 Jan'45, Highgate, London. Out of Scottish parentage, where his roots still lie as a passionate Scotland supporter. In 1963, after a time as an apprentice for Brentford F.C. and busker in Spain, he joined West Midlands group The FIVE DIMENSIONS. He played harmonica on a Jimmy Powell 45, before lending same for a live LONG JOHN BALDRY & THE HOOCHIE COOCHIE MEN a year later. He soon became singer and signed to 'Decca' as a solo artist, releasing debut single 'GOOD MORNING LITTLE SCHOOLGIRL'. In 1965, he joined STEAMPACKET, who contained 2 other singers BALDRY and JULIE DRISCOLL. This set-up finally evolved into The BRIAN AUGER TRINITY, but without ROD, who was now part of THE JEFF BECK GROUP. ROD provided vocals on a B-side 'I'VE BEEN DRINKIN'' in 1968. In the mid-60's he was also part of live group SHOTGUN EXPRESS. In 1969, ROD left JEFF BECK to join SMALL FACES evolvement into The FACES, but continued a new solo career, which was re-activated by 'Phonogram' records. His debut album 'AN OLD RAINCOAT . . . ' which featured some FACES, failed to hit in Britain, but managed to sell moderately in the States. His second 1970 album 'GASOLINE ALLEY' surprisingly broke him into the US Top 30, but he really infiltrated worldwide, when double 'A'side 'MAGGIE MAY' / 'REASON TO BELIEVE' smashed into the top slot US + UK. Its parent album 'EVERY PICTURE TELLS A STORY' also made the top, and he was soon a major star on both sides of the Atlantic. His next 5 albums 'NEVER A DULL MOMENT', SING IT AGAIN ROD', 'SMILER', 'ATLANTIC CROSSING', + 'A NIGHT ON THE TOWN', all hit UK No.1, and he also delivered over 30 major hits over the next 2 decades. • **Style:** Charismatic singer-songwriter with large sandpapery vocal range. His glamorous looks (i.e. spiky top hair, large nose and extroverted self-confidence) made him surprise star of the 70's, which was often sent up by most comics. Moved from ballads to disco anthems with incredible ease. • **Songwriters:** ROD's cover versions:- STREET FIGHTING MAN (Rolling Stones) / SWEET SOUL MUSIC (Arthur Conley) / MAN OF CONSTANT SORROW (Bob Dylan) / HANDBAGS AND GLADRAGS (Mike D'Abo) / DIRTY OLD TOWN (Ewan MacColl) / I KNOW I'M LOSING YOU (Temptations) / IT'S ALL OVER NOW (Valentinos) / MY WAY OF GIVING (Small Faces) / CUT ACROSS SHORTY (hit; Eddie Cochran) / ANGEL (Jimi Hendrix) / AMAZING GRACE (trad. / hit; Judy Collins) / I'D RATHER GO BLIND (Etta James) / ONLY A HOBO + SWEETHEART LIKE YOU (Bob Dylan) / TWISTIN' THE NIGHT AWAY + BRING IT ON HOME TO ME + YOU SEND ME + HAVING A PARTY + SOOTHE ME (Sam Cooke) / OH NO NOT MY BABY + PRETTY FLAMINGO (Manfred Mann) / THE FIRST CUT IS THE DEEPEST (Cat Stevens) / COUNTRY COMFORTS + YOUR SONG (Elton John) / WHAT MADE MILWALKEE FAMOUS (hit; Jerry Lee Lewis) / SAILING (Sutherland Brothers) / THIS OLD HEART OF MINE (Isley Brothers) / GET BACK (Beatles) / YOU KEEP ME HANGIN' ON (Supremes) / I DON'T WANT TO TALK ABOUT IT (Crazy Horse member Danny Whitten) / SOME GUYS HAVE ALL THE LUCK (Robert Palmer) / HOW LONG (Ace) / SWEET LITTLE ROCK'N'ROLLER + LITTLE QUEENIE (Chuck Berry) / THE GREAT PRETENDER (Platters) / ALL RIGHT NOW (Free) / TRY A LITTLE TENDERNESS (Otis Redding) / THE MOTOWN SONG (L.J.McNally) / IT TAKES TWO (Marvin Gaye & Tammi Terrell) / DOWNTOWN TRAIN + TOM TRAUBERT'S BLUES + HANG ON ST.CHRISTOPHER (Tom Waits) / BROKEN ARROW (Robbie Robertson) / HAVE I TOLD YOU LATELY THAT I LOVE YOU (Van Morrison) / PEOPLE GET READY (Curtis Mayfield) / RUBY TUESDAY (Rolling Stones) / SHOTGUN WEDDING (Roy C.) / WINDY

TOWN (Chris Rea) / DOWNTOWN LIGHTS (Blue Nile) / LEAVE VIRGINIA ALONE (Tom Petty) / SIMON CLIMIE began writing for him from 1988. YOU'RE THE STAR single written by Livesey, Lyle & Miller.
Trivia/Blondeography: BRITT ECKLAND (marriage 5 Mar'75-1978) / ALANA HAMILTON (marriage 6 Apr'79-1984) / KELLY EMBERG (1985-1990) / RACHEL HUNTER (marriage 15 Dec'90-now).

Recommended: STORYTELLER – THE BEST OF ROD STEWART (*8)

ROD STEWART – vocals with session people

Decca / Press

Oct 64. (7") **GOOD MORNING LITTLE SCHOOLGIRL. / I'M GONNA MOVE TO THE OUTSKIRTS OF TOWN**
(re-iss.Mar82)

In 1965, he joined STEAMPACKET, but they issued no 45's, and split Mar'66.

Columbia / not issued

Nov 65. (7") **THE DAY WILL COME. / WHY DOES IT GO ON** – | -
Apr 66. (7") **SHAKE. / I JUST GOT SOME** – | -

—— A month previous, he had joined SHOTGUN EXPRESS who released one 45, 'I COULD FEEL THE WHOLE WORLD TURN AROUND' Oct66 on 'Columbia'.

Immediate / not issued

Nov 67. (7") **LITTLE MISS UNDERSTOOD. / SO MUCH TO SAY** – | -
(re-iss.Sep80 on 'Virgin') (re-iss.Feb83)

—— In 1968, he joined JEFF BECK GROUP, appearing on 2 albums; 'TRUTH' & 'BECK-OLA'. Similtaneously joined The FACES and returned to solo work 1969.

Vertigo / Mercury

Feb 70. (lp)(c) **AN OLD RAINCOAT WON'T EVER LET YOU DOWN** (US title 'THE ROD STEWART ALBUM')
– Street fighting man / Man of constant sorrow / Blind prayer / Handbags and gladrags / An old raincoat won't ever let you down / I wouldn't ever change a thing / Cindy's lament / Dirty old town. *(re-iss.Aug83 on 'Mercury', cd-iss.Nov87 & Sep95)*
Feb 70. (7") **AN OLD RAINCOAT WON'T LET YOU DOWN. / STREET FIGHTING MAN** - |
May 70. (7") **HANDBAGS AND GLADRAGS. / MAN OF CONSTANT SORROW** - |
(re-iss. US Feb '72; hit No. 42)
Sep 70. (7") **IT'S ALL OVER NOW. / JO'S LAMENT**
Sep 70. (lp)(c) **GASOLINE ALLEY** 62 | 27 Jun 70
– Gasoline alley / It's all over now / My way of giving / Country comfort / Cut across Shorty / Lady day / Jo's lament / I don't want to discuss it. *(re-iss.Aug83 on 'Mercury', cd-iss.Oct84 & Sep95)*
Nov 70. (7") **GASOLINE ALLEY. / ONLY A HOBO** - |
Jan 71. (7") **CUT ACROSS SHORTY. / GASOLINE ALLEY** - |
Mar 71. (7") **MY WAY OF GIVING. /** - |
May 71. (7") **COUNTRY COMFORT. / GASOLINE ALLEY** - |

Mercury / Mercury

Jul 71. (7") **MAGGIE MAY. / REASON TO BELIEVE** 1 | 1 / 62

—— (above was flipped over for BBC Radio One playlist. MAGGIE MAY was now bigger played hit) *(re-iss.Oct84)*

Jul 71. (lp)(c) **EVERY PICTURE TELLS A STORY** 1 | 1 Jun 71
– Every picture tells a story / Seems like a long time / That's all right / Tomorrow is such a long time / Amazing Grace / Henry / Maggie May / Mandolin wind / (I know) I'm losing you / Reason to believe. *(re-iss.May83, cd-iss.Nov87 & Sep95)*
Nov 71. (7") **(I KNOW) I'M LOSING YOU. / MANDOLIN WIND** - | 24
Jul 72. (lp)(c) **NEVER A DULL MOMENT** 1 | 2
– True blue / Lost Paraguayos / Mama you been on my mind / Italian girls / Angel / Interludings / You wear it well / I'd rather go blind / Twisting the night away. *(re-iss.May83, cd-iss.Nov87 & Sep95)*
Aug 72. (7") **YOU WEAR IT WELL. / LOST PARAGUAYOS** 1 | -
Aug 72. (7") **YOU WEAR IT WELL. / TRUE BLUE** - | 13

—— Sep72, a ROD STEWART early recording with PYTHON LEE JACKSON; 'In A Broken Dream' hits UK No.3 / US No.56.

Nov 72. (7") **ANGEL. / WHAT MADE MILWAUKEE FAMOUS (HAS MADE A LOSER OUT OF ME)** 4 | -
Nov 72. (7") **ANGEL. / LOST PARAGUAYOS** - | 40

—— May73, older JEFF BECK & ROD STEWART recording 'I'VE BEEN DRINKIN' ' hit 27.

Aug 73. (7") **TWISTING THE NIGHT AWAY. / TRUE BLUE – LADY DAY** - | 59
Aug 73. (lp)(c) **SING IT AGAIN ROD** (compilation of covers) 1 | 31 Jul 73
– Reason to believe / You wear it well / Mandolin wind / Country comforts / Maggie May / Handbags and gladrags / Street fighting man / Twisting the night away / Lost Paraguayos / (I know) I'm losing you / Pinball wizard / Gasoline alley. *(cd-iss.Oct84)*
Aug 73. (7") **OH! NO NOT MY BABY. / JODIE** 6 | 59 Oct 73
Sep 74. (7") **FAREWELL. / BRING IT ON HOME TO ME – YOU SEND ME (Medley)** 7 | -
Oct 74. (lp)(c) **SMILER** 1 | 13
– Sweet little rock'n'roller / Lochinvar / Farewell / Sailor / Bring it on home to me – You send me (medley) / Let me be your car / A natural man / A natural man / Dixie toot / Hard road / I've grown accustomed to her face / Girl of the North Country / Mine for me. *(cd-iss.Nov87 & Sep95)*
Nov 74. (7") **MINE FOR ME. / FAREWELL** - | 91
Jan 75. (7") **LET ME BE YOUR CAR. / SAILOR** - |

Warners / Warners

Aug 75. (7") **SAILING. / STONE COLD SOBER** 1 | -
(re-activated Sep76, hit UK No.3, re-iss.Jan84) (re-iss.Jun77 on 'Riva') (re-iss.Mar87 for Channel Ferry disaster fund, hit No.41)
Aug 75. (lp)(c) **ATLANTIC CROSSING** 1 | 9
– Three time loser / Alright for an hour / All in the name of rock'n'roll / Drift away / Stone cold sober / I don't want to talk about it / It's not the spotlight / This old heart of mine / Still love you / Sailing. *(re-iss.Jan78 on 'Riva', hit UK 60) (cd-iss.Feb87 & 1989 on 'WEA') (blue-lp Jul77)*
Aug 75. (7") **SAILING. / ALL IN THE NAME OF ROCK'N'ROLL** - | 58

Riva / Warners

Nov 75. (7") **THIS OLD HEART OF MINE. / ALL IN THE NAME OF ROCK'N'ROLL** 4 | 83
May 76. (7") **TONIGHT'S THE NIGHT. / THE BALLTRAP** 5 | -
Jun 76. (lp)(c) **A NIGHT ON THE TOWN** 1 | 2
– Tonight's the night / The first cut is the deepest / Fool for you / The killing of Georgie (part 1 & 2) / The balltrap / Pretty flamingo / Big bayou / The wild side of life / Trade winds. *(re-iss.Jun83 on 'Warner Bros', cd-iss.1989 on 'WEA')*
Aug 76. (7") **THE KILLING OF GEORGIE. / FOOL FOR YOU** 2 | -
Sep 76. (7") **TONIGHT'S THE NIGHT. / FOOL FOR YOU** - | 1
Nov 76. (7") **GET BACK. / TRADE WINDS** 11 | -
Feb 77. (7") **THE FIRST CUT IS THE DEEPEST. / THE BALLTRAP** - | 21
Apr 77. (7") **THE FIRST CUT IS THE DEEPEST. / I DON'T WANT TO TALK ABOUT IT** 1 | -
Apr 77. (7") **THE KILLING OF GEORGIE. / ROSIE** - | 30
Oct 77. (7") **YOU'RE IN MY HEART. / YOU GOT A NERVE** 3 | 4
Nov 77. (lp)(c) **FOOT LOOSE AND FANCY FREE** 3 | 2
– Hot legs / You're insane / You're in my heart / Born loose / You keep me hangin' on / (If loving you is wrong) I don't want to be right / You got a nerve / I was only joking. *(re-iss.Jun83 on 'Warner Bros.', cd-iss.Jun89)*
Jan 78. (7") **HOT LEGS. / I WAS ONLY JOKING** 5 | -
Feb 78. (7") **HOT LEGS. / YOU'RE INSANE** - | 28
Apr 78. (7") **I WAS ONLY JOKING. / BORN LOOSE** | 22
May 78. (7") **OLE OLA (MUHLER BRASILEIRA). (as "ROD STEWART With The SCOTLAND WORLD CUP SQUAD") / I'D WALK A MILLION MILES FOR ONE OF YOUR GOALS** 4 | -
Nov 78. (7") **D'YA THINK I'M SEXY?. / DIRTY WEEKEND** 1 | -
Dec 78. (7")(12") **D'YA THINK I'M SEXY?. / SCARRED AND SCARED** - | 1
Dec 78. (lp)(c)(US-pic-lp) **BLONDES HAVE MORE FUN** 3 | 1
– D'ya think I'm sexy / Dirty weekend / Ain't love a bitch / The best days of my life / Is that the thanks I get / Attractive female wanted / Blondes (have more fun) / Last summer / Standing in the shadows of love / Scarred and scared. *(re-iss.Jun83 on 'Warner Bros.')*
Jan 79. (7") **AIN'T LOVE A BITCH. / SCARRED AND SCARED** 11 | -
Apr 79. (7") **AIN'T LOVE A BITCH. / LAST SUMMER** - | 22
Apr 79. (7") **BLONDES (HAVE MORE FUN). / THE BEST DAYS OF MY LIFE** 63 | -
Nov 79. (lp)(c) **GREATEST HITS VOLUME 1** (compilation) 1 | 22
– Hot legs / Maggie May / a ya think I'm sexy / You're in my heart / Sailing / I don't want to talk about it / Tonight's the night / The killing of Georgie (parts 1 & 2) / Maggie May / The first cut is the deepest / I was only joking. *(re-iss.Jun83, cd-iss.Jan84 on 'Warner Bros.')*
Dec 79. (7") **I DON'T WANT TO TALK ABOUT IT. / THE BEST DAYS OF MY LIFE** - | 46
May 80. (7") **IF LOVING YOU IS WRONG (I DON'T WANT TO BE RIGHT). / LAST SUMMER** 23 |
Nov 80. (7")(12") **PASSION. / BETTER OFF DEAD** 17 | 5
Nov 80. (lp)(c) **FOOLISH BEHAVIOR** 4 | 12
– Better off dead / Foolish behaviour / My girl / She won't dance with me / Gi' me wings / So soon we change / Somebody special / Passion / Say it ain't true / Oh God, I wish I was home tonight. *(re-iss.Jun83 on 'Warner Bros.')*
Dec 80. (7") **MY GIRL. / SHE WON'T DANCE WITH ME** 32 | -
Mar 81. (7")(c-s) **OH GOD, I WISH I WAS HOME TONIGHT. / SOMEBODY SPECIAL** | -
Mar 81. (7") **SOMEBODY SPECIAL. / SHE WON'T DANCE WITH ME** - | 71
Oct 81. (7") **YOUNG TURKS. / SONNY** - | 5
Oct 81. (7") **TONIGHT I'M YOURS (DON'T HURT ME). / SONNY** 8 | -
Nov 81. (lp)(c) **TONIGHT I'M YOURS** 8 | 11
– Tonight I'm yours (don't hurt me) / Only a boy / Just like a woman / How long / Never give up on a dream / Jealous / Tora, Tora, Tora (out with the boys) / Young Turks / Tear it up / Sonny. *(re-iss.Jun83)*
Dec 81. (7") **YOUNG TURKS. / TORA, TORA, TORA (OUT WITH THE BOYS)** 11 | -
Jan 82. (7") **TONIGHT I'M YOURS (DON'T HURT ME). / TORA, TORA, TORA (OUT WITH THE BOYS)** - | 20

Feb 82. (7") **HOW LONG. / JEALOUS** [41] [49] Apr 82

Nov 82. (d-lp)(d-c) **ABSOLUTELY LIVE (live)** [35] [46]
– The stripper / Tonight I'm yours / Sweet little rock'n'roller / Hot legs / Tonight's the night / The great pretender / Passion / She won't dance with me / Little Queenie / You're in my heart / Rock my plimsoul / Young Turks / Guess I'll always love you / Gasoline alley / Maggie May / Tear it up / D'ya think I'm sexy / Sailing / I don't want to talk about it / Stay with me. *(re-iss.Mar84 on 'Warner Bros.', cd-iss.Mar87 on 'WEA')*

Nov 82. (7") **GUESS I'LL ALWAYS LOVE YOU (live). / ROCK MY PLIMSOUL (live)** [-] [ ]

Warner Warners

May 83. (7") **BABY JANE. / READY NOW** [1] [14]
(12"+=) – If loving you is wrong (live).

Jun 83. (lp)(c) **BODY WISHES** [5] [30]
– Dancin' alone / Baby Jane / Move me / Body wishes / Sweet surrender / What am I gonna do / Ghetto blaster / Ready now / Strangers again / Satisfied. *(cd-iss.Jul84)*

Aug 83. (7")(12") **WHAT AM I GONNA DO?. / DANCIN' ALONE** [3] [35]

Dec 83. (7") **SWEET SURRENDER. / GHETTO BLASTER** [23] [-]
(12"+=)(12"pic-d+=) – Oh God I wish I was home tonight.

May 84. (7") **INFATUATION. / SHE WON'T DANCE WITH ME** [-] [6]

May 84. (7") **INFATUATION. / THREE TIME LOSER** [27] [-]
(12"+=) – Tonight's the night.

Jun 84. (lp)(c)(cd) **CAMOUFLAGE** [8] [18]
– Infatuation / All right now / Some guys have all the luck / Can we still be friends / Bad for you / Heart is on the line / Camouflage / Trouble. *(free 1-sided 7"pic-d w.a.)* – INFATUATION / (interview).

Jul 84. (7") **SOME GUYS HAVE ALL THE LUCK. / I WAS ONLY JOKING** [15] [10]
(12"+=) – The killing of Georgie.

Nov 84. (7") **TROUBLE. / TORA, TORA, TORA (OUT WITH THE BOYS)** [ ] [ ]
(12"+=) – This old heart of mine.

Dec 84. (7") **ALL RIGHT NOW. / DANCIN' ALONE** [-] [72]

— In 1985, he was credited on 45 'PEOPLE GET READY' by JEFF BECK.

Jun 86. (7") **LOVE TOUCH. / HEART IS ON THE LINE** [27] [6] May 86
(12"pic-d+=) – Hard lesson to learn.

Jun 86. (lp)(c)(cd) **EVERY BEAT OF MY HEART** (US-title 'ROD STEWART') [5] [28]
– Here to eternity / Another heartache / A night like this / Who's gonna take me home / Red hot in black / Love touch / In my own crazy way / Every beat of my heart / Ten days of rain / In my life. *(cd+=)* – Every beat of my heart (remix).

Jul 86. (7") **EVERY BEAT OF MY HEART. / TROUBLE** [2] [83] Nov 86
(12"+=) – ('A'mix).
(12"pic-d+=) – Some guys have all the luck (live)

Sep 86. (7") **ANOTHER HEARTACHE. / YOU'RE IN MY HEART** [54] [52]
(12"+=) – ('A'extended).

Jul 87. (7") **TWISTING THE NIGHT AWAY. / LET'S GET SMALL** [-] [80]

above was issued on 'Geffen' and on film 'Innerspace'.

May 88. (7")(US-c-s) **LOST IN YOU. / ALMOST ILLEGAL** [21] [12]
(12"+=)(12"pic-d+=) – ('A'extended).
(cd-s+=) – Baby Jane / Every beat of my heart.

May 88. (lp)(c)(cd) **OUT OF ORDER** [11] [20]
– Lost in you / The wild horse / Lethal dose of love / Forever young / My heart can't tell you no / Dynamite / Nobody loves you when you're down and out / Crazy about her / Try a little tenderness / When I was your man.

Jul 88. (7") **FOREVER YOUNG. / DAYS OF RAGE** [57] [12]
(12"+=)/ /(cd-s+=) – ('A'extended)./ / Every beat of my heart.

Jan 89. (7") **TRY A LITTLE TENDERNESS. / MY HEART CAN'T TELL YOU NO** [ ] [ ]
(12"+=)(cd-s+=) – Passion.

Apr 89. (7") **MY HEART CAN'T TELL YOU NO. / THE WILD HORSE** [49] [4] Nov 88
(12"+=)(cd-s+=)(12"pic-d+=) – Passion (live).

May 89. (7")(c-s) **CRAZY ABOUT HER. / DYNAMITE** [-] [11]

Nov 89. (7")(c-s)(7"pic-d) **THIS OLD HEART OF MINE. ("ROD STEWART with RONALD ISLEY") / TONIGHT I'M YOURS DON'T HURT ME)** [51] [-]
(12"+=)(cd-s+=)(12"pic-d+=) – Ain't love a bitch.

Nov 89. (d-lp)(d-c)(d-cd) **STORYTELLER – THE BEST OF ROD STEWART 1964-1990** (compilation) [3] [54]

— (was also issued UK on (7xlp)(4xc)(4xcd).

Jan 90. (7")(c-s) **DOWNTOWN TRAIN. / THE KILLING OF GEORGIE (pt.1 & 2)** [10] [3] Nov 89
(12")(cd-s) – ('A'side) / Hot legs.
(12"+=) – ('A'side) / Cindy incidentally / To love somebody.

Mar 90. (7") **THIS OLD HEART OF MINE (w/ RONALD ISLEY). / YOU'RE IN MY HEART** [-] [ ]

Mar 90. (cd)(c) **DOWNTOWN TRAIN – SELECTIONS FROM STORYTELLER** (compilation) [-] [20]

Nov 90. (7")(c-s) **IT TAKES TWO. ("ROD STEWART & TINA TURNER") / HOT LEGS (live)** [5] [ ]
(12"+=)(cd-s+=) – ('A'extended remix).

Mar 91. (7")(c-s) **RHYTHM OF MY HEART. / MOMENT OF GLORY** [3] [5] Feb 91
(12"+=)(cd-s+=) – I don't want to talk about it (re-recording).

Apr 91. (cd)(c)(lp) **VAGABOND HEART** [2] [10]
– Rhythm of my heart / Rebel heart / Broken arrow / It takes two / When a man's in love / You are everything / The Motown song / Go out dancing / No holding back / Have I told you lately that I love you / Moment of glory / Downtown train / If only.

Jun 91. (7")(c-s) **THE MOTOWN SONG. / SWEET SOUL MUSIC (live)** [10] [10]
(12"+=)(cd-s+=) – Try a little tenderness.

Aug 91. (7")(c-s) **BROKEN ARROW. / I WAS ONLY JOKING** [54] [20] Oct 91
(10"+=)(cd-s+=) – The killing of Georgie (parts 1 & 2).

Apr 92. (7")(c-s) **YOUR SONG. / BROKEN ARROW** [41] [48]
(12"+=)(cd-s+=) – Mandolin wind / The first cut is the deepest

Nov 92. (7")(c-s) **TOM TRAUBERT'S BLUES (WALTZING MATILDA). / NO HOLDING BACK** [6] [ ]
(cd-s+=) – Downtown train.
(cd-s) – ('A'side) / Sailing / I don't want to talk about it / Try a little tenderness.

Feb 93. (cd)(c)(lp) **ROD STEWART, LEAD VOCALIST** (part comp.) [3] [ ]
– I ain't superstitious / Handbags & gladrags / Cindy incidentally / Stay with me / True blue / Sweet Mary lady / Hot legs / Stand back / Ruby Tuesday / Shotgun wedding / First I look at the purse / Tom Traubert's blues.

Feb 93. (7")(c-s) **RUBY TUESDAY. / YOU'RE IN MY HEART** [11] [ ]
(cd-s+=) – Out of order / Passion.
(cd-s+=) – Crazy about her / Passion.

Apr 93. (7")(c-s) **SHOTGUN WEDDING. / EVERY BEAT OF MY HEART** [21] [ ]
(cd-s+=) – Sweet soul music (live).
(cd-s) – ('A'side) / Memphis / Maybe I'm amazed / Had me a real goodtime (all 3 by ROD STEWART & THE FACES).

— below with special guest **RONNIE WOOD** – guitar plus others **JEFF GOLUB** – guitar / **CARMINE ROJAS** – bass / **CHARLES KENTISS III** – piano, organ / **KEVIN SAVIGAR** – piano, organ & accordion / **JIM CREGAN** – guitar / **DON TESCHNER** – guitar, violin & mandolin / **PHIL PARLAPIANO** – accordion & mandolin / & backing singers

May 93. (cd)(c)(lp) **UNPLUGGED . . . AND SEATED** [2] [2]
– Hot legs / Tonight's the night / Handbags and gladrags / Cut across Shorty / Every picture tells a story / Maggie May / Reason to believe / People get ready / Have I told you lately / Tom Traubert's blues (waltzing Matilda) / The first cut is the deepest / Mandolin wind / Highgate shuffle / Stay with me / Having a party.

Jun 93. (7")(c-s) **HAVE I TOLD YOU LATELY THAT I LOVE YOU?. / LET THE DAY BEGIN** [5] [5] Apr 93
(cd-s+=) – Gasoline alley (live).
(cd-s) – ('A'side) / Love wars / One night.

Aug 93. (7")(c-s) **REASON TO BELIEVE (unplugged). / IT'S ALL OVER NOW (unplugged)** [51] [19]
(cd-s+=) – Love in the right hands.
(cd-s) – ('A'side) / Cindy incidentally / Stay with me (both w / FACES).

— In Dec '93, ROD & STING, teamed up with BRYAN ADAMS on his US Top 5 hit 'All For Love'.

Dec 93. (7")(c-s) **PEOPLE GET READY. / I WAS ONLY JOKING** [45] [ ]
(cd-s) – ('A'side) / Tonight's the night / If loving you is wrong (I don't want to be right).
(cd-s) – ('A'side) / Da ya think I'm sexy / Sweet little rock'n'roller (live) / Baby Jane.

— Late Nov '93, he BRYAN ADAMS and STING teamed up on a song from 'The Three Musketeers' film; 'ALL FOR LOVE', which hit UK No.2 (early '94) + US No.1.

Feb 94. (c-s)(cd-s) **HAVING A PARTY /** [-] [40]

May 95. (c-s) **YOU'RE THE STAR / SHOCK TO THE SYSTEM** [19] [ ]
(cd-s+=) – Have I told you lately.

May 95. (cd)(c)(lp) **A SPANNER IN THE WORKS** [4] [35]
– Windy town / Downtown lights / Leave Virginia alone / Sweetheart like you / This / Lady luck / You're the star / Muddy, Sam and Otis / Hang on St. Christopher / Delicious / Soothe me / Purple heather.

Jun 95. (c-s)(cd-s) **LEAVE VIRGINIA ALONE /** [-] [52]

Aug 95. (c-s) **LADY LUCK / HOT LEGS** [56] [ ]
(cd-s+=) – The groom still waiting at the altar / Young Turks.
(cd-s) – ('A'side) / The killing of Georgie / Sailing / The first cut is the deepest.

. . . Jan – Jun '96 stop press . . .

Jun 96. (single) **PURPLE HEATHER** [16] [ ]

— The official song for Scotland's Euro '96 football campaign. All proceeds were donated to the families of the Dunblane tragedy.

– more compilations, etc. –

Sep 72. Youngblood/ US= GNP Crescendo; (7") **IN A BROKEN DREAM. ("PYTHON LEE JACKSON") / THE BLUES** [3] [56]
(re-iss. Jul 80 +12"+=) – Cloud 9. *(re-iss.Aug87 as "PYTHON LEE JACKSON / ROD STEWART" on 'Bold Reprieve')*

— PYTHON LEE JACKSON was in fact an Australian 5-piece of the late 60s, headed by keyboard player **DAVID BENTLEY**, who employed ROD to sing on 3 tracks from their lp 'IN A BROKEN DREAM'.

1979. Lightning; (7") **IN A BROKEN DREAM. / IF THE WORLD STOPS STILL TONIGHT** [ ] [-]

Below releaes on 'Mercury' until otherwise mentioned.

Feb 76. (d-lp)(c) **THE VINTAGE YEARS 1969-70** [ ] [ ]
Feb 76. (7") **IT'S ALL OVER NOW. / HANDBAGS AND GLADRAGS** [ ] [-]
1976. (7") **EVERY PICTURE TELLS A STORY. / WHAT MADE MILWAUKEE FAMOUS (HAS MADE A LOSER OUT OF ME)** [-] [ ]
Jul 76. (lp)(c) **RECORDED HIGHLIGHTS AND ACTION REPLAYS** [ ] [ ]
Jun 77. (7"m) **MANDOLIN WIND. / GIRL FROM THE NORTH COUNTRY / SWEET LITTLE ROCK'N'ROLLER** [ ] [-]
Jun 77. (d-lp)(d-c) **THE BEST OF ROD STEWART** [18] [90]
(re-iss.1985)
Jul 77. (c) **THE MUSIC OF ROD STEWART (1970-71)** [ ] [-]
Aug 77. (d-lp)(d-c) **THE BEST OF ROD STEWART VOLUME 2** [ ] [ ]
Nov 79. (7") **MAGGIE MAY. / YOU WEAR IT WELL** [ ] [-]
(re-iss.Apr88 on 'Old Gold')
Sep 80. (lp)(c) **HOT RODS** [ ] [-]
May 81. (lp)(c) **BEST OF THE BEST** [ ] [-]
Nov 87. (cd) **THE ROD STEWART ALBUM** [ ] [-]
Jun 89. (lp)(c)(cd) **THE ROCK ALBUM** [ ] [-]
Jun 89. (cd) **THE BALLAD TIME** [ ] [-]
Feb 91. (cd)(c) **GASOLINE ALLEY / SMILER** [ ] [-]
Oct 92. (7")(c-s) **YOU WEAR IT WELL. / I WOULD RATHER GO BLIND** [ ] [ ]
(cd-s+=) – Angel.
Dec 78. St.Michael; (lp) **REASON TO BELIEVE** [ ] [-]
Sep 81. Contour; (lp)(c) **MAGGIE MAY** [ ] [-]
(cd-iss.Jul90 on 'Pickwick')
Oct 82. Contour; (lp)(c) **ROD STEWART** [ ] [-]
Sep 85. Contour; (lp)(c) **THE HITS OF ROD STEWART** [ ] [-]
Jan 87. Contour; (lp)(c) **JUKE BOX HEAVEN (14 ROCK'N'ROLL GREATS)** [ ] [-]
Jul 83. Cambra; (d-c) **ROD STEWART** [ ] [-]
Nov 83. Warners; (d-c) **ATLANTIC CROSSING / A NIGHT ON THE TOWN** [ ] [-]
Nov 84. Astan; (lp)(c) **CAN I GET A WITNESS** [ ] [-]
Jul 88. Knight; (lp)(c) **NIGHTRIDIN'** [ ] [-]
Feb 89. Venus; (c) **THE MAGIC OF ROD STEWART** [ ] [-]
Oct 89. K-Tel/ US- GNP; (lp)(c)(cd) **IN A BROKEN DREAM** [ ] [ ] 1988
Dec 92. M Classics; (cd)(c) **JUST A LITTLE MISUNDERSTOOD** [ ] [-]
Feb 93. Charly; (cd) **THE FIRST SUPER GROUP ("ROD STEWART & STEAMPACKET")** [ ] [-]
Jul 93. Ronco; (cd)(c) **THE FACE OF THE SIXTIES** [ ] [-]
Jul 94. Success; (cd)(c) **COME HOME BABY** [ ] [-]
Aug 95. Spectrum; (cd)(c) **MAGGIE MAY – THE CLASSIC YEARS** [ ] [-]

STIFF LITTLE FINGERS

Formed: Belfast, N.Ireland . . . 1977 by teenagers JAKE BURNS and co. They released a couple of singles on own 'Rigid Digit', before they moved to major indie label 'Rough Trade' in 1978. Their debut album 'INFLAMMABLE MATERIAL' hit the Top 20, due to more heavy airplay from Radio 1 DJ John Peel. In 1979, their fans cried "sell-out" when 'Chrysalis' records took them on board. They were soon chart regulars, although their loyal support soon dwindled. • **Style:** Protest punk rock (mainly about troubled homeland). In the early 80's, after SLF moved to London, England, BURNS's hoarse but effective vox had slightly succumbed to a more commercial attitude. • **Songwriters:** BURNS penned, some with OGILVIE. They also covered JOHNNY WAS (Bob Marley) / RUNNING BEAR (Johnny Preston) / WHITE CHRISTMAS (Bing Crosby) / LOVE OF THE COMMON PEOPLE (Nicky Thomas). • **Trivia:** JAKE once applied for a job of a Radio 1 producer.

Recommended: INFLAMMABLE MATERIAL (*9) / NOBODY'S HEROES (*8) / ALL THE BEST (*8).

JAKE BURNS – vocals, lead guitar / **HENRY CLUNEY** – guitar / **ALI McMORDIE** – bass / **BRIAN FALOON** – drums repl. GORDON BLAIR who later joined RUDI

Rigid Digit / not issued

Mar 78. (7") **SUSPECT DEVICE. / WASTED LIFE** [ ] [-]
(re-iss.Jun78) (re-iss.Mar79, Jan80 & Apr82 on 'Rigid Digit/Rough Trade')

Rough Trade / not issued

Oct 78. (7") **ALTERNATIVE ULSTER. / 78 R.P.M.** [ ] [-]
(above originally iss.Aug78 on 'Rigid Digit-Rough Trade')

Feb 79. (lp) **INFLAMMABLE MATERIAL** [14] [-]
– Suspect device / State of emergency / Here we are nowhere / asted life / No more of that / Barbed wire love / White noise / Breakout / Law and order / Rough trade / Johnny was / Alternative Ulster / Closed groove. *(re-iss.+c+cd.Mar89 on 'E.M.I.')*

—— **JIM REILLY** – drums repl. FALOON

May 79. (7") **GOTTA GETAWAY. / BLOODY SUNDAY** [ ] [-]

Chrysalis / Chrysalis

Sep 79. (7") **STRAW DOGS. / YOU CAN'T SAY CRAP ON THE RADIO** [44] [ ]
Feb 80. (7") **AT THE EDGE. / SILLY ENCORES: RUNNING BEAR – WHITE CHRISTMAS** [15] [ ]
Mar 80. (lp)(c) **NOBODY'S HEROES** [8] [ ]
– Gotta getaway / Wait and see / Fly the flag / At the edge / Nobody's hero / Bloody dub / Doesn't make it alright / I don't like you / No change / Suspect device / Tin soldiers. *(re-iss.+c+cd.Mar89 on 'E.M.I.')*
May 80. (7") **TIN SOLDIERS. / NOBODY'S HERO** [36] [ ]
Jul 80. (7") **BACK TO FRONT. / MR.FIRE COAL-MAN** [49] [-]
Sep 80. (lp)(c) **HANX! (live)** [9] [-]
– Nobody's hero / Gotta getaway / Wait and see / Barbed wire love / Fly the flag / Alternative Ulster / Johnny was / At the edge / Wasted life / Tin soldiers / Suspect device. *(re-iss.+c+cd.Feb89 on 'Fame-EMI')*
Mar 81. (7"m) **JUST FADE AWAY. / GO FOR IT / DOESN'T MAKE IT ALRIGHT (live)** [47] [-]
Apr 81. (lp)(c) **GO FOR IT** [14] [-]
– Roots, radicals, rockers and reggae / Just fade away / Go for it / The only one / Hits and misses / Kicking up a racket / Safe as houses / Gate 49 / Silver lining / Piccadilly Circus. *(re-iss.+c+cd.Feb89 on 'Fame-EMI', cd+=)* – Back to front.
May 81. (7") **SILVER LINING. / SAFE AS HOUSES** [68] [-]

—— **BRIAN 'DOLPHIN' TAYLOR** – drums (ex-TOM ROBINSON BAND) repl. REILLY

Jan 82. (7"ep) **R.E.P. ONE POUND TEN PENCE OR LESS** [33] [-]
– Listen / Sad-eyed people / That's when your blood bumps / Two guitars clash.
Apr 82. (7") **TALK BACK. / GOOD FOR NOTHING** [ ] [-]
Aug 82. (7") **BITS OF KIDS. / STANDS TO REASON** [73] [-]
Sep 82. (lp)(c) **NOW THEN** [24] [-]
– Falling down / Won't be told / Love of the common people / The price of admission / Touch and go / Stands to reason / Bits of kids / Welcome to the whole week / Big city night / Talkback / Is that what you fought the war for. *(re-iss.cd Dec94 on 'Fame')*
Jan 83. (d-lp)(d-c) **ALL THE BEST** (compilation) [19] [-]
– Suspect device / Wasted life / Alternative Ulster / 78 rpm / Gotta getaway / Bloody Sunday / Straw dogs / You can't say crap on the radio / At the edge / Running bear / White Christmas / Nobody's hero / Tin soldiers / Back to front / Mr. Fire coal man / Just fade away / Go for it / Doesn't make it alright / Silver lining / Safe as houses / Sad eyed people / Two guitars clash / Listen / That's when your blood bumps / Good for nothing / Talkback / Stand to reason / Bits of kids / Touch and go / The price of admission. *(d-cd-iss.Jun88) (re-iss.d-cd+d-c.Sep91 on 'E.M.I.')*
Feb 83. (7") **THE PRICE OF ADMISSION. / TOUCH AND GO** [ ] [-]

—— Had already disbanded late 1982. McMORDIE joined FICTION GROOVE and DOLPHIN joined SPEAR OF DESTINY after stint with GO WEST.

JAKE BURNS & THE BIG WHEEL

were formed by **JAKE** plus **NICK MUIR** – keyboards / **SEAN MARTIN** – bass / **STEVE GRANTLEY** – drums

Survival / not issued

Jul 85. (7")(12") **ON FORTUNE STREET. / HERE COMES THAT SONG AGAIN** [ ] [-]
Mar 86. (7")(12") **SHE GREW UP. / RACE YOU TO THE GRAVE** [ ] [-]

Jive-CBS / not issued

Feb 87. (7")('A'ext-12") **BREATHLESS. / VALENTINE'S DAY** [ ] [-]

STIFF LITTLE FINGERS

re-formed in 1987 by **BURNS, TAYLOR, CLUNEY & McMORDIE**

Kaz / not issued

May 88. (lp)(c)(cd) **NO SLEEP TILL BELFAST (live)** [ ] [-]
– Alternative Ulster / Roots radicals rockers and reggae / Silver lining / Wait and see / Gotta getaway / Just fade away / Wasted life / The only one / Nobody's hero / At the edge / Listen / Barbed wire love / Fly the flag / Tin soldiers / No sleep till Belfast / Suspect device / Johnny was.

Skunx / not issued

Jun 88. (12"ep) **NO SLEEP TILL BELFAST (live)** [ ] [-]
– Suspect device / Alternative Ulster / Nobody's hero.

Virgin / Virgin

Mar 89. (12"ep)(3"cd-ep) **ST.PATRIX** (the covers live) [ ] [-]
– The wild rover / Johnny was / Love of the common people.
Apr 89. (d-lp)(d-c)(d-cd) **SEE YOU UP THERE! (live)** [ ] [-]
– (intro: Go for it) / Alternative Ulster / Silver lining / Love of the common people / Gotta getaway / Just fade away / Piccadilly Circus / Gate 49 / Wasted

life / At the edge / Listen / Barbed wire love / Fly the flag / Tin soldiers / The wild rover / Suspect device / Johnny was.

— (Mar91) **BRUCE FOXTON** – bass (ex-JAM, ex-Solo Artist) repl. McMORDIE

		Essential	not issued
Oct 91.	(cd)(c)(lp)(pic-lp) **FLAGS AND EMBLEMS**		-
	– (It's a) Long way to Paradise (from here) / Stand up and shout / Each dollar a bullet / The cosh / Beirut Moon / The game of life / Human shield / Johnny 7 / Dread burn / No surrender. *(re-iss.cd Jul95 on 'Dojo')*		
Oct 91.	(cd-ep) **BEIRUT MOON / STAND UP AND SHOUT / (interview)**		-
Jan 94.	(12"ep) **CAN'T BELIEVE IN YOU. / SILVER LINING (unplugged) / LISTEN (unplugged) / WASTED LIFE (unplugged)**		-
	(cd-ep) – ('A'side) / ('A'extended) / Alternative Ulster (featuring RICKY WARWICK of The ALMIGHTY) / Smithers-Jones (live with BRUCE FOXTON vocals).		
Feb 94.	(cd)(c) **GET A LIFE**		-
	– Get a life / Can't believe in you / The road to kingdom come / Walk away / No laughing matter / Harp / Forensic evidence / Baby blue ((what have they been telling you?) / I want you / The night that the wall came down / Cold / When the stars fall from the sky / What if I want more?.		
Jun 94.	(12")(cd-s) **HARP. / SHAKE IT OFF / NOW WHAT WE WERE (PRO PATRIA MORI)**		

– more compilations, etc. –

Sep 86.	Strange Fruit; (12"ep) **THE PEEL SESSIONS** (12/9/78)		-
	– Johnny was / Law and order / Barbed wire love / Suspect device. *(c-ep iss. May87, cd-ep iss.Jul88)*		
Nov 89.	Strange Fruit; (lp)(c)(cd) **THE PEEL SESSIONS**		-
Apr 88.	Link; (d-lp)(green-d-lp) **LIVE AND LOUD (live)** *(cd-iss.Sep89)*		-
Oct 89.	Link; (12"ep) **THE LAST TIME. / MR.FIRE-COAL MAN / TWO GUITARS CLASH**		-
Apr 91.	Link; (cd) **GREATEST HITS LIVE (live)**		-
Oct 91.	Link; (cd) **ALTERNATIVE CHARTBUSTERS**		-
Oct 89.	Limited; (green-lp)(cd) **LIVE IN SWEDEN (live)**		-
Dec 92.	Dojo; (cd) **FLY THE FLAGS – LIVE AT BRIXTON ACADEMY (27/9/91)**		-
Aug 93.	Windsong; (cd) **BBC RADIO 1 LIVE IN CONCERT (live)**		-
Mar 95.	Dojo; (cd) **PURE FINGERS LIVE – ST.PATRIX 1993**		-

Stephen STILLS / MANASSAS

(see under ⇒ CROSBY, STILLS, NASH)

STILTSKIN

Formed: London, England . . . 1989 by LAWLOR and FINNEGAN. The latter had played with Scots act HUE AND CRY, while LAWLOR had just returned from the States. They soon found ROSS McFARLANE, who had played with SLIDE, while 1993 saw them finding singer RAY WILSON. Came to light unusually when their track 'INSIDE' was aired on a Levi jeans TV commercial (the one where the quaker girls go to lake and see what appears to be a naked man in the water, only to find he is just breaking in his new jeans). The Television company were then inundated with enquiries on who was the group or person on its soundtrack, and where could they buy it. Unfortunately it hadn't been released, but was about to due to public demand. In April 1994, a version complete with words, crashed into the UK No.5 and soon was topping the charts. However by the end of the year, bad debut album reviews made them already yesterday's men. Maybe another quality song /advert will be on the cards for '95. • **Style:** Grunge rock, cloning NIRVANA. • **Songwriters:** LAWLOR. • **Trivia:** THE AMBROSIAN CHOIR sang choral on 'INSIDE'.

Recommended: THE MIND'S EYE (*4)

RAY WILSON – vocals / **PETER LAWLOR** – guitars, mandolin, vocals / **JAMES FINNIGAN** – bass, keyboards / **ROSS McFARLANE** – drums, percussion

		Whitewater	Sony
Apr 94.	(7")(c-s) **INSIDE. / AMERICA**	1	
	(12"+=)(cd-s+=) – ('A'extended).		
Sep 94.	(7")(c-s) **FOOTSTEPS. / SUNSHINE & BUTTERFLIES (live)**	34	
	(cd-s+=) – ('A'extended).		
Oct 94.	(cd)(c)(lp) **THE MIND'S EYE**	17	
	– Intro / Scared of ghosts / Horse / Rest in peace / Footsteps / Sunshine and butterflies / Inside / An illusion / America / When my ship comes in / Prayer before birth.		
Mar 95.	(7"ep)(c-ep)(cd-ep) **REST IN PEACE. / THE POLTROON / INSIDE (acoustic)**		

— LAWLOR has now own self-named group.

STING

Born: GORDON SUMNER, 2 Oct'51, Wallsend, nr.Newcastle, England. In the early 70's he gave up his job as a primary school teacher and joined a local group. He gained his nickname after wearing black and yellow hooped T-shirt. In 1974, he joined LAST EXIT, where he became lead singer on single 'WHISPERING VOICES'. Around this time, he enrolled with RADA and began on TV ad work. He was later to become successful actor later in the 70's. Early in 1977, he formed The POLICE, who became top selling outfit until their demise in 1983. STING had earlier branched out on a solo career while starring in the film 'BRIMSTONE AND TREACLE'. In 1985 he employed American musicians, to augment his new triumphant debut album 'DREAM OF THE BLUE TURTLES'. • **Style:** Popular rock tinged artist who fused his great voice into aspects of jazz and soul. • **Songwriters:** STING penned all work, except SPREAD A LITTLE HAPPINESS + SOMEONE TO WATCH OVER ME (George Gershwin) / TUTTI FRUTTI (Little Richard) / NEED YOUR LOVE SO BAD (Little Willie John) / MACK THE KNIFE (Bertold Brecht) / PURPLE HAZE (Jimi Hendrix) / SISTERS OF MERCY (Leonard Cohen) w/ CHIEFTAINS. • **Trivia:** He divorced actress Frances Tomelty in August of '82. In 1985, he dueted on singles MONEY FOR NOTHING (Dire Straits), which he co-wrote, plus LONG WAY TO GO (Phil Collins). That year he also guested on MILES DAVIS' album 'You're Under Arrest'. He was also another one of the stars on BAND AID and LIVE AID. **Filmography:** QUADROPHENIA (1979) / RADIO ON (1980) / ARTEMIS (1981 TV movie) / BRIMSTONE AND TREACLE (1982) / DUNE (1984) / THE BRIDE (1985) / PLENTY (1985) / STORMY MONDAY (1988) / JULIA JULIA (1987). In 1988 he also narrated Stravinsky's 'Soldier's Tale', which was soon issued on own 'Pangaea' label. He followed this by writing score for documentary about Quentin Crisp 'Crisp City'. He spent much of '89, campaigning for Brazilian rain forest projects before appearing in operatic play 'MacHeath'.

Recommended: NOTHING LIKE THE SUN (*8) / THE SOUL CAGES (*9) / FIELDS OF GOLD – THE BEST OF (*9).

STING – vocals, bass, etc. (with session people)

		A & M	A & M
Aug 82.	(7") **SPREAD A LITTLE HAPPINESS. / ONLY YOU**	16	
Sep 82.	(lp)(c) **BRIMSTONE AND TREACLE (Soundtrack)**		
	– Spread a little happiness / Only you / Brimstone and treacle / You know I had the strangest dream / Brimstone 2 / (tracks by other artists).		

— Enlisted US musicians **KENNY KIRKLAND** – keyboards / **BRANFORD MARSALIS** – sax, percussion / **DARRYL JONES** – bass (ex-MILES DAVIS) / **OMAR HAKIM** – drums (WEATHER REPORT)

May 85.	(7") **IF YOU LOVE SOMEBODY SET THEM FREE. / ANOTHER DAY**	26	3
	(12"+=) – ('A'dance mix) / ('A'-Jellybean dance mix) / ('A'torch mix).		
Jun 85.	(lp)(c)(cd) **THE DREAM OF THE BLUE TURTLES**	3	2
	– If you love somebody set them free / Love is the seventh wave / Russians / Children's crusade / Shadows in the rain / We work the black seam / Consider me gone / The dream of the blue turtles / Moon over Bourbon Street / Fortress around your heart. *(pic-lp Jan86)*		
Aug 85.	(7")(12") **LOVE IS THE SEVENTH WAVE. / CONSIDER ME GONE (live)**	41	-
Aug 85.	(7") **FORTRESS AROUND YOUR HEART. / CONSIDER ME GONE**	-	8
Oct 85.	(7")(12") **FORTRESS AROUND YOUR HEART. / SHADOWS IN THE RAIN**	49	-
Nov 85.	(7") **LOVE IS THE SEVENTH WAVE. / DREAM OF THE BLUE TURTLES**	-	17
Dec 85.	(7") **RUSSIANS. / GABRIEL'S MESSAGE**	12	16
	(12"+=) – I burn for you (live).		
Feb 86.	(7") **MOON OVER BOURBON STREET. / MACK THE KNIFE**	44	
	(12"+=) – Fortress around your heart.		
Jul 86.	(d-lp)(c)(cd) **BRING ON THE NIGHT (live)**	16	-
	– Bring on the night – When the world is running down you make the best of what's still around / Consider me gone / Low life / We work the black seam / Driven to tears / The dream of the blue turtles – Demolition man / One world (not three) / Love is the seventh wave / Moon over Bourbon street / I burn for you / Another day / Children's crusade / Down so long / Tea in the Sahara.		

— He retains **KIRKLAND + MARSALIS,** and recruited **MANU KATCHE** – drums / **MINO CINELU** – percussion, vocoder / **ANDY NEWMARK** – 2nd drummer / plus guests **ERIC CLAPTON, MARK KNOPFLER, ANDY SUMMERS + GIL EVANS**

Oct 87.	(7") **WE'LL BE TOGETHER. / CONVERSATION WITH A DOG**	41	7

(12"+=)(3"cd-s+=) – ('A'extended mix) / ('A'instrumental).
Oct 87. (d-lp)(c)(cd) **NOTHING LIKE THE SUN** 1 9
– The Lazarus heart / Be still my beating heart / Englishman in New York / History will teach us nothing / They dance alone (gueca solo) / Fragile / We'll be together / Straight to my heart / Rock steady / Sister Moon / Little wing / The secret marriage.
Jan 88. (7") **BE STILL MY BEATING HEART. / GHOST IN THE STRAND** - 15
Jan 88. (7")(12") **ENGLISHMAN IN NEW YORK. / GHOST IN THE STRAND (instrumental)** 51 -
(3"cd-s+=) – Bring on the night-When the world is running down (live)
Mar 88. (7") **ENGLISHMAN IN NEW YORK. / IF YOU'RE THERE** - 84
Mar 88. (7") **FRAGILE. / FRAGIL (Portuguese mix)** 70 -
(12"+=)(cd-s+=) – Fragilidad (Spanish mix) / Mariposa libre.
Sep 88. (7") **THEY DANCE ALONE. / ELLAS DANZAN SOLAS (the Spanish version)**
(12"+=)(cd-s+=)/ /(10"+=) – We'll be together./ / Si Estamos juntos.

— He retained **MARSALIS, KIRKLAND, KATCHE.** New **DOMINIC MILLER** – guitar / **DAVID SANCIOUS** – keyboards / **KATHRYN TICKELL** – pipes / **PAOLA PAPAREUE** – oboe / **RAY COOPER, VINK, BILL SUMMERS, MUNYUNGO JACKSON, SKIP BURNEY, TONY VALCA** – percussion.

Dec 90. (7")(c-s) **ALL THIS TIME. / I MISS YOU KATE (instrumental)** 22 5
(12"+=)(cd-s+=)(pic-cd-s+=) – King of pain (live).
Jan 91. (cd)(c)(lp) **THE SOUL CAGES** 1 2
– Island of souls / All this time / Mad about you / Jeremiah blues (pt.1) / Why should I cry for you / Saint Agnes and the burning train / The wild wild sea / The soul cages / When the angels fall.
Feb 91. (7")(c-s) **MAD ABOUT YOU (remix). / TEMPTED (live)** 56
(12"+=)(cd-s+=) – If you love somebody set them free (live).
Apr 91. (7")(c-s) **THE SOUL CAGES. / WALKING IN YOUR FOOTSTEPS (live)** 57
(12"+=)(cd-s+=) – Don't stand so close to me / Oo la la Hugh (both live).
(12"+=) – The Lazarus heart / Too much inforation (live).
Aug 92. (7")(c-s)(cd-s) **IT'S PROBABLY ME. ("STING with ERIC CLAPTON") / ('A'long version)** 30

— retained on album **MILLER, SANCIOUS & TICKELL** and brought in **VINNIE COLAIUTA** – drums / **LARRY ADLER + BRENDAN POWER** – chromatic harmonicas / **SIAN BELL** – cello / **DAVE HEATH** – flute / **PAUL FRANKLIN** – pedal steel / **JAMES BOYD** – viola / **KATHRYN GREELEY + SIMON FISCHER** – violins / **GUY BARKER + JOHN BARCLAY** – trumpets / **RICHARD EDWARDS + MARK NIGHTINGALE** – trombone / **DAVID ROXXE** – narration

Feb 93. (7")(c-s) **IF I EVER LOSE MY FAITH IN YOU. / ALL THIS TIME (live)** 14 17
(cd-s+=) – Mad about you (live) / Every breath you take (live).
(cd-s) – ('A'side) / Message in a bottle (live) / Tea in the Sahara (live) / Walking on the Moon (live).
Mar 93. (cd)(c)(lp) **TEN SUMMONER'S TALES** 2 2
– Prologue (If I ever lose my faith in you) / Love is stronger than justice (the magnificent seven) / Fields of gold / Heavy cloud no rain / She's too good for me / Seven days / Saint Augustine in Hell / It's probably me / Everybody laughed but you / Shape of my heart / Something the boy said / Epilogue (Nothing 'bout me).
Apr 93. (7")(c-s) **SEVEN DAYS. / JANUARY STARS** 25
(cd-s+=) – Mad about you (live) / Ain't no sunshine (live).
(cd-s) – ('A'side) / Island of souls (live) / The wild wild sea (live) / The soul cages (live).
Jun 93. (7")(c-s) **FIELDS OF GOLD. / WE WORK THE BLACK SEAM** 16 23
(cd-s) – ('A'side) / King of pain / Fragile / Purple haze (all 3 live).
(cd-s) – ('A'side) / Message in a bottle (live) / Fortress around your heart (live) / Roxanne (live).
Aug 93. (7")(c-s) **SHAPE OF MY HEART. / WALKING ON THE MOON** 57
(cd-s) – ('A'side) / The soul cages / The wild wild sea / All this time.
Nov 93. (7")(c-s) **DEMOLITION MAN. / ('A'mix)** 21
(cd-s+=) – King of pain (live) / Shape of my heart (live).
(cd-s) – ('A'side) / It's probably me (live) / A day in the life of (live).

— Late 1993, he teamed up with BRYAN ADAMS & ROD STEWART to sing theme from 'The Three Musketeers'; ALL FOR LOVE, which hit UK No.2 & US No.1.

Feb 94. (7")(12")(c-s) **NOTHING 'BOUT ME. / IF I EVER LOSE MY FAITH IN YOU** 32 57 Sep 93
(cd-s+=) – ('B'mixes) / Demolition man (soul power mix).
Oct 94. (12")(c-s) **WHEN WE DANCE. / FORTRESS AROUND YOUR HEART** 9 38
(cd-s) – ('A'side) / If you love somebody set them free (remix) / ('A'remix).
Nov 94. (cd)(c)(d-lp) **FIELDS OF GOLD – THE BEST OF STING 1984-1994** (compilation) 2 7
– When we dance / If you love somebody set them free / Fields of gold / All this time / Englishman in New York / Mad about you / It's probably me / They dance alone / If I ever lose my faith in you / Fragile / We'll be together / Nothing 'bout me / Love is the seventh wave / Russians / Seven days / Demolition man / This cowboy song.

— Around same time, Spanish crooner JULIO IGLESIAS covered his 'FRAGILE', which he accompanied with STING.

— (below single featured PATO BANTON)

Jan 95. (c-s) **THIS COWBOY SONG. / IF YOU LOVE SOMEBODY SET THE FREE (Brothers In Rhythm mix)** 15
(cd-s+=) – Demolition man (Soul Power mix).
(12"++=) – If you love somebody set them free (extended).
(cd-s) – ('A'side) / ('A'extended) / When we dance (classic) / Take me to the sunshine.

. . . Jan – Jun '96 stop press . . .

— Jan 96, featured on PATO BANTON's UK Top 40 version of POLICE hit 'SPIRITS IN THE MATERIAL WORLD' from the film 'Ace Ventura II'.

Feb 96. (single) **LET ME BE YOUR SOUL PILOT** 15 86
Mar 96. (cd)(c)(lp) **MERCURY FALLING** 4 5
Apr 96. (single) **YOU STILL TOUCH ME** 27 60
Jun 96. (single) **LIVE AT TFI FRIDAY EP** 53 -

– compilations, others, etc. –

Jul 88. A&M; (cd-ep) **COMPACT HITS** -
– Someone to watch over me / Englishman in New York / If you love somebody set them free / Spread a little happiness.
Feb 90. A&M; (d-c) **DREAM OF THE BLUE TURTLES / NOTHING LIKE THE SUN**
Aug 90. A&M; (7")(c-s) **ENGLISHMAN IN NEW YORK (Ben Liebrand mix). / IF YOU LOVE SOMEBODY SET THEM FREE** 15 -
(12"+=)(cd-s+=)(pic-cd-s+=) – ('A'original mix) / ('A' Jellybean dance mix).
Nov 91. A&M; (cd-box)(c-box)(lp-box) **ACOUSTIC LIVE IN NEWCASTLE – LIMITED EDITION BOXED SET**

Sly STONE (see under ⇒ SLY & THE FAMILY STONE)

STONE ROSES

Formed: Sale & Chorley, Gtr.Manchester, England . . . 1984 by IAN BROWN, JOHN SQUIRE, etc, who took their name from a group called ENGLISH ROSE and The ROLLING STONES. After a MARTIN HANNETT produced 45, they signed a one-off deal with 'Black' records. In 1988, they were snapped up by ANDREW LAUDER's 'Jive' subsidiary label 'Silvertone'. They soon became darlings of the music press after indie success of single 'ELEPHANT STONE'. The following year, when their hit eponymous album was riding high in the UK charts, they exploded into the Top 10 with 'FOOL'S GOLD'. They were then chased by many record labels, but went to court many times in the 90's with Silvertone, who had tied them to a long-term contract. • **Style:** Pioneers of rave psychedelia, who were influenced by near namesakes The ROLLING STONES, LOVE or CAN. • **Songwriters:** Mainly SQUIRE but other members also collaborating. • **Trivia:** Their debut album artwork was a pastiche of a Jackson Pollock splatter job painted by the multi-talented SQUIRE.

Recommended: THE STONE ROSES (*10) / SECOND COMING (*8).

IAN BROWN (b.20 Feb'63, Ancoats, Manchester) – vocals / **JOHN SQUIRE** (b.24 Nov'62, Broadheath, Manchester) – guitar, vocals / **PETER GARNER** – rhythm guitar / **ANDY COUZENS** – bass / **RENI** (b.ALAN WREN, 10 Apr'64, Manchester) – drums

Thin Line not issued

Sep 85. (12") **SO YOUNG. / TELL ME** -
(re-dist.Mar86)

— now a quartet, when PETER departed.

Black not issued

May 87. (12"m) **SALLY CINNAMON. / HERE IT COMES / ALL ACROSS THE SANDS** -
(re-iss.Feb89, cd-s iss.Dec89, hit No.46, (+=) – ('A'demo). *(re-iss.7" – 1st 2 tracks +12"+cd-ep on 'FM Revolver')*

— (1987) **GARY 'Mannie' MOUNFIELD** (b.16 Nov'62, Crumpsall, Manchester) – bass, vocals repl. COUZENS who later joined The HIGH.

Silvertone Silvertone

Oct 88. (7") **ELEPHANT STONE. / THE HARDEST THING IN THE WORLD** -
(12"+=) – Full fathoms five. *(c+cd-s iss.Feb90 hit No.8)*
Mar 89. (7") **MADE OF STONE. / GOING DOWN** -
(12"+=) – Guernica. *(c+cd-s iss.Mar90 hit No.20)*
Apr 89. (lp)(c)(cd) **THE STONE ROSES** 19 86
– I wanna be adored / She bangs the drum / Waterfall / Don't stop / Bye bye badman / Elizabeth my dear / (Song for my) Sugar spun sister / Made of stone / Shoot you down / This is the one / I am the resurrection. *(re-iss.Aug91 as 2x12")* (+=) – Elephant stone / Fool's gold.

Jul 89. (7") **SHE BANGS THE DRUM. / STANDING HERE** [36] [-]
(12"+=) – Mersey Paradise.
(c-s+=)(cd-s+=) – Simone. *(re-iss.Mar90, hit No.34)*

Silvertone | Jive

Nov 89. (7") **FOOL'S GOLD. / WHAT THE WORLD IS WAITING FOR** [8] [ ]
(12"+=)(c-s+=)(cd-s+=) – ('A'extended). *(re-iss.Sep90, hit No.22, re-iss.May92, hit No.73) ('A'-The Top Won mix) / ('A'-The Bottom Won mix).*
Jul 90. (7")(12")(c-s)(cd-s) **ONE LOVE. / SOMETHING'S BURNING** [4] [ ]
Sep 91. (7") **I WANNA BE ADORED. / WHERE ANGELS PLAY** [20] [-]
(12"+=)(cd-s+=) – Sally Cinnamon (live).
Jan 92. (7")(c-s) **WATERFALL (remix). / ONE LOVE (remix)** [27] [ ]
(12"+=)(cd-s+=) – ('A'&'B'extended versions).
Apr 92. (7")(c-s) **I AM THE RESURRECTION. / ('A'Pan & scan radio version)** [33] [ ]
(12"+=) – Fool's gold (The Bottom Won mix).
(cd-s++=) – ('A'-5:3 Stoned Out club mix).
Jul 92. (cd)(c)(lp) **TURNS INTO STONE** (demos & rare) [32] [ ]
– Elephant stone / The hardest thing in the world / Going down / Mersey Paradise / Standing here Where angels play / Simone / Fools gold / What the world is waiting for / One love / Something's burning.

Geffen | Geffen

Nov 94. (7")(c-s) **LOVE SPREADS. / YOUR STAR WILL SHINE** [2] [ ]
(cd-s+=) – Breakout.
(12"++=) – Groove harder.
Dec 94. (cd)(c)(lp) **SECOND COMING** [4] [47] Jan 95
– Breaking into Heaven / Driving south / Ten storey love song / Daybreak / Your star will shine / Straight to the man / Begging you / Tightrope / Good times / Tears / How do you sleep? / Love spreads. *(cd+=)* – (untitled hidden track No.90).
Feb 95. (7")(c-s) **TEN STOREY LOVE SONG. / RIDE ON** [11] [ ]
(12"+=)(cd-s+=) – Moses.

— In Apr'95, RENI quit and was replaced by **ROBERT MADDIX** (ex-GINA GINA). Will there be a third coming? It looks unlikely squire.

Oct 95. (c-s) **BEGGING YOU / ('A'-Chic mix)** [15] [ ]
(cd-s+=) – ('A'-Stone Corporation mix) / ('A'-Lakota mix) / ('A'-Young American primitive remix).
(12") – ('A'-Carl Cox mix) / ('A'-Development Corporation mix).

. . . Jan – Jun '96 stop press . . .

— Late in March '96, SQUIRE leaves to pursue solo things. Could bring RENI into his team. STONE ROSES are adament they will continue on.

– compilations, etc. –

Apr 95. Silvertone; (c-s) **FOOL'S GOLD '95. / ('A'extended mix)** [23] [ ]
(12"+=)(cd-s+=) – ('A'-Tall Paul remix) / (A'-Cricklewood Ballroom mix).
May 95. Silvertone; (cd)(c) **THE COMPLETE STONE ROSES** [4] [ ]

STONE TEMPLE PILOTS

Formed: San Diego, California. USA . . . 1992 by WEILAND, etc. Signed to 'Atlantic' in 1992, and took the US charts by storm with debut US Top 3 album 'CORE'. • **Style:** Heavy laid-back 70's style rock outfit, very similar to PEARL JAM, although WEILAND's orange-haired mop top differentiated them from contemporaries. • **Songwriters:** Lyrics: WEILAND + R.DeLEO / KRETZ most of music. • **Trivia:** Brendan O'Brien produced their 1993 + '94 albums.

Recommended: CORE (*7) / PURPLE (*6).

WEILAND – vocals / **DEAN DeLEO** – guitar / **ROBERT DeLEO** – bass / **ERIC KRETZ** – drums

Atlantic | Atlantic

Mar 93. (7")(c-s) **SEX TYPE THING. / WICKED GARDEN** [60] [ ]
(12"+=)(cd-s+=) Plush (acoustic).
Aug 93. (7")(c-s) **PLUSH. / SEX TYPE THANG (swing version) / PLUSH (acoustic)** [23] [ ]
(12"+=)(cd-s+=) – ('A'side) / ('B'live version) / Sin.
Sep 93. (cd)(c)(lp) **CORE** [27] [3] Feb 93
– Dead and bloated / Sex type thang / Wicked garden / No memory / Sin / Creep / Piece of pie / Naked Sunday / Plush / Wet my bed / Crackerman / Where the river goes.
Nov 93. (12")(cd-s) **SEX TYPE THING. / PIECE OF ME** [55] [ ]
Jun 94. (cd)(c)(purple-lp) **PURPLE** [10] [1]
– Meatplow / Vasoline / Lounge fly / Interstate love song / Still remains / Pretty penny / Silvergun Superman / Big empty / Unglued / Army ants / Kitchenware & candybar!. (cd+c+=) – Gracious melodies.
Jul 94. (12"ep)(c-ep)(cd-ep) **VASOLINE / MEATPLOW. / ANDY WARHOL / CRACKERMAN** [48] [ ]
Dec 94. (7"purple)(c-s) **INTERSTATE LOVE SONG. / LOUNGE FLY** [53] [ ]
(cd-s+=) – Vasoline (live).

. . . Jan – Jun '96 stop press . . .

Mar 96. (cd)(c)(lp) **TINY MUSIC . . . SONGS FROM THE VATICAN GIFT SHOP** [31] [4]

— Had to cancel promotion tours, due to SCOTT being ordered by a Pasadena court, to attend a live-in drug rehabilitation programme.

STOOGES (see under ⇒ POP, Iggy)

STORM (see under ⇒ JOURNEY)

STRANGELOVE

Formed: Bristol, England . . . 1992 by PATRICK DUFF and ALEX LEE ex BLUE AEROPLANES. After a period of 2 years on indie labels, they secured big time signing to 'Food-EMI', who quickly issued critically approved single and album 'TIME FOR THE REST OF YOUR LIFE'. • **Style:** Re-gothic doom-laden alternative outfit, anthemic and reminiscent of The SMITHS or The BUNNYMEN. • **Songwriters:** Group penned except MOTORCYCLE NITEMARE (Bob Dylan). • **Trivia:** Produced by ANGELO BRUSCHINI also ex-BLUE AEROPLANES.

Recommended: TIME OUT FOR THE REST OF YOUR LIFE (*7) / LOVE AND OTHER DEMONS (*6)

PATRICK DUFF – vocals / **ALEX LEE** – guitar (ex-BLUE AEROPLANES) / **JOHN LANGLEY** – drums (ex-BLUE AEROPLANES) / **RODNEY ALLEN** – vocals, rhythm guitar (ex-BLUE AEROPLANES) / **JULIAN-PRANSKY POOLE** – bass

Sermon | not issued

Oct 92. (12") **VISIONARY. /** [ ] [-]
Feb 93. (7") **HYSTERIA UNKNOWN. / MY DARK** [ ] [-]
(12"+=)(cd-s+=) – Walls / Sea.

Revolver | not issued

1993. (7") **ZOO'D OUT. / CIRCLES** [ ] [-]

Food-EMI | S.B.K.

Jun 94. (7") **TIME OUT FOR THE REST OF YOUR LIFE. / IT'S SO EASY** [ ] [ ]
(12"+=)(cd-s+=) – Motorcycle nightmare.
Aug 94. (cd)(c)(lp) **TIME OUT FOR THE REST OF YOUR LIFE** [69] [ ]
– Sixer / Time out for the rest of your life / Quiet day / Sand / I will burn / Low life / World outside / The return of the real me / All because of you / Fire (show me light) / Hopeful / Kite / Is there a place?.
Oct 94. (12"ep)(cd-ep) **IS THERE A PLACE? / SAND. / NOBODY'S THERE / THE KING OF SOMEWHERE ELSE** [ ] [ ]
Apr 96. (7") **LIVING WITH HUMAN MACHINES. / MR. HONEY CATCHER** [53] [ ]
(cd-s+=) – Killing time.
(cd-s) – ('A'side) / Hysteria unknown / Chances / My dark.
Jun 96. (c-s) **BEAUTIFUL ALONE / VISIONARY** [35] [ ]
(cd-s+=) – Zoo'd out / Sea.
(cd-s) – ('A'side) / Wolf's story part 1 / Wolf's story part II / Wolf's story part III.
Jun 96. (cd)(c)(lp) **LOVE AND OTHER DEMONS** [44] [ ]
– Casualties / Spiders and flies / Living with the human machines / She's everywhere / Sway / Beautiful alone / Elin's photograph / 20th century cold / 1432 / The sea of black.

STRANGLERS

Formed: Chiddington, Surrey, England . . . Autumn 1974 as The GUILDFORD STRANGLERS by ex-science teacher HUGH CORNWALL, history graduate JEAN JACQUES BURNEL and jazz drummer JET BLACK. They were joined by DAVE GREENFIELD in the Spring of 1975 and started touring mainly local pubs. Late in 1976, after gigs supporting FLAMIN' GROOVIES and The RAMONES, they signed to 'United Artists'. Their first 45 'GRIP', gave them entry into the UK Top 50, and would have gone higher, but for a chart mistake. Their debut album in 1977 'RATTUS NORVEGICUS', gave them first of many Top 10 triumphs, and contained the banned hit single 'PEACHES'. • **Style:** Innovators of new wave/punk who moulded themselves around influences from The DOORS, ELECTRIC PRUNES or DR.FEELGOOD. Accused by critics of controversially using sexist lyrics and lurid stage shows, where they were joined by strippers. In the early 80's, they shifted into more experimental pop. • **Songwriters:** Mostly CORNWALL penned except some by BURNEL. They also covered; 96 TEARS (? & The Mysterians) / WALK ON BY (Bacharach-David) / ALL DAY AND ALL OF THE NIGHT (Kinks). • **Miscellaneous:**

On 7 Jan'80, CORNWALL was found guilty of drug possession, and was sentenced to 3 months in prison and fined. In June that year, they were all arrested in Nice, France, after being accused of inciting a riot at a gig. They were threatened with long jail sentences, but were set free and later fined, claiming it was 'NICE IN NICE'.

Recommended: RATTUS NORVEGICUS (*9) / NO MORE HEROES (*8) / BLACK AND WHITE (*8) / LIVE CERT (*8) / AURAL SCULPTURE (*6) / DREAMTIME (*7) / THE STRANGLERS' GREATEST HITS (*9).

HUGH CORNWALL (b.28 Aug'48, London, England) – vocals, guitar / **JEAN-JAQUES BURNEL** (b.21 Feb'52, London; French parents) – bass, vocals / **DAVE GREENFIELD** – keyboards / **JET BLACK** (b.BRIAN DUFFY, 26 Aug'43) – drums

		United Art	A & M
Jan 77.	(7") **(GET A) GRIP (ON YOURSELF). / LONDON LADY**	44	-
Apr 77.	(lp)(c) **STRANGLERS IV – RATTUS NORVEGICUS**	4	

– Sometimes / Goodbye Toulouse / London lady / Princess of the streets / Hanging around / Peaches / (Get a) Grip (on yourself) / Ugly / Down in the sewer: (a) Falling – (b) Down in the sewer – (c) Trying to get out again – (d) Rats rally. *(free ltd.7"w.a.)* **CHOOSEY SUSIE. / IN THE BIG SHITTY** *(re-iss.May82 on 'Fame', cd-iss.Apr88) (cd-iss.Feb88 on 'Liberty')*

May 77.	(7") **PEACHES. / GO BUDDY GO**	8	-

— Jun77; They backed CELIA & THE MUTATIONS on cover single 'MONY MONY'.

Jul 77.	(7") **SOMETHING BETTER CHANGE. / STRAIGHT-EN OUT**	9	-
Sep 77.	(7") **NO MORE HEROES. / IN THE SHADOWS**	8	-
Oct 77.	(lp)(c) **NO MORE HEROES**	2	

– I feel like a wog / Bitching / Dead ringer / Dagenham Dave / Bring on the nubiles / Something better change / No more heroes / Peasant in the big shitty / Burning up time / Dagenham Dave / English towns / School mam / In the shadows. *(re-iss.1985) (cd-iss.Feb88 on 'EMI') (re-iss.Sep87 on 'Fame', cd-iss.Aug88)*

Nov 77.	(7"pink-ep) **SOMETHING BETTER CHANGE / STRAIGHTEN OUT. / GRIP / HANGIN' AROUND**	-	
Jan 78.	(7") **FIVE MINUTES. / ROK IT TO THE MOON**	11	-
Apr 78.	(7") **NICE 'N' SLEAZY. / SHUT UP**	18	Aug 78
May 78.	(lp)(c)(US-grey-lp) **BLACK AND WHITE**	2	

– Tank / Nice 'n' sleazy / Outside Tokyo / Mean to me / Sweden (all quiet on the Eastern Front) / Hey! (rise of the robots) / Toiler on the sea / Curfew / Threatened / Do you wanna? – Death and night and blood (Yukio) / In the shadows / Enough time / Walk on by. *(free ltd.7"w.a.)* **WALK ON BY. / TITS / MEAN TO ME** *(re-iss.Jan86 on 'Epic') (cd-iss.Jul88 on 'EMI' += free 7" tracks)*

Jul 78.	(7"m) **WALK ON BY. / OLD CODGER / TANK**	21	
Mar 79.	(lp)(c) **X-CERT (live)**	7	

– (Get a) Grip (on yourself) / Dagenham Dave / Burning up time / Dead ringer / Hanging around / I feel like a wog / Straighten out / Do you wanna – Death and night and blood (Yukio) / Five minutes / Go buddy go. *(re-iss.1985) (cd-iss.Jul88)* (cd+=) – In the shadows / Peasant in the big shitty.

Aug 79.	(7") **DUCHESS. / FOOLS RUSH OUT**	14	
Sep 79.	(lp)(c) **THE RAVEN**	4	

– Longships / The raven / Dead Loss Angeles / Ice / Baroque bordello / Nuclear device / Shah shah a go go / Don't bring Harry / Duchess / Meninblack / Genetix. *(re-iss.1985 on 'Fame', cd-iss.Aug88) (cd-iss.Oct87 on 'EMI'+=)* – Bear cage.

Oct 79.	(7") **NUCLEAR DEVICE (THE WIZARD OF AUS). / YELLOWCAKE UF6**	36	
Nov 79.	(7"ep) **DON'T BRING HARRY**	41	

– Don't bring Harry / Wired / Crabs (live) / In the shadows (live).

Liberty / I.R.S.

Jan 80. (7") **DUCHESS. / THE RAVEN** [-] [ ]
Jan 80. (lp) **STRANGLERS IV** [-] [ ]
– (5 tracks from 'THE RAVEN', plus recent singles)
(above w/ free 7"ep) – Do The European / Choosie Suzie / Wired / Straighten out.
Mar 80. (7")(12") **BEAR CAGE. / SHAH SHAH A GO GO** [36] [ ]
May 80. (7") **WHO WANTS THE WORLD. / MENINBLACK** [39] [ ]
Jan 81. (7") **THROWN AWAY. / TOP SECRET** [42] [ ]
Feb 81. (lp)(c) **THE MEN• IN• BLACK** [8] [ ]
– Waltzinblack / Just like nothing on Earth / Second coming / Waiting for the men in black / Turn the centuries, turn / Two sunspots / Four horsemen / Thrown away / Manna machine / Hallo to our men. *(re-iss.1985) (re-iss.+cd.Sep88 on 'Fame'; cd+=)* – Top secret / Maninwhite.
Mar 81. (7") **JUST LIKE NOTHING ON EARTH. / MANINWHITE** [ ] [ ]
Nov 81. (7") **LET ME INTRODUCE YOU TO THE FAMILY. / VIETNAMERICA** [42] [ ]
Nov 81. (lp)(c) **LA FOLIE** [11] [ ]
– Non stop / Everybody loves you when you're dead / Tramp / Let me introduce you to the family / The man they love to hate / Pin up / It only takes two to tango / Golden brown / How to find true love and happiness in the present day / La folie. *(re-iss.Nov83 on 'Fame', cd-iss.Aug88) (cd-iss.Feb88)*
Jan 82. (7") **GOLDEN BROWN. / LOVE 30** [2] [ ]
Apr 82. (7") **LA FOLIE. / WALTZINBLACK** [47] [ ]
Jul 82. (7") **STRANGE LITTLE GIRL. / CRUEL GARDEN** [7] [ ]
Sep 82. (lp)(c) **THE COLLECTION 1977-1982** (compilation) [12] [ ]
– (Get a) Grip (on yourself) / Peaches / Hanging around / No more heroes / Duchess / Walk on by / Waltzinblack / Something better change / Nice'n'sleazy / Bear cage / Who wants the world / Golden brown / Strange little girl / La folie. *(re-iss.+cd.1985) (re-iss.+cd.Aug89 on 'Fame')*

Epic / Epic

Nov 82. (7")(7"pic-d) **THE EUROPEAN FEMALE. / SAVAGE BEAST** [9] [ ]
Jan 83. (lp)(c) **FELINE** [4] [ ]
– Midnight summer dream / It's a small world / Ships that pass in the night / The European female / Let's tango in Paris / Paradise / All roads lead to Rome / Blue sister / Never say goodbye. *(free ltd.one-sided-7"w.a.)* **AURAL SCULPTURE** *(re-iss.Apr86)* (US lp+=) – Golden brown. *(cd-iss.Dec92)*
Feb 83. (7")(12") **MIDNIGHT SUMMER DREAM. / VLADIMIR AND OLGA** [35] [-]
Jul 83. (7") **PARADISE. / PAWSHER** [48] [-]
(12"+=) – Permission.
Jul 83. (12") **MIDNIGHT SUMMER DREAM. / PARADISE** [-] [ ]
Sep84. (7") **SKIN DEEP. / HERE AND NOW** [15] [ ]
(12"+=) – Vladimir and the beast.
Nov 84. (lp)(c) **AURAL SCULPTURE** [14] [ ]
– Ice queen / Skin deep / Let me down easy / No mercy / North winds / Uptown / Punch & Judy / Spain / Laughing / Souls / Mad Hatter. *(re-iss.+cd.May87) (re-iss.cd Sep93 on 'Sony Collectors')*
Nov 84. (7")(7"sha-pic-d) **NO MERCY. / IN ONE DOOR** [37] [ ]
(12"+=)(US-c-s+=) – Hot club.
Feb 85. (7") **LET ME DOWN EASY. / ACHILLES HEEL** [48] [ ]
(12"+=) – Place des victories.
(12"++=) – Vladimir goes to Havana / Aural sculpture manifesto.
Aug 86. (7")(12")(7"sha-pic-d) **NICE IN NICE. / SINCE YOU WENT AWAY** [30] [ ]
Oct 86. (7")(7"sha-pic-d) **ALWAYS THE SUN. / NORMAN NORMAL** [30] [ ]
(12"+=) – Soul.
Oct 86. (lp)(c)(cd)(pic-lp) **DREAMTIME** [16] [ ]
– Always the sun / Dreamtime / Was it you? / You'll always reap what you sow / Ghost train / Nice in Nice / Big in America / Shakin' like a leaf / Mayan skies / Too precious. *(re-iss.Feb89)*
Dec 86. (7")(7"sha-pic-d) **BIG IN AMERICA. / DRY DAY** [48] [ ]
(12"+=) – Uptown.
Feb 87. (7")(7"sha-pic-d) **SHAKIN' LIKE A LEAF. / HIT MAN** [58] [ ]
(12"+=) – Was it you?.
Dec 87. (7")(7"sha-pic-d) **ALL DAY AND ALL OF THE NIGHT (live). / VIVA VLAD** [7] [ ]
(12"+=) – Who wants the world (live).
(cd-s+=) – Strange little girl.
Feb 88. (lp)(c)(cd) **ALL LIVE AND ALL OF THE NIGHT (live)** [12] [ ]
– No more heroes / Was it you? / Down in the sewer / Always the sun / Golden brown / North winds / The European female / Strange little girl / Nice 'n' sleazy / Toiler on the sea / Spain / London lady / All day and all of the night.
Feb 90. (7")(c-s) **96 TEARS. / INSTEAD OF THIS** [17] [ ]
(12"+=)(cd-s+=) – Poisonality.
Mar 90. (cd)(c)(lp)(pic-lp) **10** [15] [ ]
– The sweet smell of success / Someone like you / 96 tears / In this place / Let's celebrate / Man of the Earth / Too many teardrops / Where I live / Out of my mind / Never to look back. *(re-iss.cd Dec92)*
Apr 90. (7")(c-s)(7"pic-d) **THE SWEET SMELL OF SUCCESS. / MOTORBIKE** [65] [ ]
(12"+=)(cd-s+=) – Something.
Nov 90. (cd)(c)(lp) **THE STRANGLERS' GREATEST HITS 1977-1990** (complation) [4] [ ]
– Something better change / No more heroes / Walk on by / Duchess / Golden brown / Strange little girl / European female / Skin deep / Nice in Nice / Always the Sun / Big in America / All day and all of the night / 96 tears / No mercy / Peaches.
Jan 91. (7")(c-s) **ALWAYS THE SUN. / BURNHAM BEECHES** [29] [-]
(12"+=) – Straighten out.
(cd-s) – ('A'side) / Nuclear device (live) / All day and all of the night (live) / Punch and Judy (live).
Mar 91. (7")(c-s) **GOLDEN BROWN (re-mix). / YOU** [68] [-]
(cd-s+=) – Skin deep (extended) / Peaches.

—— (late 1990) **JOHN ELLIS** – guitar, vocals (once p/t member) (ex-VIBRATORS, etc.) repl. CORNWALL who has already ventured solo.

—— (Jan91) also added **PAUL ROBERTS** – vocals

China / not issued

Aug 92. (7") **HEAVEN OR HELL. / DISAPPEAR** [46] [-]
(12"ep+=)(c-ep+=)(cd-ep+=) – Brainbox / Hanging around.
Sep 92. (cd)(c)(lp) **STRANGLERS IN THE NIGHT** [33] [-]
– Time to die / Sugar bullets / Heaven or Hell / Laughing at the rain / This town / Brainbox / Southern mouintains / Gain entry to your soul / Grand canyon / Wet afternoon / Never see / Leave it to the dogs.
Oct 92. (7")(c-s) **SUGAR BULLETS. / SO UNCOOL** [ ] [-]
(12"+=)(cd-s+=) – ('A'version).

Essential / not issued

Jun 93. (cd)(c)(lp) **SATURDAY NIGHT SUNDAY MORNING** [ ] [ ]
– Toiler on the sea / 96 Tears / Always the sun / No more heroes / Golden brown / Tank / Strange little girl / Something better change / Hanging around / All day and all of the night / Duchess / *Medley / Was it you? / Down in the sewer.

—— In Jun'93, old Strangler HUGH CORNWALL released album 'WIRED' on 'Transmission' label. Nearly a year earlier as CCW, he, ROGER COOK & AND WEST issued cd 'CCW FEATURING HUGH CORNWALL • ROGER COOK • ANDY WEST' on 'UFO'.

When!-Castle / not issued

May 95. (cd)(c)(lp) **ABOUT TIME** [31] [-]
– Golden boy / Money / Sinister / Little blue lies / Still life / Paradise row / She gave it all / Lies and deception / Lucky finger / And the boat sails by.
Jun 95. (12")(cd-s) **LIES AND DECEPTION. / SWIM / DANNY COOL** [ ] [-]
(cd-s) – ('A'side) / Kiss the world goodbye / Bed of nails.

– more compilations, etc. –

Mar 84. Old Gold; (7") **GOLDEN BROWN. / STRANGE LITTLE GIRL** [ ] [-]
Sep 86. Liberty; (lp)(c) **OFF THE BEATEN TRACK** [80] [-]
Nov 88. Liberty; (lp)(c) **RARITIES** [ ] [-]
Jan 89. EMI; (7")(7"red) **GRIP '89. / WALTZINBLACK** [33] [-]
(12"+=)/ /(cd-s++=) – Tomorrow was thereafter./ / ('A'mix).
Feb 89. EMI; (lp)(c)(cd) **THE SINGLES** [57] [-]
May 92. EMI; (cd) **LIVE AT THE HOPE AND ANCHOR (live)** [ ] [-]
(re-iss.Feb95 on 'Fame')
Dec 92. EMI; (4xcd-box) **THE OLD TESTAMENT – THE U.A. STUDIO RECORDINGS (demos)** [ ] [-]
Jun 89. Nighttracks; (12"ep) **RADIO 1 SESSION (1982)** [ ] [-]
– The man they love to hate / Nuclear device / Genetix / Down in the sewer.
Feb 92. Newspeak; (cd)(c)(d-lp) **THE EARLY YEARS 74-75-76, RARE LIVE & UNRELEASED** [ ] [-]
May 94. Receiver; (cd) **DEATH AND NIGHT AND BLOOD** [ ] [-]
Jun 94. Castle; (cd) **THE EARLY YEARS 1974-76** [ ] [-]
Feb 95. Receiver; (cd) **LIVE IN CONCERT (live w/ FRIENDS)** [ ] [-]
Nov 95. Old Gold; (cd-s) **GOLDEN BROWN / NO MORE HEROES** [ ] [-]

J.J. BURNEL

solo with **BRIAN JAMES** – guitar / **CAREY FORTUNE** – drums / **LEW LEWIS** – harmonica

United Art / not issued

Mar 79. (7") **FREDDIE LAKER (CONCORDE AND EUROBUS). / OZYMANDIAS** [ ] [-]
Apr 79. (lp)(c) **EUROMAN COMETH** [40] [-]
– Euroman / Jellyfish / Freddie Laker (Concorde and Eurobus) / Euroness / Deutschland nicht uber alles / Do the European / Tout comprendre / Triumph (of the good city) / Pretty face / Crabs / Eurospeed (your own speed). *(re-iss.Feb88 on 'Mau Mau') (re-iss.+cd.Jan92 on 'EMI' with cd 35 mins extra)*

—— toured with **ELLIS, PETER HOWELLS & PENNY TOBIN.** (below withdrawn)

Jul 80. (7") **GIRL FROM SNOW COUNTRY. / ODE TO JOY (live) / DO THE EUROPEAN (live)** [-] [-]

DAVE GREENFIELD & JEAN-JAQUES BURNEL

Epic / Epic

Dec 83. (lp)(c) **FIRE AND WATER** [ ] [-]
– Liberation / Rain, dole & tea / Vladimir and Sergei / Le soir / Trois pedophiles

pour Eric Sabyr ino rap / Nuclear power (yes please) / Detective privee / Consequences.

Feb 84. (7") **RAIN, DOLE & TEA. / CONSEQUENCES** [ ] [-]

— In 1989, they with ALEX GIFFORD, MANNY ELIAS and JOHN ELLIS splintered as The PURPLE HELMUTS. They made an album RIDE AGAIN for 'New Rose' Jan89.

J.J. BURNEL

Epic Epic

1988. (7") **LE WHISKEY. / EL WHISKEY** [-] [-] France
(12"+=)(cd-s+=) – Garden of Eden.

1988. (lp)(c)(cd) **UN JOUR PARFAIT** [-] [-] France

1988. (7") **REVES. / (SHE DRIVES ME) CRAZY** [-] [-] France
(12"+=)(cd-s+=) – ('A'extended).

HUGH CORNWALL & ROBERT WILLIAMS

with **ROBERT WILLIAMS** – drums, bass, guitar, vocals, synthesizer / **MARK + BOB MOTHERSBAUGH** -synth + guitar (of DEVO) / **DAVID WALLDROOP** – guitar / **IAN UNDERWOOD** – synth, saxes

United Art not issued

Oct 79. (lp)(c) **NOSFERATU** [ ] [-]
– Nosferatu / Losers in a lost land / White room / Irate caterpillar / Rhythmic itch / Wired / Big bug / Mothra / Wrong way round / Puppets. *(cd-iss.May92 on 'EMI')*

Nov 79. (7") **WHITE ROOM. / LOSERS IN A LOST LAND** [ ] [-]

HUGH CORNWALL

— (solo with session people)

Portrait Portrait

Sep 85. (7")(12") **ONE IN A MILLION. / SIREN SONG** [ ] [-]

Sep 85. (lp)(c) **BLEEDING STAR (Various Soundtracks)** [ ] [-]

Virgin Virgin?

Jan 87. (7")(12") **FACTS AND FIGURES. / ('A'version)** [ ] [-]

Apr 88. (7") **ANOTHER KIND OF LOVE. / REAL PEOPLE** [ ] [-]
(12"+=)(cd-s+=) – Nothing but the groove / Where is this place . . .

Jun 88. (lp)(c)(cd) **WOLF** [98] [-]
– Another kind of love / Cherry rare / Never never / Real slow / Break of dawn / Clubland / Dreaming away / Decadence / All the tea in China / Getting involved.

Jul 88. (7") **DREAMING AWAY. / BLUE NOTE** [ ] [-]
(12"+=)/ /(cd-s++=) – Getting involved./ / The English walk.

In May92, ex-member HUGH CORNWALL teamed up with COOK & WEST (ex-BLUE MINK) to release single 'Sweet Sister'.

STREETWALKERS (see under ⇒ FAMILY)

Joe STRUMMER (see under ⇒ CLASH)

STYLE COUNCIL (see under ⇒ WELLER, Paul)

SUEDE

Formed: London, England . . . 1989 by BRETT ANDERSON, who put final line-up together 1991. After a single 'BE MY GOD' / 'ART', failed to appear in 1990 on 'RML', they signed to indie 'Nude'. This 12" was famous for featured ex-SMITHS drummer MIKE JOYCE. In Apr'92 with new drummer SIMON GILBERT, they featured on cover of NME just prior to release of debut top 50 hit 'THE DROWNERS'. With much hype and media attention, they scored first Top 20 hit in Sep'92 with 'METAL MICKEY'. Early in '93, 'Nude' was taken over by 'Sony' on both sides of the Atlantic. In 1993, a Top 10 follow-up preceded chartbusting No.1 eponymous album. • **Style:** Young and talented best newcomers of '93. BRETT's mannered vox and group's glitszy tunes, at times similar to MORRISSEY, BOWIE or BOLAN, whom he idolised as a boy. • **Songwriters:** ANDERSON / BUTLER, except; BRASS IN POCKET (Pretenders). • **Trivia:** Producer ED BULLER also played keyboards + synthesizers on debut album.

Recommended: SUEDE (*9) / DOG MAN STAR (*8).

BRETT ANDERSON – vocals / **BERNARD BUTLER** – guitar, piano / **MATT OSMAN** – bass / **SIMON GILBERT** – drums

Nude not issued

Apr 92. (7") **THE DROWNERS. / TO THE BIRDS** [49] [-]
(12"+=)(cd-s+=) – My insatiable one.

Sep 92. (7") **METAL MICKEY. / WHERE THE PIGS DON'T FLY** [17] [-]
(12"+=)(cd-s+=) – He's dead.

Nude-Sony Sony

Feb 93. (7")(c-s) **ANIMAL NITRATE. / THE BIG TIME** [7] [ ]
(12"+=)(cd-s+=) – Painted people.

Apr 93. (cd)(c)(lp) **SUEDE** [1] [ ]
– So young / Animal nitrate / She's not dead / Moving / Pantomime horse / The drowners / Sleeping pills / Breakdown / Metal Mickey / Animal lover / The next life.

May 93. (7")(c-s) **SO YOUNG. / HIGH RISING** [22] [ ]
(12"+=)(cd-s+=) – Dolly.

Feb 94. (7")(c-s) **STAY TOGETHER. / THE LIVING DEAD** [3] [ ]
('A'ext-12"+=) – My dark star.
(cd-s+=) -('A'extended).

— In Spring 1994, gay drummer SIMON went to House Of Commons, to air his views on the homosexual laws of consent, which were to be lowered from 21 to either 16 (the heterosexual age) or 18, as it turned out to be. Around the same time, an American jazz singer called SUEDE won her lawsuit against the band in the US. They are now to be called LONDON SUEDE, but thankfully only in the States.

Sep 94. (7")(c-s) **WE ARE THE PIGS. / KILLING OF A FLASH BOY** [18] [ ]
(12"+=)(cd-s+=) – Whipsnade.

Oct 94. (cd)(c)(lp) **DOG MAN STAR** [3] [ ]
– Introducing the band / We are the pigs / Heroine / The wild ones / Daddy's speeding / The power / New generation / This Hollywood life / The 2 of us / Black or blue / The asphalt world / Still life.

— BUTLER left July 94 and was repl. by 17 year-old **RICHARD OAKES** after recording album.

Nov 94. (12")(c-s) **THE WILD ONES. / INTRODUCING THE BAND (Eno mix) / ASDA TOWN** [18] [ ]
(cd-s) – ('A'side) / Modern boys / This world needs a father.

Jan 95. (7")(c-s) **NEW GENERATION. / BENTSWOOD BOYS** [21] [ ]
(12"+=)(cd-s+=) – Together.
(cd-s) – ('A'side) / Animal nitrate (live) / The wild ones (live) / Pantomime horse (live).

. . . Jan – Jun '96 stop press . . .

— added new member **NEIL CODLING** – keyboards, vocals

SUGAR

Formed: Minneapolis, USA . . . 1992 by former HUSKER DU frontman BOB MOULD. He had been part of this classic hard-core trio for 9 years between '78 + '87 before going solo in 1989. After 2 well-received albums for 'Virgin America' in the next couple of years, he formed SUGAR with 2 others DAVE BARBE and MALCOLM TRAVIS. Signed to UK 'Creation' in '92 and unleashed the excellent 'COPPER BLUE' album. • **Style:** Grunge in the mould of PIXIES, NIRVANA, MUDHONEY, although he could lay claim to having influenced them a decade before! • **Songwriters:** MOULD and now same with others. Covered; SHOOT OUT THE LIGHTS (Richard Thompson).

Recommended: WORKBOOK (BOB MOULD *7) / COPPER BLUE (*10) / FILE UNDER: EASY LISTENING (*8) / BEASTER (*8) / BOB MOULD (*8)

BOB MOULD

solo, with **ANTON FIER** – drums / **TONY MAIMONE** – bass, (both ex-PERE UBU) / **JANE SCARPANTONI** – cello (of TINY LIGHTS) / **STEVE HAIGLER** – cello

Virgin Virgin

Jun 89. (7") **SEE A LITTLE LIGHT. / ALL THOSE PEOPLE KNOW** [ ] [ ]
(12"+=)(cd-s+=) – Shoot out the lights / Composition for the young and the old (live).

Jul 89. (lp)(cd) **WORK BOOK** [ ] [ ]
– Sunspots / Wishing well / Heartbreak a stranger / See a little light / Poison years / Sinners and their repentances / Lonely afternoon / Brasilia crossed the Tranton / Compositions for the young and old / Dreaming, I amd / Whichever way the wind blows. *(re-iss.Sep90)*

Aug 90. (cd)(c)(lp) **BLACK SHEETS OF RAIN** [ ] [ ]
– Black sheets of rain / Stand guard / It's too late / One good reason / Stop your crying / Hanging tree / The last night / Hear me calling / Out of your life / Disappointed / Sacrifice – let there be peace.

Virgin Virgin

May 94. (cd) **THE POISON YEARS** (compilation) [ ] [ ]

SUGAR

BOB MOULD – vox, guitar, keyboards, percussion / **DAVE BARBE** – bass (ex-MERCYLAND) / **MALCOLM TRAVIS** – drums, percussion (ex-ZULUS)

		Creation	Rykodisc
Aug 92.	(12"ep)(cd-ep) **CHANGES / NEEDLE HITS E. / IF I CAN'T CHANGE YOUR MIND / TRY AGAIN**		
Sep 92.	(cd)(c)(lp) **COPPER BLUE** – The act we act / A good idea / Changes / Helpless / Hoover dam / The slim / If I can't change your mind / Fortune teller / Slick / Man on the Moon.	10	
Oct 92.	(12"ep)(cd-ep) **A GOOD IDEA. / WHERE DIAMONDS ARE HALOS / SLICK / ARMENIA CITY IN THE SKY**	65	
Jan 93.	(c-s) **IF I CAN'T CHANGE YOUR MIND. / CLOWN MASTER** (12"+=)(cd-s+=) – Anyone (live) / Hoover dam (live). (cd-s) – ('A'side) / The slim / Where diamonds are halos.	30	
Apr 93.	(cd)(c)(m-lp) **BEASTER** – Come around / Tilted / Judas cradle / JC auto / Feeling better / Walking away.	3	
Aug 93.	(7"only) **TILTED. / JC AUTO (live)**	48	
Aug 94.	(7")(c-s) **YOUR FAVORITE THING. / MIND IS AN ISLAND** (12"+=)(cd-s+=) – Frustration / And you tell me (T.V. mix).	40	
Sep 94.	(cd)(c)(lp) **FILE UNDER EASY LISTENING (F.U.E.L.)** – Gift / Company book / Your favorite thing / What you want it to be / Gee angel / Panama city hotel / Can't help it anymore / Granny cool / Believe what you're saying / Explode and make up.	7	50
Oct 94.	(7")(c-s) **BELIEVE WHAT YOU'RE SAYING. / GOING HOME** (cd-s+=) – In the eyes of my friends / And you tell me.	73	

. . . Jan – Jun '96 stop press . . .

— Disbanded and BARBE formed BUZZHUNGRY / TRAVIS went to CUSTOMIZED

BOB MOULD

		Creation	Rykodisc
Apr 96.	(cd)(c)(lp) **BOB MOULD**	52	

SUGARCUBES (see under ⇒ BJORK)

Andy SUMMERS (see under ⇒ POLICE)

SUNDAYS

Formed: London, England . . . 1988 by HARRIET, DAVID and PAUL. Signed to top indie label 'Rough Trade' in 1988, and immediately bounced into the Top 50 with debut single 'CAN'T BE SURE'. Early in 1990, their long-awaited first album 'READING, WRITING AND ARITHMETIC', soared into the UK Top 5, and also surprised many when reaching US Top 40. • **Style:** Luscious alternative rock outfit, that originally drew similarities between COCTEAU TWINS or THROWING MUSES. • **Songwriters:** HARRIET lyrics / DAVID music. Covered; WILD HORSES (Rolling Stones). • **Trivia:** PATCH now lives in Guildford, Surrey. An instrumental piece was used on the 1993 series for comedy duo NEWMAN and BADDIEL.

Recommended: READING, WRITING AND ARITHMETIC (*9) / BLIND (*7).

HARRIET WHEELER (b.26 Jun'63) – vocals (ex-JIM JIMINEE) / **DAVID GAVURIN** (b. 4 Apr'63) – guitar / **PAUL BRINDLEY** (b. 6 Nov'63, Loughborough, England) – bass / **PATRICK 'Patch' HANNAN** (b. 4 Mar'66) – drums repl. drum machine.

		Rough Trade	D.G.C.
Feb 89.	(7") **CAN'T BE SURE. / I KICKED A BOY** (12"+=)(cd-s+=) – Don't tell your mother.	45	
Jan 90.	(cd)(c)(lp)(pic-lp) **READING, WRITING AND ARITHMETIC** – Skin & bones / Here's where the story ends / Can't be sure / I won / Hideous towns / You're not the only one I know / A certain someone / I kicked a boy / My finest hour / Joy.	4	39
Jan 90.	(7") **HERE'S WHERE THE STORY ENDS. / SKIN AND BONES**	-	
		Parlophone	**D.G.C.**
Sep 92.	(7")(c-s) **GOODBYE. / WILD HORSES** (cd-s+=) – Noise.	27	
Oct 92.	(cd)(c)(lp) **BLIND** – I feel / Goodbye / Life and soul / Marc / On Earth / God made me / Love / What do you think? / 24 hours / Blood on my hands / Medieval. *(re-iss.cd+c Mar94)*	15	

SUPER FURRY ANIMALS

*** NEW ENTRY ***

Formed: Cardiff, Wales . . .1995 by GRUFF, brothers CIAN & DAFYDD, GUTO and BUMPF. Two EP singles for Welsh 'Ankst' label, led to contract with major indie 'Creation'. After a skirmish, they were banned from Welsh TV Bafta Awards and the programme 'I-Dot' on Welsh Channel 4. Early in 1996, they got stuck into the Top 50 with Creation debut 'HOMETOWN UNICORN'. **Style:** Progressive hookline acid pop outfit similar to BLUR. • **Songwriters:** Group. • **Trivia:** Known to be friends with notorious drug smuggler HOWARD MARKS.

Recommended: FUZZY LOGIC (*8)

GRUFF RHYS – vocals, guitar / **CIAN LEUAN** – keyboards / **HUW 'Bumpf' BUNFORD** – guitar / **GUTO PRYCE** – bass / **DAFYDD LEUAN** – drums

		Ankst	not issued
Jun 95.	(7"ep) **LLANFAIRPWLIGWYGYLLGOGERYCHWYRNDROBWLLANTYSILIOGOGOYOCYNYGOFOD** – Organ yn dy geg / Fix idris / Crys T. / Blerwytirhwng.		-
Oct 95.	(7"ep)(cd-ep) **MOOG DIROOG** – Pam V / God! show me magic / Sali Mali / Focus pocus – Dabiel.		-
		Creation	**Creation**
Feb 96.	(7")(c-s) **HOMETOWN UNICORN. / DON'T BE A FOOL BILLY** (cd-s+=) – Lazy life.	47	-
Apr 96.	(7")(c-s) **GOD! SHOW ME MAGIC. / DIM BENDITH** (cd-s+=) – Death by melody.	33	
May 96.	(cd)(c)(lp) **FUZZY LOGIC** – God! show me magic / Fuzzy birds / Something 4 the weekend / Frisbee / Hometown unicorn / Gathering moss / If you don't want me to destroy you / Bad behaviour / Mario man / Hangin' with Howard Marks / Long gone / For now and ever.	23	

SUPERGRASS

Formed: Oxford, England . . .1991 as The JENNIFERS by schoolboy GAZ, etc. After one single for Sam Galpern's 'Nude', they changed name to THEODORE SUPERGRASS early '94. They soon dropped first name part and appeared on Various Artists compilation 7"ep 'CRAZED AND CONFUSED' doing a demo version of 'CAUGHT BY THE FUZZ'. This was duly unleashed as their first proper 45 a month later in October and hit Top 50. 1995 started out in fine fashion, with 2 major hits and then a superb Top 3 album 'I SHOULD COCO', which soon went top. • **Style:** Teenage punk outfit, also influenced by 60's psychedelia, 70's BUZZCOCKS punk and everything under the sun, although it works just fine. • **Songwriters:** Group except; STONE FREE (Jimi Hendrix) / ITCHYCOO PARK (Small Faces). • **Trivia:** Played "T In The Park" festival early August 1995 with 4th member BOBSIE COOMBES on keyboards.

Recommended: I SHOULD COCO (*9)

JENNIFERS

GAZ COOMBES (b.1976) – vocals, guitar / **NICK GOFFEY** – guitar / **ANDY DAVIES** - bass / **DANNY GOFFEY** (b.1975) – drums

		Nude-Sony	not issued
Aug 92.	(12"ep)(cd-ep) **JUST GOT BACK TODAY / ROCKS AND BOULDERS. / DANNY'S SONG / TOMORROW'S RAIN**		-

— **MICKEY QUINN** (b.1970) – guitar repl.TARA MILTON who had repl.NICK

SUPERGRASS

— now without DAVIES who went to Bristol University.

		Parlophone	Sub Pop
Oct 94.	(7")(c-s) **CAUGHT BY THE FUZZ. / STRANGE ONES** (cd-s+=) – Caught by the fuzz (acoustic).	43	-
Feb 95.	(7")(7"red)(c-s) **MANSIZE ROOSTER. / SITTING UP STRAIGHT** (cd-s+=) – Odd.	20	-
Mar 95.	<7"yellow> **LOSE IT. / CAUGHT BY THE FUZZ (acoustic)**	75	

— (above on 'Sub Pop' also feat. on Jul95 box-set 'HELTER SHELTER')

SUPERGRA
0

Apr 95. (7"blue)(c-s) **LENNY. / WAIT FOR THE SUN** 9 -
(cd-s+=) – Sex!.

May 95. (cd)(c)(lp) **I SHOULD COCO** 1
– I'd like to know / Caught by the fuzz / Mansize rooster / Alright / Lose it / Lenny / Strange ones / Sitting up straight / She's so loose / We're not supposed to / Time / Sofa (of my lethargy) / Time to go. *(7"free w/ ltd lp)* **STONE FREE. / ODD?**

Jul 95. (7"colrd)(c-s) **ALRIGHT. / TIME** 2
(cd-s+=) – Condition / Je suis votre papa sucre.
(cd-s+=) – Lose it.

... Jan – Jun '96 stop press ...

Feb 96. (single) **GOING OUT** 5

SUPERTRAMP

Formed: London, England based ... 1969 by RICHARD DAVIES. Through sponsorship from young Dutch millionaire Stanley Miesegaes, he enlisted new members through music paper ad. Quickly obtained a deal with 'A&M' and in the early 70's, released 2 albums before their untimely demise. SUPERTRAMP (Mk.II) hit the right note, when in 1974 'CRIME OF THE CENTURY (lp)' gave them first million-seller. Continued this success on both sides of the Atlantic, until the late 80's. • **Style:** Melodic and clever progressive rock, which veered into American AOR by the late 70's. • **Songwriters:** HODGSON and/or DAVIE, except I'M YOUR HOOCHIE COOCHIE MAN (John Lee Hooker). • **Trivia:** Took their name from a 1910 W.H.Davies book 'The Autobiography Of A Supertramp'.

Recommended: CRIME OF THE CENTURY (*8) / THE AUTOBIOGRAPHY OF SUPERTRAMP (*8) / BREAKFAST IN AMERICA (*7).

RICHARD DAVIES (b.22 Jul'44) – vocals, keyboards (ex-The JOINT) / **ROGER HODGSON** (b.21 Mar'50) – bass, keyboards, vocals / **RICHARD PALMER** – guitar / **BOB MILLER** – drums

A & M A & M

Aug 70. (lp)(c) **SUPERTRAMP**
– Surely / It's a long road / Aubade / And I am not like other birds of prey / Words unspoken / Maybe I'm a beggar / Home again / Nothing to show / Shadow song / Try again / Surely (reprise). *(US-iss.Mar78) (UK re-issues Mar82, Sep89 +cd) cd-iss.Sep88) (re-iss.May84 on 'Hallmark')(re-iss.c Jan93)*

— (May71) **HODGSON** now also lead guitar, vox / **FRANK FARRELL** – bass / **KEVIN CURRIE** – drums repl. PALMER + MILLER / added **DAVE WINTHROP** – saxophone

Jun 71. (lp)(c) **INDELIBLY STAMPED**
– Your poppa don't mind / Travelled / Rosie had everything planned / Remember / Forever / Potter / Coming home to see you / Times have changed / Friend in need / Aries. *(cd-iss.1988)(re-iss.c Jan93)*

Oct 71. (7") **FOREVER. / YOUR POPPA DON'T MIND** -

— Disbanded late Summer 1971, WINTHROP later joined SECRET AFFAIR. **DAVIES + HODGSON** re-formed them Aug'73. Recruited **DOUGIE THOMPSON** – bass (ex-BEES MAKE HONEY) / **BOB BENBERG** (b.SIEBENBERG) – drums (ex-BEES MAKE HONEY) / **JOHN ANTHONY HELLIWELL** – saxophone, clarinet, vocals (ex-ALAN BOWN SET)

Mar 74. (7") **LAND HO. / SUMMER ROMANCE** -

Sep 74. (lp)(c) **CRIME OF THE CENTURY** 4 38
– School / Bloody well right / Hide in your shell / Asylum / Dreamer / Rudy / If everyone was listening / Crime of the century. *(re-iss.+cd.Apr86)*

Dec 74. (7") **DREAMER. / BLOODY WELL RIGHT** 13 35 Apr 75
(above 'B'side was US 'A'side)

Nov 75. (lp)(c) **CRISIS? WHAT CRISIS?** 20 44
– Easy does it / Sister Moonshine / Ain't nobody but me / A soapbox opera / Another man's woman / Lady / Poor boy / Just a normal day / The meaning / Two of us. *(re-iss.+cd.Apr86)*

Nov 75. (7") **LADY. / YOU STARTED LAUGHING (WHEN I HELD YOU IN MY ARMS)**

Jun 76. (7") **SISTER MOONSHINE. / AIN'T NOBODY BUT ME** -

Apr 77. (lp)(c) **EVEN IN THE QUIETEST MOMENTS** 12 16
– Give a little bit / Lover boy / Even in the quietest moments / Downstream / Babaji / From now on / Fool's overture. *(re-iss.+cd.Apr86)*

Jun 77. (7") **GIVE A LITTLE BIT. / DOWNSTREAM** 29 15

Nov 77. (7") **FROM NOW ON. / DREAMER** -

Nov 77. (7") **BABAJI. / FROM NOW ON** -

Mar 79. (lp)(c) **BREAKFAST IN AMERICA** 3 1
– Gone Hollywood / The logical song / Goodbye stranger / Breakfast in America / Oh darling / Take the long way home / Lord is it mine / Just another nervous wreck / Casual conversations / Child of vision. *(cd-iss.1983)*

Mar 79. (7") **THE LOGICAL SONG. / JUST ANOTHER NERVOUS WRECK** 7 6

Jun 79. (7") **BREAKFAST IN AMERICA. / GONE HOLLYWOOD** 9 -

Sep 79. (7") **GOODBYE STRANGER. / EVEN IN THE QUIETEST MOMENTS** 57 15 Jul 79

Oct 79. (7") **TAKE THE LONG WAY HOME. / FROM NOW ON** -

Oct 79. (7") **TAKE THE LONG WAY HOME. / RUBY** - 10

Sep 80. (d-lp)(d-c) **PARIS (live 29-11-79)** 7 8
– School / Ain't nobody but me / The logical song / Bloody well right / Breakfast in America / You started laughing / Hide in your shell / From now on / Dreamer / Rudy / A soapbox opera / Asylum / Take the long way home / Fool's overture / Two of us / Crime of the century. *(cd-iss.Apr86)*

Sep 80. (7") **DREAMER (live). / FROM NOW ON (live)** - 15

Nov 80. (7") **DREAMER (live). / YOU STARTED LAUGHING (live)** -

Nov 80. (7") **BREAKFAST IN AMERICA (live). / YOU STARTED LAUGHING (live)** - 62

Oct 82. (7") **IT'S RAINING AGAIN. / BONNIE** 26 11

Oct 82. (lp)(c) **... FAMOUS LAST WORDS** 6 5
– Crazy / Put on your brown school shoes / It's raing again / Bonnie / Know who you are / My kind of lady / C'est la bon / Waiting so long / Don't leave me now. *(cd-iss.1983)*

Jan 83. (7") **MY KIND OF LADY. / KNOW WHO YOU ARE** 31

— (Nov82) Now a quartet when HODGSON departed to go solo. (Re-joined briefly late'86 tour). HODGSON solo albums: IN THE EYE OF THE STORM (84) / HAI HAI (87).

Apr 85. (7") **CANNONBALL. / EVER OPEN DOOR** 28

May 85. (lp)(c)(cd) **BROTHER WHERE YOU BOUND** 20 21
– Cannonball / Still in love / No inbetween / Better days / Brother where you bound / Ever open door. *(re-iss.c Jan93)*

Jul 85. (7") **STILL IN LOVE. / NO INBETWEEN** Feb 85
(12"+=) – Cannonball (dance mix).

Sep 85. (7") **BETTER DAYS. / NO INBETWEEN** -

Nov 86. (lp)(c)(cd) **THE AUTOBIOGRAPHY OF SUPERTRAMP** 9
(compilation)
– Goodbye stranger / The logical song / Bloody well right / Breakfast in America / Take the long way home / Crime of the century / Dreamer / From now on / Give a little bit / It's raining again / Cannonball / Ain't nobody but me / Hide in your shell / Rudy. *(cd= 3 extra) (re-iss.cd Jan93 as 'THE VERY BEST OF SUPERTRAMP' +=)*– School.

Oct 87. (7")(12") **I'M BEGGIN' YOU. / NO INBETWEENS**

Oct 87. (lp)(c)(cd) **FREE AS A BIRD** 93
– It's alright / Not the moment / It doesn't matter / Where I stand / Free as a bird / I'm beggin' you / You never can tell with friends / Thing for you / An awful thing to waste.

Feb 88. (7") **FREE AS A BIRD. / THING FOR YOU** -

Feb 88. (7") **FREE AS A BIRD. / I'M BEGGIN' YOU** -

Oct 88. (lp)(c)(cd) **LIVE '88 (live)**
– You started laughing / It's alright / Not the moment / Oh darling / Breakfast in America / From now on / Just another nervous wreck / The logical song / I'm your hoochie coochie man / Crime of the century / Don't you lie to me. *(re-iss.cd Jan93)*

— Folded after above.

– more compilations, etc. –

May 81. A&M; (d-c) **CRISIS? WHAT CRISIS? / EVEN IN THE QUIETEST MOMENTS** -

Sep 86. A&M; (7") **THE LOGICAL SONG. / GOODBYE STRANGER** -

Aug 88. A&M; (cd-ep) **COMPACT HITS** -
– The logical song / Breakfast in America / Goodbye stranger / Hide in your shell.

Jul 92. A&M; (7")(c-s) **GIVE A LITTLE BIT (for Telethon). / ('A' original version)**
(cd-s+=) – Breakfast in America.

Sep 85. Old Gold; (7") **DREAMER. / GIVE A LITTLE BIT** -

Steve SWINDELLS (see under ⇒ HAWKWIND)

David SYLVIAN (see under ⇒ JAPAN)

SYSTEM 7 (see under ⇒ HILLAGE, Steve)

TALKING HEADS

Formed: Manhattan, New York, USA . . . May'75 by former art & design students BYRNE, WEYMOUTH and FRANTZ. Their first gig was to support The RAMONES at the CBGB's club in New York, circa mid'75. They were soon spotted by Seymour Stein, who signed them to new US label 'Sire'. Late 1976, they released debut 45 'LOVE GOES TO A BUILDING ON FIRE', which flopped. The next year, they unleashed the '77 album, which sold well enough to reach lower chart regions. The follow-up 'MORE SONGS . . . ', became their first of many US + UK Top 30 albums. • **Style:** New wave rock outfit, who later experimented with Afro-rhythms and alternative rock music. Between 1978 and 1979, BRIAN ENO (ex-ROXY MUSIC) produced a more avant-garde but soulful pop. BYRNE and ENO later (1981), collaborated on 'MY LIFE IN THE BUSH OF GHOSTS', an album of their rhythms and taped singers / speeches of various people from around the world. • **Songwriters:** Group compositions except; TAKE ME TO THE RIVER (Al Green) / SLIPPERY PEOPLE (Staple Singers). TOM TOM CLUB:- UNDER THE BOARDWALK (Drifters) / FEMME FATALE (Velvet Underground). DAVID BYRNE: – GREENBACK DOLLAR (Hoy & Axton) / GIRLS ON MY MIND (Toquinnho Vinicius) / DON'T FENCE ME IN (Cole Porter). • **Trivia:** FRANTZ and WEYMOUTH (later TOM TOM CLUB) married on 18 Jun'77. BYRNE produced The B-52's on their 1982 album 'Mesopotamia' and FUN BOY THREE on their 1983 'Waiting' album. HARRISON produced The VIOLENT FEMMES on 1986 album 'The Blind Leading The Naked'. TOM TOM CLUB started out producing in 1988 with ZIGGY MARLEY. They later worked for HAPPY MONDAYS. In 1986, BYRNE and group starred in their own film 'TRUE STORIES' which was also released as 2 separate albums.

Recommended: TALKING HEADS '77 (*9) / MORE SONGS ABOUT BUILDINGS AND FOOD (*8) / FEAR OF MUSIC (*9) / REMAIN IN LIGHT (*8) / ONCE IN A LIFETIME – THE BEST OF TALKING HEADS (*9).

DAVID BYRNE (b.14 May'52, Dumbarton, Scotland) – vocals, guitar / **TINA WEYMOUTH** (b.22 Nov'50, Coronado, California, USA) – bass, vocals / **CHRIS FRANTZ** (b.CHARLTON CHRISTOPHER FRANTZ, 8 May'51, Fort Campbell, Kentucky, USA) – drums

Sire Sire

Feb 77. (7") **LOVE GOES TO A BUILDING ON FIRE. / NEW FEELING** [ ] [ ]

— added **JERRY HARRISON** (b.JEREMIAH, 21 Feb'49, Milwalkee, Wisconsin, USA) – guitar, keyboards (ex-JONATHAN RICHMAN & THE MODERN LOVERS)

Sep 77. (lp) **TALKING HEADS '77** [60] [97]
– Uh-oh, love comes to town / New feeling / Tentative decisions / Happy day / Who is it? / No compassion / The book I read / Don't worry about the government / First week – last week . . . carefree / Psycho killer / Pulled up. *(cd-iss.Feb87)*

Oct 77. (7") **UH-OH, LOVE COMES TO TOWN. / I WISH YOU WOULDN'T SAY THAT** [-] [ ]

Dec 77. (7") **PSYCHO KILLER. / I WISH YOU WOULDN'T SAY THAT** [ ] [92]
(12"+=) – Psycho killer (acoustic version). (US; b-side)

May 78. (7") **PULLED UP. / DON'T WORRY ABOUT THE GOVERNMENT** [ ] [ ]

Jul 78. (lp)(d-c) **MORE SONGS ABOUT BUILDINGS AND FOOD** [21] [29]
– Thank you for sending me an angel / With our love / The good thing / Warning sign / Girls want to be with the girls / Found a job / Artists only / I'm not in love / Stay hungry / Take me to the river / The big country. *(double-play cass. includes debut album) (cd-iss.Jan87)*

Oct 78. (7") **TAKE ME TO THE RIVER. / THANK YOU FOR SENDING ME AN ANGEL** [-] [26]

Jun 79. (7") **TAKE ME TO THE RIVER. / FOUND A JOB** [ ] [-]
(d7"+=) – Love goes to a building on fire / Psycho killer.

Aug 79. (lp)(c) **FEAR OF MUSIC** [33] [21]
– Air / Animals / Cities / Drugs / Electric guitar / Heaven / I Zimbra / Life during wartime / Memories can't wait / Mind / Paper. *(free-7"w.a.)* – PSYCHO KILLER (live). / NEW FEELING (live) *(cd-iss.Jul84)*

Oct 79. (7") **LIFE DURING WARTIME. / ELECTRIC GUITAR** [ ] [80]

Feb 80. (7") **I ZIMBRA. / PAPER** [ ] [ ]

Jun 80. (7") **CITIES. / CITIES (live)** [ ] [ ]
(12"+=) – Artists only.

— basic 4 added **BUSTA CHERRY JONES** – bass / **ADRIAN BELEW** – guitar / **BERNIE WORRELL** – keyboards / **STEVEN SCALES** – percussion / **DONETTE McDONALD** – back.vox

Oct 80. (lp)(c) **REMAIN IN LIGHT** [21] [19]
– The great curve / Crosseyed and painless / Born under punches / Houses in motion / Once in a lifetime / Listening wind / Seen and not seen / The overlord. *(cd-iss.1983)*

Feb 81. (7")('A'ext-12") **ONCE IN A LIFETIME. / SEEN AND NOT SEEN** [14] [ ]

May 81. (7") **HOUSES IN MOTION (remix). / THE OVERLORD** [-] [ ]

May 81. (7") **HOUSES IN MOTION (remix). / AIR** [50] [-]
('A'extended-12"+=) – ('A'live version).

In 1981, all 4 diversed into own projects (see further below)

Mar 82. (7") **LIFE DURING WARTIME (live). / LIFE DURING WARTIME (lp version)** [ ] [ ]
(12"+=) – Don't worry about the government (live).

Apr 82. (d-lp)(d-c) **THE NAME OF THIS BAND IS TALKING HEADS (live)** [22] [31]
– I Zimbra / Drugs / Houses in motion / Life during wartime / Take me to the river / The great curve / Cross-eyed and painless / New feeling / A clean break / Don't worry about the government / Pulled up / Psycho killer / Artists only / Stay hungry / Air / Building on fire / Memories can't wait. *(cd-iss.1983)*

Jun 83. (lp)(c)(cd)(clear-lp) **SPEAKING IN TONGUES** [21] [15]
– Burning down the house / Making flippy floppy / Girlfriend is better / Slippery people / I get wild – Wild gravity / Swamp / Moon rocks / Pull up the roots / This must be the place (naive melody). *(c+cd+=)* – (6 extra mixes).

Jul 83. (7") **BURNING DOWN THE HOUSE. / I GET WILD – WILD GRAVITY** [ ] [9]
(12"+=) – Moon rocks.

Jan 84. (7") **THIS MUST BE THE PLACE (NAIVE MELODY). / MOON ROCKS** [51] [62] Oct 83
(d12"+=) – Slippery people (remix) / Making flippy floppy (remix). *(re-iss.7".Jun86)*

E.M.I. Sire

Oct 84. (7")('A'ext-12") **SLIPPERY PEOPLE (live). / THIS MUST BE THE PLACE (NAIVE MELODY) (live)** [68] [ ]

Oct 84. (lp)(c)(cd) **STOP MAKING SENSE (live)** [37] [41]
– Psycho killer / Swamp / Slippery people / Burning down the house / Girlfriend is better / Once in a lifetime / What a day that was / Life during wartime / Take me to the river. *(c+cd+=)* – (extra tracks) *(re-is.Mar90) (re-iss.cd+c Nov93 on 'Fame')*

Nov 84. (7")('A'ext-12") **GIRLFRIEND IS BETTER (live). / ONCE IN A LIFETIME (live)** [ ] [ ]

Dec 84. (7") **GIRLFIRIEND IS BETTER. / HEAVEN** [-] [ ]

May 85. (7")('A'ext-12") **THE LADY DON'T MIND. / GIVE ME BACK MY NAME** [ ] [ ]
(d12"+=) – Slippery people / This must be the place (naive melody).

Jun 85. (lp)(c)(cd) **LITTLE CREATURES** [10] [20]
– And she was / Give me back my name / Creatures of love / The lady don't mind / Perfect world / Stay up late / Walk it down / Television man / Road to nowhere. *(c+=)* – The lady don't mind (extended). *(re-iss.Mar90) (re-iss.cd+c Nov93 on 'Fame')*

Jun 85. (7") **ROAD TO NOWHERE. / GIVE ME BACK MY NAME** [-] [ ]

Sep 85. (7") **AND SHE WAS. / ('A' dub)** [-] [54]

Sep 85. (7")(7"pic-d) **ROAD TO NOWHERE. / TELEVISION MAN** [6] [-]
(d12"+=) – Slippery people (live) / This must be the place (naive melody) (live).

Feb 86. (7")('A'ext-12") **AND SHE WAS. / PERFECT WORLD** [17] [-]

Apr 86. (7") **ONCE IN A LIFETIME (live). / THIS MUST BE THE PLACE (live)** [-] [ ]

Aug 86. (7") **WILD WILD LIFE. / PEOPLE LIKE US** [43] [25]

Once in a lifetime. Crosseyed and painless - Facts are lazy -

facts are late. Everyone is trying get to the part. The band in heaven they

play my favorite song. Heaven is a place - where nothing

ever happens - there is a party everyone is there. Burning

down the house. Swamp. This must be the place

(Naive melody) Life during wartime. Girl

friend is better. Blind. City of Dreams. And

she was. Stay up late. Wild Wild life. Take a walk

through the peaceful meadows. I'm stuck there in

people they must stay. Lifetime

Love for Sale. Don't worry about

the Government. Warning sign. No Compassion Heaven

PSYCHO KILLER I wish you wouldn't say that.

Wild wild life. Memories can't wait

I Zimbra. Take me

to the River - drop

me in the

water. Love

Building on fire

The big country

TINA

CHRIS

DAVID

JERRY

Lost my shape

Trying to act casual

Changing my shape

I feel like an

accident

Making sense

Wild Life

My God what

have I done?

Same as it

ever was!

Where do correct ideas come from? Horses

This must be the place. Fear of Music. COMPASSION IS A VIRTUE but

I just don't have the time. REMAIN IN LIGHT. Mr. Jones. Lifetime piling

up. Life during Wartime

TALKING HEADS

No Compassion

I want to

Live.

(12"+=)(12"pic-d+=) – ('A'album version).

Sep 86. (lp)(c)(cd) **TRUE STORIES** [7] [17]
– Love for sale / Puzzlin' evidence / Hey now / Radio head / Papa Legba / Wild wild life / Radio head / Dream operator / People like us / City of dreams. *(cd+=)* – Wild (ET mix). *(re-iss.Sep89 on 'Fame')*

Nov 86. (7") **LOVE FOR SALE. / HEY NOW** [-] [ ]

Nov 86. (lp)(c) **SONGS FROM 'TRUE STORIES' (Original DAVID BYRNE Film Soundtrack; w/ other artists)** [ ] [ ]
– Cocktail desperado / Road song / Freeway son / Brownie's theme / Mall muzak: Building a highway – Puppy polka – Party girls / Dinner music / Disco hits / City of steel / Love theme from 'True Stories' / Festa para um Rei Negro / Buster's theme / Soy de Tejas / I love metal buildings / Glass operator.

Apr 87. (7") **RADIO HEAD. / HEY NOW (movie version)** [52] [ ]
(d7"+=)(12"+=)(cd-s+=) – ('A'&'B'-different versions).

Mar 88. (lp)(c)(cd) **NAKED** [3] [19]
– Blind / Mr. Jones / Totally nude / Ruby dear / (Nothing but) Flowers / The Democratic circus / The facts of life / Mommy daddy you and I / Big daddy / Bill * / Cool water. *(cd+= *) (re-iss.cd+c Nov93 on 'Fame')*

Aug 88. (7") **BLIND. / BILL** [59] [ ]
(12"+=)(cd-s+=) – ('A'mix).

Oct 88. (7") **(NOTHING BUT) FLOWERS. / RUBY DEAR (Bush mix)** [ ] [ ] Apr 88
(10"+=)(c-s+=)(cd-s+=) – Mommy daddy you and I.
(12"+=) – Facts of life.

— Cease to function as a group, after last recording. Officially split 1991.

– compilations, others, etc. –

Oct 92. EMI; (7")(c-s) **LIFETIME PILING UP. / ROAD TO NOWHERE** [50] [ ]
(cd-s+=) – Love for sale / The lady don't mind (extended).
(cd-s) – ('A'side) / Stay up late / Radio head / Take me to the river.

Oct 92. EMI; (d-cd)(d-c)(d-lp) **POPULAR FAVOURITES 1976-1992** [7] [ ]
– ONCE IN A LIFETIME:- Psycho killer / Take me to the river / Once in a lifetime / Burning down the house / This must be the place (naive melody) / Slippery people (live) / Life during wartime (live) / And she was / Road to nowhere / Wild wild life / Blind / (Nothing but) Flowers / Sax and violins / Lifetime piling up.// SAND IN MY VASELINE:- Sugar on my tongue / I want to live / Love goes to a building on fire / I wish you wouldn't say that / Don't worry about the government / The big country / No compassion / Warning sign / Heaven / Memories can't wait / I Zimbra / Crosseyed and painless / Swamp / Girlfriend is better (live) / Stay up late / Love for sale / City of dreams / Mr. Jones / Gangster of love / Popsicle.

Nov 95. EMI; (3xcd-box) **STOP MAKING SENSE / LITTLE CREATURES / TRUE STORIES** [ ] [-]

DAVID BYRNE

(solo) Earlier in the year, he had collaborated with BRIAN ENO ⇒ on album 'MY LIFE IN THE BUSH OF GHOSTS'.

Sire Sire

Dec 81. (7") **BIG BLUE PLYMOUTH (EYES WIDE OPEN). / CLOUD CHAMBER** [ ] [ ]
(12") – ('A'side) / Leg bells / Light bath.

Jan 82. (lp)(c) **SONGS FROM 'THE CATHERINE WHEEL' (Stage score)** [ ] [ ] Dec 81
– His wife refused / Two soldiers / The red house / My big hands (fall through the cracks) / Big business / Eggs in a briar patch / Poison / Cloud chamber / What a day that was / Big blue Plymouth (eyes wide open). *(US d-lp+=)* – Ade / Walking / Under the mountain / Dinosaur / Wheezing / Black flag / Combat / Leg bells / The blue flame / Danse beast / Five golden sections.

1982. (12"ep) **THREE BIG SONGS** [-] [ ]
– Big business (remix) / My big hands (fall through the cracks) / Big blue Plymouth (eyes wide open).

E.M.I. Sire

Sep 85. (lp)(c) **MUSIC FOR THE KNEE PLAYS** [ ] [ ] May 85
– Tree (today is an important occasion) / In the upper room / The sound of business / Social studies / (The gift of sound) Where the sun never goes down / Theadora is dozing / Admiral Perry / I bid you goodnight / I've tried / Winter / Jungle book / In the future.

— Rec. collaboration with RYUICHI SAKAMOTO on film 'THE LAST EMPEROR'.

BYRNE now used a plethora of Brazilian musicians.

Luaka Bop Luaka Bop

Oct 89. (lp)(c)(cd) **REI MOMO** [52] [71]
– Independence day / Make believe mambo / The call of the wild / Dirty old town / The rose tattoo / The dream police / Don't want to be part of your world / Marching through the wilderness / Lie to me / Women vs.men / Carnival eyes / I know sometimes a man is wrong.

Dec 89. (7")('A'ext-12") **MAKE BELIEVE MAMBO. / LIE TO ME** [ ] [ ]

Jun 91. (cd)(c)(lp) **THE FOREST (instrumental)** [ ] [ ]
– Ur / Kish / Dura Europus / Nineveh / Ava / Machu picchu / Teotihuaean / Asuka.

Sire-WEA Sire-WEA

Mar 92. (cd)(c)(lp) **UH-OH** [26] [ ]
– Now I'm your mom / Girls on my mind / Something ain't right / She's mad / Hanging upside down / Twistin' in the wind / A walk in the dark / The cowboy mambo (hey lookit me now) / Tiny town / Somebody. *(re-iss.cd/c Feb95)*

Apr 92. (7")(c-s) **GIRLS ON MY MIND. / MONKEY MAN** [ ] [ ]
(12"+=)(cd-s+=) – Cantode oxum.

May 92. (7")(c-s) **HANGING UPSIDE DOWN. / TINY TOWN** [ ] [ ]
(cd-s) – ('A'side) / Dirty old town (live) / (Nothing but) Flowers (live) / Girls on my mind (live).
(cd-s) – ('A'side) / Something ain't right (live) / Who we're thinking of (live) / Rockin' in the free world (live).

Jul 92. (7")(c-s) **SHE'S MAD. / SOMEBODY** [ ] [ ]
(12") – ('A'side) / Butt naked / Greenback dollar
(cd-s++=) – ('A'side) / Now I'm your man.

— with **PAUL SOCOLOW** – bass, vocals / **TODD TURKISHER** – drum, percussion / **VALERIE NARANJO** – percussion, tambourine (live: MAURO REFOSCO – percussion) / **BILL WARE** – marimba / **ARTO LINDSAY** – guitar / **JOHN MEDESKI** – organ / **BASHIRI JOHNSON** – congas, bongos / **BEBEL GILBERTO** – vocals

Luaka Bop-Sire Luaka Bop-Sire

May 94. (cd)(c) **DAVID BYRNE** [44] [ ]
– A long time ago / Angels / Crash / A self-made man / Back in the box / Sad song / Nothing at all / My love is you / Lillies of the valley / You & eye / Strange ritual / Buck naked.

Jun 94. (c-s)(cd-s) **ANGELS / PRINCESS / READY FOR THIS WORLD** [ ] [ ]

Sep 94. (c-s)(cd-s) **BACK IN THE BOX / GYPSY WOMAN (live) / GIRLS ON MY MIND (live)** [ ] [ ]

TOM TOM CLUB

CHRIS FRANTZ + TINA WEYMOUTH plus her 2 sisters + **STEVE SCALES** – percussion / **ALEX WEIR** – guitar / **TYRON DOWNIE** – keyboards

Island Sire

Jun 81. (7") **WORDY RAPPINGHOOD. / YOU DON'T STOP (WORDY RAP)** [7] [ ]
(12"+=) – L'elephant.

Sep 81. (7") **GENIUS OF LOVE. / LORELEI (instrumental)** [65] [31] Mar 82
(12"+=) – ('A'&'B'extended versions).

Oct 81. (lp)(c) **TOM TOM CLUB** [78] [23]
– Wordy rappinghood / Genius of love / Tom Tom theme / L'elephant / As above, so below / Lorelei / On, on, on, on . . . / Booming and zooming. *(re-iss.Oct86, cd-iss.May87)*

Jun 82. (7")(12") **LORELEI. / ON, ON, ON, ON . . .** [ ] [ ]

Jul 82. (7") **UNDER THE BOARDWALK. / ON, ON, ON, ON . . . (remix)** [22] [ ]
(12"+=) – Lorelei (remix).

Oct 82. (7") **GENIUS OF LOVE. / LORELEI (instrumental)** [ ] [-]
(12"+=) – Rappa rappa rhythm / Melia.

Jul 83. (7")(12") **THE MAN WITH THE 4-WAY HIPS. / ('A'dub version)** [ ] [ ]

Aug 83. (lp)(c) **CLOSE TO THE BONE** [ ] [73]
– Pleasure of love / On the line again / This is a foxy world / Bamboo town / The man with the 4-way hips / Measure up / Never took a penny / Atsababy! (life is great).

Dec 83. (7") **NEVER TOOK A PENNY. / PLEASURE OF LOVE** [-] [ ]

— **TINA + CHRIS** added **GARY POZNER** – keyboards / **MARK ROULE** – guitar, percussion

Fontana Sire

Sep 88. (7") **DON'T SAY NO. / DEVIL DOES YOUR DOG BITE?** [ ] [ ]
(12"+=) – ('A'version) / Beats and pieces.
(cd-s+=) – Beats and pieces / Percapella.

Oct 88. (lp)(c)(cd) **BOOM BOOM CHI BOOM BOOM** [ ] [ ]
– Suboceana / Shock the world / Don't say no / Challenge of the love warriors / Femme fatale / Born for love / Broken promises / She belongs to me / Little Eva / Misty teardrop.

JERRY HARRISON

Sire Sire

Oct 81. (7") **THINGS FALL APART. / WORLDS IN COLLISION** [ ] [ ]

Oct 81. (lp)(c) **THE RED AND THE BLACK** [ ] [ ]
– Things fall apart / Slink / The new adventure / Magic hymie / Fast karma / No questions / Worlds in collision / The red nights / No more returns / No warning no alarm.

Fontana Sire

Feb 88. (lp)(c)(cd) **JERRY HARRISON: CASUAL GODS** [ ] [78]
– Revi it up / Songs of angels / Man with a gun / Let it come down / Cherokee chief / A perfect lie / Are you running? / Breakdown in the passing lane / A.K.A. love / We're always talkin' / Bobby. *(cd+=)*– Bobby (12"version).

May 88. (7") **MAN WITH A GUN. / ('A'radio edit)** [ ] [ ]
(12"+=)(cd-s+=) – Breakdown on the passing line / Wire always talking.

— His backers included **BROOKS / WORRELL / BAILEY / SIEGER + WEIR**

Jun 90. (7") **WALK ON WATER. / MAN WITH A GUN** [ ] [ ]
(12"+=)(cd-s+=) – Racing the fire.

Jun 90. (cd)(c)(lp) **WALK ON WATER** [ ] [ ]
– Flying under radar / Cowboy's got to go / Kick start / I don't mind / Sleep angel / Confess / I cry for Iran / Never let it slip / If the rain returns / The doctor's lie.

TALK TALK

Formed: London, England . . . 1981 by MARK HOLLIS, who with older brother and session man ED (ex-EDDIE & THE HOT RODS), invited to studio WEBB, HARRIS and BREMNER. They soon signed to 'EMI', and employed manager Keith Aspen to hire producer Colin Thurston to work on debut. After support slot to stablemates DURAN DURAN, they soon exploded into charts with single 'TODAY' and album 'THE PARTY'S OVER'. • **Style:** At first an uptempo keyboard orientated pop band, who graduated into an intelligent but abstract rock-pop outfit. • **Songwriters:** Initially group penned, with MARK and brother ED writing most. In 1983, MARK and 4th member TIM FRIESE-GREEN wrote all material. • **Trivia:** The song 'TALK TALK', was first heard in 1978 when MARK's group The REACTION, recorded prototype of the song on Various Artists album 'Streets'.

Recommended: NATURAL HISTORY – THE VERY BEST OF TALK TALK (*9)

MARK HOLLIS (b.1955) – vocals, piano, guitar (ex-REACTION) / **SIMON BREMNER** – keyboards / **PAUL WEBB** – bass, vocals / **LEE HARRIS** – drums

E.M.I. / EMI America

Feb 82. (7") **MIRROR MAN. / STRIKE UP THE BAND** [ ] [ ]
Apr 82. (7")('A'ext-12") **TALK TALK. / ('A'version)** [52] [ ]
Jun 82. (7")('A'ext-12") **TODAY. / IT'S SO SERIOUS** [14] [ ]
Jul 82. (lp)(c) **THE PARTY'S OVER** [21] [ ]
– Talk talk / It's so serious / Today / The party's over / Hate / Have you heard the news? / Mirror man / Another word / Candy. *(re-iss.1985, cd-iss.Mar87) (re-iss.Sep87 on 'Fame', cd-iss.Apr88)*
Oct 82. (7")(7"pic-d) **TALK TALK (remix). / MIRROR MAN** [23] [75]
(12") – ('A'side) / ('A'-BBC version).
Feb 83. (7") **MY FOOLISH FRIEND. / CALL IN THE NIGHT BOYS** [57] [ ]
(12"+=) – ('A'extended).

— Now basic trio when BREMNER departed. His place was taken by 4th member **TIM FRIESE-GREEN** – keyboards, producer, co-composer. Added session people **ROBBIE McINTOSH + HENRY LOWTHER**

Jan 84. (7") **IT'S MY LIFE. / DOES CAROLINE KNOW?** [46] [31]
(12"+=) – ('A'extended).
Feb 84. (lp)(c) **IT'S MY LIFE** [35] [42]
– Dum dum girl / Such a shame / Renee / It's my life / Tomorrow started / The last time / The last time / Call in the night boy / Does Caroline know? / It's you. *(cd-iss.Feb85) (lp re-iss.1989)*
Mar 84. (7") **SUCH A SHAME. / AGAIN, A GAME . . . AGAIN** [49] [89]
(12"+=) – ('A'extended).
(d7"+=) – Talk talk (demo) / Mirror man (demo).
Jul 84. (7") **DUM DUM GIRL. / WITHOUT YOU** [74] [ ]
(12"+=) – ('A'US mix) / Such a shame (dub).

— guests on next album incl. **DAVID RHODES** – guitar / **DAVID ROACH** – saxophone / **MORRIS PERT** – percussion

Parlophone / EMI America

Jan 86. (7") **LIFE'S WHAT YOU MAKE IT. / IT'S GETTING LATE IN THE EVENING** [16] [90]
(12"+=) – ('A'extended dance mix).
(d12"+=) – It's my life / Does Caroline know?.
Feb 86. (lp)(c)(cd) **THE COLOUR OF SPRING** [8] [58]
– Happiness is easy / I don't believe in you / Life's what you make it / April 5th / Living in another world / Give it up / Chameleon day / Time it's time. *(re-iss.Mar90) (re-iss.cd+c Apr93 on 'Fame')*
Mar 86. (7")(7"sha-pic-d) **LIVING IN ANOTHER WORLD. / FOR WHAT IT'S WORTH** [48] [ ]
(12"+=)/ /(12"+=) – ('A'extended)./ / ('A'-US mix).
May 86. (7") **GIVE IT UP. / PICTURES OF BERNADETTE** [59] [ ]
(12"+=) – ('A'dance mix).
Nov 86. (7") **I DON'T BELIEVE IN YOU. / DOES CAROLINE KNOW?** [ ] [ ]
(12"+=) – Happiness is easy.

— Basic quartet added ensemble **MARTIN DITCHAM** – percussion (also on last) / **ROBBIE McINTOSH** – dobro, 12-string guitar (also on last lp) / **MARK FELTHAM** – harmonica / **SIMON EDWARDS** – Mexican bass / **HENRY LOWTHER** – trumpet / **NIGEL KENNEDY** – violin / **DANNY THOMPSON** – double bass / **HUGH DAVIS** – shozygs / **MICHAEL JEANS** – oboe / **ANDREW STOWALL** – bassoon / **ANDREW HARRINER** – clarinet / **CHRIS HOOKER** – cor anglais / plus CHOIR OF CHELMSFORD CATHEDRAL.

Sep 88. (lp)(c)(cd) **SPIRIT OF EDEN** [19] [ ]
– The rainbow / Eden / Desire / Inheritance / I believe in you / Wealth. *(re-iss.cd+c Jun93 on 'Fame')*
Sep 88. (7") **I BELIEVE IN YOU. / JOHN COPE** [ ] [ ]
(12"+=)(cd-s+=) – Eden (edit).
Dec 88. (m-lp)(c) **IT'S MY LIFE** (remixes) [-] [ ]
May 90. (7") **IT'S MY LIFE (remix). / RENEE (live)** [13] [ ]
(12"+=)(cd-s+=) – ('A'live version).
(12") – ('A'side) / Talk Talk recycled; Life's what you make it – Living in another world – Such a shame – It's my life.
Jun 90. (cd)(c)(lp) **NATURAL HISTORY – THE VERY BEST OF TALK TALK** (compilation) [3] [ ]
– Today / Talk talk / My foolish friend / Such a shame / Dum dum girl / It's my life / Give it up / Living in another world / Life's what you make it / Happiness is easy / I believe in you / Desire.
Sep 90. (7")(c-s) **LIFE'S WHAT YOU MAKE IT. / ('A'live version)** [23] [ ]
(12"+=)(cd-s+=) – Tomorrow started (live).
(12") – (3-'A' mixes).
Nov 90. (7")(c-s) **SUCH A SHAME. / DUM DUM GIRL (live)** [ ] [ ]
(12"+=)(cd-s+=) – Talk talk (live) / ('A'extended).
Feb 91. (7")(c-s) **LIVING IN ANOTHER WORLD ('91 remix). / ('A'live remix)** [ ] [ ]
(12"+=)(cd-s+=) – ('A' Mendolsohn mix).

— Basic quartet only retained **DITCHAM, EDWARDS + LOWTHER** and brought in **LEVINE ANDRADE, STEPHEN TEES, GEORGE ROBERTSON, GAVYN WRIGHT, JACK GLICKMAN, GARFIELD JACKSON + WILF GIBSON** – viola / **ERNEST MOTHLE** – acoustic bass / **ROGER SMITH + PAUL KEGG** – cello / **DAVE WHITE** – contra, bass, clarinet

Mar 91. (cd)(c)(lp) **HISTORY REVISITED – THE REMIXES** [35] [ ]
– Living in another world '91 / Such a shame / Happiness is easy (dub) / Today / Dum dum girl (spice remix) / Life's what you make it / Talk talk / It's my life (tropical rainforest mix) / Living in another world (curious world dub mix) / Life's what you make it (the Fluke remix).

Verve / Verve

Sep 91. (cd)(c)(lp) **LAUGHING STOCK** [26] [ ]
– Myrrhman / Ascension day / After the flood / Taphead / New grass / Runeii.
Sep 91. (pic-cd-s) **AFTER THE FLOOD / MYRRHMAN** [ ] [ ]
Oct 91. (pic-cd-s) **NEW GRASS. / STUMP** [ ] [ ]
Nov 91. (pic-cd-s) **ASCENTION DAY. / 5.09** [ ] [ ]

O'RANG

LEE HARRIS + PAUL WEBB

Echo / not issued

Aug 94. (cd)(c) **HERD OF INSTINCT** [ ] [-]
Nov 94. (12"ep)(cd-ep) **SPOOR** [ ] [-]
-O'rang / Little brother / Mind our pleasure / All change / And on the oasis / Loaded values / Nahoojak fejou.

TANGERINE DREAM

Formed: Berlin, Germany . . . 1967 by EDGAR FROESE. After a number of album releases on German label 'Ohr', they signed to Richard Branson's newish label 'Virgin' in 1973. Surprisingly the following year, 'PHAEDRA' made it into the UK Top 40 lists, where they were future regulars during the rest of the 70's. • **Style:** Pioneers of improvised synthesized rock, which drew influences from PINK FLOYD. Soon discovered picturesque electronic waves of sound, which were critically derided for the haunting, repetitive rhythms and drones. Obviously it wasn't long before they realised, their potential would be in film soundtracks, and thus they concentrated on this during the 80's & early 90's. • **Songwriters:** FROESE compositions. • **Trivia:** They took group name in a couple of lyrics used to describe 'Lucy In The Sky With Diamonds' BEATLES.

Recommended: PHAEDRA (*9) / RUBYCON (*9) / RICOCHET (*8) / STRATOSFEAR (*7) / SORCEROR (*7).

EDGAR FROESE (b. 6 Jun'44) – guitar, piano, organ (ex-The ONES) / **VOLKER HOMBACH** – flute, violin / **KIRT HERKENBERG** – bass / (Mar69) / **SVEN JOHANNSON** – drums repl. LANSE HAPRHASH

— In 1970, after HOMBACH became film cameraman for W.R.FASSBINDER, and brief wind instrumentalist STEVE JOLIFFE departed to join STEAMHAMMER. Group reformed **EDGAR FROESE** brought in newcomers **KLAUS SCHULTZE** – drums, percussion / **CONRAD SCHNITZLER** – cello, flute, violin. with guests **JIMMY JACKSON** – organ / **THOMAS VON KEYSERLING** – flute

Ohr / not issued

Jun 70. (lp) **ELECTRONIC MEDITATION** [-] [-] Germ'y
– Geburt (Genesis) / Reise durch ein brennendes gehirn (Journey through a burning brain) / Kalter rauch (Cold smoke) / Asche zu asche (Ashes to ashes) / Auferstehung (Resurrection).

— **FROESE** added bass to repertoire, and again supplanted new members

— **CHRISTOPHER FRANKE** – drums, percussion, synthesizer repl. CONRAD / **STEVE SCHROEDER** – organs repl. KLAUS SCHULTZE who went solo / added new guests **UDO DENNEBORG** – flute, words / **ROLAND PAULICK** – synthesizer

1971. (lp) **ALPHA CENTAURI** [ ] [-]
– Sunrise in the third system / Fly and collision of Comas Sola / Alpha Centauri. *(UK-iss.+c.1971 on 'Polydor') (re-iss.+cd.Jan87 on 'Zomba-Jive')*

— **PETER BAUMANN** – synthesizer, organ repl. SCHROYDER (guested on below)

Feb 72. (7") **ULTIMA THULE (tell 1). / ULTIMA THULE (tell 2)** [-] [-]

— More guests were added on next; **FLORIAN FRICKE** – synthesizers / cellists / **CHRISTIAN VALBRACHT / JOCKEN VON GRUMBCOW / HANS JOACHIM BRUNE / JOHANNES LUCKE**

1972. (d-lp) **ZEIT** [-] [-]
– 1st movement: Birth of liquid plejades / 2nd movement: Nebulous dawn / 3rd movement: Origins of supernatural probabilities / 4th movement: Zeit. *(UK-iss. 1976 on 'Virgin') (re-iss.+cd.Jan87 on 'Zomba-Jive')*

1973. (lp) **ATEM** [ ] [-]
– Atem / Fauni-Gena / Wahn / Circulation of events. *(UK-iss.+c.1973 on 'Polydor') (re-iss.+cd.Jan87 on 'Zomba-Jive')*

In Aug73, they recorded GREEN DESERT album, unreleased until 1986.

Virgin / Virgin

Mar 74. (lp)(c) **PHAEDRA** [15] [ ]
– Phaedra / Mysterious semblance at the strand of nightmares / Movements of a visionary / Sequent C. *(re-iss.Mar84, cd-iss.Jul87 & Feb95)*

— **MICHAEL HOENIG** – synthesizer repl. BAUMANN (on tours only 1974-75)

Mar 75. (lp)(c) **RUBYCON** [12] [ ]
– Rubycon (part 1) / Rubycon (part 2). *(re-iss.Mar84, cd-iss.Jul87 & Feb95)*

Dec 75. (lp)(c) **RICOCHET (live at Liverpool, Coventry & Yorkminster Cathedrals)** [40] [ ]
– Ricochet (part 1) / Ricochet (part 2). *(re-iss.Mar84, cd-iss.Jul87 & Feb95)*

— **BAUMANN** re-united with outfit, to depose HOENIG

Nov 76. (lp)(c) **STRATOSFEAR** [39] [ ]
– Stratosfear / The big sleep in search of Hades / 3 a.m. at the border of the marsh from Okefnokee / Invisible limits. *(re-iss.1985, cd-iss.Jul87 & Feb95)*

Jul 77. (lp)(c) **SORCERER (Soundtrack)** [25] [ ]
– Main title / Search / The call / Creation / Vengeance / The journey / Grind / Rain forest / Abyss / The mountain road / Impressions of Sorcerer / Betrayal (Sorcerer's theme). *(re-iss.Feb82)*

Above album and below 45 were from the film 'Wages Of Fear' on 'M.C.A.' records.

Aug 77. (7") **BETRAYAL. / GRIND** [-] [ ]

Nov 77. (d-lp)(c) **ENCORE (live)** [55] [ ]
– Cherokee lane / Moonlight / Coldwater canyon / Desert dream. *(cd-iss.1985 & Apr95)*

Jan 78. (7") **ENCORE. / HOBO MARCH** [ ] [-]

Mar 78. (7") **MOONLIGHT. / COLDWATER CANYON** [-] [ ]

— **STEVE JOLIFFE** – vocals, keyboards, wind returned after several years to repl. BAUMANN who went solo. Added **KLAUS KRIEGER** – drums

Mar 78. (lp)(c) **CYCLONE** [37] [ ]
– Bent cold sidewalk / Rising runner missed by endless sender / Madrigal meridian. *(re-iss.1982, cd-iss.Jul87 & Apr95)*

Feb 79. (lp)(c)(clear-lp) **FORCE MAJEURE** [27] [ ]
– Force majeure / Cloudburst flight / Thru metamorphic rocks. *(re-iss.+cd.Jul87, cd-iss.Apr95)*

— (now trio) **FROESE + FRANKE** recruited **JOHANNES SCHMOELLING** – keyboards

May 80. (lp)(c) **TANGRAM** [36] [ ]
– Tangram set 1 / Tangram set 2. *(re-iss.+cd.Oct85, cd-iss.Apr95)*

Virgin / Elektra

Apr 81. (lp)(c) **THIEF (Soundtrack)** [43] [ ]
– Beach theme / Dr. Destructo / Diamond diary / Burning bar / Scrap yard / Trap feeling / Igneous / Confrontation. *(re-iss.1985, cd-iss.Jun88 & Aug95)*

Sep 81. (lp)(c) **EXIT** [43] [ ]
– Kiwe mission / Pilots of purple twilight / Chronozon / Exit / Network 23 / Remote viewing. *(re-iss.+cd.Jun88 & Aug95)*

Sep 81. (7") **CHRONOZON. / NETWORK 23** [ ] [-]

Apr 82. (lp)(c) **WHITE EAGLE** [57] [ ]
– Midnight in Tulo / Convention of the 24 / White eagle / Mojave plan. *(cd-iss.Jun88 & Aug95)*

Dec 82. (lp)(c) **LOGOS – LIVE (At The Dominion)** [ ] [ ]
– Logos part 1 / Logos part 2 / Dominion. *(re-iss.Apr86, cd-iss.Jun88 & Aug95)*

Oct 83. (lp)(c)(cd) **HYPERBOREA** [45] [ ]
– No man's lannd / Hyperborea / Cinnamon road / Sphinx lightning. *(re-iss.cd Jun88 & Aug95)*

Dec 83. (lp)(c) **RISKY BUSINESS (Soundtrack)** [ ] [ ]
– The dream is always the same / No future / Love on a real train / Guido the killer pimp / Lana (tracks by other artists; PHIL COLLINS / JOURNEY / MUDDY WATERS / JEFF BECK / BOB SEGER). *(re-iss.+cd.Apr90)*

M.C.A. / M.C.A.

Jul 84. (lp)(c) **FIRESTARTER (Film Soundtrack)** [ ] [ ]
– Crystal voice / The run / Test lab / Charley the kid / Escaping point / Rainbirds move / Burning force / Between realities / Shop territory / Flash final / Out of the heat. *(cd-iss.Apr90)*

Jive Electro / Jive Electro

Sep 84. (7")(7"sha-pic-d) **WARSAW IN THE SUN. / POLISH DANCE** [ ] [ ]
(12"+=) – Rare bird / ('A'version).

Oct 84. (d-lp)(d-c)(d-pic-lp) **POLAND – THE WARSAW CONCERT (live)** [90] [ ]
– Poland / Tangent / Barbakane / Horizon.

Feb 85. (lp)(c)(pic-lp) **FLASHPOINT (Soundtrack)** [ ] [ ]
– Going west / Afternoon in the desert / Plane ride / Mystery tracks / Lost in the dunes / Highway patrol / Love phantasy / Madcap story / Dirty cross-roads / Flashpoint. *(cd-iss.Apr87) (re-iss.cd Sep95 on 'One Way')*

(above was on 'Jive-Heavy Metal' label).

Aug 85. (lp)(c) **LE PARC** [ ] [ ]
– Bois de Boulonge (Paris) / Central Park (New York) / Gaudi Park (Guell Garden, Barcelona) / Tiergarten (Berlin) / Zen Garden (Myoonj, Temple Kyoto) / Le Parc (L.A. Streethawk) / Hyde Park (London) / The Cliffs of Sydney (Sydney) / Yellowstone Park (Rocky Mountains). *(cd-iss.1988)*

— guest on above album **CLARE TORY** – vocals

Aug 85. (7") **STREETHAWK. / TIERGARTEN** [ ] [ ]
(12"+=) – Gaudi Park / Warsaw in the sun (part 1 & 2).

— **PAUL HASLINGER** – multi-instrumentalist repl. SCHMOELLING who went solo

Jul 86. (lp)(c)(cd) **UNDERWATER SUNLIGHT** [97] [ ]
– Song of the whale / From dawn . . . to dusk / Ride on the ray / Dolphin dance / Underwater sunlight / Scuba scuba.

Jun 87. (lp)(c)(cd) **TYGER** [88] [ ]
– Tyger / London / Alchemy of the heart / Smile. *(cd+=)*– 21st century common man I & II.

— (guest vox – **BERNADETTE SMITH**).

Jun 87. (7") **TYGER. / 21st CENTURY COMMON MAN II** [ ] [ ]
(12"+=) – ('A'version).

Jive Electro / Sil-va Screen

Feb 88. (lp)(c)(cd) **NEAR DARK (Soundtrack)** [-] [ ]
– Cabeb's blues / Pick up at high noon / Rain in the third house / Bus station / Good times / She's my sister / Father and son / Severin dies / Flight at dawn / Mae's transformation / Mae comes back. *(UK-iss.Jun90)*

Apr 88. (lp)(c)(cd) **LIVE MILES (live)** [ ] [ ]
– Live miles: (part 1) – The Albuquerque concert / Live miles: (part 2) – The West Berlin concert.

Jul 88. (lp)(c)(cd) **SHY PEOPLE (Soundtrack)** [-] [ ]
– Shy people / Joe's place / The harbor / Nightfal / Dancing on a white moon / Civilized illusion's / Swamp voices / Transparent days / Shy people (reprise).

— now a duo of **FROESE + HASLINGER**

Arista / Private . . .

Feb 89. (lp)(c)(cd) **OPTICAL RACE** [ ] [ ] Aug 88
– Marakesh / Atlas eyes / Mothers of rain / Twin soul tribe / Optical race / Cat scan / Sun gate / Turning of the wheel / The midnight trail / Ghtrezi (long song).

Jul 89. (lp)(c)(cd) **MIRACLE MILE** [-] [ ]
– Teetering scales / One for the book / After the call / On the spur of the moment / All of a dither / Final statement.

Dec 89. (lp)(c)(cd) **LILY ON THE BEACH** [-] [ ]
– Too hot for my chinchilla / Lily on the beach / Alaskan summer / Desert drive / Mount Shasta / Crystal curfew / Paradise cove / Twenty nine palms / Valley of the kings / Radio city / Blue mango cafe / Gecko / Long island sunset.

R.C.A. / R.C.A.

Dec 90. (cd)(c)(lp) **MELROSE** [ ] [ ]
– Melrose / Three bikes in the sky / Dolls in the shadow / Yucatan / Electric lion / Rolling down Cahenga / Art of vision / Desert train / Cool at heart.

Sil-va Screen / Sil-va Screen

Mar 91. (cd) **DEAD SOLID PERFECT (Soundtrack)** [ ] [ ]
– Theme from Dead Solid Perfect / In the pond / Beverly leaves / Of cads and caddies / (Tournament montage) / A whore in one / Sand trap / In the rough / Nine iron / US Open / My name is bad hair / In the hospital room / Welcome to Bushwood / Deja vu / Birdie / Divot / Kenny and Donny montage / Phone to Beverly / Nice shots / Sinking putts / Kenny's winning shot.

— Now a duo of **FROESE + JEROME FROESE** his son and **LINDA SPA** – sax / **ZLASLO PERICA** – synth.

Feb 92. (cd)(c)(lp) **ROCKOON** (on 'Essential') [ ] [ ]
– Big city dwarves / Red roadster / Touchwood / Graffiti sreeet / Funky Atlanta / Spanish love / Lifted veil / Penguin reference / Body corporate / Rockoon / Girls on Broadway.

Dec 92. (cd) **DEADLY CARE (Soundtrack)** [ ] [ ]
– Main theme / Paddles – Stolen pills / A strong drink – A bad morning / Wasted and sick / Hope for future / The hospital in bed / Annie and father / More pills / In the Head nurse's – At the father's grave / Clean and sober.

Miramar / Miramar

Jul 93. (cd) **CANYON DREAMS** [ ] [ ]
– Shadow flyer / Canyon carver / Water's gift / Canyon voices / Sudden revelation / A matter of time / Purple nightfall / Colorado dawn.

Oct 93. (cd)(c) **220 VOLT LIVE (live)** [ ] [ ]
– Oriental haze / Two bunch palms / 220 volt / Homeless / Treasure of innocence / Sundance kid / Backstreet hero / The blue bridge / Hamlet / Dreamtime / Purple haze.

Date	Release	Coast	Coast
Nov 94.	(cd) **TURN OF THE TIDES** – Pictures at an exhibition / Firetongues / Galey slave's horizon / Death of a nightingale / Twilight brigade / Jungle journey / Midwinter night / Turn of the tides.		
		Amp	
Sep 95.	(cd) **TYRANNY OF BEAUTY** –		

– compilations, others, etc. –

Date	Release	UK	US
Jul 76.	Polydor; (d-lp)(d-c) **ATEM / ALPHA CENTAURI**		-
Dec 80.	Virgin; (4xlp-box) **70-80**		-
1985.	Virgin; (lp)(c) **HEARTBREAKERS**	-	
Nov 85.	Virgin; (d-lp)(c)(cd) **DREAM SEQUENCE**		-
1983.	Varese Sara; (lp) **WAVELENGTH (Soundtrack)**	-	
1987.	Varese Sara; (lp) **THREE O'CLOCK HIGH (Soundtrack)**	-	
May 86.	MCA; (lp) **LEGEND (Soundtrack with other artists)** – Unicorn theme / Blue room / Darkness / The dance / Goblins / Fairies / The kitchen (medley).	-	96
Mar 86.	Jive Electro; (6xlp-box) **IN THE BEGINNING** – (ELECTRONIC MEDITATION / ALPHA CENTAURI / ZEIT (d-lp) / ATEM / GREEN DESERT)		-
Nov 89.	Jive; (lp)(c)(cd) **THE BEST OF TANGERINE DREAM**		-
Dec 86.	Zomba; (cd) **GREEN DESERT** (rec.1973) *(re-iss.+lp/c.May89)*		-
Mar 87.	Castle/ US= Relativity; (d-lp)(c)(cd) **THE TANGERINE DREAM COLLECTION**		Aug 87
Oct 91.	Music Club; (cd)(c)(lp) **FROM DAWN . . . TILL DUSK 1973-88**		-
Mar 93.	Silva Screen; (cd) **DREAM MUSIC** feat. selections from soundtracks; THE PARK IS MINE / DEADLY CARE / DEAD SOLID PERFECT.		
Oct 94.	Virgin; (5xcd-box) **TANGENTS**		-
Mar 95.	Emporio; (cd)(c) **ATMOSPHERICS**		-
Nov 95.	Silva Screen; (cd) **DREAM MUSIC 2**		-
Dec 95.	Essential; (d-cd) **BOOK OF DREAMS**		-

EDGAR FROESE

solo (all music by himself)

Date	Release	Virgin	Virgin
Jun 74.	(lp)(c) **AQUA** – NGC 891 / Upland / Aqua / Panorphelia. *(re-iss.Mar84, cd-iss.Jun87)*		-
Sep 75.	(lp)(c) **EPSILON IN MALAYSIAN PALE** – Epsilon in Malaysian pale / Maroubra Bay. *(re-iss.Mar84, cd-iss.Jun87)*		-
1976.	Brain Germany; (lp) **MACULA TRANSFER** – Os / Af / Pa / Quantas / If. *(re-iss.Mar82)*	-	-
Jan 78.	(d-lp) **AGES** – Metropolis / Era of the slaves / Tropic of Capricorn / Nights of automatic women / Icarus / Childrens deeper study / Ode to Granny "A" / Pizarro and Atahwallpa / Golgatha and the circle closes.		
Sep 79.	(lp)(c) **STUNTMAN** – Stuntman / It would be like Samoa / Detroit snackbar dreamer / Drunken Mozart in the desert / A Dali-esque sleep fuse / Scarlet score for Mescalero. *(re-iss.Mar84, cd-iss.1987) (cd-iss.Mar94)*		
Oct 82.	(lp)(c) **KAMIKAZE 1989 (Soundtrack)** – Videophonic / Vitamen 'C' / Krismopompas / Polizei disco / Intuition / Polizei therapie center / Blauer panther / Schlangenbad / Underwarter tod / Flying kamikaze / Der konzern / Der 31. stock. *(re-iss.+cd.1988)*		-
Aug 83.	(lp)(c) **PINNACLES** – Specific gravity of smile / The light cone / Walkabout / Pinnacles. *(re-iss.+cd.1988)*		-

– (EDGAR FROESE) compilations, others –

Date	Release	UK	US
Aug 82.	Virgin; (lp)(c) **SOLO** *(re-iss.Mar84, cd-iss.Aug88)*		-
Jun 95.	(d-cd)(d-lp) **BEYOND THE STARS**		-

TASTE (see under ⇒ GALLAGHER, Rory)

John TAYLOR (see under ⇒ DURAN DURAN)

Roger TAYLOR (see under ⇒ QUEEN)

TEARDROP EXPLODES (see under ⇒ COPE, Julian)

TEARS FOR FEARS

Formed: Bath, Avon, England . . . 1981 by SMITH and ORZABAL, after both had left ska-pop outfit GRADUATE. As TEARS FOR FEARS, they signed to 'Mercury', after A&R man Dave Bates heard a few demos. In the Autumn 1982, their CHRIS 'Merrick' HUGHES (ex-Adam & The Ants) produced single 'MAD WORLD' burst into UK Top 3. It was followed by another smash, which preceeded parent UK No.1 album 'THE HURTING'. • **Style:** Intelligent lightweight soulful rock, which progressed in the late 80's, into slight experimentation and BEATLES influenced psychedelia. • **Songwriters:** All written by ORZABAL, except CREEP (Radiohead). • **Trivia:** Took their name from Arthur Janov's book 'Prisoners Of Pain'.

Recommended: TEARS ROLL DOWN – GREATEST HITS 1982-1992 (*8)

GRADUATE

ROLAND ORZABAL (b.ROLAND ORZABAL DE LA QUINTANA, 22 Aug'61, Portsmouth, England) – vocals, guitar / **CURT SMITH** (b.24 Jun'61) – vocals, bass / **JOHN BAKER** – vocals, guitar / **STEVE BUCK** – keyboards, flute / **ANDY MARSDEN** – drums

Date	Release	Precision	not issued
Mar 80.	(7") **ELVIS SHOULD PLAY SKA. / JULIE JULIE**		-
May 80.	(7") **EVER MET A DAY?. / SHUT UP** *(re-iss.Mar81)*		-
May 80.	(10"lp)(c) **ACTING MY AGE** – Acting my age / Sick and tired / Ever met a day / Dancing nights / Shut up / Elvis should play ska / Watching your world / Love that is bad / Julie Julie / Bad dreams. *(re-iss.Jul86 on 'P.R.T.')*		-
Oct 80.	(7") **AMBITION. / BAD DREAMS**		-

TEARS FOR FEARS

ROLAND & CURT with **DAVID LORD** – synthesizers(Duo also on synthesizers)

Date	Release	Mercury	Mercury
Nov 81.	(7") **SUFFER THE CHILDREN. / WIND** ('A'remixed-12"+=) – ('A'instrumental). *(re-iss.Aug85, hit 52)*		
	— Trimmed to a basic duo of **ORZABAL & SMITH**		
Mar 82.	(7") **PALE SHELTER (YOU DON'T GIVE ME LOVE). / THE PRISONER** (12"+=) – ('A'extended). *(re-iss.Aug85, hit 73)*		
Sep 82.	(7") **MAD WORLD. / IDEAS AS OPIATES** (12"+=) – Saxophones as opiates. (d7"+=) – ('A'world remix) / Suffer the children.	3	
Jan 83.	(7") **CHANGE. / THE CONFLICT** (12"+=) – ('A'extended).	4	73 Jun 83
	— now augmented by **IAN STANLEY** – keyboards / **MANNY ELIAS** – drums		
Mar 83.	(lp)(c) **THE HURTING** – The hurting / Mad world / Pale shelter / Ideas as opiates / Memories fade / Suffer the children / Watch me bleed / Change / The prisoner / Start of the breakdown. *(cd-iss.1984)*	1	73
Apr 83.	(7")(7"red)(7"green)(7"white)(7"blue)(7"pic-d) **PALE SHELTER. / WE ARE BROKEN** (12"+=) – ('A'extended).	5	
Nov 83.	(7") **(THE) WAY YOU ARE. / THE MARAUDERS** ('A'extended-12"+=) – Start of the breakdown (live). (d7"++=) – Change (live).	24	
Aug 84.	(7")(7"green)(7"clear-pic-d) **MOTHER'S TALK. / EMPIRE BUILDING** (12"+=)/ /(12"+=) – ('A'beat of the drum mix)./ / ('A'extended). (12") – (above 2 versions + 'A'-7"version)	14	27 Mar 86
Nov 84.	(7")(10") **SHOUT. / THE BIG CHAIR** (12"+=) – ('A'extended).	4	1 May 85
	— added mainly on tour **WILLIAM GREGORY** – saxophone / **NICKY HOLLAND** – keyboards		
Mar 85.	(lp)(c)(cd) **SONGS FROM THE BIG CHAIR** – Shout / The working hour / Everybody wants to rule the world / Mother's talk / I believe / Broken / Head over heels / Broken (live) / Listen. *(c+=)* – (6 extra mixes).	2	1
Mar 85.	(7")(10") **EVERYBODY WANTS TO RULE THE WORLD. / PHAROAHS** (12"+=) – ('A'extended). (d7"+=) – ('A'urban mix) / (duo interviewed). (12") – ('A'urban mix). / ('A'instrumental)	2	1
Jun 85.	(7")(10")(7"sha-pic-d) **HEAD OVER HEELS (remix). / WHEN IN LOVE WITH A BLIND MAN** (12"+=)/ /(12"+=) – ('A'preacher mix)./ / Broken.	12	3 Sep 85
Oct 85.	(7") **I BELIEVE (A soulful re-recording). / SEA SONG** (d7"+=)(12"+=) – Shout (dub) / I believe (original version). (10"+=) – I believe (US mix).	23	
May 86.	(7")(12") **EVERYBODY WANTS TO RUN THE WORLD. / EVERYBODY . . . (Running version)**	5	
	— **ORZABAL + SMITH** retained **IAN** and **NICKY** and brought in sessioners **OLETA ADAMS** – some dual vocals, piano / **SIMON CLARK** – organ / **PINO PALLADINO** – bass / **ROBBIE McINTOSH, NEIL TAYLOR + RANDY JACOBS** – guitar / **PHIL COLLINS, CHRIS HUGHES + MANU KATCHE** – drums		

		Fontana	Fontana
Aug 89.	(7")(c-s) **SOWING THE SEEDS OF LOVE. / TEARS ROLL DOWN** (12"+=)(12"pic-d+=)(12"white+=)(3"cd-s+=) – Shout (US mix).	5	2
Sep 89.	(lp)(c)(cd) **THE SEEDS OF LOVE** – Woman in chains / Bad man's song / Sowing the seeds of love / Advice for the young at heart / Standing on the corner of the third world / Swords and knives / Year of the knife / Famous last words.	1	8

(next 'A'feat. **OLETA ADAMS** – co-vox)

Nov 89.	(7")(c-s) **WOMAN IN CHAINS. / ALWAYS IN THE PAST** (12"+=)(12"pic-d+=)(12"white+=)(3"cd-s+=)(cd-s+=) – ('A'instrumental) / My life in the suicide ranks.	26	36
Feb 90.	(7")(c-s) **ADVICE FOR THE YOUNG AT HEART. / JOHNNY PANIC AND THE BIBLE OF DREAMS** (12"+=)(cd-s+=)(12"pic-d+=) – Music for tables. (3"cd-s++=) – Johnny Panic (instrumental).	36	89
Jul 90.	(7")(c-s) **FAMOUS LAST WORDS. / MOTHER'S TALK (US remix)** (12"+=)(cd-s+=)(12"pic-d+=) – Listen.		
Feb 92.	(7")(c-s) **LAID SO LOW. / THE BODY WAH** (12"pic-d+=)(cd-s+=) – Lord of the Kharma.	17	
Mar 92.	(cd)(c)(lp) **TEARS ROLL DOWN – GREATEST HITS 1982-1992** (compilation) – Sowing the seeds of love / Everybody wants to rule the world / Woman in chains / Shout / Head over heels / Mad world / Pale shelter / I beieve / Laid so low (tears roll down) / Mothers talk / Change / Advice for the young at heart. (May93: re-entered UK charts at 37).	2	53
Apr 92.	(7")(c-s) **WOMAN IN CHAINS. / BADMAN'S SONG** (cd-s+=) – Ghost papa.	57	

(above was again credited to "TEARS FOR FEARS & OLETA ADAMS")

— **ROLAND ORZABAL** now sole survivor, when CURT SMITH launched solo career.

		Mercury	Mercury
May 93.	(7")(c-s) **BREAK IT DOWN AGAIN. / BLOODLETTING GO** (cd-s+=) – ?	20	25
Jun 93.	(cd)(c)(lp) **ELEMENTAL** – Elemental / Cold / Break it down again / Mr. Pessimist / Dog's a best friend's dog / Fish out of water / Gas giants / Power / Brian Wilson said / Goodnight song.	5	45
Jul 93.	(7")(c-s) **COLD. / NEW STAR** (cd-s+=) – Deja vu / The sins of silence.	72	

		Epic	Sony
Sep 95.	(c-s) **RAOUL AND THE KINGS OF SPAIN / QUEEN OF COMPROMISE** (cd-s) – ('A'side) / Creep / The madness of Roland.	31	
Oct 95.	(cd)(c) **RAOUL AND THE KINGS OF SPAIN** – Raoul and the Kings of Spain / Falling down / Secrets / God's mistake / Sketches of pain / Los Reyes Catolicos / Sorry / Humdrum and humble / I choose you / Don't drink the water / Me and my big ideas / Los Reyes Catolicos (reprise).	41	79

. . . Jan – Jun '96 stop press . . .

Jun 96.	(single) **GOD'S MISTAKE**	61	

TEENAGE FANCLUB

Formed: Bellshill & Motherwell, Glasgow, Scotland ... 1989 although earlier they had posed as The BOY HAIRDRESSERS. Became hitmakers in 1991, after signing to 'Creation' and scoring with album 'BANDWAGONESQUE'. • **Style:** Uptempo fun-loving punk pop outfit. • **Songwriters:** BLAKE or BLAKE-McGINLEY or group compositions except; DON'T CRY NO TEARS (Neil Young) / THE BALLAD OF JOHN AND YOKO (Beatles) / LIKE A VIRGIN (Madonna) / LIFE'S A GAS (T.Rex) / FREE AGAIN (Alex Chilton) / CHORDS OF FAME (Phil Ochs) / BAD SEEDS (Beat Happening) / HAVE YOU EVER SEEN THE RAIN? (Creedence Clearwater Revival) / BETWEEN US (Neil Innes). • **Trivia:** ALEX CHILTON (ex-BOX TOPS) guested on 1992 sessions and contributed some songs.

Recommended: BANDWAGONESQUE (*8) / THIRTEEN (*7) / GRAND PRIX (*9)

The BOY HAIRDRESSERS

NORMAN BLAKE (b.20 Oct'65) – vocals, guitar (ex-BMX BANDITS) / **RAYMOND McGINLEY** (b. 3 Jan'64, Glasgow) – bass, vocals / **FRANCIS McDONALD** (b.21 Nov'70) – drums / **JOE McALINDEN** – violin / **JIM LAMBIE** – vibraphone

		53rd & 3rd	not issued
Jan 88.	(12") **GOLDEN SHOWERS. / TIDAL WAVE / THE ASSUMPTION AS AN ELEVATOR**		-

TEENAGE FANCLUB

NORMAN + RAYMOND – guitars, vocals plus **GERARD LOVE** (b.31 Aug'67, Motherwell, Scotland) – bass, vocals / **BRENDAN O'HARE** (b.16 Jan'70) – bass repl. McDONALD who joined The PASTELS

		Paperhouse	Matador
Jun 90.	(7") **EVERYTHING FLOWS. / PRIMARY EDUCATION / SPEEDER** *(re-iss.Feb91)*(cd-ep) – Don't Cry No Tears.		
Jul 90.	(cd)(c)(lp) **A CATHOLIC EDUCATION** – Heavy metal / Everything flows / Catholic education / Too involved / Don't need a drum / Critical mass / Heavy metal II / Catholic education 2 / Eternal light / Every picture I paint / Everybody's fun. *(re-iss.cd Mar95)*		-
Oct 90.	(one-sided-7") **THE BALLAD OF JOHN AND YOKO. /**		-
Nov 90.	(7") **GOD KNOWS IT'S TRUE. / SO FAR GONE** (12"+=)(cd-s+=) – Weedbreak / Ghetto blaster.		

		Creation	Geffen
Aug 91.	(cd)(lp) **THE KING (instrumental)** – Heavy metal 6 / Mudhoney / Interstellar overdrive / Robot love / Like a virgin / The king / Opal inquest / The ballad of Bow Evil (slow and fast) / Heavy metal 9.	53	

(above originally only meant for US ears, deleted after 24 hours)

Aug 91.	(7") **STAR SIGN. / HEAVY METAL 6** (12"+=)(cd-s+=) – Like a virgin / ('A'demo version). (7"ltd) – ('A'side) / Like a virgin.	44	-
Oct 91.	(7")(c-s) **THE CONCEPT. / LONG HAIR** (12"+=)(c-s+=)(cd-s+=) – What you do to me (demo) / Robot love.	51	-
Nov 91.	(cd)(c)(lp) **BANDWAGONESQUE** – The concept / Satan / December / What you do to me / I don't know / Star sign / Metal baby / Pet rock / Sidewinder / Alcoholiday / Guiding star / Is this music?.	22	
Jan 92.	(7"ep)(12"ep)(c-ep)(cd-ep) **WHAT YOU DO TO ME / B-SIDE. / LIFE'S A GAS / FILLER**	31	
Jun 93.	(7")(c-s) **RADIO. / DON'T GONE COLUMBIA** (12"+=)(cd-s+=) – Weird horses / Chords of fame.	31	
Sep 93.	(7"ep)(12"ep)(c-ep)(cd-ep) **NORMAN 3. / OLDER GUYS / GENIUS ENVY / GOLDEN GLADES**	50	
Oct 93.	(cd)(c)(lp) **THIRTEEN** – Hang on / The cabbage / Radio / Norman 3 / Song to the cynic / 120 minutes / Escher / Commercial alternative / Fear of flying / Tears are cool / Ret live dead / Get funky / Gene Clark.	14	

— In Mar'94, they teamed up with DE LA SOUL on single 'FALLIN''. This was from the rock-rap album 'Judgement Day' on 'Epic' records (hit UK 59).

— **PAUL QUINN** – drums (ex-SOUP DRAGONS) repl. O'HARE

Mar 95.	(7")(c-s) **MELLOW DOUBT. / SOME PEOPLE TRY TO FUCK WITH YOU** (cd-s+=) – Getting real / About you. (cd-s) – ('A'side) / Have you ever seen the rain? / Between us / You're my kind.	34	
May 95.	(7")(c-s) **SPARKY'S DREAM. / BURNED** (cd-s+=) – For you / Headstand. (cd-s) – ('A'-alternative version) / Try and stop me / That's all I need to know / Who loves the sun.	40	
May 95.	(cd)(c)(lp) **GRAND PRIX** – About you / Sparky's dream / Mellow doubt / Don't look back / Verisinilitude / Neil Jung / Tears / Discolite / Say no / Going places / I'll make it clear / I gotta know / Hardcore – ballad. (lp w/ free 7") DISCOLITE (demo). / I GOTTA KNOW (demo)	7	
Aug 95.	(7")(c-s) **NEIL JUNG. / THE SHADOWS** (cd-s+=) – My life / Every step is a way through love. (cd-s) – ('A'side) / Traffic jam / Hi-fi / I heard you looking.	62	
Dec 95.	(7"ep)(c-ep)(cd-ep) **TEENAGE FANCLUB HAVE LOST IT (acoustic)** – Don't look back / Everything flows / Starsign / 120 mins.	53	-

– compilations, others, etc. –

1992.	K; (7") **FREE AGAIN. / BAD SEEDS**	-	
Nov 92.	Strange Fruit; (12"ep)(cd-ep) **THE JOHN PEEL SESSION** (FRANK BLACK & TEENAGE FANCLUB) – God knows it's true / Alcoholiday / So far gone / Long hair. *(re-iss.Dec93 & Jul95)*		-
Mar 95.	Fire; (cd)(c) **DEEP FRIED FANCLUB** – Everything flows / Primary education / Speeeder / Critical mass (orig.) / The ballad of John and Yoko / God knows it's true / Weedbreak / So far gone / Ghetto blaster / Don't cry no tears / Free again / Bad seed.		-

TELEVISION

Formed: New York, USA based . . . late '73 by VERLAINE, HELL and FICCA whom evolved from The NEON BOYS. In 1975, William Terry Ork gave them deal on own self-named indie label, for whom they issued 1 single. The following year, they transferred to 'Elektra', and unleashed their classic debut album 'MARQUEE MOON', which contained the near

10 minute UK hit single title track. • **Style:** Laid back guitar-based new wave rock, influenced by 70's fashioned ROLLING STONES and PINK FLOYD. VERLAINE tried unsuccessfully to match previous sound into more mainstream rock, which still contained his characteristic vox and guitar virtuoso. • **Songwriters:** VERLAINE lyrics / group compositions, except early live material; FIRE ENGINE (13th Floor Elevators) / KNOCKIN' ON HEAVEN'S DOOR (Bob Dylan) / SATISFACTION (Rolling Stones). • **Trivia:** VERLAINE played guitar on PATTI SMITH's 1974 single 'Hey Joe'.

Recommended: MARQUEE MOON (*10) / TOM VERLAINE – COVER (*7)

TOM VERLAINE (b.THOMAS MILLER, 13 Dec'49, Mt.Morris, New Jersey) – vocals, lead guitar / **RICHARD LLOYD** – guitar, vocals / **RICHARD HELL** – bass, vocals / **BILLY FICCA** – drums

not issued / Ork

Oct 75. (7") **LITTLE JOHNNY JEWEL. / (part 2)** [-] [ ]

— **FRED 'Sonic' SMITH** – bass, vocals (ex-BLONDIE) repl. RICHARD HELL who went solo.

Elektra / Elektra

Feb 77. (lp)(c) **MARQUEE MOON** [28] [ ]
– See no evil / Venus / Friction / Marquee moon / Elevation / Guiding light / Prove it / Torn curtain. *(cd-iss.1989)*

Mar 77. (12")(2-part-7") **MARQUEE MOON. / MARQUEE MOON (mono)** [30] [-]

Jul 77. (7")(12")(12"green) **PROVE IT. / VENUS** [25] [-]

Apr 78. (lp)(c)(red-lp) **ADVENTURE** [7] [ ]
– Glory / Days / Foxhole / Careful / Carried away / The fire / Ain't that nothin' / The dream's a dream. *(cd-iss.Nov93)*

Apr 78. (7")(12"red) **FOXHOLE. / CAREFUL** [36] [-]

Jul 78. (7") **GLORY. / CARRIED AWAY** [ ] [-]

Jul 78. (7") **GLORY. / AIN'T THAT NOTHIN'** [-] [ ]

— Broke ranks in Aug'78. FICCA joined The WAITRESSES, FRED joined The PATTI SMITH GROUP and RICHARD LLOYD went solo.

- compilations, others, etc. -

Jan 83. R.O.I.R.; (c) **THE BLOW UP (live)** [-] [ ]
(cd-iss.Feb90 on 'Danceteria')

1979. Ork-WEA; (12"m) **LITTLE JOHNNY JEWEL (part 1 & 2). / ('A'-live version)** [ ] [-]

TOM VERLAINE

went solo augmented mainly by **FRED SMITH** – bass / **JAY DEE DAUGHERTY** – drums / **BRUCE BRODY** – keyboards / **ALLAN SCHWARTZBERG** – drums, percussion

Elektra / Elektra

Sep 79. (lp)(c) **TOM VERLAINE** [ ] [ ]
– The grip of love / Souvenir from a dream / Kingdom come / Mr. Bingo / Yonki time / Flash lightning / Red leaves / Last night / Breakin' in my heart.

Warners / Warners

Sep 81. (lp)(c) **DREAMTIME** [ ] [ ]
– There's a reason / Penetration / Always / The blue robe / Without a word / Mr. Blur / Fragile / A future in noise / Down on the farm / Mary Marie.

Sep 81. (7")(12") **ALWAYS. / THE BLUE ROBE** [ ] [ ]

— **JIMMY RIPP** – guitar repl. BRODY

Virgin / Warners

May 82. (lp)(c) **WORDS FROM THE FRONT** [ ] [ ]
– Present arrived / Postcard from Waterloo / True story / Clear it away / Words from the front / Coming apart / Days on the mountain. *(re-iss.+cd.Aug88)*

May 82. (7")(12") **POSTCARD FROM WATERLOO. / DAYS ON THE MOUNTAIN** [ ] [ ]

Jun 84. (7") **LET'S GO TO THE MANSION. / ('A'version)** [ ] [ ]
(12"+=) – Lindi Lu.

Aug 84. (7") **FIVE MILES OF YOU. / YOUR FINEST HOUR** [ ] [ ]
(12"+=) – Dissolve reveal.

Sep 84. (lp)(c) **COVER** [ ] [ ]
– Five miles of you / Let's go the the mansion / Travelling / O foolish heart / Dissolve – Reveal / Miss Emily / Rotation / Swim. *(re-iss.Apr86)*

— **ANDY NEWMARK** – drums repl. JAY DEE

Fontana / Mercury

Feb 87. (7") **A TOWN CALLED WALKER. / SMOOTHER THAN JONES** [ ] [ ]
(12"+=) – ('A'version) / Caveman flashlight.

Feb 87. (lp)(c)(cd) **FLASH LIGHT** [99] [ ]
– Cry mercy, judge / Say a prayer / A town called Walker / Song / The scientist writes a letter / Bomb / 4 a.m. / The funniest thing / Annie's tellin' me / One time at sundown.

Mar 87. (7") **CRY MERCY JUDGE. / CALL ME THE CIRCLING** [ ] [ ]
(12"+=) – At this moment (live) / Lover of the night (live) / Strange things happening.

Jun 87. (7") **THE FUNNIEST THING. / ONE TIME AT SUNDOWN** [ ] [ ]
(12"+=) – Marquee Moon ('87 version).

Aug 87. (7") **THE SCIENTIST WRITES A LETTER. / ('A'-Paris version)** [ ] [ ]

Oct 89. (7") **SHIMMER. / BOMB** [ ] [ ]
(12"+=)(cd-s+=) – The scientist writes a letter.

Mar 90. (7")(c-s) **KALEIDOSCOPIN'. / SIXTEEN TULIPS** [ ] [ ]
(12"+=)(cd-s+=) – Vanity fair.

Apr 90. (cd)(c)(lp) **THE WONDER** [ ] [ ]
– Kaleidoscopin' / August / Ancient Egypt / Shimmer / Stalingrad / Pillow / Storm / 5 hours from Calais / Cooleridge / Prayer.

Rough Trade / Rough Trade

Apr 92. (cd)(c)(lp) **WARM AND COOL** [ ] [ ]
– Those harbour lights / Sleepwalkin' / The deep dark clouds / Saucer crash / Depot (1951) / Boulevard / Harley Quinn / Sor Juanna / Depot (1957) / Spiritual / Little dance / Ore.

RICHARD LLOYD

solo augmented by **JIM MAESTRO** – guitar (ex-BONGOS) / **MATTHEW MacKENZIE** – guitar, piano / **MICHAEL YOUNG** – guitar, synthesizer / **FRED SMITH** – bass / **VINNY DeNUNZIO** – drums

Elektra / Elektra

Jan 80. (lp)(c) **ALCHEMY** [ ] [ ]
– Misty eyes / In the night / Alchemy / Womans ways / Number nine / Should've known better / Blue and grey / Summer rain / Pretend / Dying words.

Apr 80. (7") **BLUE AND GREY. / PRETEND** [-] [ ]

— Enlisted new line-up.

Mistlur / Mistlur

Jan 86. (lp) **FIELD OF FIRE** [ ] [ ]

Celluloid / Celluloid

Oct 87. (lp)(c)(cd) **REAL TIME (live)** [ ] [ ]
– Fire engine / Misty eyes / Alchemy / Spider talk / Lost child / No.9 / The only feeling / Soldier blue / Field of fire / Pleading / Watch yourself / Louisinna Anna / Black to white. (cd+=) – Watch yourself / Losin' Anne / Black to white.

— LLOYD went onto join JOHN DOE (ex-X)

TELEVISION

re-formed with **VERLAINE, LLOYD, FICCA + SMITH**

Capitol / Capitol

Sep 92. (cd)(c)(lp) **TELEVISION** [ ] [ ]
– 1880 or so / Shane, she wrote this / In world / Call Mr.Lee / Rhyme / No glamour for Willi / Beauty trip / The rocket / This fire / Mars.

TEMPLE OF THE DOG (see under ⇒ SOUNDGARDEN)

10,000 MANIACS

Formed: Jamestown, New York, USA ... 1981 by NATALIE MERCHANT and J.C. LOMBARDO, who had been part of band STILL LIFE. After a few releases on US label 'Christian Burial' & 'Reflex', they signed internationally to 'Elektra' in 1984. They soon supported R.E.M. on tour, where NATALIE befriended groups' singer MICHAEL STIPE. Their debut UK album 'THE WISHING CHAIR' in 1985, set critics alike, as did their follow-up 'IN MY TRIBE', which brought them first bit of commercial credibility. • **Style:** An alternative folk-rock outfit, with a hint of country and poignant lyrics. The live experience, saw vegetarian NATALIE's 40's dress attire, proudly swirl madly into a frenzy of unmitigated beauty. • **Songwriters:** lyrics – NATALIE / music – JC LOMBARDO until his departure. MERCHANT now main writer with DREW or BUCK. Covered; PEACE TRAIN (Cat Stevens) / I HOPE THAT I DON'T FALL IN LOVE WITH YOU (Tom Waits) / STARMAN – MOONAGE DAYDREAM (David Bowie) / THESE DAYS (Jackson Browne) / EVERYDAY IS LIKE SUNDAY (Morrissey) / DON'T GO BACK TO ROCKVILLE (R.E.M.) / BECAUSE THE NIGHT (Patti Smith Group). • **Trivia:** Their 1987 & 1989 albums were produced by PETE ASHER.

Recommended: THE WISHING CHAIR (*8) / IN MY TRIBE (*9) / HOPE CHEST (*8) / BLIND MAN'S ZOO (*8) / OUR TIME IN EDEN (*8).

NATALIE MERCHANT – vocals / **ROBERT BUCK** – guitar, synths / **J.C. LOMBARDO** (b.JOHN) – rhythm guitar, bass / **STEVEN GUSTAFSON** – bass, guitar / **DENNIS DREW** – organ / **JERRY AUGUSTYNAK** – drums

not issued / ChristianB

1982. (m-lp) **HUMAN CONFLICT NUMBER FIVE** [-] [ ]
– Orange / Planed obsolescence / Anthem for doomed youth / Groove dub / Tension. *(UK-iss.Jun84 on 'Press') (cd-see compilations)*

Jan 84. (lp) **THE SECRETS OF I-CHING** [-] [ ]
– Grey victory / Pour de Chirico / Death of Manolette / Tension / Daktari / Pit

viper / Katrina's fair / The Latin one / My mother the war. *(UK-iss.Aug84 on 'Press') (cd-see compilations)*

Reflex Reflex

Mar 84. (12"m) **MY MOTHER THE WAR (remix). / PLANNED OBSOLESCENCE / NATIONAL EDUCATION WEEK** [ ] [ ]

Elektra Elektra

Jun 85. (7") **CAN'T IGNORE THE TRAIN. / DAKTARI** [ ] [ ]
(12"+=) – Grey victory / The colonial wing.

Nov 85. (lp)(c) **THE WISHING CHAIR** [ ] [ ]
– Can't ignore the train / Just as the tide was a-flowing / Scorpio rising / Lilydale / Maddox table / Everyone a puzzle lover / Arbor day / Back o' the Moon / Tension takes a tangle / Among the Americans / Grey victory / Cotton alley / My mother the war. *(cd-iss.1989)*

Nov 85. (7") **JUST AS THE TIDE WAS A-FLOWING. / AMONG THE AMERICANS** (single withdrawn) [-] [ ]

Jan 86. (7") **SCORPIO RISING. / ARBOR DAY** [ ] [ ]

— Depleted to a quintet, when LOMBARDO departed.

Aug 87. (7") **PEACE TRAIN. / PAINTED DESERT** [ ] [ ]

Aug 87. (lp)(c)(cd) **IN MY TRIBE** [ ] [37]
– What's the matter here? / Hey Jack Kerouac / Like the weather / Cherry tree / Painted desert / Don't talk / Peace train / Gun shy / Sister Rose / A campfire song / City of angels / Verdi cries.

Nov 87. (7") **DON'T TALK. / CITY OF ANGELS** [ ] [ ]
(12"+=) – Goodbye. (some included booklet instead of extra song)

Jul 88. (7") **LIKE THE WEATHER. / A CAMPFIRE SONG** [ ] [68] May 88
(12"+=) – Poison in the well (live) / Verdi cries (live).

Jul 88. (7") **WHAT'S THE MATTER HERE?. / CHERRY TREE** [-] [80]

Aug 88. (7") **WHAT'S THE MATTER HERE?. / VERDI CRIES** [ ] [-]
(12"+=)(cd-s+=) – Like the weather (live) / Gun shy (live). *(above was scheduled for release in Mar88, w/drawn)*

May 89. (lp)(c)(cd) **BLIND MAN'S ZOO** [18] [13]
– Eat for two / Please forgive us / The big parade / Trouble me / You happy puppet / Headstrong / Poison in the well / Dust bowl / The lion's share / Hateful hate / Jubilee.

Jun 89. (7")(c-s) **TROUBLE ME. / THE LION'S SHARE** [ ] [44]
(12"+=)(3"cd-s+=) – Party of God.

Sep 89. (7") **YOU HAPPY PUPPET. / GUNSHY** [-] [ ]

Nov 89. (7"ep) **EAT FOR TWO / WILDWOOD FLOWER. / DON'T CALL US / FROM THE TIME YOU SAY GOODBYE** [ ] [ ]
(12")(3"cd-s) – (1st & 2nd track) / Gun shy (acoustic) / Hello in there.
(10") – (1st & 4th track) / What's the matter here? (acoustic) / Eat for two (acoustic).

Sep 92. (7")(c-s) **THESE ARE DAYS. / CIRCLE DREAM** [58] [66]
(cd-s+=) – I hope that I don't fall in love with you.
(cd-s) – ('A'side) / Medley:- Starman – Moonage daydream / These days.

Sep 92. (cd)(c)(lp) **OUR TIME IN EDEN** [33] [28]
– Noah's dove / These are days / Eden / Few and far between / Stockton gala days / Gold rush brides / Jezebel / How you've grown / Candy everybody wants / Circle dream / If you intend / I'm not the man. (cd+=) – Tolerance.

Mar 93. (7")(c-s) **CANDY EVERYBODY WANTS. / EVERYDAY IS LIKE SUNDAY** [47] [67]
(cd-s+=) – Don't go back to Rockville (with MICHAEL STIPE co-vocals) / Sally Ann.
(cd-s+=) – Don't go back to Rockville (with MICHAEL STIPE) / ('A' MTV version).
(cd-s) – ('A'side) / Eat for two (live) / My sister Rose (live) / Hey Jack Kerouac (live).

Aug 93. (c-s)(cd-s) **FEW AND FAR BETWEEN. /** [-] [95]

Oct 93. (7") **BECAUSE THE NIGHT. / STOCKTON GALA DAYS** [65] [11]
(cd-s+=) – Let the mystery be / Sally Ann.

Oct 93. (cd)(c) **UNPLUGGED (live)** [40] [13]
– These are days / Eat for two / Candy everybody wants (MTV version) / I'm not the man / Don't talk / Hey Jack Kerouac / What's the matter here / Gold rush brides / Like the weather / Trouble me / Jezebel / Because the night / Stockton gala days / Noah's dove.

— 10,000 MANIACS split when NATALIE went solo. The rest re-formed in 1995 and added ex-original JOHN LOMBARDO and his (JOHN & MARY duo) partner MARY RAMSAY on vocals and violin.

– compilations, others, etc. –

Oct 90. Elektra; (cd)(c)(lp) **HOPE CHEST** [ ] [ ]
– (HUMAN CONFLICT NUMBER FIVE / THE SECRETS OF I-CHING)

NATALIE MERCHANT

— -vocals, keyboards / with **JENNIFER TURNER** -guitars, vocals / **BARRY MAGUIRE** -bass, guitar / **PETER YANOWITZ** -drums, percussion

Elektra Elektra

Jun 95. (cd)(c) **TIGERLILY** [39] [13]
– San Andreas fault / Wonder / Beloved wife / River / Carnival / I may know the word / The letter / Cowboy romance / Jealousy / Where I go / Seven years.

Jul 95. (c-s)(cd-s) **CARNIVAL / CARNIVAL (edit) / I MAY KNOW THE WORD** [ ] [10]

. . . . Jan – Jun '96 stop press . . .

Apr 96. (single) **WONDER** [ ] [20] Dec 95

Jun 96. (single) **JEALOUSY** [-] [37]

TERRAPLANE (see under ⇒ THUNDER)

TERRORVISION

Formed: Bradford, England ... late 1991 by (see below). In 1993 they and their label 'Total Vegas' were signed up to major 'E.M.I.'. Their first single of '94 'MY HOUSE', gave them their first deserved Top 30 hit. In August that year they were the surprise treat at Reading Festival. • **Style:** Unconventional metal outfit, fusing between THERAPY? and CHEAP TRICK. • **Songwriters:** Group penned, strings section arranged by friends AUDREY RILEY and BILLY McGHEE. Covered; PSYCHO KILLER (Talking Heads) / THE MODEL (Kraftwerk) / THE PASSENGER (Iggy Pop) / SURRENDER (Cheap Trick) / WISHING WELL (Free) / I'LL BE YOUR SISTER (Hawkwind)? • **Trivia:** Produced in New York by GIL NORTON (Pixies)

Recommended: FORMALDEHYDE (*7) / HOW TO MAKE FRIENDS AND INFLUENCE PEOPLE (*8) / REGULAR URBAN SURVIVORS (*6)

TONY WRIGHT – vocals / **MARK YATES** – guitars / **LEIGH MARKLEW** – bass / **SHUTTY** – drums

Total Vegas not issued

Feb 92. (12"ep)(cd-ep) **THRIVE EP** [ ] [-]
– Urban spacecrime / Jason / Blackbird / Pain reliever.

Oct 92. (7") **MY HOUSE. / COMING UP** [ ] [-]
(12"+=)(cd-s+=) – Tea dance.

Dec 92. (cd)(green-lp) **FORMALDEHYDE** [ ] [-]
– Problem solved / Ships that sink / American T.V. / New policy one / Jason / Killing time / Urban space crime / Hole for a soul / Don't shoot my dog / Desolation town / My house / Human being / Pain reliever / Tea dance. *(re-iss.cd,c,lp May93 on 'Total Vegas-EMI' w/out last 2 tracks, hit UK No.75)*

Jan 93. (12"ep)(cd-ep) **PROBLEM SOLVED / CORPSE FLY. / WE ARE THE ROADCREW / SAILING HOME** [ ] [ ]

Total Vegas-EMI E.M.I.

Jun 93. (12"ep) **AMERICAN T.V. / DON'T SHOOT MY DOG AGAIN / KILLING TIME** [63] [ ]
(cd-ep) – ('A'side) / Psycho killer / Hole for a soul.

Oct 93. (7"green) **NEW POLICY ONE. / PAIN RELIEVER (live)** [42] [ ]
(12") – ('A'side) / Ships that sink (live) / Problem solved (live).
(cd-s) – ('A'side) / Psycho killer (live) / Tea dance (live) / My house (live).
(cd-s) – ('A'side) / American TV (live) / New policy one (live) / Still the rhythm (live).

Jan 94. (7"green) **MY HOUSE. / TEA DANCE** [29] [ ]
(cd-s) – ('A'side) / ('A'machete mix) / Discotheque wreck.
(12") – ('A'side) / ('A'machete mix) / Psycho killer (extended).
(cd-s) – ('A'attic mix) / ('A'machete mix) / Down under.

Mar 94. (7") **OBLIVION (mix). / WHAT DO YOU DO THAT FOR?** [21] [ ]
(cd-s+=) – Problem solved (by DIE CHEERLEADER) / Oblivion (demo).
(cd-s) – ('A'side) / The model (with DIE CHEERLEADER) / Remember Zelda (written by DIE CHEERLEADER).
(12"++=) – Problem solved (by DIE CHEERLEADER).

Apr 94. (cd)(c)(lp) **HOW TO MAKE FRIENDS AND INFLUENCE PEOPLE** [18] [ ]
– Alice what's the matter / Oblivion / Stop this bus / Discotheque wreck / Middleman / Still the rhythm / Ten shades of grey / Stab in the back / Pretend best friend / Time o the signs / What the doctor ordered / Some people say / What makes you tick.

Jun 94. (c-s) **MIDDLEMAN. / OBLIVION** [25] [ ]
(cd-s) – ('A'side) / I'll be your sister / Wishing well.
(12"copper)(cd-s) – ('A'side) / Surrender / The passenger.

Aug 94. (c-s) **PRETEND BEST FRIEND. / MIDDLEMAN (live)** [25] [ ]
(12") – ('A'side) / Alice (live) / Stop the bus (live) / Discotheque wreck (live).
(cd-s) – ('A'side) / Time o' the signs (live) / Oblivion (live) / ('A'-Danny Does Vegas mix.
(cd-s) – ('A'side) / What makes you tick (live) / Still the rhythm (live) / ('A'-Alice pretends mix).

Oct 94. (c-s) **ALICE, WHAT'S THE MATTER (oh yeah mix). / SUFFOCATION** [24] [ ]
(12") – ('A'-junkie J mix) / ('B'side) / ('A'pushy bitch mix) / ('A'-all Carmen).
(cd-s) – ('A'side) / ('A'-Pop Will Eat Itself mix) / Discotheque wreck (acoustic) / ('A'demo).
(cd-s) – ('A'side) / Psycho killer (acoustic) / ('A'-kill your Terrorvision mix) / What shall we do with the drunken sailor?

Mar 95. (7")(c-s) **SOME PEOPLE SAY. / MR. BUSKERMAN / OBLIVION** [22] [ ]

(cd-s) – ('A'side) / Blood on my wheels / ('A'extended) / Oblivion.
(cd-s) – ('A'side) / This drinking will kill me / ('A'-Oblivious mix) / Oblivion.

. . . Jan – Jun '96 stop press . . .

Feb 96. (single) **PERSEVERENCE** [5] [ ]
Mar 96. (cd)(c)(lp) **REGULAR URBAN SURVIVORS** [8] [ ]
Apr 96. (single) **CELEBRITY HIT LIST** [20] [ ]

TESLA

Formed: Sacramento, California, USA ... 1985 originally as CITY KID, by JEFF KEITH, etc (see below). Signed to US label 'Geffen' in 1986, they made their mark quickly the following year, with debut album 'MECHANICAL RESONANCE'. • **Style:** Bluesy hard rock outfit, influenced by MONTROSE, BAD COMPANY or VAN HALEN. They diverted between usual two styles, of either passionate ballads or high energy heavy rock'n'roll. • **Songwriters:** KEITH-HANNON penned, except AIN'T SUPERSTITIOUS (Willie Dixon) / RUN RUN RUN (Jo Jo Gunne) / WE CAN WORK IT OUT (Beatles) / LODI (Creedence Clearwater Revival) / MOTHER'S LITTLE HELPER (Rolling Stones) / ROCK THE NATION (Montrose) / SIGNS (Five Man Electrical Band) / TRUCKIN' (Grateful Dead). • **Trivia:** Named themselves after scientist Nikola Tesla.

Recommended: THE GREAT RADIO CONTROVERY (*6).

JEFF KEITH – vox / **TOMMY SKEACH** – guitar, vocals / **FRANK HANNON** – guitar, keyboards / **BRIAN WHEAT** – bass, vocals / **TROY LUCHETTA** – drums (ex-ERIC MARTIN BAND)

Geffen Geffen

Apr 87. (7") **LITTLE SUZI (ON TEH UP). / (SEE YOU) CUMIN' ATCHA (live)** [-] [91]
Apr 87. (7") **LITTLE SUZI (ON THE UP). / BEFORE MY EYES** [ ] [-]
(12"+=) – Cumin' atcha live (remix).
Jun 87. (lp)(c)(cd) **MECHANICAL RESONANCE** [ ] [32] Jan 87
– Ez come ez go / Cumin' atcha live / Gettin' better / 2 late 4 love / Rock me to the top / We're no good together / Modern day cowboy / Changes / Little Suzi (on the up) / Love me / Cover queen / Before my eyes. *(re-iss.+cd. Jan91)*
Jun 87. (7") **MODERN DAY COWBOY. / ('A'version)** [ ] [ ]
(12"+=) – Love live / Cover queen (live).
Feb 89. (lp)(c)(cd) **THE GREAT RADIO CONTROVERSY** [34] [18]
– Hang tough / Lady luck / Heaven's trail (no way out) / Be a man / Lady days, crazy nights / Did it for the money / Yesterdaze gone / Makin' magic / The way it is / Flight to nowhere / Love song / Paradise / The party's over. *(re-iss.+cdJan91)*
Oct 89. (7") **LOVE SONG. / AIN'T SUPERSTITIOUS** [ ] [10] Sep 89
(12"+=)(cd-s+=) – Run run run.
Mar 90. (c-s)(cd-s) **THE WAY IT IS /** [-] [55]
Feb 91. (cd)(c)(d-lp) **FIVE MAN ACOUSTIC JAM** [59] [12] Nov 90
– Comin' atcha live – Truckin' – Heaven's trail (no way out) / The way it is / We can work it out / Signs / Getting better / Before my eyes / Paradise / Lodi / Mother's little helper / Modern day cowboy / Love song / Tommy's down home / Down fo' boogie.
Apr 91. (7")(US-c-s) **SIGNS. / DOWN FO' BOOGIE** [70] [8] Jan 91
(12"+=)(cd-s+=)(12"blue+=) – Little Suzi (acoustic live).
Sep 91. (7")(c-s) **EDISON'S MEDICINE. / ROCK THE NATION** [ ] [ ]
(12"+=)/ /(12"blue+=)(cd-s+=) – Had enough./ / Run run run.
Sep 91. (cd)(c)(lp) **PSYCHOTIC SUPPER** [44] [13]
– Change in the weather / Edison's medicine / Don't de-rock me / Call it what you want / Song and emotion / Time / Government personnel / Freedom slaves / Had enough / What you give / Stir it up / Can't stop / Talk about it.
Dec 91. (7")(c-s) **CALL IT WHAT YOU WANT. / FREEDOM SLAVES** [ ] [ ]
(12"+=)(cd-s+=) – Children's heritage / Cotton fields.
Apr 92. (c-s)(cd-s) **WHAT YOU GIVE. /** [-] [86]
Aug 94. (cd)(c) **BUST A NUT** [51] [20]
– The gate / Invited / Solution / Shine away / Try so hard / She want she want / I need your lovin' / Action talks / Mama's fool / Cry / Earthmover / Alot to lose / Rubberband / A wonderful world / Games people play / The ocean.

TESTAMENT

Formed: Bay Area, San Francisco, USA ... 1983 as The LEGACY. In 1985, new addition CHUCK BILLY and the lads (see below) became TESTAMENT, and soon signed to 'Atlantic' subsidiary label 'Megaforce'. Their debut (named after the original group name) arrived in 1987, but it wasn't until the 1989 set 'PRACTICE WHAT YOU PREACH', scraped the UK Top 40, that band had finally come of age. • **Style:** Thrash lightning-metal similar to MEGADETH or ANTHRAX. • **Songwriters:** Group compositions, except NOBODY'S FAULT (co-with STEVE TYLER of AEROSMITH). • **Trivia:** Original LEGACY vocalist STEVE SOUSA, fronted other metal outfit EXODUS.

Recommended: PRACTICE WHAT YOU PREACH (*6).

CHUCK BILLY – vocals / **ALEX SKOLNICK** – guitar / **ERIC PETERSON** – guitar / **GREG CHRISTIAN** – bass / **LOUIE CLEMENTE** – drums

East West Atlantic

Jun 87. (lp)(c) **THE LEGACY** [ ] [ ] 1986
– Over the wall / The haunting / Burnt offerings / Raging waters / C.O.T.L.O.D. (Curse of the legions of death) / First strikes is deadly / Do or die / Alone in the dark / Apocalyptic city.
Dec 87. (lp)(c) **LIVE IN EINDHOVEN (live)** [ ] [ ]
– Over the wall / Burnt offerings / Do or die / Apocalyptic city / Reign of terror.
Apr 88. (7") **TRIAL BY FIRE. / NOBODY'S FAULT** [ ] [ ]
(12"+=) – Reign of terror.
May 88. (lp)(c)(cd) **THE NEW ORDER** [81] [ ]
– Eerie inhabitants / The new order / Trial by fire / Into the pit / Hypnosis / Disciples of the watch / The preacher / Nobody's fault / A day of reckoning / Musical death (a dirge).
Aug 89. (lp)(c)(cd) **PRACTICE WHAT YOU PREACH** [40] [77]
– Practice what you preach / Perilous nation / Envy life / Time is coming / Blessed in contempt / Greenhouse effect / Sins of omission / The ballad (a song of hope) / Confusion fusion / Nightmare (coming back to you). *(re-iss.cd Feb95)*
Oct 90. (cd)(c)(lp) **SOULS OF BLACK** [35] [73]
– Beginning of the end / Face in the sky / Falling fast / Souls of black / Absence of light / Love to hate / Malpractise / One man's fate / The legacy / Seven days in May.
May 92. (cd)(c)(lp) **THE RITUAL** [48] [55]
– Signs of chaos / Electric crown / So many lies / Let go of my world / The ritual / Deadline / As the seasons grey / Agony / The sermon / Return to serenity / Troubled dreams.
Apr 93. (cd)(c)(lp) **RETURN TO THE APOCALYPTIC CITY** [ ] [ ]
– Over the wall / So many lies / The haunting / Disciplines of the watch / Reign of terror / Return to serenity.
Oct 94. (cd)(c) **LOW** [ ] [ ]
–

M.F.N. Megaforce

Aug 95. (cd) **LIVE AT THE FILLMORE (live)** [ ] [ ]
– The preacher / Alone in the dark / Burnt offerings / A dirge / Eerie inhabitants / The new order / Low / Vrotsvkidoji / Into the pit / Souls of black / Practice what you preach / Apocalyptic city / Hail Mary / Dog faced gods / Return to serenity / The legacy / Trail of tears.

THEM

Formed: Belfast, N.Ireland ... 1963 by MORRISON, HARRISON, HENDERSON, WRIXEN and MELLINGS. After their debut single flopped, producers TOMMY SCOTT and BERT BERNS, recruited session men JIMMY PAGE (future LED ZEPPELIN) and PETER BARDENS (future CAMEL) to feature on early '65 Top 10 'BABY PLEASE DON'T GO'. Their classic follow-up 'HERE COMES THE NIGHT' just missed the top spot in the UK, but managed a Top 30 placing in America. • **Style:** R&B rock'n'roll featuring the soulful brilliance of future solo star VAN MORRISON. • **Songwriters:** MORRISON penned (until his departure), except HERE COMES THE NIGHT + (IT WON'T HURT) HALF AS MUCH + few early songs (Bert Berns). DON'T START CRYING NOW (Slim Harpo) / BABY PLEASE DON'T GO (Big Joe Williams) / DON'T LOOK BACK (John Lee Hooker) / I PUT A SPELL ON YOU (Screaming Jay Hawkins) / IT'S ALL OVER NOW, BABY BLUE (Bob Dylan), etc. • **Trivia:** GLORIA which later became a garage-punk classic, was fortuosly covered in 1966 by US group The SHADOWS OF NIGHT.

Recommended: THE COLLECTION (*8)

VAN MORRISON (b.GEORGE IVAN, 31 Aug'45) – vocals, harmonica / **BILLY HARRISON** – guitar / **ERIC WRIXEN** – piano, keyboards / **RONNIE MELLINGS** – drums / **ALAN HENDERSON** (b.26 Nov'44) – bass

Decca London

Aug 64. (7") **DON'T START CRYING NOW. / ONE TWO BROWN EYES** [ ] [ ]

— **JACKIE McAULEY** – organ + **PATRICK McAULEY** – organ repl. ERIC and RONNIE WRIXEN who joined The WHEELS, while MELLINGS became a milkman.

Dec 64. (7") **BABY PLEASE DON'T GO. / GLORIA** [10] [93] Mar 65
US flipped over + re-dist. Apr 66 to hit 71)
(re-iss.Jul73 on 'Deram') (re-iss.May82) (re-iss.Oct83 on 'Old Gold')

Decca Parrot

Mar 65. (7") **HERE COMES THE NIGHT. / ALL FOR MYSELF** [2] [24] May 65
(re-iss.Sep73 on 'Deram') (re-iss.Oct83 on 'Old Gold')
Jun 65. (lp) **(THE ANGRY YOUNG) THEM** (US-title 'HERE COMES THE NIGHT') [ ] [54]

– Here comes the night (US-only) / Mystic eyes / If you and I could be as two / Little girl / Just a little bit / I gave my love a diamond (UK-only) / Go on home baby / Gloria / You just can't win / Don't look back / I like it like that / Bright lights big city / My little baby (UK-only) / Route 66. *(re-iss.1973 on 'Deram')* *(cd-iss.Feb89)*

above lp featured sessioners **PETER BARDENS** – keyboards + **JIMMY PAGE** – guitar

— **PETER BARDENS** – keyboards + **JOHN WILSON** (b. 6 Nov'47) – drums now repl. The McAULEY's who formed The BELFAST GYPSIES

Jun 65. (7") **ONE MORE TIME. / HOW LONG BABY?**
Aug 65. (7") **(IT WON'T HURT) HALF AS MUCH. / I'M GONNA DRESS IN BLACK**
Nov 65. (7") **MYSTIC EYES. / IF YOU AND I COULD BE AS TWO** [33] Oct 65

— **MORRISON, HENDERSON + WILSON** were joined by **RAY ELLIOTT** (b.13 Sep'43) – piano, sax repl. BARDENS to solo & later CAMEL / **JIM ARMSTRONG** (b.24 Jun'44) – guitar repl. HARRISON

Jan 66. (lp) **THEM AGAIN**
– Could you would you / Something you got / Call my name / Turn on your love light / I put a spell on you / I can only give you everything / My lonely sad eyes / I got a woman / Out of sight / It's all over now, baby blue / Bad or good / How long baby / Hello Josephine / Don't you know / Hey girl / Bring 'em on in.

Mar 66. (7") **CALL MY NAME. / BRING 'EM ON IN**

— (Jan 66) **TERRY NOONE** – drums repl. WILSON later to TASTE (RORY GALLAGHER) Apr 66, **DAVE HARVEY** – drums repl. NOONE.

May 66. (7") **RICHARD CORY. / DON'T YOU KNOW**

— Disbanded mid 1966 when VAN MORRISON went solo. In 1967, they re-formed. **KEN McDOWELL** – vocals repl. him

Major Minor / not issued

1967. (7") **GLORIA. / FRIDAY'S CHILD** [-]
1967. (7") **THE STORY OF THEM. / (pt.2)** [-]

Capitol / Tower

Jan 68. (lp) **NOW AND THEM**
– I'm your witch doctor / What's the matter baby / Truth machine / Square room / You're just what I was looking for today / Dirty old man / At the age of sixteen / Nobody loves you when you're down and out / Walking the Queen's garden / I happen to love you / Come to me. *(UK-iss.+cd.Dec88 on 'Zap!')*

Feb 68. (7") **WALKING IN THE QUEEN'S GARDEN. / HAPPEN TO LOVE YOU** [-]
Apr 68. (7") **SQUARE ROOM. / BUT IT'S ALRIGHT** [-]

— trimmed to a quartet when ELLIOTT departed

Nov 68. (lp) **TIME OUT! TIME IN FOR THEM** [-]
– Time out for time in / She put a hex on you / Bent over you / Waltz of the flees / Black widow spider / We've all agreed to help / Market place / Just one conception / Young woman / The moth. *(UK-iss.+cd.Dec88 on 'Zap!')*

Nov 68. (7") **WALTZ OF THE FLIES. / WE ALL AGREED TO HELP** [-]
Mar 69. (7") **DARK ARE THE SHADOWS. / CORINA** [-]

— added on session **JERRY COLE** – guitar, vocals / **JOHN STARK** – drums (tour)

not issued / HappyTiger

1970. (lp) **THEM** [-]
– I keep singing / Lonely weekends / Take a little time / You got me good / Jo Ann / Memphis lady / In the midnight hour / Nobody cares / I am waiting / Just a little.

1970. (7") **I AM WAITING. / LONELY WEEKENDS** [-]
1970. (7") **MEMPHIS LADY. / NOBODY CARES** [-]
1971. (lp) **THEM IN REALITY (as "THEM Featuring ALAN HENDERSON")** [-]
– Gloria / Baby please don't go / Laugh / Let my song through / California man / Lessons of the sea / Rayn / Back to the country / Can you believe.

— HENDERSON + RUFF (last lp sidemen) formed TRUTH OF TRUTHS and with session people J.SCHEFF, L.CARLTON, H.BLAINE, J.GUERRIN, J.COLE & J.OSBOURNE issued 1971 on 'Oak' (d-lp) 'TRUTH OF TRUTHS'.

— **THEM** re-formed originals **HENDERSON, HARRISON & WRIXEN + MEL AUSTIN** – vocals / **BILLY BELL** – drums

Decca / not issued

1979. (lp) **SHUT YOUR MOUTH** [-]
– Hamburg connection / I'm a lover not a worker / Shut your mouth / Needed on the farm / Streetwalking lady / Firewater / Child of the sixties / Slowdown / Losing you / Weekend entertainer / Holy roller / Cincinnati diceman.

— Split 1979 after **JIM ARMSTRONG** – guitar + **BRIAN SCOTT** – keyboards, flute repl. WRIXEN + HARRISON. The latter became BILLY WHO.

– compilations, others, etc. –

Feb 65. Decca; (7"ep) **THEM** [-]
– Don't start crying now / Philosophy / One two brown eyes / Baby please don't go.

Jan 68. Decca; (7") **GLORIA. / HERE COMES THE NIGHT** [-]
1970. Decca; (lp)(c) **THE WORLD OF THEM** [-]
Aug 72. Decca/ US= Parrot; (d-lp)(d-c) **THEM FEATURING VAN MORRISON**
– Don't start crying now / Baby please don't go / Here comes the night / One more time / It won't hurt half as much / Mystic eyes / Call my name / Richard Cory / One two brown eyes / All for myself / If you and I could be as two / Don't you know / Friday's child / The story of Them (part 1) / Philosophy / How long baby / I'm gonna dress in black / Bring 'em on in / Little girl / I gave my love a diamond / Gloria / You just can't win / Go on home baby / Don't look back / I like it like that / Bright lights big city / My little baby / Route 66.*(re-iss.Jul82, cd-iss.see below)*

May 76. Decca; (lp)(c) **ROCK ROOTS** [-]
Oct 83. Old Gold; (7") **HERE COMES THE NIGHT. / ('B'by 'Ten Years After')** [-]
Mar 85. See For Miles; (lp) **THEM** [-]
Sep 87. See For Miles; (lp)(c) **THE SINGLES** [-]
Aug 86. Castle; (d-lp)(d-c) **THE COLLECTION ("THEM featuring VAN MORRISON")** [-]
(cd-iss.Aug92)

Jan 91. London; (7")(c-s) **BABY PLEASE DON'T GO. / GLORIA** [65]
(12"+=)(cd-s+=) – Mystic eyes.

THERAPY?

Formed: Belfast, N.Ireland ... 1989 by ANDY CAIRNS, MICHAEL McKEEGAN and FYFE EWING. In Northern Ireland they issued debut 45 on own 'Multifuckingnational' label, before moving to 'Wiiija' in 1991. After their 'PLEASURE DEATH' mini-lp nearly made UK Top 50 in 1992, they signed to major 'A&M', where they progressed in to Top 40 with album 'NURSE'. • **Style:** Grunge-metal similar to HUSKER DU or BIG BLACK . • **Songwriters:** Mostly CAIRNS, or group penned, ex cept TEENAGE KICKS (Undertones) / INVISIBLE SUN (Police) / WITH OR WITHOUT YOU (U2) / BREAKING THE LAW (Judas Priest) / C.C.RIDER (Elvis Presley) / ISOLATION (Joy Division) / TATTY SEASIDE TOWN (Membranes) / NICE'N'SLEAZY (Stranglers) / REUTERS (Wire). • **Trivia:** In 1994 they featured w/ OZZY OSBORNE on 'IRON MAN' for BLACK SABBATH tribute album.

Recommended: NURSE (*8) / TROUBLEGUM (*8) / BABYTEETH (*7) / PLEASURE DEATH (*7)..

ANDY CAIRNS – vocals, guitar / **MICHAEL McKEEGAN** – bass / **FYFE EWING** – drums

Multi... / not issued

Aug 90. (7") **MEAT ABSTRACT. / PUNISHMENT KISS** [-]

Wiiija / not issued

Jul 91. (cd)(c)(m-lp) **BABYTEETH** [-]
– Meat abstract / Skyward / Punishment kiss / Animal bones / Loser cop / Innocent X / Dancin' with Manson. *(re-iss.Mar93 & Jun95 on 'Southern')*

Jan 92. (cd)(c)(m-lp) **PLEASURE DEATH** [52] [-]
– Skinning pit / Fantasy bag / Shitkicker / Prison breaker / D.L.C. / Potato junkie. *(re-iss.Sep92 on 'A&M') (re-iss.Mar93 & Jun95 on 'Southern')*

A & M / A & M

Oct 92. (7") **TEETHGRINDER. / SUMMER OF HATE** [30]
(12"+=) – ('A'dub) / ('A'unsane mix).
(12"+=)(cd-s+=) – Human mechanism / Sky high McKay.

Nov 92. (cd)(c)(lp) **NURSE** [38]
– Nausea / Teethgrinder / Disgracelands / Accelerator / Neck freak / Perversonality / Gone / Zipless / Deep skin / Hypermania.

Mar 93. (7"pink)(c-s) **SHORTSHARPSHOCK EP** [9]
– Screamager / Auto surgery.
(12"+=)(cd-s+=) – Totally random man / Accelerate.

— In May93, they appeared on the B-side of PEACE TOGETHER single 'BE STILL', covered The Police's 'INVISIBLE SUN' on 'Island' records.

Jun 93. (7"white-ep)(12"ep)(cd-ep) **FACE THE STRANGE EP** [18]
– Turn / Speedball / Bloody blue / Neckfreak (re-recording).

Aug 93. (7")(c-s)(7"colrd) **OPAL MANTRA. / ('A'live)** [13]
(cd-s+=) – Innocent X / Potato junkie / Nausea.

Sep 93. (cd)(c) **HATS OFF TO THE INSANE** (originally a US compilation)
– Screamager / Auto Surgery / Totally Random Man / Turn / Speedball / Opal Mantra

Jan 94. (7"ep)(c-ep)(cd-ep) **NOWHERE / PANTAPON ROSE. / BREAKING THE LAW / C.C.RIDER** [18]
(cd-s) – ('A'side) / ('A'-2 Andy Weatherall mixes).

Feb 94. (cd)(c)(lp)(green-lp) **TROUBLEGUM** [5]
– Knives / Screamager / Hellbelly / Stop it you're killing me / Nowhere / Die laughing / Unbeliever / Trigger inside / Lunacy booth / Isolation / Turn / Femtex / Unrequited / Brainsaw.

— above album guests **PAGE HAMILTON** – lead guitar (of HELMET) / **MARTIN McCARRICK** – cello (of THIS MORTAL COIL) / **LESLEY RANKINE + EILEEN ROSE** – vocals

Feb 94. (7"yellow-ep)(c-ep)(cd-ep) **TRIGGER INSIDE / NICE'N'SLEAZY. / REUTERS / TATTY SEASIDE TOWN** [22]

(12") – ('A'side) / ('A'mixes) / Nowhere (Sabres of Paradise mix).
May 94. (7"red-ep)(c-ep)(cd-ep) **DIE LAUGHING / STOP IT YOU'RE KILLING ME (live). / TRIGGER INSIDE (live) / EVIL ELVIS (the lost demo)** [29] [ ]

— In May95, they hit No.53 UK with ORBITAL's 'INNOCENT X', with same group covering their 'Belfast'.

May 95. (7"orange)(c-s)(cd-s) **STORIES. / STORIES (cello version) / ISOLATION (Consolidated synth mix)** [14] [ ]
Jun 95. (cd)(c)(red-lp) **INFERNAL LOVE** [9] [ ]
– Epilepsy / Stories / A moment of clarity / Jude the obscene / Bowels of love / Misery / Bad mother / Me vs you / Loose / Diane / 30 seconds.
Jul 95. (c-s)(cd-s) **LOOSE / OUR LOVE MUST DIE / NICE GUYS / LOOSE (Photek remix)** [25] [ ]
(cd-s) – ('A'side) / Die laughing (live) / Nowhere (live) / Unbeliever (live).
(7"green)(one-sided-12") – ('A'side) / ('A'-Photek remix).
Nov 95. (7"red-ep)(c-ep)(cd-ep) **DIANE / JUDE THE OBSCENE (acoustic) / LOOSE (acoustic) / 30 SECONDS (acoustic)** [26] [ ]
(cd-ep) – ('A'side) / Misery (acoustic) / Die laughing (acoustic) / Screamager (acoustic).

. . . Jan – Jun '96 stop press . . .

— Jan 96, **GRAHAM HOPKINS** – drums (ex- MY LITTLE FUNHOUSE) repl. FYFE. Also added full-time **MARTIN McCARRICK**

– compilations, etc. –

Mar 92. 1/4 Stick; (cd)(c)(lp) **CAUCASIAN PSYCHOSIS** [ ] [ ]

THE THE

Formed: Swadlincote, Derbyshire, England . . . 1979 as studio project by MATT JOHNSON, who also was part of The GADGETS at the same time. MATT signed to IVO's record label '4 a.d.' in 1980, and unleashed poignant 45 'CONTROVERSIAL SUBJECT'. After a solo project album in 1981, THE THE released another single 'COLD SPELL AHEAD' for new label 'Some Bizarre', which eventually obtained major backing from 'Epic'. The long awaited THE THE debut album in 1983, was given deserved thumbs up by critics and public alike, and soon speared into the UK Top 30. Three years later, a second album 'INFECTED' featuring the hit single 'HEARTLAND', was accompanied by a UK Channel 4 premiered hour-long video. **Style & Songwriters:** MATT was described as 'The Howard Hughes of Rock', and contributed classic but controversial alternative rock music with lyrics that dealt with subjects AIDS, the bomb, prostitution, etc. In 1989, he made THE THE into a real band who also toured and contributed to songs. In 1995, he released a collection of HANK WILLIAMS' songs on album 'HANKY PANKY'. • **Trivia:** Solo artists to be; NENEH CHERRY contributed vox to 1986 track 'SLOW TRAIN TO DAWN' and SINEAD O'CONNOR sang on 1989 track 'KINGDOM OF RAIN'. MATT is now residing in Sherman Oaks, California.

Recommended: SOUL MINING (*8) / INFECTED (*9) / MIND BOMB (*9) / MATT JOHNSON:- BURNING BLUE SOUL (*7) / DUSK (*7).

MATT JOHNSON (b.1961, Essex, England . . . raised London) – vocals, guitar, etc. (also of The GADGETS) / **KEITH LAWS** – synthesizers, drum machine / **PETER 'Triash' ASHWORTH** – drums / **TOM JOHNSTON** – bass

4 a.d. — not issued

Jul 80. (7") **CONTROVERSIAL SUBJECT. / BLACK AND WHITE** [ ] [-]

— next with guests **GILBERT & LEWIS** (of WIRE) on 2nd last track

Aug 81. (lp) **BURNING BLUE SOUL ("MATT JOHNSON" solo)** [ ] [-]
– Red cinders in the sand / Song without an ending / Time again for the golden sunset / Icing up / Like a Sun risin' thru my garden / Out of control / Bugle boy / Delirious / The river flows east in Spring / Another boy drowning. *(re-iss.Sep83, c-iss.Jun84) (re-iss.cd+c Jun93 now credited to THE THE, hit No.65)*

Some Bizzare — not issued

Sep 81. (7") **COLD SPELL AHEAD. / HOT ICE** [ ] [-]
(re-iss+/12"pic-d/cd-s. Aug 92)

— **MATT JOHNSON** was now virtually **THE THE,** although he was augmented by others on tour.

Some Bizzare — Sire

Oct 82. (7") **UNCERTAIN SMILE. / THREE ORANGE KISSES FROM KAZAN** [68] [-]
(12"+=)(12"yellow+=) – Waiting for the upturn. (US; b-side)
Feb 83. (7") **PERFECT. / THE NATURE OF VIRTUE** [ ] [-]
(12"+=) – The nature of virtue II.

Some Bizarre — Epic

Sep 83. (7") **THIS IS THE DAY. / MENTAL HEALING PROCESS** [71] [ ]
(d7"+=) – Leap into the wind / Absolute liberation.
(12") – ('A'side) / I've been waiting for tomorrow (all of my life).

— added live **ZEKE MANYIKA** – drums (of ORANGE JUICE) / **JIM THIRLWELL / JOOLS HOLLAND** – piano (ex-SQUEEZE) / **THOMAS LEER** – synthesizers, keyboards

Oct 83. (lp)(c) **SOUL MINING** [27] [ ]
– I've been waiting for tomorrow (all of my life) / This is the day / The sinking feeling / Uncertain smile / The twilight hour / Soul mining / Giant. *(free-12"ep.w.a.)* **PERFECT. / SOUP OF MIXED EMOTIONS / FRUIT OF THE HEART** (c+=) – Perfect / Three orange kisses from Kazan / Nature of virtue / Fruit of the heart / Soup of mixed emotions / Waiting for the upturn. *(cd-iss.Jun87.+= – Perfect)(re-iss.+cd.Mar90 on 'Epic')*
Nov 83. (7") **UNCERTAIN SMILE. / DUMB AS DEATH'S HEAD** [ ] [ ]
(12") – ('A'side) / Soul mining.

— Guests for next album **ROLI MOSSIMAN / NENEH CHERRY / DAVID PALMER / STEVE HOGARTH / ANNA DOMINO / JAMIE TALBOT / WAYNE LIVESEY / ZEKE MANYIKA /** etc.

May 86. (12"m) **SWEET BIRD OF TRUTH. / HARBOUR LIGHTS / SLEEPING JUICE** [ ] [ ]
Jul 86. (7") **HEARTLAND. / BORN IN THE NEW S.A.** [29] [ ]
(12"+=) – Flesh and bones.
(d12"++=) – Perfect / Fruit of the heart.
(c-s++=) – Harbour lights / Sweet bird of truth.
(12"+=) – Sweet bird of truth.
Oct 86. (7") **INFECTED. / DISTURBED** [48] [ ]
(12"+=) – ('A'energy mix).
(d12"++=) – Soul mining (remix) / The sinking feeling.
(c-s+=) – ('A'skull crusher mix) repl. ('A'energy mix)
Nov 86. (lp)(c)(cd) **INFECTED** [14] [89]
– Infected / Out of the blue (into the fire) / Heartland / Angels of deception / Sweet bird of truth / Slow train to dawn / Twilight of a champion / The mercy beat. *(cd+=) – ('A'-INFECTED singles remixed).*
Jan 87. (7") **SLOW TRAIN TO DAWN. / HARBOUR LIGHTS** [64] [ ]
(12"+=) – The nature of virtue.
May 87. (7") **SWEET BIRD OF TRUTH. / SLEEPING JUICE** [55] [ ]
(12"+=) – Harbour lights.
(c-s++=)(cd-s++=) – Soul mining (12"mix).

— **THE THE** were again a group when **MATT** retained past sessioner **DAVID PALMER** – drums (ex-ABC) / and recruited **JOHNNY MARR** – guitar (ex-SMITHS) / **JAMES ELLER** – bass (ex-JULIAN COPE, etc.)

Epic — Epic

Feb 89. (7") **THE BEAT(EN) GENERATION. / ANGEL** [18] [ ]
(12"+=)(cd-s+=)(3"cd-s+=) – Soul mining (mix).
(12"+=)(pic-cd+=) – ('A'-Palmer mix) / ('A'campfire mix).
May 89. (lp)(c)(cd) **MIND BOMB** [4] [ ]
– Good morning beautiful / Armageddon days are here (again) / The violence of truth / Kingdom of rain / The beat(en) generation / August & September / Gravitate to me / Beyond love.
Jul 89. (7")(c-s) **GRAVITATE TO ME. / THE VIOLENCE OF TRUTH** [63] [ ]
(12"+=)(cd-s+=) – I've been waiting for tomorrow (all of my life).
(12"etched-one-side) – ('A'dub). / I've been waiting for tomorrow.
Sep 89. (7")(c-s) **ARMAGEDDON DAYS ARE HERE (AGAIN). / ('A'orchestral)** [70] [ ]
(12"+=) – The nature of virtue / Perfect.
(cd-s+=) – Perfect / Mental healing process.
(10"ep) **THE THE VS.THE WORLD EP** – (all 4 tracks no 'A'orchestral)
(12"etched-one-side) – ('A'side). / Perfect.
Feb 91. (12")(c-s) **JEALOUS OF YOUTH. / ANOTHER BOY DROWNING (live)** [54] [ ]
(cd-s+=) **SHADES OF YOUTH EP** – Solitude / Dolphins.

— added **D.C. COLLARD** – instruments

Jan 93. (7"marble) **DOGS OF LUST. / THE VIOLENCE OF TRUTH** [25] [ ]
(12"pic-d+=)(cd-s+=) – Infected (live).
(cd-s) – ('A'side) / Jealous of youth (live) / Beyond love (live) / Armageddon days are here (again) (D.N.A. remix).
Jan 93. (cd)(c)(lp) **DUSK** [2] [ ]
– True happiness this way lies / Love is stronger than death / Dogs of lust / This is the night / Slow emotion replay / Helpline operator / Sodium light baby / Lung shadows / Bluer than midnight / Lonely planet.
Apr 93. (12"red-ep)(cd-ep) **SLOW MOTION REPLAY. / DOGS OF LUST (3 mixes by Jim Thirlwell)** [35] [ ]
(cd-ep) – ('A'side) / Scenes from Active Twilight (parts I-V).
Jun 93. (12"ep)(cd-ep) **LOVE IS STRONGER THAN DEATH. / THE SINKING FEELING (live) / THE MERCY BEAT (live) / ARMAGEDDON DAYS ARE HERE (AGAIN) (live)** [39] [ ]
(cd-ep) – ('A'side) / Infected / Soul mining / Armageddon days are . . .
Jan 94. (12"ep)(c-ep)(cd-ep) **DIS-INFECTED EP** [17] [ ]
– This was the day / Dis-infected / Helpline operator (sick boy mix) / Dogs of lust (germicide mix).

Jan 95. (10"ep)(c-ep)(cd-ep) **I SAW THE LIGHT / I'M FREE AT LAST. / SOMEDAY YOU'll CALL MY NAME / THERE'S NO ROOM IN MY HEART FOR THE BLUES** [31] [ ]

Feb 95. (cd)(c)(10"lp) **HANKY PANKY** [28] [ ]
– Honky tonkin' / Six more miles / My heart would know / If you'll be a baby to me / I'm a long gone daddy / Weary blues from waitin' / I saw the light / Your cheatin' heart / I can't get you off of my mind / There's a tear in my beer / I can't escape from you.

– compilations, others, etc. –

Dec 88. Epic; (d-cd) **INFECTED / SOUL MINING** [ ] [-]

GADGETS

MATT JOHNSON / COLIN TUCKER – synthesizers / **JOHN HYDE** – synthesizers (both ex-PLAIN CHARACTERS)

Final Solution / not issued

1980. (lp) **GADGETREE** [ ] [-]
– Kyleaking / Making cars / Narpath / UFO import No.1 / Slippery / Singing in the rain / Only one me / Shouting 'Nispers' / There over there / Termite mound / Sleep / Devil's dyke / Six mile bottom / UFO import No.2 / Autumn 80 / Duplicate / Bog track / Thin line. *(re-iss.+cdJun89)*

— They continued as a studio set-up with MATT's help.

1981. (lp) **LOVE, CURIOSITY, FRECKLES & DOUBT** [ ] [-]
– Bodorgan / Gadget speak / Checking to make sure / Aeron / Leave it to Charlie / Prayers / Happy endido / Quatt / Pictures of you / Aaft / Railway line through blubber houses / She's queen of toyland / Sex / It wasn't that way at all / The death and resurrection of Jennifer Gloom / Bill posters will be prosecuted. *(re-iss.+cdJun89)*

Glass / not issued

1982. (lp) **THE BLUE ALBUM** [ ] [-]
– We had no way of knowing / Space in my heart / Bodies without heads / The boyfriend / Uneasy listening / Juice of love / Discuss the sofa / Long empty train / Bite the sawdust / Broken fall. *(re-iss.+cdJun89)*

— above feat. **PETER ASHWORTH** dubbed in instead of MATT. (below withdrawn)

Jun 83. (7")(12") **WE HAD NO WAY OF KNOWING. / ACID BATH** [ ] [-]

THIEVES (see under ⇒ McALMONT & BUTLER)

THIN LIZZY

Formed: Dublin, Ireland ... 1969 by PHIL LYNOTT and DOWNEY. After suggestion of managers Ted Carroll and Brian Tuite, they moved to London late 1970 already signed for 'Decca'. With two albums under their belt and a strong live reputation, they surprisingly had a UK Top 10 hit with 'WHISKY IN THE JAR'. With change of UK label to 'Vertigo' and addition of 2nd guitarist in mid'74, they still found a follow-up unforthcoming. That is until 1976, when 'THE BOYS ARE BACK IN TOWN' cracked UK Top 10. This was a cut from the highly fruitful and acclaimed initial chart album 'JAILBREAK'. Success continued throughout the 70's and early 80's, but mainly massive in the UK. • **Style:** Initially branched out with folk-ballad type songs. Mulatto PHIL LYNOTT moved band into superior harder-laden sounds with introduction of guitarists BRIAN ROBERTSON and SCOTT GORHAM in 1974. • **Songwriters:** PHIL LYNOTT and co. except trad. arrangement WHISKEY IN THE JAR, and covers of ROSALIE (Bob Seger) / I'M STILL IN LOVE WITH YOU (Frankie Miller) / etc. • **Trivia:** On 13th Feb'80, PHIL married Caroline, daughter of UK celebrity Leslie Crowther.

Recommended: LIVE AND DANGEROUS (*9) / DEDICATION (*8)

PHIL LYNOTT (b.20 Aug'51, from Brazillian + Irish parents. Raised from 3 by granny in Crumlin, Dublin) – vocals, bass (ex-ORPHANAGE, ex-SKID ROW brief) / **ERIC BELL** (b. 3 Sep'47, Belfast, N.Ireland) – guitar, vocals (ex-DREAMS) / **BRIAN DOWNEY** (b.27 Jan'51) – drums (ex-ORPHANAGE) / **ERIC WRIXON** – keyboards

Parlophone IRELAND / not issued

1970. (7") **THE FARMER. / I NEED YOU** [-] [-]

— now trio (without WRIXON)

Decca / London

Apr 71. (lp) **THIN LIZZY** [ ] [-]
– The friendly ranger at Clontarf Castle / Honesty is no excuse / Diddy Levine ray-gun / Look what the wind blew in / Eire / Return of the farmer's son / Clifton Grange Hotel / Saga of the ageing orphan / Remembering. *(cd-iss.Jan89 on 'London')*

Aug 71. (7"ep) **NEW DAY** [ ] [-]
– Things ain't working out down on the farm / Remembering pt.II / Old Moon madness / Dublin.

Mar 72. (lp) **SHADES OF A BLUE ORPHANAGE** [ ] [-]
– The rise and dear demise of the funky nomadic tribes / Buffalo girl / I don't want to forget how to jive / Sarah / Brought down / Baby face / Chatting today / Call the police / Shades of a blue orphanage. *(re-iss.c Jul93 on 'Deram')*

Nov 72. (7") **WHISKEY IN THE JAR. / BLACK BOYS IN THE CORNER** [6] [ ]

May 73. (7") **RANDOLPH'S TANGO. / BROKEN DREAMS** [ ] [ ]

Sep 73. (lp)(c) **VAGABONDS OF THE WESTERN WORLD** [ ] [ ]
– Little girl in bloom / Hero and the madman / The rocker / Gonna creep up on you / Slow blues / Mama nature said / Vagabonds of the western world / A song for while I'm away. *(re-iss.+cd.1991 on 'Deram', +=)* – Whiskey in the jar.

Nov 73. (7") **THE ROCKER. / HERE I GO AGAIN** [ ] [-]

— **GARY MOORE** – guitar, vocals (ex-SKID ROW) repl. BELL (later MAINSQUEEZE)

Apr 74. (7") **LITTLE DARLIN'. / BUFFALO GIRL** [ ] [ ]

— (on tour May74) **JOHN CANN** – guitar (ex-ATOMIC ROOSTER, ex-BULLITT) / **+ ANDY GEE** – guitar (ex-ELLIS) both repl. GARY MOORE who joined COLOSSEUM II These temp. guitarists were deposed by **SCOTT GORHAM + BRIAN ROBERTSON**

Vertigo / Vertigo

Oct 74. (7") **PHILOMENA. / SHA LA LA** [ ] [ ]

Nov 74. (lp)(c) **NIGHTLIFE** [ ] [ ]
– She knows / Night life / It's only money / Still in love with you / Frankie Carroll / Showdown / Banshee / Philomena / Sha-la-la / Dear heart. *(re-iss.Aug83, cd-iss. Jun89)*

Jan 75. (7") **SHOWDOWN. / NIGHT LIFE** [-] [ ]

Jun 75. (7") **ROSALIE. / HALF CASTE** [ ] [-]

Aug 75. (lp)(c) **FIGHTING** [60] [ ]
– Rosalie / For those who love to die / Suicide / Wild one / Fighting my way back / King's vengeance / Spirit slips away / Silver dollar / Freedom song / Ballad of a hard man. *(re-iss.Aug83)*

Oct 75. (7") **WILD ONE. / FOR THOSE WHO LOVE TO DIE** [ ] [-]

Nov 75. (7") **WILD ONE. / FREEDOM SONG** [-] [ ]

Vertigo / Mercury

Mar 76. (lp)(c) **JAILBREAK** [10] [18]
– Jailbreak / Angel from the coast / Running back / Romeo and the lonely girl / Warriors / The boys are back in town / Fight or fall / Cowboy song / Emerald. *(re-iss.Oct83, cd-iss.Jun89)*

Apr 76. (7") **THE BOYS ARE BACK IN TOWN. / EMERALD** [8] [-]

Apr 76. (7") **THE BOYS ARE BACK IN TOWN / JAILBREAK** [-] [12]

Jul 76. (7") **JAILBREAK. / RUNNING BACK** [31] [-]

Sep 76. (7") **THE COWBOY SONG. / ANGEL FROM THE COAST** [-] [77]

Oct 76. (lp)(c) **JOHNNY THE FOX** [11] [52]
– Johnny / Rocky / Borderline / Don't believe a word / Fool's gold / Johnny the fox meets Jimmy the weed / Old flame / Massacre / Sweet Marie / Boogie woogie dance. *(re-iss.May83, cd-iss.May90)*

Nov 76. (7") **ROCKY. / HALF-CASTE** [-] [ ]

Jan 77. (7") **DON'T BELIEVE A WORD. / OLD FLAME** [12] [ ]

Jan 77. (7") **JOHNNY THE FOX MEETS JIMMY THE WEED. / OLD FLAME** [-] [ ]

— BRIAN ROBERTSON was injured and deputy GARY MOORE (for 6 mths.tour only)

Aug 77. (7") **DANCING IN THE MOONLIGHT. / BAD REPUTATION** [14] [ ]

Sep 77. (lp)(c) **BAD REPUTATION** [4] [39]
– Soldier of fortune / Bad reputation / Opium trail / Southbound / Dancing in the moonlight / Killer without a cause / Downtown sundown / That woman's gonna break your heart / Dear Lord. *(re-iss.May83, cd-iss.Apr90)*

Apr 78. (7") **ROSALIE; COWBOY'S SONG (live medley). / ME AND THE BOYS** [20] [ ]

Vertigo / Warners

Jun 78. (d-lp)(d-c) **LIVE AND DANGEROUS (live)** [2] [84]
– Jailbreak / Emerald / Southbound / The boys are back in town / Dancing in the moonlight / Massacre / Still in love with you / (me and the boys were wonderin' what you and the girls) / Johnny the fox meets Jimmy the weed / The cowboy song / Don't believe a word / Warriors / Are you ready / Suicide / Sha-la-la / Baby drives me crazy / The rocker / Rosalie – Cowgirl's song . *(re-iss.Nov84)*

— In Autumn'78 tour, DOWNEY was deputised by MARK NAUSEEF. **GARY MOORE** – guitar, vocals returned to repl. ROBERTSON who formed WILD HORSES

Feb 79. (7") **WAITING FOR AN ALIBI. / WITH LOVE** [9] [ ]

Apr 79. (lp)(c) **BLACK ROSE (A ROCK LEGEND)** [2] [81]
– Do anything you want to / Toughest street in town / S & M / Waiting for an alibi / Got to give it up / Get out of here / With love / A roisin dubh (Black rose) A rock legend: Shenandoah – Will you go lassie go – Danny boy – The mason's apron. *(re-iss.Sep86, cd-iss.Jun89)*

— Apr'79, LYNOTT's vox feat. on GARY MOORE's Top10 hit 'Parisienne Walkways'. The following year LYNOTT also combined solo career w / LIZZY's (see further on)

Jun 79. (7") **DO ANYTHING YOU WANT TO. / JUST THE TWO OF US** 14

Sep 79. (7") **SARAH. / GOT TO GIVE IT UP** 24 -

Sep 79. (7") **WITH LOVE. / GO TO GIVE IT UP** -

— (for 2 months-late'79) **MIDGE URE** – guitar (ex-SLIK, ex-RICH KIDS) repl. GARY MOORE who went solo. URE joined ULTRAVOX when repl. by **SNOWY WHITE**

May 80. (7") **CHINATOWN. / SUGAR BLUES** 1 -

Sep 80. (d7") **KILLER ON THE LOOSE. / DON'T PLAY AROUND/ / GOT TO GIVE IT UP (live). / CHINATOWN (live)** 10

Oct 80. (lp)(c) **CHINATOWN** 7
– We will be strong / Chinatown / Sweetheart / Sugar blues / Killer on the loose / Having a good time / Genocide (the killing of buffalo) / Didn't I / Hey you. *(re-is.Sep86, cd-iss.Jun89)*

Oct 80. (7") **KILLER ON THE LOOSE. / SUGAR BLUES** -

Nov 80. (7") **A MERRY JINGLE. (as The "GREEDIES") / A MERRY JANGLE** 28 -

Above also featured STEVE JONES + PAUL COOK (ex-SEX PISTOLS).

Feb 81. (7") **WE WILL BE STRONG. / SWEETHEART** -

Apr 81. (7"ep) **LIVE KILLERS (live)** 19
– Are you ready / Bad reputation / Dear Miss lonely heart.
(12"ep+=) – Opium trail.

Apr 81. (lp)(c) **ADVENTURES OF THIN LIZZY** (compilation) 6

Jul 81. (7") **TROUBLE BOYS. / MEMORY PAIN** 53

Nov 81. (lp)(c) **RENEGADE** 38
– Angel of death / Renegade / The pressure will blow / Leave this town / Hollywood (down on your luck) / No one told him / It's getting dangerous / Hollywood (down on your luck) / Fats / Mexican blood / It's getting dangerous. *(cd-iss.Jun90)*

Feb 82. (7")(7"pic-d) **HOLLYWOOD (DOWN ON YOUR LUCK). / THE PRESSURE WILL BLOW** 53
(10"-one-sided) – ('A'side only)

— **LYNOTT + DOWNEY** recruited new members **JOHN SYKES** – guitar (ex-TYGERS OF PAN TANG) repl. GORHAM **DARREN WHARTON** – keyboards repl. SNOWY WHITE to solo + re-joined PINK FLOYD

Feb 83. (d7")(12") **COLD SWEAT. / BAD HABITS / DON'T BELIEVE A WORD (live). / ANGEL OF DEATH (live)** 27

Mar 83. (lp)(c) **THUNDER AND LIGHTNING** 4
– Thunder and lightning / This is the one / The sun goes down / The holy war / Cold sweat / Someday she is going to hit back / Baby please don't go / Bad habits / Heart attack. *(cd-iss.Jun89)*

Apr 83. (7")(12") **THUNDER AND LIGHTNING. / STILL IN LOVE WITH YOU (live)** 39

Jul 83. (7") **THE SUN GOES DOWN. / BABY PLEASE DON'T GO** 52
(12"+=) – ('A'extended).

Nov 83. (d-lp)(d-c) **LIFE (live)** 29
– Thunder and lightning / Waiting for an alibi / Jailbreak / Baby please don't go / The holy war / Renegade / Hollywood (down on your luck) / Got to give it up / Angel of death / Are you ready / The boys are back in town / Cold sweat / Don't believe a word / Killer on the loose / The sun goes down / Emerald / Black rose / Still in love with you / The rocker. *(4th side featured past members).*

— Had already concluded proceedings. LYNOTT and DOWNEY formed short-lived GRAND SLAM. Tragically, PHIL LYNOTT died on 4 Jan'86 of heart failure.

– compilations, others –

Aug 76. Decca; (lp)(c) **REMEMBERING – PART ONE** -

Jan 78. Decca; (7"m) **WHISKEY IN THE JAR. / SITAMOIA / VAGABOND OF THE WESTERN WORLD** -

Aug 79. Decca; (7"m) **THINGS AIN'T WORKING OUT DOWN ON THE FARM. / THE ROCKER / LITTLE DARLIN'** -

Sep 79. Decca; (lp)(c) **THE CONTINUING SAGA OF THE AGEING ORPHANS** -

Dec 81. Decca; (lp)(c) **ROCKERS** -

Mar 83. Vertigo; (cd) **LIZZY KILLERS** -

Jan 91. Vertigo/ US= Mercury; (7")(c-s) **DEDICATION. / COLD SWEAT** 35
(12"+=)(cd-s+=) – Emerald (live) / Still in love with you.
(12"pic-d+=) – Bad reputation / China town.

Feb 91. Vertigo/ US= Mercury; (cd)(c)(lp) **DEDICATION – THE VERY BEST OF THIN LIZZY** 8
– Whiskey in the jar / The boys are back in town / Jailbreak / Don't believe a word / Dancing in the moonlight / Rosalie – Cowgirl song (live) / Waiting for an alibi / Do anything you want to / Parisienne walkways (with GARY MOORE) / The rocker / Killer on the loose / Sarah / Out in the fields (with GARY MOORE) / Dedication. *(cd+c+=)* Still in love with you (live) / Bad reputation / Emerald / Chinatown.

Mar 91. Vertigo/ US= Mercury; (7")(c-s) **THE BOYS ARE BACK IN TOWN. / SARAH** 63
(12")(cd-s)(12"pic-d) – ('A'side) / Johnny the fox / Black boys on the corner / Me and the boys.

Oct 83. Old Gold; (7") **WHISKY IN THE JAR. / THE ROCKER** -

Jan 85. Old Gold; (7") **DANCING IN THE MOONLIGHT. / DON'T BELIEVE A WORD** -

Feb 88. Old Gold; (7") **THE BOYS ARE BACK IN TOWN. / ('B'by Bachman-Turner Overdrive)** -

Nov 83. Contour; (lp)(c) **THE BOYS ARE BACK IN TOWN** -

Apr 86. Contour; (lp)(c) **WHISKEY IN THE JAR** -

Nov 85. Castle; (d-lp)(c) **THE COLLECTION** -
(cd-iss.Jul87)

Aug 86. Archive 4; (12"ep) **WHISKEY IN THE JAR / THE ROCKER. / SARAH / BLACK BOYS ON THE CORNER** -

Nov 87. Telstar; (lp)(c)(cd) **THE BEST OF PHIL LYNOTT & THIN LIZZY – SOLDIER OF FORTUNE** 55 -
(cd+=) – (3 extra tracks).

Jun 89. Grand Slam; (lp)(c)(cd) **LIZZY LIVES (1976-84)** -

Oct 92. Windsong; (cd) **BBC RADIO 1 LIVE IN CONCERT** -

Nov 94. Strange Fruit; (cd) **THE PEEL SESSIONS** -

. . Jan-Jun'96 stop press compilation . . .

Jan 96. Polygram; (cd)(c) **WILD ONE – THE VERY BEST OF THIN LIZZY** 18

PHIL LYNOTT

(solo) but with THIN LIZZY members.

Vertigo Warners

Mar 80. (7")(12") **DEAR MISS LONELY HEARTS. / SOLO IN SOHO** 32

Apr 80. (lp)(c)(pic-lp) **SOLO IN SOHO** 28
– Dear Miss lonely hearts / King's call / A child's lullaby / Tattoo / Solo in Soho / Girls / Yellow pearl / Ode to a black man / Jamaican rum / Talk in '79.. *(re-iss.Sep85, cd-iss.Jul90)*

Jun 80. (7") **KING'S CALL. / ODE TO A BLACK MAN** 35

Mar 81. (7")(12")(7"yellow) **YELLOW PEARL. / GIRLS** 56
(re-iss.Dec81)

(above was later the TV theme for 'Top Of The Pops')

Aug 82. (7") **TOGETHER. / SOMEBODY ELSE'S DREAM**
(12"+=) – ('A'dance version).

Sep 82. (7") **OLD TOWN. / BEAT OF THE DRUM**

Oct 82. (lp)(c) **THE PHIL LYNOTT ALBUM**
– Fatalistic attitude / The man's a fool / Old town / Kathleen / Growing up / Together / Little bit of water / Ode to Liberty (the protest song) / Gino / Don't talk about me baby. *(cd-iss.Jul90)*

— May'85, GARY MOORE & PHIL hit UK Top 5 with 'OUT IN THE FIELDS'.

Polydor Polydor

Nov 85. (7") **19. / 19 (dub)**
(12"+=) – A day in the life of a blues singer.
(d7"+=)(7"pic-d+=) – THIN LIZZY; Whiskey in the jar – The rocker.

– (PHIL LYNOTT) posthumous. –

Jan 87. Vertigo; (7") **KING'S CALL. / YELLOW PEARL** 68
(12"+=) – Dear Miss lonely hearts (live).

David THOMAS (see under ⇒ PERE UBU)

Ray THOMAS (see under ⇒ MOODY BLUES)

Richard THOMPSON

Born: 3 Apr'49, London, England. Founder of FAIRPORT CONVENTION from 1967, until his departure early in 1971. After session work for ex-FAIRPORT friends; SANDY DENNY and IAN MATTHEWS, he finally issued debut album HENRY THE HUMAN FLY' in 1972 for Island' records. Just prior to this, he had worked with other recently ex-FAIRPORT members; ASHLEY HUTCHINGS, DAVE MATTACKS, who as The BUNCH, released budget covers lp ROCK ON'. The following year, he teamed up with LINDA PETERS, and they became RICHARD & LINDA THOMPSON, after their marriage in 1974. Their first of many albums together I WANT TO SEE THE BRIGHT LIGHTS AGAIN', was acclaimed by many, and should have provided them with a hit title track hit single. During the recording of their next album HOKEY POKEY', they coverted to Sufism, and initiated their own religious Sufi community. In 1982, they made their last album together, due to marriage break-up. The next year, RICHARD was solo again and issued for Hannibal' records; HAND OF KINDNESS'. After many near chart breakthroughs in the second half of the 80's, he finally made UK Top 40 listings with 1991 album RUMOUR AND SIGH'. • **Style:** Accomplished and influential guitarist, lawded by many, including surprisingly Americans BOB MOULD (Sugar + Husker Du), J.MASCIS (Dinosaur Jr) and FRANK BLACK (Pixies). He blended together a rare mixture of English-folk sound with American country-rock music. Watch out for a THOMPSON tribute album in 1994, which will feature many top stars, playing their best R.T. tracks. • **Songwriters:** Self-penned compostions, collaborating for 8 between 1974-1982 with then wife LINDA. While a member of FAIRPORT CONVENTION, he contributed GENESIS HALL / MEET ON THE LEDGE + SLOTH, to name a few. • **Trivia:**

Recommended: I WANT TO SEE THE BRIGHT LIGHTS TONIGHT (*7) / WATCHING THE DARK – A HISTORY OF . . . (*7)

RICHARD THOMPSON – vocals, guitar (ex-FAIRPORT CONVENTION) with **LINDA PETERS / PAT DONALDSON** – bass / **TIM DONALD** – drums / plus **SANDY DENNY / ASHLEY HUTCHINGS / JOHN KIRKPATRICK / JOHN DEFERERI / BARRY DRANSFIELD / DAVID SNELL / CLAY TOYANI / ANDY ROBERTS / SUE DRAHEIM / JEFF COLE**

Island Reprise

Jun 72. (lp)(c) **HENRY THE HUMAN FLY**
– Roll over Vaughn Williams / Nobody's wedding / The poor ditching boy / Shaky Nancy / The angels took my racehorse away / Wheely down / The new St. George / Painted ladies / Cold feet / Mary and Joseph / The old changing ways / Twisted. *(re-iss.Jan87 on Hannibal', cd-iss.May87)*

— **RICHARD & LINDA THOMPSON**

husband & wife duo. LINDA (nee PETERS) (ex-ALBION COUNTRY BAND) with SOUR GRAPES: **SIMON NICOL** – dulcimer / **STEVE BORRELL** – bass / **WILLIAM MURRAY** – drums (ex-KEVIN AYERS)/ plus most of main musicians on above album.

Jan 74. (7") **I WANT TO SEE THE BRIGHT LIGHTS TONIGHT. / WHEN I GET TO THE BORDER**

Apr 74. (lp)(c) **I WANT TO SEE THE BRIGHT LIGHTS TONIGHT**
– When I get to the border / The Calvery Cross / Withered and died / I want to see the bright lights tonight / Down where the drunkards roll / We sing hallelujah / Has he got a friend for me? / The little beggar girl / The end of the rainbow / The Great Valero. *(cd-iss.May88) (re-iss.Oct89 on Hannibal') (cd re-iss,Mar93 on Island')*

— **IAN WHITEMAN** – keyboards, flute / **ALY BAIN** – fiddle repl. guests

Feb 75. (7") **HOKEY POKEY. / I'LL REGRET IT ALL IN THE MORNING**

Mar 75. (lp)(c) **HOKEY POKEY**
– Hokey pokey (the ice-cream song) / I'll regret it all in the morning / Smiffy's glass eye / Egypt room / Never again / Georgie on a spree / Old man inside a young man / The Sun never shines on the poor / A heart needs a home / Mole in a hole. *(cd-iss.May89) (re-iss.Jun86 on Hannibal')*

Nov 75. (lp)(c) **POUR DOWN LIKE SILVER**
– Streets of Paradise / For shame of doing wrong / The poor boy is taken away / Night comes in / Jet plane in a rocking chair / Beat the retreat / Hard luck stories / Dimming of the day / Dargai. *(re-iss.Jun86 on Hannibal', cd-iss.May89)*

— Their main band was:- **WILLIE WEEKS** – bass / **ANDY NEWMARK** – drums / **NEIL LARSON** – keyboards / **SIMON NICOL** – guitar, dulcimer / **JOHN KIRKPATRICK** – accordion

Chrysalis Chrysalis

Nov 78. (lp)(c) **FIRST LIGHT**
– Restless highway / Sweet surrender / Don't let a thief steal into your heart / The choice wife / Died for love / Strange affair / Layla / Pavanne / House of cards / First light. *(re-iss.Jun86 on Hannibal' + cd May89)*

Jan 79. (7") **DON'T LET A THIEF STEAL INTO YOUR HEART. / FIRST LIGHT**

— **TIM DONALD, PAT DONALSON + RABBIT BUNDRICK** repl. NEWMARK, WEEKS + LARSON / guests:- **DAVE MATTACKS** – drums / **DAVE PEGG** – bass

Sep 79. (lp)(c) **SUNNY VISTAS**
– Civilization / Borrowed time / Saturday rolling around / You're going to need somebody / Why do you turn your back / Sunny vista / Lonely hearts / Sisters / Justice in the streets / Traces of my love. *(re-iss.+cd.May89 on'Carthage')*

Sep 79. (7") **CIVILIZATION. / GEORGIE ON A SPREE** [-]

Elixir not issued

Sep 81. (lp) **STRICT TEMPO (RICHARD THOMPSON solo / instrumental)** [-]
– Scott Skinner medley / Banish misfortune / Dundee hornpipe / Do it for my sake / New fangled flogging reel / Vailance polka militair / Belfast polka / Rockin' in rhythm / The random jig / The grinder / Andalus / Marrakesh / The knife edge. *(re-iss.+cd Jul89 on Carthage')*

— next w / **NICOL / MATTACKS / PEGG / + bassman PETE ZORN**

Hannibal Hannibal

Apr 82. (7") **DON'T RENEGE ON YOUR LOVE. / LIVING IN LUXURY** [-]

Nov 82. (lp) **SHOOT OUT THE LIGHTS**
– Man in need / Walking on a wire / Don't renege on your love / Just the motion / Shoot out the lights / Back street slide / Did she jump or was she pushed / Wall of death. *(re-iss.+cd.Jun86)* (+=) – Living in luxury. *(re-iss.May89 on Carthage') (cd-iss.Dec94 on 'Hannibal')*

— **RICHARD THOMPSON** returned to solo work after separating with LINDA. He retained last band and label, while LINDA went on in 1985 to release an album ONE CLEAR MOMENT' for Warners'.

Jun 83. (lp) **HAND OF KINDNESS**
– A poisoned heart and a twisted memory / Tear stained letter / How I wanted to / Both ends burning / The wrong heartbeat / Hand of kindness / Devonside / Two left feet. *(re-iss.+cd Jun86)* (+=) – Where the wind don't whine.

Jul 83. (7") **THE WRONG HEARTBEAT. / DEVONSIDE** [-]

Dec 84. (lp) **SMALL TOWN ROMANCE (live)** [-]
– Time to ring some changes / Beat the retreat / A heart needs a home / Woman or a man / For shame of doin' wrong / Genesis Hall / Honky tonk blues / Small town romance / I want to see the bright lights tonight / Down where the drunkards roll / Love is bad for business / Never again / The Great Valero / Don't let a thief steal into your heart.

Polydor Polydor

Mar 85. (lp)(c) **ACROSS A CROWDED ROOM** [80]
– When the spell is broken / You don't say / I ain't going to drag my feet no more / Love in a faithless country / Fire in the engine room / Walking through a wasted land / Little blue number / She twists the knife again / Ghosts in the wind. *(re-iss.+cd Jun86) (cd re-iss.Jun92 on B.G.O.')*

Jun 85. (7") **YOU DON'T SAY. / WHEN THE SPELL IS BROKEN**

— now with **MITCHELL FROOM** – organ / **JERRY SCHEFF** – bass / **MICKEY CURRY + JIM KELTNER** – drums / **JOHN KIRKPATRICK** – accordion / **ALEX ACUNA** – percussion

Oct 86. (lp)(c)(cd) **DARING ADVENTURES** [92]
– A bone through her nose / Valerie / Missie how you let me down / Dead man's handle / Long dead love / Lover''s lane / Nearly in love / Jennie / Baby talk / Cash down / Never never / How wll I ever be simple again / Al Bowly's in Heaven. *(cd re-iss.Jun92 on B.G.O.')*

B.B.C. not issued

Oct 87. (lp)(c) **THE MARKSMAN (TV Soundtrack)** [-]
– My time / Gordon / Rude health / Night school / Cornish pastiche / Crossing the water / The marksman / Kyrie / On yer eyes / Cutters on the run / Don't ever change / Up there.

Capitol Capitol

Oct 88. (lp)(c)(cd) **AMNESIA** [89]
– Turning of the tide / Gypsy love songs / Reckless kind / Jerusalem on the jukebox / I still dream / Don't tempt me / Yankee, go home / Can't win / Waiting for dreamers / Pharoah. *(re-iss.Mar91)*

Nov 88. (7") **TURNING OF THE TIDE. / PHAROAH**

Sep 89. (7") **RECKLESS KIND (live). / TURNING OF THE TIDE (live)**
(12"+=) – Pharoah (live) / Can't win (live).
(cd-s+=) – Jerusalem on the jukebox (live).

May 91. (cd)(c)(lp) **RUMOUR AND SIGH** [32]
– Read about love / I feel so good / I misunderstood / Behind grey walls / You dream too much / Why must I plead / Vincent / Backlash love affair / Mystery wind / Jimmy Shands / Keep your distance / Mother knows best / God loves a drunk / Psycho Street. *(re-iss.cd Sep94)*

Jun 91. (7") **I FEEL SO GOOD. / HARRY'S THEME (from film 'Sweet Talker')**
(cd-s+=) – Backlash love affair.

Mar 92. (7") **I MISUNDERSTOOD. / 1952**
(cd-s+=) – Vincent / Black lightning.

— with **PETE THOMAS** – drums, percussion / **JERRY SCHEFF** – bass, double bass / **MITCHELL FROOM** – keyboards, producer / **ALISTAIR ANDERSON** – concertina, pipes / **TOM McCONVILLE** – fiddle / **MARTIN DUNN** – flute / **PHIL PICKETT** – shawms / **JOHN KIRKPATRICK** – accordion, concertina / **DANNY THOMPSON** – double bass (1) / **CHRISTINE COLLISTER + MICHAEL PARKER** – backing vocals

Jan 94. (cd)(c) **MIRROR BLUE** [23]
– For the sake of Mary / I can't wake up to save my life / MGB-GT / The way that it shows / Easy there, steady now / King of Bohemia / Shane and Dixie / Mingus eyes / I ride in your slipstream / Beeswing / Fast food / Mascara tears / Taking my business elsewhere.

— (a tribute album was released in 1995)

. . . Jan – Jun '96 stop press . . .

Apr 96. (cd)(c) **YOU? ME? US?** [32] [97]

– compilations, etc. –

(below album recorded between 1967-1976)

May 76. Island; (d-lp)(d-c) **(guitar, vocal)**
– A heart needs a home / Free as a bird / Night comes in / Pitfall / Excursion / Calvery Cross / Time will show the wiser / Throw-away street puzzle / Mr.Lacy / The ballad of Easy Rider / Poor Will and the jolly hangman / Sweet little rock'n'roller / Dark end of the street / I'll be me. (incl.Live Oxford Street concert & early demos) (US-title LIVE MORE OR LESS') *(re-iss.Jun86 on 'Hannibal', cd-iss.May89)*

Apr 93. Hannibal; (3xcd-box) **WATCHING THE DARK – A HISTORY OF . . .** [-]
– A man in need / Can't win / Waltzing's for dreamers / Crash the party / I still dream / Bird in God's garden / Lost and found / Now be thankful / A sailor's kife / Genesis Hall / The knife-edge / Walking on a wire / Small town romance / Shepherd's march – Maggie Cameron / Wall of death / For shame of doing wrong / Back street slide / Strange affair / The wrong heartbeat / Borrowed time / From Galway to Graceland / Tear-stained letter / Keep your distance / Bogie's bonnie / Poor wee Jockey Clarke / Jet plane in a rocking chair / Dimming of the day / Old man inside a young man / Never again / Hokey pokey (the ice cream

song) / A heart needs a home / Beat the retreat / Al Bowlly's in Heaven / Walking through a wasted land / When the spell is broken / Devonside / Little blue number / I ain't going to drag my feet no more / Withered and died / Nobody's wedding / The poor ditching boy / The Great Valerio / The Calvary Cross / Twisted / Jennie / Hand of kindness / Two left feet / Shoot out the lights.

Tracy THORN (see under ⇒ EVERYTHING BUT THE GIRL)

3 (see under ⇒ EMERSON, LAKE & PALMER)

THROWING MUSES

Formed: Boston, Massachusetts, USA . . . 1985 by KIRSTIN HERSH and half-sister TANYA DONNELLY, etc. They signed to British indie label '4 a.d.' alongside fellow Bostonians The PIXIES. Their eponymous debut in 1986, sold well through the cartel, due to help of Radio 1 DJ John Peel. Five years later, they broke into the UK Top 30 with album 'THE REAL RAMONA'. TANYA DONNELLY splintered not long after this, into The BREEDERS and BELLY, and she soon made the latter her new band after leaving The MUSES. • **Style:** Folky alternative band similar to 10,000 MANIACS, but centred around KIRSTIN whose vox warblings reminisced of BUFFY SAINTE-MARIE. • **Songwriters:** KIRSTIN lyrics / group compositions except; AMAZING GRACE (Judy Collins) / RIDE INTO THE SUN (Velvet Underground) / MANIC DEPRESSION (Jimi Hendrix) / WHEN THE LEVEE BREAKS (Gram Parsons). • **Trivia:** KIRSTIN later moved to Newport, Rhode Island with dad.

Recommended: THROWING MUSES (*8) / HUNKPAPA (*8) / THE REAL RAMONA (*7) / THE RED HEAVEN (*7) / HIPS AND MAKERS – KIRSTEN KERSH (*6).

KIRSTIN HERSH (b.1967) – vocals, lead guitar, piano / **ELAINE ADAMEDES** – bass / **TANYA DONNELLY** – rhythm guitar, vocals / **DAVID NARCIZO** – drums, percussion, vocals

		not issued	???
1986.	(7"ep) **STAND UP / PARTY. / SANTA CLAUS / DIRT ON THE DANCE FLOOR**	-	

—— **LESLIE LANGSTON** – bass, vocals repl. ELAINE

		4 a.d.	Relativity
Sep 86.	(lp)(c)(cd) **THROWING MUSES**		

– Call me / Green / Hate my way / Vicky's box / Rabbit's dying / America (she can't say no) / Fear / Stand up / Soul soldier / Delicious cutters.

Mar 87. (12"ep)(c-ep) **CHAINS CHANGED** [ ] [ ]
– Cry baby cry / Finished / reel / Snail head.

Aug 87. (m-lp)(c) **THE FAT SKIER** [ ] [ ]
– Soul soldier / Garoux des larmes / Pool in eyes / A feeling / You cage / Soap and water / And a she-wolf after the war.

Mar 88. (lp)(c)(cd) **HOUSE TORNADO** [ ] [ ]
– Colder / Mexican woman / The river / Juno / Marriage tree / Run letter / Saving grace / Drive / Downtown / Giant / Walking in the dark. (cd+=) – THE FAT SKIER (m-lp tracks).

Jan 89. (lp)(c)(cd) **HUNKPAPA** [59] [ ]
– Devil's roof / Bea / Dizzy / No parachutes (say goodbye) / Dragonhead / Fall down / I'm alive / Angel / Mania / The burrow / Take. *(cd+=)* – Downtown.

Feb 89. (7") **DIZZY. / SANTA CLAUS** [ ] [ ]
(10"+=)(12"+=)(cd-s+=) – Marie / Downtown.

—— TANYA with DAVID (only in '89) formed off-shoot The BREEDERS (see further). She stayed with TM until next album's completion. **FRED ABONG** – bass repl. her

Jan 91. (7") **COUNTING BACKWARDS. / SAME SUN** [70] [ ]
(12"+=)(cd-s+=) – Cotton mouth / Amazing Grace.

Feb 91. (cd)(c)(lp) **THE REAL RAMONA** [26] [ ]
– Counting backwards / Him dancing / Red shoes / Graffiti / Golden thing / Ellen West / Dylan / Hook in her head / Not too soon / Honey chain / Say goodbye / Two step

Nov 91. (7") **NOT TOO SOON. /CRY BABY CRY** [ ] [ ]
(12"+=)(cd-s+=) – Dizzy (remix) / Him dancing (remix).

—— (Sep91) **DONNELLY** and **ABONG** had now quit to form BELLY in 1992. **KIRSTEN + NARCIZO** recruited newcomer **BERNARD GEORGES** – bass

Jul 92. (12"ep)(cd-ep) **FIREPILE / MANIC DEPRESSION. / SNAILHEAD / CITY OF THE DEAD** [46] [ ]
(12"ep)(cd-ep) – ('A'remix) / Jack / Ride into the Sun / Handsome woman.

Aug 92. (cd)(c)(lp) **RED HEAVEN** [13] [ ]
– Furious / Firepile / Die / Dirty water / Stroll / Pearl / Summer Street / Vic / Backroad / The visit / Dovey / Rosetta stone / Carnival wig. (free-lp w.a.) **LIVE (live)** – Juno / Marriage tree / Pearl / Stand up – Dovey – Mexican woman / Run letter / Soap and water / Rabbit dying / Cry baby cry / Counting backwards – Handsome woman / Take / Soul soldier / Bea / Delicate cutters.

Nov 92. (cd) **THE CURSE (live)** [74] [ ]
– Manic depression / Counting backwards / Fish / Hate my way / Furious / Devil's roof / Snailhead / Firepile / Finished / Take / Say goodbye / Mania / Two step / Delicate cutters / Cottonmouth / Pearl / Vic / Bea.

Dec 94. (7")(c-s) **BRIGHT YELLOW GUN. / LIKE A DOG** [51] [ ]
(12"+=)(cd-s+=) – Red eyes / Crayon Sun.

Jan 95. (cd)(c)(lp) **UNIVERSITY** [10] [ ]
– Bright yellow gun / Start / Hazing / Shimmer / Calm down, come down / Crabtown / No way in Hell / Surf cowboy / That's all you wanted / Teller / University / Snake face / Fever few.

KRISTEN HERSH

first below featured **MICHAEL STIPE** (R.E.M.) / **JANE SCARPANTONI** – cello

		4 a.d.	4 a.d.
Jan 94.	(12")(cd-s) **YOUR GHOST / THE KEY. / UNCLE JUNE AND AUNT KIYOTI / WHEN THE LEVEE BREAKS**	45	
Jan 94.	(cd)(c)(lp) **HIPS AND MAKERS**	7	

– Your ghost / Beestung / Teeth / Sundrops / sparky / Houdini blues / A loon / Velvet days / Close your eyes / Me and my charms / Tuesday night / The letter / Lurch / The cuckoo / Hips and makers.

Apr 94. (7")(c-s) **A LOON. / VELVET DAYS** [60] [ ]
(12")(cd-ep) **'STRINGS EP'** (+=) – Sundrops / Me and my charms.

Dec 95. (cd-ep) **THE HOLY SINGLE** [ ] [-]

THUNDER

Formed: South London, England . . . mid'89 by BOWES, MORLEY and JAMES who had been part of Reading festival specialists TERRAPLANE. They had been founded around 1982 but disintegrated early 1988, when they pursued career in America. They found BEN and SNAKE and became THUNDER, and through agent Malcolm McKenzie they signed to 'EMI'. Quickly became top act for the early 90's, after breaking into the UK Top 40 with 'DIRTY LOVE', which was produced by ANDY TAYLOR (ex-DURAN DURAN). They soon played the Cathouse in New York and were given deal with EMI's US counterpart 'Capitol'. • **Style:** Heavy rock outfit suited to US – FM radio, due to similarities to BAD COMPANY, AEROSMITH or LED ZEPPELIN. • **Songwriters:** All penned by MORLEY, except; GET IT ON (T.Rex) / GIMME SOME LOVIN' (Spencer Davis Group) / WITH A LITTLE HELP FROM MY FRIENDS (Beatles) / GIMME SHELTER (Rolling Stones) / 5.15 (Who) / ALL THE WAY FROM MEMPHIS (Mott The Hoople) / IN A BROKEN DREAM (hit; Python Lee Jackson) / STAY WITH ME (Rod Stewart & The Faces). • **Trivia:** SNAKE once appeared on Top Of The Pops, as bass player on OWEN PAUL's hit 'You're My Favourite Waste Of Time'.

Recommended: BACKSTREET SYMPHONY (*6).

TERRAPLANE

DANNY BOWES – vocals / **LUKE MORLEY** – guitar / **RUDY RIVIERE** – guitar / **NICK LINDEN** – bass, piano / **GARY JAMES** – drums

		City	not issued
Mar 83.	(7") **I SURVIVE. / GIMME THE MONEY**		-
		Epic	Epic
Dec 84.	(7") **I CAN'T LIVE WITHOUT YOUR LOVE. / BEGINNING OF THE END**		-

(12"+=) – Let the wheels go round.

Mar 85. (7")(12") **I SURVIVE. / ALL NIGHT AND DAY (live)** [ ] [-]

Jul 85. (7") **WHEN YOU'RE HOT. / TOUGH KIND OF LOVE** [ ] [ ]
(12"+=) – If you could see yourself.

Oct 85. (7") **TALKING TO MYSELF. / GET YOUR FACE OUT OF MY DREAMS** [ ] [-]
(12"+=) – Gimme the money.

—— RUDY only appeared on 1 track from next album.

Jan 86. (lp)(c) **BLACK AND WHITE** [74] [ ]
– Don't walk away / When you're hot / I can't live without your love / Talking to myself / You can't hurt me anymore / I survive / Right betweeen the eyes / Black and white / I'm the one / Get your face out of my dream / Couldn't handle the tears. *(c+=)* – Tough kind of love / Beginning of the end / All night and day.

Jan 87. (7")(7"sha-pic-d) **IF THAT'S WHAT IT TAKES. / LIVING AFTER DARK** [ ] [ ]
(12"+=) – ('A'-19th nervous breakdown mix) / Drugs.

Jun 87. (7") **GOOD THING GOING. / A NIGHT OF MADNESS** [ ] [ ]
(12"+=)/ /(c++=) – The good life./ / ('A'version).

Aug 87. (7") **MOVING TARGET. / WHEN I SLEEP ALONE** [ ] [ ]
(d7"+=)(12"+=) – I survive (live) / I can't live without your love.

Sep 87. (lp)(c)(cd) **MOVING TARGET** [ ] [ ]
– If that's what it takes / Good thing going / Promised land / Moving target /

Hostage to fortune / Heartburn / Hearts on fire / I will come out fighting / Nothing on but the radio. *(cd+=)–* Moving target (extended) / When I sleep alone / I can't live without your love (live) / I survive (live).

— Disbanded early 1988. After a stint in the US,

THUNDER

BOWES + MORLEY brought back **GARY 'Harry' JAMES** – drums, with also **BEN MATTHEWS** – guitar, keyboards / **MARK 'Snake' LUCKHURST** – bass

E.M.I. | Capitol

Oct 89. (7") **SHE'S SO FINE. / GIRL'S GOING OUT OF HER HEAD** [ ] [-]
(12"+=)(cd-s+=) – Another shot of love.

Jan 90. (7")(7"pic-d) **DIRTY LOVE. / FIRED UP** [32] [-]
(12"+=)/ /(cd-s++=) – She's so fine (live)./ / Brown sugar (live).

Feb 90. (cd)(c)(lp) **BACK STREET SYMPHONY** [21] [ ] Apr 90
– She's so fine / Dirty love / Don't wait for me / Higher ground / Until my dying day / Back street symphony / Love walked in / An Englishmman on holiday / Girl's going out of her head / Gimme some lovin'. *(cd+c+=)–* Distant thunder. *(pic-lp Nov90, re-dist.Feb91, scraped UK Top 50) (re-iss.cd+c Sep94)*

Apr 90. (7")(c-s) **BACK STREET SYMPHONY. / NO WAY OUT OF THE WILDERNESS** [25] [-]
(12"+=)(12"pic-d+=) – An Englishman on holiday (live).
(cd-s++=) – Girl's going out of her head (live).

Jul 90. (7") **GIMME SOME LOVIN'. / I WANNA BE HER SLAVE** [36] [-]
(12"+=)(12"pic-d+=)(c-s+=)(cd-s+=) – Dirty love (live).
(10"red+=) – Until the night is through.

Sep 90. (7")(c-s) **SHE'S SO FINE. / I CAN STILL HEAR THE MUSIC** [34] [ ]
(12"+=) – Don't wait for me (live).
(10"blue+=) – Backstreet symphony (live).
(cd-s) – ('A'side) / (above 2 extra)

Sep 90. (c-s) **SHE'S SO FINE. / GIMME SOME LOVIN'** [-] [ ]

E.M.I. | Geffen

Feb 91. (7") **DIRTY LOVE. / GIRL'S GOING OUT OF HER HEAD** [-] [55]

Feb 91. (7")(c-s) **LOVE WALKED IN. / FLAWED TO PERFECTION (demo)** [21] [ ]
(12"+=)(cd-s+=)(12"pic-d+=) – Until my dying day (live).
(10"white+=) – World problems: a solution.

Aug 92. (7") **LOWLIFE IN HIGH PLACES. / BABY I'LL BE GONE** [22] [ ]
(cd-s) – ('A'side) / Backstreet symphony / She's so fine / Love walked in.
(cd-s) – ('A'side) / With a little help from my friends / She's my inspiration / Low life in high places (demo).

Aug 92. (cd)(c)(d-lp) **LAUGHING ON JUDGEMENT DAY** [2] [ ]
– Does it feel like love? / Everybody wants her / Low life in high places / Laughing on judgement day / Empty city / Today the world stopped turning / Long way from home / Fire to ice / Feeding the flame / A better man / The moment of truth / Flawed to perfection / Like a satellite / Baby I'll be gone. *(re-iss.cd+c Mar94)*

Oct 92. (7")(c-s) **EVERYBODY WANTS HER. / DANGEROUS RHYTHM** [36] [ ]
(12"+=) – Higher ground (acoustic).
(cd-s) – ('A'side) / Dirty love (acoustic) / Higher ground (acoustic) / Dirty love.

Feb 93. (7")(c-s) **A BETTER MAN. / LOW LIFE IN HIGH PLACES (live)** [18] [ ]
(12")(cd-s) – ('A'side) / New York, New York (Harry's theme) / Lazy Sunday (live) / Higher ground (live).

Jun 93. (12"ep)(cd-ep) **LIKE A SATELLITE / LIKE A SATELLITE (live) / GIMME SHELTER / THE DAMAGE IS DONE** [28] [ ]

Dec 94. (7"pic-d)(c-s) **STAND UP. / (interview)** [23] [ ]
(cd-s+=) – The fire is gone (demo) / Life in a day (demo).
(cd-s) – ('A'side) / One pretty woman / It happened in this town.

Jan 95. (cd)(c)(lp) **BEHIND CLOSED DOORS** [5] [ ]
– Moth to the flame / Fly on the wall / I'll be waiting / River of pain / Future train / 'Til the river runs dry / Stand up / Preaching from a chair / Castles in the sand / Too scared to live / Ball and chain / It happened in this train.

Feb 95. (c-s) **RIVERS OF PAIN / DOES IT FEEL LIKE LOVE** [31] [ ]
(cd-s+=) – Everybody wants her (live) / All the way from Memphis (live).
(cd-s) – ('A'side) / 5.15 (live) / You don't know what love is (demo).
(12"pic-d) – ('A'side) / Move on / All the way from Memphis (live).

Apr 95. (c-ep) **CASTLES IN THE SAND / A BETTER MAN / SHE'S SO FINE / DIRTY LOVE** [30] [ ]
(cd-s) – ('A'side) / Stand up (live acoustic) / Move over (live).
(cd-s) – ('A'side) / I hear you knocking (live acoustic) / River of pain (live acoustic).

Sep 95. (c-s) **IN A BROKEN DREAM / 'TIL THE RIVER RUNS DRY** [26] [ ]
(cd-s) – ('A'side) / Love walked in / Dirty love (demo).
(cd-s) – ('A'side) / Stay with me / An Englishman on holiday.

Sep 95. (cd)(c)(d-lp) **THEIR FINEST HOUR (AND A BIT)** (compilation) [22] [ ]
– Dirty love / River of pain / Love walked in / Everybody wants her / In a broken dream / Higher ground '95 / Backstreet symphony / A better man / Gimme shelter / Like a satellite / Low life in high places / Stand up / Once in a lifetime / Gimme some lovin' / Castles in the sand / She's so fine.

'TIL TUESDAY (see under ⇒ MANN, Aimee)

TIMELORDS (see under ⇒ KLF)

TINDERSTICKS

Formed: Nottingham, England ... 1988 as ASPHALT RIBBONS, by STUART STAPLES, DAVE BOULTER and DICKON HINCHCLIFFE. After 3 years, a few singles and a 1991 album, they moved to London and soon became TINDERSTICKS. With 3 others in their ranks, they soon were tipped for stardom in '94, having had their eponymous album, acclaimed by music press. • **Style:** Moved from psuedo-indie-rock outfit like TRIFFIDS or GO-BETWEENS, which progressed in TINDERSTICKS, to LOU REED or NICK CAVE like alternative rock. • **Songwriters:** Covered; KOOKS (David Bowie) / A MARRIAGE MADE IN HEAVEN (Lee Hazlewood-Nancy Sinatra) / WE HAVE ALL THE TIME IN THE WORLD (John Barry) / KATHLEEN (Townes Van Zandt). • **Trivia:** JON LANGFORD of The THREE JOHNS, produced early ASPHALT RIBBONS material.

Recommended: TINDERSTICKS (*8) / THE SECOND TINDERSTICKS ALBUM (*8)

ASPHALT RIBBONS

STUART STAPLES – vocals / **DICKON HINCHCLIFFE** – violin / **DAVE BOULTER** – keyboards / **BLACKHOUSE** – guitar / **FRASER** – bass / **WATT** – drums

In-Tape | not issued

Oct 89. (7"ep) **THE ORCHARD** [ ] [-]
– Over again / Red sauce / Greyhound / I used to live T.

May 90. (7"m) **GOOD LOVE. / LONG LOST UNCLE / THE DAY I TURNED BAD** [ ] [-]

(Alongside new stablemates MY LIFE WITH PATRICK, their new label below issued a free flexi sampler with 'Zip Code' fanzine; cat no. LILY 001)

Tiger Lily | not issued

Apr 91. (12"ep) **PASSION, COOLNESS, INDIFFERENCE, BOREDOM, MOCKERY, CONTEMPT, DISGUST** [ ] [-]

E.T.T. | not issued

Aug 91. (m-lp) **OLD HORSE & OTHER SONGS** [ ] [-]
– *(cd-iss.Apr92)*

TINDERSTICKS

were formed by **STUART, DICKON and DAVE**, plus Londoners **NEIL FRAZER** – guitar / **MARK COLWILL** – bass / **AL McCAULEY** – drums

Tippy Toe | not issued

Nov 92. (7") **PATCHWORK. / MILKY TEETH** [ ] [-]

Mar 93. (10"ep) **MARBLES / JOE STUMBLE. / FOR THOSE ... / BENN** [ ] [-]

— Below featured dual vox of **NIKI SIN** of HUGGY BEAR.

Rough Trade | not issued

Apr 93. (7") **A MARRIAGE MADE IN HEAVEN. / ('A'instrumental)** [ ] [-]

Domino | not issued

Jul 93. (7"ep) **UNWIRED EP** [ ] [-]
– Feeling relatively good / Rottweilers and mace / She / Kooks.

This Way Up | not issued

Sep 93. (7")(cd-s) **CITY SICKNESS. / UNTITLED / THE BULLRING** [ ] [-]

Oct 93. (cd)(c)(lp) **TINDERSTICKS** [56] [-]
– Nectar / Tyed / Sweet, sweet man (pt.1) / Whiskey & water / Blood / City sickness / Patchwork / Marbles / Walt blues / Milky teeth (pt.2) / Jism / Piano song / Tre dye / Drunk tank / Paco de Renaldo's dream / Not knowing. (lp+=) – Fruitless.

— In Oct'93, alongside GALLON DRUNK, they issued 'Clawfist' 7" WE HAVE ALL THE TIME IN THE WORLD. 'Tippy Toe' also gaveaway at gigs 7" 'LIVE IN BERLIN'.

Jan 94. (7"ep)(10"ep)(cd-ep) **KATHLEEN EP** [61] [-]
– Kathleen / Summat Moon / A sweet sweet man / E-type Joe.

— In Aug'94, they appeared on Various Artists EP on 'Blue Eyed Dog'; track 'LOVE BITES', and others by STRANGELOVE / GOD MACHINE + BREED.

Mar 95. (7") **NO MORE AFFAIRS. / ('A'instrumental)** [58] [ ]
(cd-s+=) – Fruitless.

Apr 95. (cd)(c)(d-lp) **THE SECOND TINDERSTICKS ALBUM** [13] [ ]
– El diablo en el ojo / My sister / Tiny tears / Snowy in F# minor / Seaweed /

Vertraven 2 / Talk to me / No more affairs / Singing / Travelling light / Cherry blossoms / She's gone / Mistakes / Vertraven 3 / Sleepy song. (some lp's w/free one-sided-7") PLUS DE LAISONS

Jul 95. (7")(cd-s) **TRAVELLING LIGHT. / WAITING 'ROUND YOU / I'VE BEEN LOVING YOU TOO LONG** 51 □

Oct 95. (cd)(d-10"lp) **THE BLOOMSBURY THEATRE 12.3.95 (live)** 32 □

– El diablo en el ojo / A night in / Talk to me / She's gone / My sister * / No more affairs / City sickness / Vertraven II / Sleepy song / Jism / Drunk tank / Mistakes / Tiny tears / Raindrops / For those . . . (d-lp+= *)

TIN MACHINE (see under ⇒ BOWIE, David)

TOM TOM CLUB (see under ⇒ TALKING HEADS)

TONES ON TAIL (see under ⇒ BAUHAUS)

TOTO

Formed: Los Angeles, California, USA ... 1977 by ex-session men, brothers JEFF and STEVE PORCARO with others (see below). Signed worldwide deal on 'CBS-Epic' in 1978, with debut single 'HOLD THE LINE', breaking through into US + UK Top 20 early 1979. • **Style:** Superstar session men, who blended together hard + soft rock, that was loved by the US mainstream audiences. • **Songwriters:** PAICH was main songwriter, with others contributing, with group taking more of a hand in the 90's. Covered; WITH A LITTLE HELP FROM MY FRIENDS (Beatles). • **Trivia:** ROSANNA was written by LUKATHER for his girlfriend; actress Rosanna Arquette.

Recommended: PAST TO PRESENT: 1977 TO 1990 (*6).

BOBBY KIMBALL (b.ROBERT TOTEAUX, 29 Mar'47, Vinton, Louisiana) – vocals / **STEVE LUKATHER** (b.21 Oct'57) – lead guitar, vocals / **STEVE PORCARO** (b. 2 Sep'57) – keyboards, vocals / **JEFF PORCARO** (b. 1 Apr'54) – drums, percussion (ex-RURAL LIFE) / **DAVID PAICH** (b.25 Jun'54) – keyboards, vocals (ex-RURAL LIFE) / **DAVID HUNGATE** – bass

C.B.S. Columbia

Jan 79. (7") **HOLD THE LINE. / TAKIN' IT BACK** 14 5 Oct 78

Mar 79. (lp)(c) **TOTO** 37 9 Oct 78

– Child's anthem / I'll supply the love / Georgy porgy / Manuela run / You are the flower / Girl goodbye / Takin' it back / Rockmaker / Hold the line / Angela. *(re-iss.Apr83 + Jun84, cd-iss.Oct86) (re-iss.cd May94 on 'Sony')*

Mar 79. (7") **I'LL SUPPLY THE LOVE. / YOU ARE THE FLOWER** □ 45 Feb 79

Apr 79. (7")(7"pic-d) **GEORGY PORGY. / CHILD'S ANTHEM** - 48

Jun 79. (7") **GEORGY PORGY. / (part 2)** □ -

Dec 79. (lp)(c) **HYDRA** □ 37 Nov 79

– Hydra / St. George and the dragon / 99 / Lorraine / All us boys / Mama / White sister / A secret love. *(re-iss.Apr83 & Feb85)*

Dec 79. (7")(7"pic-d) **ST. GEORGE AND THE DRAGON. / WHITE SISTER** - □

Dec 79. (7") **ST. GEORGE AND THE DRAGON. / A SECRET LOVE** □ -

Feb 80. (7") **99. / HYDRA** □ 26 Dec 79

Mar 80. (7") **ALL US BOYS. / HYDRA** - □

Jan 81. (lp)(c) **TURN BACK** □ 41

– Gift with a golden gun / English eyes / Live for today / A million miles away / Goodbye Elenore / I think I could stand you forever / Turn back / If it's the last night. *(re-iss.Apr83, cd-iss.May87)*

Feb 81. (7") **GOODBYE ELENORE. / TURN BACK** □ □

Apr 81. (7") **TURN BACK. / IT'S THE LAST NIGHT** - □

Apr 82. (lp)(c) **TOTO IV** (reached peak UK position Feb83) 4 4

– Rosanna / Make believe / I won't hold you back / Good for you / It's a feeling / Afraid of love / Lovers in the night / We made it / Waiting for your love / Africa. *(cd-iss.1983 & Mar91) (re-iss.+cd.Nov86) (re-iss.cd Feb95 & Dec95)*

Apr 82. (7")(7"pic-d) **ROSANNA. / IT'S A FEELING** □ 2

(re-iss.Mar83, hit UK No.12)

Aug 82. (7") **MAKE BELIEVE. / WE MADE IT** 3 30

Oct 82. (7") **AFRICA. / GOOD FOR YOU** - 1

Jan 83. (7")(7"sha-pic-d) **AFRICA. / WE MADE IT** 3 -

Jun 83. (7")(7"pic-d) **I WON'T HOLD YOU BACK. / AFRAID OF LOVE** 37 10 Mar 83

(12"+=) – 99 / Hold the line / Goodbye Elenore.

Jul 83. (7") **WAITING FOR YOUR LOVE. / LOVERS IN THE NIGHT** □ 73

— (late'82) **MIKE PORCARO** (29 May'55) – bass had already repl. HUNGATE

— (In '84) **DENNIS 'Fergie' FREDRICKSON** (b.15 May'51) – vocals repl. KIMBALL who later became part of the awful FAR CORPORATION

Nov 84. (7")(12") **STRANGER IN TOWN. / CHANGE OF HEART** □ 30

Nov 84. (lp)(c) **ISOLATION** 67 42

– Carmen / Lion / Stranger in town / Angel don't cry / How does it feel / Endless / Isolation / Mr. Friendly / Change of heart / Holyanna. *(cd-iss.1988)*

— Dec84, saw their instrumental DUNE (Film Soundtrack) released on 'Polydor'. It was accompanied by The VIENNA SYMPHONY ORCHESTRA but flopped. Around this time they laid down backing instruments for USA IN AFRICA single.

Jan 85. (7") **HOLYANNA. / MR. FRIENDLY** - 71

Feb 85. (7") **HOW DOES IT FEEL. / MR. FRIENDLY** □ □

Apr 85. (7") **ENDLESS. / ISOLATION** □ □

— **JOSEPH WILLIAMS** – vocals (ex-Solo artist) repl. FREDRICKSON

Oct 86. (7") **I'LL BE OVER YOU. / IN A WORD** □ 11 Aug 86

(12"+=) – Africa / 99.

Oct 86. (lp)(c)(cd) **FAHRENHEIT** 99 40 Sep 86

– Till the end / We can make it tonight / Without your love / Can't stand it any longer / I'll be over you / Fahrenheit / Somewhere tonight / Could this be love / Lea / Don't stop me now.

Dec 86. (7") **WITHOUT YOUR LOVE. / CAN'T STAND IT ANY LONGER** - 38

— trimmed to quintet, when STEVE PORCARO went solo.

Mar 87. (7") **TILL THE END. / DON'T STOP ME NOW** - □

Feb 88. (7") **PAMELA. / THE SEVENTH ONE** - □

Feb 88. (7") **STOP LOVING YOU. / THE SEVENTH ONE** □ □

(12"+=)/ /(cd-s+=) – ('A'version)./ / I'll be over you.

Mar 88. (lp)(c)(cd) **THE SEVENTH ONE** 73 64

– Pamela / You got me / Anna / Stop loving you / Mushanga / Stay away / Straight for the heart / Only the children / A thousand years / These chains / Home of the brave.

Apr 88. (7") **STRAIGHT FROM THE HEART. / THE SEVENTH ONE** - □

May 88. (7") **PAMELA. / STAY AWAKE** □ -

(12"+=)/ /(cd-s+=) – America./ / Africa / Rosanna.

— **KIMBALL** returned Sep'88, but was repl. by temp. **TOMMY NELSON.** He in turn was deposed by **JEAN-MICHEL BYRON** (b.South Africa) – vocals

Sep 90. (7")(12")(c-s) **CAN YOU HEAR WHAT I'M SAYING. / AFRICA** □ □

(cd-s+=) – Georgy porgy / Waiting for your love.

Oct 90. (cd)(c)(lp) **PAST TO PRESENT: 1977 TO 1990** (compilation) □ □ Sep 90

– Love has the power / Africa / Hold the line / Out of love / Georgy Porgy / I'll be over you / Can you hear what I'm saying / Rosanna / I won't hold you back / Stop loving you / 99 / Pamela / Animal.

— **KIMBALL** returned to repl. BYRON who formed self-named group.

— In Aug'92, JEFF died mysteriously of poisoning or a heart attack.

Columbia Columbia

Sep 92. (cd)(c)(lp) **KINGDOM OF DESIRE** □ □

– Gypsy train / Don't chain my heart / Never enough / How many times / 2 hearts / Wings of time / She knows the Devil / The other side / Only you / Jake to the bone.

Nov 93. (d-cd)(d-c) **ABSOLUTELY LIVE (live)** □ □

– Hydra / Rosanna / Kingdom of desire / Georgy Porgy / 99 / I won't hold you back / Don't stop me now / Africa / Don't chain my heart / I'll be over you / Home of the brave / Hold the line / With a little help from my friends.

Oct 95. (cd)(c) **TAMBU** □ □

– Gift of faith / I will remember / Slipped away / If you belong to me / Baby, he's your man / The other end of time / The turning point / Time is the enemy / Drag him to the roof / Just can't get to you / Dave's gone skiing / The road goes on.

Nov 95. (c-s) **I WILL REMEMBER / DAVE'S GONE SKIING** 64 □

(cd-s) – ('A'side) / Rosanna / Africa / Georgy porgy.

– more compilations, etc. –

Sep 84. Hallmark; (lp)(c) **HOLD THE LINE** □ -

Sep 85. Old Gold; (7") **HOLD THE LINE. / ROSANNA** □ -

Mar 90. Old Gold; (7") **AFRICA. / I WON'T HOLD YOU BACK** □ -

Dec 90. CBS; (cd-box) **TOTO / TURN BACK / HYDRA** □ □

STEVE LUKATHER

solo with **STEVE STEVENS** – guitar / **JAN HAMMER** – keyboards / **WILL LEE** – bass / **+?**

C.B.S. Columbia

Nov 89. (lp)(c)(cd) **LUKATHER** □ □

– Twist the knife / Swear your love / Fall into velvet / Drive a crooked road / Got my way / Darkest night of the year / Lonely beat of my heart / With a second chance / Turn to stone / It looks like rain / Steppin' on top of your world.

Columbia Columbia

Apr 94. (cd)(c) **CANDYMAN** □ □

– Hero with 1000 eyes / Freedom / Extinction blues / Born yesterday / Never walk alone / Party in Simon's pants / Borrowed time / Never let them see you cry / Froth / The bomber / Song for Jeff.

TOURISTS (see under ⇒ EURYTHMICS)

Pete TOWNSHEND (see under ⇒ WHO)

(see under ⇒ WHO)

TRAFFIC

Formed: based Midlands, England . . . Apr'67, by WINWOOD, MASON, CAPALDI and WOOD. Signed to 'Island' records and immediately hit the UK Top 5 with debut 45 'PAPER SUN'. Their next single 'HOLE IN MY SHOE', became regarded as a classic, after it made No.2 in the UK. After their split early in 1969, and reformation in the 70's, they concentrated on working mostly in Muscle Shoals, America, where they had huge renewed fortunes. • **Style:** Multi-talented psychedelic group who tested folk-rock and jazz in the early 70's. • **Songwriters:** Individually or group compositions, except GIMME SOME LOVIN' (Spencer Davis Group). CAPALDI covered LOVE HURTS (Everly Brothers). • **Trivia:** The album ON THE ROAD was recorded on tour in Germany.

Recommended: SMILING PHASES (*8)

STEVE WINWOOD (b.12 May'48) – vocals, keyboards (ex-SPENCER DAVIS GROUP) / **DAVE MASON** (b.10 May'47, Worcester) – guitar, vocals (ex-HELLIONS) / **JIM CAPALDI** (b.24 Aug'44, Evesham) – drums, vocals (ex-HELLIONS) / **CHRIS WOOD** (b.24 Jun'44, Birmingham) – flute, sax (ex-SOUNDS OF BLUE)

Island / United Art

May 67. (7") **PAPER SUN. / GIVING TO YOU** [5] [94] Aug 67

Aug 67. (7") **HOLE IN MY SHOE. / SMILING PHASES** [2] [ ]

Nov 67. (7") **HERE WE GO ROUND THE MULBERRY BUSH. / COLOURED RAIN** [8] [ ]

Dec 67. (lp) **MR. FANTASY** [8] [88] Apr 68
– Heaven is in your mind / Berkshire poppies / House for everyone / No name, no face, no number / Dear Mr. Fantasy / Dealer / Utterly simple / Coloured rain / Hope I never find me there / Giving to you. *(US version +=)* – Paper Sun / Hole in my shoe. *(re-iss.+c.Feb87, cd-iss.Sep89)*

Feb 68. (7") **NO NAME, NO FACE, NO NUMBER. / ROAMIN' IN THE GLOAMIN'** [40] [-]

Feb 68. (7") **NO NAME, NO FACE, NO NUMBER. / HEAVEN IS IN YOUR MIND** [-] [ ]

Sep 68. (7") **FEELING ALRIGHT. / WITHERING TREE** [ ] [ ]

Oct 68. (lp) **TRAFFIC** [9] [17]
– You can all join in / Pearly queen / Don't be sad / Who knows what tomorrow may bring / Feelin' alright / Vagabond virgin / Forty thousand headmen / Cryin' to be heard / No time to live / Means to an end. *(re-iss.+c.Feb87, cd-iss.Nov87 & 1989)*

Dec 68. (7") **MEDICATED GOO. / SHANGHAI NOODLE FACTORY** [ ] [ ]

—— Below album was recorded before their split late 1968.

May 69. (lp) **LAST EXIT (some live)** [ ] [19]
– Just for you / Shanghai noodle factory / Something's got a hold of my toe / Withering tree / Medicated goo / Feelin' good / Blind man. *(cd-iss.May88 & Sep89)*

Oct 69. (lp) **THE BEST OF TRAFFIC** (compilation) [ ] [48]
– Paper Sun / Heaven is in your mind / No face, no name, no number / Coloured rain / Smiling phases / Hole in my shoe / Medicated goo / Forty thousand headmen / Feelin' alright / Shanghai noodle factory / Dear Mr. Fantasy. *(cd-iss.Mar93)*

—— In 1969, WINWOOD formed BLIND FAITH with ERIC CLAPTON and GINGER BAKER. WOOD also joined the latter's group AIRFORCE. WOOD, MASON and CAPALDI then formed WOODEN FROG. DAVE MASON went solo as TRAFFIC re-formed as a trio.

Jul 70. (lp)(c) **JOHN BARLEYCORN MUST DIE** [5] [11]
– Glad / Freedom rider / Empty pages / Stranger to himself / John Barleycorn / Every mother's son. *(re-iss.Sep86, cd-iss.Sep89)*

Sep 70. (7") **EMPTY PAGES. / STRANGER TO HIMSELF** [-] [74]

—— added **RIC GRECH** – bass (ex-FAMILY, ex-BLIND FAITH, ex-GINGER BAKER'S AIRFORCE) / **REEBOP KWAKU-BAAH** – percussion (ex-GINGER BAKER'S AIRFORCE) / **JIM GORDON** – drums (ex-DEREK & THE DOMINOES) / **DAVE MASON** guested on some live.

Sep 71. (lp)(c) **WELCOME TO THE CANTEEN (live)** [ ] [26]
– Medicated goo / Sad and deep as you / Forty thousand headmen / Shouldn't have took more than you gave / Dear Mr. Fantasy / Gimme some lovin'. *(cd-iss.May88 & Sep89)*

Oct 71. (7") **GIMME SOME LOVIN'. / (part 2)** [-] [68]

Dec 71. (7") **GLAD. / (part 2)** [-] [ ]

Island / Island

Dec 71. (lp)(c) **THE LOW SPARK OF THE HIGH HEELED BOYS** [ ] [7]
– Hidden treasure / The low spark of the high heeled boys / Rock & roll stew / Many a mile to freedom / Light up or leave me alone / Rainmaker. *(re-iss.Sep86, cd-iss.Nov87 & Sep89)*

Jan 72. (7") **ROCK & ROLL STEW. / (part 2)** [-] [93]

—— **DAVID HOOD** – bass + ROGER HAWKINS – drums (both of JIM CAPALDI band) repl. JIM GORDON and GRECH. (The latter formed KGB)

Feb 73. (lp)(c) **SHOOT OUT AT THE FANTASY FACTORY** [ ] [6]
– Shoot out at the fantasy factory / Roll right stone / Evening blue / ragic magic / Uninspired (sometimes I feel so). *(cd-iss.May88 & Sep89)*

—— added **BARRY BECKETT** – keyboards

Oct 73. (d-lp)(d-c) **ON THE ROAD (live)** [40] [29]
– Glad / Freedom rider / Tragic magic / (Sometimes I feel so) Uninspired / Shoot out at the fantasy factory / Light up or leave me alone / The low spark of the high heeled boys. *(cd-iss.1988 & Aug91) (cd-iss.Apr94)*

—— **WINWOOD, CAPALDI & WOOD** enlisted **ROSKO GEE** – bass (ex-GONZALES)

Island / Asylum

Sep 74. (lp)(c) **WHEN THE EAGLE FLIES** [31] [9]
– Walking in the wind / Something new / Dream Gerrard / Memories of a rock'n'roller / When the eagle flies / Graveyard people / Love. *(cd-iss.1988)*

Oct 74. (7") **WALKING IN THE WIND. / ('A'instrumental version)** [ ] [ ]

—— Disbanded early 1975. STEVE WINWOOD went solo, also collaborating with STOMU YAMASHTA. WOOD and GEE took up session work. On 12 Jul'83, CHRIS WOOD died of liver failure. JIM CAPALDI continued his solo career.

– more compilations, etc. –

May 74. Island/ US= U.A.; (7") **HOLE IN MY SHOE. / HERE WE GO ROUND THE MULBERRY BUSH** [ ] [ ]

May 74. Island/ US= U.A.; (lp)(c) **YOU CAN ALL JOIN IN** [ ] [ ]

May 75. Island/ US= U.A.; (lp)(c) **HEAVY TRAFFIC** [ ] [ ]

Sep 75. Island/ US= U.A.; (lp)(c) **MORE HEAVY TRAFFIC** [ ] [ ]

Mar 78. Island; (7"ep)(7"pic-d-ep) **EXTENDED PLAY** [ ] [-]
– I'm a man / Hole in my shoe / Gimme some lovin' / No name no face no number

1992. Island; (d-cd) **SMILING PHASES** [ ] [ ]
– Paper sun / Hole in my shoe / Smiling phases / Heaven is in your mind / Coloured rain / No face, no name, no number / Here we go round the mulbury bush / Dear Mr. Fantasy / You can all join in / Feelin' alright / Pearly queen / Forty thousand headmen / Vagabond virgin / Shanghai noodle factory / Withering tree / Medicated goo / Glad / Freedom rider / Empty pages / John Barleycorn / The low spark of the high heeled boys / Light up or leave me alone / Rock & roll stew / Shoot out at the fantasy factory / Walking in the wind / When the eagle flies.

JIM CAPALDI

(solo, first 2 when member of TRAFFIC)

—— sessioners until 1978 included **JIMMY JOHNSON** – guitar / **DAVID HOOD** – bass / **ROGER HAWKINS** – drums / **BARRY BECKETT** – piano / **PETE CARR** – guitar / **STEVE WINWOOD** – various instruments / **REEBOP KWAKU BAAH** – percussion

Island / Island

Apr 72. (lp)(c) **OH HOW WE DANCED** [ ] [82] Apr 72
– Eve / Big thirst / Love is all you can try / Last day of dawn / Don't be a hero / Open your heart / How much can a man really take / Oh how we danced.

Apr 72. (7") **EVE. / GOING DOWN SLOW ALL THE WAY** [ ] [ ]

Jun 72. (7") **TRICKY DICKY RIDES AGAIN. / OH HOW WE DANCED** [ ] [ ]

Jul 72. (7") **OPEN YOUR HEART. / OH HOW WE DANCED** [-] [ ]

Feb 73. (7") **TRICKY DICKY RIDES AGAIN. / LOVE IS ALL YOU CAN TRY** [-] [ ]

May 74. (7") **WHALE MEAT AGAIN. / IT'S ALRIGHT** [-] [ ]

Jun 74. (lp)(c) **WHALE MEAT AGAIN** [ ] [ ]
– It's alright / Whale meat again / Yellow sun / I've got so much lovin' / Low rider / My brother / Summer fading.

Jun 74. (7") **IT'S ALL UP TO YOU. / WHALE MEAT AGAIN** [27] [ ]

Jul 74. (7") **IT'S ALL UP TO YOU. / I'VE GOT SO MUCH LOVIN'** [-] [ ]

Jun 75. (lp)(c) **SHORT CUT DRAW BLOOD** [ ] [ ]
– Goodbye love / It's all up to you / Love hurts / Johnny too bad / Short cut draw blood / Living on a marble / Boy on a marble / Keep on trying / Seagull.

Oct 75. (7") **LOVE HURTS. / SUGAR HONEY** [4] [97]
(re-iss.Jul81)

Jan 76. (7") **GOODBYE MY LOVE. / IT'S ALRIGHT** [ ] [ ]

Apr 76. (7") **TALKIN' ABOUT MY BABY. / STILL TALKIN'** [ ] [ ]

Apr 76. (7") **SHORT CUT DRAW BLOOD. / GOODNIGHT AND GOOD MORNING** [-] [ ]

Mar 77. (lp)(c) **PLAY IT BY EAR** [ ] [ ]

Mar 77. (7") **GOODBYE MY LOVE. / BABY YOU'RE NOT MY PROBLEM** [ ] [ ]

Polydor / Polydor

Jan 78. (7") **DAUGHTER OF THE NIGHT. / GAME OF LOVE** [ ] [ ]

Feb 78. (lp)(c) **THE CONTENDER** [ ] [ ]
– Dirty business / Sealed with a kiss / Daughter of the night (the US-title) / You burn me / Game of love / The contender / Elixir of love / Short ends / Hunger and greed.

Mar 78. (7") **SEALED WITH A KISS. / HAD A DREAM TODAY** [ ] [ ]

May 79. (lp)(c) **ELECTRIC NIGHTS** [ ] [ ]
– Shoe shine / Hotel blues / White jungle lady / Tabitha / Time / Electric nights / Wild dogs / 1890 / Wild geese.

Aug 79. (7") **SHOE SHINE. / TABITHA**

not iss. — R.S.O.

1979. (7") **DAUGHTER OF THE NIGHT. / I'M GONNA DO IT** [-]

Carrere — Carrere

Jun 80. (7") **HOLD ON TO YOUR LOVE. / FORTUNE AND FAME** [-]

Jul 80. (lp)(c) **THE SWEET SMELL OF SUCCESS**
– Hold on to your love / Take me how you find me girl / The sweet smell of success / Every man should march to the beat of his own drum / Tonight you're mine / The low spark of high heeled boys / Fortune and fame / Man with no country / Going home.

Sep 80. (7") **THE LOW SPARK OF HIGH HEELED BOYS. / BATHROOM JANE** [-]

Feb 81. (7") **CHILD IN THE STORM. / BRIGHT FIGHTER** [-]

Apr 81. (7") **OLD PHOTOGRAPHS. / MAN WITH NO COUNTRY** [-]

Apr 81. (lp)(c) **LET THE THUNDER CRY**
– Let the thunder cry / Favella music / Child in the storm / Only love / Louie Louie / Warm / Dreams do come true / Old photographs / We don't need / Anxiety.

W.E.A. — Atlantic

Jan 83. (7") **TONIGHT YOU'RE MINE. / BACK AT MY PLACE**

Jan 83. (lp)(c) **FIERCE HEART** [91]
– Tonight you're mine / Living on the edge / Bad breaks / Runaway / Back at my place / That's love / I'll always be your fool / Don't let them control you / Gifts of unknown things.

Apr 83. (7")(12") **THAT'S LOVE. / RUNAWAY** [28]

Jul 83. (7") **LIVING ON THE EDGE. / GIFTS OF UNKNOWN THINGS** [75]

Oct 84. (7") **I'LL KEEP HOLDING ON. / TALES OF POWER**
(12"+=) – Still holding on.

Jan 85. (lp)(c) **ONE MAN MISSION**
– One man mission of love / Tonight / Lost inside your love / I'll keep holding on / Nobody loves you / Young savages / Tales of power / Warriors of love / Ancient highway.

Island — Island

Jan 89. (7") **SOMETHING SO STRONG. / CHILD IN THE STORM**
(12"+=)(cd-s+=) – Tales of power.

Feb 89. (7") **SOME COME RUNNING. / FABELA MUSIC** Dec 88
(12"+=)(cd-s+=) – Love hurts.

Feb 89. (lp)(c)(cd) **SOME COME RUNNING**
– Something so strong / Love used to be a friend of mine / Dancing on the highway / Some come running / Voices in the night / You are the one / Take me home / Oh Lord, why Lord.

May 89. (7")(12") **TAKE ME HOME. / CHILD IN THE STORM**
(cd-s+=) – ('A'version) / Fabela music.

— featured old mate **STEVE WINWOOD**

All At Once — not issued

Dec 93. (cd) **PRINCE OF DARKNESS** [-]
(cd-iss.Nov94 on 'Start')

TRAFFIC

— **WINWOOD + CAPALDI** re-formed for studio.

Virgin — Virgin

May 94. (cd)(c) **FAR FROM HOME** [29]
– Riding high / Here comes a man / Far from home / Nowhere is their freedom / Holy ground / Some kinda woman / Every night, every day / This train won't stop / State of grace / Mosambique.

May 94. (7")(c-s) **HERE COMES A MAN. / GLAD (live)**
(cd-s+=) – ('A'mix).

Sep 94. (c-s) **SOME KINDA WOMAN. / FORTY THOUSAND HEADMEN**
(cd-s+=) – Low spark of high heeled boys / ('A'mix).

T.REX (see under ⇒ BOLAN, Marc)

TRICKY

Born: 1969, Knowle West, Bristol, England. Came to prominence in 1991 when taking some lead vocals on MASSIVE ATTACK's outstanding debut 'BLUE LINES'. He also guested on their 1994 follow-up 'PROTECTION', although he had already carved out own solo career, starting with single 'AFTERMATH'. Early in 1995, he unleashed the ground-breaking 'MAXINQUAYE', which hit UK Top 3 and was deservedly voted top album of the year by NME writers. • **Style:** Haunting ambient dub and jungle featured teenage MARTINA. • **Songwriters:** Self-penned except; BLACK STEEL (Public Enemy).

Recommended: MAXINQUAYE (*10) / NEARLY GOD (*7)

TRICKY -vocals (with various guests incl. **MARTINA**)

4th & Bro. — 4th & Bro.

Jan 94. (7") **AFTERMATH. / ('A'-I could be looking for people mix)** [69]
(12"+=)(cd-s+=) – (2 'A'mixes).

Apr 94. (7") **PONDEROSA. / ('A'-Dobie's roll pt.1 mix)**
(12"+=)(cd-s+=) – (3 'A'mixes; Ultragelic / Original / Dobie's roll pt.2).

Jan 95. (7")(c-s)(cd-s) **OVERCOME. / ABBA ON FAT TRACKS** [34]
(12"+=)(cd-s+=) – ('A'-Zippy & Bungle mix).

Feb 95. (cd)(c) **MAXINQUAYE** [3]
– Overcome / Ponderosa / Black steel / Hell is around the corner / Pumpkin / Aftermath (hip hop blues) / Abba on fat tracks / Brand new you're retro / Suffocated love / You don't / Strugglin' / Read me.

Mar 95. (c-s) **BLACK STEEL. / ('A'-Been caught stealing mix)** [28]
(12"+=)(cd-s+=) – ('A'live) / ('A'-In the draw mix).
(cd-s++=) – ('A'edit).

Jul 95. (7"pic-d-ep)(12"red-ep)(cd-ep) **THE HELL E.P.** [12]
– Hell is around the corner (original) / ('A'-Hell and water mix) / Psychosis / Tonite is a special nite (chaos mass confusion mix).

(above credited as "TRICKY VS. THE GRAVEDIGGAZ")

Nov 95. (c-s) **PUMPKIN / MOODY BROODY BUDHIST CAMP / NEW KINGDOM** [26]
(cd-s+=) – Brand new you're retro (Alex Reece remix).
(12"pumpkin-colrd) – ('A'side) / (above track) / Slick 66.

. . . Jan – Jun '96 stop press . . .

NEARLY GOD

— **TRICKY** with **TERRY HALL / MARTINA / BJORK / NENEH CHERRY / ALISON MOYET + CATH COFFEY**

4th & Bro — 4th & Bro

Apr 96. (single) **POEMS** [28]

Apr 96. (cd)(lp) **NEARLY GOD** [11]

— above was to have been under his DURBAN POISON project.

Robin TROWER

Born: 9 Mar'45, London, England. After initial period with 60's outfit The PARAMOUNTS (who became PROCOL HARUM), he set up his own band JUDE, with FRANKIE MILLER. Also in their ranks was JAMES DEWAR, who re-united with him after TROWER launched solo career in 1972. He signed to 'Chrysalis', and issued debut album 'TWICE REMOVED FROM YESTERDAY' in the ensuing year. Made impact in 1974, especially across the Atlantic, when the 'BRIDGE OF SIGHS' lp eased into their Top 10. They worked hard there throughout the 70's to maintain large venue audiences, though this faded in the 80's. • **Style:** HENDRIX-FREE inspired axeman, whose heavy bluesy-rock sound, combined well with DEWAR's soul-orientated vox. The facial antics of TROWER, gave music press a field-day for unjustifiably ridiculing the once great guitar hero. • **Songwriters:** Mostly TROWER-DEWAR compositions, except; MAN OF THE WORLD (Fleetwood Mac) / ROCK ME BABY (B.B.King) / I CAN'T WAIT MUCH LONGER (Frankie Miller) / FURTHER ON UP THE ROAD (?) / SAILING (Sutherland Bros.) / etc. • **Trivia:** Like so many of his rock contemporaries, he played a FENDER STRATOCASTER guitar.

Recommended: FOR EARTH BELOW (*8) / VICTIMS OF THE FURY (*6)/ PORTFOLIO (*8).

ROBIN TROWER – guitar (ex-JUDE, ex-PROCOL HARUM) / **JAMES DEWAR** – vocals, bass (ex-JUDE, ex-STONE THE CROWS) / **REG ISADORE** – drums (ex-QUIVER)

Chrysalis — Chrysalis

Mar 73. (lp)(c) **TWICE REMOVED FROM YESTERDAY**
– I can't wait much longer / Daydream / Hannah / Man of the world / I can't stand it / Rock me baby / Twice removed from yesterday / Sinner's song / Ballerina.

Mar 73. (7") **MAN OF THE WORLD. / TAKE A FAST TRAIN**

Mar 74. (7") **TOO ROLLING STONED. / MAN OF THE WORLD** [-]

Apr 74. (lp)(c) **BRIDGE OF SIGHS** [7]
– Day of the eagle / Bridge of sighs / In this place / The fool and me / Too rolling stoned / About to begin / Lady love / A little bit of sympathy. *(re-iss.Jan82, cd-iss.1980's-US) (re-iss.cd Mar94)*

May 74. (7") **TOO ROLLING STONED. / LADY LOVE**

— **BILL LORDAN** – drums (ex-SLY & THE FAMILY STONE) repl. REG to HUMMINGBIRD

Feb 75. (lp)(c) **FOR EARTH BELOW** [26] [5]
– Shame the devil / It's only money / Confessin' midnight / Fine day / Alethea / A tale untold / Gonna be more suspicious / For Earth below.

Mar 76. (lp)(c) **ROBIN TROWER LIVE (live)** [15] [10]
– Too rolling stoned / Daydream / Rock me baby / Lady love / I can't wait much

longer / Alethea / Little bit of sympathy.

Oct 76. (lp)(c) **LONG MISTY DAYS** 31 24
– Some rain falls / Long misty days / Hold me / Caledonia / Pride / Sailing / S.M.O. / I can't live without you / Messin' the blues.

Nov 76. (7") **CALEDONIA. / MESSIN' THE BLUES** 82

— added **RUSTEE ALLEN** – bass (ex-SLY & THE FAMILY STONE)

Sep 77. (lp)(c) **IN CITY DREAMS** 58 25
– Somebody calling / Sweet wine of love / Bluebird / Falling star / Further up the road / Smile / Little girl / Love's gonna bring you round / In city dreams. *(re-iss.1986)*

— added **PAULHINO DACOSTA** – percussion

Aug 78. (lp)(c) **CARAVAN TO MIDNIGHT** 37
– My love (burning love) / Caravan to midnight / I'm out to get you / Lost in love / Fool / It's for you / Birthday boy / King of the dance / Sail on.

Sep 78. (7"m-red) **IT'S FOR YOU. / MY LOVE (BURNING LOVE) / IN CITY DREAMS**

Jan 79. (7") **IT'S FOR YOU. / MY LOVE (BURNING LOVE)**

— reverted to trio of the mid-70's. (TROWER, DEWAR + LORDAN)

Jun 80. (7")(12") **VICTIMS OF THE FURY. / ONE IN A MILLION**

Jun 80. (lp)(c) **VICTIMS OF THE FURY** 61 34
– Jack and Jill / Roads to freedom / Victims of the fury / The ring / Only time / Into the flame / The shout / Madhouse / Ready for the taking / Fly low.

Aug 80. (7") **JACK AND JILL. / THE SHOUT**

BRUCE, LORDAN & TROWER

saw same line-up bar **JACK BRUCE** – vox, bass (ex-CREAM, ex-JOHN MAYALL'S BLUESBREAKERS, ex-Solo artist) repl. DEWAR

Feb 81. (lp)(c) **BLT** 37
– Into money / What it is / Won't let you down / No island lost / It's too late / Life on Earth / Once the bird has flown / Carmen / Feel the heat / End game.

Feb 81. (7") **WHAT IT IS. / INTO MONEY**

— trimmed to duo

BRUCE & TROWER

with drummer **REG ISADORE** (same label)

Jan 82. (lp)(c) **TRUCE**
– Gonna shut you down / Gone too far / Thin ice / The last train to the stars / Take good care of yourself / Fall in love / Fat gut / Shadows touching / Little boy lost.

ROBIN TROWER

went solo again, augmented by **DEWAR / DAVE BRONZE** – bass / **BOBBY CLOUTER + ALAN CLARKE** – drums

Sep 83. (lp)(c) **BACK IT UP**
– Back it up / River / Black to red / Benny dancer / Time is short / Islands / None but the brave / Captain midnight / Settling the score.

M.F.N. Passport

Jun 85. (lp)(c) **BEYOND THE MIST**
– The last time / Keeping a secret / The voice / Beyond the mist / Time is short / Back it up / Bridge of sighs.

— still retained **BRONZE,** and also with **DAVEY PATTISON** – vox (ex-GAMMA) / **PETE THOMPSON** – drums

P.R.T. GNP Cres..

Feb 87. (lp)(c)(cd) **PASSION** 100 Dec 86
– Caroline / Secret doors / If forever / Won't even think about you / Passion / No time / Night / Bad time / One more world.

— retained **PATTISON**

Atlantic Atlantic

Jun 88. (lp)(c)(cd) **TAKE WHAT YOU NEED** May 88
– Tear it up / Take what you need (from me) / Love attack / I want you home / Shattered / Over you / Careless / Second time / Love won't wait forever.

— now with **PATTISON** – vox / **JOHN REGAN** – bass / **AL FRITSCH + PEPPY CASTRO** – backing vocals / **BOBBY MAYO + MATT NOBLE** – keyboards / **TONY BEARD** – drums

Mar 90. (cd)(c)(lp) **IN THE LINE OF FIRE**
– Sea of love / Under the gun / Turn the volume up / Natural fact / If you really want to find love / Ev'rybody's watching you now / Isn't it time / (I would) Still be here for you / All that I want / (Let's) Turn this fight into a brawl / Climb above the rooftops.

— ROBIN then re-joined the reformed PROCOL HARUM in 1991.

— now w / **LIVINGSTONE BROWNE** – bass / **CLIVE MAYUYU** – drums

Demon Rykodisc

Nov 94. (cd)(c) **20th CENTURY BLUES**
– 20th century blues / Prisoner of love / Precious gift / Whisper up a storm / Extermination blues / Step into the dark / Rise up like the Sun / Secret place / Chase the bone / Promise you the stars / Don't lose faith in tomorrow / Reconsider baby.

– compilations, others, etc. –

Jul 87. Chrysalis; (d-lp)(c)(cd) **PORTFOLIO**
– Bridge of sighs / Too rolling stoned / For Earth below / Caravan to midnight / Day of the eagle / Shame the Devil / Fine day / Daydream (live) / Lady Love (live) / Alethea (live) / Caledonia (live) / Messin' the blues / Blue bird / Victims of fury / Madhouse / Into money / Gonna shut you down / Thin ice / Benny dancer. *(re-iss.cd+c Mar93)*

Aug 91. Castle; (cd)(c)(d-lp) **THE COLLECTION** -

Apr 92. Windsong; (cd)(c)(lp) **BBC RADIO 1 LIVE IN CONCERT (live)** -

May 94. Connoisseur; (cd) **ANTHOLOGY** -

TUBEWAY ARMY (see under ⇒ NUMAN, Gary)

Nik TURNER (see under ⇒ HAWKWIND)

TYRANNOSAURUS REX (see under ⇒ BOLAN, Marc)

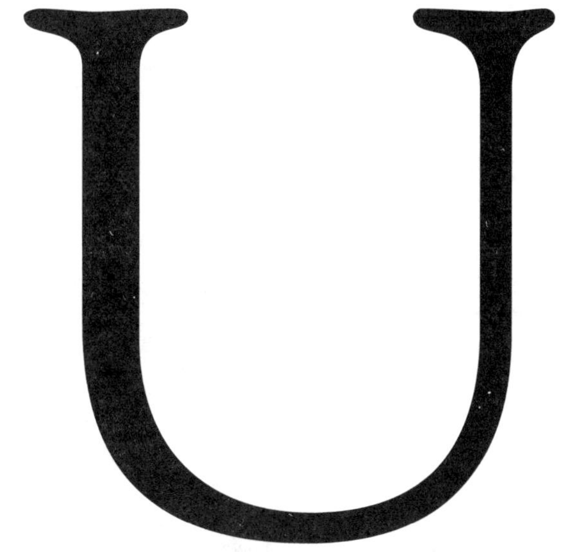

UFO

Formed: North London, England . . . 1969 briefly as HOCUS POCUS. Gained deal with 'Beacon' records and had exceptional success in Japan and Germany, before signing to 'Chrysalis' in 1974. In 1977, they had first taste of UK success, when the album LIGHTS OUT made it into Top 30. Went on to greater things throughout the late 70's and early 80's. • **Style:** Space rock heavy metal, who blew hot & cold during the tour of the decade into the 80s. • **Songwriters:** Mostly WAY / MOGG or CHAPMAN / MOGG, with both variations sometimes adding SCHENKER or CARTER, except C'MON EVERYBODY (Eddie Cochran) / ALONE AGAIN OR (Love) / and a few more. • **Trivia:** PHIL MOGG's nephew NIGEL MOGG plays in the band The QUIREBOYS.

Recommended: PHENOMENON (*6) / ANTHOLOGY (*7)

PHIL MOGG (b.1951) – vocals / **PETE WAY** – bass / **MICK BOLTON** – guitar / **ANDY PARKER** – drums

Beacon — Rare Earth

1970. (lp) **UFO** [ ] [ ]
– Unidentified flyig object / Boogie / C'mon everybody / Shake it about / Melinda / Timothy / Follow you home / Treacle people / Who do you love / Evito.

1971. (7") **COME AWAY MELINDA. / UNIDENTIFIED FLYING OBJECT** [ ] [-]

1971. (lp) **UFO 2 / FLYING** [ ] [ ]
– Silver bird / Star storm / Prince Kajaku / Coming of Prince Kajaku / Flying.

1971. (7") **BOOGIE FOR GEORGE. / TREACLE PEOPLE** [ ] [-]

1971. (7") **PRINCE KAJUKU. / THE COMING OF PRINCE KAJUKU** [ ] [-]

Nova — not issued

1972. (lp) **UFO: LIVE (live in Japan)** [-] [-] GERM.
– C'mon everybody / Who do you love / Loving cup / Prince Kajaku / The coming of Prince Kajaku / Boogie for George / Follow you home. *(UK-iss.1974 on 'Gema')*

— In 1972, they issued a few 45's in Japan, incl. 'C'MON EVERYBODY'.

— (Jun73) **MICHAEL SCHENKER** – guitar repl. BERNIE MARSDEN to WILD TURKEY. BERNIE had repl. (ex-BLODWYN PIG) LARRY WALLIS (Nov72) who had repl. BOLTON (Feb72). WALLIS went on to PINK FAIRIES.

Chrysalis — Chrysalis

Mar 74. (7") **DOCTOR DOCTOR. / LIPSTICK TRACES** [ ] [ ]

May 74. (lp)(c) **PHENOMENON** [ ] [ ]
– Too young to know / Crystal light / Doctor doctor / Space child / Rock bottom / Oh my / Time on my hands / Built for comfort / Lipstick traces / Queen of the deep. *(cd-iss.Oct91 on 'Episode')*

— Between mid'74-Jan75, they added **PAUL CHAPMAN** – guitar (ex-SKID ROW) Reverted to quartet when he joined LONE STAR.

Jul 75. (lp)(c) **FORCE IT** [ ] [71]
– Let it roll / Shoot shoot / High flyer / Love lost love / Out in the street / Mother Mary / Too much of nothing / Dance your life away / This kid's / Between the walls. *(re-iss.Jun84 on 'Fame')*

— (Sep75) added **DANNY PEYRONEL** – keyboards (ex-HEAVY METAL KIDS)

May 76. (lp)(c) **NO HEAVY PETTING** [ ] [ ]
– Natural thing / I'm a loser / Can you roll her / Belladonna / Reasons love / Highway lady / On with the action / A fool in love / Martian landscape.

— (Jul76) **PAUL RAYMOND** – keyboards, guitar (ex-SAVOY BROWN) repl. DANNY

Apr 77. (7") **ALONE AGAIN. / ELECTRIC PHASE** [ ] [ ]

May 77. (lp)(c) **LIGHTS OUT** [54] [23]
– Too hot to handle / Just another suicide / Try me / Lights out / Gettin' ready / Alone again or / Electric phase / Love to love. *(cd-iss.1987) (cd-re-iss.Jul91 on 'Episode')*

Jun 77. (7") **TOO HOT TO HANDLE. / ELECTRIC PHASE** [-] [ ]

Jun 78. (lp)(c) **OBSESSION** [26] [41]
– Only you can rock me / Pack it up (and go) / Arbory Hill / Ain't no baby / Lookin' out for No.1 / Hot 'n' ready / Cherry / You don't fool me / Lookin' out for No.1 (reprise) / One more for the rodeo / Born to lose.

Jul 78. (7")(7"red) **ONLY YOU CAN ROCK ME. / CHERRY / ROCK BOTTOM** [50] [ ]

Dec 78. (d-lp)(d-c) **STRANGERS IN THE NIGHT (live)** [8] [42]
– Natural thing / Out in the street / Only you can rock me / Doctor doctor / Mother Mary / This kid's / Love to love / Lights out / Rock bottom / Too hot to handle / I'm a loser / Let it roll / Shoot shoot. *(cd-iss.Sep91 & Mar94)*

Jan 79. (7") **DOCTOR DOCTOR (live). / ON WITH THE ACTION (live) / TRY ME (live)** [35] [ ]

Mar 79. (7")(7"clear) **SHOOT SHOOT (live). / ONLY YOU CAN ROCK ME (live) / I'M A LOSER (live)** [48] [ ]

— (Nov78) **PAUL CHAPMAN** – guitar returned to repl. SCHENKER who joined The SCORPIONS and later formed his own self-named group.

Jan 80. (7")(7"red) **YOUNG BLOOD. / LIGHTS OUT** [36] [ ]

Jan 80. (lp)(c) **NO PLACE TO RUN** [11] [51]
– Alpha Centauri / Lettin' go / Mystery train / This fire burns tonight / Gone in the night / Young blood / No place to run / Take it or leave it / Money money / Anyday.

— (Aug'80) **WAY, MOGG, CHAPMAN + PARKER** recruited **NEIL CARTER** – keyboards, guitar (ex-WILD HORSES) repl. PAUL RAYMOND who joined MICHAEL SCHENKER GROUP

Oct 80. (7")(7"colrd) **COULDN'T GET IT RIGHT. / HOT'N'READY** [ ] [ ]

Jan 81. (lp)(c) **THE WILD, THE WILLING & THE INNOCENT** [19] [77]
– Chains chains / Long gone / The wild, the willing & the innocent / It's killing me / Makin' moves / Lonely heart / Couldn't get it right / Profession of violence.

Jan 81. (7")(7"clear) **LONELY HEART. / LONG GONE** [41] [ ]

Jan 82. (7")(7"clear) **LET IT RAIN. / HEEL OF A STRANGER / YOU'LL GET LOVE** [62] [ ]

Feb 82. (lp)(c) **MECHANIX** [8] [82]
– The writer / Something else / Back into my life / You'll get love / Doing it all for you / We belong to the night / Let it rain / Terri / Feel it / Dreaming.

Apr 82. (7")(7"pic-d) **BACK INTO MY LIFE. / THE WRITER** [ ] [ ]

— (Jun82) on tour **BILLY SHEEHAN** – bass (ex-TALAS) repl. PETE WAY who formed FASTWAY and briefly joined OZZY OSBOURNE

Jan 83. (lp)(c) **MAKING CONTACT** [32] [ ]
– Blinded by a lie / Diesel in the dust / A fool for love / You and me / When it's time to rock / The way the wild wind blows / Call my name / All over you / No getaway / Push it's love.

Mar 83. (7")(7"pic-d) **WHEN IT'S TIME TO ROCK. / EVERYBODY KNOWS** [70] [ ]
(12"+=) – Push it's love.

— Disbanded when MOGG suffered a nervous breakdown on stage. He resurrected the band in 1984 with **PAUL RAYMOND / PAUL GRAY** – bass (ex-DAMNED) / **JIM SIMPSON** – drums(ex-MAGNUM) / **ATOMIK TOMMY M.** – guitar (b. Japan).

Oct 85. (7")(7"sha-pic-d) **THIS TIME. / THE CHASE** [ ] [ ]
(12"+=) – ('A'extended).

Nov 85. (lp)(c) **MISDEMEANOR** [74] [ ]
– This time / One heart / Night run / The only ones / Mean streets / Name of love / Blue / Dream the dream / Heaven's gate / Wreckless.

Feb 86. (7")(7"red) **NIGHT RUN. / HEAVEN'S GATE** [ ] [ ]
(12"+=) – ('A'extended).

— (late '86) **DAVID 'Jake' JACOBSON** – guitar (ex-ERIC MARTIN) repl. RAYMOND

FM Revolver — not issued

Mar 88. (lp)(c)(cd) **AIN'T MISBEHAVIN'** [ ] [-]
– Between a rock and a hard place / Another Saturday night / At war with the world / Hunger in the night / Easy money / Rock boyz, rock. *(cd+=)* – Lonely cities (of the heart).

— Disbanded Spring 1988. PHIL went into production mainly for his nephew NIGEL MOGG's new band QUIREBOYS.

— **MOGG & WAY** re-united **UFO** adding **LAURENCE ARCHER** – guitar (ex-GRAND SLAM) / **CLIVE EDWARDS** – drums (ex-WILD HORSES) / **JEM DAVIS** – keyboards

		Essential	Victory
Nov 91.	(12"ep)(cd-ep) **ONE OF THOSE NIGHTS. / AIN'T LIFE SWEET / LONG GONE**		-
Feb 92.	(cd)(c)(lp) **HIGH STAKES AND DANGEROUS MEN**		-

– Borderline / Primed for time / She's the one / Ain't life sweet / Don't want to lose you / Burnin' fire / Running up the highway / Back door man / One of those nights / Revolution / Love deadly love / Let the good times roll.

Feb 93. (cd)(c) **LIGHTS OUT OVER TOKYO LIVE (live)**

– Running up the highway / Borderline / Too hot to handle / She's the one / Cherry / Back door man / One of those nights / Love to love / Only you can rock me / Lights out / Doctor, doctor / Rock bottom / Shoot shoot / C'mon everybody.

– compilations, others, etc. –

1973. Decca; (d-lp) **UFO / FLYING** | | -
Dec 82. Chrysalis; (d-c) **MECHANIX / LIGHTS OUT** | | -
Aug 83. Chrysalis; (d-lp)(d-c) **HEADSTONE – THE BEST OF UFO** | 39 |

– Doctor doctor / Rock bottom / Fool for your loving / Shoot shoot / Too hot to handle / Only you can rock me / Love drive (SCORPIONS) / She said she said (LONE STAR) / Lights out / Armed and ready (MICHAEL SCHENKER GROUP) / Young blood / Criminal tendencies / Lonely heart / We belong to the night / Let it rain / Couldn't get it right / Electric phase / Doing it all for you.

Oct 92. Chrysalis; (cd) **ESSENTIAL** | | -
Nov 85. Castle; (d-lp)(d-c) **THE COLLECTION** | | -
Apr 87. Raw Power; (d-lp)(c)(cd) **ANTHOLOGY** | | -

– Rock bottom / Built for comfort / Highway lady / Can you roll her / Fool for love / Shoot shoot / Too hot to handle / Gettin' ready / Only you can rock me / Looking for number one / Hot'n'ready / Mystery train / No place to run / Profession and violence / Chains chains / Something else / Doing it for all of you / When it's time to rock / Diesel in the dust.

Apr 93. Repertoire; (cd) **THE DECCA YEARS** | | -
Mar 94. Music Club; (cd)(c) **TOO HOT TO HANDLE: THE BEST OF UFO** | | -
May 94. B.G.O.; (cd) **OBSESSION / NO PLACE TO RUN** | | -
Aug 94. B.G.O.; (cd) **NO HEAVY PETTING / LIGHTS OUT** | | -
Sep 94. B.G.O.; (cd) **THE WILD, THE WILLING AND THE INNOCENT / MECHANIX** | | -
Dec 94. B.G.O.; (cd) **PHENOMENOM / FORCE IT** | | -
Nov 94. M&M; (cd) **HEAVEN'S GATE LIVE (live)** | | -
May 95. Spectrum; (cd) **DOCTOR, DOCTOR** | | -

UGLY KID JOE

Formed: Isla Vista, North California, USA . . . 1989 by university students CRANE, EICHSTADT plus drummer MARK DAVIS. In 1991, they found the group name and signed to 'Mercury'. Their debut recording 'AS UGLY AS THEY WANNA BE' soon raced up the US billboard, helped by hit single 'EVERYTHING ABOUT YOU', which was used on 'Wayne's World' movie. • **Style:** Heavy rock/pop act, similar to a less serious MOTLEY CRUE or FAITH NO MORE. • **Songwriters:** Most by CRANE-EICHSTADT or group, except SIN CITY (Ac/Dc) / CATS IN THE CRADLE (Harry Chapin) / N.I.B. (Black Sabbath). • **Trivia:** CRANE had been a guitar technician for LOVE / HATE.

Recommended: AMERICA'S LEAST WANTED (*6).

Group: WHITFIELD CRANE – vocals / **KLAUS EICHSTADT** – guitar / **ROGER LAHR** – guitar /**CORDELL CROCKETT** – bass /**MARK DAVIS** – drums

		Mercury	Stardog
May 92.	(m-cd)(m-c)(m-lp) **AS UGLY AS THEY WANNA BE**	9	4 Feb 92

– Madman / Whiplash liquor / Too bad / Everything about you / Sweet leaf – funkyfresh country club / Heavy metal.

May 92. (7")(c-s) **EVERYTHING ABOUT YOU. / WHIPLASH LIQUOR** | 3 | 9 Mar 92

(12"+=)(cd-s+=) – Sin city.

Jul 92. (7")(c-s) **NEIGHBOR. / EVERYTHING ABOUT YOU (clean edit)** | 28 |

(12") – ('A'side) / Funky fresh country club.
(cd-s) – ('A'side) / Funky fresh country club / Cats in the cradle.

Sep 92. (cd)(c)(lp) **AMERICA'S LEAST WANTED** | 11 | 29

– Neighbor / Goddamn devil / Come tomorrow / Panhandlin' prince / Busy bee / Don't go / So damn cool / Same side / Cats in the cradle / I'll keep tryin' / Everything about you / Madman ('92 remix) / Mr. Recordman. *(will climb to No.27 in the US, early 1993) (re-iss.cd/c Apr95)*

Oct 92. (7")(c-s) **SO DAMN COOL. / NEIGHBOR** | 44 |

(cd-s+=) – Panhandlin' Prince.

Mar 93. (7")(c-s) **CAT'S IN THE CRADLE. / PANHANDLIN' PRINCE** | 7 | 6 Feb 93

(12"+=)(cd-s+=) – Whiplash liquer (live) / Neighbor (live).

Jun 93. (7")(c-s) **BUSY BEE. / CATS IN THE CRADLE (live)** | 39 |

(cd-s) – ('A'side) / Come together (live) / Don't go (live) / Everything about you (live).

— (Jun92) **DAVE FORTMAN** – guitar (ex-SUGARTOOTH) repl. LAHR

— (1994) **SHANNON LARKIN** – drums (ex-WRATHCHILD AMERICA, ex-SOULS AT ZERO) repl. DAVIS

— Nov94; WHITFIELD CRANE was credited on MOTORHEAD's single 'Born To Raise Hell' alongside ICE-T.

Jun 95. (cd)(c) **MESSAGE TO SOBRIETY** | 25 |

– Intro / God / Tomorrow's world / Clover / C.U.S.T. / Milkman's son / Suckerpath / Cloudy skies / Jesus rode a Harley / 10-10 / V.I.P. / Oompa / Candle song / Slower than nowhere.

Jun 95. (12") **MILKMAN'S SON. / CANDLE SONG (Dave - vocals) / TOMORROW'S WORLD** | 39 |

(cd-s) – (first 2 tracks) / So damn cool (live) / Neighbour (live).
(cd-s) – ('A'side) / Suckerpath (demo) / God (1994 version) / C.U.S.T. (demo).

ULTRAVOX

Formed: London, England..mid'76 after 3 years as TIGER LILY. Obtained deal with 'Island' records, who employed BRIAN ENO to produce their eponymous debut. In 1979, FOXX went solo and ULTRAVOX were without a contract until surprise replacement MIDGE URE revitalised them enough for 'Chrysalis' to give them chance. Broke the Top 30 the following year with SLEEPWALK, which paved the way for their classic VIENNA single to just miss top slot. In the early 80's, they became one of top UK bands with 7 Top 10 albums and a string of Top 30 hits. Remarkably the US surpassed them for other New Wave / British Invasion bands. • **Style:** Initially influenced by a mixture of flash-progressive ROXY MUSIC / DOCTORS OF MADNESS image/sound to new wave rock. By 1980, they had mellowed into more video-age electronic "new romantics". • **Songwriters:** FOXX and group until URE replaced FOXX. Covered only KING'S LEAD HAT (Brian Eno). MIDGE URE's solo career included NO REGRETS (Tom Rush / hit c. Walker Brothers) / THE MAN WHO SOLD THE WORLD (David Bowie) / STRANGE BREW (Cream). MIDGE also co-wrote tracks by VISAGE including hit FADE TO GREY. TIGER LILY 's first single was a strange cover of FATS WALLER's 'Ain't Misbehavin''. • **Trivia:** MIDGE URE once replaced GARY MOORE on THIN LIZZY's American tour for a couple of weeks summer '79!

Recommended: THREE INTO ONE (*8) / VIENNA (*7) / THE COLLECTION (*7).

TIGER LILY

DENNIS LEIGH (JOHN FOXX) – vocals / **STEVE SHEARS** – guitar / **BILLY CURRIE** (b. 1 Apr'52, Huddersfield, Yorkshire, England) – keyboards / **WARREN CANN** (b.20 May'52, Victoria, Canada) – drums / **CHRIS ST. JOHN** (b.14 Jul'52) – bass

		Gull	not issued
Mar 75.	(7") **AIN'T MISBEHAVIN'. / MONKEY JIVE**		-

— (w/drawn before release) *(iss.Oct77) (re-iss.Oct80 on 'Dead Good')*

ULTRAVOX!

LEIGH became **JOHN FOXX** and ST.JOHN now **CHRIS CROSS.** (CURRIE now added violin, synthesizers.)

		Island	Antilles
Feb 77.	(7") **DANGEROUS RHYTHM. / MY SEX**		-
Mar 77.	(lp)(c) **ULTRAVOX!**		-

– Saturday night in the city of the dead / Life at Rainbow End (for all the tax exiles on Main Street) / Slip away / I want to be a machine / Wide boys / Dangerous rhythm / The lonely hunter / The wild the beautiful and the damned / My sex.

May 77. (7") **YOUNG SAVAGE. / SLIPAWAY** | | -
Oct 77. (7") **ROCKWROK. / HIROSHIMA MON AMOUR** | | -

(all 3 ULTRAVOX! singles were re-iss.Jul81)

Oct 77. (lp)(c) **HA! HA! HA!** | | -

– Rockwrok / The frozen ones / Fear in the western world / Distant smile / The man who dies every day / Artificial life / While I'm still alive / Hiroshima mon amour. *(free-7"w.a.)*– **QUIRKS. / MODERN LOVE (live)**

Feb 78. (7"ep) **RETRO E.P. (live)** | | -

– The wild the beautiful and the damned / Young savage / My sex / The man who dies every day.

— **ROBIN SIMON** – guitar (ex-NEO) repl. SHEARS to COWBOYS INTERNATIONAL

Aug 78. (7")(12"violet) **SLOW MOTION. / DISLOCATION**
Sep 78. (lp)(c) **SYSTEMS OF ROMANCE**

– Slow motion / I can't stay long / Someone else's clothes / Blue light / Some of them / Quiet men / Dislocation / Maximum acceleration / When you walk through me / Just for a moment.

Oct 78. (7")(12"white) **QUIET MEN. / CROSS FADE**

— (Apr79) **MIDGE URE** (b.JAMES, 10 Oct'53, Cambuslang, Scotland) – vocals, guitar (ex-SLIK, ex-RICH KIDS, ex-THIN LIZZY, ex-VISAGE) repl. JOHN FOXX who went solo. ROBIN also departed to MAGAZINE. Now as ULTRAVOX, after dropping the exclamation mark!

Chrysalis Chrysalis

Jun 80. (7")(7"clear) **SLEEPWALK. / WAITING** 29

Sep 80. (7")(12")(7"clear) **PASSING STRANGERS. / SOUND ON SOUND** 57

Oct 80. (lp)(c) **VIENNA** 3
– Astradyne / New Europeans / Private lives / Passing strangers / Sleepwalk / Mr. X / Western promise / Vienna / All stood still. *(cd-iss.1985) (re-iss.cd Mar94 + Jul94)*

Jan 81. (7")(7"clear) **VIENNA. / PASSIONATE REPLY** 2
(12"+=) – Herr X.

Apr 81. (7")(7"clear) **PASSING STRANGERS. / FACE TO FACE** -
(12"+=) – King's lead hat.

May 81. (7")(7"clear) **ALL STOOD STILL. / ALLES KLAR** 8
(12"+=) – Keep talking.

Aug 81. (7")(12")(7"clear) **THE THIN WALL. / I NEVER WANTED TO BEGIN** 14

Sep 81. (lp)(c) **RAGE IN EDEN** 4
– The voice / We stand alone / Rage in Eden / I remember (death in the afternoon) / The thin wall / Stranger within / Accent on youth / The ascent / Your name has slipped my mind again. *(cd-iss.Jun87)*

Nov 81. (7")(7"clear) **THE VOICE. / PATHS AND ANGELS** 16
(12"+=)(12"clear+=) – All stood still (live) / Private lives (live).

Sep 82. (7")(12")(c-s)(7"clear) **REAP THE WILD WIND. / HOSANNA (IN EXCELIS DEO)** 12 71 Mar 83

Oct 82. (lp)(c)(cd)(pic-lp) **QUARTET** 6 61 Mar 83
– Reap the wild wind / Serenade / Mine for life / Hymn / Visions of blue / When the scream subsides / We came to dance / Cut and run / The song (we go).

Nov 82. (7")(7"clear) **HYMN. / MONUMENT** 11
(12"+=)(12"clear+=) – The thin wall.

Mar 83. (7")(7"clear)(7"pic-d) **VISIONS IN BLUE. / BREAK YOUR BACK** 15
(12"+=)(12"clear+=) – Reap the wild wind.

May 83. (7")(12")(7"pic-d)(7"clear)(12"clear) **WE CAME TO DANCE. / OVERLOOK** 18

Oct 83. (lp)(c) **MONUMENT – THE SOUNDTRACK (live)** 9
– Monument / Reap the wild wind / The voice / Vienna / Mine for life / Hymn.

Feb 84. (7")(12")(7"clear) **ONE SMALL DAY. / EASTERLY** 27

Apr 84. (lp)(c)(cd)(pic-lp) **LAMENT** 8
– White China / One small day * / Dancing with tears in my eyes / Lament * / Man of two worlds / Heart of the country / When the time comes / A friend I called Desire. *(c+cd+=)*– (tracks * remixed).

May 84. (7")(12")(7"clear) **DANCING WITH TEARS IN MY EYES. / BUILDING** 3

Jul 84. (7")(7"clear) **LAMENT. / HEART OF THE COUNTRY** 22
(12"+=) – ('A'instrumental).

Oct 84. (7")(12")(7"clear)(7"pic-d) **LOVE'S GREAT ADVENTURE. / WHITE CHINA** 12

Nov 84. (lp)(c)(cd) **THE COLLECTION** (compilation) 2
– Dancing with tears in my eyes / Hymn / The thin wall / The voice / Vienna / Passing strangers / Sleepwalk / Reap the wild wind / All stood still / Visions in blue / We came to dance / One small day / Love's great adventure / Lament. *(w/ free 12")*

—— guest **MARK BRZEZICKI** – drums (of BIG COUNTRY) repl. CANN to HELDEN

Sep 86. (7")(7"clear)(7"pic-d) **SAME OLD STORY. / 3** 31
(12")(12"clear) – ('A'side) / All in one day.

Oct 86. (lp)(c)(cd) **U-VOX** 9
– Same old story / Sweet surrender / Dream on / The prize / All fall down / Time to kill / Moon madness / Follow your heart / All in one day.

Nov 86. (7")(7"clear) **ALL FALL DOWN. / DREAM ON** 30
(12"+=) – ('A'version).

May 87. (7")(7"clear) **ALL IN ONE DAY. / THE PRIZE (live)**
(12"+=) – Stateless.

—— Disbanded 1987, although U-VOX was formed by BILLY CURRIE, ROBIN SIMON and MARCUS O'HIGGINS – vocals. They toured 1989 playing ULTRAVOX songs.

—— **TONY FENELLE** – vocals repl. MIDGE URE who was by now continuing solo.

D.S.B. not issued

May 93. (cd)(c)(lp) **REVELATION** -
– I am alive / Revelation / Systems of love / Perfecting the art of common ground / The great outdoors / The closer I get to you / No turning back / True believer / Unified / The new frontier.

Jun 93. (7")(c-s)(7"clear) **I AM ALIVE. / SYSTEMS OF LOVE**
(cd-s+=) – ('A'extended).

—— line-up: **CURRIE / BLUE / BURNS**

Resurgence not issued

Nov 95. (cd) **INGENUITY** -
– Ingenuity / There goes a beautiful world / Give it all back / Future picture forever / The silent cries / Distance / Ideals / Who'll save you / A way out, a way through / Majestic.

– compilations, others, etc. –

Jun 80. Island/ US= Antilles; (lp)(c) **THREE INTO ONE**
– Young savage / Rockwrok / Dangerous rhythm / The man who dies every day / The wild the beautiful and the damned / Slow motion / Just for a moment / My sex / Quiet men / Hiroshima mon amour. *(re-iss.Nov86, cd-iss.1990)*

Mar 81. Island; (12"ep)(12"clear-ep) **SLOW MOTION / DISLOCATION. / QUIET MEN / HIROSHIMA MON AMOUR** 33 -

Apr 88. Strange Fruit; (12"ep) **THE PEEL SESSIONS** (21.7.77) -
– My sex / Artificial life / Young savage.

Sep 93. Spectrum; (cd)(c) **SLOW MOTION** -

Aug 94. Chrysalis; (cd) **RARE VOLUME 2** -

Jun 95. Receiver; (cd) **FUTURE PICTURE** -

Aug 95. Old Gold; (cd-s) **VIENNA / REAP THE WILD WIND** -

Oct 95. MFP; (cd) **DANCING WITH TEARS IN MY EYES** -

Nov 95. Island; (3xcd-box) **ULTRAVOX! / HA! HA! HA! / SYSTEMS OF ROMANCE** -

MIDGE URE

had already started own solo career. Debut w / ex-COCKNEY REBEL **STEVE HARLEY** – dual vocals

Chrysalis Chrysalis

Mar 82. (7") **I CAN'T EVEN TOUCH YOU. / I CAN'T BE ANYONE** -

Jun 82. (7")(12") **NO REGRETS. / MOOD MUSIC** 9

Jul 83. (7")(12") **AFTER A FASHION ("MIDGE URE & MICK KARN"). / TEXTURES** 39 -

Above 45 on 'Musicfest' w / ex-JAPAN bassist

—— Dec'84 saw MIDGE co-write and create BAND AID with BOB GELDOF (BOOMTOWN RATS). They hit UK No.1 with famine relief single DO THEY KNOW IT'S CHRISTMAS.

Aug 85. (7")(7"clear) **IF I WAS. / PIANO** 1
(12"+=)(12"clear+=) – The man who sold the world.

Oct 85. (lp)(c)(cd) **THE GIFT** 2
– If I was / When the winds blow / Living in the past / That certain smile / The gift / Antilles / Wastelands / Edo / The chieftain / The gift (reprise). *(re-iss.cd+c Apr93)*

Nov 85. (7")(7"clear)(7"pic-d) **THAT CERTAIN SMILE. / THE GIFT** 28
(12"+=)(d12"+=)(12"clear+=) – ('A'instrumental) / Fade to grey.

Jan 86. (7")(7"clear) **WASTELANDS. / THE CHIEFTAIN** 46
(12"+=)(12"clear+=) – Dancer.

May 86. (7")(7"clear) **CALL OF THE WILD. / WHEN THE WIND BLOWS** 27
(12"+=)(12"clear+=) – After a fashion (w/ MICK KARN).

Aug 88. (7")(7"clear) **ANSWERS TO NOTHING. / HONORARE** 49
(12"+=)(12"clear+=) – Oboe.
(cd-s++=) – (excerpts from lp below).

Sep 88. (lp)(c)(cd) **ANSWERS TO NOTHING** 30 88
– Answers to nothing / Take me home / Sister and brother / Dear God / The leaving (so long) / Just for you / Hell to Heaven / Lied / Homeland / Remembrance day.

Nov 88. (7")(7"clear) **DEAR GOD. / MUSIC 1** 55 95
(12"+=) – All fall down (live) / Strange brew (live).
(cd-s+=) – Remembrance day.

—— In Apr'89, SISTERS AND BROTHERS single was withdrawn.

—— **URE** now with **MARK BRZEZICKI** – drums / **STEVE BRZEZICKI + JEREMY MEEHAN** – bass / **ROBBIE KILGORE** – keys / **SIMON PHILLIPS** – drums / **STEVE WILLIAMS** – perc./ etc

Arista Arista

Aug 91. (7")(c-s) **COLD COLD HEART. / FLOWERS** 17
(12"+=)(cd-s+=) – Supernatural *(written by GREEN; SCRITTI POLITTI)*

Sep 91. (cd)(c)(lp) **PURE** 36
– I see hope in the morning light / Cold, cold heart / Pure love / Sweet 'n' sensitive thing / Let it go? / Rising / Light in your eyes / Little one / Hands around my heart / Waiting days / Tumbling down.

Oct 91. (7")(c-s) **I SEE HOPE IN THE MORNING LIGHT. / THE MAN I USED TO BE**
(12"+=)(cd-s+=) – Madame de Sade.

. . . Jan – Jun '96 stop press . . .

May 96. (single) **BREATHE** 70

– (MIDGE URE & ULTRAVOX) compilations, etc. –

Jan 93. Chrysalis; (7")(c-s) **VIENNA. / WASTELANDS** 13
(cd-s+=) – Answers to nothing / The voice.
(cd-s) – ('A'side) / Call of the wild / One small day / Hymn.

Feb 93. Chrysalis; (cd)(c)(lp) **IF I WAS: THE VERY BEST OF MIDGE URE & ULTRAVOX** 10
– If I was / No regrets / Love's great adventure / Dear God / Cold cold heart / Vienna / Call of the wild / Dancing with tears in my eyes / All fall down / Yellow pearl / Fade to grey / Reap the wild wind / Answers to nothing / Do they know it's Christmas? (BAND AID). *(cd+=)* After a fashion (with MICK KARN) /

That certain smile.

Dec 82. Chrysalis; (d-c) **VIENNA / RAGE IN EDEN** [ ] [-]

Feb 87. Old Gold; (7") **VIENNA. / THE VOICE** [ ] [-]

Apr 87. Old Gold; (7") **DANCING WITH TEARS IN MY EYES. / REAP THE WILD WIND** *(12"-iss.Jan88)* [ ] [-]

UNDERTONES

Formed: Londonderry, N.Ireland . . . Nov'75 by the O'NEILL brothers, plus SHARKEY, BRADLEY and DOHERTY. In Aug'78, they released debut TEENAGE KICKS for Belfast label 'Good Vibrations'. Given airplay on DJ John Peel's night time radio one show, it was taken up by 'Sire' also nearly hitting Top 30. In 1979 to early 80's, they went on to have a number of UK hits and 3 Top 20 albums, with John Peel still their best-known fan. • **Style:** Intelligent new wave-pop that enthused energy and life into flagging power-pop/punk scene. In 1982, FEARGAL's quavering vocals and group's boy-next-door image had been shelved for a blend of "alternative-soul". This formula didn't work, and group drifted into other projects, both very different (see below). • **Songwriters:** O'NEILL brothers except UNDER THE BOARDWALK (Drifters). In the mid-80's, FEARGAL, solo, collaborated with DAVE STEWART of The EURYTHMICS. In 1991, he teamed up with writers SHERRILL and DiPIERO. Covered; A GOOD HEART (Maria McKee) / TAKE ME TO THE RIVER (Al Green). • **Trivia:** Band based their debut album cover on inspiration by The WHO's MY GENERATION single. • **Trivia:** In Feb'86, FEARGAL's mother and sister, while spending time in Londonderry, N.Ireland, were abducted by terrorists, but released after a number of hours.

Recommended: UNDERTONES (*9) / HYPNOTISED (*7) / CHER O'BOWLES (*9)

FEARGAL SHARKEY (b.13 Aug'58) – vocals / **DAMIEN O'NEILL** – guitar, bass / **JOHN O'NEILL** – guitar / **MIKE BRADLEY** – bass / **BILLY DOHERTY** – drums

Good Vibrations | not issued

Sep 78. (7"ep) **TEENAGE KICKS / TRUE CONFESSIONS. / SMARTER THAN U / EMMERGENCY CASES** [ ] [-]
(re-iss.Oct78 on 'Sire', hit No.31) (re-iss.Jul83 on 'Ardeck', hit 60) (re-iss.7"ep+cd-ep Apr94 on 'Dojo')

Sire | Sire

Jan 79. (7"m) **GET OVER YOU. / REALLY REALLY / SHE CAN ONLY SAY NO** [57] [ ]

Apr 79. (7")(7"lime green) **JIMMY JIMMY. / MARS BARS** [16] [ ]

May 79. (lp)(c) **THE UNDERTONES** [13] [ ] Jan 80
– Family entertainment / Girls don't like it / Male model / I gotta getta / Teenage kicks / Wrong way / Jump boys / Here comes the summer / Get over you / Billy's third / Jimmy Jimmy / True confessions / She's a runaround / I know a girl / Listening in. *(re-iss.Jul83 on 'Ardeck') (re-iss.+cd.Oct87 on 'Fame') (re-iss.cd+c May94 on 'Dojo', with 7 extra tracks)* – Smarter than u / Emergency cases / Top twenty / Really really / Mars Bars / She can only say no / One way love.

Jul 79. (7"m) **HERE COMES THE SUMMER. / ONE WAY LOVE / TOP TWENTY** [34] [ ]

Sep 79. (7") **YOU'VE GOT MY NUMBER (WHY DON'T YOU USE IT). / LET'S TALK ABOUT GIRLS** [32] [ ]

Mar 80. (7"m) **MY PERFECT COUSIN. / HARD LUCK / I DON'T WANNA SEE YOU AGAIN** [9] [ ]
(d7"+=) – Here comes the summer.

Apr 80. (lp)(c) **HYPNOTISED** [6] [ ]
– More songs about chocolate and girls / There goes Norman / Hypnotised / See that girl / Whizz kids / Under the boardwalk / The way girls talk / Hard luck / My perfect cousin / Boys will be boys / Tearproof / Wednesday week / Nine times out of ten / Girls that don't talk / What's with Terry?. *(re-iss.Mar86 on 'Fame') (re-iss.cd+c May94 on 'Dojo', with 5 extra tracks)* – You've got my number (why don't you use it?) / Hard luck (again) / Let's talk about girls / I told you so / I don't want to see you again.

Jun80. (7") **WEDNESDAY WEEK. / I TOLD YOU SO** [11] [ ]

Ardeck-EMI | Harvest

Apr 81. (7") **IT'S GOING TO HAPPEN. / FAIRLY IN THE MONEY NOW** [18] [ ]

May 81. (lp)(c) **THE POSITIVE TOUCH** [17] [ ]
– Fascination / Life's too easy / You're welcome / The positive touch / Julie Ocean / Crisis of mine / His good looking friend / When Saturday comes / It's going to happen / Sigh and explode / I don't know / Hannah Doot / Boy wonder / Forever Paradise. *(re-iss.1985) (re-iss.cd+c May94 on 'Dojo', with 4 extra tracks)* – Kiss in the dark / Beautiful friend / Life's too easy / Fairly in the money now.

Jul 81. (7") **JULIE OCEAN. / KISS IN THE DARK** [41] [ ]

Feb 82. (7") **BEAUTIFUL FRIEND. / LIFE'S TOO EASY** [ ] [-]

Jan 83. (7") **THE LOVE PARADE. / LIKE THAT** [ ] [-]
(12"+=) – You're welcome / Family entertainment / Crises of mine.

Mar 83. (7") **GOT TO HAVE YOU BACK. / TURNING BLUE** [ ] [-]
(12"+=) – Bye bye baby blue.

Mar 83. (lp)(c) **THE SIN OF PRIDE** [43] [-]
– Got to have you back / Valentine's treatment / Luxury / Love before romance / Untouchable / Bye bye baby blue / Conscious / Chain of love / Soul seven / The love parade / Save me / The sin of pride. *(re-iss.cd+c May94 on 'Dojo', with 6 extra tracks)* – Turning blue / Like that / Window shopping for new clothes / Bitter sweet / You stand so close (but you're never there) / I can only dream.

Apr 83. (7") **CHAIN OF LOVE. / WINDOW SHOPPING FOR NEW CLOTHES** [ ] [-]

—— Split mid'83 with FEARGAL SHARKEY joining The ASSEMBLY, before going solo. The O'NEILL brothers formed THAT PETROL EMOTION.

– compilations, others, etc. –

Nov 83. Ardeck-EMI; (d-lp)(c) **ALL WRAPPED UP** [67] [-]
– Teenage kicks / Get over you / Jimmy Jimmy / Here comes the summer / You've got my number (why don't you use it) / My perfect cousin / Wednesday week / It's going to happen / Julie Ocean / Beautiful friend / The love parade / Got to have you back / Chain of love.

—— (Note all singles were re-iss. on 'Ardeck-EMI')

May 86. Ardeck-EMI; (lp)(c)(cd) **CHER O'BOWLES – THE PICK OF THE UNDERTONES** [96] [-]
– Teenage kicks / True confessions / Get over you / Family entertainment / Jimmy Jimmy / Here comes the Summer / You got my number (why don't you use it) / My perfect cousin / See that girl / Tearproof / Wednesday week / It's going to happen / Julie Ocean / You're welcome / Forever Paradise / Beautiful friend / Save me / The love parade / Valentine's treatment / Love before romance. *(re-iss.+cd.Oct89 on 'Fame')*

Jun 86. Ardeck-EMI; (7") **SAVE ME. / TEARPROOF** [ ] [-]
(12"+=) – I know a girl.

Dec 86. Strange Fruit; (12"ep) **THE PEEL SESSIONS** (21.1.79) [ ] [-]
– Listening in / Family entertainment / Here comes the summer / Billy's third. *(cd-ep iss.Mar88)*

Dec 89. Strange Fruit; (lp)(c)(cd) **DOUBLE PEEL SESSIONS** [ ] [-]
(re-iss.cd Mar94 as 'THE PEEL SESSIONS ALBUM')

Sep 93. Castle; (cd)(c) **THE BEST OF THE UNDERTONES – TEENAGE KICKS** [45] [-]

Jul 95. Dojo; (cd-ep) **HERE COMES THE SUMMER / GET OVER YOU / JIMMY JIMMY / YOU'VE GOT MY NUMBER (WHY DON'T YOU USE IT)** [ ] [-]

Feargal SHARKEY

moved to California, but returned to London in 1989.

Zarjazz | not issued

Sep 84. (7")(12") **LISTEN TO YOUR FATHER. / CAN I SAY I LOVE YOU** [23] [-]

Virgin | A & M

Jun 85. (7")(12") **LOVING YOU. / IS THIS AN EXPLANATION** [26] [ ]

Sep 85. (7") **A GOOD HEART. / ANGER IS HOLY** [1] [74] Feb 86
(12"+=)/ /(cd-s+=) – Ghost train./ / ('A'original).

Nov 85. (lp)(c)(cd) **FEARGAL SHARKEY** [7] [75] Feb 86
– A good heart / You little thief / Ghost train / Ashes and diamonds / Made to measure / Someone to somebody / Don't leave it to nature / Love and hate / Bitter man / It's all over now. *(re-iss.Jun88)*

Dec 85. (7")(12") **YOU LITTLE THIEF. / THE LIVING ACTOR** [5] [ ]

Mar 86. (7")(12") **SOMEONE TO SOMEBODY. / COLD WATER** [64] [ ]

Virgin | Virgin

Jan 88. (7") **MORE LOVE. / A BREATH OF SCANDAL** [44] [ ]
(12"+=)/ /(cd-s+=) – ('A'piano version)./ / Good heart (original).

Mar 88. (lp)(c)(cd) **WISH** [ ] [ ]
– Cold, cold streets / More love / Full confession / Please don't believe in me / Out of my system / Strangest girl in Paradise / Let me be / Blue days / If this is love / Safe to touch.

Mar 88. (7") **OUT OF MY SYSTEM. / A TOUCH OF BLUE** [ ] [ ]
(12"+=) – ('A'version) / ('A'dub version).
(cd-s++=) – Blue days.

Sep 88. (7") **IF THIS IS LOVE. / A TOUCH OF BLUE** [-] [ ]

Feb 91. (7")(c-s) **I'VE GOT NEWS FOR YOU. / I CAN'T BEGIN TO STOP** [12] [ ]
(12") – ('A'side) / Loving you / A good heart / You little thief (remixes).
(cd-s+=) – Medley:- Don't leave it to nature – Take me to the river.

Apr 91. (cd)(c)(lp) **SONGS FROM THE MARDI GRAS** [27] [ ]
– After the Mardi Gras / One night in Hollywood / Miss you fever / Women and I / I've got news for you / To miss someone / Sister Rosa / I'll take it back / Cry like a rainy day / She moved through the fair.

May 91. (7")(c-s) **WOMEN AND I. / I'LL TAKE IT BACK (live)** [ ] [ ]
(12"+=)/ /(cd-s+=) – ('A'piano version)./ / Never never (ASSEMBLY).
(cd-s+=) – (2-'A'versions pt.1 & 2) / ('A'demo).

Aug 91. (7")(c-s) **TO MISS SOMEONE. / I'LL TAKE IT BACK** [ ] [ ]
(cd-s+=) – Never never (ASSEMBLY) / Miss you fever (instrumental)

(cd-s+=) – Never never (ASSEMBLY) / Women and I (piano version).

— In May93, FEARGAL appeared on PEACE TOGETHER single 'BE STILL' alongside SINEAD O'CONNOR, PETER GABRIEL & NANCI GRIFFITH.

– compilations, others, etc. –

1988. Virgin; (3"cd-ep) **YOU LITTLE THIEF / MORE LOVE / LISTEN TO YOUR FATHER** [ ] [-]

UNDERWORLD

Formed: Romford, London, England . . . 1987 by RICK, KARL, ALFIE, BRYN who had all been in Cardiff outfit FREUR (which was actually a symbol translated into a word!; no PRINCE wasn't the first!). Even before this, RICK and KARL had played in synth-pop band The SCREEN GEMS. In 1987, they were now the more conventional UNDERWORLD and hit America in the late 80's after signing for Seymour Stein's 'Sire' records. After a No.1 smash 'RADAR' in Australia, they toured the States supporting EURYTHMICS, but it was clear this was not the direction for them. Came to light once again, when newcomer DJ DARREN EMERSON was added to exploit new sounds for well-received early '94 album 'DUBNOBASS . . .'. • **Style:** Techno ambient dance /rock similar to The BELOVED with more visionary hypnobeat experiments. • **Songwriters:** SMITH / HYDE / THOMAS then SMITH / HYDE / EMERSON. • **Trivia:** Produced by RUPERT HINES in 1988. HYDE worked on a 1991 'Paisley P.' album with TERRI NUNN (ex-Berlin). GEOFF DUGMORE (ex-ART OF NOISE) was a guest on 1989 album. Also appeared on WILLIAM ORBIT's 'Watch From A Vine Leaf' & ORBITAL's 'Lush 3' and remixed BJORK's 'Human Behaviour'.

Recommended: DUBNOBASS . . . (*8) / SECOND TOUGHEST IN THE INFANTS (*9)

FREUR

RICK SMITH – keyboards, vocals / **KARL HYDE** – vocals, guitar / **ALFIE THOMAS** – guitar, vocals / **JOHN WARWICKER LE BRETON** – synthesizers / **BRYN B. BURROWS** – drums

C.B.S. Epic

Mar 83. (7"clear-pic-d)(ext-12") **DOOT DOOT. / HOLD ME MOTHER** [59] [ ]
(re-iss.Jan84)

Jun 83. (7")(7"pic-d) **MATTERS OF THE HEART. / YOU'RE A HOOVER** [ ] [ ]
(12"+=) – ('A'extended).

Sep 83. (7")(12") **RUNAWAY. / YOU'RE A HOOVER** [ ] [ ]

Nov 83. (lp)(c) **DOOT DOOT** [ ] [ ]
– Doot doot / Runaway / Riders in the night / Theme from the film of the same name / Tender surrender / Matters of the heart / My room / Steam machine / Whispering / All too much.

Apr 84. (7") **RIDERS IN THE NIGHT. / INNOCENCE** [ ] [ ]
(12"+=) – This is the way I like to live my life.

— added **JAKE BOWIE** – bass

Oct 84. (7") **DEVIL AND DARKNESS. / JAZZ 'N' KING** [ ] [ ]
(12"+=) – Devil and darkness.

Feb 85. (7") **LOOKING BACK FOR ANSWERS. / HEY HO AWAY WE GO** [ ] [ ]
(12"+=) – Uncle Jeff.

Feb 85. (lp)(c)(cd) **GET US OUT OF HERE** [ ] [ ]
– Look in the back for answers / Emeralds and pearls / Kiss me / A.O.K.O. / The Devil and darkness / The piano song / Happiness / Endless groove / This is the way I'd like to live my life / Bella Donna.

UNDERWORLD

BAZ ALLEN – bass repl. JOHN

Sire Sire

Mar 88. (lp)(c)(cd) **UNDERNEATH THE RADAR** [ ] [ ]
– Glory! glory! / Call me No.1 / Rubber ball (space kitchen) / Show some emotion / Underneath the radar / Miracle party / I need a doctor / Bright white flame / Pray / The God song.

Jul 88. (7") **UNDERNEATH THE RADAR. / BIG RED X** [ ] [74] Apr 88
(12"+=) – ('A'dub version).

Aug 88. (7") **SHOW SOME EMOTION. / SHOCK THE DOCTOR** [-] [ ]

— **PASCAL CONSOLI** – percussion, drums repl. BURROWS who joined WORLD-WIDE ELECTRIC

Aug 89. (7")(c-s) **STAND UP. / OUTSKIRTS** [ ] [67]
(12") – Stand up (and dance) / Stand up (ya house) / Outskirts.
(cd-s) – (all mixes & B-side)

Sep 89. (lp)(c)(cd) **CHANGE THE WEATHER** [ ] [ ]
– Change the weather / Stand up / Fever / Original song / Mercy / Mr.Universe / Texas / Thrash / Sole survivor / Beach.

Nov 89. (7") **CHANGE THE WEATHER. / TEXAS** [-] [ ]

— ALLEN + CONSOLI became D-INFLUENCE

LEMON INTERRUPT

— **SMITH + HYDE** brought in **DARREN EMERSON** (b.1970, Essex) – keyboards

Junior Boy not issued

Nov 91. (12") **BIG MOUTH. / DIRTY** [ ] [-]

UNDERWORLD

LEMON INTERRUPT line-up

Junior Boy Sire

Dec 92. (12"ep)(cd-ep) **DIRTY DIRTY GUITAR** [ ] [-]

Feb 93. (12"ep)(cd-ep) **REZ. / WHY WHY WHY** [ ] [-]

Jul 93. (12"ep)(cd-ep) **MMM . . .SKYSCRAPER I LOVE YOU. / ('A'-Telegraph mix 6.11.92) / ('A'-Jamscraper mix)** [ ] [ ]

Sep 93. (12")(cd-s) **REZ. / COWGIRL** [ ] [ ]
(re-iss.Aug95)

Dec 93. (12")(cd-s) **SPIKEE. / DOGMAN GO WOOF** [60] [ ]

Feb 94. (cd)(c)(d-lp) **DUBNOBASSWITHMYHEADMAN** [12] [ ]
– Dark and long / Mmm skyscraper I love you / Surfboy / Spoonman / Tongue / Dirty epic / Cowgirl / River of bass / ME.

Jun 94. (cd-ep) **DARK & LONG (mixes)** [57] [ ]
– Hall's mix / Dark train / Most 'ospitable / 215 miles.
(12") – ('A'-spoon deep mix) / ('A'-thing in a back mix).
(12") – ('A'-dark train mix) / ('A'-Burt's mix).

May 95. (12") **BORN SLIPPY (telenatic). / COWGIRL (Vinjer mix)** [52] [ ]
(12") – ('A'side) / ('A'-Nuxx mix).
(cd-s) – (above 2) / ('A'side again).

. . . Jan – Jun '96 stop press . . .

Mar 96. (cd)(c)(d-lp) **SECOND TOUGHEST IN THE INFANTS** [9] [ ]

May 96. (single) **PEARL'S GIRL** [24] [ ]

— About to hit Top 3 with re-release of 'BORN SLIPPY' due to it's use in the film 'Trainspotting' (cult book by Scotsman Irvine Welsh).

Midge URE (see under ⇒ ULTRAVOX)

URGE OVERKILL

Formed: Chicago, Illinois, USA . . .1986 by NASH KATO and BLACKIE ONASSIS. After one uneventful ep, they moved onto 'Touch & Go', where they released debut lp 'JESUS URGE SUPERSTAR'. In 1993 they signed to 'Geffen', which helped boost sales of that years' album 'SATURATION'. • **Style:** Hard imaginative punk rock, that harboured on the outlandish and freaky side of grunge scene. • **Trivia:** Cult film director Quentin Tarrantino used their version of NEIL DIAMOND's 'GIRL' on his materwork 'Pulp Fiction'. • **Songwriters:** Group except; WICHITA LINEMAN (Jimmy Webb) / GIRL YOU'LL BE A WOMAN SOON (Neil Diamond).

Recommended: STULL (*7) / EXIT THE DRAGON (*8)

NATIONAL 'Nash' KATO – vocals, guitar / **EDDIE 'King' ROESER** – bass / **BLACKIE 'Black Caesar' ONASSIS** – vocals, drums

not issued own label

1988. (12"ep) **STRANGE, I . . .** [-] [ ]

Touch & Go Touch & Go

May 89. (lp) **JESUS URGE SUPERSTAR** [ ] [ ]
– God Flintstone / Very sad trousers / Your friend is insane / Dump dump dump / Last train to Heaven / The Polaroid doll / Head on / Crown of laffs / Dubbledead / Easter '88 / Wichita lineman / Eggs.

Jun 90. (cd)(c)(lp) **AMERICRUISER** [ ] [ ]
– Ticket to L.A. / Blow chopper / 76 ball / Empire builder / Faroutski / Viceroyce / Out on the airstrip / Smokehouse. (cd+=) – JESUS URGE SUPERSTAR

Mar 91. (cd)(c)(lp) **THE SUPERSONIC STORYBOOK** [ ] [ ]
– The kids are insane / The candidate / (Today is) Blackie's birthday / Emmaline / Bionic revolution / What is artane? / Vacation in Tokyo / Henhough: The greatest story ever told / Theme from Navajo.

Roughneck Roughneck

Jun 92. (m-cd)(m-lp) **STULL** [ ] [ ]
– Girl you'll be a woman soon / Stull (part 1) / Stitches / What's this generation coming to / (Now that's) The barclouds / Goodbye to Guyville. *(re-iss.cd Mar95 on 'Fire')*

Geffen Geffen

Jun 93. (cd)(c) **SATURATION** [ ] [ ]
– Sister Havana / Tequilla sundae / Positive bleeding / Back on me / Woman 2 woman / Bottle of fur / Crackbabies / The stalker / Dropout / Erica Kane / Nite and grey / Heaven 90210.
(cd+=) – Operation: Kissinger.
Aug 93. (7")(c-s) **SISTER HAVANA. / WOMAN 2 WOMAN** [67] [ ]
(12"+=)(cd-s+=) – Operation: Kissinger.
Oct 93. (7")(c-s) **POSITIVE BLEEDING. / NITE AND GREY** [61] [ ]
(12"+=)(cd-s+=) – Quality love (Hong Kong demo).

— below from the cult Quentin Tarantino film 'Pulp Fiction' on 'M.C.A.' records.

Nov 94. (7") **GIRL YOU'LL BE A WOMAN SOON. / You Never Can Tell (by 'CHUCK BERRY')** [37] [59]
(c-s+=)(cd-s+=) – Dropout / (Bustin' Surfboards; by The TORNADOS).
Aug 95. (cd)(c) **EXIT THE DRAGON** [ ] [ ]
– Jaywalkin' / The break / Need some air / Somebody else's body / Honesty files / This is no place / The mistake / Take me / View of the rain / Last night – Tomorrow / Tin foil / Monopoly / And you'll say / Digital black epilogue.

URIAH HEEP

Formed: London, England ... 1968 as SPICE by BYRON and BOX. After one single for 'United Art', they brought in HENSLEY and became URIAH HEEP (taking the name from a Charles Dickens character in the 'David Copperfield' novel). Signed to the same label (Vertigo) as BLACK SABBATH, they unleashed debut lp in 1970 'VERY 'EAVY, VERY 'UMBLE'. By the mid-70's, they had had loads of album hits on both sides of the water. This confounded the critics, who panned them at every opportunity. • **Style:** Heavy-metal trailblazers, fronted by the near operative vox of DAVID BYRON, who has since been ripped off by many 80's styled hard rock outfits. • **Songwriters:** Majority by HENSLEY or BOX/THAIN. In 1976 all members took share of work. Covered; COME AWAY MELINDA (Tim Rose) / Live Rock'n'Roll Medley:- ROLL OVER BEETHOVEN (Chuck Berry) – BLUE SUEDE SHOES (Carl Perkins) – MEAN WOMAN BLUES + HOUND DOG (Elvis Presley) – AT THE HOP (Danny & The Juniors) – WHOLE LOTTA SHAKIN' GOIN' ON (Jerry Lee Lewis) / HOLD YOUR HEAD UP (Argent). • **Trivia:** In 1987, they were first heavy-rock outfit to play USSR.

Recommended: THE COLLECTION (*8). / URIAH HEEP LIVE (*8)

DAVID BYRON (b.29 Jan'47, Essex, England) – vocals / **MICK BOX** (b. 8 Jun'47, London, England) – guitar, vocals / **ROY SHARLAND** – organ / **PAUL NEWTON** – bass, vocals / **ALEX NAPIER** – drums

SPICE

United Art not issued

Dec 68. (7") **WHAT ABOUT THE MUSIC. / IN LOVE** [ ] [-]

URIAH HEEP

without SHARLAND who joined ARTHUR BROWN, etc. / added **KEN HENSLEY** (b.24 Aug'45) – keys, guitar, vox (ex-GODS, ex-TOE FAT) / **NIGEL OLSSON** – drums (ex-SPENCER DAVIS GROUP, ex-PLASTIC PENNY) repl. NAPIER (on all lp except 2 tracks)

Vertigo Mercury

Jun 70. (lp)(c) **VERY 'EAVY VERY 'UMBLE** (US-title 'URIAH HEEP') [ ] [ ]
– Gypsy / Real turned on / Come away Melinda / Lucy's blues / Dreammare / Walking in your shadow / I'll keep on trying / Wake up (set your sights). *(re-iss.1971 & Apr77 on 'Bronze') (re-iss.Apr86 on 'Castle', cd-iss.Dec90)*
Jul 70. (7") **GYPSY. / REAL TURNED ON** [-] [ ]
Nov 70. (7") **COME AWAY MELINDA. / WAKE UP (SET YOUR SIGHTS)** [-] [ ]

— **KEITH BAKER** – drums (ex-BAKERLOO) repl. OLSSON who joined ELTON JOHN

Jan 71. (7") **HIGH PRIESTESS. /** [-] [ ]
Jan 71. (lp)(c) **SALISBURY** [ ] [ ]
– Bird of prey * / The park / Time to live / Lady in black / High Priestess / Salisbury. *(US copies repl. * with)*– Simon the bullet freak. *(re-iss.1971 & Jul77 on 'Bronze') (re-iss.+cd Apr86 on 'Castle')*
Mar 71. (7") **LADY IN BLACK. / SIMON THE BULLET FREAK** [ ] [-]

— **IAN CLARKE** – drums (ex-CRESSIDA) repl. BAKER; guest **MANFRED MANN** – moog synthesizer / keyboards

Bronze Mercury

Nov 71. (lp)(c) **LOOK AT YOURSELF** [39] [93] Sep 71
– Look at yourself / I wanna be free / July morning / Tears in my eyes / Shadows of grief / What should be done / Love machine. *(re-iss.1977) (re-iss.+cd.Apr86 on 'Castle')*
Dec 71. (7") **LOVE MACHINE. / SIMON THE BULLET FREAK** [ ] [ ]
Dec 71. (7") **LOVE MACHINE. / LOOK AT YOURSELF** [-] [ ]
Feb 72. (7") **I WANNA BE FREE. / WHAT SHOULD BE DONE** [-] [ ]

— (Nov71) **LEE KERSLAKE** – drums, vocals (ex-GODS, ex-TOE FAT) repl. IAN (Feb'72) / **GARY THAIN** (b. New Zealand) – bass, vocals (ex-KEEF HARTLEY) repl. MARK CLARKE (ex-COLOSSEUM to TEMPEST) who had repl. NEWTON (Nov71)

May 72. (lp)(c) **DEMONS AND WIZARDS** [20] [23]
– The wizard / Traveller in time / Easy livin' / Poet's justice / Circle of hands / Rainbow demon / All my life / Paradise / The spell. *(re-iss.Apr77) (re-iss.+cd.Apr86 on 'Castle')*
Jun 72. (7") **THE WIZARD. / GYPSY** [ ] [-]
Jun 72. (7") **THE WIZARD. / WHY** [-] [ ]
Jul 72. (7") **EASY LIVIN' / ALL MY LIFE** [-] [ ]
Aug 72. (7") **EASY LIVIN'. / WHY** [ ] [-]
Nov 72. (lp)(c) **THE MAGICIAN'S BIRTHDAY** [28] [31]
– Sunrise / Spider woman / Blind eye / Echoes in the dark / Rain / Sweet Lorraine / Tales / The magician's birthday. *(re-iss.Apr77) (re-iss.+cd.Apr86 on 'Castle')*
Jan 73. (7") **BLIND EYE. / SWEET LORRAINE** [ ] [97] [91]
May 73. (d-lp)(d-c) **URIAH HEEP LIVE (live)** [23] [37]
– Sunrise / Sweet Lorraine / Traveller in time / Easy livin' / July morning / Tears in my eyes / Gypsy / Circle of hands / Look at yourself / The magician's birthday / Love machine / Rock'n'roll medley:- Roll over Beethoven – Blue suede shoes – Mean woman blues – Hound dog – At the hop – Whole lotta shakin' goin' on. *(re-iss.Apr77)*

Bronze Warners

May 73. (7") **JULY MORNING (live). / TEARS IN MY EYES (live)** [-] [ ]
Sep 73. (lp)(c) **SWEET FREEDOM** [18] [33]
– Dreamer / Stealin' / One day / Sweet freedom / If I had the time / Seven stars / Circus / Pilgrim. *(re-iss.Apr77)*
May 74. (7") **STEALIN'. / SUNSHINE** [ ] [91] Oct 73
Jun 74. (lp)(c) **WONDERWORLD** [23] [38]
– Wonderworld / Suicidal man / The shadows and the winds / So tired / The easy road / Something or nothing / I won't mind / We got we / Dreams. *(re-iss.Apr77)*
Aug 74. (7") **SOMETHING OR NOTHING. / WHAT CAN I DO** [ ] [ ]

— **JOHN WETTON** – bass, vocals (ex-KING CRIMSON, ex-ROXY MUSIC, ex-FAMILY) repl. THAIN (He died of a drug overdose 19 May'76) Line-up now **BYRON, BOX, HENSLEY, KERSLAKE & WETTON**

Jun 75. (lp)(c) **RETURN TO FANTASY** [7] [85]
– Return to fantasy / Shady lady / Devil's daughter / Beautiful dream / Prima Donna / Your turn to remember / Showdown / Why did you go / A year or a day. *(re-iss.Apr77)*
Jun 75. (7") **PRIMA DONNA. / SHOUT IT OUT** [ ] [ ]
Jun 75. (7") **PRIMA DONNA. / STEALIN'** [-] [ ]
Nov 75. (lp)(c) **THE BEST OF URIAH HEEP** (compilation) [ ] [ ]
– Gypsy / Bird of prey / July morning / Look at yourself / Easy livin' / The wizard / Sweet Lorraine / Stealin' / Lady in black / Return to fantasy. *(re-iss.Apr77) (re-iss.+cd+=.Apr90 on 'Sequel')*
May 76. (lp)(c) **HIGH AND MIGHTY** [55] [ ]
– One way or another / Weep in silence / Misty eyes / Midnight / Can't keep a good band down / Woman of the world / Footprints in the snow / Can't stop singing / Make a little love / Confession. *(re-iss.Apr77) (re-iss.+cd.Mar91 on 'Castle')*
Jun 76. (7") **ONE WAY OR ANOTHER. / MISTY EYES** [ ] [ ]

— **JOHN LAWTON** – vocals (ex-LUCIFER'S FRIEND) repl. BYRON to ROUGH DIAMOND / **TREVOR BOLDER** – bass (ex-David Bowie's SPIDERS FROM MARS, ex-WISHBONE ASH) repl. WETTON who joined BRYAN FERRY BAND, and later UK and ASIA

Feb 77. (lp)(c) **FIREFLY** [ ] [ ]
– The hanging tree / Been away too long / Who needs me / Wise man / Do you know / Rollin' on / Sympathy / Firefly. *(re-iss.+cd.Mar91 on 'Castle')*
Apr 77. (7") **WISE MAN. / CRIME OF PASSION** [ ] [ ]
Oct 77. (7") **FREE ME. / MASQUERADE** [ ] [ ]
Nov 77. (lp)(c) **INNOCENT VICTIM** [ ] [ ]
– Keep on ridin' / Flyin' high / Roller / Free 'n' easy / Illusion / Free me / Cheat 'n' lie / The dance / Choices.

Bronze Chrysalis

Sep 78. (lp)(c) **FALLEN ANGEL** [ ] [ ]
– Woman of the night / Falling in love / One more night / Put your lovin' on me / Come back to me / Whad'ya say / Save it / Love or nothing / I'm alive / Fallen angel. *(cd-iss.Feb91 on 'Castle')*
Oct 78. (7") **COME BACK TO ME. / CHEATER** [ ] [ ]

— **JOHN SLOMAN** – vocals (ex-LONE STAR) repl. LAWTON / **CHRIS SLADE** – drums (ex-MANFRED MANN'S EARTH BAND) repl. LEE to OZZY OSBOURNE

Jan 80. (7") **CARRY ON. / BEING HURT** [ ] [-]
Feb 80. (lp)(c) **CONQUEST** [ ] [ ]
– No return / Imagination / Feelings / Fools / Carry on / Won't have to wait too long / Out on the street / It ain't easy.
Jun 80. (7") **LOVE STEALER. / NO RETURN** [ ] [ ]

— **GREGG DETCHETT** – keyboards (ex-PULSAR) repl. HENSLEY to solo & BLACKFOOT

Jan 81. (7") **THINK IT OVER. / MY JOANNA NEEDS TUNING** [ ] [-]

— Split 1981 when SLOMAN developed throat infection. Later formed BADLANDS. CHRIS SLADE joined GARY NUMAN then DAVID GILMOUR. He later joined The FIRM. DETCHETT later joined MIKE + THE MECHANICS. BOLDER re-joined WISHBONE ASH. Early 1982, URIAH HEEP re-formed with **BOX** bringing back **LEE KERSLAKE** plus new **PETE GOALBY** – vocals (ex-TRAPEZE) / **JOHN SINCLAIR** – keys (ex-HEAVY METAL KIDS) / **BOB DAISLEY** – bass (ex-OZZY OSBOURNE, ex-RAINBOW, ex-WIDOWMAKER, etc.)

Bronze Mercury

Feb 82. (7"ep) **THE ABOMINATOR JUNIOR EP** [ ] [-]
– On the rebound / Tin soldier / Song of a bitch.

Mar 82. (lp)(c) **ABOMINOG** [34] [56]
– Too scared too run / Chasing shadows / On the rebound / Hot night in a cold town / Running all night (with the lion) / That's the way that it is / Prisoner / Hot persuasion / Sell your soul / Think it over. *(re-iss.+cd.Apr86 on 'Castle')*

May 82. (7") **THAT'S THE WAY THAT IT IS. / HOT PERSUASION** [ ] [-]

May 82. (7") **THAT'S THE WAY THAT IT IS. / SON OF A BITCH** [-] [ ]

May 83. (lp)(c) **HEAD FIRST** [46] [ ]
– The other side of midnight / Stay on top / Lonely nights / Sweet talk / Love is blind / Roll-overture / Red lights / Rollin' the rock / Straight through the heart / Weekend warriors.

Jun 83. (7")(7"pic-d) **LONELY NIGHTS. / WEEKEND WARRIORS** [ ] [-]

Aug 83. (7") **STAY ON TOP. / PLAYING FOR TIME** [ ] [-]
(d7"+=)(12"+=) – Gypsy / Easy livin' / Sweet Lorraine / Stealin'.

— **TREVOR BOLDER** – bass returned to repl. DAISLEY

Portrait Portrait

Mar 85. (7")(7"sha-pic-d) **ROCKERAMA. / BACK STAGE GIRL** [ ] [ ]

Mar 85. (lp)(c) **EQUATOR** [79] [ ]
– Rockerama / Bad blood / Lost one love / Angel / Holding on / Party time / Poor little rich girl / Skool's burnin' / Heartache city / Night of the wolf.

May 85. (7")(7"pic-d) **POOR LITTLE RICH GIRL. / BAD BLOOD** [ ] [-]

— **BERNIE SHAW** – vocals (ex-GRAND PRIX, ex-PRAYING MANTIS) repl. GOALBY / **PHIL LANZON** – keyboards (ex-GRAND PRIX, etc) repl. SINCLAIR (above 2 now alongside **BOX, BOLDER, KERSLAKE)**

Legacy not issued

Jul 88. (lp)(c)(cd) **LIVE IN MOSCOW (live)** [ ] [-]
– Bird of prey / Stealin' / Too scared to run / Corrina / Mister Majestic / The wizard / July morning / Easy livin' / That's the way that it is / Pacific highway. *(cd+=)*– Gypsy.

Sep 88. (7") **EASY LIVIN' (live). / CORRINA (live)** [ ] [-]
(12"+=)(12"red+=) – Gypsy (live).

Apr 89. (7") **HOLD YOUR HEAD UP. / MIRACLE CHILD** [ ] [-]
(12"+=) – ('A'extended).

Apr 89. (lp)(c)(cd)(pic-lp) **THE RAGING SILENCE** [ ] [-]
– Hold your head up / Blood red roses / Voice on my TV / Rich kid / Cry freedom / Bad bad man / More fool you / When the war is over / Lifeline / Rough justice.

Jul 89. (7") **BLOOD RED ROSES. / ROUGH JUSTICE** [ ] [-]
(12"+=) – Look at yourself.

Feb 91. (cd)(c)(lp) **DIFFERENT WORLD** [ ] [-]
– Blood on stone / Which way will the wind blow / All God's children / All for one / Different world / Step by step / Seven days / First touch / One on one / Cross that line.

– more compilations, etc. –

Apr 86. Raw Power; (d-lp)(c)(cd) **ANTHOLOGY** [ ] [-]

Mar 87. Raw Power; (lp)(c)(cd) **LIVE IN EUROPE 1979 (live)** [ ] [-]

May 88. That's Original; (d-lp)(d-cd) **LOOK AT YOURSELF / VERY 'EAVY, VERY 'UMBLE** [ ] [-]

Dec 88. Castle; (cd-ep) **LADY IN BLACK / JULY MORNING / EASY LIVIN'** [ ] [-]

Dec 88. Castle; (lp)(c)(cd) **LIVE AT SHEPPERTON '74 (live)** [ ] [-]
– Love machine / Look at yourself / Firefly / Return to fantasy / Rainbow demon / That's the way it is / Love is blind / On the rebound / Easy livin' / July morning / Running all night (with the lion) / Been away too long / Gypsy / Wake up (set your sights) / Can't keep a good band down / All of my life.

Aug 89. Castle; (d-lp)(cd) **THE COLLECTION** [ ] [-]

Jun 90. Essential; (3xcd)(5xlp) **TWO DECADES IN ROCK** [ ] [-]

Oct 91. Elite; (cd)(c) **ECHOES IN THE DARK** [ ] [-]
– Echoes in the dark / The wizard / Come away Melinda / Devil's daughter / Hot persuasion / Showdown / I'm alive / Look at yourself / Spider woman / Woman of the night / I want to be free / Gypsy / Sunrise / Bird of prey / Love machine / Lady in black *(re-iss. Sep 93)*

Nov 91. Elite; (cd)(c) **EXCAVATIONS FROM THE BRONZE AGE** [ ] [-]

Jan 92. Sequel; (cd) **RARITIES FROM THE BRONZE AGE** [ ] [-]

Jul 94. Success; (cd)(c) **LIVE (live)** [ ] [-]

Jan 95. Spectrum; (cd) **LADY IN BLACK** [ ] [-]

May 95. HTD; (cd) **SEA OF LIGHT** [ ] [-]

May 95. Spectrum; (cd) **FREE ME** [ ] [-]

KEN HENSLEY

solo while a URIAH HEEP member.

Bronze Warners

May 73. (lp)(c) **PROUD WORDS ON A DUSTY SHELF** [ ] [ ]
– When evening comes / From time to time / King without a throne / Rain / Proud words / Fortune / Blackhearted lady / Go down / Cold Autumn Sunday / The last time. *(re-iss.Oct77)*

Mar 75. (7") **IN THE MORNING. / WHO WILL SING TO YOU** [ ] [-]

Apr 75. (lp)(c) **EAGER TO PLEASE** [ ] [ ]
– Eager to please / Stargazer / Secret / Through the eyes of a child / Part three / The house on the hill / Winter or summer / Take and take / Longer shadows / In the morning / How shall I know. *(re-iss.Oct77) (cd-iss.Jun93 on 'Repertoire')*

— He left URIAH HEEP in 1980 and quickly made another solo album FREE SPIRIT *(cd-iss.Apr93 on 'Repertoire')*. Two 45's were lifted from it 'THE SYSTEM' & 'NO MORE'.

KEN HENSLEY issued new cd 'FROM TIME TO TIME' on 'Red Steel' Jun94.

DAVID BYRON

solo while a URIAH HEEP member.

Bronze Warners

Jan 76. (lp)(c) **TAKE NO PRISONERS** [ ] [ ]
– Man full of yesterday / Sweet rock and roll / Steamin' along / Silver white man / Love song / Midnight flyer / Saturday night / Roller coaster / Stop hit me with a white one.

— Later in '76, he split from HEEP to form ROUGH DIAMOND and continued solo. ROUGH DIAMOND made own self-named lp in 1977 for 'Island'.

UTOPIA (see under ⇒ RUNDGREN, Todd)

U2

Formed: Dublin, Ireland . . . 1977 by BONO, THE EDGE, CLAYTON and MULLEN. Early 1978, through A&R man Jackie Hayden, they signed to 'CBS' in 'Ireland. They arrived in UK the following year and after 2nd 45 'ANOTHER DAY' hit Irish No.1, 'Island' gave them UK contract. In 1980, STEVE LILLYWHITE produced much heralded debut album BOY, but it took the following year's OCTOBER album to give them break into Top 20. By early 1983, U2 had first top 10 hit single with appropriately titled NEW YEAR'S DAY which was culled from No.1 album WAR. Became worldwide attraction/stadium fillers by the mid-80's, progressing to No.1 rock act of that decade. • **Style:** Political hard-edged rock, fusing energy and power with message of love and peace. Their Irish-Christian beliefs were now somewhat overshadowed by their God-like status and overwhelming fan adoration. BONO's pop pin-up look has not interrupted the thought-provoking abundance of great songs U2 have created, which have not succumbed to the pop industry. • **Songwriters:** All written by BONO / THE EDGE, except HELTER SKELTER (Beatles) / ALL ALONG THE WATCHTOWER (Bob Dylan) (hit; Jimi Hendrix) / STAR SPANGLED BANNER (US National anthem) / DANCING BAREFOOT (Patti Smith) / NIGHT AND DAY (Cole Porter) / PAINT IT BLACK (Rolling Stones) / FORTUNATE SON (Creedence Clearwater Revival) / HALLELUJAH (Leonard Cohen) by BONO. • **Trivia:** BONO contributed vox to BAND AID single Dec'84. That year, the band also started own record label, mainly for other Irish groups and was a starter for HOTHOUSE FLOWERS / CACTUS WORLD NEWS / etc. In 1988, BONO and THE EDGE co-wrote for ROY ORBISON on his last living studio album 'Mystery Girl'. JOHNNY CASH was guest vocalist on 'ZOOROPA' track 'THE WANDERER'. They wrote the theme for the James Bond film 'GOLDEN EYE', which became a hit for TINA TURNER in 1995.

Recommended: BOY (*8) / OCTOBER (*6) / WAR (*9) / UNDER A BLOOD RED SKY (*6) / THE UNFORGETTABLE FIRE (*9) / WIDE AWAKE IN AMERICA (*6) / THE JOSHUA TREE (*10) / RATTLE & HUM (*8) / ACHTUNG BABY (*8) / ZOOROPA (*9) / PASSENGERS: ORIGINAL SOUNDTRACKS 1 (*7)

BONO (b.PAUL HEWSON, 10 May'60, Dublin, Ireland) – vocals / **THE EDGE** (b.DAVID EVANS, 8 Aug'61, Barking, Essex) – guitar, keyboards / **ADAM CLAYTON** (b.13 Mar'60, Chinnor, Oxfordshire, England) – bass / **LARRY MULLEN** (b.LAURENCE, 31 Oct'61, Dublin) – drums

CBS-Ireland not issued

Oct 79. (7"ep)(12"ep)(7"orange-ep)(7"yellow-ep) **U2-3** [-] [-]
– Out of control / Stories for boys / Boy-girl.

Feb 80. (7")(7"yellow)(7"white) **ANOTHER DAY. / TWILIGHT (demo)** [-] [-]

Island Island

May 80. (7")(7"red)(7"white)(7"orange)(7"yellow) **11 O'CLOCK TICK TOCK. / TOUCH** [ ] [-]

Aug 80. (7") **A DAY WITHOUT ME. / THINGS TO MAKE AND DO** [ ] [-]

Oct 80. (lp)(c) **BOY** [52] [63] Mar 81
– I will follow / Twilight / An cat dubh / Into the heart / Out of control / Stories for boys / The ocean / A day without me / Another time, another place / The Electric Co. / Shadows and tall trees. *(cd-iss.May86 & May95 +lp+c)*

Oct 80. (7")(7"white)(7"yellow) **I WILL FOLLOW. / BOY-GIRL (live)** [ ] [-]

Mar 81. (7") **I WILL FOLLOW. / OUT OF CONTROL** [-] [ ]

Jul 81. (7") **FIRE. / J.SWALLO** [35] [ ]
(d7"+=) – The ocean (live) / 11 o'clock tick tock (live). / The Electric Co. / Cry.

Sep 81. (7") **GLORIA. / I WILL FOLLOW (live)** [55] [ ]

Oct 81. (lp)(c) **OCTOBER** [11] [ ]
– Gloria / I fall down / I threw a brick through a window / Rejoice / Fire / Tomorrow / October / With a shout / Stranger in a strange land / Scarlet / Is that all?. *(cd-iss.May86) (re-iss.Jun92)*

Mar 82. (7") **A CELEBRATION. / TRASH, TRAMPOLENE AND THE PARTY GIRL** [47] [ ]

Jan 83. (7") **NEW YEAR'S DAY. / TREASURE (WHATEVER HAPPENED TO PETE THE CHOP)** [10] [53]
(d7"+=)(12"+=) – A day without me (live) / Fire (live) / I threw a brick through the window (live).

Feb 83. (lp)(c) **WAR** [1] [12]
– Sunday bloody Sunday / Seconds / Like a song / New Year's day / Two hearts beat as one / The refugee / Drowning man / Red light / '40' / Surrender. *(cd-iss.Dec85)(re-iss.cd+c.Aug91, re-iss.Jun92 hit No.51) (re-iss.all formats Aug93, hit UK No.38) (re-iss.all formats Aug93, hit UK No.38)*

Mar 83. (7") **TWO HEARTS BEAT AS ONE. / ENDLESS DEEP** [18] [ ]
(d7"+=)(12"+=) – Two hearts beat as one / New Year's day (US remixes).

Nov 83. (lp)(c) **UNDER A BLOOD RED SKY (live)** [2] [28]
– Gloria / 11 o'clock tick tock / I will follow / Party girl / Sunday bloody Sunday / The Electric Co. / New Year's day / '40'. *(cd-iss.May86) (re-iss.Jun92)*

Dec 83. (7") **I WILL FOLLOW (live). / TWO HEARTS BEAT AS ONE (live)** [-] [81]

Sep 84. (7")(7"pic-d) **PRIDE (IN THE NAME OF LOVE). / BOOMERANG II** [3] [33]
(d7"+=)(12"+=) – Boomerang II (instrumental) / 4th of July.

Oct 84. (lp)(c)(cd) **THE UNFORGETTABLE FIRE** [1] [12]
– A sort of homecoming / Pride (in the name of love) / Wire / The unforgettable fire / Promenade / 4th of July / Bad / Indian summer sky / Elvis Presley and America / MLK. *(re-iss.Jun92 hit No.38 UK)*

May 85. (7")(7"sha-pic-d) **THE UNFORGETTABLE FIRE. / A SORT OF HOMECOMING (live)** [6] [ ]
(12"+=) – The three sunrises / Bass trap / Love comes tumbling.
(d7"+=) – The three sunrises / Love comes tumbling / 60 seconds in . . .

May 85. (m-lp)(c) **WIDE AWAKE IN AMERICA** [11] [37]
– Bad (live) / A sort of homecoming (live) / The three sunrises / Love comes tumbling.

— Later in the year, BONO guested for CLANNAD on hit 'IN A LIFETIME'. In Sep'86, THE EDGE issued soundtrack album CAPTIVE (see further below).

Mar 87. (7")(12") **WITH OR WITHOUT YOU. / LUMINOUS TIMES (HOLD ON TO LOVE)** [4] [1]
(c-s+=)(cd-s+=) – Walk to the water.

Mar 87. (lp)(c)(cd)(4x7"pack) **THE JOSHUA TREE** [1] [1]
– Where the streets have no name / I still haven't found what I'm looking for / With or without you / Bullet the blue sky / Running to stand still / Red Hill mining town / In God's country / Trip through your wires / One tree hill / Exit / Mothers of the disappeared. *(re-charted UK Jan92, peaked Jun92 at No.19) (re-iss.all formats Aug93, hit UK No.27)*

May 87. (7")(12")(c-s) **I STILL HAVEN'T FOUND WHAT I'M LOOKING FOR. / SPANISH EYES / DEEP IN THE HEART** [6] [1]
(cd-s+=) – ('A'version).

Sep 87. (7"m) **WHERE THE STREETS HAVE NO NAME. / SILVER AND GOLD / SWEETEST THING** [4] [13]
(12"+=)(c-s+=)(cd-s+=) – Race against time.

Jan 88. (7"-US-imp) **IN GOD'S COUNTRY. / BULLET THE BLUE SKY** [48] [44] Dec 87
(12"+=)(cd-s+=) – Running to stand still.

Sep 88. (7") **DESIRE. / HALLELUJAH (HERE SHE COMES)** [1] [3]
(12"+=)(cd-s+=) – ('A'extended remix).
(c-s) – ('A'side) / Love comes to town / All I want is you.

Oct 88. (d-lp)(c)(cd) **RATTLE AND HUM** (some live) [1] [1]
– Helter skelter / Hawkmoon 269 / Van Diemen's land / Desire / Angel of Harlem / I still haven't found what I'm looking for / When love comes to town / God part II / Bullet the blue sky / Silver and gold / Love rescue me / Heartland / Star spangled banner / All I want is you / Freedom for my people / All along the watchtower / Pride (in the name of love). *(re-charted UK at 37 on Jun92) (re-iss.all formats Aug93, hit UK No.34)*

Oct 88. (7") **ANGEL OF HARLEM. / NO ROOM AT THE HEARTBREAK HOTEL** [9] [14]
(12"+=)(cd-s+=) – Love rescue me (live w / KEITH RICHARDS & ZIGGY MARLEY)

Apr 89. (7")(c-s) **WHEN LOVE COMES TO TOWN. ("U2 & B.B.KING") / DANCING BAREFOOT** [6] [68]
(12"+=)(cd-s+=) – ('A'live mix) / God part II (metal mix).
(12") – (3 'A'versions incl.dance version).

Jun 89. (7")(c-s) **ALL I WANT IS YOU. / UNCHAINED MELODY** [4] [83]
(12"+=)(cd-s+=) – Everlasting love.

Oct 91. (7")(c-s) **THE FLY. / ALEX DESCENDS INTO HELL FOR A BOTTLE OF MILK / KOROVA 1** [1] [61]
(12"+=)(cd-s+=) – The lounge Fly mix.

Nov 91. (cd)(c)(lp) **ACHTUNG BABY** [2] [1]
– Zoo station / Even better than the real thing / One / Until the end of the world / Who's gonna ride your wild horses / So cruel / The fly / Mysterious ways / Tryin' to throw your arms around the world / Ultra violet (light my way) / Acrobat / Love is blindness. *(re-iss.all formats Aug93, hit UK No.17)*

Dec 91. (7") **MYSTERIOUS WAYS. / ('A'solar remix)** [13] [9] Nov 91
(12"+=) – ('A'solar extended) / ('A' Apollo 440 remixes).
(cd-s++=) – ('A'-Tabla Motown mix).

Feb 92. (7")(c-s) **ONE. / THE LADY WITH THE SPINNING HEAD** [7] [10]
(12"+=)/ /(cd-s++=) – Satellite of love./ / Night and day (remix).

Jun 92. (7")(c-s) **EVEN BETTER THAN THE REAL THING. / SALOME** [12] [32]
(cd-s+=) – Where did it all go wrong (demo) / Lady with the spinning head (ext.dance).

Jul 92. (12") – ('A'perfecto remix) / ('A'trance) / ('A'sexy dub) / ('A'-Apollo 440). [8] [ ]

Nov 92. (7")(c-s) **WHO'S GONNA RIDE YOUR WILD HORSES. / PAINT IT BLACK** [14] [35]
('A'extended-cd-s+=) – ('A'-Temple bar mix) / Fortunate son.

Jul 93. (cd)(c)(lp) **ZOOROPA** [1] [1]
– Zooropa / Babyface / Numb / Lemon / Stay (faraway, so close!) / Daddy's gonna pay for your crashed car / Some days are better than others / The first time / Dirty day / The wanderer.

Aug 93. (video-ep) **NUMB / NUMB (video remix) / LOVE IS BLINDNESS** [-] [-]

Nov 93. (7")(c-s) **STAY (FARAWAY, SO CLOSE!). / ("FRANK SINATRA WITH BONO") I'VE GOT YOU UNDER MY SKIN** [4] [61]
(cd-s+=) – Lemon (mixes).
(cd-s) – ('A'side) / Slow dancing / Bullet the blue sky (live) / Love is blindness (live).

— In Mar 94, BONO teamed up with GAVIN FRIDAY (Virgin Prunes) on single 'IN THE NAME OF THE FATHER' from the film of the same name. It made No.46 in UK.

Jun 95. (7"red)(c-s) **HOLD ME, THRILL ME, KISS ME, KILL ME / (theme from 'Batman Forever')** [2] [16]
(cd-s) – ('Tell Me Now' track by MAZZY STAR).
above single from film 'Batman Forever' on 'East West' label.

PASSENGERS

aka U2, ENO + guests incl. vocalists PAVAROTTI + HOLI

Island Island

Nov 95. (cd)(c) **ORIGINAL SOUNDTRACKS 1** [12] [76]
– United colours / Slug / Your blue room / Always forever now / A different kind of blue / Beach sequence / Miss Sarajevo / Ito Okashi / One minute warning / Corpse (these chains are way too long) / Elvis ate America / Plot 180 / Theme from the swan / Theme from let's go native.

Nov 95. (7")(c-s)(cd-s) **MISS SARAJEVO. / ONE (live)** [6] [ ]
(cd-s+=) – Bottoms (Watashiitachi No Ookina Yume) (Zoo Station remix) / Viva Davidoff.

The EDGE

with guest **SINEAD O'CONNOR** – vocals

Virgin Virgin

Sep 86. (lp)(c)(cd) **CAPTIVE (Soundtrack)** [ ] [ ]
– Rowena's theme / Heroine (theme from 'Captive') / One foot in Heaven / The strange party / Hiro's theme 1 & 2 / Drift / The dream theme / Djinn / Island.

Sep 86. (7")(12") **HEROINE. / HEROINE (instrumental)** [ ] [-]

— In 1983, The EDGE had collaborated with JAH WOBBLE & HOLGER CZUKAY on m-lp 'SNAKE CHARMER'.

. . . Jan – Jun '96 stop press . . .

ADAM CLAYTON & LARRY MULLEN

Mother Mother

May 96. (single) **THEME FROM 'MISSION: IMPOSSIBLE"** [7] [7]

— above from the film 'Mission: Impossible'.

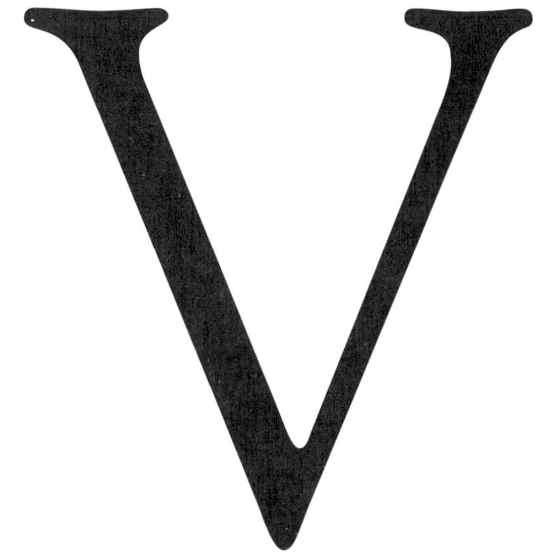

Steve VAI

Born: STEVEN CIRO VAI, 6 Jun'60, Carve Place, Long Island, New Jersey, USA. At age 20, he played guitar with FRANK ZAPPA on albums from TINSELTOWN REBELLION (1981) to FRANK ZAPPA MEETS THE MOTHERS OF PREVENTION (1986). In 1984, he also made debut solo album FLEX-ABLE for 'Relativity'. He joined ALCATRAZZ in 1985, leaving them to be part of DAVID LEE ROTH band. While a member of WHITESNAKE in 1989, he cut solo album PASSION AND WARFARE, which with incredible reviews and past C.V. gained him a Top 20 placing on both sides of the Atlantic. • **Style:** Superb guitarist, whose innovative experimentation brought new delights to the heavy-metal fraternity. • **Songwriters:** Writes all his own material. • **Trivia:** Taught as a teenager by the great JOE SATRIANI ⇒ . In 1985, he laid down all lead guitar work on PUBLIC IMAGE LTD lp 'ALBUM'. A year previous to this, he made an appearance in Walter Hill's film 'Crossroads'. VAI also co-wrote many songs for DAVID LEE ROTH.

Recommended: PASSION AND WARFARE (*7)

STEVE VAI – guitar, keyboards, bass, etc.

M.F.N. / Akashic

Aug 86. (lp) **FLEX-ABLE** [-] [ ] 1984
– Little green men / Viv women / Lovers are crazy / The boy / Salamanders in the sun / Girl song / Attitude song / Call it sleep / Junkie / Bill is private parts / Next stop Earth / There's something dead in here. *(c-iss.Sep87, cd-iss. 1989 on 'Food For Thought')*

—— now with **DAVE ROSENTHAL** – keys / **STU HAMM** – bass / **CHRIS FRAZIER** – drums

Food For Thought / Relativity

May 90. (cd)(c)(lp)(pic-lp) **PASSION AND WARFARE** [8] [18]
– Liberty / Erotic nightmares / The animal / Answers / The riddle / Ballerina 12-24 / For the love of God / The audience is listening / I would love to / Blue powder / Greasy kid's stuff / Alien water kiss / Sisters / Love secrets. *(re-iss.cd/c.Oct93)*

VAI

—— His new band were **TIM STEVENS** – bass / **TERRY BOZZIO** – drums

—— with **DEVIN TOWNSEND** – vocals / **WILL RILEY** – keyboards / **SCOTT THUNES** – bass / **ABE LABORIEL JR.** – drums

Relativity / Relativity

Jul 93. (cd)(c)(lp) **SEX & RELIGION** [17] [48]
– An Earth dweller's return / Here & now / In my dreams with you / Still my bleeding heart / Sex and religion / Dirty black hole / Touching tongues / State of grace / Survive / Pig / The road to Mt.Calvary / Deep down into the pain / Rescue me or bury me.

Epic / Epic

Aug 93. (12"pic-d) **DEEP DOWN INTO THE PAIN. (as "STEVE VAI") / ?** [ ] [ ]
(cd-s) – ('A'side) / ??

Nov 93. (12"pic-d) **IN MY DREAMS WITH YOU. / EROTIC NIGHTMARES** [ ] [ ]
(cd-s) – ('A'side) / ('A'mixes) / I would love to.

Apr 95. (cd)(c) **ALIEN LOVE SECRETS** [39] [ ]
– Mad horsie / Juice / Die to live / The boy from Seattle / Ya yo gakk / Kill the guy with the ball – The God eaters / Tender surrender.

VAN DER GRAAF GENERATOR

Formed: Manchester, England . . . 1967 by PETER HAMMILL, etc. (see below). Funnily enough, they split towards the end of '68, and although the album 'AEROSOL GREY MACHINE' looked destined to be a HAMMILL solo lp, it finally reached the shops in 1969 credited to the group. They raised the flags again, when the group/HAMMILL gained deal on 'Charisma'. Their brief liaison with the charts, came early in 1970, when album 'THE LEAST WE CAN DO . . . ' dented UK Top50. Group and HAMMILL continued together and separately for the rest of the 70's. • **Style:** Underground cult rock group, deep and gothic and often cited by 80's alternative outfits as inspiration. • **Songwriters:** HAMMILL composed all. • **Trivia:** Named after a generator built by Dr.Robert Jemison Van Der Graaf.

Recommended: AEROSOL GREY MACHINE (*8) / VITAL (*7) / PETER HAMMILL – NADIR'S BIG CHANCE (*7).

PETER HAMMILL (b. 5 Nov'48, London, England) – vocals, guitar, piano / **HUGH BANTON** – keyboards repl. NICK PEAKE / **CHRIS JUDGE SMITH** – drums, vocals, oricanos / **KEITH ELLIS** – bass (ex-KOOBAS) / **GUY EVANS** – drums (ex-MISUNDERSTOOD)

Polydor / Mercury

Dec 68. (7") **PEOPLE YOU WERE GOING TO. / FIREBRAND** [ ] [-]

—— Trimmed to a quartet when CHRIS formed HEEBALOB and later wrote for HAMMILL

Fontana / Mercury

Jan 69. (lp) **AEROSOL GREY MACHINE** [-] [ ]
– Afterwards / Orthenthian St. -part 1 & 2 / Running back / Into a game / Aerosol grey machine / Black smoke yen / Aguarian / Necromancer / Octopus. *(UK iss.Feb75)*

1969. (7") **AFTERWARDS. / NECROMANCER** [-] [ ]

—— **NIC POTTER** – bass (ex-MISUNDERSTOOD) repl. ELLIS who joined JUICY LUCY / added **DAVE JACKSON** – saxophone (ex-HEEBALOB)

Charisma / Mercury

Feb 70. (lp)(c) **THE LEAST WE CAN DO IS WAVE TO EACH OTHER** [47] [ ]
– Darkness / Refugees / White hammer / Whatever would Robert have said / Out of my book / After the flood. *(re-iss.Aug82) (cd-iss.Apr87)*

Apr 70. (7") **REFUGEES. / BOAT OF MILLIONS OF YEARS** [ ] [ ]

—— A quartet again, when POTTER left only completing half of next album. Guest on next 2 albums **ROBERT FRIPP** – guitar (of KING CRIMSON)

Charisma / Dunhill

Dec 70. (lp)(c) **H TO HE, WHO AM THE ONLY ONE** [ ] [ ]
– Killer / House with no door / The emperor in his war-room: The emperor – The room / Lost: Dance in sand and sea – Dance in frost / The pioneers over C. *(re-iss.Jun81 & Sep83) (cd-iss.Nov88)*

Charisma / Mercury

Oct 71. (lp)(c) **PAWN HEARTS** [ ] [ ]
– Lemmings / Man-erg / A plague of lighthouse keepers: 1) Eyewitness – 2) Pictures – Lighthouse – 3) Eyewitness – 4) S.H.M. – 5) Presence of the night – 6) Kosmos tours – 7) (Custards) Last stand – 8) The clot chickens – 9) Lands End – 10) We go now. *(re-iss.Oct86, cd-iss.Apr88)*

Feb 72. (7") **THEME ONE. / W** [ ] [ ]

PETER HAMMILL

had by this went solo when VAN DER GRAAF split. He continued to use VDGG members.

Charisma / Charisma

Jul 71. (lp)(c) **FOOL'S MATE** [ ] [ ]
– Imperial zeppelin / Candle / Happy / Solitude / Vision / Re-awakening / Sunshine / Child / Summer song (in the autumn) / Viking / The birds / I once wrote some poems. *(re-iss.Sep83, cd-iss.Oct88)*

May 73. (lp)(c) **CHAMELEON IN THE SHADOW OF THE NIGHT** [ ] [ ]
– German overalls / Slender threads / Rock and role / In the end / What's it worth / Easy to slip away / Dropping the torch / In the black room / The tower. *(cd-iss.Apr89)*

Feb 74. (lp)(c) **THE SILENT CORNER AND THE EMPTY STAGE** [ ] [ ]
– Modern / Wilhemina / The lie (Bernini's Saint Teresa) / Forsaken gardens / Red shift / Rubicon / A louse is not a home. *(re-iss.Oct86, cd-iss.Nov88)*

Sep 74. (lp)(c) **IN CAMERA** [ ] [ ]

– Ferret and featherbed / (No more) The sub-mariner / Tapeworm / Again / Faintheart and the sermon / The comet, the course. the tail / Gog Magog (in bromine chambers). *(re-iss.Nov80) (cd-iss.Nov88)*

Feb 75. (lp)(c) **NADIR'S BIG CHANCE**
– Nadir's big chance / The institute of mental health's burning / Open your eyes / Nobody's business / Been alone so long / Pompeii / Shingle song / Airport / People you were going to / Birthday special / Two or three spectres. *(re-iss.Mar83, cd-iss.Nov88)*

Apr 75. (7") **BIRTHDAY SPECIAL. / SHINGLE SONG**

— **HAMMILL, BANTON, JACKSON + EVANS** reformed

VAN DER GRAAF GENERATOR

Charisma Mercury

Oct 75. (lp)(c) **GODBLUFF**
– The undercover man / Scorched Earth / Arrow / The sleepwalkers. *(re-iss.Mar83) (cd-iss.Apr88)*

Apr 76. (lp)(c) **STILL LIFE**
– Pilgrims / Still life / La rossa / My room (waiting for Wonderland) / Childlike faith in childhood's end. *(re-iss.Mar83) (cd-iss.Apr87)*

Oct 76. (lp)(c) **WORLD RECORD**
– When she comes / A place to survive / Masks / Meurlys III / Songwriter's guild / Wondering. *(re-iss.Sep83) (re-iss.+cd.Aug88)*

Oct 76. (7") **WONDERING. / MEURGLYS III**

VAN DER GRAAF

GRAHAM SMITH – violin (ex-STRING DRIVEN THING) repl. JACKSON / **NIC POTTER** – bass returned after US session work to repl. BANTON

Sep 77. (lp)(c) **THE QUIET ZONE – THE PLEASURE DOME**
– Lizard play / The habit of the broken heart / The siren song / Last frame / The wave / Yellow fever (running) / The sphinx in the face / Chemical world / The sphinx returns. *(re-iss.1983) (re-iss.+cd.Aug88)*

— added **DAVE JACKSON** who returned w / **CHARLES DICKIE** – cello, piano

Charisma P.V.C.

Jul 78. (d-lp)(c) **VITAL (live)**
– Ship of fools / Still life / Mirror images / Medley: Parts of A plague of lighthouse keepers and Sleepwalkers / Pioneers over C / Door / Urban / Nadir's big chance. *(cd-iss.Apr89) (re-iss.cd Mar94 on 'Virgin')*

– (VAN DER GRAAF . . .) compilations, etc. –

Aug 72. Charisma; (lp) **68-71** -
Aug 80. Charisma; (lp)(c) **REPEAT PERFORMANCE** -
Mar 83. Charisma; (d-c) **PAWN HEARTS / STILL LIFE** -
May 85. Demi-Monde; (lp) **TIME VAULTS** (rare) -
Feb 87. Virgin; (cd) **FIRST GENERATION** -
Feb 87. Virgin; (cd) **SECOND GENERATION** -
Sep 93. Virgin; (cd) **I PROPHESY DISASTER** -
May 88. Thunderbolt; (lp)(cd) **NOW AND THEN** -
Jun 94. Band Of Joy; (cd) **MAIDA VALE** -

PETER HAMMILL

went solo after split.

Charisma P.V.C.

Sep 76. (lp)(c) **OVER**
– Crying wolf / Autumn / Time heals / Alice (letting go) / This side of the looking-glass / Betrayed (on Tuesdays she used to) / Yoga / Lost and found. *(cd-iss.Feb91 on 'Virgin')*

Sep 78. (lp)(c) **THE FUTURE NOW**
– The future now / Still in the dark / Mediaevil / A motor-bike in Africa / The cut / Palinurus / Pushing thirty / The second hand / Trappings / The mousetrap (caught in) / Energy vampires / If I could. *(re-iss.Oct86)*

Nov 79. (lp)(c) **pH7**
– My favourite / Careering / Porton Down / Mirror images / Handicap and equality / Not for Keith / The old school tie / Time for a change / Imperial walls / Mr.X gets tense / Faculty X. *(cd-iss.Apr89)*

Nov 79. (7") **THE POLAROID. (as "RICKY NADIR") / THE OLD SCHOOL TIE** -

S Type not issued

1980. (lp) **A BLACK BOX** -
– Golden promise / Losing faith in words / The Jargon king / Fog walking / The spirit / In slow time / The wipe / Flight: Flying blind – White cave fandango – Control – Cockpit – Silk worm wings / Nothing is nothing – A black box. *(re-iss.Jun83 on 'I.M.S.') (re-iss.1985 on 'Virgin')*

Virgin not issued

May 81. (7") **MY EXPERIENCE. / GLUE** -
Jun 81. (lp)(c) **SITTING TARGETS** -
– Breakthrough / My experience / Ophelia / Empress's clothes / Glue / Hesitation / Sitting targets / Stranger still / Sign / What I did for love / Central hotel. *(re-iss.+cd.Aug88) (re-iss.cd Mar94)*

— **HAMMILL** with **GUY EVANS / NIC POTTER** plus **JOHN ELLIS** – guitar (ex-VIBRATORS), formed **K**

Naive not issued

Sep 82. (7") **PARADOX DRIVE. / NOW MORE THAN EVER** -
Oct 82. (lp) **ENTER 'K'** -
– Paradox Drive / The unconscious life / Accidents / The great experiments / Don't tell me / She wraps it up / Happy hour / Seven wonders. *(cd-iss.May92 on Fie!)*

Sep 83. (lp) **PATIENCE** -
– Labour of love / Film noir / Just good friends / Jeunesse D'Oree / Traintime / Now more than ever / Comfortable / Patient. *(cd-iss.May92 on Fie!) (above 2 re-iss.d-lp,d-c.Jan86 on 'Spartan')*

Sep 83. (7") **FILM NOIR. / SEVEN WONDERS** -

Foundry not issued

Feb 85. (d-lp) **THE MARGIN (live)** -
– Future now / Porton Down / Stranger still / Sign / The Jargon king / The second hand / Empress's clothes / The sphinx in the face / Labour of love / Sitting targets / Patience / Flight. *(cd-iss.Feb91 on 'Virgin')*

Mar 86. (lp)(c) **SKIN** -
– Skin / After the show / Painting by numbers / Shell / All sais and done / A perfect date / Four pails / New lover. *(cd-iss.Feb91 on 'Virgin')*

Mar 86. (7") **PAINTING BY NUMBERS. / YOU HIT ME WHERE I LIVE** -
(12"+=) – Shell.

Virgin not issued

Nov 86. (lp)(c) **AND CLOSE TO THIS** -
– Too many of my yesterdays / Faith / Empire of delight / Silver / Beside the one you love / Other old cliches / Confident / Sleep now. *(cd-iss. Nov 88)*

PETER HAMMILL & GUY EVANS

Red Hot not issued

Jun 88. (c)(cd) **SPUR OF THE MOMENT** -
– Sweating it out / Little did he know / Without a glitch / Anatol's proposal / You think not? / Multiman / Deprogramming Archie / Always so polite / An imagined brother / Bounced / Roger and out. *(re-iss.May 93)*

PETER HAMMILL

solo again.

Enigma Enigma

Nov 88. (lp)(c)(cd) **IN A FOREIGN TOWN**
– Hemlock / Invisible ink / Sci-finance (re-visited) / This book / Time to burn / Auto / Vote brand X / Sun City night life / The play's the thing / Under cover names. (c+cd+=) – Smile / Time to burn (instrumental). *(re-iss.cd Jun95 on 'Fie!')*

Feb 90. (cd)(c)(lp) **OUT OF WATER**
– Evidently goldfish / Not the man / No Moon in the water / Our oyster / Something about Ysabel's dance / Green fingers / On the surface / A way out. *(reiss.cd Jun95 on 'Fie!')*

Some Bizzare not issued

Nov 91. (cd)(c)(lp) **THE FALL OF THE HOUSE OF USHER** -
– An unenviable role / That must be the house / Architecture / The sleeper / One thing at a time / I shun the light / Leave this house / Dreaming / A chronic catalepsy / The herbalist / The evil that is done / Five years ago / It's over now / An influence / no rot / She is dead / Beating of the heart / The haunted palace / I dared not speak / She comes towards the door / The fall

Fie! not issued

Dec 93. (cd) **THERE GOES THE DAYLIGHT (" . . . /The NOISE")** -
– Sci-finance (revisited) / The habit of a broken heart / Sign / I will find you / Lost and found / Planet Coventry / Empress's clothes / Cat's eye -Yellow fever / Primo on the parapet / Central hotel.

Virgin not issued

Sep 94. (cd) **ROARING FORTIES** -
– Sharply unclear / The gift of fire / You can't want what you always get / A headlong stretch / Your tall ship.

Golden Hind not issued

Jan 95. (cd) **OFFENSICHTLLICH GOLDFISCH** -
– Offensichtilich goldfisch / Dich zu finden / Die kalte killt den kub / Favorit / Kaufhaus Europa / Der larm / Oase / Die prominenz kubt sich / Die tunte verlischt / Auto (wieder im wagen) / Gaia / Schlaft nun.

– (PETER HAMMILL) compilations, etc. –

1978. Charisma; (lp) **VISION** -
Aug 84. (lp)(c) **THE LOVE SONGS** (remixes) -
(re-iss.Jun88)
May 85. Charisma; (7") **JUST GOOD FRIENDS. / ('A'instrumental)** -
1983. Sofa; (c) **LOOPS AND REELS** -
(cd-iss. Nov 93 on 'Fie')
Jul 93. Virgin; (cd) **THE CALM (AFTER THE STORM)** -
Jul 93. Virgin; (cd) **THE STORM (BEFORE THE CALM)** -
Jun 95. Fie!; (d-cd) **ROOM TEMPERATURE LIVE (live)** -
Nov 95. Strange Fruit; (cd) **THE PEEL SESSIONS** -

VANGELIS

Born: EVANGELOS PAPATHANASSIOU, 29 Mar'43, Valos, Greece. After 5 odd years as a member of APHRODITE'S CHILD alongside DEMIS ROUSSOS, he cut solo album early in the 70's. In 1974, he signed to 'RCA Victor', and hit UK album charts with 'HEAVEN AND HELL'. In the late 70's, he teamed up with JON ANDERSON of YES (who had earlier guested on HEAVEN lp), and scored with a hit single 'I HEAR YOU NOW'. He was then commissioned in 1980 to write score for 'CHARIOTS OF FIRE', and the following year it hit album + singles chart. It also broke him in the States, where the film also broke the box office. **Style & Songwriters:** Composer and virtuoso keyboard & synthesizer player. Neo-classical soundtrack specialist loved throughout the continent. • **Trivia:** In 1975, he was asked but refused to take the place of RICK WAKEMAN in YES, instead of PATRICK MORAZ. In 1985, he also wrote the ballet score for new version of 'Frankenstein'.

Recommended: HEAVEN & HELL (*8) / CHARIOTS OF FIRE (*7)

VANGELIS – keyboards, synthesizers (ex-APHRODITE'S CHILD, ex-FORMYNX)

Charly / not issued

1971. (lp) **THE DRAGON** [ ] [-]
– The dragon / Stuffed aubergine / Stuffed tomato. *(re-iss.1980)*

Affinity / not issued

1971. (lp) **HYPOTHESIS** [ ] [-]
– Hypothesis (part 1) / Hypothesis (part 2).

Polydor / not issued

1973. (lp) **L'APOCALYPSE DES ANIMAUX (Soundtrack)** [ ] [-]
– L'apocalypse des animaux / Generique / La petite fille / De la mer / Le singe blue / L'ours musicien / La mort / Du loop / Creation du monde / La mer recommences. *(re-iss.Oct76 + Apr84, etc.Imported, cd-iss.1988)*

— He now moved to London and signed to . . .

Vertigo / Vertigo

1974. (lp) **EARTH** [ ] [ ]
– Come on / We were all uprooted / Sunny Earth / He-o / Ritual / Let it happen / The city / My face in the rain / Watch out / A song.

RCA Victor / R.C.A.

Nov 75. (lp)(c) **HEAVEN & HELL** [31] [ ]
– Heaven and Hell pt.1 – Bacchanale symphony to the powers of B – 2nd movement – 3rd movement – So long ago so clear * / Heaven and Hell pt.2 – Intestinal heart – Needles and bones – 12 o'clock – Aries – Away. *(re-iss.Sep81 & Oct86, cd-iss.Sep89)*

— above featured The ENGLISH CHAMBER CHOIR and VANA VEROUTIS – lead vocals (track* was first to use vocals of **JON ANDERSON** (of YES).)

Aug 76. (7") **SO LONG AGO, SO CLEAR. / HEAVEN AND HELL THEME** [-] [ ]

Sep 76. (lp)(c) **ALBEDO 0.39** [18] [ ]
– Pulstar / Freefall / More tranquilillitatis / Main sequence / Sword of Orion / Alpha / Nucleogenesis (pt.1 & 2) / Albedo 0• 39. *(re-iss.Sep81) (re-iss.+cd.Sep89)*

Oct 76. (7") **PULSTAR. / ALPHA** [ ] [-]

Dec 77. (lp)(c) **SPIRAL** [ ] [ ]
– Spiral / Ballad / Dervish D / To the unknown man / 3 + 3. *(re-iss.Sep81 + Nov84)*

Jan 78. (7") **TO THE UNKNOWN MAN. / (part 2)** [ ] [-]

Jul 78. (lp)(c) **BEAUBOURG** [ ] [ ]
– Beaubourg (part 1) / Beaubourg (part 2). *(re-iss.Sep86 on 'Fame') (re-iss.+cd.Feb90)*

Polydor / Polydor

Apr 79. (lp)(c) **CHINA** [ ] [ ]
– Chung Kuo / The long march / The dragon / The plum blossom / The Tao of love / The little fete / Yin and Yang / Himalaya / Summit. *(re-iss.+cd.Aug83)*

May 79. (7") **THE LONG MARCH. / (part 2)** [ ] [-]

JON & VANGELIS

JON = **JON ANDERSON** – vocals (also of YES)

Polydor / Polydor

Dec 79. (7") **I HEAR YOU NOW. / THUNDER** [8] [58] Aug 80

Jan 80. (lp)(c) **SHORT STORIES** [4] [ ]
– Curious electic / Each and everyday / Bird song / I hear you now / The road / Far away in Bagdad / Love is / One more time / Thunder / A play within a play. *(re-iss.+cd.Jun87)*

VANGELIS

solo (same label until stated)

Jun 80. (7") **MY LOVE. / DOMESTIC LOGIC 1** [ ] [ ]

Nov 80. (lp)(c) **SEE YOU LATER** [ ] [ ]
– I can't take it anymore / Multitrack suggestion / Memories of green / Not a bit – all of it / Suffocation / See you later.

Mar 81. (lp)(c) **CHARIOTS OF FIRE (Original Motion Picture Soundtrack)** [5] [1] Oct 81
– Titles / Five circles / Abraham's theme / Eric's theme / 100 metres / Jerusalem / Chariots of fire. *(re-iss.Apr84, hit UK No.39) (cd-iss.1983)*

Apr 81. (7") **CHARIOTS OF FIRE – TITLES. / ERIC'S THEME** [12] [1] Dec 81
(re-iss.UK Feb82 hit No.41) (re-iss.Aug84)

JON & VANGELIS

were again. (same label)

May 81. (7") **THE FRIENDS OF MR.CAIRO. / BESIDE** [ ] [ ]

Jul 81. (lp)(c) **THE FRIENDS OF MR.CAIRO** [6] [64]
– The friends of Mr.Cairo / Back to school boogie / Outside of this (inside of that) / State of independence / Beside / The Mayflower. *(re-iss.+cd.Oct89)*

Jul 81. (7") **STATE OF INDEPENDENCE. / BESIDE** [ ] [ ]

Nov 81. (7") **I'LL FIND MY WAY HOME. / BACK TO SCHOOL BOOGIE** [6] [-]

Apr 82. (7") **I'LL FIND MY WAY HOME. / I HEAR YOU NOW** [-] [51]

— In 1982, he wrote unissued vinyl score for film 'Blade Runner'.

May 83. (lp)(c)(cd) **PRIVATE COLLECTION** [22] [ ]
– He is sailing / And when the night comes / Deborah / The king is coming / Horizon.

Jul 83. (7") **HE IS SAILING. / POLANAISE** [61] [ ]
(12"+=) – Song is.

— Above was last collaboration between the duo, until 1991.

– (JON & VANGELIS) compilations, etc. –

Aug 82. Polydor; (d-c) **SHORT STORIES / THE FRIENDS OF MR.CAIRO** [ ] [-]

Aug 84. Polydor; (7") **STATE OF INDEPENDENCE. /** [67] [ ]

Aug 84. Polydor; (lp)(c)(cd) **THE BEST OF JON & VANGELIS** [42] [ ]
– Italian song / I'll find my way home / State of independence / One more time / Play within a play / friends of Mr.Cairo / Outside of this (inside of that) / He is sailing / I hear you now.

Jun 88. Old Gold; (7") **I HEAR YOU NOW. / I'LL FIND MY WAY HOME** [ ] [-]

Sep 94. Spectrum; (cd)(c) **CHRONICLES (JON & VANGELIS)** [ ] [-]

VANGELIS

had continued solo. BOUNTY Soundtrack was also unissued. He continued to write unissued soundtracks throughout the 80's as well as below.

Oct 84. (lp)(c)(cd) **SOIL FESTIVITIES** [55] [ ]
– Movements 1-5. *(re-iss.Jun87)*

Mar 85. (lp)(c)(cd) **MASK (Soundtrack)** [69] [ ]
– Movements 1-6.

Mar 85. (lp)(c)(cd) **INVISIBLE CONNECTIONS** [ ] [ ]
– Invisible connections / Atom blaster / Thermo vision.

1986. (lp)(c)(cd) **RHAPSODIES** [ ] [ ]
– Ti ipermacho stratigo / O! gliki mou ear / Ton nimfona sou vlepo / Rapsodia / Tin oreotita tis partenias sou / Christos anesti / Asma asmaton.

Arista / Arista

Sep 88. (lp)(c)(cd) **DIRECT** [ ] [ ]
– The motion of stars / The will of the wind / Metallic rain / Elsewhere / Glorianna (hymn a la femme) / Rotations logic / The oracle of Apollo / Ave / First approach / Dial out / Intergallactic radio station / Message.

Sep 88. (cd-s) **THE WILL OF THE WIND / METALLIC RAIN / INTERGALACTIC RADIO STATION** [ ] [-]

East West / East West

Nov 90. (cd)(c)(lp) **THE CITY** [ ] [ ]
– Dawn / Morning papers / Nerve centre / Side streets / Good to see you / Twilight / Red lights / Procession. *(re-iss.cd Nov93 & Feb95)*

Oct 92. (cd)(c)(lp) **1492: THE CONQUEST OF PARADISE (Soundtrack)** [33] [ ]
– Opening theme / 1492: The conquest of Paradise / Monastery of la Rabida / City of Isabel / Light and shadow / Deliverance / West across the ocean sea / Eternity / Hispanola / Moxica and the horse / 28th parallel / Pinta, Nina, Santa Maria (into eternity) *(re-iss.cd Jun94)*.

Oct 92. (7")(c-s) **CONQUEST OF PARADISE. / MOXICA AND THE HORSE** [60] [ ]
(12"+=)(cd-s+=) – Line open / Landscape. *(re-iss.May95)*

Mar 93. (cd-s) **28th PARALLEL / WEST ACROSS THE OCEAN SEA** [ ] [ ]

Oct 95. (c-s)(cd-s) **VOICES / VOICES II (echoes) / VOICES III** [ ] [ ]

. . . Jan – Jun '96 stop press . . .

Feb 96. (cd)(c) **VOICES** [58] [ ]

— above featured PAUL YOUNG on vocals

Apr 96. (cd)(c) **PORTRAIT (SO LONG AGO, SO CLEAR)** [14] [ ]
(compilation)

JON & VANGELIS

re-united

Arista / Arista

Aug 91. (7") **WISDOM CHAIN. / PAGE OF LIFE** [ ] [ ]
(cd-s+=) – ('A'full version) / Sing with your eyes.

Sep 91. (cd)(c)(lp) **PAGE OF LIFE** [ ] [ ]

– Wisdom chain / Page of life / Money / Garden of senses / Is it love / Anyone can light a candle / Journey to Ixtlan / Shine for me / Genevieve.

– (VANGELIS) compilations, others –

1978. RCA; (lp)(c) **THE BEST OF VANGELIS** [ ] [ ]
(re-iss.Sep81) (cd-iss.May93)
Nov 82. RCA; (d-lp)(d-c) **TO THE UNKNOWN MAN VOLS.1 & 2** [ ] [-]
Jun 84. RCA; (c) **MAGIC MOMENTS** [ ] [ ]
Oct 89. RCA; (cd-box)(c-box) **SPIRAL / ALBEDO 0• 39 / HEAVEN AND HELL** [ ] [-]
Jul 81. BBC; (7") **HEAVEN AND HELL, THIRD MOVEMENT (THEME FROM THE BBC-TV SERIES – THE COSMOS). / ?** [48] [-]
Aug 81. Polydor; (lp)(c) **OPERA SAUVAGE – COSMOS** [ ] [-]
(US-iss.+cd Dec 86, hit No. 42)
Nov 82. Polydor; (t-lp) **CHARIOTS OF FIRE / CHINA / OPERA SAUVAGE** [ ] [-]
Nov 88. Polydor; (lp)(c)(cd) **ANTARTICA (Original Soundtrack)** [ ] [-]
Jul 89. Polydor; (lp)(c)(cd) **THEMES** [ ] [ ]
– (excerpts from films, including some from previously unissued on vinyl)
Apr 93. C.A.M.; (cd) **ENTENDS-TU LES CHEINS** [ ] [-]
Jun 94. East West; (cd)(c) **BLADE RUNNER (Soundtrack)** [20] [ ]
Apr 95. RCA; (cd) **ALBEDO 0.39 / HEAVEN AND HELL** [ ] [-]

VAN HALEN

Formed: Pasadena, California, USA . . . 1975 by brothers ALEX and EDDIE. In 1977 as MAMMOTH they were spotted by producer TED TEMPLEMAN who encouraged MO OSTIN to sign them for 'Warners'. Now as VAN HALEN, their monster debut paved the way for massive selling albums and sell-out concerts during late 70's and 80's. • **Style:** Heavy-metal/hard rock, with ROTH a hyperactive flamboyant frontman who combined and blended with supremo axeman EDDIE VAN HALEN. • **Songwriters:** ROTH lyrics until 1986, then group compositions. Covered; YOU REALLY GOT ME (Kinks) / FAIR WARNING (Aerosmith) / (OH) PRETTY WOMAN (Roy Orbison) / A POLITICAL BLUES (Little Feat) / WON'T GET FOOLED AGAIN (Who). • **Trivia:** In Apr'81, EDDIE married actress Valerie Bertinelli. He also played guitar on MICHAEL JACKSON's 'Thriller' album 1982.

Recommended: VAN HALEN (*8) / VAN HALEN II (*7) / WOMEN AND CHILDREN FIRST (*6) / FAIR WARNING (*6) / DIVER DOWN (*7) / 1984 (*7)

EDDIE VAN HALEN (b.26 Jan'57, Nijmegin, Holland) – guitar / **DAVID LEE ROTH** (b.10 Oct'55, Bloomington, Indiana, USA) – vocals / **MICHAEL ANTHONY** (b.20 Jun'55, Chicago, Illinois, USA) – bass / **ALEX VAN HALEN** (b. 8 May'55, Nijmegen, Holland) – drums

Warners Warners
Feb 78. (7") **YOU REALLY GOT ME. / ATOMIC ROCK PUNK** [ ] [36] Jan 78
Apr 78. (lp)(c) **VAN HALEN** [34] [19] Feb 78
– You really got me / Jamie's cryin' / On fire / Runnin' with the Devil / I'm the one / Ain't talkin' about love / Little dreamer / Feel your love tonight / Atomic punk / Eruption / Ice cream man. *(cd-iss.Jul86, Jun91 + Feb95)*
Apr 78. (7") **RUNNIN' WITH THE DEVIL. / ERUPTION** [ ] [84]
Jul 78. (7") **JAMIE'S CRYIN'. / I'M THE SAME** [-] [ ]
Sep 78. (7") **AIN'T TALKIN' BOUT LOVE. / FEEL YOUR LOVE TONIGHT** [-] [ ]
Apr 79. (lp)(c) **VAN HALEN II** [23] [6]
– Dance the night away / Outta love again / Somebody get me a doctor / You're no good / Bottoms up / Women in love / Light up the sky / Beautiful girls / D.O.A. / Spanish fly. *(cd-iss.Mar87) (re-iss.1989)*
May 79. (7")(7"pic-d) **DANCE THE NIGHT AWAY. / OUTTA LOVE AGAIN** [ ] [15] Apr 79
Sep 79. (7") **BEAUTIFUL GIRLS. / D. O. A.** [-] [84]
Apr 80. (lp)(c) **WOMEN AND CHILDREN FIRST** [15] [6]
– Tora! Tora! / And the cradle will rock / Romeo delight / Fools / In a simple rhyme / Could this be magic? / Loss of control / Take your whiskey home / Everybody wants some!!. *(cd-iss.Jun89)*
Apr 80. (7") **AND THE CRADLE WILL ROCK. / COULD THIS BE MAGIC** [-] [55]
Aug 80. (7") **AND THE CRADLE WILL ROCK. / EVERYBODY WANTS SOME!!** [ ] [-]
May 81. (7") **SO THIS IS LOVE. / HEAR ABOUT IT LATER** [-] [ ]
May 81. (lp)(c) **FAIR WARNING** [49] [6]
– Mean street / So this is love / Push comes to shove / Sinner's swing / Unchained / Dirty movies / Hear about it later / Sunday afternoon in the park / One foot out of the door. *(cd-iss.Jun89)*
Feb 82. (7") **(OH) PRETTY WOMAN. / HAPPY TRAILS** [ ] [12]
(re-iss.Feb85)
May 82. (7") **DANCING IN THE STREET. / THE BULL BUG** [-] [38]
May 82. (lp)(c) **DIVER DOWN** [36] [3]
– Where have all the good times gone / Hang 'em high / Cathedral / Secrets / Intruder / (Oh) Pretty woman / Dancing in the street / Little guitars / Big bad Bill (is sweet William now) / The bull bug / Happy trails. *(cd-iss.Jan84)*
May 82. (7") **DANCING IN THE STREET. / BIG BAD BILL (IS SWEET WILLIAM NOW)** [ ] [-]
Aug 82. (7") **BIG BAD BILL (IS SWEET WILLIAM NOW). / SECRETS** [-] [ ]
Jan 84. (lp)(c)(cd) **1984** [15] [2]
– 1984 / Jump / Panama / Top Jimmy / Drop dead legs / Hot for teacher / I'll wait / Girl gone bad / House of pain. *(re-iss.cd/c Feb95)*
Jan 84. (7") **JUMP. / HOUSE OF PAIN** [-] [1]
Jan 84. (7") **JUMP. / RUNNIN' WITH THE DEVIL** [7] [-]
(12"+=) – House of pain.
Apr 84. (7") **I'LL WAIT. / GIRL GONE BAD** [-] [13]
Apr 84. (7") **PANAMA. / GIRL GONE BAD** [61] [13] Jun 84
(12"+=) – Dance the night away.
Jun 84. (7") **I'LL WAIT. / DROP DEAD LEGS** [ ] [-]
(12"+=) – And the cradle will rock / (Oh) Pretty woman.
Jun 85. (7") **HOT FOR TEACHER. / LITTLE PREACHER** [ ] [56] Oct 84
(12"+=) – Hear about it later.

—— (Jun85) Trimmed to a trio, when **DAVID LEE ROTH** went solo full-time. Early '86 added **SAMMY HAGAR** – vocals (ex-MONTROSE, ex-Solo Artist)

Mar 86. (7")(12")(7"pic-d)(7"sha-pic-d) **WHY CAN'T THIS BE LOVE. / GET UP** [8] [3]
Apr 86. (lp)(c)(cd) **5150** [16] [1]
– Good enough / Why can't this be love / Get up / Dreams / Summer nights / Best of both worlds / Love walks in / 5150 / Inside. *(re-iss.cd/c Feb95)*
Jun 86. (7")(12")(7"sha-pic-d) **DREAMS. / INSIDE** [62] [22] May 86
Aug 86. (7") **LOVE WALKS IN. / SUMMER NIGHTS** [-] [22]
Oct 86. (7") **BEST OF BOTH WORLDS. / ('A' live)** [-] [ ]
May 88. (7")(12") **BLACK AND BLUE. / APOLITICAL BLUES** [ ] [34]
Jun 88. (lp)(c)(cd) **OU812** [16] [1]
– Mine all mine / When it's love / A.F.U. (naturally wired) / Cabo wabo / Source of infection / Feels so good / Finish what ya started / Black and blue / Sucker in a 3-piece. *(cd+=)*– A political blues.
Jul 88. (7") **WHEN IT LOVE. / CABO WABO** [-] [5]
Jul 88. (7") **WHEN IT'S LOVE. / APOLITICAL BLUES** [28] [-]
(12"+=)(cd-s+=)(12"pic-d+=) – Why can't this be love.
Sep 88. (7") **FINISH WHAT YA STARTED. / SUCKER IN A 3-PIECE** [-] [13]
Feb 89. (7") **FEELS SO GOOD. / SUCKER IN A 3 PIECE** [63] [35] Jan 89
(12"+=)(cd-s+=) – BEST OF BOTH WORLDS (live)
Jun 91. (7")(c-s) **POUNDCAKE. / PLEASURE DOME** [74] [ ]
(12"+=)(cd-s+=) – (interview).
Jul 91. (cd)(c)(lp) **FOR UNLAWFUL CARNAL KNOWLEDGE** [12] [1]
– Poundcake / Judgement day / Spanked / Runaround / Pleasure dome / In'n'out / Man on a mission / The dream is over / Right now / 316 / Top of the world.
Sep 91. (7") **TOP OF THE WORLD. / POUNDCAKE** [-] [27]
Oct 91. (7")(c-s) **TOP OF THE WORLD. / IN'N'OUT** [63] [-]
(12"+=)(cd-s+=) – Why can't this be love (extended) / When it's love / Dreams.
Feb 92. (c-s)(cd-s) **RIGHT NOW /** [-] [55]
Feb 93. (d-cd)(d-c) **LIVE: RIGHT HERE, RIGHT NOW (live)** [24] [5]
– Poundcake / Judgement day / When it's love / Spanked / Ain't talkin' 'bout love / In'n'out / Dreams / Man on a mission / Ultra bass / Pressure dome – Drum solo / Panama / Love walks in / Runaround/ / Right now / One way to rock / Why can't this be love / Give to love / Finished what ya started / Best of both worlds / 316 / You really got me – Cabo wabo / Won't get fooled again / Jump / Top of the world.
Mar 93. (7")(c-s) **JUMP (live). / LOVE WALKS IN (live)** [26] [ ]
(cd-s+=) – Eagles fly (live) / Mine, all mine (live).
Jan 95. (7"purple)(c-s) **DON'T TELL ME (WHAT LOVE CAN DO). / BALUCHITHERIUM** [27] [ ]
(cd-s+=) – Why can't this be love (live)/ Poundcake (live)/ Panama (live).
(cd-s) – ('A'side)/ Judgement day (live)/ Dreams (live)/ Top of the world (live).
Jan 95. (cd)(c)(lp) **BALANCE** [8] [1]
– The seventh seal / Can't stop lovin' you / Don't tell me (what love can do) / Amsterdam / Big fat money / Aftershock / Strung out / Not enough / Doin' time / Baluchitherium / Take me back (dea vu) / Feelin'.
Mar 95. (7")(c-s) **CAN'T STOP LOVIN' YOU. / CROSSING OVER** [33] [30]
(cd-s+=) – Man on a mission / Right now.
(cd-s) – ('A'side) / Best of both worlds (live) / One way to rock (live) / When it's love (live).
Jun 95. (c-s) **AMSTERDAM / RUNAROUND (live)** [ ] [ ]
(cd-s) – ('A'side) / Finish what you started (live).
Aug 95. (c-s)(cd-s) **NOT ENOUGH /** [-] [97]

– compilations, others, etc. –

Jun 80. Atlantic; (7") **RUNNIN' WITH THE DEVIL. / D.O.A.** [52] [-]

Stevie Ray VAUGHAN

Born: 3 Oct'54, Dallas, Texas. Found experience in the latter half of the 70's when playing guitar for The NIGHTCRAWLERS and The COBRAS.

In 1981 he founded own backing band DOUBLE TROUBLE who signed to 'Epic' after STEVIE guested on DAVID BOWIE's 1983 album LET'S DANCE. He quit BOWIE's band on the eve of his 'Serious Moonlight' tour. Throughout the 80's, STEVIE became renowned albums artist. • **Style:** R & B / boogie rock guitarist influenced by ERIC CLAPTON or BB KING. • **Songwriters:** Wrote half the material except TEXAS FLOOD (Davis-Scott) / CHANGE IT + LOOKING OUT THE WINDOW (D.Bramhall) / LOOK AT LITTLE SISTER (Hank Ballard) / YOU'LL BE MINE (Willie Dixon) / COME ON (E.King) / VOODOO CHILE + LITTLE WING (Jimi Hendrix) / TAXMAN (eorge Harrison) / etc. • **Miscellaneous:** Beat his booze and drugs addiction around 1987.

Recommended: GREATEST HITS (*8)

STEVIE RAY VAUGHAN & DOUBLE TROUBLE

STEVIE – vocals, guitar / **TOMMY SHANNON** – bass (ex-JOHNNY WINTER) / **CHRIS 'Whipper' LAYTON** – drums (ex-GREAZY BROTHERS)

Epic Epic

Jul 83. (7") **PRIDE AND JOY. / RUDE MOOD** [-] [ ]

Aug 83. (lp)(c) **TEXAS FLOOD** [ ] [38] Jul 83
– Love struck baby / Pride and joy / Texas flood / Tell me / Testify / Rude mood / Mary had a little lamb / Dirty pool / I'm cryin' / Lenny. *(cd-iss.Jul89 & Apr91)*

Aug 83. (7") **LOVE STRUCK BABY. / RUDE MOOD** [ ] [ ]

— added brother **JIMMIE VAUGHAN** – guitar, bass

Jun 84. (lp)(c) **COULDN'T STAND THE WEATHER** [ ] [31]
– Scuttle buttin' / Couldn't stand the weather / The things (that) I used to do / Voodoo chile (slight return) / Cold shot / Tin Pan alley / Honey bee / Stang's swang. *(cd-iss.1984, Apr91 & Feb95)*

— **JOE SUBLETT** – saxophone repl. JIMMIE / added **REESE WYNANS** – keyboards

Sep 85. (lp)(c) **SOUL TO SOUL** [ ] [34]
– Say what! / Lookin' out the window / Look at little sister / Ain't gone 'n' give up on love / Gone home / Change it / You'll be mine / Empty arms / Come on (part III) / Life without you. *(cd-iss.Apr86 & Apr91)*

Sep 85. (7") **CHANGE IT. / LOOK AT LITTLE SISTER** [-] [ ]

Mar 86. (7") **SUPERSTITION (live). / PRIDE AND JOY (live)** [-] [ ]

Jan 87. (7") **WILLIE THE WIMP. / SUPERSTITION** [-] [ ]

Jan 87. (d-lp)(d-c)(cd) **LIVE ALIVE (live)** [ ] [52] Dec 86
– Say what! / Ain't gone 'n' give up on love / Pride and joy / Mary had a little lamb / Superstition / I'm leaving you (commit a crime) / Cold shot / Willie the wimp / Look at little sister / Texas flood / Voodoo chile (slight return) / Love struck baby / Change it / Life without you. *(re-iss. cd+c Apr 93)*

Jun 87. (7") **LOVE STRUCK BABY. / PIPELINE (W/ DICK DALE)** [-] [ ]

Jun 89. (7") **TRAVIS WALK. / CROSSFIRE** [-] [ ]

Jul 89. (lp)(c)(cd) **IN STEP** [63] [33] Jun 89
– The house is rockin' / Crossfire / Tightrope / Let me love you baby / Leave my girl alone / Travis walk / Wall of denial / Scratch-n-sniff / Love me darlin' / Riviera paradise.

Aug 89. (7") **THIS HOUSE IS ROCKIN'. / TIGHTROPE** [-] [ ]

— Late in the 80's, STEVIE jammed with The ERIC CLAPTON Band. On 27 Aug'90, after a concert in Alpine Valley, Wisconsin, STEVIE and other travellers were killed in a helicopter crash. He and brother JIMMIE had just cut album below.

VAUGHAN BROTHERS

Epic Epic

Oct 90. (cd)(c)(lp) **FAMILY STYLE** [63] [7]
– Hard to be / White boots / D-FW / Good Texan / Hillbillies from Outer Space / Long way from home / Tick tock / Telephone song / Baboom / Mama said / Brothers.

Oct 90. (c-s) **TICK TOCK. / BROTHERS** [-] [65]

Jan 91. (c-s) **GOOD TEXAN. / MAMA SAID / BABOOM** [-] [ ]

– (STEVIE RAY VAUGHAN) compilations, etc. –

Nov 91. Epic; (cd)(c)(lp) **THE SKY IS CRYING** [ ] [10]
– Boot hill / The sky is crying / Empty arms / Little wing / Wham / May I have a talk with you / Chitlins con carne / So excited / Life by the drop.

Nov 92. Epic; (7") **THE SKY IS CRYING. / CHITLINS CON CARNE** [-] [ ]

Jan 92. Epic; (7") **EMPTY ARMS. / WHAM** [-] [ ]

Oct 92. Epic; (cd)(c)(lp) **IN THE BEGINNING (live)** [ ] [58]

Nov 95. Epic; (cd)(c) **GREATEST HITS** [ ] [39]
– Taxman / Texas flood / The house is rockin' / Pride and joy / Tightrope / Little wing / Crossfire / Change it / Cold shot / Couldn't stand the weather / Life without you.

Suzanne VEGA

Born: 12 Aug'59, Upper West Side, New York, USA. From half-Puerto Rican stock, she studied dance at High School of Performing Arts. With this experience, she played folk clubs throughout early 80's, finally gaining attention of Ron Fiernstein and Steve Addabbo, who became her managers. They obtained her contract with 'A&M' and employed LENNY KAYE (ex-PATTI SMITH GROUP) to produce her debut album, which was released 1985. After slow start, it became good seller the following year, paving the way for two future UK Top 10's (1987 + 1990). • **Style:** Modern folk-rock singer-songwriter, who has had usual comparisons to JONI MITCHELL, LAURA NYRO or even DORY PREVIN. • **Songwriters:** Writes all her own, except CHINA DOLL (Grateful Dead) / STORY OF ISAAC (Leonard Cohen). • **Trivia:** In 1987, she contributed 2 song lyrics for a PHILIP GLASS album 'Songs From Liquid Days'.

Recommended: SUZANNE VEGA (*8) / SOLITUDE STANDING (*7) / 99.9 F

SUZANNE VEGA – vocals, guitar with **JIM GORDON** – guitar / **FRANK CHRISTIAN** – guitar / **PAUL DUGAN + FRANK GRAVIS** – bass / **SUE EVANS** – drums / **C.P. ROTH** – synth She replaced above with touring + studio band from mid'85-late 80's. **MARC SHULMAN** – guitar / **MIKE VISCEGLIA** – bass / **ANTON SANKO** – keyboards / **STEPHEN FERRARA** – percussion / **SUE EVANS** – drums

A & M A & M

Jul 85. (lp)(c) **SUZANNE VEGA** [11] [91] Jun 85
– Cracking / Freeze tag / Marlene on the wall / Small blue thing / Straight lines / Undertow / Some journey / The queen and the soldier / Knight moves / Neighborhood girls. *(cd-iss.Feb86 & Mar93)*

Aug 85. (7") **MARLENE ON THE WALL. / NEIGHBORHOOD GIRLS** [ ] [ ]

Jan 86. (7") **SMALL BLUE THING. / THE QUEEN AND THE SOLDIER** [65] [-]
(d7"+=) – Some journey / Black widow station.

Feb 86. (7") **SMALL BLUE THING. / LEFT OF CENTER** [-] [ ]

Mar 86. (7") **MARLENE ON THE WALL. / SMALL BLUE THING** [21] [-]
(10"+=) – Neighborhood girls / Straight lines (live).

May 86. (7") **LEFT OF CENTER. / UNDERTOW** [32] [-]
(10"+=)/ /(cd-s+=) ('A'live) / Freeze tag (live)./ / Cracking.

(above 'A'side featured JOE JACKSON – piano). SUE EVANS had now left.

Oct 86. (7") **GYPSY. / CRACKING (live)** [ ] [-]
(12"+=) – Knight movies (live).

May 87. (lp)(c)(cd) **SOLITUDE STANDING** [2] [11]
– Tom's diner / Luka / Ironbound / Fancy poultry / In the eye / Night vision / Solitude standing / Calypso / Language / Gypsy / Wooden horse.

May 87. (7") **LUKA. / NIGHT VISION** [-] [3]

May 87. (7") **LUKA. / STRAIGHT LINES (live)** [23] [-]
(12"+=) – Neighbourhood girls.
(10"+=)(cd-s+=) – Cracking (alternative mix).

Jul 87. (7") **TOM'S DINER. / LEFT OF CENTER** [58] [-]
(10"+=)(12"+=)/ /(cd-s+=) – Luka (live)./ / ('A'live).

Sep 87. (7") **SOLITUDE STANDING. / TOM'S DINER** [-] [94]

Nov 87. (7") **GYPSY. / LEFT OF CENTER** [-] [ ]

Nov 87. (7")(c-s) **SOLITUDE STANDING. / LUKA** [ ] [-]
(12"+=) – Ironbound-Fancy poultry.
(10")(cd-s) – ('A'side) / Marlene on the wall (live) / Some journey (live).

— **FRANK VILARDI** – drums repl. FERRARA. Added **MICHAEL BLAIR** – percussion

Apr 90. (cd)(c)(lp) **DAYS OF OPEN HAND** [7] [50]
– Tired of sleeping / Men in a war / Rusted pipe / Institution green / Book of dreams / Those whole girls (run in grace) / Room off the street / Big space / Predictions / Fifty-fifty chance / Pilgrimage. *(re-iss.cd May95)*

Apr 90. (7")(c-s) **BOOK OF DREAMS. / BIG SPACE** [66] [ ]
(cd-s+=) – Marlene on the wall (live) / Ironbound (live).
(10"++=) – Fancy poultry.

Jun 90. (7") **TIRED OF SLEEPING. / THOSE WHOLE GIRLS (RUN IN GRACE)** [ ] [ ]
(10"+=)(cd-s+=) – Left of center / Room off the street.

Jul 90. (7")(c-s) **TOM'S DINER. ("SUZANNE VEGA & D.N.A.") / ('A'version)** [2] [5]
(12"+=)(cd-s+=) – (2 other mixes).

Sep 90. (7")(c-s) **MEN IN A WAR. / UNDERTOW (live)** [ ] [ ]
(12"+=)(cd-s+=) – ('A'live).

Aug 92. (7")(c-s) **IN LIVERPOOL. / SOME JOURNEY** [52] [ ]
(cd-s+=) – The Queen and the soldier / Luka.

Sep 92. (cd)(c)(lp) **99.9°F** [20] [86]
– Rock in this pocket (song of David) / Blood makes noise / In Liverpool / 99.9°F / Blood sings / Fat man & dancing girl / (If you were) In my movie / As a child / Bad wisdom / When heroes go down / As girls go / Songs of sand / Private goes public.

Oct 92. (7")(c-s) **99.9°F. / MEN WILL BE MEN** [46] [ ]
(cd-s+=) – Rock in this pocket (acoustic) / In Liverool (acoustic).
(cd-s) – ('A'side) / Tired of sleeping / Straight lines / Tom's diner (all live).

Dec 92. (7")(c-s) **BLOOD MAKES NOISE. / TOM'S DINER** [60] [ ]
(cd-s) – ('A'side) / Neighbourhood girls / Predictions / China doll.

(12") – ('A'side) / ('A'-Mitchell Froom remix) / ('A'house mix) / ('A'master mix).

Feb 93. (7")(c-s) **WHEN HEROES GO DOWN. / KNIGHT MOVES (live)** [58] [ ]
(cd-s+=) – Men in a war (live) / Gypsy (live).
(cd-s) – ('A'side) / Marlene on the wall / Luka / Left of center.

– compilations, others, etc. –

Oct 88. A&M; (cd-ep) **COMPACT HITS** [ ] [-]
– Luka / Left of center / Neighbourhood girls / The queen and the soldier.

Sep 91. A&M; (cd)(c)(lp) **TOM'S ALBUM** [ ] [ ]

— (above contained re-workings by other artists of the track TOM'S DINER)

VELVET UNDERGROUND

Formed: New York City, USA . . . early 1965 by LOU REED and JOHN CALE, who nearly hit as The PRIMITIVES with single 'The Ostrich'. They met modern pop artist ANDY WARHOL, who invited German chanteuse NICO to join the set-up alongside STERLING MORRISON and MO TUCKER. Early in 1966, they signed to 'MGM-Verve', and soon began what was to be their debut album 'THE VELVET UNDERGROUND AND NICO'. It featured 11 superb ahead of-their-time classics, noteably the disturbing 'HEROIN', the s+m 'VENUS IN FURS' & 'I'M WAITING FOR THE MAN', plus 3 NICO sung gems 'FEMME FATALE', 'ALL TOMORROW'S PARTIES' & 'I'LL BE YOUR MIRROR'. It only managed a brief stay in the US Top 200, as did the 1967 follow-up 'WHITE LIGHT, WHITE HEAT', which included the 17 min.'SISTER RAY'. Their self-titled 3rd album, made little impact, and the band soon disrupted with personnel clashes, etc. • **Style:** Avant-garde and disturbing band, who highlighted experimentation with drug orientated rock'n'roll. A decade later, they were cited as the inspiration for punk rock. A decade after that, alternative groups like JESUS & MARY CHAIN showed their music had not been forgotten. • **Songwriters:** REED compositions, except some by group. Many rock acts have covered their material, but so far not surprisingly, none have managed to score a major chart hit yet. • **Miscellaneous:** In 1990, REED and CALE re-united on a tribute album to the deceased ANDY WARHOL. NICO had earlier died on 18 Jul'88 of a brain haemorrhage, after falling off her bike on holiday in Ibiza. • **Trivia:** The debut lp sleeve, featured a gimmick peeling banana skin sticker. They reformed for a gig in Paris, 15 June 1990, and for an album, etc, in Dec '93. UK's Channel 4 featured a night-long session of all their previous work.

Recommended: THE VELVET UNDERGROUND AND NICO (*10) / WHITE LIGHT – WHITE HEAT (*9) / V.U. (*7) / THE VELVET UNDERGROUND (*7).

LOU REED (b.LOUIS FIRBANK, 2 Mar'44, Long Island, New York) – vocals, guitar (ex-JADES, ex-PRIMITIVES) / **JOHN CALE** (b. 5 Dec'42, Garnant, Wales, UK) – bass, viola, vocals, etc. / **STERLING MORRISON** – guitar / **MAUREEN TUCKER** – drums / plus **NICO** (b.CHRISTA PAFFGEN, Cologne, W.Germany) – vocals (also – Solo artist)

Oct 66. (7") **ALL TOMORROW'S PARTIES. / I'LL BE YOUR MIRROR** [-] [ ]

Dec 66. (7") **SUNDAY MORNING / FEMME FATALE** [-] [ ]

Verve Verve

Oct 67. (lp) **THE VELVET UNDERGROUND AND NICO** [ ] [ ] Dec 66
– Sunday morning / I'm waiting for the man / Femme fatale / Venus in furs / Run run run / All tomorrow's parties / Heroin / There she goes again / I'll be your mirror / Black angel's death song / European son to Delmore Schwartz. *(re-iss.+c.Aug83 on 'Polydor', cd-iss.1986)*

— Trimmed to a quartet when NICO preferred the solo life.

Jun 68. (lp) **WHITE LIGHT / WHITE HEAT** [ ] [ ] Dec 67
– White light – white heat / he gift / Lady Godiva's operation / Here she comes now / I heard her call my name / Sister Ray. *(re-iss.Oct71) (re-iss.+cd.Apr84 on 'Polydor')*

Mar 68. (7") **I HEARD HER CALL MY NAME. / HERE SHE COMES NOW** [-] [ ]

— **DOUG YULE** – bass, vocals, keyboards, guitar repl. CALE who went solo

M.G.M. M.G.M.

Apr 69. (lp) **THE VELVET UNDERGROUND** [ ] [ ] Mar 69
– Candy says . . . / What goes on / Some kinda love / Pale blue eyes / Jesus / Beginning to see the light / I'm set free / That's the story of my life / The murder mystery / Afterhours. *(re-iss.Nov71 & Mar76) (re-iss.Sep83 on 'Polydor', cd-iss.May86)*

1969. (7") **JESUS. / WHAT GOES ON** [-] [ ]

— **BILLY YULE** – drums repl. TUCKER who had a baby. **MO TUCKER** returned in 1970 and BILLY only appeared on MAX's live album (see compilations)

Dec 70. (7") **WHO LOVES THE SUN. / OH SWEET NUTHIN'** [-] [ ]

Atlantic Cotillion

Apr 71. (lp) **LOADED** [ ] [ ] Aug 70
– Who loves the sun / Sweet Jane / Rock and roll / Cool it down / New age / Head held high / Lonesome cowboy Bill / I found a reason / Train around the bend / Oh! sweet nuthin'. *(re-iss.May81) (cd-iss.Jun88 on 'Warners') (cd-iss.Feb93 on 'Warners')*

Apr 71. (7") **WHO LOVES THE SUN. / SWEET JANE** [ ] [ ]

— (Aug70) now with no originals The **YULE's** brought in newcomers **WALTER POWERS** – bass repl. LOU REED who went solo in 1971. (1971) **WILLIE ALEXANDER** – guitar repl. MORRISON who took a doctorate in English. MO TUCKER finally left to bring up family. She eventually had 5 kids and went solo in 1980.

Polydor Polydor

Feb 73. (lp) **SQUEEZE** [ ] [ ]
– Little Jack / Mean old man / She'll make you cry / Wordless / Dopey Joe / Crash / Friends / Jack and Jane / Send no letter / Louise.

— Folded soon after above, DOUG sessioned for ELLIOTT MURPHY and later joined AMERICAN FLYER.

– compilations, others, etc. –

Aug 72. Atlantic/ US= Cotillion; (lp) **LIVE AT MAX'S KANSAS CITY (live 22 Aug'70)** [ ] [ ] May 72
– I'm waiting for the man / Sweet Jane / Lonesome Cowboy Bill / Beginning to see the light / I'll be your mirror / Pale blue eyes / Sunday morning / New age / Femme fatale / After hours. *(cd-iss.Jun93 on 'Atlantic')*

Aug 73. Atlantic/ US= Cotillion; (7") **SWEET JANE** (live). / **ROCK AND ROLL** (live) [ ] [-]

Dec 71. MGM; (d-lp) **ANDY WARHOL'S VELVET UNDERGROUND FEATURING NICO** [ ] [-]
-I'm waiting for the man / Candy says / Run, run, run / White light -white heat / All tomorrow's parties / Sunday morning / I heard her call my name / Femme fatale / Heroin / Here she comes now / There she goes again / Sister Ray / Venus in furs / European son / Pale blue eyes / Black angel's death song / Beginning to see the light.

Jun 73. MGM; (7"m) **CANDY SAYS. / I'M WAITING FOR THE MAN / RUN RUN RUN** [ ] [-]

1974. MGM; (lp) **ARCHETYPES** [-] [ ]

Oct 73. Verve/ US= MGM; (lp) **THE VELVET UNDERGROUND AND LOU REED** [ ] [ ]

Feb 79. Mercury; (d-lp) **1969 – THE VELVET UNDERGROUND LIVE (live)** [ ] [ ] Apr 74
– I'm waiting for the man / Lisa says / What goes on / Sweet Jane / We're gonna have a real good time together / Femme fatale / New age / Rock and roll / Beginning to see the light / Ocean / Pale blue eyes / Heroin / Some kinda love / Over you / Sweet Bonnie Brown – It's just too much / I'll be your mirror / White light – white heat. *(re-iss.Nov84) (c+cd-VOL.1 & VOL.2 in 1988)*

1976. A.E.B.; (7"m) **FOGGY NOTION – INSIDE YOUR HEART. / I'M STICKING WITH YOU / FERRYBOAT BILL** [ ] [-]

Sep 88. Plastic Inev..; (lp) **THE VELVET UNDERGROUND ETC.** [-] [ ]
– The ostrich / Cycle Annie / Sneaky Pete / Noise.

Sep 88. Plastic Inev..; (lp) **THE VELVET UNDERGROUND AND SO ON** [-] [ ]
– It's alright (the way you live) / I'm not too sorry / Stephanie says.

Nov 80. Polydor; (d-lp)(d-c) **GREATEST HITS** [ ] [-]

Oct 82. Polydor; (12"ep) **HEROIN / VENUS IN FURS. / I'M WAITING FOR THE MAN / RUN RUN RUN** [ ] [-]

Feb 85. Polydor; (lp)(c) **V.U.** (rare rec.68-69) [47] [85]
– I can't stand it / Stephanie says / She's my best friend / Lisa says / Ocean / Foggy notion / Temptation inside your heart / One of these days / Andy's chest / I'm sticking with you. *(cd-iss.Jun87)*

May 86. Polydor; (5xlp-box)(5xcd-box) **BOXED SET** [ ] [ ]
– (first 3 albums, plus V.U. / ANOTHER VIEW)

Feb 87. Polydor; (lp)(c)(cd) **ANOTHER VIEW** [ ] [ ]
– We're gonna have a good time together / I'm gonna move right in / Hey Mr. Rain (version 1) / Ride into the Sun / Coney Island steeplechase / Guess I'm falling in love / Hey Mr. Rain (version 2) / Ferryboat Bill / Rock and roll (original).

Feb 88. Old Gold; (12") **I'M WAITING FOR THE MAN. / HEROIN** [ ] [-]

Mar 88. Old Gold; (12") **VENUS IN FURS. / ALL TOMORROW'S PARTIES** [ ] [-]

Nov 89. Verve/ US= Polygram; (lp)(c)(cd) **THE BEST OF THE VELVET UNDERGROUND** [ ] [ ]
– I'm waiting for the man / Femme fatale / Run run run / Heroin / All tomorrow's parties / I'll be your mirror / White light – white heat / Stephanie says / What goes on / Beginning to see the light / Pale blue eyes / I can't stand it / isa says / Sweet Jane / Rock and roll.

Oct 95. Polydor; (cd)(c) **THE BEST OF LOU REED & VELVET UNDERGROUND** [56] [ ]

Oct 95. Polydor; (5xcd-box) **PEEL SLOWLY AND SEE** [ ] [-]

— (see also LOU REED discography for other tracks on comps & B's)

VELVET UNDERGROUND

re-formed (**REED, CALE, MORRISON & TUCKER**)

		Sire	Sire
Oct 93.	(d-cd)(w/ free cd) **LIVE MCMXCII (live)** – We're gonna have a good time together / Venus in furs / Guess I'm falling in love / After hours / All tomorrow's parties / Some kinda love / I'll be your mirror / Beginning to see the light / The gift / I heard her call my name / Femme fatale / Hey Mr.Rain / Sweet Jane / Velvet nursery rhyme / White light -white heat / I'm sticking with you / Black angel's death song / Rock'n'roll / I can't stand it / I'm waiting for the man / Heroin / Pale blue eyes / Coyote.	70	
Feb 94.	(7")(c-s) **VENUS IN FURS (live). / I'M WAITING FOR THE MAN (live)** (cd-s+=) – Heroin (live) / Sweet Jane (live).	71	

— On the 30th August 1995, STERLING MORRISON died of lymponia.

. . . Jan – Jun '96 stop press . . .

— Inducted into the Rock'n'roll Hall Of Fame, and performed 'LAST NIGHT I SAID GOODBYE TO A FRIEND', REED's tribute to recently deceased STERLING.

Tom VERLAINE (see under ⇒ TELEVISION)

VERVE

Formed: Wigan, England ... 1991 by 4 schoolboys below. They soon supported the likes of RIDE and SPIRITUALIZED, after being signed by indie label 'Hut'. Made inroads into UK charts by 1993, when 'A STORM IN HEAVEN' hit 27. • **Style:** Spacey rock /pop, similar to PRIMAL SCREAM or SPIRITUALIZED fused with PINK FLOYD or The ROLLING STONES. • **Songwriters:** Group. • **Trivia:** RICHARD believes in astral travel. His nickname is MAD RICHARD, enough said!

Recommended: A STORM IN HEAVEN (*7) / A NORTHERN SOUL (*8)

RICHARD ASHCROFT (b.1971) – vocals / **NICK McCABE** – guitar / **SIMON JONES** – bass / **PETER SALISBURY** – drums

		Hut	Vernon Yard
Mar 92.	(12"ep)(cd-ep) **ALL IN THE MIND. / ONE WAY TO GO / A MAN CALLED SUN**		-
Jun 92.	(12")(cd-s) **SHE'S A SUPERSTAR. (8+mins) / FEEL (10+mins)**	66	-
Oct 92.	(10"ep)(12"ep)(cd-ep) **GRAVITY GRAVE / ENDLESS LIFE / A MAN CALLED SUN (live) / SHE'S A SUPERSTAR (live)**		-
Nov 92.	(cd)(c)(lp) **THE VERVE EP** (all above material)		
		Hut	Caroline
May 93.	(12"ep) **BLUE. / TWILIGHT / WHERE THE GEESE GO** (10"ep+=)(cd-ep+=) – No come down.	69	
Jun 93.	(cd)(c)(lp) **A STORM IN HEAVEN** – Star sail / Slide away / Already there / Beautiful mind / The Sun, the sea / Virtual world / Make it 'til Monday / Blue / Butterfly / See you in the next one (have a good time).	27	
Sep 93.	(7"ep)(12"ep)(cd-ep) **SLIDE AWAY. / MAKE IT 'TIL MONDAY (acoustic) / VIRTUAL WORLD (acoustic)**		

THE VERVE

Apr 95.	(7") **THIS IS MUSIC. / LET THE DAMAGE BEGIN** (12"+=)(cd-s+=) – You and me.	35	
Jun 95.	(7"green)(c-s) **ON YOUR OWN. / I SEE THE DOOR** (cd-s+=) – Little gun / Dance on your bones.	28	
Jul 95.	(cd)(c)(lp) **A NORTHERN SOUL** – A new decade / This is music / On your own / So it goes / A northern soul / Brainstorm interlude / Drive you home / History / No knock on my door / Life's an ocean / Stormy clouds / Stormy clouds (reprise).	13	
Sep 95.	(c-s) **HISTORY / BACK ON MY FEET AGAIN** (cd-s+=) – On your own (acoustic) / Monkey magic (Brain storm mix). (cd-s) – ('A'extended) / Grey skies / Life's not a rehearsal.	24	

This was to be their final release, due to ASHCROFT departing.

– compilations, etc. –

May 94.	Hut; (cd) **NO COMEDOWN** (rare / B-sides)		-

VICTOR (see under ⇒ RUSH)

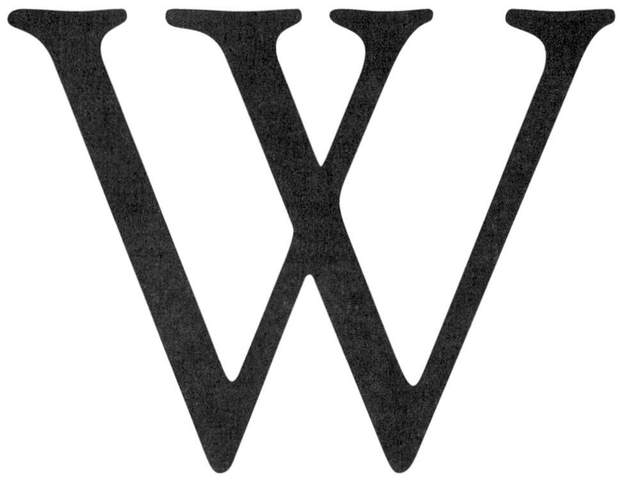

WAILERS (see under ⇒ MARLEY, Bob)

Tom WAITS

Born: 7 Dec'49, Pomona, California, USA. Signed to 'Asylum' in 1973, after being spotted at the Troubadour club. His debut album 'CLOSING TIME' produced by Jerry Yester (ex-LOVIN' SPOONFUL), didn't sell greatly, but it did contain 'OL '55' which was soon covered by The EAGLES on their album 'On The Border'. He gained much respect throughout the next decade, and finally hit the UK album charts in '83 with the great 'SWORDFISHTROMBONES'. • **Style:** Eccentric gruff voiced jazz & blues influenced balladeer. • **Songwriters:** Pens own songs except; WHAT KEEPS MAN ALIVE (Kurt Weill) / HEIGH-HO (from 'Snow White') / IT'S ALL RIGHT WITH ME (Cole Porter). From 1987, his material was co-written with wife and Irish playwright Kathleen Brennan, whom he married on 31 Dec'81. **Filmography:** PARADISE ALLEY (bit-part 1978) / WOLFEN (cameo 1979) / STONE BOY (cameo 1980) / ONE FROM THE HEART (1981 cameo + soundtrack) / THE OUTSIDERS (1983) / RUMBLEFISH (1983) / THE COTTON CLUB (1984 cameo) / DOWN BY LAW (1986) / IRONWEED (1988) / COLD FEET (1989) / NIGHT ON EARTH (1992)?. • **Trivia:** In the late 70's, he parted company with girlfriend/singer RICKIE LEE JONES. In 1991, he sued a radio ad company for using a soundalike in a chips commercial and won nearly $2.5 million.

Recommended: THE ASYLUM YEARS (*8) / SWORDFISHTROMBONES (*9) / RAIN DOGS (*9) / BIG TIME (*8) / BONE MACHINE (*8)

TOM WAITS – vocals, piano, accordion

Asylum / Elektra

May 73. (lp)(c) **CLOSING TIME** [ ] [ ]
– Ol' 55 / I hope that I don't fall in love with you / Virginia Avenue / Old shoes (and picture postcards) / Midnight lullaby / Martha / Rosie / Lonely / Ice cream man / Little trip to Heaven (on the wings of your love) / Grapefruit moon / Closing time. *(re-iss.Jun76)*

May 73. (7") **OL '55. / MIDNIGHT LULLABY** [-] [ ]

Jan 74. (lp)(c) **THE HEART OF SATURDAY NIGHT** [ ] [ ]
– New coat of paint / San Diego serenade / Semi suite / Shiver me timbers / Diamonds on my windshield / (Looking for) The heart of Saturday night / Fumblin' with the blues / Please call me baby / Depot, depot / Drunk on the Moon / The ghosts of Saturday night (after hours at Napoleon's pizza house). *(re-iss.Jun76) (cd-iss.1989 on 'WEA')*

Mar 74. (7") **DIAMONDS ON MY WINDSHIELD. / SAN DIEGO SERENADE** [-] [ ]

Jun 75. (7") **NEW COAT OF PAINT. / BLUE SKIES** [-] [ ]

Oct 75. (7") **THE HEART OF SATURDAY NIGHT. / DIAMONDS ON MY WINDSHIELD** [-] [ ]

— with **MIKE MELVOIN** – piano / **JIM HUGHART** – bass / **BILL GOODWIN** – drums

Dec 75. (d-lp)(c) **NIGHTHAWKS AT THE DINER (live)** [ ] [ ] Oct 75
– (opening intro) / Emotional weather report / (intro) / On a foggy night / (intro) / Eggs and sausage / (intro) / Better off without a wife / Nighthawk postcards (from Easy street) / (intro) / Warm beer and cold women / (intro) / Puttnam County / Spare parts 1 (a nocturnal emission) / Nobody / (intro) / Big Joe and Phantom 309 / Spare parts 2 and closing. *(re-iss.Jun76) (cd-iss.1989 on 'WEA')*

— retained **HUGHART** +new **SHELLY MANNE** – drums / **LEW TABACKIN** – tenor sax

Nov 76. (7") **STEP RIGHT UP. / THE PIANO HAS BEEN DRINKING (NOT ME)** [-] [ ]

May 77. (lp)(c) **SMALL CHANGE** [ ] [89] Nov 76
– Tom Traubert's blues / Step right up / Jitterbug boy / I wish I was in New Orleans / The piano has been drinking (not me) / Invitation to the blues / Pasties and a g-string / Bad liver and a broken heart / The one that got away / Small change / I can't wait to get off work. *(cd-iss.1989 on 'WEA')*

— **FRANK VICARI** – tenor sax / **JACK SHELDON** – trumpet repl. TABACKIN

Oct 77. (lp)(c) **FOREIGN AFFAIRS** [ ] [ ]
– Cinny's waltz / Muriel / I never talk to strangers / Jack and Neal – California here I come / A sight for sore eyes / Potter's field / Burma shave / Barber shop / Foreign affair. *(cd-iss.Mar95 on 'Warners')*

— **RICK LAWSON** – drums repl. MANNE / added **ROLAND BAUTISTA + RAY CRAWFORD** – guitar / **BYRON MILLER** – bass / **DA WILLIE CONGA** – piano / **HAROLD BATTISTE**

Apr 79. (7") **SOMEWHERE. / RED SHOES BY THE DRUGSTORE** [ ] [ ]

Aug 79. (lp)(c) **BLUE VALENTINE** [ ] [ ]
– Somewhere / Red shoes by the drugstore / Christmas card from a hooker in Minneapolis / Romeo is bleeding / Wrong side of the road / Whistlin' past the graveyard / Kentucky Avenue / A sweet little bullet from a pretty blue gun / Blue valentines. *(cd-iss.Feb93)*

— retained **HUGHART + BAUTISTA** + new **LARRY TAYLOR** – upright bass / **RONNIE BARRON** – organ / **GREG COHEN** – bass / **PLAS JOHNSON** – sax / **BIG JOHN THOMASSIE** – drums

Oct 80. (lp)(c) **HEARTATTACK AND VINE** [ ] [96]
– Saving all my love for you / On the nickel / In shades / Downtown / Jersey girl / Til the money runs out / Mr.Segal / Ruby's arms. *(cd-iss.1989 on 'WEA') (re-iss.cd May93)*

Dec 80. (7") **JERSEY GIRL. / HEARTATTACK AND VINE** [-] [ ]

Nov 81. (lp)(c) **BOUNCED CHECKS** (compilation, some live) [ ] [ ]
– Heartattack and vine / Jersey girl / Eggs and sausage / I never talk to strangers / The piano has been drinking (not me) / Whistlin' past the graveyard / Mr. Henry / Diamonds on my windshield / Burma shave / Tom Traubert's blues.

— + many session people from above incl.**VICTOR FELDMAN** – percussion

C.B.S. / Columbia

Feb 83. (lp) **ONE FROM THE HEART (Film Soundtrack) ("TOM WAITS & CRYSTAL GAYLE")** [ ] [ ]
– (opening montage): Tom's piano intro – Once upon a town – The wages of love / Is there any way out of this dream / Picking up after you / Old boyfriends / Broken bicycles / I beg your pardon / Little boy blue / (instrumental montage): The tango – Circus girl / You can't unring a bell / This one's from the heart / Take me home / Presents / (others by CRYSTAL GAYLE only.). *(cd-iss.Jan91)*

— **FRED TACKETT** – guitar + **STEPHEN TAYLOR HODGES** – drums repl. BAUTISTA + LAWSON / added **FRANCIS THUMM** – pump organ / **RANDY ALDCROFT** – horns

Island / Island

Sep 83. (lp)(c) **SWORDFISHTROMBONES** [62] [ ]
– Underground / Shore leave / Dave the butcher / Johnsburg, Illinois / 16 shells from a thirty-ought-six / Town with no cheer / In the neighbourhood / Just another sucker on the vine / Frank's wild years / Swordfishtrombones / Down, down, down / Soldier's things / Gin soaked boy / Trouble's braids / Rainbirds. *(re-iss.Sep86, cd-iss.Nov87, c+cd re-iss.Jun89) (re-iss.lp Jan94 + May94)*

Oct 83. (7") **IN THE NEIGHBOURHOOD. / FRANK'S WILD YEARS** [ ] [ ]

— **MARC RIBOT** – guitar + **MICHAEL BLAIR** – drums, percussion repl. TACKETT, THUMM + HODGES / **WILLIAM SCHIMMEL** – piano / **RAPLH CARNEY** – sax, clarinet + **BOB FUNK** – trombone repl. FELDMAN + ALDCROFT

Oct 85. (lp)(c)(cd) **RAIN DOGS** [29] [ ]
– Singapore / Clap hands / Cemetery polka / Jockey full of bourbon / Tango till they're sore / Big black Mariah / Diamonds and gold / Hang down your head / Time / Rain dogs / Midtown / Ninth and headpin / Gun Street girl / Union square / Blind love / Walking Spanish / Downtown train / Bride of Rain dog / Anywhere I lay my head. *(re-iss.cd.Aug89 & Apr91)*

Nov 85. (7")(12") **DOWNTOWN TRAIN. / TANGO 'TILL THEY'RE SORE** [ ] [ ]

Feb 86. (7")(12") **IN THE NEIGHBOURHOOD. / SINGAPORE** [ ] [ ]
(d7"+=) – Tango till they're sore (live) / Rain dogs (live).
(12") – ('A'side) / Jockey full of bourbon / Tango till they're sore (live) / 16 shells from a thirty-ought-six (live).

— Past live group **FRED TACKETT** – guitar / **RICHIE HAYWARD** – drums / **LARRY TAYLOR** – upright bass. Retained only **TAYLOR, CARNEY, SCHIMMEL** / new: **MORRIS TEPPER** – guitar / **FRANCIS THUMM** – pump organ (on some) / guest **DAVID HIDALGO** – accordion

Aug 87. (lp)(c)(cd) **FRANK'S WILD YEARS (Soundtrack)** [20] [ ]
– Hang on St. Christopher / Straight to the top (rhumba) / Blow wind blow / Temptation / Innocent when you dream (barroom) / I'll be gone / I'll take New

Well with buckshot eyes and a purple heart - I rolled down the National stroll and with
a big fat paycheck strapped to my hipsack and a shore leave wrist watch underneath my sleeve,
In a Hong Kong drizzle on Cuban Heels - I rowed down the gutter to the blood bank.....
SHORELEAVE

York / Telephone call from Istanbul / Cold cold ground / Train song / Yesterday is here / Please wake me up / Frank's theme / More than rain / Way down in the hole / Straight to the top (Vegas). *(re-iss.cd.Jun89 & Apr91)*

— 1988 live band **WILLIE SCHWARZ** – keyboards, accordion repl. SCHIMMEL + TEPPER

Sep 88. (lp)(c)(cd) **BIG TIME (live)** [84] [ ]
– 16 shells from a thirty-ought-six / Red shoes / Cold cold ground / Way down in the hole / Falling down / Strange weather / Big black Mariah / Rain dogs / Train song / Telephone call from Istanbul / Gun street girl / Time. (cd+=) Underground / Straight to the top / Yesterday is here / Johnsburg, Illinois / Ruby's arms / Clap hands.

Sep 88. (7") **16 SHELLS FROM A THIRTY-OUGHT-SIX (live). / BIG BLACK MARIAH (live)** [ ] [ ]
(12"+=) – Ruby's arms (live).

May 92. (cd)(c)(lp) **NIGHT ON EARTH – SOUNDTRACK** [ ] [ ]
– Back in the good old world / Los Angeles mood (chromium descentions) / Los Angeles theme (another private dick) / New York theme (hey, you can have that heart attack outside, buddy) / New York mood (a new haircut and a busted lip) / Baby, I'm not a baby anymore (Beatrice theme) / Good old world (waltz) / Carnival (Brunello del Montalcino) / On the old side of the world (vocal) / Good old world (gypsy instrumental) / Paris mood (un de fromage) / Dragging a dead priest / Helsinki mood / Carnival Bob's confession / Good old world (waltz vocal) / On the other side of the world (instrumental).

Aug 92. (7") **GOIN' OUT WEST. / A LITTLE RAIN** [ ] [ ]
(10"+=)(cd-s+=) – The ocean doesn't want me / Back in the good old world (gypsy).

Sep 92. (cd)(c)(lp) **BONE MACHINE** [26] [ ]
– Earth died screaming / Dirt in the ground / Such a scream / All stripped down / Who are you / The ocean doesn't want me / Jesus gonna behave / A little rain / In the Colosseum / Goin' out west / Murder in the red barn / Black wings / Whistle down the wind / I don't wanna grow up / Let me get up on it / That feel.

Nov 93. (cd)(c)(lp) **THE BLACK RIDER** [47] [ ]
– Lucky day overture / The black rider / November / Just the right bullets / Black box theme / 'T ain't no sin / Flash pan hunter intro / That's the way / The briar and the rose / Russian dance / Gospel train-orchestra / I'll shoot the Moon / Flash pan hunter / Crossroads / Gospel train / Interlude / Oily night / Lucky day / The last rose of summer / Carnival.

— 3 tracks were co-written with author WILLIAM S.BURROUGHS.

– more compilations, etc. –

Apr 84. Asylum; (d-lp)(c) **THE ASYLUM YEARS** [ ] [ ]
– Diamonds on my windshield / Looking for the heart of Saturday night / Martha / The ghosts of Saturday night / Grapefruit Moon / Small change / Burma slave / I never talk to strangers / Tom Traubert's blues / Blue valentine / Potter's field / Kentucky avenue / Somewhere / Ruby's arms. *(cd-iss.Oct86, cd-omitted 9 tracks but added 3 others)*

Mar 93. Asylum; (7")(c-s) **HEARTATTACK AND VINE. / BLUE VALENTINES** [ ] [ ]
(cd-s+=) – On a foggy night (live) / Intro to a foggy night (live).

Sep 85. Island; (lp)(c) **ANTHOLOGY** [ ] [ ]

Nov 92. Island; (d-cd) **SWORDFISHTROMBONES / RAINDOGS** [ ] [ ]

Jul 91. Edsel; (cd) **THE EARLY YEARS** (rare & demos) [ ] [-]
– Goin' down slow / Poncho's lament / I'm your late night evening prostitute / Had me a girl / Ice cream man / Rockin' chair / Virginia Ave. / Midnight lullabye / When you ain't got nobody / Little trip to Heaven / Frank's song / Looks like I'm up shit creek again / So long I'll see you.

1992. Edsel; (cd) **THE EARLY YEARS VOL.2** [ ] [-]
– Hope I don't fall in love with you / Ol' 55 / Mockin bird / In between love / Blue skies / Nobody / I want you / Shiver me timbers / Grapefruit moon / Diamonds on my windshield / Please call me, baby / So it goes / Old shoes.

Rick WAKEMAN

Born: 18 May'49, Perivale, Middlesex, England. Aged 16, he attended The Royal College of Music, but interest in playing live and doing sessions, made him drop out. His in-demand pop session work (i.e.WHITE PLAINS, EDISON LIGHTHOUSE, etc.), led him to play on albums by CAT STEVENS, DAVID BOWIE, T.REX, etc. In 1970, he joined The STRAWBS, but the following year he couldn't turn down YES, as they matched his classical ambitions. He was on-off YES member during the 70's, and started own solo career on 'A&M' records. Taking themes of history, fiction and legend, he released 3 well-received Top 10 albums between 1973-1975. His second album JOURNEY TO THE CENTRE OF THE EARTH (an adaptation of Jules Verne classic book) was premiered live at The Royal Festival Hall Jan'74, and when released hit UK No.1. He with orchestra and choir performed it at an open-air Crystal Palace Garden Party, going on to major US tours. This took its toll as RICK suffered minor heart attack nearing the end of pocket-draining tour. Nevertheless, he continued in the studio with another epic concept ' . . . KING ARTHUR' in 1975. With move into movie work, etc., his public attention drifted somewhat, thus his steady decline of commercial success. • **Style:** Virtuoso exhibitionist keyboard-player, whose flash image (long blonde hair and ankle-length silver capes) matched that of other piano-basher at the time KEITH EMERSON. Will be remembered in the next century, not for his theatrical rock albums, but for the classical style and beauty they created. • **Songwriters:** All his own work, but with little snatches of past classics interspersed with his indelible stamp. • **Trivia:** Most distinguished session work included LIFE ON MARS (David Bowie) / CHANGES (Black Sabbath) / MORNING HAS BROKEN (Cat Stevens) / LOU REED's debut album. WAKEMAN was married in the 70's to Ros and settled down in a Buckingham mansion alongside his collection of Rolls Royce's. They had 3 children, before their divorce. In the 80's, RICK then married ex-model NINA CARTER (also of twin-sister group BLONDE ON BLONDE) and fathered another 2 (so far) before finding Christianity. BILL ODDIE (of the GOODIES TV programme) guested vox on 2nd lp & 'CRIMINAL RECORD'.

Recommended: JOURNEY TO THE CENTRE OF THE EARTH (*7) / THE SIX WIVES OF HENRY VIII (*8) / THE MYTHS & LEGENDS OF KING ARTHUR . . . (*7).

RICK WAKEMAN – keyboards (a member of YES; Aug71-Jun74, Nov76-Mar80, 1990+)

— now used various YES people on sessions plus numerous choirs & ensembles.

A & M A & M

Feb 73. (lp)(c) **THE SIX WIVES OF HENRY VIII** [7] [30]
– Catherine of Aragon / Anne of Cleves / Catherine Howard / Jane Seymour / Anne Boleyn / Catherine Parr. *(re-iss.May81) (re-iss.+cd.Aug89) (also on quad-US)*

Mar 73. (7") **CATHERINE. / ANNE** [ ] [ ]

— Introduced **ASHLEY HOLT** – vocals / **ROGER NEWELL** – bass / **BARNEY JAMES** – drums / plus The ENGLISH ROCK ENSEMBLE with The LONDON SYMPHONY ORCHESTRA. Narration by actor DAVID HEMMINGS.

May 74. (lp)(c) **JOURNEY TO THE CENTRE OF THE EARTH** [1] [3]
– The journey / Recollections / The battle / The forest. *(re-iss.Feb85 on 'Hallmark') (cd-iss.1988 on 'Mobile Fidelity') (also on quad-US) (re-iss.cd+c May93 on 'Spectrum')*

Oct 74. (7") **THE JOURNEY. / THE RETURN** [-] [ ]

Dec 74. (7") **THE BATTLE. / AND NOW A WORD FROM OUR SPONSOR** [-] [ ]

Apr 75. (lp)(c) **THE MYTHS AND LEGENDS OF KING ARTHUR AND THE KNIGHTS OF THE ROUND TABLE** [2] [21]
– Arthur / Lady of the lake / Guinevere / Sir Lancelot & the Black Knight / Merlin the magician / Sir Galahad / The last battle. *(re-iss.Nov85 on 'President') (also on quad-US)*

Jun 75. (7") **MERLIN THE MAGICIAN. / SIR GALAHAD** [-] [ ]

Nov 75. (lp) **LISZTOMANIA (Soundtrack w/ ROGER DALTRY)** [ ] [ ]
– Rienzi / Chpsticks fantasia / Love's dream / Dante period / Orpheus song / Hell / Hibernation / Excelsior song / Master race / Rape, pillage and clap funerailles / Free song / Peace at last.

Jan 76. (7") **ORPHEUS SONG (w/ ROGER DALTRY). / LOVE'S DREAM** [-] [ ]

— For North & South American tour he trimmed his ENGLISH ROCK ENSEMBLE down to **ASHLEY HOLT** – vocals / **JOHN DUNSTERVILE** – guitar / **ROGER NEWELL** – bass / **TONY FERNANDEZ** – drums / **REG BROOKS + MARTYN SHIELDS** – brass section

Apr 76. (lp)(c) **NO EARTHLY CONNECTION** [9] [67]
– Music reincarnate: (part 1) The warning – (part 2) The maker – (part 3) The spaceman – (part 4) The realization – (part 5) The reaper / The prisoner / The lost cycle.

Jan 77. (lp)(c) **WHITE ROCK (Original Film Soundtrack)** [14] [ ]
– White rock / Searching for gold / The loser / The shoot / Lax'x / After the ball / Montezuma's revenge / Ice run.

— Above from 1976 Winter Olympics docu-film, narrated by James Coburn.

Jun 77. (7") **WHITE ROCK. / AFTER THE BALL** [-] [ ]

Nov 77. (lp)(c) **RICK WAKEMAN'S CRIMINAL RECORD** [25] [ ]
– Statute of justice / Crime of passion / Chamber of horrors / Birdman of Alcatraz / The breathalizer / Judas Iscariot. *(re-iss.Mar82)*

Apr 78. (7") **BIRDMAN OF ALCATRAZ. / AND NOW A WORD FROM OUR SPONSOR** [-] [ ]

Apr 79. (7") **FLACONS DE NEIGE. / BIRDMAN OF ALCATRAZ** [ ] [ ]

May 79. (d-lp)(c) **RHAPSODIES** [25] [ ]
– Pedra da Gavea / Front line / Bombay duck / Animal showdown / Big Ben / Rhapsody in blue / Wooly Willy tango / The pulse / Swan lager / March of the gladiators / Flacons de Neige / The flasher / The palais / Stand by / Sea horses / Half holiday / Summertime.

Jun 79. (7")(7"pic-d) **ANIMAL SHOWDOWN. / SEA HORSES** [ ] [-]

Nov 79. (7") **SWAN LAGER. / WOOLLY WILLY TANGO** [ ] [-]

Feb 80. (7") **I'M SO STRAIGHT I'M A WEIRDO. / DO YOU BELIEVE IN FAIRIES?** [ ] [-]

WEA not issued

Oct 80. (7") **THE SPIDER. / DANIELLE** [ ] [-]

Moon not issued

Nov 82. (7") **I'M SO STRAIGHT I'M A WEIRDO. / MAYBE '80 (edit)** [ ] [-]

Dec 82. (lp)(c) **ROCK AND ROLL PROPHET** (rec.1979) [ ] [-]
– Return of the prophet / I'm so straight I'm a weirdo / The dragon / Dark / Alpha sleep / Maybe '80 / March of the child soldiers / Early warning / Spy of '55 / Stalemate / Do you believe in fairies / Rock'n'roll prophet. *(cd-iss.Apr93 on 'President')*

RICK WAKEMAN BAND

featured **FERNANDEZ / STEVE BARNACLE** – bass / **GARY BARNACLE** – sax / **TIM STONE** – guitar / etc.

Charisma Charisma?

Jun 81. (lp)(c) **1984** [24] [ ]
– 1984 overture – part 1 & 2 / War games / Julia / The hymn / The room – part 1 & 2 / Robot man / Sorry / No name / 1984 / Forgotten memories / The proles / 1984.

Jul 81. (7") **JULIA'S SONG. / SORRY** [ ] [-]

Nov 81. (7") **ROBOT MAN. / 1984 OVERTURE (part 1)** [ ] [-]

Jan 82. (lp)(c) **THE BURNING (solo Soundtrack)** [ ] [ ]
– Themes from 'The Burning' / The chase continues / Variations on the fire / Sheer terror and more / The burning (end title theme) / Campfire story / The fire / Doin' it / Devil's creek breakdown / The chase / Sheer terror.

RICK WAKEMAN

solo with music from 1982 football World Cup in Spain (next).

Apr 83. (7") **LATIN REEL (G'OLE THEME). / NO POSSIBLA** [ ] [-]

Apr 83. (lp)(c) **G'OLE (film soundtrack)** [ ] [-]
– International flag / The dove / Wayward spirit / Red island / Latin reel (theme from G'ole) / Spanish holiday / No possibla / Shadows / Black pearls / Frustration / Spanish montage / G'ole.

1983. (lp)(c) **THE COST OF LIVING** [ ] [ ]
– Twij / Pandomonia / Gone but not forgotten / One for the road / Bedtime stories / Happening man / Shakespeare's run / Monkey nuts / Elegy (written in a country church yard). *(re-iss.Aug88)*

— Oct '84, WAKEMAN collaborated on album BEYOND THE PLANETS by KEVIN PEEK (Sky); hit 64

— His Spring 1985 tour band: **TONY FERNANDEZ** – drums / **CHAS CRONK** – bass / **RICK FENN** – lead guitar / **GORDON NEVILLE** – vocals / **LYNN SHEPHERD** – b.vocals

T.B.G. not issued

Dec 84. (7") **GLORY BOYS. / GHOST OF A ROCK AND ROLL STAR** [ ] [-]
(12"+=) – Elgin mansions.

Mar 85. (lp)(c)(cd) **SILENT NIGHTS** [ ] [-]
– Tell 'em all you know / The opening line / The opera / Man's best friend / Glory boys / Silent nights / Ghost of a rock and roll star / The dancer / Elgin mansions / That's who I am.

Jun 85. (7")(12") **THE THEME FROM 'LYTTON'S DIARY'. / DATABASE** [ ] [-]

Dec 85. (lp) **LIVE AT HAMMERSMITH (live)** [ ] [-]
– Arthur / Three wives of Henry VIII / The journey / Merlin the magician. *(cd-iss.Jan87)*

Coda not issued

Apr 86. (lp)(c)(cd) **COUNTRY AIRS** [ ] [-]
– Dandelion dreams / Stepping stones / Ducks and drakes / Morning haze / Waterfalls / Quite valleys / Nature trail / Heather carpets / Wild moors / Lakeland walks. *(re-iss.cd+c Oct92 on Art Of Language)*

Apr 86. (7") **WATERFALLS. / HEATHER CARPETS** [ ] [-]

Stylus not issued

Nov 86. (d-lp)(d-c)(cd) **THE GOSPELS** [94] [-]
– The baptism / The welcoming / The sermon on the mount / The Lord's Prayer / The way / The road to Jerusalem / Trial and error / Galilee
– The gift / The magnificat / Welcome a star / Power (the acts of the apostles) / The word / The hour / The children of mine / The last verse

President not issued

Mar 87. (lp)(c) **CRIMES OF PASSION (Soundtrack)** [ ] [-]
– It's a lovely life (featuring MAGGIE BELL) / Eastern shadows / Joanna / The stretch / Policeman's ball / Stax / Taken in hand / Paradise lost / The box / Web of love. *(cd+=)* Dangerous woman (featuring MAGGIE BELL).

Aug 87. (lp)(c)(cd) **THE FAMILY ALBUM** [ ] [-]
– Adam (Rick's second son) / Black Beauty (black rabbit) / Jemma (Rick and Nina's daughter) / Benjamin (Rick's third son) / Oscar (Rick & Nina's son) / Oliver (Rick's eldest son) / Nina (Rick's wife) / Chloe (German shepherd) / Rookie (cat) / Tilly (Golden Retriever) / Mum / Dad. (c+=) – Wiggles (black & white rabbit). (cd++=) – The day after the fair / Mackintosh.

Feb 88. (lp)(c)(cd) **A SUITE OF GODS ("RICK WAKEMAN & RAMON RAMEDIOS")** [ ] [-]

Apr 88. (lp)(c)(cd) **ZODIAQUE ("RICK WAKEMAN & TONY FERNANDEZ")** [ ] [-]
– Sagittarius / Capricorn / Gemini / Cancer / Pisces / Aquarius / Aries / Libra / Leo / Virgo / Taurus / Scorpio.

— retained **FERNANDEZ.** recruited **DAVEY PATON** – bass / **JOHN KNIGHTSBRIDGE** – guitar (2) / guest vocals – **JOHN PARR / ROY WOOD / TRACEY ACKERMAN + ASHLEY HOLT**

Jul 88. (7") **CUSTER'S LAST STAND. / OCEAN CITY** [ ] [-]
(12"+=)(c-s+=) – Ice / Open up your eyes.

Jul 88. (lp)(c)(cd) **TIME MACHINE** [ ] [-]
– Custer's last stand / Ocean city / Angel of time / Slaveman / Ice / Open up your eyes / Elizabethan rock / Make me a woman / Rock age. (cd cont. extended versions of some tracks)

Nov 89. (lp)(c)(cd) **SEA AIRS (A NEW AGE COLLECTION)** [ ] [-]
(compilation 1985-89)
– Harbour lights / The pirate / Storm clouds / Last at sea / The mermaid / Waves / The fisherman / Flying fish / The Marie Celeste / Time and tide / The lone sailor / The sailor's lament.

Nov 90. (cd)(c)(lp) **NIGHT AIRS** [ ] [-]
– The sad dream / Twilight / The sleeping child / Mr.Badger / Jack Frost / The lone star / Rain shadows / Fox by night / Night owls / An evening romance.

Ambient not issued

Feb 91. (cd)(c)(lp) **PHANTOM POWER** [ ] [-]
– The visit / Heaven / The rat / The stiff / Evil love / The voice of love / Heat of the moment / Fear of love / The love trilogy:- One night – The dream sequence – One night of love / The hangman / The sand-dance / You can't buy my love / Phantom power / The chase.

President not issued

Dec 92. (cd) **COUNTRY AIRS (re-recording)** [ ] [-]
– Lakeland walks / Wild moors / Harvest festival / The glade / Dandelion dreams / Ducks and drakes / Green to gold / Stepping stones / Morning haze / Waterfalls / The Spring / Quiet valleys / Nature trails / Heather carpets.

Feb 93. (cd)(c)(lp) **MUSIC FROM CRIMES OF PASSION** [ ] [-]

Feb 93. (cd) **WAKEMAN WITH WAKEMAN ("RICK WAKEMAN & ALAN WAKEMAN")** [ ] [ ]
– Lure of the wild / The beach comber / Meglomania / Raga and rhyme / Sync or swim / Jigajig / Caesarea / After the atom / The suicide shuiffle / Past and present / Paint it black.
(Above was with son ADAM)

Jun 93. (cd) **THE CLASSICAL CONNECTION** [ ] [-]

Jun 92. (cd) **THE CLASSICAL CONNECTION II** [ ] [-]

Jul 93. (cd)(c) **ASPIRANT SUNRISE** [ ] [-]
– Thoughts of love / Gentle breezes / Whispering cornfields / Peaceful beginnings / Dewy morn / Musical dreams / Distant thoughts / The dove / When time stood still / Secret moments / Peaceful.

Jul 93. (cd)(c) **ASPIRANT SUNSET** [ ] [-]
– Floating clouds / Still waters / The dream / The sleeping village / Sea of tranquility / Peace / Sunset / Dying embers / Dusk / Evening moods.

Jul 93. (cd)(c) **ASPIRANT SUNSHADOWS** [ ] [-]
– The nightwind / Churchyard / Tall shadows / Shadowlove / Melancholy mood / Mount Fuji by night / Hidden reflections / The evening harp / The moonraker pond / The last lamplight / Japanese sunshadows.

Sep 93. (cd) **AFRICAN BACH** (rec.1991) [ ] [-]
– African Bach / Message of mine / My homeland / Liberty / Anthem / Brainstorm / Face in the crowd / Just a game / Africa east / Don't touch the merchandise.

Sep 93. (cd) **2000 A.D. INTO THE FUTURE** [ ] [-]
– Into the future / Toward peace / 2000 A.D. / A.D rock / The time tunnel / Robot dance / A new beginning / Forward past / The seventh dimension.

Oct 93. (cd) **HERITAGE SUITE** [ ] [-]
– The chasms / Thorwald's cross / St.Michael's isle / Spanish head / The Ayres / Mona's isle / The Dhoon / The bee orchid / Chapel Hill / The Curraghs / The painted lady / The Peregrine falcon.

Nov 93. (cd) **NO EXPENSE SPARED ("WAKEMAN WITH WAKEMAN")** [ ] [-]

Apr 94. (cd) **SOFTSWORD (KING JOHN AND THE MAGNA CHARTER)** [ ] [ ]
– Magna charter / After prayers / Battle sonata / The siege / Rochester college / The story of love (King John) / March of time / Don't fly away / Isabella / Softsword / Hymn of hope.

— Below as RICK WAKEMAN & HIS BAND

May 94. (cd-ep) **LIGHT UP THE SKY / SIMPLY FREE / STARFLIGHT / THE BEAR** [ ] [ ]

Nov 94. (cd) **ROMANCE OF THE VICTORIAN AGE (with ADAM WAKEMAN)** [ ] [-]
– Burlington arcade / If only / The last teardrop / Still dreaming / Memories of the Victorian age / Lost in words / A tale of love / Mysteries unfold / Forever in my heart / Days of wonder / The swans / Another mellow day / Dance of the elves.

Jun 95. (cd) **THE SEVEN WONDERS OF THE WORLD** (with naration) [ ] [-]
– The Pharoahs Of Alexandria / The Colossus Of Rhodes / The Pyramids Of Egypt / The Gardens Of Babylon / The Temples Of Artemis / The Statue Of Zeus / The Mausoleum At Halicarnassus.

D Sharp not issued

Jul 95. (cd) **CIRQUE SURREAL –** [ ] [-]

Oct 95. (cd) **VISIONS** [ ] [-]

– compilations, others, etc. –

1978. A&M; (lp)(c) **THE ROYAL PHILHARMONIC ORCHESTRA PERFORMING BEST KNOWN WORKS OF RICK WAKEMAN** [ ] [-]
May 81. A&M; (d-c) **THE SIX WIVES OF HENRY VIII / THE MYTHS AND LEGENDS..** [ ] [-]
Feb 89. A&M; (cd-box) **20th ANNIVERSARY** [ ] [ ]
Mar 83. Charisma; (d-c) **1984 / THE BURNING** [ ] [-]
Dec 93. Fragile; (d-cd) **RICK WAKEMAN'S GREATEST HITS** (some with YES) [ ] [ ]
– Roundabout / Wondrous stories / Don't kill the whale / Going for the one / Siberian khatru / Madrigal / Starship trooper/ / Overture / The journey / The Hansbach / Lost in time / The recollection / Stream of voices / The battle / Liddenbrook / The forest / Mount Etna / Journey's end / Sea horses / Catherine of Aragon / Gone but not forgotten / Merlin the magician.
Jan 94. Sony Europe; (cd) **CLASSIC TRACKS** [ ] [ ]
Mar 94. President; (cd) **THE PRIVATE COLLECTION** [ ] [-]
Apr 94. Prestige; (cd)(c) **THE CLASSIC** [ ] [-]
Jun 94. Cyclops; (d-cd) **WAKEMAN WITH WAKEMAN** – THE OFFICIAL LIVE ALBUM (w /ADAM) [ ] [-]
Dec 94. Windsong; (cd) **LIVE ON THE TEST (live)** [ ] [-]

WALKABOUTS

Formed: Seattle, USA . . .1984 by quartet below. After a few releases on US indies (PopLlama going bust), they moved to cult label 'Sub Pop', home of NIRVANA, L7, MUDHONEY, etc. Their first for the label 'CATARACT' was welcomed by critics and public alike. • **Style:** Folk-rock (influenced by Appalachian Mountains!) which lent into the NEIL YOUNG & CRAZY HORSE for other inspiration. • **Songwriters:** Group and later ECKMAN, except covers from roster of Neil Young and Charlie Rich. • **Trivia:** The album CONTRACT featured PETER BUCK (R.E.M.), MARK LANEGAN (Screaming Trees) and IVAN KRAAL (Patti Smith Group). SCAVENGER featured NATALIE MERCHANT and BRIAN ENO.

Recommended: CATARACT (*7)

CHRIS ECKMAN – vocals, guitar / **CARLA TORGENSON** – vocals, guitar / **MICHAEL WELLS** -bass / **TERRI MOELLER** -drums / part-time 6th member **LARRY BARRETT** -banjo, mandolin, guitar

not issued / Necessity

1984. (12"ep) **WALKABOUTS** [-] [ ]
1985. (12"ep) **22 DISASTERS** [-] [ ]

Glitterhouse / Pop Llama

1987. (lp)(cd) **SEE BEAUTIFUL RATTLESNAKE GARDENS** [ ] [ ]
– Jumping off / Breakneck speed / The wellspring / John Reilly / Robert McFarlane blues / This rotten tree / Laughingstock / Glass palace / Feast or famine / Ballad of Moss Head / Who-knows-what / Rattlesnake theme / Weights and rivers. *(re-iss.cd 1995 +=)*– Linda Evans / Mai Tai time / Cyclone / Gather round / Certain gift.

—— added **GLENN SLATER** – keyboards

Sub Pop / Sub Pop

Mar 89. (lp) **CATARACT** [-] [ ]
– Whiskey XXX / Hell's soup kitchen / Whereabouts unknown / End in tow / Bones of contention / Home as found / Smokestack / The wicked skipper.
Feb 90. (12"orange-ep)(c)(cd) **RAG AND BONE** [-] [ ]
– The anvil song / Ahead of the storm / Medicine hut / Wreck of the old £9 / Mr.Clancy / Last ditch. *(cd/c +=)* – CATARACT
Sep 91. (cd)(lp) **SCAVENGER** [-] [ ]
– Dead man rise / Stir the ashes / The night watch / Hang man / Where the deep water goes / Blown away / Nothing is stranger / Let's burn down the cornfield / River blood / Train to mercy.
Jul 92. (12")(cd-s) **DEAD MAN RISE** [ ] [ ]
Feb 93. (12")(cd-s) **JACK CANDY** [ ] [ ]
Mar 93. (cd)(lp) **NEW WEST MOTEL** [ ] [ ]
May 93. (12")(cd-s) **YOUR HOPE SHINES** [ ] [ ]
Nov 93. (cd)(lp) **SATISFIED MIND** [ ] [ ]
Mar 94. (12"ep)(cd-ep) **GOOD LUCK MORNING / NIGHT DRIVE (truck stop version). / FINDLAY'S MOTEL / NOTHING IS A STRANGER** [ ] [ ]
–
May 94. (cd)(lp) **SETTING THE WOODS ON FIRE** [ ] [ ]
– Good luck morning / Firetrap / Bordertown / Feeling no pain / Old crow / Almost wisdom / Sand and gravel / Night drive (truck stop version) / Hole in the mountain / Pass me on over / Up in the graveyard / Promised.

. . . Jan – Jun '96 stop press . . .

Virgin / Virgin

Mar 96. (single) **DEVIL'S ROAD** [ ] [ ]
Apr 96. (cd)(c) **DEVIL'S ROAD** [ ] [ ]
Jun 96. (single) **THE LIGHT WILL STAY ON** [ ] [ ]

Joe WALSH

Born: 20 Nov'47, Wichita, Kansas, USA. Quit The JAMES GANG late 1971, after 4 successful albums. In 1972, he went solo backed by new band BARNSTORM. The following year he was in US Top 30 with classic 'ROCKY MOUNTAIN WAY'. He surprised the rock press in 1975, by taking up the prestigious offer of joining The EAGLES. Many would agree that his guitar contribution on album HOTEL CALIFORNIA was the superior element. • **Style:** Ace hard-rock axeman of the 70's. The 80's were more mellower but with a little experimentation. • **Songwriters:** WALSH wrote all except LOVE LETTERS (Ketty Lester ?). • **Trivia:** In 1980, he stood for US presidential election. That year he also made a cameo appearance in the 'Blues Brothers' film.

Recommended: SO FAR SO GOOD – THE BEST OF. . . (*8)

JOE WALSH – vocals, guitar (ex-JAMES GANG) with his band **BARNSTORM: KENNY PASSARELLI** – bass / **JOE VITALE** – drums

Probe / Dunhill

Sep 72. (lp) **BARNSTORM** [ ] [79]
– Midnight visitor / Here we go / One and one / Giant bohemoth / Mother says / Birdcall morning / Home / I'll tell the world about you / Turn to stone / Comin' down. *(re-iss.Oct74 on 'Anchor')*
Sep 72. (7") **MOTHER SAYS. / I'LL TELL THE WORLD ABOUT YOU** [-] [ ]

—— added **ROCKE GRACE** – keyboards / **JOE LALA** – percussion

Jun 73. (lp) **THE SMOKER YOU DRINK, THE PLAYER YOU GET** [ ] [6]
– Rocky mountain way / Bookends / Wolf / Midnight moodies / Happy ways / Meadows / Dreams / Days gone by / (Daydream) Prayer. *(re-iss.quad.Oct74 on 'Anchor')*
Aug 73. (7") **ROCKY MOUNTAIN WAY. / PRAYER** [-] [23]
(UK-iss.Jul75 on 'A.B.C.')
Jan 74. (7") **MEADOWS. / BOOKENDS** [ ] [89]
(re-iss.Mar76 on 'A.B.C.')

—— In 1974, he sessioned for EAGLES, B.B.KING, etc. Also produced DAN FOGELBERG

—— Solo; used past BARNSTORM members on a couple of tracks, plus new studio & live line-up **DAVID MASON + PAUL HARRIS** – keyboards / **BRYAN GAROFOLO** – bass / **RICKY FATAAR** – drums (ex-BEACH BOYS) / **TOM STEPHENSON** – keyboards

Anchor / Dunhill

Dec 74. (lp)(c) **SO WHAT?** [ ] [11]
– Welcome to the club / Falling down / Pavane / Time out / All night laundromat blues / Turn to stone / Help me thru the night / County fair / Song for Emma.
Feb 75. (7") **TURN TO STONE. / ALL NIGHT LAUNDROMAT BLUES** [ ] [93]

—— Although he was still a solo artist, he also joined EAGLES late '75.

A.B.C. / A.B.C.

Apr 76. (lp)(c) **YOU CAN'T ARGUE WITH A SICK MIND (live)** [28] [20]
– Rocky mountain way / Help me thru the night / Time out / Meadows / Walk away / Turn to stone. *(re-iss.Aug81 + Jun86) (re-iss.Jan83 on 'Fame') (cd-iss.Jun88)*
Apr 76. (7") **TIME OUT (live). / HELP ME THRU THE NIGHT (live)** [-] [ ]
Jun 76. (7") **WALK AWAY (live). / HELP ME THRU THE NIGHT (live)** [ ] [ ]

—— WALSH used mainly session people + VITALE.

Asylum / Asylum

Jun 78. (7") **LIFE'S BEEN GOOD. / THEME FROM BOAT WEIRDOS** [14] [12]
Jun 78. (lp)(c) **BUT SERIOUSLY, FOLKS . . .** [16] [8]
– Over and over / Second hand store / Indian summer / At the station / Tomorrow / Inner tube / Theme from Boat Weirdos / Life's been good. *(cd-iss.Feb93)*
Nov 78. (7") **OVER AND OVER. / AT THE STATION** [ ] [ ]

—— Below from the film 'Urban Cowboy'. B-side by GILLEY'S URBAN COWBOY BAND.

W.E.A. / Full Moon

Jun 80. (7") **ALL NIGHT LONG. / ORANGE BLOSSOM SPECIAL / HOEDOWN** [ ] [19] May 80

—— Now an ex-EAGLES man after their split.

Elektra / Asylum

May 81. (7") **A LIFE OF ILLUSION. / ROCKETS** [-] [34]
May 81. (7") **A LIFE OF ILLUSION. / DOWN ON THE FARM** [ ] [-]
May 81. (lp)(c) **THERE GOES THE NEIGHBORHOOD** [ ] [20]
– Things / Made your mind up / Down on the farm / Rivers (of the hidden funk) / A life of illusion / Bones / Rockets / You never know.
Jul 81. (7") **MADE YOUR MIND UP. / THINGS** [-] [ ]
Jan 82. (7") **WAFFLE STOMP. / THINGS** [-] [ ]

Full Moon / Full Moon

Jul 83. (7") **SPACE AGE WHIZ KIDS. / THEME FROM ISLAND WEIRDOS** [ ] [52] Jun 83
Jul 83. (lp)(c) **YOU BOUGHT IT - YOU NAME IT** [ ] [48]

– I can play that rock & roll / Told you so / Here we are now / The worry song / I.L.B.T.'s / Space age whiz kids / Love letters / Class of '65 / Shadows / Theme from Island weirdos. *(cd-iss.Jul84)*

Aug 83. (7") **I CAN PLAY THAT ROCK & ROLL. / HERE WE ARE NOW** [-] [ ]

Sep 83. (7") **LOVE LETTERS. / TOLD YOU SO** [ ] [-]

Nov 83. (7") **LOVE LETTERS. / I.L.B.T.'s** [-] [ ]

Jun 85. (7") **I BROKE MY LEG. / GOOD MAN DOWN** [-] [ ]

Jun 85. (lp)(c) **THE CONFESSOR** [ ] [65] May 85

– Problems / I broke my leg / Bubbles / Slow dancing / 15 years / Confessor / Rosewood bitters / Good man down / Dear John. *(cd-iss.Jul88)*

— now with **CHAD CROMWELL** – drums / **DAVID COCHRAN + RICK THE . . . PLAYER** – bass / **MARK RIVERA** – saxophone / **JOHN DAVID SOUTHER + JIMI JAMISON** – backing vocals

Aug 87. (lp)(c)(cd) **GOT ANY GUM?** [ ] [ ] Jul 87

– The radio song / Fun / In my car / Malibu / Half of the time / Got any gum? / Up to me / No peace in the jungle / Memory lane / Time.

Aug 87. (7") **THE RADIO SONG. / HOW YA DOIN'** [-] [ ]

Nov 87. (7") **IN MY CAR. / HOW YA DOIN'** [-] [ ]

Epic Pyramid

Jul 91. (cd)(c)(lp) **ORDINARY AVERAGE GUY** [ ] [ ] May 91

– Two sides to every story / Ordinary average guy / The gama goochee / All of a sudden / Alphabetical order / Look at us now / I'm actin' different / Up all night / You might need somebody / Where I grew up / Schooldays.

Jul 91. (7") **ORDINARY AVERAGE GUY. / ALPHABETICAL ORDER** [-] [ ]

— In 1995, JOE was credited on single with LITA FORD.

– compilations, others, etc. –

Jun 77. ABC; (7") **ROCKY MOUNTAIN WAY. / TURN TO STONE** [-] [ ]

Jun 77. ABC; (12"ep) **PLUS FOUR EP** [39] [-]

– Rocky mountain way / Turn to stone / Meadows / Walk away.

Oct 78. ABC; (lp)(c) **SO FAR SO GOOD – THE BEST OF JOE WALSH** [ ] [71]

– Rocky mountain way / Welcome to the club / Bookends / Walk away / Mother says / Turn to stone / Here we go / Pavane / Time out / Meadows. *(re-iss.1983 on 'M.C.A.') (cd-iss.1987)*

Aug 82. MCA; (7") **ROCKY MOUNTAIN WAY. / TURN TO STONE** [ ] [-]

(12"+=)(12"pic-d+=) – Funk 49.

Oct 87. MCA; (cd) **THE SMOKER YOU DRINK . . . / YOU CAN'T ARGUE WITH A SICK MIND** [ ] [-]

Apr 86. Old Gold; (7") **ROCKY MOUNTAIN WAY. / ('B'by Poco)** [ ] [-]

1988. Raw Power; (lp)(c) **WELCOME TO THE CLUB** [ ] [-]

Jul 95. MCA; (cd) **LOOK WHAT I DID** [ ] [-]

WANNADIES

*** NEW ENTRY ***

Formed: Skelleftea, Sweden . . .1989 by (see below). Moved to Stockholm and released two albums, the second of which, the much too commercial 'AQUANATIC', saw them working with ROXETTE songwriter PER GESSLE. Put pen to paper for 'Indolent' in 1995, and debuted that year with 'YOU & ME SONG', which finally gave them deserved Top 20 hit in the Spring of '96. • **Style:** English singing guitar pop-rock, likened to The GO-BETWEENS, NICK DRAKE, DREAM ACADEMY or even TEENAGE FANCLUB fused with BLUR. • **Songwriters:** Group, except; LEE REMICK (Go-Betweens) / NEW LIFE (Depeche Mode) / BLISTER IN THE SUN (Violent Femmes) / I'M A MAN (Spencer Davis Group) / CHILDREN OF THE REVOLUTION (T.Rex) / I GOT A RIGHT (Iggy Pop).

Recommended: BE A GIRL (*9)

PAR WILKSTEN – vocals / **CHRISTINA BERGMARK** – keyboards, vocals / **STEFAN SCHONFELT** – guitar / **FREDRIK SCHONFELT** – bass / **GUNNAR KARLSSON** – drums / **MALMQUIST**

Snap not issued

1989. (lp) **WANNADIES** [ ] [-]

– Together / Heaven / My home town / Things that you love / How beautiful is the Moon / Innocent me / So many lies / Smile / Anything / Black waters / The beast cures the lover / Children of the revolution / Lee Remick. *(re-iss.cd Jan94)*

Jan 93. (cd) **AQUANATIC** [ ] [-]

– Everything's true / Cherry man / Things that I would love to have undone / ove is dead / So hapy now / Lucky you / 1.07 / December days / Something to tell / Suddenly I missed her / God knows / Never killed anyone / I love you love me.

Apr 93. (cd-s) **SO HAPPY NOW / IN THE ALTOGETHER / BIRDS** [ ] [-]

Jul 93. (cd-ep) **CHERRY MAN** [ ] [-]

Jun 94. (cd-s) **LOVE IN JUNE / I GOT A RIGHT** [ ] [-]

— now without MALMQUIST

Indolent Geffen

Aug 95. (7"colrd)(c-s) **YOU & ME SONG. / BLISTER IN THE SUN** [ ] [-]

(cd-s+=) – Lift me up (don't let me down).

Aug 95. (cd)(c)(lp) **BE A GIRL** [ ] [ ]

– You & me song / Might be stars / Love in June / How does it feel? / Sweet nymphet / New world record / Dying for more / Soon you're dead / Do it all the time / Dreamy Wednesdays / Kid. *(re-dist.Apr96)*

Oct 95. (c-s) **MIGHT BE STARS / CHERRY MAN** [51] [ ]

(cd-s+=) – Lee Remick / Love is dead.

(cd-s) – ('A'side) / New life / So happy now / Things that I would love to have undone.

Feb 96. (c-s)(cd-s) **HOW DOES IT FEEL? / DYING FOR MORE (live) / LOVE IN JUNE (live) / MIGHT BE STARS (live)** [53] [ ]

(cd-s) – ('A'side) / Let go oh oh / I'm a man / Never killed anyone.

Apr 96. (7"colrd)(c-s) **YOU & ME SONG. / BLISTER IN THE SUN** [18] [ ]

(cd-s) – ('A'side) / Everybody loves me / I like you a lalalala lot / You & me song (lounge version).

W.A.S.P.

Formed: Los Angeles, California, USA . . . 1983 as W.A.S.P. (We Are Sexual Perverts) by 6'4 ex-New York street gangster BLACKIE LAWLESS. After one banned single for 'Music For Nations', they signed to 'Capitol' in 1984. Immediately struck up a rapport with UK audiences, where they soon became Top 30 act. • **Style:** Heavy horror-metal group, whose live shows featured codpiece-fronted BLACKIE LAWLESS, a beast of a man who simulated torture and violence at every opportunity. During the latter half of the 80's, they had mellowed into a more stereotype hard-rock outfit. • **Songwriters:** Most written by LAWLESS and PIPER, except PAINT IT BLACK (Rolling Stones) / EASY LIVIN' (Uriah Heep) / I DON'T NEED NO DOCTOR (Humble Pie) / LOCOMOTIVE BREATH (Jethro Tull) / THE REAL ME (The Who) / LONG WAY TO THE TOP + WHOLE LOTTA ROSIE (Ac-Dc) / SOMEBODY TO LOVE (Jefferson Airplane). • **Trivia:** Late in 1989, the lucky HOLMES married metal-songstress LITA FORD.

Recommended: FIRST BLOOD, LAST CUTS (*7).

BLACKIE LAWLESS (b. 4 Sep'56) – vocals, bass (ex-SISTER, ex-NEW YORK DOLLS) / **CHRIS HOLMES** (b.23 Jun'61) – lead guitar (ex-SISTER) / **RANDY PIPER** – rhythm guitar / **TONY RICHARDS** – drums

M.F.N. not issued

Apr 84. (7")(12")(7"sha-pic-d)(12"white) **ANIMAL (F**K LIKE A BEAST). / SHOW NO MERCY** [ ] [-]

*(re-iss.12"pic-d.May85) (re-iss.12".Feb88 tracks LIVE ANIMAL (F**K LIKE A BEAST). / DB BLUES / ANIMAL; hit UK 61)*

Capitol Capitol

Aug 84. (lp)(c) **W.A.S.P.** [51] [74]

– I wanna be somebody / L.O.V.E. machine / The flame / B.A.D. / School daze / Hellion / Sleeping (in the fire) / On your knees / Tormentor / The torture never stops. *(re-iss.+cdJun88 on 'Fame', cd re-iss.May89) (re-iss.cd+c Jul94)*

Sep 84. (7")(12")(12"pic-d) **I WANNA BE SOMEBODY. / TORMENTOR** [ ] [ ]

Jan 85. (7")(12") **SCHOOLDAZE. / PAINT IT BLACK** [ ] [ ]

— **STEPHEN RILEY** – drums (ex-KEEL) repl. RICHARDS

Sep 85. (lp)(c) **THE LAST COMMAND** [48] [49]

– Wild child / Ballcrusher / Fistful of diamonds / Jack action / Widow maker / Blind in Texas / Cries in the night / The last command / Running wild in the streets / Sex drive. *(re-iss.+cd.May89 on 'Fame') (re-iss.cd+c Jul94)*

Oct 85. (7")(7"pic-d) **BLIND IN TEXAS. / SAVAGE** [ ] [ ]

(12"+=)(12"pic-d+=) – I wanna be somebody (live).

Jun 86. (7") **WILD CHILD. / MISSISSIPPI QUEEN** [71] [ ]

(12"+=)/ /(d12"+=) – ('A'wild mix)./ / On your knees / Hellion.

— **JOHNNY ROD** – bass (ex-KING KOBRA) repl. PIPER

WASP

(dropped dots). **BLACKIE** now also rhythm guitar

Sep 86. (7")(7"pic-d) **9.5 -N.A.S.T.Y. / EASY LIVING** [70] [ ]

(12"+=) – Flesh and fire.

Oct 86. (lp)(c)(cd) **INSIDE THE ELECTRIC CIRCUS** [53] [60]

– The big welcome / Inside the electric circus / I don't need no doctor / 9.5 - N.A.S.T.Y. / Restless gypsy / Shoot it from the hip / I'm alive / Easy living / Sweet cheetah / Mantronic / King of Sodom and Gomorrah / The rock rolls on. *(re-iss.May89) (re-iss.+cdJul90 on 'Fame') (re-iss.cd+c Jul94)*

W.A.S.P.

Aug 87. (7") **SCREAM UNTIL YOU LIKE IT. / SHOOT IT FROM THE HIP (live)** [32] [ ]
(12"+=)(12"pic-d+=) – Sleeping (in the fire).

Sep 87. (lp)(c)(cd) **LIVE . . . IN THE RAW (live)** [23] [77]
– Inside the electric circus / I don't need no doctor / L.O.V.E. machine / Wild child / 9.5 -N.A.S.T.Y. / Sleeping (in the fire) / The manimal / I wanna be somebody / Harder faster / Blind in Texas. *(cd+=)*– Scream until you like it. *(re-iss.cd+c Jul94)*

Oct 87. (7")(7"sha-pic-d) **I DON'T NEED NO DOCTOR. / WIDOW MAKER (live)** [31] [ ]
(12"+=) – Sex drive (live).

—— now basic trio of **BLACKIE, CHRIS & JOHNNY** when STEPHEN joined L.A.GUNS. **FRANKIE BANALIE** – drums (of QUIET RIOT) filled in temp. / added guest **KEN HENSLEY** – keyboards (ex-URIAH HEEP, ex-BLACKFOOT)

Feb 89. (7")(7"pic-d)(7"purple) **MEAN MAN. / LOCOMOTIVE BREATH** [21] [ ]
(12"+=)(cd-s+=) – For whom the bells toll.

Apr 89. (lp)(c)(cd)(pic-lp) **THE HEADLESS CHILDREN** [8] [48]
– Heretic (the lost child) / The real me / The headless children / Thunderhead / Mean man / The neutron bomber / Mephisto waltz / Forever free / Maneater / Rebel in the F.D.G. *(re-iss.cd+c Jul94)*

May 89. (7")(7"pic-d)(7"blue) **THE REAL ME. / THE LAKE OF FOOLS** [23] [ ]
(12"+=)(cd-s+=) – War cry.

Aug 89. (7")(c-s)(7"sha-pic-d) **FOREVER FREE (eagle edit). / LOVE MACHINE (live'89)** [ ] [ ]
(12"+=)(cd-s+=)(12"laser-etched+=) – Blind in Texas (live'89).

—— JOHNNY ROD left in 1989 as band split. Reformed in August 1990 as BLACKIE LAWLESS & WASP, but they soon returned to original name. **BLACKIE, JOHNNY, KEN, FRANKIE** and new member **BOB GULLICK** – guitar

Parlophone Capitol

Mar 92. (7")(7"pic-d) **CHAINSAW CHARLIE (MURDERS IN THE NEW MORGUE). / PHANTOM IN THE MIRROR** [17] [ ]
(12"+=)(cd-s+=) – The story of Jonathan (prologue to the crimson idol – part I).

—— The April tour added **DAN McDADE** – guitar / **STET HOWLAND** – drums

May 92. (7")(7"pic-d)(7"crimson) **THE IDOL. / THE STORY OF JONATHAN (PROLOGUE TO THE CRIMSON IDOL – PART II)** [41] [ ]
(pic-cd+=) – The eulogy.

Jun 92. (cd)(c)(lp) **THE CRIMSON IDOL** [21] [ ]
– The Titanic overture / The invisible boy / Arena of pleasure / Chainsaw Charlie (murders in the New Morgue) / The gypsy meets the boy / Doctor Rockter / I am one / The idol / Hold on to my heart / The great misconception of me. *(re-iss.cd+c Mar94)*

Oct 92. (7")(7"pic-d) **I AM ONE. / WILD CHILD** [56] [ ]
(10"+=) – Charlie chainsaw / I wanna be somebody.
(cd-s) – ('A'side) / The invisible boy / The real me / The great misconception of me.

Oct 93. (7") **SUNSET & BABYLON. / ANIMAL (F**K LIKE A BEAST)** [38] [ ]
(cd-s+=) – Sleeping in the fire / I wanna be somebody.
(12"+=) – School daze / On your knees.
(12"pic-d+=) – Hellion / Show no mercy.

Oct 93. (cd)(c)(lp) **FIRST BLOOD, LAST CUTS** [69] [ ]
– Animal (f**k like a beast) / L.O.V.E. machine (remix) / I wanna be somebody (remix) / On your knees / Blind in Texas (remix) / Wild child (remix) / I don't need no doctor (remix) / The real me / The headless children / Mean man / Forever free / Chainsaw Charlie / The idol / Sunset and Babylon / Hold on to my heart / Rock and roll to death.

Raw Power ???

Jun 95. (7"sha-pic-d) **BLACK FOREVER. / GOODBYE AMERICA** [ ] [ ]
(cd-s+=) – Skin walker / One tribe.
(cd-s) – ('A'side) / Long way to the top / Whole lotta Rosie.

Jul 95. (cd)(c) **STILL NOT BLACK ENOUGH** [52]
– Still not black enough / Somebody to love / Black forever / Scared to death / Goodbye America / Keep holding on / Rock and roll to death / Breathe / I can't / No way out of here.

WATERBOYS

Formed: London, England ... 1982 by Scotsman MIKE SCOTT and Englishmen ANTHONY THISTLETHWAITE and KARL WALLINGER. SCOTT had previously fronted new wave Edinburgh outfit ANOTHER PRETTY FACE, with ex-Ayr school pals JOHN CALDWELL and JIM GEDDES. The WATERBOYS took their name from LOU REED lyrics (i.e. in the song 'The Kids'), and soon signed to Irish run label 'Ensign', who released their eponymous debut album in 1983. It was preceeded by an airplay favourite 45 'A GIRL CALLED JOHNNY', which nearly dented the charts. After another critically acclaimed album in '84, they broke the UK Top 40 in 1985, with 'THE WHOLE OF THE MOON' (a song that was to re-chart, peaking at No.3 in 1991). • **Style:** Adventurous peoples rock outfit, who digressed into more acoustic orientated Irish folk in the late 80's. Their live shows, however, seemed to show them a trifle harder-edged and guitar-based. • **Songwriters:** SCOTT wrote most of material, except; LOST HIGHWAY (Hank Williams). • **Trivia:** MIKE SCOTT was brough up in Ayr, and went to Edinburgh University from 1977-78.

Recommended: THE BEST OF THE WATERBOYS (*9) / DREAM REAPER (*7)

ANOTHER PRETTY FACE

MIKE SCOTT (b.14 Dec'58, Edinburgh, Scotland) – vocals, guitar, piano / **JOHN CALDWELL** – guitar / **JIM GEDDES** – bass / **CRIGG** (b.IAN WALTER GREIG) – drums

New Pleasures not issued

May 79. (7") **ALL THE BOYS LOVE CARRIE. / THAT'S NOT ENOUGH** [ ] [-]

Virgin not issued

Feb 80. (7") **WHATEVER HAPPENED TO THE WEST?. / GODDBYE 1970's** [ ] [-]

—— Trimmed to basic duo of **SCOTT + CALDWELL** plus **MAIRI ROSS** – bass / added **ADRIAN JOHNSON** – drums

Chicken Jazz not issued

Dec 80. (7") **ONLY HEROES LIVE FOREVER. / HEAVEN GETS CLOSER EVERY DAY** [ ] [-]

Mar 81. (c-ep) **I'M SORRY THAT I BEAT YOU (live)** [ ] [-]
– This could be Hell / My darkest hour / Lightning that strikes twice / Graduation day / Carrie. (on some copies, studio tracks+=) – Another kind of circus / Only heroes live forever / Out of control.

Apr 81. (7") **A WOMAN'S PLACE. / GOD ON THE SCREEN / SOUL TO SOUL** [ ] [-]

FUNHOUSE

were formed by **SCOTT + CALDWELL**

Ensign not issued

Feb 82. (7")('A'ext-12") **OUT OF CONTROL. / THIS COULD BE HELL** [ ] [-]

The WATERBOYS

were formed by **MIKE SCOTT** plus **ANTHONY THISTLETWAITE** – saxophone (ex-ROBYN HITCHCOCK / of SOFT BOYS) / **KARL WALLINGER** – keyboards, bass

Chicken Jazz not issued

May 83. (7") **A GIRL CALLED JOHNNY. / THE LATE TRAIN TO HEAVEN** [ ] [-]
(12"+=) – Ready for the monkey house / Somebody might wave back / Out of control (ANOTHER PRETTY FACE – John Peel session).

Ensign Chrysalis

Jul 83. (lp)(c) **THE WATERBOYS** [ ] [ ]
– December / A girl called Johnny / The three day man / Gala / I will not follow / It should have been you / The girl in the swing / Savage Earth heart. *(re-iss.Aug86, cd-iss.Feb87)*

Sep 83. (7") **DECEMBER. / WHERE ARE YOU NOW WHEN I NEED YOU** [ ] [ ]
(12") – ('A'side) / Red army blues / The three day man (Radio 1 session)

—— added **KEVIN WILKINSON** – drums / **RODDY LORIMER** – tru. / **TIM BLANTHORN** – violin

Apr 84. (7") **THE BIG MUSIC. / THE EARTH ONLY ENDURES** [ ] [ ]
(12"+=) – Bury my heart.

May 84. (lp)(c) **A PAGAN PLACE** [100] [ ]
– Church not made with hands / All the things she gave me / The thrill is gone / Rags / Somebody might wave back / The big music / Red army blues / A pagan place. *(cd-iss.Feb87) (re-iss.cd+c Jul94)*

—— (Oct84) **MIKE + KARL** recruited new people for tour/lp **TERRY MANN** – bass / **CHARLIE WHITTEN** – drums / **STEVE WICKHAM** – violin / **LORIMER. DELAHAYE** – organ

Sep 85. (lp)(c) **THIS IS THE SEA** [37] [ ]
– Don't bang the drum / The whole of the Moon / Spirit / The pan within / Medicine bow / Old England / Be my enemy / Trumpets / This is the sea. *(cd-iss.Feb87) (re-iss.cd Mar94)*

Oct 85. (7") **THE WHOLE OF THE MOON. / MEDICINE BOW** [26] [ ]
('A'ext-12"+=) – Spirit (extended) / The girl in the swing (live).

—— **MIKE SCOTT** now only original survivor (retained THISTLETWAITE + HUTCHISON), when KARL formed WORLD PARTY.

—— additional band **STEVE WICKHAM** – violin (ex-IN TUA NUA) / **J.D.DOHERTY** – drums / **COLIN BLAKEY** – flute (ex-WE FREE KINGS). /'88, added **SHARON**

SHANNON – accordion / **NOEL BRIDGEMAN** – drums repl. DOHERTY

Nov 88. (lp)(c)(cd) **FISHERMAN'S BLUES** [13] [76]
– Fisherman's blues / We will not be lovers / Strange boat / World party / Sweet thing / And a bang on the ear / Has anybody here seen Hank? / When we will be married? / When ye go away / The stolen child. *(cd+=)*– The lost highway.

Dec 88. (7")(12")(cd-s) **FISHERMAN'S BLUES. / THE LOST HIGHWAY** [32] [ ]

Jun 89. (7")(12")(c-s)(cd-s) **AND A BANG ON THE EAR. / THE RAGGLE TAGGLE GYPSY** [51] [ ]

— **MIKE SCOTT / THISTLETWAITE / HUTCHISON / + KEV BLEVINS** – drums repl. last additional band members

Sep 90. (cd)(c)(lp) **ROOM TO ROAM** [5] [ ]
– In search of a rose / Songs from the edge of the world / A man is in love / Bigger picture / Natural bridge blues / Something that is gone / The star and the sea / Life on Sundays / Island man / The raggle taggle gypsy / How long will I love you? / Upon the wind and waves / Spring rooms to Spiddal / Further up, further in / Trip to Broadford / Room to roam. *(cd+=)*– The kings of Kerry. *(re-iss.cd+c Sep94)*

Mar 91. (7")(c-s) **THE WHOLE OF THE MOON. / A GOLDEN AGE** [3] [ ]
(12"+=)(cd-s+=) – Higher in time / High far soon / Soon as I get home.

Apr 91. (cd)(c)(lp) **THE BEST OF THE WATERBOYS ('81-'90)** [2] [ ]
(compilation)
– A girl called Johnny / The big music / All the things she gave me / The whole of the Moon / Spirit / Don't bang the drum / Fisherman's blues / Killing my heart / Strange boat / And a bang on the ear / Old England / A man is in love.

May 91. (7")(c-s) **FISHERMAN'S BLUES. / LOST HIGHWAY** [75] [ ]
(12"+=)(cd-s+=) – Medicine bow (live).

— Disbanded soon after last studio album above. In mid'91, MIKE SCOTT re-formed group and signed for US-based label 'Geffen'. THISTLETWAITE formed The BLUE STARS.

— **MIKE SCOTT** with **CHRIS BRUCE** – guitars / **SCOTT THUNES** – bass / **CARLA AZAR** – drums / **BASHIRI JOHNSON** – percussion / **LJUBISA 'Lubi' RISTIC** – sitar / **GEORGE STATHOS** – Greek clarinet / **JAMES CAMPAGNOLA** – saxophone / **JERE PETERS** – rattles / **PAL SHAZAR + JULES SHEAR** – backing vox / **BILLY CONNOLLY**– guest 10 second voiceover

Geffen Geffen

May 93. (7")(c-s) **THE RETURN OF PAN. / KARMA** [24] [ ]
(12"+=)(cd-s+=) – Mister Powers / ('A' demo).

May 93. (cd)(c)(lp) **DREAM HARDER** [5] [ ]
– The new life / Glastonbury song / Preparing to fly / The return of Pan / Corn circles / Suffer / Winter winter / Love and death / Spiritual city / Wonders of Lewis / The return of Jimi Hendrix / Good news.

Jul 93. (7")(c-s) **GLASTONBURY SONG. / CHALICE HILL** [29] [ ]
(12"+=)(cd-s+=) – Burlington Bertie – Accrington Stanley / Corn circle symphony (extended).

– compilations –

Oct 94. Ensign/ US= Chrysalis; (cd)(c) **THE SECRET LIFE OF THE WATERBOYS** (81-85 material) [ ] [ ]

MIKE SCOTT

Chrysalis Chrysalis

Sep 95. (7")(c-s) **BRING 'EM ALL IN. / CITY FULL OF GHOSTS (DUBLIN)** [56] [ ]
(cd-s+=) – Mother Cluny / Beatles reunion blues.

Sep 95. (cd)(c)(lp) **BRING 'EM ALL IN** [23] [ ]
– Bring 'em all in / Iona song / Edinburgh Castle / What do you want me to do? / I know she's in the building / City full of ghosts (Dublin) / Wonderful disguise / Sensitive children / Learning to love him / She is so beautiful / Wonderful disguise (reprise) / Long way to the light / Building the city of light.

Nov 95. (7") **BUILDING THE CITY OF LIGHT. / WHERE DO YOU WANT THE BOOMBOX, BUDDY** [60] [ ]
(cd-s+=) – Goin' back to Glasters (live) / The whole of the Moon (live).
(cd-s) – ('A'side) / Two great waves / My beautiful guide / Building the city of light (Universal Hall demo).

Roger WATERS

Born: 6 Sep'44, Great Bookham, Cambridge, England. In 1965, he helped form PINK FLOYD, becoming mainman in 1968 when SYD BARRETT became spaced out. He was frontman and main contributor until his departure in 1983. With PINK FLOYD out of the scene in the mid 80's, fans locked on to WATERS for worthwhile material. His debut album 'PROS & CONS OF HITCH HIKING' didn't set the world alight but managed a UK Top 20 placing. In 1990, with The BERLIN WALL being dismantled, ROGER thought it neccessary to revive the 1979 PINK FLOYD album 'THE WALL'. With an array of famous guests, he played there to a live audience of 200,000, plus TV millions all contributing to The Disaster Relief Fund. • **Style:** Not surprising that his sound stems from the latter days of PINK FLOYD ⇒ (i.e. THE WALL / THE FINAL CUT). His work with said band, was his greatest contribution to rock. • **Songwriters:** WATERS wrote all material. • **Trivia:** In 1987, WATERS took members of PINK FLOYD to court, for their use of group name.

Recommended: THE PROS AND CONS OF HITCH HIKING (*7)

ROGER WATERS – vocals, bass, etc. (ex-PINK FLOYD) with **ERIC CLAPTON** – guitar / **ANDY NEWMARK** – drums / **RAY COOPER** – percussion / **MADELINE BELL** – vocals

Harvest Columbia

Apr 84. (7") **5:01 a.m. (THE PROS AND CONS OF HITCH HIKING). / 4:30 a.m. (APPARENTLY THEY WERE TRAVELLING ABROAD)** [ ] [ ]
(12"+=) – 4:33 a.m. (Running shoes).

May 84. (lp)(c)(cd) **THE PROS AND CONS OF HITCH HIKING** [13] [31]
– 4:30 a.m. (Apparently they were travelling abroad) / 4:33 a.m. (Running shoes) / 4:37 a.m. (Arabs with knives and West German skies) / 4:39 a.m. (For the first time today) / 4:41 a.m. (Sexual revolution) / 4:47 a.m. (The remains of our love) / 4:50 a.m. (Go fishing) / 4:56 a.m. (For the first time today pt.2) / 4:58 a.m. (Dunroamin' duncarin' dunlivin') / 5:06 a.m. (Every strangers eyes) / 5:11 a.m. (The moment of clarity).

Jun 84. (7") **5:06 a.m. (EVERY STRANGERS EYES). / 4:39 a.m. (FOR THE FIRST TIME TODAY)** [ ] [ ]

— In Oct'86, WATERS and his BLEEDING HEART BAND featured on 1 side of 'WHEN THE WIND BLOWS' album / animated cartoon film on 'Virgin'.

— His new band: **ANDY FAIRWEATHER-LOW** – guitar / **JAY STAPLEY** – electric guitar / **MEL COLLINS** – sax / **IAN RITCHIE** – keyboards, drum pro. / **GRAHAM BROAD** – drums

E.M.I. Columbia

May 87. (7") **RADIO WAVES (edit). / GOING TO LIVE IN L.A.** [74] [ ]
(12"+=)(cd-s+=) – ('A'demo version).

Jun 87. (lp)(c)(cd) **RADIO KAOS** [25] [50]
– Radio waves / Who needs information / Me or him / The powers that be / Sunset Strip / Home / Four minutes / The tide is turning.

Nov 87. (7") **THE TIDE IS TURNING (After Live Aid). / GET BACK ON THE RADIO (demo)** [54] [ ]
(12"+=)(cd-s+=) – Money (live).

Mercury Mercury

Sep 90. (d-cd)(d-c)(d-lp) **THE WALL: LIVE IN BERLIN (live) ("ROGER WATERS AND THE BLEEDING HEART BAND")** [27] [56]
– In the flesh? (SCORPIONS) / The thin ice (UTE LEMPER) / Another brick in the wall – part 1 / The happiest days of our lives (JOE CHEMAY) / Another brick in the wall – part 2 (CYNDI LAUPER) / Mother (SINEAD O'CONNOR) / Goodbye blue sky (JONI MITCHELL) / Empty spaces + Young lust (BRYAN ADAMS) / One of my turns / Don't leave me now / Another brick in the wall – part 3 / Goodbye cruel world / Hey you (PAUL CARRACK) / Is there anybody out there? (MICHAEL KAMEN /The RUNDFUNK ORCHESTRA +*) / Nobody home / Vera (*) / Bring the boys back home / Comfortably numb (VAN MORRISON) / In the flesh? (*) / Run like Hell / Waiting for the worms (*) / Stop to / The trial (TIM CURRY & THOMAS DOLBY) / The tide is turning (The COMPANY). *(re-iss.d-cd Sep95)*

Sep 90. (7")(12") **ANOTHER BRICK IN THE WALL (part 2). / RUN LIKE HELL (live)** [52] [ ]
(cd-s+=) – ('A'extended).

Columbia Columbia

Aug 92. (7")(c-s) **WHAT GOD WANTS, PART 1. / ('A'video edit)** [35] [ ]
(cd-s+=) – What God wants, part III.

Sep 92. (cd)(c)(lp) **AMUSED TO DEATH** [8] [21]
– The ballad of Bill Hubbard / What God wants, part 1 / Perfect sense, part I & II / The bravery of being out of range / Late home tonight, part I & II / Too much rope / What God wants, part II & III / Watching TV / Three wishes / It's a miracle / Amused to death.

Dec 92. (7")(c-s) **THE BRAVERY OF BEING OUT OF RANGE. / WHAT GOD WANTS (part 1).** [ ] [ ]
(cd-s+=) – Perfect sense. (part 1).

ROGERS WATERS w / RON GEESIN

while a member of PINK FLOYD,

Harvest Columbia

Oct 70. (lp) **MUSIC FROM THE BODY (Soundtrack)** [ ] [ ]
– Our song / Seashell and stone / Red stuff writhe / Gentle breeze through life / Lick your partners / Bridge passage for three teeth / Chain of life / Womb bit / Embryo thought / March past of the embryos / More than seven dwarfs in penis – land / Dance of the red corpuscles / Body transport / Hard dance – full evening dress / Breathe / Old folks ascensions / Bedtime climb / Piddle in perspex / Embryonic womb walk / Mrs.Throat goes walking / Seashell and soft stone / Give birth to a smile. *(re-iss.Jul85 on 'EMI') (cd-iss.Jun89)*

Ben WATT (see under ⇒ EVERYTHING BUT THE GIRL)

WEDDING PRESENT

Formed: Leeds, England . . . 1984 by ex-teachers GEDGE and SOLOWKA (father Ukrainian), plus GREGORY and CHARMAN. In 1985, they gained deal with local indie label 'Reception'. With appearances on John Peel's radio 1 show, they quickly grew enough to break the UK Top50. In 1988, they finally signed to a major record company 'R.C.A.'. Their first release on the label 'UKRAINSKI . . .', surprised many, as it was a break away from usual guitar-based style. They reverted to lovelorn lyrical fashion once again later in 1989, when releasing hit album 'BIZARRO'. In 1992, they went into the Guinness Book Of Records, when every one of their monthly single (7"only) releases hit the UK Top30. The 12 hits also contained an unusual cover version on the B-side (see below). • **Style:** Fast and furious jangly punk rock, although their musical talent was obvious on Ukrainian-style album/Peel sessions. • **Songwriters:** GEDGE compositions, except GETTING NOWHERE FAST (Girls At Our Best) / WHAT BECOME OF THE BROKEN HEARTED (Jimmy Ruffin) / I FOUND THAT ESSENCE RARE (Gang Of Four) / IT'S NOT UNUSUAL (Tom Jones) / FELICITY (Orange Juice) / MAKE ME SMILE (COME UP AND SEE ME) (Steve Harley & Cockney Rebel) / BOX ELDER (Pavement) / SHE'S MY BEST FRIEND (Velvet Underground) / MOTHERS (Jean Michel Satre) / CUMBERLAND GAP (Leadbelly) / CATTLE AND CANE (Go-Betweens) / DON'T CRY NO TEARS (Neil Young) / THINK THAT IT MIGHT (Altered Images) / FALLING (Julee Cruise) / PLEASANT VALLEY SUNDAY (Monkees) / LET'S MAKE SOME PLANS (Close Lobsters) / ROCKET (Mud) / THEME FROM SHAFT (Isaac Hayes) / CHANT OF THE EVER CIRCLING SKELETAL FAMILY (Bowie) / GO WILD IN THE COUNTRY (Bow Wow Wow) / U.F.O. (Barry Gray) / STEP INTO CHRISTMAS (Elton John) / JUMPER CLOWN (Marc Riley). • **Trivia:** STEVE ALBINI (ex-BIG BLACK) produced their early 90s material.

Recommended: GEORGE BEST (*9) / TOMMY (*8) / BIZARRO (*7) / SEA MONSTERS (*7) / THE HIT PARADE 1 (*7).

DAVID GEDGE (b.23 Apr'60) – vocals, guitar / **PETE SOLOWKA** (b.Manchester) – guitar / **KEITH GREGORY** (b. 2 Jan'63, County Durham) – bass / **SHAUN CHARMAN** (b.Brighton) – drums

Reception | not issued

May 85. (7") **GO OUT AND GET 'EM BOY. / (THE MOMENT BEFORE) EVERYTHING'S SPOILED AGAIN** [ ] [-]
(re-iss.Sep85 on 'City Slang')

Jan 86. (7") **ONCE MORE. / AT THE EDGE OF THE SEA** [ ] [-]

Apr 86. (12"ep) **DON'T TRY AND STOP ME MOTHER** [ ] [-]
– (above 4 tracks).

Jul 86. (7") **THIS BOY CAN'T WAIT. / YOU SHOULD ALWAYS KEEP IN TOUCH WITH YOUR FRIENDS** [ ] [-]
('A'extended-12"+=) – Living and learning.

Feb 87. (7")(12")(7"white) **MY FAVOURITE DRESS. / EVERY MOTHER'S SON / NEVER SAID** [ ] [-]
(2,000 copies of above single were also given free with debut lp)

Sep 87. (7") **ANYONE CAN MAKE A MISTAKE. / ALL ABOUT EVE** [ ] [-]
(12"+=)(c-s+=) – Getting nowhere fast.

Oct 87. (lp)(c)(cd) **GEORGE BEST** [47] [-]
– Everyone thinks he looks daft / What did your last servant die of? / Don't be so hard / A million miles / All this and more / Getting nowhere fast * / My favourite dress / Shatner / Something and nothing / It's what you want that matters / Give my love to Kevin / Anyone can make a mistake / You can't moan can you / All about Eve *. *(c+= *)(cd+= *)*

— **SIMON SMITH** (b. 3 May'65, Lincolnshire) – drums repl. SHAUN to POP GUNS

Feb 88. (7") **NOBODY'S TWISTING YOUR ARM. / I'M NOT ALWAYS SO STUPID** [46] [-]
(12"+=)(cd-s+=) – Nothing comes easy / Don't laugh.

Jul 88. (lp)(c)(cd) **TOMMY** – (compilation 4 singles + Peel sessions) [42] [-]
– Go out and get 'em boy / (The moment before) Everything's spolied again / Once more / At the edge of the sea / Living and learning / This boy can't wait / You should always keep in touch with your friends / Felicity / What becomes of the broken hearted? / Never said / Every mother's son / My favourite dress.

Sep 88. (7") **WHY ARE YOU BEING SO REASONABLE NOW?. / NOT FROM WHERE I'M STANDING** [42] [-]
(12"+=) – Give my love to Kevin (acoustic) / Getting better.
(c-s++=)(cd-s++=) – Pourquoi es tu devenue si raisonnable?.
(7") -Pourquoi es tu devenue si raisonnable?. / Give my love to Kevin (acoustic)

— added guest **LEN LIGGINS** – vocals, violin (ex-SINISTER CLEANERS, Solo artist) Others played assortment of instruments in Ukrainian style.

R.C.A. | R.C.A.

Apr 89. (lp)(c)(cd) **UKRAINSKI VISTUPI V JOHNA PEELA** [22] [-]
(Ukrainian style John Peel sessions)
– Davny chasy / Yikhav kozak za dunai / Tiutiunyk / Zadmav didochok svitit misyats / Katrusyai Vasya vasyl'ok / Hude dn ipro hude Verkhovyno. *(was to have been issued as 10" m-lp, late 1988 on 'Reception')*

— (Reverted to usual 4-piece & style).

Sep 89. (7")(c-s) **KENNEDY. / UNFAITHFUL** [33] [ ]
(12"+=)(cd-s+=) – One day all this will all be yours / It's not unusual.

Oct 89. (lp)(c)(cd) **BIZARRO** [22] [ ]
– Brassneck / Crushed / No / Thanks / Kennedy / What have I said now / Granadaland / Bewitched / Take me / Be honest. *(cd+=)*– Brassneck (extended) / Box elder / Don't talk, just kiss / Gone.

Feb 90. (7")(c-s) **BRASSNECK. / DON'T TALK, JUST KISS** [24] [ ]
(12"+=)(c-s+=)(cd-s+=) – Gone / Box elder.

Sep 90. (7"ep)(12"ep)(c-ep)(cd-ep) **THE 3 SONGS** [25] [ ]
– Corduroy / Make me smile (come up and see me) / Crawl.
(10"+=) – Take me (live).

Apr 91. (7")(c-s) **DALLIANCE. / NIAGRA** [29] [ ]
(12"+=)(cd-s+=) – She's my best friend.
(10"++=) – What have I said now? (live).

May 91. (cd)(c)(lp) **SEAMONSTERS** [13] [ ]
– Dalliance / Dare / Suck / Blonde / Rotterdam / Lovenest / Corduroy / Carolyn / Heather / Octopussy.

Jul 91. (12"ep)(cd-ep) **LOVENEST (edit) / MOTHERS. / DAN DARE / FLESHWORLD** [58] [ ]

— **PAUL DORRINGTON** – guitar (ex-AC TEMPLE) repl. SOLOWKA to UKRAINIANS

Jan 92. (7") **BLUE EYES. / CATTLE AND CANE** [26] [ ]

Feb 92. (7") **GO-GO DANCER. / DON'T CRY NO TEARS** [20] [ ]

Mar 92. (7") **THREE. / THINK THAT IT MIGHT** [14] [ ]

Apr 92. (7") **SILVER SHORTS. / FALLING** [14] [ ]

May 92. (7") **COME PLAY WITH ME. / PLEASANT VALLEY SUNDAY** [10] [ ]

Jun 92. (7") **CALIFORNIA. / LET'S MAKE SOME PLANS** [16] [ ]

Jun 92. (cd)(c)(lp) **THE HIT PARADE 1** [22] [ ]
– (last 6 singles 'A'&'B')

Jul 92. (7") **FLYING SAUCER. / ROCKET** [22] [ ]

Aug 92. (7") **BOING!. / THEME FROM SHAFT** [19] [ ]

Sep 92. (7") **LOVESLAVE. / CHANT OF THE EVER CIRCLING SKELETAL FAMILY** [17] [ ]

Oct 92. (7") **STICKY. / GO WILD IN THE COUNTRY** [17] [ ]

Nov 92. (7") **THE QUEEN OF OUTER SPACE. / U.F.O.** [23] [ ]

Dec 92. (7"red) **NO CHRISTMAS. / STEP INTO CHRISTMAS** [25] [ ]

— The above 12 singles, were limited to 15,000 copies, and hit peak chart position on it's first week of issue.

Jan 93. (cd)(c)(lp) **THE HIT PARADE 2** [19] [ ]
– (all last 6 'A'&'B' singles above) (free lp w/lp+=) **BBC SESSIONS** – (all 12 of the years' A-sides).

— In Oct'93, they were looking for a replacement for KEITH GREGORY.

— **DARREN BELLE** – bass repl.him

Island | Island

Sep 94. (12"ep)(c-ep)(cd-ep) **YEAH YEAH YEAH YEAH YEAH / THE BIKINI / FLAME ON / HIM OR ME (WHAT'S IT GONNA BE)** [51] [ ]
(cd-s) – ('A'side) / Gazebo / So long baby / Spangle.

Sep 94. (cd)(c)(lp) **WATUSI** [47] [ ]
– So long, baby / Click click / Yeah yeah yeah yeah yeah / Let him have it / Gazebo / Shake it / Spangle / It's a gas / Swimming pools, movie stars / Big rat / Catwoman / Hot pants.

Nov 94. (7")(c-s) **IT'S A GAS. / BUBBLES** [ ] [ ]
(12"purple+=)(cd-s+=) – ('A'acoustic) / Jumper clown.

. . . Jan – Jun '96 stop press . . .

Cooking V. | not issued

Jan 96. (m-cd)(10"m-lp) **MINI** [ ] [-]

– compilations, etc. –

Oct 86. Strange Fruit; (12"ep) **THE PEEL SESSIONS** (26.2.86) [ ] [-]
– What becomes of the broken hearted / This boy can't wait / Felicity / You should always keep in touch with your friends. *(c-ep iss.Jun87, cd-ep iss. Aug88)*

1993. Strange Fruit; (cd)(lp) **JOHN PEEL SESSIONS 1987-1990** [ ] [-]
– Give my regards to Kevin / Getting nowhere fast / A million miles / Something and nothing / Take me I'm yours / Unfaithful / Why are you being so reasonable now? / Happy birthday / Dalliance / Heather Blonde / Niagara.

Nov 88. Nighttracks; (12"ep)(cd-ep) **THE EVENING SHOW SESSIONS** (20.4.86) [ ] [-]
– Everyone thinks he looks daft / I found that essence rare / Shatner / My favourite dress.

WEEZER

Formed: Los Angeles, USA . . .1993 by CUOMO RIVERS, etc (see below). By the end of 1994, they had stormed the US album charts with the massive selling eponymous debut. • **Style:** College retro punk-pop or 'nerd' rock often described as The PIXIES meeting The BEACH BOYS. On the crest of an American 'new wave', set by GREEN DAY and OFFSPRING. • **Songwriters:** CUOMO, a few w/ WILSON. • **Trivia:** Produced by RIC OCASEK (ex-CARS).

Recommended: WEEZER (*7)

RIVERS CUOMO -vocals/ **BRIAN BELL** -guitar, vocals/ **MATT SHARP** -bass, vocals/ **PATRICK WILSON** -drums

Geffen Geffen

Jan 95. (7"blue-ep)(c-ep)(cd-ep) **UNDONE – THE SWEATER SONG. / MYKEL & CARLI / SUSANNE / HOLIDAY** [35] [57] Sep94

Feb 95. (cd)(c)(lp) **WEEZER** [23] [16] Aug94
– My name is Jonas / No one else / The world has turned and left me here / Buddy Holly / Undone – the sweater song / In the garage / Holiday / Only in dreams.

Apr 95. (7")(c-s) **BUDDY HOLLY. / JAMIE** [12] [ ]
(cd-s+=) – My name is Jonas / Surf wax America.

Jul 95. (10"ep)(c-ep)(cd-ep) **SAY IT AIN'T SO (remix). / NO ONE ELSE (live and acoustic) / JAMIE (live and acoustic)** [37] [ ]

Bob WEIR (see under ⇒ GRATEFUL DEAD)

WE KNOW WHERE YOU LIVE (see under ⇒ WONDER STUFF)

Paul WELLER

Born: London, England . . . Formed STYLE COUNCIL early 1983 with past mod MICK TALBOT. WELLER re-signed to 'Polydor', and quickly re-established themselves back in the charts with debut Top 5 hit 'SPEAK LIKE A CHILD'. PAUL went solo in 1991, and 2 years later his 'WILDWOOD' album received deserved rave reviews, resulting in a Mercury award in '94. • **Style:** Sophisticated white soul-pop, with romantic jazzy overtones mixed alongside WELLER's political socialist leanings. • **Songwriters:** WELLER penned except for TALBOT's instrumentals. They also covered MOVE ON UP (Curtis Mayfield) / PROMISED LAND (Joe Smooth) / OHIO (Neil Young). WELLER solo:- FEELIN' ALRIGHT (Traffic) / SEXY SADIE (Beatles) / I'M ONLY DREAMING (Small Faces). • **Trivia:** WELLER married his backing singer and solo star DEE C.LEE in Dec'86. He also featured on BAND AID's charity single 'DO THEY KNOW IT'S CHRISTMAS' in 1984, and 7 months later appeared in LIVE AID at Wembley.

Recommended: THE SINGULAR ADVENTURES OF THE STYLE COUNCIL (*7) / WILD WOOD (*9) / STANLEY ROAD (*8)

STYLE COUNCIL

PAUL WELLER (b.25 May'58, Woking, Surrey, England) – vocals, guitar (ex-JAM) / **MICK TALBOT** (b.11 Sep'58) – keyboards (ex-MERTON PARKAS) / **STEVE WHITE** – drums / plus various guests.

Polydor Polydor

Mar 83. (7") **SPEAK LIKE A CHILD. / PARTY CHAMBERS** [4] [ ]

May 83. (7") **MONEY GO ROUND. / (part 2)** [11] [ ]
(12") – ('A'side) / Headstart for happiness / Mick's up.

Aug 83. (7"ep)(12"ep) **LONG HOT SUMMER / PARTY CHAMBERS. / PARIS MATCH / LE DEPART** [3] [ ]

Nov 83. (7") **SOLID BOND IN YOUR HEART. / IT JUST CAME TO PIECES IN MY HAND / ('A'instrumental)** [11] [ ]

Oct 83. (lp)(c) **INTRODUCING THE STYLE COUNCIL** [-] [ ]
– (above songs)

Polydor Geffen

Feb 84. (7") **MY EVER CHANGING MOODS. / MICK'S COMPANY** [5] [29] Apr 84
(12"+=) – Spring, Summer, Autumn.

Mar 84. (lp)(c)(cd) **CAFE BLEU** [2] [56]
– Mick's blessings / My ship came in / Blue cafe / The Paris match / My ever changing moods / Dropping bombs on the Whitehouse / A gospel / Strength of your nature / You're the best thing / Here's the one that got away / Headstart for happiness / Council meetin'. *(cd+=)* – The whole point of no return. (US-album title **'MY EVER CHANGING MOODS'**) *(re-iss.cd Sep95)*

May 84. (7") **YOU'RE THE BEST THING. / BIG BOSS GROOVE** [5] [76]
(12"+=) – ('A'dub version).

Oct 84. (7") **SHOUT TO THE TOP. / GHOSTS OF DACHAU** [7] [ ]
(12"+=) – Piccadilly trail / ('A'instrumental).

Dec 84. (7") **SOUL DEEP. (as "COUNCIL COLLECTIVE") / (part 2)** [24] [-]
(12"+=) – ('A'version) / (striking miner's interview).

(above single gave proceeds to miner's strike & the deceased miner David Wilkie's widow) The COLLECTIVE featured guests JIMMY RUFFIN, JUNIOR GISCOMBE, VAUGHN TOULOUSE, DEE C.LEE and DIZZY HEIGHTS. Production handled by MARTYN WARE (Heaven 17).

May 85. (7")(12") **WALLS COME TUMBLING DOWN. / THE WHOLE POINT II / BLOODSPORTS** [6] [-]

Jun 85. (lp)(c)(cd) **OUR FAVOURITE SHOP (US title 'INTERNATIONALISTS')** [1] [ ]
– Homebreakers / All gone away / Come to Milton Keynes / Internationalists / A stone's throw away / The stand up comic's instructions / Boy who cried wolf / A man of great promise / Down in the Seine / The lodgers / Luck / With everything to lose / Our favourite shop / Walls come tumbling down. *(cd+=)*– Shout to the top. *(c+=)*– (interview).

Jun 85. (7") **COME TO MILTON KEYNES. / WHEN YOU CALL ME** [23] [-]
(12"+=) – Our favourite shop / ('A'club) / The lodgers (club mix).

Aug 85. (7") **OUR FAVOURITE SHOP. / BOY WHO CRIED WOLF** [-] [ ]

Sep 85. (7") **THE LODGERS (remix). / YOU'RE THE BEST THING (live)** [13] [ ]
(d7"+=) – Big boss groove (live) / Long hot summer (live).
(12"+=) – Big boss groove (live) / Move on up (live).
(12"+=) – Medley: Money go round – Soul deep – Strength of your nature.

Mar 86. (7")(12")(c-s) **HAVE YOU EVER HAD IT BLUE. / MR. COOL'S DREAM** [14] [ ]

May 86. (lp)(c)(cd) **HOME AND ABROAD – LIVE (live)** [8] [ ]
– The big boss groove * / My ever changing moods / The lodgers / Headstart for happiness / (When you) Call me / The whole point of no return / Our favourite shop * / With everything to lose / Homebreakers / Shout to the top / Walls come tumbling down / Internationalists. *(cd+= *)*

Jun 86. (7") **THE INTERNATIONALISTS. / (WHEN YOU) CALL ME** [-] [ ]

Polydor Polydor

Jan 87. (7")(12") **IT DIDN'T MATTER. / ALL YEAR ROUND** [9] [ ]

Feb 87. (2x12"lp)(c)(cd) **THE COST OF LOVING** [2] [ ]
– It didn't matter / Right to go / Waiting / Walking the night / The cost of loving / Heaven's above / Fairy tales / Angel / A woman's song. *(re-iss.c+cd.Oct90)*

Mar 87. (7") **WAITING. / FRANCOISE** [52] [ ]
(12"+=) – Theme from 'Jerusalem'.

Oct 87. (7") **WANTED (FOR WAITER). / THE COST OF LOVING** [20] [ ]
(12"+=)(c-s+=)/ /(cd-s+=) – There's soup in my flies./ / The cost.

May 88. (7") **LIFE AT A TOP PEOPLE'S HEALTH FARM. / SWEET LOVING WAYS** [28] [ ]
(12"+=)(cd-s+=) – Spark (live) / ('A'version).

Jun 88. (lp)(c)(cd) **CONFESSIONS OF A POP GROUP** [15] [ ]
– It's a very deep sea / The story of someone's shoe / Changing of the guard / The little boy in a castle – A dove flew down from the elephant / The gardener of Eden (a three piece suite):- In the beginning – The gardener of Eden – Mourning the passing of time / Life at a top people's health farm / Why I went missing / How she threw it all away / I was a doledads toyboy / Confessions of a pop group (parts 1, 2 & 3) / Confessions of a pop group. *(re-iss.c+cd.Oct90)*

Jul 88. (7"ep)(12"ep) **HOW SHE THREW IT ALL AWAY / IN LOVE FOR THE FIRST TIME. / LONG HOT SUMER / I DO LIKE TO BE B-SIDE THE A-SIDE** [41] [ ]

Feb 89. (7") **PROMISED LAND. / CAN YOU STILL LOVE ME** [27] [ ]
(12"+=)(cd-s+=) – ?

Mar 89. (lp)(c)(cd) **THE SINGULAR ADVENTURES OF THE STYLE COUNCIL** (compilation) [3] [ ]
– You're the best thing / Have you ever had it blue (extended) / Money go round (parts 1 & 2) / My ever changing moods (extended) / Long hot summer (extended) / The lodgers / Walls come tumbling down / Shout to the top / Wanted / It didn't matter / Speak like a child / A solid bond in your heart / Life at a top people's health farm / Promised land. *(c+=)(cd+=)*– How she threw it all away / Waiting.

May 89. (7") **LONG HOT SUMMER ('89 mix). / EVERYBODY'S ON THE RUN** [48] [ ]
(12"+=) – ('A' & 'B' different mixes).

—— Disbanded Mar'90. WELLER went solo, see below.

– more compilations, etc. –

Nov 87. Polydor; (cd-ep) **CAFE BLEU** [ ] [-]
– Headstart for happiness / Here's one that got away / Blue cafe / Strength of your nature.

Nov 87. Polydor; (cd-ep) **BIRDS AND BEES** [ ] [-]
– Piccadilly trail / It just came to pieces in my hands / Spin drifting / Spring, Summer, Autumn.

Nov 87. Polydor; (cd-ep) **MICK TALBOT IS AGENT '88** [ ] [-]
– Mick's up / Party chambers / Mick's blessing / Mick's company.

Jul 93. Polydor; (cd)(c) **HERE'S SOME THAT GOT AWAY** 39 -
Jan 90. Old Gold; (7") **YOU'RE THE BEST THING. / MY EVER CHANGING MOODS** -
Jan 90. Old Gold; (7") **LONG HOT SUMMER. / SPEAK LIKE A CHILD** -

... Jan – Jun '96 stop press ...

Feb 96. Polydor; (cd)(c) **THE STYLE COUNCIL COLLECTION** 60

PAUL WELLER MOVEMENT

with **STEVE WHITE** – drums, percussion / **JACKO PEAKE** – sax, flute, b.vox / **DEE C.LEE, DR.ROBERT + CAMELLE HINDS** – backing vocals

Freedom High / London

May 91. (7")(c-s) **INTO TOMORROW. / HERE'S NEW THING** 36 1992
(12"+=)(cd-s+=) – That spiritual feeling / ('A'demo version).

PAUL WELLER

Go! Discs / London

Aug 92. (7")(c-s) **UH HUH OH YEH. / FLY ON THE WALL** 18
(12"+=)(cd-s+=) – Always there to fool you / Arrival time.
Sep 92. (cd)(c)(lp) **PAUL WELLER** 8
– Uh huh oh yeh / I didn't mean to hurt you / Bull-rush / Round and round / Remember how we started / Above the clouds / Clues / Into tomorrow / Amongst butterflies / The strange museum / Bitterness rising / Kosmos. *(re-iss.Apr94)*
Oct 92. (7")(c-s) **ABOVE THE CLOUDS. / EVERYTHING HAS A PRICE TO PAY** 47
(12"+=)(cd-s+=) – All year round (live) / Feelin' alright.

— with **STEVE WHITE** – drums, percussion / **MARCO NELSON** – bass

Jul 93. (7")(c-s) **SUNFLOWER. / BULL-RUSH-MAGIC BUS (live)** 16
(12"+=)(cd-s+=) – Kosmo's sx dub 2000 / That spiritual feeling (new mix)
Aug 93. (7")(10")(c-s) **WILD WOOD. / ENDS OF THE EARTH** 14
Sep 93. (cd)(c)(lp) **WILD WOOD** 2
– Sunflower / Can you heal us (holy man) / Wild wood – instrumental (pt.1) / All the pictures on the wall / Has my fire really gone out? / Country / 5th season / The weaver – instrumental (pt.2) / Foot of the mountain / Shadow of the Sun – Holy man (reprise) / Moon on your pyjamas. *(re-iss.Apr94)*
Nov 93. (7"ep)(10"ep)(c-ep)(cd-ep) **THE WEAVER EP** 18
– The weaver / This is no time / Another new day / Ohio (live).
Mar 94. (7"ep)(12"ep)(c-ep)(cd-ep) **HOME OF THE CLASSIC EP** 11
– Hung up / Foot of the mountain (live) / The loved / Kosmos (Lynch Mob bonus beats).
Sep 94. (cd)(c)(lp) **LIVE WOOD (live)** 13
– Bull rush – Magic bus / This is no time / All the pictures on the wall / Remember how we started? / Dominoes / Above the clouds / Wild wood / Shadow of the Sun / (Can you hear us) Holy man – War / 5th season / Into tomorrow / Fool of the mountains / Sunflower / Has the fire really gone out?
Oct 94. (7"ep)(12"ep)(c-ep)(cd-ep) **OUT OF THE SINKING. / SUNFLOWER (Brendan Lynch dub) / SEXY SADIE** 20

— with **STEVE WHITE** -drums / **DR.ROBERT** -bass, vocals (ex-BLOW MONKEYS) / **STEVE CRADDOCK** -guitar / **MARK NELSON** -bass / **HELEN TURNER** -strings, organ / **BRENDAN LYNCH** -organ, co-producer / + guests **MICK TALBOT / CARLEEN ANDERSON / STEVE WINWOOD / NOEL GALLAGHER / YOLANDA CHARLES / CONSTANTINE WEIR**

Apr 95. (7"ep)(c-ep)(cd-ep) **THE CHANGINGMAN / I'D RATHER GO BLIND / It'S A NEW DAY, BABY / I DIDNT MEAN TO HURT YOU (live)** 7
May 95. (cd)(c)(lp)(6x7"pack) **STANLEY ROAD** 1
– The changingman / Porcelain gods / I walk on gilded splinters / You do something to me / Woodcutter's son / Time passes / Stanley Road / Broken stones / Out of the sinking / Pink on white walls / Whirlpool's end / Wings of speed.
Jul 95. (7"ep)(c-ep)(cd-ep) **YOU DO SOMETHING TO ME / A YEAR LATE. / MY WHOLE WORLD IS FALLING DOWN / WOODCUTTER'S SON** 9
Sep 95. (7")(c-s) **BROKEN STONES. / STEAM** 20
(cd-s+=) – Whirlpool's end.
(cd-s+=) – Porcelain gods.

— WELLER was also part of one-off supergroup The SMOKIN' MOJO FILTERS alongside PAUL McCARTNEY and NOEL GALLAGHER. They had a Top 20 hit with 'COME TOGETHER'.

... Jan – Jun '96 stop press ...

Feb 96. (single) **OUT OF THE SINKING EP** 16

— b-side cover; I SHALL BE RELEASED (Bob Dylan).

Paul WESTERBERG (see under ⇒ REPLACEMENTS)

WHIPPING BOY

*** NEW ENTRY ***

Formed: Dublin, Ireland . . .1989 by FERGAL McKEE and co (see below). That year, they released a single and album for 'Liquid', before moving to 'Che' early 90's. Little was heard of them until 1995, when they signed to 'Columbia', who shifted out 'TWINKLE', followed by 'HEARTWORM' album. Early in 1996, they had Top 50 debut with 45 'WHEN WE WERE YOUNG'. • **Style:** Initially noise merchants like MY BLOODY VALENTINE or The JESUS & MARY CHAIN, they tunefully progressed into a melodic SONIC YOUTH, fused with LEONARD COHEN. • **Songwriters:** Group except CAROLINE SAYS II (Lou Reed). • **Trivia:** Produced by WARREN LIVESEY. • **Note:** Not the same band from US who released in 1983 lp; THE SOUND OF NO HANDS CLAPPING.

FERGAL McKEE – vocals / **PAUL PAGE** – guitar / **MYLES McDONNELL** – bass / **COLM HASSETT** – drums

Liquid / not issued

1989. (7") **FAVOURITE SISTER. / SAFARI** - Ire
1989. (lp) **SUBMARINE** - Ire

Cheree / not issued

Aug 90. (12"ep) **WHIPPING BOY E.P.** -
– Sugar I swear / Switchblade smile / Valentine '69.
Feb 91. (7"ep) **I THINK I MISS YOU** -
– Daze / Highwayman / I think I miss you / She makes me ill.

Columbia / Columbia

Jul 95. (7")(c-s) **TWINKLE. / A NATURAL** -
(cd-s) – ('A'side) / Plaything / Favourite sister (live).
Oct 95. (cd)(c)(blue-lp) **HEARTWORM**
– Blinded / Personality / Users / Fiction / Morning rise / Twinkle / When we were young / Tripped / The honeymoon is over / We don't need nobody else.
Oct 95. (7"colrd) **WE DON'T NEED NOBODY ELSE. / TWINKLE (acoustic)** 51
(cd-s) – ('A'side) / Disappointed / Here I am.
Jan 96. (7"red)(c-s) **WHEN WE WERE YOUNG. / AS THE DAY GOES** 46
(cd-s+=) – ('A'-Philo version) / Caroline says II.
May 96. (7") **TWINKLE. / THE HONEYMOON IS OVER** 55
(cd-s+=) – Fiction / Tripped.
(cd-s) – ('A'side) / Blinded / Personality / Users.

Alan WHITE (see under ⇒ YES)

WHITESNAKE

Formed: By ex-DEEP PURPLE vocalist DAVID COVERDALE (b.22 Sep'49, Saltburn-On-Sea, Yorkshire, England). After 2 solo albums in 1977 & 1978, he soon assembled WHITESNAKE, named after debut. He/they signed to 'EMI International' and produced a Top 50 placing for album 'TROUBLE'. They grew larger with every release, culminating with re-vamped 1982 UK Top40 hit 'HERE I GO AGAIN', reaching US Top slot in summer of '87. • **Style:** Blues influenced heavy rock band that mixed usual love ballads with harder-edged mainstream rock. • **Songwriters:** COVERDALE / MOODY / MARSDEN compositions. From 1983-86, COVERDALE's writing partner was group member JOHN SYKES, who was replaced in 1989 by ADRIAN VANDENBURG. They also covered HEART OF THE CITY (Bobby Bland) / etc? • **Trivia:** On 17 Feb'89, COVERDALE married actress Tawny Kittaen, who had previously featured on their video of 'IS THIS LOVE'.

Recommended: WHITESNAKE'S GREATEST HITS (*8)

DAVID COVERDALE

(solo) – vocals (ex-DEEP PURPLE) with **MICK MOODY** – guitar (ex-JUICY LUCY, ex-SNAFU) / **TIM HINKLEY** – keyboards / **SIMON PHILLIPS** – drums / **DELISLE HARPER** – bass / plus **RON ASPERY** – sax / **ROGER GLOVER** – producer, bass, keyboards

Purple / United Art

May 77. (lp)(c) **DAVID COVERDALE'S WHITESNAKE**
– Lady / Blindman / Goldie's place / White snake / Time on my side / Peace lovin' man / Sunny days / Hole in the sky / Celebration.
May 77. (7") **HOLE IN THE SKY. / BLINDMAN** -

— **COVERDALE** retained only **MOODY** and recruited **BERNIE MARSDEN** – guitar (ex-PAICE, ASHTON & LORD, ex-UFO, ex-WILD TURKEY) / **NEIL MURRAY** – bass (ex-COLOSSEUM, ex-NATIONAL HEALTH) / **BRIAN JOHNSON** – keyboards + **DAVID DOWELL** – drums (both ex-STREETWALKERS)

Feb 78. (7") **BREAKDOWN. / ONLY MY SOUL** [ ] [-]
Mar 78. (lp)(c) **NORTHWINDS** [ ] [ ]
– Keep on giving me love / Only my soul / Breakdown / Queen of hearts / Time and again / Give me kindness / Say you love me. *(re-iss.Feb82) (re-iss.Apr84 on 'Fame')*
Jun 78. (7") **BREAKDOWN. / BLOODY MARY** [-] [ ]

DAVID COVERDALE'S WHITESNAKE

PETE SOLLEY – keyboards repl. JOHNSTON

EMI Inter... Sunburst

Jun 78. (7"ep)(7"white-ep) **SNAKEBITE** [61] [ ]
– Bloody Mary / Steal away / Come on / Ain't no love in the heart of the city.

—— **JON LORD** – keys (ex-PAICE, ASHTON & LORD, ex-DEEP PURPLE) repl. SOLLEY

Oct 78. (7") **LIE DOWN. / DON'T MESS WITH ME** [ ] [ ]
Oct 78. (lp)(c) **TROUBLE** [50] [ ]
– Take me with you / Love to keep you warm / Lie down (a modern love song) / Day tripper / Night hawl (vampire blues) / The time is right for love / Trouble / Belguin Tom's hat trick / Free flight / Don't mess with me. *(re-iss.Sep80 on 'United Art') (re-iss.May82 on 'Fame', +re+cd.May90) (re-iss.Jun87 on 'Liberty', cd-iss.Apr88 on 'EMI')*
Mar 79. (7") **THE TIME IS RIGHT FOR LOVE. / COME ON (live)** [ ] [-]
Apr 79. (7") **THE TIME IS RIGHT FOR LOVE. / BELGUIN TOM'S HAT TRICK** [-] [ ]

United Art United Art

Oct 79. (lp)(c) **LOVE HUNTER** [29] [-]
– Long way from home / Walking in the shadow of the blues / Help me through the day / Medicine man / You 'n' me / Mean business / Love hunter / Outlaw / Rock'n'roll women / We wish you well. *(re-iss.Apr84 on 'Fame', cd-iss.Apr88) (re-iss.cd+c Jul94)*
Oct 79. (7"m) **LONG WAY FROM HOME. / TROUBLE (live) / AIN'T NO LOVE IN THE HEART OF THE CITY (live)** [55] [-]
Nov 79. (7") **LONG WAY FROM HOME. / WE WISH YOU WELL** [-] [ ]

WHITESNAKE

IAN PAICE – drums (ex-PAICE, ASHTON & LORD, ex-DEEP PURPLE) repl. DOWELL

United Art Mirage

Apr 80. (7"m) **FOOL FOR YOUR LOVING. / MEAN BUSINESS / DON'T MESS WITH ME** [13] [-]
Jun 80. (lp)(c) **READY AN' WILLING** [6] [90]
– Fool for your loving / Sweet talker / Ready an' willing / Carry your load / Blindman / Ain't gonna cry no more / Love man / Black and blue / She's a woman. *(re-iss.Sep85 on 'Fame', cd-iss.Apr88) (re-iss.cd+c Jul94)*
Jul 80. (7"m) **READY AN' WILLING. / NIGHT HAWK (VAMPIRE BLUES) / WE WISH YOU WELL** [43] [ ]
Jul 80. (7") **FOOL FOR YOUR LOVING. / BLACK AND BLUE** [-] [53]
Oct 80. (7") **SWEET TALKER. / AIN'T GONNA CRY NO MORE** [-] [ ]
Nov 80. (d-lp)(d-c) **LIVE ... IN THE HEART OF THE CITY (live)** [5] [ ]
– Come on * / Sweet talker / Walking in the shadow of the blues / Love hunter / Fool for your loving / Ain't gonna cry no more / Ready an' willing / Take me with you * / Might just take your life / Lie down * / Ain't no love in the heart of the city / Trouble * / Mistreated. *(cd-iss.Jul88 on 'Underdog' US omits *) (re-iss.cd+c Jul94)*
Nov 80. (7")(12") **AIN'T NO LOVE IN THE HEART OF THE CITY (live). / TAKE ME WITH YOU (live)** [51] [ ]

Liberty Atlantic

Apr 81. (7") **DON'T BREAK MY HEART AGAIN. / CHILD OF BABYLON** [17] [-]
Apr 81. (lp)(c) **COME AN' GET IT** [2] [ ]
– Come an' get it / Hot stuff / Don't break my heart again / Lonely days, lonely nights / Wine, women an' song / Child of Babylon / Would I lie to you / Girl / Hit an' run / Till the day I die. *(re-iss.+cd.May89 on 'Fame') (cd-iss.1988 on 'EMI', re-iss.cd+c Jul94)*
May 81. (7") **WOULD I LIE TO YOU. / GIRL** [37] [-]
Jun 81. (7") **DON'T BREAK MY HEART AGAIN. / LONELY DAYS, LONELY NIGHTS** [-] [ ]

—— **COVERDALE** retained **MOODY + LORD** and brought in **MEL GALLEY** – guitar (ex-TRAPEZE) repl. MARSDEN who formed ALASKA / **COLIN 'Bomber' HODGKINSON** – bass (ex-BACK DOOR) repl. MURRAY to GARY MOORE / **COZY POWELL** – drums (ex-JEFF BECK, ex-RAINBOW, Solo Artist, ex-BEDLAM) repl. PAICE who joined GARY MOORE

Liberty Geffen

Oct 82. (7")(7"pic-d) **HERE I GO AGAIN. / BLOODY LUXURY** [34] [ ]
Nov 82. (lp)(c)(pic-lp) **SAINTS AN' SINNERS** [9] [ ]
– Young blood / Rough an' ready / Blood luxury / Victim of love / Crying in the rain / Here I go again / Love an' afection / Rock'n'roll angels / Dancing girls / Saints an' sinners. *(re-iss.1985) (re-iss.May87 on 'Fame', cd-iss.Apr88)*
Aug 83. (7")(7"sha-pic-d) **GUILTY OF LOVE. / GAMBLER** [31] [ ]

—— now a quintet, when MICK MOODY departed.

Jan 84. (7") **GIVE ME MORE TIME. / NEED YOUR LOVE SO BAD** [29] [ ]

—— **NEIL MURRAY** – bass returned to repl. HODGKINSON / added **JOHN SYKES** – guitar (ex-TYGERS OF PAN TANG)

Feb 84. (lp)(c) **SLIDE IT IN** [9] [40] Aug 84
– Gambler / Slide it in / Standing in the shadows / Give me more time / Love ain't no stranger / Slow an' easy / Spit it out / All or nothing / Hungry for love / Guilty of love. *(cd-iss.Apr88 on 'EMI')*
Apr 84. (7")(7"pic-d) **STANDING IN THE SHADOWS. / ALL OR NOTHING** [62] [ ]
(12"+=) – ('A'-US remix).
Aug 84. (7") **LOVE AIN'T NO STRANGER. / GUILTY OF LOVE** [-] [ ]
Feb 85. (7") **LOVE AIN'T NO STRANGER. / SLOW AN' EASY** [44] [ ]
(12"+=)(12"white+=) – Slide it in.

—— Split for a while in 1984 when JON LORD re-joined DEEP PURPLE. **WHITESNAKE** were re-formed by **COVERDALE + SYKES** and new musicians **TONY FRANKLIN** – bass (ex-The FIRM) repl. MURRAY and GALLEY / **CARMINE APPICE** – drums (ex-BECK, BOGERT & APPICE) repl. POWELL to E.L.P.

EMI Inter.. Geffen

Mar 87. (7")(7"white) **STILL OF THE NIGHT. / HERE I GO AGAIN (1987)** [16] [-]
(12"+=)(12"pic-d+=) – You're gonna break my heart again.
Apr 87. (lp)(c)(cd)(pic-lp) **WHITESNAKE 1987** [8] [2]
– Still of the night / Bad boys / Give me all your love / Looking for love / Crying in the rain / Is this love / Straight for the heart / Don't turn away / Children of the night. *(cd+=)*– Here I go again '87 / You're gonna break my heart again. *(re-iss.cd+c Jul94 all on 'EMI')*
May 87. (7")(7"sha-pic-d) **IS THIS LOVE. / STANDING IN THE SHADOWS** [9] [-]
(12"+=)(12"white+=) – Need your love so bad.
(cd-ep++=)(7"ep++=) – Still of the night.
Jun 87. (7") **STILL OF THE NIGHT. / DON'T TURN AWAY** [-] [79]
Jul 87. (7") **HERE I GO AGAIN. / CHILDREN OF THE NIGHT** [-] [1]
Oct 87. (7") **IS THIS LOVE. / BAD BOYS** [-] [2]
Oct 87. (7")(12")(c-s) **HERE I GO AGAIN '87 (US mix). / GUILTY OF LOVE** [9] [-]
(7"pic-d)(10"white)(cd-s) – ('A'side) / ('A'-US remix).
Jan 88. (7")(12")(12"pic-d)(7"white)(12"white) **GIVE ME ALL YOUR LOVE (edit). / FOOL FOR YOUR LOVING** [18] [48]
(cd-s+=) – Here I go again / Don't break my heart.
(3"cd-s+=) – Straight from the heart. (US; b-side)

—— **COVERDALE** completely re-modelled line-up when SYKES formed BLUE MURDER. He was replaced by **ADRIAN VANDENBURG** – guitar (ex-VANDENBERG) / **RUDY SARZO** – bass (ex-OZZY OSBOURNE, ex-QUIET RIOT) repl. FRANKLIN / **TOMMY ALDRIDGE** – drums (ex-OZZY OSBOURNE, ex-BLACK OAK ARKANSAS) repl. APPICE (Dec88) / **STEVE VAI** – guitar (solo Artist, ex-FRANK ZAPPA, DAVID LEE ROTH) repl. VIVIAN CAMPBELL

Nov 89. (lp)(c)(cd) **SLIP OF THE TONGUE** [10] [10]
– Slip of the tongue / Cheap an' nasty / Fool for your loving / Now you're gone / Kitten's got claws / Wings of the storm / The deeper the love / Judgement day / Slow poke music / Sailing ships. *(re-iss.cd+c Jul94)*
Nov 89. (7")(US-c-s) **FOOL FOR YOUR LOVIN' ('89). / SLOW POKE MUSIC** [43] [37]
(c-s+=) – ('A'version).
(12"+=)(12"white+=) – Walking in the shadow of the blues.
Jan 90. (7") **THE DEEPER THE LOVE. / SLIP OF THE TONGUE** [-] [28]
Feb 90. (7")(c-s)(7"pic-d) **THE DEEPER THE LOVE. / JUDGEMENT DAY** [35] [-]
(12"white+=) – Sweet lady luck.
(12"++=)(cd-s++=) – Fool for your lovin' (Vai voltage mix).
Aug 90. (7")(c-s)(7"sha-pic-d) **NOW YOU'RE GONE (remix). / WINGS OF THE STORM (lp version)** [31] [96] May 90
(12"+=)(cd-s+=)(12"pic-d+=) – Kittens got claws / Cheap an' nasty.

DAVID COVERDALE

Epic Epic

Sep 90. (7")(c-s) **THE LAST NOTE OF FREEDOM. / (CAR BUILDING** by HANS ZIMMER) [ ] [ ]
(12"+=)/ /(cd-s+=) – Gimme some lovin'./ / ('A'version).

COVERDALE• PAGE

DAVID COVERDALE – vocals / **JIMMY PAGE** – guitar (ex-LED ZEPPELIN, ex-solo artist) / **JORGE CASAS** – bass / **DENNY CARMASSI** – drums (ex-MONTROSE) / **RICKY PHILIPS** – bass / **LESTER MENDEL** – keyboards / **JOHN HARRIS** – acoustic harmonica / **TOMMY FUNDERBUCK** – backing vocals

E.M.I. Geffen

Mar 93. (cd)(c)(lp) **COVERDALE• PAGE** [4] [5]
– Shake my tree / Waiting on you / Take me for a little while / Pride and joy / Over now / Feeling hot / Easy does it / Take a look at yourself / Don't leave me

this way / Absolution blues / Whisper a prayer for the dying *(re-iss.cd+c Jul94)*

Jun 93. (c-s)(12"pic-d) **TAKE ME FOR A LITTLE WHILE. / EASY DOES IT** | 29 | |
(cd-s) – ('A'side) / ('A'acoustic) / Shake my tree (the crunch mix) / ('A'edit).

Sep 93. (7"pic-d)(c-s) **TAKE A LOOK AT YOURSELF. / WAITING ON YOU** | | |
(cd-s+=) – ('A'acoustic) / ('A'girls version).

– compilations, etc. –

Apr 88. Connoisseur; (d-lp)(c)(cd) **THE CONNOISSEUR COLLECTION** | | - |
– (DAVID COVERDALE's first 2 solo albums)

Jun 88. MCA; (cd) **GREATEST HITS** | - | |

Jul 94. EMI/ US= Geffen; (cd)(c)(lp) **WHITESNAKE'S GREATEST HITS** | 4 | |
– Still of the night / Here I go again / Is this love / Love ain't no stranger / Looking for love / Now you're gone / Slide it in / Slow an' easy / Judgement day / You're gonna break my heart again / The deeper the love / Crying in the rain / Fool for your loving / Sweet lady luck.

Jul 94. (7")(7"white)(c-s) **IS THIS LOVE. / SWEET LADY LUCK** | 25 | |
(cd-s+=) – Now you're gone.

Nov 95. EMI; (3xcd-box) **SLIDE IT IN / 1987 / SLIP OF THE TONGUE** | | |

WHITE ZOMBIE

Formed: New York, USA ...1985 by ROB STRAKER, female SEAN YSEULT, TOM GUAY and IVAN DePLUME. After a few indie-metal lp's in the late 80's, they had a surprise US Top 30 hit album in 1993 with an MTV favourite 'LA SEXORCISTO: ...'. • **Style:** Unconventional demon-metal grunge similar to BLACK SABBATH fused with KISS and The STOOGES. • **Songwriters:** STRAKER except CHILDREN OF THE GRAVE (Black Sabbath) / GOD OF THUNDER (Kiss). • **Trivia:** 2nd album produced by BILL LASWELL, their 3rd by ANDY WALLACE. Guested on Beavis & Butt-Head various artists album in 1993.

Recommended: LA SEXORCISTO: DEVIL MUSIC VOL.1 (*7)

ROB 'ZOMBIE' STRAKER – vocals, guitar / **TOM GUAY** – guitar / **SEAN YSEULT** – bass / **IVAN DePLUME** – drums

not issued | Silent Ex.

1987. (m-lp) **PSYCHO-HEAD BLOWOUT** | - | |

Jan 88. (lp) **SOUL CRUSHER** | - | |

—— **JOHN RICCI** -guitar repl.TOM

Caroline | Caroline

Feb 89. (lp)(c)(cd) **MAKE THEM DIE SLOWLY** | | |
– Demonspeed / Disaster blaster / Murderworld / Revenge / Acid flesh / Power hungry / Godslayer.

—— **JAY YUENGER** -guitar repl.RICCI

Jul 89. (12"ep) **GOD OF THUNDER. / LOVE RAZOR / DISASTER BLASTER 2** | | |

Geffen | Geffen

Mar 92. (cd)(c)(lp) **LA SEXORCISTO: DEVIL MUSIC VOL.1** | | |
– Welcome to Planet Mother F***** / Psychedelic slag / Knuckle duster (Radio 1-A) / Thunder kiss '65 / Black sunshine / Soul-crusher / Cosmic monsters inc. / Spiderbaby (yeah-yeah-yeah) / I am legend / Knuckle duster (Radio 2-B) / Thrust! / One big crunch / Grindhouse (a go-go) / Starface / Warp asylum. *(re-dist.Sep93, hit US No.26)*

—— **JOHN TEMPESTA** -drums (ex-TESTAMENT, ex-EXODUS) repl.PHILO, who had briefly repl.DePLUME

May 95. (c-s) **MORE HUMAN THAN HUMAN / BLOOD, MILK AND SKY (KERO KERO KEROPFI AND THE SMOOTH OPERATOR)** | 51 | |
(10"+=)(cd-s+=) – ('A'-Jeddak of the tharks super mix).

May 95. (cd)(c)(lp) **ASTRO-CREEP 2000: SONGS OF LOVE, DESTRUCTION AND OTHER SYNTHETIC DELUSIONS OF THE ELECTRIC HEAD** | 25 | 6 |
– Electric head pt.1 (the agony) / Super-charger Heaven / Real solution No.9 / Creature of the wheel / Electric head pt.2 (the ecstasy) / Grease paint and monkey brains / I, zombie / More human than human / El phantasmo and the chicken-run blast-o-rama / Blur the technicolor / Blood, milk and sky. (c+=)(cd+=) – The sidewalk ends where the bug parade begins.

... Jan – Jun '96 stop press ...

May 96. (single) **ELECTRIC HEAD PART II (THE ECSTASY)** | 31 | |

WHITFORD / ST. HOLMES (see under ⇒ AEROSMITH)

WHO

Formed: Chiswick & Hammersmith, London, England ... 1964 as The HIGH NUMBERS. After one 45 'I'M THE FACE', they changed name to The WHO and signed to 'Brunswick'. They immediately smashed the UK Top 10 with debut 'I CAN'T EXPLAIN', which was followed by a string of chartbusters starting with classics 'ANYWAY ANYHOW ANYWHERE', 'MY GENERATION' & 'SUBSTITUTE'. In May 1969, they premiered their new Top 5 double album 'TOMMY' (a concept rock opera, similar to The PRETTY THINGS' 'S.F.Sorrow'). This was later made into a film in 1975, which featured The WHO plus ELTON JOHN, TINA TURNER, ANN-MARGRET, JACK NICHOLSON and OLIVER REED. In 1973, they repeated the formula when QUADROPHENIA hit the shops, and was later made into another film in 1979. • **Style:** In the forefront of the 'mod' scene in the mid-60's, they moved into rock operas in 1969 and 1973. Were well known at the time for TOWNSHEND's windmill guitar style, which he usually smashed up after gigs. DALTREY's power vocal style and hard man looks, were later put into great use when he took up acting career in 1979. While ENTWISTLE was the quiet man on stage and off, MOON's eccentric behaviour led him to dressing up in different characters each day. His hard drinking and drug abuse, led to his eventual death on 7 Sep'78. A month previous to this, their one-time manager PETE MEADON committed suicide. **DALTREY's filmography:** LISZTOMANIA (1975) / THE LEGACY (1979) / McVICAR (1980) / BUDDY (1991 TV serial + 1992 film). • **Songwriters:** TOWNSHEND wrote most of material except I'M THE FACE (Slim Harpo's 'Got Live If You Want It') / I'M A MAN (Bo Diddley) / IN THE CITY (Speedy Keen; aka of Thunderclap Newman) / BARBARA ANN (Beach Boys) / BABY DON'T YOU DO IT (Marvin Gaye) / THE LAST TIME + UNDER MY THUMB (Rolling Stones) / SUMMERTIME BLUES (Eddie Cochran). KEITH MOON's only album featured all covers. DALTREY's solo career started with songs written for him by LEO SAYER and DAVE COURTNEY. He later covered DON'T LET THE SUN GO DOWN ON ME (Elton John) / etc. • **Trivia:** Re-grouped in 1985 for the Live Aid concert. DALTREY had run a trout farm in Dorset for the last decade or so. They are inducted into the Guinness Book Of Records, after performing the loudest concert (120 decibels) at Charlton Athletic's Football Club.

Recommended: WHO'S BETTER WHO'S BEST (*9) / TOMMY (*8) / WHO'S NEXT (*9) / QUADROPHENIA (*9). PETE TOWNSHEND:- EMPTY GLASS (*7). ROGER DALTREY:- THE BEST OF ROGER DALTREY (*6).

ROGER DALTREY (b. 1 Mar'45) – vocals / **PETE TOWNSHEND** (b.19 May'45) – guitar, vocals / **JOHN ENTWISTLE** (b. 9 Oct'44) – bass, vocals / **KEITH MOON** (b.23 Aug'47) – drums, vocals repl. DOUGIE SANDON

HIGH NUMBERS

Fontana | not issued

Jul 64. (7") **I'M THE FACE. / ZOOT SUIT** | | - |
(re-iss.Feb65) (re-iss.Mar80 on 'Back Door', hit UK No.49) (US re-iss.Mar80 as The WHO on 'Mercury')

The WHO

Brunswick | Decca

Jan 65. (7") **I CAN'T EXPLAIN. / BALD HEADED WOMAN** | 8 | 93 | Feb 65
(US re-iss.1973 on 'MCA')

May 65. (7") **ANYWAY ANYHOW ANYWHERE. / DADDY ROLLING STONE** | 10 | - |

Jun 65. (7") **ANYWAY ANYHOW ANYWHERE. / ANYTIME YOU WANT ME** | - | |

Oct 65. (7") **MY GENERATION. / SHOUT & SHIMMY** | 2 | - |

Nov 65. (7") **MY GENERATION. / OUT IN THE STREET** | - | 74 |

Dec 65. (lp) **MY GENERATION** | 5 | |
– Out in the street / I don't mind / The good's gone / La-la-la-lies / Much too much / My generation / The kid's are alright / Please please please / It's not true / I'm a man / A legal matter / The ox. *(US title 'THE WHO SING MY GENERATION') (UK re-iss.Oct80 on 'Virgin', hit No.20) (cd-iss.1990)*

Reaction | Decca

Mar 66. (7") **SUBSTITUTE. / WALTZ FOR A PIG ('B'by "WHO ORCHESTRA")** | 5 | |
(The original 'B'side on some copies were INSTANT PARTY then CIRCLES) *(The States re-iss.Mar66 single in Aug67 on 'Atco')*

Aug 66. (7") **I'M A BOY. / IN THE CITY** | 2 | | Dec 66

Dec 66. (7") **HAPPY JACK. / I'VE BEEN AWAY** | 3 | - |

Dec 66. (lp) **A QUICK ONE** (US-title 'HAPPY JACK') | 4 | 67 | May 67
– Run run run / Boris the spider / Whiskey man / I need you / Heatwave / Cobwebs and strange / Don't look away / See my way / So sad about us / A quick one,

while he's away. *(UK re-iss.c/cd.Aug88 on 'Polydor'; re-iss.cd Jun95)*

Mar 67. (7") **HAPPY JACK. / WHISKEY MAN** [-] [24]

Track Decca

Apr 67. (7") **PICTURES OF LILY. / DOCTOR DOCTOR** [4] [51] Jun 67

Jul 67. (7") **THE LAST TIME. / UNDER MY THUMB** [44] [ ]

Oct 67. (7") **I CAN SEE FOR MILES. / SOMEONE'S COMING** [10] [-]

Oct 67. (7") **I CAN SEE FOR MILES. / MARY ANN WITH THE SHAKY HANDS** [-] [9]

Jan 68. (lp) **THE WHO SELL OUT** [13] [48]
– Armenian city in the sky / Heinz baked beans / Mary-Anne with the shaky hands / Odorono / Tattoo / Our love was, is / I can see for miles / I can't reach you / Medac / Silas Stingy / Sunrise / Tattoo / Rael. *(c-iss.Oct84) (re-iss.c/cd.Aug88 on 'Polydor'; re-iss.cd Jun95)*

Mar 68. (7") **CALL ME LIGHTNING. / DR. JEKYLL & MR. HIDE** [-] [40]

Jun 68. (7") **DOGS. / CALL ME LIGHTNING** [25] [-]

Jul 68. (7") **MAGIC BUS. / SOMEONE'S COMING** [-] [25]

Oct 68. (7") **MAGIC BUS. / DR. JEKYLL & MR. HIDE** [26] [-]

Oct 68. (lp) **MAGIC BUS – (THE WHO ON TOUR) (live)** [-] [39]
– Disguises / Run run run / Dr. Jekyll & Mr. Hyde / I can't reach you / Our love was, is / Call me Lightning / Magic bus / Someone's coming / Doctor doctor / Bucket T. / Pictures of ily.

Nov 68. (lp) **DIRECT HITS** – (compilation) [ ] [-]
– Bucket T. / I'm a boy / Pictures of Lily / Doctor doctor / I can see for miles / Substitute / Happy Jack / The last time / In the city / Call me Lightning / Mary-Anne with the shaky hand / Dogs.

Mar 69. (7") **PINBALL WIZARD. / DOGS (part 2)** [4] [19]
(US re-iss.1973 on 'MCA')

May 69. (d-lp) **TOMMY** [2] [4]
– Overture / It's a boy / 1921 / Amazing journey / Sparks / Eyesight for the blind / Miracle cure / Sally Simpson / I'm free / Welcome / Tommy's holiday camp / We're not gonna take it / Christmas / Cousin Kevin / The acid queen / Underture / Do you think it's alright / Fiddle about / Pinball wizard / There's a doctor / Go to the mirror / Tommy can you hear me / Smash the mirror / Sensation. *(re-iss.1974 in 2 parts +c.) (d-lp re-iss.Jul84 on 'Polydor', d-cd-iss.Apr89)*

Jul 69. (7") **I'M FREE. / WE'RE NOT GONNA TAKE IT** [-] [37]

Mar 70. (7") **THE SEEKER. / HERE FOR MORE** [19] [44]

May 70. (lp)(c) **LIVE AT LEEDS (live)** [3] [4]
– Magic bus / My generation / Shakin' all over / Substitute / Summertime blues / Young man blues. *(re-iss.Nov83, cd-iss.May88) (re-iss.cd Feb95 on 'Polydor', hit No.59)*

Jul 70. (7") **SUMMERTIME BLUES (live). / HEAVEN AND HELL** [38] [-]

Jul 70. (7") **SUMMERTIME BLUES (live). / HERE FOR MORE** [-] [27]

Sep 70. (7") **SEE ME, FEEL ME. / WE'RE NOT GONNA TAKE IT / OVERTURE FROM TOMMY** [-] [12]
(US re-iss.1973 on 'MCA')

Sep 70. (7") **SEE ME, FEEL ME. / OVERTURE FROM TOMMY** [ ] [-]

—— In May71, JOHN ENTWISTLE brought out debut lp 'SMASH YOUR HEAD AGAINST THE WALL'. (see further on for his discography)

Jul 71. (7") **WON'T GET FOOLED AGAIN. / I DON'T EVEN KNOW MYSELF** [9] [15]

Sep 71. (lp)(c) **WHO'S NEXT** [1] [4]
– Baba O'Riley / etting in tune / Love ain't for keeping / My wife / The song is over / Bargain / Going mobile / Behind blue eyes / Won't get fooled again. *(re-iss.+cd.Nov83 on 'Polydor')*

Oct 71. (7") **LET'S SEE ACTION. / WHEN I WAS A BOY** [16] [-]

Nov 71. (7") **BEHIND BLUE EYES. / MY WIFE** [-] [34]

Dec 71. (lp)(c) **MEATY, BEATY, BIG AND BOUNCY** (compilation) [9] [11] Nov 71
– I can't explain / The kids are alright / Happy Jack / I can see for miles / Pictures of Lily / My generation / The seeker / Anyway, anyhow, anywhere / Pinball wizard / A legal matter / Boris the spider / Magic bus / Substitute / I'm a boy. *(re-iss.1974)*

Jun 72. (7") **JOIN TOGETHER. / BABY DON'T YOU DO IT** [9] [17]

—— In Oct72, PETE TOWNSHEND was another to issue debut solo album 'WHO CAME FIRST'. It scraped into UK Top30. He issued more throughout 70's-80's (see . . .) In Apr'73, ROGER DALTREY hit the singles chart with GIVING IT ALL AWAY. It was a cut from debut album DALTREY. (see further on)

Track Track

Jan 73. (7") **RELAY. / WASPMAN** [21] [39] Dec 72

Track M.C.A.

Oct 73. (7") **5:15. / WATER** [20] [-]

Oct 73. (7") **5:15. / LOVE REIGN O'ER ME** [-] [ ]

Nov 73. (d-lp)(d-c) **QUADROPHENIA** [2] [2]
– I am the sea / The real me / Quadrophenia / Cut my hair / The punk and the godfather / I'm one / Dirty jobs / Helpless dancer / Is it in my head? / I've had enough / 5:15 / Sea and sand / Drowned / Bell boy / Doctor Jimmy / The rock / Love, reign o'er me. *(re-iss.Sep79, d-cd-iss.Jan87)*

Nov 73. (7") **LOVE, REIGN O'ER ME. / WATER** [-] [76]

Jan 74. (7") **THE REAL ME. / I'M ONE** [-] [92]

—— In Apr75, KEITH MOON was the last WHO member to release solo vinyl. The dismal 'TWO SIDES OF THE MOON' sold poorly.

Polydor M.C.A.

Oct 75. (lp)(c) **THE WHO BY NUMBERS** [7] [8]
– Slip kid / However much I booze / Squeeze box / Dreaming from the waist / Imagine a man / Success story / They are all in love / Blue, red and grey / How many friends / In a hand or a face. *(re-iss.Mar84, cd-iss.Jul89)*

Jan 76. (7") **SQUEEZE BOX. / SUCCESS STORY** [10] [16] Nov 75

Aug 76. (7") **SLIP KID. / DREAMING FROM THE WAIST** [-] [ ]

Sep 76. (d-lp)(d-c) **THE STORY OF THE WHO** (compilation) [2] [ ]
– Magic bus / Substitute / Boris the spider / Run run run / I'm a boy / Heatwave / My generation / Pictures of Lily / Happy Jack / The seeker / I can see for miles / Bargain / Squeeze box / Amazing journey / The acid queen / Do you think it's alright / Fiddle about / Pinball wizard / I'm free / Tommy's holiday camp / We're not gonna take it / See me, feel me / Summertime blues / Baba O'Riley / Behind blue eyes / Slip kid / Won't get fooled again.

Jul 78. (7") **WHO ARE YOU. / HAD ENOUGH** [18] [14]

—— On 5th Aug'78, manager PETE MEADON committed suicide.

Sep 78. (lp)(c)(US-red-lp)(US-pic-lp) **WHO ARE YOU** [6] [2]
– New song / Had enough / 905 / Sister disco / Music must change / Trick of the light / Guitar and pen / Love is coming down / Who are you. *(re-iss.Aug84, cd-iss.Jul89)*

—— After a party on 7th Sep'78, KEITH MOON died on an overdose of Heminevrin.

Dec 78. (7") **TRICK OF THE LIGHT. / 509** [-] [ ]

—— Early'79, **KENNY JONES** (b.16 Sep'48) – drums (ex-SMALL FACES, ex-FACES) took place of KEITH. Added 5th tour member **JOHN 'Rabbit' BUNDRICK** – keyboards

Polydor Warners

Feb 81. (7") **YOU BETTER YOU BET. / THE QUIET ONE** [9] [18]

Mar 81. (lp)(c) **FACE DANCES** [2] [4]
– You better you bet / Don't let go the coat / Cache cache / The quiet one / Did you steal my money / How can you do it alone / Daily records / You / Another tricky day. *(re-iss.+cd.May88) (re-iss.cd Jun93)*

May 81. (7") **DON'T LET GO THE COAT. / YOU** [47] [84]

Sep 82. (lp)(c) **IT'S HARD** [11] [8]
– Athena / It's your turn / Cooks county / It's hard / Dangerous / Eminence front / I've known no war / One life's enough / One at a time / Why did I fall for that / A man is a man / Cry if you want. *(cd-iss.1983) (re-iss.cd Jun93)*

Sep 82. (7")(7"pic-d) **ATHENA. / A MAN IS A MAN** [40] [-]
(12"+=)(12"pic-d+=) – Won't get fooled again.

Sep 82. (7") **ATHENA. / IT'S YOUR TURN** [-] [28]

Dec 82. (7") **EMINENCE FRONT. / ONE AT A TIME** [-] [68]

Feb 83. (7") **IT'S HARD. / DANGEROUS** [-] [ ]

—— They officially split late 1983 from studio work. They occasionally returned for one-off live work.

– other compilations, etc. –

Below 4 on 'Brunswick' label.

Mar 66. (7") **A LEGAL MATTER. / INSTANT PARTY** [32] [-]

Aug 66. (7") **THE KIDS ARE ALRIGHT. / THE OX** [41] [-]

Aug 66. (7") **THE KIDS ARE ALRIGHT. / A LEGAL MATTER** [-] [ ]

Nov 66. (7") **LA LA LA LIES. / THE GOOD'S GONE** [ ] [-]

Nov 66. Reaction; (7"ep) **READY STEADY WHO** [ ] [-]
– Circles / Disguises / Batman / Bucket 'T' / Barbara Ann. *(re-iss.Nov83 on 'Reaction-Polydor', hit 58)*

Nov 70. Track; (7"ep) **TOMMY** [ ] [ ]
– See me, feel me / I'm free / Christmas / Overture from Tommy.

Dec 74. Track; (d-lp)(d-c) **A QUICK ONE / THE WHO SELL OUT** [ ] [ ]

Oct 74. Track; (lp)(c) **ODDS AND SODS** (rarities) [10] [15]
– Postcard / Now I'm a farmer / Put the money down / Little Billy / Too much of anything / Glow girl / Pure and easy / Faith in something bigger / I'm the face / Naked eye / Long live rock. *(re-iss.cd Jun93)*

Nov 74. Track; (7") **POSTCARD. / PUT THE MONEY DOWN** [-] [ ]

below with guest singers ELTON JOHN, TINA TURNER, OLIVER REED, ANN-MARGRET, etc

Aug 75. Polydor; (d-lp)(dc) **TOMMY (Film Soundtrack)** [30] [2]
– Prologue / Captain Walker – It's a boy / Bernie's holiday camp / 1951 – What about the boy? / Amazing journey / Christmas / Eyesight to the blind / Acid queen / Do you think it's alright / Cousin Kevin / Do you think it's alright / Fiddle about / Do you think it's alright / Sparks / Extra, extra, extra / Pinball wizard / Champagne / There's a doctor / Go to the mirror / Tommy can you hear me / Smash the mirror / I'm free / Mother and son / Sensation / Miracle cure / Sally Simpson / Welcome / T.V. studio / Tommy's holiday camp / We're not gonna take it / Listening to you – See me, feel me.

Aug 83. Track; (lp)(c) **RARITIES VOL.1 (1966-68)** [ ] [ ] 1982

Oct 83. Track; (lp)(c) **RARITIES VOL.2 (1970-73)** [ ] [ ] 1982
(re-iss.cd+c.VOL.1 & 2 Jan91)

Note; below on 'Polydor' UK/ 'MCA' US.

Oct 76. (7"m)(12"m) **SUBSTITUTE. / I'M A BOY / PICTURES OF LILY** [7] [ ]

Apr 79. (7"m) **LONG LIVE ROCK. / I'M THE FACE / MY WIFE** [48] [54]

Jun 79. (lp)(c)(US-pic-lp) **THE KIDS ARE ALRIGHT** [26] [8]
– (some live tracks with interviews) *(re-iss.cd Jun93)*

Sep 79. (7") **I'M ONE. / 5:15** [ ] [45] b-side

Sep 79. (d-lp)(d-c) **QUADROPHENIA (Film Soundtrack)** [23] [46]
– (includes tracks by other artists)

1980. (d-c) **WHO'S NEXT / THE WHO BY NUMBERS** [ ] [-]

1980. (d-c) **WHO ARE YOU / LIVE AT LEEDS** [ ] [-]

Feb 81. (lp)(c) **MY GENERATION (compilation)** [ ] [-]
May 83. (lp)(c) **WHO'S GREATEST HITS** [-] [94]
Nov 84. (lp)(c)(cd) **THE SINGLES** [ ] [ ]
Feb 88. (7") **MY GENERATION. / SUBSTITUTE** [68] [ ]
(12"+=)(c-s+=)(cd-s+=) – Baba O'Riley / Behind blue eyes.
Mar 88. (lp)(c)(cd) **WHO'S BETTER WHO'S BEST** [10] [ ]
– My generation / Anyway, anyhow, anywhere / The kids are alright / Substitute / I'm a boy / Happy Jack / Pictures of Lily / I can see for miles / Who are you / Won't get fooled again / Magic bus / Pinball wizard / I'm free / I can't explain / See me feel me / Squeeze box / Join together / You better you bet. (cd+=) – Baba O'Riley.
Jun 88. (7") **WON'T GET FOOLED AGAIN. / BONEY MORONIE (live)** [ ] [ ]
(ext-12"+=)(cd-s+=) – Dancing in the street (live) / Mary Ann with the shaky hand.
Oct 88. (lp)(c)(cd) **WHO'S MISSING** [ ] [ ]
Jul 94. (4xcd-box) **30 YEARS OF MAXIMUM R&B** [48] [ ]
Oct 81. MCA; (lp) **HOOLIGANS** [-] [52]
(UK-iss.Dec88)
Nov 84. MCA; (lp)(c) **WHO'S LAST** *(cd-iss.Dec88)* [48] [81]
Nov 84. MCA; (7") **TWIST AND SHOUT. / I CAN'T EXPLAIN** [ ] [ ]
Oct 85. Impression; (d-lp)(d-c) **THE WHO COLLECTION** [44] [-]
(d-cd-iss.Oct88 VOL.1 & 2 on 'Stylus', hit 71)
Aug 85. Karusel Gold; (c) **THE BEST OF THE SIXTIES** [ ] [-]
Apr 86. Arcade; (lp)(c) **GREATEST HITS** [ ] [-]
Mar 90. Virgin; (7") **JOIN TOGETHER. / I CAN SEE FOR MILES** [ ] [ ]
(12"+=)/ /cd-s++=) – Behind blue eyes./ / Christmas.
Mar 90. Virgin; (cd)(d-c)(d-lp) **JOIN TOGETHER** [59] [ ]
– (contains some solo material)

PETE TOWNSHEND

(solo). Before his 1972 official debut, TOWNSHEND issued 2 lp's on 'Universal'; HAPPY BIRTHDAY (1970) & I AM (1972).

Track Track
Oct 72. (lp)(c) **WHO CAME FIRST** [30] [69]
– Pure and easy / Evolution / Forever's no time at all / Let's see action / Time is passing / There's a heartache followin' me / Sheraton Gibson / Content / Parvardigar. *(cd-iss.Oct92 on 'Rykodisc')*

— next collaboration with Solo artist and ex-SMALL FACES bassman and singer.

PETE TOWNSHEND & RONNIE LANE

Polydor M.C.A.
Sep 77. (7") **MY BABY GIVES IT AWAY. / APRIL FOOL** [-] [ ]
Sep 77. (lp)(c) **ROUGH MIX** [44] [45]
– My baby gives it away / Nowhere to run / Rough mix / Annie / Keep me turning / Catmelody / Misunderstood / April fool / Street in the city / Heart to hang on to / Till the rivers all run dry. *(re-iss.Nov80 & Nov83)*
Nov 77. (7") **STREET IN THE CITY. / ANNIE (by "RONNIE LANE")** [ ] [-]
Nov 77. (7") **NOWHERE TO RUN . / KEEP ME TURNING** [-] [ ]

PETE TOWNSHEND

Island not issued
Dec 79. (12"ep) **THE SECRET POLICEMAN'S BALL** (the songs) [ ] [-]
– Drowned / Pinbal wizard / Won't get fooled again.
Atco Atco
Mar 80. (7") **ROUGH BOYS. / AND I MOVED** [39] [89] Nov 80
Apr 80. (lp)(c) **EMPTY GLASS** [11] [5]
– Rough boys / I am an animal / And I moved / Let my love open your door / Jools and Jim / Keep on working / Cat's in the cupboard / A little is enough / Empty glass / Gonna get ya. *(cd-iss.1984 + Nov93 + Oct95)*
Jun 80. (7") **LET ME LOVE OPEN THE DOOR. / AND I LOVED** [-] [9]
Jun 80. (7"m) **LET MY LOVE OPEN THE DOOR. / CLASSIFIED / GREYHOUND GIRL** [46] [-]
Oct 80. (7") **A LITTLE IS ENOUGH. / CAT'S IN THE CUPBOARD** [-] [72]
Oct 80. (7") **KEEP ON WORKING. / JOOLS AND JIM** [ ] [-]
May 82. (7") **FACE DANCES (pt.2). / MAN WATCHING** [ ] [ ]
Jun 82. (lp)(c) **ALL THE BEST COWBOYS HAVE CHINESE EYES** [32] [26]
– The sea refuses no river / Communication / Exquisitely bored / North country girl / Slit skirts / Uniforms / Prelude / Somebody saved me / Face dances 2 / Stardom in action / Stop hurting people. *(cd-iss.Nov93 & Oct95)*
Aug 82. (7")(7"pic-d) **UNIFORMS (CORPS D'ESPRIT). / DANCE IT ALL AWAY** [48] [-]
(12")(12"pic-d) – ('A'side) / Stop hurting people.
Aug 82. (7") **UNIFORMS (CORPS D'ESPRIT). / SLIT SKIRTS** [-] [ ]
Apr 83. (7") **BARGAIN. / DIRTY WATER** [-] [ ]
Oct 85. (7")(12") **FACE THE FACE. / HIDING OUT** [ ] [26]
Nov 85. (lp)(c)(cd) **WHITE CITY – A NOVEL** [70] [26]
– Give blood / Brilliant blues / Face the face / Hiding out / Secondhand love / Crashing by design / I am secure / White City fighting Come to mama. (re-iss.cd Nov93)
Jan 86. (7") **SECOND HAND LOVE. / WHITE CITY FIGHTING** [-] [ ]
Apr 86. (7") **GIVE BLOOD. / MAGIC BUS (live)** [ ] [ ]
(12"+=) – Won't get fooled again.
Oct 86. (lp)(c)(cd) **PETE TOWNSEND'S DEEP END LIVE! (live)** [-] [98]
– Barefootin' / After the fire / Behind blue eyes / Stop hurtin' people / I'm one / I put a spell on you / Save it for later / Pinball wizard / Little is enough / Eyesight to the blind.

— Next featured singers JOHN LEE HOOKER (Iron Man) / NINA SIMONE (The Dragon) / DALTREY + JOHN ENTWISTLE who play on 2 new WHO tracks.

Virgin Atlantic
Jun 89. (lp)(c)(cd) **THE IRON MAN (The Musical)** [ ] [58]
– I won't run anymore / Over the top / Man machines / Dig / A friend is a friend / I eat heavy metal / All shall be well / Was there life / Fast food / A fool says . . . / Fire / New life (reprise). *(re-iss.+cd.Mar91)*
Jul 89. (7")(c-s) **A FRIEND IS A FRIEND. / MAN MACHINES** [ ] [ ]
(12"+=)(3"cd-s+=) – Real world.
Nov 89. (7")(12") **I WON'T RUN ANYMORE. / A FOOL SAYS . . .** [ ] [ ]
Atlantic Atlantic
Jul 93. (cd)(c) **PSYCHODERELICT** [ ] [ ]
– English boy / Meher Baba M3 / Let's get pretentious / Meher Baba M4 (signal box) / Early morning dreams / I want that thing / Introduction to outlive the dinosaur / Outlive the dinosaur / Flame (demo) / Now and then / I am afraid / Don't try to make me real / Introduction to predictable / Predictable / Flame / Meher Baba M5 (Vivaldi) / Fake it / Introduction to now and then (reprise) / Now and then (reprise) / Baba O'Riley (demo) / English boy (reprise).
Jul 93. (7")(c-s) **ENGLISH BOY. / EARLY MORNING DREAMS** [ ] [ ]
(cd-s+=) – Flame (demo).
(cd-s) – ('A'side) / ('A'dialogue version) / Fake it / Psycho montage.

. . . Jan – Jun '96 stop press . . .

EastWest EastWest
May 96. (cd)(c) **COOLWALKINGSMOOTHSTRAIGHTSMOKING FIRESTOKING** [ ] [ ]

– (other PETE TOWNSHEND compilations, etc.) –

Apr 83. Atco; (d-lp) **SCOOP** [ ] [35]
– (unfinished WHO demos and solo rarities)
Jul 89. Polydor; (d-lp)(d-c) **ANOTHER SCOOP** [ ] [ ]

ROGER DALTREY

(solo)

Track Track
Apr 73. (7") **GIVING IT ALL AWAY. / THE WAY OF THE WORLD** [5] [83]
Apr 73. (lp)(c) **DALTREY** [ ] [45]
– One man band / The way of the world / You are yourself / Thinking / You and me / It's a hard life / Giving it all away / The story so far / When the music stops / Reasons. *(re-iss.Aug82) (cd-iss.Apr95 on 'Polydor')*
Jun 73. (7") **I'M FREE. / (OVERTURE)** [13] [ ]
Sep 73. (7") **THINKING. / THERE IS LOVE** [ ] [ ]
Nov 73. (7") **IT'S A HARD LIFE. / ONE MAN BAND** [ ] [ ]
Polydor M.C.A.
Mar 75. (7") **LISTENING TO YOU. / (OVERTURE)** [ ] [ ]
May 75. (7") **COME AND GET YOUR LOVE. / THE WORLD OVER** [ ] [-]
Jul 75. (lp)(c) **RIDE A ROCK HORSE** [14] [28]
– Come and get your love / Hearts right / Oceans away / Proud / The world over / Near to surrender / Feeling / Walking the dog / Milk train / I was to sing your song.
Jul 75. (7") **WALKING THE DOG. / PROUD** [ ] [ ]
Sep 75. (7") **COME AND GET YOUR LOVE. / FEELING** [-] [68]
Nov 75. (7") **OCEANS AWAY. / FEELING** [-] [ ]
Oct 75. (7") **ORPHEUS SONG. / LOVE'S DREAM** [ ] [ ]

— (above from the Ken Russell film LISTZOMANIA. Released at the same time, it was scored by RICK WAKEMAN for 'A & M' and featured some with DALTREY vocals).

Apr 77. (7") **WRITTEN ON THE WIND. / DEAR JOHN** [46] [-]
May 77. (7") **ONE OF THE BOYS. / DOING IT ALL AGAIN** [-] [ ]
May 77. (lp)(c) **ONE OF THE BOYS** [45] [46]
– Parade / Single man's dilemma / Avenging Annie / The prisoner / Leon / One of the boys / Giddy / Written on the wind / Satin and lace / Doing it all again.
Jun 77. (7") **ONE OF THE BOYS. / TO PUT SOMETHING BETTER INSIDE ME** [ ] [-]
Aug 77. (7") **SAY IT ISN'T SO, JOE. / SATIN AND LACE** [-] [ ]
Oct 77. (7") **AVENGING ANNIE. / THE PRISONER** [-] [88]
Jan 78. (7") **THE PRISONER. / LEON** [-] [ ]
Polydor Polydor
Jul 80. (7") **FREE ME. / McVICAR** [39] [53]
Jul 80. (lp)(c)(clear-lp) **McVICAR (Soundtrack)** [39] [22]
– Bitter and twisted / Just a dream away / Escape (part 1) / White City lights / Free me / My time is gonna come / Waiting for a friend / Escape (part 2) / Without your love / McVicar. *(cd-iss.Apr95)*
Sep 80. (7") **WITHOUT YOUR LOVE. / ESCAPE (part 2)** [-] [20]
Oct 80. (7") **WITHOUT YOUR LOVE. / SAY IT AIN'T SO, JOE. / FREE ME** [55] [-]

Jan 81. (7") **WAITING FOR A FRIEND. / BITTER AND TWISTED** [-] [ ]

Polydor M.C.A.

Mar 82. (lp)(c) **THE BEST OF ROGER DALTREY** (compilation) [ ] [ ]
– Martyrs and madmen / Say it isn't so, Joe / Oceans away / Treasury / Free me / Without your love / It's a hard life / Giving it all away / Avenging Annie / Proud / You put something better inside me. *(US-title* **'BEST BITS'**) *(UK cd-iss.May91)*

Apr 82. (7") **SAY IT AIN'T SO, JOE. / THE PRISONER** [ ] [-]

Apr 82. (7") **MARTYRS AND MADMEN. / AVENGING ANNIE** [-] [ ]

WEA Atlantic

Feb 84. (7") **WALKING IN MY SLEEP. / SOMEBODY TOLD ME** [56] [62]
(12"+=) – Gimme some lovin'.

Feb 84. (lp)(c) **PARTING SHOULD BE PAINLESS** [ ] [ ]
– Walking in my sleep / Parting would be painless / Is there anybody out there / Would a stranger do / Going strong / Looking for you / Somebody told me / How does the cold wind cry / Don't wait on the stairs.

Jun 84. (7") **PARTING SHOULD BE SO PAINLESS. / IS THERE ANYBODY OUT THERE** [ ] [ ]
(12"+=) – I won't be the one to say goodbye.

Ten-Virgin Atlantic

Sep 85. (7") **AFTER THE FIRE. / IT DON'T SATISFY ME** [50] [48]
(12"+=) – Love me like you do.

Oct 85. (lp)(c)(cd) **UNDER A RAGING MOON** [52] [42]
– After the fire / Don't talk to strangers / Breaking down Paradise / The pride you hide / Move better in the night / Let me down easy / Fallen angel / It don't satisfy me / Rebel / Under a raging moon. *(cd+=)–* Behind blue eyes / 5:15 / Won't get fooled again. *(re-iss.cd.1989)*

Dec 85. (7") **LET ME DOWN EASY. / FALLEN ANGEL** [-] [86]

Feb 86. (7")(12") **UNDER A RAGING MOON. / MOVE BETTER IN THE NIGHT** [43] [-]
(d7"+=) – Behind blue eyes / 5:15 / Won't get fooled again.

Apr 86. (7") **QUICKSILVER LIGHTNING. / LOVE ME LIKE YOU DO** [-] [ ]

May 86. (7") **THE PRIDE YOU HIDE. / BREAK OUT** [ ] [-]
(d7"+=) – Don't talk to strangers (live) / Pictures of Lily (live).

Jun 86. (7") **UNDER A RAGING MOON. / THE PRIDE YOU HIDE** [-] [ ]

Jun 87. (7") **HEARTS OF FIRE. / LOVERS STORM** [ ] [ ]
(12"+=) – Quick silver lightning.

Jul 87. (lp)(c)(cd) **CAN'T WAIT TO SEE THE MOVIE** [ ] [ ]
– Hearts of fire / When the thunder comes / Ready for love / Balance on wires / Miracle of love / The price of love / The heart has its reasons / Alone in the night / Lover's storm / Take me home.

Jul 87. (7") **DON'T LET THE SUN GO DOWN ON ME. / THE HEART HAS ITS REASONS** [ ] [ ]
(12"+=) – ('A'extended).

JOHN ENTWISTLE

(solo)

Track Decca

Nov 70. (lp)(c) **THE OX (by "The WHO")** [ ] [ ]
– (compilation of WHO songs written by ENTWISTLE)

May 71. (lp)(c) **BANG YOUR HEAD AGAINST THE WALL** [ ] [ ]
– My size / Pick me up (big chicken) / What kind of people are they? / Heaven and Hell / Ted end / You're mine / No.29 (external youth) / I believe in everything.

May 71. (7") **I BELIEVE IN EVERYTHING. / MY SIZE** [ ] [ ]

RIGOR MORTIS

ENTWHISTLE with **BRYAN WILLIAMS** – keys / **ALAN ROSS** – guitar / **HOWIE CASEY** – sax / **GRAHAM DEACON** – drums / **TONY ASHTON** – perc.

Track Track

Nov 72. (lp)(c) **WHISTLE RHYMES** [ ] [ ]
– Ten little friends / Mr.Bones & Mr.Apron strings / And I feel better / Thinking it over / Who cares / I wonder now / I was just being friendly / The window shopper / I found out / Nightmare.

Nov 72. (7") **WHO CARES. / I WONDER NOW** [-] [ ]

Track M.C.A.

Jun 73. (lp)(c) **RIGOR MORTIS SETS IN** [ ] [ ]
– Give me that rock and roll / Mr. Bass man / Do the dangle / Hound dog / Made in Japan / My wife / Roller skate Kate / Peg leg Peggy / Lucille / Big black Cadillac.

Jun 73. (7") **MADE IN JAPAN. / HOUND DOG** [ ] [-]

Jun 73. (7") **MADE IN JAPAN. / ROLLER SKATE KATE** [-] [ ]

JOHN ENTWISTLE'S OX

with **DEACON, ASHTON & CASEY** plus **JIM RYAN** – guitar / **MIKE WEDGWOD** – guitar / **EDDIE JOBSON** – keyboards (guest)

Feb 75. (7") **MAD DOG. / CELL NO.7** [ ] [ ]

Mar 75. (lp)(c) **MAD DOG** [ ] [ ]
– I fall to pieces / Cell number seven / You can be so mean / Lady killer / Who in the hell? / Mad dog / Jungle bunny / I'm so scared / Drowning.

JOHN ENTWISTLE

(solo, with session stars incl. **JOE WALSH** – guitar

WEA Atco

Sep 81. (7")(7"pic-d) **TOO LATE THE HERO. / COMIN' BACK** [ ] [ ]

Nov 81. (lp)(c) **TOO LATE THE HERO** [ ] [71]
– Try me / Talk dirty / Lovebird / Sleepin man / I'm coming back / Dancing master / Fallen angel / Love is a heart attack / Too late the hero.

Dec 81. (7") **TALK DIRTY. /** [-] [ ]

KEITH MOON

Polydor M.C.A.

Apr 75. (lp)(c) **TWO SIDES OF THE MOON** [ ] [ ]
– Crazy like a fox / Solid gold / Don't worry baby / One night stand / The kid's are alright / Move over Ms. L / Teenage idol / Back door Sally / In my life / Together.

May 75. (7") **DON'T WORRY BABY. / TOGETHER** [ ] [-]

May 75. (7") **DON'T WORRY BABY. / TEENAGE IDOL** [-] [ ]

Jul 75. (7") **MOVE OVER MS. L. / SOLID GOLD** [-] [ ]

Sep 75. (7") **CRAZY LIKE A FOX. / IN MY LIFE** [-] [ ]

WILD & WONDERING
(see under ⇒ POP WILL EAT ITSELF)

WILDHEARTS

Formed: London, England ... 1988 by GINGER + CJ; veterans of the 80's heavy glam scene. After difficulties with initial record label 'East West', they signed to 'Bronze' in 1991, but had to wait until their second release; 1993's 'EARTH VERSUS ... ' for their first visit into chart territory. • **Style:** Hard rock and thrash punk /pop, lying between The RUTS, The CULT and The MANICS. • **Songwriters:** GINGER, except some group. • **Trivia:** In 1993, they featured in Channel 4 play 'Comics'. Played Reading Festival in 1994, where rumours floated about a imminent split. Yeah! the same f'in ones that said The LEVELLERS were to replace SOUNDGARDEN.

Recommended: EARTH VERSUS THE WILDHEARTS (*6)

GINGER – vocals, guitar (ex-QUIREBOYS) / **BAM** – drums (ex-DOGS D'AMOUR) / **CJ** (CHRIS JAGDHAR) – guitar, vocals (ex-TATTOOED LOVE BOYS) / **DANNY McCORMICK** – bass, vocals (ex-ENERGETIC KRUSHER)

Bronze East West

Mar 92. (12"ep)(cd-ep) **MONDO AKIMBO A-GO-GO** [ ] [ ]
– (Nothing ever changes but the) Shoes / Turning American / Crying over nothing * / Liberty cap. *(re-iss.Apr94 c+cd-ep as 'DON'T BE HAPPY ... JUST WORRY' for 'East West', track * repl. by 'Splattermania')*

Sep 93. (cd)(c)(lp) **EARTH VERSUS THE WILDHEARTS** [46] [ ]
– Greetings from Shitsville / TV tan / Everlone / Shame on me / Loveshit / The miles away girl / My baby is a headf*** / Suckerpunch / News of the world / Love u til I don't.
(cd+c+=) – Drinking about life. *(re-iss.Feb94 on 'East West')*

Oct 93. (7"brown) **GREETINGS FROM SHITSVILLE. / THE BULLSHIT GOES ON** [ ] [ ]

Nov 93. (7"pic-d)(c-s) **TV TAN. / SHOW A LITTLE EMOTION** [53] [ ]
(12"+=)(cd-s+=) – Danger lust / Down on London.

—— **RITCH** – drums repl. BAM

East West East West

Feb 94. (7"green-ep)(12"ep)(c-ep)(cd-ep) **CAFFEINE BOMB / GIRLFRIENDS CLOTHES. / SHUT YOUR FUCKIN' MOUTH AND USE YOUR FUCKIN' BRAIN / AND THE BULLSHIT GOES ON** [31] [ ]

Jun 94. (10"ep)(c-ep)(cd-ep) **SUCKER PUNCH / BEAUTIFUL THING YOU. / TWO-WAY IDIOT MIRROR / 29 x THE PAIN** [38] [ ]

(Jul94) temp **DEVON TOWNSEND** – guitar repl. C.J. who formed although only briefly HONEYCRACK. He returned for Reading Festival August 1994.

Dec 94. (cd) **FISHING FOR LUCKIES** (mail order) [ ] [ ]
– Sky babies / Inglorious / Do the channel bop / Shizophronic / Geordie in wonderland / If life is like a love bank I want an overdraft.

Jan 95. (10"ep)(c-ep)(cd-ep)(cd-ep) **IF LIFE IS LIKE A LOVE BANK I WANT AN OVERDRAFT / GEORDIE IN WONDERLAND. / HATE THE WORLD DAY / FIRE UP** [31] [ ]

Apr 95. (10"ep)(c-ep)(cd-ep)(cd-ep) **I WANNA GO WHERE THE PEOPLE GO / SHANDY BANG. / CAN'T DO RIGHT FOR DOING WRONG / GIVE THE GIRL A GUN** [16] [ ]

May 95. (cd)(c)(lp) **P.H.U.Q.** [6] [ ]
– I wanna go where the people go / V-day / ust in lust / Baby strange / Nita nitro /

Jonesing for Jones / Woah shit, you got through / Cold patootie tango / Caprice / Be my drug / Naivety play / In Lilly's garden / Getting it.

— **MARK KEDS** -guitar (ex-SENSELESS THINGS) repl.C.J.

Jul 95. (10"ep)(c-ep)(cd-ep)(cd-ep) **JUST IN LUST / MINDSLIDE. / FRIEND FOR FIVE MINUTES / S.I.N. (IN SIN)** — 28 |

— **JEFF STREATFIELD** -guitar repl.KEDS who went AWOL in July

Nov 95. (cd)(c)(lp) **FISHING FOR MORE LUCKIES** (see other) — | -

— Disbanded at the end of '95, although they quickly reformed.

... Jan – Jun '96 stop press ...

		Round	Warners
Apr 96.	(single) **SICK OF DRUGS**	14	
May 96.	(3D-cd)(c)(d-lp) **FISHING FOR LUCKIES**	16	
Jun 96.	(single) **RED LIGHT, GREEN LIGHT EP**	30	

Ann WILSON (see under ⇒ HEART)

Brian WILSON / Carl WILSON / Dennis WILSON (see under ⇒ BEACH BOYS)

WINGS (see under ⇒ McCARTNEY, Paul)

Edgar WINTER

Formed: 28 Dec'46, Beaumont, Texas, USA. Having spent the latter half of the 60's playing in older brother JOHNNY's bands (i.e. BLACK PLAGUE), he went solo in 1969. His debut album 'ENTRANCE', made the US Top 200 lists, but in 1972 after forming WHITE TRASH, he made No.23 with double live album 'ROADWORK'. The following year, he surpassed brother JOHNNY's triumphs, when the THE EDGAR WINTER GROUP peaked at US No.1, with instrumental 45 'FRANKENSTEIN'. • **Style:** Experimental jazz influenced rock'n'roll, that lent on much of his stage aura to that albino EDGAR portrayed. • **Songwriters:** EDGAR penned except; I CAN'T TURN YOU LOOSE (Otis Redding) / TOGETHER album with JOHNNY featured loads of covers. • **Trivia:** A past member of his group DAN HARTMAN, went onto score disco hits such as 'Instant Replay'. In 1989, EDGAR played saxophone on TINA TURNER's hit 'Simply The Best'.

Recommended: ENTRANCE (*7) / THEY ONLY COME OUT AT NIGHT (*7)

EDGAR WINTER – (solo) – keyboards, saxophone, all (ex-JOHNNY WINTER) except guests **JOHNNY WINTER + RANDAL DOLANON** – guitar / **JIMMY GILLEN** – drums / **RAY AVONGE, EARL CHAPIN + BROOKS TILLOTSON** – horns

		Epic	Epic
Jun 70.	(lp) **ENTRANCE**		

– Entrance / Where have you gone / Rise to fall / Fire and ice / Hung and up / Back in the blues / Re-entrance / Tobacco Road / Jump right out / Peace pipe / A different game / Jimmy's gospel.

Jun 70. (7") **TOBACCO ROAD. / NOW IS THE TIME** — - |

EDGAR WINTER'S WHITE TRASH

EDGAR with **JERRY LaCROIX** – vox, sax / **JON ROBERT SMITH** – sax, vox / **MIKE McLELLAN** – trumpet, vox / **GEORGE SHECK** – bass / **FLOYD RADFORD** – guitar / **BOBBY RAMIREZ** – drums also **RICK DERRINGER** – guitar

May 71. (7") **WHERE WOULD I BE. / GOOD MORNING MUSIC** — |

Jun 71. (lp) **EDGAR WINTER'S WHITE TRASH** — | Apr 71

– Give it everything you got / Fly away / Where would I be / Let's get it on / I've got news for you / Save the planet / Dying to live / Keep playin' that rock 'n' roll / You were my light / Good morning music. *(cd-iss.Oct93 on 'Sony Europe')*

Nov 71. (7") **KEEP PLAYIN' THAT ROCK'N'ROLL. / DYING TO LIVE** — | 70

May 72. (d-lp) **ROADWORK (live)** — | 23 Mar 72

– Save the planet / Jive jive jive / I can't turn you loose / Still alive & well / Back in the U.S.A. / Rock and roll hoochie koo / Tobacco Road / Cool fool / Do yourself a favour / Turn on your lovelight.

Jun 72. (7") **I CAN'T TURN YOU LOOSE. / COOL FOOL** — | 81 May 72

— WHITE TRASH folded when on 24th Jul'72, RAMIREZ was killed in pub brawl.

EDGAR WINTER GROUP

added synthesizer to his new line-up **DAN HARTMAN** – vocals, bass / **RONNIE MONTROSE** – guitar / **CHUCK RUFF** – drums / **+ RICK**

Aug 72. (7") **FREE RIDE. / CATCHIN' UP** — |

Jan 73. (lp)(c) **THEY ONLY COME OUT AT NIGHT** — | 3 Nov72

– Hangin' around / When it comes / Alta Mira / Free ride / Frankenstein / Autumn / Round and round / Rock'n'roll boogie woogie blues / We all had a really good time. *(re-iss.quad.Sep84)*

Feb 73. (7") **ROUND AND ROUND. / CATCHIN' UP** — |

Mar 73. (7") **FRANKENSTEIN. / HANGIN' AROUND** — - | 1

(above 'B' side was original 'A' side, but flipped over after airplay)

May 73. (7") **FRANKENSTEIN. / UNDERCOVER MAN** — 18 | -

Aug 73. (7") **FREE RIDE. / WHEN IT COMES** — | 14

Feb 74. (7") **HANGIN' AROUND. / WE ALL HAD A REAL GOOD TIME** — | 65 Dec 73

— Billed on tour as EDGAR WINTER GROUP Featuring RICK DERRINGER

RICK – guitars, vocals, etc. (ex-JOHNNY WINTER, ex-McCOYS) repl. JERRY WEEMS. In Oct'74, WEEMS had repl. RONNIE who formed own band MONTROSE

Jul 74. (lp)(c) **SHOCK TREATMENT** — | 13 May 74

– Some kinda animal / Easy street / Sundown / Miracle of love / Do like me / Rock & roll woman / Someone take my heart away / Queen of my dreams / Maybe someday you'll call my name / River's risin' / Animal.

Jul 74. (7") **RIVER'S RISIN'. / ANIMAL** — | 33

Nov 74. (7") **EASY STREET. / DO LIKE ME** — | 83 Oct 74

Feb 75. (7") **SOMEONE TAKE MY HEART AWAY. / MIRACLE OF LOVE** — |

EDGAR WINTER

(solo) with **HARTMAN, RUFF, DERRINGER + J.WINTER**

		Blue Sky	Blue Sky
Jun 75.	(lp)(c) **JASMINE NIGHTDREAMS**		69

– One day tomorrow / Little brother / Hello mellow feelin' / Tell me in a whisper / Shuffle-low / Keep on burnin' / How do you like your love / I always wanted you / Outa control / All out / Sky train / Solar strut.

The EDGAR WINTER GROUP WITH RICK DERRINGER

Nov 75. (lp)(c) **THE EDGAR WINTER GROUP WITH RICK DERRINGER** — |

– Cool dance / People music / Good shot / Nothin' good comes easy / Infinite peace in rhythm / Paradise skies / Diamond eyes / Modern love / Let's do it together again / Can't tell one from the other / J.A.P. (Just Another Punk) / Chainsaw.

May 76. (7") **DIAMOND EYES. / INFINITE PEACE IN RHYTHM** — |

— Next as collaboration with brother:

EDGAR & JOHNNY WINTER

JOHNNY WINTER + RICK DERRINGER + FLOYD RADFORD – guitar / **CHUCK RUFF + RICHARD HUGHES** – drums / **RANDY JO HOBBS** – bass (DAN HARTMAN was now solo disco artist)

Jul 76. (lp)(c) **TOGETHER (live)** — | 89

– Harlem shuffle / Soul man / You've lost that lovin' feeling / Rock'n'roll medley:- Slippin' & slidin' – Jailhouse rock – Tutti frutti – Sick & tired – I'm ready – Reelin' and rockin' – Blue sude shoes – Jenny take a ride – Good golly Miss Molly / Let the good times roll / Mercy, mercy / Baby whatcha want me to do. *(cd-iss.Jun93 on 'Sony Europe')*

EDGAR WINTER

1977. (lp)(c) **RECYCLED** — |

– Puttin' it back / Leftover love / Shake it off / Stickin' it out / New wave / Open up / Parallel love / The in and out of love blue / Competition.

EDGAR WINTER GROUP

in 1979 with different line-up **CRAIG SNYDER** – guitar / **JAMES WILLIAMS** – bass / **KEITH BENSON** – drums / **LARRY WASHINGTON** – percussion (same label)

Aug 79. (7") **IT'S YOUR LIFE TO LIVE. / FOREVER IN LOVE** — |

Sep 79. (lp)(c) **THE EDGAR WINTER ALBUM** — |

– It's your life to live / Above and beyond / Take it the way it is / Dying to live / Please don't stop / Make it last / Do what / It took your love to bring me out / Forever in blue.

Mar 80. (7")(12") **ABOVE AND BEYOND. / ('A'instrumental)** — |

— now with **AL FERRANTE** – guitar / **GREG CARTER** – drums / **SCOTT SPRAY** – bass / **RONNIE LAWSON** – keyboards, vocals / **MONIQUE WINTER** – backing vocals

1981. (lp)(c) **STANDING ON ROCK** — |

– Step garbage / Standing on rock / Love is everywhere / Martians / Rock'n'roll revival / In love / Everyday man / Tomorrowland.

— EDGAR retired from solo work for the rest of the 80's.

		Thunderb.	not issued
Nov 90.	(cd) **HARLEM NOCTURNE**		-

– Searching / Tingo tango / Cry me a river / Save your love for me / Quiet gas / Satin doll / Jordu / Girl from Ipanema / Harlem nocturne / Come back baby / Before the sunset / Who dunnit / Please come home for Christmas.

Nov 91. (cd) **LIVE IN JAPAN (live with RICK DERRINGER)** [ ] [-]
– Keep playing that rock and roll / Teenage love affair / Free ride / Fly away / Blood from a stone / Undercover man / Jump jump jump / Hang on Sloopy / Against the law / Play guitar / Rock and roll hoochie koo / Frankenstein.

Jan 94. (cd) **I'M NOT A KID ANYMORE** [ ] [ ]
– Way down south / I'm not a kid anymore / Against the law / Brother's keeper / I wanta rock / Crazy / Just like you / Big city woman / Innocent lust / Wild man / Frankenstein.

— In Apr 94; his past keyboard wizard DAN HARTMAN died of a brain tumour.

– compilations, others, etc. –

1975. Epic; (7") **FRANKENSTEIN. / FREE RIDE** [ ] [-]
Jul 91. Elite; (cd)(c) **BROTHERS IN ROCK'N'ROLL (with JOHNNY)** [ ] [ ]
(re-iss. Sep93)
Aug 93. Rhino; (cd) **MISSION EARTH** [ ] [ ]
May 95. Rhino; (cd) **THE COLLECTION** [ ] [-]

Johnny WINTER

Born: JOHN DAWSON WINTER III, 23 Feb'44, Leland, Missouri, USA. After his group JOHNNY & THE JAMMERS released a single 'SCHOOLDAY BLUES' on Texas label 'Dart' in 1959, he moved to Chicago. He also formed own band BLACK PLAGUE with younger brother EDGAR (EDGAR too was born albino; white hair & born with lack of skin pigmentation). Early in 1969, after an article in The Rolling Stone magazine and a flit to New York, he signed to 'Columbia', for a record-breaking 6-figure sum. His first official debut 'JOHNNY WINTER', hit the US Top 30, and with ever increasing concert audiences, he became top live attraction of the early 70's. His full potential was curtailed when he suffered from recurring drug addiction. He issued comeback album in 1973, appropriately titled 'STILL ALIVE AND WELL'. • **Style:** White blues guitar legend, who turned great R&B standards into electrifying classics. • **Songwriters:** J.WINTER or DERRINGER, with mostly covers; JUMPIN' JACK FLASH + SILVER TRAIN + LET IT BLEED + STRAY CAT BLUES + SILVER TRAIN (Rolling Stones) / HIGHWAY 101 (Van Morrison) / IT'S ALL OVER NOW (Bobby & Shirley Womack) / GREAT BALLS OF FIRE + WHOLE LOTTA SHAKIN' GOIN' ON (Jerry Lee Lewis) / LONG TALL SALLY + SLIPPIN' & SLIDIN' (Little Richard) / BONY MORONIE (Larry Williams) / JOHNNY B.GOODE + THIRTY DAYS (Chuck Berry) / ROCK & ROLL PEOPLE (John Lennon) / IT'S MY OWN FAULT (B.B. King) / HIGHWAY 61 REVISITED (Bob Dylan) / SHAME SHAME SHAME (Shirley Ellis) / RAISED ON ROCK (Elmore James) / ROCK ME BABY (Big Bill Broozy-Arthur Crudup) / GOOD MORNING LITTLE SCHOOLGIRL (Don & Bob) / BAREFOOTIN' (Robert Parker) / PLEASE COME HOME FOR CHRISTMAS (Charles Brown) / GOT MY BRAND ON YOU (Muddy Waters) / etc. • **Trivia:** In 1977, he produced MUDDY WATERS' comeback album 'HARD AGAIN' on his 'Blue Sky' label. He also joined WATERS' touring band.

Recommended: SECOND WINTER (*8) / THE COLLECTION (*7)

JOHNNY WINTER – vocals, guitar, mandolin / with **EDGAR WINTER** – keyboards, alto saxophone / **TOMMY SHANNON** – bass, ukelele / **JOHN 'Red' TURNER** – percussion

Liberty Imperial

May 69. (lp) **WINTER, THE PROGRESSIVE BLUES EXPERIMENT** [ ] [49] Apr 69
– Rollin' and tumblin' / Tribute to Muddy / I got love if you want it / Bad luck and trouble / Help me / Mean town blues / Broke down engine / Black cat bones / It's my own fault / Forty-four. *(re-iss.1973 on 'Sunset') (re-iss.Oct79 on 'Liberty') (re-iss.Nov86 on 'Razor') (cd-iss.Sep93 on 'I.T.M.')*

C.B.S. Columbia

Jun 69. (lp) **JOHNNY WINTER** [ ] [24] May 69
– I'm yours and I'm hers / Be careful with a fool / Dallas / Mean mistreater / Leland Mississippi blues / Good morning little schoolgirl / When you got a good friend / I'll drown in my tears / Back door friend. *(re-iss.Jan76) (re-iss.Nov85 on 'Edsel')*

Jul 69. (7") **I'M YOURS AND I'M HERS. / I'LL DROWN IN MY TEARS** [ ] [ ]

Jan 70. (d-lp/3-playing sides) **SECOND WINTER** [59] [55] Nov 69
– Memory pain / I'm not sure / The good love / Slippin' and slidin' / Miss Ann / Johnny B.Goode / Highway 61 revisited / I love everybody / Hustled down in Texas / I hate everybody / Fast life rider. *(re-iss.1974) (re-iss.+cd.Apr89 on 'Edsel')*

Jan 70. (7") **JOHNNY B.GOODE. / I'M NOT SURE** [ ] [92]

— band now **RICK DERRINGER** – guitar, producer repl. EDGAR who went solo / **RANDY JO HOBBS** – bass / **RANDY ZEHRINGER** (RICK's bro) – drums (all ex-McCOYS)

Oct 70. (lp)(c) **JOHNNY WINTER AND** [29] [ ] Sep 70
– Guess I'll go away / Ain't that a kindness / No time to live / Rock and roll hoochie koo / Am I here? / Look up / Prodigal son / On the limb / Let the music play / Nothing left / Funky music. *(re-iss.+cd.Sep91 on 'B.G.O.')*

Nov 70. (7") **ROCK AND ROLL HOOCHIE KOO. / 21st CENTURY MAN** [-] [ ]

— **BOBBY CALDWELL** – drums repl. RANDY

May 71. (lp)(c) **JOHNNY WINTER AND LIVE (live)** [20] [40] Mar 71
– Good morning little schoolgirl / It's my own fault / Jumpin' Jack Flash / Rock'n'roll medley: Great balls of fire – Long tall Sally – Whole lotta shakin' goin' on – Mean town blues – Johnny B.Goode. *(re-iss.1974) (re-iss.+cd.Jan89 on 'B.G.O.')*

May 71. (7") **JUMPIN' JACK FLASH (live). / GOOD MORNING LITTLE SCHOOLGIRL (live)** [ ] [89] Apr 71

— Due to drugs problems, JOHNNY semi-retired. DERRINGER joined EDGAR WINTER Re-united w/DERRINGER in 1973, **RICHARD HUGHES** – drums repl. CALDWELL

Apr 73. (lp)(c) **STILL ALIVE AND WELL** [ ] [22]
– Rock me baby / Can't you feel it / Cheap tequila / All tore down / Rock and roll / Silver train / Ain't nothing to me / Still alive and well / Too much seconal / Let it bleed. *(also on quad.Sep74) (cd-iss.Apr93 on 'Sony Europe')*

Jun 73. (7") **SILVER TRAIN. / ROCK AND ROLL** [ ] [ ]
Sep 73. (7") **CAN YOU FEEL IT. / ROCK AND ROLL** [-] [ ]
Mar 74. (7") **BONY MORONIE. / HURTIN' SO BAD** [-] [ ]
Mar 74. (lp)(c) **SAINTS AND SINNERS** [ ] [42] Feb 74
– Stone County / Blinded by love / Thirty days / Stray cat blues / Bad luck situation / Rollin' cross the country / Riot in cell block £9 / Hurtin' so bad / Bony Moronie / Feedback on Highway 101. *(cd-iss.Apr93 on 'Sony Europe') (re-iss.cd+c Jul94)*

Apr 74. (7") **STONE COUNTY. / BAD LUCK SITUATION** [ ] [ ]

Blue Sky Blue Sky

Nov 74. (7") **MIND OVER MATTER. / PICK UP ON MY MOJO** [ ] [-]
Dec 74. (lp)(c) **JOHN DAWSON WINTER III** [ ] [78]
– Rock & roll people / Golden days of rock & roll / Self-destructable blues / Raised on rock / Stranger / Mind over matter / Roll with me / Love song to me / Pick up on my mojo / Lay down your sorrows / Sweet Papa John. *(cd-iss.Apr93 on 'Sony Europe')*

Dec 74. (7") **RAISED ON ROCK. / PICK UP ON MY MOJO** [-] [ ]
Feb 75. (7") **GOLDEN DAYS OF ROCK & ROLL. / STRANGER** [-] [ ]

— **FLOYD RADFORD** – guitar repl. DERRINGER.

Mar 76. (lp)(c) **CAPTURED LIVE! (live)** [ ] [93]
– Bony Moronie / Roll with me / Rock & roll people / It's all over now / Highway 61 revisited / Sweet Papa John.

— Mid'76, teamed up with brother EDGAR ⇒ on live album TOGETHER. Early 1977, JOHNNY also produced and joined MUDDY WATERS band.

— with **CHARLES CALMESE** – bass / **WILLIE SMITH** – drums / **MUDDY WATERS** – guitar

Aug 77. (lp)(c) **NOTHIN' BUT THE BLUES** [ ] [ ] Jul 77
– Tired of tryin' / TV mama / Everybody's blues / Sweet love and evil woman / Drinkin' blues / Mad blues / It was rainin' / Blondie Mae / Walking thru the park. *(re-iss.+cd.Aug91 on 'B.G.O.')*

— with **BOBBY TORELLO** – drums / **I.P.SWEAT** – bass / **PAT RUSH** – guitar / + **EDGAR**

Aug 78. (lp)(c) **WHITE, HOT AND BLUE** [ ] [ ]
– Walkin' by myself / Slidin' in / Divin' duck blues / One stop at a time / Nickel blues / E-Z rider / Last night / Messin' with the kid / Honest I do. *(cd-iss.Jun93 on 'Sony Europe')*

— now with **BOBBY TORTELLO** – drums / **JON PARIS** – bass, etc. /

May 80. (lp)(c) **RAISIN' CAIN** [ ] [ ]
– The crawl / Sitting in this jail house / Like a rolling stone / New York, New York / Talk is cheap / Rollin' and tumblin' / Don't hide your love. *(cd-iss.Apr93 on 'Sony Europe')*

Sonet Alligator

Mar 84. (lp) **WHOOPIN'** [ ] [ ]
– I got my eyes on you / Sonny's whoopin' the doop / Burnt child / Whoee whoee / Crow Jane / So tough with me / Whoo wee baby / I think I got the blues / Ya ya / Roll me baby.

Aug 84. (lp) **GUITAR SLINGER** [ ] [ ]
– It's my life baby / Don't like advantage / Iodine in my coffee / Trick bag / Mad dog / Boothill / I smell trouble / Lights out / My soul / Kiss tomorrow goodbye. *(cd-iss.Oct86)*

Sep 85. (lp) **SERIOUS BUSINESS** [ ] [ ]
– Master mechanic / Sound the bell / Murdering the blues / It ain't your business / Good time woman / Unseen eye / My time after a while / Serious as a heart attack / Give it back / Route 90. *(c+cd-iss.Jun88)*

Oct 86. (lp)(cd) **THIRD DEGREE** [ ] [ ]
– Mojo boogie / Love, life and money / Evil on my mind / See see baby / Tin pan alley / I'm good / Third degree / Shake your moneymaker / Bad girl blues / Broke and lonely.

— now with **JON PARIS** – bass / **TOM COMPTON** – drums

M.C.A. M.C.A.

Nov 88. (lp)(c)(cd) **WINTER OF '88** [ ] [ ]
– Close to me / Stranger blues / Lightning / Anything for your love / Rain / Ain't that just like a woman / Looking for trouble / Look away.

Point Blank Point Blank

Aug 91. (cd)(c)(lp) **LET ME IN** [ ] [ ]
– Illustrated man / Barefootin' / Life is hard / Hey you / Blue mood / Sugarlee / Medicine man / You're humbuggin' me / If you got a good woman / Got to find my baby / Shame shame shame / Let me in.

— with **JEFF GANZ** – bass / **TOM COMPTON** – drums, percussion / guests **EDGAR** – sax / **BILLY BRANCH** – harmonica

1992. (cd)(c) **HEY, WHERE'S YOUR BROTHER?** [ ] [ ]
– Johnny Guitar / She likes to boogie real low / White line blues / Please come home for Christmas / You must have a twin / You keep sayin' that you're leavin' / Hard way / Sick and tired / Blues this bad / no more dogin' / Check out her mama / Got my brand on you.

– compilations, others, etc. –

1969. GRT; (7") **ROADRUNNER. / GANGSTER OF LOVE** [-] [ ]
1971. Marble Arch/ US= GRT; (lp) **THE JOHNNY WINTER STORY** [ ] [ ] Sep 69
1970. Buddah/ US= Columbia; (lp) **FIRST WINTER** [ ] [ ]
1971. Janus; (lp) **ABOUT BLUES** [-] [ ]
1971. Janus; (lp) **EARLY TIMES** [-] [ ]
Feb 81. Blue Sky; (d-lp)(d-c) **THE JOHNNY WINTER STORY – RAISED ON ROCK** [ ] [ ]
Jul 84. President; (lp) **EARLY WINTER** [ ] [-]
(cd-iss.Jan87)
Apr 86. Showcase; (lp)(c) **LIVIN' IN THE BLUES** [ ] [-]
(re-iss.Sep86 on 'Sonet')
Mar 87. Topline; (lp)(c)(cd) **OUT OF SIGHT** [ ] [-]
1988. Castle; (d-lp)(c)(cd) **THE JOHNNY WINTER COLLECTION** [ ] [-]
– Rock and roll hoochie koo / Cheap tequila / On the lamb / Slippin' and slidin' / Johnny B.Goode / Rock me baby / Let it bleed / Stray cat blues / Riot in cell block 9 / Bony Moronie / Highway 61 revisited / Raised on rock / Pick up on my mojo / Thirty days / Good morning little school girl / Jumpin' Jack Flash / It's my own fault / Medley:- Great balls of fire – Long tall Sally – Whole lotta shakin' goin' on.
Jan 89. Relix; (lp) **BIRDS CAN'T ROW BOATS** [ ] [ ]
(cd-iss.Jun93)
Nov 89. Thunderbolt; (lp)(cd) **FIVE AFTER 4 A.M.** [ ] [-]
Apr 90. Thunderbolt; (cd)(c)(lp) **BACK IN BEAUMONT** (w / "UNCLE JOHN TURNER") [ ] [-]
Jul 91. Thunderbolt; (cd)(c) **LIVE IN HOUSTON (live)** [ ] [-]
Nov 93. Thunderbolt; (cd) **WHITE LIGHTNING** [ ] [-]
Nov 92. Fan Club; (cd) **LIVE AT LIBERTY HALL, HOUSTON, TX. 1972 (live with JIMMY REED)** [ ] [ ]
Apr 91. M.M.G.; (cd) **LIVING IN THE BLUES** [ ] [ ]
Aug 92. Sony; (cd)(c) **SEARCHIN' BLUES** [ ] [ ]
Feb 93. Charly; (cd) **THE TEXAS TORNADO** [ ] [-]
Apr 93. Pulsar; (cd) **THE GOLDEN DAYS OF ROCK'N'ROLL** [ ] [-]
Jul 94. Success; (cd)(c) **LIVIN' THE BLUES** [ ] [-]

Steve WINWOOD

Born: 12 May'48, Birmingham, England. At age 15, he joined The SPENCER DAVIS GROUP, where he had 3 massive hits 'KEEP ON RUNNING', 'SOMEBODY HELP ME' & 'GIMME SOME LOVING', between 1963 & April 1967. At this time, he formed TRAFFIC and scored 3 more UK Top 10'ers 'PAPER SUN', 'HOLE IN MY SHOE' & 'HERE WE GO ROUND THE MULBURRY BUSH'. In 1969, WINWOOD joined ERIC CLAPTON, GINGER BAKER and RIC GRECH in the supergroup BLIND FAITH, and although their stay was not long in the rock world, they managed a No.1 on both sides of the Atlantic. Early the next year, he joined GINGER BAKER'S AIRFORCE, but returned to TRAFFIC in 1971 after another 3 years stay (see further on and below). Having re-signed to 'Island' in 1976, his first solo venture was an eponymous effort in 1977. In 1988, he had his first solo No.1, when 'ROLL WITH IT' (the single and the album) peaked. • **Style:** Easy laid-back quality rock artist, whose contribution to music has only been matched by that of CLAPTON. • **Songwriters:** For his debut in 1977, he co-wrote with JIM CAPALDI (an ex-member of TRAFFIC). He collaborated on some further releases with lyricist VIV STANSHALL, WILL JENNINGS and JOE WALSH. • **Trivia:** He was also a renowned session man, having played on albums by JIMI HENDRIX (1968 + 1970) / JOE COCKER (1969) / McDONALD & GILES (1970) / LEON RUSSELL (1970) / HOWLIN' WOLF (1971) / ALVIN LEE (1973) / JOHN MARTYN (1973) / AMAZING BLONDEL (1973) / JADE WARRIOR (1975) / TOOTS & THE MAYTALS (1976) / SANDY DENNY (1977) / VIVIAN STANSHALL (1978) / GEORGE HARRISON (1979) / MARIANNE FAITHFULL (1979) / PIERRE MOERLEN'S GONG (1979) / etc. (see other 'Island' label artists).

Recommended: CHRONICLES (*7) / ROLL WITH IT (*6).

STEVE WINWOOD. Debut solo recording was actually compiled from his past bands' work.

Island Island

Jun 71. (d-lp)(d-c) **WINWOOD** [ ] [93]
– (tracks by SPENCER DAVIS GROUP / TRAFFIC / BLIND FAITH / AIRFORCE)

— Later that year, WINWOOD reformed TRAFFIC and went into numerous session work mainly for 'Island' artists. In 1976, he and ex-SANTANA drummer MIKE SHRIEVE collaborated with solo classical percussionist STOMU YAMASH'TA. As **"GO"**, they issued eponymous live album in Jun76. When WINWOOD was releasing solo albums, GO also issued live 12" CROSSING THE LINE. Another album GO LIVE IN PARIS (live), was given light in Spring'78. (watch soon for STOMU YAMASH'TA discography)

STEVE WINWOOD

STEVE WINWOOD – vocals, keyboards solo with **WILLIE WEEKS** – bass / **ANDY NEWMARK** – drums / **REEBOP KWAKU BANU** – congas

Island Island

Jun 77. (7") **TIME IS RUNNING OUT. / PENULTIMATE ZONE** [ ] [-]
Jul 77. (7") **TIME IS RUNNING OUT. / HOLD ON** [-] [ ]
Jul 77. (lp)(c) **STEVE WINWOOD** [12] [22]
– Hold on / Time is running out / Midland maniac / Vacant chair / Luck's in / Let me make something in your life. *(cd-iss.May87) (cd-iss.Mar93)*

— His next projects/albums featured WINWOOD on all instruments, vocals

Dec 80. (lp)(c) **ARC OF A DIVER** [13] [3]
– While you see a chance / Arc of a diver / Second-hand woman / Slowdown sundown / Spanish dancer / Night train / Dust. *(cd-iss.May87)*
Dec 80. (7")(c-s) **WHILE YOU SEE A CHANCE. / VACANT CHAIR** [45] [7]
Mar 81. (7")(12") **SPANISH DANCER (remix). / HOLD ON** [ ] [ ]
May 81. (7") **ARC OF A DIVER. / DUST** [-] [48]
Sep 81. (7")(12") **NIGHT TRAIN. / ('A'instrumental)** [ ] [ ]
Nov 81. (7") **THERE'S A RIVER. / TWO WAY STRETCH** [ ] [ ]
Jul 82. (7") **STILL IN THE GAME. / DUST** [ ] [47]
Aug 82. (lp)(c) **TALKING BACK TO THE NIGHT** [6] [28] Jul 82
– Valerie / Big girls walk away / And I go / While there's a candle burning / Still in the game / It was happiness / Help me angel / Talking back to the night / There's a river. *(cd-iss.May87)*
Sep 82. (7")(12") **VALERIE. / SLOWDOWN SUNDOWN** [51] [70]
Jun 83. (7") **YOUR SILENCE IS YOUR SONG. / ('A'instrumental)** [ ] [ ]

— Around the mid-80's, his work took a back seat as his marriage broke down. In 1986, he brought in session musicians to augment.

Jun 86. (7") **HIGHER LOVE. / AND I GO** [13] [1]
(extended-12"+=) – ('A'instrumental).
(c-s+=) – Valerie / While you see a chance / Talking back to the night.
Jul 86. (lp)(c)(cd) **BACK IN THE HIGH LIFE** [8] [3]
– Higher love / Take it as it comes / Freedom overspill / Back in the high life again / The finer things / Wake me up on judgement day / Split decision / My love's leavin'.
Aug 86. (7") **FREEDOM OVERSPILL. / HELP ME ANGEL** [-] [20]
Aug 86. (7") **FREEDOM OVERSPILL. / SPANISH DANCER** [69] [-]
(12"+=) – ('A'-liberty mix).
(c-s+=) – (last lp excerpts & interview)
(d7"+=) – Higher love / And I go.
Jan 87. (7") **BACK IN THE HIGH LIFE AGAIN. / HELP ME ANGEL** [53] [13]
(12"+=) – Night train (instrumental). (US; b-side)
Feb 87. (7") **THE FINER THINGS. / NIGHT TRAIN** [-] [8]
Sep 87. (7")(c-s) **VALERIE (remix). / TALKING BACK TO THE NIGHT (instrumental)** [19] [9]
(12"+=)(cd-s+=) – The finer things.
Oct 87. (lp)(c)(cd) **CHRONICLES** (compilation) [12] [26]
– Wake me up on judgement day / While you see a chance / Vacant chair / Help me angel / My love's leavin' / Valerie / Arc of a diver / Higher love / Spanish dancer / Talking back to the night.
Feb 88. (7") **TALKING BACK TO THE NIGHT. / THERE'S A RIVER** [-] [57]

Virgin Virgin

May 88. (7") **ROLL WITH IT. / THE MORNING SIDE** [53] [1]
(c-s+=)/ /(12"+=)(cd-s+=) – ('A'dub version)./ / ('A'&'B'versions).
Jun 88. (lp)(c)(cd) **ROLL WITH IT** [4] [1]
– Roll with it / Holding on / The morning side / Put on your dancing shoes / Don't you know what the night can do? / Hearts on fire / One more morning / Shining song.
Aug 88. (7") **DON'T YOU KNOW WHAT THE NIGHT CAN DO? (remix). / ('A' instrumental)** [ ] [6]

(12"+=)/ /(cd-s++=) – ('A'extended)./ / Roll with it.
Oct 88. (7") **HOLDING ON. / ('A'instrumental)** [ ] [11]
(3"cd-s+=)(12"+=) – ('A'dance version) / Go Juan.
Mar 89. (7") **HEARTS ON FIRE. / ?** [-] [53]
Oct 90. (7") **ONE AND ONLY MAN. / ALWAYS** [ ] [18]
(12"+=)(cd-s+=) – ?
Nov 90. (cd)(c)(lp) **REFUGEES OF THE HEART** [26] [27]
– You'll keep on searching / Every day (oh Lord) / One and only man / I will be here / Another deal goes down / Running on / Come out and dance / In the light of day.
Apr 91. (7") **I WILL BE HERE. / IN THE LIGHT OF DAY (Instrumental)** [ ] [ ]
(12"+=)(cd-s+=) – ?

– other compilations, etc. –

Aug 91. Island; (cd)(c)(lp) **KEEP ON RUNNING** [ ] [ ]
May 65. Fontana; (7") **INCENSE. / YOU'RE FOOLING ME** [ ] [-]
(above as "The ANGELOS")
(re-iss.May69 on 'Island')

WIRE

Formed: London, England . . . Oct'76 by LEWIS, NEWMAN, GILBERT and GOTOBED. First heard on vinyl in April 1977, when ears were subjected to their punk anthems on Various Artists lp 'LIVE AT THE ROXY'. That lp's label 'Harvest', decided to give them contract, and thus the masterful Mike Thorne produced 'PINK FLAG' album at the end of '77. It contained 21 short sharp shocks of exciting variety (see style). They followed this in 1978 with 2 classic 45's 'I AM THE FLY' & 'DOT DASH', which preceeded a gem of an album 'CHAIRS MISSING', which gave them first Top 50 entry. • **Style:** Basic but adventurous punk rock, which later degressed into electronic experimentation in the 80's. They had a non-conformist avant-garde attitude, mixed at times with a sense of future 21st century pop-rock. • **Songwriters:** Group compositions. • **Trivia:** COLIN NEWMAN produced The VIRGIN PRUNES in 1982, and FAD GADGET in 1984. He moved to India at this time, but returned to live in Belguim 1986.

Recommended: PINK FLAG (*8) / CHAIRS MISSING (*9) / 154 (*7) / ON RETURNING (*8) / THE IDEAL COPY (*8). Best solo:- COLIN NEWMAN – NOT TO (*6).

COLIN NEWMAN (b.16 Sep'54, Salisbury, England) – vox, guitar, keyboards / **BRUCE GILBERT** (b.18 May'46, Watford, England) – guitar, vocals, synths. / **GRAHAM LEWIS** (b.22 Feb'53, Grantham, England) – bass, vocals, synthesizers / **ROBERT GOTOBED** (b.MARK FIELD, 1951, Leicester, England) – drums, percussion (ex-SNAKES, ex-ART ATTACKS) / **GEORGE GILL** – guitar (left before debut)

Harvest / Harvest
Nov 77. (7m)(12"m) **MANNEQUIN. / 12XU / FEELING CALLED LOVE** [ ] [-]
Nov 77. (lp)(c) **PINK FLAG** [ ] [ ]
– Reuters / Field day for the Sundays / Three girl rhumba / Ex-lion tamer / Lowdown / Start to move / Brazil / It's so obvious / Surgeon's girl / Pink flag / The commercial / Straight line / 106 beats that / Mr.Suit / Strange / Fragile / Mannequin / Different to me / Champs / Feeling called love / 1.2.X.U. *(cd-iss.1990+=)* – Options R. *(re-iss.cd Aug94 on 'EMI')*
Feb 78. (7") **I AM THE FLY. / EX-LION TAMER** [ ] [-]
Jun 78. (7") **DOT DASH. / OPTIONS R** [ ] [-]
Sep 78. (lp)(c) **CHAIRS MISSING** [48] [ ]
– Practise makes perfect / French film blurred / Another the letter / Men 2nd / Marooned / Sand in my joints / Being sucked in again / Heartbeat / Mercy / Outdoor miner / I am the fly / I feel mysterious today / From the nursery / Used to / Too late. *(cd-iss.1990, +=)*– Go ahead / A question of degree / Former airline. *(re-iss.cd Aug94 on 'EMI')*
Jan 79. (7")(7"white) **OUTDOOR MINER. / PRACTISE MAKES PERFECT** [51] [ ]
Harvest / Warners
Jun 79. (7") **A QUESTION OF DEGREE. / FORMER AIRLINE** [ ] [-]
Sep 79. (lp)(c) **154** [39] [ ]
– I should have known better / Two people in a room / The 15th / The other window / Single k.o. / A touching display / On returning / A mutual friend / Blessed state / Once is enough / Map reference 41°N, 93°W / Indirect enquiries / 40 versions. *(free-7"ep w.a)* **SONG 1** – Get down (parts 1 & 2) / Small electric piece / Let's panic later. *(cd-iss.1990 +=)*– SONG 1 (The free ep was issued on 'Dome' records) *(re-iss.cd Aug94 on 'EMI')*
Oct 79. (7") **MAP REFERENCE 41°N, 93°W. / GO AHEAD** [ ] [-]
—— In 1980, WIRE also diversed into own activities; GILBERT & LEWIS became CUPOL and DOME, etc. The pair also joined THE THE. COLIN NEWMAN went solo taking ROBERT GOTOBED with him. The latter also became member of FAD GADGET. (see further on for these activities)

Rough Trade / not issued
May 81. (7") **OUR SWIMMER. / MIDNIGHT BAHNHOF CAFE** [ ] [-]
Jul 81. (lp)(c) **DOCUMENT AND EYEWITNESS: ELECTRIC BALLROOM (live)** [ ] [-]
– 5 10 / 12XU (fragment) / Underwater experiences / Zegk hoqp / Everything's going to be nice / Instrumental (thrown bottle) / Piano tuner (keep strumming those guitars) / And then . . . / We meet under tables / Revealing trade secrets / Eels sang lino / Eastern standard / Coda. (free 12"m-lp) **DOCUMENT AND EYE-WITNESS: NOTRE DAME HALL (live)** – Underwater experiences / Go ahead / Ally in exile / Relationship / Our swimmer / Witness to the fact / 2 people in a room / Heartbeat. *(re-iss.+c.1984) (cd-iss.1991 on 'Mute')*
Mar 83. (12"m) **CRAZY ABOUT LOVE. / CATAPULT 30 / SECOND LENGTH (OUR SWIMMER)** [ ] [-]
—— WIRE were now back to full-time membership.
Mute / Enigma
Nov 86. (12"ep) **SNAKEDRILL** [ ] [-]
– A serious of snakes / Advantage in height / Up to the Sun / Drill.
Mar 87. (7") **AHEAD. / FEED ME (live)** [ ] [-]
(12"+=) – Ambulance chasers (live) / Vivid riot of red (live).
Apr 87. (lp)(c)(cd) **THE IDEAL COPY** [87] [ ]
– Points of collapse / Ahead / Madman's honey / Feed me / Ambitious / Cheeking tongues / Still shows / Over theirs. *(cd+=)* – Ahead II / SNAKEDRILL EP tracks.
Mar 88. (7") **KIDNEY BONGOS. / PIETA** [ ] [ ]
(3"cd-s+=)/ /(12"++=) – Drill (live)./ / Over theirs (live).
May 88. (lp)(c)(cd) **A BELL IS A CUP . . . UNTIL IT IS STRUCK** [ ] [ ]
– Silk skin paws / The finest drops / The queen of Ur and the king of Um / Free falling divisions / It's a boy / Boiling boy / Kidney bongos / Come back in two halves / Follow the locust / A public place. *(cd+=)*– The queen of Ur and the king of Um (alt.take) / Pieta / Over theirs (live) / Drill (live).
Jun 88. (7") **SILK SKIN PAWS. / GERMAN SHEPHERDS** [ ] [ ]
(12"+=) – Ambitious (remix).
(3"cd-s+=) – Come back in two halves.
Apr 89. (7"clear) **EARDRUM BUZZ. / THE OFFER** [68] [ ]
(12"+=) – It's a boy (instrumental).
(cd-s) – ('A'side) / Silk skin paws / A serious of snakes / Ahead (extended).
(live-12") BUZZ BUZZ BUZZ – Eardrum buzz / Ahead / Kidney bongos.
Mute / Mute
May 89. (lp)(c)(cd) **IT'S BEGINNING TO AND BACK AGAIN (live)** [ ] [ ]
– Finest drops / Eardrum buzz / German shepherds / Public place / It's a boy / Illuminated / Boiling boy / Over theirs / Eardrum buzz (12"version) / The offer / In vivo.
Jul 89. (7") **IN VIVO. / ILLUMINATED** [ ] [ ]
(12"+=)(cd-s+=) – Finest drops (live).
May 90. (7") **LIFE IN THE MANSCAPE. / GRAVITY WORSHIP** [ ] [ ]
(12"+=)(cd-s+=) – Who has wine.
May 90. (cd)(c)(lp) **MANSCAPE** [ ] [ ]
– Patterns of behaviour / Goodbye ploy / Morning bell / Small black reptile / Torch it / Other moments / Sixth sense / What do you see? / Where's the deputation? / You hung your lights in the trees – A craftman's touch. *(US cd+=)*– Life in the manscape / Stampede / Children of groceries.
Apr 91. (cd)(c)(lp) **DRILL** [ ] [ ]
– (7 versions of out-takes from last album)

WIR

Slightly different name when GOTOBED left.
Sep 91. (7") **SO AND SLOW IT GOES. / NICE FROM HERE** [ ] [ ]
(12") – ('A'side) / ('A'-Orb mix) / Take it (for greedy)
(cd-s+=) – (all 4 tracks).
Oct 91. (cd)(c)(lp) **THE FIRST LETTER** [ ] [ ]
– Take it (for greedy) / So and slow it goes (extended) / A bargain at 3 and 20 yeah! / Rootsi-rootsy / Ticking mouth / It continues / Looking at me (stop!) / Naked, whooping and such-like / Tailor made / No cows on the ice / A big glue canal.

– compilations, others, etc. –

Mar 86. Pink -Rough Trade; (m-lp) **PLAY POP** [ ] [-]
Aug 86. Dojo; (lp) **IN THE PINK (live)** [ ] [-]
Nov 87. Strange Fruit; (12"ep) **THE PEEL SESSIONS** (18.1.78) [ ] [-]
– I am the fly / Culture vultures / Practise makes perfect / 106 beats that.
Feb 90. Strange Fruit; (cd)(c)(lp) **DOUBLE PEEL SESSIONS** [ ] [-]
Jul 89. Harvest; (lp)(c)(cd) **ON RETURNING (1977-1979)** [ ] [-]
– 1.2.X.U. / It's so obvious / Mr Suit / Three girl rhumba / Ex lion tamer / Lowdown / Strange / Reuters / Feeling called love / I am the fly / Practise makes perfect / French film blurred / I feel mysterious today / Marooned / Sand in my joints / Outdoor miner / A question of degree / I should have known better / The other window / 40 versions / A touching display / On returning. *(cd+=)*– Straight line / 106 beats that / Field day for the Sundays / Champs / Dot dash / Another the letter / Men 2nd / Two people in a room / Blessed state.
Sep 94. Materili Sonori; (cd; w/book) **EXPLODING VIEWS** [ ] [-]
May 95. EMI; (cd) **BEHIND THE CURTAIN** [ ] [-]
Dec 95. Touch; (12"w/ HAFLER TRIO) **THE FIRST LETTER. /** [ ] [-]

COLIN NEWMAN

(solo playing most instruments) **with ROBERT GOTOBED** – drums / **DESMOND SIMMONDS** – bass, guitar / **BRUCE GILBERT** – guitar / **MIKE THORNE** – keyboards

Beggar's B. not issued

Oct 80. (lp) **A-Z** [ ] [-]
– I waited for ages / And jury / Alone / Order for order / Image / Life on deck / Troisieme / S-S-S-Star eyes / Seconds to last / Inventory / But no / B. *(re-iss.+c+cd.Sep88 on 'Lowdown-Beggar's Banquet')*

Nov 80. (7"m) **B. / CLASSIC REMAINS / ALONE ON PIANO** [ ] [-]

Mar 81. (7") **INVENTORY. / THIS PICTURE** [ ] [-]

—— **COLIN** played everything.

4.a.d. not issued

Aug 81. (lp) **PROVISIONALLY TITLED THE SINGING FISH** [ ] [-]
– Fish 1 / Fish 2 / Fish 3 / Fish 4 / Fish 5 / Fish 6 / Fish 7 / Fish 8 / Fish 9 / Fish 10. *(see next album for cd! release)*

—— added **DES SIMMONDS + SIMON GILHAM** – bass, vocals

Jan 82. (lp) **NOT TO** [ ] [-]
– Lorries / Don't bring reminders / You me and happy / We meet under tables / Safe / Truculent yet / 5'10 / 1, 2, 3, beep beep / Not to / Indians / Remove for improvement / Blue Jay way. *(cd-iss.Jan88 +=)* – PROVISIONALLY TITLED lp tracks / Not to / You and your dog / The grace you know / H.C.T.F.R. / No doubt.

May 82. (7") **WE MEANS WE STARTS. / NOT TO (remix)** [ ] [-]

Crammed Discs not issued

Sep 86. (lp) **COMMERCIAL SUICIDE** [ ] [-] BELG.
– Their terrain / 2-sixes / Metakest / But I . . . / Commercial suicide / I'm still here / Feigned hearing / Can I explain the delay / I can hear you . . .

Oct 86. (7") **FEIGNED HEARING. / I CAN'T HEAR YOU . . .** [ ] [-]

Aug 87. (12") **INTERVIEW. / INTERVIEW** [ ] [-]

May 88. (12") **BETTER LATE THAN NEVER. / AT LAST** [ ] [-]

May 88. (lp)(c)(cd) **IT SEEMS** [ ] [-]
– Quite unrehearsed / Can't help being / The rite of life / An impressive beginning / It seems / Better late than never / Not being in Warsaw / At rest / Convolutions / Round and round. *(w/ free label 'Various Artists' lp)*

Swim not issued

May 95. (12") **VOICE. /** [ ] [-]

CUPOL

GILBERT & LEWIS under many guises (not initially chronological)

4.a.d. not issued

Jul 80. (12"ep) **LIKE THIS FOR AGES. / KLUBA CUPOL** [ ] [-]
(20min@'33rpm)

GILBERT & LEWIS

4 a.d. not issued

Nov 80. (m-lp) **3R4** [ ] [-]
– Barge calm / 3,4 / Barge calm / R.

Aug 81. (7") **ENDS WITH THE SEA. / HUNG UP TO DRY WHILE BUILDING AN ARCH** [ ] [-]

—— In May88, a cd-compilation '8 TIME' was issued by duo on '4 a.d.'.

DOME

Dome not issued

Aug 80. (lp) **DOME 1** [ ] [-]
– Cancel your order / Cruel when complete / And then . . . / Here we go / Rolling upon my day / Say again / Lina sixup / Airmail / Ampnoise / Madmen. (free-7") – SO. / DROP

Feb 81. (lp) **DOME 2** [ ] [-]
– The red tent 1 + 2 / Long lost life / Breathless / Reading Prof. B / Ritual view / Twist up / Keep it.

Oct 81. (lp) **DOME 3** [ ] [-]
– Jasz / Ar-gu / An-an-an-d-d-d / Ba-dr / D-o-bo / Na-drm / Dasz / Ur-ur / Danse / Roor-an.

(above with also **RUSSELL MILLS** – percussion / **DANIEL MILLER** – saxophone / **E.C.RADCLIFFE** – guitar / **PETER PRINCE** – drums)

(Early in the 90's, 1 & 2 and 3 & 4 were re-issued on 2 cd's for 'Grey Area-Mute')

Apr 83. (lp) **TO SPEAK ("BRUCE GILBERT")** [ ] [-]
– To speak / To walk, to run / To duck, to dive / This / Seven year / Atlas. *(iss.Sep84 as 'WILL YOU SPEAK THIS WORD' on 'Uniton'?)*

GILBERT, LEWIS & MILLS

Cherry Red not issued

May 82. (lp) **MZUI (WATERLOO GALLERY)** [ ] [-]
– Mzui (part 1) / Mzui (part 2).

W.M.O. not issued

Dec 95. (cd) **PACIFIC / SPECIFIC** [ ] [-]

P'O

Court not issued

Jan 83. (lp) **WHILST CLIMBING THIEVES VIE FOR ATTENTION** [ ] [-]

DUET EMMO

augmented by **DANIEL MILLER** (label boss)

Mute not issued

Aug 83. (7") **OR SO IT SEEMS. / HEART OF HEARTS (OR SO IT SEEMS)** [ ] [-]

Aug 83. (lp) **OR SO IT SEEMS** [ ] [-]
– Hill of men / Or so it seems / Friano / The first person / A.N.C. / Long sledge / Gatemmo / Last's card / Heart of hearts. *(cd-iss.Aug92 on Grey Area-Mute)*

BRUCE GILBERT

Mute not issued

Sep 84. (lp) **THIS WAY** [ ] [-]
– Work for do you me / I did / Here visit. *(see next lp for cd-iss.)*

Mar 87. (lp)(cd) **THE SHIVERING MAN** [ ] [-]
– Angel food / The shivering man / Not in the feather / There are / Hommage / Eline Court li / Epitaph for Henran Brenlar. *(cd-iss.+=THIS WAY lp tracks)*

Jan 91. (cd)(lp) **INSIDING (excerpts from 'SAVAGE WATER')** [ ] [-]
– Side 1 / Side 2 / Bloodlines (ballet).

Aug 91. (cd)(lp) **MUSIC FOR FRUIT** [ ] [-]
– Music for fruit / Push / You might be called.

Sub Pop Sub Pop

Oct 95. (7") **BI YO YO. /** [ ] [-]

. . . Jan – Jun '96 stop press . . .

Mar 96. (cd)(c) **AB OVO** [ ] [ ]

HE SAID

(aka **GRAHAM LEWIS** solo) augmented by **JOHN FRYER** – drum prog.

Mute not issued

Oct 85. (7") **ONLY ONE I. / ONLY ONE I** [ ] [-]

Apr 86. (7") **PUMP. / PUMP (instrumental)** [ ] [-]
(12"+=) – To and fro.

Aug 86. (7") **PULLING 3 G's. / PALE FEET** [ ] [-]
(12"+=) – ('A'&'B'extended versions).

—— added **BRUCE GILBERT** – guitar / **NIGEL H.KIND** – guitar / **E.C.RADCLIFFE** – prog. / **ANGELA CONWAY** – backing vocals / **ENO** (guested on 1)

Oct 86. (lp)(c)(cd) **HAIL** [ ] [-]
– Kidnap yourself / Only one I / Pump / I fall in your arms / Do you mean that? / Flagwearing / Shades to escape / Pale feet.

Nov 88. (7")(12") **COULD YOU?. / HE SAID . . . SHE SAID** [ ] [-]

Feb 89. (lp)(c)(cd) **TAKE CARE** [ ] [-]
– Could you? / ABC Dicks love / Watch-take-care / Tongue ties / Not a soul / Halfway house / Get out of that rain / Hole in the sky.

WISHBONE ASH

Formed: Torquay, Devon, England . . . summer 1969 out of the EMPTY VESSELS by MARTIN TURNER and STEVE UPTON. They quickly moved to London with other two; POWELL and TED TURNER (no relation). In 1970, they signed to 'MCA' and delivered eponymous debut into UK Top 40. Throughout the early 70's, they accrued large following peaking in 1972 when ARGUS hit Top 3. By 1974, they had crossed the Atlantic to reside and record 1974 album THERE'S THE RUB. A spate of bad luck on tour made it hard for their future albums to substantiate US breakthrough. • **Style:** Due to twin-lead guitar sound, they were described as Britain's answer to ALLMAN BROTHERS, but with mystical lyrical element. Fused heavy-rock with fine harmonies and self-indulgent solos. This sound drifted into a more countrified sound by the mid 70's. Lack of identity and introvert stage presence was cited as an excuse for decreasing sales at this time. • **Songwriters:** Group compositions / TURNERS?. • **Trivia:** The 1984 instrumental track F*U*B*B stands for 'Fucked Up Beyond Belief'. TOM DOWD produced 1976 album LOCKED IN.

Recommended: CLASSIC ASH (*8) / ARGUS (*9) / LIVE DATES (*9)

MARTIN TURNER (b. 1 Oct'47) – vocals, bass / **ANDY POWELL** (b. 8 Feb'50) – guitar, vocals repl. GLEN TURNER (no relation) / **TED TURNER** (b.DAVID, 2 Aug'50) – guitar, vocals (ex-KING BISCUIT) / **STEVE UPTON** (b.24 May'46, Wrexham, Wales) – drums

M.C.A. Decca

Dec 70. (lp)(c) **WISHBONE ASH** [34] [ ]
– Blind eye / Lady Whiskey / Error of my ways / Queen of torture / Handy /

Phoenix. *(cd-iss. Jul 91) (re-iss. Feb 74+1980) (cd-iss.Dec94 on 'B.G.O.')*

Jan 71. (7") **BLIND EYE. / QUEEN OF TORTURE**

Sep 71. (lp)(c) **PILGRIMAGE** 14
– Vas dis / The pilgrim / Jail bait / Alone / Lullaby / Valediction / Where were you tomorrow. *(re-iss. Feb 74) (re-iss.1983 on 'Fame') (cd-iss Jul 91+=)–* Baby what you want me to do / Jail bait (live).

Oct 71. (7") **JAIL BAIT. / VAS DIS** -

May 72. (lp)(c) **ARGUS** 3
– Time was / Sometime world / Blowin' free / The king will come / Leaf and stream / Warrior / Throw down the sword. *(re-iss. Feb 74 + Feb 84) (re-iss.1987 on 'Castle')*

Jun 72. (7") **BLOWIN' FREE. / NO EASY ROAD**

M.C.A. M.C.A.

May 73. (lp)(c) **WISHBONE FOUR** 12 44
– So many things to say / Ballad of the beacon / No easy road / Everybody needs a friend / Doctor / Sorrel / Sing out the song / Rock'n'roll widow. *(re-iss. Feb 74)*

Jul 73. (7") **ROCK'N'ROLL WIDOW. / NO EASY ROAD** -

Jul 73. (7") **SO MANY THINGS TO SAY. / ROCK'N'ROLL WIDOW** -

Dec 73. (d-lp)(c) **LIVE DATES (live)** 82 Nov 73
– The king will come / Warrior / Throw down the sword / Rock'n'roll widow / Ballad of the beacon / Baby what you want me to do / The pilgrim / Blowin' free / Jail bait / Lady Whiskey / Phoenix.

—— (Jun74) **LAURIE WISEFIELD** – guitar (ex-HOME) repl. TED who found religion

Nov 74. (7") **HOMETOWN. / PERSEPHONE** -

Nov 74. (lp)(c) **THERE'S THE RUB** 16 88
– Silver shoes / Don't come back / Persephone / Hometown / Lady Jay / F*U*B*B.

Feb 75. (7") **SILVER SHOES. / PERSEPHONE**

—— added on session **PETER WOODS** – keyboards

M.C.A. Atlantic

Mar 76. (lp)(c) **LOCKED IN** 36
– Rest in peace / No water in the well / Moonshine / She was my best friend / It started in Heaven / Half past lovin' / Trust in you / Say goodbye.

Nov 76. (lp)(c) **NEW ENGLAND** 22
– Mother of pearl / (In all of my dreams) You rescue me / Runaway / Lorelei / Outward bound / Prelude / When you know love / Lonely island / Candle-light. *(re-iss Jul82)*

Nov 76. (7") **OUTWARD BOUND. / LORELEI**

M.C.A. M.C.A.

Sep 77. (7") **FRONT PAGE NEWS. / DIAMOND JACK** -

Oct 77. (lp)(c) **FRONT PAGE NEWS** 31
– Front page news / Midnight dancer / Goodbye baby hello friend / Surface to air / 714 / Come in from the rain / Right or wrong / Heart beat / The day I found your love / Diamond Jack.

Oct 77. (7") **FRONT PAGE NEWS. / GOODBYE BABY HELLO FRIEND** -

Nov 77. (7") **GOODBYE BABY HELLO FRIEND. / COME IN FROM THE RAIN** -

Sep 78. (7")(12") **YOU SEE RED. / BAD WEATHER BLUES** (live)

Oct 78. (lp)(c) **NO SMOKE WITHOUT FIRE** 43
– You see red / Baby, the angels are here / Ships in the sky / Stand and deliver / Anger in harmony / Like a child / The way of the world / A stormy weather. (free live 7"w.a.) **LORELEI. / COME IN FROM THE RAIN**

Aug 79. (7") **COME ON. / FAST JOHNNY**

Jan 80. (7") **HELPLESS. / INSOMNIA** -

Jan 80. (7") **LIVING PROOF. / JAIL BAIT (live)**

Jan 80. (lp)(c) **JUST TESTING** 41
– Living proof / Haunting me / Insomnia / Helpless / Pay the price / New rising star / Masters of disguise / Lifeline.

Apr 80. (7")(12") **HELPLESS** (live). / **BLOWIN' FREE** (live)

Oct 80. (lp)(c) **LIVE DATES II (live)** 40
– Doctor / Living proof / Runaway / Helpless / F*U*B*B / The way of the world. *(ltd. w/free live lp) (re-iss Jun84)*

—— **JOHN WETTON** – bass, vocals (ex-URIAH HEEP, ex-FAMILY, ex-KING CRIMSON) repl. MARTIN TURNER to production. / Added **CLAIRE HAMILL** – vocals (solo artist)

Mar 81. (7") **UNDERGROUND. / MY MIND IS MADE UP** -

Apr 81. (lp)(c) **NUMBER THE BRAVE** 61
– Loaded / Where is the love / Underground / Kicks on the street / Open road / Get ready / Rainstorm / That's that / Rollercoaster / Number the brave.

May 81. (7") **GET READY. / KICKS ON THE STREET** -

May 81. (7") **GET READY. / LOADED** -

—— **UPTON, POWELL + WISEFIELD** recruited new member **TREVOR BOLDER** – bass (ex-SPIDERS FROM MARS / Bowie, ex-URIAH HEEP, etc. repl. WETTON to ASIA, etc.

A.V.M. Fantasy

Oct 82. (7") **ENGINE OVERHEAT. / GENEVIEVE** -

Nov 82. (lp)(c) **TWIN BARRELS BURNING** 22
– Engine overheat / Can't fight love / Genevieve / Me and my guitar / Hold on / Streets of shame / No more lonely nights / Angels have mercy / Wind up. *(cd-iss. Aug 93)*

Dec 82. (7") **NO MORE LONELY NIGHTS. / STREETS OF SHAME** -

—— **MERVYN 'Spam' SPENCER** – bass (ex-TRAPEZE) repl. BOLDER to URIAH HEEP

Neat not issued

Jan 85. (lp)(c) **RAW TO THE BONE**
– Cell of fame / People in motion / Don't cry / Love is blue / Long live the night / Rocket in my pocket / It's only love / Don't you mess / Dreams (searching for an answer) / Perfect timing. *(re-iss. Aug 93)*

—— **ANDY PYLE** – bass (ex-SAVOY BROWN, ex-BLODWYN PIG) repl. SPENCE

—— Originals (**ANDREW, STEVE, MARTIN & TED**) reformed WISHBONE ASH.

I.R.S. I.R.S.

Feb 88. (lp)(c)(cd) **NOUVEAU CALLS** (instrumental)
– Tangible evidence / Closseau / Flags of convenience / From Soho to Sunset / Arabesque / In the skin / Something's happening in Room 602 / Johnny left home without it / The spirit flies free / A rose is a rose / Real guitars have wings. *(re-iss. 1990)*

May 88. (7") **IN THE SKIN. / TANGIBLE EVIDENCE**

—— In Apr89, TED & ANDY guested on their labels' Various Artists live cd,c,d-lp, video 'NIGHT OF THE GUITAR'.

Jun 89. (7") **COSMIC JAZZ. / T-BONE SHUFFLE**
(12"+=) – Bolan's monument.

Aug 89. (lp)(c)(cd) **HERE TO HEAR**
– Cosmic jazz / Keeper of the light / Mental radio / Walk on water / Witness on wonder / Lost cause in Paradise / Why don't we / In the case / Hole in my heart (part 1 & 2).

—— **RAY WESTON** – drums repl. MARTIN

May 91. (cd)(c)(lp) **STRANGE AFFAIR**
– Strange affair / Wings of desire / Dream train / You / Hard times / Standing in the rain / Renegade / Say you will / Rollin' / Some conversion.

—— **POWELL + TED TURNER + RAY** bring in **ANDY PYLE** – bass / **DAN C.GILLOGLY** – keyboards

Permanent Griffin

Mar 92. (cd)(c)(lp) **THE ASH LIVE IN CHICAGO (live)** 1994

– compilations, others, etc. –

Apr 77. MCA; (7"ep) **PHOENIX. / BLOWIN' FREE / JAIL BAIT** -

May 77. MCA; (lp)(c) **CLASSIC ASH**
– Blind eye / Phoenix / The pilgrim / Blowin' free / The king will come / Rock'n'roll widow / Persephone / Outward bound / Throw down the sword (live). *(re-iss.Aug81) (re-iss.Jan83 on 'Fame')*

Jan 82. MCA; (lp)(c) **HOT ASH** -

Jun 82. MCA; (lp)(c) **THE BEST OF WISHBONE ASH**

Apr 82. MCA; (d-c) **PILGRIMAGE /ARGUS**

1993. MCA; (d-cd) **TIME WAS (w/ remixed 'ARGUS')** -

Apr 79. Flyover; (lp) **LIVE IN JAPAN, NOVEMBER '78 (live)** -

Oct 91. Windsong; (lp) **LIVE IN CONCERT (live)** -

Mar 94. Nectar; (cd)(c) **BLOWIN' FREE – THE VERY BEST OF WISHBONE ASH** -

Sep 94. MCA; (cd)(c) **THERE'S THE RUB / LOCKED IN**

Nov 94. Start; (cd) **IN CONCERT** -

Jah WOBBLE

Born: JOHN WORDLE. Became bassman for PUBLIC IMAGE LTD, until his sudden departure in 1980. He already went solo and had made a solo appearance, as well as 2 collaborations (see below). In 1994 after brief commercial success 2 years previous, JAH and his ever increasing INVADERS OF THE HEART scored a UK Top 20 album, which was followed by a rapturous appearance at Glastonbury Festival. • **Songwriters:** WOBBLE and /with collaborators. • **Style:** Eastern influenced quality bassman. • **Trivia:** In 1992 he appeared on 12"'ers by ONE DOVE and SECRET KNOWLEDGE FEATURING WONDER. Guested on albums by ORB, PRIMAL SCREAM, SINEAD O'CONNOR, JOOLZ, HOLGER CZUKAY, DODGY, SHAMEN, GINGER BAKER + IAN McNABB.

Recommended: INVADERS OF THE HEART (*6) / RISING ABOVE BEDLAM (*8) / TAKE ME TO GOD (*9)

JAH WOBBLE – bass, vocals

Virgin not issued

Oct 78. (12"ep) **DREADLOCK DON'T DEAL IN WEDLOCK. / PHILITUS PUBIS** -

Feb 79. (7"by; DON LETTS & JAH WOBBLE) **STEEL LEG: STRATETIME & THE WIDE MAN. / ELECTRIC DREAD: HAILE UNLIKELY** -

Oct 79. (12"by; DAN McARTHUR) **DAN McARTHUR** -

—— added **MARTIN ATKINS** – drums / **SNOWY WHITE** – vocals

Apr 80. (7")(12") **BETRAYAL OF MR.X. / THE BATTLE OF BRITAIN** -

May 80. (lp) **THE LEGEND LIVES ON . . .** -

– Betrayal / Beat the drum for me / Blueberry Hill / Today is the first day of the ? / Not another / Tales from Outer Space / Dan McArthur / Pineapple. *(cd-iss.Mar94 on 'Vinyl Vault')*

Jul 80. (12"ep) **V.I.E.P.** [ ] [-]
– Blueberry Hill / etc.

Island / not issued

Jul 81. (12"ep by; JAH WOBBLE, JAKI LIEBEZEIT & HOLGER CZUKAY) **HOW MUCH ARE THEY? / WHERE'S THE MONEY? / TRENCH WARFARE / TWILIGHT WORLD** [ ] [-]
(re-iss.1988 on 'Licensed')

Virgin / not issued

1982. (lp) **FULL CIRCLE** [ ] [-]
– (tracks as above plus; Full circle R.P.S. (No.7) / Mystery R.P.S. (No.8).

Jah Wobble / not issued

May 82. (7") **FADING. / NOCTURNAL** [ ] [-]
Oct 82. (12" by; JAH WOBBLE with ANIMAL) **LONG LONG AWAY. / ROMANY** [ ] [-]

In 1982, formed BARTOK with RAT SCABIES – drums (ex-DAMNED) / SIMON WERBER + JOHN GRANT (both ex-STRAPS). Released 7" on 'On-U-Sound' in Oct82; INSANITY. / I AM THE BOMB.

— Next with **ANIMAL** – guitar (of MOTORHEAD) / **OLLIE MARLAND** – keyboards / **ANNIE WHITEHEAD** – trombone

Lago / not issued

May 83. (m-lp) **JAH WOBBLE'S BEDROOM ALBUM** – INVADERS OF THE HEART [ ] [-]
– City / Fading / Long long way / Sense of history / Hill in Korea / Journey to death / Invaders of the heart / Sunshine / Concentration camp / Desert song / Heart of the jungle.

1983. (12") **INVADERS OF THE HEART. / ?** [ ] [-]

— next w / **THE EDGE** – guitar (of U2) / **HOLGER CZUKAY** – percussion, etc (ex-CAN) / **LIEBEZEIT** – (ex-CAN) / **BEN MENDELSON** – (ex-MAGAZINE) / **OLLIE MARLAND** – keyboards / **JIM WALKER** – drums (ex-PUBLIC IMAGE LTD) / **FRANCOIS KEVORKIAN** – electric drums

Island / Island

Oct 83. (m-lp by; JAH WOBBLE, The EDGE & HOLGER CZUKAY) **SNAKE CHARMER** [ ] [ ]
– Snake charmer / Hold on to your dreams / It was a camel / Sleazy / Snake charmer – reprise.

JAH WOBBLE & OLLIE MARLAND

with sessions **ANIMAL** – guitar / **B.J.COLE** – steel / **HARRY BECKETT** – timpani / **NEVILLE MURRAY** – percussion / **GENERAL SMUTLEY** – drums

Lago / not issued

Sep 84. (12") **VOODOO. / EAST** [ ] [-]

Island / not issued

May 85. (lp)(c) **NEON MOON** [ ] [-]
– Love mystery / Love mystery (instrumental) / Running away / Neon Moon / Life on the line / Life on the line (dub) / The beat inside / Despite.

Jul 85. (7")(12") **LOVE MYSTERY. / LOVE MYSTERY (instrumental)** [ ] [-]

JAH WOBBLE

Lago / not issued

Nov 85. (12") **BLOW OUT. / ?** [ ] [-]

General / not issued

May 86. (12" by; WOBBLE & BRETT WICKERS) **BETWEEN TWO FREQUENCIES. / 6020** [ ] [-]

Lago / not issued

Oct 86. (lp; by JAH WOBBLE & OLLIE MARLAND) **TRADE WINDS** [ ] [-]
–

Wobble / not issued

Sep 87. (12"ep) **ISLAND PARADISE / ALCOHOL. / JIHAD / ('A'remix)** [ ] [-]
Sep 87. (lp) **PSALMS** [ ] [-]
(re-iss.cd+lp Aug94 on 'Southern')

JAH WOBBLE'S INVADERS OF THE HEART

w / **JUSTIN** – guitar (ex-sessions FRANK CHICKENS) / **MICK** – drums / **NATASHA** – vocals (a Spanish/Belgian belly dancer) of TRANSGLOBAL UNDERGROUND

Boy's Own / not issued

Oct 90. (7") **BOMBA (Andy Weatherall mix). / ('A'miles away mix)** [ ] [-]
(12"+=)(cd-s+=) – ('A'live version).

— Late 1990, he also splintered in MAX with ANDY ROURKE (ex-SMITHS) on 'ZTT'.

Oval-East West / East West

Oct 91. (cd)(c)(lp) **RISING ABOVE BEDLAM** [ ] [ ]
– Visions of you / Relight the flame / Bomba / Ungodly kingdom / Rising above bedlam / Erzulie / Everyman's an island / Soledad / Sweet divinity / Wonderful world.

Nov 91. (7") **ERZULIE. / ('A'dependent mix)** [ ] [ ]
(12"+=)(cd-s+=) – Remind me to be nice to myself.

— Below 'A' + next 'B'-side featured **SINEAD O'CONNOR** – vocals

Jan 92. (7") **VISIONS OF YOU. / ('A'-Ade phases the parameters of sound mix)** [35] [ ]
(12"+=)(cd-s+=) – ('A'-secret love child of Hank & Johnny mix) / ('A' pick'n'mix 1 & 2).

Sep 92. (7") **THE UNGODLY KINGDOM. / JOSEY WALSH** [ ] [-]
(cd-s+=) – Love like / Saeta.

KK Belguim / not issued

Jun 93. (cd)(lp) **WITHOUT JUDGEMENT** [-] [-]

— next with **JUSTIN ADAMS** – guitars, vocals / **MARK FERDA** – guitars, mandolin / **NEVILLE MURRAY** – percussion / **ANNELI M.DRECKER** (of Norwegian band BEL CANTO) or **XIMENA TADSON** or **ABDEL ALI SLIMANI** or **GAVIN FRIDAY** (ex-VIRGIN PRUNES) or **ANDREA OLIVER** (ex-RIP, RIG & PANIC) or **NAJMA AKHTAR** – vocals / **KRIS NEEDS** – dub (of SECRET KNOWLEDGE) / **JAKI LIEBEZEIT** or **JOHN REYNOLDS** – drums / etc.

Island / Island

Apr 94. (7")(12")(c-s) **BECOMING MORE LIKE GOD. / ('A'mix) / WINE, WOMEN AND SONG** [36] [ ]
(cd-s+=) – Football.

May 94. (cd)(c)(d-lp) **TAKE ME TO GOD** [13] [ ]
– God in the beginning / Becoming more like God / Whisky priests / I'm an Algerian / Amor / Amor dub / Take me to God / The Sun does rise / When the storm comes / I love everybody / Yoga of the nightclub / I am the music / The bonds of love / Angels / No change is sexy / Raga / Forever.

— below 'A' track features **DOLORES O'RIORDAN** (of CRANBERRIES)

Jun 94. (7")(c-s) **THE SUN DOES RISE. / YALILI YA AINI / RAGA** [41] [ ]
(12"+=)(cd-s+=) – Om namah shiva.
(cd-s) – ('A'side) / A13 / Snake charmer (reprise) / So many years.

Oct 94. (c-s) **AMOR. / ('A'mix)** [ ] [ ]
(12"+=)(cd-s+=) – Sahara / (more rockas jungle remixes).
(cd-s) – (4-'A'mixes).

Nov 95. (cd)(c)(d-lp) **HEAVEN AND EARTH** [ ] [ ]
– Heaven and Earth / A love song / Dying over Europe / Divine mother / Gone to Croatan / Hit me / On Nanah Siva.

WONDER STUFF

Formed: Stourbridge, Midlands, England ... early 1986 by ex-EDEN drummer MILES HUNT and others (see below). After 2 indie ep's on own 'Farout' label, they signed to 'Polydor' late '87. Their 2nd single for the label 'A WISH AWAY', broke the 50 and preceeded a joyful Top 20 debut album 'THE EIGHT LEGGED GROOVE MACHINE'. The following years saw them get into Top 5 with next three albums, and hit peak spot with novelty hit 'DIZZY', helped of course by TV comics VIC REEVES and BOB MORTIMER. • **Style:** Alternative grebo punk-poppers who quickly went more commercial than their neighbours POP WILL EAT ITSELF. • **Songwriters:** Group music / HUNT lyrics except; GIMME SOME TRUTH (John Lennon) / THAT'S ENTERTAINMENT (Jam) / INSIDE YOU (Pop Will Eat Itself) / COZ I LUV YOU (Slade). • **Trivia:** Produced in the 80's by Pat Collier.

Recommended: THE EIGHT LEGGED GROOVE MACHINE (*6) / HUP (*6) / NEVER LOVED ELVIS (*7) / IF THE BEATLES HAD READ HUNTER (*8)

MILES HUNT – vocals, guitar / **MALCOLM TREECE** – guitar, vocals / **THE BASS THING** (b.ROB JONES) – bass / **MARTIN GILKS** – drums, percussion (ex-MIGHTY LEMON DROPS)

Farout / not issued

Feb 87. (7"m) **A WONDERFUL DAY / DOWN HERE. / IT'S NOT TRUE / LIKE A MERRY GO ROUND** [ ] [-]
Sep 87. (7") **UNBEARABLE. / TEN TRENCHES DEEP** [ ] [-]
(12"+=) – I am a monster / Frank.

Polydor / Polydor

Apr 88. (7") **GIVE GIVE GIVE ME MORE MORE MORE. / A SONG WITHOUT AN END** [72] [ ]
(12"+=)(cd-s+=) – Meaner than mean / See the free world.

Jul 88. (7") **A WISH AWAY. / JEALOUSY** [43] [ ]
(12"+=)(cd-s+=) – Happy-sad / Goodbye fatman.

Aug 88. (lp)(c)(cd) **THE EIGHT LEGGED GROOVE MACHINE** [18] [ ]
– Redbury joy town / No for the 13th time / It's yer money I'm after baby / Rue the day / Give give give me more more more / Like a merry go round / The animals and me / A wish away / Grin / Mother and I / Some sad someone / Ruby horse / Unbearable / Poison. *(re-iss.cd Apr95)*

Sep 88. (7"ep)(12"ep)(cd-ep) **IT'S YER MONEY I'M AFTER BABY / ASTLEY IN THE NOOSE. / OOH, SHE SAID / RAVE FROM THE GRAVE** [40] [ ]

Feb 89. (7") **WHO WANTS TO BE THE DISCO KING?. / UNBEARABLE (live)** 28
(12"+=)(cd-s+=) – Ten trenches deep (live) / No for the 13th time (live).

— added guests **JAMES TAYLOR** – organ (ex-PRISONERS) / **MARTIN BELL** – banjo

Sep 89. (7")(c-s) **DON'T LET ME DOWN, GENTLY. / IT WAS ME** 19
(12"+=)(cd-s+=) – ('A'extended).

Oct 89. (lp)(c)(cd) **HUP** 5
– 30 years in the bathroom / Radio ass kiss / Golden green / Let's be other people / Piece of sky / Can't shape up / Good night though / Don't let me down, gently / Cartoon boyfriend / Unfaithful / Them, big oak trees / Room 410. *(re-iss.cd Apr95)*

Nov 89. (7")(c-s) **GOLDEN GREEN. / GET TOGETHER** 33
(12"+=)(cd-s+=) – Gimme some truth.

— (Mar90) **PAUL CLIFFORD** – bass finally repl. The BASS THING (left '89). He later formed 8-piece The BRIDGE AND THE TUNNEL CREW.

May 90. (7")(c-s) **CIRCLESQUARE. / OUR NEW SONG** 20
(12"+=)(cd-s+=) – ('A'paranoia mix).

Mar 91. (7")(c-s) **THE SIZE OF A COW. / RADIO ASS KISS (live)** 5
(12"+=)(cd-s+=) – Give give give me more more more (live).

May 91. (7")(c-s) **CAUGHT IN MY SHADOW. / GIMME SOME TRUTH (live)** 18
(12"+=)(cd-s+=) – ('A'extended).

Jun 91. (cd)(c)(lp) **NEVER LOVED ELVIS** 3
– Mission drive / Play / False start / Welcome to the cheap seats / The size of a cow / Sleep alone / Reaction / Inertia / Maybe / Grotesque / Here come everyone / Caught in my shadow / Line poem. *(re-iss.cd Apr95)*

Aug 91. (7")(c-s) **SLEEP ALONE. / EL HERMANO DE FRANK** 43
(12"+=)(cd-s+=) – The takin' is easy.

— In Oct'91, they teamed up with comedian VIC REEVES (& BOB MORTIMER), on No.1 hit Tommy Roe cover 'DIZZY'. Next single with guest **KIRSTY MacCOLL**

Jan 92. (7"ep)(cd-ep) **WELCOME TO THE CHEAP SEATS** 8
– Welcome to the cheap seats / Me, my mum, my dad and my brother / Will the circle be unbroken / That's entertainment. (cd-ep+=) – ('A'naked mix) / Caught in my shadw (bare mix) / Circlesque (butt naked mix) / Can't shape up again.

— added **MARTIN BELL** – fiddle, accordion, mandolin, guitar, sitar, keyboards and 6th member **PETE WHITTAKER** – keyboards

Sep 93. (7"ep)(12"ep)(c-ep)(cd-ep) **ON THE ROPES EP** 10
– On the ropes / Professional disturber of the peace / Hank and John / Whites.

Oct 93. (cd)(c)(lp) **CONSTRUCTION FOR THE MODERN IDIOT** 4
– Change every light bulb / I wish them all dead / Cabin fever / Hot love now / Full of life (happy now) / Storm drain / On the ropes / Your big assed mother / Swell / A great drinker / Hush / Sing the absurd.

Nov 93. (7") **FULL OF LIFE (HAPPY NOW). / CLOSER TO FINE** 28
(cd-s+=) – Burger standing / A curious weird and ugly scene.
(cd-s) – ('A'dignity mix) / Change every light bulb (dub mix) / I wish them all dead (dub mix).

— Note: Ex-member ROB JONES (THE BASS THING) died mysteriously on 30 Jul'93 in his New York apartment.

Mar 94. (7"ep)(c-ep)(cd-ep) **HOT LOVE NOW! EP** 19
– Hot love now! / Just helicopters / I must've had something really useful to say / Room 512, all the news that's fit to print.
(cd-ep) – ('A'cardinal error mix) / Unrest song / Flour babies / The Tipperary triangle.

— Disbanded after July Phoenix Festival. MILES went onto work for MTV.

– compilations, etc.

Sep 94. Polydor; (7")(c-s)(cd-s) **UNBEARABLE. / INSIDE YOU / HIT BY A CAR** 16
(cd-s) – ('A'original) / Ten trenches deep / I am a monster / Frank.

Sep 94. Polydor; (cd)(c) **IF THE BEATLES HAD READ HUNTER . . . THE SINGLES** 8
– Welcome to the cheap seats / A wish away / Caught in my shadow / Don't let me gently / Size of a cow / Hot love now! / Dizzy / Unbearable / Circlesquare / Who wants to be the disco king? / Golden green / Give give give me more more more / Sleep alone / Coz I luv you / Full of life / On the ropes / It's yer money I'm after baby / It's not true.

Jul 95. Windsong; (cd) **LIVE IN MANCHESTER (live)** 74 -

WE KNOW WHERE YOU LIVE

TREECE / CLIFFORD / GILKS / + ANGE -vocals (ex-EAT)

H.M.D. not issued

Nov 95. (7"ep)(cd-ep) **DON'T BE TOO HONEST. / CONFESSIONS OF A THUG / EXCUSE ME?** -

Ron WOOD (see under ⇒ ROLLING STONES)

Richard WRIGHT (see under ⇒ PINK FLOYD)

WU-TANG CLAN

Formed: Staten Island, New York, USA . . .early 90's by a posse of nine young hip hop rappers under the pseudonyms; METHOD MAN, GENIUS, GZA, (SHALLAH) CHEF RAEKWON, OL' DIRTY BASTARD, PRINCE RAKEEM, REBEL INS, GHOSTFACE KILLER and U-GOD. All chess-loving wordsmiths were highly influenced by martial art movies and took their name from the WU-TANG or SHAOLIN sword. In 1991, GENIUS released debut album for 'Cold Chillin'; 'WORDS FROM THE GENIUS', while RAKEEM ousted an album for 'Tommy Boy'. The following year, the conglomerate signed for 'RCA', although each member was allowed to retain his seperate contract, if he had one. In 1993 complete with Kung-Fu style movie samples, WU-TANG CLAN's debut 'ENTER THE WU-TANG (36 CHAMBERS)', cracked the charts and showed the socially aware, wise-cracking gang in full flow. However in March the following year, tragedy struck when U-GOD's toddler son DANTE HAWKINS, was hit by a bullet in a cross-fire battle and was seriously injured. 1995 was a busy and commercially fruitful year for most of the crew, especially OL' DIRTY BASTARD, METHOD MAN, CHEF RAEKWON and the combined efforts of GENIUS / GZA (see below). • **Trivia:** GZA also works with PRINCE PAUL and FRUITKWAN (ex-STETASONIC).

Recommended: ENTER THE WU-TANG (36 CHAMBERS) (*7) / LIQUID SWORDS (GENIUS / GZA; *9) / TICAL (METHOD MAN; 7) / still assessing others and below discography is selective and not as accurate going to press

GENIUS

not issued Cold Chill

1991. (cd)(c) **WORDS FROM THE GENIUS** -

WU-TANG CLAN

METHOD MAN (r.n. JOHNNY BLAZE) / **GENIUS** (r.n. G.PRICE) / **GZA** (r.n. R. DIGGS) / **OL' DIRTY BASTARD** (r.n. D.COLES) / **CHEF RAEKWON** (r.n. LOU DIAMOND) / **GHOSTFACE KILLER** (r.n. TONY STARKS) / **U-GOD** (r.n. L. HAWKINS) / **PRINCE RAKEEM + REBEL INS** with affiliated members **SHYLEIM THE RUGGED PRINCE (PAUL) + DOLLY FINGERS + DREDDY KRUGER**

Loud-RCA Loud-RCA

May 94. (cd)(c) **ENTER THE WU-TANG (36 CHAMBERS)**
– Bring da ruckus / Shame on a nigga / Clan in da front / Wu-Tang: 7th chamber / Can it all be so simple / Intermission / Da mystery of chessboxin' / Wu-Tang Clan ain't nuthing ta f'wit / C.R.E.A.M. / Method Man / Protect ya neck / Tearz / Wu-Tang: 7th chamber – part II / Method Man (remix) skunk mix / Conclusion.

OL' DIRTY BASTARD

Elektra Elektra

Mar 95. (cd)(c) **RETURN TO THE 36 CHAMBERS** (dirty version) 7
– Intro / Shimmy shimmy ya / Baby c'mon / Brooklyn zoo / Hippa to da hoppa / Raw hide / Damage / Don't u know / The stomp / Goin' down / Drunk game (sweet sugar pie) / Snakes / Brooklyn zoo II (tiger crane) / Proteck ya neck II the zoo / Cuttin' headz / Dirty dancin' / Harlem world.

METHOD MAN

Def Jam Def Jam

Dec 94. (c-s)(cd-s) **BRING THE PAIN /** - 45

Apr 95. (c-s) **RELEASE YO SELF /** 46 98 Feb 95
(cd-s+=) –

— below A-side featured MARY J.BLIGE .

Jul 95. (c-s) **I'LL BE THERE FOR YOU / YOU'RE ALL I NEED TO GET BY** 41 May95
(12"+=)(cd-s+=) – Bring the pain (remix) / Release yo self.

Aug 95. (cd)(c) **TICAL** 4
– Tical / Biscuits / Bring the pain / All I need / What the blood clot / Meth Vs. / Chef / Sub crazy / Release yo self / P.L.O. style / I get my thang in action / Mr. Sandman / Stimulation / Method Man (remix) / I'll be there for you – You're all I need to get by (featuring MARY J. BLIGE).

Aug 95. (c-s)(cd-s) **HOW HIGH /** - 13

— above single credited with REDMAN

. . . Jan – Jun '96 stop press . . .

Jan 96. (single) **THE RIDDLER** - 56

CHEF RAEKWON

	Loud-RCA	Loud-RCA
Jul 95. (c-s)(cd-s) **GLACIERS OF ICE / CRIMINOLOGY**		43
Aug 95. (cd)(c) **ONLY BUILT 4 CUBAN LINX . . .**		4

– Striving for perfection / Knuckleheadz / Knowledge god / Criminology / Incarcerated scarfaces / Rainy dayz / Guillotine (swordz) / Can it all be so simple (remix) / Shark niggas (biters) / Ice water / Glaciers of ice / Verbal intercourse / Wisdom body / Spot rusherz / Ice cream / Wu-Gambinos / Heaven G Hell / North Star (jewels).

Oct 95. (c-s)(cd-s) **ICE CREAM /**	-	37

. . . Jan – Jun '96 stop press . . .

Jan 96. (single) **INCARCERATED SCARFACES / ICE CREAM**	-	37

— RAEKWON featured on FAT JOE's minor US hit 'FIREWATER' / 'ENVY'.

GENIUS / GZA

with some of the posse

	Geffen	Geffen
Oct 95. (c-s)(cd-s) **LIQUID SWORDS /**		48
Nov 95. (cd)(c) **LIQUID SWORDS**	73	9

– Swordsman – Unexplained / Liquid swords / Living in the world today / 4th chapter / Cold sword / Labels / Duel of the iron mic / Shadow boxin' / Killah hills 10304 / Investigate reports / Gold / I gotcha back / B.I.B.L.E. (Basic Instructions Before Leaving Earth) / Hell's wind.

. . . Jan – Jun '96 stop press . . .

— below featured D'ANGELO

Feb 96. (single) **COLD WORLD**	40	
Mar 96. (single) **SHADOWBOXIN'**	-	67

— above featured METHOD MAN

SHYHEIM

Jun 96. (single) **THE LOST GENERATION**	-	63

Bill WYMAN (see under ⇒ ROLLING STONES)

XTC

Formed: Swindon, Wiltshire, England . . . 1976 after 3 years of calling themselves The HELIUM KIDZ. Picked up by Richard Branson's 'Virgin' records in 1977. They peaked critically and commercially with 1982 double album 'ENGLISH SETTLEMENT'. Preceding this, ANDY became ill suffering a nervous breakdown. This led the band to quit the live scene and concentrate on studio work only. • **Style:** Progressed through being quirky new wave outfit to experimental pop-rock that combined folk and psychedelia. They took latter to the extreme when their alter-ego band The DUKES OF STRATOSPHEAR parodied The Beatles. • **Songwriters:** Either penned by PARTRIDGE or MOULDING or both. Covered ALL ALONG THE WATCHTOWER (Bob Dylan) / ELLA GURU (Captain Beefheart). • **Trivia:** Their 1986 album 'SKYLARKING' was produced by TODD RUNDGREN.

Recommended: ENGLISH SETTLEMENT (*8) / WHITE MUSIC (*8) / THE COMPACT XTC – THE SINGLES 1978-1985 (*9).

ANDY PARTRIDGE (b.11 Dec'53) – vocals, guitar / **COLIN MOULDING** (b.17 Aug'55) – bass, vocals / **BARRY ANDREWS** (b.12 Sep'56, London) – keyboards repl. JONATHAN PERKINS / **TERRY CHAMBERS** (b.18 Jul'55) – drums

Virgin | VirginEpic

Oct 77. (7") **SCIENCE FRICTION. / SHE'S SO SQUARE** [ ] [-]
(12"ep) **3-D**(+=) – Dance band.
Jan 78. (7") **STATUE OF LIBERTY. / HANG ON TO THE NIGHT** [ ] [-]
Feb 78. (lp)(c) **WHITE MUSIC** [38] [ ]
– Radios in motion / Cross wires / This is pop? / Do what you do / Statue of liberty / All along the watchtower / Into the atom age / I'll set myself on fire / I'm bugged / New town animal in a furnished cage / Neon shuffle. *(re-iss.Mar84) (cd-iss.Mar87+=)* – Science friction / She's so square / Dance band / Hang on to the night / Heatwave / Traffic light rock / Instant tunes.
Apr 78. (7") **THIS IS POP?. / HEATWAVE** [ ] [-]
Oct 78. (7") **ARE YOU RECEIVING ME?. / INSTANT TUNES** [ ] [-]
Oct 78. (lp)(c) **GO 2** [21] [ ]
– Mekanic dancing (oh we go!) / Battery brides / Buzzcity talking / Crowded room / The rhythm / Beatown / My weapon / Life is good in the greenhouse / Jumping in Gomorrah / My weapon / Super-tuff. *(free-12"w/lp)* **GO +** – Dance with me Germany / Beat the bible / A dictionary of modern marriage / Clap, clap, clap / We kill the beast. *(lp re-iss.Mar84) (cd-iss.Jul87 +=)* – Are you receiving me?

— **DAVE GREGORY** – synthesizers, guitar repl. ANDREWS who joined LEAGUE OF GENTLEMEN (w/**ROBERT FRIPP**). He later went solo and formed SHRIEKBACK.

May 79. (7")(7"clear) **LIFE BEGINS AT THE HOP. / HOMO SAFARI** [54] [-]

Virgin | Virgin

Aug 79. (lp)(c) **DRUMS AND WIRES** [34] [ ]
– Making plans for Nigel / Helicopter / Life begins at the hop / When you're near me I have difficulty / Ten feet tall / Roads girdle the globe / Reel by reel / Millions / That is the way / Outside world / Scissor man / Complicated game. *(free-7"w/lp)* **LIMELIGHT. / CHAIN OF COMMAND** *(US-version added track to now 7"m) (re-iss.1986) (cd-iss.1987* (+=) – (free-tracks).
Sep 79. (7"m) **MAKING PLANS FOR NIGEL. / BUSHMAN PRESIDENT (HSS 2) / PULSING, PULSING** [17] [-]
Nov 79. (7") **TEN FEET TALL. / HELICOPTER / THE SOMNAMBULIST** [-] [ ]
Feb 80. (7"m) **MAKING PLANS FOR NIGEL. / THIS IS POP? / MEKANIC DANCING (OH WE GO!)** [-] [ ]
Mar 80. (7") **WAIT TILL YOUR BOAT GOES DOWN. / TEN FEET TALL (U.S. version)** [ ] [ ]
Aug 80. (7") **GENERALS AND MAJORS. / DON'T LOSE YOUR TEMPER** [32] [ ]
(d7"+=) – Smokeless zone. / The somnambulist.
Sep 80. (lp)(c) **BLACK SEA** [16] [41]
– Respectable Street / General and majors / Living through another Cuba / Love at first sight / Rocket from a bottle / No language in our lungs / Towers of London / Paper and iron (notes and coins) / Burning with optimism's flames / Sgt. Rock (is going to help me) / Travels in Nihilon. *(re-iss.1986) (cd-iss.Mar87 +=)* – Smokeless zone / Don't lose your temper / The somnambulist.
Oct 80. (7") **TOWERS OF LONDON. / SET MYSELF ON FIRE (live)** [31] [ ]
(d7"+=) – Battery brides (live). / Scissor man.
Nov 80. (7") **TAKE THIS TOWN. / ('B'by 'The Ruts')** [ ] [ ]
— (above single was lifted from 'Times Square' film soundtrack on 'RSO')
1980. (7") **LOVE AT FIRST SIGHT. / ROCKET FROM A BOTTLE** [-] [ ]
Jan 81. (7"m) **SGT.ROCK (IS GOING TO HELP ME). / LIVING THROUGH ANOTHER CUBA (live) / GENERALS AND MAJORS (live)** [16] [ ]
Mar 81. (7"m) **RESPECTABLE STREET. / STRANGE TALES, STRANGE TAILS / OFFICER BLUE** [ ] [ ]

Virgin | Epic

Jan 82. (7"m) **SENSES WORKING OVERTIME. / BLAME THE WEATHER / TISSUE TIGERS** [10] [-]
(12"+=) – Egyptian solution. *(cd-ep iss.Jul88, see 7"tracks)*
Feb 82. (d-lp)(c)(US-lp) **ENGLISH SETTLEMENT** [5] [48]
– Runaways / Ball and chain / Senses working overtime / Jason and the Argonauts / No thugs in our house / Yacht dance / All of a sudden (it's too late) / Melt the guns / Leisure * ** / It's nearly Africa * / Knuckle down * / Fly on the wall * / Down in the cockpit * ** / English roundabout / Snowman. *(US single-lp version omits *) (cd-iss.1987 omits tracks **)*
Mar 82. (7"m) **BALL AND CHAIN. / PUNCH AND JUDY / HEAVEN IS PAVED WITH BROKEN GLASS** [58] [ ]
(12"+=) – Cockpit dance mixture.
May 82. (7"m)(9"m) **NO THUGS IN OUR HOUSE / CHAIN OF COMMAND. / LIMELIGHT / OVER RUSTY WALLS** [ ] [-]
May 82. (7") **SENSES WORKING OVERTIME. / ENGLISH ROUNDABOUT** [-] [ ]

— Trimmed to basic trio of **PARTRIDGE, MOULDING + GREGORY** plus on session **PETER PHIPPES** – drums (ex-GLITTER BAND) (CHAMBERS emigrated to Australia)

Virgin | Geffen

Apr 83. (7") **GREAT FIRE. / GOLD** [ ] [-]
(12"+=) – Frost circus / Procession towards learning land (HSS 5 & 6).
Jul 83. (7")(7"pic-d) **WONDERLAND. / JUMP** [ ] [ ]
Aug 83. (lp)(c) **MUMMER** [51] [ ]
– Beating of hearts / Wonderland / Love on a farmboy's wages / Great fire / Deliver us from the elements / Human alchemy / Ladybird / In loving memory of a name / Me and the wind / Funk pop a roll. *(re-iss.1986) (cd-iss.Mar87 +=)* – Frost circus (HSS 5) / Jump / Toys / Gold / Procession towards learning land (HSS 6) / Desert island.
Sep 83. (7") **LOVE ON A FARMBOY'S WAGES. / IN LOVING MEMORY OF A NAME** [50] [ ]
(d7"+=) – Desert island / Toys.
(12") – ('A'side) / Burning with optimist's flames (live / Cut it out (live) / English roundabout (live).
Nov 83. (7") **THANKS FOR CHRISTMAS ("THREE WISE MEN"). / COUNTDOWN TO CHRISTMAS PARTYTIME** [ ] [-]
Sep 84. (7") **ALL YOU PRETTY GIRLS. / WASHAWAY** [55] [ ]
(12"+=) – Red brick dream.
Oct 84. (lp)(c) **THE BIG EXPRESS** [38] [ ]
– Wake up / All you pretty girls / Shake you donkey up / Seagulls screaming kiss her, kiss her / This world over / Red brick dreams * / Washaway * / Blue overall * / The everyday story of Smalltown / I bought myself a liarbird / Reign of blows / You're the wish you are I had / I remember the sun / Train running low on soul coal. *(cd-iss.1987+= *)*
Oct 84. (7")(12") **THIS WORLD OVER. / BLUE OVERALL** [ ] [ ]
Jan 85. (7"m) **WAKE UP. / TAKE THIS TOWN / MANTIS ON PAROLE (HSS 4)** [ ] [ ]
(12"+=) – Making plans for Nigel / Sgt.Rock (is going to help me) / Senses working overtime.

— **IAN GREGORY** (DAVE's brother) – drums repl. PHIPPES

DUKES OF STRATOSPHEAR

Apr 85. (7") **THE MOLE FROM THE MINISTRY. / MY LOVE EXPLODES** [ ] [-]
Apr 85. (m-lp)(c) **25 O'CLOCK** [ ] [ ]
– 25 o'clock / Bike ride to the Moon / My love explodes / What in the world . . . / Your gold dress / The mole from the ministry.

XTC

Aug 86. (7") **GRASS. / DEAR GOD** [ ] [ ]
(12"+=) – Extrovert.
Oct 86. (lp)(c)(cd) **SKYLARKING** [90] [70]
– Summer's cauldron / Grass / The meeting place / That's really super, Supergirl / Ballet for a rainy day / 1000 umbrellas / Season cycle / Earn enough for us / Big day / Another satellite / Mermaid smiled / The man who sailed around his soul / Dying / Sacrificial bonfire.
Jan 87. (7")(7"clear) **THE MEETING PLACE. / THE MAN WHO SAILED AROUND HIS SOUL** [ ] [ ]
(12"+=) – Terrorism.
Aug 87. (7") **DEAR GOD. / MERMAID SMILED** [-] [ ]
Jun 87. (7") **DEAR GOD. / BIG DAY** [ ] [ ]
(12"+=) – Another satellite (live).
(cd-s) – ('A'side) / Homo safari series (HSS 1-6):- Homo safari / Bushman president / Egyptian solution / Mantis on parole / Frost circus / Procession towards learning land.

DUKES OF STRATOSPHEAR

Jul 87. (7") **YOU'RE A GOOD MAN ALBERT BROWN. / VANISHING GIRL** [ ] [-]
(12"+=) – The mole from the ministry / My love explodes.
Aug 87. (m-lp)(c) **PSONIC PSUNSPOT** [ ] [ ]
– Vanishing girl / Have you seen Jackie? / Little lighthouse / You're a good man Albert Brown (curse you red barrel) / Collideascope / You're my drug / Shiny cage / Brainiac's daughter / The affiliated / Pale and precious. *(cd-iss.as 'CHIPS FROM THE CHOCOLATE FIREBALL') (+=) – 25 O'CLOCK (m-lp tracks).*

XTC

re-grouped. **PAT MASTELOTTO** – drums (of MR. MISTER) repl. IAN
Jan 89. (7") **THE MAYOR OF SIMPLETON. / ONE OF THE MILLIONS** [46] [72]
(12"+=) – Ella guru.
(3"cd-s) – ('A'side) / Ella guru / Living in a haunted heart / The good thing.
(12") – ('A'side) / Dear God / Senses working overtime / Making plans for Nigel.
Feb 89. (lp)(c)(cd) **ORANGES AND LEMONS** [28] [44]
– Garden of earthly delights / The Mayor of Simpleton / King for a day / Here comes President Kill again / The loving / Poor skeleton steps out / One of the millions / Scarecrow people / Merely a man / Cynical days / Across this antheap / Hold me my daddy / Pink thing / Miniature sun / Chalkhills and children. *(re-iss.Oct89 as 3xcd-ep's)*
Apr 89. (7") **KING FOR A DAY. / HAPPY FAMILIES** [ ] [-]
(12"+=) – ('A'version).
(c-s+=) – Generals and majors / Towers of London.
(3"cd-s) – ('A'side) / ('A'version) / Skeletons (home demo) / My paint heroes (home demo).
May 89. (cd-s) **KING FOR A DAY (Czar mix) / ('A' Versailles mix) / TOYS / DESERT ISLAND** [-] [ ]
Aug 89. (7") **THE LOVING. / CYNICAL DAYS** [ ] [ ]
(c-s) – ('A'side) / The world is full of angry young men.
(12")(cd-s) – (all 3 tracks).
Mar 92. (7")(c-s) **THE DISAPPOINTED. / THE SMARTEST MONKEYS** [33] [ ]
(10"+=)/ /(cd-s++=) – Humble Daisy./ / ('B'demo).
May 92 (cd)(c)(d-lp) **NONESUCH** [28] [97]
– The ballad of Peter Pumpkinhead / My bird performs / Dear Madam Barnum / Humble Daisy / The smartest monkeys / The dismal / Holly up on poppy / Crocodile / Rook / Omnibus / That wave / Then she appeared / War dance / Wrapped in grey / The ugly underneath / Bungalow / Books are burning.
Jun 92. (7") **THE BALLAD OF PETER PUMPKINHEAD. / WAR DANCE** [71] [ ]
(cd-s+=) – Down a peg (demo) / ('A'demo).
(cd-s+=) – My bird performs / Always winter never Christmas (demos).

– compilations, others, etc. –

Nov 82. Virgin; (lp)(c) **WAXWORKS – A SIDES** [54] [-]
(free lp) **BEESWAX – B SIDES** (iss.on own 1983) [ ] [-]
Jan 87. Virgin; (cd) **THE COMPACT XTC – THE SINGLES 1978-1985** [ ] [ ]
– Science friction / Statue of liberty / This is pop / Are you receiving me? / Life begins at the hop / Making plans for Nigel / Wait till your boat goes down / Generals and majors / Towers of London / Sgt.Rock is going to help me / Senses working overtime / Ball and chain / Great fire / Wonderland / Love on a farmboy's wages / All you pretty girls / This world over / Wake up.
Aug 90. Virgin; (cd) **EXPLODE TOGETHER (THE DUB EXPERIMENTS 78-80)** [ ] [-]
– (included the ANDY PARTRIDGE album below)
Aug 90. Virgin; (cd) **RAG & BONE BUFFET** (rare) [ ] [-]
(c-iss.Mar91)
Nov 88. Old Gold; (7") **MAKING PLANS FOR NIGEL. / SENSES WORKING OVERTIME** [ ] [-]
Nov 94. Nighttracks; (cd) **DRUMS AND WIRELESS: BBC RADIO SESSIONS 77-89** [ ] [-]

MR. PARTRIDGE

ANDY solo.

Virgin | not issued

Feb 80. (lp)(c) **TAKE AWAY (THE LURE OF SALVAGE)** [ ] [-]
– Commerciality / The day the pulled the North Pole down / Cairo / Madhattan / The forgotten language of light / Steam fist futurist / The rotary / Shore leave ornithology (another 1950) / I sit in the snow / Work away Tokyo day / New broom. *(re-iss.Aug88)*

The COLONEL

(MOULDING + CHAMBERS)

Virgin | not issued

Oct 80. (7") **TOO MANY COOKS IN THE KITCHEN. / I NEED PROTECTION** [ ] [-]

ANDY PARTRIDGE / HAROLD BUDD

All Saints | not issued

Jun 94. (cd) **THROUGH THE HILL** [ ] [-]
– Hand 19 / Through the hill / Great valley of gongs / Western island of apples / Animal Mundi / Hand 20 / The place of odd glances / Well for the sweat of the Moon / Tenochtitlan's numberless bridges / Ceramic avenue / Hand 21 / Missing pieces in the game of salt and onyx / Mantle of peacock bones / Bronze coins showing genitals / Bearded Aphrodite / Hand 22.

YARDBIRDS

Formed: Richmond, Surrey, England . . . 1963 after stemming from METROPOLITAN BLUES QUARTET. After residency at The CRAWDADDY Club backing bluesman SONNY BOY WILLIAMSON, they gained contract with EMI's 'Columbia' label early '64. After 2 well-received singles that year, they had first of 4 consecutive Top 3 hits with 'FOR YOUR LOVE' in 1965. Became famous for introducing 3 of the greatest guitarists of all-time ERIC CLAPTON, JEFF BECK and JIMMY PAGE. • **Style:** Played R&B standards, until shift into rock-pop mid 60's. By late 1966, they progressed into psychedelia but with decreasing commercial appeal. • **Songwriters:** RELF wrote some, except covers I WISH YOU WOULD (Billy Boy Arnold) / SMOKESTACK LIGHTNING (Howlin' Wolf) / A CERTAIN GIRL (Ernie K-Doe) / GOOD MORNING LITTLE SCHOOLGIRL (Don & Bob) / TRAIN (Johnny Burnette) / FOR YOUR LOVE + HEART FULL OF SOUL (c. Graham Gouldman, ⇒ 10cc) / I'M A MAN (Bo Diddley) / TEN LITTLE INDIANS (Nilsson) / THE SUN IS SHINING (Elmore James) / plus loads of other blues greats. • **Trivia:** Made two group appearances in the 66/67 films 'SWINGING LONDON' & 'BLOW-UP'. Early in 1966, manager GIORGIO GOMELSKY was replaced by SIMON NAPIER-BELL.

Recommended: THE VERY BEST OF THE YARDBIRDS (*9)

KEITH RELF (b.22 Mar'43, Richmond) – vocals, harmonica / **ERIC CLAPTON** (b.see solo info) – lead guitar, vocals repl. ANTHONY TOPHAM / **CHRIS DREJA** (b.11 Nov'45, Surbiton, Surrey) – rhythm guitar / **PAUL SAMWELL-SMITH** (b. 8 May'43, Richmond) – bass / **JIM McCARTY** (b.25 Jul'43, Liverpool) – drums

(Columbia / Epic)

Jun 64. (7") **I WISH YOU WOULD. / A CERTAIN GIRL** [ ] [ ] Oct 64
Aug 64. (7") **A CERTAIN GIRL. / I AIN'T GOT YOU** [-] [ ]
Oct 64. (7") **GOOD MORNING LITTLE SCHOOLGIRL. / I AIN'T GOT YOU** [44] [-]
Feb 65. (lp) **FIVE LIVE YARDBIRDS (live)** [ ] [-]
– Too much monkey business / I got love if you want it / Smokestack lightning / Good morning little schoolgirl / Respectable / Five long years / Pretty girl / Louise / I'm a man / Here 'tis. *(re-iss. Aug79 +c-iss. Jan82 on 'Charly') (re-iss.+cd.Aug89 on 'Decal')*
Mar 65. (7") **FOR YOUR LOVE. / GOT TO HURRY** [3] [-]
(re-iss.Aug76 on 'Charly')
May 65. (7") **FOR YOUR LOVE. / I'M NOT TALKING** [-] [6]
Jul 65. (lp) **FOR YOUR LOVE** [-] [96]
– For your love / I'm not talking / Putty (in your hands) / I ain't got you / Got to hurry / I ain't done wrong / I wish you would / A certain girl / Sweet music / Good morning little schoolgirl / My girl Sloopy.

— (Mar65) **JEFF BECK** (b.24 Jun'44) – lead guitar repl. CLAPTON who joined JOHN MAYALL's BLUESBREAKERS. He later formed CREAM and went solo ⇒.

Jul 65. (7") **HEART FULL OF SOUL. / STEELED BLUES** [2] [9]
Oct 65. (7") **EVIL HEARTED YOU. / STILL I'M SAD** [3] [-]
(re-iss.Jul82 on 'Old Gold')
Nov 65. (7") **I'M A MAN. / STILL I'M SAD** [-] [17]
Dec 65. (lp) **HAVING A RAVE UP WITH THE YARDBIRDS (live)** [-] [53]
– You're a better man than I / Evil hearted you / I'm a man / Still I'm sad / Heart full of soul / The train kept a-rollin' / Smokestack lightning / Respectable / I'm a man / Here 'tis. *(last 4 tracks from 'FIVE LIVE YARDBIRDS')*
Feb 66. (7") **SHAPES OF THINGS. / YOU'RE A BETTER MAN THAN I** [3] [-]
Mar 66. (7") **SHAPES OF THINGS. / NEW YORK CITY BLUES** [-] [11]

— (Feb66) **JIMMY PAGE** – guitar (ex-session man, solo artist) repl. SAMWELL-SMITH who became producer. (DREJA moved to bass) KEITH issued solo 45 in May.

May 66. (7") **OVER, UNDER, SIDEWAYS, DOWN. / JEFF'S BOOGIE** [10] [13] Jun 66
Jul 66. (lp) **THE YARDBIRDS** (US title 'OVER UNDER SIDEWAYS DOWN') [20] [52]
– Lost women / Over, under, sideways, down / The Nazz are blue / I can't make your way / Rack my mind / Farewell / Hot house of Omagarashid / Jeff's boogie / He's always there / Turn into earth / What do you want / Ever since the world began. *(re-iss.UK Feb83 as 'ROGER THE ENGINEER' on 'Edsel', cd-iss.1986 +=)*– Happenings ten years time ago / Psycho daisies. *(cd-iss. US version Feb92 on 'Raven-Topic')*
Oct 66. (7") **HAPPENINGS TEN YEARS TIME AGO. / PSYCHO DAISIES** [43] [-]
Nov 66. (7") **HAPPENINGS TEN YEARS TIME AGO. / THE NAZZ ARE BLUE** [-] [30]

— (Oct66) Trimmed to a quartet when JEFF BECK left to go solo.

Apr 67. (7") **LITTLE GAMES. / PUZZLES** [ ] [51]
Apr 67. (lp) **GREATEST HITS** (compilation) [-] [28]
– Shapes of things / Still I'm sad / New York City blues / For your love / Over, under, sideways, down / I'm a man / Happenings ten years time ago / Heart full of soul / Smokestack lightning / I'm not talking.
Jun 67. (7") **HA HA SAID THE CLOWN. / TINKER, TAILOR, SOLDIER, SAILOR** [-] [45]
Aug 67. (lp) **LITTLE GAMES** [-] [80]
– Little games / Smile on me / White summer / Tinker, tailor, soldier, sailor / Glimpses / Drinking muddy water / No excess baggage / Stealing, stealing / Only the black rose / Little soldier boy. *(UK-iss.May85 on 'Fame') (re-iss.+cd.Apr91 on 'EMI')*
Oct 67. (7") **TEN LITTLE INDIANS. / DRINKIN' MUDDY WATER** [-] [96]
Mar 68. (7") **GOODNIGHT SWEET JOSEPHINE. / THINK ABOUT IT** [ ] [ ]

— Disbanded mid'68. PAGE and DREJA formed NEW YARDBIRDS, but when DREJA departed, PAGE formed LED ZEPPELIN. RELF and McCARTY formed the original RENAISSANCE. On 14 May'76, RELF was electrocuted when touching a faulty amp. In the early 90s, McCARTY was also part of PRETTY THINGS / YARDBIRD BLUES BAND collaboration.

– other compilations, etc. –

Oct 65. Columbia; (7"ep) **FIVE YARDBIRDS** [ ] [-]
– My girl Sloopy / I'm not talking / I ain't done wrong / (1).
Jan 67. Columbia; (7"ep) **OVER UNDER SIDEWAYS DOWN** [ ] [-]
Jan 66. Fontana/ US= Mercury; (lp) **SONNY BOY WILLIAMSON AND THE YARDBIRDS (live w/ SONNY)** [ ] [ ] Feb 66
– Bye bye bird / Mr. Downchild / The river Rhine / 23 hours too long / Out on the water coast / Baby don't worry / Pontiac blues / Take it easy baby / I don't care no more / Do the Weston. *(re-iss.1968) (re-iss.Jun75 on 'Philips')*
Jun 71. Regal Starline; (lp)(c) **REMEMBER THE YARDBIRDS** [ ] [-]
1971. Columbia; (lp) **LIVE YARDBIRDS FEATURING JIMMY PAGE** [-] [ ]
1972. Epic; (lp) **YARDBIRDS' FAVORITES** [-] [ ]
Aug 77. Charly; (lp) **THE YARDBIRDS FEATURING ERIC CLAPTON** [ ] [-]
(re-iss.cd+c Mar94 on 'Laserlight')
Aug 77. Charly; (lp) **THE YARDBIRDS FEATURING JEFF BECK** [ ] [-]
(above 2 re-iss.Mar83, the latter again Feb85 on 'Cambra')
Dec 77. Charly; (d-lp) **SHAPES OF THINGS** [ ] [-]
Feb 82. Charly; (10"lp) **SINGLE HITS** [ ] [-]
Jun 83. Charly; (lp) **OUR OWN SOUND** [ ] [-]
Nov 84. Charly; (lp-box) **SHAPES OF THINGS – COLLECTION OF CLASSIC RECORDINGS 1964-66** [ ] [-]
– (lp's) THE FIRST RECORDINGS / SONNY BOY WILLIAMSON & . . . / FIVE LIVE YARDBIRDS / FOR YOUR LOVE / HAVING A RAVE . . . / SHAPES OF THINGS / ODDS AND SODS *(iss.Jun91 as 4xcd-box on 'Decal')*
1986. Charly; (cd) **GREATEST HITS** (not US version) [ ] [-]
Nov 84. Topline; (lp)(c) **FOR YOUR LOVE** (not US version) [ ] [-]
Jul 82. Old Gold; (7") **FOR YOUR LOVE. / HEARTFUL OF SOUL** [ ] [-]
1989. Old Gold; (7"ep) **FOR YOUR LOVE** [ ] [-]
Feb 83. Edsel; (7") **OVER, UNDER, SIDEWAYS, DOWN. / PSYCHO DAISIES** [ ] [-]
May 84. Edsel; (7") **RACK MY MIND. / JEFF'S BOOGIE** [ ] [-]

Mar 84. Scoop; (7"ep)(c-ep) **6 TRACK HITS** [ ] [-]
1986. Castle; (d-lp)(d-c) **THE COLLECTION** [ ] [-]
(cd-iss.1988)
1986. Showcase; (lp) **GOT LIVE IF YOU WANT IT** (credited **ERIC CLAPTON)** [ ] [-]
Apr 87. Topline; (cd) **CLASSIC CUTS** [ ] [-]
1989. Instant; (lp)(c)(cd) **HITS AND MORE** [ ] [-]
Sep 89. Decal; (d-lp)(cd) **THE STUDIO SESSIONS 1964-1967** [ ] [-]
Sep 89. Decal; (lp)(cd) **THE FIRST RECORDINGS – LONDON 1963** [ ] [-]
Jun 91. Music Club; (cd) **THE VERY BEST OF THE YARDBIRDS** [ ] [-]
– For your love / Heart full of soul / Good morning little schoolgirl / Still I'm sad / Evil hearted you / A certain girl / Jeff's blues / I wish you would / New York City / I'm not talking / You're a better man than I / Shapes of things / I'm a man / Boom boom / Smokestack lightning (live) / Let it rock (live) / You can't judge a book by it's cover (live) / Who do you love (live) / Too much monkey business (live) / Respectable (live) / Pretty girl (live) / Stroll on.
Apr 91. Band Of Joy; (cd)(c)(lp) **ON AIR** (65-67) [ ] [-]
Jul 92. Repertoire; (cd) **25 GREATEST HITS** [ ] [-]
Sep 92. Promised Land; (cd) **YARDBIRDS' REUNION CONCERT (live) ("JIM McCARTY & CHRIS DREJA")** [ ] [-]
Oct 92. EMI; (cd) **LITTLE GAMES, SESSIONS & MORE** [ ] [-]
Apr 93. Pulsar; (cd) **GREATEST HITS** (not US version) [ ] [-]
Sep 93. Laserlight; (cd)(c) **HEART FULL OF SOUL** [ ] [-]
Apr 95. Top Masters; (cd) **ERIC CLAPTON & THE YARDBIRDS** [ ] [-]

KEITH RELF

solo, when a YARDBIRD.

Columbia Epic
May 66. (7") **MR.ZERO. / KNOWING** [50] [-]
Jan 67. (7") **SHAPES IN MY MIND. / BLUE SANDS** [ ] [ ]

REIGN

was formed by **RELF + McCARTY** plus **ROBIN LEMESWRIER**

Regal Zono. not issued
Nov 68. (7") **LINE OF LEAST RESISTANCE. / NATURAL LOVING WOMAN** [ ] [-]

TOGETHER

(McCARTY & RELF) with sessioners.

Columbia Epic?
1968. (7") **HENRY'S COMING HOME. / LOVE MUM AND DAD** [ ] [-]

— They evolved into RENAISSANCE the following year. McCARTY joined SHOOT in 1972 and made 1 album 'ON THE FRONTIER' for 'Capitol'. In 1976 he formed ILLUSION with JOHN KNIGHTSBRIDGE, HAWKEN and CENNAMO. The latter had previously been in ARMAGEDDON with KEITH RELF. On 22 Jul'83, The YARDBIRDS re-formed with **McCARTY, DREJA, SAMWELL-SMITH, KNIGHTSBRIDGE** plus 2 vocalists **JOHN FIDDLER** (ex-MEDICINE HEAD) + **MARK FELTON** (ex-NINE BELOW ZERO). Evolved into

BOX OF FROGS

KNIGHTSBRIDGE and FELTON having been replaced by guests **JEFF BECK** – guitar / **RORY GALLAGHER** – guitar / **MAX MIDDLETON** – keyboards

Epic Epic
Jun 84. (7") **BACK WHERE I STARTED. / THE EDGE** [ ] [ ]
(12"+=) – Nine lives.
Jul 84. (lp)(c) **BOX OF FROGS** [ ] [45]
– Back where I stand / Harder / Another wasted day / Love inside you / The edge / Two steps ahead / Into the dark / Just a boy again / Poor boy. *(cd-iss.Oct93 on 'Sony Europe')*
Aug 84. (7") **INTO THE DARK. / X TRACKS** [ ] [ ]
(12"+=) – X tracks (Medley of tracks).

— Trimmed to quartet of **FIDDLER, McCARTY, DREJA + SAMWELL-SMITH**
Jun 86. (7") **AVERAGE. / STRANGE LAND** [ ] [ ]
(12"+=) – Keep calling.
Jun 86. (lp)(c) **STRANGE LAND** [ ] [ ]
– Strange land / Get it while you can / You mix me up / House on fire / Average / Hanging from the wreckage / Heart full of soul / Asylum. *(cd-iss Jul94 on 'Sony Europe')*

YES

Formed: London, England ... mid '68 by veterans of the 60's beat era; ANDERSON and SQUIRE. They added BILL BRUFORD, PETE BANKS and TONY KAYE and soon signed to 'Atlantic', after opening for CREAM at their farewell concert at London's Royal Albert Hall. In the summer of 1969, their album debut was released, but after its flop they had first of many personnel changes; STEVE HOWE for PETE BANKS. In 1970, the follow-up 'TIME AND A WORD' hit the UK Top 50, but was surpassed early the next year, when 'THE YES ALBUM' hit the Top 10 and broke into American Top 40. The more-stylish and flamboyant RICK WAKEMAN was then drafted in to replace KAYE. The self-indulgent but well-received 'FRAGILE' was another success and was the first to feature ROGER DEAN's fantasy lp covers. At the end of the Autumn 1972, the classic 'CLOSE TO THE EDGE' was unleashed and this too was a commercial success, hitting Top 5 on both sides of the Atlantic. In 1973, their triple live lp 'YESSONGS', peaked at No.1 in the UK, and hit Top 20 in America. After another two near perfect creations 'TALES FROM TOPOGRAPHIC OCEANS' and 'RELAYER', they went on solo sojourns. WAKEMAN's was permanent, as his had started in 1973 with his album 'SIX WIVES OF HENRY VIII'. In 1977, when punk rock was king, YES returned with new keyboard wizard PATRICK MORAZ and another gem 'GOING FOR THE ONE'. Although they continued to have many successes in many shapes and forms (see below) for next two decades, they never re-created the high spots of the 70's. • **Style:** Progressive neo-classical pomp-rock dinosaurs. They blended flash-rock and superb individual musicianship, with choirboy-like vox of JON ANDERSON. • **Songwriters:** Group / individual compositions with ANDERSON lyrics. Early in the 80's, The BUGGLES boys were also contributing, much to dismay of loyal supporters. Covered EVERY LITTLE THING + I'M DOWN (Beatles) / I SEE YOU (Byrds) / NO OPPORTUNITY NECCESSARY, NO EXPERIENCE NEEDED (Stephen Stills) / SOMETHING'S COMING (Sondheim-Bernstein) / AMERICA (Simon & Garfunkel). AMAZING GRACE (trad.). JON ANDERSON recorded traditional Christmas carols on his '3 SHIPS' lp. • **Trivia:** From 1971 onwards, they employed ROGER DEAN for all album sleeve artwork. The producers were debut: co-w / PAUL CLAY / follow-up: TONY COLTON. Then untill temp. breakup 1975; EDDIE OFFORD. They produced themselves and w/HORN on '90125'). In Apr'89, HOWE appeared on Various Artists live d-lp,c,cd,video 'NIGHT OF THE GUITAR' on 'I.R.S.' label.

Recommended: CLOSE TO THE EDGE (*10) / THE YES ALBUM (*10) / YESSONGS (*9) / GOING FOR THE ONE (*8) / TALES FROM TOPOGRAPHIC OCEANS (*9) / RELAYER (*8) / FRAGILE (*7) / CLASSIC YES (*9)

JON ANDERSON (b.25 Oct'44, Accrington, England) – vocals (ex-WARRIORS) / **TONY KAYE** (b.11 Jan'46, Leicester) – keyboards (ex-FEDERALS, ex-BITTER SWEET) / **PETE BANKS** (b. 7 Jul'47, Barnet) – guitar (ex-SYN, ex-MABEL GREEN'S TOY . . .) / **CHRIS SQUIRE** (b. 4 Mar'48, Nth. London) – bass, vocals (ex-SYN) / **BILL BRUFORD** (b.17 May'48) – percussion (ex-SAVOY BROWN BLUES BAND)

Atlantic Atlantic
Jun 69. (7") **SWEETNESS. / SOMETHING'S COMING** [ ] [-]
Jul 69. (lp)(c) **YES** [ ] [ ] Oct 69
– Beyond and before / I see you / Yesterday and today / Looking around / Harold land / Every little thing / Sweetness / Survival. *(re-iss.cd Oct94)*
Oct 69. (7") **LOOKING AROUND. / EVERYDAYS** [ ] [-]
Jan 70. (7") **SWEETNESS / EVERY LITTLE THING** [-] [ ]

— **STEVE HOWE** (b. 8 Apr'47) – guitar (ex-TOMORROW, ex-IN CROWD, ex-SYNDICATS, ex-BODAST) repl. BANKS who joined BLODWYN PIG and later FLASH.
Mar 70. (7") **TIME AND A WORD. / THE PROPHET** [ ] [-]
Jun 70. (lp)(c) **TIME AND A WORD** [45] [ ] Nov 70
– No opportunity neccessary, no experience needed / Then / Everydays / Sweet dreams / The prophet / Clear days / Astral traveller / Time and a word. *(re-iss.cd Oct94)*
Jun 70. (7") **SWEET DREAMS. / DEAR FATHER** [ ] [-]
Mar 71. (lp)(c) **THE YES ALBUM** [7] [40] May 71
– Yours is no disgrace / The clap / Starship trooper; (a) Life seeker – (b) Disiilusion – (c) Wurm / I've seen good people (a) Your move – (b) All good people / A venture / Perpetual change. *(cd-iss.Jul87)*
Jul 71. (7") **YOUR MOVE. / THE CLAP** [-] [40]

— **RICK WAKEMAN** (b.18 May'49) – keyboards (ex-STRAWBS) repl. KAYE who formed BADGER
Nov 71. (lp)(c) **FRAGILE** [7] [4] Jan 72
– Roundabout / Cans and Brahms / We have Heaven / South side of the sky / Five per cent of nothing / Long distance runaround / The fish (Shindleria Praematurus) / Mood for a day / Heart of the sunrise. *(cd-iss.Dec86)*
Jan 72. (7") **ROUNDABOUT. / LONG DISTANCE RUNAROUND** [-] [13]
Jul 72. (7") **AMERICA. / TOTAL MASS RETAIN** [-] [46]
Sep 72. (lp)(c) **CLOSE TO THE EDGE** [4] [3]
– Close to the edge; (a) The solid time of change – (b) Total mass retain – (c) I get up I get down – (d) Seasons of man / And you and I; (a) Cord of life – (b) Eclipse – (c) The preacher the teacher – (d) The apocalypse / Siberian Khatru. *(cd-iss.Dec86)*
Oct 72. (7") **AND YOU AND I (part II). / (part I)** [-] [42]

— (Aug72) **ANDERSON, HOWE, WAKEMAN + SQUIRE** brought in **ALAN WHITE** (b.14 Jun'44, Pelton, Durham, England) – drums (ex-John Lennon's PLASTIC ONO BAND, ex-HAPPY MAGAZINE) repl. BRUFORD who joined KING CRIMSON, etc. (both appeared on live album below)

May 73. (t-lp)(d-c) **YESSONGS (live)** [1] [12]
– (opening excerpt from 'Firebird Suite') / Siberian Khatru / Heart of the sunrise / Perpetual change / And you and I; (a) Cord of life – (b) Eclipse – (c) The preacher the teacher – (d) The apocalypse / Mood for a day / (excerpts from 'The Six Wives Of Henry VIII') / Roundabout / I've seen all good people; Your move – All good people / Long distance runaround / The fish (Shindleria Praematurus) / Close to the edge (a) The solid time of change – (b) Total mass retain – (c) I get up I get down – (d) Seasons of man / Yours is no disgrace / Starship trooper (a) Life seeker – (b) Disillusion – (c) Wurm. *(d-cd iss.Feb87) (re-iss.d-cd Oct94)*

Dec 73. (d-lp)(c) **TALES FROM TOPOGRAPHIC OCEANS** [1] [6]
– The revealing science of God / The remembering / The ancient / Ritual. *(cd-iss.Sep89) (re-iss.d-cd Oct94)*

Jan 74. (7") **ROUNDABOUT (live). / AND YOU AND I (live)** [ ] [-]

— **PATRICK MORAZ** (b.24 Jun'48, Morges, Switzerland) – keyboards (ex-REFUGEE) repl. WAKEMAN who continued solo

Nov 74. (lp)(c) **RELAYER** [4] [5] Dec 74
– The gates of delirium / Sound chaser / To be over. *(cd-iss.Jul88) (re-iss.cd Oct94)*

Jan 75. (7") **SOON (from 'Gates of Delirium'). / SOUND CHASER** [ ] [-]

— Temporarily disbanded to release solo albums.

STEVE HOWE

augmented by **WHITE, BRUFORD, MORAZ** + many including **GRAEME TAYLOR** – guitar / **MALCOLM BENNETT + COLIN GIBSON** – bass / **DAVID OBERLE** – drums

Atlantic Atlantic

Nov 75. (lp)(c) **BEGINNINGS** [22] [63]
– Doors of sleep / Australia / The nature of the sea / The lost symphony / Beginnings / Will o' the wisp / Ram / Pleasure stole the night / Break away from it all. *(re-iss.cd Oct94)*

CHRIS SQUIRE

augmented by **BILL BRUFORD** – drums / **ANDREW BRYCE JACKMAN + BARRY ROSE** – keyboards / **MEL COLLINS** – sax / **PATRICK MORAZ** – keyboards, synthesizers / **JIMMY HASTINGS** – flute

Atlantic Atlantic

Nov 75. (lp)(c) **FISH OUT OF WATER** [25] [69]
– Hold out your hand / You by my side / Silently falling / Lucky seven / Safe (canon song).

ALAN WHITE

augmented by **PETER KIRTLEY** – guitar, vocals / **COLIN GIBSON** – bass / **KENNY CRADDOCK** – keyboards, vocals / **ANDY PHILIPS** – steel drums / **ALAN MARSHALL** vocals / **HENRY LOWTHER** – trumpet / **STEVE GREGORY + BUD BEADLE** – wind

Atlantic Atlantic

Mar 76. (lp)(c) **RAMSHACKLED** [41] [ ]
– Oooh! baby (going to pieces) / One way rag / Avakak / Spring – Song of innocence / Giddy / Silly woman / Marching into a bottle / Everybody / Darkness (parts 1, 2 & 3).

Apr 76. (7") **OOOH! BABY (GOING TO PIECES). / ONE WAY RAG** [ ] [-]

JON ANDERSON

augmented **BRIAN GAYLOR** – synths / **KEN FREEMAN** -strings

Atlantic Atlantic

Jun 76. (lp)(c) **OLIAS OF SUNHILLOW** [8] [47]
– Ocean song / Meeting (Garden of Geda) – Sound of the galleon / Dance of Ranyart – Olias (to build the Moorglade) / Qoquag en transic – Naon – Transic to / Flight of the Moorglade / Solid space / Moon Ra – Chords – Song of search / To the runner.

Oct 76. (7") **FLIGHT OF THE MOORGLADE. / TO THE RUNNER** [ ] [-]

— PATRICK MORAZ also hit UK Top 30 with his I, PATRICK MORAZ album for 'Charisma'. He had now departed YES to continue solo work & join MOODY BLUES.

YES

re-formed in 1977 the 1973 line-up w / **RICK WAKEMAN** returning, to repl. MORAZ..

Jul 77. (lp)(c)(3x12") **GOING FOR THE ONE** [1] [8]
– Going for the one / Turn of the century / Parallels / Wonderous stories / Awaken. *(cd-iss.Jul88)*

Sep 77. (7")(12")(12"blue) **WONDEROUS STORIES. / PARALLELS** [7] [-]

Sep 77. (7")(**WONDEROUS STORIES. / AWAKEN** [-] [ ]

Nov 77. (7")(12") **GOING FOR THE ONE. / AWAKEN (part 1)** [24] [-]

Sep 78. (7") **DON'T KILL THE WHALE. / ABILENE** [36] [-]

Sep 78. (lp)(c) **TORMATO** [8] [10]
– Future times / Rejoice / Don't kill the whale / Madrigal / Release, release / Arriving UFO / Circus of Heaven / Onward / On the silent wings of freedom.

Nov 78. (7") **RELEASE, RELEASE. / DON'T KILL THE WHALE** [-] [ ]

— They shocked their fans, when they replaced (solo seeking once more) WAKEMAN and ANDERSON with (ex-BUGGLES duo) :-**TREVOR HORN** – vocals, bass / + **GEOFF DOWNES** – keyboards

Aug 80. (lp)(c) **DRAMA** [2] [18]
– Machine messiah / White car / Does it really happen? / Into the lens / Run through the light / Tempus fugit. *(re-iss.cd Oct94)*

Oct 80. (7") **INTO THE LENS. / DOES IT REALLY HAPPEN?** [ ] [ ]

Jan 81. (7") **RUN THROUGH THE LIGHT. / WHITE CAR** [-] [ ]

— YES split again.

CAMERA

were formed by **SQUIRE + WHITE**

Dec 82. (7") **RUN WITH THE FOX. / (part 2)** [ ] [ ]

YES

— above partnership brought back **ANDERSON + KAYE,** plus newcomer **TREVOR RABIN** (b.South Africa) – guitar, vocals. They repl. DOWNES + HOWE (to ASIA) / and HORN who was retained as producer.

Atco Atco

Nov 83. (7")(7"pic-d)(7"sha-pic-d) **OWNER OF A LONELY HEART. / OUR SONG** [28] [1]
(12"+=)(c-s+=) – ('A'version).

Nov 83. (lp)(c)(cd) **90125** [16] [5]
– Owner of a lonely heart / Hold on / It can happen / Changes / Cinema / Leave it / Our song / City of love / Hearts.

Mar 84. (7") **LEAVE IT. / LEAVE IT (acappella)** [56] [24]
(12"+=) – ('A'version).
(US-c-s+=) – ('A'-hello goodbye mix) / Owner of a lonely heart.

Jun 84. (7") **IT CAN HAPPEN. / IT CAN HAPPEN (live)** [ ] [51]

Mar 86. (m-lp)(c) **9012LIVE – THE SOLOS (live)** [44] [81] Dec 85
– Hold on / Si / Solly's beard / Soon / Changes / Amazing Grace / Whitefish.

Sep 87. (7") **LOVE WILL FIND A WAY. / HOLY LAMB** [73] [30]
('A'extended-12"+=) – ('A'rise & fall mix)

Sep 87. (lp)(c)(cd) **BIG GENERATOR** [17] [15]
– Rhythm of love / Big generator / Shoot high aim low / Almost like love / Love will find a way / Final eyes / I'm running / Holy love.

Dec 87. (12"ep) **RHYTHM OF LOVE (dance mix) – ('A'move mix) / ('A'dub) / CITY OF LOVE** (live) [-] [40]

— In-house squabbles led to splinter of YES called . . .

ANDERSON BRUFORD WAKEMAN HOWE

Arista Arista

Jun 89. (lp)(c)(cd) **ANDERSON BRUFORD WAKEMAN HOWE** [14] [30]
– Themes: Sound – Second attention – Soul warrior / Fist of fire / Brother of mine: The big dream – Nothing can come between us – Long lost brother of mine / Quartet: I wanna learn – She gives me love – Who was the first – I'm alive / Birthright / The meeting / Teakbois / Order of the universe: Order theme – Rock gives courage – It's so hard to grow – The universe / Let's pretend. *(lp tracks edited)(re-iss.cd.Dec92)*

Jun 89. (7") **BROTHER OF MINE. / THEMES: SOUND** [63] [ ]
(12"+=) – Themes: Second attention – Soul warrior.
(3"cd-s+=)(5"cd-s+=)(10"+=)(c-s+=) – Vultures (in the city).

Aug 89. (7") **LET'S PRETEND. / QUARTET: I'M ALIVE** [-] [ ]

Nov 89. (7")(c-s) **ORDER OF THE UNIVERSE. / FIST OF FIRE** [ ] [ ]
(12"+=)(cd-s+=) – ('A'extended).

YES

now settled dispute by combining last line-up of **ANDERSON, BRUFORD, HOWE, WAKEMAN** with present YES men **SQUIRE, WHITE, RABIN + KAYE**

May 91. (cd)(c)(lp) **UNION** [7] [15]
– I would have waited forever / Shock to the system / Masquerade / Lift me up / Without hope you cannot start the day / Saving my heart / Miracle of life / Silent talking / The more we live-let go / Dangerous / Holding on / Evensong. (c+cd +=) – Angkor wat / Take the water to the mountain / Give and take. *(re-iss.cd May94)*

Jun 91. (7") **SAVING MY HEART. / LIFT ME UP (edit)** [ ] [-]
(12"+=)(cd-s+=) – America.

Aug 91. (7") **LIFT ME UP. / GIVE AND TAKE** [-] [86]

Nov 91. (c-s) **SAVING MY HEART. / THE MORE WE LIVE – LET GO** [-] [ ]

Victory Londob

Mar 94. (cd)(c) **TALK** [20] [33]
– Calling / I am waiting / Real love / State of play / Walls / Where will you be / Endless dream (Silent spring – Talk – Endless dream).

– compilations, others, etc. –

Note; on 'Atlantic' unless otherwise stated.

Feb 75. (lp)(c) **YESTERDAYS** (early rare) [27] [17]
– America / Looking around / Time and a word / Sweet dreams / Then / Survival / Astral traveller / Dear father. *(re-iss.cd Oct94)*

Dec 81. (lp)(c) **CLASSIC YES** [ ] [ ]
– Heart of the sunrise / Wonderous stories / Yours is no disgrace / Roundabout / Starship trooper (a) Life seeker (b) Disillusion (c) Wurm / Long distance runaround / The fish (schindleria praematurus) / And you and I; (a) Cord of life (b) Eclipse (c) The preacher the teacher (d) The apocalypse / I've seen all good people; (a) Your move (b) All good people. *(w/ free 7")* – **ROUNDABOUT (live). / I'VE SEEN ALL GOOD PEOPLE (live)** *(cd-iss.Dec86) (re-iss.cd Oct94)*

Oct 82. (d-c) **FRAGILE / CLOSE TO THE EDGE** [ ] [-]

Sep 93. (cd)(c) **HIGHLIGHTS – THE VERY BEST OF YES** [ ] [ ]

Dec 80. Atco; (d-lp)(c) **YESSHOWS (live 1976-1978)** [22] [43]
(re-iss.cd Oct94)

Aug 91. Atco; (4xcd-box)(4xc-box) **YES YEARS** [ ] [ ]

Oct 91. East West; (d-cd)(d-c)(t-lp) **YES STORY** [ ] [ ]

Nov 91. East West; (7")(c-s) **OWNER OF A LONELY HEART. / ('A'-wonderous mix)** [ ] [ ]
(12")(cd-s) – ('A'side) / ('A'not fragile mix) / ('A'move yourself mix) / ('A'close to the edge mix).

Sep 93. Connoiseur; (cd) **AFFIRMATIVE (YES family tree)** [ ] [-]
– Small beginnings (FLASH) / Feels good to me (BRUFORD) / Catherine Howard / Merlin the magician (RICK WAKEMAN) / Ocean song / All in a matter of time (JON ANDERSON) / I HEAR YOU NOW (JON & VANGELIS) / SPRING SONG OF INNOCENCE (ALAN WHITE) / Nature of the sea / Ram (STEVE HOWE) / Cahcaca (PATRICK MORAZ) / Hold out your hand (CHRIS SQUIRE) / Wind of change (BADGER) / Etoile noir (TREVOR RABIN).

Dec 93. Fragile; (d-cd)(video) **AN EVENING OF YES MUSIC ... PLUS** [ ] [ ]

JON ANDERSON

with more solo releases. Earlier in the year 1980, he (JON) and VANGELIS ⇒ had hit UK No.8 with single 'I HEAR YOU NOW', and 'SHORT STORIES' lp hit No.4.

—— with a plethera of session people.

Atlantic Atlantic

Sep 80. (7") **SOME ARE BORN. / DAYS** [ ] [ ]

Nov 80. (lp)(c) **SONG OF SEVEN** [38] [ ]
– For you for me / Some are born / Don't forget (nostalgia) / Heart of the matter / Hear it / Everybody loves you / Take your time / Days / Song of seven.

Nov 80. (7") **TAKE YOUR TIME. / HEART OF THE MATTER** [ ] [ ]

—— Around mid'81, JON & VANGELIS released album 'THE FRIENDS OF MR.CAIRO' which hit UK No.6. Lifted from it 'I'LL FIND MY WAY HOME' also managed to hit UK No.6 / US No.51 in Nov '81. These and his next solo releases were issued on

Polydor Atlantic

Apr 82. (7") **SURRENDER. / SPIDER** [ ] [ ]

May 82. (lp)(c) **ANIMATION** [43] [ ]
– Olympia / Animation / All in a matter of time / Unlearning / Boundaries / Pressure point / Much better reason / All Gods children.

Nov 82. (7") **ALL IN A MATTER OF TIME. / SPIDER** [ ] [ ]

—— May83, sees another JON & VANGELIS album 'PRIVATE COLLECTION' hit UK No.22. Their compilation album 'THE BEST OF . . . ' hit UK No.42 in Aug84.

Elektra Elektra

Dec 85. (lp)(c) **3 SHIPS** [ ] [ ]
– Save all your love / Easier said than done / 3 ships / Forest of fire / Ding dong merrily on high / Save all your love (reprise) / The holly and the ivy / Day of days / 2,000 years / Where were you / Oh holy night / How it hits you / Jingle bells.

Dec 85. (7") **DAY OF DAYS. / EASIER SAID THAN DONE** [-] [ ]

—— In 1986, he guested on MIKE OLDFIELD'S album 'SHINE'.

Epic Epic

Jun 88. (7")(12") **HOLD ON TO LOVE. / SUN DANCING (FOR THE HOPI-NAVAJO ENERGY)** [ ] [ ]
(cd-s+=) – In a lifetime.

Jun 88. (lp)(c)(cd) **IN THE CITY OF ANGELS** [ ] [ ]
– Hold on to love / If it wasn't for love (oneness family) / Sun dancing (for the Hopi-Navajo energy) / Is it me / In a lifetime / For you / New civilization / It's on fire / Betcha / Top of the world (the glass bead game) / Hurry home (soon from the Pleiades).

Aug 88. (7") **IS IT ME. / TOP OF THE WORLD (GLASS BEAD GAME)** [ ] [ ]
(12"+=) – For you.

—— Later that year he provided vocals for charity 45 'WHATEVER YOU BELIEVE' accompanying STEVE HARLEY & MIKE BATT.

E.M.I. not issued

Oct 94. (7")(c-s) **CHANGE WE MUST. / STATE OF INDE-PENDENCE** [ ] [ ]
(cd-s+=) – ('A'mixes) / (interview).

STEVE HOWE

with in 1979; **PATRICK MORAZ** – keyboards / **ALAN WHITE + BILL BRUFORD + CLIVE BUNKER** – drums / **RONNIE LEAHY** – keyboards / **GRAHAM PRESKETT** – violin / **CLAIRE HAMILL** – vocals

Atlantic Atlantic

Oct 79. (lp)(c) **THE STEVE HOWE ALBUM** [68] [ ]
– Pennants / Cactus boogie / All's a chord / Look over your shoulder / Diary of a man who disappeared / Meadow rag / The continental / Surface tension / Double rondo / Concerto in D (second movement). *(re-iss.cd Oct94)*

Relativity Relativity

Jan 92. (cd)(c)(lp) **TURBULENCE** [ ] [ ]
– Turbulence / Hint hint / Running the human race / The inner battle / Novalis / Fine line / Sensitive chaos / Corkscrew / While Rome's burning / From a place where time runs slow.

Road-runner Road-runner

Sep 93. (cd)(c) **THE GRAND SCHEME OF THINGS** [ ] [ ]

Jun 95. Thunderbird-RPM; (cd) **NOT NECESSARILY ACOUSTIC** [ ] [-]

—— For RICK WAKEMAN releases, see under own solo entry.

Y KANT TORI READ (see under ⇒ AMOS, Tori)

Neil YOUNG

Born: 12 Nov'45, Toronto, Canada. Raised Winnipeg until 1966 when he drove to America in his Pontiac hearse. NEIL had cut his teeth in local instrumental outfit the SQUIRES, who released one '45 'THE SULTAN'. / 'AURORA' for 'V' records in Sep 63. The following year NEIL formed the MYNHA BIRDS and joined forces with RICKY JAMES MATTHEWS (later to become RICK JAMES). Although many songs were recorded, only one saw light of day; 'MYNHA BIRD HOP' for 'Columbia' Canada. They signed to 'Motown' (first white people to do so) but were soon dropped when they found out that RICKY had dodged the draft. Met up with past acquaintance STEPHEN STILLS and formed BUFFALO SPRINGFIELD. Constant rivalry, led to YOUNG departing for solo venture after signing for new label 'Reprise' in Spring '68. His eponymous debut with arranger/producer JACK NITSCHE, then DAVID BRIGGS, was finally issued early 1969. It's lukewarm response, forced him to bring in back-up band The ROCKETS, who renamed themselves CRAZY HORSE, for follow-up second album. Early 1970, while diversing activities with CROSBY, STILLS & NASH, he recorded his third, and most successful album to date 'AFTER THE GOLDRUSH'. By 1972, he was was top of US/UK lp charts with 'HARVEST'. Throughout the 70's, part of the 80's, and early 90's he became arguably, one of the most inventive and prolific songwriters. • **Style:** Country-rock artist, who fused together his brittle, high-pitched, quavering vox, with own distinct electric guitar sound. His best work, was always with backing from CRAZY HORSE, who by the late 70's on lp 'RUST NEVER SLEEPS', transpired to a more complete, harder electric sound. In the early 80's, his shift into more synthesized music, alienated most, but not all of his long-time fans. So far in the 90's, he's reverted to his old basic rock'n'roll style, pleasing audiences reminiscing on past mid-70's 'ZUMA' album. Late in 1992, he returned with The STRAY GATORS, on excellent 'HARVEST MOON', (his 20 year follow-up to 'HARVEST'). • **Songwriters:** As said, 99% of material in his own with contributions from CRAZY HORSE members, except; FARMER JOHN (Harris-Terry). The album 'EVERYBODY'S ROCKIN'' was full of covers. • **Trivia:** 'HEY HEY MY MY..' was written about SEX PISTOL Johnny Rotten.

Recommended: HARVEST (*10) / AFTER THE GOLDRUSH (*10) / RUST NEVER SLEEPS (*9) / ZUMA (*9) / HARVEST MOON (*9) / RAGGED GLORY (*8) / WELD (*9) / SLEEPS WITH ANGELS (*9) / MIRRORBALL (*8) / EVERYBODY KNOWS THIS IS NOWHERE (*8) / TONIGHT'S THE NIGHT (*8) / DECADE (*8)

NEIL YOUNG – vocals, guitar (ex-BUFFALO SPRINGFIELD) with **JIM MESSINA** – bass / session men, etc.

Reprise Reprise

Jan 69. (lp) **NEIL YOUNG** [ ] [ ]
– The Emperor of Wyoming / The loner / If I could have her tonight / I've been waiting for you / The old laughing lady / String quartet from Whiskey Boot Hill / Here we are in the years / What did I do to my life / I've loved her so long / The last trip to Tulsa. *(re-iss.1971) (cd-iss.1987)*

Mar 69. (7") **THE LONER. / SUGAR MOUNTAIN** [-] [ ]

Sep 69. (7") **THE LONER. / EVERYBODY KNOWS THIS IS NOWHERE** [ ] [-]

LOUD
Crazy Horse

NEIL YOUNG with CRAZY HORSE

with **DANNY WHITTEN** – guitar / **BILLY TALBOT** – bass / **RALPH MOLINA** – drums / **BOBBY NOTKOFF** – violin

Jul 69. (lp) **EVERYBODY KNOWS THIS IS NOWHERE** [ ] [24] May 69
– Cinnamon girl / Everybody knows this is nowhere / Round and round (it won't be long) / Down by the river / The losing end (when you're on) / Running dry (requiem for the rockets) / Cowgirl in the sand. *(re-iss.1971) (cd-iss.1988)*

1969. (7") **DOWN BY THE RIVER (edit). / THE LOSING END (WHEN YOU'RE ON)** [-] [ ]

— Late 1969, NEIL YOUNG was also added to CROSBY, STILLS, NASH (& YOUNG).

Aug 70. (7") **DOWN BY THE RIVER (edit). / CINNAMON GIRL (alt.take)** [ ] [-]

— **NILS LOFGREN** – guitar (of GRIN) repl. NOTKOFF

Aug 70. (7") **OH LONESOME ME (extended). / I'VE BEEN WAITING FOR YOU** [-] [ ]

Sep 70. (lp)(c) **AFTER THE GOLD RUSH** [7] [8]
– Tell me why / After the gold rush / Only love can break your heart / Southern man / Till the morning comes / Oh lonesome me / Don't let it bring you down / Birds / When you dance I can really love / I believe in you / After the goldrush / Cripple Creek ferry. *(re-iss.1971) (cd-iss.Jul87)*

Sep 70. (7") **OH LONESOME ME (extended). / SUGAR MOUNTAIN** [ ] [-]

Jun 70. (7") **CINNAMON GIRL (alt.mix). / SUGAR MOUNTAIN** [-] [55]

Oct 70. (7") **ONLY LOVE CAN BREAK YOUR HEART. / BIRDS** [ ] [33]

Jan 71. (7") **WHEN YOU DANCE I CAN REALLY LOVE. / SUGAR MOUNTAIN** [-] [93]

Feb 71. (7") **WHEN YOU DANCE I CAN REALLY LOVE. / AFTER THE GOLDRUSH** [ ] [-]

NEIL YOUNG

solo with The STRAY GATORS. (CRAZY HORSE recorded on own) musicians: **JACK NITZSCHE** – piano / **BEN KEITH** – steel guitar / **TIM DRUMMOND** – bass / **KENNY BUTTREY** – drums. Guests included **CROSBY, STILLS & NASH, LINDA RONSTADT, JAMES TAYLOR** plus The LONDON SYMPHONY ORCHESTRA

Feb 72. (7") **HEART OF GOLD. / SUGAR MOUNTAIN** [10] [1]

Mar 72. (lp)(c) **HARVEST** [1] [1]
– Out on the weekend / Harvest / A man needs a maid / Heart of gold / Are you ready for the country? / Old man / There's a world / Alabama / The needle and the damage done / Words (between the lines of age). *(cd-iss.May83)*

Apr 72. (7") **OLD MAN. / THE NEEDLE AND THE DAMAGE DONE** [ ] [31]

Jun 72. (7") **WAR SONG. ("NEIL YOUNG & GRAHAM NASH") / THE NEEDLE AND THE DAMAGE DONE** [-] [61]

— **JOHNNY BARBATA** – drums (ex-CROSBY, STILLS & NASH) repl. BUTTREY

Sep 73. (lp)(c) **TIME FADES AWAY (live)** [20] [22]
– Time fades away / Journey through the past / Yonder stands the sinner / L.A. / Love in mind / Don't be denied / The bridge / Last dance.

Oct 73. (7") **TIME FADES AWAY (live). / LAST TRIP TO TULSA (live)** [-] [ ]

— now used session people including **CRAZY HORSE** members **BEN KEITH** – steel guitar had now repl. WHITTEN who o.d.'d August 1972.

Jul 74. (7") **ON THE BEACH** [42] [16]
– Walk on / See the sky about to rain / Revolution blues / For the turnstiles / Vampire blues / On the beach / Motion pictures / Ambulance blues.

Jul 74. (7") **WALK ON. / FOR THE TURNSTILES** [ ] [69]

— Had just earlier 1974, re-united with CROSBY, STILLS & NASH ⇒ .

— Even earlier (late'73)

NEIL YOUNG with CRAZY HORSE

had recorded lp. Musicians: **NILS LOFGREN / BEN KEITH / BILLY TALBOT / RALPH MOLINA**

Jun 75. (lp)(c) **TONIGHT'S THE NIGHT** [48] [25]
– Tonight's the night (part I) / Speakin' out / World on a string / Borrowed tune / Come on baby let's go downtown / Mellow my mind / Roll another number (for the road) / Albuquerque / New mama / Lookout Joe / Tired eyes / Tonight's the night (part II). *(re-iss.cd Jul93)*

— (Mar75) **FRANK 'Poncho' SAMPEDRO** – guitar, vocals repl. KEITH + LOFGREN The latter earlier went solo, and later joined BRUCE SPRINGSTEEN band.

Nov 75. (lp)(c) **ZUMA** [44] [25]
– Don't cry no tears / Danger bird / Pardon my heart / Lookin' for a love / Barstool blues / Stupid girl / Drive back / Cortez the killer / Through my sails. *(re-iss.cd Jul93)*

Mar 76. (7") **LOOKIN' FOR A LOVE. / SUGAR MOUNTAIN** [ ] [ ] Dec 75

Mar 76. (7") **DRIVE BACK. / STUPID GIRL** [-] [ ]

May 76. (7") **DON'T CRY NO TEARS. / STUPID GIRL** [ ] [-]

— Mid 1976, he teamed up as STILLS-YOUNG BAND with STEPHEN STILLS on album LONG MAY YOU RUN. (see under ⇒ CROSBY, STILLS, NASH & YOUNG)

Jun 77. (lp)(c) **AMERICAN STARS'N'BARS** [17] [21]
– The old country waltz / Saddle up the Palomino / Hey babe / Hold back the tears / Bite the bullet / Star of Bethlehem / Will to love / Like a hurricane / Homegrown.

Jul 77. (7") **HEY BABE. / HOMEGROWN** [-] [ ]

Sep 77. (7") **LIKE A HURRICANE (edit). / HOLD BACK THE TEARS** [ ] [ ]

NEIL YOUNG

solo with loads on session incl.**NICOLETTE LARSON** – vox

Oct 78. (7") **COMES A TIME. / MOTORCYCLE MAMA** [-] [ ]

Oct 78. (lp)(c) **COMES A TIME** [42] [7]
– Goin' back / Comes a time / Look out for my love / Lotta love / Peace of mind / Human highway / Already one / Field of opportunity / Motorcycle mama / Four strong winds. *(re-iss.cd Jul93)*

Nov 78. (7") **FOUR STRONG WINDS. / MOTORCYCLE MAMA** [57] [-]

Dec 78. (7") **FOUR STRONG WINDS. / HUMAN HIGHWAY** [-] [61]

NEIL YOUNG with CRAZY HORSE

(YOUNG w / **SAMPEDRO, TALBOT & MOLINA)**

Jun 79. (lp)(c) **RUST NEVER SLEEPS** [13] [8]
– My my, hey hey (out of the blue) / Thrasher / Ride my llama / Pocahontas / Sail away / Powderfinger / Welfare mothers / Sedan delivery / Hey hey, my my (into the black). *(re-iss.Oct81) (re-iss.cd Jul93)*

Aug 79. (7") **HEY HEY, MY MY (INTO THE BLACK). / MY MY, HEY HEY (OUT OF THE BLUE)** [ ] [79]

Nov 79. (d-lp)(d-c) **LIVE RUST (live)** [55] [15]
– Sugar mountain / I am a child / Comes a time / After the gold rush / My my, hey hey (out of the blue) / When you dance I can really love / The loner / The needle and the damage done / Lotta love / Sedan delivery / Powderfinger / Cortez the killer / Cinnamon girl / Like a hurricane / Hey hey, my my (into the black) / Tonight's the night. *(re-iss.Oct81) (re-iss.cd Jul93)*

Dec 79. (7") **CINNAMON GIRL (live). / THE LONER (live)** [-] [ ]

NEIL YOUNG

solo with **TIM DRUMMOND + DENNIS BELFIELD** – bass / **LEVON HELM + GREG THOMAS** – drums / **BEN KEITH** – steel, dobro / **RUFUS THIBODEAUX** – fiddle

Oct 80. (lp)(c) **HAWKS & DOVES** [34] [30]
– Little wing / The old homestead / Lost in space / Captain Kennedy / Stayin' power / Coastline / Union power / Comin' apart at every nail / Hawks & doves.

Nov 80. (7") **HAWKS & DOVES. / UNION MAN** [ ] [ ]

Feb 81. (7") **STAYIN' POWER. / CAPTAIN KENNEDY** [-] [ ]

NEIL YOUNG with CRAZY HORSE

(see last CRAZY HORSE line-up)

Oct 81. (lp)(c) **RE• AC• TOR** [69] [27]
– Opera star / Surfer Joe and Moe the sleaze / T-bone / Get back on it / Southern Pacific / Motor city / Rapid transit / Shots.

Nov 81. (7")(10"sha-red-d) **SOUTHERN PACIFIC. / MOTOR CITY** [-] [70]

Jan 82. (7") **OPERA STAR. / SURFER JOE AND MOE THE SLEAZE** [-] [ ]

NEIL YOUNG

solo adding synthesizers, drum machine (sessioners) **BRUCE PALMER** – bass (ex-BUFFALO SPRINGFIELD)

Geffen Geffen

Jan 83. (7") **LITTLE THING CALLED LOVE. / WE'R IN CONTROL** [ ] [71] Dec 82

Jan 83. (lp)(c) **TRANS** [29] [19]
– Little thing called love / Computer age / We'r in control / Transformer man / Computer cowboy (aka Syscrusher) / Hold on to your love / Sample and hold / Mr. Soul / Like an Inca. *(re-iss.Sep86)*

Feb 83. (7") **MR. SOUL. / MR. SOUL (part 2)** [-] [ ]
(12") – ('A'extended) / Sample and hold (extended).

NEIL YOUNG & The SHOCKING PINKS

w / **BEN KEITH** – guitar / **TIM DRUMMOND** – bass / **KARL HIMMEL** – drums / **LARRY BYROM** – piano, vocals / **RICK PALOMBI + ANTHONY CRAWFORD** – b.vocals

Sep 83. (lp)(c) **EVERYBODY'S ROCKIN'** [50] [46] Aug 83
– Betty Lou's got a new pair of shoes / Rainin' in my heart / Payola blues / Wonderin' / Kinda fonda Wanda / Jellyroll man / Bright lights, big city / Cry, cry, cry / Mystery train / Everybody's rockin'. *(re-iss.Sep86, cd-iss.1988)*

Sep 83. (7") **WONDERIN'. / PAYOLA BLUES** [ ] [ ]

Oct 83. (7") **CRY, CRY, CRY. / PAYOLA BLUES** [-] [ ]

— Jul85, with country singer WILLIE NELSON he duets on his ARE THERE ANY MORE REAL COWBOYS single issued on 'Columbia'.

NEIL YOUNG

solo again with loads of session people.

Aug 85. (lp)(c) **OLD WAYS** [39] [75]
– The wayward wind / Get back to the country / Are there any more real cowboys? / Once an angel / Misfits / California sunset / Old ways / My boy / Bound for glory / Where is the highway tonight?.

Sep 85. (7") **BACK TO THE COUNTRY. / MISFITS** [-] □

Nov 85. (7") **OLD WAYS. / ONCE AN ANGEL** [-] □

—— w / **STEVE JORDAN** – drums, synths, vox / **DANNY KORTCHMAR** – guitar, synth

Aug 86. (lp)(c)(cd) **LANDING ON WATER** [52] [46]
– Weight of the world / Violent side / Hippie dream / Bad news beat / Touch the night / People on the street / Hard luck stories / I got a problem / Pressure / Drifter. *(re-iss.Apr91)*

Sep 86. (7")(12") **WEIGHT OF THE WORLD. / PRESSURE** □ □ Jul86

NEIL YOUNG & CRAZY HORSE

(see last **CRAZY HORSE, + BRYAN BELL** – synth)

May 87. (lp)(c)(cd) **LIFE** [71] [75]
– Mideast vacation / Long walk home / Around the world / Inca queen / Too lonely / Prisoners of rock'n'roll / Cryin' eyes / When your lonely heart breaks / We never danced.

Jun 87. (7") **MIDEAST VACATION. / LONG WALK HOME** [-] □

Jun 87. (7") **LONG WALK HOME. / CRYIN' EYES** □ [-]

NEIL YOUNG & THE BLUENOTES

with **SAMPEDRO** – keyboards plus others **CHAD CROMWELL** – drums / **RICK ROSAS** – bass / **STEVE LAWRENCE** – tenor sax / **BEN KEITH** – alto sax / **LARRY CRAIG** – baritone sax / **CLAUDE CAILLIET** – trombone / **JOHN FUMO** – trumpet / **TOM BRAY** – trumpet

Reprise Reprise

Apr 88. (7") **TEN MEN WORKIN'. / I'M GOIN'** [-] □

May 88. (lp)(c)(cd) **THIS NOTE'S FOR YOU** [56] [61]
– Ten men workin' / This note's for you / Coupe de ville / Life in the city / Twilight / Married man / Sunny inside / Can't believe you're lyin' / Hey hey / One thing. *(re-iss.cd Feb95)*

May 88. (7") **THIS NOTE'S FOR YOU (live). / THIS NOTE'S FOR YOU** [-] □

—— Nov88, NEIL re-joined CROSBY, STILLS, NASH & YOUNG for 'AMERICAN DREAM' lp.

NEIL YOUNG

solo again with **SAMPEDRO, ROSAS, CROMWELL,** etc.

Oct 89. (lp)(c)(cd) **FREEDOM** [17] [35]
– Rockin' in the free world / Crime in the city (sixty to zero part 1) / Don't cry / Hangin' on a limb / Eldorado / The ways of love / Someday / On Broadway / Wreckin' ball / No more / Too far gone / Rockin' in the free world (live). *(re-iss.cd/c Feb95)*

Apr 90. (7") **ROCKIN' IN THE FREE WORLD. / ('A'live version)** □ □ Oct 89
(UK-12"+=)(cd-s+=) – Cocaine eyes.

NEIL YOUNG & CRAZY HORSE

with **SAMPEDRO, TALBOT + MOLINA**

Sep 90. (cd)(c)(lp) **RAGGED GLORY** [15] [31]
– Country home / White line / Fuckin' up / Over and over / Love to burn / Farmer John / Mansion on the hill / Days that used to be / Love and only love / Mother Earth (natural anthem). *(re-iss.cd/c Feb95)*

Sep 90. (cd-s) **MANSION ON THE HILL (edit) / MANSION ON THE HILL / DON'T SPOOK THE HORSE** [-] □

Oct 91. (d-cd)(d-c)(d-lp) **WELD (live)** [20] □
– Hey hey, my my (into the black) / Crime in the city / Blowin' in the wind / Live to burn / Welfare mothers / Cinnamon girl / Mansion on the hill / F+!£in' up / Farmer John / Cortez the killer / Powderfinger / Love and only love / Roll another number / Rockin' in the free world / Like a hurricane / Tonight's the night. (free-cd-ep w.a.+=) – ARC EP – (feedback).

NEIL YOUNG

solo, with The STRAY GATORS (**KENNY BUTTREY, TIM DRUMMOND, BEN KEITH & SPOONER OLDHAM**) plus **JAMES TAYLOR, LINDA RONSTADT, NICOLETTE LARSON, ASTRID YOUNG & LARRY CRAGG** – backing vocals

Oct 92. (cd)(c)(lp) **HARVEST MOON** [9] [16]
– Unknown legend / From Hank to Hendrix / You and me / Harvest moon / War of man / One of these days / Such a woman / Old king / Dreamin' man / Natural beauty.

Feb 93. (7")(c-s) **HARVEST MOON. / WINTERLONG** [36] □
(cd-s+=) – Deep forbidden lake / Campaigner.
(cd-s) – ('A'side) / Old king / The needle and the damage done / Goin' back.

Jun 93. (cd)(c)(lp) **UNPLUGGED** [4] [23]
– The old laughing lady / Mr.Soul / World on a string / Pocahontas / Strongman / Like a hurricane / The needle and the damage done / Helpless / Harvest Moon / Transformer man / Unknown legend / Look out for my love / Long may you run / From Hank to Memphis.

Jul 93. (7")(c-s) **THE NEEDLE AND THE DAMAGE DONE (live). / YOU AND ME** [75] □
(cd-s+=) – From Hank to Hendrix.

Oct 93. (7")(c-s) **LONG MAY YOU RUN (live). / SUGAR MOUNTAIN (live)** [71] □
(cd-s+=) – Cortez the killer (live) / Cinnamon girl (live).

Feb 94. (7")(c-s) **ROCKIN' IN THE FREE WORLD. / ('A'mixes)** □ □
(cd-s+=) – Weld.

Apr 94. (cd-s) **PHILADELPHIA / SUCH A WOMAN / STRINGMAN (unplugged)** [62] □

—— Above 'A'side was another to be taken from the film 'Philadelphia' on 'Epic'.

NEIL YOUNG & CRAZY HORSE

Aug 94. (cd)(c)(d-lp) **SLEEPS WITH ANGELS** [2] [9]
– My heart / Prime of life / Drive by / Sleeps with angels / Western hero / Change your mind / Blue Eden / Safeway cart / Train of love / Trans Am / Piece of crap / A dream that can last.

Aug 94. (c-s)(cd-s) **PIECE OF CRAP / TONIGHT'S THE NIGHT** □ □

Oct 94. (c-s)(cd-s) **MY HEART / ROLL ANOTHER NUMBER (FOR THE ROAD)** □ □
(cd-s+=) – Tired eyes.

Nov 94. (c-s) **CHANGE YOUR MIND / SPEAKIN' OUT** □ □
(cd-s+=) – ('A'full version).

Neil YOUNG

—— with backing from all of PEARL JAM; 8th track written w/ EDDIE VEDDER

Warners Warners

Jun 95. (cd)(c)(lp) **MIRROR BALL** [4] [5]
– Song x / Act of love / I'm the ocean / Big green country / Truth be known / Downtown / What happened yesterday / Peace and love / Throw your hatred down / Scenery / Fallen angel.

Sep 95. (c-s) **DOWNTOWN / BIG GREEN COUNTRY** □ □
(cd-s+=) – ('A'-lp version).

. . . Jan – Jun '96 stop press . . .

Feb 96. (cd) **Music From And Inspired By The Motion Picture DEAD MAN** □ □

—— above was instrumental YOUNG, and based on Jim Jarmusch's film starring Johnny Depp.

NEIL YOUNG AND CRAZY HORSE

Jun 96. (cd)(c)(lp) **BROKEN ARROW** [17] □

– compilations, others, etc. –

Note; on 'Reprise' until otherwise stated.

1971. (7") **CINNAMON GIRL (alt.mix). / ONLY LOVE CAN BREAK YOUR HEART** [-] □

Nov 72. (d-lp)(d-c) **JOURNEY THROUGH THE PAST (Soundtrack featuring live & rare material with past bands)** □ [45]
– For what it's worth – Mr. Soul / Rock & roll woman / Find the cost of freedom / Ohio / Southern man / Are you ready for the country / Let me call you sweetheart / Alabama / Words / Relativity invitation / Handel's Messiah / King of kings / Soldier / Let's go away for a while.

Jan 73. (7") **HEART OF GOLD. / OLD MAN** [-] □

Mar 74. (7") **ONLY LOVE CAN BREAK YOUR HEART. / AFTER THE GOLDRUSH** □ [-]

May 74. (7"ep) **SOUTHERN MAN / TILL MORNING COMES. / AFTER THE GOLDRUSH / HEART OF GOLD** □ [-]

Nov 77. (t-lp) **DECADE** [46] [43]
– Down to the wire + Burned + Mr.Soul + Broken arrow + Expecting to fly (BUFFALO SPRINGFIELD) / Sugar mountain / I am a child / The loner / The old laughing lady / Cinnamon girl / Down by the river / Cowgirl in the sand / I believe in you / After the goldrush / Southern man / Helpless + Ohio (CROSBY, STILLS, NASH & YOUNG) / A man needs a maid / Harvest / Heart of gold / Star of Bethlehem / The needle and the damage done / Tonight's the night (part 1) / Turnstiles / Winterlong / Deep forbidden lake / Like a hurricane / Love is a rose / Cortez the killer / Campaigner / Long may you run (w / STEPHEN STILLS). *(re-iss.d-cd Jul93)*

Jan 78. (7") **SUGAR MOUNTAIN. / THE NEEDLE AND THE DAMAGE DONE** [-] □

Oct 82. (d-c) **NEIL YOUNG / EVERYBODY KNOWS THIS IS NOWHERE** □ [-]

Oct 82. (d-c) **AFTER THE GOLDRUSH / HARVEST** □ [-]

Feb 87. (cd) **THE BEST OF NEIL YOUNG** □ □

Jan 93. Movieplay Gold; (cd) **THE LOST TAPES** □ [-]

Jan 93. Geffen; (cd)(c) **LUCKY THIRTEEN** (80's material) 69 ☐
– Sample and hold / Transformer man / Depression blues / Get gone / Don't take your love away from me / Once an angel / Where is the highway tonight / Hippie dream / Pressure / Around the world / East vacation / Ain't it the truth / This note's for you.

— Note that 1980's 'Where The Buffalo Roam' film contained several YOUNG songs

Frank ZAPPA

Born: 21 Dec'40, Baltimore, Maryland, USA. From Sicilian and Greek parents, who moved to California in 1950. In 1956, he formed The BLACKOUTS with school chum DON VAN VLIET (aka CAPTAIN BEEFHEART). After marrying in the late 50's, he wrote a soundtrack for B-movie 'The World's Greatest Sinner'. In 1963, after writing another B-movie soundtrack 'Run Home Slow', he set up own Studio Z. He also initiated local groups The MASTERS and The SOUL GIANTS, who recorded some extremely rare 45's. In 1964, he was arrested and sentenced to 10 days in prison and put on probation for 3 years, having made a pornographic tape. He moved to Los Angeles and formed again The SOUL GIANTS who soon became The MOTHERS OF INVENTION. Early in 1966, after a residency at The Whiskey A-Go-Go, they were signed to 'MGM' by producer Tom Wilson. Their debut album (a double!) 'FREAK OUT!' peaked at No.130 in the States. Later in 1967 their follow-up 'ABSOLUTELY FREE', nearly scratched the Top 40, and on 23 Sep'67, they played London's Albert Hall with a 15-piece orchestra. ZAPPA and the MOTHERS continued as a unit throughout the late 60's and early 70's, with ZAPPA also maintaining a solo career. After many more albums, in the 80's he tragically died of prostate cancer on 4th Dec '93. • **Style:** Avant-garde satirical rocker, who mixed together psychedelia, doo-wop and sexually explicit lyrics. ZAPPA was never typecast into any one style, and sometimes his brilliant guitar picking was overlooked on his more eccentric jazz and modern classical albums. • **Songwriters:** ZAPPA compositions, augmented by MOTHERS. Covered WHIPPING BOY (Allman Brothers Band) / STAIRWAY TO HEAVEN (Led Zeppelin) / etc. • **Trivia:** In 1969, he married for a second time and soon was the father of sons Dweezil (who became a singer in the 80's), AHMET RODAN, and daughters MOON UNIT and DIVA. In 1976, ZAPPA produced GRAND FUNK on their lp 'Good Singin', Good Playin''.

Recommended: FREAK OUT (*9) / ABSOLUTELY FREE (*8) / WE'RE ONLY IN IT FOR THE MONEY (*8) / HOT RATS (*9) / ZOOT ALLURES (*8) / TINSEL TOWN REBELLION (*8) / THEM OR US (*9) / THING FISH (*6) / STRICTLY COMMERCIAL – THE BEST OF FRANK ZAPPA (*9)

The MOTHERS OF INVENTION

FRANK ZAPPA – guitar, vocals / with **RAY COLLINS** – vocals (had been temp.repl. by JIM GUERCIO; later a producer) / **ELLIOTT INGBER** – guitar repl. STEVE MANN who had repl. HENRY VESTINE. Before he moved onto CANNED HEAT he had repl. MOTHERS original ALICE STUART. / **ROY ESTRADA** – bass / **JIM BLACK** – drums

Verve | Verve-MGM

1966. (7") **HELP, I'M A ROCK. / HOW COULD I BE SUCH A FOOL?** [-] [ ]

Nov 66. (7") **IT CAN'T HAPPEN HERE. / HOW COULD I BE SUCH A FOOL?** [ ] [-]

1966. (7") **TROUBLE EVERY DAY. / WHO ARE THE BRAIN POLICE?** [-] [ ]

Mar 67. (lp) **FREAK OUT!** [ ] [ ] Aug 66
– Hungry freaks, daddy / I ain't got no heart / Who are the brain police? / Go cry on somebody else's shoulder * / Motherly love / How could I be such a fool * / Wowie Zowie / You didn't try to call me / Any way the wind blows * / I'm not satisfied / You're probably wondering why I'm here / Trouble every day / Help, I'm a rock / The return of the son of monster magnet. *(US d-lp+= *)* (UK re-iss.Dec71 as d-lp) (cd-iss.Oct87 on 'Zappa'UK /'Rykodisc'US) (re-iss.cd/c May95 on Rykodisc')

— **JIM FIELDER** – guitar repl. INGBER who joined FRATERNITY OF MAN. He later changed his name and joined CAPTAIN BEEFHEART / added **BILLY MUNDI** – drums / **DON PRESTON** – keyboards / **BUNK GARDNER** – horns

Apr 67. (7") **BIG LEG EMMA. / WHY DON'T YOU DO ME RIGHT?** [ ] [ ]

Oct 67. (lp) **ABSOLUTELY FREE** [ ] [41] May 67
– Plastic people / The Dukes of Prunes / Amnesia vivace / The Duke regains his chops / Call any vegetable / Invocation and ritual dance of the young pumpkin / Soft-cell conclusion and ending of side 1 / America drinks / Status back baby / Uncle Bernie's farm / Son of Suzy Creamcheese / Brown shoes don't make it / America drinks and goes home. *(re-iss.Jun72) (cd-iss.Jan89 on 'Zappa' UK / 'Rykodisc' US version +=) (re-iss.cd/c May95 on 'Rykodisc' +=)* – Big leg Emma / Why don'tcha do me right?.

— **ZAPPA, ESTRADA, MUNDI, PRESTON, GARDNER & JIMMY CARL BLACK** recruited **JIM 'Motorhead' SHERWOOD** – sax (ex-roadie) repl. FIELDER to BUFFALO SPRINGFIELD / **IAN UNDERWOOD** – piano, wind repl. COLLINS

Dec 67. (7") **MOTHER PEOPLE. / LONELY LITTLE GIRL (version)** [-] [ ]

Jun 68. (lp) **WE'RE ONLY IN IT FOR THE MONEY** [32] [30] Jan 68
– Are you hung up? / Who needs the peace corps? / Concentration Moon / Mom and dad / Telephone conversation / Bow tie daddy / Harry, you're a beast / What's the ugliest part of your body? / Absolutely free / Flower punk / Hot poop / Nasal retentive calliope music / Let's make the water turn black / The idiot bastard son / Lonely little girl / Take your clothes off when you dance / What's the ugliest part of your body (reprise) / Mother people / The chrome plated megaphone of destiny. *(re-iss.Jun72) (cd-iss.Dec88 on 'Zappa' UK / Oct87 on 'Rykodisc') (re-iss.cd/c/lp Apr95 on 'Rykodisc')*

— (now with The ABNUCEALS EMUUKHA ELECTRIC SYMPHONY ORCHESTRA & CHORUS; a 50+ piece orchestra incl. some MOTHERS)

Oct 68. (lp) **LUMPY GRAVY ("FRANK ZAPPA" solo)** [ ] [ ] May 68
– Lumpy gravy (part one): The way I see it, Barry – Duodenum – Oh no – Bit of nostalgia – It's from Kansas – Bored out 90 over – Almost Chinese – Switching girls – Oh no again – At the gas station – Another pickup – I don't know if I can go through this again / Lumpy gravy (part two): Very distrautening – White ugliness – Amen – Just one more time – A vicious circle – Kink Kong – Drums are too noisy – Kangaroos – Envelopes the bath tub – Take your clothes off. *(re-iss.Jun72) (cd-iss.Apr95 on 'Rykodisc')*

Dec 68. (7") **DESERI. / JELLY ROLL GUM DROP** [-] [ ]

— (above single and below album credited to **"RUBEN AND THE JETS"**)

— **ARTHUR TRIPP III** – drums repl. MUNDI who formed RHINOCEROS / added again **RAY COLLINS** – vocals

Feb 69. (lp) **CRUISING WITH RUBEN & THE JETS** [ ] [ ] Nov 68
– Cheap thrills / Love of my life / How could I be such a fool / Deseri / I'm not satisfied / Jelly roll gum drop / Anything / Later that night / You didn't try to call me / Fountain of love / No no no / Anyway the wind blows * / Stuff up the cracks. *(re-iss.Jun73) (cd-iss.Oct87 on 'Zappa' UK/'Rykodisc' US) (re-iss.cd May95 on 'Rykodisc')*

— added **BILLY MUNDI** – drums / **RUTH KOMANOFF** (UNDERWOOD) – marimba, vibes / **NELCY WALKER** – soprano vocals

Trans-atlantic | Bizarre

Sep 69. (d-lp) **UNCLE MEAT** [ ] [43] Apr 69
– Uncle Meat (main title theme) / The voice of cheese / Nine types of industrial pollution / Zolar Czakl / Dog breath in the year of the plague / The legend of the golden arches / Louie Louie (at the Royal Albert Hall in London) / The dog breath variations / Sleeping in a jar / Our bizarre relationship / The Uncle Meat variations / Electric Aunt Jemima // Prelude to King Kong / God bless America (live at the Whisky A Go Go) / A pound for a brown on the bus / Ian Underwood whips it out (live on stage in Copenhagen) / Mr.Green genes / We can shoot you / If we'd all been living in California / The air / Project X / Cruising for burgers / Uncle Meat film excerpt part 1 * / Tengo na minchia tanta * / Uncle Meat film excerpt part II * / King Kong itself (as played by The Mothers in a studio) / King Kong II (it's magnificence as interpreted by Dom Dewild) / King Kong III (as Motorhead explains it) / King Kong IV (the Gardner varieties) / King Kong V (as played by 3 deranged good humor trucks) / King Kong VI (live on a flat bed diesel in the middle of a race track at a Miami pop festival . . . the Underwood ramifications). *(d-cd iss.Oct87 on 'Zappa' += *) (re-iss.d-cd/c May 95 on 'Rykodisc')*

Sep 69. (7") **MY GUITAR. / DOG BREATH** [-] [ ]

FRANK ZAPPA

solo w/**IAN UNDERWOOD / LOWELL GEORGE** – guitar / **JEAN-LUC PONTY** – violin (solo artist) / **SUGAR-CANE HARRIS** – vocals / **MAX BENNETT + SHUGGY OTIS** – bass / **PAUL HUMPHREY + RON SELICO** – drums

Reprise Bizarre

Jan 70. (7") **PEACHES EN REGALIA. / LITTLE UMBRELLAS** [-] [ ]

Feb 70. (lp)(c) **HOT RATS** [9] [ ] Oct 69
– Peaches en regalia / Willie the wimp / Son of Mr.Green genes / Little umbrellas / The Gumbo variations / It must be a camel. *(re-iss.Sep70 + Jul71) (remixed cd-iss.Oct87 on 'Zappa') (re-iss.cd/c May95 on 'Rykodisc')*

The MOTHERS OF INVENTION

(see last line-up) added **BUZZ GARDNER** – horns / **SUGAR-CANE HARRIS** – vocals

Mar 70. (lp)(c) **BURNT WEENIE SANDWICH** [17] [94] Feb 70
– WPLJ / Ivor's boogie – phase 1 / Overture to a holiday in Berlin / Theme from Burnt Weenie Sandwich / Igor's boogie – phase 2 / Holiday in Berlin, full blown / Aybe sea / The little house I used to live in / Valarie. *(re-iss.Sep70 & Jul71) (cd-iss.Nov91 on 'Zappa') (re-iss.cd May95 on 'Rykodisc')*

Mar 70. (7") **WPLJ. / MY GUITAR** [-] [ ]

Sep 70. (lp)(c) **WEASELS RIPPED MY FLESH** [28] [ ]
– Didja get any onya? / Directly from my heart to you / Prelude to the afternoon of a sexually aroused gas mask / Toads of the short forest / Get a little / Eric Dolphy memorial barbecue / Dwarf Nebula processional march and dwarf Nebula / My guitar wants to kill your mama / oh no / The Orange County lumber truck / Weasels ripped my flesh. *(re-iss.Jul71) (cd-iss.May95 on 'Rykodisc')*

— (above album used rare material from 1967-69, as The MOTHERS OF INVENTION officially disbanded Oct69).

— LOWELL and ROY formed LITTLE FEAT. ART TRIPP became ED MARIMBA and joined CAPTAIN BEEFHEART & HIS MAGIC BAND. BUNK GARDNER and JIMMY CARL BLACK formed GERONIMO BLACK.

FRANK ZAPPA

formed solo band with **IAN UNDERWOOD, SUGAR-CANE HARRIS & MAX BENNETT.** He introduced **JEFF SIMMONS** – guitar, bass / **JOHN GUERIN** – drums / **AYNSLEY DUNBAR** – drums / **GEORGE DUKE** – keyboards, trombone / **MARK VOLMAN + HOWARD KAYLAN** (aka The PHLORESCENT LEECH AND EDDIE) – vocals (ex-TURTLES)

Nov 70. (lp)(c) **CHUNGA'S REVENGE** [43] [ ]
– Transylvania boogie / Road ladies / Twenty small cigars / The Nancy and Mary music (part 1, 2 & 3) / Tell me you love me / Would you go all the way? / Chunga's revenge / Rudy wants to buy yez a drink / The clap / Sharleena. *(re-iss.Jul71) (cd-iss.May95 on 'Rykodisc')*

Nov 70. (7") **TELL ME YOU LOVE ME. / WOULD YOU GO ALL THE WAY?** [-] [ ]

The MOTHERS

re-formed early 1971. Re-instated **DON PRESTON** – keys. Recruited **JIM PONS** – bass (ex-TURTLES) / **BOB HARRIS** – keyboards

Aug 71. (lp)(c) **FILLMORE EAST – JUNE 1971 (live)** [ ] [38]
– Little house I used to live in / The mud shark / What kind of girl do you think we are? / Bwana Dik / Latex solar beef / Willie the wimp (part 1) / Do you like my new car? / Happy together / Lonesome electric turkey / Peaches en regalia / Tears began to fall. *(re-iss.cd/c May 95 on 'Rykodisc')*

FRANK ZAPPA & THE MOTHERS OF INVENTION

Aug 71. (7") **TEARS BEGAN TO FALL. / JUNIER MINTZ BOOGIE** [ ] [ ]

FRANK ZAPPA

solo, with MOTHERS:- **IAN + RUTH UNDERWOOD / GEORGE DUKE / AYNSLEY DUNBAR / VOLMAN + KAYLAN / MARTIN LICKERT** – bass / guests were **JIM PONS + JIMMY CARL BLACK / THEODORE BIKEL** – narrator + ROYAL PHILHARONIC

United Art United Art

Oct 71. (d-lp) **200 MOTELS (live studio soundtrack)** [ ] [59]
– Semi-fraudulent – Direct-from-Hollywood overture / Mystery roach / Dance of the rock & roll interviewers / This town is a sealed tuna sandwich (prologue) / Tuna fish promenade / Dance of the just plain folks / This town is a sealed tuna fish sandwich (reprise) / The sealed tuna bolero / Lonesome cowboy Burt / Tiuring can make you crazy / Would you like a snack? / Redneck eats / Centerville / She painted up her face / Janet's big dance number / Half a dozen provocative squats / Mysterioso / Shove it right in / Lucy's seduction of a bored violinist & postlude / I'm stealing the towels / Dental hygeine dilemma / Does this kind of life look interesting to you? / Daddy, daddy, daddy / Penis dimension / What will this evening bring me this morning / A nun suit painted on some old boxes / Magic fingers / Motorhead's midnight ranch / Dew on the newts we got / The lad searches the night for his newts / The girl wants to fix him some broth / The girl's dream / Little green scratchy sweaters & corduroy ponce / Strictly genteel (the finale). *(re-iss.+d-c.Jan89 on 'MCA')*

Oct 71. (7") **MAGIC FINGERS. / DADDY, DADDY, DADDY** [-] [ ]

Nov 71. (7") **WHAT WILL THIS EVENING BRING ME THIS MORNING?. / DADDY, DADDY, DADDY** [ ] [-]

Aug 72. (lp)(c) **WAKA / JAWAKA** [ ] [ ] 
– Big Swifty / Your mouth / It just might be a one-shot deal / Waka-Jawaka. *(cd-iss.Jan89 on 'Zappa') (re-iss.cd May95 on 'Rykodisc')*

— (above featured **PRESTON, DUNBAR, DUKE, SIMMONS** & others also on next).

The MOTHERS

recorded live 7th August'71. (see last ZAPPA line-up) Re-formed earlier that year.

Reprise Bizarre

Jun 72. (lp)(c) **JUST ANOTHER BAND FROM L.A.** [ ] [85]
– Billy the mountain / Call any vegetable / Eddie, are you kidding? / Magdalena / Dog breath. *(cd-iss.May95 on 'Rykodisc')*

— The MOTHERS added **TONY DURAN** – slide guitar / **ERRONEOUS** – bass repl. SIMMONS / **KEN SHROYER** – trombone / **JOEL PESKIN** – tenor saxophone / **SAL MARQUEZ** – timpani / **BILL BYERS** – trombone / **MIKE ALTSCHUL** – wind / **JANET NEVILLE-FERGUSON** – vocals / **CHUNKY** – vocals / **EARL DUMLER, FRED JACKSON + TONY ORTEGA** – wind / **ERNIE WATTS** – sax / **ERNIE TACK + MALCOLM McNABB** – horns / **JOHNNY ROTELLA, BOB ZIMMITTI + LEE CLEMENT** – percussion / **JOANNE CALDWELL McNABB** – violin

Dec 72. (lp)(c) **THE GRAND WAZOO** [ ] [ ]
– The grand Wazoo / For Calvin (and his next two hitch-hikers) / Cletus-awreetus-awrightus / Eat that question / Blessed relief. *(cd-iss.Sep86 & May95 on 'Rykodisc')*

Dec 72. (7") **CLETUS-AWREETUS-AWRIGHTUS. / EAT THAT QUESTION** [-] [ ]

— **ZAPPA** brought back **IAN + RUTH UNDERWOOD** (They were on '72 tour) / **GEORGE DUKE / JEAN-LUC PONTY / SAL MARQUEZ.** He introduced **TOM FOWLER** – bass / **BRUCE FOWLER** – trombone / **RALPH HUMPHREY** – drums

Discreet Discreet

Jan 73. (lp) **OVERNITE SENSATION** [ ] [32]
– Camarillo brillo / I'm the slime / Dirty love / Fifty-fifty / Zomby woof / Dinah-Moe humm / Montana. *(cd-iss.Oct87 w / 'APOSTROPHE' tracks on 'Rykodisc') (re-iss.cd/c Apr95 on 'Rykodisc')*

Feb 73. (7") **I'M THE SLIME. / MONTANA** [-] [ ]

FRANK ZAPPA

solo retaining current MOTHERS except RUTH. He also brought back past MOTHERS: **AYNSLEY DUNBAR / RAY COLLINS / ERRONEOUS / JOHN GUERIN / SUGAR CANE HARRIS / RUBEN GUEVARA + ROBERT CAMARENA** – b.vocals (of RUBEN &..JETS) **NAPOLEON BROCK** – saxophone / guest **JACK BRUCE** – bass (ex-CREAM)

May 74. (lp)(c) **' (APOSTROPHE)** [ ] [10] Apr 74
– Don't eat the yellow snow / Nanook rubs it / St.Alphonso's pancake breakfast / Father O'Blivion / Cosmik debris / Excentrifugal forz / Apostrophe / Uncle

Remus / Stink-foot. *(cd-iss.see last lp) (re-iss.cd/c Apr95 on 'Rykodisc')*

Aug 74. (7") **DON'T EAT THE YELLOW SNOW. / COSMIK DEBRIS** - 86

Aug 74. (7") **COSMIK DEBRIS. / UNCLE REMUS** -

Sep 74. (7") **DON'T EAT THE YELLOW SNOW. / CAMARILLO BRILLO** -

ZAPPA / MOTHERS

were now basically **GEORGE DUKE / TOM FOWLER / NAPOLEON / RUTH UNDERWOOD** and new drummer **CHESTER THOMPSON**. Temp. old members were also used **DON PRESTON / BRUCE FOWLER / JEFF SIMMONS + RALPH HUMPHREY**

Oct 74. (d-lp) **ROXY & ELSEWHERE (live + unreleased)** 27 Sep 74

– Preamble / Penguin in bondage / Pygmy twylyte / Dummy up / Preamble / Village of the sun / Echidna's arf (of you) / Don't you ever wash that thing? / Preamble / Cheepnis / Son of Orange County / More trouble every day / Be-bop tango (of old Jazzmen's church). *(re-iss.1977) (cd-iss.Feb92 on 'Zappa') (re-iss.cd/c May95 on 'Rykodisc')*

FRANK ZAPPA AND THE MOTHERS OF INVENTION

— temp.members above repl. by **JOHNNY GUITAR WATSON** – guitar / **JAMES YOUMAN** – bass / **BLOODSHOT ROLLIN RED** (DON WATSON) – harmonica

Aug 75. (lp)(c) **ONE SIZE FITS ALL (live)** 26

– Inca roads / Can't afford no shoes / Sofa No.1 / Po-jama people / Florentine pogen / Evelyn, a modified dog / San Ber'dino / Andy / Sofa No.2. *(cd-iss.Jan89 on 'Zappa') (re-iss.cd May95 on 'Rykodisc')*

Sep 75. (7") **STINK-FOOT. / DU BIST MEIN SOFA** -

FRANK ZAPPA and CAPTAIN BEEFHEART / MOTHERS

collaborated with also **G.DUKE / B.+ T.FOWLER / N.BROCK / C.THOMPSON** plus **TERRY BOZZIO** – drums / **DENNY WHALLEY**

Nov 75. (lp) **BONGO FURY (live + 2 studio)** - 66

– Debra Kadabra / Caroline hard-core ecstasy / Sam with the showing scalp flat top / Poofter's froth Wyoming plans ahead / 200 years old / Cucamonga / Advance romance / Man with the woman head / Muffin man. *(cd-iss.Jan89 on 'Zappa') (re-iss.cd May95 on 'Rykodisc')*

FRANK ZAPPA

finally disbanded The MOTHERS and went solo. Augmented by **TERRY BOZZIO** – drums / **ROY ESTRADA, DAVE PARLATO + RUTH UNDERWOOD** – bass / **DAVEY MOIRE** – b.vocals / **LU ANN NEIL** – harp

Warners Warners

Oct 76. (7") **FIND HER FINER. / ZOOT ALLURES** -

Nov 76. (lp)(c) **ZOOT ALLURES** 61

– Wind up workin' in a gas station / Black napkins / The torture never stops / Ms. Pinky / Find her finer / Friendly little finger / Wonderful wino / Zoot allures / Disco boy. *(cd-iss.Jun90 on 'Zappa') (re-iss.cd May95 on 'Rykodisc')*

Dec 76. (7") **DISCO BOY. / MS. PINKY** -

— His basic band were **EDDIE JOBSON** – keyboards, violin (ex-ROXY MUSIC) / **RAY WHITE** – guitar, vocals / **PAT O'HEARN** – bass / **RUTH UNDERWOOD** - / **TERRY BOZZIO** – drums. Plus brass section – **RANDY + MICHAEL BRECKER / LOU MARINI / RONNIE CUBER / TOM MALONE / DAVID SAMUELS** – percussion

Discreet Discreet

Jun 78. (d-lp) **ZAPPA IN NEW YORK (live 1976)** 55 57

– Titties & beer / Cruisin' for burgers * / I promise not to come in your mouth / Punky's whips / Honey, don't you want a man like me? / The Illinois enema bandit // I'm the slime * / Pound for a brown * / Manx needs women / The black page drum solo – Black page #1 / Big leg Emma / Sofa / Black page #2 / The torture never stops * / The purple lagoon – approximate. *(d-cd-iss.1990 May95 on 'Rykodisc' += *)*

— He retained only **BOZZIO + O'HEARN,** bringing back **NAPOLEON, ANDRE LEWIS + MOIRE.** New musicians:- **ADRIAN BELEW** – rhythm guitar, some lead vox / **TOMMY MARS** – keyboards, vocals / **PETER WOLF** – keyboards / **ED MANN** – percussion, vocals / **RANDY THORNTON** – b.vocals / **DAVID OCKER** – clarinet (1)

C.B.S. Zappa

Mar 79. (d-lp)(d-c) **SHIEK YERBOUTI** 32 21

– I have been in you / Flakes / Broken heart are for assholes / I'm so cute / Jones crusher / What ever happened to all the fun in the world / Rat tomago / We've gotta get into something real / Bobby Brown / Rubber shirt / The Sheik Yerbouti tango / Baby snakes / Tryin' to grow a chin / City of tiny lites / Dancin' fool / Jewish princess / Yo' mama. *(re-iss.Feb86 on 'EMI') (cd-iss.Apr88) (re-iss.cd/c May95 on 'Rykodisc')*

Apr 79. (7") **DANCIN' FOOL. / BABY SNAKES** 45

— **WARREN CUCURILLO** – rhythm guitar repl. BELEW (later to BOWIE + TALKING HEADS) /**IKE WILLIS** – lead vocals repl. MARS / **ARTHUR BARROW** – bass repl. O'HEARN / **VINNIE COLAIUTA** – drums repl. TERRY BOZZIO. Others in line-up **DALE BOZZIO** – vocals / **DENNIS WHALLEY** – slide guitar / **MARGINAL CHAGRIN** – sax / **WOLF + MANN.**

Sep 79. (lp)(c) **JOE'S GARAGE ACT I** 62 27

– Central scrutinizer / Joe's garage / Catholic girls / Crew slut / Wet T-shirt nite / Toad-o-line / Why does it hurt when I pee? / Lucille has messed my mind up. *(US cd-iss.Oct87 on 'Rykodisc'; UK May95)*

Jan 80. (7") **JOE'S GARAGE. / CENTRAL SCRUTINIZER** -

Jan 80. (7") **JOE'S GARAGE. / CATHOLIC GIRLS** -

Jan 80. (d-lp)(d-c) **JOE'S GARAGE ACT II & III** 75 53

– ACT II:- A token of my extreme / Stick it out / Sy Borg / Dong work for Yuda / Keep it greasey / Outside now / ACT III:- He used to cut the grass / Packard goose / Watermelon in Easter hay / A little green Rosetta. *(US d-cd-iss.Oct87 on 'Rykodisc'; UK May95 w/ ACT I)*

Jun 80. (7") **I DON'T WANT TO GET DRAFTED. / ANCIENT ARMAMENTS**

— added **STEVE VAI + RAY WHITE** – rhythm guitar, vocals / **TOMMY MARS** – keyboards

C.B.S. B.Pumpkin

May 81. (d-lp)(d-c) **TINSELTOWN REBELLION (live)** 55 66

– Fine girl / Easy meat / For the young sophisticate / Love of my life / I ain't got no heart / Panty rap / Tell me you love me / Now you see it – now you don't / Dance contest / The blue light / Tinseltown rebellion / Pick me, I'm clean / Bamboozled by love / Brown shoes don't make it / Peaches III. *(re-iss.Feb86 on 'EMI') (d-cd-iss.Apr88) (cd-iss.Jun90 on 'Zappa') (re-iss.cd May95 on 'Rykodisc')*

— **JIMMY CARL BLACK** – drums returned to repl. RAY WHITE

Oct 81. (d-lp)(d-c) **YOU ARE WHAT YOU IS** 51 93

– Teenage wind / Harder than your husband / Doreen / Goblin girl / Theme from the 3rd movement of sinister footwear / Society pages / I'm a beautiful guy / Beauty knows no pain / Charlie's enormous mouth / Any downers? / Conehead / You are what you is / Mudd club / The meek shall inherit nothing / Dumb all over / Heavenly bank account / Suicide chump / Jumbo go away / If only she woulda / Drafted again. *(re-iss.Feb86 on 'EMI') (d-cd-iss.Apr88) (cd-iss.Jun90 on 'Zappa') (re-iss.cd May95 on 'Rykodisc')*

Nov 81. (12"pic-d) **GOBLIN GIRL. / PINK NAPKINS** -

Feb 82. (7") **YOU ARE WHAT YOU IS. / HARDER THAN YOUR HUSBAND**

(12"pic-d+=) – Pink napkins / Soup'n'old clothes.

— added **SCOTT THUNES** – bass / **CHAD WACKERMAN** – drums / **BOBBY MARTIN** – keys, sax

Jun 82. (lp)(c) **SHIP ARRIVING TO LATE TO SAVE A DROWNING WITCH** 61 23

– No not now / Valley girl / I come from nowhere / Drowning witch / Envelopes / Teen-age prostitute. *(free 7"w.a.)* – SHUT UP 'N' PLAY YER GUITAR (excerpts) *(lp re-iss.Feb86 on 'EMI') (re-iss.Jun87 on 'Fame') (cd-iss.Aug91 on 'Zappa') (re-iss.cd May95 on 'Rykodisc')*

Aug 82. (7") **VALLEY GIRL. ("FRANK & MOON ZAPPA" his daughter) / TEENAGE PROSTITUTE** 32 Jul 82

(re-iss.12"/cd-s Jul93 on 'Zappa')

— **ROY ESTRADA** – falsetto + **BOB HARRIS** – soprano returned to repl. WOLF / **MARTY KRYSTAL** – sax / **DICK PEGY** – mandolin / **CRAIG STEWARD** – harmonica repl. WHALLEY

Jun 83. (lp)(c) **THE MAN FROM UTOPIA** 87

– Cocaine decisions / Sex / Tink walks amok / The radio is broken / We are not alone / The dangerous kitchen / The man from Utopia meets Mary Lou / Stick together / The jazz discharge party hats / Luigi & the wise guys * / Moggio. *(re-iss.Feb86 on 'EMI') (re-iss.Apr88 on 'Fame') (cd-iss.Feb93 on 'Zappa' += *) (re-iss.cd May95 on 'Rykodisc')*

— **JOHNNY GUITAR WATSON + NAPOLEON MURPHY BROCK** – vocals repl. BOB + VINNIE

E.M.I. E.M.I.

Sep 84. (7") **BABY TAKE YOUR TEETH OUT. / STEVIE'S SPANKING**

Oct 84. (d-lp)(d-c) **THEM OR US** 53

– The closer you are / In France / Ya hozna / Sharleena / Sinister footwear II / Truck driver divorce / Stevie's spanking / Baby take your teeth out / Marqueson's chicken / Planet of my dreams / Be in my video / Them or us / Frogs with dirty, little lips / Whippin' post. *(cd-iss.Apr88) (re-iss.cd May95 on 'Rykodisc')*

— **ZAPPA** with band: **VAI, MARS, WHITE, MANN, WACKERMAN, BARROW, THUNES** plus **STEVE DE FURIA** – programming. Characters: **IKE WILLIS** (Thing Fish) / **TERRY BOZZIO** (Harry) / His wife **DALE BOZZIO** (Rhonda) / **NAPOLEON MURPHY BROCK** (The Prince) / **BOB HARRIS** (Harry as a boy) / **JOHNNY GUITAR WATSON** (Brown Moses) / **RAY WHITE** (Owl Gonkwin Jane Cowhoon)

E.M.I. Capitol

Mar 85. (t-lp)(d-c) **THING FISH**

– Prologue / The mammy nuns / Harry & Rhonda / Galoot up-date / The 'torchum never stops / That evil prince / You are what you is / Mudd club / The meek shall inherit nothing / Clowns on velvet / Harry-as-a-boy / He's so gay / The massive improve'lence / Artificial Rhonda / The crab-grass baby / The white boy troubles / No not now / Briefcase boogie / Wistful with a fist-full / Drop dead / Won ton on. *(d-cd-iss.Apr88) (d-cd-iss.Feb90 on 'Zappa') (re-iss.d-cd May95 on 'Rykodisc')*

— Musicians; as last but without BOZZIO's, ESTRADA, BARROW, BROCK,

HARRIS **BOBBY MARS** – vocals, keyboards repl. DE FURIA

Mar 86. (lp)(c)(cd) **FRANK ZAPPA MEETS THE MOTHERS OF PREVENTION** ☐ ☐
– I didn't even care * / One man one vote * / Little biege Sambo / Aerobics in bondage / We're turning again / Alien orifice / Aerobics in bondage / Yo' cats / What's new in Baltimore? / Porn wars / H.R. 2911 *. *(cd repl. Porn wars; w/ *) (cd-iss.May95 on 'Rykodisc')*

— **FRANK** still with **WILLIS, WACKERMAN, THUNES, MANN, MARTIN,** plus new **MIKE KENEALLY** – guitar, synth., vocals repl. VAI who went solo, etc. / **WALT FOWLER** – trumpet / **BRUCE FOWLER** – trombone / **PAUL CARMAN** – alto sax / **ALBERT WINO** – tenor sax / **KURT McGETTRICK** – baritone sax / guest vox – **ERIC BUXTON**

Zappa Zappa

Dec 88. (lp)(c)(cd) **BROADWAY THE HARD WAY (live)** ☐ ☐
– Elvis has just left the building / Planet of the baritone women / Any kind of pain / Dickie's such an asshole / When the lie's so big / Rhymin' man / Promiscuous / The untouchables / Why don't you like me? * / Bacon fat * / Stolen moments * / Murder by numbers * / Jezebel boy * / Outside now * / Hot plate heaven at the green hotel * / What kind of a girl? * / Jesus thinks you're a jerk. *(cd+= *) (re-iss.cd May95 on 'Rykodisc')*

— Late '91, it was announced FRANK had been diagnosed with prostrate cancer. He was to die of this on 4 Dec '93.

Feb 93. (12")(cd-s) **STAIRWAY TO HEAVEN. / BOLERO** ☐ ☐

Oct 93. (cd)(c) **YELLOW SHARK** ☐ ☐
– Intro / Dog breath variations / Uncle Meat / Outrage at Valdez / Times beach II / III revised / The girl in the magnesium dress / Be bop tango / Ruth is sleeping / None of the above / Pentagon afternoon / Questi cazzi di piccione / Times beach III / Food gathering in post industrial America 1992 / Welcome to the united States / Pound for a brown / Exercise 4 / Get Whitey / G-spot tornado. *(re-iss.cd/c May95 on 'Rykodisc')*

— an opera-pantomime with pre-recorded voices and music supplied by THE PIANO PEOPLE: **F.Z. / SPIDER / JOHN / MOTORHEAD / LARRY / ROY / LOUIS / MONICA / GILLY / GIRL 1 / GIRL 2 / MOON / MIKE / ALI / TODD / DARYL / JESUS**

Feb 95. (d-cd)(d-c) **CIVILIZATION PHAZE III** ☐ ☐
– ACT ONE; This is phaze III / Put a motor in yourself / Oh-umm / They made me eat it / Reagan at Bitburg / A very nice body / Navanax / How the pigs' music works / Xmas values / Dark water / Amnerika / Have you ever heard their band / Religious superstition / Saliva can only take so much / Buffalo voice / Someplace else ight now / Get a life / A kayak (on snow) / N-lite (I) Negative light (II) Venice submerged (III) The new world order (IV) The lifestyle you deserve (V) Creationism (VI) He is risen / / ACT TWO; I wish Motorhead would come back / Secular humanism / Attack! attack! attack! / I was in a drum / A different octave / This ain't CNN / The pigs' music / A pig with wings / This is all wrong / Hot & putrid / Flowing inside-out / I had a dream about that / Gross man / A tunnel into muck / Why not? / Put a little motor in 'em / You're just insultin' me, aren't you! / Cold light generation / Dio fa / That would be the end of that / Beat the reaper / Waffenspiel.

– compilations, others, etc. –

Apr 69. Verve; (lp)(c) **MOTHERMANIA: THE BEST OF THE MOTHERS** ☐ ☐
(re-iss.Feb72 & Mar73)

1975. Verve; (lp) **ZAPPA & THE MOTHERS: ROCK FLASHBACKS** ☐ ☐

Nov 78. Discreet; (lp) **STUDIO TAN (instrumental 74-76)** ☐ ☐
– The adventures of Greggery Peccary / Revised music for guitar and low budget orchestra / Let me take you to the beach / RDNZL. *(cd-iss.May95 on 'Rykodisc')*

Feb 79. Discreet; (lp)(c) **SLEEP DIRT (instrumental 74-76)** ☐ ☐
– Filthy habits / Flambay / Spider of destiny / Regymptian strut / Time is money / Sleep dirt / The ocean is the ultimate solution. *(cd-iss.May95 on 'Rykodisc')*

Jun 79. Discreet; (lp) **ORCHESTRAL FAVORITES (live 1975)** ☐ ☐
– Strictly genteel / Pedro's dowry / Naval aviation in art? / Duke of prunes / Bogus pomp. *(cd-iss.May95 on 'Rykodisc')*

— Next vocal-less **ZAPPA** – lead guitar plus usual ensemble.

Aug 82. CBS-Barking Pumpkin; (t-lp) **SHUT UP 'N PLAY YER GUITAR** (rec.1977-80 live) ☐ ☐
– Five, five, five / Hog heaven / Pink napkins / Stucco homes / Variations on the Carlos Santana secret chord progression / Gee I like your pants / Soup 'n old clothes / The deathless horsie / Shut up 'n play yer guitar (x2) / Heavy duty Judy / The return of shut up 'n play yer guitar / Canard du joir / While you were out / Pinocchio's furniture / Beat it with your fist / Why Johnny can't read / Canarsie / Treacherous cretins. *(re-iss.Apr88 on 'EMI') (d-cd-iss.Jan90 on 'Zappa') (re-iss.t-cd May95 on 'Rykodisc')*

Sep 82. CBS-Barking Pumpkin; (7") **SHUT UP 'N' PLAY YER GUITAR. / VARIATION ON THE C SANTANA SECRET** ☐ ☐

Feb 86. EMI/ US= Capitol; (cd) **DOES HUMOR BELONG IN MUSIC** ☐ ☐
(re-iss.Apr95 on 'Rykodisc')

Dec 86. (lp)(c) **JAZZ FROM HELL (instrumental live 1982)** ☐ ☐
– Night school / The Beltaway bandits / While you were art II / Jazz from Hell / G-spot tornado / Damp ankles / St.Etienne / Massaggio galore. *(d-cd-iss.of 1986 albums May88) (cd-iss.May95 on 'Rykodisc')*

Apr 88. EMI/ US= Capitol; (cd) **THE MAN FROM UTOPIA / SHIP ARRIVING TOO LATE TO SAVE..** ☐ -

Apr 88. CBS; (2xt-cd-box) **JOE'S GARAGE ACTS I / II / II / SHUT UP AND PLAY YER GUITAR** ☐ ☐

1986. Rykodisc; (d-cd) **WE'RE ONLY IN IT FOR THE MONEY / LUMPY GRAVY** ☐ ☐

Oct 87. Rykodisc; (cd) **APOSTROPHE / OVERNITE SENSATION** - ☐

Oct 87. Rykodisc; (3"cd-ep) **PEACHES EN REGALIA / I'M NOT SATISFIED / LUCILLE HAS MESSED UP MY MIND** - ☐

Apr 88. Rykodisc; (3"cd-s) **SEXUAL HARASSMENT IN THE WORKPLACE / WATERMELON IN EASTER HAY** - ☐

May 88. Rykodisc; (3"cd-s) **ZOMBY WOOF / YOU DIDN'T TRY TO CALL ME** - ☐

May 88. Rykodisc; (3"cd-s) **MONTANA (WHIPPING FLOSS) / CHEEPNIS** - ☐

Jul 87. Barking Pumpkin; (lp-box) **OLD MASTERS – BOX ONE** - ☐
– FREAK OUT / ABSOLUTELY FREE / WE'RE ONLY IN IT FOR THE MONEY / LUMPY GRAVY / CRUISIN' WITH RUBEN & THE JETS / (Mystery Disc – rare).

Jul 87. Barking Pumpkin; (lp-box) **OLD MASTERS – BOX TWO** - ☐
– UNCLE MEAT / HOT RATS / BURNT WEENIE SANDWICH / WEASELS RIPPED MY FLESH / CHUNGA'S REVENGE / LIVE AT THE FILLMORE EAST / JUST ANOTHER BAND FROM L.A. / (Mystery Disc – live in London 1968).

Nov 87. Barking Pumpkin; (lp-box) **OLD MASTERS – BOX THREE** - ☐
– OVERNITE SENSATION / ONE SIZE FITS ALL / WAKA JAWAKA / THE GRAND WAZOO / APOSTROPHE / BONGO FURY / ZOOT ALLURES / ROXY AND ELSEWHERE.

Jan 88. MFN/ US= Zappa; (lp)(c) **THE LONDON SYMPHONY ORCHESTRA VOL.II** ☐ ☐
– (out-takes from '200 Motels') Bob in Dacron / Strictly genteel / Bogus bomp (cd+=) – (2 extra tracks).

Apr 88. MFN/ US= Barking Pumpkin; (d-lp)(c)(d-cd) **GUITAR** (rec.live 1979-84) 82 ☐
– Sexual harassment in the workplace / Which one is it? * / Republicans / Do not pass go / Chalk pie * / In-a-gadda-Stravinsky * / That's not really reggae / When no one was no one / Once again, without the net / Outside now (original solo) / Jim and Tammy's upper room / Were we ever really safe in San Antonio? / That ol' G minor thing again / Hotel Atlanta incidentals * / That's not really a shuffle * / Move it or park it // Sunrise redeemer // Variations on sinister #3 * / Orrin Hatch on skis * / But who was Fulcanelli? / For Duane / Goa / Winos do not march / Swans? what swans? * / Too ugly for show business * / Systems of edges / Do not try this at home * / Things that look like meat / Watermelon in Easter hay / Canadian customs * / Is that all there is? * / It ain't necessarily the St.James Infirmary *. *(cd+= *) (re-iss.cd May95 on 'Rykodisc')*

Apr 88. Barking Pumpkin; (d-lp) **YOU CAN'T DO THAT ON STAGE ANYMORE** ☐ ☐
(d-cd-iss.Jan90) (re-iss.May95 on 'Rykodisc')

Oct 88. Zappa; (d-cd) **YOU CAN'T DO THAT ON STAGE ANYMORE VOL.2** ☐ ☐
(re-iss.May95 on 'Rykodisc')

Jan 89. Zappa; (cd) **BABY SNAKES** ☐ ☐
(re-is.May95 on 'Rykodisc')

Jan 90. Zappa; (d-cd) **JOE'S GARAGE ACT I / II / III** ☐ ☐
(re-iss.May95 on 'Rykodisc')

— FRANK decided to bootleg the bootleggers by releasing 10 best sellers that had fleeced him in the past. They were limited on 'Rhino'.

Apr 91. Zappa; (d-cd)(d-c)(d-lp) **THE BEST BAND YOU NEVER HEARD IN YOUR LIFE** ☐ ☐
(re-iss.May95 on 'Rykodisc')

Jun 91. Zappa; (d-cd)(d-c)(t-lp) **MAKE A JAZZ NOISE HERE** ☐ ☐
(re-iss.d-cd May95 on 'Rykodisc')

Jun 91. Zappa; (d-cd) **YOU CAN'T DO THAT ON STAGE ANYMORE VOL.3** ☐ ☐
(re-iss.d-cd May95 on 'Rykodisc')

Jun 91. Zappa; (d-cd)(dc)(d-lp) **YOU CAN'T DO THAT ON STAGE ANYMORE VOL.4** ☐ ☐
(re-iss.May95 on 'Rykodisc')

May 92. Zappa; (cd) **BOULEZ CONDUCTS ZAPPA: THE PERFECT STRANGER** ☐ ☐
(re-iss.May95 on 'Rykodisc')

May 92. Zappa; (cd) **FRANCESCO ZAPPA** ☐ ☐
(re-iss.May95 on 'Rykodisc')

Nov 92. Zappa; (cd) **PLAYGROUND PSYCHOTICS** ☐ ☐
(re-iss.May95 on 'Rykodisc')

Nov 92. Zappa; (d-cd) **YOU CAN'T DO THAT ON STAGE ANYMORE VOL.5** ☐ ☐
(re-iss.May95 on Rykodisc')

Nov 92. Zappa; (d-cd) **YOU CAN'T DO THAT ON STAGE ANYMORE VOL.6** ☐ ☐
(re-iss.May95 on 'Rykodisc')

Note; below releases on 'Essential' UK/ 'Zappa' US.

Sep 91. (cd)(lp) **AS AN AM**
Sep 91. (cd)(lp) **THE ARK (live Boston 1968)**
Sep 91. (cd)(lp) **FREAKS & MOTHERFU*£'%!**
Sep 91. (cd)(lp) **UNMITAGATED AUDACITY**
Sep 91. (d-cd)(d-lp) **ANYWAY THE WIND BLOWS**
Sep 91. (cd)(d-lp) **SAARBRUCKEN 1978**
Sep 91. (cd)(lp) **PIQUANTIQUE**
Sep 91. (cd)(lp) **L.S.D. VOL. 1** -
Apr 95. Rykodisc; (d-cd) **LONDON SYMPHONY ORCHESTRA VOLUMES 1 & 2**
May 95. Rykodisc; (cd) **AHEAD OF THEIR TIME**
May 95. Sonora; (cd; w/mag) **MAGAZINE & CD**
Aug 95. Rykodisc; (cd)(c)(d-lp) **STRICTLY COMMERCIAL (THE BEST OF FRANK ZAPPA)** 45
– Peaches en regalia / Don't eat the yellow snow / Dancin' fool / San Ber'dino / Dirty love / My guitar wants to kill your mama / Cosmik debris / Trouble every day / Disco boy / Fine girl / Sexual harassment in the workplace / Let's make the water turn black / I'm the slime / Joe's garage / Bobby Brown goes down / Montana / Valley girl / Be in my video / Muffin man.
. . .Jan-Jun'96 stop press compilation . . .
Feb 96. Rykodisc; (cd) **THE LOST EPISODES**

ZEE (see under ⇒ PINK FLOYD)

ZOO (see under ⇒ FLEETWOOD MAC)

ZZ TOP

Formed: Houston, Texas, USA . . . as The MOVING SIDEWALKS by BILLY GIBBONS. The now famous trio/line-up finally emerged in 1970, when HILL and BEARD joined them. After one-off 45 on manager BILLY HAM's new 'Scat' label, they moved to 'London' where they stayed for 8 years. In this time they built up huge following which stemmed from supporting many huge acts (i.e. STONES). After new contract with 'Warners' during the early 80's, they suffered slight lull, but took off worldwide especially in UK when 'ELIMINATOR' and its 45's hit charts. • **Style:** Powerful Southern hard-rocking boogie and blues trio, who featured the cultivated beards of GIBBONS and HILL (FRANK BEARD didn't have one!). • **Songwriters:** Group penned (plus some early w / manager BILL HAM) except; FRANCINE (trad.) / JAILHOUSE ROCK + VIVA LAS VEGAS (hits; Elvis Presley) / I THANK YOU (Isaac Hayes) / DUST MY BROOM (Elmore James) / etc. • **Trivia:** On the 1st Jan'85, HILL accidentally shot himself in the stomach but he soon recovered.

Recommended: GREATEST HITS (*9) / ELIMINATOR (*8) / TRES HOMBRES (*7) / FANDANGO (*7) /

MOVING SIDEWALKS

BILLY GIBBONS (b.12 Dec'49) – vocals, guitar / **TOM MOORE** – keyboards / **DON SUMMERS** – bass / **DAN MITCHELL** – drums

not issued / Tantara
1967. (7") **99th FLOOR. / WHAT ARE YOU GOING TO DO?** -
(re-iss.1967 on 'Wand')

not issued / Wand
1967. (7") **NEED ME. / EVERY NIGHT A NEW SURPRISE** -
(above tracks were re-iss.1980 as EP on 'Movie' US)

—— **LANIER GREIG** – keyboards repl. MOORE

not issued / Tantara
1968. (7") **I WANT TO HOLD YOUR HAND. / JOE BLUES** -
1968. (lp) **FLASH** -
– Flashback / Crimson witch / Pluto -Sept.31 / Eclipse / Scoun da be / No good to cry / You don't know the life / You make me shake / Reclipse.
1969. (7") **FLASHBACK. / NO GOOD TO CRY** -

ZZ TOP

(GIBBONS, MITCHELL & GREIG)

not issued / ScatLondon
1970. (7") **SALT LICK. / MILLER'S FARM** -

—— **GIBBONS** now sole survivor when LANIER and DAN departed. Newcomers were **DUSTY HILL** (b.JOE, 1949) – bass, vocals (ex-WARLOCKS, ex-AMERICAN BLUES) / **FRANK BEARD** (b.10 Dec'49) – drums (ex-CELLAR DWELLARS)

London / London
Jan 71. (lp) **FIRST ALBUM** -
– (Somebody else been) Shakin' your tree / Brown sugar / Squank / Goin' down to Mexico / Old man / Neighbor, neighbor / Certified blues / Bedroom thang / Just got back from baby's / Backdoor love affair. *(UK-iss.+c.Sep84 on 'Warners', cd-iss.Jan87) (cd-iss.Mar94 on 'Warners')*
Feb 71. (7") **(SOMEBODY ELSE BEEN) SHAKIN' YOUR TREE. / NEIGHBOR, NEIGHBOR** -
May 72. (7") **FRANCENE. / FRANCENE (Spanish)** - 69
Jul 72. (lp) **RIO GRANDE MUD** Apr 72
– Francene / Just got paid / Mushmouth shoutin' / Ko ko blue / Chevrolet / Apologies to Pearly / Bar-b-q / Sure got cold after the rain fell / Whiskey'n mama / Down Brownie. *(re-iss.+c.Sep84 on 'Warners', cd-iss.Jan87) (cd-iss.Mar94 on 'Warners')*
Jul 72. (7") **FRANCENE. / DOWN BROWNIE** -
Nov 73. (lp)(c) **TRES HOMBRES** 8 Aug 73
– Waitin' for the bus / Jesus just left Chicago / Beer drinkers & Hell raisers / Master of sparks / Hot, blue and righteous / Move me on down the line / Precious and Grace / La Grange / Shiek / Have you heard?. *(re-iss.cd+c Mar94 on 'Warners')*
Jun 74. (7") **BEER DRINKERS & HELL RAISERS. / LA GRANGE** -
Jan 75. (7") **LA GRANGE. / JUST GOT PAID** 41 Mar 74
Jun 75. (lp)(c) **FANDANGO! (live Warehouse, New Orleans + studio)** 60 10 May 75
– Thunderbird / Jailhouse rock / Back door medley / Nasty dogs and funky kings / Blue jean blues / Balinese / Mexican blackbird / Heard it on the X / Tush. *(re-iss.Nov83 on 'Warners', cd-iss.Jan87) (re-iss.cd+c Mar94 on 'Warners')*
Jul 75. (7") **TUSH. / BLUE JEAN BLUES** 20
Aug 76. (7") **IT'S ONLY LOVE. / ASLEEP IN THE DESERT** 44
Feb 77. (lp)(c) **TEJAS** 17 Jan 77
– It's only love / Arrested for driving while blind / El Diablo / Snappy kakkie / Enjoy and get it on / Ten dollar man / Pan Am highway blues / Avalon hideaway / She's a heartbreaker / Asleep in the desert. *(re-iss.Sep84 on 'Warners', cd-iss.Mar87) (cd-iss.Mar94 on 'Warners')*
Mar 77. (7") **ARRESTED FOR DRIVING WHILE BLIND. / IT'S ONLY LOVE** - 91
Apr 77. (7") **ARRESTED FOR DRIVING WHILE BLIND. / NEIGHBOR, NEIGHBOR** -
May 77. (7") **EL DIABLO. / ENJOY AND GET IT ON** -
Dec 77. (lp)(c) **THE BEST OF ZZ TOP** (compilation) 94
– Tush / Waitin' for the bus / Jesus just left Chicago / Francene / Just got paid / La grange / Blue jean blues / Backdoor love affair / Beer drinkers and Hell raisers / Heard it on the X. *(re-iss.Dec83 on 'Warners', cd-iss.Jan86)*

Warners / Warners
Dec 79. (lp)(c) **DEGUELLO** 24 Nov 79
– I thank you / She loves my automobile / I'm bad, I'm nationwide / A fool for your stockings / Manic mechanic / Dust my broom / Lowdown in the street / Hi-fi mama / Cheap sunglasses / Esther be the one. *(re-iss.+cd Jan85) (re-iss.cd+c Mar94 on 'Warners')*
Mar 80. (7") **I THANK YOU. / A FOOL FOR YOUR STOCKINGS** 34 Jan 80
Jun 80. (7") **CHEAP SUNGLASSES. / ESTHER BE THE ONE** 89
Jul 81. (7") **LEILA. / DON'T TEASE ME** - 77
Jul 81. (lp)(c) **EL LOCO** 88 17
– Tube snake boogie / I wanna drive you home / Ten foot pole / Leila / Don't tease me / It's so hard / Pearl necklace / Groovy little hippy pad / Heaven, Hell or Houston / Party on the patio. *(cd-iss.Mar87) (cd-iss.Mar94 on 'Warners')*
Jan 82. (7") **TUBE SNAKE BOOGIE. / HEAVEN, HELL OR HOUSTON** -
Jun 83. (7")(7"sha-pic-d) **GIMME ALL YOUR LOVIN'. / IF I COULD ONLY FLAG HER DOWN** 61 37 Mar 83
(12") – ('A'side) / Jesus just left Chicago / Heard it on the x / Arrested for driving while blind. *(re-iss.UK Sep84, hit No.10)*
Jun 83. (lp)(c) **ELIMINATOR** 3 9 Apr 83
– Gimme all your lovin' / Got me under pressure / Sharp dressed man / I need you tonight / I got the six / Legs / Thug / TV dinners / Dirty dog / If I could only flag her down / Bad girl. *(cd-iss.1984) (pic-lp Aug85) (re-iss.cd+c Mar94)*
Nov 83. (7") **SHARP DRESSED MAN. / I GOT THE SIX** 53 56 Jul 83
(12"+=) – La Grange. *(re-iss.UK Sep84, hit No.22)*
Mar 84. (7")(12") **TV DINNERS. / CHEAP SUNGLASSES** 67
(d12"+=)(c-s+=) – A fool for your stockings / Legs.
Feb 85. (7") **LEGS (remix). / BAD GIRL** 16 8 May 84
(12") – ('A'side) / La grange / A fool for your stocking
Jul 85. (d7")(12"ep)(c-ep) **THE ZZ TOP SUMMER HOLIDAY EP** 51
– Beer drinkers and Hell raisers / I'm bad, I'm nationwide / Tush / Got me under pressure.
Oct 85. (7")(7"sha-pic-d)(7"interlocking jigsaw pic-d pt.1) **SLEEPING BAG. / PARTY ON THE PATIO** 27 8
(d7"+=) – Sharp dressed man / I got the six.
Nov 85. (lp)(c)(cd) **AFTERBURNER** 2 4
– Sleeping bag / Stages / Woke up with wood / Rough boy / Can't stop rockin' / Planet of women / I got the message / Velcro fly / Dipping low (in the lap of luxury) / Delirious. *(re-iss.cd+c Mar94)*
Feb 86. (7")(7"jigsaw pic-d pt.2) **STAGES. / HI-FI MAMA** 43 21 Jan 86
(12"+=) – ('A'version).
Apr 86. (7")(7"pic-d)(7"jigsaw pic-d pt.3) **ROUGH BOY. / DELIRIOUS** 23 22 Mar 86
(12"shrinkwrapped to free jigsaw 'SLEEPING BAG' pic-d+=) – Legs (mix)
Aug 86. (7") **VELCRO FLY. / CAN'T STOP ROCKIN'** - 35
Sep 86. (7") **VELCRO FLY. / WOKE UP WITH WOOD** 54 -

LOUD
VERY LOUD
EXTREME PAIN

(12"+=) – Can't stop rockin' ('86 remix).
Jul 90. (7")(12")(c-s) **DOUBLEBACK. / PLANET OF WOMEN** [29] [50] May 90
(cd-s+=) – ('A'-AOR mix).
Oct 90. (cd)(c)(lp) **RECYCLER** [8] [6]
– Concrete and steel / Lovething / Penthouse eyes / Tell it / My head's in Mississippi / Decision or collision / Give it up / 2000 blues / Burger man / Doubleback. *(re-iss.cd+c Mar94)*
Nov 90. (7")(c-s) **GIVE IT UP. / SHARP DRESSED MAN** [ ] [79] Jan 91
(12"+=)(cd-s+=) – Cheap sunglasses (live).
Apr 91. (7")(c-s)(7"sha-pic-d) **MY HEAD'S IN MISSISSIPPI. / A FOOL FOR YOUR STOCKINGS** [37] [ ]
(12"+=)(cd-s+=) – Blue Jean blues.
Mar 92. (7")(c-s) **VIVA LAS VEGAS. / 2000 BLUES** [10] [ ]
(cd-s+=) – Velcro fly / Stages / Legs.
May 92. (cd)(c)(lp) **GREATEST HITS** (compilation) [5] [9]
– Gimme all your lovin' / Sharp dressed man / Rough boy / Tush / My head's in Mississippi / Pearl necklace / I'm bad, I'm nationwide / Viva Las Vegas / Doubleback / Gun love / Got me under pressure / Give it up / Cheap sunglasses / Sleeping bag / Planet of women / La Grange / Tube snake boogie / Legs.
Jun 92. (7")(c-s) **ROUGH BOY. / VIVA LAS VEGAS (Remix)** [49] [ ]
(cd-s+=) – Velcro fly (extended) / Doubleback (AOR mix).
(cd-s) – ('A'side) / TV dinners / Jesus has just left Chicago / Beer drinkers and Hell raisers.
R.C.A. R.C.A.
Jan 94. (7")(c-s) **PINCUSHION. / CHERRY RED** [15] [ ]
(cd-s+=) – ('A'mix).
Jan 94. (cd)(c)(lp) **ANTENNA** [3] [14]
– Pincushion / Breakaway / World of swirl / Fuzzbox voodoo / Girl in a T-shirt / Antenna head / Pch / Cherry red / Cover your rig / Lizard life / Deal goin' down / Everything.
Apr 94. (c-s)(12")(cd-s) **BREAKAWAY. / MARY'S** [60] [ ]
. . . Jan – Jun '96 stop press . . .
Jun 96. (single) **WHAT'S UP WITH THAT** [58] [ ]

– other compilations, etc. –

Nov 83. Warners; (d-c) **TRES HOMBRES / FANDANGO** [ ] [-]
1987. (3xcd-box) **FIRST ALBUM / RIO GRANDE MUD/ / TRES HOMBRES / FANDANGO!/ / TEJAS / EL LOCO** [ ] [ ]
Nov 94. Warners; (cd)(c) **ONE FOOT IN THE BLUES** [ ] [ ]

The 1990s Great Rock Survey

Who are the best groups/artists... and what are the best songs of the 90s?

In the second edition of THE GREAT ROCK DISCOGRAPHY I launched a competition to find the best bands and best tracks in the history of rock. The response was phenomenal – our post bag bulged like Russell Grant's corset – and the results and winners are printed in the third edition. Being a glutton for punishment I've decided to do it all again – this time, however, our search is restricted to music from the 90s.

Below is a chart (1990–1995) culled from readers' listings in the original Great Rock Survey. This is how your entries should look (without the points in the brackets!) – five tracks for each of your top ten artists and three tracks for each of the next ten. IN ADDITION to these, you can also choose up to 50 bonus tracks in groups of ten. Points will be awarded as follows:

- your top 50 tracks will be awarded between 100 and 51 points (e.g. in the example below, R.E.M.'s "Losing my Religion" would receive 100 points, while "Signe" by Eric Clapton would get 51)
- the next 30 tracks (for artists 11–20) will be awarded between 50 and 21 points
- bonus tracks, arranged in tens, will be graded points between 10 and 1.

You can pick any track released in the 90s up to the end of 1996 (by either new or old artists) – although a single from 1990 on an album from 1989 will not count. Also excluded are remixes, compilation tracks and exploitation releases of tracks recorded before the 90s. Obviously JIMI HENDRIX, THE DOORS and ELVIS PRESLEY should not feature in your lists. I think you know why. The lists will be printed in THE GREAT ROCK DISCOGRAPHY: FOURTH EDITION.

There will also be a prize for the person who can predict – or come nearest to – the top 10 groups/artists. She or he will receive every new edition of THE GREAT ROCK DISCOGRAPHY for as long as they can keep breathing.

So, send in your surveys and top 10 predictions right away: I'd like to receive them before 1 February 1997 – entries arriving on, or after, this date will not be taken into account. Only one entry per household will be accepted. Please send your listings to:

The 90s Great Rock Survey, Canongate Books, 14 High Street, Edinburgh EH1 1TE.

1 R.E.M.
1. **LOSING MY RELIGION** (2958)
2. **MAN ON THE MOON** (1592)
3. **EVERYBODY HURTS** (1536)
4. **DRIVE** (1353)
5. **THE SIDEWINDER SLEEPS TONIGHT** (1165)

2 OASIS
1. **LIVE FOREVER** (1281)
2. **WONDERWALL** (1230)
3. **SUPERSONIC** (1162)
4. **ROCK'N'ROLL STAR** (701)
5. **CHAMPAGNE SUPERNOVA** (682)

3 U2
1. **ONE** (1644)
2. **THE FLY** (628)
3. **MYSTERIOUS WAYS** (522)
4. **ZOOROPA** (334)
5. **EVEN BETTER THAN THE REAL THING** (216)

4 NIRVANA
1. **SMELLS LIKE TEEN SPIRIT** (1015)
2. **LITHIUM** (632)
3. **COME AS YOU ARE** (615)
4. **HEART-SHAPED BOX** (530)
5. **DUMB** (459)

5 PEARL JAM
1. **ALIVE** (1168)
2. **BETTER MAN** (608)
3. **BLACK** (566)
4. **EVEN FLOW** (537)
5. **DAUGHTER** (509)

6 QUEEN
1. **THE SHOW MUST GO ON** (1038)
2. **INNUENDO** (916)
3. **HEADLONG** (308)
4. **HITMAN** (185)
5. **THESE ARE THE DAYS OF OUR LIVES** (161)

7 NEIL YOUNG
1. **HARVEST MOON** (639)
2. **I'M THE OCEAN** (628)
3. **CHANGE YOUR MIND** (609)
4. **MANSION ON THE HILL** (525)
5. **LOVE TO BURN** (465)

8 BLUR
1. **GIRLS AND BOYS** (696)
2. **PARKLIFE** (617)
3. **TO THE END** (603)
4. **THE UNIVERSAL** (586)
5. **END OF A CENTURY** (390)

9 NICK CAVE
1. **MERCY SEAT** (703)
2. **PAPA WON'T LEAVE YOU HENRY** (543)
3. **THE WEEPING SONG** (513)
4. **THE SHIP SONG** (399)
5. **BROTHER MY CUP IS EMPTY** (342)

10 ERIC CLAPTON
1. **TEARS IN HEAVEN** (1301)
2. **ALBERTA** (432)
3. **SAN FRANCISCAN BAY BLUES** (424)
4. **MALTED MILK** (157)
5. **SIGNE** (142)

11 METALLICA
1. **ENTER SANDMAN** (725)
2. **THE UNFORGIVEN** (506)
3. **WHEREVER I MAY ROAM** (369)

12 PULP
1. **COMMON PEOPLE** (562)
2. **BABIES** (476)
3. **DO YOU REMEMBER THE FIRST TIME** (470)

13 PINK FLOYD
1. **HIGH HOPES** (923)
2. **KEEP TALKING** (449)
3. **COMING BACK TO LIFE** (319)

14 BRUCE SPRINGSTEEN
1. **STREETS OF PHILADELPHIA** (799)
2. **HUMAN TOUCH** (456)
3. **57 CHANNELS (AND NOTHING ON)** (197)

15 CROWDED HOUSE
1. **FOUR SEASONS IN ONE DAY** (608)
2. **WEATHER WITH YOU** (436)
3. **DISTANT SUN** (333)

16 RADIOHEAD
1. **FAKE PLASTIC TREES** (466)
2. **CREEP** (427)
3. **JUST** (415)

17 PET SHOP BOYS
1. **GO WEST** (668)
2. **CAN YOU FORGIVE HER** (421)
3. **I WOULDN'T NORMALLY DO THIS KIND OF THING** (313)

18 GUNS N' ROSES
1. **NOVEMBER RAIN** (612)
2. **CIVIL WAR** (394)
3. **ESTRANGED** (341)

19 SOUNDGARDEN
1. **BLACK HOLE SUN** (592)
2. **FELL ON BLACK DAYS** (399)
3. **4th OF JULY** (312)

20 PIXIES
1. **PLANET OF SOUND** (506)
2. **IS SHE WEIRD?** (384)
3. **DIG FOR FIRE** (349)

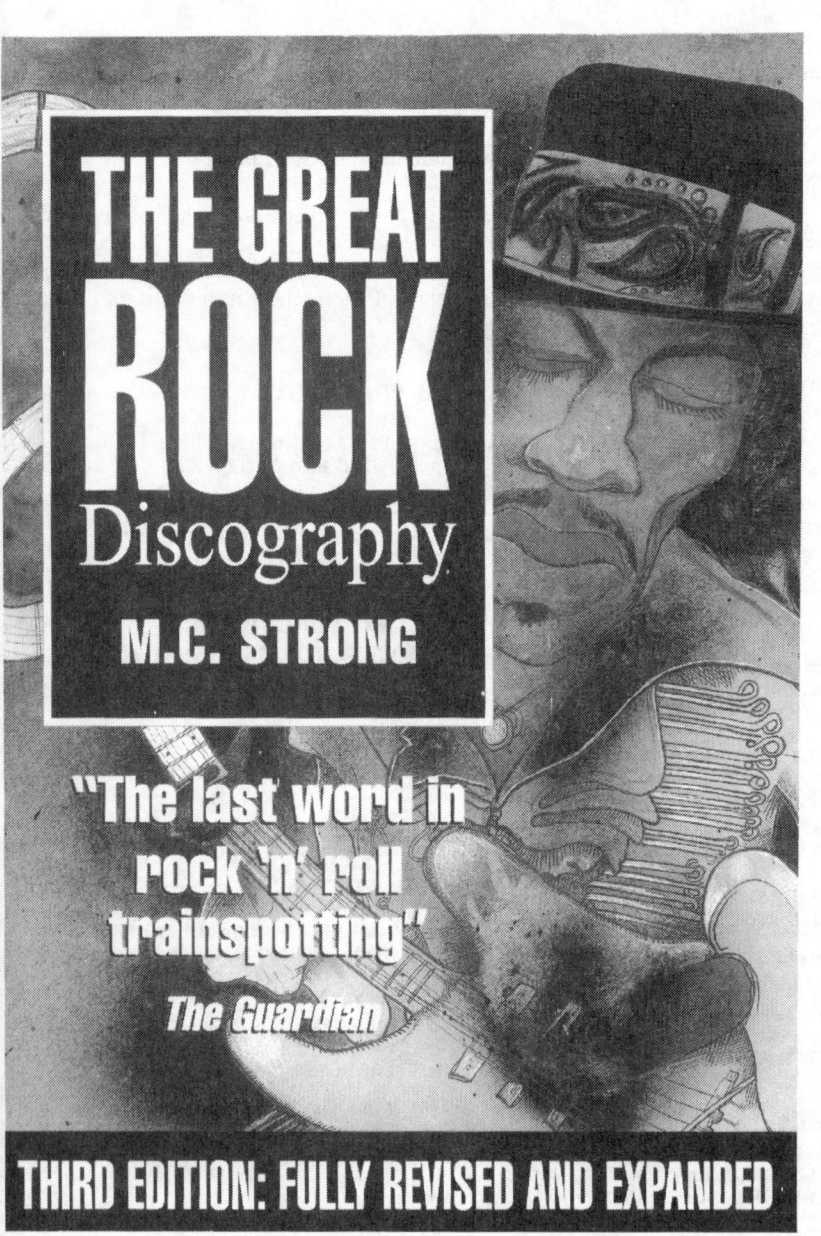

music is what i require

Can you imagine what it would be like if you could access any of the information contained in this book at the flick of a button?

Maybe all you want is quick access to a particular band's entire discography or biography? Possibly you can only remember the name of a song but have no idea who recorded it and are desperate to know so you can buy the album?

All of these questions can be easily and quickly answered thanks to the **music is what i require** web site. Canongate Books in conjunction with the internet wizards at 4th-edge have databased the entire contents of The Great Rock Discography (plus a profusion of additional material that won't fit in the book) and made it open to all who use the internet.

The site is still in its infancy but rapid growth is planned. Naturally, with a beast of this size, some teething trouble is to be expected. What we would like from you is input and suggestions. **require** is an organic site, not static, and we want it to develop the way that you as the user will want it to. The site's future is the most exciting thing of all. Check it out for yourself:

http://www.4th-edge.co.uk/require.htm

We should add that any parties willing or wishing to contribute to the development of the site, financially or otherwise, should contact Canongate Books.

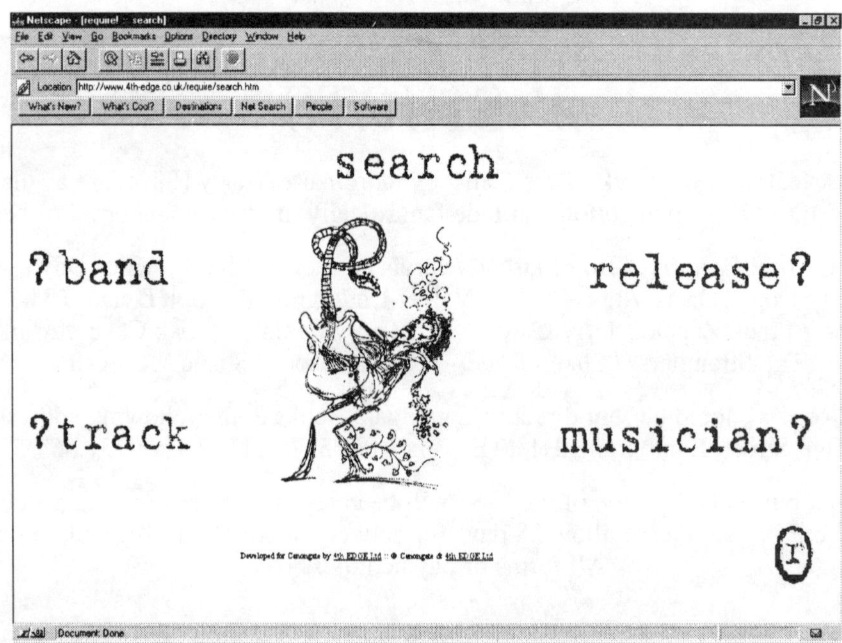